ROGET A to Z

Edited by
Robert L. Chapman

HarperPerennial
A Division of HarperCollins*Publishers*

A hardcover edition of this book was published in 1994 by HarperCollins Publishers, Inc.

First HarperPerennial edition published 1995.

Designed by C. Linda Dingler

The Library of Congress has catalogued the hardcover edition as follows:
Roget A to Z / edited by Robert L. Chapman. — 1st ed.
p. cm.
Roget's international thesaurus in alphabetical format.
ISBN 0-06-270058-8
1. English language—Synonyms and antonyms. 2. English language—Dictionaries. 3. Roget's international thesaurus. I. Chapman, Robert L. II. Roget's international thesaurus.
PE1591.R712 1994
423'.1—dc20 94-9501

ISBN 0-06-272059-7
97 98 ❖/RRD 10 9 8 7 6 5 4

Publisher's Preface

For many years, HarperCollins, publisher of the definitive Roget's International Thesaurus®, has been extensively researching how words are actually used in order to be able to provide the most current reflection for the users of its thesaurus books.

After the successful publication of the latest edition of Roget's International Thesaurus®, many readers asked us to provide this wealth of material from our database in an alphabetical form and Roget A to Z is the result of that effort.

Here are the useful features:

Headwords in boldface

Complete, in-depth entries requiring no cross references

Words identified by part of speech with closely associated words grouped together

Most frequently used words printed in boldface for quick reference

Quotations from literature conveying the essence of many entry words, with their attributions

Common foreign words with clear language identification

Slang words identified as <nonformal> with groupings in shaded boxes

As always, a book such as this would not be possible without the contributions of many. The publisher wishes to particularly thank Eugene Ehrlich who did the lion's share of the editorial work and George Alexander for his valuable computer technology work. Special thanks also to John Day, Manager, Electronic Publishing for Reference, for supervising this complex project; to C. Linda Dingler, Senior Art Director of Interior Design, for design and composition of these pages; to Elaine Verriest, Supervisor, Reference Production; to Dennis Sawicki for running computer programs against the files; and to Joe Ford and Jim Hornfischer for proofreading.

CAROL COHEN
Vice President and Publisher
HarperReference

A

abandon NOUNS 1 unrestraint, unconstraint, noncoercion, nonintimidation; **unreserve,** irrepressibleness, irrepressibility, uninhibitedness, exuberance VERBS 2 **desert, forsake; quit, leave,** leave behind, take leave of, depart from, absent oneself from, turn one's back upon, say goodbye to, bid a long farewell to, walk away, **walk** *or* **run out on** <nonformal>, **leave flat** *and* leave high and dry *or* holding the bag *or* in the lurch <all nonformal>, leave one to one's fate, throw to the wolves <nonformal>

abandoned ADJS 1 **neglected,** unattended to, untended, unwatched, unchaperoned, uncared-for; **ignored, slighted;** half-done, undone, left undone; deserted 2 **unrestrained, unconstrained, unforced,** uncompelled, uncoerced; unmeasured, **uninhibited, unsuppressed, unrepressed, unreserved,** go-go <nonformal>, exuberant; **uncurbed, unchecked, unbridled,** unmuzzled; **unreined,** reinless

abashed ADJS perturbed, disquieted, discomforted, discomposed, agitated; **chagrined, embarrassed,** discomfited, **disconcerted, upset, confused,** mortified, **put-out,** out of countenance, cast down, chapfallen

aabbé NOUNS **clergyman,** man of the cloth, **divine, ecclesiastic, churchman, cleric,** clerical; parson, pastor, *curé* <Fr>, **rector,** curate, man of God, servant of God, shepherd

abbess NOUNS prioress; **mother superior,** lady superior, superioress, the reverend mother, holy mother; canoness, regular *or* secular canoness

abbey NOUNS **cloister, monastery, house,** friary; priory, priorate; lamasery; **convent, nunnery**

abbreviate VERBS **shorten, cut; reduce; abridge, condense,** compress, contract, **boil down,** abstract, sum up, synopsize, epitomize, encapsulate, capsulize; **curtail,** truncate, retrench; bowdlerize; elide, **cut short,** cut down

abdicate VERBS renounce the throne, give up the crown; **give up, relinquish, surrender, yield,** waive, **forgo, resign, renounce,** throw up, **abjure, forswear, give up on, have done with,** wash one's hands of, **write off,** drop, drop all idea of, drop like a hot potato

abdomen NOUNS **stomach, belly** <nonformal>, **midriff,** diaphragm; swollen *or* distended *or* protruding *or* prominent belly, *embonpoint* <Fr>, **paunch,** ventripotence

abdominal ADJS **digestive;** stomachal, stomachic; ventral, celiac, **gastric,** ventricular; big-bellied

abduct VERBS **kidnap,** snatch <nonformal>, carry off; shanghai

aberration NOUNS **deviation,** deviance *or* deviancy, deviousness, **departure, digression,** diversion, **divergence,** divarication, branching off, divagation, declination, aberration, aberrancy, **variation,** indirection, exorbitation; **straying,** errantry, pererration

abet VERBS **advance, further,** expedite, **encourage, hearten, embolden,** pat *or* clap on the back, stroke <nonformal>; **foster, nurture,** nourish, feed, **aid, help, assist,** comfort, **succor,** relieve, **ease,** doctor, remedy; be of some help, put one's oar in <nonformal>; do good, do a world of good, **benefit, avail;** aid and abet, encourage, hearten, embolden, comfort <old>

abhor VERBS **dislike,** disrelish, have no taste for, not stomach, not have the stomach for, not be one's cup of tea; be hostile to, have it in for <nonformal>; **hate, detest, loathe,** execrate, **abominate,** take an aversion to, be death on, not stand the sight of, not stomach, scorn, **despise**

abhorrent ADJS **offensive, objectionable, odious, repulsive,** repellent, rebarbative, **repugnant, revolting,** forbidding; **disgusting, sickening, loathsome,** gross *and* yucky *and* grungy *and* scuzzy <all nonformal>, beastly <nonformal>, **vile, foul, nasty, nauseating;** fulsome, mephitic, miasmal, miasmic, malodorous, stinking, fetid, noisome, noxious

abide VERBS **await,** wait, wait for, wait on *or* upon; have *or* keep an eye out for, lie in wait for; watch, watch and wait; **bide one's time,** bide, **mark time;** cool one's heels <nonformal>; be on tenterhooks, be on pins and needles, hold one's breath, bite one's nails, sweat *or* sweat out *or* sweat it *or* sweat it out <all nonformal>; **endure, bear, stand,** support, sustain, **suffer, tolerate,** live with; **bear up under, bear the brunt, bear with, put up with, stand for,** carry *or* bear one's cross, take what comes, take the bitter with the sweet

ability NOUNS **skill,** skillfulness, **expertness, expertise, proficiency,** craft, **cleverness; dexterity,** dexterousness *or* dextrousness; **adroitness, adeptness, deftness,** handiness; **competence,** capability, capacity, ability; **facility, prowess**

abject ADJS **penitent, repentant; penitential,** penitentiary; **contrite,** abject, humble, humbled, **sheepish, apologetic,** touched, softened, melted

able ADJS **competent, capable, efficient, qualified, fit, fitted, suited, worthy;** fit *or* fitted for; effective, effectual, efficient, efficacious; productive; **proficient, equal to, up to;** up to snuff <nonformal>, up to the mark <nonformal>, *au fait* <Fr>

ably ADVS **skillfully, expertly, proficiently,** excellently, well; **dexterously, adroitly, deftly, adeptly,** aptly, handily; agilely, nimbly, featly, spryly; **competently, capably,** efficiently; **masterfully**

abnormal ADJS unnatural, irregular, divergent, deviative, deviant, different, exceptional; unconventional; **irregular,** deviative, divergent, **different**; **aberrant,** stray, straying, wandering; heteroclite, heteromorphic

abnormality NOUNS 1 anomaly, unnaturalness, irregularity, deviation, deviancy, differentness, divergence, aberration; **nonconformity,** unconventionality
2 **oddity, curiosity, wonder,** funny *or* peculiar *or* strange thing; **anomaly**

aboard ADVS **on board,** on shipboard, on board ship, all aboard, afloat; **on deck,** topside; aloft; in sail; before the mast

abode NOUNS **habitation, place, dwelling,** dwelling place, abiding place, place to live, where one lives *or* resides, where one is at home, roof, roof over one's head, **residence,** place of residence, **domicile,** *domus* <L>; **lodging,** lodgment, lodging place

abolish VERBS **repeal, revoke, rescind, reverse, strike down, abrogate;** renege, renig *and* go back on *and* welsh <all nonformal>; suspend; do away with; **invalidate,** vacate, void, make void, declare null and void

abominable ADJS **wicked, evil, vicious, bad, naughty, wrong, sinful, iniquitous,** peccant, reprobate; dark, black; **base, low, vile,** foul, rank, flagrant, arrant, nefarious, **heinous,** villainous, criminal, up to no good, knavish, flagitious

aborigine NOUNS **primitive, aboriginal,** bushman, autochthon; **cave man,** cave dweller, troglodyte; bog man, bog body, Lindow man; Stone Age man, Bronze Age man, Iron Age man

abort VERBS **miscarry,** be stillborn, die aborning; **go amiss,** go astray, **go wrong,** go on a wrong tack, take a wrong turn, derail, go off the rails

abortion NOUNS 1 **miscarriage,** miscarrying, abortive attempt, vain attempt; glitch <nonformal>; **dud** <nonformal>
2 **monstrosity, monster,** miscreation, teratism, abnormal *or* defective birth, abnormal *or* defective fetus

abortive ADJS **fruitless,** gainless, profitless, bootless, otiose, **unrewarding,** rewardless; barren, sterile, unproductive; failed, *manqué* <Fr>; fruitless, bootless, no-win <nonformal>, futile, useless; lame, **ineffectual,** ineffective, inefficacious

abound VERBS **teem with,** overflow with, **abound with,** burst with, bristle with, pullulate with, **swarm with,** throng with, creep with, **crawl with, be alive with,** be lousy with <nonformal>, bristle with; **have coming out of one's ears** *and* **have up the gazoo** *and* **kazoo** <both nonformal>

about ADVS 1 **approximately,** nearly, some, circa; more or less, *plus ou moins* <Fr>, by and large, upwards of
2 **near, nigh, close;** hard, at close quarters; **nearby, close by,** hard by, fast by, not far *or* far off, in the vicinity *or* **neighborhood of,** at hand, at close range, **near** *or* **close at hand;** thereabout *or* thereabouts, hereabout *or* hereabouts

above ADJS 1 **superior, greater,** better, finer; **higher,** ascendant, in the ascendant, in ascendancy, coming <nonformal>; **previous, prior, early, earlier,** *ci-devant* or *ci-dessus* <Fr>, **former,** fore, prime, first, **preceding,** foregoing, anterior, **anticipatory,** antecedent; **preexistent**

ADVS 2 **on high,** high up, high; **aloft,** aloof; **up,** upward, upwards, straight up, to the zenith; on the shoulders of; supra, *ubi supra* <L>, hereinabove, hereinbefore, *supra* <L>, *ante* <L>
3 **beyond, plus; extra,** on the side <nonformal>, for lagniappe; **more, moreover,** *au reste* <Fr>, *en plus* <Fr>, thereto, farther, further, **furthermore,** at the same time, then, again, yet; similarly, likewise, by the same token, by the same sign; item; therewith, withal <old>; all included, altogether; among other things, *inter alia* <L>

aboveboard ADJS 1 **straight, square,** foursquare, straight-arrow <nonformal>, honest and aboveboard, right as rain; **fair and square; square-dealing,** square-shooting, straight-shooting, up-and-up, **on the up-and-up** *and* **on the level,** *and* on the square <all nonformal>
ADVS 2 **openly, overtly,** before one, **before one's eyes** *or* very eyes, under one's nose <nonformal>; **publicly,** in public; **in the open,** out in the open, **in plain sight,** in broad daylight, for all to see, in public view, in plain view

abrasion NOUNS 1 **trauma, wound, injury,** hurt, lesion; **laceration,** mutilation; scuff, scrape, chafe, gall; frazzle, fray; run, **rip,** rent, slash, **tear; bruise, contusion,** ecchymosis, **black-and-blue mark; black eye,** shiner *and* mouse <both nonformal>
2 **attrition, erosion, wearing away, wear,** detrition, ablation; rubbing away *or* off *or* out; **grinding, filing,** rasping, limation; fretting; galling; **chafing, chafe**

abrasive ADJS **unpleasant, disagreeable; unlikable,** dislikable; unattractive, unappealing, unengaging, uninviting, unalluring

abreast ADJS 1 **informed, enlightened, instructed,** versed, well-versed, educated, schooled, **taught;** posted, briefed, primed, trained; **up on,** up-to-date, abreast of, *au courant* <Fr>
ADVS 2 **in parallel;** side-by-side, alongside; equidistantly, nonconvergently, nondivergently

abridge VERBS **shorten, condense, cut, clip; summarize,** synopsize, wrap up <nonformal>; **sketch,** sketch out, hit the high spots; capsule, capsulize, encapsulate; **put in a nutshell**

abridgment NOUNS **condensation,** compression, conspectus, epitome, epitomization, summary, summation, précis, abstract, recapitulation, recap <nonformal>, wrapup, synopsis, encapsulation; **curtailment,** truncation, retrenchment; elision, ellipsis, syncope, apocope; foreshortening; **deletion,** erasure, cancellation, omission; editing, blue-penciling, striking *or* striking out; expurgation, bowdlerization, censoring *or* censorship; abbreviation

abroad ADJS 1 **nonresident,** not in residence, from home, **away from home,** on leave *or* vacation *or* holiday, on tour, on the road; overseas
ADVS 2 **far and wide,** far and near, distantly and broadly, widely

abrogate VERBS **abolish,** void, annihilate, annul, tear up, repeal, revoke, negate, invalidate, **undo, cancel,** cancel out, bring to naught, put *or* lay to rest; **repeal, revoke, rescind, reverse, strike down,** suspend

abrupt ADJS **sudden,** precipitant, **precipitate; hasty,** headlong, impulsive, impetuous; **unexpected**, unanticipated, unpredicted, unforeseen, unlooked-for; **gruff, brusque, curt,** short, sharp, snippy <nonformal>, **blunt,** bluff, brash, cavalier

abruptly ADVS **precipitately,** precipitantly, slap-bang; **suddenly,** abruptly; **impetuously, impulsively, rashly; headlong,** headfirst, head over heels, *à corps perdu* <Fr>; **gruffly, brusquely, curtly,** shortly, sharply, snippily <nonformal>, bluntly, bluffly, brashly, cavalierly

abscess NOUNS **sore, lesion;** pustule, papule, papula, fester, **pimple,** hickey *and* zit <both nonformal>; pock; ulcer, ulceration; fistula; suppuration

abscond VERBS **flee, fly, take flight,** take wing, fugitate, **run, cut and run** <nonformal>, make a precipitate departure, **run off** *or* **away,** run away from, bug out <nonformal>, **decamp,** pull up stakes, **take to one's heels,** make off, **depart**, do the disappearing act, make a quick exit, **beat a retreat** *or* **a hasty retreat, turn tail**

absence NOUNS 1 **nonattendance, absenting, leaving,** taking leave, **departure**; **truancy, hooky** <nonformal>, French leave, **cut** <nonformal>;

absence without leave *or* AWOL; **absenteeism,** truantism

to leave is to die a little
FRENCH SAYING

Say, is not absence death to those who love?
POPE

2 **want, lack, need, deficiency, deficit, shortage, shortfall,** wantage, **incompleteness,** defectiveness, shortcoming, imperfection

absent ADJS not present, nonattendant, **away, gone,** departed, disappeared, vanished, absconded, out of sight; **missing,** among the missing, wanting, **lacking,** not found, nowhere to be found, omitted, taken away, subtracted, deleted

absentminded ADJS **forgetful, forgetting,** inclined to forget, **memoryless, unremembering, unmindful, oblivious,** insensible to the past, with a mind *or* memory like a sieve; amnesic, amnestic; **abstracted, bemused,** museful <old>, **musing, preoccupied, absorbed, engrossed,** taken up; **absent,** faraway, elsewhere, somewhere else, not there; pensive, meditative; **lost in thought,** wrapped in thought

absolute ADJS 1 **downright, outright, out-and-out; utter, perfect, consummate,** superlative, surpassing, the veriest, positive, definitive, classical, pronounced, decided, regular <nonformal>, proper <Brit nonformal>, precious, profound, stark; **unmitigated,** unqualified, unrelieved, unspoiled, undeniable, unquestionable, unequivocal
2 **unrestricted, unconfined, uncircumscribed,** unbounded, unmeasured; **unlimited,** limitless, illimitable

absolutely ADVS 1 **certainly, surely, assuredly, positively, definitely,** decidedly; without batting an eye <nonformal>; decisively, distinctly, clearly, unequivocally, unmistakably
2 **exactly, precisely,** to a T, expressly; **just, dead,** right, straight, even, square, **plumb,** directly, squarely, point-blank; unerringly, undeviatingly; in every respect, in all respects, for all the world, neither more nor less

absolve VERBS 1 **acquit, clear, exculpate, exonerate,** give absolution, bring in *or* return a verdict of not guilty; **pardon, excuse, forgive;** remit, grant remission, remit the penalty of; wipe the slate clean; **whitewash,** decontaminate; destigmatize
2 **confess,** make confession, receive absolution; **shrive,** hear confession; administer absolution; administer extreme unction

absorb VERBS 1 **assimilate,** engross, digest, **drink,** imbibe, take up *or* in, drink up *or* in, slurp up, swill up; blot, **blot up, soak up,** sponge; osmose; infiltrate, filter in; **soak in, seep in,** percolate in
2 **understand, comprehend, apprehend,** have, **know, conceive, realize,** appreciate, have no problem with, ken <Scots>, savvy <nonformal>, sense, make sense out of, make something of; **fathom, follow; grasp, seize**

absorbed ADJS **engrossed,** single-minded, **occupied, preoccupied, engaged,** devoted, devoted to, intent, intent on, monopolized, obsessed, monomaniacal, swept up, taken up with, **involved, caught up in,** wrapped in, **wrapped up in,** engrossed in, **absorbed in** *or* with *or* by, **lost in, immersed in,** submerged in, buried in

absorbing ADJS **deep, profound;** pervasive, pervading; **engrossing,** consuming, **gripping,** riveting, holding, **arresting,** engaging, attractive, **fascinating, enthralling, spellbinding,** enchanting, magnetic, hypnotic, mesmerizing, mesmeric; obsessive, obsessing

abstain VERBS refrain, **refrain from, forbear, forgo,** spare, withhold, hold back, **avoid, shun,** eschew, **pass up** <nonformal>, **keep from,** keep *or* stand *or* hold aloof from, have nothing to do with, take no part in, have no hand in, **let alone,** let well enough alone, let go by, **deny oneself,** do without, go without, make do without, not *or* never touch, keep hands off

abstinence NOUNS **asceticism, austerity, self-denial,** self-abnegation, **rigor; puritanism,** eremitism, anchoritism, anchorite *or* anchoritic monasticism, monasticism, monachism; **continence** *or* continency; abstemiousness, abstaining; celibacy; **virginity,** intactness, maidenhood, maidenhead

abstract NOUNS 1 **abridgment,** compendium, *abrégé* <Fr>, **condensation,** condensed version, abbreviation, abbre-

viature, brief, digest, epitome, **précis, capsule,** capsulization, encapsulation, thumbnail sketch, **synopsis,** conspectus, syllabus, *aperçu* <Fr>, **survey, review,** pandect; **outline,** skeleton
VERBS 2 **abbreviate, cut; reduce**; **abridge, condense,** compress, contract, **boil down,** abstract, sum up, summarize, recapitulate, recap <nonformal>, synopsize, epitomize, encapsulate, capsulize; **curtail,** truncate, retrench; bowdlerize
ADJS 3 **recondite, abstruse,** transcendental; **profound, deep; hidden**; arcane, **esoteric,** occult; **secret; general, generalized, nonspecific,** generic, **indefinite,** indeterminate, vague, nebulous, unspecified, undifferentiated, featureless, uncharacterized, bland, neutral

abstracted ADJS absorbed *or* engrossed in thought, **absorbed, engrossed,** introspective, rapt, **wrapped in thought, lost in thought,** immersed in thought, buried in thought, engaged in thought, occupied, **preoccupied**

abstraction NOUNS 1 **abstract idea,** general idea, generality, abstract; **generalization,** general idea, generalized proposition
2 **thoughtfulness,** contemplativeness, speculativeness, reflectiveness; **pensiveness,** wistfulness, reverie, musing, melancholy; **preoccupation, absorption, engrossment,** brown study, intense *or* deep *or* profound thought

absurd ADJS 1 **humorous, funny, amusing; witty**; **droll, whimsical,** quizzical; **laughable,** risible, good for a laugh; **ludicrous, ridiculous, hilarious, absurd,** quaint, eccentric, incongruous, bizarre; **nonsensical,** insensate, ridiculous, laughable, ludicrous
2 **impossible, not possible,** beyond the bounds of possibility *or* reason, contrary to reason, at variance with the facts; **inconceivable, unimaginable, unthinkable, not to be thought of, out of the question**

abundance NOUNS **plenty,** plenitude, plentifulness, plenteousness; myriad, myriads, numerousness; **amplitude,** ampleness; substantiality, substantialness; **copiousness; wealth, opulence** *or* opulency, richness, affluence; **prevalence,** profuseness, **profusion,** riot; **superabundance**

abundant ADJS **much, many,** beaucoup <nonformal>, ample, copious, generous, overflowing, superabundant, multitudinous, plentiful, **numerous**, countless; **plentiful,** plenty, **plenteous,** plenitudinous; **bountiful,** bounteous, **lavish, generous, liberal, extravagant, prodigal; luxuriant,** fertile, productive, **rich,** fat, **wealthy, opulent, affluent**

abuse NOUNS 1 misuse, misusage, abuse; misapplication; **mishandling,** mismanagement, poor stewardship; malversation, breach of public trust, maladministration; diversion, defalcation, misappropriation, conversion, **embezzlement,** peculation, pilfering
2 **mistreatment, ill-treatment, maltreatment, ill-use,** ill-usage; **molesting, molestation,** child abuse *or* molestation; **berating,** rating, tongue-lashing; **revilement, vilification,** blackening, **execration, vituperation,** invective, contumely, hard *or* cutting *or* bitter words; **tirade, diatribe,** jeremiad, screed, philippic
VERBS 3 **exploit, take advantage of, use,** make use of, **use for one's own ends; manipulate,** work on, work upon, stroke, play on *or* upon; play both ends against the middle; **impose upon,** presume upon
4 **misuse, misemploy, misapply; mishandle,** mismanage, maladminister; divert, misappropriate, convert, defalcate <old>, embezzle, pilfer, peculate, feather one's nest <nonformal>; pervert, prostitute; profane, violate, pollute, foul, foul one's own nest, befoul, desecrate, defile, debase
5 **vilify, revile,** vituperate, blackguard, call names, epithet, epithetize; **swear at,** damn, cuss out <nonformal>

abusive ADJS **condemnatory, censorious,** censorial, damnatory, **denunciatory, reproachful,** blameful, reprobative, objurgatory, priggish; reviling; **disparaging, derogatory,** derogative, depreciative, deprecatory, slighting, belittling, minimizing, detractory, pejorative, backbiting, catty *and* bitchy <both nonformal>, contumelious, contemptuous, derisive, derisory, ridiculing

abut VERBS adjoin, **join, conjoin,** connect, **butt, abut on *or* upon, be contiguous, be in contact;** neighbor, **border,** border on *or* upon, **verge on *or* upon**

abyss NOUNS 1 **pit, deep, depth, hole,** hollow, **cavity,** shaft, well, **gulf, chasm,** abysm

2 **ocean depths, the deep sea, the deep,** trench, deep-sea trench, hadal zone, **the deeps, the depths,** bottomless depths, inner space; bottom waters

academic NOUNS 1 **professor,** member of academy; don <Brit>, fellow; guide, docent; rabbi, *melamed* <Heb>, pandit, pundit, guru, *mullah* <Persian>, *starets* <Russ>

ADJS 2 **studious, scholarly,** scholastic, professorial, tweedy, donnish <Brit>; owlish; rabbinic, mandarin; pedantic, dry as dust; bookish; diligent

accelerate VERBS **speed up, step up** <nonformal>, **hurry up, quicken; hasten**; **rush,** quicken, hustle <nonformal>, bustle, bundle, precipitate, forward; **dispatch, expedite; intensify, heighten, deepen,** enhance, **strengthen,** aggravate, exacerbate; **reinforce,** double, redouble; **complicate,** ramify, make complex; give a boost to, **step up** <nonformal>

accent NOUNS 1 brogue, twang, burr, drawl, broad accent; **foreign accent;** accentuation, stress accent; **emphasis, stress, word stress;** ictus, beat, rhythmical stress; rhythm, rhythmic pattern, **cadence**

VERBS 2 emphasize, stress, lay emphasis or stress upon, feature, highlight, place emphasis on, give emphasis to, **accentuate, punctuate, point up,** bring to the fore, put in the foreground

accept VERBS 1 **condone, countenance;** overlook, not make an issue of, let go by, let pass; **reconcile oneself to,** resign oneself to, yield *or* submit to, obey; accustom *or* accommodate *or* adjust oneself to, sit through; accept one's fate, lay in the lap of the gods, take things as they come, roll with the punches <nonformal>

2 <nonformal> **take it,** take it on the chin, take it like a man, not let it get one down, stand the gaff; bite the bullet; hold still *or* stand still for, swallow, stick, **hang in, hang in there, hang tough,** tough *or* stick it out; lump it

3 **assent,** give *or* yield assent, **acquiesce, consent**, **comply, accede, agree,** agree to *or* with, have no problem with; find it in one's heart; take kindly to *and* hold with <both nonformal>; buy <nonformal>, take one up on <nonformal>; **subscribe to,** acquiesce in, abide by; **say 'yes' to; ratify, endorse,** sign off on, second, support, **certify, confirm, validate, authenticate,** give the nod *or* the green light *or* the go-ahead *or* the OK <all nonformal>, give one's imprimatur, permit, give permission, **approve**; sanction, **authorize,** warrant, accredit

acceptable ADJS **tolerable, goodish, fair, fairish,** moderate, tidy <nonformal>, **decent,** respectable, presentable, good enough, **pretty good, not bad,** not amiss, not half bad, not so bad, **adequate, satisfactory, all right,** OK *or* okay <nonformal>; better than nothing; admissible, **passable,** unobjectionable, unexceptionable

accepted ADJS 1 **approved,** received; acknowledged, admitted, allowed, granted, conceded, recognized, professed, confessed, avowed, warranted; self-confessed; **ratified, endorsed, certified,** confirmed, validated, authenticated

2 **customary, wonted,** consuetudinary; traditional, time-honored; familiar, everyday, ordinary, **usual; established,** received, accepted; set, prescribed, prescriptive; **conventional**; conformist, conformable

accepting ADJS 1 **patient,** armed with patience, with a soul possessed in patience, patient as Job, Job-like, Griselda-like

like patience on a monument
smiling at grief
Shakespeare

2 **submissive, compliant,** compliable <old>, complaisant, complying, **acquiescent,** consenting; **assenting,** agreeable; subservient, abject, **obedient**

access NOUNS 1 entree, entrée, in <nonformal>, entry, **entrance,** opening, **open door,** open arms; a foot in the door, an opening wedge, the camel's nose under the wall of the tent; **opening**

2 accessibility, approachability, openness, reachableness, come-at-ableness *and* get-at-ableness <both nonformal>; **penetrability,** perviousness; **availability, donability, procurability,** procur-

ableness, securableness, getableness, acquirability
VERBS 3 **enter, go in** *or* **into,** cross the threshold, **come in,** find one's way into, put in *or* into; be admitted, gain admission *or* admittance, have an entree, have an in <nonformal>; **set foot in,** step in, walk in

accessible ADJS 1 **handy, convenient; available, ready, at hand,** to hand, **on hand,** on tap, on deck <nonformal>, on call, at one's call *or* beck and call, at one's elbow, at one's fingertips, just around the corner, at one's disposal
2 **communicative, talkative**, gossipy, newsy; **sociable; unreserved, unreticent,** unshrinking, **unrestrained, unconstrained,** unhampered, unrestricted; demonstrative, expansive, effusive

accessory NOUNS 1 **belongings, appurtenances,** trappings, paraphernalia, appointments, accessories, perquisites, appendages, appanages, choses local
2 **attendant,** concomitant, corollary, appendage; **adjunct; accomplice,** cohort, confederate, fellow conspirator, coconspirator, partner *or* accomplice in crime; *particeps criminis, socius criminis* <both L>; accessory before the fact, accessory after the fact
ADJS 3 **additional, supplementary, supplemental; extra,** plus, further, farther, fresh, **more,** new, **other,** another, ulterior; **auxiliary,** ancillary, supernumerary, contributory, collateral; **surplus,** spare
4 **accompanying, attending, attendant, concomitant,** collateral

accident NOUNS **misfortune, mishap,** ill hap, **misadventure, mischance,** *contretemps* <Fr>, grief; **disaster, calamity, catastrophe,** meltdown, cataclysm, **tragedy; happening,** hap, happenstance; **fortuity,** casualty, adventure, hazard

accidental ADJS 1 **incidental, occasional, casual;** parenthetical, by-the-way; **unessential,** inessential *or* nonessential, unnecessary, nonvital, superfluous; **accessory, extra,** collateral, auxiliary, supernumerary; adventitious, appurtenant, adscititious
2 **circumstantial,** conditional, provisional; **incidental,** occasional, contingent, adventitious, **accidental, chance,** fortuitous, casual, aleatory, unessential *or* inessential *or* nonessential

acclaim NOUNS 1 **applause,** plaudit, éclat, **acclamation; popularity;** ovation, standing ovation; **repute, reputation; fame,** famousness, **renown; kudos,** report, **glory; celebrity,** recognition, a place in the sun; popular acceptance *or* favor, vogue

the bubble reputation
Shakespeare

that last infirmity of noble mind
Milton

VERBS 2 **applaud, hail; clap,** clap one's hands, give a hand *or* big hand, have *or* hear a hand *or* big hand for, hear it for <nonformal>; root for <nonformal>, cheer on

acclaimed ADJS **distinguished,** distingué; **famous,** famed, honored, **renowned, celebrated, popular,** much acclaimed, sought-after, hot *and* world-class <both nonformal>, **notorious, well-known,** best-known, on everyone's tongue *or* lips

accommodate VERBS 1 **be kind,** show kindness; treat well, do right by; favor, oblige; **conform, comply, correspond,** accord, harmonize; **adapt,** adjust, bend, meet, suit, fit, shape; **adapt to,** adjust to, gear to, assimilate to, **accommodate to** *or* **with; reconcile,** settle, compose
2 **provide, supply,** find, dish up *and* rustle up <both nonformal>, **furnish;** invest, endow, fund, subsidize

accommodating ADJS **considerate, thoughtful,** mindful, heedful, regardful, solicitous, attentive, delicate, tactful, mindful of others; complaisant, accommodative, at one's service, **helpful,** agreeable, **obliging,** indulgent, tolerant, lenient; **courteous, polite, civil, urbane, gracious,** graceful, agreeable, affable, fair

accommodation NOUNS 1 **compromise,** adjustment, settlement, mutual concession, give-and-take; bargain, deal <nonformal>, arrangement, understanding; **concession,** giving way, yielding
2 accommodations, facilities; **lodgings; room and board,** bed and board; **subsistence,** keep, fostering

accompaniment NOUNS **supplement,** complement, continuation, extrapolation, extension; offshoot, side issue, corollary, sidebar <nonformal>, side effect, spin-off <nonformal>, **concomi-**

tant, additive, adjuvant; **adjunct, addition,** increase, **increment**

accompany VERBS 1 **agree,** match, go along with, go hand in hand, keep pace with, keep in step; **coincide,** concur; **coexist;** coextend; **synchronize,** isochronize
2 **result, ensue, issue, follow,** attend; **turn out, come out,** fall out, redound, **work out,** pan out <nonformal>, fare

accomplice NOUNS **participator, participant, partaker, player, sharer;** party, **a party to,** accessory; cohort, confederate, coconspirator, partner in crime; *particeps criminis, socius criminis* <both L>; **abettor**

accomplish VERBS 1 **achieve, effect, effectuate,** compass, consummate, **do, execute, produce, deliver, make;** enact, **perform, discharge, fulfill, realize, attain,** run with *and* hack *and* swing <all nonformal>; **work,** work out
2 **complete,** bring to completion *or* fruition, mature; **fill in, fill out,** piece out, top off, eke *or* eke out, round out

accomplished ADJS 1 **achieved, effected,** effectuated, implemented, **consummated, executed, discharged, fulfilled, realized,** compassed, **attained**
2 **skilled; practiced;** trained, coached, prepared, primed, finished; at one's best, at concert pitch

accomplishment NOUNS **act, action, deed, doing,** thing, thing done; **turn; feat, stunt** *and* **trick** <both nonformal>; **master stroke,** *tour de force* <Fr>, **exploit,** adventure, gest, **enterprise, initiative,** track record <nonformal>; accomplished fact, *fait accompli* <Fr>, done deal <nonformal>; **achievement, fulfillment, performance, execution, effectuation,** implementation, carrying out *or* through, **discharge, dispatch, consummation, realization, attainment,** production, fruition

accord NOUNS 1 **unanimity,** unanimousness, universal *or* univocal *or* unambiguous assent; **like-mindedness, meeting of minds,** one *or* same mind; **concurrence, consent,** general consent, common assent *or* consent, consentaneity, accordance, **concord,** concordance, **agreement,** general agreement; **consensus;** *consensus omnium* <L>, universal agreement *or* accord, *consensus gentium* <L>, agreement of all, shared sense, sense of the meeting
2 **compact, pact, contract,** legal contract, valid contract, **covenant,** convention, transaction, paction <Scots>, formal agreement, legal agreement, undertaking, stipulation; adjustment, accommodation; **understanding, arrangement, bargain,** dicker *and* **deal** <both nonformal>
VERBS 3 **permit, allow, admit, let,** leave <nonformal>, give permission, give leave, make possible; **allow** *or* **permit of;** give *or* leave room for, open the door to; consent; **grant,** vouchsafe
4 **agree, harmonize, concur**, have no problem with, go along with <nonformal>, **cooperate**, **correspond, conform,** coincide, parallel, intersect, overlap, **match,** tally, hit, register, lock, interlock, check <nonformal>, square, dovetail, jibe <nonformal>; **assent**, come to an agreement, be of one *or* the same *or* like mind, see eye to eye, sing in chorus, have a meeting of the minds, climb on the bandwagon

accordingly ADVS **in that case, in that event, at that rate,** that being the case, such being the case, that being so, **under the circumstances,** the condition being such, as it is, as matters stand, as the matter stands, **therefore, consequently; hence, wherefore,** wherefrom, whence, then, thence, *ergo* <L>, for which reason; **consequently**

account NOUNS 1 **record, recording,** documentation, written word; **chronicle, annals,** history, story; letters, correspondence; **vestige, trace,** memorial, token, relic, remains; **story, tale, yarn, narrative,** narration, chronicle; **anecdote,** anecdotage; **epic,** epos, **saga**
2 **reckoning, tally, score;** account current; account rendered, *compte rendu* <Fr>; **reckoning, check,** *l'addition* <Fr>, score *or* tab <both nonformal>

accountable ADJS **responsible, answerable; liable,** amenable, unexempt from, chargeable, on one's head, at one's doorstep, on the hook <nonformal>; **attributable, assignable, ascribable, imputable,** traceable, referable, explicable

accountant NOUNS cost accountant, cost keeper; certified public accountant *or* CPA; chartered accountant *or* CA <Brit>; **auditor,** bank examiner

accrue VERBS 1 **grow, increase, advance,** appreciate; **spread, widen,**

broaden; **intensify, develop,** gain strength, strengthen; accumulate; **multiply, proliferate,** breed, teem; run *or* shoot up, **boom, explode**
2 **result from,** be the effect of, be due to, originate in *or* from, **come from,** come out of, grow from, **grow out of,** follow from *or* on, proceed from, descend from, emerge from, issue from, ensue from, emanate from, flow from, **derive from,** accrue from, rise *or* arise from, take its rise from, **spring from, stem from,** sprout from; **depend on,** hinge *or* pivot *or* turn on, hang on, be contingent on

accumulate VERBS cumulate, **amass,** mass, bulk, batch; agglomerate, conglomerate, aggregate; **combine, network, join, bring together,** get together, **gather together,** draw *or* lump *or* batch *or* bunch together, pack, pack in, cram, cram in; **bunch,** bunch up; **cluster,** clump

accuracy NOUNS **correctness,** care for truth, attention to fact, right, subservience to the facts *or* the data, **rightness, rigor, rigorousness, exactness, exactitude**

accurate ADJS **meticulous, exacting, scrupulous, conscientious,** religious, punctilious, punctual, **particular, fussy, critical, attentive,** scrutinizing; **thorough,** thoroughgoing, thoroughpaced; **finical,** finicking, finicky; **exact, precise,** precisionistic, precisianistic, prissy, **correct**

accurately ADVS **meticulously, exactingly, scrupulously, conscientiously,** religiously, punctiliously, punctually, fussily; strictly, rigorously

accusation NOUNS finger-pointing <nonformal>, accusal, **charge, complaint,** plaint, count, **blame, imputation,** delation, reproach, taxing; **accusing, bringing of charges,** laying of charges, bringing to book; **denunciation,** denouncement; **impeachment, arraignment, indictment,** bill of indictment, true bill

accuse VERBS 1 **charge, press charges, prefer** *or* **bring charges,** lay charges; complain, **lodge a complaint,** lodge a plaint; **impeach, arraign, indict,** bring in *or* hand up an indictment, return a true bill, article, **cite,** cite on several counts; book; **denounce,** denunciate; **finger** *and* point the finger at *and* put *or* lay the finger on <all nonformal>, **inform on** *or* **against**
2 **censure,** reprehend; **blame,** lay *or* cast blame upon; **bash** *and* trash *and* rubbish <all nonformal>; **reproach,** impugn; **condemn,** damn, take out after; damn with faint praise; fulminate against, anathematize, anathemize

accuser NOUNS accusant, accusatrix; incriminator, delator, allegator, impugner; informer; impeacher, indictor; **plaintiff, complainant,** claimant, appellant, petitioner, libelant, suitor; **prosecutor,** the prosecution

accustomed ADJS **wont, wonted, used to; conditioned,** trained, seasoned; experienced, **familiarized,** naturalized <old>, broken-in, run-in <nonformal>; **usual, regular; customary,** habitual, **normative,** prescriptive, standard, regulation, conventional

ache NOUNS 1 aching, throbbing, throbbing ache *or* pain; **pain, distress, grief,** stress, stress of life, suffering, passion, dolor; pang, wrench, throes, cramp, spasm; wound, injury, hurt; **sore,** sore spot, tender spot, lesion; cut, stroke; shock, blow, hard *or* nasty blow
VERBS 2 **suffer, feel pain,** feel the pangs, anguish; **hurt,** have a misery <nonformal>, ail; **smart,** tingle; throb, pound; shoot; twinge, thrill, twitch; **wince,** blanch, shrink, make a wry face, grimace; **agonize,** writhe; **suffer anguish; agonize;** go hard with, have a bad time of it, go through hell; quaff the bitter cup, drain the cup of misery to the dregs, be nailed to the cross
3 **wish for, hope for, yearn for,** yen for *and* have a yen for <both nonformal>, **itch for,** lust for, pant for, **long for, pine for,** hone for <nonformal>, ache for, be hurting for <nonformal>, weary for, languish for, **be dying for,** thirst for, sigh for, gape for <old>; cry for, clamor for; spoil for <nonformal>

achieve VERBS 1 **succeed with,** crown with success; **make a go of it; accomplish,** compass, **achieve**; **bring off, carry off, pull off** <nonformal>, turn *or* do the trick <nonformal>, **put through,** bring through; **put over** *or* **across** <nonformal>; get away with it *and* get by <both nonformal>
2 **arrive,** arrive at, arrive in, come, **come** *or* **get to,** approach, access, **reach, hit** <nonformal>; find, **gain,** attain, attain to, accomplish, make, **make it** <nonformal>, fetch, fetch up

at, get there, reach one's destination, come to one's journey's end, end up
3 **perform, do,** work, act, execute, **accomplish, deliver,** come through with, realize, engineer, effectuate, **bring about,** bring to fruition *or* into being, cause; mass-produce, volume-produce, industrialize; overproduce; underproduce; **be productive**

achievement NOUNS **exploit, feat, deed, enterprise, adventure,** gest, **bold stroke,** heroic act *or* deed; aristeia; **performance, execution, doing, accomplishment,** productive effort *or* effect, realization, bringing to fruition, fructification, effectuation, operation

Achilles' heel NOUNS weak point, vulnerable place, chink in one's armor, weak link; **fault,** *faute* <Fr>, **defect, deficiency, inadequacy,** imperfection, kink, defection <old>; **flaw,** hole, bug <nonformal>; something missing; catch <nonformal>, fly in the ointment, problem, little problem, curate's egg <Brit>, snag, drawback; **crack,** rift; **weakness,** frailty, infirmity, failure, **failing, foible, shortcoming; blemish,** taint

acid NOUNS 1 **bitterness, bitter resentment,** bitterness of spirit, heartburning; **rancor,** virulence, **acrimony,** acerbity, asperity; causticity; **choler,** gall, bile, spleen, acidity, acidulousness

2 <nonformal terms for LSD> big D, blotter, blue acid, blue cheer, blue heaven, California sunshine, cap, cubes, D, deeda, dots, electric Kool-Aid, haze, L, mellow yellows, orange cubes, pearly gates, pink owsley, strawberry fields, sugar, sunshine, tabs, yellow

ADJS 3 acidulous, acidulent, acidulated; acetic, acetous, acetose
4 **pungent, piquant, poignant; sharp, keen,** piercing, penetrating, nose-tickling, stinging, **biting, acrid,** astringent, irritating, harsh, rough, severe, asperous, cutting, trenchant; **caustic,** vitriolic, mordant, escharotic; **bitter**; acerbic, **sour**

acknowledge VERBS 1 **admit, own, confess, allow,** avow, **grant,** warrant, **concede,** yield <old>; **accept, recognize**
2 **thank, extend gratitude** *or* **thanks,** bless; give one's thanks, **express one's appreciation; offer** *or* **give thanks,** tender *or* render thanks, return thanks

acknowledged ADJS **accepted, approved,** received; admitted, allowed, granted, conceded, recognized, professed, confessed, avowed, warranted; self-confessed; **ratified, endorsed, certified,** confirmed, validated, authenticated; certificatory, confirmatory, validating, warranting; **signed,** sealed, signed and sealed, countersigned, underwritten; stamped; sworn to, notarized, affirmed, sworn and affirmed

acme NOUNS **summit,** top; **tip-top, peak,** pinnacle; **crest, brow;** ridge, edge; **crown,** cap, **tip,** point, spire, pitch; highest pitch, no place higher, **apex,** vertex, *ne plus ultra* <Fr>, **zenith, climax,** apogee; **culmination**

acoustic ADJS acoustical, phonic; **auditory,** audio, audile, **hearing, aural,** auricular, otic; **sonic;** subsonic, supersonic, ultrasonic, hypersonic; transonic *or* transsonic

acquaint VERBS **inform, tell, speak on** *or* **for,** apprise, **advise, advertise,** advertise of, **give word,** mention to, **enlighten,** familiarize, brief, verse, give the facts, give an account of, give by way of information

acquaintance NOUNS 1 casual acquaintance; pickup <nonformal>; close acquaintance; confidant, confidante, repository; **intimate,** familiar, **close friend,** intimate *or* familiar friend; **bosom friend,** friend of one's bosom, inseparable friend, **best friend**
2 **knowledge,** knowing, knowingness, ken; **command,** reach; **familiarity,** intimacy; private knowledge, privity

acquiesce VERBS **be willing, be game** <nonformal>, be ready; be of favorable disposition, take the trouble, find it in one's heart, find one's heart <old>, have a willing heart; **incline, lean;** look kindly upon; **bite the bullet; knuckle down** *or* **under,** take it, swallow it; grin and bear it, make the best of it, take the bitter with the sweet, shrug, shrug off, **live with it;** obey

acquiescent ADJS **assenting, agreeing,** acquiescing, **compliant,** consenting, consentient, consensual, submissive, unmurmuring, conceding, concessive, assentatious, **agreed, content**

acquire VERBS **get, gain, obtain, secure, procure; win,** score; **earn,** make; **reap, harvest; receive,** have, come by, be in receipt of, be on the receiving end; **obtain**

acquisition NOUNS **taking,** possession, taking possession, taking away; **claiming,** staking one's claim; **reception**

acquit VERBS **clear, exculpate, exonerate, absolve,** bring in *or* return a verdict of not guilty; **vindicate,** justify; grant *or* extend amnesty; **discharge, release, dismiss, free, set free,** let off <nonformal>, let go; withdraw the charge; shrive, purge; wipe the slate clean

acquittal NOUNS acquittance; **exculpation,** disculpation, verdict of not guilty; **exoneration, absolution, vindication, remission,** compurgation, purgation, purging; **discharge, release,** dismissal, setting free; quashing of the charge *or* indictment

acrimonious ADJS **harsh,** fierce, **rigorous,** severe, rough, stringent, astringent, strident, **sharp, keen,** sharpish, incisive, trenchant, **cutting,** biting, stinging, **scathing,** stabbing, **piercing, poignant,** penetrating, edged, double-edged

across ADJS 1 **transverse,** crosswise *or* crossways, thwart, athwart; **diagonal,** bendwise; catercorner *or* **catercornered** *or* cattycorner *or* cattycornered *or* kittycorner *or* kittycornered
ADVS 2 **crosswise** *or* crossways *or* crossway, decussatively; **cross, crisscross,** thwart, thwartly, thwartways, **athwart,** athwartwise, overthwart; **transverse,** transversely, transversally; obliquely; **sideways** *or* sidewise; across the grain, against the grain

act NOUNS 1 **process, procedure,** proceeding, course; step, measure, initiative, *démarche* <Fr>, move, maneuver, motion
2 **law,** *lex, jus* <both L>, **statute,** rubric, **canon,** institution; **ordinance;** measure, legislation; **rule, ruling; prescript,** prescription; **regulation,** *règlement* <Fr>; **dictate,** dictation; bylaw; **edict, decree**; **bill**
VERBS 3 **perform, do,** work, execute, **bring about,** bring to fruition *or* into being, cause; **be productive; behave,** go on; **behave oneself, conduct oneself,** manage oneself, **handle oneself,** guide oneself, **comport oneself, deport oneself**
4 **take action, take steps** *or* **measures; proceed,** proceed with, go ahead with, go with, go through with; do something, go *or* swing into action, **do something about,** take it on, run with it <nonformal>, get off the dime *or* one's ass *or* one's dead ass <nonformal>
5 **play,** playact, tread the boards, strut one's stuff <nonformal>; appear, **appear on the stage;** emote <nonformal>; pantomime, mime

acting NOUNS 1 **action, activity**, act, willed action *or* activity; **sham, fakery,** faking, falsity, feigning, pretending; feint, pretext, **pretense,** hollow pretense, **pretension, false pretense** *or* **pretension**
ADJS 2 performing, practicing, serving, functioning, functional, operating, operative, operational, working; **deputy,** deputative

action NOUNS **activity**, act, willed action *or* activity; **acting, doing,** activism, direct action, not words but action; **undertaking, enterprise, operation,** work, **venture, project,** proposition *and* deal <both nonformal>; **program, plan**; **affair, business, matter, task**, concern, interest; **initiative,** effort, attempt

active ADJS 1 **operating, operational, working, functioning,** operant, functional, running, **going,** going on, ongoing; **in operation,** in action, **in practice, in force,** in play, in exercise, at work, on foot
2 **lively, animated, spirited,** bubbly, ebullient, effervescent, **vivacious, sprightly,** chipper *and* perky <both nonformal>, pert; **spry, breezy, brisk, energetic,** eager, keen, can-do <nonformal>; full of life, **peppy** *and* snappy *and* zingy <all nonformal>; frisky, bouncing, bouncy

activist NOUNS 1 **man** *or* **woman of action, doer; hustler** *and* self-starter <both nonformal>, bustler; go-getter *and* ball of fire *and* live wire *and* powerhouse *and* human dynamo *and* spitfire <all nonformal>; **eager beaver** <nonformal>; take-charge guy <nonformal>
ADJS 2 **enterprising, aggressive, dynamic,** proactive, driving, forceful, **pushing,** pushful, **pushy, up-and-coming, go-ahead** *and* **hustling** <both nonformal>

activity NOUNS 1 **action,** activeness; **movement,** motion, **stir; proceedings, doings, goings-on**
2 **occupation, work,** business, **function,** enterprise, undertaking, **work,**

affairs, labor; thing *and* bag <both nonformal>

actor NOUNS **actress, player,** stage player *or* performer, playactor, histrion, histrio, thespian, theatrical <nonformal>, trouper; mummer, pantomime, pantomimist; monologist, diseur, diseuse, reciter; mime, mimer, mimic; character actor *or* actress; **villain,** antagonist, **bad guy** *or* **heavy** *or* black hat <all nonformal>; juvenile, ingenue; soubrette; straight man; matinee idol <nonformal>; romantic lead

actual ADJS **real,** factual, veritable, for real <nonformal>, de facto, simple, sober, **hard; self-evident,** axiomatic; accepted, conceded, stipulated, given; admitted, well-known, **established, inescapable, indisputable, undeniable; demonstrable,** provable; empirical, **objective,** historical

actuality NOUNS **fact, reality**, the real world; the true, ultimate truth; eternal verities; truthfulness, veracity; **the present,** presentness, present time, the here and now; **now,** the present juncture *or* occasion, the present hour *or* moment, this instant *or* second *or* moment

actually ADVS **truly, really, in truth,** in good *or* very truth, historically, objectively, impersonally, rigorously, strictly, strictly speaking, unquestionably, without question, **in reality, in fact,** factually, technically, in point of fact, as a matter of fact

acute ADJS 1 **painful;** hurtful, **hurting,** distressing, afflictive; **sharp,** piercing, stabbing, shooting, stinging, biting, gnawing; **poignant,** pungent, **severe,** cruel, harsh, grave, hard; **agonizing, excruciating,** martyrizing, **harrowing, cutting,** knifelike; sharp as a razor *or* needle *or* tack

sharp as a two-edged sword
BIBLE

2 **sagacious, astute,** longheaded, argute; **understanding, discerning,** penetrating, incisive, trenchant, cogent, piercing; **perspicacious,** perspicuous; **perceptive, percipient,** apperceptive, appercipient
3 **urgent, imperative,** imperious, **compelling, pressing,** high-priority, high-pressure, crying, clamorous, insistent, exigent; crucial, critical, pivotal

adamant ADJS **unyielding, unbending, inflexible, hard, hard-line,** inelastic, impliable, ungiving, **firm, stiff, rigid,** rigorous, stuffy; rock-ribbed, rock-hard, rock-like; adamantine; unmoved, unaffected; iron, cast-iron, flinty, steely

adapt VERBS **accustom, habituate,** wont; **condition,** season, **train;** familiarize, naturalize <old>, break in <nonformal>, orient, orientate; acclimatize, acclimate; inure, harden, case harden; adjust, accommodate

adaptable ADJS **versatile, ambidextrous,** two-handed, **all around** <nonformal>, broad-gauge, **well-rounded, many-sided,** generally capable; **pliant, pliable, flexible,** flexile, flexuous, **plastic, elastic**, **ductile,** sequacious *or* facile <both old>, tractile, **tractable, yielding,** giving, bending; **malleable,** moldable

add VERBS 1 **combine, unite, unify,** couple, link, yoke, yoke together; **incorporate, amalgamate, consolidate,** assimilate, **integrate,** solidify, coalesce, compound, put *or* lump together, roll into one, come together, make one, unitize
2 **calculate, compute, estimate, reckon, figure,** reckon at, put at, cipher, cast, tally, score

addict NOUNS 1 **drug addict, narcotics addict, user, drug user,** drug abuser, junkie *and* head *and* druggy *and* doper *and* toker *and* fiend *and* freak *and* space cadet <all nonformal>; cocaine user, cokie *and* coke head *and* crackhead *and* sniffer *and* snow drifter *and* flaky <all nonformal>
2 **enthusiast, zealot,** infatuate, energumen, rhapsodist; faddist; **fanatic; devotee,** votary, aficionada, aficionado, **fancier**

addiction NOUNS **substance abuse, drug abuse,** narcotics abuse, drug use, glue-sniffing, solvent abuse; **addictedness, drug addiction,** narcotic addiction, drug habit, drug habituation, drug dependence, physical addiction *or* dependence, psychological addiction *or* dependence, jones *and* monkey on one's back *and* Mighty Joe Young <all nonformal>

addition NOUNS accession, annexation, affixation, suffixation, prefixation, agglutination, attachment, junction, **joining**, adjunction, uniting; **increase**; **augmentation, supplementation, complementation,** reinforcement

additional ADJS **supplementary, supplemental; extra,** plus, further, farther, fresh, **more,** new, **other**; **auxiliary,** ancillary, supernumerary, contributory, **accessory,** collateral

addled ADJS **muddled,** in a muddle; fuddled <nonformal>, **befuddled;** muddleheaded, fuddlebrained <nonformal>; adrift, at sea, foggy, fogged, in a fog, hazy, muzzy <nonformal>, misted, misty, cloudy, beclouded

address NOUNS 1 **remark, statement,** earful *and* crack *and* one's two cents' worth <all nonformal>, **word,** say, **saying, utterance, observation, reflection, expression; assertion,** averment, allegation, affirmation, pronouncement, position, dictum
2 **speech,** speeching, speechification <nonformal>, **talk, oration,** declamation, harangue; public speech *or* address, formal speech, set speech, prepared speech *or* text; **tirade,** screed, **diatribe,** jeremiad, philippic, invective
VERBS 3 **speak to, talk to,** bespeak, beg the ear of; **appeal to,** invoke; apostrophize; **approach; buttonhole,** take by the button *or* lapel; take aside, talk to in private, closet oneself with; **greet, hail, accost; salute,** make one's salutations
4 **make a speech, give a talk, deliver an address,** speechify <nonformal>, **speak, talk, discourse;** stump <nonformal>, go on *or* take the stump; platform, soapbox; take the floor

add up VERBS 1 **sum up,** sum, summate, say it all <nonformal>; **figure up,** cipher up, reckon up, **count up,** foot up, cast up, score up, **tally up**
2 **be right, be correct,** be just right, get it straight; **hit the nail on the head,** hit it on the nose *or* on the money *and* say a mouthful <all nonformal>, hit the bull's-eye, score a bull's-eye

adept NOUNS 1 **expert; artist, craftsman,** artisan, skilled workman, journeyman; technician; seasoned *or* experienced hand; shark *or* sharp *or* sharpy *and* no slouch *and* tough act to follow <all nonformal>
ADJS 2 **skillful, good,** goodish, excellent, **expert, proficient; dexterous,** callid <old>, **adroit, deft, coordinated,** well-coordinated, **apt,** no mean, **handy;** quick, ready; **clever,** cute *and* slick *and* slick as a whistle <all nonformal>, neat, clean

adequate ADJS 1 **satisfactory, satisfying; sufficient**, sufficing, **enough,** commensurate, proportionate, ample, equal to
2 **tolerable, goodish, fair, fairish,** moderate, tidy <nonformal>, **decent,** respectable, presentable, good enough, **pretty good, not bad,** not amiss, not half bad, not so bad, **satisfactory, all right,** OK *or* okay <nonformal>; **acceptable,** admissible, **passable,** workmanlike

adhere VERBS 1 **join, connect, unite, meet,** meet up, link up, merge, converge, **come together;** knit, grow together; cohere, hang *or* hold together
2 **stick, cling,** cleave, hold; **persist,** stay, stay put <nonformal>; cling to, freeze to <nonformal>; hang on, hold on; take hold of, clasp, grasp, hug, embrace, clinch; **stick together**

adhesive NOUNS 1 **fastening, binding,** bonding, gluing, sticking, tying, lashing, splicing, knotting, linking, trussing, girding, hooking, clasping, zipping, buckling, buttoning
ADJS 2 **viscous, viscid,** viscose, slabby; **sticky, tacky,** tenacious, clingy, clinging, tough; gluey, gluelike, **gummy, syrupy;** treacly <Brit>; mucilaginous, clammy, slimy, slithery; gooey *and* gunky *and* gloppy *and* goopy *and* gooky <all nonformal>

adjacent ADJS **next,** immediate, contiguous, **adjoining, abutting; neighboring,** neighbor; **juxtaposed,** juxtapositional; **bordering,** conterminous *or* coterminous, connecting

adjoin VERBS 1 **connect,** butt, **abut,** abut on *or* upon, be contiguous, be in contact; **neighbor,** border, **border on** *or* **upon,** verge on *or* upon; lie by, stand by
2 **border, edge, bound, rim, skirt, hem, hem in, ringe,** befringe, lap, list, margin, marge, marginate, march, verge, line, side

adjoining ADJS **adjacent,** contiguous, **abutting; neighboring; juxtaposed,** juxtapositional; **bordering,** connecting

adjourn VERBS **postpone, delay, defer, put off,** give one a rain check <nonformal>, shift off, hold off *or* up <nonformal>, prorogue, put on hold *or* ice *or* the back burner <all nonformal>, reserve, waive, **suspend,** hang up, stay, hang fire

adjunct NOUNS 1 **addition,** increase, **increment,** augmentation, supplemen-

tation, complementation, *additum* <L>, additament, additory, addendum, addenda <pl>, accession, fixture; **appendage,** appendant, pendant, appanage, coda
2 **component, constituent, ingredient,** integrant, makings *and* fixings <both nonformal>, **element, factor, part,** player, module, part and parcel; appurtenance
ADJS 3 **added,** affixed, add-on, **attached,** annexed, appended, appendant; adjoined, conjoined, subjoined

adjust VERBS 1 **reconcile, bring to terms, bring together,** reunite, heal the breach; bring about a détente; **harmonize,** restore harmony, put in tune; **iron** *or* **sort out,** settle, compose, accommodate, arrange matters, settle differences, resolve, compromise; **patch things up**
2 **modify;** adapt; modulate, accommodate, fine-tune, fit, **qualify; vary, diversify; convert, renew, recast, revamp** <nonformal>, change over, exchange, **revive;** remake, reshape, re-create, redesign, **rebuild,** reconstruct, restructure

adjustable ADJS 1 **conformable, adaptable,** adaptive; **compliant,** pliant, complaisant, malleable, flexible, plastic, acquiescent, unmurmuring, other-directed, submissive, tractable, obedient
2 **changeable, alterable,** alterative, modifiable; mutable, permutable, impermanent, transient, **transitory; variable,** checkered, ever-changing, many-sided, kaleidoscopic

adjusted ADJS **used to; conditioned,** trained, seasoned; experienced, **familiarized,** broken-in, run-in <nonformal>, oriented, orientated; acclimated, acclimatized; **fitted, adapted, suited; qualified, fit, competent, able, capable,** proficient; checked out <nonformal>; well-qualified, well-fitted, well-suited

adjustment NOUNS accommodation, resolution, composition of differences, compromise, arrangement, settlement; **alteration, modification; realignment, adaptation,** accommodation, fitting

ad lib NOUNS 1 **improvisation, extemporization,** improvision, improvising, extempore <old>, **impromptu, ad-lib,** ad-libbing *and* playing by ear <both nonformal>; temporary measure *or* arrangement, **stopgap, makeshift**
ADVS 2 **extemporaneously, extemporarily,** extempore, *à l'improviste* <Fr>, **impromptu, offhand,** by ear, off the top of one's head *and* off the cuff <both nonformal>

ad-lib VERBS 1 **improvise, extemporize,** improvisate, improv *and* tapdance *and* talk off the top of one's head <all nonformal>, speak off the cuff, think on one's feet, make it up as one goes along, play it by ear <nonformal>, throw away *or* depart from the prepared text, throw away the speech, scrap the plan, **do offhand,** wing it <nonformal>, vamp, fake <nonformal>, play by ear <nonformal>
ADJS 2 **extemporaneous, extemporary,** extempore, **impromptu,** unrehearsed, **improvised,** improvisatory, improvisatorial, improviso, *improvisé* <Fr>; *ad libitum* <L>; **ad-hoc,** stopgap, makeshift, jury-rigged; **offhand,** off the top of one's head *and* off-the-cuff <both nonformal>, **spur-of-the-moment**

administer VERBS 1 **govern, regulate; wield authority; command, head, lead,** be master, be at the head of, **preside over,** chair; **direct, manage, supervise**
2 **bestow, confer, award, allot, render,** bestow on; **grant,** accord, **allow,** vouchsafe, yield, afford, make available; **tender,** proffer, offer, extend, come up with <nonformal>; **issue, dispense;** serve, help to; **distribute;** deal, dole, mete; **give out, deal out, dole out, mete out, hand** *or* dish out <nonformal>, fork *or* shell out <nonformal>

administration NOUNS **governance, authority, jurisdiction, control, command, power, rule, reign,** regnancy, **dominion, sovereignty,** empire, empery, raj <India>, imperium, **swa;** direction, management, dispensation, disposition, oversight, **supervision**

administrator NOUNS **director,** *directeur* <Fr>, director general, **governor,** rector, **manager,** intendant, **conductor**

admirable ADJS **endearing, lovable, likable, adorable, lovely,** lovesome, sweet, winning, winsome; **charming; praiseworthy,** worthy, **commendable,** estimable, **laudable,** meritorious, creditable; exemplary, model, unexceptionable

admire VERBS 1 **respect,** entertain respect for, accord respect to, **regard, esteem,** hold in esteem *or* consideration, favor, think much of, think highly of, have *or* hold a high opinion of; think well of, take kindly to; **sanction, accept;** endorse, bless, sign off on <nonformal>, OK

admirer NOUNS 1 **enthusiast, zealot,** infatuate, energumen, rhapsodist; **fanatic; devotee,** votary, aficionada, aficionado, **fancier, follower; disciple,** worshiper, idolizer, idolater
2 infatuate, **suitor, wooer,** pursuer, follower; **flirt,** coquette

admission NOUNS 1 admittance, acceptance; **installation,** installment, inauguration, initiation; baptism, investiture, ordination; enrollment, induction
2 **acknowledgment, admission,** avowal, self-admission, self-concession, self-avowal, owning, owning up *and* coming clean <both nonformal>, unbosoming, unburdening oneself, getting a load off one's mind <nonformal>, fessing up <nonformal>, making a clean breast, baring one's breast

admit VERBS 1 **take in; let in,** intromit, give entrance *or* admittance to; **welcome,** bid welcome, give a royal welcome, roll out the red carpet
2 **acknowledge,** tell all, avow, concede, grant, **own, own up** <nonformal>, let on, implicate *or* incriminate oneself, come clean <nonformal>; spill *and* spill it *and* spill one's guts <all nonformal>; **tell the truth,** tell all, admit everything, let it all hang out <nonformal>
3 **permit, allow, let,** give permission, give leave, make possible; **allow** *or* **permit of;** give *or* leave room for, open the door to; consent; say *or* give the word <nonformal>

admonish VERBS **warn, caution, advise; give warning,** give fair warning, utter a caveat, address a warning to, put a flea in one's ear <nonformal>, have a word with one, say a word to the wise; tip *and* tip off <both nonformal>

ado NOUNS **hubbub, Babel, tumult,** turmoil, **uproar, racket,** riot, **disturbance, rumpus** <nonformal>, ruckus *and* ruction <both nonformal>, commotion, **fracas, hassle,** shindy <nonformal>, rampage; to-do <nonformal>, trouble, bother, pother, dustup <Brit nonformal>, stir <nonformal>, **fuss,** brouhaha, foofaraw <nonformal>

adolescent NOUNS 1 **youth, juvenile,** youngling, young'un <nonformal>; **stripling,** slip, sprig, sapling; fledgling; hopeful, young hopeful; **teenager,** teener, teenybopper <nonformal>
ADJS 2 **immature, unripe,** underripe, unripened, impubic, **raw, green,** callow, wet behind the ears, unseasoned, unmellowed; half-grown, juvenile, puerile; half-baked <nonformal>; half-cocked *and* at half cock <both nonformal>

adopt VERBS **appropriate, assume, usurp,** arrogate, accroach; **take possession of,** possess oneself of, take for oneself, arrogate to oneself, take up, **take over, help oneself to,** make use of, make one's own, make free with, dip one's hands into

adorable ADJS **desirable,** sought-after, much sought-after, to be desired, **much to be desired; enviable,** worth having; **likable, pleasing,** after one's own heart; **attractive,** taking, winning, sexy <nonformal>, dishy <Brit nonformal>, **seductive, provocative,** tantalizing, exciting; appetizing, tempting, toothsome, mouth-watering; **lovable**

adore VERBS **cherish, hold dear,** hold in one's heart *or* affections, think much *or* the world of, prize, treasure; **admire, regard,** esteem, revere; **appreciate, value,** prize; **revere, reverence,** hold in reverence, **venerate, honor, look up to, defer to, bow to,** exalt, put on a pedestal, worship the ground one walks on

adorn VERBS **decorate, dress, trim, garnish,** array, **deck,** bedeck, dizen <old>, bedizen; prettify, **beautify; embellish, furbish,** embroider, enrich, grace, set off *or* out, paint, color, blazon, emblazon, paint in glowing colors; **spruce up** *and* gussy up *and* doll up *and* fix up <all nonformal>, **primp up,** prink up, prank up, trick up *or* out, deck out

adrift ADJS 1 **unanchored,** afloat, floating, free, free-floating; **unfastened, unbound,** uncaught, unfixed, **undone, loose, free,** loosened, unloosened, clear
2 **bewildered, dismayed,** distracted, distraught, abashed, **disconcerted, embarrassed,** discomposed, **put-out, disturbed, upset,** perturbed, **bothered,** all hot and bothered <nonformal>
ADVS 3 **separately,** severally, piecemeal, one by one; **apart,** asunder, **in two,** in twain; apart from, away from, aside from; abstractly, in the abstract, objectively, impersonally

adult NOUNS 1 **grownup,** mature man *or* woman, grown man *or* woman, big boy *and* big girl <both nonformal>; *legalis homo* <L>
ADJS 2 **mature, of age,** grown, **grown-up;** old enough to know better; **marriageable,** of marriageable age, nubile

adulterate VERBS **corrupt,** contaminate, **debase,** denaturalize, pollute, denature, bastardize, **tamper with,** doctor *and* doctor up <both nonformal>

adulterer NOUNS **cheater, fornicator; adulteress,** fornicatress, fornicatrix

adulterous ADJS freeloving; illicit, extramarital, premarital; incestuous

adultery NOUNS **love affair, affair,** affair of the heart, **amour, romance,** something between, thing <nonformal>, liaison, entanglement, intrigue; **dalliance,** amorous play, hanky-panky, lollygagging <nonformal>; adulterous affair, **unfaithfulness, infidelity, cuckoldry**

advance NOUNS 1 advancement; upward mobility; **promotion, furtherance,** preferment; **rise,** ascent, **lift, uplift,** uptick <nonformal>, upswing, uptrend, upbeat; **enhancement, enrichment; restoration,** revival, recovery
2 **offer,** offering, proffer, presentation, **bid,** submission; **overture,** approach, invitation; hesitant *or* tentative *or* preliminary approach, feeling-out, **feeler** <nonformal>
VERBS 3 **progress, proceed, go,** go *or* move forward, step forward, go on, **go ahead,** go along, push ahead, pass on *or* along; move, travel; go fast; **make progress,** come on, **get along,** come along <nonformal>, **get ahead;** further oneself
4 **improve, better,** change for the better, make an improvement; transform, transfigure; improve upon, refine upon, **mend, amend,** emend; meliorate, **ameliorate; promote,** foster, favor, nurture, forward, bring forward
5 **propose, submit,** prefer; **suggest,** recommend, commend to attention, **propound, pose, put forward,** bring forward, put *or* set forth, put it to, put *or* set *or* lay *or* bring before, dish up *and* come out *or* up with <both nonformal>; put a bee in one's bonnet, put ideas into one's head
6 **lend, loan,** accommodate with

advanced ADJS **contemporary, present-day,** present-time, latter-day, space-age, neoteric, now <nonformal>, **newfashioned,** fashionable, modish, mod, *à la mode* <Fr>, **up-to-date, up-to-the-minute, in,** abreast of the times; **avant-garde**

advancement NOUNS **progress,** going, going forward; **furtherance,** furthering; **promotion, advance,** step-up *and* upping <both nonformal>, rise, elevation, upgrading, jump, step up, step up the ladder

advantage NOUNS 1 vantage, odds, leg up *and* inside track *and* pole position <all nonformal>; **upper hand,** whip hand; start, head *or* flying *or* running start; **edge,** bulge *and* jump *and* drop <all nonformal>
2 **benefit, use, service, avail, profit,** point, percentage *and* mileage <all nonformal>, what's in it for one <nonformal>, convenience

advantageous ADJS **helpful,** of help; **to one's advantage** *or* **profit, profitable,** remuneratory, beneficial; **gainful,** productive, **profitable, remunerative, lucrative,** fat, **paying,** worthwhile

advent NOUNS **coming,** forthcoming; flowing toward, afflux, affluxion; imminence

adventure NOUNS **exploit, feat, deed, enterprise, achievement,** gest, **bold stroke,** heroic act *or* deed; aristeia; **happening,** hap, happenstance; **fortuity, accident,** casualty, hazard; contingent, contingency

adventurer NOUNS **daredevil, madcap,** harumscarum *and* fire-eater <both nonformal>; adventuress, adventurist; brazen-face

adversary NOUNS 1 **enemy, foe,** foeman, **antagonist;** bitter enemy; sworn enemy; open enemy; public enemy; archenemy, devil; **bane,** bête noire
ADJS 2 **oppositional, opponent, opposing, opposed;** contra, confrontational, confrontive; at odds, at loggerheads; **adverse,** adversarial, adversative, oppugnant, antithetic, antithetical, repugnant, **set** *or* **dead set against**

adverse ADJS **untoward, detrimental, unfavorable;** sinister; hostile, antagonistic, inimical; contrary, counter, counteractive, conflicting, opposing, opposed, opposite, in opposition

adversity NOUNS adverse circumstances, difficulties, hard knocks *and* rough going <both nonformal>, **hardship,**

trouble, troubles, **rigor,** vicissitude, care, stress, pressure, stress of life; hard case *or* plight, **hard life,** dog's life, vale of tears; wretched *or* miserable *or* hard *or* unhappy lot, tough *or* hard row to hoe <nonformal>

sea of troubles
SHAKESPEARE

advertise VERBS **promote,** build up, cry up, sell, puff <nonformal>, **boost** <nonformal>, **plug** <nonformal>, **ballyhoo** <nonformal>; **publicize,** give publicity; go public with <nonformal>; bring *or* drag into the limelight, throw the spotlight on <nonformal>

advice NOUNS **counsel, recommendation, suggestion; direction, instruction,** guidance, briefing; **exhortation,** hortation <old>, enjoinder, expostulation, remonstrance; **tip** *and* tip-off *and* **pointer** <all nonformal>, clue, cue; steer <nonformal>; whisper, passing word, **word to the wise,** word in the ear, bug in the ear <nonformal>, bee in the bonnet <nonformal>

advisable ADJS **expedient, desirable,** to be desired, much to be desired, **politic,** recommendable; **appropriate, meet, fit, fitting,** befitting, **right, proper,** good, **becoming,** seemly, likely, congruous, **suitable,** sortable, feasible, doable, swingable <nonformal>, **convenient,** happy, heaven-sent, felicitous

advise VERBS **counsel, recommend, suggest, advocate,** propose, submit; **instruct,** coach, guide, direct, brief; prescribe; weigh in with advice <nonformal>, give a piece of advice, give a hint *or* broad hint, hint at, intimate, insinuate, put a flea in one's ear <nonformal>, have a word with one, speak words of wisdom

adviser NOUNS **counsel, counselor, consultant,** professional consultant, expert, maven <nonformal>, boffin <Brit nonformal>; instructor, guide, **mentor,** nestor, orienter; confidant, personal adviser; Polonius <Shakespeare>, preceptist

advisory ADJS **consultative,** consultatory; directive, instructive; **admonitory,** monitory, monitorial, cautionary, **warning**

advocate NOUNS 1 **lawyer, attorney, attorney-at-law,** barrister, barrister-at-law, **counselor,** counselor-at-law, **counsel,** legal counsel *or* counselor, legal adviser, legal expert, **solicitor;** member of the bar, legal practitioner, officer of the court; smart lawyer, pettifogger, Philadelphia lawyer; **defender,** pleader; successful advocate *or* defender, proponent, **champion**
VERBS 2 **urge, press, push,** work on <nonformal>, twist one's arm <nonformal>; **sell,** flog <Brit>; **insist,** push for, not take no for an answer, **importune, nag, pressure, high-pressure,** bring pressure to bear upon, throw one's weight around, jawbone *and* build a fire under <both nonformal>, talk round *or* around; **encourage,** hearten, embolden, comfort <old>; hold a brief for <nonformal>, countenance, keep in countenance, **endorse**

aerate VERBS **air,** air out, **ventilate,** cross-ventilate, wind, refresh, freshen

aerosol NOUNS **solution;** decoction, infusion, mixture; chemical solution; lixivium, leach, leachate; **suspension,** colloidal suspension; atomizer, spray

aesthete NOUNS person of taste, lover of beauty

aesthetic ADJS **tasteful, in good taste,** in the best taste; excellent, of quality, of the best, of the first water; artistic, pleasing, well-chosen, choice, of choice; pure, chaste; classic *or* classical, Attic, restrained, understated, unobtrusive, quiet, subdued, simple, unaffected

aesthetics NOUNS **aesthetic** *or* **artistic taste,** virtuosity, virtu, **expertise,** expertism, connoisseurship; aesthetic *or* artistic criticism, aesthetic *or* artistic evaluation, aesthetic *or* artistic analysis, aesthetic *or* artistic interpretation

afar ADVS **far, far off,** far away, afar off, a long way off, a good ways off <nonformal>, a long cry to, as far as the eye can see, out of sight

over the hills and far away
JOHN GAY

affable ADJS 1 **good-natured,** well-natured, **good-humored, good-tempered,** bonhomous, **sweet, sweet-tempered; courteous, polite, civil, urbane, gracious,** graceful, agreeable, fair; complaisant; obliging, accommodating; **thoughtful, considerate,** tactful, solicitous
2 **sociable, social,** social-minded, fit for

society, fond of society, **gregarious; companionable,** companionate, compatible, *gemütlich* <Ger>, **congenial**

affair NOUNS 1 **concern, matter,** thing, concernment, interest, **business,** job <nonformal>, **transaction,** proceeding; cause célèbre, matter of moment
2 **social gathering, social,** sociable, social affair, social hour, hospitality hour, affair, gathering, get-together <nonformal>; **reception,** at home, salon, levee, soiree; matinee; reunion, family reunion; wake
3 **love affair, romance,** romantic tie *or* bond, liaison, entanglement, intrigue; **dalliance,** amorous play, the love game, hanky-panky; illicit *or* unlawful love, adulterous affair, adultery, unfaithfulness, infidelity, cuckoldry

affect NOUNS 1 **feeling, emotion, sentiment,** affection, affections; affective faculty, affectivity; emotional charge, cathexis
VERBS 2 **touch, move, stir; melt, soften,** melt the heart, choke one up, give one a lump in the throat; **penetrate,** pierce, go through one, go deep; touch a chord, **touch a sympathetic chord, touch one's heart,** tug at the heart *or* heartstrings
3 **impress, strike, hit,** smite, rock; **make an impression, get to one** <nonformal>; make a dent in, make an impact upon, sink in <nonformal>, strike home; **influence,** make oneself felt, weigh with, **sway,** bias, bend, incline, dispose, predispose, **move,** prompt, lead
4 **assume, put on,** assume *or* put on airs, wear, **pretend, simulate, counterfeit, sham, fake** <nonformal>, **feign,** make out like <nonformal>, make a show of, play, playact <nonformal>, act *or* play a part, put up a front <nonformal>, dramatize

affectation NOUNS **affectedness; pretension, pretense, airs,** putting on airs, put-on <nonformal>; **show, false show,** mere show; front, false front <nonformal>, **facade,** mere facade, **image,** public image; **pretentiousness, mannerism,** posiness <Brit>, manneredness, artifice, artfulness, **artificiality,** unnaturalness

affection NOUNS **friendship, friendliness; amicability,** amicableness, amity, peaceableness, unhostility; **amiability,** amiableness, **congeniality; attachment, devotion, fondness,** sentiment, warm feeling, soft spot in one's heart, weakness <nonformal>, like, **liking,** fancy, shine <nonformal>; **partiality, predilection; passion,** tender feeling *or* passion, **ardor,** ardency, fervor, heart, flame

affectionate ADJS **kind, kindly, benign,** benignant; good as gold, **good, nice, decent; gracious; kindhearted, warm, warmhearted,** softhearted, tenderhearted, tender, loving

affiliate NOUNS 1 **branch, organ, division,** wing, arm, offshoot; **chapter,** lodge, post; chapel; **local;** branch office
2 **member,** insider, initiate, one of us, cardholder, card-carrier, card-carrying member
VERBS 3 **join,** join up <nonformal>, **enter, go into,** come into, get into, make oneself part of, swell the ranks of; **enlist, enroll, sign up** *or* **on** <nonformal>, take up membership, take out membership
4 band, league, ally, **combine, unite,** fuse, merge, coalesce, amalgamate, federate, confederate, consolidate; hook up *and* tie up *and* tie in <all nonformal>; **join together,** club together, league together, band together

affiliation NOUNS **alliance, allying, alignment, association,** consociation, combination, **union,** unification, **coalition,** fusion, merger, coalescence, coadunation, amalgamation, **league, federation, confederation,** confederacy, consolidation, incorporation, inclusion, integration; hookup *and* tie-up *and* tie-in <all nonformal>

affinity NOUNS 1 **inclination, penchant, partiality, fancy, favor, predilection, preference,** propensity, proclivity, **leaning, bent,** turn, tilt, bias; special affinity, mutual affinity
2 **kinship,** family resemblance *or* likeness, generic *or* genetic resemblance

affirm VERBS 1 **assert,** asseverate, **aver,** protest, avow, **declare,** say loud and clear, sound off <nonformal>, have one's say, speak one's piece *or* one's mind, speak up *or* out, **state,** put in one's two-cents worth <nonformal>; **allege,** profess
2 **ratify, endorse,** sign off on, second, support, **certify, confirm, validate, authenticate, accept,** give the nod *or*

the green light *or* the go-ahead *or* the OK <all nonformal>, give a nod of assent, give one's imprimatur, permit, give permission, **approve**

affirmative NOUNS 1 **yes,** yea, aye, amen; nod, nod of assent; thumbs-up; **affirmativeness,** affirmative attitude, yea-saying
ADJS 2 affirming, affirmatory, certifying, certificatory; **assertive, declarative,** declaratory; **consenting, assenting,** amenable, persuaded, approving, agreeing, favorable, accordant; sanctioning, endorsing, ratifying; **acquiescent, compliant,** submissive

afflict VERBS **sicken, indispose; weaken, enfeeble,** enervate, reduce, debilitate, devitalize; **invalid,** incapacitate, **disable;** lay up; **distress, afflict, trouble,** burden, give one a tough row to hoe, **perturb, disquiet, discomfort, agitate, upset; pain,** give *or* inflict pain, **hurt, wound; irritate, inflame,** harshen, exacerbate, intensify

affliction NOUNS 1 **disease, illness, sickness, malady, ailment, indisposition, disorder,** complaint, morbidity, affection, **infirmity; disability,** defect, handicap
2 **adversity,** adverse circumstances, difficulties, hard knocks *and* rough going <both nonformal>, **hardship, trouble,** troubles, **rigor,** vicissitude, care, stress, pressure, stress of life

affluent ADJS **wealthy, rich, moneyed** *or* **monied,** in funds, **well-to-do, well-off, well-situated, prosperous,** comfortable, provided for, well provided for, fat, **flush,** flush with *or* of money, abounding in riches, worth a great deal, rich as Croesus

afford VERBS 1 **provide, supply,** find, dish up *and* rustle up <both nonformal>, **furnish;** invest, endow, fund, subsidize; donate, give, contribute, kick in <nonformal>, yield, present; make available
2 **have money,** command money, **be loaded** *and* have deep pockets <both nonformal>, have the wherewithal, have means, have independent means

affordable ADJS **cheap, inexpensive,** unexpensive, **low, low-priced,** frugal, reasonable, sensible, manageable, modest, moderate, to fit the pocketbook, budget, easy, economy, economic, economical; within means, within reach *or* easy reach

affront NOUNS **provocation, offense;** *casus belli* <L>, raw nerve, the quick, where one lives; **indignity, injury,** humiliation; scurrility, contempt, contumely, despite, flout, flouting, mockery, jeering, jeer, mock, scoff, gibe, taunt, brickbat <nonformal>; **insult, aspersion,** slap *or* kick in the face, left-handed *or* backhanded compliment, damning with faint praise; cut

head and front of one's offending
SHAKESPEARE

afire ADJS **fervent, fervid, passionate, impassioned,** intense, **ardent; hearty, cordial,** enthusiastic, exuberant, unrestrained, vigorous; keen, breathless, **excited; lively**

afraid ADJS fearful; **cowardly;** timid, timorous, overtimorous, overtimid, rabbity *and* mousy <both nonformal>; **fainthearted,** weakhearted, chicken-hearted, henhearted, pigeonhearted; white-livered *and* lily-livered *and* chicken-livered *and* milk-livered <all nonformal>; **yellow** *and* yellow-bellied *and* with a yellow streak <all nonformal>

afresh ADVS **newly,** freshly, **anew,** once more, from the ground up, from scratch <nonformal>, *ab ovo* <L>, *de novo* <L>, **again**

African American NOUNS **black man** *or* **woman, black,** colored person, person of color, Negro

aft ADJS 1 **rear,** rearward, **back,** backward, retrograde, **posterior,** postern, tail; after; **hind; hindmost,** rearmost
ADVS 2 **after;** abaft, baft, astern; aback

after ADJS 1 **subsequent, later,** after-the-fact, *post factum* and *ex post facto* <both L>, posterior, **following, succeeding,** successive, sequent, consecutive, attendant
ADVS 2 **subsequently, afterwards, later, next,** since; **thereafter,** thereon, thereupon, therewith, **then;** at a subsequent *or* later time, in the aftermath; *ex post facto* <L>; hard on the heels *or* on the heels

afterlife NOUNS **the hereafter,** the afterworld, the afterlife, life after death

aftermath NOUNS **sequel, follow-up,** sequelae; **consequence, effect,** result, resultant, **consequence,** consequent, sequent, sequence, sequel, sequela, sequelae; **upshot, outcome,** logical outcome, possible outcome

afternoon NOUNS 1 *post meridiem* <L> *or* **PM;** this afternoon, this PM <nonformal>
ADJS 2 postmeridian

afterthoughts NOUNS **change of mind;** second thoughts, better thoughts, mature judgment

afterwards ADVS **in the future, afterward** *or* afterwards, **later,** at a later time, after a time *or* while, anon; **by and by,** in the sweet by-and-by <nonformal>; **in the near** *or* **immediate future,** just around the corner, **imminently, soon, before long**

afterworld NOUNS **the hereafter,** the great hereafter, Paradise, Heaven, Elysian Fields, Happy Isles, the Land of Youth *or* Tir na n'Og, Valhalla; Hades, the Underworld, Hell, Gehenna; **the next world,** the world to come, life *or* world beyond the grave, the great beyond, the great unknown, **the grave,** home *or* abode *or* world of the dead

the good hereafter
WHITTIER

again ADVS 1 another time, **once more,** once again, over again, yet again, *encore, bis* <both Fr>; **anew,** afresh, freshly, newly
2 **additionally, in addition, also,** and then some, even more, more so, and also, and all <nonformal>, and so, **as well, too,** else, beside, **besides, to boot, not to mention, let alone, into the bargain**

against ADJS **disapproving,** unapproving, turned-off, **displeased, dissatisfied,** less than pleased, discontented, disgruntled

agape ADJS **astonished, amazed, surprised, astounded,** flabbergasted <nonformal>, **bewildered,** puzzled, confounded, **dumbfounded,** dumbstruck, staggered, overwhelmed, unable to believe one's senses *or* eyes; **in awe,** in awe of; spellbound, fascinated, captivated, beguiled, enthralled, enraptured, enchanted, entranced, bewitched, hypnotized, mesmerized, stupefied, lost in wonder *or* amazement

age NOUNS 1 years; time of life; **lifetime, life,** life's duration, life expectancy, lifespan, expectation of life, all the days of one's life; all one's born days *or* natural life <nonformal>

the days of our years
BIBLE

the measure of my days
BIBLE

2 **era, epoch**
VERBS 3 **grow old, get on** *or* **along in years,** be over the hill <nonformal>, turn gray *or* white; **decline,** wane, fade, fail, sink, waste away; **live to a ripe old age,** cheat the undertaker <nonformal>; be in one's dotage *or* second childhood

ageless ADJS **perpetual, everlasting,** everliving, permanent, perdurable, indestructible; **eternal,** sempiternal, **infinite;** dateless, timeless, immemorial; **endless,** unending, never-ending, without end, **interminable**

agency NOUNS 1 **instrumentality;** machinery, **mechanism,** modality; gadgetry <nonformal>; mediation, going between, intermediation, service; **expedient,** recourse, resort, device
2 **deputation; assignment,** consignment; **errand, task, office; responsibility,** purview, jurisdiction; **mission,** legation, embassy

agenda NOUNS **schedule** *or* program of operation, **order of the day,** things to be done; protocol; laundry list *and* wish list <both nonformal>

agent NOUNS 1 **intermediary,** link, **connecting link,** tie, connection, **go-between,** liaison; **instrument, tool, implement, appliance,** device; contrivance, lever, mechanism; **vehicle, organ;** medium, mediator, intermedium, intermediary, intermediate, interagent, liaison, go-between
2 **actor's agent,** playbroker, ten-percenter <nonformal>; **booking agent;** publicity man *or* agent

aggrandize VERBS **increase, enlarge, amplify, augment, extend,** maximize, **add to; expand, inflate; raise,** exalt, boost <nonformal>, hike *and* hike up *and* jack up *and* jump up <all nonformal>; **build, build up**

aggravate VERBS 1 **worsen,** make worse; **exacerbate,** embitter, sour; deteriorate; **intensify, heighten,** step up, sharpen, make acute *or* more acute, bring to a head, deepen,

increase, enhance, amplify, enlarge, magnify, build up; augment; rub salt in the wound, twist the knife, add insult to injury, pour oil on the fire, add fuel to the fire *or* flame
2 **vex, irk, annoy,** exasperate, provoke; **trouble, worry,** give one gray hair, plague, harass, bother, hassle

aggravating ADJS aggravative; **exasperating,** exasperative; **annoying, irritating**; provocative; contentious

aggravation NOUNS 1 **worsening; exacerbation,** embittering, embitterment, souring; deterioration; **intensification, heightening,** magnification, augmentation
2 **annoyance, vexation,** exasperation, *tracasserie* <Fr>; **nuisance, pest, bother,** botheration <nonformal>, public nuisance, **trouble, problem,** pain <nonformal>, difficulty, hot potato <nonformal>

aggregate NOUNS 1 **sum,** summation, **number, count;** account, cast, **score, reckoning, tally,** tale, the bottom line <nonformal>, **amount,** quantity; **whole, total**; box score <nonformal>
ADJS 2 **whole, total, entire,** gross, all; **inclusive,** all-inclusive, **exhaustive,** comprehensive, omnibus, all-embracing

aggression NOUNS **aggressiveness,** killer instinct, force, forcefulness, **pushiness, push, drive, hustle, go,** getup, get-up-and-get *or* **get-up-and-go** <both nonformal>, go-ahead, go-getting, go-to-itiveness <nonformal>

aggressive ADJS 1 **enterprising, dynamic,** activist, proactive, driving, forceful, **pushing,** pushful, **pushy, up-and-coming, go-ahead** *and* **hustling** <both nonformal>
2 **harsh,** rough, severe; **combative, contentious; belligerent, pugnacious, truculent, bellicose,** scrappy <nonformal>, full of fight; offensive; **antagonistic,** inimical; unfriendly; **quarrelsome**

aggressor NOUNS invader, raider; **assailant,** assailer, **attacker;** mugger <nonformal>

aghast ADJS **appalled, astounded; terrified,** terror-stricken; awestricken, awestruck; **horrified,** horror-stricken, horror-struck; frightened out of one's wits *or* mind, **scared to death, scared stiff** *or* **shitless** *or* spitless <nonformal>; unnerved, unstrung, unmanned, undone, **cowed,** awed, **intimidated; stunned, petrified, stupefied,** white as a sheet, ashen, pallid

agile ADJS **nimble, spry,** sprightly, fleet, pert, graceful, nimble-footed, light-footed, sure-footed

aging NOUNS 1 senescence, **maturation, development,** growth, ripening, blooming, blossoming, flourishing; **mellowing,** seasoning, tempering
ADJS 2 growing old, senescent, **getting on** *or* **along,** getting on *or* along *or* up in years, not as young as one used to be, long in the tooth; **declining,** wasting

agitated ADJS **perturbed, disturbed, troubled, disquieted, upset,** antsy <nonformal>, unsettled, **discomposed, flustered,** ruffled, **shaken**; **jittery** <nonformal>, **jumpy,** twittery, skittish, skittery, **agitated;** shaking, trembling, shook up *and* all shook up <both nonformal>

agitation NOUNS **perturbation,** ferment, **turbulence, turmoil,** tumult, uproar, **commotion,** disturbance, ado, *brouhaha* <Fr>

agitator NOUNS **fomenter, instigator, inciter,** exciter; **provoker,** *provocateur* <Fr>, *agent provocateur* <Fr>, catalyst; agitprop; **rabble-rouser,** firebrand, incendiary

agnostic NOUNS 1 **skeptic, doubter, doubting Thomas,** scoffer
ADJS 2 **skeptical, doubtful, dubious, incredulous,** from Missouri <nonformal>; **distrustful, mistrustful, untrustful,** mistrusting, untrusting

ago ADJS 1 **past, gone,** by, **gone-by, bygone,** departed, passed, passed away, elapsed, lapsed, vanished, faded, no more, irrecoverable, never to return, not coming back
ADVS 2 **since,** gone by; back, back when; backward, to *or* into the past; **retrospectively,** reminiscently, retroactively

agog ADJS **eager, anxious,** all agog; **avid, keen,** forward, prompt, quick, ready, ready and willing, alacritous, bursting to, dying to, raring to; impatient

agonize VERBS excruciate, **torture, torment,** desolate

agony NOUNS **anguish, torment, torture,** exquisite torment *or* torture, the rack, excruciation, crucifixion, martyrdom, martyrization, excruciating *or* agonizing *or* atrocious pain

agree VERBS **concur, accord,** coincide, **agree with,** agree in opinion; **see eye to**

eye, be at one with, be of one mind with, go with, **go along with,** fall *or* chime *or* strike in with, conform to, side with, join *or* identify oneself with

agreeable ADJS 1 **pleasant, pleasing, pleasureful, pleasurable;** fair, fair and pleasant, **enjoyable,** pleasure-giving; **likable, desirable,** to one's liking, to one's taste, to *or* after one's fancy, after one's own heart; genial, congenial, cordial, *gemütlich* <Ger>
2 **acceptable,** admissible, unobjectionable, unexceptionable, tenable, viable; **OK** *and* okay *and* all right <all nonformal>; **passable,** good enough
3 **willing, willinghearted, ready, game** <nonformal>; **disposed, inclined, minded, willed,** fain *and* prone <both old>; **well-disposed,** well-inclined, favorably inclined *or* disposed; predisposed; amenable, tractable, docile, pliant

agreement NOUNS 1 **accord**, accordance; **concord,** concordance; **harmony, cooperation**, peace, *rapport* <Fr>, concert, consort, **consonance,** unisonance, **unison,** union, chorus, oneness
2 **similarity, likeness,** alikeness, **sameness,** similitude; **resemblance,** semblance; **analogy, correspondence,** conformity, accordance, comparability, comparison, **parallelism, parity,** community, alliance

agree to VERBS 1 **assent,** give *or* yield assent, **acquiesce, consent**, **comply, accede, agree,** agree to *or* with, have no problem with; find it in one's heart; take kindly to *and* hold with <both nonformal>
2 **strike a bargain,** make a bargain, **make a deal,** put through a deal, shake hands, shake on it <nonformal>; **come to terms**

agree with VERBS 1 **concur, accord,** coincide, **agree,** agree in opinion; **see eye to eye, be at one with,** be of one mind with, go with, **go along with,** join *or* identify oneself with; cast in one's lot, fall in *or* into line, lend oneself to, play *or* go along, take kindly to; get on the bandwagon <nonformal>
2 **make for health,** conduce to health, **be good for**

agricultural ADJS **rustic, rural, country, provincial, farm, pastoral, bucolic,** Arcadian, **agrarian,** agrestic

agriculture NOUNS **farming,** husbandry; cultivation, culture, tillage, tilth

ahead ADJS 1 **front, frontal, anterior; full-face, full-frontal; fore, forward,** forehand; foremost, headmost; first, earliest, **pioneering, trail-blazing, advanced; leading,** up-front <nonformal>, **in front,** one-up, one jump *or* move ahead
2 **superior, greater,** better, finer; **higher,** upper, over, super, above; ascendant, in the ascendant, in ascendancy, coming <nonformal>
ADVS 3 **before,** out *or* up ahead, **in front,** in the front, in the lead, in the van, in advance, **in the forefront,** in the foreground; **to the fore,** to the front

aid NOUNS 1 **help, assistance, support, succor, relief, comfort,** ease, remedy; mutual help *or* assistance; **service, benefit**
VERBS 2 **help, assist,** comfort, abet <old>, **succor,** relieve, **ease,** doctor, remedy; be of some help, put one's oar in <nonformal>; do good, do a world of good, **benefit, avail**; **favor, befriend; give help,** render assistance, offer *or* proffer aid, come to the aid of, rush *or* fly to the assistance of, lend aid, **give** *or* **lend** *or* **bear a hand** *or* **helping hand,** stretch forth *or* hold out a helping hand

aide NOUNS **assistant, helper,** auxiliary, paraprofessional; **help, helpmate, helpmeet;** deputy, **agent**; **attendant, second,** acolyte

ail VERBS **feel ill,** feel under the weather, feel awful <nonformal>, feel something terrible, not feel like anything <nonformal>, look green about the gills <nonformal>

ailment NOUNS **disease, illness, sickness, malady, indisposition, disorder,** complaint, morbidity, *morbus* <L>, **affliction,** affection, **infirmity**

aim NOUNS 1 **direction,** directionality; **line,** direction line, line of direction, point, quarter, **way,** track, range, **bearing,** azimuth, compass reading, **heading, course**
2 **motive, reason, cause,** source, spring, mainspring; matter, score, consideration; end, end in view, telos, final cause
VERBS 3 **direct, point, turn, bend, train,** fix, set, determine; point to *or* at, hold on, fix on, sight on; take aim, aim at
4 **intend, purpose, plan,** purport, **mean,** think, **propose; resolve,** determine; project, **design,** destine; aim at,

take aim at, draw a bead on, set one's sights on, have designs on, go for, drive at, aspire to *or* after

aimless ADJS 1 **useless,** of no use, no go <nonformal>; meaningless, **purposeless,** of no purpose, **pointless,** feckless
2 **causeless,** designless, driftless, undirected, objectless, unmotivated, mindless; **haphazard, random,** stray, inexplicable, unaccountable, promiscuous, indiscriminate

air NOUNS 1 ether; ozone <nonformal>; thin air; **milieu, ambience, atmosphere, climate,** aura, spirit, feeling, feel, quality, color, sense
2 manner, manners, demeanor, mien, *maintien* <Fr>, **carriage, bearing,** port, poise, posture, guise, address, presence; tone, style, lifestyle
3 aria, **tune, melody,** line, melodic line, refrain, note, **song,** solo, lay, descant, lilt, **strain,** measure
VERBS 4 air out, **ventilate,** cross-ventilate, refresh, freshen; **aerate,** airify; oxygenate, oxygenize
5 **divulge, reveal, make known, tell,** breathe, utter, vent, ventilate, give vent to, **give out,** let get around, come out with; let in on *or* to, **confide,** confide to, let one's hair down <nonformal>, unbosom oneself, let into the secret
6 **discuss, debate, reason, deliberate,** deliberate upon, exchange views *or* opinions, talk, **talk over, hash over** <nonformal>, talk of *or* about, rap <nonformal>, comment upon, **consider, treat,** dissertate on, handle, deal with, take up, **go into, examine,** investigate, talk out, **analyze,** sift, **study,** canvass, review, ventilate, consider pro and con; **kick** *or* **knock around** <nonformal>

airing NOUNS 1 **walk,** ramble, amble, **hike, tramp,** traipse <nonformal>; **stroll,** saunter; **promenade;** *passeggiata* <Ital>; jaunt; **constitutional** <nonformal>, stretch; turn
2 **debate, deliberation,** exchange of views, canvassing, ventilation, review, **treatment, consideration,** investigation, **examination, study, analysis, forum,** open forum, town meeting

airless ADJS **stuffy,** breathless, breezeless, windless; **close, oppressive, stifling, suffocating;** ill-ventilated, unventilated, unvented

airlift VERBS ferry, **fly,** be airborne, wing, take wing, wing one's way, take *or* make a flight, take to the air, volitate

air out VERBS **ventilate,** cross-ventilate, refresh, air, freshen; **aerate**

airplane NOUNS aeroplane <Brit>, **aircraft, plane, ship,** fixed-wing aircraft, flying machine <old>, *avion* <Fr>; aerodyne, heavier-than-air craft

air pollution NOUNS atmospheric pollution, smog, **miasma, mephitis,** malaria <old>; effluvium, exhaust, exhaust gas

airport NOUNS **airdrome,** aerodrome <Brit>, drome, port, air harbor <Can>, aviation field, **landing field,** airship station; **air terminal, jetport; air base,** air station, naval air station; airpark; **heliport,** helidrome

airs NOUNS lofty airs, airs and graces, highfalutin *or* highfaluting ways <nonformal>, side; **pretensions,** vain pretensions; **show, false show,** mere show; front, false front <nonformal>, **facade,** mere facade, **image,** public image; artificiality, unnaturalness, insincerity

airship NOUNS **aerostat,** lighter-than-air craft; ship, dirigible balloon, **blimp** <nonformal>; rigid airship, semirigid airship; **dirigible,** zeppelin, Graf Zeppelin; gasbag, ballonet; **balloon,** *ballon* <Fr>

airsick NOUNS **nauseated, queasy,** squeamish, qualmish, qualmy; **sick to one's stomach**

airtight ADJS **close, tight, compact,** fast, shut fast, **snug,** staunch, firm; **sealed;** hermetically sealed; dustproof

airy ADJS 1 **lighthearted,** light, lightsome; **buoyant, jaunty,** perky, **debonair, carefree,** free and easy; **breezy**
2 **light,** unheavy, imponderous; **weightless; ethereal; volatile;** frothy, foamy, spumy, spumous, spumescent, bubbly, yeasty
3 **immaterial,** nonmaterial; **unsubstantial**, insubstantial, **intangible,** impalpable, imponderable; **incorporeal,** incorporate, incorporeous; **bodiless,** unembodied, **disembodied**

aisle NOUNS **alley, lane; channel, conduit;** opening, aperture; access

ajar ADJS half-open, cracked; **gaping, yawning,** agape, oscitant, slack-jawed, openmouthed

akimbo ADJS **angular;** cornered, **crooked, hooked, bent,** flexed, flexural; knee-shaped, geniculate, geniculated; crotched, furcate, furcal, forked; sharp-cornered, **sharp, pointed**

akin ADJS **related, kindred;** consanguineous *or* consanguinean *or* consanguineal, consanguine, by *or* of the blood; allied, affiliated, congeneric; intimately *or* closely related, remotely *or* distantly related

alarm NOUNS 1 **fear, fright,** affright; **scare, consternation, dismay; dread,** unholy dread, **awe; terror, horror,** horrification, mortal *or* abject fear
2 **warning, caution,** caveat, **admonition,** monition, admonishment; alarum, alarm signal *or* bell, **alert;** hue and cry
VERBS 3 **frighten,** fright, affright, funk <nonformal>, frighten *or* scare out of one's wits; **scare,** spook <nonformal>, scare one stiff *or* shitless *or* spitless <nonformal>, scare the life out of, scare the pants off of *and* scare the hell out of *and* scare the shit out of <all nonformal>

alarming ADJS 1 **frightening, frightful; fearful,** fearsome, fear-inspiring, nightmarish, hellish; **scary,** scaring, chilling; **startling,** disquieting, dismaying, disconcerting; **unnerving, daunting**
2 **dangerous,** dangersome <nonformal>, **perilous,** periculous, parlous, jeopardous, bad, ugly, serious, critical, explosive, attended *or* beset *or* fraught with danger

albino NOUNS **whiteness, white, whitishness;** albescence; **lightness, fairness;** paleness; silveriness; snowiness, frostiness; chalkiness; pearliness

album NOUNS photograph album; scrapbook; **compilation,** omnibus; symposium; collection, collectanea, miscellany; **miscellanea,** analects; chrestomathy, delectus

alchemy NOUNS **sorcery, necromancy, magic,** sortilege, **wizardry,** theurgy, gramarye <old>, rune

alcohol NOUNS **spirits, liquor,** intoxicating liquor, adult beverage, **hard liquor, whiskey,** whisky, firewater, spiritus frumenti, usquebaugh <Scots>, schnapps, ardent spirits, strong waters, **intoxicant,** toxicant, inebriant, **potable,** potation, **beverage, drink, strong drink,** strong liquor, alcoholic drink *or* beverage, aqua vitae, water of life, brew, **grog,** social lubricant, nectar of the gods

the luscious liquor
MILTON

alcoholic NOUNS 1 **drinker,** imbiber, **social drinker,** tippler, bibber; winebibber, oenophilist; **drunkard, drunk, inebriate, sot,** toper, guzzler, swiller, soaker, lovepot, tosspot, barfly, thirsty soul, **serious drinker,** devotee of Bacchus; **dipsomaniac, problem drinker,** chronic alcoholic
ADJS 2 **spirituous, ardent, strong, hard,** with a kick <nonformal>

alcoholism NOUNS **dipsomania,** oenomania, alcoholic psychosis *or* addiction, pathological drunkenness, problem drinking, heavy drinking, habitual drunkenness, ebriosity

alcove NOUNS **recess,** recession, **niche, nook,** inglenook, corner; cove; bay

alert NOUNS 1 **warning sign, premonitory sign, danger sign;** preliminary sign *or* signal *or* token; **symptom,** early symptom, premonitory symptom, prodrome, prodroma, prodromata <pl>; **precursor**; **omen**
VERBS 2 **tip** *and* tip off *and* **give one a tip** <all nonformal>; confide to, entrust with information, give confidential information, mention privately *or* confidentially, whisper, buzz, breathe, whisper in the ear, **put a bug in one's ear** <nonformal>
ADJS 3 **attentive, heedful, mindful, regardful,** advertent; observant; watchful, aware, conscious; open-eared, open-eyed, **all eyes, all ears,** all eyes and ears

alfresco ADVS **outdoors, out of doors, outside,** abroad; in the open, **in the open air,** *en plein air* <Fr>

alias NOUNS **pseudonym,** anonym, **assumed name,** false *or* fictitious name, *nom de guerre* <Fr>; **pen name, nom de plume;** stage name, *nom de théâtre* <Fr>

alibi NOUNS 1 **pretext, pretense, pretension,** lying pretension, **show,** ostensible *or* announced *or* public *or* professed motive; **sham**; **excuse,** apology, protestation, poor excuse, lame excuse; cover story
VERBS 2 **excuse,** offer excuse for, give as an excuse, cover with excuses, **explain,** offer an explanation; alibi out of <nonformal>, crawl *or* worm *or* squirm out of, lie out of, have an out *or* alibi *or* story <all nonformal>

alien NOUNS 1 **stranger, foreigner, outsider,** non-member, not one of us, not our sort, not the right sort, the other,

outlander, *Uitlander* <Afrikaans>, tramontane, ultramontane, barbarian, foreign devil <China>, *gringo* <Sp Amer>
ADJS 2 **unrelated, unconnected,** unallied, unlinked, **unassociated,** unaffiliated *or* disaffiliated; **isolated,** insular; **foreign,** strange, exotic, outlandish
3 **extraterrestrial,** exterrestrial, extraterrene, extramundane, space

alienate VERBS 1 **antagonize,** set against, set at odds, set at each other's throat, sick on each other <nonformal>; estrange; be alienated *or* estranged, draw *or* grow apart
2 **separate, divide, disjoin, disunite,** draw apart, dissociate, disassociate, grow apart, **disjoint,** disengage, disarticulate, **disconnect;** uncouple, unyoke

alienation NOUNS 1 **falling-out, breach of friendship,** parting of the ways, bust-up <nonformal>; **estrangement, disaffection,** disfavor; **breach, break, rupture, schism, split, rift,** cleft, **disunity, disunion, disruption,** separation, cleavage, divergence, division, dividedness
2 **aloneness,** loneness, **loneliness, lonesomeness,** singleness; separateness, aloofness, detachment, seclusion, sequestration, **withdrawal,** standing *or* moving *or* keeping apart, **isolation**

align VERBS **level, flatten, even, equalize,** smooth *or* smoothen, level out, smooth out, flush

alike ADJS 1 **identical,** identic; **same, selfsame,** one, **one and the same,** all the same, all one, of the same kidney; **indistinguishable,** without distinction, without difference, undifferent, undifferentiated
ADVS 2 **identically,** synonymously; coincidentally, correspondingly, congruently; **likewise,** the same way, just the same, as is, ditto, same here <nonformal>; *ibid* and *ibidem* <both L>

alive ADJS 1 **living,** having life, live, very much alive, alive and well, alive and kicking <nonformal>, conscious, breathing, quick <old>, **animate,** animated, **vital,** zoetic, instinct with life, imbued *or* endowed with life, vivified, enlivened, inspirited; capable of life *or* survival, viable
2 **alert, on the alert,** on the *qui vive* <Fr>, **on one's toes, on top** *and* **on the job** *and* on the ball <all nonformal>, **attentive;** quick on the trigger *or* draw *or* uptake <all nonformal>; **smart, bright, keen, sharp**
3 **remembered, recollected, recalled; retained,** kept in remembrance, enduring, lasting, **unforgotten;** lodged in one's mind, stamped on the memory; vivid, eidetic, fresh, green

all NOUNS 1 **the whole, the entirety, everything,** all the above *or* all of the above <both nonformal>, the aggregate, the assemblage, one and all, all and sundry, each and every <nonformal>; A to Z, A to izzard, everything from soup to nuts *and* everything but the kitchen sink <both nonformal>

alpha and omega
BIBLE

2 <nonformal> **whole bunch, whole mess, whole caboodle, the kit and caboodle, whole kit and caboodle,** whole kit and boodle, whole bit *or* shtick, whole megillah, **whole shooting match,** whole hog, whole animal [old], **whole deal,** whole schmear, **whole shebang,** whole works, the works, whole ball of wax, whole show, whole nine yards

3 **limit, end, extremity,** extreme, **acme,** apogee, climax, **maximum,** max <nonformal>, ceiling, **peak,** summit, **pinnacle,** crown, top; **utmost,** uttermost, utmost extent, highest degree, nth degree *or* power, *ne plus ultra* <L>; **the whole**
4 **everyone, everybody, each and everyone, one and all,** all comers *and* all hands *and* every man Jack *and* every mother's son <all nonformal>, every living soul, **all the world,** *tout le monde* <Fr>, totality; you name it *and* what have you *and* all the above <all nonformal>
ADJS 5 **whole, total, entire,** aggregate, gross; integral, integrated; **exhaustive,** comprehensive, omnibus, all-embracing
6 **every,** any, whichever, whichsoever; **each,** each one; every one, each and every, each and all, **one and all, all and sundry**
ADVS 7 **wholly, entirely**; **totally,** *in toto* <L>, from start to finish, from soup to nuts <nonformal>, from A to Z, from A to izzard, across the board; **altogether,**

all put together, in its entirety, *tout ensemble* <Fr>; lock, stock, and barrel; hook, line, and sinker

allay VERBS **relieve,** give relief; **ease,** ease matters; **relax,** slacken; **alleviate, mitigate, palliate,** soften, pad, cushion, assuage, subdue, soothe; salve, pour balm into, pour oil on; temper the wind to the shorn lamb; **pacify, conciliate, placate, propitiate, appease, mollify,** dulcify; **calm, settle, soothe,** tranquilize; smooth one's feathers; pour oil on troubled waters, pour balm on, take the edge off of, take the sting out of; cool <nonformal>, defuse; clear the air

allege VERBS 1 **state, declare, assert,** aver, affirm, asserverate; **say,** make a statement, send a message; proclaim
2 **accuse,** bring accusation; **charge, press charges, prefer** *or* **bring charges,** lay charges; complain, **lodge a complaint, impeach, arraign, indict,** bring in *or* hand up an indictment, return a true bill, article, **cite; finger** *and* point the finger at *and* put *or* lay the finger on <all nonformal>

alleged ADJS 1 **affirmed, asserted,** asseverated, avouched, avowed, averred, **declared;** professed; predicated
2 **supposed,** suppositive, **assumed, presumed, conjectured, inferred,** understood, deemed, **reputed,** putative, accounted as; **presumptive;** given, granted, taken as *or* for granted, agreed, stipulated

allegiance NOUNS 1 **deference**, servility; eagerness *or* readiness *or* willingness to serve, **dutifulness,** duteousness; fealty, **loyalty,** faithfulness, faith
2 **fidelity, constancy, steadfastness,** staunchness, firmness; good faith, *bona fides* <L>, *bonne foi* <Fr>

allegorical ADJS 1 **symbolic,** symbolical, allegoric, figural, figurative, **metaphoric,** metaphorical, anagogic, anagogical
2 **fictional,** fictionalized; mythical, mythological, **legendary, fabulous; romantic,** romanticized; historicized

allergic ADJS anaphylactic; **sensitive,** responsive, sympathetic, compassionate; empathic, empathetic; **oversensitive, thin-skinned;** oversensible, hyperesthetic, hyperpathic, hypersensitive, supersensitive, overtender, overrefined; **irritable, touchy,** quick on the draw *or* trigger *or* uptake, itchy, ticklish, prickly

allergy NOUNS allergic disorder; allergic rhinitis, **hay fever,** rose cold, pollinosis; **asthma,** bronchial asthma; **hives,** urticaria; eczema

alleviate VERBS **mitigate, palliate,** soften, pad, cushion, assuage, allay, defuse, lay, appease, mollify, subdue, soothe; salve, pour balm into, pour oil on; **dull, deaden,** dull *or* deaden the pain, numb, benumb, anesthetize; sedate, narcotize, dope *or* dope up <nonformal>

alley NOUNS **passageway, pass, passage, defile; avenue, artery; corridor, aisle, lane; channel, conduit**; access, inlet; exit, outlet; connection, communication; covered way, gallery, arcade, portico, colonnade, cloister, ambulatory

alliance NOUNS 1 **coalition, league, union;** council; **bloc, partnership; federation, confederation,** confederacy; grouping, assemblage; **combination,** combine
2 **treaty,** international agreement, *entente, entente cordiale* <both Fr>, concord, concordat, cartel, convention, paction, capitulation; **league**

allied ADJS 1 **joined, united, connected,** copulate, **coupled,** linked, knit, bridged, tight-knit, knitted, bracketed, associated, conjoined, incorporated, integrated, **merged,** gathered, assembled, accumulated, **collected**
2 **affiliated,** affiliate, associate, corporate; federated, confederated, federate, confederate; **in league,** in cahoots <nonformal>, in with, coupled, linked, linked up

allocate VERBS **allot,** lot, **assign, appoint, set,** detail; make assignments *or* allocations; **set apart** *or* **aside, earmark,** tag, mark out for

allocation NOUNS **allotment, assignment, appointment,** setting aside, **earmarking,** tagging

allot VERBS **bestow, confer, award, render,** bestow on; **grant,** accord, **allow,** vouchsafe, yield, afford, make available; **tender,** proffer, offer, extend; deal, dole, mete; **give out, deal out, dole out, mete out, hand** *or* dish out <nonformal>, fork *or* shell out <nonformal>

allotment NOUNS **portion, share, interest, part,** stake, stock, **piece,** bit, segment; **bite** *and* **cut** *and* **slice** *and* **chunk** *and* slice of the pie *or* melon *and* piece of the action <all nonformal>, **lot, pro-**

portion, **percentage,** measure, quantum, **quota,** deal *or* dole <both old>, meed, moiety, mess, helping

all-out ADVS **actively, busily; lively,** sprightly, **briskly, breezily, energetically, animatedly, vivaciously, spiritedly,** with life and spirit, with gusto; full tilt, in full swing; like a house afire

allow VERBS 1 **grant,** accord, yield, afford, make available; make a present of, give as a gift; **give generously,** give the shirt off one's back; be generous *or* liberal with, give freely; heap, lavish
2 **acknowledge, admit, own, confess,** avow, **grant,** warrant, **concede; accept, recognize;** agree in principle, express general agreement, go along with, agree provisionally *or* for the sake of argument; assent grudgingly *or* under protest
3 **make allowance for,** make room for, provide for, open the door to, take account of, **take into account** *or* **consideration, consider,** consider the circumstances; admit exceptions, **waive, set aside,** ease, lift temporarily

allowable ADJS **permissible, admissible;** justifiable, warrantable, sanctionable; licit, **lawful, legitimate, legal,** legitimized, legalized

allowance NOUNS 1 **fee, stipend,** emolument, tribute; retainer, retaining fee
2 **discount, cut, deduction,** slash, abatement, price reduction, price-cut, rollback <nonformal>; **rebate**

allowed ADJS **permitted,** admitted; tolerated, on sufferance; unregulated, unchecked

alloy NOUNS **compound, mixture, admixture,** intermixture, immixture, commixture, **composite, blend,** meld, amalgam

all-powerful ADJS **omnipotent, almighty;** plenipotentiary, absolute, unlimited, **sovereign**

all right 1 tolerable, fair, moderate, tidy <nonformal>, **decent,** respectable, presentable, good enough, **pretty good, not bad,** not amiss, not half bad, not so bad, **adequate, satisfactory,** OK *or* okay <nonformal>; better than nothing; **acceptable,** admissible, **passable**
2 **well,** doing nicely, up and about, sitting up and taking nourishment, alive and well

all things considered PHRS **on the whole, taking one thing with another,** on balance, taking everything into consideration *or* account; everything being equal, other things being equal, *ceteris paribus* <L>, taking into account

allude to VERBS **call attention to,** direct attention to, **bring under** *or* **to one's notice,** hold up to notice, bring to attention, **mention,** mention in passing, touch on; mention in passing, touch on, cite

alluring ADJS **fascinating, captivating, riveting, charming, glamorous,** exotic, **enchanting,** spellbinding, **entrancing,** ravishing, **intriguing, enthralling, bewitching; attractive, interesting, appealing,** dishy <Brit nonformal>, sexy <nonformal>, engaging, taking, eye-catching, catching, fetching, winning, winsome, prepossessing

allusion NOUNS **implication, connotation, import,** latent *or* underlying *or* implied meaning, ironic suggestion *or* implication, what is read between the lines; **suggestion;** coloration, tinge, undertone, overtone, undercurrent, more than meets the eye *or* ear, something between the lines, intimation, touch, nuance, innuendo; undermeaning, **subtext;** cryptic *or* hidden *or* esoteric *or* arcane meaning

ally NOUNS 1 military ally, cobelligerent, treaty partner; satellite; **associate, confederate, colleague,** bedfellow, cohort, comrade in arms, **comrade**
VERBS 2 **affiliate, associate,** consociate; **federate, confederate,** federalize, centralize; **join forces,** join *or* unite with, join *or* come together, join up with <nonformal>, hook up with <nonformal>, tie up *or* in with <nonformal>, **throw in with** <nonformal>, stand up with, be in cahoots <nonformal>, **pool one's interests, join fortunes with,** stand together, close ranks, make common cause with

alma mater NOUNS **college, university,** institution of higher education *or* learning; academe, academia, the groves of Academe, **the campus,** the halls of learning *or* ivy, ivied halls

almighty ADJS 1 **omnipotent, all-powerful;** absolute, unlimited, **sovereign; supreme**
ADVS 2 **exceedingly,** awfully *and* terribly *and* terrifically <all nonformal>, **quite,** just, so, **really,** real *and* right <both nonformal>, mightily, **mighty**

and almighty *and* powerfully *and* powerful <all nonformal>

almost ADVS **nearly, near,** pretty near <nonformal>, close, **closely;** all but, not quite, as good as; **well-nigh, just about;** nigh

alms NOUNS pittance, **charity, dole, handout** <nonformal>, widow's mite; Peter's pence; **offering,** offertory, votive offering; tithe

almsgiver NOUNS **giver, donor,** bestower, grantor, vouchsafer; fairy godmother, Lady Bountiful, Santa Claus, sugar daddy <nonformal>

aloft ADVS **on high,** high up, high; **above, over,** o'er, **overhead;** supra

aloha NOUNS Godspeed; **adieu,** one's adieus, **farewell, good-bye;** parting *or* Parthian shot; swan song; viaticum; stirrup cup, one for the road, *doch-an-dorrach* or *doch-an-dorris* <Gaelic>

alone ADJS 1 **solitary,** solo, *solus* <L>; **isolated,** insular, apart, separate, separated, alienated, withdrawn, aloof, standoffish, detached, removed; **private,** reserved, reticent, reclusive, shy, nonpublic, ungregarious
ADVS 2 **independently, by oneself,** all by one's lonesome <nonformal>, under one's own power *or* steam, **on one's own** *and* **on one's own hook** <both nonformal>, on one's own initiative; **on one's own account** *or* **responsibility,** on one's own say-so <nonformal>; of one's own accord, of one's own volition, at one's own discretion
3 **singly, individually,** particularly, severally, one by one, one at a time; **singularly,** in the singular; **by oneself,** by one's lonesome <nonformal>, under one's own steam, **single-handedly, solo, unaided;** separately

along ADVS **forward, forwards, onward, onwards, forth, on, ahead;** on the way to, on the road *or* high road to, en route to *or* for

alongside ADJS 1 **side, lateral;** flanking, skirting; **beside,** to the side, off to one side; **parallel**
ADVS 2 **aside,** on one side, **to one side,** to the side, sidelong, on the side, on the one hand, on the other hand; in parallel, side-by-side

aloof ADJS 1 **standoffish, distant, remote,** withdrawn, removed, detached, Olympian; **cool,** cold, cold-fish, frigid, chilly, icy, frosty
ADVS 2 **at a distance, away, off,** at arm's length; distantly, remotely

aloud ADVS **loudly,** loud, lustily; **boomingly, thunderously, thunderingly; noisily,** uproariously; at the top of one's voice, in full cry

alp NOUNS **mountain,** mount, hump, tor, height, dizzying height, nunatak, dome; **peak, pinnacle, summit**, mountaintop, point, topmost point *or* pinnacle, **crest,** *pic* <Fr>, *pico* <Sp>; crag, spur, the roof of the world

the beginning and the end
of all natural scenery
RUSKIN

alphabet NOUNS **writing system, script, letters;** letters of the alphabet, **ABC's; phonetic alphabet,** International Phonetic Alphabet *or* IPA; Initial Teaching Alphabet *or* ITA

alphabetize VERBS **catalog,** list, file, tabulate, rationalize, **index,** digest, codify; **categorize,** put down as, **pigeonhole,** place, **group, arrange**, range; **order**, put in order, rank, rate, **grade; sort,** assort

alpine ADJS **mountainous,** mountained, alpen, alpestrine, alpigene; subalpine

already ADVS **until now, hitherto,** till now, thitherto, **hereunto,** heretofore, until this time, by this time, **up to now,** up to the present, up to this time, to this day, to the present moment, to this very instant, **so far,** thus far, **as yet, to date**

also ADVS **additionally, in addition,** and then some, even more, more so, and also, and all <nonformal>, and so, **as well, too,** else, beside, **besides, to boot, not to mention, let alone, into the bargain**

altar NOUNS **Lord's table,** holy table, **Communion table,** chancel table, table of the Lord, God's board; rood altar

alter VERBS 1 **change, mutate; modify;** adapt; modulate, accommodate, adjust, fine-tune, fit, **qualify; vary, diversify; convert, renew, recast, revamp** <nonformal>, change over, exchange, **revive; about-face,** do an about-face, do a 180 <nonformal>, reverse oneself, turn one's coat, sing *or* dance to a different tune, flip-flop <nonformal>
2 **castrate,** geld, emasculate, eunuchize, neuter, spay, fix <nonformal>, unsex, deball <nonformal>

alteration NOUNS **modification, change; variation,** variety, difference, diversity, diversification; **deviation,** diversion, aberrance *or* aberrancy, **divergence; switch, switchover, changeover, turn,** turnabout, about-face, **reversal,** flip-flop <nonformal>; realignment, **adaptation, adjustment,** accommodation, fitting; **reform,** reformation, **improvement,** amelioration, melioration, mitigation, constructive change, **betterment,** change for the better

alternate NOUNS 1 **substitute,** sub <nonformal>, **substitution, replacement,** backup, second *or* third string <nonformal>, secondary, utility player, succedaneum; fill-in, **stand-in, understudy, pinch hitter** *or* runner <nonformal>
VERBS 2 reciprocate, swing, **go to and fro,** to-and-fro, **come and go,** ebb and flow, wax and wane, ride and tie, hitch and hike, back and fill
ADJS 3 **reciprocal,** reciprocative; **back-and-forth, to-and-fro,** up-and-down

alternative NOUNS 1 **option, discretion, pleasure,** possible choice, alternate choice
ADJS 2 **elective;** volitional, voluntary; **optional,** discretional

although ADVS, CONJ **notwithstanding,** all the same <nonformal>, still, yet, even; **however, nevertheless,** nonetheless; when, though; **at all events,** in any event, **in any case,** at any rate; **be that as it may,** for all that, even so, **on the other hand,** rather, again, at the same time, all the same, just the same, **however, that may be;** after all, after all is said and done

altitude NOUNS **height,** vertical *or* perpendicular distance; **highness, tallness, elevation,** ceiling; **loftiness,** sublimity, exaltation; hauteur, toploftiness

altogether ADVS 1 **in addition,** and then some, even more, more so, and also, and all <nonformal>, and so, **as well, too,** else, beside, **besides, to boot, not to mention, let alone, into the bargain; beyond, plus; moreover,** thereto, farther, further, **furthermore,** at the same time, then, again, yet; similarly, likewise, by the same token, by the same sign
2 **wholly, entirely,** all; **totally,** *in toto* <L>, from start to finish, from soup to nuts <nonformal>, from A to Z, from A to izzard, across the board; *tout ensemble* <Fr>; **in all,** on all counts, in all respects, at large; **as a whole, in the aggregate,** in bulk, in the mass, *en masse* <Fr>, *en bloc* <Fr>; lock, stock, and barrel; hook, line, and sinker
3 **generally, in general; generally speaking,** speaking generally, **broadly,** broadly speaking, **roughly,** roughly speaking, as an approximation; **usually, as a rule, ordinarily, commonly, normally,** routinely, as a matter of course; **by and large,** at large, overall, over the long haul <nonformal>, **all things considered,** taking one thing with another, taking all things together, **all in all,** taking all in all, **on the whole,** as a whole, **in the long run,** for the most part, for better or for worse

altruistic ADJS 1 **benevolent, charitable, beneficent, philanthropic,** humanitarian; **bighearted,** greathearted; **generous**; eleemosynary
2 **unselfish, selfless;** self-unconscious, self-forgetful, self-abasing, self-effacing; **humble; unpretentious, modest**; **self-denying,** self-renouncing, self-abnegating; **self-sacrificing,** devoted, dedicated, committed, consecrated, unsparing of self, disinterested

alumna *and* **alumnus** NOUNS **graduate,** grad <nonformal>; alumni, alumnae; old boy <Brit>; **graduate student,** grad student <nonformal>, **postgraduate,** postgrad <nonformal>; college graduate, college man *or* woman

always ADVS 1 **all along, all the time,** all the while, at all times, *semper et ubique* <L, always and everywhere>; **invariably,** without exception, *semper eadem* <L, ever the same; Elizabeth I>
2 **constantly, continually**, **steadily,** sustainedly, **regularly,** as regular as clockwork, every time one turns around, right along <nonformal>, unvaryingly, uninterruptedly, **incessantly,** unceasingly, **ceaselessly,** without cease *or* ceasing, perennially, all the time, at all times, ever, ever and anon, without letup *or* break *or* intermission, without stopping

amalgamation NOUNS **affiliation, alliance, allying, alignment, association,** consociation, combination, **union,** unification, **coalition,** fusion, merger, coalescence, **league, federation, confederation,** confederacy, consolidation, incorporation, inclusion, integration

amass VERBS **store up, stock up, lay up,** put up, **save up,** hoard up, treasure up, garner up, **heap up,** pile up, build up a stock *or* an inventory; **accumulate,** cumulate, **collect, stockpile**

amateur NOUNS 1 **nonprofessional, layman,** member of the laity, laic
2 **dilettante, half scholar,** sciolist, **dabbler,** dabster, trifler, smatterer
ADJS 3 **avocational,** hobby, nonprofessional

amateurish ADJS **unskilled, unaccomplished, untrained,** untaught, unschooled, untutored, uncoached, unimproved, uninitiated, **unprepared,** unprimed, unfinished, unpolished; **untalented, ungifted, unendowed;** unprofessional, unbusinesslike, semiskilled

amaze VERBS **astonish, astound, surprise,** startle, stagger, **bewilder, perplex**, flabbergast <nonformal>, confound, overwhelm, **boggle, boggle the mind; dumbfound,** strike dumb, strike dead; knock one's socks off *and* bowl down *or* over <both nonformal>, dazzle, bedazzle, daze, bedaze

amazement NOUNS **wonder,** wonderment, sense of wonder, marveling, **astonishment;** stupefaction; **surprise; awe,** sense of mystery, admiration; beguilement, fascination; bewilderment

ambassador NOUNS **diplomat,** diplomatist, diplomatic agent; **emissary, envoy, legate, minister,** foreign service officer; ambassador-at-large; envoy extraordinary, plentipotentiary, **minister plenipotentiary;** nuncio, internuncio, apostolic delegate

ambidextrous ADJS ambidextral, ambidexter; dextrosinistral, sinistrodextral

ambience NOUNS 1 **environment, surroundings, environs,** surround, circumambiencies, **circumstances,** environing circumstances, *alentours* <Fr>; **precincts,** ambit, purlieus; **neighborhood, vicinity,** vicinage
2 **milieu, atmosphere, climate, air,** aura, spirit, feeling, feel, quality, color, local color, sense, sense of place, note, tone, overtone, undertone

ambiguity NOUNS ambiguousness; **equivocalness,** equivocacy; **double meaning,** amphibology, multivocality, polysemy, polysemousness; double entendre; inexplicitness, uncertainty

ambiguous ADJS **equivocal,** multivocal, polysemous, polysemantic; two-edged, two-sided, either-or, betwixt and between; obscure, enigmatic; self-contradictory, **paradoxical,** antinomic, oxymoronic, ambivalent, **ironic**

ambition NOUNS 1 ambitiousness, vaulting ambition; climbing, status-seeking, social climbing, careerism; opportunism; power-hunger

the mind's immodesty
D'AVENANT

the way in which a vulgar man aspires
HENRY WARD BEECHER

2 **aim, goal**, end, end in view, telos, final cause; aspiration, inspiration, guiding light *or* star, lodestar

ambitious ADJS 1 **aspiring,** upward-looking, high-reaching; high-flying, social-climbing, careerist, careeristic, on the make <nonformal>; power-hungry
2 **ostentatious, pretentious;** vaunting, **lofty, highfalutin** *and* highfaluting <both nonformal>, **high-flown; high-toned,** tony <both nonformal>

ambivalence NOUNS **irresolution, indecision,** unsettledness, irresoluteness, **indecisiveness,** undecidedness, infirmity of purpose; mugwumpery, mugwumpism, fence-sitting, fence-straddling; capriciousness, mercuriality, fickleness; change of mind, second thoughts, tergiversation

amble NOUNS 1 ramble, **hike, tramp,** traipse <nonformal>; **stroll,** saunter; **promenade;** *passeggiata* <Ital>; **constitutional** <nonformal>
VERBS 2 **go slow** *or* **slowly,** go at a snail's pace, take it slow, get no place fast <nonformal>; **drag,** drag out; **creep, crawl;** laze, idle; get nowhere fast; inch, inch along; shuffle *or* stagger *or* totter *or* toddle along; traipse *and* **mosey** <both nonformal>; **saunter, stroll,** waddle, toddle <nonformal>

ambush NOUNS 1 **ambuscade,** *guet-apens* <Fr>; blind, stalking-horse; booby trap, trap
VERBS 2 ambuscade, **waylay; lie in ambush,** lay wait for, **lie in wait for,** lay for <nonformal>; stalk; set a trap for

ameliorate VERBS **improve, better,** change for the better, make an improvement; transform, transfigure; improve upon, refine upon, **mend, amend,**

emend; meliorate; **civilize,** acculturate, socialize; enlighten, edify; **educate**

amenable ADJS 1 **consenting, assenting,** affirmative, persuaded, approving, agreeing, favorable, accordant, consentient, consentual; **acquiescent, compliant, willing, agreeable,** content
2 **persuadable,** persuasible, open-minded, pervious, accessible, receptive, responsive; **plastic, pliant,** pliable, malleable; **suggestible, susceptible, impressionable,** weak

amend VERBS **revise,** redact, **revamp, rewrite,** redraft, **rework,** work over; **emend,** emendate; **edit,** blue-pencil; **redress,** make good *or* right, **put right,** set right, put *or* set to rights, put *or* set straight, make all square; requite, restitute

amendment NOUNS **revision,** revise, **emendation, correction, corrigenda, rectification;** editing, redaction, recension, revampment; touching up, putting on the finishing touches, putting the gloss on, finishing, perfecting, tuning, fine-tuning

amenities NOUNS 1 **creature comforts, comforts, conveniences,** good things of life, cakes and ale, egg in one's beer <nonformal>, all the comforts of home; all the heart can desire, luxuries, the best
2 **etiquette,** social code, rules *or* code of conduct; **formalities,** social procedures, social conduct, what is done, what one does; **manners,** good manners, exquisite manners, quiet good manners, **politeness,** *politesse* <Fr>, natural politeness, comity, civility; civilities, **social graces, mores, proprieties;** decorum, good form

amiable ADJS affable, genial, cordial; gentle, mild, mild-mannered; easy, easy-natured, easy to get along with, able to take a joke, **agreeable, good-natured,** well-natured, **good-humored, good-tempered,** bonhomous, **sweet, sweet-tempered**

amicable ADJS **in accord, harmonious, in harmony,** congruous, congruent, in tune, attuned, agreeing, in concert, **in rapport,** *en rapport* <Fr>; friendly, frictionless; **sympathetic,** simpatico <nonformal>, empathic, empathetic, **understanding**

amiss ADJS 1 **disorderly, in disorder,** disordered, **disorganized, disarranged, discomposed,** dislocated, deranged, convulsed; **upset, disturbed,** perturbed, unsettled, discomfited, disconcerted
2 **erroneous, untrue,** not true, **not right;** unfactual, **wrong,** all wrong; peccant, perverse, corrupt; straying, astray, adrift
ADVS 3 **astray, beside the mark,** beside the point, far from it, to no purpose, in vain, vainly, fruitlessly, bootlessly; **erroneously, falsely,** by mistake, fallaciously; **mistakenly;** on the wrong track

amity NOUNS **concord,** concordance, **harmony,** symphony; **rapport;** good vibrations <nonformal>, good vibes <nonformal>, good karma; **fellowship,** kinship, togetherness, **affinity; congeniality, compatibility**

ammunition NOUNS **ammo** <nonformal>, **powder and shot**

amnesia NOUNS **loss of memory, memory loss,** memory failure; **memory gap,** blackout <nonformal>; fugue

amnesty NOUNS 1 **pardon,** excuse, sparing, indemnity, exemption, immunity, reprieve, grace; **absolution,** shrift, remission, remission of sin
VERBS 2 **forgive, pardon, excuse,** give *or* grant forgiveness, spare; grant amnesty to, grant immunity *or* exemption; **absolve,** remit, give absolution, shrive, grant remission

amok ADJS **rabid, maniac** *or* **maniacal,** raving mad, stark-raving mad, **frenzied, frantic,** frenetic; **berserk,** running wild

amoral ADJS **unconscientious,** unconscienced, conscienceless, unconscionable, shameless, without shame *or* remorse, **unscrupulous, unprincipled,** unethical, immoral

amorous ADJS amatory, amative, erotic; **sexual; passionate, ardent,** impassioned; desirous; lascivious

amortization NOUNS **payment, paying,** paying off, paying up <nonformal>, payoff; **defrayment,** defrayal; **discharge, settlement, clearance, liquidation,** amortizement, retirement, satisfaction

amount NOUNS 1 quantity, **sum, number,** count, group, total, reckoning, **measure,** parcel, passel <nonformal>, **part, portion,** clutch, ration, share, issue, allotment, lot, deal
2 **price, cost, expense,** expenditure, **charge,** damage *and* score *and* tab <all nonformal>

amphibian NOUNS batrachian, croaker, paddock <nonformal>; **frog,** tree toad *or* frog, bullfrog; **toad,** hoptoad *or* hoppytoad; newt, salamander; **tadpole, polliwog**

ample ADJS **spacious, roomy, commodious, capacious; extensive,** expansive, extended; **abundant,** copious, plenteous, **plentiful, sufficient,** sufficing; **enough,** substantial, **plenty, satisfactory, adequate,** decent, due

amplify VERBS **expatiate, dilate, expand,** enlarge, **enlarge on,** expand on, **elaborate;** relate *or* rehearse in extenso; detail, particularize

amputate VERBS **sever, dissever,** cut off *or* away *or* loose, shear off, hack through, hack off, ax; **cleave, split**

amulet NOUNS **talisman, charm, fetish,** periapt, phylactery; **voodoo, hoodoo,** juju, obeah, mumbo jumbo; **good-luck charm,** good-luck piece, **lucky piece,** rabbit's-foot, lucky bean, four-leaf clover, whammy <nonformal>

amusement NOUNS **entertainment, diversion,** solace, divertisement, *divertissement* <Fr>, **recreation, relaxation,** regalement; **pastime,** *passe-temps* <Fr>; **mirth**; **pleasure, enjoyment**

amusing ADJS **entertaining, diverting,** beguiling; **fun,** funsome *and* more fun than a barrel of monkeys <both nonformal>; recreative, recreational; **delightful,** titillative, titillating; humorous

anachronism NOUNS chronological *or* historical error, **mistiming, misdating,** misdate, postdating, antedating; parachronism, metachronism, prochronism; prolepsis

anagram NOUNS logogram, logogriph, metagram; acrostic, double acrostic; amphiboly, amphibologism

analogy NOUNS **likening,** comparing; **comparison,** compare, examining side by side, matching, matchup, holding up together, proportion <old>, comparative judgment *or* estimate; parallelism; correlation

analysis NOUNS 1 analyzation, **breakdown,** breaking down, breakup, breaking up; anatomy, anatomizing, dissection; separation, **division, subdivision,** segmentation, reduction to elements *or* parts; **examination, study,** logical analysis; logical discussion, dialectic
2 a priori reasoning, a fortiori reasoning, a posteriori reasoning; discursive reasoning; **deduction, deductive reasoning,** syllogism, syllogistic reasoning; hypothetico-deductive method; **induction, inductive reasoning,** epagoge
3 **psychoanalysis,** the couch <nonformal>; psychoanalytic therapy, psychoanalytic method

analyst NOUNS 1 **analyzer, examiner**; taxonomist; **critic,** interpreter, exegete, explicator, theoretician, aesthetician; reviewer
2 **psychoanalyst; shrink** *and* headshrinker *and* shrinker <all nonformal>; **counselor,** psychological counselor; **psychologist; psychotherapist, therapist,** psychotherapeutist; **psychiatrist,** alienist, somatist; neuropsychiatrist; psychopathist, psychopathologist

analytic ADJS 1 **analytical;** segmental; classificatory, enumerative; schematic; **inquiring, questioning, querying,** quizzing; **rational,** ratiocinative *or* ratiocinatory
2 dialectic, dialectical, maieutic; syllogistic, syllogistical, enthymematic, enthymematical, soritical, epagogic, inductive, deductive, inferential, synthetic, synthetical, discursive

analyze VERBS 1 **break down,** break up, anatomize, dissect, atomize, unitize; **divide, subdivide,** segment; assay; separate, make discrete, isolate, reduce, reduce to elements, resolve; **reason; deduce, infer, generalize; synthesize; theorize,** hypothesize; philosophize; syllogize
2 **discuss, debate, reason, deliberate,** deliberate upon, exchange views *or* opinions, talk, **talk over, hash over** <nonformal>, talk of *or* about, **consider, treat,** dissertate on, **go into, examine,** investigate, talk out, sift, **study,** review, ventilate, thresh out, consider pro and con; **kick** *or* **knock around** <nonformal>

anarchist NOUNS anarch; antinomian; **nihilist,** syndicalist *and* anarcho-syndicalist <both old>

anarchy NOUNS anarchism; **disorderliness, unruliness,** misrule, **disorder,** disruption, disorganization, confusion, **turmoil, chaos,** primal chaos, tohubohu; antinomianism; **nihilism;** syndicalism *and* anarcho-syndicalism *and* criminal syndicalism <all old>, lynch law, mob rule *or* law, mobocracy, ochlocracy; **law of the jungle**

anatomy NOUNS 1 **body,** frame, bodily *or* corporal *or* corporeal entity, physical self, physical *or* bodily structure, physique, soma; organism, organic complex
2 form; **morphology,** science of structure; **structure, construction,** architecture, tectonics, architectonics, **frame,** make, **build,** fabric, tissue, warp and woof *or* weft, web, weave, texture, contexture, mold, **shape, pattern, plan,** fashion, arrangement, **organization**; organism, organic structure, **constitution, composition**

ancestor NOUNS procreator, begetter; natural *or* birth *or* biological parent; grandparent; ancestress, progenitress, progenitrix; **predecessor,** forebear, precedent, antecedent

ancestry NOUNS progenitorship; parentage, parenthood; patrocliny, matrocliny; patrilineage, matrilineage; patriliny, matriliny; **blood relationship,** blood, ties of blood, consanguinity, common descent *or* ancestry, biological *or* genetic relationship, **kinship,** kindred, **relation, relationship,** sibship

anchor NOUNS 1 mooring, hook *and* mudhook <both nonformal>; **anchorage,** moorings; **berth,** slip; mooring buoy
2 newscaster, sportscaster; commentator, news commentator, news reader <Brit>; news anchor, anchor man *or* woman
VERBS 3 come to anchor, lay anchor, **cast anchor,** let go the anchor, drop the hook; carry out the anchor; kedge, kedge off; **dock, tie up; moor,** pick up the mooring

ancient NOUNS 1 man *or* woman *or* person of old, **prehistoric mankind;** preadamite, antediluvian; **primitive, aboriginal,** aborigine, bushman, autochthon; **caveman,** cave dweller, troglodyte
ADJS 2 **aged, elderly, old,** grown old in years, along *or* up *or* advanced *or* on in years, years old, advanced, advanced in life, **at an advanced age,** geriatric, gerontic; **venerable,** old as Methuselah *or* as God *or* as the hills

anemic ADJS 1 **feeble,** debilitated; **strengthless,** sapless, marrowless, pithless, sinewless, listless, out of gas <nonformal>, nerveless, lustless; **impotent, powerless**
2 dull, flat, mat, dead, dingy, muddy, leaden, lusterless, lackluster; **faded, washed-out,** dimmed, discolored, etiolated; **pale, dim,** weak, **faint; pallid, wan, sallow**

anesthetic NOUNS 1 general anesthetic, local anesthetic, analgesic, anodyne, balm, ointment, **pain killer,** pain-reliever, antiodontalgic
ADJS 2 **deadening,** numbing, dulling; analgesic, narcotic; stupefying, stunning, numbing, mind-boggling *or* -numbing; anesthetizing, narcotizing

anesthetize VERBS **deaden, numb,** benumb, blunt, dull, obtund, **desensitize; put to sleep,** slip one a Mickey *or* Mickey Finn <nonformal>, chloroform, etherize; narcotize, drug, dope <nonformal>

angel NOUNS 1 celestial, celestial *or* heavenly being; messenger of God; **seraph,** seraphim <pl>, angel of love; **cherub, cherubim** <pl>, angel of light
2 **innocent,** baby, babe, babe in arms, newborn babe, infant, babe in the woods, lamb, dove
3 **backer, sponsor, patron, supporter,** Maecenas; cash cow *and* staker *and* grubstaker <all nonformal>, meal ticket <nonformal>

angelic ADJS 1 **seraphic, cherubic; heavenly, celestial**
2 **endearing, lovable, likable, adorable,** admirable, **lovely,** lovesome, sweet, winning, winsome

anger NOUNS 1 **wrath, ire,** *saeva indignatio* <L>; angriness, irateness, wrathfulness, soreness <nonformal>; infuriation, enragement

a transient madness
HORACE

VERBS 2 **lose one's temper,** become irate, forget oneself, let one's angry passions rise; get one's blood up, **bridle,** bridle up, **bristle,** bristle up, raise one's hackles, get one's back up; reach boiling point, boil over, climb the wall, go through the roof

3 <nonformal> **get mad** *or* **sore,** get one's Irish *or* dander *or* hackles up, get one's monkey up <Brit>; **see red, get hot under the collar,** flip out, work oneself into a lather *or* sweat *or* stew, get oneself in a tizzy, do a slow burn; **work oneself up,** work oneself into a sweat, lather, have a short fuse, get hot

under the collar, run a temperature, race one's motor, get into a dither *or* tizzy *or* swivet *or* pucker *or* stew; blow up, **blow one's top** *or* stack *or* cool, **flip,** flip out, flip one's lid *or* wig, pop one's cork, wig out, blow a gasket, fly off the handle, **hit the ceiling,** go ape, go hog wild, go bananas, lose one's cool, go off the deep end

4 **make angry, make mad,** raise one's gorge *or* choler; make one's blood boil

5<nonformal> **piss** *or* tee off, tick off, piss, **get one's goat, get one's Irish** *or* back *or* dander *or* hackles up, **make sore,** get one's mad up, make one hot under the collar, put one's nose out of joint, burn one up, burn one's ass *or* butt, steam

angle NOUNS 1 **viewpoint, standpoint, point of view,** vantage, vantage point, point *or* coign of vantage, where one stands
2 **slant,** spin <nonformal>; bias, leaning, inclination, tendentiousness; unequal *or* preferential treatment, discrimination, inequality

angry ADJS 1 angered, **incensed, indignant, irate,** ireful; **livid,** livid with rage, beside oneself, **wroth, wrathful,** wrathy, **cross,** wrought-up, worked up, riled up <nonformal>; **out of humor,** out of temper, out of sorts

2 <nonformal> **mad, sore,** mad as a hornet *or* as a wet hen *or* as hell, sore as a boil, pissed; **pissed-off** *or* PO'd; teed off *or* TO'd; ticked off, browned-off, waxy *and* stroppy <both Brit>, **hot,** het up, **hot under the collar,** burned up, hot and bothered, boiling, boiling *or* hopping *or* fighting *or* roaring mad, fit to be tied, good and mad, steamed, hacked, bent out of shape, in a lather *or* lava *or* pucker, red-assed

anguish NOUNS 1 **wretchedness, despair,** bitterness, infelicity, **misery, agony, woe,** woefulness, woesomeness <old>, bale, balefulness
VERBS 2 **suffer, hurt, ache, bleed; suffer anguish; agonize,** writhe; have a bad time of it, go through hell; aggrieve, oppress, **grieve, sorrow,** plunge one into sorrow, embitter; **break one's heart, make one's heart bleed;** desolate

animal NOUNS 1 **creature,** critter <nonformal>, living being *or* thing; **brute, beast,** varmint <nonformal>, dumb animal *or* creature, dumb friend
ADJS 2 **ruthless**; **brutal,** brutish, brute, bestial, beastly, animalistic; **mindless, soulless,** insensate, senseless, subhuman, dehumanized, brutalized

animal kingdom NOUNS **animal life, brute creation, fauna, Animalia** <zoology>, **animality; wild animals** *or* **beasts, beasts of field, wildlife, denizens of the forest** *or* **jungle** *or* **wild, furry creatures**

animate VERBS 1 **energize,** dynamize; **invigorate, enliven, liven, liven up,** vitalize, quicken, goose *or* jazz up <nonformal>; **exhilarate, stimulate,** hearten, galvanize, electrify, charge up, psych *or* pump up <nonformal>, **pep** *or* snap *or* jazz *or* zip *or* perk up <nonformal>
ADJS 2 **living, alive,** having life, live, very much alive, alive and well, alive and kicking <nonformal>, conscious, breathing, quick <old>, animated, **vital,** zoetic; viable

animated ADJS **active, lively, spirited,** bubbly, ebullient, effervescent, **vivacious, sprightly,** chipper *and* perky <both nonformal>, pert; **spry, breezy, brisk, energetic,** eager, keen, can-do <nonformal>; **peppy** *and* snappy *and* zingy <all nonformal>; frisky, bouncing, bouncy

animism NOUNS **animistic religion** *or* cult; voodooism, voodoo, hoodoo, wanga, juju, jujuism, obeah, obeahism; shamanism; fetishism, totemism; nature worship, naturism; primitive religion

animosity NOUNS animus; **ill will,** ill feeling, bitter feeling, **hard feelings,** no love lost; **bitterness,** sourness, soreness, **rancor,** acrimony, virulence, venom, vitriol

annals NOUNS **chronicle, chronology, register,** registry, record; journal, diary

annex NOUNS 1 **adjunct, addition,** increase, **increment,** augmentation, *additum* <L>, addendum, addenda <pl>, accession; annexation; **appendage,** appendant, pendant, appanage, tailpiece, coda
2 <building> wing, **addition,** extension, ell *or* L

VERBS 3 **take possession, appropriate, take up,** take over, make one's own, move in *or* move in on <nonformal>

annihilate VERBS **exterminate**, eradicate, extirpate, **eliminate,** liquidate, **wipe out, stamp out,** waste *and* take out *and* nuke *and* zap <all nonformal>, put an end to

annihilation NOUNS **extinction, extermination, elimination, eradication,** extirpation; rooting out, deracination, uprooting, tearing up root and branch; **snuffing out; liquidation, purge; suppression**

anniversary NOUNS **commemoration;** immovable feast, annual holiday; jubilee, silver jubilee, golden jubilee, diamond jubilee; centennial, centenary

annotation NOUNS **comment, word of explanation;** notation, **note,** note of explanation, footnote, gloss, scholium; exegesis; *apparatus criticus* <L>; commentary

announce VERBS 1 **herald, harbinger, forerun,** run before; give notice, notify, talk about; **state, declare, assert,** aver, affirm, asseverate, allege; make a statement, send a message; tell the world; nuncupate

announcement NOUNS **pronouncement, proclamation,** annunciation, enunciation; predication, predicate; utterance, dictum, *ipse dixit* <L>; **affirmation,** affirmance, **assertion, asseveration,** averment, **declaration,** vouch <old>, allegation; manifesto, position paper; statement of principles, **creed**

annoy VERBS **irk, vex, nettle, provoke, pique,** miff *and* peeve <both nonformal>, distemper, **ruffle, disturb,** discompose, **roil,** rile, **aggravate,** make a nuisance of oneself, **exasperate,** exercise, try one's patience, try the patience of a saint; **put one's back up,** make one bristle; **bug** <nonformal>, be on the back of *and* be at *and* ride <all nonformal>, **pester, tease, needle,** devil, get after *or* get on <nonformal>, **bedevil, pick on** <nonformal>, **plague,** beset, beleaguer

annoyance NOUNS **vexation,** exasperation, *tracasserie* <Fr>, **aggravation; nuisance, pest, bother,** botheration <nonformal>, public nuisance, **trouble, problem,** pain <nonformal>, difficulty, hot potato <nonformal>; **pain in the neck** *or* **in the ass** <nonformal>; **harassment,** molestation, harrying; bedevilment; vexatiousness

annoying ADJS **irritating,** galling, **provoking, aggravating** <nonformal>, **exasperating; vexatious,** vexing, irking, **irksome,** tiresome, wearisome; **troublesome, bothersome, worrisome,** bothering, troubling, **pesky** *and* pesty *and* pestiferous <all nonformal>; tormenting, harassing, worrying

annual NOUNS 1 **periodical, serial, journal,** gazette; ephemeris; yearbook
ADJS 2 **yearly;** biennial, triennial, decennial, etc

annuity NOUNS **subsidy,** subvention, subsidization, support; **allowance, stipend,** allotment; pension, old-age insurance, retirement benefits, social security, remittance; **insurance,** variable annuity

annul VERBS **abolish, nullify,** void, abrogate, annihilate, tear up, repeal, revoke, negate, invalidate, **undo, cancel,** cancel out, bring to naught, put *or* lay to rest; countermand, **abolish,** do away with; vacate, declare null and void; **overrule,** override

annulment NOUNS 1 **divorce,** civil divorce, **separation,** legal *or* judicial separation, separate maintenance; interlocutory decree; dissolution of marriage
2 **neutralization, nullification,** cancellation, voiding, invalidation, vitiation, frustration, thwarting, undoing

annunciation NOUNS **announcement,** enunciation; **proclamation,** pronouncement, pronunciamento; public declaration *or* statement, **notice, notification,** public notice; encyclical, encyclical letter; manifesto, position paper; broadside; ukase, edict

anoint VERBS 1 **install,** instate, induct, **inaugurate,** invest, put in, place, **place in office;** crown, throne, enthrone
2 **perform a rite,** perform service *or* divine service; administer a sacrament
3 **oil,** grease; salve, unguent, embrocate, dress, pour oil *or* balm upon; smear, daub

anonymity NOUNS **privacy,** retirement, isolation, sequestration, seclusion; **confidentialness,** confidentiality; **anonymousness, namelessness; incognito**

anonymous ADJS **private, privy, closed-door; intimate, inmost,** innermost, interior, inward, **personal; privileged,** protected; **secluded, sequestered,** isolated, withdrawn, retired; incognito

another NOUNS 1 **a different thing,** a different story <nonformal>, **something else,** something else again <nonformal>, *tertium quid* <L, a third something>, *autre chose* <Fr>, another kettle of fish <nonformal>, another tune, different breed of cat <nonformal>, horse of a different color
ADJS 2 **other,** whole nother <nonformal>, else, otherwise, other than *or* from; not the same, not the type <nonformal>, not that sort, of another sort, of a sort *and* of sorts <both nonformal>

answer NOUNS 1 **reaction, response,** respondence, feedback; reply, **rise** <nonformal>; **reflex,** reflection, **reflex action;** reverberation, resonance, sympathetic vibration; riposte, **uptake** <nonformal>, **retort, rejoinder,** reaction, return, **comeback** *and* **take** <both nonformal>, back talk
2 **solution,** resolution, **reason, explanation**; **finding,** conclusion, determination, ascertainment, verdict, judgment; **outcome, upshot,** denouement, **result,** issue, end, end result
VERBS 3 respond *or* reply to, get back to; **communicate with, get in touch** *or* **contact with, contact** <nonformal>, **make contact with,** raise, reach, get to, get through to, get hold of, make *or* establish connection, get in connection with; **refute, confute, confound, rebut,** parry, **answer conclusively,** dismiss, dispose of
4 **avail,** be of use, be of service, serve, **suffice, do, answer** *or* **serve one's purpose,** serve one's need, fill the bill *and* do the trick <both nonformal>

answerable ADJS **responsible; liable, accountable,** amenable, unexempt from, chargeable, on one's head, at one's doorstep, on the hook <nonformal>; responsible for, at the bottom of; to blame

ant NOUNS emmet <nonformal>, pismire, pissant *and* antymire <both nonformal>; red ant, black ant, fire ant, house ant, agricultural ant, carpenter ant, army ant; slave ant, slave-making ant; **termite,** white ant; queen, worker, soldier

antagonism NOUNS **hostility,** oppugnancy, oppugnance *and* oppugnation <both old>, **antipathy,** enmity, bad blood, inimicalness; **contrariness, contrariety,** orneriness <nonformal>, repugnance *or* repugnancy, perverseness, **obstinacy**; fractiousness, refractoriness, recalcitrance; **disagreement, discord,** discordance *or* discordancy; **disharmony,** unharmoniousness; dissonance, dissidence; **dissent**, negation, contradiction

antagonist NOUNS **opponent, adversary, assailant, foe, enemy,** archenemy; opposite *or* opposing side, **the opposition,** the loyal opposition; **combatant**

antagonize VERBS set against, set at odds, set at each other's throat, sick on each other <nonformal>; **provoke,** envenom, **embitter,** infuriate, madden; **alienate,** estrange; be alienated *or* estranged, draw *or* grow apart

ante NOUNS 1 **bet, wager, stake,** hazard, lay; long shot; parlay, double or nothing; **poker bet**
VERBS 2 **bet, wager, gamble, hazard, stake,** punt, lay, lay down, put up, **make a bet, lay a wager,** give *or* take *or* lay odds, make book, get a piece of the action <nonformal>; plunge <nonformal>

antebellum ADJS prewar, before the war; prerevolutionary

antecedent NOUNS 1 **precursor, forerunner,** *voorlooper* <Dutch>, vaunt-courier, avant-courier; trailblazer *or* trailbreaker, guide; **predecessor,** forebear, precedent, **ancestor;** innovator, groundbreaker
ADJS 2 **prior,** antecedent, anterior, **leading**; **preliminary,** precursory, prevenient, prefatory, exordial, prelusive, preludial, proemial, preparatory, initiatory, propaedeutic, inaugural; **preceding**, foregoing, above, anterior, **anticipatory,** antecedent; **preexistent**

antedate VERBS **predate,** backdate; **be prior,** be before *or* early *or* earlier, come on the scene *or* appear earlier, **precede, antecede, forerun,** come *or* go before, set a precedent; **herald,** usher in, proclaim, announce

anthem NOUNS 1 **paean,** laud; hosanna, hallelujah, alleluia; **hymn,** hymn of praise, **doxology, psalm,** motet, canticle, chorale; **chant,** versicle; antiphon, antiphony; offertory, offertory sentence *or* hymn

anthology NOUNS **compilation,** omnibus; symposium; collection, collectanea, miscellany; **miscellanea,** analects; ana; chrestomathy; garland, florilegium; *Festschrift* <Ger>

anthropoid NOUNS 1 preadamite, antediluvian; humanoid, primate, fossil man, protohuman, prehuman, missing link, apeman, hominid; **primitive, aboriginal,** aborigine, bushman, autochthon; **caveman,** cave dweller, troglodyte
ADJS 2 **manlike,** humanoid, hominid; anthropomorphic

antibiotic NOUNS 1 ampicillin, bacitracin, penicillin, etc; **miracle drug, wonder drug,** magic bullets; bacteriostat; **sulfa drug,** sulfa, sulfanilamide, sulfonamide
ADJS 2 **antidotal,** alexipharmic; **antitoxic;** bacteriostatic, antimicrobial

antic NOUNS **prank, trick, practical joke,** waggish trick, *espièglerie* <Fr>, caper, frolic; **monkeyshines** *and* **shenanigans** <both nonformal>

anticipate VERBS **foresee,** previse, see the handwriting on the wall, pave the way for; forerun, go before, get a head start, steal a march on, beat someone to the punch *or* the draw <nonformal>; **jump the gun,** go off half-cocked <nonformal>; take the words out of one's mouth

anticipation NOUNS 1 **carefulness, care, heed, concern, regard; attention**; **heedfulness,** regardfulness, mindfulness, **thoughtfulness;** circumspection; forethought
2 **prevision,** divination, forecast; **prediction**; **foreglimpse, prospect;** sagacity, providence, discretion, preparation, provision, prudence

antidepressant ADJS **psychochemical,** psychoactive; ataractic; mood drug

antidote NOUNS counterpoison, alexipharmic, theriaca *or* theriac; **counteractant,** counteractive, **counteragent;** counterirritant; **neutralizer,** nullifier, offset

antipathy NOUNS **hostility,** antagonism, **enmity**; **hatred, hate**; **aversion, repugnance,** repulsion, allergy <nonformal>, grudge, abomination, **abhorrence, horror,** mortal horror

antipodes NOUNS 1 **opposites,** polar opposites, contraries; **poles,** opposite poles, antipoles, counterpoles, North Pole, South Pole
2 jumping-off place *and* godforsaken place *and* God knows where *and* the middle of nowhere <all nonformal>, remotest corner of the world; outpost, outskirts; the sticks *and* the boondocks *and* the boonies <all nonformal>

antiquarian NOUNS antiquary, *laudator temporis acti* <L>; dryasdust, the Rev Dr Dryasdust, Jonathan Oldbuck <both Sir Walter Scott>, Herr Teufelsdröckh <Carlyle>; antique dealer, antique collector, antique-car collector; archaist

antiquated ADJS 1 **past, gone,** by, **gone-by, bygone,** gone glimmering, bypast, ago, **over,** departed, passed, passed away, elapsed, lapsed, vanished, faded, no more, irrecoverable, never to return, not coming back; dead as a dodo, expired, extinct, dead and buried, defunct, deceased; **passé, obsolete,** has-been, dated, antique
2 grown old, **superannuated, old,** age-encrusted; antediluvian; **fossil,** fossilized, petrified

antique NOUNS **antiquity,** archaism; **relic,** relic of the past; **remains,** survival, vestige, ruin *or* ruins; old thing, oldie *and* golden oldie <nonformal>
ADJS 2 **ancient,** venerable, hoary; of old, of yore; dateless, timeless, ageless; **immemorial,** old as Methuselah *or* Adam, old as God, old as the hills

antiquity NOUNS 1 **ancient times,** time immemorial, ancient history, remote age *or* time, remote *or* far *or* dim *or* **distant past,** distance of time
2 **oldness, age,** eld <old>, hoary eld; **ancientness,** dust of ages, rust *or* cobwebs of antiquity; venerableness, eldership, primogeniture, great *or* hoary age

anti-Semitism NOUNS **discrimination,** social discrimination, minority prejudice; xenophobia, know-nothingism; **chauvinism,** ultranationalism, superpatriotism; fascism

antiseptic NOUNS 1 microbicide, germicide, antiseptic, disinfectant
ADJS 2 **sanitary, hygienic, prophylactic; sterile,** aseptic, **uninfected;** disinfected, decontaminated, sterilized; pasteurized

antisocial ADJS **misanthropic,** people-hating, Timonist, Timonistic, cynical; unsociable; **man-hating,** misandrist; **woman-hating,** misogynic, misogynistic, misogynous; solitary, reclusive

anus NOUNS rectum; **asshole** *and* bumhole *and* bunghole <all nonformal>; bung

anxiety NOUNS **anxiousness; apprehension, apprehensiveness,** antsyness <nonformal>, misgiving, foreboding, forebodingness, suspense, strain, tension, stress, nervous strain *or* tension; **dread, fear**; **concern,** concernment, anxious concern, **solicitude**; perturbation, disturbance, upset, **agitation, disquiet,** disquietude, inquietude, unquietness; **nervousness**; malaise, angst

anxious ADJS **concerned, apprehensive,** foreboding, misgiving, suspenseful, strained, tense, tensed up <nonformal>, nail-biting, white-knuckle <nonformal>; **fearful**; uneasy, perturbed, disturbed, disquieted, agitated; **on pins and needles,** on tenterhooks, on shpilkes <nonformal>, on the anxious seat *or* bench

any NOUNS 1 **anything,** any one, aught, either; **anybody, anyone**
ADJS 2 **every, all,** whichever, whichsoever; **each,** each one; every one, each and every, each and all, **one and all, all and sundry,** all and some

anybody NOUNS any one, aught, either; **anyone**

anyhow ADVS **anyway,** anywise, in any way, **by any means, by any manner of means;** in any event, at any rate, leastways <nonformal>, in any case; **nevertheless, nonetheless, however, regardless**

anyone NOUNS **whoever,** whoso, **whosoever, whomever,** whomso, **whomsoever,** no matter who

anything NOUNS **any,** any one, aught, either

anytime ADVS **whenever,** whene'er, whensoever, whensoe'er, **at whatever time,** at any time, no matter when; if ever, once; **imminently,** impendingly; any time now, any moment, any second, any minute, any hour, any day; **to be expected,** as may be expected, as may be

anywhere ADVS anyplace <nonformal>; **wherever,** where'er, **wheresoever,** wheresoe'er, whithersoever, wherever it may be

apart ADJS 1 **secluded, seclusive, retired, withdrawn; isolated,** shut off, insular, **separate,** separated, detached, removed
ADVS 2 **away, aside,** wide apart; **separately,** severally, piecemeal, one by one; apart from, away from, aside from

apartheid NOUNS **discrimination,** social discrimination, minority prejudice; **color line,** color bar; **segregation**

apartment NOUNS **flat,** tenement, chambers <Brit>, rooms; studio apartment *or* flat; bed-sitter <Brit>, granny flat, flatlet; garden apartment; duplex apartment; railroad flat

apathy NOUNS **indifference, unconcern,** lack of caring, disinterest; withdrawnness, **aloofness, detachment,** ataraxy *or* ataraxia; **passiveness,** passivity, supineness, insouciance, nonchalance; **listlessness, spiritlessness,** burnout, blah *or* blahs <nonformal>; **lethargy,** hebetude, **dullness,** sluggishness, languor, languidness

ape NOUNS 1 **primate, simian; monkey**
2 **imitator,** simulator, me-tooer <nonformal>, **impersonator, impostor, mimic,** mimicker, mimer, mime, **mocker; parrot,** polly, poll-parrot *or* polly-parrot, aper
VERBS 3 **mimic, impersonate,** mime, **parrot,** copycat <nonformal>; take off, hit off, hit off on, take off on

aperture NOUNS **opening, hole,** hollow, **cavity, orifice; slot,** split, crack, check, leak

apex NOUNS **summit,** top; **tip-top, peak,** pinnacle; **crest, brow;** ridge, edge; **crown,** cap, **tip,** point, spire, pitch; **acme,** *ne plus ultra* <Fr>, **zenith, climax,** apogee, pole

aphorism NOUNS **maxim, apothegm, epigram, dictum, adage, proverb,** gnome, words of wisdom, **saw, saying,** witticism, sentence, expression, phrase, catchword, catchphrase, word, byword, mot, motto, moral

aphrodisiac NOUNS 1 **love potion, philter,** love philter; cantharis, blister beetle, Spanish fly
ADJS 2 aphroditous, **arousing,** stimulating, eroticizing, venereal

aplomb NOUNS **equanimity,** equilibrium, equability, balance; **levelheadedness,** level head, well-balanced *or* well-regulated mind; **poise, self-possession, self-control,** self-command, self-restraint, restraint, possession, **presence of mind**

apocalypse NOUNS **revelation, divine revelation; inspiration,** afflatus, divine inspiration; theophany, theophania, epiphany; **prophecy,** prophetic revelation

apocryphal ADJS **unauthoritative, unauthentic, unofficial,** nonofficial; **uncertified, unverified,** unchecked, unconfirmed, uncorroborated, unauthenticated, unvalidated, unattested, unwarranted; **undemonstrated, unproved**

apologetic ADJS **penitent, repentant; penitential,** penitentiary; **contrite,** abject, humble, humbled, **sheepish,** touched, softened, melted

apologize VERBS **beg pardon, ask forgiveness,** beg indulgence, express regret; take back; get *or* fall down on one's knees

apology NOUNS **excuse,** regrets; acknowledgment, penitence, contrition, breast-beating, *mea culpa* <L>, confession; abject apology, apologia, apologetic

apoplexy NOUNS **paralysis,** palsy, impairment of motor function; **stroke;** motor paralysis, sensory paralysis; hemiplegia, paraplegia, diplegia, quadriplegia

apostate NOUNS 1 **turncoat,** turnabout, **recreant, renegade,** renegado, renegate *or* runagate <old>, **defector,** tergiversator, tergiversant
ADJS 2 **recreant,** renegade, tergiversating, tergiversant; **treasonous, treasonable, traitorous,** forsworn; collaborating; faithless, **disloyal**

apostle NOUNS 1 **disciple, follower;** convert, proselyte; **evangelist, disciple,** saint

appall VERBS **horrify,** shock; make the flesh creep *or* crawl, make one shudder; **repel,** put off, turn off <nonformal>, **revolt, disgust,** nauseate, sicken, make one sick, make one sick to *or* in the stomach, make one vomit *or* puke *or* retch, turn the stomach, gross out <nonformal>

appalling ADJS **terrible,** terrific, tremendous; **horrid, horrible, horrifying,** horrific, horrendous; **dreadful, dread,** dreaded; **hideous, ghastly,** morbid, grim, grisly, gruesome, ghoulish, macabre

apparatus NOUNS **device,** contrivance, contraption <nonformal>, gadget, gizmo, gimcrack, gimmick <nonformal>, means

apparel NOUNS 1 **clothing, clothes, wear, wearing apparel, daywear, dress,** dressing, **raiment,** garmenture, **garb, attire, array,** habit, habiliment, fashion, style, guise, **costume,** costumery, gear; **vestment,** vesture, investment, investiture; **garments,** robes, robing, rags <nonformal>, drapery, finery, feathers; toggery *or* togs *or* **duds** *or* threads <all nonformal>

apparent ADJS **manifest, evident, self-evident,** axiomatic, indisputable, **obvious, plain, clear,** perspicuous, distinct, palpable, patent, tangible; **visible, perceptible, perceivable, discernible,** seeable, observable, **noticeable, much in evidence**

apparently ADVS 1 **seemingly, ostensibly,** to *or* by all appearances, to *or* by all accounts, to the eye; on the face of it, *prima facie* <L>; on the surface, outwardly, superficially; at first sight *or* view, at first blush
2 **manifestly, evidently, obviously, patently, plainly, clearly,** distinctly, **unmistakably,** expressly, explicitly, palpably, tangibly; **visibly, perceptibly,** perceivably, discernibly, observably, **noticeably**

appeal NOUNS 1 **delightfulness,** exquisiteness, loveliness; **charm,** winsomeness, grace, **attractiveness;** sexiness <nonformal>; **glamour;** captivation, enchantment, entrancement, bewitchment, witchery, enravishment, **fascination**
2 **entreaty, plea, bid,** suit, call, cry, clamor, *cri du c<oe>ur* <Fr>, beseeching, impetration, obtestation; **supplication, prayer,** rogation, **beseechment,** imploring, imploration, obsecration, obtestation, adjuration, imprecation
VERBS 3 **attract, interest, engage,** impress, charismatize, fetch <nonformal>, catch *or* get one's eye, command one's attention, rivet one, attract one's interest, be attractive, take *or* tickle one's fancy
4 **entreat, implore, beseech, beg,** crave, **plead, pray, supplicate,** impetrate, obtest; adjure, conjure; invoke, imprecate <old>, **call on** *or* **upon,** cry on *or* upon, **appeal to,** cry to, run to; go cap *or* hat in hand to

appealing ADJS 1 **delightful, exquisite, lovely; thrilling,** titillative; **charming, attractive, endearing, engaging,** prepossessing, heartwarming, sexy <nonformal>, **enchanting,** bewitching, witching, entrancing, enthralling, intriguing, fascinating
2 **imploring, entreating, beseeching, begging, pleading,** precatory, precative, adjuratory

appear VERBS 1 become visible; **arrive, make one's appearance,** make *or* put in an appearance, appear on the scene, **show up** <nonformal>, **turn up,** come, **materialize,** present oneself, present

oneself to view, **come to light,** see the light, see the light of day; **emerge,** issue, issue forth, stream forth, come forth, come to the fore, come out, come forward, come one's way, come to hand
2 be published, **come out,** break, hit the streets <nonformal>, **issue,** go *or* come forth, find vent, **see the light,** see the light of day, become public; **circulate, spread,** spread about, have currency, **get around** *or* about, **go the rounds,** pass from mouth to mouth, be on everyone's lips

appearance NOUNS 1 **appearing,** showing-up, coming forth, coming on the scene, making the scene <nonformal>, putting in an appearance; **emergence,** issuing, issuance; **disclosure, exposure,** opening, unfolding, showing
2 exterior, externals, **mere externals, facade,** outside, **show, outward show, image,** display, front <nonformal>, outward *or* external appearance, surface appearance, surface show, vain show, apparent character, public image, window dressing, cosmetics
3 <thing appearing> **apparition,** phenomenon; **vision, image, shape, form,** figure, presence; false image, mirage, specter, **phantom**

appease VERBS **pacify, conciliate, placate, propitiate, mollify,** dulcify; **calm, settle, soothe,** tranquilize; smooth over *or* out, smooth down, smooth one's feathers; pour oil on troubled waters, pour balm on, take the sting out of

append VERBS affix, attach, annex, adjoin, conjoin, subjoin, prefix, suffix, infix, postfix, tag, tag on, **tack on** <nonformal>, slap on <nonformal>, hitch on <nonformal>

appendage NOUNS 1 **external organ; head, arm, leg,** etc
2 **adjunct, addition,** increase, **increment,** augmentation, supplementation, complementation, *additum* <L>, addendum, addenda <pl>, accession, fixture; **annex,** annexation; appurtenance, appurtenant; **accessory,** attachment; **supplement,** complement, continuation, extrapolation, extension

appendix NOUNS vermiform appendix *or* process; **sequel,** sequela *or* sequelae, sequelant, sequent, sequitur, **consequence**; **continuation,** continuance, **follow-up** *or* **follow-through** <nonformal>; **supplement,** addendum, back matter

appetite NOUNS 1 **craving, coveting, lust; hunger, thirst, appetency** *or* appetence; aching void; **itch, itching,** prurience *or* pruriency; **sexual desire; mania**

appetite, an universal wolf
SHAKESPEARE

2 **eagerness, enthusiasm, avidity,** avidness, keenness <chiefly Brit>, forwardness, prothymia, **readiness,** promptness, quickness, **alacrity,** cheerful readiness, *empressement* <Fr>; **zest,** zestfulness, gusto

appetizer NOUNS *apéritif* <Fr>; foretaste, *antipasto* <Ital>, *Vorspeise* <Ger>; **hors d'oeuvre;** *crostato* <Ital>; smorgasbord; canapé; **dip**

appetizing ADJS mouth-watering, piquant; **alluring, fascinating, captivating, riveting, charming, glamorous,** exotic, **enchanting,** spellful, spellbinding, **entrancing,** ravishing, **enravishing, intriguing, enthralling,** witching, **bewitching; tempting**

applaud VERBS 1 **cheer,** give a cheer, give three cheers, **cry, shout, yell,** cry for joy, yell oneself hoarse; shout hosanna *or* hallelujah
2 **congratulate, felicitate,** bless, **compliment,** tender *or* offer one's congratulations *or* felicitations *or* compliments; shake one's hand, pat one on the back

applause NOUNS plaudit, éclat, **acclaim, acclamation; clapping,** handclapping, clapping of hands; **cheer**; burst of applause; **round of applause, hand, big hand; ovation,** standing ovation

appliance NOUNS **implement,** device; contrivance, lever, mechanism; fixture; labor-saving device

applicable ADJS 1 **usable, utilizable;** appliable; practical, operable
2 **relevant, pertinent,** appertaining, **germane, apposite,** cogent, material, admissible, applying, pertaining, belonging, involving, appropriate, **apropos,** *à propos* <Fr>, to the purpose, **to the point**

applicant NOUNS **petitioner, supplicant,** suppliant, suitor; solicitant, claimant; **aspirant, candidate,** postulant

application NOUNS 1 **industry,** industriousness, assiduousness, **assiduity, diligence,** concentration, laboriousness, sedulity, **sedulousness,** unsparingness,

relentlessness, zealousness, ardor, fervor, vehemence
2 **use, employment,** utilization, employ <old>, **usage; exercise, exertion,** active use; good use; expenditure, expending, using up, exhausting, dissipation, dissipating, **consumption**
3 **request,** asking; desire, wish, expressed desire; **petition,** petitioning, impetration, address

apply VERBS 1 **put to use** *or* **good use,** carry out, put into execution, **put into practice** *or* **operation,** put in force, enforce; bring to bear upon
2 **petition,** present *or* prefer a petition, sign a petition, circulate a petition; **pray,** sue
3 **relate, associate, connect,** interconnect, ally, link, link up, wed, marry, marry up, weld, bind, tie, couple, bracket, equate, identify

appoint VERBS 1 **elect, vote in,** place in office
2 **equip, furnish, outfit,** gear, **prepare, fit,** fit up *or* out, fix up <nonformal>, **rig,** rig up *or* out, **turn out,** accouter, clothe, dress; man, staff

appointment NOUNS 1 **engagement, date** <nonformal>, double date *and* blind date <both nonformal>
2 **position, job,** employment, gainful employment, situation, **office, post, place,** station, berth, billet, engagement, gig <nonformal>

apportion VERBS **portion, parcel, partition, part, divide,** share; share with, cut *or* deal one in <nonformal>, share and share alike, divide with; divide into shares, divide up, divvy *or* divvy up *or* out <nonformal>, **split,** split up, carve, cut, slice, carve up, slice up, cut up, cut *or* slice the pie *or* melon <nonformal>

appraisal NOUNS **stocktaking, assay,** assaying; **assessment,** determination, rating, valuation, evaluation

appreciable ADJS **substantial,** substantive; **solid, concrete; tangible,** sensible, palpable, ponderable; **material**; **real**

appreciate VERBS 1 **enjoy,** be pleased with, receive *or* derive pleasure from, take delight *or* pleasure in, get a kick *or* boot *or* bang *or* charge *or* lift *or* rush out of <nonformal>; feast on, gloat over *or* on; **relish,** savor, smack the lips
2 **be grateful, be obliged,** feel *or* be *or* lie under an obligation, be obligated *or* indebted, be in the debt of, give credit *or* due credit; **be thankful,** thank one's lucky stars, thank *or* bless one's stars; be appreciative of
3 **grow, increase, advance; gain,** get ahead; wax, swell, balloon, bloat, mount, **rise,** go up, crescendo, snowball

appreciative ADJS **grateful, thankful; obliged, much obliged,** beholden, indebted to, crediting, under obligation, acknowledging, cognizant of; **approbatory, approbative, commendatory, complimentary, laudatory,** acclamatory, eulogistic, panegyric, panegyrical, encomiastic

apprehend VERBS 1 **arrest,** make an arrest, put under arrest, pick up; catch flat-footed; catch with one's pants down *or* hand in the till <nonformal>, catch one in the act *or* red-handed *or* in flagrante delicto, catch *or* have one dead to rights
2 **know, perceive,** prehend, cognize, recognize, discern, see, make out; conceive, conceptualize; **realize, appreciate, understand, comprehend,** fathom; dig <nonformal>

apprehension NOUNS 1 apprehensiveness, **misgiving, qualm,** qualmishness, funny feeling; foreboding; **misgiving,** chill *or* quiver along the spine
2 **arrest,** pinch *and* bust *and* collar <all nonformal>; **capture, seizure**

apprehensive ADJS **concerned,** foreboding, misgiving, suspenseful, strained, tense, tensed up <nonformal>, nail-biting, white-knuckle <nonformal>; **fearful**; **on pins and needles,** on tenterhooks

apprentice NOUNS 1 **novice,** novitiate *or* noviciate, **tyro,** abecedarian, alphabetarian, **beginner**, entrant, **neophyte, tenderfoot** *and* **greenhorn** <both nonformal>, freshman, **fledgling;** catechumen, initiate, debutant
VERBS 2 **train; drill, exercise; prepare,** ready, **condition, groom,** fit, put in tune, form, **lick into shape** <nonformal>; indenture, article, bind, bind over
ADJS 3 **indentured,** articled, bound over; **apprenticed**

apprise VERBS **inform, advise, advertise,** mention to, **acquaint, enlighten,** familiarize, brief, verse, give the facts, give an account of, give by way of information; **give** *or* **lead one to believe** *or* **understand;** notify, give notice *or* notification, serve notice; **communicate**; bring *or* send *or* leave word; **disclose**

approach NOUNS 1 **approaching, coming** *or* going toward, coming *or* going near, **access,** accession, nearing; **advent, coming,** forthcoming; imminence; approximation
2 **entrance,** entry, gate, door, portal, **entranceway,** entryway; **inlet,** ingress, intake, adit, **access,** means of access, in <nonformal>, way in; a foot in the door, an opening wedge, the camel's nose under the wall of the tent
3 **manner, way, means, mode,** modality, **fashion, style,** tone, guise <old>; **method,** methodology, **system;** algorithm <math>
4 **offer,** proffer, presentation, **bid; advance, overture,** approach, invitation; **feeler** <nonformal>; asking price
VERBS 5 **near, draw near** *or* nigh, go *or* come near, go *or* come toward, come closer *or* nearer; **accost,** encounter, confront
6 **communicate with, get in touch** *or* **contact with, contact** <nonformal>, **make contact with,** raise, reach, get to, get through to, get hold of, make *or* establish connection, get in connection with
7 **bribe,** throw a sop to; grease *and* **grease the palm** *or* **hand** *and* oil the palm *and* tickle the palm <all nonformal>; buy *and* **buy off** *and* pay off <all nonformal>; suborn, **corrupt,** tamper with; reach *and* get at *and* get to <all nonformal>

appropriate VERBS 1 **steal, thieve, purloin, take,** snatch, palm, **make off with,** walk off with, run off *or* away with, abstract; have one's hand in the till; **pilfer, filch**
ADJS 2 **apposite, suitable;** applicable, relevant, likely, sortable, seasonable, opportune; **fitting,** befitting, **suiting,** becoming; **fit,** fitted, qualified, **suited,** adapted, geared, tailored, dovetailing, meshing

approval NOUNS 1 **respect, regard,** consideration, appreciation, favor; **esteem,** estimation, prestige
2 **approbation; sanction,** acceptance, countenance, **favor; admiration, esteem, respect**; endorsement

Our polite recognition of another's resemblance to ourselves
AMBROSE BIERCE

approve VERBS **adopt;** ratify, pass, carry, endorse, sign off on <nonformal>; accept, **embrace,** espouse; **approve of,** think well of, take kindly to; **sanction, accept; admire, esteem, respect; favor,** view with favor

approximate VERBS 1 approach, near, come near, come close; **compare with,** stack up with <nonformal>; **correspond, match, parallel**
ADJS 2 **approaching,** nearing, approximating, proximate, proximal

approximately ADVS nearly, some, about, circa; more or less, *plus ou moins* <Fr>, by and large

approximation NOUNS **estimation,** estimate, rough measure, ballpark figure <nonformal>; **appraisal,** appraisement, **assay,** assaying; rough idea, sketch; coordinate, reciprocal, obverse, equivalent; correlate, correlative; **likeness,** like, the like of *or* **the likes of** <nonformal>; suchlike, such; simulacrum; **close match, match-up**

apropos ADJS 1 **germane, apposite,** cogent, material, admissible, applicable, applying, pertaining, belonging, involving, **appropriate,** *à propos* <Fr>, to the purpose, **to the point,** in point, *ad rem* <L>
ADVS 2 **incidentally, by the way, by the by;** speaking of, *à propos* <Fr>; **in passing,** *en passant* <Fr>; parenthetically, by way of parenthesis

apt ADJS 1 **apposite, appropriate, suitable;** applicable, relevant, likely, sortable, seasonable, opportune; **fitting,** befitting, **suiting,** becoming; to the point, to the purpose, on the button *and* on the money <both nonformal>
2 **teachable, instructable, educable,** schoolable, trainable; quick, **ready,** ripe for instruction; **receptive, willing,** motivated; docile, **malleable, moldable,** pliable, facile, plastic, **impressionable,** susceptible, formable

aptitude NOUNS 1 flair; **bent, turn,** propensity, **leaning,** inclination, tendency; turn for, capacity for, gift for, genius for; an eye for, an ear for, a hand for, a way with; ready wit, quick wit, sprightly wit, *esprit* <Fr>
2 **fitness** *or* fittedness, **suitability, appropriateness,** propriety, admissibility; **aptness,** qualification

aquatic ADJS **water-dwelling,** water-living, water-growing, water-loving; **swim-**

ming, balneal, natant, natatory, natatorial; **watery,** waterish, **aqueous**

aqueous ADJS watery, aquatic; **liquid;** splashy, **plashy, sloppy; hydraulic**

arbiter NOUNS **connoisseur,** *connaisseur* <Fr>, *cognoscente* <Ital>; **judge,** good judge, **critic, expert,** authority, maven <nonformal>, arbiter, arbiter of taste, *arbiter elegantiarum* <L>, tastemaker, trend-setter; **epicure,** epicurean; **gourmet, gourmand,** *bon vivant* <Fr>

arbitrary ADJS **capricious, whimsical,** freakish; **fanciful, notional,** fantastic *or* fantastical, maggoty, **crotchety,** kinky, harebrained, cranky, flaky <nonformal>, quirky; petulant; unrestrained

arbitrator NOUNS arbiter, impartial arbitrator, third party, unbiased observer; **moderator; umpire, referee, judge; go-between, middleman, intermediary, medium,** intermediate, **internuncio,** broker; **negotiator;** mediator

arc NOUNS 1 **curve,** sinus; **bow; crook, hook;** parabola, hyperbola; ellipse; catenary, festoon, swag
VERBS 2 **curve, turn,** sweep; **crook, hook,** loop; incurve, incurvate; recurve, decurve, bend back, retroflex; sag, swag <nonformal>; **bend,** flex; deflect, inflect; reflect, reflex; **bow,** embow; **arch,** vault; dome; **hump**

arcade NOUNS **corridor, hall,** hallway; passage, **passageway; gallery,** loggia; colonnade, pergola, cloister, peristyle; areaway; breezeway

arcane ADJS esoteric, occult, cabalistic, hermetic; enigmatic, mysterious; **secret,** close, closed, closet; cryptic, dark; unuttered, unrevealed, undivulged, undisclosed, unspoken, untold

arch NOUNS 1 **span, vault,** vaulting, concameration, camber; ogive; apse; **dome,** cupola; arched roof, ceilinged roof
2 **pillar,** stele *or* stela, shaft, column, memorial column, rostral column, manubial column; war memorial; memorial arch, triumphal arch
VERBS 3 vault; dome; **hump,** hunch; wind, curl; round; **curve, turn,** arc, sweep; **crook, hook,** loop; incurve, incurvate; recurve, decurve, bend back, retroflex; sag, swag <nonformal>; **bend,** flex; deflect, inflect; reflect, reflex; **bow**
ADJS 4 **chief, main, principal,** paramount, **foremost,** headmost, **leading, dominant,** crowning, capital, **cardinal;** master, magisterial; central, focal, prime, **primary,** primal, first; **preeminent**
5 **cunning, crafty, artful, wily,** guileful, **sly,** insidious, **shifty, smooth, slick** *and* slick as a whistle <both nonformal>, **slippery,** snaky, serpentine, **foxy,** vulpine, feline; **canny, shrewd,** knowing, sharp, razor-sharp, cute, acute, astute, **clever**

archdiocese NOUNS **diocese, see,** bishopric, archbishopric; province

architecture NOUNS 1 architectural design, building design, the art and technique of building; **architectural science,** architectural engineering, architectural technology

frozen music
GOETHE

the art of significant forms in space
CLAUDE BRAGDON

2 **structure, construction,** tectonics, architectonics, **frame,** make, **build,** fabric, tissue, texture, contexture, mold, **shape, pattern, plan,** fashion, arrangement, **organization**; organism, organic structure

archives NOUNS public records, government archives, government papers, presidential papers, historical documents, historical records, memorabilia

arctic ADJS 1 **northern,** north, northernmost, northerly, northbound, boreal, hyperborean; **southern,** south, southernmost, southerly, southbound, meridional, **antarctic,** austral
2 **cold, freezing,** freezing cold, **crisp, brisk,** nipping, **nippy, snappy** <nonformal>, **raw, bleak, keen, sharp,** bitter, biting, pinching, cutting, **piercing,** penetrating; **frigid,** bitter *or* bitterly cold, gelid, algid; numbing; Siberian, boreal, hyperborean

ardent ADJS 1 **industrious, assiduous, diligent, sedulous,** laborious, **hardworking;** hard, unremitting, unsparing, relentless, zealous, fervent, vehement; tireless, unwearied, unflagging, indefatigable
2 **amorous,** amatory; **passionate,** impassioned

arduous ADJS **laborious, toilsome, strenuous,** operose, onerous, oppressive, burdensome; wearisome; tough <non-

formal>, uphill, **backbreaking,** grueling, punishing, crushing, killing, Herculean

area NOUNS 1 **region, zone,** belt, **territory,** terrain; **district, quarter, section,** department, division; precincts, environs, milieu
2 **vocation**; **forte, métier, strong point,** long suit; specialism, specialization; cup of tea *and* bag *and* thing *and* weakness <all nonformal>

arena NOUNS **scene of action, site,** scene, setting, background, **field, ground,** terrain, sphere, place, locale, milieu, precinct, purlieu; athletic field, field, playing field; stamping ground, turf, bailiwick

argue VERBS **dispute,** polemicize, **bandy words, plead,** pettifog <nonformal>, join issue, give and take, cut and thrust, try conclusions, cross swords, lock horns, **contend, contest,** spar, **bicker, wrangle,** hassle <nonformal>, have it out

argument NOUNS 1 **quarrel, dispute,** polemic, **controversy,** altercation, **fight, squabble, contention,** strife, **tussle,** bicker, wrangle, snarl, **tiff, spat,** fuss
2 *argumentum* <L>; **case, plea,** pleading, *plaidoyer* <Fr>, brief

aria NOUNS **air, tune, melody,** line, melodic line, refrain, note, **song, strain**

arise VERBS 1 **emerge, come out, issue,** issue forth, come into view, extrude, **come forth; surface,** rise to the surface; **originate,** be born, come into the world, **become,** come to be, get to be <nonformal>, see the light of day
2 **rise,** ascend, mount, uprise, **rise up, get up,** get to one's feet; **revolt, rebel,** kick over the traces, reluct, reluctate; rise up, rise up in arms, mount the barricades

aristocracy NOUNS **nobility,** titled aristocracy, hereditary nobility, noblesse; **elite, upper classes** *or* circles, **upper crust** <nonformal>

aristocrat NOUNS **patrician,** Brahmin, blue-blood, socialite, swell *and* uppercruster <both nonformal>, grandee, grand dame, dowager, magnifico, lord of creation

aristocratic ADJS **upper-class, patrician, upscale; highborn,** highbred; born to the purple, born with a silver spoon in one's mouth; **noble,** of rank, high, exalted

to the manner born
SHAKESPEARE

arm VERBS **equip, furnish, outfit,** gear, **prepare, fit,** fit up *or* out, fix up <nonformal>, **rig,** rig up *or* out

armada NOUNS **fleet,** flotilla, argosy, squadron, escadrille, division, task force, task group

armed ADJS armed and ready, in arms, up in arms; in battle array, mobilized; **provided, equipped; readied,** available

arms NOUNS **weapons,** instruments of destruction, offensive weapons, **military hardware,** matériel, **weaponry, armament, munitions, ordnance,** munitions of war, *apparatus belli* <L>

army NOUNS forces, troops, host, array, legions; ranks, rank and file; **standing army, regular army,** professional *or* career soldiers

aroma NOUNS **fragrance, perfume,** scent, redolence, **incense, bouquet, odor;** muskiness; fruitiness

aromatic ADJS **fragrant,** odoriferous, redolent, **perfumed, scented,** sweet-smelling, sweet-scented, savory, balmy, ambrosial; **odorous**; fruity; musky

around ADVS round, **about,** in the neighborhood *or* vicinity *or* vicinage

arouse VERBS **excite, impassion, rouse, stir, stir up,** set astir, stir the feelings, stir the blood, cause a stir *or* commotion, play on the feelings; **foment, incite**; turn on <nonformal>

arrange VERBS 1 **prepare, make** *or* **get ready,** prep <nonformal>, **ready, fix** <nonformal>; fix *or* ready up <both nonformal>, put in *or* into shape, get one's ducks in a row <nonformal>; **put** *or* **set to rights, get it together** <nonformal>, **pull it together,** put in *or* into shape, whip into shape <nonformal>
2 **settle; adjust,** fine-tune, accommodate, reshuffle, rejigger <nonformal>, **compose,** fix, make up, straighten out, put *or* set straight

arrangement NOUNS **ordering,** structuring, shaping, forming, configurating, configuration, constitution; **disposition, disposal, deployment,** placement, **formation,** formulation, **configuration,** form, array; **order; organization**; **disposition,** disposal, deployment, marshaling

arrears NOUNS arrearage, back debts, back payments; **deficit,** default, deferred payments; cash *or* credit crunch <nonformal>

arrest VERBS 1 **slow, slow down** *or* **up,**

let down *or* **up, ease off** *or* **up, slack off** *or* **up, slacken,** relax, moderate, taper off, lose speed *or* momentum; **put on the brakes**
2 make an arrest, put under arrest, pick up; take prisoner, apprehend, capture, seize, net <nonformal>, **take into custody**

3<nonformal> **bust, pinch,** make a pinch, nab, pull in, **run in,** collar

4 **impede, inhibit, check,** countercheck, scotch, **curb,** snub; **resist, oppose**

arrive VERBS arrive at, arrive in, come, **come** *or* **get to,** approach, access, **reach, hit** <nonformal>; find, **gain,** attain, attain to, accomplish, achieve, make, **make it** <nonformal>, reach one's destination

arrogant ADJS **overbearing, superior,** domineering, **proud, haughty;** high-flown, high-falutin *and* high-faluting <both nonformal>; **condescending, patronizing,** *de haut en bas* <Fr>

arsonist NOUNS **incendiary,** torcher <nonformal>; pyromaniac, firebug <nonformal>

art NOUNS 1 **representation, delineation,** presentment, drawing, **portrayal, portraiture, depiction,** depictment, rendering, rendition, limning, imaging; **realization;** imagery
2 **visual arts; artwork,** the arts; **fine arts,** *beaux arts* <Fr>; **design,** art form; abstract art, representational art
3 **artistry, talent,** artistic skill, artistic flair, artistic invention
4 craftiness, **artfulness, artifice, wiliness,** wiles, guile, **slyness,** insidiousness, **foxiness,** slipperiness, shiftiness, trickiness

artery NOUNS **passageway, pass,** passage, defile; **avenue;** corridor, aisle, alley, lane; **channel,** conduit

artful ADJS **wily,** guileful, **sly,** insidious, **shifty,** pawky <Brit>, arch, **smooth, slick** *and* slick as a whistle <both nonformal>, **slippery,** snaky, serpentine, **foxy,** vulpine, feline; **canny, shrewd,** knowing, sharp, manipulative, manipulatory; **deceitful**

article NOUNS 1 **news item,** piece of news; **story,** piece; copy
2 **object, thing,** material thing, affair, something; artifact

artifact NOUNS **relic, fossil; product,** end product, production, manufacture; **work,** *œhuvre* <Fr>, **handiwork; object, thing,** material thing

artificial ADJS **affected, pretentious, mannered,** *maniéré* <Fr>; **unnatural,** insincere

artillery NOUNS **cannon,** cannonry, ordnance, engines of war, howitzer; field artillery; heavy artillery, mountain artillery, coast artillery, anti-aircraft artillery

artisan NOUNS **skilled worker, journeyman,** mechanic; **craftsman, handicraftsman;** artificer; *fabbro* <Ital>

artist NOUNS **entertainer,** public entertainer, performer; artiste; **musician,** performer, interpreter, concert artist, **virtuoso; vaudevillian,** dancer, **stripteaser,** singer

artistic ADJS **aesthetic,** pleasing, choice; pure, chaste; classic *or* classical, Attic, restrained, understated, unobtrusive, quiet, subdued, simple, unaffected; painterly

artistry NOUNS **competence,** capability, capacity, ability; **facility, prowess;** grace, style, finesse; **art, talent,** artistic skill, artistic flair, artistic invention

artwork NOUNS **work of art,** objet d'art, art object, piece, **work, study, design, composition;** creation, brainchild; virtu, article *or* piece of virtu; **masterpiece,** *chef d'œhuvre* <Fr>, masterwork, old master, classic

ascend VERBS **rise, mount,** arise, up, uprise, levitate, upgo, **go up,** rise up, come up; stand up, **rear,** rear up, **tower,** loom

ascending ADJS in the ascendant, **mounting, rising,** uprising, upgoing, upcoming; climbing, scandent, scansorial; **uphill, upgrade;** acclivous, acclivitous, acclinate

ascertain VERBS **learn, gain knowledge,** pick up information, gather *or* collect *or* glean knowledge *or* learning; **find out, discover,** find, determine; **become informed,** gain knowledge *or* understanding of, acquire information *or* intelligence about, **learn about, find out about**

ascetic NOUNS 1 **recluse, loner,** solitary; cloistered monk *or* nun; **hermit,** eremite, anchorite; stylite
2 **abstainer,** abstinent; **teetotaler,** teetotalist

ADJS 3 austere, self-denying, self-abnegating, **rigorous, puritanical,** eremitic, anchoritic

aseptic ADJS **sanitary, hygienic, prophylactic; sterile,** antiseptic, **uninfected;** disinfected, decontaminated, sterilized

asexual ADJS **sexless, neuter,** neutral; castrated, emasculated, eunuchized; **cold, frigid**

ashamed ADJS **humiliated,** humbled, mortified <old>, **embarrassed, chagrined, abashed, crushed, red-faced,** shamed, ashamed of oneself, shamefaced

ashen ADJS **colorless, hueless,** toneless, uncolored, achromic, achromatic, achromatous; **faded, washed-out,** dimmed, discolored, etiolated; **pale, dim,** weak, **faint; pallid, wan, sallow;** white as a sheet; ashy, ashen-hued, cinereous, cineritious, gray, griseous

ashore ADVS **on land,** on dry land, on terra firma

asinine ADJS **foolish, fatuous,** fatuitous, inept, **inane;** futile; **senseless, witless, thoughtless,** insensate, brainless

ask VERBS 1 **request,** make a request, **ask for,** order, put in an order for, bespeak, call for, trouble one for; demand

2 **invite, call, summon,** extend *or* issue an invitation, request the presence of, request the pleasure of one's company

askance ADVS 1 **warily, charily,** cagily <nonformal>; distrustfully

2 **disapprovingly, unfavorably;** critically, reproachfully, rebukingly; captiously

askew ADVS 1 **awry,** askance, askant, asquint, squinting, **cockeyed** <nonformal>; **crooked**

2 **disorderly, in disorder,** disordered, **disorganized, disarranged, discomposed,** dislocated, deranged, convulsed; **out of kilter** *or* **kelter** <nonformal>, **out of whack** <nonformal>, out of gear, out of joint, out of tune, on the fritz <nonformal>

asleep ADJS 1 **sleeping, slumbering,** in the arms *or* lap of Morpheus, in the land of Nod; **sound asleep, fast asleep,** dead to the world

2 **unalert, unwary, unwatchful, unvigilant,** uncautious, incautious; nodding, napping, **asleep at the switch** *and* asleep on the job *and* **not on the job** *and* goofing off; daydreaming, woolgathering

aspect NOUNS look, view; effect, impression, **form, shape,** figure, configuration, gestalt; **respect, regard,** reference, light

aspersion NOUNS slur, **remark, reflection,** imputation, **insinuation,** suggestion, innuendo, disparaging *or* uncomplimentary remark, slap *or* kick in the face

asphalt NOUNS **pavement,** paving; macadam, blacktop, bitumen, tarmacadam, tarmac, tarvia, bituminous macadam

asphyxiation NOUNS **suffocation,** smothering, asphyxia; **choking**

aspirant NOUNS **applicant,** solicitant, claimant; seeker; postulant; **candidate,** hopeful *and* political hopeful <both nonformal>, office seeker *or* hunter, baby kisser <nonformal>

aspire VERBS **be ambitious;** aspire to, try to reach; aim high, keep one's eyes on the stars, raise one's sights, set one's sights, reach for the sky

hitch one's wagon to a star
EMERSON

aspiring ADJS **ambitious,** on the make <nonformal>; **hopeful, hoping, in hopes,** full of hope

ass NOUNS 1 **donkey, burro,** Rocky Mountain canary <W US>; **jackass,** jenny; **mule,** sumpter mule, sumpter; hinny, jennet

2 **fool, damn fool,** tomfool, perfect fool, born fool; *schmuck* <Yiddish>; jackass, stupid ass

3 **sex object;** piece *and* meat *and* piece of meat *and* piece of ass *and* hot number <all nonformal>

4 <nonformal> arse *and* bum <both chiefly Brit>, behind, backside, **butt, can,** cheeks, hind end, nether cheeks, stern, tail, rusty-dusty, **fanny,** prat, keister, popo, rear, rear end, tuchis *or* tushy *or* tush

assail VERBS 1 **attack, assault,** harry, assume *or* take the offensive; commit an assault upon

2 criticize, reprove, **castigate, flay,** skin alive <nonformal>, lash, slash, **excoriate,** fustigate, **roast** <nonformal>, blister

assailant NOUNS assailer, **attacker;** assaulter, mugger <nonformal>; **aggressor**

assassin NOUNS **killer, slayer, slaughterer, butcher, murderer, cutthroat,** gorilla <nonformal>, hired killer, hit man *or* button man *or* gun *or* trigger man *or* torpedo *or* gunsel <all nonformal>; **hatchet man**

assassination NOUNS murder, bloody murder <nonformal>; serial killing; hit *and* bump-off *and* bumping-off <all nonformal>, gangland-style execution; kiss of death; foul play

assault NOUNS 1 **attack; offense, offensive; strike;** surgical strike, first strike
2 **berating,** rating, tongue-lashing; **revilement, vilification,** blackening, **execration, abuse, vituperation,** invective, contumely, hard *or* cutting *or* bitter words; **tirade, diatribe,** screed, philippic
VERBS 3 **attack, assail,** harry, assume *or* take the offensive; commit an assault upon; **strike, hit, pound; launch out against, fall on** *or* **upon, set on** *or* **upon, descend on** *or* upon, come down on, swoop down on; pounce upon; blitz

assay NOUNS 1 **analysis,** chemical analysis, assaying, resolution, titration, qualitative analysis, quantitative analysis, volumetric analysis, gravimetric analysis
2 **test, trial, try;** essay; acid test, litmus *or* litmus-paper test; ordeal, crucible
VERBS 3 **measure, guage, quantify,** quantitate, quantize, take the measure of, mensurate,triangulate, apply the yardstick to; **estimate,** make an approximation; **assess, rate, appraise, valuate, value,** evaluate, appreciate, prize

ass-backwards ADJS 1 **backward,** reversed, reflex, **turned around,** back; wrong-way, wrong-way around, counter, bassackwards <nonformal>; misinterpreted
ADVS 2 **backwards,** backward, **hindwards,** hindward, **rearwards,** rearward, arear, astern

assemble VERBS gather; drum up, muster, rally, **mobilize; accumulate,** cumulate, **amass,** mass, bulk, batch; agglomerate, conglomerate, aggregate; **combine, gather together,** draw *or* lump *or* batch *or* bunch together, pack, pack in, cram, cram in; **bunch,** bunch up; **cluster,** clump

assembly NOUNS 1 **council,** conclave, *concilium* <L>, deliberative *or* advisory body; deliberative assembly, consultative assembly
2 **collection, gathering,** ingathering, **congregation;** concourse, concurrence, conflux, confluence, convergence; assemblage

assent NOUNS 1 acquiescence, concurrence, concurring, concurrency, **compliance, agreement,** acceptance, accession
VERBS 2 **acquiesce, consent, comply, accede, agree,** agree to *or* with, have no problem with; find it in one's heart; take kindly to *and* hold with <both nonformal>; **accept,** receive, buy <nonformal>, take one up on <nonformal>; **subscribe to,** acquiesce in

assert VERBS assever <old>, asseverate, **aver,** protest, lay down, avouch, avow, **declare,** say loud and clear, sound off <nonformal>, have one's say, speak one's piece *or* one's mind, speak up *or* out, **state,** set down, put in one's two-cents worth <nonformal>; **maintain, contend,** argue, **insist, hold,** submit, maintain with one's last breath

assertive ADJS **affirmative,** affirming, affirmatory; **positive,** absolute, emphatic, decided, table-thumping <nonformal>, unambiguously, unmistakably

assess VERBS **price,** place a value on, **value, evaluate,** valuate, **appraise, rate,** prize, apprize; **classify,** class, **categorize**

assets NOUNS **means, resources, worth,** net worth, what one is worth; circumstances, funds; wealth

asshole NOUNS

<nonformal> **jerk, horse's ass,** creep, **shit,** shithead, shitface, fart, **louse, meanie, heel, shitheel, rat, stinker,** dirtbag, dork, geek, dweeb, twerp, sleaze

assiduous ADJS **diligent, sedulous,** industrious; dogged, plodding, slogging, plugging; **pertinacious, tenacious, stick-to-itive** <nonformal>; **unswerving,** unremitting, unabating, unintermitting, uninterrupted; **unfaltering, unwavering,** relentless, **indefatigable,** undaunted, indomitable

assign VERBS 1 **allot,** lot, **appoint, set,** detail; **allocate,** tag, mark out for; set off, mark off, portion off; assign to, appropriate to *or* for; give *or* make an assignment, set a task

2 **transfer, convey, deliver,** hand, pass, negotiate; **hand over, turn over, pass over; consign,** confer, settle, settle on; cede, bequeath; **make over, sign over,** sign away; **deed,** deed over, give title to

assignment NOUNS 1 **allotment, appointment,** setting aside, **earmarking,** tagging; **allocation; task, work, stint, job,** labor, piece of work, **chore,** chare, odd job; homework
2 **transfer,** transference; **conveyance,** conveyancing; **consignment,** settling, settlement; entailment

assist NOUNS 1 **helping hand, hand, lift; boost** *and* leg up <both nonformal>; help in time of need
VERBS 2 minister to, act for, act in the interests of, **promote, advance, forward,** facilitate; **aid, help,** comfort, **succor,** relieve, **ease,** doctor, remedy; give help, render assistance, come to the aid of, rush *or* fly to the assistance of, **give** *or* **lend** *or* **bear a hand** *or* **helping hand,** hold out a helping hand

assistance NOUNS 1 **aid, help, support, succor, relief, comfort,** ease, remedy; mutual help *or* assistance; **service, benefit**
2 **subsidy,** subvention, subsidization, support, **allowance, stipend,** allotment; financial assistance; **help,** pecuniary aid

assistant NOUNS **helper,** auxiliary, aide, paraprofessional; **help, helpmate, helpmeet;** deputy, **agent**; **attendant, second,** acolyte

associate NOUNS 1 **confederate,** consociate, **colleague,** fellow member, **companion, fellow,** bedfellow, **crony,** consort, cohort, compatriot, **ally,** adjunct, coadjutor
ADJS 2 **related, connected; associated, affiliated,** filiated, **allied,** affiliate; interlocked, **interrelated,** interlinked, involved, implicated, overlapping, interpenetrating, **correlated**

association NOUNS 1 **association of ideas,** chain of ideas, concatenation, mental linking
2 **society,** body; **alliance, coalition, league, union;** council; **bloc,** axis; **partnership; federation, confederation,** confederacy; grouping, assemblage

assorted ADJS 1 **diversified, varied,** heterogeneous; **various,** divers <old>, diverse, sundry, **several, many;** of all sorts *or* conditions *or* kinds *or* shapes *or* descriptions *or* types
2 **classified, cataloged,** indexed, sorted, **graded, grouped,** ranked, rated, stratified, hierarchic

assortment NOUNS 1 **miscellany,** miscellanea, collectanea; **medley, variety, mixture**; hodgepodge, conglomerate, **conglomeration, odds and ends**
2 **grouping, classification**, categorization, taxonomy; **sorting,** sorting out, sifting, screening, triage, culling

assume VERBS 1 **undertake,** accept, **take on, take upon oneself,** take upon one's shoulders
2 **appropriate, adopt, usurp,** arrogate, accroach; **take possession of,** possess oneself of, take for oneself, arrogate to oneself
3 **suppose, presume, surmise,** expect, **suspect, infer, understand, gather, conclude, deduce, consider,** reckon, divine, imagine, **fancy,** dream, conceive, **believe, deem,** repute, feel, **think,** be inclined to think, opine, daresay

assumed name NOUNS **alias, pseudonym,** anonym, false *or* fictitious name, *nom de guerre* <Fr>; **pen name, nom de plume;** stage name, *nom de thé[aca]tre* <Fr>, professional name

assumption NOUNS 1 **appropriation, taking over, takeover** <nonformal>, **adoption, usurpation,** arrogation
2 **presumption, imposition; license,** licentiousness, **undue liberty,** liberties

assurance NOUNS 1 **confidence,** confidentness, conviction, belief, fixed *or* settled belief, **sureness, assuredness,** surety, security, certitude
2 **insurance; annuity, social security**

assure VERBS 1 **secure, guarantee, guaranty, warrant, insure,** ensure, bond, **certify; endorse**
2 **satisfy;** put one's mind at rest on; sell *and* sell one on <both nonformal>; make *or* carry one's point, bring *or* drive home to; inspire belief *or* confidence

assuring ADJS 1 **comforting, consoling,** consolatory, of good comfort; **reassuring,** supportive; **encouraging, heartening; cheering**
2 **persuasive,** impressive, satisfying, satisfactory, confidence-building; decisive, absolute, conclusive, determinative

astonish VERBS **amaze, astound, surprise,** startle, stagger, **bewilder, perplex**, flabbergast <nonformal>, confound, overwhelm, **boggle the mind; awe,** strike with wonder *or* awe; **dumb-**

found, strike dumb; knock one's socks off *and* bowl down *or* over <all nonformal>, dazzle, bedazzle; **stun, stupefy**

astonishing ADJS **amazing, surprising,** startling, **astounding,** confounding, staggering, stunning <nonformal>, eye-opening, breathtaking, overwhelming, mind-boggling *or* -numbing; **remarkable, outstanding,** extraordinary, **superior**, **marked,** of mark, signal, conspicuous, **striking; marvelous,** wonderful, formidable, exceptional, uncommon, appalling, humongous <nonformal>, fabulous, fantastic, incredible, egregious

astound VERBS **dismay, disconcert, appall,** confound, abash, discomfit, put out, take aback; **stun, stupefy**

astounding ADJS **terrible,** terrific, tremendous; **dreadful, dread,** dreaded; **awful;** awesome, awe-inspiring; **shocking, appalling; dire,** direful, fell; formidable, redoubtable

astray ADJS 1 **lost,** abroad, adrift, **at sea,** off the track, out of one's bearings, disoriented
ADVS 2 **amiss, beside the mark,** beside the point, to no purpose, vainly, fruitlessly, bootlessly; on the wrong track

astrology NOUNS astromancy, **horoscopy;** astrodiagnosis; natural astrology; judicial *or* mundane astrology

astronaut NOUNS astronavigator, cosmonaut, **spaceman, spacewoman,** space crew member, space traveler, rocketeer, rocket pilot

astronomical ADJS **vast, enormous,** astronomic, humongous *and* jumbo <both nonformal>, tremendous, prodigious, stupendous; **innumerable, numberless,** unnumbered, **countless,** uncounted, uncountable, unreckonable, untold, incalculable, immeasurable, unmeasured, measureless, inexhaustible, endless, infinite, without end *or* limit, more than you can shake a stick at <nonformal>

astronomy NOUNS **stargazing,** uranology, astrognosy, astrography, uranography, uranometry

astute ADJS **sagacious,** longheaded, argute; **understanding, discerning,** penetrating, incisive, acute, trenchant, cogent, piercing; **perspicacious,** perspicuous; **perceptive, percipient,** apperceptive, appercipient

asunder ADJS 1 **distant, remote, removed, far, far-off,** away, **faraway,** way-off, at a distance, separated, apart
ADVS 2 **separately,** severally, piecemeal, one by one; **apart,** adrift, **in two,** in twain

asylum NOUNS 1 **insane asylum,** lunatic asylum, **madhouse,** mental institution, mental home, bedlam; **bughouse** *and* nuthouse *and* laughing academy *and* **loonybin** *and* **booby hatch** *and* funny farm <all nonformal>
2 **refuge, sanctuary,** safehold, **haven, port,** harborage, **harbor;** port in a storm, snug harbor, safe haven; stronghold

asymmetry NOUNS 1 unsymmetry, disproportion, lopsidedness, imbalance, irregularity, **deviation**
2 **inconsistency, incongruity,** inconsonance, incoherence; **incompatibility,** irreconcilability, incommensurability

atavistic ADJS **reversionary, regressive, retrogressive, retrograde;** recidivist *or* recidivistic, recidivous, lapsarian

atelier NOUNS **study,** studio, *atelier* <Fr>, workroom; **office,** workplace

atheist NOUNS 1 **unbeliever, disbeliever,** nonbeliever; **infidel, pagan, heathen;** nullifidian
ADJS 2 **unbelieving, disbelieving, faithless; infidel,** infidelic; **pagan, heathen; atheistic;** nullifidian

athlete NOUNS jock <nonformal>, **player,** competitor, sportsman; letter man

athletics NOUNS **sport, sports,** athletic competition, game, sports activity

atmosphere NOUNS 1 aerosphere, gaseous envelope *or* environment *or* medium *or* blanket, welkin, lift <nonformal>; atmospheric layer *or* stratum *or* belt
2 **milieu, ambience, climate, air,** aura, spirit, feeling, feel, quality, local color, sense, note, tone, overtone, undertone

atoll NOUNS **island, isle; islet,** holm; oceanic island; **reef,** coral reef, coral head; coral island

atomic energy NOUNS **nuclear energy** *or* **power,** thermonuclear power

atomize VERBS 1 **disintegrate, decompose, decay,** dissolve, come apart, disorganize, **break up**, go to rack and ruin, crack up, disjoin, unknit, split, fission, **come** *or* **fall to pieces**
2 **vaporize, evaporate,** volatilize, **gasify;** sublimate, sublime; distill, fractionate; etherify; **etherize**

atom smasher NOUNS **accelerator, parti-**

cle accelerator, atomic accelerator, atomic cannon

atone VERBS **atone for, propitiate, expiate,** compensate, restitute, recompense, redress, redeem, repair, satisfy, give satisfaction, **make amends, make reparation** *or* **compensation** *or* **expiation** *or* **restitution,** make good *or* right, set right

atonement NOUNS **reparation, amends,** making amends, **restitution, propitiation, expiation, redress, recompense,** compensation, setting right, making right *or* good, making up, squaring, redemption, reclamation, satisfaction, quittance; expiatory offering *or* sacrifice, piaculum, peace offering

atop ADVS **on top,** at *or* on the top, topside <nonformal>; on top of the roost *or* heap; on the crest *or* crest of the wave; at the peak *or* pinnacle *or* summit

atrocious ADJS **horrible,** horrific, **horrifying,** horrendous, unspeakable, beyond words; **dreadful, terrible, rotten,** awful *and* beastly <both nonformal>

atrocity NOUNS 1 **act of cruelty,** cruelty, brutality, bestiality, barbarity, inhumanity
2 **iniquity, evil,** bad, wrong, error, obliquity, villainy, knavery, reprobacy, peccancy, **abomination, infamy,** shame

atrophy VERBS **waste, waste away, wither away,** consume, emaciate

attach VERBS 1 **annex; confiscate,** sequester, sequestrate, impound; expropriate, exercise the right of eminent domain
2 **fasten, fix, affix,** annex, put to, set to; graft, engraft; **secure,** anchor, moor; cement, knit, set, grapple, belay, **make fast**

attaché NOUNS commercial attaché, military attaché, **consul,** consular agent; chargé, chargé d'affaires ad interim

attachment NOUNS 1 **affection, devotion, fondness,** sentiment, warm feeling, soft spot in one's heart, weakness <nonformal>, like, **liking,** fancy, shine <nonformal>; **partiality, predilection; passion,** tender feeling *or* passion, **ardor,** ardency, fervor; charity, *caritas* <L>, brotherly love, Christian love, agape, loving concern, **caring**
2 **addition,** accession, annexation, affixation, suffixation, prefixation, agglutination, junction, **joining,** adjunction, uniting; **binding,** bonding, gluing, sticking, tying, lashing, splicing, knotting, linking, trussing

attack NOUNS 1 **seizure,** access, visitation; arrest; blockage, stoppage, occlusion, thrombosis, thromboembolism; **stroke,** ictus, apoplexy; **spasm, throes, fit, paroxysm, convulsion,** eclampsia, frenzy
2 **assault, offense, offensive; aggression; onset, onslaught; strike;** descent on *or* upon; **charge,** rush, dead set at, run at *or* against; **drive, push** <nonformal>; **sally, sortie;** *coup de main* <Fr>; frontal attack *or* assault, head-on attack, flank attack; mass attack, kamikaze attack; banzai attack *or* charge, suicide attack *or* charge; hit-and-run attack
3 **berating,** rating, tongue-lashing; **revilement, vilification,** blackening, **execration, abuse, vituperation,** invective, contumely, hard *or* cutting *or* bitter words; **tirade, diatribe,** jeremiad, screed, philippic
VERBS 4 **tackle;** engage *or* contract *or* obligate *or* commit oneself; **put** *or* **set** *or* **turn one's hand to, engage in, devote oneself to, apply oneself to,** address oneself to, give oneself up to; busy oneself with; **go** *or* **swing into action, set to, turn to, buckle to, fall to; pitch into** <nonformal>, plunge into, fall into, **launch into** *or* **upon**
5 **assault,** assume *or* take the offensive; commit an assault upon; **strike, hit, pound; go at, come at,** have at, **launch out against,** make a set *or* dead set at; gang up on, attack in force; surprise, **ambush; blitz**
6 **assail; castigate, flay,** skin alive <nonformal>, lash, slash, **excoriate,** fustigate, scathe, **roast** <nonformal>, scorch, blister

7 <nonformal> **pitch into, light into, lambaste,** pile into, sail into, wade into, lay into, plow into, tie into, rip into; **let one have it,** let one have it with both barrels; **land on,** land on like a ton of bricks, climb all over, crack down on, lower the boom on, tee off on; **mug,** jump, bushwhack, sandbag, scrag; swipe at, lay at, **go for, go at;** blindside, blind-pop, sucker-punch; **take a swing** *or* **crack** *or* **swipe** *or* **poke** *or* punch *or* **shot at**

attacker NOUNS **assailant,** rapist, mugger <nonformal>; **aggressor;** invader, raider

attain VERBS **achieve, effect, effectuate, compass, consummate, do, execute, produce, deliver, make,** enact, **perform, discharge, fulfill, realize,** run with *and* hack *and* swing <all nonformal>

attainable ADJS **practicable, practical, feasible; workable,** realizable, operable, negotiable, doable; **viable; achievable;** surmountable, superable

attempt NOUNS 1 **trial, effort, essay,** *coup d'essai* <Fr>; **endeavor, undertaking;** approach, move; coup, stroke, step

2 <nonformal> **try, whack, fling, shot, crack,** bash, belt, go, stab, lick, rip, ripple, cut, hack, smack

3 VERBS **try, essay,** try one's hand *or* wings, **undertake**, come to grips with, engage, take the bull by the horns; venture, chance; **make an attempt** *or* **effort,** lift a finger *or* hand

4 <nonformal> **tackle, take on, make a try, give a try,** have a go <chiefly Brit>, take a shot *or* stab *or* crack *or* try *or* whack at; try on for size, **go for it,** go for the brass ring, **have a fling** *or* **go at,** give a fling *or* a go *or* a whirl, **make a stab at,** have a shot *or* stab *or* crack *or* try *or* whack at

attend VERBS 1 **be at,** be present at, find oneself at, **go** *or* **come to; appear**, turn up, set foot in, show up <nonformal>, show one's face, make *or* put in an appearance, give the pleasure of one's company, make a personal appearance, **visit, take in** *and* do *and* catch <all nonformal>
2 **serve, work for,** be in service with; minister *or* administer to, pander to, do service to; **help**; **care for,** do for <nonformal>, **look after,** wait on hand and foot, take care of
3 **heed,** be heedful, tend, **mind, watch, observe, regard,** look, see, view, mark, remark, **note, notice,** take note *or* notice, get a load of <nonformal>

attendant NOUNS **assistant, helper,** auxiliary, aide; **help, helpmate, helpmeet;** deputy, **agent; second,** acolyte; adjutant, aide-de-camp; lieutenant, executive officer

attention NOUNS **attentiveness,** mindfulness, regardfulness, heedfulness; **heed,** ear; consideration, thought, mind; **observation,** observance, advertence, advertency, **note, notice,** remark, **regard,** respect; **intentness,** intentiveness, concentration

attentive NOUNS **heedful, mindful, regardful,** advertent; intent, on top of <nonformal>, diligent, assiduous, intense, earnest, concentrated; watchful, aware, conscious, alert; **meticulous**, nice, finical, finicky, finicking, niggling

attest VERBS **depose,** depone; **testify,** take the stand, witness; **warrant,** certify, **guarantee, assure; vouch, vouch for, swear, swear to,** swear the truth, **assert under oath;** make *or* take one's oath, **vow;** swear by bell, book, and candle

attic NOUNS attic room, **garret, loft,** sky parlor; cockloft, hayloft

Attic ADJS **elegant, tasteful, graceful, polished,** finished, round, terse; **restrained; clear,** lucid, limpid, pellucid, perspicuous; **simple, unaffected, natural,** unlabored, fluent, flowing, **easy; pure,** chaste

Attila NOUNS **brute,** monster, monster of cruelty, **devil,** devil incarnate; **sadist,** torturer, tormenter

attitude NOUNS mental attitude; psychology; **position, posture,** stance; **way of thinking; feeling, sentiment,** the way one feels; opinion

attorney NOUNS **lawyer, attorney-at-law,** barrister, **counselor,** counselor-at-law, **counsel,** legal counsel *or* counselor, legal adviser, legal expert, **solicitor, advocate, pleader;** member of the bar, legal practitioner, officer of the court

attract VERBS 1 **interest, appeal, engage,** impress, charismatize, fetch <nonformal>, catch *or* get one's eye, command one's attention, rivet one, attract one's interest, be attractive, take *or* tickle one's fancy; **invite,** summon, beckon
2 **pull, draw,** drag, tug, pull *or* draw towards, have an attraction; **lure;** adduct

attraction NOUNS 1 **allurement, allure, enticement, inveiglement,** invitation, come-hither <nonformal>, blandishment, cajolery; **temptation,** tantalization; **seduction,** seducement; **beguilement,** beguiling; **fascination, captivation,** enthrallment, entrapment, snaring
2 mutual attraction *or* magnetism; magnetism; gravity, gravitation; centripetal force; capillarity, capillary attraction

attractive ADJS 1 **delightful, exquisite, lovely; thrilling,** titillative; **charming, endearing, engaging, appealing,** prepossessing, heartwarming, sexy <nonformal>, **enchanting,** bewitching, witching, entrancing, enthralling, intriguing, fascinating; **beautiful, beauteous,** endowed with beauty; **pretty, handsome,** pulchritudinous, **lovely, graceful,** gracile
2 drawing, pulling, dragging, tugging; **magnetic;** charismatic; **alluring;** adductive, adducent

attribute NOUNS 1 **characteristic, peculiarity, singularity,** particularity, specialty, individualism, **character,** nature, **trait,** quirk, point of character, bad point, good point, saving grace, redeeming feature, mannerism, keynote, trick, **feature,** distinctive feature, lineament
VERBS 2 **assign, ascribe, impute,** give, place, put, apply, attach, refer

attrition NOUNS 1 **weakening, enfeeblement, debilitation,** exhaustion, inanition; **devitalization,** enervation; attenuation, extenuation
2 **reduction, diminution,** decrease, build-down, phasedown, drawdown, decrement, impairment, **cut** *or* **cutting,** curtailment, shortening, truncation
3 **abrasion, erosion, wearing away, wear,** detrition, ablation; ruboff; erasure, erasing, rubbing away *or* off *or* out; **grinding, filing,** rasping, limation; fretting; galling

attune VERBS **harmonize,** coordinate, bring into line, accord, make uniform, equalize, assimilate, homologize; **adjust, set,** regulate, **accommodate, reconcile,** synchronize, sync <nonformal>

attuned ADJS **harmonious,** harmonic, symphonious; harmonizing, **concordant,** consonant, accordant, according, **in accord,** in concord, in concert; synchronous, synchronized

atypical ADJS **unusual,** unordinary, **uncustomary,** unwonted, **uncommon, unfamiliar,** atypic, unheard-of, *recherché* <Fr>; **out of the ordinary,** out of this world, out-of-the-way, **off the beaten track,** offbeat

auction NOUNS 1 auction sale, vendue, outcry, sale at *or* by auction, sale to the highest bidder
VERBS 2 **auction off, auctioneer,** sell at auction, sell by auction, put up for auction, **put on the block,** bring under the hammer; knock down, sell to the highest bidder

audible ADJS hearable; **distinct, clear,** plain, definite, articulate

audience NOUNS 1 **audition,** hearing, tryout, call <all nonformal>, **interview,** conference; attention, favorable attention, ear
2 **house, congregation;** studio audience, live audience

audit NOUNS 1 **auditing; accounting, accountancy**
VERBS 2 **be taught, receive instruction,** be tutored, undergo schooling, pursue one's education, attend classes, go to *or* attend school, take lessons, matriculate; monitor
3 **verify, confirm,** test, prove, validate, **check,** check up *or* on *or* out <nonformal>, check over *or* through, **double-check,** triple-check, cross-check, recheck, check and doublecheck

audition NOUNS 1 **hearing;** sense of hearing, auditory *or* aural sense, ear; listening, heeding, attention
2 **tryout,** workout, **rehearsal,** practice; **dry run,** road test; **trial run,** practical test

auditorium NOUNS **theater, playhouse, house,** odeum; **opera house,** opera; **hall,** music hall, concert hall

auditory ADJS **aural,** auricular, otic; audio-visual; audible; acoustic, acoustical, phonic

augment VERBS **increase, enlarge,** aggrandize, **amplify, extend,** maximize, supplement, **add to; expand,** lengthen, broaden, fatten, fill out, thicken; build up; **reinforce,** strengthen, fortify, beef up <nonformal>; swell the ranks of

augur NOUNS 1 prophesier, soothsayer, *vates* <L>; **diviner,** divinator; prophetess, seeress, divineress, pythoness; Druid; **fortuneteller,** haruspex *or* aruspex, astrologer; Cassandra
VERBS 2 hint, divine <old>; **foretoken, preindicate,** presignal, **prefigure,** betoken, token, typify, **signify, mean,** spell, **indicate,** point to, **be a sign of,** show signs of

augury NOUNS 1 **omen, portent;** auspice, soothsay, prognostic, prognostication; foreshadowing, adumbration
2 **divination,** divining; haruspication, haruspicy, pythonism; **fortunetelling,** crystal gazing, palm-reading, palmistry; crystal ball; sorcery; clairvoyance

august ADJS worthy, **venerable; dignified, stately, imposing, grand, courtly,** magisterial, aristocratic

aura NOUNS 1 **ambience, atmosphere, climate, air,** spirit, feeling, feel, quality, color, sense, tone, overtone, undertone
2 **luster,** brilliance, radiance, splendor, resplendence *or* resplendency, refulgence *or* refulgency, **glory,** blaze of glory, nimbus, halo, envelope; charisma, mystique, glamour, numinousness

aurora NOUNS 1 **dawn, daybreak, sunrise, sunup** <nonformal>, cockcrowing *or* cocklight <Brit nonformal>, light, first light, daylight; **break of day,** peep of day, **crack of dawn,** first blush *or* flush of the morning, brightening *or* first brightening
2 polar lights; **northern lights, aurora borealis;** southern lights, **aurora australis;** aurora polaris

auspices NOUNS **patronage, fosterage, tutelage, sponsorship, backing,** aegis, coattails <nonformal>, care, guidance, **championing, championship,** seconding; **backing**

auspicious ADJS of good omen, of happy portent; **propitious, favorable,** favoring, fair, good; **promising,** of promise, full of promise

austere ADJS 1 self-denying, self-abnegating, **rigorous, rigoristic; puritanical,** eremitic, anchoritic
2 **simple, plain,** bare, bare-bones *and* no-frills <both nonformal>, mere; **single,** uniform, homogeneous, of a piece; **pure,** simon-pure, pure and simple

austerity NOUNS **severity, harshness, stringency,** astringency, **hard line; discipline,** strict *or* tight *or* rigid discipline, regimentation, spit and polish; Spartanism; demandingness, exactingness

authentic ADJS **genuine,** veridic, veridical, **real, natural, realistic, naturalistic,** true to reality, **true to nature, lifelike,** true to life, verisimilar, veristic

authenticate VERBS **confirm,** affirm, **substantiate, authenticate, validate, certify,** ratify, **verify; document;** probate, prove

authenticity NOUNS **genuineness,** bona fides, bona fideness, **legitimacy; honesty, sincerity**

author NOUNS **writer,** scribe <nonformal>, composer, inditer; authoress, penwoman; **creative writer,** *littérateur* <Fr>, literary artist, literary craftsman *or* artisan *or* journeyman, belletrist, man of letters, literary man

authoritarian ADJS **strict, exacting,** exigent, demanding, not to be trifled with, **stringent,** astringent; **severe, harsh,** dour, unsparing; despotic, **dictatorial; totalitarian**

authoritative ADJS 1 clothed *or* vested *or* invested with authority, **commanding, imperative; governing, controlling, ruling; preeminent, supreme,** leading, **superior; influential, prestigious, weighty,** momentous, consequential, eminent, substantial, considerable
2 **authentic,** magisterial, **official;** ex cathedra; standard, approved, accepted, received, pontific; from *or* straight from the horse's mouth

authority NOUNS 1 **prerogative, right, power,** faculty, competence *or* competency; **mandate,** popular authority *or* mandate, people's mandate, electoral mandate
2 **expert,** savant, scholar, connoisseur, maven <nonformal>; pundit
3 **influence,** influentiality; **power,** force, clout <nonformal>, potency, pressure, effect, indirect *or* incidental power, **say,** the final say, the last word, say-so *and* a lot to do with *or* to say about <all nonformal>, veto power

authorize VERBS **sanction, warrant;** give official sanction *or* warrant, legitimize, validate, legalize; empower, give power, enable, entitle; **license**

autocratic ADJS **arbitrary, peremptory,** imperative; absolute, absolutist, absolutistic; **dictatorial, authoritarian; bossy** <nonformal>, **domineering, high-handed, overbearing,** overruling; **despotic, tyrannical;** tyrannous

autograph NOUNS **signature,** hand, **John Hancock** <nonformal>

automatic ADJS **unpremeditated,** unmeditated, **uncalculated,** undeliberated, **spontaneous, undesigned, unstudied;** unintentional, unintended, inadvertent, unwilled, undeliberate; **unconsidered,** unadvised, snap, casual, offhand, throwaway <nonformal>; **involuntary, instinctive, mechanical,** reflex, reflexive, knee-jerk <nonformal>, conditioned

automation NOUNS automatic control;

robotization, cybernation; **self-action,** self-activity; self-movement, self-motion, **self-propulsion;** self-direction

automobile NOUNS **car, auto,** motorcar, motocar, autocar, **machine,** motor, motor vehicle, *voiture* <Fr>

automotive ADJS **vehicular,** transportational

autonomous ADJS **independent,** self-dependent; free-spirited, freewheeling, free-floating, free-standing; **self-determined,** self-directing, one's own man; self-governed, **self-governing,** sovereign

autonomy NOUNS **independence, self-determination, self-government,** self-direction, home rule; autarky, autarchy, self-containment, self-sufficiency; **self-reliance,** self-dependence

autopsy NOUNS **postmortem, inquest,** postmortem examination, ex post facto examination, necropsy, necroscopy

autumn NOUNS **fall,** fall of the year, harvest time

Season of mists and mellow fruitfulness!
KEATS

ADJS 2 autumnal; **seasonal,** in season and out of season

auxiliary NOUNS 1 **helper,** aide, paraprofessional; **help, helpmate, helpmeet; attendant, second,** acolyte
ADJS 2 **helping,** assisting, serving; **assistant,** adjuvant, subservient, subsidiary, ancillary, accessory; fostering, nurtural

availability NOUNS **accessibility,** access, **approachability, openness,** reachableness; **penetrability,** perviousness

available ADJS 1 **idle,** fallow, otiose; **unemployed, unoccupied,** disengaged, **jobless, out of work,** out of a job, out of harness; free, at liberty, at leisure; at loose ends
2 **accessible, approachable, reachable,** within reach; **open, penetrable,** pervious; **obtainable, attainable,** procurable, securable

avalanche NOUNS 1 **snowslide,** snowslip <Brit>; **slide; slip,** slippage; **landslide,** mudslide, landslip, subsidence
VERBS 2 **slide, slip,** slip *or* slide down

avant-garde NOUNS 1 vanguard, avant-gardist, innovator, groundbreaker; **precursor, forerunner,** foregoer, *voorlooper* <Dutch>; pathfinder, explorer, point, point man, trailblazer *or* trailbreaker, guide
ADJS 2 **advanced,** progressive, forward-looking, modernizing, ultramodern, ahead of its time, far out, way out

avenge VERBS **take** *or* **exact revenge,** have one's revenge, wreak one's vengeance; **retaliate, even the score, get even with**

avenger NOUNS **vindicator;** revanchist

avenue NOUNS **artery; corridor, aisle, alley, lane; channel, conduit;** opening, aperture; access

average NOUNS 1 **mean, median, middle; golden mean,** *juste milieu* <Fr>; **medium,** happy medium; middle of the road, middle course, *via media* <L>; middle state *or* ground *or* position *or* echelon *or* level *or* point, midpoint; **run of the mill;** any Tom, Dick, or Harry <nonformal>; Everyman
VERBS 2 average out, **split the difference,** take the average, strike a balance, pair off; strike *or* hit a happy medium
ADJS 3 **ordinary,** normal, **common, commonplace,** garden *and* garden-variety <both nonformal>, run-of-the-mill; **unexceptional, unremarkable, unnoteworthy,** unspectacular, nothing *or* nobody special *and* no great shakes <all nonformal>, no prize, no prize package, no brain surgeon, no rocket scientist

aversion NOUNS 1 **repugnance,** repulsion, **antipathy,** abomination, **abhorrence, horror,** mortal horror; **disgust, loathing;** nausea; distaste
2 **anathema, abomination,** detestation, abhorrence, antipathy, execration, hate; peeve, pet peeve; phobia

avert VERBS **prevent, prohibit, forbid; bar;** save, help, **keep from; deter, discourage,** dishearten; **parry, keep off, ward off, stave off, fend off,** fend, repel, deflect, turn aside; **forestall,** foreclose, **preclude,** exclude, debar, **obviate**

avoid VERBS **evade, dodge,** duck <nonformal>, shun, turn aside *or* to the side, draw aside, **turn away,** jib, shy, shy off; **avert; steer clear of,** make way for, get out of the way of

avoidable ADJS **escapable,** eludible; evadable; preventable

await VERBS have *or* keep an eye out for, lie in wait for; wait around *or* about, watch, watch and wait; **wait up for,** stay up for, sit up for; **loom,** threaten; lie ahead

awake VERBS 1 **awaken, wake, wake up, get up,** rouse, come alive <nonformal>; open one's eyes, stir <nonformal>
2 **come to life,** come into existence *or* being, come into the world, see the light; **revive, come to,** come alive, show signs of life
ADJS 3 conscious, **up;** alert, **on the alert,** on the *qui vive* <Fr>, **on one's toes, on top** *and* **on the job** *and* on the ball <all nonformal>, **attentive;** wakeful, **wide-awake,** sleepless, unsleeping, unblinking, alive, ready, prompt, quick, agile, nimble, quick on the trigger *or* draw *or* uptake <all nonformal>

awaken VERBS 1 **waken, rouse, arouse,** awake, wake, **wake up,** shake up, roust out <nonformal>
2 **excite, impassion, arouse, rouse, stir, stir up,** set astir, stir the feelings, stir the blood, cause a stir *or* commotion, play on the feelings; **foment, incite**; turn on <nonformal>
3 **disillusion, disenchant,** unspell, uncharm, break the spell *or* charm; **disabuse, undeceive;** correct, **set right** *or* **straight,** put straight, tell the truth, enlighten, let in on, put one wise <nonformal>; open one's eyes

awakening NOUNS 1 **wakening,** rousing, **arousal;** rude awakening, rousting out <nonformal>
2 **disillusionment,** disillusion, **disenchantment,** return to reality, loss of innocence, cold light of reality, enlightenment, bursting of the bubble; debunking <nonformal>

award NOUNS 1 **giving, donation,** bestowal, bestowment; **endowment, presentation,** presentment; awarding; grant, granting
2 **reward, prize;** first prize, second prize, etc; blue ribbon; consolation prize; booby prize; Nobel Prize, Pulitzer Prize; Oscar, Academy Award
VERBS 3 **give, present, donate,** slip <nonformal>, let have; **bestow, confer, allot, render,** bestow on; **grant,** accord, **allow,** vouchsafe, yield, afford, make available; **tender,** proffer, offer, extend, come up with <nonformal>; **give out, deal out, dole out, mete out, hand** *or* dish out <nonformal>, fork *or* shell out <nonformal>

aware ADJS **perceptive; conscious,** cognizant, sensitive to, alive to, **attentive, heedful, mindful, regardful,** advertent; on top of <nonformal>, diligent, assiduous, intense, earnest, concentrated; watchful, conscious, alert

away ADJS 1 **gone,** gone away, past and gone, extinct, missing, lost to sight *or* view, long-lost, **out of sight; unaccounted for**
ADVS 2 **elsewhere,** somewhere else, not here

awe NOUNS 1 **wonder,** wonderment, sense of wonder, marveling, marvel, **astonishment, amazement;** dumbfoundment, stupefaction
2 dread, unholy dread; **terror, horror,** horrification, mortal *or* abject fear
VERBS 3 **astonish, amaze, astound, surprise,** startle, stagger, **bewilder, perplex**, flabbergast <nonformal>, confound, overwhelm, **boggle, boggle the mind;** strike with wonder *or* awe; **dumbfound; stun, stupefy**

awe-inspiring ADJS 1 **awesome,** awful, awing; **mysterious,** numinous; weird, eerie, uncanny, bizarre
2 **imposing, impressive,** larger-than-life, awful, awesome; **sumptuous, elegant, elaborate, luxurious,** extravagant, deluxe

awesome ADJS 1 **magnificent, splendid, glorious,** superb, fine, superfine, fancy, superfancy, swell <nonformal>; **imposing, impressive,** larger-than-life, awful, awe-inspiring
2 **sacred, holy,** numinous, **sacrosanct, religious, spiritual,** heavenly, divine; **venerable,** awful; **ineffable,** unutterable, unspeakable, inexpressible

awful ADJS **terrible, dreadful,** dire, horrible, horrid; atrocious, outrageous, heinous, villainous, nefarious; monstrous; **deplorable,** lamentable, regrettable, pitiful, pitiable, woeful, grievous; flagrant, **scandalous,** shameful, **shocking,** infamous, **notorious,** arrant, **egregious**

awkward ADJS **bungling, blundering,** blunderheaded, bumbling, fumbling, mistake-prone, accident-prone; **clumsy, uncoordinated,** maladroit, unhandy, **all thumbs; ungainly,** uncouth, **ungraceful,** graceless, inelegant, *gauche* <Fr>; **inconvenient, incommodious**

awning NOUNS **shade,** shader, **screen, light shield, curtain,** drape, drapery, blind

ax VERBS **sever, dissever,** cut off *or* away

or loose, shear off, hack through, hack off, amputate; **cleave, split,** fissure; sunder, cut in two, dichotomize, halve, bisect; **chop, hew,** hack, **slash;** gash, whittle, butcher

axiomatic ADJS **evident, self-evident,** indisputable, **obvious, plain, clear,** perspicuous, distinct, palpable, patent, tangible; **aphoristic, proverbial,** epigrammatic, epigrammatical, **axiomatical; sententious, pithy,** gnomic, pungent, succinct, terse, crisp, pointed

axis NOUNS 1 **center,** centrum; **middle, heart, core, nucleus; core of one's being, where one lives; kernel; pith,** marrow, medulla; **nub, hub,** nave, pivot 2 **alliance, coalition, league, union;** council; **bloc; federation, confederation,** confederacy; **combination,** combine

B

babble NOUNS 1 **chatter, jabber,** gibber, babblement, prate, **prating, prattle, palaver,** chat, natter <Brit>, **gabble,** blab, **blabber, blather,** cackle
VERBS 2 **chatter, chat, prate, prattle, patter,** palaver, **gab** <nonformal>, natter <Brit>, **gabble, jabber, blab, blabber, blather,** spout *or* **spout off** <nonformal>, pour forth, **gush,** have a big mouth <nonformal>, love the sound of one's own voice

baby NOUNS 1 **newborn; infant, babe,** babe in arms, little darling *or* angel *or* doll *or* cherub, bouncing baby, puling infant, mewling infant, babykins <nonformal>, baby bunting; **toddler**
ADJS 2 **infant, infantile, babyish; newborn,** neonatal; tied to mother's apron strings

bachelor NOUNS bach <nonformal>, confirmed bachelor, **single man**

back NOUNS 1 dorsum, ridge; dorsal region, lumbar region; hindquarter; loin
VERBS 2 **secure, guarantee, guaranty, warrant, assure, insure,** ensure, bond, **certify; back up, sponsor, endorse;** sign, cosign, **underwrite; stand behind, stand back of** *or* in back of, get behind; **stand by,** stick by *and* **stick up for** <both nonformal>, **champion; finance, fund, sponsor, patronize, support,** provide capital *or* money for, pay for, bankroll <nonformal>
3 **bet, wager, gamble, hazard, stake,** punt, lay, lay down, put up, **make a bet, lay a wager,** get a piece of the action <nonformal>; plunge <nonformal>
ADJS 4 **backward, reversed,** reflex, **turned around**
5 **rear,** rearward, backward, retrograde, **posterior**

backbone NOUNS 1 **pluck, spunk** <nonformal>, **mettle, grit,** true grit, spirit, **stamina, guts** *and* moxie <both nonformal>, bottom, **toughness** <nonformal>
2 **support; mainstay,** spine

backbreaking ADJS **strenuous,** painful, effortful, operose, troublesome, onerous, oppressive, burdensome

backdrop NOUNS **setting, background,** ground, surround, field, scene, arena, theater, locale; back, rear, hinterland, distance

backer NOUNS **supporter, upholder,** maintainer, sustainer; support, **mainstay, standby** <nonformal>, stalwart, reliance, dependence

background NOUNS 1 **setting,** backdrop, scene, arena, theater, locale; stage setting, stage set, *mise-en-scène* <Fr>
2 **experience, practice,** practical knowledge *or* skill, hands-on experience <nonformal>
3 **source, origin,** genesis, original, origination, **derivation, rise, beginning,** conception, inception, provenance, provenience

backhanded ADJS **circuitous, roundabout, out-of-the-way, devious, oblique, indirect,** meandering; equivocatory; evasive; vacillating

backlash NOUNS **counteraction, counterworking; opposition, antipathy, conflict, friction;** reaction, repercussion, recoil

backlog NOUNS 1 **reserve, reserves,** reservoir, resource; **stockpile, cache,** backup, reserve supply, something in reserve *or* in hand, something to fall back on, reserve fund, **nest egg, savings,** sinking fund
VERBS 2 **store up, stock up, lay up,** put up, **save up,** hoard up, treasure up, garner up, **heap up,** pile up, build up a stock *or* an inventory

backslapper NOUNS **flatterer; cajoler, wheedler;** back scratcher; ass-kisser <nonformal>, brown-noser, **sycophant**

backslide VERBS **relapse, lapse, slip back,** sink back, **fall back,** have a relapse, **revert to,** yield again to, fall again into, recidivate

back talk NOUNS **retort, rejoinder,** reaction, return, **comeback** *and* **take** <both nonformal>, clever *or* ready *or* witty reply *or* retort, snappy comeback <nonformal>; sass *and* lip <both nonformal>

backtrack VERBS backpedal, back off *or* away; reverse one's field; have second thoughts, think better of it, cut one's losses

backup NOUNS 1 **support, backing, aid; upholding, upkeep,** carrying, carriage, maintenance, **sustaining,** sustainment, sustenance; **reinforcement;** subsidy, subvention
ADJS 2 **substitute, alternate, alterna-**

tive, equivalent, token, dummy, pinch, utility, secondary

backward ADJS 1 **reversed,** reflex, **turned around,** back, **backward;** wrong-way, wrong-way around, counter, ass-backwards *and* bassackwards <both nonformal>
2 **undeveloped, unfinished,** unlicked, unformed; unfashioned, unwrought, unlabored, unworked, unprocessed, untreated; **underdeveloped;** arrested, stunted
ADVS 3 **inversely, conversely,** contrarily, contrariwise, **vice versa,** the other way around, **backwards,** turned around
4 **rearward,** rearwards, to the rear, **hindward,** hindwards, backwards

backwater NOUNS back stream, gurge, **swirl,** twirl, whirl; countercurrent, counterflow, counterflux, backflow, reflux, refluence, regurgitation, backwash, snye <Can>

backwoods NOUNS 1 **hinterland, back country,** outback <Australia>, up-country, boonies *and* boondocks <both nonformal>, outback <Australia>, wilderness

bacterial ADJS **microbic,** microbial, **microorganic;** animalcular; microzoic

bad NOUNS 1 **evil, wrong, ill; harm, hurt, injury, damage, detriment; destruction**; abomination, grievance, vexation, blight; ills the flesh is heir to

something rotten in the state of Denmark
SHAKESPEARE

ADJS 2 **evil, ill,** untoward, black, sinister; **wicked, wrong,** peccant, iniquitous, **vicious; sinful**

bad person NOUNS 1 disreputable person, **undesirable, good-for-nothing, no-good, rascal**

2 <nonformal> **asshole, prick, bastard, son of a bitch** *or* SOB, **jerk, horse's ass,** creep, motherfucker, mother, dork, **shit,** turd, birdturd, shithead, shitface, cuntface, dickhead, fart, **louse, meanie, heel, shitheel, rat, stinker,** stinkard, pill, bugger, dirtbag, dork, geek, dweeb, twerp, sleaze, sleazoid, sleazebag, bad lot <Brit>; **hood, hooligan**

bad-mouth VERBS <nonformal> put down, trash, rubbish, dump on, dig at, dis, roast, slam, hurl a brickbat

bad taste NOUNS **tastelessness, impropriety,** indecorousness, unseemliness; **coarseness, unrefinement,** roughness, grossness, rudeness, crudeness, uncouthness

baffled ADJS **at an impasse, at one's wit's end, at a loss, perplexed, bewildered,** mystified, stuck *and* stumped <both nonformal>, stymied

bag NOUNS **sack,** sac, poke <nonformal>; **pocket,** fob; **purse, wallet, pocketbook, handbag,** porte-monnaie; **take, catch,** seizure, **haul;** booty

bagatelle NOUNS **trifle, triviality, oddment,** fribble, **gimcrack, gewgaw,** frippery, **trinket,** bibelot, curio, **bauble,** gaud, toy, **knickknack,** knickknackery, kickshaw, folderol

baggage NOUNS 1 **impedimenta, luggage, dunnage,** bag and baggage, traps, tackle, apparatus, truck, gear, kit, outfit, duffel
2 **strumpet, trollop, wench, hussy, slut, jade,** *cocotte* <Fr>, grisette

baggy ADJS **drooping, droopy,** limp, loose, nodding, floppy <nonformal>; **sagging,** saggy; **bagging,** ballooning; **shapeless,** nondescript, lumpy, lumpish

bail NOUNS 1 bond, vadimonium; surety; **pledge, gage,** *pignus, vadium* <both L>
VERBS 2 **ladle, dip, scoop;** bucket; **dish, shovel, pour**

bail out VERBS 1 **parachute, jump,** make a parachute jump, hit the silk, sky-dive
2 **get out, get out of,** get well out of; **break loose,** cut loose, break away, break one's bonds *or* chains, shake off the yoke; **jump** *and* **skip** <both nonformal>; fly the coop <nonformal>
3 **give an assist, give a leg up** *or* lift *or* boost <nonformal>; **save,** redeem, **rescue**; see one through

bait NOUNS 1 **lure,** charm, **come-on** <nonformal>, attention-getter *or* -grabber, **attraction, draw** *or* drawer *or* crowd-drawer, crowd-pleaser; drawing card; **decoy**
VERBS 2 **heckle,** pick *or* prod at, badger, hector, bullyrag, worry, worry at, nip at the heels of, chivy, hardly give one time to breathe, make one's life miserable, keep on at, **pester, tease, needle,** devil, get after *or* get on <nonformal>, **bedevil**

baker NOUNS *boulanger* <Fr>, pastry cook, pastry chef, *patissier* <Fr>

balance NOUNS 1 **moderation,** moderateness; **restraint,** constraint, control;

judiciousness, prudence; steadiness, evenness, equilibrium, **stability**; **temperateness**
2 **stability, firmness, soundness, substantiality, solidity; security,** reliability; **steadiness,** steadfastness; constancy, invariability, undeflectability; **imperturbability,** unflappability <nonformal>
3 **remainder, leftover, extra, spare,** something extra *or* to spare
VERBS 4 regularize, balance off, compensate; harmonize; **proportion,** equalize; **offset**, set off, **counteract,** countervail, **counterbalance,** counterweigh, counterpoise, play off against
5 balance accounts, balance the books, strike a balance; close the books, close out

balcony NOUNS gallery, terrace; **peanut gallery**

bald ADJS 1 **hairless,** depilous; acomous; bald as a coot, bald as an egg; **baldheaded,** bald-pated
2 **plain,** common; **simple,** unadorned, unvarnished, pure, neat; bare, stark, Spartan

ball NOUNS 1 **sphere;** orb, orbit, **globe,** rondure; geoid; spheroid, globoid, ellipsoid, oblate spheroid, prolate spheroid
2 **dance,** *bal* <Fr>; masked ball, masque, mask, *bal masqué* <Fr>, *bal costumé* <Fr>, fancy-dress ball, cotillion; promenade, **prom** <nonformal>, formal <nonformal>
3 **fun,** action, big time *and* **high time** *and* high old time, picnic *and* laughs *and* lots of laughs, time of one's life <all nonformal>

ballad NOUNS popular song *or* air *or* tune, hit, song hit, hit tune; lay, *Lied* <Ger>, *chanson* <Fr>, carol, **ditty,** canticle, ballade, *ballata* <Ital>; *canzone* <Ital>; canzonet, *canzonetta* <Ital>

ballerina NOUNS **ballet dancer;** danseuse, coryphée; *première danseuse* <Fr>; figurante

balloon NOUN 1 **aerostat,** lighter-than-air craft; **airship,** ship, dirigible balloon, **blimp** <nonformal>; **dirigible,** zeppelin, *ballon* <Fr>
VERBS 2 **grow, increase, advance,** appreciate; **spread, widen,** broaden; wax, swell, bloat, mount, **rise,** go up, crescendo, snowball; **multiply, proliferate,** breed, teem

ballooning NOUNS lighter-than-air aviation

ballot NOUNS 1 **vote,** voting, **suffrage,** franchise, enfranchisement, right to vote; **voice, say;** representation; **poll,** polling, canvass, canvassing, counting heads *or* noses, exit poll; **plebiscite, referendum;** voice vote, *viva voce* vote; rising vote; show of hands
2 **slate, ticket,** proxy <nonformal>
VERBS 3 **vote, cast one's vote,** cast a ballot; exercise one's suffrage *or* franchise, stand up and be counted

ballroom NOUNS **dance hall,** dancery; dance palace; casino

balls NOUNS 1 **genitals,** genitalia, sex organs, reproductive organs, pudenda, private parts, privy parts, privates, meat <nonformal>; gonads; **testes, testicles,** balls *and* nuts *and* rocks *and* ballocks *and* family jewels <all nonformal>

2 <nonformal> **guts,** intestinal fortitude, spunk, brass balls, cojones, moxie, **backbone,** chutzpah

balm NOUNS 1 **lotion, salve, ointment, unguent,** *unguentum* <L>, cerate, unction, balsam, oil, emollient, demulcent
2 **condolence, condolences,** condolement, **consolation,** comfort, soothing words, **commiseration, sympathy**

balmy ADJS **bright, sunny,** fair, mild; halcyon

baloney NOUNS

<nonformal> **bunk**, **bunkum;** hooey, hoke, **hokum**, **bosh**, bull, **bullshit**, crap, flimflam, smoke and mirrors, claptrap, moonshine, eyewash, hogwash

bamboozle VERBS **dupe, gull,** pigeon, play one for a fool *or* sucker, snow *and* **hornswoggle** *and* diddle *and* scam <all nonformal>, **humbug, take in, put something over** *or* **across,** slip one over on <nonformal>, pull a fast one on

ban NOUNS 1 **prohibition, forbidding,** forbiddance; **ruling out, disallowance,** denial, rejection; refusal; injunction, **proscription,** inhibition, **interdict,** *interdictum* <L>, interdiction
VERBS 2 **prohibit, forbid; disallow, rule out** *or* **against;** deny, **reject**; say no to, **refuse**; **bar,** debar, preclude, exclude, exclude from, shut out, shut *or* close the door on, **prevent**; put under the ban, **outlaw, inhibit, interdict**
3 **ostracize,** exclude, send down, **black-**

ball, spurn, turn thumbs down on, snub, cut, give the cold shoulder, send to Coventry, give the silent treatment; **excommunicate;** rusticate

banal ADJS **trite;** corny *and* square <both nonformal>, platitudinous, **stereotyped,** stock, set, **commonplace, common,** twice-told, **familiar,** bromidic <nonformal>, old hat <nonformal>, back-number, bewhiskered, warmed-over, **cut-and-dried; hackneyed, stale,** moth-eaten

bandage NOUNS 1 bandaging, **tourniquet;** tape, **adhesive tape**
VERBS 2 **gird,** girt, belt, girdle, cinch; **tie up,** bind up, do up; **bandage,** bandage up, swathe, swaddle

band-aid NOUNS 1 **front,** mask, cloak, veil; **cosmetics,** mere cosmetics, gloss, varnish, color, coat of paint, whitewash <nonformal>; **cover,** cover-up, cover story, alibi; expedient
ADJS 2 **makeshift, stopgap,** improvised, improvisational, **jury-rigged; last-ditch; ad hoc;** quick and dirty <nonformal>

bandit NOUNS **brigand,** dacoit; **thug, hoodlum**

bane NOUNS 1 **curse, affliction, plague, pestilence,** pest, calamity, scourge, **torment,** open wound, running sore, grievance, woe, burden, crushing burden; thorn in the flesh *or* side, pea in the shoe; bugbear, **bête noire,** nemesis
2 **destroyer, ruiner, wrecker,** demolisher; **vandal,** hun; exterminator

bang NOUNS 1 **detonation, blast, explosion,** fulmination, **discharge, burst, pop, crack;** volley, salvo, fusillade
VERBS 2 **crack, clap, crash,** wham, slam, clash; **knock, rap, tap,** smack, whack, thwack, whop, whap, whomp, splat
ADVS 3 **suddenly,** sudden, **all of a sudden, all at once: abruptly,** sharp; precipitately, precipitantly, impulsively, impetuously, hastily; dash; on short notice, without notice *or* warning, like a bolt from the blue

banish VERBS **expel, cast out, ostracize,** exclude, send down, **blackball,** spurn, turn thumbs down on, snub, cut, give send to Coventry, **excommunicate; expatriate, deport**

bank NOUNS 1 **slope, declivity,** steep, versant, incline, rise, talus
2 **shoal, shallow,** shallows, **bar,** sandbank, sandbar, tombolo
3 **lending institution,** savings and loan association *or* thrift *or* thrift institution *or* savings institution
VERBS 4 **store, stow,** lay in store; **lay in, deposit, cache,** stash <nonformal>, bury away

banker NOUNS **money dealer,** moneymonger; money broker; moneylender

bankroll VERBS **finance, back, fund, sponsor, patronize, support,** provide for, capitalize, provide capital *or* money for, **stake** *or* **grubstake** <both nonformal>; subsidize

bankrupt NOUNS 1 **insolvent,** failure; **loser**
VERBS 2 **ruin, break,** bust *and* wipe out <both nonformal>; put out of business, drive to the wall, impoverish
ADJS **insolvent,** in receivership, in the hands of receivers, belly-up <nonformal>, broken, **broke** *and* busted <both nonformal>, **ruined,** failed, on the rocks

bankruptcy NOUNS **insolvency,** receivership, Chapter 11, **failure; crash,** collapse, bust <nonformal>

banner NOUNS 1 **flag,** oriflamme, **standard, pennant,** pennon, pennoncel, banneret, banderole, swallowtail, burgee, **streamer; bunting**
ADJS 2 **leading, dominant,** crowning, capital, **cardinal; preeminent, predominant,** preponderant, prevailing

banquet NOUNS **feast,** festal board; lavish *or* Lucullan feast; blow *or* blowout <nonformal>, groaning board

banter NOUNS 1 **badinage, persiflage, pleasantry, raillery,** rallying, **sport,** good-natured banter, harmless teasing; **byplay**

2 <nonformal> **kidding,** joshing, jollying, jiving, fooling around; **ribbing,** ragging, razzing, **roasting**

VERBS 3 **twit, chaff,** rally, **joke, jest,** jape, **tease,** haze

baptize VERBS 1 **christen;** dip, immerse; sprinkle, asperge
2 **name, denominate,** nominate, **designate, call, term, style, dub,** specify; christen

bar NOUNS 1 **stripe, striping, streak, streaking;** striation, striature, stria
2 barroom, *bistro* <Fr>, **tavern, pub,** gin mill <nonformal>, **saloon,** watering hole <nonformal>
3 **obstruction, clog, block,** blockade,

sealing off, **blockage,** strangulation, choking, choking off, **stoppage,** stop, **barrier, obstacle,** impediment
4 legal profession, members of the bar; representation, counsel
VERBS 5 **exclude,** debar, lock out, **shut out, keep out,** close the door on, close out, cut off, preclude; **reject, repudiate,** blackball *and* turn thumbs down on <both nonformal>; **ban,** prohibit, proscribe
6 **obstruct, get** *or* **stand in the way; block,** put up a roadblock, blockade, occlude; **debar,** shut out

barbarian NOUNS 1 brute; troglodyte; **alien, stranger, foreigner, outsider,** ultramontane, foreign devil <China>, *gringo* <Sp Amer>
ADJS 2 **unrefined, unpolished, uncouth,** unkempt, uncombed, unlicked; **uncultivated, uncultured; uncivilized, barbarous,** barbaric, troglodytic

barbaric ADJS sadistic; **ruthless; brutal,** brutish, brute, bestial, beastly, animal, subhuman; **barbarous,** uncivilized, unchristian; **savage, ferocious,** feral

barber NOUNS hairdresser, *coiffeur, coiffeuse* <both Fr>

barbiturates NOUNS

<nonformal> barbs, black beauties, candy, dolls, downers, downs, goofballs, nimbies, pink ladies, purple hearts

bare ADJS 1 **naked, nude; in the raw** <nonformal>, *in puris naturalibus* <L>, in a state of nature, in one's birthday suit, **in the buff** *and* stripped to the buff *and* **in the altogether** <all nonformal>, **stark-naked,** bare-ass <nonformal>, naked as a jaybird <nonformal>

bare-bones ADJS **plain,** bare, no-frills <nonformal>, mere; of a piece; **pure,** simon-pure, pure and simple; **austere,** chaste, unadorned, uncluttered, spare, stark, severe

barefoot ADJS barefooted, unshod; discalced, discalceate

barely ADVS **scarcely, hardly,** not hardly <nonformal>, only just, **narrowly,** closely, nearly, **by the skin of one's teeth,** by a hair, **slightly,** exiguously, scantily, inconsequentially, **insignificantly, negligibly,** minimally, inappreciably, **little**

bargain NOUNS 1 **compromise,** accommodation, settlement, mutual concession, give-and-take
2 advantageous purchase, **buy** <nonformal>, **good buy, steal** <nonformal>; money's worth
VERBS 3 **treat with, negotiate,** make terms, sit down with, sit down at the bargaining table; **drive a bargain, haggle,** chaffer, **deal, dicker,** hack out *or* work out *or* hammer out a deal

barker NOUNS **pitchman, pitchwoman,** spieler, ballyhooer

bar mitzvah NOUNS **confirmation;** bas mitzvah

barn NOUNS **stable,** stall; **cowbarn,** cowshed, byre

barnacle NOUNS **parasite,** leech, limpet, remora; **sponger,** sponge <nonformal>, freeloader <nonformal>

barometer NOUNS **feeler, probe,** sound, sounder; **trial balloon,** *ballon d'essai* <Fr>, pilot balloon; weather vane

barracks NOUNS **camp, encampment,** *Lager* <Ger>; bivouac; barrack *or* **barracks,** casern, *caserne* <Fr>

barrage NOUNS 1 **volley, salvo,** burst, spray, **fusillade, cannonade,** cannonry, **broadside,** enfilade
VERBS 2 **bombard, blast, strafe, shell,** cannonade, mortar, blitz; pepper, fusillade, fire a volley; rake, enfilade; pour a broadside into

barren NOUNS 1 **wasteland, waste,** desolation, **barrens,** barren land
ADJS 2 **fruitless,** profitless, bootless, otiose, **unprofitable,** unremunerative, sterile, unproductive

barricade VERBS **fortify,** garrison, man the garrison *or* trenches *or* barricades; bulwark, wall, palisade, fence; castellate, crenellate

barrier NOUNS 1 **boundary, bound, limit,** limitation, extremity; block, claustrum; delimitation, hedge, break *or* breakoff point, cutoff, cutoff point, terminus; **limiting factor,** determinant, limit *or* boundary condition
2 **obstruction, clog, block,** blockade, sealing off, **blockage,** strangulation, choking, choking off, **stoppage,** stop, **bar, obstacle,** impediment; **bottleneck,** chokepoint

bartender NOUNS mixologist, barkeeper, barkeep, barman <Brit>, tapster

barter NOUNS 1 **trading, swapping** <nonformal>; trade, swap <nonformal>, even trade, even-steven trade

VERBS 2 **trade, deal, traffic, truck, do business; exchange,** give in exchange, take in exchange, **swap** <nonformal>; horse-trade <nonformal>

base NOUNS 1 **bottom**, lowest point, nadir
2 **pedestal; stand,** standard
3 **headquarters** *or* **HQ,** central office, main office, central administration, seat, **base of operations,** center of authority
VERBS 4 **establish, fix, plant, site,** pitch, seat, **set; found,** ground, lay the foundation
ADJS 5 **low, mean, ignoble,** vile, scurvy, sorry, scrubby, beggarly; low-minded, base-minded; below par, sub-par, not up to scratch *or* snuff *or* the mark, **worthless**

baseless ADJS **groundless,** ungrounded, **without foundation,** unfounded, built on sand; ill-founded, unbased, **untenable, unsupportable,** unsustainable

basement NOUNS **cellar,** cellarage; sub-basement; wine cellar, potato cellar, storm cellar, cyclone cellar

bash NOUNS

1 <nonformal> **brawl,** blast, clambake, wingding, blowout, shindig

VERBS 2 **injure, hurt;** rough up <nonformal>, make mincemeat of, maul, batter, savage; maul, pound, beat, beat black and blue

3 <nonformal> **sock,** bang, bat, belt, bust, clip, clout, duke, swat, larrup, paste, lick, biff, wallop, whop, slam, slug

4 **censure,** reprehend; trash *and* rubbish <both nonformal>; **reproach,** impugn

bashful ADJS **shy, timid,** timorous, **coy, demure,** self-conscious

basic ADJS 1 basal, **underlying, essential,** of the essence, **fundamental; substantive,** substantial, material; **vital, all-important,** crucial, of vital importance, life-and-death *or* life-or-death; **central,** focal
2 **original, primary,** primal, primitive, pristine, primeval, aboriginal, **rudimentary,** germinal, seminal

basics NOUNS **essentials, rudiments, elements, nuts and bolts** <nonformal>; **principles,** principia, first principles, first steps, **outlines, primer, ABC's,** abecedarium

basis NOUNS **motive, reason, cause,** source, spring, mainspring; **foundation,** *fond* <Fr>, firm foundation, **base, footing,** grounds, **principle, premise**

bask VERBS insolate; **sun,** bask in the sun, sun oneself, sunbathe

basket NOUNS **container, receptacle;** receiver, holder, vessel, utensil; box, case

bass ADJS **deep,** deep-toned, deep-pitched, deep-sounding, deepmouthed, deep-echoing; low, low-pitched, low-toned, grave, heavy

bastard NOUNS 1 illegitimate *or* bastard child, whoreson, by-blow, child born out of wedlock *or* without benefit of clergy *or* on the wrong side of the blanket, natural *or* love child, *nullius filius* <L>
ADJS 2 **illegitimate, spurious,** false; misbegot, **misbegotten,** miscreated, baseborn, born out of wedlock

bastion NOUNS **stronghold,** strong point, **fastness,** keep, ward, donjon, **citadel, castle,** tower, tower of strength, strong point

batch NOUNS 1 **amount,** quantity, **sum, number,** count, group, total, reckoning, **measure,** parcel, passel <nonformal>, bunch, heap <nonformal>, gob *and* chunk *and* hunk <all nonformal>
VERBS 2 **assemble, gather; accumulate,** cumulate, **amass,** mass, bulk; agglomerate, conglomerate, aggregate; pack, pack in, cram, cram in; **bunch,** bunch up; **cluster,** clump

bathe VERBS 1 **wash,** bath <Brit>, lave; **steep**
2 **swim,** go in swimming *or* bathing; skinny-dip

bathing suit NOUNS **swimwear;** swim suit, swimming suit, tank suit, tank top, *maillot* <Fr>; **trunks;** bikini, string bikini *or* string

bathroom NOUNS **latrine,** convenience, **toilet,** water closet *or* WC <nonformal>; **john** *and* johnny *and* **can** *and* crapper <all nonformal>; loo <Brit nonformal>; **lavatory,** washroom, **rest room,** powder room <nonformal>; men's *or* boys' *or* little boys' room <nonformal>; head; privy, outhouse

baths NOUNS **health resort, spa, watering place;** mineral spring, warm *or* hot spring

baton NOUNS **staff,** stave; **cane, stick, walking stick,** handstaff, shillelagh

batten VERBS **secure,** make sure *or* secure, tie up, chain, tether; **make fast, fasten,** fasten down; batten down
4 **thrive, flourish,** boom; blossom, bloom, flower

battered ADJS **dilapidated, ramshackle, tumbledown, broken-down, run-down,** in ruins, derelict; beaten up, **beat-up** <nonformal>, bruised, wounded

battery NOUNS 1 **artillery, cannon,** cannonry, ordnance, engines of war, Big Bertha, howitzer
2 **corporal punishment, whipping, beating, thrashing, flogging,** flagellation, flailing, trouncing, basting, drubbing, buffeting

battle NOUNS 1 **fight, fray,** affray, combat, action, conflict, embroilment; **clash; brush, skirmish,** scrimmage; tussle, **scuffle, struggle,** scramble
VERBS 2 **contend against,** combat, clash with, rival, compete with *or* against, vie with *or* against; **resist, offer resistance**

battle-ax NOUNS **shrew, vixen,** virago, termagant, fury, witch, beldam, cat, tigress, she-wolf, she-devil, spitfire; **scold,** common scold

battle cry NOUNS **call to arms, call-up,** call to the colors, **rally;** war cry, war whoop, rebel yell; banzai, gung ho, Geronimo, go for broke; remember the Maine *or* the Alamo *or* Pearl Harbor

battlefield NOUNS **battleground,** battle site, **field,** combat zone, **field of battle;** field of slaughter, field of blood *or* bloodshed, aceldama, killing ground *or* field, shambles

battleship NOUNS battlewagon <nonformal>, capital ship; **cruiser,** battlecruiser; **destroyer,** can *or* tin can <nonformal>

bauble NOUNS **trinket,** gewgaw, **knickknack** *or* nicknack, **gimcrack**

bawdy ADJS **obscene, lewd, adult,** ithyphallic, **ribald, pornographic, salacious,** lurid, **dirty, smutty,** raunchy <nonformal>, blue, unclean, **foul, filthy, nasty,** vile, fulsome, offensive, unprintable, **foulmouthed**

bay NOUNS **inlet, cove,** arm of the sea, loch <Scots>, **fjord,** bight; cove; **estuary,** firth *or* frith, bayou, mouth
VERBS 2 cry, call; **howl,** yowl, yawp, yawl <nonformal>, ululate; bay at the moon

bayonet VERBS **stab, stick** <nonformal>, **run through, impale,** spit, **transfix,** transpierce

bazaar NOUNS rummage sale, white elephant sale, garage sale, flea market, flea fair, street market, **mart, market, open market**

beach NOUNS 1 **shore, coast,** *côte* <Fr>; **strand,** *playa* <Sp>, beachfront, plage, lido, riviera
VERBS 2 **shipwreck,** wreck, **go** *or* **run aground,** strand, run on the rocks

beachcomber NOUNS **vagabond, vagrant,** loafer, idler; beach bum, surf bum

beacon NOUNS **signal, sign;** signal fire, beacon fire, parachute flare; rocket, signal rocket, Roman candle

beaded ADJS **beady,** bead-shaped, beadlike; **ornamented, adorned, decorated, embellished, bedecked,** decked out, tricked out, garnished, spangled, jeweled, bejeweled; studded

beaked ADJS **hooked, crooked, aquiline,** aduncous; **hook-shaped,** hooklike, uncinate, unciform

beam NOUNS 1 **smile,** smiling; bright smile, gleaming *or* glowing smile; **grin,** ear-to-ear grin
2 **timber,** pole, spar
3 **ray,** radiation, **gleam, pencil, patch,** ray of light, beam of light
VERBS 4 exude cheerfulness, radiate cheer, not have a care in the world, glow; **smile**
5 **broadcast,** radiate, **transmit,** send

beanery NOUNS eating place, eating house; eatery *and* hashery *and* hash house *and* greasy spoon <all nonformal>; **fast-food restaurant,** hamburger joint <nonformal>

beanpole NOUNS <thin person> **slim, lanky; skeleton,** walking skeleton, beanstalk, broomstick

bear NOUNS 1 bar <nonformal>; grizzly, polar bear
2 short, short seller
VERBS 3 **give birth,** bear *or* have young, **have; have a baby,** bear a child; lie in, be confined, labor
4 **endure, stand,** support, sustain, **suffer, tolerate, abide,** bide, persevere; **bear up under, bear the brunt, bear with, put up with, stand for,** tolerate
5 **transport, convey,** freight, conduct, **take; carry,** pack, tote *and* lug <both nonformal>

6 **yield, produce,** furnish; **bring forth;** fruit, **bear fruit,** fructify
7 **support,** carry, **hold, sustain, maintain, bolster, reinforce,** back, back up, shoulder, give *or* furnish *or* afford *or* supply *or* lend support
bearable ADJS **tolerable, endurable, supportable, sufferable**
bear arms VERBS **serve,** do duty; fulfill one's military obligation, wear the uniform; **soldier,** see *or* do active duty
beard NOUNS 1 **whiskers;** beaver <nonformal>; chin whiskers, side whiskers; **sideburns,** burnsides, **muttonchops; goatee, Vandyke**
VERBS 2 **brave, face, confront,** affront, front, look one in the eye, say to one's face, **face up to, meet head-on** *or* boldly, stand up to *or* against, go eyeball-to-eyeball *or* one-on-one with <nonformal>
bearing NOUNS 1 **look, air, mien,** demeanor, carriage, port, posture, stance, poise, presence
2 **direction,** directionality; **orientation,** lay, lie
bearings NOUNS **position, orientation,** lay, lie, set, **attitude,** aspect, position line *or* line of position; **fix**
bear market NOUNS **declining market,** sagging market, retreating market, **slump,** sag; break in the market
bear witness VERBS 1 **be pious, be religious; have faith,** trust in God, love God, fear God
2 **testify, attest, give evidence, give** *or* **bear witness; depose,** depone, **warrant, swear,** allege, asseverate
beastly ADJS 1 **offensive, objectionable, odious, repulsive,** repellent, rebarbative, **repugnant, revolting**
2 **gruff, brusque, curt,** short, sharp, snippy <nonformal>, abrupt, **blunt,** bluff, brash, bearish, churlish
3 **brutish, brutal,** brute; **bestial,** beastlike; swinish
beast of burden NOUNS **pack** *or* **draft animal,** pack horse *or* mule, sumpter, sumpter horse *or* mule
beat NOUNS 1 **pulsation, pulse, throb;** beating, throbbing; systole, diastole
VERBS 2 **best, beat out, defeat, whip,** give a whipping *or* beating *or* thrashing, **thrash, flog,** whale; **smite,** thump, trounce, baste, **pummel,** lay on
3 <nonformal> beat all hollow, trounce, clobber, take to the cleaners, smoke, skin, skin alive, worst, whip, lick, have it all over, cut down to size
4 **pulsate, pulse, throb, palpitate,** go pit-a-pat

ADJS 5 <nonformal> **pooped, bushed,** frazzled, tuckered, tuckered out, done in, all in, dead, dead beat, dead on one's feet, gone; **pooped out,** knocked out, wiped out, run ragged, played out

6 <nonformal> **clobbered, licked, whipped,** trimmed, sandbagged, banjaxed, done in, lathered, creamed, shellacked, trounced, lambasted, settled, fixed; skinned alive; thrown for a loss

beaten ADJS **defeated, worsted, bested, outdone; discomfited,** put to rout, **routed,** scattered, stampeded, panicked; **undone, done for** <nonformal>, **ruined,** kaput *and* on the skids <both nonformal>, *hors de combat* <Fr>
beater NOUNS **agitator,** shaker, jiggler, vibrator; paddle, whisk, eggbeater; churn; blender
beatify VERBS **sanctify, hallow; purify,** cleanse, wash one's sins away; **bless; glorify,** exalt, ensky; saint, canonize; deify, apotheosize
beating NOUNS 1 **defeat;** drubbing, thrashing; clobbering *and* hiding *and* lathering *and* whipping *and* lambasting *and* trimming *and* licking <all nonformal>, trouncing; Waterloo; failure
2 **corporal punishment, whipping, thrashing, spanking, flogging,** flagellation, scourging, flailing, trouncing, basting, drubbing, buffeting, belaboring
ADJS 3 **drumming, thrumming, pounding, thumping; throbbing;** sputtering, spattering, spluttering
beat it VERBS

<nonformal> **split,** scram, buzz off, buzz along, bug out, fuck off *or* f off, get rolling, hightail it, pull up stakes, check out, clear out, cut out, haul ass, hit the road *or* trail, get lost, get going, shove off, push along, push off, get the hell out, make oneself scarce, vamoose

beatitude NOUNS **sanctification, hallowing; purification;** blessing; **glorification,** exaltation, enskying; **consecration,** dedication, canonization, enshrinement

beatnik NOUNS **nonconformist, original,** eccentric, gonzo <nonformal>, deviant, maverick <nonformal>, Bohemian, hippie, hipster, freak <nonformal>, flower child, street people, yippie

beat up VERBS

<nonformal> rough up, clobber, marmelize <Brit>, work over, lick, larrup, wallop, whop, swinge, beat one's brains out, whale, whale the tar out of, beat *or* kick the shit out of, beat to a jelly, **beat black and blue, knock one's lights out, nail,** welt, trim, flax, lather, leather, **hide,** tan, **tan one's hide,** dress down, **kick ass,** give a dressing-down, knock head, knock heads together; **paddle; lambaste, clobber,** dust one's jacket, give a dose of birch oil *or* strap oil *or* hickory oil *or* hazel oil, take it out of one's hide *or* skin

beau NOUNS **inamorato, swain,** man, gallant, cavalier, squire, *caballero* <Sp>; *amoroso, cavaliere servente* <both Ital>; gigolo; **boyfriend** *and* **fellow** *and* young man *and* flame <all nonformal>; old man <nonformal>; Prince Charming, Lothario, Romeo; Casanova, Don Juan; Beau Brummel

beautified ADJS **improved, bettered;** changed for the better, adorned, decorated

beautiful ADJS **artistic,** painterly; **aesthetic; decorative, ornamental**; **beauteous,** endowed with beauty; **pretty, handsome, attractive**, pulchritudinous, **lovely, graceful,** gracile; elegant; aesthetically appealing

beautiful people NOUNS **society,** *société* <Fr>, fashionable society, **polite society, high society,** *beau monde, haut monde* <both Fr>; best people, right people; **smart set** <nonformal>; the Four Hundred, **upper crust** <nonformal>; café society, jet set, beautiful people, in-crowd, the glitterati <nonformal>

beauty NOUNS 1 **beautifulness,** beauteousness, **prettiness, handsomeness, attractiveness**, **loveliness, pulchritude, charm,** grace, elegance, exquisiteness
2 **charmer, glamour girl,** cover girl, sex goddess; **belle,** reigning beauty, great beauty, enchantress

3 <nonformal> **doll, dish, cutie,** angel, angelface, babyface, beaut, honey, dream, looker, good-looker, stunner, dazzler, dreamboat, fetcher, bird *and* crumpet <both Brit>, peach, knockout, raving beauty, centerfold, pinup girl, pinup, bunny, cutie *or* cutesy pie, cute *or* slick chick, pussycat, sex kitten, ten

4 <famous beauties> Venus, Venus de Milo; Aphrodite, Hebe; Adonis, Appollo, Apollo Belvedere, Hyperion, Antinoüs, Narcissus; Astarte; Balder, Freya; Helen of Troy, Cleopatra; the Graces, houri, peri

truth's smile when she beholds her own face in a perfect mirror
TAGORE

God's handwriting
EMERSON

beckon VERBS attract one's interest, be attractive, take *or* tickle one's fancy; **invite,** summon; **tempt, tantalize, titillate,** whet the appetite, make one's mouth water, dangle before one

become VERBS 1 **originate,** come into the world, get to be <nonformal>, see the light of day, rise, **arise,** take rise, **come forth, issue,** issue forth
2 be converted into, **turn into** *or* **to, change into, grow into,** ripen into, **develop** *or* **evolve into,** merge *or* blend *or* melt into

becoming ADJS **decorous,** proper, **seemly,** fitting, appropriate, suitable, meet, happy, felicitous; **decent, modest,** delicate, elegant, proper

bedazzle VERBS **confuse,** throw into confusion *or* chaos, entangle, **mix up, fluster;** flummox <nonformal>, **flutter,** put into a flutter, **flurry, rattle, ruffle**

bedding NOUNS **bedclothes, blanket, coverlet,** cover, covers, **spread,** robe, **afghan, bedspread; bedcover; linen,** bed linen

bedlam NOUNS 1 **racket, din, clamor; cacophony,** din, noise, static, racket; outcry, **uproar,** hue and cry, noise and shouting
2 **insane asylum,** lunatic asylum, **madhouse,** mental institution, mental home; **bughouse** *and* nuthouse *and* laughing academy *and* **loonybin** *and* **booby hatch** *and* funny farm <all nonformal>; mental hospital

bedraggled ADJS **untidy, unsightly,** unneat, slobby *and* scuzzy <both non-

formal>, **unkempt; sloppy** <nonformal>, scraggly, poky, seedy <nonformal>, **shabby,** grubby <nonformal>, **frowzy, blowzy,** tacky <nonformal>

bedridden ADJS **bedfast, sick abed; down,** prostrate, flat on one's back; **laid up, invalided,** hospitalized

bedrock NOUNS 1 **rock bottom,** bed, hardpan; **grass roots;** substratum, underlayer, lowest level *or* layer *or* stratum, the pits <nonformal>
ADJS 2 **bottom,** bottommost, **undermost,** nethermost, lowermost, deepest, deepmost, profoundest, **lowest**

bedroom NOUNS **boudoir,** chamber, sleeping chamber, **bedchamber,** cubicle, cubiculum

bedtime NOUNS **sleep, slumber; repose,** silken repose, *somnus* <L>, the arms of Morpheus; bye-bye *or* beddy-bye <both nonformal>; **land of Nod,** slumberland, sleepland, dreamland; sack time <nonformal>

beef NOUNS 1 *bœuf* <Fr>; roast beef, *rosbif* <Fr>; Kobe beef
2 **power, potency, might;** oomph *and* punch *and* bang *and* clout *and* steam <all nonformal>; **strength; energy;** muscle power, sinew, might and main
3 **objection, protest;** protestation; **remonstrance, remonstration,** expostulation; **reservation, scruple,** compunction, qualm, twinge *or* qualm of conscience; **complaint, grievance; exception**
VERBS 4 **object, protest, kick** <nonformal>, put up a struggle *or* fight; **bitch** *and* **squawk** *and* howl *and* holler *and* put up a squawk <all nonformal>; make *or* create *or* raise a stink about <all nonformal>; yell bloody murder <nonformal>; **remonstrate,** expostulate

beef up VERBS **intensify, heighten, deepen,** enhance, **strengthen; exaggerate,** blow up *and* puff up <both nonformal>, **magnify;** augment, supplement; swell the ranks of

beep NOUNS 1 **blare,** shriek, peal; **toot,** tootle, **honk,** blat, trumpet
VERBS 2 **blare;** shriek; **toot,** tootle, sound, peal, wind, blow, blat; **honk,** honk *or* sound *or* blow the horn

beeper NOUNS **alarm, alert;** buzzer; automobile alarm; fire alarm

beer NOUNS lager, light beer; brew *and* brewskie *and* suds <all nonformal>, bitter <Brit>

befitting ADJS **expedient, desirable,** to be desired, much to be desired, **advisable, politic,** recommendable; **appropriate, meet, fit, fitting, right, proper, becoming,** seemly, likely, congruous, **suitable,** sortable, feasible, doable, swingable <nonformal>, **convenient,** happy, heaven-sent, felicitous; worthwhile, worth one's while

beforehand ADVS **early, beforetime,** early on, betimes, **ahead of time,** foresightedly, in advance, in anticipation, **with time to spare**

befriend VERBS 1 **make friends with,** gain the friendship of, **strike up a friendship,** take up with <nonformal>, **get acquainted,** make acquaintance with

2 <nonformal> **be buddy-buddy** *or* **palsy-walsy with,** click, have good *or* great chemistry, team up; **get next to, get palsy** *or* **palsy-walsy with,** get cozy with, cozy *or* snuggle up to, get close to, get chummy with, buddy *or* pal up with, play footsie with

beg VERBS 1 **entreat, implore, beseech,** crave, **plead, appeal, pray, supplicate,** impetrate, obtest; clamor for, cry for, cry out for
2 **scrounge, cadge; mooch** *and* **bum** *and* **panhandle** <all nonformal>; **hit** *and* hit up *and* **touch** *and* put the touch on *and* make a touch <all nonformal>

beget VERBS 1 **procreate, generate, breed,** get, **engender; propagate, multiply;** proliferate; sire; reproduce in kind
2 **cause,** be the cause of, lie at the root of; **bring about, bring to pass,** effectuate, **effect,** bring to effect, realize; establish, inaugurate, institute

beggar NOUNS 1 **mendicant,** scrounger, **cadger; bum** *and* bummer *and* **moocher** *and* **panhandler** <all nonformal>; *schnorrer* <Yiddish>
2 **wretch, poor devil,** *pauvre diable* <Fr>, poor creature, *mauvais sujet* <Fr>; **sad case,** sad sack *and* sad sack of shit <both nonformal>

begin VERBS **commence, start; start in, start off, start out, set out,** set to *or* about, go *or* swing into action, get to *or* down to, **turn to,** fall to, pitch in <nonformal>, dive in <nonformal>, plunge into, head into <nonformal>, **go**

ahead, fire *or* blast away <nonformal>, get the show on the road <nonformal>, get *or* set *or* start the ball rolling <nonformal>

beginner NOUNS **neophyte, tyro;** newcomer, new arrival, Johnny-come-lately <nonformal>; **novice,** novitiate, probationer, catechumen; **recruit,** raw recruit, rookie <nonformal>

beginning NOUNS 1 **commencement, start,** running *or* flying start, starting point, square one <nonformal>, **outset,** outbreak, **onset,** oncoming; **origin,** genesis
ADJS 2 **initial,** initiatory *or* initiative; **incipient,** inceptive, **introductory,** inchoative, inchoate; inaugural *or* inauguratory

begrudge VERBS 1 **envy,** be envious *or* covetous of, **covet,** cast envious eyes, desire for oneself; resent; **grudge**
2 **stint, scrimp, skimp, scamp,** scant, **pinch, pinch pennies,** rub the print off a dollar bill

beguile VERBS **fascinate, captivate, charm,** becharm, spell, spellbind, cast a spell, put under a spell, **intrigue, enthrall,** infatuate, **enrapture, transport, enravish, entrance, enchant,** witch, **bewitch**, astound

beguiling ADJS **alluring, fascinating, captivating, riveting, charming, glamorous,** exotic, **enchanting,** spellbinding, **entrancing,** ravishing, **enravishing, intriguing, enthralling, bewitching**

behave VERBS **behave oneself, conduct oneself,** manage oneself, **handle oneself,** guide oneself, **comport oneself, deport oneself,** demean oneself, **bear oneself, carry oneself**

behavior NOUNS **conduct, deportment, comportment, manner, manners, demeanor, mien, carriage, bearing,** poise, posture, guise, **air,** address, presence

behead VERBS decapitate, decollate, guillotine, bring to the block

behest NOUNS **command, commandment, order,** direct order, command decision, **bidding,** imperative, **dictate,** dictation, **will, pleasure,** say-so <nonformal>, **authority**

behind NOUNS 1 **rear, rear end, hind end,** hind part, hinder part, afterpart, rearward, **posterior,** breech, stern, tail, tail end
2 <nonformal> **ass,** backside, **butt, can,** cheeks, hind end, tail, **fanny,** prat, keister
ADJS 3 **retarded,** slowed-down, eased, slackened; set back, backward
ADVS 4 **after,** in the rear, in the train *or* wake of; in back of; behind one's back
5 **late, behindhand, belatedly,** backward, slow, in arrears *or* arrear, **behind time;** none too soon, in the nick of time, under the wire

beholden ADJS **grateful, thankful; appreciative,** appreciatory, sensible; **obliged, much obliged,** indebted to, under obligation

being NOUNS 1 **person, human, human being, man, woman, child,** member of the human race *or* family, Adamite, daughter of Eve
2 **existence;** subsistence, entity, essence, *Ding-an-sich* <Ger, thing-in-itself>, noumenon; **occurrence,** presence

belabor VERBS overemphasize, overstress, overaccentuate, harp on, dwell on; make a big deal *or* Federal case of <nonformal>

belch NOUNS 1 **burp** <nonformal>, belching, wind, gas, eructation
VERBS 2 **erupt, burst forth** *or* **out, break out, blow out** *or* **open,** eruct, **burp** <nonformal>, eructate

belfry NOUNS **tower; turret,** *tour* <Fr>; campanile, bell tower, **spire,** church spire

belief NOUNS 1 religious belief *or* faith, teaching, doctrine, creed, credo, theology, orthodoxy; system of beliefs
2 credence, credit, trust; **confidence,** assuredness, convincedness, persuadedness, **assurance; credulity**

believable ADJS **credible; tenable,** conceivable, **plausible,** colorable; reliable; unimpeachable, unexceptionable, **unquestionable**

believe VERBS 1 **have faith,** bear witness, affirm; keep the faith, fight the good fight, be observant, follow righteousness
2 credit, trust, accept, receive, buy <nonformal>; give credit *or* credence to, put faith in, take stock in *or* set store by <nonformal>, take to heart, attach weight to; **buy** *and* **buy into** <both nonformal>, **swallow**; **be certain**

believer NOUNS pietist, religionist, saint, theist; **devotee,** devotionalist, votary;

zealot, zealotist, fundamentalist, militant; **disciple,** follower, servant, faithful servant; **fanatic**

belittle VERBS **disparage, depreciate,** slight, minimize, make little of, degrade, debase, **run** *or* **knock down** <nonformal>, **put down** <nonformal>; **discredit,** bring into discredit

belle NOUNS **beauty, charmer,** *charmeuse* <Fr>; reigning beauty, great beauty, lady fair; toast of the town; enchantress

belles lettres NOUNS **literature, letters,** humane letters, *litterae humaniores* <L>, republic of letters

belligerent NOUNS 1 **combatant, fighter, battler,** scrapper <nonformal>; **contestant, contender, competitor, rival;** disputant, wrangler, squabbler
ADJS 2 **contentious, quarrelsome; disputatious,** controversial, litigious, polemic, polemical; **argumentative,** scrappy <nonformal>; **quarrelsome**

bellow NOUNS 1 **cry, call, shout, yell,** hoot
VERBS 2 **bawl,** roar; cry *or* yell *or* scream bloody murder *or* blue murder

belly NOUNS 1 **abdomen; stomach, midriff,** diaphragm, **paunch**

2 <nonformal> goozle, guzzle; tum, tummy, tum-tum, breadbasket, **gut,** bulge, fallen chest <nonformal>, corporation, spare tire, bay window, **pot,** potbelly, potgut, beerbelly, German *or* Milwaukee goiter, pusgut, swagbelly; **guts,** tripes, stuffings

VERBS 3 **bulge,** balloon, **pouch, swell, swell up, dilate, distend,** billow; swell out, **belly out**

belong VERBS hold membership, be a member, be on the rolls, be inscribed, subscribe, hold *or* carry a card, be in <nonformal>

belongings NOUNS **personal effects,** chattels personal, movables, choses transitory

beloved NOUNS 1 **sweetheart, loved one,** dearly beloved, well-beloved, object of one's affections, light of one's eye *or* life
ADJS 2 **loved, dear, darling, precious;** pet, favorite; **adored, admired, cherished,** prized, treasured, held dear

below ADVS **down, downward, downwards,** from the top down, *de haut en bas* <Fr>; down below

bemused ADJS **abstracted,** museful <old>, **musing, preoccupied, absorbed, engrossed,** taken up; **absentminded, absent,** faraway, elsewhere, somewhere else, not there; lost, **lost in thought,** wrapped in thought; **daydreaming,** daydreamy

bench NOUNS 1 **seat of justice, judgment seat,** mercy seat, siege of justice <old>
2 reserves, second team, second string, third string
3 workbench; **counter,** bar, buffet; **desk,** writing table; **lectern,** reading stand, ambo, reading desk

bend VERBS 1 **comply with,** agree with, tally with, chime *or* fall in with, go by, be guided *or* regulated by, observe, follow, yield, take the shape of; straighten, rectify, correct, **discipline**
2 **crouch, duck,** cringe, **cower; stoop, stoop down, squat,** squat down, get down, hunker *and* hunker down *and* get down on one's hunkers <all nonformal>

Benedict Arnold NOUNS **traitor,** treasonist, **betrayer, quisling, rat** <nonformal>, **snake in the grass, double-crosser** <nonformal>, double-dealer; Judas, Judas Iscariot, Quisling, Brutus

benediction NOUNS **thanks, thanksgiving,** praise, laud, hymn, paean; **blessing,** benison, invocation, benedicite

benefactor NOUNS benefactress, **benefiter,** succorer, befriender; ministrant, ministering angel; Samaritan, **good Samaritan; helper,** aider, assister, help, aid, helping hand

beneficial ADJS 1 **healthful, healthy, salubrious, salutary, wholesome,** health-enhancing, life-promoting, benign, bracing, refreshing, invigorating, tonic
2 **helpful, useful,** utile; **profitable, salutary,** good for; remedial, therapeutic; **serviceable, useful**; **constructive, positive**

benefit NOUNS 1 benefaction, benevolence, **blessing, favor, boon,** grace; **good, welfare,** well-being
2 benefit performance, **performance, show, presentation,** presentment, **production,** entertainment
VERBS 3 **avail,** be of use, be of service, serve, **suffice, do,** answer, **answer** *or* **serve one's purpose,** serve one's need, fill the bill *and* do the trick <both nonformal>

benevolent ADJS **beneficent, philanthropic, altruistic,** humanitarian; **big-**

hearted, greathearted; **generous**; eleemosynary; **magnanimous**

benign ADJS 1 **kind, kindly;** benignant; kindhearted, warm, warmhearted, soft-hearted, tenderhearted, tender, loving, affectionate
2 **harmless,** unhurtful; well-meaning, well-meant; **innocuous,** nonmalignant

bent NOUNS 1 **disposition, character, nature, temper, temperament,** mettle, constitution, stamp, type, stripe, kidney, make, mold; **turn, bias,** slant, cast, warp, twist
ADJS 2 **distorted, contorted, warped, twisted, crooked;** tortuous, labyrinthine, buckled, sprung, bowed; unsymmetric, unsymmetrical, asymmetric, asymmetrical, nonsymmetric, non-symmetrical; irregular, deviative

bequeath VERBS **will, leave, devise, will to,** hand down, hand on, pass on, transmit; make a bequest

bequest NOUNS bequeathal, **legacy,** devise; inheritance; patrimony, birthright; heirloom

berserk ADJS **amok,** running wild; **rabid, maniac** *or* **maniacal,** raving mad, stark-raving mad, **frenzied, frantic,** frenetic; **raving, raging,** ranting; frothing *or* foaming at the mouth

berth NOUNS **anchor,** mooring, **anchorage,** moorings; slip; mooring buoy

beseech VERBS **entreat, implore, beg,** crave, **plead, appeal, pray, supplicate,** impetrate, obtest; **plead for,** clamor for, cry for, cry out for

besiege VERBS **lay siege to,** encompass, surround, **encircle,** set upon on all sides, get in a pincers, close the jaws of the pincers *or* trap

besmirch VERBS **vilify, revile, defile, sully, soil, smear,** smirch, bespatter, tarnish, **blacken,** denigrate, blacken one's good name, give a black eye <nonformal>; stigmatize; **muckrake, throw mud at,** heap dirt upon, drag through the mud

bespoke ADJS tailored, custom-made

best NOUNS 1 **the best,** the very best, the best ever, the top of the heap *or* the line <nonformal>, the tops <nonformal>; cream of the crop, *crème de la crème* <Fr>, salt of the earth; *pièce de résistance* <Fr>; paragon, nonpareil
VERBS 2 **defeat**; beat all hollow <nonformal>, trounce, clobber *and* take to the cleaners *and* smoke *and* skin *and* skin alive <all nonformal>, worst, whip *and* lick *and* have it all over *and* cut down to size <all nonformal>; **triumph over**
ADJS 3 very best, greatest *and* top-of-the-line <both nonformal>, **prime,** optimum, optimal; **choice, select, elect,** elite, **picked,** handpicked; **prize, champion; unsurpassed,** surpassing, unparalleled, unmatched, unmatchable, matchless, **peerless**

bestial ADJS **brutal,** brutish, brute, beastly, animal; insensate, senseless, subhuman, dehumanized, brutalized; **barbarous,** barbaric, uncivilized, **inhuman,** inhumane, unhuman; fiendish, fiendlike

bestow VERBS **give, present, donate,** slip <nonformal>, let have; **confer, award, allot, render,** bestow on; impart, let one know, communicate; **grant,** accord, **allow,** vouchsafe, yield, afford, make available

bet NOUNS 1 **wager, stake,** hazard, **ante;** parlay, double or nothing
VERBS 2 **wager, gamble, hazard, stake,** punt, lay, lay down, put up, **make a bet, lay a wager,** give *or* take *or* lay odds, make book, get a piece of the action <nonformal>; plunge <nonformal>

bête noire NOUNS **bane, curse,** infliction, visitation, **plague, pestilence,** pest, calamity, scourge, **torment,** crushing burden; bugbear, bogy, bogeymen, nemesis, arch-nemesis

betray VERBS inform, **inform on**, talk *and* peach <both nonformal>; rat *and* stool *and* sing *and* squeal <all nonformal>, turn state's evidence; leak <nonformal>, spill <nonformal>, **spill the beans** <nonformal>; **let the cat out of the bag** <nonformal>, speak before one thinks, be unguarded *or* indiscreet, kiss and tell, **give away** *and* give the show away *and* give the game away <all nonformal>, betray a confidence, tell secrets, reveal a secret; have a big mouth *or* bazoo <nonformal>, **blab** *or* blabber <nonformal>; babble, **tattle,** tell *or* tattle on, tell tales, **tell tales out of school;** talk out of turn, let slip, let fall *or* drop; **blurt, blurt out**

betrayer NOUNS **informer, betrayer,** double-crosser <nonformal>, delator <old>; **snitch** *and* snitcher <both nonformal>; whistle-blower <nonformal>; **tattler,**

tattletale, telltale, talebearer; blab *or* blabber *or* blabberer *or* blabbermouth <all nonformal>; **squealer** *and* preacher *and* **stool pigeon** *and* stoolie *and* **fink** *and* rat <all nonformal>, nark <Brit nonformal>; **spy**

betrothed NOUNS 1 **fiancé, fiancée,** bride-to-be, affianced, future, intended <nonformal>
ADJS 2 **engaged, plighted, affianced,** intended; **promised, pledged, bound, committed,** compromised, **obligated; sworn**

better VERBS 1 **improve,** change for the better, make an improvement; transform, transfigure; improve upon, refine upon, **mend, amend,** emend; meliorate, **ameliorate**
ADJS 2 **superior, greater,** finer; **higher,** upper, over, above; ascendant, in the ascendant, in ascendancy, coming <nonformal>; **ahead,** a cut *or* stroke above, more than a match for

bettor NOUNS **gambler, player,** gamester, wagerer, punter; high-stakes gambler, money player, high roller, plunger; petty gambler, low roller, piker *and* tinhorn *and* tinhorn gambler <all nonformal>

beverage NOUNS drink, thirst quencher, potation, potable, **liquor,** liquid

bevy NOUNS **company, group,** grouping, groupment, network, **party, band, knot, gang, crew,** complement, cast, outfit, pack, cohort, troop, troupe, tribe, **body,** corps, stable, bunch *and* mob *and* crowd <all nonformal>

bewildered ADJS **dismayed,** distracted, distraught, abashed, **disconcerted, embarrassed,** discomposed, **put-out, disturbed, upset,** perturbed, **bothered,** all hot and bothered <nonformal>; clueless, without a clue, guessing, like a chicken with its head cut off <nonformal>; **nonplussed, baffled, perplexed,** mystified

bewildering ADJS **confusing, distracting, disconcerting,** discomposing, **dismaying, embarrassing,** disturbing, **upsetting, perplexing, baffling, mystifying, mysterious, puzzling,** confounding; **enigmatic**

bewitching ADJS **alluring, fascinating, captivating, riveting, charming, glamorous,** exotic, **enchanting,** spellful, spellbinding, **entrancing,** ravishing, **enravishing, intriguing, enthralling,** witching; **tantalizing,** teasing, titillating, titillative, tickling; **provocative,** *provoquant* <Fr>

bias NOUNS 1 **bend,** bent, **crook, warp, twist, turn, skew,** slue, **veer,** sheer, **swerve,** lurch
2 **partiality, onesidedness;** leaning, inclination, tendentiousness; partisanship, **slant,** angle, spin <nonformal>
VERBS 3 **prejudice,** prejudice against, **jaundice, influence, sway,** bias one's judgment; warp, twist, bend, distort
ADJS 4 **slant, biased, biaswise** *or* biasways; **transverse,** crosswise *or* crossways, thwart, athwart, across; **diagonal**
ADVS 5 **diagonally, on the bias,** biaswise; catercornerways *or* **catercorner** *or* cattycorner *or* kittycorner

bicker VERBS **quibble, cavil,** boggle, chop logic, **split hairs,** nitpick, pick nits; **shuffle, dodge,** shy, **evade,** sidestep, hedge, skate around <nonformal>, pussyfoot <nonformal>, evade the issue

bid NOUNS 1 **offer,** offering, proffer, presentation, submission; **invitation**
VERBS 2 **command, order, dictate, direct, instruct,** mandate, **enjoin, charge,** commission, call on *or* upon; give an order *or* a direct order, issue a command
3 make a bid, offer, offer to buy, make an offer; give the asking price; bid up; bid in

bier NOUNS litter, catafalque

big ADJS 1 **large, sizable, great, grand, substantial,** bumper; as big as all outdoors; numerous; largish, biggish
2 **adult, mature, of age,** out of one's teens, grown, **grown-up;** old enough to know better
3 **magnanimous,** great-souled *or* -spirited; **generous,** generous to a fault, openhanded, **liberal; bighearted**

bigamous ADJS digamous; **polygamous,** polygynous, polyandrous; morganatic

bighearted ADJS openhearted, greathearted, **magnanimous; liberal, free,** free with one's money, free-spending; **generous, munificent,** large, princely, handsome; **openhanded,** freehanded, open; **giving**

bigmouthed ADJS **talkative, loquacious, talky,** overtalkative, garrulous, chatty; gabby *and* windy *and* gassy <all nonformal>, all jaw <nonformal>; **longwinded, prolix, verbose**

bigot NOUNS **racist,** racial supremacist, white *or* black supremacist; **chauvinist,** ultranationalist, jingo, superpatriot

big shot NOUNS 1 **superior, chief, head, boss**, honcho <nonformal>, commander, **ruler, leader,** dean, *primus inter pares* <L, first among equals>

2 <nonformal> wheel, **big wheel,** big cheese, big noise, big-timer, big-time operator, **bigwig,** big man, big gun, **high-muck-a-muck** *or* high-muckety-muck, **VIP,** brass hat, high man on the totem pole

bile NOUNS 1 digestive secretion, gastric juice, pancreatic juice, intestinal juice
2 **bitterness, bitter resentment,** bitterness of spirit, heartburning; **rancor,** virulence, **acrimony,** acerbity, asperity; causticity

bilge NOUNS 1 garbage, swill, slop, slops
2 **sink;** sump, **cesspool,** cesspit, septic tank; catchbasin; **sewer,** drain, *cloaca* and *cloaca maxima* <both L>

bilk VERBS **cheat, victimize, gull, swindle, defraud,** euchre, **con,** finagle, **fleece,** mulct, **cheat out of, do out of,** obtain under false pretenses

bill NOUNS 1 **snout, proboscis,** antlia, **trunk;** rostrum; **bill** *and* pecker <both nonformal>
2 **statute,** rubric, **canon,** institution; **ordinance; act, enactment, measure,** legislation
3 **paper money;** dollar bill, etc; **note,** negotiable note, legal-tender note; **bank note,** Federal Reserve note
4 statement, account, ledger, books
VERBS 5 send a statement; **invoice;** call, call in, demand payment, **dun**

billboard NOUNS **poster, bill, placard, sign,** show card, banner, *affiche* <Fr>; highway sign

billow VERBS **surge, swell,** heave, lift, rise, toss, **roll,** wave, **undulate;** comb, break, dash, crash, smash; rise and fall, ebb and flow; balloon, distend

bin NOUNS storage, **depository, repository,** conservatory <old>, reservoir, repertory; bunker, bay, crib; rack, rick; crate, box; chest, **locker,** hutch

bind NOUNS 1 **predicament, plight,** spot of trouble, **strait,** straits, parlous straits, tightrope, knife-edge, thin edge; **embarrassment,** embarrassing position *or* situation; **complication,** imbroglio; the devil to pay
VERBS 2 **edge, bound, rim, skirt, hem, hem in,** fringe, lap, line, side
3 **restrain, tie,** tie up, put the clamps on, **strap,** lash, leash, pinion, fasten, secure, make fast
4 **obligate, oblige, require,** make incumbent *or* imperative, tie, pledge, commit, saddle with, put under an obligation
5 **stick together, cement, colligate, paste, glue,** agglutinate, conglutinate, gum

binding NOUNS 1 **edging, bordering, trimming,** skirting; fringe, fimbriation, fimbria; **hem,** selvage, frill, frilling
ADJS 2 **obligatory, imperative,** peremptory, mandatory, must, *de rigueur* <Fr>; **necessary,** required

binge NOUNS

<nonformal> **drunk,** bust, tear, **bender, toot, bat,** jag, brannigan, guzzle, rip

binoculars NOUNS **spy glass,** terrestrial telescope, glass, **field glass;** zoom binoculars, opera glasses

biodegradable ADJS degradable, decomposable, putrefiable, putrescible, disintegrable

biography NOUNS memoir, **life,** story, **life story,** adventures, fortunes, experiences; **autobiography, profile, biographical sketch**

biologist NOUNS **naturalist,** life scientist; **botanist,** plant scientist, plant biologist, phytobiologist, phytologist; **zoologist,** animal biologist, animal scientist

biology NOUNS biological science, life science, the science of life, the study of living things; **botany,** plant biology, phytobiology, phytology, plant science; **zoology,** animal biology, animal science

bionics NOUNS autonetics, automatic *or* automation technology, automatic electronics, automatic engineering, automatic control engineering, servo engineering, **servomechanics,** system engineering

biorhythm NOUNS **life force, soul,** spirit, indwelling spirit, force of life, living force, *vis vitae* or *vis vitalis* <both L>, **vital force** *or* energy, animating force *or* power *or* principle, biological clock, life cycle

biotic ADJS **organic,** organismic; organized; **animate, living,** vital, zoetic

birdbrained ADJS **superficial, shallow, unprofound;** shallow-witted, shallow-minded, shallow-brained, shallow-headed, shallow-pated; **frivolous,** dizzy *and* ditzy <both nonformal>, flighty, light, volatile, frothy, fluffy, **feather-brained, birdwitted**

birth NOUNS 1 **nativity,** nascency, **childbirth, childbearing, having a baby, giving birth, birthing,** parturition, the stork <nonformal>; **confinement,** lying-in, being brought to bed, **childbed,** *accouchement* <Fr>; **labor,** travail, birth throes *or* pangs; **delivery,** blessed event <nonformal>; the Nativity; multiparity; **hatching;** littering, whelping, farrowing
2 **generation, genesis; development;** procreation; **heredity, heritage, inheritance;** patrocliny, matrocliny; endowment, inborn capacity *or* tendency *or* susceptibility *or* predisposition; diathesis; inheritability, heritability, hereditability
ADJS 3 **kindred, akin;** consanguineous *or* consanguinean *or* consanguineal, consanguine, by *or* of the blood; **biological,** genetic; **natural,** by birth; cognate, uterine, agnate, enate; intimately *or* closely related, remotely *or* distantly related

birth control device NOUNS **contraceptive,** prophylactic; condom; **rubber** *and* skin *and* bag <all nonformal>; oral contraceptive, **birth control pill, the pill** <nonformal>, morning-after pill, abortion pill; diaphragm, pessary; spermicide, spermicidal jelly, contraceptive foam; intrauterine device *or* IUD, Dalkon shield <trademark>, Lippes loop

birth defect NOUNS congenital defect; abnormality, condition, pathological condition; complication, secondary disease *or* condition

birthmark NOUNS strawberry mark, port-wine stain, vascular nevus, nevus, hemangioma; beauty mark *or* spot

birthplace NOUNS **fatherland,** *Vaterland* <Ger>, *patria* <L>, *la patrie* <Fr>, **motherland,** mother country, **native land,** native soil, one's native heath *or* ground *or* soil *or* place, the old country, country of origin, **birthplace,** cradle; **home, homeland,** homeground, God's country

home is where one starts
T S Eliot

biscuit NOUNS sinker <nonformal>; hardtack, sea biscuit, ship biscuit, pilot biscuit *or* bread; **cracker,** soda cracker *or* saltine, graham cracker, *biscotto* <Ital>, cream cracker, nacho, potato chip, potato crisp <Brit>, sultana, water biscuit, butter cracker, oyster cracker, pilot biscuit; wafer; rusk, zwieback, melba toast, Brussels biscuit; pretzel

bisexuality NOUNS bisexualism, ambisexuality, ambisextrousness, amphierotism, swinging both ways <nonformal>; **sexual preference; sexual orientation**

bishop NOUNS <Mormon> deacon, teacher, priest, elder, Seventy, high priest, patriarch, apostle; Aaronic priesthood, Melchizedek priesthood

bisque NOUNS **ceramic ware, ceramics; pottery, crockery; china, porcelain;** enamelware; refractory, cement; biscuit

bistro NOUNS **bar,** barroom, *bistro* <Fr>, cocktail lounge; taproom; **tavern, pub,** pothouse, alehouse, rumshop, grogshop, dramshop, groggery, gin mill <nonformal>, **saloon,** drinking saloon, saloon bar <Brit>; café

bit NOUNS 1 **distance;** stone's throw, spitting distance <nonformal>, bowshot, gunshot, pistol shot; earshot, earreach, a whoop *and* a whoop and a holler *and* two whoops and a holler <all nonformal>, ace
2 **little,** little *or* wee *or* tiny bit <nonformal>, bite, **particle,** fragment, spot, **speck,** flyspeck, fleck, point, dot, jot, tittle, **iota,** ounce, **dab** <nonformal>, mote, **mite** <nonformal>; whit, ace, **hair,** scruple, groat, farthing, pittance, dole, trifling amount, **smidgen** *and* skosh *and* smitch <all nonformal>, pinch, gobbet, dribble, driblet, dram, drop, drop in a bucket *or* in the ocean, nutshell
3 **piece, particle, scrap**, bite, **fragment, morsel, crumb,** shard, potsherd, snatch, snack; **cut,** cutting, clip, clipping, paring, shaving, rasher, snip, snippet, chip; **tatter, shred,** stitch; **splinter,** sliver; **shiver, smithereen** <nonformal>
4 **short time, little while,** little, **instant, moment**, mo <nonformal>, small space, span, spurt, **short spell;** no time, less than no time; bit *or* **little bit,** a breath, the wink of an eye, pair of winks <nonformal>; **two shakes** *and* two shakes of a lamb's tail <both nonformal>

5 **binary digit,** infobit, kilobit, megabit, gigabit, terbit; **byte,** kilobyte, megabyte

bitch NOUNS 1 **shrew, vixen,** virago, termagant, brimstone, fury, witch, beldam, cat, tigress, she-wolf, she-devil, spitfire; fishwife; **scold,** common scold; battle-ax <nonformal>
2 **dog, canine, pooch** *and* bow-wow <both nonformal>; **pup, puppy,** puppy-dog *and* perp <both nonformal>, **whelp;** gyp <S US>, slut
3 **tough proposition** *and* tough one *and* toughie <all nonformal>, large *or* tall order <nonformal>; **hard job, tough job** *and* heavy lift <both nonformal>, backbreaker, ballbuster <nonformal>, **chore,** man-sized job; brutal task, Herculean task, Augean task; **uphill work** *or* **going,** rough go <nonformal>, **heavy sledding,** hard pull <nonformal>, dead lift <old>; tough lineup to buck <nonformal>, hard road to travel; hard *or* tough nut to crack *and* hard *or* tough row to hoe *and* hard row of stumps <all nonformal>
VERBS 4 **object, protest, kick** *and* **beef** <both nonformal>, put up a struggle *or* fight; **bitch** *and* **beef** *and* **squawk** *and* howl *and* holler *and* put up a squawk *and* raise a howl <all nonformal>; exclaim *or* cry out against, make *or* create *or* raise a stink about <all nonformal>; yell bloody murder <nonformal>; **remonstrate,** expostulate; raise *or* press objections, raise one's voice against, enter a protest; **complain,** exclaim at, state a grievance, air one's grievances; **dispute, challenge,** call in question

bitchy ADJS 1 **spiteful,** despiteful; **catty,** cattish; **snide**

2 <nonformal> **crabby, grouchy,** cantankerous, crusty, grumpy *or* grumpish, cussed, huffy *or* huffish, mean, mean as a junkyard dog, ornery, cussed, feisty, ugly, miffy, salty, scrappy, shirty <Brit>, soreheaded

bite NOUNS 1 **morsel, taste,** swallow; mouthful, gob <nonformal>; a nibble, a bite, munchies; cud, quid; bolus; **chew,** chaw <nonformal>; nip, nibble; munch; gnash; champ, chomp <nonformal>; snap
2 **light meal, refreshments,** light repast, light lunch, spot of lunch <nonformal>, collation, **snack** *and* nosh <both nonformal>, *casse-croûte* <Fr>
3 **zest,** zestfulness, zestiness, **briskness,** liveliness, raciness; **nippiness, tanginess,** snappiness; **spiciness,** pepperiness, hotness, fieriness; **tang, spice,** relish; **nip;** punch, snap, zip, ginger; **kick,** guts <nonformal>
4 **bit, scrap, fragment, morsel, crumb,** shard, potsherd, snatch; cutting, clip, clipping, paring, shaving, rasher, snip, snippet, chip
VERBS 5 **pain,** sting; nip, tweak, pinch; pierce, prick, stab, cut, lacerate; **irritate, inflame,** harshen, exacerbate, intensify

biting ADJS 1 **painful;** hurtful, **hurting,** distressing, afflictive; **acute, sharp,** piercing, stabbing, shooting, stinging, gnawing; **poignant,** pungent, **severe,** cruel, harsh, grave, hard; griping, cramping, spasmic, spasmatic, spasmodic, paroxysmal; **agonizing, excruciating,** exquisite, atrocious, torturous, tormenting, martyrizing, racking, **harrowing**
2 **pungent, piquant, poignant; sharp, keen,** piercing, penetrating, nose-tickling, stinging, **acrid,** astringent, irritating, harsh, rough, severe, asperous, cutting, trenchant; **caustic,** vitriolic, mordant, escharotic; **bitter**; acerbic, acid, **sour**

bitter ADJS 1 **sharp, keen,** piercing, penetrating, nose-tickling, stinging, **biting, acrid,** astringent, irritating, harsh, rough, severe, asperous, cutting, trenchant; **caustic,** vitriolic, mordant, escharotic
2 **resentful,** resenting; embittered, rancorous, virulent, **acrimonious,** acerb, acerbic, acerbate; caustic; **choleric,** splenetic, acid, acidic, acidulous, acidulent; **sore** <nonformal>, rankled, burning *and* stewing <both nonformal>

bitterly ADVS **caustically,** mordantly, mordaciously, corrosively, corrodingly; **acrimoniously,** acridly, acidly, acerbly, acerbically, tartly; **sharply,** keenly, incisively, trenchantly, **cuttingly,** penetratingly, piercingly, bitingly, **stingingly,** stabbingly, **scathingly,** scorchingly, witheringly, thersitically, scurrilously, abusively

bivouac NOUNS 1 campground *or* campsite, camp, encampment, tented field
VERBS 2 **camp, encamp,** tent; pitch,

pitch camp, pitch one's tent, drive stakes <nonformal>; camp out, sleep out, rough it

bizarre ADJS 1 **humorous, funny, amusing; witty; droll, whimsical,** quizzical; **laughable,** risible, good for a laugh; **ludicrous, ridiculous, hilarious,** quaint, eccentric, incongruous
2 **absurd, nonsensical,** insensate, ridiculous, laughable, ludicrous; **foolish, crazy;** preposterous, cockamamie <nonformal>, fantastic, fantastical, grotesque, monstrous, wild, weird, **outrageous,** incredible, beyond belief, *outré* <Fr>, extravagant

blabbermouth NOUNS **informer, betrayer,** double-crosser <nonformal>, delator <old>; **snitch** *and* snitcher <both nonformal>; whistle-blower <nonformal>; **tattler, tattletale, telltale, talebearer; blab** *or* blabber *or* blabberer *or* blabbermouth <all nonformal>; **squealer** *and* preacher *and* **stool pigeon** *and* stoolie *and* **fink** *and* rat <all nonformal>, nark <Brit nonformal>

black NOUNS 1 **blackness,** nigritude, nigrescence; inkiness; **sable, ebony;** melanism; darkness
ADJS 2 **ebony;** deep black, of the deepest dye; **pitch-black, pitch-dark,** pitchy, black *or* dark as pitch, tar-black, tarry; night-black, night-dark, black *or* dark as night; midnight, black as midnight; **inky,** inky-black, atramentous, ink-black, black as ink; **jet-black,** jetty; **coal-black,** coaly, black as coal, coal-black; sloe, sloe-black, sloe-colored; raven, **raven-black,** black as a crow; **dark**

cyprus black as e'er was crow
SHAKESPEARE

3 <comparisons> ebony *or* ebon <old>, jet, ink, sloe, pitch, tar, coal, charcoal, smoke, soot, smut, raven, crow, night, hell, sin, one's hat <Brit>
4 **dark-skinned,** black-skinned, **dark-complexioned; colored;** melanian, melanic, melanotic, melanistic, melanous
5 **bad, evil, ill,** untoward, sinister; **wicked, wrong,** peccant, iniquitous, **vicious**

blackball VERBS **ostracize,** turn thumbs down, disfellowship; **reject, repudiate,** blackball *and* turn thumbs down on <both nonformal>, read *or* drum out, ease *or* freeze out *and* leave *or* keep out in the cold <all nonformal>, **exile, banish; proscribe, ban, outlaw,** put under the ban; **boycott,** blacklist

blacken VERBS 1 black, nigrify, melanize, denigrate; **darken,** bedarken; shade, shadow; blackwash, ink, charcoal, cork; **smudge,** smutch, **smirch,** besmirch, murk, blotch, blot, dinge; smut, soot; smoke, oversmoke; ebonize
2 **vilify, revile, defile, sully, soil, smear,** smirch, besmirch, bespatter, tarnish, denigrate, blacken one's good name, give a black eye <nonformal>; **call names,** give a bad name, give a dog a bad name, stigmatize; **muckrake, throw mud at,** mudsling, heap dirt upon, drag through the mud; engage in personalities
3 **darken,** bedarken; **obscure,** obfuscate, adumbrate; **eclipse,** occult, occultate, block the light; **black out,** brown out

black eye NOUNS **stigma,** stigmatism, onus; **brand,** badge of infamy; **slur,** reproach, censure, reprimand, imputation, aspersion, reflection, stigmatization; pillorying; black mark; **disparagement; stain, taint,** attaint, **tarnish,** blur, **smirch,** smutch *or* smooch, smudge, **smear,** spot, blot, blot on *or* in one's escutcheon *or* scutcheon; shiner *and* mouse <both nonformal>

black humor NOUNS **humor,** sick humor, gallows humor

blacklist VERBS **ostracize,** turn thumbs down, disfellowship; **reject, exile, banish; proscribe, ban, outlaw,** put under the ban; **boycott, blackball**

black magic NOUNS **Satanism,** diabolism, devil-worship, **demonism, devilry, diablerie, demonry;** demonomy, demonianism; the black art; Black Mass; sorcery; demonolatry, demon *or* devil *or* chthonian worship; demonomancy; demonology, diabolology *or* diabology, demonography, devil lore

blackmail NOUNS 1 **extortion, shakedown** <nonformal>, bloodsucking, vampirism; protection racket; badger game
VERBS 2 **extort, exact,** squeeze, screw, **shake down** <nonformal>, levy blackmail, badger *and* play the badger game <both nonformal>

black-market ADJS **illegal, unlawful, illegitimate, illicit,** nonlicit, nonlegal, lawless, wrongful, fraudulent, creative <nonformal>, **against the law; outlaw, outlawed; contraband,** bootleg; under-the-table, under-the-counter

blackout NOUNS 1 **unconsciousness, loss of memory, memory loss, amnesia,** failure; **memory gap;** fugue; agnosia, unrecognition, body-image agnosia, ideational agnosia, astereognosis *or* astereocognosy; paramnesia, retrospective falsification, false memory, misremembrance; amnesiac
2 **power failure,** power cut, power loss; **brownout,** dimout, voltage drop, voltage loss

blade NOUNS 1 **leaf, frond;** lamina, spear, spire, pile, flag; **needle,** pine needle
2 **sword,** good *or* trusty sword; steel, **cold steel;** Excalibur; **knife; dagger; axe**
3 **dandy, fop,** coxcomb, macaroni, gallant, dude *and* swell *and* sport <all nonformal>, ponce *and* toff <both Brit nonformal>, exquisite, blood, fine gentleman, puppy, jackanapes, jack-a-dandy, fribble, clotheshorse, fashion plate; beau, Beau Brummel, spark, ladies' man, lady-killer <nonformal>, masher, cocksman <nonformal>; man-about-town, boulevardier

blahs NOUNS **listlessness, spiritlessness,** burnout, blah *or* blahs <nonformal>, heartlessness, plucklessness, spunklessness; **blues** *and* blue devils *and* mulligrubs <all nonformal>, mumps, **dumps** <nonformal>, **doldrums,** dismals, dolefuls <nonformal>, blahs *and* mopes *and* megrims *and* sulks <all nonformal>

blame NOUNS 1 **censure, reprehension,** stricture, reprobation, **denunciation,** denouncement, decrying, decrial, bashing *and* trashing <both nonformal>, impeachment, arraignment, indictment, **condemnation,** damnation, fulmination, anathema; castigation, flaying, skinning alive <nonformal>, fustigation, excoriation; pillorying
VERBS 2 **censure,** reprehend; lay *or* cast blame upon; **bash** *and* trash *and* rubbish <all nonformal>; **reproach,** impugn; **condemn,** damn, take out after; damn with faint praise; fulminate against, anathematize, anathemize, put on the Index; **denounce,** denunciate, **accuse, decry,** cry down, impeach, arraign, indict, call to account, exclaim *or* declaim *or* inveigh against, peg away at, cry out against, cry out on *or* upon, cry shame upon, raise one's voice against, raise a hue and cry against, shake up <old>; reprobate, hold up to reprobation; animadvert on *or* upon, reflect upon, cast reflection upon, cast a reproach *or* slur upon, complain against; throw a stone at, cast *or* throw the first stone

blameless ADJS **innocent;** unfallen, unlapsed, prelapsarian; **unguilty,** not guilty, **guiltless, faultless,** reproachless, **sinless,** offenseless, with clean hands; clear, in the clear; without reproach, *sans reproche* <Fr>; innocent as a lamb, lamblike, dovelike, angelic, childlike; unacquainted with *or* untouched by evil, uncorrupted, incorrupt, pristine, undefiled

bland ADJS 1 **insipid, tasteless, flavorless,** spiceless, **savorless,** sapless, unsavory, unflavored; pulpy, pappy, gruelly; **weak, thin,** mild, **wishy-washy,** milktoast, washy, watery, watered, watered-down, diluted, dilute, milk-and-water; **flat, stale,** dead, *fade* <Fr>; vapid, inane, jejune; indifferent, neither one thing nor the other, featureless, unrelieved, characterless, insipid

weary, flat, stale, and unprofitable
SHAKESPEARE

2 **mild,** soft, **gentle,** tame; mild as milk *or* mother's milk, mild as milk and water, gentle as a lamb

blank ADJS **inexpressive,** unexpressive, impassive, po-faced <Brit>; uncommunicative; **expressionless; vacant, empty;** glassy, glazed, glazed-over, fishy, wooden; deadpan, poker-faced <nonformal>

blanket NOUNS 1 **coverlet,** coverlid <nonformal>, space blanket, cover, covers, **spread,** robe, buffalo robe, **afghan,** rug <Brit>; lap robe; **bedspread; bedcover;** counterpane, counterpin <nonformal>; comfort, **comforter, down comforter, duvet, continental quilt** <Brit>, **quilt,** feather bed, eiderdown; patchwork quilt; **bedding, bedclothes,** clothes; **linen,** bed linen; **sheet,** sheeting, bedsheet, fitted sheet, contour sheet; **pillowcase,** pillow slip, case, slip; duvet cover
VERBS 2 **conceal, hide,** ensconce; **cover, cover up,** blind, **screen, cloak,**

veil, screen off, curtain, shroud, enshroud, envelop; **disguise, camouflage, mask,** dissemble; plain-wrap, wrap in plain brown paper; whitewash <nonformal>; **paper over,** gloss over, varnish, slur over; distract attention from; **obscure,** obfuscate, cloud, becloud, befog, throw out a smoke screen, shade, throw into the shade
ADJS 3 **comprehensive, sweeping, complete**; whole; **all-comprehensive,** all-inclusive; without omission *or* exception, **overall,** universal, global, wall-to-wall <nonformal>, around-the-world, **total,** omnibus, across-the-board; encyclopedic, compendious; synoptic; bird's-eye, panoramic

blare NOUNS 1 **blast,** shriek, peal; **toot,** tootle, **honk,** beep, blat, trumpet; bay, bray; **whistle,** tweedle, squeal; trumpet call, trumpet blast *or* blare, sound *or* flourish of trumpets, Gabriel's trumpet *or* horn, **fanfare,** tarantara, tantara, tantarara; tattoo; taps
VERBS 2 blast; shriek; **toot,** tootle, sound, peal, wind, blow, blat; pipe, trumpet, bugle, clarion; bay, bell, bray; **whistle,** tweedle, squeal; **honk,** honk *or* sound *or* blow the horn, beep; sound taps, sound a tattoo

blaring ADJS **noisy,** noiseful, rackety, clattery, clangorous, clanging, **clamorous,** clamoursome <Brit nonformal>, clamant, blatant, brassy, brazen, blatting; uproarious, **tumultuous,** turbulent, blustering, brawling, **boisterous,** riproaring, rowdy, mafficking <Brit>, strepitous, strepitant, obstreperous; vociferous

blasé ADJS 1 **nonchalant, indifferent,** insouciant, unconcerned; **casual, offhand, relaxed, laid-back** *and* throwaway <both nonformal>; **easygoing,** easy, free and easy, devil-may-care, lackadaisical, *dégagé* <Fr>; splenetic <old>, melancholy, melancholic, life-weary, world-weary, tired of living; **listless, dispirited**
2 **disillusioned, disenchanted,** unspelled, uncharmed, **disabused,** undeceived, stripped *or* robbed of illusion, enlightened, set right, put straight

blasphemy NOUNS **sacrilege,** blaspheming, impiety; **profanity,** profaneness; sacrilegiousness, blasphemousness; **desecration, profanation;** tainting, pollution, contamination

blast NOUNS 1 **noise,** loud noise, tintamarre, **racket, din, clamor;** outcry, **uproar,** hue and cry, noise and shouting; howl; clangor, clatter, clap, jangle, rattle; roar, thunder, thunderclap; **crash, boom,** sonic boom; **bang,** percussion; brouhaha, **tumult, hubbub,** bobbery <India>; fracas, **brawl,** commotion, drunken brawl; **pandemonium,** bedlam, hell *or* bedlam let loose; charivari, shivaree <nonformal>; discord
2 **detonation, explosion,** fulmination, **discharge, burst, bang, pop, crack,** bark; **shot,** gunshot; volley, salvo, fusillade
3 **gust,** wind gust, blow, flaw, **flurry,** scud <Scots>
VERBS 4 **blare;** shriek; **toot,** tootle, sound, peal, wind, blow, blat; pipe, trumpet, bugle, clarion; bay, bell, bray; **whistle,** tweedle, squeal; **honk,** honk *or* sound *or* blow the horn, beep; sound taps, sound a tattoo
5 **detonate, explode, discharge, burst,** go off, **bang, pop, crack,** bark, fulminate; burst on the ear
6 **blow; blow up a storm;** bluster, squall; **storm,** rage, blow great guns, blow a hurricane

blow, winds, and crack your cheeks, rage, blow
SHAKESPEARE

blastoff NOUNS **rocket launching** *or* **firing,** ignition, launch, shot, shoot; countdown; **lift-off;** guided *or* automatic control, programming; flight, trajectory; **burn; burnout,** end of burning

blaze NOUNS 1 **fire; flame,** ingle, devouring element; **combustion, ignition,** ignition temperature *or* point, flash *or* flashing point; **conflagration;** flicker, wavering *or* flickering flame; smoldering fire, sleeping fire; marshfire, fen fire, ignis fatuus, will-o'-the-wisp; fox fire; witch fire, St Elmo's fire, corposant; **cheerful fire,** cozy fire, crackling fire; **roaring fire,** blazing fire; **raging fire,** sheet of fire, sea of flames

whirlwinds of tempestuous fire
MILTON

2 **flash, flare, gleam, glint, glance;** blaze *or* flash *or* gleam of light; green flash; solar flare, solar prominence, facula; Bailey's beads

VERBS 3 **mark,** make a mark, put a mark on; blaze a trail
4 **burn,** torrefy, **scorch, parch, sear; singe,** swinge; **blister,** vesicate; **cauterize,** brand, burn in; **char,** coal, carbonize
5 **flame,** fulgurate; **radiate,** shoot, shoot out rays, send out rays; spread *or* diffuse light; be bright, shine brightly, beacon

bleach NOUNS 1 bleacher, bleaching agent *or* substance; decolorant, decolorizer, achromatizer
VERBS 2 decolor, decolorize, discolor, achromatize, etiolate; **fade, wash out; dim, dull, tarnish,** tone down; **pale, whiten,** blanch, drain, drain of color; **lose color, fade**

bleak ADJS 1 **gloomy, dismal, murky, grim, somber,** sombrous, **solemn, grave;** sad, *triste* <Fr>, **funereal,** funebrial, crepehanging <nonformal>, saturnine; **dark,** black, gray; **dreary,** drear, drearisome; weary, weariful, wearisome
2 **hopeless,** unhopeful, without hope, affording no hope, worst-case, grim, dismal, cheerless, comfortless; **desperate, despairing, in despair;** despondent; disconsolate
3 **windblown,** blown; **windswept,** raw, exposed

bleat VERBS cry, call; **howl,** yowl, yawp, yawl <nonformal>, ululate; wail, whine, pule; **squeal,** squall, scream, screech, screak, squeak; blate, blat

bleed VERBS 1 **hemorrhage,** lose blood, **shed blood,** spill blood; bloody; ecchymose
2 **suffer, hurt, ache;** anguish, **suffer anguish; agonize,** writhe; go hard with, have a bad time of it, go through hell; quaff the bitter cup, drain the cup of misery to the dregs, be nailed to the cross
3 **draw off, draft off,** draft, draw, draw from; **suck,** suck out *or* up, **siphon off;** pipette; pump, pump out; tap, broach; let, let out; let blood, venesect, phlebotomize; milk; **drain,** decant; exhaust, empty
4 **take advantage of, use,** make use of, **use for one's own ends;** make a paw *or* cat's-paw of, sucker *and* play for a sucker <both nonformal>; **manipulate,** work on, work upon, stroke, play on *or* upon; play both ends against the middle; **impose upon,** presume upon; use ill, ill-use, abuse, misuse; batten on; milk, bleed white <nonformal>; drain, suck the blood of *or* from, suck dry; exploit one's position, feather one's nest <nonformal>, **profiteer, strip,** strip bare *or* clean, **fleece** <nonformal>, skin *and* pluck <both nonformal>, flay, **despoil, divest,** pick clean, pick the bones of

blemish NOUNS **disfigurement,** disfiguration, **defacement;** scar, keloid, cicatrix; needle scar, track *or* crater <both nonformal>; scratch; scab; blister, vesicle, bulla, bleb; weal, wale, welt, wen, sebaceous cyst; port-wine stain *or* mark, hemangioma, strawberry mark; pock, pustule; pockmark, pit; nevus, birthmark, mole; freckle, lentigo; milium, whitehead, blackhead, comedo, pimple, hickey, sty; wart, verruca; **crack,** craze, check, rift, split; **deformity,** deformation, warp, twist, kink, **distortion; flaw, defect, fault, stigma; eyesore,** blot, blot on the landscape

blend NOUNS 1 **compound, mixture, admixture,** intermixture, immixture, commixture, **composite,** meld, composition, confection, concoction, **combination,** combo <nonformal>, ensemble, marriage; amalgam, alloy
VERBS 2 **mix,** admix, commix, immix, **intermix, mingle,** bemingle, commingle, immingle, **intermingle,** interlace, interweave, intertwine, interlard; syncretize; interblend, stir in; **amalgamate, integrate,** alloy, coalesce, **fuse, merge,** meld, compound, compose, conflate, concoct; **combine**; mix up, hash, stir up, **scramble,** conglomerate, shuffle, **jumble,** jumble up, mingle-mangle, throw *or* toss together; knead, work; homogenize, emulsify

bless VERBS **sanctify, hallow; purify,** cleanse, wash one's sins away; beatify; **glorify,** exalt, ensky; **consecrate,** dedicate, devote, set apart; **beatify, saint, canonize;** enshrine

blessed ADJS 1 **sanctified, hallowed;** consecrated, devoted, dedicated, set apart; **glorified, exalted,** enskied; **saintly,** sainted, beatified, canonized
2 **fortunate, lucky, providential; in luck;** blessed with luck, favored; born under a lucky star, born with a silver spoon in one's mouth, born on the sunny side of the hedge; out of the woods, over the hump; **auspicious**

blessing NOUNS 1 **approval, approba-**

tion; sanction, acceptance, countenance, **favor;** endorsement, vote, favorable vote, yea vote, yea, voice, adherence, seal of approval, nod, stamp of approval, **OK**
2 **benediction,** benison, invocation, benedicite; sign of the cross; laying on of hands
3 **good fortune** *or* **luck,** happy fortune, **fortune, luck,** the breaks <nonformal>; **fortunateness, luckiness,** felicity <old>; smiles of fortune, fortune's favor

blighted ADJS **ruined, destroyed, wrecked, blasted, undone,** down-and-out, broken, bankrupt; spoiled; irremediable; fallen, overthrown; **devastated, desolated, ravaged,** wasted; ruinous, in ruins; gone to wrack and ruin

blind NOUNS 1 **stratagem, artifice,** art <old>, **craft, wile,** strategy, **device,** wily device, **contrivance, expedient, design, scheme, trick,** cute trick, fetch, fakement <nonformal>, gimmick <nonformal>, **ruse, red herring, shift,** tactic, **maneuver, stroke,** stroke of policy, master stroke, **move,** coup, gambit, **ploy, dodge,** artful dodge; **game,** little game, racket *and* grift <both nonformal>; **plot,** conspiracy, **intrigue;** sleight, feint, jugglery; method in one's madness; **subterfuge,** dust in the eyes; chicanery, knavery, deceit, trickery
2 **shade,** shader, **screen, light shield, curtain,** drape, drapery, veil; cover
VERBS 3 **hoodwink,** blindfold, blind one's eyes, blear the eyes of <old>, throw dust in one's eyes, **pull the wool over one's eyes**
ADJS 4 **sightless, unsighted,** ablepticai, eyeless, visionless, **unseeing,** undiscerning, unobserving, unperceiving; in darkness, rayless, bereft of light, dark <nonformal>; **stone-blind,** stark blind, **blind as a bat,** blind as a mole *or* an owl; amaurotic; dim-sighted; hemeralopic; nyctalopic; color-blind; mind-blind, soul-blind, mentally *or* psychically *or* spiritually blind, benighted, unenlightened

dark, dark, dark, amid the blaze of noon
MILTON

5 **unpersuadable,** deaf; closed-minded; positive; dogmatic
6 **undiscerning, unperceptive,** imperceptive, impercipient, insensible, unapprehending, uncomprehending, nonunderstanding; **shortsighted,** myopic, nearsighted, dim-sighted; purblind, mind-blind, blind as a bat; blinded, blindfold, blindfolded

blinding ADJS obscuring; **dazzling,** bedazzling; **bright, brilliant, vivid, splendid,** splendorous, splendent, **resplendent,** bright and shining; fulgid <old>, fulgent, effulgent, refulgent; **flamboyant,** flaming; **glaring,** glary, garish

blind spot NOUNS **narrow-mindedness, small-mindedness, shortsightedness,** nearsightedness, purblindness; blind side, tunnel vision, blinders; closed mind, mean mind, petty mind, shut mind; narrow views *or* sympathies, cramped ideas; *parti pris* <Fr>, an ax to grind

blink VERBS 1 **wink,** nictitate, bat the eyes <nonformal>
2 **flinch, shrink, shy,** shy away from, draw back, recoil, funk <nonformal>, **quail, cringe, wince, blench,** say *or* cry uncle; put one's tail between one's legs

blip NOUNS radar signal; trace, reading, return, **echo, bounce, pip;** spot, CRT spot

blissful ADJS 1 **cheerful, gay**; blessed; thrice happy; happy as a lark, happy as a king, happy as the day is long, happy as a baby boy, happy as a clam at high water, happy as a pig in shit <nonformal>, happy as a sand boy <Brit>

thrice and four times blessed
VERGIL

2 beatific, saintly, divine; sublime; **heavenly,** paradisal, paradisiac, paradisiacal, paradisic, paradisical, empyreal *or* empyrean, Elysian; out of sight *or* of this world <nonformal>

blister NOUNS 1 **bubble,** bleb, **globule;** vesicle, bulla, blood blister, fever blister; balloon, bladder
VERBS 2 **sear; singe,** swinge; vesicate; **cauterize,** brand, burn in; **char,** coal, carbonize; scorify; calcine; pyrolyze

blithe ADJS **cheerful, cheery,** of good cheer, in good spirits, vogie <Scots>; in high spirits, exalted, elated, exhilarated, high <nonformal>; irrepressible; blithesome; **glad, gladsome; happy,** happy as a clam *or* a sand boy *or* a lark, on top of the world

blithering ADJS babbling, driveling, slobbering, drooling, dithering, maundering, burbling

blitz NOUNS 1 blitzkrieg, lightning attack, lightning war, panzer warfare, sudden *or* devastating *or* crippling attack, deep strike, shock tactics; **pass rush** <football>
VERBS 2 **attack, assault, strike, hit, pound;** attack in force; surprise; attack *or* hit like lightning; **blow up,** blast, spring, explode, blow to pieces *or* bits *or* smithereens *or* kingdom come, bomb, bombard

blizzard NOUNS **snowstorm,** snow blast, snow squall, snow flurry, flurry

bloated ADJS 1 **distended, dilated, inflated,** sufflated, **blown up, puffed up, swollen,** swelled, turgid, tumid, plethoric, incrassate; **puffy,** pursy; flatulent, gassy, windy, ventose; tumefacient; dropsical, edematous; enchymatous; fat; puffed out, bouffant, bouffed up *and* bouffy <both nonformal>; **bulging, swelling,** distended, potbellied, bellying, pouching; bagging, baggy
2 **pompous, stuffy** <nonformal>, **self-important,** impressed with oneself, pontific, pontifical; **inflated, swollen,** tumid, turgid, flatulent, gassy <nonformal>, stilted; grandiloquent, **bombastic**; solemn, formal

blob NOUNS **ball;** globule, globelet, orblet; glomerulus; **pellet;** boll; knob, knot; **gob,** glob <nonformal>, gobbet; **lump,** clump, bunch

bloc NOUNS **alliance, coalition, league;** axis; **partnership; federation, confederation,** confederacy; grouping, assemblage; **combination,** combine; *Bund, Verein* <both Ger>

block NOUNS 1 **obstacle, obstruction,** obstructer; **hang-up** <nonformal>; blockade, cordon, curtain; **difficulty,** hurdle, hazard; **deterrent,** determent; **drawback,** objection; **stumbling block,** stumbling stone, stone in one's path; fly in the ointment, one small difficulty, **hitch, catch,** joker <nonformal>, a "but,"a "however"
VERBS 2 **delay, retard, detain,** make late, slacken, lag, drag, drag one's feet *and* stonewall <both nonformal>, slow down, **hold up** <nonformal>, hold *or* keep back, check, **stay, stop,** arrest, impede, hinder, obstruct, throw a monkey wrench in the works <nonformal>, confine; tie up with red tape
3 **obstruct, get** *or* **stand in the way; dog,** block the way, put up a roadblock, blockade, block up, occlude; **jam,** crowd, pack; **bar,** barricade, bolt, lock; **debar,** shut out; shut off, **close,** close off *or* up, close tight, shut tight; constrict, squeeze, squeeze shut, **strangle,** strangulate, **stifle,** suffocate, **choke,** choke off, chock; stop up

blockade NOUNS 1 **siege, besiegement, beleaguerment;** encompassment, investment, encirclement, envelopment; blockading; cutting of supply lines; vertical envelopment; pincer movement
2 block, block the way, put up a roadblock, block up, occlude; shut off, **close,** close off *or* up, close tight, shut tight; constrict, squeeze, squeeze shut, **strangle,** strangulate, **stifle,** suffocate, **choke,** choke off

blockage NOUNS 1 stoppage, occlusion, thrombosis, thromboembolism; embolism, embolus; infarct, infarction; **stroke,** ictus, apoplexy; constipation, obstipation, costiveness
2 **obstruction,** blocking, blockage, clogging, occlusion; **bottleneck,** traffic jam, gridlock; constriction, squeeze, stricture, cramp, stranglehold; **closure,** closing up *or* off; obstructionism, bloody-mindedness <Brit>, negativism, foot-dragging <nonformal>; nuisance value

blockbuster NOUNS **surprise,** surprisal; surpriser, startler, shocker, **blow,** staggerer <nonformal>, **eye-opener,** revelation; **bolt out of** *or* **from the blue,** thunderbolt, thunderclap; **bombshell,** bomb; earthshaker; sudden turn *or* development, *peripeteia* <Gk>, switch; surprise ending, kicker *or* joker *or* catch <all nonformal>; surprise package; surprise party

bloodbath NOUNS **carnage, massacre, decimation,** saturnalia of blood; **mass murder, mass destruction,** mass extermination, wholesale murder, pogrom, race-murder, genocide, race extermination, **the Holocaust,** the final solution, ethnic cleansing

bloodcurdling ADJS **terrifying,** terrorful, terror-striking, terror-inspiring, terror-bringing, terror-giving, terror-breeding, terror-breathing, terror-bearing, terror-fraught; **hair-raising** <nonformal>; petrifying, paralyzing, stunning, stupefying; **terrorizing, terror, terroristic;** *schrecklich* <Ger>

bloodsucker NOUNS 1 parasite; **leech;**

tick, wood tick, deer tick; **mosquito,** skeeter <nonformal>, culex; bedbug, housebug <Brit>
2 **extortionist,** extortioner, **blackmailer,** racketeer, shakedown artist <nonformal>, leech, **vampire; predator,** raptor, bird of prey, beast of prey; **vulture,** shark; profiteer

bloodthirsty ADJS **murderous,** slaughterous; cutthroat; redhanded; **homicidal,** man-killing, death-dealing; biocidal, genocidal; suicidal, self-destructive; soul-destroying; cruel; bloody-minded; **bloody, gory,** sanguineous, sanguinary; Draconian, Tartarean

blood vessel NOUNS **artery,** aorta, pulmonary artery, carotid; **vein,** jugular vein, vena cava, pulmonary vein; portal vein, varicose vein; venation; **capillary;** arteriole, veinlet, veinule, venule

bloody ADJS 1 **sanguine,** sanguineous, **blood-red,** blood-colored, bloody-red, gory, red as blood; **bloodstained,** blood-spattered, sanguinary, ensanguined; **bleeding,** hemorrhaging; ecchymosed
2 **savage, fierce, ferocious, vicious, murderous, cruel, atrocious, mindless, brutal,** brutish, **bestial,** mindless, insensate, monstrous, mutant, inhuman, pitiless, ruthless, merciless, sanguinary, kill-crazy <nonformal>

bloom NOUNS 1 **flower, posy, blossom,** blow <old>; floweret, floret, floscule; **wildflower**
2 **glow,** incandescence, fieriness; **flush, blush,** redness, rubicundity, rosiness
VERBS 3 **enjoy good health,** have a clean bill of health, be in the pink; be in the best of health; **feel good,** feel fine, feel fit, feel like a million dollars *or* like a million <nonformal>, never feel better; feel one's oats, be full of pep; burst with health, glow, flourish
4 **flower,** be in flower, **blossom,** be in bloom, blow, effloresce, floreate, burst into bloom

blooper NOUNS

<nonformal> **goof, boo-boo,** muff, flub, foozle, bloomer, bloop, boot, bobble, boner, bonehead play *or* trick, dumb trick, boob stunt, fool mistake; howler, clanger <Brit>, screamer; fuck-up, screw-up, foul-up, snafu, muck-up, balls-up <Brit>, louse-up; pratfall, whoops

blossom NOUNS 1 **flowering,** florescence, efflorescence, flowerage, **blossoming, blooming;** inflorescence; **bloom,** blowing, blow; unfolding, unfoldment; anthesis, full bloom
VERBS 2 **grow, develop,** wax, **increase**; gather, brew; **grow up,** mature, maturate, spring up, ripen, come of age, **shoot up,** sprout up, upshoot, upspring, upsprout, upspear, overtop, tower; grow like a weed <nonformal>; burgeon, **sprout**, reproduce, procreate, grow out of, germinate, pullulate; vegetate; **flourish, thrive;** mushroom, balloon

blot NOUNS 1 **stain, taint, tarnish;** mark, brand, **stigma;** maculation, macule, macula; **spot,** blur, **blotch,** patch, speck, speckle, fleck, flick, flyspeck; daub, dab; **smirch, smudge,** smutch *or* smouch, smut, **smear;** splotch, splash, splatter, spatter; bloodstain; eyesore
VERBS 2 **absorb,** adsorb, chemisorb *or* chemosorb, **assimilate,** engross, digest, **drink,** imbibe, take up *or* in, drink up *or* in, slurp up, swill up; **blot up, soak up,** sponge; osmose; infiltrate, filter in; **soak in, seep in,** percolate in

blotchy ADJS **spotted, spotty,** maculate, maculated, macular, blotched, splotched, splotchy; **speckled,** speckly, bespeckled; freckled, freckly, freckle-faced; spattered, splattered, splashed

blow NOUNS 1 **slap,** smack, whack, whomp, **cuff, box,** buffet, belt, sock; **rap on the knuckles,** box on the ear, slap in the face; slap on the wrist, token punishment
2 **misfortune, mishap,** ill hap, **misadventure, mischance,** *contretemps* <Fr>, grief; **disaster, calamity, catastrophe,** meltdown, cataclysm, **tragedy; shock,** hard *or* nasty *or* staggering blow
VERBS 3 **blare,** blast; shriek; **toot,** tootle, sound, peal, wind, blat; pipe, trumpet, bugle, clarion
4 **squander, lavish,** slather, play ducks and drakes with; **dissipate,** scatter <old>, sow broadcast, scatter to the winds; **run through,** go through; **throw away,** throw one's money away, throw money around, **spend money like water,** hang the expense, let slip *or* flow through one's fingers, spend as if money grew on trees, spend money as if it were going out of style, throw money around, spend like a drunken sailor; gamble away; burn the candle at both ends;

seize the day, live for the day, let tomorrow take care of itself

blow one's mind VERBS

1 <nonformal> **go crazy, go bats,** go cuckoo, go bughouse, go nuts, go nutso, go out of one's gourd *or* skull *or* tree, go off one's nut *or* rocker, go off the track *or* trolley, go off the deep end, blow one's top *or* stack, pop one's cork, flip one's lid *or* wig, wig out, go ape *or* apeshit, schiz out, go bananas, go crackers *and* go bonkers <both Brit>, go bonzo, freak out, flip out, go hog wild, go round the bend <Brit>, lose one's marbles

2 **go on a trip**, freak out <both nonformal>; **hallucinate;** expand one's consciousness

blowout NOUNS 1 **explosion, discharge,** blowup, detonation, fulmination, **blast, burst, report**; flat tire
2 **eruption,** eructation, extravasation, **outburst;** outpour, jet, spout, spurt

blow the whistle VERBS 1 **have no patience with,** be out of all patience; **lose patience,** run out of patience, call a halt, have had it <nonformal>

2 <nonformal> tell on, blab, snitch, squeal, peach <old>, sell out, sing, rat, stool, fink, nark, finger, put the finger on, shop <Brit>, dime, drop a dime, spill one's guts, spill the beans, squawk, weasel

blowup NOUNS 1 **outburst,** outburst of anger, burst, **explosion,** eruption, blowup *and* **flare-up** <both nonformal>, access, blaze of temper; **storm, scene,** high words
2 **explosion, discharge, blowout,** detonation, fulmination, **blast, burst, report;** backfire
3 **enlargement; print,** photoprint, positive

blowzy ADJS **slovenly, slipshod, careless, loose, slack,** nonformal, negligent; **untidy, unsightly,** unneat, slobby *and* scuzzy <both nonformal>, **unkempt; messy** <nonformal>, mussy <nonformal>, **sloppy** <nonformal>, scraggly, poky, seedy <nonformal>, **shabby,** shoddy, schlocky <nonformal>, lumpen, chintzy, grubby <nonformal>, **frowzy,** tacky <nonformal>; **slatternly, sluttish, frumpish,** frumpy, draggletailed, drabbletailed, draggled, bedraggled

blue ADJS 1 **melancholy,** melancholic, splenetic <old>, funky <nonformal>; atrabilious, atrabiliar; **pensive, wistful,** tristful; **nostalgic,** homesick
2 **obscene, lewd, adult, bawdy,** ithyphallic, **ribald, pornographic, salacious,** sultry <nonformal>, lurid, **dirty, smutty,** raunchy <nonformal>, smoking-room, impure, unchaste, unclean, **foul, filthy, nasty,** vile, fulsome, offensive, unprintable, unrepeatable, not fit for mixed company; scurrilous, scurrile, Fescennine; **foulmouthed,** foul-tongued, foul-spoken; Rabelaisian

blue blood NOUNS **aristocrat, patrician,** Brahmin, thoroughbred, member of the upper class, socialite, swell *and* upper-cruster <both nonformal>, grandee, grand dame, dowager, magnifico, lord of creation; **gentleman, lady,** person of breeding

blue-collar worker NOUNS **worker, toiler,** moiler; member of the working class, proletarian, prole <Brit nonformal>, blue-collar *or* lunch-bucket worker, laboring man, stiff *and* working stiff <both nonformal>; **workman, workingman; workwoman, workingwoman,** workfolk, workpeople; working girl, workgirl; **factory worker,** industrial worker; autoworker, steelworker; construction worker; **laborer,** common laborer, **unskilled laborer,** navvy <Brit>, day laborer, roust-about; casual, casual laborer; **labor force, work force,** shop floor <Brit>; labor market

blueprint NOUNS **plan, scheme, design,** method, **program,** device, contrivance, game, envisagement, conception, enterprise, **idea, notion;** organization, rationalization, systematization, schematization; charting, mapping, graphing; **planning,** calculation, figuring; **master plan,** the picture *and* the big picture <both nonformal>; approach, attack, plan of attack; way, procedure; **arrangement,** prearrangement, system, disposition, layout, setup, lineup; **schedule,** timetable, time-scheme, time frame; deadline; plan of work; **schema,** schematism, scheme of arrangement; **guideline, guidelines,** program of action; methodology; working plan, ground plan, tactical plan, strategic plan; tactics, **strategy,** game plan <nonformal>; contingency plan

blue ribbon NOUNS 1 **award, reward, prize;** first prize, second prize, etc; sweepstakes; jackpot; Oscar, Academy Award; **decoration,** decoration of honor, order, ornament; ribbon

blues NOUNS

1 <nonformal> blue devils, mulligrubs, mumps, **dumps, doldrums,** dismals, dolefuls, blahs, mopes, sullens, megrims, sulks

2 music; the blues, talking blues, country blues, city blues

bluff NOUNS 1 **precipice, cliff, sheer** *or* yawning cliff *or* precipice *or* drop, steep, wall, face, scar; crag, craig <Scots>; scarp, **escarpment; palisade,** palisades
2 **sham, fakery,** faking, falsity, feigning, pretending; feint, pretext, **pretense,** hollow pretense, **pretension, false pretense** *or* **pretension;** humbug, humbuggery; bluffing, four-flushing <nonformal>; speciousness, meretriciousness; cheating, fraud; imposture; deception, delusion; acting, playacting; representation, **simulation,** simulacrum; dissembling, **dissemblance, dissimulation;** seeming, semblance, appearance, face, ostentation, **show, false show,** outward show, false air; window dressing, front, **false front, facade,** gloss, varnish; color, coloring, false color; masquerade, disguise; posture, pose, posing, attitudinizing
3 **bluster,** blustering, hectoring, bullying, **swagger,** swashbucklery, side; **bravado,** rant, rodomontade, fanfaronade; sputter, splutter; fuss, bustle, fluster, flurry; bluster and bluff; intimidation; **boastfulness**
VERBS 4 swear falsely; **bluster,** hector; **swagger,** swashbuckle; bully; bounce, vapor, roister, rollick, gasconade, kick up a dust <nonformal>; sputter, splutter; rant, rage, rave, rave on, storm; slang <Brit>; bluster and bluff, put up a bluff <nonformal>

out-herod Herod
SHAKESPEARE

blunder NOUNS 1 **bungle, botch,** flub, boner *and* bonehead play <both nonformal>, boggle, bobble *and* boo-boo *and* screw-up *and* fuck-up <all nonformal>, foozle <nonformal>, bevue; **fumble, muff,** fluff, miscue <nonformal>; **faux pas,** gaffe, solecism; stupidity, indiscretion; **slip,** trip, stumble; *gaucherie, étourderie, balourdise* <all Fr>; **hash** *and* **mess** <both nonformal>; bad job, sad work, clumsy performance; off day; **error, mistake**
VERBS 2 **make a blunder, make a faux pas,** blot one's copy book, make a colossal blunder, make a false *or* wrong step, make a misstep; **misspeak,** misspeak oneself, trip over one's tongue; embarrass oneself, have egg on one's face <nonformal>; blunder into; **botch, bungle**

blundering ADJS **bungling,** blunderheaded, bumbling, fumbling, mistake-prone, accident-prone; **clumsy, awkward, uncoordinated,** maladroit, unhandy, left-hand, left-handed, heavy-handed, ham-handed <nonformal>, ham-fisted *and* cack-handed <both Brit nonformal>, clumsy-fisted, butterfingered <nonformal>, **all thumbs,** fingers all thumbs, with a handful of thumbs; stiff; **ungainly,** uncouth, **ungraceful,** graceless, inelegant, *gauche* <Fr>; **gawky,** gawkish; **lubberly, loutish, oafish,** boorish, clownish, lumpish, slobbish <nonformal>; **sloppy, careless; ponderous, cumbersome,** lumbering, hulking, hulky; **unwieldy**

blunt ADJS 1 **dull,** obtuse, obtundent; bluntish, dullish; **unsharp,** unsharpened; **unedged,** edgeless; rounded, faired, smoothed, streamlined; **unpointed,** pointless; blunted, dulled; blunt-edged, dull-edged; blunt-pointed, dull-pointed, blunt-ended; bluff, abrupt
2 straight <both nonformal>, **forthright,** downright, straight-out <nonformal>; plain, broad, round; **unreserved,** unrestrained, unconstrained, unchecked; unguarded, uncalculating; free; **outspoken, plain-spoken,** free-spoken, free-speaking, free-tongued; explicit, unequivocal; bluff, brusque; heart-to-heart

blur NOUNS 1 **indistinctness, unclearness,** unplainness, **faintness,** paleness, feebleness, weakness, **dimness,** bedimming, bleariness, darkness, shadowiness, **vagueness,** vague appearance, indefiniteness, obscurity, uncertainty, indistinguishability; **blurriness,** soft

focus, defocus, **fuzziness, haziness,** mistiness, filminess, fogginess
VERBS 2 **dim, pale,** soften, film, mist, fog; defocus, lose resolution *or* sharpness *or* distinctness, go soft at the edges; **confound, confuse,** mix, mix up, muddle, tumble, jumble, jumble together, blur distinctions, overlook distinctions

blurred ADJS **formless, shapeless,** featureless, characterless, nondescript, inchoate, lumpy, lumpish, blobby *and* baggy <both nonformal>, inform; amorphous, **chaotic, orderless,** disorderly, unordered, unorganized, confused, anarchic; kaleidoscopic; **indeterminate, indefinite,** undefined, indecisive, vague, misty, hazy, fuzzy, blurred *or* blurry, unclear, obscure; obfuscatory

blush VERBS **flush,** mantle, **color,** change color, color up, redden, crimson, turn red, have a red face, get red in the face, blush up to the eyes; stammer; squirm with self-consciousness *or* embarrassment

bluster NOUNS 1 blustering, hectoring, bullying, **swagger,** swashbucklery, side; **bravado,** rant, rodomontade, fanfaronade; sputter, splutter; fuss, bustle, fluster, flurry; bluff, bluster and bluff; intimidation; **boastfulness**
VERBS 2 swagger, **show** *or* **put up a bold front,** throw out one's chest, strut, crow, look big, stand with arms akimbo; **boast, brag,** make a boast of, vaunt, flourish, gasconade, vapor, toot one's own horn, sing one's own praises, exaggerate one's own merits

board NOUNS 1 food and drink, sustenance, kitchen stuff, victualage, **comestibles, edibles,** eatables, viands; **fare,** cheer, creature comfort; provision, provender; table, spread <nonformal>
VERBS 2 **feed, dine,** wine and dine, mess; sustain; provision; mess with, break bread with; furnish accommodations; house, lodge
3 **go aboard,** go on board; go on shipboard, take ship

boarder NOUNS board-and-roomer, **transient,** transient guest *or* boarder; **lodger, roomer,** paying guest

boardinghouse NOUNS **lodging house,** rooming house; *pension* <Fr>, *pensione* <Ital>

boardwalk NOUNS walkway, catwalk, skybridge *or* skywalk *or* flying bridge *or* walkway; **sidewalk, walk,** fastwalk, *trottoir* <Fr>, foot pavement <Brit>

boastful ADJS **boasting, braggart, bragging,** thrasonical, thrasonic, bigmouthed <nonformal>, vaunting, vaporing, gasconading, Gascon, fanfaronading, fanfaron; vain, conceited; **vainglorious**

boat NOUNS ark, canoe, gondola, kayak, lifeboat, motorboat, shell, skiff, whaleboat, workboat; vessel, craft, bottom, bark, argosy, hull, hulk, keel, watercraft; tub *and* bucket *and* rustbucket *and* hooker <all nonformal>, packet

boating NOUNS water travel, travel by water, marine *or* ocean *or* sea travel, **navigation,** navigating, passage-making, voyaging, **cruising,** coasting, gunkholing <nonformal>; **yachting,** motorboating, canoeing, rowing, sculling

bob VERBS **shorten, cut; cut short,** cut off short; **dock,** shear, shave, trim, clip, snub, nip; mow, reap, **crop; prune,** poll, pollard; stunt, check the growth of; telescope; foreshorten

bode VERBS **forebode,** portend, croak; **threaten, menace, lower,** look black, spell trouble; **warn, forewarn,** raise a warning flag, give pause; have a premonition *or* presentiment, apprehend, preapprehend, fear for

body NOUNS 1 **person, human, human being, man, woman, child,** member of the human race *or* family, Adamite, daughter of Eve; ethnic; **mortal,** life, **soul,** living soul; **being,** creature, clay, ordinary clay; **individual;** somebody, one, someone
2 **corpse,** dead body, dead man *or* woman, dead person, **cadaver, carcass;** *corpus delicti* <L>; **stiff** <nonformal>; **the dead,** the defunct, **the deceased,** the departed, the loved one; **decedent,** late lamented; **remains,** mortal *or* organic remains, bones, skeleton, dry bones, relics, reliquiae; dust, ashes, earth, clay, tenement of clay
3 **substantiality,** substantialness; materiality; **substance,** mass; **solidity,** density, concreteness, **tangibility,** palpability, ponderability; **sturdiness, stability,** soundness, firmness, steadiness, stoutness, toughness, **strength,** durability

bodybuilding NOUNS **exercise,** motion, movement, maneuver; **program,** routine, drill, work-out; **exercise systems;**

warm-up, stretching, warm-down; **calisthenics,** free exercise, setting-up exercise *or* set-ups, physical jerks <Brit>, daily dozen <nonformal>, constitutional; weightlifting, weight training, pumping iron <nonformal>, bench press, arm raise, curl, wrist curl

bodyguard NOUNS safeguard; **convoy, escort;** guards, praetorian guard; guardsman; yeoman *or* yeoman of the guard *or* beefeater, gentleman-at-arms, Life Guardsman <all England>; Secret Service agent

body language NOUNS **gesture, gesticulation; motion,** movement; carriage, bearing, posture, poise, pose, stance, way of holding oneself

bog NOUNS **marsh,** marshland, **swamp,** swampland, fen, fenland, **morass,** mere *or* marish <both old>, *marais* <Fr>, *maremma* <Ital>, **bog, mire, quagmire,** sump <nonformal>, wash, baygall; glade, everglade; slough, swale, wallow, hog wallow, buffalo wallow, sough <Brit>; bottom, **bottoms,** bottomland, slob land, holm <Brit>, water meadow, meadow; **moor,** moorland, moss <Scots>, peat bog; salt marsh; quicksand; taiga; mud flat

bogeyman NOUNS **frightener, scarer, hair-raiser;** scarebabe, **bogey, bugaboo,** bugbear; hobgoblin; **scarecrow; horror, terror,** holy terror; **ogre,** ogress, **monster,** vampire, werewolf, ghoul, bête noire, fee-faw-fum; incubus, succubus, nightmare; witch, goblins; **ghost,** specter, phantom, revenant; Frankenstein, Dracula, Wolf-man; mythical monsters

boggle the mind VERBS 1 **astonish, amaze, astound, surprise,** startle, stagger, **bewilder, perplex**, flabbergast <nonformal>, confound, overwhelm, **boggle; awe,** strike with wonder *or* awe; **dumbfound** *or* dumbfounder, strike dumb, strike dead; strike all of a heap *and* throw on one's beam ends *and* knock one's socks off *and* bowl down *or* over <all nonformal>, dazzle, bedazzle, daze, bedaze; **stun, stupefy,** petrify, paralyze

2 **be unbelievable,** be incredible, be hard to swallow, defy belief, pass belief, be hard to believe, strain one's credulity, **stagger belief;** shake one's faith, undermine one's faith; stagger, fill with doubt

bogus ADJS **false, untrue, truthless, not true,** void *or* devoid of truth, contrary to fact, in error, **fallacious, erroneous**; unfounded; disinformative; **vicarious,** ersatz, mock, phony *and* fake *and* bogus <all nonformal>, counterfeit, imitation

Bohemian NOUNS 1 **nonconformist,** unconformist, **original,** eccentric, gonzo <nonformal>, deviant, deviationist, maverick <nonformal>, dropout, beatnik, hippie, hipster, freak <nonformal>, flower child, street people, yippie; **misfit,** square peg in a round hole, ugly duckling, fish out of water

ADJS 2 **unconventional, unorthodox, eccentric,** gonzo <nonformal>, heterodox, heretical; offbeat <nonformal>, way out *and* far out *and* kinky *and* out in left field <all nonformal>, fringy, breakaway, **out-of-the-way; original,** maverick, beat, hippie, counterculture; **nonformal,** free and easy <nonformal>

at ease and lighthearted
WHITMAN

boil NOUNS 1 furuncle, furunculus; carbuncle; canker; canker sore; cold sore, fever blister; sty; abscess, gathering, aposteme <old>; gumboil, parulis; whitlow, felon, paronychia; bubo; chancre; soft chancre, chancroid

2 **agitation, perturbation,** fidgets *and* jitters *and* ants in the pants <all nonformal>, antsiness *and* jitteriness <both nonformal>, jumpiness, nervousness, yips <nonformal>, nerviness <Brit>, nervosity, twitter, upset; **disquiet,** disquietude, inquietude, discomposure; **stir, churn, ferment,** fermentation, foment; seethe, seething, ebullition, boiling; embroilment, roil, turbidity, fume, **disturbance, commotion,** moil, **turmoil, turbulence**, **swirl, tumult,** tumultuation, hubbub, shemozzle <Brit nonformal>, rout, fuss, row, to-do, bluster, fluster, flurry, flutteration, hoo-ha *and* flap <both nonformal>, bustle, brouhaha, bobbery, hurly-burly; maelstrom; **disorder**

3 VERBS **seethe, fume,** foam, simmer, stew, ferment, stir, churn

boisterous ADJS 1 **noisy,** noiseful, rackety, clattery, clangorous, clanging, **clamorous,** clamoursome <Brit nonformal>, clamant, blatant, blaring, brassy, brazen, blatting; uproarious, **tumultuous,** turbu-

lent, blustering, brawling, rip-roaring, mafficking <Brit>, strepitous, strepitant, obstreperous; vociferous
2 **rampageous, rambunctious** <nonformal>, rumbustious, roisterous, wild, rollicking, **rowdy,** rough, hoody <nonformal>, harum-scarum <nonformal>; knockabout, rough-and-tumble, knockdown-and-drag-out <nonformal>

bold ADJS 1 **courageous, plucky, brave, valiant, valorous, gallant, intrepid,** doughty, **hardy,** stalwart, stout, stouthearted, ironhearted, lionhearted, greathearted, bold-spirited, bold as a lion; **heroic, manly,** manful, virile, macho; **audacious;** forward, bold, **presumptuous; daring,** daredevil, fire-eating, death-defying; adventurous
2 **immodest,** unmodest; exhibitionistic; **shameless,** dead *or* lost to shame, unashamed, unembarrassed, unabashed, unblushing, **brazen,** brazenfaced, brassy, bold as brass <nonformal>; **forward,** bold, pert, procacious <old>, bumptious; **flagrant,** notorious, scandalous

bolt NOUNS 1 **lock,** bar, padlock, catch, safety catch; barrier
2 **lightning, flash** *or* **stroke of lightning,** fulguration, fulmination, lightning strike, **bolt of lightning,** bolt from the blue, **thunderbolt,** thunderstroke, thunderball, fireball, firebolt, levin bolt *or* brand
VERBS 3 **gobble, gulp,** wolf, gobble *or* gulp *or* bolt *or* wolf down
4 **flee, fly, take flight,** take to flight, take wing, fugitate, **run, cut and run** <nonformal>, make a precipitate departure, **run off** *or* **away,** run away from, bug out <nonformal>, **decamp,** pull up stakes, **take to one's heels,** make off, **depart**, do the disappearing act, make a quick exit, **beat a retreat** *or* **a hasty retreat, turn tail,** show the heels, show a clean *or* light pair of heels; **run for it, run for one's life;** make a run for it; **take French leave,** go AWOL, slip the cable; **desert; abscond,** levant <Brit>, **elope,** run away with; skip *or* jump bail

show it a fair pair of heels and run for it
SHAKESPEARE

6 **hook,** hitch; lock, latch; **pin,** skewer, peg, nail, nail up, tack, staple, toggle, screw, rivet; batten, batten down; cleat

bomb NOUNS 1 bombshell; antipersonnel bomb, atomic bomb *or* atom bomb *or* A-bomb, atomic warhead, blockbuster, depth charge *or* depth bomb *or* ash can <nonformal>, fire bomb *or* incendiary bomb *or* incendiary, grenade, hand grenade, hydrogen bomb *or* H-bomb, letter bomb, Molotov cocktail, napalm bomb, neutron bomb, nuclear warhead, pipe bomb, plastic *or* plastique bomb, plutonium bomb, smart bomb, stench *or* stink bomb, time bomb; clean bomb, dirty bomb; **mine**
VERBS 2 drop a bomb, lay an egg <nonformal>; dive-bomb, glide-bomb, skip-bomb, pattern-bomb, etc; atom-bomb, hydrogen-bomb; **blow up,** blast, spring, explode, blow to pieces *or* bits *or* smithereens *or* kingdom come, bombard, blitz; mine; self-destruct

3 <nonformal> **lose out,** get left, **not make it,** not hack it, not get to first base, drop the ball, go for a Burton *and* come a cropper <both Brit>, **flop,** flummox, fall flat on one's ass, lay an egg, go over like a lead balloon, draw a blank, drop a bomb; fold, fold up; take it on the chin, take the count; crap out; take the collar, strike out, fan, whiff

bombastic ADJS 1 **stiff, stilted, formal,** Latinate, *guindé* <Fr>, **labored,** ponderous, elephantine, lumbering, cumbrous, leaden, heavy, unwieldy, sesquipedalian, inkhorn, pompous; **forced,** awkward, cramped, halting; crabbed
2 fustian, mouthy, **inflated, swollen,** swelling, turgid, turgescent, tumid, tumescent, flatulent, windy *and* gassy <both nonformal>; overadorned, fulsome

bomber NOUNS **destroyer, ruiner, wrecker, bane,** wiper-out, demolisher; **vandal,** hun; exterminator, annihilator; **iconoclast,** idoloclast, idol breaker; biblioclast; nihilist; terrorist, syndicalist; **bomber,** bombardier, dynamiter, dynamitard; burner, arsonist

bombshell NOUNS **eye-opener,** revelation; **bolt out of** *or* **from the blue,** thunderbolt, thunderclap; bomb; blockbuster, earthshaker; sudden turn *or* development, *peripeteia* <Gk>, switch; surprise ending, kicker *or* joker *or* catch <all nonformal>; surprise package; surprise party

bona fide ADJS **genuine, authentic,**

veridic, veridical, **real, natural, realistic, naturalistic,** true to reality, **true to nature, lifelike,** true to life, verisimilar, veristic; **literal,** following the letter, letter-perfect, *au pied de la lettre* <Fr>, true to the letter; verbatim, verbal, word-perfect, **word-for-word;** true to the spirit; **legitimate,** rightful, lawful; card-carrying <nonformal>, **good,** sure-enough <nonformal>, **sincere, honest; unadulterated**; **pure,** simon-pure; **sterling,** twenty-four carat, all wool and a yard wide <nonformal>

bond NOUNS 1 **security, surety,** indemnity, **guaranty, guarantee, warranty, insurance,** warrant, assurance; **obligation**, full faith and credit; **bond,** tie; stocks and bonds
2 **relation, relationship, connection;** relatedness, connectedness, **association**, **affiliation,** filiation, union, alliance, **tie,** tie-in <nonformal>, link, linkage, linking, linkup, liaison
VERBS 3 **put together, join,** conjoin, **unite,** unify, **connect,** associate, league, band, merge, **assemble,** accumulate; **join up,** become a part of, associate oneself, enter into, come aboard <nonformal>; **couple,** pair, accouple, copulate, conjugate, marry, wed, tie the knot <nonformal>, **link,** link up, build bridges, yoke, knot, splice, tie, chain, bracket; glue, tape, cement, solder, weld

bone ADJS **skeleton, skeletal;** osteal; **bony,** osseous, ossiferous; ossicular; ossified; **spinal,** myelic; cartilage, cartilaginous

bonehead NOUNS

<nonformal> **blockhead, airhead,** bubblehead, fluffhead, featherhead, woodenhead, dolthead, dumbhead, dummy, dum-dum, dumbo, dumb cluck, dodo head, doodoohead, dumbbell, dumb bunny, stupidhead, dullhead, bufflehead, jughead, thickhead, thickskull, numskull, putz, lunkhead, chucklehead, knucklehead, chowderhead, headbanger *and* jolterhead <both Brit>, muttonhead, beefhead, meathead, noodlehead, thimblewit, pinhead, pinbrain, peabrain, cabbagehead, pumpkin head, fathead, blubberhead, muddlehead, puzzlehead, addlebrain, addlehead, addlepate, tottyhead <old>, puddinghead, stupe, mushhead, blunderhead, dunderhead, dunderpate, clodpate, clodhead, clodpoll, jobbernowl *and* gaby *and* gowk <all Brit>

bonfire NOUNS **cheerful fire,** crackling fire; **roaring fire,** blazing fire

bright-flaming, heatfull fire
DU BARTAS

bonnet NOUNS **hat,** bonnet, cap, hood, coif

bonus NOUNS 1 **extra,** something extra, extra dash, extra added attraction, something into the bargain, something for good measure, baker's dozen; **padding,** stuffing, filling; trimming, **frill,** flourish, filigree, decoration, ornament; bells
2 **premium, fringe benefit** *or* **benefits,** bounty, perquisite, perquisites, perks <nonformal>, gravy <nonformal>, lagniappe, solatium; **tip**; overtime pay

bon voyage! PHRS **farewell!, pleasant journey!, have a nice trip!,** *tsetchem leshalom!* <Heb>, *glückliche Reise!* <Ger>, happy landing!; Godspeed!, peace be with you!, *pax vobiscum!* <L>; all good go with you!, God bless you!

boo VERBS **hiss, hoot,** catcall, give the raspberry *or* Bronx cheer <nonformal>, give the bird <nonformal>, whistle at

boob NOUNS

<nonformal> **chump,** booby, sap, prize sap, klutz, basket case, dingbat, dingdong, ding-a-ling, **ninny,** ninnyhammer, **nincompoop,** looby, noddy, saphead, mutt, jerk, jerk-off, asshole, goof, schlemiel, sawney <Brit>, galoot, gonzo, dumbo, dweeb, dropshop, dipshit, nerd, twerp, yo-yo

boo-boo NOUNS **bungle, blunder, botch,** flub, **error, mistake**

booby trap NOUNS **ambush,** ambushment, **ambuscade,** *guet-apens* <Fr>; surveillance, shadowing; lurking hole *or* place; blind, stalking-horse; **trap, gin; pitfall,** trapfall, deadfall; flytrap, mousetrap, mole trap, rattrap, bear trap; deathtrap, firetrap; Venus's flytrap, Dionaea; spring gun, set gun; baited trap; **mine; decoy;** springe, snare, tripwire

book NOUNS 1 **volume, tome;** publication, writing, **work, opus, production; title;** opusculum, opuscule; **trade book; textbook,** schoolbook; **reference book,**

playbook; songbook; notebook; storybook, **novel; best seller;** coffee-table book; nonbook; **children's book,** juvenile book, juvenile; picture book; coloring book, sketchbook; prayer book, psalter, psalmbook; **classic,** the book, the bible, magnum opus, great work, standard work, definitive work
VERBS 2 **charge, press charges, prefer** *or* **bring charges,** lay charges; complain, **lodge a complaint,** lodge a plaint; **impeach, arraign, indict,** bring in *or* hand up an indictment
3 **schedule, line up** <nonformal>, **slate,** book in, bill, program, calendar, docket, budget, put on the agenda; arrange for, reserve, prearrange

bookie NOUNS **bookmaker,** turf accountant; **tout,** turf consultant

booking NOUNS **engagement,** playing engagement, booking; **run; stand,** one-night stand *or* one-nighter; **circuit,** vaudeville circuit, borscht circuit; **tour, bus-and-truck, production tour;** date

bookish ADJS 1 **studious,** devoted to studies, **scholarly,** scholastic, academic, professorial, tweedy, donnish <Brit>; owlish; rabbinic, mandarin; pedantic, dryasdust; diligent
2 **book-learned,** book-read, **literary,** book-taught, book-fed, book-wise, book-smart, booky, book-minded; book-loving, bibliophilic, bibliophagic; **pedantic,** inkhorn; **bluestocking**

bookkeeper NOUNS **accountant; clerk,** actuary <old>, registrar, recorder, journalizer; calculator, reckoner; cost accountant, cost keeper; **auditor,** bank examiner; bank accountant; accountant general; comptroller *or* controller

booklet NOUNS **pamphlet, brochure, chapbook, leaflet, folder, tract;** circular; comic book

booklover NOUNS philobiblist, bibliophile, bibliolater, book collector, bibliomane, bibliomaniac, bibliotaph; **bookworm,** bibliophage; book-stealer, biblioklept

books NOUNS **account book, ledger, journal,** daybook; **register,** registry, **record book;** inventory, catalog; **log,** logbook; **cashbook; bankbook,** passbook; balance sheet; cost sheet, cost card

bookshelf NOUNS **bookholder, bookrest,** book support, **book end; bookcase,** revolving bookcase *or* bookstand, bookrack, bookstand; stack, bookstack; book table, book tray, book truck

bookstore NOUNS **bookshop,** *librairie* <Fr>, bookseller's; **bookstall,** bookstand; **book club**

bookworm NOUNS 1 **booklover,** philobiblist, bibliophile, bibliolater, book collector, bibliomane, bibliomaniac, bibliotaph
2 **nerd** *and* grind *or* greasy grind <all nonformal>, swotter *or* mugger <both Brit nonformal>

boomerang NOUNS 1 **missile, projectile,** bolt; brickbat, stone, rock, alley apple *and* Irish confetti <both nonformal>; bola; throwing-stick, throw stick, waddy <Austral>
VERBS 2 **recoil, rebound,** resile; **bounce, bound, spring; spring** *or* **fly back,** bounce *or* bound back, snap back; repercuss, have repercussions; **kick,** kick back, kick like a mule <nonformal>, recalcitrate <old>; **backfire;** backlash, lash back; ricochet, carom, cannon *and* cannon off <both Brit>

booming ADJS 1 **thundering, thunderous,** thundery, fulminating, tonitruous, tonitruant, thunderlike; pealing, rumbling, rolling, roaring; cannonading, volleying
2 **thriving, flourishing, prospering;** vigorous, exuberant; in full swing, going strong <nonformal>; halcyon, palmy, balmy, rosy, piping, clear, fair; blooming, blossoming, flowering, fruiting; fat, sleek, in good case; fat, dumb, and happy <nonformal>

boon NOUNS **godsend, blessing;** manna, manna from heaven, loaves and fishes, gift from on high; **benefit,** benefaction, benevolence, **favor,** grace

boondocks NOUNS **hinterland, back country,** outback <Australia>, up-country, boonies *and* boondocks <both nonformal>; **the bush,** bush country, bushveld, **woods,** woodlands, **backwoods,** forests, timbers, the big sticks <nonformal>, brush; wilderness, wilds, uninhabited region, virgin land *or* territory; **wasteland**

boorish ADJS 1 **churlish,** carlish, **loutish,** redneck <nonformal>, lubberly, lumpish, cloddish, clownish, loobyish, yokelish; rowdy, **rowdyish, ruffianly,** roughneck <nonformal>, hooliganish, raffish, raised in a barn
2 **ill-bred, ungenteel,** ungentle, cad-

dish; **ungentlemanly,** ungentlemanlike; **unladylike,** unfeminine; **vulgar, unrefined**, **inconsiderate, unsolicitous, tactless, insensitive; gross,** offensive, crass, **coarse, crude,** loutish, nasty

boost NOUNS 1 **promotion, preferment, advancement, advance,** step-up *and* upping <both nonformal>, rise, elevation, upgrading, jump, step up, step up the ladder; **raise;** kicking *or* bumping upstairs <nonformal>; exaltation, aggrandizement; pay raise
2 **commendation,** good word, acknowledgment, recognition, appreciation; boost *and* buildup <both nonformal>
VERBS 3 **cheer, gladden, brighten,** put in good humor; **encourage, hearten,** pick up <nonformal>; **inspire,** inspirit, warm the spirits, **raise the spirits,** elevate one's mood, buoy up, give a lift <nonformal>, put one on top of the world *and* on cloud nine <both nonformal>; **exhilarate,** animate, invigorate, liven, enliven, vitalize; **rejoice,** rejoice the heart, do the heart good
4 **publicize, advertise, promote,** build up, cry up, sell, puff <nonformal>, **plug** <nonformal>, **ballyhoo** <nonformal>
5 **elevate, raise, rear,** escalate, up, boost *and* hike <both nonformal>; **erect, heighten, lift,** levitate, boost <nonformal>, **hoist,** heist <nonformal>, heft, heave; raise up, rear up, lift up, hold up, set up; stick up, cock up, perk up; buoy up, upbuoy; **upraise, uplift**

booster NOUNS 1 injection; broken dose; booster dose, recall dose, booster shot
2 **promoter,** plugger <nonformal>; **ballyhooer** *or* **ballyhoo man** <nonformal>; **barker,** spieler <nonformal>, skywriter; billposter; sign-painter; sandwich boy *or* man

booth NOUNS **stall, stand;** newsstand, kiosk, news kiosk

bootlegger NOUNS **black marketeer,** gray marketeer; bootlegger, moonshiner <nonformal>; pusher *and* dealer <both nonformal>

bootlicker NOUNS

<nonformal> **apple-polisher, ass-kisser, brown-nose,** brown-noser, brownie, ass-licker, ass-wiper, suck-ass; **backslapper,** backscratcher, clawback, back-patter; bootlick; **handshaker; yes-man, stooge**

booty NOUNS spoil, **spoils, loot, swag** <nonformal>, ill-gotten gains, **plunder,** prize, haul, take, pickings, stealings, stolen goods, hot goods *or* items <nonformal>; **boodle** *and* squeeze *and* **graft** <all nonformal>

booze NOUNS 1 **spirits, liquor,** intoxicating liquor, adult beverage, **hard liquor, whiskey,** firewater, spiritus frumenti, usquebaugh <Scots>, schnapps, ardent spirits, strong waters, **intoxicant,** toxicant, inebriant, **potable,** potation, **beverage, drink, strong drink,** strong liquor, alcoholic drink *or* beverage, **alcohol,** aqua vitae, water of life, brew, **grog,** social lubricant, nectar of the gods; **rum,** the Demon Rum, John Barleycorn; the bottle, the cup, the cup that cheers, little brown jug; punch bowl, the flowing bowl

the ruddy cup
SIR WALTER SCOTT

VERBS 2 <nonformal> swig, swill, moisten *or* wet one's whistle; **liquor, liquor up,** lush, souse, tank up, **hit the booze** *or* **bottle** *or* **sauce,** exercise *or* bend *or* crook *or* raise the elbow, dip the beak, splice the main brace; chug-a-lug, chug

border NOUNS 1 **frontier, borderland,** border ground, marchland, march, marches; outskirts, outpost; frontier post; iron curtain, bamboo curtain, Berlin wall; Pillars of Hercules; three-mile *or* twelve-mile limit
2 bed, **flower bed,** ornamental border
VERBS 2 **edge, bound, rim, skirt, hem, hem in, ringe,** befringe, lap, list, margin, marge, marginate, march, verge, line, side; **adjoin**; **frame,** enframe, set off; trim, bind; purl; purfle

bore NOUNS 1 crashing bore <nonformal>, frightful bore; **pest, nuisance;** dryasdust; proser, twaddler; buttonholer

2 <nonformal> **wet blanket; drag, drip, pill,** flat tire, deadass, deadfanny, dull tool; **headache,** pain in the neck *or* ass

VERBS 3 leave one cold, set *or* send to sleep; **bore stiff** *or* to tears *or* to death *or* to extinction <nonformal>, bore to distraction, bore out of one's life, bore out of all patience; buttonhole

4 **excavate, dig,** dig out, **scoop,** scoop out, **gouge,** gouge out, grub, shovel, spade, dike, delve, scrape, scratch, scrabble; dredge; **trench,** trough, furrow, groove; **tunnel, burrow;** drive <min>, sink, lower; **mine,** sap; quarry; drill

boring ADJS **wearying,** wearing, **tiring; wearisome,** weariful, fatiguing, **tiresome, irksome; boresome,** stupefyingly boring, stuporific, yawny <nonformal>; **monotonous, humdrum,** unrelieved, repetitive, drab, gray, ho-hum <nonformal>, samey <Brit nonformal>, usual, as usual; tedious

born ADJS given birth; **hatched;** cast, dropped, whelped, foaled, calved, etc; née; newborn; stillborn

cast naked upon the naked earth
PLINY THE ELDER

born-again ADJS **redeemed, saved,** converted, regenerated, regenerate, justified, reborn, renewed; circumcised, spiritually purified *or* cleansed, sanctified

borrow VERBS borrow the loan of, get on credit *or* trust, get on tick *and* get on the cuff <both nonformal>; get a loan, float *or* negotiate a loan, go into the money market, **raise money; touch** *and* **hit up** *and* hit one for *and* put the arm *or* bite *or* touch on <all nonformal>; run into debt; pawn

bosom NOUNS 1 **heart, soul, spirit,** *esprit* <Fr>, **breast,** inmost heart *or* soul, heart of hearts, secret *or* inner recesses of the heart, secret places, heart's core, heartstrings, cockles of the heart, bottom of the heart, being, innermost being, core of one's being

2 **breast, bust, chest,** crop, brisket; **breasts,** dugs, teats; **nipple,** papilla, pap, mammilla, *mamelon* and *téton* <both Fr>; mammillation, mamelonation; mammary gland, udder, bag

boss NOUNS 1 **superior, chief, head, superintendent; supervisor, foreman,** monitor, **head,** headman, overman, chief, gaffer *and* ganger <both Brit nonformal>, taskmaster; sirdar <India>, **overseer,** overlooker; **straw boss** <nonformal>; slave driver; **master, lord, lord and master,** overlord, seigneur, paramount, lord paramount, liege, liege lord, *padrone* <Ital>, *patron* and *chef* <both Fr>, patroon; sahib <India>, *bwana* <Swah>; employer

2 <nonformal> **honcho,** big enchilada, biggest frog in the pond, top *or* high man on the totem pole, top dog, Mr Big, head cheese, his nibs, himself, man upstairs

VERBS 3 **direct, manage, supervise, superintend, oversee,** overlook, ride herd on <nonformal>, stand over, keep an eye on *or* upon, keep in order; cut work out for; straw-boss <nonformal>; take care of; **regulate, conduct, carry on, handle, run** <nonformal>; **control, command, head, govern**, head up *and* pull the strings *and* **mastermind** *and* quarterback *and* call the signals <all nonformal>; lay down the law, make the rules, call the shots *or* tune <nonformal>

bossy ADJS arrogant; **arbitrary, peremptory,** imperative; **dictatorial, authoritarian; domineering, high-handed, overbearing,** overruling; autocratic, monocratic; **tyrannical**, tyrannous, grinding, oppressive; repressive, suppressive; strict, severe

botany NOUNS plant biology, phytobiology, phytology, plant science; **plant kingdom,** vegetable kingdom; **plants**, flora, plant life, vegetation; vegetable life; herbage, flowerage, verdure, greenery, greens

botch VERBS 1 **do carelessly,** do by halves, do in a half-assed way <nonformal>, do in a slip-shod fashion, do anyhow, do in any old way <nonformal>; **bungle**; **do offhand,** dash off, knock off *and* throw off <both nonformal>, **toss off** *or* **out** <nonformal>; **roughhew,** roughcast, rough out; **knock out** <nonformal>, hammer *or* pound out, bat out <nonformal>; toss *or* **throw together,** knock together, throw *or* slap together, cobble up, patch together, patch, patch up, fudge up, fake up, whomp up <nonformal>, lash up <Brit nonformal>, slap up <nonformal>

2 **blunder, make a blunder, make a faux pas,** blot one's copy book, make a colossal blunder, make a false *or* wrong step, make a misstep; embarrass oneself, have egg on one's face <nonformal>; **bungle**

bother NOUNS 1 **nuisance, pest,** botheration <nonformal>, public nuisance, **trouble, problem,** pain <nonformal>, difficulty, hot potato <nonformal>;

inconvenience; headache <nonformal>; **pain in the neck** *or* **in the ass** <nonformal>

VERBS 2 **annoy, irk, vex, nettle, provoke, pique,** miff *and* peeve <both nonformal>, distemper, **ruffle, disturb,** discompose, **roil,** rile, **aggravate,** make a nuisance of oneself, **exasperate,** exercise, try one's patience, try the patience of a saint; give one a pain <nonformal>; get, get one down, **get one's goat,** get under one's skin, get in one's hair, tread on one's toes; burn up *and* brown off <both nonformal>; **torment, molest,** pother; **harass,** harry, drive up the wall <nonformal>, **hound,** dog, nag, nobble <Brit nonformal>, nudzh <nonformal>; **heckle,** pick *or* prod at, rub it in *and* rub one's nose in it <both nonformal>, badger, hector, bait, bullyrag, worry, worry at, nip at the heels of, chivy, hardly give one time to breathe, make one's life miserable, keep on at, fash <Scots>; **bug** <nonformal>, be on the back of *and* be at *and* ride <all nonformal>, **pester, tease, needle,** devil, get after *or* get on <nonformal>, **bedevil, pick on** <nonformal>, tweak the nose, pluck the beard, give a bad time to <nonformal>

bottle NOUNS **container, receptacle;** basin, pot, pan, cup, glass, ladle; cask

bottleneck NOUNS **hindrance,** hindering, **hampering; check, arrest,** arrestment, arrestation; fixation; **impediment,** holdback; **resistance, opposition**; suppression, **repression, restriction, restraint**; **obstruction,** blocking, blockage, clogging, occlusion; traffic jam, gridlock; **interruption,** interference; **retardation,** retardment, **detention,** detainment, **delay,** holdup, setback; **inhibition;** constriction, squeeze, stricture, cramp, stranglehold; **closure,** closing up *or* off; obstructionism, bloody-mindedness <Brit>, negativism, foot-dragging <nonformal>

bottomless ADJS 1 **piggish, hoggish,** swinish, a hog for, greedy as a hog; **gluttonous**; omnivorous, all-devouring; insatiable, insatiate, unsatisfied, unsated, unappeased, unappeasable, limitless, unquenchable, quenchless, unslaked, unslakeable, slakeless

2 **abysmal,** abyssal, yawning, cavernous, gaping, plunging; without bottom, soundless, unsounded, plumbless, **fathomless,** unfathomed, unfathomable; deep as a well, deep as the sea *or* ocean, deep as hell

3 **plentiful, full,** replete, well-filled, running over, overflowing; inexhaustible, exhaustless; **profuse,** profusive, effuse, diffuse

the bottom line NOUNS **salient point,** cardinal point, high point, great point; important thing, chief thing, **the point, main point,** main thing, essential matter, **essence,** the name of the game *and* what it's all about *and* where it's at <all nonformal>, substance, gravamen, *sine qua non* <L>, issue, real issue, front-burner issue <nonformal>, prime issue; **essential,** fundamental, substantive point, material point; **gist, nub** <nonformal>, **heart,** meat, pith, kernel, **core; crux,** crucial *or* pivotal *or* critical point, pivot; turning point, **climax, cusp, crisis;** summation, **score, reckoning, tally,** tale, the story *and* whole story *and* all she wrote <all nonformal>

boudoir NOUNS **bedroom,** chamber, sleeping chamber, **bedchamber,** sleeping room

bough NOUNS **branch,** fork, **limb; twig, sprig,** switch; spray; **shoot,** offshoot, spear, frond; scion; **sprout,** sprit, slip, burgeon, thallus; sucker

bounce NOUNS 1 **buoyancy,** buoyance, resilience, resiliency, springiness; springy step; **jauntiness,** perkiness, debonairness, carefreeness; **breeziness,** airiness, pertness, chirpiness, light heart

VERBS 2 **bound, spring; spring** *or* **fly**

bouncer NOUNS **ejector,** expeller; **ouster,** evictor; chucker <nonformal>, chucker-out <Brit nonformal>

bound VERBS 1 circumscribe, surround, limit, enclose, divide, separate; **border, edge, rim, skirt, hem, hem in, ring,**

2 **leap, jump, vault, spring, skip, hop,** bounce; upleap, upspring, updive; leap over, jump over, etc; overleap, overjump, overskip, leapfrog; **hurdle,** clear, negotiate

ADJS 3 **limited, restricted, bounded, finite; confined**

4 **promised, pledged, committed,** compromised, **obligated; sworn,** warranted, **guaranteed,** assured, underwritten; contracted; **engaged, plighted, affianced, betrothed,** intended

5 **joined, united, connected, coupled,** linked, knit, bridged, tight-knit, knitted, bracketed, associated, conjoined, incorporated, integrated, **merged,** gathered,

assembled, accumulated, **collected; associated,** joined up, on board; **allied,** leagued, banded together; hand-in-hand, hand-in-glove, intimate; unseparated, undivided; **wedded,** matched, married, paired, yoked, mated; **tied,** knotted, spliced, lashed

boundary NOUNS **limitation, limiting, restriction,** restricting, confinement, prescription, proscription, restraint, discipline, moderation, continence; bounds, limit; time-limit, time constraint; small space; **fence, wall, barrier;** stone wall; paling, palisade; rail, railing

boundless ADJS **infinite, endless, limitless,** termless, shoreless; unbounded, uncircumscribed, **unlimited,** illimited, infinitely continuous *or* extended, stretching *or* extending everywhere, without bound, without limit *or* end, no end of *or* to; illimitable, **interminable,** interminate; **immeasurable,** incalculable, unreckonable, innumerable, incomprehensible, unfathomable; measureless, countless, sumless; **unmeasured,** unmeasurable, immense, unplumbed, untold, unnumbered, without measure *or* number *or* term; exhaustless, inexhaustible; **all-inclusive,** all-comprehensive, **universal**; **perpetual, eternal**

as boundless as the sea
SHAKESPEARE

bounty NOUNS bountifulness, bounteousness; **openhandedness,** freehandedness, open *or* free hand, easy purse strings; **givingness;** open-heartedness, bigheartedness, largeheartedness, greatheartedness, freeheartedness; open heart, big *or* large *or* great heart, heart of gold; **magnanimity**

bouquet NOUNS 1 **fragrance,** fragrancy <old>, **perfume, aroma,** scent, redolence, balminess, **incense,** nosegay <old>, sweet smell, sweet savor; **odor**; spice, spiciness; muskiness; fruitiness
2 **nosegay, posy,** boughpot, flower arrangement; **boutonniere,** buttonhole <Brit>; **corsage; spray; wreath;** festoon; **garland,** chaplet, lei

bourgeois NOUNS 1 member of the middle class, white-collar worker, salaried worker; pillar of society, solid citizen
2 **conformist,** conformer, sheep, trimmer, parrot, yes-man, organization man; **conventionalist,** Mrs Grundy, Babbitt, Philistine, middle-class type, button-down *or* white-bread type <nonformal>, Middle American, *parvenu, arriviste, nouveau riche* <all Fr>; plastic person *and* clone *and* square <all nonformal>, three-piecer *and* yuppie <both nonformal>, Barbie Doll <trademark> <nonformal>
ADJS 3 **capitalist, capitalistic,** individualistic, nonsocialistic, free-enterprise, private-enterprise
4 **conformist, conventional**, plastic *and* square *and* straight *and* white-bread *and* white-bready *and* button-down *and* buttoned-down <all nonformal>

bout NOUNS **fight, match,** battle, duel, slugfest

bow NOUNS 1 **obeisance,** reverence, homage; **nod, bob,** bend, inclination, inclination of the head, **curtsy, salaam, kowtow,** scrape, bowing and scraping, making a leg; **genuflection,** kneeling, bending the knee; prostration; salute, salutation, namaste; presenting arms, dipping the colors *or* ensign, standing at attention
2 **prow, stem,** rostrum, figurehead, nose, beak; bowsprit, jib boom
VERBS 3 **make obeisance, salaam, kowtow,** make one's bow, bow down, **nod,** incline *or* bend *or* bow the head, bend the neck, **bob,** bob down, **curtsy,** bob a curtsy, bend, make a leg, scrape, **bow and scrape; genuflect, kneel,** bend the knee, get down on one's knees, throw oneself on one's knees, fall on one's knees, fall down before, fall at the feet of, prostrate oneself, kiss the hem of one's garment

bowel movement NOUNS **defecation,** dejection, **evacuation,** voidance; movement, BM, number two <nonformal>, **stool, feces,** feculence, **ordure,** night soil, jakes <Brit nonformal>, shit *and* crap <both nonformal>, turd <nonformal>; dingleberry <nonformal>; **diarrhea,** loose bowels, flux; trots *and* runs *and* shits *and* GI's *and* GI shits <all nonformal>; tourista *and* Montezuma's revenge <both nonformal>; lientery; **dysentery,** bloody flux; catharsis, purgation, purge

bowels NOUNS 1 small intestine, odenum, jejunum, ileum; blind gut, cecum; foregut, hindgut; midgut, mesogaster;

large intestine, colon, sigmoid flexure, rectum; anus
2 **depths,** deeps, bowels of the earth; bottomless pit; infernal pit, hell, nether world, underworld; dark *or* unknown *or* yawning *or* gaping depths, unfathomed deeps

bowl NOUNS 1 **cavity,** concavity, concave; **hollow,** hollow shell, shell; **hole, pit, depression, basin,** trough; **crater;** antrum
2 **arena, theater, amphitheater,** circus, **hippodrome, coliseum,** colosseum, **stadium**; Cotton Bowl, Gator Bowl, Orange Bowl, Rose Bowl, Sugar Bowl, Super Bowl

bowlegged ADJS bandy-legged, bandy; rickety, rachitic

box NOUNS 1 **container, receptacle;** receiver, holder, vessel, utensil; case
VERBS 2 **package, pack, parcel;** box up, case, encase, crate, carton; enwrap, bundle; shrink-wrap
3 **cuff,** buffet; strike; box the ears; **fight,** punch, spar, mix it up <nonformal>, shadowbox

boxer NOUNS **fighter,** pugilist, prizefighter, pug *and* palooka <both nonformal>, slugger, mauler

boxing NOUNS **prizefighting,** fighting, pugilism, noble *or* manly art of self-defense, the noble *or* sweet science, fisticuffs, the fistic sport, the fights *and* the fight game <both nonformal>, the ring

box office NOUNS **attendance,** frequenting, frequence; number present; turnout *and* box office *and* draw <all nonformal>

boy NOUNS **lad, youth,** manchild, manling, young man, *garçon* <Fr>, *muchacho* <Sp>, schoolboy, schoolkid <nonformal>, fledgling, hobbledehoy

boycott NOUNS 1 **proscription, ban;** boycottage; **blackball,** blackballing, blacklist; **rejection, exclusion, barring,** debarring, debarment, preclusion
VERBS 2 **ostracize,** turn thumbs down; **proscribe, ban, outlaw**, put under the ban; **blackball,** blacklist

boyfriend NOUNS **fellow** *and* young man *and* flame <all nonformal>

boyish ADJS **childish,** childlike, kiddish <nonformal>, **puerile;** boylike, beardless; puppyish, puppylike, puplike, calflike, coltish, coltlike; ungrown, half-grown, juvenile, puerile

bra NOUNS **brassiere,** bandeau, underbodice, *soutien-gorge* <Fr>, uplift brassiere

brace NOUNS 1 **two,** twain <old>; **couple, pair, matching pair, twosome,** set of two, duo, duet, team, span, yoke, double harness
VERBS 2 **strengthen, invigorate, fortify,** beef up <nonformal>, buttress, prop, shore up, support, undergird, brace up; refresh, revive, recruit one's strength

bracelet NOUNS armlet, wristlet, wristband, anklet

bracket VERBS parenthesize, precede and follow, bookend; interconnect, ally, link, marry, marry up, weld, bind, tie, couple

brag VERBS 1 **boast,** make a boast of, vaunt, flourish, gasconade, vapor, puff, draw the longbow, advertise oneself, **blow one's own trumpet, toot one's own horn,** sing one's own praises, exaggerate one's own merits; bluster, swagger

2 <nonformal> **blow,** blow off, mouth off, **blow hard, talk big,** sound off, blow off *and* toot *or* blow one's own horn, **bullshit,** shoot the shit, spread oneself, lay it on thick, brag oneself up; jaw, talk trash

Brahman NOUNS **nobleman, noble, gentleman; peer; aristocrat, patrician, blue blood,** thoroughbred, silk-stocking, lace-curtain, swell *and* upper-cruster <both nonformal>

Brahmin NOUNS **elitist; highbrow** *and* egghead <both nonformal>, mandarin; **intellectual, intellect,** intellectualist, literate, member of the intelligentsia, white-collar intellectual; wise man

someone whose mind watches itself
CAMUS

braid NOUNS 1 plait, twist; **pigtail,** rat's-tail *or* rat-tail, tail; **wreath,** wreathwork
VERBS 2 plait, pleach, **wreathe,** raddle, **knit,** twist, mat, wattle

brain NOUNS 1 seat *or* organ of thought; sensory, sensorium; encephalon; gray matter, noodle *or* noggin *or* bean *or* upper story <all nonformal>
2 **intellectual, intellect,** intellectualist, member of the intelligentsia; rocket scientist <all nonformal>

VERBS 3 blow *or* knock *or* dash one's brains out, poleax

brainstorm NOUNS **good idea, great idea,** not a bad idea; **bright thought,** bright *or* brilliant idea, **insight; inspiration**

brainwash VERBS **condition, program, indoctrinate,** reindoctrinate, counterindoctrinate

braise VERBS **cook, brown,** embrown, infuscate; sauté, scorch

bramble NOUNS **thorn, brier, nettle,** burr, prickle, sticker <nonformal>; scrub, brier bush

branch NOUNS 1 **ramification,** stem, offshoot; fork, **limb, bough**
2 **stream, waterway, watercourse, channel**; meandering stream, flowing stream, lazy stream, racing stream, braided stream
3 arm, offshoot, **affiliate; chapter,** lodge, post; branch office, local office
VERBS 4 **fork,** furcate, bifurcate, trifurcate, divaricate; ramify, branch off *or* out

brand NOUNS 1 **stamp,** feather, color, stripe, line, grain, kidney; **make,** mark, label, shape, cast, form, mold
VERBS 2 **stigmatize; disparage, defame**; censure, reprimand, **give a black eye** <nonformal>, give a black mark, put in one's bad *or* black books; **skewer,** impale, crucify

brass NOUNS 1 **rashness, brashness, imprudence, indiscretion,** injudiciousness, improvidence; overconfidence, oversureness, overweeningness; **impudence,** insolence; **gall** *and* brass *and* cheek *and* chutzpah <all nonformal>; hubris
2 top brass; top people, the great; ruling circle, lords of creation

brassy ADJS **brazen,** brazenfaced, boldfaced, barefaced, **bold,** bold as brass <nonformal>, unblushing, unabashed, **shameless;** swaggering

brat NOUNS **urchin; minx, imp,** puck, elf, gamin, little monkey, **whippersnapper,** young whippersnapper, *enfant terrible* <Fr>, little terror, holy terror

bravado NOUNS **audacity,** boldness, bold front, brash bearing, brashness, brassiness <nonformal>, brazenness, bravado, insolence; rant, rodomontade, fanfaronade

brave ADJS **courageous, plucky, bold, valiant, valorous, gallant, intrepid,** doughty, **hardy,** stalwart, stout, stouthearted, ironhearted, lionhearted, greathearted, bold-spirited, bold as a lion

bravery NOUNS **courage,** courageousness, **nerve,** pluck, braveness, ballsiness *and* gutsiness *or* guttiness <all nonformal>, **boldness, valor**

brawl NOUNS 1 free-for-all, knock-down-and-drag-out <nonformal>**, broil, melee, scrimmage,** fracas, **riot**
VERBS 2 be quarrelsome *or* contentious, be thin-skinned, be touchy *or* sensitive, get up on the wrong side of the bed; broil; riot; **fight, battle, put up a fight** <nonformal>**; wage war**

brawny ADJS well-built, well-set, well-set-up <nonformal>, well-knit, of good *or* powerful physique, broad-shouldered; **muscular,** well-muscled, heavily muscled, thickset, burly

brazen VERBS 1 **brave, face, confront,** affront, look one in the eye, say to one's face, **meet head-on** *or* boldly, square up to, stand up to *or* against, go eyeball-to-eyeball *or* one-on-one with <nonformal>; brazen out *or* through
ADJS 2 loud <nonformal>, **blatant, flagrant,** shameless, brazenfaced, lurid, extravagant, sensational, **spectacular,** glaring, flaring, flaunting, screaming <nonformal>, obtrusive, vulgar, crude

breach NOUNS 1 **violation, infraction,** breaking; **infringement, transgression, trespass,** contravention; breach of promise, breach of contract, breach of trust *or* faith, breach of the peace
2 **break,** breakage, burst, **rupture, fracture; crack,** cleft, **fissure, cut, split,** slit; slash, slice; **gap, rift,** rent, rip, tear; chip, splinter, scale
VERBS 3 **violate, break; infringe, transgress, trespass,** contravene, trample on *or* upon, trample
4 rupture; **break open,** force *or* pry *or* prize open, crack *or* split open, rip *or* tear open; break in, burst in, bust in <nonformal>

breadth NOUNS **width,** broadness, wideness, fullness, amplitude, latitude, distance across *or* crosswise *or* crossways, extent, **span, expanse, spread;** beam; broad gauge, latitude

breadwinner NOUNS **worker, workman, workingman; workwoman, workingwoman; jobholder,** wageworker, **wage earner,** salaried worker

break NOUNS 1 breakage, **breach,** burst,

rupture, fracture; crack, cleft, fissure, cut, split, slit
2 **interruption, suspension,** gap, hiatus, lacuna, caesura; **interval, pause,** interim, lull, cessation, letup <nonformal>, **intermission**
3 **stroke of luck,** piece of good luck; **fluke** *and* lucky strike *and* **break** <all nonformal>, **good** *or* **lucky break** <nonformal>
VERBS 4 **break up,** fracture, **come apart,** come unstuck, **come** *or* **fall to pieces, fall apart; shatter,** fragment, fragmentize, fragmentate, fall to pieces, shard, **disintegrate**
5 **take a rest, take a break, take time out** *and* grab some R and R <both nonformal>, pause, lay off, **knock off** <nonformal>, recess, **take a recess,** take ten *and* take five <both nonformal>
6 **domesticate, tame,** bust *and* gentle <both nonformal>, break in, break to harness

breakable ADJS **fragile,** frangible, destructible, shattery, crumbly, brittle, fragmentable, fracturable; **unsubstantial, flimsy;** delicate, flimsy, frangible

breakdown NOUNS **collapse, crackup** <nonformal>, **prostration,** exhaustion; nervous prostration *or* breakdown *or* exhaustion, neurasthenia

breakfast NOUNS *petit déjeuner* <Fr>, continental breakfast, English breakfast

breakthrough NOUNS progress, headway; quantum jump *or* leap; **advance,** advancement; **innovation,** leap

break wind VERBS **fart** <nonformal>, let *or* lay *or* cut a fart <nonformal>, let wind

breast NOUNS 1 **bosom, bust, chest,** crop, brisket; thorax; pigeon breast; **breasts,** dugs, teats

2 <nonformal> **tits,** titties, **boobs,** boobies, bubbies, jugs, headlights, **knockers,** knobs, *nénés* <Fr>, bazooms, bags, bazongas, coconuts, hooters

breath NOUNS 1 **murmur,** murmuring, murmuration; sigh, exhalation, aspiration
2 **puff,** puff of air *or* wind, breath of air, flatus, waft, capful of wind, whiff, whiffet, stir of air

breathtaking ADJS **exciting, thrilling,** thrilly <nonformal>, **stirring, moving,** eye-popping <nonformal>; suspensive, **suspenseful,** cliff-hanging <nonformal>; mind-boggling

breed NOUNS 1 **kind, sort, ilk, type,** breed of cat <nonformal>, lot <nonformal>, **variety, species, genus,** *genre* <Fr>, phylum; tribe, clan, race, strain, blood, kin, breed
VERBS 2 **raise,** rear, grow, hatch, feed, nurture, fatten

breeze NOUNS light *or* gentle wind *or* breeze, softblowing wind, **zephyr,** gale <old>, air, light air, moderate breeze; fresh *or* stiff breeze; cool *or* cooling breeze; sea breeze, onshore breeze, ocean breeze

breezy ADJS 1 **lighthearted,** light; **jaunty,** perky, **debonair, carefree,** free and easy
2 **windy, blowy; drafty,** airy, airish; brisk, fresh

brevity NOUNS **conciseness,** concision, briefness, brachylogy; **pithiness,** succinctness

the soul of wit
SHAKESPEARE

brew NOUNS 1 **beer,** brew *and* brewskie *and* suds <all nonformal>, swipes <Brit nonformal>; small beer
2 **concoction,** decoction, *decoctum* <L>, **confection; mixture**, combination
VERBS 3 **distill;** bootleg, moonshine <nonformal>; **plot, scheme, intrigue,** be up to something; **conspire, connive,** collude; gather

bribable ADJS corruptible, purchasable, buyable; approachable; fixable; on the take *and* on the pad <both nonformal>; **venal, corrupt,** bought and paid for, in one's pocket

bribe NOUNS 1 bribe money, sop, sop to Cerberus, gratuity, gratification <old>, payoff <nonformal>, boodle <nonformal>; payola <nonformal>

2 VERBS <nonformal>grease, **grease the palm**, oil the palm, tickle the palm; **purchase, take care of buy, buy off**, pay off; **fix**

bribery NOUNS bribing, subornation, **corruption, graft**

bridal ADJS **matrimonial, marital, conjugal, connubial, nuptial,** wedded, married, hymeneal; epithalamic

bride NOUNS **newlywed;** plighted bride, blushing bride

bridegroom NOUNS **newlywed; groom**

bridesmaid NOUNS wedding attendant;

bridemaiden, maid *or* matron of honor

bridge NOUNS 1 **span, viaduct;** cantilever bridge, clapper bridge, drawbridge, footbridge, pontoon bridge, rope bridge, skybridge *or* skywalk *or* flying bridge *or* walkway *or* skywalk, suspension bridge, toll bridge; overpass
2 auction bridge, contract bridge, rubber bridge, duplicate *or* tournament bridge
VERBS 3 **extend over,** span, bestride, bestraddle, arch over, overarch, hang over, overhang

bridle VERBS 1 **anger, get one's gorge up,** get one's blood up, bridle up, **bristle,** bristle up, raise one's hackles, get one's back up
2 **restrain, curb, check, arrest,** get under control, rein, snub, snub in

brief NOUNS 1 **argument,** *argumentum* <L>; **case, plea,** pleading, *plaidoyer* <Fr>; special pleading
VERBS 2 give a briefing; debrief; **acquaint, enlighten,** familiarize, verse, give the facts, give an account of, give by way of information
ADJS 3 **short, abbreviated,** abbreviatory; **concise**; **succinct, summary,** synoptic, synoptical, compendious, compact

short and sweet
THOMAS LODGE

briefing NOUNS **instructions, directions, orders;** final instructions

briefly ADVS **shortly,** summarily, *tout court* <Fr>, in brief compass, economically, sparely, curtly, succinctly, in a nutshell, in two *or* a few words

brier NOUNS **thorn, bramble, nettle,** burr, prickle, sticker <nonformal>; shrub, bush; scrub, bramble, brier bush

brig NOUNS **military prison, guardhouse, stockade; prison camp,** internment camp, detention camp

bright ADJS 1 **sunny,** fair, mild, balmy; halcyon, Saturnian; **brilliant, vivid, splendid,** splendorous, splendent, **resplendent,** bright and shining
2 **smart, brainy** <nonformal>, **brilliant,** scintillating; **clever,** apt, **gifted,** talented; **sharp,** keen; smart as a whip, sharp as a tack <nonformal>; nobody's fool *and* no dumbbell *and* not born yesterday <all nonformal>

brilliant ADJS 1 **bright, vivid,** intense, **rich,** exotic, burning, **gorgeous**
2 **illustrious,** lustrous, glorious, radiant, splendid, splendorous, splendrous, splendent, resplendent, bright, shining; charismatic, glamorous; scintillating; **gifted,** talented; **dazzling,** bedazzling

brim NOUNS **border, edge, verge, brink,** brow, **rim, margin,** marge, **skirt, fringe, lip,** flange

brindle ADJS **striped,** stripy; **streaked,** streaky; brindled, brinded; marbled, marbleized

brine NOUNS **saltiness, salinity,** brininess; brackishness; **salt; preservative,** preservative medium

bring VERBS **fetch, go get,** go and get, go to get, **go after,** go fetch, **go for,** call for, pick up; **get,** obtain, procure, secure; **bring back, retrieve;** chase after, run after, shag, fetch and carry; **be sold, sell,** bring, realize, sell for

brink NOUNS **verge, brim, rim, margin,** marge, **skirt, fringe,** side

brinkmanship NOUNS **foreign policy,** playing with fire, flirting with death, courting disaster, stretching one's luck, going for broke <nonformal>, tightrope walking

brisk ADJS **refreshing,** refreshful, **fresh,** crisp, crispy, zesty, zestful, **bracing, tonic, exhilarating, stimulating, invigorating,** energizing

bristle NOUNS **spike,** spikelet, spicule, spiculum; **spine;** quill; **needle**
VERBS **anger, get one's blood up, bridle,** bridle up, bristle up, get one's back up; **ruffle,** rub the wrong way, go against the grain, set on edge

Britain NOUNS **Great Britain, United Kingdom, the UK,** Britannia, Albion, Blighty <Brit nonformal>, Tight Little Island, Land of the Rose

This royal throne of kings, this scepter'd isle, This earth of majesty, this seat of Mars, This other Eden, demi-paradise
SHAKESPEARE

britches NOUNS **pants, trousers,** pair of trousers *or* pants, trews <Scots>, **breeches,** breeks <Scots>

brittle ADJS 1 **fragile,** frangible, **breakable,** destructible, shattery, crumbly, fragmentable, fracturable
2 <comparisons> eggshell, matchwood, old paper, piecrust, glass, glass jaw, china, parchment, ice, bubble, glass house, house of cards, hothouse plant

broad NOUNS

1 <nonformal> **gal, dame,** hen, biddy, skirt, jane, doll, babe, chick, wench, bird <Brit>, tomato, bitch, minx, momma, mouse, sister, squaw, toots

ADJS 2 **wide,** deep; wide-ranging, exhaustive, comprehensive, in-depth, extensive; spread-out, **expansive;** widespread; **loose, lax, inexact,** inaccurate, imprecise; nonspecific, unspecified; **general,** sweeping; inchoate, disordered, orderless, chaotic, incoherent

broad as the world
JAMES RUSSELL LOWELL

broadcast NOUNS 1 **publication, promulgation,** evulgation, **propagation, dissemination, diffusion, broadcasting, spread, spreading,** spreading abroad, **circulation,** ventilation, airing; **dispersion** *or* **dispersal, scattering; radiobroadcast,** radiocast, **radio program**
VERBS 2 **communicate, impart, tell,** lay on one <nonformal>, **convey, transmit,** transfer, send, send word, deliver *or* send a signal *or* message, **disseminate,** pass, **pass on** *or* **along, publish, promulgate, propagate, circulate,** circularize, **diffuse, disseminate,** distribute, **spread,** spread around *or* about, spread far and wide, publish abroad, **pass the word around,** put about, **bandy about, noise about,** cry about *or* abroad, noise *or* sound abroad

broadly ADVS **generally, in general; generally speaking,** speaking generally, broadly speaking, **roughly,** roughly speaking, as an approximation; **vaguely, indefinitely,** indeterminably, indefinably, **indistinctly,** indecisively

broad-minded ADJS wide-minded, large-minded, **broad, wide,** wide-ranging, broad-gauged, catholic, spacious of mind; cosmopolitan, ecumenistic, ecumenical

brochure NOUNS circular; **booklet, pamphlet, chapbook, leaflet, folder, tract**

brogue NOUNS **accent,** regional accent, twang, burr, drawl, broad accent

broke ADJS 1 **insolvent, bankrupt,** in receivership, in the hands of receivers, belly-up <nonformal>, broken, **ruined,** failed, out of business, unable to pay one's creditors, unable to meet one's obligations, on the rocks; destitute

2 <nonformal> **dead broke,** busted, **flat, flat broke,** flat on one's ass, flat-ass, down for the count, stone *or* stony broke, stony, **strapped,** skint <Brit>, beat; down to one's last penny *or* cent, cleaned out, tapped out, Tap City, oofless, wasted, wiped out, without a pot to piss in

broken ADJS 1 **subdued, quelled,** crushed, reduced, mastered, overmastered, humbled, humiliated, brought to one's knees, brought low, made to grovel; **tamed, domesticated,** broken to harness, gentled
2 **in disrepair,** out of working order, out of condition, out of repair, inoperative

brokenhearted ADJS **overcome,** crushed, borne-down, overwhelmed, inundated, **stricken, cut up** <nonformal>, **desolated,** prostrate *or* prostrated, undone; **heart-stricken,** heart-struck; heartbroken

broken-in ADJS **accustomed, wont, wonted, used to; conditioned,** trained, seasoned; experienced, **familiarized,** naturalized <old>, run-in <nonformal>, oriented

broker NOUNS **go-between, middleman, intermediary, medium,** intermediate; connection <nonformal>, **contact;** arbitrator, mediator; **stockbroker,** sharebroker <Brit>, stockjobber, dealer, stock dealer; Wall Streeter; stock-exchange broker, *agent de bourse* <Fr>

brokerage NOUNS **stockbrokerage,** brokerage house, brokerage office; wire house; bucket shop *and* boiler room <both nonformal>

brooch NOUNS **gem,** pin, stickpin, breastpin, scatter pin, chatelaine

brood NOUNS 1 **family,** progeny, issue, offspring, fruit, seed, breed; heirs, inheritors, sons, **children, kids** <nonformal>
VERBS 2 introspect, be abstracted; fall into a brown study, retreat into one's mind *or* thoughts; **grieve, sorrow; mope, fret**

brook NOUNS 1 **stream,** branch; kill, bourn, run <Brit nonformal>, **creek,** crick <nonformal>; **rivulet,** rill, **streamlet,** brooklet, runlet, runnel

brothel NOUNS **house of prostitution,** house of assignation, house of joy *or* ill repute *or* ill fame, **whorehouse,** bawdy-house, massage parlor, sporting house, disorderly house, **cathouse, bordello,** bagnio, stew, dive, den of vice, den *or* sink of iniquity, crib, joint

brotherhood NOUNS fellow feeling, **sympathy,** fraternal feeling, feeling of kinship; compassion; humaneness, humanity; charitableness; **fellowship, fraternity,** fraternalism, sodality, confraternity

brotherly love NOUNS charity, *caritas* <L>, Christian love, agape, loving concern, **caring**

brow NOUNS **countenance,** face, visage, feature, favor, physiognomy; **forehead,** lofty brow

brownie NOUNS **elf, pixie, gremlin,** ouphe, hob, cluricaune, puca *or* pooka *or* pwca, kobold, nisse, peri

brown-nose NOUNS 1 **yes-man,** toady, creature, ass-licker *and* ass-kisser *and* brown-nose *and* brown-noser *and* bootlicker <all nonformal>
VERBS 2 **fawn, truckle; flatter; toady; bootlick** <nonformal>, lick one's shoes, lick the feet of; **grovel,** crawl, creep, cower, cringe, crouch, stoop, kneel, bend the knee, fall on one's knees, prostrate oneself, throw oneself at the feet of, fall at one's feet, kiss *or* lick *or* suck one's ass *and* brown-nose <all nonformal>; **kowtow, bow and scrape**

browse VERBS 1 **dip into,** thumb over *or* through, run over *or* through, glance *or* run the eye over *or* through, turn over the leaves, have a look at, hit the high spots
2 **shop, market, go shopping,** go marketing; **shop around;** window-shop, comparison-shop

bruise NOUNS 1 contusion, ecchymosis, **black-and-blue mark; black eye,** shiner *and* mouse <both nonformal>; **discoloration,** discolorment, discolor <old>
VERBS 2 **hurt, wound, hurt one's feelings; injure, traumatize;** contuse, bung *and* bung up <both nonformal>; **buffet,** batter, bash <nonformal>, maul, pound, beat, beat black and blue; give a black eye

bruiser NOUNS

<nonformal> **roughneck, tough,** mug, mugger, bozo, ugly customer, **hoodlum, hood, hooligan,** gorilla, ape, plug-ugly, strong-arm man, muscle man, **goon**

brunt NOUNS **shock; impact, collision, clash; concussion,** percussion

brush NOUNS 1 **touch;** graze, grazing; stroke, gentle *or* tentative contact, caress, nudge
2 skirmish, scrimmage; tussle, **scuffle, struggle,** shoving match; **quarrel**
3 barren land, treeless plain; bush, outback <Australia>
VERBS 4 graze, brush by, glance, scrape, skim, sideswipe, skirt, shave
5 **sweep,** sweep up *or* out, brush off, whisk, broom

brush up VERBS **refresh the memory, review,** restudy, **rub up,** polish up *and* bone up <both nonformal>, get up on

brutal ADJS **savage, fierce, ferocious, vicious, murderous, cruel, atrocious, mindless,** brutish, **bestial,** mindless, insensate, monstrous, mutant, inhuman, pitiless, ruthless, merciless, bloody, sanguinary

brutality NOUNS mindless *or* senseless brutality, brutalness, **brutishness, bestiality, animality,** beastliness; **savagery, viciousness, violence,** fiendishness

brutalize VERBS **terrorize,** sow terror, vandalize, barbarize; **rape,** violate; **attack, assault,** batter, savage, mug, maul, hammer

brute NOUNS 1 **beast, animal, monster,** monster of cruelty, **devil,** devil incarnate; **sadist,** torturer, tormenter; Attila, Torquemada, the Marquis de Sade; **savage, barbarian, beast, animal, devil, demon, fiend; rapist, mugger, killer**
ADJS 2 **brutish, brutal,** brutelike; **bestial, beastly,** beastlike

bubble NOUNS 1 **globule;** vesicle, bulla, **blister,** blood blister, fever blister; balloon, bladder; air bubble, soap bubble
VERBS 2 bubble up, burble; **effervesce, fizz, fizzle;** bubble over

bubbly ADJS frothy, foamy, spumy, spumous, spumescent, bubbly, yeasty; burbly, **bubbling,** burbling; **effervescent,** spumescent, **fizzy, sparkling,** *mousseux* <Fr>, *spumante* <Ital>

buck VERBS **contend against,** strive against, struggle against, labor against, **take on** <nonformal>, grapple with, join battle with, close with, come to close quarters with, go the the mat with <nonformal>, antagonize <old>, **fight, counter**

buckle VERBS 1 **distort, twist,** turn,

screw, wring, wrench, wrest; writhe; **warp**
2 **hook,** hitch; **clasp,** hasp, clip, snap; **button,** zipper; lock, latch

Buddha NOUNS the Blessed One, the Teacher, **the Lord Buddha,** bodhisattva, Gautama Buddha

budding NOUNS 1 germination, pullulation; burgeoning, sprouting
ADJS 2 unseasoned, unfledged, callow, unripe, ripening, raw, green, virginal, naive, ingenuous, undeveloped

buddy NOUNS **coworker, workfellow, workmate, fellow worker,** butty <Brit nonformal>; **teammate,** shopmate

budge VERBS **move, stir; progress,** advance; shift, change, shift *or* change place

budget NOUNS 1 **funds, finances, moneys,** exchequer, purse, pocket
VERBS 2 **ration;** allowance, put on an allowance; schedule, cost, cost out
ADJS 3 **cheap, inexpensive,** unexpensive, **low, low-priced,** frugal, reasonable, sensible, manageable, modest, moderate, affordable, to fit the pocketbook, budget, easy, economy, economic, economical

buff NOUNS 1 devotee, **zealot, enthusiast,** fancier, follower

2 <nonformal> **fan, freak,** hound, fiend, demon, nut, bug, head, junkie, groupie, rooter, booster

VERBS 3 **burnish, polish,** rub up, smooth, dress, shine, furbish

buffer NOUNS 1 **guard; bulwark**; backstop; **fender,** mudguard, **bumper, cushion,** pad, padding
VERBS 2 **neutralize, nullify, annul, cancel,** cancel out, negate, negative, invalidate, vitiate, void, frustrate, thwart, come *or* bring to nothing, undo; **offset, counterbalance**

buffer zone NOUNS demilitarized zone, neutral territory

bug NOUNS 1 **germ,** pathogen, contagium, bug <nonformal>, disease-causing agent, disease-producing microorganism
2 **insect, beetle, mite, tick**
3 **fault,** *faute* <Fr>, **defect, deficiency, inadequacy,** imperfection, kink, defection <old>; **flaw,** hole; fly in the ointment, problem, little problem, snag, drawback; **malfunction,** glitch <nonformal>
VERBS 4 **listen in; eavesdrop,** wiretap, tap, intercept, bug <nonformal>
5 **harass,** badger, hector, be on the back of *and* be at *and* ride <all nonformal>, **pester, tease, needle,** devil, get after *or* get on <nonformal>; hassle <nonformal>

build NOUNS 1 **muscularity,** brawn, sinew, sinews, thew, thews; physique, body-build; body
VERBS 2 put up, set up; expand, extend, widen, broaden, build up; **construct**

building NOUNS **structure, edifice, construction,** construct, erection, establishment, fabric

buildup NOUNS development, widening, spread, broadening, elevation, **extension,** aggrandizement, access, accession, **increment,** accretion; **addition**; **expansion**; proliferation, productiveness; appreciation, waxing, snowballing, **rise** *or* raise, fattening *and* boost *and* hike <all nonformal>; **promotion, buildup** *and* promo <both nonformal>

bulging ADJS swelling, distended, bloated, potbellied, bellying, pouching; bagging, baggy; rounded, hillocky, hummocky, moutonnée; billowing, billowy, bosomy, ballooning, pneumatic; **swollen**, bursting, bursting at the seams, ready to burst, full to bursting, fit to bust <nonformal>

bulk NOUNS 1 mass, substance, matter, magnitude, amplitude, **extent; bulkiness,** hulkingness *or* hulkiness, **massiveness,** lumpishness, clumpishness; **substance,** gist, meat, essence, thrust, gravamen
VERBS 2 develop, bulk up; inflate, sufflate, **blow up,** puff up, pump up

bulkhead NOUNS **partition, wall, barrier;** brattice <mining>; diaphragm, septum; **buffer; bulwark,** rampart; **embankment,** bank, retaining wall, bulkheading, piling

bulky ADJS **hulky,** hulking, lumpish, lumpy, lumping <nonformal>, clumpish, lumbering, lubberly; **massive,** massy; **ponderous,** cumbrous, cumbersome; **clumsy,** awkward, **unwieldy;** clunky <nonformal>

bull NOUNS

1 <nonformal> **humbug, bunk, bunkum;** hooey, hoke, **hokum, bullshit**, crap, baloney

2 **decree,** decreement <old>, decretum, decretal, rescript, fiat, **edict,** *edictum* <L>; **proclamation,** pronouncement, pronunciamento, **declaration,** ukase; diktat
VERBS 3 **talk nonsense, gas** *and* bull *and* **bullshit** *and* throw the bull *and* shoot off one's mouth *and* shoot the bull <all nonformal>

bulldoze VERBS **intimidate,** bully, **cow,** walk all over, **browbeat,** bludgeon, dragoon; **demoralize;** steamroller, flatten, smash, prostrate, raze to the ground

bulletin NOUNS **report,** news report, flash; **brief, statement, account,** accounting

bullfighter NOUNS toreador, *torero* <Sp>; banderillero, picador, matador

bullion NOUNS ingot, bar

bull session NOUNS **chinfest** *and* **chinwag** *and* **talkfest** *and* **bull session** <all nonformal>; **dialogue,** duologue, trialogue

bullshit NOUNS 1 **absurdity,** absurdness, **ridiculousness;** ludicrousness; **nonsense,** nonsensicality, stuff and nonsense, codswallop <Brit nonformal>, horseshit <nonformal>
VERBS 2 **talk nonsense, twaddle, piffle,** waffle <Brit>, **blather, blabber, babble, gabble,** gibble-gabble, **jabber, gibber,** prate, **prattle,** rattle; gas *and* bull *and* throw the bull *and* shoot off one's mouth *and* shoot the bull <all nonformal>

bully NOUNS 1 **tormentor,** torturer; harasser, harrier, badgerer, **heckler,** plaguer, persecutor; molester
VERBS 2 **intimidate, cow, browbeat, hector, harass,** huff; **terrorize,** threaten; **demoralize**

bulwark NOUNS 1 **fortification,** work, defense work, **rampart, fence, barrier; enclosure; safeguard,** palladium, **guard; shield, screen;** umbrella, protective umbrella

bum NOUNS 1 **vagabond, vagrant,** vag <nonformal>; **bum** *or* bummer <nonformal>, loafer, wastrel, losel <old>, *lazzarone* <Ital>; **tramp,** turnpiker, piker, knight of the road, easy rider, **hobo** *or* bo <nonformal>, rounder <nonformal>, stiff *or* bindlestiff <nonformal>; ski bum, beach bum, surf bum, tennis bum
VERBS 2 **tramp,** hobo, go on the bum <nonformal>, vagabond, vagabondize, take to the road, beg, **scrounge, cadge; mooch** *and* **panhandle** <both nonformal>; **hit** *and* hit up *and* **touch** *and* put the touch on *and* make a touch <all nonformal>

travel the open road
WHITMAN

bumbler NOUNS **bungler, blunderer,** blunderhead, boggler, slubberer, **fumbler, botcher**

bump NOUNS 1 **knock, rap, tap,** smack, whack, thwack, whop, whap, swap <nonformal>, whomp, splat, crump <Brit nonformal>, slap, slat <Brit nonformal>, flap, flop
2 **rising, lump,** clump, bunch, blob; thank-you-ma'am *and* whoopdedoo <both nonformal>, cahot <Can>; speed bump, sleeping policeman <Brit>
VERBS 3 **knock, rap, tap,** smack, whack, thwack, whop, whap, swap <nonformal>, whomp, splat, crump <Brit nonformal>, slat <Brit nonformal>, slap, flap; **collide,** come into collision, be on a collision course, **clash,** meet, encounter, confront each other, impinge; **hit, strike, knock, bang; run into, bump into,** bang into, slam into, smack into, **crash into, impact,** smash into; rear-end

bumper NOUNS 1 **buffer, cushion,** pad, padding
ADJS 2 **large, sizable, considerable, goodly,** healthy, tidy <nonformal>, **substantial**

bumpy ADJS **rough, unsmooth; uneven,** ununiform, unlevel, inequal, **broken,** irregular, textured; jolty, rutty, rutted, pitted, pocky, potholed; **jolting,** jolty, **joggling,** joggly, jogglety, jouncy, **bouncy,** choppy, rough; **jarring,** bone-bruising

bunch NOUNS 1 **batch,** heap <nonformal>, pack, mess <nonformal>, gob *and* chunk *and* hunk <all nonformal>; agglomeration, cluster, mass, clot
2 **clique, coterie,** group; **crew** *and* mob *and* **crowd** *and* **bunch** *and* outfit <all nonformal>; ingroup, we-group
VERBS 3 **cluster,** mass, **cohere, adhere, stick, cling,** cleave, hold; **stick together, hang** *or* **hold together;** solidify, set, conglomerate, agglomerate, conglobate; **congeal,** coagulate, clabber <nonformal>, **clot**

bundle NOUNS 1 bindle <nonformal>, **pack, package,** packet, deck, budget,

parcel, fardel <nonformal>, sack, bag, poke <nonformal>, rag-bag <nonformal>, bale, truss, **roll,** rouleau, bolt; fagot, fascine, fasces

2 hoard, store; wealth; **big bucks,** megabucks, gigabucks, big money, serious money, gobs, heaps, heavy lettuce, heavy jack, heavy money, important money, pot, potful, power, mint, barrel, raft, load, **loads,** pile, wad, wads, nice hunk of change, packet <Brit> <all nonformal>

VERBS 3 bundle up, **package,** parcel, parcel up, **pack,** bag, sack, truss, truss up; bale; wrap, **wrap up,** do *or* tie *or* bind up; roll up

4 **snuggle, nestle, cuddle,** cuddle up, curl up; nest; snuggle up to, snug up *or* together <old>

bungalow NOUNS **cottage,** cot *or* cote, box; **cabin,** log cabin; **second home, vacation home;** chalet, lodge, snuggery

bungle NOUNS 1 **blunder, botch,** flub, boner *and* bonehead play <both nonformal>, boggle, bobble *and* boo-boo *and* screw-up *and* fuck-up <all nonformal>, foozle <nonformal>, bevue; **fumble, muff,** fluff, miscue <nonformal>; **slip,** trip, stumble; *gaucherie, étourderie, balourdise* <all Fr>; **hash** *and* **mess** <both nonformal>; bad job, sad work, clumsy performance

VERBS 2 **blunder,** bumble, boggle, **muff,** muff one's cue *or* lines, **fumble,** be all thumbs, have a handful of thumbs; **flounder,** muddle, lumber; stumble, **slip,** trip, trip over one's own feet, get in one's own way, miss one's footing, miscue; commit a *faux pas,* commit a gaffe; **botch,** mar, **spoil, butcher, murder,** make sad work of; play havoc with, play mischief with

3 <nonformal> **goof, pull a boner,** bobble, lay an egg, put *or* stick one's foot in it, stub one's toe, step on one's schvantz *or* pecker, drop the ball, drop a brick, bonehead into it; **blow,** blow it, bitch, bitch up, hash up, **mess up,** flub, flub the dub, **make a mess** *or* **hash of,** foul up, fuck up, goof up, bollix up, **screw up, louse up, gum up,** gum up the works, bugger, bugger up, play the deuce *or* devil *or* hell *or* merry hell with; go at it ass-backwards; put one's foot in one's mouth

bunk NOUNS

1<nonformal>**humbug,** humbuggery; **bunkum;** hooey, hoke, **hokum, bosh,** bull, **bullshit,** crap, baloney, flimflam, flam, smoke and mirrors, claptrap, moonshine, eyewash, hogwash, gammon <Brit nonformal>, *blague* <Fr>, jiggery-pokery <Brit>

VERBS 2 **room,** crash <nonformal>, berth, doss down <Brit>; perch *and* roost *and* squat <all informal>

bunker NOUNS **bastion,** donjon; pillbox, blockhouse, garrison *or* trenches *or* barricades; garrison house; air-raid shelter, bomb shelter

bunny NOUNS **rabbit, bunny** *and* bunny rabbit <both nonformal>, lapin; cottontail

bunting NOUNS **flag, banner,** oriflamme, **standard,** gonfalon *or* gonfanon, guidon, *vexillum* <L>, *labarum* <L>; **pennant,** pennon, pennoncel, banneret, banderole, swallowtail, burgee, **streamer**

buoy NOUNS **marker,** aid to navigation, bell, gong, lighted buoy, nun, can, spar buoy, wreck buoy, junction buoy

burden NOUNS 1 **affliction,** infliction; **curse, woe,** distress, grievance, **sorrow,** *tsures* <Yiddish>; **trouble,** peck *or* pack of troubles; **care,** burden of care, cankerworm of care; **oppression, cross, cross to bear** *or* **be borne, load,** fardel <old>, encumbrance, weight, albatross around one's neck, millstone around one's neck

all the ills that men endure
ABRAHAM COWLEY

2 **duty, obligation,** charge, **onus,** mission, devoir, must, ought, imperative, bounden duty, proper *or* assigned task, what ought to be done, what one is responsible for, where the buck stops <nonformal>, workload

stern daughter of the voice of God
WORDSWORTH

VERBS 3 **distress, afflict, trouble,** give one a tough row to hoe, load with care, **bother, disturb, perturb, disquiet, discomfort, agitate, upset,** put to it; **worry,** give one gray hair

4 **load, lade,** freight; **encumber,** cumber, lumber, **saddle with,** weigh *or* weight down, press down

burdened ADJS **weighted, weighed** *or* **weighted down; oppressed, laden,** cumbered, **encumbered,** charged, loaded, fraught, freighted, taxed, saddled, hampered; **overburdened,** overloaded, overladen, overcharged, overfreighted, overfraught, overweighted, overtaxed; borne-down, sinking, foundering

burdensome ADJS **onerous, oppressive,** incumbent *or* superincumbent, **cumbersome,** cumbrous; massive; lumpish, **unwieldy**

bureau NOUNS **office, department;** secretariat, ministry, commissariat; municipality, bailiwick

bureaucracy NOUNS **officialism; red-tapeism** *and* red-tapery *and* **red tape** <all nonformal>

bureaucratic ADJS **executive, administrative,** ministerial; official; **supervisory, directing, managing**

burglar NOUNS yegg *and* cracksman <both nonformal>; housebreaker, cat burglar, cat man, second-story thief *or* worker; **safecracker,** safebreaker, safeblower; pete blower *or* pete man *or* peterman <all nonformal>

burglary NOUNS burglarizing, housebreaking, **breaking and entering,** break and entry, break-in, unlawful entry; second-story work <nonformal>; safebreaking, **safecracking, safeblowing**

burial NOUNS **interment,** burying, inhumation, sepulture, **entombment;** encoffinment, inurning, inurnment, urn burial; disposal of the dead; burial *or* funeral *or* funerary customs

buried ADJS **concealed, hidden, hid,** occult, recondite <old>, blind; **covered**; **covert, under cover,** under wraps <nonformal>; code-named; **obscured,** obfuscated, clouded, beclouded, befogged; secluded, secluse, sequestered; **obscure,** abstruse, mysterious; **secret**; unknown, latent

burlesque NOUNS **exaggeration,** travesty, caricature; **lampoon,** squib, **parody, satire, farce,** mockery, imitation, wicked imitation *or* pastiche, takeoff <nonformal>, **caricature**
VERBS 2 **lampoon,** satirize, parody, caricature, travesty, hit *or* take off on; send up <nonformal>; dip the pen in gall
ADJS 3 **farcical, broad,** slapstick; parodic, caricatural, macaronic, doggerel

burly ADJS muscular, well-muscled, heavily muscled, thickset, **brawny;** muscle-bound, all muscle

burn VERBS **catch fire,** catch on fire, catch, take fire, **flame,** combust, blaze, **blaze up, burst into flame; shine,** shine forth, **give light,** incandesce; scald, scorch, singe, sear

burnish NOUNS 1 **polish, gloss, glaze, shine, luster,** finish; **patina**
VERBS 2 **polish, shine, furbish,** sleek, slick, slick down, gloss, glaze, glance, luster; **rub,** scour, **buff;** wax, varnish; finish

burnout NOUNS **fatigue, weariness;** end of one's tether, overtiredness, overstrain; jadedness; lassitude, languor; combat fatigue; mental fatigue, brain fag <nonformal>; **listlessness, spiritlessness,** blah *or* blahs <nonformal>

burn out VERBS **get tired, grow weary, tire, weary,** fatigue, jade; **flag, droop,** faint, sink, feel dragged out, wilt; **play out,** run out, run down; **go out, die,** die out *or* down *or* away; fizzle *and* **fizzle out** <both nonformal>

burp NOUNS 1 **belch,** belching, wind, gas, eructation; **hiccup**
VERBS 2 **belch,** eruct, eructate; **hiccup**

burrow NOUNS 1 **lair, den,** cave, **hole,** covert, mew, form; tunnel, earth, run, couch, lodge
VERBS 2 **excavate, scoop,** scoop out, **gouge,** gouge out, grub, shovel, spade, dike, delve, scrape, scratch, scrabble; dredge; **trench,** trough, furrow; **tunnel**, dig

burst NOUNS 1 **report, crash, crack, clap, bang,** wham, slam, clash; **detonation, blast, explosion,** fulmination, **discharge, bang, pop, crack,** bark; **shot,** gunshot; volley, salvo, fusillade
VERBS 2 **break, break up,** fracture, **come apart,** come unstuck, **come** *or* **fall to pieces, fall apart, explode, blow up,** go off, go up, blow out, blast, bust <nonformal>; **detonate,** fulminate
ADJS 3 **broken,** busted <nonformal>, **ruptured,** dissilient; sprung; **shattered,** broken up, broken to pieces *or* bits, fragmentized, fragmented, in shards, in smithereens <nonformal>

bursting ADJS **teeming, swarming,**

crowding, thronging, overflowing, overcrowded, overwhelming, **crawling, alive with,** lousy with <nonformal>, populous, prolific, proliferating, crowded, packed, jammed, bumper-to-bumper <nonformal>, jam-packed, like sardines in a can <nonformal>, thronged, studded, bristling, rife, lavish, prodigal, superabundant, **profuse,** in profusion, thick

bury VERBS **inter,** inhume, sepulture, inearth <old>, **lay to rest, consign to the grave,** lay in the grave *or* earth, lay under the sod, put six feet under <nonformal>; tomb, **entomb,** ensepulcher, hearse; enshrine; inurn; encoffin, coffin; hold *or* conduct a funeral
2 **secrete, hide away,** keep hidden, put away, store away, stow away, file and forget, bottle up, lock up, seal up, put out of sight; **keep secret**; **cache,** stash <nonformal>, deposit, plant <nonformal>

bus NOUNS omnibus, chartered bus, autobus, motorbus, motor coach, articulated bus, jitney <nonformal>; express bus, local bus; schoolbus

bush NOUNS 1 **the bush,** bush country, bushveld, **woods,** woodlands, **backwoods,** forests, timbers, the big sticks <nonformal>, brush
2 **shrub;** scrub, bramble, brier, brier bush; topiary

business NOUNS 1 **undertaking, enterprise, operation,** work, **venture, project,** proposition *and* deal <both nonformal>; **affair, matter, task**, concern, interest; **vocation, occupation, work, line, line of work,** line of business *or* endeavor, number <nonformal>, walk, **walk of life, calling**
2 **company, firm, business firm, concern, house,** *compagnie* <Fr>, *compañía* <Sp>, *Aktiengesellschaft* <Ger>, *aktiebolag* <Swed>; **industry,** business establishment, commercial enterprise
3 business dealings *or* affairs *or* relations, commercial affairs *or* relations; the business world, the world of trade *or* commerce, the marketplace
ADJS 4 **commercial,** mercantile; entrepreneurial; **mercantile,** merchant

businessman NOUNS businesswoman, businessperson, businesspeople; enterpriser, entrepreneur; big businessman, magnate, tycoon <nonformal>, baron, king, top executive, business leader

bust NOUNS 1 **breast, bosom, chest,** crop, brisket; pigeon breast; **breasts,** dugs, teats
VERBS 2 **domesticate, tame, break,** bust *and* gentle <both nonformal>, break in, break to harness; housebreak
3 **go bankrupt, fail,** break, bust <nonformal>, crash, collapse, **fold, fold up,** belly up *and* go up *and* go belly up *and* **go under** <all nonformal>, shut down, shut one's doors, go out of business

bustle NOUNS 1 **haste, hurry, scurry, rush, race,** dash, drive, scuttle, scamper, **scramble,** hustle <nonformal>, flutter, **flurry,** hurry-scurry, helter-skelter; no time to be lost
VERBS 2 **hurry up,** hustle up <nonformal>, **rush,** quicken, hustle <nonformal>, bundle, precipitate, forward; rush along, speed along, **speed on its way; push through,** railroad through <nonformal>, steamroll

busy ADJS **occupied,** working; workaday, workday, prosaic

busybody NOUNS **meddler,** intermeddler; **pry,** Paul Pry, prier, Nosey Parker *or* nosey Parker *or* Nosy Parker <all nonformal>, snoop *or* snooper, *yenta* <Yiddish>, **kibitzer** *and* backseat driver <both nonformal>

butch NOUNS 1 <mannish female> **amazon,** virago, androgyne; lesbian, butch *and* dyke <both nonformal>; **tomboy,** hoyden, romp
ADJS 2 lesbian, sapphic, tribadistic; mannish, butch *and* dykey <both nonformal>

butcher NOUNS 1 **killer, slayer, slaughterer,** bloodshedder; massacrer; **murderer, cutthroat,** gorilla <nonformal>; professional killer, hired killer, hit man *or* button man *or* gun *or* trigger man *or* torpedo *or* gunsel <all nonformal>; **hatchet man;** exterminator, eradicator
VERBS 2 **slaughter, massacre, decimate,** commit carnage, depopulate, murder *or* kill *or* slay en masse; commit mass murder *or* destruction, murder wholesale, commit genocide
3 **botch,** mar, **spoil, murder,** make sad work of; play havoc with

butchered ADJS **botched, bungled,** fumbled, muffed, spoiled, murdered; **ill-managed,** ill-done, **mutilated,** garbled, hashed, **mangled**

butler NOUNS **major-domo, steward,** house steward, chamberlain, *maître d'hôtel* <Fr>, seneschal

butt NOUNS 1 **cigarette;** cig *and* **fag** *and* coffin nail *and* cancer stick <all nonformal>; cigarette butt, stub; snipe <nonformal>
2 **laughingstock, figure of fun,** joke, target, stock, **goat** <nonformal>, **fair game,** victim, dupe, fool, everybody's fool, monkey, mug <Brit nonformal>
VERBS 3 **adjoin,** join, conjoin, **connect, abut,** abut on *or* upon, be contiguous, be in contact; **border on** *or* **upon,** verge on *or* upon; lie by, stand by
4 **push, shove,** thrust; bunt; shunt; pole, row; pedal, treadle

butterfingers NOUNS

<nonformal> **goof,** goofer, goofball, goofus, foul-up, bonehead, dub, foozler, clumsy, fumble-fist, klutz, stumblebum, stumblebunny, duffer, lummox, **slob,** lump, dub

butterflies NOUNS

<nonformal> **jitters,** willies, **heebie-jeebies,** jimjams, **jumps, shakes,** quivers, trembles, dithers, collywobbles, butterflies, shivers, cold shivers, creeps, sweat, cold sweat; antsyness, ants in one's pants, yips

butt in VERBS **talk out of turn,** speak inopportunely, interrupt, **put one's foot in one's mouth** <nonformal>, intrude, butt in *and* stick one's nose in <both nonformal>, **go off half-cocked** <nonformal>, open one's big mouth *or* big fat mouth <nonformal>

buttocks NOUNS 1 **rump,** bottom, posterior, derrière; croup, crupper; podex; haunches; gluteal region; nates

2 <nonformal> **ass,** arse *and* bum <both chiefly Brit>, behind, backside, **butt, can,** cheeks, hind end, nether cheeks, stern, tail, rusty-dusty, **fanny,** prat, keister, popo, rear, rear end, tuchis *or* tushy *or* tush

button VERBS **fasten,** secure; button up; put *or* slap the lid on, **cover**

butt out VERBS

<nonformal> **get off one's back** *or* **one's case** *or* **one's tail,** get out of one's face *or* hair, **back off,** leave be, call off the dogs, keep one's nose out, get lost, take a walk

buxom ADJS **shapely,** well-built, built, well-shaped, well-proportioned, well-made, well-formed, stacked *or* well-stacked <both nonformal>, curvaceous, curvy <nonformal>, pneumatic, amply endowed, built for comfort *or* built like a brick shithouse <both nonformal>

buy NOUNS 1 **bargain,** advantageous purchase, **buy** <nonformal>, **good buy, steal** <nonformal>; money's worth
VERBS 2 **purchase,** procure, make *or* complete a purchase, make a buy, make a deal for, blow oneself to <nonformal>; buy out; buy in, buy into, buy a piece of; buy back; buy on credit, buy on the installment plan
3 **believe, credit, trust, accept,** give credit *or* credence to, put faith in, take stock in *or* set store by <nonformal>, take to heart, attach weight to; believe without reservation, take for granted, take as gospel truth <nonformal>, take on faith, take on trust *or* credit, pin one's faith on; take at face value; **take one's word for,** trust one's word, take at one's word; **buy** *and* **buy into** <both nonformal>, **swallow**

buyer NOUNS purchaser, emptor, **consumer,** vendee; **shopper,** marketer; window-shopper, browser; purchasing agent, customer agent

buzz NOUNS 1 **rasp, scratch, scrape,** grind; crunch, craunch, scranch <old>, scrunch, crump; burr, chirr
2 **report, rumor,** flying rumor, unverified *or* unconfirmed report, **hearsay,** *on-dit* <Fr>, **scuttlebutt** *and* latrine rumor <both nonformal>; **talk, whisper, rumble**
VERBS 3 whisper, buzz, breathe, whisper in the ear, **put a bug in one's ear** <nonformal>

bypass NOUNS 1 **detour,** roundabout way; back way, back road, back street
VERBS 2 **go roundabout,** meander, deviate, go around Robin Hood's barn, take *or* go the long way around, twist and turn; **detour,** make a detour, **go around,** go round about, go out of one's way

by-product NOUNS **effect, result,** resultant, **consequence,** consequent, sequent, sequence, sequel, sequela, sequelae; development, corollary; derivative, derivation; secondary *or* incidental product, spin-off, outgrowth, offshoot; **residue,** leavings, waste, waste product, industrial waste, solid waste, lees, dregs, ash

bystander NOUNS **witness, eyewitness,** spectator, earwitness; passerby

byte NOUNS **bit, binary digit,** infobit, kilobit, megabit, gigabit, terbit; kilobyte, megabyte

byword NOUNS **catchword,** catch phrase, shibboleth, slogan, cry; **pet expression,** cliché; **buzzword,** vogue word, fad word, in-word

Byzantine ADJS **scheming, calculating, designing, contriving, plotting, intriguing;** manipulatory, **manipulative;** opportunist, **opportunistic;** Machiavellian; insinuating, insidious, devious, calculating

C

cab NOUNS taxicab, taxi, hack <nonformal>, gypsy cab <nonformal>; rental car; hired car, limousine, limo *and* stretch limo <both nonformal>

cabal NOUNS **intrigue,** web of intrigue, **plot, scheme,** deep-laid plot *or* scheme; **conspiracy,** confederacy, covin, complot <old>; junta

cabaret NOUNS **tavern, roadhouse; nightclub,** night spot *or* nitery *and* hot spot <all nonformal>, *boîte, boîte de nuit* <both Fr>; juke joint <nonformal>, discothèque *or* disco <nonformal>

cabdriver NOUNS **driver,** Jehu; cabman, cabby <nonformal>, hackman, hack *or* hacky <nonformal>

cabin NOUNS **cottage,** cot *or* cote, **bungalow,** box; log cabin; **second home, vacation home;** chalet, lodge, snuggery

cabinet NOUNS 1 **container, receptacle;** receiver, holder; box, case; cupboard
2 **council,** conclave, *concilium* <L>, deliberative *or* advisory body; divan, council of ministers, council of state, US Cabinet, British Cabinet; kitchen cabinet, camarilla; staff

cable NOUNS 1 **cord, line, rope, wire,** braided rope, twisted rope, flattened-strand rope, wire rope, locked-wire rope, wire cable
2 **telegram, telegraph, wire** <nonformal>, telex; **cablegram; radiogram,** radiotelegram; **day letter, night letter;** fast telegram
VERBS 3 **telegraph,** telegram, flash, **wire** *and* send a wire <both nonformal>, telex; Teletype

cache NOUNS 1 **hiding place,** stash <nonformal>; cubbyhole, cubby, pigeonhole
2 **stockpile,** backup, reserve supply, something in reserve *or* in hand, something to fall back on, reserve fund
VERBS 3 **secrete, hide away,** keep hidden, put away, bury away, store away, stow away, stash <nonformal>, deposit, plant <nonformal>

cad NOUNS bounder *and* rotter <nonformal>; **boor,** churl, clown, **lout,** looby

cadaver NOUNS **corpse,** dead body, dead man *or* woman, dead person, **body;** *corpus delicti* <L>; **stiff** <nonformal>; **the dead, remains,** mortal *or* organic remains, bones, skeleton, dry bones, relics, reliquiae

cadaverous ADJS **deathly, deathlike,** deadly; pale, deathly pale, wan, lurid, blue, livid, haggard; corpselike

café NOUNS **restaurant,** *trattoria* <Ital>; *caffè* <Ital>; *bistro* <Fr>; **coffeehouse,** coffeeroom, **coffee shop,** coffee bar, coffee-pot <nonformal>; pub, tavern; **bar,** barroom, *bistro* <Fr>; waterhole *or* watering hole <nonformal>; **nightclub**

cafeteria NOUNS **restaurant,** eating place, eating house; eatery *and* beanery *and* hashery *and* hash house *and* greasy spoon <all nonformal>; **fast-food restaurant,** hamburger joint <nonformal>; **lunchroom; tearoom,** *bistro* <Fr>; **coffee shop; tea shop,** tea-room, tea-garden, teahouse; **lunch counter,** quick-lunch counter; **snack bar,** *buvette* <Fr>, *cantina* <Sp>; milk bar; automat

cage NOUNS 1 **place of confinement,** close quarters, not enough room to swing a cat; pound, pinfold *or* penfold; **enclosure,** pen, coop
VERBS 2 **confine, shut in,** shut away, coop in, hem in, fence in *or* up, wall in *or* up, rail in; **shut up, coop up, pen up,** box up, mew up, bottle up, cork up, seal up, **impound;** pen, coop, pound <old>, crib, mew, cloister, immure, cage in, encage; **hold, keep in,** hold *or* keep in custody, keep in detention, constrain, ground, **restrain,** hold in restraint; check, inhibit; restrict

cagey ADJS **wary, chary, cagey** <nonformal>, **leery** <nonformal>, **suspicious,** suspecting, **distrustful,** mistrustful, shy

cajole VERBS **wheedle, blandish,** palaver; slaver *or* slobber over, beslobber, beslubber

calamity NOUNS **disaster, catastrophe,** meltdown, cataclysm, **tragedy; shock, blow,** hard *or* nasty *or* staggering blow

calculate VERBS **compute, estimate, reckon, figure,** reckon at, put at, cipher, cast, tally, score; **figure out,** work out, dope out <nonformal>; take account of, figure in *and* figure on <both nonformal>

calculating ADJS **scheming, designing, contriving, plotting, intriguing;** manipulatory, **manipulative;** opportunist, **opportunistic;** Machiavellian, Byzantine; **conniving,** connivent <old>, conspiring, collusive

calf NOUNS dogie, leppy <both W US>, weaner; heifer, yearling, fatling, stirk <Brit>

call NOUNS 1 **cry, shout, yell,** hoot; bawl, bellow, roar; **scream, shriek,** screech, squeal, squall, caterwaul; summons; whistle; moose call, bird call, duck call, hog call, goose call, crow call, hawk call, dog whistle; **bugle call,** trumpet call
2 **visit, social call;** formal visit, duty visit, required visit; look-in
VERBS 3 **cry, shout, yell, holler** <nonformal>, hoot; **bawl, bellow,** roar, roar *or* bellow like a bull; cry *or* yell *or* scream bloody murder *or* blue murder; caterwaul
4 **invite, ask, summon, call in, bid come,** extend *or* issue an invitation

calligraphy NOUNS **handwriting, hand, script,** fist <nonformal>, chirography, autography; fine writing, elegant penmanship, **good hand,** fine hand, good fist <nonformal>

calling NOUNS **vocation, occupation, business, work, line, line of work,** line of business *or* endeavor, number <nonformal>, walk, **walk of life,** mission, **profession, practice, pursuit, specialty,** specialization, *métier* <Fr>, **trade,** racket *and* game <both nonformal>; **career,** lifework, life's work

callous ADJS **calloused, insensitive,** Philistine; **thick-skinned,** pachydermatous; **hard, hard-hearted, hardened,** case-hardened, coarsened, brutalized, indurated, stony, stony-hearted, flint-hearted, flinty, steely, impervious, inured, armored *or* steeled against; **uncontrite,** unabject; untouched, unsoftened, unmelted

calm NOUNS 1 **lull,** lull *or* calm before the storm
VERBS 2 calm down, **stabilize, tranquilize, pacify,** mollify, appease, dulcify; **quiet,** hush, still, rest, compose, **lull, soothe,** gentle, rock, cradle, rock to sleep; cool, **subdue,** quell; keep the peace, be the dove of peace, pour oil on troubled waters
ADJS 3 **placid,** quiet, **tranquil, serene,** peaceful; **cool, coolheaded,** cool as a cucumber <nonformal>; philosophical

camaraderie NOUNS **fellowship, companionship, comradeship,** colleagueship; comradery, male bonding; community of interest, *esprit de corps* <Fr>

camouflage NOUNS 1 **cover, disguise,** protective coloration; **false colors, false front**; smoke screen; masking, dissimilation
VERBS 2 **cover, disguise,** dissimilate, **mask,** dissemble; plain-wrap, wrap in plain brown paper; whitewash <nonformal>; **paper over,** gloss over, varnish, slur over; distract attention from; **obscure,** obfuscate, cloud, throw out a smoke screen; do a cosmetic job on

camp NOUNS 1 **encampment,** *Lager* <Ger>; bivouac; barrack *or* **barracks,** casern, *caserne* <Fr>, cantonment, lines <Brit>; hobo jungle *or* camp; detention camp, concentration camp, *Konzentrationslager* <Ger>; campground *or* campsite
2 **vulgarity,** campiness, high *or* low camp; kitsch
3 **party, interest, side; faction,** division, **sect,** wing, splinter, splinter group, breakaway group, offshoot; **political party**
VERBS 4 **encamp,** tent; pitch, **pitch camp,** pitch one's tent, drive stakes <nonformal>; bivouac; go camping, camp out, sleep out, rough it
ADJS 5 **comic, light;** tragicomical, **farcical, slapstick;** camp *or* campy <nonformal>

campaign NOUNS 1 war, **drive, expedition,** hostile expedition; **crusade,** holy war, jihad
2 all-out campaign, hard-hitting campaign, hoopla *or* hurrah campaign <nonformal>; **canvass, solicitation;** front-porch campaign; grass-roots campaign; **whistle-stop campaign** <nonformal>; TV *or* media campaign
VERBS 3 **electioneer; stump** *and* take the stump *and* take to the stump *and* stump the country *and* take to the hustings *and* hit the campaign trail *and* **whistle-stop** <all nonformal>

camp follower NOUNS **follower,** hanger-on, satellite, creature, lackey, flunky, stooge <nonformal>, jackal, minion, myrmidon; yes-man <nonformal>, sycophant

canal NOUNS **trench, trough, channel, ditch,** dike <old>, fosse, cut, gutter, kennel <Brit>

cancel VERBS **nullify,** void, abrogate, annul, tear up, repeal, revoke, negate, invalidate, **undo,** cancel out, bring to naught, put *or* lay to rest; strike out, cross out, scratch, scratch out, rule out;

blue-pencil; **delete** *or* dele, kill; write off; expunge, censor, censor out, blank out

cancer NOUNS **growth,** neoplasm; **tumor,** intumescence; malignant tumor, malignant growth, metastatic tumor, sarcoma, carcinoma; **blight,** blast; canker

cancerous ADJS tumorous; malignant; **carcinogenic,** tumorigenic

candid ADJS **frank, sincere,** genuine, ingenuous, frankhearted; **open,** openhearted, transparent, open-faced; artless; **straightforward, direct,** up-front *and* straight <both nonformal>, **forthright,** downright, straight-out <nonformal>; plain, broad, round; **unreserved,** unrestrained, unconstrained, unchecked; unguarded, uncalculating; free; **outspoken, plain-spoken,** free-spoken, free-speaking, free-tongued; explicit, unequivocal; **blunt,** bluff, brusque; heart-to-heart

candidate NOUNS **aspirant,** hopeful *and* political hopeful *and* wannabee <all nonformal>, office seeker *or* hunter, baby kisser <nonformal>; running mate; leading candidate, head of the ticket *or* slate; **dark horse;** stalking-horse; favorite son; presidential timber

candor NOUNS **candidness, frankness,** plain dealing; sincerity, genuineness, authenticity; ingenuousness; artlessness; **openness,** openheartedness; freedom, freeness; **unreserve,** unrestraint, unconstraint; **forthrightness, directness, straightforwardness; outspokenness,** plain speaking; **bluntness,** bluffness, brusqueness

candy NOUNS **sweets,** sweet stuff, **confectionery; sweet; confection**

cane NOUNS 1 **staff,** stave; **stick, walking stick,** handstaff, shillelagh; Malacca cane
2 rush, reed, bamboo

cannibal NOUNS **man-eater,** anthropophagite

cannon NOUNS **artillery,** cannonry, ordnance, engines of war, Big Bertha, howitzer

canny ADJS **cunning, crafty, artful, wily,** callid <old>, guileful, **sly,** insidious, supple <Scots>, **shifty,** pawky <Brit>, arch, **smooth, slick** *and* slick as a whistle <both nonformal>, **foxy, shrewd,** knowing, sharp, razor-sharp

canon NOUNS 1 **rule, law, maxim,** dictum, moral, moralism; **norm, standard;** formula, form; rule of action *or* conduct, moral precept; commandment, *mitzvah* <Heb>; **guideline,** ground rule, rubric, protocol, working rule, working principle, standard procedure; guiding principle
2 **literary works, complete works, oeuvre, literary canon, author's canon, body of knowledge,** corpus, body of learning, store of knowledge, system of knowledge; literature of a field, publications; bibliography

cant NOUNS 1 **hypocrisy,** hypocriticalness; Tartuffery, Tartuffism, Pecksniffery, pharisaism, **sanctimony**, sanctimoniousness, religiosity, false piety; mummery, snuffling <old>, **mouthing;** sweet talk *and* soft soap <both nonformal>
2 **jargon, slang, argot, patois, patter, vernacular;** vocabulary, phraseology

cantankerous ADJS **perverse, contrary, wrongheaded, wayward, froward, difficult,** cross-grained, feisty, ornery <nonformal>; sullen, sulky, stuffy; irascible; bloody-minded <Brit>, contrary, crosswise

canter NOUNS 1 lope; **trot,** extended trot, dogtrot, jog trot
VERBS 2 amble, pace, tittup, lope

cantilever NOUNS **overhang, overhanging,** impendence *or* impendency, **projection,** beetling, jutting

canvass NOUNS 1 **survey, inquiry, questionnaire,** questionary; exit poll; **poll, public-opinion poll,** opinion poll *or* survey, statistical survey, opinion sampling
VERBS 2 go to the voters *or* electorate, solicit votes, ring doorbells; shake hands and kiss babies

canyon NOUNS **ravine, gorge,** box canyon, *arroyo* <Sp>, barranca, bolson, coulee, gully, gulch, combe <Brit>, dingle, rift, rift valley, kloof, donga, graben, gully, draw, wadi, basin, cirque, corrie, hanging valley

cap NOUNS 1 **headdress,** headgear, headwear, headclothes, headtire; **millinery;** headpiece, **chapeau, hat;** lid <nonformal>
2 top; **crown, tip,** point, spire, pitch; upper extremity, highest point, very top
3 **cover, lid, top, screw-top;** operculum; stopper
VERBS 4 **top,** put the lid on, cork, stopper, plug; roof, roof in *or* over

5 crown, climax, culminate; **give the finishing touches** *or* **strokes,** put the finishing touches *or* strokes on, finalize, put the icing on the cake

capable ADJS **competent, able, efficient, qualified, fit, fitted, suited, worthy; equal to, up to;** up to snuff <nonformal>, up to the mark <nonformal>, *au fait* <Fr>; well-qualified, well-fitted, well-suited

capacity NOUNS 1 **ability, capability,** faculty, facility, fitness, qualification, talent; mental capacity, **mentality,** caliber, reach *or* compass *or* scope of mind
2 **volume, content,** holding capacity, cubic footage *or* yardage etc, accommodation, room, space, measure, limit; gallonage, tankage; poundage, tonnage, cordage; stowage

caper NOUNS **prank, trick, practical joke,** waggish trick, *espièglerie* <Fr>, antic, frolic; **monkeyshines** *and* **shenanigans** <both nonformal>; frisk, gambol, dido <nonformal>

capital NOUNS 1 **architectural topping,** head, crown, cap; bracket capital; cornice
2 capital city, **seat,** seat of government; **county seat** *or* county site, county town *or* shiretown <Brit>
3 **fund;** moneyed capital; principal, corpus; circulating capital, floating capital; fixed capital, working capital, equity capital, **risk** *or* **venture capital**

capitalism NOUNS capitalistic system, **free enterprise,** private enterprise, free-enterprise economy, free-enterprise system, free economy; finance capitalism; *laissez-faire* <Fr>, laissez-faireism

capitalize VERBS **finance, back, fund, sponsor, patronize, support,** provide for, provide capital *or* money for, pay for, bankroll <nonformal>, angel <nonformal>, put up the money; subsidize; set up, set up in business

capital punishment NOUNS **execution;** legal *or* judicial murder; **hanging,** the gallows, the rope *or* noose; summary execution; **electrocution,** the chair <nonformal>, the hot seat <nonformal>; gassing, the gas chamber; lethal injection; **decapitation,** decollation, beheading, the guillotine, the ax, the block; **shooting,** fusillade, firing squad; **burning,** burning at the stake; stoning, lapidation; defenestration

capitol NOUNS **statehouse;** city hall

capricious ADJS **whimsical,** freakish, humorsome, vagarious; **fanciful, notional,** fantasied <old>, fantastic *or* fantastical, maggoty, **crotchety,** kinky, harebrained, cranky, flaky <nonformal>, quirky; wanton, wayward, vagrant; **arbitrary, unreasonable,** motiveless; **moody, temperamental;** petulant

capsize VERBS **upset,** overset, **overturn,** turn over, turn turtle, upset the boat, keel, keel over *or* up; **sink, founder,** be lost, go down, go to the bottom, go to Davy Jones's locker; scuttle

capsule NOUNS 1 **pill,** bolus, **tablet,** lozenge, troche
2 **condensation,** condensed version, digest, **abstract,** epitome, **précis,** nutshell *or* capsule version, capsulization, encapsulation
VERBS 3 **abridge, shorten, condense, cut, clip; summarize,** synopsize, wrap up <nonformal>; capsulize, encapsulate; **put in a nutshell**
ADJS 4 abridged, compressed, condensed, epitomized, digested, abstracted, capsulized, encapsulated

captivate VERBS **fascinate, charm,** becharm, spell, spellbind, cast a spell, put under a spell, **beguile, intrigue, enthrall,** infatuate, **enrapture, transport, enravish, entrance, enchant,** witch, **bewitch;** carry away, sweep off one's feet, turn one's head, knock one's socks off <nonformal>

captivating ADJS **alluring, fascinating, riveting, charming, glamorous,** exotic, **enchanting,** spellful, spellbinding, **entrancing,** ravishing, **enravishing, intriguing, enthralling,** witching, **bewitching; attractive, interesting, appealing,** dishy <Brit nonformal>, sexy <nonformal>, engaging, taking, eye-catching, catching, fetching, winning, winsome, prepossessing; **seductive,** seducing, **beguiling, enticing, inviting,** come-hither <nonformal>

captive NOUNS 1 **prisoner,** *détenu* <Fr>, cageling; arrestee; **convict,** con <nonformal>; **jailbird** <nonformal>, gaolbird <Brit nonformal>, stir bird <nonformal>; **detainee; internee; prisoner of war** *or* POW
ADJS 2 **in subjection, in bondage, in captivity,** in slavery, in bonds, in chains; under the lash, under the heel; **in one's power,** in one's control, in one's hands *or* clutches, in one's pocket, **under one's**

thumb, at one's mercy, at one's beck and call

capture VERBS 1 **apprehend, collar** <nonformal>, run down, run to earth, **nab** <nonformal>, grab <nonformal>, lay by the heels, take prisoner; **arrest,** place *or* put under arrest, take into custody; pick up *or* take in *or* run in <all nonformal>

car NOUNS 1 **automobile, auto,** motorcar, motocar, autocar, **machine,** motor, motor vehicle, motorized vehicle, *voiture* <Fr>

2 <nonformal> **jalopy,** banger, bus, buggy, wheels, tub, tuna wagon, heap, boat, short, crate, wreck, clunker, junker, junkheap, junkpile

caravan NOUNS **procession, train, column, line, string, cortege;** cavalcade, motorcade

carbohydrate NOUNS carbo *or* carbs <nonformal>, simple carbohydrate, complex carbohydrate; **sugar; starch**

carbonated ADJS **bubbly,** burbly, **bubbling,** burbling; **effervescent,** spumescent, **fizzy, sparkling,** *mousseux* <Fr>, *spumante* <Ital>

carbuncle NOUNS pock, furuncle, boil, wen

carcinogenic ADJS tumorous; cancerous, malignant; tumorigenic

cardholder NOUNS **member,** affiliate, belonger, insider, initiate, card-carrier, card-carrying member

cardinal ADJS **principal,** paramount, **foremost,** headmost, **leading, dominant,** crowning, capital; central, focal, prime, **primary,** primal, first; **preeminent,** supereminent

cardsharp NOUNS **cheat, cheater; skillful gambler, sharp, shark,** sharper, dean *and* professor *and* river gambler *and* dice gospeller *and* sharpie <all nonformal>; cardshark, cardsharper; **card counter**

care NOUNS 1 **custody,** custodianship, keep <old>, **keeping, change, ward,** guarding, hold, protective *or* preventive custody; protection, safekeeping; **support, maintenance, nurture, fostering,** nurturance, nourishment, mothering, parenting, rearing, fosterage, foster-care, **caring,** care-giving, tender loving care *or* TLC <nonformal>
2 **caution, cautiousness;** slowness to act *or* commit oneself *or* make one's move; **heed, solicitude; carefulness, heedfulness,** mindfulness, regardfulness, thoroughness; paying mind *or* attention
VERBS 3 **mind, heed,** reck, think, consider, regard, pay heed to, take heed *or* thought of; **take an interest,** be concerned; **pay attention**

careen VERBS **list, heel,** tilt, tip, cant, heave *or* lay down, stagger, totter, trip, flounder; set on its beam ends, set on its ears

career NOUNS lifework, life's work

carefree ADJS **lighthearted,** light, lightsome; **buoyant,** corky <nonformal>, resilient; **jaunty,** perky, **debonair,** free and easy; **breezy,** airy, without care, *sans souci* <Fr>

careful ADJS 1 **heedful, regardful, mindful, thoughtful, considerate, caring,** solicitous, loving, tender, curious <old>; circumspect; **attentive**; **cautious**
2 **economical, thrifty, frugal,** economic, unwasteful, conserving, **saving,** economizing, spare, **sparing; prudent,** prudential, provident, forehanded

caregiver NOUNS **nurse,** sister *or* nursing sister <both Brit>; hospice caregiver; practical nurse; registered nurse *or* RN; steward, **keeper, caretaker,** warder <Brit>, attendant

careless ADJS **heedless, unheeding, unheedful, disregardful,** disregardant, regardless, **unsolicitous, uncaring;** tactless, respectless, **thoughtless, unthinking, inconsiderate,** untactful, undiplomatic, mindless of, **unmindful,** forgetful, oblivious; **reckless**; **indifferent**; perfunctory, cursory, casual, offhand; **lax, slack, loose,** relaxed; imprecise, sloppy <nonformal>, slipshod; remiss, negligent; indifferent

caress NOUNS 1 gentle *or* tentative contact, brush, nudge, kiss, rub, graze
VERBS 2 **pet,** pat; feel *or* feel up <nonformal>, **fondle,** dandle, coddle, cocker, cosset; pat on the head *or* cheek, chuck under the chin

caretaker NOUNS **guardian, warden,** governor; **custodian,** steward, **keeper,** warder <Brit>, attendant; **curator,** conservator; janitor; castellan

cargo NOUNS payload; lading, load; freight, charge, burden; payload

caricature NOUNS 1 **burlesque, lampoon,** squib, **parody, satire, farce,**

mockery, imitation, wicked imitation *or* pastiche, takeoff <nonformal>, **travesty; cartoon**
VERBS 2 **misrepresent,** overstate, exaggerate, overdraw, blow up, blow out of all proportion; travesty, parody, burlesque

caring NOUNS 1 **sympathy, fellow feeling, sympathetic response,** responsiveness, relating, warmth, concern; **empathy,** identification; involvement, sharing; pathos; charity, *caritas* <L>, brotherly love, Christian love, agape, loving concern
2 **nurture, fostering,** nurturance, nourishment, nutriture <old>, mothering, parenting, rearing, fosterage, fostercare, **care,** care-giving
ADJS 3 regardful, mindful, thoughtful, considerate, solicitous, loving, tender; circumspect; **attentive**

carnage NOUNS **massacre, bloodbath, decimation,** saturnalia of blood; **mass murder, mass destruction**

carnal ADJS 1 carnal-minded, fleshly, bodily, physical; Adamic, fallen, lapsed, postlapsarian; animal, animalistic; brutish, brutal, brute; bestial, beastly, beastlike; Circean; coarse, gross; swinish; orgiastic; earthy, unspiritual, nonspiritual, material, materialistic
2 **lascivious, lecherous, sexy, salacious, sexual, lustful,** ithyphallic, **hot,** horny *and* sexed-up *and* hot to trot <all nonformal>; prurient, itching, itchy <nonformal>; concupiscent, libidinous, randy, horny <nonformal>, lubricious

carnival NOUNS **festival, fair;** kermis; *Oktoberfest* <Ger>; Mardi Gras; Saturnalia; **amusement park,** Tivoli, fun fair; fairground

carnivorous ADJS **flesh-eating, meat-eating,** omophagous, predacious

carom VERBS **rebound,** resile; ricochet, cannon *and* cannon off <both Brit>

carouse VERBS **go on a spree; go on a binge** *or* **drunk** *or* **toot** *or* **bat** *or* **bender** <nonformal>, **spree, revel,** roister, wassail, debauch, paint the town red <nonformal>

eat, drink, and be merry
BIBLE

carousel NOUNS merry-go-round, roundabout, ride, whirligig, whip, flying horses

carp VERBS **pick** *or* **pull** *or* **tear to pieces; tear down, cavil,** quibble, **nitpick,** pick nits, pettifog

carpet NOUNS **rug,** floor cover *or* covering; carpeting, wall-to-wall carpet *or* carpeting

carpetbagger NOUNS **defrauder,** shyster *and* pettifogger <both nonformal>; land shark, land pirate, land grabber

carping NOUNS **faultfinding,** taking exception, caviling, pettifogging, quibbling, captiousness, niggling, nitpicking, pestering, nagging; hypercriticism, hairsplitting

carriage NOUNS 1 **look, air, mien,** demeanor, bearing, port, posture, stance, poise, presence
2 **vehicle, conveyance,** carrier, means of carrying *or* transporting, means of transport, medium of transportation

carrier NOUNS 1 vector, biological vector, mechanical vector; Typhoid Mary
2 conveyer; transporter, hauler, carter, wagoner, drayman, shipper, trucker, common carrier, truck driver; letter carrier; cupbearer, Ganymede, Hebe; **dispatch-bearer,** nuncio <old>, **courier,** diplomatic courier, **runner,** express <Brit>, dispatch-rider, pony-express rider, *estafette* <Fr>; bicycle *or* motorcycle messenger

carry VERBS bear, pack, tote *and* lug <both nonformal>, manhandle

carry on VERBS 1 **misbehave,** get into mischief; **act up**
2 <nonformal> **kick up a row,** kick up a shindy *or* a fuss *or* a storm, piss up a storm, **raise the devil,** raise the deuce *or* dickens, raise a rumpus *or* a storm, raise a ruckus, raise Cain, **raise hell,** raise sand, raise the roof, whoop it up, hell around, horse around *or* about; go on, maffick <Brit>; **cut up,** cut up rough, **roughhouse**
3 **continue**, keep *or* stay with it, keep *or* stay at it; **go on,** go along, **keep on,** keep on keeping on, keep going, see it through, stay on, hold on, hold one's way *or* course *or* path, hold steady, slog on, plug away <nonformal>

cart NOUNS oxcart, horsecart, ponycart, dogcart; dumpcart; **handcart;** jinrikisha, ricksha

carte blanche NOUNS blank check <nonformal>, **full authority,** full power, free hand, open mandate; no holds barred; rope, long rope *or* tether, rope enough to hang oneself

cartel NOUNS **combination,** combine, **amalgamation, consolidation, alliance,** affiliation, **association,** hookup <nonformal>; **synthesis,** syncretism, syneresis; **conspiracy,** cabal

cartographer NOUNS mapmaker, mapper; chorographer, topographer, oceanographer

carve VERBS **shape,** whittle, cut, chisel, hew, hew out; **slice,** carve up, slice up, **cut up,** cut *or* slice the pie *or* melon <nonformal>

Casanova NOUNS **libertine, swinger** <nonformal>, **profligate, rake,** rakehell, rip <nonformal>, **roué,** wanton, womanizer, cocksman <nonformal>, walking phallus, debauchee, rounder <old>, **wolf** <nonformal>, woman chaser, skirt chaser <nonformal>, gay dog, gay deceiver, gallant, philanderer, lover-boy <nonformal>, lady-killer, Lothario, Don Juan

cascade NOUNS 1 **waterfall, cataract,** fall, **falls, Niagara,** force <Brit>, linn <Scots>, sault; nappe; watershoot
VERBS 2 **overflow,** inundate, engulf, swamp, sweep, whelm, overwhelm, **flood,** deluge, submerge

case NOUNS 1 **lawsuit, court case,** cause, cause in court, legal case
2 casing, encasement; **sheath,** sheathing; **box,** crate, **package,** container
3 **instance,** relevant instance, typical example *or* case, case in point, object lesson

cash NOUNS 1 **money, currency, legal tender, medium of exchange,** circulating medium, sterling <Brit>, hard cash, cold cash
VERBS 2 cash in <nonformal>, liquidate, convert into cash

cashier NOUNS 1 financial officer, bursar, purser, purse bearer, cashkeeper
VERBS 2 **dismiss, discharge, expel,** drum out, disemploy, outplace, separate forcibly *or* involuntarily, **lay off,** suspend, surplus, furlough, turn off, make redundant, riff <nonformal>, turn out, release, let go, let out, remove, displace, replace, strike off the rolls, give the pink slip

casino NOUNS 1 **ballroom, dance hall,** dancery; dance palace
2 **gambling house, house,** store *and* shop <both nonformal>, gaming house, betting house, betting parlor, gambling den, gambling hall; luxurious casino

casket NOUNS **coffin,** burial case, box, kist <Scots>; wooden kimono *or* overcoat <nonformal>; **sarcophagus;** mummy case

Cassandra NOUNS **pessimist, cynic,** malist, nihilist; killjoy, gloomy Gus *and* calamity howler *and* worrywart <all nonformal>, seek-sorrow, Job's comforter, prophet of doom, Eeyore

one who is always building dungeons in the air
JOHN GALSWORTHY

cassette NOUNS **recording,** tape recording; tape, tape cassette; tape cartridge, cartridge; video-cassette recorder *or* VCR

cast NOUNS 1 cast of characters, characters, persons of the drama, *dramatis personae* <L>; supporting cast
2 **disposition, bent, turn, bias,** slant, warp, twist
VERBS 3 **throw, fling, sling, pitch, toss, hurl, heave, chuck,** chunk *and* peg <both nonformal>, lob, shy, fire, burn, pepper <nonformal>, launch, dash, let fly, let go, let rip, let loose

caste NOUNS **rank, standing, level,** footing, **status,** station; **social class,** social group *or* grouping, status group, accorded status, social category, order, grade, estate, rank

castle NOUNS **mansion,** palatial residence, stately home <Brit>; **villa, château,** *hôtel* <Fr>, tower; **stronghold,** hold, safehold, fasthold, strong point, **fastness,** keep, ward, **bastion,** donjon, **citadel**

castoff NOUNS **reject,** throwaway, castaway, rejectamenta <pl>

castrate VERBS geld, emasculate, eunuchize, unman, neuter, spay, fix *or* alter <both nonformal>, unsex, deball <nonformal>

casual ADJS **nonchalant, blasé, indifferent,** unconcerned; **offhand, relaxed, laid-back** *and* throwaway <both nonformal>; **easygoing,** easy, free and easy, devil-may-care, lackadaisical, *dégagé* <Fr>; perfunctory, cursory, offhand; **occasional, incidental**

cat NOUNS **feline,** pussy *and* **puss** *and* **pussycat** <all nonformal>, tabby, grimalkin; house cat; **kitten, kitty** *and* kitty-cat <both nonformal>; **tomcat,** tom; mouser; ratter; Cheshire cat, Chessycat <nonformal>; Maltese cat; tiger cat, tabby cat; tortoise-shell cat, calico cat; alley cat

cataclysm NOUNS **debacle, disaster, catastrophe; breakup,** breaking up; **upheaval, convulsion; tragedy**

catacombs NOUNS **tomb, sepulcher; crypt, vault,** burial chamber; ossuary *or* ossuarium

catalog NOUNS 1 **description,** specification, particularization, details, itemization, cataloging; **narration**
VERBS 2 **classify,** class, **categorize,** sort, sort out, sift, group, factor, winnow, thrash out; **list, enumerate, itemize, tabulate,** tally

catalyst NOUNS **alterant,** alterer, alterative, **agent,** catalytic agent; **instigator, inciter,** exciter, urger; **provoker,** *provocateur* <Fr>, *agent provocateur* <Fr>

catapult NOUNS 1 arbalest, ballista, trebuchet
VERBS 2 **throw, fling, sling,** launch, let fly, let go, let rip, let loose

catastrophe NOUNS **debacle, disaster, cataclysm; disaster, calamity,** meltdown, **tragedy; shock, blow,** hard *or* nasty *or* staggering blow

catch NOUNS 1 **trick, artifice,** gimmick, joker; curve ball; **Catch-22,** kicker, zinger, snag <all nonformal>; fly in the ointment
2 **good thing,** find <nonformal>, *trouvaille* <Fr>; godsend, windfall; conquest
VERBS 3 **trap,** entrap, gin, catch out, catch in a trap; **ensnare, snare,** hook, **hook in,** sniggle, noose; inveigle

catchword NOUNS catch phrase, shibboleth, slogan, cry; **pet expression,** byword, cliché; **buzzword,** vogue word, fad word, in-word; euphemism, **code word**

catchy ADJS **melodious,** melodic; fine-toned, **pleasant-sounding,** agreeable-sounding, pleasant, appealing, agreeable, singable; **euphonious** *or* euphonic, **lyric, lyrical,** melic

catechism NOUNS creedal *or* doctrinal statement, formulated *or* stated belief; gospel

categorical ADJS **classificational, taxonomic** *or* **taxonomical,** typologic *or* typological; **unrestricted,** uncircumscribed, unmitigated, straight, **unreserved,** without reserve

categorize VERBS **classify,** class, catalog, sort, sort out, sift, group, factor, winnow, thrash out; weigh, weigh up, **evaluate, judge,** gauge, assess, appraise

category NOUNS **class, head, order, division,** branch, set, **group,** grouping, bracket, pigeonhole; **subdivision,** subgroup

cater to VERBS **wait on** *or* **upon,** wait on hand and foot, dance attendance, do service, fetch and carry, do the dirty work of, do *or* jump at the bidding of; favor, please, gratify, satisfy; **pamper,** cosset, **coddle,** mollycoddle

catharsis NOUNS purgation, abreaction, motor abreaction, psychocatharsis, **emotional release,** relief of tension, outlet; release therapy, acting-out, psychodrama; imaging

cathartic NOUNS 1 **laxative, physic, purge, purgative,** aperient, carminative, diuretic
ADJS 2 laxative, purgative, aperient; carminative; diuretic
3 **relieving, easing, alleviative,** alleviating, alleviatory, **mitigative,** mitigating

catholic ADJS **universal, all-inclusive,** all-including, **all-embracing,** all-encompassing, all-comprehensive, all-comprehending, all-pervading; **broad-minded,** wide-minded, large-minded, **broad, wide,** wide-ranging, broad-gauged

catty ADJS **spiteful,** despiteful; cattish, bitchy <nonformal>; **snide; disparaging, derogatory,** slighting, belittling, minimizing, pejorative, back-biting, catty *and* bitchy <both nonformal>

caught ADJS **stuck, fast,** stuck fast, **fixed, transfixed,** fastened, tied, chained, tethered, anchored, moored, held, inextricable; **fascinated,** enthralled, rapt, spellbound, charmed, enchanted, mesmerized, **hypnotized,** fixed, riveted, **arrested,** switched on <nonformal>

caulk VERBS **stop, stop up; obstruct, clog,** clog up; **dam,** dam up; stanch, stench <Scots>; chink

cause NOUNS 1 **occasion,** antecedents, **grounds,** ground, background, stimulus, base, **basis,** element, principle, factor; **determinant,** determinative; causation, causality, cause and effect; etiology
2 **principle,** interest, issue, burning issue, commitment, faith, great cause, lifework; reason for being, *raison d'être* <Fr>; **movement,** mass movement,

activity; **drive, campaign, crusade;** zeal, passion, fanaticism
VERBS 3 **compel, force, make;** have, cause to; **constrain, bind,** tie, tie one's hands; **restrain**; enforce, **drive,** impel; dragoon, use force upon, force one's hand, hold a pistol *or* gun to one's head

caustic ADJS mordant, mordacious, corrosive, corroding; **acrimonious,** acrid, acid, acidic, acidulous, acidulent, acerb, acerbate, acerbic, **bitter,** tart; **sharp,** sharpish, keen, incisive, trenchant, **cutting,** penetrating, piercing, biting, **stinging,** stabbing, **scathing, scorching,** withering, scurrilous, abusive, thersitical, foulmouthed, harsh-tongued

cauterize VERBS **burn,** torrefy, **sear; singe,** swinge; brand, burn in; **char,** scorify

caution NOUNS 1 **warning,** caveat, **admonition,** monition, admonishment; **notice,** notification; **word to the wise,** *verbum sapienti* <L>, verb sap, enough said
2 **cautiousness;** slowness to act *or* commit oneself *or* make one's move; **care, heed, solicitude; carefulness, heedfulness,** mindfulness, regardfulness, thoroughness; paying mind *or* attention; **guardedness; prudence,** prudentialness, **circumspection, discretion,** canniness <Scots>
VERBS 3 **warn, advise, admonish; give warning,** give fair warning, utter a caveat, address a warning to, put a flea in one's ear <nonformal>, have a word with one, say a word to the wise; tip *and* tip off <both nonformal>; **alert,** warn against, put on one's guard, warn away *or* off; **give the high sign** <nonformal>; **put on alert,** cry havoc, sound the alarm

cautious ADJS **careful, heedful, regardful, mindful, thoughtful, considerate, caring,** solicitous, loving, tender, curious <old>; circumspect; **attentive**

cave NOUNS 1 **cavern,** cove <Scots>, **hole, grotto,** grot, antre, subterrane; lair; **tunnel, burrow,** warren; subway; bunker, foxhole, dugout, *abri* <Fr>; sewer
VERBS 2 **collapse, cave in,** fall in; fold, fold up; implode; **deflate**

cavity NOUNS concavity, concave; **hollow,** hollow shell, shell; **hole, pit, depression, dip,** sink, fold <Brit>; scoop, pocket; **basin,** trough, **bowl, crater**

cavort VERBS **frolic, rollick, gambol, frisk, romp, caper,** cut capers <nonformal>, lark about <Brit nonformal>, antic, curvet, caracole, flounce, trip, skip, dance; **cut up** <nonformal>, cut a dido <nonformal>, horse around <nonformal>, fool around, carry on <nonformal>

cease NOUNS 1 **cessation, discontinuance,** discontinuation, phaseout, phasedown, scratching *and* scrubbing *and* breakoff <all nonformal>; **desistance,** desinence, surcease, **ceasing,** ending, halting, stopping, termination
VERBS 2 **discontinue, end, stop, halt,** end-stop, terminate, close the books on, close the books, put paid to <Brit>, abort, cancel, scratch *and* scrub <both nonformal>, hold, **quit,** stay, belay <nonformal>; **desist, refrain,** leave off, lay off <nonformal>, give over, **have done with**

ceaseless ADJS **endless,** unending, neverending, without end, **interminable,** nonterminous, nonterminating; **continual,** continuous, steady, **constant, ceaseless,** nonstop, unceasing, neverceasing, **incessant,** unremitting, unintermitting, uninterrupted

cede VERBS **surrender,** renounce, abandon, relinquish, give over, hand over

ceiling NOUNS **limit, end, extremity,** extreme, **acme,** apogee, climax, **maximum,** max <nonformal>, roof, **peak,** summit, **pinnacle,** crown, top; *plafond* <Fr>, overhead

celebrate VERBS **observe, keep, mark,** solemnly mark, **honor; commemorate,** memorialize; **solemnize,** signalize, hallow, mark with a red letter; **make merry;** kill the fatted calf; sound a fanfare, blow the trumpet, beat the drum, fire a salute; sound *or* resound the praises of, ring one's praises, sing the praises of, trumpet; praise to the skies, *porter aux nues* <Fr>

celebrated ADJS **notable, noteworthy, remarkable, marked, standout** <nonformal>, of mark, signal; **memorable,** unforgettable, never to be forgotten; striking, telling, salient; **eminent, prominent,** conspicuous, noble, **outstanding, distinguished;** prestigious, esteemed, estimable, reputable; **extraordinary,** *extraordinaire* <Fr>, out of the ordinary, **exceptional, special,** rare

celebration NOUNS celebrating; **observance,** formal *or* solemn *or* ritual observance, **solemnization;** marking *or* honoring the occasion; **commemoration,** memorialization, remembrance, memory; jubilee; red-letter day, **holiday**; anniversaries; **festivity; revel**; rejoicing; **ceremony,** rite; religious rites; ovation, triumph; **tribute;** testimonial, testimonial banquet *or* dinner; toast; roast; **salute;** salvo; flourish of trumpets, fanfare, fanfaronade

celebrity NOUNS 1 **publicity,** publicness, **notoriety, fame,** famousness, notoriousness, notice, public notice, *réclame, éclat* <both Fr>
2 man *or* woman of mark *or* note, person of note *or* consequence, **notable, notability, luminary, great man** *or* **woman,** master spirit, worthy, name, **big name,** figure, public figure, **somebody; important person, VIP** *and* **standout** <both nonformal>, personage, one in a hundred *or* thousand *or* million etc; **star, superstar,** megastar, hot stuff <nonformal>

celestial ADJS **heavenly,** heavenish; **paradisal, paradisaic, paradisaical,** paradisiac, paradisiacal, paradisic, paradisical; supernal, ethereal; Elysian, Olympian

celibate ADJS **monastic,** monachal, **monkish;** misogamic, misogynous; sexually abstinent *or* continent, abstinent, abstaining

cellar NOUNS cellarage, **basement;** subbasement; wine cellar, potato cellar, storm cellar, cyclone cellar; coal bin *or* hole, hold, hole, bunker

cemetery NOUNS **graveyard, burial ground** *or* **place,** burying place *or* ground, *campo santo* <Ital>, boneyard *and* bone orchard <both nonformal>, burial yard, necropolis, polyandrium, **memorial park,** city *or* village of the dead; **churchyard,** God's acre; **potter's field;** Golgotha, Calvary

censor NOUNS 1 **critic**, captious critic, criticizer, **nitpicker** <nonformal>, smellfungus, belittler, censurer, carper, caviler, quibbler, petti-fogger
VERBS 2 bowdlerize, expurgate; bleep *or* bleep out <nonformal>, silence; sit on *and* sit down on *and* slap *or* smack down <all nonformal>

censorship NOUNS expurgation, bowdlerization, censoring; blackout <nonformal>; bleeping *or* bleeping out <nonformal>

censure VERBS **condemn, damn, doom; denounce,** denunciate; reprimand, **give a black eye** <nonformal>, give a black mark, put in one's bad *or* black books; pick holes in, pick to pieces

census NOUNS head count; population statistics, demography, demographics; **numeration, enumeration, numbering, counting,** tallying

centennial NOUNS **anniversary,** centenary; centennium

center NOUNS 1 **middle ground,** neutral ground *or* territory, center; meeting ground, interface; **middle of the road**
2 **moderate,** moderatist, moderationist, **centrist,** middle-of-the-roader <nonformal>; independent
3 nucleus, focus, kernel, **core, pith,** meat; **heart,** soul, heart and soul, spirit, sap, marrow
VERBS 4 **converge, come together,** approach, run together, **meet,** unite, connect, merge; centralize, **come to a center;** center on *or* around, concentralize, concenter, **concentrate**

central ADJS centric, **middle**; centermost, middlemost, **midmost; equidistant;** centralized, concentrated; axial, **essential,** fundamental, indispensable, basic, substantive, bedrock, material; **central,** focal, **pivotal,** key; core, nuclear; equidistant, halfway, midway, equatorial

centrifuge VERBS **separate, whirl, spin,** spin like a top *or* teetotum, whirl like a dervish; centrifugate

centrist NOUNS **moderate,** moderatist, moderationist, middle-of-the-roader, neutral, compromiser

ceramics NOUNS **pottery;** potting; **ceramic ware**

cereal NOUNS 1 breakfast food, dry cereal, hot cereal
2 cereal plant, farinaceous plant, **grain,** corn <Brit>

cerebral ADJS **mental, intellectual, rational, reasoning, thinking,** noetic, conceptive, conceptual, phrenic

ceremonious ADJS **ceremonial; red-carpet; ritualistic, ritual;** hieratic, hieratical, sacerdotal, liturgic; **grave, solemn**; **pompous**; **stately**; well-mannered; **conventional,** decorous

ceremony NOUNS 1 **formality, form, formalness;** ceremonial, **ceremoniousness; the red carpet; ritual,** rituality;

dignity, gravity, *gravitas* <L>, weighty dignity, staidness, reverend seriousness, **solemnity**; **pomp**
2 **rite, ritual,** rituality, **liturgy,** holy rite; order of worship; observance, ritual observance; **sacrament,** sacramental

certain ADJS **sure,** sure-enough <nonformal>; bound; **positive, absolute, definite,** perfectly sure, apodictic; decisive, conclusive; clear, clear as day, clear and distinct, unequivocal, unmistakable, unambiguous, nonambiguous, univocal; **necessary,** determinate, ineluctable, predetermined, predestined, **inevitable**; **true**

certainty NOUNS 1 **certitude,** certainness, **sureness,** surety, **assurance, assuredness,** certain knowledge; **positiveness, absoluteness, definiteness,** dead *or* moral *or* absolute certainty; unequivocalness, unmistakableness, unambiguity, nonambiguity, univocity, univocality; **infallibility,** infallibilism, inerrability, inerrancy; **necessity,** determinacy, determinateness, noncontingency, Hobson's choice, ineluctability, predetermination, predestination, **inevitability**; **truth**; **proved fact,** probatum

2 <nonformal> **sure thing,** dead certainty, dead-sure thing, sure bet, sure card, aces wired, cinch, lead-pipe cinch, dead cinch, lock, mortal lock, shoo-in, open-and-shut case

certificate NOUNS certification, **ticket; authority,** authorization; **credential, voucher, warrant,** warranty, testimonial; note; **affidavit,** sworn statement, notarized statement, deposition, witness, attestation, *procès-verbal* <Fr>; **visa,** *visé* <Fr>; **bill of health,** clean bill of health; navicert <Brit>; **diploma,** sheepskin <nonformal>; certificate of proficiency, testamur <Brit>; birth certificate, death certificate

certify VERBS substantiate, **verify, ratify, endorse,** sign off on, second, support, **confirm, validate, authenticate, accept,** give the nod *or* the green light *or* the go-ahead *or* the OK <all nonformal>, give a nod of assent, give one's imprimatur, permit, give permission, **approve**; sanction, **authorize,** warrant, vouch for, accredit; **sign,** undersign, sign on the dotted line, put one's John Hancock on <nonformal>, initial, put one's mark *or* X *or* cross on; **set one's hand and seal**

cesspool NOUNS sump, cesspit, septic tank; bilge *or* bilges; **sewer,** drain, *cloaca* and *cloaca maxima* <both L>

chafe VERBS 1 **pain,** gall, fret, rasp, rub, grate; gnaw, grind; fester, rankle <old>
2 **be impatient,** hardly wait; itch to, burn to; **champ at the bit, pull at the leash,** not be able to sit down *or* stand still; **fret, fuss,** squirm; **stew,** sweat, sweat and stew, get into a dither, get into a stew <nonformal>, work oneself into a lather *or* sweat <nonformal>, get excited

chagrin NOUNS **distress; embarrassment, abashment, discomfiture,** egg on one's face <nonformal>, disconcertion, disconcertment, discountenance, discomposure, disturbance, confusion; **humiliation, shame,** shamefacedness, mortification, red face

chain NOUNS 1 **series, succession, connection, concatenation,** catenation, catena, chaining, linkup, articulation, reticulation, nexus
2 **curb, check,** countercheck, arrest, **stay, stop,** damper, holdback; **brake,** clog, drag, drogue, remora; shackle, fetter, trammel
VERBS 3 **bind, restrain,** put the clamps on, **strap,** lash, pinion, fasten, secure, make fast; **hamper, trammel,** entrammel; rope; enchain; **shackle, fetter, manacle,** gyve, **put in irons**

chair NOUNS 1 **chairman,** chairwoman, convener <Brit>, speaker, presiding officer
VERBS 2 **officiate; preside,** preside over, preside at the board; occupy the chair

challenge NOUNS 1 **dare,** double dare; fighting words; **defy** *or* defi; gage, gage of battle, gauntlet, glove, chip on one's shoulder, slap of the glove, invitation *or* bid to combat
VERBS 2 dare, defy, fly in the teeth of, throw down the gauntlet, ask for trouble, start something, do something about it
3 **dispute,** call in question; **demur, scruple,** boggle, dig in one's heels; contest; cast doubt on, greet with skepticism, keep one's eye on, treat with reserve, bring *or* call into question, raise a question, throw doubt upon, awake a doubt *or* suspicion

4 **contend, vie, compete with** *or* **against, vie with,** enter into competition with, give a run for one's money

challenging ADJS **provocative, provoking,** piquant, **exciting,** prompting, **rousing, stirring, stimulating, defiant,** defying

chamber NOUNS 1 **compartment,** space, enclosed space; **cavity,** hollow, hole, concavity; **cell, crypt, vault**
2 **bedroom, boudoir,** sleeping chamber, **bedchamber,** cubicle, cubiculum
3 **council,** conclave, *concilium* <L>, deliberative *or* advisory body, **assembly;** deliberative assembly, consultative assembly; house

champion NOUNS 1 champ <nonformal>, title-holder, world champion; **record holder,** world-record holder; laureate; medal winner, Olympic medal winner, medalist, award winner, prizeman, prizetaker, **prizewinner;** hall of famer
2 **defender, advocate; upholder; guardian angel, supporter**; vindicator, apologist; **protector**; paladin; **justifier,** proponent
VERBS 3 **safeguard, protect**; stand by the side of; **advocate,** go to bat for <nonformal>, espouse, join *or* associate oneself with, stand *or* stick up for, speak up for, contend for, speak for, argue for, urge reasons for, put in a good word for

chance NOUNS 1 happenstance, hap; **luck;** good luck *or* fortune, serendipity, happy chance, dumb luck <nonformal>, rotten *and* tough luck <both nonformal>; **fortune,** fate, **destiny,** whatever comes, *moira* <Gk>, lot; **fortuity, randomness,** fortuitousness, adventitiousness, flip of a coin, the breaks <nonformal>, run of luck, the luck of the draw, the way the cards fall, the way the cookie crumbles *or* the ball bounces <both nonformal>

heedless hap
Spenser

VERBS 2 **take chances, take a chance, risk, gamble,** hazard, press *or* push one's luck, **run the chance** *or* **risk** *or* **hazard;** risk one's neck, run a risk, go out on a limb, stick one's neck out<nonformal>, **expose oneself,** bare one's breast, lower one's guard, **lay oneself open to,** leave oneself wide open, open the door to, let oneself in for; **tempt Providence** *or* **fate,** forget the odds, **defy danger,** skate on thin ice, dance on the razor's edge, put one's head in the lion's mouth, throw caution to the wind
ADJS 3 chancy <nonformal>, dicey <Brit nonformal>, **risky** <nonformal>; **fortuitous, accidental,** aleatory

change NOUNS 1 **alteration, modification; variation,** variety, difference, diversity, diversification; **deviation,** diversion, aberrance *or* aberrancy, **divergence; switch, switchover, changeover, turn,** turnabout, about-face, **reversal,** flip-flop <nonformal>
VERBS 2 **fluctuate, vary; shift; alternate, vacillate,** oscillate, pendulate, waffle <Brit nonformal>, blow hot and cold <nonformal>; ebb and flow, wax and wane; go through phases, waver, shuffle, swing, sway, wobble, wobble about, flounder, stagger, teeter, totter, **seesaw,** back and fill, turn, blow hot and cold
3 **change over,** switch *and* switch over <both nonformal>, **shift; transform,** transmute; **change into, turn into, become,** resolve into, assimilate to, change one's tune, sing a different tune, dance to another tune

changeable ADJS **alterable,** alterative, modifiable; mutable, permutable, impermanent, transient, **transitory; variable,** checkered, ever-changing, many-sided, kaleidoscopic; **movable,** mobile, motile; plastic, malleable, rubbery, fluid; **inconstant, shifting,** uncertain, inconsistent; whimsical, **capricious, fickle**, off-again-on-again; **erratic, eccentric,** freakish; volatile, giddy, dizzy, ditzy <nonformal>, scatterbrained, mercurial, moody, flighty, impulsive, impetuous

change of life NOUNS **menopause,** climacteric, grand climacteric

channel NOUNS 1 **conduit, duct,** canal, course; **way, passage, passageway;** trough, troughway, troughing; tunnel; ditch, trench; adit; ingress, entrance; egress, exit; **stream**
2 **informant, informer, source,** news source, teller, interviewee, enlightener; the grapevine
VERBS 3 **conduct, convey,** put through; pipe, funnel, siphon; trench; direct; **guide, steer, drive, run** <nonformal>; herd, shepherd

chant NOUNS 1 **refrain,** burden, undersong, chorus, bob; versicle
VERBS 2 intone, intonate; **croon**

chaos NOUNS **formlessness,** confusion, messiness, mess, muddle, orderlessness, untidiness; **anarchy,** anarchism; **disorderliness, unruliness,** misrule, **disorder,** disruption, disorganization, confusion, **turmoil,** primal chaos, tohubohu; **turbulence, turmoil,** upset

chaotic ADJS **anarchic, anarchical,** anarchial, anarchistic; **unruly, disorderly,** disorganized; **turbulent, tumultuous, raging,** hellish, **storming,** stormy, **tempestuous,** troublous; **confused, muddled, jumbled,** in a mess

chaperon NOUNS 1 duenna; **governess;** escort
VERBS 2 **escort, conduct,** have in tow <nonformal>, marshal, **usher,** shepherd, **guide, lead; convoy,** guard; **squire,** esquire, **attend**

chaplain NOUNS **clergyman,** clergywoman, man *or* woman of the cloth, **divine, ecclesiastic, churchman, cleric,** minister, pastor, parson

chapter NOUNS **branch, organ, division,** wing, arm, offshoot, **affiliate;** lodge, post; chapel; **local**

character NOUNS 1 **letter, written character, sign, symbol,** graph, digraph, grapheme, allograph, alphabetic character *or* symbol, phonetic character *or* symbol
2 **disposition, nature, temper, temperament,** mettle, constitution, complexion *and* humor <both old>, makeup, stamp, type, stripe

characteristic NOUNS 1 **peculiarity, singularity,** particularity, specialty, individualism, **character,** nature, **trait,** quirk, point of character, bad point, good point, saving grace, redeeming feature, mannerism, keynote, trick, **feature,** distinctive feature, lineament
ADJS 2 **peculiar, singular,** single, quintessential, intrinsic, unique, qualitative, **distinctive,** marked, distinguished, notable, nameable; appropriate, proper; idiosyncratic, idiocratic, **in character, true to form**

charade NOUNS dumb show, **pantomime; riddle, conundrum**

charge NOUNS 1 **power, potency** *or* potence, prepotency, **force, might,** mightiness, **vigor,** vitality, vim, push, drive, puissance <old>
2 <nonformal> **kick,** boot, bang, belt, blast, flash, hit, jolt, large charge, rush, upper, lift; jollies
3 **injunction,** commission, **mandate**
4 **dependent, ward,** client, protégé, encumbrance; public charge, ward of the state; foster child
5 **attack, assault,** assailing, assailment; **offense, offensive; aggression;** rush, drive, push <nonformal>
6 **accusation,** accusal, finger-pointing <nonformal>, **complaint,** plaint, count, **blame, imputation,** delation, reproach, **bringing of charges,** laying of charges, bringing to book
7 **fee, dues, toll, charges, demand, exaction,** exactment, scot, shot, scot and lot; duty, tax, task; **burden,** weight, freight, cargo, load, onus
8 **electric** *or* **electrical charge,** positive charge, negative charge; live wire
VERBS 9 **exhilarate, stimulate,** hearten, galvanize, electrify, fire, build a fire under, inflame, warm, kindle, charge up, psych *or* pump up <nonformal>, rouse, arouse, act like a tonic, be a shot in the arm <nonformal>, **pep** *or* snap *or* jazz *or* zip *or* perk up <nonformal>, put pep *or* zip into it <nonformal>
10 **burden,** burthen <old>, **load,** load down *or* up, lade, cumber, **encumber, freight,** tax, handicap, hamper, saddle
11 **command, order, dictate, direct, instruct,** mandate, **bid, enjoin,** commission, call on *or* upon; issue a writ *or* an injunction
12 rush, **rush at, fly at,** run at, dash at, make a dash *or* rush at; tilt at, go full tilt at, make *or* run a tilt at, ride full tilt against; **jump off,** go over the top <nonformal>
13 **accuse,** bring accusation; **press charges, prefer** *or* **bring charges,** lay charges
14 charge to one's account, keep an account with, go on tick <nonformal>, buy on credit, buy on the cuff <nonformal>, buy on the installment plan, buy on time, put on the lay-away plan

charisma NOUNS **allure, attraction, interest, charm, glamour, appeal,** magnetism; star quality; personality, leadership, enchantment

charismatic ADJS **alluring, persuasive,**

suasive, personable, **winning,** magnetic, charming, enchanting, **attractive, magnetic**

charitable ADJS 1 philanthropic, eleemosynary; giving, generous to a fault, liberal, **generous**
2 **tolerant**, tolerating; **indulgent, lenient**, **condoning;** compassionate, sympathetic, sensitive

charity NOUNS **benevolence,** benevolentness, benevolent disposition, well-disposedness, **beneficence,** charitableness, **philanthropy; altruism,** philanthropy, philanthropism, almsgiving; **goodwill,** grace, brotherly love, Christian charity *or* love, *caritas* <L>, love of mankind, good will to *or* toward man, love, *agape* <Gk>; **generosity**; giving

charm NOUNS 1 **loveableness, likeableness,** lovability, likability, loveliness; attractiveness, desirability, agreeability; **appeal,** allurement; winsomeness, winning ways
2 **spell,** magic spell, glamour, weird *or* cantrip <both Scots>, wanga
3 **amulet, talisman, fetish,** periapt, phylactery; **voodoo, hoodoo,** juju, obeah, mumbo jumbo; **good-luck charm,** good-luck piece, **lucky piece,** rabbit's-foot, four-leaf clover, whammy <nonformal>; love charm, philter; scarab, scarabaeus, scarabee
VERBS 4 **fascinate, captivate,** becharm, spell, spellbind, cast a spell, put under a spell, **beguile, intrigue, enthrall,** infatuate, **enrapture, transport, enravish, entrance, enchant,** witch, **bewitch**

charmer NOUNS entrancer, **enchanter,** befuddler, hypnotizer, mesmerizer; **tempter, seducer, enticer,** inveigler, fascinator, tantalizer, teaser; coquette, **temptress,** enchantress, seductress, **siren;** Siren, Circe, Lorelei, Parthenope

charming ADJS **delightful, exquisite, lovely; attractive, endearing, engaging, appealing,** prepossessing, heartwarming, sexy <nonformal>, **enchanting,** bewitching, witching, entrancing, enthralling, intriguing, fascinating; **winning,** winsome, taking, fetching

chart NOUNS 1 **diagram, plot, blueprint,** graph, bar graph, pie *or* circle graph *or* chart, area graph; flow diagram, flow chart; **map**
VERBS 2 **plot; map, blueprint; diagram,** graph; map out, plot out, **lay out,** set out, mark out; lay off, mark off

chase NOUNS 1 **pursuit,** pursuing, pursuance, prosecution <old>; **quest,** seeking, hunting, searching; **following,** follow, follow-up; tracking, trailing, tracking down, dogging, shadowing, stalking; hot pursuit; hue and cry
VERBS 2 **pursue, follow,** go after *or* behind, come after *or* behind, move behind; **shadow** *and* **tail** <both nonformal>, **trail,** trail after, follow in the trail of, camp on the trail of, breathe down the neck of, follow in the wake of

chasm NOUNS **gap,** gape, **abyss,** abysm, **gulf,** void; **breach, break,** fracture, rupture

chassis NOUNS **frame,** underframe, infrastructure, **skeleton; mounting,** mount

chaste ADJS **immaculate, spotless, pure; clean,** squeaky-clean <nonformal>; guiltless, **innocent; abstinent,** abstentious, sexually abstinent, celibate

chastened ADJS **subdued, tame,** tamed, broken, housebroken, domesticated; **restrained,** constrained, limited, controlled, tempered, **softened,** hushed, quelled

chastise VERBS **correct,** rap on the knuckles, spank, turn over one's knees; **take to task,** give one a tongue-lashing, tonguelash

chastity NOUNS **virtue,** virtuousness, honor; **purity,** cleanness, cleanliness; **immaculacy,** immaculateness, spotlessness, stainlessness; sexual innocence, innocence

chat NOUNS 1 **talk,** gab *and* jaw-jaw <both nonformal>, blab, **blabber, blather,** blether, blethers <Scots>, clatter, talkee-talkee
VERBS 2 **talk,** gossip, **gab, blab, blabber, blather,** blether, clatter, twaddle, twattle, rattle, clack, natter *and* haver <both Brit>, dither

château NOUNS **villa,** *hôtel* <Fr>, **castle**

chattel NOUNS 1 **subject, vassal,** liege, liege man, liege subject, homager; **slave,** servant, chattel slave, **bondsman,** bondman, **bondslave,** theow, thrall
2 **property, properties, possessions, holdings,** havings, goods, chattels, goods and chattels, **effects,** household possessions *or* effects, lares and penates

chatter NOUNS 1 clack, clacket <nonformal>; racket; conversation; **palaver, prattle, gab** *and* jaw-jaw <both nonfor-

mal>; rapping *and* yakking *and* yakkety-yak <all nonformal>
VERBS 2 **chat, prate, prattle, patter,** palaver, **babble, gab** <nonformal>, natter <Brit>, **gabble, gibble-gabble,** tittle-tattle, **jabber,** gibber, **blab, blabber, blather,** blether, clatter, twaddle, twattle, rattle, clack
3 quake, shake, tremble, shudder, didder <Brit nonformal>; have a chill, have the cold shivers

chauvinist NOUNS 1 **patriot;** nationalist; ultranationalist; chauvin, **jingo,** jingoist; patrioteer <nonformal>, flag waver, superpatriot; **bigot, racist, sexist,** male chauvinist, male chauvinist pig *or* MCP <nonformal>, female chauvinist, womanist, **dogmatist,** fanatic
ADJS 2 **chauvinistic,** chauvinist, **jingoistic,** jingoist, jingoish, jingo

cheap ADJS 1 shoddy, trashy
2 **stingy, illiberal, ungenerous, chintzy, miserly,** save-all, **tight** *and* narrow <both nonformal>, **closefisted,** closehanded <old>, tightfisted, **penny-pinching**
3 **inexpensive,** unexpensive, **low, low-priced,** frugal, reasonable, sensible, manageable, modest, moderate, affordable, to fit the pocketbook, budget, easy, economy, economical; within means, within reach *or* easy reach; nominal, token; worth the money, well worth the money; cheap *or* good at the price, cheap at half the price
ADVS 4 **cheaply,** on the cheap <Brit nonformal>; **inexpensively,** reasonably, moderately, nominally; **at a bargain,** *à bon marché* <Fr>, for a song *or* mere song <nonformal>, for pennies *or* nickels and dimes *or* peanuts <all nonformal>

cheapen VERBS depreciate, devaluate, lower, reduce, **mark down, cut prices, cut,** slash, shave, trim, pare, underprice, knock the bottom out of <nonformal>; devalue, coarsen, vulgarize, drag in the mud; adulterate, water, water down

cheat NOUNS 1 **cheater;** two-timer <nonformal>; **swindler, defrauder,** cozener, juggler; **sharper, sharp, confidence man, confidence trickster; cardsharp,** cardsharper
2 chicanery, chicane, **skulduggery** <nonformal>, **trickery,** dodgery, pettifogging, pettifoggery, *supercherie* <Fr>, **artifice,** sleight, machination; **sharp practice, underhand dealing, foul play;** connivery, connivance, collusion, conspiracy, covin <law>

3 <nonformal> **gyp,** diddle, diddling, scam, flimflam flam, ramp <Brit>, scam, snow job, song and dance, number, bill of goods, burn, the business, dipsy-doodle, double cross, fiddle, hosing, the old army game, reaming, suckering, sting

VERBS 4 **victimize, gull,** pigeon, fudge, **swindle, defraud,** practice fraud upon, euchre, **con,** finagle, **fleece,** mulct, fob <old>, **bilk,** cozen, cog <old>, chouse, **cheat out of, do out of,** chouse out of, beguile of *or* out of; deceive; falsify

5 <nonformal> **gyp, clip, scam,** rope in, hose, shave, beat, rook, flam, flimflam, diddle, dipsy-doodle, do a number on, hustle, fuck, screw, have, pull something, pull a trick *or* stunt, give the business, ramp <Brit>, stick, sting, burn, gouge, chisel, hocus, hocus-pocus, play *or* take for a sucker, make a patsy of, do, run a game on, slicker, take for a ride

6 **be promiscuous,** sleep around *and* swing <both nonformal>; **debauch, wanton,** rake, chase women, womanize, whore, sow one's wild oats; **philander; commit adultery,** get a little on the side <nonformal>

check NOUNS 1 **restraint, constraint; control, curb,** rein, arrest, arrestation; **retardation,** deceleration, slowing down; clampdown *and* crackdown <both nonformal>, proscription, **prohibition**
2 **negotiable instrument** *or* **paper,** cheque <Brit>; blank check; bank check, teller's check; treasury check; cashier's check, certified check; traveler's check *or* banker's check
VERBS 3 look after; **check out,** scope, scope on *or* out <all nonformal>, check into, check on, check out, nose into, see into; poke about, root around *or* about, scratch around *or* about, cast about *or* around; keep under observation, spy on, have an eye out, keep an eye out, keep an eye on, keep a weather eye on, follow, tail *and* shadow <both nonformal>, stake out
4 **curb, arrest, bridle,** get under con-

trol, rein, snub, snub in; **retard,** slow down, decelerate; **cool** *and* **cool off** *and* **cool down** <all nonformal>; retrench, curtail; **hold** *or* **keep in check, hold at bay,** hold in leash, tie one down, tie one's hands
5 **verify, confirm,** test, prove, audit, **collate,** validate, check up *or* on *or* out <nonformal>, check over *or* through, **double-check,** triple-check, cross-check, recheck, check and doublecheck, check up and down

make assurance double sure
SHAKESPEARE

cheek NOUNS **brashness, impudence,** insolence; **gall** *and* brass *and* cheek *and* chutzpah <all nonformal>; **temerity,** temerariousness

cheer NOUNS 1 **cry, call, shout, yell,** hoot; **whoop, holler** <nonformal>; **hurrah;** burst of applause, peal *or* thunder of applause; **round of applause, hand, big hand; ovation,** standing ovation
2 **cheerfulness,** cheeriness, **good cheer,** cheery vein *or* mood; **happiness**; sanguinity, sanguine humor, euphoric *or* eupeptic mein
VERBS 3 **cry, call, shout, yell, holler** <nonformal>, hoot; **whoop, applaud, acclaim, hail;** clap one's hands, give a hand *or* big hand, have *or* hear a hand *or* big hand for, hear it for <nonformal>; root for <nonformal>, cheer on
4 **gladden, brighten,** put in good humor; **encourage, hearten,** pick up <nonformal>; **inspire,** inspirit, warm the spirits, **raise the spirits,** elevate one's mood, buoy up, boost, give a lift <nonformal>, put one on top of the world *and* on cloud nine <both nonformal>; do the heart good

cheerful ADJS **happy, glad, joyful, joyous,** flushed with joy, radiant, beaming, glowing, starry-eyed, sparkling, laughing, smiling, smirking, smirky, chirping, purring, singing, dancing, leaping, capering, **cheerful, gay**

cheerless ADJS **pathetic,** affecting, touching, moving, saddening, poignant; comfortless, discomforting, uncomfortable; **desolate,** dreary, joyless, dismal, bleak

cheesecake NOUNS **photograph,** pinup <nonformal>, beefcake <nonformal>

chef NOUNS **cook,** *cuisinier* or *cuisinière* <Fr>, kitchener, culinarian, culinary artist; **chief cook, head chef,** *chef de cuisine* <Fr>

cherish VERBS 1 **hold dear,** hold in one's heart *or* affections, think much *or* the world of, prize, treasure; **admire, regard,** esteem, revere; **adore, idolize,** worship, dearly love, think worlds *or* the world of, love to distraction
2 **foster, nurture,** nourish, mother, care for, lavish care on, feed, parent, rear, sustain, cultivate; take to the bosom

chestnut NOUNS **platitude, cliché, saw, old saw, commonplace, banality,** bromide, corn <nonformal>, tired phrase, trite saying, hackneyed *or* stereotyped saying; old joke

chew VERBS chew up, chaw <nonformal>, bite into; **masticate,** manducate; ruminate, chew the cud; **bite,** grind, champ, chomp <nonformal>; **munch;** gnash; nibble, **gnaw;** mouth, mumble; gum

chic NOUNS 1 **smartness,** elegance
ADJS 2 **well-dressed,** well-groomed, *soignée* or *soigné* <both Fr>, stylish, modish, well-turned, well turned-out, **smart,** elegant; style-conscious, clothes-conscious

chicanery NOUNS **trick, artifice, device,** ploy, gambit, stratagem, **scheme,** design, *ficelle* <Fr>, **subterfuge,** blind, **ruse, wile,** chouse <nonformal>, shift, **dodge,** artful dodge, sleight, pass, feint, fetch

chicken NOUNS 1 chick, chicky *and* chickabiddy <both nonformal>; **cock, rooster,** chanticleer; **hen,** biddy <nonformal>, partlet; cockerel, pullet; setting hen, brooder, broody hen; capon, poulard
2 **coward,** jellyfish, invertebrate, **weakling,** weak sister <nonformal>, milksop, milquetoast, mouse, **sissy, wimp** <nonformal>, baby, **big baby**
VERBS 3 **lose one's nerve,** lose courage, **get cold feet** <nonformal>, **show the white feather;** falter, boggle, funk <nonformal>; put one's tail between one's legs, back out, funk out <nonformal>, **wimp** *or* **chicken out** <both nonformal>
ADJS 4 **afraid, fearful;** timid, timorous, overtimorous, overtimid, rabbity *and* mousy <both nonformal>; **fainthearted,** weakhearted, chicken-hearted, henhearted, pigeonhearted; **weak-kneed,** afraid of one's shadow; weak, soft; **wimpy** *or* wimpish <nonformal>

chide VERBS **reprove, rebuke, reprimand,** reprehend, put a flea in one's ear, **scold,** rate, **admonish, upbraid,** objurgate, have words with, take a hard line with

chief NOUNS 1 **superior, boss,** honcho <nonformal>, commander, **ruler, leader,** dean, *primus inter pares* <L, first among equals>, **master**; higher-up <nonformal>, senior, principal, big shot <nonformal>; chieftain, high chief
ADJS 2 **main, principal,** paramount, **foremost,** headmost, **leading, dominant,** crowning, capital, **cardinal, first, foremost,** front, up-front <nonformal>, **head, principal,** premier, **leading, main,** flagship

chiefly ADVS **mainly, in the main,** in chief; dominantly, **predominantly; mostly, for the most part; principally, especially, particularly,** peculiarly; **primarily, in the first place,** first of all, **above all; indeed,** even, more than ever, all the more, *a fortiori* <L>; substantially, essentially, effectually, **for the most part,** almost entirely, for all practical purposes, **virtually;** approximately, nearly, all but; **broadly,** broadly speaking, **roughly,** roughly speaking, as an approximation; **usually, as a rule, ordinarily, commonly, normally,** routinely, as a matter of course, in the usual course; **by and large,** at large, altogether, overall, over the long haul <nonformal>, **all things considered,** taking one thing with another

child NOUNS **simple soul,** unsophisticate, naïf, **ingenue, innocent, babe,** baby, newborn babe, babe in the woods, babe in arms, mere child, lamb, dove, angel

childhood NOUNS babyhood, **boyhood; girlhood**

childlike ADJS **artless, ingenuous, unsophisticated, naive;** born yesterday; **innocent,** innocent as a lamb

children NOUNS **young people, youth,** young, **younger generation,** rising *or* new generation, young blood, young fry <nonformal>, *ragazze* <Ital>; tots, childkind; small fry *and* **kids** *and* **little kids** *and* little guys <all nonformal>

chill NOUNS 1 **aloofness, remoteness,** coolness, coldness, frigidity, chilliness, iciness, frostiness; cold shoulder
VERBS 2 **discourage; pour** *or* **dash** *or* **throw cold water on,** throw *or* lay a wet blanket on, damp, dampen, demotivate, **cool,** quench, blunt; **refrigerate**

chilly ADJS **aloof, standoffish,** offish, standoff, **distant, remote,** withdrawn, removed, detached, Olympian; **cool,** cold, cold-fish, frigid, icy, frosty; shivering, shivery, shaky, dithery; chilled to the bone

chime NOUNS 1 **ringing,** tintinnabulation, **pealing, chiming, tinkling,** tingling, **jingling,** dinging, donging; **ring, peal**
VERBS 2 tintinnabulate, **peal,** sound; **toll,** knell, sound a knell; **tinkle,** tingle, **jingle,** ding, dingdong, dong

china NOUNS **ceramic ware, ceramics; pottery, crockery; porcelain**

chink NOUNS **crack,** cranny, check, craze, chap, **crevice,** fissure, scissure, incision, notch, score, cut, gash, slit, split, **rift,** rent; vulnerable point, **weak link, weak point, soft spot,** heel of Achilles, chink in one's armor

chintzy ADJS **stingy, illiberal, ungenerous, miserly,** save-all, **cheap** *and* **tight** *and* narrow <all nonformal>, **near, close, closefisted,** closehanded <old>, tightfisted; messy <nonformal>, mussy <nonformal>, **sloppy** <nonformal>, scraggly, poky, seedy <nonformal>, **shabby,** shoddy, schlocky <nonformal>, lumpen, grubby <nonformal>

chip NOUNS 1 **cut,** cutting, clip, clipping, paring, shaving, rasher, snip, snippet, slice, collop, dollop, scoop
VERBS 2 split, check, craze, fissure; scale, exfoliate

chirp VERBS **stridulate;** crick, creak, chirk, cheep, peep, pip, chirrup

chivalry NOUNS chivalrousness, knightliness; military *or* martial spirit, soldierly quality *or* virtues; **gallantry,** gallantness; courtliness, courtly behavior *or* politeness; *noblesse oblige* <Fr>; errantry, knight-errantry

choice NOUNS 1 **selection, election,** preference, decision, **pick, choosing,** free choice; alternativity; co-option, co-optation; **will,** volition, free will; preoption, first choice; the pick; **discrimination**
2 **pick, select, elect, elite,** *corps d'élite* <Fr>, chosen; **cream, flower,** fat; cream of the crop, *crème de la crème* <Fr>, salt of the earth
ADJS 3 **best,** greatest *and* top-of-the-line <both nonformal>, **prime,** optimum, optimal; **select, elect,** elite, **picked,** handpicked; **prize, champion; supreme,** paramount, **unsurpassed,**

unmatched, matchless, **peerless;** quintessential

choke VERBS 1 strangle, strangulate, choke off; garrote, **throttle,** burke; **suffocate, stifle, smother, asphyxiate**
2 **overload, overfill,** stuff, crowd, cram, jam, pack, jam-pack, **congest,** constrict, squeeze, squeeze shut; stop up

choked ADJS contracted, constricted, choked off, choked up, squeezed shut, strangulated, **obstructed,** infarcted, **blocked; plugged,** plugged up; **clogged,** clogged up; choked up, strangulated, strangled; packed, jammed, bumper-to-bumper <nonformal>, jam-packed, like sardines; **congested,** stuffed up

choose VERBS **select, elect,** pick, go with <nonformal>, opt, opt for, co-opt, make *or* take one's choice, make choice of, have one's druthers <nonformal>, use *or* take up *or* exercise one's option; **shop around** <nonformal>, pick and choose

choosy ADJS **fastidious, particular, scrupulous, meticulous, conscientious,** exacting, precise, punctilious, spit-and-polish; **sensitive, discriminating**, discriminative; **selective,** picky <nonformal>, choicy <nonformal>; critical

nothing if not critical
SHAKESPEARE

chop NOUNS 1 **whack, smack, thwack,** smash, dash, swipe, swing, **punch, poke, jab,** dig, drub, thump, pelt, cut, slog
VERBS 2 **sever, dissever,** cut off *or* away *or* loose, shear off, hack through, hack off, ax, amputate; hew, hack, **slash**

choppy ADJS **rough, unsmooth; uneven, nonuniform,** irregular, ragged, erose, jerky, jagged, rough, disorderly, unsystematic; **sporadic,** patchy, spotty, scrappy, snatchy, catchy, **broken, disconnected, discontinuous**

choral ADJS **vocal,** singing; choric

chorale NOUNS **hymn,** hymn of praise, **doxology, psalm, anthem,** motet, canticle; choral fantasy, anthem

chore NOUNS 1 **task, work, stint, job,** labor, piece of work, chare, odd job; **assignment, charge,** project, errand, **mission,** commission, **duty,** service, exercise
2 **hard job, tough job** *and* heavy lift <both nonformal>, backbreaker, ballbuster <nonformal>

chorus NOUNS 1 general voice, vox pop, *vox populi* <L>, ensemble; agreement, accord, *rapport* <Fr>, concert, consort, **consonance,** unisonance, **unison,** union, oneness, harmony, one *or* single voice
2 **verse, stanza;** burden, bourdon; **refrain,** response

chosen NOUNS 1 **choice, pick, select, elect, elite,** *corps d'élite* <Fr>; cream of the crop, *crème de la crème* <Fr>, salt of the earth
ADJS 2 **selected, picked;** select, elect; handpicked, singled-out; **elected,** unanimously elected, elected by acclamation

chow NOUNS

<nonformal> **grub,** grubbery, **eats,** chuck, groceries, the nosebag, scarf *or* scoff, tuck, victuals *or* vittles

chronic ADJS **confirmed, inveterate, established,** long-established, **fixed, settled, rooted,** thorough; incorrigible, irreversible; **deep-rooted, deep-seated, infixed, ingrained,** fast

chronicle NOUNS 1 **chronology, register,** registry, record; **annals,** journal, diary; story, tale, yarn, narrative
VERBS 2 write history, historify; historicize; biograph, biography, biographize; immortalize; **record**

chronology NOUNS 1 **history, annals, chronicles,** memorabilia, record; **chronicle, register,** registry, record; journal, diary

chubby ADJS **chunky** <nonformal>, **fat,** tubby <nonformal>, dumpy; **squat,** squatty, squattish; **pudgy,** podgy

chuckle NOUNS 1 **laugh;** chortle; cackle; **snicker,** snigger, snort
VERBS 2 **laugh,** chortle; cackle; **snicker,** snigger, snort

chum NOUNS

<nonformal> **pal, buddy,** bud, buddy-boy, bosom buddy, ace, mate *and* butty <both Brit>

chummy ADJS

<nonformal> pally, palsy, palsy-walsy, buddy-buddy

chump NOUNS

<nonformal> **sucker, patsy,** pigeon, chicken, fall guy, pushover, mark, easy pickings, boob, schlemiel, sap, saphead, prize sap, easy touch, soft touch

chunk NOUNS **lump,** clump, wodge <Brit nonformal>; **bite**
chunky ADJS **stubby, thickset, stocky,** blocky, **chubby,** tubby <nonformal>, dumpy; **squat, pudgy,** podgy
churn NOUNS 1 **mixer, blender,** beater, agitator, food processor
VERBS 2 **seethe, boil, fume,** foam, simmer, stew, ferment, stir
3 whip, whisk, beat, paddle; work up, shake up, churn up, whip up, beat up; roil, rile <nonformal>
chutzpah NOUNS **impudence,** insolence; **gall** *and* brass *and* cheek <all nonformal>; hubris; **temerity,** temerariousness
cigar NOUNS seegar <nonformal>; rope *and* stinker <both nonformal>; **cheroot, stogie,** corona, belvedere, Havana, panatella, colorado, trichinopoly; cigarillo
cigarette NOUNS

<nonformal>butt, cig, **fag**, coffin nail, cancer stick

cinch NOUNS 1 sure success, foregone conclusion, sure-fire proposition <nonformal>; **winner** *and* **natural** <both nonformal>; shoo-in *and* **sure thing** *and* sure bet *and* lead-pipe cinch <all nonformal>; **snap,** pushover, breeze, waltz, duck soup, velvet, picnic, pie, cherry pie, apple pie, cakewalk, piece of cake <all nonformal>
2 VERBS **set at rest;** clinch *and* cinch *and* nail down <all nonformal>; **prove one's point,** make one's case, bring home to, make good, have *or* make out a case
cinema NOUNS **motion-picture theater, movie theater,** movie palace, dream palace <nonformal>, **motion picture, movie, film**
cipher NOUNS 1 **code; secret writing,** coded message, cryptogram, cryptograph
2 **a nobody, insignificancy,** hollow man, jackstraw <old>, **nonentity,** empty suit *and* nebbish <both nonformal>, a nothing; lightweight, mediocrity
circa ADVS **approximately,** nearly, some, about; more or less, *plus ou moins* <Fr>, by and large
circle NOUNS 1 **sphere,** hemisphere, orb, **orbit,** ambit; **clique, coterie, set,** ring, group
VERBS 2 **encircle,** ensphere, belt, belt in, zone, cincture, encincture; **girdle,** ring, band
circuit NOUNS **route, path, way, itinerary, course,** track, run, line, road; tour; walk, beat, round, **round,** revolution, **circle,** full circle, go-round, **cycle,** orbit, ambit; round trip; **network,** circuit network
circular NOUNS 1 **booklet, pamphlet, brochure, chapbook, leaflet, folder, tract**
ADJS 2 **round,** rounded, circinate, annular, annulate ring-shaped, ringlike; **circuitous, roundabout**
circulate VERBS **publish, promulgate, propagate,** circularize, **diffuse, disseminate,** distribute, **broadcast,** televise, telecast, videocast, air, **spread,** spread around *or* about, spread far and wide, publish abroad, **spread a report,** launch a rumor, whisper, **rumor about,** whisper *or* buzz about
circumference NOUNS **periphery, fringe,** outline, lineaments, border; periphery; **compass,** circumscription
circumscribe VERBS **bound,** surround, limit, enclose, divide, separate; **mark off** *or* mark out, stake out, lay off, rope off; **demarcate,** delimit, delimitate, draw *or* mark *or* set *or* lay out boundaries, circle in, hedge in, set the limit, mark the periphery; **restrict, limit, narrow, confine,** tighten
circumstance NOUNS **pomp,** pride, **state,** solemnity, formality; **pomp and circumstance,** condition, occurrence, occasion, event, **incident**
circumstantial ADJS conditional, provisional; **incidental,** occasional, contingent, adventitious, **accidental, chance,** fortuitous, casual, aleatory, unessential *or* inessential *or* nonessential
circumvent VERBS **avoid, shun, fight shy of, shy away from,** keep from, **keep away from,** keep clear of, avoid like the plague, **steer clear of** <nonformal>, skate around <Brit informal>, **give a wide berth,** keep remote from, stay detached from; get round *or* around, **evade,** stonewall <nonformal>,

elude, frustrate, foil, give the slip *or* runaround <nonformal>

circus NOUNS **amphitheater, hippodrome, coliseum,** colosseum, **stadium, bowl; carnival**

cite VERBS 1 **impeach, arraign, indict,** bring in *or* hand up an indictment, return a true bill, article, cite on several counts; book
2 **itemize, specify,** circumstantiate, particularize, **spell out, detail,** go *or* enter into detail, descend to particulars, give full particulars; instance, adduce, document, give *or* quote chapter and verse; **mention,** specify, mention in passing, touch on, **refer to,** allude to

citizen NOUNS **national,** subject; **naturalized citizen,** nonnative citizen, citizen by adoption; hyphenated American, citizen of the world

city NOUNS 1 metropolis, metro, metropolitan area, greater city, megalopolis, supercity, conurbation, urban complex, spread city, urban sprawl, urban corridor, strip city, **municipality,** *urbs* <L>, *polis* <Gk>
ADJS 2 **urban, metropolitan, municipal,** metro, burghal, **civic,** oppidan; citywide; downtown, uptown, midtown; **inner-city,** core, core-city, ghetto; small-town; boom-town

civic ADJS **public-spirited; patriotic; nationalistic; political,** politic; governmental

civil ADJS **courteous, polite, urbane, gracious,** graceful, agreeable, affable, fair; complaisant; obliging, accommodating; **thoughtful, considerate,** tactful, solicitous; respectful, deferential, attentive

civilization NOUNS **culture, society; folkways, mores,** system of values, **ethos, culture pattern**

civilized ADJS **cultivated,** cultured, **refined,** polished; **learned, erudite, educated, cultured,** cultivated, lettered, literate

civil servant NOUNS **official, officer,** officiary, functionary, *fonctionnaire* <Fr>, apparatchik; **public official,** public servant; government *or* public employee; **bureaucrat,** mandarin

claim NOUNS 1 **demand, call; requisition,** requirement, stated requirement, order; legal claim, lien
VERBS 2 **demand, ask, ask for,** make a demand; **call for,** call on *or* upon one for, appeal to one for; call out for, cry *or* cry out for, clamor for; challenge, **require; requisition,** make *or* put in requisition; **demand,** ask, exact

clairvoyance NOUNS **extrasensory perception** *or* ESP; lucidity, second sight, insight, precognition, sixth sense; intuition; foresight; premonition; clairsentience, clairaudience

clammy ADJS **sweaty,** perspiry <nonformal>; sweating, perspiring; wet with sweat, beaded with sweat, **sticky** <nonformal>; bathed in sweat, drenched with sweat; sudatory, sudoric, sudorific, diaphoretic

clamor NOUNS **outcry, vociferation;** hullabaloo, hubbub, brouhaha, **uproar; hue and cry**

clan NOUNS **people, folk, family, house, tribe, nation; caste,** race, strain, blood, kin, sept; **subdivision,** subgroup, suborder

clank NOUNS 1 **ringing,** clang, clangor, twang, twanging
VERBS 2 clank, clang, clangor, twang

clannish ADJS **exclusive,** selective, **select,** elect, elite; **cliquish, snobbish,** snobby

clap NOUNS 1 **report, crash, crack, bang,** wham, slam, clash, burst; handclap, **clapping,** handclapping, clapping of hands
VERBS 2 **crack, crash,** wham, slam, **bang,** clash; clap one's hands, give a hand *or* big hand; **poke, punch, jab,** thwack, **smack,** crack, swipe, **whack**

claque NOUNS **booster** <nonformal>, puffer, promoter; **applauder,** *claqueur* <Fr>; rooter *and* fan *and* buff <all nonformal>, adherent

clarity NOUNS **clearness; plainness, distinctness,** explicitness, definition; **lucidity,** limpidity, pellucidity, crystal *or* crystaline clarity, crystallinity, perspicuity, transpicuity, transparency; **simplicity,** straightforwardness, directness, unequivocalness, unambiguousness

clash NOUNS 1 **jangle, jar; noise,** mere noise, confusion *or* conflict *or* jarring *or* jostling of sounds; jangle, clashing; **fight, battle, fray,** affray, combat, action, conflict, **brush, skirmish,** scrimmage; tussle, **scuffle, struggle,** scramble, shoving match; exchange of blows, *passage d'armes* <Fr>, passage at *or* of arms, clash of arms; **quarrel**
VERBS 2 **jangle, clash, jar;** conflict, collide, fight, jostle; **disagree, differ,** vary, not see eye-to-eye, be at cross-pur-

poses, tangle assholes <nonformal>, **disaccord**, jostle, collide

clasp NOUNS 1 **grasp, grip, hug, embrace,** bear hug; tight grip, iron grip, grip of iron *or* steel
VERBS 2 hug, embrace; cling, cling to, cleave to, stick to, adhere to, freeze to; **hold on to,** hold fast *or* tight, hang on to, keep a firm hold upon; **enfold,** bosom, embosom, put *or* throw one's arms around, take to *or* in one's arms, press to the bosom

class NOUNS 1 **social class, economic class,** social group *or* grouping, status group, accorded status, social category, order, grade, caste, estate, rank; **status, social status, economic status,** socioeconomic status *or* background, standing, footing, prestige, rank, ranking, place, station, position, level, degree, stratum; **category, group,** grouping, bracket, pigeonhole
2 **goodness, excellence, quality,** class <nonformal>; **virtue,** grace; **merit,** desert; **value, worth**
VERBS 3 **classify,** assign, designate; **categorize,** type, put down as, **pigeonhole,** place, **group, arrange**, range; **order**, rank, rate

classic ADJS 1 **model, exemplary,** precedential, typical, paradigmatic, representative, standard, normative; ideal
2 classic *or* classical, Attic, restrained, understated, unobtrusive, quiet, subdued, simple, unaffected; masterly, masterful, expert, proficient; **consummate,** quintessential, archetypical, exemplary, model

classification NOUNS **categorization,** classing, placement, ranging, **pigeonholing, sorting, grouping; grading,** stratification, ranking, rating, classing; division, subdivision; **cataloging,** codification, tabulation, rationalization, indexing, filing; **taxonomy,** typology; analysis, **arrangement**

classify VERBS class, **categorize,** catalog, sort, sort out, sift, group, factor, winnow, thrash out; weigh, weigh up, **evaluate, judge,** gauge, assess, appraise

classy ADJS **high-toned,** tony <both nonformal>, **fancy, dapper,** dashing, jaunty, braw <Scots>; sharp *and* spiffy *and* nifty *and* snazzy <all nonformal>

clean VERBS 1 **cleanse, purge,** deterge, depurate; **purify,** lustrate; sweeten, **freshen;** whiten, bleach; clean up *or* out, clear out, sweep out, clean up after; houseclean, clean house, spring-clean; spruce, **tidy**; scavenge; **wipe,** wipe up *or* out, wipe off; dust, dust off; steam-clean, **dry-clean, wash,** launder
ADJS 2 **pure; immaculate, spotless,** stainless, white, fair, dirt-free, soil-free; **unsoiled, unsullied,** unmuddied, unsmirched, unbesmirched, unblotted, unsmudged, unstained, untarnished, **unspotted,** unblemished; **unpolluted,** nonpolluted, untainted, unadulterated; **sqeaky-clean** *and* clean as a whistle *or* a new penny *or* a hound's tooth <all nonformal>

clean up VERBS 1 **make money;** rake it in *and* coin money *and* make a bundle *or* pile *or* killing *or* mint *and* clean up <all nonformal>
2 tidy, **tidy up,** neaten, trim, **put in trim,** trim up, trig up <chiefly Brit>, **straighten up,** fix up <nonformal>, police *and* police up <both nonformal>

clear VERBS 1 **extricate, free, release,** get out; **disengage,** disentangle, untangle, unsnarl, unravel, disentwine, disinvolve, unknot, disembarrass, disembroil; dislodge
2 **profit, make** *or* **draw** *or* **realize** *or* **reap profit, come out ahead, make money;** realize; make a fast *or* quick buck <nonformal>
3 **acquit, exculpate, exonerate, absolve,** give absolution, bring in *or* return a verdict of not guilty; **vindicate,** justify; **pardon, excuse, forgive;** remit, grant remission, remit the penalty of
ADJS 4 **distinct, plain, obvious, evident, patent,** unmistakable, not to be mistaken, much in evidence, plain to be seen, for all to see, showing for all to see, plain as a pikestaff, plain as the nose on one's face, plain as day, clear as day, plain as plain can be, big as life and twice as ugly; **crystal-clear,** clear as crystal, clear as day
5 **transparent,** transpicuous, light-pervious; show-through, see-through, peekaboo, revealing; **lucid,** pellucid, limpid

clearance NOUNS 1 **latitude, scope, room,** range, way, field, maneuvering space *or* room, room to swing a cat <nonformal>; **margin, space,** open space *or* field, elbowroom, breathing space, **leeway** <nonformal>
2 **authorization, authority, sanction, licensing,** countenance, **warrant,** war-

ranty, fiat; empowerment, security clearance

clear-cut ADJS **definite,** defined, well-defined, clean-cut, crisp; **direct, literal;** simple, **straightforward; explicit, express; unmistakable, unequivocal,** univocal, unambiguous, unconfused

clearing NOUNS opening up, unstopping, uncorking, throwing open, laying open, broaching, cutting through; **gap,** gape, yawn, hiatus, lacuna, gat, space, interval; **clearance,** clearage

clearly ADVS 1 **distinctly,** with clarity *or* crystal clarity, **plainly,** obviously, patently, definitely, unmistakably; conspicuously, undisguisedly, unconcealedly, prominently, pronouncedly, glaringly, starkly, staringly; **positively, decidedly,** manifestly, unambiguously, decisively, distinctly, patently, **obviously,** visibly, audibly, unquestionably, observably, **noticeably,** demonstrably, sensibly, quite

clear up VERBS **clarify, elucidate,** clear the air, **cover** *and* cover the waterfront *or* the territory <all nonformal>, **make clear,** make plain; **illuminate,** enlighten, **shed** *or* **throw light upon**

cleft NOUNS **crack,** cranny, chink, check, craze, chap, **crevice,** fissure, scissure, incision, notch, score, cut, gash, slit, split, **rift,** rent
2 **breach, break, rupture, schism, split, rift, disunity, disunion, disruption,** separation, cleavage, divergence, division

clemency NOUNS **leniency** *or* lenience, lenientness, lenity; clementness, **mercifulness,** mercy, **humaneness,** humanity, pity, **compassion**

clench VERBS **hold, grip, grasp, clutch,** clip, **clinch; clasp, hug, embrace; cling, cling to,** cleave to, stick to, adhere to, freeze to; **hold on to,** hold fast *or* tight, keep a firm hold upon

clergy NOUNS **ministry,** the cloth; clerical order, clericals; **priesthood;** priestery; presbytery; prelacy; Sacred College; rabbinate

clerical ADJS **ecclesiastic, ecclesiastical, churchly; ministerial,** sacerdotal, **pastoral; priestly,** priestish; episcopal, episcopalian; canonical; rabbinic, rabbinical

clever ADJS 1 **skillful, cute** *and* slick *and* slick as a whistle <all nonformal>, neat; **canny, shrewd,** knowing, sharp, razor-sharp, cute *or* cutesy *or* cutesy-poo <nonformal>, acute, astute
2 smart, brilliant, scintillating, sparkling, sprightly; keen, sharp, rapier-like, pungent, pointed, biting, mordant

cliché NOUNS 1 **platitude, saw, old saw, commonplace, banality,** bromide, **chestnut** <nonformal>, corn <nonformal>, triticism <old>, tired phrase, trite saying, hackneyed *or* stereotyped saying, *lieu commun* <Fr>, *locus communis* <L>, **familiar tune** *or* **story, old song** *or* **story,** twice-told tale
ADJS 2 banal, tired, trite, tritical <old>, **platitudinous**

client NOUNS **advisee,** counselee; **customer, patron**

cliff NOUNS **precipice, sheer** *or* yawning cliff *or* precipice *or* drop, steep, bluff, wall, face, scar; crag, craig <Scots>; scarp, **escarpment; palisade,** palisades

climate NOUNS **weather,** clime; **the elements,** forces of nature; microclimate, macroclimate; mental *or* intellectual climate, spiritual climate, moral climate, mores, norms, climate of opinion

climax NOUNS 1 **crucial moment,** critical moment, loaded *or* charged moment, decisive moment, kairotic moment, kairos, pregnant moment, defining moment, turning point, climax, **moment of truth,** crunch *and* when push comes to shove <both nonformal>, when the balloon goes up <Brit nonformal>; **orgasm,** sexual climax
VERBS 2 **come,** achieve satisfaction, achieve *or* reach orgasm; **ejaculate,** get off <nonformal>; **culminate,** consummate

climb NOUNS 1 **ascent,** climbing, upclimb, anabasis, clamber, escalade
VERBS 2 climb up, upclimb, **mount,** clamber, **clamber up,** scramble *or* scrabble up, claw one's way up, struggle up, inch up, shin, shinny *or* shin up <nonformal>, work *or* inch one's way up, climb the ladder; **scale,** escalade, scale the heights

clinch VERBS 1 **hold, grip, grasp, clutch,** clip, **clench; clasp, hug, embrace; cling, cling to,** cleave to, stick to, adhere to, freeze to; **hold on to,** hold fast *or* tight, hang on to, keep a firm hold upon
2 **make sure, make certain,** make sure of, make no doubt; lock in *and* nail down *and* clinch *and* cinch <all nonformal>

cling VERBS **hold, cling to,** cleave to, stick to, adhere to, freeze to; **hold on to,** hold fast *or* tight, hang on to, keep a firm hold upon; **hold on, hang on** <nonformal>, hold on like a bulldog, stick like a leech; **cohere, adhere, stick,** cleave, hold; hug, embrace, clinch

clip NOUNS 1 **extract,** film clip, outtake, sound bite <nonformal>
VERBS 2 **cut off** *or* **away,** shear *or* take *or* strike *or* knock *or* lop off, truncate; **amputate,** mutilate, abscind; **prune,** pare, peel, crop, bob, dock, lop, nip, shear
3 **overcharge; hold up** *and* **soak** *and* **stick** *and* **sting** *and* **clip** <all nonformal>, **make pay through the nose, gouge**

clique NOUNS **coterie, set, circle,** ring, junto, junta, cabal, camarilla, **clan,** group; cadre, inner circle; closed *or* charmed circle; ingroup, we-group; elite, elite group; leadership group; **old-boy network**

clobber VERBS **best, beat, beat out, defeat**; beat all hollow <nonformal>, trounce, take to the cleaners *and* smoke *and* skin *and* skin alive <all nonformal>, worst, whip *and* lick *and* have it all over *and* cut down to size <all nonformal>

clock NOUNS 1 horologe, horologium; Big Ben, ticker <nonformal>, **watch,** turnip; **timepiece,** timekeeper, **timer, chronometer**
VERBS 2 **time, fix** *or* **set the time,** mark the time; **keep time,** mark time, measure time, beat time

clod NOUNS 1 **lump,** clump, **hunk** *and* **chunk** <both nonformal>, wodge <Brit nonformal>; **mass,** piece, **gob** *and* glob <both nonformal>, gobbet
2 **bungler,** clodhopper, clodknocker, yokel; clot <Brit>, **dolt,** blockhead; awkward squad; **oaf, lout,** boor, lubber, oik <Brit>, **gawk,** gawky, **lummox,** yokel, rube, hick, hayseed, bumpkin

clog NOUNS 1 **obstruction, block,** blockade, sealing off, **blockage,** strangulation, choking, choking off, **stoppage,** stop, **bar, barrier, obstacle,** impediment; **bottleneck,** chokepoint; **congestion,** jam, traffic jam, gridlock
VERBS 2 **obstruct, bar,** stay; **block,** block up; clog up, foul; **choke,** choke up *or* off; **congest,** stuff up; **plug,** plug up; constipate, obstipate, bind

cloister NOUNS 1 **monastery, house, abbey,** friary; priory, priorate; lamasery; **convent, nunnery**
VERBS 2 **confine, immure;** pen, coop, pound <old>, crib, mew, cage, cage in, encage

clone NOUNS 1 **duplicate, duplication; double,** cookie-cutter copy
VERBS 2 **reproduce,** copy, reduplicate, **duplicate,** ditto <nonformal>; replicate

close NOUNS 1 **completion,** completing, **finish,** finishing, **conclusion, end,** ending, **termination,** terminus, cessation, **windup** <nonformal>, topping off, wrapping up, wrap-up, finalization
VERBS 2 **shut,** occlude; close up, shut up, contract, constrict, strangle, strangulate, choke, choke off, squeeze, squeeze shut; put *or* slap the lid on, **cover; shut the door; end, terminate,** determine, close out, close the books on, phase out *or* down, **finish, conclude,** finish with, resolve, finish *or* wind up <nonformal>; **put an end to,** put a period to, put paid to <Brit>, put *or* lay to rest, **make an end of,** bring to an end
ADJS 3 **stuffy, airless,** breathless, breezeless, windless; **oppressive, stifling, suffocating;** stirless, unstirring, not a breath of air, not a leaf stirring
4 **tight, confined,** constricted; **cramped;** intimate, cheek-by-jowl, side-by-side, hand-in-hand, arm-in-arm, *bras-dessus-bras-dessous* <Fr>
5 **imminent, near,** immediate, instant, soon to be, **at hand,** near at hand, close at hand; **in the offing,** on the horizon, **in prospect, in the wind,** in the cards <nonformal>
ADVS 6 **near, nigh;** hard, at close quarters; **nearby, close by,** hard by, fast by, not far *or* far off, in the vicinity *or* **neighborhood of,** at hand, at close range, **near** *or* **close at hand; within reach** *or* **range,** a stone's throw away

closed-minded ADJS **unpersuadable,** positive; dogmatic; **narrow-minded,** narrow, narrow-gauged, closed, cramped, constricted; provincial, insular, parochial

closemouthed ADJS **secretive,** close-lipped, secret, close, dark; discreet; evasive, shifty; **uncommunicative**

close shave NOUNS **narrow escape,** hair-breadth escape, **close call** <nonformal>, **near miss,** near go *or* thing <Brit nonformal>, near *or* narrow squeak <Brit

nonformal>, close *or* tight squeeze <nonformal>, squeaker <nonformal>

closet NOUNS 1 clothes closet, wardrobe, cloakroom; checkroom; linen closet
VERBS 2 **confine, immure;** cramp, straiten, encase; cloister, cabin, crib
ADJS 3 **secret,** close, closed; unuttered, unrevealed, undivulged, undisclosed, unspoken, untold; undisclosable, unbreatheable, unutterable

closure NOUNS **completion, fulfillment, consummation,** culmination, perfection, realization, actualization, **accomplishment**

clot VERBS **thicken,** thick <old>; inspissate, incrassate; **congeal, coagulate,** set, concrete; **curdle,** curd, clabber, lopper <nonformal>; cake, lump, clump, cluster, knot

cloth NOUNS **material, fabric, textile,** textile fabric, texture, tissue, stuff, weave, weft, woof, web, **material, goods,** *étoffe, tissu* <both Fr>

clothe VERBS enclothe, **dress, garb, attire,** tire, array, **apparel,** raiment, garment, habilitate, **tog** *and* tog out <both nonformal>, dud <nonformal>, robe, enrobe, invest, endue, **deck,** bedeck, dight, rag out *or* up <nonformal>

clothes NOUNS **clothing, apparel, wear, wearing apparel, daywear, dress,** dressing, **raiment,** garmenture, **garb, attire, array,** habit, habiliment, fashion, style, guise, **costume,** costumery, gear, fig *or* full fig <both Brit>, toilette, trim, bedizenment; **garments,** robes, robing, rags <nonformal>, drapery, finery, feathers; toggery *or* togs *or* **duds** *or* threads <all nonformal>

cloud NOUNS high fog; fleecy cloud, cottony cloud, billowy cloud; haze, fog, mist

islands on a dark-blue sea
SHELLEY

cloudless ADJS **clear,** serene; unclouded, unobscured

cloud nine NOUNS **bliss,** blissfulness; paradise, heaven, seventh heaven

cloudy ADJS nebulous, nubilous, nimbose, nebulosus; **clouded,** overclouded, **overcast;** dirty, heavy, lowering *or* louring; dark; **gloomy**; cloud-flecked; cirrous, cirrose; cumulous, cumuliform, stratous, stratiform

clout NOUNS **influence,** influentiality; **power**, force, potency, pressure, effect, indirect *or* incidental power, **say,** the final say, the last word, say-so *and* a lot to do with *or* to say about <all nonformal>, veto power; **weight,** moment, consequence, importance, eminence

clown NOUNS 1 **bungler, blunderer,** blunderhead, boggler, slubberer, bumbler, **fumbler, botcher;** oaf, gawk, boor, **clod,** clot <Brit>, **dolt,** blockhead; **fool, damn fool,** tomfool, perfect fool, born fool
2 **buffoon,** *buffo* <Ital>, **fool, jester, zany, merry-andrew,** jack-pudding, pickle-herring, **motley fool,** motley, wearer of the cap and bells; harlequin
VERBS 3 **be foolish;** be stupid; **act** *or* **play the fool; fool** *or* **horse around** <nonformal>, dick around <nonformal>, clown around; **make a fool of oneself,** make a monkey of oneself <nonformal>, play the buffoon

club NOUNS 1 **haunt,** purlieu, **hangout** <nonformal>, **stamping ground** <nonformal>; gathering place, rallying point, meeting place, clubhouse; casino, gambling house; country club
2 **rod, stick, switch; paddle,** ruler, ferule, pandybat
3 **fellowship, brotherhood, fraternity,** confraternity, confrerie, fraternal order *or* society; **sisterhood, sorority**
VERBS 4 cudgel, blackjack, sandbag, cosh <Brit>

clue NOUNS **cue, key,** tip-off <nonformal>, telltale, smoking gun <nonformal>, straw in the wind; **trace, vestige, spoor,** scent, whiff; **lead** *and* hot lead <both nonformal>; **hint,** gentle hint, **intimation, indication, suggestion, mere** *or* **faint suggestion, suspicion, inkling,** whisper

clump NOUNS 1 **bunch, cluster,** knot; tuft, wisp; tussock, hassock; shock
VERBS 2 **congeal, coagulate, clot,** set, concrete; **curdle,** curd, clabber, lopper <nonformal>; cake, lump, cluster, knot

clumsy ADJS **awkward, uncoordinated,** maladroit, unhandy, left-hand, left-handed, heavy-handed, ham-handed <nonformal>, ham-fisted *and* cack-handed <both Brit nonformal>, clumsy-fisted, butterfingered <nonformal>, **all thumbs**

clunk NOUNS 1 **thud,** dull thud; **thump,** flump, crump, clop, clump, plunk, tunk, plump, bump

VERBS 2 **thud, thump,** clop, clump, plunk, flump, crump

cluster NOUNS 1 **bunch, group,** grouping, groupment, crop, **clump,** knot; **batch, lot,** slew <nonformal>, **mess** <nonformal>; agglomeration, bunch, mass, clot
VERBS 2 **come together, assemble, congregate, collect,** come from far and wide; muster, **meet, gather, forgather,** gang up <nonformal>, mass; bunch, bunch up, clot, clump; gather around, gang around <nonformal>

clutch NOUNS 1 **hold, purchase, grasp, grip, clamp, clinch, clench;** seizure; **clasp, hug, embrace,** bear hug; firm hold, tight grip, iron grip, grip of iron *or* steel, death grip
2 **predicament, pinch, bind,** pass, situation, emergency; pretty pass, nice *or* pretty predicament, pretty *or* fine state of affairs, **sorry plight; complication,** imbroglio
VERBS 3 **hold, grip, grasp,** clip, **clinch, clench; clasp, hug, embrace; cling, cling to,** cleave to, stick to, adhere to, freeze to; **hold on to,** hold fast *or* tight, hang on to, keep a firm hold upon

clutter NOUNS 1 **jumble, litter, hodgepodge**, rat's nest, mare's nest, hurrah's nest <nautical>
VERBS 2 **litter,** scatter, crowd, jam, pack, overwhelm, overflow

coach NOUNS 1 trainer, instructor, mentor, teacher; **tutor,** tutorer; coacher; athletic coach
VERBS 2 **instruct,** guide, direct, **tutor; prime, cram** <nonformal>

coagulate VERBS **congeal, clot; cluster,** mass, bunch; **thicken,** inspissate, incrassate, curdle, clot, clabber *and* lopper <both nonformal>

coalition NOUNS **front, movement,** political front; popular front, people's front, grass-roots movement, ground swell; **alliance, league, union;** council; **bloc,** axis

coarse ADJS **gross, rude, crude, crass,** offensive, crass, loutish, nasty, raw, rough, **earthy;** ribald; raunchy <nonformal>, **obscene**; meretricious, **loud** <nonformal>, **gaudy**

coast NOUNS 1 **shore,** *côte* <Fr>; **strand,** *playa* <Sp>, **beach,** beachfront, plage, lido, riviera, sands, berm; **waterfront;** shoreline, coastline; **seashore, seacoast, seaside, seaboard,** seabeach, seacliff, seabank, sea margin, oceanfront, oceanside, seafront, seaside, shorefront, coastland, littoral
VERBS 2 **glide, skim,** sweep, flow; **slide,** slip, skid, skitter, sideslip, slither, glissade
3 **not lift a finger** *or* **hand, sit back, sit on one's hands** *or* ass *or* dead ass *or* butt *or* duff <nonformal>, sit on the sidelines, drift, lay down on the job <nonformal>, idle; **take it easy,** take things as they come, go with the flow, eat the bread of idleness, lie *or* rest on one's oars

coat NOUNS 1 **overcoat,** greatcoat, **topcoat,** surcoat; raincoat, slicker
VERBS 2 **cover,** spread on, **spread with;** smear, **smear on,** besmear, slap on, dab, daub, bedaub, plaster, beplaster; flow on, pour on; lay on, lay it on thick, slather; undercoat, prime

coax VERBS **urge,** wheedle, cajole, blandish, plead with, sweet-talk and soft-soap <both nonformal>, exhort, call on or upon, advocate, recommend, put in a good word, buck for and hype <both nonformal>

cobweb NOUNS **filament; web,** gossamer, spider *or* spider's web

cocaine NOUNS

<nonformal> basuco, bernice, big C, blow, C, charlie, coke, crack, crack cocaine, jumps, dust, flake, girl, gold dust, her, jay, joy powder, lady, lady snow, nose candy, snow, star dust, toot, white, white girl, white lady

cockeyed ADJS **cross-eyed,** swivel-eyed <nonformal>, goggle-eyed, bug-eyed *and* popeyed <both nonformal>, **walleyed;** askance, askant, asquint, squinting; in disorder, skewgee *and* slaunchways *and* skygodlin <all nonformal>; **silly,** knocked silly; **groggy** <nonformal>, **dopey** <nonformal>, woozy <nonformal>

cocksure ADJS **confident, convinced,** persuaded, positive; **unhesitating,** unfaltering, unwavering; **undoubting**; **self-confident, self-assured, self-reliant,** sure of oneself; poised; unafraid

cocktail NOUNS **drink,** mixed drink; *apéritif* <Fr>

cocky ADJS **conceited,** big-headed *and* too big for one's shoes *or* britches *and* biggety <all nonformal>, jumped-up <chiefly Brit nonformal>; **impudent,** bumptious, cheeky *and* **fresh** *and* facy *and* crusty *and* nervy <all nonformal>; **saucy,** sassy <nonformal>; smart *or* smart-alecky <nonformal>, smart-ass *or* wise-ass <nonformal>

coddle VERBS **pamper,** cosset, mollycoddle, pet, make a lap dog of, **spoil;** spare the rod

code NOUNS 1 **canon, maxim,** dictum, moral, moralism; **norm, standard;** formula, form; rule of action *or* conduct, moral precept; ethical *or* moral code, **ethic,** code of morals *or* ethics, ethical system, value system, axiology
VERBS 2 encode, encipher, cipher

codify VERBS **classify,** rationalize, **index; normalize, standardize, regularize;** formalize

coerce VERBS use violence, ride roughshod, intimidate, bully, bludgeon, blackjack; bully, cow, bulldoze <nonformal>, walk over, walk all over; keep down, hold *or* keep a tight hand upon, rule with a rod of iron, rule with an iron hand *or* fist; compel

cogent ADJS striking, telling, effective, impactful, valid, operative, in force; **relevant, pertinent,** appertaining, **germane, apposite,** material, admissible, applicable, applying, pertaining, belonging, involving, appropriate, **apropos,** *à propos* <Fr>, to the purpose, **to the point,** in point, *ad rem* <L>; weighty, authoritative

cognizant ADJS **knowing,** knowledgeable, informed; **conscious, aware, mindful, sensible; perceptive,** insightful, apperceptive, percipient, perspicacious, appercipient

coherent ADJS **clear, crystal-clear,** clear as crystal, clear as day, clear as the nose on one's face; **plain, distinct,** microscopically distinct, plain as pikestaffs; defined, well-defined, **clear-cut,** clean-cut; connected, consistent

cohesive ADJS cohering, coherent; adhering, **sticking, clinging,** inseparable, cleaving, holding together; **indivisible,** nondivisible, undividable, **inseparable,** indissoluble; unified

cohort NOUNS **henchman,** hanger-on, buddy *and* sidekick <both nonformal>; **accomplice,** confederate, fellow conspirator, coconspirator, partner *or* accomplice in crime

coiffure NOUNS **hairdo, hairstyle, haircut,** coif, headdress; wave; marcel, marcel wave; **permanent,** permanent wave

coil NOUNS **whorl,** roll, **curl,** curlicue, ringlet, pigtail, **spiral,** helix, volute, volution, involute, evolute, gyre, scroll; **kink, twist, twirl;** screw, corkscrew; tendril, cirrus; whirl, swirl, vortex

coin NOUNS 1 **specie,** hard money; piece, piece of money, piece of silver *or* gold
VERBS 2 **mint; counterfeit, forge**
3 innovate, invent, **make from scratch *or* from the ground up, new-mint, mint, inaugurate; neologize, neoterize**

coincide VERBS 1 **correspond,** agree, chime with, match, tally, go hand in glove with, twin
2 co-occur, concur; **coexist;** coextend; **synchronize,** isochronize, put *or* be in phase, be in time, keep time, time; contemporize; **accompany, agree,** match, go along with, go hand in hand, keep pace with, keep in step

coitus NOUNS **copulation, sex act,** having sex, having intercourse, *le sport* <Fr>, coupling, mating, coition, pareunia, venery, copula <law>, **sex, intercourse, sexual intercourse,** cohabitation, commerce, sexual commerce, congress, sexual congress, sexual union, sexual relations, relations, marital relations, marriage act, act of love, sleeping together *or* with; screwing *and* balling *and* nookie *and* diddling *and* making it with <all nonformal>

making the beast with two backs
SHAKESPEARE

colander NOUNS **filter; strainer, sifter, sieve, screen,** riddle, cribble, bolter, grate, grating

cold ADJS 1 **cool, chill,** nippy, crisp, brisk, sharp
2 **freezing;** frigid, icy, **shivering,** shivery, shaky, dithery; algid, aguish, aguey; **frozen**, half-frozen, frozen to death, chilled to the bone, blue with cold

3 <nonformal> **cold as hell,** cold as a welldigger's ass, cold as a witch's tit *or* kiss, cold enough to freeze the tail *or* balls off a brass monkey, cold as a bastard *or* a bitch, colder than hell *or* the deuce *or* the devil

4 **unfeeling, unemotional,** nonemotional, emotionless, affectless, emotionally dead *or* numb *or* paralyzed, anesthetized, drugged, narcotized; **unpassionate, frigid, unresponsive,** unresponding, **unsympathetic**
5 **aloof, standoffish, distant, remote,** withdrawn, removed, detached, Olympian; inaccessible, unapproachable; **unfriendly, inimical, uncordial,** unsociable

cold feet NOUNS weak knees, **faintheart,** chicken heart, **yellow streak** <nonformal>, white feather

coldhearted ADJS **unfeeling, unemotional,** nonemotional, emotionless, affectless, emotionally dead *or* numb *or* paralyzed, anesthetized, drugged, narcotized; passionless, **spiritless, heartless,** soulless; lukewarm, Laodicean; **cold, cool, frigid,** frozen, chill, chilly, arctic, frosty, frosted, icy, **cold-blooded,** cold as charity

cold shoulder NOUNS **aloofness, standoffishness,** offishness, withdrawnness, **remoteness,** distance, detachment; **repulse, rebuff; dismissal,** snub, spurning, brush-off, cut; kiss-off <nonformal>; turn-off <nonformal>; **ostracism,** ostracization, thumbs-down, thumbing-down, *pollice verso* <L>, blackballing, silent treatment, sending to Coventry

cold turkey NOUNS **withdrawal, withdrawal sickness,** withdrawal syndrome, withdrawal symptoms, bogue *and* coming down *and* crash <both nonformal>, abrupt withdrawal *and* cold turkey <both nonformal>; **detoxification** *or* detox <nonformal>, drying out, taking the cure

colicky ADJS **aching,** achy, **throbbing;** stomachachy, griping

collaborate VERBS 1 **cooperate,** do business *and* **play ball** <both nonformal>, coact, concur; concert, harmonize, concord; be in league, **go into partnership with,** go partners <nonformal>, go *or* be in cahoots with; **work together,** get together *and* team up *and* buddy up <all nonformal>, work as a team, act together, act in concert, **pull together; hold together, hang together,** keep together, **stand together,** stand shoulder to shoulder
2 **act the traitor,** turn against, go over to the enemy, turn one's coat, sell oneself, sell out <nonformal>; fraternize

collaborator NOUNS 1 **subversive; saboteur, fifth columnist, collaborationist,** fraternizer; fifth column, underground; Trojan horse
2 cooperator; coauthor; **collaborationist**

collapse NOUNS **breakdown, crackup** <nonformal>, **prostration,** exhaustion, cave-in; nervous prostration *or* breakdown *or* exhaustion, neurasthenia; circulatory collapse
2 **defeat; fall, downfall,** smash, crash, **undoing, ruin,** debacle, derailing, derailment; **destruction**; deathblow, quietus; Waterloo; failure; **insolvency, bankruptcy,** receivership, **failure;** bust <nonformal>
VERBS 3 **weaken,** crumble, go to pieces, disintegrate; go downhill, hit the skids <nonformal>, give way, break, cave in <nonformal>, **break down, founder;** crash <nonformal>, cave *or* fall in, come crashing *or* tumbling down, topple, totter, sway
4 **go bankrupt, go broke** <nonformal>, go into receivership, become insolvent *or* bankrupt, **fail,** break, bust <nonformal>, crash, **fold, fold up,** belly up *and* go up *and* go belly up *and* **go under** <all nonformal>, shut down, shut one's doors, go out of business, **be ruined,** go to ruin, go on the rocks, go to the wall

collapsible ADJS **contractive, compressible,** condensable, reducible; foldable; deflationary

collar NOUNS 1 **arrest,** arrestment, arrestation, pinch *and* bust <nonformal>; **capture, apprehension, seizure,** netting <nonformal>
VERBS 2 **capture, apprehend, collar** <nonformal>, run down, run to earth, **nab** <nonformal>, grab <nonformal>, lay by the heels, take prisoner; **arrest,** place *or* put under arrest, take into custody; pick up *or* take in *or* run in <all nonformal>

colleague NOUNS **associate, confederate,** consociate, fellow member, **companion, fellow,** bedfellow, **crony,** consort, cohort, compeer, compatriot, confrere, brother, brother-in-arms, **ally,** adjunct, coadjutor; comrade in arms, **comrade, partner**

collect VERBS **gather, glean, pick, pluck,** cull, **take up,** pick up, get *or* gather in, gather to oneself, bring *or* get together, scrape together; heap up, amass, assemble, accumulate

collection NOUNS 1 **gathering,** gleaning, bringing together, assembling, putting *or* piecing together, **accumulation,** cumulation, **amassment,** heaping up, grubbing
2 **donation,** donative; **contribution, subscription; alms,** pittance, **charity, dole, handout** <nonformal>, alms fee, widow's mite; Peter's pence; **offering,** offertory, votive offering
3 **compilation,** omnibus; collectanea, miscellany; collected works, *œuvres* <Fr>, canon; **miscellanea,** analects; chrestomathy, delectus; **anthology,** *Festschrift* <Ger>
4 collector's items, collectibles; **holdings,** fund, treasure; collectanea

collective bargaining NOUNS **negotiation, bargaining, haggling,** higgling, **dickering, chaffering,** chaffer, haggle; hacking out *or* working out *or* hammering out a deal, coming to terms; package bargaining, pattern bargaining

collector NOUNS gatherer, accumulator, connoisseur, fancier, enthusiast, pack rat *and* magpie <both nonformal>

college NOUNS **university,** institution of higher education *or* learning, degree-granting institution; academe, academia, the groves of Academe, **the campus,** the halls of learning *or* ivy, ivied halls; alma mater

collegiate ADJS **scholastic, academic,** institutional, **school,** classroom; **university;** intercollegiate, extramural; intramural

collide VERBS come into collision, be on a collision course, **clash,** meet, encounter, confront each other, impinge; percuss, concuss; **bump, hit, strike, run into, bump into,** bang into, slam into, smack into, **crash into, impact,** smash into, dash into, carom into; rear-end; **sideswipe** <nonformal>; **crash,** smash, crump, whomp; smash up *or* crack up *or* crunch <all nonformal>

collision NOUNS **crash, crack-up,** prang <Brit nonformal>; **impact, clash,** appulse, **encounter,** meeting, impingement, **bump, crash,** crump, whomp; **carom,** carambole, cannon; sideswipe <nonformal>; smash *and* crunch <both nonformal>

colloquial ADJS **vernacular, conversational, unliterary, nonformal,** demotic, spoken, vulgar, vulgate

collusion NOUNS **chicanery,** connivery, connivance, conspiracy, covin <law>; **intrigue,** web of intrigue, **plot, scheme,** deep-laid plot *or* scheme, underplot, game *or* little game <both nonformal>, trick, stratagem, finesse; counterplot; **conspiracy,** confederacy, covin, complot <old>, cabal; **complicity,** finagling <nonformal>, machination, manipulation

cologne NOUNS **toilet water,** Florida water; rose water, *eau de rose* <Fr>; lavender water, *eau de lavande* <Fr>; *eau de jasmin* <Fr>; cologne water, eau de Cologne; bay rum

color NOUNS 1 **hue; tint,** tinct, tincture, **tinge, shade, tone,** cast; key; **coloring, coloration; colorfulness,** bright color, pure color; coloring, colorant, tinction, tincture, **pigment, stain**
VERBS 2 **redden,** turn *or* grow red, color up, **mantle, blush, flush, crimson;** flame, glow

colored ADJS 1 hued, in color, in Technicolor <trademark>; **tinged, tinted,** tinctured, tinct, toned; **painted, enameled; stained, dyed;** tie-dyed; imbued
2 **dark-skinned, dark-complexioned;** melanian, melanic, melanotic, melanistic, melanous

colorful ADJS **bright, vivid,** intense, **rich,** exotic, **brilliant,** burning, **gorgeous, gay,** bright-hued, bright-colored, rich-colored, gay-colored, high-colored, deep-colored

colorless ADJS 1 **hueless,** toneless, uncolored, achromic, achromatic, achromatous; neutral; dull, flat, mat, dead, dingy, muddy, leaden, lusterless, lackluster; **faded, washed-out,** dimmed, discolored, etiolated; **pale, dim,** weak, **faint; pallid, wan, sallow,** fallow; pale *or* blue *or* green around the gills
2 **dull, dry,** dusty, dry as dust; **stuffy, stodgy,** wooden, stiff; characterless, pointless

colossal ADJS **huge,** great big, larger than life, Homeric, mighty, titanic, monumental, heroic, heroical, epic, epical, towering, mountainous

colt NOUNS **horse;** foal, filly

column NOUNS **pillar,** post, pier, pilaster; colonnette, columella; caryatid; atlas, atlantes <pl>; telamon, telamones

coma NOUNS **stupor,** sopor, **swoon,** lethargy <old>, soporifousness, comatoseness, torpidness, torpor, torpidity, stupefaction, **trance;** narcosis, narcohypnosis, narcoma, narcotization, narcotic stupor *or* trance; catalepsy, catatony *or* catatonia

comatose ADJS **unconscious, senseless, oblivious,** asleep, **dead to the world,** cold, out, **out cold;** catatonic, cataleptic; **lethargic, phlegmatic,** hebetudinous, **dull,** desensitized, sluggish, torpid, languid, slack, soporific, **stupefied,** in a stupor, **numb,** numbed, benumbed

combat NOUNS 1 **contention, contest,** contestation, **fighting, conflict, strife, war, struggle,** blood on the floor, cut and thrust; fighting at close quarters, infighting; **warfare**; **hostility,** enmity; **fighting,** scrapping *and* hassling <both nonformal>; **quarreling, bickering, wrangling, squabbling;** oppugnancy, contentiousness
VERBS 2 **contend, contest,** jostle; **fight, battle, war, declare** *or* **go to war,** take *or* take up arms, put up a fight <nonformal>; wage war; make the fur *or* feathers fly, **tussle, scuffle;** clash, collide; **come to blows,** close, **mix it up** *and* go toe-to-toe <both nonformal>, exchange blows

combatant NOUNS **fighter, battler,** scrapper <nonformal>; **contestant, contender, competitor, rival;** disputant, wrangler, squabbler, bickerer, quarreler; struggler, tussler, scuffler; **belligerent,** militant

combative ADJS **offensive,** on the offensive *or* attack; **aggressive, contentious, quarrelsome,** testy, feisty <nonformal>, ill-humored

combination NOUNS combine, combo <nonformal>, composition; **union, unification,** linking, linkage, yoking; **amalgamation, consolidation,** assimilation, **integration,** solidification, **encompassment,** inclusion, ecumenism; **alliance,** affiliation, reaffiliation, **association, merger,** league, hookup <nonformal>, tie-up <nonformal>

combine VERBS **unite, unify,** marry, wed, couple, link, yoke, yoke together; **incorporate, amalgamate, consolidate,** assimilate, **integrate,** solidify, coalesce, compound, put *or* lump together, roll into one, come together, make one, unitize; **connect, join**; **mix; add**; **merge,** meld, **blend,** stir in, merge *or* blend *or* meld *or* shade into, **fuse,** flux, melt into one, conflate

combustible ADJS **flammable, inflammable,** burnable

come VERBS 1 **appear,** become visible; **arrive, make one's appearance,** make *or* put in an appearance, appear on the scene, make the scene *and* weigh in <both nonformal>, appear to one's eyes, meet *or* catch *or* strike the eye, **come in sight** *or* **view, show,** show oneself, show one's face, nip in <nonformal>, **show up** <nonformal>, **turn up,** come, **materialize,** present oneself, present oneself to view, **manifest oneself,** become manifest, **reveal oneself,** discover oneself, uncover oneself, declare oneself, expose *or* betray oneself
2 **climax,** achieve satisfaction, achieve *or* reach orgasm; **ejaculate,** get off <nonformal>

comeback NOUNS 1 **recovery, rally,** return; **recuperation, convalescence; retaliation, reciprocation,** exchange, interchange, give-and-take; **retort, reply,** return, comeback <nonformal>
2 **gibe, cut,** cutting remark, verbal thrust; gibing retort, rude reproach, short answer, back answer, parting shot, Parthian shot

comedian NOUNS comedienne, **comic, funnyman;** farcist, farcer, *farceur, farceuse* <both Fr>; stand-up comic *or* comedian <nonformal>, light comedian, genteel comedian, low comedian, slapstick comedian

comedown NOUNS **disappointment,** setback, **letdown** <nonformal>; failure, fizzle <nonformal>, fiasco; **disillusionment;** descent, deflation, wounded or humbled pride; self-abasement, shamefacedness

comedy NOUNS **humor,** black humor, sick humor, gallows humor; comic relief, comedy relief; comic muse, Thalia; sock, coxcomb, cap and bells, motley, bladder, slapstick

comeuppance NOUNS **desserts,** just desserts, deservings, merits, dues, due reward *or* punishment, all that is coming to one; retaliation, vengeance

comfort NOUNS 1 **ease, well-being;** contentment; clover, velvet <nonformal>, bed of roses; life of ease; solid comfort
2 **consolation, solace,** solacement, easement, heart's ease, **encouragement,** aid and comfort, **assurance, reassur-**

ance, support, crumb *or* shred of comfort, condolence, sympathy; **relief**

kind words and comfortable
WILLIAM COWPER

VERBS 3 **console, solace,** give *or* bring comfort, bear up; condole with, sympathize with, extend sympathy; ease, **put** *or* **set at ease;** bolster, support; relieve; **assure, reassure; encourage, hearten,** pat on the back; **cheer**; wipe away the tears

comfortable ADJS comfy <nonformal>; contented; **easy,** easeful; **restful,** reposeful, peaceful, **relaxing;** soft, cushioned, cushy <nonformal>, cushiony; comfortable as an old shoe; **cozy, snug,** snug as a bug in a rug; **homelike,** homey *and* down-home <both nonformal>, homely, lived-in; **commodious,** roomy, convenient; luxurious; comfortably situated, **easy;** on Easy Street *and* in Fat City *and* in hog heaven <all nonformal>, **in clover** *and* **on velvet** <both nonformal>, on a bed of roses, in luxury, high on the hog <nonformal>

comic NOUNS 1 **comedian,** comedienne, **funnyman;** stand-up comic *or* comedian <nonformal>, light comedian, low comedian, slapstick comedian
ADJS 2 **comical; farcical,** slapstick, broad; **burlesque**; tragicomic, seriocomic, mock-heroic; **light;** tragicomical

comics NOUNS **comic strip;** comic section, funny paper *and* funnies <both nonformal>; comic book

command NOUNS 1 **commandment, order,** direct order, command decision, **bidding,** behest, hest <old>, imperative, **dictate,** dictation, **will, pleasure,** say-so <nonformal>, word, word of command, *mot d'ordre* <Fr>; special order; **authority**
2 **control, mastery, mastership, power, jurisdiction, dominion, domination; hold, grasp,** grip, gripe; hand, hands, iron hand, clutches; talons, claws; helm, reins of government
3 **understanding, comprehension, apprehension,** intellection, prehension; **grasp,** mental grasp, grip, mastery
VERBS 4 **order, dictate, direct, instruct,** mandate, **bid, enjoin, charge,** commission, call on *or* upon; issue a writ *or* an injunction; **decree, rule, ordain,** promulgate; give an order *or* a direct order, issue a command, say the word, give the word *or* word of command; call the shots *or* tune *or* signals *or* play <nonformal>; order about *or* around

commanding ADJS imperious, imperative, jussive, peremptory, abrupt; **directive, instructive; mandating,** dictating, compelling, obligating, **prescriptive,** preceptive; decretory, decretive, decretal; **authoritative; governing, controlling, regulating,** regulative, regulatory; **ruling, reigning, sovereign,** regnant

commemorative ADJS **celebrative,** celebratory, celebrating; commemorating; memorial; solemn

commencement NOUNS 1 **beginning, start,** running *or* flying start, starting point, square one <nonformal>, **outset,** outbreak, **onset,** oncoming; dawn; **launching,** launch; **opening,** jump-off *and* send-off *and* start-off *and* take-off *and* blast-off *and* git-go *and* square one <all nonformal>
2 commencement exercises, graduation, graduation exercises, baccalaureate service

commend VERBS **speak well** *or* **highly of,** speak in high terms of, speak warmly of, have *or* say a good word for; boost *and* give a boost to <both nonformal>, puff, promote, cry up; plug *and* tout *and* hype; pour *or* spread *or* lay it on thick <all nonformal>

commendable ADJS **praiseworthy,** worthy, estimable, **laudable,** admirable, meritorious, creditable; exemplary, model, unexceptionable; deserving, well-deserving; beyond all praise, *sans peur et sans reproche* <Fr>

commensurate ADJS **comparative, relative**, **comparable,** commensurable, parallel, matchable, **analogous;** analogical; **correlative**

comment NOUNS **1 word of explanation; annotation,** notation, **note,** note of explanation, footnote, gloss, scholium; exegesis; *apparatus criticus* <L>; commentary, commentation <old>
VERBS 2 **remark, observe, note; mention,** speak <old>, let drop *or* fall, say by the way, make mention of; refer to, allude to, touch on, make reference to, call attention to; interject; blurt, blurt out, exclaim

commentary NOUNS commentation <old>; **comment, remark; criticism,**

critique, *compte-rendu critique* <Fr>, analysis; **review,** critical review, **report,** notice, **write-up** <nonformal>; **editorial,** leading article *or* leader <both Brit>; gloss, running commentary

commerce NOUNS **trade, traffic,** truck, intercourse, **dealing, dealings; business,** business dealings *or* affairs *or* relations, commercial affairs *or* relations; the business world, the world of trade *or* commerce, the marketplace; merchantry

commercial NOUNS 1 **advertisement, ad** <nonformal>, advert <Brit nonformal>, notice; **commercial,** message, important message, message *or* words from the sponsor; spot commercial *or* spot, network commercial; commercial announcement, commercial message, plug <nonformal>
ADJS 2 **business, trade,** trading, **mercantile,** merchant; commercialistic, mercantilistic; **salable, marketable,** merchandisable

commiserate VERBS **condole with, sympathize with,** feel with, empathize with, express sympathy for, send one's condolences; pity; **console,** wipe away one's tears, comfort

commission VERBS **authorize,** empower, accredit; **delegate,** devolute, devolve, devolve upon, vest, invest; depute, **deputize; assign,** consign, **commit, charge, entrust,** give in charge; license, charter, warrant

commit VERBS 1 consign, commit to prison, send to jail, send up *and* send up the river <both nonformal>; commit to an institution, institutionalize; recommit, remit, remand
2 **engage,** undertake, obligate, bind, **agree to,** answer for, be answerable for, take on oneself, be responsible for, be security for, go bail for, accept obligation *or* responsibility, bind oneself to, put oneself down for; have an understanding; enter into a gentlemen's agreement; shake hands on; contract; **obligate, oblige,** make incumbent *or* imperative, tie, **bind,** pledge, saddle with, put under an obligation; call to account, hold responsible *or* accountable *or* answerable

commitment NOUNS 1 **devotion,** devoutness, devotedness, dedication, committedness; **earnestness, seriousness,** sincerity; loyalty, faithfulness, faith, fidelity
2 **obligation, agreement, engagement,** undertaking, recognizance; **understanding,** gentlemen's agreement; verbal agreement, nonformal agreement, pactum <law>; tacit *or* unspoken agreement; **contract;**

commit suicide VERBS **take one's own life, kill oneself,** die by one's own hand, do away with oneself, put an end to oneself; blow one's brains out, take an overdose <of a drug>, overdose *or* OD <nonformal>; commit hara-kiri *or* seppuku; sign one's own death warrant, doom oneself

committed ADJS **devoted,** dedicated, **fast,** steadfast, constant, faithful, staunch; tried, true, **tried and true,** true-blue, tested; bound, duty-bound, in duty bound, tied, pledged, saddled, beholden, bounden; **obliged to,** beholden to, bound *or* bounden to, **indebted to**

commodity NOUNS **ware,** vendible, **product, article, item,** article of commerce *or* merchandise; staple, staple item, standard article

common ADJS 1 **commonplace, ordinary;** plebeian; homely, homespun; **general, public, popular,** pop <nonformal>; prosaic, prosy, **matter-of-fact,** everyday, workaday, household, garden, common- *or* garden-variety; **unexceptional, unremarkable, unnoteworthy,** unspectacular, nothing *or* nobody special *and* no great shakes <all nonformal>; **prevalent, prevailing, current,** running
2 **mutual,** commutual, **joint, communal,** shared, sharing, conjoint; respective, two-way

common man NOUNS **commoner,** little man, **little fellow, average man,** ordinary man, typical man, **man in the street,** one of the people, man of the people, Everyman; **plebeian,** pleb <slang>; **proletarian,** prole <Brit nonformal>, *roturier* <Fr>; ordinary *or* average Joe *and* Joe Doakes *and* Joe Sixpack <all nonformal>, John Doe, Jane Doe, John Smith, Mr *or* Mrs Brown *or* Smith; a nobody

commonplace ADJS 1 **trite;** corny *and* square *and* square-John *and* Clyde <all nonformal>, fade, **banal,** unoriginal, platitudinous, **stereotyped,** stock, set, **common,** truistic, twice-told, **familiar,** bromidic <nonformal>, old hat <nonformal>, back-number, bewhiskered,

warmed-over, **cut-and-dried; hackneyed,** hackney; **stale,** musty, fusty; **worn,** timeworn, well-worn, motheaten, threadbare, **worn thin**
2 **common, ordinary;** plebeian; homely, homespun; pedestrian, **unimaginative**; insipid, vapid, flat; **general, public, popular,** pop <nonformal>; Babbittish, Philistine, bourgeois; **simple**, **plain, ordinary, nondescript, prosaic,** prosy, **matter-of-fact, homely, homespun,** everyday, humdrum, tiresome

common sense NOUNS **reasonableness,** reasonability, **logicalness,** logicality, **rationality, sensibleness, soundness,** justness, justifiability, admissibility, cogency; **sense,** sound sense, sweet reason, **logic, reason;** plausibility

commonwealth NOUNS community, society, **nation,** constituency, body politic, electorate; **republic,** people's republic, commonweal

commotion NOUNS **hubbub, Babel, tumult,** turmoil, **uproar, racket,** riot, **disturbance, rumpus** <nonformal>, ruckus *and* ruction <both nonformal>, **fracas, hassle,** shemozzle <Brit nonformal>, shindy <nonformal>, rampage; **row** *and* hassle <both nonformal>

commune NOUNS **community, family,** extended family, nuclear family, binuclear family; colony, settlement; communal ownership; ashram

communicate VERBS 1 **be in touch** *or* **contact,** be in connection *or* intercourse, have intercourse, hold communication; **intercommunicate,** interchange, commune with; grok <nonformal>; commerce with, **deal with, traffic with, have dealings with, have truck with** <nonformal>; **speak, talk,** be in a speech situation, **converse**, pass the time of day
2 **impart, tell,** lay on one <nonformal>, **convey, transmit,** transfer, send, send word, deliver *or* send a signal *or* message, **disseminate,** broadcast, pass, **pass on** *or* **along, hand on; report, render, make known,** get across *or* over; give *or* send *or* leave word; **signal;** share, share with; **leak,** let slip out, **give**; tell

communication NOUNS communion, congress, **commerce, intercourse; speaking, speech**, utterance, speech act, talking, linguistic intercourse, speech situation, speech circuit, converse, **conversation**; **contact, touch, connection; interpersonal communication, intercommunication,** intercommunion, grokking <nonformal>, **interplay,** interaction; **exchange,** interchange; answer, response, reply; one-way communication, two-way communication; **dealings,** dealing, **traffic, truck** <nonformal>; information; message; correspondence; social intercourse

communicative ADJS **talkative**, gossipy, newsy; **sociable; unreserved, unreticent,** unshrinking, **unrestrained, unconstrained,** unhampered, unrestricted; demonstrative, expansive, effusive; **candid, frank**; **open,** free, outspoken, free-speaking, free-spoken, free-tongued; **accessible, approachable,** easy to speak to

communiqué NOUNS **message, dispatch, word, communication,** advice, press release, release

communism NOUNS **Bolshevism, Marxism,** Marxism-Leninism, Leninism, Trotskyism, Stalinism, Maoism, Titoism, Castroism

Communist NOUNS 1 Bolshevist; Bolshevik, **Red** *and* commie *and* bolshie <all nonformal>; Marxist, Leninist, Marxist-Leninist, Trotskyite *or* Trotskyist, Stalinist, Maoist, Titoist, Castroite; card-carrying Communist, avowed Communist; fellow traveler, Communist sympathizer, comsymp <nonformal>
ADJS 2 **communistic,** Bolshevik, Bolshevist, commie *and* bolshie *and* Red <all nonformal>; **Marxist,** Leninist, Marxist-Leninist, Trotskyite *or* Trotskyist, Stalinist, Maoist, Titoist, Castroite

community NOUNS **society, commonwealth;** body; **kinship group, clan,** sept <Scots>, moiety, totemic *or* totemistic group, phyle, phratry *or* phratria, gens, caste, subcaste, endogamous group; **family,** extended family, nuclear family, binuclear family; order, **class, social class**, economic class; colony, settlement; **commune,** ashram

commuter NOUNS **traveler, passenger,** straphanger <nonformal>

compact VERBS 1 compress, **consolidate, concentrate,** squeeze, press, crowd, cram, jam, ram down
ADJS 2 **compressed,** cramped, compacted, concentrated, condensed, consolidated, solidified

companion NOUNS 1 **fellow,** fellow com-

panion, **comrade,** *camarade* <Fr>, amigo <nonformal>, mate <Brit>, comate, company, **associate**, consociate, compeer, confrere, consort, **colleague, partner,** copartner, side partner, **crony;** girlfriend <nonformal>; boyfriend <nonformal>
2 **escort, chaperon,** duenna; travel companion

company NOUNS 1 **fellowship, companionship, society;** fraternity, **fraternization**
2 **firm, business firm, concern, house,** *compagnie* <Fr>, *compañía* <Sp>, *Aktiengesellschaft* <Ger>, *aktiebolag* <Swed>; **business, industry, enterprise,** business establishment, commercial enterprise; cast, acting company, troupe, repertory company, stock company

comparable ADJS commensurable; correlative; **like,** homologous, **similar; analogous**

compare VERBS **liken,** assimilate, similize, liken to, compare with; **make** *or* **draw a comparison,** run a comparison, do a comparative study, bring into comparison; **analogize,** bring into analogy; **relate**; metaphorize; **draw a parallel,** parallel; **be comparable, compare to** *or* **with,** not compare with, admit of comparison, be commensurable, be of the same order *or* class, be worthy of comparison, be fit to be compared; **measure up to, come up to,** stack up with <nonformal>, hold a candle to <nonformal>

comparison NOUNS compare, examining side by side, matching, matchup, holding up together, proportion <old>, comparative judgment *or* estimate; **likening,** comparing, **analogy;** correlation; simile, similitude, metaphor, allegory, figure *or* trope of comparison

compassion NOUNS **sensitivity, sensitiveness;** perceptivity, perceptiveness; responsiveness; **sympathy;** empathy, identification; **concern,** solicitousness, solicitude; **pity, mercy; humaneness,** humanity; charitableness

compatible ADJS **in accord,** accordant <old>, **harmonious, in harmony,** congruous, congruent, in tune, attuned, agreeing, in concert, **in rapport,** *en rapport* <Fr>; frictionless; **sympathetic,** simpatico <nonformal>, empathic, empathetic, **understanding; like-minded,** akin, of the same mind, of one mind, at one, united, together; concordant, corresponding; agreeable, congenial

compel VERBS 1 **force, make;** have, cause, cause to; **constrain, bind,** tie, tie one's hands; **restrain**; enforce, **drive,** impel; dragoon, use force upon, force one's hand, hold a pistol *or* gun to one's head; **necessitate, oblige,** dictate, **constrain;** insist upon

2 <nonformal> **twist one's arm, arm-twist, twist arms, knock** *or* bang heads, knock *or* bang heads together, strong-arm, steamroller, bulldoze, **pressure,** high-pressure, lean on, squeeze; put the screws on *or* to, get one over a barrel *or* under one's thumb, hold one's feet to the fire, put the heat on; pull rank; ram *or* cram down one's throat

compensate VERBS make compensation, make good, set right, restitute, make up for, counterpoise; countervail, counterbalance, cancel, rectify, **make up for; make amends,** expiate, do penance, atone; **recompense,** pay back, repay, indemnify, cover; **trade off,** give and take; **retaliate; pay,** render, tender; **recompense, remunerate,** satisfy

compete VERBS **contend, vie,** try conclusions *or* the issue, jockey <nonformal>; **compete with** *or* **against, vie with, challenge,** cope <old>, enter into competition with, give a run for one's money, **meet;** try *or* test one another; **rival,** emulate, outvie; keep up with the Joneses

competent ADJS **capable, able, efficient, qualified, fit, fitted, suited, worthy;** journeyman; fit *or* fitted for; **equal to, up to;** up to snuff <nonformal>, up to the mark <nonformal>, *au fait* <Fr>; well-qualified, well-fitted, well-suited

competitive ADJS competing, **vying,** rivaling, **rival,** rivalrous, emulous, in competition, in rivalry; **cutthroat**

competitor NOUNS **contestant, contender,** corrival, vier, player, entrant; **rival,** arch-rival; emulator

compilation NOUNS omnibus; symposium; collection, collectanea, miscellany; **miscellanea,** analects; ana; chrestomathy, delectus; **anthology,** garland, florilegium

compile VERBS **put together,** make up,

compile, colligate; **codify,** digest; publish

complacent ADJS **smug, self-complacent, self-satisfied,** self-content, **self-contented**; self-sufficient

complain VERBS 1 **groan; grumble, murmur, mutter,** growl, clamor, croak, grunt, yelp; **fret,** fuss, make a fuss about, fret and fume; air a grievance, lodge *or* register a complaint; fault, find fault; **object, protest,** remonstrate, **dispute,** challenge, complain loudly, exclaim at

2 <nonformal> **beef, bitch, kick, kvetch,** bellyache, crab, gripe, grouch, grouse, grump, have an attitude, kick, holler, howl, moan, piss, make a stink, squawk, yap; raise a howl, put up a squawk *or* howl, take on, cry *or* yell *or* scream bloody murder, give one a hard time, piss *or* kick up a storm *or* row *or* fuss, raise a stink

complainer NOUNS 1 **malcontent,** *frondeur* <Fr>; complainant, **faultfinder, grumbler,** growler, smellfungus, griper, croaker, peevish *or* petulant *or* querulous person, whiner

2 <nonformal> **grouch, kvetch,** kicker, griper, moaner, moaning Minnie <Brit>, crank, crab, grouser, beefer, bellyacher, bitcher, sorehead, picklepuss, sourpuss

complaint NOUNS 1 **grievance, peeve,** pet peeve, **groan; dissent,** objection, **protest**; hard luck story <nonformal>, tale of woe; **complaining,** scolding, groaning, **faultfinding**, sniping, destructive criticism, **grumbling, murmuring;** whining, petulance, peevishness, querulousness

2 <nonformal> **beef, kick, gripe,** kvetch, grouse, bellyache, howl, holler, **squawk,** bitch; **beefing, grousing, kicking, griping,** kvetching, **bellyaching,** squawking, **bitching,** yapping

complementary ADJS **reciprocal,** reciprocative, tit-for-tat, seesaw, seesawing; **completing, fulfilling,** filling; completive *or* completory, consummative *or* consummatory, culminative, perfective; complemental

complete VERBS 1 **perfect, finish, finish off, conclude, terminate, end,** bring to a close, carry to completion, prosecute to a conclusion; **get through, get done; round off** *or* **out, wind up** <nonformal>, **top off;** top out, crown, cap; climax, culminate; **give the finishing touches** *or* **strokes,** put the finishing touches *or* strokes on, lick *or* whip into shape, finalize, put the icing on the cake

ADJS 2 **undivided,** uncut, unsevered, unclipped, uncropped, unshorn; **undiminished,** unreduced; **whole, total,** global, **entire,** intact, solid; **full, full-fledged,** full-dress, **full-scale;** full-grown, mature, matured, ripe, developed; unabbreviated, undiminished, unexpurgated; **terminated,** concluded, finished, perfected, settled, decided, set at rest; **over, all over,** all up <nonformal>; **finished**

completely ADVS **fully, in full, in detail,** minutely, specifically, particularly, in particular, wholly, *in toto* <L>, **at length,** *in extenso* <L>, *ad nauseam* <L>

completion NOUNS completing, **finish,** finishing, **conclusion, end,** ending, **termination,** terminus, **close, windup** <nonformal>, rounding off *or* out, topping off, wrapping up, wrap-up, finalization; **perfection,** culmination; **fulfillment,** consummation, culmination, perfection, realization, actualization, **accomplishment**, closure

complex ADJS **complicated,** many-faceted, multifarious, ramified, perplexed, **confused,** confounded, **involved,** implicated, crabbed, **intricate,** elaborate, involuted, convoluted, multilayered, multilevel; **tangled,** entangled, tangly, embrangled, **snarled,** knotted, matted, twisted, raveled; **labyrinthine,** labyrinthian, meandering; **devious,** roundabout, deep-laid, Byzantine, subtle

complicate VERBS **involve, perplex,** ramify; **confound, confuse,** muddle, **mix up,** mess up *and* ball up *and* bollix up *and* screw up *and* foul up *and* fuck up *and* snafu *and* muck up *and* louse up <all nonformal>, implicate; **tangle,** entangle, embrangle, **snarl, snarl up,** ravel, knot, tie in knots

complication NOUNS **abstruseness,** reconditeness; crabbedness, crampedness, knottiness; **complexity,** intricacy; **profundity,** profoundness, deepness; esotericism, esotery; **complexity,**

involvement, complexness, involution, convolution, tortuousness, Byzantinism, *chinoiserie* <Fr>, tanglement, **entanglement,** perplexity, **intricacy,** intricateness, ramification, crabbedness, technicality, subtlety; **predicament, embarrassment,** embarrassing position *or* situation; imbroglio

complicity NOUNS **collusion,** connivance; artifice; **contrivance,** contriving; **guilt, guiltiness;** guilty *or* wrongful *or* criminal involvement; censurability, censurableness, reproachability, reproachableness, reprovability, reprovableness, inculpation, implication, involvement, impeachability, impeachableness, indictability

compliment NOUNS 1 polite commendation, complimentary *or* flattering remark, stroke <nonformal>; **bouquet** *and* posy <both nonformal>
VERBS 2 **pay a compliment,** make one a compliment, give a bouquet *or* posy <nonformal>, say something nice about; hand it to *and* have to hand it to <both nonformal>, pat on the back, take off one's hat to, doff one's cap to, congratulate

complimentary ADJS **approbatory, approbative, commendatory, laudatory,** acclamatory, eulogistic, panegyric, panegyrical, encomiastic, **appreciative, appreciatory; admiring, regardful, respectful**; flattering
2 **gratuitous, gratis, free, free of charge,** for free, **for nothing,** free for nothing, free for the asking, free gratis *and* free gratis for nothing <both nonformal>, for love, free as air; on the house

comply VERBS **acquiesce, comply with,** fall in with, take one up on <nonformal>, be persuaded, come round *or* around, come over, come to <nonformal>, see one's way clear to; **conform, correspond,** accord, harmonize; **comply with,** agree with, tally with, chime *or* fall in with, go by, be guided *or* regulated by, observe, follow, bend, yield, take the shape of

component NOUNS **constituent, ingredient,** integrant, makings *and* fixings <both nonformal>, **element, factor, part**, player, module, part and parcel; appurtenance, adjunct; **feature,** aspect, specialty, circumstance, detail, item

composed ADJS 1 **collected,** recollected, **levelheaded; poised,** together <nonformal>, in equipoise, equanimous, equilibrious, **balanced,** well-balanced; **self-possessed,** self-controlled, self-restrained; confident, assured, **self-confident, self-assured**
2 **arranged, ordered, disposed,** configured, constituted, fixed, placed, aligned, ranged, arrayed, marshaled

composite NOUNS 1 **compound, mixture, admixture,** intermixture, immixture, commixture, **blend,** meld, composition, confection, concoction; amalgam, alloy
ADJS 2 blended, compounded, amalgamated; **combined**; compound; **conglomerate,** pluralistic, heterogeneous, varied, **miscellaneous,** medley, motley, dappled, patchy; **scrambled, jumbled,** thrown together; syncretic, eclectic

composition NOUNS 1 **constitution, construction, formation,** fabrication, fashioning, shaping, organization; **embodiment,** incorporation, incarnation; **make, makeup,** getup *or* setup <both informal>; **assembly,** assemblage, putting *or* piecing together; synthesis, syneresis; **mixture**
2 **creation; invention,** origination, coinage, mintage *or* new mintage, brainchild; **concoction,** opus

compost NOUNS **fertilizer,** dressing, top dressing, enricher, richener; organic fertilizer, manure, muck, night soil, dung, guano, leaf litter, leaf mold, humus, peat moss, castor-bean meal, bone meal

composure NOUNS countenance; **calm, calmness,** calm disposition, **placidity, serenity,** tranquility, soothingness, peacefulness; mental composure, peace *or* calm of mind; calm *or* quiet mind, easy mind; **quiet,** quietness of mind *or* soul, quietude; **coolness,** coolheadedness, cool <nonformal>, sangfroid; possession, aplomb

compound NOUNS 1 **mixture, admixture,** intermixture, immixture, commixture, **composite, blend,** meld, composition, confection, concoction, **combination**
VERBS 2 **combine, consolidate,** assimilate, **integrate,** solidify, coalesce, put *or* lump together, roll into one, come together, make one, unitize; **synthesize,** syncretize

comprehensive ADJS **sweeping, complete**; whole; **all-comprehensive,** all-inclusive; without omission *or* exception, **overall,** universal, global, wall-to-wall <nonformal>, around-the-world, **total,** blanket, omnibus, across-the-board; encyclopedic, compendious; thorough

compress VERBS 1 **squeeze,** clamp, cramp, cramp up, tighten; **press,** pressurize, crush
2 **abridge, condense, boil down,** abstract, sum up, summarize, recapitulate, recap <nonformal>, synopsize, epitomize, encapsulate, capsulize

compressed ADJS **contracted,** cramped, compact *or* compacted, concentrated, condensed, consolidated, solidified; **squeezed; abridged,** condensed, epitomized, digested, abstracted, capsule, capsulized, encapsulated, **concise, brief, short**

compromise NOUNS 1 adjustment, accommodation, settlement, mutual concession, give-and-take; abatement of differences; bargain, deal <nonformal>, arrangement, understanding; **concession,** giving way, yielding; adaptation, mutual adjustment, coaptation, arbitration, arbitrament
VERBS 2 make *or* reach a compromise, compound, compose, accommodate, adjust, settle, make an adjustment *or* arrangement, **make a deal** <nonformal>, do a deal <Brit nonformal>, come to an understanding, strike a bargain, do something mutually beneficial; plea-bargain; strike a balance, take the mean, **meet halfway,** split the difference, go fifty-fifty <nonformal>
3 **endanger, jeopardize,** put in danger, **put in jeopardy,** put on the spot *and* lay on the line <both nonformal>; **expose,** lay open; incur danger, run into *or* encounter danger

compulsion NOUNS **obligation,** obligement; **command**; **necessity**; **inevitability**; **irresistibility, compulsiveness; forcing,** enforcement; command performance; **constraint,** coaction; **restraint; impulse,** impulsion, impelling force, impellent; **drive,** driving force *or* power, urge

compulsive ADJS **compelling; overfastidious,** queasy, **overparticular, overscrupulous, overconscientious,** overmeticulous, **overnice,** overprecise; **compulsive,** anal, anal-compulsive, **obsessive,** obsessional

compulsory ADJS **mandatory,** mandated, **imperative,** prescript, prescriptive, **obligatory,** must <nonformal>; compulsive, compulsatory, **compelling;** constraining, coactive; restraining; irresistible

compute VERBS **calculate, estimate, reckon, figure,** reckon at, put at, cipher, cast, tally, score; **figure out,** work out, dope out <nonformal>; **add, subtract, multiply, divide,** multiply out, algebraize, extract roots

computer NOUNS electronic data processor, information processor, electronic brain, digital computer, general purpose computer, analog computer, hybrid computer, machine, **hardware,** computer hardware, microelectronics device

comrade NOUNS **companion, fellow,** fellow companion, *camarade* <Fr>, amigo <nonformal>, mate <Brit>, comate, company, **associate**, consociate, compeer, confrere, consort, **colleague, partner,** copartner, side partner, **crony**

con NOUNS 1 **cheating,** cheating scheme, cheating method, angle, grift *and* move *and* racket *and* scam *and* sting <all nonformal>; deception
VERBS 2 **cheat, victimize, gull,** pigeon, fudge, **swindle, defraud,** practice fraud upon, euchre, finagle, **fleece,** mulct, fob <old>, **bilk,** cozen, cog <old>, chouse, **cheat out of, do out of,** chouse out of, beguile of *or* out of

concave ADJS concaved, **incurved,** incurving, incurvate; **sunk,** sunken; retreating, recessed, retiring; **hollow,** hollowed, empty; palm-shaped; dish-shaped, dished, dishing, dishlike, bowl-shaped; bowllike, crater-shaped, craterlike, saucer-shaped

conceal VERBS **hide,** ensconce; **cover, cover up,** blind, **screen, cloak, veil,** screen off, curtain, blanket, shroud, enshroud, envelop; **disguise, camouflage, mask,** dissemble; **paper over,** gloss over, varnish, slur over; **obscure,** obfuscate, cloud, becloud, befog, throw out a smoke screen, shade, throw into the shade; **eclipse,** occult

concede VERBS **acknowledge, admit, own, confess, allow,** avow, **grant,** warrant, yield <old>; go along with, not oppose *or* deny, agree provisionally *or* for the sake of argument; bring oneself to agree, assent grudgingly *or* under protest

conceited ADJS **vain,** vogie <Scots>; haughty, **arrogant**; **boastful, boasting, braggart, bragging,** thrasonical, thrasonic, big-mouthed <nonformal>, vaunting, vaporing, gasconading, Gascon, fanfaronading, fanfaron

conceivable ADJS **knowable,** recognizable, **understandable, comprehensible,** apprehendable, apprehensible, graspable, seizable, discernible, appreciable, perceptible, ascertainable, discoverable; credible, reasonable; **plausible,** colorable, apparent <old>; **imaginable, thinkable, supposable**

conceive VERBS 1 **understand, realize,** appreciate, have no problem with, ken <Scots>, savvy <nonformal>, sense, make sense out of, make something of; grasp, seize, get hold of, grasp *or* seize the meaning, be seized of, take, **take in,** catch, **catch on,** get the meaning of, get the hang of
2 **imagine, fancy,** conceptualize, ideate, figure to oneself; **invent, create, originate, make,** think up, dream up, shape, mold, coin, hatch, concoct, fabricate, produce

concentrate NOUNS 1 **extract,** extraction; **essence, quintessence, spirit, elixir;** decoction; **distillate,** distillation; concentration; infusion; refinement, purification
VERBS 2 concentrate the mind *or* thoughts, concentrate on *or* upon, attend closely to, brood on, **focus on** *or* **upon,** give *or* devote the mind to, glue the mind to, cleave to the thought of, fix the mind *or* thoughts upon, bend the mind upon, bring the mind to bear upon; get to the point; gather *or* collect one's thoughts, pull one's wits together, focus *or* fix one's thoughts, marshal *or* arrange one's thoughts *or* ideas
3 **intensify, heighten, condense, compress,** compact, **consolidate,** come to a head; **congest; squeeze, press, crowd,** cram, jam, ram down; steeve; pack *or* jam in; **solidify**

concept NOUNS **idea; thought,** mental *or* intellectual object, **notion,** conception, conceit, fancy; **opinion**; supposition, **theory**

conception NOUNS 1 **source, origin,** genesis, original, origination, **derivation, rise, beginning,** inception, commencement
2 invention, originating, engenderment, engendering, genesis, beginning; **devising,** hatching, fabrication, **concoction,** coinage, mintage, **contriving,** contrivance
3 **creative thought; visualization, envisioning,** envisaging, picturing, objectification, imaging, calling to *or* before the mind's eye, figuring *or* portraying *or* representing in the mind; depicting *or* delineating in the imagination; conceptualization; **picture, vision, image,** mental image, mental picture, visual image, vivid *or* lifelike image, eidetic image, concept, mental representation *or* presentation, *Vorstellung* <Ger>

concern NOUNS 1 **sympathy, fellow feeling, sympathetic response,** responsiveness, relating, warmth, **caring**; concernment, anxious concern, **solicitude,** zeal
2 **affair, matter,** thing, concernment, interest, **business,** job <nonformal>, **transaction,** proceeding, doing; cause célèbre, matter of moment; subject, subject of thought, **matter, subject matter,** what it is about, focus of interest *or* attention, discrete matter, topic of the day
VERBS 3 give concern, **trouble, bother, distress, disturb, upset,** frazzle, **disquiet, agitate;** rob one of ease *or* sleep *or* rest, keep one on edge *or* on tenterhooks *or* on pins and needles *or* on shpilkes <nonformal>
4 **interest,** involve in *or* with, affect the interest, give pause; pique one's interest, excite interest, excite *or* whet one's interest, arouse one's passion *or* enthusiasm, turn one on <nonformal>

concert NOUNS 1 **performance,** musical performance, **program,** musical program, program of music; symphony concert, chamber concert; philharmonic concert, philharmonic; popular concert, pops *and* pop concert <both nonformal>; promenade concert; band concert; **recital**
2 **harmony, cooperation**, peace, *rapport* <Fr>, **consonance,** unisonance, **unison,** union, chorus, oneness

concession NOUNS giving way, yielding; surrender, desertion of principle, evasion of responsibility, cop-out <nonformal>

concise ADJS **brief, short, condensed, compressed,** tight, close, compact; compendious; **curt,** brusque, **crisp,**

terse, summary; taciturn; reserved; **pithy, succinct; laconic,** Spartan; **abridged, abbreviated,** vest-pocket, synopsized, shortened, clipped, cut, pruned, contracted, truncated, docked; elliptic; sententious, epigrammatic, epigrammatical, gnomic, aphoristic<al>, **pointed,** to the point

short and sweet
THOMAS LODGE

conclude VERBS draw a conclusion, be forced to conclude, **come to** *or* **arrive at a conclusion, come up with a conclusion** *and* **end up** <both nonformal>; find, hold; deduce, derive, take as proved *or* demonstrated, extract, **gather,** collect, glean, fetch; **infer,** draw an inference; put two and two together

conclusion NOUNS 1 **end,** end point, ending, perfection, be-all and end-all, **termination, terminus, terminal,** terminating, term, period, **expiration,** expiry, phaseout, phasedown, discontinuation, closeout, **cessation**, ceasing, consummation, culmination, **finish, finis, finale,** the end, finishing, finalizing *or* finalization, a wrap <nonformal>, quietus, stoppage, windup *and* payoff <both nonformal>, curtain, curtains <nonformal>, all she wrote <nonformal>, fall of the curtain, end of the road *or* line <nonformal>
2 **deduction, inference,** consequence, consequent, corollary; derivation, illation; induction

conclusive ADJS 1 **completing,** completive, completory, **finishing,** consummative, culminating, terminative, **concluding,** fulfilling, finalizing, crowning; ultimate, **last, final,** terminal
2 **convincing,** convictional, well-founded, **persuasive,** assuring, impressive, satisfying, satisfactory, confidence-building; decisive, absolute, determinative; authoritative

concoct VERBS 1 **plot, hatch, hatch up,** cook up <nonformal>, brew, hatch *or* lay a plot
2 **invent, create, originate, make,** think up, dream up, shape, mold, coin, hatch, fabricate, produce; **suppose**; **fantasize;** fictionalize

concrete ADJS **substantial,** substantive; **solid; tangible,** sensible, appreciable, palpable, ponderable; **material, dense, compact;** compacted, consolidated, concentrated

concur VERBS **collaborate,** coact, **co-work,** synergize; **cooperate**; conspire, collude, connive, be in cahoots <nonformal>; **combine**, **unite, associate**, coadunate, join, conjoin; harmonize; **coincide,** synchronize, happen together; **accord**, correspond, **agree**

condemn VERBS **damn, doom; denounce,** denunciate; **censure**; **convict,** find guilty, bring home to; proscribe, excommunicate, anathematize; blacklist, put on the Index; pronounce judgment; **sentence,** pronounce sentence, pass sentence on; penalize; attaint; sign one's death warrant

condense VERBS 1 **abridge, shorten**, **cut, clip; summarize,** synopsize, wrap up <nonformal>; **outline, sketch,** sketch out, hit the high spots; capsule, capsulize, encapsulate; **put in a nutshell**
2 **densify,** inspissate, densen; **compress,** compact, **consolidate, concentrate,** come to a head; **congest; squeeze, press, crowd,** cram, jam, ram down; steeve; pack *or* jam in; **solidify**

condiment NOUNS **flavoring, flavor,** flavorer; **seasoning,** seasoner, **relish, spice,** condiments

condition NOUNS 1 **stipulation, provision,** proviso; **terms;** exception, reservation; **qualification**
VERBS 2 **accustom, habituate,** wont; season, **train;** familiarize, naturalize <old>, break in <nonformal>, orient, orientate
3 **train; prepare,** ready, **groom,** fit, put in tune, form, **lick into shape** <nonformal>
4 **make conditional,** make contingent; make it a condition, attach a condition *or* proviso, **stipulate;** insist upon, make a point of

conditional ADJS **undecided, undetermined, unsettled,** unfixed, unestablished; pendent, dependent, **pending,** depending, contingent, conditioned

conditioning NOUNS **habituation, accustoming;** seasoning, training; **familiarization,** naturalization <old>, breaking-in <nonformal>, orientation; **domestication, taming,** breaking, housebreaking; **inculcation, indoctrination,** catechization, inoculation, **implantation,** infixation, infixion, **impression, instillment,** instillation, impregnation, brainwashing; reindoctrination

condolence NOUNS **condolences,** condolement, **consolation,** comfort, balm, soothing words, **commiseration, sympathy,** sharing of grief *or* sorrow

condom NOUNS **contraceptive,** birth control device, prophylactic; **rubber** *and* skin *and* bag <all nonformal>

condone VERBS **overlook, disregard, ignore,** accept, take *and* swallow *and* let go <all nonformal>, pass over, give one another chance, let one off this time *and* let one off easy <both nonformal>, close *or* shut one's eyes to, **blink** *or* **wink at,** connive at; allow for, make allowances for; bear with, endure, regard with indulgence; pocket the affront, leave unavenged, turn the other cheek, bury *or* hide one's head in the sand

conducive ADJS **instrumental, implemental;** agential, agentive, agentival; **useful,** utile, handy, **helpful; contributory,** contributing, **constructive, positive,** promotional

conduct NOUNS 1 **behavior, deportment, comportment, manner, manners, demeanor, mien,** *maintien* <Fr>, **carriage, bearing,** port, poise, posture, guise, **air,** address, presence; tone, style, lifestyle; modus vivendi; **actions,** acts, goings-on, doings, what one is up to, movements, moves, tactics
VERBS 2 **channel,** channelize, canalize, **convey,** put through; **direct, manage, regulate, carry on, handle, run** <nonformal>; **control, command, head, govern, boss** *and* head up *and* pull the strings *and* **mastermind** *and* quarterback *and* call the signals <all nonformal>; **escort,** have in tow <nonformal>, marshal, **usher,** shepherd, **guide, lead; convoy,** guard

conduit NOUNS **channel, duct,** canal, course; **way, passage, passageway;** trough, troughway, troughing; tunnel; ditch, trench; adit; ingress, entrance; egress, exit

confederacy NOUNS **affiliation, alliance,** consociation, combination, union, unification, **coalition,** fusion, merger, coalescence, coadunation, **federation, confederation,** consolidation, incorporation, inclusion, integration

confederate NOUNS **associate,** consociate, **colleague,** fellow member, **companion, fellow,** bedfellow, **crony,** consort, cohort, compeer, compatriot, confrere, brother, brother-in-arms, **ally,** adjunct, coadjutor; comrade in arms, **comrade; accomplice,** cohort, fellow conspirator, coconspirator, partner *or* accomplice in crime; *particeps criminis, socius criminis* <both L>

confer VERBS 1 hold a conference, parley, palaver, powwow, sit down together, meet around the conference table, **go into a huddle** <nonformal>, deliberate, take counsel, counsel, **lay** *or* **put heads together;** collogue; **confer with,** sit down with, **consult with, advise with, discuss with, take up with,** reason with; **discuss,** talk over; **consult,** refer to, call in; **compare notes,** exchange observations *or* views; have conversations; negotiate, bargain
2 **transfer, convey, deliver,** hand, pass, negotiate; **hand over, turn over, pass over; assign, consign,** settle, settle on; bequeath; entail; **make over, sign over,** sign away; transmit, **hand down, hand on, pass on,** devolve upon; **deed,** deed over, give title to

conference NOUNS 1 **congress, convention, parley, palaver, confab** <nonformal>, confabulation, **conclave, powwow, huddle** <nonformal>, **consultation,** *pourparler* <Fr>, **meeting; council,** council of war; **discussion; interview, audience; news conference,** press conference; high-level talk, conference at the summit, summit, summit conference; summitry
2 **discussion, deliberation,** panel discussion, open discussion, joint discussion, symposium, colloquium, seminar; forum, open forum, **assembly,** *assemblée* <Fr>, **gathering, forgathering, congregation,** congress, convocation, concourse, **meeting,** meet, **get-together** *and* turnout <both nonformal>

confess VERBS break down and confess, **admit, acknowledge,** tell all, avow, concede, grant, **own, own up** <nonformal>, let on, implicate *or* incriminate oneself, come clean <nonformal>; spill *and* spill it *and* spill one's guts <all nonformal>; **tell the truth,** tell all, admit everything, let it all hang out <nonformal>, throw off all disguise; **unbosom oneself, make a clean breast, get it off one's chest** <nonformal>, **get it out of one's system** <nonformal>, disburden *or* unburden one's mind *or* conscience *or* heart, **get a load off one's mind** <nonformal>, fess up <nonformal>; out with it *and* spit it out *and* open up <all nonformal>

confession NOUNS confessing, shrift, **acknowledgment, admission,** concession, avowal, self-admission, self-concession, self-avowal, owning, owning up *and* coming clean <both nonformal>, unbosoming, unburdening oneself, getting a load off one's mind <nonformal>, fessing up <nonformal>, making a clean breast, baring one's breast; rite of confession

confidant NOUNS **counselor, mentor,** nestor, orienter; personal adviser; admonisher, monitor, Dutch uncle; **friend, acquaintance,** close acquaintance; confidante, repository; **intimate,** familiar, **close friend,** intimate *or* familiar friend; **bosom friend,** friend of one's bosom, inseparable friend, **best friend**

confide VERBS **divulge, reveal,** let in on, confide to, let one's hair down <nonformal>, unbosom oneself, let into the secret; entrust with information, give confidential information, mention privately *or* confidentially, whisper, buzz, breathe, whisper in the ear, **put a bug in one's ear** <nonformal>

confidence NOUNS 1 **poise,** aplomb, **self-possession, self-control,** self-command, self-restraint, restraint, possession, **presence of mind;** assurance, **self-confidence, self-assurance**
2 **secret,** private *or* personal matter, privity <old>; confidential *or* **privileged information** *or* **communication;** dark secret; solemn secret; guarded secret, hush-hush matter, classified information, eyes-only *or* top-secret information, restricted information; inside information

confident ADJS **sure,** secure, **assured,** reassured, decided, determined; **convinced,** persuaded, positive, **cocksure; unhesitating,** unfaltering, unwavering; **undoubting**; **self-confident, self-assured, self-reliant,** sure of oneself; poised; unafraid; **overconfident, oversure,** overweening, hubristic

confidential ADJS auricular, **inside** <nonformal>, esoteric; *in petto* <Ital>, close to one's chest *or* vest <nonformal>, under one's hat <nonformal>; **off the record,** not for the record, within these four walls, for no other ears, eyes-only, between us; not to be quoted, not for publication *or* release

configuration NOUNS **arrangement, ordering,** structuring, shaping, forming, configurating, constitution; **formation,** formulation, form, array; **constellation**

confine VERBS **shut in,** shut away, coop in, hem in, fence in *or* up, wall in *or* up, rail in; **shut up, coop up, pen up,** box up, mew up, bottle up, cork up, seal up, **impound;** pen, coop, pound <old>, crib, mew, cloister, immure, cage, cage in, encage; **enclose**; **hold, keep in,** hold *or* keep in custody, **detain,** keep in detention, constrain, ground, **restrain,** hold in restraint; check, inhibit; restrict; shackle

confinement NOUNS 1 **birth, childbirth, childbearing, having a baby, giving birth, birthing,** parturition, the stork <nonformal>; lying-in, being brought to bed, **childbed,** *accouchement* <Fr>; **labor,** travail, birth throes *or* pangs; **delivery,** blessed event <nonformal>
2 locking-up, lockup, caging, penning, putting behind bars, impoundment, **restraint,** restriction; check, **restraint, constraint**

confirm VERBS affirm, **attest,** warrant, uphold <Brit nonformal>, **substantiate, authenticate, validate, certify,** ratify, **verify;** circumstantiate, **corroborate, bear out,** support, buttress, **sustain,** fortify, bolster, back, back up, reinforce, undergird, strengthen; **document;** probate, prove

confirmation NOUNS **substantiation,** proof, proving, proving out, bearing out, affirmation, attestation, **authentication, validation, certification,** ratification, **verification; corroboration, support,** supporting evidence, corroboratory evidence, fortification, buttressing, bolstering, backing, backing up, reinforcement, undergirding, strengthening, circumstantiation, fact sheet; **documentation**

confirmed ADJS **inveterate, chronic, established,** long-established, **fixed, settled, rooted,** thorough; incorrigible, irreversible; **deep-rooted,** deep-set, deep-settled, **deep-seated,** deep-fixed, deep-dyed; **infixed, ingrained,** fast, dyed-in-the-wool; implanted, inculcated, instilled; set, **set in one's ways,** settled in habit

confiscate VERBS **attach, annex;** sequester, sequestrate, impound; **commandeer,** press, **impress;** expropriate, nationalize, socialize, communalize, communize, collectivize; exercise the right of eminent domain, exercise the right of angary; replevy, replevin; garnishee, garnish

conflict NOUNS 1 **disaccord, discord,** open conflict *or* war, **friction,** rub; jar, **jarring,** jangle, clash, clashing; touchiness, strained relations, **tension;** bad blood; **unpleasantness;** mischief; **contention**; **enmity**; psychological stress VERBS 2 **disagree, differ**, vary, not see eye-to-eye, be at cross-purposes, tangle assholes <nonformal>, **disaccord**, clash, **jar,** jangle, jostle, collide, square off, cross swords, break, break off

conform VERBS observe the proprieties, play the game, follow the rules, fall in *or* into line; comply, correspond, accord, harmonize; **adapt,** adjust, **accommodate,** bend, meet, suit, fit, shape; **comply with,** agree with, tally with, chime *or* fall in with, go by, be guided *or* regulated by, observe, follow, bend, yield, take the shape of; **adapt to,** adjust to, gear to, assimilate to, **accommodate to** *or* **with; reconcile,** settle, compose; rub off corners; **make conform,** shape, lick into shape, mold, force into a mold; straighten, rectify, correct, **discipline**

conformist NOUNS conformer, sheep, trimmer, parrot, yes-man, organization man; **conventionalist,** Mrs Grundy, Babbitt, Philistine, middle-class type, button-down *or* white-bread type <nonformal>, **bourgeois,** Middle American, plastic person *and* clone *and* square <all nonformal>, three-piecer *and* yuppie <both nonformal>, Barbie Doll <trademark> <nonformal>

confound VERBS **confuse,** mix, mix up, muddle, tumble, jumble, jumble together, **blur,** blur distinctions, overlook distinctions; **thwart, frustrate, foil, cross, balk; discomfit,** upset, **disrupt,** flummox <nonformal>, **disconcert, baffle,** nonplus, perplex, stump <nonformal>

confront VERBS **meet, meet with,** meet up with <nonformal>, come face to face with, meet head-on *or* eyeball to eyeball, be on a collision course; **accost,** encounter; front, fly in the teeth *or* face of, **face up to,** face down, face out; affront, say right to one's face, square up to, go eyeball-to-eyeball *or* one-on-one with <nonformal>;

confused ADJS **chaotic,** anarchic, **muddled, jumbled,** scattered, helter-skelter <nonformal>, higgledy-piggledy, hugger-mugger, skimble-skamble, in a mess; **topsy-turvy,** arsy-varsy, upside-down, ass-backwards <nonformal>; **mixed up, balled** *or* **bollixed up** <nonformal>, **screwed up** <nonformal>, mucked up <nonformal>, **fouled up** *and* fucked up *and* snafu <all nonformal>; **bewildered, dismayed,** distracted, distraught, abashed, **disconcerted, embarrassed,** discomposed, **put-out, disturbed, upset,** perturbed, **bothered,** all hot and bothered <nonformal>

confusion NOUNS **fluster,** flummox <nonformal>, **flutter,** flurry, ruffle; disorientation, **muddle, muddlement,** fuddle *and* fuddlement <both nonformal>, befuddlement, muddleheadedness, daze, maze <nonformal>; unsettlement, disorganization, **disorder,** chaos, **mess** *and* mix-up *and* snafu <all nonformal>, balls-up *and* shemozzle <both Brit nonformal>, shuffle, jumble, **discomfiture, discomposure, disconcertion,** discombobulation <nonformal>, **bewilderment, embarrassment, disturbance,** perturbation, **upset,** frenzy, pother, bother, botheration *and* stew <both nonformal>, pucker <old>; tizzy *and* swivet *and* sweat <all nonformal>; haze, fog, mist, cloud; maze; **perplexity**

con game NOUNS **confidence game, skin game** <nonformal>, **bunco game; shell game,** thimblerig, thimblerigging; bucket shop, boiler room <nonformal>; bait-and- switch, the wire

congeal VERBS **cohere,** coagulate, clabber <nonformal>, **clot; freeze; thicken,** thick <old>; inspissate, incrassate; set, concrete; gelatinize, gelatinate, jelly, jellify, **jell,** gel

congenial ADJS **friendly,** friendlike; **amicable, peaceable,** unhostile; **harmonious**; **amiable,** *simpático* <Sp>, *simpatico* <Ital>, *sympathique* <Fr>, compatible, pleasant, agreeable, favorable, well-intentioned, well-meaning, well-meant; sociable; symbiotic

congenital ADJS **innate, inborn; born, consummate,** unmitigated, unalloyed, perfect, veritable, egregious, deep-dyed, dyed-in-the-wool; **native, natural,** natural to, connatural, native to, indigenous; hereditary, inherited, bred in the bone, in the blood, running in the blood *or* race *or* strain, radical, rooted; connate, connatal, coeval

congested ADJS **glutted,** gorged, overfed, bloated, replete, swollen, **satiated, stuffed,** overstuffed, **crowded, overcrowded, crammed,** jammed, packed, jam-packed, like sardines in a can *or* tin, bumper-to-bumper <nonformal>; choked, stuffed up; overblown, distended, **swollen, bloated**

conglomeration NOUNS 1 **hodgepodge,** hotchpotch, hotchpot; **medley, miscellany,** mélange, pastiche, *pasticcio* <Ital>, **assortment,** assemblage, mixed bag, ragbag, grab bag, olio, *olla podrida* <Sp>, **scramble, jumble,** mingle-mangle, **mix,** mishmash, **mess,** can of worms <nonformal>, dog's breakfast <Can nonformal>, mare's nest, rat's nest, hurrah's nest <nautical nonformal>, hash, patchwork, salad, gallimaufry, salmagundi, **potpourri,** stew, sauce, slurry, omnium-gatherum
2 **combination, incorporation,** aggregation, agglomeration, congeries; **amalgamation, consolidation,** assimilation, **integration,** solidification, **encompassment,** inclusion, ecumenism

congratulate VERBS **felicitate,** bless, **compliment,** tender *or* offer one's congratulations *or* felicitations *or* compliments; shake one's hand, pat one on the back; **rejoice with one,** wish one joy; **applaud, praise,** flatter

congratulations NOUNS 1 **felicitation,** blessing, **compliment,** pat on the back; good wishes, best wishes; **applause, praise,** flattery

2 <nonformal> **congrats!, all right!, aw right!, right on!,** way to go!, attaboy!, attagirl!, good deal!, looking good!, nice going!, that's my boy!, that's my girl!

congregate VERBS **come together, assemble, collect,** come from far and wide, come *or* arrive in a body; league, ally; **unite**; muster, **meet, gather, forgather,** gang up <nonformal>, mass; **merge,** converge, flow together, fuse; flock together; herd together; **throng, crowd,** swarm, teem, hive, surge, seethe, mill, stream, horde

congregation NOUNS **lay persons,** flock, fold, sheep; parishioners, churchgoers, assembly; *minyan* <Heb>; **parish,** society; **assembly,** *assemblée* <Fr>, **gathering, forgathering,** congress

congress NOUNS **legislature,** legislative body; **parliament, assembly,** general assembly, house of assembly, legislative assembly, **national assembly, chamber of deputies,** federal assembly, diet; **upper chamber** *or* **house**

conjecture NOUNS 1 **guess,** unverified supposition, perhaps, speculation, guesswork, surmise, educated guess; guesstimate *and* hunch *and* shot *and* stab <all nonformal>; rough guess, wild guess, blind guess, bold conjecture, shot in the dark <nonformal>
VERBS 2 **guess,** guesstimate <nonformal>, give a guess, talk off the top of one's head <nonformal>, hazard a conjecture, venture a guess, risk assuming *or* stating, tentatively suggest, go out on a limb <nonformal>

conjugal ADJS **matrimonial, marital, connubial, nuptial,** wedded, married, hymeneal; epithalamic; **spousal;** husbandly, uxorious; bridal, wifely, uxorial

conjure VERBS **conjure up,** evoke, invoke, raise, summon, call up; **call up spirits,** conjure *or* conjure up spirits, summon spirits, raise ghosts, evoke from the dead

call spirits from the vasty deep
SHAKESPEARE

conjurer NOUNS **trickster,** tricker; **juggler,** sleight-of-hand performer, magician, illusionist, **prestidigitator,** *escamoteur* <Fr>; **sorcerer, necromancer, wizard,** warlock, theurgist; diviner

con man NOUNS

<nonformal> **gyp,** gypper, gyp artist, flimflammer, flimflam man, blackleg, bilker, fleecer, diddler, crook, sharpie, shark, jackleg, slicker, con artist, bunco, bunco artist, bunco steerer, scammer, hustler

connect VERBS **adjoin,** join, conjoin, butt, **abut,** abut on *or* upon, be contiguous, be in contact; border, **border on** *or* **upon,** verge on *or* upon; lie by, stand by; unite, meet, meet up, link up, merge, converge, **come together;** communicate, intercommunicate

connection NOUNS 1 **intermediary,** intermedium, mediary, medium; link, **connecting link,** tie, **go-between,** liaison; **mediator; contact, touch; passageway, conduit**; access, communication; alliance, **family connection** *or* tie; **marriage relationship,** affinity, marital affinity; marriage connection, matrimonial connection; **relation, relationship, association**
2 **relevance, pertinence,** pertinency, cogency, relatedness, materiality, **appositeness,** germaneness; reference, **bearing,** concern; **continuum,** plenum; concatenation, catenation

connive VERBS **conspire,** collude, be in cahoots <nonformal>, complot <old>, cabal; **hatch, hatch up,** cook up <nonformal>, brew, concoct, hatch *or* lay a plot; **maneuver,** machinate, finesse, operate <nonformal>, engineer, rig, wangle <nonformal>, angle, finagle <nonformal>

connoisseur NOUNS *connaisseur* <Fr>, *cognoscente* <Ital>; **judge,** good judge, **critic, expert,** authority, maven <nonformal>, arbiter, arbiter of taste, *arbiter elegantiarum* <L>, tastemaker, trend-setter; **epicure,** epicurean; **gourmet, gourmand,** *bon vivant* <Fr>, good *or* refined palate

connotation NOUNS **implication, import,** latent *or* underlying *or* implied meaning, ironic suggestion *or* implication, more than meets the eye, what is read between the lines; meaning; **suggestion,** allusion; coloration, tinge, undertone, overtone, undercurrent, more than meets the eye *or* ear, something between the lines, intimation, touch, nuance, innuendo; **inference, supposition,** presupposition, assumption, presumption; secondary *or* transferred *or* metaphorical sense; undermeaning, undermention, subsidiary sense, subsense, **subtext**

connubial ADJS **matrimonial, marital, conjugal, nuptial,** wedded, married, hymeneal; epithalamic; **spousal;** husbandly, uxorious; bridal, wifely, uxorial

conquer VERBS **vanquish,** quell, **suppress, put down, subdue, subjugate,** put under the yoke, master; **reduce,** prostrate, fell, **flatten, break, smash, crush, humble,** bend, **bring to terms, humble,** humiliate, take down a notch *or* peg, bend, **bend to one's will**

conqueror NOUNS **victor, winner,** victress, victrix, triumpher; defeater, **vanquisher,** subduer, subjugator, *conquistador* <Sp>; master of the situation; conquering hero

conscience NOUNS grace, **sense of right and wrong;** inward monitor, inner arbiter, moral censor, censor, ethical self, superego; **voice of conscience,** still small voice within, guardian *or* good angel; tender conscience; clear *or* clean conscience; social conscience; conscientiousness; twinge of conscience

conscientious ADJS **meticulous, exacting, scrupulous,** religious, punctilious, punctual, **particular, fussy, critical, attentive,** scrutinizing; **thorough,** thoroughgoing; **finical,** finicking, finicky; **strict,** rigid, **rigorous,** exigent, demanding

conscious ADJS 1 **living, alive,** having life, live, very much alive, alive and well, alive and kicking <nonformal>, breathing, quick <old>, **animate,** animated, **vital,** zoetic, instinct with life, imbued *or* endowed with life, viable
2 **intentional,** considered, studied, advised, calculated, contemplated, envisaged, envisioned, premeditated, knowing, witting; watchful, aware, alert

conscript VERBS **call to arms, call up,** call to the colors; recruit; draft, induct, press, impress, commandeer; **mobilize,** call to active duty; **muster,** levy, raise, muster in

consecrate VERBS **dedicate, commit, devote,** set apart; **ordain,** frock, **canonize**

consecutive ADJS **successive,** successional, back-to-back <nonformal>; progressive; **serial,** ordinal, seriate, catenary; sequent, **sequential;** linear, lineal, in-line

consensus NOUNS general agreement, *consensus omnium* <L, consent of all> *and consensus gentium* <L, consent of the people>, sense, **unanimity**; **like-mindedness,** meeting *or* intersection *or* confluence of minds, sense of the meeting

consent NOUNS 1 **assent, agreement,** accord <old>, acceptance, approval, blessing, approbation, sanction, **endorsement,** ratification, backing; affirmation, affirmative, affirmative voice *or* vote, yea, aye, **nod** *and* **okay** *and* **OK** <all nonformal>; **leave, per-**

mission, readiness, promptness, promptitude, eagerness, tacit *or* unspoken *or* silent *or* implicit consent
VERBS 2 **assent,** give *or* yield assent, **acquiesce, comply, accede, agree,** agree to *or* with, have no problem with; find it in one's heart; take kindly to *and* hold with <both nonformal>; **subscribe to,** acquiesce in, abide by; yes, **say 'yes'**

consequence NOUNS **effect, result,** resultant, consequent, sequent, sequence, sequel, sequela, sequelae; event, eventuality, eventuation, **upshot, outcome,** logical outcome, possible outcome, scenario; **outgrowth,** spin-off, offshoot, offspring, issue, aftermath, legacy; **weight,** moment, importance, eminence

conservation NOUNS **preservation,** preserval, **saving, salvation,** salvage, **keeping, safekeeping,** maintenance, upkeep, support; environmental conservation; nature conservation *or* conservancy, soil conservation, forest conservation, etc

conservationist NOUNS **environmentalist,** preservationist, nature-lover, environmental activist, doomwatcher <Brit>, duck-squeezer *and* ecofreak *and* tree-hugger *and* eagle freak <all nonformal>

conservative NOUNS **rightist, rightwinger;** dry <Brit nonformal>, standpat *and* standpatter <both nonformal>; hard hat; social Darwinist; ultraconservative, arch-conservative, extreme right-winger, **reactionary,** reactionarist, reactionist, diehard; **royalist, monarchist,** Bourbon, Tory, imperialist; **right, right wing; radical right**

the leftover progressive of an earlier generation
EDMUND FULLER

2 **moderate,** moderatist, moderationist, middle-of-the-roader, **centrist,** neutral, compromiser
ADJS 3 **right-wing,** right of center, dry <Brit nonformal>; old-line, die-hard, unreconstructed, standpat <nonformal>, unprogressive, nonprogressive; ultraconservative, **reactionary,** reactionist

consider VERBS 1 **care, mind, heed,** reck, think, regard, pay heed to, take heed *or* thought of; **take an interest,** be concerned; **pay attention**
2 **discuss, debate, reason, deliberate,** deliberate upon, exchange views *or* opinions, talk, **talk over, hash over** <nonformal>, talk of *or* about, rap <nonformal>, comment upon, reason about, discourse about, **treat,** dissertate on, handle, deal with, take up, **go into, examine,** investigate, talk out, **analyze,** sift, **study,** canvass, review
3 **allow for, make allowance for,** make room for, provide for, open the door to, take account of, **take into account** *or* **consideration,** consider the circumstances

considerable NOUNS 1 **lot, lots,** deal, no end of, **good** *or* **great deal,** sight, **heap, pile, stack,** loads, **raft, slew,** whole slew, spate, wad, **batch,** mess, mint, peck, pack, pot, **tidy sum,** quite a little
ADJS 2 **sizable, big, great, grand,** tall <nonformal>, **goodly,** healthy, tidy <nonformal>, **substantial,** bumper; **numerous, many, manifold,** not a few, no few; **very many,** full many, **ever so many,** quite some <nonformal>

considerably ADVS **greatly, largely,** to a large *or* great extent, in great measure, on a large scale; **much,** muchly <nonformal>, pretty much, very much, so, so very much, ever so much, ever so, never so; considerable <nonformal>; abundantly, plenty <nonformal>, no end of, no end, not a little, galore <nonformal>, **a lot,** a deal <nonformal>, **a great deal,** *beaucoup* <Fr>

considerate ADJS **thoughtful,** mindful, heedful, regardful, solicitous, attentive, delicate, tactful, mindful of others; complaisant, **accommodating,** accommodative, at one's service, **helpful,** agreeable, **obliging,** indulgent, tolerant, lenient

consign VERBS **assign,** confer, settle, settle on; **make over, sign over,** sign away; transmit, **hand down, hand on, pass on,** devolve upon

consistent ADJS **connected;** continuous, **serial,** uninterrupted, contiguous, sequential, sequent, **consecutive**; orderly, tight; **joined; sound, well-grounded, well-founded,** conforming to the facts *or* the data *or* the evidence *or* reality, hard, solid, substantial; self-consistent, logical

consolation NOUNS **solace,** solacement, easement, heart's ease, **encouragement,** aid and comfort, **assurance, reassur-**

ance, support, **comfort,** crumb *or* shred of comfort, condolence, sympathy; **relief**

kind words and comfortable
William Cowper

console VERBS **comfort, solace,** give *or* bring comfort, bear up; condole with, sympathize with, extend sympathy; ease, **put** *or* **set at ease;** bolster, support; relieve; **assure, reassure; encourage, hearten,** pat on the back; **cheer**; wipe away the tears

rejoice with them that do rejoice, and weep with them that weep
Bible

consolidate VERBS **incorporate, amalgamate,** assimilate, **integrate,** solidify, coalesce, compound, put *or* lump together, roll into one, come together, make one, unitize

conspicuous ADJS **noticeable, notable,** ostensible, **prominent, bold, pronounced, salient,** in relief, in bold *or* high *or* strong relief, **striking, outstanding,** in the foreground, sticking *or* hanging out

conspiracy NOUNS **intrigue,** web of intrigue, **plot, scheme,** deep-laid plot *or* scheme, underplot, game *or* little game <both nonformal>, trick, stratagem, finesse; counterplot; confederacy, covin, complot <old>, cabal; **scheming,** schemery, plotting; finagling <nonformal>, **machination,** manipulation, **maneuvering,** engineering, rigging; frame-up <nonformal>; wire-pulling <nonformal>

conspirator NOUNS **schemer, plotter,** counterplotter, finagler <nonformal>, Machiavellian; **intriguer,** *intrigant, intrigante* <both Fr>, cabalist; **conspirer,** coconspirator, **conniver;** maneuverer, machinator, operator <nonformal>, opportunist, exploiter; wire-puller <nonformal>

conspire VERBS **plot, scheme, intrigue,** be up to something; **connive,** collude, complot <old>, cabal; **hatch, hatch up,** cook up <nonformal>, brew, concoct, hatch *or* lay a plot; **maneuver,** machinate, finesse, operate <nonformal>, engineer, rig, wangle <nonformal>, angle, finagle <nonformal>

constant ADJS 1 **faithful, loyal,** devoted, allegiant; **true, true-blue,** true to one's colors; **steadfast,** unswerving, steady, consistent, stable, unfailing, staunch, firm, solid
2 **continual, perennial; steady,** sustained, **regular; incessant, ceaseless, unceasing,** unintermitting, unintermittent *or* unintermitted, unremitting, relentless, unrelenting, unchanging, unvarying, uninterrupted, unstopped, unbroken

constellation NOUNS **configuration,** asterism; zodiacal constellation; **star cluster,** galactic cluster, open cluster, globular cluster, stellar association, supercluster; Magellanic clouds

consternation NOUNS **fear, fright,** affright; **scare, alarm, dismay; dread,** unholy dread, **awe; terror, horror,** horrification, mortal *or* abject fear; **phobia** <see list>, funk *or* blue funk <both nonformal>; **panic,** panic fear *or* terror; stampede; **cowardice**

constituency NOUNS **electorate,** electors; constituents; bailiwick, vantage, stamping ground, footing, **territory,** turf, home turf, **power base**

constituent NOUNS **component, ingredient,** integrant, makings *and* fixings <both nonformal>, **element, factor, part**, player, module, part and parcel; appurtenance, adjunct; **feature,** aspect, specialty, circumstance, detail, item; elector

constitute VERBS **compose,** construct, fabricate; **incorporate,** embody, incarnate; **form, organize,** structure, shape, shape up; **consist of,** be a feature of, form a part of, combine *or* unite in, merge in; **consist,** be made up of, be constituted of, contain

constraint NOUNS **restraint; inhibition;** legal restraint, injunction, enjoining, enjoinder, interdict; **control, curb, check,** rein, arrest, arrestation; **retardation,** deceleration, slowing down; cooling *and* cooling off *and* cooling down <all nonformal>; retrenchment, curtailment; self-control; **hindrance**

constrict VERBS **narrow,** constrict, diminish, draw in, go in; restrict, limit, straiten, confine; shut off, **close,** close off *or* up, close tight, shut tight; constrict, squeeze, **stifle,** stop up

construct VERBS **build; structure; organize; form**, fabricate

construction NOUNS 1 **structure, formation,** conformation, **format; arrangement**, configuration; **composition**; making, building, creation, production, forging, fashioning, molding, fabrication, manufacture
2 **interpretation, reading,** way of seeing *or* understanding *or* putting; **explanation, definition,** sense-distinction; **phrase, expression, locution, utterance,** usage, term, verbalism

constructive ADJS **helpful, useful,** utile, aidful <old>; **profitable, salutary,** good for, **beneficial**; remedial, therapeutic; **serviceable, useful**; **contributory,** contributing, conducive, **positive,** promotional

construe VERBS **interpret,** put a construction on, **take;** understand, **understand by, take to mean,** take it that; **read; read into,** read between the lines; see in a special light, read in view of, take an approach to, **define, describe**; **translate, render**

consular ADJS **diplomatic,** ambassadorial, ministerial, plenipotentiary

consulate NOUNS **office, embassy,** legation, chancery, chancellery

consult VERBS **confer,** sit down together, **go into a huddle** <nonformal>, deliberate, take counsel, counsel, **lay** *or* **put heads together;** collogue; **consult with, advise with, discuss with, take up with,** reason with; **discuss,** talk over; refer to, call in

consultant NOUNS **adviser, counsel, counselor,** professional consultant, expert, maven <nonformal>, boffin <Brit nonformal>; instructor, guide, **mentor,** nestor, orienter; confidant, personal adviser

consultation NOUNS **conference, congress, convention, parley, palaver, confab** <nonformal>, confabulation, **conclave, powwow, huddle** <nonformal>, *pourparler* <Fr>, **meeting;** interview, audience

consume VERBS **spend, expend, use up;** absorb, assimilate, digest, ingest, eat, **eat up,** swallow, swallow up, gobble, gobble up; burn up; **finish,** finish off; **exhaust, deplete,** impoverish, drain, drain of resources; suck dry, bleed white <nonformal>, suck one's blood; wear away, erode, erode away, ablate; waste away; **throw away, squander**

consumer NOUNS **user,** employer; **buyer,** purchaser, emptor, vendee; **shopper,** marketer

consumption NOUNS 1 **consuming, using** *or* **eating up;** burning up; absorption, assimilation, digestion, ingestion, **expenditure,** expending, spending; squandering, wastefulness; finishing; **depletion,** drain, exhausting, **exhaustion,** impoverishment; **waste,** wastage, wasting away, erosion, ablation, wearing down, wearing away, attrition; throwing away
2 **tuberculosis** *or* **TB,** white plague, phthisis

contact NOUNS 1 **touch,** touching, *attouchement* <Fr>, taction, tangency, contingence; gentle *or* tentative contact, caress, brush, glance, nudge, kiss, rub, graze; impingement, impingence; osculation; **communication,** communion, congress, **commerce, intercourse**
2 **go-between, middleman, intermediary, medium,** intermedium, intermediate, interagent, **internuncio,** broker; connection <nonformal>; **negotiator,** negotiant; interpleader; arbitrator, mediator
VERBS 3 **come in contact, touch, feel, impinge,** bump up against, hit; osculate; **graze,** caress, kiss, nudge, rub, brush, glance, scrape, sideswipe, skim, skirt, shave; grope *and* feel up *and* cop a feel <all nonformal>; have a near miss, brush *or* graze *or* squeak by
4 **communicate with, get in touch** *or* **contact with, make contact with,** raise, reach, get to, get through to, get hold of, make *or* establish connection, get in connection with; **make advances,** make overtures, **approach,** make up to <nonformal>; relate to; keep in touch *or* contact with, maintain connection; **answer,** respond *or* reply to, get back to; **question,** interrogate; **correspond,** drop a line

contagious ADJS **infectious,** infective, **catching,** taking, spreading, **communicable,** zymotic, inoculable; pestiferous, pestilential, **epidemic,** epidemial, pandemic; epizootic, epiphytotic; endemic; sporadic

contain VERBS **enclose,** close in, bound, include; compass, encompass; **surround,** encircle; **shut** *or* **pen in,** coop in; **fence in,** wall in, wall up, rail in, rail off, screen off, curtain off; **hem** *or* **hedge in,** box in, pocket; shut *or* coop *or* mew up; pen, coop, corral, cage, impound, mew; **imprison,** incarcerate, jail, lock up, lock down; **besiege,** beset, beleaguer, leaguer, cordon, cordon off, quarantine, blockade

container NOUNS **receptacle;** receiver, holder, vessel, utensil; basin, pot, pan, cup, glass, ladle, bottle; cask; box, case; basket

contaminate VERBS **defile, foul, befoul; sully;** foul one's own nest, shit where one eats <nonformal>, nasty *or* benasty <both nonformal>, mess *and* mess up <both nonformal>; **pollute, corrupt, infect; taint,** tarnish; **adulterate, debase,** denaturalize, pollute, denature, bastardize, **tamper with, doctor** *and* doctor up <both nonformal>; **irradiate**

contemplate VERBS **consider, speculate, reflect, study, ponder,** perpend, **weigh, deliberate, debate, meditate, muse, brood, ruminate,** chew the cud <nonformal>, digest; introspect, be abstracted; wrinkle one's brow; fall into a brown study, retreat into one's mind *or* thoughts; **toy with, play with,** play around with, flirt *or* coquet with the idea

contemporary ADJS **modern, present-day,** present-time, twentieth-century, latter-day, space-age, neoteric, now <nonformal>, **newfashioned,** fashionable, modish, mod, *à la mode* <Fr>, **up-to-date,** up-to-datish, **up-to-the-minute, in,** abreast of the times; **advanced,** progressive, forward-looking, modernizing, **avant-garde;** ultramodern, ultra-ultra, ahead of its time, far out, way out, modernistic

contempt NOUNS **disdain, scorn,** contemptuousness, disdainfulness, superciliousness, snootiness, snottiness, sniffiness, toploftiness, scornfulness, despite, contumely, sovereign contempt; snobbishness; clannishness, cliquishness, exclusiveness, exclusivity; hauteur, airs, arrogance; **ridicule**; **insult**; **disparagement**

contemptible ADJS **offensive, objectionable, odious, repulsive,** repellent, rebarbative, **repugnant, revolting,** forbidding; **obnoxious, abhorrent, hateful, abominable,** heinous, **despicable,** detestable, execrable, beneath *or* below contempt, **base,** ignoble

contemptuous ADJS **disdainful,** dismissive, **supercilious,** contumelious, cavalier, you-be-damned <nonformal>; **arrogant**, uppish *and* uppity <both nonformal>; abusive, offensive, humiliating, degrading, calumnious; **disparaging, derogatory,** derogative, **depreciatory,** depreciative, deprecatory, slighting, belittling, minimizing, detractory, pejorative, backbiting

content NOUNS 1 **contents,** what is contained *or* included *or* comprised; **insides**, innards <nonformal>, guts; **components, constituents, ingredients,** elements, **items, parts, divisions,** subdivisions
2 **capacity, volume,** holding capacity, cubic footage *or* yardage etc, accommodation, room, space, measure, limit, burden; gallonage, tankage; poundage, tonnage, cordage; stowage; **quantity**
3 **contentment,** contentedness, satisfiedness; **satisfaction,** entire satisfaction, fulfillment; ease, peace of mind, composure; comfort; well-being, euphoria; **happiness**; **acceptance,** resignation, reconcilement, reconciliation
ADJS 4 **contented, satisfied; pleased**; happy; **easy, at ease,** at one's ease, easygoing; composed; **comfortable**, of good comfort; euphoric, eupeptic; carefree, without care, *sans souci* <Fr>; accepting, resigned, reconciled; uncomplaining, unrepining; **willing, agreeable**

contest NOUNS 1 **game,** play, engagement, **match,** trial, test; **fight,** bout
VERBS 2 **deny, not admit, not accept,** refuse to admit *or* accept; **disclaim, disown, disaffirm, disavow, disallow, dispute,** gainsay, **oppose, counter,** go counter to, take issue with, join issue upon, run counter to

context NOUNS **circumstances,** total situation, existing conditions *or* situation, set of conditions, terms of reference, **environment**, environing circumstances, frame, setting, surrounding conditions, parameters; **the picture,** the whole picture, full particulars

contingent ADJS **dependent, depending;** contingent on, **dependent on, depending on,** predicated on, based on, hanging *or* hinging on, turning on, revolving on; depending on circumstances; circumscribed by, hedged *or* hedged about by; boxed in <nonformal>; **subject to,** incidental to, incident to; adventitious, incidental, iffy <nonformal>

continual ADJS continued, continuing;

cyclical, repetitive, **recurrent,** periodic; **constant, perennial**

continuation NOUNS **sequel,** continuance, **follow-up** *or* **follow-through** <nonformal>; **protraction, prolongation,** extension, lengthening, **postponement, deferment** *or* **deferral,** prorogation, putting-off, tabling, protraction, extension of time; **adjournment** *or* adjournal, adjournment sine die; **persistence, perseverance**; **endurance, stamina,** staying power; **continuity**; **repetition**

continue VERBS 1 **lengthen, prolong,** prolongate, **elongate, extend,** produce, **protract;** lengthen out, let out, **draw** *or* drag *or* stretch *or* string *or* spin out; last, **endure,** go *or* run *or* flow on
2 **postpone, delay, defer, put off,** give one a rain check <nonformal>, shift off, hold off *or* up <nonformal>, prorogue, put on hold *or* ice *or* the back burner <all nonformal>, reserve, waive, **suspend,** hang up, stay, hang fire; protract, drag *or* stretch out <nonformal>; **hold over,** lay over, stand over, let the matter stand, **put aside,** lay *or* set *or* push aside, lay *or* set by, **table,** lay on the table, pigeonhole, **shelve,** put on the shelf, put on ice <nonformal>

continuing ADJS **durable,** perdurable, **lasting, enduring,** perduring, **abiding,** remaining, staying, **stable**, persisting, **persistent,** perennial; inveterate, agelong; **steadfast, constant,** intransient, immutable, unfading, evergreen, sempervirent, **permanent**, perennial, **long-lasting,** long-standing, of long duration *or* standing; long-term; **long-lived**

continuity NOUNS logical order, serial order; **degree**; **hierarchy, gradation,** subordination, superordination, rank, place; **sequence**

continuous ADJS continued, **continual,** continuing; **uninterrupted, unintermittent,** unintermitted, featureless, unrelieved, monotonous; **connected, joined**, linked, chained, concatenated, catenated, articulated; **unbroken,** serried, **uniform**, **incessant, constant,** steady, stable, **ceaseless,** unceasing, **endless,** unending, never-ending, **interminable,** perennial; **perpetual, everlasting,** everliving, ever-being, ever-abiding, ever-during, ever-durable, permanent, perdurable, indestructible; **infinite, abiding**

contortion NOUNS **distortion,** torsion, twist, twistedness, **crookedness,** tortuosity; unsymmetry, disproportion, lopsidedness, imbalance, irregularity, **deviation; twist,** quirk, turn, screw, wring, wrench, wrest; **warp,** buckle; knot, gnarl

contraband NOUNS smuggled goods; narcotics, drugs, dope <nonformal>, jewels, cigarettes; bootleg liquor; stolen goods *or* property, hot goods *or* items <nonformal>

contraceptive NOUNS birth control device, prophylactic; condom; **rubber** *and* skin *and* bag <all nonformal>; oral contraceptive, **birth control pill, the pill** <nonformal>, morning-after pill, abortion pill; diaphragm, pessary; spermicide, spermicidal jelly, contraceptive foam; intrauterine device *or* IUD

contract NOUNS 1 **compact, pact,** legal contract, valid contract, **covenant,** convention, transaction, paction <Scots>, accord, **agreement,** mutual agreement, agreement between *or* among parties, signed *or* written agreement, formal agreement, legal agreement, undertaking, stipulation; bond, binding agreement, ironclad agreement, covenant of salt
VERBS 2 **catch, get,** take, sicken for <Brit>, **come down with** <nonformal>, be stricken *or* seized by, fall a victim to; catch cold; take one's death <nonformal>
3 **compress,** cramp, compact, condense, concentrate, consolidate, solidify; **reduce, decrease**; abbreviate, curtail, **shorten**; **constrict, narrow,** draw, draw in *or* together; choke, choke off

contraction NOUNS 1 contracture; systole; **compression,** compressure, pressurizing, pressurization; **compacting,** compaction, compactedness; **condensation, concentration,** consolidation, solidification; **circumscription, narrowing;** reduction, diminuendo, **decrease**; abbreviation, curtailment, shortening; **constriction,** stricture *or* striction, astriction, strangulation, **choking,** choking off; bottleneck, chokepoint, hourglass, hourglass figure
2 **abbreviation,** shortening, clipping, cutting, pruning, truncation

contradict VERBS **deny, not admit, not accept,** refuse to admit *or* accept; **disclaim, disown, disaffirm, disavow,**

disallow, abjure, forswear, **renounce, retract,** take back, recant; revoke, nullify, **repudiate;** fly in the face of, cross, assert the contrary, contravene, controvert, impugn, **dispute,** gainsay, **oppose, counter,** go counter to, contest, take issue with, join issue upon, run counter to; belie, give the lie to, give one the lie direct *or* in his throat

contradiction NOUNS **denial, disavowal, disaffirmation, disownment,** disallowance; disclamation, disclaimer; **renunciation, retraction,** retractation, **repudiation,** recantation; revocation, nullification, annulment, abrogation; abjuration, abjurement, forswearing; flat *or* absolute contradiction, contravention, contrary assertion, controversion, countering, crossing, gainsaying, impugnment; **refutation, disproof**

contraption NOUNS **tool, instrument, implement, utensil; apparatus, device,** mechanical device, contrivance, contraption <nonformal>, gadget, gizmo, gimcrack, gimmick <nonformal>, means, mechanical means; gadgetry

contrary ADJS 1 perverse, **opposite,** antithetic, antithetical, **contradictory,** counter, contrapositive, contrasted; **converse, reverse,** obverse, inverse; **adverse,** adversative *or* adversive, adversarial, **opposing, opposed,** oppositive, oppositional; **antagonistic,** repugnant, oppugnant, perverse, contrarious, ornery <nonformal>, nay-saying, negative, hostile, combative, bellicose, belligerent, inimical, antipathetic, antipathetical, discordant

ADVS 2 **opposite, poles apart,** at opposite extremes; contrariwise, counter; just opposite, **face-to-face,** vis-à-vis, *front à front* <Fr>, nose to nose, one on one, eyeball-to-eyeball, back to back

contrast VERBS **make** *or* **draw a comparison,** run a comparison, do a comparative study, bring into comparison; weigh *or* measure against; confront, bring into confrontation, **oppose,** set in opposition, set off against, set in contrast, **put** *or* **set over against,** set *or* place against, counterpose

contribute VERBS 1 **participate, take part, partake,** chip in, involve *or* engage oneself, get involved; **have** *or* **take a hand in,** get in on, have a finger in, have a finger in the pie, have to do with, have a part in, be an accessory to, be implicated in, be a party to, be a player in; **join, join in,** figure in, make oneself part of, join oneself to, associate oneself with, play *or* perform a part in, play a role in, get in the act <nonformal>

2 **subscribe, chip in** *and* kick in *and* pony up *and* pay up <all nonformal>, give one's share *or* fair share; put oneself down for, pledge; contribute to, give to, **donate to,** gift *and* gift with <both nonformal>; put something in the pot, sweeten the kitty

contribution NOUNS 1 **participation, partaking, sharing,** having a part *or* share *or* voice, association; **involvement,** engagement; complicity

2 **donation,** donative; **subscription; alms,** pittance, **charity, dole, handout** <nonformal>, alms fee, widow's mite; Peter's pence; **offering,** offertory, votive offering, collection; tithe

contrite ADJS **penitent, repentant; penitential,** penitentiary; abject, humble, humbled, **sheepish, apologetic,** touched, softened, melted

contrive VERBS **plan, devise, design,** frame, shape, cast, concert, lay plans; **arrange,** prearrange, make arrangements, set up, work up, work out; **maneuver, manipulate,** pull strings *or* wires; **machinate,** angle <nonformal>, **jockey, engineer;** play games <nonformal>

control NOUNS 1 **mastery, mastership, command, power, jurisdiction, dominion, domination; hold, grasp,** grip, gripe; hand, hands, iron hand, clutches; talons, claws; helm, reins of government

VERBS 2 **restrain, constrain, govern,** guard, contain, keep under control, put *or* lay under restraint; **inhibit,** straiten <old>; enjoin, clamp *or* crack down on <nonformal>, proscribe, prohibit; **curb, check, arrest, bridle,** get under control, rein, snub, snub in; **retard,** slow down, decelerate; **cool** *and* **cool off** *and* **cool down** <all nonformal>; hold, **hold in,** keep, withhold, hold up <nonformal>; **direct, manage, regulate, conduct, carry on, handle, run** <nonformal>; **command, head, govern, boss** *and* head up *and* pull the strings *and* **mastermind** *and* quarterback *and* call the signals <all nonformal>

controlling ADJS **restraining, constraining; inhibiting,** inhibitive; **suppressive, repressive,** stultifying; controlling, on top of <nonformal>; **managing, managerial; commanding, governing**; leading, guiding

controversial ADJS 1 **contentious, quarrelsome; disputatious,** litigious, polemic, polemical; **argumentative,** argumental; on the warpath, looking for trouble; scrappy <nonformal>; cat-and-doggish, cat-and-dog; **bellicose, belligerent**
2 **debatable,** moot, arguable, disputable, contestable, controvertible, refutable, confutable, deniable; suspect; open to question *or* doubt

controversy NOUNS **quarrel,** open quarrel, dustup, **dispute, argument,** polemic, argy-bargy *and* slanging match <both Brit>, fliting <old>, altercation, **fight, squabble, contention,** strife, **tussle,** bicker, wrangle, snarl, **tiff, spat,** fuss

convalescence NOUNS **recovery, rally, comeback** <nonformal>, return; **recuperation**

convene VERBS **meet,** hold a meeting *or* session, sit; **convoke,** summon, call together

convenience NOUNS 1 **facility, accommodation, appliance,** amenity, appurtenance; advantage
2 **handiness, wieldiness, manageability,** manageableness, maneuverability; practicality; **flexibility,** pliancy, **pliability;** adaptability, feasibility

convenient ADJS **handy; available,** accessible, **ready, at hand,** to hand, **on hand,** on tap, on deck <nonformal>, on call, at one's call *or* beck and call, at one's elbow, at one's fingertips, just around the corner, at one's disposal; **timely, well-timed, seasonable, opportune; expedient,** meet, fit, fitting, befitting, suitable, sortable, appropriate

convent NOUNS **cloister, house, abbey;** priory, priorate; lamasery; **nunnery**

convention NOUNS 1 **custom,** use, **usage,** standard usage, standard behavior, **wont,** wonting, **way,** established way, time-honored practice, **tradition,** standing custom, **folkway,** manner, **practice,** praxis, prescription, **observance,** ritual, consuetude, what is done, **social convention; rule, law, canon, maxim,** dictum, moral, moralism; **norm, standard;** formula, form; rule of action *or* conduct, moral precept; commandment, *mitzvah* <Heb>; **principle,** principium, settled principle, general principle *or* truth, tenet
2 **conference, congress, parley, palaver, confab** <nonformal>, confabulation, **conclave, powwow, huddle** <nonformal>, **consultation,** *pourparler* <Fr>, **meeting**

conventional ADJS **decorous,** orthodox, **correct,** right, **right-thinking, proper,** decent, seemly, meet; **accepted, recognized,** acknowledged, received, admitted, approved, being done; *comme il faut, de rigueur* <both Fr>; **traditional, customary;** formal; **conformist,** bourgeois, plastic *and* square *and* straight *and* white-bread *and* white-bready *and* button-down *and* buttoned-down <all nonformal>

converge VERBS **come together,** approach, run together, **meet,** unite, connect, merge; **cross, intersect**; fall in with, link up with; be on a collision course; go toward, narrow the gap, close with, close, close up, close in; funnel; taper, pinch, nip; centralize, center, **come to a center;** center on *or* around, concentralize, concenter, **concentrate,** come *or* tend to a point; **come to a focus**

conversation NOUNS conversing; interlocution, colloquy; **exchange;** verbal intercourse, conversational interchange, interchange of speech, give-and-take, cross-talk, rapping <nonformal>, **repartee,** backchat; **discourse,** colloquial discourse; **communion, intercourse, communication**

convert NOUNS 1 **proselyte,** neophyte, catechumen, disciple
VERBS 2 **redeem,** regenerate, reform, save, give salvation
3 **convince; win over,** lead one to believe, bring over, bring round, talk over, talk around, bring to reason, bring to one's senses, **persuade, lead to believe, give to understand**

convertible ADJS changeable, resolvable, transmutable, **transformable, transitional, modifiable;** reformable, reclaimable, renewable; liquid, negotiable

convex ADJS **rotund, round,** rounded, rounded out, round as a ball; bellied, bellylike; bulging

convey VERBS 1 **transport,** freight, conduct, **take; carry, bear,** pack, tote *and* lug <both nonformal>; **channel,** channelize, canalize, **conduct,** put through; pipe, funnel, siphon
2 **communicate, impart, tell,** lay on one <nonformal>, **transmit,** transfer, send, send word, deliver *or* send a signal *or* message, **disseminate,** broadcast, pass, **pass on** *or* **along, hand on; report, render, make known,** get across *or* over

convict NOUNS 1 **prisoner, captive,** *détenu* <Fr>, cageling; con <nonformal>; **jailbird** <nonformal>, gaolbird <Brit nonformal>, stir bird <nonformal>; political prisoner, prisoner of conscience; lifer <nonformal>; trusty
VERBS 2 **bring in a verdict, pass** *or* **pronounce sentence**; penalize

conviction NOUNS 1 **trust, confidence, faith,** assured faith, belief, fixed *or* settled belief, **reliance,** dependence; assurance
2 **condemnation, damnation, doom,** guilty verdict, verdict of guilty; judgment

convince VERBS **persuade,** wean, bring over, sweep off one's feet <nonformal>, **win over;** seem true, ring true, sound true, **carry conviction,** hold *or* have the ring of truth

convocation NOUNS **summons,** convoking; calling forth, **ecclesiastical council, conclave, consistory, convention; assembly**

convoy NOUNS **escort, guard;** outrider

convulsion NOUNS **spasm, paroxysm,** throes; **seizure,** grip, attack, **fit,** access, ictus

cool NOUNS 1 **composure,** countenance; **calm, calmness,** calm disposition, **placidity, serenity,** tranquility, soothingness, peacefulness; mental composure, peace *or* calm of mind; calm *or* quiet mind, easy mind; **coolness,** coolheadedness, sangfroid; icy calm
VERBS 2 **calm, settle, soothe,** tranquilize; smooth, smooth over *or* out, smooth down, smooth one's feathers; allay, lay, lay the dust; pour oil on troubled waters, pour balm on, take the edge off of, take the sting out of; defuse; clear the air
3 **refrigerate; chill;** refresh, freshen; water-cool, air-cool; **air-condition;** ventilate
ADJS 4 **indifferent, halfhearted,** perfunctory, fervorless; **cold**; tepid, **lukewarm,** Laodicean; neither hot nor cold, neither one thing nor the other, **neuter, neutral; calm, placid,** quiet, **tranquil, serene,** peaceful; **coolheaded,** cool as a cucumber <nonformal>; philosophical
5 **aloof, standoffish,** standoff, offish <nonformal>, chilly, distant, remote, above all that; Olympian
6 coolish, temperate; chill, **chilly,** parky <Brit nonformal>; **fresh,** brisk, crisp, bracing, sharpish, **invigorating,** stimulating

cooperation NOUNS **collaboration, coaction,** concurrence, synergy, synergism; **consensus, commonality; community,** harmony, concordance, concord, fellowship, fellow feeling, solidarity, concert, **teamwork;** pulling *or* working together, communal *or* community activity, joining of forces, pooling, pooling of resources, joining of hands; joint effort, common effort, combined *or* joint operation, common enterprise *or* endeavor, collective *or* united action, mass action; **cooperativeness,** team spirit, morale, esprit, *esprit de corps* <Fr>

cooperative ADJS **cooperating,** cooperant, **hand in glove; collaborative,** coactive, coacting, coefficient, synergistic

coordinate VERBS 1 **harmonize,** bring into line, accord, make uniform, equalize, similarize, assimilate, homologize; **adjust, set,** regulate, **accommodate, reconcile,** synchronize, sync <nonformal>, integrate, proportion
2 **organize,** methodize, **systematize,** rationalize, regularize, get *or* put one's house in order; **regulate,** fix, settle; **plan,** chart, codify

cop NOUNS

<nonformal> copper, John Law, bluecoat, bull, flatfoot, gumshoe, gendarme, shamus, dick, pig, flattie, bizzy *and* bobby *and* peeler <all Brit>; the cops, the law, the fuzz; New York's finest

cope VERBS **support oneself,** make one's way; **make ends meet, keep body and soul together, keep the wolf from the door,** keep *or* hold one's head above water, keep afloat; **survive, subsist, eke out,** make out, scrape along, manage, get by; **deal with,** come to grips with, take on, tackle <nonformal>, contend with, do with

copious ADJS **abundant,** ample, plenteous, **plentiful**, thick on the ground <Brit>; **prolific,** proliferous, uberous, **teeming,** swarming, bursting, bursting out, plenteous, **plentiful,** generous, bountiful, **abundant, luxuriant, exuberant, lush,** superabundant

copulate VERBS couple, **mate,** unite in sexual intercourse, **have sexual relations, have sex,** make out <nonformal>, perform the act of love *or* marriage act, come together, cohabit, shack up <nonformal>, be intimate; sleep with, lie with, go to bed with; fuck *and* screw *and* lay *and* ball *and* frig *and* diddle *and* **make it with** <all nonformal>, go all the way, go to bed with, lie together; cover, mount, serve *or* service <of animals>; **make love**

copy NOUNS 1 **reproduction, duplication, imitation**, dummy, mock-up, **replica,** facsimile, representation, paraphrase, approximation, model, version, knockoff <nonformal>; **counterfeit**, forgery, fake *and* phony <both nonformal>
2 **the same, selfsame,** carbon copy, very same, one and the same, identical same, a distinction without a difference, the same difference <nonformal>; **duplicate,** double, clone *and* cookie-cutter dead ringer <nonformal>, the image of, the picture of, spitting image *and* spit and image <both nonformal>, facsimile
VERBS 3 **imitate, repeat,** ditto <nonformal>; do like <nonformal>, do <nonformal>, act *or* go *or* make like <nonformal>; **mirror, reflect; echo,** reecho, chorus; **borrow,** steal one's stuff <nonformal>, take a leaf out of one's book; assume, **affect;** counterfeit, fake <nonformal>, hoke *and* hoke up <both nonformal>, forge, plagiarize, crib, lift <nonformal>; **parody,** pastiche; **paraphrase,** approximate
4 **reproduce,** replicate, **duplicate,** dupe <nonformal>; clone; reduplicate; **transcribe;** trace; double; triplicate, quadruplicate, etc; stat <nonformal>, facsimile, fax <nonformal>, Xerox <trademark>; microcopy, microfilm

copycat NOUNS **imitator,** simulator, me-tooer <nonformal>, **impersonator, impostor**, **mimic,** mimicker, mimer, mime, **mocker;** mockingbird, cuckoo; **parrot,** polly, poll-parrot *or* polly-parrot, **ape,** aper, monkey; **copier,** copyist, counterfeiter, forger, plagiarist

cord NOUNS **line, rope, wire,** braided rope, twisted rope, flattened-strand rope, wire rope, locked-wire rope, **cable,** wire cable; **yarn,** spun yarn, skein, hank; **string, twine;** electric wire, electric cord, power cord, power cable

cordial NOUNS 1 **liqueur,** brandy, flavored brandy
ADJS 2 amiable, affable, genial; gentle, mild, mild-mannered; easy, easy-natured, easy to get along with, able to take a joke, **agreeable; genial,** hearty, ardent, warm, warmhearted, affable; hospitable

core NOUNS **center,** centrum; **middle, heart, nucleus; core of one's being, where one lives; kernel; pith,** marrow; **nub, hub,** nave, axis, pivot; **essence, substance,** stuff, very stuff, inner essence, essential nature, quiddity; crux, crucial *or* pivotal *or* critical point, pivot

corner NOUNS 1 **nook, cranny, niche, recess,** cove, bay, oriel, alcove
2 **angle,** point, bight; vertex, apex; quoin, coin, nook; **crook, hook,** crotchet
VERBS 3 run *and* drive into a corner <both nonformal>, **tree** <nonformal>, chase up a tree *or* stump <nonformal>, drive *or* force to the wall, push one to the wall, put one's back to the wall, have one on the ropes <nonformal>; get a corner on, **corner the market;** monopolize, engross; buy up, absorb

cornerstone NOUNS **foundation stone,** footstone; **keystone,** headstone, first stone, quoin; **salient point,** cardinal point, high point, great point; important thing, chief thing, **the point, main point,** main thing, essential matter, **essence,** the name of the game *and* the bottom line *and* what it's all about *and* where it's at <all nonformal>, substance, gravamen

cornucopia NOUNS horn of plenty, horn of Amalthea, endless supply, bottomless well

corny ADJS **trite;** corny *and* square *and* square-John *and* Clyde <all nonformal>, fade, **banal,** unoriginal, platitudinous, **stereotyped,** stock, set, **commonplace, common,** truistic, twice-told, **familiar,** bromidic <nonformal>, old hat <nonfor-

mal>, back-number, bewhiskered, warmed-over, **cut-and-dried; hackneyed,** hackney; **stale,** musty, fusty

coronation NOUNS **installation,** installment, **instatement,** induction, placement, **inauguration,** investiture, taking office; **accession,** accedence; enthronement

corpse NOUNS dead body, dead man *or* woman, dead person, **cadaver, carcass, body;** *corpus delicti* <L>; **stiff** <nonformal>; **the dead,** the defunct, **the deceased,** the departed, the loved one; **decedent,** late lamented; **remains,** mortal *or* organic remains, **mummy**

corpulent ADJS **stout, fat, overweight,** fattish, **obese,** adipose, gross, fleshy, beefy, meaty, hefty, porky, porcine; paunchy, paunched, bloated, puffy, blowzy, distended, swollen, pursy; abdominous, big-bellied, full-bellied, potbellied, gorbellied <old or dial>, swag-bellied, pot-gutted *and* pussle-gutted <both nonformal>

corral VERBS **enclose,** pen, coop, cage, impound, mew; round up, drive together; **drive, herd,** drove <Brit>, herd up, punch cattle, ride herd on; spur, goad, prick, lash, whip; wrangle

correct VERBS 1 **revise,** redact, recense, **revamp, rewrite,** redraft, **rework,** work over; **emend, amend,** emendate, **rectify, edit,** blue-pencil

2 rap on the knuckles, **chastise,** spank, turn over one's knees; **take to task,** call to account, bring to book, call on the carpet, read the riot act, give one a tongue-lashing, tonguelash; straighten out

ADJS 3 **meticulous, thorough,** thoroughgoing, thoroughpaced; prissy, **accurate; strict,** rigid, **rigorous,** spit-and-polish; **mannerly, well-mannered,** good-mannered, **well-behaved,** well- *or* fair-spoken; correct in one's manners *or* behavior

4 **orthodox,** orthodoxical; received, approved; right, proper; **accurate, right,** proper, just; dead right, on target *and* on the money *and* on the nose <all nonformal>, bang on <Brit nonformal>, straight, straight-up-and-down

correction NOUNS 1 **revision, emendation, amendment, corrigenda, rectification;** editing, redaction, recension, revampment; **polishing,** touching up, putting on the finishing touches, putting the gloss on, finishing, perfecting, tuning, fine-tuning; retrofitting

2 **reproof,** reproval; **punishment,** punition, **chastisement, chastening, correction, discipline,** disciplinary measure *or* action, **castigation,** infliction, scourge, ferule, what-for <nonformal>

correlation NOUNS **reciprocation,** reciprocity, reciprocality, two-edged sword, relativity; **mutuality,** communion, community, commutuality; **correspondence, equivalence,** equipollence, coequality

correspondence NOUNS letter writing, written communication, exchange of letters, epistolary intercourse *or* communication; personal correspondence, business correspondence

correspondent NOUNS 1 **letter writer,** writer, communicator; pen pal <nonformal>; addressee; **foreign correspondent,** war correspondent, special correspondent, stringer

ADJS 2 **reciprocal, corresponding,** answering, analogous, homologous, equipollent, tantamount, equivalent, coequal; **complementary,** complemental

corridor NOUNS 1 **airway, air lane, air line,** air route, skyway, flight path, lane, path

2 **hall,** hallway; passage, **passageway; gallery,** loggia; arcade, colonnade, pergola, cloister, peristyle; areaway; breezeway

corrosion NOUNS **disintegration, decomposition, erosion,** crumbling, dilapidation, wear, wear and tear, waste, wasting, wasting away, ablation, ravagement, ravages of time

corrosive ADJS **caustic,** mordant, mordacious, corroding; **acrimonious,** acrid, acid, acidic, acidulous, acidulent, acerb, acerbate, acerbic, **bitter,** tart; corroding; erosive, eroding, **damaging, injurious**; pollutive; corruptive, corrupting, corroding

corrugated ADJS **rugged,** ragged, harsh; rugose, rugous, wrinkled, crinkled, crumpled; **furrowed, grooved,** scratched, scored, incised, cut, gashed, gouged, slit, striated

corrupt VERBS 1 **debase, degrade,** degenerate, **deprave, debauch, defile,** violate, desecrate, deflower, ravish, ravage, despoil; **contaminate,** confound, **pollute, vitiate, poison, infect, taint;**

pervert, warp, twist, distort; prostitute, misuse; denature; **cheapen,** devalue; coarsen, vulgarize, drag in the mud; adulterate, alloy, water, water down; **sully, soil, defile;** demoralize
ADJS 2 corrupted, vice-corrupted, polluted, morally polluted, rotten, tainted, contaminated, vitiated; warped, perverted; **decadent,** debased, degraded, reprobate, **depraved, debauched, dissolute, degenerate,** profligate, abandoned, gone to the dogs, sunk *or* steeped in iniquity, rotten at *or* to the core, in the sewer *or* gutter

corruption NOUNS 1 **perversion,** misdirection, misrepresentation, misinterpretation, misconstruction; **falsification**; **twisting,** false coloring, bending the truth, **spin,** spin control, slanting, straining, torturing; misuse
2 **bribery,** bribing, subornation, **graft,** bribery and corruption; corruptedness, corruptness, rottenness, moral pollution, lack *or* absence of moral fiber

corset NOUNS foundation garment, corselet; **girdle,** undergirdle, panty girdle

cosmetic ADJS 1 **shallow, surface,** on *or* near the surface, merely surface; **superficial, cursory,** slight, light, merely cosmetic, thin, jejune, trivial
2 **beautifying;** decorative; cosmetized, cosmeticized, beautified, made-up, mascaraed, titivated

cosmetics NOUNS **makeup, beauty products, beauty-care products;** war paint *and* drugstore complexion <both nonformal>

cosmic ADJS **universal,** cosmic *or* cosmical, heaven-wide, galactic, planetary, world-wide, transnational, planet-wide, **global; total, all-inclusive,** all-including, **all-embracing,** all-encompassing, all-comprehensive, all-comprehending, all-filling, all-pervading, all-covering

cosmopolitan NOUNS 1 **sophisticate,** man of experience, **man of the world;** slicker *and* city slicker <both nonformal>; man-about-town; cosmopolite, citizen of the world
ADJS 2 **traveled,** well-traveled, **worldly, worldly-wise,** world-wise, wise in the ways of the world, knowing, **sophisticated,** cosmopolite, blasé

cosmos NOUNS **universe, world;** creation, created universe, created nature, all, **all creation,** all tarnation <nonformal>, all *or* everything that is, all being, totality, totality of being, sum of things; omneity, allness

cost NOUNS 1 **expense,** burden of expenditure; **price,** expenditure, **charge,** damage *and* score *and* tab <all nonformal>; rate, figure, amount
VERBS 2 **sell for, fetch, bring,** bring in, stand one *and* set *or* move one back <all nonformal>, knock one back <Brit nonformal>; **come to,** run to *or* into, **amount to,** mount up to, come up to, total up to

costly ADJS **expensive, dear,** of great cost, dear-bought, **high, high-priced,** premium, at a premium, top; big ticket <nonformal>, **fancy** *and* stiff *and* steep <all nonformal>, pricey; beyond one's means, not affordable, more than one can afford; upmarket, upscale <nonformal>, rich, sumptuous, executive *and* posh <both nonformal>, **luxurious,** gold-plated

costume NOUNS 1 **clothing, wearing apparel, raiment, garb, attire, array,** habit, habiliment, fashion, style, guise, costumery, gear, fig *or* full fig <both Brit>, toilette, trim, bedizenment; **vestment,** vesture, investment, investiture; habit, bib and tucker <nonformal>
VERBS 2 **outfit;** equip, **accouter,** uniform, caparison, rig, rig out *or* up, fit, **fit out,** turn out, habit, suit; **tailor,** tailor-make, make to order; order, bespeak

couch NOUNS sofa, **bed;** the sack *and* the hay *and* kip *and* doss <all nonformal>; bedstead; **litter, stretcher,** gurney

counsel NOUNS 1 **advice, recommendation, suggestion;** proposal; advising, advocacy; **direction, instruction,** guidance, briefing; **exhortation,** hortation <old>, enjoinder, expostulation, remonstrance; **admonition,** monition, monitory *or* monitory letter, caution, caveat, **warning; idea,** thought, opinion; **counseling;** guidance counseling, educational counseling, vocational guidance
2 **adviser, counselor, consultant,** professional consultant, expert, maven <nonformal>, boffin <Brit nonformal>; instructor, guide, **mentor,** nestor
3 **lawyer, attorney, attorney-at-law,** barrister, barrister-at-law, **counselor,** counselor-at-law, legal counsel *or* counselor, legal adviser, legal expert, **solicitor, advocate, pleader;** member of the bar, legal practitioner, officer of the court

VERBS 4 **advise, recommend, suggest, advocate,** propose, submit; **instruct,** coach, guide, direct, brief; prescribe; weigh in with advice <nonformal>, give a piece of advice

count NOUNS 1 **sum,** summation, difference, product, **number;** account, cast, **score, reckoning, tally,** tale, the story *and* whole story *and* all she wrote <all nonformal>, the bottom line <nonformal>
VERBS 2 **matter,** import <old>, signify, **tell, weigh, carry weight,** cut ice *and* cut some ice <both nonformal>, be prominent, stand out, mean much; be something, be somebody, amount to something; have a key to the executive washroom; be featured, star, get top billing
3 **enumerate, tell, tally,** give a figure to, put a figure on, call off, name, call over, run over; **count noses** *or* **heads** <nonformal>, call the roll

counter NOUNS 1 **token,** slug; **coupon; check, ticket,** tag
2 workspace, working space; **bench,** workbench, worktable; worktop; bar, buffet
VERBS 3 **retaliate, retort, strike back,** hit back at <nonformal>, give in return; **reciprocate,** give in exchange, give and take; **get** *or* **come back at** <nonformal>, turn the tables upon
4 **go contrary to, run counter to, contradict,** contravene, controvert, fly in the face of, be *or* play at cross-purposes, go against; **oppose,** be opposed to, go *or* run in opposition to, side against
ADJS 5 contrary, counteractive, conflicting, opposing, opposed, opposite, in opposition

counteract VERBS **offset**, set off, countervail, **counterbalance,** counterweigh, counterwork, counterpoise, **balance,** play off against, set against, set over against, equiponderate; **square,** square up

counterfeit NOUNS 1 counterfeit money, funny *or* phony *or* bogus money <nonformal>, false *or* bad money, queer <nonformal>, base coin, green goods <nonformal>; **forgery,** bad check, rubber check *and* bounced check *and* kite <all nonformal>
2 **copy, imitation**, forgery, fake *and* phony <both nonformal>
VERBS 3 **imitate,** copy, **simulate,** fake; forge; phony up <nonformal>, fabricate
ADJS 4 **imitation, mock, sham,** copied, fake *and* phony <both nonformal>, forged, plagiarized, unoriginal, ungenuine; **pseudo,** synthetic, synthetical, ersatz, hokey *and* hoked-up <both nonformal>, quasi; **vicarious,** ersatz, mock

counterpart NOUNS **analogue, parallel;** cognate, congener; **complement, correspondent,** pendant, similitude, tally

counterproductive ADJS counteractive *or* counteractant, **counteracting, counterworking,** countervailing; **opposing,** oppositional; **inexpedient, undesirable, inadvisable,** impolitic, impolitical, unpolitic, not to be recommended, contraindicated; **impractical, impracticable,** dysfunctional, unworkable; **ill-advised, ill-considered, unwise;** distressing, **injurious, damaging, detrimental,** deleterious, **pernicious,** mischievous

countless ADJS 1 **much, many,** beaucoup <nonformal>, ample, **abundant,** copious, generous, overflowing, superabundant, multitudinous, plentiful, **numerous**
2 **innumerable, numberless,** unnumbered, uncounted, uncountable, unreckonable, untold, incalculable, immeasurable, unmeasured, measureless, inexhaustible, endless, infinite, without end *or* limit, more than one can tell, more than you can shake a stick at <nonformal>, no end of *or* to; countless as the stars *or* sands

country NOUNS 1 land; **nation,** nationality, **state,** nation-state, sovereign nation *or* state, polity, **body politic; power,** superpower, world power; microstate; **republic,** people's republic, **commonwealth,** commonweal; **kingdom,** sultanate; **empire,** empery; **realm,** dominion, domain; **principality,** principate; duchy, dukedom
ADJS 2 **rustic, rural, provincial, farm, pastoral, bucolic,** Arcadian, **agrarian,** agrestic; **agricultural**

countryman NOUNS **fellow citizen,** fellow countryman, **compatriot,** congener, countrywoman, *landsman* <Yiddish>, *paesano* <Ital>, *paisano* <Sp>; fellow townsman, home boy *and* home girl *and* hometowner <all nonformal>

countryside NOUNS **the country,** agricultural region, farm country, farmland, arable land, grazing region *or* country, rural district, rustic region, province *or* **provinces,** woodland, grassland, woods and fields, meadows and pastures, the soil, grass roots; **the sticks** *and* the tall corn *and* yokeldom *and* hickdom <all nonformal>

coup NOUNS **attempt, trial, effort, essay,** assay <old>, first attempt, *coup d'essai* <Fr>; **endeavor, undertaking;** stroke, step; gambit; **stratagem, artifice,** art <old>, **craft, wile,** strategy, **device,** wily device, **contrivance, expedient, design, scheme, move,** gambit, **ploy, dodge,** artful dodge; **plot,** conspiracy, **intrigue**
2 **seizure,** power grab <nonformal>, coup d'état, seizure of power

couple NOUNS 1 **two,** twain <old>; **pair, matching pair, twosome,** set of two, duo, duet, brace, team, span, yoke, double harness; match, matchup, mates
VERBS 2 **copulate, mate,** unite in sexual intercourse, **have sexual relations, have sex,** make out <nonformal>, perform the act of love *or* marriage act, come together, cohabit, shack up <nonformal>, be intimate; commit adultery, fornicate
3 **put together, join,** conjoin, **unite,** unify, bond, **connect,** associate, league, band, merge, **assemble,** accumulate; **join up,** become a part of, associate oneself, enter into, come aboard <nonformal>; pair, accouple, **link,** link up, build bridges, yoke, knot, splice, tie, chain, bracket

coupon NOUNS **scrip, check, ticket,** tag; hat check, baggage check

courage NOUNS courageousness, **nerve,** pluck, **bravery,** braveness, ballsiness *and* gutsiness *or* guttiness <all nonformal>, **boldness, valor,** valorousness, valiance, valiancy, **gallantry,** conspicuous gallantry, gallantry under fire *or* beyond the call of duty, gallantness, **intrepidity,** intrepidness, **prowess,** virtue; doughtiness, stalwartness, stoutness, **manliness,** manfulness, **manhood,** virility, machismo

fear holding on a minute longer
George Patton

doing without witnesses that which we would be capable of doing before everyone
La Rochefoucauld

courageous ADJS **plucky, brave, bold, valiant, valorous, gallant, intrepid,** doughty, **hardy,** stalwart, stout, stouthearted, ironhearted, lionhearted, greathearted, bold-spirited, bold as a lion; **heroic,** herolike

course NOUNS 1 **serving,** service; **portion, helping,** help; second helping; dish, plate
2 heading, vector; compass heading *or* course, compass direction, magnetic heading, true heading *or* course
3 onward course, **surge, gush, rush,** onrush, spate, run, race; **route, path, way, itinerary,** track, run, line, road
4 **policy,** polity, principles, guiding principles; **procedure,** line, plan of action
5 **study,** branch of learning; course of study, **curriculum; subject; major, minor;** requirement *or* required course, elective course, refresher course; gut course <nonformal>

court VERBS 1 **curry favor, pay court to,** make court to, run after <nonformal>, dance attendance on; **shine up to,** make up to <nonformal>; **suck up to** *and* **play up to** *and* act up to <all nonformal>; be a yes-man <nonformal>, agree to anything; fawn upon, fall over *or* all over <nonformal>; **handshake** *and* back-scratch *and* **polish the apple** <all nonformal>
2 **solicit, canvass; seek, bid for,** look for; **fish for,** angle for
3 **woo,** sue, press one's suit, **pay court** *or* **suit to,** make suit to, cozy up to <nonformal>, eye up *and* chat up <Brit nonformal>, pay one's court to, address, pay one's addresses to, pay attention to, lay siege to, fling oneself at, throw oneself at the head of; **pursue,** follow; chase <nonformal>; set one's cap at *or* for <nonformal>; serenade; spark <nonformal>

courteous ADJS polite, civil, urbane, gracious, graceful, agreeable, affable, fair; complaisant; obliging, accommodating; **thoughtful, considerate,** tactful, solicitous; respectful, deferential, attentive

courtesy NOUNS courteousness, common courtesy, **politeness, civility,** *politesse* <Fr>, amenity, agreeableness, urbanity, comity, affability; **graciousness,** gracefulness; complaisance; **thoughtfulness, considerateness, tactfulness,** tact, consideration, **solicitousness, solicitude; respect,** respectfulness, deference

courtly ADJS **dignified, stately, imposing, grand,** magisterial, aristocratic; **noble,** lordly, princely; **majestic,** regal; worthy, **august, venerable;** statuesque; **sedate, solemn**, sober, grave

courtship NOUNS **courting, wooing;** court, suit, suing, amorous pursuit, addresses

cove NOUNS **inlet,** creek <Brit>, arm of the sea, arm, armlet, canal, reach, loch <Scots>, **bay, fjord,** bight; **gulf; estuary,** firth *or* frith, bayou, mouth, *boca* <Sp>; **harbor,** natural harbor; road *or* roads, roadstead; **strait** *or* straits, kyle <Scots>, **narrow** *or* **narrows,** euripus, belt, gut, narrow seas; **sound**

cover NOUNS 1 **covering,** coverage, covert, coverture, housing, hood, cowl, cowling, **shelter; screen,** shroud, shield, veil, pall, mantle, curtain, hanging, drape, drapery; **coat,** cloak, mask, guise; vestment
2 **lid, top, cap, screw-top;** operculum; stopper
3 **blanket, coverlet,** coverlid <nonformal>, space blanket, covers, **spread,** robe, buffalo robe, **afghan,** rug <Brit>; lap robe; **bedspread; bedcover;** counterpane, counterpin <nonformal>; comfort, **comforter, down comforter, duvet, continental quilt** <Brit>, **quilt,** feather bed, eiderdown; patchwork quilt
4 **concealment, hiding, secretion;** burial, burying, interment, putting away; **covering,** covering up, masking, screening; mystification, obscuration; darkening, obscurement, clouding; **subterfuge, deception, disguise, camouflage,** protective coloration
VERBS 5 **extend, reach, stretch,** sweep, spread, run, **go** *or* **go out,** carry, **range,** lie; **reach** *or* stretch *or* thrust out; span, straddle, take in, hold, encompass, surround, environ
6 **traverse, cross, travel over** *or* through, pass through, **go** *or* **pass over,** measure, transit, track, range, range over *or* through, course, do, perambulate, peregrinate, overpass, go over the ground
7 cover up; apply to, **put on,** lay on; **superimpose,** superpose; **lay over,** overlay; **spread over,** overspread; **clothe, cloak,** mantle, muffle, blanket, canopy, cope, cowl, hood, **veil,** curtain, **screen, shield,** screen off, mask, cloud, obscure, fog, befog, fuzz; block, eclipse, occult
8 **include, comprise, contain, comprehend,** hold, **take in;** cover a lot of ground <nonformal>, occupy, take up, fill; fill in *or* out, build into, **complete**

cover-up NOUNS **veil of secrecy, veil,** curtain, pall, wraps; iron curtain, bamboo curtain; wall *or* barrier of secrecy; **suppression,** repression, stifling, smothering; **censorship,** blackout <nonformal>, **hush-up**

covet VERBS **crave, hunger after,** thirst after, crave after, **lust after,** have a lech for <nonformal>, pant after, run mad after, **hanker for** *or* **after** <nonformal>; crawl after; aspire after, be consumed with desire; have an itchy *or* itching palm *and* have sticky fingers <all nonformal>; **envy,** be envious *or* covetous of, cast envious eyes, desire for oneself

coward NOUNS jellyfish, invertebrate, **weakling,** weak sister <nonformal>, milksop, milquetoast, mouse, **sissy, wimp** <nonformal>, baby, **big baby, chicken** <nonformal>; **yellow-belly,** *and* white-liver *and* lily-liver *and* chicken-liver <all nonformal>, white feather; fraid-cat *and* **fraidy-cat** *and* scaredy-cat <all nonformal>; funk *and* funker <both nonformal>

one who in a perilous emergency thinks with his legs
AMBROSE BIERCE

cowardly ADJS **fearful,** fearing, fearsome, **in fear, afraid; timorous, timid, shy,** rabbity *and* mousy <both nonformal>, afraid of one's own shadow; **skittish,** skittery <nonformal>, gun-shy, jumpy, goosy <nonformal>; **tremulous,** trembling, trepidant, shaky, shivery; **yellow** *and* yellow-bellied *and* with a yellow streak <all nonformal>; **weak-kneed, chicken** <nonformal>, afraid of one's shadow; weak, soft;

cowboy NOUNS cowgirl, puncher *or* cowpuncher *or* cowpoke <all nonformal>, *vaquero, gaucho* <both Sp>; broncobuster <nonformal>, buckaroo

cower VERBS **quail, cringe, crouch, skulk, sneak, slink, crouch, duck,** cringe; hunch, hunch down, hunch over, scrooch *or* scrouch down <nonformal>

coy ADJS **shy, timid,** timorous, **bashful,** shamefaced, shamefast, pudibund *and* verecund *and* verecundious <all old>; **demure,** skittish, mousy; self-conscious,

conscious, confused; stammering, inarticulate; **coquettish,** come-hither

cozy ADJS snug, snug as a bug in a rug; friendly, warm; **homelike,** homey *and* down-home <both nonformal>, homely, lived-in; **commodious,** roomy, convenient; **intimate, familiar,** chatty, *tête-à-tête* <Fr>

crack NOUNS 1 **cleft,** cranny, chink, check, craze, chap, **crevice,** fissure, scissure, incision, notch, score, cut, gash, slit, split, **rift,** rent; **opening,** excavation, cavity, concavity, hole; **breach, break,** fracture, rupture; fault, flaw, craze, check, rift, split
2 **witticism, crack** *and* smart crack *and* **wisecrack** <all nonformal>; **quip, mot, bon mot,** smart saying, stroke of wit, one-liner *and* zinger <both nonformal>; **gibe, dirty** *or* **nasty crack** <nonformal>; persiflage
VERBS 3 **cleave,** check, incise, craze, **cut, cut apart,** gash, slit, **split,** rive, rent, rip open; **open; gap,** breach, break, fracture, rupture; slot, groove, furrow, ditch, trench
ADJS 4 **skillful,** excellent, **expert,** crackerjack <nonformal>

cracked ADJS **impaired, damaged,** chipped, crazed, checked

crackle NOUNS 1 **snap, crack;** snapping, cracking, crackling, crepitation, decrepitation, sizzling, spitting; rale
VERBS 2 **snap, crack;** crepitate, decrepitate; spit

crackpot NOUNS

<nonformal> freak, character, nut, screwball, weirdie, weirdo, kook, queer potato, oddball, flake, strange duck, odd fellow, crank, bird, goofus, wack, wacko

craft NOUNS 1 **skill,** skillfulness, **expertness, expertise, proficiency,** dexterity, dexterousness *or* dextrousness; **craftsmanship,** workmanship, artisanship; skill; technique, art, handicraft
2 **cunning,** cunningness, **craftiness,** callidity <old>, **artfulness, art, artifice, wiliness,** wiles, guile, **slyness,** insidiousness, **foxiness**

crafty ADJS **cunning, artful, wily,** callid <old>, guileful, **sly,** insidious, supple <Scots>, **shifty,** pawky <Brit>, arch, **smooth, slick** *and* slick as a whistle <both nonformal>, **slippery,** snaky, serpentine, **foxy,** vulpine, feline; **canny, shrewd,** knowing, sharp, razor-sharp, cute *or* cutesy *or* cutesy-poo <nonformal>, acute, astute, **clever;** resourceful, ingenious, inventive, **scheming, designing; manipulative,** manipulatory; **deceitful**

cram VERBS 1 **stuff, gorge,** pig out <nonformal>, engorge, glut, guttle, eat one's fill, stuff *or* gorge oneself, gluttonize
2 **study up, get up,** study up on, read up on, get up on; **review, brush up,** polish up <nonformal>, rub up, **cram** *or* cram up <nonformal>, **bone up** <nonformal>
3 **fill, charge, load,** lade, freight, weight; **stuff, wad,** pad, **pack,** crowd, am, jam-pack, ram in, chock; **fill up,** fill to the brim, brim, top up *or* top off, fill to overflowing

cramp NOUNS **pain, distress, grief,** stress, stress of life, suffering, passion, dolor; ache, aching; pang, wrench, throes, spasm

cramped ADJS **limited, restricted,** bound, **bounded, finite; confined,** prescribed, proscribed, strait, straitened, narrow; close-fitting; **restricted,** limited, circumscribed, **confined,** constricted; incapacious, incommodious, crowded; **forced,** awkward; crabbed

cranky ADJS 1 **crotchety,** quirky, dotty, maggoty <Brit>, crank, crankish, whimsical, twisted

2 <nonformal> **grouchy, kvetchy,** beefing, crabby, crabbing, grousing, griping, bellyaching, bitching

cranny NOUNS **nook, corner, niche, recess,** cove, bay, oriel, alcove; cubicle, roomlet, carrel, hole-in-the-wall <nonformal>, cubby, **cubbyhole,** snuggery, hidey-hole <nonformal>

crap NOUNS 1 **feces,** feculence; defecation, movement, bowel movement *or* **BM; stool, shit** <nonformal>, **ordure,** night soil, jakes <Brit nonformal>, crap *and* ca-ca *and* doo-doo <all nonformal>; turd <nonformal>; dingleberry <nonformal>; **manure, dung, droppings;** cow pats, cow flops <nonformal>; cow chips, buffalo chips; guano; coprolite, coprolith

2 <nonformal> **bullshit,** shit, horseshit, horsefeathers, bull, poppycock, bosh, tosh <Brit>, applesauce, bunkum, bunk,

garbage, guff, jive, bilge, piffle, moonshine, flapdoodle, a crock *or* a crock of shit, claptrap, tommyrot, rot, hogwash, malarkey, double Dutch, hokum, hooey, bushwa, blah, balls <Brit>, baloney, blarney, tripe, hot air, gas, wind, waffle <Brit>

VERBS 3 **defecate, shit** <nonformal>, **evacuate,** void, **stool,** dung, have a bowel movement *or* BM, take a shit *or* crap <nonformal>, ca-ca *or* number two <both nonformal>

crash NOUNS 1 **noise,** loud noise, roar, thunder, thunderclap; **boom,** sonic boom
2 **crack-up,** prang <Brit nonformal>; crash landing; collision, mid-air collision
3 **collapse,** smash, comedown, breakdown, derailment, **fall,** pratfall <nonformal>, stumble, tumble, **downfall,** cropper <chiefly Brit nonformal>; nose dive *and* tailspin <both nonformal>; bursting of the bubble, **bear market,** bearishness; break in the market; selloff

VERBS 4 <nonformal> **hit the hay, hit the sack,** turn in, crawl in, flop, sack out, sack up, kip down *or* doss down <both Brit>

5 **crack up,** prang <Brit nonformal>, spin in, fail to pull out
6 **collapse;** cave *or* fall in, come crashing *or* tumbling down, topple, topple down *or* over; **go bankrupt, go broke** <nonformal>, go into receivership, become insolvent *or* bankrupt, **fail,** break, bust <nonformal>, **fold, fold up,** belly up *and* go up *and* go belly up *and* **go under** <all nonformal>, shut one's doors, go out of business, **be ruined,** go to ruin, go on the rocks, go to the wall; take a bath *and* be taken to the cleaners *and* be cleaned out *and* lose one's shirt *and* tap out <all nonformal>

crave VERBS **covet, hunger after,** thirst after, crave after, **lust after,** have a lech for <nonformal>, pant after, run mad after, **hanker for** *or* **after** <nonformal>; crawl after; aspire after, be consumed with desire; have an itchy *or* itching palm *and* have sticky fingers <all nonformal>

crawl NOUNS 1 **slow motion, leisurely gait,** snail's *or* tortoise's pace; **creep**

VERBS 2 **feel creepy,** feel funny, **have the creeps** *or* **cold creeps** *or* the heebie-jeebies <nonformal>; have gooseflesh *or* goose bumps; give one the creeps *or* the willies <nonformal>
3 **go slow** *or* **slowly,** go at a snail's pace, take it slow, get no place fast <nonformal>; **drag,** drag out; **creep;** inch, inch along; worm, worm along; poke, **poke along;** shuffle *or* stagger *or* totter *or* toddle along; **linger on,** linger, tarry, go on, **go on and on, wear on,** drag, **drag on,** drag along

craze NOUNS 1 **infatuation, enthusiasm,** passion, fascination, crazy fancy, bug <nonformal>, rage, furor
VERBS 2 **madden,** dement, make mad, send mad, **unbalance,** unhinge, undermine one's reason, **derange,** distract, frenzy, shatter, **drive insane** *or* mad *or* **crazy,** put *or* send out of one's mind, overthrow one's mind *or* reason, drive up the wall <nonformal>

crazy ADJS 1 **mentally deficient,** mentally defective, mentally handicapped, retarded, **mentally retarded,** backward, arrested, subnormal, not right in the head, **not all there** <nonformal>; **simpleminded,** simplewitted, simple, simpletonian; **half-witted,** half-baked <nonformal>; **idiotic, moronic, imbecile,** imbecilic, cretinous, cretinistic; crackbrained, cracked; babbling, driveling, slobbering, drooling, blithering, dithering, maundering, burbling

2 <nonformal> **nutty,** daffy, dotty, dippy, crazy as a bedbug *or* coot *or* loon, loony, loony-tune, goofy, wacky, balmy *or* barmy, flaky, kooky, potty, batty, ape, apeshit, wiggy, lunchy, out to lunch, bonzo, bats, nuts, nutso, nutty as a fruitcake, fruity, fruitcakey, screwy, screwball, screwballs, crackers, bananas, bonkers <Brit>, loopy, beany, buggy, bughouse, bugs, cuckoo, slaphappy, flipped, freaked-out, off-the-wall, gaga, haywire, off in the upper story, off one's nut *or* rocker, off the track *or* trolley, off the hinges, round the bend <Brit>, minus some buttons, nobody home, with bats in the belfry, just plain nuts, loco, mental <Brit>, psycho, cracked, not right in the head, tetched, off one's head, out of one's head, out of one's gourd *or* skull, out of one's tree, not all there, *meshuggah*

<Yiddish>, not tightly wrapped, three bricks shy of a load, rowing with one oar in the water, up the wall, off the wall, schizzy, schizoid, schizo

cream NOUNS 1 lotion, cold cream, cleansing cream; **ointment, balm, salve, unguent,** unguentum, inunction, inunctum, unction, chrism
2 **the best,** flower, fat; cream of the crop, *crème de la crème* <Fr>, salt of the earth; *pièce de résistance* <Fr>; nonesuch, paragon, nonpareil; gem of the first water

create VERBS **originate, invent; innovate; occasion, make, engender,** generate, give origin to, give occasion to, **give rise to,** spark, spark off, set off, trigger, trigger off

creation NOUNS **work of art, object of art,** objet d'art, art object, art work, artistic production, piece, **work, study, design, composition;** brainchild

creative ADJS **originative,** causative, **productive, constructive,** formative, fabricative, demiurgic; inventive; generative; **imaginative,** conceptual, conceptive, ideational, ideative, notional; originative, ingenious; productive, fertile, fecund, prolific, seminal, germinal, teeming, pregnant; **inspired,** visioned

creativity NOUNS **originality, novelty,** newness, innovation, freshness, uniqueness; inventiveness, creativeness, originality, **ingenuity;** productivity, **fertility,** fecundity

credential NOUNS **recommendation, reference,** letter of reference, voucher, **testimonial; identification; voucher, warrant,** warranty; **diploma,** sheepskin <nonformal>

credible ADJS **believable; tenable,** conceivable, **plausible,** colorable; worthy of faith, trustworthy, trusty; reliable; unimpeachable, unexceptionable, **unquestionable**

credit NOUNS 1 **trust,** tick <nonformal>; borrowing power *or* capacity; commercial credit, cash credit, bank credit, book credit, tax credit, investment credit; credit line, line of credit; installment plan, installment credit, consumer credit, store credit, hire purchase plan <Brit>, never-never <Brit nonformal>
2 **due,** one's due, what one merits *or* is entitled to, what one has earned, what is owing, what one has coming, what is coming to one, acknowledgment, cognizance, recognition, crediting
VERBS 3 acknowledge, make acknowledgments of, recognize, give *or* render credit *or* recognition; credit with; credit to one's account, place to one's credit *or* account
4 **believe, trust, accept,** receive, buy <nonformal>; give credit *or* credence to, give faith to, put faith in, take stock in *or* set store by <nonformal>, take to heart, attach weight to

creditable ADJS **praiseworthy,** worthy, **commendable,** estimable, **laudable,** admirable, meritorious, **reputable,** noble, sterling, manly, yeomanly; **respectable,** highly respectable

creed NOUNS **system of belief; religion, faith**, belief-system; **school, cult, ism, ideology,** *Weltanschauung* <Ger>, world view; political faith *or* belief *or* philosophy; **credo,** credenda; articles of religion, articles of faith, formulated *or* stated belief

creek NOUNS **waterway,** crick <nonformal>; rivulet, rill, streamlet, brooklet, runlet, runnel, rundle <nonformal>, rindle <Brit nonformal>, beck <Brit>, gill <Brit>, burn <Scots>, sike <Brit nonformal>

creep VERBS **crawl,** scramble, scrabble, grovel, **go on hands and knees,** go on all fours; worm, worm along, worm one's way, snake; inch, inch along; **sneak, steal,** steal along; pussyfoot *and* gumshoe <both nonformal>, slink, sidle, pad, prowl, nightwalk; **tiptoe,** tippytoe, go on tiptoe

creepy ADJS **spooky, eerie, weird, uncanny,** unco *or* uncolike <both Scots>

cremation NOUNS **incineration, burning,** reduction to ashes; suttee, self-cremation, self-immolation; the stake, burning at the stake, *auto da fé* <Pg>

crescendo NOUNS **loudness,** intensity, volume, amplitude, fullness; sonorousness, sonority; surge of sound, surge, swell, swelling

crescent NOUNS 1 **semicircle,** scythe, sickle, meniscus; crescent moon, half-moon; lunula, lunule; horseshoe
ADJS 2 **increasing, rising,** on the upswing, on the increase, on the rise; growing, fast-growing, flourishing, burgeoning, blossoming, waxing, swelling; **crescent-shaped,** crescentlike, crescen-

tic, crescentiform; **semicircular,** semilunar; horn-shaped, hornlike, horned, corniform

crest NOUNS **summit,** top; **tip-top, peak,** pinnacle; **brow;** ridge, edge; **crown,** cap, **tip,** point, spire, pitch; **apex,** vertex

crevice NOUNS **crack, cleft,** cranny, chink, check, craze, chap, fissure, scissure, incision, notch, score, cut, gash, slit, split, **rift,** rent

crew NOUNS **aircrew,** flight crew; **staff, personnel, employees,** help, hired help, the help, **gang,** men, force, servantry, retinue; rowing crew; **cast,** company; complement, outfit, pack, cohort, troupe, tribe, stable, bunch *and* mob *and* crowd <all nonformal>

crib NOUNS 1 booth, stall, manger
2 **translation, pony** *and* trot <both nonformal>; interlinear, interlinear translation
3 **storeroom,** bin, bunker, bay; corncrib
VERBS 4 **borrow,** steal one's stuff <nonformal>, take a leaf out of one's book; counterfeit, fake <nonformal>, hoke *and* hoke up <both nonformal>, forge, plagiarize, lift <nonformal>, cheat

crime NOUNS **wrongdoing, evildoing, wickedness,** misdoing <old>, wrong conduct, **misbehavior, misconduct,** misdemeaning, misfeasance, malfeasance, malversation, **malpractice,** evil courses, machinations of the devil; **sin, criminality,** lawbreaking, feloniousness; misdemeanor, felony

the transgression of the law
BIBLE

criminal NOUNS 1 **felon, perpetrator, crook** *and* perp <both nonformal>, public enemy, **lawbreaker,** scofflaw; **gangster** *and* mobster *and* wiseguy <all nonformal>, **racketeer; swindler;** thief; thug; **desperado,** desperate criminal; **outlaw,** fugitive, **convict,** jailbird, gaolbird <Brit>; gallows bird <nonformal>
ADJS 2 **illegal, unlawful, illegitimate, illicit,** nonlicit, nonlegal, lawless, wrongful, fraudulent, creative <nonformal>, **against the law; felonious; outlaw, outlawed**

cringe VERBS **flinch, shrink, shy,** shy away from, draw back, recoil, funk <nonformal>, **quail, wince, blench, blink,** say *or* cry uncle; **cower**

crinkle NOUNS 1 **wrinkle, corrugation,** ridge, **furrow, crease, crimp,** ruck, **pucker,** cockle; crankle, rimple, ripple, wimple; crumple, rumple; crow's-feet
VERBS 2 **wrinkle, corrugate,** shirr, ridge, **furrow, crease,** crimp, crimple, cockle, cocker, **pucker, purse; knit;** ruck, ruckle; **crumple,** rumple; rimple, ripple, wimple

cripple NOUNS 1 **handicapped person,** incapable; amputee; paraplegic, quadriplegic, paralytic; deformity; the crippled, the handicapped
VERBS 2 **lame,** maim; **hamstring,** hobble; wing; emasculate, castrate; incapacitate, **disable; handicap,** put at a disadvantage; hamstring

crisis NOUNS **critical point,** crunch, crucial period, climax, climacteric; **turning point,** hinge, turn, turn of the tide, cusp; **emergency, exigency,** juncture *or* conjuncture *or* convergence of events, critical juncture, crossroads; **pinch,** clutch <nonformal>, rub, push, pass, strait, extremity, spot <nonformal>; **emergency,** state of emergency, red alert, race against time

crisp ADJS 1 **refreshing,** refreshful, **fresh,** brisk, zesty, zestful, **bracing, tonic,** cordial; analeptic; **exhilarating, stimulating, stimulative, stimulatory, invigorating,** rousing, energizing; **cool,** coolish, temperate; chill, **chilly,** parky <Brit nonformal>
2 **brittle,** crispy; **fragile, frail,** delicate, flimsy, **breakable,** frangible, crushable, crackable, crunchable, fracturable; crumbly; fissile, scissile; brittle as glass

criterion NOUNS 1 **measure,** measuring instrument, **meter, instrument, gauge,** barometer, **rule, yardstick,** measuring rod *or* stick, **standard,** norm, canon, test, touchstone, check
2 **model, pattern, standard,** classic example, rule, mirror, paradigm

critic NOUNS 1 interpreter, exegete, analyst, explicator, theoretician, aesthetician; reviewer
2 criticizer; connoisseur, *cognoscente* <Ital>; literary critic, man of letters; textual critic; editor; social critic, muckraker; captious critic, smellfungus, caviler, carper, faultfinder; criticaster, criticule, critickin

critical ADJS 1 **faultfinding,** carping, picky *and* nitpicky <both nonformal>, caviling, quibbling, pettifogging, cap-

tious, cynical; nagging, niggling; hypercritical, ultracritical, overcritical, hairsplitting, trichoschistic
2 evaluative, interpretive, exegetical, analytical, explicative
3 **crucial,** pivotal, climactic, climacteric *or* climacterical, decisive; pregnant, kairotic, loaded, charged; exigent, emergent

criticism NOUNS 1 adverse *or* harsh *or* hostile criticism, flak <nonformal>, bad notices, bad press, animadversion, imputation, reflection, **aspersion,** stricture, obloquy; **knock** *and* **swipe** *and* **slam** *and* **rap** *and* hit <all nonformal>, home thrust; minor *or* petty criticism, niggle, cavil, quibble, exception, nit <nonformal>; **faultfinding,** taking exception, carping, caviling, pettifogging, quibbling, captiousness, niggling, nitpicking, pestering, nagging; hypercriticism, hypercriticalness, hairsplitting, trichoschistism
2 **censure**; **approval**; **critique,** review, notice, critical notice, report, comment

criticize VERBS **pan** *and* **knock** *and* **slam** *and* hit *and* rap *and* take a rap *or* swipe at <all nonformal>, snipe at, strike out at, tie into *and* tee off on *and* rip into *and* open up on *and* plow into <all nonformal>; critique, evaluate, interpret, explicate, analyze, judge; theorize; pick holes in, pick to pieces; **approve**; **review;** comment upon, annotate; moralize upon; pontificate

crony NOUNS **companion, fellow,** fellow companion, **comrade,** *camarade* <Fr>, amigo <nonformal>, mate <Brit>, comate, company, **associate**, consociate, compeer, confrere, consort, **colleague**

crook NOUNS 1 **staff,** pastoral staff, **crosier, cross,** cross-staff, paterissa
2 **criminal, crook** *and* perp <both nonformal>, public enemy, **lawbreaker,** scofflaw; **gangster** *and* mobster *and* wiseguy <all nonformal>, **racketeer; swindler**; thief; thug

crop NOUNS 1 **harvest,** harvesting, **reaping, gleaning,** gathering, cutting; yield; cash crop, root crop
VERBS 2 **cut off** *or* **away,** shear *or* take *or* strike *or* knock *or* lop off, truncate; **amputate,** mutilate, abscind; **prune,** pare, peel, clip, bob, dock, lop, nip, shear, shave, strip, strip off *or* away

cross NOUNS 1 crux, cruciform; **crucifix,** rood, tree *or* rood tree <old>; X *or* ex, exing, T, Y; **swastika,** gammadion, fylfot, *Hakenkreuz* <Ger>; crossbones
VERBS 2 **oppose, counter,** go *or* act in opposition to, **go against,** run against, **run counter to,** fly in the face of, fly in the teeth of
3 **hybridize, crossbreed, interbreed,** miscegenate, mongrelize
ADJS 4 **angry,** angered, **incensed, indignant, irate,** ireful; **livid,** livid with rage, beside oneself, **wroth, wrathful,** wrathy, wrought-up, worked up, riled up <nonformal>

cross-eyed ADJS **cockeyed,** swivel-eyed <nonformal>, goggle-eyed, bug-eyed *and* popeyed <both nonformal>, **walleyed,** saucer-eyed, glare-eyed; moon-eyed

crossroads NOUNS 1 **village, hamlet;** ham *and* thorp *and* wick <all old>; country town, wide place in the road

a little one-eyed, blinking sort o' place
THOMAS HARDY

2 **crisis, critical point,** crunch, crucial period, climax, climacteric; **turning point,** hinge, turn, turn of the tide, cusp; **emergency, exigency,** juncture *or* conjuncture *or* convergence of events, critical juncture

cross section NOUNS sample, random sample, sampling

crotch NOUNS 1 **genitals,** crutch <Brit>, groin, pubic region, perineum, pelvis
2 **fork, prong,** trident; **branch, ramification,** stem, offshoot; crutch

crotchety ADJS **capricious,** kinky, harebrained, cranky, flaky <nonformal>, quirky; dotty, maggoty <Brit>, crank, crankish, whimsical, twisted; antisocial

crouch VERBS duck, cringe, **cower; stoop, bend, stoop down, squat,** squat down, get down, hunker *and* hunker down *and* get down on one's hunkers <all nonformal>; hunch, hunch down, hunch over, scrooch *or* scrouch down <nonformal>

crow VERBS **exult,** triumph, glory, delight, joy, jubilate; **crow** *or* crow over, crow like a rooster *or* cock; **gloat,** gloat over

crowd NOUNS 1 **clique, coterie, set, circle,** ring, junto, junta, cabal, camarilla, **clan,** group; **crew** *and* mob *and* **bunch** *and* outfit <all nonformal>; inner circle;

closed *or* charmed circle; ingroup, we-group; **old-boy network**
2 **throng,** press, crush, flood, spate, deluge, mass; mob, rabble, rout, ruck, jam, *cohue* <Fr>, everybody and his uncle *or* his brother <nonformal>
VERBS 3 **throng,** swarm, teem, hive, surge, seethe, mill, stream, horde; **be crowded,** be mobbed, burst at the seams, be full to overflowing

crown NOUNS 1 **summit,** top; cap, **tip,** point, spire, pitch; highest pitch, no place higher, **apex,** vertex, **acme,** *ne plus ultra* <Fr>, **zenith, climax,** apogee, pole; **culmination**
2 **championship,** laurels, palms, first prize, blue ribbon, new high, record
3 royal crown, coronet, tiara, diadem
VERBS 4 **top,** top off, **cap,** crest, **head,** tip, peak, surmount; overtop *or* outtop, have the top place *or* spot, over-arch; **culminate,** consummate, climax
5 **install,** instate, induct, **inaugurate,** invest, put in, place, **place in office;** throne, enthrone, anoint

crowning ADJS **topping,** heading, surmounting, overtopping *or* outtopping, overarching; **culminating,** consummating, perfecting, climaxing

crucial ADJS **critical,** pivotal, climactic, decisive

crucify VERBS **torture, torment, agonize, harrow,** savage, **rack,** scarify, impale, excruciate, prolong the agony, kill by inches, martyr, martyrize

crude ADJS **unfinished,** rude, coarse, unpolished, unrefined; uncultivated, uncultured

cruel ADJS cruel-hearted, sadistic; **ruthless; brutal,** brutish, brute, bestial, beastly, animal, animalistic; **mindless, soulless,** insensate, senseless, subhuman, dehumanized, brutalized

cruelty NOUNS cruelness, sadistic *or* insensate cruelty, sadism, wanton cruelty; **brutality,** mindless *or* senseless brutality, brutalness, **brutishness, bestiality, animality,** beastliness

cruise NOUNS 1 **voyage,** ocean *or* sea trip, sail; course, **run, passage; crossing;** shakedown cruise
VERBS 2 **navigate, sail,** steam, run, **seafare, voyage,** ply, go on shipboard, go by ship, go on *or* take a voyage

crumb NOUNS **scrap,** tatter, snip, **snippet,** snick, chip, nip; **morsel,** *morceau* <Fr>

crumble VERBS **weaken,** go to pieces, disintegrate; go downhill, hit the skids <nonformal>, give way, break, collapse, cave in <nonformal>, surrender, cry uncle <nonformal>

crumbly ADJS **pulverable, pulverizable,** pulverulent, triturable; **friable**

crummy ADJS **base, low,** low rent *and* low ride *and* low-down *and* cotton-picking <all nonformal>, **mean**

crunch NOUNS 1 **embarrassed** *or* **reduced** *or* **straitened circumstances,** tight squeeze, hard pinch, crunch <nonformal>, cash *or* credit crunch <nonformal>
2 **crucial moment,** critical moment, **moment of truth,** when push comes to shove <nonformal>; **pickle,** pretty pickle, fine kettle of fish <all nonformal>

crusade NOUNS 1 **campaign,** war, **drive, expedition,** hostile expedition; holy war, jihad
VERBS 2 **campaign for, crusade for,** put on a drive for, devote *or* dedicate oneself to, spend *or* give *or* sacrifice oneself for

crush NOUNS 1 **infatuation;** case <nonformal>; **puppy love** *and* calf love <both nonformal>; love at first sight
2 **crowd,** press, flood, spate, deluge, mass
VERBS 3 **deject, depress,** press down, hit one like a ton of bricks <nonformal>, **cast down,** lower, lower the spirits, get one down <nonformal>, take the wind out of one's sails, rain on one's parade, burst one's bubble, **discourage, dishearten,** take the heart out of, **dispirit,** overcome, prostrate
4 **subdue, master,** overmaster, **quell, reduce,** beat down, **break,** break down, overwhelm; tread underfoot, trample on *or* down, trample underfoot, roll in the dust, trample in the dust

crusty ADJS **surly,** bearish, beastly, churlish; **crusted,** incrusted

crutch NOUNS **supporter, support;** staff, stave, cane, stick, walking stick, alpenstock, crook

crux NOUNS **salient point,** cardinal point, high point, great point; **gist, nub** <nonformal>, **heart,** meat, pith, kernel, **core;** knotty point, knot, node, nodus

cry NOUNS 1 **call, shout, yell, whoop, holler** <nonformal>; **cheer, hurrah; howl,** yowl, yawl <Brit nonformal>;

scream, shriek, screech, squeal, squall, caterwaul
2 **appeal, plea,** call, clamor, *cri du cœur* <Fr>, beseeching, impetration, obtestation
VERBS 3 **weep, sob, bawl;** whimper, snivel; **shed tears,** burst into tears, burst out crying, dissolve in tears, cry one's eyes out
4 **call, shout, yell, holler** <nonformal>, hoot; hail, halloo, hollo; **whoop; cheer**; **howl,** yowl, yammer, yawl <Brit nonformal>; squawk, yawp; **bawl, bellow,** roar, roar *or* bellow like a bull; cry *or* yell *or* scream bloody murder *or* blue murder

crypt NOUNS **tomb, vault,** burial chamber; ossuary *or* ossuarium; charnel house, bone house; **mausoleum**

cryptic ADJS **secret,** close, closed, closet; dark; unuttered, unrevealed, undivulged, undisclosed, unspoken, untold; arcane, esoteric, occult, enigmatic, mysterious

cryptography NOUNS cryptoanalysis, cryptoanalytics; **code, cipher;** secret language; code book, code word, code name; **secret writing,** coded message, cryptogram, cryptograph

crystallize VERBS 1 **form, take form,** take order, **take shape, shape up;** arrange *or* range itself, **fall** *or* **drop into place,** come together
2 **solidify, set,** thicken; granulate; petrify, lithify, harden

cubbyhole NOUNS **nook,** cubicle, roomlet, carrel, hole-in-the-wall <nonformal>, cubby, snuggery, hidey-hole <nonformal>

cuddle VERBS **snuggle, nestle,** nuzzle; lap; bundle

cuddly ADJS **endearing, lovable, likable, adorable,** admirable, **lovely,** lovesome, sweet, winning, winsome; **charming;** caressable, kissable; cuddlesome

cue NOUNS **reminder,** remembrancer; **prompt,** prompter, tickler; prompting, hint; jogger <nonformal>, flapper

cuff NOUNS 1 **slap, smack,** flap; **box,** buffet; **spank**
VERBS 2 **slap,** smack, whack, whomp, **box,** buffet; strike; box the ears, give a rap on the knuckles

cuisine NOUNS **cooking, cookery, culinary art;** food preparation; culinary science; catering; nutrition

culinary ADJS **cooking,** kitchen

cull VERBS **collect, pick, pluck, take up,** pick up, get *or* gather in, gather to oneself, bring *or* get together, scrape together; isolate, set on the side

culmination NOUNS **completion, fulfillment, consummation,** perfection, height, top, acme, ultimate, summit, pinnacle, realization, actualization, **accomplishment**, topping-off, closure

culpable ADJS **blameworthy,** blamable, to blame, at fault, much at fault; chargeable, impeachable, accusable, indictable, arraignable, imputable

culprit NOUNS **wrongdoer, malefactor, sinner,** transgressor, delinquent; offender; evildoer

cult NOUNS **ism;** cultism; cultus; **mystique**

cultivate VERBS 1 cultivate the friendship of, **court,** pay court to, pay addresses to, seek the company of, **run after** <nonformal>, **shine up to,** make up to <nonformal>, play up to *and* suck up to <both nonformal>, hold out *or* extend the right of friendship *or* fellowship
2 **grow,** culture, **dress, work, till,** till the soil, dig, delve, spade

cultivated ADJS cultured, **refined,** polished, civilized; **educated, learned, erudite, scholarly,** scholastic, studious

cultural ADJS **educational,** educative, educating, teaching, **instructive,** instructional, **tuitional,** tuitionary; **edifying, enlightening,** illuminating

culture NOUNS **society, civilization; ethos, culture pattern;** cultural change; cultural lag; culture conflict; **cultivation, refinement, polish,** civility; cultivation of the mind; **refinement,** finesse, refined *or* cultivated *or* civilized taste

cultured ADJS **improved, bettered;** changed for the better, advanced, ameliorated, enhanced, enriched; developed, perfected; beautified, embellished; upgraded; gentrified; **reformed; transformed,** transfigured, converted; **cultivated, refined,** polished, civilized; **educated**

culvert NOUNS **watercourse, waterway, aqueduct,** water channel, water gate, water carrier, irrigation ditch

cumbersome ADJS **onerous, oppressive, burdensome,** incumbent *or* superincumbent, cumbrous; massive; lumpish, **unwieldy**

cumulative ADJS **additive,** additional,

additory; accumulative; summative *or* summational

cunning ADJS **crafty, artful, wily,** callid <old>, guileful, **sly,** insidious, supple <Scots>, **shifty,** pawky <Brit>, arch, **smooth, slick** *and* slick as a whistle <both nonformal>, **slippery,** snaky, serpentine, **foxy,** vulpine, feline

cup NOUNS 1 **container, receptacle;** receiver, holder, vessel, utensil; basin, pot, pan, glass
2 **trophy,** loving cup, pot <nonformal>

Cupid NOUNS Love, Amor, Eros, Kama; Venus, Aphrodite, Astarte, Freya

curable ADJS **remediable;** medicable, treatable; emendable, amendable, **correctable,** rectifiable, corrigible; **reparable,** repairable, **mendable, fixable**

curb NOUNS 1 **pavement,** curbstone, kerbstone <Brit>, edgestone; kerb <Brit>, curbing; gutter, kennel <Brit>
VERBS 2 **control, check,** rein, arrest; **retard,** slow down; **hinder, impede, inhibit,** countercheck, scotch, snub

cure NOUNS 1 **remedy, corrective,** alterative, remedial measure, sovereign remedy; **relief, help, aid, assistance,** succor; balm, balsam; healing agent; restorative, analeptic; healing quality *or* virtue; specific, specific remedy; **prescription,** recipe, receipt
VERBS 2 remedy; prescribe; treat
3 **preserve,** salt, brine, marinate *or* marinade, pickle, corn, **dry, dry-cure,** jerk, dry-salt; dehydrate, anhydrate, evaporate, desiccate; vacuum-pack; **smoke,** fume, **smoke-cure,** smoke-dry, kipper

cure-all NOUNS **panacea,** universal remedy, theriac, catholicon; broad-spectrum drug *or* antibiotic; elixir, elixir of life, *elixir vitae* <L>

curio NOUNS conversation piece; museum piece; **oddity, curiosity, wonder,** funny *or* peculiar *or* strange thing; **abnormality, anomaly**

curiosity NOUNS 1 intellectual curiosity, thirst for knowledge, lust for learning; eagerness; interest, **concern,** concernment; **enthusiasm,** passion, ardor, zeal; cathexis; matter of interest, special interest
2 **oddity, abnormality, anomaly; rarity,** improbability, exception, one in a thousand *or* million; **prodigy,** prodigiosity

curious ADJS 1 **odd, queer, peculiar, absurd, singular, oddball** <nonformal>, weird *and* kooky *and* freaky *and* freaked-out <all nonformal>, quaint, **eccentric,** gonzo <nonformal>, funny, rum <Brit nonformal>; **strange, outlandish,** off-the-wall <informal>, surreal, not for real <nonformal>, passing strange, **weird,** unearthly; off, out

wondrous strange
SHAKESPEARE

2 **inquisitive,** inquiring, interested, quizzical; **alert,** tuned in <nonformal>, **attentive**; burning with curiosity, eaten up *or* consumed with curiosity, curious as a cat; gossipy; overcurious, supercurious; morbidly curious, **morbid, ghoulish**

curl NOUNS 1 **lock, tress;** flowing locks, flowing tresses; **ringlet,** earlock, *payess* <Yiddish>; lovelock
VERBS 2 wind, **curve, turn,** arc, sweep; **crook, hook,** loop; incurve, incurvate; recurve, decurve, bend back, retroflex; **hump,** hunch; coil; kink, crimp

curly ADJS **curled; kinky,** kinked; **frizzly,** frizzy, frizzled, frizzed

currency NOUNS **money, legal tender, medium of exchange,** circulating medium, sterling <Brit>, **cash,** hard cash, cold cash; specie, coinage, mintage, coin of the realm, gold; **silver; the wherewithal,** the wherewith; lucre, **filthy lucre** <nonformal>, the almighty dollar, pelf, root of all evil, mammon

current NOUNS 1 **electric current,** current flow, amperage, electric stream *or* flow, juice <nonformal>
ADJS 2 **fashionable, in fashion, smart, in style, in vogue; all the rage,** all the thing; **popular,** prevalent, current; **up-to-date,** up-to-datish, up-to-the-minute, switched-on *and* hip *and* with-it <all nonformal>, trendy <nonformal>, new-fashioned, modern; **in the swim;** sought-after, much sought-after

curry VERBS **tend; groom,** rub down, brush, currycomb; gentle, handle, manage; tame, train, break

curse NOUNS 1 **affliction,** infliction; **woe,** distress, grievance, **sorrow,** *tsures* <Yiddish>; **trouble,** peck *or* pack of troubles, **burden, oppression, cross, cross to bear** *or* **be borne, load,** fardel <old>, encumbrance, weight, albatross around one's neck, millstone around one's neck;

thorn, thorn in the side, crown of thorns

2 **malediction,** malison, damnation, denunciation, commination, imprecation, execration; blasphemy; anathema, fulmination, thundering, excommunication; ban, proscription; hex, evil eye, *malocchio* <Ital>, whammy <nonformal>; **hex, jinx**

3 **oath,** profane oath; cuss *or* cuss word *and* dirty word *and* four-letter word *and* **swearword** <all nonformal>, naughty word, no-no <nonformal>, foul invective, **expletive, epithet,** dirty name <nonformal>, dysphemism, obscenity

VERBS 4 accurse, **damn,** darn, **confound,** blast, anathematize, fulminate *or* thunder against, execrate, imprecate; excommunicate; call down evil upon, call down curses on the head of; put a curse on; curse up hill and down dale; curse with bell, book, and candle; blaspheme; hex, give the evil eye, throw a whammy <nonformal>

5 **swear, cuss** <nonformal>, curse and swear, execrate, rap out *or* rip out an oath, take the Lord's name in vain; swear like a trooper, cuss like a sailor, make the air blue, swear till one is blue in the face; **talk dirty** <nonformal>, scatologize, coprologize, dysphemize, use strong language

curt ADJS **gruff, brusque,** short, sharp, snippy <nonformal>, abrupt, **blunt,** bluff, brash, cavalier; **harsh,** rough, severe; truculent, aggressive; **surly,** crusty, bearish, beastly, churlish

curtain NOUNS **veil,** curtain, **cover, screen**; fig leaf; **wraps** <nonformal>; **disguise, veil of secrecy,** pall, wraps; iron curtain, bamboo curtain; wall *or* barrier of secrecy; **suppression,** repression, stifling, smothering; **censorship,** blackout <nonformal>, **hush-up, cover-up**

curtsy NOUNS 1 **bow, nod, bob,** bend, inclination, inclination of the head, **salaam, kowtow,** scrape, bowing and scraping, making a leg; **genuflection,** kneeling, bending the knee; salute, salutation, namaste

VERBS 2 **bow, make obeisance, salaam, kowtow,** make one's bow, bow down, **nod,** incline *or* bend *or* bow the head, bend the neck, **bob,** bob down, bob a curtsy, bend, make a leg, scrape, **bow and scrape**

curve NOUNS 1 **bend,** curve, swerve, veer, inflection, deflection; ell, L; cant

VERBS 2 **turn,** arc, sweep; **crook, hook,** loop; incurve, incurvate; recurve, decurve, bend back, retroflex; sag, swag <nonformal>; **bend,** flex; deflect, inflect; reflect, reflex; **bow,** embow; **arch,** vault; dome; **hump,** hunch; wind, curl; round

ADJS 3 **curved,** curvate, curvated, **curving,** curvy, curvaceous <nonformal>, curvesome, curviform; curvilinear, curvilineal; wavy, undulant, billowy, billowing; sinuous, tortuous, serpentine, mazy, labyrinthine, meandering

cushion NOUNS 1 **pillow,** bolster; **safeguard, fender,** mudguard, **bumper, buffer,** pad, padding

VERBS 2 absorb the shock, **soften the blow,** break the fall, deaden, damp *or* dampen, soften, suppress, neutralize, offset; show pity *or* mercy *or* consideration *or* sensitivity, temper the wind to the shorn lamb; **soften,** soften up; **ease**

custodian NOUNS 1 **cleaner,** cleaner-up, cleaner-off, cleaner-out; **janitor,** janitress; cleaning woman *or* lady *or* man, daily *or* daily woman *and* charwoman *or* char <all Brit>

2 **guardian, warden,** governor; steward, **keeper, caretaker,** warder <Brit>, attendant; caregiver; next friend, prochein ami, guardian *ad litem;* **curator,** conservator; janitor; castellan

custody NOUNS **preservation,** preserval, **conservation, saving, salvation,** salvage, **keeping, safekeeping,** maintenance, upkeep, support; custodianship, keep <old>, **keeping, care, change, ward,** guarding, hold, protective *or* preventive custody; protection, safekeeping

custom NOUNS **convention,** use, **usage,** standard usage, standard behavior, **wont,** wonting, **way,** established way, time-honored practice, **tradition,** standing custom, **folkway,** manner, **practice,** praxis, prescription, **observance,** ritual, consuetude, **mores;** proper thing, what is done, **social convention**; bon ton, **fashion**; manners, etiquette; way of life, lifestyle; conformity; **generalization,** labeling, stereotyping

customary ADJS **wonted;** traditional, time-honored; familiar, everyday, ordinary, **usual; established,** received, accepted; set, prescribed, prescriptive; **normative, normal; standard,** regular, stock, regulation; prevalent, prevailing, widespread, obtaining, generally accepted, popular, **current**; **conventional**; conformist, conformable

cut NOUNS 1 incision, scratch, gash; puncture, stab, stab wound; flesh wound; **laceration,** mutilation; abrasion, scuff, scrape, chafe, gall; frazzle, fray; run, **rip,** rent, slash, **tear**
2 **indignity, affront, offense, injury,** humiliation; scurrility, contempt, contumely, despite, flout, flouting, mockery, jeering, jeer, mock, scoff, gibe, taunt, brickbat <nonformal>; **insult, aspersion,** uncomplimentary remark, slap *or* kick in the face, left-handed *or* backhanded compliment, damning with faint praise

most unkindest cut of all
SHAKESPEARE

3 **portion, share, bite** *and* **cut** *and* **slice** *and* **chunk** *and* slice of the pie *or* melon *and* piece of the action <all nonformal>, **lot, allotment; commission,** rake-off <nonformal>
4 **discount, deduction,** slash, abatement, reduction, price reduction, price-cutting, price-cut, rollback <nonformal>; underselling
VERBS 5 **pain,** give *or* inflict pain, **hurt, wound, afflict, distress; burn;** sting; nip, bite, tweak, pinch; pierce, prick, stab, lacerate; **offend, give offense, give umbrage,** affront, outrage; grieve, aggrieve; wound, hurt, cut to the quick, hit one where one lives <nonformal>, **sting,** hurt one's feelings; step *or* tread on one's toes
6 **delete,** erase, expunge, **cancel,** omit; **edit,** edit out, blue-pencil; strike, strike out *or* off, rub *or* blot out, cross out *or* off, kill; void, rescind; **censor,** bowdlerize, expurgate; abridge, abbreviate
7 **notch, nick, incise, gash,** slash, chop, crimp, scotch, **score,** blaze, jag, scarify; **indent**; **scallop,** crenellate, crenulate, machicolate; serrate, pink, mill, knurl, tooth, picot
8 **cheapen, depreciate, devaluate,** lower, reduce, **mark down, cut prices,** slash, shave, trim, pare, underprice, knock the bottom out of <nonformal>
9 **adulterate, corrupt,** contaminate, **debase,** denaturalize, pollute, denature, bastardize, **tamper with, doctor** *and* doctor up <both nonformal>; **fortify,** spike <nonformal>, lace; **dilute,** water, water down <nonformal>
10 **turn off, shut off,** shut, shut down, close; **phase out,** phase down, taper off, wind up *or* down; **kill,** cut off short, switch off
ADJS 11 **diluted, reduced, thinned,** rarefied, attenuated; adulterated; watered, watered-down
12 **pained, grieved,** aggrieved; **wounded, hurt,** injured, **bruised,** mauled; cut to the quick; **stung;** anguished, aching, bleeding
13 **cleft,** cloven, **cracked,** sundered, rift, rent, chinky, chapped, crazed; **slit, split;** gaping, gappy; hiatal, caesural, lacunar; fissured, fissural
14 **abridged, abbreviated,** vest-pocket, synopsized, shortened, clipped, pruned, contracted, truncated, docked

cut back VERBS **retrench, cut down,** cut *or* pare down expenses, **curtail expenses; cut corners, tighten one's belt,** roll back, take a reef, slow down; downsize

cute ADJS pretty as a picture, **pretty, attractive, lovely, graceful,** gracile

cutoff NOUNS **stop,** stoppage, **halt, stay, arrest,** check; stand, **standstill;** full stop, dead stop, screaming *or* grinding *or* shuddering *or* squealing halt

cut-rate ADJS **reduced,** cut, cut-price, slashed, **marked down;** giveaway <nonformal>, sacrificial

cutthroat NOUNS 1 **killer,** thug, desperado, bravo, gorilla <nonformal>, apache, gunman; professional killer, hired killer, hit man *or* button man *or* gun *or* trigger man *or* torpedo *or* gunsel <all nonformal>
ADJS 2 **competitive,** extortionate, **gouging, usurious,** exacting

cutting ADJS **acrimonious, harsh,** fierce, **rigorous,** severe, rough, stringent, astringent, strident, **sharp, keen,** sharpish, incisive, trenchant, biting, stinging, **scathing,** stabbing, **piercing, poignant,** penetrating, edged, double-edged

cycle NOUNS **succession, round,** rotation, routine, the daily grind <nonformal>, recurrence, periodicity, revolution, **circle,** full circle, go-round, orbit, ambit

cyclical ADJS **continuous,** continued, **continual,** repetitive, **recurrent,** periodic; **recurrent,** recurring, **returning,**

reappearing, revenant, ubiquitous, ever-recurring, periodic, serial, isochronal, metronomic

cyclone NOUNS **whirlwind,** whirlblast, tourbillon, wind eddy; **tornado, twister,** rotary storm, typhoon, *baguio* <Sp>; **storm, tempest,** squall, line squall, **tornado, hurricane,** tropical cyclone, typhoon, storm-center, tropical storm

cynic NOUNS **pessimist,** malist, nihilist; killjoy, gloomy Gus *and* calamity howler *and* worrywart <all nonformal>, seek-sorrow, Job's comforter, prophet of doom, Cassandra, Eeyore; doubter, doubting Thomas

a man who feels bad when he feels good for fear he'll feel worse when he feels better
GEORGE BURNS

cynical ADJS **pessimistic,** pessimist, downbeat <nonformal>, nihilistic; **critical, faultfinding,** carping, picky *and* nitpicky <both nonformal>, caviling, quibbling, pettifogging, captious; **gloomy,** dismal, crapehanging, funereal, lugubrious; negative, negativistic; defeatist; Cassandran *or* Cassandrian, Cassandra-like

D

daily NOUNS 1 **newspaper,** news, **paper,** sheet *or* rag <both nonformal>, **gazette,** daily newspaper
ADJS 2 **recurrent,** recurring, **returning,** reappearing, revenant, ubiquitous, ever-recurring, circadian, thick-coming, frequent, incessant

dainty ADJS **delicate, gossamer, diaphanous; subtle,** subtile, tenuous, thin, rarefied; **fine, exquisite,** flowerlike

dairy NOUNS **larder, pantry,** buttery <nonformal>; dairy house *or* room, creamery

dais NOUNS **platform; stage,** estrade, floor; **rostrum, podium, pulpit,** speaker's platform *or* stand, **soapbox** <nonformal>; hustings, **stump**

dam NOUNS 1 **barrier,** weir, barrage, milldam, beaver dam, cofferdam, wicket dam, shutter dam
VERBS 2 **stop, stop up; obstruct, bar,** stay; **block,** block up; **clog,** clog up, foul; **choke,** choke up *or* off; dam up

damage NOUNS 1 **impairment, injury, harm,** mischief, scathe, **hurt, detriment,** loss, weakening, sickening; disablement, incapacitation; **malfunction,** glitch <nonformal>; mayhem, mutilation, crippling, hobbling, hamstringing
VERBS 2 **impair, injure, harm, hurt,** irritate; **worsen,** make worse, disimprove, deteriorate, put *or* set back, aggravate, exacerbate, embitter; **weaken; dilapidate;** add insult to injury, rub salt in the wound

dame NOUNS **noblewoman, peeress, gentlewoman**

damn VERBS 1 doom, send *or* consign to hell, cast into hell, doom to perdition, condemn to hell *or* eternal punishment
ADJS 2 **cursed,** accursed, bloody <Brit nonformal>, **damned, damnable,** goddamned, goddamn, **execrable**

damned ADJS **cursed,** accursed, bloody <Brit nonformal>, **damn, damnable,** goddamned, goddamn, **execrable; execrable, damnable;** accursed, cursed; infernal, hellish, devilish, fiendish

damp NOUNS 1 **moisture,** wet; **dampness, moistness,** moistiness, **wetness,** wettedness, wettishness, **wateriness,** humor *or* humectation <both old>; soddenness, soppiness, soppingness, sogginess
ADJS 2 **moist,** moisty; dampish; **wet,** wettish; **humid, dank, muggy, sticky**

dance NOUNS 1 **dancing,** terpsichore; the light fantastic; **choreography; ball,** *bal* <Fr>; masked ball, masque, mask, masquerade ball, masquerade, *bal masqué* <Fr>, *bal costumé* <Fr>, fancy-dress ball, cotillion
VERBS 2 **trip the light fantastic,** trip, skip, hop, foot, prance <nonformal>, **hoof** <nonformal>, clog

trip it as we go, on the light fantastic toe
MILTON

dancer NOUNS danseur, terpsichorean, **hoofer** <nonformal>, step dancer, tap dancer, clog dancer, **ballet dancer; ballerina,** danseuse, coryphée; **chorus girl, chorine,** chorus boy *or* man; nautch

dandruff NOUNS **flake,** flock, floccule, flocculus; **scale, scurf**

dandy NOUNS 1 **fop,** coxcomb, macaroni, gallant, dude *and* swell *and* sport <all nonformal>, ponce *and* toff <both Brit nonformal>, exquisite, blood, clotheshorse, fashion plate; beau, Beau Brummel, spark, blade, ladies' man, man-about-town, boulevardier

ADJS 2 <nonformal> **great,** swell, jim dandy, neat, cool, super, super-duper, groovy, out of sight, something else, hot, nifty, sexy, spiffy, spiffing, ripping

danger NOUNS **peril, endangerment, imperilment, jeopardy, hazard, risk,** cause for alarm, **menace, threat**; **crisis, emergency,** hot spot, nasty *or* tricky spot, pass, pinch, strait, plight, predicament; powder keg, time bomb

dangerous ADJS dangersome <nonformal>, **perilous,** periculous, parlous, jeopardous, ugly, serious, critical, explosive, attended *or* beset *or* fraught with danger

dangle VERBS **hang,** hang down, fall; **depend,** pend; swing, flap, flop <nonformal>; flow, drape, cascade; **droop**

dangling ADJS **pendent,** pendulous, pendulant, pendular, penduline, pensile; swinging, falling loosely; shaky, rickety; hanging, drooping

dank ADJS **humid, muggy, sticky;** dewy, bedewed

dapper ADJS 1 dashing, jaunty, braw <Scots>

2 <nonformal> sharp, spiffy, classy, nifty, snazzy; swank, swanky, swell

dapple ADJS **mottled, motley; pied, piebald,** skewbald, pinto; **dappled**

dare NOUNS 1 **challenge,** double dare; fighting words; gage, gauntlet, glove, chip on one's shoulder, slap of the glove
VERBS 2 **venture, make bold to,** make so bold as to, take risks, walk the tightrope, **have the nerve, have the guts** *or* the balls <nonformal>, have the courage of one's convictions

daring NOUNS 1 derring-do, deeds of derring-do; **bravado,** bravura; daredeviltry, daredevilry, fire-eating; playing with fire, flirting with death, courting disaster, stretching one's luck, going for broke <nonformal>, **audacity,** audaciousness, overboldness; **venturousness,** venturesomeness, risk-taking, tightrope walking, funambulism
ADJS 2 **audacious,** overbold; **adventurous, venturous, venturesome,** adventuresome, enterprising; foolhardy, daredevil, fire-eating, death-defying; adventurous

dark NOUNS 1 **dark, lightlessness; obscurity,** tenebrosity, tenebrousness; **night**, dead of night, deep night; **pitch-darkness,** pitch-blackness, Cimmerian *or* Stygian *or* Egyptian darkness, Erebus

darkness visible
MILTON

ADJS 2 dark-colored, **darkish,** darksome, blackish; nigrescent; darksome, darkling; **lightless,** beamless, rayless, unlighted, **unilluminated,** unlit; **swarthy,** swart; **dusky,** dusk; **somber,** sombrous, **sober, grave,** sad, funereal; hostile, sullen, angry

dark horse NOUNS **small chance,** little chance, **poor prospect** *or* prognosis, poor lookout <nonformal>, little opportunity, poor possibility, **unlikelihood, improbability**, hardly a chance, not half a chance; **off chance, outside chance** <nonformal>, **remote possibility,** bare possibility, a ghost of a chance, slim chance, long shot <nonformal>, hundred-to-one shot <nonformal>

dark-skinned ADJS black-skinned, **dark-complexioned;** melanian, melanic, melanotic, melanistic, melanous

darling ADJS **beloved, loved, dear, precious;** pet, favorite; **adored, admired,** esteemed, revered; **cherished,** prized, treasured, held dear

darn VERBS **repair, mend, fix,** put in repair, set to rights, put in order *or* condition; patch, **patch up;** sew up

dash NOUNS 1 **vim, verve,** fire, adrenalin, **drive; aggressiveness, enterprise,** initiative, proactiveness, thrust, spunk
2 **rush,** plunge, headlong rush *or* plunge, **race, scurry, scamper,** scud, scuttle, **spurt,** burst, **burst of speed**
3 **showiness, flashiness,** flamboyance, panache, jazziness <nonformal>, jauntiness, sportiness <nonformal>, gaiety, glitter, glare, dazzle
VERBS 4 **sadden,** damp *or* dampen the spirits; knock down, beat down; plunge one into despair; **unnerve, unman, undo, unstring,** unbrace, reduce to jelly, **demoralize, shake, upset,** psych out <nonformal>, knock down *or* flat, **crush,** overcome, prostrate; throw a wrench in the machinery, upset one's applecart; take the wind out of one's sails, cut the ground out from under one
5 **rush, tear,** dart, shoot, hurtle, bolt, fling, **scamper, scurry,** scour, scud, scuttle, scramble, **race,** careen

dashing ADJS **showy, flaunting, flashy,** snazzy, jaunty, rakish

dastardly ADJS dastard; hit-and-run; **pusillanimous,** base, craven, recreant, caitiff

data NOUNS **information,** database, data capture, database management, file, record, data bank

date NOUNS 1 **appointment, engagement,** double date *and* blind date <both nonformal>; point of time, time, day
VERBS 2 be dated, date at *or* from, date back, bear a date of, bear the date of; fix *or* set the date, make a date; **predate,** backdate, antedate; **postdate; update**
3 **age,** grow old, grow *or* have whiskers; **antiquate,** fossilize, **superannuate,** outdate; obsolesce, go out of use *or* style, lose currency *or* novelty; become obsolete *or* extinct

dated ADJS **old-fashioned,** old-fangled, old-timey <nonformal>, **out-of-date, outdated, outmoded,** out of style *or* fashion, out of use, disused, out of season, **unfashionable, behind the times,**

old hat *and* back-number *and* has-been <all nonformal>

daunt VERBS **deter,** shake, stop, stop in one's tracks, set back; **discourage, dishearten;** faze <nonformal>, terrorize; **awe, overawe**

dawdle VERBS **linger, loiter, tarry, delay, dally, dillydally,** shilly-shally, lollygag, waste time, **take one's time,** take one's own sweet time

dawn NOUNS the dawn of day, dawning, **daybreak,** dayspring, day-peep, **sunrise, sunup** <nonformal>, cockcrowing *or* cocklight <Brit nonformal>, light, first light, daylight, aurora; **break of day, crack of dawn,** first blush *or* flush of the morning

day NOUNS **period, point, juncture,** stage; **time,** while, **moment,** minute, instant, hour, **season;** psychological moment; **age, generation,** time, date, cycle; **daylight,** dayshine, day glow, light of day

daydream NOUNS 1 fantasy, pipe dream <nonformal>; reverie
VERBS 2 **muse, moon** <nonformal>, **dream,** pipe-dream <nonformal>, fantasy; abstract oneself, be lost in thought, let one's attention wander, let one's mind run on other things, dream of *or* muse on other things; **woolgather,** be somewhere else, be out of it *and* be not with it <both nonformal>

daze NOUNS **trance,** stupor; dream state, reverie, daydreaming; hypnotic trance; fugue, fugue state; disorientation, **muddle, muddlement,** fuddle *and* fuddlement <both nonformal>, befuddlement, muddleheadedness, maze <nonformal>

dazed ADJS **stupefied, stunned,** bedazed; **dazzled,** fuddled

dazzle NOUNS 1 **showiness, flashiness,** flamboyance, panache, dash, jazziness <nonformal>, jauntiness, sportiness <nonformal>, gaiety, glitter, glare
VERBS 2 **astonish, amaze, astound, surprise,** startle, stagger, **bewilder, perplex**, flabbergast <nonformal>, confound, overwhelm, **boggle, boggle the mind;** knock one's socks off *and* bowl down *or* over <all nonformal>, bedazzle

dazzling ADJS **gorgeous, ravishing; brilliant,** bright, radiant, shining, beaming, glowing, blooming, abloom, sparkling

deactivate VERBS **demilitarize, demobilize, disband,** reconvert, decommission

dead ADJS 1 **inanimate,** inanimated, unanimated, exanimate, azoic, nonliving, **lifeless,** soulless; inert; insentient, unconscious, nonconscious, **insensible,** insensate, senseless, unfeeling; **defunct,** extinct; **ended, at an end, terminated, concluded, finished, complete**, perfected, settled, decided, set at rest; **over, all over,** all up <nonformal>; **extinct,** gone out, gone-by, past
2 **lackluster, lusterless; dull,** deadened, **lifeless,** somber, **drab,** wan, **flat,** mat

deadbeat NOUNS **parasite,** barnacle, leech; **sponger,** sponge <nonformal>, freeloader <nonformal>, smell-feast

deaden VERBS 1 **numb,** benumb, blunt, dull, obtund, **desensitize;** paralyze, palsy; **anesthetize, put to sleep,** slip one a Mickey *or* Mickey Finn <nonformal>, chloroform, etherize
2 **muffle, mute, dull, soften,** quietize, cushion, baffle, damp, **dampen, soft-pedal,** put on the soft pedal

dead end NOUNS impasse, corner *and* box *and* hole <all nonformal>, **cleft stick;** cul-de-sac, blind alley, **dead-end street;** extremity, end of one's rope *or* tether, **wit's end, nowhere to turn;** stalemate, **deadlock; stand, standoff, standstill, halt, stop**

deadline NOUNS **bound, limit,** limitation, extremity; cutoff, cutoff point, terminus; time limit, time frame, term, deadline, target date, terminal date, time allotment

deadly ADJS **deathly,** deathful, **killing, destructive,** death-dealing, death-bringing, feral <old>; internecine; **fatal, mortal, lethal, malignant,** malign, **virulent, pernicious,** baneful; **life-threatening, terminal**

deaf ADJS **hard-of-hearing,** dull *or* thick of hearing, deaf-eared, dull-eared; surd <old>; deafened, stunned; **stone-deaf,** deaf as a stone, deaf as a door *or* a doorknob *or* doornail, **deaf as a post,** deaf as an adder; **unhearing;** earless; word-deaf; tone-deaf

deafening ADJS **loud,** loud-sounding, forte, fortissimo; loudish; **resounding,** ringing, plangent, pealing; full, sonorous; ear-deafening, **ear-splitting,** head-splitting, ear-rending, ear-piercing, piercing; **thunderous, crashing, booming**; window-rattling, earthshaking, enough to wake the dead *or* the seven sleepers

deal NOUNS 1 **undertaking, enterprise, operation,** work, **venture, project,** proposition <nonformal>; **understanding, arrangement, bargain; settlement,** negotiated settlement; binding agreement, ironclad agreement, covenant of salt; gentleman's *or* gentlemen's agreement

VERBS 2 **trade, traffic, truck, buy and sell, do business; barter; exchange,** change, interchange, give in exchange, take in exchange, **swap** <nonformal>, switch; swap horses *and* horse-trade <both nonformal>; **bargain, drive a bargain, negotiate, haggle,** higgle, chaffer, huckster, **dicker,** make a deal, hack out *or* work out *or* hammer out a deal

dealer NOUNS 1 **merchant,** merchandiser, marketer, **trader,** trafficker, monger, chandler; **tradesman,** tradeswoman; **storekeeper, shopkeeper**

2 pusher <nonformal>, narcotics *or* dope *or* drug pusher <nonformal>; **drug lord**

dear NOUNS 1 **sweetheart, loved one, love, beloved, darling, dear one,** dearly beloved, well-beloved, truelove, beloved object, **object of one's affections,** light of one's eye *or* life, light of love

ADJS 2 **beloved, loved, darling, precious;** pet, favorite; **adored, admired,** esteemed, revered; **cherished,** prized, treasured, held dear

3 **expensive, costly,** of great cost, dear-bought, **high, high-priced,** premium, at a premium, top; **fancy** *and* stiff *and* steep <all nonformal>, pricey; upmarket, upscale <nonformal>

ADVS 4 **dearly;** at a high price, at great cost, at a premium, at a great rate, at heavy cost, at great expense

death NOUNS 1 somatic death, clinical death, biological death, abiosis, **decease, demise;** brain death; **passing away,** passing, passing over, leaving life, ending, **end**, end of life, cessation of life, end of the road *or* line <nonformal>; **sleep, rest,** eternal rest *or* sleep, last sleep, last rest; reward, last debt; last muster, last roundup, curtains <nonformal>

the undiscovered country from whose bourn no traveler returns
SHAKESPEARE

a debt we all must pay
EURIPIDES

that good night
DYLAN THOMAS

deathless ADJS **immortal,** everlasting, undying, never-dying, **imperishable,** incorruptible, amaranthine; **indestructible, imperishable;** immortal, undying

debacle NOUNS **disaster, cataclysm, catastrophe; breakup,** breaking up; **breakdown, collapse; fall, downfall,** collapse, smash, crash, **undoing, ruin, destruction**

debase VERBS **abase, crush,** abash, **degrade, reduce,** diminish, **demean,** lower, **bring low,** bring down, trip up, take down, set down, put in one's place, put down, dump *and* dump on <both nonformal>; take down a peg *or* notch or two <nonformal>, make a fool *or* an ass *or* a monkey of one <nonformal>

debatable ADJS **doubtful,** iffy <nonformal>; **in doubt,** *in dubio* <L>; dubitable, doubtable, **dubious, questionable, problematic, problematical, speculative,** conjectural, suppositional; moot, arguable, disputable, contestable, controvertible, **controversial,** refutable, confutable, deniable

debate NOUNS 1 **discussion,** debating, **deliberation, nonformalogue,** exchange of views, canvassing, ventilation, airing, review, **examination, study, analysis,** logical analysis; logical discussion, dialectic; **argumentation, argument, controversy, dispute, disputation, polemic, contention, wrangling, bickering,** hubbub, bicker, verbal engagement *or* contest

VERBS 2 **discuss, reason, deliberate,** deliberate upon, exchange views *or* opinions, **talk over, consider, treat,** dissertate on, take up, **go into, examine,** investigate, talk out, **analyze,** sift, **study,** pass under review, controvert

debauch VERBS **corrupt, debase, degrade,** degenerate, **deprave, defile,** violate, desecrate, deflower, ravish, ravage, despoil; **be promiscuous,** sleep around *and* swing <both nonformal>; **wanton,** rake, womanize, whore, sow one's wild oats; **philander; dissipate**; fornicate, **cheat, commit adultery**

debilitated ADJS **decrepit, infirm,** weak,

feeble, the worse for wear, run to seed; **doddering,** doddery, doddered, tottering, tottery, rickety, shaky, palsied; on one's last legs, with one foot in the grave

debit NOUNS **loss, privation, expense, cost, debit;** detriment, injury, damage; **ruin,** perdition, total loss, dead loss; **expenditure, spending,** expense, disbursal, **disbursement**

debris NOUNS detritus, ruins, **remainder, residue,** residuum; refuse, trash, odds and ends, scraps, rags, **rubbish, waste,** orts, candle ends; scourings

debt NOUNS **indebtedness, obligation, liability,** financial commitment, due, **dues,** score, pledge, unfulfilled pledge, amount due, outstanding debt

debug VERBS **straighten out, iron out,** sort out, puzzle out; unscramble, undo, untangle, disentangle, untwist, unspin, unweave, **unravel,** ravel, ravel out

debunk VERBS **disabuse, undeceive;** correct, **set right** *or* **straight,** put straight, tell the truth, enlighten, let in on, put one wise <nonformal>; knock the props out from under, take the ground from under; expose, show up

debut NOUNS 1 **coming out** <nonformal>, presentation; premiere, premier performance; **launching,** unveiling; first appearance; maiden speech, inaugural address

VERBS 2 make one's debut *or* bow, come out; **enter on** *or* **upon** *or* **into, embark in** *or* **on** *or* **upon,** take up, go into, have a go at <chiefly Brit>, take a crack *or* whack *or* shot at <nonformal>

decay NOUNS 1 **decomposition, disintegration, dissolution,** resolution, degradation, biodegradation, breakup, disorganization, **corruption, spoilage, dilapidation; rot, rottenness, foulness, putridness,** putridity, rancidness, rancidity, rankness, **putrefaction,** putrescence, spoilage

VERBS 2 **decompose, disintegrate;** go *or* fall into decay, go *or* fall to pieces, break up, crumble, crumble into dust; **spoil,** corrupt, canker, **go bad; rot, putrefy,** putresce; molder, molder away, rot away, rust away, mildew

deceased NOUNS 1 dead person, **cadaver, carcass, body; the dead,** the defunct, **the deceased,** the departed, the loved one; **decedent,** late lamented; **remains,** mortal *or* organic remains, bones, skeleton, dry bones, relics, reliquiae

ADJS 2 **dead,** without life, inanimate, exanimate, without vital functions; **demised, defunct,** croaked <nonformal>, departed, departed this life, destitute of life, **gone, passed on,** gone the way of all flesh, dead and gone, done for <nonformal>, dead and done for <nonformal>, **at rest,** out of one's misery; **called home,** gone to a better world *or* place *or* land, gone to glory, joined the choir invisible, with the saints, sainted, numbered with the dead

gathered to his fathers
BIBLE

deceitful ADJS **false; fraudulent, sharp, guileful, insidious,** slippery, slippery as an eel, **shifty, tricky,** trickish, cute, finagling, chiseling <nonformal>; underhand, **underhanded, furtive, surreptitious,** indirect; **falsehearted, two-faced**

deceive VERBS **beguile, trick, hoax, dupe,** gammon, **gull,** pigeon, play one for a fool *or* sucker, **bamboozle** *and* snow *and* **hornswoggle** *and* diddle *and* scam <all nonformal>, take in, put on <nonformal>, string along, **put something over** *or* **across,** slip one over on <nonformal>, pull a fast one on

decent ADJS **kind, kindly, benign,** benignant; good as gold, **good, nice; kindhearted, warm, warmhearted,** humane, human; **honest, upright,** uprighteous, **upstanding,** erect, right, **righteous, virtuous, good,** clean, squeaky-clean <nonformal>; **modest, decorous,** delicate, elegant, proper, becoming, seemly

deception NOUNS 1 calculated deception, **deceptiveness, subterfuge,** gimmickry *or* gimmickery, **trickiness; fooling,** befooling, tricking, **kidding** *and* putting on <both nonformal>; bluffing; ensnarement, entrapment, enmeshment, entanglement

2 **hoax,** spoof <nonformal>, **humbug,** flam, **fake** *and* fakement, **rip-off** <nonformal>, **sham;** mare's nest

deceptive ADJS **deceiving, misleading,** beguiling, **false, fallacious,** delusive, delusory; hallucinatory, illusive, **illusory;** tricky, **fishy** <nonformal>, questionable, dubious

decide VERBS **determine; find,** hold, ascertain; **resolve, settle,** fix; make a decision, come to a decision, **make up one's mind,** settle one's mind, come down <nonformal>

decision NOUNS **resolution,** resolve, resolvedness, **determination,** fixed *or* firm resolve, **will,** purpose; **resoluteness, determinedness,** determinateness, decisiveness, decidedness, **purposefulness;** definiteness; **judgment, verdict**

decisive ADJS **resolute, resolved, determined,** bound *and* bound and determined <both nonformal>, **decided, purposeful;** single-minded, relentless, persistent, tenacious, persevering; **critical, crucial,** pivotal, climactic, climacteric *or* climacterical

deck NOUNS 1 **platform; terrace,** step terrace
VERBS 2 **fell, drop, bring down,** fetch down, down <nonformal>, take down, take down a peg, lay low; **raze,** rase, raze to the ground; **level,** lay level; **knock down,** dash down, send headlong, **floor,** lay out <nonformal>, **bowl down** *or* **over** <nonformal>

declaration NOUNS **statement,** allegation, allegation *or* statement of facts, procès-verbal; **deposition,** affidavit

declare VERBS **state, assert,** swear, swear to God <nonformal>, **affirm,** vow, avow, avouch, warrant, asseverate, confess, profess, express the belief, swear to a belief; depose, make an affidavit *or* a sworn statement

decline NOUNS 1 **deterioration, decadence** *or* decadency, **degradation, debasement,** derogation, deformation; **degeneration,** degeneracy, degenerateness, effeteness; declination, declension, comedown, **descent,** downtick <nonformal>, downtrend, downward trend, downturn, depreciation, **decrease**, **drop, fall, plunge,** free-fall, falling-off, lessening, slippage, slump, lapse, fading, dying, failing, failure, wane, ebb
VERBS 2 sink, fail, fall, slip, fade, die, wane, ebb, subside, lapse, **run down,** go down, **go downhill, fall away, fall off,** go off <nonformal>, slide, slump, hit a slump, take a nose dive <nonformal>, go into a tailspin, take a turn for the worse; hit the skids <nonformal>; reach the depths, hit *or* touch bottom, hit rock bottom, have no lower to go
3 **refuse,** refuse consent, **reject, turn down** <nonformal>, decline to accept, **not have,** not buy <nonformal>; not hold with, not think *or* hear of; **say no,** say nay, vote nay, vote negatively *or* in the negative, side against, disagree, beg to disagree, dissent; **turn thumbs down on;** be unwilling

decode VERBS **solve, resolve,** find the solution *or* answer, **clear up,** get, get right, do, work, **work out, find out, figure out,** dope *and* dope out <both nonformal>; **straighten out, iron out,** sort out, puzzle out; **unriddle,** riddle, unscramble, undo, untangle, disentangle, untwist, unspin, unweave, **unravel,** ravel, ravel out; **decipher,** decrypt, crack

decompose VERBS **disintegrate, decay,** dissolve, come apart, disorganize, **break up**, go to rack and ruin, crack up, disjoin, unknit, split, fission, atomize, **come** *or* **fall to pieces;** wear *or* waste away, molder, crumble, crumble into dust

decor NOUNS **decoration, adornment, embellishment,** embroidery, elaboration; **interior decoration** *or* decorating, room decoration, interior design

decorate VERBS 1 **ornament, adorn, embellish, embroider,** enrich; paint in glowing colors, tell in glowing terms; elaborate, convolute, involve
2 **honor, do honor,** pay regard to, give *or* pay *or* render honor to, **recognize;** pin a medal on; crown, crown with laurel; hand it to *or* take off one's hat to one <nonformal>, pay tribute, praise

decoration NOUNS 1 **adornment, embellishment,** embroidery, elaboration; **interior decoration** *or* decorating, room decoration, interior design
2 **insignia, regalia,** ensign, **emblem, badge,** marking, attribute; badge of office, mark of office, chain, chain of office, collar; medal

decorative ADJS **ornamental,** adorning, embellishing

decorum NOUNS **decorousness,** decency, properness, propriety, rightness, right thinking, **seemliness,** becomingness, fittingness, fitness, appropriateness, suitability, meetness, civility, urbanity; **social convention, convention,** conventional usage, what is done, what one does, **social usage, form, formality; custom**; **conformism, conformity**; **propriety**

decoy NOUNS **lure,** charm, **come-on**

<nonformal>, attention-getter *or* -grabber, **attraction, draw** *or* drawer *or* crowd-drawer, crowd-pleaser, headliner; hook *and* gimmick <both nonformal>; **bait, snare,** trap

decrease NOUNS 1 **diminishment,** diminution, **reduction, lessening, lowering,** waning, shrinking *or* shrinkage, withering, withering away, scaling down, scaledown, downsizing, builddown; **letup** <nonformal>, abatement, easing, easing off
VERBS 2 **diminish, lessen; let up,** bate, abate; **decline, subside,** shrink, wane, wither, ebb, ebb away, dwindle, languish, sink, sag, die down *or* away, wind down, taper off *and* trail off *or* away *and* tail off *or* away <all nonformal>; **reduce,** shorten, curtail, retrench, lessen, **decrease,** phase down, impair, bate, abate; **depreciate,** disparage, detract, derogate; **erode,** abrade, eat *or* wear *or* rub *or* shave *or* file away; **extract,** leach, drain, wash away; thin, thin out, weed; **refine,** purify

decree NOUNS 1 decretum, decretal, rescript, fiat, **edict,** *edictum* <L>; **law**; **rule, ruling,** dictum, ipse dixit; **proclamation,** pronouncement, pronunciamento, **declaration,** ukase; bull; **verdict,** holding
VERBS 2 **rule, ordain,** promulgate; give an order *or* a direct order, issue a command, say the word, give the word *or* word of command; proclaim, declare, pronounce; **pass judgment, pronounce judgment,** utter a judgment, deliver judgment; pronounce on, act on, **pronounce,** report; **sentence,** pass sentence, hand down a sentence, doom, condemn

decrepit ADJS **dilapidated, ramshackle,** tottery, **tumbledown, broken-down, run-down,** in ruins, ruinous, ruined, derelict, gone to wrack and ruin, the worse for wear; **senile,** doddering, doddery

decriminalize VERBS **legalize, legitimize,** legitimatize, legitimate, make legal, declare lawful; **authorize, sanction**

dedicate VERBS **commit, devote, consecrate,** set apart; **consecrate**

dedicated ADJS **devoted,** committed, **fast,** steadfast, constant, faithful, staunch; **tried and true,** true-blue, tested; **blessed,** consecrated, devoted, set apart

dedication NOUNS resolve, **determination,** fixed *or* firm resolve, **will,** purpose; **earnestness, seriousness,** sincerity, devotion, commitment, total commitment; single-mindedness, relentlessness, persistence, tenacity, perseverance; **self-sacrifice,** sacrifice, self-immolation, self-devotion, consecration

deduce VERBS **conclude,** draw a conclusion, **come to** *or* **arrive at a conclusion; derive, infer,** draw an inference; put two and two together

deduct VERBS **subtract,** subduct, take away, take from, **remove,** withdraw, abstract; **reduce,** shorten, curtail, retrench, lessen, **diminish, decrease,** phase down; **discount, cut, take off,** write off, charge off; **depreciate,** reduce

deduction NOUNS 1 **conclusion, inference,** consequence, consequent, corollary
2 **subtraction,** subduction, **removal,** taking away; **discount, cut,** slash, abatement, reduction, price reduction, price-cutting, price-cut, rollback <nonformal>; **depreciation**

deed NOUNS 1 **exploit, feat, enterprise, achievement, adventure,** gest, **bold stroke,** heroic act *or* deed; aristeia
VERBS 2 **transfer, convey,** deed over, give title to; exchange, barter, trade, trade away

deemphasize VERBS **minimize,** minify, **belittle,** detract from; dwarf, bedwarf; play down, underplay, downplay; deprecate, depreciate; **trivialize**

deep ADJS 1 deep-toned, deep-pitched, deep-sounding, deepmouthed, deep-echoing; **hollow, sepulchral; low,** low-pitched, low-toned, grave, heavy
2 **profound,** deep-down; deepish, deepsome; **deep-going,** deep-lying, deep-reaching; **deep-set,** deep-laid; **deep-seated, deep-rooted; recondite, abstruse,** abstract, transcendental
3 **wise, sage,** sapient, seasoned, **knowing; learned**; wise as Solomon; **learned, erudite, educated, cultured,** cultivated, lettered, literate, civilized, **scholarly,** studious

deepen VERBS **intensify, heighten,** enhance, **strengthen,** beef up <nonformal>, aggravate, exacerbate; **broaden, widen; lower, depress, sink**

deep-seated ADJS **confirmed, inveterate, chronic, established,** long-established, **fixed, settled, rooted,** thorough; incorrigible, irreversible; **deep-rooted,** deep-set, **infixed, ingrained,** fast, dyed-in-the-wool; **entrenched,** vested, **confirmed, inveterate**

deface VERBS **blemish, disfigure, flaw, mar;** scab; scar, cicatrize, scarify; **crack,** craze, check, split; blot, spoil; dysphemize

de facto ADJS 1 **real, actual,** factual, veritable, for real <nonformal>, **established, inescapable, indisputable, undeniable; empirical, objective**
ADVS 2 **really, actually; factually; genuinely,** veritably, **truly; in reality,** in actuality, in effect, in fact, in point of fact, as a matter of fact

default NOUNS 1 **nonpayment, delinquency,** nondischarge of debts, nonremittal, failure to pay; defection
VERBS 2 **not pay;** dishonor, repudiate, disallow, protest, stop payment, refuse to pay; **welsh** <nonformal>, levant

defeat NOUNS 1 **beating,** drubbing, thrashing; clobbering *and* hiding *and* lathering *and* whipping *and* lambasting *and* trimming *and* licking <all nonformal>, trouncing; **vanquishment, conquest, conquering,** mastery, subjugation, subduing, subdual; **frustration, thwarting, balking, foiling; discomfiture, disconcertion,** bafflement, confounding; upset
VERBS 2 **triumph over, prevail over,** best, **get the better** *or* **best of; surmount, overcome,** outmatch, rise above; **thwart, frustrate, baffle,** foil, cross

3 <nonformal> **clobber, trim, skin alive, beat,** skunk, drub, massacre, marmelize <Brit nonformal>, lick, whip, thrash, knock off, trim, hide, cut to pieces, run rings *or* circles around, throw for a loss, lather, trounce, **lambaste,** skin alive; fix, settle, settle one's hash, make one say 'uncle,' do in, lick to a frazzle, beat all hollow, beat one's brains out, cook one's goose, make hamburger *or* mincemeat out of, mop up the floor with, sandbag, banjax, bulldoze, steamroller, **smear,** paste, cream, **shellac,** whup, whop, whomp, shut out

defect NOUNS 1 **fault, deficiency, inadequacy,** imperfection, kink; **flaw,** hole, bug <nonformal>; **failing, foible, shortcoming;** weak point, Achilles' heel, chink in one's armor, weak link; **blemish,** taint; **blemish, disfigurement; malfunction,** glitch <nonformal>
VERBS 2 secede, bolt, break away; pull out <nonformal>, withdraw one's support; sell out *and* sell down the river <both nonformal>, **betray**; turn one's back on; apostatize

defective ADJS **imperfect, faulty, inadequate, deficient,** short, flawed, not all it's cracked up to be <nonformal>, lacking, wanting, found wanting

defend VERBS offer *or* say in defense, allege in support *or* vindication, **support, uphold, sustain, maintain,** assert; **plead for,** make a plea, offer as a plea, plead one's case *or* cause, put up a front *or* a brave front; **advocate,** champion, go to bat for <nonformal>, espouse, speak up for, put in a good word for; **protect, guard, safeguard, secure, keep,** bless, make safe, keep from harm

defendant NOUNS **accused,** respondent, codefendant, corespondent, libelee, suspect, prisoner

defender NOUNS **champion, advocate; upholder; guardian angel, supporter**; vindicator, apologist; **protector**; **guard**; paladin

defense NOUNS 1 **protection**; self-defense, self-protection, self-preservation; deterrent capacity; defense in depth; the defensive; covering one's ass *or* rear-end <nonformal>; psychological defenses, defense mechanism, avoidance reaction
2 **bulwark, rampart,** buffer, bulkhead, parapet, breastwork, work, earthwork, mound

defensive ADJS defending, **guarding,** shielding, screening; **protective**; self-defensive, self-protective, self-preservative

defer VERBS **postpone, delay, put off,** give one a rain check <nonformal>, hold off *or* up <nonformal>, prorogue, put on hold *or* ice *or* the back burner <all nonformal>, reserve, waive, **suspend,** hang up, stay, hang fire

deference NOUNS **respect, regard,** consideration, appreciation, favor; approbation, approval; **esteem,** estimation, prestige; **reverence, veneration,** awe; deferential *or* reverential regard; self-abnegation, submission, submissiveness; servility

defiance NOUNS **refractoriness, recalcitrance** *or* recalcitrancy, recalcitration, defiance of authority, defying, contumacy, **contumaciousness, obstreperousness, unruliness,** restiveness, fractiousness, orneriness *and* feistiness <both nonformal>; wildness; **obstinacy, stubbornness**

deficiency NOUNS **inadequacy, mediocrity**, imperfection, insufficiency; **incompetence,** *or* incompetency, maladroitness, unskillfulness; underdevelopment, hypoplasia; want, **lack, need, deficit,** defect, **shortage,** shortfall, underage; **shortcoming**

deficient ADJS **inadequate, mediocre,** imperfect, **insufficient; incompetent,** unskillful, maladroit; half-assed <nonformal>, botched; **incomplete, uncompleted,** defective, unfinished, imperfect, unperfected, **inadequate; wanting, lacking,** needing, missing, **partial,** part, failing

deficit NOUNS default, deferred payments; cash *or* credit crunch <nonformal>; unfavorable trade balance *or* balance of payments; **shortfall; shortage,** short measure, underage

define VERBS **characterize, distinguish, differentiate, describe; mark, earmark,** mark off, mark out, demarcate, **set apart,** make special *or* unique; keynote <nonformal>, sound the keynote, set the tone *or* mood, set the pace; be characteristic, **be a feature** *or* **trait of**

definite ADJS **fixed, defined,** distinct, different as night and day, determinate, certain, absolute; detailed; **particular, special, especial, specific, express,** precise, **concrete; singular, individual,** individualist *or* individualistic; **positive, absolute, flat,** definitive, determinate, decided, decisive, conclusive

definition NOUNS **circumscription, limiting,** circumscribing, **bounding, demarcation,** delimitation, determination, specification; **interpretation, construction, reading,** way of seeing *or* understanding *or* putting; description; **meaning**; **explanation,** sense-distinction, **interpretation**

deflate VERBS **humiliate, humble;** mortify <old>, **embarrass**; put out, put out of face *or* countenance; prick one's balloon; **reduce, decrease, diminish, lessen,** take from; depreciate, let the air out of, take the wind out of; puncture, **shoot** *or* **poke full of holes, cut to pieces, cut the ground from under;** cut the ground from under one's feet, not leave a leg to stand on

deformity NOUNS deformation, **malformation,** malconformation, monstrosity, teratology, freakishness, misproportion, **misshapenness,** misshape; **disfigurement, defacement;** mutilation, truncation; warp, twist, kink, **distortion; flaw, defect, fault**

defray VERBS **finance, fund**; defray expenses; pay the bill, **foot the bill** *and* pick up the check *or* tab *and* spring *or* pop for <all nonformal>; pay one's way; pay one's share, chip in <nonformal>

defrock VERBS **unfrock,** unchurch; strike off the roll, read out of; **unseat,** unsaddle; **dethrone,** disenthrone, unthrone, uncrown, discrown; **humiliate**; **degrade, debase**, deplume, displume, bring low

deft ADJS **skillful, expert, proficient; dexterous, adroit, adept, coordinated,** well-coordinated, **apt,** no mean, **handy; masterly, masterful; ingenious,** resourceful, daedal, Daedalian

defuse VERBS **alleviate, mitigate, palliate,** soften, pad, cushion, assuage, allay, lay, appease, mollify, subdue, soothe; take the edge off of, take the sting out of; cool <nonformal>; **moderate, restrain,** constrain, control, **keep within bounds; modulate,** abate, **diminish, reduce,** de-escalate, slacken, lessen, slow down

defy VERBS **confront, challenge,** dare, fly in the teeth of, throw down the gauntlet, ask for trouble, start something, do something about it; **disobey,** not mind, not heed, not keep *or* observe, not listen *or* hearken, pay no attention to, **ignore, disregard,** set at defiance, fly in the face of, snap one's fingers at, scoff at, flout

degenerate NOUNS 1 **reprobate,** recreant, **miscreant,** bad egg *and* wrongo *and* wrong number <all nonformal>, pervert

VERBS 2 **deteriorate, sicken, worsen, get** *or* **grow worse,** get no better fast <nonformal>, disimprove; **fall on evil days, go** *or* **come down in the world,** go downhill, be on the skids <nonformal>; run *or* go to seed, sink, decline; **go to pot** <nonformal>, go to the dogs

ADJS 3 **decadent,** debased, degraded, reprobate, **depraved, debauched, dissolute,** profligate, abandoned, gone to the bad *or* dogs, rotten at *or* to the core

degrade VERBS **abase, debase, crush,** abash, **demean,** lower, **bring low,** bring down, trip up, take down, set down, put in one's place, put down, dump *and* dump on <both nonformal>; **corrupt, debase,** degenerate, **deprave, debauch, defile,** violate, desecrate, deflower, ravish, ravage, despoil

degree NOUNS **extent, measure,** amount, proportion, stint, standard, height, pitch, reach, remove, compass, range, scale, scope, caliber; **shade,** shadow, nuance

deify VERBS **exalt,** elevate, ensky, raise, uplift, set up, **ennoble,** aggrandize, magnify, exalt to the skies; apotheosize, apotheose; **lionize**

deity NOUNS **divinity,** divineness; **godliness,** godlikeness; **god,** *deus* <L>; immortal, heathen god, pagan deity *or* divinity; **idol,** false god, devil-god

dejected ADJS **depressed, downhearted, down, downcast, cast down,** bowed down, subdued; **discouraged, disheartened, dispirited,** dashed; **low, feeling low,** low-spirited, **in low spirits; down in the mouth** <nonformal>, **in the doldrums, down in the dumps** *and* **in the dumps** <both nonformal>, in the depths; **despondent,** desponding; **despairing**, weary of life, suicidal, world-weary; pessimistic; spiritless, heartless, **woebegone**

delay NOUNS 1 stoppage, jam *and* logjam <both nonformal>, obstruction, tie-up *and* bind <both nonformal>, **block,** blockage, **hang-up** <nonformal>; **wait, halt, stay, stop,** down-time, break, pause, interim, respite; reprieve, moratorium; **retardation,** retardment, **detention,** detainment, holdup, setback

VERBS 2 **retard, detain,** make late, slacken, lag, drag, drag one's feet *and* stonewall <both nonformal>, slow down, **hold up** <nonformal>, hold *or* keep back, check, **stay, stop,** arrest, impede, **block,** hinder, obstruct, throw a monkey wrench in the works <nonformal>, **postpone, defer, put off,** prorogue, put on hold *or* ice *or* the back burner <all nonformal>, reserve, waive, **suspend,** hang up, stay, hang fire

delegation NOUNS **deputation, commission, mission**

delete VERBS **erase, expunge, cancel,** omit; **edit,** edit out, blue-pencil; strike, strike out *or* off, rub *or* blot out, cross out *or* off, kill, cut; void, rescind; **censor,** bowdlerize, expurgate; abridge, abbreviate

deliberate VERBS 1 **consider, contemplate, speculate, reflect, study, ponder,** perpend, **weigh, debate, meditate,** chew the cud <nonformal>, digest; introspect, be abstracted; wrinkle one's brow

ADJS 2 **intentional, intended,** proposed, purposed, telic, **projected, designed,** of design, aimed, aimed at, **meant, purposeful,** purposive, **willful, voluntary; leisurely, unhurried,** laid-back <nonformal>, unhasty, hasteless, easy, relaxed

delicacy NOUNS 1 **dainty, goody** <nonformal>, treat, kickshaw, **tidbit,** titbit; **morsel,** choice morsel

2 **sensibility, sensitivity, sensitiveness,** fineness of feeling, tenderness, affectivity, susceptibility, impressionability; attentiveness, **solicitousness,** solicitude, thought, regard, concern, **sensitivity,** tact, tactfulness

3 **sickliness,** peakedness <nonformal>, **feebleness,** fragility, **frailty**; **infirmity, unsoundness,** chronic ill health, invalidity, **invalidism**

delicious ADJS **tasty,** good, fit to eat *and* finger-lickin' good <both nonformal>, good-tasting, **savory,** savorous, **palatable, toothsome,** sapid, **good,** good to eat, nice, agreeable, likable, pleasing, to one's taste, delightful, delectable, exquisite; succulent, **luscious,** lush; ambrosial, nectarous, nectareous; scrumptious *and* yummy <both nonformal>

delight NOUNS 1 **happiness, felicity, gladness,** delectation; **cheer,** cheerfulness, exhilaration, **exuberance, high spirits, glee,** sunshine; **enchantment,** unalloyed happiness; elation, exaltation

VERBS 2 **tickle, titillate, thrill, enrapture, enthrall, enchant,** entrance, fascinate, captivate, bewitch, **charm,** becharm; enravish, ravish, imparadise; ecstasiate, transport, carry away; tickle, titillate, tickle the fancy; **rejoice,** jubilate, **exult**

3 <nonformal> **give one a bang** *or* kick *or* charge *or* rush, knock out, knock off one's feet *or* dead *or* for a loop, knock

one's socks off, thrill to death *or* to pieces, tickle to death, tickle pink, **wow,** slay, send, freak out; **stroke,** massage one's ego

delinquent NOUNS 1 **defaulter,** nonpayer; **welsher** <nonformal>, levanter; tax evader, tax dodger *or* cheat <nonformal>; **wrongdoer, malefactor, sinner,** transgressor; malfeasor, misfeasor, nonfeasor; misdemeanant, misdemeanist ADJS 2 **defaulting,** nonpaying, in arrear *or* arrears; criminal, illegal, unlawful; fraudulent

delirious ADJS out of one's head <nonformal>, off one's head <nonformal>, off; **giddy,** dizzy, lightheaded; **wandering, rambling, raving, ranting,** babbling, incoherent

deliver VERBS 1 **transfer, convey,** hand, pass, negotiate; **hand over, turn over, pass over; assign, consign,** confer, settle, settle on; transmit, **hand down, hand on, pass on,** devolve upon 2 **perform, do,** work, act, execute, **accomplish, achieve**, come through with, realize, engineer, effectuate, **bring about,** bring to fruition *or* into being; formulate, put into words, couch, phrase; **present**

deliverer NOUNS **savior, redeemer, liberator,** rescuer, freer, **emancipator,** manumitter

delusion NOUNS **deception,** self-deception, fond illusion, wishful thinking, willful misconception; vision, hallucination, phantasm, mirage, will-o'-the-wisp, delusiveness, illusion

deluxe ADJS **sumptuous, elegant, elaborate, luxurious,** extravagant; plush *and* posh *and* ritzy *and* swank *and* swanky <all nonformal>, Corinthian

demagogue NOUNS **instigator, inciter,** exciter, urger; **agitator, fomenter,** inflamer; **rabble-rouser,** rouser

demand NOUNS 1 **claim, call; ultimatum,** nonnegotiable demand; notice, warning; **question, query, inquiry, interrogation,** interrogatory; interrogative VERBS 2 ask, ask for, make a demand; **call for,** call on *or* upon one for, appeal to one for; call out for, cry *or* cry out for, clamor for; **oblige, necessitate, require,** exact, **dictate,** impose, call for; leave no option *or* escape, admit of no option; **levy, exact**

demanding ADJS **exacting,** exigent; draining, taxing, exorbitant, extortionate, grasping; **insistent,** instant, **importunate,** urgent, pertinacious, pressing, loud, clamant, crying, clamorous; persistent; **strict, exacting,** exigent, not to be trifled with, **stringent,** astringent; **difficult,** difficile; no picnic; rigorous, brutal, severe

demeaning ADJS **disgraceful, shameful,** pitiful, deplorable, opprobrious, sad, sorry, too bad; degrading, debasing, beneath one, beneath one's dignity, *infra indignitatem* <L>, infra dig <nonformal>, unbecoming, unworthy of one

demented ADJS **insane,** unsane, **mad,** stark-mad, mad as a hatter, mad as a march hare, **stark-staring mad,** maddened, **sick,** crazed, **lunatic,** moonstruck, **daft, non compos mentis,** non compos, *baca* <Japanese>, **unsound,** of unsound mind, **deranged,** deluded, disoriented, unhinged, **unbalanced,** unsettled, distraught, wandering, mazed, crackbrained, brainsick, sick *or* soft in the head, not right, not in one's right mind, **touched,** touched in the head, **out of one's mind,** out of one's senses *or* wits, bereft of reason, reasonless, irrational, deprived of reason, senseless, witless

demobilize VERBS **demilitarize,** deactivate, **disband,** decommission, demob <nonformal>, muster out

democracy NOUNS representative government, representative democracy, direct *or* pure democracy, town-meeting democracy

government of the people, by the people, for the people
LINCOLN

the recurrent suspicion that more than half of the people are right more than half of the time
E B WHITE

demolish VERBS **wreck,** total *and* rack up <both nonformal>, undo, unbuild, unmake, **dismantle, disassemble; take apart, tear apart, tear asunder, rend, take** *or* **pull** *or* **pick** *or* **tear to pieces,** pull in pieces, tear to shreds *or* rags *or* tatters; sunder, cleave, **split; disintegrate, fragment,** break to pieces, make mincemeat of, reduce to rubble, atomize, pulverize, **smash,** shatter

demon NOUNS **fiend,** fiend from hell, **devil,** Satan, daeva, rakshasa, dybbuk, shedu, gyre <Scots>, bad *or* evil *or* unclean spirit; **ghoul,** lamia, Lilith, yogini, Baba Yaga, **vampire,** the undead

demonstrate VERBS 1 **protest, kick** *and* **beef** <both nonformal>, put up a struggle *or* fight; demonstrate against, rally, march, sit-in, teach-in, boycott, strike, picket; **rebel**
2 **manifest, show, exhibit, display,** breathe, unfold, develop; **present,** represent <old>, **evince, evidence; indicate,** give sign *or* token, token, betoken, mean; illustrate, exhibit, manifest, display, express, set forth; **prove,** afford proof of, prove to be, prove true

demonstration NOUNS **objection, protest; kick** *and* **beef** *and* **bitch** *and* squawk *and* howl <all nonformal>, protestation; **remonstrance, remonstration,** expostulation; protest demonstration, counterdemonstration, **rally,** march, boycott, strike, picketing; **explanation,** explication, unfolding, **elucidation,** illumination, enlightenment, light, **clarification,** *éclaircissement* <Fr>; **illustration,** exemplification

demoralize VERBS **unnerve, unman, undo, unstring,** unbrace, reduce to jelly, **shake, upset,** psych out <nonformal>, dash, knock down *or* flat, **crush,** overcome, prostrate; vitiate, drive to the dogs

demote VERBS **degrade,** disgrade, downgrade, debase, abase, humble, humiliate, **lower, reduce,** bump *and* bust <both nonformal>; strip of rank, cut off one's spurs, deplume, displume

demure ADJS **shy, timid,** timorous, **bashful,** shamefaced, **coy,** skittish, **overmodest, straitlaced, puritanical**

den NOUNS 1 **lair,** cave, **hole,** covert, mew, form; **burrow,** tunnel, earth, run, couch, lodge
2 **retreat,** recess, hiding place, **hideaway,** hideout, hidey-hole <nonformal>; **sanctum, inner sanctum, sanctum sanctorum,** holy ground, holy of holies, adytum; private place, **ivory tower;** study, library

denial NOUNS **disavowal, disaffirmation, disownment,** disallowance; disclamation, disclaimer; **renunciation, retraction,** retractation, **repudiation,** recantation; revocation, nullification, annulment, abrogation; palinode, palinody

denomination NOUNS **sect,** sectarism, religious order, **persuasion,** faction, **church,** communion, community, group, fellowship, affiliation, order, school, party, society, body, organization; branch, variety, version, segment

denote VERBS **mean, signify,** spell, have the sense of, be construed as, have the force of; mean something, mean a lot, indicate, signify, signalize, symptomatize, mark, **betoken, point to,** give indication of

denounce VERBS **condemn, damn, doom;** denunciate; **censure**; blacklist, put on the Index; pronounce judgment

dense ADJS **compact, close;** close-textured, close-knit, close-woven, tight-knit; **condensed, compressed,** compacted, concrete, consolidated, concentrated; **crowded, jammed,** packed, jam-packed, packed *or* jammed in, packed *or* jammed in like sardines; **solid,** firm, substantial, massive; impenetrable, impermeable

dent NOUNS 1 **indentation,** indent, indention, indenture, dint; gouge, **furrow**; sunken part *or* place, **dimple; pit,** pock, pockmark; impression, impress
VERBS 2 **indent,** dint, **depress,** press in, stamp, tamp, punch, punch in, impress, imprint; **pit;** pock, pockmark; dimple

deny VERBS 1 **recant, retract, repudiate, withdraw, take back,** unswear, renege, welsh <nonformal>, **abjure, disavow, disown;** disclaim, unsay, unspeak; **back down** *or* **out,** climb down, crawfish out <nonformal>, backwater, weasel; **withhold,** hold back; grudge, begrudge; close the hand *or* purse; deprive one of

depart VERBS 1 **deviate, depart from, vary, diverge,** divaricate, branch off, angle, angle off; **digress,** divagate, turn aside, go out of the way, detour, take a side road
2 make off, begone, be off, take oneself off *or* away, take one's departure, take leave *or* take one's leave, **leave, go, go away, go off, get off** *or* **away,** get under way, **pull out;** decamp, pull up stakes, **take to one's heels,** make off, **depart**, do the disappearing act, make a quick exit, **beat a retreat** *or* **a hasty retreat, turn tail,** show the heels

3 <nonformal> **beat it, split,** scram, up and go, trot, toddle, stagger along,

mosey *or* sashay along, buzz off, buzz along, bug out, bugger off <Brit>, fuck off *or* f off, get rolling, hightail it, pull up stakes, check out, clear out, cut out, haul ass, hit the road *or* trail, piss off <chiefly Brit>, get lost, flake off, get going, shove off, push along, push off, get out, get *or* git, clear out, get the hell out, make oneself scarce, vamoose, take off, skip, skip out, lam, take it on the lam, powder, take a powder, take a runout powder, skedaddle, absquatulate <old>

departure NOUNS 1 **leaving, going,** passing, **parting; exit,** walkout <nonformal>; egress; **withdrawal,** removal, retreat, retirement; evacuation, abandonment, desertion; decampment; escape, flight, getaway <nonformal>; exodus, hegira; defection, voting with one's feet
2 **digression,** deviation, **discursion,** excursion, excursus, sidetrack

depend VERBS hang, rest, hinge; **depend on** *or* **upon, hang on** *or* **upon, rest on** *or* **upon,** rest with, repose upon, lie on, lie with, stand on *or* upon, be based on, be contingent *or* conditional on, hang in the balance, be touch and go

dependable ADJS **reliable, sure,** surefire <nonformal>, **trustworthy, trusty,** faithworthy, **to be depended** *or* **relied upon,** to be counted *or* reckoned on; predictable, calculable; **secure, solid, sound, firm,** fast, **stable, substantial,** staunch, steady, **steadfast, faithful, unfailing;** true to one's word

dependent NOUNS 1 **charge, ward,** client, protégé, encumbrance; pensioner, pensionary; **retainer,** follower; myrmidon, yeoman
ADJS 2 **subject,** tributary, client; **subservient, subordinate, inferior;** servile; relying, depending, reliant; **contingent, depending;** contingent on, **dependent on, depending on,** predicated on, based on, hanging *or* hinging on, turning on, revolving on

deplete VERBS **exhaust,** impoverish, drain, drain of resources; suck dry, bleed white <nonformal>, suck one's blood; **throw away, squander**

deplore VERBS **regret, repine; rue,** rue the day; **bemoan, bewail; lament, mourn, moan, grieve,** give sorrow words

deploy VERBS **locate, situate, site, place, position;** emplace, spot <nonformal>, **install,** put in place; **allocate,** collocate, **dispose,** assign; spread, **spread out,** outspread, splay, fan out; mobilize, marshal, marshal *or* deploy one's forces *or* resources

deport VERBS **banish, expel, cast out,** thrust out, exile, expatriate, transport, send away, **extradite**

deposit NOUNS 1 down payment, earnest, earnest money, binder
2 mineral deposit, pay dirt; **vein, lode,** seam, dike, ore bed
VERBS 3 **store, stow,** lay down, salt down *or* away *and* sock away *and* squirrel away <all nonformal>; reposit, lodge; **cache,** stash <nonformal>, bury away

deposition NOUNS 1 **placement, positioning, emplacement, situation, location, siting,** localization, **locating, placing,** putting; reposition, **deposit,** disposal, dumping
2 **sworn statement, affidavit,** statement under oath, notarized statement, sworn testimony, affirmation; **vouching, swearing; attestation;** certification; **testimony, declaration, statement,** allegation, allegation *or* statement of facts, procès-verbal

depot NOUNS **storehouse, storeroom,** stock room, lumber room, store, storage, **depository, repository,** conservatory <old>, reservoir, repertory, supply depot, supply base, magazine, *magasin* <Fr>, warehouse, godown; bonded warehouse, entrepôt

depravity NOUNS **turpitude, moral turpitude; decadence** *or* decadency, debasement, **degradation,** demoralization, abjection; **degeneracy,** degenerateness, degeneration, reprobacy, **dissoluteness, profligacy;** abandonment, abandon

depreciate VERBS 1 **subtract, deduct,** subduct, take away, take from, **remove,** withdraw, abstract; **reduce,** shorten, curtail, retrench, lessen, **diminish, decrease,** phase down, impair, bate, abate
2 **cheapen, devaluate,** lower, reduce, **mark down, cut prices, cut,** slash, shave, trim, pare, underprice, knock the bottom out of <nonformal>

depress VERBS 1 **sadden,** darken, cast a pall *or* gloom upon, weigh *or* weigh heavy upon; **deject, oppress, crush,**

press down, hit one like a ton of bricks <nonformal>, **cast down,** lower, lower the spirits, get one down <nonformal>, take the wind out of one's sails, rains on one's parade, burst one's bubble, **discourage, dishearten,** take the heart out of, **dispirit**
2 **lower,** let *or* take down, debase, **sink,** bring low, reduce, couch; pull *or* haul down, take down a peg <nonformal>; thrust *or* press *or* push down, detrude

depression NOUNS 1 **dejection, oppression,** dejectedness, **downheartedness,** downcastness; **discouragement, disheartenment,** dispiritedness; *Schmerz* and *Weltschmerz* <both Ger>; lowness *or* depression *or* oppression of spirit, downer *and* down trip <both nonformal>; **low spirits,** drooping spirits, sinking heart; despondence *or* **despondency,** spiritlessness
2 **hard times,** bad times, sad times; **recession,** slow-down, cooling off, slump *and* bust <both nonformal>, downturn, downtick <nonformal>
3 **lowering; sinking;** ducking, submergence, pushing *or* thrusting under, down-thrust, down-thrusting, detrusion, pushing *or* pulling *or* hauling down

deprivation NOUNS **loss, losing, privation,** getting away, losing hold of; **bereavement,** taking away, stripping, dispossession, despoilment, despoliation, spoliation, robbery; divestment, denudation; **destitution, privation, deprivation; neediness, want,** need, lack, pinch, impoverishment

deprive VERBS **take from,** take away from, **deprive of,** do out of <nonformal>, relieve of, disburden of, lighten of, ease of; **bereave, divest;** tap, milk, mine, drain, bleed, curtail

depth NOUNS **deepness;** deep-downness, deep-seatedness, deep-rootedness; bottomlessness; **profundity,** profoundness, **wisdom,** wiseness, sageness, sapience

deputy NOUNS 1 **proxy, representative, substitute,** vice, vicegerent, **alternate,** backup *and* stand-in <both nonformal>, alter ego, **surrogate,** procurator, secondary, understudy, pinch hitter <nonformal>, utility man *or* woman, the bench <nonformal>; second in command, executive officer
2 peace officer, law enforcement agent, arm of the law; deputy sheriff

derelict NOUNS 1 **bum,** stiff <nonformal>, skid-row bum, Bowery bum, *lazzarone* <Ital>; drifter, vagrant, hobo, tramp; beggar; castoff; jetsam, flotsam, lagan, **flotsam and jetsam;** waifs and strays
ADJS 2 **negligent, neglectful,** neglecting, culpably negligent; inadvertent, uncircumspect; **inattentive**; unwary, unwatchful, asleep at the switch, off-guard, unguarded; **remiss,** lax
3 **abandoned, forsaken, deserted,** left; disused; castaway, jettisoned; marooned; junk, junked, discarded

deride VERBS **ridicule,** ride <nonformal>, make a laughingstock *or* a mockery of; roast <nonformal>, **insult**; **make fun** *or* **game of, poke fun at,** make merry with, put one on *and* pull one's leg <both nonformal>; **laugh at,** laugh in one's face, hold in derision, hoot down; point the finger of scorn; pillory

derivation NOUNS 1 **etymology, origin,** word origin, word history, semantic history
2 **source, origin,** genesis, original, origination, **rise, beginning,** conception, inception, commencement, provenance, provenience

derive VERBS **elicit,** educe, deduce, induce, obtain, procure, secure; **get from,** get out of; **draw out** *or* **forth,** bring out *or* forth, pry *or* prize out; extract, **gather,** collect, glean

derogatory ADJS **disparaging,** derogative, **depreciatory,** depreciative, deprecatory, slighting, belittling, minimizing, detractory, pejorative, back-biting, catty *and* bitchy <both nonformal>, contumelious, contemptuous, derisive, derisory, ridiculing

derrick NOUNS **lifter, erector;** crane, gantry crane, crab; **hoist,** lift, hydraulic lift

descend VERBS **go** *or* **come down,** down, dip down, lose altitude, dump altitude <nonformal>; gravitate; **fall, drop,** precipitate, rain, rain *or* pour down, fall *or* drop down; **collapse,** crash; **swoop,** stoop, pounce; **pitch, plunge, plummet;** cascade, cataract; parachute; come down a peg <nonformal>; **fall off,** drop off; go downhill

descendant NOUNS **offspring, child, scion; son,** son and heir, a chip of *or* off the old block, sonny; **daughter,** heiress; grandchild, grandson, granddaughter; stepchild, stepson, stepdaughter; foster child

descent NOUNS 1 **descending, dropping, falling,** plummeting, **drop, fall, free-fall,** *chute* <Fr>, **downfall,** debacle, **collapse,** crash; **decline,** declination, declension, comedown, downtrend, downward trend, downturn, depreciation, **decrease, drop, fall, plunge,** free-fall, falling-off, lessening, slippage, slump, lapse, fading, dying, failing, failure, wane, ebb
2 **lineage, line, bloodline,** descendancy, line of descent, ancestral line, succession, **extraction,** derivation, birth, **blood,** breed, **family,** house, **strain,** sept, **stock,** race, stirps, seed

describe VERBS **portray, picture,** render, **depict, represent, delineate,** limn, **paint,** draw; evoke, bring to life, make one see; outline, sketch; **characterize,** character; **express,** set forth, give words to; **write**

descriptive ADJS **depictive,** expositive, **representative, delineative; expressive, vivid, graphic,** well-drawn; realistic, naturalistic, true to life, lifelike, faithful

desecrate VERBS **profane,** dishonor, unhallow, commit sacrilege; **corrupt, debase, degrade,** degenerate, **deprave, debauch, defile,** violate, deflower, ravish, ravage, despoil

desensitize VERBS **deaden, numb,** benumb, blunt, dull, obtund, hebetate; freeze, **stupefy, stun,** bedaze, besot

desert NOUNS wilderness, back country, boonies *and* boondocks <both nonformal>, outback <Austral>; Sahara, karroo <Africa>, badlands, dust bowl, salt flat, Death Valley, Arabia Deserta, lunar waste *or* landscape

a barren waste, a wild of sand
ADDISON

desert VERBS **abandon, forsake; quit, leave,** leave behind, take leave of, depart from, absent oneself from, turn one's back upon, turn one's tail upon, say goodbye to, bid a long farewell to, walk away, **walk** *or* **run out on** <nonformal>, **leave flat** *and* leave high and dry *or* holding the bag *or* in the lurch <all nonformal>, leave one to one's fate, throw to the wolves <nonformal>; **withdraw, back out, drop out** <nonformal>, pull out, stand down <nonformal>; **go back on, go back on one's word; vacate,** evacuate; quit cold <nonformal>, toss aside; jilt, throw over <nonformal>; **defect,** renege, wimp *or* chicken *or* cop out <nonformal>, turn one's coat, apostatize, change one's colors, turn against, turn traitor; leave *or* desert a sinking ship

deserter NOUNS **apostate, turncoat,** turnabout, **recreant, renegade,** renegado, renegate *or* runagate <old>, **defector,** tergiversator, tergiversant; **bolter, seceder,** secessionist, **separatist,** schismatic

deserts NOUNS **reprisal, requital, retribution; recompense, compensation, reward,** comeuppance <nonformal>, **just deserts,** what is merited, what is due *or* condign, what's coming to one *and* a dose of one's own medicine <both nonformal>; quittance, return of evil for evil; **punishment**

deserve VERBS **merit,** earn, rate *and* be in line for <both nonformal>, **be worthy of,** be deserving, richly deserve

deserving ADJS **due, entitled to,** with a right to; **deserving,** well-deserving, **meriting, meritorious, worthy of**

design NOUNS **treatment; composition,** arrangement; styling, patterning, planning, shaping

the conscious effort to impose meaningful order
VICTOR PAPANEK

VERBS 2 **plan, devise, contrive,** frame, shape, cast, concert, lay plans; organize, rationalize, systematize, schematize, methodize, configure, pull together, sort out; make up, get up, prepare, compose, write, indite, devise, concoct, compound, churn out *and* crank out *and* pound out *and* hammer out *and* grind out *and* rustle up *and* gin up <all nonformal>; think up, think out, dream up, set one's wits to work

designate VERBS **specify;** denominate, name, denote; **symbolize, stand for,** typify, be taken as, symbol, emblematize, figure <old>; **point to,** refer to, advert to, allude to, make an allusion to; pick out, select; **point out,** point at, put *or* lay one's finger on, finger <nonformal>; **classify,** class, assign

desirable ADJS sought-after, much sought-after, to be desired, **much to be desired; enviable,** worth having; **lik-**

able, pleasing, after one's own heart; **agreeable,** acceptable, unobjectionable; palatable; **attractive,** taking, winning, sexy <nonformal>, **seductive, provocative,** tantalizing, exciting; appetizing, tempting, toothsome, mouth-watering; **lovable,** adorable

desire NOUNS 1 **wish,** wanting, **want, need,** desideration; **hope; fancy; will, mind, pleasure,** will and pleasure; heart's desire; **urge,** drive, libido; concupiscence; passion, ardor, sexual desire; something to be desired
VERBS 2 be desirous of, **wish,** lust after, bay after, kill for *and* give one's right arm for <both nonformal>, die for <nonformal>, **want,** have a mind to, choose <nonformal>; would fain do *or* have <old>, would be glad of; **like,** have *or* acquire a taste for, fancy, take to, **take a fancy** *or* a shine to, have a fancy for; have an eye to, have one's eye on

desirous ADJS desiring, **wanting, wishing,** needing, hoping; dying to <nonformal>; tempted; appetitive, desiderative, optative, libidinous, libidinal; **eager;** lascivious, **lustful, passionate, ardent,** impassioned

desk NOUNS **table,** board, **stand;** writing table, **secretary,** *secrétaire* <Fr>, escritoire; **lectern,** reading stand, ambo, reading desk

desolation NOUNS 1 **wretchedness, despair,** bitterness, infelicity, **misery, anguish, agony, woe,** woefulness, bale, balefulness; **melancholy,** melancholia, **depression, sadness, grief**; suicidal despair, black night of the soul, **despondency,** despond, prostration; depth of misery; **destruction, ruin, ruination,** rack, **rack and ruin,** blue ruin <nonformal>; devastation, ravage, havoc, holocaust, firestorm, hecatomb, carnage, shambles, slaughter, bloodbath

Slough of Despond
BUNYAN

2 **wasteland, waste,** barren *or* **barrens,** barren land, **depopulation,** dispeoplement, unpeopling

despair NOUNS 1 **desperation,** desperateness; no way <nonformal>, no way out, no exit, despondency; disconsolateness; forlornness
VERBS 2 despair of, **despond**, falter, lose hope, **lose heart, abandon hope,** give up hope, **give up,** give up all hope *or* expectation, give way *or* over, fall *or* sink into despair, give oneself up *or* yield to despair, throw up one's hands in despair, turn one's face to the wall; curse God and die

desperate ADJS **hopeless,** unhopeful, without hope, affording no hope, worst-case, bleak, grim, dismal, cheerless, comfortless; **despairing, in despair;** despondent; disconsolate; forlorn; **reckless,** devil-may-care; **furious,** wild, wanton; **at the end of one's rope** *or* **tether**

despicable ADJS **offensive, objectionable, odious, repulsive,** repellent, rebarbative, **repugnant, revolting,** forbidding; detestable, execrable, beneath *or* below contempt, **base,** ignoble, pitiable, pathetic, **contemptible,** beneath contempt, **miserable, wretched,** beggarly, vile, **shabby**

despise VERBS **disdain, scorn,** hold in contempt, contemn, vilipend, disprize, misprize, rate *or* rank low, be contemptuous of, feel contempt for, **hold in contempt,** hold cheap, look down upon, think little *or* nothing of, feel superior to, be above, hold beneath one *or* beneath contempt, look with scorn upon

despondent ADJS **hopeless,** unhopeful, without hope, affording no hope, worst-case, bleak, grim, dismal, cheerless, comfortless; **desperate, despairing, in despair;** disconsolate; forlorn; apathetic

destination NOUNS **goal,** bourn <old>; port, haven, harbor, anchorage, **journey's end;** end of the line, terminus, **terminal,** terminal point; stop, stopping place, last stop; **objective, object, aim, end, goal**

destiny NOUNS **fate,** doom, karma, kismet, what bodes *or* looms, what is fated *or* destined *or* doomed, what is written, what is in the books

whatever limits us
EMERSON

destroy VERBS **devastate, desolate,** waste, **lay waste, ravage,** havoc, wreak havoc, despoil, depredate; deal *or* unleash destruction, unleash the hurricane, nuke <nonformal>; **ruin,** ruinate <nonformal>, bring to ruin, lay in ruins, play *or* raise hob with

destroyer NOUNS **ruiner, wrecker, bane,**

demolisher; exterminator, annihilator; **iconoclast;** terrorist

destructive ADJS destroying; **ruinous,** ruining; demolishing, demolitionary; **devastating, desolating,** ravaging, wasting, wasteful, spoliative, depredatory; subversive, subversionary; nihilist, nihilistic; internecine

detach VERBS **remove,** disengage, take *or* lift off, doff; **unfasten, undo,** unattach, unfix; **untie,** unbind, unknit, unbandage, unlace, unzip, unstrap, unchain

detached ADJS **separated,** disjoined, disjoint, disjointed, disjunct, **disconnected,** disengaged, **disunited, divided,** removed, divorced, **alienated,** estranged, distanced, **segregated,** sequestered, isolated, cloistered, withdrawn, aloof, standoffish

detail NOUNS **particular, instance, item,** point, count, case, fact, matter, article, datum, element, part, ingredient, factor, facet, aspect, thing; minutia, minutiae <pl>, trifle, petty *or* trivial matter; incidental, minor detail; **feature,** aspect, specialty, circumstance

detain VERBS **delay, retard,** make late, slacken, lag, drag, drag one's feet *and* stonewall <both nonformal>, slow down, **hold up** <nonformal>, hold *or* keep back, check, **stay, stop,** arrest, impede, **block,** hinder, obstruct, throw a monkey wrench in the works <nonformal>, confine; tie up with red tape

detectable ADJS **visible,** visual, **perceptible,** perceivable, **discernible, seeable,** viewable, witnessable, beholdable, observable, noticeable, recognizable, to be seen; **in sight,** in view, in plain sight, in full view, **evident,** in evidence, **manifest, apparent;** revealed, disclosed, unhidden, unconcealed, unclouded, undisguised

detective NOUNS 1 **operative, investigator, sleuth,** Sherlock Holmes <A Conan Doyle>; **plainclothesman;** private detective, private investigator *or* PI

2 <nonformal> **dick,** gumshoe, gumshoe man, hawkshaw, sleuthhound, beagle, flatfoot, tec; eye, private eye; skip tracer, spotter

detention NOUNS **jailing,** incarceration, **internment,** immurement, immuration; **captivity,** duress, durance, durance vile; suspension, holdup <nonformal>, detainment, **delay,** holdup, setback

deter VERBS **daunt,** shake, stop, stop in one's tracks, set back; **discourage, dishearten;** faze <nonformal>; **disincline, indispose,** disaffect, repel, turn from, turn away *or* aside; divert, deflect; distract, put off *and* turn off <both nonformal>; **discourage; pour** *or* **dash** *or* **throw cold water on,** take the starch out of, take the wind out of one's sails

deteriorate VERBS **sicken, worsen, get** *or* **grow worse,** get no better fast <nonformal>, disimprove, **degenerate;** slip back, **retrogress,** retrograde, regress, relapse, fall back

determined ADJS **resolute, resolved,** bound *and* bound and determined <both nonformal>, **decided,** decisive, **purposeful; earnest, serious,** sincere; devoted, dedicated, committed, wholehearted; single-minded, relentless, persistent, tenacious, persevering; fixed, **settled,** nailed down <nonformal>, ascertained; predetermined, **predestined,** predestinate, foreordained; foregone

deterrent NOUNS **obstacle, obstruction,** obstructer; **hang-up** <nonformal>; **difficulty,** hurdle, hazard; determent; **stumbling block,** fly in the ointment, **hitch, catch**

detest VERBS **hate, loathe, abhor,** execrate, **abominate,** hold in abomination, take an aversion to, shudder at, utterly detest, be death on, not stand, not stand the sight of, not stomach; scorn, **despise**

detestable ADJS **offensive, objectionable, odious, repulsive,** repellent, rebarbative, **repugnant, revolting,** forbidding; **obnoxious, abhorrent, hateful, abominable,** heinous, **contemptible, despicable,** execrable

detour NOUNS 1 **bypass, roundabout way,** roundabout, circuit, the long way around, digression, deviation, excursion
VERBS 2 **go roundabout,** meander, deviate, take *or* go the long way around; make a detour, **go around,** go round about, go out of one's way, **bypass**

detrimental ADJS **disadvantageous,** unadvantageous, **unfavorable;** deleterious, injurious, harmful, prejudicial, counterproductive, **pernicious,** mischievous; **adverse, untoward, unfavorable**

devalue VERBS **corrupt, cheapen,**

coarsen, vulgarize, drag in the mud; adulterate, alloy, water, water down

devastate VERBS **destroy,** desolate, waste, **lay waste, ravage,** havoc, wreak havoc, despoil, depredate; vandalize; **decimate;** gut, gut with fire, incinerate, vaporize, ravage with fire and sword; **depopulate,** dispeople, unpeople

devastation NOUNS **destruction, ruin, ruination,** rack, **rack and ruin,** ravage, havoc, holocaust, firestorm, hecatomb, carnage, shambles, slaughter, bloodbath, **desolation;** decimation; **depopulation,** dispeoplement, unpeopling; desolation

develop VERBS **intensify,** gain strength, strengthen; accrue, accumulate; **grow,** wax, **increase**; burgeon, **sprout**, blossom, **flourish, thrive,** grow like a weed; mushroom; **mature,** flourish, unfold; elaborate; open out, fill in, flesh out, evolve, unfold; work out, explicate

development NOUNS **refinement,** elaboration, **perfection;** beautification, embellishment; maturation, coming-of-age, ripening, evolution, seasoning; **training, preparation,** readying <nonformal>, **conditioning, grooming,** cultivation, improvement; growth, rise, incremental change, developmental change, natural growth *or* development; flowering, blossoming

deviant NOUNS 1 sexual pervert; **pervert,** deviate, sex *or* sexual pervert, sexual psychopath; sodomist, sodomite, pederast
ADJS 2 **perverted, deviative,** deviatory, deviating, aberrant, aberrational, aberrative, shifting, turning, swerving, veering; abnormal, aberrant, deviationist

deviate VERBS **depart from, vary, diverge,** divaricate, branch off, angle, angle off; **digress,** divagate, turn aside, go out of the way, detour, take a side road; **swerve, veer,** sheer, curve, **shift, turn,** trend, bend, heel, bear off; alter one's course, make a course correction, tack

device NOUNS 1 **trick, artifice,** ploy, gambit, stratagem, **scheme,** design, *ficelle* <Fr>, **subterfuge,** blind, **ruse, wile,** tactic, contrivance, sleight, pass, feint, fetch, chicanery
2 **mark, earmark,** hallmark, **badge,** banner, stamp, signature, sigil, seal
3 apparatus, mechanical device, contraption <nonformal>, gadget, gizmo, gimcrack, gimmick <nonformal>, means, mechanical means

devil NOUNS 1 **mischief-maker, rogue,** knave, **rascal,** rapscallion, scapegrace, **scamp; imp, elf, puck,** pixie, **minx,** bad boy, bugger <nonformal>, little devil, little rascal, little monkey, *enfant terrible* <Fr>
2 **demon, fiend,** fiend from hell, Satan, daeva, rakshasa

devious ADJS **oblique;** deviant, deviative, divergent, digressive, divagational, deflectional, excursive; **indirect,** left-handed, sinister, sinistral, shady <nonformal>, up to no good, not kosher <nonformal>, unsavory, dark, sinister, insidious, indirect, slippery, devious, tricky, shifty, evasive, unstraightforward

devoted ADJS dedicated, committed, **fast,** steadfast, constant, faithful, staunch; tried, true, **tried and true,** true-blue, tested; **devout,** worshipful, **reverent,** reverential, venerative, venerational, adoring, solemn

devour VERBS **swallow,** ingest, **consume,** take in, tuck in *or* away *and* tuck into <all nonformal>, down, take down, get down, put away <nonformal>; **eat up;** dispatch *or* dispose of *and* get away with <all nonformal>; surround *and* put oneself outside of <both nonformal>

devout ADJS **pious,** pietistic; **religious,** religious-minded; theistic; devoted, worshipful, prayerful, reverential, venerative, venerational; faithful, dutiful; **observant, practicing**

diagnosis NOUNS **examination, physical examination; interpretation, construction, reading,** way of seeing *or* understanding *or* putting; **determination, finding,** holding; prognosis

diagonal ADJS oblique, transverse, bias, bend <heraldry>, oblique line, slash, **slant,** virgule, scratch comma, separatrix, solidus

diagram NOUNS 1 **plot, chart, blueprint,** graph, bar graph, pie *or* circle graph *or* chart, area graph; flow diagram, flow chart; **outline, delineation,** skeleton, figure, profile
VERBS 2 **plot; map, chart, blueprint,** graph; **sketch,** sketch in *or* out, draw up a plan; map out, plot out, **lay out,** set out, mark out; lay off, mark off

dialect NOUNS **diction,** words, wordage, verbiage, word-usage, **usage,** *usus loquendi* <L>, use *or* choice of words, formulation, way of putting *or* couching, word garment, word dressing; parlance, locution, expression; **idiom;** class dialect; regional *or* local dialect, subdialect; patois

dialogue NOUNS **talk, palaver, speech, words;** confabulation, **confab** <nonformal>; **chinfest** *and* **chinwag** *and* **talkfest** *and* **bull session** <all nonformal>; duologue, trialogue; **interview,** question-and-answer session; reasoning together, dialectic

diarrhea NOUNS loose bowels, flux; trots *and* runs *and* shits *and* GI's *and* GI shits <all nonformal>; turistas *and* Montezuma's revenge <both nonformal>; **dysentery,** bloody flux

diary NOUNS **chronicle, chronology, annals,** journal

dice NOUNS 1 <nonformal> **bones**, rolling bones, ivories, babies, cubes, devil's bones *or* teeth, galloping dominoes, golf balls, marbles, Memphis dominoes, Mississippi marbles, Missouri marbles
VERBS 2 **square, quadrate,** form *or* make four; form fours *or* squares; **cube**

dicker VERBS **bargain, drive a bargain, negotiate, haggle,** higgle, chaffer, huckster, **deal,** make a deal, hack out *or* work out *or* hammer out a deal

dictate VERBS 1 **command, order, direct, instruct,** mandate, **bid, enjoin, charge,** commission, call on *or* upon; issue a writ *or* an injunction; **decree, rule, ordain,** promulgate; give an order *or* a direct order, issue a command, say the word, give the word *or* word of command; call the shots *or* tune *or* signals *or* play <nonformal>; order about *or* around
2 **oblige, necessitate, require,** exact, demand, impose, call for; take *or* brook no denial; leave no option *or* escape, admit of no option

dictatorial ADJS **authoritarian; lordly, imperious,** aristocratic, totally self-assured; hubristic; masterful, magisterial, **high-and-mighty;** elitist

diction NOUNS words, wordage, verbiage, word-usage, **usage,** *usus loquendi* <L>, use *or* choice of words, formulation, way of putting *or* couching, word garment, word dressing; locution, expression

dictionary NOUNS word list, **lexicon, glossary, wordbook, Webster's; glossary,** gloss, **vocabulary,** onomasticon, nomenclator; **thesaurus**

die NOUNS 1 **mold, form**, cast, template, matrix, negative; punch, stamp, intaglio, seal, mint
VERBS 2 **decease, succumb, expire, perish,** be taken by death, up and die <nonformal>, cease to be *or* live, part, depart, quit this world, make one's exit, go, go the way of all flesh, go out, pass, pass on *or* over, **pass away, meet one's death** *or* **end** *or* **fate,** end one's life *or* days, depart this life

3 <nonformal> **croak,** go west, kick the bucket, kick in, pop off, conk off, conk out, cop it, drop off, step off, go to the wall, go home feet first, knock off, pipe off, kick off, shove off, bow out, pass out, peg out, push up daisies, go for a burton <Brit>, belly up, go belly up, bite the dust, take the last count; check out, check in, cash in, hand *or* pass *or* cash in one's checks *or* chips; turn up one's toes; slip one's cable; buy the farm *or* the ranch, farm, have one's time *and* have it *and* buy it <all Brit>

4 **come to an end, draw to a close,** end up, land up; lapse, become void *or* extinct *or* defunct, run out, run its course, have its time *and* have it <both nonformal>, die away, wear off *or* away, go out, blow over, be all over, be no more

diet VERBS **slenderize, reduce,** reduce *or* lose *or* take off weight, watch one's weight, lose flesh, weight-watch, count calories; slim, **slim down,** thin down

dietary ADJS dietetic, dietic <old>; regiminal

differ VERBS **vary,** diverge, stand apart, be distinguished *or* distinct; **deviate from,** diverge from, divaricate from, depart from; **disagree with,** disaccord with, conflict with, contrast with, clash with, jar with; not be like, bear no resemblance to, not square with, not accord with

difference NOUNS **disagreement, difficulty, misunderstanding,** difference of opinion, agreement to disagree, **variance,** division, dividedness; cross-purposes; polarity of opinion, polarization; **disparity,** diversity, divergence, gap, **contrast**

different ADJS differing; unlike, not like, **dissimilar**; **distinct,** distinguished, differentiated, discriminated, discrete, separated, separate, disjoined, widely apart; **various,** variant, varying, varied, heterogeneous, multifarious, motley, assorted, variegated, diverse, divers, **diversified; novel, original, unique;** strange, unusual, uncommon; unfamiliar, unheard-of

differentiate VERBS **distinguish, make a distinction, discriminate, secern; separate,** sever, severalize, segregate, divide; **demarcate,** mark, mark out *or* off, set off, set apart, draw a line, set limits; **characterize, define**

difficult ADJS 1 **perverse, contrary, wrongheaded, wayward, froward,** cross-grained, cantankerous, feisty, ornery <nonformal>; irascible
2 **hard to understand, hard,** tough <nonformal>, beyond one, **over one's head,** beyond *or* out of one's depth; knotty, cramp, crabbed; intricate, **complex,** overtechnical, perplexed, **complicated**
3 troublesome, troublous, hard, trying, rigorous, stressful; wretched, miserable; **not easy;** harmful

difficulty NOUNS 1 **disagreement, misunderstanding, difference,** difference of opinion, agreement to disagree, **variance,** division, dividedness; cross-purposes
2 **abstruseness,** reconditeness; crabbedness, crampedness, knottiness; **complexity,** intricacy, **complication**; **hardness; profundity,** profoundness
3 **adversity,** adverse circumstances, difficulties, hard knocks *and* rough going <both nonformal>, **hardship, trouble,** troubles, **rigor,** vicissitude, care, stress, pressure

diffuse ADJS 1 diffusive; **formless**, unstructured; **profuse,** profusive; **redundant,** pleonastic, repetitive, reiterative, iterative, tautologous, parrotlike
2 **dispersed, scattered, distributed,** dissipated, disseminated, strown, strewn, broadcast, **spread,** dispread; **widespread,** discrete, sparse; **diluted,** thinned, thinned-out, watered, watered-down, weakened; **sporadic**

dig VERBS 1 **excavate,** dig out, **scoop,** scoop out, **gouge,** gouge out, grub, shovel, spade, dike, delve, scrape, scratch, scrabble; dredge; **trench,** trough, furrow, groove; **tunnel, burrow**
2 **prod, goad, poke, punch, jab,** nudge

digest NOUNS 1 **abridgment, condensation,** short *or* shortened version, condensed version, abbreviation, abbreviature, brief, **abstract,** epitome, **précis, capsule,** encapsulation, **synopsis,** conspectus, pandect
VERBS 2 **absorb,** adsorb, chemisorb *or* chemosorb, **assimilate,** engross, ingest
3 **consider, contemplate, speculate, reflect, study, ponder,** perpend, **weigh, deliberate, debate, meditate, muse, brood, ruminate,** chew the cud <nonformal>

dignified ADJS **stately, imposing, grand, courtly,** magisterial, aristocratic; worthy, **august, venerable; sedate, solemn**, sober, grave

dignify VERBS **honor,** confer *or* bestow honor upon; adorn, grace; **distinguish,** signalize, confer distinction on, give credit where credit is due

dignity NOUNS **stiffness, stiltedness,** primness, prissiness, rigidness, starchiness, buckram <old>, gravity, weight, *gravitas* <L>, weighty dignity, staidness, reverend seriousness, **solemnity**; **pomp**; pomposity

digression NOUNS **obliquity,** obliqueness; **deviation**, deviance, divergence, divagation, vagary, excursion, skewness, aberration, squint, declination; deflection, deflexure

dike NOUNS **barrier,** bank, embankment, levee

dilapidated ADJS **ramshackle,** decrepit, shacky, tottery, slummy <nonformal>, **tumbledown, broken-down, rundown,** in ruins, ruinous, ruined, derelict, gone to wrack and ruin, the worse for wear

dilemma NOUNS Scylla and Charybdis, the devil and the deep blue sea; *embarras de choix* <Fr>; choice of Hercules; Hobson's choice, **no choice,** only choice, zero option; horns of a dilemma, double bind, damned-if-you-do-and-damned-if-you-don't, no-win situation, **quandary,** nonplus

dilettante NOUNS **half scholar,** sciolist, **dabbler,** dabster, amateur, trifler, smatterer; grammaticaster, philologaster, criticaster, philosophaster, Latinitaster

diligent ADJS **industrious, assiduous, sedulous,** laborious, **hardworking;** hard, unremitting, unsparing, relentless, zealous, ardent, fervent, vehement; **energetic,** strenuous; tireless, unwearied, unflagging, indefatigable

dilute VERBS **cut** <nonformal>, **reduce, thin,** thin out, attenuate, rarefy; **water,** water down, adulterate, **weaken,** dilute, attenuate, extenuate; **dissipate, dispel,** dissolve

dim VERBS 1 **blur, pale,** soften, film, mist, fog; defocus, lose resolution *or* sharpness *or* distinctness, go soft at the edges; **darken,** bedarken; **obscure,** obfuscate, obumbrate
ADJS 2 **dim-sighted,** dull-sighted, dim-eyed, half-blind, sand-blind; bleary-eyed, blear-eyed
3 half-visible, semivisible, low-profile; **indistinct, unclear,** unplain, **indefinite,** undefined, ill-defined, ill-marked, **faint,** pale, feeble, weak, dark, **shadowy, vague, obscure,** indistinguishable, half-seen, merely glimpsed
4 **dull,** dull of mind, **dopey** <nonformal>, **obtuse,** blunt, wooden, heavy, sluggish, slow, **slow-witted,** hebetudinous, **dim-witted, dull-witted, thick-witted,** thick-headed

dimension NOUNS **extent,** spread, breadth; proportion; **dimensions, proportions,** caliber, scantling, proportion; **measure,** expanse, **scope,** reach, range, ballpark <nonformal>, spread, coverage, area, cirumference, ambit, girth, diameter, radius, boundary, border, periphery

diminish VERBS **decrease, lessen; let up,** bate, abate; **decline, subside,** shrink, wane, wither, ebb, ebb away, dwindle, languish, sink, sag, die down *or* away, wind down, taper off *and* trail off *or* away *and* tail off *or* away <all nonformal>; **reduce, lower, depress,** damp, dampen, **step down** *and* tune down *and* phase down *or* out *and* scale back *or* down *and* roll back *or* down <all nonformal>

din NOUNS **noise,** loud noise, **blast**, tintamarre, **racket, clamor;** outcry, **uproar,** hue and cry, noise and shouting; howl; clangor, clatter, clap, jangle, rattle; **pandemonium,** bedlam, hell *or* bedlam let loose

dine VERBS **feed,** wine and dine, mess; satisfy, gratify; regale

diner NOUNS 1 **eater,** feeder, consumer, devourer; gourmand, trencherman, **glutton**
2 **restaurant,** eating place, eatery *and* beanery *and* hashery *and* hash house *and* greasy spoon <all nonformal>; **fast-food restaurant,** hamburger joint <nonformal>; **lunch counter,** quick-lunch counter; dog wagon <nonformal>; **kitchen;** dining car

dingy ADJS **grimy, smoky,** sooty, fuliginous, **smudgy,** smutty, blotchy, dirty, **muddy,** murky, smirched, besmirched

dining room NOUNS *salle à manger* <Fr>, dinette, dining hall, refectory, mess *or* messroom *or* mess hall, commons

diocese NOUNS **see,** archdiocese, bishopric, archbishopric; province; synod, conference; **parish**

dip NOUNS 1 **bath;** acid bath, mercury bath, fixing bath; sheepdip; duck, souse
2 **declivity, descent,** drop, fall, falling-off *or* -away, **decline; downgrade, downhill**
VERBS 3 **incline, descend, decline,** drop, fall, fall off *or* away, **go downhill**
4 **submerge,** submerse, **immerse,** immerge, merge, **sink,** bury, engulf, **inundate,** deluge, drown, overwhelm, whelm; **duck, dunk** <nonformal>, douse, souse, plunge in water; baptize

diploma NOUNS **certificate,** sheepskin <nonformal>; certificate of proficiency, testamur <Brit>

diplomacy NOUNS **tact, tactfulness, diplomacy;** *savoir-faire* <Fr>; diplomatics; shirt-sleeve diplomacy; shuttle diplomacy; dollar diplomacy, gunboat diplomacy; brinkmanship

the police in grand costume
NAPOLEON

diplomatic ADJS tactful, politic, statesmanlike

dire ADJS grim, baleful, baneful; appalling, shocking, disgusting; direful, fell; **ill-fated,** ill-starred, evil-starred, star-crossed; **terrible, dreadful,** awful <nonformal>, horrible, horrid; fatal, doomful, **ominous, inauspicious**

direct VERBS 1 **govern, rule, control**, order, **regulate,** guide; **determine,** decide, dispose; have the say *or* say-so, have veto power over, have the last word, call the shots *and* be in the driver's seat *and* wear the pants <all nonformal>
ADJS 2 undeviating, unswerving, unbending, undeflected; single-hearted, single-minded; bluff, blunt, outspoken; **unaffected, unpretentious,** unpretending, unassuming, unfeigning, straightforward, honest, candid; unadorned,

gracile, no-frills *and* vanilla *and* plain vanilla <all nonformal>, up-front *and* straight <both nonformal>, **forthright,** downright, straight-out <nonformal>
ADVS 3 **directly, straight, straightforward, undeviatingly,** unswervingly, unveeringly; straight as an arrow

direction NOUNS 1 **line,** direction line, line of direction, point, quarter, **aim, way,** track, range, **bearing,** azimuth, compass reading, **heading, course**
2 **directive, instruction, rule, regulation;** prescript, prescription, **precept; management, managing,** handling, **running** <nonformal>, **conduct;** governance, **command, control, chiefdom, government**, controllership
3 **trend, drift, course, current,** *Tendenz* <Ger>, flow, stream, mainstream, main current, movement, motion, run, **tenor,** tone, **set,** set of the current, swing, bearing, line, the general tendency *or* drift, the course of events, the way the wind blows, **the way things go**

director NOUNS *directeur* <Fr>, director general, **governor,** rector, **manager, administrator,** intendant, **conductor;** person in charge, responsible person; impresario, producer; auteur

dirge NOUNS **funeral** *or* **death song,** coronach, keen, elegy, epicedium, requiem, monody, threnody, threnode, knell, death knell, passing bell, funeral march, muffled drums

dirt NOUNS 1 **grime;** dust; soot, smut; **mud**
2 **land, ground,** landmass, earth, glebe <old>, **sod,** clod, **soil,** dust, clay, marl
3 **scandal, malicious gossip,** juicy morsel, tidbit, choice bit of dirt <nonformal>; **scandalmongering;** character assassination

gossip made tedious by morality
OSCAR WILDE

dirty VERBS 1 dirty up, grime, **begrime;** muck, muck up <nonformal>; **muddy,** mire, bemire; **stain,** bestain, **discolor,** smirch, besmirch, **taint,** attaint, **tarnish; mark, stigmatize,** brand; smear, besmear, daub, bedaub, slubber <Brit nonformal>; blur, slur <nonformal>; **darken, blacken; soil**
ADJS 2 **dingy, grimy, smoky,** sooty, fuliginous, **smudgy,** smutty, blotchy, **muddy,** murky, smirched, besmirched
3 blasphemous, **profane, foul, foulmouthed, vile,** thersitical, **obscene,** dysphemistic, scatologic, scatological, coprological, toilet, sewer, cloacal; ribald, Rabelaisian, raw, risqué
4 **unfair,** not fair; **unsporting,** unsportsmanly, **unsportsmanlike,** not done, not kosher <nonformal>, not cricket <Brit nonformal>; foul, below the belt; **base, low, mean,** crummy

disabled ADJS **incapacitated; crippled,** hamstrung; disqualified, invalidated; disarmed; paralyzed; hog-tied <nonformal>; prostrate, **on one's back,** on one's beam-ends

disadvantage NOUNS **drawback, liability; detriment,** impairment, prejudice, loss, damage, hurt, harm, mischief, injury; **a step back** *or* **backward,** a loss of ground; **handicap**, disability; drag, millstone around one's neck

disagree VERBS **differ,** differ in opinion, hold opposite views, disaccord, **be at variance,** not get along, pull different ways, be at cross-purposes, have no measures with, misunderstand one another

disagreeable ADJS **unsavory, unpalatable, unappetizing,** untasteful, untasty, ill-flavored, foul-tasting, **distasteful,** dislikable, unlikable, uninviting, unpleasant, unpleasing, displeasing; perverse, fractious, cross-grained

disappear VERBS **vanish,** vanish from sight, do a vanishing act <nonformal>, depart, fly, **flee**, go, be gone, **go away,** pass, pass out *or* away, pass out of sight, exit, pull up stakes <nonformal>, leave the scene *or* stage, clear out, pass out of the picture, pass *or* retire from sight, become lost to sight, be seen no more; dematerialize, evaporate, evanesce, **vanish into thin air,** go up in smoke

disappointed ADJS bitterly *or* sorely disappointed; **let down,** betrayed, ill-served, ill done-by; **dashed,** blighted, blasted, crushed; **balked,** bilked, **thwarted, frustrated,** baffled, crossed, defeated, foiled

disapprove VERBS **disapprove of,** not approve, raise an objection, go *or* side against, go contra; **disfavor, view with disfavor, raise one's eyebrows, frown at** *or* **on,** look black upon, look askance at, make a wry face at, grimace at, **turn up one's nose at,** shrug one's shoulders at; **take a dim view of** <nonformal>, not think much of, think ill of, think little of, not take kindly to, not hold with, hold no brief for *and* not sign off on <both nonformal>

disarm VERBS lay down one's arms, unarm, turn in one's weapons, down *or* ground one's arms, sheathe the sword, turn swords into plowshares; **demilitarize,** deactivate, **demobilize, disband,** reconvert, decommission

disaster NOUNS **debacle, cataclysm, catastrophe; breakup,** breaking up; **breakdown, collapse; crash,** smash, **smashup,** crack-up <nonformal>; **wreck,** wrack, shipwreck; cave-in, cave; washout; total loss

disastrous ADJS **calamitous, catastrophic, cataclysmic,** cataclysmal, **tragic,** ruinous, wreckful <old>, fatal, dire, black, woeful, sore, baneful, grievous

disbelief NOUNS **unbelief,** nonbelief, discredit; refusal *or* inability to believe; **incredulity**; **unpersuadedness,** lack of conviction; misbelief, heresy; infidelity, atheism, **agnosticism**; minimifidianism, nullifidianism

discard VERBS **reject, throw away, throw out,** chuck *or* chuck away *and* shit-can *and* eighty-six <all nonformal>, cast, cast off *or* away *or* aside; **get rid of,** get quit of, get shut *or* shet of <nonformal>, rid oneself of, shrug off, **dispose of,** slough, **dump, ditch** <nonformal>, **jettison, throw** *or* **heave** *or* **toss overboard,** deep-six <nonformal>, throw out the window, throw *or* cast to the dogs, cast to the winds

discharge NOUNS 1 **detonation, blast, explosion,** fulmination, **burst, bang, pop, crack,** bark; **shot,** gunshot; volley, salvo, fusillade

2 **exculpation,** disculpation, verdict of acquittal *or* not guilty; **pardon, excuse, forgiveness, free pardon; release, dismissal,** setting free; quashing of the charge *or* indictment

3 **dismissal,** forced separation, *congé* <Fr>; outplacement; **firing** *and* canning <both nonformal>, **cashiering,** drumming out, dishonorable discharge; **layoff,** removal, suspension; **the sack** *and* the chuck <both Brit nonformal>; the boot *and* the gate *and* the ax <all nonformal>; walking papers *or* ticket <nonformal>, pink slip <nonformal>

VERBS 4 **blast, detonate, explode, burst,** go off, **bang, pop, crack,** bark, fulminate

5 **emit,** give off; eject, throw *or* hurl forth

6 **perform, practice,** do, execute, carry out *or* through, do one's duty, do one's office, fulfill one's role, discharge one's function

7 release, dismiss, free, set free, let off <nonformal>, let go; quash the charge *or* indictment, withdraw the charge

disciple NOUNS **worshiper,** idolizer, idolater; **evangelist, apostle,** follower, servant, faithful servant

discipline NOUNS 1 **self-control,** control, restraint, constraint; composure, possession, aplomb; strict *or* tight *or* rigid discipline, regimentation, spit and polish; **punishment,** punition, **chastisement, chastening, correction,** disciplinary measure *or* action, **castigation,** infliction

2 **field,** field of inquiry, concern, province, domain, area, arena, sphere, branch *or* field of study, branch *or* department of knowledge, specialty, academic specialty, academic discipline

VERBS 3 **punish, chastise, chasten, correct, castigate, penalize; take to task,** bring to book, bring *or* call to account; deal with, settle with, settle *or* square accounts, teach *or* give one a lesson; pillory; **make conform,** shape, lick into shape, mold, force into a mold; straighten, rectify, correct

disclosure NOUNS disclosing; **revelation,** revealing, making public, publicizing, broadcasting; apocalypse; manifestation; exposure, **exposé; baring,** stripping, stripping *or* laying bare; outing <nonformal>

discomfort NOUNS displeasure, dissatisfaction, uncomfortableness, malaise, **painfulness; disquiet,** inquietude, **uneasiness,** unease, discomposure, vexation of spirit

disconnected ADJS 1 **separated,** disjoined, disjoint, disjointed, disjunct, disengaged, detached, **disunited, divided,** removed, divorced, **alienated,** estranged, distanced, **segregated,** sequestered, isolated, cloistered, shut off; **incoherent, inconsistent, uncohesive, unconsolidated,** tenuous

2 **sporadic,** patchy, spotty, scrappy, snatchy, catchy, choppy, **broken, discontinuous**

discontent NOUNS 1 **dissatisfaction,** unsatisfaction, unfulfillment; **resentment, envy**; **restlessness, restiveness, uneasiness,** unease; malaise; **disgruntlement,** sulkiness, sourness, petulance, peevishness, querulousness
VERBS 2 **dissatisfy, disgruntle, displease,** fail to satisfy, be inadequate, not fill the bill, disappoint, leave much *or* a lot to be desired, dishearten, put out <nonformal>

discontinue VERBS **cease, end, stop, halt,** terminate, close the books on, close the books, put paid to <Brit>, abort, cancel, scratch *and* scrub <both nonformal>, hold, **quit,** stay, belay <nonformal>

discord NOUNS discordance *or* discordancy, **dissonance** *or* dissonancy, diaphony, **cacophony;** stridor; **inharmoniousness,** unharmoniousness; **disaccord, conflict,** open conflict *or* war, **friction,** rub; jar, **jarring,** jangle, clash, clashing; touchiness, strained relations, **tension;** bad blood; **unpleasantness;** mischief; **contention**; **enmity**

discount NOUNS 1 **cut, deduction,** slash, abatement, reduction, price reduction, price-cutting, price-cut, rollback <nonformal>; underselling; **rebate,** rebatement
VERBS 2 disregard, leave out of account; consider the source, take with a grain of salt; waive, ignore, not hear of, wave aside, brush away *or* aside, refuse to consider; **cut, deduct,** bate, abate; **take off,** write off, charge off; **depreciate,** reduce; rebate, **refund,** kick back <nonformal>

discourage VERBS **daunt, deter,** shake, stop, stop in one's tracks, set back; **dishearten;** faze <nonformal>; **awe, overawe; pour** *or* **dash** *or* **throw cold water on,** throw *or* lay a wet blanket on, damp, dampen, demotivate, **cool, chill,** quench, blunt; take the starch out of, take the wind out of one's sails

discover VERBS **find,** get; strike, hit; put *or* lay one's hands on, lay one's fingers on, **locate**; **hunt down,** search out, trace down, track down, **run down, run** *or* **bring to earth;** trace; **learn, find out,** determine, become cognizant *or* conscious of, become aware of; discover *or* find oneself; invent

discreet ADJS **reticent, reserved,** restrained, nonassertive, low-key, low-keyed, constrained; guarded; **secretive,** close-lipped, secret, close, dark; **uncommunicative, close-mouthed**

discrepancy NOUNS inconsistency, inconsonance, incongruity, discongruity, unconformity *or* nonconformity, disconformity, **strangeness**, unorthodoxy, incompatibility, irreconcilability; **disparity,** inequality

discrete ADJS **separate, distinct; unjoined, unconnected, unattached,** unaccompanied, unattended, unassociated; discontinuous, noncontiguous, divergent; **isolated,** insular, detached, detachable, free-standing, free-floating, autonomous

discretion NOUNS **volition; free choice,** one's own will *or* choice *or* discretion *or* initiative, **option, pleasure, free will**; **reserve,** reservedness, restraint, low key, **constraint;** guardedness, discreetness, **uncommunicativeness**; **circumspection**

discriminate VERBS **distinguish,** draw *or* make distinctions, contradistinguish, secern, distinguish in thought, **separate,** separate out, divide, analyze, subdivide, **segregate,** sever, severalize, **differentiate,** demark, demarcate, set off, **set apart,** sift, sift out, sieve, sieve out, winnow, screen, screen out, sort, classify, sort out

discriminating ADJS **discriminate,** discriminative, selective; discriminatory; **tactful, sensitive;** appreciative, appreciatory; **critical; distinguishing;** differential; precise, accurate, exact; nice, fine, delicate, subtle, subtile, refined; fastidious; distinctive, contrastive

discuss VERBS **debate,** reason, deliberate, deliberate upon, exchange views *or* opinions, talk, **talk over, hash over** <nonformal>, talk of *or* about, rap <nonformal>, comment upon, reason about, discourse about, **consider, treat,** dissertate on, handle, deal with, take up, **go into, examine,** investigate, talk out, **analyze,** sift, **study,** canvass, review, pass under review, controvert, ventilate, air, thresh out, consider pro and con; **kick** *or* **knock around** <nonformal>

discussion NOUNS **debate,** debating, **deliberation,** exchange of views, canvassing, ventilation, airing, review, **treatment, consideration,** investigation, **examination, study, analysis,** logical analysis; logical discussion, dialectic

disease NOUNS **illness, sickness, malady, ailment, indisposition, disorder,** complaint, morbidity, *morbus* <L>, **affliction,** affection, **infirmity**

disengage VERBS **extricate, free, release, clear,** get out; disentangle, untangle, unsnarl, unravel, disentwine, disinvolve, unknot, disembarrass, disembroil; dislodge, break out *or* loose, cut loose, tear loose

disfavor NOUNS **falling-out, breach of friendship,** parting of the ways, bust-up <nonformal>; **alienation, estrangement, disaffection; disapproval, disapprobation,** disesteem, disrespect; rejection, thumbs-down, exclusion, ostracism, blackballing, blackball, ban

disgrace NOUNS 1 **scandal, humiliation; shame,** dirty shame *and* low-down dirty shame <both nonformal>, crying *or* burning shame; **reproach,** byword, byword of reproach, a disgrace to one's name
VERBS 2 **dishonor, discredit,** reflect discredit upon, bring into discredit, reproach, cast reproach upon, be a reproach to; **shame, put to shame,** impute shame to, hold up to shame; hold up to public shame *or* public scorn *or* public ridicule, pillory, bring shame upon, **humiliate**; **degrade, debase**, deplume, displume, defrock, unfrock, bring low

disgruntled ADJS **discontented, dissatisfied,** unaccepting, unaccommodating, **displeased,** less than pleased, let down, disappointed; resentful, dog-in-the-manger; malcontent, malcontented, **complaining,** sour, **faultfinding,** grumbling, growling, murmuring, muttering, griping, croaking, **peevish, petulant,** sulky, **querulous,** querulant, whiny

disguise NOUNS 1 **cover, camouflage,** protective coloration; **false colors, false front**; dissimilation, masking
VERBS 2 **conceal, hide,** ensconce; **cover, cover up,** blind, **screen, cloak, veil,** shroud, enshroud; **camouflage, mask,** dissemble; plain-wrap, wrap in plain brown paper; **obscure,** obfuscate, cloud, becloud, befog, throw out a smoke screen, shade

disgust NOUNS 1 **aversion, repugnance,** repulsion, **antipathy,** allergy <nonformal>, abomination, **abhorrence, horror,** mortal horror; **loathing**
VERBS 2 **repel,** turn one's stomach, nauseate; make one's gorge rise; gross one out <nonformal>; **offend,** give offense, **repel,** put off, turn off <nonformal>, **revolt,** sicken, make one sick

disgusting ADJS **odious, repulsive,** repellent, rebarbative, **repugnant, revolting, sickening, loathsome,** gross *and* yucky *and* grungy *and* scuzzy <all nonformal>, beastly <nonformal>, **vile, foul, nasty, nauseating**; fulsome, mephitic, miasmal, miasmic, malodorous, stinking, fetid, noisome, noxious

dish NOUNS 1 **serving,** service; **portion, helping,** help; second helping; **course;** plate; *plat du jour* <Fr>
VERBS 2 **ladle, dip, scoop;** dish out *or* up

dishevel VERBS **disorder, disarrange, disorganize,** rumple, ruffle; tousle <nonformal>, muss *and* **muss up** <both nonformal>, mess *and* **mess up** <both nonformal>; **litter, clutter,** scatter

dishonest ADJS **dishonorable; unconscientious,** unconscienced, conscienceless, unconscionable, shameless, without shame *or* remorse, **unscrupulous, unprincipled,** unethical, immoral, amoral; **corrupt,** corrupted, rotten; **crooked, criminal,** felonious, **fraudulent,** underhanded; shady <nonformal>, up to no good, not kosher <nonformal>, unsavory, dark, sinister, slippery, devious, tricky, shifty; fishy <nonformal>, questionable, suspicious

dishonor VERBS **disgrace, discredit,** reflect discredit upon, bring into discredit, reproach, cast reproach upon, be a reproach to; hold up to public shame *or* public scorn *or* public ridicule, pillory, bring shame upon, **humiliate**; **degrade, debase, desecrate, profane,** unhallow, commit sacrilege

disillusion NOUNS 1 **disillusionment, disenchantment,** undeception, unspelling, return to reality, loss of one's illusions, loss of innocence, cold light of reality, bursting of the bubble; awakening, rude awakening, bringing back to earth
VERBS 2 **disenchant,** unspell, uncharm, break the spell *or* charm; **disabuse, undeceive;** correct, **set right** *or* **straight,** put straight, tell the truth, enlighten, let in on, put one wise <nonformal>; open one's eyes, awaken, wake up, rob *or* strip one of one's illusions; bring one back to earth

disinfectant NOUNS 1 **antiseptic,** fumigant, fumigator, **germicide,** bactericide, microbicide, antibiotic
ADJS 2 **antiseptic, germicidal,** bactericidal

disinherit VERBS disendow; **disown,** cut out of one's will, **cut off,** cut off without a cent

disintegrate VERBS **decompose, decay,** dissolve, come apart, disorganize, **break up**, go to rack and ruin, crack up, disjoin, unknit, split, fission, atomize, **come** *or* **fall to pieces; erode,** corrode, ablate, consume, wear *or* waste away, molder, molder away, crumble, crumble into dust

disinterested ADJS **impartial, impersonal, evenhanded,** equitable, **dispassionate,** detached, objective, lofty, Olympian; **unbiased,** uninfluenced, unswayed; **neutral; unprejudiced, unbiased, unprepossessed, unjaundiced**

disk NOUNS **circle,** circus, rondure, **ring,** annulus; discus, saucer; halo, glory, areola, aureole; **computer disk,** diskette, floppy disk *or* floppy, hard disk, compact disk *or* CD

disk jockey NOUNS **broadcaster,** DJ <nonformal>; master of ceremonies, MC *or* emcee <both nonformal>

dislike NOUNS 1 **distaste,** disrelish, scunner; disaffection, **disfavor,** disinclination; disaffinity; **displeasure, disapproval,** disapprobation
VERBS 2 disfavor, not like, have no liking for, be no love lost between, **have no use for** <nonformal>, **not care for,** have no time for, have a disaffinity for, want nothing to do with, not think much of, entertain *or* conceive *or* take a dislike to, take a scunner to, not be able to bear *or* endure *or* abide, not give the time of day to <nonformal>, **disapprove of; disrelish,** have no taste for, not stomach, not have the stomach for, not be one's cup of tea

dislodge VERBS unplace; evict; **uproot,** root up *or* out, deracinate; depose, **unseat;** throw off, buck off; displace, delocalize, break out *or* loose, cut loose, tear loose

disloyal ADJS **unfaithful,** faithless, of bad faith, trothless; **inconstant, unsteadfast,** fickle; unloyal; false, **untrue,** not true to; disaffected, recreant, derelict, barratrous

dismal ADJS **gloomy, murky, bleak, grim, somber,** sombrous, **solemn, grave;** sad, *triste* <Fr>, **funereal,** funebrial, crepe-hanging <nonformal>, saturnine; **dreary,** drear, drearisome; **hopeless,** unhopeful, without hope, affording no hope, worst-case, cheerless, comfortless

dismantle VERBS **disassemble,** take apart *or* down, tear down; **demolish**

dismay NOUNS 1 **scare, alarm, consternation; dread,** unholy dread, **awe**
VERBS 2 **distress,** grieve, mourn, lament, sorrow; pain, discomfort, try one's patience, give one a hard time *or* a pain *or* a pain in the neck *or* ass *or* butt <nonformal>; **disconcert, appall, astound, confound, abash, discomfit, put out, take aback**

dismember VERBS **tear** *or* **rip apart,** take *or* pull apart, **pick** *or* **rip** *or* **tear to pieces,** tear to rags *or* tatters, **shred,** rip to shreds; tear limb from limb, draw and quarter; **mangle, disjoin,** unknit, unravel

dismiss VERBS 1 **send off** *or* **away, turn off** *or* **away,** bundle, bundle off *or* out, hustle out, pack off, **send packing,** send about one's business, send to the showers <nonformal>; **show the door,** show the gate; **give the gate** *or* the air <nonformal>; **discharge, expel, cashier,** drum out, disemploy, outplace, separate forcibly *or* involuntarily, **lay off,** suspend, surplus, furlough, turn out, release, let go, let out, remove, strike off the rolls, give the pink slip; break, bust <nonformal>; **retire,** superannuate, put out to pasture
2 dismiss *or* drive from one's thoughts; **put out of mind,** put out of one's head *or* thoughts, **think no more of, forget,** not give it another *or* a second thought, **drop the subject,** give it no more thought; turn one's back upon, abandon, leave out in the cold <nonformal>; put *or* set *or* lay aside, put on the back burner *or* on hold <nonformal>

disobedience NOUNS nonobedience, **noncompliance; undutifulness,** unduteousness; willful disobedience; **insubordination,** indiscipline; **unsubmissiveness, intractability,** indocility, recusancy; **nonconformity**; **disrespect**; **lawlessness,** waywardness, frowardness, **dereliction,** delinquency, nonfeasance

disorder NOUNS **disorderliness, disar-**

rangement, derangement, disarticulation, disjunction, **disorganization; disarray,** upset, disturbance, discomfiture, disconcertedness; turbulence, perturbation; **disruption**, destabilization; **confusion,** chaos, **mess** *and* mix-up *and* snafu <all nonformal>

disoriented ADJS **bewildered,** distracted, distraught, **disconcerted,** discomposed, in a fix *or* stew *or* pickle *or* jam *or* scrape <nonformal>; **lost,** astray, abroad, adrift, **at sea, confused, mixed-up, flustered,** fluttered, **ruffled, rattled, upset, unsettled,** off-balance, off one's stride; **disorganized, disordered,** disorientated, in a jumble

disown VERBS disendow; **disinherit,** disherison, cut out of one's will, **cut off,** cut off with a cent

disparity NOUNS **inequality, unevenness, contrariety**, **difference**; **irregularity,** nonuniformity, heterogeneity; **disproportion,** asymmetry; **unbalance,** imbalance, disequilibrium, overbalance, overcompensation, tippiness; **injustice,** inequity

dispatch NOUNS 1 **speed; rapidity,** celerity, **swiftness,** fastness, **quickness,** snappiness <nonformal>, **speediness;** haste, hurry, flurry, rush, precipitation; **expedition, promptness,** promptitude, instantaneousness
2 **message, word, communication, communiqué,** advice
VERBS 3 **send,** send off *or* away, send forth; transmit, remit, consign, forward; **mail, post**

dispensable ADJS **superfluous, redundant; excess, in excess;** unnecessary, unessential, expendable, **needless,** unneeded, gratuitous, uncalled-for

dispense VERBS **parcel out, dole out, hand out, mete out,** ration out, give out, hand around, pass around; **distribute,** disperse; issue, administer; disburse, pay out

disperse VERBS **scatter,** diffract; **distribute, broadcast, sow,** narrowcast, disseminate, propagate, pass around *or* out, publish; **diffuse, spread,** dispread, circumfuse, strew, bestrew, dot; **radiate,** diverge; scatter to the winds; **disband, scatter, separate, part,** break up, split up; part company, go separate ways

displace VERBS **remove, move, relocate, shift,** send, shunt; dislodge; **take away,** cart off *or* away, carry off *or* away; succeed, replace, take the place of, **step into** *or* **fill the shoes of,** don the mantle of, assume the robe of

displaced person NOUNS stateless person, homeless person, man without a country, exile, drifter, vagabond, deportee; expatriate

display NOUNS 1 **demonstration, show, showing; presentation, exhibition, exhibit, exposition, showcase,** showcasing, unveiling, exposure, manifestation
VERBS 2 **manifest, show, exhibit, demonstrate,** breathe, unfold, develop; **present, evince, evidence; make public,** go public with <nonformal>; bring *or* lay *or* drag before the public, take one's case to the public, **give** *or* **put out,** give to the world, **make known; divulge**; **ventilate,** air, get out in the open, open up

displeasure NOUNS **resentment,** resentfulness; disapproval, disapprobation, dissatisfaction, **discontent; vexation,** irritation, **annoyance,** aggravation <nonformal>, exasperation

dispossess VERBS disseise, expropriate, foreclose; **evict, oust,** dislodge, put out, turn out, **turn out of doors,** turn out of house and home, throw into the street

disprove VERBS **invalidate,** disconfirm, discredit, prove the contrary, belie, give the lie to; **negate,** negative; **expose, show up; explode,** blow up, blow sky-high, **puncture,** deflate, **shoot** *or* **poke full of holes, cut to pieces, cut the ground from under; knock the bottom out of** <nonformal>, knock the props *or* chocks out from under, cut the ground from under one's feet, not leave a leg to stand on, put *or* lay to rest

disputable ADJS doubtable, **dubious, questionable,** moot, arguable, contestable, controvertible, controversial, refutable, confutable, deniable; open to question *or* doubt; in question, in dispute, at issue

dispute NOUNS 1 **quarrel,** open quarrel, **argument,** polemic, **controversy,** altercation, **fight, squabble, contention,** strife, **tussle,** bicker, wrangle, snarl, **tiff, spat,** fuss; disputation; **quarreling, bickering, wrangling, squabbling;** oppugnancy
VERBS 2 **contest,** oppugn, take issue with; **fight over, quarrel over, wrangle over, squabble over,** bicker over, strive

or contend about; **question,** query, **challenge, contest,** cast doubt on, greet with skepticism, keep one's eye on, bring *or* call into question, raise a question, throw doubt upon

disqualify VERBS **invalidate,** knock the bottom out of <nonformal>, **make impossible, rule out,** disenable, close out, **bar,** prohibit, put out of reach, leave no chance

disregard VERBS **overlook, ignore,** accept, take *and* swallow *and* let go <all nonformal>, pass over, give one another chance, let one off this time *and* let one off easy <both nonformal>, close *or* shut one's eyes to, **blink** *or* **wink at,** connive at; **neglect, overlook,** not heed, not attend to, take for granted; lose sight of, pay no regard to; **flout, slight,** treat with contempt, fly in the teeth *or* face of, **snap one's fingers at; thumb one's nose at**

disreputable ADJS **discreditable, dishonorable,** unsavory, shady, **seamy, sordid; unrespectable, ignoble, ignominious, infamous,** inglorious; notorious; unpraiseworthy

disrespect NOUNS 1 **disrespectfulness,** lack of respect, low estimate *or* esteem, **disesteem,** dishonor, **irreverence; ridicule**; **disparagement**; **discourtesy**; **impudence,** insolence
VERBS 2 not respect, disesteem, hold a low opinion of, rate *or* rank low, hold in low esteem, not care much for, pay a lefthanded *or* backhanded compliment, damn with faint praise; **show disrespect for,** show a lack of respect for, **be disrespectful,** treat with disrespect, be overfamiliar with; trifle with, make bold *or* free with, take liberties with, play fast and loose with; **disparage**

disruption NOUNS **dissolution,** abruption, cataclasm; destabilization, **disintegration**, breakup, crack-up, shattering, splintering, fragmentizing, fragmentation; **bursting, scattering,** dispersal, diffusion

dissatisfaction NOUNS **unpleasantness**, **lack of pleasure,** joylessness, cheerlessness; discontent; displeasure, disapproval, disapprobation, **discomfort,** uncomfortableness, malaise, **painfulness; disquiet,** inquietude, **uneasiness,** unease, discomposure, unfulfillment

dissect VERBS **analyze, break down,** break up, anatomize, atomize, vivisect; **divide, subdivide,** segment; reduce to elements

dissent NOUNS 1 **dissidence,** dissentience; nonassent, nonconsent, nonconcurrence, nonagreement, agreement to disagree; **disagreement, difference, variance,** diversity, disparity; **dissatisfaction, disapproval,** disapprobation; repudiation, **rejection;** dissension, discord; bickering, infighting, factiousness
VERBS 2 dissent from, be in dissent, say nay, **disagree,** discord with, **differ,** not agree, disagree with, agree to disagree *or* differ; divide on, be at variance; **take exception,** withhold assent, **take issue, beg to differ,** raise an objection, march to *or* hear a different drummer, swim against the tide *or* against the current *or* upstream

dissident NOUNS 1 **dissenter,** dissentient, recusant; **objector,** demurrer; minority *or* opposition voice; **protester,** protestant; **separatist,** schismatic; sectary, sectarian, opinionist; nonconformist; apostate
ADJS 2 **dissenting,** dissentient, recusant; **disagreeing, differing; opposing**, in opposition; at variance with, at odds with; nonconforming

dissipate VERBS 1 **squander, lavish,** slather, blow <nonformal>; scatter to the winds; **run through,** go through; **throw away,** throw one's money away, throw money around, **spend money like water,** spend as if money grew on trees, spend money as if it were going out of style, throw money around; burn the candle at both ends; **be promiscuous,** sleep around *and* swing <both nonformal>; **debauch, wanton,** rake, chase women, womanize, whore, sow one's wild oats
2 **dispel,** dissolve, attenuate, dilute, thin, thin out, water, water down, weaken; **evaporate,** volatilize; drive away, clear away, cast forth, blow off

dissolve VERBS **disintegrate, decompose, decay,** come apart, disorganize, **break up**, go to rack and ruin, crack up, disjoin, unknit, split, fission, atomize, **come** *or* **fall to pieces; liquefy,** liquidize, **melt,** colliquate; deliquesce; solve

distance NOUNS **remoteness,** farness, faroffness, longinquity; **separation,** separatedness, divergence, clearance, margin, leeway; **extent, length,** space, **reach,** stretch, range, compass, span, stride, haul, a way, ways *and* piece <both nonformal>; **aloofness, standoffishness,** offishness, withdrawnness, **remoteness,** detachment; **coolness,** coldness, cold shoulder; inaccessibility, unapproachability

distant ADJS **aloof, standoffish,** offish, standoff, **remote,** withdrawn, removed, detached, Olympian; **cool,** cold, frigid, chilly, icy, frosty; inaccessible, unapproachable; tight-assed <nonformal>; remote, out-of-the-way

distasteful ADJS **unsavory, unpalatable, unappetizing,** untasteful, untasty, ill-flavored, foul-tasting, unlikable, uninviting, displeasing, disagreeable; **uncongenial,** unpleasant; **not to one's taste,** not one's cup of tea

distill VERBS **brew;** bootleg, moonshine <nonformal>, **simplify,** streamline, purify, refine; strip, strip down

distinct ADJS **plain, clear, obvious, evident, patent,** unmistakable, not to be mistaken, much in evidence, plain to be seen, for all to see, plain as the nose on one's face, plain as day, plain as plain can be, big as life and twice as ugly; **definite, defined, well-defined,** well-marked, well-resolved, in focus; **clear-cut,** clean-cut; crystal-clear, clear as crystal; **audible,** hearable; **express, explicit, unmistakable**

distinction NOUNS **notability, noteworthiness,** remarkableness, salience, memorability; **prominence, eminence, greatness;** prestige, esteem, repute, reputation, honor, glory, renown, dignity, **fame**; celebrity

distinguish VERBS **discriminate,** draw *or* make distinctions, secern, **separate,** separate out, divide, analyze, subdivide, **segregate,** sever, severalize, **differentiate,** demark, demarcate, **set apart,** sift, sift out, sieve, sieve out, winnow, screen, sort; separate the sheep from the goats, separate the men from the boys; **split hairs,** draw *or* make a fine *or* overfine *or* nice *or* subtle distinction

distinguished ADJS distingué; **noted, notable,** marked, of note, of mark; **famous,** famed, honored, **renowned, celebrated, popular,** acclaimed, much acclaimed, sought-after, hot *and* world-class <both nonformal>, on everyone's tongue *or* lips; fabled, legendary

distort VERBS **contort,** turn awry; **twist,** turn, screw, wring, wrench, wrest; writhe; **warp,** buckle, crumple; knot, gnarl; **crook,** bend, spring; **misinterpret, misunderstand,** misconceive, **mistake, misapprehend; get backwards,** have the wrong way round, put the cart before the horse; quote out of context; misquote, miscite, give a false coloring, give a false impression *or* idea; **garble, pervert,** twist the words *or* meaning

distress NOUNS 1 **chagrin; embarrassment, abashment, discomfiture,** egg on one's face <nonformal>, disconcertment, discomposure, **humiliation,** mortification
2 **pain, grief,** stress, stress of life, suffering, passion, dolor; ache, aching; pang, wrench, throes, cramp, spasm; wound, injury, hurt; **sore,** sore spot, tender spot; **curse, woe,** grievance, **sorrow**
VERBS 3 afflict, trouble, burden, give one a tough row to hoe, load with care, **bother, disturb, perturb, disquiet, discomfort, agitate, upset,** put to it; **worry,** give one gray hair; dismay, grieve, mourn, lament, sorrow; pain, discomfort, give one a hard time *or* a pain *or* a pain in the neck *or* ass *or* butt <nonformal>

distribute VERBS **bestow, confer, award, allot, render,** bestow on; **tender,** proffer, offer, extend, come up with <nonformal>; **issue, dispense,** administer; serve, help to; broadcast, sow, disseminate, propagate, pass around *or* out, publish

district NOUNS **location, area, region**; **locality, locale,** locus; quarter, section, department, division; **neighborhood,** vicinity, vicinage, neck of the woods <nonformal>, purlieus; precincts, environs, milieu

distrust NOUNS 1 **suspiciousness,** suspicion, doubt, misdoubt, mistrust, distrustfulness, **wariness, chariness, cageyness** *and* **leeriness** <both nonformal>; **suspicion,** suspiciousness; **distrust,** distrustfulness, mistrust, mistrustfulness
VERBS 2 **doubt, be doubtful, be dubious, be skeptical,** doubt the truth of, beg leave to doubt, **have one's doubts,** have *or* harbor *or* entertain doubts *or* suspicions, half believe, have reservations, **take with a grain of salt,** be

from Missouri <nonformal>, mistrust, misgive, cross one's fingers

disturb VERBS **trouble,** beset; **bother,** pother, get one down, <nonformal>, **perturb,** irk, plague, **torment,** drive one up the wall <nonformal>, give one gray hair, make one lose sleep; **harass, vex, distress**; inconvenience, **put out,** discommode

disturbed ADJS **neurotic, psychoneurotic,** disordered; neurasthenic, psychasthenic; stressed; **bothered, troubled, ruffled, roiled,** riled; **irked, vexed, piqued, nettled, provoked, peeved** *and* miffed <both nonformal>, **griped, aggravated, exasperated;** burned-up *and* browned-off <both nonformal>; **agitated, perturbed, disquieted, upset,** antsy <nonformal>, unsettled, **discomposed, shaken**

ditch NOUNS 1 **trench, trough, channel, ditch,** dike <old>, fosse, **canal,** cut, gutter, kennel <Brit>; moat
VERBS 2 **discard, get rid of,** get quit of, get shut *or* shet of <nonformal>, rid oneself of, shrug off, **dispose of,** slough, **dump, jettison, throw** *or* **heave** *or* **toss overboard,** deep-six <nonformal>, throw out the window, throw to the dogs, cast to the winds

ditto NOUNS **duplicate, duplication, double,** cookie-cutter copy, clone; **reproduction, replica,** facsimile, model, **counterpart;** a chip off the old block

dive NOUNS 1 **tumble, fall,** *culbute* <Fr>, cropper *and* **spill** <both nonformal>, **flop** <nonformal>; **header** <nonformal>; **sprawl; pratfall** <nonformal>; **stumble,** trip; **plunge**
2 **den, lair,** den of thieves; hole *and* dump *and* **joint** <all nonformal>; gyp *or* clip joint <nonformal>
VERBS 3 **plunge, pitch, plummet, drop, fall;** skydive; bungee jump; freefall; plump, plunk, plop; nose-dive, make *or* take a nose dive; take a header <nonformal>

diversify VERBS **vary,** variegate, chop and change; **differentiate,** divaricate, ramify; **differ**; dissent; **disunify,** break up, break down, fragment, partition, **analyze;** change form, change shape, shift shape, ring changes, cover the spectrum

diversity NOUNS **difference,** otherness, separateness, discreteness, distinctness, **distinction;** unlikeness, **dissimilarity**; **variation,** variance, variegation, variety, **mixture**, **heterogeneity**

divert VERBS **amuse, entertain,** regale, beguile, solace, recreate, refresh, enliven, exhilarate, put in good humor; **delight, tickle, titillate,** tickle pink *or* to death <nonformal>, tickle the fancy; **distract,** detract, distract the attention, divert *or* detract attention, divert the mind *or* thoughts, draw off the attention, take the mind off of, relieve the mind of

divide VERBS 1 **partition,** set apart, separate; **wall off,** fence off, screen off, curtain off; tear open, rent, tear, rip, rip open, part, dispart, separate, divaricate; **break with, split,** separate, **diverge, part company,** come to *or* reach a parting of the ways; **alienate, estrange, disunite,** disaffect, **come between; set against,** pit against
2 **apportion, portion, parcel,** share; share with, cut *or* deal one in <nonformal>, share and share alike, divide with, go halvers *or* fifty-fifty *or* even stephen with <nonformal>

dividend NOUNS **return, yield,** return on investment, payout, payback

divine VERBS 1 **augur,** hint; **prefigure,** betoken, token, typify, **signify, mean,** spell, **indicate,** point to, look like, **be a sign of,** show signs of
ADJS 2 **blissful,** beatific, saintly; sublime; **heavenly,** paradisal, paradisiac, paradisiacal, paradisic, paradisical, empyreal *or* empyrean, Elysian; **sacred, holy,** numinous, **sacrosanct, religious, spiritual; venerable, ineffable, marvelous, wonderful,** glorious, terrific, sensational
3 **gorgeous, ravishing; glorious,** heavenly; **resplendent,** splendorous *or* splendrous, splendiferous, **splendid,** resplendently beautiful

division NOUNS **separation,** decentralization; **disunity, disunion, disruption,** separation, cleavage, divergence, dividedness; **apportionment, apportioning, portioning,** partitioning, parceling, budgeting, rationing; **denomination, persuasion,** faction, branch, variety, version, segment; **segregation, separationism, differentiation,** differencing, **discrimination,** distinguishing

divorce NOUNS 1 divorcement, grasswidowhood, civil divorce, **separation,** legal *or* judicial separation, separate maintenance; interlocutory decree

VERBS 2 **separate,** part, split up *and* split the sheets <both nonformal>, unmarry, put away, untie the knot, sue for divorce

dizzy ADJS **tiddly, giddy,** muddled, addled, flustered, bemused, reeling, seeing double, muzzy, foggy, vertiginous

dock NOUNS 1 dockage, marina, basin; dry dock; shipyard, dockyard; **wharf, pier,** quay
VERBS 2 **land,** moor, tie up, anchor, drop anchor; go ashore, **disembark,** debark, unboat

doctor NOUNS 1 **physician,** Doctor of Medicine *or* **MD, medical practitioner, medical man, medico** <nonformal>, leech <old>, croaker *and* sawbones <both nonformal>
VERBS 2 **treat,** minister to, care for, give care to, physic; **cure, remedy, heal; undergo treatment,** take medicine
3 **falsify, belie, misrepresent,** miscolor; distort, strain, warp, **slant, twist,** impart spin <nonformal>; put a false appearance upon, give a false coloring, **color, tamper with**

doctrine NOUNS **dogma**; **creed,** credo; credenda, tenet, precept, **principle, principle** *or* **article of faith,** canon, teaching

document NOUNS 1 official document, legal document, legal paper, legal instrument, **instrument,** writ, **paper,** parchment, scroll, roll, **writing**
VERBS 2 **itemize, specify,** circumstantiate, particularize, **spell out, detail,** go *or* enter into detail, give full particulars; **cite,** instance, adduce, give *or* quote chapter and verse; **substantiate**

documentation NOUNS **evidence, proof; reason to believe,** grounds for belief; **ground, grounds,** material grounds, **facts, data,** premises, basis for belief; piece *or* item of evidence, **fact,** datum, relevant fact; body of evidence; chain of evidence

dodge NOUNS 1 **trick, artifice, device,** ploy, gambit, stratagem, **scheme,** design, *ficelle* <Fr>, **subterfuge,** blind, **ruse, wile,** chouse <nonformal>, shift, artful dodge, sleight, pass, feint, fetch, chicanery
VERBS 2 **duck;** take evasive action, zigzag; **sidestep,** parry, fence, ward off; **hedge,** pussyfoot <nonformal>, be *or* sit on the fence, beat around *or* about the bush, hem and haw, beg the question, tapdance <nonformal>, dance around, equivocate

dog NOUNS 1 **canine, pooch** *and* bowwow <both nonformal>; **pup, puppy,** puppy-dog *and* perp <both nonformal>, **whelp;** bitch, toy dog, lap dog; working dog
VERBS 2 **pursue,** prosecute <old>, **follow,** follow up, bay after, run after, **chase, give chase,** chivy; hound

dogged ADJS **unfaltering, unwavering,** unflinching; relentless, **unrelenting; obstinate, stubborn**; **unrelaxing,** unfailing, **untiring,** unwearying, unflagging, never-tiring, **tireless,** weariless, **indefatigable; tenacious, persevering**

dogmatic ADJS didactic, **positive,** peremptory, pontifical, oracular; **opinionated,** opinionative, conceited; doctrinaire

dole NOUNS 1 **welfare,** public welfare, public assistance, relief, relief *or* welfare payments, welfare aid, aid to dependent children; **pittance**
VERBS 2 **parcel out, portion out,** measure out, serve out, spoon *or* ladle *or* dish out, **deal out, dole out, hand out, mete out,** ration out, give out, hand around, pass around; mete, deal; disburse, pay out

doll NOUNS

<nonformal> cutie, angel, angelface, babyface, beaut, honey, dream, looker, good-looker, stunner, dazzler, dreamboat, knockout, raving beauty, centerfold, pinup, pussycat <all nonformal>

domain NOUNS **sphere, realm,** demesne, dominion, jurisdiction, bailiwick; **province,** precinct, **field,** pale, arena, turf <nonformal>, area, discipline, subdiscipline, orb, orbit, walk; **specialty**

dome NOUNS **mountain,** mount, alp, hump, tor, height, dizzying height, nunatak, cupola, geodesic dome; stadium, sports dome, **arena**

domestic NOUNS 1 **servant,** servitor, help; domestic help, domestic servant, house servant; live-in help, day help
ADJS 2 **residential,** residentiary; domiciliary, domal; **household;** stay-at-home, homebound

domesticate VERBS **set up housekeeping,** keep house; domesticize; tame, break, bust *and* gentle <both nonfor-

mal>, break in, break to harness; housebreak

dominant ADJS **chief, main, principal,** paramount, **foremost,** headmost, **leading,** crowning, capital, **cardinal;** ascendant, in the ascendant, in ascendancy, sitting on top of the world *and* sitting pretty <both nonformal>; predominant, preponderant, **paramount, supreme,** number one <nonformal>, hegemonic, hegemonistic

dominate VERBS **predominate,** preponderate, prevail; **have the ascendancy, have the upper** *or* **whip hand,** get under control, dictate, lay down the law; **rule the roost** *and* wear the pants *and* crack the whip *and* ride herd <all nonformal>; take the lead

domineering ADJS **arrogant, overbearing, superior, proud, haughty; lofty, condescending, patronizing,** *de haut en bas* <Fr>, **bossy** <nonformal>, **highhanded**

donate VERBS **give, present, distribute;** deal, dole, mete; **give out, dole out, hand** *or* dish out <nonformal>; make a present of, gift *or* gift with <nonformal>, give as a gift; **give generously,** give the shirt off one's back

done ADJS **completed, finished, concluded, terminated, ended,** finished up; signed, sealed, and delivered; **through,** done with; all over with, all said and done, all over but the shouting; **produced, made, caused, brought about;** effectuated, executed, performed; grown, raised

Don Juan NOUNS **tempter, seducer, enticer,** inveigler, **charmer,** enchanter, fascinator, tantalizer, teaser; **philanderer,** woman chaser, **ladies' man,** heartbreaker; lady-killer, wolf, skirt chaser; libertine, lecher, cocksman <nonformal>, Casanova

donkey NOUNS **ass, burro,** Rocky Mountain canary <W US>; **jackass,** jack; jenny, jenny ass, jennet; **mule,** sumpter mule, sumpter; hinny

donor NOUNS **giver,** donator, presenter, bestower, conferrer, grantor, awarder, imparter, vouchsafer; fairy godmother, Lady Bountiful, Santa Claus, sugar daddy <nonformal>; **contributor, subscriber,** supporter, backer, financer, funder, angel <nonformal>; subsidizer; patron, patroness

doodle VERBS **scribble,** scrabble, **scratch, scrawl,** make hen tracks *or* hen *or* chicken scratches <nonformal>

doom NOUNS 1 **end,** death, death knell, bane, deathblow, death warrant, *coup de grâce* <Fr>, final blow, quietus, cutoff; **destiny, fate,** karma, kismet, what bodes *or* looms, what is fated *or* destined *or* doomed, what is written, what is in the books
VERBS 2 **damn,** send *or* consign to hell, cast into hell, doom to perdition, condemn to hell *or* eternal punishment; **pass judgment, sentence,** pass sentence, hand down a sentence, condemn

door NOUNS **entrance,** entry, gate, portal, **entranceway,** entryway; **inlet,** ingress, intake, adit, approach, **access,** means of access, in <nonformal>, way in; **outlet,** egress, **exit,** outgo, outcome, out <nonformal>, way out

doormat NOUNS **weakling,** pushover <nonformal>, **wimp,** poor *or* weak *or* dull tool <nonformal>; **nonentity,** hollow man, empty suit *and* nebbish *and* sad sack <all nonformal>

dope NOUNS 1 **drug, narcotic,** dangerous drug, controlled substance, abused substance, illegal drug, addictive drug, **hard drug**
2 **stupid person, dolt, dunce,** clod, **dullard,** *niais* <Fr>, donkey, yahoo, thickwit, **nitwit,** dimwit, lackwit, halfwit, lamebrain, putz
VERBS 3 **deaden, numb,** benumb, blunt, dull, obtund, **desensitize; anesthetize, put to sleep,** slip one a Mickey *or* Mickey Finn <nonformal>; narcotize, drug, **medicate,** drug, sedate, dope *or* dope up <nonformal>

dormant ADJS **inert, inactive, static,** passive, sedentary; **latent,** unaroused, suspended, abeyant, in suspense *or* abeyance; sleeping, slumbering, smoldering; **inert,** immobile, vegetative, **inactive, idle**; quiescent; hibernating, sleeping

dose NOUNS 1 **draft, potion,** portion, **shot,** injection; broken dose; booster, booster dose, recall dose, booster shot
2 **venereal disease** *or* VD, gonorrhea *or* clap *or* the clap *or* claps <nonformal>; dose <nonformal>
VERBS 3 **medicate,** drug, dope <nonformal>; **administer,** dose with, dish out <nonformal>, mete out, prescribe

dot NOUNS 1 **fleck, speckle; spot,** polka dot, macula, macule; little *or* wee *or* tiny

bit <nonformal>, bite, **particle,** fragment, spot, **speck,** flyspeck, point, jot, tittle, **iota,** ounce, **dab** <nonformal>, mote, **mite** <nonformal>
VERBS 2 **mottle, dapple,** stipple, **fleck,** flake, **speck, speckle,** bespeckle, freckle, **spot,** bespot, sprinkle, spangle, bespangle, pepper, stud, maculate

dotty ADJS **eccentric, queer,** queer in the head, **odd, peculiar,** strange, fey, **crotchety,** quirky, whimsical, twisted; solitary, reclusive, antisocial

double NOUNS 1 **perfect** *or* **exact likeness, duplicate;** match, **twin;** living image, very image, very picture, living picture, dead ringer <nonformal>, spitting image *or* spit and image <nonformal>; cookie-cutter copy, clone
2 etheric double *or* self, co-walker, *Doppelgänger* <Ger>, doubleganger, fetch, wraith
VERBS 3 **turn back,** double back, retrace one's steps; **return,** go *or* come back
4 **intensify, reinforce,** redouble, add fuel to the flame *or* the fire; **fold,** fold on itself, fold up; fold over, double over, lap over, turn over *or* under

double-cross VERBS **betray, double-cross** *and* two-time <both nonformal>, sell out *and* sell down the river <both nonformal>, turn in; let down *and* let down one's side <both nonformal>; inform on

double-dealing NOUNS 1 **treachery,** treacherousness; **perfidy,** perfidiousness, falseheartedness, two-facedness, doubleness; **duplicity, dirty work** *and* dirty pool *and* dirty trick <all nonformal>
ADJS 2 **manipulated, cooked** *and* **doctored** <both nonformal>, juggled, **rigged,** engineered; packed; **shifty,** slippery, tricky; **two-faced**

double-edged ADJS **sharp, keen, edged, acute,** fine, **cutting,** knifelike; razor-edged, knife-edged, sharp as broken glass; two-edged

double-talk NOUNS 1 **gibberish,** jargon, mumbo jumbo, amphigory, gobbledegook <nonformal>; claptrap, moonshine, empty words, double-speak
VERBS 2 **equivocate,** mystify, obscure, prevaricate, tergiversate, double-speak, tap-dance <nonformal>, palter, fence, parry, shift, **shuffle, dodge,** shy, **evade,** sidestep, hedge, skate around, pussyfoot <nonformal>, evade the issue

doubt NOUNS 1 **doubtfulness, dubiousness,** dubiety, dubitancy; half-belief; **reservation, question,** question in one's mind; **skepticism,** Pyrrhonism; **suspicion,** suspiciousness, wariness, leeriness, **distrust, mistrust, misdoubt,** distrustfulness, mistrustfulness, disbelief
VERBS 2 **be doubtful, be dubious, be skeptical,** doubt the truth of, beg leave to doubt, **have one's doubts,** have *or* harbor *or* entertain doubts *or* suspicions, half believe, have reservations, **take with a grain of salt,** be from Missouri <nonformal>, **distrust, mistrust,** misgive, cross one's fingers; **question,** query, **challenge, contest, dispute,** cast doubt on, greet with skepticism, keep one's eye on, treat with reserve, bring *or* call into question, raise a question, throw doubt upon, awake a doubt *or* suspicion

doubtful ADJS iffy <nonformal>; **in doubt,** *in dubio* <L>; dubitable, doubtable, **dubious, questionable, problematic, problematical, speculative,** conjectural, suppositional; **unsure, uncertain,** unpredictable

doubtless ADVS unquestionably, without question, undoubtedly, beyond the shadow of a doubt, beyond a reasonable doubt, indubitably, admittedly, undeniably, unarguably, indisputably, doubtlessly, without doubt

doughnut NOUNS friedcake, sinker <nonformal>, cymbal <old>, olykoek <nonformal>; French doughnut, raised doughnut; glazed doughnut; fastnacht; **cruller,** twister; jelly doughnut

dour ADJS **sullen, sulky, surly, morose,** mumpish, dumpish, **glum,** grum, grim; **moody,** moodish; **mopish,** mopey <nonformal>, moping; **glowering,** lowering, **scowling, frowning;** dark, black; black-browed, beetle-browed; dejected, melancholy; **severe,** austere, harsh, hard, stern, unsparing, hard-shell, obdurate, **inflexible,** ironhanded, inexorable, **unyielding,** unbending, **relentless,** unrelenting, procrustean

douse VERBS **submerge, dip, duck, dunk** <nonformal>, souse, plunge in water; extinguish, put out, quench, out, **snuff,** snuff out, blow out, stamp out

dove NOUNS **pigeon,** squab; **pacifist,** pacificist, peacenik <nonformal>, **peace lover; innocent**, angel

dovetail VERBS **harmonize, concur**, have no problem with, go along with <nonformal>, **correspond, conform,** coincide, parallel, intersect, overlap, **match,** tally, hit, register, lock, interlock, square, jibe <nonformal>; **be consistent,** cohere, stand *or* hold *or* hang together, fall in together, fit together

dowager NOUNS **woman, matron, widow,** relict; **patrician,** grand dame, lady, person of breeding

dowdy ADJS **shabby, shoddy, seedy,** scruffy, **tacky** <nonformal>, tatty, ratty; **out at the elbows,** out at the heels, **down-at-heel**

down NOUNS 1 **fluff,** flue, floss, **fuzz, fur,** pile; eiderdown, eider; swansdown; thistledown
2 **plain, moor,** moorland, **downs, heath**
3 **fell, drop, bring down,** fetch down, take down a peg, lay low
ADJS 4 **fallen,** floored, **undone, done for** <nonformal>, **ruined,** kaput *and* on the skids <both nonformal>, *hors de combat* <Fr>

down-and-out ADJS **destitute,** in the gutter; **penniless,** moneyless, fortuneless, out of funds, **without a sou,** without one dollar to rub against another; homeless

downbeat ADJS **pessimistic,** pessimist, **cynical,** nihilistic; uncheerful; negative, negativistic; defeatist

downcast ADJS **dejected, depressed, downhearted, down, cast down,** bowed down, subdued; **discouraged, disheartened, dispirited,** dashed; **in low spirits; down in the mouth** <nonformal>, **in the doldrums, down in the dumps** *and* **in the dumps** <both nonformal>, in the depths

downfall NOUNS **collapse, crash,** comedown, breakdown, derailment, **fall,** pratfall <nonformal>, stumble, tumble; nose dive *and* tailspin <both nonformal>; **undoing, ruin,** debacle

downgrade VERBS **demote, degrade,** disgrade, debase, abase, humble, humiliate, **lower, reduce,** strip of rank, deplume, displume

downhearted ADJS **dejected, depressed, down,** bowed down, subdued; **discouraged, disheartened, dispirited,** dashed; down in the mouth <nonformal>, **in the doldrums, down in the dumps** *and* **in the dumps** *and* in the doleful dumps <all nonformal>, in the depths

downhill ADJS 1 descending, falling, dropping, dipping; **declining,** declined; declivous, declivitous, declivate
ADVS 2 **down, downward, downwards,** from the top down, *de haut en bas* <Fr>; downgrade

downplay VERBS **minimize,** minify, **belittle,** detract from; play down, underplay, deemphasize, tone *or* tune down; **attach little importance to,** give little weight to; make little of, make light of, think little of, throw away, **make** *or* **think nothing of,** take no account of, set little by, set no store by, set at naught

downpour NOUNS **rainstorm, cloudburst,** rainburst, burst of rain, torrent of rain, torrential rain *or* downpour; waterspout, spout, rainspout, downfall, pour, pouring *or* pelting *or* teeming *or* drowning rain, **deluge,** heavy rain, driving *or* gushing rain, drenching *or* soaking rain, lovely weather for ducks

smoky rain
CHAUCER

downstairs ADVS **down, downward, downwards,** from the top down, *de haut en bas* <Fr>

downtime NOUNS **delay,** stoppage, **wait, halt, stay, stop,** break, pause, interim, respite

down-to-earth ADJS **unidealistic,** unideal, **unromantic, unsentimental, practical-minded,** sober-minded, sobersided, **hardheaded,** straight-thinking, **with both feet on the ground;** sensible, sane, reasonable, rational, sound, sound-thinking

downtrodden ADJS **oppressed;** kept down *or* under, ground down, overborne, trampled; henpecked, browbeaten, ordered *or* kicked around <nonformal>, regimented, tyrannized; treated like dirt under one's feet

downturn NOUNS **decline,** declension, **subsidence,** slump <nonformal>, lapse, **drop,** downtick <nonformal>; dwindling, wane, ebb; downtrend, retreat, remission; declination, comedown, downward trend, depreciation, **decrease**, **drop, fall, plunge,** free-fall, falling-off, lessening, slippage, slump

downward ADJS 1 descending, sinking, plunging, down-trending; descendant, on the descendant; declivitous; decurrent, deciduous; **downgoing,** downcom-

ing; down-reaching; plummeting, **sinking,** foundering, setting; declining, **subsiding**
ADVS 2 **downwards,** from the top down, *de haut en bas* <Fr>

dowry NOUNS **settlement,** *dot* <Fr>, portion, marriage portion; **dower,** widow's dower

doze VERBS **slumber,** rest in the arms of Morpheus; **drowse; nap, catnap,** take a nap, catch a wink

drab ADJS **lackluster, lusterless; dull, dead,** deadened, **lifeless,** somber, wan, **flat,** mat

draft NOUNS 1 **air current,** current of air, movement of air, stream, stream of air, flow of air
2 **conscription, drafting, induction,** impressment, press; draft call, call-up, summons, call to the colors, letter from Uncle Sam <nonformal>
VERBS 3 **draw off,** draw, draw from; **suck,** suck out *or* up, **siphon off;** tap, broach
4 **sketch,** trace; block in *or* out; rough in, rough out; **write, draw up, write out,** make out; **write down, record**
5 **conscript, induct,** press, impress, commandeer; call up, call to the colors; **recruit, muster,** levy, raise, muster in

drag NOUNS 1 **disadvantage, detriment,** impairment; **handicap**, disability; millstone around one's neck
VERBS 2 **pull, draw, heave, haul,** hale, lug, **tug, tow,** take in tow; draggle, snake <nonformal>; troll, trawl
3 **lag, lag behind, straggle,** lag back, trail, **trail behind,** hang back *or* behind, loiter, linger, **loiter** *or* **linger behind,** dawdle, get behind, let grass grow under one's feet, **linger on,** linger, tarry, go on, **go on and on, wear on,** crawl, creep, **drag on,** drag along

drain NOUNS 1 **depletion,** exhausting, **exhaustion,** sapping, depreciation, dissipation, impoverishment; **waste,** wastage, wasting away; using up, consumption, expenditure
VERBS 2 **draw off,** draft, draw, draw from; **suck,** suck out *or* up, **siphon off;** decant; exhaust, empty
3 **waste, deplete, depreciate,** dissipate, wear, wear away, erode, ablate, consume, **shrink,** dribble away; squander

dramatic ADJS emotive, melodramatic, theatrical, histrionic, overdramatic, hammy <nonformal>, nonrational, unreasoning; overemotional, hyperthymic

dramatize VERBS play up <nonformal>, splash, make a production of; overact

drape NOUNS 1 screen, shroud, shield, veil, pall, mantle, curtain, hanging, drapery
VERBS 2 **clothe,** enclothe, **dress, garb, attire,** tire, array, **apparel,** raiment, garment, habilitate, **tog** *and* tog out <both nonformal>, robe, enrobe, invest, endue, **deck,** bedeck, wrap, enwrap, lap, envelop, sheathe, shroud, enshroud

drastic ADJS **extreme,** outrageous, excessive, exorbitant, unconscionable, intemperate, immoderate, extravagant

draw NOUNS 1 **lure,** charm, **come-on** <nonformal>, attention-getter *or* -grabber, **attraction,** crowd-pleaser, headliner; hook *and* gimmick <both nonformal>, drawing card; **decoy,** decoy duck; **bait,** ground bait, baited trap, baited hook; **snare,** trap; **endearment**; the song of the Sirens, the voice of the tempter, honeyed words; forbidden fruit
2 **tie,** dead heat, wash <nonformal>
VERBS 3 **portray, picture,** render, **depict, represent, delineate,** limn, **paint**
4 **attract, pull,** drag, tug, pull *or* draw towards, have an attraction; **lure**

draw and quarter VERBS **dismember,** tear limb from limb; **mangle,** lacerate, mutilate, maim

drawback NOUNS **disadvantage, liability; detriment,** impairment, prejudice, loss, damage, hurt, harm, mischief, injury; **a step back** *or* **backward,** a loss of ground; **handicap**, disability; drag, millstone around one's neck; objection; **stumbling block,** fly in the ointment, one small difficulty, **hitch, catch,** joker <nonformal>

drawing NOUNS 1 **representation, delineation,** presentment, **portrayal, portraiture, depiction,** depictment, rendering, rendition, characterization, limning, imaging
2 **lottery,** sweepstakes *or* sweepstake *or* sweep; draft lottery; **raffle;** grab bag *or* barrel *or* box
3 **pulling,** tractional, tractive, hauling, tugging, towing, towage

drawing card NOUNS **lure,** charm, **come-on** <nonformal>, attention-getter *or* -grabber, **attraction, draw** *or* drawer *or* crowd-drawer, crowd-pleaser, headliner;

hook *and* gimmick <both nonformal>

drawl NOUNS **accent,** regional accent, brogue, twang, burr, broad accent

drawn ADJS **tired-looking, weary-looking, tired-eyed, tired-faced, haggard, hollow-eyed, ravaged, cadaverous, worn, wan, zombiish**

dread NOUNS 1 **anxiety, apprehension,** foreboding, tension, stress; **fear; agitation, disquiet,** disquietude, inquietude, unquietness; **nervousness; consternation, dismay;** unholy dread, **terror, horror,** horrification, mortal *or* abject fear; **phobia**

VERBS 2 stand in dread *or* awe of, be in mortal dread *or* terror of, stand in awe of, stand aghast; be on pins and needles, break out in a cold sweat, sweat bullets <nonformal>

ADJS 3 **terrible, horrid, horrible, horrifying,** horrific, horrendous; **dreadful,** dreaded; **awful;** awesome, grim, grisly, gruesome, ghoulish, macabre

dreadful ADJS **horrid, horrible,** horrific, **horrifying,** horrendous, unspeakable, beyond words; **atrocious, terrible, rotten,** awful *and* beastly <both nonformal>, **hideous; tragic;** dire, grim, baneful; appalling, shocking, disgusting

dream NOUNS 1 **reverie, daydream, pipe dream** <nonformal>; **brown study**; **vision; nightmare,** incubus, bad dream

VERBS 2 **muse, moon** <nonformal>, **daydream,** pipe-dream <nonformal>, fantasy; be lost in thought, let one's attention wander, let one's mind run on other things, dream of *or* muse on other things; **wander, stray, ramble,** divagate, let one's thoughts *or* mind wander, give oneself up to reverie, **woolgather,** be absent, be somewhere else, stargaze

dreamland NOUNS **sleep, slumber;** the arms of Morpheus; **land of Nod,** dreamworld, dreamscape; lotus land, land of dreams, land of enchantment, land of heart's desire, wonderland, cloudland, fairyland, slumberland; light sleep, fitful sleep, **doze, drowse,** snoozle <nonformal>

dreamy ADJS **dreamful; dreamy-eyed,** dreamy-minded, dreamy-souled; dreamlike; day-dreamy, **dreaming, daydreaming,** pipe-dreaming <nonformal>, castle-building

dreary ADJS **dull, dingy,** dismal, **somber, sober, sad; desolate,** cheerless, joyless, dismal, bleak, **gloomy, murky, grim, somber,** sombrous, **solemn, grave;** drear, drearisome; weary, weariful, wearisome; blah <nonformal>, dryasdust, dusty, **dull**

dregs NOUNS 1 **grounds, lees,** dross, slag, draff, scoria, feces; **residue,** leavings, waste, waste product, industrial waste, solid waste, lees, ash; **sediment, settlings, deposits,** deposition

2 **riffraff, trash,** raff, chaff, **rubbish,** sordes, offscourings, off-scum, **scum, scum of the earth, dregs** *or* **scum of society**

drench VERBS **soak,** imbrue, **souse, sop,** sodden; **saturate,** permeate; water-soak, waterlog; **steep,** seethe, macerate, infuse, imbue, brew, impregnate, inject; infiltrate, percolate, leach, lixiviate

dress NOUNS 1 **clothing, clothes, apparel, wear, wearing apparel, daywear,** dressing, **raiment,** garmenture, **garb, attire, array,** habit, habiliment, fashion, style, guise, **costume,** costumery, gear, toilette, trim

VERBS 2 **clothe,** enclothe, **garb, attire,** tire, array, **apparel,** raiment, garment, habilitate, robe, enrobe, invest, endue, **deck,** bedeck, **groom, brush up, ornament, decorate, adorn, trim, garnish,** array

3 **prepare, make** *or* **get ready,** prep <nonformal>, trim <old>, **ready, fix** <nonformal>; treat, pretreat, process

dress up VERBS **get up, doll** *or* **spruce up** <nonformal>, **primp** *and* prink *and* prank <all nonformal>, gussy up <nonformal>, spiff *or* fancy *or* slick up <nonformal>, pretty up <nonformal>, deck out *or* up, trick out *or* up, tog out *or* up <nonformal>

drift VERBS **stray,** go astray, lose one's way, err; take a wrong turn *or* turning; go adrift; **wander,** wander off, ramble, rove, straggle, divagate, excurse; meander, wind, twist, snake, twist and turn; **take it easy,** take things as they come, drift with the current, go with the flow, lie *or* rest on one's oars

drill NOUNS 1 **exercise,** motion, movement, maneuver; **program,** practice, routine, workout

VERBS 2 **dig,** excavate, tunnel, mine; pierce to the depths; **bore,** auger; **ream,** ream out, countersink, gouge, gouge out; trepan, trephine; punch full of holes, make look like Swiss cheese *or* a sieve, **riddle, honeycomb**

3 **study,** apply oneself to, hit the books <nonformal>; **review; dig** *and* **grind** *and* **bone** *and* bone up on <all nonformal>, **practice**

drink NOUNS 1**beverage,** thirst quencher; **soft drink,** nonalcoholic beverage; cold drink; alcoholic beverage, liquor
2 potation, potion, libation; draft, **swig** <nonformal>, swill *and* guzzle <both nonformal>, quaff, **sip,** tot, snort *and* slug <both nonformal>, pull <nonformal>, slurp <nonformal>; nip
VERBS 3 drink in, **imbibe,** wet one's whistle <nonformal>; **quaff, sip, sup,** bib, swig *and* swill *and* guzzle *and* pull <all nonformal>; toss off *or* down, tipple, **booze, tipple, down,** toss off *or* down, knock back, throw one back, **drink hard,** drink like a fish, drink seriously, **tope**

follow strong drink
Bible

drip NOUNS 1 **trickle,** tricklet, **dribble,** dripping, drop, spurtle; seeping, seepage
VERBS 2 **trickle, dribble,** dripple, drop, spurtle; seep, ooze, weep; **gurgle**

drive NOUNS 1 **vigor, force,** power, strength, vitality, sinew, sinewiness, nervousness, nervosity, vigorousness, forcefulness, pizzazz *and* punch *and* clout <all nonformal>; driving force *or* power; **motive power**
VERBS 2 **move, actuate,** motivate, push, shove, nudge, impel, propel; **hustle** <nonformal>, drive oneself, **push, scramble,** go all out <nonformal>, **make things hum,** step lively <nonformal>, make the sparks *or* chips fly <nonformal>; enforce, give an impetus, **set going** *or* agoing, put *or* set in motion, give momentum; motivate, incite; compel

drivel NOUNS **nonsense, stuff and nonsense,** pack of nonsense, **folderol, balderdash,** *niaiserie* <Fr>, flummery, trumpery, **rubbish,** trash, **humbug,** hocus-pocus; claptrap, fustian, rodomontade, bombast, absurdity

driver NOUNS **motorist,** automobilist; **chauffeur;** speeder, road hog <nonformal>, Sunday driver, joyrider <nonformal>; hit-and-run driver

driving ADJS **enterprising, aggressive, dynamic,** activist, proactive, forceful, pushing, pushy, up-and-coming, go-ahead *and* hustling <both nonformal>; ambitious; motivating, motivational, motive, moving, animating, actuating, **impelling,** impulsive; **urgent, pressing;** imperative

droll ADJS facetious, funny, joshing <nonformal>, **whimsical,** salty, salt, Attic

drone NOUNS 1 **nonworker; sponger,** freeloader, lounge lizard <nonformal>, social parasite, parasite
VERBS 2 **hum,** thrum, bombilate, bombinate, **buzz,** whiz, whir, burr, purr; **mumble, mutter,** maunder; drone on; swallow one's words, jabber, gibber, gabble

drool NOUNS 1 **saliva, spittle, sputum, spit, expectoration;** salivation, ptyalism, sialorrhea, sialagogue, **slobber,** slabber, slaver, **drivel,** dribble
VERBS 2 **salivate,** ptyalize; **slobber,** slabber, slaver, **drivel,** dribble, dither, blither, blather, maunder, dote, burble

droop VERBS **languish, pine, flag, wilt; decline,** lower, **subside,** give way, lapse, cave, cave in; slouch, **sag, slump,** slump down

drop NOUNS 1 **descent, descending, dropping, falling,** plummeting, **fall, free-fall,** *chute* <Fr>, **downfall,** debacle, **collapse,** crash
2 **trickle,** tricklet, **dribble, drip,** dripping, seeping, seepage; droplet, **trace,** trace amount, snip, snippet
VERBS 3 **faint, swoon,** succumb, keel over <nonformal>, fall in a faint, fall senseless, **pass** *or* zonk out <nonformal>,
4 **descend, go** *or* **come down,** down, dip down, lose altitude, dump altitude <nonformal>; **fall, fall** *or* drop down; **collapse,** crash, plunge, **plummet; decline,** dip, fall off *or* away, **go downhill; decline, drop off,** fall off, fall away, fall to a low ebb, run low
5 **fell, bring down,** fetch down, down <nonformal>, take down, take down a peg, lay low; **knock down,** dash down, send headlong, **floor,** deck *and* lay out <both nonformal>, lay by the heels, ground, **bowl over** <nonformal>; strike dead, shoot

drop in VERBS **visit,** look in, drop by, pop in <nonformal>; **breeze in,** come breezing in; **barge in** *or* come barging in *and* wade in <all nonformal>; intrude; make *or* pay a visit, **call on** *or* **upon,** run *or* stop in, look in, drop around *or* round

drop in the bucket NOUNS **pittance,** dole, scrimption <nonformal>; drop in the ocean; **mite,** bit; short allowance, short commons, half rations, cheeseparings and candle ends; mere subsistence, starvation wages; widow's mite

drop out VERBS **withdraw, back out,** pull out, stand down <nonformal>; quit cold *and* leave flat <both nonformal>, opt out

drought NOUNS **dryness, aridness,** aridity, waterlessness

drown VERBS go to a watery grave, go to Davy Jones's locker <nonformal>; **immerse,** immerge, merge, **sink,** bury, engulf, **inundate,** deluge

drowsy ADJS **sleepy,** dozy, snoozy <nonformal>, **slumberous,** slumbery, dreamy; **half asleep,** asleep on one's feet; yawny, stretchy <nonformal>, oscitant, yawning, napping, **nodding,** ready for bed

drub VERBS **beat, smite,** thump, trounce, baste, **pummel,** pommel, **buffet, belabor,** lay on, **batter,** baste, lambaste; thrash

drudge NOUNS 1 **menial,** slavey <nonformal>; scullion
VERBS 2 **grind** *and* **dig** <both nonformal>, fag <Brit>, **grub, toil,** moil, toil and moil, travail, **slog,** peg away *or* along, plug away *or* along <nonformal>, hammer away, pound away, struggle along, struggle on, work away

drug NOUNS 1 **medicine, medicament, medication,** medicinal, theraputant, **physic,** preparation, mixture; prescription drug, nonprescription drug; **narcotic drug, controlled substance**
2 narcotic, dope <nonformal>, dangerous drug, controlled substance, abused substance, illegal drug, addictive drug, **hard drug;** soft drug, gateway drug; **opiate; sedative, depressant,** sedative hypnotic, **antipsychotic tranquilizer; hallucinogen,** psychedelic, psychedelic drug, psychoactive drug, psychoactive chemical *or* psychochemical, psychotropic drug, psychotomimetic drug, mind-altering drug, mind-expanding drug, mind-blowing drug; **stimulant; antidepressant; inhalant,** volatile inhalant
VERBS 3 **put to sleep; lull to sleep,** rock to sleep; narcotize, dope <nonformal>; anesthetize, put under; sedate; **medicate,** dope <nonformal>, dose

drug abuse NOUNS **substance abuse,** narcotics abuse, drug use, glue-sniffing, solvent abuse; **addiction, addictedness, habit,** drug habit, drug habituation, drug dependence

drugstore NOUNS **pharmacy,** chemist *and* chemist's shop <both Brit>, apothecary's shop, dispensary, dispensatory

drum VERBS **beat time,** keep time, tap, tap out the rhythm; count, count the beats; beat the drum, play drum *or* the drums, thrum, beat, thump, pound; tomtom; ruffle; beat *or* sound a tattoo

drunk NOUNS 1 **drunkard, inebriate, sot,** toper, guzzler, swiller, soaker, love-pot, tosspot, barfly, thirsty soul, **serious drinker,** devotee of Bacchus; swigger; hard drinker, heavy drinker, **alcoholic, dipsomaniac, problem drinker,** chronic alcoholic, chronic drunk, pathological drinker; wino <nonformal>

2 <nonformal> **lush,** lusher, **soak,** sponge, hooch hound, **boozer, boozehound,** booze fighter, booze freak, dipso, juicehead, loadie, ginhound, elbow bender *or* crooker, shikker, bottle sucker, swillbelly, swillpot, swillbowl; **souse, stew,** bum, rummy, rumhound, stewbum; wino

ADJS 3 **intoxicated, inebriated,** inebriate, inebrious, **drunken,** *shikker* <Yiddish>, **tipsy**

4 <nonformal> **in one's cups, under the influence,** the worse for liquor; **tiddly, giddy, dizzy,** muddled, addled, flustered, bemused, reeling, seeing double; **besotted,** sotted, sodden, drenched, fargone; drunk as a lord; staggering drunk; **fuddled,** muzzy, **boozy,** overtaken; **swacked, plastered,** shnockered, stewed, **pickled,** pissed, **soused,** soaked, boiled, fried, canned, tanked, potted, corned, bombed, ripped, smashed; bent, **crocked,** crocko, shellacked, sloshed, sozzled, zonked, tight, lushy, squiffy, afflicted, jug-bitten, oiled, lubricated, feeling no pain, polluted, raddled, organized, **high,** elevated, high as a kite, lit, **lit up,** lit to the gills, illuminated, **loaded, stinko,** tanked, tanked-up, stinking drunk, pie-eyed, pissy-eyed, shitfaced, cockeyed, cockeyed drunk, roaring or rip-roaring

drunk, skunk-drunk; half-seas over, three sheets to the wind, **blotto, stiff** blind, paralyzed, **stoned**

dry VERBS 1 **desiccate,** exsiccate, dry up, **dehydrate,** anhydrate; evaporate; dehumidify; torrefy, burn, fire, kiln, **bake, parch,** scorch, sear
ADJS 2 unsweet, unsweetened, sec; **thirsty,** thirsting, athirst; parched, droughty <nonformal>
3 blah <nonformal>, **dreary,** drearisome, dryasdust, dusty, **dull; satiric, satirical; sarcastic, ironic, ironical, sardonic, cynical,** Rabelaisian; caustic
4 **unproductive, barren,** dried-up, sere, exhausted, drained, leached, sucked dry, wasted, gaunt, **waste, desolate,** jejune; arid; **bone-dry,** dry as dust, dry as a bone

drying NOUNS 1 **desiccation,** drying up; **dehydration,** anhydration
ADJS 2 **dehydrating, desiccative,** desiccant, exsiccative, exsiccant, siccative, siccant; evaporative

dry run NOUNS **tryout,** workout, **rehearsal,** practice; pilot plan *or* program; dummy run; **trial run,** practical test; shakedown, shakedown cruise, bench test; flight test, test flight *or* run; audition, hearing

dry up VERBS **shrivel, wither,** sear, parch; **wizen,** weazen; consume, waste, waste away, attenuate, thin, emaciate, macerate; **be consumed, be used up,** waste; **run out, give out,** peter out <nonformal>; run dry

dubious ADJS **doubting; skeptical, distrustful, mistrustful,** mistrusting, untrusting; **suspicious,** suspecting, wary, leery
2 **improbable, unlikely,** unpromising, logic-defying, scarcely to be expected *or* anticipated; statistically improbable; **doubtful, questionable,** dubitable, **implausible,** incredible

duck VERBS 1 **avoid, evade, dodge,** turn aside *or* to the side, draw aside, **turn away,** jib, shy, shy off; **steer clear of,** tapdance <nonformal>, get out of the way of; **shrink,** wince, cringe, flinch
2 **dip, duck, dunk** <nonformal>, douse, souse, plunge in water; baptize

dud NOUNS 1 thing of naught, nullity, zero; **nonentity, nobody** *and* nonstarter *and* nebbish <all nonformal>, nonperson, unperson, cipher, man of straw, jackstraw <old>, lay figure, puppet, dummy, hollow man
2 **flop,** flopperoo, **bust, fizzle,** lemon, clinker, non-starter, **loser, washout,** turkey, bomb, flat failure, dull thud, total loss <all nonformal>

dude NOUNS **dandy, fop,** coxcomb, macaroni, gallant, dude *and* swell *and* sport <all nonformal>, ponce *and* toff <both Brit nonformal>, blood, fine gentleman, clotheshorse, fashion plate

due NOUNS 1 one's due, what one merits *or* is entitled to, what one has earned, what is owing, what one has coming, what is coming to one, acknowledgment, cognizance, recognition, credit, crediting; **right**
ADJS 2 **owed, owing, payable,** receivable, redeemable, mature, **outstanding, unpaid,** in arrear *or* arrears, back
3 fit, suitable; **proper, correct, decorous,** good, nice, decent, seemly, **appropriate,** fitting, condign, **right and proper,** as it should be, as it ought to be, *comme il faut* <Fr>; kosher *and* according to Hoyle <both nonformal>
4 **attributable, assignable, ascribable, imputable,** traceable, referable, accountable, explicable

duel NOUNS 1 single combat, monomachy, satisfaction, **affair of honor,** *affaire d'honneur* <Fr>; **fight, match, bout,** battle, slugfest <nonformal>
VERBS 2 fight a duel, give satisfaction; feud; skirmish; fight the good fight

dues NOUNS **fee, toll, charge, charges, demand, exaction,** exactment, scot, shot, scot and lot; **deserts,** just deserts, deservings, merits, due reward *or* punishment, **comeuppance** <nonformal>, all that is coming to one

duet NOUNS **couple, pair, matching pair, twosome,** set of two, duo, brace, team, span, yoke, double harness; match, matchup, mates

duffer NOUNS 1 **incompetent,** incapable; mediocrity, hacker <nonformal>, no great shakes, no prize, no prize package, no brain surgeon, no rocket scientist
2 **golfer,** player, dub *or* hacker <nonformal>

dugout NOUNS **shelter, cover, covert,** coverture; concealment; *abri* <Fr>, cave, earth, foxhole; **bunker**

dull ADJS 1 flat, mat, dead, dingy, muddy, leaden, lusterless, lackluster; **faded,**

washed-out, dimmed, discolored, etiolated; **pale, dim,** weak, **faint**
2 **lethargic, phlegmatic,** hebetudinous, desensitized, sluggish, torpid, languid, slack, soporific, comatose, **stupefied,** in a stupor, **numb,** numbed, benumbed; blah <nonformal>, **dreary,** drearisome, dry as dust, dusty; humdrum, tiresome
3 dull of mind, **dopey** <nonformal>, **obtuse,** blunt, dim, wooden, heavy, sluggish, slow, **slow-witted,** hebetudinous, **dim-witted, dull-witted, thick-witted,** thick-headed

dumb ADJS 1 **mute, mum,** voiceless, tongueless, **speechless,** wordless, breathless, at a loss for words, choked up; inarticulate; **tongue-tied,** dumb-struck, dumbstricken, stricken dumb, **dumbfounded**
2 instinctual *or* instinctive, mindless, nonrational, animal
3 **foolish,** fool <nonformal>, foolheaded <nonformal>, **stupid,** clueless <Brit nonformal>, **asinine, silly,** fatuous, fatuitous, inept, **inane;** futile

dumbfound VERBS **astonish, boggle the mind; dumbfound** *or* dumbfounder, strike dumb, strike dead; knock one's socks off *and* bowl over <both nonformal>, **stun, stupefy**

dummy NOUNS 1 **figure, figurine; mannequin** *or* manikin, model, lay figure; **fake, rip-off** <nonformal>, **sham, mock, imitation,** simulacrum
ADJS 2 **substitute, alternate, alternative,** other, tother <nonformal>, equivalent, token, pinch, utility, backup, secondary; ad hoc, provisional

dump NOUNS 1 **hovel,** rathole, hole, sty, pigsty, pigpen, tumbledown shack
2 **trash pile,** rubbish heap, junkheap *and* junkpile <both nonformal>, scrap heap, dustheap, midden, kitchenmidden; wasteyard, **junkyard** <nonformal>, scrapyard, dumpsite, garbage dump, landfill, sanitary landfill, toxic waste dump
VERBS 3 **discard, reject, throw away, throw out,** chuck *or* chuck away *and* shit-can *and* eighty-six <all nonformal>, cast, cast off *or* away *or* aside; **get rid of, dispose of,** slough, **ditch** <nonformal>, **jettison, throw** *or* **heave** *or* **toss overboard,** deep-six <nonformal>, throw to the dogs, cast to the winds
4 **sell,** unload, flood the market with; sacrifice, sell at a sacrifice *or* loss; undersell, undercut, **unload**

dumpling NOUNS ravioli, *kreplach* <Yiddish pl>, won ton; spaetzle, dim sum, gnocchi, matzo balls, *knaydlach* <Yiddish>

dumps NOUNS **sulks,** sullens, mumps, grumps <nonformal>, frumps <Brit nonformal>, **blues,** blue devils, mulligrubs, dorts *or* dods <both Scots>, **pouts, doldrums,** dismals, dolefuls <nonformal>, blahs *and* mopes *and* megrims <all nonformal>

dumpy ADJS **stubby,** stubbed, stumpy <nonformal>, undergrown, **thickset, stocky,** blocky, **chunky** <nonformal>, **fat, chubby,** tubby <nonformal>; **squat,** squatty, squattish

dun VERBS **importune, press,** pressure <nonformal>, prod, prod at, apply *or* exert pressure, push, **ply; beset, buttonhole,** besiege, take *or* grasp by the lapels; pester, plague, nag, nag at, make a pest *or* nuisance of oneself, try one's patience, bug <nonformal>, nudge; **bill,** send a statement; demand payment

dunce NOUNS **stupid person, dolt,** clod, Boeotian, **dullard,** *niais* <Fr>, donkey, yahoo, thickwit, **dope, nitwit,** dimwit, lackwit, half-wit, lamebrain, putz, lightweight, witling; **ignoramus, know-nothing;** no scholar, puddinghead, fool

dune NOUNS **hill, knoll,** hummock, hammock, eminence, rise, mound, swell, barrow, tumulus, kop, tel, jebel; sand dune, sandhill

dung NOUNS **feces,** feculence; **manure, droppings;** cow pats, cow flops <nonformal>; cow chips, buffalo chips; guano

dunghill NOUNS **manure pile,** midden, mixen <Brit nonformal>, colluvies

dunk VERBS **submerge,** submerse, **immerse,** immerge, merge, **sink,** bury, engulf, **inundate,** deluge, drown, overwhelm, whelm; **dip, duck,** douse, souse

dupe NOUNS 1 **gull,** gudgeon, *gobemouches* <Fr>; **victim;** gullible *or* dupable *or* credulous person, trusting *or* simple soul, innocent, *näif* <Fr>, babe, babe in the woods; **figure of fun, butt,** target, stock, **goat** <nonformal>, **fair game,** fool, everybody's fool, monkey, mug <Brit nonformal>; trusting soul; sucker *and* patsy *and* easy mark *and* pushover <all nonformal>
VERBS 2 **deceive, trick, hoax,** gammon, **gull,** pigeon, play one for a fool *or* sucker, **bamboozle** *and* snow *and*

hornswoggle *and* diddle *and* scam <all nonformal>, **take in,** put on *and* hocus-pocus <both nonformal>, string along, **put something over** *or* **across,** slip one over on <nonformal>, pull a fast one on

duplicate NOUNS 1 **copy, duplication,** dupe *and* ditto <both nonformal>; **double,** cookie-cutter copy, clone; representation, **reproduction, replica,** repro <nonformal>, facsimile, model
VERBS 2 **copy, reproduce,** replicate, dupe <nonformal>; clone
ADJS 3 **identical,** identic; **alike,** just alike, exactly alike, like two peas in a pod; reduplicated, twin

durable ADJS **lasting, enduring,** perduring, **abiding, continuing,** remaining, staying, **stable**, persisting, **persistent,** perennial; inveterate, agelong; **steadfast, constant,** intransient, immutable, unfading, evergreen, sempervirent, **permanent**, perennial, **long-lasting,** of long duration *or* standing, diuturnal; **tough, resistant;** shockproof, shock-resistant, impactproof, impact-resistant; **heavy-duty;** hard *or* tough as nails; **strong, hardy,** vigorous

duration NOUNS **time,** *durée* <Fr>, lastingness, continuity, term, while, tide, space; **period**, time frame; **chronology**, **term, tenure,** spell

duress NOUNS **coercion,** intimidation, scare tactics, headbanging *and* arm-twisting <both nonformal>; **the strong arm** *and* strong-arm tactics <both nonformal>, a pistol *or* gun to one's head, the sword, the mailed fist, the bludgeon, the boot in the face, the jackboot, the big stick, the club, *argumentum baculinum* <L>; **pressure, high pressure,** high-pressure methods; **compulsion**

dusk NOUNS dusking time *or* -tide, dusk-dark *and* dust-dark *and* dusty-dark <all nonformal>, **twilight,** evening twilight, crepuscule, crepuscular light, **semidarkness,** semidark, partial darkness, bad light, dim light, half-light, *demi-jour* <Fr>; gloam, **gloaming,** glooming; owl-light *or* owl's light

the pale dusk of the impending night
LONGFELLOW

dust NOUNS 1 **dirt, grime; powder, soot, smut; particle, particulate,** particulates, airborne particles, air pollution; fallout; cosmic dust
VERBS 2 **clean, cleanse, purge,** deterge, depurate; clean house, spruce, **tidy**; dust off

dusty ADJS 1 **dirty, grimy, grubby,** grungy <nonformal>, smirchy, dingy, messy <nonformal>; scruffy, slovenly, untidy; **stale, fusty, musty,** rusty
2 **powdery,** pulverulent, pulverous, lutose; **pulverized,** pulverant, powdered, disintegrated, comminute, gone to dust, reduced to powder; sandy

duty NOUNS 1 **obligation,** charge, **onus, burden,** mission, devoir, must, ought, imperative, bounden duty, proper *or* assigned task, what ought to be done, what one is responsible for, where the buck stops <nonformal>

stern daughter of the voice of God
WORDSWORTH

2 **task, work, stint, job,** labor, piece of work, **chore,** chare, odd job; **assignment, charge,** project, errand, **mission,** commission; things to do, matters in hand, irons in the fire, fish to fry; homework; busywork, makework

dwarf NOUNS 1 **midget,** midge, **pygmy,** manikin, homunculus, atomy, micromorph, hop-o'-my-thumb; Lilliputian, Tom Thumb; **gnome**
VERBS 2 **minimize,** minify, **belittle,** detract from; bedwarf; play down, underplay, downplay, deemphasize

dwell VERBS **reside, live, live in, lodge, stay,** remain, abide, hang *or* hang out <nonformal>, domicile, domiciliate

dwelling NOUNS **abode, habitation, place,** dwelling place, abiding place, place to live, where one lives *or* resides, where one is at home, roof, roof over one's head, **residence,** place of residence, **domicile,** *domus* <L>; **lodging,** lodgment, lodging place

dwindle VERBS **decrease, diminish, lessen; let up,** bate, abate; **decline, subside,** shrink, wane, wither, ebb, ebb away, languish, sink, sag, die down *or* away, wind down, taper off *and* trail off *or* away *and* tail off *or* away <all nonformal>; **drop,** drop off, fall off, fall away, fall to a low ebb, run low

dying ADJS **terminal,** expiring, going, slipping, slipping away, sinking, sinking fast, low, despaired of, given up, given up for dead, not long for this world, hopeless, bad, **moribund,** near death, near one's end, at the end of one's rope <nonformal>, done for <nonformal>, at the point of death, **at death's door,** at the portals of death, *in articulo mortis* <L>, *in extremis* <L>, in the jaws of death, facing *or* in the face of death; **on one's last legs** <nonformal>, with one foot in the grave

dyke NOUNS lesbian, butch <nonformal>; **amazon,** virago, androgyne

dynamic ADJS **kinetic, kinetical, kinematic, kinematical;** geodynamic, radiodynamic, electrodynamic, etc; **enterprising, aggressive,** activist, proactive, driving, forceful, **pushing, up-and-coming, go-ahead** *and* **hustling** <both nonformal>

dynasty NOUNS **posterity,** offspring, descendant, heir, inheritor; **successor;** replacement, line, **lineage,** family

E

eager ADJS **active, lively, animated, spirited,** bubbly, ebullient, effervescent, **vivacious, sprightly,** chipper *and* perky <both nonformal>, pert; **spry, breezy, brisk, energetic,** keen, can-do <nonformal>; **enterprising,** venturesome, adventurous, plucky; psyched *or* pumped up <nonformal>, champing at the bit

eagle eye ADJS **sharp eye,** keen eye, piercing *or* penetrating eye, gimlet eye, X-ray eye; hawkeye, peeled eye <nonformal>, watchful eye; **weather eye; guard,** guardedness

earlier ADJS 1 **previous, prior, early**, *ci-devant* or *ci-dessus* <Fr>, **former,** fore, prime, first, **preceding**, foregoing, above, anterior, **anticipatory,** antecedent; **preexistent**
ADVS 2 **formerly, previously, before,** before now, erenow, erst, whilom, erewhile, **hitherto, heretofore,** thitherto, aforetime, beforetime, **in the past,** in times past

early ADJS 1 **former,** past, fore, **previous,** late, recent, **once, onetime,** sometime, **erstwhile,** then, quondam; **prior**; **ancient, immemorial,** primitive, primeval, prehistoric; **old,** olden
ADVS 2 **bright and early, beforehand, beforetime,** early on, betimes, precociously, **ahead of time,** foresightedly, in advance, in anticipation, ahead, before, **with time to spare**

earmark VERBS **allot,** lot, **assign, appoint, set,** detail; **allocate,** make assignments *or* allocations, schedule; **set apart** *or* **aside,** tag, mark out for; set off, mark off, portion off; assign to, appropriate to *or* for; reserve, restrict to, restrict; **ordain, destine, fate**

earn VERBS 1 **deserve, merit,** rate *and* be in line for <both nonformal>, **be worthy of,** be deserving, richly deserve
2 **be paid, draw wages,** be salaried, work for wages, be remunerated, collect for one's services, get an income, pull down *and* drag down <both nonformal>

earnest ADJS **sincere, serious;** loyal, faithful; intent, intent on, resolute; on top of <nonformal>, diligent, assiduous, intense, concentrated

earnings NOUNS **gains, profits,** winnings, return, returns, proceeds, **bottom line** <nonformal>, **income; pay,** remuneration, compensation, salary, wage, **wages,** hire

earth NOUNS 1 **land, ground,** landmass, **sod,** clod, **soil, dirt,** dust, clay, marl; *terra* <L>, **terra firma;** terrain
ADJS 2 **terrestrial,** earthly, telluric, tellurian

earthly ADJS **secular, worldly,** earthy, terrestrial, **mundane,** here-and-now, temporal; **unspiritual, profane,** carnal, materialistic; humanistic, secular-humanistic

earthy ADJS **vulgar, uncouth, coarse, gross,** rank, raw, broad, low, foul, gutter; frank, pulling no punches

ease NOUNS 1 **rest, repose, relaxation,** slippered *or* unbuttoned ease, decompression <nonformal>; **comfort**; restfulness, quiet, tranquility; inactivity; peace of mind, composure; well-being; contentment; clover, velvet <nonformal>, bed of roses; life of ease; **smoothness, facility; casualness,** offhandedness, **easiness**
VERBS 2 **extenuate, mitigate, palliate,** soften, lessen, diminish, mince; **relax,** unbend; **ease up,** ease off, **let up,** let down; abate, bate, remit, mitigate; **facilitate, grease the wheels** <nonformal>, **smooth, smooth** *or* **pave the way,** ease the way, cushion

easy ADJS **slow, leisurely,** slack, moderate, gentle, deliberate, unhurried, laid-back <nonformal>, relaxed, gradual, tentative, cautious, reluctant, foot-dragging <nonformal>; facile, effortless, smooth, painless

2 <nonformal> **cinch, snap,** pushover, breeze, waltz, duck soup, velvet, picnic, pie, cherry pie, apple pie, cakewalk, piece of cake <Brit>, kid stuff, turkey shoot, no-brainer, setup

easygoing ADJS **casual, offhand, relaxed, laid-back** *and* throwaway <both nonformal>; easy, free and easy, devil-may-care, lackadaisical, *dégagé* <Fr>

eat VERBS **feed,** fare, take, partake, partake of, break bread, break one's fast; refresh *or* entertain the inner man, feed one's face *and* put on the feed bag <both nonformal>, fall to, pitch in <nonformal>

eavesdrop VERBS **listen in;** wiretap, tap, intercept, bug <nonformal>; **keep one's ears open,** be all ears <nonformal>, listen with both ears, strain one's ears

ebb VERBS **diminish,** decline, sink, shrink, dwindle, **fade,** wane; go out with the tide, fade into the distance; **subside,** wither, ebb away, dwindle, languish, sink, sag, die down *or* away, wind down, taper off *and* trail off *or* away *and* tail off *or* away <all nonformal>

eccentric NOUNS 1 erratic, character; odd person; **nonconformist**, recluse
ADJS 2 **erratic,** idiocratic, idiocratical, idiosyncratic, idiosyncratical, **queer,** queer in the head, **odd, peculiar,** strange, fey, singular, anomalous, freakish, funny; unnatural, abnormal, irregular, divergent, deviative, deviant, different, exceptional; unconventional; solitary, reclusive, antisocial

3 <nonformal> **kooky, goofy,** birdy, funny, kinky, loopy, goofus, haywire, squirrely, screwy, screwball, nutty, wacky, flaky, oddball, wacky, wacko, lunch, out to lunch, nobody home, weird

ecclesiastic ADJS **ecclesiastical, churchly; ministerial, clerical,** sacerdotal, **pastoral**

echo NOUNS 1 **reverberation, resounding;** rebound, resound, reecho
VERBS 2 **reverberate, resound,** sound, **rumble,** roll, boom, reecho, rebound, bounce back, be reflected, be sent back, echo back, send back, return; **respond, react,** be moved, be affected *or* touched, be inspired, catch the flame *or* infection, be in tune; **mirror, reflect; reproduce, duplicate**, reduplicate, double, redouble, ditto <nonformal>, **parrot**

eclipse NOUNS 1 occultation; total eclipse, partial eclipse, central eclipse, annular eclipse; solar eclipse, lunar eclipse; blocking, blotting out, eclipsing
VERBS 2 **overshadow, throw into the shade,** extinguish; **cover,** cover up; obscure, block, occult, occultate, block the light

economical ADJS **thrifty, frugal,** unwasteful, conserving, **saving,** economizing, spare, **sparing; prudent,** prudential, provident, forehanded; careful, chary, canny; scrimping, skimping <nonformal>, cheeseparing; penny-wise; **parsimonious**; **cost-effective, cost-efficient; efficient,** labor-saving, time-saving, money-saving

economics NOUNS economic science, the dismal science; political economy; dynamic economics; theoretical economics, plutology; classical economics; Keynesian economics, Keynesianism; supply side economics

economy NOUNS 1 **thrift, thriftiness, frugality,** frugalness; tight purse strings; parsimony, **parsimoniousness**; care, chariness, canniness; **prudence,** providence, forehandedness; **husbandry,** management, good management *or* stewardship, prudent administration; **austerity,** austerity program, belt-tightening
2 **economic system,** capitalist *or* capitalistic economy, free-enterprise *or* private-enterprise economy, market economy, socialist *or* socialistic economy, collectivized economy

ecstasy NOUNS 1 **passion,** passionateness, strong feeling, powerful emotion; **ardor, ardency,** *empressement* <Fr>, warmth of feeling, **warmth, heat, fire, excitement**
2 **trance,** ecstasis, transport, mystic transport; **rapture;** yoga trance, dharana, dhyana, samadhi

ecstatic ADJS **overjoyed,** brimming *or* bursting with happiness, on top of the world; **rapturous,** raptured, **enraptured, enchanted,** entranced, enravished, ravished, rapt, possessed; sent *and* high *and* freaked-out <all nonformal>, **in raptures,** transported, in a transport of delight, **carried away,** rapt *or* ravished away, beside oneself, beside oneself with joy, all over oneself <nonformal>; **elated,** elate, exalted, jubilant, exultant, flushed

edge NOUNS **border,** limbus, bordure <heraldry>, limb, **verge, brink,** brow, **brim, rim, margin, fringe,** selvage *or* selvedge; **advantage,** vantage, odds, leg up *and* inside track *and* pole position <all nonformal>; **upper hand,** whip hand
2 **sharpness, keenness,** acuteness, acuity; **pointedness,** acumination
VERBS 3 **border, bound, rim, skirt, hem in,** befringe, marginate, verge, trim, bind
4 **go sideways, sidle,** lateral, lateralize, **veer, angle, slant, skew,** sidestep

edgy ADJS **nervous, uneasy, apprehensive,** qualmish, nail-biting, white-knuckle <nonformal>, nervous as a cat; **irritable, on edge,** nerves on edge, on the ragged edge <nonformal>, panicky, **fearful, frightened**

edible ADJS **eatable,** comestible, gustable, esculent; **palatable**

edict NOUNS **decree,** decretum, decretal, rescript, fiat, *edictum* <L>; **proclamation,** pronouncement, pronunciamento, **declaration,** ukase; bull, brevet <old>; diktat

edit VERBS **comment upon,** commentate, remark upon; **annotate,** gloss; **revise,** redact, recense, **revamp, rewrite,** redraft, **rework,** work over; blue-pencil

edition NOUNS issue; volume, number; **printing,** impression, print order, print run; copy; library edition; **trade edition,** subscription edition; school edition, text edition

editorial NOUNS **commentary,** criticism, critique, *compte-rendu critique* <Fr>, analysis; **review,** critical review, **report,** notice, **write-up** <nonformal>; leading article *or* leader <both Brit>

educate VERBS **teach, instruct,** give instruction, give lessons in, **school; edify, enlighten,** civilize, illumine; **direct, guide; inform**; enlarge *or* broaden the mind; **ground,** teach the rudiments *or* elements *or* basics; catechize

educated ADJS **informed, enlightened, instructed,** versed, well-versed, schooled, **taught; learned, erudite, cultured,** cultivated, lettered, literate, civilized, **scholarly,** scholastic, studious

education NOUNS **teaching, instruction, schooling, tuition; edification, enlightenment,** illumination; tutelage, **pedagogy,** pedagogics, didactics, didacticism; catechization; **learning,** acquisition of knowledge

educational ADJS **informative,** informing, informational; **instructive, enlightening;** educative, advisory, monitory

eerie ADJS **creepy, weird, uncanny,** unco *or* uncolike <both Scots>; unearthly, unworldly, otherworldly; fey; mysterious, macabre; **spooky** *and* spookish *and* hairy <all nonformal>

effect NOUNS 1 **result,** resultant, **consequence,** consequent, sequent, sequence, sequel, sequela, sequelae; event, eventuality, eventuation, **upshot, outcome,** logical outcome, possible outcome, scenario; **outgrowth,** spin-off, offshoot, offspring, issue, aftermath, legacy; **product**, **fruit,** first fruits, development, by-product
VERBS 2 effectuate, **make; bring about,** bring to pass, **bring off, produce, deliver** <nonformal>, **do the trick,** put across *or* through; swing *or* swing it *and* hack it *and* cut it *and* cut the mustard <all nonformal>; **cause,** be the cause of, lie at the root of; **bring about, bring to pass,** realize; **occasion, engender,** generate, breed, **induce,** lead, procure, get, obtain, contrive, **bring on**

effective ADJS **effectual,** active, efficient, efficacious, operative, telling; **practical,** practicable, pragmatic *or* pragmatical, banausic; feasible, workable, operable, realizable

effects NOUNS **property, possessions, holdings,** havings, goods, chattels, goods and chattels, estate and effects, what one can call one's own, what one has to one's name, all one owns *or* has, all one can lay claim to, one's all; household possessions *or* effects, lares and penates

effeminate ADJS **frail, slight, delicate, dainty,** puny; light, lightweight; womanish, **unmanly,** soft, prissy, **sissified,** sissy, **sissyish**

delicately weak
POPE

effervescent ADJS **bubbly,** burbly, **bubbling,** burbling; spumescent, **fizzy, sparkling,** *mousseux* <Fr>, *spumante* <Ital>; carbonated; ebullient, lively, animated, spirited, **vivacious, sprightly,** chipper *and* perky <both nonformal>, pert; alive, live, full of life, **peppy** *and* snappy *and* zingy <all nonformal>; frisky, bouncing, bouncy

efficiency NOUNS **capacity,** potentiality, faculty, facility, fitness, qualification, talent, flair, genius, caliber, **competence,** competency, adequacy, sufficiency, efficacy; **utility, usefulness,** avail, good, serviceability, functionality, **practicability,** practicality, practical utility, **effectiveness**

efficient ADJS 1 **competent, capable, able, qualified, fit, fitted, suited, worthy;** up to snuff <nonformal>, up to the mark <nonformal>, *au fait* <Fr>

2 **practical,** practicable, pragmatic *or* pragmatical, banausic; feasible, workable, operable, realizable; effective, **effectual**

effort NOUNS **endeavor,** striving, struggle, strain; **all-out effort,** best effort, college try *or* old college try <nonformal>; **exertion, energy,** elbow grease; **trouble, pains;** great *or* mighty effort, might and main, muscle, one's back, nerve, and sinew, hard *or* strong *or* long pull

a long pull, a strong pull, and a pull all together
DICKENS

egghead NOUNS **intellectual, intellect,** member of the intelligentsia, white-collar intellectual; **brain** *and* rocket scientist *and* brain surgeon <all nonformal>; pointy-head <nonformal>; **highbrow** <nonformal>

someone whose mind watches itself
CAMUS

ego NOUNS **egotism, egoism,** egoisticalness, egotisticalness, self-interest, individualism, **egocentricity,** egocentrism, self-centeredness, self-centerment, self-obsession; selfishness; **self, oneself,** the self, the I

the tongue of vanity
CHAMFORT

egotistical ADJS **egotistic,** egoistic, egoistical, self-interested; **egocentric,** egocentristic, self-centered, self-obsessed, narcissistic

ego trip NOUNS **self-satisfaction, self-content,** self-approbation, self-congratulation, self-gratulation, self-complacency, **smugness,** complacency; **narcissism, self-love,** self-devotion, self-jealousy, **self-consideration,** self-absorption, self-occupation

eject VERBS **expel, discharge,** extrude, obtrude, detrude, exclude, **reject,** cast, remove; **oust, bounce** *and* give the hook <both nonformal>, **put out, turn out,** thrust out; **throw out,** run out <nonformal>, cast out, chuck out, toss out, heave out; kick *or* boot out <nonformal>; give the bum's rush *or* give the old heave-ho *or* throw out on one's ear <all nonformal>; defenestrate; jettison

eke out VERBS **support oneself,** make one's way; **make ends meet, keep body and soul together, keep the wolf from the door,** keep *or* hold one's head above water, keep afloat; **survive, subsist, cope,** make out, scrape along, manage, get by; fill out, piece out, top off, round out

elaborate VERBS **develop, work out,** enlarge, enlarge on *or* upon, amplify, **expand,** expand on *or* upon, detail, go *or* enter into detail, go into, flesh out, **pursue,** spell out <nonformal>; complete

elaborate ADJS 1 **painstaking, diligent, assiduous,** sedulous, **thorough, thoroughgoing,** operose, industrious
2 **complex, ramified, intricate,** involuted, convoluted, multilayered, multilevel

elapse VERBS lapse, **pass, expire,** run its course, run out, go *or* pass by; **flow,** tick away *or* by *or* on, run, proceed, advance, roll *or* press on, flit, fly, slip, slide, glide; **continue**, last, **endure,** go *or* run *or* flow on

elastic ADJS resilient, springy, bouncy; **stretchable, stretchy,** stretch; extensile; **flexible**; flexile; **adaptable,** adaptive, responsive; buoyant; lively

elate VERBS **exalt,** elevate, lift, uplift, flush; **make proud,** do one's heart good, do one proud <nonformal>, **gratify,** turn one's head

elbow VERBS **bump,** jog, joggle, jolt, shake, rattle; **jostle,** shoulder

elder ADJS **older,** senior, major, dean

elect NOUNS 1 **the best,** the very best, the best ever, the top of the heap *or* the line <nonformal>, the tops <nonformal>; **choice, pick, select, elite,** chosen; **cream, flower,** cream of the crop, *crème de la crème* <Fr>, salt of the earth
VERBS 2 **choose,** pick, go with <nonformal>, opt, opt for, co-opt, make *or* take one's choice, make choice of, have one's druthers <nonformal>, use *or* take up *or* exercise one's option; vote in, place in office

election NOUNS **choice, selection,** preference, decision, **pick, choosing,** free choice; appointment; general election, by-election; congressional election, presidential election

elective ADJS volitional, voluntary, volitive; **optional,** discretional; **alternative,** disjunctive

electric chair NOUNS death chair, the chair <nonformal>, hot seat <nonformal>

electrify VERBS **stimulate,** hearten, **galvanize,** fire, build a fire under, inflame, charge up, psych *or* pump up <nonformal>, rouse, arouse, act like a tonic, be a shot in the arm <nonformal>, pep *or* snap *or* jazz *or* zip *or* perk up <nonformal>, put pep *or* zip into it <nonformal>

elegance NOUNS elegancy; **grace,** gracefulness, gracility; **taste,** tastefulness, good taste; **correctness,** seemliness, comeliness, **propriety,** aptness, fittingness; **refinement,** precision, exactitude, lapidary quality, finish; **smartness, chic**

elegant ADJS graceful, gracile, gracious; **refined, polished, cultivated,** civilized, **cultured;** nice, fine, delicate, dainty, **subtle, sophisticated, discriminating**, fastidious

elegy NOUNS **dirge, funeral** *or* **death song,** coronach, keen, epicedium, requiem, monody, threnody, threnode, muffled drums

element NOUNS **component, constituent, ingredient,** integrant, makings *and* fixings <both nonformal>, **factor, part**, module, part and parcel; appurtenance, adjunct; **feature,** aspect, specialty, circumstance, detail, item

elementary ADJS **original, primary,** primal, primitive, pristine, primeval, aboriginal, elemental, **basic,** basal, **rudimentary,** crucial, central, radical, **fundamental;** embryonic, germinal, seminal

elementary school NOUNS **grade school** *or* graded school, the grades; **primary school;** junior school <Brit>; **grammar school;** folk school, *Volksschule* <Ger>

elevate VERBS **raise, rear,** escalate, up, boost *and* hike <both nonformal>; **erect, heighten, lift,** levitate, boost <nonformal>, **hoist,** heft, heave; raise up, rear up, lift up, hold up, set up; stick up, cock up, perk up; buoy up, upbuoy; **upraise, uplift, exalt,** ensky; deify, apotheosize; put on a pedestal

elicit VERBS educe, deduce, induce, derive, obtain, procure, secure; **get from,** get out of; rouse, arouse, stimulate; **draw out** *or* **forth,** bring out *or* forth, pry *or* prize out, drag out, worm out, bring to light; **prompt, provoke, evoke,** call forth, inspire; bring about, cause

eligible ADJS **qualified, fit,** fitted, **suitable,** acceptable, admissible, worthy, desirable; with voice, with vote, with voice and vote, enfranchised

eliminate VERBS get rid of, rid oneself of, **get quit of,** get shut of <nonformal>, **dispose of, remove,** abstract, eject, expel, give the bum's rush <nonformal>, cast off *or* out, chuck <nonformal>, throw over *or* overboard <nonformal>; **weed out,** pick out; **cut out,** strike off *or* out, elide; eradicate, root up *or* out; **purge, liquidate**

elite NOUNS 1 **the best,** the very best, the best ever, the top of the heap *or* the line <nonformal>, the tops <nonformal>; nonesuch, paragon, nonpareil; gem of the first water
ADJS 2 **exclusive,** selective, **select,** elect; socially prominent, in society, high-society; jet-set; lace-curtain, silk-stocking; **choice, select, elect,** handpicked

eloquence NOUNS **rhetoric, silver tongue,** eloquent tongue; **articulateness;** gift of gab <nonformal>, **glibness,** smoothness, slickness; **felicitousness,** felicity; **oratory**; expression, **expressiveness,** command of words *or* language, gift of gab *or* of the gab <nonformal>, gift of expression

elude VERBS **evade,** get away from, give the runaround *or* the slip <nonformal>; throw off the scent; lead one a merry chase, frustrate, foil, **circumvent**

emancipated ADJS **liberated, freed, released;** delivered, rescued, ransomed, redeemed; extricated, unbound, untied, unshackled

emasculate VERBS **unman, unnerve, enervate,** exhaust, incapacitate, **disable**, etiolate; cut the balls off <nonformal>, demasculinize, effeminize; castrate, geld, eunuchize, neuter, spay, fix *or* alter <both nonformal>, unsex, deball <nonformal>

embankment NOUNS **shore,** bank; roadway, roadbed, retaining wall, bulkhead, bulkheading, plank buttress, piling, levee, dike

embargo NOUNS **ban, enjoinder, injunction,** prohibitory injunction, **proscription,** inhibition, **interdict,** *interdictum* <L>, interdiction; **restriction,** prohibition

embark VERBS **go aboard,** board, go on board; go on shipboard, take ship; hoist the blue Peter; **entrain,** enplane *or* emplane, embus; weigh anchor, up-anchor, put to sea

embarrass VERBS **chagrin, abash, discomfit, disconcert,** discompose, confuse, throw into confusion *or* a tizzy, **upset,** pother, **bother,** flummox <nonformal>, confound, cast down, mortify, put out, put out of face *or* countenance, put to the blush; **mortify,** humiliate, disturb; **hamper, impede, cramp, put in a hole** <nonformal>, put in a spot <nonformal>

embarrassed ADJS **distressed, uncomfortable,** uneasy, ill at ease; **chagrined,** abashed, discomfited, **disconcerted, upset, confused,** mortified, **put-out,** out of countenance, cast down, chapfallen; in debt, plunged in debt, in difficulties, in embarrassed circumstances, in the hole *and* in hock <both nonformal>, in the red; **bewildered, dismayed,** distracted, distraught, discomposed, perturbed, **bothered,** all hot and bothered <nonformal>

embassy NOUNS **foreign office, legation;** consulate, chancery, chancellery

embattled ADJS battled, **engaged,** at grips, in combat; **arrayed, deployed,** ranged, in battle array, in the field; war-ravaged, war-torn

embed VERBS internalize, put in, keep within; enclose, surround, contain, comprise, include, enfold, take to heart, assimilate; infix, ingrain, set in, plant, implant, engraft, bed

embellish VERBS **develop,** elaborate; beautify, furbish, embroider, enrich, grace, set off *or* out, paint, color, blazon, emblazon, paint in glowing colors; **dress up; spruce up** *and* gussy up *and* doll up *and* fix up <all nonformal>, **ornament, decorate, adorn,** enrich; paint in glowing colors, tell in glowing terms

to gild refined gold, to paint the lily, to throw a perfume on the violet
SHAKESPEARE

embellishment NOUNS **ornamentation, decoration, adornment,** embroidery, elaboration; nonfunctional addition *or* adjunct; garnish, garnishment, garniture; **ornament,** grace, arabesque, *fioritura* <Ital>; **padding, filling;** pleonasm, tautology; verbosity, prolixity

ember NOUNS live coal, brand, firebrand, burning ember

embezzle VERBS divert, **misappropriate,** convert, defalcate <old>, peculate, feather one's nest <nonformal>; pervert, prostitute; have one's hand in the till; **pilfer, filch**

emblem NOUNS **symbol, icon, token, insignia, regalia,** ensign, **badge,** logo <nonformal>, marking, attribute

embodiment NOUNS **incarnation,** materialization, substantiation, concretization, hypostasis, reification; **essence, substance,** stuff, very stuff, inner essence, essential nature, quiddity; **quintessence, epitome,** perfect example *or* exemplar; **whole, totality, entirety,** collectivity; integration, incorporation

embody VERBS incarnate, **materialize,** concretize, lend substance to, reify, entify, hypostatize; **compose, constitute,** construct, fabricate; **incorporate,** embody, corporify, personify

embossed ADJS **in relief,** chased, bossed, hammered, toreutic; *repoussé* <Fr>; **infixed,** inwrought; impressed, indelibly impressed, imprinted; engraved, etched, graven

embrace NOUNS 1 **hug, squeeze,** fond embrace, embracement, clasp, enfoldment, bear hug <nonformal>
VERBS 2 **hug, clasp, press, squeeze** <nonformal>, fold, **enfold,** bosom, embosom, put *or* throw one's arms around, take to *or* in one's arms, fold to the heart, press to the bosom
3 **comprise, comprehend,** hold, **take in;** encompass, enclose, encircle, incorporate, assimilate, embody, admit, receive, envisage

embroider VERBS **ornament, embellish,** enrich; festoon, weight down with ornament, gild the lily, trick out, varnish; paint in glowing colors, tell in glowing terms

embryo NOUNS zygote, oösperm, oöspore, blastula; *Anlage* <Ger>; **fetus,** germ, rudiment; **larva,** nymph

emerge VERBS **come out, issue,** issue forth, come into view, extrude, **come forth; surface,** rise to the surface; sally, sally forth, come to the fore; emanate, effuse, arise, come; debouch, disembogue; jump out, leap out, hop out; bail out; **burst forth, break forth, erupt;** break cover, **come out in the open;** protrude

emergency NOUNS exigency, juncture *or* conjuncture *or* convergence of events, critical juncture, crossroads; **pinch,** clutch <nonformal>, rub, push, pass, strait, extremity, spot <nonformal>; state of emergency, red alert, race against time; **crisis,** hot spot, nasty *or* tricky spot, pass, pinch, strait, plight, predicament

emergent ADJS **emerging, issuing,** arising, surfacing, coming, forthcoming; emanating, emanent, emanative, transient; projected, plotted, planned, looked- *or* hoped-for, desired, **predicted,** prophesied, foreseen, anticipated, anticipatory, previsional, prevenient, envisioned, envisaged, probable, extrapolated

emigrant NOUNS **migrant,** migrator, trekker; out-migrant, *émigré* <Fr>; expatriate; **evacuee,** exile; outgoer, leaver, departer

emigrate VERBS **leave home,** go from home; leave the country, out-migrate, expatriate, defect; vote with one's feet; burn one's bridges

eminent ADJS **prominent,** outstanding, standout, high, elevated, towering, soaring, overtopping, exalted, **lofty,** sublime; august, majestic, noble, distinguished; **magnificent,** magnanimous, heroic, godlike, superb; famous, renowned, lauded, glorious; **distinguished;** prestigious, esteemed, estimable, reputable; **extraordinary,** *extraordinaire* <Fr>, out of the ordinary, **exceptional, special,** rare

emissary NOUNS envoy, legate, minister, foreign service officer; envoy extraordinary, plentipotentiary, nuncio, internuncio, apostolic delegate

emit VERBS **exude,** transude; effuse, extravasate; **issue, bring out, put out, get out,** put *or* give *or* send forth; put *or* set forth, pour forth; give vent to, give out *or* off, throw off, blow off

emotion NOUNS **feeling, affect, sentiment,** affection, affections; affective faculty, affectivity; emotional charge, cathexis; **feelings, sensitiveness, sensibility,** susceptibility, thin skin; the logic of the heart; feeling tone, affectivity, emotivity

emotional ADJS **affective,** emotive, affectional, **feeling;** soulful, of soul, of heart, of feeling, of sentiment; visceral, gut <nonformal>; demonstrative, overdemonstrative; **excitable,** highly emotional, overemotional, hyperthymic, perturbable, flappable <nonformal>, agitable

empathy NOUNS **affinity,** identification; involvement, sharing; pathos; identity, feeling of identity, fellow feeling, **fellowship,** kinship, togetherness

emphasis NOUNS **accent,** accentuation, rhythmical accent *or* accentuation, ictus, stress arsis, thesis

emphasize VERBS **stress,** lay emphasis *or* stress upon, feature, highlight, brightline, place emphasis on, give emphasis to, **accent, accentuate, punctuate, point up,** bring to the fore, put in the foreground; prioritize; **highlight,** spotlight; harp on; dwell on, belabor; attach too much importance to, make a big deal *or* Federal case of <nonformal>, make a mountain out of a molehill

emphatic ADJS **decided, positive, forceful,** forcible; **emphasized, stressed,** accented, accentuated, punctuated, pointed; underlined, underscored, italicized; red-letter, in red letters, in letters of fire

employ VERBS 1 **use, utilize, make use of,** do with; practice, ply, work, manage, handle, manipulate, operate, **wield,** play; **occupy, engage, busy,** devote, spend, occupy oneself, busy oneself, go about one's business, devote oneself
2 **hire,** give a job to, take into employment, take into one's service, take on <nonformal>, recruit, headhunt <nonformal>, **engage,** sign up *or* on <nonformal>

employee NOUNS hired man, hired hand, man *or* girl Friday, right-hand man, assistant; **worker, laborer, toiler,** moiler; member of the working class, blue-collar *or* lunch-bucket worker, stiff *and* working stiff <both nonformal>; staff member

empower VERBS **enable;** invest, clothe, invest *or* clothe with power, deputize; enfranchise; endue, endow, **commission, authorize,** accredit; arm

empty ADJS **vacant,** hollow, inane, **bare, vacuous, void,** without content, with nothing inside, devoid, null, null and void; **blank,** clear, white, bleached; featureless, unrelieved, characterless, bland, insipid; **barren, vain, futile,** hollow, fatuous, fatuitous; **baseless, groundless,** ungrounded, **unfounded,**

ill-founded, unbased, **unsupported,** unsustained, **without foundation,** without basis *or* sound basis; **untenable, unsupportable,** unsustainable; **unwarranted,** idle, inane, vacuous

enable VERBS **empower,** give power, entitle; **license; make possible, permit, clear the road** *or* path for, smooth the way for, open the way for, open the door to, open up the possibility of

enact VERBS **perform, execute; transact; discharge, dispatch;** conduct, **manage, handle;** dispose of, take care of, **deal with,** cope with; **make, accomplish,** complete; effect, effectuate, compass, consummate, do, deliver, fulfill, realize, attain; **legislate,** make *or* enact laws, **pass,** constitute, ordain, put in force; **put through, jam** *or* **steamroller** *or* **railroad through** <nonformal>, lobby through

enamored ADJS **charmed,** becharmed, **fascinated, captivated,** bewitched, enraptured, enchanted; **infatuated,** infatuate; **smitten,** heartsmitten, heartstruck, lovestruck

enchant VERBS **delight,** delectate, **tickle, titillate, thrill, enrapture, enthrall,** entrance, fascinate, captivate, bewitch, **charm,** becharm; enravish, ravish, imparadise; ecstasiate, transport, carry away

enchanted ADJS **charmed,** becharmed, charmstruck, charm-bound; **spellbound,** spell-struck, spell-caught; **fascinated,** captivated; **hypnotized, mesmerized;** under a spell, in a trance

enclose VERBS **close in,** bound, include, **contain;** compass, encompass; **surround,** encircle; **shut** *or* **pen in,** coop in; **fence in,** wall in, wall up, rail in, rail off, screen off, curtain off; **hem** *or* **hedge in,** box in, pocket; shut *or* coop *or* mew up; **embrace,** encompass, encircle, incorporate, assimilate, embody

enclosure NOUNS 1 **confinement,** containing, containment, circumscription, immurement, walling- *or* hedging- *or* hemming- *or* boxing- *or* fencing- *or* walling-in; **imprisonment,** incarceration, jailing, locking-up, lockdown; inclusion; **envelopment**
2 close, **confine,** precinct, enclave, pale, paling, list, cincture; **cloister; pen, coop,** fold

encompass VERBS **extend,** span, straddle, take in, hold, surround, environ; **envelop,** enfold, lap, wrap, enwrap, embrace, **encircle**, girdle; **include, number, comprise, contain, comprehend; cover,** incorporate, assimilate, embody, admit, receive, envisage; **total, amount to, come to, run to** *or* **into,** mount up to, add up to, tot *or* tot up to <nonformal>, tote *or* tote up to <nonformal>, reckon up to <nonformal>, aggregate to; aggregate

encore NOUNS 1 repeat performance, repeat, **reprise;** replay, replaying, return match
ADVS 2 **again,** over, over again, **once more,** *encore, bis* <both Fr>, two times, twice over, ditto; **anew,** *de novo* <L>, afresh; from the beginning, *da capo* <Ital>
INTER 3 **bravo!,** bravissimo!, **well done!,** *¡ole!* <Sp>, *bene!* <Ital>, hear, hear!, bis!

encounter NOUNS 1 **meeting,** meeting up, joining, joining up; near-miss, collision course, near thing, narrow squeak *or* brush; **contest, engagement, match, trial, test,** *concours* and *rencontre* <both Fr>
VERBS 2 **meet, come across, run across,** meet up, fall across, cross the path of; **come upon,** run upon, fall upon, light *or* alight upon; come among, fall among; **meet with,** meet up with <nonformal>, come face to face with, **come** *or* **go up against**

encourage VERBS **hearten, embolden,** give encouragement, pat *or* clap on the back, stroke <nonformal>; **invite,** ask for; **abet,** aid and abet, countenance, keep in countenance; **foster, nurture,** nourish, feed; **inspire,** inspirit; buck *or* brace up <nonformal>

encouraging ADJS **heartening,** heartwarming; **inspiring,** inspiriting; **exhilarating,** animating, enlivening, invigorating; cheerful, cheery, glad, joyful; **auspicious, propitious**; cheering, reassuring, supportive

encroach VERBS **intrude,** obtrude, **interlope;** infringe, impinge, **trespass,** trespass on *or* upon, trench, entrench, overstep the bounds, go too far, know no bounds, invade, infiltrate; **break in upon,** break in, burst in, charge in, crash in, smash in, storm in; **barge in**

encumbered ADJS **burdened, oppressed,** laden, cumbered, charged, loaded, fraught, freighted, taxed, saddled, hampered; **overburdened,** overloaded, overladen, overfraught, overweighted, overtaxed; **in debt,** plunged in debt, in difficulties, embarrassed, in embarrassed circumstances, in the hole *and* in hock <both nonformal>, in the red, mortgaged, mortgaged to the hilt, tied up, involved

encyclopedic ADJS **comprehensive, sweeping, complete**; whole; **all-comprehensive,** all-inclusive; without omission *or* exception, **overall,** universal, global, wall-to-wall <nonformal>, around-the-world, **total,** blanket, omnibus, across-the-board; compendious; synoptic; pansophic, polymath *or* polymathic, polyhistoric

end NOUNS 1 end point, ending, perfection, be-all and end-all, **termination, terminus, terminal,** terminating, term, period, **expiration,** expiry, phaseout, phasedown, discontinuation, closeout, **cessation**, ceasing, consummation, culmination, **conclusion, finish, finis, finale,** the end, finishing, finalizing *or* finalization, a wrap <nonformal>, quietus, stoppage, windup *and* payoff <both nonformal>, curtain, curtains <nonformal>, end of the road *or* line <nonformal>

VERBS 2 **put an end to,** make an end of, **finish,** finish off <nonformal>, put paid to <Brit>, give the *coup de gr[aca]ce* <Fr> to, give the quietus to, deal a deathblow to, dispose of, get rid of, do in, do away with; **complete, perfect, finish, finish off, conclude, terminate,** bring to a close, carry to completion, prosecute to a conclusion

3 **cease, discontinue, stop, halt,** terminate, close the books, put paid to <Brit>, abort, cancel, scratch *and* scrub <both nonformal>, hold, **quit,** stay; **desist, refrain,** leave off, lay off <nonformal>, **have done with;** cut it out *and* drop it *and* knock it off <all nonformal>

endeavor NOUNS 1 **effort,** striving, struggle, strain; **all-out effort,** best effort, college try *or* old college try <nonformal>; **exertion**; determination, resolution; **enterprise,** undertaking

VERBS 2 **strive, struggle,** strain, sweat, sweat blood, labor, get one's teeth into, come to grips with, take it on, make an all-out effort, move heaven and earth, **exert oneself,** apply oneself, use some elbow grease <nonformal>; **try**

endless ADJS **infinite, boundless, limitless,** termless, shoreless; unbounded, uncircumscribed, **unlimited,** illimited, stretching *or* extending everywhere, without bound, without limit *or* end, no end of *or* to; **interminable,** interminate; **immeasurable,** incalculable, unreckonable, innumerable, incomprehensible, unfathomable; **perpetual, everlasting,** permanent, perdurable, indestructible; sempiternal, **infinite**, aeonian *or* eonian; dateless, ageless, timeless, immemorial; continuous, steady, **constant, ceaseless,** nonstop, unceasing, never-ceasing, **incessant,** unremitting

continuous as the stars that shine
WORDSWORTH

endorse VERBS **ratify,** sign off on, second, support, **certify, confirm, validate, authenticate, accept,** give the nod *or* the green light *or* the go-ahead *or* the OK <all nonformal>, give a nod of assent, give one's imprimatur, permit, give permission, **approve**; sanction, **authorize,** warrant, accredit; **sign,** undersign, sign on the dotted line, put one's John Hancock on <nonformal>, cosign, countersign; advocate, hold a brief for <nonformal>, countenance, keep in countenance, **lend oneself to,** lend one's name to, give one's support *or* countenance to, **support, back** *and* **back up** <both nonformal>, come out for

endow VERBS invest, vest; endow with, favor with, bless with, grace with, vest with; **settle on** *or* **upon; dower; establish, found,** constitute, institute

endowed ADJS **talented, gifted,** with a flair; dowered, invested

endurance NOUNS fortitude, intestinal fortitude <nonformal>, **toughness**, **stamina,** staying *or* sticking power, stick-to-it-iveness <nonformal>; **sufferance, stoicism,** patience of Job; **perseverance, persistence** *or* persistency, insistence *or* insistency, singleness of purpose; **pertinacity, tenacity,** tenaciousness, **doggedness**

a minor form of despair, disguised as a virtue
AMBROSE BIERCE

endure VERBS 1 **last** *or* **last out,** bide,

abide, dwell, perdure, **continue,** run, extend, **go on,** carry on, hold on, keep on, stay on, run on, stay the course, go the distance, go through with, grind *or* slog on, grind *or* plug away; live, **live on,** continue to be, subsist, exist, tarry; get *or* keep one's head above water; **persist;** hang in *and* hang in there *and* hang tough <all nonformal>; maintain, sustain, **remain, stay,** keep, hold, stand, prevail, last long, hold out; **survive,** defy *or* defeat time; live to fight another day; perennate; **survive,** live on, live through; wear, wear well

2 <nonformal> **take it,** take it on the chin, take it like a man, not let it get one down, stand the gaff; bite the bullet; hold still *or* stand still for, swallow, stick, **hang in, hang in there, hang tough,** tough *or* stick it out; lump it

enemy NOUNS **foe,** foeman, **adversary, antagonist;** bitter enemy; sworn enemy; open enemy; public enemy; archenemy, devil; the other side, the opposition; **bane**, bête noire

energetic ADJS **vigorous, strenuous, forceful, forcible, strong, dynamic,** kinetic, intense, acute, keen, incisive, trenchant, vivid, vibrant; **enterprising, aggressive,** proactive, activist, can-do *and* gung ho *and* take-over *and* take-charge <all nonformal>; **active, lively,** living, **animated, spirited,** go-go <nonformal>, **vivacious,** brisk, bright-eyed and bushy-tailed <nonformal>, lusty, **robust,** hearty, enthusiastic, mettlesome, zesty, zestful, impetuous, spanking, smacking; pumped *and* pumped up *and* jazzed-up *and* charged up *and* switched on <all nonformal>

energy NOUNS 1 **vigor, force, power, vitality,** strenuousness, **intensity, dynamism,** demonic energy; **potency**; **strength**; actual *or* kinetic energy; dynamic energy; potential energy

2 <nonformal> **pep,** bang, biff, get-up-and-go, ginger, gism, jazz, sizzle, kick, moxie, oomph, pepper, piss and vinegar, **pizzazz,** poop, punch, push, snap, spizzerinctum, starch, steam, zing, zip, zizz

enforce VERBS **discharge, fulfill,** render, administer; **carry out,** carry through, put through, prosecute; effect, effectuate, set in motion, implement; put in force; **abide by, honor, live up to,** adhere to, live by, **observe**

enfranchise VERBS **liberate, free, deliver, set free,** set at liberty, set at large; **emancipate,** manumit, disenthrall; affranchise; empower, give power, enable, entitle; charter, patent, franchise

engage VERBS 1 **take on** <nonformal>, go against *or* up against, close with, try conclusions with, enter the ring *or* arena with, put on the gloves with, match oneself against; **join issue** *or* **battle, do** *or* **give battle,** engage in battle *or* combat

2 **engross, absorb,** immerse, **occupy, preoccupy,** involve, monopolize, exercise, take up; **grip, hold, arrest, hold the interest, fascinate, enthrall,** spellbind, **hold spellbound,** grab <nonformal>, charm, enchant, mesmerize, hypnotize, catch; absorb the attention, claim one's thoughts, engage the attention, involve the interest, occupy the attention, monopolize one's attention, engage the mind *or* thoughts

engaging ADJS **engrossing, absorbing,** consuming, **gripping, arresting,** attractive, **fascinating,** enchanting, magnetic

engrave VERBS **grave, tool, enchase, incise, sculpture, inscribe,** character, **mark,** line, crease, score, scratch, scrape, cut, carve, chisel

engrossed in VERBS **absorbed,** totally absorbed, single-minded, **occupied, preoccupied, engaged,** devoted, devoted to, intent, intent on, monopolized, obsessed, monomaniacal, swept up, taken up with, **involved, caught up in,** wrapped in, **wrapped up in, absorbed in** *or* with *or* by, **lost in, immersed in,** submerged in, buried in

enhance VERBS **intensify, heighten, deepen, strengthen,** beef up <nonformal>, **magnify; reinforce,** change for the better, make an improvement; transform, transfigure; improve upon, refine upon, **mend, amend,** emend; meliorate, **ameliorate; enrich,** fatten

enigma NOUNS **mystery, puzzle,** puzzlement; **matter of ignorance,** sealed book, riddle, conundrum, **vexed question,** thorny problem, knotty point, knot, crux, node, nodus, Gordian knot, poser, teaser, perplexity

a riddle wrapped in a mystery inside an enigma
Winston Churchill

enigmatic ADJS enigmatical, cryptic, cryptical; sphinxlike; **perplexing, puzzling;** riddling; logogriphic, anagrammatic; obscure, mysterious

enjoy VERBS pleasure in, be pleased with, receive *or* derive pleasure from, take delight *or* pleasure in, get a kick *or* boot *or* bang *or* charge *or* lift *or* rush out of <nonformal>; **like, love,** adore <nonformal>; **delight in, rejoice in,** indulge in, luxuriate in, revel in, riot in, bask in, wallow in, swim in; groove on *and* get high on *and* freak out on <all nonformal>; feast on, gloat over *or* on; **relish, appreciate,** roll under the tongue, do justice to, savor, smack the lips; devour, eat up

enjoyment NOUNS **pleasure,** quiet pleasure, euphoria, well-being, good feeling, **contentment,** content, **ease, comfort**; **gratification, satisfaction,** great satisfaction, hearty enjoyment, keen pleasure *or* satisfaction; **self-gratification,** self-indulgence; **relish, zest, gusto,** *joie de vivre* <Fr>; sweetness of life, *douceur de vivre* <Fr>; intellectual pleasure, pleasures of the mind; **strokes** *and* stroking *and* ego massage <all nonformal>

enlarge VERBS **increase,** aggrandize, **amplify, augment, extend,** maximize, **add to; expand, inflate; build, build up;** pyramid, parlay; develop, bulk *or* bulk up; **stretch, distend, dilate, swell, inflate,** sufflate, **blow up,** puff up, huff, puff, bloat; pump, pump up; **amplify, expatiate, dilate, expand, enlarge on,** expand on, **elaborate**

enlightening ADJS **educational, cultural, edifying,** illuminating; informative; didactic, preceptive; **liberalizing, liberating, broadening**

enlist VERBS **install,** instate, inaugurate, initiate, invest, ordain; enroll, induct, sign up, sign on; **participate, take part, partake, contribute,** chip in, involve *or* engage oneself, get involved; **join up,** sign on; **conscript, draft,** press, impress

enmity NOUNS **unfriendliness,** inimicality; **uncordiality,** unamiability, ungeniality, disaffinity, incompatibility, incompatibleness; personal conflict, strain, **tension;** coolness, coldness, chilliness, chill, frost, iciness, the freeze; inhospitality, unsociability

enormity NOUNS **outrage, atrocity, baseness, lowness, meanness, vileness,** foulness, rankness, fulsomeness, grossness, nefariousness, heinousness, **atrociousness,** monstrousness

enormous ADJS **large, immense, huge**; **gigantic,** mountainous, titanic, colossal, mammoth, Gargantuan, gigantesque, monstrous, outsize, sizable, larger-than-life, overgrown, king-size, monumental; **massive,** massy, weighty, bulky, voluminous; **vast,** vasty, boundless, **infinite,** immeasurable, cosmic, astronomical, galactic; **tremendous,** stupendous, awesome, prodigious; astronomical, humongous *and* jumbo <both nonformal>, prodigious, stupendous, larger than life, Homeric, mighty

enough NOUNS 1 **sufficiency,** sufficientness, **adequacy,** adequateness, competence *or* competency; satisfactoriness, satisfaction, satisfactory amount, enough to go around; good *or* adequate supply
ADJS 2 **sufficient,** sufficing; **ample,** substantial, **plenty, satisfactory, adequate,** decent, due;
ADVS 3 **sufficiently, amply,** substantially, **satisfactorily;** competently, **adequately**

enraptured ADJS **overjoyed, rapturous,** raptured, **enchanted,** entranced, enravished, ravished, rapt, possessed; **in raptures,** transported, in a transport of delight, **carried away,** rapt *or* ravished away, beside oneself, beside oneself with joy, **ecstatic,** in ecstasies, **enamored, charmed,** becharmed, **fascinated, captivated,** bewitched, enchanted

enrich VERBS **improve, better,** change for the better, make an improvement; **enhance,** fatten, enlighten, edify; **embellish, furbish,** embroider, grace, **ornament, decorate, adorn, gild,** trick out; paint in glowing colors, tell in glowing terms; elaborate; **fertilize,** richen, fatten, feed

enroll VERBS **install,** instate, inaugurate, initiate, invest, ordain; enlist, induct, sign up, sign on; **enlist, sign up** *or* **on** <nonformal>

ensemble NOUNS 1 **furniture,** furnishings, **suite, set of furniture,** decor
2 **cast,** cast of characters, characters,

persons of the drama, *dramatis personae* <L>; supporting cast; **company,** acting company, **troupe; orchestra, band,** combo <nonformal>, group; **chorus, chorale, choir,** choral group, choral society

enslave VERBS **subjugate, subject, subordinate; dominate**; enthrall, hold in thrall, make a chattel of; take captive, lead captive *or* into captivity; **hold in subjection,** hold in bondage, **hold captive,** hold in captivity; **conquer,** overrun, occupy

ensue VERBS **succeed, follow,** come *or* go after, **come next;** issue, emanate, attend, result; follow up, trail, track, come close on *or* tread on the heels of

ensure VERBS **guarantee, assure, insure,** bond, **certify;** countersecure; **sponsor,** be sponsor for, sign for, sign one's note, **back,** stand behind *or* back of, stand up for; **endorse;** sign, cosign, **underwrite,** undersign, subscribe to; confirm, attest

entail VERBS **imply, implicate, involve,** import, connote; involve, assume, presume, presuppose, subsume, affect, take in, contain, comprise, **call for, require,** lead to; **necessitate,** require; contribute to, lead to, conduce to

enter VERBS **go in** *or* **into,** access, cross the threshold, **come in,** find one's way into, put in *or* into; be admitted, gain admission *or* admittance, have an entree, have an in <nonformal>; **set foot in,** step in, walk in; **get in,** jump in, leap in, hop in; **drop in,** look in, drop by *or* in, pop in <nonformal>; **barge in** *or* come barging in *and* wade in <all nonformal>; thrust in, push *or* press in, crowd in, jam in, wedge in, pack in, squeeze in; irrupt, intrude; take in, admit; insert, **penetrate; put in, stick in,** interject; make an entry, insert, write in

enterprise NOUNS 1 dynamism, **initiative,** aggression, **aggressiveness,** killer instinct, force, forcefulness, pushfulness, pushingness, **pushiness, push, drive, hustle, go,** getup, **get-up-and-go** <nonformal>, go-ahead, go-getting, go-to-itiveness <nonformal>
2 **undertaking, venture, project,** proposition *and* deal <both nonformal>; **exploit, feat, deed, achievement, adventure,** gest, **bold stroke,** heroic act *or* deed; **business, industry,** business establishment, commercial enterprise

entertain VERBS entertain guests, guest; host, preside, do the honors <nonformal>; give a party, throw a party <nonformal>; **amuse, divert,** regale, beguile, solace, recreate, refresh, enliven, exhilarate, put in good humor

entertainment NOUNS **amusement, diversion,** divertisement, *divertissement* <Fr>, **recreation, relaxation,** regalement; **pastime,** *passe-temps* <Fr>; **mirth**; **pleasure, enjoyment**

enthusiasm NOUNS **eagerness, avidity,** avidness, forwardness, prothymia, **readiness,** promptness, quickness, **alacrity,** cheerful readiness, *empressement* <Fr>; keen desire, **appetite; zest,** zestfulness, gusto, **liveliness,** life, **vitality,** vivacity, élan, spirit, animation; **vehemence, passion,** impassionedness, **ardor,** ardency

enthusiastic ADJS 1 **energetic, active, lively,** living, **animated, spirited,** go-go <nonformal>, **vivacious,** brisk, bright-eyed and bushy-tailed <nonformal>, lusty, **robust,** hearty, mettlesome, zesty, zestful, impetuous; snappy *and* zingy *and* zippy *and* peppy <all nonformal>, hearty, cordial, exuberant, unrestrained, vigorous; enthused <nonformal>, glowing, full of enthusiasm; enthusiastic about, infatuated with

2 <nonformal> **gung ho, wild about, crazy about, mad about,** ape about *or* over, gone on, all in a dither over, gaga over, starry-eyed over, all hopped up about, hepped up over, hot about *or* for *or* on, steamed up about, **turned-on, switched-on;** hipped on, **cracked on,** bugs on, freaked-out, **nuts on** *or* **over** *or* **about, keen on** *or* **about,** crazy *or* mad *or* nuts about; spanking, smacking; pumped, pumped up, jazzed-up, charged up

entice VERBS **lure,** allure, **seduce, inveigle, lead on;** come on to *and* give the come-on *and* give a come-hither look *and* bat the eyes at *and* make goo-goo eyes at <all nonformal>, flirt with, flirt; coax, cajole, blandish; draw in, suck in *and* rope in <both nonformal>; bait, offer bait to, bait the hook

entire ADJS **complete, whole, total,** global, intact, solid; **full, full-fledged,** full-dress, **full-scale; uncut,** unabbreviated, undiminished, unexpurgated

entitled ADJS **authorized,** empowered; **warranted, sanctioned; justified,** qualified, worthy; **deserved, merited,** richly deserved, earned, well-earned

entity NOUNS **something, thing,** an existence; **being,** unit, individual, entelechy, monad; **person,** persona, personality, body, soul; **creature,** created being, contingent being; **organism,** life form, living thing, **individual**

entourage NOUNS **following, cortege, retinue,** suite, followers, followership, rout, train, body of retainers; **court**

entrance NOUNS **entry,** access, entree, entrée; **ingress,** ingression; **admission, reception;** infiltration, percolation, seepage, leakage; insinuation; intrusion; introduction, **insertion**

entrance VERBS **fascinate, captivate, charm,** becharm, spell, spellbind, cast a spell, put under a spell, **beguile, intrigue, enthrall,** infatuate, **enrapture, transport, enravish, enchant,** witch, **bewitch;** carry away, sweep off one's feet, turn one's head, knock one's socks off <nonformal>

entrust VERBS assign, consign, **commit, charge,** give in charge; license, charter, warrant; sell on credit, trust

entry NOUNS 1 **entrance,** access, entree, entrée; **ingress,** ingression; **admission, reception**; gate, door, portal, **entranceway,** entryway; **opening; vestibule, portico, entrance hall, threshold; lobby, foyer**
2 item, line item, minute, note, notation; single entry, double entry; **credit, debit**

enumerate VERBS **itemize,** factorize, number, detail, break out; tabulate, catalog, tally; **register,** post, enter; **count noses** *or* **heads** <nonformal>, call the roll; quantify, quantitate, quantize

envelop VERBS **surround, environ,** compass, **encompass,** enclose, close; go round *or* around, compass about; enfold, lap, wrap, enwrap, embrace, enclasp, embosom, embay, involve, invest; **screen, cloak, veil,** screen off, curtain, blanket, shroud, enshroud

envious ADJS envying, **invidious,** green with envy; **jealous; covetous,** desirous of; resentful; **grudging, begrudging;** mean, mean-spirited, ungenerous

environment NOUNS **surroundings, environs,** surround, ambience, entourage, circle, circumjacencies, circumambiencies, **circumstances,** environing circumstances, *alentours* <Fr>, total situation, existing conditions *or* situation, set of conditions, terms of reference, context, frame, setting, surround, surrounding conditions

the environment NOUNS the natural world, global ecosystem, the biosphere, the ecosphere, the balance of nature

envision VERBS **visualize,** vision, **envisage, picture, image,** objectify; picture in one's mind, picture to oneself, **view with the mind's eye,** contemplate in the imagination, form a mental picture of, represent, **see,** have a picture of; **call up,** summon up, conjure up, **call to mind,** realize

envoy NOUNS **diplomat,** diplomatist, diplomatic agent; **emissary, legate, minister,** foreign service officer; **ambassador,** ambassadress, ambassador-at-large; envoy extraordinary, plentipotentiary, **minister plenipotentiary;** nuncio, internuncio, apostolic delegate; chargé d'affaires; **attaché,** commercial attaché, military attaché, **consul,** consul general, vice-consul

envy NOUNS 1 enviousness, **covetousness;** invidia, deadly sin of envy, **invidiousness;** grudging, grudgingness; resentment, resentfulness; meanness, meanspiritedness, ungenerousness

the tax which all distinction must pay
EMERSON

a kind of praise
JOHN GAY

VERBS 2 be envious *or* covetous of, **covet,** cast envious eyes, desire for oneself; resent; **grudge, begrudge**

epic NOUNS 1 **account, narrative,** narration, chronicle; epos, **saga**
ADJS 2 larger than life, Homeric, mighty, **titanic, colossal, monumental,** heroic, heroical, epical, towering

epidemic NOUNS 1 **plague, pestilence,** pest, pandemic, pandemia, scourge
ADJS 2 **infectious,** infective, **catching,** taking, spreading, **communicable,** zymotic; pestiferous, pestilential, epidemial, pandemic; epizootic, epiphytotic; rife, rampant, pandemic, besetting

epiphany NOUNS **manifestation, appearance;** theophany, angelophany, Satanophany, Christophany, pneumatophany, avatar; revelation, disclosure, showing forth, moment of illumination; **insight,** inspiration, *aperçu* <French>; *satori* <Japanese>, *buddhi* <Skt>

episode NOUNS **event, occurrence, incident, experience, adventure,** hap, **happening,** happenstance, **phenomenon,** fact, matter of fact, reality, particular, circumstance, **occasion,** turn of events

epitaph NOUNS inscription, *hic jacet* <L>, tombstone marking

epithet NOUNS **oath,** profane oath, curse; cuss *or* cuss word *and* dirty word *and* four-letter word *and* **swearword** <all nonformal>, naughty word, no-no <nonformal>, foul invective, **expletive,** dirty name <nonformal>, dysphemism, obscenity; **nickname, sobriquet,** agnomen

epitome NOUNS **quintessence,** embodiment, incarnation, model, pattern, purest type, typification, perfect example *or* exemplar, paragon; archetype, prototype, exemplar, mirror

equal NOUNS 1 **match,** mate, twin, fellow, **like, equivalent,** opposite number, counterpart, answer <nonformal>, vis à vis, equipollent, coequal, parallel, ditto <nonformal>; **peer,** compeer, colleague, peer group
VERBS 2 match, rival, correspond, be even-steven, be tantmount to, be equal to; **keep pace with, keep step with, run abreast; amount to,** come to, come down to, run to, reach, touch; **measure up to,** come up to, stack up with <nonformal>, match up with; lie on a level with, **balance, parallel**
ADJS 3 **equalized,** like, **alike, even,** level, par, **on a par,** at par, at parity, au pair, commensurate, proportionate; on the same level, on the same plane, on the same *or* equal footing; on terms of equality, **on even** *or* **equal terms,** on even ground; on a level playing field

equality NOUNS **parity,** par, equation, **identity**; equivalence *or* equivalency, convertibility, **correspondence,** parallelism , equipollence, coequality; **likeness,** levelness, evenness, coextension; **balance,** poise, equipoise, **equilibrium,** equiponderance

equalize VERBS **equate; even,** equal out, even up, even off, square, level, level out, level off, make both ends meet; **balance,** strike a balance, poise, balance out, balance the accounts, balance the books; **compensate,** make up for, counterpoise; countervail, counterbalance, cancel

equate VERBS **relate, associate, connect,** interconnect, ally, link, link up, wed, marry, marry up, weld, bind, tie, couple, bracket, identify; bring into relation with, bring to bear upon, apply; **interrelate,** relativize, **correlate**

equilibrium NOUNS **harmony, proportion,** symmetry, **balance,** order, orderedness, measure, measuredness, concinnity, poise, equipoise, equiponderance; steadiness, evenness, **stability**; **temperateness,** temperance, sobriety; **happy medium, golden mean,** *juste-milieu* <Fr>, middle way *or* path, *via media* <L>, balancing act <nonformal>

equip VERBS **furnish, outfit,** gear, **prepare, fit,** fit up *or* out, fix up <nonformal>, **rig,** rig up *or* out, **turn out,** appoint, accouter, clothe, dress

equipment NOUNS matériel, equipage, munitions; **fixtures, fittings, appointments, accouterments, appurtenances,** installations; outfit, apparatus, rig, machinery; paraphernalia, things, **gear, stuff** <nonformal>, impedimenta <pl>, **tackle**

equivalent NOUNS 1 **equal, match,** mate, twin, fellow, **like,** opposite number, counterpart, answer <nonformal>, vis à vis, equipollent, coequal, parallel, ditto <nonformal>; **peer,** compeer, colleague, peer group
ADJS 2 **tantamount,** equiparant, equipollent, coequal, coordinate; **identical**; corresponding *or* correspondent; convertible, much the same, as broad as long, neither more nor less, **all one,** all the same, neither here nor there

eradicate VERBS **annihilate, exterminate**, extirpate, **eliminate,** liquidate, **wipe out, stamp out,** waste *and* take out *and* nuke *and* zap <all nonformal>, put an end to; root up *or* out; **purge, liquidate**

erase VERBS **obliterate, expunge, efface, wipe out,** wipe off the map, rub out, **blot out,** sponge out, wash away; cancel, strike out, cross out, scratch, scratch out, rule out; blue-pencil; **delete** *or* dele, kill

erect VERBS 1 **elevate, rear, raise,** pitch, **set up,** raise *or* lift *or* cast up; raise *or* heave *or* rear aloft; uprear, upraise,

uplift, upheave; upright; **upend,** stand upright *or* on end; set on its feet *or* legs *or* base *or* bottom
ADJS 2 **vertical, upright,** bolt upright, ramrod straight, upstanding, standing up, stand-up; rearing, rampant; **upended,** upraised, upreared; downright

erode VERBS **decrease, waste,** wear, waste *or* wear away, crumble, ablate, corrode, consume, consume away, be eaten away; melt away, deliquesce; abrade, eat *or* wear *or* rub *or* shave *or* file away; **corrode,** eat, gnaw, eat into, eat away, nibble away

erogenous ADJS **erotic,** erogenic, erotogenic

erosion NOUNS **wear, wear and tear; weathering,** ablation, ravages of time; **waste,** wastage, **exhaustion, depletion,** sapping, depreciation, dissipation, diffusion, **wearing, wearing away,** leaching away

erotic ADJS **sexual,** sexy, amorous; **carnal, sensual**, voluptuous, fleshly; **lascivious, lecherous, salacious,** animal, **sexual, lustful,** ithyphallic, **hot,** horny *and* sexed-up *and* hot to trot <all nonformal>; prurient, itching, itchy <nonformal>; concupiscent, lickerish, libidinous, randy, horny <nonformal>, lubricious

erotica NOUNS erotic literature; pornographic literature, pornography, porn *and* hard porn *and* soft porn <all nonformal>, obscene literature, scatological literature

err VERBS fall into error, **go wrong, go amiss,** go astray, go *or* get out of line, go awry, stray, get off-base <nonformal>, **deviate,** wander; **lapse, slip, slip up,** trip, stumble; **miscalculate**

errand NOUNS **task, assignment, charge,** project, **mission,** commission, **duty,** service, exercise

errant ADJS **deviative,** deviatory, deviating, **deviant,** departing, aberrant, aberrational, aberrative, shifting, turning, swerving, veering; **digressive,** discursive, excursive, **circuitous; devious,** indirect, out-of-the-way; erratic, zigzag, doglegged, **wandering,** rambling, roving, winding, twisting, meandering

erratic ADJS **capricious,** whimsical, variable, wavering, **changeable**; **indecisive, irresolute** unnatural, abnormal, irregular, divergent, deviative, deviant, different, exceptional; unconventional; **eccentric,** idiocratic, idiocratical, idiosyncratic, idiosyncratical, **queer,** queer in the head, **odd, peculiar,** strange, fey, singular, anomalous, freakish, funny

erroneous ADJS **untrue,** not true, **not right;** unfactual, **wrong,** all wrong; peccant, perverse, corrupt; **false, fallacious,** self-contradictory; **illogical**; **fallible; faulty,** faultful, flawed, defective, **at fault;** out, off, all off, off the track *or* rails

error NOUNS 1 **erroneousness; untrueness,** untruthfulness, **untruth; wrongness, wrong; falseness, falsity; fallacy, fallaciousness,** self-contradiction; fault, **faultiness,** defectiveness; misdoing, misfeasance; errancy, aberrancy, aberration, **deviancy; heresy,** unorthodoxy, heterodoxy; **mistake,** *erratum* <L>, *corrigendum* <L>; misidentification; **misjudgment, miscalculation**; misplay

2 <nonformal> **goof, boo-boo,** muff, flub, foozle, bloomer, bloop, blooper, boot, bobble, boner, bonehead play *or* trick, dumb trick, boob stunt, fool mistake; howler, clanger <Brit>, screamer; fuck-up, screw-up, foul-up, snafu, muck-up, balls-up <Brit>, louse-up; pratfall, whoops

erupt VERBS **burst forth,** break forth, debouch, irrupt, explode; **pop up, bob up** <nonformal>, start up, spring up, burst upon the view; flare up, flash, gleam; **find vent,** issue forth, come forth, exit, **emerge, issue,** break out, break through; **spew,** jet, spout, squirt, **spurt**

escapade NOUNS **revel, lark, party**; **spree, bout, fling,** wingding *and* randan <both nonformal>; **carouse, drinking bout**

escape NOUNS 1 **getaway** *and* break *and* breakout <all nonformal>; **deliverance; delivery,** riddance, **release,** setting-free, freeing, **liberation, extrication, rescue;** emergence, issuance, issue, outlet, vent
VERBS 2 make *or* effect one's escape, make good one's escape; **get away, make a getaway** <nonformal>; **free oneself,** deliver oneself, gain one's liberty, **get free, get clear of,** bail out, **get out, get out of,** get well out of; **break loose,** cut loose, break away, break one's

bonds *or* chains, slip the collar, shake off the yoke; **jump** *and* **skip** <both nonformal>; **break jail** *or* **prison,** fly the coop <nonformal>

escort NOUNS 1 **conductor, usher,** shepherd; **guide,** tourist guide, cicerone; **chaperon,** duenna; **bodyguard,** guard, **convoy;** companion, sidekick <nonformal>, travel companion
VERBS 2 **conduct,** have in tow <nonformal>, marshal, **usher,** shepherd, **guide, lead; convoy,** guard; **squire, attend,** wait on *or* upon, **take out** <nonformal>; **chaperon**

esoteric ADJS **occult, esoterical, mysterious,** mystic, mystical, anagogic, anagogical; metaphysic, metaphysical; cabalic, cabalistic; **paranormal, supernatural**; theosophical, theosophist, anthroposophical

ESP NOUNS **extrasensory perception; clairvoyance,** lucidity, second sight, insight, sixth sense; intuition; foresight; premonition; clairsentience, clairaudience, crystal vision, psychometry, metapsychosis

espionage NOUNS **spying,** espial, **intelligence,** military intelligence, intelligence work, cloak-and-dagger work <nonformal>; counterespionage, counterintelligence; wiretap, wiretapping, bugging <nonformal>, electronic surveillance

esprit NOUNS **liveliness, vivacity, vitality,** life, **animation, spiritedness, spirit,** élan, **sprightliness,** high spirits, zestfulness, zest, vim, zip <nonformal>, vigor, verve, gusto, **exuberance,** heartiness; solidarity, team spirit, *esprit de corps* <Fr>

essence NOUNS 1 **substance,** stuff, very stuff, inner essence, essential nature, quiddity, **core,** kernel, marrow, pith, sap, spirit, quintessence, elixir, distillate, **extract,** distillation, distilled essence; sine qua non, irreducible *or* indispensable content

2 <nonformal> **meat and potatoes,** nuts and bolts, the nitty-gritty, the guts, the name of the game, the bottom line, where it's at, what it's all about, the ball game, the payoff, the score, where the rubber meets the road

essential NOUNS 1 **requirement, necessity,** desideratum, desideration; prerequisite, prerequirement; **must,** must item; indispensable; the necessary, the needful; necessities, necessaries, essentials, bare necessities
ADJS 2 of the essence, **fundamental; primary,** primitive, primal, elementary, elemental, simple, bare-bones *and* no-frills *and* bread-and-butter <all nonformal>, original, *ab ovo* <L>, **basic, gut** <nonformal>, basal, underlying; **substantive,** substantial, material; constitutive, constituent

establish VERBS **found,** constitute, institute, install, form, **set up, organize,** equip, endow, inaugurate, realize, materialize, effect, effectuate; fix, **determine, ascertain,** make out, remove all doubt; **settle,** settle the matter

establishment NOUNS **foundation,** constitution, institution, installation, formation, **organization,** inauguration, **inception, setting-up,** realization, materialization, effectuation; **determination, settlement, proof**

the Establishment NOUNS **the authorities, the powers that be,** ruling class, the lords of creation, the interests, the power elite, **the power structure;** the inner circle; the ins *and* the in-group *and* those on the inside <all nonformal>; **top brass** <nonformal>; higher-ups *and* the people upstairs *or* in the front office <all nonformal>; the corridors of power

esteem NOUNS 1 estimation, **honor, regard, respect,** approval, approbation, account, favor, consideration, **credit,** points *and* Brownie points <both nonformal>; prestige, repute, reputation, honor, glory, renown, dignity, **fame**
VERBS 2 **respect,** entertain respect for, accord respect to, **regard,** hold in esteem *or* consideration, favor, **admire,** think much of, think well of, think highly of, have *or* hold a high opinion of; **appreciate, value,** prize, **rate highly, think much of,** set store by

estimate NOUNS 1 **estimation; view, opinion**; **assessment,** assessing, **appraisal,** appraisement, appraising, appreciation, reckoning, **stocktaking,** valuation, valuing, **evaluation,** evaluating, value judgment, evaluative criticism, analyzing, weighing, weighing up, gauging, ranking, rank-ordering, **rating;** measurement; comparison
VERBS 2 form an estimate, make an estimation; **reckon,** call, guess, figure

<nonformal>; **assess, appraise,** give an appreciation, **gauge, rate, rank,** rank-order, put in rank order, class, mark, **value, evaluate,** place *or* set a value on, weigh, weigh up, prize, appreciate; size up *or* take one's measure <nonformal>, **measure**

et cetera NOUNS **etc, and so forth, and so on,** *und so weiter* <Ger>; **et al,** *et alii* <L>, and all <nonformal>, and others, and other things, *cum multis aliis* <L, with many others>; and everything else, **and more of the same, and the rest, and the like;** and stuff like that *and* and all that jazz <both nonformal>; **and what not** *and* and what have you *and* and I don't know what *and* and God knows what *and* and then some *and* you name it<all nonformal>; and the following, *et sequens* <L>, et seq

eternal ADJS **perpetual, everlasting,** everliving, ever-being, ever-abiding, ever-during, ever-durable, permanent, perdurable, indestructible; sempiternal, **infinite**, aeonian *or* eonian; dateless, ageless, timeless, immemorial; **endless,** unending, never-ending, without end, **interminable,** nonterminous, nonterminating; **continual,** continuous, steady, **constant, ceaseless,** nonstop, unceasing, never-ceasing, **incessant,** unremitting, unintermitting, uninterrupted

eternity NOUNS **perpetuity,** perpetualness; eternalness, sempiternity, infinite duration; everness, foreverness, **everlastingness, permanence**, perdurability, indestructibility; timelessness; **endlessness,** never-endingness, **interminability; infinity**

ethical ADJS **moral,** moralistic; **honest, upright,** uprighteous, **upstanding,** erect, right, **righteous, virtuous, good,** clean, squeaky-clean <nonformal>, **decent; honorable,** full of integrity, **reputable,** estimable, creditable, worthy, noble, sterling, manly, yeomanly; **respectable,** highly respectable; principled, high-principled, high-minded, right-minded; uncorrupt, uncorrupted, inviolate

ethics NOUNS **principles,** standards, norms, principles of conduct *or* behavior, principles of professional practice; **morals,** moral principles; code, ethical *or* moral code, **ethic,** code of morals *or* ethics, ethical system, value system, axiology; moral climate, **ethos,** *Zeitgeist* <Ger>

ethnic ADJS **racial, tribal, national, family,** clannish, totemic, **lineal;** phyletic, phylogenetic, genetic

etiquette NOUNS social code, rules *or* code of conduct; **formalities,** social procedures, social conduct, what is done, what one does; **manners,** good manners, exquisite manners, quiet good manners, **politeness,** *politesse* <Fr>, natural politeness, comity, civility; **amenities,** decencies, civilities, elegancies, **social graces, mores, proprieties;** decorum, good form

eulogy NOUNS **praise,** bepraisement; **laudation,** laud; *éloge* and *hommage* <both Fr>, eulogium; **encomium,** accolade, kudos, panegyric; paean; **tribute,** homage; funeral oration

euphemism NOUNS **overniceness,** overpreciseness, **overrefinement, elegance,** exquisiteness, preciousness, preciosity; goody-goodyism *and* goody-goodness <both nonformal>; purism

euphoric ADJS **in high spirits,** exalted, **elated,** exhilarated, high <nonformal>; irrepressible; **blithe,** blithesome; **happy,** happy as a clam *or* a lark, on top of the world, sitting on top of the world, sitting pretty; sanguine, sanguineous, eupeptic; **irrepressible**

evacuate VERBS **vacate,** abandon, desert, turn one's back on, walk away from, leave to one's fate, leave flat *or* high and dry; **withdraw,** retreat, **beat a retreat,** retire, remove; walk away, abscond, disappear, vanish; **bow out** <nonformal>, make one's exit; jump ship

evade VERBS **elude,** beg, **get out of,** shuffle out of, skirt, **get around** <nonformal>, circumvent; give one the runaround; ditch *and* shake *and* shake off <all nonformal>, get away from, give the runaround *or* the slip <nonformal>; lead one a chase *or* merry chase; **equivocate,** prevaricate, tergiversate, doubletalk, doublespeak, tap-dance <nonformal>, palter, **shuffle, dodge,** shy, sidestep, hedge, evade the issue; **beat about** *or* **around the bush,** not come to the point, **beg the question**

evaluate VERBS **estimate,** form an estimate, make an estimation; **reckon,** call, guess, figure <nonformal>; **assess, appraise,** give an appreciation, **gauge, rate, rank,** rank-order, put in rank order, class, mark, **value,** valuate, place *or* set a value on, weigh, weigh up, prize, appreciate

evangelical ADJS evangelic, evangelistic, gospel; **strict,** scripturalistic; hyperorthodox, puritanical, purist *or* puristic, straitlaced

evangelist NOUNS revivalist, evangel, evangelicalist; **missionary,** missioner; missionary apostolic, missionary rector, colporteur; television *or* TV evangelist, televangelist <nonformal>

evaporate VERBS **vanish,** dematerialize, evanesce, **vanish into thin air,** go up in smoke; disperse, dispel, dissipate; cease, cease to exist, **cease to be;** leave no trace, disappear, fade, fade away *or* out, fly, flee, dissolve, melt away, die out *or* away, pass, pass away, pass out of the picture <nonformal>, turn to nothing *or* naught, peter out <nonformal>, come to an end, wind down, tail off *and* trail off <both nonformal>; volatilize

evasion NOUNS **prevarication, equivocation,** hedging, pussyfooting <nonformal>, **sidestepping,** tergiversation, shuffle, fencing, dodging, parrying, waffling *and* tap-dancing <both nonformal>; *suppressio veri* <L>; weasel words; elusion; **evasiveness,** subterfuge; hugger-mugger, hugger-muggery

even ADJS 1 **smooth;** smooth-textured *or* -surfaced, **level, plane, flat,** regular, uniform, **unbroken**
2 **equal, equalized,** like, **alike,** par, **on a par,** at par, at parity, au pair, commensurate, proportionate; **drawn, tied,** neck-and-neck <nonformal>, too close to call
ADVS 3 **exactly, precisely,** to a T, expressly; **just,** right, straight, square, **plumb,** directly, squarely, point-blank; unerringly, undeviatingly; **faithfully, strictly, rigorously,** rigidly; in every respect, in all respects, for all the world, neither more nor less

evening NOUNS **eve,** even, evensong time *or* hour, **eventide,** vesper; **close of day,** decline *or* fall of day, when day is done; **nightfall, sunset, sundown,** setting sun

event NOUNS **occurrence, incident, episode, experience, adventure,** hap, **happening,** happenstance, **phenomenon,** fact, matter of fact, reality, particular, circumstance, **occasion,** turn of events

eventuality NOUNS **possibility,** possibleness, **the realm of possibility,** the domain of the possible, conceivableness, **conceivability,** thinkability, thinkableness, imaginability; contingency, **chance, prospect; outside chance** <nonformal>, off chance, remote possibility

ever ADVS **forever, forevermore, for ever and ever,** forever and aye; forever and a day <nonformal>, now and forever, *ora e sempre* <Ital>, **evermore,** ever and anon, ever and again; **constantly, continually, steadily,** sustainedly, **regularly,** as regular as clockwork, with every other breath, every time one turns around, unvaryingly, uninterruptedly, **incessantly, ceaselessly,** without letup *or* break *or* intermission, without stopping; **perpetually, always, at all,** if at all

yesterday and today and forever
BIBLE

evergreen ADJS **perennial,** indeciduous, sempervirent, ever-new, ever-young; ever-blooming, ever-bearing

everlasting ADJS **perpetual,** everliving, permanent, perdurable, indestructible; **immortal, deathless,** undying, neverdying, **imperishable,** incorruptible, amaranthine; **endless,** unending, neverending, without end, **interminable, constant, ceaseless,** nonstop, unceasing, never-ceasing, **incessant,** unremitting, uninterrupted

every ADJS **all,** any, whichever, whichsoever; **each,** each one; every one, each and every, each and all, **one and all, all and sundry**

everybody NOUNS **all, everyone, each and everyone, one and all,** all comers *and* all hands *and* every man Jack *and* every mother's son <all nonformal>, every living soul, **all the world,** *tout le monde* <Fr>, **whole, totality**

everyday ADJS **usual, regular; common, commonplace, ordinary, average,** mediocre, familiar, household, vernacular, stock; **prevailing, predominating,** current, popular

everyone NOUNS **the populace, the public,** the general public, people in general, everybody; **the population,** the citizenry, the whole people, the polity, the body politic; ordinary people, **persons, folk, folks,** gentry; plain people *or* folks, the rank and file, **all, each and everyone, one and all,** every living soul

everything NOUNS **all, the whole, the**

entirety, all the above *or* all of the above <both nonformal>, the aggregate, the assemblage, one and all, all and sundry, each and every <nonformal>; everything from soup to nuts *and* everything but the kitchen sink <both nonformal>

everywhere ADJS 1 **omnipresent, all-present,** ubiquitous; continuous, uninterrupted, infinite
ADVS 2 **here, there, and everywhere;** in every place, in all places, in every quarter, in all quarters; **all over,** all over hell *and* all over the map *and* all over the place *and* all over town <all nonformal>, all over the world, the world over, on the face of the earth, under the sun, throughout the world

evict VERBS **oust,** dislodge, dispossess, put out, turn out, **turn out of doors,** turn out of house and home, turn *or* put out bag and baggage, throw into the street; unhouse, unkennel

evidence NOUNS **proof; reason to believe,** grounds for belief; **ground, grounds,** material grounds, **facts, data,** premises, basis for belief; piece *or* item of evidence, **fact,** datum, relevant fact; **indication, manifestation, sign, symptom,** mark, token, mute witness; body of evidence, documentation

evil NOUNS 1 **iniquity,** bad, wrong, error, obliquity, villainy, knavery, reprobacy, peccancy, **abomination, atrocity, infamy,** shame, disgrace, scandal, unforgivable *or* cardinal *or* mortal sin, **sin**
ADJS 2 **wicked, vicious, bad, naughty, wrong, sinful, iniquitous,** peccant, reprobate; dark, black; **base, low, vile,** foul, rank, flagrant, arrant, nefarious, **heinous,** villainous, criminal, up to no good, knavish, flagitious; abominable, atrocious, monstrous, unspeakable, execrable, damnable; shameful, disgraceful, scandalous, **infamous, unpardonable,** unforgivable

evil eye NOUNS **spell,** *malocchio* <Ital>, whammy <nonformal>; **hex,** evil genius, **hoodoo** *and* **jinx** <both nonformal>, **Jonah; curse,** enchantment, whammy *and* double *or* triple whammy <all nonformal>

evince VERBS **evidence, show,** tend to show, witness to, testify to; **demonstrate, illustrate,** exhibit, manifest, display, express, set forth; **indicate, signify,** signalize, mark, **denote, betoken, point to,** give indication of, show signs of, bear on, touch on

evocative ADJS elicitory, arousing; **reminiscent, mindful, remindful, suggestive,** redolent

evoke VERBS **call up, summon up,** call *or* summon forth, call out; rouse, arouse, stimulate; **draw out** *or* **forth,** bring out *or* forth, pry *or* prize out, drag out, worm out, bring to light; **prompt, provoke,** muster up, inspire; put one in mind of <nonformal>, remind one of, bring to mind, be reminiscent of, suggest

evolution NOUNS **evolving,** evolvement; evolutionary change, gradual change, step-by-step change, peaceful *or* nonviolent change; **development, growth,** rise, incremental change, natural growth *or* development; flowering, blossoming; ripening, coming of age, maturation; **advance,** advancement, furtherance

evolve VERBS **develop, grow,** wax, change gradually *or* step-by-step; **progress, advance,** come a long way; ripen, mellow, mature, maturate; flower, bloom, blossom

exact ADJS **precise,** express; even, square; absolutely *or* definitely *or* positively right; **faithful;** direct; **unerring,** undeviating, constant; **infallible,** inerrant, inerrable

exacting VERBS **meticulous, scrupulous, conscientious,** religious, punctilious, punctual, **particular, fussy, critical, attentive,** scrutinizing; **thorough,** thoroughgoing, thoroughpaced; **exact, precise,** precisionistic, precisianistic, prissy, **accurate, correct; strict,** exigent, demanding, not to be trifled with, **stringent,** astringent; disciplined, spit-and-polish; **severe, harsh,** dour, unsparing

exaggerate VERBS hyperbolize; **overstate,** overspeak <old>, overreach, **overdraw,** overcharge; overstress; **overdo, carry too far, go to extremes;** push to the extreme, indulge in overkill, overestimate; overpraise, oversell, tout, puff *and* ballyhoo <both nonformal>; **stretch,** stretch the truth, stretch the point, draw the longbow; **magnify, inflate;** pile *or* lay it on *and* pour *or* spread *or* lay it on thick *and* lay it on with a trowel <all nonformal>; talk big <nonformal>, make much of; make a

Federal case out of it <nonformal>, something out of nothing, make a mountain out of a molehill; caricature, travesty, burlesque

exaggeration NOUNS **overstatement,** big *or* tall talk <nonformal>, **hyperbole,** hyperbolism; **magnification, enlargement,** dilation, dilatation, **inflation,** expansion, blowing up, puffing up, aggrandizement; **stretching, heightening,** enhancement; burlesque, travesty, caricature; sensationalism, puffery *and* ballyhoo <both nonformal>, touting, huckstering; grandiloquence

exalted ADJS **eminent, prominent,** outstanding, standout, high, elevated, towering, soaring, overtopping, **lofty,** sublime; august, majestic, noble, distinguished; **magnificent,** magnanimous, heroic, godlike, superb; famous, renowned, lauded, glorious; blessed, consecrated, devoted; **glorified,** enskied; **saintly,** sainted, beatified, canonized

examination NOUNS **discussion, debate,** debating, **deliberation,** exchange of views, canvassing, ventilation, airing, review, **treatment, consideration,** investigation, **study, analysis,** logical analysis; logical discussion, dialectic; survey, **discourse,** disquisition, lucubration, étude; school examination, examen, **test, quiz;** oral examination, viva voce examination, viva <nonformal>; inspection, scrutiny

examine VERBS **discuss, debate, reason, deliberate,** exchange views *or* opinions, **talk over, hash over** <nonformal>, talk of *or* about, comment upon, **consider, treat,** dissertate on, handle, deal with, take up, **go into,** investigate, talk out, **analyze,** sift, **study,** canvass, review, pass under review, scrutinize, inspect, controvert, ventilate, air, thresh out, **kick** *or* **knock around** <nonformal>

example NOUNS exemplar; **representative,** type, symbol, emblem, exponent; **exemplification,** illustration, demonstration, explanation; **instance,** relevant instance, **case,** typical example *or* case, case in point, object lesson

exasperate VERBS **provoke, incense,** arouse, inflame, embitter; **vex, irritate, annoy, aggravate** <nonformal>, **nettle,** fret, chafe; **pique, peeve** *and* miff <both nonformal>, huff; **ruffle, roil, rile** <nonformal>, ruffle one's feathers, **rankle;** bristle, put *or* get one's back up, stick in one's craw <nonformal>

excavation NOUNS **deepening, lowering, depression;** digging, mining, tunneling; drilling, probing; **pit, well, shaft,** sump; dig, diggings, workings; mine, quarry

exceed VERBS **surpass, pass, top, transcend, go beyond;** overpass, overstep, overrun, **overreach,** overshoot, overshoot the mark

excel VERBS **surpass, exceed, transcend,** get *or* have the ascendancy, get *or* have the edge, have it all over <nonformal>, overcome, overpass, best, **better,** improve on, perfect, go one better <nonformal>; **cap,** trump; top, tower above *or* over, overtop; **predominate,** prevail, preponderate; **excel in** *or* **at, shine in** *or* **at** <nonformal>, be master of; **have a gift** *or* **flair** *or* **talent** *or* **bent** *or* **faculty** *or* **turn for,** be a natural *and* be cut out *or* born to be <both nonformal>

excellence NOUNS **goodness, quality,** class <nonformal>; **virtue,** grace; **superiority,** first-rateness, **skillfulness**

excellent ADJS **surpassing, exceeding, excelling, rivaling, eclipsing,** capping, topping, **transcending,** transcendent *or* transcendental; a cut *or* stroke above, one up on <nonformal>; more than a match for

exception NOUNS **exemption, immunity;** special case *or* privilege; privilege; **exclusion, barring,** debarring, debarment, preclusion, omission, nonadmission, cutting-out, leaving-out; **restriction, circumscription,** narrowing, demarcation; **reservation,** waiver

excerpt NOUNS **extract, selection,** extraction, excerption, snippet; passage, selected passage; **clip** <nonformal>, film clip, outtake, sound bite <nonformal>
VERBS 2 **select,** make a selection; **pick,** handpick, **pick out, single out,** choose out, smile on, give the nod <nonformal>, jump at, seize on; extract, cull, glean, winnow, sift

excess NOUNS 1 **surplus,** surplusage, overplus, overage; superfluity, redundancy; overestimation; exaggerated lengths, **extreme,** exorbitance, inordinacy, **overkill;** grandiloquence; **excessiveness,** too much, too-muchness <nonformal>
ADJS 2 **superfluous, redundant; in excess;** unnecessary, unessential, nonessential, expendable, dispensable,

needless, unneeded, gratuitous, uncalled-for; verbose, prolix; *de trop* <Fr>, supererogatory, supererogative

exchange NOUNS 1 **retaliation, reciprocation,** interchange, give-and-take; **retort, reply,** return, comeback <nonformal>; counterblow, counterblast, recoil, boomerang, backlash; **substitution, change,** switch, switcheroo <nonformal>, commutation, subrogation; tit for tat, *quid pro quo* <L>
VERBS 2 **interchange,** change, counterchange; alternate; **transpose;** convert, commute, permute; **trade, swap** <nonformal>, **switch;** bandy, bandy about, play at battledore and shuttlecock; **reciprocate, trade off,** compromise, settle, settle for, respond, keep a balance; give tit for tat, **retaliate**

excitement NOUNS emotion, excitedness, **arousal, stimulation, exhilaration;** a high <nonformal>, manic state *or* condition; **excitation, arousal,** arousing, **stirring,** stirring up, working up, working into a lather <nonformal>, lathering up, whipping up, steaming up, **agitation, perturbation**

exciting ADJS **thrilling,** thrilly <nonformal>, **stirring, moving, breathtaking,** eye-popping <nonformal>; agitating, agitative, perturbing, disturbing, upsetting, troubling, disquieting, unsettling, distracting, jolting, jarring; heart-stirring, heart-swelling, heart-expanding, soul-stirring, spirit-stirring, deep-thrilling, mind-blowing <nonformal>; **stimulating,** stimulative, stimulatory; exhilarating, heady, intoxicating, maddening, ravishing

exclaim VERBS give an exclamation, burst out, blurt, blurt out, jerk out, spout out; stammer out

exclamation NOUNS outburst, blurt, ecphonesis; expletive, interjection

exclude VERBS **bar,** debar, bar out, lock out, **shut out, keep out,** count out <nonformal>, close the door on, close out, cut out, cut off, preclude; **reject, repudiate,** blackball *and* turn thumbs down on <both nonformal>, read *or* drum out, ease *or* freeze out *and* leave *or* keep out in the cold <all nonformal>, ostracize, wave off *or* aside

exclusive ADJS selective, **select,** elect, elite; **cliquish,** clannish; **snobbish,** snobby; excluding, exclusory; seclusive, preclusive, exceptional, inadmissible, prohibitive, preventive, prescriptive, restrictive; narrow, insular, parochial, ethnocentric, xenophobic, snobbish

excrement NOUNS dejection, dejecta, **discharge,** ejection; matter; **waste,** waste matter; **excreta,** egesta, ejecta, ejectamenta; exudation, exudate; transudation, transudate; extravasation, extravasate; effluent

excruciating ADJS **agonizing, harrowing,** racking, rending, **desolating,** consuming; **tormenting,** torturous; **heartbreaking,** heartrending, **heartsickening**

excursion NOUNS **journey, jaunt, junket, outing,** pleasure trip; sight-seeing trip *or* tour, rubberneck tour <nonformal>; day-trip; round trip, circuit, turn; **cruise,** package cruise, cruise to nowhere

excuse NOUNS 1 **cop-out** *and* **alibi** *and* **out** <all nonformal>; lame excuse, poor excuse, likely story; escape hatch, way out; **apology,** regrets
VERBS 2 **forgive, pardon,** give *or* grant forgiveness, spare; grant amnesty to, grant immunity *or* exemption; **exonerate, exculpate;** spare, except, grant immunity, make a special case of; absolve

execute VERBS 1 **complete,** transact, promulgate, **make;** make out, fill out; **discharge, fulfill,** render, administer; **carry out,** carry through, put through, prosecute; effect, effectuate, set in motion, implement; enforce, put in force; **abide by, honor, live up to,** adhere to, live by, **observe**
2 **put to death,** inflict capital punishment; **electrocute,** burn *and* fry <nonformal>; send to the gas chamber; **behead, decapitate,** decollate, guillotine, bring to the block; **shoot,** execute by firing squad; burn, **burn at the stake; strangle,** garrote, bowstring; stone, lapidate; defenestrate

execution NOUNS 1 **completion;** transaction; carrying out, discharge, fulfillment, prosecution, effectuation; enforcement; observance
2 **capital punishment; hanging,** the gallows, the rope *or* noose; summary execution; **electrocution,** the chair <nonformal>, the hot seat <nonformal>; gassing, the gas chamber; lethal injection; **decapitation,** decollation, beheading, the guillotine, the ax, the block

executive NOUNS 1 officer, official; **president,** prexy <nonformal>, chief executive officer; policy-maker, agenda-setter
ADJS 2 **administrative, administrating;** ministerial; **officiating, presiding;** supervisory, directing, managing

exempt VERBS **free, release,** discharge, **let go** *and* **let off** <both nonformal>, set at liberty, spring <nonformal>; **excuse,** spare, except, grant immunity, make a special case of; grandfather; **dispense,** dispense from, give dispensation from; dispense with, save the necessity; remit, remise; absolve

exemption NOUNS exception, **immunity; release,** discharge; diplomatic immunity, congressional *or* legislative immunity; special case *or* privilege; privilege; permission

exercise NOUNS 1 exercising; **practice, drill, workout;** yoga; constitutional <nonformal>, stretch; violent exercise; physical education
VERBS 2 **work out,** warm up, aerobicize, stretch, lift weights, pump iron <nonformal>, jog, run, bicycle, walk, fitness-walk, power-walk
3 **use, utilize, make use of,** do with; **employ,** practice, ply, work, manage, handle, manipulate, operate, **wield,** play; **have** *or* **enjoy the use of**

exert VERBS **exercise, ply, employ, use, put forth,** put out *and* make with <both nonformal>; practice

exertion NOUNS **effort, energy,** elbow grease; **endeavor**; **trouble, pains;** great *or* mighty effort, might and main, muscle, one's back, hard *or* strong *or* long pull

exhaust VERBS 1 **fatigue, tire, weary,** wilt, flag, jade, harass; **wear,** wear on *or* upon, **wear down; tire out, wear out, burn out; use up; do in; wind,** put out of breath; overtire, overstrain; weaken, enervate, debilitate; weary *or* tire to death; prostrate
2 **run out,** empty, find vent; **drain,** drain out; **draw off,** draft, draw, draw from; **suck,** suck out *or* up, **siphon off**

exhaustion NOUNS 1 exhaustedness, draining; **collapse, prostration,** breakdown, crack-up <nonformal>, nervous exhaustion *or* prostration
2 **depletion,** drain, exhausting, impoverishment; **waste,** sapping, depreciation, dissipation, diffusion, **wearing, wearing away, erosion,** ablation, leaching away

exhaustive ADJS **thorough, thoroughgoing,** thorough-paced, intensive, broad-based, house-to-house *and* door-to-door <both nonformal>, A-to-Z, comprehensive, all-embracing, all-encompassing, omnibus, radical, sweeping

exhibit NOUNS 1 presentation, presentment, **exhibition, exposition,** retrospective
VERBS 2 **evidence, evince,** furnish evidence, **show, go to show, mean,** tend to show, witness to, testify to; **demonstrate, illustrate,** manifest, display, express, set forth; **attest; indicate, signify,** signalize, symptomatize, mark, **denote, betoken, point to,** give indication of, show signs of, bear on, touch on

exhibition NOUNS **display, show, demonstration,** manifestation, **parade,** *étalage* <Fr>; **pageantry,** pageant, **spectacle;** vaunt, fanfaronade, blazon, flourish, flaunt, flaunting

exhilarate VERBS **stimulate,** invigorate, fortify, enliven, liven up, animate, vivify, quicken; brace, **brace up,** buck up *and* pick up <both nonformal>, set on one's legs *or* feet <nonformal>; renew one's strength, put *or* breathe new life into, give a breath of fresh air, give a shot in the arm <nonformal>; **animate,** enliven

exigency NOUNS **urgency,** imperativeness, exigence *or* exigency; **momentousness, crucialness, cruciality;** consequentiality, consequentialness; **press,** pressure, high pressure, **stress,** tension, **pinch;** clutch *and* crunch <both nonformal>

exile NOUNS 1 **banishment, expatriation,** exilement; outlawing *or* outlawry; **ostracism,** ostracization, thumbs-down, thumbing-down, *pollice verso* <L>, blackballing; **deportation,** transportation, **extradition**
VERBS 2 **banish, expatriate, deport,** transport, send away, **extradite; deport; outlaw,** ban, proscribe

exist VERBS **be,** be in existence, be extant, have being; breathe, **live**; subsist, stand, obtain, hold, prevail, be the case; **occur,** be present, be there, be found, be met with, happen to be

existence NOUNS **being;** subsistence, entity, essence, absolute *or* transcendental essence, *l'être* <Fr>, pure being, *Ding-an-sich* <Ger, thing-in-itself>, noumenon; **occurrence,** presence

exit NOUNS 1 **egress,** egression; exodus;

outgoing, outgo, going out; emersion *or* egress <astronomy>; **departure**; extraction
VERBS 2 make an exit, **make one's exit;** egress, **go out,** get out, walk out, march out, run out, pass out, bow out *and* include oneself out <both nonformal>; walk out on, leave cold <nonformal>; **depart**

exodus NOUNS **egress,** egression; **exit,** outgoing, outgo, going out; **departure**; extraction; hegira

exonerate VERBS **acquit, clear, exculpate, absolve,** bring in *or* return a verdict of not guilty; **pardon, excuse, forgive;** remit, grant remission, remit the penalty of; amnesty, grant *or* extend amnesty

exorbitant ADJS **overpriced,** grossly overpriced, **excessive, extravagant, inordinate, immoderate,** undue, unwarranted, unreasonable, fancy, unconscionable, outrageous, preposterous, out of bounds, out of sight <nonformal>, **prohibitive; extortionate,** cutthroat, **gouging, usurious,** exacting

exotic ADJS **distant,** distal, **remote, removed, far, far-off,** away, **faraway,** way-off, at a distance, separated, apart, asunder; **alluring, fascinating, captivating, riveting, charming, glamorous, enchanting,** spellful, spellbinding, **entrancing,** ravishing, **enravishing, intriguing, enthralling,** witching, **bewitching; foreign, alien,** strange, foreign-looking

expand VERBS **enlarge, extend, widen, broaden,** build, build up, aggrandize, **amplify,** crescendo, **magnify, increase**, augment, add to, raise, up, scale up, hike *or* hike up; **stretch, distend, dilate, swell, inflate,** sufflate, **blow up,** puff up, huff, puff, bloat; pump, pump up; rarefy

expanse NOUNS **immensity,** enormousness, **vastness,** vastitude, tremendousness, boundlessness, infinity; stupendousness, formidableness, prodigiousness, humongousness <nonformal>

expansive ADJS **extensive;** expansional, extensional; expansile, extensile, elastic; expansible, inflatable; distensive, dilatant; inflationary; spacious, **roomy;** ample, full

expect VERBS be expectant, **anticipate, have in prospect,** face, think, **contemplate,** have in contemplation *or* mind, envision, envisage; **hope**; presume; dread; **take for granted;** not be surprised *or* a bit surprised; foresee

expectation NOUNS expectance *or* **expectancy,** state of expectancy; **predictability,** predictableness; **anticipation, prospect,** thought; probability; confidence, reliance, overreliance; certainty

expedient ADJS **desirable,** to be desired, much to be desired, **advisable, politic,** recommendable; **appropriate, meet, fit, fitting,** befitting, **right, proper,** good, seemly, likely, congruous, **suitable,** sortable, feasible, doable, **convenient,** happy, heaven-sent, felicitous; timely, seasonable, opportune, well-timed, in the nick of time

expedite VERBS **advance, further, promote,** forward, hasten, contribute to, foster, aid, facilitate, abet; **send, dispatch,** transmit, remit, consign

expedition NOUNS **journey, trip,** *jornada* <Sp>, peregrination, sally, **trek; adventure,** emprise, **mission;** quest, pilgrimage; exploration

expel VERBS **banish, cast out,** thrust out, exclude, **excommunicate; exile, expatriate, deport,** transport, send away, **extradite; deport; dismiss, discharge, cashier,** drum out, throw out, **cast forth,** send out *or* forth

expendable ADJS **consumable,** spendable; exhaustible; replaceable; disposable, throwaway, no-deposit, no-deposit-no-return; **superfluous, redundant;** unnecessary, unessential, nonessential, dispensable, **needless,** unneeded, gratuitous, uncalled-for

expensive ADJS **dear, costly,** of great cost, dear-bought, **high, high-priced,** premium, at a premium, top; big ticket <nonformal>, **fancy** *and* stiff *and* steep <all nonformal>, pricey; upmarket, upscale <nonformal> rich, sumptuous, **luxurious**, gold-plated

experience NOUNS 1 **practice,** practical knowledge *or* skill, hands-on experience <nonformal>, field-work; background, past experience, seasoning, tempering; **worldly wisdom,** knowledge of the world, blaséness, **sophistication; occurrence, incident, episode, adventure**
VERBS 2 **have, know, feel,** taste; **encounter, undergo, go through,** pass through, be subjected to, be exposed to, **endure, suffer,** sustain

experienced ADJS **practiced,** mature, matured, ripe, ripened, **seasoned,** tried, well-tried, tried and true, **veteran,** an old dog at <nonformal>; **worldly, worldly-wise,** world-wise, wise in the ways of the world, knowing, **sophisticated,** cosmopolitan, cosmopolite, blasé, dry behind the ears, not born yesterday, long in the tooth

experiment NOUNS 1 **experimentation;** testing, trying, trying-out, **trial; trial and error,** cut and try <nonformal>; empiricism, experimentalism, pragmatism, instrumentalism

VERBS 2 **research,** make an experiment, **run an experiment,** run a sample *or* specimen; **test, try,** essay, cut and try <nonformal>, **test** *or* **try out,** have a dry run *or* dummy run *or* rehearsal *or* test run; put to the test, **put to the proof, prove, verify,** validate, substantiate, confirm

expert NOUNS 1 **adept,** proficient; **specialist,** specializer, **authority,** savant, scholar, connoisseur, maven <nonformal>; technical expert, technician; pundit

ADJS 2 **skillful, good,** goodish, excellent, **proficient; dexterous, adroit, deft, adept, coordinated,** well-coordinated, **apt,** no mean, **handy;** authoritative, professional; **virtuoso,** bravura, technically superb; **brilliant**

expertise NOUNS **profound knowledge,** deep knowledge, total command *or* mastery; specialized *or* special knowledge; proficiency; wide *or* vast *or* extensive knowledge

expire VERBS 1 **perish, succumb, die, cease, end,** come to an end, go, pass, **pass away, vanish, disappear,** fade away, run out, peg *or* conk out <nonformal>, come to nothing *or* naught, be no more, be done for

2 **elapse,** lapse, **pass,** run its course, run out, go *or* pass by; **endure,** go *or* run *or* flow on

explain VERBS **explicate, expound,** make of, exposit; **give the meaning,** tell the meaning of; **spell out,** unfold; **account for,** give reason for; **clarify, elucidate,** clear up, clear the air, **cover** *and* cover the waterfront *or* the territory <all nonformal>, **make clear,** make plain; **simplify,** popularize; **illuminate,** enlighten, **shed** *or* **throw light upon;** rationalize, euhemerize, demythologize

explanation NOUNS explication, unfolding, **elucidation,** illumination, enlightenment, light, **clarification,** *éclaircissement* <Fr>, simplification; **exposition,** expounding, exegesis; **justification, vindication;** rationalization

expletive NOUNS **oath,** profane oath, curse; cuss *or* cuss word *and* dirty word *and* four-letter word *and* **swearword** <all nonformal>, naughty word, no-no <nonformal>, foul invective, **epithet,** dysphemism, obscenity

explicit ADJS **crystal-clear,** clear as crystal; **express, unmistakable,** not to be mistaken, open-and-shut <nonformal>, unequivocal; self-explanatory, self-explaining; **indubitable**

explode VERBS **blow up, burst,** go off, go up, blow out, blast, bust <nonformal>; **detonate,** fulminate; **expose, show up;** blow sky-high, **puncture,** deflate, **shoot** *or* **poke full of holes, cut to pieces**

exploit NOUNS 1 **feat, deed, enterprise, achievement, adventure,** gest, **bold stroke,** heroic act *or* deed; aristeia

VERBS 2 **take advantage of,** use, make use of, **use for one's own ends;** make a paw *or* cat's-paw of, sucker *and* play for a sucker <both nonformal>; **manipulate,** work on, work upon, stroke, play on *or* upon; exploit one's position, feather one's nest <nonformal>, **profiteer**

exploration NOUNS **expedition; reconnaissance; reconnoitering,** reconnoiter, **scouting; search,** searching, **quest, hunt,** stalk, stalking

exploratory ADJS **preceding**; preliminary, pioneering, trailblazing, door-opening, kickoff, inaugural

explore VERBS **seek, look for,** look around *or* about for, look for high and low, look high and low, search out, **search for,** seek for, **hunt for,** cast *or* beat about for

explosion NOUNS **detonation, blast,** fulmination, **discharge, burst, bang; outburst,** outburst of anger, burst, eruption, blowup *and* **flare-up** <both nonformal>, access, blaze of temper

explosive NOUNS 1 high explosive; cellulose nitrate, cordite, dynamite, gelignite, guncotton, gunpowder, nitroglycerin, plastic explosive *or* plastique, powder, trinitrotoluene *or* trinitrotoluol *or* TNT

ADJS 2 **excitable, emotional,** highly emotional, overemotional, hyperthymic, perturbable, flappable <nonformal>, volcanic, eruptive, inflammable; **dangerous, perilous,** ugly, serious, critical, attended *or* beset *or* fraught with danger

export NOUNS 1 **transferal, transfer; transmission,** transference, transmittal, transmittance; translocation, **transplantation,** translation; exportation, exporting

VERBS 2 **transfer, transpose,** translocate, hand on, send abroad

expose VERBS **disclose, reveal, let out, show,** impart, discover, **leak,** let slip out, let the cat out of the bag *and* spill the beans <both nonformal>; bring out of the closet; **show up; take the lid off, bring to light,** bring into the open, hold up to view; **unmask,** tear off the mask, **uncover,** unveil, take the lid off <nonformal>, ventilate, lift *or* draw the veil, raise the curtain, let daylight in

exposé NOUNS **disclosure,** disclosing; **revelation,** revealment, revealing, making public, publicizing, broadcasting; **uncovering,** unwrapping, uncloaking, taking the wraps off, removing the veil, **unveiling, unmasking; exposure, baring,** stripping *or* laying bare; outing <nonformal>

exposure NOUNS **unclothing,** divestment, stripping, denudation; baring, stripping *or* laying bare, uncovering, exposing; indecent exposure, exhibitionism, flashing <nonformal>; **disclosure,** disclosing; **revelation,** revealing, making public, publicizing, broadcasting; **unveiling, unmasking; spotlight** <nonformal>, daylight, public eye *or* consciousness, **currency,** common *or* public knowledge

express VERBS **phrase,** find a phrase for, give expression *or* words to, **word,** state, **frame,** conceive, style, couch, **put in** *or* **into words,** clothe *or* embody in words, couch in terms, express by *or* in words

expression NOUNS **phrase, locution, utterance,** usage, term, verbalism; **saying,** witticism, sentence, catchword, catchphrase, word, byword, mot, motto, moral; golden saying, proverbial saying

expressive ADJS **graphic, vivid,** suggestive, imaginative; well-turned; **meaningful**

expurgate VERBS expunge, **edit,** edit out, blue-pencil; strike out *or* off, void, rescind; **censor,** bowdlerize

exquisite ADJS **delightful, lovely; thrilling,** titillative; **charming, attractive, endearing, engaging, appealing,** prepossessing, heartwarming, sexy <nonformal>, **enchanting,** bewitching, witching, entrancing, enthralling, intriguing, fascinating; *recherché* <Fr>; **overnice,** overprecise, precious, *précieuse* <Fr>, **overrefined, elegant, fine,** flowerlike, **dainty, delicate**

extant ADJS **remaining, surviving,** vestigial, over, left, **leftover, still around, remnant,** remanent, odd; **spare,** to spare; unused, unconsumed; **outstanding,** unmet, unresolved; **present, immediate,** current, running, existent, **existing,** actual

extemporaneous ADJS **extemporary,** extempore, **impromptu,** unrehearsed, **improvised,** improvisatory, improvisatorial, improviso, *improvisé* <Fr>; **ad-lib,** *ad libitum* <L>; **ad-hoc,** stopgap, makeshift, jury-rigged; **offhand,** off the top of one's head *and* off-the-cuff <both nonformal>, **spur-of-the-moment, quick and dirty** <nonformal>

extend VERBS **reach, stretch,** sweep, spread, run, **go** *or* **go out,** cover, carry, **range,** lie; **reach** *or* stretch *or* thrust out; span, straddle, take in, hold, encompass, surround, environ; **enlarge, expand, increase,** greaten, crescendo, **develop, widen, broaden,** bulk

extension NOUNS **expansion, enlargement, increase**, uptick, crescendo, upping, raising, hiking, magnification, aggrandizement, amplification, ampliation <old>, broadening, widening; **spread,** spreading, creeping, fanning out, dispersion, ripple effect; **flare,** splay; deployment; augmentation, **addition**; adjunct

extensive ADJS **broad, wide,** liberal, diffuse, large-scale, broad-scale, broadscope, broadly-based, wide-scale, **sweeping; widespread, far-reaching,** far-ranging, **far-flung,** wide-ranging

extenuating ADJS **justifying,** justificatory; **vindicative,** vindicatory, rehabilitative; refuting; **excusing,** excusatory; extenuative, **palliative, mitigating,** mitigative, assuasive, lenitive, softening

exterior NOUNS 1 **appearance,** externals, **mere externals, facade,** outside, **show, outward show, image,** display, front <nonformal>, outward *or* external appearance, surface appearance, surface show, vain show, apparent charac-

ter, public image, window dressing, cosmetics
ADJS 2 **external;** extrinsic; **outer, outside, out, outward,** outward-facing, outlying, outstanding; **outermost,** outmost

exterminate VERBS **eliminate, eradicate,** deracinate, **extirpate, annihilate; do away with, wipe out** <nonformal>; uproot, pull *or* pluck up by the roots, strike at the root of; **liquidate, purge;** remove, sweep away

external ADJS **exterior;** extrinsic; **outer, outside, out, outward,** outward-facing, outlying, outstanding; **outermost,** outmost; surface, superficial, peripheral, **fringe,** apparent, seeming; **extraneous**

extinct ADJS **no more, defunct, dead,** expired, passed away; vanished, gone glimmering; perished, annihilated; all over with, had it <nonformal>, down the tube *and* down the drain <both nonformal>, done for *and* dead and done for <both nonformal>; **obsolete, passé,** gone-by, past, outworn

extinguish VERBS **quench, snuff out,** put out, stamp *or* trample out, trample underfoot; **smother,** choke, stifle, strangle, suffocate; silence; **suppress, quash,** squash *and* squelch <both nonformal>, **quell,** put down

extort VERBS **exact,** squeeze, claim, demand, screw, **shake down** <nonformal>, **blackmail,** levy blackmail, badger *and* play the badger game <both nonformal>; **wrest, wring from, wrench from, rend from,** wrest *or* tear from

extra NOUNS 1 **bonus, premium,** something extra, extra dash, extra added attraction, lagniappe, something into the bargain, something for good measure, baker's dozen; **surplus; supernumerary,** spear carrier <nonformal>
ADJS 2 **additional, supplementary, supplemental;** plus, further, farther, fresh, **more,** new, **other,** another, ulterior; **auxiliary,** ancillary, supernumerary, contributory, **accessory,** collateral; **surplus,** spare
ADVS 3 **in addition, also,** and then some, even more, more so, and also, and all <nonformal>, and so, **as well, too,** else, beside, **besides, to boot, not to mention, let alone, into the bargain;** on top of, over, above; **beyond, plus;** on the side <nonformal>

extract NOUNS 1 extraction; **essence, quintessence, spirit, elixir;** decoction; **distillate,** distillation; infusion
2 **excerpt, selection,** snippet; passage, selected passage; **clip** <nonformal>, film clip, outtake, sound bite <nonformal>
VERBS 3 **take out,** get out, **withdraw, remove;** pull, draw; **pull out, draw out,** tear out, rip out, wrest out, pluck out; smelt
4 **select, pick,** handpick, **pick out, single out,** excerpt; separate the wheat from the chaff *or* tares, separate the sheep from the goats; **free,** set free, **release, extricate, liberate**

extradite VERBS deport, expel; repatriate; recommit, remand; transport, send away

extramarital ADJS freeloving; **adulterous,** illicit

extraneous ADJS **foreign, alien,** strange, exotic, foreign-looking; unearthly, extraterrestrial; exterior, **external;** extrinsic; ulterior, outside, outland, outlandish; **irrelevant, unessential,** nonessential, extrinsic; incidental, parenthetical

extraordinary ADJS **exceptional, remarkable,** noteworthy, **wonderful, marvelous,** fabulous, mythical, legendary; **stupendous,** stupefying, prodigious, portentous, phenomenal; unprecedented, unexampled, unparalleled, indescribable, unspeakable, ineffable

extrapolate VERBS **predict,** foresee, envision, envisage, see ahead, previse, foretell, prophesy; **anticipate, expect,** hope, hope for, look for, look forward to, **project,** plot, plan, scheme, think ahead

extrasensory ADJS psychosensory; **psychic, psychical, spiritual; spiritualistic,** spiritistic; mediumistic; **clairvoyant,** second-sighted, clairaudient, clairsentient, **telepathic; telekinetic, psychokinetic**

extraterrestrial ADJS foreign, outlandish, **alien; otherworldly,** extramundane, transmundane, transcendental, unearthly, exterrestrial, extraterrene

extravagant ADJS **prodigal, lavish,** profuse, **overliberal,** overgenerous, overlavish, **spendthrift, wasteful,** profligate, dissipative; pound-foolish, penny-wise and pound-foolish; easy come, easy go; elaborate, luxurious

extreme NOUNS 1 **limit, end, extremity, acme,** apogee, climax, **maximum,** ceiling, **peak,** summit, **pinnacle,** crown,

top; **utmost,** uttermost, utmost extent, highest degree, nth degree *or* power, *ne plus ultra* <L>; excess
ADJS 2 **radical,** out of this world, way *or* far out <nonformal>, too much <nonformal>; **greatest,** furthest, **most, utmost,** uttermost, the max <nonformal>; **ultra,** ultra-ultra; at the height *or* peak *or* limit *or* summit *or* zenith

extremist NOUNS 1 **radical,** ultra, ultraist; **revolutionary,** revolutionist; subversive; extreme left-winger, left-wing extremist; **anarchist,** nihilist; mild radical, parlor Bolshevik <nonformal>, pink *and* parlor pink *and* pinko <all nonformal>; lunatic fringe
ADJS 2 **radical, extreme,** revolutionary, revolutionist; subversive; ultraconservative; extreme left-wing, anarchistic, nihilistic

extrinsic ADJS **external,** outward, outside, outlying; **extraneous,** foreign; **objective,** nonsubjective, impersonal, extraorganismic *or* extraorganismal; **unessential,** nonessential, extraneous; incidental, parenthetical

extroverted ADJS extrovert, extroversive, **outgoing,** extrospective; other-directed

exuberant ADJS **unrestrained, unconstrained, uninhibited, unreserved,** go-go <nonformal>; **uncurbed, unchecked, unbridled,** unmuzzled; **unreined,** reinless; **uncontrolled,** unsubdued, **unruly;** irrepressible, **effusive,** gushing, gushy; extravagant

exult VERBS **rejoice,** jubilate, **glory, joy, delight,** bless *or* thank one's stars *or* lucky stars, congratulate oneself, hug oneself, rub one's hands, clap hands; dance *or* skip *or* jump for joy, caper, gambol, caracole, romp; triumph, glory, delight, **crow** *or* crow over, crow like a rooster *or* cock; **gloat,** gloat over

eye NOUNS 1 **look, sight,** the eye *and* a look-see *and* a gander <all nonformal>, regard; sidelong look; connoisseurship, savvy <nonformal>, selectiveness, fastidiousness; **view,** sight, light
VERBS 2 **scrutinize, survey,** contemplate, look over, give the eye *or* the once-over <nonformal>; **ogle,** ogle at, **leer,** leer at, give one the glad eye; examine, **inspect**; take a close *or* careful look; take a long, hard look; size up <nonformal>; take stock of

eyeglasses NOUNS **spectacles, specs** <nonformal>, **glasses,** pair of glasses *or* spectacles, cheaters *and* peepers <both nonformal>; reading glasses, bifocals, trifocals, pince-nez, lorgnette, *lorgnon* <Fr>; dark glasses, shades <nonformal>; goggles, blinkers; thick glasses, Coke-bottle glasses <nonformal>; **contacts,** contact lenses, hard lenses, soft lenses

F

fabric NOUNS **substance, stuff, material, matter**, medium, the tangible; **elements,** constituent elements, constituents, ingredients, components, atoms, building blocks, parts

fabulous ADJS **marvelous,** wonderful, formidable, exceptional, uncommon, astonishing, fantastic, incredible, egregious; fabulous, mythic, mythical, mythological, **legendary; mythopoeic, mythopoetic** *or* mythopoetical

facade NOUNS **exterior, face,** outer face *or* side, **front; show, false show,** outward show, false air; window dressing, front, **false front,** gloss, varnish; masquerade, disguise; posture, pose, posing, attitudinizing; mannerism, affectation

face NOUNS 1 **countenance,** visage; cast of countenance, facial appearance *or* expression, cast, turn; **look, air, mien,** demeanor; seeming, semblance, appearance, ostentation, **show, false show,** outward show, false air; **false front, façade,** posture, mannerism, affectation VERBS 2 **expect,** be expectant, **anticipate, have in prospect,** think, **contemplate,** have in contemplation *or* mind, envision, envisage; **brave, confront,** affront, front, look one in the eye, say to one's face, **face up to,** meet, **meet head-on** *or* boldly, square up to, stand up to *or* against, go eyeball-to-eyeball *or* one-on-one with <nonformal>

facet NOUNS **particular, instance, item, detail,** point, count, case, fact, matter, article, datum, element, part, ingredient, factor, aspect, thing; **respect, regard,** angle; minutia, minutiae <pl>, trifle, petty *or* trivial matter; incidental, minor detail

facetious ADJS **jocular, jesting, jocose, tongue-in-cheek;** joshing <nonformal>, **whimsical, droll,** humorsome; satiric, **satirical, sarcastic, ironic,** ironical; salty, salt, Attic

facile ADJS **glib, smooth,** smooth-spoken, smooth-tongued, **slick; felicitous;** slick as a whistle <nonformal>, pleasing, **easy, graceful, effortless,** painless

facilitate VERBS **ease; grease the wheels** <nonformal>; **smooth, smooth** *or* **pave the way,** ease the way, grease *or* soap the ways <both nonformal>, prepare the way, **clear the way,** make all clear for, make way for; run interference for <nonformal>, open the way, open the door to; **speed, expedite,** quicken, hasten; **help along,** help on its way

facilitator NOUNS animator; **agent, instrument,** implement, implementer; expediter

facility NOUNS 1 **accommodation, appliance, convenience,** amenity, appurtenance; advantage
2 **ease, easiness,** facileness, **effortlessness;** lack of hindrance, **smoothness,** freedom; easy going, plain sailing, smooth *or* straight sailing; **tractability,** amenability, adaptability, **suppleness,** willowiness, **litheness**

facing ADJS **opposite,** opposing, confronting, confrontive, eyeball-to-eyeball, one-on-one; **fronting,** looking on *or* out on, opposite, contrapositive

facsimile NOUNS representation, **reproduction, replica,** reduplication, model, **counterpart;** a chip off the old block

fact NOUNS the case, the truth of the matter, not opinion, not guesswork, what's what *and* where it's at <both nonformal>; **matter of fact, bare fact,** naked fact, bald fact, **simple fact,** sober fact, simple *or* sober truth; **cold fact,** hard fact, **brutal fact,** painful fact, the nitty-gritty *and* the bottom line <both nonformal>

plain, plump fact
R Browning

faction NOUNS **party, interest, camp, side;** interest group, pressure group, ethnic group; minority group, vocal minority; silent majority; division, **sect,** wing, **caucus,** splinter, splinter group, breakaway group, offshoot, schism

factor NOUNS **particular, instance, item, detail,** point, count, case, fact, matter, article, datum, element, part, ingredient, facet, aspect, thing; **element, part,** player, module, part and parcel; **feature,** aspect, circumstance

facts NOUNS **information,** data, knowledge; general information; factual information, hard information; **evidence, proof; reason to believe,** grounds for belief; **grounds,** material grounds

factual ADJS **real, actual,** veritable, for real <nonformal>, de facto, simple, sober, **hard; absolute, positive; self-evident,** axiomatic; accepted, conceded, stipulated, given; admitted, well-known, **established, inescapable, indisputable, undeniable; demonstrable,** provable; empirical, **objective, true**; genuine, **authentic**

faculties NOUNS **wits, senses,** parts, capacities, intellectual gifts *or* talents, mother wit; consciousness

faculty NOUNS 1 **ability, capability, capacity,** potentiality, facility, fitness, qualification, talent, flair, genius, caliber, **competence,** competency, adequacy, sufficiency, **efficiency,** efficacy; **proficiency**; the stuff *and* the goods *and* what it takes <all nonformal>
2 faculty members, professorate, professoriate, professors, professordom, teaching staff

fad NOUNS **craze, rage;** wrinkle <nonformal>; new take <nonformal>; novelty; faddishness, faddiness <nonformal>, faddism

fade VERBS **weaken, languish, wilt,** faint, **droop,** drop, **sink, decline, flag, pine, tail away** *or* off, fail, fall *or* drop by the wayside; give out, have no staying power, run out of gas <nonformal>, conk *or* peter *or* poop *or* peg *or* fizzle out <nonformal>; come apart at the seams, come unstuck *or* unglued <both informal>; wear thin *or* away; die out *or* away, dwindle, wane, **fade out** *or* **away, lose color, pale, turn pale,** grow pale, **change color,** turn white, **whiten, blanch,** wan

fail VERBS 1 **weaken, sink, decline,** run down, lose strength, lose one's grip, dwindle, droop, flag, wilt, wither, wither away, fade, **languish,** waste, waste away, pine, peak, be unsuccessful, fail of success, not work *and* not come off <both nonformal>, come to grief, **lose,** not make the grade, be found wanting, not come up to the mark; not pass

2 <nonformal> **lose out,** get left, **not make it,** not hack it, not get to first base, drop the ball, go for a Burton *and* come a cropper <both Brit>, **flop,** flummox, fall flat on one's ass, lay an egg, go over like a lead balloon, draw a blank, bomb, drop a bomb; fold, fold up; take it on the chin, take the count; crap out; strike out, fan, whiff; **flunk** *and* **flunk out**

failing NOUNS **vice, weakness,** weakness of the flesh, **flaw,** moral flaw *or* blemish, **frailty, infirmity;** failure; weak point, weak side, foible; bad habit, besetting sin; **fault, imperfection**

failure NOUNS 1 **unsuccessfulness,** unsuccess; no go <nonformal>; ill success; futility, uselessness; **defeat**; losing game, **no-win situation;** nonaccomplishment; **bankruptcy, insolvency,** receivership, Chapter 11

2 <nonformal> **flop,** flopperoo, megaflop, gigaflop, **bust,** frost, **fizzle,** lemon, clinkler, dud, non-starter, **loser, washout,** turkey, bomb, flat failure, dull thud, total loss

3 <nonformal> **loser, non-starter,** born loser, **flop,** washout, false alarm, **dud,** also-ran, bum, dull tool, bust, schlemiel, turkey

faint NOUNS 1 **unconsciousness, senselessness;** swoon, blackout, syncope, athymia, lipothymy *or* lipothymia; **coma; stupor;** semiconsciousness, grayout
VERBS 2 **swoon,** drop, succumb, keel over <nonformal>, fall in a faint, fall senseless, **pass** *or* zonk out <nonformal>, **black out,** go out like a light; gray out
ADJS 3 faintish, lightheaded, dizzy, gone
4 **indistinct, unclear,** ill-defined, ill-marked, pale, feeble, weak, **dim,** dark, **shadowy, vague, obscure,** indistinguishable, unrecognizable

fair NOUNS 1 **festival, festivity,** festive occasion, *fiesta* <Sp>, **fete,** gala, **gala affair, blowout** <nonformal>, **jamboree** <nonformal>; carnival; kermis; *Oktoberfest* <Ger>; Mardi Gras; Saturnalia; gala day, feria
ADJS 2 **bright, sunny,** mild, balmy, rainless, fine, bright and fair, pleasant
3 **just,** square, **fair and square; equitable,** balanced, level <nonformal>, **even,** evenhanded; deserved, merited; meet, meet and right, right and proper, fit, **proper, good,** as it should *or* ought to be; lawful, legal
4 **mediocre, middling, indifferent, fairish, fair to middling** <nonformal>, moderate, modest, medium, betwixt and between; respectable, passable, **tolera-**

ble; so-so, *comme ci comme ça* <Fr>
ADVS 5 **justly, fairly,** in a fair manner; **equitably, equally, evenly,** upon even terms; **impartially, disinterestedly,** without distinction, without regard *or* respect to persons, without fear or favor

fairy NOUNS **sprite, fay,** fairy man *or* woman; **elf, brownie, pixie, gremlin,** ouphe, hob, cluricaune, puca *or* pooka *or* pwca, kobold, nisse, peri; **imp, goblin**; **gnome; banshee; leprechaun**

faith NOUNS 1 **religion,** religious belief *or* faith, **belief,** teaching, doctrine, creed, credo, theology, orthodoxy; system of beliefs; tradition
2 **confidence,** confidentness, conviction, belief, fixed *or* settled belief, **sureness, assurance, assuredness,** surety, security, certitude; subjective certainty; trust

faithful ADJS 1 **loyal,** devoted, allegiant; **true, true-blue,** true to one's colors; **constant, steadfast,** unswerving, steady, consistent, stable, unfailing, staunch, firm, solid; dutiful; affirming, witnessing, believing; **observant, practicing**
2 **lifelike,** speaking, living, breathing, to the life, **true to life** *or* nature; **realistic, natural**

faith healer NOUNS **healer,** theotherapist; Christian *or* spiritual *or* divine healer; Christian Science practitioner

fake NOUNS 1 **hoax, deception,** spoof <nonformal>, **humbug,** flam, **rip-off** <nonformal>, **sham;** mare's nest
2 **impostor, ringer;** sham, shammer, **humbug,** *blagueur* <Fr>, **fraud** <nonformal>, **faker** *and* **phony** <both nonformal>, **fourflusher** <nonformal>, bluff, bluffer; **charlatan, quack,** quacksalver, quackster, **mountebank,** saltimbanco
3 **copy, imitation**, **counterfeit**, forgery, phony <nonformal>; ersatz
VERBS 4 **counterfeit,** hoke *and* hoke up <both nonformal>, forge, plagiarize, crib, lift <nonformal>; **tamper with, manipulate, juggle,** sophisticate, **doctor** *and* **cook** <both nonformal>, rig, cook *or* juggle the books *or* the accounts <nonformal>
ADJS 5 **imitation, mock, sham,** copied, phony <nonformal>, counterfeit, forged, plagiarized, unoriginal, ungenuine; synthetic, synthetical, ersatz, hokey *and* hoked-up <both nonformal>

fall NOUNS 1 **downfall,** prostration; **overthrow, overturn, upset, upheaval,** *bouleversement* <Fr>; convulsion, **subversion,** sabotage, monkey-wrenching <nonformal>; **collapse, crash,** smash, comedown, breakdown, derailment, pratfall <nonformal>, stumble, tumble, cropper <chiefly Brit nonformal>
VERBS 2 **fall down** <nonformal>, fall *or* drop by the wayside, fall flat, fall flat on one's face; fall down on the job <nonformal>; **fall short, fall through,** fall to the ground; fall between two stools; **fall dead; collapse,** fall in; **crash,** go to smash <nonformal>

fallacy NOUNS logical fallacy, formal fallacy, material fallacy, verbal fallacy; fallaciousness, self-contradiction; heresy, unorthodoxy, heterodoxy; mistaking, misconstruction, misapplication, misjudgment; **misinterpretation**

fall off VERBS **diminish, lessen; drop,** drop off, dive, take a nose dive, plummet, plunge, fall, fall away, fall to a low ebb, run low

fall short VERBS **come short, run short,** stop short, not make the course, not reach; not measure up, not hack it *and* not make the grade *and* not make the cut <all nonformal>, not make it, not make out; **be found wanting,** not fill the bill, not suffice

false ADJS **deceitful; fraudulent, sharp, guileful, insidious,** slippery, slippery as an eel, **shifty, tricky,** trickish, cute, finagling, chiseling <nonformal>; underhand, **underhanded, furtive, surreptitious,** indirect; **falsehearted, two-faced; treacherous**

falsehood NOUNS **lie,** falsity, **untruth,** untruism, mendacity, **prevarication, fib,** taradiddle <nonformal>, flimflam *or* flam, a crock *and* a crock of shit <both nonformal>, *blague* <Fr>; **trumped-up story,** farrago; tall tale *and* **tall story** <both nonformal>, **cock-and-bull story,** fish story <nonformal>; half-truth, stretching of the truth, slight stretching, white lie, little white lie; a pack of lies

falsify VERBS **pervert, twist, garble, put a false construction upon, give a spin, give a false coloring,** color, varnish, slant, strain, torture; misrepresent, misconstrue; **fabricate, invent, manufacture, trump up, make up, hatch, concoct, cook up** *and* make out of whole cloth <both nonformal>

falter VERBS **despair,** despair of, **despond**, lose hope, **lose heart, abandon hope,** give oneself up *or* yield to despair; **hesitate, pause, hang back,** hover; wait to see how the cat jumps *or* the wind blows, scruple, jib, stick at, stickle, strain at; **lose one's nerve,** lose courage, **get cold feet** <nonformal>, boggle, funk <nonformal>, **chicken** <nonformal>; **flounder,** flounce, **stagger,** totter, stumble, blunder

fame NOUNS **repute,** famousness, **renown, kudos,** report, **glory;** éclat, **celebrity, popularity,** recognition, a place in the sun; popular acceptance *or* favor, vogue; **acclaim, public acclaim,** réclame, **publicity; notoriety,** notoriousness, talk of the town; prestige, esteem, repute, reputation, honor, renown, dignity

that last infirmity of noble mind
MILTON

familiar ADJS 1 **intimate, close,** near, inseparable, on familiar *or* intimate terms; just between the two, one-on-one, man-to-man, woman-to-woman; hand-in-hand, hand and glove *or* hand in glove; **thick, thick as thieves** <nonformal>
2 familiar as household words, household, **common, current; proverbial**

familiarize VERBS **inform,** apprise, advise, advertise of, **give word,** mention to, **acquaint, enlighten,** brief, verse, give the facts, give an account of, give by way of information; possess *or* seize one of the facts; notify, give notice *or* notification, serve notice; **accustom, habituate,** orient

family NOUNS **kinfolk** *and* **kinfolks** <both nonformal>, **kinsmen, kin,** kith and kin, **relatives, relations, people,** folks <nonformal>, connections; **posterity, progeny, issue, offspring,** fruit, seed, brood, breed; extended family, nuclear family

famished ADJS **hungry, ravenous,** voracious, **starved,** starving, famishing, perishing *or* pinched with hunger; unfed, underfed, undernourished

famous ADJS **distinguished,** distingué; **noted, notable,** marked, of note, of mark; famed, honored, **renowned, celebrated, popular,** acclaimed, much acclaimed, sought-after, hot *and* world-class <both nonformal>, **well-known,** on everyone's tongue *or* lips, talked-of, talked-about

fan NOUNS **supporter, upholder, follower,** maintainer, sustainer; well-wisher, favorer, encourager, sympathizer; **partisan,** sider <old>, sectary, votary; buff <nonformal>, freak *and* nut <both nonformal>, aficionado, devotee, **zealot, enthusiast**

fanatic NOUNS 1 infatuate, **bug** <nonformal>, **nut** <nonformal>, **buff** *and* **fan** <both nonformal>, freak <nonformal>, *fanatico, aficionado* <both Sp>, devotee, **zealot, enthusiast,** energumen; **monomaniac,** crank <nonformal>; lunatic fringe
ADJS 2 **fanatical, rabid; overzealous, overenthusiastic,** bigoted, perfervid; **extreme,** extremist, extravagant, inordinate; **unreasonable, irrational; wild-eyed**

fanciful ADJS **capricious, whimsical,** notional, kinky, harebrained, cranky, flaky <nonformal>, quirky; **fantastic,** fantastical, antic, **unbelievable, impossible, incredible,** logic-defying, incomprehensible, unimaginable, inconceivable

fancy NOUNS 1 **inclination, penchant, partiality, favor, predilection, preference,** propensity, proclivity, **leaning, bent,** turn, tilt, bias, **affinity;** mutual affinity *or* attraction; **sympathy,** fascination; **attachment,** fondness, sentiment, warm feeling, soft spot in one's heart, weakness <nonformal>, **liking,** shine <nonformal>
VERBS 2 **desire, want,** have a mind to, **like,** have *or* acquire a taste for, take to, **take a fancy** *or* a shine to, have a weakness *or* soft spot in one's heart for; prefer, favor
3 **imagine, conceive,** conceptualize, ideate, figure to oneself
ADJS 4 **ornate, elegant,** fine, chichi, pretty-pretty; picturesque; **elaborate,** overornamented, overornate, overelegant, labored, high-wrought; **ostentatious,** flossy <nonformal>

fanfare NOUNS **blare,** sound *or* flourish of trumpets, fanfaronade, Gabriel's trumpet *or* horn, tarantara, tantara, tantarara; **celebration,** celebrating; rejoicing; **ceremony,** rite

fantastic ADJS fantastical, fanciful, antic, **unbelievable, impossible, incredible,**

logic-defying, incomprehensible, unimaginable, unexpected, unaccountable, inconceivable; preposterous, grotesque, monstrous, wild, weird, **outrageous,** beyond belief, *outré* <Fr>, extravagant, **bizarre**

fantasy NOUNS wildest dream; **figment of the imagination**, phantom of the mind; **apparition, appearance; vision,** waking dream; eidolon, idolum; **imagination,** imagining, **fancy,** conceit <old>; flight of fancy, fumes of fancy; make-believe

such stuff as dreams are made on
SHAKESPEARE

far ADJS 1 **distant,** distal, **remote, removed, far-off,** away, **faraway,** way-off, at a distance, separated, apart, asunder
ADVS 2 **far off,** far away, **afar,** afar off, a long way off, a good ways off <nonformal>, as far as the eye can see, out of sight; clear to hell and gone <nonformal>

farce NOUNS **humor, slapstick,** mere farce, slapstick humor, broad humor; visual humor; mockery, imitation, wicked imitation *or* pastiche, takeoff <nonformal>

farewell NOUNS 1 **leave-taking, send-off,** Godspeed; **adieu,** one's adieus, aloha, **good-bye;** valedictory address, valedictory, valediction, parting words; parting *or* Parthian shot
VERBS 2 say *or* bid good-bye *or* farewell, take leave, make one's adieus; bid Godspeed, give one a send-off *or* a big send-off, see off *or* out

speed the parting guest
POPE

ADJS 3 **departing, leaving; parting,** last, final; valedictory; outward-bound

farfetched ADJS **remote,** distant, out-of-the-way, strained, forced, dragged in, neither here nor there, brought in from nowhere; **imaginary**; improbable

far-flung ADJS **extensive,** widespread, **far-reaching,** far-ranging, wide-ranging

farm NOUNS 1 farmplace, farmstead, farmhold <old>, farmery <Brit>, **grange,** location <Austral>, pen <Jamaica>; **plantation,** *hacienda* <Sp>; croft; **homestead,** steading; collective farm, *kibbutz* <Heb>
VERBS 2 **ranch; grow, raise,** rear; crop; dryfarm; sharecrop
ADJS 3 **rustic, rural, country, provincial, pastoral, bucolic,** Arcadian, **agrarian,** agrestic; **agricultural**

farmer NOUNS **agriculturist,** granger, husbandman, **yeoman,** cultivator, tiller, sodbuster, **tiller of the soil;** boutique farmer, contour farmer, crop-farmer, dirt farmer <nonformal>, gentleman-farmer; **grower,** raiser; **planter;** tenant farmer, crofter <Brit>; sharecropper, cropper, collective farm worker, *kibbutznik* <Yiddish>; **agricultural worker, farm worker,** farmhand, farm laborer, migrant *or* migratory worker *or* laborer, bracero, picker

farsighted ADJS longsighted, presbyopic; **farseeing,** sagacious, prepared, ready, prudent

fart NOUNS 1 **flatulence** *or* flatulency, flatuosity, flatus, gas, wind
VERBS 2 let *or* lay *or* cut a fart <nonformal>, let *or* break wind

farther ADJS **extra,** plus, further, fresh, **more,** new, **other,** another, ulterior; **auxiliary,** ancillary, supernumerary, contributory; remoter, more distant
ADVS 2 **more, moreover,** *au reste* <Fr>, *en plus* <Fr>, thereto, further, **furthermore,** at the same time, then, again, yet

fascinate VERBS **captivate, charm,** becharm, spell, spellbind, cast a spell, put under a spell, **beguile, intrigue, enthrall,** infatuate, **enrapture, transport, enravish, entrance, enchant,** witch, **bewitch;** sweep off one's feet, turn one's head, knock one's socks off <nonformal>

fascinating ADJS **charming, enchanting, entrancing, spellbinding,** glamorous, Circean; **engrossing, absorbing,** consuming, **gripping,** riveting, holding, **arresting,** engaging, attractive, **enthralling, spellbinding,** magnetic, hypnotic, mesmerizing, mesmeric

fascination NOUNS **captivation,** enthrallment, entrapment, snaring; **enchantment,** witchery, bewitchery, bewitchment; **attraction, interest, charm, glamour, appeal,** magnetism; charisma; **obsession,** prepossession, preoccupation, **hang-up** <nonformal>, **fixation**

fashion NOUNS 1 **manner, way,** wise, **means,** modality, tone; **style,** mode, vogue, trend, prevailing taste; the swim

<nonformal>, height of fashion; the new look, the season's look; high fashion, *haute couture* <Fr>
VERBS 2 **produce, create, make, manufacture, form,** formulate, evolve, mature, elaborate, **fabricate,** prefabricate, cast, shape, configure, carve out, mold, extrude, frame; **construct,** devise, design, concoct, compound, churn out *and* crank out *and* pound out *and* hammer out *and* grind out *and* rustle up *and* gin up <all nonformal>; **put together, assemble,** piece together, slap up *or* together <both nonformal>, improvise

fast NOUNS 1 **abstinence,** abstention, abstainment, **abstemiousness,** refraining, refrainment, avoidance, eschewal, denying *or* refusing oneself, saying no to, passing up <nonformal>
VERBS 2 not eat, go hungry, dine with Duke Humphrey; eat sparingly
ADJS 3 **swift, speedy, rapid; fastened, fixed,** secure, firm, close, tight, set; **bonded,** glued, cemented, taped; **jammed,** wedged, stuck, frozen, seized, seized up
4 **devoted,** dedicated, committed, steadfast, constant, faithful, staunch; tried, true, **tried and true,** true-blue, tested
5 **wild,** gallant, gay, rakish; rakehell, rakehellish, rakehelly
ADVS 6 **swiftly, rapidly, quickly,** snappily <nonformal>, **speedily,** apace; at a good clip <nonformal>, **by leaps and bounds,** trippingly; **posthaste, hastily,** expeditiously, promptly, double-quick; **securely, firmly,** tight; **inseparably,** indissolubly

7 <nonformal> **like a shot, as if shot out of a cannon, like a flash,** like a streak, like a blue streak, like a streak of lightning, like lightning, like greased lightning, **like a bat out of hell, like a scared rabbit,** like a house afire, like sixty, like mad *and* **crazy** *and* fury, like sin, to beat the band *or* the Dutch *or* the deuce *or* the devil; **lickety-split**; hell-bent *and* hell-bent for election *and* hell-bent for leather

fasten VERBS **fix, attach, affix,** annex, put to, set to; graft, engraft; **secure,** anchor, moor; cement, knit, set, grapple, belay, **make fast;** clinch, clamp, cramp; tighten, trim, trice up, screw up; cinch *or* cinch up

fastidious ADJS **particular, scrupulous, meticulous, conscientious,** exacting, precise, punctilious, spit-and-polish; **sensitive, discriminating**, discriminative; **selective,** picky <nonformal>, choosy; **strict**, perfectionistic; puritanic, puritanical, priggish, prudish, prissy, strait-laced

fasting NOUNS abstinence from food; starvation; punishment of Tantalus; hunger strike; **asceticism, austerity, self-denial,** belt-tightening

fat ADJS **corpulent, stout, overweight,** fattish, **obese,** adipose, gross, fleshy, beefy, meaty, hefty, porky, porcine; paunchy, bloated, puffy, blowzy, distended, swollen, pursy; abdominous, big-bellied, potbellied, **plump, buxom,** *zaftig* <Yiddish>, pleasantly plump, full, **tubby** <nonformal>, roly-poly; **pudgy,** podgy; sleek; fat, dumb, and happy <nonformal>

fatal ADJS **deadly,** death-bringing, mortal, lethal, malignant, malign, **virulent, pernicious,** baneful

fatality NOUNS fatal accident, violent death, **casualty,** disaster, calamity; DOA *or* dead-on-arrival; **deadliness, lethality,** mortality

fate NOUNS **destiny**, doom, karma, kismet, what bodes *or* looms, what is fated *or* destined *or* doomed, what is written, what is in the books

whatever limits us
EMERSON

father NOUNS 1 **sire,** genitor, paternal ancestor, pater <nonformal>, governor <nonformal>, *abba* <Heb>; patriarch, paterfamilias; stepfather; foster father, adoptive father; birth father

2 <nonformal> **papa,** pa, pap, pappy, **pop,** pops, **dad, daddy,** daddums, daddyo, big daddy, the old man, the governor, pater

3 **priest,** *gallach* <Heb>, father in Christ, **padre,** cassock, presbyter; curé, parish priest; confessor, father confessor, spiritual father *or* director *or* leader
VERBS 3 **engender, beget, procreate; originate,** give origin to, give occasion to, **give rise to,** spark, spark off, set off, trigger, trigger off; sire, sow the seeds of; **conceive,** have the idea, have a bright

idea <nonformal>; found, establish, inaugurate, institute

fatigue NOUNS 1 **tiredness, weariness,** wearifulness; **burnout,** end of one's tether, overtiredness, overstrain; lassitude, languor; combat fatigue; mental fatigue, mental strain
VERBS 2 **tire, weary, exhaust,** wilt, flag, jade, harass; **wear,** wear on *or* upon, **wear down; tire out, wear out, burn out; use up; do in;** overtire, overweary, weaken, enervate, debilitate

fatten VERBS **nourish, nurture,** nutrify, aliment, foster; **nurse, suckle,** lactate, breast-feed, wet-nurse, dry-nurse; fatten up, stuff, force-feed; **raise, breed,** rear, grow, hatch, feed, nurture

fault NOUNS 1 **defect, deficiency, inadequacy,** imperfection, kink, **flaw; weakness,** frailty, infirmity, failure, **failing, foible, shortcoming;** weak point, Achilles' heel, vulnerable place, chink in one's armor, weak link; **malfunction,** glitch <nonformal>
VERBS 2 **deprecate,** discommend, dispraise, disvalue, not be able to say much for, denigrate, faultfind, find fault with, put down <nonformal>, pick at *or* on, pick holes in, pick to pieces; **depreciate, disparage**

faulty ADJS **imperfect,** not perfect; **defective,** flawed, **inadequate, deficient,** short, not all it's cracked up to be <nonformal>, lacking, wanting, found wanting

fauna NOUNS **animal life, animal kingdom,** brute creation, Animalia <zoology>, animality; wild animals *or* beasts, beasts of field, wildlife, denizens of the forest *or* jungle *or* wild, furry creatures

favor NOUNS 1 **inclination, penchant, partiality, fancy, predilection, preference,** propensity, proclivity, **leaning, bent,** turn, tilt, bias, **affinity; act of kindness, kindness,** mercy, **benefit,** benefaction, benevolence, benignity, blessing, **service,** turn, break <nonformal>, **good turn, good** *or* **kind deed,** *mitzvah* <Heb>, office, good *or* kind offices, obligation, courtesy, kindly act
2 **esteem,** estimation, **honor, regard, respect,** approval, approbation, account, consideration, **credit**
3 **token, souvenir, keepsake,** token of remembrance
VERBS 4 **prefer,** have preference, **like better** *or* **best,** prefer to, set before *or* above, regard *or* honor before; rather <nonformal>, **had** *or* **have rather;** think proper, see *or* think fit, think best, please; tilt *or* incline *or* lean *or* tend toward, have a bias *or* partiality *or* penchant
5 **resemble,** be like, bear resemblance; put one in mind of <nonformal>, remind one of, bring to mind, be reminiscent of, suggest, evoke, call up, call to mind; **look like,** mirror; **take after**

favorable ADJS **propitious, advantageous;** kind, kindly, kindly-disposed, all for <nonformal>, **well-disposed,** well-intentioned, well-meant, **well-meaning; approving,** favoring, in favor of, well-disposed, well-inclined, supporting, backing, **advocating**

favorite NOUNS 1 preference; **darling,** idol, jewel, apple of one's eye, fair-haired boy, man after one's own heart; teacher's pet; tin god, little tin god
ADJS 2 **beloved, loved, dear, darling, precious;** pet; **adored, admired,** esteemed, revered; **cherished,** prized, treasured, held dear; **well-liked,** popular; dear to one's heart, after one's heart *or* own heart

favoritism NOUNS **partiality,** partisanship, onesidedness, undispassionateness, undetachment

fawning ADJS **obsequious, flattering,** sycophantic, sycophantical, toadyish, flattering, truckling, ingratiating, smarmy <nonformal>, toadying, toadeating, **bootlicking** *and* back scratching *and* backslapping *and* ass-licking *and* brown-nosing <all nonformal>; **groveling,** sniveling, cringing, cowering, crouching, crawling

fay NOUNS 1 **fairy, sprite,** fairy man *or* woman; **elf, brownie, pixie, gremlin,** gnome, ouphe, hob, cluricaune, puca *or* pooka *or* pwca, kobold, nisse, peri
ADJS 2 **fairy,** faery, **fairylike,** fairyish; **elfin,** elfish, elflike; gnomish, gnomelike; pixieish

faze VERBS **daunt, deter,** shake, stop, stop in one's tracks, set back; **discourage, dishearten; awe, overawe**

fear NOUNS 1 **fright,** affright; **scare, alarm, consternation, dismay; dread,** unholy dread, **awe; terror, horror,** horrification, mortal *or* abject fear; **phobia;** funk *or* blue funk <both nonformal>
VERBS 2 **be afraid; apprehend,** have qualms, misgive, eye askance; **dread,**

stand in dread *or* awe of, be in mortal dread *or* terror of, stand in awe of, stand aghast; have one's heart in one's mouth, have one's heart stand still, have one's heart skip *or* miss a beat

fearful ADJS fearing, fearsome, **in fear; cowardly**; **timorous, timid, shy,** rabbity *and* mousy <both nonformal>, afraid of one's own shadow; scary; **skittish,** skittery <nonformal>, jumpy, goosy <nonformal>

feasible ADJS **practicable, practical, workable,** realizable, operable, doable; **viable; achievable, attainable;** adaptable

feast NOUNS 1 **banquet,** festal board; lavish *or* Lucullan feast; blowout <nonformal>, groaning board
VERBS 2 **banquet,** regale; eat heartily, have a good appetite, eat up, lick the platter *or* plate, do oneself proud <nonformal>, do one's duty, do justice to, polish the platter, put it away <nonformal>

feat NOUNS **exploit, deed, enterprise, achievement, adventure,** gest, **bold stroke,** heroic act *or* deed

feather NOUNS **plume,** pinion; **quill;** pinfeather; contour feather, penna, down feather, plume feather, plumule; filoplume

feature NOUNS 1 **component,** aspect, specialty, circumstance, detail, item; **characteristic, peculiarity, singularity,** particularity, specialty, individualism, **character,** nature, **trait,** quirk, point of character, bad point, good point, saving grace, redeeming feature, mannerism, keynote, trick, distinctive feature, lineament; **highlight,** high spot, main attraction, centerpiece, pièce de résistance; outstanding feature
VERBS 2 **emphasize, stress,** lay emphasis *or* stress upon, highlight, brightline, place emphasis on, give emphasis to, **accent, accentuate, punctuate, point up,** bring to the fore, put in the foreground; headline <nonformal>; **star,** give top billing to

feces NOUNS feculence; defecation, movement, bowel movement *or* **BM; stool, shit** <nonformal>, **ordure,** night soil, crap *and* ca-ca *and* doo-doo <all nonformal>; turd <nonformal>; dingleberry <nonformal>; **dregs, grounds, lees,** dross, slag, draff, scoria

federation NOUNS **affiliation, alliance, allying, alignment, association,** consociation, combination, **union,** unification, **coalition,** fusion, merger, coalescence, coadunation, amalgamation, **league, confederation,** confederacy, consolidation, incorporation, inclusion, integration

fee NOUNS **stipend, allowance,** emolument, tribute; initiation fee; retainer, retaining fee; **dues,** toll, charge, charges, demand, exaction, exactment, scot, shot, scot and lot

feeble ADJS 1 **weak,** weakly, debilitated, imbecile; **doddering,** doddery, doddered, tottering, tottery, rickety, shaky, on one's last legs, with one foot in the grave; **strengthless,** sapless, marrowless, pithless, sinewless, listless, frail, out of gas <nonformal>, nerveless, lustless; **impotent, powerless; soft, flabby,** flaccid, unhardened; **limp,** limber, limp *or* limber as a dishrag, floppy, rubbery
2 **faint, low, soft, gentle, subdued, dim, weak,** faint-sounding, low-sounding, soft-sounding; faint-voiced, weak-voiced; half-heard, scarcely heard; barely audible, subaudible

feebleminded ADJS **weak-minded,** weak, feeble, infirm, soft, soft in the head, weak in the upper story <nonformal>

feed NOUNS 1 **fodder, provender;** forage, pasture, eatage, pasturage; grain; corn, oats, barley, wheat; ensilage, silage
VERBS 2 **dine,** wine and dine, mess; nibble, snack, graze <nonformal>; satisfy, gratify; regale; fare, take, partake, partake of, break bread; feed one's face *and* put on the feed bag <both nonformal>, fall to, pitch in <nonformal>; **foster, nurture,** nourish

feel VERBS **sense,** experience, **perceive,** apprehend, intuit, be sensible of, be conscious *or* aware of, apperceive; respond, respond to stimuli; be sensitive to, have a thing about <nonformal>; entertain *or* harbor *or* cherish *or* nurture a feeling; have a sensation, get *or* receive an impression

feeler NOUNS **offer,** offering, proffer, presentation, **bid,** submission; hesitant *or* tentative *or* preliminary approach, feeling-out; **probe,** sound, sounder; **trial balloon,** *ballon d'essai* <Fr>, pilot balloon, barometer; weather vane; straw vote

feeling NOUNS 1 **emotion, affect, sentiment,** affection, affections; **feelings, sensitiveness, sensibility,** susceptibil-

ity, thin skin; emotional life; the logic of the heart; **sense,** deep *or* profound sense, gut sense *or* sensation <nonformal>; **sensation**; **impression,** undercurrent
2 **hunch** <nonformal>, sense, **presentiment, premonition,** preapprehension, intimation, foreboding; suspicion, **impression,** intuition, intuitive impression, vague feeling *or* idea, funny feeling <nonformal>, feeling in one's bones
ADJS 3 **emotional, affective,** emotive, affectional; visceral, gut <nonformal>; **intuitive,** intuitional, sensing

feisty ADJS **plucky, spunky** *and* gutty *or* gutsy <all nonformal>, gritty, **mettlesome,** dauntless, **game,** game to the last *or* end; **perverse, contrary, wrongheaded, wayward, froward, difficult,** cantankerous, ornery <nonformal>

feline NOUNS 1 **cat,** pussy *and* **puss** *and* **pussycat** <all nonformal>, tabby, grimalkin; house cat; **kitten, kitty** *and* kitty-cat <both nonformal>; **tomcat,** tom; mouser; ratter; tiger cat, tabby cat; calico cat; alley cat
ADJS 2 felid, cattish, catty, catlike; kittenish; leonine, lionlike; tigerish, tigerlike

fellow NOUNS 1 **companion,** fellow companion, **comrade,** *camarade* <Fr>, amigo <nonformal>, mate <Brit>, comate, company, **associate**, consociate, compeer, confrere, consort, **colleague, partner,** copartner, side partner, **crony,** old crony
ADJS 2 **accompanying, twin, joint, joined**, conjoint, hand-in-hand, hand-in-glove, mutual

fellowship NOUNS **companionship, comradeship,** colleagueship, chumship <nonformal>, palship <nonformal>, freemasonry, consortship, boon companionship; camaraderie; scholarship

felon NOUNS **criminal, perpetrator, crook** *and* perp <both nonformal>, public enemy, **lawbreaker,** scofflaw

felony NOUNS **crime; offense, wrong,** illegality; **violation**; **wrongdoing**; much to answer for

feminine ADJS **female;** gynic, gynecic, gynecoid; muliebral, distaff, **womanly, womanish, womanlike,** petticoat; **ladylike,** gentlewomanlike, gentlewomanly; **matronly,** matronal, matronlike; **girlish,** little-girlish, kittenish; maidenly

femininity NOUNS **womankind, woman, women, womanhood,** womenfolk *or* womenfolks <nonformal>, the distaff side; **the female sex;** the second sex, **the fair sex,** the gentle sex, the softer sex, **the weaker sex,** the weaker vessel

feminism NOUNS **women's rights,** rights of women; **women's liberation,** women's lib <nonformal>, womanism, women's movement *or* liberation movement, sisterhood

fence NOUNS 1 **wall,** boundary, **barrier;** stone wall; paling, palisade; rail, railing; balustrade, balustrading; arcade
2 receiver, **receiver of stolen goods,** swagman *and* swagsman <both nonformal>, bagman, bagwoman
VERBS 3 **wall,** fence in, fence up; pale, rail, bar; hem, hem in, hedge, hedge in, hedge out; picket, palisade; bulkhead in
4 push *and* shove <both nonformal>; **sell under the counter; black-market,** black-marketeer; bootleg, moonshine <nonformal>

fend VERBS **fend off, ward off, stave off, hold off, fight off,** keep off, beat off, parry, counter, turn aside; **hold** *or* **keep at bay,** keep at arm's length; **hold the fort, hold the line,** stop, check, block, hinder, obstruct; **repel, repulse, rebuff, drive back,** put back, push back

ferment VERBS work; **bubble,** bubble up, burble; **effervesce, fizz, fizzle;** hiss, **sparkle; foam, froth,** froth up; have a head, foam over

ferocious ADJS **savage, fierce, vicious, murderous, cruel, atrocious, mindless, brutal,** brutish, **bestial,** mindless, insensate, monstrous, mutant, inhuman, pitiless, ruthless, merciless, bloody, sanguinary, kill-crazy <nonformal>

fertile ADJS **productive, fruitful,** fructiferous, fecund; **pregnant,** seminal, **rich,** flourishing, thriving, blooming; **prolific,** proliferous, uberous, **teeming,** swarming, bursting, bursting out, plenteous, **plentiful,** copious, generous, bountiful, **abundant**, **luxuriant, exuberant, lush,** superabundant; creative

fervent ADJS **fervid, passionate, impassioned,** intense, **ardent; hearty, cordial,** enthusiastic, exuberant, unrestrained, vigorous; keen, breathless, **excited**; **zealous,** perfervid, **spirited, vehement, abandoned**

fervor NOUNS **zeal, ardor,** ardency, fervency, fervidness, spirit, warmth, fire, heat, heatedness, **passion,** passionateness, impassionedness, heartiness, intensity, **abandon,** vehemence

festering ADJS 1 suppurating, suppurative, rankling, mattering; pussy, purulent
2 haunting, persistent, recurrent, nagging, plaguing, rankling; obsessing, obsessive

festival NOUNS **festivity,** festive occasion, *fiesta* <Sp>, **fete,** gala, **gala affair, blowout** <nonformal>, **jamboree** <nonformal>; **high jinks,** do, great doings <all nonformal>

festive ADJS **festal; merry,** gay, jolly, jovial, joyous, joyful, gladsome, convivial, gala, hilarious; merrymaking, on the loose <nonformal>

festivity NOUNS **merrymaking, merriment, gaiety, jollity,** jollification <nonformal>, **joviality, conviviality,** whoopee *and* hoopla <both nonformal>; cavorting, skylarking; **revelry,** reveling, revels; **festival,** festive occasion, gala, **gala affair;** *fête champêtre* <Fr>; *Oktoberfest* <Ger>; Mardi Gras; Saturnalia

fetal ADJS **embryonic, germinal,** germinant, germinative, germinational; larval; in the bud; germiparous

fetch VERBS **bring, go get,** go and get, go to get, **go after,** go fetch, **go for,** call for, pick up; **get,** obtain, procure, secure; **bring back, retrieve;** chase after, run after, shag, fetch and carry

fetching ADJS **attractive,** interesting, **appealing,** engaging, taking, eye-catching, winning, winsome, prepossessing

fete NOUNS **party, festivity**, at home, housewarming, soiree, reception, shindig *and* brawl <both nonformal>

fetish NOUNS **amulet, talisman,** periapt, phylactery; totem, joss

fetter VERBS **shackle, manacle,** gyve, **put in irons; handcuff, tie one's hands; tie hand and foot,** hog-tie <nonformal>; straitjacket; hobble, hopple, tether; **hamper, impede, cramp, handicap,** put at a disadvantage; hamstring

fetus NOUNS **embryo,** zygote, oösperm, oöspore, blastula; germ, **larva,** nymph

feud NOUNS 1 **vendetta,** blood feud; **quarrel,** squabble, contention, strife, **tussle,** bicker, wrangle, snarl, **tiff, spat,** fuss
VERBS 2 **quarrel, dispute,** oppugn, flite <old>, altercate, **fight, squabble,** tiff, spat, **bicker, wrangle,** spar, broil, have words, set to, join issue, make the fur fly; cross swords

feudal ADJS 1 **imperious,** imperial, **masterful,** authoritative, aristocratic, **lordly,** magistral, **magisterial**
2 liege, **vassal,** feudatory, feodal

fever NOUNS 1 **feverishness,** febrility, febricity, pyrexia; hyperpyrexia, hyperthermia; **heat, fire, fever heat;** flush, hectic flush; calenture; **fever of excitement, fever pitch,** heat, fever heat, fire; sexual excitement, rut
2 **frenzy, furor,** fury, maniacal excitement, **rage; amok,** murderous insanity *or* frenzy, homicidal mania, hemothymia

fey ADJS **eccentric, erratic,** idiocratic, idiocratical, idiosyncratic, idiosyncratical, **queer,** queer in the head, **odd, peculiar,** strange, singular, anomalous, freakish, funny

fiancé NOUNS **fiancée,** bride-to-be, affianced, betrothed, intended <nonformal>

fiasco NOUNS **botch,** botch-up, bungle, hash, mess, muddle, foozle *and* bollix *and* bitch-up *and* screw-up *and* fuck-up <all nonformal>

fiat NOUNS 1 **decree,** decretum, decretal, rescript, **edict,** *edictum* <L>; **proclamation,** pronouncement, pronunciamento, **declaration,** ukase; bull, brevet <old>; diktat
2 **authorization, authority, sanction, licensing,** countenance, **warrant,** warranty

fibrous ADJS **stringy,** ropy, wiry; fibered, fibroid, fibrilliform

fickle ADJS **flighty,** skittish, **light;** coquettish, flirtatious, toying; versatile, **inconstant, changeable**; vacillating; volatile, mercurial, quicksilver

fiction NOUNS narrative, narrative literature, imaginative narrative, prose fiction; **storytelling,** tale-telling, yarn-spinning *and* yarning <both nonformal>; fictionalization; **figment of the imagination,** creature of the imagination, creation *or* coinage of the brain, fiction of the mind; myth, romance

fictitious ADJS **make-believe, figmental,** fictional, fictive, fabricated, fictionalized; nonhistorical, nonfactual, nonactual, nonrealistic

fidelity NOUNS **faithfulness, loyalty,** faith; **constancy, steadfastness,** staunchness, firmness; trueness, troth, true blue; good faith, *bona fides* <L>, *bonne foi* <Fr>; **allegiance, fealty, homage;** bond, tie; attachment, adherence, adhesion; devotion, devotedness

fidget VERBS have the fidgets; jitter, have the jitters, etc; **tense up; tremble; twitch, jerk,** vellicate; **jig, jiggle,** jigger *or* jigget <nonformal>

field NOUNS 1 **sphere,** profession, province, bailiwick, turf <nonformal>, department, area, discipline, subdiscipline, orb, orbit, realm, arena, domain, walk
2 **tract,** plat, **plot, patch,** piece *or* parcel of land; cultivated land; clearing

fiend NOUNS 1 **monster,** fiend from hell, **demon, devil,** devil incarnate, hellhound, hellkite; **vampire,** lamia, **harpy, ghoul**
2 **brute,** hellcat, **beast,** wild beast, mad dog, wolf, monster, mutant, savage; **rapist, mugger, killer**

fierce ADJS **savage, ferocious,** feral, **vicious, atrocious,** truculent, fell; **inhuman,** inhumane, unhuman; fiendish, fiendlike; **violent, virulent, severe, furious, intense,** sharp, acute, keen, cutting, splitting, piercing

fiery ADJS **heated, inflamed,** flaming, scorching, hot, red-hot, white-hot; **fanatic, zealous,** totally committed, hard-core, hard-line, ardent, passionate; **hotheaded**

fiesta NOUNS **festivity,** fete, festive occasion, celebration, merrymaking, revel, revelry, jubilation, joyance

fight NOUNS 1 **battle, fray,** affray, combat, action, conflict, embroilment; **clash; brush, skirmish,** scrimmage; tussle, **scuffle, struggle,** scramble, shoving match; exchange of blows, clash of arms; **quarrel**; pitched battle; battle royal; **fistfight,** punch-out *and* duke-out <both nonformal>, punch-up <Brit nonformal>; **struggle,** hassle <nonformal>
VERBS 2 **struggle, strive, contend, battle,** buffet, scuffle, tussle, wrestle, hassle <nonformal>; **box,** punch, spar, mix it up <nonformal>, knock out, slug, maul

fighter NOUNS **combatant, battler,** scrapper <nonformal>; **contestant, contender, competitor, rival;** disputant, wrangler, squabbler, bickerer, quarreler; tussler, scuffler; brawler, **boxer,** pugilist, prizefighter, pug *and* palooka <both nonformal>, slugger, mauler

figurative ADJS **representational, representative, depictive, delineatory, illustrative,** pictorial, graphic, ideographic, pictographic; **symbolizing,** personifying, embodying; imitative, mimetic, simulative, apish, mimish; **symbolic,** metaphorical, allegorical, figural

figurehead NOUNS 1 **prow, bow, stem,** rostrum, nose, beak
2 nominal head, dummy, lay figure, front man *and* front <both nonformal>, stooge *and* Charlie McCarthy <both nonformal>, puppet, creature

figure of speech NOUNS **figure, image,** trope, turn of expression, manner *or* way of speaking, ornament, device, flourish, flower

fill NOUNS 1 **full measure,** full house, bellyful *and* skinful <both nonformal>; more than enough

> *good measure, pressed down, and shaken together, and running over*
> BIBLE

VERBS 2 fill up, **pack, load; pad,** wad, **stuff;** extend throughout, leave no void, occupy; creep *or* crawl *or* swarm with, be lousy with <nonformal>, teem with; honeycomb

filler NOUNS **filling, packing,** padding, wadding, **stuffing**

filling ADJS **completing, fulfilling,** completive *or* completory, consummative *or* consummatory; **complementary,** complemental; **satiating,** sating, satisfying, surfeiting, overfilling; jading, **cloying,** cloysome

film NOUNS 1 covering, **coat,** coating, veneer, patina, scum, membrane, pellicle, peel, skin, rind, hide; slick, oil slick
2 **motion picture, movie, picture,** flick *and* flicker <both nonformal>, picture show; motion-picture film, panchromatic film, monochromatic film, orthochromatic film, black-and-white film, color film

filter VERBS **clarify,** clear, purify, rectify, depurate, decrassify; **strain;** elute, elutriate; filtrate; **percolate,** leach, lixiviate; **sift,** separate, sieve, **screen,** bolt, winnow

filth NOUNS **muck,** slime, mess, sordes, foul matter; ordure, **excrement**; mucus, snot <nonformal>; scurf, furfur, dandruff; putrid matter, pus, corruption, gangrene, decay, carrion, **rot**; **obscenity,**

smut <nonformal>; **dirtiness,** bawdry, raunch <nonformal>, **ribaldry, pornography,** porno *and* porn <both nonformal>, hard *or* hard-core pornography, soft *or* soft-core pornography, salacity, **smut, dirt**

filthy ADJS **obscene, lewd, adult, bawdy,** ithyphallic, **ribald, pornographic, salacious,** sultry <nonformal>, lurid, **dirty, smutty,** raunchy <nonformal>, blue, smoking-room, impure, unchaste, unclean, **foul, nasty,** vile, fulsome, offensive, unprintable, unrepeatable, not fit for mixed company

finagle VERBS **maneuver, manipulate,** pull strings *or* wires; **machinate, contrive,** angle <nonformal>, **jockey, engineer;** play games <nonformal>; **plot, scheme, intrigue; wangle;** gerrymander

final ADJS **terminal,** terminating *or* terminative, determinative, definitive, **conclusive; last,** last-ditch <nonformal>, last but not least, eventual, farthest, extreme, boundary, border, limbic, limiting, polar, **endmost, ultimate;** caudal, tail, tail-end

finale NOUNS ending, **termination, terminus,** expiry, phaseout, phasedown, discontinuation, closeout, cessation, ceasing, consummation, culmination, **conclusion, finish, finis,** the end, finishing, finalizing *or* finalization, windup *and* payoff <both nonformal>, curtains <nonformal>, end of the road *or* line <nonformal>

finalize VERBS **complete, round off** *or* **out, wind up** <nonformal>, **top off;** top out, crown, cap; climax, culminate; **give the finishing touches** *or* **strokes,** put the finishing touches *or* strokes on, lick *or* whip into shape, put the icing on the cake

finally ADVS in fine; **ultimately, eventually, as a matter of course; lastly,** last, **at last,** at the last *or* end *or* conclusion, at length, at long last; **in conclusion, in sum;** conclusively, once and for all; **after all is said and done,** the way the cookie crumbles <nonformal>

finance NOUNS 1 **finances, money matters;** world of finance, financial world, financial industry, **high finance,** investment banking, international banking
VERBS 2 **subsidize, back, fund, sponsor, support,** provide for, capitalize, provide capital *or* money for, pay for, bankroll <nonformal>, angel <nonformal>, put up the money; **stake** *or* **grubstake** <both nonformal>; set up, set up in business

find NOUNS 1 finding, **discovery;** catch, trove, *trouvaille* <Fr>; treasure trove, buried treasure; **windfall,** windfall money, windfall profit, found money, money in the bank, **bonus, gravy** <nonformal>
VERBS 2 **discover,** get; strike, hit; put *or* lay one's hands on, lay one's fingers on, **locate**; **hunt down,** search out, trace down, track down, **run down, run** *or* **bring to earth;** trace; **learn, find out,** determine, become cognizant *or* conscious of, become aware of; discover *or* find out the hard way, discover to one's cost; discover *or* find oneself; **draw a conclusion,** hold, ascertain
3 agree on a verdict, return a verdict, hand down a verdict, **bring in a verdict,** find for *or* against

finding NOUNS conclusion, determination, ascertainment, judgment, **verdict, decision,** resolution <old>, **determination,** holding; **learning, finding out,** determining, becoming conscious *or* cognizant of, becoming aware of; self-discovery

fine ADJS 1 **healthy, healthful,** enjoying health, in health, in shape, in condition, **fit,** fit and fine; **in good** *or* **fine shape, in fine fettle,** bursting with health
2 flimsy, slight, **unsubstantial** *or* **insubstantial**; **thin, tenuous,** subtile, subtle, evanescent, fastidious, overfine, refined, rarefied
3 **good, excellent,** *bueno* <Sp>, *bon* <Fr>, bonny <Brit>, **nice,** goodly, fair; **splendid, capital, grand,** elegant <nonformal>
ADVS 4 **excellently, nicely,** finely, **capitally, splendidly, famously,** royally; **well,** very well, right, aright

finesse NOUNS 1 **skill,** grace, style; **tact, tactfulness, diplomacy;** *savoir-faire* <Fr>; **craftsmanship,** workmanship, technical skill, **technique, touch,** technical brilliance, technical mastery, **virtuosity,** bravura, wizardry; refinement, delicacy; **tact, tactfulness,** feel, feeling, sense, **sensitivity**, **sensibility**
VERBS 2 **maneuver,** machinate, operate <nonformal>, engineer, rig, wangle <nonformal>, angle, finagle <nonformal>; use one's fine Italian hand

finger NOUNS 1 **digit;** forefinger, index

finger, index; ring finger, annulary; middle finger, medius, dactylion; little finger, pinkie <nonformal>, minimus; thumb, pollex
VERBS 2 **touch, feel,** feel of, palpate; pass *or* run the fingers over, feel with the fingertips, thumb; **point out,** point at, put *or* lay one's finger on
3 **denounce,** denunciate; point the finger at *and* put *or* lay the finger on <all nonformal>, **inform on** *or* **against; condemn to death,** sign one's death warrant, give the kiss of death to

finicky ADJS **finical,** finicking, finikin; **fussy,** fuss-budgety <nonformal>; **squeamish,** pernickety *and* persnickety <both nonformal>, difficult, hard to please; **meticulous**, nice, niggling

finish NOUNS 1 **completion,** completing, finishing, **conclusion, end,** ending, **termination,** terminus, **close, windup** <nonformal>, rounding off *or* out, topping off, wrapping up, wrap-up, finalization; **refinement,** precision, exactitude, lapidary quality; **discrimination,** choice; **restraint; polish; conclusion, finis, finale,** the end
VERBS 2 **complete, perfect, finish off, conclude, terminate, end,** bring to a close, carry to completion, prosecute to a conclusion; **get through, get done; polish, burnish;** get it over with, **finish up; give the finishing touches** *or* **strokes,** put the finishing touches *or* strokes on, lick *or* whip into shape, finalize, put the icing on the cake

finished ADJS 1 **used up, consumed,** concluded, terminated, ended, finished up; signed, sealed, and delivered; **skilled, accomplished;** trained, coached, prepared, primed; **elegant, polished,** round, terse; neat, trim, **refined, exact,** lapidary *or* lapidarian; wound up <nonformal>

2 <nonformal> **belly-up, dead meat,** kaput, shot, done for, SOL *or* shit out of luck, scragged, shot down, shot down in flames, down in flames, wasted, zapped, pffft *or* phut, wiped out, washed up, down and out, down the tubes, totaled; all over but the shouting

finite ADJS **limited, restricted,** bound, **bounded; confined**, prescribed, proscribed, cramped, strait, straitened, narrow

fire NOUNS 1 **zeal, ardor, ardency, fervor, fervency, fervidness, spirit, passion,** impassionedness, intensity, **abandon,** vehemence; **inspiration,** spark; afflatus, divine afflatus
2 **blaze, flame,** ingle, devouring element; **combustion, ignition,** ignition temperature *or* point, flash *or* flashing point; **conflagration**
VERBS 3 **excite, impassion, kindle,** enkindle, light up, light the fuse, **inflame,** set fire to, set on fire, fire *or* warm the blood; fan the fire *or* flame, raise to a fever heat *or* pitch; **fire one's imagination; animate, exhilarate,** enliven
4 **shoot,** fire off, let off, let fly, **discharge,** eject; detonate; **launch,** project, blast off
5 **discharge, dismiss,** expel, **lay off,** furlough, let go, make redundant, **retire;** kick upstairs

6 <nonformal> **can, sack, bump,** bounce, kick, boot, give the ax, give the gate, give one the sack *or* the ax *or* the boot *or* the gate *or* the air *or* one's walking papers, send one to the showers, show one the door *or* gate

firearm NOUNS **gun;** shooting iron *and* gat *and* rod *and* heater *and* piece <all nonformal>; shoulder weapon *or* gun *or* arm

firebrand NOUNS **hothead,** revolutionary, **terrorist,** incendiary, bomber, guerrilla; brand, **ember,** burning ember

fireworks NOUNS **pyrotechnics** *or* pyrotechny; **gunfire, fire, firing,** musketry, **shooting,** gunplay <nonformal>; gunfight, shootout

firm NOUNS 1 **company, business firm, concern, house,** *compagnie* <Fr>, *compañía* <Sp>, *Aktiengesellschaft* <Ger>, *aktiebolag* <Swed>; **business, industry, enterprise,** business establishment, commercial enterprise
ADJS 2 **sound, stout,** sturdy, tough, hard-boiled <nonformal>, solid; sound as a dollar, solid as a rock, firm as Gibraltar, made of iron; rigid, unbreakable, infrangible; **staunch,** standup <nonformal>, steady, steadfast, constant, not to be shaken, unflappable <nonformal>; undeflectable, **unswerving,** immovable, unbending, inflexible, **unyielding**; true, loyal

first NOUNS 1 first ever, prime, primal,

primary, **initial,** alpha; initialization, first move, opening move, gambit, **first step,** baby step, *le premier pas* <Fr>, openers, starters
ADJS 2 **foremost,** front, up-front <nonformal>, **head, chief, principal,** premier, **leading, main,** flagship; maiden
ADVS 3 firstly, **at first,** first off, first thing, for openers *or* starters <nonformal>, as a gambit, up front <nonformal>, **in the first place,** first and foremost, before everything, *primo* <L>; **originally, in the beginning,** *in limine* <L>, **at the start,** at first glance *or* first blush, at the outset; from the ground up, from the beginning, **from scratch** <nonformal>, from the first, **from the word 'go'** <nonformal>, *ab origine* <L>, *ab initio* <L>; *ab ovo* <L>

first-class ADJS **first-rate,** in a class by itself; of the first *or* highest degree; unmatched, matchless; champion, record-breaking; of the first water, top of the line, highest-quality, best-quality, far and away the best, the best by a long shot *or* long chalk, head and shoulders above, of the highest type

firsthand ADJS **unused, original;** authentic, reliable, eye-witness

first name NOUNS **forename, Christian name, given name,** baptismal name

first-rate ADJS 1 **superlative,** top, topmost, uppermost, tip-top, top-level, top-echelon, first-class, of the first water, top of the line, in a class by itself; of the first *or* highest degree

2 <nonformal> **A-1, A number one,** primo, first-chop, tip-top, top-notch, topflight, top-drawer, tops; topping *or* top-hole <both Brit>

fiscal ADJS **monetary, pecuniary,** nummary, **financial;** capital

fish VERBS go fishing, **angle;** cast one's hook *or* net; shrimp, whale, clam, grig, still-fish, fly-fish, troll, bob, dap, dib *or* dibble, gig, jig

fisherman NOUNS **fisher, angler,** *piscator* <L>, piscatorian, piscatorialist; Waltonian, dibber, dibbler, troller, trawler, trawlerman, dragger, jacker, jigger, bobber, guddler, tickler, drifter, drift netter, whaler, clam digger, lobsterman

The Compleat Angler
IZAAK WALTON

fission NOUNS **severance,** disseverment *or* disseverance, **sunderance,** scission, cleavage, dichotomy; **nuclear fission,** fission reaction; **atom-smashing,** atom-chipping, **splitting the atom;** atomic reaction; thermonuclear reaction; **chain reaction**

fissure NOUNS **crack, cleft,** cranny, chink, check, craze, chap, **crevice,** scissure, incision, notch, score, cut, gash, slit, split, **rift,** rent; **interruption, suspension, break,** breach, gap, hiatus, lacuna, caesura

fit NOUNS 1 **seizure, spasm, throes, paroxysm, convulsion,** eclampsia, frenzy; **epilepsy,** falling sickness; fit of anger, fit of temper, rage, **tantrum,** temper tantrum
VERBS 2 **equip, furnish, outfit,** gear, **prepare,** fit up *or* out, fix up <nonformal>, **rig,** rig up *or* out, **turn out,** appoint, accouter, clothe, dress; adapt, tailor, measure, proportion, adjust to, trim to, cut to, gear to, key to
3 **suit,** suit *or* fit to a tee, fit like a glove, **qualify, do,** serve, answer, be OK <nonformal>, do the job *and* do the trick *and* fill the bill <all nonformal>
ADJS 3 **healthy, healthful,** enjoying health, **fine,** in health, in shape, in condition, fit and fine; **in good health,** in the pink of condition, in mint condition, **in good** *or* **fine shape, in fine fettle,** bursting with health, full of life and vigor
4 **eligible, qualified,** fitted, **suitable,** acceptable, admissible, worthy, desirable; **appropriate,** fitting, proper, correct, seemly

fitful ADJS **discontinuous,** broken off, fragmentary, **interrupted,** suspended; disjunctive, discrete, discretive; **intermittent,** spotty, patchy, jagged; choppy, chopped-off, herky-jerky <nonformal>, jerky, spasmodic; episodic

fitting ADJS **decorous,** decent, proper, right, right-thinking, **seemly, becoming,** appropriate, meet, happy, felicitous; genteel; civil, urbane; **expedient,** fit, befitting, suitable

fix NOUNS 1 **predicament,** plight, pass, pickle *and* picklement *and* jam *and* spot *and* bind <all nonformal>; **temporary expedient, improvisation,** ad hoc measure, **quick fix** <nonformal>, **makeshift,** stopgap, shake-up, jury-rig

2 <nonformal> **put-up job,** packed *or* rigged game *or* jury, packed deal, stacked deck, cold deck, boat race, tank job; **frame-up,** frame, setup

VERBS 3 **repair, mend,** fix up <nonformal>, do up, doctor <nonformal>, put in repair, put in shape, set to rights, put in order *or* condition; **condition, recondition, service, overhaul;** patch, **patch up;** tinker, tinker up, fiddle, fiddle around; cobble
4 **fasten, attach, affix,** annex, put to, set to; **secure,** anchor, moor; belay, **make fast; determine,** decide, **establish,** settle, lock in *and* nail down *and* clinch *and* cinch <all nonformal>, clear up, sort out, set at rest

5 <nonformal> **rig,** pack, cook, cook up; **stack the cards,** cold-deck, pack the deal; put in the bag, sew up; frame, frame-up, set up; **throw,** tank, go in the tank, hold a boat race

fixation NOUNS **fixity,** fixedness, fixture; infixion, implantation, embedment; **obsession,** prepossession, preoccupation, **hang-up** <nonformal>, complex, fascination; **compulsion,** morbid drive, obsessive compulsion, irresistible impulse

fixer NOUNS **mender,** doctor <nonformal>, restorer, renovator, repairer, **repairman, repairwoman,** maintenance man *or* woman, **serviceman, servicewoman;** trouble man *and* **troubleshooter** <both nonformal>; **wire-puller** <nonformal>; **influence peddler,** power broker

fixings NOUNS **constituents, ingredients,** makings *and* fixings <both nonformal>, **elements**

fizz NOUNS 1 **bubbling,** bubbliness, **effervescence** *or* effervescency, **sparkle,** spumescence, frothiness, frothing, foaming; fizzle, carbonation; **fermentation,** ferment
VERBS 2 **bubble,** bubble up, burble; **effervesce, fizzle;** hiss, **sparkle; ferment,** work; **foam, froth,** froth up; have a head, foam over

flabbergast VERBS **astonish, amaze, astound, surprise,** startle, stagger, **bewilder, perplex**, confound, overwhelm, **boggle, boggle the mind; awe,** strike with wonder *or* awe; **dumbfound** *or* dumbfounder, strike dumb, strike dead; knock one's socks off *and* bowl over <both nonformal>, dazzle

flabby ADJS **flaccid, limp,** rubbery, flimsy, floppy; **loose,** lax, relaxed; feeble, soft, **weak**, weak as a kitten, wimpy *or* wimpish <nonformal>

flag NOUNS **banner,** oriflamme, **standard,** gonfalon *or* gonfanon, guidon, *vexillum* <L>, *labarum* <L>; **pennant,** pennon, pennoncel, banneret, banderole, swallowtail, burgee, **streamer; bunting**

flagrant ADJS **outright,** arrant, shocking, shattering, egregious, intolerable, unbearable, unconscionable, glaring, stark-staring, rank, crass, gross; **blatant,** shameless, **brazen,** brazenfaced, lurid, glaring, flaring, flaunting, screaming <nonformal>, obtrusive, vulgar, crude

flail VERBS **whip,** give a whipping *or* beating *or* thrashing, **beat, thrash, spank, flog,** scourge, flagellate, whale

flair NOUNS **talent,** strong flair, **gift, endowment,** dowry, dower, natural gift *or* endowment, **genius,** instinct, **faculty; forte,** specialty, métier, long suit, strong point; **aptitude,** inborn *or* innate aptitude, aptness, felicity, **bent**

flak NOUNS **criticism,** adverse criticism, harsh *or* hostile criticism, bad notices, bad press, animadversion, imputation, reflection, **aspersion,** stricture, obloquy; **knock** *and* **swipe** *and* **slam** *and* **rap** *and* hit <all nonformal>

flaky ADJS 1 **fanciful, notional,** fantastic *or* fantastical, maggoty, **crotchety,** kinky, harebrained, cranky, quirky; wanton, wayward, vagrant; **arbitrary, unreasonable,** motiveless; **moody, temperamental,** prima-donnaish; petulant; unrestrained
2 flocculent; **scaly,** scurfy, squamous, lentiginous, furfuraceous, lepidote

flamboyant ADJS **showy, flashy, ostentatious,** gaudy, glitzy <nonformal>, meretricious, flaming, bedizened, flaunting, garish

flame NOUNS 1 **boyfriend** *and* **girlfriend** <both nonformal>; sweetheart, passion
2 **fire; blaze,** ingle, devouring element; **combustion, ignition,** ignition temperature *or* point, flash *or* flashing point; **conflagration;** flicker, wavering *or* flickering flame

lambent flame
Dryden

VERBS 3 **catch fire,** catch on fire, catch, take fire, **burn,** combust, blaze, **blaze up, burst into flame**

flaming ADJS **fiery, heated, inflamed,** scorching, hot, red-hot, white-hot; **fanatic, zealous,** totally committed, hard-core, hard-line, ardent, passionate; **hotheaded**

flap NOUNS 1 **bustle,** brouhaha, hurly-burly, **fuss, flurry, flutter,** fluster, scramble, ferment, stew, sweat, whirl, swirl, vortex, maelstrom, **stir,** hubbub, hullabaloo, hoo-ha *and* foofaraw <both nonformal>, ado, to-do <nonformal>, bother, botheration <nonformal>, pother
VERBS 2 **hang,** hang down, fall; **dangle,** swing, flop <nonformal>; **droop,** lop; **trail, drag, draggle,** drabble, daggle

flare NOUNS 1 flareup, **flash,** flash fire, **blaze,** burst, outburst; deflagration; **torch,** flaming torch, flambeau, cresset; signal flare, beacon
VERBS 2 **spread,** spread out, outspread, outstretch; flare out, broaden out, splay; spraddle, sprangle, sprawl
3 **blaze,** combust, spark, **catch fire, flame**, flame up, flare up

flareup NOUNS **outburst,** outburst of anger, burst, **explosion,** eruption, blowup <nonformal>, access, blaze of temper; **storm, scene,** high words

flashy ADJS **showy, flaunting,** snazzy, flashing, glittering, **ostentatious,** gaudy, **jazzy** *and* **glitzy** *and* gimmicky *and* splashy *and* splurgy <all nonformal>; exhibitionistic, showoffy <nonformal>, bravura; **sporty** *or* dressy <both nonformal>; **frilly, flouncy,** frothy, chichi

flat NOUNS 1 **apartment, rooms;** studio apartment; suite, suite *or* set of rooms; walkup, cold-water flat; railroad flat
ADJS 2 dull, mat, dead, dingy, muddy, leaden, lusterless, lackluster; **insipid, tasteless, flavorless,** bland, spiceless, **savorless,** sapless, unsavory, unflavored; stale, dead, *fade* <Fr>; vapid, inane, jejune; insipid, vapid
3 **horizontal, level,** flattened; **even,** smooth, smoothened, smoothed out

flatten VERBS **level, even, equalize,** align, smooth *or* smoothen, level out, smooth out, flush; grade, roll, roll flat, steamroller *or* steamroll; **raze,** rase, **fell,** smash, prostrate, raze to the ground *or* dust

flatter VERBS 1 adulate, conceit; **cajole, wheedle, blandish,** palaver; slaver *or* slobber over, beslobber, beslubber; oil the tongue, lay the flattering unction to one's soul, make fair weather; **praise, compliment**, praise to the skies; scratch one's back, kiss ass <nonformal>, fawn upon

2 <nonformal> **soft-soap,** butter, honey, **butter up,** soften up; stroke, massage the ego; **blarney,** jolly, pull one's leg; lay it on, pour *or* spread *or* lay it on thick *or* with a trowel, overdo it, soap, oil; string along, kid along; play up to, get around

flatterer NOUNS 1 commender, eulogist, eulogizer; **praiser,** lauder, extoller, encomiast, panegyrist, **booster** <nonformal>, puffer, promoter

2 <nonformal> **apple-polisher, ass-kisser, brown-nose,** brown-noser, brownie, ass-licker, ass-wiper, suck-ass; **backslapper,** backscratcher, clawback, back-patter; **bootlicker,** bootlick; **handshaker; yes-man, stooge**

flattery NOUNS **adulation; praise**; **blandishment,** palaver, **cajolery,** cajolement, wheedling; **blarney** *and* bunkum *and* **soft soap** <all nonformal>, oil, grease, eyewash <nonformal>; strokes *and* stroking *and* ego massage <all nonformal>, sweet talk, fair *or* sweet *or* honeyed words, pretty lies, sweet nothings

flatulence NOUNS **distension,** puffing, puff, puffiness, **bloating,** bloat, flatulency, gassiness, **gas,** stomach gas, gassiness, flatus, windiness, farting <nonformal>, windiness; **turgidity,** turgidness, turgescence; **vaporousness,** vaporiness

flaunt VERBS vaunt, **parade, display, demonstrate,** manifest, make a great show of, **exhibit,** air, put forward, put forth, hold up, flash *and* sport <both nonformal>; **wave, brandish, flourish,** shake, swing, wield

flavor NOUNS 1 **taste,** sapor; **smack, tang; savor, relish,** sapidity; palate, tongue, tooth, stomach
2 **flavoring,** flavorer; **seasoning,** sea-

soner, **relish, condiment, spice,** condiments
VERBS 3 savor; **season,** salt, pepper, **spice,** sauce; **tinge, tincture**

flavorsome ADJS **flavorful,** flavorous, flavory, well-flavored; full-flavored, full-bodied; rich-flavored; **delectable, delicious,** luscious; tasty, savory; succulent

flaw NOUNS **fault,** *faute* <Fr>, **defect,** imperfection, kink, hole, bug <nonformal>; fly in the ointment, problem, snag, drawback; **blemish, malfunction,** glitch <nonformal>

flawed ADJS **illogical, irrational, invalid,** inauthentic, unauthentic, faulty, paralogical, fallacious; defective, **blemished, disfigured,** defaced, **marred,** scarred

flawless ADJS **perfect, ideal, faultless,** unflawed, defectless, not to be improved, **impeccable,** absolute; **just right;** spotless, stainless, taintless, unblemished, untainted, unspotted, immaculate, **pure,** uncontaminated, unadulterated; sinless; chaste; infallible; irreproachable

fleabag NOUNS **flophouse** *and* fleabag <both nonformal>, dosshouse <Brit nonformal>

fledgling NOUNS **novice,** novitiate *or* noviciate, **tyro,** abecedarian, alphabetarian, **beginner**, entrant, **neophyte, tenderfoot** *and* **greenhorn** <both nonformal>, freshman, **rookie** *and* yardbird <both nonformal>, boot

flee VERBS **fly, take flight,** take to flight, take wing, fugitate, **run, cut and run** <nonformal>, run away from, bug out <nonformal>, **decamp,** pull up stakes, **take to one's heels,** make off, **depart**, do the disappearing act, make a quick exit, **beat a retreat** *or* **a hasty retreat, turn tail,** show the heels, show a clean *or* light pair of heels; **bolt, run for one's life**

fleeting ADJS **transient, transitory,** transitive; **temporary,** temporal; **passing,** flitting, flying, fading, dying; fugitive, fugacious

flexible ADJS **adaptable,** adjustable, resourceful, supple; **resilient, adaptable,** adjustable, able to roll with the punches *or* bend without breaking; **compliant,** pliant, complaisant, malleable, plastic, acquiescent, submissive, tractable, obedient

flickering ADJS **fluctuating,** alternating, **vacillating, wavering,** wavery, wavy, mazy, flitting, guttering, fitful, shifting, shuffling

flier NOUNS 1 **aviator, pilot,** air pilot, licensed pilot, private pilot, airline pilot, commercial pilot, aeronaut, flyboy *and* airplane driver *and* birdman <all nonformal>
2 **advertising matter,** leaflet, leaf, folder, handbill, bill, throwaway, handout, circular, broadside, broadsheet
3 **gamble,** chance, risk, risky thing, hazard; **speculation, venture,** plunge <nonformal>; calculated risk

flight NOUNS 1 **trip, run; hop** *and* **jump** <both nonformal>; powered flight; solo flight, **solo;** supersonic flight; test flight, **test hop** <nonformal>
2 exit, quick exit, making oneself scarce *and* getting the hell out <both nonformal>, bolt, disappearing act <nonformal>, hasty retreat; **decampment;** skedaddle *and* skedaddling <both nonformal>; French leave, absence without leave *or* AWOL; **desertion**; hegira

flighty ADJS **fickle,** skittish, **light;** coquettish, flirtatious, toying; volatile, mercurial, quicksilver; faddish; **scatterbrained**, unpredictable; **impulsive;** unreliable, undependable; whimsical, **capricious,** off-again-on-again

flimflam VERBS

<nonformal> **gyp, clip, scam,** rope in, hose, shave, beat, rook, diddle, do a number on, hustle, fuck, screw, have, pull something, pull a trick *or* stunt, give the business, stick, sting, burn, gouge, chisel, play *or* take for a sucker, make a patsy of, take for a ride

flimsy ADJS **fragile,** frangible, **breakable,** destructible, shattery, crumbly, brittle, fragmentable, fracturable; **unsubstantial,** sleazy, tacky <nonformal>, wispy, cobwebby, gossamery, papery, pasteboardy; gimcrack *and* gimcracky *and* cheap-jack *and* ticky-tacky <all nonformal>; jerry-built, jerry

flinch VERBS **shrink, shy,** shy away from, draw back, recoil, funk <nonformal>, **quail, cringe, wince, blench, blink,** say *or* cry uncle; put one's tail between one's legs

fling NOUNS 1 **revel, lark, escapade,** ploy; **celebration**; **party**; **spree, bout,**

wingding *and* randan <both nonformal>; **carouse, drinking bout**
2 **throw, toss, sling, cast, hurl,** chuck, chunk <nonformal>, lob, **heave,** shy, **pitch, toss,** peg <nonformal>
VERBS 3 **throw, sling, pitch, toss, cast, hurl, heave, chuck,** chunk *and* peg <both nonformal>, lob, shy, fire, burn, pepper <nonformal>, launch, dash, let fly, let go, let rip, let loose

flip NOUNS 1 **reverse, reversal,** flip-flop *and* U-turn <both nonformal>, turnabout, turnaround, **about-face,** about turn <Brit>, *volte-face* <Fr>; tergiversation, tergiversating; **change of mind;** second thoughts, better thoughts, afterthoughts, mature judgment
VERBS 2 **reverse,** transpose; **throw, fling, sling, pitch, toss, cast, hurl, heave, chuck,** chunk *and* peg <both nonformal>, lob, shy, fire, burn, pepper <nonformal>, launch, dash, let fly, let go, let rip, let loose

3 <nonformal> **blow one's top** *or* stack *or* cool, flip out, flip one's lid *or* wig, pop one's cork, blow a gasket, fly off the handle, **hit the ceiling,** go ape, go hog wild, go bananas, lose one's cool, go off the deep end

ADJS 4 **impudent, impertinent, pert,** flippant, **cocky** *and* cheeky *and* **fresh** *and* facy *and* crusty *and* nervy <all nonformal>; uncalled-for, gratuitous, biggety <nonformal>; **disrespectful,** derisive, brash, bluff; **saucy,** sassy <nonformal>; **glib,** smooth

flirt NOUNS 1 **coquette,** gold digger *and* vamp <both nonformal>; **trifler, dallier**
VERBS 2 **coquet; philander,** gallivant, play the field <nonformal>, run *or* play around, sow one's oats; **make eyes at, ogle,** eye, cast coquettish glances, cast sheep's eyes at, make goo-goo eyes at <nonformal>, *faire les yeux doux* <Fr>, look sweet upon <nonformal>; **trifle, dally**

flitter NOUNS 1 **flutter,** flit, **flicker, waver,** dance; shake, quiver; **sputter, splutter; palpitation,** throb, pit-a-pat, pitter-patter
VERBS 2 **flutter,** flit, flick, **flicker,** gutter, bicker, wave, **waver,** dance; **sputter, splutter; palpitate,** pulse, throb, pitter-patter, go pit-a-pat

float NOUNS 1 **raft;** balsa, balsa raft; life raft; boom; pontoon; buoy, life buoy; **life preserver**; surfboard
VERBS 2 ride, drift; **sail, scud, run,** shoot; skim, foot; ride the sea, walk the waters; float on one's back, do the dead-man's float
3 **issue,** put on the market; issue stock, go public <nonformal>; float a bond issue

flock NOUNS 1 **tuft,** fleck; forelock, widow's peak, fetlock, cowlick
2 fold, sheep; **congregation,** parishioners, churchgoers, assembly
3 **bunch, pack,** colony, host, troop, army, **herd, drove,** drive, drift, trip; flight, **swarm,** cloud

flood NOUNS 1 **torrent, river,** flash flood, wall of water, waterflood, **deluge;** spate, **pour,** freshet, fresh; **overflow,** spillage, spill, spillover, overflowing, overrunning, alluvion, alluvium, **inundation,** whelming, overwhelming, engulfment, submersion; washout
VERBS 2 **overflow,** inundate, engulf, swamp, sweep, whelm, overwhelm, deluge, submerge

floor NOUNS 1 **story,** level, flat; first floor *or* story, ground *or* street floor, *rez-de-chaussée* <Fr>; mezzanine, mezzanine floor, *entresol* <Fr>
2 **foundation,** *fond* <Fr>, firm foundation, **base, basis, footing,** basement, pavement, **ground,** grounds, **groundwork, seat,** sill, flooring, fundament
VERBS 3 **knock down,** dash down, send headlong, deck *and* lay out <both nonformal>, lay by the heels, ground, **bowl down** *or* **over** <nonformal>; **prostrate,** supinate; **throw,** pin, pin down; **stump** *or* buffalo *or* bamboozle <all nonformal>, beat the shit out of *or* lick <both nonformal>

floozy NOUNS **tart** *and* **chippy** *and* broad <all nonformal>, wanton, **loose woman,** easy woman <nonformal>, easy lay <nonformal>, woman of easy virtue

flop NOUNS 1 **tumble, fall,** *culbute* <Fr>, cropper *and* **spill** <both nonformal>; **header** <nonformal>; **pratfall** <nonformal>
2 failure; flopperoo, megaflop, gigaflop, **bust,** frost, **fizzle,** lemon, dud, nonstarter, **loser, washout,** turkey, bomb, dull thud, total loss <all nonformal>
VERBS 3 **go down, slump,** flop down <nonformal>; plump, plop *or* plop

down, plunk *or* plunk down <both nonformal>; founder

4 <nonformal> **not make it,** not hack it, not get to first base, fall flat on one's ass, lay an egg, go over like a lead balloon, draw a blank, bomb; fold, fold up; take it on the chin, take the count; crap out; strike out, fan, whiff

floppy ADJS **drooping, droopy,** limp, loose, nodding, loppy, lop; **sagging,** saggy, swag, sagging in folds; **bagging,** baggy, ballooning; lop-eared

floral ADJS **flowery; flowered,** floreate, floriate, floriated; **flowering, blossoming, blooming,** abloom, bloomy, florescent, inflorescent, efflorescent, in flower, in bloom, in blossom; horticultural, hortulan, floricultural

flotsam NOUNS **derelict,** castoff; jetsam, lagan, **flotsam and jetsam;** waifs and strays; abandonee, waif, throwaway, orphan, dogie <nonformal>; **castaway;** foundling

flounce VERBS **caper, cut capers,** cut a dido <nonformal>, curvet, cavort, capriole, **gambol,** gambado, **frisk, trip, skip,** bob, bounce, jump about; **romp,** ramp <nonformal>; **prance;** caracole

flounder VERBS 1 **pitch, toss, tumble,** toss and tumble, pitch and toss, **plunge,** hobbyhorse, pound, **rear, rock, roll, reel, swing, sway, lurch, yaw, heave,** scend, **welter, wallow;** make heavy weather
2 **have difficulty, struggle**

3 <nonformal> have one's back to the wall, not know where to turn, come to a dead end *or* standstill, not know whether one is coming or going, go around in circles, swim against the current; walk a tightrope, walk on eggshells *or* hot coals, dance on a hot griddle

flourish NOUNS 1 **display,** vaunt, fanfaronade, blazon, flaunt, flaunting; daring, brilliancy, éclat, bravura, flair; dash *and* splash *and* splurge <all nonformal>
2 turn of expression, manner *or* way of speaking, ornament, device, flower; Gongorism, floridity, euphuism
VERBS 3 **grow, develop,** wax, **increase**; grow like a weed <nonformal>; burgeon, thrive; mushroom, balloon; **enjoy good health,** burst with health, bloom, glow
4 **display,** make a great show of, brandish, wave

flourishing ADJS **thriving, prospering, booming** <nonformal>; vigorous, exuberant; in full swing, going strong <nonformal>; halcyon, palmy, balmy, rosy, piping, clear, fair

flout VERBS disregard, **slight,** slight over, treat with contempt, set at defiance, fly in the teeth *or* face of, **snap one's fingers at; thumb one's nose at,** cock a snook at, bite the thumb at; **disdain, despise, scorn**; hold in derision, scout, scoff at, **deride**

flow NOUNS 1 flowing, **flux,** fluency, profluence, fluid motion *or* movement; **stream, current,** set, trend, tide, water flow; drift, driftage; **course,** onward course, **surge, gush, rush,** onrush, spate, run, race
VERBS 2 **stream, issue, pour, surge, run, course, rush, gush, flush, flood;** empty into, flow into, join; tick away *or* by *or* on, run, proceed, advance, roll *or* press on, flit, fly, slip, slide, glide; **go easily, run smoothly,** work well, work like a machine, go like clockwork

flower NOUNS 1 **posy, blossom, bloom;** floweret, floret, floscule
VERBS 2 be in flower, **blossom, bloom,** be in bloom, blow, effloresce, floreate, burst into bloom; **thrive, flourish,** boom; batten

flowery ADJS **floral; flowered,** floreate, floriate, floriated; **flowering, blossoming, blooming,** abloom, bloomy, florescent, inflorescent, efflorescent, in flower, in bloom, in blossom; florid; flamboyant, fussy, frilly, frilled, flouncy, gingerbread *or* gingerbready; mannered, figured, ornamented

flowing ADJS **streaming, running, pouring,** fluxive, fluxional, coursing, racing, gushing, rushing, onrushing, surging, surgy, torrential, rough, whitewater; **fluent,** profluent, affluent, defluent, decurrent, confluent, diffluent

flub NOUNS 1 **bungle, blunder, botch,** boner *and* bonehead play <both nonformal>, boggle, bobble *and* boo-boo *and* screw-up *and* fuck-up <all nonformal>; **fumble, muff,** fluff, miscue <nonformal>; **error, mistake**

VERBS 2 <nonformal> **goof, pull a**

boner, bobble, lay an egg, put *or* stick one's foot in it, stub one's toe, drop the ball, drop a brick; **blow,** blow it, bitch up, hash up, **mess up,** flub the dub, **make a mess** *or* **hash of,** foul up, fuck up, goof up, bollix up, **screw up, louse up, gum up,** go at it ass-backwards; put one's foot in one's mouth

fluctuate VERBS **vacillate, waver, waffle** <nonformal>, pendulate, oscillate, wobble, wobble about, teeter, dither, swing from one thing to another, **shilly-shally,** back and fill, keep *or* leave hanging in midair; blow hot and cold

fluent ADJS **flowing,** tripping; **smooth,** pleasing, facile, **easy, graceful, elegant**

fluff NOUNS 1 **down,** flue, floss, **fuzz, fur,** pile; eiderdown, eider; swansdown; thistledown; lint
2 **fumble, muff,** miscue <nonformal>; **slip,** trip, stumble; *gaucherie, étourderie, balourdise* <all Fr>; **hash** *and* **mess** <both nonformal>; **error, mistake**
VERBS 3 massage, knead, plump, plump up, fluff up, shake up

fluffy ADJS flossy, **downy,** pubescent, feathery; fleecy, woolly, lanate; furry

fluid NOUNS 1 **liquid;** liquor, drink, beverage; liquid extract, fluid extract; **juice, sap,** latex; milk, whey; water; **body fluid, blood;** semiliquid
ADJS 2 **changeable,** impermanent, transient, transitory; **variable,** plastic, malleable, fluidal, fluidic, **fluent, flowing,** runny; **liquid**

fluke NOUNS **fortuity, accident,** casualty, adventure, hazard; freak, freak occurrence *or* accident; chance hit, lucky shot, long shot, one in a million, lucky strike *and* scratch hit *and* **break** <all nonformal>

flunk VERBS **flunk out** <nonformal>; **fail,** bust *and* wash out <both nonformal>

flunky NOUNS **lackey,** livery *or* liveried servant; **footman,** *valet de pied* <Fr>; henchman, camp follower, hanger-on, satellite, creature, stooge <nonformal>, jackal, minion, myrmidon; menial

flurry NOUNS 1 haste, hurry, commotion, rush, precipitation
2 **gust,** wind gust, **blast,** blow, flaw, scud <Scots>; snow flurry

flush NOUNS 1 **blushing, flushing,** coloring, mantling, reddening, rubicundity, rosiness; **blush,** suffusion, red face; rush, **gush; glow,** incandescence, fieriness
ADJS 2 flushed, **rosy,** rosy-cheeked, apple-cheeked, ruddy, pink, pink-cheeked
3 **prosperous,** comfortable, provided for, well provided for, fat, flush with money, worth a great deal; **full,** filled, **replete,** plenary, capacity

fluster VERBS **confuse,** throw into confusion *or* chaos, entangle, **mix up;** flummox <nonformal>, **flutter,** put into a flutter, **flurry,** rattle, ruffle, **disconcert,** discomfit, **discompose,** discombobulate <nonformal>, **embarrass,** put out, disturb, perturb, bother, pother, bug <nonformal>

flutter NOUNS 1 **dither, tizzy** <nonformal>, swivet, foofaraw, **pucker** <nonformal>, **twitter,** twitteration <nonformal>, **fluster, fret, fuss,** pother, bother; **bustle, flurry,** scramble, ferment, stew, sweat; **palpitation,** arrhythmia, pitter-patter, pit-a-pat
2 **flicker, dance, quiver;** flickering, fluttering, bickering, guttering, dancing, quivering, lambency
VERBS 3 **agitate, disturb, perturb,** shake up, perturbate, **disquiet, discompose, upset, trouble, unsettle, stir,** swirl, flurry, flutter the dovecot, fret, roughen, ruffle, rumple, ripple, ferment, convulse; flitter, flit, flick, **flicker,** gutter, bicker, wave, **waver,** dance; **palpitate,** pulse, throb, pitter-patter, go pit-a-pat

fly VERBS 1 be airborne, wing, take wing, wing one's way, take *or* make a flight, take to the air, take the air, volitate, be wafted; **pilot,** control, be at the controls, fly left seat; **copilot,** fly right seat; solo; **barnstorm** <nonformal>; fly blind, fly by the seat of one's pants <nonformal>
2 **flee, take flight,** take to flight, take wing, fugitate, **run, cut and run** <nonformal>, make a precipitate departure, **run off** *or* **away,** run away from, bug out <nonformal>, **decamp,** pull up stakes, **take to one's heels,** make off, **depart,** make a quick exit, **beat a retreat** *or* **a hasty retreat, turn tail**

fly-by-night ADJS **untrustworthy,** unfaithworthy, untrusty, trustless, **unreliable, undependable,** irresponsible, unsure, not to be trusted, not to be depended *or* relied upon; **short-lived, ephemeral,** evanescent, volatile

foam NOUNS 1 **froth; spume,** sea foam, scud; **spray, surf,** breakers, white water, spoondrift *or* **spindrift, suds, lather,** soap-suds; beer-suds, head; head, collar

stinging, ringing spindrift
KIPLING

VERBS 2 **froth,** spume, cream; **lather,** suds, sud; scum, mantle; **aerate,** whip, beat, whisk; **seethe, fume,** stew, ferment, stir, churn

focus NOUNS 1 focal point, prime focus, point of convergence; **center of interest** *or* attention, focus of attention; center of consciousness; **center of attraction, centerpiece,** clou, mecca, cynosure, cynosure of all eyes; polestar, lodestar; magnet; **gist,** gravamen, **nub** <nonformal>, nucleus, center, kernel, **core, pith**
VERBS 2 focalize, come to a point *or* focus, bring to *or* into focus; bring *or* come to a head, get to the heart of the matter home in on; zero in on; draw a bead on *and* get a handle on <nonformal>; **concentrate,** concenter, get it together <nonformal>; **channel,** direct, canalize, channelize; converge

focus on VERBS **concentrate,** concentrate the mind *or* thoughts, concentrate on *or* upon, attend closely to, brood on, give *or* devote the mind to, glue the mind to, cleave to the thought of, fix the mind *or* thoughts upon, bend the mind upon, bring the mind to bear upon; get to the point; gather *or* collect one's thoughts, pull one's wits together, focus *or* fix one's thoughts, marshal *or* arrange one's thoughts *or* ideas

foe NOUNS **enemy,** foeman, **adversary, antagonist;** bitter enemy; sworn enemy; archenemy; the other side, the opposition; **bane**, bête noire

fog NOUNS 1 pea soup *and* peasouper *and* pea-soup fog <all nonformal>; London fog, London special <Brit nonformal>; **smog,** smaze <smoke-haze>; murkiness, murk, mistiness, mist, fogginess
VERBS 2 **blur, dim, pale,** soften, film, mist; defocus, lose resolution *or* sharpness *or* distinctness, go soft at the edges; befog; fog in; smog; **mist,** mist over, mist up, bemist, enmist; **obscure,** muddle, muddy, fuzz, **confuse**

foggy ADJS 1 soupy *or* pea-soupy <nonformal>, nubilous; fog-bound, fogged-in; smoggy; hazy, misty; so thick you can cut it with a knife; **murky,** cloudy, nebulous
2 **muddled,** in a muddle; adrift, at sea, fogged, in a fog, hazy, muzzy <nonformal>, misted, misty, cloudy, beclouded

foible NOUNS **vice, weakness,** weakness of the flesh, **flaw,** moral flaw *or* blemish, **frailty, infirmity; failing,** failure; weak point, weak side, Achilles' heel, vulnerable place, chink in one's armor, weak link

foil VERBS **thwart, frustrate, cross, balk;** spike, scotch, checkmate; **counter,** contravene, counteract, countermand, counterwork; **derail;** take the wind out of one's sails, steal one's thunder, cut the ground from under one

foliage NOUNS **leafage,** leafiness, umbrage, foliation; frondage, frondescence; vernation

folk NOUNS **family,** brood, **house, household,** hearth, hearthside, ménage, people, homefolk, folks *and* homefolks <both nonformal>; **common people, ordinary people** *or* **folk, persons, folks,** gentry; plain people *or* folks

folklore NOUNS **legend, lore,** mythical lore; myth, mythology, folktale, folk motif; racial memory, archetypal myth *or* image *or* pattern; **superstition,** popular belief, **old wives' tale**

folksy ADJS **informal, natural,** simple, plain, homely, homey, down-home *and* folksy <both nonformal>, *haymish* <Yiddish>; **unaffected, unassuming**; unconstrained

follow VERBS 1 **pursue, shadow** *and* **tail** <both nonformal>, **trail,** trail after, follow in the trail of, camp on the trail of, **heel,** tread close upon, breathe down the neck of, follow in the wake of, tailgate <nonformal>, go in the rear of, bring up the rear, eat the dust of, take *or* swallow one's dust; tag *and* **tag after** *and* tag along <all nonformal>; string along <nonformal>; **dog,** bedog, **hound,** chase, get after, take out *or* take off after, **pursue**
2 **emulate,** follow in the steps *or* footsteps of, walk in the shoes of, put oneself in another's shoes, follow in the wake of, follow the example of, follow suit; pattern after, pattern on, take after, take a leaf out of one's book
3 **observe, keep, heed,** keep the faith; **live up to,** act up to, practice what one preaches, **be faithful to,** keep faith with, do justice to, do the right thing by
4 **succeed, ensue,** come *or* go after,

come next; inherit, take the mantle of, step into the shoes *or* place of, take over

follower NOUNS **hanger-on, adherent,** dangler, appendage, **dependent, satellite,** cohort, retainer, servant, man, shadow, tagtail, **henchman,** heeler <nonformal>; successor; **disciple,** adherent, votary

following ADJS trailing, on the track *or* trail; succeeding, successive, sequent, lineal, consecutive, ensuing, attendant; back-to-back <nonformal>, consecutive; **pursuing,** pursuant; **questing, seeking, searching**; **in pursuit,** in hot pursuit, in full cry

follow-through NOUNS **sequel,** sequela *or* sequelae, sequelant, sequent, sequitur, **consequence**; **continuation,** continuance, **follow-up** <nonformal>

follow up VERBS **pursue, follow, go after,** take out *or* off after <nonformal>, bay after, run after, run in pursuit of, make after, go in pursuit of; **go to all lengths, go all out, go the limit** <nonformal>, go the whole way, **go the whole hog** <nonformal>, cover a lot of ground, make a federal case of *and* make a big deal of *and* do up brown *and* do with a vengeance <all nonformal>, **see it through** <nonformal>, follow *or* prosecute to a conclusion

folly NOUNS **foolishness,** foolery, foolheadedness, **stupidity, asininity,** *niaiserie* <Fr>; *bêtise* <Fr>; **inanity, fatuity,** fatuousness; act of folly, absurdity, *sottise* <Fr>, foolish *or* stupid thing, dumb thing to do <nonformal>; fool *or* fool's trick, dumb trick <nonformal>; **imprudence, indiscretion,** imprudent *or* unwise step; blunder

foment VERBS **incite, instigate, put up to** <nonformal>; ferment, **agitate, arouse,** excite, stir up, work up, whip up; **inflame,** incense, **fire,** heat, heat up, impassion; **provoke,** wave the bloody shirt

fond ADJS **loving,** lovesome, **adoring, devoted, affectionate,** demonstrative, **romantic, sentimental, tender,** soft <nonformal>, melting; infatuated, doting

fondle VERBS **stroke, pet, caress**; **nuzzle,** nose, rub noses; feel up <nonformal>; rub, rub against, massage, knead; **cherish,** entertain, treasure

fond of VERBS 1 **enamored of,** partial to, **in love with,** attached to, wedded to, devoted to, wrapped up in; **taken with,** smitten with, struck with

2 <nonformal> **crazy about,** mad *or* nuts *or* nutty *or* wild about, swacked on, sweet on, stuck on, gone on

food NOUNS 1 foodstuff, food and drink, sustenance, kitchen stuff, victualage, **comestibles, edibles,** eatables, viands, **cuisine,** tucker <Australia>, ingesta <pl>; **fare,** cheer, creature comfort; provision, provender

2 <nonformal> **grub,** grubbery, **eats, chow,** chuck, grits, groceries, the nosebag, scarf *or* scoff, tuck, victuals *or* vittles

fool NOUNS 1 **damn fool,** tomfool, perfect fool, born fool; *schmuck* <Yiddish>; **ass,** jackass, stupid ass, egregious ass; zany, **clown, buffoon,** doodle; sop, milksop; mome <old>, mooncalf, softhead; figure of fun; **lunatic**; **ignoramus**

2 <nonformal> **blockhead, airhead,** bubblehead, fluffhead, featherhead, woodenhead, dolthead, dumbhead, dummy, dum-dum, dumbo, dumb cluck, dodo head, doodoohead, dumbbell, dumb bunny, stupidhead, dullhead, bufflehead, bonehead, jughead, thickhead, thickskull, numbskull, putz, lunkhead, chucklehead, knucklehead, chowderhead, headbanger *and* jolterhead <both Brit>, muttonhead, beefhead, meathead, noodlehead, thimblewit, pinhead, pinbrain, peabrain, cabbagehead, pumpkin head, fathead, blubberhead, muddlehead, puzzlehead, addlebrain, addlehead, addlepate, tottyhead <old>, puddinghead, stupe, mushhead, blunderhead, dunderhead, dunderpate, clodpate, clodhead, clodpoll, jobbernowl *and* gaby *and* gowk <all Brit>

VERBS 3 befool, make a fool of, practice on one's credulity, **pull one's leg,** make an ass of; **trick; spoof** *and* **kid** *and* put one on <all nonformal>; **play a trick on,** play a practical joke upon, send on a fool's errand; fake one out <nonformal>; sell one a bill of goods, give one a snow job; toy with, fiddle with, fool with, play with

fool around VERBS

<nonformal> **monkey, monkey around,** fiddle, fiddle around, fiddle-faddle, frivol, horse around, fool around, play around, mess around, kid around, **screw around,** muck around, muck about <Brit>, fart around, piss around, bugger around, diddle around, frig around, mess around; jerk off

foolhardy ADJS **harebrained,** madcap, **wild,** wild-ass <nonformal>, madbrain, madbrained; **audacious;** forward, bold, **presumptuous; daring,** daredevil, fire-eating, death-defying; adventurous

foolish ADJS fool <nonformal>, fool-headed <nonformal>, **stupid, dumb** <nonformal>, clueless <Brit nonformal>, **asinine; silly,** apish, dizzy <nonformal>; **fatuous,** fatuitous, inept, **inane; senseless, witless, thoughtless,** insensate, brainless; **idiotic, insane**

foolproof ADJS **convenient,** goofproof <nonformal>, practical, untroublesome, user-friendly; adaptable, feasible

foothold NOUNS **footing, toehold,** hold, perch, **purchase**; **standing,** stand, stance, standing place, *point d'appui* <Fr>, *locus standi* <L>

footloose ADJS **free; at liberty, at large,** on the loose, **loose,** unengaged, disengaged, detached, unattached, uncommitted, uninvolved, clear, in the clear, go-as-you-please, easygoing, footloose and fancy-free, free and easy

fop NOUNS **dandy,** coxcomb, macaroni, gallant, dude *and* swell *and* sport <all nonformal>, ponce *and* toff <both Brit nonformal>, exquisite, blood, fine gentleman, puppy, jackanapes, jack-a-dandy, fribble, clotheshorse, fashion plate

forage VERBS **plunder, pillage,** spoliate, despoil, depredate, prey on *or* upon, **raid,** reive <Scots>, ravage, ravish, raven, maraud, foray

foray NOUNS **raid,** razzia; **invasion, incursion,** inroad, irruption; **pillage, plunder,** sack; **marauding,** foraging; **venture**

forbearance NOUNS **patience, tolerance,** toleration, **acceptance; indulgence,** longaninimity, lenience, leniency; sweet reasonableness; forbearing, refraining, forbearingness; **sufferance, endurance; temperance,** nothing in excess, sobriety, soberness, frugality, abnegation

forbid VERBS **prohibit; disallow, rule out** *or* **against;** deny, **reject**; say no to, **refuse**; **bar,** debar, preclude, exclude, exclude from, shut out, shut *or* close the door on, **prevent**; **ban,** put under the ban, **outlaw; repress, suppress**; **enjoin,** put under an injunction, issue an injunction against, issue a prohibitory injunction; **proscribe,** inhibit, embargo, **lay** *or* **put an embargo on; taboo**

forbidding ADJS **offensive, objectionable, odious, repulsive,** repellent, rebarbative, **repugnant, revolting; prohibitive,** prohibitory, prohibiting; inhibitive, inhibitory, **repressive, suppressive**; proscriptive, interdictive, interdictory; preclusive, exclusive, **preventive**

force NOUNS 1 **strength, might,** mightiness, powerfulness, stamina; **potency, power**; **energy**; **vigor, vitality,** vigorousness, heartiness, lustiness

2 **meaning, significance, signification,** *significatum* <L>, *signifié* <Fr>, point, **sense,** idea, **purport, import,** where one is coming from <nonformal>; effect, impact, consequence, practical consequence, response; **validity, soundness,** solidity, substantiality, **justness;** authority, **authoritativeness; cogency,** weight, persuasiveness

VERBS 3 **compel, make;** cause, cause to; enforce, **drive,** impel; dragoon, use force upon, force one's hand, hold a pistol *or* gun to one's head; **force upon,** impose by force *or* main force, strong-arm <nonformal>, force down one's throat, enforce upon

forceful ADJS **powerful, potent,** prepotent, powerpacked, **mighty,** irresistible, avalanchine, forcible, dynamic; **cogent,** striking, telling, effective, impactful, valid, incisive, trenchant

forcible ADJS **strong, forceful, mighty, powerful,** puissant <nonformal>, **potent**; **stout, sturdy, stalwart, rugged,** hale; **energetic, vigorous, strenuous, strong, dynamic,** kinetic, intense, acute, keen, incisive, trenchant, vivid, vibrant; **enterprising, aggressive,** proactive, activist, can-do *and* gung ho *and* take-over *and* take-charge <all nonformal>; **coercive,** steamroller *and* bulldozer *and* sledgehammer *and* strong-arm <all nonformal>; violent

foreboding ADJS **anxious, concerned, apprehensive,** misgiving, suspenseful, strained, tense, tensed up <nonformal>, nail-biting, white-knuckle <nonformal>; **ominous,** premonitory, **portentous,** portending; boding, **bodeful; inauspicious, ill-omened,** ill-boding, of ill *or* fatal omen, of evil portent, loaded *or* laden *or* freighted *or* fraught with doom, looming, looming over; **unpropitious, unpromising, unfavorable, threatening, menacing, lowering;** dire, baleful, baneful, **ill-fated,** ill-starred, evil-starred, star-crossed

forecast NOUNS 1 **prediction, foretelling,** foreshowing, forecasting, **prognosis,** prognostication, presage <old>, presaging; **prophecy,** prophesying, vaticination

VERBS 2 **predict,** make a prediction, **foretell, soothsay,** prefigure, **prophesy, prognosticate,** call <nonformal>, make a prophecy *or* prognosis, vaticinate, forebode, presage, see ahead, see *or* tell the future, read the future, see in the crystal ball; **foresee**

forefathers NOUNS **ancestors, antecedents, predecessors,** ascendants, **fathers, forebears,** progenitors, primogenitors

forefront NOUNS front, point, **leading edge, cutting edge, vanguard,** van; cutting edge, front line, **fore,** forepart, forequarter, foreside, forehand; **priority,** anteriority

foregoing ADJS **former;** aforesaid, aforementioned, beforementioned, abovementioned, aforenamed, forenamed, forementioned, said, named, same; aforegoing, **preceding**; last, latter

foreign ADJS **alien,** strange, exotic, foreign-looking; exterior, **external;** extrinsic; ulterior, outside, outland, outlandish; barbarian, barbarous, barbaric; foreign-born; intrusive

foreigner NOUNS **alien, stranger, outsider,** nonmember, not one of us, not our sort, not the right sort, the other, outlander, *Uitlander* <Afrikaans>, tramontane, ultramontane, barbarian, foreign devil <China>, *gringo* <Sp Amer>

foremost ADJS 1 **first,** headmost; **preceding,** antecedent; **prior**; **chief**, **leading,** up-front <nonformal>, head, prime, primary; principal, paramount, **foremost, leading, dominant,** crowning, capital, **cardinal; predominant,** preponderant, prevailing, hegemonic *or* hegemonical

ADVS 2 **before**, in front, out in front, outfront, headmost, in the the van, in the forefront, in advance

forerunner NOUNS **harbinger, precursor,** messenger <old>, **herald,** announcer, *buccinator novi temporis* <L>; presager, premonitor, foreshadower; **trailblazer, pathfinder;** *voorlooper* <Dutch>, vaunt-courier, avant-courier, frontrunner; ancestor

foresee VERBS see beforehand *or* ahead, foreglimpse, foretaste, **anticipate,** contemplate, envision, envisage, **look forward to,** look ahead, look beyond, look *or* pry *or* peep into the future; **predict**; think ahead *or* beforehand; dope *and* dope out <both nonformal>; call the turn *and* call one's shot <both nonformal>

foreseeable ADJS **predictable, divinable, foretellable, calculable,** anticipatable; **foreknowable,** precognizable; **probable**

foresight NOUNS foreseeing, looking ahead, **prevision,** divination, forecast; **prediction**; **foreglimpse,** foreglance, foregleam; **prospect,** prospection; **anticipation,** contemplation, envisionment, envisagement; **foresightedness;** sagacity, provision, forehandedness, readiness, prudence

forest NOUNS 1 **woodland, wood, woods, timberland; timber,** stand of timber, forest land, forest cover, forest preserve, state *or* national forest

ADJS 2 **sylvan, woodland,** forestal; dendrologic, dendrological, silvicultural, afforestational, reforestational; **wooded,** timbered, forested, arboreous; **woody,** woodsy, bosky, bushy, shrubby, scrubby; copsy, braky

forestall VERBS cajole, **circumvent,** get around; **monopolize,** hog *and* grab all of *and* gobble up <all nonformal>, take it all, have all to oneself, have exclusive possession of *or* exclusive rights to; engross, tie up, foreclose, **preclude,** exclude, debar, **obviate,** anticipate; rule out

foretell VERBS **predict,** make a prediction, **soothsay,** prefigure, **forecast, prophesy, prognosticate,** call <nonformal>, vaticinate, forebode, presage, see ahead, see *or* tell the future, read the future, see in the crystal ball; dope *and* dope out <both nonformal>; call the turn *and* call one's shot <both nonformal>

forethought NOUNS **foresight,** foresightedness, forehandedness, forethoughtfulness; **providence,** provision, forearming; precautions, steps, measures, steps and measures; **premeditation,** predeliberation, preconsideration; caution

forever NOUNS 1 **an eternity,** endless time, **time without end**

a short parenthesis in a long period
DONNE

ADVS 2 **forevermore, for ever and ever,** forever and aye; forever and a day <nonformal>, now and forever, **eternally, evermore,** ever and anon, ever and again; **for good,** for keeps <nonformal>, for all time; **to the end of time,** till time stops *or* runs out, till hell freezes over <nonformal>, till the cows come home <nonformal>

forewarned ADJS **expectant,** forearmed, forestalling, ready, prepared; **looking forward to,** looking for, watching for, on the watch *or* lookout for

foreword NOUNS **prelude, preamble, preface,** prologue, introduction, *avant-propos* <Fr>, protasis, proem, proemium, prolegomenon *or* prolegomena, exordium

forfeit VERBS **lose,** incur loss, **suffer loss,** undergo privation *or* deprivation, be bereaved *or* bereft of, have no more, let slip, let slip through one's fingers; default; **sacrifice;** go broke *and* lose one's shirt *and* take a bath *or* to the cleaners *and* tap out <all nonformal>

forgery NOUNS fakery, plagiarism, plagiarizing, plagiary; **fake, counterfeit,** counterfeit money, funny *or* phony *or* bogus money <nonformal>, false *or* bad money, queer <nonformal>, green goods <nonformal>; bad check, rubber check *and* bounced check *and* kite <all nonformal>

forget VERBS **forgive and forget,** dismiss from one's thoughts, think no more of, not give it another *or* a second thought, let it go <nonformal>, let it pass, **let bygones be bygones;** write off, charge off, charge to experience; bury the hatchet; **drop the subject,** give it no more thought; turn one's back upon, turn away from, turn one's attention from, walk away; disremember *and* disrecollect <both nonformal>, fail to remember, forget to remember, **have no remembrance** *or* **recollection of,** be unable to recollect *or* recall, draw a blank <nonformal>

forgetful ADJS **forgetting,** inclined to forget, **memoryless, unremembering, unmindful,** absentminded, **oblivious,** insensible to the past, with a mind *or* memory like a sieve; suffering from *or* stricken with amnesia, amnesic, amnestic; blocked, repressed, suppressed, sublimated, converted; heedless; Lethean

forgive VERBS **pardon, excuse,** give *or* grant forgiveness, spare; amnesty, grant amnesty to, grant immunity *or* exemption; hear confession, **absolve,** remit, give absolution, shrive, grant remission; **exonerate, exculpate**; blot out one's sins, wipe the slate clean, **write off,** absolve, **cancel,** nullify; wipe out, obliterate

forgone ADJS **relinquished,** released, disposed of; waived, dispensed with; forsworn, renounced, abjured, **abandoned**; recanted, retracted; **surrendered,** ceded, yielded; sacrificed

forgotten ADJS clean forgotten <nonformal>, **unremembered,** disremembered *and* disrecollected <both nonformal>, **unrecollected, unretained, unrecalled,** past recollection *or* recall, out of the mind, lost, erased, effaced, obliterated, gone out of one's head *or* recollection, consigned to oblivion, buried *or* sunk in oblivion; out of sight out of mind; misremembered, misrecollected

fork NOUNS 1 **prong,** trident; **branch, ramification,** stem, tributary, offshoot; **crotch,** crutch; **delta; groin,** inguen; furcula, furculum, **wishbone**

VERBS 2 furcate, bifurcate, trifurcate, divaricate; **branch,** stem, ramify, branch off *or* out

forlorn ADJS lorn; **abandoned, forsaken, deserted, desolate,** godforsaken <nonformal>, friendless, unfriended, kithless, fatherless, motherless, homeless; helpless, defenseless; outcast

form NOUNS 1 **shape, figure;** figuration, **configuration;** formation, **conformation; structure**; **build,** make, frame; **arrangement**; makeup, format, layout; **composition**; cut, set, stamp, type, turn, cast, mold, impression, pattern, matrix, model, mode, modality

VERBS 2 formalize, **shape, fashion,** tailor, frame, figure, **lick into shape** <nonformal>; work, knead; set, fix; **forge, mold,** model, take form, shape, **shape up, take shape;** materialize; **organize,** structure, shape up; take form, take order, crystallize, **fall** *or* **drop into place,** fall into line *or* order *or* series, fall into rank, take rank; come together, draw up, gather around

formal NOUNS 1 **dance, ball,** *bal* <Fr>; masked ball, masque, mask, masquerade ball, masquerade, *bal masqué* <Fr>, *bal costumé* <Fr>, fancy-dress ball, cotillion; promenade, **prom** <nonformal> ADJS 2 **orderly,** ordered, **regular, well-regulated,** uniform, **systematic, harmonious;** businesslike, routine, steady, normal, habitual, usual, en règle, in hand; **nominal,** cognominal; **titular, in name only,** nominative; **stiff, stilted,** Latinate, *guindé* <Fr>, **labored,** ponderous, elephantine, lumbering, cumbrous, leaden, heavy, unwieldy, sesquipedalian, inkhorn, turgid, bombastic, pompous

formality NOUNS **form, formalness; ceremony,** ceremonial, **ceremoniousness; dignity,** gravity, weight, *gravitas* <L>, weighty dignity, staidness, reverend seriousness, **solemnity**; **pomp**; pomposity

formalize VERBS ritualize, solemnize, **celebrate,** dignify; **observe;** conventionalize, stylize; **normalize,** standardize, regularize; **codify**

format NOUNS **form, shape, figure;** figuration, **configuration;** formation, **conformation; structure**; **arrangement**; makeup, layout; **composition**

formation NOUNS **composition, constitution, construction,** fabrication, fashioning, shaping, organization; structure, configuration, array, makeup, lineup, setup, layout; formulation, **configuration,** form, array

former ADJS foregoing; aforesaid, aforementioned, beforementioned, abovementioned, aforenamed, forenamed, forementioned, said, named, same; past, fore, **previous,** late, recent, **once, onetime,** sometime, **erstwhile,** then, quondam; **prior**

formidable ADJS **difficult,** difficile; **not easy,** no picnic; **hard, tough** *and* **rough** *and* **rugged** <all nonformal>, rigorous, brutal, severe; wicked *and* mean *and* **hairy** <all nonformal>; **arduous, strenuous, toilsome, laborious,** operose, Herculean; easier said than done, like pulling teeth; exacting, demanding

formula NOUNS **rule,** form; rule of action *or* conduct, moral precept; ordinance, imperative, **regulation,** *règlement* <Fr>; **principle,** principium, settled principle, general principle *or* truth, tenet, convention; **guideline,** ground rule, rubric, protocol, working rule, working principle, standard procedure; guiding principle, golden rule; **code; recipe,** receipt; **prescription;** formulary

formulate VERBS **say, express,** give expression, verbalize, put in words, find words to express; **word,** put into words, couch, phrase; find a phrase for, give expression *or* words to, state, **frame,** conceive, style, couch, clothe *or* embody in words, express by *or* in words; put, present, set out; formularize; **write, indite,** produce, prepare

fornicate VERBS **be promiscuous,** sleep around *and* swing <both nonformal>; **debauch, wanton,** rake, chase women, womanize, whore, sow one's wild oats; **philander; dissipate**; **cheat, commit adultery,** get a little on the side <nonformal>

forsake VERBS **abandon, desert; quit, leave,** leave behind, take leave of, depart from, absent oneself from, turn one's back upon, turn one's tail upon, say goodbye to, bid a long farewell to, walk away, **walk** *or* **run out on** <nonformal>, **leave flat** *and* leave high and dry *or* holding the bag *or* in the lurch <all nonformal>, leave one to one's fate, throw to the wolves <nonformal>

forsaken ADJS **abandoned, deserted,** left; disused; **derelict,** castaway, jettisoned; marooned; junk, junked, discarded; **desolate,** godforsaken <nonformal>, friendless, unfriended, fatherless, motherless, homeless

fort NOUNS **fortress,** post; **stronghold,** hold, safehold, fasthold, strong point, **fastness,** keep, ward, **bastion,** donjon, **citadel, castle,** tower, tower of strength, strong point

forte NOUNS **métier, strong point,** long suit; **specialty, line, pursuit, pet subject, field,** area, main interest; **vocation**

forth ADVS **forward, forwards, onward, onwards, on,** along, **ahead; out,** outward, outwards, outwardly

forthcoming ADJS **approaching, nearing,** advancing; attracted to, drawn to; **com-**

ing, oncoming, upcoming, to come; proximate, near; **issuing,** arising, surfacing

forthright ADJS **candid, frank, sincere,** genuine, ingenuous, frankhearted; **open,** openhearted, transparent, open-faced; artless; **straightforward, direct,** up-front *and* straight <both nonformal>, downright, straight-out <nonformal>; **outspoken, plain-spoken,** free-spoken, free-speaking, free-tongued; explicit, unequivocal; **blunt,** bluff, brusque

fortify VERBS **strengthen, invigorate,** beef up <nonformal>, brace, buttress, prop, shore up, support, undergird, brace up; steel, harden, caseharden, anneal, stiffen, **toughen,** temper, nerve; confirm, sustain; **doctor** *and* **doctor up** <both nonformal>; spike <nonformal>, lace

fortitude NOUNS **hardihood,** hardiness; **pluckiness; spunkiness** *and* grittiness *and* nerviness <all nonformal>, mettlesomeness; **gameness,** grit, **stamina,** toughness, **mettle,** bottom; **heart,** spirit, stout heart, heart of oak; **resolution**, resoluteness, tenaciousness, tenacity, pertinaciousness, pertinacity, bulldog courage

fortress NOUNS **stronghold,** hold, safehold, fasthold, strong point, **fastness,** keep, ward, **bastion,** donjon, **citadel, castle,** tower; **fort**

fortuitous ADJS **incidental,** adventitious, **accidental, chance,** casual, aleatory, unessential *or* inessential *or* nonessential; **circumstantial,** conditional, provisional

fortunate ADJS **lucky, providential; in luck; blessed,** blessed with luck, favored; born under a lucky star, born with a silver spoon in one's mouth, born on the sunny side of the hedge; out of the woods, over the hump; **auspicious**

fortune NOUNS **wealth, treasure,** handsome fortune; full *or* heavy *or* well-lined *or* bottomless *or* fat *or* bulging purse, deep pockets <nonformal>; **chance,** happenstance, fate, **destiny,** whatever comes, *moira* <Gk>, lot; **good fortune** *or* **luck,** happy fortune, **luck,** the breaks <nonformal>, fortune's favor

forum NOUNS **conference,** discussion group, buzz session <nonformal>, **round table, panel;** open forum, colloquium, symposium; town meeting; **powwow** <nonformal>; agora, marketplace, open forum, public square; **tribunal, board,** curia, Areopagus

forward VERBS 1 **advance, promote,** forward, hasten, contribute to, foster, aid, facilitate, expedite, abet; **dispatch,** transmit, remit, consign

ADJS 2 **insolent,** insulting; pushy <nonformal>, obtrusive, familiar; **self-assertive,** self-asserting, importunate; bold, pert, bumptious; **precocious, advanced,** far ahead, born before one's time

ADVS 3 **forwards, onward, onwards, forth, on,** along, **ahead;** on the way to, on the road *or* high road to, en route to *or* for; **frontward,** frontwards, vanward, **headward,** headwards

foster VERBS **nurture,** nourish, mother, care for, lavish care on, feed, parent, rear, sustain, cultivate, **cherish;** pamper, coddle, cosset, spoon-feed; provide for, support; take charge of, **take under one's wing,** look *or* watch out for <nonformal>, have *or* keep an eye on *or* upon, keep a sharp eye on *or* upon, **watch over,** keep watch over, **watch, mind, tend**

foul VERBS 1 **defile, befoul; sully;** foul one's own nest, shit where one eats <nonformal>, mess *and* mess up <both nonformal>; **pollute, corrupt, contaminate, infect; taint,** tarnish, profane, violate, desecrate, defile, debase

ADJS 2 **filthy, vile,** mucky, **nasty,** icky *and* yecchy *and* yucky *and* gross *and* grungy *and* scuzzy <all nonformal>; malodorous, mephitic, rank, **fetid; putrid, rotten;** pollutive; **offensive, objectionable,** repellent, rebarbative, **repugnant, revolting,** forbidding, nauseating, disgusting; **odious, repulsive, obscene,** ithyphallic, **ribald, pornographic, salacious,** lurid, **dirty, smutty,** raunchy <nonformal>, blue, smoking-room, impure, unchaste, unclean, fulsome, offensive, unprintable, unrepeatable, not fit for mixed company

foulmouthed ADJS **cursing, maledictory,** imprecatory, **damnatory,** denunciatory, epithetic, epithetical; **abusive,** vituperative, contumelious; calumnious, calumniatory; **scurrilous;** blasphemous, **profane, foul, vile,** thersitical, **dirty** <nonformal>, **obscene,** dysphemistic, scatologic, scatological, coprological, ribald, Rabelaisian, raw, risqué; foul-tongued, foul-spoken

found VERBS **inaugurate,** institute, **establish,** set up <nonformal>; constitute, install, form, **set up, organize,** equip, endow, realize, materialize, effect, effectuate

foundation NOUNS 1 **warrant, reason,** good reason, **cause,** call, **right, basis,** substantive *or* material basis, **ground, grounds,** substance
2 **organization,** creation, establishment

founder NOUNS 1 **originator,** initiator, inaugurator, introducer, institutor, motive force, instigator; **organizer,** founding father, founding *or* founder member, founding partner, cofounder
VERBS 2 **sink,** be lost, go down, go to the bottom, go to Davy Jones's locker; scuttle; **break down, collapse; slip,** go downhill, be on the skids <nonformal>

fountain NOUNS **fountainhead,** headwater, headstream, riverhead, springhead, headspring, **mainspring,** wellspring, wellhead, well, **spring,** fount, font; **source of supply,** source, staple, resource; **spout,** rush, gush, geyser spouter <nonformal>

the fourth estate NOUNS **the press,** journalism, the public press, print medium, the print media, print journalism, the print press, the public print; mass media, the communications industry, public communication

fracas NOUNS **commotion, hubbub, Babel, tumult,** turmoil, **uproar, racket,** riot, **disturbance, rumpus** <nonformal>, ruckus *and* ruction <both nonformal>, **hassle,** shindy <nonformal>, rampage; **brawl,** free-for-all <nonformal>, donnybrook *or* donnybrook fair, broil, embroilment, melee

fraction NOUNS **part, portion;** percentage; **division**; **share,** parcel, dole, quota, piece *or* piece of the action <nonformal>; cut *and* slice *and* vigorish <all nonformal>; **ratio, rate, proportion; quota,** quotum; **percentage**

fracture NOUNS 1 **break,** bone-fracture, comminuted fracture, compound *or* open fracture, greenstick fracture, spiral *or* torsion fracture; rupture
VERBS 2 **cleave, crack,** breach, **break, break up, come apart,** come unstuck, **come** *or* **fall to pieces,** fall apart, rupture

fragile ADJS 1 **flimsy,** shaky, weak, papery, paper-thin, **unsound,** infirm; **impermanent,** unenduring, undurable, nondurable, nonpermanent; frail, brittle, delicate, insubstantial, **breakable,** frangible, crushable, crackable, crunchable, fracturable
2 <comparisons> eggshell, matchwood, old paper, piecrust, glass, glass jaw, china, parchment, ice, bubble, glass house, house of cards, hothouse plant

fragment NOUNS **piece, particle, bit, scrap**, bite, **morsel, crumb,** shard, potsherd, snatch, snack; **tatter, shred,** stitch; **splinter,** sliver; **shiver, smithereen** <nonformal>

fragmentary ADJS **unsound, unsubstantial,** unsturdy, unsolid, decrepit, crumbling, fragmented, disintegrating; **shattered,** broken up, broken to pieces *or* bits, fragmentized, in shards, in smithereens <nonformal>; **discontinuous,** nonlinear, nonsequential, discontinued, broken, broken off, **interrupted,** disjunctive, discrete, discretive; **intermittent, fitful**

fragrance NOUNS **perfume, aroma,** scent, redolence, balminess, **incense, bouquet,** nosegay <old>, sweet smell, sweet savor; **odor**; spice, spiciness; muskiness; fruitiness

frail ADJS **slight, delicate, dainty,** puny; light, lightweight; **fragile,** frangible, **breakable,** destructible, shattery, crumbly, brittle, fragmentable, fracturable; **unsubstantial, flimsy,** tacky <nonformal>, wispy, cobwebby, gossamery, papery, pasteboardy; in poor health; **sickly,** peaked <nonformal>; **run-down,** reduced in health

delicately weak
POPE

frame NOUNS 1 **body,** the person, carcass, anatomy, bodily *or* corporal *or* corporeal entity, physical self, physical *or* bodily structure, physique, soma
2 put-up job *and* frame-up <both nonformal>, put-on <nonformal>; **trumped-up charge,** false witness; stacked deck *or* cold deck <both nonformal>, setup
VERBS 3 **border, edge, bound, hem in,** befringe, margin, marginate, line; enframe, set off; trim, bind; **form,** formalize, **shape, fashion,** tailor; **plan, devise, contrive, design,** shape, cast, concert, lay plans; organize, rationalize, systematize, schematize, methodize,

configure, pull together, sort out
4 **phrase, express,** find a phrase for, give expression *or* words to, **word,** state, conceive, style, couch, **put in** *or* **into words,** clothe *or* embody in words, couch in terms, express by *or* in words, find words to express; **formulate,** formularize
5 **trump up a charge, bear false witness;** frame up *and* set up *and* put up a job on <all nonformal>

framework NOUNS **frame,** framing; **skeleton,** fabric, cadre, chassis, shell, armature; **frame of reference,** intellectual *or* ideational frame of reference, arena, world, universe, world *or* universe of discourse, system, reference system

franchise NOUNS 1 **vote,** voting, **suffrage,** enfranchisement, voting right, right to vote; **voice, say;** representation; charter, liberty, diploma, patent, letters patent, brevet
2 **dealership, distributorship;** concession

frank ADJS **candid, sincere,** genuine, ingenuous, frankhearted; **open,** openhearted, transparent, open-faced; artless; **straightforward, direct,** up-front *and* straight <both nonformal>, **forthright,** downright, straight-out <nonformal>; **unreserved,** unrestrained, unconstrained, unchecked; **outspoken, plain-spoken,** free-spoken, free-speaking; explicit, unequivocal

frantic ADJS **frenzied; ecstatic,** transported, enraptured, ravished, in a transport *or* ecstasy; intoxicated, abandoned; carried away, **distracted, delirious, beside oneself,** out of one's wits; uncontrollable, running mad, amok, berserk, hog-wild <nonformal>; hectic, frenetic

fraternity NOUNS **affiliation,** colleagueship, collegialism, collegiality; confraternity, fraternization, fraternalism; sisterhood, sorority; **fellowship,** brotherhood, sodality; comradeship, camaraderie

fraternize VERBS **associate with,** assort with, sort with, consort with, hobnob with, fall in with, go around with, **mingle with, mix with, touch** *or* **rub elbows** *or* **shoulders with,** eat off the same trencher; join in fellowship; flock together, herd together, club together

fraud NOUNS 1 **fraudulence** *or* fraudulency, **dishonesty; imposture; imposition, cheat, cheating,** cozenage, **swindle,** dodge, fishy transaction, piece of sharp practice
2 **impostor, ringer;** sham, shammer, **humbug,** *blagueur* <Fr>, **fake** *and* **faker** *and* **phony** <all nonformal>, **four-flusher** <nonformal>, bluff, bluffer; **charlatan, quack,** quacksalver, quackster, **mountebank,** saltimbanco

fraudulent ADJS **illegal, unlawful, illegitimate, illicit,** nonlicit, nonlegal, lawless, wrongful, creative <nonformal>, **against the law; unauthorized,** unallowed, impermissible, unwarranted; **criminal, felonious**

fray NOUNS 1 **fight, battle,** affray, combat, action, conflict, embroilment; **clash; brush, skirmish,** scrimmage; tussle, **scuffle, struggle,** scramble, shoving match; **quarrel**; pitched battle; battle royal; **internal struggle**
VERBS 2 **wear, wear away, wear down, wear off;** abrade, fret, whittle away, rub off; frazzle, tatter, wear ragged

freak NOUNS 1 **monstrosity, monster;** miscreation, abortion, teratism, abnormal *or* defective birth, abnormal *or* defective fetus; freak of nature, *lusus naturae* <L>
2 **fanatic, bug** <nonformal>, **nut** <nonformal>, **buff** *and* **fan** <both nonformal>, *fanatico, aficionado* <both Sp>, devotee, **zealot, enthusiast,** energumen
3 **fluke** <nonformal>, freak occurrence *or* accident; chance hit, lucky shot, one in a million

freakish ADJS freak *or* freaky <nonformal>; **eccentric, erratic,** idiocratic, idiocratical, idiosyncratic, idiosyncratical, **queer,** queer in the head, **odd, peculiar,** strange, fey, singular, anomalous, funny; unnatural, abnormal, irregular, divergent, deviative, deviant, different, exceptional

freak out VERBS **crack, crack up,** go haywire, **blow one's cork** *or* mind *or* stack, **flip,** flip one's lid *or* wig, wig out, freak out, go out of one's skull; come unglued *or* unstuck, go up the wall, **go on a trip** *and* **blow one's mind** <all nonformal>; **hallucinate;** expand one's consciousness

freckle NOUNS **mark, marking;** lentigo; blemish, macula, **spot,** blotch, splotch, flick, patch, splash; mottle, dapple

free VERBS 1 **extricate, release, clear,** get out; **disengage,** disentangle, untangle, unsnarl, unravel, disentwine, disinvolve, unknot, disembarrass, disembroil; dislodge, break out *or* loose, cut loose, tear loose; grant *or* extend amnesty; **discharge, release, dismiss, set free,** let off <nonformal>, let go
ADJS 2 **at liberty, at large,** on the loose, **loose,** unengaged, disengaged, detached, unattached, uncommitted, uninvolved, clear, in the clear, go-as-you-please, easygoing, footloose, footloose and fancy-free, free and easy; free as air, free as a bird, free as the wind; scot-free; **freed, liberated, emancipated,** manumitted, released, uncaged, sprung <nonformal>; **liberal,** free with one's money, free-spending; **gratuitous, gratis,** free of charge, for free, **for nothing,** free for nothing, free for the asking, for love; **profligate, licentious,** unbridled, untrammeled, uninhibited

afoot and lighthearted
WHITMAN

ADVS 3 **freely, without restraint,** without stint, **unreservedly,** with abandon; **gratuitously, gratis,** free, free of charge, for nothing, for the asking, at no charge, without charge, on the house

freebie NOUNS **gift, present;** free gift, gimme <nonformal>; oblation; handsel; free ride <nonformal>; gimme <nonformal>; labor of love

freedom NOUNS **liberty; license, civil liberty,** the Four Freedoms <F D Roosevelt>: freedom of speech and expression, freedom of worship, freedom from want, freedom from fear; academic freedom

the right to live as we wish
EPICTETUS

free-for-all NOUNS **knock-down-and-drag-out** <nonformal>, **brawl,** broil, melee, scrimmage, **fracas,** riot

free hand NOUNS 1 **latitude, leeway** <nonformal>, free scope, full *or* ample scope, free play, free course; **carte blanche,** blank check; **full authority,** full power, open mandate
2 **liberality,** liberalness, freeness, freedom; **generosity,** generousness, largeness, **unselfishness, munificence,** largess; **openhandedness,** freehandedness, open hand, easy purse strings

free-lance VERBS **stand on one's own two feet, shift for oneself, fend for oneself,** stand on one's own, strike out for oneself; **go it alone, be one's own man,** pull a lone oar, play a lone hand <nonformal>, **paddle one's own canoe** <nonformal>; **be one's own boss** <nonformal>, answer only to oneself; do on one's own, do on one's own initiative, do on one's own hook *or* say-so <nonformal>, do in one's own sweet way <nonformal>; be a free agent

freeloader NOUNS **parasite,** barnacle, leech; **sponger,** sponge <nonformal>; cadger, bummer *and* moocher <both nonformal>, free rider, deadhead <nonformal>

freewheeling ADJS **independent,** self-dependent; free-spirited, free-floating, free-standing; stand-alone, self-reliant, self-sufficient, self-subsistent, self-supporting, self-contained, autarkic, autarchic

free will NOUNS **free choice, discretion,** option, choice, say, say-so *and* druthers <both nonformal>, free decision; absolute *or* unconditioned *or* noncontingent free will

freeze VERBS 1 **take fright,** be paralyzed with fear, throw up one's hands in horror; shit in one's pants *and* shit green <both nonformal>; **immobilize,** keep, retain; **transfix, stick,** stick fast; seize, seize up
2 be cold, grow cold, lose heat; **shiver, quiver,** chill, have a chill, have the cold shivers; freeze to death, freeze one's balls off <nonformal>, die *or* perish with the cold; ice, glaciate, congeal

freezing ADJS **cold, raw,** bitter, biting, **piercing,** penetrating; **frigid,** bitter *or* bitterly cold, gelid, algid; **frozen,** half-frozen, frozen to death, chilled to the bone, blue with cold, congealing

freight NOUNS **load, burden; payload; burden,** burthen <old>, pressure, **oppression, deadweight;** charge, **load,** loading, lading, cargo, bale; **encumbrance;** handicap, drag, millstone

frenzied ADJS feverish, perfervid, febrile, at fever *or* fevered pitch; hectic, frenetic, furious, frantic, **wild,** hysteric, hysterical, delirious; **insane**; **fanatical**

frenzy NOUNS **furor,** fury, maniacal excitement, fever, **rage; seizure,** attack, acute episode, episode, **fit,** paroxysm, spasm, **convulsion; snit,** *crise* <Fr>; amok, murderous insanity *or* frenzy, homicidal mania, hemothymia

frequent VERBS 1 **haunt,** resort to, hang *and* hang around *and* hang about *and* hang out <all nonformal>
ADJS 2 oftentime, many, many times, **recurrent, oft-repeated,** thick-coming; **common,** of common occurrence, not rare, **prevalent,** usual, routine, habitual, ordinary, everyday

fresh ADJS 1 **refreshing,** refreshful, brisk, crisp, crispy, zesty, zestful, **bracing, tonic,** cordial; **sweet, cleanly,** fastidious, dainty, of cleanly habits; **new,** original, pristine, fresh off the assembly line, mint, in mint condition, factory-fresh; wet behind the ears, not dry behind the ears, **untried,** fresh as a daisy, fresh as the morning dew
2 **impudent, impertinent, pert,** flip <nonformal>, flippant, **cocky** *and* cheeky *and* nervy <all nonformal>, **disrespectful,** derisive, brash, bluff; **saucy,** sassy <nonformal>; smart *or* smart-alecky <nonformal>, smart-ass *or* wise-ass <nonformal>

freshen VERBS **refresh,** freshen up, **air,** air out, **ventilate,** fresh up <nonformal>; **revive,** revivify, **reinvigorate,** reanimate; brace, **brace up,** buck up *and* pick up <both nonformal>, perk up *and* chirk up <both nonformal>, set up, set on one's legs *or* feet <nonformal>; renew one's strength, put *or* breathe new life into, give a breath of fresh air, give a shot in the arm <nonformal>

fret VERBS **sulk, mope,** mope around; grump *and* **grouch** *and* **bitch** <all nonformal>; air a grievance, lodge *or* register a complaint; fret and fume, **chafe, fuss,** squirm; **stew,** sweat, sweat and stew, get into a dither, get into a stew <nonformal>, work oneself into a lather *or* sweat <nonformal>, get excited; **nettle,** chafe; **pique, peeve** *and* miff <both nonformal>, huff; **ruffle, roil, rile** <nonformal>, ruffle one's feathers, **rankle**

fretful ADJS peevish, petulant, **pettish,** querulous, **resentful;** impatient, **fretting,** chafing, antsy-pantsy *and* antsy <both nonformal>, squirming, squirmy, about to pee *or* piss one's pants <nonformal>; fidgety, **restless, jumpy, unquiet, unsettled**

friction NOUNS 1 **discord, conflict,** open conflict *or* war, rub; contention, collision, clash, clashing
2 **rubbing,** rub, frottage; frication *and* confrication *and* perfrication <all old>; **drag,** skin friction; **resistance,** frictional resistance

friend NOUNS **acquaintance,** close acquaintance; confidant, confidante, repository; **intimate,** familiar, **close friend,** intimate *or* familiar friend; **bosom friend,** friend of one's bosom, inseparable friend, **best friend;** alter ego, other self

friendly ADJS friendlike; **amicable, peaceable,** unhostile; **harmonious**; **amiable, congenial,** *simpático* <Sp>, *simpatico* <Ital>, *sympathique* <Fr>, pleasant, agreeable, favorable, well-disposed, well-intentioned, well-meaning, well-meant

fright NOUNS **fear,** affright; **scare, alarm, consternation, dismay; dread,** unholy dread, **awe; terror, horror,** horrification, mortal *or* abject fear; **phobia**

frighten VERBS affright, frighten *or* scare out of one's wits; **scare,** spook <nonformal>, scare one stiff *or* shitless *or* spitless <nonformal>, scare the life out of, scare the pants off of *and* scare hell out of *and* scare the shit out of <all nonformal>; scare one to death, scare the daylights *or* the living daylights *or* the wits *or* the shit out of <nonformal>; give one a fright *or* scare *or* turn; **startle; unnerve, unman,** unstring; make one's flesh creep, chill one's spine, curl one's hair <nonformal>, make one's hair stand on end, make one's blood run cold

frightening ADJS **frightful; fearful,** fearsome, fear-inspiring, nightmarish, hellish; **scary,** scaring, chilling; **alarming, startling,** disquieting, dismaying, disconcerting; **unnerving, daunting,** deterring, disheartening, fazing, awing, overawing

frightful ADJS **hideous, horrid, horrible, dreadful, terrible, awful** <nonformal>; **repulsive**, repellent, repelling, rebarbative, **repugnant,** offensive, foul, forbidding, loathsome, revolting

frigid ADJS bitter *or* bitterly cold, gelid, algid; **unsexual,** unsexed; **unfeeling, unemotional,** nonemotional, emotionless, affectless, emotionally dead *or* numb *or* paralyzed, **unpassionate, unaffectionate,** unloving; **unrespon-**

sive, unresponding, **unsympathetic; aloof, standoffish,** offish, standoff, **distant, remote,** withdrawn, removed, detached

cold as the north side of a gravestone in winter
ANON

frill NOUNS trimming, flourish, filigree, decoration, ornament

frilly ADJS **showy, flaunting, flashy,** snazzy, flashing, glittering, **jazzy** *and* **glitzy** *and* gimmicky *and* splashy *and* splurgy <all nonformal>; exhibitionistic, showoffy <nonformal>, bravura; flouncy, frothy, chichi

fringe NOUNS 1 **periphery,** circumference, outline, lineaments, border; **edging, bordering,** bordure <heraldry>, **trimming,** binding, skirting; fimbriation, fimbria; **hem,** selvage, list, welt
ADJS 2 **exterior, external;** extrinsic; peripheral, roundabout

frisk VERBS **play, sport, disport; frolic,** rollick, **gambol, romp, caper,** cut capers <nonformal>, antic, curvet, cavort, caracole, flounce, trip, skip, dance; **cut up** <nonformal>, cut a dido <nonformal>, horse around <nonformal>, fool around, carry on <nonformal>

frisky ADJS **spirited,** sprightly, **lively, animated, vivacious,** vital, zestful, zippy <nonformal>, **exuberant,** hearty; antic, bouncing, bouncy, skittish, coltish, rompish, capersome; **full of beans** *and* **feeling one's oats** <both nonformal>, full of piss and vinegar <nonformal>; **sportive, playful,** playful as a kitten, kittenish, **frolicsome,** gamesome

frivolous ADJS **haphazard,** desultory, **erratic,** sporadic, spasmodic, fitful, promiscuous, indiscriminate, casual, capricious, random, hit-or-miss, vague, dispersed, wandering, planless, undirected, **aimless,** straggling, straggly; senseless, meaningless, gratuitous; **superficial,** light, windy, airy, frothy, dizzy *and* ditzy <both nonformal>, flighty, light, volatile, frothy, fluffy, **featherbrained, birdwitted, birdbrained**

frizzy ADJS **curly, curled; kinky,** kinked; **frizzly,** frizzled, frizzed

frock NOUNS **garment,** vestment, vesture, robe, gown, rag <nonformal>, togs *and* duds <both nonformal>, dress, rig <nonformal>, **gown**

frolic NOUNS 1 **play,** romp, rollick, frisk, gambol, caper, dido <nonformal>
VERBS 2 **play, sport, disport; rollick, gambol, frisk, romp, caper,** cut capers <nonformal>, antic, curvet, cavort, caracole, flounce, trip, skip, dance; **cut up** <nonformal>, cut a dido <nonformal>, horse around <nonformal>, fool around, carry on <nonformal>

front NOUNS 1 **fore,** forepart, forequarter, foreside, forefront, forehand; **priority,** anteriority; front office; **frontier**; **foreground;** proscenium; frontage
2 **pretext, pretense, pretension,** lying pretension, **show,** ostensible *or* announced *or* public *or* professed motive; facade, **sham; cover,** cover-up, cover story
VERBS 3 **confront, face, meet, encounter,** breast, brave, meet squarely, square up to, come to grips with, head *or* wade into, meet face to face *or* eyeball to eyeball *or* one-on-one, come face to face with, look in the face *or* eye, stare in the face, stand up to, stand fast, hold one's ground, hang tough *and* tough it out *and* gut it out <all nonformal>
ADJS 4 **frontal, anterior; full-face, full-frontal; ahead, in front,** one-up, one jump *or* move ahead

frontier NOUNS 1 **border, borderland,** border ground, marchland, march, marches; outskirts, outpost; frontier post; **the unknown,** frontiers of knowledge
ADJS 2 **bordering, fringing,** rimming, skirting; **bounding,** boundary, **limiting,** limit, determining *or* determinant *or* determinative; threshold, liminal, limbic; **marginal, borderline;** coastal, littoral

front runner NOUNS **leader,** first in line; pacesetter; **precursor,** foregoer, *voorlooper* <Dutch>, vaunt-courier, avant-courier; **vanguard,** avant-garde, avant-gardist, innovator, groundbreaker

frosty ADJS **unfeeling, cold, cool, frigid,** frozen, chill, chilly, arctic, frosted, icy, **coldhearted, cold-blooded,** cold as charity; **unaffectionate,** unloving; **aloof, standoffish,** offish, standoff, **distant, remote,** withdrawn, removed, detached, Olympian; cold-fish, inaccessible, unapproachable

frothy ADJS **light,** unheavy, imponderous; foamy, spumy, spumous, spumescent, bubbly, yeasty; **frilly, flouncy,** chichi; **superficial, shallow, unprofound;** light, volatile, fluffy

frown NOUNS 1 **scowl,** lower, **glower, pout,** moue, mow, grimace, wry face; sullen looks, black looks, **long face; reproving look,** dirty *or* nasty look <nonformal>
VERBS 2 **look sullen,** pull *or* make a long face; **scowl,** knit the brow, lower, **glower, pout,** make a moue *or* mow, grimace, make a wry face, make a lip, hang one's lip, thrust out one's lower lip

frozen ADJS frozen solid, glacial, gelid, congealed; **icy,** ice-cold, icy-cold, ice, icelike; frostbitten, frostnipped;
2 **stunned,** petrified, stupefied, paralyzed; white as a sheet, pale as death *or* a ghost, deadly pale, ashen, blanched, pallid, gray with fear; **immobile, static,** stationary, **rigid**
3 **stuck, fast,** stuck fast, **jammed,** impacted, congested, packed, wedged; seized, seized up

frugal ADJS **parsimonious, sparing,** cheeseparing, **stinting, scamping, scrimping,** skimping; too frugal, overfrugal, frugal to excess; **economical, thrifty,** economic, unwasteful, conserving, **saving,** economizing, spare, **sparing; prudent,** prudential, provident, forehanded

fruit NOUNS **yield, output,** make, production; **proceeds,** produce, product; **crop, harvest,** vintage, bearing; **posterity, progeny, issue, offspring,** seed, brood, breed, family

fruitful ADJS **productive,** fructiferous, fecund; **fertile, pregnant,** seminal, **rich,** flourishing, thriving, blooming; **prolific,** proliferous, uberous, **teeming,** swarming, bursting, bursting out, plenteous, **plentiful,** copious, generous, bountiful, **abundant, luxuriant, exuberant, lush,** superabundant; creative

fruitless ADJS gainless, profitless, bootless, otiose, **unprofitable,** unremunerative, nonremunerative; uncommercial; **unrewarding,** bootless, no-win <nonformal>, futile, useless; abortive; **barren,** sterile, unproductive

frump NOUNS **slob** <nonformal>, **slattern, sloven,** sloppy Joe, schlep, schlump, *Strüwelpeter* <Ger>

frustrate VERBS **thwart,** dash, check, deal a check to, checkmate; **circumvent,** get round *or* around, **evade,** stonewall <nonformal>, **elude, foil,** give the slip *or* runaround <nonformal>; negate, invalidate, vitiate, void, stultify, come *or* bring to nothing, undo

frustration NOUNS **thwarting, balking, foiling; discomfiture, disconcertion,** bafflement, confounding; **defeat,** upset; check, checkmate, balk; derailing, derailment

fry VERBS prepare food, cook up, fry up, deep-fry *or* deep-fat fry, griddle, pan, pan-fry; stir-fry

fuck VERBS **copulate,** couple, **mate,** unite in sexual intercourse, **have sexual relations, have sex,** make out <nonformal>, perform the act of love *or* marriage act, come together, cohabit, shack up <nonformal>, be intimate; sleep with, lie with, go to bed with; screw *and* lay *and* ball *and* frig *and* diddle *and* **make it with** <all nonformal>, go all the way, go to bed with, lie together

fucked-up ADJS **confused, chaotic, mixed up,** balled *or* bollixed up <nonformal>, screwed up <nonformal>, mucked up <nonformal>, fouled up *and* snafu <both nonformal>

fuck up VERBS 1 **complicate, confound, confuse,** muddle, **mix up**

2 <nonformal> **goof, pull a boner,** bobble, lay an egg, put *or* stick one's foot in it, stub one's toe, step on one's schvantz *or* pecker, drop the ball, blow it, bitch, bitch up, hash up, **mess up,** flub, flub the dub, **make a mess** *or* **hash of,** goof up, **louse up, gum up,** gum up the works, bugger, bugger up, play the deuce *or* devil *or* hell *or* merry hell with; go at it ass-backwards; put one's foot in one's mouth; mess up *and* ball up *and* bollix up *and* screw up *and* foul up *and* snafu *and* muck up *and* louse up

fuddy-duddy NOUNS 1 **fussbudget, fusspot** <nonformal>, fuss, fusser, granny, old woman, old maid; back number <nonformal>; pop *and* pops *and* dad <all nonformal>, dodo *and* old dodo <both nonformal>; fossil *and* antique *and* relic <all nonformal>; **fogy, old fogy,** regular old fogy, old poop *or* crock <nonformal>
ADJS 2 **old-fogyish,** fogyish, old-fogy; square *and* corny *and* cornball <all non-

formal>; **stuffy, stodgy; aged**, senile, bent *or* wracked *or* ravaged with age

fudge VERBS **tamper with, manipulate, fake, juggle,** sophisticate, **doctor** *and* **cook** <both nonformal>, rig, cook *or* juggle the books *or* the accounts <nonformal>; **cheat, victimize, gull,** pigeon, **swindle, defraud,** practice fraud upon, euchre, **con,** finagle, **fleece,** mulct, **bilk,** cozen, chouse, **cheat out of, do out of**

fuel NOUNS 1 energy source; heat source, firing, combustible *or* inflammable *or* flammable material, burnable, combustible, inflammable, flammable; fossil fuel, nonrenewable energy *or* fuel source; alternate *or* alternative energy source, renewable energy *or* fuel source; solar energy, solar radiation, insolation; wind energy; geothermal energy, geothermal heat, synthetic fuels *or* synfuels
VERBS 2 fuel up; fill up, top off; refuel; coal, oil; **stoke, feed,** add fuel to the flame

fugitive NOUNS **escapee,** escaper, evader; escape artist; escapologist, runaway

führer NOUNS **dictator,** duce, commissar, pharaoh, caesar, czar

fulfill VERBS **carry out,** carry through, go through, work out; **put through,** get through; **implement; put into effect,** put in or into practice, translate into action; come through <nonformal>; consummate, do, execute, produce, deliver, make, enact, **perform, discharge, realize,** fill, meet, satisfy

fulfillment NOUNS **accomplishment, achievement, performance,** execution, effectuation, implementation, carrying out *or* through, **discharge, dispatch, consummation, realization, attainment,** production, fruition; dutifulness, acquittal, satisfaction

full ADJS 1 **resonant, reverberant, vibrant, sonorous,** plangent, rolling; mellow, rich; **total,** plenary, comprehensive, exhaustive; **absolute,** perfect, unequivocal, plenary; **teeming, swarming, crawling,** bristling, populous
2 filled, **replete,** plenary, capacity, flush, round; **brimful,** brimming; **chock-full,** chock-a-block, chuck-full, **jam-packed, overcrowded;** stuffed, overstuffed, **packed, crammed,** *farci* <Fr>; **glutted; cloyed,** jaded; full of, with one's fill of, **overfull,** saturated, oversaturated, supersaturated

full-blown ADJS **full-grown, full-fledged,** full-formed, in full bloom, in one's prime; **mellow** *or* mellowed, seasoned, tempered, aged

full-fledged ADJS **full-grown, grown-up,** developed, well-developed, fully developed, **mature, adult; complete, whole, entire,** solid; **full,** full-dress, **full-scale**

fumble NOUNS 1 **muff,** fluff, miscue <nonformal>; **bungle, blunder, botch,** flub, boner *and* bonehead play <both nonformal>, boggle, bobble *and* boo-boo *and* screw-up *and* fuck-up <all nonformal>, foozle <nonformal>; *gaucherie, étourderie, balourdise* <all Fr>; bad job, sad work, clumsy performance; **error, mistake**
VERBS 2 **bungle, blunder,** bumble, boggle, **muff,** muff one's cue *or* lines, be all thumbs, have a handful of thumbs; **flounder,** muddle, lumber; commit a *faux pas,* commit a gaffe; **botch,** mar

fume VERBS 1 **burn, seethe, simmer,** sizzle, smoke, reek, smolder, steam; be pissed *or* pissed off *or* browned off <all nonformal>, be livid, be beside oneself, stew <nonformal>, boil, fret, chafe; breathe fire and fury; **rage, storm, rave,** rant, bluster; take on *and* go on *and* carry on <all nonformal>
2 **let out, give vent to,** give out *or* off, throw off, blow off, **emit, exhaust,** evacuate, let go; **exhale,** expire, breathe out, let one's breath out, blow, puff; steam, vapor, smoke, reek

fumigate VERBS **sanitize,** sanitate, hygienize; **disinfect, decontaminate,** sterilize; disinfest, delouse; **deodorize**

fun NOUNS funmaking, fun and games, **play, sport,** game; **good time,** lovely time, pleasant time; big time *and* **high time** *and* high old time <all nonformal>, picnic *and* laughs *and* lots of laughs *and* ball <all nonformal>, great fun, time of one's life; wild oats
ADJS 2 **amusing, entertaining, diverting,** beguiling; funsome *and* more fun than a barrel of monkeys <both nonformal>; recreative, recreational; **delightful,** titillative, titillating; humorous

function NOUNS 1 **use, purpose, role,** part, end use, immediate purpose, ultimate purpose, operational purpose, operation; work, duty, **office,** province, place, **role,** *rôle* <Fr>, part; obligation, charge, **onus, burden,** mission, devoir, must, ought, imperative, bounden duty,

proper *or* assigned task, what ought to be done, what one is responsible for
VERBS 2 **operate, run, work; manage, direct, conduct; carry on** *or* **out** *or* **through,** make go *or* work, carry the ball <nonformal>, perform; **handle,** manipulate, maneuver; deal with, see to, take care of; occupy oneself with; be responsible for; be effective, go into effect, have effect, take effect

functional ADJS **acting,** performing, practicing, serving, functioning, operating, operative, operational, working; in action; **practical,** banausic, pragmatical, **utilitarian,** of general utility *or* application

functioning ADJS **operating, operational, working,** operant, functional, acting, active, running, **going,** going on, ongoing; **in operation,** in action, **in practice, in force,** in play, in exercise, at work, on foot; **in process,** in the works, in the pipe *or* pipeline <nonformal>

fund NOUNS 1 **supply, resource, resources; means, assets,** liquid assets, balance, pluses <nonformal>, black-ink items, **capital,** capitalization, available means *or* resources *or* funds, cash flow, stock in trade; venture capital
VERBS 2 **finance, back, sponsor, patronize, support,** provide for, capitalize, provide capital *or* money for, pay for, bankroll <nonformal>, angel <nonformal>, put up the money; **stake** *or* **grubstake** <both nonformal>; subsidize; set up, set up in business; refinance

fundamental NOUNS 1 **essential,** principle, essential principle, premise, substantive point, material point, hypostasis, postulate, axiom; **gist,** gravamen, **nub** <nonformal>, nucleus, center, focus, kernel, **core, pith,** meat; **heart,** soul, heart and soul, spirit, sap, marrow
ADJS 2 **essential,** of the essence; **primary,** primitive, primal, elementary, elemental, foundational, simple, barebones *and* no-frills *and* bread-and-butter <all nonformal>, original, *ab ovo* <L>, **basic, gut** <nonformal>, basal, **rudimentary,** crucial, central, underlying; **substantive,** substantial, material; constitutive, constituent; radical

funds NOUNS **finances, moneys,** exchequer, purse, budget, pocket; treasury, treasure, substance, **assets,** resources, total assets, worth, net worth, **pecuniary resources, means,** available means *or* resources *or* funds, cash flow, wherewithal, command of money; balance; war chest; reserves, cash reserves; savings, savings account, nest egg <nonformal>

funny ADJS 1 **humorous, amusing; witty; droll, whimsical,** quizzical; **laughable,** risible, good for a laugh
2 **ludicrous, ridiculous, hilarious, absurd,** quaint, eccentric, incongruous, bizarre, **inexplicable, unexplainable,** uninterpretable, undefinable, indefinable, **unaccountable; suspicious,** suspect

fur NOUNS **pelt, hide,** fell, fleece, vair <heraldry>; imitation fur, fake fur, synthetic fur; peltry, skins

furious ADJS hectic, frenetic, **frenzied,** frantic, **wild,** hysteric, hysterical, delirious; **violent,** fierce, ferocious, feral; feverish; desperate, mad, wild, wanton, harum-scarum <nonformal>

furlough NOUNS **leave, leave of absence, liberty,** shore leave; **sabbatical,** sabbatical leave *or* year; layoff

furnace NOUNS **kiln, oven, stove;** fiery furnace, inferno, hell; **reactor, nuclear reactor, pile,** atomic pile, reactor pile, chain-reacting pile, chain reactor, atomic *or* nuclear furnace, neutron factory

furnish VERBS **supply, provide, afford,** provide for; **make available to,** put one in the way of; **accommodate with,** favor with, indulge with; **heap upon,** pour on, shower down upon, **lavish upon; bear, yield, produce; bring forth,** usher into the world; fruit, **bear fruit,** fructify

furniture NOUNS furnishings, movables, home furnishings, house furnishings, household effects, household goods, office furniture, school furniture, church furniture, library furniture, furnishments <old>; **fixtures,** fittings, **appointments,** accouterments, appurtenances, installations

furor NOUNS **fury,** furore <Brit>, fire and fury; **turbulence, turmoil,** chaos, upset, **frenzy,** maniacal excitement, fever, tempestuousness, storminess, wildness, tumultuousness, tumult, uproar, racket, cacophony, pandemonium, hubbub, **commotion, disturbance, agitation,** bluster, broil, brawl, embroilment, brouhaha, fuss, flap <nonformal>, **row, rumpus,** ruckus <nonformal>, **ferment,** fume, boil, boiling, seething, ebullition, fomentation; rabidness, **mania**

furrow NOUNS **groove,** scratch, crack, cranny, chase, chink, score, **cut,** gash, striation, streak, stria, **gouge,** slit, incision; sulcus, sulcation; **rut,** wheel track, well-worn groove; **wrinkle, corrugation,** ridge, **crease, crimp,** ruck, **pucker,** cockle; **crinkle,** crankle, rimple, ripple, wimple

furry ADJS furred; villous; villose; ciliate, cirrose; hispid, hispidulous; **woolly, fleecy,** lanate, bushy, tufty, **shaggy,** shagged, wooly; **downy,** fluffy, nappy, velvety, peachy, fuzzy, flossy

further VERBS **advance, promote,** forward, hasten, contribute to, foster, aid, facilitate, expedite, abet; **be useful,** stand in good stead, encourage, boost <nonformal>, favor, advantage, **facilitate,** set *or* put *or* push forward
ADJS 2 **additional, supplementary, supplemental; extra,** plus, fresh, **more,** new, **other,** another, ulterior; **auxiliary,** ancillary, supernumerary, contributory, **accessory,** collateral
ADVS 3 **additionally, in addition, also,** and then some, even more, more so, and also, and all <nonformal>, and so, **as well, too,** else, beside, **besides, to boot, not to mention, let alone, into the bargain;** on top of, over, above; **beyond, plus; extra,** on the side <nonformal>, for lagniappe; **more, moreover,** *au reste* <Fr>, *en plus* <Fr>, thereto, **furthermore,** at the same time, then, again, yet; similarly, likewise, by the same token, by the same sign; all included, altogether; among other things, *inter alia* <L>

furtive ADJS **stealthy,** indirect, privy, backstairs, **sly, shifty, sneaky,** sneaking, skulking, slinking, slinky, feline; **covert, clandestine,** quiet, unobtrusive, hugger-mugger, **surreptitious, undercover,** underground, under-the-counter, under-the-table, **cloak-and-dagger,** backdoor, hole-and-corner <nonformal>, underhand, **underhanded**

fury NOUNS **furor,** fire and fury; **ecstasy,** transport, **rapture,** ravishment; intoxication, abandon; **passion, rage,** blind *or* burning rage, raging *or* tearing passion, livid *or* towering rage *or* passion; **frenzy,** orgy, orgasm; madness, craze, **delirium,** hysteria

fuse NOUNS 1 **detonator,** exploder; **cap,** blasting cap, percussion cap, mercury fulminate, fulminating mercury; electric detonator *or* exploder; detonating powder; **primer,** priming; primacord; circuit breaker
VERBS 2 **come together, cluster,** bunch, bunch up, clot; **amalgamate, integrate,** alloy, coalesce, **merge,** meld, **blend,** stir in, merge *or* blend *or* meld *or* shade into, melt into one, compound, compose, conflate, concoct; **combine,** unite, unify, marry, wed, couple, link, yoke, yoke together; conflate; interfuse, interblend; **encompass,** include, comprise

fusion NOUNS **interfusion, conflation;** blend, blending, meld, melding; **amalgamation, integration,** coalescence; **merger,** unification, uniting, integration, combination; **admixture,** composition, commixture, immixture, intermixture, **mingling,** minglement, commingling, intermingling, interlarding; **pluralism,** melting pot, multiculturalism, ethnic *or* racial *or* cultural diversity; **melting,** liquefaction, liquefying, liquescence

fuss NOUNS 1 **dither, tizzy** <nonformal>, swivet, foofaraw, **pucker** <nonformal>, **twitter,** twitteration <nonformal>, **flutter, fluster,** flusteration *and* flustration <both nonformal>, **fret,** pother, bother, lather *and* stew *and* snit <all nonformal>, flap; **quarrel,** open quarrel, dustup, **dispute, argument,** polemic, **controversy,** altercation, **fight, squabble, contention,** strife, **tussle,** bicker, wrangle, snarl, **tiff, spat**
VERBS 2 **bustle,** make a fuss, stir, stir about, rush around *or* about, tear around, hurry about, buzz *or* whiz about, dart to and fro, run *or* go around like a chicken with its head cut off; **be hard to please,** want everything just so, fuss over; pick and choose; **turn up one's nose,** disdain, scorn, spurn

fussy ADJS **bustling,** fussing; **meticulous, exacting, scrupulous, conscientious,** religious, punctilious, punctual, **particular, critical, attentive,** scrutinizing; **thorough,** thoroughgoing; **finical,** finicking, finicky, fuss-budgety <nonformal>; difficult, hard to please, picayune, picky <nonformal>

fusty ADJS **malodorous,** fetid, olid, odorous, stinking, reeking, reeky, nidorous, smelling, bad-smelling, **evil-smelling,** ill-smelling, heavy-smelling, **smelly,** stenchy; **foul,** vile, putrid, **musty,** funky, frowzy, stuffy, moldy, mildewed, mildewy; **stale**

futile ADJS **ineffective, ineffectual, inefficacious,** feckless; **vain, inutile, useless,** unavailing, bootless, fruitless; doomed, foredoomed; hollow, empty, idle; **abortive,** miscarrying, miscarried, stillborn, died aborning; no-win <nonformal>

weary, stale, flat, and unprofitable
SHAKESPEARE

futility NOUNS vanity, emptiness, hollowness; **fruitlessness,** bootlessness, unprofitableness, otiosity, worthlessness; triviality, nugacity, nugaciousness; unproductiveness; **ineffectuality,** ineffectiveness, inefficacy; **impotence**; **pointlessness,** meaninglessness, purposelessness, aimlessness, fecklessness; the absurd, absurdity; inanity, fatuity; **much ado about nothing,** tempest in a teapot, much cry and little wool

future NOUNS 1 **the future,** futurity, what is to come, imminence, subsequence, eventuality, **hereafter,** aftertime, afteryears, years to come, etc; **tomorrow,** the morrow, the morning after, *mañana* <Sp>; **immediate** *or* **near future,** time just ahead, immediate prospect, offing, next period; **distant future,** remote *or* deep *or* far future; **by-and-by,** the sweet by-and-by <nonformal>; **prospect,** outlook, anticipation, expectation, project, probability, prediction, extrapolation, forward look, foresight, prevision, prevenience; what is to be *or* come

ADJS 2 **later,** hereafter; **coming, forthcoming, imminent**, approaching, nearing, **prospective; eventual**, ultimate, to-be, **to come; projected,** plotted, planned, looked- *or* hoped-for, desired, emergent, **predicted,** prophesied, foreseen, anticipated, anticipatory, previsional, prevenient, envisioned, envisaged, probable, extrapolated; **in the offing,** on the horizon, **in prospect,** already in sight, just around the corner, in view, in one's eye, in store, in reserve, **in the wind**

fuzz NOUNS **down, fluff,** flue, floss, **fur,** pile; **downiness,** fluffiness, velvet, velvetiness, fuzziness, peach fuzz, pubescence

G

gab NOUNS 1 **chatter, jabber,** gibber, **babble,** babblement, prate, **prating, prattle, palaver,** chat, **gabble,** jaw-jaw <nonformal>, blab, **blabber, blather,** blether, clatter, clack, cackle, talkee-talkee; twaddle, twattle, **gibble-gabble, chitter-chatter, tittle-tattle,** mere talk, idle talk *or* chatter; **guff** *and* **gas** *and* **hot air** *and* blah-blah *and* yak *and* yakkety-yak <all nonformal>; **gossip**
VERBS 2 **chatter, chat, prate, prattle, patter,** palaver, **babble,** natter <Brit>, **gabble,** tittle-tattle, **jabber,** gibber, **blab, blabber, blather,** blether, clatter, twaddle, twattle, rattle, clack, dither, spout *or* **spout off** <nonformal>, pour forth, **gush,** have a big mouth <nonformal>, love the sound of one's own voice; **jaw** *and* **gas** *and* yak *and* **yakkety-yak** *and* run off at the mouth *and* beat one's gums <all nonformal>, **shoot off one's mouth** *or* **face** <nonformal>; run on, rattle on

gad about VERBS **wander, roam, rove,** range, nomadize, **gad,** gad around, follow the seasons, wayfare, flit, traipse <nonformal>, gallivant, knock around *or* about *and* bat around *or* about <all nonformal>, prowl, **drift, stray,** float around, straggle, **meander, ramble,** stroll, saunter, jaunt, peregrinate, divagate, go *or* run about

gadfly NOUNS **goad, spur, prod,** sting; **prompter, mover, prime mover,** motivator, impeller, energizer, galvanizer, inducer, **actuator, animator,** moving spirit; spark plug <nonformal>; persuader; **stimulator;** coaxer, wheedler, cajoler

gadget NOUNS 1 **tool, instrument, implement, utensil; apparatus, device,** mechanical device, contrivance, contraption <nonformal>, gimcrack, means, mechanical means

2 <nonformal> **thingumabob, thingumajig, doodad, dohickey,** flumadiddle, gigamaree, **gimmick, gizmo,** dingus, hickey, jigger, widget

gaffe NOUNS **blunder, faux pas,** solecism; stupidity, indiscretion; **botch, bungle**

gag NOUNS 1 **silencer, muffler,** muffle, **mute,** baffle *or* baffler, quietener, cushion; **damper,** damp; dampener; **soft pedal,** sordine, sourdine, *sordino* <Ital>; hushcloth, silence cloth; **muzzle**
2 **joke, jest,** one-liner <nonformal>, **wheeze,** jape; story, yarn, **funny story,** good story; punch line, gag line
VERBS 3 muzzle, silence, muffle, stop one's mouth, cut one short, strike dumb *or* mute, dumbfound; tonguetie; squash, squelch <nonformal>, stifle, choke, choke off, throttle, put the kibosh on <nonformal>, put the lid on *and* shut down on <both nonformal>, put the damper on <nonformal>
4 be nauseated, **sicken at,** choke on, have a bellyful of <nonformal>; **retch,** keck, heave, vomit, puke, hurl *and* upchuck *and* barf <all nonformal>

gain NOUNS 1 **profit,** percentage <nonformal>, **take** *or* take-in *and* piece *and* slice *and* end *and* rakeoff *and* skimmings <all nonformal>; **gains, profits,** earnings, winnings, return, returns, proceeds, bottom line <nonformal>; **income**; **receipts**; **fruits,** pickings, gleanings; **pile** *and* bundle *and* cleanup *and* killing *and* mint <all nonformal>; net *or* neat profit, clean *or* clear profit, net
VERBS 2 get ahead; wax, swell, balloon, bloat, mount, **rise,** go up, crescendo, snowball; accrue, accumulate; **improve, grow better,** look better, show improvement, meliorate, ameliorate; **advance, progress,** make progress, make headway, gain ground, go forward, get *or* go ahead, come on, come along *and* come along nicely <both nonformal>, get along; make strides *or* rapid strides, **acquire,** get, obtain, secure, procure; **receive, secure,** have, come by, be in receipt of, be on the receiving end

gait NOUNS **pace, walk, step, stride, tread;** saunter, stroll, strolling gait; shuffle, shamble, hobble, limp, hitch, waddle; totter, stagger, lurch; toddle, paddle; mince, mincing steps, scuttle, prance, flounce, stalk, strut, swagger; trot, gallop

gal NOUNS

<nonformal> **dame, chick,** tomato, **babe** *or* baby, **broad,** frail, **doll,** skirt, jill, chit, cutie, filly

gala NOUNS 1 **fete, gala affair, blowout** <nonformal>, **jamboree** <nonformal>; gala day, *fiesta* <Sp>
ADJS 2 **festive,** festal; merry, gay, jolly, jovial, joyous, joyful, gladsome, convivial, hilarious

galaxy NOUNS **island universe,** galactic nebula; spiral galaxy *or* nebula, spiral; barred spiral galaxy *or* nebula, barred spiral; elliptical *or* spheroidal galaxy; disk galaxy; irregular galaxy; radio galaxy; **the Milky Way,** the galactic circle, *Via Lactea* <L>

gale NOUNS **windstorm,** big *or* great *or* fresh *or* strong *or* stiff *or* high *or* howling *or* spanking wind, ill *or* dirty *or* ugly wind; **tempest,** tempestuous wind; williwaw; **blow,** violent *or* heavy blow; **squall,** thick squall, black squall, white squall; half a gale, whole gale; **hurricane,** typhoon, tropical storm

gall NOUNS 1 **rancor,** virulence, **acrimony,** acerbity, asperity; hard feelings, **animosity**; soreness, rankling, slow burn <nonformal>; gnashing of teeth

2 <nonformal> **cheek,** face, brass, **nerve, chutzpah,** crust

VERBS 3 **irritate, aggravate,** exacerbate, worsen, rub salt in the wound, twist the knife in the wound, step on one's corns, barb the dart; touch a soft spot *or* tender spot, touch a raw nerve, touch where it hurts; provoke, **chafe, fret,** grate, rasp; **get on one's nerves, grate on,** set on edge; **set one's teeth on edge,** go against the grain; **rub one** *or* **one's fur the wrong way**

gallant ADJS **chivalrous,** chivalric, knightly; **courtly; formal,** ceremonious; old-fashioned, old-world

gallery NOUNS **corridor, hall,** hallway; passage, **passageway;** loggia; arcade, colonnade, pergola, cloister, peristyle; areaway; breezeway; **balcony,** terrace

gallop NOUNS 1 **run, sprint; dash, rush,** plunge, headlong rush *or* plunge, **race, scurry, scamper,** scud, scuttle, **spurt,** burst, **burst of speed;** canter, lope; hand gallop, full gallop; **trot**
VERBS 2 **go on horseback, ride;** ride hard, clap spurs to one's horse; trot, amble, pace, canter, tittup, lope

gallows NOUNS **scaffold;** gallows-tree, gibbet, tree, drop; hangman's rope, noose, rope, halter, hemp, hempen collar *or* necktie *or* bridle <nonformal>; the necklace <nonformal>

galvanize VERBS **stimulate, whet, sharpen,** pique, provoke, quicken, enliven, liven up, animate, **exhilarate,** invigorate, give a fillip to; infuse life into, give new life to, revive, renew, resuscitate; **motivate, move,** set in motion, **actuate,** move to action, **impel,** propel; **stimulate,** energize, **animate, spark;** promote, foster

gambit NOUNS **trick, artifice, device,** ploy, stratagem, **scheme,** design, *ficelle* <Fr>, **subterfuge,** blind, **ruse, wile,** shift, **dodge,** artful dodge, sleight, pass, feint, fetch, chicanery; offer, **bid,** strong bid; experiment, tentative; tentation, trial and error

gamble NOUNS 1 **chance, risk, risky thing, hazard; gambling** *or* **gambler's chance,** betting proposition, bet, matter of chance, sporting chance, **luck of the draw,** hazard of the die, roll *or* cast *or* throw of the dice, turn *or* roll of the wheel, turn of the cards, fall of the cards, flip *or* toss of a coin, toss-up, toss; **speculation,** venture, flier *and* plunge <both nonformal>; calculated risk; uncertainty; fortune, luck
VERBS 2 **try one's luck** *or* **fortune; speculate; run** *or* **bank a game;** draw lots, draw straws, lot, cut lots, **cast lots;** cut the cards *or* deck; match coins, toss, flip a coin, call, call heads or tails; shoot craps, play at dice, roll the bones <nonformal>; play the ponies <nonformal>; punt, lay, lay down, put up, **make a bet, lay a wager,** give *or* take *or* lay odds, make book; plunge <nonformal>; **bet on** *or* **upon, back;** bet *or* play against; play *or* follow the ponies <nonformal>
3 **take chances, take a chance, chance, risk,** hazard, press *or* push one's luck, **run the chance** *or* **risk** *or* **hazard;** risk one's neck, run a risk, go out on a limb, stick one's neck out<nonformal>, **expose oneself,** bare one's breast, lower one's guard, **lay oneself open to,** leave oneself wide open, open the door to, let oneself in for; **tempt Providence** *or* **fate,** forget the odds, **defy danger,** skate on thin ice, court destruction, dance on the razor's edge, go in harm's way, hang by a hair *or* a thread, put one's head in the lion's mouth, play with fire, risk one's life, throw caution to the wind

gambol VERBS **caper, cut capers,** cut a dido <nonformal>, curvet, cavort, capriole, gambado, **frisk,** flounce, **trip, skip,** bob, bounce, jump about; **romp; prance;** caracole

game NOUNS 1 **contest, engagement, encounter, match,** matching, meet, meeting, derby, pissing match <nonformal>, **trial, test,** *concours* and *rencontre* <both Fr>; card game; board game; parlor game; **gambling game**, game of chance, friendly game
ADJS 2 **willing,** ready; **disposed, inclined, minded, well-disposed,** well-inclined, favorably inclined *or* disposed; predisposed; compliant, **consenting**; **eager;** keen, prompt, quick, ready and willing, zealous, ardent, enthusiastic, resolute, tough; in the mood *or* vein *or* humor *or* mind, in a good mood; receptive, responsive; amenable, tractable, docile, pliant; **plucky, spunky** *and* feisty *and* gutty *or* gutsy <all nonformal>, gritty, **mettlesome,** dauntless, game to the last *or* end

gamin NOUNS **waif,** homeless waif, dogie, stray, waifs and strays; ragamuffin, tatterdemalion; gamine, urchin, street urchin, dead-end kid <nonformal>, mudlark, guttersnipe <nonformal>

gamut NOUNS **range, scope, compass, reach, stretch, expanse** radius, sweep, carry, fetch; **scale,** register, diapason; **spectrum**

gamy ADJS **strong,** strong-flavored, strong-tasting; **high,** high-flavored, high-tasted; **rank,** high; **rancid, tainted, off,** blown, turned

gang NOUNS **staff, personnel, employees,** help, hired help, the help, **crew,** men, force, servantry, retinue; **unholy alliance, ring** *and* mob <both nonformal>; **company, group,** band, knot, complement, cast, outfit, pack, cohort, troop, troupe, tribe, **body,** corps, stable, bunch *and* mob *and* crowd <all nonformal>

gangly ADJS **lean,** lean-looking, **skinny** <nonformal>, fleshless, lean-fleshed, thin-fleshed, **spare,** meager, **scrawny,** scraggy, thin-bellied, **gaunt, lank,** rangy, **lanky,** tall as a maypole; **gangling** <nonformal>, gawky, **spindling,** spindly; all skin and bones, nothing but skin and bones; **long-legged,** long-limbed, leggy

gangster NOUNS **criminal, felon, perpetrator, crook** *and* perp <both nonformal>, public enemy, **lawbreaker,** scofflaw; mobster *and* wiseguy <both nonformal>, **racketeer**

gap NOUNS **interval, space**, intervening *or* intermediate space, **interspace,** distance *or* space between, interstice; **clearance,** margin, leeway, **room**; discontinuity, jump, leap, interruption; hiatus, caesura, lacuna; time interval, interim; **disparity,** diversity, divergence, gap, contrast, difference

gape NOUNS 1 **gaze, stare,** goggle, glare, glower; **gaping, yawning,** oscitation, oscitancy, dehiscence, pandiculation; **yawn**
VERBS 2 stare, stare at, stare hard, look, goggle, **gawk** *or* gawp <nonformal>, gaze open-mouthed; look straight in the eye, look full in the face, hold one's eye *or* gaze, stare down; **gaze,** drop one's jaw, look *or* stand aghast *or* agog; gap <nonformal>, **yawn,** oscitate, dehisce, hang open

garb NOUNS **clothing, clothes, apparel, wear, wearing apparel, daywear, dress,** dressing, **raiment,** garmenture, **attire, array,** habit, habiliment, fashion, style, guise, **costume,** costumery, gear, trim, bedizenment; **garments,** robes, robing, rags <nonformal>, drapery, finery

garbage NOUNS **refuse, leavings,** sweepings, **scraps,** orts; gash <nonformal>, swill, pig-swill, slop, slops, hogwash <nonformal>; rags, bones, wastepaper, shard, potsherd

garble VERBS **pervert, falsify, twist, put a false construction upon, give a spin, give a false coloring,** twist the words *or* meaning, color, varnish, slant, strain, torture; misrepresent, misconstrue, misinterpret, misrender, misdirect, **make unintelligible, scramble,** jumble; send *or* deliver the wrong signal *or* message

garden NOUNS 1 *jardin* <Fr>; bed, **flower bed,** border, ornamental border; paradise; garden spot
VERBS 2 **grow, raise;** cultivate; have a green thumb
ADJS 3 horticultural, hortulan, floricultural

gardening NOUNS horticulture, floriculture; landscape gardening; truck gardening, market gardening, olericulture

garden-variety ADJS **simple, plain, ordinary, nondescript, common, com-**

monplace, prosaic, prosy, **matter-of-fact, homely, homespun,** garden, everyday, workaday, **average**

gargantuan ADJS **gigantic,** mountainous, titanic, colossal, mammoth, gigantesque, monster, monstrous, outsize, sizable, larger-than-life, overgrown, king-size, monumental

garish ADJS **lurid,** loud, screaming, shrieking, glaring, flaring, flashy, glitzy <nonformal>, flaunting, crude, blinding, overbright, raw, gaudy

garland NOUNS **bouquet,** festoon; **trophy,** laurel, **laurels,** bays, palm, palms, crown, chaplet, lei, wreath, **feather in one's cap** <nonformal>

garment NOUNS vestment, vesture, robe, frock, gown, rag <nonformal>, togs *and* duds <both nonformal>

garnish NOUNS **adornment, embellishment,** embroidery, elaboration; nonfunctional addition *or* adjunct; garnishment, garniture; trimming, trim

garret NOUNS **attic,** attic room, **loft,** sky parlor; storeroom, junk room

garrison NOUNS **stronghold,** hold, safehold, fasthold, strong point, **fastness,** keep, ward, **bastion,** donjon, **citadel, castle,** tower, tower of strength, strong point; **bunker, pillbox,** blockhouse, trenches *or* barricades

garrulous ADJS **talkative, loquacious, talky,** big-mouthed <nonformal>, gabby *and* windy *and* gassy <all nonformal>, all jaw <nonformal>; **longwinded,** prolix, verbose; **voluble,** fluent; **effusive,** gushy; expansive

gas NOUNS 1 **chatter, jabber,** gibber, **babble,** babblement, prate, prating, prattle, palaver, gabble, gab *and* jaw-jaw <both nonformal>, blab, **blabber, blather; guff** *and* **hot air** *and* blah-blah *and* yak *and* yakkety-yak <all nonformal>
2 **belch, burp** <nonformal>, belching, wind, eructation; **fart** <nonformal>, **flatulence** *or* flatulency, flatuosity, flatus, wind
3 **atmosphere, air**
VERBS 4 **jaw** *and* yak *and* **yakkety-yak** *and* run off at the mouth *and* beat one's gums <all nonformal>, **shoot off one's mouth** *or* **face** <nonformal>; **talk on,** talk away, **go on** <nonformal>, run on, rattle on, ramble on; talk oneself hoarse, talk till one is blue in the face

gasp NOUNS 1 **breathing;** insufflation, exsufflation; **breath,** wind, breath of air; pant, puff; wheeze, asthmatic wheeze; gulp
VERBS 2 murmur, mutter, mumble, whisper, breathe, buzz, sigh; pant

gastronomy NOUNS gastronomics, gastrology, **epicurism,** epicureanism, gourmandise; *friandise* <Fr>

gate NOUNS 1 **entrance,** entry, door, portal, **entranceway,** entryway; gateway, portcullis
2 **floodgate,** flood-hatch, **head gate,** penstock, water gate, **sluice,** sluice gate; tide gate, aboiteau <Can>; weir; **lock,** lock gate, dock gate; air lock
3 **receipts,** gate receipts, box office

gate-crasher NOUNS **intruder,** interloper, trespasser; crasher <nonformal>, unwelcome *or* uninvited guest; moocher *and* freeloader <both nonformal>

gather VERBS 1 **fold,** fold on itself, fold up; **double,** ply, plicate; fold over, double over, lap over, turn over *or* under; **crease, crimp; pleat,** plait, plat <nonformal>; **tuck,** tuck up, ruck, ruck up; flounce
2 **collect, glean, pick, pluck,** cull, **take up,** pick up, get *or* gather in, gather to oneself, bring *or* get together, scrape together; heap up, amass, accumulate; **come together, congregate,** come from far and wide, come *or* arrive in a body; muster, **meet, forgather,** gang up <nonformal>, mass; flock together; herd together
3 **be imminent, impend, overhang,** hang *or* lie over, **loom,** hang over one's head, hover, **threaten, menace,** lower; brew
4 **suppose,** assume, presume, surmise, expect, suspect, infer, understand, **conclude, deduce, consider,** reckon, divine, imagine, **fancy,** dream, conceive, **believe, deem,** repute, feel, **think,** be inclined to think, opine

gathering NOUNS **social gathering, social,** sociable, social affair, social hour, hospitality hour, affair, get-together <nonformal>; **reception,** at home, salon, levee, soiree

gauche ADJS **ungainly,** uncouth, **ungraceful,** graceless, inelegant; **green,** callow, innocent, ingenuous, awkward, naive, unripe, raw

gaudy ADJS **tawdry;** gorgeous, colorful; **garish, loud** <nonformal>, **blatant, flagrant,** shameless, **brazen,** brazenfaced, lurid, extravagant, sensational, **spectac-**

ular, glaring, flaring, flaunting, screaming <nonformal>, obtrusive, vulgar, crude; **showy, flashy, ostentatious,** glitzy <nonformal>, meretricious, flamboyant, flaming, bedizened

gauge NOUNS 1 **measure,** measuring instrument, **meter, instrument,** barometer, **rule, yardstick,** measuring rod *or* stick, **standard,** norm, canon, **criterion,** test, touchstone, check
VERBS 2 **measure, quantify,** quantize, take the measure of, mensurate, apply the yardstick to; **estimate,** make an approximation; **assess,** rate, appraise, valuate, value, evaluate, appreciate, prize; size *or* size up <nonformal>

gaunt ADJS **lean,** lean-looking, **skinny** <nonformal>, fleshless, lean-fleshed, thin-fleshed, **spare,** meager, **scrawny,** scraggy, thin-bellied, **lank, lanky; gangling** *and* gangly <both nonformal>, gawky, **spindling,** spindly; nothing but skin and bones

gawk VERBS **ogle; stare,** stare at, stare hard, look, goggle, **gape,** gawp <nonformal>, gaze *or* stare open-mouthed, drop one's jaw, look *or* stand aghast *or* agog, rubber *and* rubberneck <both nonformal>

gay ADJS 1 **colorful, bright, vivid,** exotic, **brilliant,** burning, **gorgeous,** bright-hued, bright-colored
2 **homosexual,** homoerotic, queer *and* limp-wristed *and* faggoty <all nonformal>; lesbian, sapphic, tribadistic; effeminate
3 gay as a lark; **spirited,** sprightly, **lively, animated, vivacious,** vital, zestful, zippy <nonformal>, **exuberant,** hearty; **frisky,** antic, skittish, coltish, rompish, capersome; **full of beans** *and* **feeling one's oats** <both nonformal>, full of piss and vinegar <nonformal>; **jovial, jolly,** hearty, festive

gaze NOUNS 1 **stare,** gape, goggle; sharp *or* piercing *or* penetrating look; **ogle,** glad eye, come-hither look <nonformal>, bedroom eyes <nonformal>
VERBS 2 fix one's gaze, fix *or* fasten *or* rivet one's eyes upon, keep one's eyes upon, feast one's eyes on; **eye, ogle; stare,** stare at, stare hard, look, goggle, **gape, gawk** *or* gawp <nonformal>, gaze open-mouthed; strain one's eyes; look straight in the eye, look full in the face, hold one's eye *or* gaze, stare down

gazebo NOUNS **summerhouse,** arbor, bower, pergola, kiosk, alcove, retreat

gear NOUNS 1 **equipment,** paraphernalia, things, **stuff** <nonformal>, impedimenta <pl>, **tackle; kit,** duffel, effects, personal effects
2 gearing, gear train; gearwheel, cogwheel, rack; **gearshift; transmission,** gearbox; automatic transmission

gel NOUNS 1 **semiliquid,** semifluid; **jelly,** gelatin, jell, jam; **emulsion**
VERBS 2 **thicken, congeal,** coagulate, clot, set, concrete; gelatinize, gelatinate, jelly, jellify, **jell**

geld VERBS **castrate,** emasculate, eunuchize, neuter, spay, fix *or* alter <both nonformal>, unsex, deball <nonformal>

gem NOUNS 1 good person, fine person, good *or* fine man *or* woman *or* child, worthy, prince, nature's nobleman *or* -woman, man *or* woman after one's own heart; **treasure,** jewel, pearl, diamond
2 **precious stone, gemstone;** semiprecious stone; gem of the first water

gender NOUNS **sex;** maleness, masculinity, femaleness, femininity; masculine, feminine, neuter, common gender; grammatical gender, natural gender

genealogy NOUNS **pedigree,** stemma, *Stammbaum* <Ger>, genealogical tree, **family tree,** tree; genogram

general ADJS **generalized, nonspecific,** generic, **indefinite,** indeterminate, vague, abstract, nebulous, unspecified, undifferentiated, featureless, uncharacterized, bland, neutral

generalization NOUNS universalization, globalization, ecumenization, internationalization; **labeling,** stereotyping; general idea, **abstraction,** generalized proposition; glittering generality, sweeping statement

generally ADVS **in general; generally speaking,** speaking generally, **broadly,** broadly speaking, **roughly,** roughly speaking, as an approximation; **usually, as a rule, ordinarily, commonly, normally,** routinely, as a matter of course, in the usual course; **by and large,** at large, altogether, overall, over the long haul <nonformal>, **all things considered,** taking one thing with another, taking all things together, on balance, **all in all,** taking all in all, **on the whole,** as a whole, **in the long run,** for the most part, for better or for worse

generate VERBS **cause,** be the cause of,

lie at the root of; **bring about, bring to pass,** effectuate, **effect,** bring to effect, realize; **occasion, make, create,** engender, produce, breed, work, do; **originate,** give origin to, give occasion to, **give rise to,** spark, spark off, set off, trigger, trigger off; set afloat, **set on foot;** found, establish, inaugurate, institute

generation NOUNS **lifetime, life,** life's duration, life expectancy, lifespan, expectation of life, period of existence, all the days of one's life; **age**

generous ADJS **magnanimous,** great-souled *or* -spirited; generous to a fault, openhanded, **liberal; big, bighearted,** greathearted, largehearted, great of heart *or* soul; plenteous, **plentiful,** copious, bountiful, **abundant, luxuriant, exuberant, lush,** superabundant

genesis NOUNS **origin,** origination, **inception,** incipience *or* incipiency, inchoation; **divine creation,** creationism, creation science; **birth,** birthing, bearing, parturition, pregnancy, nascency *or* nascence, nativity; **source, origin,** original, origination, **derivation, rise, beginning,** conception, inception, commencement, **head;** provenance, provenience, background

genetic ADJS **hereditary,** patrimonial, **inherited, innate;** genic; patroclinous, matroclinous; **inbred,** bred in the bone, in the blood, running in the blood *or* race *or* strain, radical, rooted; connate, connatal, coeval

genial ADJS **pleasant,** congenial, cordial, *gemütlich* <Ger>, affable, amiable, amicable, gracious; good, goodly, nice, fine; cheerful, **good-natured, good-humored,** bonhomous, **sweet-tempered; agreeable; hospitable, receptive,** welcoming; **friendly,** neighborly, hearty, open, openhearted, warm, warmhearted

genie NOUNS **jinni,** genius, jinniyeh, afreet

genitalia NOUNS **genitals,** sex organs, reproductive organs, pudenda, private parts, privy parts, privates meat <nonformal>; **male organs; penis, phallus,** *lingam* <Skt>; gonads; **testes, testicles,** balls *and* nuts *and* rocks *and* ballocks *and* family jewels <all nonformal>, cullions <old>; spermary; scrotum, bag *and* basket <both nonformal>, cod <old>; **female organs; vulva,** *yoni* <Skt>, cunt <nonformal>; **vagina;** clitoris; labia, labia majora, labia minora, lips, nymphae

genius NOUNS **talented person, talent,** man *or* woman of parts, gifted person, prodigy, natural <nonformal>, mental genius, intellectual genius, intellectual prodigy, mental giant; rocket scientist *and* brain surgeon <both nonformal>; gifted child, **child prodigy,** wunderkind, whiz kid *and* boy wonder <both nonformal>

genocide NOUNS **carnage, massacre, bloodbath, decimation,** saturnalia of blood; **mass murder, mass destruction,** mass extermination, wholesale murder, pogrom, race extermination, **the Holocaust,** the final solution

genre NOUNS **kind, sort, ilk, type,** breed of cat <nonformal>, lot <nonformal>, **variety, species, genus,** *genre* <Fr>, phylum, denomination, designation, description, style, manner, **nature, character,** persuasion, the like *or* likes of <nonformal>

genteel ADJS **well-bred,** highbred, **well-brought-up; cultivated,** cultured, polished, refined, gentle; gentlemanly, gentlemanlike, ladylike

gentile NOUNS non-Christian; **non-Jew,** goy, goyim, non-Jewish man *or shegets* <Yiddish>, non-Jewish woman *or shiksa* <Yiddish>; non-Muslim, non-Muhammadan, *giaour* <Turk>, kaffir; non-Mormon; infidel; unbeliever

gentle ADJS **light, soft, delicate,** dainty, tender, **easy; lenient, mild,** mild-mannered, tender, humane, compassionate, **clement,** merciful

gentleman NOUNS good person, fine person, good *or* fine man, worthy, prince, nature's nobleman, man after one's own heart; **good fellow,** capital fellow, **good sort,** right sort, a decent sort of fellow; real person, real man, mensch <nonformal>; perfect gentleman, a gentleman and a scholar

gentry NOUNS gentlefolk, gentlefolks, gentlepeople, better sort; lesser nobility, *petite noblesse* <Fr>; *samurai* <Japanese>; landed gentry, squirearchy

genuine ADJS **authentic,** veridic, veridical, **real, natural, realistic, naturalistic,** true to reality, **true to nature, lifelike,** true to life, verisimilar, veristic; **bona fide,** card-carrying <nonformal>, **good,** sure-enough <nonformal>, **sin-**

cere, **honest;** unflattering, unvarnished, uncolored, unqualified; **unadulterated**

geriatric ADJS **aged, elderly, old,** grown old in years, along *or* up *or* advanced *or* on in years, years old, advanced, advanced in life, **at an advanced age, ancient,** gerontic; **venerable,** old as Methuselah *or* as God *or* as the hills

germ NOUNS pathogen, contagium, bug <nonformal>, disease-causing agent, disease-producing microorganism; **microbe,** microorganism; **virus,** filterable virus, nonfilterable virus, adenovirus, echovirus, reovirus, rhinovirus, enterovirus, picornavirus, retrovirus; rickettsia; bacterium, **bacteria,** coccus, streptococcus, staphylococcus, bacillus, spirillum, vibrio, spirochete, gram-positive bacteria, gram-negative bacteria, aerobe, aerobic bacteria, anaerobe, anaerobic bacteria

germane ADJS **relevant, pertinent,** appertaining, **apposite,** cogent, material, admissible, applicable, applying, pertaining, belonging, involving, appropriate, **apropos,** *à propos* <Fr>, to the purpose, **to the point,** in point, *ad rem* <L>

germicide NOUNS **antiseptic, disinfectant,** fumigant, fumigator, antibiotic, bactericide, microbicide

germinate VERBS **grow, develop,** wax, **increase**; burgeon, **sprout**, blossom, reproduce, procreate, grow out of, pullulate

gesture NOUNS 1 **gesticulation; motion,** movement; carriage, bearing, posture, poise, pose, stance, way of holding oneself; beck, beckon; shrug; charade, dumb show, **pantomime;** broad hint, signal, nod, wink, look, nudge, kick, prompt
VERBS 2 **gesticulate; motion,** motion to; beckon, wiggle the finger at; wave the arms, wig-wag, saw the air; shrug, shrug the shoulders; pantomime, mime, ape, take off

get VERBS **fetch, bring, go get,** go and get, go to get, **go after,** go fetch, **go for,** call for, pick up; obtain, procure, secure; **bring back, retrieve;** chase after, run after, shag, fetch and carry; **learn,** get hold of <nonformal>, get into one's head, get through one's thick skull <nonformal>; gain, acquire

getaway NOUNS **escape;** break *and* breakout <both nonformal>; **deliverance; release,** setting-free, freeing, **liberation, extrication, rescue;** jailbreak, prisonbreak, break, breakout; **flight**

get-together NOUNS **social gathering, social,** sociable, social affair, social hour, hospitality hour, affair, gathering

get up VERBS **get out of bed, arise,** rise, **rise and shine** <nonformal>, greet the day, **turn out** <nonformal>; roll out *and* pile out *and* **show a leg** *and* hit the deck <all nonformal>

get-up-and-go NOUNS **enterprise,** dynamism, **initiative,** aggression, **aggressiveness,** killer instinct, force, forcefulness, pushfulness, pushingness, **pushiness, push, drive, hustle, go,** getup, get-up-and-get <nonformal>, go-ahead, go-getting, go-to-itiveness <nonformal>, **up-and-comingness;** spirit, gumption *and* spunk <both nonformal>

geyser NOUNS **jet, spout, spurt,** spurtle, squirt, spit, spew, spray, spritz <nonformal>; rush, **gush,** flush; hot *or* warm *or* thermal spring, thermae; Old Faithful

ghastly ADJS **deathly, deathlike,** deadly; ghostly, ghostlike; **grisly, gruesome, macabre;** pale, deathly pale, wan, lurid, blue, livid, haggard; **cadaverous,** corpselike

ghetto NOUNS **slum,** the inner city, the ghetto, the slums; urban ghetto

ghost NOUNS **specter,** spectral ghost, **spook** <nonformal>, **phantom,** phantasm, phantasma, **wraith, shade,** shadow, fetch, **apparition,** appearance, presence, shape, form, eidolon, idolum, revenant, larva; **spirit;** sprite, shrouded spirit, disembodied spirit, departed spirit, restless *or* wandering spirit *or* soul, soul of the dead, dybbuk

ghostly ADJS **spectral,** specterlike; ghostish, ghosty, ghostlike; **phantomlike,** phantom, phantomic *or* phantomical, phantasmal, phantasmic, **wraithlike,** wraithy, shadowy; etheric, ectoplasmic, astral, ethereal; incorporeal

ghoulish ADJS **hideous, ghastly,** grim, grisly, gruesome, macabre; morbidly curious, **morbid;** infernal, hellish, devilish, fiendish, satanic, demoniac, demonic, demonical, diabolic, diabolical, unholy, ungodly

giant NOUNS 1 amazon, colossus, titan, *nephilim* <Heb pl>
ADJS 2 gigantic, colossal, statuesque, king-size, very large

gibberish NOUNS **nonsense, stuff and nonsense,** pack of nonsense, **folderol,**

balderdash, *niaiserie* <Fr>, flummery, trumpery, **rubbish,** trash, *narrishkeit* <Yiddish>, vaporing, fudge; jargon, mumbo jumbo, **double-talk,** amphigory, gobbledegook <nonformal>; glossolalia, speaking in tongues

giddy ADJS **dizzy,** vertiginous, spinning, swimming, turned around, going around in circles; lightheaded, tiddly <nonformal>, **drunk, drunken**

gift NOUNS 1 **present,** presentation, *cadeau* <Fr>, **offering;** tribute, **award;** free gift, freebie *and* gimme <both nonformal>; oblation; handsel; Christmas present *or* gift, birthday present *or* gift
2 peace offering; **talent, flair,** strong flair, **endowment,** dowry, dower, natural gift *or* endowment, **genius,** instinct, **faculty**

gifted ADJS **talented, endowed,** clever, apt, with a flair; born for, made for, cut out for <nonformal>, with an eye for, with an ear for, with a bump for <nonformal>; **smart, brainy** <nonformal>, **bright, brilliant**

gig NOUNS **engagement, job,** employment, gainful employment, situation, **office, post, place,** station, berth, billet, **appointment**

gigantic ADJS **huge,** mountainous, titanic, colossal, mammoth, Gargantuan, gigantesque, monster, monstrous, outsize, sizable, larger-than-life, overgrown, king-size, monumental; giant, giantlike, gigantean

giggle NOUNS 1 **laughter, titter; chuckle, chortle;** cackle, crow; **snicker,** snigger, snort; fit of laughter
VERBS 2 **laugh, titter; chuckle, chortle;** cackle, crow; **snicker,** snigger, snort

gigolo NOUNS fancy man; **inamorato;** lovemaker, lover-boy <nonformal>; lady-killer, ladies' man, sheik, cocksman <nonformal>; Lothario, Casanova, Don Juan

gild VERBS begild, engild; aurify; gild the lily, trick out, varnish; paint in glowing colors, tell in glowing terms; brighten, sweeten

gimmick NOUNS 1 **stratagem,** artifice, craft, wile, strategy, device, wily device, contrivance, expedient, design, **scheme, trick,** cute trick, **ruse, red herring,** tactic, **maneuver, stroke,** gambit, **ploy, dodge,** artful dodge; **device,** mechanical device, contrivance, contraption <nonformal>, gadget, gizmo, gimcrack, means, mechanical means

gingerbread NOUNS **ornamentation, embellishment**; frippery, froufrou, overadornment, bedizenment

gingerly ADVS **cautiously,** prudently, circumspectly, discreetly, judiciously; guardedly, easy <nonformal>, with caution, with care

gird VERBS **strengthen, invigorate,** beef up <nonformal>, brace, buttress, prop, shore up, support, undergird, brace up; gird up one's loins; steel, harden, case harden, anneal, stiffen, **toughen,** temper, nerve
2 **encircle,** begird, engird; **bind,** girt, belt, girth, girdle, band, cinch; **tie up,** bind up, do up

girl NOUNS 1 **maid,** maiden, **lass, lassie,** young thing, young creature, young lady, damsel in distress, **damsel,** damoiselle, demoiselle, *jeune fille* <Fr>, *mademoiselle* <Fr>, *muchacha* <Sp>, miss, missy, little missy, slip, colleen <Irish>; girlie <nonformal>; girlfriend

2 <nonformal> **gal,** dame, **chick,** tomato, **babe** *or* baby, **broad,** frail, **doll,** skirt, jill, chit, cutie, filly, heifer; teenybopper *and* weenybopper

girlfriend NOUNS

<nonformal> **doll, angel,** baby, babydoll, doll-baby, buttercup, ducks, ducky, pet, snookums, snooky, **girl,** best girl, dream girl; old lady

girlish ADJS **girl-like,** maiden, maidenly; little-girlish, kittenish; **slim,** gracile, thinnish, slenderish, slimmish; **immature,** half-grown, adolescent, juvenile, puerile

girth NOUNS **extent,** extension, expansion, expanse, **scope,** reach, range, spread, coverage, area, cirumference, ambit, boundary, periphery

gist NOUNS **substance,** pith, spirit, essence, gravamen, main point; last word, name of the game *and* meat and potatoes *and* bottom line <all nonformal>; **drift,** tenor; sum, sum and substance; **heart, soul, meat, nub**

give NOUNS 1 **elasticity, resilience** *or* resiliency; snap, **bounce,** bounciness; **stretch, stretchiness,** stretchability; extensibility; **spring, springiness;** rebound; **flexibility**; **adaptability,** responsiveness; **buoyancy** *or* buoyance

VERBS 2 yield; bounce, spring, spring back
3 **present, donate,** slip <nonformal>, let have; **bestow, confer, award, allot, render,** bestow on; impart, let one know, communicate; **grant,** accord, **allow,** vouchsafe, yield, afford, make available; **tender,** proffer, offer, extend, come up with <nonformal>; **give out, deal out, dole out, mete out, hand** *or* dish out <nonformal>, fork *or* shell out <nonformal>; **give generously,** give the shirt off one's back

give birth VERBS **bear,** bear *or* have young, **have; have a baby,** bear a child; drop, cast, throw, pup, whelp, kitten, foal, calve, fawn, lamb, yean, farrow, litter; lie in, be confined, labor, travail

give in VERBS **yield, cede, give way, give ground, back down, give up,** cave in <nonformal>, withdraw from *or* quit the field, break off combat, cease resistance, have no fight left

give off VERBS **exude,** exudate, transude, transpire, reek; **emit, discharge,** send out, give out, throw off, blow off, evacuate, let go

give up VERBS **relinquish, surrender, yield,** yield up, waive, **forgo, resign, renounce,** throw up, abdicate, **abjure, forswear, give up on, have done with,** give up as a bad job, cede, hand over, lay down, wash one's hands of, **write off,** drop, drop all idea of, drop like a hot potato; **cease**, **desist from,** leave off, give over; hold *or* stay one's hand, cry quits, acknowledge defeat, **throw in the towel** *or* **sponge**

glacial ADJS **icy,** icelike, **ice-cold,** ice-encrusted; **frigid,** bitter *or* bitterly cold, gelid, algid; **frozen,** frozen solid, congealed

glad ADJS **happy, joyful, joyous,** flushed with joy, radiant, beaming, glowing, starry-eyed, sparkling, laughing, smiling, smirking, smirky, chirping, purring, singing, dancing, leaping, capering, **cheerful, blissful,** happy as a lark, happy as a king, happy as the day is long, happy as a pig in shit <nonformal>

glade NOUNS **open space,** clear space; **clearing,** clearance; everglade

glamorous ADJS **alluring, fascinating,** captivating, riveting, charming, exotic, **enchanting,** spellbinding, **entrancing,** ravishing, **enravishing, intriguing, enthralling,** witching, **bewitching; attractive, interesting, appealing,** sexy <nonformal>, engaging, taking, eye-catching, catching, fetching, winning, winsome, prepossessing; **provocative,** *provoquant* <Fr>; irresistible, Circean

glamour NOUNS **allurement, allure, enticement, inveiglement,** invitation, come-hither <nonformal>, blandishment, cajolery; inducement; **temptation,** tantalization; **attraction,** interest, charm, appeal, magnetism; star quality

glance NOUNS 1 **glimpse,** flash, quick sight; **peek, peep;** wink, blink, flicker *or* twinkle of an eye; casual glance, **half an eye;** *coup d'œil* <Fr>; quick *or* cursory inspection, quick look, first look, once-over-lightly <nonformal>
VERBS 2 **glimpse,** glint, cast a glance, glance at *or* upon, give a *coup d'œil* <Fr>, take a glance at, take a squint at <nonformal>; sweep, **graze,** brush by, scrape, skim

glandular ADJS glandulous; **endocrine,** humoral, exocrine, eccrine, apocrine, holocrine, merocrine; **hormonal** *or* hormonic; adrenal, pancreatic, gonadal; ovarian; luteal; prostatic; splenetic; thymic; thyroidal

glare NOUNS **gaze,** sharp *or* piercing *or* penetrating look; **glower,** glaring *or* glowering look; withering look, hostile look, chilly look, the fisheye <nonformal>
VERBS 2 **glower,** look daggers, look black; give a dirty look <nonformal>, give one the evil eye, give one a whammy <nonformal>; give one the fish eye <nonformal>
3 **be bright,** shine brightly, beacon; daze, blind, dazzle, bedazzle

glaring ADJS 1 **conspicuous,** staring, **prominent,** pronounced, well-pronounced, in bold *or* strong *or* high relief, **flagrant,** arrant, shocking, shattering, egregious, intolerable, unbearable, unconscionable, **rank,** crass, high-profile
2 flashy, blinding, overbright

glass NOUNS 1 **mirror, looking glass,** reflector, speculum; cheval glass, pier glass; pane, windowpane, light, windowlight, shopwindow; vitrine
ADJS 2 **glassy,** glasslike, clear as glass, vitric, vitreous, vitriform, hyaline, hyalescent; hyalinocrystalline

glasses NOUNS **spectacles, eyeglasses,** cheaters <nonformal>; reading glasses, readers; bifocals, divided spectacles, trifocals, pince-nez, nippers <nonformal>; lorgnette, *lorgnon* <Fr>

glaze NOUNS 1 **polish, gloss,** burnish, **shine, luster,** finish; **patina**
VERBS 2 **sugarcoat,** candy; **polish, shine, burnish, furbish,** sleek, slick, slick down, gloss, luster

glazed ADJS 1 **polished,** burnished, furbished; buffed, rubbed, finished; varnished, lacquered, shellacked, *glacé* <Fr>; **glassy,** smooth as glass
2 **expressionless; vacant,** empty, blank; glassy, glazed-over, fishy, wooden; deadpan, poker-faced <nonformal>

gleam NOUNS 1 **shine,** shininess, **luster, sheen, gloss,** glint; **glow,** flush, sunset glow; lambency; **incandescence,** candescence
VERBS 2 **shine,** shine forth, **burn, give light,** incandesce; **glow, beam,** glint, luster

glean VERBS **collect, gather, pick, pluck,** cull, **take up,** pick up, get *or* gather in, gather to oneself, bring *or* get together, scrape together; **harvest, reap,** crop, gather in

glee NOUNS **merriment,** merriness; **joy,** joyfulness, joyousness; gleefulness, high glee; **jollity,** jolliness, **joviality,** jocularity, jocundity

glen NOUNS **valley,** vale, dale, dell, dingle; bottom, bottoms, bottom glade, intervale, wadi, grove

glib ADJS **eloquent, silver-tongued,** silver; **smooth,** smooth-spoken, **slick; felicitous;** facile, slick as a whistle <nonformal>, spellbinding

glide VERBS **coast, skim,** sweep, flow; **sail, fly,** flit; **slide,** slip, skid, slither, glissade; sailplane, sail, volplane

glimmer NOUNS 1 **hint,** gentle hint, intimation, indication, suggestion, **mere** *or* **faint suggestion,** suspicion, inkling, whisper, **glimmering; cue, clue,** index, **symptom, sign,** spoor, track, scent, sniff, whiff, telltale, tip-off <nonformal>
2 **glitter,** shimmer, twinkle, blink; **sparkle,** spark; **scintillation,** scintilla; coruscation; **glisten,** glister, spangle, tinsel, glittering, glimmering, shimmering, twinkling
VERBS 3 **glitter,** shimmer, twinkle, blink, spangle, tinsel, coruscate; **sparkle,** spark, **scintillate; glisten,** glister

glimpse NOUNS **glance,** glance *or* flick of the eye, rapid glance, cast, side-glance; flash, quick sight; **peek, peep;** wink, blink, flicker *or* twinkle of an eye; casual glance, **half an eye**

glint NOUNS 1 **flash,** blaze, flare, flame, gleam, glance; blaze *or* flash *or* gleam of light
VERBS 2 **shine,** shine forth, burn, give light, incandesce; **glow,** beam, gleam, luster, flash, flare, blaze, flame, fulgurate; **radiate,** shoot, shoot out rays, send out rays

glisten VERBS **glitter,** glimmer, shimmer, twinkle, blink, spangle, tinsel, coruscate; **sparkle,** spark, **scintillate;** glister

glitch NOUNS **malfunction, misfire,** flash in the pan; **dud** <nonformal>; **fault,** *faute* <Fr>, defect, deficiency, inadequacy, imperfection, kink, **flaw,** bug <nonformal>; fly in the ointment, problem, little problem, snag, drawback

glitter NOUNS 1 **showiness, flashiness,** flamboyance, panache, dash, jazziness <nonformal>, jauntiness, sportiness <nonformal>, gaiety, glare, dazzle, dazzlingness; **gaudiness,** gaudery, glitz *and* gimmickry *and* razzmatazz *and* razzledazzle <all nonformal>, **tawdriness,** meretriciousness
VERBS 2 **cut a dash,** make a show, put on a show, make one's mark, cut a swath, **cut** *or* **make a figure;** make a splash *or* a splurge <nonformal>; shine, glare, dazzle, gleam, glow

glitz NOUNS tinsel <nonformal>, gaudiness, speciousness, meretriciousness, **superficiality; garishness**

gloat VERBS **exult,** triumph, glory, delight, joy, jubilate; **crow** *or* crow over, crow like a rooster *or* cock; gloat over

glob NOUNS **lump,** clump, **hunk** *and* **chunk** <both nonformal>; **mass,** piece, **gob** <nonformal>, gobbet; batch, **wad,** block, loaf

global ADJS **comprehensive,** sweeping, complete; whole; **all-comprehensive,** all-inclusive; without omission *or* exception, **overall,** universal, wall-to-wall <nonformal>, around-the-world, **total,** blanket, omnibus, across-the-board; **universal,** cosmic *or* cosmical, heaven-wide, galactic, planetary, world-wide, transnational, planet-wide; **total,** allover, holistic

globe NOUNS **sphere; ball,** orb, orbit, rondure; oblate spheroid, prolate spheroid; globule, globelet, orblet; glomerulus; terrestrial globe, the blue planet

gloom NOUNS **gloominess,** darkness, murk, murkiness, dismalness, bleakness, grimness, somberness, gravity, solemnity; **dreariness,** drearisomeness; wearifulness, wearisomeness

gloomy ADJS **dismal,** murky, bleak, grim, somber, sombrous, **solemn, grave;** sad, *triste* <Fr>, **funereal,** funebrial, crepe-hanging <nonformal>, saturnine; **dark,** black, gray; **dreary,** drear, drearisome; weary, weariful, wearisome; **pessimistic,** pessimist, downbeat <nonformal>, **cynical,** nihilistic; uncheerful; dismal, lugubrious; negative, negativistic; defeatist

glorified ADJS ennobled, magnified, aggrandized; enthroned, throned; immortalized, shrined, enshrined; beatified, canonized, sainted, sanctified; **idolized, godlike, deified,** apotheosized

glorify VERBS glamorize; **exalt,** elevate, ensky, raise, uplift, set up, **ennoble,** aggrandize, magnify, exalt to the skies; crown; throne, enthrone; immortalize, enshrine, hand one's name down to posterity, make legendary; praise, laud, extol, magnify, bless, celebrate; beatify, canonize, saint, sanctify; **deify,** apotheosize, apotheose; **lionize**

glorious ADJS **grandiose,** grand, magnificent, splendid, splendiferous, superb, fine, superfine, fancy, superfancy, swell <nonformal>; **imposing, impressive,** larger-than-life, awful, awe-inspiring, awesome; **illustrious,** lustrous, brilliant, radiant, splendorous, splendrous, splendent, resplendent, bright, shining

glory NOUNS 1 **eminence, preeminence, majesty, loftiness, prominence,** distinction, outstandingness, consequence, notability; **magnanimity,** nobility, sublimity; **fame,** renown, **kudos,** report, celebrity; **grandeur,** grandness, grandiosity, **magnificence,** gorgeousness, splendidness, splendiferousness, resplendence, brilliance; **honor,** great honor, distinction, credit, ornament; **illustriousness, luster,** brilliance *or* brilliancy, radiance, splendor, resplendence *or* resplendency, refulgence *or* refulgency, blaze of glory
VERBS 2 **rejoice,** jubilate, **exult, joy, delight,** bless *or* thank one's stars *or* lucky stars, congratulate oneself, hug oneself

gloss NOUNS 1 **polish, glaze,** burnish, **shine, luster,** finish; **patina;** window dressing, front, **false front, façade, pretext,** guise, semblance; mask, cloak, veil; **cosmetics,** mere cosmetics, coat of paint, whitewash <nonformal>; **cover,** cover-up, cover story, alibi; band-aid
2 amplification, restatement, rewording; **comment,** word of explanation; **annotation,** notation, **note,** note of explanation, footnote, scholium; exegesis; *apparatus criticus* <L>; commentary
VERBS 3 **comment upon,** commentate, remark upon; **annotate**

glossary NOUNS **dictionary,** word list, **lexicon,** thesaurus, Roget's, vocabulary, terminology, nomenclator; promptorium, gradus

glow NOUNS 1 **health, well-being;** bloom, flush, rosiness
2 **shine,** shininess, **luster,** sheen, gloss, glint; **gleam,** flush, sunset glow; lambency; **incandescence,** candescence; afterglow; air glow, night glow, day glow, twilight glow
VERBS 3 **enjoy good health,** have a clean bill of health, be in the pink; be in the best of health; **feel good,** feel fine, feel fit, feel like a million dollars *or* like a million <nonformal>, never feel better; feel one's oats, be full of pep; burst with health, bloom, flourish; **look good;** look like a million *and* look fit to kill *and* knock dead *and* knock one's eyes out <all nonformal>; shine, beam
4 **thrill,** tingle, **tingle with excitement;** swell, swell with emotion, be full of emotion; thrill to; turn on to *and* get high on *and* freak out on <all nonformal>; exude cheerfulness, radiate cheer, not have a care in the world, **beam,** burst *or* brim with cheer, radiate, sparkle
5 **flush, blush,** crimson, mantle, color, redden, turn *or* get red; incandesce, bloom

glowing ADJS 1 **rosy,** rosy-cheeked; blooming; flushed, flush; flushed with joy, radiant, beaming; **bright, sunny,** bright and sunny, **radiant,** riant, sparkling, beaming, glowing, smiling, laughing
2 **burning,** heated, hot, volcanic, red-hot, fiery, flaming, ablaze, afire, on fire;

alight, aglow, lambent, suffused with light

glue NOUNS 1 **adhesive,** cement, mucilage, epoxy resin, paste, stickum *and* gunk <both nonformal>; **plaster,** adhesive plaster, court plaster
VERBS 2 **stick together,** cement, bind, colligate, paste, agglutinate, conglutinate, gum

glum ADJS **morose, sullen,** sulky, mumpish, dumpish, long-faced, crestfallen, chapfallen; **moody,** moodish, **brooding,** broody; mopish, mopey <nonformal>, **moping**

glut NOUNS **satiety,** satiation, satisfaction, fullness, surfeit, repletion, engorgement; **saturation,** supersaturation; saturation point; more than enough, all one can stand *or* take; too much of a good thing, much of a muchness <nonformal>

glutton NOUNS greedy eater, big *or* hefty *or* husky eater <nonformal>, trencherman, trencherwoman, belly-god, gobbler, greedygut *or* greedyguts <nonformal>, gorger, **gourmand,** gourmandizer, gormand, gormandizer; **hog** *and* **pig** *and* chowhound *and* khazer <all nonformal>

gnarl VERBS **distort, contort,** turn awry; **twist,** turn, screw, wring, wrench, wrest; writhe; knot

gnaw VERBS **chew,** chew up, chaw <nonformal>, bite into; **masticate,** manducate; ruminate, chew the cud; **bite,** grind, champ, chomp <nonformal>; **munch;** gnash; nibble; **pain,** give *or* inflict pain, **hurt, wound, afflict, distress**

gnome NOUNS **fairy,** sprite, fay, fairy man *or* woman; **elf,** brownie, pixie, gremlin, ouphe, hob, cluricaune, puca *or* pooka *or* pwca, kobold, nisse, peri; **imp, goblin**; dwarf; **sylph,** sylphid; **banshee; leprechaun**

go VERBS 1 **disappear, vanish,** vanish from sight, do a vanishing act <nonformal>, depart, fly, **flee,** be gone, **go away,** pass, pass out *or* away, pass out of sight, exit, pull up stakes <nonformal>, leave the scene *or* stage, clear out, pass out of the picture, pass *or* retire from sight, become lost to sight, be seen no more
2 **progress, advance, proceed,** go *or* move forward, step forward, go on, **go ahead,** go along, push ahead, pass on *or* along; move, travel

goad NOUNS 1 **spur, prod,** prick <old>, sting, **gadfly;** oxgoad; rowel; whip, lash, whiplash, gad <nonformal>
VERBS 2 **prod,** poke, nudge, prod at, goose <nonformal>, **spur,** prick, sting, needle; whip, lash; pick at *or* on, nibble at, nibble away at

goal NOUNS **objective,** object, aim, end, destination, mark, object in mind, **end in view,** telos, final cause, ultimate aim; end in itself; **score,** hit, bull's-eye; touchdown

go away VERBS 1 **disappear, vanish,** vanish from sight, do a vanishing act <nonformal>, depart, fly, **flee**, go, be gone, pass, pass out *or* away, pass out of sight, exit, pull up stakes <nonformal>, leave the scene *or* stage, clear out, pass out of the picture, pass *or* retire from sight, become lost to sight, be seen no more; **perish, die,** die off; die out *or* away, dwindle, wane, fade, **fade out** *or* **away,** do a fade-out <nonformal>; sink, sink away, dissolve, melt, melt away, dematerialize, evaporate, evanesce, **vanish into thin air,** go up in smoke; disperse, dispel, dissipate; cease, cease to exist, **cease to be;** leave no trace, waste, waste away, erode, be consumed, wear away; undergo *or* suffer an eclipse; **hide**
2 **depart,** make off, begone, be off, take oneself off *or* away, take one's departure, take leave *or* take one's leave, **leave, go, go off, get off** *or* **away,** get under way, come away, go one's way, go *or* get along, be getting along, go on, get on; **pull out;** decamp; exit; take *or* break *or* tear oneself away, take oneself off, take wing *or* flight

go-between NOUNS **middleman, intermediary, medium,** intermedium, intermediate, broker; connection <nonformal>, **contact; negotiator,** negotiant; interpleader; arbitrator, mediator

goblin NOUNS **elf,** brownie, pixie, gremlin, cluricaune, puca *or* pooka *or* pwca, kobold, nisse, peri; **hobgoblin,** hob, ouphe

gobs NOUNS **lots,** deal, no end of, **good** *or* **great deal, considerable,** sight, **heap, pile, stack,** loads, **raft, slew,** whole slew, spate, wad, **batch,** mess, mint, peck, pack, pot, **tidy sum,** quite a little; **oodles, scads**

go crazy VERBS

<nonformal> go bats, go cuckoo, go

bughouse, go nuts, go nutso, go out of one's gourd *or* skull *or* tree, go off one's nut *or* rocker, go off the track *or* trolley, go off the deep end, blow one's top *or* stack, pop one's cork, flip one's lid *or* wig, wig out, go ape *or* apeshit, schiz out, go bananas, go crackers *and* go bonkers <both Brit>, go bonzo, blow one's mind, freak out, flip out, go hog wild, go round the bend <Brit>, have a screw loose, have bats in one's belfry, have rocks in one's head, lose one's marbles

god NOUNS **hero, demigod,** phoenix; **heroine, goddess,** demigoddess; **idol** 2 *deus* <L>; **deity, divinity,** immortal, heathen god, pagan deity *or* divinity; **goddess,** *dea* <L>; deva, devi, the shining ones

God NOUNS Jehovah; *Yahweh, Adonai, Elohim* <all Heb>; **Allah;** the Great Spirit, Manitou

God-fearing ADJS faithful <old>, pious, pietistic, observant, **devout**

God forbid! INTER Heaven forbid!, Heaven forfend!, forbid it Heaven!; by no means!, not for the world!, not on your life!, over my dead body!, not if I know it!, nothing doing!, no way! *and* no way José! <both nonformal>, perish the thought!, I'll be hanged *or* damned if!, **shame!,** for shame!, tuttut!

godforsaken ADJS **out-of-the-way,** back of beyond, upcountry; out of reach, **inaccessible; abandoned,** deserted, desolate, forlorn, lorn; helpless, defenseless

godless ADJS **ungodly,** irreligious, unrighteous, unholy, unsaintly, unangelic, unangelical; impious; **unregenerate,** unredeemed, **unconverted,** reprobate, graceless, shriftless, **lost, damned;** lapsed, fallen, recidivist, recidivistic

godlike ADJS **divine, godly; magnificent,** magnanimous, heroic, superb; immortalized, shrined, enshrined; beatified, canonized, sainted, sanctified; **idolized, deified,** apotheosized

godsend NOUNS **boon, blessing;** manna, manna from heaven, loaves and fishes, gift from on high; windfall

go Dutch VERBS pay one's way; pay one's share, chip in <nonformal>, share and share alike, go halfers <nonformal>

gofer NOUNS **underling,** understrapper, low man on the totem pole <nonformal>, flunky, errand boy *or* girl, office boy *or* girl

go for it VERBS

<nonformal> **knock oneself out, break one's neck,** break *or* bust one's balls, bust a gut, bust one's ass *or* hump, rupture oneself, do it or know why not, do it or break a leg, do it or bust a gut, do *or* try one's damndest *or* darndest, go all out, go the limit, go for broke, shoot the works, give it all one's got, give it one's best shot

go-getter NOUNS **man** *or* **woman of action, doer,** man of deeds; **hustler** *and* self-starter <both nonformal>; ball of fire *and* live wire *and* powerhouse *and* human dynamo *and* spitfire <all nonformal>; beaver, busy bee, **eager beaver** <nonformal>; operator *and* big-time operator *and* wheeler-dealer <all nonformal>; take-charge guy <nonformal>

goggles NOUNS **spectacles,** specs <nonformal>, glasses, eyeglasses, pair of glasses *or* spectacles, cheaters *and* peepers <both nonformal>; blinkers; eyeshield

gold NOUNS **wealth, money,** lucre, pelf, mammon; **substance,** property, possessions, material wealth; yellow stuff <nonformal>; nugget, gold nugget

goldbrick NOUNS 1 **shirker,** shirk, **slacker,** goldbricker, goof-off <nonformal>; clock watcher; **malingerer** VERBS 2 **shirk, slack,** not pull fair, not pull one's weight; **lie down on the job** <nonformal>; duck duty, dog it <nonformal>; **malinger**

golden ADJS **precious, dear, valuable,** worthy, rich, worth a pretty penny <nonformal>, worth a king's ransom, worth its weight in gold, good as gold, precious as the apple of one's eye; **gold,** gilt, aureate; benign, benignant, bright, happy

golden rule NOUNS rule of action *or* conduct, moral precept; commandment, *mitzvah* <Heb>; **principle,** principium, settled principle, general principle *or* truth, tenet, convention; **guideline,** ground rule, rubric, protocol, working rule, working principle, standard procedure; guiding principle

gold mine NOUNS **source of supply,** mine, rich lode, mother lode, **bonanza,** luau <nonformal>; quarry, lode, vein; Eldorado, Golconda

gone ADJS 1 away, gone away, past and gone, extinct, missing, no more, lost, lost to sight *or* view, long-lost, **out of sight; absent,** not present, nonattendant, departed, disappeared, vanished, absconded, out of sight
2 **missing,** among the missing, wanting, **lacking,** not found, nowhere to be found, omitted, taken away, no longer present *or* with us *or* among us

goner NOUNS **lost cause, fool's errand, wild-goose chase; hopeless case;** gone goose *or* gosling *and* dead duck <all nonformal>; terminal case

goo NOUNS 1 **sentimentality,** mawkishness, cloyingness, maudlinness, mushiness *or* sloppiness <both nonformal>; **mush** *and* slush *and* slop *and* schmaltz <all nonformal>
2 **semiliquid,** goop *and* gook *and* gunk *and* glop <all nonformal>, sticky mess, gaum <nonformal>

good NOUNS 1 **welfare,** well-being, **benefit; interest,** advantage; **behalf,** behoof; blessing, benison, boon; **profit,** avail <old>, gain; world of good
ADJS 2 **healthful, healthy, salubrious, salutary, wholesome,** health-preserving, health-enhancing, life-promoting, **beneficial,** benign
3 **excellent,** *bueno* <Sp>, *bon* <Fr>, bonny <Brit>, fine, nice, goodly, fair; **splendid, capital, grand,** elegant <nonformal>, braw <Scots>, famous <nonformal>; very good, *très bon* <Fr>; commendable, laudable, **estimable**

good-bye NOUNS 1 **leave-taking,** leave, parting, departure, congé; **send-off,** Godspeed; **adieu,** one's adieus, **farewell,** aloha; valedictory address, valedictory, valediction, parting words; swan song; viaticum; stirrup cup, one for the road, *doch-an-dorrach* or *doch-an-dorris* <Gaelic>
INTER 2 **farewell!, adieu!, so long!, I'm outa here** <both nonformal>, cheerio! <Brit>, *au revoir!* <Fr>, *¡adios!* <Sp>, *¡hasta la vista!* <Sp>, *¡hasta luego!* <Sp>, *¡vaya con Dios!* <Sp>, *auf Wiedersehen!* <Ger>, *addio!* <Ital>, *arrivederci!, arrivederla!* <both Ital>, *ciao!* <Ital nonformal>, *do svidanye!* <Russ>, *shalom!* <Heb>, *sayonara!* <Japanese>, *vale!, vive valeque!* <both L>, aloha!

good-for-nothing NOUNS 1 good-for-naught, **ne'er-do-well,** wastrel; drifter, vagrant, hobo, tramp; no-good <nonformal>, *vaurien* <Fr>, worthless fellow
ADJS 2 **worthless, valueless,** good-for-naught, no-good *or* NG <nonformal>, no-account <nonformal>, dear at any price, worthless as tits on a boar <nonformal>, not worth a dime *or* a red cent *or* a hill of beans *or* shit *or* bubkes <nonformal>, not worthwhile, not worth having, not worth mentioning *or* speaking of, not worth the powder to blow it to hell, of no earthly use, fit for the junk yard <nonformal>

good-looking ADJS **comely,** fair, **nice-looking,** well-favored, **personable,** presentable, agreeable, becoming, pleasing, goodly, bonny, likely <nonformal>, **sightly,** braw <Scots>; pleasing to the eye, lovely to behold

good luck NOUNS **good fortune,** happy fortune, **fortune, luck,** the breaks <nonformal>; **fortunateness, luckiness,** felicity <old>; blessing, smiles of fortune, fortune's favor

good-natured ADJS **good-humored, good-tempered,** bonhomous, **sweet,** sweet-tempered; **amiable, affable,** genial, cordial; **gentle,** mild, mild-mannered; easy, easy-natured, easy to get along with, able to take a joke, **agreeable**

goodness NOUNS **excellence, quality,** class <nonformal>; **virtue,** grace; **merit,** desert; **value, worth; fineness,** goodliness, fairness, niceness; **superiority,** first-rateness, **skillfulness**; wholeness, **soundness,** healthiness; **virtuousness**; **kindness,** benevolence

good person NOUNS

<nonformal> **good guy,** crackerjack, brick, trump, good egg, stout fellow, nice guy, Mr Nice Guy, good Joe, likely lad, no slouch, doll, living doll, pussycat, **sweetheart, sweetie**

goods NOUNS 1 **property, properties, possessions, holdings,** havings, chattels, goods and chattels, **effects,** estate and effects, what one can call one's own, what one has to one's name, all one owns *or* has, all one can lay claim to, one's all; household possessions *or* effects, lares and penates
2 **merchandise,** commodities, wares, effects, vendibles; **consumer goods,** consumer items, retail goods, goods for sale

good Samaritan NOUNS **benefactor,** benefactress, **benefiter,** succorer, befriender; ministrant, ministering angel; Samaritan, **helper,** aider, assister, help, aid, helping hand, Johnny-on-the-spot <nonformal>

a very present help in time of trouble
BIBLE

goodwill NOUNS **benevolence,** grace, brotherly love, charity, Christian charity *or* love, *caritas* <L>, love of mankind, good will to *or* toward man, love, *agape* <Gk>

goody-goody NOUNS 1 **prude, prig,** priss, puritan, bluenose; Victorian
ADJS 2 **overnice,** overprecise, precious, *précieuse* <Fr>, exquisite, **overrefined, elegant,** mincing, simpering, namby-pamby

gooey ADJS 1 **sentimental,** sentimentalized, soft, **mawkish, maudlin,** cloying; sticky *and* schmaltzy *and* sappy *and* soppy <all nonformal>, oversentimental, oversentimentalized, bathetic; **mushy** *or* sloppy *or* gushing *or* teary *or* beery <all nonformal>, tearjerking <nonformal>
2 **viscous, sticky, tacky,** tenacious, adhesive, clingy, clinging, tough; gunky *and* gloppy *and* goopy *and* gooky <all nonformal>; **gelatinous,** jellylike, jellied, jelled

goof NOUNS 1 **mistake,** error, blunder

2 <nonformal> **boo-boo,** muff, flub, foozle, bloomer, bloop, blooper, boot, bobble, boner, bonehead play *or* trick, dumb trick, boob stunt, fool mistake; howler, screamer; fuck-up, screw-up, foul-up, snafu, muck-up, louse-up

VERBS 3 **miss, miss the mark,** miss one's aim; slip, slip up <nonformal>; blunder, foozle <nonformal>, **err**; botch, bungle; waste one's effort, run around in circles, spin one's wheels

goof off VERBS **idle,** do nothing, **laze,** lazy <nonformal>, take one's ease *or* leisure, take one's time, **loaf, lounge; lie around,** lounge around, loll around, sit on one's ass *or* butt *or* duff <nonformal>, stand *or* hang around, **loiter about** *or* **around,** slouch, slouch around, **bum around** *and* mooch around <both nonformal>; **shirk,** avoid work, fuck off *and* **lie down on the job** <both nonformal>

goof-off NOUNS **idler, loafer, lounger,** loller, couch potato <nonformal>, lotus-eater, *flâneur, flâneuse* <both Fr>, **do-nothing,** do-little, *fainéant* <Fr>, fuck-off *and* goldbrick *and* goldbricker <all nonformal>, clock watcher

goofy ADJS

<nonformal> **kooky,** funny, kinky, loopy, goofus, haywire, screwy, screwball, nutty, wacky, flaky, oddball, wacky, wacko, out to lunch, nobody home, weird

goose NOUNS 1 gander, gosling
2 **silly,** silly Billy <nonformal>, **silly ass**
VERBS 3 poke, nudge, prod at, **spur,** prick, sting, needle

goose bumps NOUNS **creeps** *and* **cold creeps** *and* shivers *and* **cold shivers** <all nonformal>, creeping of the flesh; horripilation, gooseflesh, goose pimples; formication

gore NOUNS 1 **bloodshed,** bloodletting, blood, flow of blood
VERBS 2 **perforate, pierce,** drill, auger; **ream,** ream out, countersink, gouge, gouge out; trepan, trephine

gorge NOUNS 1 **ravine, canyon,** box canyon, *arroyo* <Sp>, barranca, bolson, coulee, gully, gulch, combe <Brit>, dingle, rift, rift valley, kloof, donga, graben, gully, draw, wadi, basin, cirque, corrie
VERBS 2 **stuff,** pig out <nonformal>, engorge, glut, guttle, cram, eat one's fill, stuff *or* gorge oneself, gluttonize
3 **satiate,** sate, satisfy, slake, allay; **surfeit,** glut, saturate, oversaturate, supersaturate

gorgeous ADJS 1 **ravishing; glorious,** heavenly, divine, sublime; **resplendent,** splendorous *or* splendrous, splendiferous, **splendid,** resplendently beautiful; **brilliant,** bright, radiant, shining, beaming, glowing, blooming, abloom, sparkling, **dazzling; glamorous**

2 <nonformal> **eye-filling, easy on the eyes,** not hard to look at, long on looks, looking fit to kill, dishy <chiefly Brit>; cutesy, cutesy-poo; **raving,** devastating, **stunning,** killing

gorilla NOUNS

<nonformal> **roughneck, tough,** bruiser, mug, mugger, bimbo, bozo, ugly

customer, **hoodlum, hood, hooligan,** ape, plug-ugly, strong-arm man, muscle man, **goon**

gory ADJS **bloodstained,** blood-spattered, **bloody,** sanguinary, ensanguined

gospel NOUNS **the truth,** the absolute truth, the intrinsic truth, the unalloyed truth, the cast-iron truth, the hard truth, the stern truth, gospel truth, Bible truth, revealed truth

gossamer ADJS **frail,** dainty, delicate, diaphanous, light, airy, wispy, lacy, gauzy, papery, insubstantial, ethereal, misty, vague, flimsy, wafer-thin, **fine; threadlike,** slender as a thread; **tenuous,** subtle, rare, **rarefied;** attenuated, attenuate

gossip NOUNS 1 gossiping, gossipmongering, back-fence gossip <nonformal>, newsmongering; **talebearing,** taletelling; **tattle,** tittle-tattle, chitchat, **talk,** idle talk, small talk, by-talk; piece of gossip, groundless rumor, tale, story
2 **newsmonger,** rumormonger, scandalmonger, gossipmonger, gossiper, *yenta* <Yiddish>, quidnunc, **busybody,** tabby <nonformal>; **talebearer,** taleteller, telltale, **tattletale** <nonformal>, tattler, tittle-tattler
VERBS 3 talk over the back fence <nonformal>; **tattle,** tittle-tattle; clatter; retail gossip, **dish the dirt** <nonformal>, tell idle tales

Gothic ADJS **unrefined,** unpolished, uncouth, unkempt, uncombed, unlicked; **uncultivated, uncultured; barbarous,** barbaric, barbarian; outlandish, **fanciful, notional,** whimsical, **fantastic, fantastical,** preposterous, outlandish, wild, baroque, rococo, Alice-in-Wonderland, bizarre, grotesque

gouge NOUNS 1 **furrow, groove,** scratch, crack, cranny, chase, chink, score, **cut,** gash, striation, streak, stria, slit
VERBS 2 **excavate, dig,** dig out, **scoop,** scoop out, gouge out, grub, shovel, spade, dike, delve, scrape, scratch, scrabble; dredge; **trench,** trough, furrow, groove; **tunnel, burrow**
3 **overcharge, hold up** *and* **soak** *and* **stick** *and* **sting** *and* **clip** <all nonformal>, **make pay through the nose,** victimize, swindle; exploit, skin <nonformal>, **fleece,** screw *and* put the screws to <both nonformal>, bleed, bleed white

gourmand NOUNS **glutton,** greedy eater, big *or* hefty *or* husky eater <nonformal>, trencherman, trencherwoman, belly-god, gobbler, greedygut *or* greedyguts <nonformal>, gorger, gormand, gormandizer, guttler, cormorant; **hog** *and* **pig** *and* chow hound *and* khazer <all nonformal>

gourmet NOUNS 1 gastronome, epicure, connoisseur of food *or* wine, bon vivant, high liver, Lucullus, Brillat-Savarin
ADJS 2 **savory,** savorous, **palatable, toothsome,** sapid, pleasing, to one's taste, **delicious,** delightful, delectable, exquisite; for the gods, ambrosial, nectarous, nectareous; fit for a king, gourmet, fit for a gourmet, of gourmet quality

govern VERBS **regulate; wield authority; command,** officer, captain, **head, lead,** be master, be at the head of, **preside over,** chair; **direct, manage, supervise, administer,** administrate; discipline; **rule, control,** order, **regulate,** direct, guide

governess NOUNS **chaperon,** duenna; escort

government NOUNS governance, **discipline, regulation; direction, management, administration,** dispensation, disposition, oversight, **supervision; regime,** regimen; **rule, sway, sovereignty, reign,** regnancy; empire, empery; social order, civil government, political government

governor NOUNS **ruler; captain, master, commander,** commandant, commanding officer, intendant, castellan, chatelain, chatelaine; **director, manager, executive**

gown NOUNS **garment,** vestment, vesture, robe, frock, rag <nonformal>, mantle, cloak

grab VERBS **seize,** take *or* get hold of, **lay hold of,** catch *or* grab hold of, glom *or* latch on to <nonformal>, **get** *or* **lay hands on,** clap hands on <nonformal>, put one's hands on, get into one's grasp *or* clutches; get one's fingers *or* hands on; **grasp, grip, grapple, snatch,** snatch up, nip, nail <nonformal>, **clutch,** claw, clinch, clench

grab bag NOUNS **hodgepodge,** hotchpotch, hotchpot; **medley, miscellany,** mélange, pastiche, *pasticcio* <Ital>, **conglomeration, assortment,** assemblage, mixed bag, ragbag, olio, *olla podrida* <Sp>, **scramble, jumble,** mingle-mangle, **mix,** mishmash, **mess,** can of worms <nonformal>, dog's breakfast <Can nonformal>, mare's nest, rat's nest, hash, patchwork, salad, gallimaufry, salmagundi, **potpourri,** stew, sauce, slurry, omnium-gatherum, **odds and ends,** oddments, all sorts, everything but the kitchen sink <nonformal>

grace NOUNS 1 **charm,** winsomeness, **attractiveness, appeal, elegance,** elegancy; gracefulness, gracility; **loveliness, pulchritude,** exquisiteness
2 **benevolence, goodwill,** brotherly love, charity, Christian charity *or* love, *caritas* <L>, love of mankind, good will to *or* toward man, love, *agape* <Gk>, state of grace
3 **pardon,** excuse, sparing, **amnesty,** indemnity, exemption, immunity, reprieve; **exoneration, exculpation**
4 **prayer, invocation,** silent prayer, meditation, contemplation, communion; thanks, thanksgiving

graceful ADJS **agile, nimble, spry,** sprightly, fleet, featly, light, nimble-footed, light-footed, sure-footed; **elegant,** gracile, gracious

graceless ADJS **inelegant, clumsy, clunky** *and* **klutzy** <both nonformal>, heavy-handed, heavy-footed, ham-handed, ungraceful, ungainly, infelicitous, unfelicitous; **tasteless,** in bad taste, indecorous, unseemly, uncourtly, undignified; **unpolished, unrefined**

gracious ADJS **courteous, polite, civil, urbane,** graceful, agreeable, affable, fair; complaisant; obliging, accommodating; **thoughtful, considerate,** tactful, solicitous; respectful, deferential, attentive; **cordial,** amiable, **friendly,** neighborly, genial, hearty, open, openhearted, warm, warmhearted

grade NOUNS 1 **incline,** inclination, **slope,** gradient, pitch, **ramp,** launching ramp, bank, talus, gentle *or* easy slope, glacis; rapid *or* steep slope
2 **rank,** rating, status, estate, stratum, level, station, position
VERBS 3 **level, flatten, even, equalize,** align, smooth *or* smoothen, level out, smooth out; roll, roll flat, steamroller *or* steamroll
4 **classify,** class, assign, designate; **categorize,** type, put down as, **pigeonhole,** place, **group, arrange**, range; **order**, put in order, rank, rate, **sort,** assort

gradual ADJS **slow, leisurely,** slack, moderate, gentle, **easy,** deliberate, go-slow, unhurried, relaxed, gradual, circumspect, tentative, cautious, reluctant, foot-dragging <nonformal>; **gradational,** calibrated, graduated, phased, staged, tapered, scalar

graduate NOUNS 1 grad <nonformal>; **alumnus,** alumni, alumna, alumnae; **graduate student,** grad student <nonformal>, **postgraduate,** postgrad <nonformal>; college graduate
VERBS 2 **promote, advance,** up *and* boost <both nonformal>, elevate, upgrade; pass

graduation NOUNS **convocation;** commencement, commencement exercises; graduation exercises; baccalaureate service

graffito NOUNS **inscription,** epigraph

graft NOUNS 1 grafting, engrafting, transplant, transplantation; infixing, implantation, embedment, tessellation, impactment, impaction; **insert,** insertion; **inset, inlay;** scion *or* cion
2 **bribery,** bribing, subornation, **corruption,** bribery and corruption; **spoils of office;** boodle <nonformal>; slush fund <nonformal>; public tit *and* public trough <both nonformal>; spoils system
VERBS 3 engraft, **implant,** bud; inarch

grain NOUNS 1 **particle,** fragment, spot, **speck,** flyspeck, fleck, point, dot, jot, tittle, **iota,** ounce, **dab** <nonformal>, mote, **mite** <nonformal>; granule, pebble
2 **texture,** surface texture; **surface; finish,** feel; granular texture, fineness *or* coarseness of grain
3 **cereal,** cereal plant, farinaceous plant; **kernel,** berry

grammar NOUNS rules of language, linguistic structure, syntactic structure; **traditional grammar, school grammar;** descriptive grammar, **structural grammar**

the rule and pattern of speech
HORACE

grammar school NOUNS **elementary school, grade school** *or* graded school, the grades; **primary school;** junior school <Brit>; folk school, *Volksschule* <Ger>

grammatical ADJS **syntactical,** formal, structural; correct, well-formed; tagmemic, glossematic

granary NOUNS **garner,** grain bin, elevator, grain elevator, **silo;** mow, haymow, hayloft, hayrick; crib, corncrib

grand ADJS 1 **great, considerable,** consequential; **mighty,** powerful, strong, irresistible, intense; main, maximum, **total, full,** plenary, comprehensive, exhaustive
2 **grandiose, magnificent, splendid,** splendiferous, **glorious,** superb, fine, superfine, fancy, superfancy, swell <nonformal>; **noble, proud, stately, majestic,** princely; **sumptuous, elegant, elaborate, luxurious,** extravagant, deluxe; palatial, Babylonian

grandeur NOUNS grandness, grandiosity, **magnificence,** gorgeousness, **splendor,** splendidness, splendiferousness, resplendence, brilliance, glory; nobility, proudness, **state, stateliness, majesty;** impressiveness, imposingness; **sumptuousness, elegance, elaborateness, lavishness, luxuriousness;** barbaric *or* Babylonian splendor

grandfather NOUNS 1 grandsire, grandpa, gramps; old man; great-grandfather

2 <nonformal> **grandpa,** grampa, gramper, gramp, gramps, grandpapa, grandpap, grandpappy, **granddad,** granddaddy, granddada, granfer, gramfer, granther, pop, grandpop

grandiose ADJS **imposing, impressive,** larger-than-life, awful, awe-inspiring, awesome; **sumptuous, elegant, elaborate, luxurious,** extravagant, deluxe; executive *and* plush *and* posh *and* ritzy *and* swank *and* swanky <all nonformal>

grandmother NOUNS 1 grandam; old woman, old lady, dowager, matriarch; great-grandmother

2 <nonformal> **grandma,** granma, old woman, grandmamma, grandmammy, **granny,** grammy, gammy, grannam, gammer

grandstand NOUNS 1 **stands,** boxes, lower deck, upper deck, outfield stands, bleachers
VERBS 2 **show off** <nonformal>, hotdog *and* showboat <both nonformal>, play to the gallery *or* galleries <nonformal>, please the crowd; strut one's stuff <nonformal>, go through one's paces, show what one has

grange NOUNS **farm,** farmplace, farmstead, farmhold <old>, farmery <Brit>, location <Austral>, pen <Jamaica>

grant NOUNS 1 **concession;** charter, franchise, liberty, diploma, patent, letters patent, brevet; royal grant
2 **subsidy,** subvention, subsidization, support, grant-in-aid, bounty; **allowance, stipend,** allotment; scholarship, fellowship; honorarium
VERBS 3 **give,** present, bestow, confer, award, allot, render, bestow on; accord, **allow,** vouchsafe, yield, afford, make available; **tender,** proffer, offer, extend, come up with <nonformal>; **issue, dispense,** administer; serve, help to; **distribute**, give out, deal out, dole out, mete out, hand *or* dish out <nonformal>, fork *or* shell out <nonformal>; make a present of, gift *or* gift with <nonformal>, give as a gift
4 allow, **concede,** admit, admit exceptions, see the special circumstances; **waive, set aside,** ease, lift temporarily, pull one's punches <nonformal>

granulated ADJS **granular, grainy,** granulate, **sandy, gritty,** sabulous, arenarious, arenaceous

grapevine NOUNS **report, rumor,** flying rumor, unverified *or* unconfirmed report, **hearsay,** *on-dit* <Fr>, **scuttlebutt** *and* latrine rumor <both nonformal>; grapevine telegraph, bush telegraph <Australia>; **pipeline;** a little bird *or* birdie

graph NOUNS 1 **diagram,** plot, chart, blueprint, bar graph, pie *or* circle graph *or* chart, area graph; flow diagram, flow chart
VERBS 2 **plot; map, chart, blueprint; diagram,** plot out, **lay out,** set out

graphic ADJS **descriptive, depictive,** expositive, representative, delineative; expressive, vivid, suggestive, imaginative, well-drawn; realistic, naturalistic, true to life, lifelike, faithful

grapple VERBS **contend, wrestle,** rassle <nonformal>, grapple with, go to the mat with; **seize, grab, grasp, grip,** gripe <old>, **snatch,** snatch up, nip, nail <nonformal>, **clutch,** claw, clinch, clench

grasp NOUNS 1 **hold,** purchase, grip, clutch, clamp, clinch, clench; **clasp,** hug, embrace, firm hold, tight grip
2 **understanding, comprehension, apprehension,** intellection, prehension; mental grasp, grip, **command,** mastery; intelligence, wisdom

VERBS 3 **seize,** take *or* get hold of, **lay hold of,** catch *or* grab hold of, glom *or* latch on to <nonformal>, **grab,** grip, gripe <old>, grapple, snatch, snatch up, nip, nail <nonformal>, **clutch,** claw, clinch, clench; **clasp,** hug, embrace
4 **understand,** comprehend, apprehend, have, **know, conceive, realize,** appreciate, have no problem with, ken <Scots>, savvy <nonformal>, sense, make sense out of, make something of; **fathom, follow; seize,** get hold of, grasp *or* seize the meaning, **catch on,** get the meaning of, get the hang of; **master, learn**

grasping ADJS **greedy,** avaricious, avid, voracious, rapacious, cupidinous, esurient, ravening, **grabby** <nonformal>, graspy, acquisitive, mercenary, sordid, overgreedy; miserly, money-hungry, money-grubbing, money-mad, venal

grass NOUNS

> <nonformal terms for marijuana> Acapulco gold, aunt mary, bomb, boo, bush, doobie, gage, ganja, grefa, hay, hemp, herb, Indian hay, J, jane, kif, mary, maryjane, mary warner, meserole, mighty mezz, moota, muggles, pod, pot, smoke, snop, tea, Texas tea, weed, yerba

grassland NOUNS grass; parkland; **meadow,** meadow land, mead <old>, swale, lea, vega; **pasture,** pastureland, pasturage, pasture land, park <Brit nonformal>; **range,** grazing, grazing land; **prairie, savanna, steppe,** steppeland, **pampas,** pampa, campo, llano, **veld,** grass veld

grate VERBS 1 **rasp, scratch, scrape,** grind; crunch, craunch, scranch <old>, scrunch, crump
2 **irritate,** touch a soft spot *or* tender spot, touch a raw nerve, touch where it hurts; provoke, **gall,** chafe, fret, rasp; **get on one's nerves, grate on,** set on edge; set one's teeth on edge, go against the grain; **rub one** *or* **one's fur the wrong way**

grateful ADJS **thankful; appreciative,** appreciatory, sensible; **obliged, much obliged,** beholden, indebted to, crediting, under obligation, acknowledging, cognizant of; gratifying, pleasing

gratify VERBS **satisfy,** sate, satiate; slake, appease, allay, assuage, quench; regale, feed, feast; do one's heart good, warm the cockles of the heart; **make proud,** do one's heart good, do one proud <nonformal>, **elate,** flush, turn one's head; favor, please, **cater to**

gratifying ADJS **pleasing,** satisfying, rewarding, heartwarming, grateful; **agreeable,** desirable, acceptable

grating ADJS **irritating,** irritative, irritant; **chafing, galling,** fretting, rasping, boring, grinding, stinging, scratchy; **jarring; rasping,** raspy; strident, shrill, harsh, raucous

gratis ADJS 1 **gratuitous,** free, free of charge, for free, **for nothing,** free for nothing, free for the asking, complimentary, **on the house,** comp
ADVS 2 **gratuitously,** free, **free of charge,** for nothing, for the asking, at no charge, without charge, with the compliments of the management, as our guest, on the house

gratitude NOUNS **gratefulness,** thankfulness, appreciation, appreciativeness; obligation, sense of obligation *or* indebtedness

gratuitous ADJS unnecessary, unessential, nonessential, expendable, dispensable, **needless,** unneeded, uncalled-for

gratuity NOUNS **largess, bounty,** liberality, donative, sportula; perquisite, perks <Brit nonformal>; consideration, fee <old>, **tip,** *pourboire* <Fr>, *Trinkgeld* <Ger>, sweetener, inducement; grease *and* salve *and* palm oil <all nonformal>; honorarium

grave NOUNS 1 **tomb, sepulcher;** gravesite, burial, pit, deep six <nonformal>; resting place, last home, long home, narrow house, house of death, low house, low green tent; **crypt, vault,** burial chamber

> *the lone couch of his*
> *everlasting sleep*
> SHELLEY

ADJS 2 **solemn,** dignified, sober, unsmiling, weighty, somber, frowning, **grim; sedate, staid;** demure, decorous; **serious, earnest, thoughtful; sober-minded,** sober-sided; straight-faced, long-faced, grim-faced, grim-visaged, stone-faced; sober as a judge, grave as an undertaker; **formal**

graven ADJS **engraved,** graved, tooled, enchased, inscribed, incised, marked, lined, creased, cut, carved, glyphic, **sculptured,** insculptured, **printed,** imprinted, impressed, stamped

graveyard NOUNS **cemetery, burial ground** *or* **place,** burying place *or* ground, *campo santo* <Ital>, boneyard *and* bone orchard <both nonformal>, burial yard, necropolis, polyandrium, **memorial park,** city *or* village of the dead; **churchyard,** God's acre; **potter's field;** Golgotha, Calvary

gravitate VERBS **descend**, drop, plunge, precipitate, sink, settle, subside; tend, tend to go, **incline,** point, head, lead, lean

gravity NOUNS **importance, significance, consequence,** consideration, **import,** note, mark, **moment, weight;** graveness, seriousness, solemnity, weightiness; *gravitas* <L>; no joke, no laughing matter, hardball <nonformal>

gray ADJS dull, flat, mat, dead, dingy, muddy, leaden, lusterless, lackluster; **faded, washed-out,** dimmed, discolored, etiolated; **pale, dim,** weak, **faint; pallid, wan, sallow,** fallow; pale *or* blue *or* green around the gills; **ashen,** ashy, ashen-hued, cinereous, cineritious, griseous; **grayish,** gray-colored, gray-hued, gray-toned, grayed, **grizzly,** grizzled

gray area NOUNS **ambiguity,** ambiguousness; **equivocalness,** equivocacy, equivocality; **double meaning,** amphibology; twilight zone, inexplicitness, uncertainty, borderline case

gray matter NOUNS **intellect, mind,** *mens* <L>; mental *or* intellectual faculty, nous, **reason, rationality,** rational *or* reasoning faculty, power of reason, *Vernunft* <Ger>, *esprit* <Fr>, *raison* <Fr>, **intelligence,** mentality, mental capacity, **understanding,** reasoning, intellection, conception; **brain, brains,** brainpower, smarts <nonformal>

graze VERBS **touch lightly,** touch upon; kiss, **brush,** sweep, brush by, glance, scrape, skim

grease NOUNS 1 **flattery, adulation; blarney** *and* bunkum *and* **soft soap** *and* soap *or* butter salve <all nonformal>, oil, eyewash <nonformal>; strokes *and* stroking *and* ego massage <all nonformal>, sweet talk, fair *or* sweet *or* honeyed words, soft *or* honeyed phrases, ass-kissing <nonformal>, **fawning, sycophancy; gratuity,** sweetener, inducement; salve *and* palm oil <both nonformal>
2 **oil,** *oleum* <L>; **fat,** lipid, sebum, tallow, vegetable oil, animal oil
VERBS 3 **bribe,** throw a sop to; **grease the palm** *or* **hand** *and* oil the palm *and* tickle the palm <all nonformal>; buy *and* **buy off** *and* pay off <all nonformal>; suborn, **corrupt,** tamper with; reach *and* get at *and* get to <all nonformal>; approach, try to bribe; **fix, take care of**
4 **facilitate, ease; grease the wheels** <nonformal>; grease *or* soap the ways <both nonformal>, prepare the way, **clear the way,** make all clear for, make way for; open the way, open the door to; **lubricate,** make frictionless *or* dissipationless, remove friction, oil; **speed, expedite,** quicken, hasten; **help along,** help on its way; **aid; explain,** make clear; **simplify**

grease paint NOUNS theatrical makeup, **makeup,** cosmetics, beauty products, beauty-care products; war paint <nonformal>; pancake makeup

greasy ADJS 1 **slippery,** slippy, **slick,** slithery *and* sliddery <both nonformal>, slippery as an eel; lubricious, lubric, oily, oleaginous, buttery, soaped; lubricated, oiled, greased
2 **oily; unctuous,** unctional; unguinous; **oleaginous,** oleic; unguentary, **unguent,** unguentous

greasy spoon NOUNS eatery *and* beanery *and* hashery *and* hash house <all nonformal>; hamburger joint <nonformal>; **lunchroom,** luncheonette; lunch wagon, dog wagon <nonformal>

great ADJS 1 **grand, considerable,** consequential; **mighty,** powerful, strong, irresistible, intense; main, maximum, **total, full,** plenary, comprehensive, exhaustive; grave, **serious,** heavy, deep; arch, banner, master, magisterial; topflight, highest-ranking, ranking; **star,** superstar, stellar, world-class
2 **important,** major, consequential, momentous, significant, substantial, material, big; superior, world-shaking, earthshaking; big-time *and* big-league *and* major-league *and* heavyweight <all nonformal>; high-powered <nonformal>, double-barreled <nonformal>

3 <nonformal> swell, dandy, bitchin', jim dandy, neat, cool, super, superduper, bully <old>, tough, mean, gnarly, heavy, bad, groovy, out of sight, fab, fantabulous, marvy, gear, something

else, ducky, dynamite, keen, killer, hot, nifty, sexy, spiffy, spiffing, ripping, nobby, peachy, peachy-keen, delicious, scrumptious, not too shabby, tits, out of this world, hunky-dory, crackerjack, boss, stunning, corking, smashing, solid, all wool and a yard wide; rum *or* wizard <both Brit>, bonzer <Austral>; bang-up, jam-up, slap-up, ace-high, fine and dandy, just dandy, but good, OK, okay, A-OK

greed NOUNS greediness, graspingness, **avarice,** cupidity, avidity, voracity, rapacity, lust, avariciousness, *avaritia and cupiditas* <both L>; money-grubbing; avidness, esurience, wolfishness; voraciousness, ravenousness, rapaciousness, sordidness, **covetousness,** acquisitiveness; itching palm; grasping; **piggishness,** hoggishness, swinishness; **gluttony**, *gula* <L>; inordinate desire, furor, craze, fury *or* frenzy of desire, overgreediness; insatiable desire, insatiability; incontinence, intemperateness

greedy ADJS **avaricious,** avid, voracious, rapacious, cupidinous, esurient, **ravening, grasping, grabby** <nonformal>, graspy, acquisitive, mercenary, sordid, overgreedy; ravenous, gobbling, devouring; miserly, money-hungry, money-grubbing, money-mad, venal; **covetous,** coveting; **piggish, hoggish,** swinish, a hog for, greedy as a hog; **gluttonous**; omnivorous, all-devouring; insatiable, insatiate, unsatisfied, unsated, unappeased, unappeasable, limitless, bottomless, unquenchable, quenchless, unslaked, unslakable, slakeless

green NOUNS 1 **lawn;** grassplot, greenyard; grounds; **common, park, village green;** golf course *or* links, fairway; bowling green, putting green
ADJS 2 **verdant,** verdurous; grassy, leafy, leaved, foliaged; springlike, summerlike, summery, vernal, vernant, aestival; **greenish,** viridescent, virescent; **grass-green,** green as grass; glaucous, glaucescent, glaucous-green
3 **jealous, jaundiced,** jaundice-eyed, yellow-eyed, green-eyed, yellow, green with jealousy; invidious, **envious**
4 **immature, unripe,** underripe, unripened, impubic, **raw,** callow, wet behind the ears, unfledged, fledgling, unseasoned, unmellowed; **ignorant, inexperienced**; innocent, ingenuous, gauche, awkward, naive

greenery NOUNS **plants, vegetation;** herbage, flowerage, verdure, greens

greenhorn NOUNS **newcomer, new arrival,** *novus homo* <L>; *arriviste* <Fr>, Johnny-come-lately <nonformal>, new boy <Brit>; **tenderfoot;** settler, immigrant; recruit, rookie <nonformal>

greenhouse NOUNS **nursery; conservatory,** glasshouse <Brit>, forcing house, summerhouse, lathhouse, **hothouse,** coolhouse

greenroom NOUNS **anteroom,** antechamber; **waiting room,** *salle d'attente* <Fr>; **reception room,** presence chamber *or* room, audience chamber; lounge, wardroom

greet VERBS **hail, accost,** address; **salute,** make one's salutations; **bid** *or* **say hello,** bid good day *or* good morning, etc; exchange greetings, **pass the time of day; give one's regards**; shake hands, shake *and* give one some skin *and* give a high *or* a low five <all nonformal>, press the flesh <nonformal>, press *or* squeeze one's hand

greetings NOUNS **regards, compliments, respects,** *égards, devoirs* <both Fr>; **salutations,** salaams; **best wishes,** one's best, good wishes, best regards, kind *or* kindest regards, love, best love; remembrances, kind remembrances; compliments of the season

gregarious ADJS **sociable, social,** social-minded, fit for society, fond of society, **affable; companionable,** companionate, compatible, genial, *gemütlich* <Ger>, **congenial; communicative**; amiable, **friendly;** civil, urbane, courteous

gremlin NOUNS **imp, pixie,** sprite, elf, puck, kobold, *diablotin* <Fr>, tokoloshe, poltergeist, Dingbelle, Fifinella, **bad fairy,** bad peri

grid NOUNS **network,** hachure *or* hatchure, hatching, cross-hatching; grate, grating; grille, grillwork; gridiron

griddle VERBS fry, deep-fry *or* deep-fat fry, pan, pan-fry; sauté, stir-fry; broil, grill, pan-broil

gridlock NOUNS **blockage,** strangulation, choking, choking off, **stoppage,** stop, **bar, barrier, obstacle,** impediment; **bottleneck,** chokepoint; **congestion,** jam, traffic jam, bottleneck; impasse

grief NOUNS **pain, distress,** stress, stress of life, suffering, passion, dolor; **melan-**

choly, melancholia, depression, sadness, heartache, aching heart, heavy heart, bleeding heart, broken heart, agony of mind *or* spirit; **distressfulness,** distress, grievousness; **painfulness,** pain; **sorrow,** sorrowing, **care, woe;** heartgrief, heartfelt grief; prostrating grief, prostration; **lamentation**

grievance NOUNS **complaint, peeve,** pet peeve, **groan; dissent, protest**; hard luck story <nonformal>, tale of woe; **complaining,** scolding, groaning, **faultfinding**, sniping, destructive criticism, grumbling, murmuring; **injustice,** wrong, injury, disservice; raw *or* rotten deal *and* bad rap <all nonformal>; imposition; mockery *or* miscarriage of justice; great wrong, grave *or* gross injustice

grieve VERBS **sorrow; weep,** mourn; be dumb with grief; **pine,** pine away; **brood over,** mope, fret, take on <nonformal>; **eat one's heart out,** break one's heart over; **agonize,** ache, bleed; **lament,** moan, keen, weep over, bewail, bemoan, deplore, repine

grill VERBS 1 fry, deep-fry *or* deep-fat fry, griddle, pan, pan-fry; sauté, stir-fry; sear, blacken, braise, brown; broil, pan-broil
2 **interrogate,** question, **pump,** pump for information, shoot questions at, pick the brains of, worm out of; interview; draw one out

grille NOUNS **network, net,** netting; **mesh,** meshes; **web,** webbing; lattice, latticework; hachure *or* hatchure, hatching, cross-hatching; grillwork; **grid,** gridiron; tracery, fretwork

grim ADJS **sullen,** sulky, surly, morose, dour, mumpish, dumpish, **glum, moody,** moping; **glowering,** lowering, **scowling, frowning; gloomy,** dismal, murky, bleak, somber, sombrous, **solemn,** grave; **hopeless,** unhopeful, without hope, affording no hope, worst-case, bleak, dismal, cheerless, comfortless

grimace NOUNS 1 **wry face,** wry mouth, rictus, snarl; moue, mow, pout
VERBS 2 **make a face,** make a wry face *or* mouth, pull a face, **screw up one's face,** mug <nonformal>, mouth, make a mouth, mop, mow <old>, mop and mow <old>; pout

grime NOUNS **dirt;** dust; soot, smut; **mud**

grimy ADJS **dirty, grubby,** grungy <nonformal>, smirchy, dingy, messy <nonformal>; scruffy, slovenly, untidy; miry, **muddy**; **dusty;** smutty, smutchy, smudgy; sooty, smoky; snuffy

grin NOUNS 1 **smile,** silly smile *or* grin; grinning; broad grin, ear-to-ear grin, toothful grin; stupid grin, idiotic grin; sardonic grin, **smirk, simper**
VERBS 2 **smile,** beam, smile brightly; grin like a Cheshire cat *or* chessy-cat <nonformal>; **smirk, simper**

grind NOUNS 1 **routine,** rut, groove, well-worn groove; **treadmill,** squirrel cage; the working day, nine-to-five, the daily grind <nonformal>; **study, studying,** application; **brainwork, headwork,** lucubration, mental labor; grinding *and* boning <both nonformal>, **cramming** *and* cram <both nonformal>
2 **drudge,** grub, hack, fag, plodder, slave, galley slave, **workhorse,** beast of burden, slogger; greasy grind <nonformal>; **bookworm**
VERBS 3 **grate,** rasp, scratch, scrape; **sharpen, edge,** acuminate, aculeate, spiculate, taper; **whet, hone,** oilstone, file; **pulverize, powder,** comminute, triturate, contriturate, levigate, bray, pestle, disintegrate, reduce to powder *or* dust, grind to powder *or* dust, grind up

grip NOUNS 1 **control,** mastery, mastership, command, power, jurisdiction, dominion, domination; hold, grasp, hand, hands, iron hand, clutches; talons, claws; steady hand; firm hold, tight grip, iron grip, grip of iron *or* steel, death grip; **handle, hold,** grasp, haft, helve
VERBS 2 **hold,** grasp, clutch, clip, clinch, clench; bite, nip; **clasp,** hug, embrace; **cling, cling to,** cleave to, stick to, adhere to, freeze to; **hold on to,** hold fast *or* tight, hang on to, keep a firm hold upon; **hold on, hang on** <nonformal>, hold on like a bulldog, stick like a leech, hang on for dear life; keep hold of, never let go; **seize**
3 **engross,** absorb, immerse, occupy, preoccupy, engage, involve, monopolize, exercise, take up; **obsess; hold,** arrest, hold the interest, fascinate, enthrall, spellbind, hold spellbound, grab <nonformal>, charm, enchant, mesmerize, hypnotize, catch; absorb the attention, claim one's thoughts, monopolize one's attention, engage the mind *or* thoughts

gripe NOUNS

<nonformal> **beef, kick, gripe,** kvetch, grouse, bellyache, howl, holler, **squawk,** bitch; **beefing,** grousing, kicking, griping, kvetching, bellyaching, squawking, **bitching,** yapping

gripping ADJS **engrossing,** absorbing, consuming, riveting, holding, arresting, engaging, attractive, fascinating, enthralling, **spellbinding,** enchanting, magnetic, hypnotic, mesmerizing, mesmeric; obsessive, obsessing

grisly ADJS **deathly, deathlike,** deadly; **weird,** eerie, uncanny, unearthly; ghostly, ghostlike; **ghastly,** gruesome, macabre; **repulsive**, repellent, repelling, rebarbative, **repugnant,** offensive, foul, forbidding, loathsome, revolting

grit NOUNS **pluck, spunk** <nonformal>, mettle, backbone <nonformal>, true grit, spirit, **stamina, guts** *and* moxie <both nonformal>, bottom, **toughness** <nonformal>; pluckiness, spunkiness <nonformal>, **gameness,** feistiness <nonformal>, mettlesomeness; courage

gritty ADJS **rough**, coarse, gross, unrefined, coarse-grained; grained, **grainy,** granular, granulated, gravelly; **plucky, spunky** *and* feisty *and* gutty *or* gutsy <all nonformal>, **mettlesome,** dauntless, **game,** game to the last *or* end; **courageous**

grizzled ADJS **white, hoary,** hoar, grizzly, canescent; **gray, grayish,** griseous; grizzle

groan NOUNS 1 **lament,** plaint, *planctus* <L>; **murmur,** mutter; **moan,** whine, wail, wail of woe; **sob,** *cri du coeur* <Fr>, **cry,** outcry, scream, **howl,** yowl, bawl, yawp, keen, ululation; **complaint,** grievance
VERBS 2 **moan, howl,** yowl, **cry,** squall, bawl, yawp, yell, scream, shriek; cry out, make an outcry; **complain,** grumble, murmur, mutter, growl, clamor, croak, grunt, yelp

groceries NOUNS **provisions,** provender, supplies, stores, larder, food supply; food items, edibles, victuals, baked goods, packaged goods, canned goods

groggy ADJS **dazed,** in a daze; **silly,** knocked silly, **dopey** <nonformal>, woozy <nonformal>; **punch-drunk** *and* punchy *and* **slap-happy** <all nonformal>

groom NOUNS 1 **stableman,** stableboy, hostler, equerry
VERBS 2 dress, fettle <Brit nonformal>, **brush up; preen,** plume, titivate; manicure; **prepare,** ready, **condition,** fit, put in tune, form, **lick into shape** <nonformal>; rub down, brush, curry, currycomb

groomed ADJS **prepared, ready,** well-prepared, prepped <nonformal>, in readiness *or* ready state, all ready, good and ready, prepared and ready; coached; **readied,** available

groove NOUNS **furrow,** scratch, crack, cranny, chase, chink, score, **cut,** gash, striation, streak, stria, **gouge,** slit, incision; sulcus, sulcation; **rut,** wheeltrack, well-worn groove; wrinkle; **corrugation;** flute, fluting; rifling

groovy ADJS

<nonformal> **hep, hip,** on the beam, go-go, **with it,** into, really into; chic, clued-up, clued in, in the know, trendy

grope VERBS 1 **touch, feel, impinge,** bump up against, hit; osculate; **graze,** nudge, rub, brush, glance, scrape, sideswipe, skim, skirt, shave; feel up *and* cop a feel <both nonformal>; **search, hunt, explore;** dig, delve, burrow, root, pick over, poke, pry; look round *or* around, poke around, nose around, smell around; beat the bushes
2 **be uncertain, feel unsure;** be at one's wit's end, not know which way to turn, be of two minds, be at sixes and sevens, not know where one stands, be in a dilemma *or* quandary, flounder, beat about, thrash about, not know whether one is coming or going

gross NOUNS 1 **receipts,** revenue, profits, earnings, returns, proceeds, **take,** takings; gate receipts, gate, box office; gross receipts
VERBS 2 **make money;** rake it in *and* coin money *and* make a bundle *or* pile *or* killing *or* mint *and* clean up <all nonformal>; **realize**
ADJS 3 **offensive,** coarse, crude, obscene; obnoxious, abhorrent, hateful, abominable, heinous, **contemptible, despicable,** detestable, execrable, beneath *or* below contempt, **base,** ignoble

grotesque ADJS **freakish,** freak *or* freaky <nonformal>; **monstrous, deformed,**

malformed, misshapen, **misbegotten,** teratogenic, teratoid; **bizarre,** baroque, rococo; preposterous, cockamamie <nonformal>, fantastic, fantastical, wild, weird, **outrageous,** incredible, beyond belief, *outré* <Fr>, extravagant

grotto NOUNS **cave,** cavern, hole, grot, antre, subterrane

grouch NOUNS **sorehead,** curmudgeon, grump, crank, crosspatch, wasp, **bear,** grizzly bear, pit bull, junkyard dog <nonformal>; **spoilsport,** malcontent

grouchy ADJS

<nonformal> **crabby,** cantankerous, crusty, grumpy *or* grumpish, huffy *or* huffish, mean, mean as a junkyard dog, ornery, bitchy, cussed, feisty, ugly, miffy, salty, scrappy, shirty <Brit>, soreheaded

groundless ADJS **baseless,** ungrounded, **unfounded,** ill-founded, unbased, **unsupported,** unsustained, **without foundation,** without basis *or* sound basis; **untenable, unsupportable,** unsustainable; **unwarranted,** idle, empty, vain

grounds NOUNS 1 **dregs, lees,** dross, slag, draff, scoria, feces; **sediment, settlings, deposits,** deposition; alluvium, alluvion, diluvium
2 **evidence, proof; reason to believe,** grounds for belief; **ground,** material grounds, **facts, data,** premises, basis for belief

group NOUNS 1 **bunch,** grouping, groupment, crop, **cluster, clump,** knot; **batch, lot,** slew <nonformal>, **mess** <nonformal>; **set**
VERBS 2 **classify**, categorize; **grade,** gradate, rank, subordinate; **sort,** sort out <chiefly Brit>, assort; **separate,** divide; collate

groupie NOUNS

<nonformal> **fan, buff, freak,** hound, fiend, demon, nut, bug, head, junkie, rooter, booster, great one for

grouping NOUNS **classification**, categorization, taxonomy; **gradation,** subordination, superordination, **ranking,** placement; **sorting,** sorting out, assortment, sifting, screening, triage, culling, selection, shakeout

grove NOUNS **woodlet;** holt <nonformal>, hurst, tope <India>, shaw <nonformal>, bosk <old>; **orchard;** wood lot; coppice, copse; *bocage* <Fr>

grovel VERBS **fawn,** truckle; **toady,** toadeat; **bootlick** <nonformal>, lickspittle, lick one's shoes, lick the feet of; **crawl,** creep, cower, cringe, crouch, stoop, kneel, bend the knee, fall on one's knees, prostrate oneself, throw oneself at the feet of, fall at one's feet, kiss *or* lick *or* suck one's ass *and* brown-nose <all nonformal>, kiss one's feet, kiss the hem of one's garment, lick the dust, make a doormat of oneself; **kowtow,** bow, **bow and scrape**

grow VERBS **develop,** wax, **increase**; gather, brew; **grow up,** mature, maturate, spring up, ripen, come of age, **shoot up,** sprout up, upshoot, upspring, upsprout, upspear, overtop, tower; grow like a weed <nonformal>; burgeon, **sprout**, blossom, reproduce, procreate, grow out of, germinate, pullulate; **flourish, thrive;** mushroom, balloon

growl VERBS **snarl,** grumble, gnarl, snap; show one's teeth, spit

grownup NOUNS **adult,** mature man *or* woman, grown man *or* woman, big boy *and* big girl <both nonformal>; **man, woman;** no chicken *and* no spring chicken <both nonformal>

growth NOUNS **development;** bodily development, **maturation,** maturing, coming of age, growing up, upgrowth; burgeoning, sprouting; budding, gemmation; outgrowth, excrescence; overgrowth

grow up VERBS **mature,** grow, **develop, ripen,** flower, flourish, bloom, blossom; fledge, leave the nest, put up one's hair, not be in pigtails, put on long pants; **come of age,** come to maturity, attain majority, **reach one's majority,** reach the age of consent, reach manhood *or* womanhood, put on long trousers *or* pants, assume the toga virilis, come into years of discretion, be in the prime of life, cut one's wisdom teeth *or* eyeteeth <nonformal>, have sown one's wild oats, settle down; **mellow,** season, temper

grubby ADJS **dirty, grimy,** grungy <nonformal>, smirchy, dingy; smutty, smutchy, smudgy; **messy** <nonformal>, mussy <nonformal>, **sloppy** <nonformal>, scraggly, poky, seedy <nonformal>, **shabby,** shoddy, schlocky <nonformal>, lumpen, chintzy, grubby <nonformal>, **frowzy, blowzy,** tacky <nonformal>; **infested,** wormy, ratty

grudge NOUNS **aversion, repugnance,** repulsion, **antipathy,** allergy <nonformal>, abomination, **abhorrence; spite,** crow to pick *or* pluck *or* pull, bone to pick

grudging ADJS **envious,** envying, **invidious,** green with envy; **jealous**; **covetous,** desirous of; resentful; **begrudging;** mean, mean-spirited, ungenerous; **reluctant,** renitent, **loath;** unenthusiastic, unzealous, indifferent, apathetic, perfunctory; balky, balking, restive; **niggardly,** niggard, pinchpenny, penurious, **mean,** mingy, shabby, sordid

grueling ADJS **fatiguing, wearying,** wearing, **tiring,** straining, stressful, trying, **exhausting,** draining, punishing, killing; **tiresome,** fatiguesome, **wearisome,** weariful; **backbreaking,** punishing, crushing, killing, Herculean

gruesome ADJS **deathly,** deathlike, deadly; **ghastly,** grisly, macabre; **repulsive**, repellent, repelling, rebarbative, **repugnant,** offensive, foul, forbidding, loathsome

gruff ADJS **brusque, curt,** short, sharp, snippy <nonformal>, abrupt, **blunt,** bluff, brash, cavalier; **harsh,** rough, severe; truculent, aggressive; **surly,** crusty, bearish, beastly, churlish

grumble VERBS **complain,** groan; **murmur, mutter,** growl, clamor, croak, grunt, yelp; **fret,** fuss, make a fuss about, fret and fume; air a grievance, lodge *or* register a complaint; fault, find fault

grumbling ADJS malcontent, malcontented, **complaining,** sour, **faultfinding,** growling, murmuring, muttering, griping, croaking, **peevish, petulant,** sulky, **querulous,** querulant, whiny; out of humor

grump NOUNS 1 **sorehead,** grouch, curmudgeon, crank, crosspatch, grizzly bear, pit bull, junkyard dog <nonformal>
VERBS 2 **sulk, mope,** mope around; grizzle <chiefly Brit nonformal>, **grouch** *and* **bitch** <both nonformal>, **fret;** get oneself in a sulk

grungy ADJS **offensive,** repellent, rebarbative, repugnant, revolting, forbidding; **disgusting, sickening, loathsome,** gross *and* yucky *and* scuzzy <all nonformal>, beastly <nonformal>, **vile, foul, nasty, nauseating**

guarantee NOUNS 1 **oath,** vow, word, assurance, **warrant,** solemn oath *or* affirmation *or* word *or* declaration; **pledge**
VERBS 2 **secure,** warrant, assure, insure, ensure, bond, certify; countersecure; **sponsor,** be sponsor for, sign for, sign one's note, **back,** stand behind *or* back of, stand up for; **endorse;** sign, cosign, **underwrite**

guaranty NOUNS **security, surety,** indemnity, **warranty, insurance,** warrant, assurance; **obligation**, full faith and credit

guard NOUNS 1 **defender,** champion, advocate; upholder; guardian angel, supporter; vindicator, apologist; **protector;** paladin; **bodyguard, convoy; safeguard,** palladium, shield, screen, aegis; umbrella, protective umbrella
VERBS 2 **defend, shield,** screen, secure, guard against; defend tooth and nail *or* to the death *or* to the last breath; **safeguard, protect**; stand by the side of, flank; **advocate, champion**; **defend oneself,** cover one's ass *or* rear-end <nonformal>, CYA *or* cover your ass <nonformal>

guarded ADJS **vigilant, wary,** prudent, **watchful,** lidless, sleepless, observant; **on the watch, on the lookout,** *aux aguets* <Fr>; **on guard,** on one's guard; discreet; **suspicious, suspecting,** wary, leery, cautious; **protected,** safeguarded, defended; **sheltered, shielded,** screened, covered, cloaked

guardian NOUNS **warden,** governor; **custodian,** steward, **keeper, caretaker,** warder <Brit>, attendant; caregiver; next friend, prochein ami, guardian *ad litem;* **curator,** conservator; janitor; castellan; **shepherd,** herd, cowherd; **game warden,** gamekeeper; guardian angel

guardian angel NOUNS **defender,** champion, advocate; upholder; **supporter**; vindicator, apologist; **protector**; **guard**; paladin; **voice of conscience,** still small voice within; guardian spirit, good angel, ministering angel, **fairy godmother**

guerrilla NOUNS **irregular,** casual; partisan, franctireur; **bushfighter,** bushwhacker <nonformal>; underground, resistance, maquis; *maquisard* <Fr>, underground *or* resistance fighter

guess NOUNS 1 **conjecture,** unverified supposition, perhaps, speculation,

guesswork, surmise, educated guess; guesstimate *and* hunch *and* shot *and* stab <all nonformal>; rough guess, wild guess, blind guess, bold conjecture, shot in the dark <nonformal>
VERBS 2 **conjecture,** guesstimate <nonformal>, talk off the top of one's head <nonformal>, hazard a conjecture, venture a guess, risk assuming *or* stating, tentatively suggest, go out on a limb <nonformal>

guest NOUNS **visitor,** visitant; **caller,** company; invited guest, invitee; uninvited guest, gate-crasher <nonformal>; moocher *and* freeloader <both nonformal>

guidance NOUNS **advice,** counsel, recommendation, suggestion; proposal; **direction,** instruction, briefing; **counseling;** guidance counseling, educational counseling, vocational guidance

guide NOUNS 1 guider; **shepherd,** tour guide, tour director *or* conductor, cicerone, tourist guide, dragoman; **escort, conductor, usher**
VERBS 2 **steer, drive, run** <nonformal>; channel; **escort, conduct,** have in tow <nonformal>, marshal, **usher,** shepherd, **lead; convoy,** guard; **govern, rule, control**, order, **regulate,** direct

guidebook NOUNS **handbook, manual,** enchiridion, vade mecum, gradus, how-to book <nonformal>; field guide; travel book, handbook, Baedeker

guideline NOUNS **rule,** ground rule, rubric, protocol, working rule, working principle, standard procedure; guiding principle, golden rule; code

guidepost NOUNS **pointer,** index, **direction, guide; signpost,** finger post, direction post; milepost; blaze; guideboard, signboard

guild NOUNS **fellowship,** sodality; **society,** order; **brotherhood, fraternity,** confraternity, confrerie, fraternal order *or* society; **sisterhood, sorority**

guilt NOUNS **guiltiness; criminality,** peccancy; guilty *or* wrongful *or* criminal involvement; **culpability,** reprehensibility, blameworthiness; bloodguilt *or* -guiltiness, red-handedness, dirty hands, red *or* bloody hands

guiltless ADJS **innocent;** unfallen, unlapsed, prelapsarian; **unguilty,** not guilty, **faultless, blameless,** reproachless, **sinless,** offenseless, with clean hands, clear, in the clear; innocent as a lamb, lamblike, dovelike, angelic, childlike; uncorrupted, incorrupt, pristine, undefiled

blameless in life and pure of crime
HORACE

guilty ADJS 1 guilty as hell, peccant, **criminal, to blame, at fault, culpable,** reprehensible, censurable, reproachable, reprovable, inculpated; red-handed, bloodguilty; caught in the act *or* flat-footed *or* red-handed, caught with one's pants down *or* with one's hand in the till *or* with one's hand in the cookie jar <nonformal>

guinea pig NOUNS **subject, experimental subject,** experimentee, testee, patient, sample; laboratory animal, experimental *or* test animal

guise NOUNS **pretext,** pretense, pretension, lying pretension, show, ostensible *or* announced *or* public *or* professed motive; **front,** facade, **sham**; **excuse,** apology, protestation, poor excuse, lame excuse; **subterfuge,** refuge, device, stratagem, feint, dipsy-doodle <nonformal>, **trick**; dust thrown in the eye, smoke screen, **screen, cover,** stalking-horse, **blind;** semblance; mask, cloak, veil; **cover,** cover-up, cover story, alibi

gulf NOUNS **sea,** tributary sea, bay, arm of the sea, fjord, bight; cove; **chasm, abyss,** abysm

gull VERBS **deceive,** beguile, trick, hoax, **dupe,** gammon, pigeon, play one for a fool *or* sucker, **bamboozle** *and* snow *and* **hornswoggle** *and* diddle *and* scam <all nonformal>, take in, put on *and* hocus-pocus <both nonformal>, string along, **put something over** *or* **across,** slip one over on <nonformal>, pull a fast one on, **cheat,** victimize, **swindle,** defraud, practice fraud upon, euchre, **con,** finagle, **fleece,** mulct, fob <old>, **bilk,** cozen, chouse, **cheat out of, do out of,** chouse out of; **make a fool of,** make a monkey of <nonformal>

gullible ADJS **dupable,** cullible <old>, deceivable, exploitable, seducible, persuadable, **simple; ingenuous,** unsophisticated, green, naive

gullible person NOUNS **dupe, gull,** gudgeon, *gobe-mouches* <Fr>; **victim;** dupable *or* credulous person, trusting *or* simple soul, innocent, *naïf* <Fr>, babe, babe in the woods

gully NOUNS **ravine,** gorge, canyon, box

canyon, *arroyo* <Sp>, barranca, bolson, coulee, gulch, combe <Brit>, dingle, rift, rift valley, kloof, donga, graben, draw, wadi, basin, cirque, corrie, hanging valley

gulp NOUNS 1 draft, dram, drench, **swig** <nonformal>, swill *and* guzzle <both nonformal>, quaff, **sip,** sup, suck, tot, bumper, snort *and* slug <both nonformal>, pull <nonformal>, lap, slurp <nonformal>; swallow
VERBS 2 **gobble, bolt,** wolf, gobble *or* gulp *or* bolt *or* wolf down; gulp down, swill, swill down

gum NOUNS **resin;** gum resin; oleoresin; hard *or* varnish resin, vegetable resin; synthetic resin, plastic, resinoid; chewing gum, bubble gum; chicle, chicle gum

gummy ADJS **adhesive,** sticky, tacky, gluey, **viscid,** glutinous; **resinous,** gummous, gumlike; gooey *and* gunky *and* gloppy *and* goopy *and* gooky <all nonformal>

gumption NOUNS **adventurousness,** venturousness, venturesomeness, adventuresomeness; spirit, **spunk** <nonformal>

gun NOUNS **firearm;** shooting iron *and* gat *and* rod *and* heater *and* piece <all nonformal>; shoulder weapon *or* gun *or* arm; stun gun; automatic, BB gun, blunderbuss

gunfire NOUNS **fire, firing,** musketry, **shooting,** fireworks *or* gunplay <both nonformal>; gunfight, shoot-out; **shot,** discharge; detonation; **salvo, volley,** fusillade, tattoo, spray; bowshot, gunshot, stoneshot, potshot

gung-ho ADJS **enthusiastic,** enthused *and* big <both nonformal>, glowing, full of enthusiasm; enthusiastic about, infatuated with

gunk NOUNS **slime, slop,** scum, sludge, slush; glop <nonformal>, **muck, mire,** ooze

gunman NOUNS **killer,** slayer, slaughterer, butcher, bloodshedder; massacrer; **manslayer, homicide, murderer,** mankiller, bloodletter, Cain; **assassin,** assassinator; **cutthroat,** thug, desperado, bravo, gorilla <nonformal>, apache; professional killer, hired killer, hit man *or* button man *or* gun *or* trigger man *or* torpedo *or* gunsel <all nonformal>; **hatchet man**

gunrunning NOUNS **smuggling,** contrabandage, contraband

gunshot NOUNS **shot,** discharge; ejection; detonation; gunfire; gun, cannon; bullet; **salvo, volley,** fusillade, tattoo, spray; bowshot, stoneshot, potshot

guru NOUNS **mentor;** pandit, pundit, *mullah* <Persian>, *starets* <Russ>; holy man; great soul, mahatma; *rishi* <Skt>; Brahman, pujari, purohit, bashara, vairagi *or* bairagi, sannyasi; yogi, yogin; bhikshu, bhikhari

gush NOUNS 1 **flow,** flowing, **flux,** fluency, profluence, fluid motion *or* movement; **course,** onward course, **surge, rush,** onrush, spate, run, race
VERBS 2 **be enthusiastic, rave, enthuse** *and* be big for <both nonformal>; **rhapsodize, carry on over** *and* rave on <both nonformal>, make much of, **make a fuss over,** make an ado *or* much ado about, make a to-do over *and* take on over <both nonformal>, be *or* go on over *or* about <nonformal>, rave about *and* whoop it up about <both nonformal>; go nuts *or* gaga *or* ape over <nonformal>; gush over; effervesce, bubble over

gushing ADJS 1 **sentimental,** sentimentalized, soft, **mawkish, maudlin,** cloying; sticky *and* gooey *and* schmaltzy *and* sappy *and* soppy <all nonformal>, oversentimental, oversentimentalized, bathetic; **mushy** *or* sloppy *or* teary *or* beery <all nonformal>; fulsome, slobbery, protesting too much, smarmy <nonformal>, **unctuous**
2 **flowing, streaming, running, pouring,** coursing, racing, rushing, onrushing, surging, surgy, torrential

gust NOUNS wind gust, **blast,** blow, flaw, **flurry,** scud <Scots>

gusto NOUNS **relish,** zest, *joie de vivre* <Fr>; taste, gust <Scots>; **liveliness,** vivacity, vitality, life, animation, spiritedness, spirit, esprit, élan, **sprightliness,** high spirits, zestfulness, zest, vim, zip <nonformal>, vigor, verve, **exuberance,** heartiness

gusty ADJS **windy,** blowy; **breezy,** drafty, airy, airish; brisk, fresh; blasty, puffy, flawy; **squally;** blustery, blustering, blusterous

gut NOUNS 1 goozle, guzzle; tum, tummy, tum-tum, breadbasket, bulge, fallen chest <nonformal>, corporation, spare tire, bay window, **pot,** potbelly, potgut, beerbelly, German *or* Milwaukee goiter, swagbelly <all nonformal>

VERBS 2 **eviscerate,** disembowel; **devastate,** desolate, waste, lay waste, ravage, havoc, wreak havoc, despoil, depredate; gut with fire, incinerate, vaporize, ravage with fire and sword; dissolve, lyse
ADJS 3 **emotional, affective,** emotive, affectional, **feeling;** soulful, of soul, of heart, of feeling, of sentiment; visceral
4 **primary,** primitive, primal, elementary, elemental, simple, bare-bones *and* no-frills *and* bread-and-butter <all nonformal>, original, *ab ovo* <L>, **basic,** basal, underlying; **substantive,** substantial, material

gutless ADJS **uncourageous,** unvalorous, unheroic, undaring, unable to say 'boo' to a goose; **pluckless,** spunkless *and* gritless <both nonformal>, spiritless, heartless

gut reaction NOUNS **impulse;** natural impulse, blind impulse, **instinct,** urge, drive; vagrant *or* fleeting impulse; hunch; involuntary impulse, reflex, knee jerk, automatic response

guts NOUNS 1 **insides, innards** <nonformal>, inwards, internals; inner mechanism, what makes it tick *and* works <both nonformal>; **vitals, viscera,** *kishkes* <Yiddish>, giblets; entrails, bowels
2 **pluck,** spunk <nonformal>, mettle, backbone <nonformal>, **grit,** true grit, spirit, **stamina,** moxie <nonformal>; pluckiness, spunkiness <nonformal>, **gameness,** feistiness <nonformal>, mettlesomeness; courage; **balls,** intestinal fortitude, spunk, brass balls, cojones, moxie, spizzerinctum, **backbone,** chutzpah <all nonformal>

gutsy ADJS 1 **gritty, mettlesome,** dauntless, **game,** game to the last *or* end; **courageous**

2 <nonformal> **plucky, spunky** *and* feisty; **ballsy,** gutty, stand-up, dead game, gritty, spunky, nervy

gutter NOUNS 1 **trough,** eave *or* eaves trough; **flume,** chute, shoot; pentrough, penstock; guide; **drain,** sluice, scupper; kennel
ADJS 2 **vulgar, uncouth, coarse, gross,** rank, raw, broad, low, foul; **earthy,** frank, pulling no punches

guttersnipe NOUNS **waif,** homeless waif, ragamuffin, tatterdemalion; **gamin,** gamine, urchin, street urchin, dead-end kid <nonformal>, mudlark

guy NOUNS

1 <nonformal> **fellow,** feller, lad, chap, cat, bird, duck, stud, joker, jasper, bugger, bastard, customer, party, character, warm body, bean, cookie, dude, gent, Joe

2 **stay, prop,** fulcrum, **bracket, brace,** bracer, guywire *or* guyline, shroud, rigging, standing rigging

guzzle VERBS **tipple, drink,** nip; grog, gargle; **imbibe,** have a drink *or* nip *or* dram *or* guzzle *or* gargle, soak, bib, quaff, sip, sup, lap, lap up, take a drop, slake one's thirst, cheer *or* refresh the inner man, drown one's troubles *or* sorrows, commune with the spirits

gymnasium NOUNS **gym** <nonformal>, **fitness center, health club,** health spa, work-out room, weight room, exercise track *or* trail, *parcourse* or *parcours* <both Fr>

gymnastics NOUNS **exercise,** free exercise, setting-up exercise *or* set-ups, daily dozen <nonformal>, constitutional; **gymnastic exercise; isometrics,** isometric *or* no-movement exercise; **aerobic exercise, aerobics,** aerobic dancing *or* dance, dancercize *or* dancercizing, fitaerobics, jazz ballet *or* jazzercise *and* popmobility <all Brit>; **bodybuilding,** weightlifting, weight training, pumping iron <nonformal>; calisthenics, eurythmics

gyp NOUNS 1 trick, hoax, deceptive, fraud
VERBS 2 **cheat, deceive, trick, hoax,** dupe

3 <nonformal> **clip,** scam, beat, rook, flam, flimflam, diddle, do a number on, hustle, fuck, screw, have, pull something, pull a trick *or* stunt, give the business, stick, sting, burn, gouge, chisel, play *or* take for a sucker, make a patsy of, run a game on, slicker, take for a ride

gypsy NOUNS Bohemian, Romany, *zingaro* <Ital>, *Zigeuner* <Ger>, *tzigane* <Fr>

gyrate VERBS **rotate, revolve, spin, turn,** round, **go round** *or* **around,** turn round *or* around; **spiral,** gyre; circumrotate, circumvolute; pirouette, turn a pirouette; wind, twist, screw, crank; wamble

H

habit NOUNS 1 **clothing,** clothes, apparel, wear, wearing apparel, daywear, dress, dressing, **raiment,** garmenture, **garb, attire, array,** habiliment, **costume**
2 **substance abuse, drug abuse,** narcotics abuse, drug use, glue-sniffing, solvent abuse; drug habit, drug habituation, drug dependence, physical addiction *or* dependence, psychological addiction *or* dependence, jones *and* monkey on one's back *and* Mighty Joe Young <all nonformal>
3 **mannerism,** *minauderie* <Fr>, **trick of behavior,** trick, **quirk,** peculiarity, peculiar trait, idiosyncrasy, trademark

habitat NOUNS home, **range,** stamping grounds, locality, native environment

habitual ADJS **regular,** frequent, constant, persistent; repetitive, recurring, recurrent; stereotyped; knee-jerk <nonformal>, goose-step, lockstep, automatic; **routine,** nine-to-five, workaday, well-trodden, well-worn, beaten

habitué NOUNS **frequenter,** haunter

hack NOUNS 1 **cabdriver,** cabman, cabby <nonformal>, hackman, hacky <nonformal>; **cab, taxicab, taxi,** gypsy cab <nonformal>
2 **hack writer,** literary hack, penny-a-liner, scribbler <nonformal>, potboiler <nonformal>; **drudge,** grub, plodder
3 **two-bit** *or* **peanut politician** <nonformal>, politicaster, political dabbler; **party hack**
ADJS 4 **incompetent,** incapable; dull tool, mediocrity, dub *and* duffer <both nonformal>, no great shakes, no prize, no prize package, no brain surgeon, no rocket scientist
VERBS 5 **sever, dissever,** cut off *or* away *or* loose, shear off, hack through, hack off, ax, amputate; **chop,** hew, slash; gash, butcher

hack it VERBS **achieve one's purpose, gain one's end** *or* **ends,** secure one's object, attain one's objective, do what one set out to do, reach one's goal, bring it off, pull it off *and* swing it <both nonformal>; **pass muster,** get by <nonformal>, make it *and* cut the mustard <both nonformal>, meet *or* satisfy requirements

hackneyed ADJS **trite;** corny *and* square *and* square-John *and* Clyde <all nonformal>, fade, **banal,** unoriginal, platitudinous, **stereotyped,** stock, set, **commonplace, common,** truistic, twice-told, **familiar,** bromidic <nonformal>, old hat <nonformal>, back-number, bewhiskered, warmed-over, **stale,** musty, fusty

hag NOUNS **crone,** witch, beldam, frump <nonformal>, old wife; **witch, vixen,** hellhag, hellcat, she-devil, virago, brimstone, termagant, grimalkin, Jezebel, she-wolf, tigress, wildcat, siren, fury

haggard ADJS tired-looking, weary-looking, tired-eyed, tired-faced, hollow-eyed, ravaged, drawn, cadaverous, worn, wan, zombiish

haggle VERBS **bargain,** drive a bargain, negotiate, higgle, chaffer, huckster, **deal, dicker,** make a deal, hack out *or* work out *or* hammer out a deal; drive a hard bargain

hail NOUNS 1 hailstone; soft hail, graupel, snow pellets, tapioca snow; **hailstorm**
VERBS 2 **applaud,** acclaim; **cheer**; root for <nonformal>, cheer on; **signal,** give a signal, make a sign; hail and speak; **accost, call to,** halloo, greet, salute, speak
3 sleet, snow

hair NOUNS pile, **fur**, coat, pelt, **fleece,** wool, camel's hair, horsehair; **mane;** shag, tousled *or* matted hair, **mat of hair;** pubic hair; hairlet, villus, capillament, cilium, ciliolum; seta, setula; bristle

haircut NOUNS **hairdo, hairstyle, coiffure,** coif, headdress

hairdresser NOUNS **beautician,** beautifier, cosmetologist; *coiffeur, coiffeuse* <both Fr>; barber

hairless ADJS depilous; **bald,** acomous; bald as a coot, bald as an egg; **baldheaded,** bald-pated, tonsured

hairpiece NOUNS **wig, peruke, toupee,** rug *and* divot *and* doormat <all nonformal>; **periwig**

hairsplitting NOUNS **quibbling, caviling,** boggling, captiousness, nit-picking, **bickering; logic-chopping,** trichoschistism; **equivocation,** tergiversation, prevarication, **evasion, hedging, pussyfooting** <nonformal>, **sidestepping,** dodging, shifting, shuffling, fencing, parrying, boggling, paltering

hairy ADJS 1 **hirsute,** barbigerous, crinose, crinite, pubescent; pilose, pilous, pileous; **furry,** furred; villous; villose; ciliate, cirrose; hispid, hispidulous; woolly-headed, woolly-haired, ulotrichous; bushy, tufty, **shaggy,** shagged; matted, tomentose
2 **difficult,** difficile; **not easy,** no picnic; **hard, tough** *and* **rough** *and* **rugged** <all nonformal>, rigorous, brutal, severe; wicked *and* mean <both nonformal>, **formidable; arduous,** strenuous, toilsome, laborious, operose, Herculean; delicate, ticklish, tricky, sticky <nonformal>, critical, easier said than done, like pulling teeth; exacting, demanding; intricate, complex; abstruse

hale ADJS **hearty,** hale and hearty, **robust,** robustious, robustuous, vital, **vigorous, strong,** strong as a horse *or* an ox, bionic <nonformal>, stalwart, stout, sturdy, **rugged,** rude, hardy, lusty, bouncing, well-knit; **fit,** in condition *or* shape

half NOUNS 1 moiety; hemisphere, semisphere, semicircle, **fifty percent;** half-and-half *and* fifty-fifty <both nonformal>
ADJS 2 **part, partly, partial,** halfway

half-assed ADJS **slipshod,** slipshoddy, **slovenly,** sloppy *and* **messy** <both nonformal>, sluttish, untidy; **clumsy, bungling**; **haphazard, promiscuous, hit-or-miss,** hit-and-miss; deficient, botched

half-baked ADJS **premature,** unpremeditated, unmeditated, ill-considered, **half-cocked** <nonformal>, immature, undeveloped, unjelled, uncrystallized, not firm; **precocious, forward, advanced,** far ahead, born before one's time

halfhearted ADJS **indifferent,** zealless, perfunctory, fervorless; **cool, cold**; tepid, **lukewarm,** Laodicean; neither hot nor cold, neither one thing nor the other

half-truth NOUNS exaggeration; stretching of the truth, slight stretching, white lie, little white lie

halfway ADJS 1 **middle, medial, intermediate,** intermediary; equidistant, midway, equatorial; partly, partial
ADVS 2 **midway, in the middle,** betwixt and between <nonformal>, halfway in the middle <nonformal>; plump *or* smack *or* slap- *or* smack-dab in the middle <nonformal>; half-and-half, neither here nor there, *mezzo-mezzo* <Ital>

half-wit NOUNS **stupid person, dolt,** dunce, clod, Boeotian, **dullard,** *niais* <Fr>, donkey, yahoo, thickwit, dope, **nitwit,** dimwit, lamebrain, putz, lightweight, witling

hall NOUNS 1 assembly hall, exhibition hall, convention hall; gallery; meetinghouse, meeting room; **auditorium; concert hall; theater,** music hall; dance hall; ballroom, grand ballroom
2 **corridor,** hallway; passage, **passageway; gallery,** loggia; arcade, colonnade, pergola, cloister, peristyle

hallelujah NOUNS hosanna, alleluia, paean, paean *or* chorus of cheers

hallmark NOUNS **sign,** telltale sign, sure sign, tip-off <nonformal>, **index,** indicant, **indicator,** signal <old>, measure; **symptom;** note, keynote, **mark,** earmark, badge, device, banner, stamp, signature, sigil, seal, trait, **characteristic,** character, peculiarity, idiosyncrasy, **property,** differentia

hallow VERBS **sanctify; purify,** cleanse, wash one's sins away; **bless**; **glorify,** exalt, ensky; **consecrate,** dedicate, devote, set apart; **beatify,** saint, canonize; enshrine

hallucinate VERBS **go on a trip** *and* **blow one's mind** <both nonformal>, freak out <nonformal>; expand one's consciousness

hallucinogen NOUNS **psychoactive drug, psychedelic,** psychedelic drug, psychoactive drug, psychoactive chemical *or* psychochemical, psychotropic drug, psychotomimetic drug, mind-altering drug, mind-expanding drug, mind-blowing drug

halo NOUNS nimbus, aura, **aureole,** circle, ring, glory; **rainbow,** solar halo, lunar halo, ring around the sun *or* moon; **illustriousness, luster,** brilliance *or* brilliancy, radiance, splendor, resplendence *or* resplendency, refulgence *or* refulgency, refulgentness, **glory,** blaze of glory

halt VERBS 1 **put a stop to, call a halt to,** get it over with, blow the whistle on <nonformal>, **put an end to**, put paid to <Brit nonformal>, call off the dogs <nonformal>; **stop,** stay, arrest, check, flag down, wave down; block, brake, dam, stem, stem the tide *or* current; pull up, draw rein, put on the brakes, hit the

brake pedal; **bring to a stand** *or* **standstill,** bring to a close *or* halt, bring up short, **stop dead** *or* dead in one's tracks, set one back on his heels, stop cold, stop short, cut short, check in full career
ADJS 2 **crippled,** game <nonformal>, bad, handicapped, **lame,** halting, hobbling, limping; **disabled, incapacitated**

halve VERBS **bisect,** divide in half *or* by two, transect, subdivide; cleave, fission, **divide** *or* split *or* **cut in two,** share and share alike, go halfers *or* go Dutch <both nonformal>, **dichotomize;** bifurcate, fork, ramify, branch

ham NOUNS ham actor <nonformal>; grimacer; **amateur radio operator,** ham operator <nonformal>, radio amateur

hamlet NOUNS **village;** country town, crossroads, wide place in the road

a little one-eyed, blinking sort o' place
THOMAS HARDY

hammer VERBS **attack, assault,** batter, savage, mug, maul; plug away *or* along <nonformal>, hammer away, pound away, struggle along, struggle on, work away; drum, beat, pound; drum into, say over and over

hamper VERBS **impede, cramp,** embarrass; trammel, entrammel, enmesh, entangle, ensnarl, entrap, entwine, involve, entoil, toil, net, lime, tangle, snarl; fetter, shackle; **handcuff,** tie one's hands; **encumber,** cumber, **burden,** lumber, **saddle with,** weigh *or* weight down, press down; hang like a millstone round one's neck; **handicap,** put at a disadvantage

hamstring VERBS **cripple, lame,** cripple, maim; hobble; wing; emasculate, castrate; incapacitate, **disable**

hand NOUNS **worker, laborer, toiler,** moiler; employee, servant; workhand

handbook NOUNS **manual,** enchiridion, vade mecum, gradus, how-to book <nonformal>; nature book, field guide; travel book, **guidebook,** gazetteer, reference book

handcuff VERBS **hamper, impede, cramp,** embarrass; fetter, shackle; tie one's hands

handful NOUNS 1 **a few,** too few, mere *or* piddling *or* piddly few, only a few, **small number,** limited *or* piddling *or* piddly number, not enough to count *or* matter, not enough to shake a stick at, **scattering,** sprinkling, trickle
2 **tough proposition** *and* tough one *and* toughie <all nonformal>, large *or* tall order <nonformal>; **uphill work** *or* **going,** rough go <nonformal>, **heavy sledding,** hard pull <nonformal>; bitch <nonformal>; all one can manage

handicap NOUNS 1 **impediment,** embarrassment, hamper; encumbrance, cumbrance; **trouble,** difficulty; disadvantage, inconvenience, penalty; white elephant; **burden,** imposition, onus, cross, weight, deadweight, ball and chain, millstone around one's neck; disability
VERBS 2 **penalize,** put *or* impose *or* inflict a penalty *or* sanctions on; **punish**; put at a disadvantage; **encumber,** cumber, **burden,** lumber, **saddle with,** weigh *or* weight down, press down

handicraft NOUNS **craft, manual art,** industrial art, artisan work, craftwork, artisanship; woodcraft, woodwork, metalcraft, stonecraft; handiwork, handwork, crafting

handkerchief NOUNS headcloth, **kerchief,** coverchief

handle NOUNS 1 **hold,** grip, grasp, haft, helve; **name, moniker** <nonformal>; **label, tag; epithet,** byword; **title, honorific**
VERBS 2 **touch, finger,** pass *or* run the fingers over, feel with the fingertips, thumb; palm, paw
3 **manipulate,** wield; **deal with,** cope with, conduct, **manage; employ,** practice, ply, work, manage, operate
4 **deal in,** trade in, traffic in, carry, be in; market, merchandise, **sell,** retail, wholesale, job

handmade ADJS **made,** man-made; **homemade,** homespun, handcrafted, handicrafted, self-made, DIY *or* do it yourself; **custom-made,** custom-built, made to order, bespoke

hand-me-down ADJS **secondhand, used,** worn, previously owned, unnew, not new, pawed-over; reach-me-down <nonformal>

handout NOUNS **press release,** release, bulletin, official bulletin, notice; **leaflet,** leaf, folder, handbill, bill, flier, throwaway, **circular,** broadside
2 alms, pittance, **charity,** dole, alms fee, widow's mite; Peter's pence; **offering,** offertory, votive offering

handsome ADJS 1 **generous, munificent,** large, princely; **unsparing, unstinting,** stintless, unstinted; **openhanded,** freehanded, open; **giving**
2 **attractive**, pulchritudinous, **lovely, graceful,** gracile; elegant; aesthetically appealing; **cute;** pretty as a picture; tall, dark and handsome

handwriting NOUNS **hand, script,** fist <nonformal>, chirography, **calligraphy,** autography; **manuscript; autograph,** holograph; **penmanship,** penscript, pencraft; stylography

handy ADJS **convenient; available,** accessible, **ready, at hand,** to hand, **on hand,** on tap, on deck <nonformal>, on call, at one's call *or* beck and call, at one's elbow, at one's fingertips, just around the corner, at one's disposal; versatile, adaptable, all-around <nonformal>, of all work; crude but effective, quick and dirty <nonformal>

hang NOUNS 1 **knack, art, trick,** way; **touch,** feel
VERBS 2 hang down, fall; **depend,** pend; **dangle,** swing, flap, flop <nonformal>; flow, drape, cascade; **droop,** lop; nod, weep; **sag,** swag, bag; **trail, drag, draggle,** drabble, daggle
3 hang by the neck; **string up** *and* scrag *and* stretch <all nonformal>; gibbet, noose, neck, bring to the gallows; **lynch;** hang, draw, and quarter
4 **depend,** all depend, be contingent *or* conditional on, hang on *or* upon; **hang in the balance,** be touch and go, tremble in the balance, **hang in suspense; hang by a thread,** cliffhang, hang by a hair, hang by the eyelids

hangar NOUNS housing, dock, airdock, shed, airship shed; mooring mast

hanger-on NOUNS **adherent,** dangler, appendage, **dependent, satellite, follower,** cohort, retainer, servant, man, shadow, tagtail, **henchman,** heeler <nonformal>; camp follower, groupy <nonformal>

hang in VERBS **persist, persevere,** keep at it, stick it out, stick to it, stick with it, never say die, see it through, hang tough *and* not know when one is licked <both nonformal>; survive, make out, manage, get along, get on, eke out an existence, keep the even tenor of one's way; go on with the show <nonformal>, press on

hanging NOUNS 1 **pendency,** pendulousness *or* pendulosity, pensileness *or* pensility; **suspension,** dangling *or* danglement, suspense, dependence *or* dependency
2 **screen,** shroud, shield, veil, pall, mantle, curtain, drape, drapery
3 the gallows, the rope *or* noose; summary execution; **lynching,** necktie party *or* sociable <nonformal>, vigilanteism, vigilante justice; the necklace
ADJS 4 **pendent,** pendulous, pendulant, pendular, penduline, pensile; **suspended,** hung; pending, depending, dependent; **dangling,** swinging, falling loosely

hangman NOUNS **executioner,** executionist, deathsman <old>; **lyncher**

hang on VERBS **keep alive,** keep body and soul together, endure, survive, persist, last, last out, hang in <nonformal>, cheat death; **stay with it, hold on,** hold fast, hang on like a bulldog *or* leech, **stick to one's guns;** not give up, **never say die,** not give up the ship, not strike one's colors; **stay it out, stick out, hold out;** hold up, last out, **bear up,** stand up; stay the distance *or* the course; brazen it out

hangout NOUNS **resort, haunt,** purlieu, **stamping ground** <nonformal>; gathering place, meeting place, clubhouse, club

hang out VERBS 1 **frequent, haunt,** resort to, hang *and* hang around *and* hang about <all nonformal>
2 **be manifest,** be there for all to see, make an appearance, be no secret *or* revelation, **surface,** lie on the surface, be seen with half an eye; stand out, stick out, stick out a mile, stick out like a sore thumb

hang tough VERBS **remain firm, stand fast** *or* **firm, hold out,** hold fast, get tough <nonformal>, **take one's stand,** set one's back against the wall, **stand** *or* **hold one's ground,** keep one's footing, hold one's own, hang in *and* hang in there <both nonformal>, dig in, dig one's heels in; **stick to one's guns,** stick, stick with it, stick fast, stick to one's colors, adhere to one's principles

hang-up NOUNS 1 **delay,** stoppage, jam *and* logjam <both nonformal>, obstruction, tie-up *and* bind <both nonformal>, **block,** blockage
2 **obsession,** prepossession, preoccupation, **fixation,** complex, fascination; hypercathexis

hankering NOUNS 1 **yearning, yen** <nonformal>; **longing,** desiderium, **pining,** aching
ADJS 2 **wistful,** wishful; **longing,** yearning, yearnful, languishing, pining

hanky-panky NOUNS **affair,** affair of the heart, **amour, romance,** romantic tie *or* bond, something between, thing <nonformal>, liaison, entanglement, intrigue; **dalliance,** amorous play, the love game, flirtation, lollygagging <nonformal>

haphazard ADJS **slipshod,** sloppy *and* **messy** *and* half-assed <all nonformal>; **promiscuous;** deficient, botched; **irregular,** desultory, **erratic,** sporadic, spasmodic, fitful, indiscriminate, casual, frivolous, capricious, random, hit-or-miss, vague, dispersed, wandering, planless, undirected, **aimless,** straggling, straggly

hapless ADJS **unfortunate, unlucky, unprovidential,** unblessed, **unprosperous,** sad, unhappy, luckless; **out of luck,** short of luck; **down on one's luck** <nonformal>, badly *or* ill off, down in the world, in adverse circumstances

happen VERBS **occur,** hap, eventuate, **take place,** come *or* go down <nonformal>, go on, **transpire,** be realized, come, **come off** <nonformal>, **come about,** come true, **come to pass,** pass, pass off, go off, fall, **befall,** betide; fall to one's lot, be one's fate

happening NOUNS 1 **event,** occurrence, incident, episode, experience, adventure, hap, happenstance, **phenomenon,** fact, matter of fact, reality, particular, circumstance, **occasion,** turn of events
ADJS 2 **occurring, current, actual,** passing, taking place, on, **going on,** ongoing <nonformal>, **prevalent, prevailing,** that is, that applies, in the wind, afloat, afoot, under way

happy ADJS **glad, joyful, joyous,** flushed with joy, radiant, beaming, glowing, starry-eyed, sparkling, laughing, smiling, smirking, smirky, chirping, purring, singing, dancing, leaping, capering, **cheerful, gay**; **blissful;** happy as a lark, happy as a king, happy as the day is long, happy as a pig in shit <nonformal>

happy-go-lucky ADJS **improvident, prodigal,** unproviding; **thriftless, unthrifty,** uneconomical; grasshopper; **shiftless, feckless, thoughtless, heedless**

hara-kiri NOUNS **disembowelment,** ritual suicide, *seppuku* <Jap>, suttee, sutteeism; **suicide,** autocide, self-murder, self-homicide, self-destruction, death by one's own hand, felo-de-se, self-immolation, self-sacrifice; car of Jagannath *or* Juggernaut

harangue NOUNS 1 **speech,** speeching, speechification <nonformal>, **talk, oration, address,** declamation; **tirade,** screed, **diatribe,** jeremiad, philippic, invective; peroration
VERBS 2 **declaim,** hold forth, **orate,** spout <nonformal>, spiel <nonformal>, mouth; **rant,** tub-thump, perorate, rodomontade; demagogue, rabble-rouse

harass VERBS harry, drive up the wall <nonformal>, **hound,** dog, nag, nudzh <nonformal>, **persecute; heckle,** pick *or* prod at, rub it in *and* rub one's nose in it <both nonformal>, badger, hector, bait, bullyrag, worry, worry at, nip at the heels of, chivy, hardly give one time to breathe, make one's life miserable, keep on at; **bug** <nonformal>, be on the back of *and* be at *and* ride <all nonformal>, **pester, tease, needle,** devil, get after *or* get on <nonformal>, **bedevil, pick on** <nonformal>, give a bad time to <nonformal>; **plague,** beset, beleaguer

harbor NOUNS **haven, port, seaport,** port of call, free port, treaty port, home port; hoverport; harborage, **anchorage,** anchorage ground, protected anchorage, moorage, moorings; **roadstead,** road, roads; berth, slip; **dock,** dockage, marina, basin; dry dock; shipyard, dockyard; **wharf, pier,** quay

hard ADJS 1 **hardened,** case-hardened, **obdurate,** inured, indurated; **callous,** calloused, **seared; hardhearted,** heartless; **shameless,** lost to shame, blind to virtue, lost to all sense of honor, conscienceless, unblushing, **brazen; difficult,** troublesome, troublous, trying, rigorous, stressful; wretched, miserable; **solid,** lacking give, **tough**; resistive, resistant, steely, steellike, iron-hard, ironlike
2 <comparisons> stone, rock, adamant, granite, flint, marble, diamond; steel, iron, nails; concrete, cement; brick; oak, heart of oak; bone

hard-boiled ADJS **firm, obdurate,** tough, **hard,** hard-set, hard-mouthed, hard-bitten, hard-nosed <nonformal>, hard as nails

hard-core ADJS **unyielding, unbending, inflexible, hard, hard-line,** inelastic, impliable, ungiving, **firm, stiff, rigid,** rigorous, stuffy; rock-ribbed, rock-hard, rock-like; **immovable,** not to be moved; **uncompromising,** intransigent, irreconcilable, hard-shell <nonformal>; **fanatic, zealous,** totally committed, hard-line, ardent, passionate

harden VERBS indurate, stiffen, work-harden, firm, **toughen**; **callous; temper,** anneal, oil-temper, heat-temper, **case-harden,** steel; season; **petrify,** fossilize; lithify; vitrify; calcify; ossify; cornify, hornify

hardened ADJS **hard,** steeled, case-hardened, **obdurate,** inured, indurated, **toughened,** tempered, annealed; seasoned; **callous,** calloused, **seared; hardhearted,** heartless; **shameless,** lost to shame, blind to virtue, lost to all sense of honor, conscienceless, unblushing, **brazen**

hard feelings NOUNS **animosity,** animus; **ill will,** ill feeling, bitter feeling, no love lost; **bad blood,** ill blood, feud, blood feud, vendetta; **bitterness,** sourness, soreness, **rancor,** acrimony, virulence, venom, vitriol

hard hat NOUNS **patriot; chauvinist,** chauvin, **jingo,** jingoist; patrioteer <nonformal>, flag waver, superpatriot, hundred-percenter, hundred-percent American; hawk; **helmet,** crash helmet

hardheaded ADJS **obstinate,** stubborn, pertinacious, restive; willful, self-willed, strong-willed, headstrong, strong-headed, *entêté* <Fr>; **dogged,** bull-dogged, **tenacious,** persevering; **bull-headed,** bulletheaded, **pigheaded, mulish** <nonformal>, stubborn as a mule; set, **set in one's ways,** case-hardened, stiff-necked; balky, balking; unregenerate, uncooperative; dogmatic, opinionated, **sophisticated, wise,** practical, realistic, tough-minded; nobody's fool, not born yesterday, nobody's sucker *or* patsy <nonformal>

hardhearted ADJS **callous, calloused, insensitive,** Philistine; **thick-skinned,** pachydermatous; **hard, hardened,** coarsened, brutalized, indurated, stony, stony-hearted, flinthearted, flinty, steely, impervious, inured, armored *or* steeled against, as hard as nails

hard-line ADJS **unyielding, unbending,** inflexible, inelastic, ungiving, firm, stiff, rigid, rigorous; rock-ribbed, rock-hard, rock-like; **adamant,** adamantine; **immovable,** not to be moved; **uncompromising,** intransigent, irreconcilable, hard-shell *and* hard-core <both nonformal>; authoritarian

hard-nosed ADJS **obdurate,** tough, **hard,** hard-set, hard-mouthed, hard-bitten, hard-boiled <nonformal>

hard-pressed ADJS **straitened,** reduced to dire straits, in desperate straits, **pinched,** sore *or* sorely pressed, **hard up** <nonformal>, **up against it** <nonformal>; **desperate,** at the end of one's rope *or* tether; **hurried, rushed,** pushed, pressed, crowded, **pressed for time**

hard sell NOUNS **persuasion,** suasion; exhortation, hortation, preaching, preachment; **selling,** sales talk, salesmanship, high pressure, huckstering; jawboning *and* arm-twisting <both nonformal>; **lobbying; coaxing,** wheedling, working on <nonformal>, cajolery, cajolement, conning, snow job *and* smoke and mirrors <both nonformal>

hardworking ADJS **industrious,** assiduous, diligent, sedulous, laborious; unremitting, unsparing, relentless, zealous, ardent, fervent, vehement; never idle; tireless, unwearied, unflagging, indefatigable

hardy ADJS **hale, robust,** robustious, robustuous, vital, **vigorous, strong,** strong as a horse *or* an ox, bionic <nonformal>, stalwart, stout, sturdy, **rugged,** rude, lusty, bouncing; **fit,** in condition *or* shape

harebrained ADJS **capricious, whimsical,** freakish, vagarious; **fanciful, notional,** fantastic *or* fantastical, maggoty, **crotchety,** kinky, cranky, flaky <nonformal>, quirky; **foolhardy,** madcap, **wild,** daredevil; **scatterbrained,** rattlebrained, rattleheaded, rattlepated, scramblebrained, featherbrained, featherheaded; **witless,** empty-headed

harem NOUNS **seraglio,** serai, gynaeceum; zenana, purdah

harlot NOUNS **prostitute, whore,** *fille de joie* <Fr>, call girl *and* B-girl <both nonformal>, **scarlet woman,** unfortunate woman, painted woman, fallen woman, erring sister, **streetwalker,** hustler *and* **hooker** <both nonformal>, stew, meretrix

harm NOUNS 1 **impairment,** damage,

injury, mischief, scathe, **hurt, detriment,** loss, weakening, sickening; **worsening,** disimprovement; disablement, incapacitation; encroachment, inroad, infringement; evil
VERBS 2 **impair, damage,** endamage, injure, hurt, irritate; disadvantage; work evil, do ill; **injure,** scathe, wound, **damage; wrong,** do wrong, do wrong by, aggrieve, do evil, do a mischief, do an ill office to; **molest,** afflict; lay a hand on; **abuse,** bash <nonformal>, batter, outrage, violate, maltreat, mistreat

harmful ADJS **hurtful,** scatheful, **baneful,** baleful, distressing, **injurious, damaging, detrimental,** deleterious, counterproductive, **pernicious,** mischievous; **malignant,** malign, malevolent, malefic, vicious; prejudicial, disadvantageous, disserviceable; corruptive, corrupting, corrosive, corroding; deadly, lethal; ominous

harmless ADJS hurtless, unhurtful; well-meaning, well-meant; **uninjurious,** undamaging, **innocuous,** innoxious, innocent; inoffensive; nonmalignant, **benign**

harmonious ADJS **in accord, in harmony,** congruous, congruent, in tune, attuned, agreeing, in concert, amicable; frictionless; **sympathetic,** simpatico <nonformal>, empathic, empathetic, **understanding; like-minded,** akin, of the same mind, of one mind, at one, united, together; concordant, corresponding; agreeable, congenial, **compatible; peaceful**

harmonize VERBS **reconcile, bring to terms, bring together,** reunite, heal the breach; bring about a détente; restore harmony, put in tune; **iron** *or* **sort out,** adjust, settle, compose, accommodate, arrange matters, settle differences, resolve, compromise; **patch things up,** fix up <nonformal>, patch up a friendship *or* quarrel; **agree,** accord, concur, have no problem with, go along with <nonformal>, **cooperate, correspond, conform,** coincide, parallel, intersect, overlap, **match,** tally, hit, register, lock, interlock, check <nonformal>, square, dovetail, jibe <nonformal>

harmony NOUNS **cooperation, collaboration,** concurrence, synergy, synergism; **consensus, commonality; community,** concordance, concord, fellowship, fellow feeling, solidarity, concert, **teamwork;** pulling *or* working together, communal *or* community activity, joining of forces, pooling, pooling of resources, joining of hands; **accord,** accordance, **rapport;** good vibrations <nonformal>, good vibes <nonformal>, good karma; **proportion,** symmetry, **balance,** equilibrium, order, orderedness, measure, measuredness, concinnity; **euphony,** sweetness, beauty

harness NOUNS 1 caparison, trappings, **tack,** tackle; panoply
VERBS 2 **yoke, hitch up,** hook up; harness up; halter, bridle; saddle; tether, fetter

harp on VERBS **harp upon, dwell on** *or* **upon,** harp upon one *or* the same string, play *or* sing the same old song *or* tune, play the same broken record, beat a dead horse, have on the brain, constantly recur *or* revert to, labor, belabor, hammer away at, always trot out, never hear the last of; **thrash** *or* **thresh over,** cover the same ground, go over again and again, go over and over

harried ADJS **tormented,** plagued, harassed, dogged, hounded, persecuted, beset; nipped at, worried, chivied, **heckled,** badgered, hectored, baited, bullyragged, ragged, **pestered,** teased, needled, deviled, bedeviled, picked on <nonformal>, **bugged** <nonformal>

harrowing ADJS **agonizing,** excruciating, racking, rending, desolating, consuming; **tormenting,** torturous; **heartbreaking,** heartrending, heartsickening

harsh ADJS 1 fierce, **rigorous,** severe, rough, stringent, astringent, strident, **sharp, keen,** sharpish, incisive, trenchant, **cutting,** biting, stinging, **scathing,** stabbing, **piercing, poignant,** penetrating, edged, double-edged; **discordant,** strident, shrill, raucous
2 **oppressive, burdensome, crushing,** trying, onerous, heavy, weighty; wearing, wearying, exhausting; overburdensome, tyrannous, grinding; **heartless,** hard, hard as nails, steely, flinty, savage, **cruel**

harvest NOUNS 1 **yield, output,** make, production; **proceeds,** produce, product; **crop,** fruit, vintage, bearing; second crop, aftermath; bumper crop; harvesting, **reaping, gleaning,** gathering, cutting
VERBS 2 **reap,** crop, **glean, gather,** gather in, bring in, get in the harvest,

reap and carry; **pick,** pluck; dig, grabble <S US>; mow, cut

has-been NOUNS back number <nonformal>; dodo *and* old dodo <both nonformal>; fossil *and* antique *and* relic <all nonformal>; **mossback** <nonformal>, antediluvian; old liner, old believer, conservative, hard-shell, traditionalist, reactionary; **fogy, old fogy,** regular old fogy, **fud** *and* **fuddy-duddy** <both nonformal>

hash NOUNS **medley, miscellany,** mélange, pastiche, mixed bag, ragbag, jumble, mingle-mangle, **mix,** mishmash, can of worms <nonformal>, dog's breakfast <Can nonformal>, mare's nest, rat's nest, patchwork, gallimaufry, salmagundi, **potpourri,** everything but the kitchen sink <nonformal>

hashish NOUNS <nonformal> black hash, black Russian, hash

hassle NOUNS 1 **commotion,** hubbub, Babel, tumult, turmoil, uproar, racket, riot, **disturbance, rumpus** <nonformal>, ruckus *and* ruction <both nonformal>, **fracas,** shindy <nonformal>, rampage; **ado,** to-do <nonformal>, trouble, bother, pother, stir <nonformal>; **contention,** wrangling, bickering, hubbub, bicker, set-to <nonformal>, rhubarb <nonformal>
VERBS 2 **trouble, worry,** give one gray hair, plague, harass, bother, pick on *and* pick at <all nonformal>, bug <nonformal>; **contend,** contest, spar, bicker, wrangle

haste NOUNS **hurry,** scurry, rush, race, dash, drive, scuttle, scamper, **scramble,** hustle <nonformal>, **bustle,** flutter, **flurry,** hurry-scurry, helter-skelter; no time to be lost; **hastiness,** hurriedness, overeagerness, overzealousness, overenthusiasm

hasty ADJS **hurried,** festinate, **quick,** flying, **expeditious,** prompt; quick-and-dirty <nonformal>, **immediate,** instant, on the spot; onrushing, swift, speedy; **urgent;** furious, feverish; slap-bang, slapdash, **cursory,** passing, cosmetic, snap <nonformal>, superficial; spur-of-the-moment, last-minute

hat NOUNS **headdress,** headgear, headwear, headpiece, **chapeau, cap;** lid <nonformal>

hatch VERBS **be born,** have birth, come forth, issue forth, see the laight of day, come into the world; **breed,** engenger, beget, spawn, give rise to

hatchet man NOUNS **killer,** slayer; **disparager,** depreciator, decrier, detractor, basher *and* trasher <both nonformal>, belittler, debunker, deflater, slighter, derogator, **knocker** <nonformal>, caustic critic; **slanderer,** libeler, defamer, backbiter; calumniator, traducer; **muckraker, mudslinger,** social critic

hate NOUNS 1 **hatred;** dislike; **detestation,** abhorrence, aversion, antipathy, repugnance, **loathing,** execration, **abomination,** odium; **spite,** spitefulness, despite, despitefulness, **malice, malevolence,** malignity; vials of hate *or* wrath; scorn, despising, **contempt**
VERBS 2 **detest,** loathe, abhor, execrate, abominate, hold in abomination, take an aversion to, shudder at, utterly detest, be death on, not stand, not stand the sight of, not stomach; scorn, **despise**

hateful ADJS **loathsome,** detestable; despiteful; unlikable; **contemptible; malicious,** maleficent, malefic; **malignant,** malign; **mean** *and* ornery *and* cussed *and* bitchy <all nonformal>, nasty, baleful, beneath contempt, invidious; **wicked,** iniquitous; **harmful,** noxious

hatred NOUNS **hate;** dislike; **detestation,** abhorrence, aversion, antipathy, repugnance, **loathing,** execration, **abomination,** odium; **spite,** spitefulness, malice, **malevolence,** malignity; vials of hate *or* wrath; scorn, despising, **contempt**

haughty ADJS **arrogant,** overbearing, superior, domineering, proud; high-flown, high-falutin *and* high-faluting <both nonformal>; **stuck-up** *and* **uppish** *and* uppity *and* **upstage** <all nonformal>; **hoity-toity,** big, big as you please, six feet above contradiction; on one's high horse; **condescending,** patronizing, *de haut en bas* <Fr>

haul NOUNS 1 **booty,** spoil, spoils, loot, swag <nonformal>, ill-gotten gains, **plunder,** prize, take, pickings, stealings, stolen goods, hot goods *or* items <nonformal>; **boodle** *and* squeeze *and* **graft** <all nonformal>
VERBS 2 **strain, pull,** tug, heave; strain the muscles, strain every nerve *or* every nerve and sinew; put one's back into it <nonformal>; sweat blood; take on too much, spread oneself too thin, overexert, overstrain, overtax, overextend

haunt NOUNS 1 **hangout** <nonformal>,

stamping ground <nonformal>; gathering place, rallying point, meeting place, clubhouse, club
VERBS 2 **frequent,** hang *and* hang around *and* hang about *and* hang out <all nonformal>
3 **worry,** upset, vex, fret, agitate, get to <nonformal>, **torment,** dog, hound, plague, persecute, beset

haunted ADJS 1 **worried,** tormented, dogged, hounded, persecuted, beset, plagued; worried sick, worried to a frazzle, worried stiff <nonformal>; unable to forget, obsessed, nagged, rankled
2 spooked *and* spooky <both nonformal>, spirit-haunted, ghost-haunted, specter-haunted; **possessed,** ghost-ridden

haunting ADJS **unforgettable,** never to be forgotten, never to be erased from the mind, **indelible,** indelibly impressed on the mind, fixed in the mind; persistent, recurrent, nagging, plaguing, rankling, festering; obsessing, obsessive

haven NOUNS **refuge, sanctuary,** safehold, asylum, **port,** harborage, **harbor;** harbor of refuge, port in a storm, snug harbor, safe haven; game sanctuary, bird sanctuary, preserve, forest preserve, game preserve; stronghold

havoc NOUNS **detriment;** destruction; despoliation; mischief; outrage, atrocity

hawk NOUNS 1 **militarist, warmonger,** war dog *or* hound, war hawk
VERBS 2 **vend,** dispense, **peddle, huckster**

haze NOUNS 1 gauze, film; vapor; confusion
VERBS 2 **banter,** twit, chaff, rally, joke, jest, jape, **tease**

hazy ADJS **indistinct, unclear,** unplain, **indefinite,** undefined, ill-defined, **blurred, blurry,** bleared, bleary, blear, **fuzzy,** misty, filmy, foggy; **murky,** cloudy, foggy, fogbound, nebulous

head NOUNS 1 **supervisor,** foreman, monitor, headman, overman, **boss,** chief, taskmaster
2 **brain**, gray matter, pate *and* sconce *and* noddle <all nonformal>; noodle *or* noggin *or* bean *or* upper story <all nonformal>; **intelligence, intellect,** mentality, consciousness
VERBS 3 **direct,** manage, regulate, conduct, carry on, handle, run <nonformal>; **control,** command, govern, boss *and* head up *and* pull the strings *and* mastermind *and* quarterback *and* call the signals <all nonformal>; head up, office, captain, skipper <nonformal>
ADJS 4 headmost, capital, chief, paramount, supreme, preeminent; **top-level,** highest level, top-echelon, top-flight, top-ranking, top-drawer <nonformal>; **principal,** premier, **leading, main,** flagship

headache NOUNS 1 cephalalgia, misery in the head <nonformal>; splitting headache, **sick headache, migraine,** megrim, hemicrania
2 **nuisance,** pest, bother, botheration <nonformal>, public nuisance, **trouble, problem,** pain <nonformal>, difficulty, hot potato <nonformal>; **pain in the neck** *or* **in the ass** <nonformal>

head count NOUNS **roll call,** muster, **census,** nose count <nonformal>, **poll,** questionnaire, returns, census report *or* returns

headhunter NOUNS executive search agency *or* firm; executive recruiter, executive recruitment consultant, executive development specialist; body snatcher *and* flesh peddler *and* talent scout <all nonformal>

heading NOUNS 1 **direction,** directionality; **line,** direction line, line of direction, point, quarter, **aim, way,** track, range, **bearing,** azimuth, compass reading, **course**
2 **caption,** title, head, superscription, rubric; **headline**

headline NOUNS 1 banner, banner head *or* line, streamer; **scarehead,** screamer; drop head, running head *or* title; **subhead, subheading**
VERBS 2 **star, feature** <nonformal>, bill, give top billing to

headlong ADJS 1 **reckless,** devil-may-care; careless; **impetuous,** hotheaded; **hasty**, hurried, overeager, overzealous, overenthusiastic; **furious,** desperate, mad, wild, wanton, harum-scarum <nonformal>; precipitate, **precipitous,** precipitant; **breakneck**
ADVS 2 **impulsively,** impetuously, hastily, suddenly, quickly, **precipitately,** recklessly, rashly

headquarters NOUNS **HQ,** central station, central office, main office, central administration, seat, base, **base of operations,** center of authority; general headquarters *or* **GHQ,** command post *or* **CP,** company headquarters

head start NOUNS **earliness,** early hour, time to spare; running start, ground floor, first crack, beginnings, first *or* early stage, very beginning, preliminaries; advance notice, lead time, a stitch in time, readiness, preparedness, preparation

headstrong ADJS **obstinate,** stubborn, pertinacious, restive; willful, self-willed, strong-willed, hardheaded, strong-headed, *entêté* <Fr>; bullheaded, bullet-headed, **pigheaded, mulish** <nonformal>, stubborn as a mule; **set in one's ways,** case-hardened, stiff-necked

headway NOUNS **improvement,** betterment, bettering, change for the better; melioration, amelioration; **progress,** progression; **advance,** advancement; **rise,** ascent, **lift, uplift,** uptick <nonformal>, upswing, uptrend, upbeat

headwear NOUNS **headdress,** headgear, headclothes, headtire; **millinery;** headpiece, chapeau, cap, **hat;** lid <nonformal>; headcloth, **kerchief,** coverchief

heady ADJS **exciting,** thrilling, stirring, moving, breathtaking, eye-popping <nonformal>; heart-stirring, heart-swelling, heart-expanding, soul-stirring, mind-blowing <nonformal>; **stimulating,** stimulative, stimulatory; exhilarating, intoxicating, maddening, ravishing; self-willed, willful, headstrong

heal VERBS 1 **cure,** work a cure, **remedy, restore to health,** heal up, knit up, bring round *or* around, pull round *or* around, give a new *or* fresh lease on life, make better, make well, fix up, pull through, set on one's feet *or* legs; snatch from the jaws of death
2 **heal over,** close up, scab over, cicatrize, granulate; heal *or* right itself; **knit, set**

health NOUNS **well-being; fitness,** health and fitness, physical fitness; bloom, flush, glow, rosiness; mental health, emotional health; physical condition; **wholesomeness,** propriety, regularity

healthy ADJS 1 enjoying health, **fine,** in health, in shape, in condition, **fit,** fit and fine; **in good health,** in the pink of condition, in mint condition, **in good** *or* **fine shape, in fine fettle,** bursting with health, full of life and vigor, feeling one's oats; eupeptic

2 <nonformal> **in the pink,** in fine whack, in fine *or* high feather, chipper, **fit as a fiddle;** alive and kicking, bright-eyed and bushy-tailed; full of beans *or* of piss and vinegar

heap NOUNS 1 **lot, lots,** deal, no end of, **good** *or* **great deal, considerable,** sight, **pile, stack,** loads, **raft, slew,** whole slew, spate, wad, **batch,** mess, mint, peck, pack, pot, **tidy sum,** quite a little; **oodles, gobs, scads**
VERBS 2 **pile,** pile on, stack, heap *or* pile *or* stack up; mound, hill, bank, bank up; rick; pyramid; drift

hear VERBS 1 catch, get <nonformal>, take in; **overhear; hear of,** hear tell of <nonformal>; get an earful <nonformal>, get wind of; have an ear for
2 **sit in judgment,** hold the scales, hold court; give a hearing to; **try; referee, umpire,** officiate; arbitrate

hearing NOUNS 1 sense of hearing, auditory *or* aural sense, ear; heeding, attention, hushed attention, rapt attention, eager attention; auscultation, aural examination, examination by ear; audibility, **earshot,** earreach, range, auditory range, reach, carrying distance, **sound of one's voice**
2 **audition,** tryout, call <all nonformal>, **audience, interview,** conference; attention, favorable attention, ear; **listening,** listening in; **eavesdropping,** wiretapping, electronic surveillance, bugging <nonformal>
3 **trial,** jury trial, trial by jury, trial at the bar, inquiry, inquisition, inquest, assize; court-martial; **examination,** cross-examination

hearsay NOUNS 1 **report, rumor,** flying rumor, unverified *or* unconfirmed report, *on-dit* <Fr>, **scuttlebutt** *and* latrine rumor <both nonformal>; **talk, whisper,** idea afloat, news stirring; common talk, town talk, **talk of the town,** topic of the day, *cause célèbre* <Fr>; **grapevine; canard,** roorback
ADJS 2 circumstantial, presumptive, nuncupative, cumulative, ex parte

heart NOUNS 1 **soul, spirit,** *esprit* <Fr>, **breast, bosom,** inmost heart *or* soul, heart of hearts, secret *or* inner recesses of the heart, secret places, heart's core, heartstrings, cockles of the heart, bottom of the heart, being, innermost being, core of one's being; viscera, pit of one's stomach, **gut** *or* guts <nonformal>; bones

2 **passion,** tender feeling *or* passion, **ardor,** ardency, fervor, flame; **regard,** admiration
3 **sum and substance,** stuff, material, matter, medium, building blocks, fabric; **gist,** soul, meat, nub; the nitty-gritty *and* the bottom line *and* the name of the game <all nonformal>, **core,** kernel, marrow, pith, sap, spirit, **essence,** quintessence

heartache NOUNS **wretchedness,** aching heart, heavy heart, bleeding heart, broken heart, agony of mind *or* spirit; suicidal despair, black night of the soul, **despondency,** despond

heartbreaker NOUNS **philanderer,** philander, woman chaser, **ladies' man;** man chaser; masher, lady-killer, wolf, skirt chaser, man *or* woman on the make *and* make-out artist <both nonformal>

heartening ADJS **cheering,** gladdening; **encouraging,** heartwarming; **inspiring,** inspiriting; **exhilarating,** animating, enlivening, invigorating; cheerful, cheery, glad, joyful

heartfelt ADJS **deep-felt,** deepgoing, from the heart; **deep, profound;** indelible; pervasive, pervading, absorbing; penetrating, penetrant, piercing; **poignant,** keen, sharp, acute

hearth NOUNS **home,** home sweet home; **fireside,** hearth and home, hearthstone, fireplace, *foyer* <Fr>, chimney corner, ingle, ingleside *or* inglenook; **household,** ménage; **homestead,** home place, home roof, roof, rooftree; paternal roof *or* domicile, family homestead, ancestral halls

heartland NOUNS the Middle West, Middle America; the Great Plains, the heartlands

heartless ADJS **unfeeling,** unnatural, unresponsive, insensitive, **cold,** cold of heart, coldhearted, **cold-blooded; hard,** hardened, hard of heart, hardhearted, stony-hearted, marble-hearted, flinthearted; **callous,** calloused; obdurate, indurated; **unmerciful; shameless,** lost to shame, blind to virtue, lost to all sense of honor, conscienceless

heartrending ADJS **agonizing,** excruciating, harrowing, racking, rending, **desolating,** consuming; **heartsickening,** heartwounding, **pitiful,** pitiable, pathetic, piteous, touching, moving, affecting, grievous, doleful

heartsick ADJS **disconsolate,** inconsolable, unconsolable, comfortless, prostrate *or* prostrated, **forlorn; desolate,** *désolé* <Fr>; sick, **sick at heart,** soul-sick, heartsore

heartstrings NOUNS **heart, bosom,** inmost heart *or* soul, heart of hearts, secret *or* inner recesses of the heart, secret places, heart's core, cockles of the heart, bottom of the heart, being, innermost being, core of one's being

heartthrob NOUNS

<nonformal> **sweetie, honey,** honeybunch, honeypie, sweetie-pie, sweet patootie, tootsie, tootsy-wootsy, dearie, baby, dreamboat, poopsy, sugar, sugarbun, sweets

heart-to-heart NOUNS 1 **chat,** cozy chat, friendly chat *or* talk, **little talk,** coze, causerie, *tête-à-tête* <Fr>, **heart-to-heart talk;** pillow-talk, intimate discourse
ADJS 2 **candid, frank, sincere,** genuine, ingenuous, frankhearted; **open,** openhearted, transparent, open-faced; **unreserved,** unrestrained, unconstrained, unchecked; unguarded, uncalculating

heartwarming ADJS **cheering,** gladdening; **encouraging,** heartening; **inspiring,** inspiriting; **exhilarating,** animating, enlivening, invigorating; cheerful, cheery, glad, joyful

hearty ADJS **vigorous,** nervy, **lusty,** bouncing, full- *or* red-blooded; **active,** lively, living, animated, spirited, go-go <nonformal>, vivacious, brisk, bright-eyed and bushy-tailed <nonformal>, lusty, **robust,** enthusiastic, mettlesome, zesty, zestful, impetuous, spanking, smacking; **hale,** hale and hearty

heat NOUNS 1 **fever of excitement, fever pitch,** fever, fever heat, fire; sexual excitement, rut; **anger,** more heat than light <nonformal>; **hotness,** heatedness; **warmth,** warmness
VERBS 2 raise *or* increase the temperature, **warm,** warm up, fire, fire up, stoke up

heated ADJS **passionate, warm, hot,** red-hot, flaming, burning, glowing, fervent, fervid; **fiery,** inflamed, flaming, scorching, white-hot; **fanatic, zealous,** totally committed, hard-core, hard-line, ardent; **hotheaded**

heathen NOUNS 1 **unbeliever,** disbeliever,

nonbeliever; **atheist,** infidel, pagan; nullifidian, minimifidian; secularist
ADJS 2 **pagan, paganish,** paganistic; **heathenish; unbelieving,** disbelieving, faithless; **infidel,** infidelic; **atheistic,** atheist; nullifidian, minimifidian

heat up VERBS **incite, stir up,** work up, whip up; **inflame,** incense, **fire,** heat, impassion; lash into a fury *or* frenzy; feed the fire, fan the flame; **aggravate,** exacerbate, heat up, **provoke,** envenom, **embitter,** infuriate, madden

heave VERBS **throw,** fling, sling, pitch, toss, cast, hurl, chuck, peg <nonformal>, lob, shy, fire, burn, pepper <nonformal>, launch, dash, let fly, let go, let rip, let loose

heaven NOUNS 1 **utopia,** paradise, heaven on earth
2 **the heavens,** heaven, **sky, firmament;** vault, cope, vault *or* canopy of heaven, celestial sphere, starry heaven *or* heavens

this majestical roof fretted with golden fire
SHAKESPEARE

Heaven NOUNS **the hereafter,** the great hereafter, a better place, Paradise, Heaven, Elysian Fields; **the afterworld,** the otherworld, **the next world,** the world to come, life *or* world beyond the grave, **the beyond,** the great beyond, the unknown, the great unknown, eternal home; **afterlife, postexistence,** future state, **life to come,** life after death

the good hereafter
WHITTIER

heavenly ADJS 1 **blissful,** beatific, saintly, divine; sublime; paradisal, paradisiac, paradisiacal, paradisic, paradisical, empyreal *or* empyrean, Elysian; **sacred, holy,** numinous, **sacrosanct,** religious, spiritual, divine; out of sight *or* of this world <nonformal>
2 **glorious,** heavenly, divine, sublime; **resplendent,** splendorous *or* splendrous, splendiferous, **splendid,** resplendently beautiful; **brilliant,** bright, radiant, shining, beaming, glowing, blooming, abloom, sparkling, **dazzling; glamorous**

heavy NOUNS 1 **actor, villain,** antagonist, **bad guy** *or* black hat <both nonformal>; villainess
ADJS 2 **ponderous, massive,** massy, weighty, hefty <nonformal>, fat; **leaden,** heavy as lead; deadweight; overweight

heavy-handed ADJS **inelegant,** clumsy, clunky and klutzy <both nonformal>, heavy-footed, ham-handed, graceless, ungraceful, infelicitous, unfelicitous; **tasteless,** in bad taste, offensive to polite ears; indecorous, unseemly, uncourtly, undignified; **unpolished, unrefined**

heckle VERBS **harass,** harry, drive up the wall <nonformal>, **hound,** dog, nag, pick *or* prod at, rub it in *and* rub one's nose in it <both nonformal>, badger, hector, bait, bullyrag, worry, worry at, nip at the heels of, chivy, hardly give one time to breathe, make one's life miserable, **pester, tease, needle,** devil, get after *or* get on <nonformal>, **bedevil, pick on** <nonformal>, tweak the nose, pluck the beard, give a bad time to <nonformal>

hectic ADJS **overactive,** hyperactive, hyper <nonformal>; frenzied, frantic, frenetic; hyperkinetic

hedge NOUNS 1 **qualification, limitation, limiting, restriction,** circumscription, **modification,** hedging, hedging one's bets, cutting one's losses; setting conditions, conditionality, provisionality, circumstantiality
VERBS 2 **condition,** qualify, hedge about; pussyfoot <nonformal>, be *or* sit on the fence, beat around *or* about the bush, hem and haw, beg the question, tapdance <nonformal>, dance around, equivocate; provide a hedge, hedge one's bets, cut one's losses; keep something for a rainy day

heed VERBS **obey, mind, keep, observe,** listen *or* hearken to; **comply, conform,** walk in lockstep; stay in line *and* not get out of line *and* not get off base <all nonformal>, **toe the line** *or* mark, fall in, fall in line, obey the rules, follow the book, **do what one is told**

heedless ADJS **careless, unheeding, unheedful, disregardful,** disregardant, regardless, **unsolicitous, uncaring;** tactless, respectless, **thoughtless, unthinking, inconsiderate,** untactful, undiplomatic, mindless of, **unmindful,** forgetful, oblivious

heft NOUNS 1 **weight, heaviness, weight-**

iness, ponderousness, ponderosity, ponderability, leadenness, heftiness <nonformal>; body weight, avoirdupois <nonformal>, fatness, beef *and* beefiness <both nonformal>
VERBS 2 **weigh,** weight; **balance,** weigh in the balance, strike a balance, hold the scales, put on the scales, lay in the scales; **elevate, raise, rear,** escalate, up, boost *and* hike <both nonformal>; **erect, heighten, lift,** levitate, boost <nonformal>, **hoist,** heist <nonformal>, heave; raise up, rear up, lift up, hold up, set up

hefty ADJS **heavy, ponderous, massive,** massy, weighty, fat; **leaden,** heavy as lead; deadweight; heavyweight; overweight

heifer NOUNS **calf,** yearling, fatling, stirk <Brit>

heights NOUNS **elevation,** eminence, **rise,** raise, **uprise,** lift, rising ground, vantage point *or* ground; soaring *or* towering *or* Olympian heights, aerial heights, dizzy *or* dizzying heights; upmost *or* uppermost *or* utmost *or* extreme height; sky, stratosphere, ether, heaven *or* heavens; **zenith, apex, acme**

heir NOUNS heritor, inheritor, *heres* <L>; **heiress,** inheritress, inheritrix; coheir, joint heir, fellow heir, coparcener; **heir apparent,** apparent heir; **heir presumptive,** presumptive heir; statutory next of kin; **successor,** next in line

heirloom NOUNS **inheritance,** heritance <old>, heritage, patrimony, birthright, legacy, bequest, bequeathal; hereditament, corporeal *or* incorporeal hereditament; **heritable**

heist NOUNS

<nonformal> **stickup,** job, stickup job, bag job, boost, burn, knockover, **ripoff**

held ADJS **possessed, owned;** in seisin, in fee, in fee simple, **free and clear; own,** of one's own; **in one's possession, in hand,** in one's grip *or* grasp, at one's command *or* disposal; on hand, by one, in stock, in store; **believed,** credited, trusted, accepted; received, of belief; **obsessed, possessed,** prepossessed, **infatuated,** preoccupied, fixated, **hung up** <nonformal>, besotted, gripped; **fascinated, enthralled, rapt, spellbound,** charmed, enchanted, mesmerized, **hypnotized,** fixed, caught, riveted, **arrested,** switched on <nonformal>

hell NOUNS 1 **depths,** deeps, bowels, bowels of the earth; bottomless pit; dark *or* unknown *or* yawning *or* gaping depths, unfathomed deeps; **perdition, inferno,** the pit, **the bottomless pit,** the abyss, **nether world,** lower world, underworld, infernal regions, abode *or* world of the dead, abode of the damned, place of torment, the grave, shades below; **purgatory; limbo**

a vast, unbottom'd, boundless pit
ROBERT BURNS

2 **Hades** Sheol, Gehenna, Tophet, Abaddon, Naraka, jahannan, avichi, **perdition,** Pandemonium, **inferno,** the pit, **the bottomless pit,** the abyss

hellcat NOUNS 1 **daredevil,** devil, hellraiser, **madcap,** madbrain, wild man, hotspur, rantipole, harum-scarum *and* fire-eater <both nonformal>; **adventurer,** adventuress, adventurist; brazenface
2 **witch, hag, vixen,** hellhag, she-devil, virago, brimstone, termagant, grimalkin, Jezebel, beldam, she-wolf, tigress, wildcat, bitch-kitty <nonformal>, siren, fury

hellish ADJS **fearful,** fearsome, fear-inspiring, nightmarish; **scary,** scaring, chilling; demoniac *or* demoniacal, diabolic, diabolical, devilish, satanic, infernal; sulfurous, brimstone, fire-and-brimstone; chthonic, chthonian

helm NOUNS **control, grasp,** grip, hand, hands, iron hand, clutches; reins of government

help NOUNS 1 **aid,** assistance, support, succor, relief, comfort, ease, remedy; mutual help *or* assistance; **bailout** <nonformal>, **rescue; financial assistance;** pecuniary aid; scholarship, fellowship; **welfare,** public welfare, public assistance, relief, relief *or* welfare payments, welfare aid, dole, aid to dependent children
2 **staff,** personnel, employees, hired help, the help, **crew, gang,** men, force, servantry, retinue
VERBS 3 **aid, assist,** comfort, abet <old>, **succor,** relieve, **ease,** doctor, remedy; be of some help, put one's oar in <nonformal>; do good, do a world of

good, **benefit, avail**; **favor, befriend; give help,** render assistance, offer *or* proffer aid, come to the aid of, rush *or* fly to the assistance of, lend aid, **give** *or* **lend** *or* **bear a hand** *or* **helping hand,** stretch forth *or* hold out a helping hand; **give an assist, give a leg up** *or* lift *or* boost <nonformal>

helper NOUNS **assistant,** auxiliary, aider, aide, paraprofessional; **help,** helpmate, helpmeet; **servant, employee**

helpful ADJS **useful,** utile; **profitable,** salutary, good for, beneficial; remedial, therapeutic; serviceable, **useful**; **contributory,** contributing, conducive, **constructive, positive,** promotional

helping NOUNS 1 **serving,** service; **portion,** help; second helping; **course;** dish, plate; **portion,** share, interest, part, stake, stock, piece, bit, segment; **bite** *and* **cut** *and* **slice** *and* **chunk** *and* slice of the pie *or* melon *and* piece of the action <all nonformal>, **lot, allotment, end** <nonformal>, **proportion, percentage,** measure, quantum, **quota,** deal *or* dole <both old>, meed, moiety, mess
ADJS 2 assisting, serving; **assistant, auxiliary,** adjuvant, subservient, subsidiary, ancillary, accessory; ministerial, ministering, ministrant; fostering, nurtural; care, caring, care-giving; instrumental

helpless ADJS **defenseless, unprotected;** vulnerable, like a sitting duck <nonformal>, aidless, friendless, unfriended; fatherless, motherless; leaderless, guideless; **untenable,** pregnable, vulnerable

helter-skelter ADJS 1 **confused, chaotic,** anarchic, **muddled, jumbled,** scattered, higgledy-piggledy, hugger-mugger, skimble-skamble, in a mess; **mixed up, balled** *or* **bollixed up** <nonformal>, **screwed up** <nonformal>, mucked up <nonformal>, **fouled up** *and* fucked up *and* snafu <all nonformal>
ADVS 2 **in disorder, in disarray, in confusion,** Katy bar the door <nonformal>, in a jumble, in a tumble, in a muddle, in a mess; higgledy-piggledy, hugger-mugger, skimble-skamble, willy-nilly <nonformal>, all over, all over hell <nonformal>, **all over the place, all over the shop** <nonformal>

hem NOUNS **edging,** fringe, fimbriation, fimbria; selvage, list, welt; frill, frilling

hemisphere NOUNS **half,** moiety; semisphere, semicircle, **fifty percent;** half-and-half *and* fifty-fifty <both nonformal>

hemmed-in ADJS **restricted,** limited, confined; circumscribed, hedged in *or* about, boxed in; landlocked; **shut-in, enclosed,** closed-in; bound, immured, cloistered, pent-up, penned, cooped, mewed, walled- *or* hedged- *or* fenced-in, fenced, walled, paled, railed, barred

hemorrhage NOUNS 1 hemorrhea, **bleeding;** nosebleed; ecchymosis, petechia
VERBS 2 **bleed,** lose blood, **shed blood,** spill blood; bloody; ecchymose

henchman NOUNS cohort, hanger-on, buddy *and* sidekick <both nonformal>; heeler *and* **ward heeler** <both nonformal>; hanger-on, satellite, creature, lackey, flunky, stooge <nonformal>, jackal, minion, myrmidon

henpeck VERBS **nag,** niggle, **carp at, fuss at, fret at,** yap *or* **pick at** <nonformal>, peck at, nibble at, **pester, pick on** *and* pick at <all nonformal>, bug *and* hassle <nonformal>

henpecked ADJS **tied to one's apron strings,** on a string, on a leash, in leading strings; wimpish <nonformal>; milk-toast *or* milquetoast, Caspar Milquetoast

hep ADJS

< nonformal> **hip,** on the beam, go-go, **with it,** into, really into, groovy; chic, clued-up, clued in, in the know, trendy

herald NOUNS 1 **harbinger,** forerunner, vaunt-courier; evangel, evangelist, bearer of glad tidings; herald angel, Gabriel, *buccinator* <L>
VERBS 2 **harbinger, forerun,** run before; speak of, announce, proclaim, preannounce; give notice, notify, talk about; usher in, **anticipate,** antedate, predate; **preexist**

heraldry NOUNS **pomp,** circumstance, pride, **state,** solemnity, formality; **pomp and circumstance;** armory, blazonry, sigillography, sphragistics

trump and solemn heraldry
COLERIDGE

herbicide NOUNS **poison,** defoliant, Agent Orange, paraquat, weed killer

herculean ADJS **arduous,** strenuous, toilsome, laborious, operose

herd NOUNS 1 **the masses,** *hoi polloi* <Gk>, the many, **the multitude,** the crowd, the horde, the million, the mass of the people, the great unnumbered, the great unwashed, **the vulgar** *or* **common herd**
VERBS **guide,** steer, drive, run <nonformal>; herd up, punch cattle, **shepherd,** ride herd on; wrangle, round up

hereafter NOUNS 1 **the future,** future, futurity, what is to come, imminence, subsequence, eventuality, aftertime, afteryears, **time to come,** years to come; **distant future,** remote *or* deep *or* far future; **by-and-by,** the sweet by-and-by <nonformal>
ADVS 2 in future, hereinafter, thereafter, **henceforth, henceforward** *or* henceforwards, thence, **thenceforth,** thenceforward *or* thenceforwards, over the long haul *or* short haul <nonformal>, from this time forward, from this day on *or* forward, from this point, from this *or* that time, from then on, **from here** *or* **now on, from now on in** <nonformal>, from here in *or* out <nonformal>, from this moment on

the hereafter NOUNS the afterworld, the afterlife, life after death; **destiny, fate,** doom, karma, kismet, what bodes *or* looms, what is fated *or* destined *or* doomed, what is written, what is in the books, the great hereafter, **the next world,** the world to come, life *or* world beyond the grave, **the beyond,** the great beyond, the unknown, the great unknown

hereditary ADJS patrimonial, **inherited, innate;** genetic, genic; bred in the bone, in the blood, running in the blood *or* race *or* strain, radical, rooted; patroclinous, matroclinous

heredity NOUNS **heritage, inheritance, birth;** patrocliny, matrocliny; endowment, inborn capacity *or* tendency *or* susceptibility *or* predisposition

heresy NOUNS false doctrine, **misbelief; fallacy, error;** heterogeneity, heterodoxy, unorthodoxy, **unconventionality**

heritage NOUNS **inheritance,** heritance <old>, patrimony, birthright, legacy, bequest, bequeathal

hermaphrodite NOUNS 1 **intersex,** sex-intergrade, epicence; pseudohermaphrodite; androgyne, gynandroid; transsexual
ADJS 2 hermaphroditic, pseudohermaphrodite, pseudohermaphroditic, epicene, monoclinous; androgynous, androgynal, gynandrous, gynandrian

hermit NOUNS **recluse,** eremite, anchorite, anchoret; marabout; hermitess, anchoress; ascetic; stylite, pillarist, pillar saint

hero NOUNS **god, demigod,** phoenix; **heroine, goddess,** demigoddess; **idol,** popular idol, tin god *or* little tin god <nonformal>; popular hero, pop hero <nonformal>, folk hero, superhero; **star, superstar,** megastar, hot stuff <nonformal>; cult figure; **immortal;** brave, stalwart, man *or* woman of courage *or* mettle, **celebrity,** person of note *or* consequence, **notable, notability, luminary, great woman,** worthy, name, **big name,** figure, public figure, **somebody**

heroic ADJS **valorous,** gallant, intrepid, doughty, **hardy,** stalwart, stout, stouthearted, ironhearted, lionhearted, greathearted, bold-spirited, bold as a lion; herolike

heroin NOUNS

<nonformal> big H, boy, brown, caballo, crap, doojee, flea powder, garbage, H, hard stuff, henry, him, his, horse, hombre, jones, junk, mojo, P-funk, scag, schmeck, smack, white stuff

heroism NOUNS **courage,** courageousness, **nerve,** pluck, **bravery,** braveness, ballsiness *and* gutsiness *or* guttiness <all nonformal>, **boldness, valor,** valorousness, valiance, valiancy, **gallantry,** conspicuous gallantry, gallantry under fire *or* beyond the call of duty, gallantness, **intrepidity,** intrepidness, **prowess,** virtue; stoutheartedness, lionheartedness, greatheartedness; heroicalness

hero worship NOUNS overpraise, excessive praise, idolizing, idolatry, deification, apotheosis, adulation, lionizing

hesitant ADJS hesitating, pikerish; faltering; shilly-shallying; diffident, tentative, timid, cautious; scrupling, jibbing, sticking, straining, stickling; **tentative,** unprecipitate, cool; **deliberate**

hesitate VERBS **pause, falter, hang back,** hover; shilly-shally, hum and haw, **hem and haw;** wait to see how the cat jumps *or* the wind blows, scruple, jib, stick at, stickle, strain at; think twice about, stop to consider, ponder, wrinkle one's brow; pull back, drag one's feet; **flinch, shy**

away from, shy, back off <nonformal>; not face up to, hide one's head in the sand; **procrastinate,** be dilatory, let something slide, hang, hang back, hang fire

heterogeneous ADJS **various,** variant, varying, varied, multifarious, motley, assorted, variegated, diverse, divers, **diversified; conglomerate,** pluralistic, multiracial, multicultural, multiethnic, multinational, **miscellaneous**

heterosexual NOUNS **straight** *and* breeder <both nonformal>

hex NOUNS 1 **curse, malediction,** malison, damnation, denunciation, commination, imprecation, execration; blasphemy; anathema, fulmination, thundering, excommunication; ban, proscription; evil eye, *malocchio* <Ital>, whammy <nonformal>
2 **spell,** magic spell, **charm,** glamour, wanga; evil eye, *malocchio* <Ital>, whammy <nonformal>; jinx, curse
VERBS 3 bring bad luck; hoodoo *and* jinx *and* Jonah *and* put the jinx on <all nonformal>; put the evil eye on, whammy <nonformal>

hiatus NOUNS **interruption, suspension, break,** fissure, breach, gap, lacuna, caesura; **interval, pause,** interim, lull, cessation, letup <nonformal>, **intermission**

hibernate VERBS **lie idle, lie fallow;** aestivate, lie dormant; lie *or* lay off, charge *or* recharge one's batteries <nonformal>; have nothing to do

hick NOUNS **oaf, lout,** boor, lubber, oik <Brit>, **gawk,** gawky, **lummox,** yokel, rube, hayseed, bumpkin, clod, clodhopper

hick town NOUNS

> <nonformal terms> **one-horse town,** jerkwater town, one-gas-station, **tank town** or station, **whistle-stop,** jumping-off place; rube town podunk; hoosier town; wide place in the road

hickey NOUNS **sore, lesion;** pustule, papule, papula, fester, **pimple,** zit <both nonformal>; pock; blister, bleb, bulla, blain

hidden ADJS **secret,** close, closed, closet; cryptic, dark; unuttered, unrevealed, undivulged, undisclosed, unspoken, untold; **hush-hush, top secret,** supersecret, eyes-only, classified, restricted, under wraps <nonformal>, under security *or* security restrictions; latent, ulterior, concealed

hide NOUNS 1 **fur, pelt,** fell, fleece; peltry, skins; **leather,** rawhide
VERBS 2 **conceal,** ensconce; **cover, cover up,** blind, **screen, cloak, veil,** screen off, curtain, blanket, shroud, enshroud, envelop; **disguise, camouflage, mask,** dissemble; plain-wrap, wrap in plain brown paper; whitewash <nonformal>; **obscure,** obfuscate, cloud, becloud, befog, throw out a smoke screen, shade, throw into the shade; put out of sight, sweep under the rug, keep under cover
3 **hide out**, **conceal oneself, take cover,** hide away, **go into hiding,** go to ground; stay in hiding, **lie hid** *or* **hidden,** lie *or* lay low <nonformal>, lie *perdue,* lie snug *or* close <nonformal>, lie doggo *and* sit tight <both nonformal>, burrow <old>, **hole up** <nonformal>, **go underground**

hideaway NOUNS **retreat**, **cell, ivory tower,** hidey-hole <nonformal>, lair, sanctum, sanctum sanctorum, inner sanctum

hideous ADJS **horrid, horrible,** frightful, dreadful, terrible, awful <nonformal>; **repulsive**, repellent, repelling, rebarbative, **repugnant,** offensive, foul, forbidding, loathsome, loathly <old>, revolting; **ghastly,** gruesome, grisly

hideout NOUNS **hiding place, hideaway,** hiding, concealment, **cover,** secret place; safe house; drop, accommodation address <Brit>; **asylum,** sanctuary, retreat, refuge

hierarchy NOUNS class structure, power structure, pyramid, establishment, pecking order; natural hierarchy, order *or* chain of being

high NOUNS 1 **intoxication, inebriation, inebriety,** insobriety, besottedness, sottedness, **drunkenness, tipsiness,** befuddlement, fuddle, fuddlement, fuddledness, tipsification *and* tiddliness <both nonformal>; **excitement,** emotion, excitedness, **arousal, stimulation, exhilaration;** manic state *or* condition
ADJS 2 **overjoyed,** overjoyful, overhappy, brimming *or* bursting with happiness, on top of the world; **rapturous,** raptured, **enraptured, enchanted,** entranced, enravished, ravished, rapt, possessed; sent *and* freaked-out <both

nonformal>, **in raptures,** transported, in a transport of delight, **carried away,** rapt *or* ravished away, beside oneself, beside oneself with joy, all over oneself <nonformal>; **ecstatic,** in ecstasies, ecstasiating; rhapsodic, rhapsodical; imparadised, **in paradise,** in heaven, in seventh heaven, on cloud nine <nonformal>; **elated,** elate, exalted, jubilant, exultant, flushed
3 **intoxicated,** under the influence, **drugged**

4 <nonformal> bent, blasted, blind, bombed out, bonged out, buzzed, coked, coked out, flying, fried, geared, geared up, geezed, gonged, gorked, hopped-up, in a zone, junked, luded out, maxed, noddy, ripped, smashed, snowed, spaced, space out, spacey, stoned, strung out, switched on, tanked, totaled, tranqued, tripping, trippy, wired, zoned, zoned out, zonked, zonked out

ADVS 5 **on high,** high up; **aloft,** aloof; **up,** upward, upwards, straight up, to the zenith; **above, over,** o'er, **overhead;** above one's head, over head and ears; skyward, airward, in the air, in the clouds; on the peak *or* summit *or* crest *or* pinnacle

highball NOUNS **drink,** long drink, mixed drink; **eye-opener** <nonformal>, **nightcap** <nonformal>, sundowner <Brit nonformal>

highbrow NOUNS **snob, prig; elitist;** egghead <nonformal>, Brahmin, mandarin; **intellectual, intellect,** intellectualist, literate, member of the intelligentsia, white-collar intellectual; namedropper, tufthunter <chiefly Brit old>

high-class ADJS **superior,** above par, head and shoulders above, **crack** <nonformal>; **high-grade,** high-quality, high-caliber, high-test, **world-class**

highest ADJS **superlative, supreme, greatest, best,** maximal, maximum, most, utmost, outstanding, stickout <nonformal>; top, topmost, **uppermost,** tip-top, top-level, top-echelon, top-notch *and* top-of-the-line <both nonformal>, **first-rate,** first-class, of the first water, top of the line, highest-quality, best-quality, far and away the best, the best by a long shot *or* long chalk, head and shoulders above

highfalutin ADJS **ostentatious, pretentious;** vaunting, **lofty,** highfaluting <nonformal>, **high-flown,** high-flying; **high-toned,** tony <both nonformal>, **fancy,** classy <nonformal>, flossy <nonformal>

high-handed ADJS **imperious,** bossy <nonformal>, domineering, overbearing, overruling; tyrannous, grinding, oppressive; repressive, suppressive; strict, severe

highlands NOUNS **uplands,** highland, upland, high country, elevated land, dome, **plateau, tableland,** upland area, piedmont, moor, moorland, **hills, heights,** hill *or* hilly country, downs, wold, foothills, rolling country, **mountains,** mountain *or* mountainous country, high terrain, peaks, range, *massif* <Fr>

highlight NOUNS 1 **feature,** high spot, main attraction, centerpiece, pièce de résistance; outstanding feature
VERBS 2 **illuminate, spotlight, feature,** bring to the fore, place in the foreground, bring out in bold *or* strong *or* high relief; **flaunt,** dangle, wave, **flourish,** brandish, parade; make a show *or* a great show of; **single out,** pick out, lift up, focus on, call *or* bring to notice, direct to the attention

high-minded ADJS **principled,** high-principled, right-minded; true-dealing, true-disposing, true-devoted; noble-minded, **idealistic**

high society NOUNS **society,** fashionable society, **polite society,** high life, *beau monde, haut monde* <both Fr>, good society; best people, people of fashion, right people; *monde* <Fr>, world of fashion, Vanity Fair; **smart set** <nonformal>; the Four Hundred, **upper crust** *and* upper cut <both nonformal>; **cream of society,** *crème de la crème* <Fr>, elite, carriage trade; café society, jet set, beautiful people, the glitterati <nonformal>

high-spirited ADJS **high-strung,** highly strung, mettlesome, high-mettled; **mischievous,** mischief-loving, full of mischief, full of the devil *or* old nick; **playful,** sportive

high-strung ADJS **excitable, emotional,** highly emotional, overemotional, hyperthymic, perturbable, flappable <nonformal>, agitable; highly strung, high-spirited, mettlesome, high-mettled; irritable, edgy, **on edge,** nerves on edge, on the ragged edge <nonformal>

hijack VERBS shanghai, dragoon; **coerce,** use violence, ride roughshod, intimidate, bully

hike NOUNS 1 **walk,** ramble, amble, **tramp,** traipse <nonformal>
VERBS 2 **march,** mush, footslog, **tramp,** backpack, trail-hike; route-march
3 **increase, raise,** exalt, boost <nonformal>, hike up *and* jack up *and* jump up <all nonformal>, mark up, put up, **up** <nonformal>

hilarious ADJS **merry,** mirthful; **joyful, joyous,** rejoicing; **gleeful,** gleesome; **jolly,** buxom; **jovial,** jocund, jocular; **frivolous**

hill NOUNS down <chiefly Brit>; brae *and* fell <both Scots>; **hillock, knob,** butte, kopje, kame, monticle, monticule, monadnock, **knoll,** hummock, hammock, eminence, rise, mound, swell, barrow, tumulus, kop, tel, jebel; **dune,** sand dune

hillbilly NOUNS **provincial, hick** *and* yokel *and* rube *and* hayseed *and* shitkicker <all nonformal>, **bumpkin,** country bumpkin, clod, **clodhopper** <nonformal>, **boor,** clown, lout, looby

hill of beans NOUNS **trifle, triviality,** pin, button, hair, straw, rush, feather, fig, bean, molehill, row of pins *or* buttons <nonformal>, pinch of snuff; a continental, a hoot *and* a damn *and* a darn *and* a shit <all nonformal>, a tinker's damn

hilly ADJS **rolling,** knobby, undulating; **mountainous,** montane, alpine

hindrance NOUNS hindering, **hampering,** let, let or hindrance; **check, arrest,** arrestment, arrestation; fixation; **impediment,** holdback; **resistance, opposition**; suppression, **repression, restriction, restraint**; **obstruction,** blocking, blockage, clogging, occlusion; **interruption,** interference; **retardation,** retardment, **detention,** detainment, **delay,** holdup, setback

hindsight NOUNS **remembering, remembrance, recollection,** recollecting, exercise of memory, **recall,** recalling; reflection, reconsideration; **retrospect,** retrospection, looking back

hinge NOUNS 1 **joint,** join, joining, **juncture, union, connection,** link, connecting link, **coupling, accouplement;** clinch, embrace; **pivot**
VERBS 2 **depend,** hang, rest; **depend on** *or* **upon, hang on** *or* **upon, rest on** *or* **upon,** rest with, repose upon, lie on, lie with, stand on *or* upon, be based on, be

hint NOUNS 1 gentle hint, **intimation, indication, suggestion,** mere or faint suggestion, suspicion, inkling, whisper, **glimmer, glimmering; cue, clue,** index, **symptom, sign,** spoor, track, scent, sniff, whiff, telltale, tip-off <nonformal>; **implication, insinuation, innuendo;** broad hint, gesture, signal, nod, wink, look, nudge, kick, prompt
VERBS 2 **intimate,** suggest, insinuate, imply, indicate, adumbrate, lead *or* leave one to gather, justify one in supposing, give *or* drop *or* throw out a hint, give an inkling of, **hint at; leak,** let slip out; allude to, make an allusion to

hinterland NOUNS **back country,** outback <Australia>, up-country, boonies *and* boondocks <both nonformal>; **the bush,** bush country, bushveld, **woods,** woodlands, **backwoods,** forests, timbers, the big sticks <nonformal>, brush; wilderness, wilds, uninhabited region, virgin land *or* territory; **wasteland**; **frontier,** borderland, outpost

hip ADJS **fashionable, all the rage,** all the thing; **popular,** prevalent, current; **up-to-date,** up-to-datish, up-to-the-minute, switched-on *and* with-it <both nonformal>, trendy <nonformal>, newfashioned, modern, new; **in the swim;** sought-after, much sought-after; **hep,** on the beam, **with it,** into, really into, groovy <all nonformal>

hippie NOUNS 1 **nonconformist,** unconformist, **original,** eccentric, gonzo <nonformal>, deviant, deviationist, maverick <nonformal>, dropout, Bohemian, beatnik, hipster, freak <nonformal>, flower child, street people, yippie
ADJS 2 **unconventional, unorthodox, eccentric,** gonzo <nonformal>, heterodox, heretical; offbeat <nonformal>, way out *and* far out *and* kinky *and* out in left field <all nonformal>, fringy, breakaway, Bohemian, beat, counterculture

hire VERBS **employ,** give a job to, take into employment, take into one's service, take on <nonformal>, recruit, headhunt <nonformal>, **engage,** sign up *or* on <nonformal>; retain, **rent,** lease, job, **charter; sublease,** sublet

hiss NOUNS 1 **hissing,** siss, sissing, white

noise; **boo,** booing, hoot, catcall; **Bronx cheer** *and* **raspberry** *and* razz <all nonformal>; the bird <nonformal>
VERBS 2 **boo, hoot,** catcall, give the raspberry *or* Bronx cheer <nonformal>, give the bird <nonformal>

historical ADJS **historic,** historied, historically accurate; fact-based; historicized; historiographical; cliometric; **chronicled,** empirical, **objective, real,** actual

history NOUNS the historical discipline, the investigation of the past, the record of the past, the story of mankind; **annals, chronicles,** memorabilia, chronology; chronicle, record; **the past,** past, foretime, former times, past times, times past, water under the bridge, **days** *or* **times gone by,** bygone times *or* days, yesterday, yesteryear; recent past, just *or* only yesterday

a set of lies agreed upon
NAPOLEON

hit NOUNS 1 **blow,** stroke, knock, rap, slam, bang, crack, whack, smack, thwack, smash, dash, swipe, swing, punch, poke, jab, dig, drub, thump, pelt, cut, chop
2 hit show, success, critical success, audience success, word-of-mouth success; song hit, hit tune
VERBS 3 **strike, knock,** knock down *or* out, smite; land a blow, draw blood; **poke, punch, jab,** thwack, **smack,** clap, crack, swipe, **whack;** deal, fetch, swipe at, take a punch at, throw one at <nonformal>, deal *or* fetch a blow, hit a clip <nonformal>, let have it

4 <nonformal> **sock,** bang, bash, bat, belt, bonk, bust, clip, clout, duke, swat, yerk , plunk larrup, paste, lick, biff, clump, clunk, clonk, wallop, whop, bonk, slam, slug

hitch NOUNS 1 **obstacle, obstruction,** obstructer; **hang-up** <nonformal>; **difficulty,** hurdle, hazard; **drawback,** objection; **stumbling block,** stumbling stone, stone in one's path; fly in the ointment, one small difficulty, **catch,** joker <nonformal>
2 **term,** time; **tenure,** continuous tenure, tenure in *or* of office; **enlistment,** tour; prison term, stretch <nonformal>

hitchhike VERBS **hitch** <nonformal>, **thumb** *or* **thumb one's way** <nonformal>, **catch a ride;** hitch *or* hook *or* bum *or* cadge *or* thumb a ride <nonformal>

hit man NOUNS **killer,** slayer, slaughterer, butcher, bloodshedder; **homicide, murderer,** man-killer, bloodletter, Cain; **assassin,** assassinator; professional killer, contract killer, hired killer, hired gun, button man *or* gun *or* trigger man *or* torpedo *or* gunsel <all nonformal>; **hatchet man**

hit-or-miss ADJS **slipshod,** haphazard, hit-and-miss; half-assed <nonformal>, indiscriminate, casual, frivolous, capricious, random, vague, dispersed, wandering, planless, undirected, trial-and-error, cut-and-try

hit the spot VERBS

<nonformal> be just the ticket, be just what the doctor ordered, **make a hit,** go over big, go over with a bang

hoard NOUNS 1 **store, treasure,** wealth, treasury; plenty, plenitude, abundance, cornucopia; heap, mass, stack, pile, dump, rick; **collection, accumulation,** cumulation, amassment, stockpile
VERBS 2 **store up,** stock up, lay up, put up, **save up,** hoard up, treasure up, garner up, **heap up,** pile up, build up a stock *or* an inventory; **accumulate,** cumulate, **collect, amass, stockpile;** treasure, save, keep, hold, squirrel, squirrel away; hide, secrete

hoarse ADJS **raucous,** raucid, **harsh,** harsh-sounding; coarse, rude, rough, gruff, ragged; **husky,** cracked, dry; **guttural,** thick, throaty, croaky, croaking

hoary ADJS hoar, **grizzled,** grizzly, griseous, canescent; **gray-haired,** gray-headed, silver-headed; **old, age-old,** old-time, **ancient, antique,** venerable; **frosty, frosted,** rimed, hoar-frosted, rime-frosted

hoax NOUNS **deception,** spoof <nonformal>, **humbug,** flam, **fake** *and* fakement, **rip-off** <nonformal>, **sham;** mare's nest

hobby NOUNS **avocation,** hobbyhorse <old>, sideline, by-line, side interest, pastime, spare-time activity; amateur pursuit, amateurism; unpaid work, volunteer work

hobgoblin NOUNS **frightener, bogey,**

bogeyman, **bugaboo,** bugbear; **goblin,** hob, ouphe

hobo NOUNS drifter, vagrant, tramp; vagabond, drifter, derelict, homeless person, bum <nonformal>

hock VERBS **pledge, pawn,** put in pawn, **put in hock** <nonformal>; mortgage, hypothecate, bond

hodgepodge NOUNS hotchpotch, hotchpot; **medley, miscellany,** mélange, pastiche, *pasticcio* <Ital>, **conglomeration, assortment,** assemblage, mixed bag, ragbag, grab bag, jumble, mingle-mangle, **mix,** mishmash, **mess,** can of worms <nonformal>, rat's nest, hash, patchwork, everything but the kitchen sink <nonformal>

hog NOUNS 1 **swine, pig,** porker; **shoat,** piggy, piglet, pigling; sucking *or* suckling pig; gilt; **boar, sow;** barrow; wild boar, tusker, razorback; warthog, babirusa
2 **glutton,** greedy eater, big *or* hefty *or* husky eater <nonformal>, trencherman, trencherwoman, gorger, **gourmand,** gourmandizer, gormand, gormandizer; **pig** *and* chow hound *and* khazer <all nonformal>
VERBS 3 **monopolize,** grab all of *and* gobble up <both nonformal>, take it all, have all to oneself, have exclusive possession of *or* exclusive rights to

hogwash NOUNS

<nonformal> **humbug,** humbuggery; **bunk, bunkum;** hooey, hoke, **hokum, bosh,** bull, **bullshit,** crap, baloney, flimflam, flam, smoke and mirrors, claptrap, eyewash

hoist NOUNS 1 **lift, boost** *and* **hike** <both nonformal>, heave; hydraulic lift; forklift; hydraulic tailgate; lever; windlass
VERBS 2 **elevate, lift,** levitate, boost <nonformal>, heist <nonformal>, heft, heave; raise up, rear up, lift up

hokey ADJS **imitation, mock, sham,** copied, fake *and* phony <both nonformal>, counterfeit, forged, plagiarized, unoriginal, ungenuine; ersatz, hoked-up <nonformal>

hold NOUNS 1 **purchase,** grasp, grip, clutch, clamp, clinch, clench; toehold, foothold, footing; **clasp, hug, embrace,** bear hug; firm hold, tight grip, iron grip, grip of iron *or* steel, death grip
2 **influence, authority,** control, domination; **sway,** reign, rule; **mastery,** ascendancy, supremacy, dominance, predominance, preponderance; upper hand, whip hand, trump card; leverage
VERBS 3 **keep, harbor,** bear, have, have and hold, hold on to; **cherish,** embrace, hug, cling to

holding NOUNS 1 **retention,** retainment, **keeping,** maintenance, preservation; **share, lot;** holdings, stockholding, stockholdings
2 **verdict,** decision, determination, finding; dictum

holdover NOUNS **remainder,** remains, remnant, residue, residuum, rest, balance; lame duck

holdup NOUNS 1 bank robbery; **armed robbery,** assault and robbery
2 **delay,** stoppage, tie-up *and* bind <both nonformal>, **block,** blockage, **hang-up** <nonformal>; **detention,** suspension, obstruction, hindrance; delaying action; **wait,** halt, stay, stop, downtime, pause

hole NOUNS 1 **perforation,** penetration, piercing, empiercement, **puncture,** goring, boring, puncturing, punching, pricking, lancing, broach, transforation, terebration; bore, borehole, drill hole
2 **omission,** gap, hiatus, vacuum, break, lacuna, discontinuity, interval

holiday NOUNS 1 **day off; red-letter day,** gala day, fete day, festival day, day of festivities; national holiday, legal holiday, bank holiday <Brit>
VERBS 2 **vacation,** get away from it all, take a holiday, weekend

holier-than-thou ADJS **sanctimonious,** sanctified, **pious,** pietistic, pietistical, self-righteous, pharisaic, pharisaical

holistic ADJS **whole, total, entire,** aggregate, gross, all; integral, integrated; **one,** one and indivisible; **inclusive,** all-inclusive, **exhaustive,** comprehensive, omnibus, all-embracing; universal

hollow NOUNS 1 **valley,** vale, glen, dale, dell, holler <nonformal>, flume
2 **opening,** aperture, hole, cavity, orifice
ADJS 3 **vacant, empty,** inane, **bare, vacuous, void,** without content, with nothing inside, devoid, null, null and void; hollowed, empty

holocaust NOUNS extermination, destruction, mass killing, genocide; mass murder

holy ADJS **sacred,** numinous, **sacrosanct, religious, spiritual,** heavenly, divine; inviolable, **inviolate,** untouchable; **inef-**

fable, unutterable, unspeakable, inexpressible, inenarrable; **godly**

homage NOUNS **respect,** approbation, approval; **reverence, veneration,** awe; **deference,** deferential *or* reverential regard; **honor,** duty; great respect, high regard, **admiration; service,** servitium, fealty, **allegiance, loyalty,** faithfulness, faith; **encomium,** accolade, kudos, panegyric; paean; **tribute**

home NOUNS 1 home sweet home; **fireside, hearth,** hearth and home, hearthstone; **household,** ménage; **homestead,** home place, roof; family homestead, ancestral halls; **habitat, range,** stamping grounds, locality, native environment

the place where, when you go there,
They have to take you in
ROBERT FROST

ADJS 2 **residential,** residentiary; domestic, domiciliary, domal; **household**

homeland NOUNS **fatherland,** *Vaterland* <Ger>, *patria* <L>, *la patrie* <Fr>, **motherland,** mother country, **native land,** native soil, one's native heath *or* ground *or* soil *or* place, the old country, country of origin, **birthplace,** cradle; **home,** homeground, God's country

homeless ADJS **destitute, down-and-out,** in the gutter; **penniless,** moneyless, fortuneless, out of funds, **without a sou,** without a penny to bless oneself with, without one dollar to rub against another; propertyless, landless; **friendless,** kithless, rootless, companionless

the homeless NOUNS **the underprivileged,** the disadvantaged, the poor, the wretched of the earth, outcasts, the dispossessed, the powerless, the underclass

homely ADJS **unattractive, unhandsome,** unpretty, unlovely, uncomely, inelegant; **plain;** not much to look at, not much for looks, short on looks <nonformal>, hard on the eyes <nonformal>; homely as a mud fence, homely enough to sour milk, homely enough to stop a clock

homemade ADJS homespun, **handmade,** handcrafted, handicrafted, self-made, DIY *or* do it yourself

homemaker NOUNS housewife, househusband, houseperson, goodwife <Scots>, lady of the house

homeowner NOUNS **householder,** house-owner, proprietor, freeholder; cottager, cotter, cottier, crofter; head of household

homesick ADJS **wistful,** wishful; **longing, yearning,** yearnful, **hankering** <nonformal>, **languishing, pining,** honing <nonformal>; **nostalgic**

homespun ADJS **simple,** plain, ordinary, nondescript, common, commonplace, prosaic, prosy, **matter-of-fact, homely,** everyday, workday, workaday, household, garden, common- *or* garden-variety; rustic

homesteader NOUNS **settler,** *habitant* <Canadian & Louisiana Fr>; **colonist,** colonizer, colonial, immigrant, planter; **squatter,** nester; **pioneer;** sooner

homestretch NOUNS **close,** closing, cessation; decline, lapse; **last lap** *or* **round** *or* **inning** <nonformal>, last stage; beginning of the end

homework NOUNS **assignment, exercise,** task, set task

homey ADJS **comfortable,** comfy <nonformal>; contented; **restful,** reposeful, peaceful, **relaxing;** comfortable as an old shoe; **cozy, snug,** snug as a bug in a rug; friendly, warm; **homelike,** down-home <nonformal>, homely, lived-in; simple, plain, unpretending

homicidal ADJS **murderous,** slaughterous; man-killing, death-dealing; biocidal, genocidal; cruel; **bloodthirsty,** bloody-minded; **bloody, gory,** sanguinary

homicide NOUNS **manslaughter; negligent homicide; murder,** bloody murder <nonformal>; serial killing; hit *and* bump-off *and* bumping-off <all nonformal>, gangland-style execution; kiss of death; foul play; **assassination;** removal, elimination; liquidation, purge, purging; justifiable homicide

homily NOUNS **lesson,** teaching, instruction, lecture, discourse, talk, **sermon,** preachment; **moral,** morality, moralization, moral lesson

homogeneous ADJS **identical,** identic; **same,** selfsame, one, one and the same, all the same, all one, of the same kidney; **indistinguishable,** without distinction, without difference, undifferent, undifferentiated; **alike, all alike, like,** just alike, exactly alike, like two peas in a pod; consubstantial, consonant, **alike,** all alike, all of a piece, of a piece, monolithic

homosexual NOUNS 1 gay person, homosexualist, homophile; catamite, *mignon* <Fr>, Ganymede; **bisexual,** bi-guy <nonformal>; **lesbian,** sapphist, tribade, fricatrice <old>
ADJS 2 homoerotic, gay, queer *and* limp-wristed *and* faggoty <all nonformal>; **bisexual,** bisexed, ambisexual, ambisextrous, amphierotic, AC-DC <nonformal>, autoerotic; lesbian, sapphic, tribadistic; mannish, butch *and* dykey <both nonformal>; effeminate; transvestite

3 <nonformal> homo, queer, faggot, fag, fruit, flit, fairy, pansy, nance, auntie, queen, drag queen, closet queen, fruitcake, poof *and* poofter *and* poove <all Brit>; <nonformal terms for female homosexuals> dyke, bull dyke, butchfemme, boondagger, diesel-dyke, lesbo, lez

honcho NOUNS

<nonformal> **boss,** big enchilada, biggest frog in the pond, top *or* high man on the totem pole, top dog, Mr Big, head cheese, his nibs, himself, man upstairs

hone VERBS **sharpen, edge,** acuminate, aculeate, spiculate, taper; **whet,** oilstone, file, grind; strop, strap; set, reset; **point;** barb, spur, file to a point

honest ADJS **veracious, truthful,** true, true to one's word, veridical; truth-telling, truth-speaking, truth-declaring, truth-passing, truth-bearing, truth-loving, truth-seeking

honesty NOUNS **veracity,** veraciousness, verity, **truthfulness,** truth, veridicality, truth-telling, truth-speaking; truth-loving; credibility, absolute credibility

honk NOUNS 1 **blare, blast,** shriek, peal; **toot,** tootle, beep, blat, trumpet
VERBS 2 **blare,** blast; shriek; **toot,** tootle, sound, peal, wind, blow, blat; honk *or* sound *or* blow the horn, beep

honor NOUNS 1 great honor, distinction, glory, credit, ornament; **esteem,** estimation, **prestige; dignity; rank, standing,** stature, high place, position, station, face, **status; chastity, virtue,** virtuousness; sexual innocence, innocence
VERBS 2 confer *or* bestow honor upon; **dignify,** adorn, grace; **distinguish,** signalize, confer distinction on, give credit where credit is due; hold in high esteem, crown with laurels

honorable ADJS **reputable,** highly reputed, **estimable, esteemed,** much *or* highly esteemed, honored; **meritorious,** worth one's salt, noble, worthy, creditable; respected, respectable, highly respectable; revered, reverend, venerable, venerated, worshipful; **well-thought-of,** highly regarded, held in esteem, in good odor, in favor, in high favor

honorary ADJS **honorific, honorable; titular,** titulary; honorific

hood NOUNS 1 **cover, covering,** coverage, covert, coverture, housing, cowl, cowling, **shelter;** cloak, mask, guise; vestment
2 **gangster, roughneck, tough**

3 <nonformal> bruiser, mug, mugger, bimbo, bozo, ugly customer, **hoodlum, hooligan,** gorilla, ape, plug-ugly, strong-arm man, muscle man, **goon;** gun, gunsel, trigger man, rodman, torpedo, hatchet man <all nonformal>

hoodlum NOUNS **rowdy,** ruffian, hood <nonformal>, hooligan; **gangster** *and* mobster <both nonformal>; racketeer; **thug**

hoodwink VERBS blindfold, blind, blind one's eyes, throw dust in one's eyes, **pull the wool over one's eyes**

hoofer NOUNS **dancer,** danseur, terpsichorean, step dancer, tap dancer, clog dancer, etc; **chorus girl, chorine,** chorus boy *or* man

hook NOUNS 1 **lure,** charm, **come-on** <nonformal>, attention-getter *or* -grabber, **attraction, draw** *or* drawer *or* crowd-drawer, crowd-pleaser, headliner; clou, gimmick <nonformal>, drawing card, drawcard; **decoy,** decoy duck; **bait, snare**
VERBS 2 **trap,** entrap, gin, catch, catch out, catch in a trap; **ensnare, snare,** hook in, sniggle, noose; inveigle; **set** *or* **lay a trap for,** bait the hook, spread the toils; **lure,** allure, **decoy**

hooked ADJS 1 **addicted,** on the needle <nonformal>; dependency-prone
2 **crooked, aquiline,** aduncous; **hook-shaped,** hooklike, uncinate, unciform; hamulate, hamate, hamiform; **hook-nosed,** beak-nosed, parrot-nosed,

aquiline-nosed, Roman-nosed, crooknosed, crookbilled

hooker NOUNS **prostitute, harlot, whore,** *fille de joie* <Fr>, call girl *and* B-girl <both nonformal>, **streetwalker,** hustler <nonformal>, *poule* <Fr>, stew, meretrix, Cyprian, Paphian

hooky NOUNS **absence,** nonattendance, **absenting, leaving,** taking leave, **departure**; **truancy,** French leave, **cut** <nonformal>; **absence without leave** *or* AWOL; **absenteeism,** truantism

hooligan NOUNS **mischief-maker, rowdy,** ruffian, hoodlum, hood <nonformal>

hoopla NOUNS **publicity,** publicness, **notoriety, fame,** famousness, notoriousness, notice, public notice, **celebrity,** *réclame, éclat* <both Fr>; **limelight** *and* **spotlight** <both nonformal>, daylight, bright light, glare, public eye *or* consciousness, **exposure, currency,** common *or* public knowledge, widest *or* maximum dissemination; **ballyhoo** <nonformal>; **festivity,** merrymaking, merriment, gaiety, jollity, jollification <nonformal>, **joviality, conviviality,** whoopee <nonformal>

hope NOUNS 1 **hopefulness,** hoping, **hopes,** fond *or* fervent hope, good hope, good cheer; aspiration, **desire**; prospect, **expectation**; sanguine expectation, happy *or* cheerful expectation; the light at the end of the tunnel; **possibility,** possibleness, **the realm of possibility,** the domain of the possible, conceivableness, **conceivability,** thinkability, thinkableness, imaginability; outside hope, small hope, slim odds; **good possibility, good chance,** even chance; bare possibility

the second soul of the unhappy
GOETHE

VERBS 2 be *or* live in hopes, have reason to hope, entertain *or* harbor the hope, cling to the hope, cherish *or* foster *or* nurture the hope; look for, prognosticate, **expect**; **trust,** confide, presume, feel confident, rest assured; pin one's hope upon, put one's trust in, hope in, rely on, count on, lean upon, bank on, set great store on; hope for, **aspire to, desire**; **hope against hope,** hope and pray, hope to God <nonformal>

hopeful ADJS **hoping, in hopes,** full of hope, in good heart, of good hope, of good cheer; **aspiring**; **expectant**; **sanguine,** fond; **confident,** assured; undespairing; **promising,** fair

hopeless ADJS unhopeful, without hope, affording no hope, worst-case, bleak, grim, dismal, cheerless, comfortless; **desperate, despairing, in despair;** despondent; disconsolate; forlorn; apathetic; **dying, terminal,** sinking, sinking fast, low, despaired of, given up, given up for dead, not long for this world, **moribund,** near death, near one's end, at the end of one's rope <nonformal>, done for <nonformal>

horde NOUNS **throng, multitude,** host, heap <nonformal>, army, panoply, legion; **crowd,** press, crush, flood, spate, deluge, mass; **mob,** rabble, rout, ruck, jam, *cohue* <Fr>, everybody and his uncle *or* his brother <nonformal>

horizon NOUNS **skyline,** rim of the horizon; sea line; the far horizon, where the earth meets the sky, vanishing point, background

horizontal ADJS **level, flat,** flattened; **even,** smooth, smoothened, smoothed out; table-like, tabular; **plane,** plain; flat as a pancake, flat as a board

horn NOUNS 1 **projection,** spur, jag, **snag,** snaggle; antler; cornicle
2 **alarm,** fog signal *or* alarm, foghorn

horny ADJS **lustful,** prurient, hot, steamy, sexy, concupiscent, lickerish, libidinous, salacious, **passionate,** hot-blooded, itching, hot to trot *and* sexed-up <both nonformal>, randy, goatish; sex-starved, unsatisfied; lascivious

horrendous ADJS **terrible,** horrid, horrible, horrifying, horrific; **dreadful,** dread, dreaded; **awful; shocking,** appalling, astounding; **hideous, ghastly,** morbid, grim, grisly, gruesome, ghoulish, macabre

horrible ADJS **hideous,** horrid, frightful, dreadful, terrible, awful <nonformal>; **repulsive**, repellent, repelling, rebarbative, **repugnant,** offensive, foul, forbidding, loathsome, revolting; **ghastly,** gruesome, grisly

horrified ADJS **terrified,** terror-stricken, terror-struck, terror-smitten, terror-ridden; horror-stricken, horror-struck; frightened out of one's wits *or* mind, **scared to death, scared stiff** *or* **shitless** *or* spitless <nonformal>; unnerved, unstrung, unmanned, undone, **cowed,** awed, **intimidated; stunned, petrified, stupefied,** paralyzed, frozen

horrify VERBS **terrify, awe,** strike terror into; **appall, shock,** make one's flesh creep; **frighten out of one's wits** *or* **senses;** strike dumb, **stun, stupefy, paralyze, petrify,** freeze

horror NOUNS 1 **aversion,** repugnance, repulsion, antipathy, allergy <nonformal>, grudge, abomination, **abhorrence,** mortal horror; **terror, mortal** *or* abject fear; **phobia**
2 **abomination,** terrible thing; **scandal,** disgrace, shame, pity, atrocity, profanation, desecration, violation, sacrilege, infamy, ignominy; **eyesore,** blot, blot on the landscape, blemish, **sight** <nonformal>, **fright**

horseplay NOUNS **misbehavior, misconduct,** unsanctioned *or* nonsanctioned behavior; **rowdiness,** rowdyism, riotousness, ruffianism, hooliganism, roughhouse; shenanigans *and* monkey tricks *and* monkeyshines <all nonformal>

horse racing NOUNS **the turf,** the sport of kings, the turf sport, the racing world *or* establishment; **flat racing; harness racing,** trotting, pacing; steeplechase, the jumps

horticulture NOUNS **gardening;** landscape gardening, landscape architecture, groundskeeping; truck gardening, market gardening, olericulture; flower gardening, flower-growing, floriculture; viniculture, viticulture; orcharding, fruit-growing, pomiculture

hospice NOUNS youth hostel, elder hostel; **asylum, home,** retreat; hospitium; rest home, nursing home, old soldiers' home, sailors' snug harbor; halfway house; life-care home, continuing-care retirement community *or* CCRC

hospitable ADJS **receptive,** welcoming; **cordial,** amiable, gracious, **friendly,** neighborly, genial, hearty, open, openhearted, warm, warmhearted; **generous,** liberal

hospital NOUNS **clinic,** *hôpital* <Fr>, treatment center; infirmary; sanitarium; sick bay *or* berth; trauma center; wellness center

hospitality NOUNS hospitableness, receptiveness; honors *or* freedom of the house; **cordiality,** amiability, graciousness, **friendliness,** neighborliness, geniality, heartiness, bonhomie, **generosity,** liberality, openheartedness, warmth, warmness, warmheartedness; open door

host NOUNS 1 mine host; hostess, receptionist, greeter; landlord
2 **throng, multitude, horde,** heap <nonformal>, army, panoply, legion; **crowd,** press, crush, flood, spate, deluge, mass; an abundance of, all kinds *or* sorts of, no end of, quite a few
VERBS 3 **entertain,** entertain guests; preside, do the honors <nonformal>; give a party, throw a party <nonformal>; spread oneself <nonformal>

hostile ADJS **antagonistic,** repugnant, antipathetic, set against, snide, spiteful, despiteful, malicious, malevolent, malignant, hateful, full of hate *or* hatred; virulent, **bitter,** sore, rancorous, acrid, caustic, venomous, vitriolic; conflicting, clashing, colliding; quarrelsome; **provocative,** off-putting; belligerent

hot ADJS 1 **heated, torrid; sweltering,** sweltry, canicular; **burning,** parching, scorching, searing, scalding, blistering, baking, roasting, toasting, broiling, grilling, simmering; **boiling,** seething, ebullient; **piping hot,** scalding hot, burning hot, roasting hot, scorching hot, sizzling hot, smoking hot; **red-hot,** white-hot; hot as hell *or* blazes, hot as the hinges of hell, so hot you can fry eggs on the sidewalk <nonformal>
2 **passionate,** fiery, glowing, fervent, fervid; **sexually excited,** in rut, lustful, ithyphallic, horny *and* sexed-up *and* hot to trot <all nonformal>; prurient, itching, itchy <nonformal>; randy, horny <nonformal>, lubricious; burning with excitement, het up <nonformal>, hot under the collar <nonformal>; seething, boiling, boiling over, steamy, steaming
3 **stolen,** pilfered, purloined; pirated, plagiarized

hot-blooded ADJS warm-blooded; **lustful, prurient, hot,** steamy, sexy, concupiscent, lickerish, libidinous, **salacious, passionate,** itching, **horny** *and* hot to trot *and* sexed-up <all nonformal>, randy, goatish

hot dog VERBS **exercise skill,** handle oneself well, demonstrate one's ability, **strut one's stuff <nonformal>,** go through one's paces, show what one has, grandstand *and* showboat *and* show off <all nonformal>, play to the gallery *or* galleries <nonformal>, please the crowd; exhibit *or* parade one's wares <nonformal>

hotel NOUNS **inn,** hostel, hostelry, **tavern,** *posada* <Sp>; tourist hotel, *parador* <Sp>; **roadhouse,** caravansary *or* caravanserai

hotheaded ADJS **hot-tempered, passionate,** hot, fiery, peppery, feisty, spunky <nonformal>, **quick-tempered, short-tempered;** hasty, quick, explosive, volcanic, combustible

sudden and quick in quarrel
SHAKESPEARE

hothouse NOUNS **nursery; conservatory, greenhouse,** glasshouse <Brit>, forcing house, summerhouse, lathhouse, coolhouse

hound VERBS **pursue, follow,** follow up, **go after,** take out *or* off after <nonformal>, bay after, run after, run in pursuit of, make after, go in pursuit of; **chase, give chase,** chivy; dog; **worry, upset, vex,** fret, agitate, get to <nonformal>, **harass,** harry, **torment,** plague, persecute, haunt, beset

house NOUNS 1 **dwelling,** dwelling house, *casa* <Sp & Ital>; house and grounds, house and lot, homesite; **building, structure, edifice,** manor house, hall; town house, *rus in urbe* <L>; country house, *dacha* <Russ>, country seat; ranch house, farmhouse, sod house, adobe house; split-level; parsonage, **rectory,** vicarage, deanery, manse; official residence, White House, 10 Downing Street
VERBS 2 domicile, domiciliate; provide with a roof, **accommodate,** furnish accommodations; have as a guest *or* lodger, shelter, harbor; **lodge, quarter, put up,** billet, room, bed, berth, bunk; stable

housebreaker NOUNS **burglar,** yegg *and* cracksman <both nonformal>; cat burglar, cat man, second-story thief *or* worker

housebroken ADJS **conditioned,** trained, seasoned; domesticated, **subdued, tame,** tamed, broken, housebroke; potty-trained

household NOUNS 1 **family,** brood, nuclear family, binuclear family, extended family, one-parent *or* single-parent family; **house,** hearth, hearthside, ménage, people, **folk,** homefolk, folks *and* homefolks <both nonformal>; **children,** issue, descendants, progeny, **offspring,** kids <nonformal>
ADJS 2 **well-known,** well-recognized, **widely known,** commonly known, universally recognized, generally *or* universally admitted; **familiar,** familiar as household words, **common, current; proverbial;** public, notorious; known by every schoolboy; talked-of, talked-about, in everyone's mouth, **on everyone's tongue** *or* **lips**

housekeeping NOUNS **domestic management,** homemaking, housewifery, ménage, househusbandry; domestic economy, home economics

housewarming NOUNS **gathering, get-together** *and* turnout <both nonformal>; **party, festivity,** fete, at home, reception

housewife NOUNS **matron,** homemaker, goodwife <Scots>, lady of the house, chatelaine

housing NOUNS **shelter, living quarters; lodgings,** lodging, lodgment; diggings *and* digs <both Brit nonformal>, pad *and* crib <both nonformal>, room; **rooms,** berth, roost, accommodations; shelter, *gîte* <Fr>; **cover, covering,** coverage

hovel NOUNS **dump** <nonformal>, rathole, hole, sty, pigsty, pigpen, tumbledown shack

hover VERBS **be imminent, impend, overhang,** hang *or* lie over, **loom,** hang over one's head, **threaten, menace,** lower; be on the horizon, be in the offing, be just around the corner, await, face, stare one in the face, be in store, breathe down one's neck, be about to be borning; float, levitate

howl NOUNS 1 **screech, whine,** wail, ululation, yammer; waul, caterwaul
VERBS 2 **screech, whine,** wail, wrawl <Brit nonformal>, yammer, ululate; waul, caterwaul

hub NOUNS **center,** centrum; **middle,** heart, core, nucleus; core of one's being, where one lives; **pith, nub,** nave, axis, pivot; bull's-eye; dead center

hubris NOUNS overconfidence, oversureness, overweeningness; **gall** *and* brass *and* cheek *and* chutzpah <all nonformal>; pride, arrogance, pomposity, self-importance

huckster NOUNS **vendor, peddler, hawker,** butcher <old>, higgler, cadger <Scots>, colporteur, chapman <Brit>; adman *and* pitchman <both nonformal>

huddle VERBS **stay near,** keep close to; **cling to,** clasp, hug; go into a huddle, close ranks

hue NOUNS **color; tint,** tinct, tincture, **tinge, shade, tone,** cast; **way, habit,** tenor, cast, grain, vein, streak, stripe, mold, brand, stamp; **kind,** sort, type, ilk

huffy ADJS **provoked,** vexed, piqued; **peeved** *and* miffed <both nonformal>, **nettled, irritated, annoyed,** aggravated <nonformal>, exasperated, put-out

hug NOUNS 1 **embrace, squeeze,** fond embrace, embracement, clasp, enfoldment, bear hug <nonformal>
VERBS 2 **embrace,** clasp, press, squeeze <nonformal>, fold, **enfold,** bosom, embosom, put *or* throw one's arms around, take to *or* in one's arms, fold to the heart, press to the bosom; take hold of, clinch

huge ADJS 1 **immense, vast, enormous,** astronomic, astronomical, humongous *and* jumbo <both nonformal>, king-size, queen-size, tremendous, prodigious, stupendous, macro, mega, giga; great big, larger than life, Homeric, mighty, **titanic, colossal, monumental,** heroic, heroical, epic, epical, towering, mountainous

2 <nonformal> **whopping, walloping, whaling, whacking,** spanking, slapping, lolloping, thumping, thundering, bumping, banging

hulking ADJS **bulky, hulky,** lumpish, lumpy, lumping <nonformal>, clumpish, lumbering, lubberly; **massive,** massy; **ponderous,** cumbrous, cumbersome; **clumsy,** awkward, **unwieldy;** clunky <nonformal>

hullabaloo NOUNS **outcry,** vociferation, clamor; hubbub, brouhaha, **uproar**; **hue and cry**

hum NOUNS 1 **humming,** thrumming, low rumbling, booming, bombilation, bombination, **droning, buzzing,** whizzing, whirring, purring
VERBS 2 thrum, boom, bombilate, bombinate, **drone, buzz,** whiz, whir, burr, purr

human NOUNS 1 **person,** human being, man, woman, child, member of the human race *or* family, Adamite, daughter of Eve; **mortal,** life, **soul,** living soul; **being,** creature, clay, ordinary clay; **individual,** personage, **personality, personhood,** individuality
ADJS 2 hominal; creaturely, creatural; Adamite *or* Adamitic; **frail, weak,** fleshly, finite, **mortal; only human;** earthborn, of the earth, earthy, tellurian, unangelic; humanistic; homocentric, anthropocentric

humane ADJS **kind, kindly,** kindly-disposed; **benign,** benignant; good as gold, good, nice, **decent; kindhearted,** warm, warmhearted, softhearted, tenderhearted, tender, loving, affectionate; **sympathetic,** sympathizing, **compassionate**, merciful; **lenient,** mild, gentle, mild-mannered, tender, compassionate, **clement,** merciful

humanitarian NOUNS 1 **philanthropist, altruist,** benevolist, person of good will, **do-gooder,** bleeding heart <nonformal>, well-doer, power for good; almsgiver, almoner; Robin Hood, Lady Bountiful
ADJS 2 **benevolent,** charitable, beneficent, philanthropic, altruistic; **bighearted,** largehearted, greathearted, freehearted; **generous**; almsgiving, eleemosynary

humanity NOUNS **humankind,** mankind, man, human species, **human race,** race of man, human family, the family of man, human beings, mortals, mortality, flesh, mortal flesh, clay; **human nature;** frail *or* fallen humanity, Adam, the generation of Adam, Adam's seed *or* offspring; **humanness,** mortality

humankind NOUNS **mankind, man,** human species, **human race,** race of man, human family, the family of man, **humanity,** human beings, mortals, mortality, flesh, mortal flesh, clay; homo, genus Homo, **Homo sapiens**

the plumeless genus of bipeds
PLATO

human nature NOUNS **humanity;** frail *or* fallen humanity, Adam, the generation of Adam, Adam's seed *or* offspring; the way you are; human frailty, weakness, **human weakness,** weakness of the flesh, the weaknesses human flesh is heir to; human equation

humble VERBS 1 **humiliate,** bring low, **bring to terms,** take down a notch *or* peg, bend, **bring one to his knees,** bend to one's will; mortify <old>, **embarrass**; put out, put out of face *or*

countenance; **deflate,** prick one's balloon; tread *or* trample underfoot, trample down, ride down, ride *or* run roughshod over, override; have one's way with
ADJS 2 **lowly,** low, **poor, mean,** small, inglorious, undistinguished; unimportant; innocuous; **modest, unpretentious**; **plain, simple,** homely; humble-looking, humble-visaged; humblest, lowliest, lowest, least

humbug NOUNS

<nonformal> **bunk bunkum;** hooey, hoke, **hokum, bosh,** bull, **bullshit,** crap, baloney, flimflam, flam, smoke and mirrors, claptrap, moonshine, eyewash, hogwash, jiggery-pokery <Brit>

humdinger NOUNS

<nonformal> **dandy,** jim dandy, dilly, pip, pippin, peach, beaut, **lulu,** doozy, honey, sweetheart, dream, lollapaloosa, crackerjack, hot shit *or* poo, pisser, pistol, corker, whiz, **crackerjack,** knockout, something else, something else again, barn-burner, killer, killer-diller, the nuts, the cat's pajamas *or* balls *or* meow, whiz, whizbang, wow

humdrum ADJS **tedious, monotonous,** singsong, jog-trot, treadmill, unvarying, invariable, uneventful, broken-record, parrotlike, harping, everlasting, too much with us <nonformal>; tiresome, blah <nonformal>, **dreary,** drearisome, dry, dryasdust, dusty, **dull**

humidity NOUNS humidness, **dankness,** dankishness, **mugginess,** stickiness, sweatiness; absolute humidity, relative humidity; dew point; humidification

humiliate VERBS 1 **humble;** mortify <old>, **embarrass**; put out, put out of face *or* countenance; **shame, disgrace,** put to shame, put to the blush, give one a red face; **deflate;** dishonor, treat with indignity; **add insult to injury**

2 <nonformal> beat *or* knock *or* **cut one down to size,** take the shine *or* starch out of, take the wind out of one's sails; put one's nose out of joint, put a tuck in one's tail, make one sing small; prick one's balloon

humility NOUNS **humbleness,** meekness; **lowliness,** lowlihood, poorness, meanness, smallness, ingloriousness; unimportance; innocuousness; **modesty,** unpretentiousness

humor NOUNS 1 **wit,** pleasantry, *esprit* <Fr>, salt, spice *or* savor of wit; Attic wit *or* salt, Atticism; ready wit, quick wit, nimble wit, agile wit, pretty wit; dry wit, subtle wit; **comedy**; black humor, sick humor, gallows humor; slapstick humor, broad humor; visual humor
2 **mood,** feeling, feelings, temper, frame of mind, state of mind, morale, tone, note, **vein**
VERBS 3 **indulge, oblige;** favor, please, gratify, satisfy, **cater to; give way to,** yield to, let one have his own way; **pamper,** cosset, **coddle,** mollycoddle

humorist NOUNS **wit,** satirist, ironist; burlesquer, caricaturist, parodist, lampooner

humorless ADJS **unhappy, uncheerful,** uncheery, **cheerless, joyless, unjoyful,** unsmiling; mirthless, unmirthful, infestive; funny as a crutch <nonformal>; **out of humor,** out of sorts, in bad humor *or* spirits

humorous ADJS **funny,** amusing; witty; droll, whimsical, quizzical; **laughable,** risible, good for a laugh; **ludicrous,** ridiculous, hilarious, absurd, quaint, eccentric, incongruous, bizarre

hump NOUNS **bulge,** bilge, bow, convex; **bump;** thank-you-ma'am *and* whoopdedoo <both nonformal>, cahot <Can>; speed bump, sleeping policeman <Brit>; hill, mountain; hunch

hunch NOUNS **guess, conjecture,** unverified supposition, perhaps, speculation, guesswork, surmise, educated guess; guesstimate *and* shot *and* stab <all nonformal>; blind guess, bold conjecture, shot in the dark <nonformal>

hunchbacked ADJS **humpbacked,** bunchbacked, crookbacked, crookedbacked, camelback, humped, gibbous, kyphotic

hung ADJS **pendent,** pendulous, pendulant, pendular, penduline, pensile; **suspended**

hunger NOUNS **appetite,** stomach, relish, taste; hungriness; the munchies <nonformal>; **yen,** lech <nonformal>, thirst; instinct *or* feeling for, sensitivity to

hungry ADJS hungering, peckish <Brit nonformal>; empty <nonformal>, unfilled; ravening, **ravenous,** voracious, sharp-set, **wolfish,** dog-hungry <nonfor-

mal>, hungry as a bear; **starved, famished,** starving, famishing, perishing *or* pinched with hunger; fasting; half-starved, half-famished

hunk NOUNS

1 <nonformal> **he-man,** *and* two-fisted man <both nonformal>, jockstrap *and* jock <both nonformal>, man with hair on his chest; caveman *and* bucko <both nonformal>

2 **batch,** bunch, heap <nonformal>, pack, mess <nonformal>, gob *and* chunk <both nonformal>

hunt NOUNS 1 **search,** searching, **quest,** hunting, stalk, stalking, still hunt, dragnet, posse, search party
VERBS 2 go hunting, hunt down, chase, run, shikar <India>, sport; engage in a blood sport; shoot, gun; course; ride to hounds, follow the hounds; **track,** trail; **stalk; search for,** seek for, **hunt for,** cast *or* beat about for

hunter NOUNS **huntsman,** sportsman, **Nimrod;** huntress, sportswoman; stalker; courser; trapper; big game hunter, shikari <India>, white hunter; jacklighter, jacker

hurdle NOUNS **obstacle, obstruction,** obstructer; **hang-up** <nonformal>; **block,** blockade, cordon, curtain; **difficulty,** hazard; **stumbling block,** stumbling stone, stone in one's path; fly in the ointment, one small difficulty, **hitch**

hurl VERBS **throw,** fling, sling, pitch, toss, cast, heave, chuck, chunk *and* peg <both nonformal>, lob, shy, fire, burn, pepper <nonformal>, launch, dash, let fly, let go, let rip, let loose

hurrah NOUNS 1 **cheer, huzzah,** hurray, hooray, yippee, rah; **cry, shout, yell;** hosanna, hallelujah, alleluia, paean, paean *or* chorus of cheers; **applause**

hurricane NOUNS **storm, tempest,** squall, line squall, **tornado, cyclone,** tropical cyclone, typhoon, storm-center, tropical storm, eye of the storm *or* hurricane, war of the elements

Nature's elemental din
THOMAS CAMPBELL

hurried ADJS **rushed,** pushed, pressed, crowded, **pressed for time,** hard-pushed *or* -pressed, hard-run; double-time, double-quick, on *or* at the double

hurry NOUNS 1 **haste, scurry, rush, race,** dash, drive, scuttle, scamper, **scramble,** hustle <nonformal>, **bustle,** flutter, **flurry,** hurry-scurry, helter-skelter
VERBS 2 **hasten,** haste, make haste, hie, post; march in quick *or* double-quick time; **make time,** make good time, **cover ground,** get over the ground, **make strides** *or* **rapid strides**

hurry up VERBS 1 **accelerate,** speed up, step up <nonformal>, **quicken; hasten;** crack on, put on, put on steam, pour on the coal, put on more speed, open the throttle; quicken one's pace; pick up speed

2 <nonformal> **step on it, snap to it,** hop to it, hotfoot, bear down on it, shake it up, **get moving** *or* **going,** get a move on, get cracking <chiefly Brit>, get *or* shake the lead out, get the lead out of one's ass, get one's ass in gear, give it the gun, hump, hump it, hump oneself, shag ass, tear ass, **get a hustle** *or* **move** *or* **wiggle on,** stir one's stumps, not spare the horses

hurt VERBS 1 **pain,** give *or* inflict pain, **wound, afflict, distress; chafe,** gall, fret, rasp, rub, grate; gnaw, grind; **gripe; torture, torment,** rack, put to torture, put *or* lay on the rack, **agonize, harrow,** crucify, martyr, martyrize, excruciate; **suffer, feel pain,** feel the pangs, anguish; **ache,** have a misery <nonformal>, ail
ADJS 2 **pained,** in pain, hurting, **suffering,** afflicted, wounded, distressed, in distress; **tortured,** tormented, racked, agonized, harrowed, lacerated; **impaired, damaged,** injured, harmed

hurtle VERBS **speed, rush, tear,** dash, dart, shoot, bolt, fling, **scamper, scurry,** scour, scud, scuttle, scramble, **race,** careen

husband NOUNS 1 **married man,** man, benedict, goodman <old>, old man <nonformal>
VERBS 2 **manage,** husband one's resources; live frugally, get along on a shoestring, get by on little; keep *or* stay within one's means *or* budget, balance income with outgo, live within one's income, make ends meet, cut one's coat according to one's cloth, keep *or* stay ahead of the game; **save up,** save for a rainy day

hush NOUNS **silence,** silentness, **soundlessness,** noiselessness, **stillness, quietness,** quietude, quiescence, **quiet, still,** peace, mum; golden silence; hush *or* dead of night

lucid stillness
T S ELIOT

hushed ADJS **silent, still,** stilly, **quiet,** quiescent, **soundless,** noiseless; quiet as a mouse, silent as the grave *or* tomb; hushed-up

husky ADJS **strong,** hunky *and* hefty *and* beefy <all nonformal>, strapping, doughty <nonformal>, **hardy,** hard, hard as nails, cast-iron, iron-hard, steely; **robust,** robustious, gutty *and* gutsy <both nonformal>; **hoarse,** roupy <Scots>, cracked, dry; **guttural,** thick, throaty, croaky, croaking

hussy NOUNS **strumpet,** trollop, wench, slut, jade, baggage, *cocotte* <Fr>, grisette; **tart** *and* **chippy** *and* **floozy** *and* broad <all nonformal>, bitch, drab, trull, quean, harridan, Jezebel, wanton, whore <nonformal>, bad woman, **loose woman,** easy woman <nonformal>

hustle NOUNS 1 **enterprise,** dynamism, **initiative,** aggression, aggressiveness, pushiness, push, drive, go, **get-up-and-go** <both nonformal>, go-ahead, go-getting, go-to-itiveness <nonformal>, **up-and-comingness**
VERBS 2 drive oneself, **push, scramble,** go all out <nonformal>, **make things hum,** step lively <nonformal>, make the sparks *or* chips fly <nonformal>; go full steam ahead, **hasten,** haste, **hurry, speed; work hard; scratch** *and* **sweat** <both nonformal>, slave away, toil away

3 <nonformal> **hump,** get cutting, break one's neck, bear down on it, put one's back into it, get off the dime, get off one's ass *or* duff *or* dead ass, **hit the ball,** pour it on, lean on it, shake a leg, go to town, get the lead out, floor it

hustler NOUNS 1 **man** *or* **woman of action,** doer; self-starter <nonformal>, bustler; go-getter *and* ball of fire *and* live wire *and* powerhouse *and* human dynamo *and* spitfire <all nonformal>; beaver, busy bee, **eager beaver** <nonformal>
2 **streetwalker, hooker** <nonformal>; **cheater,** cheat, grifter *and* mechanic *and* mover *and* rook *and* worker <all nonformal>

hut NOUNS hutch, **shack, shanty,** crib, hole-in-the-wall <nonformal>, **shed; lean-to;** Quonset hut *or* Nissen hut; hutment

hybrid NOUNS **crossbreed,** cross, mixed-blood, mixblood, **half-breed,** half-bred, half blood, half-caste

hygiene NOUNS hygienics; sanitation; public health, epidemiology; health physics; **preventive medicine,** prophylaxis, preventive dentistry, prophylactodontia

hygienic ADJS **healthful,** healthy, salubrious, salutary, wholesome, health-preserving, health-enhancing, life-promoting, **beneficial,** benign, good, **good for; hygienical,** hygeian, sanitary

hymn NOUNS **thanks, thanksgiving,** praise, laud, paean, benediction; grace, prayer of thanks; hymn of praise, **doxology, psalm, anthem,** motet, canticle, chorale; offertory, offertory sentence *or* hymn; hymnody, hymnology, hymnography, psalmody

hype NOUNS 1 **commendation,** good word, acknowledgment, recognition, appreciation; boost *and* buildup <both nonformal>; **puff,** promotion; **blurb** *and* **plug** *and* promo <all nonformal>
VERBS 2 boost *and* give a boost to <both nonformal>, puff, promote, cry up; plug *and* tout; pour *or* spread *or* lay it on thick <all nonformal>; **recommend, advocate,** put in a word *or* good word for, support, back, lend one's name *or* support *or* backing to, make a pitch for <nonformal>

hyperactive ADJS **overactive,** hyper <nonformal>; hectic, frenzied, frantic, frenetic; hyperkinetic

hypnotic ADJS 1 **mesmeric;** odylic; narcohypnotic; soporific, somniferous, somnifacient, sleep-inducing
2 **engrossing, absorbing,** consuming, **gripping,** riveting, holding, **arresting,** engaging, attractive, **fascinating, enthralling, spellbinding,** enchanting, magnetic, mesmerizing, mesmeric; obsessive, obsessing

hypnotist NOUNS **mesmerist,** hypnotizer, mesmerizer; Svengali, Mesmer

hypnotize VERBS **mesmerize,** magnetize; **entrance,** trance, put in a trance; **cast a**

spell, spell, **spellbind; have influence** *or* power *or* a hold over, lead by the nose, **twist** *or* **turn** *or* **wind around one's little finger; grip,** hold, arrest, hold the interest, fascinate, enthrall, hold spellbound, grab <nonformal>, charm, enchant

hypochondria NOUNS hypochondriasis, valetudinarianism; morbid anxiety

hypocrisy NOUNS hypocriticalness; Tartuffery, Tartuffism, Pecksniffery, pharisaism, **sanctimony**, sanctimoniousness, religiosity, false piety, ostentatious devotion, pietism, Bible-thumping <nonformal>; **falseness,** insincerity, duplicity, two-facedness

hypocrite NOUNS **phony** <nonformal>, sanctimonious fraud, pharisee, whited sepulcher, **canter,** snuffler, mealy-mouth; Tartuffe <Molière>, Pecksniff *and* Uriah Heep <both Charles Dickens>; **pietist,** religionist, religious hypocrite, canting hypocrite, pious fraud, religious *or* spiritual humbug, **pharisee**

a saint abroad and a devil at home
BUNYAN

hypocritical ADJS **insincere,** mealy-mouthed, unctuous, oily, disingenuous, smarmy <nonformal>; dishonest; **empty, hollow; sanctimonious,** sanctified, pious, pietistic, pietistical, self-righteous, pharisaic, pharisaical, **holier-than-thou, false**

hypodermic NOUNS **injection,** hypodermic injection, shot *and* bing <both nonformal>, hypospray *or* jet injection; booster, booster shot <nonformal>, needle <nonformal>

hypothesis NOUNS **theory, explanation,** proposed *or* tentative explanation, proposal, proposition, statement covering the facts or evidence; working hypothesis

hypothetical ADJS **theoretical,** hypothetic; postulatory, notional; **speculative, conjectural;** merely theoretical, academic, moot; impractical, armchair

hysteria NOUNS **fury, furor,** furore <Brit>, fire and fury; **passion, rage,** raging *or* tearing passion, towering rage *or* passion; madness, craze, **delirium**

hysterical ADJS **emotionalistic,** emotive, overemotional, hysteric, sensational, sensationalistic, melodramatic, theatric, theatrical, histrionic, dramatic, overdramatic, hammy <nonformal>, nonrational, unreasoning; overemotional, hyperthymic, in hysterics

I

ice NOUNS 1 frozen water; ice needle *or* crystal; **icicle**
VERBS 2 **refrigerate; cool, chill;** ice-cool; ice up, ice over, glaze, glaze over

iced ADJS **cooled, chilled; air-conditioned,** ice-cooled

icing NOUNS **topping,** frosting

icky ADJS

<nonformal> **nasty,** yecchy, yucky, gross, grungy, scuzzy

icon NOUNS **image, likeness; effigy,** idol; **symbol,** emblem, token, type; **alterpiece,** diptych, triptych

iconoclast NOUNS **destroyer, ruiner, wrecker, bane,** wiper-out, demolisher; idoloclast, idol breaker; **irreligionist**

idea NOUNS **thought,** mental *or* intellectual object, **notion, concept,** conception, conceit, fancy; **perception, sense, impression,** mental impression, image, **mental image,** picture in the mind, mental picture, representation, recept; imago; memory trace; **sentiment,** apprehension; reflection, observation; **opinion**; supposition, **theory**

ideal NOUNS 1 ideal type, acme, highest *or* perfect *or* best type; cynosure, apotheosis, idol; **shining example, hero, superhero; model,** the very model, role model, mirror, paragon, epitome
ADJS 2 **idealized;** utopian, Arcadian, Edenic, paradisal; pie in the sky <nonformal>; heavenly, celestial; millennial; **perfect, faultless, flawless,** unflawed, defectless, not to be improved, **impeccable,** absolute; **just right;** beyond all praise, irreproachable, unfaultable, *sans peur et sans reproche* <Fr>, **matchless, peerless**

idealist NOUNS **visionary;** utopian, utopianist, utopianizer

idealize VERBS utopianize, quixotize, rhapsodize; **romanticize,** romance; paint pretty pictures of, paint in bright colors; see through rose-colored glasses; **build castles in the air** *or* **Spain**

identical ADJS **same, selfsame,** one, **one and the same,** all the same, all one, of the same kidney; **indistinguishable,** without distinction, without difference, undifferent, undifferentiated; **alike, all alike, like,** just alike, exactly alike, like two peas in a pod

identification NOUNS identification mark; **badge,** identification badge, identification tag, dog tag <military>, personal identification number *or* PIN number *or* PIN, **identity card** *or* **ID card** *or* **ID; card,** business card, calling card, visiting card, *carte de visite* <Fr>, press card
2 likening, unification, coalescence, combination, union, fusion, merger, melding, synthesis

identify VERBS **signify, betoken,** stand for, differentiate, note <old>, speak of, talk, **indicate,** be indicative of, be an indication of, be significant of, connote, denominate, argue, bespeak, be symptomatic *or* diagnostic of, symptomize, **characterize, mark,** highlight, be the mark *or* sign of, give token, **denote, mean; define; place,** have; spot *and* nail *and* peg *and* cotton on <all nonformal>

identify with VERBS **sympathize,** empathize, respond to, understand one another, enter into one's views, enter into the ideas *or* feelings of; **accord,** correspond

identity NOUNS **sameness,** identicalness, selfsameness, indistinguishability, undifferentiation, nondifferentiation, two peas in a pod; **equality, parity,** par, equation; **personality,** personship, personal identity; **oneness,** unity, singleness, singularity, individuality

ideology NOUNS system of ideas, body of ideas, system of theories; world view, *Weltanschauung* <Ger>; philosophy; **ethos**

idiom NOUNS **phrase, expression, locution, utterance,** usage, term, verbalism; idiotism, phrasal idiom; turn of phrase *or* expression, peculiar expression, manner *or* way of speaking; set phrase *or* term; conventional *or* common *or* standard phrase

idiosyncrasy NOUNS **mannerism,** *minauderie* <Fr>, **trick of behavior,** idiocrasy, trick, **quirk,** habit, peculiarity, peculiar trait, trademark; **characteristic,** character, peculiarity, **property,** differentia, **eccentricity**

idiot NOUNS driveling *or* blithering *or* adenoidal *or* congenital idiot; **imbecile,**

moron, **half-wit,** natural, natural idiot, born fool, natural-born fool, mental defective, defective; cretin, basket case <nonformal>

idiotic ADJS **foolish, inane;** futile; **senseless, witless, thoughtless,** insensate, brainless; moronic, imbecile, imbecilic

idle VERBS 1 **fritter away,** fool away, fribble away, dribble away, drivel away, **trifle away,** dally away, potter away, piss away <nonformal>, muddle away, diddle away <nonformal>, squander in dribs and drabs; idle away, while away
2 **trifle, dally; flirt, coquet; toy,** fribble, **play, fool,** play at, **putter, potter,** tinker, **piddle; dabble,** smatter; toy with, fiddle with, fool with, play with
ADJS 3 **sluggish,** languid, languorous, lazy, slothful, indolent, slouchy; **inactive,** unactive; fallow, otiose; **unemployed, unoccupied,** disengaged, *désœvré* <Fr>, **jobless, out of work,** out of a job, out of harness; free, available, at liberty, at leisure; at loose ends

idol NOUNS 1 **hero, god, demigod,** phoenix; **heroine, goddess,** demigoddess; false god
2 fetish, totem, joss; **graven image, golden calf;** devil-god, Baal, Jaganatha *or* Juggernaut; sacred cow

the god of my idolatry
SHAKESPEARE

idolize VERBS **cherish, hold dear,** hold in one's heart *or* affections, think much *or* the world of, prize, treasure; **admire, regard,** esteem, revere; **adore,** worship, dearly love, think worlds *or* the world of, love to distraction; **revere, reverence,** hold in reverence, **venerate,** honor, look up to, defer to, bow to, exalt, put on a pedestal, hero-worship, deify, apotheosize, worship the ground one walks on, stand in awe of

idyllic ADJS **pacific,** peaceful, peaceable; **tranquil, serene;** pastoral, bucolic, eclogic

iffy ADJS **doubtful, in doubt,** *in dubio* <L>; dubitable, doubtable, **dubious,** questionable, problematic, problematical, speculative, conjectural, suppositional; **debatable,** moot, arguable, disputable, contestable, controvertible, **controversial,** refutable, confutable, deniable; **casual,** adventitious, incidental, contingent

ignite VERBS **set fire to, fire, set on fire, kindle,** enkindle, inflame, **light,** light up, strike a light, apply the match *or* torch to, torch <nonformal>, touch off, **burn,** conflagrate; **build a fire;** rekindle, relight, relume; feed, feed the fire, **stoke,** stoke the fire, add fuel to the flame; bank; poke *or* stir the fire, blow up the fire, fan the flame; open the draft

ignominious ADJS **disreputable,** discreditable, dishonorable, unsavory, shady, **seamy, sordid; unrespectable,** ignoble, infamous, inglorious; unpraiseworthy; derogatory

ignoramus NOUNS **know-nothing;** no scholar, puddinghead, dunce, fool; **illiterate; lowbrow** <nonformal>; unintelligentsia, illiterati

ignorance NOUNS **unknowingness,** unknowing, nescience; lack of information, knowledge-gap, hiatus of learning; empty-headedness, blankmindedness, vacuousness, vacuity, inanity; tabula rasa; **unacquaintance,** unfamiliarity; **greenness,** greenhornism, rawness, callowness, unripeness, green in the eye, **inexperience**; crass *or* gross *or* primal *or* pristine ignorance

ignorant ADJS nescient, **unknowing,** uncomprehending, **know-nothing;** simple, **dumb** <nonformal>, empty, empty-headed, blankminded, vacuous, inane, **unintelligent**; **ill-informed,** uninformed, unenlightened, unilluminated, unapprized, unposted <nonformal>, clueless *or* pig-ignorant <both Brit nonformal>

ignore VERBS **slight,** pooh-pooh <nonformal>, make little of, dismiss, pretend not to see, disregard, overlook, neglect, pass by, pass up *and* give the go-by <both nonformal>, leave out in the cold <nonformal>, take no note *or* notice of, look right through <nonformal>, pay no attention *or* regard to, refuse to acknowledge *or* recognize

ignored ADJS **neglected,** unattended to, untended, unwatched, unchaperoned, uncared-for; **disregarded,** unconsidered, unregarded, **overlooked, missed,** omitted, passed by, passed over, passed up <nonformal>, gathering dust, **slighted;** half-done, undone, left undone; deserted, abandoned

ilk NOUNS **kind, sort, type,** breed of cat <nonformal>, lot <nonformal>, **variety, species, genus,** *genre* <Fr>, phylum, denomination, designation, description, style, manner, **nature, character,** persuasion, the like *or* likes of <nonformal>

ill ADJS **ailing, sick, unwell, indisposed,** taken ill, down, bad, on the sick list; **sickish, seedy** *and* rocky <both nonformal>, **under the weather, out of sorts** <nonformal>, below par <nonformal>, off-color, off one's feed <nonformal>; not quite right, not oneself; faint, faintish, feeling faint; feeling awful *and* feeling something terrible <both nonformal>; sick as a dog *or* a pig <nonformal>, laid low; in a bad way, critically ill, in danger, on the critical list, on the guarded list, in intensive care; mortally ill, sick unto death
ADVS 2 **unkindly, unbenignly,** unbenignantly; **unamiably,** disagreeably, uncordially, ungraciously, inhospitably, ungenially, unsympathetically, uncompassionately; **badly,** bad <nonformal>, evil, evilly, wrong, wrongly, amiss

ill-advised ADJS **unwise,** injudicious, **imprudent,** unpolitic, impolitic, contraindicated, **counterproductive;** indiscreet; **ill-considered,** ill-gauged, ill-judged, ill-imagined, on the wrong track, unconsidered

illegal ADJS **unlawful, illegitimate, illicit,** nonlicit, nonlegal, lawless, wrongful, fraudulent, creative <nonformal>, **against the law; unauthorized,** unallowed, impermissible, unwarranted, unwarrantable, unofficial; **criminal, felonious**

illegality NOUNS **unlawfulness,** illicitness, lawlessness, wrongfulness; unauthorization, impermissibility; legal *or* technical flaw, legal irregularity; **outlawry;** collapse *or* breakdown *or* paralysis of authority, anomie

illegible ADJS **unreadable, unclear; undecipherable,** indecipherable

illegitimate ADJS **spurious,** false; **bastard,** misbegot, **misbegotten,** miscreated, gotten on the wrong side of the blanket, baseborn, born out of wedlock, without benefit of clergy

ill-equipped ADJS **unfitted, unfit,** ill-fitted, **unsuited, unadapted, unqualified,** disqualified, incompetent, incapable; **unequipped, unfurnished,** unarmed, ill-furnished, **unprovided,** ill-provided

ill-fated ADJS **ominous, portentous,** portending; **foreboding,** boding, **bodeful; inauspicious, ill-omened,** ill-boding, of ill *or* fatal omen, of evil portent, loaded *or* laden *or* freighted *or* fraught with doom, looming, looming over; fateful, doomful; apocalyptic; **unpropitious, unpromising, unfavorable, unfortunate, unlucky; sinister,** dark, black, gloomy, somber, dreary; **threatening, menacing, lowering;** bad, evil, ill, untoward; dire, baleful, baneful, ill-starred, evil-starred, star-crossed

ill health NOUNS **unhealthiness,** healthlessness; poor health, delicate *or* shaky *or* frail *or* fragile health; **sickliness,** peakedness <nonformal>, **feebleness,** delicacy, weakliness, fragility, **frailty; infirmity, unsoundness,** debility, debilitation, enervation; chronic ill health, invalidity, **invalidism**

illicit ADJS **illegal, unlawful, illegitimate,** nonlicit, nonlegal, lawless, wrongful, fraudulent, creative <nonformal>, **against the law; unauthorized,** unallowed, impermissible, unwarranted, unwarrantable, outlaw, outlawed; **adulterous,** extramarital, premarital; incestuous

ill-informed ADJS **uninformed,** unenlightened, unilluminated, unapprised, unposted <nonformal>, clueless <nonformal>; **unversed,** uninitiated, **unfamiliar,** strange to

illiterate NOUNS 1 **ignoramus, know-nothing;** no scholar, puddinghead, dunce, fool
ADJS 2 **uneducated,** unschooled, uninstructed, untutored, unbriefed, untaught, unedified, unguided; ill-educated, functionally illiterate, unlettered, grammarless

illness NOUNS **disease, sickness,** malady, ailment, indisposition, disorder, complaint, morbidity, *morbus* <L>, **affliction,** affection, **infirmity; sickishness,** malaise, seediness *and* rockiness <both nonformal>; complication, secondary disease *or* condition

illogical ADJS **unreasonable, irrational, reasonless,** contrary to reason, **senseless,** without reason, **without rhyme or reason; unscientific,** nonscientific, unphilosophical; **invalid,** inauthentic, unauthentic, faulty, flawed, paralogical, fallacious; **inconsistent,** incongruous, contradictory, **self-contradictory,** self-annulling, self-refuting, oxymoronic

ill repute NOUNS **disrepute,** bad repute,

bad *or* poor reputation, evil repute *or* reputation, ill fame, shady *or* unsavory reputation, **bad name,** bad odor, bad report, bad character; **disesteem, dishonor,** public dishonor, **discredit; disfavor,** ill-favor; disapprobation

ill-suited ADJS **inappropriate, inapt,** unapt, inapposite, misplaced, **irrelevant,** malapropos, *mal à propos* <Fr>; **unsuited, unfitted,** ill-fitted; **maladjusted,** ill-chosen; ill-matched, ill-mated, mismatched, mismated, mismarried, misallied; **unfit,** inept, unqualified; unfitting, unbefitting; **unsuitable,** improper, **unbecoming,** unseemly; **out of place,** out of line, out of keeping, out of character, out of proportion, out of joint, out of tune, out of time, out of season, out of its element

illuminated ADJS luminous, **lightened,** enlightened, brightened, **lighted,** lit, **lit up,** flooded *or* bathed with light, floodlit; irradiated, irradiate; **alight, glowing,** aglow, lambent, suffused with light; lamplit, lanternlit, candlelit, torchlit, gaslit, firelit; sunlit, moonlit, starlit

illuminating ADJS **explanatory,** explaining, exegetic, exegetical, **explicative,** explicatory; **expository,** expositive; **clarifying, elucidative, elucidatory;** illuminative, enlightening; illumining, **lighting, lightening,** brightening

illusion NOUNS **delusion,** deluded belief; **deception, trick;** self-deception, self-deceit, self-delusion; dereism, autism; **misconception, misbelief,** false belief, wrong impression, warped *or* distorted conception; **bubble, chimera,** vapor, *ignis fatuus* <L>, will-o'-the-wisp; **dream,** dream vision; dreamworld, dreamland, dreamscape; **daydream;** pipe dream *and* trip <nonformal>; fool's paradise

airy nothing
Shakespeare

illusionary ADJS **bewitching, witching;** illusory, illusive; **enchanting, entrancing, spellbinding, fascinating,** glamorous, Circean

illusory ADJS **deceptive, deceiving, misleading,** beguiling, **false, fallacious,** delusive, delusory; hallucinatory, illusive, illusionary; **unreal,** unrealistic, **immaterial**; **imaginary,** imagined, fantastic, fanciful, fancied

illustrate VERBS **demonstrate, show,** exemplify; exhibit, manifest, display, express, set forth

illustration NOUNS **representation, delineation,** presentment, drawing, portrayal, portraiture, depiction, depictment, rendering, rendition, characterization; exemplification, demonstration; **picture**

illustrative ADJS **explanatory,** clarifying, elucidative; illuminating, illuminative, enlightening; **demonstrative,** exemplificative; illustrational; pictorial, graphic, vivid

ill will NOUNS **animosity,** animus; ill feeling, bitter feeling, **hard feelings,** no love lost; **bitterness,** sourness, soreness, **rancor,** acrimony, virulence, venom, vitriol

image NOUNS **likeness; resemblance,** semblance, similitude, simulacrum; **effigy,** icon, idol; **copy**, fair copy; **portrait,** likeness; **perfect** *or* **exact likeness,** representation, duplicate, double; match, fellow, mate, companion, **twin;** living image, very image, very picture, living picture, dead ringer <nonformal>, spitting image *or* spit and image *or* spit 'n' image <all nonformal>; **figure of speech,** trope

imaginable ADJS fanciable, **conceivable, thinkable,** cogitable; **supposable**

imaginary ADJS notional; **imagined, fancied; unreal,** unrealistic, nonexistent, never-never; visional, supposititious, **all in the mind; illusory**

imagination NOUNS imagining, imaginativeness, **fancy, fantasy,** conceit <old>; mind's eye, flight of fancy, fumes of fancy

that inward eye which is the bliss of solitude
Wordsworth

imaginative ADJS conceptual, conceptive, ideational, ideative, notional; **inventive, original,** originative, esemplastic, shaping, **creative, ingenious; productive, fertile,** fecund, prolific, seminal, germinal, teeming, pregnant; **inspired,** visioned

imagine VERBS **fancy, conceive,** conceptualize, ideate, figure to oneself; **invent,** create, originate, make, think up, dream up, shape, mold, coin, hatch, concoct, fabricate, produce; **suppose**; **fantasize;**

give free rein to the imagination, let one's imagination run riot *or* run wild, allow one's imagination to run away with one; experience imaginatively *or* vicariously

imaging NOUNS **visualization, envisioning,** envisaging, picturing, objectification, calling to *or* before the mind's eye, figuring *or* portraying *or* representing in the mind; depicting *or* delineating in the imagination; conceptualization

imbalance NOUNS **inequality,** disparity, unevenness, contrariety, difference; **disproportion,** asymmetry; **unbalance,** disequilibrium, overbalance, inclination of the balance, overcompensation, tippiness; **injustice,** inequity

imbecile NOUNS 1 **idiot,** driveling *or* blithering *or* adenoidal *or* congenital idiot; **moron, half-wit,** born fool, natural-born fool, mental defective, defective; **simpleton,** simp <nonformal> ADJS 2 **foolish,** fool <nonformal>, foolheaded <nonformal>, **stupid, dumb** <nonformal>, **asinine;** buffoonish; **senseless,** witless, thoughtless, insensate, brainless; **idiotic,** moronic, imbecilic, **insane**

imbue VERBS **suffuse,** inform, transfuse, perfuse, diffuse, leaven; **infuse, infect,** inject, inoculate; **inculcate,** indoctrinate, catechize, **instill,** impregnate, **implant,** infix, impress

imitate VERBS **copy, repeat,** do like <nonformal>, do <nonformal>, act *or* go *or* make like <nonformal>; **mirror, reflect; echo,** reecho, chorus; **borrow,** steal one's stuff <nonformal>, take a leaf out of one's book; assume, **affect; simulate;** counterfeit, fake <nonformal>, hoke *and* hoke up <both nonformal>, forge, plagiarize, crib, lift <nonformal>; **parody,** pastiche; **paraphrase,** approximate

imitation NOUNS 1 **copying,** counterfeiting, repetition; **me-tooism** <nonformal>, emulation, the sincerest form of flattery, following, mirroring; copycat crime <nonformal>; **simulation**, modeling; fakery, forgery, plagiarism, plagiarizing, plagiary; **imposture, impersonation, takeoff** *and* hit-off <both nonformal>, **impression,** burlesque, pastiche, *pasticcio* <Ital>; mimesis; parody, onomatopoeia
ADJS 2 **mock, sham,** copied, fake *and* phony *and* bogus <all nonformal>, counterfeit, forged, plagiarized, unoriginal, ungenuine; **pseudo,** synthetic, synthetical, ersatz, hokey *and* hoked-up <both nonformal>

immaculate ADJS **chaste,** spotless, virtuous, pure; **clean,** squeaky-clean <nonformal>; blotless, stainless, taintless, white, snowy, pure *or* white as driven snow, guiltless, **innocent**

immature ADJS unadult; **inexperienced,** unseasoned, unfledged, new-fledged, **callow, unripe,** ripening, unmellowed, **raw, green,** vernal, primaveral, dewy, juicy, sappy, budding, tender, virginal, intact, innocent, naive, ingenuous, **undeveloped,** growing, unformed, unlicked, wet *or* not dry behind the ears; **minor,** underage, **puerile, childish;** childlike; **infantile**

immeasurable ADJS **vast,** vasty, boundless, **infinite**, cosmic, astronomical, galactic; **spacious,** amplitudinous, extensive; **tremendous,** stupendous, awesome, prodigious; incalculable, unreckonable, innumerable, incomprehensible, unfathomable; measureless, inexhaustible, endless, infinite, without end *or* limit, more than one can tell, more than you can shake a stick at <nonformal>, no end of *or* to

immediate ADJS **present,** attendant; immanent, indwelling, inherent, **available, accessible, at hand,** in view, within reach *or* sight *or* call, in place; **nearest,** nighest, **closest,** nearmost, next; **prompt, punctual, instant,** instantaneous, **quick**, speedy, swift, expeditious, summary, decisive, apt, alert, **ready,** Johnny-on-the-spot <nonformal>

immense ADJS **huge, vast, enormous,** astronomic, astronomical, humongous *and* jumbo <both nonformal>, king-size, queen-size, tremendous, prodigious, stupendous, macro, mega, giga; great big, larger than life, Homeric, mighty, **titanic, colossal, monumental,** heroic, heroical, epic, epical, towering, mountainous; **mammoth,** mastodonic; **gigantic, giant,** giantlike, gigantesque, gigantean

immersion NOUNS **submergence, submersion,** immergence, engulfment, **inundation,** burial; **dipping, ducking,** dousing, sousing, dunking <nonformal>, sinking; **baptism, baptizement; christening;** total immersion; **engross-**

ment, absorption, intentness, single-mindedness, **concentration, application,** study, studiousness, **preoccupation,** engagement, **involvement**

immigrant NOUNS **settler,** *habitant* <Canadian & Louisiana Fr>; **newcomer,** new arrival, *novus homo* <L>; greenhorn

immigration NOUNS in-migration, incoming population, foreign influx; border-crossing

imminent ADJS **impending,** impendent, **overhanging,** hanging over one's head, waiting, lurking, **threatening, looming,** lowering, **menacing,** lying in ambush; **brewing,** gathering, preparing; **coming, forthcoming, upcoming, to come,** about to be, about *or* going to happen, **approaching, nearing,** looming up, looming in the distance *or* future; **near, close,** immediate, instant, soon to be, **at hand,** near at hand, close at hand; **in the offing,** on the horizon, **in prospect,** already in sight, just around the corner, in view, in one's eye, in store, in reserve, **in the wind**

immobile ADJS **immovable,** unmovable, immotile, unmoving, **stationary,** frozen, not to be moved, at a standstill, on dead center; **firm, unyielding,** adamant, adamantine, rigid, **inflexible**

immodest ADJS unmodest; exhibitionistic; **shameless,** unashamed, unembarrassed, unabashed, unblushing, **brazen,** brazenfaced, brassy; **forward,** bold, pert, bumptious; **flagrant,** notorious, scandalous

immolation NOUNS **extermination,** destruction, destruction of life, taking of life, death-dealing, dealing of death, bane; ritual murder *or* killing, sacrifice; *auto-da-fé* <Sp, literally, act of faith>, martyrdom, martyrization; **oblation, offering, sacrifice,** incense; self-sacrifice, self-immolation; sutteeism

immoral ADJS **dishonorable;** unconscionable, shameless, without shame *or* remorse, **unscrupulous, unprincipled,** unethical, amoral; **corrupt,** corrupted, rotten

immortal ADJS everlasting, **deathless,** undying, never-dying, **imperishable,** incorruptible, amaranthine; fadeless, **unfading,** never-fading, ever-fresh

immortality NOUNS eternal life, **deathlessness,** imperishability, undyingness, incorruptibility *or* incorruption, athanasy *or* athanasia; eternal youth, fountain of youth; lasting *or* undying fame, secure place in history

immortalize VERBS **glorify,** glamorize; **exalt,** elevate, ensky, raise, uplift, set up, **ennoble,** aggrandize, magnify, exalt to the skies; crown; throne, enthrone; enshrine, make legendary, **perpetuate, preserve,** preserve from oblivion, keep fresh *or* alive, perennialize, **eternalize,** eternize

immovable ADJS unmovable, **immobile,** irremovable, stationary, frozen, not to be moved, at a standstill, on dead center; **firm, unyielding,** stubborn, adamant, adamantine, rigid, **inflexible**; pat, standpat <nonformal>

immune ADJS **resistant,** nonprone *or* nonsusceptible to disease; **exempt;** exempted, **released, excused,** immunized, excepted, let off <nonformal>, spared; grandfathered; permitted; dispensed; **unliable,** unsubject, irresponsible, unaccountable, unanswerable

immunity NOUNS **resistance,** nonproneness *or* nonsusceptibility to disease; **immunization; pardon,** excuse, impunity, sparing, **amnesty,** indemnity, exemption, reprieve, grace; **absolution,** shrift, remission, remission of sin; redemption; **exoneration, exculpation**

immunize VERBS **inoculate, vaccinate,** shoot <nonformal>

immutable ADJS **unchangeable,** not to be changed, changeless, unchanged, unchanging, unvarying, unvariable, **unalterable,** unaltered, unalterative, incommutable, inconvertible, unmodifiable; insusceptible of change; **inflexible,** unmalleable, intractable, untractable, intractile, **unbending, unyielding**, ungiving, **stubborn,** unalterable; irrevocable, indefeasible, **irreversible**

imp NOUNS **brat, minx,** puck, elf, gamin, little monkey, **whippersnapper,** young whippersnapper, *enfant terrible* <Fr>, little terror, holy terror; **pixie,** sprite, puck, kobold, *diablotin* <Fr>, tokoloshe, poltergeist, **gremlin**

impact NOUNS 1 **collision, clash,** appulse, **encounter,** meeting, impingement, **bump, crash,** crump, whomp; **carom,** carambole, cannon; sideswipe <nonformal>; smash *and* crunch <both nonformal>; **shock,** brunt; **concussion,** percussion

VERBS 2 operate on, **act on** *or* **upon, work on, affect, influence,** bear on, impact on; have to do with, treat, focus *or* concentrate on; bring to bear on; **run into,** bump into, bang into, slam into, smack into, **crash into,** smash into, carom into, **hit against,** strike against, knock against

impacted ADJS **stuck, jammed,** congested, packed, wedged

impaired ADJS **damaged,** hurt, injured, harmed; **deteriorated, worsened,** cut to the quick, aggravated, exacerbated, irritated, embittered; weakened; imperfect

impale VERBS **pierce, run through,** spit, **transfix,** transpierce; **spear,** lance, poniard, bayonet, saber, sword, put to the sword; spike

impart VERBS **communicate, tell,** lay on one <nonformal>, **convey, transmit,** transfer, send, send word, deliver *or* send a signal *or* message, **disseminate,** broadcast, pass, **pass on** *or* **along, hand on; report, render, make known,** get across *or* over; **disclose, reveal, let out, show,** discover, **leak,** let slip out, let the cat out of the bag *and* spill the beans <both nonformal>

impartial ADJS **impersonal, evenhanded,** fair, just, equitable, **dispassionate, disinterested,** detached, objective, lofty, Olympian; **unbiased,** uninfluenced, unswayed; **neutral**; selfless, unselfish

impasse NOUNS **corner** *and* **box** *and* **hole** <all nonformal>, cleft stick; cul-de-sac, blind alley, **dead end,** dead-end street; **extremity, end of one's rope** *or* **tether,** wit's end, nowhere to turn; **stalemate,** deadlock; stand, standoff, standstill, halt, stop

impassioned ADJS **fervent,** fervid, passionate, intense; **hearty, cordial,** enthusiastic, exuberant, unrestrained, vigorous; **zealous, ardent,** perfervid, **spirited,** vehement, abandoned, **warm,** heated, hot, hot-blooded, red-hot, fiery, white-hot, flaming, burning, afire, aflame, on fire

impassive ADJS **stolid,** inexcitable, **imperturbable,** undisturbable, **inexpressive,** unexpressive, unflappable <nonformal>; **dispassionate,** unpassionate; **steady;** stoic, stoical; **even-tempered;** bovine, expressionless, blank, dull; **patient**

impatient ADJS breathless; champing at the bit, rarin' to go <nonformal>; dying, **anxious, eager;** hopped-up *and* in a lather *and* in a sweat *or* stew <all nonformal>, excited; edgy, **on edge; restless,** restive, unquiet, uneasy, on *shpilkes* <Yiddish>; **fretful,** fretting, chafing, antsy-pantsy *and* antsy <both nonformal>, squirming, squirmy, about to pee *or* piss one's pants <nonformal>

impeach VERBS **denounce,** denunciate, **accuse**, decry, cry down, arraign, indict, call to account, exclaim *or* declaim *or* inveigh against, peg away at, cry out against, cry out on *or* upon, cry shame upon, raise one's voice against, raise a hue and cry against, shake up <old>

impeachable ADJS **blameworthy,** blamable, to blame, at fault, much at fault; **reprehensible,** censurable, reproachable, reprovable, open to criticism *or* reproach; **culpable,** chargeable, indictable, arraignable, imputable

impeachment NOUNS **arraignment,** indictment; **complaint, charge**; presentment; information; bill of indictment, true bill

impeccable ADJS **perfect, ideal, faultless, flawless,** unflawed, defectless, not to be improved, absolute; **just right;** spotless, stainless, taintless, unblemished, untainted, unspotted, immaculate, **pure,** uncontaminated, unadulterated, unmixed; chaste; beyond all praise, irreproachable, unfaultable, *sans peur et sans reproche* <Fr>, **matchless, peerless**

impede VERBS **hamper, cramp,** embarrass; trammel, entrammel, enmesh, entangle, ensnarl, entrap, entwine, involve, entoil, toil, net, lime, tangle, snarl; **encumber,** cumber, **burden,** lumber, **saddle with,** weigh *or* weight down, press down; hang like a millstone round one's neck; **handicap,** put at a disadvantage; cripple, hobble, hamstring

impediment NOUNS embarrassment, hamper; encumbrance, cumbrance; **trouble,** difficulty; **handicap,** disadvantage, inconvenience, penalty; **burden,** imposition, onus, cross, weight, deadweight, ball and chain, millstone around one's neck

impel VERBS give an impetus, **set going** *or* agoing, put *or* set in motion, give momentum; **drive, move,** animate, actuate, forward; **thrust,** power; drive *or* whip on; goad; motivate, incite; compel

impending ADJS **imminent,** impendent, **overhanging,** hanging over one's head, waiting, lurking, **threatening, looming,** lowering, **menacing,** lying in ambush, **brewing,** gathering, preparing; **coming, forthcoming, upcoming, to come,** about to be, about *or* going to happen, **approaching, nearing,** looming, looming up, looming in the distance *or* future; **near, close,** immediate, instant, soon to be, **at hand,** near at hand, close at hand; **in the offing,** on the horizon, **in prospect,** already in sight, just around the corner, in view, in one's eye, in store, in reserve, **in the wind**

impenetrable ADJS **impregnable, invulnerable,** inviolable, inexpugnable; **unassailable,** unattackable, insuperable, unsurmountable; resistless, **irresistible; invincible,** indomitable, **unconquerable,** incontestable, unbeatable; **dense,** thick, heavy, overgrown, overrun; **unfathomable,** inscrutable, ambiguous; **incoherent,** unconnected, rambling; **past comprehension,** beyond one's comprehension, beyond understanding; Greek to one

imperative NOUNS 1 **urgent need,** dire necessity; **exigency** *or* exigence, **urgency,** imperativeness, immediacy, pressingness, pressure; matter of necessity, case of need *or* emergency, **matter of life and death**

ADJS 2 **mandatory,** mandated, **compulsory,** prescript, prescriptive, **obligatory,** must <nonformal>; decisive, final, peremptory, absolute, eternal, written, hard-and-fast, carved in stone, set in concrete <nonformal>, ultimate, conclusive, binding, irrevocable, without appeal; **urgent,** imperious, **compelling, pressing,** high-priority, high-pressure, crying, clamorous, insistent, instant, exigent

imperfect ADJS not perfect; unperfected; **defective, faulty, inadequate, deficient,** short, not all it's cracked up to be <nonformal>, lacking, wanting, found wanting, erroneous, **fallible;** inaccurate, inexact, imprecise; **unsound, incomplete,** unfinished, partial, patchy, sketchy, uneven, unthorough; **damaged,** impaired; **blemished**; half-baked <nonformal>, immature, undeveloped; impure, adulterated, mixed

imperious ADJS imperial, **lordly,** magisterial; arrogant; **arbitrary,** peremptory, imperative; absolute, absolutist, absolutistic; **dictatorial,** authoritarian; **bossy** <nonformal>, **domineering,** high-handed, overbearing, overruling; autocratic, monocratic, **despotic, tyrannical;** tyrannous, grinding, oppressive

impermeable ADJS **impervious,** impenetrable; **impassable,** unpassable; unpierceable, unperforable

impersonal ADJS **reticent, reserved,** restrained, nonassertive, low-key, low-keyed, constrained; guarded, discreet; backward, **retiring,** shrinking; **aloof, standoffish,** offish <nonformal>, standoff, **distant,** remote, removed, **detached,** Olympian, withdrawn; **cool,** cold, frigid, icy, frosty, chilled, chilly; **impartial, evenhanded,** equitable, **dispassionate, disinterested,** detached, objective, lofty

impersonate VERBS **mimic,** ape, parrot, copycat <nonformal>; do an impression; take off, hit off, hit off on, take off on

impersonator NOUNS **imitator,** impostor, **mimic,** mimicker, mimer, mime, **mocker; faker,** pretender; sham, shammer, **humbug,** *blagueur* <Fr>, **fraud** <nonformal>, **fake** *and* **faker** *and* **phony** <all nonformal>, **fourflusher** <nonformal>, bluff, bluffer; poser, poseur; female impersonator

impertinent ADJS **impudent,** flip <nonformal>, flippant, **cocky** *and* cheeky *and* **fresh** *and* facy *and* crusty *and* nervy <all nonformal>, *chutzpadik* <Yiddish>; **rude, disrespectful,** derisive, brash, bluff; **saucy,** sassy <nonformal>; smart *or* smart-alecky <nonformal>, smart-ass *or* wise-ass <nonformal>

impervious ADJS **impenetrable,** impermeable; **impassable,** unpassable; unpierceable, unperforable; **uninfluenceable,** unswayable, unmovable

impetuous ADJS **impulsive, hasty,** overhasty, quick, sudden; quick on the draw *or* trigger *or* uptake, hair-trigger; **precipitate,** headlong; **reckless, rash**; impatient; **reckless,** devil-may-care; careless; hotheaded, volatile, giddy, dizzy, ditzy <nonformal>, scatterbrained, mercurial, moody, flighty

impetus NOUNS **acceleration,** quickening; step-up, speedup; thrust, drive, momentum

impiety NOUNS **impiousness; irrever-**

ence, undutifulness; **sacrilege,** blasphemy, blaspheming; **profanity,** profaneness; sacrilegiousness, blasphemousness; **desecration,** profanation

impinge VERBS **intrude,** encroach, infringe, trespass, trespass on *or* upon, trench, entrench, invade, infiltrate; **break in upon,** break in, **collide,** come into collision, be on a collision course, **clash,** meet, encounter, confront each other

impish ADJS **puckish, elfish,** elvish; mischievous

implant VERBS transplant; infix; fit in, **inlay; inculcate, indoctrinate,** catechize, inoculate, **instill, infuse,** imbue, impregnate, infix, impress; **impress upon the mind** *or* **memory,** urge on the mind, beat into, beat *or* knock into one's head, grind in, drill into, drum into one's head *or* skull

implement NOUNS 1 **instrument, tool, appliance,** device; contrivance, mechanism; **agent**; medium, mediator, intermedium, intermediary, intermediate, interagent, liaison, go-between; expediter, facilitator, animator; **cat's-paw,** puppet, dummy, pawn, creature, minion VERBS 2 **carry out,** carry through, go through, fulfill, work out; **bring off,** carry off; **put through,** get through; put into effect, **put in** *or* **into practice,** carry into effect, translate into action; effect, effectuate, set in motion, put in force

implicate VERBS **involve,** tangle, **entangle,** embarrass, enmesh, engage, **draw in,** drag *or* hook *or* suck into, catch up in, **make a party to;** interest, concern; **absorb**

implication NOUNS **connotation, import,** latent *or* underlying *or* implied meaning, ironic suggestion *or* implication, what is read between the lines; **suggestion,** allusion; coloration, tinge, undertone, overtone, undercurrent, more than meets the eye *or* ear, something between the lines, intimation, touch, nuance, innuendo; **hint**; **inference, supposition,** presupposition, assumption, presumption; undermeaning, subsidiary sense, **subtext;** cryptic *or* hidden *or* esoteric *or* arcane meaning

implicit ADJS **tacit, implied,** understood, taken for granted, intrinsic, **inherent,** resident, immanent, indwelling; unquestioning, undoubting, unhesitating

implied ADJS implicated, involved; **meant,** indicated; **suggested,** intimated, insinuated, hinted; **tacit,** implicit, understood, taken for granted

implode VERBS **collapse,** cave, cave in, fall in; fold, fold up; **deflate,** let the air out of, take the wind out of; puncture

implore VERBS **entreat,** beseech, **beg,** crave, **plead,** appeal, pray, **supplicate,** impetrate, obtest; adjure, conjure; **call on** *or* **upon,** cry on *or* upon, **appeal to,** cry to, run to; go cap *or* hat in hand to; kneel to, go down on one's knees to, fall on one's knees to, go on bended knee to, throw oneself at the feet of; **plead for,** clamor for, cry for, cry out for; call for help

imply VERBS **implicate, involve,** import, connote, entail; mean; **suggest, connote,** lead one to believe, bring to mind; **hint,** insinuate, infer, intimate; **allude to,** point to from afar, point indirectly to; write between the lines; **suppose, presuppose,** assume, presume, take for granted; mean to say *or* imply *or* suggest

impolite ADJS **discourteous,** uncourteous; unpolite; **rude, uncivil,** ungracious, ungallant, uncourtly, inaffable, uncomplaisant, unaccommodating; disrespectful; **insolent**

import NOUNS 1 **meaning, significance,** signification, *significatum* <L>, *signifié* <Fr>, point, **sense,** idea, where one is coming from <nonformal>; **implication, connotation,** latent *or* underlying *or* implied meaning, ironic suggestion *or* implication, what is read between the lines; meaning; **suggestion,** allusion; coloration, tinge, undertone, overtone, undercurrent, more than meets the eye *or* ear, something between the lines, intimation, touch, nuance, innuendo VERBS 2 **transfer,** transmit, transpose, translocate, transplace; **transplant,** translate; **pass,** pass over, **hand over,** turn over, carry over, make over, consign, assign; **deliver**; pass on, hand forward, hand on, relay; transfuse, perfuse, transfer property *or* right

importance NOUNS **significance, consequence,** consideration, **import,** note, mark, moment, weight, **gravity;** materiality; concern, concernment, interest; **first order,** high order, high rank; **priority,** primacy, precedence, preeminence, paramountcy, superiority, **supremacy;** value, worth, merit

important ADJS **major,** consequential, momentous, **significant, considerable,** substantial, material, **great,** grand, big; superior, world-shaking, earthshaking; big-time *and* big-league *and* major-league *and* heavyweight <all nonformal>; high-powered <nonformal>

important person NOUNS 1 **personage,** person of importance *or* consequence, **great man** *or* **woman,** man *or* woman of mark *or* note, **somebody, notable,** notability, figure; **celebrity,** famous person, person of renown, personality; name, big name, nabob, **mogul,** panjandrum, person to be reckoned with, very important person; mover and shaker, lord of creation; **worthy,** pillar of society, **dignitary, magnate;** tycoon <nonformal>, baron; power; brass, top brass; top people, the great; ruling circle, lords of creation

2 < nonformal> **big shot,** wheel, **big wheel,** big boy, big cat, big fish, big shot, biggie, big cheese, big noise, big-timer, big-time operator, **bigwig,** big man, big gun, **high-muck-a-muck** *or* high-muckety-muck, lion, something, **VIP** brass hat, high man on the totem pole, suit; sacred cow, little tin god, tin god; big man on campus *or* BMOC; 800-pound gorilla; queen bee, heavy mama

impose VERBS **prescribe,** require, demand, dictate, lay down, set, fix, appoint, make obligatory *or* mandatory; **oblige, necessitate, require,** exact, demand, **dictate,** call for; **exact,** assess, levy, **tax,** assess a tax upon, slap a tax on <nonformal>, lay *or* put a duty on, make dutiable, subject to a tax *or* fee *or* duty, collect a tax *or* duty on; tithe

impose upon VERBS **impose on,** take advantage of; **presume upon**; use ill, ill-use, abuse, misuse; **inconvenience,** put to inconvenience, **put out,** discommode, incommode, disoblige, **burden, embarrass; trouble, bother,** put to trouble, put to the trouble of

imposing ADJS **dignified, stately,** grand, courtly, magisterial, aristocratic; worthy, **august, venerable;** impressive, larger-than-life, awful, awe-inspiring, awesome; **sumptuous,** elegant, elaborate, luxurious, extravagant, deluxe; executive *and* plush *and* posh *and* ritzy *and* swank *and* swanky <all nonformal>; formidable, awe-inspiring

imposition NOUNS **infliction,** laying on *or* upon, charging, taxing, tasking; burdening, weighting *or* weighting down, freighting, loading *or* loading down, heaping on *or* upon, imposing an onus; **exaction, demand**; unwarranted demand, obtrusiveness, presumptuousness; inconvenience, trouble, bother; inconsiderateness

impossibility NOUNS impossibleness, the realm *or* domain of the impossible, **inconceivability,** unthinkability, unimaginability, what cannot be, what can never be, what cannot happen, hopelessness, Chinaman's chance *and* a snowball's chance in hell <both nonformal>, **no chance**; **self-contradiction,** absurdity, paradox, oxymoron, logical impossibility; impossible, the impossible

impossible ADJS **not possible,** beyond the bounds of possibility *or* reason, contrary to reason, at variance with the facts; **inconceivable,** unimaginable, unthinkable, not to be thought of, out of the question; hopeless; **absurd,** ridiculous, preposterous; **self-contradictory,** paradoxical, oxymoronic, logically impossible; **ruled-out,** excluded, closed-out, **barred,** prohibited

impostor NOUNS **ringer; impersonator; pretender;** sham, shammer, humbug, *blagueur* <Fr>, fraud <nonformal>, **fake** *and* **faker** *and* **phony** <all nonformal>, fourflusher <nonformal>, bluff, bluffer; **wolf in sheep's clothing,** ass in lion's skin, jackdaw in peacock's feathers; poser, poseur

impotent ADJS **powerless,** forceless, out of gas <nonformal>; **uninfluential;** feeble, soft, flabby, **weak**, weak as a kitten, wimpy *or* wimpish <nonformal>; **unsexual,** unsexed; **sexless,** asexual, **neuter,** neutral; castrated, emasculated, eunuchized; **cold, frigid**

impound VERBS **confine, shut in,** shut away, coop in, hem in, fence in *or* up, wall in *or* up, rail in; **shut up, coop up, pen up,** box up, mew up, bottle up, cork up, seal up; **confiscate,** sequester, sequestrate

impoverished ADJS **indigent,** poverty-stricken; **needy,** poor, necessitous, **in need, in want,** disadvantaged, deprived, underprivileged; **pauperized,**

starveling; **down at heels,** down at the heel, on *or* down on one's uppers, out at the heels, out at elbows, in rags; on welfare, on relief, on the dole <Brit>

impractical ADJS **impracticable,** unpragmatic, unfeasible; **unachievable,** unattainable, unrealizable, uncompassable; unpractical, inconvenient, unrealistic; dysfunctional, unworkable; **ill-advised,** ill-considered, unwise

impregnable ADJS impenetrable, **invulnerable,** inviolable, inexpugnable; **unassailable,** unattackable, insuperable, unsurmountable; resistless, **irresistible; invincible,** indomitable, **unconquerable,** unyielding, incontestable, unbeatable, more than a match for; overpowering, overwhelming

impregnate VERBS 1 **inseminate,** spermatize, knock up <nonformal>, **get with child** *or* **young; pollinate** *or* pollinize, pollen; cross-fertilize, cross-pollinate *or* cross-pollinize
2 **inculcate, indoctrinate,** catechize, inoculate, instill, infuse, imbue, **implant,** infix, impress

impresario NOUNS **showman,** exhibitor, **producer**

impress VERBS 1 **affect, strike, hit,** smite, rock; **make an impression, get to one** <nonformal>; make a dent in, make an impact upon, sink in <nonformal>, strike home, come home to, hit the mark <nonformal>; tell, have a strong effect, traumatize, strike hard, impress forcibly; **inculcate, indoctrinate,** catechize, inoculate, **instill, infuse,** imbue, **implant,** infix; **impress upon the mind** *or* **memory,** urge on the mind, beat into, beat *or* knock into one's head, grind in, drill into, drum into one's head *or* skull; **condition, brainwash, program**
2 **mark,** make a mark, put a mark on; **brand,** stigmatize; stamp, seal, punch, imprint, **print, engrave**
3 **conscript,** draft, induct, press, commandeer; **recruit, muster,** levy, raise, muster in

impressed ADJS 1 **affected,** moved, touched; impressed with *or* by, penetrated with, seized with, imbued with, devoured by, obsessed, obsessed with *or* by; wrought up by; stricken, wracked, racked, torn, agonized, tortured; worked up, all worked up, **excited**
2 **printed,** imprinted, stamped; indelibly impressed; engraved, etched, graven, embossed; **dyed-in-the-wool**

impression NOUNS **sense,** deep *or* profound sense, gut sense *or* sensation <nonformal>; **sensation**; undercurrent; hunch, feeling in one's bones, presentiment; foreboding; **perception,** mental impression, image, **mental image,** picture in the mind, mental picture, representation; intuition, intuitive impression; **opinion, sentiment,** reaction, **notion, idea, thought,** mind, thinking, **way of thinking, attitude,** stance, posture, position, mindset, **view,** point of view

impressionable ADJS **teachable,** instructable, educable, schoolable, trainable; docile, **malleable, moldable,** pliable, facile, plastic, susceptible, formable; **suggestible, susceptible**

impressive ADJS **exciting, thrilling,** thrilly <nonformal>, **stirring, moving, breathtaking,** eye-popping <nonformal>; striking, telling; **imposing,** larger-than-life, awful, awe-inspiring, awesome; **convincing,** convictional, well-founded, **persuasive,** assuring, satisfying, satisfactory, confidence-building

imprison VERBS **incarcerate, intern,** immure; **jail,** gaol <Brit>, jug <nonformal>, throw into jail, throw under the jailhouse <nonformal>; throw *or* cast in prison, clap in jail *or* prison, send up the river <nonformal>; **lock up,** hold captive, hold prisoner, hold in captivity; hold under close *or* house arrest

improbable ADJS **unlikely,** unpromising, hardly possible, logic-defying, scarcely to be expected *or* anticipated; statistically improbable; **doubtful,** dubious, **questionable,** doubtable, dubitable, more than doubtful; **implausible,** incredible; unlooked-for, unexpected, unpredictable

impromptu ADJS 1 **extemporaneous, extemporary,** extempore, unrehearsed, **improvised,** improvisatory, improvisatorial, improviso, *improvisé* <Fr>; **ad-lib,** *ad libitum* <L>; **ad-hoc,** stopgap, makeshift, jury-rigged; **offhand,** off the top of one's head *and* off-the-cuff <both nonformal>, **spur-of-the-moment, quick and dirty** <nonformal>
ADVS 2 **extemporaneously, extemporarily,** extempore, *à l'improviste* <Fr>, **ad lib, offhand,** out of hand; off the top of one's head *and* off the cuff <both nonformal>

improper ADJS **wrong,** wrongful; **incorrect, indecorous,** undue, unseemly; unfit, unfitting, unsuitable; **inappropriate; indecent,** indelicate, inelegant, unseemly, unbecoming, indiscreet

impropriety NOUNS **unfitness,** inappropriateness, unsuitability; **inaptness,** inaptitude, **inappositeness, irrelevance** *or* irrelevancy, infelicity, uncongeniality, inapplicability, inadmissibility; **awkwardness,** unfitness, unfittingness, wrongness, unsuitability

improve VERBS 1 **grow better,** look better, show improvement, **mend,** meliorate, ameliorate; **look up** *or* **pick up** *or* **perk up** <all nonformal>; **develop,** shape up; **advance, progress, make progress, make headway, gain,** gain ground, go forward, get *or* go ahead, come on, come along *and* come along nicely <both nonformal>, get along; make strides *or* rapid strides, take off *and* skyrocket <both nonformal>
2 **train; prepare,** ready, **condition, groom,** fit, put in tune, form, **lick into shape** <nonformal>; **cultivate,** develop, improve; **nurture, foster,** nurse; **discipline,** take in hand; ameliorate, meliorate, mitigate

improvement NOUNS **betterment,** bettering, change for the better; melioration, **amelioration; mend,** mending, **amendment; progress,** progression, headway; breakthrough, quantum jump *or* leap; **advance,** advancement; upward mobility; **promotion, furtherance,** preferment; **rise,** ascent, **lift, uplift,** uptick <nonformal>, upswing, uptrend, upbeat; **increase**, upgrade, upping *and* boost *and* pickup <all nonformal>; gentrification; **enhancement, enrichment;** euthenics, eugenics; **restoration,** revival, retro, recovery

improvident ADJS **prodigal,** unproviding; **thriftless, unthrifty,** uneconomical; grasshopper; hand-to-mouth; **shiftless, feckless, thoughtless, heedless;** happy-go-lucky; negligent

improvisation NOUNS **extemporization,** improvision, improvising, extempore <old>, **impromptu, ad-lib,** ad-libbing *and* playing by ear <both nonformal>, **ad hoc measure** *or* solution, adhocracy <nonformal>, ad hockery *or* hocery *or* hocism <nonformal>; temporary measure *or* arrangement, *pro tempore* measure *or* arrangement, **stopgap, makeshift,** jury-rig <naut>; cannibalization; bricolage

improvise VERBS **extemporize,** improv *and* tapdance *and* talk off the top of one's head <all nonformal>, speak off the cuff, think on one's feet, make it up as one goes along, play it by ear <nonformal>, throw away *or* depart from the prepared text, throw away the speech, scrap the plan, **ad-lib** <nonformal>, **do offhand,** wing it <nonformal>, vamp, fake <nonformal>, play by ear <nonformal>; **dash off, strike off,** knock off, throw off, toss off *or* out; make up, whip up, **cook up,** run up, rustle up *or* whomp up <nonformal>, slap up *or* together *and* throw *or* slap together <all nonformal>, lash up <Brit>, cobble up; jury-rig; cannibalize

improvised ADJS **makeshift,** makeshifty, **stopgap,** band-aid <nonformal>, improvisational, **jury-rigged; last-ditch; ad hoc;** quick and dirty <nonformal>; temporary, provisional, tentative

imprudent ADJS **unwise,** injudicious, unpolitic, impolitic, contraindicated, **counterproductive;** indiscreet; inconsiderate, thoughtless, mindless, witless, unthoughtful, unthinking, unreflecting, unreflective; **unreasonable, unsound, unsensible,** senseless, insensate, reasonless, **irrational,** reckless, inadvisable; inexpedient; **ill-advised,** ill-considered, on the wrong track, unconsidered; unadvised, misadvised, misguided

impudent ADJS **impertinent, pert,** flip <nonformal>, flippant, **cocky** *and* cheeky *and* **fresh** *and* facy *and* crusty *and* nervy <all nonformal>, *chutzpadik* <Yiddish>; uncalled-for, gratuitous, biggety <nonformal>; **rude, disrespectful,** derisive, brash, bluff; **saucy,** sassy <nonformal>; smart *or* smart-alecky <nonformal>, smart-ass *or* wise-ass <nonformal>

impulse NOUNS natural impulse, blind impulse, **instinct,** urge, drive; vagrant *or* fleeting impulse; involuntary impulse, reflex, knee jerk, automatic response; gut response *or* reaction <nonformal>; **notion, fancy; sudden thought,** flash, inspiration, brainstorm, brain wave, quick hunch

impulsive ADJS **impetuous, hasty,** overhasty, quick, sudden; quick on the draw *or* trigger *or* uptake, hair-trigger; **pre-**

cipitate, headlong; **reckless, rash**; impatient

impure ADJS **unclean, unwashed,** unbathed, unscrubbed, unscoured, unswept, unwiped; unpure; **polluted,** contaminated, infected, corrupted; ritually unclean *or* impure *or* contaminated, *tref* <Yiddish>, *terefah* <Heb>, nonkosher; not to be handled without gloves; **uncleanly; unchaste, unvirtuous,** unvirginal; indecent; soiled, sullied, smirched, besmirched, defiled, tainted, maculate

impurity NOUNS **uncleanness,** immundity; unpureness; **dirtiness,** grubbiness, dinginess, griminess, messiness *and* grunginess *and* scuzziness <all nonformal>, scruffiness, slovenliness, sluttishness, untidiness; miriness, muddiness; uncleanliness; **unchastity,** unchasteness; unvirtuousness; **indecency**

impute VERBS **attribute,** assign, ascribe, give, place, put, apply, attach, refer

in NOUNS 1 **entrée,** entry, **entrance**, **access,** opening, **open door,** open arms; a foot in the door, opening wedge, the camel's nose under the wall of the tent
ADJS 2 **participating, participative,** participant, participatory; involved, engaged, **in on** <nonformal>; implicated, accessory; **partaking, sharing; on good terms,** on a good footing, on friendly *or* amicable terms, **on speaking terms,** on a first-name basis, on visiting terms; **in good with,** in with *and* on the in with <both nonformal>, **in favor, in one's good graces,** in one's good books, on the good *or* right side of <nonformal>
ADVS 3 inward, inwards, inwardly; thereinto; inside, within; herein, therein, wherein

inability NOUNS **incapability, incapacity,** incapacitation, **incompetence** *or* incompetency, inadequacy, insufficiency, ineptitude, **inferiority**, inefficiency, unfitness; disability, disablement, disqualification; legal incapacity, wardship, minority, infancy

inaccessible ADJS **out-of-the-way,** godforsaken, back of beyond, upcountry; **out of reach,** unapproachable, untouchable, hyperborean, antipodean; **aloof, standoffish,** offish, standoff, **distant, remote,** withdrawn, removed, detached, Olympian

inaccurate ADJS **incorrect, inexact,** unfactual, **unprecise,** imprecise, unspecific, loose, lax, unrigorous; negligent; **vague;** approximate, approximative; out of line, out of plumb, out of true, out of square

inactivate VERBS **disarm,** unarm, put out of action, put *hors de combat;* **put out of order,** put out of commission <nonformal>, throw out of gear; bugger *and* bugger up *and* queer *and* queer the works *and* gum up *or* screw up <all nonformal>, throw a wrench *or* monkey wrench in the machinery <nonformal>, sabotage, wreck; kibosh *and* put the kibosh on <both nonformal>; spike, spike one's guns, put a spoke in one's wheels

inactive ADJS unactive; stationary, static, at a standstill; sedentary; **quiescent,** motionless

inadequacy NOUNS **unskillfulness, incompetence** *or* incompetency, inability, incapability, incapacity; ineffectiveness, **ineffectuality; shortcoming,** falling short, not measuring up, coming up short, **shortfall; insufficiency,** inadequateness, **deficiency,** lack, want, shortage

inadequate ADJS **insufficient,** unsufficing; found wanting, defective, incomplete, imperfect, deficient, lacking, failing, wanting; **too few,** undersupplied; **too little,** not enough, precious little, a trickle *or* mere trickle; **unsatisfactory,** unsatisfying

inadmissible ADJS **unacceptable,** unsuitable, undesirable, **objectionable,** exceptionable, impossible, untenable, indefensible; **intolerable**

inadvertent ADJS **unthinking,** unreasoning, unreflecting, uncalculating, unthoughtful, **thoughtless,** heedless, careless, inconsiderate; unguarded; arbitrary, capricious

inadvisable ADJS **inexpedient,** undesirable, counterproductive, impolitic, impolitical, unpolitic, not to be recommended, contraindicated; **impractical, impracticable,** dysfunctional, unworkable; **ill-advised,** ill-considered, unwise; **inappropriate,** unsuitable, unmeet, inapt, inept, unseemly, **improper, wrong,** bad, out of place, out of order, incongruous, ill-suited; malapropos, *mal à propos* <Fr>, inopportune, untimely, ill-timed, badly timed, unseasonable;

infelicitous, unfortunate, unhappy; unprofitable; futile

inalienable ADJS **inherent,** resident, implicit, immanent, indwelling; unalienable, unquestionable, unchallengeable, irreducible, **inseparable,** impartible, **indivisible,** undividable, indissoluble, bound up in *or* with

inalterable ADJS **permanent, unchanged,** unchangeable, unvaried, **unaltered,** inviolate, undestroyed, intact; **constant, persistent,** sustained, fixed, firm, solid, steadfast, like the Rock of Gibraltar, faithful

inane ADJS **empty-headed,** empty-minded, empty-noddled, empty-pated, empty-skulled; **vacuous,** vacant, empty, hollow, vapid, jejune, blank, airheaded *and* bubbleheaded <both nonformal>; **rattlebrained,** rattleheaded; scatter-brained; **fatuous,** fatuitous, inept

inanimate ADJS inanimated, unanimated, exanimate, azoic, nonliving, dead, **lifeless,** soulless; inert; insentient, unconscious, nonconscious, **insensible,** insensate, senseless, unfeeling

inappropriate ADJS **vulgar,** inelegant, indelicate, indecorous, indecent, improper, unseemly, unbeseeming, unbecoming, unfitting, unsuitable, **ungenteel,** undignified; **untasteful,** tasteless, in bad *or* poor taste, tacky *and* chintzy *and* Mickey Mouse <all nonformal>; **offensive,** offensive to gentle ears; malapropos, *mal à propos* <Fr>, infelicitous, unfortunate, unhappy

inarticulate ADJS **indistinct,** blurred, muzzy; incomprehensible

inattentive ADJS **unmindful,** inadvertent, thoughtless, **incurious**, **indifferent**; **heedless,** unheeding, unheedful, regardless, *distrait* <Fr>, **disregardful,** disregardant; **unobserving,** inobservant, unobservant, unnoticing, unnoting, unremarking, unmarking; **distracted**; **careless,** negligent; **scatter-brained,** giddy, flighty

inaudible ADJS **silent, still,** stilly, quiet, quiescent, hushed, soundless, noiseless; subaudible, below the limen *or* threshold of hearing, unhearable; quiet as a mouse, mousy; silent as a post *or* stone, so quiet that one might hear a feather *or* pin drop; **unsounded, unvoiced,** unvocalized, unpronounced, unuttered, unarticulated

inaugurate VERBS institute, **found, establish,** set up <nonformal>; **install,** initiate, induct; **introduce,** broach, bring up, lift up, raise; **launch,** float; **usher in,** ring in <nonformal>; **set on foot,** set abroach, set agoing, turn on, kick-start *and* jump-start <both nonformal>, start up, start going, start the ball rolling <nonformal>

inauguration NOUNS **establishment,** foundation, constitution, institution, installation, formation, **organization,** inception, setting-up, realization, materialization, effectuation

inborn ADJS **innate,** born, congenital; **native, natural,** natural to, connatural, native to, indigenous; **inbred,** genetic, hereditary, inherited, bred in the bone, in the blood, running in the blood *or* race *or* strain, radical, rooted; connate, connatal, coeval; **instinctive,** instinctual, atavistic, primal

inbred ADJS **innate, inborn,** born, congenital; **genetic,** hereditary, inherited, bred in the bone, in the blood, running in the blood *or* race *or* strain, radical, rooted; connate, connatal, coeval; **instinctive,** instinctual, atavistic, primal

incalculable ADJS **infinite,** boundless, endless, limitless, termless, shoreless; illimitable, **interminable,** interminate; **immeasurable,** unreckonable, innumerable, incomprehensible, unfathomable; measureless, countless, sumless; unmeasurable, immense, unplumbed, untold, unnumbered, without measure *or* number *or* term

incandescent ADJS **burning, ignited,** kindled, enkindled, **blazing,** ablaze, ardent, flaring, flaming, aflame, inflamed, alight, **afire, on fire,** in flames, in a blaze; **glowing,** aglow, in a glow, candescent, candent; sparking, scintillating, scintillant, ignescent

incantation NOUNS **conjuration,** magic words *or* formula; hocus-pocus, abracadabra, mumbo jumbo

incapable ADJS **incompetent,** unable, inadequate, unequipped, unqualified, ill-qualified, out of one's depth, outmatched, **unfit, unfitted,** unadapted, not equal *or* up to, not cut out for <nonformal>; ineffective, **ineffectual;** maladjusted

incapacitated ADJS **disabled; crippled,** hamstrung; disqualified, invalidated; disarmed; paralyzed; hog-tied <nonformal>; prostrate, **on one's back,** on one's beam-ends

incarcerated ADJS **jailed,** jugged <nonformal>, **imprisoned, interned,** immured; **in prison,** in stir <nonformal>, in captivity, **behind bars,** locked up, under lock and key, in durance vile

incendiary ADJS **incitive,** inciting, incentive; **instigative,** instigating; **agitative,** agitational; **inflammatory,** fomenting, rabble-rousing; incendive; arsonous

incense NOUNS joss stick; pastille; frankincense *or* olibanum; agalloch *or* aloeswood, calambac, lignaloes *or* linaloa, sandalwood

incense VERBS **provoke,** arouse, inflame, embitter; **vex,** irritate, annoy, exasperate, **nettle,** fret, chafe; **pique, peeve** *and* miff <both nonformal>, huff; **ruffle,** roil, rile <nonformal>, ruffle one's feathers, **rankle;** bristle, put *or* get one's back up, set up, put one's hair *or* fur *or* bristles up; stick in one's craw <nonformal>; **stir up, work up,** stir one's bile, stir the blood; wave the bloody shirt

incentive NOUNS **inducement, encouragement,** persuasive, invitation, provocation, incitement; **stimulus, stimulation,** stimulative, fillip, whet; carrot; reward, payment; bait, **lure**; palm oil <nonformal>, bribe; sweetening *and* sweetener <both nonformal>, interest, percentage, what's in it for one <nonformal>

inception NOUNS **origin,** origination, **genesis,** incipience or incipiency, inchoation; **birth,** birthing, bearing, parturition, pregnancy, nascency *or* nascence, nativity; beginnings, cradle; **establishment,** foundation, constitution, institution, installation, formation, **organization,** inauguration, **setting-up,** realization, materialization, effectuation

incessant ADJS **endless,** unending, never-ending, without end, **interminable,** nonterminous, nonterminating; **continual,** continuous, steady, **constant, ceaseless,** nonstop, unceasing, neverceasing, unremitting, unintermitting, uninterrupted

incest NOUNS incestuousness, **sex crime; sexual abuse,** carnal abuse, molestation

incident NOUNS **event,** occurrence, episode, experience, adventure, **happening,** happenstance, **phenomenon,** fact, matter of fact, reality, particular, circumstance, **occasion,** turn of events; **nonevent,** pseudo-event, media event *or* happening, photo opportunity; what's happening

incidental NOUNS 1 **contingency,** contingent, accidental, accident, happenstance, mere chance; **superfluity,** superfluousness; fifth wheel *and* tits on a boar <both nonformal>
ADJS 2 **occasional, casual,** accidental; parenthetical, by-the-way; odd, sometime, extra, side, off, off-and-on, out-of-the-way; adventitious, **unexpected, unpredictable,** unforeseeable, unlooked-for, **unforeseen**

incinerate VERBS **cremate, burn,** reduce to ashes; **burn up,** incendiarize, consume, **burn to a crisp,** burn to a cinder

incinerator NOUNS cinerator, burner; solid-waste incinerator, garbage incinerator; **crematory,** cremator, crematorium, burning ghat; calcinatory

incise VERBS **engrave,** grave, tool, enchase, **inscribe, mark,** line, crease, score, scratch, scrape, cut, carve, chisel; groove, furrow; **cut,** carve, **slice,** pare, prune, trim, trim away, resect, excise; slit, snip, lance

incision NOUNS **furrow, groove,** scratch, crack, cranny, chase, chink, score, **cut,** gash, striation, streak, stria, **gouge,** slit

incisive ADJS **energetic,** vigorous, strenuous, forceful, forcible, strong, dynamic, kinetic, intense, **sharp, keen,** sharpish, trenchant, **cutting,** biting, stinging, **scathing,** stabbing, **piercing, poignant,** penetrating, edged, double-edged; **sagacious, astute,** longheaded, argute; **understanding, discerning,** penetrating, acute, cogent, **perspicacious,** perspicuous; **perceptive, percipient,** apperceptive, appercipient

incite VERBS **instigate, put up to** <nonformal>; set on, sic on; **foment,** ferment, **agitate,** arouse, excite, **stir up,** work up, whip up; rally; **inflame,** incense, **fire,** heat, heat up, impassion; **provoke,** pique, whet, tickle; nettle; lash into a fury *or* frenzy; wave the bloody shirt; pour oil on the fire, feed the fire, add fuel to the flame, fan, fan the flame, blow the coals, stir the embers

inclement ADJS **raw,** bleak, keen, sharp, bitter, biting, pinching, cutting, **piercing,** penetrating; severe, rigorous

inclination NOUNS **leaning,** lean, angularity; **slant,** rake, **slope; tilt, tip,** pitch, **list, cant,** swag, sway; partiality, **penchant,** fancy, favor, predilection, preference, propensity, proclivity, leaning, **bent,** turn, bias, **affinity;** mutual affinity *or* attraction; **sympathy,** fascination; **disposition,** liking, appetence, appetency, **desire**; half a mind *or* notion, idle wish, velleity; **appetite,** passion

incline NOUNS 1 inclination, **slope, grade,** gradient, pitch, **ramp,** launching ramp, bank, talus, gentle *or* easy slope, glacis; rapid *or* steep slope

VERBS 2 **lean; slope, slant,** rake, pitch, grade, bank, shelve; **tilt,** tip, list, cant, careen, keel, sidle, swag, sway; **ascend, rise,** uprise, climb, go uphill; **descend, decline,** dip, drop, fall, fall off *or* away, **go downhill;** retreat

3 **be willing, be game** <nonformal>, be ready; be of favorable disposition, take the trouble, find it in one's heart, look kindly upon; be open to, bring oneself, **agree,** be agreeable to; **acquiesce, consent**; not hesitate to, would as lief, would as leave <nonformal>, would as lief as not, not care *or* mind if one does <nonformal>; **play** *or* **go along** <nonformal>, do one's part *or* bit

inclined ADJS **moved, motivated,** prompted, impelled, actuated; stimulated, animated; minded, of a mind to, with half a mind to, **disposed,** dispositioned, predisposed, prone, given, bent, bent on, apt, likely, **minded, in the mood** *or* **humor**

include VERBS **comprise,** contain, comprehend, hold, take in; **cover,** cover a lot of ground <nonformal>, occupy, take up, fill; fill in *or* out, build into, **complete**; **embrace,** encompass, enclose, encircle, incorporate, assimilate, embody, admit, receive, envisage; **legitimize,** legitimatize; **share power,** enable, enfranchise, cut in *and* deal in *and* give a piece of the action <all nonformal>; **number among,** take into account *or* consideration

including ADJS **composed of,** formed of, **made of,** made up of, made out of, consisting of; composing, comprising, constituting, inclusive of, containing, incarnating, embodying, subsuming; contained in, embodied in

inclusive ADJS **including,** containing, comprising, covering, embracing, encompassing, enclosing, encircling, assimilating, incorporating, envisaging; counting, numbering; broad-brush *and* ballpark <both nonformal>

incognito ADJS **disguised,** camouflaged, in disguise; masked, masquerading; incog <nonformal>; in plain wrapping *or* plain brown paper <nonformal>; **anonymous; nameless, unnamed,** unidentified, undesignated, unspecified, innominate, without a name, **unknown**

incoherent ADJS 1 uncoherent, noncoherent, **inconsistent,** uncohesive, like grains of sand, **untenacious,** unconsolidated, tenuous; disconnected, unconnected, **disordered, chaotic, anarchic,** anomic, confused; **discontinuous**, broken, detached, discrete, disarticulated

2 **delirious,** out of one's head <nonformal>, off one's head <nonformal>, off; **giddy,** dizzy, lightheaded; **wandering,** rambling, raving, ranting, babbling

incombustible ADJS **noncombustible,** uninflammable, noninflammable, noncombustive, nonflammable

income NOUNS **pay,** payment, remuneration, compensation, total compensation, financial remuneration; **salary,** wage, wages, earnings; **receipts,** revenue, profits, earnings, returns, proceeds, **take,** takings, intake; net income, gross income; earned income, unearned income; dividends, royalties, commissions; disposable income

incomparable ADJS **peerless,** matchless, **unmatched,** unmatchable, unrivaled, **unequaled,** unapproachable, **unsurpassed, unexcelled;** unsurpassable; **uncomparable,** not comparable, not to be compared, inimitable, beyond compare *or* comparison, **apples and oranges, unique;** without equal *or* parallel, *sans pareil* <Fr>; in a class by itself, *sui generis* <L>, easily first, *facile princeps* <L>; second to none, *nulli secundus* <L>; **unbeatable,** invincible

incompatible ADJS **unfriendly,** inimical, unamicable; **disagreeable,** cross, cranky, ornery <nonformal>, negative, uncongenial; **discrepant,** inconsistent, inconsonant, incongruous, incongruent, unconformable, irreconcilable; strained, tense; disaccordant, unharmonious

incompetence NOUNS **inability,** incapability, incapacity, incapacitation, incompetency, inadequacy, insufficiency, ineptitude, **inferiority**, inefficiency, unfitness, imbecility; disability, disablement, disqualification; maladroitness, unskillfulness; legal incapacity

incompetent ADJS **incapable,** unable,

inadequate, unequipped, unqualified, ill-qualified, out of one's depth, outmatched, **unfit, unfitted,** unadapted, not equal *or* up to, not cut out for <nonformal>; ineffective, **ineffectual;** unadjusted, maladjusted

incomplete ADJS **uncompleted, deficient,** defective, unfinished, imperfect, unperfected, **inadequate; undeveloped,** underdeveloped, undergrown, stunted, hypoplastic, **immature,** callow, infant, arrested, embryonic, **wanting, lacking,** needing, missing, **partial,** part, failing; in default, in arrear *or* arrears; **in short supply,** scanty; **short,** scant, shy <nonformal>; **sketchy,** patchy, scrappy

incomprehensible ADJS **unintelligible,** ungraspable, unseizable, ununderstandable, unknowable; **unfathomable, inscrutable,** impenetrable, unsearchable, numinous; **ambiguous; incoherent,** unconnected, rambling; **inarticulate; past comprehension,** beyond one's comprehension, beyond understanding; Greek to one

inconceivable ADJS **fantastic,** fantastical, fanciful, antic, **unbelievable**, impossible, incredible, logic-defying, incomprehensible, unimaginable, unexpected, unaccountable

inconclusive ADJS **unsound, unsubstantial,** insubstantial, weak, feeble, poor, flimsy, unrigorous, unproved, unsustained, poorly argued, indecisive; **moot**

incongruous ADJS **ludicrous,** ridiculous, hilarious, absurd, quaint, eccentric, bizarre; **inconsistent,** inconsonant, inconsequent, incoherent, **incompatible,** irreconcilable; self-contradictory, paradoxical, oxymoronic, **absurd**

inconsequential ADJS **insignificant**, immaterial; nonessential, unessential, inessential, **not vital,** back-burner <nonformal>, dispensable; unnoteworthy, unimpressive; **inconsiderable,** inappreciable, negligible; irrelevant

inconsiderate ADJS **unthoughtful,** unmindful, unheedful, disregardful, **thoughtless,** heedless, respectless, mindless, unthinking, forgetful; **tactless,** insensitive; **unhelpful,** unaccommodating, unobliging, disobliging, uncooperative

inconsistent ADJS **incongruous, inconsonant,** inconsequent, incoherent, **incompatible,** irreconcilable; incommensurable, incommensurate; disproportionate, out of proportion, self-contradictory, paradoxical, oxymoronic, **absurd**

inconsolable ADJS unconsolable, **disconsolate,** comfortless, prostrate or prostrated, forlorn; **desolate,** *désolé* <Fr>; sick, **sick at heart, heartsick,** soul-sick, heartsore

inconspicuous ADJS half-visible, semivisible, low-profile; **indistinct, unclear,** unplain, **indefinite,** undefined, ill-defined, ill-marked, **faint,** pale, feeble, weak, **dim,** dark, **shadowy, vague, obscure,** indistinguishable, unrecognizable; half-seen, merely glimpsed; uncertain, confused, out of focus, **blurred, blurry,** bleared, bleary, blear, **fuzzy, hazy,** misty, filmy, foggy

inconstant ADJS **changeable,** changeful, changing, shifting, uncertain, inconsistent; **shifty,** unreliable, undependable; **unstable, unfixed,** infirm, restless, **unsettled,** unstaid, **unsteady,** wishy-washy, spineless, shapeless, amorphous, indecisive, irresolute, waffling <nonformal>, blowing hot and cold <nonformal>, like a feather in the wind, unsteadfast, unstable as water; **capricious, fickle**, off-again-on-again; **erratic, eccentric,** freakish; volatile, giddy, dizzy, ditzy <nonformal>, scatterbrained, mercurial, moody, flighty, impulsive, impetuous; **fluctuating,** alternating, **vacillating, wavering,** wavery, wavy, mazy, flitting, flickering, guttering, fitful, shifting, shuffling

incontrovertible ADJS **conclusive,** determinative, **decisive,** final, irresistible, sure, certain, absolute; indubitable, unarguable, indisputable, incontestable, **irrefutable,** unrefutable, unconfutable, irrefragable, unanswerable, unimpeachable; admitting no question *or* dispute *or* doubt *or* denial

inconvenience NOUNS 1 **impediment,** embarrassment, **trouble,** difficulty; **handicap,** disadvantage, penalty; white elephant; headache <nonformal>, problem, besetment; the bad part, the downside <nonformal>; **unwieldiness,** unmanageability; **unhandiness,** impracticality; **awkwardness,** clumsiness
VERBS 2 put to inconvenience, **put out, discommode,** incommode, disoblige, **burden, embarrass; trouble, bother,** put to trouble, put to the trouble of, **impose upon;** harm, disadvantage

inconvenient ADJS **unhandy, awkward,**

clumsy, unwieldy, troublesome; **incommodious,** discommodious; impractical

incorporate VERBS **embrace,** encompass, enclose, encircle, assimilate, embody, admit, receive, envisage; **number among,** take into account *or* consideration; **amalgamate,** consolidate, integrate, solidify, coalesce, compound, put *or* lump together, roll into one, come together, make one, unitize

incorrect ADJS **inaccurate, inexact,** unfactual, **unprecise,** imprecise, unspecific, loose, lax, unrigorous; negligent; **vague;** off-base <nonformal>; **ungrammatical,** solecistic, solecistical, barbarous; faulty, erroneous; infelicitous, improper; loose, imprecise

incorrigible ADJS **past hope, beyond recall,** past praying for; **irretrievable, irrecoverable, irreclaimable,** irredeemable, unsalvageable, unsalvable; irreformable; **irremediable, irreparable,** inoperable, **incurable,** cureless, remediless, immedicable, beyond remedy, terminal; recidivist, recidivistic; beyond control, out of hand, irreversible; unredeemable, unregenerate

incorruptible ADJS **trustworthy, trusty,** faithworthy, reliable, dependable, responsible, straight <nonformal>, sure, to be trusted, **to be depended** *or* **relied upon,** to be counted *or* reckoned on, as good as one's word; tried, true, **tried and true,** tested, proven; inviolable

increase NOUNS 1 **gain,** augmentation, greatening, **enlargement, amplification, growth,** development, widening, spread, broadening, elevation, **extension,** aggrandizement, access, accession, **increment,** accretion; **expansion,** proliferation, productiveness; **advance,** appreciation, ascent, mounting, crescendo, waxing, snowballing, **rise** *or* raise, fattening *and* boost *and* hike <all nonformal>, **up** *and* upping <both nonformal>, buildup; **upturn,** uptick <nonformal>, uptrend, upsurge, upswing VERBS 2 **grow, advance,** appreciate; **spread, widen,** broaden; **gain,** get ahead; wax, swell, balloon, bloat, mount, **rise,** go up, crescendo, snowball; **intensify, develop,** gain strength, strengthen; accrue, accumulate; **multiply, proliferate,** breed, teem; run *or* shoot up, **boom, explode**

increased ADJS **heightened,** raised, elevated, stepped-up <nonformal>; **intensified,** deepened, reinforced, strengthened, fortified, beefed-up <nonformal>, tightened, stiffened; **enlarged, extended,** augmented, aggrandized, amplified, **enhanced,** boosted, hiked <nonformal>; broadened, widened, spread; **magnified, inflated, expanded,** swollen, bloated; **multiplied,** proliferated; **accelerated,** hopped-up *and* jazzed-up <both nonformal>

incredible ADJS **unbelievable,** unthinkable, **implausible,** unimaginable, inconceivable, not to be believed, **hard to believe,** hard of belief, beyond belief, unworthy of belief, not meriting *or* not deserving belief, tall <nonformal>; **defying belief,** staggering belief, passing belief; **mind-boggling,** preposterous, absurd, ridiculous, unearthly, ungodly; **doubtful, dubious,** doubtable, dubitable, **questionable,** problematic, problematical, **unconvincing,** open to doubt *or* suspicion

incredulous ADJS uncredulous, **hard of belief,** shy of belief, disposed to doubt, indisposed *or* disinclined to believe, unwilling to accept; impervious to persuasion, unconvincible, unpersuadable, unpersuasible; **suspicious, suspecting,** wary, leery, cautious, guarded; **skeptical**

increment NOUNS **increase, gain,** augmentation, greatening, enlargement, amplification, growth, development, widening, spread, broadening, elevation, **extension,** aggrandizement, access, accession, accretion; **adjunct, addition,** supplementation, complementation, *additum* <L>, additament, addendum, addenda <pl>, accession

incriminate VERBS **inculpate, implicate,** involve; cry out against, cry out on *or* upon, cry shame upon, raise one's voice against; attack, assail, impugn

incubate VERBS **be pregnant,** be gravid; gestate, breed, carry, carry young; **hatch; brood,** sit, set, cover

inculcate VERBS **indoctrinate,** catechize, inoculate, **instill, infuse,** imbue, impregnate, **implant,** infix, impress; **impress upon the mind** *or* **memory,** urge on the mind, beat into, beat *or* knock into one's head, grind in, drill into, drum into one's head *or* skull; **condition,** brainwash, program

incumbent NOUNS **officeholder,** officebearer <Brit>, jack-in-office, public servant, public official; holdover, lame duck; benefice-holder, beneficiary

incur VERBS **contract,** invite, welcome, run, **bring on, bring down,** bring upon *or* down upon, bring upon *or* down upon oneself; fall into, fall in with; get, gain, acquire

incurable ADJS **past hope, beyond recall,** past praying for; irrevocable, **irreversible; irremediable,** irreparable, inoperable, cureless, remediless, immedicable, beyond remedy, terminal; unrelievable, unmitigable; **ruined,** undone, kaput <nonformal>; lost, gone, gone to hell *and* gone to hell in a handbasket <both nonformal>

incursion NOUNS **raid,** foray, razzia; **invasion,** inroad, irruption; **air raid, air strike,** air attack, shuttle raid, fire raid, saturation raid

indecency NOUNS **indelicacy,** inelegance *or* inelegancy, **indecorousness,** indecorum, **impropriety**, inappropriateness, unseemliness, indiscretion, indiscreetness; **unchastity**

indecent ADJS **indelicate,** inelegant, indecorous, improper, inappropriate, unseemly, unbecoming, indiscreet

indecisive ADJS **wishy-washy,** tasteless, bland, **insipid,** vapid, neutral, watery, milky, milk-and-water, mushy; halfhearted, infirm of will *or* purpose, irresolute, changeable; **inconclusive, moot**

indefatigable ADJS **persevering,** perseverant, **persistent,** persisting, insistent; relentless, **unrelenting; unrelaxing,** unfailing, **untiring,** unwearying, unflagging, never-tiring, **tireless,** weariless, unwearied; undiscouraged, undaunted, indomitable, unconquerable, invincible, game to the last *or* to the end; **patient,** patient as Job

indefensible ADJS **unacceptable,** inadmissible, unsuitable, undesirable, **objectionable,** exceptionable, impossible, untenable, **unjustifiable,** unwarrantable, unallowable, unreasonable

indefinite ADJS **vague, indecisive,** indeterminate, indeterminable, undetermined, unpredetermined, undestined; amorphous, shapeless, blobby; inchoate, disordered, orderless, chaotic, incoherent

indelible ADJS **unforgettable, never to be forgotten,** never to be erased from the mind, indelibly impressed on the mind, fixed in the mind; haunting, persistent, recurrent, nagging, plaguing, rankling, festering; obsessing, obsessive

indelicacy NOUNS **indecency,** inelegance *or* inelegancy, **indecorousness,** indecorum, **impropriety**, inappropriateness, unseemliness, indiscretion, indiscreetness

indemnify VERBS **compensate,** make compensation, make good, set right, restitute, pay back, rectify, **make up for; recompense,** pay back, repay, cover

indemnity NOUNS **compensation, recompense,** repayment, payback, indemnification, measure for measure, rectification, restitution, **reparation; amends,** expiation, atonement

independence NOUNS **self-determination, self government,** self-direction, **autonomy,** home rule; autarky, autarchy, self-containment, self-sufficiency; **individualism,** rugged individualism, individual freedom; **self-reliance,** self-dependence; inner-direction

independent NOUNS 1 **nonpartisan,** neutral, mugwump, undecided or uncommitted voter
ADJS 2 self-dependent; free-spirited, freewheeling, free-floating, free-standing; **self-determined,** self-directing, one's own man; inner-directed, **individualistic;** self-governed, **self-governing, autonomous,** sovereign; stand-alone, self-reliant, self-sufficient, self-subsistent, self-supporting, self-contained, autarkic, autarchic; nonpartisan, neutral, **nonaligned**

indescribable ADJS **ineffable,** inenarrable, inexpressible, unutterable, unspeakable, noncommunicable, incommunicable, indefinable, undefinable, unnameable, innominable, unwhisperable, unmentionable

indestructible ADJS undestroyable, **imperishable,** nonperishable, incorruptible; **deathless,** immortal, undying; **invulnerable, invincible,** inexpugnable, impregnable, indivisible; **ineradicable,** indelible, ineffaceable, inerasable; **inextinguishable,** unquenchable, quenchless, undampable

index NOUNS 1 **mark,** marking, **earmark,** hallmark; listing, tabulation
VERBS 2 **catalog,** list, file, tabulate, rationalize, alphabetize, digest, codify

Indian summer NOUNS St Martin's summer, St Luke's summer, little summer of St Luke, St Austin's *or* St Augustine's summer

the dead Summer's soul
MARY CLEMMER

indicate VERBS **signify, mean**, spell, point to, look like, **be a sign of,** show signs of; **imply,** suggest, argue, breathe, bespeak, betoken

indication NOUNS signification, identification, differentiation, denotation, **designation,** denomination; characterization, highlighting; **specification,** naming, pointing, pointing out *or* to, fingering <nonformal>, picking out, selection; indicativeness; **meaning**; hint, suggestion; **expression, manifestation**; show, showing, disclosure

indicative ADJS indicatory; connotative, indicating, signifying, signalizing; **significant,** significative, meaningful; symptomatic, symptomatologic, symptomatological, diagnostic, pathognomonic, pathognomonical; evidential, **designative,** denotative, denominative, naming; **suggestive,** implicative; **expressive,** demonstrative, exhibitive; identifying; **emblematic, symbolic,** emblematical, symbolical

indicator NOUNS **sign,** telltale sign, sure sign, tip-off <nonformal>, **index,** indicant, measure; tip of the iceberg

indict VERBS **arraign, impeach,** find an indictment against, present a true bill, prefer *or* file a claim, have *or* pull up <nonformal>, bring up for investigation; **prefer charges**

indictment NOUNS **censure, reprehension,** stricture, reprobation, **blame, denunciation,** denouncement, decrying, decrial, bashing *and* trashing <both nonformal>, **condemnation,** damnation, fulmination, anathema; **impeachment, arraignment,** bill of indictment, true bill; **allegation**

indifference NOUNS 1 indifferentness; unconcern, halfheartedness, perfunctoriness; **coolness,** coldness, chilliness, chill, iciness, frostiness; tepidness, **lukewarmness**

2 **carelessness,** heedlessness, unheedfulness, *je-m'en-fichisme* and *je-m'en-foutisme* <both Fr>; perfunctoriness; cursoriness, hastiness, offhandedness, casualness

indifferent ADJS **halfhearted,** zealless, perfunctory, fervorless; **cool, cold**; tepid, **lukewarm;** neither hot nor cold, neither one thing nor the other, **nonchalant,** blasé, unconcerned; **casual,** offhand, relaxed, laid-back *and* throwaway <both nonformal>; **easygoing,** easy, free and easy, devil-may-care, lackadaisical, *dégagé* <Fr>

indigent ADJS **poverty-stricken; needy,** necessitous, **in need, in want,** disadvantaged, deprived, underprivileged; **impoverished, pauperized,** starveling; **down at heels,** down at the heel, on *or* down on one's uppers, out at the heels, out at elbows, in rags; on welfare, on relief, on the dole <Brit>

indigestible ADJS **innutritious,** unassimilable

indignant ADJS **disapproving, disapprobatory,** unapproving, turned-off, **displeased, dissatisfied,** less than pleased, discontented, disgruntled, **unhappy**

indignity NOUNS **affront, offense, injury,** humiliation; scurrility, contempt, contumely, despite, flout, flouting, mockery, jeering, jeer, mock, scoff, gibe, taunt, brickbat <nonformal>; **insult, aspersion,** uncomplimentary remark, slap *or* kick in the face, left-handed *or* backhanded compliment, damning with faint praise; cut

most unkindest cut of all
SHAKESPEARE

indirect ADJS **circuitous,** roundabout, out-of-the-way, devious, oblique, ambagious <old>, meandering, backhanded; **deviative**, **deviating,** digressive, discursive, excursive; equivocatory; evasive

indiscreet ADJS **rash,** brash, incautious, overbold, imprudent, injudicious, improvident; **unwary, unchary;** overconfident, oversure, overweening, **impudent,** insolent, brazenfaced, brazen

indiscretion NOUNS **rashness, brashness,** brazen boldness, incautiousness, overboldness, imprudence, injudiciousness, improvidence; **impropriety,** slight *or* minor wrong, venial sin, peccadillo, misstep, trip, slip, lapse; **blunder, faux pas,** gaffe, solecism; stupidity

indiscriminate ADJS **undiscriminating,** indiscriminative, undiscriminative, unselective; wholesale, general, blanket;

uncritical, uncriticizing, undemanding, nonjudgmental; **casual, promiscuous;** unexacting, unmeticulous

indispensable ADJS **vital, all-important,** crucial, of vital importance, life-and-death *or* life-or-death; earth-shattering, epoch-making; **essential,** fundamental, basic, substantive, bedrock, material

indisposed ADJS 1 **ill,** ailing, sick, unwell, taken ill, down, bad, on the sick list; **sickish, seedy** *and* rocky <both nonformal>, **under the weather, out of sorts** <nonformal>, below par <nonformal>, off-color, off one's feed <nonformal>; not quite right, not oneself
2 **unwilling, disinclined,** not in the mood, averse; **unconsenting**

indisputable ADJS **real, actual,** factual, veritable, for real <nonformal>, de facto, admitted, well-known, established, inescapable, undeniable; **demonstrable,** provable

indistinct ADJS **obscure, vague,** indeterminate, fuzzy, shapeless, amorphous; unclear, unplain, opaque, muddy, **clear as mud** *and* clear as ditch water <both nonformal>; **indistinguishable,** undistinguishable, undistinguished, indiscernible

indistinguishable ADJS undistinguishable, undistinguished, indiscernible, **indistinct,** indistinctive, **without distinction,** not to be distinguished, undiscriminated, unindividual, unindividualized, undifferentiated, **alike,** six of one and half a dozen of the other <nonformal>; standard, interchangeable, stereotyped, uniform

individual NOUNS 1 **person,** human, human being, man, woman, child, member of the human race *or* family, Adamite, daughter of Eve; **mortal, being,** creature, clay, ordinary clay; personage, **personality, personhood,** individuality; somebody, one, someone
ADJS 2 **personal,** private, peculiar, idiosyncratic; person-to-person, one-to-one, one-on-one; **singular,** individualist *or* individualistic; **personal,** private, intimate, inner, solipsistic, esoteric; **one, single,** singular, sole, unique, a certain, **solitary, lone**

individualist NOUNS **egotist,** egoist, egocentric; **free agent,** independent, free lance; rugged individualist; free spirit; loner *and* lone wolf <both nonformal>

indivisible ADJS nondivisible, undividable, **inseparable,** impartible, infrangible, indiscerptible, indissoluble; cohesive, coherent; unified; insoluble, indissolvable, infusible

indoctrinate VERBS **brainwash,** reindoctrinate, counterindoctrinate; subvert, alienate, win away, corrupt

indoctrination NOUNS **inculcation,** catechization, inoculation, **implantation,** infixation, infixion, **impression, instillment,** instillation, impregnation, **infusion,** imbuement; conditioning, brainwashing; reindoctrination

indolence NOUNS **laziness, sloth,** slothfulness, bone-laziness; inexertion, inertia; **shiftlessness,** spring fever; ergophobia

indolent ADJS **lazy,** bone-lazy, **slothful,** workshy, ergophobic; **do-nothing,** *fainéant* <Fr>, **laggard,** slow, **dilatory,** procrastinative, remiss, slack, lax; **shiftless,** do-less <nonformal>; **unenterprising,** nonaggressive; good-for-nothing, ne'er-do-well; dronish, parasitic, cadging, sponging, scrounging

indomitable ADJS **invincible, unconquerable,** unsubduable, unyielding, unbeatable, more than a match for; **persevering,** undiscouraged, undaunted, game to the last *or* to the end

indubitable ADJS **unarguable,** indisputable, incontestable, **irrefutable,** unrefutable, unconfutable, incontrovertible, irrefragable, unanswerable, inappealable, unimpeachable, absolute; admitting no question *or* dispute *or* doubt *or* denial

induce VERBS **prompt,** move one to, influence, sway, incline, dispose, carry, bring, lead, **lead one to; persuade**, jawbone *and* twist one's arm *and* hold one's feet to the fire <all nonformal>, work *or* bend to one's will; lead by the nose <nonformal>, wear down, soften up

inducement NOUNS enlistment, engagement, solicitation, **persuasion,** suasion; exhortation, hortation, preaching, preachment; **selling,** sales talk, salesmanship, hard sell, high pressure, hawking, huckstering; jawboning *and* arm-twisting <both nonformal>; **lobbying; coaxing,** wheedling, working on <nonformal>, cajolery, cajolement, conning, snow job *and* smoke and mirrors <both nonformal>, blandishment, sweet talk *and* soft soap <both nonformal>, soft sell <nonformal>

induct VERBS **install,** instate, inaugurate, initiate, invest, ordain; enlist, enroll, sign up, sign on

indulge VERBS 1 **humor, oblige;** favor, please, gratify, satisfy, **cater to; give way to,** yield to, let one have his own way; **pamper,** cosset, **coddle,** mollycoddle, pet, make a lap dog of, **spoil;** spare the rod

2 indulge oneself, indulge one's appetites, deny oneself nothing *or* not at all; **give oneself up to,** give free course to, give free rein to; live well *or* high, live high on the hog <nonformal>, live off the fat of the land; indulge in, luxuriate in, wallow in; roll in

indulge in easy vices
SAMUEL JOHNSON

indulgent ADJS 1 **compliant,** complaisant, **obliging, accommodating, agreeable,** amiable, gracious, generous, benignant, affable, decent, kind, kindly, benign, benevolent; **hands-off** <nonformal>, permissive, overpermissive, overindulgent

2 **intemperate, self-indulgent; overindulgent,** overindulging, unthrifty, unfrugal, **immoderate,** inordinate, **excessive,** too much, prodigal, extravagant, extreme, unmeasured, unlimited; crapulous, crapulent; undisciplined, uncontrolled, unbridled, unconstrained, uninhibited, **unrestrained; incontinent**; bibulous

industrial ADJS **manufacturing,** manufactural, fabricational, smokestack

industrious ADJS **assiduous,** diligent, sedulous, laborious, hardworking; **energetic,** strenuous; never idle; tireless, unwearied, unflagging, indefatigable; **painstaking,** thorough, thoroughgoing, operose

inedible ADJS **uneatable,** not fit to eat, unfit for human consumption

ineducable ADJS **stupid, dumb,** dullard, **doltish,** blockish, klutzy *and* klutzish <both nonformal>; **dense,** thick <nonformal>, opaque; unteachable

ineffective ADJS **ineffectual, inefficacious,** counterproductive, feckless, not up to scratch *or* up to snuff <nonformal>, **inadequate**; **invalid, inoperative,** of no force; nugatory, nugacious; fatuous, fatuitous; **vain, futile, inutile, useless,** unavailing, bootless, fruitless

inefficiency NOUNS **inability,** incapacity, incompetence *or* incompetency, inadequacy, insufficiency, ineptitude, **inferiority**, inexpertness, unproficiency, uncleverness

inefficient ADJS **unable,** incapable, incompetent, ineffective; **unqualified,** inept, unendowed, ungifted, untalented, **unfit,** unfitted; **unskillful,** artless, inexpert, unproficient, unclever

inept ADJS **incompetent,** inefficient, ineffective; **unqualified,** unendowed, ungifted, untalented, **unfit,** unfitted; out of one's depth, in over one's head; **unapt,** inapt, hopeless, half-assed *and* clunky <both nonformal>

inequality NOUNS **disparity, unevenness,** contrariety, difference; **irregularity,** nonuniformity, heterogeneity; **disproportion,** asymmetry; **unbalance,** imbalance, disequilibrium, overbalance, inclination of the balance, overcompensation, tippiness; **inadequacy,** insufficiency, shortcoming; **odds,** handicap; **injustice,** inequity, unfair discrimination, second-class citizenship, untouchability

inequity NOUNS **injustice, unjustness;** iniquity, inequitableness, iniquitousness; inequality, inequality of treatment *or* dealing; **wrong, wrongness,** wrongfulness, unmeetness, improperness, **impropriety;** what should not be, what ought not *or* must not be

inert ADJS **inactive, static, dormant,** passive, sedentary; **latent,** unaroused, suspended, abeyant, in suspense *or* abeyance; sleeping, slumbering, smoldering; **stagnant,** standing, foul; **torpid, languorous, languid,** apathetic, phlegmatic, **sluggish,** logy, dopey <nonformal>, groggy, heavy, leaden, **dull,** flat, slack, tame, **dead,** lifeless

inertia NOUNS **inertness, dormancy;** passiveness, passivity; suspense, abeyance, latency; torpor, apathy, indifference, indolence, lotus-eating, languor; **stagnation,** stagnancy, **vegetation;** stasis; entropy

inescapable ADJS **inevitable, unavoidable,** necessary, unpreventable, undeflectable, ineluctable, irrevocable, indefeasible; uncontrollable, unstoppable; relentless, inexorable, unyielding, inflexible; irresistible, resistless; sure as death, sure as death and taxes

inestimable ADJS **precious, valuable,**

worthy, rich, golden, of great price <old>, worth a pretty penny <nonformal>, worth a king's ransom, worth its weight in gold, good as gold, precious as the apple of one's eye; **priceless, invaluable,** without *or* **beyond price,** not to be had for love or money, not for all the tea in China

inevitable ADJS **unavoidable,** necessary, **inescapable,** unpreventable, undeflectable, ineluctable, irrevocable, indefeasible; uncontrollable, unstoppable; relentless, inexorable, unyielding, inflexible; irresistible, resistless; **certain,** fateful, **sure,** sure as fate, sure as death, sure as death and taxes

inexcitable ADJS **imperturbable,** undisturbable, unflappable <nonformal>; **unirritable; dispassionate,** unpassionate; **steady;** stoic, stoical; **even-tempered; impassive,** stolid; bovine, dull; **patient**

inexcusable ADJS **unjustifiable, unwarrantable,** unallowable, unreasonable, indefensible; unconscionable, **unpardonable, unforgivable,** inexpiable, irremissible

inexhaustible ADJS **infinite,** boundless, endless, limitless; unbounded, uncircumscribed, **unlimited,** illimited, infinitely continuous *or* extended, without bound, without limit *or* end, no end of *or* to; **immeasurable,** incalculable, unreckonable, innumerable, measureless, countless; **unmeasured,** unmeasurable, immense, unplumbed, untold, unnumbered, without measure *or* number *or* term; exhaustless

inexorable ADJS **firm,** rigid, rigorous, rigorist, rigoristic, stiff, **hard,** iron, steel, steely, hard-shell, obdurate, **inflexible,** ironhanded, dour, **unyielding,** unbending, impliable, **relentless,** unrelenting, procrustean; **uncompromising;** ironbound, rockbound, musclebound, hidebound

inexpedient ADJS **undesirable,** inadvisable, counterproductive, impolitic, impolitical, unpolitic, not to be recommended, contraindicated; **impractical, impracticable,** dysfunctional, unworkable; **ill-advised, ill-considered, unwise; unfit, unfitting,** unbefitting, **inappropriate, unsuitable,** unmeet, inapt, inept, unseemly, **improper, wrong,** bad, out of place, out of order, incongruous, ill-suited; inopportune, ill-timed, badly timed, unseasonable; unprofitable; futile

inexpensive ADJS **cheap,** unexpensive, **low, low-priced,** frugal, reasonable, sensible, manageable, modest, moderate, affordable, to fit the pocketbook, budget, easy, economy, economic, economical; within means, within reach *or* easy reach; nominal, token; worth the money, well worth the money; cheap at half the price; shabby, shoddy

inexperienced ADJS **unexperienced,** unversed, unconversant, **unpracticed;** undeveloped, unseasoned; **raw, green,** green as grass, unripe, callow, unfledged, immature, unmatured, fresh, wet behind the ears, not dry behind the ears, **untried;** unskilled in, unpracticed in, unversed in, unconversant with, unaccustomed to, unused to, unfamiliar *or* unacquainted with, new to, uninitiated in, a stranger to, a novice *or* tyro at; ignorant

inexplicable ADJS **unexplainable,** uninterpretable, undefinable, indefinable, funny, **unaccountable; insolvable,** unsolvable, insoluble, inextricable; mysterious, mystic, mystical, shrouded *or* wrapped *or* enwrapped in mystery

infallible ADJS **inerrable,** inerrant, unerring

infamous ADJS **abominable,** terrible, scandalous, disgraceful, shameful, shameless, atrocious, sacrilegious, ignoble, ignominious, inglorious, flagrant, **shocking, notorious,** arrant, **egregious,** unpardonable, unforgivable

infamy NOUNS infamousness; **ignominy,** ignominiousness; ingloriousness, **ignobility,** odium, obloquy, opprobrium; depluming, displuming, loss of honor *or* name *or* repute *or* face; degradation, comedown <nonformal>

infant NOUNS 1 **baby, babe,** babe in arms, little darling *or* angel *or* doll *or* cherub, bouncing baby, puling infant, mewling infant, babykins <nonformal>, baby bunting; papoose, *bimbo* <Ital> or *bambino* <Ital>; **toddler; suckling,** nursling, fosterling, weanling; neonate
2 **innocent,** child, mere child, newborn babe, babe in the woods, lamb, dove
ADJS 3 **infantile,** infantine, **babyish,** baby; **newborn,** neonatal; in the cradle *or* crib *or* nursery, in swaddling clothes, in diapers, in nappies <Brit>, in arms, at the breast, tied to mother's apron

strings; **undeveloped,** underdeveloped, **immature,** callow, arrested, embryonic

infantile ADJS **infant,** infantine, **babyish,** baby; **puerile,** immature, **childish;** childlike; incunabular, infantine

infatuated ADJS **enamored, charmed,** becharmed, **fascinated, captivated,** bewitched, enraptured, enchanted; **smitten,** heartsmitten, heartstruck, lovestruck, besotted, credulous, gulled, befooled, beguiled, fond, doting, gaga; **obsessed, possessed,** prepossessed, preoccupied, fixated, **hung up** <nonformal>, infatuate, gripped, held; sentimental, maudlin; dazed, fuddled

infatuation NOUNS infatuatedness, passing fancy; **crush** *and* mash *and* pash *and* case <all nonformal>; **puppy love** *and* calf love <both nonformal>; love at first sight; fondness, dotage; one's blind side

infect VERBS 1 **contaminate,** tarnish, confound, **pollute,** vitiate, poison, taint; **corrupt,** debase, degrade, degenerate, deprave, debauch, defile, violate, desecrate

2 **inspire,** inspirit, spirit, spirit up; fire, fire one's imagination; **animate, exhilarate,** enliven; **infuse,** inject, inoculate, imbue, inform

infected ADJS **diseased,** morbid, pathological, **contaminated,** tainted, peccant, **poisoned,** polluted, corrupted, septic

infection NOUNS **contagion,** contamination, taint, virus; **contagiousness,** infectiousness, communicability; carrier, vector

infectious ADJS **contagious,** infective, **catching,** taking, spreading, **communicable,** zymotic, inoculable; pestiferous, pestilential, **epidemic,** epidemial, pandemic; epizootic, epiphytotic; endemic

infelicitous ADJS **inelegant,** clumsy, clunky *and* klutzy <both nonformal>, heavy-handed, heavy-footed, ham-handed, graceless, ungraceful, inconcinnate *and* inconcinnous <both old>, unfelicitous, inapplicable, inadmissible; **faulty,** erroneous; **improper; careless,** slovenly, slipshod; ungrammatic, **ungrammatical,** solecistic, solecistical, **incorrect,** barbarous

infer VERBS **deduce,** generalize; **conclude,** draw a conclusion, **come to** *or* **arrive at a conclusion,** draw an inference; put two and two together

inference NOUNS **conclusion, deduction,** consequence, consequent, corollary; **connotation, import,** latent *or* underlying *or* implied meaning, more than meets the eye, what is read between the lines; undermeaning

inferior NOUNS 1 **underling, subordinate,** subaltern, **junior;** second fiddle *and* second stringer *and* third stringer *and* benchwarmer *and* low man on the totem pole <all nonformal>, loser *and* nonstarter <both nonformal>; lightweight, follower, pawn, cog, flunky, yes-man, creature

ADJS 2 **subordinate,** subaltern, sub, small-scale, **secondary; junior, minor;** second *or* third string *and* one-horse *and* penny-ante *and* dinky <all nonformal>, second *or* third rank, low in the pecking order, low-rent *and* downscale <both nonformal>; **subservient,** subject, servile, low, **lowly,** humble, modest; **lesser,** less, lower; **beneath one's dignity** *or* station, infra dig, demeaning; **poor,** punk <nonformal>, **base, mean, common,** coarse, cheesy *and* tacky <both nonformal>, tinny; shabby, seedy; cheap, Mickey Mouse <nonformal>, paltry

inferiority NOUNS 1 **subordinacy,** subordination, secondariness; **juniority,** minority; **subservience, subjection,** servility, lowliness, humbleness, humility; back seat *and* second fiddle <both nonformal>, second *or* third string <nonformal>

2 inferiorness, **poorness,** lowliness, humbleness, **baseness, meanness, commonness,** coarseness, tackiness, tack; **second-rateness,** third-rateness, fourth-rateness

inferiority complex NOUNS **complex; self-effacement, self-depreciation,** self-deprecation, self-detraction, undervaluing of self, self-doubt, **diffidence;** hiding one's light under a bushel; low self-esteem, weak ego, lack of self-confidence *or* self-reliance, self-distrust

infernal ADJS **cruel, inhuman,** fiendish, fiendlike; demoniac *or* demoniacal, diabolic, diabolical, devilish, satanic; **hellish,** sulfurous, brimstone, fire-and-brimstone; chthonic, chthonian

inferno NOUNS **hell, Hades,** Sheol, Gehenna, Tophet, Abaddon, Naraka, jahannan, avichi, **perdition,** Pandemonium, the pit, **the bottomless pit,** the abyss, **nether world,** lower world, underworld, infernal regions, abode *or* world of the dead, abode of the damned, place of torment, the grave, shades below; **purgatory; oven, furnace,** fiery furnace

inferred ADJS **supposed,** suppositive, assumed, presumed, **conjectured,** understood, deemed, **reputed,** putative, alleged, accounted as; suppositional, supposititious

infertility NOUNS **unproductiveness,** unproductivity, ineffectualness; **unfruitfulness, barrenness,** nonfruition, dryness, aridity, dearth, famine; sterileness, **sterility,** unfertileness, infecundity; wasted *or* withered loins, dry womb; impotence, incapacity

infest VERBS **beset,** invade, swarm, ravage, plague; **overrun, overswarm,** overspread; **creep with, crawl with,** swarm with; seize

infestation NOUNS **invasion,** swarming, swarm, teeming, ravage, plague; **overrunning, overswarming,** overspreading

infidel NOUNS **unbeliever,** disbeliever, nonbeliever; **atheist, pagan, heathen;** nullifidian, minimifidian; **gentile**

infidelity NOUNS **unfaithfulness,** unfaith, faithlessness, trothlessness, illicit *or* unlawful love, forbidden *or* unsanctified love, adulterous affair, adultery, unfaithfulness, cuckoldry; **inconstancy, unsteadfastness,** fickleness; **disloyalty,** unloyalty; **falsity,** falseness, untrueness; disaffection, recreancy, dereliction; bad faith, *mala fides* <L>, Punic faith; breach of promise, breach of trust *or* faith, barratry; breach of confidence

infighting NOUNS **dissension, dissent,** dissidence, bickering, factiousness, partisanship, partisan spirit; **divisiveness; quarrelsomeness;** fighting at close quarters

infiltrate VERBS **filter in, seep in,** percolate into, leak in, soak in, perfuse; **encroach, infringe,** impinge, **trespass,** trespass on *or* upon, trench, entrench, invade

infinite ADJS **boundless, endless, limitless,** termless, shoreless; unbounded, uncircumscribed, **unlimited,** illimited, infinitely continuous *or* extended, stretching *or* extending everywhere, without bound, without limit *or* end, no end of *or* to; illimitable, **interminable,** interminate; **immeasurable,** incalculable, unreckonable, innumerable, incomprehensible, unfathomable; **all-inclusive,** all-comprehensive, **universal**; **perpetual, eternal**

infinitesimal ADJS **microscopic,** ultramicroscopic; evanescent, thin, tenuous; inappreciable; impalpable, imponderable, intangible; imperceptible, indiscernible, invisible, unseeable

infinity NOUNS infiniteness, infinitude, the all, the be-all and end-all; **boundlessness, limitlessness, endlessness; immeasurability,** unmeasurability, immensity, incalculability, innumerability, incomprehensibility; measurelessness, countlessness, exhaustlessness, inexhaustibility; universality

world without end
BIBLE

infirmity NOUNS **unsoundness,** incapacity, unfirmness, unsturdiness, **instability, unsubstantiality;** decrepitude; **unsteadiness, shakiness,** ricketiness, wobbliness, wonkiness <Brit nonformal>, caducity, senility, invalidism; wishy-washiness, insipidity, vapidity, wateriness; **illness,** sickness, malady, ailment, indisposition, disorder, complaint, morbidity, affliction

inflame VERBS **incite, instigate,** put up to <nonformal>; set on, sic on; **foment,** ferment, **agitate, arouse, excite, stir up,** work up, whip up; rally; incense, **fire,** heat, heat up, impassion; pour oil on the fire, feed the fire, add fuel to the flame, fan, fan the flame, blow the coals, stir the embers; **ignite,** set fire to, set on fire, kindle, enkindle, **light,** light up, strike a light, apply the match *or* torch to, torch <nonformal>, touch off, **burn,** conflagrate

inflamed ADJS **fiery, heated,** flaming, scorching, hot, red-hot, white-hot; **fanatic, zealous,** totally committed, hard-core, hard-line, ardent, passionate; **hotheaded**

inflammable NOUNS 1 **fuel,** energy source; heat source, firing, combustible *or* inflammable *or* flammable material, burnable, combustible, flammable ADJS 2 **flammable, combustible,** burnable; explosive, volcanic, eruptive

inflammation NOUNS **soreness, irritation,** tenderness, sensitiveness; algesia; festering; sore; sore spot; inflammatory disease

inflammatory ADJS inflammative, **inflaming, kindling,** enkindling, lighting; **incendiary,** incendive; arsonous; **incitive, instigative,** instigating; **agitative,** agitational; fomenting, rabble-rousing

inflate VERBS **puff up,** swell; go to one's head, turn one's head; **stretch, distend, dilate,** sufflate, **blow up,** huff, puff, bloat; pump, pump up; **exaggerate,** hyperbolize; **overstate,** overspeak <old>, overreach, **overdraw,** overcharge; **magnify,** amplify <old>; **heat** *or* **heat up the economy;** reflate

inflated ADJS **magnified, expanded,** swollen; **multiplied,** proliferated; **distended, dilated,** sufflated, blown up, puffed up, swollen, swelled, **bloated,** turgid, tumid, plethoric, incrassate; **exaggerated,** hyperbolical, aggrandized; **stretched,** disproportionate, blown up out of all proportion, **extravagant**; high-flown, grandiloquent, windy *and* gassy <both nonformal>, **bombastic, pretentious**

inflexible ADJS unflexible, **unpliable,** unpliant, unmalleable, **intractable,** untractable, intractile, **unbending,** unlimber, **unyielding**, ungiving, **stubborn,** unalterable, immutable; **immovable**; **adamant,** adamantine; **inelastic,** nonelastic, irresilient

inflict VERBS **wreak, do to,** bring, bring upon, bring down upon, bring on *or* down on one's head, visit upon

influence NOUNS 1 **machination, manipulation,** wire-pulling <nonformal>; political influence, behind-the-scenes influence *or* pressure; **prestige,** authority, influentialness; pressure, **weight,** weightiness, moment, **consequence**
2 make oneself felt, **affect,** weigh with, **sway,** bias, bend, incline, dispose, predispose, **move,** prompt, lead; color, tinge, tone, slant, impart spin; **persuade**, jawbone *and* twist one's arm *and* hold one's feet to the fire <all nonformal>, work, work *or* bend to one's will; lead by the nose <nonformal>, wear down, soften up

influence peddler NOUNS **wire-puller;** wheeler-dealer <nonformal>, lobby, lobbyist, influencer, **powerbroker; power behind the throne,** gray eminence, *éminence grise* <Fr>, hidden hand, manipulator, friend at *or* in court, kingmaker; **pressure group,** special-interest group, special interests, single-issue group, PAC *or* political action committee

influential ADJS **powerful**, potent, strong, to be reckoned with; **effective,** effectual, efficacious, telling; **weighty,** momentous, important, consequential, substantial, **prestigious,** estimable, authoritative, reputable; **persuasive,** suasive, personable, **winning,** magnetic, charming, enchanting, charismatic

influx NOUNS **inflow,** inflooding, incursion, indraft, indrawing, inpour, inrun, inroad, infiltration, inrush

inform VERBS **tell, speak on** *or* **for,** apprise, **advise, advertise,** advertise of, **give word,** mention to, **acquaint, enlighten,** familiarize, brief, verse, give the facts, give an account of, give by way of information; **instruct;** possess *or* seize one of the facts; let know, **give** *or* **lead one to believe** *or* **understand;** tell once and for all; notify, give notice *or* notification, serve notice; **report**; **disclose**; shed new *or* fresh light upon

inform on VERBS

<nonformal> **sell one out** *or* **down the river,** tell on, blab, snitch, squeal, peach <old>, sell out, sing, rat, stool, fink, nark, finger, put the finger on, blow the whistle, shop <Brit>, dime, drop a dime, spill one's guts, spell the beans, squawk, weasel

informality NOUNS **informalness,** unceremoniousness; **casualness,** offhandedness, **ease, easiness,** easygoingness; affability, graciousness, cordiality, sociability; Bohemianism, unconventionality; **familiarity; naturalness,** simplicity, plainness, homeliness, homeyness, folksiness <nonformal>, common touch, **unaffectedness,** unpretentiousness; unconstraint, unconstrainedness

informant NOUNS **informer, source,** teller, interviewee, enlightener; **adviser,** monitor; **reporter,** notifier, **announcer,** annunciator; spokesperson, spokeswoman, spokesman, press secretary, press officer, information officer, mouthpiece; **authority,** witness, expert witness; **tipster** <nonformal>, **tout** <nonformal>; newsmonger, gossipmonger; public relations officer

information NOUNS info <nonformal>, **facts, data, knowledge**; public knowledge, open secret, common knowledge;

general information; factual information, hard information; **enlightenment,** light; incidental information, sidelight; **intelligence; the dope** *and* the goods *and* **the scoop** *and* the skinny *and* the straight skinny *and* the inside skinny <all nonformal>; **communication**; **report, word,** message, presentation, account, **statement,** mention; **data,** database, **file,** data set, record, data record, data file, text file

informative ADJS informing, informational; **instructive, enlightening;** educative, educational; advisory, monitory; **communicative**

informed ADJS **enlightened, instructed,** versed, well-versed, educated, schooled, **taught;** posted, briefed, primed, trained; **up on,** up-to-date, abreast of, *au courant* <Fr>; informed of, in the know, clued-in *or* clued-up <nonformal>; **versed in, informed in,** read *or* well-read in, up on, strong in, at home in, master of, expert *or* authoritative in, proficient in, **familiar with,** at home with, **conversant with, acquainted with,** intimate with

informer NOUNS **betrayer,** double-crosser <nonformal>; **snitch** *and* snitcher <both nonformal>; whistle-blower <nonformal>; **tattler,** tattletale, telltale, talebearer; **blab** *or* blabber *or* blabberer *or* blabbermouth <all nonformal>; **squealer** *and* preacher *and* **stool pigeon** *and* stoolie *and* **fink** *and* rat <all nonformal>, nark <Brit nonformal>; **spy**

infraction NOUNS **violation, breach,** breaking; **infringement, transgression, trespass,** contravention; offense; breach of promise, breach of contract, breach of trust *or* faith, bad faith, breach of privilege; breach of the peace; **lawbreaking, violation,** breach *or* violation of law

infrequent ADJS unfrequent, **rare,** scarce, scarce as hens' teeth, scarcer than hens' teeth, **uncommon,** unique, unusual, almost unheard-of, seldom met with, seldom seen, few and far between, **sparse**; one-time, one-shot, once in a lifetime; **slow**

infringe VERBS **overstep,** transgress, trespass, intrude, break bounds, overstep the bounds, go too far, know no bounds, **encroach,** invade, irrupt, make an inroad *or* incursion *or* intrusion, advance upon

infringement NOUNS **overstepping,** transgression, trespass, incursion, intrusion, **encroachment,** infraction, **usurpation,** arrogation, appropriation, assumption

infuriate VERBS **enrage, madden,** drive one mad, frenzy, lash into fury, work up into a passion, make one's blood boil, **provoke,** envenom, **embitter,** madden

infuriated ADJS in a rage *or* passion *or* fury; **furious,** fierce, wild, savage; raving mad <nonformal>, **rabid,** foaming *or* frothing at the mouth; **fuming,** in a fume; **enraged,** raging, raving, ranting, storming

infusion NOUNS **insertion, introduction,** insinuation, injection, perfusion, inoculation, intromission; **steeping,** soaking, brewing; **imbuement, impregnation,** suffusion, decoction, infiltration, instillment, instillation, permeation, pervasion, interpenetration, penetration

ingenue NOUNS **simple soul,** unsophisticate, naïf, **innocent;** juvenile, *jeune première* <Fr>; soubrette

ingenuity NOUNS ingeniousness, resource, resourcefulness, wit; invention, **inventiveness,** originality, **creativity,** creativeness; rich *or* teeming imagination, fertile *or* pregnant imagination, seminal *or* germinal imagination, fertile mind

ingenuous ADJS **artless, simple,** plain, **guideless;** simplehearted, simple-minded; *ingénu* <Fr>; **unsophisticated, naive;** childlike, born yesterday; **innocent;** trustful, trusting, unguarded, unwary, unreserved, confiding, unsuspicious; **open,** openhearted, sincere, candid, **frank**; single-hearted, single-minded; direct, bluff, blunt, outspoken

ingest VERBS **eat,** tuck away, put away; imbibe, **drink; swallow, devour,** ingurgitate; **engulf,** engorge; **gulp,** gulp down, swill, swill down, wolf down, gobble; **absorb,** assimilate, digest, **eat up,** swallow, swallow up, gobble up

ingrained ADJS **confirmed, inveterate,** chronic, established, long-established, fixed, settled, rooted, thorough; incorrigible, irreversible; **deep-rooted,** deep-set, deep-settled, **deep-seated,** deep-dyed; **infixed,** fast, dyed-in-the-wool; in the very grain; infixed, implanted, inwrought

ingratiating ADJS **obsequious, flattering,** sycophantic, sycophantical, toadyish, fawning, flattering, truckling, smarmy <nonformal>, toadying, toadeating, **bootlicking** *and* back scratching *and* backslapping *and* ass-licking *and* brown-nosing <all nonformal>; **groveling,** sniveling, cringing, cowering, crouching, crawling

ingratitude NOUNS **ungratefulness, unthankfulness,** thanklessness, unappreciation, **unappreciativeness;** nonrecognition, denial of due *or* proper credit; grudging *or* halfhearted thanks

benefits forgot
SHAKESPEARE

ingredient NOUNS **component, constituent,** integrant, makings *and* fixings <both nonformal>, **element, factor, part**, player, module, part and parcel; appurtenance, adjunct; **feature,** aspect, specialty, circumstance, detail, item

in-group NOUNS **clique, coterie, set, circle,** ring, junto, junta, cabal, camarilla, **clan,** group; **crew** *and* mob *and* **crowd** *and* **bunch** *and* outfit <all nonformal>; cadre, inner circle; closed *or* charmed circle; elite, elite group; leadership group; **old-boy network;** the Establishment, powers that be, lords of creation

ingrown ADJS **entrenched,** vested, firmly established; **well-established,** well-founded, **well-grounded,** in *or* on bedrock; old-line, long-established; **confirmed, inveterate; infixed,** implanted, engrafted, embedded, inwrought

inhabit VERBS **occupy,** tenant, move in *or* into, take up one's abode, make one's home; rent, lease; **reside, live, live in, dwell, lodge, stay,** remain, abide, domicile, domiciliate; **room,** bunk, crash <nonformal>, berth, doss down <Brit>; **exist in, consist in,** subsist in, lie in, rest in, repose in, reside in, abide in, dwell in, **inhere in,** be present in, be a quality of, be comprised in, be contained in, be constituted by, be coextensive with

inhabitant NOUNS inhabiter, habitant; **occupant,** occupier, **dweller, tenant, denizen,** inmate; **resident,** residencer, residentiary, resider

inhale VERBS **draw in, suck,** suckle, suck in *or* up, aspirate; **inspire,** breathe in, puff, draw, drag <nonformal>, pull; snuff, snuffle, sniff, sniffle, snuff in *or* up, slurp

inherent ADJS **immediate,** immanent, indwelling, **available, accessible, at hand,** in view, within reach *or* sight *or* call, in place; **intrinsic,** resident, implicit, indwelling; **ingrained,** in the very grain; **instinctive,** natural, **innate,** unlearned

inherit VERBS be heir to, **come into,** come in for, come by, fall *or* step into; step into the shoes of, succeed to, take the mantle of, take over

inheritance NOUNS **heritage,** patrimony, birthright, legacy, bequest, bequeathal; reversion; entail; heirship; **succession,** line of succession, mode of succession, law of succession; primogeniture, ultimogeniture; **heritable; heirloom**

inherited ADJS **inbred, genetic, hereditary,** bred in the bone, in the blood, running in the blood *or* race *or* strain, radical, rooted; connate, connatal, coeval

inhibit VERBS **hinder, impede,** arrest, check, countercheck, scotch, **curb,** snub; damp, dampen, pour *or* dash *or* throw cold water; **retard,** slacken, **delay,** detain, **hold back, keep back,** set back, hold up <nonformal>; **restrain**; keep *or* hold in check, bottle up, dam up

inhibition NOUNS **suppression, repression,** resistance, restraint, censorship; block, psychological block, blockage, blocking; reaction formation; rigid control; **suppressed desire**

inhospitable ADJS unhospitable; **unreceptive,** closed; **uncordial,** ungracious, **unfriendly,** unneighborly

inhuman ADJS **cruel,** cruel-hearted, sadistic; **ruthless**; **brutal,** brutish, brute, bestial, beastly, animal, animalistic; inhumane, **savage,** fierce, ferocious, vicious, murderous, atrocious, mindless, insensate, monstrous, pitiless, merciless, bloody, sanguinary

inimitable ADJS **matchless, unmatched,** unmatchable, unrivaled, unparalleled, **unequaled,** unapproached, unapproachable, **unsurpassed,** unexcelled; **incomparable,** beyond compare *or* comparison, without equal *or* parallel, *sans pareil* <Fr>

initial VERBS 1 **ratify, endorse, sign,** undersign, sign on the dotted line, put one's John Hancock on <nonformal>, put one's mark *or* X *or* cross on; **letter, inscribe,** character, sign, mark
ADJS 2 **beginning,** initiatory *or* initia-

tive; **introductory,** inaugural *or* inauguratory; **original, first,** first ever, first of all; aboriginal, autochthonous

initiate VERBS **originate, create,** invent; **precede**, take the initiative, take the first step, take the lead, pioneer; **lead,** lead off, lead the way; **break the ice,** take the plunge, break ground, cut the first turf, lay the first stone

initiation NOUNS **installation,** installment, inauguration, investiture, placing in office; initialization, first move, opening move, gambit, **first step,** baby step, *le premier pas* <Fr>

initiative NOUNS **undertaking,** enterprise, operation, work, venture, project, proposition *and* deal <both nonformal>; **effort,** attempt, **act,** step, measure, *démarche* <Fr>, move, maneuver, motion

inject VERBS **insert, introduce,** insinuate, infuse, perfuse, inoculate, intromit; **enter**; **penetrate; put in, stick in,** set in, throw in, pop in, tuck in, whip in; slip in, ease in; interject

injection NOUNS **inoculation,** hypodermic, hypodermic injection, shot *and* bing <both nonformal>, hypospray *or* jet injection; booster, booster shot <nonformal>
2 **intrusion,** obtrusion, interposition, interposal, imposition, insinuation, **interference,** intervention, interventionism, interruption, interjection

injunction NOUNS **court order,** legal order; **instruction,** direction, charge, commission, dictate; **order,** command; **restraint,** constraint; **inhibition;** legal restraint, enjoining, enjoinder, interdict; proscription, **prohibition, forbidding,** forbiddance; **ban,** embargo, prohibitory injunction, *interdictum* <L>, interdiction

injure VERBS **mistreat,** maltreat, ill-treat, ill-use, abuse, molest; buffet, batter, bruise, **savage,** manhandle, maul, knock about, rough, rough up; **impair, damage,** endamage, **harm, hurt,** irritate

injured ADJS **pained, grieved,** aggrieved; **wounded,** hurt, **bruised,** mauled; **cut,** cut to the quick; **impaired,** damaged, harmed

injurious ADJS **harmful, hurtful,** scatheful, **baneful,** baleful, distressing, **damaging, detrimental,** deleterious, counterproductive, **pernicious,** mischievous; **malignant,** malign, malevolent, malefic, vicious

injury NOUNS **indignity,** affront, offense, humiliation; **violation,** outrage, violence, atrocity; **impairment,** damage, harm, mischief, scathe, detriment, loss, weakening, sickening; **offense,** injustice, **wrong; detriment,** loss, mischief

injustice NOUNS **unjustness; inequity,** iniquity, inequitableness, iniquitousness; inequality, inequality of treatment *or* dealing; **wrong, wrongness,** wrongfulness, unmeetness, improperness, **impropriety;** undueness; what should not be, what ought not *or* must not be; unlawfulness, illegality

inkling NOUNS **suggestion,** bare suggestion, suspicion, hint, sense, feeling, **feeling in one's bones, intuition,** intimation, impression, notion, mere notion, hunch *and* sneaking suspicion <both nonformal>, trace of an idea, half an idea, vague idea, hazy idea

inlay NOUNS 1 **insert,** insertion; **inset;** gore, godet, gusset; inlayer, inside layer, inlaying; **filling,** filler
VERBS 2 **inset;** infix; fit in; **fill,** pack, load; **line,** interline, interlineate

inlet NOUNS **cove,** creek <Brit>, arm of the sea, arm, armlet, canal, reach, loch <Scots>, **bay, fjord,** bight; **gulf; estuary,** firth *or* frith, bayou, mouth, *boca* <Sp>; **passageway,** opening, aperture; access

inmate NOUNS **occupant,** occupier, dweller, tenant, **denizen; prisoner,** jailbird <nonformal>, convict

inmost ADJS **interior,** innermost, intimate; visceral, gut <nonformal>; **intrinsic**; deep; central; **private,** privy, closed-door

innards NOUNS **viscera,** vitals, internal organs, insides, inwards, internals; inner mechanism, works <nonformal>; **guts** *and* kishkes *and* giblets <all nonformal>

innate ADJS **inborn,** born, congenital; **native, natural,** natural to, connatural, native to, indigenous; **constitutional,** bodily, physical, temperamental, organic; **inbred, genetic, hereditary,** inherited, bred in the bone, in the blood, running in the blood *or* race *or* strain, radical, rooted; connate, connatal, coeval; **instinctive,** instinctual, atavistic, primal

inner ADJS **intrinsic,** internal, inward; **inherent,** resident, implicit, immanent, indwelling; **ingrained,** in the very grain; infixed, implanted, inwrought, deep-seated; **subjective,** esoteric, private, secret

inner circle NOUNS **clique,** coterie, set, circle, ring, junto, junta, cabal, camarilla, **clan,** group; closed *or* charmed circle; ingroup, we-group; elite, elite group; **old-boy network**

innermost ADJS **interior,** inmost, intimate, private; visceral, gut <nonformal>; **intrinsic**; deep; central; **private,** inward, personal; protected

innocence NOUNS innocentness; unfallen *or* unlapsed *or* prelapsarian state; **guiltlessness,** faultlessness, blamelessness, reproachlessness, **sinlessness; spotlessness,** stainlessness, taintlessness, unblemishedness; **purity,** cleanness, cleanliness, whiteness, immaculateness, immaculacy, impeccability; clean hands, clean slate, clear conscience, nothing to hide; **chastity, virtue;** ingenuousness

innocent ADJS **artless, simple,** plain, **guileless;** simplehearted, simpleminded; **unsophisticated,** green, callow, ingenuous, naive, unripe, raw; childlike, born yesterday; trustful, trusting, unguarded, unwary, unreserved, confiding, unsuspicious; **open,** openhearted, sincere, candid, **frank**

innocuous ADJS **harmless,** hurtless, unhurtful; well-meaning, well-meant; **uninjurious,** undamaging, innoxious, innocent, unobjectionable; inoffensive; nonmalignant, **benign;** nontoxic, nonvenomous

innovation NOUNS **novelty,** newfangled device *or* contraption <nonformal>, neoism, neonism, **new** *or* **latest wrinkle** <nonformal>, **the last word** *or* **the latest thing** <both nonformal>, *dernier cri* <Fr>; **introduction,** discovery, invention, launching; neologism, neoterism, coinage; **breakthrough,** leap, quantum jump *or* leap

innovator NOUNS **transformer,** transmogrifier, innovationist, introducer; precursor; **alterant,** alterer, alterative, **agent,** catalytic agent, catalyst; **vanguard,** avant-garde, avant-gardist, groundbreaker

innuendo NOUNS **aspersion,** slur, **remark, reflection,** imputation, **insinuation,** suggestion, sly suggestion, whispering campaign; disparaging *or* uncomplimentary remark, allusion; coloration, tinge, undertone, overtone, undercurrent, more than meets the eye *or* ear, something between the lines, intimation, touch, nuance

innumerable ADJS **numberless,** unnumbered, **countless,** uncounted, uncountable, unreckonable, untold, incalculable, immeasurable, unmeasured, measureless, inexhaustible, endless, infinite, without end *or* limit, more than one can tell, more than you can shake a stick at <nonformal>, no end of *or* to; countless as the stars *or* sands

inoculate VERBS **immunize, vaccinate,** shoot <nonformal>; **insert, introduce,** inform, insinuate, inject, infuse, perfuse, intromit

inoculation NOUNS **vaccination; injection,** hypodermic, hypodermic injection, shot *and* bing <both nonformal>, hypospray *or* jet injection; booster, booster shot <nonformal>; antitoxin, vaccine; **insertion, introduction,** insinuation, perfusion, intromission

inoffensive ADJS **harmless,** hurtless, unhurtful; well-meaning, well-meant; **uninjurious,** undamaging, **innocuous,** innoxious, innocent; **benign**

inoperative ADJS **unusable,** unemployable, inoperable, unworkable; out of order, out of whack *and* on the blink *and* on the fritz <all nonformal>, in disrepair; **malfunctioning,** out of working order, out of condition, out of repair, out of tune, out of gear; out of joint; **broken**

inopportune ADJS **untimely,** unseasonable, badly timed, ill-timed, mistimed, unripe, unready, ill-considered, too late *or* soon, out of phase *or* time *or* sync; **inconvenient,** unhandy; malapropos, *mal à propos* <Fr>

inquest NOUNS **hearing, inquiry, inquisition,** inquiring, probing, inquirendo; inquisition; inquiring mind

inquire VERBS **be curious, want to know, take an interest in,** take a lively interest, burn with curiosity; interrogate, quiz, question, query; seek, dig up, dig around for, nose out, nose around for

inquirer NOUNS **asker, prober,** querier, querist, **questioner,** questionist, interrogator; examiner, catechist; inquisitor, inquisitionist; cross-questioner, cross-interrogator, **cross-examiner;** interlocutor; **pollster,** poller, sampler, opinion sampler; **interviewer; busybody,** gossip, **pry,** Paul Pry, **snoop,** snooper, nosy Parker <nonformal>

inquiring ADJS **curious, inquisitive,** interested, quizzical; **alert,** tuned in <nonformal>, **attentive**; burning with curiosity, eaten up *or* consumed with curiosity, curious as a cat; overcurious, supercurious; morbidly curious

inquiry NOUNS inquiring, probing, **inquest**, inquirendo; inquisition; **question,** query, interrogation, interrogatory; interrogative; vexed *or* knotty question, burning question; **canvass,** survey, questionnaire, questionary

inquisition NOUNS **trial, jury trial,** trial by jury, trial at the bar, **hearing, inquiry,** inquest, assize; **examination,** cross-examination; **grilling,** the grill <nonformal>; police interrogation; **the third-degree** <nonformal>

inquisitive ADJS **curious,** inquiring, interested, quizzical; **alert,** tuned in <nonformal>, **attentive**; burning with curiosity, eaten up *or* consumed with curiosity, curious as a cat; morbidly curious

inroad NOUNS **intrusion,** impingement, **infringement,** invasion, incursion, influx, irruption, infiltration; encroachment; **overstepping, transgression, trespass,** usurpation, infraction

insane ADJS **mad,** stark-mad, mad as a hatter, mad as a March hare, **stark-staring mad,** maddened, **sick,** crazed, **lunatic,** moonstruck, **daft, non compos mentis,** non compos, **unsound,** of unsound mind, **demented, deranged,** deluded, disoriented, unhinged, **unbalanced,** unsettled, distraught, wandering, mazed, crackbrained, brainsick, sick *or* soft in the head, not right, not in one's right mind, **touched,** touched in the head, **out of one's mind,** out of one's senses *or* wits, bereft of reason, reasonless, irrational, deprived of reason, senseless, witless; queer, queer in the head, odd, strange, off

insanity NOUNS insaneness, **lunacy, madness,** *folie* <Fr>, **craziness, daftness,** oddness, strangeness, queerness, abnormality; loss of touch *or* contact with reality, loss of mind *or* reason; dementia, athymia, brainsickness, mindsickness, mental sickness; **mental illness,** alienation, aberration, mental disturbance, **derangement,** distraction, disorientation, mental derangement *or* disorder, unbalance, mental instability, unsoundness, **unsoundness of mind**

insatiable ADJS **gluttonous, greedy,** voracious, ravenous, edacious, rapacious, polyphagic, bulimic, hyperphagic, Apician; **piggish, hoggish,** swinish; insatiate, unsatisfied, unsated, unappeased, unappeasable, limitless, bottomless, unquenchable, quenchless, unslaked, unslakable, slakeless

inscribe VERBS 1 **write out,** make out; **write down, record,** put *or* place upon record; enscroll; **register, enroll,** matriculate, check in; impanel; **print,** imprint, **stamp, etch,** engrave, impress; instill, infix, inculcate, impress, imprint, stamp, etch, grave, engrave
2 **impress on the mind, get into one's head,** drive *or* hammer into one's head, get across, get into one's thick head *or* skull <nonformal>

inscription NOUNS **epitaph,** tombstone marking; epigraph, graffito; **writing,** scrivening <old>, lettering; engrossment; inscript

inscrutable ADJS **unfathomable,** impenetrable, unsearchable, numinous; **unintelligible, incomprehensible,** inapprehensible, ungraspable, unknowable, incognizable; **past comprehension,** beyond one's comprehension, beyond understanding

insecure ADJS **unconfident,** unsure, unassured, unsure of oneself; unself-confident, unself-assured, unself-reliant; **unreliable,** undependable, untrustworthy, treacherous, **unsound,** unstable, unsteady, shaky, tottery, rocky

inseminate VERBS **fertilize,** fructify, fecundate, fecundify; **impregnate,** spermatize, knock up <nonformal>, **get with child** *or* **young; pollinate** *or* pollinize, pollen; cross-fertilize, cross-pollinate *or* cross-pollinize

insensitive ADJS **callous, calloused,** Philistine; **thick-skinned,** pachydermatous; **hard, hard-hearted, hardened,** case-hardened, coarsened, brutalized, indurated, stony, stony-hearted, marble-hearted, flinthearted, flinty, steely, impervious, inured, armored *or* steeled against, proof against, as hard as nails; **inconsiderate, unthoughtful,** unmindful, unheedful, disregardful, **thoughtless,** heedless, mindless, unthinking; **tactless**

inseparable ADJS impartible, **indivisible,** undividable, indissoluble, inalienable, inseverable, bound up in *or* with; **thick, thick as thieves** <nonformal>

insert NOUNS 1 insertion; **inset, inlay;** gore, godet, gusset; **graft,** scion *or* cion; tessera
VERBS 2 **introduce,** insinuate, inject, infuse, perfuse, inoculate, intromit; **enter**; **penetrate; put in, stick in,** set in, throw in, pop in, tuck in, whip in; slip in, ease in; **enter,** make an entry, write in

inside ADJS 1 **internal,** inner, inward; **innermost,** inmost, **intimate,** private; visceral, gut <nonformal>; **intrinsic**; deep; central; indoor; **confidential,** auricular, esoteric; **off the record,** not for the record, not to be minuted, within these four walls, eyes-only, between us; not for attribution; sensitive, privileged, under privilege
ADVS 2 **in, within;** herein, therein, wherein

insider NOUNS **member,** affiliate, belonger, initiate, one of us, cardholder, card-carrier, card-carrying member

insides NOUNS **innards** <nonformal>, inwards, internals; inner mechanism, what makes it tick *and* works <both nonformal>; **guts** <nonformal>, **vitals, viscera,** *kishkes* <Yiddish>, giblets; entrails, bowels, guts

insight NOUNS **discernment,** critical discernment, penetration, **perception,** perceptiveness, perspicacity; **flair; judgment,** acumen

insightful ADJS **understanding,** comprehending, perceptive, discerning, apperceptive, percipient, perspicacious, appercipient, shrewd, sagacious, wise; omniscient, all-knowing

insignia NOUNS **regalia,** ensign, **emblem, badge, symbol,** logo <nonformal>, marking, attribute; badge of office, mark of office, chain, chain of office, collar; wand, verge, *fasces* <L>, **mace, staff, baton**

insignificance NOUNS **unimportance,** inconsequence, inconsequentiality, indifference, **immateriality;** inessentiality; ineffectuality; unnoteworthiness, unimpressiveness; inferiority, secondariness, low order of importance, low priority, dispensability, expendability, marginality; **smallness,** littleness, slightness, inconsiderableness, negligibility; irrelevancy, meaninglessness; **pettiness,** puniness, pokiness, picayune, picayunishness; irrelevance

insignificant ADJS **small, inconsiderable,** inconsequential, immaterial, negligible, no great shakes, footling, one-horse *and* pint-size *and* vest-pocket <all nonformal>; unimportant, no skin off one's nose *or* ass, **trivial,** trifling, nugacious, nugatory, petty, mean, niggling, picayune *or* picayunish, nickel-and-dime *and* penny-ante *and* Mickey-Mouse *and* chickenshit <all nonformal>; **small, little,** minute, footling, minor, inferior; irrelevant

insincere ADJS **affected, pretentious,** la-di-da, posy <Brit nonformal>; **artificial,** unnatural; **deceitful;** unsincere, uncandid, unfrank, disingenuous; **false, hypocritical**

insinuate VERBS **hint,** intimate, suggest, imply, indicate, adumbrate, lead *or* leave one to gather, justify one in supposing, give *or* drop *or* throw out a hint, give an inkling of, **hint at; allege**

insipid ADJS **tasteless, flavorless,** bland, spiceless, savorless, sapless, unsavory, unflavored; pulpy, pappy, gruelly; **weak, thin,** mild, **wishy-washy,** milktoast, washy, watery, watered, watered-down, diluted, dilute, milk-and-water; **flat, stale,** dead, *fade* <Fr>; vapid, inane, jejune, hollow, empty, superficial; indifferent, neither one thing nor the other

insist VERBS **insist on** *or* **upon,** stick to <nonformal>, set one's heart *or* mind upon; **take one's stand upon,** stand on *or* upon, put *or* lay it on the line <nonformal>, make no bones about it; stand upon one's rights, **put one's foot down** <nonformal>; brook *or* take no denial, not take no for an answer; **maintain, contend,** assert; urge, press; **persist**

insistence NOUNS **exigence, importunity,** importunateness, importunacy, **demandingness,** pertinaciousness, pertinacity; pressure, pressingness, **urgency,** exigency; **persistence**

insistent ADJS **persevering,** perseverant, **persistent,** persisting; dogged, plodding, slogging, plugging; **pertinacious,** tenacious, stick-to-itive <nonformal>; **unswerving,** unremitting, unabating, unintermitting, uninterrupted; single-minded, utterly attentive; undiscouraged, undaunted, indomitable, game to the last *or* to the end; **importunate,**

urgent, pressing, loud, clamant, crying, clamorous

insolence NOUNS 1 **presumption,** presumptuousness; **audacity, effrontery,** boldness, assurance, hardihood, bumptiousness; overweeningness; **contempt, contemptuousness,** contumely; **disdain**, *sprezzatura* <Ital>; **arrogance**, uppishness *and* uppityness <both nonformal>; **impudence,** disrespect, disrespectfulness

2 <nonformal> **cheek,** face, brass, **nerve, gall, chutzpah,** crust

insolent ADJS insulting; **presumptuous,** presuming, overpresumptuous, overweening; **audacious, bold,** assured, hardy, bumptious; **contemptuous**, contumelious; **disdainful**, **arrogant**, uppish *and* uppity <both nonformal>; forward, pushy <nonformal>, obtrusive, pushy <nonformal>, **impudent**

insolvent ADJS **bankrupt,** in receivership, in the hands of receivers, belly-up <nonformal>, broken, **broke** *and* busted <both nonformal>, **ruined,** failed, out of business, unable to pay one's creditors, unable to meet one's obligations, on the rocks; destitute

insomnia NOUNS **wakefulness,** wake; **sleeplessness,** restlessness, tossing and turning; insomnolence *or* insomnolency, white night, all-night vigil, lidless vigil, *per vigilium* <L>

inspect VERBS **scrutinize, survey, eye,** contemplate, look over, give the eye *or* the once-over <nonformal>; examine, vet <Brit nonformal>; **pore,** pore over, peruse; take a close *or* careful look; take a long, hard look; size up <nonformal>; take stock of

inspection NOUNS **examination, scrutiny; survey, review, perusal,** look-over, once over *and* look-see <both nonformal>, perlustration, **study,** look-through, scan, run-through

inspector NOUNS **examiner,** examinant, **tester;** scrutinizer, scrutator, scrutineer, quality-control inspector; **monitor,** reviewer

inspiration NOUNS **encouragement, heartening,** inspiriting, inspiritment, emboldening, assurance, reassurance, pat *or* clap on the back; afflatus, divine inspiration

inspire VERBS inspirit, spirit, spirit up; fire, **fire one's imagination; animate, exhilarate,** enliven; **infuse, infect,** inject, inoculate, imbue, inform

inspired ADJS **fired,** afire, on fire; **well-put,** well-expressed, inspired, theopneustic

inspiring ADJS **inspirational,** inspiriting; infusive; animating, exhilarating, enlivening

instability NOUNS **inconstancy,** changefulness, unstableness, **unsteadiness,** unsteadfastness, unfixedness, unsettledness, rootlessness; **uncertainty,** undependability, inconsistency, shiftiness, unreliability; **variability,** variation, variety, restlessness, deviability; unpredictability, irregularity

install VERBS emplace, spot <nonformal>, put in place; **invest,** vest, place in office, put in, instate, induct, inaugurate, initiate, invest, ordain, **place in office**

installation NOUNS installment, **instatement,** induction, placement, **inauguration,** investiture, taking office; **accession,** accedence; coronation, enthronement

instance NOUNS **particular, item, detail,** point, count, fact, matter, article, datum, element, part, ingredient, factor, facet, aspect, thing; **example,** exemplar; relevant instance, **case,** typical example *or* case, case in point, object lesson

instant NOUNS 1 **moment, second,** split second, millisecond, microsecond, nanosecond, half a second, minute, **trice,** twinkle, **twinkling, twinkling** *or* **twinkle of an eye,** twink, **wink,** bat of an eye <nonformal>, **flash,** crack, tick, stroke, coup, breath, twitch; two shakes of a lamb's tail *and* two shakes *and* shake *and* half a shake *and* **jiffy** *and* jiff *and* half a jiffy <all nonformal>

ADJS 2 **hasty, hurried,** festinate, **quick,** flying, **expeditious,** prompt; quick-and-dirty <nonformal>, **immediate,** on the spot; onrushing, **swift, speedy; instantaneous,** momentary, **immediate,** presto, quick as thought *or* lightning; lightning-like, lightning-swift

instantaneous ADJS instant, momentary, **immediate,** lightning-like, lightning-swift; nearly simultaneous; simultaneous

instigate VERBS **incite, put up to** <nonformal>; set on, sic on; **foment,** ferment, **agitate,** arouse, excite, stir up, work up, whip up; rally; **inflame,**

incense, **fire,** heat, heat up, impassion; **provoke,** pique, whet, tickle; nettle; feed the fire, add fuel to the flame, fan, fan the flame

instigator NOUNS **inciter,** exciter, urger; **provoker,** *provocateur* <Fr>, *agent provocateur* <Fr>, catalyst; **agitator, fomenter,** inflamer; agitprop; **rabble-rouser,** rouser, **demagogue; firebrand, incendiary; troublemaker,** mischief-maker, ringleader

instill VERBS **inculcate, indoctrinate,** catechize, inoculate, **infuse,** imbue, impregnate, **implant,** infix, impress; **impress upon the mind** *or* **memory,** urge on the mind, beat into, beat *or* knock into one's head, grind in, drill into, drum into one's head *or* skull; **condition, brainwash**

instinct NOUNS **impulse;** natural impulse, blind impulse, urge, drive; vagrant *or* fleeting impulse

instinctive ADJS natural, **inherent, innate,** unlearned; unconscious, subliminal; **involuntary, automatic,** spontaneous, impulsive; **instinctual**

institute NOUNS 1 **organization,** establishment, foundation, **institution,** school, **educational institution,** teaching institution, academic *or* scholastic institution, teaching and research institution, **academy**
VERBS 2 **inaugurate,** found, establish, set up <nonformal>; **introduce,** broach, bring up, lift up, raise; **launch,** float; **usher in,** ring in <nonformal>; **set on foot,** set agoing, turn on, kick-start *and* jump-start <both nonformal>, start up, start going, start the ball rolling <nonformal>

institution NOUNS **organization,** establishment, foundation, institute; **creation,** establishing, origin, origination, setting-up, setting in motion; constitution, installation, formation, inauguration, **inception,** realization, materialization, effectuation

institutionalize VERBS **commit,** consign, commit to prison, send to jail, send up *and* send up the river <both nonformal>; commit to an institution, recommit, remit, remand

instruct VERBS **advise,** coach, brief; **teach,** give instruction, give lessons in, **educate, school; edify,** enlighten, civilize, illumine; **direct, guide;** get across, **inform; show,** show how, show the ropes, demonstrate; enlarge *or* broaden the mind; sharpen the wits, open the eyes *or* mind; teach a lesson, give a lesson to; **ground,** teach the rudiments *or* elements *or* basics; catechize; teach an old dog new tricks; reeducate

instruction NOUNS **teaching,** education, schooling, tuition; edification, **enlightenment,** illumination; tutelage, tutorage, tutorship; tutoring, coaching, private teaching, teacher; spoon-feeding; **pedagogy,** pedagogics, didactics, didacticism; catechization; computer-aided instruction, programmed instruction; self-teaching, self-instruction; **school**; **formal education,** coursework, schoolwork

instructive ADJS **informative,** informing, informational; **enlightening;** educative, educational; advisory, monitory; **communicative**

instructor NOUNS **teacher, educator,** preceptor, **mentor; master,** maestro; **pedagogue,** pedagogist, educationist; schoolman; **schoolteacher,** schoolmaster, schoolkeeper; **professor, academic,** member of academy; don <Brit>, fellow; guide, docent; rabbi, *melamed* <Heb>, pandit, pundit, guru, *mullah* <Persian>, *starets* <Russ>

instrument NOUNS **tool, implement, appliance,** device; contrivance, lever, mechanism; **vehicle,** organ; **agent**; medium, mediator, intermedium, intermediary, intermediate, interagent, liaison, go-between; expediter, facilitator, animator; **cat's-paw,** puppet, dummy, pawn, creature, minion, stooge <nonformal>; stalking horse; dupe

instrumental ADJS 1 **helping,** assisting, serving; **assistant, auxiliary,** adjuvant, subservient, subsidiary, ancillary, accessory; ministerial, ministering, ministrant; fostering, nurtural
2 orchestral, symphonic, concert

insubordinate ADJS **unsubmissive,** indocile, uncompliant, uncooperative, noncooperative, noncooperating, **intractable;** mutinous, disobedient

insubordination NOUNS **disobedience,** nonobedience, **noncompliance; undutifulness,** unduteousness; willful disobedience; indiscipline; mutiny

insubstantial ADJS **unsubstantial,** nonsubstantial, unsubstanced; intangible, impalpable, imponderable; **immaterial**; **bodiless,** incorporeal, unsolid, unconcrete; weightless; **transient**, ephemeral, fleeting, fugitive

insufferable ADJS **intolerable,** insupportable, unendurable, unbearable, past bearing, not to be borne *or* endured, for the birds <nonformal>, **too much** *or* a bit much <nonformal>, more than flesh and blood can bear, enough to drive one mad, enough to provoke a saint, enough to make a preacher swear <nonformal>, enough to try the patience of Job

insufficiency NOUNS **inadequacy,** insufficientness, inadequateness; short supply, seller's market; none to spare; nonsatisfaction, nonfulfillment, coming *or* falling short *or* shy; **undercommitment;** too little too late; a band-aid <nonformal>, a drop in the bucket *or* the ocean, a lick and a promise, a cosmetic measure; **incompetence,** incompetency, unqualification, unsuitability

insufficient ADJS unsufficing, **inadequate;** found wanting, defective, incomplete, imperfect, deficient, lacking, failing, wanting; **too few,** undersupplied; **too little,** not enough, precious little, a trickle *or* mere trickle; **unsatisfactory,** unsatisfying; cosmetic, merely cosmetic, surface, superficial, symptomatic, merely symptomatic; **incompetent,** unequal to, unqualified, not up to

insular ADJS insulated, isolated; island, islandy *or* islandish, islandlike; islanded, isleted, island-dotted; **remote, out-of-the-way,** up-country, in a backwater, out-of-the-world, out-back *and* back of beyond <both Austral>; **narrow,** parochial

insulate VERBS **segregate,** separate, separate out *or* off, divide, cordon, cordon off; **isolate,** seclude; **set apart,** keep apart; **quarantine,** put in isolation

insulated ADJS **insular,** isolated; **segregated,** separated, cordoned-off, divided; **isolated,** secluded; **set apart,** sequestered; **quarantined**

insult NOUNS 1 **indignity,** affront, offense, injury, humiliation; scurrility, contempt, contumely, despite, flout, flouting, mockery, jeering, jeer, mock, scoff, gibe, taunt, brickbat <nonformal>; **aspersion,** uncomplimentary remark, slap *or* kick in the face, left-handed *or* backhanded compliment, damning with faint praise; cut
VERBS 2 **offend, affront,** give offense to, disoblige, outrage, step *or* tread on one's toes; dishonor, humiliate, treat with indignity; call names, kick *or* slap in the face, take *or* pluck by the beard; **add insult to injury**

insulting ADJS **insolent, abusive, offensive,** humiliating, degrading, contemptuous, contumelious, calumnious; scurrilous, scurrile

insurance NOUNS **security, surety,** indemnity, guaranty, guarantee, warranty, warrant; assurance <Brit>; **annuity,** variable annuity; **social security**

insure VERBS **secure,** guarantee, guaranty, warrant, assure, ensure, bond, **certify; make sure, make certain,** make sure of, make no doubt, make no mistake; remove *or* dismiss *or* expunge *or* erase all doubt; **underwrite**

insured ADJS **secured,** covered, **guaranteed, warranted,** certified, ensured, **assured;** certain, sure

insurer NOUNS **guarantor,** warrantor, guaranty, guarantee; mortgagor; underwriter; sponsor, surety

insurgent NOUNS 1 **rebel,** revolter; insurrectionary, insurrecto, **insurrectionist;** malcontent, *frondeur* <Fr>; **mutineer,** agitator; extremist; revolutionary, revolutionist; traitor, subversive; freedom fighter
ADJS 2 **rebellious,** rebel, breakaway; **mutinous,** mutineering; **insurrectionary,** riotous, turbulent; factious, **seditious,** seditionary; revolutionary, revolutional; traitorous, treasonable, subversive; extreme, extremistic

insurmountable ADJS **unachievable,** unattainable, unrealizable, uncompassable; unsurmountable, **insuperable; beyond one,** beyond one's power, beyond one's control, out of one's depth, too much for

insurrection NOUNS **revolt,** rebellion, revolution, mutiny, insurgence *or* insurgency, *émeute* <Fr>, **uprising,** rising, **riot,** civil disorder; peasant revolt, *jacquerie* <Fr>; putsch, coup d'état; intifada

intact ADJS untouched, undamaged, all in one piece <nonformal>, unimpaired, virgin, pristine, unspoiled; **sound,** whole, entire, complete, integral; unhurt, unharmed, unscathed, with a whole skin

intangible ADJS **unsubstantial**, insubstantial, impalpable, imponderable; **incorporeal,** incorporate, incorporeous;

unphysical, nonphysical; **unfleshly;** airy, ghostly, spectral, phantom, shadowy, ethereal

integral ADJS integrated; **one,** one and indivisible; **inclusive,** all-inclusive, **unitary, unified,** united, rolled into one, composite; **intact,** whole, entire, complete

integrate VERBS **form** *or* **make a whole,** constitute a whole; unite, form a unity; **amalgamate,** alloy, coalesce, **fuse, merge,** meld, compound, compose, conflate, concoct; **combine, incorporate, consolidate,** assimilate, put *or* lump together, roll into one, come together, make one, unitize

integrated ADJS **combined,** united, amalgamated, incorporated, consolidated, assimilated, one, unitary, unitive, unitized, **joined**, joint, conjoint; **merged,** blended, fused; **mixed; unified,** rolled into one, composite

integration NOUNS **affiliation,** alliance, allying, alignment, **association,** consociation, combination, **union,** unification, **coalition,** fusion, merger, coalescence, coadunation, amalgamation, **league, federation, confederation,** confederacy, consolidation, incorporation, inclusion

integrity NOUNS **probity,** assured probity, **honesty,** rectitude, uprightness, upstandingness, erectness, **virtue,** virtuousness, **righteousness, goodness;** cleanness, **decency; honor,** honorableness, worthiness, estimableness, reputability, nobility; unimpeachableness, unimpeachability, irreproachableness, irreproachability, blamelessness; **soundness,** intactness, wholeness, entireness, completeness

intellect NOUNS **mind,** *mens* <L>; mental *or* intellectual faculty, nous, **reason, rationality,** rational *or* reasoning faculty, power of reason, *Vernunft* <Ger>, *esprit* <Fr>, *raison* <Fr>, ratio, discursive reason, **intelligence,** mentality, mental capacity, **understanding,** reasoning, intellection, conception; intellectual

discourse of reason
Shakespeare

intellectual NOUNS 1 **intellect,** intellectualist, literate, member of the intelligentsia, white-collar intellectual; **brain** *and* rocket scientist *and* brain surgeon <all nonformal>; **pundit, Brahmin, mandarin,** egg-head *and* pointy-head <both nonformal>; **highbrow** <nonformal>; wise man
ADJS 2 **mental,** rational, reasoning, thinking, noetic, conceptive, conceptual, phrenic; intelligent; noological; cerebral

intelligence NOUNS 1 **secret service,** intelligence service, intelligence bureau *or* department; military intelligence, naval intelligence; **counterintelligence**
2 **intellect,** head, brain, mentality, consciousness; wise man, wisdom

intelligence agent NOUNS **secret agent,** operative, cloak-and-dagger operative, **undercover man,** inside man <nonformal>; **spy,** espionage agent; counterspy, double agent; **spotter; scout,** reconnoiterer; **intelligence officer;** spymaster; spy-catcher <nonformal>, counterintelligence agent

intelligent ADJS ideational, conceptual, conceptive, discursive; sophic, noetic; **knowing,** understanding, reasonable, rational, sensible, bright; sane; not so dumb <nonformal>, strong-minded

intelligentsia NOUNS literati, illuminati; intellectual elite; clerisy

intelligible ADJS **comprehensible, apprehensible,** prehensible, graspable, **knowable,** cognizable, scrutable, **fathomable,** decipherable, plumbable, penetrable, interpretable; **understandable,** easily understood, easy to understand, exoteric; readable; articulate

intemperance NOUNS intemperateness, **indulgence,** self-indulgence; **overindulgence,** overdoing; **unrestraint,** unconstraint, indiscipline, uncontrol; **immoderation,** immoderacy, immoderateness; inordinacy, inordinateness; **excess,** excessiveness, too much, too-muchness <nonformal>; prodigality, extravagance; crapulence *or* crapulency, crapulousness; **incontinence**; **swinishness,** gluttony; **drunkenness**

intend VERBS **purpose, plan,** purport, **mean,** have in mind, think, **propose; resolve,** determine; project, **design,** destine; **aim,** aim at, take aim at, draw a bead on, set one's sights on, have designs on, go for, drive at, aspire to *or* after, be after, set before oneself, purpose to oneself; harbor a design; **desire**

intended NOUNS 1 **fiancé, fiancée,** bride-to-be, affianced, betrothed, future

ADJS 2 **intentional,** proposed, purposed, telic, **projected, designed,** of design, aimed, aimed at, **meant, purposeful,** purposive, **willful,** voluntary, deliberate; **engaged,** plighted, affianced, betrothed

intense ADJS **fervent,** fervid, passionate, impassioned, ardent; **zealous,** spirited, hearty, vehement, abandoned, **passionate,** impassioned, **warm,** heated, hot, hot-blooded, red-hot, fiery, white-hot, flaming, burning, afire, aflame, on fire, like a house afire <nonformal>

intensify VERBS **heighten, deepen,** enhance, **strengthen,** beef up <nonformal>, aggravate, exacerbate; **exaggerate,** blow up *and* puff up <both nonformal>, **magnify;** whet, sharpen; **reinforce,** double, redouble, triple; **concentrate,** condense, consolidate; **develop,** gain strength, strengthen

intensity NOUNS **energy,** vigor, force, power, vitality, strenuousness, **dynamism,** demonic energy; **potency; strength; zeal,** ardor, ardency, fervor, fervency, fervidness, spirit, warmth, fire, heat, heatedness, **passion,** passionateness, impassionedness, heartiness, **abandon,** vehemence

intensive ADJS **thorough, thoroughgoing,** thorough-paced, exhaustive, broad-based, wall-to-wall <nonformal>, house-to-house *and* door-to-door <both nonformal>, A-to-Z, comprehensive, all-embracing, all-encompassing, omnibus, radical, sweeping

intent NOUNS **intention,** purpose, aim, object, design, plan

intention NOUNS **intent,** intendment, mindset, **aim,** effect, meaning, view, study, animus, **point, purpose,** function, set *or* settled *or* fixed purpose; **design, plan, project,** idea, notion; **quest,** pursuit; **resolve,** resolution, mind, will; **motive**

interact VERBS interwork, **interplay;** mesh, intermesh, engage, fit, fit like a glove, dovetail, mortise; **interweave,** interlace, intertwine; **interchange;** coact, **cooperate;** codepend

interacting ADJS interactive, interworking, interplaying; in gear, in mesh; dovetailed, mortised; **cooperative,** cooperating

intercede VERBS **mediate,** intermediate, go between; **intervene,** interpose, step in, step into the breach, declare oneself a party, involve oneself, put oneself between disputants, use one's good offices, act between; butt in *and* put one's nose in <both nonformal>; **negotiate,** bargain, **treat with,** make terms, meet halfway; **arbitrate,** moderate; **umpire, referee,** judge

intercept VERBS **listen in; eavesdrop,** wiretap, tap, bug <nonformal>

interchangeable ADJS 1 **exchangeable,** changeable, standard; equivalent; **even,** equal; returnable, **convertible,** commutable, permutable; commutative; retaliatory, equalizing; reciprocal, traded-off; mutual, give-and-take; **exchanged, transposed,** switched, **swapped** <nonformal>, traded, **interchanged**

2 **indistinguishable,** undistinguishable, indiscernible, not to be distinguished, undiscriminated, undifferentiated, **alike,** six of one and half a dozen of the other <nonformal>; standard

interconnect VERBS **interjoin,** intertie, interassociate, interaffiliate, **interlink,** interlock, interdigitate

intercourse NOUNS 1 **copulation, sex act,** having sex, having intercourse, *le sport* <Fr>, coupling, mating, coition, **coitus,** pareunia, venery, copula <law>, **sex, sexual intercourse,** cohabitation, commerce, sexual commerce, congress, sexual congress, sexual union, sexual relations, relations, marital relations, marriage act, act of love, sleeping together *or* with; screwing *and* balling *and* nookie *and* diddling *and* making it with <all nonformal>; meat *and* ass <both nonformal>, intimacy, connection, carnal knowledge

making the beast with two backs
SHAKESPEARE

2 **communication,** communion, congress, **commerce; speaking, speech**, utterance, speech act, talking, linguistic intercourse, speech situation, speech circuit, converse, **conversation;** social intercourse

interdict VERBS **prohibit, proscribe,** inhibit, put *or* lay under an interdict *or* interdiction; embargo, **lay** *or* **put an embargo on; taboo**

interest NOUNS 1 **premium, price, rate;** interest rate, rate of interest, prime interest rate *or* **prime rate,** bank rate,

lending rate, borrowing rate, the price of money; discount rate
2 **concern,** concernment; **curiosity**; **enthusiasm,** passion, ardor, zeal; cathexis; matter of interest, special interest
VERBS 3 **concern,** involve in *or* with, affect the interest, give pause; **pique, titillate,** tantalize, tickle, tickle one's fancy, **attract,** invite, **fascinate, provoke, stimulate, arouse, excite,** pique one's interest, excite interest, excite *or* whet one's interest, arouse one's passion *or* enthusiasm, turn one on <nonformal>

interested ADJS concerned; **alert to, sensitive to, on the watch; curious**; tantalized, piqued, titillated, tickled, **attracted,** fascinated, excited, turned-on <nonformal>; keen on *or* about, enthusiastic, passionate; fixating, cathectic

interesting ADJS **stimulating, provocative,** provoking, thought-provoking, thought-challenging, thought-inspiring; **titillating,** tickling, **tantalizing, inviting, exciting; piquant,** lively, racy, juicy, succulent, spicy, rich; readable

interfere VERBS **intrude,** obtrude, **interlope;** come between, **interpose**, insert oneself, insinuate, impose; **encroach, infringe,** impinge, **trespass,** trespass on *or* upon

interference NOUNS **intrusion,** obtrusion, **interloping;** interposition, interposal, imposition, insinuation, intervention, interventionism, interruption, injection, interjection; **encroachment,** entrenchment, trespass, trespassing, unlawful entry; impingement, **infringement,** invasion, incursion, inroad, influx, irruption, infiltration

interfering ADJS **intrusive,** obtrusive, intervenient, invasive, interruptive

interim NOUNS 1 **interval, interlude,** pause, break, **time-out,** recess, coffee break, halftime *or* halftime intermission, interruption; **lull,** quiet spell, resting point, point of repose, plateau, letup, relief; **respite**; **intermission,** entr'acte; *intermezzo* <Ital>
ADJS 2 **temporary,** tentative, provisional, provisory

interior NOUNS 1 **inside,** inner, inward, internal, intern; inner recess, recesses, **innermost** *or* **deepest recesses,** penetralia, intimate places, secret place *or* places; bosom, secret heart, heart, heart of hearts, soul, vitals, vital center; inner self, inner life, inner landscape, inner *or* interior man, inner nature; core, center
2 **inland,** inlands, up-country; heartland; hinterland; Middle America
ADJS 3 **internal, inner, inside, inward;** intestine; **innermost,** inmost, **intimate,** private

interject VERBS **interpose, interpolate,** intercalate, interjaculate; **intervene; insert in,** stick in, introduce in, insinuate in, sandwich in, slip in, inject in, implant in; **remark, mention,** let drop *or* fall, say by the way, make mention of; refer to, allude to, touch on, make reference to, call attention to

interlace VERBS **mix,** admix, commix, immix, **intermix, mingle,** bemingle, commingle, immingle, **intermingle,** interweave, intertwine, interlard

interlocking NOUNS **interconnection,** interjoinder, **interlinking,** interdigitation; **interassociation,** interaffiliation

interloper NOUNS **intruder, trespasser;** crasher *and* gate-crasher <both nonformal>, unwelcome *or* uninvited guest; invader, encroacher, infiltrator

interlude NOUNS **respite, recess,** rest, pause, halt, stay, lull, **break,** surcease, suspension, **intermission,** spell <Australia>, letup <nonformal>, **time out** <nonformal>, time to catch one's breath; **breathing spell,** breathing time, breathing place, breathing space, breath, **breather**

intermarriage NOUNS mixed marriage, interfaith marriage, interracial marriage; miscegenation; misalliance, *mésalliance* <Fr>, ill-assorted marriage

intermarry VERBS interwed, miscegenate

intermediary NOUNS **go-between, middleman,** medium, intermedium, intermediate, interagent, **internuncio,** broker; connection <nonformal>, **contact; negotiator,** negotiant; interpleader; arbitrator, mediator

intermediate NOUNS 1 **mediator,** intermediator, intermediate agent, intermedium, **intermediary,** interagent, internuncio; **intercessor,** interceder; ombudsman; **go-between, middleman**; connection <nonformal>; **negotiator,** negotiant, negotiatress *or* negotiatrix
ADJS 2 **intervening,** intermediary, intermedial, medial, mean, medium, mesne, median, **middle**

interment NOUNS **burial,** burying, inhumation, sepulture, **entombment;** encoffinment, inurning, inurnment, urn burial; disposal of the dead; burial *or* funeral *or* funerary customs

interminable ADJS **perpetual, everlasting,** everliving, ever-being, ever-abiding, ever-during, ever-durable, permanent, perdurable, indestructible; **endless,** unending, never-ending, without end, nonterminous, nonterminating; **continual,** continuous, steady, **constant, ceaseless,** nonstop, unceasing, never-ceasing, **incessant,** unremitting

intermingle VERBS **mix,** admix, commix, immix, **intermix, mingle,** bemingle, commingle, immingle, interlace, interweave, intertwine, interlard

intermission NOUNS **respite, recess, rest, pause,** halt, stay, lull, **break,** surcease, suspension, interlude, letup <nonformal>, **time out** <nonformal>, time to catch one's breath; **breathing spell, breather;** coffee break, tea break, cigarette break

intermittent ADJS **irregular,** unregular, unsystematic, unmethodical *or* immethodical; intermitting, **desultory, fluctuating, wavering,** wandering, rambling, veering; flickering, guttering

intern VERBS **imprison, incarcerate,** immure; **jail,** gaol <Brit>, jug <nonformal>, throw into jail, send up the river <nonformal>; hold captive, hold prisoner, hold in captivity; hold under close *or* house arrest

internal ADJS **interior,** inner, inside, inward; **innermost,** inmost, **intimate,** private; **intrinsic, inherent,** resident, implicit, immanent, indwelling

internalize VERBS put in, **keep within;** enclose, embed, surround, contain, comprise, include, enfold, take to heart, assimilate

international ADJS **universal,** worldwide, transnational, planet-wide, **global,** cosmopolitan, supernational, supranational

interplay NOUNS **interaction,** interworking, intercourse, intercommunication, **interweaving,** interlacing, intertwining; interpersonal communication, intercommunication, intercommunion, **exchange,** interchange

interpose VERBS **interject, interpolate,** intercalate, interjaculate; **mediate,** go between, **intervene;** put between, sandwich; **insert in,** stick in, introduce in, insinuate in, sandwich in, slip in, inject in, implant in; **intrude**

interpret VERBS **diagnose; construe,** put a construction on, **take;** understand, understand by, **take to mean,** take it that; **read; read into,** read between the lines; see in a special light, read in view of, take an approach to, **define, describe; criticize,** critique, evaluate, explicate, analyze, judge

interpretation NOUNS **construction, reading,** way of seeing *or* understanding *or* putting; constructionism, strict constructionism, loose constructionism; **diagnosis; definition,** description; **meaning; explanation,** sense-distinction

interrogate VERBS **inquire,** ask, question, query; ask after, inquire after, ask about, ask questions, put queries; inquire of, require an answer, ask a question, put a question to, pose *or* set *or* propose *or* propound a question

interrogation NOUNS **questioning, querying,** asking, seeking, pumping, probing, inquiring; **quiz,** quizzing, **examination;** interpellation, bringing into question; catechizing, catechization; catechetical method, Socratic method *or* induction

interrogator NOUNS **inquirer, asker, prober,** querier, querist, **questioner,** questionist; interviewer; interrogatrix; interpellator; **quizzer,** examiner, catechist; inquisitor, inquisitionist

interrupt VERBS **put in, cut in, break in;** jump in, chime in *and* chip in *and* put in one's two-cents worth <all nonformal>; **talk out of turn,** speak inopportunely, intrude, butt in *and* stick one's nose in <both nonformal>, open one's big mouth *or* big fat mouth <nonformal>; **suspend,** intermit, **break, break off,** take a break <nonformal>, cut off, break *or* snap the thread

interruption NOUNS **intrusion,** obtrusion; **interference,** intervention, interventionism, injection, interjection; **suspension,** interval, pause, interim, lull, cessation, letup <nonformal>, **intermission;** time-out, break in the action, breathing spell, cooling-off period; **postponement**

intersect VERBS **cross, crisscross,** cruciate; intercross, decussate; **cut across,** crosscut; **traverse,** transverse, lie across

intersecting ADJS **cross,** crossing,

crossed; **crisscross,** crisscrossed; **intersected,** intersectional; **meeting,** converging, convergent, uniting, merging; concurrent, confluent, mutually approaching, approaching

intersperse VERBS **interfuse,** interlard, interpenetrate; intersow, intersprinkle

intertwine VERBS **interweave, interlace,** interknit, interthread, intertissue, intertie, intertwist; **mix,** admix, commix, immix, **intermix, mingle,** bemingle, commingle, immingle, **intermingle,** interlard

intertwined ADJS **webbed,** webby, weblike, woven, interwoven, interlaced, interknit, intertissued, intertied, intertwisted

interval NOUNS **gap, space**, intervening *or* intermediate space, **interspace,** distance *or* space between, interstice; **clearance,** margin, leeway, **room;** discontinuity, jump, leap, interruption; hiatus, caesura, lacuna; lapse of time, time frame, space, span, timespan, stretch

intervene VERBS **intrude,** obtrude, **interlope;** come between, **interpose**, insert oneself, **interfere,** insinuate, impose; step in, step into the breach, declare oneself a party, involve oneself, put oneself between disputants, use one's good offices, act between; butt in *and* put one's nose in <both nonformal>

intervening ADJS intervenient, **interjacent,** intercurrent; **intermediate,** intermediary, medial, mean, medium, mesne, median, **middle**

intervention NOUNS intervenience, intercurrence, slipping-in, sandwiching; **intrusion,** interposition, **interposing,** interposal, interlocation, intermediacy, interjacence; putting oneself between, stepping in, declaring oneself in, involvement, interagency; interventionism

interview NOUNS 1 press conference, press opportunity, photo opportunity, photo op <nonformal>; **audition,** hearing, tryout, call <all nonformal>, **audience**
VERBS 2 **question, query; make inquiry,** take up *or* institute *or* pursue *or* follow up *or* conduct *or* carry on an inquiry, ask after, inquire after, ask about, ask questions, put queries; inquire of, ask a question, put a question to, pose *or* set *or* propose *or* propound a question

interviewer NOUNS **inquirer,** asker, prober, querier, querist, **questioner,** questionist, interrogator; talk-show host *or* hostess

interweave VERBS **mix,** admix, commix, immix, **intermix, mingle,** bemingle, commingle, immingle, **intermingle,** interlace, intertwine, interlard

interwoven ADJS **webbed,** webby, weblike, woven, interlaced, intertwined

intimacy NOUNS **familiarity,** intimate acquaintance, closeness, nearness, inseparableness, inseparability; affinity, special affinity, mutual affinity; **sex, sexual intercourse,** sexual relations, relations

intimate NOUNS 1 **friend, acquaintance,** close acquaintance; confidant, confidante; familiar, **close friend,** intimate *or* familiar friend; **bosom friend,** friend of one's bosom, inseparable friend, **best friend**
ADJS 2 **familiar, close,** near, inseparable, personal, on familiar *or* intimate terms; just between the two, one-on-one, man-to-man, woman-to-woman; hand-in-hand, hand and glove *or* hand in glove; **thick, thick as thieves** <nonformal>

intimate VERBS **hint,** suggest, insinuate, imply, indicate, adumbrate, lead *or* leave one to gather, justify one in supposing, give *or* drop *or* throw out a hint, give an inkling of, **hint at**

intimidate VERBS **cow, browbeat, bulldoze** <nonformal>, bludgeon, dragoon; **bully, hector, harass,** huff; **coerce,** use violence, ride roughshod, intimidate, bully, blackjack; hold a pistol to one's head, twist one's arm *and* arm-twist <both nonformal>; **terrorize,** put in bodily fear, use terror *or* terrorist tactics, pursue a policy of *Schrecklichkeit,* systematically terrorize; threaten; **demoralize**

intimidated ADJS **terrified,** frightened out of one's wits *or* mind, **scared to death,** scared stiff *or* shitless *or* spitless <nonformal>; unnerved, unstrung, unmanned, undone, **cowed,** awed, daunted, dismayed, unmanned

intimidating ADJS **threatening, menacing,** threatful, minatory, minacious; fear-inspiring, bludgeoning, muscle-flexing, saber-rattling, bulldozing, browbeating, bullying, hectoring, blustering, terrorizing, terroristic

intolerable ADJS **insufferable,** insupportable, unendurable, unbearable, past bearing, not to be borne *or* endured, for the birds <nonformal>, **too much** *or* a bit much <nonformal>, more than flesh and blood can bear, enough to drive one mad, enough to provoke a saint, enough to make a preacher swear <nonformal>, enough to try the patience of Job

intolerant ADJS bigoted, overzealous, fanatic, fanatical; dogmatic, opinionated; **unindulgent,** uncondoning, unforbearing

intonation NOUNS **inflection, modulation;** intonation pattern *or* contour, intonation *or* inflection of voice, speech tune *or* melody

intoxicate VERBS 1 **inebriate, addle, befuddle,** bemuse, besot, go to one's head, make one see double, make one tiddly; **fascinate,** titillate, take one's breath away

2 <nonformal> **plaster,** pickle, swack, crock, stew, souse, stone, polluute, tipsify, booze up, boozify, fuddle, overtake

intoxicated ADJS **inebriated,** inebriate, inebrious, **drunk, drunken,** *shikker* <Yiddish>, **tipsy,** in liquor, **in one's cups, under the influence,** the worse for liquor; **tiddly, giddy, dizzy,** muddled, addled, flustered, bemused, reeling, seeing double; **besotted,** sotted, sodden, drenched, far-gone; drunk as a lord, drunk as a fiddler *or* piper, drunk as an owl; crapulent, crapulous

2 <nonformal> **high,** bent, blasted, blind, bombed out, bonged out, buzzed, coked, coked out, flying, fried, geared, geared up, geezed, gonged, gorked, hopped-up, in a zone, junked, luded out, maxed, noddy, ripped, smashed, snowed, spaced, space out, spacey, stoned, strung out, switched on, tanked, totaled, tranqued, tripping, trippy, wired, zoned, zoned out, zonked, zonked out

intoxicating ADJS intoxicative, **inebriating,** inebriative, inebriant; **exhilarating,** heady, maddening, ravishing

intractable ADJS **inflexible,** unflexible, **unpliable, unpliant, unmalleable,** untractable, intractile, **unbending,** unlimber, **unyielding**, ungiving, **stubborn, unalterable,** immutable; **immovable**; **adamant,** adamantine

intransigent ADJS **unyielding,** unbending, inflexible, hard, hard-line, inelastic, impliable, ungiving, **firm, stiff, rigid,** rigorous, stuffy; **uncompromising,** irreconcilable, hard-shell *and* hard-core <both nonformal>; implacable, inexorable, **relentless,** unrelenting

intrepid ADJS **courageous,** plucky, brave, bold, valiant, valorous, **gallant,** doughty, **hardy,** stalwart, stout, stouthearted, ironhearted, lionhearted, greathearted, bold-spirited, bold as a lion

intricacy NOUNS **complexity, complication, involvement,** complexness, involution, convolution, tortuousness, Byzantinism, *chinoiserie* <Fr>, tanglement, **entanglement,** perplexity, intricateness, ramification, crabbedness, technicality, subtlety

intricate ADJS **complex, complicated,** many-faceted, multifarious, ramified, perplexed, **confused,** confounded, **involved,** elaborate, involuted, convoluted, multilayered, multilevel; **tangled,** entangled, tangly, embrangled, **snarled,** knotted, matted, twisted, raveled; mazy, daedal, **labyrinthine,** labyrinthian

intrigue NOUNS 1 web of intrigue, **plot, scheme,** deep-laid plot *or* scheme, underplot, game *or* little game <both nonformal>, trick, stratagem, finesse; **conspiracy,** confederacy, covin, cabal; finagling <nonformal>, **machination,** manipulation, **maneuvering,** engineering, rigging; frame-up <nonformal>; wire-pulling <nonformal>
VERBS 2 **fascinate, captivate, charm,** becharm, spell, spellbind, cast a spell, put under a spell, **beguile, enthrall,** infatuate, **enrapture, transport, enravish, entrance, enchant,** witch, **bewitch**
3 **plot, scheme,** be up to something; **conspire, connive,** collude; **maneuver,** machinate, finesse, operate <nonformal>, engineer, rig, wangle <nonformal>, angle, finagle <nonformal>; frame *or* frame up <both nonformal>

intriguing ADJS **charming,** attractive, endearing, engaging, appealing, prepossessing, heartwarming, sexy <nonformal>, **enchanting,** bewitching, witching, entrancing, enthralling, fascinating; **captivating,** irresistible, ravishing; **scheming,** calculating, designing, contriving, plotting; manipulatory, **manip-**

ulative; conniving, conspiring, collusive
intrinsic ADJS internal, **inner,** inward; **inherent,** resident, implicit, immanent, indwelling; **ingrained,** in the very grain; infixed, implanted, inwrought, deep-seated
introduce VERBS **insert,** insinuate, inject, infuse, perfuse, inoculate, intromit; **bring up, broach,** open up, launch, start, kick off <nonformal>; **present,** acquaint, make acquainted, give an introduction, give a knockdown <nonformal>, do the honors <nonformal>; **herald,** count down, run up, lead in, forerun, usher in; **pioneer**
introductory ADJS **beginning, initial,** initiatory *or* initiative; **incipient,** inceptive, inchoative, inchoate; inaugural *or* inauguratory; **elementary,** elemental, **fundamental,** foundational; **rudimentary,** rudimental
introspective ADJS absorbed *or* engrossed in thought, **absorbed, engrossed,** rapt, wrapped in thought, **lost in thought,** abstracted, immersed in thought, buried in thought, engaged in thought, occupied, **preoccupied**
introverted ADJS **reticent, reserved,** restrained, nonassertive, low-key, low-keyed, constrained; repressed, subdued; backward, **retiring,** shrinking; **undemonstrative,** unexpansive, unaffable, uncongenial, ungenial; modest, verecund, verecundious, *pudique* <Fr>, bashful
intrude VERBS obtrude, **interlope;** come between, **interpose**, insert oneself, **intervene, interfere,** insinuate, impose; **encroach, infringe,** impinge, **trespass,** trespass on *or* upon, invade, infiltrate; **break in upon,** break in, **barge in**
intruder NOUNS **interloper, trespasser;** crasher *and* gate-crasher <both nonformal>, unwelcome *or* uninvited guest; invader, encroacher, infiltrator
intrusion NOUNS obtrusion, **interloping;** interposition, interposal, imposition, insinuation, **interference,** intervention, interventionism, interruption, injection, interjection; **encroachment,** trespass, trespassing, unlawful entry; impingement, **infringement,** invasion, incursion, inroad, influx, irruption, infiltration
intrusive ADJS obtrusive, **interfering,** intervenient, invasive, interruptive
intuition NOUNS **intuitiveness, sixth sense;** intuitive reason *or* knowledge, direct perception *or* apprehension, immediate apprehension *or* perception, unmediated perception *or* apprehension, subconscious perception, unconscious *or* subconscious knowledge, immediate cognition, knowledge without thought *or* reason, flash of insight; intuitive understanding
intuitive ADJS intuitional, sensing, feeling; second-sighted, precognitive, clairvoyant; impressionistic, general, generalized, abstract
inundate VERBS **overflow,** engulf, swamp, sweep, whelm, overwhelm, **flood,** deluge, submerge; **oversupply, overprovide,** overlavish, overfurnish, overequip; flood the market, oversell
inundated ADJS **flooded,** deluged, engulfed, swamped, swept, whelmed, drowned, overwhelmed, afloat, awash; **overrun, overspread,** buried
inured ADJS **callous, hardened,** case-hardened, coarsened, brutalized, indurated, stony, stony-hearted, marble-hearted, flinthearted, flinty, steely, impervious, armored *or* steeled against, proof against, as hard as nails
invade VERBS **intrude,** obtrude, interlope; **encroach, infringe,** impinge, **trespass,** trespass on *or* upon, infiltrate; **break in upon,** break in, burst in, charge in; make an inroad, make an irruption into; storm, take by storm; **infest, beset,** swarm, ravage, plague
invader NOUNS **intruder,** interloper, trespasser; crasher *and* gate-crasher <both nonformal>, unwelcome *or* uninvited guest; encroacher, infiltrator; raider
invalid NOUNS **sick person,** ill person, sufferer; valetudinarian, **shut-in; patient,** case; **the sick, the infirm**
invalid ADJS **illogical,** unreasonable, irrational, reasonless, contrary to reason, **senseless,** without reason, **without rhyme or reason; unscientific,** nonscientific, unphilosophical; **inauthentic,** unauthentic, faulty, flawed, paralogical, fallacious; **repealed, revoked, rescinded,** struck down, set aside; void, **null and void**
invalidate VERBS **disprove,** disconfirm, discredit, prove the contrary, belie, give the lie to; **negate,** explode, blow up, blow sky-high, **puncture,** deflate, **shoot** *or* **poke full of holes,** cut to pieces, cut

the ground from under; **knock the bottom out of** <nonformal>, knock the props *or* chocks out from under, take the ground from under, cut the ground from under one's feet, not leave a leg to stand on

invaluable ADJS **precious, priceless,** inestimable, without *or* **beyond price,** not to be had for love or money, not for all the tea in China

invariable ADJS **unchangeable, constant,** undeviating, undeflectable; **irreversible,** nonreversible, reverseless

invasion NOUNS **raid, incursion,** inroad, irruption; **usurpation, arrogation,** seizure, unlawful seizure, **appropriation,** assumption, adoption, infringement, encroachment, trespass, trespassing; **infestation,** infestment; swarming, swarm, teeming, ravage, plague

invasive ADJS **intrusive,** obtrusive, **interfering,** intervenient, interruptive; **invading,** invasionary, incursive, incursionary, irruptive

invective NOUNS **vilification, abuse,** revilement, **vituperation,** opprobrium, obloquy, contumely, calumny, scurrility, blackguardism; **disparagement**

invent VERBS **innovate,** make from scratch *or* from the ground up, coin, new-mint, mint, inaugurate, neologize, neoterize; **originate,** conceive, discover, make up, devise, contrive, concoct, fabricate, frame, hatch, hatch *or* cook up, strike out; think up, think out, dream up, **design,** plan, set one's wits to work; **generate, develop**

inventive ADJS **creative,** originative, causative, productive, **constructive,** formative, fabricative, demiurgic; generative; **original,** esemplastic, shaping, **ingenious; productive, fertile,** fecund, prolific, seminal, germinal, teeming, pregnant; **inspired,** visioned

inventor NOUNS discoverer, deviser; developer

inventory NOUNS 1 **list, enumeration, itemization,** listing, shopping list *and* laundry list *and* want list *and* wish list *and* hit list *and* shit list *and* drop-dead list <all nonformal>, items, **schedule, register,** registry; repertory, tally; summation, **reckoning, count,** bean-counting <nonformal>, census, head count, nose count, body count

VERBS 2 **list, enumerate, itemize,** tabulate, catalog, tally; **register,** post, enter, enroll, book; score, keep score; **schedule,** program; take stock

inverse NOUNS 1 **reverse, converse, opposite,** other side of the coin *or* picture, the flip side *and* B side <both nonformal>

ADJS 2 contrapositive, **opposite,** opposing, **opposed,** on opposite sides; **reverse,** obverse, converse; **antipodal**

inversion NOUNS turning over *or* around *or* upside down, the other way round; **reversing, reversal,** turning front to back *or* side to side; **reversion,** turning back *or* backwards, retroversion, retroflexion, revulsion

invest VERBS place, put, sink; **risk, venture;** make an investment, lay out money, place out *or* put out at interest; reinvest, roll over, plow back into <nonformal>; **invest in, put money in,** sink money in, pour money into, tie up one's money in; buy in *or* into, buy a piece *or* share of; financier; plunge <nonformal>, speculate

investigation NOUNS **research,** legwork <nonformal>, inquiry into; data-gathering, gathering *or* amassing evidence; perscrutation, **probe,** searching investigation, close inquiry, exhaustive study; police inquiry *or* investigation, criminal investigation, detective work, detection, sleuthing

investigator NOUNS **detective,** operative, sleuth, Sherlock Holmes <A Conan Doyle>; police detective, **plainclothesman;** private detective *or* dick, private investigator *or* PI, hotel detective, house detective, house dick <nonformal>, store detective

investiture NOUNS **installation,** installment, **instatement,** induction, placement, **inauguration,** taking office; **accession,** accedence; coronation, enthronement; calling, election, nomination, appointment, preferment, induction, institution, endowment, enfranchisement

investment NOUNS **endowment,** investment, **settlement,** foundation; **venture,** risk, plunge <nonformal>, speculation

investor NOUNS **financier,** moneyman, **capitalist,** finance capitalist; Wall Streeter

invidious ADJS **envious,** envying, green with envy; **jealous; covetous,** desirous of; resentful; **grudging, begrudging;** mean, mean-spirited, ungenerous

invigorate VERBS **strengthen, fortify,** beef up <nonformal>, brace, buttress, prop, shore up, support, undergird, brace up; gird, gird up one's loins; steel, harden, anneal, stiffen, **toughen,** temper, nerve; confirm, sustain; **restrengthen,** reinforce; **reinvigorate,** refresh, revive, recruit one's strength; **energize,** dynamize; **animate, enliven, liven, liven up,** vitalize, quicken, goose *or* jazz up <nonformal>

invigorating ADJS **refreshing,** refreshful, **fresh,** brisk, crisp, crispy, zesty, zestful, **bracing, tonic,** cordial; analeptic; **exhilarating,** stimulating, stimulative, stimulatory, rousing, energizing; regaling, cheering

invincible ADJS **indestructible,** undestroyable, **imperishable,** nonperishable, incorruptible; **invulnerable,** inexpugnable, impregnable, indivisible; **ineradicable,** indelible, ineffaceable, inerasable; **inextinguishable**

invisible ADJS **imperceptible,** unperceivable, **indiscernible,** undiscernible, undetectable, **unseeable,** viewless, unbeholdable, unapparent, insensible; **out of sight,** *à perte de vue* <Fr>; **secret; unseen,** sightless, unbeheld, unviewed, unwitnessed, unobserved, unnoticed, unperceived; disguised, camouflaged, hidden, **concealed**

invitation NOUNS **invite** *and* **bid** <both nonformal>, engraved invitation, bidding, biddance, **call,** calling, **summons**

invite VERBS 1 **ask,** call, summon, call in, bid come, extend *or* issue an invitation, request the presence of, request the pleasure of one's company, send an engraved invitation
2 **bring on, bring down,** bring upon *or* down upon, bring upon *or* down upon oneself

inviting ADJS **interesting,** stimulating, provocative, provoking, thought-provoking, thought-challenging, thought-inspiring; **titillating,** tickling, **tantalizing,** exciting; **piquant,** lively, racy, juicy, succulent, spicy, rich; readable

invocation NOUNS **prayer, supplication,** imploration, impetration, entreaty, beseechment, appeal, petition, suit, aid prayer, bid *or* bidding prayer, orison, obsecration, obtestation, rogation, **devotions; benediction, blessing,** benison, benedicite

invoice NOUNS 1 **bill,** statement, account; **bill of lading,** manifest, waybill
VERBS 2 **bill,** send a statement; demand payment, **dun**

invoke VERBS **summon, call,** demand, preconize; **conjure, conjure up,** evoke, raise, summon, call up; **call up spirits,** conjure *or* conjure up spirits, summon spirits, raise ghosts, evoke from the dead; **pray, supplicate,** petition, make supplication, *daven* <Yiddish>

involuntary ADJS **instinctive, automatic, mechanical,** reflex, reflexive, knee-jerk <nonformal>, conditioned; **unconscious,** unthinking, blind; **unwitting,** unintentional, independent of one's will, unwilling, unwilled, against one's will; **compulsive;** forced; **impulsive**

involve VERBS **implicate,** tangle, **entangle,** embarrass, enmesh, engage, **draw in,** drag *or* hook *or* suck into, catch up in, **make a party to;** interest, concern; **absorb**

involved ADJS **implicated;** interested, concerned, a party to; **included**

invulnerable ADJS **impregnable,** impenetrable, inviolable, inexpugnable; **unassailable,** unattackable, insuperable, unsurmountable; **invincible,** indomitable, **unconquerable,** unsubduable, unyielding, incontestable, unbeatable, more than a match for

inward ADJS 1 **interior,** internal, inner, inside; **innermost,** inmost, **intimate,** private; visceral, gut <nonformal>; **intrinsic**
ADVS 2 **inwards, inwardly,** withinward, withinwards; inland, inshore

iota NOUNS **little, bit,** little *or* wee *or* tiny bit <nonformal>, bite, **particle,** fragment, spot, **speck,** flyspeck, fleck, point, dot, jot, tittle, **dab** <nonformal>, mote, **mite** <nonformal>; whit, ace, **hair,** scruple, groat, farthing, pittance, dole, trifling amount, **smidgen** *and* skosh *and* smitch <all nonformal>, pinch

irate ADJS **angry,** angered, incensed, indignant, ireful; **livid,** livid with rage, beside oneself, **wroth, wrathful,** wrathy, **cross,** wrought-up, worked up, riled up <nonformal>

ire NOUNS **anger,** wrath, *saeva indignatio* <L>; angriness, irateness, wrathfulness, soreness <nonformal>

a transient madness
HORACE

iridescent ADJS **rainbowy,** rainbowlike; **opalescent,** opaline, opaloid; nacreous, nacry, *nacré* <Fr>, nacred, **pearly,** pearlish, mother-of-pearl; iridal, iridial, iridine, iridian; irised, irisated

irk VERBS **vex, annoy, aggravate,** exasperate, provoke; **trouble, worry,** give one gray hair, plague, harass, bother, hassle

irksome ADJS **troublesome,** besetting; **bothersome,** vexatious, painful, plaguey <nonformal>, annoying; **burdensome,** oppressive, onerous, heavy *and* hefty <both nonformal>, crushing, backbreaking; **trying,** grueling

iron VERBS 1 **press,** hot-press, **mangle,** calender; roll
ADJS 2 **firm,** rigid, rigorous, rigorist, rigoristic, stiff, **hard,** steel, steely, hardshell, obdurate, **inflexible,** ironhanded, inexorable, dour, **unyielding,** unbending, impliable, **relentless,** unrelenting, procrustean

ironclad ADJS **uncompromising;** stubborn, obstinate; purist, puristic; puritan, puritanic, puritanical, fundamentalist, orthodox; ironbound, rockbound, musclebound; straitlaced, hidebound

ironic ADJS **satiric,** satirical; **sarcastic,** ironical, sardonic, cynical, Rabelaisian, dry; caustic; self-contradictory, **paradoxical,** antinomic, oxymoronic, ambivalent

irony NOUNS **sarcasm,** cynicism, satire, satiric wit *or* humor, invective, innuendo; causticity; self-contradiction, **paradox**, antinomy, oxymoron, ambivalence, enantiosis, equivocation

irrational ADJS 1 **unreasonable,** unsound, unsensible, senseless, insensate, reasonless, reckless, inadvisable; inexpedient; **ill-advised, ill-considered,** ill-gauged, ill-judged, ill-imagined, ill-contrived, ill-devised, on the wrong track, unconsidered
2 **unsound,** of unsound mind, **demented, deranged,** deluded, disoriented, unhinged, **unbalanced,** unsettled, distraught, wandering, mazed, crackbrained, brainsick, sick *or* soft in the head, not right, not in one's right mind, **touched,** touched in the head, **out of one's mind,** out of one's senses *or* wits, bereft of reason, reasonless, deprived of reason, senseless, witless

irreconcilable ADJS **inconsistent,** incongruous, inconsonant, inconsequent, incoherent, **incompatible;** disproportionate, out of proportion, self-contradictory, paradoxical, oxymoronic, **absurd**

irreducible ADJS **requisite,** needful, required, needed, necessary, wanted, called for, indicated; **essential,** vital, indispensable, unforgoable, irreplaceable; irreductible; prerequisite

irrefutable ADJS **conclusive,** determinative, **decisive,** final, incontrovertible, irresistible, indisputable, sure, certain, absolute; documented, documentary; authentic, reliable, indubitable, unarguable, incontestable, unrefutable, unconfutable, irrefragable, unanswerable, inappealable, unimpeachable

irregular NOUNS 1 casual; **guerrilla,** partisan, franctireur; **bushfighter,** bushwhacker <nonformal>; underground, resistance, maquis; *maquisard* <Fr>, underground *or* resistance fighter
ADJS 2 unregular, unsystematic, unmethodical *or* immethodical; **inconstant, unsteady, uneven, unrhythmical,** unmetrical, rough, unequal, uncertain, unsettled; **variable,** deviative, heteroclite; **capricious, erratic,** off-again-on-again, eccentric; **sporadic,** patchy, spotty, scrappy, snatchy, catchy, choppy, broken, disconnected, discontinuous; **intermittent,** intermitting, **desultory,** fluctuating, wavering

irregularity NOUNS **asymmetry,** unsymmetry, disproportion, lopsidedness, imbalance, quirk; **nonuniformity,** unevenness, raggedness, crazy-quilt, choppiness, jerkiness, **disorder**; **inconstancy, inconsistency,** variability, changeability, changeableness, mutability, capriciousness, mercuriality, wavering, **instability, unsteadiness**

irrelevant ADJS **impertinent, inapposite,** ungermane, uncogent, inconsequent, inapplicable, immaterial, inappropriate, inadmissible; wide of *or* away from the point, *nihil ad rem* <L>, **beside the point,** beside the mark, wide of the mark, **beside the question,** off the subject, not to the purpose, **nothing to do with the case,** not at issue, out-of-the-way; incidental, parenthetical

irreligious ADJS **ungodly,** godless, **unrighteous, unholy,** unsaintly, unangelic, unangelical; impious; **wicked, sinful**

irreplaceable ADJS **requisite,** needful,

required, needed, necessary, wanted, called for, indicated; **essential, vital, indispensable,** unforgoable, prerequisite

irrepressible ADJS **unrestrained,** unconstrained, unforced, uncompelled, uncoerced; unmeasured, **uninhibited,** unsuppressed, unrepressed, unreserved, go-go <nonformal>, exuberant; **unreined,** reinless; lax

irreproachable ADJS **inculpable,** unblamable, unblameworthy, irreprovable, **irreprehensible,** uncensurable, unimpeachable, unindictable, unarraignable, unobjectionable, unexceptionable, above suspicion; beyond all praise, unfaultable, *sans peur et sans reproche* <Fr>

irresistible ADJS **overpowering,** overcoming, overwhelming, overmastering, overmatching, avalanchine; **enchanting,** bewitching, entrancing, enthralling, intriguing, fascinating

irresolute ADJS irresolved, **unresolved; undecided, indecisive, undetermined,** unsettled, infirm of purpose; at loose ends, at a loose end; **of two minds,** in conflict, double-minded, ambivalent, ambitendent; capricious, mercurial, fickle

irrespective of ADVS in spite of, spite of <nonformal>, **despite,** in despite of, with, even with; **regardless of,** regardless, irrespective of, without respect *or* regard to; cost what it may, regardless of cost, at any cost, at all costs, whatever the cost

irresponsible ADJS **untrustworthy,** unfaithworthy, untrusty, trustless, **unreliable, undependable,** fly-by-night, unsure, not to be trusted, not to be depended *or* relied upon; **unrestrained, undisciplined,** uncontrolled, fast and loose

irretrievable ADJS **irrecoverable, irreclaimable,** irredeemable, unsalvageable, unsalvable; irrevocable, **irreversible; past hope, beyond recall,** past praying for; unrestorable

irreverent ADJS **disrespectful,** aweless; **discourteous; insolent, impudent;** ridiculing, **derisive; disparaging; impious,** undutiful; **profane,** profanatory; sacrilegious, blasphemous

irreversible ADJS **confirmed,** incorrigible; deep-rooted, deep-set, deep-settled, **deep-seated,** deep-fixed, deep-dyed; **infixed, ingrained,** fast, dyed-in-the-wool; **irrevocable,** indefeasible, nonreversible, reverseless

irrevocable ADJS **decisive,** final, peremptory, absolute, eternal, written, hard-and-fast, carved in stone, set in concrete <nonformal>, ultimate, conclusive, binding, without appeal

irrigate VERBS **water; wash,** bathe, **rinse,** rinse out, flush, flush out, sluice, sluice out

irritable ADJS **irascible,** excitable, flappable <nonformal>; **cross, cranky, testy;** cankered, crabbed, spiteful, spleeny, splenetic, churlish, bearish, snappish, waspish; **gruff,** grumbly, grumbling, growling; **disagreeable; perverse,** fractious, cross-grained

irritant NOUNS **irritation,** exacerbation, salt in the wound, twisting the knife in the wound, embitterment, **provocation;** pea in the shoe

irritate VERBS **aggravate,** exacerbate, worsen, rub salt in the wound, twist the knife in the wound, step on one's corns, barb the dart; touch a soft spot *or* tender spot, touch a raw nerve, touch where it hurts; provoke, **gall, chafe, fret,** grate, grit *and* gravel <both nonformal>, rasp; **get on one's nerves,** grate on, set on edge; **set one's teeth on edge,** go against the grain; **rub one** *or* **one's fur the wrong way**

irritated ADJS **annoyed,** bugged <nonformal>; galled, chafed; **bothered,** troubled, disturbed, ruffled, roiled, riled; **irked,** vexed, piqued, nettled, provoked, peeved *and* miffed <both nonformal>, **griped,** aggravated, exasperated; burnt-up *and* browned-off <both nonformal>, resentful, angry

irritating ADJS irritative, irritant; **chafing, galling,** fretting, rasping, boring, grating, grinding, stinging, scratchy; **annoying,** provoking, aggravating <nonformal>, **exasperating; vexatious,** vexing, irking, **irksome,** tiresome, wearisome

irritation NOUNS **aggravation,** exacerbation, worsening, salt in the wound, twisting the knife in the wound, embitterment, **provocation;** fret, gall, chafe; irritant; pea in the shoe

Islam NOUNS **Muslimism,** Islamism, Moslemism, Muhammadanism, Mohammedanism; Sufism, Wahabiism, Sunnism, Shiism; Black Muslimism; Muslim fundamentalism, militant Muslimism

Islamic ADJS **Muslim,** Moslem, Islamitic, Islamistic, Muhammadan, Mohammedan; Shiite, Sunni, Sunnite

island NOUNS 1 **isle; islet,** holm; continental island; oceanic island; **key,** cay; sandbank, sandbar, bar; **reef,** coral reef, coral head; coral island, atoll; archipelago, island group *or* chain
ADJS 2 **insular,** insulated, isolated; islandy *or* islandish, islandlike; islanded, isleted, island-dotted; seagirt; archipelagic *or* archipelagian

isolate VERBS **quarantine,** insulate, segregate, separate, seclude; **set apart,** keep apart; **put beyond the pale,** ghettoize; **cordon, cordon off,** seal off, rope off; wall off, set up barriers, put behind barriers; **reduce,** reduce to elements, resolve

isolated ADJS cloistered, **sequestered,** sequestrated, secluded, sheltered; **insular,** insulated; shut off, **separate,** separated, **apart,** detached, removed; **remote, out-of-the-way,** up-country, in a backwater, out-of-the-world, out-back *and* back of beyond <both Austral>; **unfrequented,** unvisited, off the beaten track; untraveled

isolation NOUNS **privacy,** retirement, sequestration, seclusion; **quarantine,** cordoning off, segregation, separation

issue NOUNS 1 **posterity, progeny, offspring,** fruit, seed, brood, breed, family
2 **cause, principle,** interest, burning issue, commitment, faith, great cause, lifework; **problem, topic**, case *or* point in question, bone of contention, controversial point, question before the house, debating point, question *or* point at issue, **moot point** *or* case, question mark, *quodlibet* <L>; vexed *or* knotty question, burning question
VERBS 3 **emerge, come out,** issue forth, come into view, extrude, **come forth; surface,** rise to the surface; come to the fore; emanate, effuse, arise, come; debouch, disembogue; **burst forth,** break forth, erupt; **come out in the open;** protrude
4 **bring out,** put out, get out, **launch** get off, emit, put *or* give *or* send forth, offer to the public, pass out

itch NOUNS 1 **sexual desire,** sensuous *or* carnal desire, bodily appetite, **biological urge,** venereal appetite *or* desire, sexual longing, **lust,** desire, lusts *or* desires of the flesh, lech <nonformal>; **craving,** coveting
2 lust; hunger, thirst, appetite
VERBS 3 **tingle,** thrill; scratch; **prickle,** prick, sting

item NOUNS **commodity, ware,** vendible, **product, article,** article of commerce *or* merchandise; **entry,** line item, minute, note, notation; **feature,** aspect, specialty, circumstance, detail

itemize VERBS **specify,** circumstantiate, particularize, **spell out, detail,** go *or* enter into detail, descend to particulars, give full particulars, atomize, anatomize; **descend to particulars,** get precise, get down to brass tacks *or* to cases <nonformal>, get down to the nitty-gritty <nonformal>, come to the point, lay it on the line <nonformal>

itinerary NOUNS **route, path, way, course,** track, run, line, road; road map, roadbook

ivories NOUNS 1 **teeth,** dentition
2 **piano keys,** eighty-eight <nonformal>
3 **dice; bones**, rolling bones, cubes, devil's bones *or* teeth, galloping dominoes, golf balls, marbles, Memphis dominoes, Mississippi marbles, Missouri marbles <all nonformal>

J

jab NOUNS 1 **thrust, pass,** lunge, swing, cut, stab; **prod,** poke, **punch,** dig, nudge
VERBS 2 **thrust, push,** shove, boost <nonformal>; **prod,** goad, poke, punch, dig, nudge, thwack, **smack,** clap, crack, swipe, **whack**

jabber NOUNS 1 **chatter,** gibber, **babble,** babblement, prate, prating, prattle, **palaver,** chat, natter <Brit>, **gabble, gab** *and* jaw-jaw <both nonformal>, blab, **blabber, blather,** blether, clatter, clack, cackle, talkee-talkee; twaddle, twattle, **gibble-gabble,** bibble-babble, **chitter-chatter,** prittle-prattle, **tittle-tattle,** mere talk, idle talk *or* chatter
VERBS 2 **talk nonsense,** twaddle, piffle, blather, **blabber, babble,** gabble, gibble-gabble, jabber, gibber, prate, **prattle,** rattle; gas *and* bull *and* **bullshit** *and* throw the bull *and* shoot off one's mouth *and* shoot the bull <all nonformal>; **drivel,** vapor, run off at the mouth <nonformal>

jaded ADJS **worn-out, exhausted,** tired, fatigued, pooped <nonformal>, **spent,** effete, etiolated, played out, *ausgespielt* <Ger>, emptied, done *and* done up <both nonformal>; **run-down,** dragged-out <nonformal>, laid low, at a low ebb, in a bad way, far-gone, on one's last legs; **cloyed, fed up** *and* fed to the gills *or* fed to the teeth *and* stuffed to the gills <all nonformal>

jag NOUNS **binge, drunk,** bust, tear, **bender, toot, bat,** brannigan, guzzle, randan, rip

jagged ADJS **nonuniform,** ununiform, **uneven, irregular,** ragged, erose, choppy, jerky, rough, disorderly, unsystematic; scrappy, snatchy, spotty, patchy

jail NOUNS 1 **prison,** gaol <Brit>, jailhouse, lockup, toolbooth <Scots>, bridewell <Brit>; maximum- *or* minimum-security prison

2 <nonformal> **slammer, slam,** can, coop, cooler, hoosegow, stir, clink, pokey, brig, tank

VERBS 3 **imprison, incarcerate, intern,** immure; gaol <Brit>, jug <nonformal>, throw into jail, clap in jail *or* prison, send up the river <nonformal>; **lock up,** lock in, bolt in, put *or* keep under lock and key

jailbreak NOUNS **escape; getaway** *and* break *and* breakout <all nonformal>; prisonbreak

jailer NOUNS **gaoler** <Brit>, correctional *or* correction *or* corrections officer; **keeper, warder,** prison guard, **turnkey,** bull *and* screw <both nonformal>; **warden,** custodian, guardian; **guard**

jalopy NOUNS

<nonformal> banger, bus, buggy, wheels, tub, tuna wagon, heap, boat, short, crate, wreck, clunker, junker, junkheap, junkpile

jam NOUNS 1 comfit, confiture; **jelly,** preserve, conserve
2 **delay,** stoppage, logjam <nonformal>, obstruction, tie-up *and* bind <both nonformal>, **block,** blockage, **hang-up** <nonformal>;
3 **predicament,** fix *and* pickle *and* scrape *and* stew <all nonformal>; perturbation, **disturbance**
VERBS 4 **stop, stop up; block,** block up; **clog,** clog up, foul; **choke,** choke up *or* off; **fill,** fill up; **stuff,** pack; **congest,** stuff up; **plug,** plug up; **catch,** lodge, foul; **squeeze,** press, crowd, cram, ram down; pack *or* jam in

jamboree NOUNS **festival, festivity,** festive occasion, *fiesta* <Sp>, **fete,** gala, **gala affair, blowout** <nonformal>; **field day**

jammed ADJS **stuck, fast,** stuck fast, **fixed, transfixed, caught,** fastened, tied, chained, tethered, anchored, moored, held, inextricable; **impacted,** congested, packed, wedged; seized, seized up, frozen; aground, grounded, stranded, high and dry

jangle NOUNS 1 **clash, jar; noise,** mere noise, confusion *or* conflict *or* jarring *or* jostling of sounds; Babel
VERBS 2 **clash,** jar; **disagree, differ,** vary, not see eye-to-eye, be at cross-purposes, tangle assholes <nonformal>, **disaccord, conflict,** jostle, collide, square off, cross swords, break, break off

janitor NOUNS **cleaner,** cleaner-up, cleaner-off, cleaner-out; janitress, custodian; cleaning woman *or* lady *or* man

jar VERBS 1 **startle,** shock, electrify, jolt, shake, stun, stagger, **give one a turn** <nonformal>, take aback, take one's breath away; frighten
2 **differ,** differ in opinion, hold opposite views, disaccord, **be at variance,** not get along, pull different ways, be at cross-purposes, have no measures with, misunderstand one another; **conflict, clash,** collide, jostle, jangle

jargon NOUNS **lingo** <nonformal>, **slang,** cant, argot, patois, patter, vernacular; vocabulary, phraseology; **lingua franca, pidgin,** trade language

jarring ADJS **clashing, jangling,** jangly, confused, conflicting, jostling, warring, ajar; **harsh,** grating; **startling, shocking,** electrifying, staggering, stunning, jolting

jaunt NOUNS **walk,** ramble, amble, **hike, tramp,** traipse <nonformal>; slog, trudge, schlep <nonformal>; **stroll,** saunter; **promenade;** *passeggiata* <Ital>; airing; **constitutional** <nonformal>, stretch

jaunty ADJS **lighthearted,** light, lightsome; **buoyant,** corky <nonformal>, resilient; perky, **debonair, dapper,** dashing, **carefree,** free and easy, **gay,** rakish, **dashing; breezy,** airy

jaw NOUNS 1 **muzzle,** lips, embouchure; **jaws,** mandibles, chops, chaps, jowls
VERBS 2 **berate,** rate, betongue, clapper-claw <nonformal>, **tongue-lash, rail at,** rag, thunder *or* fulminate against, rave against, yell at, bark *or* yelp at

jawbreaker NOUNS long word, hard word, jawtwister *and* two-dollar *or* five-dollar word <all nonformal>, polysyllable; sesquipedalian, sesquipedalia <pl>

jaws NOUNS **clutches, claws, talons,** pounces, unguals; **pincers,** nippers, chelae; **tentacles;** mandibles, maxillae

jazz NOUNS 1 hot jazz, Dixieland, Basin Street; **swing,** jive <nonformal>; bebop, bop <nonformal>; mainstream jazz; avant-garde jazz, the new music <nonformal>; boogie *or* boogie-woogie; walking bass, stride *or* stride piano
ADJS 2 **syncopated; ragtime,** ragtimey <nonformal>; jazzy *and* jazzed *and* jazzed up <all nonformal>, hot, swingy <nonformal>

jazz up VERBS **stimulate,** whet, sharpen, pique, provoke, quicken, enliven, liven up, pick up, animate, **exhilarate,** invigorate, galvanize, fillip, give a fillip to; infuse life into, give new life to, revive, renew, resuscitate; key up, hop up *and* soup up <both nonformal>

jazzy ADJS **showy, flaunting, flashy,** snazzy, flashing, glittering, **glitzy** *and* gimmicky *and* splashy *and* splurgy <all nonformal>; exhibitionistic, showoffy <nonformal>, bravura; **syncopated; ragtime,** ragtimey <nonformal>; **jazz;** jazzed *and* jazzed up <both nonformal>, hot, swingy <nonformal>

jealous ADJS **jaundiced,** jaundice-eyed, yellow-eyed, green-eyed, yellow, green, green with jealousy; horn-mad; invidious, **envious**; **suspicious,** distrustful

jealousy NOUNS *jalousie* <Fr>, jealousness, heartburning, heartburn, **jaundice,** jaundiced eye, green in the eye <nonformal>, Othello's flaw, horn-madness

green-eyed monster
Shakespeare

jeer VERBS **scoff,** gibe, barrack <Brit>, **mock,** revile, rail at, rally, chaff, twit, taunt, jape, flout, scout, have a fling at, cast in one's teeth

jellied ADJS **thickened,** inspissate *or* inspissated, incrassate; **congealed, coagulated, clotted,** grumous; **curdled,** curded, clabbered; jelled, gelatinized; coagulant, coagulating

jeopardize VERBS **endanger, imperil,** peril; **risk, hazard, gamble, gamble with;** jeopard, jeopardy, compromise, put in danger, **put in jeopardy,** put on the spot *and* lay on the line <both nonformal>; **expose,** lay open; incur danger, run into *or* encounter danger

jeopardy NOUNS **danger,** peril, endangerment, imperilment, hazard, risk, cause for alarm, **menace, threat**; **crisis, emergency,** hot spot, nasty *or* tricky spot, pass, pinch, strait, plight, predicament; dangerous ground, yawning *or* gaping chasm, quicksand, thin ice; hornet's nest; house of cards, hardball <nonformal>, no tea party, no picnic

Jeremiah NOUNS **warner,** cautioner, admonisher, monitor; prophet *or* messenger of doom, Cassandra

jerk NOUNS 1 **yank** <nonformal>, quick *or* sudden pull; **twitch,** tweak, pluck, hitch, wrench, snatch, start, bob; **flip,**

flick, flirt, flounce; jig, **jiggle;** jog, joggle
VERBS 2 **twitch,** vellicate; itch; **jig, jiggle,** jigger *or* jigget <nonformal>; **fidget,** have the fidgets

jerky ADJS herky-jerky <nonformal>, twitchy *or* twitchety, jerking, **twitching, fidgety, jumpy,** jiggety <nonformal>, vellicative; **spastic, spasmodic,** eclamptic, orgasmic, convulsive; fitful, saltatory

jerry-built ADJS **unsubstantial, flimsy,** sleazy, tacky <nonformal>, wispy, cobwebby, gossamery, papery, pasteboardy; gimcrack *and* gimcracky *and* cheap-jack *and* ticky-tacky <all nonformal>; jerry

jest NOUNS 1 **gibe, scoff, jeer,** fleer, flout, mock, barracking <Brit>, **taunt, twit,** quip, jape, put-on *and* leg-pull <both nonformal>, foolery
VERBS 2 **joke, wisecrack** *and* crack wise <both nonformal>, utter a mot, **quip,** jape, josh <nonformal>, make fun, **kid** *or* **kid around** <both nonformal>; **crack a joke,** get off a joke, tell a good story; **make fun of,** gibe at, fleer at, mock; **banter, twit, chaff,** rally, jape, **tease,** haze

jester NOUNS **buffoon,** *buffo* <Ital>, clown, fool, zany, merry-andrew, jack-pudding, pickle-herring, motley fool, motley, wearer of the cap and bells

jet NOUNS 1 **jet plane, turbojet,** ramjet, pulse-jet, blowtorch <nonformal>; single-jet, twin-jet, multi-jet; supersonic jet, supersonic transport *or* SST, Concorde
2 **spout, spurt,** spurtle, squirt, spit, spew, spray, spritz <nonformal>; rush, **gush,** flush
VERBS 3 **fly,** be airborne, wing, take wing, wing one's way, take *or* make a flight, take to the air, take the air, volitate, be wafted
4 **spout, spurt,** spurtle, **squirt,** spit, spew, spray, spritz <nonformal>, play, **gush,** well, surge; vomit, vomit out *or* forth

jetsam NOUNS **derelict,** castoff; flotsam, lagan, **flotsam and jetsam;** waifs and strays; abandonee, waif, throwaway, orphan, dogie <nonformal>; **castaway**

jet set NOUNS **society,** *société* <Fr>, fashionable society, **polite society, high society,** high life, *beau monde, haut monde* <both Fr>, good society; best people, people of fashion, right people; *monde* <Fr>, world of fashion, Vanity Fair; **smart set** <nonformal>; the Four Hundred, **upper crust** *and* upper cut <both nonformal>; **cream of society,** *crème de la crème* <Fr>, elite, carriage trade; café society, beautiful people, in-crowd, the glitterati <nonformal>

jettison VERBS **discard, reject, throw away, throw out,** chuck *or* chuck away *and* shit-can *and* eighty-six <all nonformal>, cast, cast off *or* away *or* aside; **get rid of,** get quit of, get shut *or* shet of <nonformal>, rid oneself of, shrug off, **dispose of,** slough, **dump, ditch** <nonformal>, **throw** *or* **heave** *or* **toss overboard,** deep-six <nonformal>, throw *or* cast to the dogs, cast to the winds

jetty NOUNS **barrier,** seawall, groin, mole, breakwater; bulwark, rampart, defense, buffer, bulkhead, parapet, breastwork, work, earthwork, mound; bank, embankment, levee, dike

Jew NOUNS **Hebrew,** Judaist, Israelite; Orthodox *or* Conservative *or* Reform Jew, Reconstructionist; Hasid; Rabbinist, Talmudist; Pharisee; Sadducee

jewel NOUNS 1 bijou, **gem,** stone, precious stone; rhinestone
2 **good thing,** a thing to be desired, **treasure,** boast, pride, **pride and joy;** prize, trophy, plum; winner *and* no slouch *and* nothing to sneeze at <all nonformal>; catch, find <nonformal>, *trouvaille* <Fr>; godsend, windfall

jewelry NOUNS bijouterie, ice <nonformal>; costume jewelry, glass, paste, junk jewelry <nonformal>

Jewish ADJS **Hebrew,** Judaic, Judaical, Israelite, Israelitic, Israelitish; Orthodox, Conservative, Reform, Reconstructionist; Hasidic

Jezebel NOUNS **strumpet,** trollop, wench, hussy, slut, jade, baggage, *cocotte* <Fr>, grisette; **tart** *and* **chippy** *and* **floozy** *and* broad <all nonformal>, bitch, drab, trull, quean, harridan, wanton, whore <nonformal>, bad woman, **loose woman**

jibe VERBS **agree,** accord, harmonize, concur, have no problem with, go along with <nonformal>, **cooperate, correspond, conform,** coincide, parallel, intersect, overlap, **match,** tally, hit, register, lock, interlock, check <nonformal>, square, dovetail; **be consistent,** cohere, stand *or* hold *or* hang together, fall in together, fit together, chime, chime with, chime in with

jiffy NOUNS **instant,** moment, second,

half a second, half a mo <Brit nonformal>, minute, **trice,** twinkle, **twinkling** *or* **twinkle of an eye,** twink, **wink,** bat of an eye <nonformal>, **flash,** crack, tick, stroke, coup, breath, twitch; two shakes of a lamb's tail *and* two shakes *and* half a shake *and* jiff *and* half a jiffy <all nonformal>

jigger NOUNS **drink,** dram, potation, potion, libation, **nip,** draft, drop, spot, finger or two, sip, sup, suck, drench, guzzle, gargle, peg, swig, swill, pull; **snort,** jolt, **shot,** snifter, quickie

jiggle NOUNS 1 **shake,** quake, quiver, quaver, falter, tremor, tremble, **shiver, shudder,** twitter, didder, dither; **wobble; bob,** bobble; **jerk, twitch,** tic, grimace, rictus; jig
VERBS 2 **twitch, jerk,** vellicate; itch; **jig,** jigger *or* jigget <nonformal>

jilt VERBS **abandon, desert, forsake;** turn one's back upon, turn one's tail upon, say goodbye to, walk or run out on <nonformal>, **leave flat** *and* leave high and dry *or* holding the bag *or* in the lurch <all nonformal>, leave one to one's fate, throw to the wolves <nonformal>; quit cold *and* leave flat <both nonformal>, toss aside; throw over <nonformal>; **junk,** deep-six <nonformal>, **discard**

jilted ADJS **unloved,** unbeloved, uncherished, loveless; **lovelorn,** forsaken, **rejected,** thrown over <nonformal>, spurned, crossed in love

Jim Crow NOUNS **segregation,** separation, separationism, division; racial segregation, apartheid, color bar, race hatred; **discrimination,** social discrimination, **social barrier**

jimmy NOUNS 1 **lever; pry,** prize <nonformal>; **bar,** pinch bar, **crowbar,** crow, pinchbar
VERBS 2 **pry,** prize, **lever,** wedge; pry *or* prize out; crowbar, pinchbar

jingle NOUNS 1 **ringing, tinkle,** tingle, dingle, ding, dingdong, ding-a-ling, ting-a-ling; **rhythm, cadence,** movement, lilt
VERBS 2 **ring, tinkle,** tingle, ding, dingdong, dong; clink, tink, ting, chink

jingoistic ADJS **chauvinistic,** chauvinist, jingoist, jingoish, jingo; **hard-line, hawkish** <nonformal>; patriotic; **nationalistic;** ultranationalist, ultranationalistic; overpatriotic, superpatriotic, flag-waving

jinx NOUNS 1 **bad influence,** malevolent influence, evil star, **ill wind;** evil genius, **hoodoo** <nonformal>, **Jonah; curse,** enchantment, whammy *and* double *or* triple whammy <all nonformal>, spell, hex, voodoo; **evil eye,** *malocchio* <Ital>
VERBS 2 bring bad luck; hoodoo *and* hex *and* Jonah *and* put the jinx on <all nonformal>; put the evil eye on, whammy <nonformal>

jitters NOUNS **agitation,** perturbation, trepidation, trepidity, fidgets *and* ants in the pants <both nonformal>, antsiness *and* jitteriness <both nonformal>, jumpiness, nervousness, yips <nonformal>, nervosity, twitter, upset

jittery ADJS **jumpy,** twittery, skittish, skittery, trigger-happy <nonformal>, gun-shy; **shaky,** shivery, quivery, in a quiver; tremulous, tremulant, trembly; jumpy as a cat on a hot tin roof; **fidgety,** fidgeting; shaking, trembling, quivering, shivering; shook up *and* all shook up <both nonformal>

jive NOUNS 1 **jazz; swing,** bebop, bop <nonformal>
VERBS 2 **syncopate,** play jazz, swing, rag <nonformal>
3 **kid,** jolly, josh, fool around, rub, put on, **razz, roast,** ride, needle <all nonformal>

job NOUNS 1 **position,** employment, gainful employment, situation, **office, post, place,** station, berth, billet, **appointment,** engagement, gig <nonformal>
VERBS 2 **sell, wholesale,** sell wholesale, be jobber *or* wholesaler for

Job NOUNS **stoic,** Spartan, man of iron; Griselda

jock NOUNS **athlete; real man, he-man,** *and* two-fisted man <both nonformal>, hunk *and* jockstrap <both nonformal>, man with hair on his chest; caveman *and* bucko <both nonformal>; athletic supporter, G-string <nonformal>

jockey NOUNS 1 **rider,** equestrian, horseman, horserider, horseback rider, horsebacker
VERBS 2 **maneuver,** manipulate, contrive, angle <nonformal>

jocularity NOUNS **facetiousness,** pleasantry, jocoseness, jocosity; **joking,** japery, joshing <nonformal>

jog NOUNS 1 **bump,** joggle, jolt; **jostle,** hustle
VERBS 2 **exercise,** run; **bump,** joggle, jolt, shake, rattle; **jostle,** hustle, hurtle

jogger NOUNS **reminder,** remembrancer;

prompt, prompter, tickler; prompting, cue, hint; *aide-mémoire* <Fr>, **memorandum**; **runner**

john NOUNS **latrine,** convenience, **toilet,** water closet *or* WC <nonformal>; johnny *and* **can** *and* crapper <all nonformal>; loo <Brit nonformal>; **lavatory,** washroom, public convenience

John Doe NOUNS 1 **alias, pseudonym,** anonym, **assumed name,** false *or* fictitious name, *nom de guerre* <Fr>; **pen name, nom de plume;** Jane Doe, Richard Roe
2 **common man, commoner,** little man, **little fellow, average man,** ordinary man, typical man, **man in the street,** one of the people, man of the people, Everyman; ordinary *or* average Joe *and* Joe Doakes *and* Joe Sixpack *and* Joe Blow <all nonformal>

John Hancock NOUNS **signature,** autograph, hand, mark, mark of signature, cross, christcross, X

Johnny-come-lately NOUNS **newcomer, new arrival,** *novus homo* <L>; *arriviste* <Fr>, new boy; **latecomer,** late arrival

joie de vivre <Fr> NOUNS **animation, vivacity,** liveliness, **ardor,** glow, warmth, enthusiasm, lustiness, robustness, mettle, **zest,** zestfulness, **gusto, élan,** *brio* <Ital>, spiritedness, **briskness,** perkiness, pertness, **life, spirit,** life force, vital force *or* principle, *élan vital* <Fr>

join VERBS 1 **adjoin,** conjoin, **connect,** butt, **abut,** abut on *or* upon, be contiguous, be in contact; **neighbor,** border, **border on** *or* **upon,** verge on *or* upon; lie by, stand by
2 band, league, **associate, affiliate,** ally, **combine, unite,** fuse, merge, coalesce, amalgamate, federate, confederate, consolidate; hook up *and* tie up *and* tie in <all nonformal>; be in league, **go into partnership with,** go partners <nonformal>, go *or* be in cahoots with; **join together,** club together, league together, band together; **work together,** get together *and* team up *and* buddy up <all nonformal>, work as a team, act together, act in concert, **pull together; hold together, hang together,** keep together, **stand together,** stand shoulder to shoulder
3 **marry,** wed, nuptial, **unite, hitch** *and* **splice** <both nonformal>, couple, match, match up, make *or* arrange a match, join together, **unite in marriage,** join *or* unite in holy wedlock, tie the knot, tie the nuptial *or* wedding knot, make one
4 **enlist,** enroll, sign up *or* on <nonformal>

joiner NOUNS mixer *and* **good mixer** <both nonformal>, good *or* pleasant company, excellent companion, life of the party, bon vivant; clubman, clubwoman

joint NOUNS 1 **dive** <nonformal>, **den, lair,** den of thieves; hole *and* dump <both nonformal>; gyp *or* clip joint <nonformal>; **whorehouse,** cathouse <nonformal>, sporting house, brothel, bordello, stews, fleshpots
2 **marijuana cigarette;** roach, joy stick, kick stick, reefer, stick, twist <all nonformal>
3 **jail; slammer, slam, jug,** can, coop, cooler, hoosegow, stir, clink, pokey, big house, big school, big cage, big joint, brig, tank <all nonformal>
ADJS 4 **combined,** joined, **conjoint,** conjunct, conjugate, corporate, compact, cooperative, cooperating; concurrent, coincident; inclusive, comprehensive

joke NOUNS 1 **jest, gag** *and* one-liner <both nonformal>, **wheeze,** jape; **fun, sport, play;** story, yarn, **funny story,** good story; dirty story *or* joke, blue story *or* joke, *double entendre* <Fr>; shaggy-dog story; sick joke <nonformal>; ethnic joke; laugh, belly laugh, rib tickler, sidesplitter, thigh-slapper, howler, wow, scream, riot, panic; visual joke, sight gag <nonformal>
2 **laughingstock,** jestingstock, gazingstock, derision, mockery, **figure of fun,** byword, byword of reproach, jest, **butt,** target, stock, **goat** <nonformal>, game, **fair game,** victim, dupe, fool, everybody's fool
VERBS 3 **jest, wisecrack** *and* crack wise <both nonformal>, utter a mot, **quip,** jape, josh <nonformal>, fun <nonformal>, make fun, **kid** *or* **kid around** <both nonformal>; **make a funny** <nonformal>; **crack a joke,** get off a joke, tell a good story; **make fun of,** gibe at, fleer at, mock, scoff at, poke fun at, make the butt of one's humor, be merry with; ridicule

joker NOUNS **mischief-maker,** mischief, **rogue, devil,** knave, **rascal,** rapscallion, scapegrace, **scamp; wag**; buffoon; funmaker, jokester, practical joker, prankster, life of the party, **cutup** <nonformal>; gimmick, catch; curve, curveball, googly *or* bosey *or* wrong'un <all Brit nonformal>; **fooler, hoaxer,** practical joker; spoofer *and* **kidder** *and* ragger *and* leg-puller <all nonformal>

joking ADJS **jocular,** joky <nonformal>, **jesting,** jocose, tongue-in-cheek; **facetious,** joshing <nonformal>, **whimsical, droll,** humorsome; satiric, satirical, sarcastic, **ironic,** ironical; **keen-witted,** quick-witted, nimble-witted

jolly VERBS 1 **kid,** josh, fool around, jive, rub, put on; **razz, roast,** ride, needle <all nonformal>
2 **make merry, revel,** roister, lark <nonformal>, skylark, **make whoopee** <nonformal>, let oneself go, **blow** *or* **let off steam**
ADJS 3 **jovial,** hearty, festive, gay; **convivial,** boon, free and easy, hail-fellow-well-met

jolt NOUNS 1 **prod,** poke, punch, jab, dig, nudge; **bump,** jog, joggle, **jostle,** butt
VERBS 2 **startle,** shock, electrify, jar, shake, stun, **stagger, give one a turn** <nonformal>, give the shock of one's life, make one jump out of his skin, take aback, take one's breath away, bowl down *or* over <nonformal>, strike all of a heap <nonformal>
3 **prod,** goad, poke, punch, jab, dig, nudge; **bump,** jog, joggle, shake, rattle; **jostle,** hustle, **butt**

jostle NOUNS 1 **prod,** poke, punch, jab, dig, nudge; **bump,** jog, joggle; hustle; **shock, jolt,** jar
VERBS 2 **contend,** contest, **tussle, scuffle;** clash, collide; **wrestle,** rassle <nonformal>, grapple, grapple with; **disagree, differ**, vary, not see eye-to-eye, be at cross-purposes, tangle assholes <nonformal>, **conflict,** clash, **jar,** jangle, collide, square off; pick pockets

jot NOUNS minutia, **minutiae** <pl>, minim, **drop,** droplet, **mite** <nonformal>, mote, fleck, **speck,** flyspeck, tittle, jot nor tittle, iota, **trace,** trace amount, suspicion, *soupçon* <Fr>

jounce VERBS **shake,** quake, vibrate, jactitate; **tremble,** quiver, quaver, falter, shudder, shiver, twitter, didder, chatter; **shock, jolt,** jar, hustle, bounce, bump

journal NOUNS **periodical, magazine,** gazette; ephemeris; trade journal, trade magazine; daybook, diary; **account book,** ledger; **chronicle, annals**

journalism NOUNS **the press,** the public press, **the fourth estate;** print medium, the print media, print journalism, the print press, the public print; newspaper writing, editorial-writing, feature-writing, rewriting

journalist NOUNS **newspaperman, newspaperwoman,** newsman, newswoman, inkstained wretch, newswriter, gentleman *or* representative of the press; **reporter,** newshawk *and* newshound <both nonformal>; leg man <nonformal>; investigative reporter; **cub reporter; correspondent, foreign correspondent,** war correspondent, special correspondent, stringer; paparazzo

journey NOUNS 1 **trip,** *jornada* <Sp>, peregrination, sally, **trek;** progress, course, run; **tour,** grand tour; **excursion,** jaunt, junket, outing, pleasure trip; sight-seeing trip *or* tour; **pilgrimage,** hajj; **voyage**
VERBS 2 **travel,** make *or* take *or* go *or* go on a journey, **take** *or* **make a trip,** trek, jaunt, peregrinate; junket, go on a junket; **tour;** hit the trail <nonformal>, take the road, go on the road; go abroad, go to foreign places *or* shores, range the world, globe-trot <nonformal>; go on *or* make a pilgrimage

journeyman NOUNS 1 **skilled worker,** skilled laborer, mechanic; **craftsman, handicraftsman;** craftswoman; craftsperson; craftspeople; **artisan,** artificer
ADJS 2 **competent,** capable, able, efficient, qualified, fit, fitted, suited, worthy; well-qualified, well-fitted, well-suited

jovial ADJS **festive, festal; merry,** gay, jolly, joyous, joyful, gladsome, convivial, gala, hilarious

joy NOUNS **happiness,** joyfulness, cheer, cheerfulness, exhilaration, **exuberance,** high spirits, glee, sunshine; gaiety

joyful ADJS **happy, glad, joyous,** flushed with joy, radiant, beaming, glowing, starry-eyed, sparkling, laughing, smiling, smirking, smirky, chirping, purring, singing, dancing, leaping, capering, **cheerful,** gay; cheering, gladdening; **exhilarating,** animating, enlivening, invigorating; cheerful, cheery

joyless ADJS **pleasureless,** cheerless, depressed, grim; **sad, unhappy**; unsatisfied, unfulfilled, ungratified; **bored; desolate,** dreary, cheerless, dismal, bleak

jubilant ADJS **overjoyed,** brimming *or* bursting with happiness, on top of the world; **rapturous,** raptured, **enraptured, enchanted,** entranced, enravished, ravished, rapt, possessed; **in raptures,** transported, in a transport of delight, **carried away,** beside oneself with joy; **elated,** elate, exalted, exultant, flushed

jubilee NOUNS **celebration,** celebrating; **observance, commemoration,** memorialization, remembrance, memory; red-letter day, **festivity, revel**; rejoicing; **anniversary,** silver jubilee, golden jubilee, diamond jubilee

Judaism NOUNS Orthodox Judaism, Conservative Judaism, Reform Judaism, Reconstructionism; Hasidism

Judas NOUNS **traitor,** treasonist, **betrayer, quisling,** rat <nonformal>, serpent, snake, cockatrice, snake in the grass, **double-crosser** <nonformal>, double-dealer; Judas Iscariot

judge NOUNS 1 **magistrate,** justice, adjudicator, moderator; umpire, referee; good judge, **critic, expert,** authority, maven <nonformal>, arbiter
VERBS 2 **administer justice,** sit in judgment; **try,** try a case, conduct a trial, **hear,** give a hearing to, sit on; **criticize,** critique, evaluate, interpret, explicate, analyze; exercise judgment *or* the judgment; make a judgment call <nonformal>; adjudge, adjudicate

judgment NOUNS 1 **decision,** landmark decision; **verdict, sentence**; acquittal; condemnation, penalty, rap <nonformal>; punishment that fits the crime, condign punishment, well-deserved punishment
2 **judiciousness,** good *or* sound judgment, cool judgment, soundness of judgment; **prudence,** consideration, circumspection, circumspectness, reflection, reflectiveness, **thoughtfulness; discretion,** discernment, critical discernment, penetration, perception, perceptiveness, **insight,** perspicacity; acumen

judgmental ADJS **judicial, judiciary,** judicative; **evaluative,** critical; **disapproving, censorious**

Judgment Day NOUNS **doomsday,** doom, day of doom, day of reckoning, crack of doom, trumpet *or* trump of doom; Day of Judgment, the Judgment; eschatology, last things, **last days**

judiciary NOUNS judicial *or* legal *or* court system, judicature, judicatory, court, the courts; criminal-justice system; **justice,** the wheels of justice, judicial process

judicious ADJS **prudent,** prudential, politic, careful, provident, **considerate,** circumspect, **thoughtful,** reflective, reflecting; **discreet;** astute, discriminative, discriminating; **well-advised,** well-judged, enlightened

jug NOUNS 1 crock, vase, urn, bowl; prison

juggle VERBS **falsify, belie, misrepresent,** miscolor; misstate, misquote, misreport, miscite; **slant, twist,** impart spin <nonformal>; put a false appearance upon, give a false coloring, fudge <nonformal>; **play games** <nonformal>, **swindle,** defraud; conjure; **bluff**

juggler NOUNS **trickster,** tricker; sleight-of-hand performer, **swindler, defrauder,** cozener

juice NOUNS 1 **fluid, liquid;** liquor, drink, beverage; liquid extract, fluid extract; **sap,** latex
2 **current,** electric current, current flow, amperage, electric stream *or* flow

juicy ADJS **interesting,** stimulating, provocative, provoking, thought-provoking, thought-challenging, thought-inspiring; **titillating,** tickling, tantalizing, inviting, exciting; **piquant,** lively, racy, succulent, spicy, rich; sappy

jumble NOUNS **conglomeration, assortment,** assemblage, mixed bag, ragbag, grab bag, olio, *olla podrida* <Sp>, **scramble,** mingle-mangle, mishmash, **mess,** can of worms <nonformal>, everything but the kitchen sink <nonformal>, disorganization, **disorder,** chaos, **mess** *and* mix-up <both nonformal>

jumbled ADJS **confused, chaotic,** anarchic, **muddled,** scattered, helter-skelter <nonformal>, higgledy-piggledy, hugger-mugger, skimble-skamble, in a mess; **topsy-turvy,** arsy-varsy, upside-down, ass-backwards <nonformal>; **mixed up, balled** *or* **bollixed up** <nonformal>, **screwed up** <nonformal>, mucked up <nonformal>, **fouled up** *and* fucked up *and* snafu <all nonformal>

jumbo ADJS **huge, immense, vast, enormous,** astronomic, astronomical, humongous <nonformal>, king-size, queen-size, tremendous, prodigious, stupendous

jump NOUNS 1 **leap,** forward leap *or* jump, quantum jump *or* leap, spring, forward spring; **discontinuity,** interruption; **advantage,** vantage, odds, leg up *and* inside track *and* pole position <all nonformal>; **edge,** bulge *and* drop <both nonformal>
VERBS 2 **leap, vault, spring, skip, hop, bound,** bounce; **start,** startle, jump out of one's skin, jump a mile; have at, **attack**

jumper NOUNS leaper, hopper; broad jumper, high jumper; bungee jumper; parachute jumper, sky diver, sport jumper, paratrooper, smoke jumper

jumping-off place NOUNS **extremity, extreme; limit**, ultimacy, definitiveness, **boundary,** farthest bound, Thule, *Ultima Thule* <L>

jumpy ADJS **jittery** <nonformal>, twittery, skittish, skittery, trigger-happy <nonformal>, gun-shy; **shaky,** shivery, quivery, in a quiver; tremulous, tremulant, trembly; jumpy as a cat on a hot tin roof; **fidgety,** fidgeting; fluttery, all of a flutter *or* twitter; twitchy; **agitated;** shaking, trembling, quivering, shivering; shook up *and* all shook up <both nonformal>

junction NOUNS **joining,** joinder, jointure, **connection, union,** unification, bond, bonding, connectedness *or* connectivity, conjunction, conjoining, conjugation, liaison, marriage, hookup <nonformal>, splice, tie, tie-up *and* tie-in <both informal>, knotting

juncture NOUNS **circumstance,** conjuncture, contingency, eventuality; **joint,** join, joining, **union, connection,** link, connecting link, coupling, accouplement; **period, point,** stage; **time,** while, **moment,** minute, instant, hour, day, **season**

jungle NOUNS **labyrinth;** webwork, mesh; **wilderness,** morass, quagmire; mare's nest, rat's nest, can of worms <nonformal>, snake pit

junior NOUNS 1 **subordinate,** secondary, second-in-command, lieutenant, **inferior; underling,** understrapper, low man on the totem pole <nonformal>, errand boy, flunky, gofer <nonformal>; assistant, personal assistant, helper; **upperclassman**
ADJS 2 **inferior,** subordinate, secondary; **minor;** low in the pecking order; cadet, puisne <law>, younger

junk NOUNS 1 **rubbish,** rubble, trash, scrap, debris, litter
VERBS 2 **scrap,** consign to the scrap heap, throw on the junk heap <nonformal>; jettison, throw overboard, discard, throw away
ADJS 3 **abandoned, forsaken, deserted,** left; disused; **derelict,** castaway, jettisoned; junked, discarded; **worthless,** valueless, good-for-nothing; **cheap,** shoddy, trashy, **shabby**

junket NOUNS **tour,** excursion, jaunt, outing, pleasure trip; sight-seeing trip *or* tour

junkie NOUNS **addict,** drug addict, narcotics addict, user, drug user, drug abuser; head *and* druggy *and* doper *and* toker *and* freak <all nonformal>

junkyard NOUNS wasteyard, scrapyard, **dump,** dumpsite, garbage dump, landfill, sanitary landfill, toxic waste dump

Junoesque ADJS **shapely,** well-built, built, well-shaped, well-proportioned, well-made, well-formed, stacked *or* well-stacked <both nonformal>, curvaceous, curvy <nonformal>, pneumatic, amply endowed, built for comfort *or* built like a brick shithouse <both nonformal>, buxom, callipygian, callipygous; statuesque, goddess-like

junta NOUNS **clique,** conspiracy, ring, junto, cabal, camarilla, **clan,** group

jurisdiction NOUNS legal authority *or* power *or* right *or* sway, the confines of the law; **control,** mastery, mastership, command, dominion, domination; hold, grasp, grip, gripe

jurisprudence NOUNS **law,** legal science; nomology, nomography

jurist NOUNS legist, jurisprudent, jurisconsult; law member of a court-martial

juror NOUNS **juryman, jurywoman,** venireman *or* venirewoman, talesman; foreman of the jury, foreman; grand juror, petit juror, petty juror

jury NOUNS **panel,** jury of one's peers, sessions <Scots>, twelve men in a box; inquest; jury panel, jury list, venire facias; hung *or* deadlocked jury

jury-rigged ADJS **makeshift,** makeshifty, **stopgap,** band-aid <nonformal>, improvised, improvisational; **ad hoc;** quick and dirty <nonformal>; temporary, provisional, tentative

just ADJS 1 **fair,** square, **fair and square;**

equitable, balanced, level <nonformal>, **even,** evenhanded; **right, rightful;** justifiable, justified, warranted, warrantable, defensible; **due,** deserved, merited; meet, meet and right, right and proper, fit, **proper, good,** as it should *or* ought to be; lawful, legal
ADVS 2 **very, exceedingly,** awfully *and* terribly *and* terrifically <all nonformal>, **quite,** so, **really,** real *and* right <both nonformal>, **pretty,** only too, mightily, **mighty** *and* almighty *and* powerfully *and* powerful <all nonformal>

justice NOUNS 1 **justness; equity,** equitableness, level playing field <nonformal>; **evenhandedness,** measure for measure, give-and-take; balance, equality; **right, rightness,** rightfulness, meetness, properness, propriety, what is right; dueness; justification, **justifiableness,** justifiability, warrantedness, warrantability, defensibility; poetic justice; retributive justice, nemesis; summary justice, drumhead justice, rude justice; scales of justice; lawfulness, legality; **judge, magistrate,** adjudicator

justifiable ADJS **vindicable,** defensible; **excusable, pardonable, forgivable,** expiable, remissible, exemptible, venial; **condonable,** dispensable; **warrantable,** allowable, admissible, reasonable, colorable, legitimate

justified ADJS **warranted, entitled,** qualified, worthy; **deserved, merited,** richly deserved, earned, well-earned; **redeemed, saved,** converted, regenerated, regenerate, reborn, born-again, renewed

justify VERBS **vindicate,** do justice to, make justice *or* right prevail; **warrant,** account for, show sufficient grounds for, give good reasons for; **rationalize,** explain

jut VERBS **protrude,** protuberate, project, extrude; **stick out,** jut out, poke out, stand out, shoot out; **stick up,** bristle up, start up, cock up, shoot up

jutting ADJS **protruding, protrusive,** protrudent; protrusile, protrusible; **protuberant,** protuberating; **projecting, extruding,** outstanding; prominent, eminent, salient, bold; prognathous; protrusile, emissile

juvenile NOUNS 1 **youngster,** young person, **youth,** youngling, young'un <nonformal>, juvenal <old>; **stripling,** slip, sprig, sapling; fledgling; hopeful, young hopeful; **minor,** infant; **adolescent,** pubescent; **ingenue**
ADJS 2 **young,** youngling, juvenal, juvenescent, **youthful;** ungrown, half-grown, adolescent, puerile, boyish, girlish

K

kaput ADJS **past hope, beyond recall,** past praying for; **ruined,** undone, gone to hell *and* gone to hell in a handbasket <both nonformal>

karma NOUNS **destiny**, **fate,** doom, kismet, what bodes *or* looms, what is fated *or* destined *or* doomed, what is written, what is in the books

kayo VERBS knock unconscious, knock senseless, **knock out,** KO *and* lay out *and* coldcock *and* knock stiff <all nonformal>

keen VERBS 1 **lament, mourn,** moan, grieve, sorrow, weep over, bewail, bemoan, deplore, **repine, sigh,** give sorrow words; elegize, dirge
ADJS 2 **eager, anxious,** agog, all agog; **avid,** forward, prompt, quick, ready, ready and willing, alacritous, bursting to, dying to, raring to; **zestful, lively,** full of life, vital, vivacious, vivid, spirited, **animated; impatient**
3 **sharp,** sharpish, incisive, trenchant, **cutting,** penetrating, piercing, biting, **stinging,** stabbing, **scathing, scorching,** withering, scurrilous, abusive, thersitical, foulmouthed, harsh-tongued
4 **smart, brainy** <nonformal>, **bright, brilliant,** scintillating; **clever,** apt, **gifted,** talented; **sharp,** smart as a whip, sharp as a tack <nonformal>; nobody's fool *and* no dumbbell *and* not born yesterday <all nonformal>

keen on ADJS **desirous of** *or* **to,** set on <nonformal>, bent on; fond of, with a liking for, partial to <nonformal>; inclined toward, leaning toward; **itching for** *or* **to,** aching for *or* to, **dying for** *or* **to;** spoiling for <nonformal>; mad on *or* for, wild to *or* for <nonformal>, crazy to *or* for <nonformal>; hipped on, **cracked on,** bugs on, freaked-out, **nuts on** *or* **over** *or* **about, keen about,** crazy *or* mad *or* nuts about <all nonformal>

keep NOUNS 1 **accommodations,** accommodation, facilities; **lodgings;** bed, board, full board; **room and board,** bed and board; **subsistence,** fostering
2 **prison,** correctional *or* correction facility, **penitentiary,** pen <nonformal>, penal institution, bastille, state prison, federal prison; house of detention, detention center, detention home; **jail, gaol** <Brit>, jailhouse, lockup
3 **stronghold,** hold, safehold, fasthold, strong point, **fastness,** ward, **bastion,** donjon, **citadel, castle,** tower, tower of strength, strong point
VERBS 4 **obey, mind,** heed, observe, listen or hearken to; comply, conform, walk in lockstep; stay in line *and* not get out of line *and* not get off base <all nonformal>; **observe, keep, heed, follow,** keep the faith
5 provide for, make provision *or* due provision for; prepare; support, maintain; **preserve, conserve, save,** spare; keep safe, keep inviolate *or* intact
6 **raise, breed,** rear, grow, hatch, feed, nurture, fatten; run; ranch, farm; culture

keeper NOUNS **jailer,** gaoler <Brit>, correctional *or* correction *or* corrections officer; **warder,** prison guard, **turnkey,** bull *and* screw <both nonformal>; **guard; protector,** protectress, safekeeper

keep out VERBS **exclude, bar,** debar, bar out, lock out, **shut out,** count out <nonformal>, close the door on, close out, cut out, cut off, preclude; **reject, repudiate,** blackball *and* turn thumbs down on <both nonformal>, read *or* drum out, ease *or* freeze out *and* leave *or* keep out in the cold <all nonformal>, ostracize, wave off *or* aside

keep quiet VERBS **be still,** lie still; stand, **stand still,** be at a standstill; stand like a post; **not stir,** not stir a step, not move a muscle; not breathe, hold one's breath

keepsake NOUNS **memento,** remembrance, token, trophy, souvenir, relic, favor, token of remembrance; *memento mori* <L>; **memories, memorabilia,** memorials

keep the faith VERBS **be hopeful,** keep one's spirits up, never say die, take heart, be of good hope, be of good cheer, keep hoping, keep hope alive; **hope for the best,** keep one's fingers crossed, allow oneself to hope; fight the good fight, let one's light shine, praise and glorify God, walk humbly with one's God

keep the peace VERBS remain at peace, wage peace; refuse to shed blood, keep one's sword in its sheath; forswear violence, beat one's swords into plowshares; pour oil on troubled waters; defuse

keep time VERBS **beat time,** tap out the rhythm; count, count the beats; mark time, measure time

kelp NOUNS **seaweed,** sea moss, rockweed, gulfweed, sargasso *or* sargassum, sea lentil, wrack, sea wrack

ken NOUNS 1 **knowledge,** knowing, knowingness; **familiarity,** intimacy; private knowledge, privity
VERBS 2 **understand, comprehend,** apprehend, have, know, conceive, realize, appreciate, have no problem with, savvy <nonformal>, sense, make sense out of, make something of

kennel NOUNS 1 **doghouse;** pound, dog pound; cattery
2 **drain,** sough <Brit nonformal>, sluice, scupper; **sink,** sump; piscina; **gutter, sewer,** cloaca, headchute

kept ADJS **reserved, preserved, saved,** conserved, put by, retained, held, withheld, held back, kept *or* held in reserve; **well-preserved,** well-conserved, **well-kept,** in a good state of preservation

kept woman NOUNS **mistress,** woman, kept mistress, **paramour,** concubine, doxy, playmate, spiritual *or* unofficial wife; live-in lover <nonformal>

kerchief NOUNS **headdress,** headcloth, coverchief; **handkerchief**

kernel NOUNS **substance,** sum and substance, stuff, material, matter, medium, building blocks, fabric; **gist,** heart, soul, meat, nub; the nitty-gritty *and* the bottom line *and* the name of the game <all nonformal>, **core,** marrow, pith, sap, spirit, **essence,** quintessence

key NOUNS 1 **island, isle; islet,** holm, cay; sandbank, sandbar, bar
2 clavis; latchkey; passkey, *passe-partout* <Fr>; master key, skeleton key; open sesame; plastic key
3 **clue, cue,** tip-off <nonformal>, telltale, smoking gun <nonformal>, straw in the wind; **lead** *and* hot lead <both nonformal>
ADJS 4 **central,** centric, **middle**; centermost, middlemost, **midmost;** axial, **pivotal**

keyed up ADJS **excited, stirred,** stirred up, wrought up, **worked up,** worked up into a lather <nonformal>, steamed up, hopped up <nonformal>, carried away

keynote NOUNS 1 **characteristic, peculiarity, singularity,** particularity, specialty, individualism, **character,** nature, **trait,** quirk, point of character, bad point, good point, saving grace, redeeming feature, mannerism, trick, **feature,** distinctive feature
VERBS 2 **characterize,** distinguish, differentiate, define, describe; **mark, earmark,** mark off, mark out, demarcate, **set apart,** make special *or* unique; sound the keynote, set the tone *or* mood, set the pace; be characteristic, **be a feature** *or* **trait of**

keystone NOUNS **foundation stone,** footstone; **cornerstone,** headstone, first stone, quoin; **salient point,** cardinal point, high point, great point; **essence,** linchpin, the name of the game *and* the bottom line *and* what it's all about *and* where it's at <all nonformal>, substance, gravamen

khan NOUNS **prince,** *Prinz, Fürst* <both Ger>, knez, atheling, sheikh, sherif, mirza, emir, shahzada <India>

kibbutz NOUNS **community,** communal effort *or* enterprise, cooperative society; **collectivity,** collectivism, collective enterprise, collective farm

kibitz VERBS **advise, counsel,** recommend, suggest, advocate, propose, submit; weigh in with advice <nonformal>, give a piece of advice, give a hint *or* broad hint, meddle

kibitzer NOUNS **meddler,** intermeddler; **busybody, pry,** Paul Pry, prier; buttinsky *and* yenta *and* backseat driver <all nonformal>

kick NOUNS 1

thrill, sensation; **charge,** boot, bang, belt, blast, flash, hit, jolt, large charge, rush, upper, lift; jollies

2 **boot;** punt, drop kick, place kick, kicking; **recoil, rebound,** resilience, repercussion, *contrecoup* <Fr>; **bounce, bound, spring,** bounce-back; **backlash,** backlashing, kickback, a kick like a mule <nonformal>; **backfire, boomerang**
VERBS 3 **object, protest, remonstrate,** expostulate; **complain,** exclaim at, state a grievance, air one's grievances
4 <nonformal> put up a struggle *or* fight; **bitch** *and* **beef** *and* **squawk** *and* howl *and* holler *and* put up a squawk *and* raise a howl; exclaim *or* cry out against, make *or* create *or* raise a stink about; yell bloody murder

5 **break the habit, cure oneself of,** disaccustom oneself, wean oneself from, break the pattern, break one's chains *or* fetters; **give up,** leave off, **abandon,** drop, stop, discontinue, shake <nonformal>, throw off, rid oneself of; get on the wagon, swear off
6 boot, kick about *or* around; kick downstairs <old>; kick out; **recoil, rebound,** resile; **bounce, bound, spring; spring** *or* **fly back,** bounce *or* bound back, snap back; kick back, kick like a mule <nonformal>, **backfire, boomerang;** backlash, lash back

kicker NOUNS **condition, provision, proviso, stipulation,** whereas; **catch** *and* joker *and* string *and* a string to it <all nonformal>

kickoff NOUNS 1 **beginning, commencement, start,** running *or* flying start, starting point, square one <nonformal>, **outset,** outbreak, **onset,** oncoming; **creation, foundation, establishment, establishing, institution, origin,** origination, establishment, setting-up, setting in motion; **launching,** launch, jump-off *and* send-off *and* start-off *and* take-off *and* blast-off *and* git-go *and* square one <all nonformal>, the word 'go' <nonformal>
ADJS 2 preliminary, exploratory, pioneering, trailblazing, door-opening, inaugural

kick off VERBS **start,** start off, start up, give a start, crank up, give a push *or* shove <nonformal>, jump-start, kick-start, **put** *or* **set in motion, set on foot,** set going *or* agoing, start going; **start the ball rolling** <nonformal>; get off the ground *or* off the mark, **launch**

kid NOUNS 1 **child,** nipper, kiddy *and* kiddo <both nonformal>, **little one,** little fellow *or* guy, little bugger <nonformal>, shaver *and* little shaver <both nonformal>, little squirt <nonformal>, **tot, little tot,** wee tot, pee-wee, tad *or* little tad, tyke, moppet
VERBS 2 **joke, jest, wisecrack** *and* crack wise <both nonformal>, utter a mot, **quip,** jape, josh <nonformal>, fun <nonformal>, make fun, **kid around** <both nonformal>; put on, razz, roast, ride, heckle <all nonformal>

kidding ADJS 1 **bantering,** chaffing, twitting; **fooling, teasing,** japing

kidnap VERBS **snatch** <nonformal>, hold for ransom; **abduct,** abduce, spirit away, **carry off** *or* **away,** run off *or* away with; skyjack; **shanghai,** crimp, impress

kidnapper NOUNS **abductor; shanghaier,** snatcher *and* baby-snatcher <both nonformal>; crimp, crimper

kidnapping NOUNS **abduction,** snatching <nonformal>; **shanghaiing,** impressment, crimping

kill NOUNS 1 bourn, run <Brit nonformal>, **creek,** crick <nonformal>
2 **quarry, game, prey,** venery, beasts of venery, victim, the hunted; big game
VERBS 3 **slay, put to death,** deprive of life, bereave of life, **take life,** take the life of, take one's life away, **do away with,** make away with, **put out of the way,** put to sleep, end, **put an end to,** end the life of, **dispatch,** do for, murder, finish, finish off, kill off, take out, **dispose of, exterminate, destroy,** annihilate; **liquidate,** purge; carry off *or* away, remove from life; put down, put away, put one out of one's misery; launch into eternity, send to glory, send to kingdom come <nonformal>; euthanatize; **execute**

4 <nonformal> **waste, zap,** nuke, rub out, croak, snuff, bump off, knock off, bushwhack, lay out, polish off, blow away, blot out, erase, wipe out, blast, do in, off, hit, ice, gun down, pick off, put to bed with a shovel, scrag, take care of, take out, take for a ride, give the business *or* works, get, fix, settle

5 **quash,** squash *and* **squelch** <both nonformal>; **smother, stifle,** suffocate, asphyxiate, strangle, throttle, choke off, **muzzle, gag;** censor, bleep *or* bleep out <nonformal>, silence; jump on *and* crack down on *and* clamp down on <all nonformal>, put *or* keep the lid on <nonformal>; **veto,** put one's veto upon, decide *or* rule against, **turn thumbs down on** <nonformal>

killer NOUNS **slayer, slaughterer, butcher,** bloodshedder; massacrer; **manslayer, homicide, murderer,** mankiller, bloodletter, Cain; **assassin,** assassinator; **cutthroat,** thug, desperado, bravo, gorilla <nonformal>, apache, gunman; professional killer, hired killer, hit man *or* button man *or* gun *or* trigger man *or* torpedo *or* gunsel <all nonformal>; **hatchet man**

killing NOUNS 1 **slaying, slaughter, dispatch, extermination, destruction,**

destruction of life, taking of life, death-dealing, dealing of death, bane; kill; **bloodshed,** bloodletting, blood, gore, flow of blood; mercy killing, euthanasia, negative *or* passive euthanasia; ritual murder *or* killing, immolation, sacrifice; *auto-da-fé* <Sp, literally, act of faith>, martyrdom, martyrization; lynching; stoning, lapidation; defenestration; braining; shooting; poisoning; execution; mass killing, biocide, ecocide, genocide; Holocaust; mass murder
2 **gain, profit; pile** *and* bundle *and* cleanup *and* mint <all nonformal>
ADJS 3 **fatiguing, wearying,** wearing, **tiring,** straining, stressful, trying, **exhausting,** draining, **grueling,** punishing; **deadly, deathly,** deathful, **destructive,** death-dealing, savage, brutal; internecine; **fatal, mortal, lethal, malignant,** malign, **virulent, pernicious,** baneful

killjoy NOUNS **spoilsport,** grinch *and* crapehanger *and* drag <all nonformal>; damp, damper, **wet blanket,** party pooper; gloomster *and* doomster <both nonformal>, doomsdayer, apocalypticist, Moaning Minnie <Brit nonformal>; skeleton at the feast; gloomy Gus *and* calamity howler *and* worrywart <all nonformal>, seek-sorrow, Job's comforter, prophet of doom, Cassandra

one who is always building dungeons in the air
JOHN GALSWORTHY

kill oneself VERBS **commit suicide, take one's own life,** die by one's own hand, do away with oneself, put an end to oneself; blow one's brains out, take an overdose <of a drug>, overdose *or* OD <nonformal>; commit hara-kiri *or* seppuku; sign one's own death warrant, doom oneself

kiln NOUNS **oven;** acid kiln, brick kiln, cement kiln, enamel kiln, muffle kiln, limekiln, reverberatory, reverberatory kiln

kin NOUNS **kinfolk** *and* **kinfolks** <both nonformal>, **kinsmen, kinsfolk, kindred,** kith and kin, **family, relatives, relations, people,** folks <nonformal>, connections; **blood relation** *or* **relative,** flesh, blood, flesh and blood, uterine kin, consanguinean; cognate; agnate, enate; kinsman, kinswoman, sib, sibling; german; next of kin

kind NOUNS 1 **sort, ilk, type,** breed of cat <nonformal>, lot <nonformal>, **variety, species, genus,** *genre* <Fr>, phylum, denomination, designation, description, style, manner, **nature, character,** persuasion, the like *or* likes of <nonformal>; **stamp, brand,** feather, color, stripe, line, grain, kidney; **make,** mark, label, shape, cast, form, mold; tribe, clan, race, strain, blood, kin, breed
ADJS 2 **kindly,** kindly-disposed; **benign,** benignant; good as gold, **good, nice, decent; gracious; kindhearted, warm, warmhearted,** softhearted, tenderhearted, tender, loving, affectionate; **sympathetic,** sympathizing, **compassionate**, merciful; brotherly, fraternal; humane, human; charitable, caritative

kindergarten NOUNS **preschool,** infant school <Brit>, nursery, **nursery school;** day nursery, **day-care center,** crèche; playschool

kindhearted ADJS **kind, kindly,** kindly-disposed; **benign,** benignant; good as gold, **good, nice, decent; warm, warmhearted,** softhearted, tenderhearted, tender, loving, affectionate; **compassionate**, merciful; charitable, caritative

kindle VERBS **excite, impassion,** arouse, rouse, stir, stir up, set astir, stir the feelings, stir the blood, cause a stir *or* commotion, play on the feelings; **work up,** work into a lather <nonformal>, whip up, **key up,** steam up; **move**; **foment, incite**; turn on <nonformal>; **awaken,** awake, wake, waken, wake up; light the fuse, **fire, inflame,** heat, warm, set fire to, set on fire, fire *or* warm the blood; fan, fan the fire *or* flame, add fuel to the fire *or* flame; raise to a fever heat *or* pitch; **ignite**

kindred NOUNS 1 **blood relationship,** blood, ties of blood, consanguinity, common descent *or* ancestry, biological *or* genetic relationship, **kinship, relation, relationship,** sibship; propinquity; cognation; agnation, enation; filiation, affiliation; **kinfolk** *and* **kinfolks** <both nonformal>, **kinsmen, kinsfolk,** kinnery <nonformal>, **kin,** kith and kin, **family,** relatives, relations, people, folks <nonformal>
ADJS 2 **akin, related,** of common source *or* stock *or* descent *or* ancestry, agnate, cognate, enate, connate, connatural, congeneric *or* congenerous, con-

sanguine *or* consanguineous, genetically related, related by blood, affinal
kindred soul NOUNS soul mate, kindred spirit, **companion, twin,** brother, sister; *mon semblable* <Fr>, second self, alter ego
kinetic ADJS **dynamic,** dynamical, kinetical, kinematic, kinematical
king NOUNS **potentate,** sovereign, monarch, ruler, prince, dynast, crowned head, anointed king, majesty, royalty, royal, royal personage
kingmaker NOUNS operator *and* finagler *and* **wire-puller** <all nonformal>; behind-the-scenes operator, gray eminence, *éminence grise* <Fr>, power behind the throne, **powerbroker**
kingpin NOUNS

<nonformal> **top dog,** boss man, big boy, Big Daddy, big cheese, kingfish, el supremo, honcho *or* head honcho, top banana, big enchilada, himself, herself, man *or* woman upstairs, queen bee, heavy momma, Big Momma

king-size ADJS **oversize,** oversized; **outsize,** outsized, giant-size, **queen-size,** record-size, **overlarge,** overbig, too big; **overgrown,** overdeveloped; **overweight,** overheavy; overfleshed, overstout, overfat, overplump, overfed, obese
kink NOUNS 1 **pang,** crick, hitch, cramp *or* cramps
2 **quirk, twist,** crank, quip, trick, mannerism, **crotchet,** conceit, whim, maggot, maggot in the brain, bee in one's bonnet *or* head <nonformal>
kinky ADJS 1 **curly, curled;** kinked; **frizzly,** frizzy, frizzled, frizzed
2 **capricious, whimsical,** freakish, humorsome, vagarious; **fanciful, notional,** maggoty, **crotchety,** harebrained, cranky, flaky <nonformal>, quirky; wanton, wayward, vagrant
3 **unconventional, unorthodox, eccentric,** gonzo <nonformal>, offbeat <nonformal>, way out *and* far out *and* out in left field <all nonformal>
kismet NOUNS **destiny, fate,** doom, karma, what bodes *or* looms, what is fated *or* destined *or* doomed, what is written, what is in the books
kiss NOUNS 1 **contact, touch,** gentle *or* tentative contact, caress, brush, glance, nudge, rub, graze; impingement, impingence; buss, smack, smooch <nonformal>, **osculation;** French kiss, soul kiss
VERBS 2 **touch lightly,** touch upon; **brush,** sweep, graze, brush by, glance, scrape, skim; buss, smack, smooch <nonformal>, **osculate;** blow a kiss
kit NOUNS **baggage,** bag and baggage, traps, tackle, apparatus, truck, gear, outfit, duffel; **set,** suit, suite, series
kite NOUNS 1 box kite, Eddy kite, Hargrave *or* cellular kite, tetrahedral kite
2 bad check, rubber check *and* bounced check <both nonformal>
kitsch NOUNS **vulgarity,** vulgarness, vulgarism, commonness, **untastefulness,** tastelessness, unaestheticness, unaestheticism, tackiness <nonformal>; low *or* bad *or* poor taste, *mauvais goût* <Fr>; vulgar taste, bourgeois taste, Babbittry, philistinism; popular taste, pop culture *and* pop <both nonformal>; campiness, camp, high *or* low camp
kitten NOUNS **cat, feline,** pussy *and* **puss** *and* **pussycat** <all nonformal>, tabby, grimalkin; **kitty** *and* kitty-cat <both nonformal>
kittenish ADJS **frisky,** antic, skittish, coltish, rompish, capersome; **full of beans** *and* **feeling one's oats** <both nonformal>, full of piss and vinegar <nonformal>; **sportive, playful,** playful as a kitten, **frolicsome,** gamesome; kittenlike
kitty NOUNS **funds, means,** available means *or* resources *or* funds, wherewithal, command of money; **pot,** jackpot, pool, stakes
kittycornered ADJS 1 **transverse,** crosswise *or* crossways, thwart, athwart, across; **diagonal,** bendwise; catercorner *or* **catercornered** *or* cattycorner *or* cattycornered *or* kittycorner; slant, bias, biased, biaswise *or* biasways
ADVS 2 **diagonally,** diagonalwise; **on the bias,** bias, biaswise; **cornerwise,** cornerways; catercornerways *or* **catercorner** *or* cattycorner *or* kittycorner
klutzy ADJS **clumsy, clunky** <nonformal>, heavy-handed, heavy-footed, hamhanded, ham-fisted <chiefly Brit>, graceless, ungraceful, inconcinnate *and* inconcinnous <both old>, infelicitous, unfelicitous; **stupid, dumb,** dullard, **doltish,** blockish, klutzish <nonformal>, duncish, duncical, cloddish, lumpish, **oafish,** boobish, sottish, **asinine,** lamebrained

knave NOUNS **rascal,** precious rascal, rogue, **scoundrel,** villain, blackguard, **scamp, scalawag** <nonformal>, spalpeen <Ir>, rapscallion, **devil**

knead VERBS **mix, blend,** interblend, work; **massage,** caress, pet, stroke; plump, plump up, fluff, fluff up, shake up; **mash, smash,** squash, pulp

knee-high ADJS **little, small**, smallish; **slight,** exiguous; pintsized <nonformal>, half-pint; knee-high to a grasshopper; petite; short

kneel VERBS **bow, bend,** genuflect, bend the knee, **curtsy,** make a low bow, make a leg, make a reverence *or* an obeisance, salaam, bob, duck; **kowtow,** prostrate oneself; crawl, grovel; wallow, welter

knell NOUNS 1 passing bell, death bell, funeral ring, tolling, tolling of the knell; **dirge, funeral** *or* **death song**
VERBS 2 **ring,** tintinnabulate, **peal,** sound; **toll,** sound a knell; **elegize,** dirge

knickknack NOUNS **trinket,** gewgaw, nicknack, **gimcrack,** kickshaw, whim-wham, **bauble,** fribble, bibelot, toy, gaud; bric-a-brac

knife NOUNS 1 blade, cutter, whittle; steel, cold steel, naked steel; shiv *and* pig-sticker *and* toad stabber *and* toad sticker <all nonformal>; dirk, dagger, stiletto
VERBS 2 **stab, stick** <nonformal>, **pierce,** plunge in; **run through, impale,** spit, **transfix,** transpierce

knight NOUNS **cavalier,** chevalier, *caballero* <Sp>, *Ritter* <Ger>, **knight-errant,** knight-adventurer

a verray parfit gentil knight
CHAUCER

knightly ADJS **courageous, valiant,** valorous, gallant, intrepid, stalwart, stouthearted, ironhearted, lionhearted, greathearted, bold-spirited, bold as a lion; **chivalrous,** chivalric, knightlike

knit VERBS 1 **heal, heal over,** close up, scab over, cicatrize, granulate; heal *or* right itself; **set; braid,** plait, pleach, **wreathe,** raddle, twist, mat, wattle, grow together
ADJS 2 **joined, united, connected,** copulate, **coupled,** linked, bridged, tight-knit, knitted, bracketed, associated, conjoined, incorporated, integrated, **merged,** gathered, assembled, accumulated, **collected; tied, bound,** knotted, spliced, lashed

knob NOUNS **hill,** brae *and* fell <both Scots>; **hillock,** butte, kopje, kame, monticle, monticule, monadnock, **knoll,** hummock, hammock, eminence, rise, mound, swell, barrow, tumulus, kop, tel, jebel; **boss,** bulla, button, bulb

knock NOUNS 1 **blow,** stroke, pound, bang, crack, **whack,** smack, thwack, smash, dash, **punch, poke, jab,** dig, drub, thump; **criticism,** adverse criticism, harsh *or* hostile criticism, flak <nonformal>, bad notices, bad press, animadversion, imputation, reflection, **aspersion,** stricture, obloquy; **swipe** *and* **slam** *and* **rap** *and* hit <all nonformal>
VERBS 2 **hit, strike,** knock down *or* out, smite; **criticize; pan** *and* **slam** *and* hit *and* rap *and* take a rap *or* swipe at <all nonformal>, snipe at, strike out at

knockoff NOUNS **reproduction,** duplication, imitation, copy, dummy, mock-up, **replica,** facsimile, representation, paraphrase, approximation, model, version; **parody,** burlesque, pastiche, *pasticcio* <Ital>, travesty

knock off VERBS 1 **take a break, take time out** *and* grab some R and R <both nonformal>, pause, lay off, take ten *and* take five <both nonformal>; stop work, suspend operations, call it a day
2 **do carelessly,** do by halves, do in a half-assed way <nonformal>, do in a slipshod fashion, do in any old way <nonformal>; **do offhand,** dash off, **toss off** *or* **out** <nonformal>; toss *or* **throw together,** knock together, throw *or* slap together

knockout NOUNS 1 **unconsciousness, senselessness;** stupor; KO *or* kayo <both nonformal>; semiconsciousness, grayout
2 **finishing stroke, finisher,** clincher, equalizer, crusher, settler; knockout blow <nonformal>; sockdolager, KO *or* kayo *and* kayo punch <all nonformal>; final stroke, finishing *or* perfecting *or* crowning touch, last dab *or* lick <nonformal>
3 **the best,** first-rater, wonder, world-beater
4 <nonformal> **dandy,** jim dandy, dilly, humdinger, pip, pippin, **peach,** ace, beaut, **lulu,** doozy, honey, sweetheart, dream, lollapaloosa, hot shit *or* poo, pisser, pistol, corker, whiz, blinger, **crackerjack,** something else, something

else again, barn-burner, killer, killer-diller, the nuts, the cat's pajamas *or* balls *or* meow, whiz, whizbang, wow, wowser

knock out VERBS 1 **anesthetize, put to sleep,** slip one a Mickey *or* Mickey Finn <nonformal>, chloroform, etherize; narcotize, drug, dope <nonformal>; freeze, **stupefy, stun,** bedaze, besot; knock unconscious, knock senseless, KO *and* kayo *and* lay out *and* coldcock *and* knock stiff <all nonformal>
2 **do carelessly,** do by halves, do in a half-assed way <nonformal>, do in a slipshod fashion, do anyhow, do in any old way <nonformal>; botch, **bungle; do offhand,** dash off, **toss off** *or* **out** <nonformal>; hammer *or* pound out, bat out <nonformal>; toss *or* **throw together,** knock together, throw *or* slap together, slap up <nonformal>

knoll NOUNS **hillock, knob,** butte, kopje, kame, monticle, monticule, monadnock, hummock, hammock, eminence, rise, mound, swell, barrow, tumulus, kop, tel, jebel; **dune,** sand dune, sandhill

knot NOUNS 1 knur, knurl, gnarl, burl, gall
2 **bunch,** group, grouping, groupment, crop, cluster, **clump**
3 **vexed question,** thorny problem, knotty point, crux, node, nodus, Gordian knot, poser, teaser, perplexity, puzzle, enigma
VERBS 4 **tangle,** entangle, embrangle, **snarl,** snarl up, ravel, tie in knots; **couple,** pair, accouple, copulate, conjugate, marry, wed, tie the knot <nonformal>, **link,** link up, build bridges, yoke, splice, tie, chain, bracket; **thicken,** cake, lump, clump, cluster

knotty ADJS **knotted;** knobbly, nodose, nodular, studded, lumpy; gnarled, knurled, knurly, burled, gnarly; **hard to understand, difficult, hard,** tough <nonformal>; exacting, demanding; intricate, complex; abstruse

know VERBS **perceive, apprehend,** prehend, cognize, recognize, discern, see, make out; conceive, conceptualize; **realize, appreciate, understand, comprehend,** fathom; dig *and* savvy <both nonformal>; ken <Scots>; have, possess, **grasp,** seize, have hold of; have knowledge of, be informed, be apprised of, have a good command of, have information about, be acquainted with, be conversant with, be cognizant of, be conscious *or* aware of; know something by heart *or* by rote *or* from memory

know-how NOUNS **skill,** skillfulness, expertness, expertise, proficiency, cleverness; **competence,** capability, capacity, ability; **craftsmanship,** workmanship, artisanship; savvy *and* bag of tricks <both nonformal>; technical skill, **technique, touch,** technical brilliance, technical mastery, **virtuosity,** bravura, wizardry

knowing ADJS 1 experienced, practiced, mature, matured, ripe, ripened, **seasoned,** tried, well-tried, tried and true, **veteran,** old, an old dog at <nonformal>; sagacious; **worldly, worldly-wise,** world-wise, wise in the ways of the world, knowing, **sophisticated,** cosmopolitan, cosmopolite, blasé, dry behind the ears, not born yesterday, long in the tooth
2 **knowledgeable, informed; cognizant, conscious,** aware, mindful, sensible; intelligent; **understanding, comprehending,** apprehensive, apprehending; **perceptive,** insightful, apperceptive, percipient, perspicacious, appercipient, prehensile; shrewd, sagacious, wise; all-knowing

know-it-all NOUNS 1 **swellhead** <nonformal>, **braggart**, know-all, smart-ass *and* wise-ass <both nonformal>, smart aleck, no modest violet
ADJS 2 **conceited, self-conceited,** immodest, self-opinionated; swollen-headed, **swelled-headed, big-headed** *and* too big for one's shoes *or* britches *and* biggety *and* **cocky** <all nonformal>; know-all, smart-ass *and* wise-ass <both nonformal>, smarty, smart-alecky, overwise, wise in one's own conceit; aggressively self-confident, obtrusive, bumptious

knowledge NOUNS knowing, knowingness, ken; **command,** reach; **acquaintance, familiarity,** intimacy; private knowledge, privity; **information,** data, database, datum, items, facts, factual base, corpus; **certainty, sure** *or* **certain knowledge**; practical knowledge, **experience, know-how, expertise**

knowledgeable ADJS **knowing,** informed; **cognizant,** conscious, aware, mindful, sensible; **perceptive,** insightful, apperceptive, percipient, perspicacious, appercipient, prehensile; shrewd, sagacious, wise; omniscient, all-knowing

know-nothing NOUNS **ignoramus;** no scholar, puddinghead, dunce, fool; **illiterate; lowbrow** <nonformal>; unintelligentsia, illiterati

kook NOUNS

<nonformal> freak, character, crackpot, nut, screwball, weirdie, weirdo, oddball, flake, strange duck, bird, goofus, wack, wacko

kooky ADJS **odd,** queer, peculiar, absurd, singular, curious, **oddball** <nonformal>, weird *and* freaky *and* freaked-out <all nonformal>, quaint, **eccentric,** gonzo <nonformal>, funny; **strange, outlandish,** off-the-wall <informal>, surreal, not for real <nonformal>, passing strange; **weird,** unearthly

kosher ADJS 1 **clean, pure; undefiled;** *tahar* <Heb>, ritually pure *or* clean; glatt kosher
2 **legal, legitimate,** legit <nonformal>, competent, **licit, lawful,** rightful, according to law, within the law

kowtow VERBS **bow, make obeisance, salaam,** make one's bow, bow down, scrape, **bow and scrape; genuflect, kneel,** bend the knee, get down on one's knees, throw oneself on one's knees, fall on one's knees, fall down before, fall at the feet of, prostrate oneself, kiss the hem of one's garment; crawl, grovel; wallow, welter

kudos NOUNS **praise,** bepraisement; **laudation,** laud; **glorification,** glory, exaltation, magnification, **honor; eulogy,** *éloge* and *hommage* <both Fr>, eulogium; **encomium,** accolade, panegyric; paean; **tribute,** homage, meed of praise; **citation,** mention, honorable mention

kvetch NOUNS 1 **malcontent, complainer,** grumbler, griper, whiner
2 <nonformal> **grouch,** kicker, moaner, moaning Minnie <Brit>, crank, crab, grouser, grump, beefer, bellyacher, bitcher, sorehead, picklepuss, sourpuss <all nonformal>
3 VERBS **be discontented, complain,** be disgruntled; **beef, bitch,** bellyache, crab, gripe, grouch, grouse, grump <all nonformal>

L

label NOUNS 1 **tag;** ticket, docket <Brit>, tally; **stamp, sticker; seal,** sigil, signet; cachet; **brand, brand name,** trade name, **trademark; epithet,** byword
VERBS 2 **tag,** tab, ticket; stamp, seal; **brand, earmark; name,** denominate, nominate, designate, call, term, style, dub, color <nonformal>; specify; define, identify; stereotype

labor NOUNS 1 **work,** employment, industry, toil, moil, travail, toil and trouble, sweat of one's brow; **drudgery, sweat,** slavery, spadework, rat race <nonformal>; treadmill; unskilled labor, hewing of wood and drawing of water; dirty work, grunt work *and* donkey work *and* shit-work *and* scut work <all nonformal>; **makework,** tedious *or* stupid *or* idiot *or* tiresome work, humdrum toil, grind <nonformal>
VERBS 2 **work;** busy oneself; turn a hand, do a hand's turn, do a lick of work, earn one's keep; chore, do the chores

laboratory NOUNS **lab** <nonformal>, research laboratory, research establishment *or* facility *or* institute, experimental station, field station, research and development *or* R and D establishment; **proving ground**

labored ADJS 1 **elaborate,** overornamented, overornate, overelegant, highwrought; **overelegant,** overelaborate, overlabored, overworked, overwrought, busy
2 **stiff, stilted, formal,** Latinate, *guindé* <Fr>, ponderous, elephantine, lumbering, cumbrous, leaden, heavy, unwieldy, sesquipedalian, inkhorn, turgid, bombastic, pompous; **forced,** strained, awkward, cramped, halting; crabbed

laborer NOUNS **worker, toiler,** moiler; member of the working class, proletarian, prole <Brit nonformal>, blue-collar *or* lunch-bucket worker, laboring man, stiff *and* working stiff <both nonformal>; **workman, workingman; workwoman, workingwoman,** workfolk, workpeople; **factory worker,** industrial worker; **jobholder,** wageworker, **wage earner,** salaried worker; common laborer, **unskilled laborer,** navvy <Brit>, day laborer, roustabout

laborious ADJS **toilsome, arduous, strenuous,** painful, effortful, operose, troublesome, onerous, oppressive, burdensome; wearisome; **heavy,** hefty <nonformal>, tough <nonformal>, uphill, **backbreaking,** grueling, punishing, crushing, killing, Herculean

labor-saving ADJS **economical, efficient,** time-saving, money-saving

labor union NOUNS trade union, trades union <Brit>; organized labor; **craft union,** horizontal union; **industrial union,** vertical union; **local,** union local, local union; company union

labyrinth NOUNS **complex,** perplex <nonformal>, **tangle,** tangled skein, **mess** *and* snafu *and* fuck-up <all nonformal>, ravel, snarl, snarl-up; **maze,** meander, Chinese puzzle; mare's nest, rat's nest, can of worms <nonformal>, snake pit

lace NOUNS 1 lacery, lacing, lacework; lattice, latticework; hachure *or* hatchure, hatching, cross-hatching
VERBS 2 **interweave, interlace, intertwine,** interknit, interthread, intertissue, intertie, intertwist; web, net; enlace
3 **tamper with, doctor** *and* doctor up <both nonformal>; **fortify,** spike <nonformal>

laceration NOUNS **cutting, slitting,** slashing, **splitting,** slicing; **rending, tearing,** ripping, hacking, chopping, butchering, mutilation

lack NOUNS 1 **want, need,** deficiency, deficit, shortage, shortfall, wantage, **incompleteness,** defectiveness, shortcoming, imperfection; **absence**, omission
VERBS 2 **want, need, require;** miss, feel the want of, be sent away empty-handed; run short of

lackadaisical ADJS **casual,** offhand, relaxed, **laid-back** *and* throwaway <both nonformal>; **easygoing,** easy, free and easy, devil-may-care, *dégagé* <Fr>

lackey NOUNS **flunky,** livery *or* liveried servant; **footman,** *valet de pied* <Fr>; **minion,** creature, hanger-on, stooge <nonformal>; henchman, camp follower, satellite, jackal, myrmidon

lacking ADJS **absent, missing,** among the missing, not found, nowhere to be found, omitted, taken away, subtracted, deleted; **undeveloped,** underdeveloped, undergrown, stunted, hypoplastic, **immature,** callow, infant, arrested, embryonic, **wanting,** needing, missing, **partial,** part, failing; **in short supply,** scanty; found wanting

lackluster ADJS **colorless,** dull, flat, mat, dead, dingy, muddy, leaden, lusterless, insipid, tedious; **lifeless,** somber, **drab,** wan

laconic ADJS **taciturn, untalkative,** unloquacious, indisposed to talk; curt, brief, terse, brusque, short, concise, **sparing of words,** economical of words, of few words

lacquered ADJS varnished, shellacked, glazed, *glacé* <Fr>; **glassy,** smooth as glass

lacuna NOUNS **omission,** gap, hole, vacuum, break, discontinuity, interval; **interruption, suspension, break,** fissure, breach, gap, hiatus, caesura; **interval, pause,** interim, lull, cessation, letup <nonformal>, **intermission**

lad NOUNS **boy,** laddie, **youth,** manchild, manling, young man, *garçon* <Fr>, *muchacho* <Sp>, schoolboy, schoolkid <nonformal>, fledgling, hobbledehoy; fellow; sonny, sonny boy

laden ADJS burdened, oppressed, cumbered, **encumbered,** charged, loaded, fraught, freighted, taxed, saddled, hampered; heavy-laden; full-laden

ladies' man NOUNS **philanderer,** philander, woman chaser, heartbreaker; masher, lady-killer, wolf, skirt chaser, man on the make *and* make-out artist <both nonformal>; libertine, lecher, cocksman <nonformal>, seducer, Casanova, Don Juan

ladle NOUNS 1 **container,** basin, pot, pan, cup, glass, bottle
VERBS 2 **dip, scoop; bail,** bucket; spoon

lady NOUNS matron; dowager, person of breeding, perfect lady

ladylike ADJS **well-bred,** highbred, **well-brought-up; cultivated,** cultured, polished, refined, genteel, gentle; quite the lady; **wellborn,** blue-blooded

ladylove NOUNS **inamorata,** *amorosa* <Ital>, lady, mistress, ladyfriend

Lady Luck NOUNS Chance, Fortune, Lady *or* Dame Fortune, wheel of fortune, Fortuna, the fickle finger of fate <nonformal>; Luck

lag VERBS **lag behind, straggle,** lag back, drag, trail, **trail behind,** hang back *or* behind, loiter, linger, **loiter** *or* **linger behind,** dawdle, get behind, fall behind *or* behindhand, let grass grow under one's feet

laggard NOUNS **slowpoke** *and* slowcoach <both nonformal>, plodder, slow goer, **lingerer, loiterer, dawdler,** dawdle, procrastinator, foot-dragger, stick-in-the-mud <nonformal>, drone, slug, sluggard, lie-abed, goof-off <nonformal>, goldbrick <nonformal>; tortoise, snail

lagoon NOUNS **lake,** salt pond, salina, tidal pond *or* pool; *laguna* <Sp>

laid-back ADJS **nonchalant,** blasé, indifferent, unconcerned; **casual,** offhand, relaxed, throwaway <nonformal>; **easygoing,** free and easy, devil-may-care, lackadaisical, *dégagé* <Fr>; **leisurely, unhurried,** unhasty, hasteless, easy; deliberate

laid up ADJS 1 **invalided,** hospitalized, in hospital <Brit>; **sick,** ill; **bedridden, bedfast, sick abed; down,** prostrate, flat on one's back; in childbed, confined
2 **stored, accumulated,** amassed; gathered, garnered, collected; **stockpiled;** backlogged; **hoarded,** treasured

lair NOUNS **den,** cave, **hole,** covert, mew, form; **burrow,** tunnel, earth, run, couch, lodge; **retreat, hideaway, cell, ivory tower,** hidey-hole <nonformal>, sanctum, sanctum sanctorum, inner sanctum

laissez-faire NOUNS 1 **noninterference, nonintervention; isolationism; laissez-faireism,** let-alone principle *or* doctrine *or* policy, deregulation; *laissez-aller* <Fr>; liberalism, free enterprise, free competition, self-regulating market; capitalism; free trade
ADJS 2 **passive; neutral,** neuter; standpat <nonformal>, **do-nothing;** *laissez-aller* <Fr>; permissive, overly permissive; noninterfering, nonrestrictive, hands-off; noninvasive, noninterventionist

lake NOUNS landlocked water, loch <Scots>, lough <Ir>, nyanza <Africa>, mere, freshwater lake; oxbow lake, bayou lake, glacial lake; volcanic lake; tarn; inland sea

lake dweller NOUNS **lacustrian, lacustrine dweller** *or* inhabitant, **pile dweller** *or* builder; laker

lakefront NOUNS 1 **shore, strand,** *playa* <Sp>, **beach,** beachfront, waterside, **waterfront;** lakeshore
ADJS 2 **littoral,** lakeshore; shorefront, shoreline; beachfront, beachside

lambaste VERBS **pound, beat, hammer, maul,** sledgehammer, **knock, rap, bang,** thump, **drub,** buffet, **batter,** pulverize, paste <nonformal>, patter, pommel, pummel, pelt, baste

lame ADJS **crippled,** game <nonformal>, bad, handicapped, maimed; **halt,** halting, hobbling, limping; **disabled,** incapacitated; **ineffectual,** ineffective, inefficacious, of no effect

lamebrain NOUNS **stupid person,** dolt, dunce, clod, Boeotian, dullard, *niais* <Fr>, donkey, yahoo, thickwit, **dope, nitwit,** dimwit, lackwit, half-wit, putz, lightweight

lame duck NOUNS **officeholder,** public official, **incumbent;** holdover

lament NOUNS 1 **plaint,** *planctus* <L>; **murmur,** mutter; **moan, groan; whine, whimper; wail,** wail of woe; **sob,** *cri du coeur* <Fr>, **cry,** outcry, scream, **howl,** yowl, bawl, yawp, keen, ululation
VERBS 2 **mourn, moan, grieve, sorrow,** keen, weep over, **bewail, bemoan, deplore, repine, sigh,** give sorrow words; sing the blues <nonformal>, elegize, dirge, knell

laminate VERBS 1 **layer,** lay down, lay up, **stratify,** arrange in layers *or* levels *or* strata *or* tiers
ADJS 2 **layered,** in layers; **laminated,** laminous; lamellated, lamellate, lamellar, lamelliform; **stratified,** stratiform; foliated, foliaceous, leaflike

lamination NOUNS **stratification,** lamellation; foliation; flakiness, scaliness

lamp NOUNS **light source,** source of light, **luminary,** illuminator, luminant, illuminant, incandescent body *or* point, **light,** glim; light bulb, electric light bulb, lantern, candle, taper, torch, flame; **fluorescent light, fluorescent tube,** fluorescent lamp

lampoon NOUNS 1 send-up <nonformal>, pasquinade, pasquin, pasquil, squib, lampoonery, **satire,** malicious parody, **burlesque**; poison pen, hatchet job
VERBS 2 **satirize,** pasquinade; parody, send up <nonformal>; dip the pen in gall, **burlesque**

lance VERBS **perforate, pierce,** empierce, **penetrate, puncture, punch, hole,** prick; **tap, broach; stab, stick,** pink, run through; **transfix,** transpierce, fix, **impale,** spit, skewer; gore, spear, spike, needle; slit, snip, scissor

land NOUNS 1 **ground,** landmass, earth, glebe <old>, **sod,** clod, **soil, dirt,** dust, clay, marl, mold <Brit nonformal>; *terra* <L>, **terra firma;** terrain; **dry land;** arable land; marginal land; grassland, woodland; crust, earth's crust, lithosphere; **real estate,** real property, landholdings, acres, territory, freehold; region; **country**
VERBS 2 set down <nonformal>, **alight, light,** touch down; **descend,** come down, dump altitude <nonformal>, fly down; come in, come in for a landing; **crash-land;** ditch <nonformal>; come to land, make a landfall, set foot on dry land; reach *or* make land, make port; put in *or* into, put into port; **disembark,** debark, unboat; **detrain,** debus, **deplane, disemplane**

landed ADJS **propertied,** proprietary; property-owning, landowning, landholding

landed gentry NOUNS **gentry,** gentlefolk, gentlefolks, gentlepeople, better sort; lesser nobility, *petite noblesse* <Fr>; *samurai* <Japanese>; squirearchy

landlocked ADJS **restricted, limited, confined;** circumscribed, hemmed in, hedged in *or* about, boxed in; cramped, stinted

landlubber NOUNS **landsman,** landman, **lubber**

landmark NOUNS **marker, mark;** bench mark; **milestone,** milepost; cairn, menhir, capstone; **salient point,** cardinal point, high point, great point; important thing, chief thing, **the point, main point,** main thing, essential matter, **essence,** the name of the game *and* the bottom line *and* what it's all about *and* where it's at <all nonformal>, substance, gravamen, *sine qua non* <L>, issue, real issue, front-burner issue <nonformal>, prime issue

landowner NOUNS **landlord, landlady;** lord of the manor; squire, country gentleman; landholder, property owner, propertied *or* landed person, man of property, freeholder; landed interests, landed gentry; slumlord, rent gouger; absentee landlord

landscape NOUNS **scene, view, scape;** waterscape, riverscape, seascape, seapiece; airscape, skyscape, cloudscape; snowscape; cityscape, townscape; farmscape

landslide NOUNS 1 **slide; slip,** slippage; mudslide, landslip, subsidence;

snowslide, snowslip <Brit>; **avalanche**
2 **victory,** total victory, grand slam; election returns, tidal wave

language NOUNS speech, tongue, *lingua* <L>, spoken language, natural language; **talk, parlance, locution,** phraseology, **idiom, lingo** <nonformal>; dialect; idiolect, personal usage, individual speech habits *or* performance, parole

languish VERBS **pine, droop, flag, wilt; fade,** fade away; **wither, shrivel,** shrink, diminish, wither *or* die on the vine

languishing ADJS **drooping,** sinking, declining, flagging, pining, fading, failing, **dying, terminal,** moribund; lovelorn, lovesick

lanky ADJS **lean,** lean-looking, **skinny** <nonformal>, fleshless, lean-fleshed, thin-fleshed, **spare,** meager, **scrawny,** scraggy, thin-bellied, **gaunt, lank, gangling** *and* gangly <both nonformal>, gawky, **spindling,** spindly

lantern NOUNS **light source,** source of light, **luminary,** illuminator, luminant, illuminant, incandescent body *or* point, **light,** glim; **lamp,** candle, taper, torch, flame

lap NOUNS **circuit, round,** revolution, **circle,** full circle, go-round, **cycle,** orbit, ambit; pass; round trip, *aller-retour* <Fr>; **beat,** rounds, **walk,** tour, turn, loop; bell lap, victory lap

lapse NOUNS 1 **decline,** declension, **subsidence,** slump <nonformal>, **drop,** downtick <nonformal>; **backsliding,** relapse, recidivism, recidivation, fall *or* lapse from grace; **omission,** nonfeasance, nonperformance, failure, **default; impropriety,** slight *or* minor wrong, venial sin, **indiscretion,** peccadillo, misstep, trip, slip
VERBS 2 **relapse, backslide,** slide back, lapse back, **slip back,** sink back, **fall back,** have a relapse, devolve, **return to, revert to,** recur to, yield again to, fall again into, recidivate; revert, **regress; fall,** fall from grace
3 **elapse, pass, expire,** run its course, run out, go *or* pass by

lapsed ADJS 1 erring, **fallen,** Adamic, postlapsarian; **relapsing, backsliding,** recidivist, recidivistic, fallen from grace; of easy virtue
2 **past, gone,** by, **gone-by, bygone,** gone glimmering, bypast, ago, **over,** departed, passed, passed away, elapsed, vanished, faded, no more, never to return, not coming back

larboard NOUNS 1 **left side, left, left hand,** left-hand side, wrong side <nonformal>, portside, port
ADJS 2 **left, left-hand,** sinister, sinistral; **port**
ADVS 3 **leftward,** leftwards, leftwardly, **left, to the left,** sinistrally, sinister, sinistrad; on the left; port, aport

larcenous ADJS **thievish,** thieving, light-fingered, sticky-fingered; fraudulent

larceny NOUNS **theft;** petit *or* petty larceny, petty theft, grand larceny, grand theft, simple larceny, mixed *or* aggravated larceny

larder NOUNS **provisions, groceries,** provender, supplies, stores, food supply; commissariat, **commissary; pantry,** buttery <nonformal>; spence <Brit nonformal>, stillroom <Brit>

large ADJS **sizable, big,** great, grand, tall <nonformal>, considerable, goodly, healthy, tidy <nonformal>, **substantial,** bumper; as big as all outdoors; numerous; largish, biggish; large-scale, larger than life; man-sized <nonformal>; large-size *or* -sized, man-sized, king-size, queen-size; good-sized, life-size *or* -sized

largess NOUNS **gratuity, bounty,** liberality, donative, sportula; perquisite, perks <nonformal>; consideration, fee <old>, **tip,** *pourboire* <Fr>, *Trinkgeld* <Ger>, sweetener, inducement; **liberality,** liberalness, freeness, freedom; **generosity,** generousness, largeness, **unselfishness, munificence; openhandedness,** freehandedness, open *or* free hand, easy purse strings; open-heartedness, bigheartedness, largeheartedness, greatheartedness, freeheartedness; open heart, big *or* large *or* great heart, heart of gold; **magnanimity**

lark NOUNS **revel, escapade,** ploy; **spree,** bout, fling, wingding and randan <both nonformal>, randy <Scots>; **carouse; songbird**

larva NOUNS **chrysalis,** aurelia, **cocoon,** pupa; nymph, nympha; wriggler, wiggler; caterpillar, maggot, grub

larynx NOUNS voice box, Adam's apple

lascivious ADJS **lecherous, sexy, salacious, carnal,** animal, **sexual, lustful,** ithyphallic, **hot,** horny *and* sexed-up *and* hot to trot <all nonformal>; prurient, itching, itchy <nonformal>; concupiscent, lickerish, libidinous, randy, lubricious; **lewd, bawdy,** adult, X-rated, hard, pornographic, porno <nonformal>, **dirty, obscene**; erotic, **sensual,** fleshly; goatish, satyric, priapic, nymphomaniacal

lash NOUNS 1 **whip, scourge,** flagellum, strap, thong, rawhide, cowhide, blacksnake, kurbash, sjambok, belt, razor strap; knout; bullwhip, bullwhack; horsewhip; crop; quirt; rope's end; cat, cat-o'-nine-tails; whiplash
VERBS 2 **whip,** give a whipping *or* beating *or* thrashing, **beat, thrash, spank, flog,** scourge, flagellate, flail, whale; **smite,** thump, trounce, baste, **pummel,** pommel, **drub, buffet, belabor,** lay on; **lace,** cut, stripe; horsewhip; knout; **strap,** belt, rawhide, cowhide

lass NOUNS **girl,** girlie <nonformal>, maid, maiden, **lassie,** young thing, young creature, young lady, damsel in distress, **damsel,** damoiselle, demoiselle, *jeune fille* <Fr>, *mademoiselle* <Fr>, *muchacha* <Sp>, miss, missy, little missy, slip, wench <dial or nonformal>, colleen <Irish>

lasso NOUNS 1 noose, **lariat; snare,** springe
VERBS 2 **catch, take,** land *and* nail <both nonformal>, hook, **snag, snare,** sniggle, ensnare, enmesh, **net,** mesh; **bag,** sack; **trap,** entrap; rope, noose

last NOUNS 1 **end,** last gasp *or* breath, final twitch, last throe, last legs, last hurrah <nonformal>; omega, izzard; **fate, destiny,** last things, eschatology, last trumpet, Gabriel's trumpet, crack of doom, doom
VERBS 2 **endure, last out,** bide, **abide,** dwell, perdure, **continue,** run, extend, **go on,** carry on, hold on, keep on, stay on, run on, stay the course, go the distance, go through with, grind *or* slog on, grind *or* plug away; live, **live on,** continue to be, subsist, exist, tarry; **persist;** hang in *and* hang in there *and* hang tough <all nonformal>; **survive,** defy *or* defeat time; live to fight another day
ADJS 3 **final, terminal,** terminating *or* terminative, determinative, definitive, **conclusive;** last-ditch <nonformal>, last but not least, eventual, farthest, extreme, boundary, border, limbic, limiting, polar, **endmost, ultimate**
ADVS 4 **finally,** in fine; **ultimately,** eventually, as a matter of course; **at last,** at the last *or* end *or* conclusion, at length, at long last; **in conclusion, in sum;** conclusively, once and for all

lasting ADJS **durable,** perdurable, **enduring,** perduring, **abiding, continuing,** remaining, staying, **stable**, persisting, **persistent,** perennial; inveterate, age-long; **steadfast, constant,** intransient, immutable, unfading, evergreen, sempervirent, **permanent**, **long-lasting,** long-standing, of long duration *or* standing, diuturnal; **long-lived,** tough, hardy, vital, longevous *or* longeval

last-minute ADJS **hasty, hurried,** festinate, **quick,** flying, **expeditious,** prompt; quick-and-dirty <nonformal>, **immediate,** instant, on the spot; eleventh-hour, deathbed

last name NOUNS **surname, family name,** cognomen, byname; **maiden name;** married name; patronymic, matronymic

last resort NOUNS **expedient,** means to an end, last expedient, last resource, *pis aller* <Fr>, last shift, trump, **recourse, resource, resort; hope**

last rites NOUNS **last offices,** last honors, funeral rites, last duty *or* service, funeral service, burial service, exequies, **obsequies; extreme unction;** viaticum

last straw NOUNS provocation, straw that broke the camel's back, match in the powder barrel

Last Supper NOUNS **Eucharist, Lord's Supper,** Communion, Holy Communion, **the Sacrament,** the Holy Sacrament

last word NOUNS 1 **authority**, directorship, management, jurisdiction, power, say <nonformal>; **ultimatum,** final word *or* offer, firm bid *or* price, sticking point; **substance, gist,** pith, spirit, essence, gravamen, name of the game *and* meat and potatoes *and* bottom line <all nonformal>
2 **the rage,** the thing, *le dernier cri* <Fr>, **the latest thing,** the in thing *and* the latest wrinkle <both nonformal>; **acme of perfection,** pink, pink of perfection, culmination, perfection, height, top, acme, ultimate, summit, pinnacle, peak, highest pitch, climax, consummation, *ne plus ultra* <L>, a dream come true

latch VERBS **fasten,** secure; **lock,** lock up, lock out, key, padlock, bolt, bar

late ADJS 1 **belated, tardy,** slow, slow on the draw *or* uptake *or* trigger <all nonformal>, **behindhand,** never on time,

backward, back, **overdue,** long-awaited, untimely; **unpunctual,** unready; latish; **delayed,** detained, **held up** <nonformal>, **retarded, arrested,** blocked, **hung up** *and* in a bind <both nonformal>; **postponed, in abeyance,** held up, put off, **on hold** *or* put on hold <nonformal>, on the back burner *or* put on the back burner <nonformal>
ADVS 2 **behind,** behindhand, belatedly, backward, slow, **behind time,** after time; far on, deep into; late in the day, at the last minute, at the eleventh hour, none too soon, in the nick of time, under the wire

latecomer NOUNS late arrival, Johnny-come-lately; slow starter, dawdler, dallier, dillydallier; late bloomer *or* developer; retardee

latent ADJS **concealed,** hidden, invisible; unrealized, submerged; ulterior; unknown

later ADJS 1 **subsequent, after,** after-the-fact, *post factum* and *ex post facto* <both L>, posterior, **following, succeeding,** successive, sequent, lineal, consecutive, ensuing, attendant; **future,** hereafter; **coming,** forthcoming, imminent, approaching, nearing, latter, **prospective**
ADVS 2 **subsequently, after, afterwards,** after that, after all, **next,** since; **thereafter,** thereon, thereupon, therewith, **then;** in the process *or* course of time, at a subsequent *or* later time, in the aftermath; *ex post facto* <L>; hard on the heels *or* on the heels; in the future

latest ADJS **state-of-the-art, newest,** the very latest, up-to-the-minute, last, most recent, newest of the new, farthest out

lather NOUNS 1 **dither, tizzy** <nonformal>, swivet, foofaraw, **pucker** <nonformal>, **twitter,** twitteration <nonformal>, **flutter, fluster,** flusteration *and* flustration <both nonformal>, **fret, fuss,** pother, bother, stew *and* snit <both nonformal>, flap; emotional crisis, *crise* <Fr>
2 **foam, froth; spume,** sea foam, scud; **suds,** soapsuds
VERBS 3 **foam, froth,** spume, cream; suds, sud

latitude NOUNS **scope, room,** range, way, field, maneuvering space *or* room, room to swing a cat <nonformal>; **margin,** clearance, **space,** open space *or* field, elbowroom, breathing space, **leeway** <nonformal>, sea room, wide berth; **tolerance; free scope,** full *or* ample scope, **free hand,** free play, free course; **carte blanche,** blank check; no holds barred; rope, long rope *or* tether, rope enough to hang oneself

lattice NOUNS **network,** interlacement, intertwinement, intertexture, texture, reticulum, reticulation; **net,** netting; **mesh,** meshes; **web,** webbing; weave, weft; latticework; hachure *or* hatchure, hatching, crosshatching; **grid,** gridiron

laud VERBS **praise,** bepraise, talk one up <nonformal>; belaud; **eulogize,** panegyrize, pay tribute, salute, hand it to one <nonformal>; **extol, glorify,** magnify, exalt, bless; cry up, blow up, puff, puff up; boast of, brag about <nonformal>, make much of; sound *or* resound the praises of, ring one's praises, sing the praises of, trumpet; overpraise, praise to excess, idolize, deify, apotheosize, adulate; put on a pedestal

laudable ADJS **praiseworthy,** worthy, **commendable,** estimable, admirable, meritorious, creditable; exemplary, model, unexceptionable; deserving, well-deserving;

laudatory ADJS **approbatory,** approbative, commendatory, **complimentary,** acclamatory, eulogistic, panegyric, panegyrical, encomiastic, **appreciative,** appreciatory; **admiring,** regardful, respectful; flattering

laugh NOUNS 1 **joke,** capital joke, good one, belly laugh, rib tickler, sidesplitter, thigh-slapper, howler, wow, scream, riot, panic
VERBS 2 burst out laughing, burst into laughter, burst out, laugh outright; laugh it up <nonformal>; **titter; giggle; chuckle, chortle;** cackle, crow; **snicker,** snigger, snort; **guffaw,** belly laugh, horselaugh; cachinnate, roar with laughter, shake with laughter, shake like jelly; be convulsed with laughter, go into convulsions, break up *and* crack up <both nonformal>, **split one's sides,** laugh fit to burst *or* bust <nonformal>, bust a gut *and* pee in *or* wet one's pants laughing <both nonformal>, **be in stitches** <nonformal>, hold one's sides, roll in the aisles <nonformal>; laugh oneself sick *or* silly *or* limp, die laughing; laugh in one's sleeve, laugh up one's sleeve

laughable ADJS **absurd, nonsensical,** insensate, ridiculous, ludicrous; **foolish, crazy;** preposterous, cockamamie <nonformal>, fantastic, fantastical, grotesque, monstrous, wild, weird, **outrageous,** incredible, beyond belief, *outré* <Fr>, extravagant, **bizarre**

laugh at VERBS **ridicule, deride,** ride <nonformal>, make a laughingstock *or* a mockery of; roast <nonformal>; **make fun** *or* **game of, poke fun at,** make merry with, put one on *and* pull one's leg <both nonformal>; laugh in one's face, grin at, smile at, snicker *or* snigger at; **laugh to scorn,** hold in derision, laugh out of court, hoot down

laughter NOUNS **laughing, hilarity**, risibility; **laugh;** boff *and* boffola *and* yuck <all nonformal>; **titter; giggle; chuckle, chortle;** cackle, crow; **snicker,** snigger, snort; guffaw, **horselaugh; hearty laugh, belly laugh** <nonformal>, Homeric laughter, cachinnation; gales of laughter; fit of laughter, convulsion

laughter holding both his sides
MILTON

launch NOUNS 1 **beginning, commencement, start,** running *or* flying start, starting point, square one <nonformal>, **outset,** outbreak, **onset,** oncoming; **foundation,** establishing, institution, origin, origination, establishment, setting-up, setting in motion; **launching,** launch *or* launching pad
VERBS 2 **inaugurate,** institute, **found, establish,** set up <nonformal>; **start,** start off, start up, give a start, crank up, give a push *or* shove <nonformal>, jump-start, kick-start, **put** *or* **set in motion, set on foot,** set going *or* agoing, start going; **kick off** *and* **start the ball rolling** <both nonformal>; get off the ground *or* off the mark

launder VERBS **wash,** tub; **wash up** *or* out *or* away; **rinse,** rinse out, flush, flush out, irrigate, sluice, sluice out; **scrub; clean,** cleanse

laundress NOUNS **washer,** launderer; laundrywoman, **washerwoman,** washwoman, washerwife <Scots>

laundry NOUNS **washery,** washhouse, washshed; **coin laundry, Laundromat** <trademark>, **launderette,** coin-operated laundry, laundrette <Brit>, washateria; automatic laundry; hand laundry

laundry list NOUNS schedule *or* program of operation, **order of the day,** things to be done, **agenda,** list of agenda; wish list <both nonformal>

laurels NOUNS **championship,** crown, palms, first prize, blue ribbon, trophy, chaplet, wreath, garland, **feather in one's cap** <nonformal>; civic crown *or* garland *or* wreath; **cup,** loving cup

lavatory NOUNS **latrine,** convenience, **toilet,** toilet room, water closet *or* WC <nonformal>; loo <Brit nonformal>; washroom, public convenience; **bathroom, rest room,** comfort station *or* room; ladies' *or* women's *or* girls' *or* little girls' *or* powder room <nonformal>; men's *or* boys' *or* little boys' room <nonformal>

lavish VERBS 1 **give freely,** give cheerfully, give with an open hand, give with both hands, put one's hands in one's pockets, open the purse, loosen *or* untie the purse strings; **spare no expense,** spare nothing, not count the cost, let money be no object; **heap upon,** lavish upon, shower down upon; **squander,** slather, blow <nonformal>, play ducks and drakes with; **throw away,** throw one's money away, throw money around, **spend money like water,** hang the expense, spend as if money grew on trees, spend money as if it were going out of style, throw money around, spend like a drunken sailor
ADJS 2 **liberal, free,** free with one's money, free-spending; **generous, munificent,** large, princely, handsome; **unselfish,** ungrudging; **unsparing,** unstinting, stintless, unstinted; **bountiful,** bounteous, profuse; **openhanded,** freehanded, open; **prodigal,** extravagant, overliberal, overgenerous, overlavish, **spendthrift, wasteful,** profligate, dissipative; penny-wise and pound-foolish; easy come, easy go
3 **ornate,** purple <nonformal>, colored, **fancy; embellished, embroidered,** adorned, decorated, festooned, overcharged, overloaded, befrilled; **flowery, florid,** lush, luxuriant

law NOUNS **rule, canon, maxim,** dictum, moral, moralism; **norm, standard;** formula, form; rule of action *or* conduct, moral precept; guiding principle, golden rule; **code; legal system,** system of laws

the Law NOUNS **Old Testament,** Tenach;

Hexateuch, Octateuch; Pentateuch, Chumash, Five Books of Moses, **Torah,** the Jewish *or* Mosaic Law, Law of Moses

the law NOUNS

<nonformal> cop, copper, John Law, bluecoat, bull, flatfoot, gumshoe, gendarme, shamus, dick; the cops, the fuzz; New York's finest

law-abiding ADJS **honest, upright,** uprighteous, **upstanding,** erect, right, **righteous, virtuous, good,** clean, squeaky-clean <nonformal>, **decent; respectable,** highly respectable; **principled, high-principled,** high-minded, right-minded; uncorrupt, uncorrupted, inviolate; law-loving, law-revering

law and order NOUNS **peacefulness,** tranquillity, serenity, calmness, quiet, peace and quiet, quietude, quietness, quiet life, restfulness; order, orderliness

lawbreaker NOUNS **criminal,** felon, perpetrator, crook *and* perp <both nonformal>, public enemy, scofflaw

lawful ADJS **legal, legitimate,** legit *and* kosher <both nonformal>, competent, **licit,** rightful, according to law, within the law

lawless ADJS **illegal,** unlawful, illegitimate, **illicit,** nonlicit, nonlegal, lawless, wrongful, fraudulent, creative <nonformal>, **against the law; licentious, ungoverned,** undisciplined, unrestrained; insubordinate, mutinous, disobedient; **uncontrolled,** uncurbed, unbridled, unchecked, rampant, untrammeled, unreined, reinless, anything goes; **irresponsible,** wildcat, unaccountable

lawmaker NOUNS **legislator,** solon, lawgiver; **congressman,** congresswoman, Member of Congress; **senator; representative;** state senator, assemblyman, assemblywoman, freeholder, councilman, councilwoman, councilperson

lawyer NOUNS 1 **attorney, attorney-at-law,** barrister, barrister-at-law, **counselor,** counselor-at-law, **counsel,** legal counsel *or* counselor, legal adviser, legal expert, **solicitor, advocate, pleader;** member of the bar, legal practitioner, officer of the court; smart lawyer, pettifogger, Philadelphia lawyer; sea lawyer, latrine *or* guardhouse lawyer <nonformal>

2 <nonformal> **shyster, mouthpiece, ambulance chaser,** lip, fixer, legal eagle

lax ADJS **slack, loose,** relaxed; imprecise, sloppy <nonformal>, careless, slipshod; remiss, negligent; indifferent; weak; impotent; untrammeled, unrestrained

laxative NOUNS **cathartic, physic, purge, purgative,** aperient, carminative, diuretic

lay NOUNS 1 **song,** *Lied* <Ger>, *chanson* <Fr>, carol, **ditty,** canticle, lilt; **ballad,** ballade, *ballata* <Ital>; *canzone* <Ital>; canzonet, *canzonetta* <Ital>
ADJS 2 laic *or* laical; **nonecclesiastical,** nonclerical, nonministerial, nonpastoral, nonordained; nonreligious; **secular,** secularist; secularistic; temporal, popular, civil

lay down VERBS **store, stow,** lay in store; lay in a supply *or* stock *or* store, store away, stow away, **put away, lay away,** put *or* lay by, pack away, bundle away, salt away *and* sock away *and* squirrel away <all nonformal>

layer NOUNS 1 thickness; **level, tier,** stage, story, floor, gallery, step, ledge, deck; **stratum,** seam, *couche* <Fr>, belt, band, **bed, course,** measures; zone; shelf; **overlayer, superstratum,** overstory, topsoil; **underlayer, substratum,** understratum, understory
VERBS 2 lay down, lay up, **stratify,** arrange in layers *or* levels *or* strata *or* tiers, **laminate;** flake, scale; delaminate, desquamate, exfoliate

layman NOUNS 1 laic, member of the laity, secular, churchman, **parishioner,** church member; brother, sister, lay brother, lay sister; laywoman, churchwoman; catchumen; communicant; **amateur,** nonprofessional

layoff NOUNS **dismissal, discharge,** forced separation, *congé* <Fr>; outplacement; **firing** *and* canning <both nonformal>, **cashiering,** drumming out, dishonorable discharge, rogue's march; disemployment, removal, surplusing, displacing, furloughing; suspension; **retirement;** the bounce, **the sack** <nonformal>; the boot *and* the gate *and* the ax <all nonformal>; walking papers *or* ticket <nonformal>, pink slip <nonformal>

lay off VERBS 1 **discontinue, desist, refrain,** leave off, give over, **have done with;** cut it out *and* drop it *and* knock it off <all nonformal>, relinquish, renounce, abandon

2 **dismiss, discharge, expel, cashier,** drum out, disemploy, outplace, separate involuntarily, suspend, surplus, furlough, turn off, make redundant, riff <nonformal>, turn out, release, let go, let out, remove, displace, replace, strike off the rolls, give the pink slip

layout NOUNS **arrangement, formation,** structure, configuration, array, makeup, lineup, setup

layover NOUNS **sojourn,** sojourning, sojournment, temporary stay; **stay,** stop; **stopover,** stopoff, stayover

lazy ADJS **indolent,** bone-lazy, **slothful,** workshy, ergophobic; **shiftless,** do-less <nonformal>; drony, dronish, parasitic, cadging, sponging, scrounging; lackadaisical; remiss, slack

lazybones NOUNS lazyboots, lazylegs, indolent, lie-abed, slugabed

leach VERBS **percolate,** lixiviate, edulcorate <old>; **trickle, dribble,** dripple, **drip,** drop, spurtle; **filter, extract,** drain, wash away

lead NOUNS 1 **superiority,** preeminence, greatness, transcendence *or* transcendency, ascendancy *or* ascendance, prestige, favor, prepotence *or* prepotency, preponderance; predominance *or* predominancy

2 **clue,** hot lead <nonformal>; **evidence; hint,** intimation, suggestion

3 **role,** starring *or* lead *or* leading role, fat part, leading man, leading woman *or* lady, hero, heroine; romantic lead; juvenile lead

VERBS 4 **head,** spearhead, stand at the head, stand first, be way ahead <nonformal>, head the line; take the lead, go in the lead, **lead the way,** break the trail, be the bellwether, lead the pack; be the point *or* point man; **light the way,** show the way, beacon, guide

5 **rule, command,** possess authority, have the authority, have the say *or* the last word, have the whip hand *and* hold all the aces <both nonformal>; **govern,** regulate; **wield authority**

leaden ADJS 1 **colorless,** dull, flat, mat, dead, dingy, muddy, lusterless, lackluster; livid, lead-gray

2 **torpid,** languorous, languid, apathetic, phlegmatic, **sluggish,** logy, dopey <nonformal>, groggy, heavy, slack, tame, **dead,** lifeless

3 **stiff, stilted, formal,** Latinate, *guindé* <Fr>, **labored,** ponderous, elephantine, lumbering, cumbrous, heavy, unwieldy, sesquipedalian, inkhorn, turgid, bombastic, pompous

leader NOUNS pacemaker, pacesetter; bellwether, bell mare, bell cow, Judas goat; standard-bearer, torchbearer; **leader of men,** born leader, charismatic leader *or* figure, inspired leader; **conductor,** symphonic conductor, **music director,** director, *Kapellmeister* <Ger>; **orchestra leader,** band leader, bandmaster, band major, drum major

leadership NOUNS **supremacy, primacy,** paramountcy, **first place,** height, acme, zenith, be-all and end-all, summit, top spot <nonformal>; **influence,** influentiality; **prestige,** favor, good feeling, credit, esteem, repute, personality, charisma, magnetism, charm, enchantment; **weight,** moment, consequence, importance, eminence

leading ADJS 1 **heading,** precessional, precedent, precursory, foregoing; **first, foremost,** headmost; **preceding,** antecedent; prior; up-front <nonformal>, first, chief, head, prime, primary; **ahead, in front,** one-up, one jump *or* move ahead

2 **dominant,** predominant, predominate, preponderant, preponderate, **paramount,** supreme, number one <nonformal>, hegemonic, hegemonistic; ascendant, in the ascendant, in ascendancy; at the head, in chief; in charge

leaf NOUNS lamina, lamella; **sheet,** *feuille* <Fr>, foil; frond; leaflet, foliole; **blade,** spear, spire, pile, flag; **needle**

leaflet NOUNS **folder, handbill,** bill, flier, throwaway, handout, circular, broadside, broadsheet; **booklet,** pamphlet, brochure, chapbook, **tract**

leafy ADJS foliated, foliate, foliose, foliaged, leaved

league NOUNS affiliation, **alliance,** allying, alignment, association, consociation, combination, union, unification, **coalition,** fusion, merger, coalescence, coadunation, amalgamation, **federation, confederation,** confederacy, consolidation, incorporation, inclusion, integration

leak NOUNS 1 **leakage,** leaking, weeping <nonformal>; **dripping,** drippings, **drip,** dribble, drop, trickle

2 **divulgence, divulging,** divulgement, divulgation, letting out; **betrayal,** unwitting disclosure, indiscretion; communi-

cation leak; **blabbing** *and* blabbering <both nonformal>, babbling; **tattling**
VERBS 3 **leak out, drip,** dribble, drop, trickle, trill, distill
4 **disclose,** reveal, let out, show, impart, discover, let slip out, let the cat out of the bag *and* spill the beans <both nonformal>; take the lid off, **bring to light,** bring into the open, hold up to view

leakproof ADJS **watertight, waterproof,** moistureproof, seepproof, dripproof, stormproof, stormtight, rainproof, raintight

leaky ADJS exudative, exuding, transudative; percolative; porous, permeable, pervious, oozy, runny, weepy

lean VERBS 1 **incline; slope, slant,** slaunch <nonformal>, rake, pitch, grade, bank, shelve; **tilt, tip, list, cant,** careen, keel, sidle, swag, sway; **gravitate,** tend, tend to go, point, head, lead; **be willing, be game** <nonformal>, be ready; be disposed, **trend,** have a penchant
ADJS 2 lean-looking, **skinny** <nonformal>, fleshless, lean-fleshed, thin-fleshed, **spare,** meager, **scrawny,** scraggy, thin-bellied, gaunt, lank, lanky; **bony, rawboned,** bare-boned, rattleboned <nonformal>, skeletal, **mere skin and bones, all skin and bones, nothing but skin and bones;** twiggy; thin, slim, slender

leaning NOUNS 1 **inclination,** lean, angularity; **slant,** slaunch <nonformal>, rake, **slope; tilt, tip,** pitch, **list, cant,** swag, sway; leaning tower, tower of Pisa; **preference, predilection,** proclivity, bent, affinity, prepossession, predisposition, partiality, penchant, bias, tendency, taste
ADJS 2 **inclining,** inclined, inclinatory, inclinational; recumbent; **sloping,** sloped, aslope; raking, pitched; **slanting,** slanted, slant, aslant, slantways, slantwise; **tilting,** tilted, atilt, tipped, **tipping,** tipsy, listing, **canting,** careening

lean-to NOUNS **hut,** hutch, **shack, shanty,** crib, hole-in-the-wall <nonformal>, **shed**

leap NOUNS 1 forward leap *or* jump, quantum jump *or* leap, spring, forward spring; **increase, gain,** augmentation, greatening, **enlargement, amplification, growth,** development, widening, spread, broadening, elevation, **extension,** aggrandizement, access, accession, **increment,** accretion
2 **jump,** hop, spring, skip, bound, bounce; pounce; upleap, upspring, jump-off; **hurdle; vault,** pole vault; jeté, grand jeté, tour jeté, saut de basque
VERBS 3 **jump,** vault, spring, skip, hop, bound, bounce; leap over, jump over; leapfrog; **hurdle,** clear, negotiate

learn VERBS **come to know, be informed** *or* **apprised of,** have it reported, get the facts, **get wise to** <nonformal>, **get hep to** *and* **next to** *and* **on to** <all nonformal>; become conscious *or* aware of, become alive *or* awake to, awaken to, tumble to <nonformal>, open one's eyes to; get into one's head, get through one's thick skull <nonformal>; **gain knowledge,** pick up information, gather *or* collect *or* glean knowledge *or* learning; stock *or* store the mind, improve *or* broaden the mind; stuff *or* cram the mind; **find out, ascertain, discover,** find, determine

learned ADJS **erudite, educated, cultured,** cultivated, lettered, literate, civilized, **scholarly,** scholastic, studious; wise; **profound,** deep, abstruse; **encyclopedic,** pansophic, polymath *or* polymathic, polyhistoric

learner NOUNS **student, pupil,** scholar, studier, educatee, **trainee,** *élève* <Fr>; tutee; **beginner,** neophyte, tyro; **apprentice**

learning NOUNS **enlightenment, education, schooling,** instruction, edification, illumination; attainments, accomplishments, skills; sophistication; store of knowledge; liberal education; acquisition of knowledge

lease NOUNS 1 **occupancy,** occupation; **tenancy,** tenantry, charter, leasehold, sublease, underlease, undertenancy; **rental, rent;** let <Brit>
VERBS 2 **rent out, rent;** lease out; let *and* let off *and* let out <all Brit>; charter; **sublease, sublet,** underlet

leash NOUNS 1 **tether,** spancel, lead, leading string; **rein;** hobble, hopple
VERBS 2 **bind, restrain, tie,** tie up, put the clamps on, **strap,** lash, pinion, fasten, secure, make fast; hobble, hopple, fetter, put on a lead, spancel; tether, picket, moor, anchor

least ADJS **smallest,** littlest, slightest, **lowest,** shortest; minimum, minimal, minim

leatherneck NOUNS **marine,** gyrene *and* devil dog <both nonformal>; horse marine; boot <nonformal>

leave NOUNS 1 **vacation,** holiday; **time off;** leave of absence, furlough; liberty, shore leave; **sabbatical,** sabbatical leave *or* year

2 **leave-taking, parting, departure,** congé; **send-off,** Godspeed; **adieu,** one's adieus, **farewell,** aloha, **good-bye;** valedictory address, valedictory, valediction, parting words; parting *or* Parthian shot

3 **permission, allowance,** vouchsafement; **consent**; permission to enter, admission, ticket, ticket of admission; **license,** liberty; **okay** *and* **OK** *and* **nod** *and* **go-ahead** *and* **green light** *and* **go sign** *and* **thumbs-up** <all nonformal>

VERBS 4 **depart,** make off, begone, be off, take oneself off *or* away, take one's departure, take leave *or* take one's leave, **go, go away, go off, get off** *or* **away,** get under way, come away, go one's way, go *or* get along, be getting along, go on, get on; move off *or* away, move out, march off *or* away; **pull out;** decamp; exit; take *or* break *or* tear oneself away, take oneself off, take wing *or* flight

5 <nonformal> **split,** bugger off, fuck off, f off, make tracks, pull up stakes, push along, scarper <Brit>, push off, skedaddle *or* absquatulate <old> **haul ass,** bag ass, **beat it, blow,** boogie, bug out, cut, **cut out,** cut and run, make tracks, peel out, piss off, *and* scarper <Brit nonformal>, scram, shove off

6 **abandon,** desert, forsake; **quit,** leave behind, take leave of, depart from, absent oneself from, turn one's back upon, turn one's tail upon, say goodbye to, bid a long farewell to, walk away, **walk** *or* **run out on** <nonformal>, **leave flat** *and* leave high and dry *or* holding the bag *or* in the lurch <all nonformal>, leave one to one's fate, throw to the wolves <nonformal>

7 **bequeath, will,** will and bequeath, **devise, will to,** hand down, hand on, pass on, transmit

leave of absence NOUNS **vacation, time off;** day off, week off, month off, etc; paid vacation; weekend; **leave, furlough; liberty,** shore leave; **sabbatical,** sabbatical leave *or* year

leave-taking NOUNS **leave, parting, departure,** congé; **send-off,** Godspeed; **adieu,** one's adieus, **farewell,** aloha, **good-bye**

leavings NOUNS **remainder,** remains, remnant, residue, residuum, rest, balance; **leftovers, refuse,** odds and ends, scraps, rags, **rubbish, waste,** orts, candle ends; scourings, offscourings; parings, sweepings, filings, shavings, sawdust; chaff, straw, stubble, husks; **debris,** detritus, ruins; end, fag end

lecher NOUNS **satyr, goat,** old goat, **dirty old man;** whorer *or* whoremonger <both old>, whoremaster, whorehound <nonformal>; Priapus; gynecomaniac; erotomaniac, eroticomaniac, aphrodisiomaniac

lechery NOUNS **philandering,** philander, lady-killing <nonformal>; **lasciviousness, lecherousness, lewdness,** bawdiness, **dirtiness,** salacity, salaciousness, **carnality,** animality, fleshliness, **sexuality, sexiness, lust, lustfulness**

an expense of spirit in a waste of shame is lust in action
SHAKESPEARE

lectern NOUNS **reading stand,** ambo, reading desk; **table,** board, **stand**

lecture NOUNS 1 **lesson, teaching, instruction,** lecture-demonstration, harangue, **discourse,** disquisition, exposition, **talk,** homily, **sermon,** preachment

2 **rebuke, reprimand, reproach,** reprehension, **scolding, chiding,** rating, **upbraiding,** objurgation; **admonishment, admonition**

VERBS 3 **expound,** exposit; explain; **discourse,** harangue, hold forth, give *or* read a lesson; **preach,** sermonize; **reprove, rebuke, reprimand,** reprehend, put a flea in one's ear, **scold, chide,** rate, **admonish, upbraid,** objurgate, have words with, take a hard line with

lecturing NOUNS **public speaking, declamation, speechmaking, speaking,** speechification <nonformal>, speeching; **oratory,** platform oratory *or* speaking

ledge NOUNS **shelf,** shoulder, corbel, beam-end; mantel, mantelshelf, mantelpiece; retable, superaltar, gradin, *gradino* <Ital>, predella

ledger NOUNS **account book, journal,**

daybook; **register,** registry, **record book,** books; **cashbook**

leech NOUNS 1 **parasite,** barnacle; **sponger,** sponge <nonformal>, freeloader <nonformal>, smell-feast; beat *and* deadbeat <both nonformal>; **extortionist,** extortioner, **blackmailer,** racketeer, shakedown artist <nonformal>, **bloodsucker,** vampire; profiteer
VERBS 2 bleed, let blood, phlebotomize

leer NOUNS 1 **look,** the eye *and* a look-see *and* a gander <all nonformal>, eye, view, regard; sidelong look; leering look; snigger, **smirk,** sardonic grin, fleer, **sneer,** snort
VERBS 2 **scrutinize, survey, eye,** contemplate, look over, give the eye *or* the once-over <nonformal>; **ogle,** ogle at, leer at, give one the glad eye; take a long, hard look; size up <nonformal>; take stock of; wink, glance, raise one's eyebrows

leery ADJS **wary,** chary, cagey <nonformal>, **suspicious,** suspecting, **distrustful,** mistrustful, shy, cautious, guarded; **skeptical**

leeway NOUNS **room, latitude,** swing, play, way; room to spare, room to swing a cat <nonformal>, **elbowroom, margin;** breathing space; sea room; headroom, clearance

left NOUNS 1 **left side, left hand,** left-hand side, wrong side <nonformal>, near *or* nigh side <of a horse or vehicle>, portside, port, larboard; Gospel side, cantorial side, verso <of a book>
2 left wing, left-winger, radical, liberal, progressive
ADJS 3 **left-hand,** sinister, sinistral; near, nigh; **larboard, port;** left-wing, left-wingish, left-of-center, radical, liberal, progressive, wet <Brit nonformal>
4 **remaining, surviving, extant,** vestigial, over, **leftover,** still around, remnant, remanent, odd; **spare,** to spare; unused, unconsumed; **surplus,** superfluous; **outstanding,** unmet, unresolved; **abandoned,** forsaken, deserted
ADVS 5 **leftward,** leftwards, leftwardly, **to the left,** sinistrally, sinister, sinistrad; on the left; larboard, port, aport

left-handed ADJS 1 **oblique; devious,** deviant, deviative, divergent, digressive, divagational, deflectional, excursive; **indirect,** side, sidelong; sinister, sinistral, sinistromanual, sinistral, lefty *and* southpaw <both nonformal>; backhand, backhanded; circuitous; insulting
2 <nonformal> **southpaw** *and* lefty *and* portsider

leftist NOUNS 1 **liberal,** liberalist, wet <Brit nonformal>, **progressive,** progressivist, **left-winger; left**
ADJS 2 **liberal, liberalistic,** liberalist, wet <Brit nonformal>, bleeding-heart <nonformal>; **progressive,** progressivistic; **left-wing,** on the left, left of center

leftover NOUNS 1 **surplus,** surplusage, leftovers, plus, **overplus,** overstock, **overage,** overset, overrun, **overmeasure, oversupply;** margin; **remainder, balance,** extra, spare, something extra *or* to spare; bonus, dividend
ADJS 2 **remaining, surviving, extant,** vestigial, over, left, still around, remnant, remanent, odd; **spare,** to spare; unused, unconsumed; **surplus,** superfluous; **outstanding,** unmet, unresolved; net

left wing NOUNS **liberalism, progressivism,** leftism; **left,** progressiveness

left-wing ADJS **liberal, liberalistic,** liberalist, wet <Brit nonformal>, bleeding-heart <nonformal>; **progressive,** progressivistic; **leftist,** on the left, left of center

leg NOUNS 1 **limb, shank;** hind leg, foreleg; gamb, jamb <heraldry>

2 <nonformal> gams, stems, trotters, hind legs, underpinnings, wheels, shanks, sticks, pins, stumps

legacy NOUNS **bequest,** bequeathal, devise; inheritance, **heritage,** patrimony, birthright; **outgrowth,** spin-off, offshoot, offspring, issue, aftermath

legal ADJS **legitimate,** legit *and* kosher <both nonformal>, competent, **licit, lawful,** rightful, according to law, within the law; within the scope of the law; **enforceable,** legally binding

legality NOUNS **legitimacy, lawfulness,** legitimateness, licitness, rightfulness, validity, scope, applicability; **jurisdiction**; legal process, legal form, **due process**

legalize VERBS **legitimize,** legitimatize, legitimate, make legal, declare lawful, **decriminalize;** wash or launder money; validate; **authorize, sanction;** constitute, ordain, establish, put in force; prescribe, formulate; regulate, make a regulation

legal system NOUNS **law,** system of laws, legal branch *or* specialty; **judiciary,** judicial *or* court system, judicature, judicatory, court, the courts; criminal-justice system; the wheels of justice, judicial process

legatee NOUNS **beneficiary,** allottee, donee, grantee, patentee; assignee, **assign; devisee,** legatary <old>; stipendiary; pensioner, pensionary; annuitant

legation NOUNS **mission,** diplomatic mission, diplomatic staff *or* corps, *corps diplomatique* <Fr>; **embassy,** consular service; consulate, chancery, chancellery

legend NOUNS 1 **memory, remembrance,** blessed *or* sacred memory, heroic legend *or* myth; **immortality,** lasting *or* undying fame, niche in the hall of fame, secure place in history
2 **mythology,** mythicism; **lore, folklore,** folktale, myth, mythical lore; fairy lore, fairyism
3 **caption,** title, heading, head, superscription, rubric; motto, **epigraph**

legendary ADJS **famous,** famed, honored, **renowned, celebrated, popular,** acclaimed, much acclaimed, sought-after, hot *and* world-class <both nonformal>, **notorious, well-known,** best-known, in everyone's mouth, on everyone's tongue *or* lips; **extraordinary, exceptional, remarkable,** noteworthy, **wonderful, marvelous,** fabulous; fabled, mythical, folkloric; **traditional;** mythological, heroic; unwritten, oral, handed down

legible ADJS **decipherable, readable,** fair; uncoded, unenciphered, in the clear, clear, plaintext

legion NOUNS **throng, multitude, horde,** host, heap <nonformal>, army, panoply; flock, cluster, galaxy

legislate VERBS make *or* enact laws, **enact, pass,** constitute, ordain, put in force; **put through,** jam *or* steamroller *or* railroad through <nonformal>, lobby through; **filibuster; logroll,** roll logs

legislation NOUNS **lawmaking,** legislature <old>; **enactment,** enaction, constitution, passage, passing; **law,** *lex, jus* <both L>, **statute,** rubric, **canon,** institution; **ordinance; measure**

legislator NOUNS **lawmaker,** solon, lawgiver; **congressman,** congresswoman, Member of Congress; **senator; representative;** state senator, assemblyman, assemblywoman, freeholder, councilman, councilwoman, councilperson, city father

legislature NOUNS legislative body; **parliament, congress, assembly,** general assembly, house of assembly, legislative assembly, **national assembly, chamber of deputies,** federal assembly, diet, soviet, court; legislative chamber, **upper chamber** *or* **house, lower chamber** *or* **house;** state legislature, state assembly; provincial legislature, provincial parliament; city council, city board, common council, commission; representative town meeting, town meeting

legitimate ADJS **justifiable,** vindicable, defensible; **warrantable,** allowable, admissible, reasonable, colorable; **legal,** legit *and* kosher <both nonformal>, competent, **licit, lawful,** rightful, according to law, within the law

leisure NOUNS 1 **ease, convenience,** freedom; retirement, semiretirement; rest, repose; **free time, spare time,** goof-off time <nonformal>, odd moments, idle hours; **vacation, holiday,** time off, day off, recess, playtime
ADJS 2 **leisured;** idle, unoccupied, free, open, spare; retired, semiretired

lend VERBS **loan, advance,** accommodate with; loan-shark <nonformal>; float *or* negotiate a loan; lend-lease, lease-lend

length NOUNS longness, lengthiness, overall length; wheelbase; **extent,** extension, **measure,** span, reach, stretch; **distance**

lengthen VERBS **prolong,** prolongate, **elongate, extend,** produce, **protract,** continue; make prolix; lengthen out, let out, **draw** *or* drag *or* stretch *or* string *or* spin out; **stretch,** draw, pull

lengthy ADJS **long;** longish, longsome; **extensive, far-reaching,** fargoing, far-flung; sesquipedalian, sesquipedal; **time-consuming,** interminable, without end, no end of *or* to, **protracted,** extended, *de longue haleine* <Fr>, **long-drawn-out,** long-spun, spun-out, endless, unrelenting

leniency NOUNS lenience, lenientness, lenity; **clemency,** clementness, **mercifulness,** mercy, **humaneness,** humanity, pity, **compassion**; **mildness, gentleness,** tenderness, softness, moderateness; **easiness,** easygoingness; laxness; **forbearance,** forbearing, patience; acceptance, **tolerance**

lenient ADJS **tolerant,** tolerative, tolerating, accepting; condoning, understanding, **indulgent, forbearing; accommodating,** accommodative, at one's service, **helpful,** agreeable, **obliging,** indulgent

leper NOUNS **outcast,** social outcast, outcast of society, **pariah,** untouchable; outcaste; *déclassé* <Fr>; undesirable; *persona non grata* <L>, unacceptable person

leprechaun NOUNS **fairy, sprite, fay,** fairy man *or* woman; **elf,** brownie, pixie, gremlin, ouphe, hob, cluricaune, puca *or* pooka *or* pwca, kobold, nisse, peri; **imp,** goblin; **gnome,** dwarf

lesbian NOUNS 1 **homosexual,** gay person, homosexualist, sapphist, tribade, fricatrice <old>; butch *and* dyke <both nonformal>
ADJS 2 **homosexual,** homoerotic, sapphic, tribadistic; mannish, butch *and* dykey <both nonformal>

lesion NOUNS **trauma,** wound, injury, hurt; **cut,** incision, scratch, gash; puncture, stab, stab wound; flesh wound; **laceration,** mutilation; **sore,** sore spot, tender spot

less ADJS 1 **reduced, decreased,** diminished, lowered, dropped, fallen; bated, **abated; deflated,** contracted, shrunk, shrunken; **simplified**; scaled-down, miniaturized; minimized, belittled; **lower,** lesser, smaller, shorter
ADVS 2 **decreasingly,** diminishingly, less and less, ever less; on a declining scale, at a declining rate

lessee NOUNS **tenant, occupant,** occupier, incumbent, **resident; renter,** hirer <Brit>, leaseholder; subtenant, sublessee, underlessee, undertenant

lessen VERBS **relieve,** give relief; **ease,** ease matters; **relax,** slacken; **reduce,** abate, remit; **alleviate, mitigate, palliate,** soften, pad, cushion, assuage, allay, defuse, lay, appease, mollify, subdue, soothe; **decrease, diminish; decline, subside,** shrink, wane, wither, ebb, ebb away, dwindle, languish, sink, sag, die down *or* away, wind down, taper off *and* trail off *or* away *and* tail off *or* away <all nonformal>; **extenuate**

lesser ADJS **inferior, subservient,** subject, servile, low, **lowly,** humble, modest; less, lower, smaller, shorter; in the shade, thrown into the shade; **common,** vulgar, ordinary; **reduced,** decreased, diminished, lowered, fallen

lesson NOUNS **warning,** object lesson, **example,** deterrent example, warning piece; moral, moral of the story; **correction,** castigation, chastisement, spanking, rap on the knuckles; lecture, teaching, instruction, **talk,** homily, **sermon,** preachment

let VERBS **permit, allow,** admit, give permission, give leave, make possible; **allow** *or* **permit of;** give *or* leave room for, open the door to; consent; **grant,** accord, vouchsafe; **rent, lease,** hire, job, **charter; sublease, sublet,** underlet

letdown NOUNS **disappointment, comedown,** setback; **disillusionment,** descent, deflation, wounded *or* humbled pride; **slowdown,** slowup, **letup, slackoff,** ease-off, ease-up; bursting of the bubble

let down VERBS **disappoint,** defeat expectation *or* hope; **dash,** dash *or* blight *or* blast *or* crush one's hope; cast down; **disillusion; betray, doublecross** *and* two-time <both nonformal>, sell out *and* sell down the river <both nonformal>, turn in; let down one's side <nonformal>

let go VERBS 1 let pass, **let slip, let slide** *and* let ride <both nonformal>; **neglect,** overlook, disregard, not heed, not attend to, take for granted, **ignore;** not care for, not take care of
2 **exempt, free, release,** discharge, **let off** <nonformal>, set at liberty, set free, spring <nonformal>; **excuse,** spare, except, grant immunity, make a special case of; absolve
3 **let oneself go,** let loose *and* cut loose *and* let one's hair down <all nonformal>, **give way to,** open up, let it all hang out <nonformal>; go all out, pull out all the stops; go unrestrained, run wild, have one's fling, sow one's wild oats
4 **dismiss, discharge, expel, cashier,** drum out, disemploy, outplace, separate forcibly *or* involuntarily, **lay off,** suspend, surplus, furlough, turn off, make redundant, riff <nonformal>, turn out, release, let out, remove, displace, replace, strike off the rolls, give the pink slip

lethal ADJS **deadly, deathly,** deathful, killing, destructive, death-dealing, death-bringing; savage, brutal; internecine; **fatal, mortal,** malignant, malign, virulent, pernicious, baneful; **life-threatening,** terminal

lethargic ADJS **languid, languorous, list-**

less, lifeless, inanimate, enervated, debilitated, **pepless** <nonformal>, lackadaisical, slow, wan, logy, hebetudinous, supine, lymphatic, apathetic, **sluggish,** dopey <nonformal>, drugged, nodding, droopy, **dull,** heavy, leaden, lumpish, **torpid,** stultified, stuporous, **inert,** stagnant, stagnating, phlegmatic

lethargy NOUNS **languor,** languidness, languorousness, lackadaisicalness, lotus-eating; **listlessness,** lifelessness, inanimation, enervation, **dullness, sluggishness,** heaviness, dopiness <nonformal>, hebetude, supineness, **lassitude,** loginess

letter NOUNS **epistle, message,** communication, dispatch, missive; personal letter, business letter; **note, line,** chit

letter carrier NOUNS **postman, mailman,** mail carrier; postmaster, postmistress; postal clerk

lettered ADJS **learned, erudite, educated, cultured,** cultivated, literate, civilized, **scholarly,** scholastic, studious; **encyclopedic,** pansophic, polymath *or* polymathic, polyhistoric

letter of credit NOUNS **credit instrument;** paper credit; *lettre de créance* <Fr>, circular note; credit slip, credit memorandum, **negotiable instrument** *or* **paper,** commercial paper, paper, commercial letter of credit

letters NOUNS **literature, belles lettres,** polite literature, humane letters, *litterae humaniores* <L>, republic of letters; **scholarship, erudition,** eruditeness, learnedness

letter writer NOUNS **correspondent,** writer, communicator; pen pal <nonformal>

letting go NOUNS **relinquishment, release,** giving up, dispensation; **renunciation,** forgoing, forswearing, swearing off, resignation, abjuration, **abandonment; surrender,** cession, handover, turning over, **yielding**

letup NOUNS **pause, rest, break,** caesura, **recess, intermission,** interim, intermittence, interval, interlude, *intermezzo* <Ital>; **respite; interruption, suspension,** time-out, break in the action, breathing spell, cooling-off period

levee NOUNS **barrier, bar;** bank, embankment, dike

level NOUNS 1 **tier,** stage, story, floor, gallery, step, ledge, deck
2 **status, social status, economic status,** socioeconomic status *or* background, standing, footing, prestige, rank, ranking, place, station, position, degree, stratum
VERBS 3 **flatten, even,** align, smooth *or* smoothen, level out, smooth out, flush; grade, roll, roll flat, steamroller *or* steamroll; **raze,** rase, lay level, lay level with the ground; lay low *or* flat; **equalize;** equal out, even up, even off, square, level off, make both ends meet
ADJS 4 **horizontal, flat,** flattened; **even,** smooth, smoothened, smoothed out; table-like, tabular; **flush; plane,** rolled, trodden, squashed, rolled *or* trodden *or* squashed flat; flat as a pancake, flat as a board
5 **uniform, equable,** equal, **even; unvarying,** undeviating, unchanging, steady, stable; **consistent,** consonant, correspondent, accordant, homogeneous, **alike,** all alike, all of a piece, of a piece, consubstantial, monolithic
ADVS 6 **horizontally, flat,** flatly, flatways, flatwise; **evenly,** flush; **on a level**

levelheaded ADJS **sensible,** reasonable, rational, logical; **practical,** pragmatic; philosophical; commonsense, commonsensical <nonformal>; balanced, coolheaded, cool, **sound, sane,** sober, **sober-minded,** well-balanced

leverage NOUNS **influence,** influentiality; **power**, force, clout <nonformal>, potency, pressure, effect, indirect *or* incidental power, **say,** the final say, the last word, say-so *and* a lot to do with *or* to say about <all nonformal>, veto power; purchase; fulcrumage

leviathan NOUNS **behemoth, monster;** mammoth, mastodon; elephant, jumbo <nonformal>; whale; hippopotamus, hippo <nonformal>; **dinosaur**

levitate VERBS **ascend, rise, mount,** arise, hover, float, up, uprise, upgo, **go up,** rise up, come up

levity NOUNS **lightheartedness,** lightsomeness, lightness; **waggishness,** waggery; **playfulness,** sportiveness, **frivolity,** flippancy, merriment; panning *and* razzing *and* roasting *and* ragging <all nonformal>, **scoffing, jeering, sneering,** snickering, sniggering, smirking, grinning, leering, fleering, snorting, smart-aleckiness *and* joshing <both nonformal>, fooling, japery

levy NOUNS 1 **tax, taxation, duty,** tribute, taxes, rates <Brit>, contribution, assess-

ment, revenue enhancement, toll, **impost,** imposition
VERBS 2 **impose,** exact, demand; tax, task, charge, burden with, weight *or* freight with, weight down with, yoke with, **fasten upon,** saddle with, stick with <nonformal>; subject to

lewd ADJS **obscene,** adult, bawdy, ithyphallic, **ribald, pornographic, salacious,** sultry <nonformal>, lurid, **dirty, smutty,** raunchy <nonformal>, blue, smoking-room, impure, unchaste, unclean, **foul, filthy, nasty,** vile, fulsome, offensive, unprintable, unrepeatable, not fit for mixed company; **foulmouthed,** foul-tongued, foul-spoken; Rabelaisian

lexicon NOUNS **vocabulary,** lexis, words, word stock, wordhoard, stock of words; phraseology; **thesaurus,** Roget's; **dictionary,** wordbook, Webster's; glossary, onomasticon, nomenclator; storehouse *or* treasury of words

liability NOUNS **disadvantage,** drawback; **detriment,** impairment, prejudice, loss, damage, hurt, harm, mischief, injury; **a step back** *or* **backward,** a loss of ground; **handicap**, disability; drag, millstone around one's neck; **exposure, openness,** nonimmunity, susceptibility

liable ADJS **likely,** prone; **probable; responsible,** legally responsible, answerable; **exposed,** susceptible, at risk, overexposed, open, like a sitting duck, **vulnerable**

liaison NOUNS 1 **love affair, affair,** affair of the heart, **amour, romance,** romantic tie *or* bond, something between, thing <nonformal>, entanglement, intrigue
2 **intermediary,** intermedium, mediary, medium; link, **connecting link,** tie, connection, **go-between**

liar NOUNS **fibber,** fibster, fabricator, fabulist, pseudologist; falsifier; **prevaricator,** equivocator, waffler <nonformal>, palterer; consummate liar, dirty liar; pathological liar, mythomaniac, pseudologue, confirmed *or* habitual liar; **perjurer,** false witness

libel NOUNS 1 **slander, scandal,** traducement; calumny, calumniation; backbiting, cattiness *and* bitchiness <both nonformal>
VERBS 2 **slander;** calumniate, traduce; stab in the back, backbite, speak ill of behind one's back

liberal NOUNS 1 **leftist,** left-winger; liberalist; libertarian; freethinker, latitudinarian, ecumenist, ecumenicist; bleeding heart, bleeding-heart liberal
ADJS 2 **free,** free with one's money, free-spending; **generous, munificent,** large, princely, handsome; **unselfish,** ungrudging; **unsparing, unstinting,** stintless, unstinted; **bountiful,** bounteous, **lavish,** profuse; **openhanded,** freehanded, open; **giving;** openhearted, **bighearted,** largehearted, greathearted, freehearted; **magnanimous**
3 **liberalistic,** liberalist, wet <Brit nonformal>, bleeding-heart <nonformal>; **progressive,** progressivistic; **leftist, left-wing,** on the left, left of center

liberate VERBS **free, deliver, set free,** set at liberty, set at large; **emancipate,** manumit, disenthrall; enfranchise, affranchise; **rescue; release,** loose, unloose, unleash, unfetter

liberated ADJS **freed, emancipated, released;** delivered, rescued, ransomed, redeemed; extricated, unbound, untied, unshackled, etc; free; on parole

liberator NOUNS **savior, redeemer,** deliverer, rescuer, freer, **emancipator,** manumitter

libertarian NOUNS 1 individualist, rugged individualist; free spirit; **liberal,** latitudinarian
ADJS 2 **liberal, liberal-minded,** liberalistic; freethinking, latitudinarian

libertine NOUNS **swinger** <nonformal>, **profligate, rake,** rakehell, rip <nonformal>, **roué,** wanton, womanizer, cocksman <nonformal>, walking phallus, debauchee, rounder <old>, **wolf** <nonformal>, woman chaser, skirt chaser <nonformal>, gay dog, gay deceiver, gallant, philanderer, lover-boy <nonformal>, lady-killer, Lothario, Don Juan, Casanova

liberty NOUNS **freedom; license,** run *and* the run of <both nonformal>; **civil liberty,** constitutional freedom; academic freedom

libido NOUNS **sexuality,** sexual nature, sexualism, love-life; sex drive, sexual instinct *or* urge

library NOUNS book depository; media center, media resource center, information center; **public library,** town *or* city *or* municipal library, county library, state library; school library, college library, university library; **special**

library, circulating library, lending library <Brit>; rental library; **book wagon, bookmobile**

license NOUNS 1 **lawlessness; licentiousness,** uncontrol, anything goes, unrestraint; indiscipline, insubordination, mutiny, disobedience; **profligacy, dissoluteness,** unbridledness, wildness, fastness, rakishness, gallantry, **libertinism,** libertinage
2 **franchise,** charter, patent, dispensation, release, waiver; **permit, warrant;** nihil obstat, imprimatur
VERBS 3 **authorize, sanction, warrant;** give official sanction *or* warrant, legitimize, validate, legalize; empower, give power, enable, entitle; charter, patent, enfranchise, franchise; accredit, certificate, certify

licentious ADJS **dissipated,** riotous, dissolute, debauched; free-living, high-living <nonformal>

licit ADJS **lawful, legitimate, legal,** legitimized, legalized, legitimated, decriminalized

lick VERBS 1 **lap up,** sponge *or* soak up, lap, slurp <nonformal>

2 <nonformal> **clobber, trim, skin alive, beat,** skunk, drub, massacre, whip, thrash, trim, hide, cut to pieces, lather, trounce, **lambaste**

lid NOUNS **cover,** top, cap, screw-top; operculum; stopper

lie NOUNS 1 **falsehood,** falsity, **untruth,** untruism, mendacity, **prevarication, fib,** flimflam *or* flam, a crock *and* a crock of shit <both nonformal>, *blague* <Fr>; **fiction,** pious fiction, legal fiction; half-truth, stretching of the truth, slight stretching, white lie, little white lie; a pack of lies
VERBS 2 **lie down, recline, repose,** lounge, sprawl, loll, drape *or* spread oneself, splay, lie limply; **lie flat** *or* prostrate *or* prone *or* supine, lie on one's face *or* back, lie on a level, hug the ground *or* deck
3 **fabricate,** invent, manufacture, trump up, make up, hatch, concoct, cook up *and* make out of whole cloth <both nonformal>, fudge <nonformal>, fake, hoke up <nonformal>

lie detector NOUNS polygraph, psychogalvanometer

lie down VERBS **recline**; prostrate, supinate, prone <nonformal>; flatten oneself, prostrate oneself; hit the ground *or* the dirt <nonformal>

lieutenant NOUNS **assistant, helper,** auxiliary, aider, **aid,** aide, paraprofessional; **attendant, second,** acolyte; adjutant, aide-de-camp; executive officer

life NOUNS **living, vitality,** being alive, having life, animation, animate existence; breath; liveliness, animal spirits, vivacity, spriteliness; **spirit,** verve, energy, adrenalin; pep *and* moxie *and* oomph *and* pizzazz *and* piss and vinegar <all nonformal>, **vim;** long life, longevity; life expectancy, life span; viability; lifetime; existence; **biography, memoir,** memorial, story, **life story,** adventures, fortunes, experiences

one dem'd horrid grind
DICKENS

a comedy to those who think, a tragedy to those who feel
H WALPOLE

life force NOUNS **soul,** spirit, indwelling spirit, force of life, living force, *vis vitae* or *vis vitalis* <both L>, **vital force** *or* energy, animating force *or* power *or* principle, inspiriting force *or* power *or* principle, archeus, élan vital, impulse of life, vital principle, **vital spark** *or* **flame,** spark of life, divine spark, life principle, vital spirit, vital fluid, anima

lifeless ADJS 1 **dead,** breathless, without life, inanimate, exanimate, without vital functions; **deceased, demised, defunct,** croaked <nonformal>, departed, departed this life, destitute of life, **gone, passed on,** gone the way of all flesh, gone west <nonformal>, dead and gone, done for <nonformal>, dead and done for <nonformal>, no more, finished <nonformal>, taken off *or* away, released, fallen, bereft of life
2 **lackluster,** lusterless; dull, dead, deadened, somber, **drab,** wan, **flat,** mat

lifelike ADJS **representative,** delineative; **expressive,** realistic, natural, naturalistic, true to life, faithful, verisimilar, veristic

lifesaver NOUNS **rescuer,** lifeguard; coast guard, lifesaving service, air-sea rescue; savior; lifeboat; salvager, salvor

lifestyle NOUNS **behavior, conduct,** deportment, comportment; tone, style;

way of life, habit of life, modus vivendi; **way, way of acting, ways;** culture pattern, behavioral norm, folkway, **custom**

life-threatening ADJS **deadly, deathly,** deathful, **killing, destructive,** death-dealing, death-bringing, feral <old>; **fatal,** mortal, lethal, malignant, malign, virulent, pernicious, baneful; **terminal**

lifetime NOUNS 1 **life,** life's duration, life expectancy, lifespan, expectation of life, period of existence, all the days of one's life; all one's born days *or* natural life <nonformal>

threescore years and ten
BIBLE

ADJS 2 **lifelong,** livelong, for life

lift NOUNS 1 **assist,** helping hand, hand; boost *and* leg up <both nonformal>; help in time of need; **elevator,** *ascenseur* <Fr>
VERBS 2 **elate, exalt,** elevate, uplift; waft, whisk, wing; **improve, better,** change for the better, make an improvement; meliorate, **ameliorate; advance, promote,** foster, favor, nurture, forward, bring forward; raise

liftoff NOUNS **rocket launching** *or* **firing,** ignition, launch, shot, shoot; blast-off

light NOUNS 1 radiant *or* luminous energy, visible radiation, radiation in the visible spectrum, **illumination, radiation, radiance** *or* radiancy, irradiance *or* irradiancy, irradiation, emanation; highlight; sidelight; light source; **invisible light,** black light, infrared light, ultraviolet light
2 **light source,** source of light, **luminary,** illuminator, luminant, illuminant, incandescent body *or* point, glim
VERBS 3 **ignite, set fire to,** fire, set on fire, kindle, enkindle, inflame, light up, strike a light, apply the match *or* torch to, torch <nonformal>, touch off, **burn,** conflagrate; **grow light,** grow bright, **lighten,** brighten
ADJS 4 **frail,** delicate, airy, wispy, lacy, gauzy, papery, gossamer, diaphanous, insubstantial, ethereal, misty, vague, flimsy, wafer-thin, **fine**
5 **agile, nimble, spry,** sprightly, fleet, featly, peart <nonformal>, graceful, nimble-footed, light-footed, sure-footed
6 **superficial, frivolous,** dizzy *and* ditzy <both nonformal>, flighty, volatile, frothy, fluffy; unburdensome

lighten VERBS 1 **disburden,** unburden, unweight, unload, unfreight, disencumber, disembarrass, ease one's load; **set one's mind at ease** *or* **rest,** set at ease, **take a load off one's mind,** smooth the ruffled brow of care; relieve oneself, let one's hair down, pour one's heart out, talk it out, let it all hang out *and* go public <both nonformal>, get it off one's chest; make light *or* lighter, reduce weight
2 **grow light,** grow bright, brighten; dawn, break; **illuminate,** illumine, illume, luminate, **light, light up,** enlighten, brighten, brighten up, irradiate; bathe *or* flood with light

lightheaded ADJS **dizzy, giddy,** vertiginous, spinning, swimming, turned around, going around in circles; tiddly <nonformal>, **drunk, drunken**

lightning NOUNS **flash** *or* **stroke of lightning,** fulguration, fulmination, bolt, lightning strike, **bolt of lightning,** bolt from the blue, **thunderbolt,** thunderstroke, thunderball, fireball, firebolt

lightweight NOUNS 1 **nonentity,** hollow man, doormat *and* empty suit *and* nebbish *and* sad sack <all nonformal>; **a nobody, insignificancy,** hollow man, jackstraw <old>, an obscurity, a nothing, cipher; mediocrity; small potato, small potatoes
ADJS 2 **uninfluential, powerless,** forceless, impotent; **weak,** wimpy *or* wimpish <nonformal>; unauthoritative; **ineffective,** ineffectual, inefficacious; **of no account,** no-account, without any weight, featherweight

likable ADJS **endearing,** lovable, adorable, admirable, **lovely,** lovesome, sweet, winning, winsome; **charming;** angelic, seraphic; caressable, kissable; cuddlesome, cuddly

like NOUNS 1 **equal, match,** mate, twin, fellow, **equivalent,** opposite number, counterpart, answer <nonformal>, vis à vis, equipollent, coequal, parallel, ditto <nonformal>
VERBS 2 **savor, relish,** love, be fond of, be partial to, enjoy, delight in, have a soft spot for, appreciate; have *or* acquire a taste for, fancy, take to, **take a fancy** *or* a shine to, have a fancy for; have an eye to, have one's eye on
ADJS 3 **similar, alike,** something like, not unlike; **resembling,** resemblant, following, favoring <nonformal>, savoring

or smacking of, suggestive of, **on the order of;** consimilar; **on a par,** at par, at parity, au pair, on the same level, on the same plane, on the same *or* equal footing
ADVS 4 **similarly,** correspondingly, **likewise,** either; in the same manner, **in like manner,** in kind; in that way, like that, like this; **thus**; so; by the same token, by the same sign; identically

likelihood NOUNS **probability,** likeliness, liability, aptitude, verisimilitude; **chance, odds; expectation, outlook,** prospect; favorable prospect, well-grounded hope, some *or* reasonable hope, fair expectation; **good chance**; presumption, tendency; probable cause, reasonable ground *or* presumption

likely ADJS 1 **probable, liable, apt,** verisimilar, in the cards, odds-on; **promising, hopeful,** fair, in a fair way; foreseeable, **predictable; presumable,** presumptive; **statistical,** actuarial; predictable within limits
ADVS 2 **probably, in all probability** *or* **likelihood,** most likely, very likely; as likely as not, very like *and* like enough *and* like as not <all nonformal>; **doubtlessly,** doubtless, **no doubt,** indubitably; **presumably,** presumptively; by all odds, ten to one, a hundred to one, dollars to doughnuts

likely story NOUNS **excuse, cop-out** *and* **alibi** *and* **out** <all nonformal>; lame excuse, poor excuse; escape hatch, way out

like-minded ADJS **agreeing, in agreement; in accord, concurring,** positive, affirmative, in rapport, *en rapport* <Fr>, **in harmony,** in accordance, in sync <nonformal>, **at one,** on all fours, of one *or* the same *or* like mind, consentient, consentaneous, **unanimous**, unisonous *or* unisonant; **harmonious,** accordant, **concordant,** consonant

liken VERBS **compare,** assimilate, similize, liken to, compare with; **make** *or* **draw a comparison,** run a comparison, do a comparative study, bring into comparison; **analogize,** bring into analogy; **draw a parallel,** parallel; **match,** match up; examine side by side, view together, hold up together

likeness NOUNS 1 **image, resemblance,** semblance, similitude, simulacrum; **effigy,** icon, idol; **copy**, fair copy; **portrait,** perfect *or* exact likeness, duplicate, double
2 **similarity,** alikeness, **sameness,** similitude; **analogy, correspondence,** conformity, accordance, agreement, comparability, comparison, **parallelism, parity,** community, alliance, consimilarity

likewise ADVS **similarly,** correspondingly, **like,** either; in the same manner, **in like manner,** in kind; in that way, like that, like this; **thus**; so; by the same token, by the same sign; identically

lilt NOUNS **rhythm,** beat, meter, measure, number *or* numbers, movement, **swing;** prosody, metrics; rhythmic pattern *or* phrase

limb NOUNS **branch,** fork, **bough; arm,** leg; **wing,** pinion

limbo NOUNS **hell,** purgatory; **place of confinement**

limelight NOUNS **publicity, celebrity,** *réclame, éclat* <both Fr>; **spotlight** <both nonformal>, daylight, bright light, glare, public eye *or* consciousness, **exposure, currency,** common *or* public knowledge, widest *or* maximum dissemination; **ballyhoo** *and* hoopla <both nonformal>

limit NOUNS 1 **end**, **extremity,** extreme, **acme,** apogee, climax, **maximum,** max <nonformal>, ceiling, **peak,** summit, **pinnacle,** crown, top; **utmost,** uttermost, utmost extent, highest degree, nth degree *or* power, *ne plus ultra* <L>; **the last straw,** the straw that breaks the camel's back, all one can bear *or* stand
VERBS 2 **restrict,** restrain, bound, confine, ground <nonformal>; straiten, narrow, tighten; specialize; stint, scant; **condition,** qualify, hedge, hedge about; draw the line, set an end point *or* a stopping place; discipline, moderate, contain; restrain oneself, pull one's punches <nonformal>

limited ADJS **restricted,** bound, **bounded, finite; confined**, prescribed, proscribed, cramped, strait, straitened, narrow; conditioned, qualified, hedged; disciplined, moderated; **deprived,** in straitened circumstances, pinched, on short commons, on short rations, strapped

limiting ADJS **restricting,** defining, determining, determinative, confining; limitative, limitary, definitive, exclusive; enclosing, **cloistered,** cloisterlike, claustral, parietal, surrounding; **restrictive,** narrowing, cramping; **qualifying, modifying,** modificatory, altering

limitless ADJS **unrestricted,** unconfined, uncircumscribed, unbounded, unmeasured; **unlimited,** illimitable; unqualified, unconditioned, **unconditional,** without strings, no strings, no strings attached; **infinite,** boundless, endless

limp NOUNS 1 hobble, claudication; shuffle, shamble, hitch, waddle; halt
VERBS 2 hobble, claudicate; **go slow** *or* **slowly,** go at a snail's pace, take it slow, get no place fast <nonformal>; **drag,** drag out; inch, inch along; poke, **poke along;** shuffle *or* stagger *or* totter *or* toddle along; drag along, drag one's feet
ADJS 3 **flaccid, flabby,** flimsy; limber, limp *or* limber as a dishrag, floppy, rubbery; **drooping, droopy,** loose, nodding, loppy, lop

limpid ADJS **clear, lucid,** pellucid, crystal-clear, crystalline, perspicuous, transpicuous, **transparent,** translucent, luminous; **coherent,** connected, consistent

line NOUNS 1 **strip,** cord, string, bar; stripe
2 **policy,** polity, principles, guiding principles; **party line,** party principle *or* doctrine *or* philosophy, **position**
3 **route,** path, way, itinerary, course, track, run, road; **railway, railroad,** rail, track, trackage, railway *or* railroad *or* rail line; **procession,** train, column, cortege
4 **lineage,** bloodline, descent, descendancy, line of descent, ancestral line, succession, **extraction,** derivation, birth, **blood,** breed, **family,** house, **strain, stock,** stirps, seed
5 **occupation,** business, work, **line of work,** line of business *or* endeavor, calling, mission, **pursuit,** *métier* <Fr>, **trade,** racket *and* game <both nonformal>; **specialty,** speciality, **field,** area, main interest; cup of tea *and* bag *and* thing <all nonformal>
VERBS 6 **border,** edge, bound, rim, skirt, hem, hem in, lap, list, margin, marge, marginate, march, verge, side; **align, line up,** string out, rank, array, range, get *or* put in a row

lineage NOUNS **line,** blood, strain, stock, stem, species, stirps, **breed,** brood, kind; **descent,** dynasty, family, succession; bloodline

linear ADJS **straight;** lineal, in a line; **direct, undeviating, unswerving,** unbending, undeflected; **sequential**

lineup NOUNS **arrangement,** prearrangement, system, disposition, layout, setup; **roll,** batting order, **roster,** rota <chiefly Brit>

line up VERBS 1 **align, line,** string out, rank, array, range, get *or* put in a row; **get in** *or* **get on line,** queue *or* queue up <Brit>, make *or* form a line, get in formation, **fall in,** fall in *or* into line, fall into rank, take one's place
2 **schedule, slate, book,** book in, bill, program, calendar, docket, budget, put on the agenda

linger VERBS **dawdle,** loiter, tarry, delay, dally, dillydally, shilly-shally, lollygag, waste time, **take one's time,** take one's own sweet time; goof off *or* around <nonformal>; lag, drag, trail; flag, falter, halt

lingerer NOUNS **slowpoke** *and* slowcoach <both nonformal>, plodder, slow goer, **loiterer, dawdler,** dawdle, **laggard,** procrastinator, foot-dragger, stick-in-the-mud <nonformal>, drone, slug, sluggard

lingerie NOUNS **underclothes,** underclothing, undergarments, bodywear, **underwear, undies** <nonformal>, skivvies, body clothes, smallclothes, unmentionables <nonformal>, **linen,** underlinen

lingering ADJS **dawdling,** loitering, tarrying, dallying, dillydallying, shilly-shallying, lollygagging, procrastinatory *or* procrastinative, dilatory, delaying, **lagging,** dragging; **protracted, prolonged,** extended, lengthened; lasting, languishing; long-continued, long-continuing, long-pending; drawn- *or* stretched- *or* dragged- *or* spun-out, long-drawn, **long-drawn-out**

lingo NOUNS **jargon,** slang, cant, argot, patois, patter, vernacular; vocabulary, phraseology

lingua franca NOUNS jargon, **pidgin,** trade language; auxiliary language, interlanguage; creolized language, creole language, creole; koine; pidgin English, talkee-talkee

linguist NOUNS linguistic scientist, linguistician, linguistic scholar; philologist, philologer, philologian; philologaster; **grammarian,** grammatist; grammaticaster; **etymologist,** etymologer; **lexicologist; polyglot,** bilingual *or* diglot, trilingual, multilingual

linguistic ADJS lingual, glottological; **philological;** lexicological, lexicographic, lexicographical; syntactic, syntactical, **grammatical**

liniment NOUNS **balm,** lotion, salve, ointment, unguent, *unguentum* <L>, cerate, unction, balsam, oil, emollient, demulcent; **embrocation**

link NOUNS 1 **relation, relationship, connection;** relatedness, connectedness, **association, affiliation,** filiation, bond, union, alliance, **tie,** tie-in <nonformal>, linkage, linking, linkup, liaison, **addition**, adjunct, junction, **combination**, assemblage
VERBS 2 **put together, join,** conjoin, **unite,** unify, bond, **connect,** associate, league, band, merge, **assemble,** accumulate; **couple,** pair, accouple, copulate, conjugate, marry, wed, tie the knot <nonformal>, link up, build bridges, yoke, knot, splice, tie, chain, bracket

linkage NOUNS **union, unification,** marriage, wedding, coupling, accouplement, linking, yoking; **fusion,** blend, blending, meld, melding; coalescence, coalition; **synthesis,** syncretism, syneresis

linked ADJS **joined, united,** connected, copulate, coupled, knit, bridged, tight-knit, knitted, bracketed, associated, conjoined, incorporated, integrated, **merged,** gathered, assembled, accumulated, **collected; associated,** joined up, on board

lint NOUNS **fluff,** flue, floss, **fuzz,** pile

lion NOUNS 1 **big cat, jungle cat;** Leo <nonformal>, *simba* <Swah>
2 **celebrity,** man *or* woman of mark *or* note, person of note *or* consequence, **notable, big name,** figure, public figure, somebody; **important person, VIP** *and* **standout** <both nonformal>, personage; social lion

lionhearted ADJS **courageous,** plucky, brave, bold, valiant, valorous, gallant, **intrepid,** doughty, stalwart, stout, stouthearted, ironhearted, greathearted, bold-spirited, bold as a lion

lionize VERBS **praise,** overpraise, praise to excess, idolize, deify, apotheosize, adulate, hero-worship; put on a pedestal

lip NOUNS 1 **border,** limbus, **edge,** verge, brink, brow, brim, rim, margin, marge, skirt, fringe, hem, list, selvage *or* selvedge, side; **labium,** labrum, labellum
2 **sauce** *and* sass, **back talk,** backchat <nonformal>

lip service NOUNS **mouth honor,** mouthing, lip homage *or* worship *or* devotion *or* praise *or* reverence; formalism, solemn mockery

liquefy VERBS liquidize, liquesce, fluidify, fluidize; **melt, run,** thaw, colliquate; melt down; deliquesce; **dissolve,** solve; solubilize; unclot, decoagulate; **infuse,** decoct, steep, soak, brew

liqueur NOUNS **cordial;** brandy, flavored brandy

liquid NOUNS 1 **fluid;** liquor, drink, beverage; liquid extract, fluid extract; **juice,** sap, body fluid
ADJS 2 **fluid,** fluidal, fluidic, **fluent, flowing,** fluxional, fluxionary, runny; watery; **juicy,** sappy
3 **convertible,** negotiable

liquid assets NOUNS **cash, ready money** *or* **cash,** the ready <nonformal>, available funds, money in hand, cash in hand, balance in hand, immediate resources, cash supply, **cash flow**

liquidate VERBS 1 **murder,** commit murder; **assassinate;** remove, **purge,** eliminate, get rid of
2 **pay in full,** discharge, settle, square, clear, **amortize,** retire, take up, lift, take up and pay off, honor, acquit oneself of <old>; **cash,** cash in <nonformal>, convert into cash; **sell,** convert, sell out, terminate the account

liquor NOUNS 1 **spirits,** intoxicating liquor, **hard liquor, whiskey,** firewater, spiritus frumenti, usquebaugh <Scots>, schnapps, ardent spirits, strong waters, **intoxicant,** toxicant, inebriant, **potable,** potation, **drink,** strong drink, grog, social lubricant, nectar of the gods; **alcohol,** aqua vitae, water of life, brew, **grog;** the cup that cheers

the luscious liquor
Milton

2 <nonformal> **booze, likker, hooch, juice, sauce,** tiger milk, pig *or* tiger sweat, sheepdip, moonshine, white lightning; **medicine,** snake medicine, corpse reviver; **rotgut, poison,** rat poison, formaldehyde, embalming fluid, shellac, **panther piss**

list NOUNS 1 **leaning,** slant, tilt, tip, pitch, **cant,** swag, sway
2 **enumeration, itemization,** listing, shopping list *and* laundry list *and* want list *and* wish list *and* hit list *and* shit list *and* drop-dead list <all nonformal>,

items, **schedule, register,** registry; waiting list; blacklist; short list
VERBS 3 **careen, heel,** tip, cant, heave *or* lay down, lie along; **stumble,** stagger, totter, tilt, trip, flounder; **incline,** lean; slope
4 **inscribe,** enscroll; **register,** enroll, catalog, calendar, **tabulate,** docket; **chronicle**

listen VERBS hark, **hearken,** heed, hear, attend, give attention, give ear, give *or* lend an ear, bend an ear; **listen to,** attend to, give a hearing to, give audience to, sit in on; **listen in; eavesdrop,** wiretap, tap, intercept, bug <nonformal>; **keep one's ears open,** be all ears <nonformal>, listen with both ears, hang on every word; hear out

listener NOUNS hearer, auditor, audient, hearkener; **eavesdropper,** overhearer, little pitcher with big ears, snoop, listener-in <nonformal>; fly on the wall

listless ADJS **languid, languorous,** lifeless, inanimate, enervated, debilitated, **pepless** <nonformal>, lackadaisical, slow, wan, **lethargic,** logy, hebetudinous, supine, lymphatic, apathetic, **sluggish,** dopey <nonformal>, droopy, **dull,** heavy, leaden, lumpish, **torpid,** stultified, stuporous, dormant; phlegmatic

lit ADJS **illuminated,** luminous, **lightened,** enlightened, brightened, lighted, lit up, flooded *or* bathed with light, floodlit; **alight, glowing,** aglow, lambent, suffused with light

litany NOUNS **prayer, supplication, invocation,** imploration, impetration, entreaty, beseechment, appeal, petition, suit, orison, obsecration, obtestation, rogation, **devotions;** silent prayer, meditation, contemplation, communion

literacy NOUNS **scholarship, erudition,** eruditeness, **learnedness,** reading, letters; **intellectuality,** intellectualism; computer literacy, computeracy, numeracy; **culture, literary culture, high culture,** book learning, booklore

literal NOUNS following the letter, letter-perfect, *au pied de la lettre* <Fr>, true to the letter; verbatim, verbal, word-perfect, **word-for-word;** literal-minded

literary ADJS belletristic; classical; **bookish,** booky, book-minded; book-loving, bibliophilic, bibliophagic

literate ADJS **learned,** erudite, educated, cultured, cultivated, lettered, civilized, **scholarly,** scholastic, studious

literature NOUNS **letters, belles lettres,** polite literature, humane letters, *litterae humaniores* <L>, republic of letters; **work, literary work,** text, literary text; works, complete works, oeuvre, canon, literary canon, author's canon; serious literature

lithe ADJS **supple,** willowy, **limber;** lithesome, lissome, loose-limbed; resilient, springy

as lissome as a hazel wand
TENNYSON

litigate VERBS **sue, prosecute,** go into litigation, **bring suit,** put in suit, sue *or* prosecute at law, **go to law,** seek in law, appeal to the law, seek justice *or* legal redress, implead, **bring action against,** prosecute a suit against, take *or* institute legal proceedings against; take to court, bring into court, hale *or* haul *or* drag into court, bring to justice, bring to trial, **put on trial,** bring to the bar, take legal action

litigation NOUNS **lawsuit, suit,** suit in *or* at law; countersuit; **prosecution, action,** legal action, proceedings, legal proceedings, legal process; legal remedy; **case, court case,** cause, cause in court, legal case; **judicial process**

litter NOUNS 1 **rubbish,** rubble, trash, junk <nonformal>, shoddy, riffraff, **scrap,** dust <Brit>, **debris,** clamjamfry <Scots>; **clutter,** rat's nest, mare's nest, hurrah's nest <nautical>
VERBS 2 **disorder, disorganize,** throw out of order, put out of gear, dislocate, upset the apple-cart, **disarray;** mess *and* **mess up** <both nonformal>; **clutter,** scatter

little ADJS 1 **small,** smallish; **slight,** exiguous; **puny, trifling,** poky, piffling *and* pindling *and* piddling *and* piddly <all nonformal>, **dinky** <nonformal>; cramped, limited; one-horse, two-by-four <nonformal>; pintsized <nonformal>, half-pint; knee-high, knee-high to a grasshopper; petite; short
2 **ungenerous, illiberal,** unchivalrous, mean, small, paltry, mingy, petty; **niggardly, stingy; narrow-minded,** narrow, narrow-gauged, closed, closed-minded, cramped, constricted, small-minded, mean-minded, narrow-hearted, mean-spirited
ADVS 3 **small, slightly,** fractionally; **on**

a small scale, in a small compass, in a small way, on a minuscule *or* infinitesimal scale; **in miniature,** in a nutshell

liturgy NOUNS **rite, ritual,** rituality, holy rite; order of worship; **ceremony, ceremonial; observance,** ritual observance; solemnity; **form,** formula, formulary, form of worship *or* service, mode of worship; prescribed form; service, function, duty, office, practice; **sacrament,** sacramental, mystery

live VERBS 1 **exist, be,** be in existence, be extant, have being; breathe; subsist, stand, obtain, hold, prevail, be the case; **occur,** be present, be there, be found, be met with, happen to be; **endure, last** *or* **last out,** bide, **abide,** dwell, perdure, **continue,** run, extend, **go on,** carry on, hold on, keep on, stay on, run on, stay the course, go the distance, go through with, grind *or* plug away; **live on,** continue to be, subsist, exist, tarry; **persist; survive,** defy *or* defeat time; live to fight another day
ADJS 2 **living, alive,** having life, very much alive, alive and well, alive and kicking <nonformal>, conscious, breathing, quick <old>, **animate,** animated, **vital,** zoetic, instinct with life, imbued *or* endowed with life, vivified, enlivened, inspirited; in the flesh, among the living, in the land of the living, on this side of the grave, aboveground; existent, viable; full of life, full of pep *or* go *and* pizzazz *or* moxie <nonformal>; **charged, electrified,** hot

lived-in ADJS **comfortable,** comfy <nonformal>; **cozy, snug,** snug as a bug in a rug; friendly, warm; **homelike,** homey *and* down-home <both nonformal>, homely

live-in ADJS **resident,** residing, living, dwelling, commorant, lodging, **staying,** remaining, abiding, cohabiting

livelihood NOUNS **support,** maintenance, sustainment, sustentation, sustenance, subsistence, keep, upkeep; **living,** meat, bread, daily bread

lively ADJS 1 **active, animated,** spirited, bubbly, ebullient, effervescent, vivacious, **sprightly,** chipper *and* perky <both nonformal>, pert; **spry,** breezy, brisk, energetic, eager, keen, can-do <nonformal>; full of life, full of pep *or* go *and* pizzazz *or* moxie <nonformal>; **peppy** *and* snappy *and* zingy <all nonformal>; frisky, bouncing, bouncy
ADVS 2 **actively, busily;** sprightly, **briskly,** breezily, energetically, animatedly, vivaciously, **spiritedly,** with life and spirit, with gusto; full tilt, in full swing, all out <nonformal>

liven VERBS **invigorate, animate,** enliven, liven up, vitalize, quicken, goose *or* jazz up <nonformal>; **exhilarate, stimulate,** hearten, galvanize, electrify, fire, build a fire under, inflame, warm, kindle, charge, charge up, psych *or* pump up <nonformal>, rouse, arouse, act like a tonic, be a shot in the arm <nonformal>

live off VERBS **sponge** *and* **sponge on** *and* **sponge off of** <all nonformal>; feed on, fatten on, batten on, use as a meal ticket

live wire NOUNS **man** *or* **woman of action, doer,** man of deeds; **hustler** *and* self-starter <both nonformal>, bustler; go-getter *and* ball of fire *and* powerhouse *and* human dynamo *and* spitfire <all nonformal>

live with VERBS **endure, bear up under,** bear the brunt, bear with, put up with, tolerate, carry *or* bear one's cross, take what comes, take the bitter with the sweet, abide with, brook, brave, brave out, hang in there, keep it up

livid ADJS 1 **ghastly,** lurid, **haggard,** cadaverous, sickly, deadly *or* deathly pale; pale as death *or* a ghost *or* a corpse, pale-faced, tallow-faced, wheyfaced; black and blue
2 **angry,** angered, **incensed, indignant, irate,** ireful; livid with rage, beside oneself, **wroth, wrathful,** wrathy, **cross,** wrought-up, worked up, riled up <nonformal>

living NOUNS 1 **support,** keep, upkeep; **livelihood, benefice,** incumbency, glebe, advowson
ADJS 2 **alive,** having life, live, very much alive, alive and well, alive and kicking <nonformal>, conscious, breathing, quick <old>, **animate,** animated, **vital,** zoetic, instinct with life, imbued *or* endowed with life, vivified, enlivened, inspirited

load NOUNS 1 **lading,** cargo, freight, charge, burden; **payload;** boatload, busload, carload, cartload, container-load, shipload, trailerload, trainload, truckload, vanload, wagonload
2 **full measure, capacity,** complement, the whole bit <nonformal>; bellyful *and*

snootful <both nonformal>, skinful *or* mouthful <both nonformal>

VERBS 3 **lade,** freight, burden; fill; **stow,** store, put in storage, warehouse; **pack,** pack away; pile, dump, heap, heap up, stack, mass; bag, sack, pocket

4 **burden,** load down *or* up, lade, cumber, **encumber,** charge, freight, tax, handicap, hamper, saddle; **weigh on** *or* **upon,** weigh heavy on, bear or rest hard upon, lie hard *or* heavy upon, press hard upon

loaded ADJS 1 **weighted, weighed** *or* **weighted down; burdened,** oppressed, laden, cumbered, encumbered, charged, fraught, freighted, taxed, saddled, hampered; **primed,** cocked, **loaded for bear** <nonformal>

2 well-heeled *and* filthy rich *and* in the money *or* dough *and* well-fixed *and* made of money *and* **rolling in money** *and* big-rich *and* rich-rich *and* lousy rich

loaf VERBS **idle,** do nothing, **laze,** lazy <nonformal>, take one's ease *or* leisure, **lounge; lie around,** lounge around, loll around, sit on one's ass *or* butt *or* duff <nonformal>, stand *or* hang around, **loiter about** *or* **around,** slouch, slouch around, **bum around** *and* mooch around <both nonformal>; let the grass grow under one's feet; twiddle one's thumbs

loafer NOUNS **idler, lounger,** loller, layabout <Brit nonformal>, couch potato <nonformal>, lotus-eater, *flâneur, flâneuse* <both Fr>, **do-nothing,** *fainéant* <Fr>, goof-off *and* fuck-off *and* goldbrick *and* goldbricker <all nonformal>, clock watcher; **sluggard,** slug, slouch, sloucher, lubber, stick-in-the-mud <nonformal>, gentleman of leisure

loan shark NOUNS **moneylender,** moneymonger; **usurer,** shylock <nonformal>

loathe VERBS **hate, detest, abhor,** execrate, **abominate,** hold in abomination, take an aversion to, shudder at, utterly detest, be death on, not stand, not stand the sight of, not stomach; scorn, **despise**

loathsome ADJS **offensive,** objectionable, odious, repulsive, repellent, rebarbative, **repugnant, revolting,** forbidding; **disgusting, sickening,** gross *and* yucky *and* grungy *and* scuzzy <all nonformal>, beastly <nonformal>, **vile, foul, nasty, nauseating**; fulsome, mephitic, miasmal, miasmic, malodorous, stinking, fetid, noisome, noxious

lob VERBS **throw,** fling, sling, pitch, toss, cast, hurl, heave, chuck

lobby NOUNS 1 legislative lobby, special-interest lobby; **pressure group,** special-interest group, special interests, single-issue group, PAC *or* political action committee

2 **vestibule,** entrance hall, entranceway, **foyer**

VERBS 3 **exercise** *or* **exert influence,** use one's influence, bring pressure to bear upon, lean on <nonformal>, act on, **work on,** bear upon, throw one's weight around *or* into the scale, say a few words to the right person *or* in the right quarter; get at *or* get the ear of <nonformal>; **pull strings** *or* **wires** *or* **ropes,** lobby through

lobbyist NOUNS **person** *or* **woman** *or* **man of influence,** a mover and shaker <nonformal>, wheeler-dealer <nonformal>, influencer, **wire-puller** <nonformal>; **powerbroker; influence peddler**

local ADJS **localized,** of a place, geographically limited, topical, vernacular, parochial, provincial, insular, limited, confined

locale NOUNS **location,** situation, place, position, spot, *lieu* <Fr>, placement, emplacement, stead; **whereabouts,** whereabout, ubicity; **area,** district, region; **locality,** locus; **setting, background,** backdrop, ground, surround, field, scene, arena, theater

locate VERBS 1 **situate,** site, place, position; emplace, spot <nonformal>, **install,** put in place; narrow *or* pin down; **map, chart,** put on the map *or* chart; put one's finger on, **fix,** assign *or* consign *or* relegate to a place; **pinpoint,** zero in on, home in on; **discover, find,** get; **hunt down,** search out, trace down, track down, **run down, run** *or* **bring to earth;** trace

2 **settle, settle down,** sit down, park <nonformal>, ensconce, ensconce oneself; take up one's abode *or* quarters, make one's home, **reside, inhabit**

location NOUNS **situation, place, position,** *lieu* <Fr>, placement, emplacement, stead; **whereabouts,** whereabout, ubicity; **site,** situs; **spot, point,** pinpoint, exact spot *or* point, very spot *or* point; *locus classicus* <L>; locale

lock NOUNS 1 **tress;** flowing locks, flowing tresses; **curl, ringlet,** earlock, *payess*

<Yiddish>; lovelock; frizz, frizzle; dreadlocks
2 bolt, bar, padlock, catch, safety catch; barrier
VERBS 3 **close, shut,** lock up, lock out, key, padlock, latch, bolt, bar, barricade

lockup NOUNS **confinement,** locking-up, caging, penning, putting behind barriers, impoundment, **restraint,** restriction; **prison,** correctional *or* correction facility, penal institution, **jail, gaol** <Brit>, jailhouse

lock up VERBS **secrete, hide away,** keep hidden, put away, store away, stow away, file and forget, seal up, put out of sight; **imprison, incarcerate, intern,** immure; **jail,** jug <nonformal>, throw into jail; lock in, bolt in, put *or* keep under lock and key; hold captive, hold prisoner, hold in captivity

lode NOUNS **deposit,** mineral deposit, pay dirt; **vein,** seam, dike, ore bed; rich lode, mother lode

lodestar NOUNS **ideal,** principle, **ambition,** aspiration, inspiration, guiding light *or* star; **guiding star,** cynosure <old>, **polestar,** polar star, Polaris, **North Star**

lodestone NOUNS **magnet,** artificial magnet, field magnet, bar magnet, horseshoe magnet, electromagnet; magnetite

lodge NOUNS 1 **cabin,** log cabin; chalet, snuggery; **burrow,** tunnel, earth, run, couch
VERBS 2 **deposit,** repose, reposit, rest, **lay, put down,** set down, lay down
3 **house,** domicile, domiciliate; provide with a roof, have as a guest *or* lodger, shelter, harbor; **quarter, put up,** billet, room, bed, berth, bunk; stable

lodger NOUNS **roomer,** paying guest; **boarder,** board-and-roomer, **transient,** transient guest *or* boarder

lodging NOUNS **quarters, living quarters; lodgings,** lodgment; diggings *and* digs <both Brit nonformal>, pad *and* crib <both nonformal>, room; **rooms,** berth, roost, accommodations; **housing,** shelter, *gîte* <Fr>

loft NOUNS **attic,** attic room, **garret,** sky parlor; cockloft, hayloft; storeroom, junk room

lofty ADJS 1 **elevated,** triumphal, high, high-flown, highfalutin *and* highfaluting <both nonformal>, high-toned <nonformal>; high-minded, lofty-minded; high-headed, high-nosed <nonformal>
2 **eminent, prominent,** outstanding, standout, towering, soaring, overtopping, exalted, sublime; august, majestic, noble, distinguished; **haughty,** toplofty

log NOUNS 1 **journal,** ship's log, **logbook;** diary; time sheet, time book, daybook; timecard, time ticket, clock card, check sheet; datebook
VERBS 2 **make an entry,** enter, post, post up, journalize, book, docket, note, minute

logic NOUNS **reasonableness,** reasonability, **logicalness,** logicality, **rationality,** sensibleness, soundness, justness, justifiability, admissibility, cogency; **sense,** common sense, sound sense, sweet reason, **reason;** plausibility

logical ADJS **reasonable,** rational, cogent, sensible, sane, sound, well-thought-out, legitimate, just, justifiable, admissible; credible; plausible; as it should be, as it ought to be; well-argued, **well-founded,** well-grounded; consistent, self-consistent

logjam NOUNS **delay,** stoppage, jam <nonformal>, obstruction, tie-up *and* bind <both nonformal>, **block,** blockage, **hang-up** <nonformal>; gridlock

logo NOUNS **trademark,** logotype, registered trademark, trade name, service mark

logy ADJS **torpid,** languorous, languid, apathetic, phlegmatic, **sluggish,** dopey <nonformal>, groggy, heavy, leaden, **dull,** flat, slack, tame, **dead,** lifeless

loiter VERBS **dawdle, linger,** tarry, delay, dally, dillydally, shilly-shally, lollygag, waste time, **take one's time,** take one's own sweet time; goof off *or* around <nonformal>; lag, drag, trail; flag, falter, halt

loiterer NOUNS **lingerer, dawdler,** dawdle, laggard, procrastinator, foot-dragger, stick-in-the-mud <nonformal>, drone, slug, sluggard, lie-abed, sleepyhead, goof-off <nonformal>, goldbrick <nonformal>

loll VERBS **lie, lie down,** recline, repose, lounge, sprawl, drape *or* spread oneself, splay, lie limply

lolling NOUNS 1 **idling, loafing,** lazing, *flânerie* <Fr>, goofing off <nonformal>, goldbricking <nonformal>; *dolce far niente* <Ital>; dallying, dillydallying, mopery, dawdling; lounging

ADJS 2 **lying, reclining,** reposing, flat on one's back; sprawling, lounging; sprawled, spread, splay, splayed, draped

lone ADJS **solitary,** alone; **in solitude,** by oneself, all alone; **lonely,** lonesome; sole, unique, a certain

loneliness NOUNS **aloneness,** loneness, **lonesomeness,** soleness, singleness; **privacy,** solitariness, **solitude;** separateness, aloofness, detachment, seclusion, sequestration, **withdrawal, alienation,** standing *or* moving *or* keeping apart, **isolation**

lonely ADJS **solitary,** alone; **in solitude,** by oneself, all alone; **lonesome, lone;** lonely-hearts

loner NOUNS **recluse,** solitaire, solitary, solitudinarian; cloistered monk *or* nun; **hermit,** eremite, anchorite, anchoret; marabout; hermitess, anchoress; **ascetic;** closet cynic; stylite, pillarist, pillar saint; **individualist,** lone wolf <nonformal>

lonesomeness NOUNS **aloneness,** loneness, **loneliness,** soleness, singleness; **privacy,** solitariness, **solitude;** separateness, aloofness, detachment, seclusion, sequestration, **withdrawal, alienation,** standing *or* moving *or* keeping apart, **isolation**

long ADJS 1 **lengthy;** longish, longsome; tall; **extensive, far-reaching,** fargoing, far-flung; sesquipedalian, sesquipedal; as long as one's arm, a mile long; **time-consuming,** interminable, without end, no end of *or* to, overlong, marathon, lasting, **lingering,** languishing
ADVS 2 **for a long time, for long, interminably,** unendingly, undyingly, persistently, protractedly, enduringly; for ever so long <nonformal>, for many a long day, for life *or* a lifetime, for an age *or* ages, for a coon's *or* dog's age <nonformal>, for a month of Sundays <nonformal>, **forever and a day, forever and ever,** for years on end, **for days on end, etc;** morning, noon, and night; hour after hour, day after day, month after month, year after year; day in day out, month in month out, year in year out; till hell freezes over <nonformal>, till you're blue in the face <nonformal>, till the cows come home <nonformal>, from here to eternity, till the end of time; since time began

longevity NOUNS **durability, endurance,** duration, durableness, **lastingness,** *longueur* <Fr>, perenniality, abidingness, long-lastingness, perdurability; long-livedness

longing NOUNS 1 **yearning, yen** <nonformal>; desiderium, **hankering** <nonformal>, **pining,** honing <nonformal>, aching; **nostalgia, homesickness,** *Heimweh* <Ger>, *mal du pays* and *maladie du pays* <both Fr>; nostomania
ADJS 2 **wistful,** wishful; **yearning,** yearnful, **hankering** <nonformal>, languishing, pining, honing <nonformal>; **nostalgic, homesick**

long-lived ADJS **durable,** perdurable, **lasting, enduring,** perduring, **abiding, continuing,** remaining, staying; **stable,** persisting, **persistent,** perennial; long-term; tough, hardy, vital, longevous *or* longeval

long shot NOUNS **fluke** <nonformal>, freak, freak occurrence *or* accident; chance hit, lucky shot, one in a million, long odds, poor bet, hundred-to-one shot <nonformal>

long-term ADJS **steadfast, constant,** intransient, immutable, unfading, evergreen, sempervirent, **permanent**, perennial, **long-lasting,** long-standing, of long duration *or* standing, diuturnal

long-winded ADJS **wordy, verbose; talkative**; **prolix,** windy <nonformal>, longiloquent; **protracted,** extended, *de longue haleine* <Fr>, lengthy, long, **long-drawn-out,** long-spun, spun-out, endless, unrelenting

long word NOUNS hard word, jawbreaker *or* jawtwister *and* two-dollar *or* five-dollar word <all nonformal>, polysyllable; sesquipedalian, sesquipedalia <pl>; lexiphanicism, grandiloquence

look NOUNS 1 **sight,** the eye *and* a look-see *and* a gander <all nonformal>, eye, view, regard; sidelong look; leer, leering look; aspect, view; feature, lineaments
2 **air,** mien, demeanor, carriage, bearing, port, posture, stance, poise, presence; guise, garb, complexion, color
VERBS 3 **peer,** have a look, take a gander *and* take a look <both nonformal>, direct the eyes, turn *or* bend the eyes, cast one's eye, lift up the eyes; **look at,** take a look at, eye, **eyeball** <nonformal>, have a look-see <nonformal>, look on *or* upon, gaze at *or* upon; **watch, observe, view, regard;** keep one's eyes peeled *or* skinned, be watch-

ful *or* observant *or* vigilant, keep one's eyes open; keep in sight *or* view, hold in view; look after; **check** *and* **check out** <both nonformal>, scope <nonformal>, scope out <nonformal>; keep under observation, spy on, have an eye out, keep an eye out, keep an eye on, keep a weather eye on; **reconnoiter,** scout, get the lay of the land; **peek, peep,** pry, take a peep *or* peek

look-alikes NOUNS **set,** group, matching pair *or* set, his and hers <nonformal>, couple, pair, twins, two of a kind, birds of a feather, peas in a pod

lookout NOUNS 1 **vigilance, wariness,** prudence, **watchfulness,** watching, observance, **surveillance; watch,** vigil; *qui vive* <Fr>; **sharp eye,** weather eye, peeled eye, watchful eye, eagle eye
2 **warner,** cautioner, admonisher, monitor; **lookout man; sentinel,** sentry; **signalman,** signaler, flagman; lighthouse keeper; **watchman, watch,** watcher; watchkeeper

looks NOUNS **features, lineaments,** traits, lines; **countenance,** face, visage, feature, favor, brow, physiognomy; cast of countenance, **cut of one's jib** <nonformal>, facial appearance *or* expression, cast, turn

loom VERBS 1 **weave,** tissue; **interweave, interlace, intertwine,** interknit, interthread, intertissue, intertie, intertwist; inweave, intort
2 **appear,** become visible; heave in sight, appear on the horizon; **bulk,** loom large, bulk large, stand out; **tower above,** rise above, overtop; **exceed, transcend,** outstrip; **lower,** spell *or* mean trouble, look threatening, loom up; **be imminent**; **forebode**; **warn**

looming ADJS **imminent, impending,** impendent, overhanging, hanging over one's head, waiting, lurking, **threatening,** lowering, **menacing,** lying in ambush, **brewing,** gathering, preparing; **coming, forthcoming,** upcoming, to come, about to be, about *or* going to happen, **approaching, nearing,** looming up, looming in the distance *or* future; **near, close,** immediate, instant, soon to be, **at hand,** near at hand, close at hand; **in the offing,** on the horizon, **in prospect,** already in sight, just around the corner, in view, in one's eye, in store, in reserve, **in the wind,** in the womb of time; on the knees *or* lap of the gods, in the cards <nonformal>; that will be, that is to be; future

in danger imminent
Spenser

loonybin NOUNS **insane asylum,** asylum, lunatic asylum, **madhouse,** mental institution, mental home, bedlam; **bughouse** *and* nuthouse *and* laughing academy *and* **booby hatch** *and* funny farm <all nonformal>; mental hospital, psychiatric hospital *or* ward

loop NOUNS 1 **circuit, round,** revolution, **circle,** full circle, go-round, **cycle,** orbit, ambit; pass; round trip, *aller-retour* <Fr>; **beat,** rounds, **walk,** tour, turn, lap
VERBS 2 **encircle, circle,** ensphere, belt, belt in, zone, cincture, encincture; **girdle,** gird, begird, engird; ring, band; wreathe, wreathe *or* twine around

loophole NOUNS **way out,** way of escape, hole to creep out of, escape hatch, escape clause, saving clause; pretext; **alternative,** choice

loose VERBS 1 **loosen, slacken, relax;** slack, slack off; ease, ease off, let up; **free,** let go, unleash; **disjoin,** unknit, unravel, dismember; **sow confusion,** open Pandora's box; unstick, unglue; **scatter,** disperse, diffuse; **open up, unclog,** unblock, unjam, unbar
ADJS 2 **adrift, afloat,** unmoored, untied, unanchored; **drooping, droopy,** limp, nodding, floppy <nonformal>, loppy, lop; **sagging,** saggy, swag, sagging in folds; baggy; **lax, slack,** relaxed; imprecise, sloppy <nonformal>, careless, slipshod; remiss, negligent; untrammeled, unrestrained
3 **wanton, wayward,** Paphian; **lax,** slack, loose-moraled, of loose morals, of easy virtue, easy <nonformal>, **light,** no better than she should be, whorish, chambering, **promiscuous**
4 **inaccurate, incorrect, inexact,** unfactual, **unprecise,** imprecise, unspecific, lax, unrigorous

loosen VERBS **loose,** let loose, cut loose *or* free, unloose, unloosen; **unbind, untie,** unstrap, unbuckle, unlash; **unfetter, unshackle,** unchain, unhandcuff, untie one's hands; **unleash,** untether, unhobble; unharness, unyoke, unbridle; unlock, unlatch, unbolt, unbar
2 **slacken, relax;** slack, slack off; ease,

ease off, let up; **loose, free,** let go, unleash; unstick, unglue

loot NOUNS 1 **booty,** spoil, **spoils, swag** <nonformal>, ill-gotten gains, **plunder,** prize, haul, take, pickings, stealings, stolen goods, hot goods *or* items <nonformal>; pork barrel, spoils of office, public trough; till, public till
VERBS 2 **plunder, pillage, sack,** ransack, rifle, freeboot, spoil, spoliate, despoil, depredate, prey on *or* upon, **raid,** reive <Scots>, ravage, ravish, raven, sweep, gut

looter NOUNS **plunderer, pillager, marauder,** rifler, sacker, spoiler, despoiler, spoliator, depredator, **raider,** moss-trooper, reiver <Scots>, forayer, forager, ravisher, ravager

lop VERBS **amputate,** mutilate, abscind; **prune,** pare, peel, clip, crop, bob, dock, nip, shear, strip, strip off *or* away

lopsided ADJS **unbalanced, ill-balanced,** overbalanced, off-balance, tippy, listing, heeling, leaning, canted, top-heavy; slaunchways *and* cockeyed *and* skewgee *and* skygodlin <all nonformal>

lord NOUNS **nobleman,** noble, gentleman; **peer; aristocrat, patrician,** Brahman, **blue blood,** thoroughbred, silk-stocking, lace-curtain, swell *and* upper-cruster <both nonformal>; **grandee,** magnifico, magnate, optimate; laird <Scots>, lordling; seignior, seigneur, *hidalgo* <Sp>; **master,** lord and master

lordly ADJS **imperious,** aristocratic, totally self-assured; hubristic; masterful, magisterial, **high-and-mighty;** elitist

lore NOUNS **body of knowledge,** corpus, body of learning, store of knowledge, system of knowledge, treasury of information; **superstition,** superstitiousness; popular belief, **old wives' tale;** tradition, folklore

lose VERBS lose out <nonformal>, lose the day, come off second best, **get** *or* **have the worst of it, meet one's Waterloo; fall,** succumb, tumble, bow, go down, go under, **bite** *or* **lick the dust,** take the count <nonformal>; snatch defeat from the jaws of victory; throw in the towel, say 'uncle'; have enough; incur loss, **suffer loss,** undergo privation *or* deprivation, be bereaved *or* bereft of, have no more, meet with a loss; kiss good-bye <nonformal>; let slip through one's fingers; **forfeit,** default; **mislay,** misplace; **lose everything,** go broke *and* lose one's shirt *and* take a bath *or* to the cleaners *and* tap out *and* go to Tap City <all nonformal>

lose face VERBS **incur disgrace,** incur disesteem *or* dishonor *or* discredit, get a black eye <nonformal>, be shamed, earn a bad name *or* reproach *or* reproof, forfeit one's good opinion, fall into disrepute, seal one's infamy; lose one's good name, lose countenance, lose credit, **lose caste; disgrace oneself,** lower oneself, demean oneself, drag one's banner in the dust, degrade *or* debase oneself, act beneath oneself, dirty *or* soil one's hands, get one's hands dirty, sully *or* lower oneself, derogate, stoop, descend, ride to a fall, fall from one's high estate, foul one's own nest

loser NOUNS the vanquished; good loser, game loser, sport *or* **good sport** <nonformal>; poor sport, poor loser; **underdog,** also-ran; **unfortunate,** poor unfortunate, the plaything *or* toy *or* sport of fortune, fortune's fool; sure loser *and* nonstarter <both nonformal>; hard case *and* sad sack *and* hard-luck guy <all nonformal>

loss NOUNS **losing, privation,** getting away, losing hold of; **deprivation, bereavement,** taking away, stripping, dispossession, despoilment, despoliation, spoliation, robbery; divestment, denudation; **sacrifice, forfeit, forfeiture,** giving up *or* over, denial; **destruction, ruin,** perdition, total loss, dead loss; **disadvantage,** drawback, liability; **detriment,** impairment, damage, hurt, harm, mischief, injury; **a step back** *or* **backward,** a loss of ground

lost ADJS **gone;** forfeited, forfeit; by the board, out the window *and* down the drain *or* tube <all nonformal>; **nonrenewable;** long-lost; lost to; wasted, consumed, depleted, squandered, dissipated, diffused, **expended; worn away, eroded,** ablated, used, used up, shrunken; stripped, clear-cut; squandered; irretrievable; **gone to waste,** run *or* gone to seed; down the drain *or* spout *or* rathole <nonformal>; misspent; **irreclaimable,** irredeemable, unredeemable, unregenerate, **irreformable,** incorrigible, past praying for; shriftless, graceless; **astray,** abroad, adrift, **at sea,** off the track, out of one's reckoning, out of one's bearings, disoriented

lost cause NOUNS **fool's errand,** wild-goose chase; **hopeless case; goner** *and* gone goose *or* gosling *and* dead duck <all nonformal>

lot NOUNS 1 **land,** property, grounds; parcel, plot, plat, quadrat; **portion, share,** interest, part, stake, stock, piece, bit, segment; **bite** *and* **cut** *and* **slice** *and* **chunk** *and* slice of the pie *or* melon *and* piece of the action <all nonformal>, **allotment, proportion, percentage,** measure, quantum, **quota**
2 **fate,** fatality, **fortune,** cup, **portion,** appointed lot, karma, kismet, weird, *moira* <Gk>, future; **destiny,** destination, **end,** final lot; the way the cards fall, the way the cookie crumbles *or* the ball bounces <both nonformal>

the lot NOUNS **all, the whole,** the entirety, everything, all the above *or* all of the above <both nonformal>, the aggregate, the assemblage, one and all, all and sundry, each and every <nonformal>; the corpus, everything from soup to nuts *and* everything but the kitchen sink <both nonformal>

lotion NOUNS **balm, salve,** ointment, unguent, *unguentum* <L>, cerate, unction, balsam, oil, emollient, demulcent, inunction, chrism

lots NOUNS **lot,** deal, no end of, **good** *or* **great deal, considerable,** sight, **heap,** pile, stack, loads, raft, slew, whole slew, spate, wad, **batch,** mess, mint, peck, pack, pot, **tidy sum,** quite a little; **oodles, gobs, scads;** bumper crop, rich harvest, bonanza, enough and to spare, enough and then some; fat of the land

lottery NOUNS drawing, sweepstakes *or* sweepstake *or* sweep; draft lottery; **raffle; state lottery,** Lotto, Pick Six, Pick Four; tombola <Brit>; number lottery, numbers pool, **numbers game** *or* **policy,** Chinese lottery <nonformal>; interest lottery, Dutch *or* class lottery; tontine

loud ADJS 1 loud-sounding, forte, fortissimo; loudish; **resounding,** ringing, plangent, pealing; full, sonorous; **deafening,** ear-deafening, **ear-splitting,** head-splitting, ear-rending, ear-piercing, piercing; **thunderous,** thundering, window-rattling, earthshaking, enough to wake the dead; **insistent,** instant, **importunate,** urgent, pertinacious, pressing, clamant, crying, clamorous; persistent
2 **gaudy, tawdry;** gorgeous, colorful; **garish, blatant, flagrant,** shameless, **brazen,** brazenfaced, lurid, extravagant, sensational, **spectacular,** glaring, flaring, flaunting, screaming <nonformal>, obtrusive, vulgar, crude; meretricious
ADVS 3 **loudly, aloud,** lustily; **boomingly,** thunderously, thunderingly; **noisily,** uproariously; ringingly, resoundingly; with a loud voice, at the top of one's voice, forte, *fortemente* <Ital>, fortissimo

loudmouthed ADJS **loud-voiced,** full-mouthed, full-throated, big-voiced, clarion-voiced, **stentorian,** stentorious, like Stentor

lounge NOUNS 1 **anteroom,** antechamber; side room, byroom; **waiting room,** *salle d'attente* <Fr>; **reception room,** presence chamber *or* room, audience chamber; greenroom, wardroom
VERBS 2 **lie, lie down,** recline, repose, sprawl, loll, drape *or* spread oneself, splay, lie limply; **idle,** do nothing, **laze,** lazy <nonformal>, take one's ease *or* leisure, take one's time, **loaf; lie around,** lounge around, loll around, sit on one's ass *or* butt *or* duff <nonformal>, stand *or* hang around, **loiter about** *or* **around,** slouch, slouch around, **bum around** *and* mooch around <both nonformal>

I loafe and invite my soul, I lean and loafe at my ease
WALT WHITMAN

lousy ADJS

<nonformal> punk, bum, badass, shitty, crappy, cruddy, cheesy, gross, raunchy, piss-poor, rat-ass, **crummy,** grim, icky, yecchy, stinking, stinky, creepy, hairy, god-awful, gosh-awful

lout NOUNS **oaf,** boor, lubber, **gawk,** yokel, rube, hick, hayseed, bumpkin, clod, clodhopper

lovable ADJS **endearing,** likable, adorable, admirable, lovely, lovesome, sweet, winning, winsome; **charming**

love NOUNS 1 **affection, attachment,** devotion, fondness, sentiment, warm feeling, soft spot in one's heart, weakness <nonformal>, like, **liking,** fancy, shine <nonformal>; passion, tender feeling *or* passion, **ardor,** ardency, fervor, heart, flame; physical love, Amor, Eros, bodily love, libido, sexual love, sex;

desire, yearning; charity, *caritas* <L>, brotherly love, Christian love, agape, loving concern, **caring;** spiritual love, platonic love; married love, conjugal love; **sweetheart, loved one,** beloved, darling, dear, dear one, dearly beloved, well-beloved, truelove, beloved object, **object of one's affections,** light of one's eye *or* life, light of love

an insatiate thirst of enjoying a greedily desired object
MONTAIGNE

a spiritual coupling of two souls
BEN JOHNSON

VERBS 2 **be fond of,** be in love with, **care for, like, fancy,** have a fancy for, take an interest in, **dote on** *or* **upon,** be desperately in love, burn with love; be partial to, have a soft spot in one's heart for, have a weakness *or* fondness for

3 <nonformal> **go for,** have an eye *or* eyes for, only have eyes for, be sweet on, have a crush *or* mash *or* case on; have it bad, carry a torch *or* the torch for

love affair NOUNS **affair,** affair of the heart, **amour, romance,** romantic tie *or* bond, something between, thing <nonformal>, liaison, entanglement, intrigue; **dalliance,** amorous play, the love game, flirtation, hanky-panky, lollygagging <nonformal>; illicit *or* unlawful love, forbidden *or* unsanctified love, adulterous affair, adultery, unfaithfulness, infidelity, cuckoldry

love child NOUNS **bastard,** illegitimate, illegitimate *or* bastard child, whoreson, by-blow, child born out of wedlock *or* without benefit of clergy *or* on the wrong side of the blanket, natural child, *nullius filius* <L>

loveless ADJS **unloved,** unbeloved, uncherished; **lovelorn,** forsaken, **rejected,** jilted, thrown over <nonformal>, spurned, crossed in love

love letter NOUNS billet-doux, mash note <nonformal>; valentine

love life NOUNS **sexuality,** sexual nature, sexualism; **love**, sexual activity, lovemaking, marriage; **carnality, sensuality**; **libido,** sex drive, sexual instinct *or* urge

lovelorn ADJS **unloved,** unbeloved, uncherished, loveless; forsaken, **rejected,** jilted, thrown over <nonformal>, spurned, crossed in love; lovesick, languishing

lovely ADJS **delightful,** exquisite; **charming, attractive,** endearing, engaging, appealing, prepossessing, heartwarming, **captivating,** irresistible, ravishing, enravishing; **winning,** winsome, taking, fetching, heart-robbing; inviting, tempting, tantalizing; **pretty,** pulchritudinous, **graceful**

lovemaking NOUNS 1 dalliance, amorous dalliance, billing and cooing; **fondling, caressing,** hugging, kissing; cuddling, snuggling, nestling, nuzzling; bundling; sexual intercourse

2 <nonformal> **making out, necking, petting,** spooning, smooching, lollygagging, canoodling, playing kissy-face *or* kissy-kissy *or* kissy-poo *or* kissy-huggy *or* lickey-face *or* spacky-lips, pitching *or* flinging woo, sucking face, swapping spit

lover NOUNS **admirer,** adorer, amorist; infatuate, paramour, **suitor, wooer,** pursuer, follower; **flirt,** coquette; vampire, vamp; conquest, catch; devotee; date *and* steady <both nonformal>; significant other

loving ADJS lovesome, **fond, adoring,** devoted, affectionate, demonstrative, romantic, **sentimental, tender,** soft <nonformal>, melting; **careful,** heedful, regardful, mindful, thoughtful, considerate, caring, solicitous; **attentive**

low ADJS 1 **deep,** deep-toned, deep-pitched, deep-sounding, deepmouthed, deep-echoing; **hollow, sepulchral;** low-pitched, low-toned, grave, heavy
2 feeling low, low-spirited, **in low spirits; down in the mouth** <nonformal>, in the doldrums, **down in the dumps** *and* **in the dumps** *and* in the doleful dumps <all nonformal>, in the depths; **despondent,** desponding; **despairing**, weary of life, suicidal, world-weary; pessimistic; spiritless, heartless, **woebegone; humble, lowly,** poor, mean, small, inglorious, undistinguished
3 **unelevated,** flat, low-lying; short, squat, squatty, stumpy, runty; **lowered,** debased, depressed; demoted; **reduced**; prone, supine, prostrate *or* prostrated,

couchant, crouched, stooped, recumbent; laid low, knocked flat, decked <nonformal>; low-set, low-hung; **low-built,** low-sized, low-statured, low-bodied; low-level, low-leveled; neap; knee-high, knee-high to a grasshopper <nonformal>
4 **base, mean, ignoble,** vile, scurvy, sorry, scrubby, beggarly; low-minded, base-minded
ADVS 5 **faintly, softly,** gently, subduedly, hushedly, dimly, feebly, weakly; near the ground; at a low ebb

lowbrow NOUNS 1 **ignoramus, know-nothing;** no scholar, puddinghead, dunce, fool
ADJS 2 **unlearned, inerudite,** unerudite, **uneducated,** unschooled, uninstructed, untutored, unbriefed, untaught, unedified, unguided; ill-educated, unlettered, **unscholarly,** unread, unbookish, bookless <old>, unbooked; nonintellectual, **unintellectual;** lowbrowed *and* lowbrowish <both nonformal>

low-class ADJS **inferior, poor,** punk <nonformal>, **base, mean, common,** coarse

low-cut ADJS low-necked, décolleté, strapless, half-clothed

lowdown ADJS **base,** low, mean, crummy

the lowdown NOUNS **inside information,** private *or* confidential information; **the inside dope** *and* inside wire *and* **hot tip** <all nonformal>

lower VERBS 1 **reduce,** decrease, diminish, lessen, take from; **depress,** de-escalate, damp, dampen, **step down** *and* tune down *and* phase down *or* out *and* scale back *or* down *and* roll back *or* down <all nonformal>; depreciate, **deflate; curtail,** retrench; deduct; **deepen, sink;** countersink; **demote, degrade,** debase, abase, humble, humiliate, bust <nonformal>
ADJS 2 **inferior, subordinate,** secondary; junior; second *or* third string *and* one-horse *and* penny-ante *and* dinky <all nonformal>, second *or* third rank, low in the pecking order; **lesser;** in the shade, thrown into the shade; **common,** vulgar; **reduced,** decreased, diminished, dropped, fallen

lower class NOUNS **lower classes,** lower orders, plebs, workers, working class, working people, proletariat, proles <Brit nonformal>, laboring class *or* classes

lowest ADJS **humble, lowly,** low, **poor, mean,** small, inglorious, undistinguished; humblest, lowliest; **least, smallest,** littlest, slightest, shortest; rock-bottom, bottom

low-grade ADJS **inferior, poor,** punk <nonformal>, base, mean, common, coarse, cheesy *and* tacky <both nonformal>, tinny; shabby, seedy; cheap, Mickey Mouse <nonformal>, paltry; low-class, low-quality

low key NOUNS **reserve, restraint,** constraint, backwardness, retiring disposition; low visibility, low profile

lowlife NOUNS **wretch,** mean *or* miserable wretch; **bum** *and* bummer *and* lowlifer *and* **mucker** <all nonformal>, caitiff, pilgarlic; **good-for-nothing,** good-for-naught, no-good <nonformal>, ne'er-do-well, wastrel, *vaurien* <Fr>, worthless fellow

loyal ADJS **faithful,** devoted, allegiant; **true, true-blue,** true to one's colors; **constant, steadfast,** unswerving, steady, consistent, stable, unfailing, staunch, firm, solid

loyalist NOUNS **partisan, party member,** party man *or* woman; regular, stalwart; wheelhorse, party wheelhorse; heeler, ward heeler, **party hack;** party faithful

loyal opposition NOUNS **political party, party,** minor party, opposition party

loyalty NOUNS **fidelity,** faithfulness, faith; constancy, **steadfastness,** staunchness, firmness; trueness, troth, true blue; **allegiance, fealty,** homage; bond, tie; attachment, adherence, adhesion; devotion, devotedness

lozenge NOUNS **pill,** bolus, **tablet, capsule,** troche

LSD NOUNS

<nonformal> acid, big D, blotter, blue acid, blue cheer, blue heaven, California sunshine, cap, cubes, D, deeda, dots, electric Kool-Aid, haze, L, mellow yellows, orange cubes, pearly gates, pink owsley, strawberry fields, sugar, sunshine, tabs, yellow

lubricant NOUNS **lubricator,** lubricating oil, lubricating agent, antifriction; graphite, plumbago, black lead; silicone; glycerin; wax, cerate

lubricate VERBS **facilitate,** ease; **grease the wheels** <nonformal>; smooth, **smooth** *or* **pave the way,** ease the way, grease *or* soap the ways <both nonformal>, prepare the way, **clear the way,** run interference for <nonformal>, open the way, open the door to; make frictionless *or* dissipationless, remove friction, grease, oil; **speed, expedite,** quicken, hasten; **help along,** help on its way

lucid ADJS 1 **clear, crystal-clear,** clear as crystal, clear as day, clear as the nose on one's face; **plain, distinct,** pellucid, limpid, perspicuous, transpicuous, **transparent,** translucent, luminous; **coherent,** connected, consistent; lucent, luculent
2 **sane,** sane-minded, **rational,** reasonable, sensible, normal, wholesome, clearheaded, clearminded, balanced, **sound,** mentally sound, of sound mind, *compos mentis* <L>, right, right in the head, **in one's right mind,** in possession of one's faculties *or* senses, together *and* all there <both nonformal>; in touch with reality

luck NOUNS **good fortune** *or* **luck,** happy fortune, **fortune,** the breaks <nonformal>; **fortunateness,** luckiness, smiles of fortune, fortune's favor

lucky ADJS **fortunate, providential;** in luck; blessed with luck, favored; born under a lucky star, born on the sunny side of the hedge; **auspicious**

lucrative ADJS **gainful,** productive, **profitable,** remunerative, remuneratory, fat, paying, well-paying, high-yield, high-yielding; advantageous, worthwhile; banausic, moneymaking, breadwinning

lucre NOUNS **wealth, riches,** opulence *or* opulency, richness, wealthiness; **prosperity,** prosperousness, **affluence,** comfortable *or* easy circumstances, independence; **money,** pelf, gold, mammon; **the wherewithal,** filthy lucre <nonformal>, the almighty dollar, root of all evil

ludicrous ADJS **absurd, nonsensical,** insensate, ridiculous, laughable; **foolish, crazy;** preposterous, cockamamie <nonformal>, fantastic, fantastical, grotesque, monstrous, wild, weird, **outrageous,** incredible, beyond belief, *outré* <Fr>, extravagant, **bizarre**

lug VERBS **pull,** carry, draw, heave, haul, hale, tote, tug, tow, take in tow

luggage NOUNS **impedimenta,** dunnage, **baggage,** bag and baggage, traps, tackle, apparatus, truck, gear, kit, outfit, duffel

lukewarm ADJS **indifferent, halfhearted,** zealless, perfunctory, fervorless; **cool, cold**; tepid, Laodicean; neither hot nor cold, neither one thing nor the other

lull NOUNS 1 **respite, recess, rest, pause,** halt, stay, **break,** surcease, suspension, interlude, **intermission,** spell <Australia>, letup <nonformal>, **time out** <nonformal>, time to catch one's breath; **breathing spell,** breathing time, breathing place, breathing space, breath; **breather;** rest; **calm,** calm before the storm
VERBS 2 **quiet,** quieten, **soothe,** quiesce, **calm,** calm down, tranquilize, pacify, passivize, pour oil on troubled waters; hush, still, rest, compose, gentle, rock, cradle, rock to sleep; ease, steady, smooth, smoothen, smooth over, smooth down, even out; pour oil on troubled waters

lullaby NOUNS **sleep-inducer,** sleep-producer, sleep-provoker, sleep-bringer, hypnotic, soporific, somnifacient; song

lumber NOUNS 1 **wood, timber,** hardwood, softwood; pole, post, beam, **board,** plank
VERBS 2 **plod,** plug <nonformal>, peg, shamble, **trudge,** tramp, stump, plod along, plug along <nonformal>, schlep <nonformal>; **flounder,** muddle; stumble, **slip; encumber,** cumber, burden, saddle with, weigh *or* weight down

lumbering NOUNS 1 **forestry,** arboriculture, tree farming, silviculture, forest management; Christmas tree farming; forestation, afforestation, reforestation; logging
ADJS 2 **poking,** poky, slow-poky <nonformal>; tottering, staggering, toddling, trudging, ambling, waddling, shuffling; **slow-moving,** slow-creeping, snail-paced, snail-like, tortoiselike, turtlelike, slow as slow, slow as molasses *or* molasses in January, slow as death; **bulky, hulky,** hulking, lumpish, lumpy, clumpish, lubberly; **clumsy,** awkward, **unwieldy; stiff, stilted, formal,** Latinate, *guindé* <Fr>, **labored,** ponderous, elephantine, cumbrous, leaden, heavy

luminary NOUNS **celebrity,** man *or* woman of mark *or* note, person of note *or* consequence, **notable,** great man *or* woman, master spirit, worthy, name, **big name,** figure, public figure, **somebody; important person, VIP** *and* **standout** <both nonformal>, personage, **idol,** popular idol, tin god *or* little tin god <nonformal>; lion, social lion; **star, superstar,** megastar, hot stuff <nonfor-

mal>; leading light, hard *or* tough act to follow <nonformal>

luminous ADJS **incandescent,** candescent; **lustrous, radiant,** irradiative; **shining,** shiny, burning, lamping, streaming; **beaming,** beamy; **gleaming,** gleamy, glinting

lummox NOUNS **oaf, lout,** boor, lubber, **gawk,** gawky, yokel, rube, hick, hayseed, bumpkin, clod, clodhopper

lump NOUNS clump, **hunk** *and* **chunk** <both nonformal>, **mass,** piece, **gob** *and* glob <both nonformal>, gobbet; batch, **wad,** block, loaf; pat <of butter>; clod; nugget

lumpy ADJS **bulky, hulky,** hulking, lumpish, lumping <nonformal>, clumpish; **congealed,** coagulated, clotted, grumous; **curdled,** curded, clabbered

lunacy NOUNS **insanity,** insaneness, unsaneness, **madness,** *folie* <Fr>, **craziness,** daftness, oddness, strangeness, queerness, abnormality; loss of touch *or* contact with reality, loss of mind *or* reason; dementedness, dementia, athymia, brainsickness, mindsickness, mental sickness, sickness

lunar ADJS **crescent-shaped,** crescentlike, crescent, crescentic, crescentiform; sickle-shaped, sickle-like, falcate, falciform; moon-shaped, moonlike, lunate, lunular, luniform

lunatic NOUNS 1 **madman, madwoman** dement, *fou* and *aliéné* <both Fr>, non compos, *bacayaro* <Japanese>; bedlamite, Tom o' Bedlam; **maniac,** raving lunatic; homicidal maniac, psychopathic killer, berserk *or* berserker
ADJS 2 **insane,** unsane, **mad,** stark-mad, mad as a hatter, mad as a march hare, **stark-staring mad,** maddened, **sick,** crazed, moonstruck, **daft,** non compos mentis, non compos, *baca* <Japanese>, **unsound,** of unsound mind, **demented, deranged,** deluded, disoriented, unhinged, **unbalanced,** unsettled, distraught, wandering, mazed, crackbrained, brainsick, sick *or* soft in the head, not right, not in one's right mind, **touched,** touched in the head, **out of one's mind,** out of one's senses *or* wits, bereft of reason, reasonless, irrational, deprived of reason, senseless, witless

lunchroom NOUNS **cafeteria,** eating place, eatery *and* beanery *and* hashery *and* hash house *and* greasy spoon <all nonformal>; luncheonette; **café,** *caffè* <Ital>; **coffee shop, lunch counter,** quick-lunch counter; **snack bar,** *buvette* <Fr>, *cantina* <Sp>; automat; **diner**

lunge NOUNS **thrust, pass,** swing, cut, stab, jab; feint; home thrust

lurch NOUNS 1 totter, stagger, **swing,** swinging, **sway,** swag; **rock,** roll, reel, careen; toss, tumble, pitch, plunge
VERBS 2 **pitch,** toss, tumble, toss and tumble, pitch and toss, **plunge,** hobbyhorse, pound, **rear,** rock, roll, reel, swing, **sway,** yaw, heave, scend, flounder, welter, **wallow; topple, stumble,** stagger, totter, careen, list, tilt, trip, flounder

lure NOUNS 1 charm, **come-on** <nonformal>, attention-getter *or* -grabber, **attraction, draw** *or* drawer *or* crowd-drawer, crowd-pleaser, headliner; **decoy,** decoy duck; **bait,** ground bait, baited trap, baited hook; **snare,** trap; **endearment**; the song of the Sirens, the voice of the tempter, honeyed words; forbidden fruit
VERBS 2 allure, **entice, seduce, inveigle, decoy,** draw, **draw on, lead on;** come on to *and* give the come-on *and* give a come-hither look *and* bat the eyes at *and* make goo-goo eyes at <all nonformal>, flirt with, flirt; **woo;** coax, cajole, blandish; **ensnare;** draw in, suck in *and* rope in <both nonformal>; bait, offer bait to, bait the hook, angle with a silver hook

lurid ADJS **sensational,** yellow, **melodramatic,** Barnumesque; spine-chilling, eye-popping <nonformal>; pale, deathly pale, wan, blue, livid, haggard; **cadaverous,** corpselike; **garish, loud** <nonformal>, blatant, flagrant, shameless, brazen, brazenfaced, extravagant, sensational, **spectacular,** glaring, flaring, flaunting, screaming <nonformal>, obtrusive, vulgar, crude; meretricious, **obscene,** lewd, adult, bawdy, ithyphallic, ribald, **pornographic, salacious,** sultry <nonformal>, **dirty, smutty,** raunchy <nonformal>

lurk VERBS couch; **lie in wait,** lay wait; **sneak, skulk, slink, prowl,** nightwalk, **steal, creep,** pussyfoot <nonformal>, gumshoe <nonformal>, tiptoe; stalk, shadow; **lie under the surface,** lie low, lie beneath, lie dormant, smolder

lurking ADJS **latent,** lying low, delitescent, **hidden**, obscured, obfuscated, veiled, muffled, covert, occult, cryptic; **underlying, under the surface,** submerged; **between the lines; imminent, impending,** impendent, **overhanging,** hanging over one's head, waiting, **threatening, looming,** lowering, **menacing,** lying in ambush

luscious ADJS **tasty,** delectable, delicious, flavorsome, savory; juicy, succulent

lush NOUNS 1 **drunk; soak,** boozer, boozehound, dipso, juicehead, loadie, ginhound, elbow bender *or* crooker, shikker, bottle sucker, swillbelly, swillpot, swillbowl; **souse, stew,** bum, rummy, rumhound, stewbum; wino <all nonformal>
ADJS 2 **luxuriant,** flourishing, **rank,** riotous, exuberant; dense, impenetrable, thick, heavy, gross; overgrown, overrun; **flowery, florid; exuberant,** superabundant

lust NOUNS 1 **craving,** coveting; **hunger,** thirst, appetite; **itch, itching,** prurience *or* pruriency; lech <nonformal>, **sexual desire,** lasciviousness, lechery, lecherousness, lewdness, bawdiness, dirtiness, salacity, salaciousness, carnality, animality, fleshliness, **sexuality,** sexiness, lustfulness
VERBS 2 **lust after,** itch for, have a lech *and* have hot pants for <both nonformal>, **desire; be in heat** *or* **rut,** rut, come in; get physical <nonformal>; **desire,** desiderate, be desirous of, **wish,** lust after, bay after, kill for *and* give one's right arm for <both nonformal>, die for <nonformal>, **want,** have a mind to, choose <nonformal>; **hanker for** *or* **after** <nonformal>; aspire after, be consumed with desire; have an itchy *or* itching palm *and* have sticky fingers <all nonformal>

luster NOUNS **illustriousness,** brilliance *or* brilliancy, radiance, splendor, resplendence *or* resplendency, refulgence *or* refulgency, refulgentness, **glory,** blaze of glory, nimbus, halo, aura, envelope; charisma, mystique, glamour, numinousness, magic; **shine,** shininess, **sheen, gloss,** glint

lustrous ADJS **illustrious,** glorious, brilliant, radiant, splendid, splendorous, splendrous, splendent, resplendent, bright, shiny, shining; charismatic, glamorous, numinous, magic, magical

lusty ADJS **strong,** vigorous, hearty, nervy, bouncing, full- *or* red-blooded, **animated, spirited, robust,** hearty, enthusiastic, mettlesome, zesty, zestful, impetuous, spanking, smacking; stalwart, stout, strapping, sturdy, **rugged,** rude, hardy, well-knit

luxuriant ADJS flourishing, **rank, lush,** riotous, exuberant; dense, impenetrable, thick, heavy, gross; jungly, jungled; overgrown, overrun; **rich, luxurious**

luxuriate VERBS **superabound,** overabound, **know no bounds, swarm,** pullulate, run riot, **teem; delight in, rejoice in,** indulge in, revel in, riot in, bask in, wallow in, swim in; groove on *and* get high on *and* freak out on <all nonformal>; feast on, gloat over *or* on; **relish, appreciate,** do justice to, savor, smack the lips

luxurious ADJS **ornate, elegant,** ostentatious; rich, luxuriant; **sumptuous,** elaborate, extravagant, deluxe; executive *and* plush *and* posh *and* ritzy *and* swank *and* swanky <all nonformal>, Corinthian; palatial, Babylonian, gold-plated

luxury NOUNS **splendor,** splendidness, splendiferousness, resplendence, brilliance, glory; impressiveness, imposingness; **sumptuousness,** elegance, elaborateness, lavishness; ritziness *or* poshness *or* plushness *or* swankness *or* swankiness <all nonformal>

lynch VERBS **hang,** hang by the neck; **string up** *and* scrag *and* stretch <all nonformal>; gibbet, noose, neck; hang, draw, and quarter

lynching NOUNS **hanging,** the rope *or* noose; summary execution; necktie party *or* sociable <nonformal>, vigilantism, vigilante justice; the necklace

lyric ADJS **melodious,** melodic; **musical,** music-like; **tuneful,** tunable; **euphonious** *or* euphonic, **lyrical,** melic; **lilting,** songful, songlike

lyricist NOUNS song writer, songsmith, librettist, lyrist

M

macabre ADJS **hideous, ghastly,** morbid, grim, grisly, gruesome, ghoulish; **weird, eerie,** eldritch, **uncanny,** unearthly; **spooky** *and* spookish *and* hairy <all nonformal>

Machiavellian ADJS **scheming, calculating,** designing, contriving, plotting, intriguing; manipulatory, **manipulative;** opportunist, **opportunistic;** Byzantine; **conniving,** conspiring, collusive

machination NOUNS **manipulation, wire-pulling** <nonformal>; influence, political influence, behind-the-scenes influence *or* pressure; **maneuvering,** maneuvers, tactical maneuvers

machismo NOUNS **virility,** virileness, potence *or* **potency,** sexual power, manly vigor; ultramasculinity; **manliness,** manfulness, **manhood**

macho ADJS **virile, potent,** viripotent; ultramasculine, **he-mannish** *and* hunky <both nonformal>, two-fisted <nonformal>, broad-shouldered, hairy-chested; **manly,** manful

mad ADJS 1 **insane,** mad as a hatter, mad as a march hare, **stark-staring mad,** maddened, crazed, **lunatic,** moonstruck, **demented, deranged,** deluded, disoriented, unhinged, **unbalanced,** unsettled, distraught, wandering, mazed, crackbrained, brainsick, sick *or* soft in the head, not right, not in one's right mind, **touched,** touched in the head, **out of one's mind,** out of one's senses *or* wits, bereft of reason, reasonless, irrational

2 <nonformal> **sore,** mad as a hornet *or* as a wet hen *or* as hell, pissed; **pissed-off** *or* PO'd; teed off *or* TO'd; ticked off, browned-off, het up, **hot under the collar,** burned up, hot and bothered, boiling *or* hopping *or* fighting *or* roaring mad, fit to be tied, good and mad, steamed, bent out of shape, in a lather

mad about VERBS

< nonformal>**wild about, crazy about,** gone on, gaga over, all hopped up about, hot about *or* for *or* on, steamed up about, **turned-on,** freaked-out, **nuts on** *or* **over** *or* **about,** crazy *or* nuts about

madam NOUNS **procurer, pimp,** pander *or* panderer, *maquereau* <Fr>, mack *or* mackman, ponce <Brit nonformal>; **bawd;** procuress; white slaver

maddening ADJS **inflammatory; stimulating,** stimulative, stimulatory; exhilarating, heady, intoxicating, ravishing

made ADJS man-made; **manufactured,** created, crafted, formed, shaped, molded, cast, forged, machined, milled, fashioned, **built, constructed,** fabricated

made-up ADJS **invented,** originated, **conceived,** discovered, newfound; fabricated, coined, minted, new-minted; made out of whole cloth; cosmetized, cosmeticized, beautified, titivated

madhouse NOUNS **insane asylum,** asylum, lunatic asylum, mental institution, mental home, bedlam; **bughouse** *and* nuthouse *and* **loonybin** *and* **booby hatch** *and* funny farm <all nonformal>; mental hospital, psychopathic hospital *or* ward

madman NOUNS **lunatic,** dement, *fou* and *aliéné* <both Fr>, non compos, *bacayaro* <Japanese>; bedlamite, Tom o' Bedlam; **maniac,** raving lunatic; homicidal maniac, psychopathic killer

maelstrom NOUNS **eddy,** back stream, gurge, **swirl,** twirl, whirl; **whirlpool,** vortex, Charybdis; **bustle, fuss, flurry, flutter,** fluster, scramble, ferment, stew, sweat, **stir,** hubbub, hullabaloo, hoo-ha *and* foofaraw *and* flap <all nonformal>

maestro NOUNS **teacher,** instructor, educator, preceptor, **mentor; master**

Mafia NOUNS **the rackets** <nonformal>, the syndicate, **organized crime,** Cosa Nostra

magazine NOUNS **periodical,** serial, journal, gazette; ephemeris; review; organ, **house organ; trade journal,** trade magazine

magic NOUNS **sorcery, necromancy,** sortilege, **wizardry,** theurgy, gramarye <old>, rune, glamour; **witchcraft,** spellcraft, spellbinding, spellcasting; **witchery,** witchwork, bewitchery, enchantment; spell, charm; illusionism, sleight of hand, prestidigitation, magic show, magic act

magical ADJS **illustrious,** charismatic, glamorous, numinous; sorcerous, necromantic, **magic,** magian, numinous, thaumaturgic, thaumaturgical, **miraculous, wondrous,** wonder-working, **prodigious;** enchanted, bewitched

magician NOUNS mage, magus, magian; Merlin; prestidigitator, illusionist, conjurer, sleight-of-hand artist; mummer, guiser <Scots>, guisard

magisterial ADJS **dignified,** stately, imposing, grand, courtly, aristocratic; **noble,** lordly, princely; **majestic,** regal, royal, kingly, queenly; worthy, **august, venerable;** statuesque; **sedate, solemn**, sober, grave

magistrate NOUNS **judge, justice,** adjudicator, bencher, man *or* woman on the bench, **justice of the peace** *or* JP; arbiter, arbitrator, moderator

magnanimous ADJS great-souled *or* -spirited; **generous,** generous to a fault, openhanded, **liberal; big, bighearted,** greathearted, largehearted, great of heart *or* soul; noble-minded, **high-minded,** idealistic; **benevolent**, **noble,** princely, handsome, great, high, elevated, **lofty,** exalted, sublime; charitable, compassionate, sympathetic; sensitive

magnate NOUNS **businessman,** businesswoman, businessperson, big businessman, tycoon <nonformal>, baron, king, top executive, business leader; **industrialist,** captain of industry

magnetic ADJS **engrossing, absorbing,** consuming, **gripping,** riveting, holding, **arresting,** engaging, attractive, **fascinating,** enthralling, spellbinding, enchanting, hypnotic, mesmerizing, mesmeric; obsessive, obsessing; appealing, seductive, charismatic

magnetize VERBS **attract, pull, draw,** drag, tug, pull *or* draw towards, have an attraction; magnet, be magnetic; **lure;** electromagnetize

magnificence NOUNS **grandeur,** grandness, grandiosity, gorgeousness, **splendor,** splendidness, splendiferousness, resplendence, brilliance, glory; nobility, proudness, **state, stateliness, majesty;** impressiveness, imposingness

magnificent ADJS **grandiose,** grand, splendid, splendiferous, splendacious <nonformal>, **glorious,** superb, fine, superfine, fancy, superfancy, swell <nonformal>; **imposing, impressive,** larger-than-life, awful, awe-inspiring, awesome; **noble, proud,** stately, majestic, princely

magnified ADJS **exaggerated,** hyperbolical, amplified <old>, **inflated,** aggrandized; **stretched,** disproportionate, **blown up out of all proportion;** overstated, overdrawn; overdone, overwrought; overestimated; overlarge, overgreat; high-flown, grandiloquent

magnify VERBS **aggravate, intensify, heighten,** step up, sharpen, make acute *or* more acute, bring to a head, deepen, **increase,** enhance, enlarge, build up; augment; **exaggerate,** blow up *and* puff up <both nonformal>, **enlarge, expand,** extend, widen, broaden, build, build up, aggrandize; **extol, glorify,** exalt

magnitude NOUNS **size,** largeness, bigness, greatness, vastness, vastitude, order of magnitude, amplitude; mass, bulk, **volume,** body; **dimensions, proportions,** dimension, caliber, scantling, proportion; **extent,** extension, expansion, expanse, square footage *or* yardage etc, **scope,** reach, range

maid NOUNS **maidservant,** servitress, **girl,** servant girl, *bonne* <Fr>, serving girl, wench, biddy <nonformal>, hired girl; au pair girl, ayah <India>, amah <China>; live-in maid, live-out maid; **handmaid,** handmaiden; **lady's maid,** waiting maid *or* woman, gentlewoman, abigail, soubrette

maiden NOUNS 1 **single** *or* unmarried woman, spinster, spinstress, **old maid,** maid, bachelor girl, single girl, single woman, lone woman, maiden lady, feme sole

ADJS 2 **unmarried,** unwedded, unwed, single, sole, spouseless, husbandless; **spinsterly,** spinsterish, spinsterlike; **old-maidish,** old-maidenish; maidenly

maidenhead NOUNS **virginity,** maiden *or* virgin state, intactness, maidenhood

mail VERBS **post,** dispatch, send; airmail

maim VERBS **cripple,** lame; **hamstring,** hobble; wing; emasculate, castrate; incapacitate, **disable**

main ADJS **chief, principal,** paramount, **foremost,** headmost, **leading,** dominant, crowning, capital, cardinal; central, focal, prime, **primary,** primal, first

mainland NOUNS **continent,** landform, continental landform, landmass

mainline VERBS **inject,** shoot *and* shoot up *and* jab *and* get down *and* get off <all nonformal>, pop *and* skin pop <both nonformal>

mainspring NOUNS **fountainhead,** headwater, headstream, riverhead, springhead, headspring, wellspring, wellhead, well, **spring, fountain,** fount, font, *fons et origo* <L>

mainstay NOUNS **supporter, upholder,** maintainer, sustainer; support, standby <nonformal>, stalwart, reliance, dependence; **abettor, seconder,** second; endorser, sponsor; **backer, promoter,** angel <nonformal>, rabbi <nonformal>; **patron,** Maecenas; **champion,** defender, apologist, **advocate,** exponent, **protagonist**

maintain VERBS **affirm, assert,** asseverate, **aver,** protest, lay down, avouch, avow, **declare,** say, say loud and clear, say out loud, sound off <nonformal>, have one's say, speak, speak one's piece *or* one's mind, speak up *or* out, **state,** set down, express, put, put it, put in one's two-cents worth <nonformal>; **allege,** profess; **contend,** argue, **insist, hold,** submit, maintain with one's last breath
2 support, keep; sustain, uphold, **keep up,** keep alive

maintenance NOUNS **support, sustainment,** sustentation, **sustenance, subsistence,** provision, total support, meal ticket <nonformal>; **keep, upkeep; livelihood, living,** meat, bread, daily bread; **nurture, fostering,** nurturance, nourishment, mothering, parenting, rearing, fosterage, foster-care, **care, caring,** care-giving, tender loving care *or* TLC <nonformal>; preservation, **conservation**

majestic ADJS **lofty, elevated,** sublime, grand, noble, stately, grave, solemn, dignified; serious, weighty; moving, inspiring

majesty NOUNS **loftiness,** elevation, sublimity; grandeur, **nobility,** stateliness, gravity, *gravitas* <L>, solemnity, **dignity**

major ADJS **important,** consequential, momentous, significant, considerable, substantial, material, **great,** grand, big; superior, world-shaking, earthshaking; big-time *and* big-league *and* major-league *and* heavyweight <all nonformal>; high-powered <nonformal>

majority NOUNS 1 **maturity, adulthood,** grown-upness, full growth, mature age, legal age, voting age, driving age, drinking age, *legalis homo* <L>; age of consent; **manhood,** man's estate, virility, *toga virilis* <L>, **womanhood,** womanness, femininity, femaleness, womanliness
2 plurality, more than half, the greater number, the greatest number, **most,** preponderance *or* preponderancy, **bulk, mass;** lion's share

make NOUNS 1 **kind, sort, ilk, type,** breed of cat <nonformal>, **stamp, brand,** feather, color, stripe, line, grain, kidney; mark, label, shape, cast, form, mold
VERBS 2 **produce, create,** manufacture, form, formulate, evolve, mature, elaborate, fashion, **fabricate,** prefabricate, cast, shape, configure, carve out, mold, extrude, frame; **construct, build,** erect, put up, set up, run up, raise, rear

make-believe NOUNS 1 **fantasy; fiction,** myth, romance; wildest dreams, stretch of the imagination; **chimera, bubble, illusion**
ADJS 2 **fictitious, figmental,** fictional, fictive, fabricated, fictionalized; nonfactual, nonactual, nonrealistic; **fabulous, mythic, mythical,** mythological, legendary

make do VERBS **make shift,** make out <nonformal>, cope, manage, manage with, get along on, get by on, do with; do as well as *or* the best one can; use a last resort, scrape the bottom of the barrel

make ends meet VERBS **support oneself,** make one's way; **keep body and soul together,** *or* hold one's head above water, keep afloat; **survive, subsist, cope, eke out,** make out, scrape along, manage, get by

makeshift ADJS makeshifty, **stopgap,** band-aid <nonformal>, improvised, improvisational, **jury-rigged; last-ditch; ad hoc;** quick and dirty <nonformal>; temporary, provisional, tentative

make sure VERBS **make certain,** make sure of, make no doubt, make no mistake; remove *or* dismiss *or* expunge *or* erase all doubt; **assure, ensure,** insure, **certify; ascertain, get a fix** *or* **lock on** <nonformal>; **find out,** get at, see to it, see that; **determine,** decide, **establish,** settle, fix, lock in *and* nail down *and* clinch *and* cinch <all nonformal>, clear up, sort out, set at rest

makeup NOUNS 1 **disposition, character,** nature, temper, temperament, mettle, constitution, complexion *and* humor <both old>, stamp, type, stripe, kidney, make, mold; **turn of mind, inclination,** mind, **tendency,** grain, vein, set, mental

set, mindset, **leaning,** animus, propensity, proclivity, predilection, preference, predisposition
2 **cosmetics, beauty products, beauty-care products;** war paint *and* drugstore complexion <both nonformal>; pancake makeup

make up VERBS 1 **compose, constitute,** construct, fabricate; **incorporate,** embody, incarnate; **form, organize,** structure, shape, shape up; **enter into,** go into, go to make up; **make, build,** build up, assemble, put *or* piece together; **consist of,** be a feature of, form a part of, combine *or* unite in, merge in; **consist,** be made up of, be constituted of, contain; **synthesize; combine**; join; **mix**
2 **kiss and make up** *and* make it up *and* make matters up <all nonformal>, **shake hands,** come round, come together, come to an understanding, **come to terms,** let the wound heal, let bygones be bygones, forgive and forget, put it all behind one, settle *or* compose one's differences, meet halfway
3 **beautify, prettify,** cutify <nonformal>, pretty up *or* gussy up *or* doll up <all nonformal>, grace, **adorn; glamorize;** paint *and* put on one's face <both nonformal>, titivate, cosmetize, cosmeticize

makings NOUNS **component, constituent,** ingredient, integrant, fixings <nonformal>, **element, factor, part**, player, module, part and parcel; appurtenance, adjunct

maladjusted ADJS **incompetent, incapable,** unable, inadequate, unequipped, unqualified, ill-qualified, out of one's depth, outmatched, **unfit, unfitted,** unadapted, not equal *or* up to, not cut out for <nonformal>; ineffective, **ineffectual;** unadjusted

malady NOUNS **disease, illness,** sickness, ailment, indisposition, disorder, complaint, morbidity, *morbus* <L>, **affliction,** affection, distemper <old>, **infirmity**

malaise NOUNS **anxiety,** anxiousness; **uneasiness,** perturbation, disturbance, upset, agitation, disquiet, disquietude, inquietude, unquietness; **nervousness**; angst; **sickishness,** seediness *and* rockiness <both nonformal>

malapropism NOUNS antiphrasis, **solecism,** ungrammaticism, **misusage,** missaying, misconstruction, infelicity; corruption

malcontent NOUNS 1 **complainer,** complainant, **faultfinder, grumbler,** growler, smellfungus, **murmurer,** mutterer, griper, croaker, peevish *or* petulant *or* querulous person, whiner, *frondeur* <Fr>; reactionary, reactionist; rebel
ADJS 2 **discontented,** malcontented, complaining, complaintful, sour, **faultfinding,** grumbling, growling, murmuring, muttering, griping, croaking, **peevish, petulant,** sulky, **querulous,** querulant, whiny

male NOUNS 1 male being, **man,** male person, *homme* <Fr>, *hombre* <Sp>; **gentleman,** gent <nonformal>
ADJS 2 **masculine,** bull, **manly,** manlike, mannish, manful, andric; uneffeminate; **gentlemanly,** gentlemanlike

male chauvinist NOUNS **sexist,** male chauvinist pig *or* MCP <nonformal>, manist, masculist

male organs NOUNS **genitals,** genitalia, sex organs, reproductive organs, pudenda, private parts, privy parts; **crotch,** pubic region, perineum, pelvis; **male organs; penis,** phallus, *lingam* <Skt>; gonads; **testes, testicles,** balls *and* nuts *and* rocks *and* ballocks *and* family jewels <all nonformal>; spermary; scrotum, cod <old>

malevolent ADJS **ill-disposed,** evil-disposed, **ill-natured,** ill-affected, ill-conditioned, ill-intentioned, **hostile, antagonistic,** repugnant, antipathetic, set against, snide, spiteful, despiteful, malefic, malicious, malignant, hateful, full of hate *or* hatred; virulent, **bitter,** sore, rancorous, acrid, caustic, venomous, vitriolic

malformed ADJS **deformed, misshapen,** misbegotten, misproportioned, ill-proportioned, ill-made, ill-shaped, **out of shape;** dwarfed, stumpy; bloated; grotesque, **monstrous**

malfunction NOUNS 1 **fault,** *faute* <Fr>, **defect,** deficiency, inadequacy, imperfection, kink, defection <old>; **flaw,** hole, bug <nonformal>; **blemish,** taint; glitch <nonformal>
VERBS 2 **get out of order,** get out of gear; get out of joint; go wrong

malice NOUNS **maliciousness,** maleficence; malignance *or* **malignancy,** malignity; **meanness** *and* orneriness *and* cussedness *and* bitchiness <all non-

formal>, hatefulness, nastiness, invidiousness; **wickedness,** iniquitousness; deviltry, devilry, devilment; malice prepense *or* aforethought, evil intent; **noxiousness**

malicious ADJS maleficent, malefic; **malignant,** malign; **mean** *and* **ornery** *and* cussed *and* bitchy <all nonformal>, hateful, nasty, baleful, invidious; **wicked,** iniquitous; **harmful, noxious**

malign VERBS **defame, bad-mouth** *and* poor-mouth <both nonformal>; asperse, cast aspersions on, cast reflections on, injure one's reputation, damage one's good name, give one a black eye <nonformal>; **slur,** cast a slur on, do a number *or* a job on <nonformal>, tear down

malignancy NOUNS **virulence** *or* virulency, noxiousness, destructiveness, deadliness; **lethality,** mortality, fatality; **malignity, perniciousness,** banefulness; cancer

malignant ADJS **virulent, noxious,** malign, malevolent, malefic, vicious, destructive, deadly; mephitic, miasmal, miasmic, miasmatic; cancerous

malingerer NOUNS **slacker,** shirker, dodger, goof-off *and* goldbrick <both nonformal>, idler

malingering NOUNS **shirking, slacking,** goldbricking <nonformal>, soldiering, goofing *and* goofing off *and* fucking off <all nonformal>; **dodging,** ducking

mall NOUNS **marketplace, mart,** market, open market, market overt; **shopping center, shopping plaza** *or* **mall,** plaza, shopping *or* shop *or* commercial complex; public walk, promenade, esplanade, alameda, parade, *prado* <Sp>

malleable ADJS **docile, tractable,** biddable, unmurmuring, **yielding,** pliant, pliable, flexible, moldable, ductile, plastic, like putty in one's hands

malnutrition NOUNS undernourishment, undernutrition; **dietary deficiency,** vitamin deficiency

malodorous ADJS **fetid,** olid, **odorous, stinking, reeking,** reeky, nidorous, smelling, bad-smelling, **evil-smelling,** ill-smelling, heavy-smelling, **smelly,** smellful <Australia>, stenchy; **foul,** vile, putrid, bad, fulsome, noisome, fecal, feculent, excremental, offensive, repulsive, noxious, sulfurous; **rank,** strong, high, gamy; **rancid, musty,** funky, fusty, frowzy, stuffy, moldy, mildewed, mildewy; mephitic, miasmic, miasmal

malpractice NOUNS **misuse,** misusage, abuse; abuse of office, misconduct, malfeasance, misfeasance, malversation, wrongdoing; **negligence,** neglect; **misbehavior, misconduct**

mammoth ADJS **gigantic,** mountainous, titanic, colossal, Gargantuan, gigantesque, monster, monstrous, outsize, sizable, larger-than-life, overgrown, king-size, monumental; **massive,** massy, weighty, bulky, voluminous; **tremendous,** stupendous, awesome, prodigious

man NOUNS 1 **male,** male being; male person, *homme* <Fr>, *hombre* <Sp>; **gentleman,** gent <nonformal>; **husband, married man,** benedict, goodman <old>, old man <nonformal>; manservant, serving man, butler; valet, *valet de chambre* <Fr>, gentleman's gentleman

2 <nonformal > **guy,** fellow, felle, lad, chap, guy, cat, bird, duck, stud, joker, jasper, bugger, bastard, bloke *and* cove *and* johnny *and* bod, <all Brit nonformal> customer, party, character, warm, body, bean, cookie, dude, gent, Joe

VERBS 3 staff; garrison, man the garrison *or* trenches *or* barricades

man about town NOUNS **sophisticate,** man of experience, **man of the world;** boulevardier, playboy, social lion, slicker *and* city slicker <both nonformal>; **cosmopolitan,** cosmopolite

manacle NOUNS 1 **shackle,** restraint, **restraints, fetter, hamper,** trammel, trammels, gyves, bond, **bonds,** irons, chains, Oregon boat; **handcuffs,** cuffs
VERBS 2 **shackle, fetter,** gyve, put in irons; **handcuff,** tie one's hands; **tie hand and foot,** hog-tie <nonformal>

manacled ADJS **bound, tied,** bound hand and foot, tied up, tied down, strapped, hampered, trammeled, shackled, handcuffed, fettered, tethered; **in bonds,** in irons *or* chains, ironbound

manage VERBS 1 **direct, regulate,** conduct, carry on, handle, run <nonformal>; **control,** command, head, govern, **boss** *and* head up *and* pull the strings *and* **mastermind** *and* quarterback *and* call the signals <all nonformal>;
2 **economize, save,** make *or* enforce economies; **husband,** husband one's resources; live frugally, get along on a

shoestring, get by on little; keep *or* stay within one's means *or* budget, balance income with outgo, live within one's income, make ends meet, cut one's coat according to one's cloth, keep *or* stay ahead of the game

manageable ADJS **governable, controllable,** manipulable, corrigible, restrainable, untroublesome; domitable, tamable, domesticable; milk-toast *or* milquetoast; **workable,** operable, performable, actable, doable, negotiable, maneuverable; **practicable, feasible,** practical, viable

management NOUNS **direction, managing,** handling, running <nonformal>, conduct; governance, **regulation,** ordering, husbandry; manipulation

manager NOUNS **director,** *directeur* <Fr>, director general, **governor,** rector, **administrator,** intendant, **conductor;** person in charge, responsible person; executive

mandarin NOUNS **intellectual, intellect,** intellectualist, literate, member of the intelligentsia, white-collar intellectual; **pundit,** Brahmin, egghead *and* pointy-head <both nonformal>; **highbrow** <nonformal>; wise man; **bureaucrat,** red-tapist, *rond-de-cuir* <Fr>

mandate NOUNS 1 **authority, prerogative,** popular authority *or* mandate, people's mandate, electoral mandate; **injunction,** charge, commission; **dependency,** colony
VERBS 2 **command, order,** dictate, direct, instruct, bid, enjoin, charge, commission, call on *or* upon; **decree,** rule, ordain, promulgate; give an order *or* a direct order, issue a command, say the word, give the word *or* word of command; call the shots *or* tune *or* signals *or* play <nonformal>

mandatory ADJS **obligatory, compulsory,** must <nonformal>, imperative, required, dictated, **binding; preceptive,** didactic, instructive, moralistic, **prescriptive;** prescript, prescribed, hard-and-fast; formulary, standard, regulation, official, authoritative, canonical, statutory, rubric, rubrical, protocolary, protocolic

maneuver NOUNS 1 **stratagem, artifice,** craft, wile, strategy, device, wily device, contrivance, expedient, design, scheme, trick, cute trick, gimmick <nonformal>, **ruse,** red herring, shift, tactic, stroke, stroke of policy, master stroke, **move,** coup, gambit, **ploy, dodge,** artful dodge; **act,** step, measure, initiative, *démarche* <Fr>
VERBS 2 **manipulate,** pull strings *or* wires; **machinate,** contrive, angle <nonformal>, jockey, engineer; play games <nonformal>; **plot,** scheme, intrigue; **finagle,** wangle

man Friday NOUNS **right-hand man,** right hand, strong right hand *or* arm, fidus Achates, second self, alter ego, confidant

manger NOUNS **compartment,** booth, stall, crib

mangle VERBS **tear** *or* **rip apart,** take *or* pull apart, **pick** *or* **rip** *or* **tear to pieces,** tear to rags *or* tatters, **shred,** rip to shreds; lacerate, mutilate, maim

mangled ADJS **injured,** lacerated, cut, split, rent, torn, slit, slashed, mutilated, chewed-up; **smashed,** in bits, in pieces, in shards, burst, busted <nonformal>, ruptured, butchered, hacked

manhandle VERBS **mistreat,** maltreat, ill-treat, ill-use, abuse, injure, **molest;** do wrong to, do wrong by; outrage, do violence to, do one's worst to; mishandle; buffet, batter, bruise, **savage,** maul, knock about, rough, rough up

man-hater NOUNS **misanthrope,** misanthropist, people-hater, cynic, Timon, Timonist; misandrist; **sexist,** female chauvinist, chauvinist

manhood NOUNS **masculinity,** masculineness, maleness; **manliness,** manlihood, manfulness, manlikeness; mannishness; gentlemanliness, gentlemanlikeness; **maturity, adulthood, majority,** grown-upness, man's estate, virility, machismo, *toga virilis* <L>

mania NOUNS **craze, infatuation, enthusiasm,** passion, fascination, crazy fancy, bug <nonformal>, rage, furor; manic psychosis

maniac NOUNS **lunatic, madman, madwoman,** raving lunatic; homicidal maniac, psychopathic killer, berserk *or* berserker

manic ADJS **psychotic, psychopathic,** psychoneurotic, mentally ill, mentally sick, certifiable; disturbed, neurotic; schizophrenic, schizoid; manic-depressive; uncontrollable, running amok, wild

manifest NOUNS 1 **statement, bill,** itemized bill, invoice, bill of lading
VERBS 2 **show, exhibit,** demonstrate, display, breathe, unfold, develop;

evince, evidence; **indicate,** give sign *or* token, token, betoken, mean; **make plain,** make clear; bring to notice, expose to view, bring to *or* into view; **reveal,** divulge, disclose; **flaunt,** dangle, wave, **flourish,** brandish, parade; affect, make a show *or* a great show of; perform, enact, dramatize; **embody,** incarnate, **materialize**
ADJS 3 **apparent, evident,** self-evident, axiomatic, indisputable, obvious, plain, clear, perspicuous, distinct, palpable, patent, tangible; **visible,** perceptible, perceivable, discernible, observable, noticeable, **much in evidence; to be seen,** easy to be seen, plain to be seen; plain as day, plain as the nose on one's face, big as life; **crystal-clear,** clear as crystal; **express,** explicit, unmistakable, not to be mistaken, open-and-shut <nonformal>; self-explanatory, self-explaining; **indubitable**

manifestation NOUNS **appearance; expression,** evincement; **indication, evidence,** proof; embodiment, incarnation, bodying forth, materialization; epiphany, theophany, Christophany, avatar; **revelation, disclosure**, showing forth; dissemination, **publication**

manifesto NOUNS **statement of belief** *or* **principles,** position paper; solemn declaration; deposition, affidavit, sworn statement

manikin NOUNS **figure, figurine; mannequin,** model, dummy, lay figure

manipulate VERBS **maneuver,** pull strings *or* wires; **machinate,** contrive, angle <nonformal>, jockey, **engineer;** play games <nonformal>; **plot,** scheme, intrigue; finagle, wangle

manipulative ADJS **using, exploitive,** exploitative, manipulatory, scheming

mankind NOUNS **humankind, man,** men and women, people, human species, **human race,** human family, the family of man, **humanity,** human beings, mortals, mortality, flesh, mortal flesh, clay; generation of man <old>, *le genre humain* <Fr>, genus Homo, **Homo sapiens,** Hominidae, hominids

manlike ADJS **anthropoid,** humanoid, hominid; anthropomorphic, anthropopathic, therioanthropic

manly ADJS **masculine, male,** bull, **manlike, mannish,** manful, andric; uneffeminate; **gentlemanly,** gentlemanlike; virile, macho

man-made ADJS **made, manufactured,** created, crafted, formed, shaped, molded, cast, forged, machined, milled, fashioned, **built, constructed,** fabricated

manna NOUNS **godsend,** boon, blessing; manna from heaven, manna in the wilderness, gift from on high

manned ADJS staffed, readied, in place, **prepared; garrisoned**

mannequin NOUNS artist's model, dressmaker's model, photographer's model; dummy, lay figure

manner NOUNS **way,** wise, means, mode, modality, fashion, **style,** tone, guise <old>; **method,** methodology, **system; approach,** attack, tack; **technique,** procedure, process, proceeding, course, practice; *modus operandi* <L>, mode of operation *or* MO, manner of working, mode of procedure; **routine;** manner of speaking, mode of expression

mannered ADJS **affected, pretentious,** la-di-da; *maniéré* <Fr>; **artificial, unnatural,** insincere; theatrical, stagy, histrionic; overdone, overacted, hammed up <nonformal>; precious, *précieux, précieuse* <both Fr>, overnice, overrefined, overelegant, overelaborate; Gongoristic, Gongoresque

mannerism NOUNS *minauderie* <Fr>, **trick of behavior,** trick, **quirk,** habit, peculiar trait, idiosyncrasy, trademark; **characteristic, peculiarity, singularity,** particularity, specialty, individualism, **character,** nature, **trait**

manners NOUNS **mannerliness, good manners,** excellent *or* exquisite manners, good *or* polite deportment, good *or* polite behavior, *bienséance* <Fr>; *savoir-faire, savoir-vivre* <both Fr>; correctness, correctitude, **etiquette**

mannish ADJS **mannified; unwomanly,** unfeminine, uneffeminate, viraginous; **tomboyish,** hoyden, rompish

man of the world NOUNS person of fashion, fashionable, man-about-town, nob, *mondain* <Fr>; fashion plate, clotheshorse, Beau Brummel; **socialite;** clubman; jet setter; swinger <nonformal>

the glass of fashion and the mold of form
SHAKESPEARE

man-of-war NOUNS **warship,** war vessel, naval vessel; warship; man-o'-war, ship of war, armored vessel

manse NOUNS **parsonage,** pastorage, pastorate, **church house,** clergy house; presbytery, **rectory,** vicarage, deanery

mansion NOUNS **estate;** palatial residence, stately home <Brit>; **villa,** château, palace, *palais* <Fr>, *palazzo* <Ital>

mantle NOUNS **cover, covering,** screen, shroud, shield, veil, pall, curtain, hanging, drape, drapery; **robe,** frock, gown, cloak

manual NOUNS **handbook,** enchiridion, vade mecum, gradus, how-to book <nonformal>; **textbook,** text, schoolbook, manual of instruction

manual labor NOUNS **work, labor,** employment, industry, toil, moil, travail, toil and trouble, sweat of one's brow; **drudgery, sweat,** slavery, spadework, rat race <nonformal>; handwork, handiwork

manufacture VERBS **produce, create, make, form,** formulate, evolve, mature, elaborate, fashion, **fabricate,** prefabricate, cast, shape, configure, carve out, mold, extrude, frame; **put together, assemble,** piece together, patch together, whomp up *and* fudge together *and* slap up *or* together <all nonformal>

manufactured ADJS **made,** man-made; created, crafted, formed, shaped, molded, cast, forged, machined, milled, fashioned, **built, constructed,** fabricated; **mass-produced,** volume-produced, assembly-line; **assembled,** put together; **concocted, trumped-up, doctored**

manufacturing NOUNS **production, manufacture,** producing, devising, fashioning, framing, forming, formation, formulation; engineering, tooling-up; processing, conversion; **fabrication,** prefabrication

manure NOUNS **fertilizer,** dressing, top dressing, enricher, richener; organic fertilizer, muck, night soil, dung, guano, **droppings;** cow pats, cow flops <nonformal>; cow chips, buffalo chips; coprolite, coprolith

many ADJS **numerous, manifold,** not a few, no few; **very many,** full many, **ever so many,** considerable *and* quite some <both nonformal>; **multitudinous,** multitudinal, multifarious, multifold, multiple, **myriad;** numerous as the stars, a dime a dozen

map NOUNS 1 **chart; projection,** map projection, azimuthal equidistant projection *or* azimuthal projection, conic projection, Mercator projection
VERBS 2 **plot; chart, blueprint; diagram,** graph; **sketch,** sketch in *or* out, draw up a plan; map out, plot out, **lay out,** set out, mark out; lay off, mark off

mapmaker NOUNS **cartographer,** mapper; chorographer, topographer, oceanographer, photogrammetrist; **surveyor,** land surveyor

mapped ADJS **surveyed,** plotted, admeasured, triangulated; known by measurement

mar VERBS **spoil,** botch, **ruin,** wreck, blight, play havoc with, play mischief with; **blemish, disfigure**

marathon ADJS **protracted, prolonged,** extended, lengthened; **long,** overlong, time-consuming, interminable, lasting, **lingering,** languishing; long-continued, long-continuing

marauder NOUNS **plunderer, pillager, looter,** rifler, sacker, spoiler, despoiler, spoliator, depredator, **raider,** moss-trooper, free-booter, rapparee, reiver <Scots>, forayer, forager, ravisher, ravager; wrecker

marble NOUNS 1 **plaything,** mig, agate, steelie, taw
VERBS 2 **streak,** striate, band, bar, vein; marbleize
ADJS 3 **milk-white,** milky, lactescent; marmoreal

march NOUNS 1 quick *or* quickstep march, quickstep, quick time; lockstep; double march, double-quick, double time; slow march, slow time; half step; goose step
VERBS 2 mush, footslog, **tramp, hike,** backpack, trail-hike; route-march; file, defile, file off; **parade,** go on parade; goose-step, do the goose step; do the lock step

margin NOUNS 1 **room, latitude,** swing, play, way; room to spare, room to swing a cat <nonformal>, **elbowroom, leeway;** breathing space; headroom, clearance
2 **border,** limbus, bordure <heraldry>, **edge,** limb, **verge, brink,** brow, **brim, rim,** marge, **skirt, fringe, hem,** list, selvage *or* selvedge, side

marginal ADJS **borderline,** frontier; secondary, of a low order of importance, low-priority, expendable

marijuana NOUNS

1 <nonformal> Acapulco gold, aunt mary, bomb, boo, bush, doobie, gage, ganja, grass, grefa, hay, hemp, herb, Indian hay, J, jane, kif, mary, maryjane, mary warner, meserole, mighty mezz, moota, muggles, pod, pot, smoke, snop, tea, Texas tea, weed, yerga

2 <nonformal> joint, joy stick, kick stick, reefer, roach, stick, twist

marina NOUNS **harbor, dock,** dockage, basin

marinate VERBS **preserve, cure,** season, brine, marinade, pickle, corn

marine ADJS **nautical,** maritime, naval, navigational; **seafaring,** seagoing, oceangoing, seaborne, water-borne; **oceanic,** pelagic, thalassic; nautical; oceanographic, oceanographical

mariner NOUNS **seaman, sailor,** sailorman, **navigator, seafarer,** seafaring man, bluejacket, sea *or* water dog <nonformal>, crewman, shipman, jack, jacky, jack afloat, jack-tar, **tar, salt** <nonformal>, hearty, lobscouser <nonformal>, *matelot* <Fr>, windsailor, windjammer

marionette NOUNS **puppet,** *fantoche* <Fr>, *fantoccino* and *fantoccio* <both Ital>, hand puppet, glove puppet

marital ADJS **matrimonial, conjugal,** connubial, nuptial, wedded, married, hymeneal; epithalamic; **spousal;** husbandly, uxorious; bridal, wifely, uxorial

maritime ADJS **nautical,** marine, naval, navigational; **seafaring,** seagoing, oceangoing, seaborne, water-borne; seamanly, seamanlike, **salty** <nonformal>; pelagic, oceanic

mark NOUNS **marking;** watermark; **scratch,** scratching, engraving, graving, **score,** scotch, cut, hack, gash, blaze; bar code; nick, notch; **scar,** cicatrix, scarification, cicatrization; **brand,** earmark; **stigma; stain,** discoloration; blemish, macula, **spot,** blotch, splotch, flick, patch, splash; mottle, dapple; **dot,** point; polka dot; tittle, jot; **speck, speckle,** fleck; tick, **freckle,** lentigo, mole; **birthmark,** strawberry mark, port-wine stain, vascular nevus, nevus, hemangioma; beauty mark *or* spot; caste mark; **check,** checkmark; prick, puncture; tattoo, tattoo mark
2 **dupe, victim;** coll *and* flat *and* john *and* lamb *and* lobster *and* monkey *and* patsy *and* **sucker** <all nonformal>
VERBS 3 make a mark, put a mark on; pencil, chalk; mark out, demarcate, delimit, define; **mark off, check, check off,** tick, tick off, chalk up; punctuate, point; **dot, spot,** blotch, splotch, dash, **speck, speckle,** fleck, freckle; mottle, dapple; blemish; **brand,** stigmatize; **stain, discolor**; stamp, seal, punch, impress, imprint, **print, engrave; score, scratch,** gash, scotch, scar, scarify, cicatrize; nick, notch; **blaze,** blaze a trail; **line, seam,** trace, **stripe, streak, striate;** hatch; **underline, underscore;** prick, puncture, tattoo, riddle, pepper
4 **destine, predestine,** necessitate, **ordain,** fate, appoint; come with the territory <nonformal>; have in store for; **doom,** foredoom

mark down VERBS **write down,** jot down, put down, set down, take down; **cheapen,** depreciate, devaluate, lower, reduce, **cut prices, cut,** slash, shave, trim, pare, underprice, knock the bottom out of <nonformal>

marked ADJS 1 **designated,** flagged; signed, signposted; monogrammed, individualized, personal; own-brand, own-label
2 **distinguished,** distingué; **noted, notable,** of note, of mark; **characteristic, peculiar, singular,** single, quintessential, intrinsic, unique, qualitative, **distinctive; destined, fated,** fateful, ordained, written in the cards, in store; **doomed,** foredoomed

marker NOUNS **mark;** bookmark; **landmark,** seamark; bench mark; **milestone,** milepost; cairn, menhir, catstone; **buoy,** aid to navigation, bell, gong, lighted buoy, nun, can, spar buoy, wreck buoy, junction buoy, special-purpose buoy; **monument; IOU**

market NOUNS 1 **mart, store, shop,** salon, boutique, emporium, house, establishment, *magasin* <Fr>; **retail store;** discount store, discount house, outlet store; **shopping center, shopping plaza** *or* **mall,** plaza, mall, shopping *or* shop *or* commercial complex
VERBS 2 **sell, merchandise,** move, turn over, sell off, make *or* effect a sale

marketable ADJS **salable,** retailable, merchandisable, merchantable, commercial, vendible; in demand

marketplace NOUNS **mart, market,** open

market, market overt; **shopping center, shopping plaza** *or* **mall,** plaza, mall, shopping *or* shop *or* commercial complex; emporium, rialto; **bazaar, fair,** trade fair, show, flea market, flea fair, street market, *marché aux puces* <Fr>

market value NOUNS **worth, value,** account, rate; street value; **price, quotation**

mark off VERBS **circumscribe, bound;** mark out, stake out, rope off; **demarcate,** delimit, draw *or* mark *or* set *or* lay out boundaries, circle in *or* out, hedge in, set the limit, mark the periphery; **define,** determine, fix, specify; **measure off, lay off,** set off, rule off; **step off,** pace off *or* out

marksman NOUNS **shooter,** shot; **gunner,** gun, **gunman; rifleman,** musketeer, carabineer; Nimrod, hunter; trapshooter; **markswoman,** targetshooter, **sharpshooter,** sniper; good shot, dead shot, deadeye, **crack shot**

marooned ADJS **stranded, grounded,** aground, **on the rocks,** high and dry; **stuck,** stuck *or* set fast; castaway, wrecked, shipwrecked

marred ADJS **spoiled** *or* spoilt, botched, blighted, **ruined,** wrecked; **blemished, disfigured,** defaced, scarred, scarified, scabbed, scabby; **faulty, flawed, defective**

marriage NOUNS 1 **matrimony, wedlock,** married status, holy matrimony, holy wedlock, match, matching, match-up, splicing <nonformal>, union, matrimonial union, alliance, marriage sacrament, sacrament of matrimony, bond of matrimony, wedding knot, conjugal bond *or* tie *or* knot, nuptial bond *or* tie *or* knot; misalliance, *mésalliance* <Fr>, ill-assorted marriage

a world-without-end bargain
SHAKESPEARE

2 **wedding,** marriage ceremony, nuptial mass; church wedding, civil wedding, civil ceremony; **nuptials,** spousals, espousals, hymeneal rites; white wedding; forced marriage, shotgun wedding; Gretna Green wedding, elopement

marriageable ADJS nubile, ripe, of age, of marriageable age, marriable

marriage broker NOUNS **matchmaker,** matrimonial agent, *shadchen* <Yiddish>; matrimonial agency *or* bureau

marriage vow NOUNS **betrothal,** betrothment, espousal, **engagement,** handfasting *and* affiance <both old>, troth, marriage contract, plighted troth *or* faith *or* love; banns, banns of matrimony; prenuptial agreement *or* contract

married ADJS **wedded,** one, one bone and one flesh, mated, matched, coupled, partnered, paired, hitched *and* spliced <both nonformal>; **linked,** tied, coupled, knotted, twinned, wed, married up, welded, conjugate, bracketed, bound, yoked, spliced, conjoined, conjoint, conjunct, joined

marrow NOUNS **center,** centrum; **middle,** heart, core, nucleus; **core of one's being,** where one lives; kernel; **pith,** medulla; **nub, hub,** nave, axis, pivot

marry VERBS wed, nuptial, **join, unite, hitch** *and* **splice** <both nonformal>, couple, match, match up, make *or* arrange a match, join together, **unite in marriage,** join *or* unite in holy wedlock, tie the knot, tie the nuptial *or* wedding knot, make one; give away, give in marriage; marry off, find a mate for, find a husband *or* wife for

marsh NOUNS marshland, **swamp,** swampland, fen, fenland, **morass,** *marais* <Fr>, *maremma* <Ital>, **bog, mire, quagmire,** sump <nonformal>, wash, baygall; glade, everglade; slough, swale, wallow, hog wallow, buffalo wallow, sough <Brit>

marshal VERBS **order, arrange**, get it together <nonformal>, **organize, regulate;** dispose, deploy; **form,** form up, configure, structure, array, pull it together, get *or* put one's ducks in a row <nonformal>, straighten it out, get *or* put one's house in order, line up, set up, lay out; rally

martial ADJS **warlike, militant,** fighting, warring, battling; **military,** soldierly, soldierlike; **combative, contentious,** gladiatorial

martyr NOUNS 1 **sufferer,** victim, prey; **wretch,** poor devil <nonformal>, object of compassion; redeemed *or* saved soul, soul in glory

VERBS 2 **torture, torment,** rack, put to torture, put *or* lay on the rack, **agonize, harrow,** crucify, martyrize, excruciate, wring, twist, contorse, convulse; prolong the agony, kill by inches

marvel NOUNS 1 **wonder, prodigy, miracle, phenomenon,** phenom <nonfor-

mal>; astonishment, amazement, marvelment, wonderment, wonderful thing, nine days' wonder, amazing *or* astonishing thing, quite a thing, really something, **sensation,** rocker *and* stunner <both nonformal>; one for the book *and* something to brag about *and* something to shout about *and* something to write home about *and* something else <all nonformal>
VERBS 2 **wonder,** be astonished *or* amazed *or* astounded, be seized with wonder; **gaze, gape,** drop one's jaw, look *or* stand aghast *or* agog, gawk, **stare,** stare openmouthed, open one's eyes, rub one's eyes, hold one's breath; not be able to account for, not know what to make of, not believe one's eyes *or* ears *or* senses

marvelous ADJS **wonderful, wondrous, miraculous,** fantastic, fabulous, phenomenal, **prodigious, stupendous,** unheard-of, unprecedented, extraordinary, exceptional, rare, unique, singular, **remarkable,** striking, **sensational; beguiling, fascinating**

masculine ADJS **male,** bull; **manly, manlike, mannish,** manful, andric; uneffeminate; **gentlemanly,** gentlemanlike

masculinity NOUNS masculineness, maleness; **manliness,** manlihood, **manhood,** manfulness, manlikeness; mannishness; gentlemanliness, gentlemanlikeness

mash NOUNS 1 **pulp, paste, mush,** smash, squash, crush
VERBS 2 **beat, pound, smash, crush,** crunch, flail, squash, scrunch <nonformal>

mask NOUNS 1 **cover, disguise, camouflage,** protective coloration; **masquerade,** masque, mummery; visor, vizard, false face, domino, domino mask
VERBS 2 **cover,** cloak, mantle, muffle, blanket, canopy, cope, cowl, hood, **veil,** curtain, **screen, shield,** screen off, cloud, obscure, fog, befog, fuzz
3 **disguise,** camouflage

masque NOUNS **ball,** *bal* <Fr>; masked ball, mask, masquerade ball, masquerade, *bal masqué* <Fr>, *bal costumé* <Fr>, fancy-dress ball, cotillion

masquerade VERBS **disguise oneself,** take an assumed name, assume a cover, change one's identity, go under an alias, remain anonymous, be incognito, go *or* sail under false colors, wear a mask

mass NOUNS 1 **bulk,** substance, matter, magnitude, amplitude, **extent, sum; volume,** mountain, load
2 **lump,** clump, **hunk** *and* **chunk** <both nonformal>, piece, **gob** *and* glob <both nonformal>, gobbet; batch, **wad,** block, loaf
3 **sacred music,** requiem mass, requiem, missa brevis, missa solemnis
4 **throng, multitude, horde,** host, heap <nonformal>, army, panoply, legion; **crowd,** press, crush, flood, spate, deluge
VERBS 5 **come together, assemble, congregate, collect,** come from far and wide, come *or* arrive in a body; **unite**; muster, **meet, gather, forgather,** gang up <nonformal>; **merge,** converge, flow together, fuse; **throng, crowd,** swarm, teem, hive, surge, seethe, mill, stream, horde
ADJS 6 **popular,** public, grass-roots, **common,** common as dirt, commonplace, **plain, ordinary, lowly,** low, mean, base

massacre NOUNS 1 **carnage, bloodbath, decimation,** saturnalia of blood; **mass murder, mass destruction,** mass extermination, wholesale murder, pogrom, race-murder, genocide, race extermination, **the Holocaust,** the final solution
VERBS 2 **slaughter, butcher, decimate,** commit carnage, depopulate, murder *or* kill *or* slay en masse; commit mass murder *or* destruction, murder wholesale, commit genocide

massage NOUNS massaging, stroking, kneading; **rubdown;** massotherapy; vibrator; facial massage, facial

the masses NOUNS **the hoi polloi,** *hoi polloi* <Gk>, the many, **the multitude,** the crowd, **the mob,** the horde, the million, the mass of the people, the herd, the great unnumbered, the great unwashed, **the vulgar** *or* **common herd;** *profanum vulgus, ignobile vulgus, mobile vulgus* <all L>

the booboisie
H L MENCKEN

massive ADJS 1 **large, immense, enormous, huge**; **gigantic,** mountainous, titanic, colossal, mammoth, Gargantuan, gigantesque, monster, monstrous, outsize, sizable, larger-than-life, overgrown, king-size, monumental; massy, weighty, bulky, voluminous; **vast,** vasty, boundless, **infinite**, immeasurable, cos-

mic, astronomical, galactic; **spacious,** amplitudinous, extensive; **tremendous,** stupendous, awesome, prodigious
2 **heavy, ponderous,** hefty <nonformal>, fat; **solid,** firm, substantial

mass-produced ADJS **manufactured,** volume-produced, assembly-line

mast NOUNS **spar,** timber; pole, stick *and* tree <both nonformal>; bare pole; radio *or* television mast, antenna tower; sprit, yard, yardarm

master NOUNS 1 lord, lord and master, overlord, seigneur, paramount, lord paramount, liege, liege lord, *padrone* <Ital>, *patron* and *chef* <both Fr>, patroon; **chief, boss,** sahib <India>, *bwana* <Swah>; employer; husband, man of the house, master of the house, goodman <old or nonformal>, paterfamilias; teacher, rabbi, guru, starets; master craftsman, master workman, master carpenter, etc
2 **wise man, wise woman, sage,** sapient, man *or* woman of wisdom; **mistress,** authority, mastermind, master spirit of the age, oracle
VERBS 3 **subdue,** overmaster, **quell, crush, reduce,** beat down, **break,** break down, overwhelm; **conquer**; bring low, **bring to terms, humble,** humiliate, take down a notch *or* peg, bend, bring one to his knees, bend to one's will
4 attain mastery of, make oneself master of, **gain command of, become adept in,** become familiar *or* conversant with, become versed *or* well-versed in, **get up in** *or* **on,** gain a good *or* thorough knowledge of, **learn all about, get down pat** <nonformal>, get down cold <nonformal>, get to the bottom *or* heart of; **get the hang** *or* **knack of; learn the ropes,** learn the ins and outs; know well
ADJS 5 highest, uppermost, topmost, toprank, ranking, of the first rank, world-class, **dominant,** predominant, controlling, **overruling,** overriding, all-absorbing

masterful ADJS **perfected, finished,** polished, refined; done to a T *or* to a turn; **classic, classical,** masterly, expert, proficient; **consummate,** quintessential, archetypical, exemplary, model

mastermind NOUNS 1 **master, past master;** master hand, world-class performer, **good hand,** skilled *or* practiced hand; **prodigy; virtuoso; genius,** man *or* woman of genius
VERBS 2 **control, command,** head, govern, boss *and* head up *and* pull the strings *and* quarterback *and* call the signals <all nonformal>; **order, prescribe;** lay down the law, make the rules, call the shots *or* tune <nonformal>; manipulate, maneuver, engineer; take command; be responsible for

master of ceremonies NOUNS **MC** *or* **emcee** <both nonformal>, compère <Brit>, marshal; **toastmaster;** host, master of the revels, revel master; social director

masterpiece NOUNS **masterwork,** *chef d'œuvre* <Fr>; **master stroke,** *coup de maître* <Fr>; **feat,** *tour de force* <Fr>, **epitome;** perfect specimen, highest type; **classic,** showpiece; **paragon**

masturbation NOUNS autoeroticism, self-abuse, onanism, manipulation, playing with oneself, jacking off *and* pulling off *and* hand job <all nonformal>; sexual fantasy; wet dream

mat NOUNS pad, rug; litter, bedstraw

matador NOUNS **bullfighter,** toreador, *torero* <Sp>; banderillero, picador

match NOUNS 1 **contest,** engagement, encounter, matching, meet, meeting, derby, pissing match <nonformal>, **trial, test,** *concours* and *rencontre* <both Fr>; **close contest, hard contest,** closely fought contest, close *or* tight one, horse race *and* crapshoot <all nonformal>; **fight, bout,** battle, duel, slugfest <nonformal>
2 **equal,** mate, twin, fellow, **like, equivalent,** opposite number, counterpart, answer <nonformal>, vis à vis, equipollent, coequal, parallel, ditto <nonformal>
3 matchstick, lucifer; friction match, locofoco *and* vesuvian *and* vesta *and* fusee *and* Congreve *or* Congreve match <all old>; safety match
VERBS 4 **equal,** rival, correspond, be even-steven, be tantmount to, be equal to; **keep pace with,** keep step with, run abreast; **measure up to,** come up to, stack up with <nonformal>, match up with; **accompany**, **agree,** go along with, go hand in hand, keep pace with, keep in step

matching ADJS **analogous,** comparable; **corresponding,** correspondent, equivalent; **parallel,** paralleling; cast in the same mold, of a kind, of a size, of a piece; duplicate, twin, of the same hue *or* stripe

matchless ADJS **peerless,** champion; **unmatched,** unmatchable, unrivaled, unparagoned, unparalleled, immortal, **unequaled,** never-to-be-equaled, unpeered, unexampled, unapproached, unapproachable, **unsurpassed, unexcelled;** unsurpassable; inimitable, **incomparable,** beyond compare *or* comparison, **unique;** without equal *or* parallel, *sans pareil* <Fr>; in a class by itself, *sui generis* <L>, easily first, *facile princeps* <L>; second to none, *nulli secundus* <L>; **unbeatable,** invincible

matchmaker NOUNS **marriage broker,** matrimonial agent, *shadchen* <Yiddish>; matrimonial agency *or* bureau

mate NOUNS 1 **spouse,** yokemate, partner, consort, **better half** <nonformal>

bone of my bones, and flesh of my flesh
BIBLE

2 **equal, match,** twin, fellow, **like, equivalent,** opposite number, counterpart, answer <nonformal>, **peer,** compeer, colleague
VERBS 3 **copulate,** couple, unite in sexual intercourse, **have sexual relations,** come together, cohabit, shack up <nonformal>, be intimate; cover, mount, serve *or* service <of animals>

material NOUNS 1 **fabric, cloth, textile,** textile fabric, texture, tissue, stuff, weave, weft, woof, web, **goods,** drapery, *étoffe, tissu* <both Fr>; **substance,** matter, medium, the tangible; **elements,** constituent elements, constituents, ingredients, components, atoms, building blocks, parts
ADJS 2 **relevant, pertinent,** appertaining, **germane, apposite,** cogent, admissible, applicable, applying, pertaining, belonging, involving, appropriate, **apropos,** *à propos* <Fr>, to the purpose, **to the point,** in point, *ad rem* <L>; telling, convincing, weighty

materialistic ADJS **earthy,** unspiritual, nonspiritual, material, **secularist,** secularistic, worldly, earthly, terrestrial, **mundane,** temporal; practical, realistic; banausic, moneymaking, breadwinning, utilitarian

materialize VERBS 1 **turn up, show up,** be found; discover itself, expose *or* betray itself; hang out <nonformal>; materialize, **come to light,** come out; come along, come to hand
2 **embody,** incarnate, concretize, body forth, lend substance to, reify, entify, hypostatize

matériel NOUNS **equipment,** equipage, munitions; armament, munition; **arms, weapons,** deadly weapons, instruments of destruction, offensive weapons, **military hardware,** weaponry, ordnance, munitions of war, *apparatus belli* <L>

maternal ADJS **native,** natal, **indigenous,** endemic, autochthonous; mother, original, aboriginal, primitive; **motherly,** motherlike

mathematical ADJS numeric *or* numerical, numerary, arithmetic *or* arithmetical, algebraic *or* algebraical, geometric *or* geometrical, trigonometric *or* trigonometrical, analytic *or* analytical

mathematics NOUNS math <US nonformal>, maths <Brit nonformal>, mathematic, **numbers, figures;** pure mathematics, abstract mathematics, applied mathematics, higher mathematics, elementary mathematics

matriarch NOUNS genetrix, dam, maternal ancestor, materfamilias; **matron,** lady of the house, chatelaine; great lady, first lady; dowager

matriculate VERBS **register, enroll,** check in

matrimonial ADJS **marital, conjugal,** connubial, nuptial, wedded, married, hymeneal; epithalamic; **spousal;** husbandly, uxorious; bridal, wifely, uxorial

matrimony NOUNS **marriage,** wedlock, married status, holy matrimony, holy wedlock, match, matching, match-up, splicing <nonformal>, union, matrimonial union, alliance, marriage sacrament, sacrament of matrimony, bond of matrimony, conjugal bond *or* tie *or* knot, nuptial bond *or* tie *or* knot; married state *or* status, wedded state *or* status, wedded bliss, weddedness; intermarriage, mixed marriage, interfaith marriage, interracial marriage; misalliance, *mésalliance* <Fr>, ill-assorted marriage

a world-without-end bargain
SHAKESPEARE

matrix NOUNS **mold, form,** cast, template, negative; **die,** punch, stamp, intaglio, seal, mint; last, shoe last

matronly ADJS **womanly,** matronal, matronlike; **middle-aged,** mid-life, *entre deux âges* <Fr>, fortyish

matter NOUNS 1 **substance, sum and substance,** stuff, material, medium, building blocks, fabric; **gist, heart,** soul, meat, nub; the nitty-gritty *and* the bottom line *and* the name of the game <all nonformal>, **core,** kernel, marrow, pith, sap, spirit, **essence,** quintessence, elixir, distillate, distillation, distilled essence; **affair, business, task**, concern, interest; printed matter, reading matter
VERBS 2 signify, **count, tell,** weigh, carry weight, cut ice *and* cut some ice <both nonformal>, be prominent, stand out, mean much; be something, be somebody, amount to something

matter-of-fact ADJS **prosaic,** prose, prosy, prosing, plain; unimaginative, unimpassioned, everyday, workday, workaday, household, garden, common- *or* garden-variety; unpoetical, dull, dry, unromantic, unidealistic, unimpassioned; pedestrian

mature VERBS 1 **grow up,** grow, **develop, ripen,** flower, flourish, bloom, blossom; fledge, leave the nest, put up one's hair, not be in pigtails, put on long pants; **come of age,** come to maturity, attain majority, **reach one's majority,** reach twenty-one, reach voting age, reach the age of consent, reach manhood *or* womanhood, put on long trousers *or* pants, come into years of discretion, cut one's wisdom teeth *or* eyeteeth <nonformal>, settle down
ADJS 2 **adult, of age,** out of one's teens, big, grown, **grown-up;** old enough to know better; **ripe,** matured, maturated, seasoned; blooming, abloom; **mellow,** full-grown, fully developed

maturity NOUNS **adulthood, majority,** grown-upness, full growth, mature age, legal age, voting age, driving age, drinking age, *legalis homo* <L>; age of consent; ripe age, riper years, full age *or* growth *or* bloom, flower of age, **prime, prime of life,** age of responsibility, age *or* years of discretion, age of matured powers; **manhood,** man's estate, virility, *toga virilis* <L>; **womanhood,** womanness

maul VERBS **pound, beat,** hammer, sledgehammer, knock, rap, bang, thump, **drub,** buffet, **batter,** pulverize, paste <nonformal>, patter, pommel, pummel, pelt, baste, lambaste; thresh, thrash; flail; spank, flap

mausoleum NOUNS **tomb, sepulcher;** resting place, last home, long home, narrow house, house of death, low house, low green tent; **crypt, vault,** burial chamber

the lone couch of his everlasting sleep
SHELLEY

maven NOUNS **specialist,** specializer, **expert, authority,** savant, scholar, connoisseur; technical expert; pundit, critic; amateur, dilettante; fan, buff, freak *and* nut <both nonformal>, aficionado

maverick NOUNS 1 **nonconformist,** unconformist, **original,** eccentric, gonzo <nonformal>, deviant, deviationist; **misfit,** square peg in a round hole, **dissenter**
ADJS 2 **unconventional,** unorthodox, eccentric, gonzo <nonformal>, original, Bohemian

mawkish ADJS **oversweet,** saccharine, rich, **cloying,** sickly-sweet; **sentimental,** sentimentalized, soft, **maudlin,** oversentimental, oversentimentalized, bathetic; **mushy** *or* sloppy *or* gushing *or* teary *or* beery <all nonformal>

maxim NOUNS **aphorism,** apothegm, epigram, dictum, adage, proverb, gnome, words of wisdom, saw, saying, witticism, sentence, expression, phrase, catchword, catchphrase, word, byword, mot, motto, moral

maximize VERBS **increase, enlarge,** aggrandize, **amplify,** augment, extend, **add to; expand**, inflate; **build,** build up; pyramid, parlay

maximum NOUNS 1 **limit, end**, extremity, extreme, **acme,** apogee, climax, max <nonformal>, ceiling, **peak,** summit, **pinnacle,** crown, top; **utmost,** uttermost, utmost extent, highest degree, nth degree *or* power, *ne plus ultra* <L>
ADJS 2 **superlative,** supreme, greatest, best, highest, veriest, maximal, most, utmost, outstanding

mayhem NOUNS **mutilation,** crippling, hobbling, hamstringing, laming, maiming; destruction

maze NOUNS **complex,** meander, Chinese puzzle, **labyrinth; perplexity**

meadow NOUNS **grassland,** meadow land, mead <old>, swale, lea, haugh *or* haughland <Scots>, vega; bottomland, water meadow; **pasture,** pastureland, pasturage, pasture land

meager ADJS **slight,** scrimpy, skimp,

skimpy, exiguous; scant, **scanty,** spare; miserly, niggardly, stingy, narrow <nonformal>, parsimonious, mean; austere, Lenten, Spartan, abstemious, ascetic; stinted, frugal, sparing; poor, impoverished; small, puny, paltry

meal NOUNS **repast,** feed *and* sit-down <both nonformal>, mess, spread <nonformal>, table, board, meat, *repas* <Fr>; **refreshment,** refection

mealymouthed ADJS **flattering,** adulatory; smooth-spoken, smooth-tongued, honey-mouthed, honey-tongued, honeyed, oily-tongued; fulsome, slimy, slobbery, gushing, protesting too much, smarmy <nonformal>, insinuating, oily, buttery <nonformal>, soapy <nonformal>, **unctuous,** smooth, bland; canting, sniveling

mean NOUNS 1 **median, middle**; **golden mean,** *juste milieu* <Fr>; **medium,** happy medium; middle of the road, middle course, *via media* <L>; middle state *or* ground *or* position *or* echelon *or* level *or* point, midpoint; **average,** balance, par, normal, norm, rule, run, generality
VERBS 2 **signify,** denote, connote, import, spell, have the sense of, be construed as, have the force of; **stand for,** symbolize; imply, suggest, argue, breathe, bespeak, betoken, **indicate; mean something,** mean a lot, have impact, come home, hit one where one lives *and* hit one close to home <both nonformal>
ADJS 3 **intermediate,** intermediary, medial, medium, mesne, median, **middle**
4 **low, base, ignoble,** vile, scurvy, sorry, scrubby, beggarly; low-minded, base-minded; **ungenerous, illiberal,** unchivalrous, small, little, paltry, mingy, petty; **niggardly, stingy**

meander VERBS **go roundabout,** deviate, go around Robin Hood's barn, take *or* go the long way around, twist and turn; digress; **talk in circles,** say in a roundabout way; equivocate, shilly-shally; dodge

meandering ADJS **circuitous,** roundabout, out-of-the-way, devious, oblique, indirect, ambagious <old>, backhanded; **deviating,** digressive, discursive, excursive

meaning NOUNS **significance, signification,** *significatum* <L>, *signifié* <Fr>, point, **sense,** idea, purport, import, where one is coming from <nonformal>; **denotation;** dictionary meaning, lexical meaning; emotive *or* affective meaning, undertone, overtone, coloring; relevance, bearing, **relation,** pertinence *or* pertinency; literal meaning, true *or* real meaning, unadorned meaning; **secondary meaning,** connotation; more than meets the eye, what is read between the lines; syntactic *or* structural meaning, grammatical meaning; symbolic meaning

meaningful ADJS **significant,** significative; **denotative, connotative,** denotational, connotational, intensional, extensional, associational; **referential; symbolic, metaphorical,** figurative, allegorical; **suggestive,** indicative, **expressive; pregnant,** full of meaning, loaded *or* laden *or* fraught *or* freighted *or* heavy with significance; **pithy, meaty,** sententious, substantial, full of substance; pointed

meaningless ADJS **senseless,** purportless, importless, **insignificant,** unsignificant; empty, inane, null; **purposeless,** aimless, designless, without rhyme or reason

means NOUNS 1 ways, **ways and means,** means to an end; **wherewithal,** wherewith; funds; **resources,** disposable resources, capital; bankroll <nonformal>; assets, liquid assets, balance, **capital,** available means *or* resources *or* funds, holdings, property
2 **expedient,** means to an end, provision, measure, step, action, effort, **stroke,** stroke of policy, coup, **move,** countermove, **maneuver,** demarche, course of action

meant ADJS **intentional, intended,** proposed, purposed, telic, projected, designed, of design, aimed, aimed at, **purposeful,** purposive, willful, voluntary, deliberate; deliberated; considered, studied, advised, **calculated,** contemplated, envisaged, envisioned, meditated, **conscious,** knowing, witting; planned; teleological

meanwhile ADVS **meantime, in the meanwhile** *or* **meantime,** in the interim, *ad interim* <L>; between acts *or* halves *or* periods, betweentimes, between now and then; till *or* until then; *en attendant* <Fr>, in the intervening time, at the same time, for the nonce, for a time *or* season

measly ADJS **base, low,** low rent *and* low ride *and* low-down *and* cotton-picking <all nonformal>, **mean,** crummy, shabby, mangy <nonformal>, cheesy <nonformal>

measure NOUNS 1 **amount,** quantity, large amount, small amount, **sum, number,** count, group, total, reckoning, parcel, passel <nonformal>, **part, portion,** clutch, ration, share, issue, allotment, lot, deal
2 measuring instrument, **meter, instrument, gauge,** barometer, **rule, yardstick,** measuring rod *or* stick, **standard,** norm, canon, **criterion,** test, touchstone, check
3 **act, enactment,** legislation; **rule, ruling; prescript,** prescription; **regulation,** *règlement* <Fr>; edict, decree; **bill**
VERBS 4 **gauge, quantify,** quantitate, quantize, mete <old>, take the measure of, mensurate, triangulate, apply the yardstick to; **estimate,** make an approximation; **assess,** rate, appraise, valuate, value, evaluate, appreciate, prize; **assay**

measurement NOUNS **measure;** mensuration, measuring, **gauging; estimation,** estimate, rough measure, approximation, ballpark figure <nonformal>; **quantification,** quantitation, quantization; **appraisal,** appraisement, **stocktaking, assay,** assaying

meat NOUNS 1 flesh, red meat, *viande* <Fr>; butcher's meat, *viande de boucherie* <Fr>
2 **gist,** heart, soul, nub; the nitty-gritty *and* the bottom line *and* the name of the game <all nonformal>, **core,** kernel

meat-eating ADJS **flesh-eating, carnivorous,** omophagous, predacious

meaty ADJS **meaningful, pithy,** sententious, substantial, full of substance; pointed

mechanic NOUNS **skilled worker,** skilled laborer, **journeyman, artisan,** artificer

mechanical ADJS **involuntary,** instinctive, automatic, reflex, reflexive, knee-jerk <nonformal>, conditioned; **unconscious,** unthinking, blind; **unwitting,** unintentional, machinelike

mechanism NOUNS machinery, **movement,** movements, **action, motion, works,** workings, inner workings, what makes it work, innards, what makes it tick

medal NOUNS **military honor,** medallion; military medal, service medal, war medal, soldier's medal

meddle VERBS **pry, snoop,** peep, peek, spy, nose, nose into, have a long *or* big nose, poke *or* stick one's nose in; intervene, interfere, intermeddle

meddler NOUNS **busybody, pry,** Paul Pry, prier, Nosey Parker *or* nosey Parker *or* Nosy Parker <all nonformal>, snoop *or* snooper, **kibitzer** *and* backseat driver <both nonformal>

meddlesome ADJS meddling; **officious,** overofficious, self-appointed, impertinent, presumptuous; **busybody,** busy; pushing, pushy, forward; **prying,** nosy *or* nosey *and* snoopy <both nonformal>; inquisitive

media NOUNS **communications,** electronic communications, communications industry, communications medium *or* media, communications network

median NOUNS 1 **middle,** midmost, **midst; mean**
ADJS 2 **intermediate,** intermediary, medial, mean, medium, mesne, **middle; average,** normal, standard, par for the course

mediate VERBS intermediate, **intercede,** go between; **intervene,** interpose, step in, step into the breach, declare oneself a party, involve oneself, put oneself between disputants, use one's good offices, act between; **negotiate,** bargain, **treat with,** make terms, meet halfway; **arbitrate,** moderate; **umpire, referee,** judge

mediator NOUNS intermediator, intermediate agent, intermediate, intermedium, **intermediary,** interagent, internuncio; **intercessor,** interceder; ombudsman; **intervener,** intervenor; **go-between, middleman**; negotiator

medicate VERBS **give medicine,** drug, dope <nonformal>, dose; salve, oil, anoint, embrocate

medication NOUNS **medicine, medicament,** medicinal, theraputant, **drug,** physic, preparation; **therapy, therapeutics,** therapeusis, treatment, medical care *or* treatment

medicine man NOUNS **shaman,** shamanist; **voodoo,** voodooist, wangateur, **witch doctor,** obeah doctor, mundunugu, isangoma

mediocre ADJS **middling,** indifferent, fair, fairish, fair to middling <nonformal>, moderate, modest, medium, betwixt and between; respectable, passable, **tolerable; so-so,** *comme ci comme ça* <Fr>

meditate VERBS **consider, contemplate,** speculate, reflect, study, ponder, perpend, weigh, deliberate, debate, muse, brood, ruminate, chew the cud <nonformal>, digest; introspect, be abstracted; wrinkle one's brow

medium NOUNS 1 **psychic; spiritualist,** spiritist, ecstatic, spirit rapper, automatist, psychographist; necromancer
2 **substance,** stuff, fabric, material, matter, the tangible; **elements,** constituent elements, constituents, ingredients, components, atoms, building blocks, parts
ADJS 3 mean, **intermediate,** intermediary, median, medial, mid-level, middle-echelon; **average,** normal, standard, par for the course; middle-of-the-road, moderate; **middling, ordinary,** usual, routine, common, mediocre, merely adequate, passing, banal, so-so

medley NOUNS **miscellany,** miscellanea, collectanea; **assortment,** variety, mixture; hodgepodge, conglomerate, **conglomeration,** omnium-gatherum <nonformal>

meek ADJS **gentle, mild,** mild-mannered, peaceable, pacific, quiet; **subdued, chastened, tame,** tamed, broken, housebroken, domesticated; lamblike, gentle as a lamb, dovelike; humble

meet NOUNS 1 **contest, engagement, encounter, match,** matching, meeting, derby, pissing match <nonformal>, **trial, test,** *concours* and *rencontre* <both Fr>; tournament, tourney; rally; **game**; **games,** Olympic games, Olympics, gymkhana
2 **assembly,** *assemblée* <Fr>, **gathering, forgathering, congregation,** congress, conference, convocation, concourse, **meeting, get-together** *and* turnout <both nonformal>
VERBS 3 **encounter; come across, run across,** meet up, fall across, cross the path of; **come upon,** run upon, fall upon, light *or* alight upon; come among, fall among; **meet with,** meet up with <nonformal>, experience, come face to face with, **confront,** meet head-on *or* eyeball to eyeball; **run into, bump into** *and* run smack into <both nonformal>, join up with, come *or* run up against <nonformal>, run *and* fall foul of; be on a collision course
4 **come together, assemble, congregate, collect,** come from far and wide, come *or* arrive in a body; league, ally; **unite**; muster, **gather, forgather,** gang up <nonformal>, mass; **merge,** converge, flow together, fuse

meeting NOUNS 1 meeting up, joining, joining up, **encounter;** confrontation; rencontre; near-miss, collision course, near thing, narrow squeak *or* brush; **conference,** congress, convention, parley, palaver, confab <nonformal>, confabulation, **conclave, powwow, huddle** <nonformal>, **consultation,** *pourparler* <Fr>; **rendezvous,** tryst, assignation
ADJS 2 **in contact,** contacting, **touching,** contingent; impinging, impingent; tangent, tangential; osculatory; grazing, kissing, glancing, brushing, rubbing, nudging; **assembled,** collected, gathered; **joining, connecting**

melancholy NOUNS 1 **melancholia,** melancholiness; gentle melancholy, romantic melancholy; **pensiveness, wistfulness,** tristfulness; **nostalgia,** homesickness, *mal du pays* <Fr>
ADJS 2 melancholic, **blue** <nonformal>, life-weary, world-weary, tired of living; atrabilious, atrabiliar; **pensive, wistful,** tristful; **nostalgic,** homesick

melee NOUNS **commotion, hubbub,** Babel, tumult, turmoil, uproar, racket, riot, **disturbance, rumpus** <nonformal>, ruckus *and* ruction <both nonformal>, **fracas, hassle; row** *and* hassle <both nonformal>, **brawl,** free-for-all <nonformal>, donnybrook *or* donnybrook fair, broil, embroilment, scramble; **roughhouse, rough-and-tumble**

meliorate VERBS **improve, grow better,** look better, show improvement, **mend,** ameliorate; **look up** *or* **pick up** *or* **perk up** <all nonformal>; **advance, progress,** make progress, make headway, gain, gain ground, go forward, get *or* go ahead, come on, come along *and* come along nicely <both nonformal>, get along; make strides *or* rapid strides, take off *and* skyrocket <both nonformal>

mellow VERBS 1 **mature, grow up,** grow, **develop, ripen,** flower, flourish, bloom, blossom; season, temper
ADJS 2 **resonant, reverberant, vibrant, sonorous,** plangent, rolling;

rich, full; **merry,** jolly, happy, gay; **agreeable,** complaisant, harmonious, *en rapport* <Fr>, compatible; **mature, ripe,** ripened, of full *or* ripe age, **developed,** fully developed, well-developed, **full-grown,** full-fledged, fully fledged, full-blown, in full bloom, in one's prime; mellowed, seasoned, tempered, aged

melodrama NOUNS **theatrics,** theatricality, histrionics, dramatics, hamminess *and* chewing up the scenery <both nonformal>; **sensationalism,** emotionalism, melodramatics, blood and thunder

melodramatic ADJS **emotionalistic,** emotive, overemotional, hysteric, hysterical, sensational, sensationalistic, theatric, theatrical, histrionic, dramatic, overdramatic, hammy <nonformal>, nonrational, unreasoning; hyperthymic

melody NOUNS **tune, tone,** musical sound, musical quality, tonality; sweetness, dulcetness, mellifluence, mellifluousness

melt VERBS **liquefy,** liquidize, liquesce, fluidify, fluidize; **run,** thaw, colliquate; **affect, touch, move, soften,** melt the heart, choke one up, give one a lump in the throat; touch a chord, **touch a sympathetic chord,** touch one's heart, tug at the heart *or* heartstrings

member NOUNS 1 **appendage,** external organ; **arm; leg,** limb, wing
2 affiliate, belonger, insider, initiate, one of us, cardholder, card-carrier, card-carrying member; **enrollee,** enlistee; **associate,** socius, **fellow;** brother, sister; comrade; honorary member; life member; member in good standing, dues-paying member; charter member

membership NOUNS participation, partaking, sharing, cooperation; members, associates, affiliates, body of affiliates, constituency

memento NOUNS **remembrance,** token, trophy, souvenir, keepsake, relic, favor, token of remembrance; *memento mori* <L>; **memories, memorabilia,** memorials

memoir NOUNS **history, biography,** memorial, life, story, life story, adventures, fortunes, experiences; **autobiography, memoirs,** memorials

memorabilia NOUNS **archives,** public records, government archives, government papers, presidential papers, historical documents, historical records; biographical records, life records, biographical material, papers, ana; **annals, chronicles,** chronology; notabilia, great doings

memorable ADJS **notable,** noteworthy, celebrated, remarkable, marked, **standout** <nonformal>, of mark, signal; rememberable, unforgettable, never to be forgotten; striking, telling, salient

memorandum VERBS **memo** <nonformal>, memoir, *aide-mémoire* <Fr>, memorial; **reminder**; **note, notation,** annotation, jotting, docket, marginal note, marginalia, scholium, scholia, adversaria

memorial NOUNS 1 **monument,** monumental *or* memorial record; necrology, obituary, **memento,** remembrance, testimonial; **marker;** inscription; **tablet,** stone, hoarstone <Brit>, boundary stone, memorial stone; **pillar,** stele *or* stela, shaft, column, memorial column, rostral column, manubial column; war memorial; arch, memorial arch, triumphal arch; memorial statue, bust; monolith, obelisk, **pyramid; gravestone, tombstone;** memorial tablet, brass; cenotaph; cairn, mound, barrow, cromlech, dolmen, megalith, menhir, cyclolith; **shrine,** reliquary, tope, stupa
ADJS 2 **celebrative,** celebratory, celebrating; **commemorative,** commemorating

memorialize VERBS **celebrate,** observe, keep, mark, solemnly mark, honor; **commemorate; solemnize,** signalize, hallow, mark with a red letter

memorize VERBS **commit to memory,** con; **learn by heart,** get by heart, learn *or* get by rote, get word-perfect *or* letter-perfect, learn word for word, learn verbatim; know by heart *or* from memory, have by heart *or* rote, have at one's fingertips

memory NOUNS 1 **engram,** memory trace, traumatic trace *or* memory; unconscious memory; **remembrance,** recollection, reminiscence, fond remembrance, retrospection, musing on the past, looking back

the remembrance of things past
SHAKESPEARE

la recherche du temps perdu
PROUST

2 **computer memory, storage,** memory bank, memory chip, firmware; **main memory,** main storage *or* store, random access memory *or* RAM, core, core storage *or* store, disk pack, magnetic disk, primary storage, backing store, read/write memory, optical disk memory, bubble memory; read-only memory *or* ROM, programmable read-only memory *or* PROM

men NOUNS **work force,** hands, staff, personnel, employees, help, hired help, the help, **crew, gang,** force; **fighting force,** troops, units, firepower; human resources; **forces; mankind,** menfolk *or* menfolks <nonformal>, the sword side

menace NOUNS 1 **threat,** threateningness, threatfulness, promise of harm, knife poised at one's throat, arrow aimed at one's heart, sword of Damocles; **foreboding; warning**; saber-rattling, muscle-flexing, woofing <nonformal>, bulldozing, scare tactics, **intimidation**, arm-twisting <nonformal>

VERBS 2 **threaten,** bludgeon, bulldoze, put the heat *or* screws *or* squeeze on <nonformal>, lean on <nonformal>; hold a pistol to one's head, terrorize, **intimidate,** twist one's arm *and* arm-twist <both nonformal>; utter threats against, shake *or* double *or* clench one's fist at; hold over one's head; **lower,** spell *or* mean trouble, look threatening, loom, loom up; **be imminent**

menacing ADJS **threatening,** threatful, minatory, minacious; **lowering; imminent**; **ominous,** foreboding; denunciatory, comminatory, abusive; fear-inspiring, **intimidating,** bludgeoning, muscle-flexing, saber-rattling, bulldozing, browbeating, bullying, hectoring, blustering, terrorizing, terroristic

ménage NOUNS **family,** household, hearth, hearthside, people, **folk,** homefolk, folks *and* homefolks <both nonformal>

menagerie NOUNS **zoo,** *Tiergarten* <Ger>, zoological garden *or* park

mend VERBS 1 **get well,** recover, be oneself again, feel like a new person, get back on one's feet, get over it; recuperate; **improve, better,** change for the better

2 **repair,** fix, fix up <nonformal>, do up, doctor <nonformal>, put in repair, put in shape, set to rights, put in order *or* condition; **condition,** recondition, commission, put in commission, ready; **service, overhaul;** patch, **patch up**

menial NOUNS 1 **servant,** servitor, help; **domestic,** domestic help, domestic servant, house servant; live-in help, day help; drudge, slavey <nonformal>; scullion, turnspit

ADJS 2 **servile,** slavish, subservient, **base,** mean

menopause NOUNS **change of life,** climacteric, grand climacteric

mental ADJS **intellectual,** rational, reasoning, thinking, noetic, conceptive, conceptual, phrenic; intelligent; noological; **cognitive,** prehensive, thought, conceptualized, ideative, ideational

mental block NOUNS **block,** blocking, memory obstruction; repression, suppression, defense mechanism

mental deficiency NOUNS **insanity,** alienation, aberration, mental disturbance, **derangement,** distraction, disorientation, mental derangement *or* disorder, unbalance, mental instability, unsoundness, **unsoundness of mind;** unbalanced mind, diseased *or* unsound mind

mental hospital NOUNS psychopathic hospital *or* ward, **psychiatric hospital** *or* ward, **insane asylum,** asylum, lunatic asylum, **madhouse,** mental institution, mental home, bedlam; **bughouse** *and* nuthouse *and* laughing academy *and* **loonybin** *and* **booby hatch** *and* funny farm <all nonformal>

mental illness NOUNS **mental disorder,** emotional disorder, psychonosema, psychopathyfunctional nervous disorder; emotional instability; **maladjustment,** social maladjustment; nervous breakdown, crack-up <nonformal>; **insanity; psychosis;** schizophrenia; paranoia; **manic-depressive psychosis, depression,** melancholia; **neurosis, psychoneurosis,** neurotic *or* psychoneurotic disorder

mentality NOUNS **intellect,** mind, *mens* <L>; mental *or* intellectual faculty, nous, **reason, rationality,** rational *or* reasoning faculty, power of reason, *Vernunft* <Ger>, *esprit* <Fr>, *raison* <Fr>, ratio, discursive reason, **intelligence,** mental capacity, **understanding,** reasoning, intellection, conception

discourse of reason
SHAKESPEARE

mental telepathy NOUNS **telepathy,** mind reading, thought transference, telepathic transmission; telepathic dream, telepathic hallucination

mention NOUNS 1 **remark,** statement, earful *and* crack *and* one's two cents' worth <all nonformal>, **word,** say, **saying,** utterance, observation, reflection, expression; note, thought; assertion, averment, allegation, affirmation, pronouncement, position, dictum; **declaration; citation,** eulogy, honorable mention, kudos, accolade, tribute, praise
VERBS 2 **remark,** comment, observe, note; let drop *or* fall, say by the way, make mention of; refer to, allude to, touch on, make reference to, call attention to; opine <nonformal>; interject; blurt, blurt out, exclaim; direct attention to, **bring under** *or* **to one's notice,** hold up to notice, bring to attention, mention in passing

mentor NOUNS **adviser,** counsel, counselor, consultant, expert, maven <nonformal>; instructor, guide, nestor, orienter; confidant, personal adviser

menu NOUNS **bill of fare,** *carte du jour* <Fr>

mercantile ADJS **commercial,** business, trade, trading, merchant; commercialistic, mercantilistic

mercenary NOUNS 1 **hireling,** *condottiere* <Ital>, free lance, free companion, **soldier of fortune,** adventurer, myrmidon
ADJS 2 **greedy, avaricious,** avid, voracious, rapacious, cupidinous, esurient, **ravening,** grasping, grabby <nonformal>, graspy, acquisitive, sordid, overgreedy; ravenous, gobbling, devouring; miserly, money-hungry, money-grubbing, money-mad, venal; **piggish,** hoggish, swinish, a hog for, greedy as a hog; **gluttonous; employed,** hired, hireling, paid

merchandise NOUNS 1 **commodities,** wares, goods, effects, vendibles; **items,** oddments; **consumer goods,** consumer items, retail goods, goods for sale; **stock, stock-in-trade;** staples; **inventory; line,** line of goods; mail-order goods, catalog goods; **luxury goods,** high-ticket *or* big-ticket *or* upscale items
VERBS 2 **sell, market,** move, turn over, sell off, make *or* effect a sale

merchandising NOUNS **selling,** marketing; direct selling; mail-order selling, direct-mail selling, catalog selling; television *or* video selling; **vending,** peddling, hawking, huckstering

merchant NOUNS merchandiser, marketer, **trader,** trafficker, **dealer,** monger, chandler; **tradesman,** tradeswoman; **storekeeper,** shopkeeper

merciful ADJS **pitying, sympathetic,** sympathizing, commiserative, condolent, understanding; **compassionate,** ruthful, rueful, **clement,** gentle, soft, melting, bleeding, tender, **tenderhearted,** softhearted, warmhearted; **humane,** human; lenient, forbearant; charitable

merciless ADJS **pitiless,** unpitying, unpitiful; blind *or* deaf to pity; **unsympathetic,** unsympathizing; **uncompassionate,** uncompassioned; **unmerciful,** without mercy, unruing, **ruthless,** dog-eat-dog; unfeeling, bowelless, inclement, relentless, inexorable, unyielding, unforgiving; **heartless,** hard, hard as nails, steely, flinty, harsh, savage, **cruel**, brutal, brutish, **bestial,** mindless, insensate, monstrous, mutant, inhuman, bloody, sanguinary, kill-crazy <nonformal>; malign, malignant

mercy NOUNS **clemency,** clementness, mercifulness, **humaneness,** humanity, pity, **compassion**; **mildness, gentleness,** tenderness, softness, moderateness; **easiness,** easygoingness; laxness; acceptance, **tolerance**

mercy killing NOUNS euthanasia, negative *or* passive euthanasia

merge VERBS **converge,** come together, approach, run together, **meet,** unite, connect; **join,** band, league, **associate, affiliate,** ally, **combine, unite,** fuse, coalesce, amalgamate, federate, confederate, consolidate; hook up *and* tie up *and* tie in <all nonformal>; be in league, **go into partnership with,** go partners <nonformal>, go *or* be in cahoots with; **join together,** club together, league together, band together; **blend,** interblend, stir in

merger NOUNS **combination,** combine, combo <nonformal>, composition; **amalgamation,** consolidation, assimilation, **integration,** solidification, encompassment, inclusion, ecumenism; **alliance,** affiliation, reaffiliation, association, league, hookup <nonformal>, tie-up <nonformal>; buyout, takeover, leveraged buyout

merit NOUNS 1 **importance,** value, worth, excellence; **goodness,** quality, class <nonformal>; **virtue,** grace; desert; **fineness,** goodliness, fairness, niceness; **superiority,** first-rateness, **skillfulness**
VERBS 2 **deserve,** earn, rate *and* be in line for <both nonformal>, **be worthy of,** be deserving, richly deserve

meritorious ADJS **praiseworthy,** worthy, **commendable,** estimable, **laudable,** admirable, creditable; exemplary, model, unexceptionable; well-deserving; beyond all praise, *sans peur et sans reproche* <Fr>; **deserving,** meriting, worthy of, worth one's salt, **well-thought-of,** highly regarded, held in esteem, in good odor, in favor, in high favor; in one's good books

mermaid NOUNS **swimmer, bather,** natator, merman; bathing girl; bathing beauty; undine, nix, nixie, kelpie; **naiad,** limniad, fresh-water nymph; sea nymph, ocean nymph, sea-maid, sea-maiden, siren

merry ADJS **mirthful,** hilarious; joyful, joyous, rejoicing; **gleeful,** gleesome; **jolly,** buxom; **jovial,** jocund, jocular; **frivolous;** laughter-loving, mirth-loving, risible

as merry as the day is long
SHAKESPEARE

merry-go-round NOUNS **round of pleasure,** mad round, **whirl,** the rounds, the dizzy rounds; carousel, roundabout, ride, whirligig, whip, flying horses

merrymaking NOUNS **conviviality,** joviality, jollity, gaiety, heartiness, cheer, good cheer, festivity, partying, merriment, revelry

mesa NOUNS **plateau,** tableland, high plateau, table, table mountain, butte, moor, fell <Brit>, hammada

mescaline NOUNS

<nonformal> beans, big chief, buttons, cactus, mesc

mesh NOUNS 1 **interaction,** interworking, intercourse, intercommunication, **interplay;** meshing, intermeshing, engagement; **network, computer network,** communications network, local area network *or* LAN, workgroup computing
VERBS 2 **interact,** interwork, **interplay;** intermesh, engage, fit, fit like a glove, dovetail, mortise; **interweave,** interlace, intertwine; **interchange;** coact, **cooperate;** codepend

mesmerize VERBS **grip,** hold, arrest, hold the interest, fascinate, enthrall, spellbind, **hold spellbound,** grab <nonformal>, charm, enchant, hypnotize, catch; absorb the attention, claim one's thoughts, engross the mind *or* thoughts, engage the attention, involve the interest, occupy the attention, monopolize one's attention, engage the mind *or* thoughts

mess NOUNS 1 **meal,** repast, feed *and* sit-down <both nonformal>, spread <nonformal>, table, board, meat, *repas* <Fr>; **rations,** board, meals, commons <chiefly Brit>, allowance, allotment, food allotment, tucker <Australia>
2 **dining room,** *salle à manger* <Fr>, dining hall, refectory, messroom *or* mess hall, commons
3 **jumble,** scramble, tumble, snarl-up, bloody *or* holy *or* unholy *or* god-awful mess <nonformal> **turmoil,** welter, mishmash, hash, helter-skelter, farrago, crazy-quilt, higgledy-piggledy; **clutter,** litter, **disorder,** chaos, mix-up *and* snafu <both nonformal>;
4 **eyesore,** blot, blot on the landscape, blemish, **sight** <nonformal>, **fright, horror,** no beauty, no beauty queen, ugly duckling
5 **disarrange,** derange, misarrange; **disorder,** disorganize, throw out of order, put out of gear, dislocate, upset the applecart, **disarray; dishevel,** rumple, ruffle; tousle <nonformal>, muss *and* **muss up** <both nonformal>, **mess up** <nonformal>; **litter, clutter,** scatter

message NOUNS **dispatch,** word, communication, communiqué, advice, press release, release; **letter,** epistle; personal letter, business letter; **commercial,** commercial announcement, commercial message, **spot announcement,** spot *and* plug <both nonformal>

messed up ADJS 1 **disheveled,** mussed up <nonformal>, **rumpled,** tumbled, ruffled, snarled, snaggy; **tousled,** tously; uncombed, shaggy, matted

2 <nonformal> **goofed-up, bobbled,** bitched, bitched-up, hashed-up, **fouled-**

up, fucked-up, screwed-up, bollixed-up, loused-up, gummed-up, buggered, buggered-up, snafued; clunky, half-assed; ass-backwards

3 <nonformal> **queered, screwed up, fouled up,** loused up, snafued, buggered, buggered up, gummed up, snarled up, balled up, bollixed up, hashed up, mucked up, botched up; beat up, clapped-out <Brit>; totaled, kaput, finished, packed-up <Brit>, done for, cooked, sunk, shot

messenger NOUNS message-bearer, **dispatch-bearer,** commissionaire <Brit>, nuncio <old>, **courier,** diplomatic courier, carrier, **runner,** express <Brit>, dispatch-rider, pony-express rider, post-boy, postrider, *estafette* <Fr>; bicycle *or* motorcycle messenger; **go-between,** emissary; Mercury, Hermes, Iris, Pheidippides, Paul Revere

mess hall NOUNS **dining room,** *salle à manger* <Fr>, dinette, dining hall, refectory, mess *or* messroom, commons; **cafeteria**

messiah NOUNS **leader of men,** born leader, charismatic leader *or* figure, inspired leader; Mahdi

messy ADJS **dirty,** grimy, grubby, grungy <nonformal>, smirchy, dingy; scruffy, slovenly, untidy; **slipshod,** slipshoddy, **slovenly,** sloppy *and* half-assed <both nonformal>, sluttish

metabolize VERBS **digest,** assimilate, absorb; predigest

metallic ADJS **metal,** metallike, metalline, metalloid *or* metalloidal, metalliform

metamorphosis NOUNS **transformation,** transmogrification; **translation;** metamorphism; **transfiguration** *or* transfigurement; **transubstantiation,** consubstantiation

metaphor NOUNS **comparison,** likening, comparing, **analogy;** simile, similitude, allegory, figure *or* trope of comparison

metaphorical ADJS **symbolic,** symbolical, allegoric, allegorical, figural, figurative, tropological, metaphorical, anagogic, anagogical, trolatitious; allusive, referential

mete VERBS **administer,** give, bestow; apply, put on *or* upon, lay on *or* upon, dose, dose with, dish out <nonformal>, mete out, prescribe; **force, force upon,** impose by force *or* main force, strongarm <nonformal>, force down one's throat, enforce upon

meteoric ADJS **brief,** short, short-time, quick, brisk, swift, fleet, speedy, cometary, flashing, flickering; short-term, short-termed

meteorology NOUNS weather science, aerology, aerography, air-mass analysis, weatherology, climatology, climatography, microclimatology, forecasting, long-range forecasting; barometry; anemology; nephology

meter NOUNS **measure,** numbers; **rhythm,** cadence, movement, lilt, jingle, swing; **accent,** accentuation, metrical accent, stress, emphasis, ictus, **beat**

method NOUNS 1 **plan,** scheme, design, **program,** device, contrivance, game, envisagement, conception, enterprise, **idea,** notion; organization, rationalization, systematization, schematization; tactics, **strategy,** game plan <nonformal>; methodology, **system;** algorithm <math>; **approach,** attack, tack
2 **approach,** attack, tack; **technique, procedure, process,** proceeding, course, practice; *modus operandi* <L>, mode of operation *or* MO, manner of working, mode of procedure

methodical ADJS **orderly,** ordered, regular, well-regulated, well-ordered, formal, regular as clockwork, uniform, **systematic,** symmetrical, **harmonious;** businesslike, routine, steady, normal, habitual, usual, *en règle,* in hand; **arranged**

meticulous ADJS **exacting,** scrupulous, conscientious, religious, punctilious, punctual, **particular,** fussy, critical, attentive, scrutinizing; **thorough,** thoroughgoing, thoroughpaced; **finical,** finicking, finicky; **exact,** precise, precisionistic, precisianistic, prissy, accurate, correct; **strict,** rigid, **rigorous,** spit-and-polish, exigent, demanding; nice, delicate, subtle, fine, refined, minute, detailed, exquisite; **fastidious**

metropolis NOUNS **capital;** metropolitan area, greater city, megalopolis, supercity, conurbation, urban complex; urban center, art center, cultural center, medical center, shopping center, shipping center, railroad center, garment center, manufacturing center, tourist center, trade center, etc

mettle NOUNS **pluck, spunk** <nonformal>, backbone <nonformal>, **grit,** true grit, spirit, **stamina,** guts *and* moxie <both nonformal>, pith <old>

mettlesome NOUNS **plucky,** spunky *and* feisty *and* gutty *or* gutsy <all nonformal>, gritty, dauntless, **game,** game to the last *or* end; **courageous**

mews NOUNS **barn,** stable, stall; **cowbarn,** cowhouse, cowshed, cowbyre, byre; street

Mickey Finn NOUNS **anesthetic,** sleeping pill *or* tablet, Mickey *and* knockout drops <both nonformal>, chloral hydrate; drug, dope <nonformal>, narcotic, opiate

Mickey Mouse ADJS **vulgar,** tasteless, in bad *or* poor taste, tacky *and* chintzy <both nonformal>; cheap, paltry

microbe NOUNS **germ,** pathogen, contagium, bug <nonformal>, disease-causing agent, disease-producing microorganism; microorganism

microcosm NOUNS **miniature,** mini; scaled-down *or* miniaturized version; microcosmos

microorganism NOUNS **germ,** pathogen, contagium, disease-causing agent, disease-producing microorganism, bug <nonformal> **microbe, virus,** filterable virus, nonfilterable virus, adenovirus, echovirus, reovirus, rhinovirus, enterovirus, picornavirus, retrovirus; rickettsia; bacterium, **bacteria,** streptococcus, staphylococcus, bacillus, spirillum, vibrio, spirochete

microphone NOUNS **mike** <nonformal>; radiomicrophone; concealed microphone, **bug** <nonformal>

microscopic ADJS **infinitesimal,** ultramicroscopic; evanescent, thin, tenuous; inappreciable; impalpable, imponderable, intangible; imperceptible, indiscernible, invisible, unseeable

microwave VERBS **cook,** prepare food, heat, micro-cook, nuke <nonformal>

midday NOUNS 1 **noon,** noonday, noontide, nooning <nonformal>, noontime, **high noon,** meridian, *meridiem* <L>, twelve o'clock, 1200 hours, eight bells; noonlight
ADJS 2 **noon,** noonday, noonish, meridian, twelve-o'clock; noonlit

middle NOUNS 1 median, midmost, **midst;** thick, thick of things; **center**; **heart,** core, nucleus, kernel; **mean**; interior; midriff, diaphragm; **waist,** waistline, zone, girth
ADJS 2 **medial,** median, mesial, middling, mediocre, average, **medium**, mezzo <music>, **mean,** mid; **midmost,** middlemost; **central**, core, nuclear; interior; **intermediate,** intermediary; centrist, moderate, middle-of-the-road

middle age NOUNS middle life, meridian of life, the middle years, the wrong side of forty, the dangerous age

middle-class ADJS bourgeois, *petit-bourgeois* <Fr>, petty-bourgeois, suburban

middleman NOUNS **go-between,** intermediary, medium, intermedium, intermediate, interagent, **internuncio,** broker; connection <nonformal>, **contact; negotiator,** negotiant; interpleader; arbitrator, mediator; wholesaler, jobber

middle school NOUNS **secondary school,** middle school, **junior high school,** junior high <nonformal>, intermediate school

middling ADJS **mediocre,** indifferent, fair, fairish, fair to middling <nonformal>, moderate, modest, medium, betwixt and between; respectable, passable, **tolerable; so-so,** *comme ci comme ça* <Fr>; of a kind, of a sort, of sorts <nonformal>; nothing to brag about, not much to boast of, nothing to write home about

midget NOUNS 1 **dwarf,** dwarfling, midge, **pygmy,** manikin, homunculus, atomy, micromorph, hop-o'-my-thumb
ADJS 2 **dwarf,** dwarfed, dwarfish, **pygmy,** nanoid, elfin; Lilliputian, Tom Thumb; **undersized,** undersize, squat, dumpy; **stunted,** undergrown, runty, pint-size *or* -sized *and* sawed-off <all nonformal>; **small,** tiny

midnight NOUNS 1 **dead of night,** hush of night, the witching hour

the very witching time of night
SHAKESPEARE

ADJS 2 **nocturnal,** night, **nightly,** nighttime; nightlong, all-night; night-fallen

midst NOUNS **middle,** median, midmost; thick, thick of things; **center; heart, core,** nucleus, kernel; **mean**; interior

midtown NOUNS 1 city center, city centre <Brit>, urban center, central *or* center city, core, core city, inner city, business district *or* section, shopping center
ADJS 2 **urban,** municipal, **inner-city,** core, core-city

midway ADVS **halfway, in the middle,** betwixt and between <nonformal>, halfway in the middle <nonformal>; plump *or* smack *or* slap- *or* smack-dab in the middle <nonformal>; half-and-half, neither here nor there, *mezzo-mezzo* <Ital>; medially, mediumly; **in the midst of,** in the thick of

mien NOUNS **look, air,** demeanor, carriage, bearing, port, posture, stance, poise, presence; guise, garb, complexion, color; appearance, outward appearance, seeming, **front,** manner

miff VERBS **provoke, incense,** arouse, inflame, embitter; **vex, irritate, annoy, aggravate** <nonformal>, **exasperate, nettle,** fret, chafe; **pique, peeve** <nonformal>, huff; **ruffle, roil, rile** <nonformal>, ruffle one's feathers, **rankle;** put *or* get one's back up, stick in one's craw <nonformal>; **stir up, work up**

might NOUNS **strength,** mightiness, powerfulness, stamina; **force,** potency, power; **energy; vigor,** vitality, vigorousness, heartiness, lustiness, lustihood; **stoutness, sturdiness,** stalwartness, robustness, hardiness, ruggedness

mighty ADJS 1 **strong, forceful,** forcible, forcy <Scots>, powerful, puissant <nonformal>, potent; **stout,** sturdy, stalwart, rugged, hale; hunky *and* husky *and* hefty *and* beefy <all nonformal>, strapping, doughty <nonformal>, **hardy,** hard, hard as nails, cast-iron, iron-hard, steely; **robust,** robustious, gutty *and* gutsy <both nonformal>; strong-willed, obstinate; **vigorous, hearty,** nervy, **lusty,** bouncing, full- *or* red-blooded; bionic, sturdy as an ox, strong as a lion *or* an ox *or* a horse

ADVS 2 **very, exceedingly,** awfully *and* terribly *and* terrifically <all nonformal>, **quite,** just, so, **really,** real *and* right <both nonformal>, **pretty,** only too, mightily, almighty *and* powerfully *and* powerful <all nonformal>

migrate VERBS **transmigrate,** trek; flit, take wing; run <of fish>, swarm <of bees>; **emigrate,** out-migrate, expatriate; **immigrate,** in-migrate; remigrate; intermigrate

mild ADJS 1 **lenient, gentle,** mild-mannered, tender, humane, compassionate, **clement,** merciful; soft, moderate, **easy,** easygoing; lax; forgiving; **forbearing,** forbearant, patient; accepting, **tolerant**

2 **warm,** fair, genial; **temperate,** warmish; **tepid,** lukewarm, room-temperature

mildew NOUNS 1 **fetidness, mustiness,** funkiness, must, moldiness, fustiness, frowziness, stuffiness; mold, fungus, smut, rust

VERBS 2 mold, molder, molder away, rot away, rust away

mileage NOUNS distance; footage, yardage; infinity; perpetuity; long time; linear measures; oblongness; longitude

milestone NOUNS **marker,** mark; **landmark,** seamark; benchmark; milepost; cairn, menhir

milieu NOUNS **ambience,** atmosphere, climate, air, aura, spirit, feeling, feel, quality, color, local color, sense, sense of place, note, tone, overtone, undertone; **neighborhood,** vicinity, vicinage, neck of the woods <nonformal>, purlieus; premises, confines, precincts, environs

militant ADJS **warlike,** fighting, warring, battling; **martial,** military, soldierly, soldierlike; **combative,** contentious, gladiatorial; **belligerent,** pugnacious, truculent, bellicose, scrappy <nonformal>, full of fight; **aggressive,** offensive; **activist,** activistic

military ADJS **warlike,** militant, fighting, warring, battling; **martial,** soldierly, soldierlike

militia NOUNS organized militia, national militia, mobile militia, territorial militia, reserve militia; home reserve; **National Guard,** Air National Guard, state guard; minutemen

milk VERBS **exploit,** take advantage of, use, make use of, **use for one's own ends;** make a paw *or* cat's-paw of, sucker *and* play for a sucker <both nonformal>; **manipulate,** work on, work upon, stroke, play on *or* upon; play both ends against the middle; **impose upon,** presume upon; batten on; bleed, bleed white <nonformal>; drain, suck the blood of *or* from, suck dry; exploit one's position, feather one's nest <nonformal>, **profiteer**

mill NOUNS 1 **plant, factory, works,** manufacturing plant, *usine* <Fr>; sawmill, flour mill, etc

2 **pulverizer,** comminutor, triturator, levigator; crusher; grinder; granulator, pepper grinder, pepper mill

VERBS 3 **throng,** crowd, swarm, teem, hive, surge, seethe, stream, horde; gather around, gang around <nonfor-

mal>; **seethe,** mill around *or* about, stir, roil, moil, be turbulent
4 **process,** convert; machine; **pulverize, powder,** comminute, triturate, contriturate, levigate, bray, pestle, disintegrate, reduce to powder *or* dust, grind to powder *or* dust, grind up; flour

millennium NOUNS **thousand,** M, chiliad; **utopia** *or* Utopia <Sir Thomas More>, paradise, heaven, **heaven on earth;** kingdom come; **good times,** piping times, bright *or* palmy *or* halcyon days, days of wine and roses, rosy era; heyday; prosperity, era of prosperity; age of Aquarius

millinery NOUNS **headdress,** headgear, headwear, headclothes, headtire; headpiece, chapeau, cap, hat; hatmaking, hatting

millstone NOUNS **burden,** pressure, oppression, deadweight; handicap, drag; grinder; quern, quernstone

Milquetoast NOUNS **weakling,** weak *or* meek soul, weak sister <nonformal>, hothouse plant, softy <nonformal>, softling, **jellyfish,** invertebrate, gutless wonder <nonformal>, **baby,** big baby, crybaby, chicken <nonformal>, sop, **milksop,** namby-pamby, mollycoddle, mama's boy, mother's boy, mother's darling, teacher's pet; **wimp,** poor *or* weak *or* dull tool <nonformal>; **nonentity,** hollow man, doormat *and* empty suit *and* nebbish *and* sad sack <all nonformal>

mime NOUNS **imitator,** simulator, impersonator, impostor, **mimic,** mimicker, mimer; **impersonation,** personation; mimicry, mimicking, miming, mummer, pantomimist; pantomime, pantomiming, aping, dumb show; mimesis, **imitation**

mimic NOUNS 1 **imitator,** simulator, metooer <nonformal>, impersonator, impostor, mimicker, mimer, mime, **mocker;** mockingbird, cuckoo
VERBS 2 **impersonate,** mime, **ape, parrot,** copycat <nonformal>; do an impression; take off, hit off, hit off on, take off on; **imitate, simulate,** copy, counterfeit

mince VERBS 1 **strut,** swagger; sashay <nonformal>, prance, tittup, flounce, trip, skip
2 **pulverize**, grind, cut to pieces, make mincemeat of, make hamburger of <nonformal>

mind NOUNS 1 **will,** pleasure, will and pleasure; heart's desire; **wish, fancy,** discretion, pleasure, inclination, disposition, liking, appetence, appetency, **desire;** half a mind *or* notion; **resolve,** resolution; **turn of mind,** tendency, grain, vein, set, mental set, mindset, **leaning,** animus, propensity, proclivity, predilection, preference, predisposition
VERBS 2 **care, heed,** reck, think, consider, regard, pay heed to, take heed *or* thought of; **take an interest,** be concerned; **pay attention; care for,** take care of; **look after,** see after, attend to, minister to, look *or* see to, look *or* watch out for <nonformal>, have *or* keep an eye on *or* upon, keep a sharp eye on *or* upon, **watch over,** keep watch over, **watch**, tend

mind-altering drug NOUNS **hallucinogen,** psychedelic, psychedelic drug, psychoactive drug, psychoactive chemical *or* psychochemical, psychotropic drug, psychotomimetic drug, mind-expanding drug, mind-blowing drug

mind-blowing ADJS **hallucinatory,** hallucinative, hallucinational; hallucinogenic, psychedelic, consciousness-expanding, mind-expanding

mind-boggling ADJS **astonishing,** amazing, surprising, startling, **astounding,** confounding, staggering, stunning <nonformal>, eye-opening, breathtaking, overwhelming, mind-numbing; **spectacular**

minded ADJS **moved,** motivated, prompted, impelled, actuated; stimulated, animated; inclined, disposed, of a mind to, with half a mind to

mindful ADJS **attentive,** heedful, regardful, advertent; intent, intentive, on top of <nonformal>, diligent, assiduous, intense, earnest, concentrated; **careful**; **observing,** observant; watchful, aware, conscious, alert

mindless ADJS **purposeless, causeless,** designless, aimless, driftless, undirected, objectless, unmotivated; **haphazard,** random, dysteleological, stochastic, stray, inexplicable, unaccountable, promiscuous, indiscriminate, casual, leaving much to chance

mind reader NOUNS **telepathist,** mental telepathist, thought reader

mine NOUNS 1 mine of wealth, **gold mine,** bonanza, luau <nonformal>, lode, rich lode, mother lode, Eldorado,

Golconda, Seven Cities of Cibola
2 pit; **quarry; diggings, workings;** open cut, opencast; coal mine, colliery; strip mine; gold mine, silver mine, etc
VERBS 3 **undermine,** sap, sap the foundations of, honeycomb; plant a mine, trigger a mine
4 **take from,** tap, milk, drain, bleed, curtail; extract, pump

mineral NOUNS 1 inorganic substance, lifeless matter found in nature; extracted matter *or* material; mineral resources; **ore,** mineral-bearing material; unrefined *or* untreated mineral; natural *or* native mineral
ADJS 2 **inorganic,** unorganic, nonorganic; nonbiological; ore-bearing, ore-forming

mingle VERBS **mix,** admix, commix, immix, **intermix,** bemingle, commingle, immingle, **intermingle,** interlace, interweave, intertwine, interlard; syncretize; **amalgamate,** integrate, alloy, coalesce, **fuse,** merge, meld, compound, compose, conflate, concoct

miniature NOUNS 1 mini; scaled-down *or* miniaturized version; microcosm, microcosmos; baby; doll, puppet, model
ADJS 2 **diminutive,** minuscule, minuscular, mini, micro, miniaturized, subminiature, minikin <old>, **small-scale,** minimal; pocket, pocket-sized, **vest-pocket**

minimal ADJS **least,** smallest, littlest, slightest, **lowest,** shortest; minimum, minim; **miniature,** diminutive, minuscule, minuscular, miniaturized, subminiature, **small-scale;** barely sufficient

minimize VERBS minify, **belittle,** detract from; play down, underplay, downplay, de-emphasize; **attach little importance to,** give little weight to; make little of, make light of, think little of, throw away, **make** *or* **think nothing of,** take no account of, set little by, set no store by; not give a shit *or* a hoot *or* two hoots for <nonformal>, not give a damn about, bad-mouth <nonformal>, deprecate, depreciate; **trivialize**

minimum NOUNS 1 **sufficiency,** sufficientness, **adequacy,** adequateness, **enough,** a competence *or* competency; exact measure, right amount, no more and no less; bare sufficiency, bare minimum, just enough, enough to get by on
ADJS 2 **least,** smallest, littlest, slightest, **lowest,** shortest; minimal, minim; few; sufficient for *or* to *or* unto, up to, equal to; barely sufficient

minion NOUNS **sycophant,** flatterer, toady, toad, toadeater, lickspit, lickspittle, **truckler, fawner,** courtier, flunky; creature, **puppet,** lap dog, **tool,** cat's-paw, dupe, instrument, hanger-on, lackey, flunky, stooge <nonformal>; peon, serf, slave, jackal, myrmidon; yes-man <nonformal>

minister NOUNS 1 **emissary,** envoy, legate, foreign service officer; envoy extraordinary, plentipotentiary, **minister plenipotentiary;** nuncio, internuncio, apostolic delegate
2 **clergyman,** clergywoman, man *or* woman of the cloth, divine, ecclesiastic, churchman, cleric, clerical; minister of the Gospel; chaplain
VERBS 3 **officiate,** do duty, **perform a rite,** perform service *or* divine service; administer a sacrament, administer the Eucharist, etc; anoint, chrism

minor NOUNS 1 **youngster,** young person, **youth, juvenile,** youngling, young'un <nonformal>; **stripling,** slip, sprig, sapling; fledgling; hopeful, young hopeful; infant; **adolescent,** pubescent; **teenager,** teener, teenybopper <nonformal>; junior, younger, youngest, baby
ADJS 2 **inferior,** subordinate, subaltern, sub, small-scale, **secondary;** junior; underage; **inconsiderable,** inappreciable, negligible

minority NOUNS 1 **immaturity,** undevelopment, inexperience, **callowness,** unripeness, greenness, rawness, sappiness, freshness, juiciness, dewiness; juniority, infancy, nonage; least
2 the minority, the few; racial *or* ethnic minority, minority group; persons of color

minstrel NOUNS **ballad singer,** balladeer, **bard,** rhapsode, rhapsodist; wandering *or* strolling minstrel, **troubadour,** trovatore, trouvère, minnesinger, scop, gleeman, fili, jongleur; street singer, wait

mint ADJS **new,** original, pristine, fresh, fresh off the assembly line, in mint condition, factory-fresh, **new-made,** new-built, new-wrought, new-shaped, new-minted, new-coined, uncirculated, new-begotten, untouched,

mint condition NOUNS **fine fettle,** fine whack <nonformal>, fine *or* high feather <nonformal>, **good shape,** good trim, fine shape, top shape <nonformal>, good condition; **newness,** freshness, maidenhood, dewiness, pristineness

minus ADJS **out of,** wanting, lacking; missing, less than nothing; negative, electronegative

minuscule ADJS **miniature,** diminutive, minuscular, mini, micro, miniaturized, subminiature, minikin <old>, **small-scale,** minimal; small-lettered, **lowercase**

minute NOUNS 1 **instant,** moment, second, sec <nonformal>, split second, **trice,** twinkle, twinkling, twinkling *or* twinkle of an eye, twink, **wink,** bat of an eye <nonformal>, **flash,** crack, tick, stroke, coup, breath, twitch; two shakes of a lamb's tail *and* two shakes *and* shake *and* half a shake *and* **jiffy** *and* jiff *and* half a jiffy <all nonformal>
2 ADJS **detailed,** full, particular, meticulous, fussy, finicky *or* finicking *or* finical, picayune, picky <nonformal>, nice <old>, precise, exact, specific, special

minutes NOUNS **report,** the record, proceedings, transactions, acta

minutiae NOUNS minim, **drop,** droplet, **mite** <nonformal>, **point,** vanishing point, mathematical point, point of a pin, pinpoint, pinhead, **dot;** trifle, petty *or* trivial matter; incidental, minor detail, details, minor details

miracle NOUNS **sign,** signs and portents, prodigy, wonder, wonderwork; thaumatology, thaumaturgy; fantasy, enchantment

miraculous ADJS **wondrous,** wonderworking, thaumaturgic *or* thaumaturgical, necromantic, **prodigious; magical,** enchanted, bewitched

mirage NOUNS **deception,** vision, hallucination, phantasm, fata morgana, looming, will-o'-the-wisp, **delusion,** delusiveness, illusion

mire NOUNS **swamp,** bog, quagmire, marsh; **mud,** muck, slush, slosh, sludge, slob <Ir>, squash, swill, **slime;** slop, ooze

mirror NOUNS 1 glass, **looking glass,** seeing glass <Brit nonformal>, reflector, speculum; hand mirror, window mirror, rear-view mirror, cheval glass, pier glass, shaving mirror; steel mirror; convex mirror, concave mirror, distorting mirror
VERBS 2 **image,** hold the mirror up to nature, reflect, figure; **embody,** body forth, incarnate, **personify,** personate, impersonate; **illustrate,** demonstrate, exemplify; **look like,** favor <nonformal>; **take after,** partake of, follow, appear *or* seem like, sound like; savor *or* smack of, be redolent of; **have all the earmarks of,** have every appearance of, have all the features of, have all the signs of, have every sign *or* indication of

mirth NOUNS **merriment,** merriness; **hilarity,** hilariousness; **joy,** joyfulness, joyousness; **glee,** gleefulness, high glee; **jollity,** jolliness, joviality, jocularity, jocundity; frivolity, **levity;** mirthfulness, amusement; fun; laughter

misanthrope NOUNS misanthropist, people-hater, cynic, Timon, Timonist; **man-hater,** misandrist; **woman-hater,** misogynist; **sexist,** male *or* female chauvinist, chauvinist

misapprehension NOUNS **misinterpretation,** misunderstanding, *malentente* <Fr>, misintelligence, misreading, misconstruction, mistaking, malobservation, **misconception; misrendering,** mistranslation, eisegesis; misexplanation, misexplication, misexposition; **perversion, distortion,** wrenching, twisting, contorting, torturing, squeezing, garbling

misbegotten ADJS **deformed,** malformed, misshapen, misproportioned, ill-proportioned, ill-made, ill-shaped, **out of shape; illegitimate,** spurious, false; **bastard,** misbegot, miscreated, gotten on the wrong side of the blanket, baseborn, born out of wedlock, without benefit of clergy

misbehave VERBS **misbehave oneself,** misconduct oneself, behave ill; get into mischief; **act up** *and* make waves *and* **carry on** *and* carry on something scandalous <all nonformal>, sow one's wild oats; **cut up** <nonformal>, horse around <nonformal>, roughhouse *and* cut up rough <both nonformal>; **do wrong, err,** offend; **sin,** commit sin; **transgress,** trespass

miscalculate VERBS **misjudge,** judge amiss, misestimate, misreckon, misappreciate, misperceive, get a wrong impression, misesteem, misthink, misconjecture; **misread,** misconstrue, put the wrong construction on things, misread the situation *or* case; **misinterpret;** err; fly in the face of facts

miscellany NOUNS **miscellanea,** collectanea; **assortment,** medley, variety, mixture; hodgepodge, conglomerate, mélange, pastiche, *pasticcio* <Ital>, **conglomeration,** omnium-gatherum <nonformal>; **sundries,** oddments, odds and ends

mischief NOUNS **mischievousness; devilment,** deviltry, devilry; **roguishness,** roguery, scampishness; **waggery,** waggishness; **impishness,** devilishness, puckishness, elfishness; **prankishness,** pranksomeness; sportiveness, playfulness, *espièglerie* <Fr>; high spirits, youthful spirits; foolishness

mischievous ADJS mischief-loving, full of mischief, full of the devil *or* old nick; **roguish,** scampish, scapegrace, arch, knavish; **devilish;** impish, puckish, elfish, elvish; **waggish,** prankish, pranky, pranksome, trickish, tricksy; **playful,** sportive, high-spirited, *espiègle* <Fr>

misconception NOUNS **misinterpretation,** misunderstanding, *malentente* <Fr>, misintelligence, misapprehension, misreading, misconstruction; misrendering, mistranslation, eisegesis; **perversion,** distortion, misuse of words, catachresis; misquotation

misconduct NOUNS **misbehavior,** unsanctioned *or* nonsanctioned behavior; frowned-upon behavior; **naughtiness,** badness; impropriety; venial sin; **disorderly conduct,** disorder, disorderliness, disruptiveness, disruption, **rowdiness,** rowdyism, riotousness, ruffianism, hooliganism; misfeasance, malfeasance, misdoing, delinquency, **wrongdoing**

misconstrue VERBS **pervert,** falsify, twist, garble, put a false construction upon, give a spin, give a false coloring, color, varnish, slant, strain, torture; put words in someone's mouth; **bias;** misrepresent, misinterpret, misrender, misdirect; misread, miss the point, **take wrong, get wrong,** get one wrong, take amiss, take the wrong way; **get backwards,** reverse, have the wrong way round, put the cart before the horse

misdated ADJS **anachronous** *or* anachronistical *or* **anachronistic,** parachronistic, metachronistic, prochronistic, unhistorical, unchronological; **mistimed;** antedated, foredated, postdated; ahead of time, **beforehand, early;** behind time, **behindhand, late,** unpunctual, tardy; **overdue,** past due

misdemeanor NOUNS **offense, wrong,** illegality; violation; wrongdoing; much to answer for; tort; delict, delictum

misdirect VERBS **mislead,** misguide, lead astray, lead up the garden path, **give a bum steer** <nonformal>; feed one a line <nonformal>, throw off the scent, throw off the track *or* trail, put on a false scent, drag *or* draw a red herring across the trail; throw one a curve *or* curve ball <nonformal>; **mismanage,** mishandle, misconduct, **misgovern,** misrule; be negligent

miser NOUNS **niggard,** tightwad *and* cheapskate <both nonformal>, hard man with a buck <nonformal>, **skinflint,** scrooge, penny pincher, pinchfist, churl, curmudgeon <old>, muckworm, save-all <nonformal>

miserable ADJS **wretched; woeful,** woebegone; crushed, stricken, **cut up** <nonformal>, heartsick, heart-stricken, heart-struck; deep-troubled; desolate, disconsolate, pleasureless; **paltry,** poor, common, **mean,** sorry, sad, pitiful, pitiable, pathetic, despicable, contemptible, beneath contempt, vile, **shabby,** scrubby, scruffy, shoddy, scurvy, crummy *and* cheesy <both nonformal>, **trashy,** rubbishy, garbagey <nonformal>, trumpery, gimcracky <nonformal>

miserly ADJS **stingy,** illiberal, ungenerous, chintzy, save-all, **cheap** *and* **tight** *and* narrow <all nonformal>, near, close, closefisted, tightfisted, pinchfisted, hardfisted; pinching, penny-pinching; avaricious

misery NOUNS **wretchedness,** despair, bitterness, infelicity, anguish, agony, woe, woefulness, bale, balefulness; **heartache,** aching heart, heavy heart, bleeding heart, broken heart, agony of mind *or* spirit; suicidal despair, black night of the soul, **despondency**

Slough of Despond
BUNYAN

misfire VERBS **come to nothing,** fail miserably *or* ignominiously; fizz out *and* **fizzle** *and* **fizzle out** *and* peter out *and* poop out <all nonformal>; flash in the pan, hang fire; **blow up in one's face,** explode, end *or* go up in smoke, go up

like a rocket and come down like a stick
misfit NOUNS **nonconformist,** individualist, inner-directed person, oddball <nonformal>; a fish out of water, a square peg in a round hole <nonformal>
misfortune NOUNS **mishap,** ill hap, misadventure, mischance, *contretemps* <Fr>, grief; **disaster,** calamity, catastrophe, meltdown, cataclysm, **tragedy; shock, blow,** hard *or* nasty *or* staggering blow; **accident**
misgiving NOUNS **apprehension,** apprehensiveness, **qualm,** qualmishness, funny feeling; **anxiety**; doubt; foreboding, chill *or* quiver along the spine, creeping *or* shudder of the flesh
misguided ADJS **misdirected;** impolitic, ill-considered, ill-advised; negligent; **botched,** bungled, fumbled, muffed, spoiled, butchered, murdered; **ill-managed,** ill-done, ill-conducted, ill-devised, ill-contrived, ill-executed; mismanaged, misconducted
mishandle VERBS **mismanage,** misconduct, misdirect, misguide, **misgovern,** misrule; misadminister, maladminister; be negligent
mishap NOUNS **misfortune,** ill hap, **misadventure, mischance,** *contretemps* <Fr>, grief; shock, blow, hard *or* nasty *or* staggering blow; **accident,** casualty, collision, crash, smash *and* smashup *and* crack-up *and* pileup <all nonformal>
misinform VERBS **misteach,** misinstruct, miseducate; misadvise, **misguide,** misdirect, **mislead;** pervert, corrupt
misinterpret VERBS **misunderstand,** misconceive, mistake, misapprehend; misread, misconstrue, put a false construction on, miss the point, **take wrong, get wrong,** get one wrong, take amiss, take the wrong way; **get backwards,** reverse, have the wrong way round, put the cart before the horse; misapply; **misrender,** mistranslate; quote out of context; misquote, miscite, give a false coloring, give a false impression *or* idea; **garble,** pervert, distort, wrench, contort, torture, squeeze, twist the words *or* meaning, stretch *or* strain the sense *or* meaning, misdeem, **misjudge**; bark up the wrong tree
misjudge VERBS judge amiss, **miscalculate,** misestimate, misperceive, get a wrong impression, misevaluate, misesteem, misthink, misconjecture; **misread,** misconstrue, put the wrong construction on things, misread the situation *or* case; **misinterpret;** err; fly in the face of facts
misleading ADJS **deceptive,** deceiving, beguiling, **false, fallacious,** delusive, delusory; misteaching, misinstructive, miseducative, **misinforming;** misguiding, misdirecting
mismanage VERBS **mishandle,** misconduct, misdirect, misguide, **misgovern,** misrule; misadminister, maladminister; be negligent
mismatched ADJS **unsuited,** ill-suited; **unfitted,** ill-fitted; **maladjusted,** unadapted, ill-adapted; ill-sorted, ill-assorted, ill-chosen; ill-matched, ill-mated, mismated, mismarried, misallied; disproportionate, **out of proportion,** skew, skewed, asymmetric *or* asymmetrical
misogynist NOUNS **woman-hater; sexist,** male chauvinist, chauvinist; **misanthrope,** misanthropist, people-hater
misogyny NOUNS **woman-hating; sexism,** sex discrimination, sexual stereotyping, male chauvinism; **misanthropy,** misanthropism, people-hating
misplace VERBS **mislay,** misput; **lose,** incur loss, **suffer loss,** let slip through one's fingers
misplaced ADJS **mislaid,** misput; out of one's element, like a fish out of water, in the wrong place, in the wrong box *or* pew *and* in the right church but the wrong pew <all nonformal>; **inappropriate,** inapt, unapt, inapposite, **irrelevant,** malapropos, *mal à propos* <Fr>; shuffled; **out of line,** out of keeping, out of order *or* place, **out of step,** out of turn <nonformal>
misprint NOUNS **mistake,** error, *erratum* <L>, *corrigendum* <L>; misstatement, misquotation; misreport; **typographical error,** typo <nonformal>, printer's error, typist's error; clerical error
misquote VERBS **misrepresent,** misstate, misreport, put words into one's mouth, quote out of context; overstate, exaggerate
misrepresent VERBS **belie,** give a wrong idea, pass *or* pawn *or* foist *or* fob off as, send *or* deliver the wrong signal *or* message; put in a false light, **pervert,** distort, garble, twist, warp, wrench, slant, put a spin on, twist the meaning of;

color, miscolor, give a false coloring, put a false construction *or* appearance upon, falsify; **disguise,** camouflage; misstate, misreport, misquote, put words into one's mouth, quote out of context; overstate, exaggerate, overdraw, blow up, blow out of all proportion; understate

miss NOUNS 1 **girl,** girlie <nonformal>, **maid, maiden, lass,** girlchild, **lassie,** young thing, young creature, young lady, damsel in distress, **damsel,** damoiselle, demoiselle, *jeune fille* <Fr>, *mademoiselle* <Fr>, *muchacha* <Sp>, missy, little missy, slip, wench <dial or nonformal>, colleen <Irish>
2 near-miss; **slip, slipup** <nonformal>, slip 'twixt cup and lip; **error, mistake**
VERBS 3 **miss the mark,** miss one's aim; slip, slip up <nonformal>; goof <nonformal>, blunder, foozle <nonformal>, err; **botch,** bungle; **miscarry,** go amiss, go astray, miss by a mile <nonformal>; misfire; **miss out,** miss the boat *or* bus
4 **be inattentive,** pay no attention, pay no mind <nonformal>, not attend, not notice, **take no note** *or* **notice of,** take no thought *or* account of, not heed, give no heed, pay no regard to, not listen, hear nothing, not hear a word; **disregard,** overlook, ignore, pass over *or* by, have no time for, let pass *or* get by *or* get past; **want,** lack, need, require; feel the want of, be sent away empty-handed; run short of

misshapen ADJS **deformed, malformed,** misbegotten, misproportioned, ill-proportioned, ill-made, ill-shaped, **out of shape;** sway-backed, round-shouldered; bowlegged, bandy-legged, bandy; knock-kneed; flatfooted, splayfooted, pigeon-toed

missile NOUNS **projectile,** bolt; brickbat, stone, rock, alley apple *and* Irish confetti <both nonformal>; boomerang; bola; throwing-stick, throw stick, waddy <Austral>; **ballistic missile,** cruise missile, Exocet missile, surface-to-air missile *or* SAM, surface-to-surface missile, Tomahawk missile; **rocket; torpedo**

missing ADJS **absent,** not present, nonattendant, **away, gone,** departed, disappeared, vanished, absconded, out of sight; among the missing, wanting, **lacking,** not found, nowhere to be found, omitted, taken away, subtracted, deleted; no longer present *or* with us *or* among us; long-lost

mission NOUNS 1 **delegation,** deputation, commission; legation, embassy; **duty,** obligation, charge, onus, burden, devoir, must, ought, imperative, bounden duty, proper *or* assigned task, what ought to be done, what one is responsible for, where the buck stops <nonformal>; duties and responsibilities, assignment
2 **vocation,** occupation, business, work, line, line of work, line of business *or* endeavor, number <nonformal>, walk, **walk of life,** calling, **profession,** practice, pursuit, specialty, specialization, *métier* <Fr>, **trade,** racket *and* game <both nonformal>; **career,** lifework, life's work

missionary NOUNS **evangelist,** revivalist, evangel, evangelicalist; missioner; missionary apostolic, missionary rector, colporteur; television *or* TV evangelist, televangelist <nonformal>; **converter,** proselyter, proselytizer, apostlet

misspeak VERBS **blunder,** make a blunder, make a faux pas, make a colossal blunder, misspeak oneself, trip over one's tongue; embarrass oneself, have egg on one's face <nonformal>

misspent ADJS **wasted,** squandered, dissipated, consumed, spent, used, lost; **gone to waste,** run *or* gone to seed; down the drain *or* spout *or* rathole <nonformal>

misstep NOUNS **impropriety,** slight *or* minor wrong, venial sin, indiscretion, peccadillo, trip, slip, lapse; **transgression,** trespass; **sin,** cardinal *or* deadly *or* mortal sin, grave *or* heavy sin, unutterable sin, unpardonable *or* unforgivable *or* inexpiable sin; trip, **stumble,** false *or* wrong step, wrong *or* bad *or* false move

mist NOUNS 1 **drizzle,** mizzle; misty rain, Scotch mist; evening mist; fog drip; drizzling mist, drisk <nonformal>; mistiness, haze, fog, cloud
VERBS 2 **blur,** dim, pale, soften, film, fog; defocus, lose resolution *or* sharpness *or* distinctness, go soft at the edges; mist over, mist up, bemist, enmist; **haze**

mistake NOUNS **error,** *erratum* <L>, *corrigendum* <L>; **fault,** *faute* <Fr>; **misconception,** misapprehension, misunderstanding; misstatement, misquotation; misreport; **misprint,** typographical error, typo <nonformal>, printer's error, typist's error; clerical error; **misjudg-**

ment, miscalculation; misplay; misdeal; miscount; misuse; failure, miss, miscarriage

mistaken ADJS **in error, erring,** under an error, wrong, all wet <nonformal>, full of bull *or* shit *or* hot air *or* it *or* prunes *or* crap *or* beans <all nonformal>; off in one's reckoning; in the right church but the wrong pew

mistreat VERBS 1 **maltreat,** ill-treat, ill-use, abuse, injure, **molest;** do wrong to, do wrong by; outrage, do violence to, do one's worst to; mishandle, manhandle; buffet, batter, bruise, **savage,** maul, knock about, rough, rough up

2 <nonformal> **screw,** screw over, shaft, stiff, give the short *or* the shitty end of the stick, fuck, fuck over

mistress NOUNS 1 woman, **kept woman,** kept mistress, **paramour,** concubine, doxy, playmate, spiritual *or* unofficial wife; live-in lover <nonformal>
2 governess, duenna, madam; **matron, housewife,** homemaker, goodwife <Scots>, lady of the house, chatelaine; housemistress, housemother
3 instructress, educatress, preceptress; **schoolmistress; schoolma'am** *or* **schoolmarm**

mistrust NOUNS 1 **suspiciousness,** suspicion, doubt, misdoubt, distrust, distrustfulness; **wariness,** chariness, cageyness *and* leeriness <both nonformal>, mistrustfulness
VERBS 2 suffer pangs of jealousy, have green in the eye <nonformal>, be possessive *or* overpossessive, view with a jaundiced eye; **suspect,** distrust, doubt, **have one's doubts,** have *or* harbor *or* entertain doubts *or* suspicions, half believe, have reservations, **take with a grain of salt,** be from Missouri <nonformal>, misgive, cross one's fingers; **be uncertain; doubt one's word,** give one the lie

misty ADJS uncertain, confused, out of focus, **blurred, blurry,** bleared, bleary, blear, **fuzzy, hazy,** filmy, foggy; misty-moisty; **murky,** cloudy, foggy, fogbound, nebulous

misunderstand VERBS **misinterpret,** misconceive, mistake, misapprehend; misread, misconstrue, put a false construction on, miss the point, **take wrong, get wrong,** get one wrong, take amiss, take the wrong way; **get backwards,** reverse, have the wrong way round, put the cart before the horse; **confuse,** mix up, not distinguish

misunderstanding NOUNS **misinterpretation,** *malentente* <Fr>, misintelligence, **misapprehension,** misreading, misconstruction, mistaking, **misconception; misrendering,** mistranslation, eisegesis; **perversion,** distortion, wrenching, twisting, contorting, torturing, squeezing, garbling; misjudgment; **error; disagreement,** difficulty, difference, difference of opinion, agreement to disagree, **variance,** division, dividedness

misuse VERBS **misemploy,** abuse, misapply; mishandle, mismanage, maladminister; divert, misappropriate, convert, defalcate <old>, embezzle, pilfer, peculate, feather one's nest <nonformal>; pervert, prostitute; profane, violate, pollute, foul, foul one's own nest, befoul, desecrate, defile, debase

mite NOUNS 1 **little, bit,** little *or* wee *or* tiny bit <nonformal>, bite, **particle,** fragment, spot, **speck,** flyspeck, fleck, point, dot, jot, tittle, **iota,** ounce, **dab** <nonformal>, mote; whit, ace, **hair,** scruple, groat, farthing, pittance, dole, trifling amount, **smidgen** *and* skosh *and* smitch <all nonformal>, pinch, gobbet, dribble, driblet, dram, drop, drop in a bucket *or* in the ocean, tip of the iceberg; grain, granule, pebble
2 **flea,** sand flea, dog flea, cat flea, chigoe, chigger, jigger, red bug, harvest mite
3 **pittance,** drop in the bucket *or* the ocean; bit; widow's mite

mitigate VERBS **extenuate,** palliate, soften, lessen, diminish, **ease,** mince; **soft-pedal;** slur over, ignore, pass by in silence, give the benefit of the doubt, not hold it against one, **explain away,** gloss *or* smooth over, put a gloss upon, put a good face upon, varnish, **whitewash,** color, lend a color to, put the best color *or* face on, show in the best colors, show to best advantage; **modulate,** dampen, blunt, defuse, abate, weaken, reduce, de-escalate, slacken

mitigating ADJS assuaging, abating, **diminishing,** reducing, lessening, allaying, **alleviating,** relaxing, easing; tempering, **softening,** chastening, **subduing;** deadening, dulling, blunting, damping, dampening, cushioning

mix NOUNS 1 **medley, miscellany,** mélange, pastiche, *pasticcio* <Ital>, conglomeration, assortment, assemblage, mixed bag, ragbag, grab bag, olio, *olla podrida* <Sp>, **scramble, jumble,** mingle-mangle, mishmash, **mess,** can of worms <nonformal>, rat's nest, hash, patchwork, salad, gallimaufry, salmagundi, **potpourri,** stew, sauce, slurry, omnium-gatherum, Noah's ark, **odds and ends,** oddments
VERBS 2 admix, commix, immix, **intermix, mingle,** bemingle, commingle, immingle, **intermingle,** interlace, interweave, intertwine, interlard; syncretize; **blend,** interblend, stir in; amalgamate, integrate, alloy, coalesce, **fuse, merge,** meld, compound, compose, conflate, concoct; **combine**; mix up, hash, stir up, **scramble,** conglomerate, shuffle, **jumble,** jumble up, mingle-mangle, throw *or* toss together

mixed ADJS **mingled,** blended, compounded, amalgamated; combined; **composite,** compound, **complex,** many-sided, multifaceted, intricate; **conglomerate,** pluralistic, multiracial, multicultural, multiethnic, multinational, heterogeneous, varied, **miscellaneous,** medley, motley, dappled, patchy; promiscuous, indiscriminate, **scrambled, jumbled,** thrown together; syncretized, syncretistic, eclectic

mixed bag NOUNS **hodgepodge,** hotchpotch, hotchpot; **medley, miscellany,** mélange, pastiche, *pasticcio* <Ital>, **assortment,** assemblage, ragbag, grab bag, olio, *olla podrida* <Sp>, mishmash, **mess,** can of worms <nonformal>, dog's breakfast <Can nonformal>, hash, patchwork, salad, gallimaufry, salmagundi, **potpourri,** stew, omnium-gatherum, Noah's ark, **odds and ends,** oddments, all sorts, everything but the kitchen sink <nonformal>, what you will

mixed marriage NOUNS **marriage,** coverture, cohabitation; intermarriage, interfaith marriage, interracial marriage; miscegenation; misalliance, *mésalliance* <Fr>, ill-assorted marriage

mixed-up ADJS **confused,** crazy mixed-up <nonformal>; **flustered,** fluttered, ruffled, rattled, fussed <nonformal>; **upset, unsettled,** off-balance, off one's stride; **disorganized,** disordered, disoriented, disorientated, chaotic, jumbled, in a jumble, shuffled; **disconcerted,** discomposed, discombobulated <nonformal>, embarrassed, put-out, disturbed, perturbed, bothered, all hot and bothered <nonformal>; in a tizzy *or* swivet *or* sweat <nonformal>, in a pother; **perplexed**

mixer NOUNS 1 **blender,** beater, agitator, food processor; cement mixer, eggbeater, churn; homogenizer, colloid mill, emulsifier; crucible, melting pot
2 **dance, hop** <nonformal>, dancing party, **shindig** *and* shindy <both nonformal>

mixture NOUNS **assortment,** medley, variety; hodgepodge, conglomerate, **conglomeration,** omnium-gatherum <nonformal>; **compound,** admixture, intermixture, immixture, commixture, **composite,** blend, meld, composition, confection, concoction, **combination,** amalgam, alloy

mix up VERBS **confound,** confuse, muddle, mess up *and* ball up *and* bollix up *and* screw up *and* foul up *and* fuck up *and* snafu *and* muck up *and* louse up <all nonformal>, implicate; **tangle,** entangle, embrangle, **snarl, snarl up,** ravel, knot, tie in knots

mix-up NOUNS **confusion,** chaos, anarchy, misrule, license; **Babel,** cognitive dissonance; **muddle,** morass, foul-up *and* fuck-up *and* snafu *and* screw-up <all nonformal>, ball-up <nonformal>, hoo-ha *and* fine how-de-do <all nonformal>, pretty kettle of fish, pretty piece of business, nice piece of work

moan NOUNS 1 **lament,** plaint, *planctus* <L>; **murmur,** mutter; **groan; whine,** whimper; wail, wail of woe; **sob,** *cri du coeur* <Fr>, **cry,** outcry, scream, **howl,** yowl, bawl, yawp, keen, ululation
VERBS 2 **lament,** mourn, grieve, groan, sorrow, keen, weep over, **bewail,** bemoan, deplore, repine, sigh, give sorrow words; sing the blues <nonformal>, elegize, dirge, knell; **wail,** ululate

moat NOUNS **trench,** trough, channel, ditch, fosse, **canal,** cut, gutter, kennel <Brit>; sunk fence, ha-ha

mob NOUNS **throng,** multitude, horde, host, heap <nonformal>, army, panoply, legion; flock, cluster, galaxy; **crowd,** press, crush, flood, spate, deluge, mass; rabble, rout, ruck, jam, *cohue* <Fr>, everybody and his uncle *or* his brother <nonformal>

the mob NOUNS 1 **the masses, the hoi polloi,** *hoi polloi* <Gk>, the many, **the multitude,** the crowd, the horde, the million, **the majority,** the mass of the people, the herd, the great unnumbered, the great unwashed, **the vulgar** *or* **common herd;** *profanum vulgus, ignobile vulgus, mobile vulgus* <all L>

the hateful, hostile mob
PETRARCH

2 **the underworld,** gangland, gangdom, **organized crime,** organized crime family, the rackets, the syndicate, the Mafia, Cosa Nostra

mobile ADJS **moving,** stirring, in motion; transitional; motive, motile, movable

mobilize VERBS **set in motion,** move, actuate, motivate, push, shove, nudge, **drive,** impel, propel; **militarize,** activate, go on a wartime footing, gird *or* gird up one's loins, muster one's resources; reactivate, remilitarize, take out of mothballs *and* retread <both nonformal>

mobster NOUNS **criminal,** outlaw, felon, **crook** <nonformal>, lawbreaker, perpetrator, perp <nonformal>, gangster *and* wiseguy <both nonformal>, racketeer, thief; **bad person**; deceiver

mock VERBS 1 **scoff, jeer,** gibe, barrack <Brit>, revile, rail at, rally, chaff, **twit, taunt,** jape, flout, scout, have a fling at, cast in one's teeth; sneer, **sneer at,** fleer, curl one's lip
ADJS 2 **imitation, sham,** copied, fake *and* phony <both nonformal>, counterfeit, forged, plagiarized, unoriginal, ungenuine; **pseudo,** synthetic, synthetical, ersatz, hokey *and* hoked-up <both nonformal>, quasi

mockery NOUNS 1 **indignity,** affront, offense, injury, humiliation; scurrility, contempt, contumely, despite, flout, flouting, jeering, jeer, mock, scoff, gibe, taunt, brickbat <nonformal>; **insult, aspersion,** uncomplimentary remark, slap *or* kick in the face, left-handed *or* backhanded compliment; cut

most unkindest cut of all
SHAKESPEARE

2 **mimicry,** apery, parrotry, mimetism; hollow mockery; **insincerity,** uncandidness, uncandor, unfrankness, disingenuousness; **ridicule,** derision, raillery, rallying, chaffing; panning *and* razzing *and* roasting *and* ragging <all nonformal>, scoffing, sneering, snickering, sniggering, smirking, grinning, leering, fleering, snorting
3 **burlesque,** lampoon, squib, parody, satire, farce, imitation, wicked imitation *or* pastiche, takeoff <nonformal>, **travesty, caricature**

mock-up NOUNS **reproduction,** duplication, imitation, **copy**, dummy, **replica,** facsimile, representation, approximation, model, version, knockoff <nonformal>

mode NOUNS 1 **fashion,** style, vogue, trend, prevailing taste; proper thing, ton, bon ton; custom; convention; the swim <nonformal>, current *or* stream of fashion; height of fashion; the new look, the season's look; high fashion, *haute couture* <Fr>
2 **manner, way,** tenor, vein, lifestyle, way of life, preference, thing *and* bag <both nonformal>

model NOUNS 1 **pattern,** standard, criterion, classic example, rule, mirror, paradigm; showpiece, showplace; **original,** urtext, *locus classicus* <L>; **type,** prototype, antetype, **archetype,** genotype, biotype, type specimen, type species; **precedent**
2 **beauty,** beauty queen, beauty contest winner, Miss America, bathing beauty; **glamor girl,** cover girl; **belle,** reigning beauty, great beauty, lady fair
VERBS 3 **form,** formalize, shape, fashion, tailor, frame, figure, lick into shape <nonformal>; **mold,** sculpt *or* sculpture; carve, whittle, cut, chisel, hew, hew out; roughhew, roughcast, rough out, block out, lay out, sketch out
ADJS 4 **exemplary,** precedential, typical, paradigmatic, representative, standard, normative, classic; ideal

moderate NOUNS 1 moderatist, moderationist, **centrist,** middle-of-the-roader <nonformal>; independent; center, centrist, neutral; conservative
ADJS 2 centrist, middle-of-the-road <nonformal>, independent; **temperate,** sober, frugal, restrained, **sparing,** stinting, measured; nonviolent, peaceable, peaceful, pacifistic; judicious, prudent

moderate VERBS **restrain,** constrain, control, **keep within bounds; modulate,** mitigate, defuse, abate, weaken, diminish, reduce, de-escalate, slacken, lessen, slow down; **alleviate,** assuage, allay, lay, lighten, palliate, extenuate, **temper,** lenify; **soften,** subdue, tame, hold in check, keep a tight rein, chasten, underplay, play down, downplay, de-emphasize, tone *or* tune down

moderator NOUNS **mitigator,** modulator, stabilizer, temperer, assuager; **mediator,** bridge-builder, calming *or* restraining hand, wiser head; **alleviator,** alleviative, palliative, lenitive; **pacifier,** soother, comforter, peacemaker, pacificator, dove of peace, mollifier

modern ADJS **contemporary,** present-day, present-time, twentieth-century, latter-day, space-age, neoteric, now <nonformal>, **newfashioned,** fashionable, modish, mod, *à la mode* <Fr>, **up-to-date,** up-to-datish, up-to-the-minute, in, abreast of the times; **advanced,** progressive, forward-looking, modernizing, avant-garde

modernize VERBS streamline; update, **bring up to date,** keep *or* stay current, move with the times

modest ADJS 1 **meek;** humble; **unpretentious,** unpretending, unassuming, unpresuming, unpresumptuous, **unostentatious,** unobtrusive, unimposing, unboastful; unambitious, unaspiring; verecund, verecundious, *pudique* <Fr>, bashful; **decent, decorous,** delicate, elegant, proper, becoming, seemly
2 **cheap, inexpensive,** unexpensive, low, low-priced, frugal, reasonable, sensible, manageable, moderate, affordable, to fit the pocketbook, budget, easy, economy, economic, economical; within means, within reach *or* easy reach; **mediocre,** middling, indifferent, fair, fairish, fair to middling <nonformal>, medium, betwixt and between

modesty NOUNS 1 **humility,** unpretentiousness; plainness, simpleness, homeliness; **meekness;** unassumingness, unpresumptuousness, **unostentatiousness,** unambitiousness, unobtrusiveness, unboastfulness; bashfulness, pudicity, shame, pudency; expressionlessness, blankness, impassiveness, impassivity; straight *or* poker face, mask
2 **mediocrity,** mediocreness, fairishness, modestness, moderateness, middlingness, **indifference**

modicum NOUNS minim; **minimum; little, bit,** little *or* wee *or* tiny bit <nonformal>, bite, **particle,** fragment, moiety, spot, **speck,** flyspeck, fleck, point, dot, jot, tittle, **iota,** ounce, **dab** <nonformal>, mote, **mite** <nonformal>; whit, ace, **hair,** scruple, groat, farthing, pittance, dole, trifling amount, **smidgen** *and* skosh *and* smitch <all nonformal>, pinch, gobbet, dribble, driblet, dram, drop, drop in a bucket *or* in the ocean, grain, granule, pebble; small share

modification NOUNS **qualification,** limitation, limiting, restriction, circumscription, hedge, hedging; setting conditions, conditionality, provisionality, circumstantiality; specification; **allowance,** concession, cession, grant

modify VERBS **qualify, limit,** condition <old>, hedge, hedge about, restrict, restrain, circumscribe, set limits *or* conditions, box in <nonformal>, narrow; adjust to, regulate by; alter; **temper,** season, leaven, soften, modulate, moderate, assuage, **mitigate,** palliate, abate, reduce, diminish

module NOUNS **component,** constituent, ingredient, integrant, makings *and* fixings <both nonformal>, **element,** factor, part, player, part and parcel; appurtenance, adjunct; **feature,** aspect, specialty, circumstance, detail, item

mogul NOUNS **personage,** important person, somebody, notable, notability, figure; **celebrity,** famous person, person of renown, personality; name, big name, nabob, panjandrum, person to be reckoned with, very important person; mover and shaker, lord of creation; **dignitary,** dignity; **magnate;** tycoon <nonformal>, baron

moisten VERBS **dampen,** moisturize, damp, **wet,** wet down; humidify; dew, bedew; **sprinkle,** besprinkle, **spray,** spritz <nonformal>, sparge, asperge; **splash,** dash, swash, slosh, splatter, spatter, bespatter; hose, hose down; syringe, douche; sponge

moisture NOUNS damp, wet; **dampness,** moistness, moistiness, **wetness,** wettedness, wettishness, **wateriness;** soddenness, soppiness, soppingness, sogginess; dewiness; mistiness, raininess

moisturizer NOUNS wetting agent, wetting-out agent, liquidizer; humidifier

mold NOUNS 1 **original,** model, archetype, prototype, **pattern,** pilot model; **form,** cast, template, matrix,

negative; **die,** punch, stamp, intaglio, seal, mint; last, shoe last
2 **decay,** decomposition, disintegration, dissolution, resolution, degradation, biodegradation, breakup; mildew, fungus, smut, must, rust; rot, dry rot
VERBS 3 **form,** formalize, **shape, fashion,** tailor, frame, figure, **lick into shape** <nonformal>; work, knead; carve, whittle, cut, chisel, hew, hew out; roughhew, roughcast, rough out, block out, lay out, sketch out; **invent,** create, originate, make, think up, dream up, coin, hatch, concoct, fabricate, produce
4 **decay,** decompose, disintegrate; go *or* fall into decay, go *or* fall to pieces, break up, crumble, crumble into dust; **spoil,** corrupt, canker, **go bad; rot,** putrefy, putresce; molder, molder away, rot away, rust away, mildew

moldy ADJS **malodorous,** fetid, musty, funky, fusty, frowzy, stuffy, mildewed, mildewy; mephitic, miasmic, miasmal

molehill NOUNS **trifle,** triviality, pin, button, hair, straw, rush, feather, fig, bean, hill of beans <nonformal>, row of pins *or* buttons <nonformal>, pinch of snuff

molest VERBS **annoy,** torment, bother, pother; **harass,** harry, drive up the wall <nonformal>, **hound,** dog, nag, **persecute; mistreat,** maltreat, ill-treat, ill-use, abuse, injure; do wrong to, do wrong by; outrage, do violence to, do one's worst to; mishandle, manhandle

mollify VERBS **calm,** calm down, **stabilize, tranquilize, pacify,** appease, dulcify; **quiet,** hush, still, rest, compose, **lull, soothe,** gentle, rock, cradle, rock to sleep; ease, steady, smooth, smoothen, smooth over, smooth down, even out; keep the peace, be the dove of peace, pour oil on troubled waters, pour balm into

mollycoddle VERBS **indulge,** cater to; give way to, yield to, let one have his own way; **pamper,** cosset, **coddle,** pet, make a lap dog of, **spoil;** spare the rod

molt VERBS **shed, cast,** throw off, **slough,** slough off, exuviate

molten ADJS **melted,** fused, liquefied; liquated; meltable, fusible; thermoplastic

moment NOUNS **time,** while, minute, instant; psychological moment; pregnant *or* fateful moment, fated moment, kairos, moment of truth; **short time,** little while, mo <nonformal>, span, **short spell;** no time, less than no time; bit *or* **little bit,** a breath, the wink of an eye, pair of winks <nonformal>; **two shakes** *and* two shakes of a lamb's tail <both nonformal>

momentary ADJS **instantaneous,** instant, **immediate,** presto, quick as thought *or* lightning; lightning-like, lightning-swift; nearly simultaneous; simultaneous

momentous ADJS **important,** major, consequential, significant, considerable, substantial, material, **great,** grand, big; superior, world-shaking, earthshaking; big-time *and* big-league *and* major-league *and* heavyweight <all nonformal>; high-powered <nonformal>, double-barreled <nonformal>

momentum NOUNS **motion; movement,** stir, unrest, restlessness; **going,** running, stirring; **operation,** operating, **working,** ticking; **course,** passage, progress, trend, **advance,** forward motion, going *or* moving on; **motive power,** power; **force,** irresistible force; clout <nonformal>; **impetus**

monastery NOUNS **cloister,** house, abbey, friary; priory, priorate; lamasery

money NOUNS 1 **wealth,** lucre, pelf, gold, mammon; **substance,** property, possessions, material wealth; **assets;** *embarras de richesses* <Fr>, money to burn <nonformal>; **currency,** legal tender, medium of exchange, circulating medium, **cash,** hard cash, cold cash; specie, coinage, mintage, coin of the realm

2 <nonformal> **dough, bread, jack, kale,** scratch, sugar, change, mazuma, mopus, gelt, gilt, coin, spondulics, oof, ooftish, wampum, possibles, moolah, boodle, blunt, dinero, do-re-mi, **sugar,** brass, tin, rocks, simoleons, shekels, berries, chips, bucks, green, green stuff, the needful, grease, ointment, oil of palms, cabbage, whip-out, the nesessary, loot

3 <nonformal> **folding money, green stuff,** the long green, folding green, lean green, mint leaves, lettuce, greenbacks, frogskins, skins

moneylender NOUNS **lender,** loaner; loan officer; commercial banker; moneymonger; money broker; banker; **usurer,** Shylock *and* loan shark <both nonformal>

mongrel NOUNS 1 **cur,** lurcher <Brit>, **mutt** <nonformal>; pariah dog, hound, whelp
ADJS 2 **hybrid,** interbred, **crossbred,** crossed, cross; **half-breed,** half-bred, half-blooded, half-caste

monitor NOUNS 1 **warner,** cautioner, admonisher; prophet *or* messenger of doom, Cassandra, Jeremiah; **lookout,** lookout man; sentinel, sentry; signalman, signaler, flagman; reviewer
VERBS 2 **probe,** sound, plumb, fathom; check into, check on, check out, nose into, see into; poke about, root around *or* about, scratch around *or* about, cast about *or* around; **review,** pass under review, oversee

monk NOUNS **religious,** *religieux* <Fr>; monastic; brother, lay brother; cenobite, conventual; caloyer, hieromonach; **mendicant,** friar; beadsman; prior, claustral *or* conventual prior, grand prior, general prior; abbot; hermit; ascetic; celibate

monolith NOUNS **monument,** monumental *or* memorial record, **memorial; tablet,** stone, boundary stone, memorial stone; **pillar,** stele *or* stela, shaft, column, memorial column, rostral column, manubial column; obelisk; **gravestone,** tombstone; headstone, footstone; cenotaph; cairn, mound, barrow, cromlech, dolmen, megalith, menhir, cyclolith

monolithic ADJS **uniform, consistent,** consonant, correspondent, accordant, homogeneous, **alike,** all alike, all of a piece, of a piece, consubstantial; undifferentiable *or* undifferentiated, undifferenced

monologue NOUNS **soliloquy,** monology, self-address; aside; solo; monodrama; apostrophe; monotone, drone, ding-dong, singsong

monopolize VERBS hog *and* grab all of *and* gobble up <all nonformal>, take it all, have all to oneself, have exclusive possession of *or* exclusive rights to; engross, forestall, tie up; **corner** *and* get a corner on *and* corner the market <all nonformal>; **take possession of,** possess oneself of, take for oneself, arrogate to oneself, take up, **take over,** help oneself to, make use of, make one's own, make free with, dip one's hands into; take all of, sit on

monopoly NOUNS monopolization; **corner** *and* cornering *and* a corner on <all nonformal>; exclusive possession; engrossment, forestallment; restraint of trade, corner on the market

monotonous ADJS **tedious, humdrum,** singsong, jog-trot, treadmill, unvarying, unrelieved, invariable, uneventful, broken-record, parrotlike, harping, everlasting, too much with us <nonformal>; **dreary,** drearisome, dry, dryasdust, dusty, **dull**; protracted, prolonged

monotony NOUNS **tedium,** humdrum, irksomeness, irk; **sameness,** sameliness, more of the same, the same old thing, the same damn thing <nonformal>; broken record, parrot; the daily round *or* grind, the weary round, the treadmill, the squirrel cage, the rat race <nonformal>, the beaten track *or* path; time on one's hands, time hanging heavily on one's hands

monster NOUNS 1 **fiend,** fiend from hell, **demon, devil,** devil incarnate, hellhound, hellkite; **vampire,** lamia, **harpy, ghoul;** werewolf, ape-man; ogre, ogress; Frankenstein's monster
ADJS 2 **huge,** immense, vast, enormous, humongous *and* jumbo <both nonformal>, tremendous, prodigious, stupendous; great big, larger than life, Homeric, mighty, **titanic,** colossal, monumental; monstrous; **mammoth,** mastodonic; **gigantic**

monstrosity NOUNS 1 **freakishness,** grotesqueness, grotesquerie, strangeness, weirdness, gonzo <nonformal>, monstrousness, malformation, deformity, teratism; miscreation, abortion, abnormal *or* defective birth, abnormal *or* defective fetus; **freak,** freak of nature, *lusus naturae* <L>
2 **eyesore,** blot, blot on the landscape, blemish, sight <nonformal>, fright, horror, mess, no beauty, no beauty queen, ugly duckling

monstrous ADJS **wicked,** abominable, atrocious, unspeakable, execrable, damnable; shameful, disgraceful, scandalous, **infamous,** unpardonable, unforgivable; **bestial,** mindless, insensate, inhuman, pitiless, ruthless, merciless; **deformed,** malformed, misshapen, **misbegotten,** teratogenic, teratoid

monument NOUNS **shaft,** pillar, column; sphinx, obelisk, pyramid; colossus; memorial arch, gravestone, mausoleum; cairn, menhir

monumental ADJS **immense,** enormous, huge; **gigantic,** mountainous, titanic, colossal, mammoth, Gargantuan, gigantesque, outsize, sizable, larger-than-life; **massive,** massy, weighty, bulky, voluminous; **spacious,** amplitudinous, extensive; **tremendous,** stupendous, awesome, prodigious, Olympian

moocher NOUNS **drone;** cadger, bummer *and* panhandler <nonformal>, **sponger,** freeloader, lounge lizard <nonformal>, social parasite, parasite; *schnorrer* <Yiddish>; uninvited guest, gate-crasher <nonformal>

mood NOUNS **humor,** feeling, feelings, temper, frame of mind, state of mind, morale, tone, note, **vein; mind,** heart, spirit *or* spirits

moody ADJS **glum,** grum, **morose,** sullen, sulky, mumpish, dumpish, long-faced, crestfallen, chapfallen; moodish, **brooding,** broody; mopish, mopey <nonformal>, **moping; temperamental,** primadonnaish; petulant; **volatile,** mercurial, flighty, impulsive, impetuous

moon NOUNS 1 **satellite;** orb of night, queen of heaven, queen of night, silvery moon; **new moon,** wet moon; **crescent moon,** crescent, increscent moon, increscent, waxing moon, waxing crescent moon; decrescent moon, decrescent, waning moon, waning crescent moon; gibbous moon; **half-moon,** demilune; **full moon,** harvest moon, hunter's moon

that orbèd maiden
SHELLEY

VERBS 2 **lie around,** lounge around, loll around, moon around, sit around, sit on one's ass *or* butt *or* duff <nonformal>, stand *or* hang around, **loiter about** *or* **around,** slouch, slouch around, **bum around** *and* mooch around <both nonformal>; **muse,** dream, daydream, pipe-dream <nonformal>, fantasy; abstract oneself, be lost in thought, let one's attention wander, let one's mind run on other things, dream of *or* muse on other things; **woolgather,** go woolgathering, let one's wits go bird's nesting, **be in a brown study,** be absent, be somewhere else, stargaze, be out of it *and* be not with it <both nonformal>

moor NOUNS 1 **plateau,** tableland, high plateau, table, mesa, table mountain, butte, moorland, moss <Scots>

VERBS 2 **anchor,** come to anchor, lay anchor, **cast dock,** tie up, drop anchor; pick up the mooring; lash, lash and tie; **secure,** make fast

mooring NOUNS **landing,** landfall; docking, tying up, dropping anchor; **getting off,** disembarkation, disembarkment, debarkation, coming *or* going ashore

moot ADJS **unproved,** not proved, unproven, **undemonstrated,** unshown, not shown; **untried,** untested; **unestablished,** unfixed, unsettled, undetermined, unascertained; **inconclusive,** sub judice; **debatable,** arguable, disputable, contestable, controvertible, **controversial,** refutable, confutable, deniable

mop VERBS **wash, rinse,** rinse out, flush, flush out, irrigate, sluice, sluice out; sponge, sponge down *or* off; **scrub,** scrub up *or* out, **swab,** mop up; hose out *or* down; rinse off *or* out

mope VERBS **sulk,** mope around; grizzle <Brit nonformal>, grump *and* grouch *and* bitch <all nonformal>, **brood over,** fret, take on <nonformal>; get oneself in a sulk, **eat one's heart out,** ache, bleed

mopey ADJS **glum,** grum, **morose,** sullen, sulky, mumpish, dumpish, long-faced, crestfallen, chapfallen; **moody,** moodish, brooding, broody; mopish, moping

moral NOUNS 1 **maxim,** aphorism, apothegm, epigram, dictum, adage, proverb, gnome, words of wisdom, **saying,** sentence, expression, phrase, catchword, catchphrase, word, byword, mot, motto

ADJS 2 **ethical,** moralistic; ethological; axiological; principled, high-principled, high-minded, right-minded; **virtuous,** good, upright, honest; **righteous,** just, straight, rightminded, right-thinking; **angelic,** seraphic; **saintly,** saintlike; **godly**

morale NOUNS **morality,** moral fiber *or* rectitude *or* virtue; **mood,** humor, feeling, feelings, temper, frame of mind, state of mind, tone, note, **vein**

moralistic ADJS **preceptive,** didactic, instructive, prescriptive; prescript, prescribed, mandatory, hard-and-fast, binding, dictated; **exhortative,** exhortatory, hortative, hortatory, preachy <nonformal>, **didactic,** sententious; **ethical,** moral; ethological; axiological

morals NOUNS **ethics, principles,** standards, norms, principles of conduct *or* behavior, principles of professional practice; morality, moral principles; ethical *or* moral code, **ethic,** code of morals *or* ethics, ethical system, value system, axiology; ethicality, ethicalness

morass NOUNS **marsh,** marshland, swamp, swampland, fen, fenland, bog, mire, quagmire, quicksand, slough; **muddle,** mix-up *and* foul-up *and* fuck-up *and* snafu *and* screw-up <all nonformal>, pretty kettle of fish; **predicament, plight,** spot of trouble, **strait,** straits, parlous straits, tightrope, knife-edge, thin edge; pretty *or* fine state of affairs, **sorry plight**

moratorium NOUNS **grace period;** suspension, holdup <nonformal>, **wait,** halt, stay, stop, downtime, break, pause, interim, respite; reprieve

morbid ADJS **unwholesome, unhealthy,** unsound, diseased, pathological, pathological, **infected, contaminated,** tainted, peccant, **poisoned,** septic; **hideous, ghastly,** grim, grisly, gruesome, ghoulish, macabre; overcurious, supercurious; morbidly curious

more ADVS **additionally,** in addition, also, and then some, even more, more so, and also, and all <nonformal>, and so, **as well,** too, else, beside, **besides,** to boot, not to mention, let alone, into the bargain; on top of, over, above; **beyond,** plus; extra, on the side <nonformal>, for lagniappe; **moreover,** *au reste* <Fr>, *en plus* <Fr>, thereto, farther, further, **furthermore,** at the same time, then, again, yet; similarly, likewise, by the same token, by the same sign

mores NOUNS **etiquette,** social code, rules *or* code of conduct; **formalities,** social procedures, social conduct, what is done, what one does; **amenities,** decencies, civilities, elegancies, social graces, proprieties; decorum, good form; **protocol,** convention, social usage

morgue NOUNS **mortuary,** charnel house, lichhouse <Brit nonformal>; ossuary *or* ossuarium; **funeral home** *or* **parlor,** undertaker's establishment; **crematorium,** crematory, cinerarium

moribund ADJS **dying, terminal,** expiring, going, slipping, slipping away, sinking, sinking fast, low, despaired of, given up, given up for dead, not long for this world, hopeless, bad, languishing, failing, near death, near one's end, at the end of one's rope <nonformal>, done for <nonformal>, at the point of death, **at death's door,** at the portals of death, *in articulo mortis* <L>, *in extremis* <L>, in the jaws of death, facing *or* in the face of death; **on one's last legs** <nonformal>, with one foot in the grave, tottering on the brink of the grave; nonviable, unviable, incapable of life

morning NOUNS morn, morningtide, morning time, morntime, matins, waking time, reveille, get-up time <nonformal>, **forenoon;** *ante meridiem* <L> *or* AM, this morning, this AM <nonformal>

rosy-finger'd morn
HOMER

moron NOUNS **idiot,** driveling *or* blithering *or* adenoidal *or* congenital idiot; **imbecile,** half-wit, natural, natural idiot, born fool, natural-born fool, mental defective, defective; **simpleton**

moronic ADJS **mentally deficient,** mentally defective, mentally handicapped, retarded, **mentally retarded,** backward, arrested, subnormal, not right in the head, **not all there** <nonformal>; **idiotic,** imbecile, imbecilic; **foolish,** fool <nonformal>, foolheaded <nonformal>, **stupid, dumb** <nonformal>, clueless <Brit nonformal>, **asinine**

morose ADJS **glum,** grum, **sullen,** sulky, mumpish, dumpish, long-faced, crestfallen, chapfallen; **moody,** moodish, **brooding,** broody; mopish, mopey <nonformal>, **moping**

morphine NOUNS

<nonformal> big M, emm, hocus, M, miss emma, miss morph, morph, moocah, white stuff

morsel NOUNS **bite, taste,** swallow; mouthful, gob <nonformal>; a nibble, a bite, munchies; **delicacy,** dainty, goody <nonformal>, treat, kickshaw, **tidbit,** titbit; choice morsel, *bonne bouche* <Fr>; *morceau* <Fr>, **crumb; piece,** particle, bit, scrap, **fragment,** shard, potsherd, snatch

mortal NOUNS 1 **person,** human, human being, man, woman, child, member of the human race *or* family, Adamite, daughter of Eve; life, **soul,** living soul; **being,** creature, clay, ordinary clay; **individual**

ADJS 2 **perishable,** subject to death, ephemeral, transient, mutable; **deadly,** deathly, deathful, killing, destructive, death-dealing, death-bringing; **fatal,** lethal, malignant, malign, virulent, pernicious, baneful; **life-threatening,** terminal
3 **human; frail,** weak, fleshly, finite, only human; earthborn, of the earth, earthy, tellurian, unangelic

mortality NOUNS **deadliness,** lethality, mortality, fatality; **death rate,** death toll; **humanness,** humanity; **death,** perishability, corruptibility, caducity

mortifying ADJS humiliating, humiliative, humbling, chastening, **embarrassing,** crushing, disconcerting, awkward, disturbing

mosaic ADJS **checked, checkered,** checkedy, check, **plaid,** plaided; tessellated, tessellate

most NOUNS 1 **maximum,** highest, *ne plus ultra* <Fr, no more beyond>, the max <nonformal>; **major part,** best part, better part; **majority,** generality, plurality; **bulk, mass,** body, main body; **lion's share; substance,** gist, meat, essence, thrust, gravamen
ADJS 2 **greatest,** furthest, **utmost,** uttermost; **ultra,** ultra-ultra; at the height *or* peak *or* limit *or* summit *or* zenith; **superlative,** supreme, greatest, best, highest, veriest, maximal, maximum, outstanding, stickout <nonformal>; **majority,** the greatest number
ADVS 3 **extremely, utterly, totally** in the extreme, *à outrance* <Fr, to the utmost>; **immeasurably,** incalculably, indefinitely, **infinitely;** beyond compare *or* comparison, **beyond measure,** beyond all bounds, all out <nonformal>, flat out <nonformal>; unconditionally, with no strings attached, unequivocally, downright, dead; with a vengeance

mot NOUNS **witticism,** pleasantry, *plaisanterie, boutade* <both Fr>; **play of wit,** *jeu d'esprit* <Fr>; crack *and* smart crack *and* wisecrack <all nonformal>; **quip,** conceit, bright *or* happy thought, bright *or* brilliant idea; **bon mot,** smart saying, stroke of wit, one-liner *and* zinger <both nonformal>; epigram, turn of thought, aphorism, apothegm

mote NOUNS fleck, **speck,** flyspeck, jot, tittle, jot nor tittle, iota, **trace,** trace amount, suspicion, *soupçon* <Fr>; **particle,** crumb, scrap, bite, snip, snippet

motel NOUNS motor court, motor inn, motor hotel, auto court

mother NOUNS 1 genetrix, dam, maternal ancestor, matriarch, materfamilias; stepmother; foster mother, adoptive mother; birth mother; surrogate mother

2 <nonformal> **mama,** mater, the old woman, mammy, mam, **ma, mom, mommy,** mummy, mumsy, mimsy, motherkin, motherkins

VERBS 3 **foster, nurture,** nourish, care for, lavish care on, feed, parent, rear, sustain, cultivate, **cherish;** pamper, coddle, cosset, fondle <old>; **nurse,** suckle, cradle
ADJS 4 **native,** natal, **indigenous,** endemic, autochthonous; maternal, original, aboriginal, primitive; native-born, home-grown, homebred, native to the soil *or* place *or* heath

motherhood NOUNS **maternity,** mothership; natural *or* birth *or* biological motherhood; motherliness, maternalness; adoptive motherhood; surrogate motherhood

mothering NOUNS **nurture, fostering,** nurturance, nourishment, parenting, rearing, fosterage, foster-care, **care, caring,** care-giving, tender loving care *or* TLC <nonformal>

motif NOUNS 1 ornamental motif, **figure, detail,** form, touch, repeated figure; **pattern, theme,** design, ornamental theme, ornamental *or* decorative composition; foreground detail, background detail; **background,** setting, foil, **style,** ornamental *or* decorative style, national style, **period style**
2 **passage, phrase,** musical phrase, strain, part, motive, theme, subject, figure; leitmotiv; **theme, text,** matter in hand

motion NOUNS 1 **movement,** moving, **momentum; stir,** unrest, restlessness; **going,** running, stirring; **operation,** operating, **working,** ticking; **activity**; kinesis, kinetics, kinematics; dynamics; kinesiatrics, kinesipathy, kinesitherapy; **actuation,** motivation; mobilization
VERBS 2 **gesture,** gesticulate; motion to; beckon, wiggle the finger at; wave the arms, wigwag, saw the air

motionless ADJS **unmoving,** unmoved, moveless, **immobile,** immotive; **still,** fixed, stationary, static, at a standstill; **stock-still,** dead-still; statuelike; still as a mouse

motion picture NOUNS **motion pictures, movies,** the movies, the pictures, moving pictures, films, the film, the cinema, the screen, the big screen, the silver screen, the flicks *and* the flickers <both nonformal>; **movie,** picture, film, flick *and* flicker <both nonformal>, picture show, motion-picture show, moving-picture show, photoplay, photodrama; cinéma vérité *or* direct cinema; vérité; magic realism; **documentary film** *or* **movie,** docudrama, docutainment; **feature,** feature film, feature-length film, main attraction; **educational film** *or* **movie,** training film, promotional film, trigger film; **underground film** *or* **movie,** experimental film *or* movie, avant-garde film *or* movie, representational film, art film *or* movie, surrealistic film *or* movie

motivate VERBS **move,** set in motion, **actuate,** move to action, **impel,** propel; **stimulate,** energize, galvanize, **animate, spark;** promote, foster; force, compel; ego-involve

motivated ADJS **moved,** prompted, impelled, actuated; stimulated, animated; minded, inclined, of a mind to, with half a mind to; inner-directed, other-directed

motive NOUNS **reason, cause,** source, spring, mainspring; matter, score, consideration; **ground, basis**; sake; **aim, goal**, end, end in view, telos, final cause; **ideal,** principle, **ambition,** aspiration, inspiration, guiding light *or* star, lodestar; intention; ulterior motive

motley ADJS **mottled; pied, piebald,** skewbald, pinto; **dappled,** dapple; calico; marbled; pepper-and-salt; **conglomerate,** pluralistic, multiracial, multicultural, multiethnic, multinational, heterogeneous, varied, **miscellaneous,** medley, patchy; promiscuous, indiscriminate, **scrambled, jumbled,** thrown together

motor VERBS **ride,** go for a ride *or* drive; go for a spin <nonformal>, take *or* go for a Sunday drive; **drive,** chauffeur; joyride *or* take a joyride <nonformal>

motorcade NOUNS **procession,** cavalcade, caravan; **parade,** pomp

mottled ADJS **motley; pied, piebald,** skewbald, pinto; **dappled,** dapple; calico; marbled; clouded; pepper-and-salt

motto NOUNS **slogan,** watchword, catchword, catchphrase, tag line; **device;** epithet; inscription, epigraph

mound NOUNS 1 **hillock, knob,** butte, kopje, kame, monticle, monticule, monadnock, **knoll,** hummock, hammock, eminence, rise, swell, barrow, tumulus, kop, tel, jebel; **dune,** sand dune
VERBS 2 **pile,** pile on, heap, stack, heap *or* pile *or* stack up; hill, bank, bank up; rick

mount NOUNS 1 **mountain,** alp, hump, tor, height, dizzying height, nunatak, dome; **peak, pinnacle, summit**, mountaintop, point, topmost point *or* pinnacle, **crest,** tor, *pic* <Fr>, *pico* <Sp>
2 **horse;** hoss <nonformal>, critter <nonformal>; **equine,** nag <nonformal>; **steed,** prancer, dobbin; charger, courser, war-horse; **pony,** Shetland pony, Shetland, shelty, Iceland pony, Galloway; cowcutting horse, stock horse, roping horse, cow pony
VERBS 3 **climb,** climb up, upclimb, clamber, **clamber up,** scramble *or* scrabble up, claw one's way up, struggle up, inch up, shin, shinny *or* shin up <nonformal>, ramp <nonformal>, work *or* inch one's way up, climb the ladder; **scale,** escalade, scale the heights
4 **get on,** climb on, back; **bestride,** bestraddle
5 **grow,** increase, advance, appreciate; **spread, widen,** broaden; **gain,** get ahead; wax, swell, balloon, bloat, **rise,** go up, crescendo, snowball; **intensify, develop,** gain strength, strengthen

mountain NOUNS mount, alp, hump, tor, height, dizzying height, nunatak; crag, spur, cloud-capped *or* cloud-topped *or* snow-clad peak, the roof of the world

mourn VERBS **lament,** moan, grieve, sorrow, keen, weep over, **bewail,** bemoan, deplore, repine, sigh, give sorrow words; sing the blues <nonformal>, elegize, dirge, knell

mourner NOUNS **griever,** lamenter, keener; mute, professional mourner; **pallbearer,** bearer

mourning NOUNS **lamentation,** lamenting, moaning, grieving, sorrowing, wailing, bewailing, bemoaning, keening, howling, ululation, **weeds,** widow's weeds, crape, black; deep mourning; sackcloth, sackcloth and ashes

weeping and gnashing of teeth
BIBLE

mouth VERBS **speak,** talk; patter *or* gab *or* wag the tongue <all nonformal>; chatter; converse; declaim

mouthful NOUNS 1 **bite,** morsel, taste, swallow; gob <nonformal>; a nibble, a bite, munchies; cud, quid; bolus; **chew,** chaw <nonformal>
2 **sesquipedalian word,** big *or* long word, two- dollar *or* five-dollar word <nonformal>, **jawbreaker,** jawtwister, polysyllabism, sesquipedalianism, sesquipedality

mouthpiece NOUNS **spokesman,** spokeswoman, spokesperson, spokespeople, official spokesman *or* -woman *or* -person, press officer, speaker, **voice**

mouth-watering ADJS **appetizing,** tempting, tantalizing, provocative, piquant

mouthy ADJS **bombastic,** fustian, inflated, swollen, swelling, turgid, turgescent, tumid, tumescent, flatulent, windy *and* gassy <both nonformal>; overadorned, fulsome

movable ADJS mobile, motile; **influenceable,** swayable, persuadable, persuasible, suasible, open, open-minded, pervious, accessible, receptive, responsive, amenable

move NOUNS 1 **operation,** proceeding, step, measure, maneuver, movement; **endeavor,** undertaking; approach, coup, stroke, step; gambit, offer, **bid,** strong bid; **expedient,** means, means to an end, **provision,** action, effort, countermove, demarche, course of action
VERBS 2 **affect,** touch, stir; melt, soften, melt the heart, choke one up, give one a lump in the throat; **penetrate,** pierce, go through one, go deep; touch a chord, **touch a sympathetic chord,** touch one's heart, tug at the heart *or* heartstrings, go to one's heart, get under one's skin; **touch to the quick,** smart, sting
3 locate, relocate, establish residence, make one's home, **take up residence,** take residence at, put up *or* live *or* stay at, quarter *or* billet at, move in, hang up one's hat <nonformal>
4 **set in motion,** actuate, motivate, push, shove, nudge, **drive,** impel, propel; mobilize

moved ADJS **motivated,** prompted, impelled, actuated; stimulated, animated; minded, inclined, of a mind to, with half a mind to; inner-directed, other-directed

movement NOUNS 1 **exercise,** motion, maneuver; moving, **momentum; stir,** unrest, restlessness; **going,** running, stirring; **operation,** operating, **working,** ticking; activity; **travel,** traveling, going, journeying, touring, moving, locomotion, transit, progress, passage, course, crossing
2 **gesture,** gesticulation; motion, beck, beckon; shrug
3 **trend,** drift, course, current, *Tendenz* <Ger>, flow, stream, mainstream, main current, glacial movement, motion, run, **tenor,** tone, **set,** set of the current, the way the wind blows, **the way things go,** trend of the times, spirit of the age *or* time, time spirit, *Zeitgeist* <Ger>

mover NOUNS **prompter,** prime mover, motivator, impeller, energizer, galvanizer, inducer, **actuator, animator,** moving spirit; **encourager,** abettor, **inspirer,** firer, spark, sparker, spark plug <nonformal>; persuader; stimulator, gadfly; **producer,** maker, creator, fabricator, **author**

moving ADJS 1 **pitiful,** pitiable, pathetic, piteous, touching, affecting, heartrending, grievous, doleful
2 **stirring,** in motion; transitional; **mobile,** motive, motile, motor, motorial, motoric; motivational, impelling, propelling, propellant, driving; traveling; **active**
3 **lofty,** elevated, sublime, grand, majestic, noble, stately, grave, solemn, dignified; serious, weighty; inspiring

moxie NOUNS **pluck,** spunk <nonformal>, mettle, backbone <nonformal>, **grit,** true grit, spirit, **stamina,** guts <nonformal>, pith <old>, bottom, **toughness** <nonformal>; pluckiness, spunkiness <nonformal>, **gameness,** feistiness <nonformal>, mettlesomeness; courage

Mrs Grundy NOUNS conventionalist, Grundy; conformist

much NOUNS 1 **plenty,** plenitude, plentifulness, plenteousness; great abundance, great plenty, quantities, as much as one could wish, more than one can shake a stick at, lots, a fistful <nonformal>, **scads**; an ample sufficiency, enough and to spare, enough and then some; fat of the land

ADJS 2 **many,** beaucoup <nonformal>, ample, **abundant,** copious, generous, overflowing, superabundant, multitudinous, plentiful, **numerous**, countless
ADVS 3 **greatly, largely,** to a large *or* great extent, in great measure, on a large scale; pretty much, very much, so, so very much, ever so much, ever so, never so; **considerably**

muck NOUNS **filth,** slime, mess, sordes, foul matter; ordure, **excrement**; **mud,** mire, slush, slosh, sludge, squash, swill

muckraking NOUNS **smear campaign,** mudslinging campaign, negative campaign; **whispering campaign;** mudslinging *and* dirty politics *and* dirty tricks *and* dirty pool <all nonformal>, character assassination; political canard, roorback

muddle NOUNS 1 **confusion, fluster,** flummox <nonformal>, flutter, flurry, ruffle; disorientation, muddlement, fuddle *and* fuddlement <both nonformal>, befuddlement, muddleheadedness, daze, maze <nonformal>; unsettlement, disorganization, **disorder,** chaos, **mess** *and* mix-up *and* snafu <all nonformal>, discomfiture, discomposure, disconcertion, discombobulation <nonformal>, **bewilderment,** embarrassment, disturbance, perturbation, **upset,** frenzy, pother, bother, botheration *and* stew <both nonformal>
VERBS 2 **confound, confuse,** mix, mix up, tumble, jumble, jumble together, **blur,** blur distinctions, overlook distinctions; **perplex, baffle,** daze, addle, fuddle, **mystify, puzzle,** nonplus, put to one's wit's end; **make uncertain,** obscure, muddy, fuzz, fog, **confuse**

muddled ADJS **confused,** in a muddle; fuddled <nonformal>, **befuddled;** muddleheaded, **addled,** addlepated, addlebrained; adrift, at sea, foggy, fogged, in a fog, hazy, muzzy <nonformal>, misted, misty, cloudy, beclouded

muddle through VERBS **manage,** make out, get on *or* along <nonformal>, **scrape along,** worry along, get by, **manage somehow;** make it <nonformal>, **make the grade,** cut the mustard *and* hack it <both nonformal>

muddy VERBS 1 **make uncertain,** obscure, muddle, fuzz, fog, **confuse**
ADJS 2 **dingy,** grimy, smoky, sooty, fuliginous, smudgy, smutty, blotchy, dirty, murky, smirched, besmirched
3 **obscure,** vague, indistinct, indeterminate, fuzzy, shapeless, amorphous; unclear, unplain, opaque, **clear as mud** *and* clear as ditch water <both nonformal>

mudslinging NOUNS **smear campaign,** mudslinging campaign, negative campaign; **whispering campaign;** muckraking, dirty politics *and* dirty tricks *and* dirty pool <all nonformal>, character assassination; political canard, roorback

muffle NOUNS 1 **silencer,** muffler, mute, baffle *or* baffler, quietener, cushion; **damper,** damp; dampener; **soft pedal,** sordine, sourdine, *sordino* <Ital>; hushcloth, silence cloth; **gag, muzzle**
VERBS 2 **mute,** dull, soften, deaden, quietize, cushion, baffle, damp, **dampen,** deafen; subdue, stop, tone down, **soft-pedal,** put on the soft pedal

mufti NOUNS civilian dress *or* clothes, **civvies** *and* cits <both nonformal>, plain clothes

mug NOUNS 1 **face,** facies, **visage;** physiognomy, phiz *and* dial <both nonformal>; **countenance,** features, lineaments, favor; mush *and* pan *and* kisser *and* map *and* puss <all nonformal>
VERBS 2 **make a face,** make a wry face *or* mouth, pull a face, **screw up one's face,** mouth, make a mouth, mop, mow, mop and mow; pout
3 **overact,** overdramatize, chew up the scenery <nonformal>, act all over the stage; **ham** *and* ham it up <both nonformal>; grimace; milk a scene
4 **rob;** roll, stick up <nonformal>, **attack**

mugger NOUNS **assailant,** assailer, attacker; assaulter; **robber,** holdup man *and* stickup man <both nonformal>; sandbagger

muggy ADJS **moist,** moisty; **damp,** dampish; **wet,** wettish; **humid,** dank, sticky

mulish ADJS **obstinate,** stubborn, pertinacious, restive; willful, self-willed, strong-willed, hardheaded, **headstrong,** strongheaded, *entêté* <Fr>; **dogged,** bulldogged, tenacious, perserving; bullheaded, bulletheaded, **pigheaded,** stubborn as a mule; set, **set in one's ways,** balky, balking

mull over VERBS **think over,** ponder over, brood over, muse over, reflect over, con over, **deliberate over,** run over, **meditate over,** ruminate over, chew over, digest, turn over, **revolve,** revolve *or* turn over in the mind, deliberate upon, meditate upon, muse on *or* upon, bestow thought *or* consideration upon

multicolor ADJS **variegated, many-colored,** many-hued, diverse-colored, **multicolored,** varicolored, polychrome, polychromic, polychromatic; parti-colored, parti-color; of all manner of colors, of all the colors of the rainbow; versicolor, versicolored

multilateral ADJS **many-sided,** multifaceted, polyhedral

multilingual NOUNS **polyglot,** linguist, **bilingual** *or* diglot, trilingual

multiple ADJS multiplied, multifold, **manifold**; **increased**; multinomial, polynomial <both mathematics>; **multitudinous,** multitudinal, multifarious, **myriad,** numerous as the stars, numerous as the sands, numerous as the hairs on the head

numerous as glittering gems of morning dew
EDWARD YOUNG

multiplied ADJS **increased, heightened,** raised, elevated, stepped-up <nonformal>; **intensified,** deepened, reinforced, strengthened, fortified, beefed-up <nonformal>, tightened, stiffened; **enlarged,** extended, augmented, aggrandized, amplified, **enhanced,** boosted, hiked <nonformal>; **magnified,** inflated, expanded, swollen, bloated; proliferated; **multiple,** multifold, **manifold**

multiply VERBS proliferate, **increase,** duplicate; **produce,** be productive, pullulate, fructify, be fruitful, spin off, engender, beget, teem; **reproduce**

multiracial ADJS **mixed, mingled,** blended, compounded, amalgamated; **conglomerate,** pluralistic, multicultural, multiethnic, multinational, heterogeneous, varied, **miscellaneous,** medley, motley

multitude NOUNS **throng, horde,** host, heap <nonformal>, army, panoply, legion; flock, cluster, galaxy; **crowd,** press, crush, flood, spate, deluge, mass; **mob,** rabble, rout, ruck, jam, *cohue* <Fr>, everybody and his uncle *or* his brother <nonformal>

mum ADJS **mute, dumb,** voiceless, tongueless, **speechless,** wordless, breathless, at a loss for words, choked up; inarticulate; close, **closemouthed,** close-tongued, snug <nonformal>, **tight-lipped;** close-lipped, tongue-tied, wordbound

mumble NOUNS 1 **murmur,** murmuring, murmuration; **mutter,** muttering; mumbling; soft voice, low voice, small *or* little voice

still small voice
BIBLE

VERBS 2 **murmur,** mutter, maunder; **lower one's voice,** speak under one's breath; swallow one's words

mumbo jumbo NOUNS 1 **incantation, conjuration,** magic words *or* formula; hocus-pocus, abracadabra; open sesame; **voodoo, hoodoo,** juju, obeah
2 **nonsense, gibberish,** jargon, doubletalk, amphigory, gobbledegook <nonformal>; glossolalia, speaking in tongues

mummy NOUNS **corpse,** dead body, dead man *or* woman, dead person, cadaver, body; embalmed corpse

munch VERBS **chew,** chew up, chaw <nonformal>, bite into; **masticate,** manducate; ruminate, chew the cud; **bite,** grind, champ, chomp <nonformal>; nibble, **gnaw**

mundane ADJS **secularist,** secularistic, worldly, earthly, earthy, terrestrial, temporal; **plain,** common, commonplace, ordinary, unembellished; **matter-of-fact,** unromantic, unidealistic, unimpassioned; pedestrian, **unimaginative**; insipid, vapid, flat; humdrum, tiresome, **dull**

munitions NOUNS **arms, weapons,** deadly weapons, instruments of destruction, offensive weapons, **military hardware,** matériel, **weaponry,** armament, ordnance, munitions of war, *apparatus belli* <L>

murder NOUNS 1 **homicide,** manslaughter; negligent homicide; bloody murder <nonformal>; serial killing; hit *and* bump-off *and* bumping-off <all nonformal>, gangland-style execution; kiss of death; foul play; **assassination;** removal, elimination; liquidation, purge, purging; justifiable homicide
VERBS 2 commit murder; **assassinate;** remove, **purge, liquidate,** eliminate, get rid of
3 **botch,** mar, spoil, butcher, make sad work of; play havoc with, play mischief with

murderer NOUNS **killer,** slayer, slaughterer, butcher, bloodshedder; manslayer, homicide, man-killer, bloodletter, Cain; **assassin,** assassinator; **cutthroat,** thug, desperado, bravo, gorilla <nonformal>, apache, gunman; professional killer, hired killer, hit man *or* button man *or* gun *or* trigger man *or* torpedo *or* gunsel <all nonformal>; **hatchet man;** thrill killer, homicidal maniac; serial killer; executioner; exterminator, eradicator; death squad

murderous ADJS slaughterous; cutthroat; **homicidal,** man-killing, death-dealing; biocidal, genocidal; **savage,** fierce, ferocious, vicious, cruel, **atrocious,** mindless, brutal, brutish, **bestial,** insensate, monstrous, inhuman, pitiless, ruthless, merciless, bloody, sanguinary

murky ADJS **gloomy,** dismal, bleak, grim, somber, sombrous, solemn, grave; cloudy, **foggy,** fogbound, hazy, misty, nebulous; indefinable, undefined, ill-defined, **unclear,** unplain, **indistinct,** fuzzy, **obscure,** confused, hazy, shadowy, shadowed forth, misty, blurred, blurry, veiled; **loose, lax, inexact,** inaccurate, imprecise; nonspecific, unspecified

murmur NOUNS 1 murmuring, murmuration, sough; **mutter,** muttering; **mumble,** mumbling; susurration, susurrus; **whisper,** whispering, stage whisper, breathy voice
VERBS 2 **mutter,** mumble; susurrate; lower one's voice, **speak under one's breath;** whisper, whisper in the ear; **sigh,** sough

muscle NOUNS 1 **muscularity,** brawniness; beefiness *and* huskiness *and* heftiness *and* hunkiness <all nonformal>, thewiness, sinewiness; **brawn,** beef <nonformal>; **sinew,** sinews, thew, thews; musculature, build, physique; great *or* mighty effort, might and main, one's back, nerve and sinew, hard *or* strong *or* long pull
VERBS 2 **exert strength,** put beef *or* one's back into it <nonformal>; use force, get tough <nonformal>, manhandle *and* strong-arm <both nonformal>; bull, bulldoze, steamroller, railroad; elbow, shoulder; **butt,** bunt, buck <nonformal>, run *or* bump *or* butt against, bump up against, knock *or* run one's head against; assault

muscular ADJS **able-bodied, well-built,** well-set, well-set-up <nonformal>, well-knit, of good *or* powerful physique, broad-shouldered, barrel-chested, **athletic;** well-muscled, heavily muscled, thickset, burly, **brawny;** thewy, sinewy, **wiry;** muscle-bound, all muscle

muse NOUNS 1 **inspiration,** afflatus, divine afflatus; genius, animus, moving *or* animating spirit; the Muses; **brown study,** study, reverie, dreamy abstraction, quiet *or* muted ecstasy, trance
VERBS 2 **consider,** contemplate, speculate, reflect, study, ponder, perpend, **weigh,** deliberate, debate, meditate, brood, ruminate, chew the cud <nonformal>; **moon** <nonformal>, **dream,** daydream, pipe-dream <nonformal>, fantasy; abstract oneself, be lost in thought, let one's attention wander, let one's mind run on other things, dream of *or* muse on other things; **wander,** stray, ramble, divagate, let one's thoughts *or* mind wander, give oneself up to reverie, **woolgather,** go woolgathering, **be in a brown study,** be absent, be somewhere else, stargaze, be out of it *and* be not with it <both nonformal>

museum NOUNS **gallery,** art gallery, picture gallery, pinacotheca; Metropolitan Museum, National Gallery, Museum of Modern Art, Guggenheim Museum, Tate Gallery, British Museum, Louvre, Hermitage, Prado, Uffizi, Rijksmuseum; **library;** repository

mushy ADJS **wishy-washy,** tasteless, bland, **insipid,** vapid, neutral, watery, milky, milk-and-water; halfhearted, infirm of will *or* purpose, **indecisive,** irresolute, changeable; **sentimental,** sentimentalized, soft, **mawkish,** maudlin, cloying; oversentimental, oversentimentalized, bathetic; sloppy *or* gushing *or* teary *or* beery <all nonformal>, treacly <Brit nonformal>; tear-jerking <nonformal>

music NOUNS harmonious sound, **score,** musical score *or* copy, notation, musical notation, written music, copy, draft, transcript, transcription, version, edition, text, arrangement; **harmonics,** harmony; melodics; musicality

the speech of angels
CARLYLE

musical NOUNS 1 **musical theater,** music theater, lyric theater, musical stage, lyric

stage; **music drama,** lyric drama; **musical comedy;** Broadway musical
ADJS 2 **musically inclined,** musicianly, with an ear for music; **music-loving,** music-mad, musicophile, philharmonic; **melodious,** melodic; music-like; **tuneful,** lilting; fine-toned, **pleasant-sounding,** agreeable-sounding, pleasant, appealing, agreeable, catchy, singable; euphonious *or* euphonic, **lyric,** lyrical, melic; **sweet, dulcet,** sweet-sounding, achingly sweet

musician NOUNS **music maker,** professional musician; performer, executant, interpreter, tunester, artiste, artist, concert artist, **virtuoso,** virtuosa; maestro; recitalist; **soloist,** duettist; street musician, busker <chiefly Brit>

must NOUNS 1 **fetidness,** fetidity, malodourousness, **smelliness,** stinkingness, **odorousness,** noisomeness, **rankness, foulness,** putridness, offensiveness; **mustiness,** funkiness, moldiness, smut, rust, fungus, mildew, mildew, fustiness, frowziness, stuffiness
VERBS 2 **be necessary,** lie under a necessity, be one's fate; be a must <nonformal>; be obliged, **have to,** have got to <nonformal>, should, need, **need to,** have need to; not able to keep from, not able to help, **cannot help but,** cannot do otherwise; be forced *or* driven
ADJS 3 **obligatory,** binding, imperative, imperious, peremptory, mandatory, *de rigueur* <Fr>; **necessary,** required; carved in stone, set in concrete <nonformal>

mustache NOUNS mustachio, soup-strainer <nonformal>, toothbrush, handle bars *or* handlebar mustache, Fu Manchu mustache, Zapata mustache, walrus mustache

muster NOUNS 1 **enlistment,** enrollment; conscription, draft, drafting, induction, impressment, press; call, draft call, call-up, summons, call to the colors, letter from Uncle Sam <nonformal>; **recruitment,** recruiting; mustering, mustering in, levy, levying
2 **roll call,** nose *or* head count <nonformal>, **poll,** questionnaire, returns, census report *or* returns

musty ADJS **stale,** fusty, rusty, dusty, moldy, mildewed; **worn,** timeworn, time-scarred; **moth-eaten,** moss-grown, crumbling, moldering, gone to seed, dilapidated

mutate VERBS **change,** work *or* make a change, alter, modify; **adapt;** vary, **diversify; convert,** renew, recast, revamp <nonformal>, change over, exchange, remake, reshape, re-create, redesign, rebuild, reconstruct, restructure

mute NOUNS 1 **silencer,** muffler, muffle, baffle *or* baffler, quietener, cushion; **damper,** damp; dampener; **soft pedal,** sordine, sourdine, *sordino* <Ital>; **gag,** muzzle; soundproofing
VERBS 2 **muffle,** dull, soften, deaden, quietize, cushion, baffle, damp, **dampen,** deafen; subdue, stop, tone down, **soft-pedal,** put on the soft pedal
ADJS 3 **mum, dumb,** voiceless, tongueless, speechless, wordless, breathless, at a loss for words, choked up; inarticulate; **tongue-tied,** dumbstruck, dumbstricken, stricken dumb, **dumbfounded;** anaudic, aphasic, aphonic

muted ADJS **muffled,** softened, dampened, damped, **smothered,** stifled, bated, dulled, deadened, subdued; **dull,** dead, flat, *sordo* <Ital>

mutilate VERBS **tear** *or* **rip apart,** take *or* pull apart, pick *or* rip *or* tear to pieces, **shred,** rip to shreds; **dismember,** tear limb from limb, draw and quarter; **mangle,** lacerate, maim; **damage**

mutinous ADJS **rebellious,** rebel, breakaway; mutineering; **insurgent, insurrectionary,** riotous, turbulent; factious, **seditious,** seditionary; revolutionary, revolutional; traitorous, treasonable, subversive; extreme, insubordinate, disobedient

mutiny NOUNS 1 **revolt,** rebellion, revolution, insurrection, insurgence *or* insurgency, *émeute* <Fr>, **uprising,** rising, outbreak, general uprising, *levée en masse* <Fr>, **riot,** civil disorder; peasant revolt, *jacquerie* <Fr>; putsch, coup d'état; indiscipline, insubordination, disobedience
VERBS 2 **revolt, rebel,** kick over the traces, reluct, reluctate; **rise up,** rise, arise, rise up in arms, mount the barricades; mount *or* make a coup d'état

mutter VERBS **mumble,** maunder; drone, drone on; swallow one's words, speak drunkenly *or* incoherently; jabber, gibber, gabble

mutual ADJS commutual, **common,** joint, communal, shared, sharing, conjoint; respective, two-way; give-and-take;

exchanged, transposed, switched, swapped <nonformal>, traded, **interchanged**

muzzle NOUNS 1 **silencer, gag,** muffle, **mute,** baffle *or* baffler, quietener, cushion; **damper,** damp; dampener; **soft pedal**
2 **snout,** snoot <nonformal>, nozzle <nonformal>; **mouth;** maw, oral cavity, gob <nonformal>, gab <Scots>; jaw, lips, embouchure; bazoo *or* kisser *or* mug *or* mush *or* trap *or* yap <all nonformal>
VERBS 3 **silence,** squash, squelch <nonformal>, stifle, choke, choke off, throttle, put the kibosh on <nonformal>, put the lid on *and* shut down on <both nonformal>, put the damper on <nonformal>, **gag,** muffle, stop one's mouth, cut one short

mysterious ADJS **awesome,** awful, awing, awe-inspiring; **transcendent,** transcending, surpassing; numinous; weird, eerie, uncanny, bizarre; enigmatic; **inexplicable, unexplainable,** uninterpretable, undefinable, indefinable; mystic, mystical, shrouded *or* wrapped *or* enwrapped in mystery; **occult,** paranormal, supernatural; arcane, esoteric

mystery NOUNS **enigma,** puzzle, puzzlement; **perplexity;** mysteriousness, miraculousness, strangeness; problem, riddle, conundrum

mystic NOUNS 1 **occultist,** esoteric, mystagogue, cabalist, supernaturalist, transcendentalist; adept, mahatma; yogi, yogin, yogist; theosophist, anthroposophist
ADJS 2 **occult,** esoteric, esoterical, mysterious, mystical, anagogic, anagogical; metaphysic, metaphysical; cabalic, cabalistic; theosophical, theosophist, anthroposophical

mystify VERBS **perplex,** baffle, confound, daze, maze, addle, fuddle, muddle, **puzzle,** nonplus, put to one's wit's end; keep one guessing, keep in suspense

mystifying ADJS **bewildering,** confusing, distracting, disconcerting, discomposing, **dismaying,** embarrassing, disturbing, **upsetting,** perturbing, bothering; **perplexing,** baffling, mysterious, puzzling, funny, funny peculiar, confounding; **problematic** *or* problematical; intricate; **enigmatic**

mystique NOUNS **illustriousness,** luster, brilliance *or* brilliancy, radiance, splendor, resplendence; charisma, glamour, numinousness, magic

myth NOUNS **fabrication,** invention, concoction, disinformation; canard, base canard; **fiction,** figment, fable, romance, extravaganza; mythology, legend, lore, folklore, folktale, folk motif; racial memory, archetypal myth *or* image *or* pattern

mythical ADJS **fictional,** mythological, **legendary,** fabulous; mythopoeic, mythopoetic *or* mythopoetical; **allegorical** *or* allegoric, parabolic *or* parabolical; **romantic,** romanticized; **extraordinary,** exceptional, remarkable, noteworthy, **wonderful,** marvelous; mythified, mythicized

N

nadir NOUNS **boundary,** lower limit, floor, low-water mark, the pits <nonformal>; **base, bottom**, lowest point; the lowest of the low

nag NOUNS 1 **nuisance, pest,** pesterer, pain *and* pain in the neck *or* ass <nonformal>, nudzh <nonformal>, *nudnik* <Yiddish>; annoyer, harasser, harrier, badgerer, **heckler,** plaguer, persecutor
2 horse; **plug,** hack, jade, crock, garron <Scots & Ir>, crowbait <nonformal>, scalawag, rosinante; balky horse, balker, jughead; stack of bones
VERBS 3 **importune,** beset, buttonhole, besiege, take *or* grasp by the lapels; work on <nonformal>, **tease,** pester, plague, nag at, make a pest *or* nuisance of oneself, try one's patience, bug <nonformal>, nudge; niggle, **carp at, fuss at,** fret at, yap *or* pick at <nonformal>, peck at, nibble at, **henpeck,** pick on *and* pick at <all nonformal>, bug *and* hassle <nonformal>

nagging ADJS 1 **importunate; teasing,** pesty, pesky <nonformal>, pestering, plaguing, dunning; **insistent,** demanding, urgent; **critical, faultfinding,** carping, caviling, quibbling, pettifogging, captious, cynical; niggling; hypercritical, ultracritical, overcritical, hairsplitting, trichoschistic
2 **unforgettable, never to be forgotten,** never to be erased from the mind, **indelible,** indelibly impressed on the mind, fixed in the mind; haunting, persistent, recurrent, plaguing, rankling, festering; obsessing, obsessive

nail VERBS 1 **catch, take,** catch flatfooted, land <nonformal>, hook, **snag, snare,** sniggle, spear, harpoon; **bag,** sack; **trap,** entrap
2 **pin,** skewer, peg, nail up, tack, staple, toggle, screw, bolt, rivet

naive ADJS **immature,** unadult; **inexperienced,** unseasoned, unfledged, newfledged, **callow,** unripe, **raw, green,** vernal, primaveral, dewy, juicy, sappy, budding, tender, virginal, intact, ingenuous, **undeveloped,** growing, unformed, unlicked, wet *or* not dry behind the ears; **unsophisticated,** childlike, born yesterday; **innocent;** trustful, trusting, unguarded, unwary, unreserved, confiding, unsuspicious

naked ADJS 1 **nude; bare,** peeled, raw <nonformal>, **in the raw** <nonformal>, *in puris naturalibus* <L>, in a state of nature, in nature's garb; in one's birthday suit, **in the buff** *and* in native buff *and* stripped to the buff *and* **in the altogether** <all nonformal>, with nothing on, without a stitch, without a stitch to one's name *or* on one's back; **stark-naked,** bare-ass <nonformal>, naked as the day one was born, naked as a jaybird <nonformal>
2 **open,** overt, open to all, open as day, out of the closet <nonformal>; **revealed,** disclosed, exposed; bare, bald

name NOUNS 1 **appellation,** appellative, **denomination,** designation, style, *nomen* <L>, **cognomen,** cognomination, full name; proper name *or* noun; moniker *and* handle <both nonformal>; **title,** honorific; **label,** tag; epithet, byword; middle name; eponym; namesake; secret name, cryptonym, euonym
2 **celebrity,** man *or* woman of mark *or* note, person of note *or* consequence, **notable,** notability, luminary, great man *or* woman, master spirit, worthy, **big name,** figure, public figure, **somebody**
VERBS 3 **designate, specify;** denominate, denote; stigmatize; **appoint,** assign, **nominate,** select, tab <nonformal>; **ordain**
ADJS 4 **important,** major, consequential, momentous, significant, considerable, substantial, material, **great,** grand, big; big-time *and* big-league *and* major-league *and* heavyweight <all nonformal>; high-powered <nonformal>, double-barreled <nonformal>; big-name <nonformal>, self-important

name-dropper NOUNS **social climber,** climber, tufthunter, status seeker, fortune hunter

nanny NOUNS **nurse, nursemaid,** nurserymaid, amah, ayah, mammy <nonformal>; **baby-sitter,** baby-minder <Brit>, sitter <nonformal>

nap NOUNS 1 **snooze** <nonformal>, **catnap,** wink, **forty winks** *and* some Zs <both nonformal>; **siesta,** blanket drill *and* sack *or* rack time <all nonformal>
2 **texture,** surface texture; **finish,** feel; **grain,** granular texture, fineness *or* coarseness of grain; pile, shag, nub, knub

VERBS 3 **sleep, slumber,** rest in the arms of Morpheus; **doze,** drowse; **catnap,** take a nap, catch a wink, sleep soundly, **sleep like a top** *or* **log,** sleep like the dead

napping ADJS **sleepy, slumberous,** slumbery, dreamy; **half asleep,** asleep on one's feet; yawny, stretchy <nonformal>, oscitant, yawning, **nodding,** ready for bed; asleep, **off one's guard,** caught napping, caught tripping, **asleep at the switch** *and* asleep on the job *and* **not on the job** *and* goofing off *and* looking out the window <all nonformal>; daydreaming, woolgathering

narc NOUNS **detective,** operative, investigator, narcotics agent; treasury agent *or* T-man <nonformal>

narcissistic ADJS **egotistic,** egotistical, **egocentric,** egocentristic, self-centered, self-obsessed, narcistic; selfish, self-esteeming, self-admiring; **self-centered**

narcotic NOUNS 1 **drug,** dope <nonformal>, dangerous drug, controlled substance, abused substance, illegal drug, addictive drug, **hard drug; opiate; sedative,** depressant, sedative hypnotic, antipsychotic tranquilizer
ADJS 2 hypnotic, **soporific,** somniferous, somnifacient; sedative, **anesthetic,** analgesic; stupefying, stunning, numbing, mind-boggling *or* -numbing; anesthetizing, narcotizing; **palliative,** alleviative, alleviatory, assuasive, lenitive, **calmative,** calmant, demulcent, anodyne

narcotics addict NOUNS **addict, drug addict,** user, drug user, drug abuser, junkie *and* head *and* druggy *and* doper *and* toker *and* fiend *and* freak *and* space cadet <all nonformal>; cocaine user, cokie *and* coke head *and* crackhead *and* sniffer *and* snow drifter *and* flaky <all nonformal>; opium user, opium addict, hophead *and* hopdog *and* tar distiller <all nonformal>; heroin user *or* addict, smackhead *and* smack-sack *and* schmecker <all nonformal>; methedrine user *or* methhead <nonformal>; amphetamine user, pillhead *and* pill popper *and* speed freak <all nonformal>; LSD user, acidhead *and* acid freak *and* tripper *and* cubehead <all nonformal>; marijuana smoker *and* pothead <both nonformal>

narcotize VERBS **numb, benumb,** paralyze, deaden, anesthetize, freeze, **stun, stupefy,** drug, sedate, dope *or* dope up <nonformal>, tranquilize, deaden, dull, blunt, obtund, take the edge off, take the sting *or* bite out

narrate VERBS **tell, relate,** recount, report, **recite,** rehearse, give an account of; tell a story, unfold a tale, a tale unfold, fable, fabulize

narrative NOUNS **story,** tale, yarn, account, narration, chronicle; **anecdote,** anecdotage; **epic,** epos, **saga**

narrator NOUNS **relator,** reciter, recounter, *raconteur* <Fr>; **anecdotist; storyteller,** storier, taleteller, teller of tales, spinner of yarns *and* yarn spinner <both nonformal>; word painter; **persona,** central consciousness, the I of the story

narrow VERBS 1 constrict, diminish, draw in, go in; restrict, limit, straiten, confine; **taper; contract**
ADJS 2 **slender;** narrowish, narrowy; **close,** near; **tight, strait,** isthmic, isthmian; close-fitting; **restricted,** limited, circumscribed, **confined,** constricted; **cramped,** cramp; incapacious, incommodious, crowded

narrow-minded ADJS **prudish,** priggish, prim, prissy, smug, stuffy <nonformal>, old-maidish, **overmodest,** demure, **straitlaced,** stiff-necked, hide-bound, censorious, sanctimonious, **puritanical,** Victorian, mid-Victorian; **insular,** parochial, ethnocentric, xenophobic, snobbish; narrow-gauged, closed, closed-minded, cramped, constricted, *borné* <Fr>, little-minded, small-minded, mean-spirited; **small,** little, mean, petty; uncharitable, ungenerous; bigot, **bigoted,** fanatical; **illiberal,** unliberal, uncatholic

nasal ADJS **stopped,** muted, checked, occlusive, nasalized, twangy, continuant, liquid, lateral, affricated; **twangy,** breathy, adenoidal, snuffling

nasty ADJS 1 **offensive**, fulsome, noisome, noxious, rebarbative, mawkish, cloying, brackish, **foul, vile,** bad; gross *and* icky *and* yucky <all nonformal>, **sickening, nauseating,** nauseous, nauseant, vomity *and* barfy <both nonformal>; rank, rancid, maggoty, weevily, spoiled, overripe, high, rotten, stinking, putrid, malodorous, fetid
2 **malicious,** maleficent, malefic; **malignant,** malign; **mean** *and* **ornery** *and* cussed *and* bitchy <all nonformal>, hateful, baleful, invidious; **wicked,** iniq-

uitous; **harmful,** noxious; gross, offensive, crass, **coarse, crude,** loutish

nation NOUNS **country,** land; nationality, **state,** nation-state, sovereign nation *or* state, polity, **body politic; power,** superpower, world power; **republic,** people's republic, **commonwealth,** commonweal; free nation, captive nation, nonaligned *or* unaligned *or* neutralist nation; developed nation, industrial *or* industrialized nation; underdeveloped nation, third-world nation

national ADJS **public,** general, common; communal, societal, social; state; societal; **popular,** public, mass, grass-roots; nation-wide, country-wide

nationality NOUNS **nativeness,** nativity, native-bornness, indigenousness *or* indigenity, aboriginality, autochthonousness; **nation,** state, nation-state, sovereign nation *or* state, polity, body politic; nationhood, peoplehood

native NOUNS 1 indigene, autochthon, earliest inhabitant, first comer, primitive settler; primitive; **aborigine,** aboriginal; local *and* local yokel <both nonformal>
ADJS 2 natal, **indigenous,** endemic, autochthonous; mother, maternal, original, aboriginal, primitive; native-born, home-grown, homebred, native to the soil *or* place *or* heath
3 **innate,** inborn, born, congenital; **natural,** natural to, connatural, native to, indigenous; **constitutional,** bodily, physical, temperamental, organic; **inbred,** genetic, hereditary, inherited, bred in the bone, in the blood, running in the blood *or* race *or* strain, radical, rooted; connate, connatal, coeval; **instinctive,** instinctual, atavistic, primal

native land NOUNS **fatherland,** *Vaterland* <Ger>, *patria* <L>, *la patrie* <Fr>, **motherland,** mother country, native soil, one's native heath *or* ground *or* soil *or* place, the old country, country of origin, **birthplace,** cradle; **home, homeland,** homeground, God's country

home is where one starts
T S Eliot

nativity NOUNS **birth,** genesis, nascency, **childbirth,** childbearing, having a baby, giving birth, birthing, parturition, the stork <nonformal>; **delivery,** blessed event <nonformal>; the Nativity

natty ADJS **tidy,** trim, neat, spruce, sleek, slick *and* slick as a whistle <nonformal>, smart, trig, snug, **well-kept,** well-kempt, well-cared-for, well-groomed; neat as a button *or* pin <nonformal>

natural NOUNS 1 **talented person,** talent, man *or* woman of parts, gifted person, prodigy, **genius,** mental genius, intellectual genius, intellectual prodigy, mental giant; rocket scientist *and* brain surgeon <both nonformal>; phenom <nonformal>; gifted child, **child prodigy,** wunderkind, whiz kid *and* boy wonder <both nonformal>
ADJS 2 naturelike, native; in the state of nature; primitive, primal, pristine, unspoiled, untainted, uncontaminated; **unaffected, unassuming, unpretending,** unpretentious, unfeigning, undisguising, undissembling, undesigning; **genuine,** inartificial, unadorned, unvarnished, unembellished; homespun
3 **instinctive,** inherent, innate, unlearned; unconscious, subliminal; **involuntary,** automatic, spontaneous, impulsive; **instinctual,** libidinal

naturalize VERBS grant *or* confer citizenship, adopt, admit, affiliate, **assimilate;** Americanize, Anglicize, etc; acculturate, acculturize; indigenize, go native <nonformal>; **domesticate,** domesticize, **tame,** break, gentle, housebreak; acclimatize, acclimate

nature NOUNS **character, quality,** suchness; **constitution,** composition, **characteristics,** makeup, constituents; **temperament,** temper, fiber, **disposition,** spirit, ethos, genius, dharma; **way, habit,** tenor, cast, hue, tone, grain, vein, streak, stripe, mold, brand, stamp
2 physical world, natural world

naughty ADJS **misbehaving,** unbehaving; bad; improper, not respectable; out-of-order *and* off-base *and* out-of-line <all nonformal>; **disorderly,** disruptive, **disobedient,** transgressive, uncomplying, wayward, froward

nauseating ADJS **offensive,** objectionable, odious, repulsive, repellent, rebarbative, **repugnant, revolting,** forbidding; **disgusting,** sickening, loathsome, gross *and* yucky *and* grungy *and* scuzzy <all nonformal>, beastly <nonformal>, **vile,** foul, nasty; **obnoxious,** abhorrent, hateful, abominable

nauseous ADJS **nasty, offensive**, fulsome, noisome, noxious, rebarbative, mawkish, cloying, brackish, **foul, vile,** bad;

gross *and* icky *and* yucky <all nonformal>, **sickening, nauseating,** nauseant; **nauseated,** queasy, squeamish, qualmish, qualmy; **sick to one's stomach;** pukish *and* puky *and* barfy <all nonformal>; seasick, carsick, airsick

nautical ADJS **marine,** maritime, naval, navigational; seafaring, seagoing, oceangoing, seaborne, water-borne; seamanly, seamanlike, **salty** <nonformal>; pelagic, oceanic

naval ADJS **nautical,** marine, maritime, navigational; seafaring, seagoing, oceangoing, seaborne, water-borne; seamanly, seamanlike

navigate VERBS **sail, cruise,** steam, run, seafare, voyage, ply, go on shipboard, go by ship, go on *or* take a voyage, cross, traverse, make a passage *or* run; sail round, circumnavigate; **pilot,** helm, coxswain, **steer,** guide, be at the helm *or* tiller, direct, manage, handle, run, operate, shape *or* chart a course

navy NOUNS naval forces, **first line of defense; fleet,** flotilla, argosy, armada, squadron, escadrille, division, task force, task group; mosquito fleet

Neanderthal ADJS **unrefined,** unpolished, uncouth, unkempt, uncombed, unlicked; **uncivilized,** noncivilized; **barbarous,** barbaric, barbarian; outlandish, Gothic; **savage,** brutish, bestial, animal, **mindless;** troglodytic

near VERBS 1 **come near,** draw near *or* nigh, **approach**, come within shouting distance; come within an ace *or* an inch; **be imminent,** impend, overhang, hang *or* lie over, **loom,** hang over one's head, hover, **threaten, menace,** lower; brew, gather; rush up on one, forthcome, be on the horizon, be in the offing, be just around the corner
ADJS 2 **close, nigh,** close-in, nearish, nighish, intimate, cheek-by-jowl, side-by-side, hand-in-hand, arm-in-arm, *bras-dessus-bras-dessous* <Fr>; **approaching,** nearing, approximate *or* approximating, proximate, proximal
ADVS 3 **nearly,** pretty near <nonformal>, close, **closely; almost,** all but, not quite, as good as, as near as makes no difference; **well-nigh,** just about; nigh, nigh hand

nearby ADJS 1 **handy, convenient,** neighboring, vicinal, propinquant *or* propinquous, ready at hand, easily reached *or* attained
ADVS 2 **aside,** on one side, **to one side,** to the side, sidelong, on the side, on the one hand, on one hand, on the other hand; **alongside,** in parallel, side-by-side; in juxtaposition; away

nearest ADJS nighest, **closest,** nearmost, next, immediate

nearsighted ADJS **undiscerning,** unperceptive, imperceptive, impercipient, insensible, unapprehending, uncomprehending, nonunderstanding; **shortsighted,** myopic, dim-sighted, purblind

neat ADJS **tidy,** trim, natty, spruce, sleek, slick *and* slick as a whistle <nonformal>, smart, trig, snug, tight, **shipshape; well-kept,** well-kempt, well-cared-for, well-groomed; neat as a button *or* pin <nonformal>

necessary ADJS **obligatory,** compulsory, entailed, mandatory; **exigent,** urgent, necessitous, importunate, **imperative;** choiceless, without choice, out of one's hands *or* control; **requisite,** needful, required, needed, **wanted,** called for, indicated; **essential,** vital, indispensable, unforgoable, irreplaceable

necessity NOUNS **obligation,** obligement; compulsoriness, **compulsion,** duress; **requirement,** requisite, requisition; **need,** want, occasion; desideratum, desideration; **prerequisite,** essential, indispensable; the necessary, the needful; necessities, necessaries, essentials, bare necessities

need NOUNS 1 **want,** lack, deficiency, deficit, shortage, shortfall, wantage, **incompleteness,** defectiveness, shortcoming, imperfection; **destitution,** impoverishment, beggary, deprivation
VERBS 2 **want,** lack, require; miss, feel the want of, be sent away empty-handed; run short of

needle NOUNS 1 **thorn,** bramble, brier, nettle, burr, prickle, sticker <nonformal>; **spike,** spikelet, spicule, spiculum; **spine;** bristle; quill; nib, neb
VERBS 2 **annoy, bug** <nonformal>, be on the back of *and* be at *and* ride <all nonformal>, **pester, tease,** devil, get after *or* get on <nonformal>, **bedevil, pick on** <nonformal>, tweak the nose, pluck the beard, give a bad time to <nonformal>; **goad, prod,** poke, nudge, prod at, goose <nonformal>, **spur,** prick, sting

needless ADJS **unnecessary,** unessential, nonessential, **unneeded,** gratuitous, uncalled-for, unrequired; unrecognized, neglected

the needy NOUNS **the poor,** the have-nots <nonformal>, the down-and-out, the disadvantaged, the underprivileged, the distressed, the underclass; the urban poor, the homeless, the ranks of the homeless; the other America; the forgotten man

the forgotten man at the bottom of the economic pyramid
F D Roosevelt

negate VERBS abnegate, **say 'no';** shake the head, wag *or* waggle the beard; **abolish,** nullify, void, abrogate, annihilate, annul, tear up, repeal, revoke, invalidate, **undo, cancel,** cancel out, bring to naught, put *or* lay to rest; **belie,** be contrary to, come in conflict with

negative ADJS **contrary;** contrarious, perverse, **opposite,** antithetic, antithetical, **contradictory,** counter, contrapositive, contrasted; **antagonistic,** repugnant, oppugnant, perverse, contrarious, ornery <nonformal>, nay-saying, hostile, combative, bellicose, belligerent, inimical, antipathetic, antipathetical, discordant; **disagreeable,** cross, cranky, ornery <nonformal>, uncongenial, incompatible

neglect NOUNS 1 neglectfulness, **negligence,** inadvertence *or* inadvertency, malperformance, dereliction, *culpa* <L>, culpable negligence, criminal negligence; **remissness,** laxity, laxness, slackness, looseness, laches; **disregard,** airy disregard, slighting; **inattention**; **oversight,** overlooking; **omission,** nonfeasance, nonperformance, lapse, failure, **default;** poor stewardship *or* guardianship *or* custody; procrastination
VERBS 2 **overlook, disregard,** not heed, not attend to, take for granted, **ignore;** not care for, not take care of; **pass over,** gloss over; **let slip, let slide** <nonformal>, let the chance slip by, **let go,** let ride <nonformal>, let take its course; not give a thought to, take no thought *or* account of, blind oneself to, turn a blind eye to, leave out of one's calculation; lose sight of, lose track of; **be neglectful** *or* **negligent,** fail in one's duty, **fail,** lapse, **default**

neglected ADJS unattended to, untended, unwatched, unchaperoned, uncared-for; **disregarded,** unconsidered, unregarded, **overlooked, missed,** omitted, passed by, passed over, passed up <nonformal>, gathering dust, **ignored, slighted;** half-done, undone, left undone; deserted, abandoned; in the cold *and* out in the cold <both nonformal>; on the shelf, shelved, pigeonholed, on hold *and* on the back burner <both nonformal>, **put** *or* **laid aside,** sidetracked *and* sidelined <both nonformal>, shunted

negligee NOUNS **dishabille,** *déshabillé* <Fr>, **undress,** something more comfortable; *néglig*é <Fr>; **wrap,** wrapper

negligent ADJS **neglectful,** neglecting, derelict, culpably negligent; inadvertent, uncircumspect; **inattentive**; unwary, unwatchful, asleep at the switch, off-guard, unguarded; **remiss,** slack, lax, relaxed, laid-back <nonformal>, loose, loosey-goosey <nonformal>, unrigorous, permissive, overly permissive; slighting; slurring, scamping, skimping <nonformal>; procrastinating

negligible ADJS **insignificant,** small, inconsiderable, inconsequential, no great shakes, footling, one-horse *and* pint-size *and* vest-pocket <all nonformal>; unimportant, no skin off one's nose *or* ass, **trivial**

negotiable ADJS 1 **transferable,** conveyable, alienable; **assignable,** consignable; devisable, bequeathable; heritable, inheritable
2 **practicable,** practical, feasible; workable, actable, performable, realizable, compassable, operable, doable, swingable, bridgeable; **viable; achievable, attainable;** surmountable, superable

negotiate VERBS **manage,** contrive, succeed in; make out, get on *or* along <nonformal>, come on *or* along <nonformal>, go on; **scrape along,** worry along, **muddle through,** get by, manage somehow; make it <nonformal>, **make the grade,** cut the mustard *and* hack it <both nonformal>; **clear,** clear the hurdle; **engineer; swing** <nonformal>, put over <nonformal>, put through; **treat with,** bargain, make terms, sit down with, sit down at the bargaining table

negotiation NOUNS **bargaining,** haggling, higgling, **dickering,** chaffering, chaffer, haggle; hacking out *or* working out *or* hammering out a deal, coming to terms; collective bargaining

negotiator NOUNS **mediator,** intermediator, intermediate agent, intermediate, intermedium, **intermediary,** interagent, internuncio; **intercessor,** interceder; **go-between,** middleman; negotiant, negotiatress *or* negotiatrix

neighborhood NOUNS **vicinity,** vicinage, environs, surroundings, surround, setting, grounds, purlieus, confines, precinct; neck of the woods <nonformal>, precincts, milieu

neighboring ADJS **nearby,** handy, convenient, vicinal, propinquant *or* propinquous, ready at hand, easily reached *or* attained; **adjacent,** next, immediate, contiguous, **adjoining,** abutting; neighbor; **bordering,** conterminous *or* coterminous, connecting

neighborly ADJS **hospitable,** receptive, welcoming; **cordial,** amiable, gracious, **friendly,** genial, hearty, open, openhearted, warm, warmhearted; **generous,** liberal; neighborlike; sociable

nemesis NOUNS **bane,** curse, affliction, infliction, visitation, **plague,** pestilence, pest, calamity, scourge, **torment,** open wound, running sore, grievance, woe, burden, crushing burden; bugbear, **bête noire,** bogy, bogeymen, arch-nemesis

nepotism NOUNS **partiality,** onesidedness; **favoritism,** preference, unequal *or* preferential treatment, discrimination

nerd NOUNS **specialist,** specializer, **expert, authority,** savant, scholar, connoisseur, maven <nonformal>; technical expert, technician, techie <nonformal>; fan, buff, freak *and* nut <both nonformal>, aficionado

nervous ADJS **high-strung,** overstrung, highly strung, all nerves; **uneasy, apprehensive,** qualmish, nail-biting, white-knuckle <nonformal>; nervous as a cat; **excitable; irritable,** edgy, **on edge,** nerves on edge, on the ragged edge <nonformal>, panicky, **fearful, frightened;** jittery, jumpy, agitated, shook up, shaking, trembling

nervous breakdown NOUNS **collapse,** breakdown, crackup <nonformal>, **prostration,** exhaustion; nervous prostration *or* exhaustion, neurasthenia

nervy ADJS **impudent,** impertinent, pert, flip <nonformal>, flippant, **cocky** *and* cheeky *and* **fresh** *and* facy *and* crusty <all nonformal>, *chutzpadik* <Yiddish>; **rude,** disrespectful, derisive, brash, bluff; **saucy,** sassy <nonformal>; smart *or* smart-alecky <nonformal>, smart-ass *or* wise-ass <nonformal>

nest egg NOUNS **reserves,** stockpile, cache, backup, reserve supply, something in reserve *or* in hand, something to fall back on, reserve fund, **savings,** sinking fund; proved reserves; life savings

nestle VERBS **snuggle,** cuddle, cuddle up, curl up; nestle, nest; bundle; snuggle up to, snug up *or* together <old>

net NOUNS 1 **network, webwork, weaving, meshwork,** tissue, crossing over and under, interlacement, intertwinement, intertexture, texture, reticulum, reticulation; netting; **mesh; web,** webbing; trawl, dragnet, seine, purse seine, pound net, gill net; **meshes, toils**
2 **gain,** profit, take *or* take-in *and* piece *and* slice *and* end *and* rakeoff *and* skimmings <all nonformal>; net *or* neat profit, clean *or* clear profit
VERBS 3 **trap,** entrap, gin, catch, **ensnare, snare,** hook, **hook in,** sniggle, noose; mesh, enmesh, ensnarl, wind, tangle, entangle, entoil, enweb; run down, run to earth, **take captive, take prisoner,** apprehend, capture, seize, **take into custody**
4 **profit,** make *or* draw *or* realize *or* reap profit, come out ahead, make money; rake it in *and* coin money *and* make a bundle *or* pile *or* killing *or* mint *and* clean up <all nonformal>; **realize,** clear; make a fast *or* quick buck <nonformal>; **yield,** bring in, afford, pay, pay off <nonformal>, **return**
ADJS 5 **remaining,** over, left, leftover; **spare,** to spare; unused, unconsumed; **surplus**

network NOUNS 1 **webwork,** weaving, meshwork, tissue, crossing over and under, interlacement, intertwinement, intertexture, texture, reticulum, reticulation; **net,** netting; **mesh,** meshes; **web,** webbing; wicker, wickerwork; basketwork, basketry; lattice, latticework; hachure *or* hatchure, hatching, crosshatching; trellis, trelliswork, treillage; grate, grating; grille, grillwork; **grid,** gridiron

Any thing reticulated or decussated, at equal distances, with interstices between the intersections
SAMUEL JOHNSON

2 **source,** information medium *or* media, mass media, print media, electronic media, the press, radio, television; channel, the grapevine; information network, in-group, old-boy network; coterie, salon, clique, **set**

neurological ADJS **neural,** nervous, nerval; neurologic

neurosis NOUNS **mental disorder,** emotional disorder, emotional instability; **psychoneurosis,** neuroticism, neurotic *or* psychoneurotic disorder

neurotic ADJS **psychoneurotic,** disturbed, disordered; neurasthenic, psychasthenic; hysteric<al>, hypochondriac, phobic; stressed, disturbed, depressive; manic; manic-depressive

neuter VERBS 1 **castrate,** geld, emasculate, eunuchize, spay, fix *or* alter <both nonformal>, unsex, deball <nonformal>
ADJS 2 **unsexual,** unsexed; **sexless,** asexual, neutral; castrated, emasculated, eunuchized; **cold,** frigid; impotent

neutral NOUNS 1 **nonpartisan,** independent, mugwump, undecided *or* uncommitted voter; **moderate,** moderatist, moderationist, middle-of-the-roader, **centrist,** compromiser
ADJS 2 **impartial,** impersonal, evenhanded, equitable, dispassionate, **disinterested,** detached, objective, lofty, Olympian; **unbiased,** uninfluenced, unswayed; indifferent

neutralize VERBS **nullify,** annul, cancel, cancel out, negate, negative, negativate, invalidate, vitiate, void, frustrate, stultify, thwart, come *or* bring to nothing, undo; **offset,** counterbalance; buffer

never ADVS ne'er, **not ever,** at no time, on no occasion, not at all; **nevermore;** never in the world, never on earth; never in all one's born days <nonformal>, never in my life, *jamais de la vie* <Fr>

never-ending ADJS **perpetual, everlasting,** everliving, ever-being, ever-abiding, ever-during, ever-durable, permanent, perdurable, indestructible; **eternal,** sempiternal, infinite, **endless,** unending, without end, **interminable, continual,** continuous, steady, **constant, ceaseless,** nonstop, unceasing, neverceasing, **incessant,** unremitting, unintermitting, uninterrupted

nevertheless ADVS **notwithstanding,** but, all the same <nonformal>, still, yet, even; **however,** regardless, nonetheless; **although,** when, though; howbeit, albeit; **at all events,** in any event, **in any case,** at any rate; **be that as it may,** for all that, even so, **on the other hand,** rather, again, at the same time, just the same, after all, after all is said and done

new ADJS 1 young, **fresh,** fresh as a daisy, fresh as the morning dew; **unused,** firsthand, original; untried, untouched, unhandled, untrodden, unbeaten; virgin, virginal, intact; dewy, pristine, evernew, sempervirent, evergreen; **immature,** undeveloped, raw, callow, fledgling, unfledged, nestling

2 <nonformal> **brand-new**, fire-new, **brand-spanking new,** spanking,, **spanking new; just out; hot,** hottest, hot off the fire *or* griddle *or* spit, hot off the press; newfangled *or* newfangle

ADVS 3 **newly,** freshly, **anew,** once more, from the ground up, from scratch <nonformal>, *ab ovo* <L>, *de novo* <L>, **afresh, again;** as new

newborn ADJS **born,** given birth; hatched; **infant, infantile,** infantine, **babyish,** baby; neonatal, new-fledged; in the cradle *or* crib *or* nursery, in swaddling clothes, at the breast, tied to mother's apron strings

newcomer NOUNS **new arrival,** *novus homo* <L>; *arriviste* <Fr>, Johnny-come-lately <nonformal>, new boy <Brit>; **tenderfoot,** greenhorn; settler, emigrant, immigrant; recruit, rookie <nonformal>

news NOUNS **tidings, intelligence,** information, word, advice; newsiness <nonformal>; newsworthiness; a nose for news; **journalism,** reportage, coverage, news coverage; **the press,** the fourth estate, the press corps, print journalism, electronic journalism, broadcast journalism, broadcast news, radio journalism, television journalism

newscaster NOUNS **broadcaster,** radiobroadcaster, radiocaster; commentator, news commentator; anchor, news anchor, anchor man *or* woman; news reader <Brit>

newsman NOUNS **journalist,** newspaperman, newspaperwoman, newswoman, newspeople, inkstained wretch, newswriter, gentleman *or* representative of the press; **reporter,** newshawk *and* newshound <both nonformal>; leg man

<nonformal>; interviewer; investigative reporter; **cub reporter; correspondent,** foreign correspondent, war correspondent, special correspondent, own correspondent, stringer; **editor,** managing editor, city editor, news editor, sports editor, woman's editor, feature editor, **copy editor,** copyman, copy chief, slotman; **columnist**

newspaper NOUNS news, **paper,** sheet *or* rag <both nonformal>, **gazette,** daily newspaper, daily, weekly newspaper, weekly, neighborhood newspaper, national newspaper; newspaper of record; **tabloid,** extra, special, special edition

next ADJS 1 **adjacent,** immediate, contiguous, **adjoining,** abutting; neighboring, neighbor; **juxtaposed,** juxtapositional; **bordering,** conterminous *or* coterminous, connecting; **nearest,** nighest, **closest,** nearmost, immediate; **succeeding,** successive, following, ensuing, sequent, sequential, sequacious, posterior, **subsequent,** consequent; proximate
ADVS 2 **subsequently,** after, afterwards, after that, after all, **later,** since; **thereafter,** thereon, thereupon, therewith, **then;** in the process *or* course of time, as things worked out, in the sequel; at a subsequent *or* later time, in the aftermath; *ex post facto* <L>; hard on the heels *or* on the heels

nibble NOUNS 1 **bite,** morsel, taste, swallow; mouthful, a nibble, a bite, munchies; **chew,** chaw <nonformal>; nip, munch
VERBS 2 **pick,** peck <nonformal>, **snack** <nonformal>, munch, nosh <nonformal>; pick at, peck at <nonformal>, eat like a bird, show no appetite; gnaw

nice ADJS **dainty, delicate,** *délicat* <Fr>, fine, refined, exquisite, subtle; minute, detailed, exquisite; **meticulous**, finical, finicky, finicking, niggling

nice guy NOUNS **good guy,** crackerjack, brick, trump, good egg, stout fellow, Mr Nice Guy, good Joe, likely lad, no slouch, doll, living doll, pussycat, **sweetheart,** sweetie <all nonformal>

nicety NOUNS niceness, **delicacy,** delicateness, daintiness, exquisiteness, fineness, refinement, subtlety

niche NOUNS **nook,** corner, cranny, recess, cove, bay, oriel, alcove; cubicle, roomlet, carrel, hole-in-the-wall <nonformal>, cubby, **cubbyhole**

nick NOUNS 1 **notch,** nock, **cut,** cleft, **incision, gash,** hack, blaze, scotch, **score,** kerf, crena, depression, jag; **indentation**
VERBS 2 **notch,** cut, incise, gash, slash, chop, crimp, scotch, **score,** blaze, jag, scarify; **indent**; **scallop,** crenellate, crenulate, machicolate

nickname NOUNS **sobriquet,** byname, cognomen; epithet, agnomen; **pet name,** diminutive, hypocoristic, affectionate name

nifty ADJS **chic, dapper,** dashing, jaunty, braw <Scots>; sharp *and* spiffy *and* classy *and* snazzy <all nonformal>

niggling ADJS **insignificant,** unimportant, no skin off one's nose *or* ass, **trivial,** trifling, nugacious, nugatory, petty, mean, picayune *or* picayunish, nickel-and-dime *and* penny-ante *and* Mickey-Mouse *and* chickenshit <all nonformal>; shallow, depthless, cursory, superficial, skin-deep; **critical, faultfinding,** carping, picky *and* nitpicky <both nonformal>, caviling, quibbling, pettifogging, captious, cynical; nagging; hypercritical, ultracritical, overcritical, hairsplitting, trichoschistic

night NOUNS 1 **nighttime,** nighttide, lights-out, taps, bedtime, sleepy time <nonformal>, **darkness**, blackness, dark, lightlessness; tenebrosity, tenebrousness; dead of night, deep night

sable-vested Night, eldest of things
MILTON

ADJS 2 **nocturnal,** nightly, nighttime; nightlong, all-night; night-fallen; midnight

nightclub NOUNS **cabaret;** club, night spot; nitery *and* hot spot <both nonformal>, *boîte, boîte de nuit* <both Fr>; discothèque *or* disco <nonformal>

nightfall NOUNS **close of day,** decline *or* fall of day, shut of day, gray of the evening, grayness, evening's close, when day is done; **sunset, sundown,** setting sun, going down of the sun, cockshut *and* cockshut time *and* cockshut light <all nonformal>, retreat; shank of the evening <nonformal>, the cool of the evening

the evening is spread out against the sky, Like a patient etherized upon a table
T S ELIOT

nightgown NOUNS **nightwear,** night clothes; **nightdress,** nightie *and* shortie nightie <both nonformal>, bedgown; nightshirt; **pajamas,** pyjamas <Brit>, pj's <nonformal>; sleepers

nightmare NOUNS **frightener,** scarer, hair-raiser; **bogey,** bogeyman, **bugaboo,** bugbear; hobgoblin; **incubus,** succubus, bad dream

nimble ADJS **agile, spry,** sprightly, fleet, featly, peart <nonformal>, light, graceful, nimble-footed, light-footed, surefooted; nimble-fingered, neat-fingered, neat-handed; **quick,** adroit, dexterous; **sharp-witted,** keen-witted, needle-witted, **quick-witted,** quick-thinking, steel-trap, nimble-witted, quick on the trigger *or* uptake <nonformal>

nincompoop NOUNS **chump, boob,** booby, sap, prize sap, klutz, dingbat, dingdong, ding-a-ling, **ninny,** saphead, mutt, jerk, goof, schlemiel, galoot, gonzo, dumbo, dweeb, nerd, twerp, yo-yo <all nonformal>

nip NOUNS 1 **drink,** dram, potation, potion, libation, draft, drop, spot, finger or two, sip, sup, suck, drench, guzzle, gargle, jigger; peg, swig, swill, pull; **snort,** jolt, **shot,** snifter, quickie
2 **chilliness,** nippiness, crispness, briskness, sharpness, bite; **chill,** sharp air
VERBS 3 **bite,** cut, penetrate, bite the tongue, sting, make the eyes water, go up the nose; **chill; prune,** pare, peel, clip, crop, bob, dock, lop, shear, shave, strip, strip off *or* away; **put an end to,** nip in the bud; cut short
4 **tipple,** drink, **guzzle, imbibe,** have a drink *or* nip *or* dram *or* guzzle *or* gargle, soak, bib, quaff, sip, sup, lap, lap up, take a drop, slake one's thirst, cheer *or* refresh the inner man, drown one's troubles *or* sorrows, commune with the spirits; **down,** toss off *or* down, knock back, throw one back, drink off *or* up

nippy ADJS 1 **zestful,** zesty, **brisk,** lively, racy, zippy, **tangy,** with a kick; spiced, seasoned, high-seasoned; **spicy,** curried, **peppery,** hot, burning
2 **cold,** crisp, brisk, nipping, **snappy** <nonformal>, raw, bleak, keen, sharp, bitter, biting, pinching, cutting, **piercing,** penetrating

nit ADJS **louse,** head louse, body louse, grayback, cootie <nonformal>

nitpick VERBS **find fault,** take exception, fault-find, pick holes, cut up, pick *or* pull *or* tear apart, pick *or* pull *or* tear to pieces; tear down, **carp,** cavil, quibble, pick nits, pettifog, catch at straws, **split hairs**

nitpicker NOUNS **perfectionist,** precisian, precisianist, stickler, captious critic, **faultfinder,** smellfungus, carper, caviler, quibbler, pettifogger

the nitty-gritty NOUNS **sum and substance,** gist, heart, soul, meat, nub; the bottom line *and* the name of the game <both nonformal>, **core,** kernel, marrow, pith, sap, spirit, essence; sober *or* grim reality, hardball <nonformal>, not a dream, more truth than poetry; **meat and potatoes** *and* nuts and bolts *and* where the rubber meets the road <all nonformal>

nitwit NOUNS **stupid person,** dolt, dunce, clod, Boeotian, **dullard,** *niais* <Fr>, donkey, yahoo, thickwit, **dope,** dimwit, lackwit, half-wit, lamebrain, putz, lightweight, witling

no INTERJS 1 **nay,** *non* <Fr>, *nein* <Ger>, *nyet* <Russ>, certainly not, no sir, no ma'am, to the contrary, **by no means,** under no circumstances, never

2 <nonformal> nope, nix, no dice, unhunh, no sirree; no way, no way Jose, not on your life, not by a long chalk, not by a long shot *or* sight, not by a darn *or* damn sight, not a bit of it, not much, not a chance, fat chance, nothing doing, forget it, that'll be the day

noble NOUNS 1 **nobleman,** gentleman; peer; aristocrat, patrician, Brahman, **blue blood,** thoroughbred, silk-stocking, lace-curtain, swell *and* upper-cruster <both nonformal>
2 **aristocracy,** titled aristocracy, hereditary nobility, noblesse
ADJS 3 **lofty,** elevated, sublime, grand, majestic, stately, grave, solemn, dignified; **meritorious,** worth one's salt, worthy, creditable; respected, respectable, highly respectable; **well-thought-of,** highly regarded, held in esteem, in good odor, in favor, in high favor; **eminent,** prominent, conspicuous, **outstanding,** distinguished

nobody NOUNS **no one,** no man, not one, not a single one *or* person, **not a soul** *or* **blessed soul** *or* **living soul,** never a one, ne'er a one, nary one <nonformal>, nobody on earth *or* under the sun, nobody present; **nonentity,** nonstarter *and* nebbish <both nonformal>, nonperson, unperson, cipher, man of straw, puppet, hollow man; **mediocrity, second-rater,** third-rater, fourth-rater, nothing *or* nobody special, no great shakes <nonformal>, no prize package, no brain surgeon, no rocket scientist, small potatoes <nonformal>

nocturnal ADJS night, **nightly,** nighttime; nightlong, all-night; night-fallen; midnight

no-good NOUNS 1 **wretch, good-for-nothing,** good-for-naught, ne'er-do-well, wastrel, *vaurien* <Fr>, worthless fellow ADJS 2 **worthless,** valueless, good-for-nothing, good-for-naught, NG <nonformal>, no-account <nonformal>, dear at any price, worthless as tits on a boar <nonformal>, not worth a dime *or* a red cent *or* a hill of beans *or* shit *or* bubkes <nonformal>, not worthwhile, not worth having, not worth a rap *or* a continental *or* a damn, not worth the powder to blow it to hell, of no earthly use

noise NOUNS loud noise, **blast**, tintamarre, **racket, din, clamor;** outcry, **uproar,** hue and cry, noise and shouting; howl; clangor, clatter, clap, jangle, rattle; roar, thunder, thunderclap; **crash, boom,** sonic boom; **bang,** percussion; brouhaha, **tumult,** hubbub; fracas, **brawl,** commotion, drunken brawl; **pandemonium,** bedlam, hell *or* bedlam let loose; charivari, shivaree <nonformal>; discord

noisemaker NOUNS snapper, cricket, clapper, clack, clacker, cracker; firecracker, cherry bomb

noisy ADJS noiseful, rackety, clattery, clangorous, clanging, **clamorous,** clamant, blatant, blaring, brassy, brazen, blatting; uproarious, **tumultuous,** turbulent, blustering, brawling, **boisterous,** riproaring, rowdy, strepitous, strepitant; vociferous

nomad NOUNS Bedouin; gypsy, tinker <Brit>, Bohemian, Romany, *zingaro* <Ital>, *Zigeuner* <Ger>, *tzigane* <Fr>

nomadic ADJS **wandering, nomad,** floating, drifting, gypsyish *or* gypsylike; **vagrant,** vagabond, vagabondish; **footloose,** footloose and fancy-free; **migratory,** migrational, transmigrant, transmigratory

no-man's-land NOUNS forbidden ground *or* territory, **battlefield,** battleground, battle site, **field,** combat area, **field of battle**

nom de plume NOUNS **pseudonym,** assumed name, **pen name**

nomenclature NOUNS **terminology,** orismology, glossology <old>; onomatology, onomastics; **taxonomy,** classification, binomial nomenclature, binomialism, Linnaean method, trinomialism

nominate VERBS **name, designate;** put up, propose, submit, name for office; **denominate,** call, term, style, dub, color <nonformal>; specify; define, identify; **title,** entitle; **label,** tag

nominee NOUNS **assignee,** appointee, selectee, candidate; licensee, licentiate; deputy, agent

nonaggressive ADJS **unbelligerent,** unhostile, unbellicose, **uncontentious,** unmilitant, unmilitary, noncombative, nonmilitant; **antiwar,** pacific, peaceable, peace-loving, dovish <nonformal>; meek, lamblike; **pacifistic,** pacifist, irenic; **nonviolent;** conciliatory

nonalcoholic beverage NOUNS **soft drink,** cold drink; carbonated water, soda water, sparkling water, **soda,** pop, soda pop, tonic; milk shake, frosted shake, thick shake, shake *and* frosted <both nonformal>; malted milk, malt <nonformal>

nonaligned ADJS **independent,** free-spirited, freewheeling, free-floating, free-standing; **self-determined,** self-directing, one's own man; self-governed, **self-governing,** autonomous, sovereign; stand-alone, self-reliant, self-sufficient, self-subsistent, self-supporting, self-contained, autarkic, autarchic; nonpartisan, neutral; third-world, third-force

nonbeliever NOUNS **unbeliever,** disbeliever; **atheist,** infidel, pagan, heathen; nullifidian, minimifidian; secularist; **gentile**

nonchalant ADJS **blasé,** indifferent, unconcerned; **casual,** offhand, relaxed, laid-back *and* throwaway <both nonformal>; **easygoing,** easy, free and easy, devil-may-care, lackadaisical, *dégagé* <Fr>

noncombatant NOUNS nonbelligerent, nonresistant, nonresister; **civilian,** citizen

noncommittal ADJS **cautious,** careful, heedful, mindful, regardful, **thorough; prudent,** circumspect, slow to act *or* commit oneself *or* make one's move, uncommitted; **discreet,** politic, judicious, Polonian; guarded, on guard, on one's guard; uncommunicative; **tentative,** hesistant, unprecipitate, cool; **deliberate**

noncommunicable ADJS **indescribable,** ineffable, inexpressible, unutterable, unspeakable, indefinable, undefinable, unnameable

nonconformist NOUNS unconformist, **original,** eccentric, gonzo <nonformal>, deviant, deviationist, maverick <nonformal>, dropout, Bohemian, beatnik, hippie, hipster, freak <nonformal>, flower child, street people, yippie; **misfit,** square peg in a round hole, ugly duckling, fish out of water; **dissenter**

nondenominational ADJS **nonsectarian,** undenominational; interdenominational, ecumenic *or* ecumenical

nondescript ADJS **simple**, plain, ordinary, common, commonplace, prosaic, prosy, **matter-of-fact,** homely, homespun, everyday, workday, workaday, household, garden, common- *or* garden-variety

nonentity NOUNS **a nobody, insignificancy,** hollow man, jackstraw <old>, empty suit *and* nebbish <both nonformal>, an obscurity, a nothing, cipher; lightweight; **small fry; mediocrity,** second-rater, third-rater, fourth-rater, nothing *or* nobody special, no great shakes <nonformal>, no prize, no prize package

nonessential NOUNS 1 inessential *or* unessential, nonvitalness, carrying coals to Newcastle, gilding the lily; **accessory, extra,** collateral; the other, not-self; **appendage,** appurtenance, auxiliary, supernumerary, **supplement,** addition, addendum, superaddition, adjunct; **subsidiary,** subordinate, secondary; **contingency,** contingent, incidental, accidental, accident, happenstance, mere chance; **superfluity,** superfluousness; fifth wheel <nonformal>
ADJS 2 **needless,** unnecessary, unessential, **unneeded,** uncalled-for, unrequired; unrecognized, neglected

nonetheless ADVS **nevertheless,** however, regardless; at all, nohow <nonformal>

nonexistent ADJS without being, nowhere to be found; **minus, missing,** lacking, wanting; **null, void,** devoid, empty, inane, vacuous; **negative,** less than nothing; **unreal,** unrealistic, unactual, never-never; supposititious, **illusory**

nonflammable ADJS **incombustible,** noncombustible, uninflammable, noninflammable, noncombustive

nonliving ADJS **inanimate,** inanimated, unanimated, exanimate, azoic, dead, **lifeless,** soulless; inert; insentient, unconscious, nonconscious, **insensible,** insensate, senseless, unfeeling

no-no NOUNS **prohibition,** forbidding, forbiddance; thou-shalt-not *and* don't <both nonformal>; forbidden fruit, contraband; cuss *or* cuss word *and* dirty word *and* four-letter word *and* swearword <all nonformal>, naughty word, foul invective, **expletive, epithet,** dirty name <nonformal>, dysphemism, obscenity

nonpartisan NOUNS 1 **independent,** neutral, mugwump, undecided *or* uncommitted voter, centrist; swing vote
ADJS 2 **independent,** neutral, mugwumpian *and* mugwumpish <both nonformal>, **on the fence**

nonperishable ADJS **indestructible,** undestroyable, **imperishable,** incorruptible; **ineradicable,** indelible, ineffaceable, inerasable; **inextinguishable,** unquenchable, quenchless, undampable

nonplussed ADJS **in a dilemma,** on the horns of a dilemma; **perplexed,** confounded, mystified, puzzled, baffled, bamboozled <nonformal>, buffaloed <nonformal>; **at a loss,** at one's wit's end, fuddled, addled, muddled, dazed, stymied

nonpoisonous ADJS **innocuous,** innoxious, innocent; nontoxic, nonvirulent, nonvenomous

nonproductive ADJS **unproductive,** nonproducing; **infertile,** sterile, unfertile *or* nonfertile, **unfruitful,** unfructuous, infecund, unprolific *or* nonprolific; **ineffectual**

nonprofessional NOUNS **amateur,** layman, layperson, member of the laity, laic

nonsectarian ADJS **undenominational,** nondenominational; interdenominational; ecumenic *or* ecumenical

nonsense NOUNS 1 **stuff and nonsense,** pack of nonsense, folderol, balderdash, *niaiserie* <Fr>, flummery, trumpery, **rubbish,** trash, vaporing, fudge; **humbug,** gammon, hocus-pocus; rant, claptrap, fustian, rodomontade, bombast, absurdity; stultiloquence, **twaddle**

2 <nonformal> **bullshit,** shit, crap, horseshit, horsefeathers, bull, poppycock, bosh, tosh <Brit>, applesauce, bunkum, bunk, garbage, guff, jive, bilge, piffle, moonshine, flapdoodly, moonshine, a crock *or* a crock of shit, claptrap, tommyrot, rot, hogwash, malarkey, double Dutch, hokum, hooey, bushwa, blah, balls <Brit> blah, baloney, blarney tripe, hot air, gas, wind, waffle <Brit>

nonstop ADJS **continuous,** ceaseless, unceasing, **endless,** unending, never-ending, **interminable,** perennial; straight, running; **round-the-clock,** twenty-four-hour, steady, **constant,** never-ceasing, **incessant,** unremitting, unintermitting, uninterrupted

nontoxic ADJS **harmless,** hurtless, unhurtful; **uninjurious,** undamaging, **innocuous,** innoxious, innocent; nonpoisonous, nonvirulent, nonvenomous

nonviolent ADJS **moderate,** temperate, sober; **mild,** soft, bland, **gentle,** tame; mild as milk *or* mother's milk, gentle as a lamb; peaceable, peaceful, pacifistic; **judicious, prudent**

nook NOUNS **corner,** cranny, niche, recess, cove, bay, oriel, alcove; cubicle, roomlet, carrel, hole-in-the-wall <nonformal>, cubby, **cubbyhole,** snuggery; **hiding place,** hideaway, hideout, hidey-hole <nonformal>

noon NOUNS **noonday,** noontide, nooning <nonformal>, noontime, **high noon, midday,** meridian, *meridiem* <L>, twelve o'clock, 1200 hours, eight bells

noose NOUNS lasso, lariat; **hangman's rope,** rope, halter, hemp, hempen collar *or* necktie *or* bridle <nonformal>; the necklace <nonformal>

norm NOUNS **rule,** procedure, **common practice,** the way things are done, form, prescribed *or* set form; common *or* ordinary run of things, matter of course, par for the course <nonformal>; standard operating procedure *or* SOP, drill <Brit>

normal ADJS 1 **natural; general**; typical, unexceptional; **normative,** prescribed, model, ideal, desired
2 **sane,** sane-minded, **rational,** reasonable, sensible, **lucid,** wholesome, clear-headed, clearminded, balanced, **sound,** mentally sound, of sound mind, *compos mentis* <L>, sound-minded, healthy-minded, right, right in the head, **in one's right mind,** in possession of one's faculties *or* senses, together *and* all there <both nonformal>

normalize VERBS **regulate,** regularize, stabilize, damp; **systematize,** methodize, standardize, routinize; **codify,** formalize

northern lights NOUNS polar lights, **aurora; aurora borealis,** merry dancers; aurora polaris; aurora glory; streamer *or* curtain *or* arch aurora; polar ray

North Star NOUNS **guiding star,** cynosure <old>, **polestar,** polar star, lodestar, Polaris

nose NOUNS 1 olfactory organ; **snout, snoot** <nonformal>, nozzle <nonformal>, **muzzle; proboscis,** antlia, **trunk; beak,** rostrum; **bill** *and* pecker <both nonformal>; nib, neb; smeller *and* beezer *and* bugle *and* schnozzle *and* schnoz *and* schnozzola *and* conk <all nonformal>
VERBS 2 **smell,** scent; **sniff,** snuff, snuffle, inhale, breathe, breathe in; get a noseful of, smell of, catch a smell of, get *or* take a whiff of, whiff
3 **pry,** Paul-Pry, snoop, **stick** *or* **poke one's nose in,** stick one's long nose into

nosh NOUNS 1 **light meal,** refreshments, light repast, light lunch, spot of lunch <nonformal>, collation, **snack** *and* **bite** <both nonformal>, *casse-croûte* <Fr>
VERBS 2 **nibble; snack** <nonformal>, pick at, peck at <nonformal>

no-show NOUNS **absentee,** truant

nostalgia NOUNS **sentimentality,** sentiment, sentimentalism, oversentimentality, oversentimentalism, bathos; nostomania; romanticism; **wistfulness,** wishfulness, yearnfulness; **homesickness,** *Heimweh* <Ger>, *mal du pays* and *maladie du pays* <both Fr>

nostalgic ADJS **sentimental,** sentimentalized, soft, **mawkish, maudlin,** cloying; nostomanic, **longing,** yearning, yearnful, hankering <nonformal>, languishing, pining, **homesick**

nosy ADJS **meddlesome,** meddling; **officious,** overofficious, self-appointed, impertinent, presumptuous; **busybody,** busy; pushing, pushy, forward; **prying,**

snooping, nosey *and* snoopy <both nonformal>; inquisitive

notable NOUNS 1 **celebrity,** man *or* woman of mark *or* note, person of note *or* consequence, notability, luminary, great man *or* woman, name, **big name,** figure, public figure, **somebody;** important person, VIP *and* standout <both nonformal>, personage; lion, social lion
ADJS 2 **noteworthy,** celebrated, remarkable, marked, standout <nonformal>, of mark, signal; **memorable,** rememberable, unforgettable, never to be forgotten; striking, telling, salient; **eminent,** prominent, conspicuous, noble, **outstanding,** distinguished; prestigious, esteemed, estimable, reputable; **extraordinary,** *extraordinaire* <Fr>, out of the ordinary, **exceptional,** special, rare

notarized statement NOUNS **deposition,** sworn statement, affidavit, statement under oath, sworn testimony, affirmation

notary NOUNS **notary public;** endorser, subscriber, ratifier, approver, upholder, certifier, confirmer

notched ADJS **nicked,** incised, gashed, scotched, scored, chopped, blazed; **indented**; serrate, serrated, serrulated, **saw-toothed,** saw-edged, sawlike; crenate, crenated, crenulate, crenellated, battlemented, embrasured; scalloped; dentate, dentated, **toothed,** toothlike, tooth-shaped; lacerate, lacerated; **jagged,** jaggy; erose

note NOUNS 1 **remark,** statement, thought, **mention;** letter, message, communication, missive, line, chit, billet <old>; **reply,** answer, acknowledgment
2 **distinction,** mark; importance, consequence, significance; **notability,** prominence, eminence, preeminence, greatness, conspicuousness, outstandingness; **stardom;** loftiness, high and mightiness <nonformal>
3 musical note, notes of a scale; tone; sharp, flat, natural; accidental
VERBS 4 **heed, attend,** be heedful, tend, **mind,** watch, observe, regard, look, see, view, mark, remark, **notice,** take note *or* notice, get a load of <nonformal>

notebook NOUNS pocket notebook, blankbook; loose-leaf notebook, spiral notebook; **memorandum book,** memo book <nonformal>, commonplace book, adversaria; address book

noteworthy ADJS **notable,** celebrated, remarkable, marked, standout <nonformal>, of mark, signal; striking, telling, salient; **eminent,** prominent, conspicuous, noble, **outstanding,** distinguished; prestigious, esteemed, estimable, reputable; **extraordinary,** *extraordinaire* <Fr>, out of the ordinary, **exceptional,** special, rare

nothing NOUNS 1 **nil,** *nihil* <L>, *nichts* <Ger>, *nada* <Sp>, **naught, aught;** zero, cipher; nothing whatever, nothing at all, nothing on earth *or* under the sun, no such thing; thing of naught, nullity
2 **nonentity, nobody** *and* nonstarter *and* nebbish <all nonformal>, nonperson, unperson, cipher, man of straw, hollow man

3 <nonformal> **ziltch, zip,** zippo, nix, goose egg, Billy be damn, diddly, shit, diddly shit, squat, diddly squat, Sweet Fanny Adams <Brit>, bubkes, beans, a hill of beans, a hoot, **a fart,** a fuck, fuck all *and* bugger all <both Brit>, jack shit, a rat's ass

notice NOUNS 1 **press release,** release, handout, bulletin, official bulletin; **publicity,** publicness, notoriety, fame, famousness, notoriousness, public notice, **celebrity,** *réclame, éclat* <both Fr>; **review,** critical review, report, **write-up** <nonformal>
2 **cognizance;** cognition, noesis; **recognition,** realization; **consciousness,** awareness, mindfulness, note; **observation,** observance, advertence, advertency, **note,** remark, regard, respect; **intentness,** intentiveness, concentration
VERBS 3 **see,** behold, observe, view, witness, perceive, discern, spy, espy, **sight,** have in sight, make out, pick out, descry, spot <nonformal>, discover, take notice of, have one's eye on, distinguish, recognize, **catch sight of,** get a load of <nonformal>, take in, get an eyeful of <nonformal>, **set** *or* **lay eyes on,** clap eyes on <nonformal>; **glimpse,** get *or* catch a glimpse of

noticeable ADJS **conspicuous,** notable, ostensible, **prominent,** bold, pronounced, salient, in relief, in bold *or* high *or* strong relief, **striking,** outstanding, in the foreground, sticking *or* hanging out

notify VERBS **inform,** tell, speak on *or* for,

apprise, **advise, advertise,** advertise of, give word, mention to, **acquaint,** enlighten, familiarize, brief, verse, give the facts, give an account of, give by way of information; give notice *or* notification, serve notice; **report,** disclose

notion NOUNS 1 **caprice,** whim, *capriccio* <Ital>, *boutade* <Fr>, humor, **whimsy,** freak, whim-wham; **fancy,** fantasy, conceit, flimflam, toy, freakish inspiration, crazy idea, fantastic notion, fool notion <nonformal>, harebrained idea, brainstorm, **vagary,** megrim; **design,** plan, project, idea

2 **suggestion,** bare suggestion, suspicion, inkling, hint, sense, feeling, feeling in one's bones, intuition, intimation, impression, mere notion, hunch *and* sneaking suspicion <both nonformal>, trace of an idea, half an idea, vague idea, hazy idea

notoriety NOUNS **disreputability,** disreputableness; discreditableness, dishonorableness, unsavoriness, **unrespectability;** disgracefulness, shamefulness; talk of the town

notorious ADJS **disreputable,** discreditable, dishonorable, unsavory, shady, **seamy,** sordid; unrespectable, ignoble, ignominious, infamous, inglorious; unpraiseworthy; derogatory; talked about

notwithstanding ADVS **however,** nevertheless, nonetheless; **although,** when, though; howbeit, albeit; **at all events,** in any event, in any case, at any rate; **be that as it may,** for all that, even so, on the other hand, rather, again, at the same time, all the same, just the same, **however that may be;** after all, after all is said and done

nourish VERBS feed, sustain, nurture; nutrify, aliment, foster; **sustain,** strengthen; **nurse,** suckle, lactate, breast-feed, wet-nurse, dry-nurse; fatten, fatten up, stuff, force-feed

nourishment NOUNS **nutrition,** nourishing, feeding, nurture; alimentation; **food** *or* **nutritive value,** food intake; food chain *or* cycle; **fostering,** nurturance

nouveau riche NOUNS **vulgarian,** low *or* vulgar *or* ill-bred fellow, *épicier* <Fr>; *parvenu, arriviste* <both Fr>, upstart; parvenu, **new-rich,** pig in clover <nonformal>; **social climber,** climber, namedropper, tufthunter, status seeker

novel ADJS **original,** unique, different; strange, unusual, uncommon; unfamiliar, unheard-of; **first,** first ever

novelty NOUNS **innovation,** newfangled device *or* contraption <nonformal>, neoism, neonism, **new** *or* **latest wrinkle** <nonformal>, the last word *or* the latest thing <both nonformal>, *dernier cri* <Fr>; what's happening *and* what's in *and* the in thing *and* where it's at <all nonformal>; new ball game; new look, latest fashion *or* fad

novice NOUNS novitiate *or* noviciate, **tyro,** abecedarian, alphabetarian, **beginner,** entrant, **neophyte,** tenderfoot *and* greenhorn <both nonformal>, freshman, **fledgling;** catechumen, initiate, debutant; postulant; newcomer; **recruit**

noway ADVS noways, **nowise,** in no wise, in no case, in no respect, **by no means,** by no manner of means, on no account, not on any account, not for anything in the world, under no circumstances, nohow <nonformal>, **not in the least,** not much, not at all, never, not by a damn sight <nonformal>, not by a long shot <nonformal>; not nearly, **nowhere near;** not a bit, not a bit of it, not a whit, not a speck, not a jot, not an iota

nowhere ADVS in no place, neither here nor there; nowhither

noxious ADJS **nasty, offensive**, fulsome, noisome, rebarbative, mawkish, cloying, brackish, **foul, vile,** bad; **sickening,** nauseating, nauseant, vomity *and* barfy <both nonformal>; poisonous, rank, rancid, maggoty, weevily, spoiled, overripe, high, rotten, stinking, putrid, malodorous, fetid

nth degree NOUNS **limit,** end, extremity, extreme, **acme,** apogee, climax, **maximum,** ceiling, **peak,** summit, **pinnacle,** crown, top; **utmost,** uttermost, utmost extent, highest degree, *ne plus ultra* <L>

nuance NOUNS **suggestion,** allusion; coloration, tinge, undertone, overtone, undercurrent, more than meets the eye *or* ear, something between the lines, intimation, touch, innuendo; **nicety, subtlety,** refinement, delicacy, nice *or* fine *or* delicate *or* **subtle distinction,** fine point; shade *or* particle of difference, hairline

nubby ADJS **studded,** knobbed, knobby, knoblike, nubbled, nubbly, torose; **knotty, knotted**

nuclear power NOUNS **atomic energy,**

nuclear energy, thermonuclear power; activation energy, binding energy, mass energy; energy level

nuclear reactor NOUNS **reactor, pile,** atomic pile, reactor pile, chain-reacting pile, chain reactor, **furnace,** atomic *or* nuclear furnace, neutron factory; fast pile, intermediate pile, slow pile

nuclear weapons NOUNS **atomic weapons,** thermonuclear weapons, A-weapons; weapons of mass destruction

nucleus NOUNS 1 **center,** centrum; **middle**, heart, core; pith, marrow, medulla; **nub, hub,** nave, axis, pivot, **gist,** gravamen, focus, kernel, meat; **heart,** soul, heart and soul, spirit, sap, marrow
2 **atomic nucleus;** cell nucleus; macronucleus, meganucleus; micronucleus; nucleolus

nude NOUNS 1 **work of art,** art work, artistic production, piece, **work,** study, design, composition; still life
ADJS 2 **naked,** bare, peeled, raw <nonformal>, **in the raw** <nonformal>, *in puris naturalibus* <L>, in a state of nature, in nature's garb; in one's birthday suit, **in the buff** *and* in native buff *and* stripped to the buff *and* **in the altogether** <all nonformal>, with nothing on, without a stitch; **stark-naked,** bare-ass <nonformal>, naked as the day one was born, naked as a jaybird, **undressed,** undecked, unarrayed

in naked beauty more adorned
MILTON

nudge NOUNS 1 **hint,** broad hint, gesture, signal, nod, wink, look, kick, prompt; **prod,** poke, punch, jab, dig
VERBS 2 **set in motion,** move, actuate, motivate, push, shove, **drive,** impel, propel; **goad, prod,** poke, prod at, goose <nonformal>, **spur,** prick, sting, needle; work on <nonformal>, **tease,** pester, plague, nag, nag at, make a pest *or* nuisance of oneself, try one's patience, bug <nonformal>

nudity NOUNS **nakedness,** bareness, undress, beauty unadorned; **the nude,** the altogether *and* the buff <both nonformal>, **the raw** <nonformal>; state of nature, **birthday suit** <nonformal>; not a stitch, not a stitch to one's name *or* back; full-frontal nudity; décolleté, décolletage, toplessness; nudism, naturism, gymnosophy

nugget NOUNS **lump,** clump, **hunk** *and* **chunk** <both nonformal>; **mass,** piece, gob *and* glob <both nonformal>, gobbet

nuisance NOUNS **annoyance,** vexation, bothersomeness, exasperation, *tracasserie* <Fr>, **aggravation; pest,** bother, botheration <nonformal>, public nuisance, **trouble,** problem, pain <nonformal>, difficulty, hot potato <nonformal>; **trial; bore,** crashing bore <nonformal>; **headache** <nonformal>; **pain in the neck** *or* **in the ass** <nonformal>

nullify VERBS **abolish,** void, abrogate, annihilate, annul, tear up, repeal, revoke, negate, negative, invalidate, **undo, cancel,** cancel out, put *or* lay to rest; **neutralize,** vitiate, frustrate, stultify, thwart, come *or* bring to nothing

numb VERBS 1 **benumb,** paralyze, **deaden,** anesthetize, freeze, **stun,** stupefy, drug, narcotize, **dull,** dull *or* deaden the pain; sedate, dope *or* dope up <nonformal>
ADJS 2 **insensible,** numbed, benumbed, dead, **deadened,** asleep, unfelt; **unfeeling,** apathetic, affectless; callous; anesthetized, narcotized; **lethargic,** phlegmatic, apathetic, hebetudinous, **dull,** desensitized, sluggish, torpid, languid, slack, soporific, comatose, **stupefied,** in a stupor

number NOUNS 1 **sum,** count, group, total, reckoning, **measure,** parcel, passel <nonformal>, part, **portion,** clutch, ration, share, issue, allotment, lot, deal
VERBS 2 numerate, number off, **enumerate, count,** tell, tally, give a figure to, put a figure on, call off, name, call over, run over; **count noses** *or* **heads** <nonformal>, call the roll; census, poll; page, paginate, foliate

numerable ADJS **calculable,** computable, **reckonable,** estimable, countable, numberable, enumerable; **measurable,** mensurable, quantifiable

numeral NOUNS 1 **number,** *numero* <Sp and Ital>, no *or* n, digit, binary digit *or* bit, **cipher,** character, symbol, sign, notation
ADJS 2 **numeric** *or* numerical, numerary, numerative

numerous ADJS **many,** manifold, not a few, no few; **very many,** full many, **ever so many,** considerable *and* quite some <both nonformal>; **multitudinous,** multitudinal, multifarious, multifold, multiple, **myriad,** numerous as the stars

nun NOUNS sister, *religieuse* <Fr>, clergywoman, conventual; abbess, prioress; **mother superior,** lady superior, superioress, the reverend mother, holy mother; canoness, regular *or* secular canoness; novice, postulant

nunnery NOUNS **convent, cloister,** house; priory, priorate

nuptial ADJS **matrimonial,** marital, conjugal, connubial, wedded, married, hymeneal; epithalamic; **spousal;** husbandly, uxorious; bridal, wifely, uxorial

nuptials NOUNS **wedding, marriage,** marriage ceremony, nuptial mass; church wedding, civil wedding, civil ceremony; spousals, espousals, hymeneal rites; white wedding; forced marriage, shotgun wedding; Gretna Green wedding, elopement

nurse NOUNS 1 sister *or* nursing sister <both Brit>; **probationer,** probationist; caregiver, hospice caregiver; practical nurse; registered nurse *or* RN
2 **nursemaid,** nurserymaid, nanny <chiefly Brit>, amah, ayah, mammy <nonformal>; dry nurse, wet nurse; **baby-sitter,** baby-minder <Brit>, sitter <nonformal>
VERBS 3 **foster, nurture,** nourish, mother, care for, lavish care on, feed, parent, rear, sustain, cultivate, **cherish;** suckle, cradle; dry-nurse, wet-nurse; spoon-feed; **harbor,** hold on to, bear, cling to

nursery NOUNS **conservatory,** greenhouse, glasshouse <Brit>, forcing house, summerhouse, lathhouse, **hothouse,** coolhouse; potting shed; force *or* forcing bed, forcing pit, **hotbed,** cold frame; **cradle,** bedroom

nurture NOUNS 1 **nutrition, nourishment,** nourishing, feeding; **support,** maintenance, sustainment, sustentation, **sustenance, subsistence,** provision; **fostering,** nurturance, mothering, parenting, rearing, fosterage, **care, caring,** care-giving, tender loving care *or* TLC <nonformal>; **upbringing,** bringing-up, fetching-up <nonformal>, raising, breeding
VERBS 2 **foster,** nourish, mother, care for, lavish care on, feed, parent, rear, sustain, cultivate, **cherish; nurse,** suckle, cradle; dry-nurse, wet-nurse; spoon-feed

nut NOUNS 1 **seed; stone,** pit; pip; fruit; **grain,** kernel, berry
2 **fanatic,** infatuate, **buff** *and* **fan** <both nonformal>, freak <nonformal>, *fanatico, aficionado* <both Sp>, devotee, **zealot, enthusiast,** energumen; **monomaniac,** crank <nonformal>; lunatic fringe

3 <nonformal> **nut,** nutso, nutter, nutball, nutbar, nutcase, loon, loony, headcase <Brit>, crazy, psycho, crackpot, screwball, weirdie, weirdo, kook, flake, crackbrain, *meshugana* <Yiddish>, fruitcake, schizo, wack, wacko, sickie, sicko

nutrient NOUNS nutritive, **nutriment,** food; **natural food,** health food; roughage, fiber

nutrition NOUNS **nourishment,** nourishing, feeding, nurture; alimentation; **food** *or* **nutritive value,** food intake; food chain *or* cycle

nutritious ADJS nutritive, nutrient, **nourishing;** alimentary, alimental; digestible, assimilable

nutty ADJS

<nonformal> **crazy,** daffy, dotty, dippy, crazy as a bedbug *or* coot *or* loon, loony, goofy, wacky, flaky, kooky, potty, batty, ape, out to lunch, bats, nuts, nutty as a fruitcake, screwy, screwball, bananas, cuckoo, flipped, freaked-out, off-the-wall, off one's nut *or* rocker, round the bend <Brit>, minus some buttons, nobody home, with bats in the belfry, cracked, not right in the head, tetched, out of one's head, out of one's gourd *or* skull, not all there, *meshuggah* <Yiddish>, three bricks shy of a load, rowing with one oar in the water

nuzzle VERBS **stroke,** pet, caress, fondle; **nose,** rub noses; feel up <nonformal>; rub, rub against, massage; **cuddle,** snuggle, nestle; bundle

nymph NOUNS nymphet, nymphlin; **dryad,** hamadryad, wood nymph; vila *or* willi; tree nymph; oread, mountain nymph; **larva**

O

oaf NOUNS **lout,** boor, lubber, oik <Brit>, **gawk,** gawky, **lummox,** yokel, rube, hick, hayseed, bumpkin, clod, clodhopper

oath NOUNS 1 **vow,** word, assurance, guarantee, warrant, solemn oath *or* affirmation *or* word *or* declaration; **pledge**; Bible oath, ironclad oath; judicial oath, extrajudicial oath; oath of office, official oath; oath of allegiance, loyalty oath, test oath
2 **profane oath,** curse; cuss *or* cuss word *and* dirty word *and* four-letter word *and* **swearword** <all nonformal>, naughty word, no-no <nonformal>, foul invective, **expletive, epithet,** dirty name <nonformal>, dysphemism, obscenity

obedient ADJS **compliant,** complying, allegiant; **acquiescent,** consenting, **submissive**, deferential, self-abnegating; willing, **dutiful,** duteous; loyal, faithful, devoted; uncritical, unshakable, doglike; conforming, in conformity; law-abiding

obese ADJS **corpulent,** stout, fat, big, overweight, fattish, adipose, gross, dumpy, fleshy, beefy, meaty, hefty, porky, porcine; paunchy, paunched, bloated, puffy, blowzy, distended, swollen, pursy; abdominous, big-bellied, full-bellied, potbellied, swag-bellied, rotund, **tubby** <nonformal>, roly-poly; **pudgy,** podgy; **portly,** stocky, imposing; well-fed, corn-fed, grain-fed

obey VERBS **mind,** heed, keep, observe, listen *or* hearken to; **submit, comply,** conform, walk in lockstep; stay in line *and* not get out of line *and* not get off base <all nonformal>, **toe the line** *or* mark, fall in, fall in line, obey the rules, follow the book, **do what one is told;** do as one says, defer to, do one's bidding, lie down and roll over for <nonformal>

obituary NOUNS obit <nonformal>, necrology, necrologue; register of deaths, roll of the dead, death roll, mortuary roll, bill of mortality; casualty list

object NOUNS 1 **article, thing,** material thing, affair, something; whatsit <nonformal>, what's-its-name; something or other, *etwas* <Ger>, *eppes* <Yiddish>, *quelque chose* <Fr>; artifact
2 **intent,** intention, purpose, aim, design, plan

object VERBS **protest, kick** *and* **beef** <both nonformal>, put up a struggle *or* fight; bitch *and* squawk *and* howl *and* holler *and* put up a squawk *and* raise a howl <all nonformal>; exclaim *or* cry out against, make *or* create *or* raise a stink about <all nonformal>; yell bloody murder <nonformal>; **remonstrate,** expostulate; raise *or* press objections, raise one's voice against, enter a protest; **complain,** exclaim at, state a grievance, air one's grievances; **dispute,** challenge, call in question; **demur,** scruple, boggle, dig in one's heels; **demonstrate,** demonstrate against, rally, march, sit-in, teach-in, boycott, strike, picket; **rebel**

objectionable ADJS **offensive,** odious, repulsive, repellent, rebarbative, **repugnant, revolting,** forbidding; **disgusting,** sickening, loathsome, gross *and* yucky *and* grungy *and* scuzzy <all nonformal>, beastly <nonformal>, **vile,** foul, nasty, nauseating; fulsome, mephitic, miasmal, miasmic, malodorous, stinking, fetid, noisome, noxious; **obnoxious,** abhorrent, hateful, abominable, heinous, **contemptible, despicable,** detestable, execrable, beneath *or* below contempt, **base,** ignoble

objective NOUNS 1 **object,** aim, end, goal, destination, mark, object in mind, **end in view,** telos, final cause, ultimate aim; end in itself; **target,** butt, bull's-eye, quintain; quarry, prey, game; reason for being, *raison d'être* <Fr>
ADJS 2 **extrinsic,** external, outward, outside, outlying; **unprejudiced,** unbiased, unprepossessed, unjaundiced; impartial, evenhanded, **fair, just**, equitable, **dispassionate,** impersonal, detached, disinterested; indifferent, neutral; **unswayed,** uninfluenced, undazzled

objector NOUNS **dissenter,** dissident, dissentient, recusant; demurrer; minority *or* opposition voice; **protester,** protestant, dissident, dissentient; obstructionist, obstructive, negativist, naysayer; contra; **resister;** die-hard, bitter-ender, last-ditcher, intransigent, irreconcilable

obligated ADJS **obliged,** obligate, under obligation; bound, duty-bound, in duty bound, tied, pledged, committed, saddled, beholden, bounden; **obliged to,**

beholden to, bound *or* bounden to, **indebted to**

obligation NOUNS 1 **commitment,** agreement, engagement, undertaking, recognizance; **understanding,** gentlemen's agreement; verbal agreement, nonformal agreement, pactum <law>; tacit *or* unspoken agreement; **contract**; designation, committal, earmarking
2 **debt,** indebtedness, indebtment, **liability,** financial commitment, due, **dues,** score, pledge, unfulfilled pledge, amount due, outstanding debt; **bill, bills,** chits <nonformal>, **charges**

obligatory ADJS **compulsory,** imperative, mandatory, required, dictated, **binding;** involuntary; necessary; *de rigueur* <Fr>

obliging ADJS **considerate,** thoughtful, mindful, heedful, regardful, solicitous, attentive, delicate, tactful, mindful of others; complaisant, **accommodating,** accommodative, at one's service, **helpful,** agreeable, indulgent, tolerant, lenient

oblique ADJS **devious,** deviant, deviative, divergent, digressive, divagational, deflectional, excursive; **indirect,** side, sidelong; left-handed, sinister, sinistral; backhand, backhanded; circuitous

obliterate VERBS **expunge,** efface, erase, raze <old>, blot, sponge, **wipe out,** wipe off the map, rub out, **blot out,** sponge out, wash away; cancel, strike out, cross out, scratch, scratch out, rule out; blue-pencil; **delete** *or* dele, kill

oblivion NOUNS **insensibility,** insensibleness, **unconsciousness,** unawareness, obliviousness, nirvana; anesthesia, narcosis; unthinkingness, unmindfulness, forgetfulness, lack *or* loss of memory, amnesia; quietism, passivity, apathy; blank mind, fallow mind, tabula rasa; unintelligence

oblivious ADJS **unconscious, out,** out like a light, out cold; comatose; dormant; dead, **dead to the world;** inconsiderate, untactful, undiplomatic, mindless of, **unmindful,** forgetful; out of it *and* not with it <both nonformal>; **preoccupied**

obnoxious ADJS **offensive,** odious, offensive, gross, **disgusting,** repulsive, loathsome, **abominable,** detestable, despicable, contemptible, beneath contempt, hateful

obscene ADJS **lewd,** adult, bawdy, ithyphallic, **ribald,** pornographic, salacious, sultry <nonformal>, lurid, **dirty, smutty,** raunchy <nonformal>, blue, smoking-room, impure, unchaste, unclean, **foul, filthy,** nasty, vile, fulsome, offensive, unprintable, unrepeatable, not fit for mixed company; **foulmouthed,** foul-tongued, foul-spoken; Rabelaisian

obscenity NOUNS **coarseness,** grossness, *grossièreté* <Fr>, rudeness, crudeness, crudity, **crassness,** rawness, roughness, **earthiness;** ribaldness, ribaldry; raunchiness <nonformal>; **cursing,** cussing <nonformal>, **swearing, profanity,** profane swearing, foul *or* profane *or* obscene *or* blue *or* bad *or* strong *or* unparliamentary *or* indelicate language, vulgar language, vile language, colorful language, unrepeatable expressions, dysphemism, billingsgate, evil speaking, **dirty language** *or* **talk** <nonformal>, scatology, coprology, filthy language, filth

obscure VERBS 1 **cover,** cover up; **clothe,** cloak, mantle, muffle, blanket, canopy, cope, cowl, hood, **veil,** curtain, **screen, shield,** screen off, mask, darken, obfuscate, cloud, fog, befog, fuzz; block, eclipse, occult; film, film over, scum; **make unintelligible, scramble,** jumble, garble; mystify, shadow; **complicate**
ADJS 2 **vague, indistinct,** indeterminate, fuzzy, shapeless, amorphous; unclear, unplain, opaque, muddy, **clear as mud** *and* clear as ditch water <both nonformal>; **dark,** dim, shadowy; **murky,** cloudy, foggy, fogbound, hazy, misty, nebulous; mysterious, enigmatic
3 **unrenowned,** renownless, nameless, inglorious, **unnotable,** unnoted, unnoticed, unremarked, undistinguished, unfamed, uncelebrated, unsung, unhonored, unglorified, unpopular; **unknown,** little known, unheard-of, *ignotus* <L>

observant ADJS respectful, regardful, mindful; **faithful,** devout, devoted, true, loyal, constant; dutiful, duteous; as good as one's word; **practicing,** active; compliant, conforming; punctual, punctilious, scrupulous, meticulous, conscientious

observation NOUNS 1 observance; **looking,** watching, viewing, seeing, witnessing, espial; **notice,** note, respect, **regard;** watch, lookout; surveillance, spying, espionage

2 **remark, statement,** earful *and* crack *and* one's two cents' worth <all nonformal>, **word,** say, saying, utterance, reflection, expression; assertion, averment, allegation, affirmation, pronouncement, position, dictum; **declaration; opinion**; supposition, **theory**

observe VERBS 1 **keep, heed,** follow, keep the faith; regard, defer to, **respect**, attend to, comply with, conform to; hold by, **abide by,** adhere to; **live up to,** act up to, practice what one preaches, **be faithful to,** keep faith with, do justice to, do the right thing by; **fulfill,** fill, meet, satisfy; **make good,** keep *or* make good one's word *or* promise, be as good as one's word

2 **celebrate,** keep, mark, solemnly mark, **honor; commemorate,** memorialize; **solemnize,** kill the fatted calf; sound a fanfare, blow the trumpet, beat the drum, fire a salute

3 **remark,** comment, note; mention, let drop *or* fall, say by the way, make mention of; refer to, allude to, touch on, make reference to, call attention to; muse, reflect; opine <nonformal>; interject; blurt, blurt out, exclaim

observer NOUNS **spectator,** looker, onlooker, looker-on, **watcher,** gazer, gazer-on, gaper, goggler, **viewer,** seer, beholder, perceiver, percipient; **witness,** eyewitness; sidewalk superintendent; kibitzer; girl-watcher, ogler, drugstore cowboy <nonformal>

obsessed ADJS 1 **possessed,** prepossessed, **infatuated,** preoccupied, fixated, **hung up** <nonformal>, besotted, gripped, held; monomaniac *or* monomaniacal; unable to forget, haunted, plagued, nagged, rankled

2 **engrossed, absorbed,** totally absorbed, single-minded, **occupied,** preoccupied, engaged, devoted, devoted to, intent, intent on, monopolized, swept up, taken up with, **involved,** caught up in, **wrapped up in**

obsession NOUNS prepossession, preoccupation, **hang-up** <nonformal>, **fixation,** tic, complex, fascination; hypercathexis; **compulsion,** morbid drive, obsessive compulsion, irresistible impulse; **monomania,** ruling passion, fixed idea, *idée fixe* <Fr>, one-track mind; **possession**, spirit control

obsessive ADJS obsessional; **obsessing,** possessing, preoccupying, gripping, holding; driving, impelling, **compulsive,** compelling; haunting, persistent, recurrent, nagging, plaguing, rankling, festering

obsolete ADJS **passé,** extinct, gone out, gone-by, dead, past, run out, **outworn**

obstacle NOUNS **obstruction,** obstructer; **hang-up** <nonformal>; **block,** blockade, cordon, curtain; **difficulty,** hurdle, hazard; **deterrent,** determent; **drawback,** objection; **stumbling block,** stumbling stone, stone in one's path; fly in the ointment, **hitch, catch,** joker <nonformal>

obstinate ADJS **stubborn,** pertinacious, restive; willful, self-willed, strong-willed, hardheaded, **headstrong,** strongheaded, *entêté* <Fr>; **dogged,** bulldogged, tenacious, perserving; bullheaded, bulletheaded, **pigheaded, mulish** <nonformal>, stubborn as a mule; **set in one's ways,** case-hardened, stiff-necked; balky, balking

obstreperous ADJS **defiant,** refractory, recalcitrant, contumacious, unruly, restive, impatient of control *or* discipline; fractious, ornery *and* feisty <both nonformal>; wild, untamed

obstruct VERBS **get** *or* **stand in the way;** dog, block, block the way, put up a roadblock, blockade, block up, occlude; **jam,** crowd, pack; **bar,** barricade, bolt, lock; **debar,** shut out; shut off, **close,** close off *or* up, close tight, shut tight; strangle, suffocate

obstruction NOUNS **clog, block,** blockade, sealing off, **blockage,** strangulation, choking, choking off, **stoppage,** stop, **bar, barrier, obstacle,** impediment; **bottleneck,** chokepoint; **congestion,** jam, traffic jam, gridlock, rush hour; constipation, obstipation, costiveness; infarct, infarction; embolism, embolus; **blind alley,** blank wall, **dead end,** cul-de-sac, dead-end street, impasse

obtain VERBS **acquire,** get, gain, secure, procure; win, score; **earn,** make; **reap,** harvest; come *or* enter into possession of, **come into, come by,** come in for, be seized of; draw, derive

obverse NOUNS opposite side, other side, the other side of the picture *or* coin, other face; **reverse,** inverse, converse; flip side *and* B-side <both nonformal>; **front,** head <of a coin>

obvious ADJS **patent,** unquestionable, unexceptionable, undeniable, self-evident, axiomatic; indubitable, unarguable, indisputable, incontestable, **irrefutable,** unrefutable, unconfutable, incontrovertible, irrefragable, unanswerable, unimpeachable, absolute; admitting no question *or* dispute *or* doubt *or* denial; **demonstrable,** provable, verifiable, testable, confirmable; well-founded, well-established, well-grounded; factual, **real,** historical, actual

occasion NOUNS **circumstance,** occurrence, event, **incident;** juncture, conjuncture, contingency, eventuality; **condition; opportunity,** chance, time; **necessity,** need, want

occasionally ADVS on occasion, **sometimes,** at times, at odd times, every so often <nonformal>, at various times, on divers occasions, **now and then,** every now and then <nonformal>, now and again, every once in a while <nonformal>, every now and again, once or twice, **from time to time;** only when the spirit moves, only now and then, at infrequent intervals, once in a blue moon <nonformal>; irregularly, sporadically, once in a while

occult ADJS **esoteric,** esoterical, mysterious, mystic, mystical, anagogic, anagogical; metaphysic, metaphysical; cabalic, cabalistic; **paranormal, supernatural**; theosophical, theosophist, anthroposophical

the occult NOUNS **supernaturalism,** supernaturalness, supernaturality, supranaturalism, supernormalness, **preternaturalism,** supersensibleness, superphysicalness, superhumanity; **the paranormal;** numinousness; **unearthliness,** unworldliness, **otherworldliness,** eeriness; the supernatural, the supersensible; **paranormality;** supernature, supranature; **mystery,** mysteriousness, miraculousness, strangeness; faerie, witchery, elfdom

occupant NOUNS **inhabitant,** inhabiter, habitant; occupier, **dweller,** tenant, denizen, inmate; **resident,** residencer, residentiary, resider; incumbent, *locum tenens* <L>; sojourner; addressee; squatter; homesteader

occupation NOUNS 1 **habitation,** inhabiting, inhabitation, habitancy, inhabitancy, **tenancy,** occupancy, residence *or* residency, residing, abiding, **living,** nesting, **dwelling,** commorancy <law>, lodging, staying, stopping, sojourning, staying over
2 **appropriation,** taking over, takeover <nonformal>, **adoption,** assumption, usurpation, arrogation; **conquest,** subjugation, enslavement, colonization
3 **vocation,** business, work, line, line of work, line of business *or* endeavor, number <nonformal>, walk, walk of life, calling, mission, **profession,** practice, pursuit, specialty, specialization, *métier* <Fr>, **trade,** racket *and* game <both nonformal>

occupied ADJS 1 **inhabited,** tenanted; **peopled,** empeopled, populated, colonized, settled; populous
2 **busy, engaged,** employed, working; at it; **at work,** on duty, on the job, in harness; hard at work, **hard at it;** on the move, on the go, on the run, **on the hop** *or* **jump** <nonformal>; busy as a bee *or* beaver, busier than a one-armed paper hanger <nonformal>; up to one's ears *or* elbows *or* asshole *or* neck *or* eyeballs in <nonformal>; tied up
3 absorbed *or* engrossed in thought, **absorbed,** engrossed, introspective, rapt, wrapped in thought, lost in thought, abstracted, immersed in thought, buried in thought, engaged in thought, **preoccupied**

occupy VERBS 1 **engage, busy,** devote, spend, **employ,** occupy oneself, busy oneself, go about one's business, devote oneself; pass *or* employ *or* spend the time; **occupy the mind** *or* **thoughts,** fasten itself on the mind, seize the mind, fill the mind; **engross, absorb,** immerse, preoccupy, involve, monopolize, exercise, take up; **obsess;** absorb the attention, claim one's thoughts, engross the mind *or* thoughts, engage the attention, monopolize one's attention, engage the mind *or* thoughts
2 **inhabit,** tenant, move in *or* into, make one's home, rent, lease, **reside, live in,** dwell, lodge, stay

occur VERBS **happen**, hap, eventuate, **take place,** come *or* go down <nonformal>, go on, **transpire,** be realized, come, **come off** <nonformal>, **come about,** come true, **come to pass,** pass, pass off, go off, fall, **befall,** betide; **be found,** be met with; **occur to,** come to mind, come into one's head, impinge on one's consciousness, claim one's mind *or* thoughts, pass through one's head *or* mind, dawn upon one, **enter one's mind,** cross one's mind; **strike,** strike one, strike the mind, grab one <nonformal>, **suggest itself**

occurrence NOUNS **event,** incident, episode, experience, adventure, hap, **happening,** happenstance, **phenomenon,** fact, matter of fact, reality, particular, circumstance, **occasion,** turn of events

ocean NOUNS **sea,** ocean sea, great *or* main sea, *thalassa* <Gk>, main *or* ocean main, the bounding main, tide, salt sea, salt water, blue water, deep water, open sea, the brine, the briny *and* the big pond <both nonformal>, the briny deep, **the deep,** the deep sea, the deep blue sea, drink *and* big drink <both nonformal>, **high sea, high seas**

the great naked sea shouldering a load of salt
SANDBERG

the wine-dark sea
HOMER

oceanic ADJS **marine, maritime,** pelagic, thalassic; nautical; deep-sea

ocular ADJS **visual,** eye, eyeball <nonformal>; **sighted,** seeing, having sight *or* vision; **optic,** optical; ophthalmic, ophthalmological; binocular, monocular

odd ADJS 1 **queer, peculiar,** absurd, singular, curious, oddball <nonformal>, kooky *and* freaky *and* freaked-out <all nonformal>, quaint, **eccentric,** gonzo <nonformal>, funny; **strange, outlandish,** off-the-wall <informal>, surreal, not for real <nonformal>, passing strange; **weird,** unearthly

wondrous strange
SHAKESPEARE

2 **sole, unique,** singular, absolute, unrepeated, **alone,** lone, **only,** only-begotten, **one and only,** first and last; unpaired, azygous

oddball NOUNS **misfit, nonconformist,** individualist, inner-directed person; **freak,** sport, anomaly; a fish out of water, a square peg in a round hole <nonformal>

oddity NOUNS 1 **eccentricity,** idiosyncrasy, idiocrasy, **erraticism,** erraticness, **queerness, peculiarity,** strangeness, singularity, freakishness, freakiness, quirkiness, crotchetiness, dottiness, crankiness, crankism, crackpotism; abnormality, anomaly, unnaturalness, irregularity, deviation, deviancy, differentness, divergence, aberration
2 **curiosity,** funny *or* peculiar *or* strange thing; **abnormality,** anomaly; rarity, improbability, exception, one in a thousand *or* million; curio, conversation piece

odds NOUNS **gambling odds; short odds, long odds,** long shot; even chance, good chance, small chance, no chance; **probability, likelihood,** likeliness, liability, aptitude, verisimilitude; **chance**

odious ADJS **offensive,** objectionable, repulsive, repellent, rebarbative, **repugnant, revolting,** forbidding; **obnoxious,** abhorrent, hateful, abominable, heinous, **contemptible, despicable,** detestable, execrable, beneath *or* below contempt, **base,** ignoble

odor NOUNS **smell, scent,** aroma, flavor <old>, savor; **essence,** definite odor, redolence, effluvium, emanation, exhalation, fume, breath, subtle odor, whiff, trace, detectable odor; trail, spoor; **fragrance**; stink, stench

odyssey NOUNS **travels,** journeys, **journeyings,** wanderings, voyagings, transits, peregrinations, peripatetics, migrations, transmigrations

off ADJS 1 **tainted,** blown; **stale; sour,** soured, turned; **rank,** rancid, strong <nonformal>, **high,** gamy
2 **unbalanced,** unsettled, distraught, wandering, mazed, crackbrained, brainsick, sick *or* soft in the head, not right, not in one's right mind, **touched,** touched in the head, **out of one's mind,** out of one's senses *or* wits, irrational, queer, queer in the head, odd, strange
3 **below par,** below standard, below the mark <nonformal>, substandard, **not up to scratch** *or* snuff *or* the mark <nonformal>, not up to sample *or* standard *or* specification
ADVS 4 **at a distance,** away, aloof, at arm's length; distantly, remotely

off-base ADJS **misbehaving,** naughty, bad; improper, not respectable; out-of-order *and* out-of-line <both nonformal>; **disorderly,** disruptive, **rowdy,** rowdyish, **ruffianly**

offbeat ADJS **unconventional,** way out *and* far out *and* kinky *and* out in left field <all nonformal>, fringy, breakaway,

out-of-the-way; original, maverick, Bohemian, **nonformal,** free and easy <nonformal>

offend VERBS give offense, **repel,** put off, turn off <nonformal>, **revolt, disgust,** nauseate, sicken, make one sick; stick in one's throat, stick in one's crop *or* craw *or* gizzard <nonformal>; **horrify, appall,** shock; give umbrage, affront, outrage; grieve, aggrieve; wound, hurt, cut, cut to the quick, hit one where one lives <nonformal>, **sting,** hurt one's feelings; step *or* tread on one's toes; offend the eye, offend one's aesthetic sensibilities, **look bad**

offense NOUNS **indignity,** affront, injury, humiliation; **insult,** aspersion, uncomplimentary remark, slap *or* kick in the face, left-handed *or* backhanded compliment, damning with faint praise; **outrage,** atrocity, enormity; **misdeed, misdemeanor,** misfeasance, malfeasance, malefaction, criminal *or* guilty *or* sinful act, injustice, injury, **wrong,** iniquity, evil, peccancy, *malum* <L>; tort; **impropriety,** slight *or* minor wrong, venial sin, **indiscretion,** peccadillo, misstep, trip, slip, lapse; **transgression,** trespass

offensive NOUNS 1 **attack, assault,** assailing, assailment; **offense,** aggression; onset, onslaught; strike; surgical strike, first strike, preventive war; **charge,** rush, dead set at, run at *or* against; breakthrough; **counterattack,** counteroffensive; blitzkrieg, blitz, lightning attack, lightning war, panzer warfare, sudden *or* devastating *or* crippling attack

ADJS 2 **objectionable,** odious, repulsive, repellent, rebarbative, **repugnant, revolting,** forbidding; **disgusting,** sickening, loathsome, beastly <nonformal>, **vile,** foul, filthy, bawdy, nasty, nauseating; fulsome, mephitic, miasmal, miasmic, malodorous, stinking, fetid, noisome, noxious; coarse, gross, crude, obscene; **insulting,** insolent, abusive, humiliating, degrading, contemptuous, contumelious, calumnious; scurrilous

offer NOUNS 1 offering, proffer, presentation, **bid,** submission; **advance, overture,** approach, invitation; hesitant *or* tentative *or* preliminary approach, feeling-out, **feeler** <nonformal>; asking price; **counteroffer,** counterproposal

VERBS 2 **proffer, present,** tender, offer up, **put up, submit,** extend, prefer <old>, **hold out,** hold forth, place in one's way, lay at one's feet, put *or* place at one's disposal, put one in the way of; **bid,** make a bid, offer to buy, make an offer

offering NOUNS **oblation,** sacrifice, immolation, incense; burnt offering, votive *or* ex voto offering; peace offering, sacramental offering; **donation,** donative; **contribution,** subscription; alms, pittance, **charity,** dole, handout <nonformal>, alms fee, widow's mite; Peter's pence; collection; tithe

off-guard ADJS **unalert,** unwary, unwatchful, unvigilant, uncautious, incautious; **unprepared,** unready; **off one's guard,** napping, asleep at the switch *and* asleep on the job *and* not on the job *and* goofing off *and* looking out the window <all nonformal>; daydreaming, woolgathering

office NOUNS **bureau,** department; secretariat, ministry; **function,** duty, job, province, place, **role,** *rôle* <Fr>, part; **capacity,** character, **position**

officer NOUNS 1 **executive,** official; chief executive officer, chief executive, managing director <Brit>; functionary, *fonctionnaire* <Fr>, apparatchik; **public official,** public servant; officeholder; **commissioned officer**

2 **policeman,** constable, police officer, *flic* <Fr nonformal>, *gendarme* <Fr>, *carabiniere* <Ital>; peace officer, law enforcement agent, arm of the law; policewoman, police matron; patrolman, police constable <England>; trooper, mounted policeman; chief of police

official ADJS **recorded,** registered; **filed,** indexed, enrolled, **entered,** logged, booked, posted; documented; **on record,** on file, on the books; legal, of record; **authoritative, authentic,** magisterial; cathedral, ex cathedra; standard, approved, accepted, received, pontific; from *or* straight from the horse's mouth

officiate VERBS **function,** serve; perform as, act as, act *or* play one's part, **do duty,** discharge *or* perform *or* exercise the office *or* duties *or* functions of, serve in the office *or* capacity of; **referee, umpire,** arbitrate; **minister,** perform a rite, perform service *or* divine service; administer a sacrament, administer the Eucharist, etc; anoint, chrism

off-limits ADJS **prohibited,** forbidden,

forbade, *verboten* <Ger>, **barred; unpermissible,** not permitted *or* allowed, unchartered; beyond the pale, out of bounds; unauthorized, **unsanctioned,** unlicensed; banned, under the ban, **outlawed,** contraband; taboo, tabooed, untouchable; **illegal,** unlawful, illicit

offset VERBS set off, **counteract,** countervail, **counterbalance,** counterweigh, counterpoise, **balance,** play off against, set against, set over against, equiponderate; **square,** square up; **cushion,** absorb the shock, **soften the blow,** break the fall, deaden, damp *or* dampen, soften, suppress, neutralize

offshoot NOUNS **branch,** fork, limb, bough; **shoot,** spear, frond; scion; **sprout,** sprit, slip, burgeon; **branch,** organ, division, wing, arm, **affiliate; chapter,** lodge, post; branch office

offspring NOUNS **descendant; child,** scion; son, son and heir, a chip off the old block; **daughter,** grandchild, grandson, granddaughter

often ADVS **repeatedly,** frequently, recurrently, every time one turns around, with every other breath, **again and again, over and over,** over and over again, many times over, time and again, **time after time,** times without number, **ad nauseam;** year in year out, week in week out, etc, year after year, day after day, day by day; **many times,** several times, a number of times, many a time

ogle VERBS **scrutinize,** survey, eye, contemplate, look over, give the eye *or* the once-over <nonformal>; ogle at, **leer,** leer at, gape, give one the glad eye; take a long, hard look; size up <nonformal>; take stock of; **make eyes at,** make goo-goo eyes at <nonformal>, *faire les yeux doux* <Fr>, look sweet upon <nonformal>

ogre NOUNS **monster,** vampire, werewolf, ghoul, *bête noire;* **fiend,** fiend from hell

oil VERBS grease, **lubricate; anoint,** salve, unguent, embrocate, dress, pour oil *or* balm upon; smear, daub; slick, slick on <nonformal>

oily ADJS **greasy; unctuous,** unctional; unguinous; **oleaginous,** oleic; unguentary, **unguent,** unguentous; chrismal, chrismatory; **fat, fatty,** adipose; pinguid, pinguedinous, pinguescent; blubbery, tallowy, suety; lardy, lardaceous

ointment NOUNS **balm,** salve, lotion, cream, unguent, unguentum, inunction, inunctum, unction, chrism; lenitive, embrocation, demulcent, emollient

okay NOUNS 1 **permission,** leave, consent; **license,** liberty; **OK** *and* **nod** *and* **go-ahead** *and* **green light** *and* **go sign** *and* **thumbs-up** <all nonformal>; special permission, charter, patent, dispensation, release, waiver; zoning variance, variance

VERBS 2 **consent, assent,** give consent, say yes *or* aye *or* yea, vote affirmatively, vote aye, nod, nod assent; accept, play *or* go along <nonformal>, **agree to, sign off on** <nonformal>, go along with <nonformal>; **approve,** give one's blessing to, **OK** <nonformal>; sanction, **endorse,** ratify; **wink at,** connive at; be willing, turn a willing ear; deign, condescend; have no objection, not refuse; permit

ADJS 3 **tolerable,** goodish, fair, fairish, moderate, **decent,** respectable, presentable, good enough, **pretty good,** not bad, not amiss, not half bad, not so bad, **adequate,** satisfactory, all right, OK <nonformal>; better than nothing; **acceptable,** admissible, **passable,** unobjectionable, unexceptionable

old ADJS 1 **aged, elderly,** grown old in years, along *or* up *or* advanced *or* on in years, years old, advanced, advanced in life, **at an advanced age,** ancient, geriatric, gerontic; **venerable,** old as Methuselah *or* as God *or* as the hills; patriarchal; hoary, hoar, **gray,** white, gray- *or* white-haired, gray with age; wrinkled, prune-faced <nonformal>; wrinkly, with crow's feet, marked with the crow's foot

2 **antiquated,** grown old, superannuated, antique, age-encrusted, of other times

old age NOUNS **oldness,** elderliness, senectitude, advanced age *or* years; **ripe old age,** the golden years, senior citizenship, hoary age, gray *or* white hairs; **decline of life,** declining years; sunset *or* twilight *or* evening *or* autumn *or* winter of one's days; **dotage,** second childhood; senility, anility

an incurable disease
SENECA

old-fashioned ADJS old-fangled, **dated,** out-of-date, outdated, **outmoded,** out of style *or* fashion, out of use, **unfashionable,** styleless, **behind the times,** of the old school, old hat *and* back-number *and* has-been <all nonformal>

old-line ADJS **conservative,** diehard, standpat <nonformal>, opposed to change; backward, backward-looking, old-fashioned, **unprogressive,** nonprogressive, unreconstructed, status-quo, stuck-in-the-mud; long-established; **confirmed,** inveterate, **dyed-in-the-wool**

omen NOUNS **portent; augury,** auspice, soothsay, prognostic, prognostication; **warning sign,** premonitory sign, danger sign; preliminary sign *or* signal *or* token; **handwriting on the wall;** straw in the wind; presentiment, foreboding

ominous ADJS **portentous,** portending; **foreboding,** boding, **bodeful; inauspicious,** ill-omened, ill-boding, of ill *or* fatal omen, of evil portent, loaded *or* laden *or* freighted *or* fraught with doom, looming, looming over; fateful, doomful; **unpropitious,** unpromising, unfavorable, unfortunate, unlucky; sinister, dark, black, gloomy, somber, dreary; **threatening,** menacing, lowering; dire, baleful, baneful, **ill-fated,** ill-starred, evil-starred, star-crossed

omit VERBS **leave undone,** leave, **let go,** leave half-done, pretermit, **skip,** jump, **miss,** pass over, pass up <nonformal>, abandon; **ban,** prohibit, proscribe, taboo, **leave out,** ignore

omnipotent ADJS **almighty,** all-powerful; plenipotentiary, absolute, unlimited, **sovereign**; **supreme**; omnicompetent

omnipresent ADJS **all-present,** ubiquitous, everywhere; continuous, uninterrupted, infinite; **pervasive,** all-pervading, **universal**

omniscient ADJS **all-wise,** all-knowing, all-seeing

omnivorous ADJS all-devouring, pantophagous; **gluttonous**

onerous ADJS **oppressive,** burdensome, incumbent *or* superincumbent, **cumbersome,** cumbrous; **laborious,** toilsome, arduous, strenuous, painful, operose, troublesome, oppressive

one-sided ADJS **discriminatory; prejudiced,** prepossessed, biased, jaundiced, colored; **partial,** partisan; interested, nonobjective, **undetached,** undispassionate

one-upmanship NOUNS **cunning,** low cunning, animal cunning; gamesmanship <nonformal>; **canniness, shrewdness,** sharpness, acuteness, astuteness, **cleverness;** lifemanship, **competitive advantage**

one-way ADJS unidirectional, irreversible

ongoing ADJS **happening,** occurring, current, actual, passing, taking place, on, **going on, prevalent,** prevailing, that is, that applies, in the wind, afloat, afoot, under way, in hand, **on foot,** ado, doing; **operating,** operational, working, functioning, operant, functional, acting, active, running

onset NOUNS **beginning,** commencement, start, running *or* flying start, starting point, square one <nonformal>, **outset,** outbreak, oncoming

onslaught NOUNS **attack,** assault, assailing, assailment; **offense,** offensive; aggression; onset

onus NOUNS **duty,** obligation, charge, **burden,** mission, devoir, must, ought, imperative, bounden duty, proper *or* assigned task, what ought to be done, what one is responsible for, where the buck stops <nonformal>; **stigma,** stigmatism; burden of proof, *onus probandi* <L>; the proof of the pudding

ooze NOUNS 1 **slime, slop,** scum, sludge, slush; glop *and* gunk <both nonformal>, **muck,** mire; **seepage,** seep; perfusion; **oozing,** weeping

VERBS 2 **exude,** exudate, transude, transpire, reek; **emit,** discharge, give off; leach, lixiviate; effuse, extravasate; **seep,** bleed, weep

opalescent ADJS pearly, nacreous, mother-of-pearl, iridescent, opaline, opaloid

opaque ADJS intransparent, nontranslucent, adiaphanous, impervious to light; **dark, obscure**, cloudy, roiled, roily, turbid; **dense,** thick <nonformal>

open VERBS 1 **disclose,** open up, lay open, break the seal, bring into the open, get out in the open

ADJS 2 **unclosed,** uncovered; **unobstructed,** unstopped, unclogged; clear, cleared, free; wide-open, unrestricted; **disclosed**; bare, exposed, unhidden, naked, bald; candid, **frank**; self-revealing, self-revelatory; outspoken, free-speaking, free-spoken, free-tongued; **accessible, approachable,** conversable, easy to speak to; **extroverted,** outgoing

3 overt, open to all, open as day, out of the closet <nonformal>; unclassified;

revealed, bare, **exposed,** out in the open, naked; out on a limb <nonformal>; liable, susceptible, nonimmune

openhearted ADJS **open,** sincere, candid, **frank; giving,** bighearted, largehearted, greathearted; **cordial,** amiable, gracious, **friendly,** neighborly, genial, hearty, warm, warmhearted; heart-to-heart

opening NOUNS 1 **aperture, hole,** hollow, cavity, **orifice; slot,** split, crack, check, leak; opening up, unstopping, uncorking, clearing, throwing open, laying open, broaching, cutting through; passageway; inlet; outlet; **gap,** gape, yawn, hiatus, lacuna, gat, space, interval; **chasm,** gulf; cleft; fontanel; foramen, fenestra

2 **opportunity,** chance, time, occasion; room, scope, space, place, liberty

open-minded ADJS **open, receptive,** rational, admissive; **persuadable,** persuasible; **unopinionated,** unopinioned, unwedded to an opinion; **undogmatic**

operable ADJS **workable,** performable, actable, **doable,** manageable, compassable, negotiable, maneuverable; **practicable, feasible,** practical, viable

operate VERBS 1 **function,** perform, go, run, be in action *or* operation *or* commission; be effective, go into effect, have effect, take effect, militate

2 **work, move,** practice, do one's stuff *or* one's thing <all nonformal>; **plot, scheme,** intrigue, be up to something; **conspire, connive,** collude, complot <old>, cabal; **maneuver,** engineer, rig, wangle <nonformal>, angle, finagle <nonformal>

operation NOUNS 1 **surgery,** surgical treatment, surgical operation, surgical intervention, surgical technique *or* measure, the knife <nonformal>; unnecessary surgery, tomomania

2 **function,** use, purpose, role, part, end use, immediate purpose, ultimate purpose, operational purpose; **functioning,** action, performance, performing, **working,** work, workings, exercise, practice; **management,** direction, conduct, running, carrying-on *or* -out, execution, seeing to, overseeing, oversight

3 action; **mission; operations,** military operations, naval operations

operative NOUNS 1 **secret agent,** cloak-and-dagger operative, **undercover man,** inside man <nonformal>; **spy,** espionage agent; counterspy, double agent; **detective,** investigator, sleuth

ADJS 2 **operational,** go <nonformal>, functional, practical; effective, effectual, efficient, efficacious

operator NOUNS 1 **telephone operator,** switchboard operator, telephonist, **central;** long distance; PBX operator

2 **conniver;** maneuverer, machinator, opportunist, pot-hunter, exploiter; strategist, machinator, wheeler-dealer <nonformal>; finagler *and* **wire-puller** <both nonformal>; behind-the-scenes operator, gray eminence, *éminence grise* <Fr>, power behind the throne, kingmaker <nonformal>, **powerbroker**

opiate NOUNS **sleep-inducer,** sleep-producer, sleep-provoker, sleep-bringer, hypnotic, soporific, somnifacient; poppy, mandrake, mandragora, narcotic, opium, morphine, morphia; sedative; anesthetic

opinion NOUNS **sentiment,** feeling, sense, impression, reaction, **notion,** idea, thought, mind, thinking, **way of thinking,** attitude, stance, posture, position, mindset, **view,** point of view, eye, sight, lights, observation, **conception,** concept, conceit, **estimation,** estimate, consideration, **theory**, assumption, presumption, **conclusion,** judgment, personal judgment; **point of view**

opinionated ADJS **dogmatic,** dogmatical, dogmatizing, pronunciative, didactic, **positive,** positivistic, peremptory, pontifical, oracular; **opinioned,** opinionative, conceited; **self-opinionated,** self-opinioned; doctrinaire

opium NOUNS 1 **sleep-inducer,** sleep-producer, sleep-provoker, sleep-bringer, hypnotic, soporific, somnifacient; poppy, mandrake, mandragora, opiate, morphine, morphia; sedative; anesthetic

2 <nonformal> black pills, brown stuff, hop, O, tar

opponent NOUNS **adversary,** antagonist, assailant, foe, foeman, **enemy,** archenemy; adverse *or* opposing party, opposite camp, opposite *or* opposing side, **the opposition,** the loyal opposition

opportune ADJS **timely,** well-timed, in the nick of time, seasonable, convenient; **propitious,** ripe, auspicious, lucky, providential, heaven-sent, fortunate, happy, felicitous

opportunist NOUNS **intriguer,** *intrigant, intrigante* <both Fr>, cabalist; maneuverer, machinator, operator <nonformal>, pot-hunter, exploiter

opportunity NOUNS **chance,** time, occasion; opening, room, scope, space, place, liberty; equal opportunity, nondiscrimination, affirmative action; a leg up, stepping-stone, rung of the ladder; time's forelock; break <nonformal>, the breaks <nonformal>

oppose VERBS **counter, cross,** go *or* act in opposition to, **go against,** run against, **run counter to,** fly in the face of, fly in the teeth of; kick out against, make waves <nonformal>, **protest**; set oneself against, set one's face *or* heart against; be *or* play at cross-purposes, **obstruct,** traverse, sabotage; **take issue with,** take one's stand against, lift *or* raise a hand against, declare oneself against, stand and be counted against, side against, vote against, vote nay, veto; make a stand against; not put up with, not abide, not be content with; counteract, counterwork, countervail; **resist,** withstand

opposed ADJS contrapositive, **opposite,** opposing, **facing,** confronting, confrontational, confrontive, eyeball-to-eyeball, one-on-one; on opposite sides, adversarial, at loggerheads, at daggers drawn, antithetic, antithetical; **unconsenting**; dead set against

opposing ADJS **contradictory,** contradicting, contrary, contra, nay-saying, adversative, repugnant; **opposed,** oppositive, oppositional; anti <nonformal>, dead against

opposite NOUNS 1 **the opposite,** the contrary, the antithesis, the reverse, the other way round *or* around, the inverse, the converse, the obverse, the counter; **the other side,** the mirror *or* reverse image, the other side of the coin, the flip *or* B side <nonformal>; the direct *or* polar opposite, the other *or* opposite extreme; antipode, antipodes; **antonym,** opposite term, counterterm
ADJS 2 **adverse,** untoward, detrimental, unfavorable; sinister; hostile, antagonistic, inimical; contrary, counter, counteractive, conflicting, opposing, opposed, in opposition
ADVS 3 **poles apart,** at opposite extremes; contrary, contrariwise, counter; just opposite, **face-to-face,** vis-à-vis, *front à front* <Fr>, nose to nose, one on one, eyeball-to-eyeball

opposition NOUNS **contrariety,** oppositeness, antithesis, contrast, contraposition, counterposition, contradiction, contraindication, contradistinction; **antagonism,** repugnance, resistance, oppugnance, oppugnancy, **hostility,** perversity, nay-saying, negativeness, orneriness <nonformal>, inimicalness, **antipathy**

oppress VERBS 1 **burden,** weigh upon, weight down, wear one down, be heavy on one, crush one; **tire, exhaust,** weary, wear out, wear upon one; prey on the mind, prey on *or* upon; **haunt,** haunt the memory, obsess; **anguish,** afflict, torment
2 **persecute,** torment, victimize, play cat and mouse with, **harass,** get *or* keep after, get *or* keep at, harry, hound, beset

oppressed ADJS **weighted,** weighed *or* weighted down; burdened, laden, cumbered, **encumbered,** charged, loaded, fraught, freighted, taxed, saddled, hampered; **overburdened,** overloaded, overladen; **subjugated,** subjected, enslaved, enthralled, in thrall, captive, bond, unfree; **downtrodden,** kept down *or* under, ground down, overborne, trampled, ordered *or* kicked around <nonformal>, regimented, tyrannized; treated like dirt under one's feet

oppression NOUNS **persecution,** harrying, hounding, tormenting, bashing <nonformal>, harassment, victimization; **despotism,** tyranny, fascism, domineering, domination; heavy hand, high hand, iron hand, iron heel *or* boot; big stick, *argumentum baculinum* <L>

oppressive ADJS 1 **burdensome,** crushing, trying, onerous, heavy, weighty; **harsh,** wearing, wearying, exhausting; overburdensome, tyrannous, grinding, repressive
2 **stuffy,** airless, breathless, breezeless, windless; **close,** stifling, suffocating; stirless, unstirring, not a breath of air, not a leaf stirring

not wind enough to twirl the one red leaf
COLERIDGE

oppressor NOUNS **tyrant,** despot, hard master, driver, **slave driver,** Simon Legree <Harriet B Stowe>; **martinet,** disciplinarian, stickler

opt VERBS **choose,** elect, pick, go with <nonformal>, opt for, co-opt, make *or* take one's choice, make choice of, have one's druthers <nonformal>, use *or* take up *or* exercise one's option

optimal ADJS **best,** very best, greatest *and* top-of-the-line <both nonformal>, **prime,** optimum; **choice,** paramount, **unsurpassed,** surpassing, unparalleled, unmatched, unmatchable, matchless, makeless <old>, **peerless;** quintessential

optimist NOUNS hoper, Pollyanna <Eleanor Porter>, ray of sunshine <nonformal>, irrepressible optimist, Dr Pangloss <Voltaire>; utopian, perfectionist; millenarian, chiliast, millennialist, millennian

a proponent of the doctrine that black is white
AMBROSE BIERCE

optimistic ADJS upbeat <nonformal>, bright, sunny; **cheerful**; **rosy,** roseate, rose-colored, *couleur de rose* <Fr>; pollyannaish, Panglossian; utopian, perfectionist, millenarian, chiliastic, millennialistic

optimum NOUNS 1 **the best,** the very best, the best ever, the top of the heap *or* the line <nonformal>, the tops <nonformal>; **quintessence,** prime, superlative; **cream,** flower, fat; cream of the crop, *crème de la crème* <Fr>, salt of the earth; *pièce de résistance* <Fr>; nonesuch, paragon, nonpareil; gem of the first water
ADJS 2 **best,** very best, greatest *and* top-of-the-line <both nonformal>, **prime,** optimal; supreme, paramount, **unsurpassed,** surpassing, unparalleled, unmatched, unmatchable, matchless, makeless <old>, **peerless;** quintessential

option NOUNS 1 **discretion,** pleasure, will and pleasure; optionality; possible choice, alternative, alternate choice, say, say-so *and* druthers <both nonformal>, free decision
2 stock option, right, **put, call,** put and call, right of put and call; straddle, spread

optional ADJS **discretionary,** discretional, nonmandatory, elective; arbitrary; **self-determined,** self-determining, autonomous, independent, self-active, self-acting; **unforced,** uncoerced, unpressured, unrequired, uncompelled; unprompted, uninfluenced

opulence NOUNS **wealth,** riches, opulency, luxuriousness; richness, wealthiness; **prosperity,** prosperousness, **affluence,** comfortable *or* easy circumstances, independence; **money,** lucre, pelf, gold, mammon; **substance,** property, possessions, material wealth; **assets; fortune,** treasure, handsome fortune; *embarras de richesses* <Fr>, money to burn <nonformal>

opulent ADJS **luxuriant,** fertile, productive, **rich,** fat, **wealthy,** affluent

opus NOUNS publication, writing, **work,** production; opusculum, opuscule; **piece,** composition, production, work; **masterwork,** masterpiece, *chef d'œuvre* <Fr>, *Meisterstück* <Ger>

oracle NOUNS **master,** mistress, authority, mastermind, master spirit of the age; Delphic *or* Delphian oracle, Python, Pythian oracle; Delphic tripod, tripod of the Pythia; Dodona, oracle *or* oak of Dodona

oral NOUNS 1 **examination,** school examination, examen, **exam** <nonformal>, **test, quiz;** oral examination
ADJS 2 **speech; spoken,** uttered, said, vocalized, **voiced,** verbalized, pronounced, sounded, articulated, enunciated; vocal, voiceful; verbal, **unwritten,** *viva voce* <L>, nuncupative, parol

orate VERBS **declaim,** hold forth, elocute <nonformal>, spout <nonformal>, spiel <nonformal>, mouth; **harangue, rant,** tub-thump, perorate, rodomontade; demagogue, rabble-rouse

oration NOUNS **speech,** speeching, speechification <nonformal>, **talk, address,** declamation, harangue; public speech *or* address, formal speech; campaign speech, stump speech; **tirade,** screed, **diatribe,** jeremiad, philippic, invective; after-dinner speech; funeral oration, eulogy; allocution, exhortation, hortatory address; salutatory, salutatory address; valediction, valedictory, valedictory address; inaugural address, inaugural; peroration

orator NOUNS **public speaker,** platform orator *or* speaker; rhetorician, rhetor; silver-tongued orator, spellbinder; **soapbox orator,** soapboxer, stump orator

oratory NOUNS 1 **public speaking,** declamation, speechmaking, speaking,

speechification <nonformal>, lecturing, speeching; after-dinner speaking; platform oratory *or* speaking; campaign oratory, stump speaking, the stump, the hustings; the soap box; **elocution; rhetoric,** art of public speaking; **eloquence**; forensics, **debating; preaching,** pulpit oratory, Bible-thumping <nonformal>, the pulpit, homiletics
2 **chapel,** oratorium; chantry; sacellum, sacrarium

orb NOUNS **sphere,** hemisphere, **orbit,** ambit, circle; **circuit,** judicial circuit, **beat, round,** walk; **realm,** demesne, **domain,** dominion, jurisdiction, bailiwick; **province,** precinct, department; **field,** pale, arena

orbit NOUNS 1 **sphere of influence,** orb, ambit; bailiwick, vantage, stamping ground, footing, **territory,** turf, home turf, constituency, power base
2 **circuit,** round, revolution, **circle,** full circle, go-round, **cycle; trajectory;** circle of the sphere, great circle, small circle
VERBS 3 **circle, circuit,** describe a circle, make a circuit, move in a circle, **circulate; go round** *or* **around,** go about; **wheel,** round; make a pass; come full circle, close the circle, make a round trip, return to the starting point; circumnavigate, girdle, girdle the globe

ordain VERBS 1 **install,** instate, inaugurate, initiate, invest; frock, **canonize, consecrate;** saint
2 **command,** order, dictate, direct, instruct, mandate, **bid,** enjoin, charge, commission, call on *or* upon; **decree,** rule, promulgate; **proclaim,** declare, pronounce; **destine,** predestine, necessitate, fate, mark, appoint; constitute, establish, put in force

ordained ADJS 1 in orders, in holy orders, of the cloth
2 **destined, fated,** fateful, written, in the cards, marked, in store; **doomed,** foredoomed, devoted; inevitable

ordeal NOUNS **trial, tribulation,** trials and tribulations; fiery ordeal, the iron entering the soul; crucial test; acid test, litmus test; crucible

order NOUNS 1 **harmony,** proportion, symmetry, **balance,** equilibrium, orderedness, measure, measuredness, concinnity
2 **fellowship,** sodality; **society,** guild; **brotherhood,** fraternity, confraternity, confrerie, fraternal order *or* society; **sisterhood,** sorority; **sect,** sectarism, religious order, **denomination,** persuasion, faction, **church,** communion, community, group, affiliation, school, party, body, organization
3 **sequence,** logical sequence, **succession,** successiveness, consecution, **consecutiveness,** following, coming after; descent, lineage, line; order of succession; **priority**
VERBS 4 **command,** dictate, direct, instruct, mandate, **bid,** enjoin, charge, commission, call on *or* upon; issue a writ *or* an injunction; **decree,** rule, ordain, promulgate; give an order *or* a direct order, issue a command, say the word, give the word *or* word of command; call the shots *or* tune *or* signals *or* play <nonformal>; order about *or* around; put in *or* place an order, order up
5 **arrange,** reduce to order, **put** *or* **get** *or* **set in order,** right, prioritize, put first things first, get one's ducks in a row <nonformal>; **put** *or* **set to rights,** get it together <nonformal>, **pull it together,** put in *or* into shape, whip into shape <nonformal>, sort out <chiefly Brit>, unsnarl, make sense out of <nonformal>

orderly ADJS ordered, **regular,** well-regulated, well-ordered, methodical, formal, regular as clockwork, uniform, **systematic,** symmetrical, **harmonious;** businesslike, routine, steady, normal, habitual, usual, en règle, in hand; **arranged**

ordinance NOUNS **law;** imperative, **regulation,** *règlement* <Fr>; **decree,** decretum, decretal, rescript, fiat, **edict,** *edictum* <L>; *ordonnance* <Fr>; **proclamation,** pronouncement, pronunciamento, **declaration,** ukase; bull, diktat

ordinary ADJS **average,** normal, **common, commonplace,** garden *and* garden-variety <both nonformal>, run-of-the-mill; **unexceptional,** unremarkable, unnoteworthy, unspectacular, nothing *or* nobody special *and* no great shakes <all nonformal>; conventional

ordnance NOUNS **arms, weapons,** deadly weapons, instruments of destruction, offensive weapons, **military hardware,** matériel, **weaponry,** armament, munitions, munitions of war, *apparatus belli* <L>; **artillery, cannon,** cannonry, engines of war

organic ADJS **anatomic,** anatomical,

organismal; organized; **animate, living,** vital, zoetic; **biological,** biotic; physiological; **constitutional,** bodily, physical, temperamental; connate, connatal, coeval; **instinctive,** instinctual, atavistic, primal

organism NOUNS organization, organic being, life-form, form of life, **living being** *or* **thing,** being, creature, created being, **individual,** genetic individual, physiological individual, morphological individual; zoon, zooid; virus; aerobic organism, anaerobic organism; heterotrophic organism, autotrophic organism; microbe, microorganism

organization NOUNS 1 establishment, foundation, institution, institute; **composition,** constitution, construction, formation, fabrication, fashioning, shaping; **methodization,** ordering, planning, charting, codification, regulation, regularization, routinization, normalization, rationalization; **systematization,** ordination, coordination

organize VERBS methodize, **systematize,** rationalize, regularize, get *or* put one's house in order; **harmonize,** synchronize, **tune,** tune up; **regularize,** routinize, normalize, standardize; **regulate,** adjust, coordinate, fix, settle; **plan,** chart, codify; **establish, found,** constitute, institute, install, form, **set up,** equip, endow, inaugurate, realize, materialize, effect, effectuate; **unionize**

organized ADJS **arranged,** ordered, disposed, configured, composed, constituted, fixed, placed, aligned, ranged, arrayed, marshaled, grouped, ranked, **graded;** methodized, **regularized,** routinized, normalized, standardized, **systematized;** regulated, harmonized, synchronized; **classified**, categorized, **sorted,** assorted; **orderly**

organized crime NOUNS **the underworld,** gangland, gangdom, organized crime family, the rackets, the mob, the syndicate, the Mafia, Cosa Nostra

organizer NOUNS **planner, designer,** deviser, contriver, framer, projector; enterpriser, entrepreneuer; promoter, developer, expediter, facilitator, animator; **founder,** founding father, founding *or* founder member, founding partner, cofounder; union *or* labor organizer

orgy NOUNS **debauch,** saturnalia; **frenzy,** orgasm; madness, craze, **delirium,** hysteria

orientation NOUNS **habituation,** accustoming; conditioning, seasoning, training; **familiarization,** breaking-in <nonformal>; acclimation, acclimatization; adaption, adjustment, accommodation, adaptation; alignment, collimation; **bearings**

origin NOUNS origination, **genesis, inception,** incipience *or* incipiency, inchoation; **divine creation,** creationism, creation science; **birth,** birthing, bearing, parturition, pregnancy, nascency *or* nascence, nativity; **source,** origination, **derivation,** rise, beginning, conception, commencement

original ADJS **novel,** unprecedented; unique, *sui generis* <L>; new, fresh; underived, **firsthand; authentic,** genuine, veridic, veridical; imaginative, creative; **avant-garde,** revolutionary; **pioneer,** bellwether, trail-blazing

originate VERBS **invent, conceive,** discover, make up, devise, contrive, concoct, fabricate, coin, mint, frame, hatch, hatch *or* cook up, strike out; think up, think out, dream up, **design,** plan, set one's wits to work; **generate, develop,** mature, **evolve;** engender, beget, spawn, hatch, bring forth, give rise to, bring *or* call into being; procreate

ornament NOUNS 1 ornamentation, **adornment,** embellishment, elegant variation, **embroidery, frill,** colors *or* colors of rhetoric <both old>, figure, figure of speech; musical flourish, ruffles and flourishes, grace note
VERBS 2 **decorate,** adorn, dress, trim, garnish, array, **deck,** bedeck, bedizen; **redecorate,** refurbish, redo; gimmick *or* glitz *or* sex up <nonformal>; **embellish, furbish,** embroider, enrich, grace, set off *or* out, paint, color, blazon, emblazon, paint in glowing colors; **gild,** gild the lily, trick out, varnish; **dress up; spruce up** *and* gussy up *and* doll up *and* fix up <all nonformal>, **primp up,** prink up, prank up, trick up *or* out, deck out; smarten, smarten up, dandify, titivate

ornamental ADJS **decorative,** adorning, embellishing

ornate ADJS **elegant, fancy,** fine, chichi, pretty-pretty; picturesque; **elaborate,** overornate, labored; **ostentatious**; **rich,** luxurious, luxuriant; **flowery,** florid; flamboyant, fussy, frilly, frilled, befrilled, flouncy, gingerbread *or* gingerbready; **overelegant,** overelaborate, overlabored, overworked, overwrought, overornamented, busy; cluttered; **baroque,** rococo, arabesque, moresque; purple, colored, adorned, **embellished, embroidered,** lavish, festooned

ornery ADJS **perverse,** contrary, wrong-headed, wayward, froward, difficult, cross-grained, cantankerous, feisty; sullen, sulky, stuffy; irascible

orphan NOUNS abandonee, waif, dogie <nonformal>; foundling; wastrel, reject, **discard**

orthodox ADJS of the faith, of the true faith; **sound,** firm, faithful, true, true-blue, right-thinking; **evangelical; scriptural,** canonical; traditional, traditionalistic; literal, textual; standard, customary, conventional; **authoritative,** authentic, accepted, received, approved; correct, right, proper

oscillate VERBS **vibrate,** librate, nutate; pendulate; **fluctuate,** vacillate, waver, wave; resonate; **swing,** sway, swag, dangle, **reel,** rock, lurch, roll, careen, toss, pitch; **wag,** waggle; **wobble,** wamble; shake, flutter

ostentatious ADJS **pretentious; ambitious,** vaunting, lofty, highfalutin *and* highfaluting <both nonformal>, **high-flown,** high-flying; **high-toned,** tony <both nonformal>, **fancy,** classy <nonformal>, flossy <nonformal>, gaudy, glitzy <nonformal>, meretricious, flamboyant, flaming, bedizened, flaunting, garish

ostracize VERBS turn thumbs down; **reject,** exile, banish; **proscribe,** ban, outlaw, put under the ban; **boycott,** blackball, blacklist, snub, cut, give the cold shoulder, send to Coventry, give the silent treatment; **excommunicate**

other ADJS **another,** whole nother <nonformal>, else, otherwise, other than *or* from; not the same, not the type <nonformal>, not that sort, of another sort, of a sort *and* of sorts <both nonformal>; **fresh,** additional, further; **substitute,** alternate, alternative, tother <nonformal>, equivalent, token, dummy, pinch, utility, backup, secondary

otherwise ADVS in other ways, **in other respects;** elsewise, else, or else; than; other than; **on the other hand;** contrarily; alias

otherworldly ADJS **heavenly;** extraterrestrial, extramundane, transmundane, transcendental; Elysian, Olympian; **unearthly,** unworldly, eerie; fey; starry-eyed, dewy-eyed; in the clouds, with one's head in the clouds; airy; supernatural; **occult**

oust VERBS **eject,** expel, discharge, extrude, obtrude, detrude, exclude, **reject,** cast, remove; **bounce** *and* give the hook <both nonformal>, **put out, turn out,** thrust out; **throw out,** run out <nonformal>, cast out, chuck out, **evict,** dislodge, dispossess, put out, turn out, **turn out of doors,** turn out of house and home, turn *or* put out bag and baggage, throw into the street; unhouse, unkennel

out NOUNS 1 **excuse,** cop-out *and* alibi <both nonformal>; lame excuse, poor excuse, likely story; escape hatch, way out
ADJS 2 **asleep,** sleeping, **sound asleep,** fast asleep, in a sound sleep, flaked-out <nonformal>; **unconscious,** oblivious, out like a light, out cold; comatose; **dead to the world;** drugged, narcotized; doped *and* stoned *and* spaced out *and* strung out *and* zonked *and* zonked out *and* out of it <all nonformal>; **dead-drunk,** blind drunk, overcome, passed out <nonformal>, under the table
3 **extinguished,** quenched, snuffed; contained, under control
ADVS 4 outward, outwards, outwardly; **without,** outside
5 **at a loss, unprofitably,** to the bad <nonformal>; in the red <nonformal>; out-of-pocket

outback NOUNS **hinterland,** back country, up-country, boonies *and* boondocks <both nonformal>; **the bush,** bush country, bushveld, **woods,** woodlands, **backwoods,** forests, timbers, the big sticks <nonformal>, brush; wilderness, wilds, uninhabited region, virgin land *or* territory; **wasteland**; **frontier,** borderland, outpost

outburst NOUNS outburst of anger, burst, **explosion,** eruption, blowup *and* **flare-up** <both nonformal>, access, blaze of temper; **storm, scene,** high words

outcast NOUNS social outcast, outcast of society, **castaway, derelict,** Ishmael; **pariah,** untouchable, leper; outcaste; *déclassé* <Fr>; **outlaw; expellee,** evictee; displaced person *or* DP; exile, expatriate, man without a country; undesirable; *persona non grata* <L>, unacceptable person

outcome NOUNS **event, eventuality,** eventuation, effect, issue, result, denouement, end, end result, aftermath, **upshot,** logical outcome, possible outcome, scenario; consequence; **realization,** materialization, coming to be *or* pass, incidence

outcry NOUNS **vociferation,** clamor; hullabaloo, hubbub, brouhaha, uproar; **hue and cry**

outdated ADJS **old-fashioned,** old-fangled, old-timey <nonformal>, **dated,** out, out-of-date, **outmoded,** obsolete, out of style *or* fashion, out of use, disused, out of season, **unfashionable,** styleless, **behind the times,** of the old school, old hat *and* back-number *and* has-been <all nonformal>; superannuated, superannuate

outdo VERBS **outrival,** outvie, outachieve, edge out, **outclass, outshine,** overmatch, outgun <nonformal>; **outstrip,** outgo, outrange, outreach, outpoint, **outperform;** outplay, outmaneuver, outwit; outrun, outstep, outpace, outmarch, run rings *or* circles around <nonformal>; outride, outjump, outleap, outgeneral, outpoint, outsail, outfight

outdoor ADJS **out-of-door,** out-of-doors, **outside,** without-doors; open-air, alfresco; out and about

outdoors NOUNS outside, **the out-of-doors,** the great out-of-doors, the open, **the open air;** outland

outfit NOUNS 1 **costume,** costumery, character dress; getup *and* rig <both nonformal>; masquerade, disguise; **apparatus,** rig, machinery; paraphernalia, things, **gear, stuff** <nonformal>, impedimenta <pl>, **tackle; kit,** duffel, effects, personal effects
VERBS 2 **equip, furnish,** gear, prepare, fit, fit up *or* out, fix up <nonformal>, **rig,** rig up *or* out, **turn out,** appoint, accouter, clothe, dress

outgoing ADJS **unreserved,** unreticent, unshrinking, **unrestrained,** unconstrained, unhampered, unrestricted; demonstrative, expansive, effusive; **accessible, approachable,** conversable, easy to speak to; **extroverted**

outgrowth NOUNS **effect, result,** resultant, **consequence,** consequent, sequent, sequence, sequel, sequela, sequelae; event, eventuality, eventuation, **upshot, outcome,** logical outcome, possible outcome, scenario; **spin-off,** offshoot, offspring, issue, aftermath, legacy; derivative, derivation, by-product

outhouse NOUNS **latrine,** convenience, **toilet, john** *and* johnny *and* **can** *and* crapper <all nonformal>; loo <Brit nonformal>; privy, backhouse, shithouse <nonformal>

outing NOUNS 1 **excursion,** jaunt, junket, pleasure trip; day-trip
2 **disclosure,** disclosing; **revelation,** revealment, revealing, making public, publicizing, broadcasting

outlandish ADJS **strange,** off-the-wall <informal>, surreal, not for real <nonformal>, passing strange; **fantastic, fantastical,** fantasque, extravagant, preposterous, wild, baroque, rococo, florid; Alice-in-Wonderland, bizarre, grotesque

outlast VERBS **outstay,** last out, outwear, **outlive,** survive; **outtalk,** outspeak, **talk down,** filibuster

outlaw NOUNS 1 **criminal,** felon, **crook** <nonformal>, lawbreaker, perpetrator, perp <nonformal>, gangster *and* mobster <both nonformal>, racketeer, thief
VERBS 2 **prohibit, forbid; disallow,** rule out *or* against; **bar,** debar, preclude, exclude, exclude from, shut out, shut *or* close the door on, **prevent; ban, proscribe,** inhibit, interdict, put *or* lay under an interdict *or* interdiction

outlay NOUNS **spendings,** disbursements, payments, outgoings, outgo, outflow, money going out

outlet NOUNS egress, **exit,** outgo, outcome, out <nonformal>, way out; loophole, escape; **opening**; outfall, estuary; chute, flume, sluice, weir, floodgate; **vent,** ventage, venthole, port; **exhaust;** door

outline NOUNS 1 **contour,** delineation, lines, lineaments, shapes, figure, figuration, **configuration,** gestalt; **features,** main features; **profile,** silhouette
2 **plan,** scheme, schema, chart, flow chart, graph; table of contents
VERBS 3 contour; **delineate;** silhouette, profile, limn; **sketch,** sketch out, hit the high spots; capsule, capsulize, encapsulate; **put in a nutshell**

outlook NOUNS mental outlook; *Anschauung* <Ger>, **point of view,** viewpoint, standpoint, **perspective,** *optique* <Fr>; position, stand, place, situation; side; footing, basis; where one is *or* sits *or* stands; **view,** sight, light, eye; respect, regard; **frame of reference,** intellectual *or* ideational frame of reference, framework, arena, world, universe, world *or* universe of discourse, system, reference system

out of order ADJS **in disrepair, malfunctioning,** out of working order, out of condition, out of repair, inoperative; **out of kilter** *or* **kelter** <nonformal>, out of whack <nonformal>, out of gear, on the fritz <nonformal>, on the blink *and* haywire <both nonformal>

out-of-pocket ADJS **at a loss,** unprofitably, to the bad <nonformal>; in the red <nonformal>; out, short, **short of money** *or* **funds** *or* **cash**

out of shape ADJS **out of practice,** out of training *or* form, soft <nonformal>, out of condition, stiff, **rusty;** gone *or* run to seed *and* over the hill *and* not what one used to be <all nonformal>, losing one's touch, slipping, on the downgrade

out-of-the-way ADJS godforsaken, back of beyond, upcountry; **out of reach,** inaccessible, remote, ungetatable, unapproachable, untouchable, hyperborean, antipodean; **unfrequented,** unvisited, off the beaten track; untraveled

outpouring NOUNS **overflow,** flood, inundation, flow, shower, spate, stream, gush, avalanche; **prevalence,** profuseness, **profusion,** riot; **superabundance;** an ample sufficiency, enough and to spare, enough and then some

output NOUNS **yield,** make, production; **proceeds,** produce, product; **crop, harvest,** fruit, vintage, bearing; second crop, aftermath; bumper crop

outrage NOUNS 1 **injustice,** wrong, injury, grievance, disservice; raw *or* rotten deal *and* bad rap <all nonformal>; imposition; mockery *or* miscarriage of justice; great wrong, grave *or* gross injustice; atrocity, enormity
VERBS 2 **offend, affront,** give offense to, disoblige, step *or* tread on one's toes; dishonor, humiliate, treat with indignity; flout, mock, jeer at, scoff at, fleer at, gibe at, taunt; **insult,** call names, kick *or* slap in the face, take *or* pluck by the beard; **add insult to injury**

outrageous ADJS **disgraceful, shameful,** pitiful, deplorable, opprobrious, sad, sorry, too bad; degrading, debasing, demeaning, beneath one, beneath one's dignity, *infra indignitatem* <L>, infra dig <nonformal>, unbecoming, unworthy of one; cheap, gutter; **humiliating,** humiliative; **scandalous,** shocking, incredible, beyond belief, *outré* <Fr>

outset NOUNS **beginning,** commencement, start, running *or* flying start, starting point, square one <nonformal>, outbreak, **onset,** oncoming

outside NOUNS 1 **exterior,** external, surface
2 **outdoors,** the out-of-doors, the great out-of-doors, the open, **the open air**
ADJS 3 **exterior,** external; extrinsic; **outer,** out, outward, outward-facing, outlying, outstanding; **outermost,** outmost; surface, superficial, epidermic, cortical; cosmetic, merely cosmetic
4 **outdoor,** out-of-door, out-of-doors, without-doors; open-air, alfresco; out and about
ADVS 5 **outdoors,** out of doors, abroad; in the open, **in the open air,** alfresco, *en plein air* <Fr>

outsider NOUNS **alien, stranger,** foreigner, non-member, not one of us, not our sort, not the right sort, the other, outlander, *Uitlander* <Afrikaans>, tramontane, ultramontane, barbarian, foreign devil <China>, *gringo* <Sp Amer>

outsmart VERBS **outwit, outfox,** outguess, outfigure, **outmaneuver,** outgeneral, outflank, outplay; get the better *or* best of, go one better; pull a fast one <nonformal>, steal a march on; make a fool of, make a sucker *or* patsy of <nonformal>; be too much for, throw a curve <nonformal>

outspoken ADJS **communicative, open,** free, free-speaking, free-spoken, free-tongued; candid, frank; direct, bluff, blunt

outstanding ADJS 1 **eminent, prominent,** standout, high, elevated, towering, soaring, overtopping, exalted, **lofty,** sublime; august, majestic, noble, distinguished; **magnificent,** magnanimous, heroic, godlike, superb; famous, renowned, lauded, glorious
2 **remaining, surviving,** extant, vestigial, over, left, **leftover,** still around, remnant, remanent, odd; **spare,** to spare; unused, unconsumed; **surplus,** superfluous; unmet, unresolved

outward ADJS 1 **exterior,** external; **outer,** outside, out, outward-facing, outlying, outstanding; **outermost,** outmost; surface, superficial; apparent, seeming; open, public
ADVS 2 **forth; out,** outwards, outwardly

outwit VERBS **outfox, outsmart,** outguess, outfigure, **outmaneuver,** outgeneral, outflank, outplay; get the better *or* best of; get round *or* around, **evade,** stonewall <nonformal>, **elude, frustrate, foil,** give the slip *or* runaround <nonformal>; pull a fast one <nonformal>, steal a march on; be too much for, be too deep for; throw a curve <nonformal>

oval ADJS ovate, ovoid, oviform, egg-shaped, obovate

ovation NOUNS **applause,** plaudit, éclat, **acclaim, acclamation;** popularity; clap, handclap, **clapping,** handclapping, clapping of hands; **cheer**; burst of applause, peal *or* thunder of applause; **round of applause,** hand, big hand; standing ovation

oven NOUNS **kiln,** stove, furnace

over ADJS 1 **higher,** superior, greater; **above;** upper, upmost *or* uppermost, outtopping, overtopping
2 **past, gone,** by, gone-by, bygone, gone glimmering, bypast, ago, departed, passed, passed away, elapsed, lapsed, vanished, faded, no more, irrecoverable, never to return, not coming back; over and above; extra, spare, supernumerary
ADVS 3 **again,** over again, **once more,** *encore, bis* <both Fr>, two times, twice over, ditto; **anew,** *de novo* <L>, afresh; from the beginning, *da capo* <Ital>
4 **excessively,** inordinately, immoderately, intemperately, overweeningly, hubristically, **overly,** overmuch, too much; **too,** too-too <nonformal>; **exorbitantly,** unduly, unreasonably, unconscionably, outrageously

overact VERBS overdramatize, chew up the scenery <nonformal>, act all over the stage; **ham** *and* ham it up <both nonformal>; **mug** <nonformal>, grimace; spout, rant, roar, declaim; milk a scene

overactive ADJS hyperactive, hyper <nonformal>; hectic, frenzied, frantic, frenetic; hyperkinetic; intrusive, officious

overall ADVS **throughout,** all over, inside and out, through and through; **at full length,** *in extenso* <L>, *ad infinitum* <L>; every inch, every whit, every bit; **in every respect,** in all respects, you name it <nonformal>; **on all counts,** at all points, for good and all

overbearing ADJS **arrogant, superior,** domineering, proud, haughty; lofty, toplofty <nonformal>; high-nosed *and* stuck-up *and* uppish *and* uppity *and* upstage <all nonformal>; **hoity-toity,** big, big as you please, six feet above contradiction; **condescending,** patronizing, *de haut en bas* <Fr>

overcast ADJS **cloudy,** nebulous, nubilous, nimbose, nebulosus; **clouded,** overclouded; dirty, heavy, lowering *or* louring; dark; **gloomy,** glooming, dark and gloomy, Acheronian, Acherontic, **somber,** sombrous

overcharge NOUNS 1 surcharge, overassessment; gouging *or* price-gouging, highway robbery <nonformal>
VERBS 2 **overprice,** set the price tag too high; surcharge, overtax; **hold up** *and* **soak** *and* **stick** *and* **sting** *and* **clip** <all nonformal>, make pay through the nose, gouge; victimize, swindle; exploit, skin <nonformal>, **fleece,** screw *and* put the screws to <both nonformal>, bleed, bleed white; profiteer

overcoat NOUNS **outerwear; coat,** greatcoat, **topcoat,** surcoat

overcome VERBS 1 **unnerve,** undo, unstring, unbrace, reduce to jelly, **demoralize,** shake, upset, psych out <nonformal>, dash, knock down *or* flat, **crush,** prostrate
2 surmount; **overpower, overmaster,** overmatch; **overthrow, overturn,** overset; put the skids to <nonformal>; **upset,** trip, trip up, lay by the heels, send flying *or* sprawling; silence, floor, deck, make bite the dust; overcome oneself, master oneself; kick the habit <nonformal>
ADJS 3 crushed, borne-down, overwhelmed, inundated, **stricken,** cut up <nonformal>, **desolated,** prostrate *or* prostrated, broken-down, undone; **heart-stricken,** heart-struck; **brokenhearted,** heartbroken

overcrowded ADJS **teeming, swarming,** crowding, thronging, overflowing, overwhelming, bursting, **crawling, alive with,** lousy with <nonformal>, populous, prolific, proliferating, crowded, packed, jammed, bumper-to-bumper <nonformal>, jam-packed, like sardines in a can <nonformal>, thronged, studded, bristling, rife, lavish, prodigal, superabundant, **profuse,** in profusion, thick, **thick with,** thick-coming, thick as flies

overdo VERBS **go too far,** do it to death <nonformal>, pass all bounds, know no bounds, overact, **carry too far,** overcarry, go to an extreme, **go to extremes,** go overboard, go *or* jump off the deep end; **run** *or* **drive into the ground; overemphasize,** overstress; overplay, overplay one's hand <nonformal>; **overreact,** protest too much; overreach oneself; **overtax,** overtask, overexert, overexercise, overstrain, overdrive, overspend, exhaust, overexpend, overuse; burn the candle at both ends; **spread oneself too thin,** take on too much, have too much on one's plate, have too many irons in the fire; exaggerate; **overindulge**

overdue ADJS **late,** belated, tardy, slow, slow on the draw *or* uptake *or* trigger <all nonformal>, **behindhand,** never on time, backward, back, **long-awaited,** untimely; unpunctual, unready; latish; **delayed,** detained, **held up** <nonformal>, retarded, arrested, blocked, hung up *and* in a bind <both nonformal>, obstructed, stopped, jammed, congested; weather-bound

overeat VERBS overgorge, **overindulge,** make a pig *or* hog of oneself, pig out *or* pork out *or* scarf out <nonformal>; stuff oneself

overflow NOUNS 1 spillage, spill, spillover, overflowing, overrunning, alluvion, alluvium, **inundation, flood,** deluge, whelming, overwhelming, engulfment, submersion, cataclysm; **outpouring,** superabundance; enough and to spare, enough and then some
VERBS 2 flow over, wash over, **run over, well over,** brim over, lap, lap at, lap over, overbrim, overrun, pour out *or* over, **spill,** slop, slosh, spill out *or* over; **cataract,** cascade; inundate

overgrown ADJS 1 **gigantic,** mountainous, titanic, colossal, mammoth, Gargantuan, gigantesque, monster, monstrous, outsize, sizable, larger-than-life, king-size, monumental; hypertrophied
2 **luxuriant,** flourishing, **rank,** dense, impenetrable, thick, heavy, gross; jungly, jungled; overrun; **weedy,** unweeded, weed-choked, weed-ridden

overhang NOUNS 1 **overhanging,** impendence *or* impendency, **projection,** beetling, jutting; cantilever
VERBS 2 hang over, hang out, **impend,** impend over, **project,** project over, beetle, **jut,** beetle *or* jut *or* thrust over, stick out over; **overlie,** lie over
3 **be imminent,** loom, hang over one's head, hover

overhaul NOUNS 1 **repair,** repairing, **fixing,** mending, making *or* setting right, repair work; servicing, maintenance; overhauling
2 VERBS **repair,** mend, fix, fix up <nonformal>, do up, doctor <nonformal>, put in repair, put in shape, set to rights, put in order *or* condition; **recondition,** put in commission, ready; **service**

overhead NOUNS 1 **expenses, costs,** charges, disbursals, liabilities; expense, cost, burden of expenditure; operating expense *or* expenses *or* costs *or* budget, general expenses
ADVS 2 **on high,** high up, high; **aloft,** aloof; **up,** upward, upwards, straight up, to the zenith; **above, over,** o'er

overhear VERBS **hear,** catch, get <nonformal>, take in; **hear of,** hear tell of <nonformal>; get an earful <nonformal>, get wind of

overjoyed ADJS overjoyful, overhappy, brimming *or* bursting with happiness, on top of the world; **rapturous,** raptured, **enraptured,** enchanted, entranced, enravished, ravished, rapt, possessed; sent *and* high *and* freaked-out <all nonformal>, **in raptures,** transported, in a transport of delight, **carried away,** beside oneself, beside oneself with joy, in seventh heaven, on cloud nine <nonformal>; **elated,** elate, exalted, jubilant, exultant, flushed

overkill NOUNS **overdoing,** overcarrying, **overreaching,** supererogation; piling on <nonformal>, overimportance, overemphasis; overuse; overreaction; too much on one's plate, too many irons in the fire, too much at once

overlap VERBS **overlie,** lie over; lap, **lap over,** override, imbricate, jut, shingle; **extend over,** span, bridge, bestride, bestraddle, arch over, overarch, hang over, overhang

overlook VERBS 1 **condone,** disregard, ignore, accept, take *and* swallow *and* let go <all nonformal>, pass over, give one another chance, let one off this time *and* let one off easy <both nonformal>, close *or* shut one's eyes to, **blink** *or* **wink at,** connive at; allow for, make allowances for; bear with, endure, regard with indulgence; pocket the affront, leave unavenged, turn the other cheek, bury *or* hide one's head in the sand

2 **slight, ignore,** pooh-pooh <nonformal>, make little of, dismiss, pretend not to see, disregard, neglect, miss, pass by, pass up *and* give the go-by <both nonformal>, leave out in the cold <nonformal>, take no note *or* notice of, look right through <nonformal>, pay no attention *or* regard to, refuse to acknowledge *or* recognize

overpowering ADJS **irresistible,** overcoming, overwhelming, overmastering, overmatching, avalanchine

overpriced ADJS grossly overpriced, **exorbitant,** excessive, extravagant, inordinate, immoderate, undue, unwarranted, unreasonable, fancy, unconscionable, outrageous, preposterous, out of bounds, out of sight <nonformal>, **prohibitive; extortionate,** cutthroat, gouging, usurious

overrated ADJS **overestimated,** puffed up, pumped up <nonformal>, overvalued, on the high side; **exaggerated**

overreact VERBS make a Federal case out of it <nonformal>, make something out of nothing, make a mountain out of a molehill, protest too much

overriding ADJS **paramount,** highest, uppermost, topmost, toprank, ranking, of the first rank, world-class, **dominant,** predominant, master, controlling, **overruling,** all-absorbing

overrule VERBS **repeal,** revoke, rescind, reverse, strike down, abrogate; suspend; **waive,** set aside; countermand, counterorder; **cancel,** write off; **annul,** nullify, disannul, withdraw, **invalidate,** void, vacate, make void, declare null and void; override

overseas ADVS **abroad,** in foreign parts; **oversea,** beyond seas, over the water, transmarine, across the sea; on one's travels

oversee VERBS **supervise,** superintend, boss, ride herd on <nonformal>, stand over, keep an eye on *or* upon, keep in order; straw-boss <nonformal>; take care of

overshadow VERBS **eclipse,** throw into the shade, top, extinguish, take the shine out of <nonformal>; put to shame, show up <nonformal>, put one's nose out of joint, put down <nonformal>, fake out <nonformal>; **command,** dominate, overarch, command a view of; bestride, bestraddle

oversight NOUNS 1 **neglect,** neglectfulness, **negligence,** inadvertence *or* inadvertency, malperformance, dereliction, *culpa* <L>, culpable negligence, criminal negligence; **remissness,** laxity, laxness, slackness, looseness, laches; unrigorousness; **inattention;** overlooking; **omission,** nonfeasance, nonperformance, lapse, failure, **default;** poor stewardship *or* guardianship *or* custody

2 **supervision,** superintendence, **surveillance,** eye; **charge,** care, auspices, jurisdiction; responsibility, accountability

overspend VERBS spend more than one has, spend what one hasn't got; overdraw, overdraw one's account, live beyond one's means, have champagne tastes on a beer budget

overstep VERBS **transgress, trespass,** intrude, break bounds, overstep the bounds, go too far, know no bounds, **encroach, infringe,** invade, irrupt, make an inroad *or* incursion *or* intrusion, advance upon; usurp

overt ADJS **open,** open to all, open as day, out of the closet <nonformal>; **revealed,** disclosed, exposed; bare, bald, naked

overtake VERBS **outstrip, overhaul,** catch up, **catch up with,** come up with *or* to, gain on *or* upon, pass, lap; outpace, outrun, outsail; leave behind, leave standing *or* looking *or* flatfooted

overthrow VERBS **overturn; upset,** overset, upend, **subvert,** throw down *or* over; undermine, honeycomb, **sap,** sap the foundations, **weaken**

overtone NOUNS **meaning, signification,** emotive *or* affective meaning, coloration, coloring, tinge, undertone, undercurrent, intimation, touch, nuance, innuendo; connotation, **implication, import,** latent *or* underlying *or* implied meaning, ironic suggestion *or* implication, more than meets the eye, what is read between the lines

overture NOUNS 1 **prelude,** *Vorspiel* <Ger>, **introduction,** operatic overture, dramatic overture, concert overture, voluntary, descant, vamp; curtain raiser

2 **offer, advance,** approach, invitation; hesitant *or* tentative *or* preliminary approach, feeling-out, **feeler** <nonformal>

overview NOUNS **abstract,** epitome, **précis,** capsule, nutshell *or* capsule version, capsulization, encapsulation, sketch, thumbnail sketch, **synopsis,** conspectus, syllabus, *aperçu* <Fr>, **survey,** review, pandect, bird's-eye view

overweight ADJS **corpulent, stout,** fat, fattish, **obese,** adipose, gross, fleshy, beefy, meaty, hefty, porky, porcine; **heavyset,** thickset, chubby, chunky <nonformal>, dumpy; pyknic, endomorphic, overheavy; overfleshed, overstout, overfat, overplump, overfed

overwhelmed ADJS 1 **overcome,** crushed, borne-down, inundated, **stricken,** cut up <nonformal>, **desolated,** prostrate *or* prostrated, broken-down, undone; **heart-stricken,** heart-struck; **broken-hearted,** heartbroken; **astonished,** amazed, surprised, astounded, flabbergasted <nonformal>, **bewildered,** puzzled, confounded, **dumbfounded,** dumbstruck, staggered, unable to believe one's senses *or* eyes
2 **defeated,** worsted, bested, outdone; beaten, discomfited, put to rout, **routed,** scattered, stampeded, panicked; confounded; **overcome,** overthrown, upset, overturned, overmatched, **overpowered,** whelmed, **overmastered,** overborne, overridden; **undone,** done for <nonformal>, **ruined,** kaput *and* on the skids <both nonformal>, *hors de combat* <Fr>

overwhelming ADJS **exciting,** overpowering, overcoming, overmastering, more than flesh and blood can bear; **astonishing,** amazing, surprising, startling, **astounding,** confounding, staggering, stunning <nonformal>, eye-opening, breathtaking, mind-boggling *or* -numbing; incontrovertible, irresistible, indisputable, irrefutable, sure, certain, absolute

owe VERBS **be indebted,** be obliged *or* obligated for, be financially committed, lie under an obligation, be bound to pay

owing ADJS **due,** owed, payable, receivable, redeemable, mature, **outstanding, unpaid,** in arrear *or* arrears, back

own VERBS **have title to,** have for one's own *or* very own, have to one's name, call one's own, have the deed for, hold in fee simple

owner NOUNS **proprietor,** proprietary; *rentier* <Fr>; titleholder, deedholder; proprietress, proprietrix; **master,** mistress, lord, laird <Scots>

ownership NOUNS **title,** possessorship, *dominium* <L>, **proprietorship,** proprietary, property right *or* rights; **dominion,** sovereignty; landownership, landowning, landholding, land tenure

oxymoron NOUNS self-contradiction, **paradox**, antinomy, ambivalence, **irony,** enantiosis, equivocation, **ambiguity**, absurdity, logical impossibility

P

pacifier NOUNS **soother,** comforter, peacemaker, pacificator, dove of peace, mollifier; **moderator,** mitigator, modulator, stabilizer, temperer, assuager; **mediator,** bridge-builder, calming *or* restraining hand, wiser head; **alleviator,** alleviative, palliative, lenitive

pacify VERBS **conciliate,** placate, propitiate, appease, mollify, dulcify; **calm,** settle, soothe, tranquilize; smooth, smooth over *or* out, smooth one's feathers; allay, lay, lay the dust; pour oil on troubled waters, pour balm on, take the edge off of, take the sting out of; cool <nonformal>, defuse

pack VERBS 1 **bundle,** bundle up, **package,** parcel, parcel up, bag, sack, truss, truss up; bale; wrap, **wrap up,** do *or* tie *or* bind up; **box, case,** encase, crate, embox; containerize; encapsulate
2 **gather together,** draw *or* lump *or* batch *or* bunch together, pack in, cram, cram in; **fill,** charge, load, lade, freight, weight; **stuff,** wad, pad, jam, jam-pack, ram in, chock; **fill up,** fill to the brim, brim, top up *or* top off, fill to overflowing, fill the measure of

package NOUNS **bundle,** bindle <nonformal>, pack, packet, deck, budget, **parcel,** fardel <nonformal>, sack, bag, poke <nonformal>, ragbag <nonformal>, bale, truss, **roll,** rouleau, bolt

packed ADJS **crowded,** crammed; bumper-to-bumper <nonformal>, jam-packed, packed *or* crammed like sardines <nonformal>; **compact,** firm, solid, dense, close, serried; **teeming,** swarming, crawling, bristling, populous, **full**

pact NOUNS **compact,** contract, legal contract, valid contract, **covenant,** convention, transaction, accord, **agreement,** mutual agreement, agreement between *or* among parties, signed *or* written agreement, formal agreement, legal agreement, undertaking, stipulation; **understanding,** arrangement, bargain, dicker *and* deal <both nonformal>; bond, binding agreement, ironclad agreement, covenant of salt; gentleman's *or* gentlemen's agreement

pad NOUNS 1 **quarters,** living quarters; lodgings, lodging, lodgment; diggings *and* digs <both Brit nonformal>, crib <nonformal>, room; **rooms,** berth, roost, accommodations; **housing,** shelter; **scratch pad**
VERBS 2 **alleviate,** mitigate, palliate, soften, cushion, assuage, allay, defuse, lay, appease, mollify, subdue, soothe
3 **protract,** extend, spin out, string out, draw out, stretch out, go on *or* be on about, **drag out,** run out, drive into the ground <nonformal>; fill out, **tautologize,** battologize

paddy wagon NOUNS **police van,** patrol wagon; wagon *and* Black Maria <both nonformal>

padlock NOUNS 1 **lock,** bolt, bar, catch, safety catch
VERBS 2 **fasten,** secure; **lock,** lock up, lock out, key, latch, bolt, bar

paean NOUNS laud; hosanna, hallelujah, alleluia; **hymn,** hymn of praise, **doxology,** psalm, anthem, motet, canticle, chorale; **chant,** versicle; antiphon, antiphony; offertory, offertory sentence *or* hymn

pagan NOUNS 1 **heathen;** allotheist; animist; idolater, idolist; **unbeliever,** disbeliever, nonbeliever; **atheist,** infidel; nullifidian, minimifidian
ADJS 2 **paganish,** paganistic; **heathen,** heathenish; pagano-Christian; allotheistic; animist, animistic; idolatrous; **unbelieving,** disbelieving, faithless; infidel, infidelic; **atheistic,** atheist; nullifidian, minimifidian

page NOUNS 1 **attendant,** usher, squire; errand boy *or* girl, gofer <nonformal>, office boy *or* girl, copyboy; footboy
2 **paper,** sheet, leaf
VERBS 3 **summon,** call; call for, send for *or* after, bid come

pageant NOUNS **display,** show, demonstration, manifestation, **exhibition,** parade, *étalage* <Fr>; **pageantry,** spectacle; vaunt, fanfaronade, blazon, flourish, flaunt, flaunting

paid ADJS **paid-up,** discharged, settled, liquidated, acquitted <old>, paid in full, receipted, remitted; prepaid, postpaid

pain NOUNS 1 **suffering,** hurt, hurting, misery <nonformal>, **distress,** *Schmerz* <Ger>, dolor <old>; **discomfort,** malaise; aches and pains
2 **grief,** stress, stress of life, passion
VERBS 3 give *or* inflict pain, **hurt,**

wound, afflict, distress; burn; sting; nip, bite, tweak, pinch; pierce, prick, stab, cut, lacerate; **irritate,** chafe, gall, fret, rasp, rub, grate; **torture,** torment, rack, put to torture, put *or* lay on the rack, **agonize,** harrow, crucify, martyr, martyrize, excruciate, wring, twist, contorse, convulse; wrench, tear, rend
4 **dismay,** grieve, mourn, lament, sorrow; discomfort, get in one's hair, try one's patience, give one a hard time *or* a pain *or* a pain in the neck *or* ass *or* butt <nonformal>

painful ADJS hurtful, **hurting,** distressing, afflictive; **acute,** sharp, piercing, stabbing, shooting, stinging, biting, gnawing; **poignant,** pungent, **severe,** cruel, harsh, grave, hard; griping, cramping, spasmic, spasmatic, spasmodic, paroxysmal; **agonizing,** excruciating, exquisite, atrocious, torturous, tormenting, martyrizing, racking, **harrowing**

pain killer NOUNS **anesthetic,** general anesthetic, local anesthetic, analgesic, anodyne, balm, ointment, pain-reliever, antiodontalgic, soothing syrup; tranquilizer, **sedative,** drug, dope <nonformal>, narcotic, opiate

painless ADJS **easy,** facile, effortless, smooth; plain, uncomplicated, straightforward, **simple**, Mickey Mouse <nonformal>, simple as ABC <nonformal>, easy as pie *and* easy as falling off a log <both nonformal>, downhill all the way, like shooting fish in a barrel, like taking candy from a baby; nothing to it

painstaking ADJS **diligent,** assiduous, sedulous, **thorough,** thoroughgoing, operose, industrious, elaborate

paint VERBS 1 **color,** hue, lay on color; apply paint, paint up, **coat,** cover, face; dab, **daub,** dedaub, smear, besmear, brush on paint, slap *or* slop on paint; **embellish, furbish,** embroider, enrich, grace, set off *or* out, blazon, emblazon, paint in glowing colors
2 **portray,** picture, render, **depict,** represent, delineate, limn; evoke, bring to life, make one see

pair NOUNS **set,** matching pair *or* set, his and hers <nonformal>, twins, lookalikes, two of a kind, birds of a feather, peas in a pod; **two,** twain <old>; **couple,** twosome, set of two, duo, duet, brace, team, span, yoke, double harness; match, matchup, mates

pal NOUNS

<nonformal terms> **buddy,** bud, buddy-boy, bosom buddy, asshole buddy, main man, home boy, goombah, landsman, paesan, paesano, pally, palsy-walsy, road dog, walkboy, cobber <Austral>, pardner, pard, sidekick, tillicum, **chum,** ace, mate *and* butty <both Brit>

palatable ADJS **tasty,** good, fit to eat *and* finger-lickin' good <both nonformal>, good-tasting, **savory,** savorous, **toothsome,** gusty <Scots>, sapid, **good,** good to eat, nice, agreeable, likable, pleasing, to one's taste, **delicious,** delightful, delectable, exquisite; fit for a king, gourmet, fit for a gourmet, of gourmet quality; scrumptious *and* yummy <both nonformal>

palatial ADJS **imposing,** impressive, larger-than-life, awe-inspiring, awesome; **noble,** proud, stately, majestic, princely; **sumptuous,** elegant, elaborate, luxurious, extravagant, deluxe; executive *and* plush *and* posh *and* ritzy *and* swank *and* swanky <all nonformal>, Babylonian

pale VERBS 1 **lose color,** fade, fade out; **bleach,** bleach out; **turn pale,** grow pale, change color, turn white, whiten, blanch, wan
ADJS 2 **colorless,** faded, washed-out, dimmed, discolored, etiolated; **dim,** weak, faint; pallid, wan, sallow, fallow; pale *or* blue *or* green around the gills; **white,** white as a sheet; **pasty,** mealy, waxen; deathly pale, lurid, haggard; **cadaverous**

pall NOUNS 1 **veil of secrecy,** veil, curtain, wraps; wall *or* barrier of secrecy; **suppression,** repression, stifling, smothering
VERBS 2 **be tedious,** drag on, go on forever; have a certain sameness, be infinitely repetitive; **weary,** tire, irk, wear, wear on *or* upon, **make one tired,** fatigue, weary *or* tire to death, jade; give one a swift pain in the ass *and* give one a bellyful *and* make one fed-up <all nonformal>, **satiate,** glut

palliative NOUNS **alleviative,** alleviatory, lenitive, assuasive, assuager; soothing, abirritant, extenuative, saving grace; **alleviator,** pacifier, soother, comforter, peacemaker, pacificator, dove of peace, mollifier; **drug,** anodyne, dolorifuge, soothing syrup, **tranquilizer,** calmative; **sedative**; balm, salve; cushion, shock absorber

pallor NOUNS **paleness,** dimness, weakness, **faintness,** fadedness; pallidity, pallidness, prison pallor, **wanness, sallowness,** pastiness, ashiness; wheyface; grayness, griseousness; **haggardness,** lividness, sickly hue, sickliness, deadly *or* deathly pallor, deathly hue, cadaverousness

palpable ADJS **manifest,** apparent, evident, self-evident, axiomatic, indisputable, **obvious,** plain, clear, perspicuous, distinct, patent, tangible, sensible, appreciable, ponderable

palpitation NOUNS **trepidation,** trepidity, perturbation, fear and trembling; **uneasiness,** disquiet, disquietude, inquietude; nervousness; heartquake; flutter, **arrhythmia,** throb, pitter-patter, pit-a-pat; fibrillation, ventricular fibrillation, tachycardia, ventricular tachycardia <all medicine>

palsy NOUNS **paralysis,** impairment of motor function; shaking, quaking, **quivering,** quavering, shivering, trembling, tremulousness, **shuddering,** vibration; jactation, jactitation; the shakes *and* the shivers *and* the cold shivers <all nonformal>, ague, chattering

paltry ADJS **poor,** common, mean, sorry, sad, pitiful, pitiable, pathetic, **despicable,** contemptible, beneath contempt, **miserable, wretched,** beggarly, vile, **shabby,** scrubby, scruffy, shoddy, scurvy, scuzzy <nonformal>, scummy, crummy *and* cheesy <both nonformal>, **trashy,** rubbishy, gimcracky <nonformal>; **cheap,** worthless, valueless; tawdry, meretricious, gaudy

pamper VERBS **indulge,** humor, oblige; favor, please, gratify, satisfy, **cater to; give way to,** yield to, let one have his own way; cosset, **coddle,** mollycoddle, pet, make a lap dog of, **spoil;** spare the rod

pamphlet NOUNS **booklet,** brochure, chapbook, leaflet, folder, tract; circular

pan VERBS 1 **criticize; knock** *and* **slam** *and* hit *and* rap *and* take a rap *or* swipe at <all nonformal>, snipe at, strike out at, tie into *and* tee off on *and* rip into *and* open up on *and* plow into <all nonformal>
2 **mine;** pan for gold; prospect

panacea NOUNS **cure-all,** universal remedy, theriac, catholicon; polychrest, broad-spectrum drug *or* antibiotic; elixir, elixir of life, *elixir vitae* <L>

pancake NOUNS griddlecake, **hot cake,** battercake, flapcake, **flapjack,** flannel cake; buckwheat cake; chapatty <India>; blintz, cheese blintz, *crêpe, crêpe suzette* <both Fr>, *palacsinta* <Hung>, *Pfannkuchen* <Ger>, Swedish pancake

pandemonium NOUNS **turbulence,** turmoil, chaos, upset, **fury, furor,** *furore* <Ital>, **rage,** frenzy, passion, fanaticism, zealousness, zeal, tempestuousness, storminess, wildness, tumultuousness, **tumult,** uproar, racket, cacophony, hubbub, **commotion,** disturbance, agitation, bluster, broil, brawl, embroilment, brouhaha, fuss, flap <nonformal>, **row, rumpus,** ruckus <nonformal>, foofaraw <nonformal>, **ferment,** bedlam, hell *or* bedlam let loose; charivari, shivaree <nonformal>

pander to VERBS **toady to,** truckle to, cater to; **wait on** *or* **upon,** wait on hand and foot, dance attendance, do service, fetch and carry, do the dirty work of, do *or* jump at the bidding of

Pandora's box NOUNS **trouble,** peck of troubles; hornet's nest, can of worms <nonformal>; **evil**

panel NOUNS 1 **forum,** conference, discussion group, panel discussion, open discussion, buzz session <nonformal>, **round table;** open forum, colloquium, seminar, symposium; **powwow** <nonformal>
2 **jury,** jury of one's peers, sessions <Scots>, country, twelve men in a box; inquest; jury panel, jury list, venire facias

pang NOUNS **compunction,** qualm, qualms, qualmishness, scruples, scrupulosity, scrupulousness, pangs, **pangs of conscience,** throes, sting *or* pricking *or* twinge *or* twitch of conscience, touch of conscience, **voice of conscience,** pricking of heart, better self

panhandle VERBS beg, **scrounge,** cadge; mooch *and* bum <both nonformal>; **hit** *and* hit up *and* **touch** *and* put the touch on *and* make a touch <all nonformal>; pass the hat <nonformal>

panhandler NOUNS **beggar,** mendicant, scrounger, cadger; bum *and* bummer *and* **moocher** <all nonformal>; hobo, tramp; loafer

panic NOUNS 1 **fear, fright,** affright; **scare,** alarm, consternation, dismay; dread, unholy dread, **awe; terror,** horror, horrification, mortal *or* abject fear; panic fear *or* terror; stampede; **cowardice**
VERBS 2 **put in fear,** put the fear of God into, **throw a scare into** <nonformal>; stampede, send scuttling, throw blind fear into

panicky ADJS panic-prone, panicked, in a panic, panic-stricken, panic-struck, terror-stricken, out of one's mind with fear, prey to blind fear

panoramic ADJS **comprehensive,** sweeping, complete; encyclopedic, compendious; synoptic; bird's-eye

pantomime VERBS **impersonate,** personate; **mimic,** mime, take off, do *or* give an impression of, mock; ape, copy; **pose as, masquerade as,** affect the manner *or* guise of, pass for, pretend to be, represent oneself to be

pantry NOUNS **larder,** buttery <nonformal>; spence <Brit nonformal>, stillroom <Brit>

pants NOUNS **trousers,** pair of trousers *or* pants, trews <Scots>, **breeches,** britches <nonformal>, breeks <Scots>, **pantaloons,** jeans, **slacks**

papal ADJS **pontific, pontifical,** apostolic, apostolical; **popish** *or* papist *or* papistic *or* papistical *or* papish <all nonformal>

paper NOUNS 1 **document,** official document, legal document, legal paper, legal instrument, **instrument,** writ, parchment, scroll, roll, **writing,** script, scrip; holograph, chirograph; **papers,** ship's papers; docket, **file,** personal file, **dossier;** blank, form
2 **newspaper,** news, sheet *or* rag <both nonformal>, **gazette,** daily newspaper, daily, weekly newspaper, weekly, neighborhood newspaper, national newspaper; newspaper of record; **tabloid,** extra, special, extra edition, special edition
3 **treatise,** piece, treatment, handling, tractate, tract; contribution; examination, survey, **discourse, discussion,** disquisition, descant, exposition, screed; homily; memoir; dissertation, **thesis; essay,** theme; pandect; excursus; **study,** lucubration, étude; research paper, term paper; **monograph,** research monograph

papers NOUNS **archives,** public records, government archives, government papers, presidential papers, historical documents, historical records, memorabilia; cartulary; biographical records, life records, biographical material, ana; parish rolls *or* register *or* records; citizenship papers

par NOUNS 1 **average,** balance, normal, norm, rule, run, generality; **mediocrity,** averageness, passableness, adequacy; par value
2 **equality, parity,** equation, identity; equivalence *or* equivalency, convertibility, **correspondence,** parallelism, equipollence, coequality; **balance,** poise, equipoise, **equilibrium,** equiponderance; symmetry, proportion; level playing field
ADJS 3 **equal, equalized,** like, **alike, even,** level, **on a par,** at par, at parity, au pair, commensurate, proportionate; on the same level, on the same plane, on the same *or* equal footing; on terms of equality, **on even** *or* **equal terms,** on even ground; on a level, on a level playing field, in the same boat

parade NOUNS 1 display, show, demonstration, manifestation, exhibition, *étalage* <Fr>; **pageantry,** pageant, pomp, spectacle; **procession,** train, column, line, string, cortege; cavalcade, caravan, motorcade; dress parade; promenade, review, march-past, funeral
VERBS 2 **flaunt,** vaunt, display, demonstrate, manifest, make a great show of, **exhibit,** air, put forward, put forth, hold up, flash *and* sport <both nonformal>; **file,** defile, file off; go on parade, promenade, march past

paradise NOUNS **bliss,** blissfulness; **heaven,** seventh heaven, cloud nine, **utopia, heaven on earth;** millennium, kingdom come; dreamland, lotus land, land of dreams, land of enchantment, land of heart's desire, wonderland, cloudland, fairyland, land of faerie, faerie; Eden, Garden of Eden; the Promised Land, land of promise, land of plenty, land of milk and honey, Canaan, Goshen; Shangri-la

paradox NOUNS **self-contradiction,** antinomy, oxymoron, ambivalence, **irony,** enantiosis, equivocation, ambiguity, equivocality, equivocalness, mixed message *or* signal, absurdity, logical impossibility

paradoxical ADJS **inconsistent,** incongruous, inconsonant, inconsequent, incoherent, **incompatible,** irreconcilable; disproportionate, out of proportion, self-contradictory, oxymoronic, **absurd;** abnormal, anomalous

paragon NOUNS **ideal,** beau ideal, nonpareil, nonesuch, person to look up to, *chevalier sans peur et sans reproche* <Fr>, **good example, role model,** shining example; exemplar, epitome; **model,** pattern, standard, norm, mirror; **standout,** one in a thousand *or* ten thousand, man of men, a man among men, woman of women, a woman among women

parallel VERBS 1 be parallel, coextend; run parallel, go alongside, go beside, run abreast; match, equal, **compare with,** stack up with <nonformal>; **agree,** accord, harmonize, concur, have no problem with, go along with <nonformal>, **cooperate**, correspond, conform, coincide, intersect, overlap, **match,** tally, hit, register, lock, interlock, check <nonformal>, square, dovetail, jibe <nonformal>
ADJS 2 paralleling; coextending, coextensive, nonconvergent, nondivergent, **equidistant,** equispaced, collateral, concurrent; lined up, aligned; equal, even; analogous; in the same category, of that kind *or* sort *or* ilk; **congenial,** *en rapport* <Fr>, sympathetic, compatible, affinitive

paralyzed ADJS **disabled,** incapacitated; crippled, hamstrung; disqualified, invalidated; hog-tied <nonformal>; prostrate, **on one's back,** on one's beam-ends; **stunned,** petrified, stupefied, frozen; **inert,** like a bump on a log <nonformal>, immobile, dormant, stagnant, stagnating, vegetative, vegetable, static, stationary, motionless, immobile, unmoving, paralytic

parameter NOUNS **specification,** given, *donnée* <Fr>, **limitation,** limiting condition, boundary condition; **contingency,** circumstance; **terms,** provisions; grounds; small *or* fine print *and* fine print at the bottom <all nonformal>

paramount ADJS **principal,** leading, foremost, main, chief, number one <nonformal>, premier, **prime, primary,** preeminent, **supreme,** cardinal; highest, uppermost, topmost, toprank, ranking, of the first rank, world-class, **dominant,** predominant, master, controlling, **overruling,** overriding, all-absorbing; **unsurpassed,** surpassing, unparalleled, unmatched, unmatchable, matchless, **peerless;** quintessential

paranoid NOUNS 1 **psychotic,** psycho <nonformal>, mental, mental case, certifiable case, **psychopath,** psychopathic case; psychopathic personality; paranoiac
ADJS 2 **psychotic,** psychopathic, psychoneurotic, mentally ill, mentally sick, certifiable; paranoiac

paraphernalia NOUNS things, **gear,** stuff <nonformal>, impedimenta <pl>, **tackle; belongings,** appurtenances, trappings, appointments, accessories, perquisites, appendages

paraphrase NOUNS **rephrase,** reword, restate, rehash; give a free *or* loose translation; approximate

parasite NOUNS 1 **nonworker,** drone; **sponger,** sponge <nonformal>, freeloader <nonformal>, social parasite, smell-feast, cadger, bummer *and* moocher <both nonformal>, beat *and* deadbeat <both nonformal>; **attendant**, satellite, hanger-on, dangler, adherent, appendage, dependent, stooge <nonformal>, flunky
2 bloodsucker; **leech; tick,** wood tick, deer tick; **mosquito,** skeeter <nonformal>, culex; bedbug, housebug <Brit>; parasitic plant, saprophyte

parcel NOUNS 1 **bundle,** pack, package, packet, deck, budget, fardel <nonformal>, sack, bag, poke <nonformal>, **roll,** rouleau, bolt
VERBS 2 **apportion,** divide, divide up, divvy *and* divvy up <both nonformal>, parcel up *or* out, **split,** split up, cut up, subdivide; district, zone

parched ADJS **dried,** dehydrated, desiccated, dried-up, exsiccated; **baked,** sunbaked, burnt, scorched, **seared,** sere, sun-dried, adust; **withered,** shriveled, wizened, weazened; **thirsty,** thirsting, athirst

parchment NOUNS **codex;** scroll; palimpsest, *codex rescriptus* <L>; papyrus

pardon NOUNS 1 excuse, sparing, **amnesty,** indemnity, exemption, immunity, reprieve, grace; **absolution,** shrift, remission, remission of sin; redemption; **exoneration, exculpation**
VERBS 2 **forgive,** excuse, give *or* grant forgiveness, spare; amnesty, grant amnesty to, grant immunity *or* exemp-

tion; hear confession, **absolve,** remit, give absolution, shrive, grant remission; **exonerate,** exculpate; blot out one's sins, wipe the slate clean

pardonable ADJS **excusable,** forgivable, expiable, remissible, exemptible, venial; **condonable,** dispensable; **warrantable,** allowable, admissible, reasonable, colorable, legitimate; innocuous, unobjectionable, inoffensive

pare VERBS 1 **peel,** skin, strip, flay, excoriate, decorticate, bark; scalp
2 **reduce,** decrease, diminish, lessen, take from; **lower,** curtail, retrench; **cut,** cut down *or* back, trim away, chip away at, whittle away *or* down, roll back <nonformal>

parent NOUNS 1 **progenitor, ancestor,** procreator, begetter; natural *or* birth *or* biological parent; grandparent; ancestress, progenitress, progenitrix; stepparent; adoptive parent; surrogate parent
VERBS 2 **foster, nurture,** nourish, mother, care for, lavish care on, feed, rear, sustain, cultivate, **cherish**

parental ADJS **ancestral,** ancestorial, patriarchal; parent; **paternal,** fatherly, fatherlike; **maternal,** motherly, motherlike; fostering

pariah NOUNS **outcast,** social outcast, outcast of society, castaway, derelict, Ishmael; **untouchable,** leper; outcaste; *déclassé* <Fr>; undesirable; *persona non grata* <L>, unacceptable person

parish NOUNS **diocese,** see, archdiocese, bishopric, archbishopric; province; synod, conference; **congregation,** parishioners, churchgoers, assembly

parishioner NOUNS **layman,** laic, secular, churchman, church member; brother, sister, lay brother, lay sister; laywoman, churchwoman; catchumen; communicant

parity NOUNS **equality,** par, equation, **identity**; equivalence *or* equivalency, convertibility, **correspondence,** parallelism , equipollence, coequality; **likeness,** levelness, evenness, coextension; **balance,** poise, equipoise, **equilibrium,** equiponderance; symmetry, proportion; level playing field; **justice**, equity

parliamentary ADJS **legislative,** legislatorial, lawmaking; deliberative; **congressional;** senatorial; bicameral, unicameral

parlor NOUNS **living room,** sitting room, morning room, drawing *or* withdrawing room, best room <nonformal>, salon

parochial ADJS **local, localized,** of a place, geographically limited, topical, vernacular, provincial, insular, limited, confined; narrow, insular, ethnocentric, xenophobic, snobbish

parochial school NOUNS **religious school,** church-related school, church school; Sunday school

parody NOUNS 1 **burlesque, lampoon,** squib, **satire, farce,** mockery, imitation, wicked imitation *or* pastiche, takeoff <nonformal>, travesty, caricature
VERBS 2 **burlesque, lampoon,** satirize, caricature, travesty, hit *or* take off on, send up <nonformal>; dip the pen in gall

parole VERBS **release,** put on parole, release from prison, spring <nonformal>; let out, let off, let go free; let out on bail

parrot NOUNS 1 **imitator,** simulator, metooer <nonformal>, **impersonator, impostor**, **mimic,** mimicker, mimer, mime, **mocker;** mockingbird, cuckoo; polly, poll-parrot *or* polly-parrot, **ape,** aper, monkey; **echo,** echoer, echoist
VERBS 2 **mimic,** impersonate, mime, **ape,** copycat <nonformal>; do an impression; take off, hit off, hit off on, take off on; **echo**

parry VERBS **fend off,** ward off, stave off, hold off, fight off, keep off, beat off, fend, counter, turn aside; **hold** *or* **keep at bay,** keep at arm's length; **hold the fort,** hold the line, stop, check, block, hinder, obstruct; **repel, repulse,** rebuff, drive back, put back, push back

parsimonious ADJS **sparing,** cheeseparing, **stinting,** scamping, scrimping, skimping; frugal; too frugal, overfrugal, frugal to excess; penny-wise, penny-wise and pound-foolish

parson NOUNS **clergyman,** clergywoman, man *or* woman of the cloth, divine, ecclesiastic, churchman, cleric, minister, pastor, rector, curate

parsonage NOUNS **pastorage,** pastorate, manse, **church house,** clergy house; presbytery, **rectory,** vicarage, deanery; glebe; chapter house

part NOUNS 1 **portion,** share, interest, stake, stock, **piece,** bit, segment; **bite** *and* **cut** *and* **slice** *and* **chunk** *and* slice of the pie *or* melon *and* piece of the action <all nonformal>, **lot, allotment,** end <nonformal>, **proportion,** percent-

age, measure, quantum, **quota,** meed, moiety, mess, helping
2 **role, lines,** side; bit, bit part, minor role; feeder, straight part; walking part, walk-on; top banana, second banana
3 **component,** constituent, ingredient, integrant, makings *and* fixings <both nonformal>, **element,** factor, player, module, part and parcel; appurtenance, adjunct
VERBS 4 **part company,** split up, dispel, disband, scatter, **disperse,** break up, break it up <nonformal>, **go separate ways,** diverge
ADJS 5 **incomplete, uncompleted, deficient,** defective, unfinished, imperfect, unperfected, **inadequate; partial,** failing; **half,** halfway; **in short supply,** scanty; **short,** scant, shy <nonformal>; **sketchy,** patchy
ADVS 6 **partly,** partially, **in part**

partial ADJS 1 **interested,** involved, **partisan,** unneutral, **one-sided,** all on *or* way over to one side, **biased,** tendentious, slanted
2 part; **fractional,** sectional, componential; segmentary, segmental, modular; **fragmentary;** incomplete, open-ended

partial to ADJS fond of, enamored of, **in love with,** attached to, wedded to, devoted to, wrapped up in; **taken with,** smitten with, struck with

participant NOUNS **participator,** partaker, player, sharer; party, **a party to,** accomplice, accessory; partner, copartner; shareholder

participate VERBS **take part,** partake, contribute, chip in, involve *or* engage oneself, get involved; **have** *or* **take a hand in,** get in on, have a finger in, have a finger in the pie, have to do with, have a part in, be an accessory to, be implicated in, be a party to, be a player in; **participate in,** partake of *or* in, **take part in,** take an active part in, **join, join in,** figure in, make oneself part of, play a part in, play a role in, get in the act <nonformal>; climb on the bandwagon; **have a voice in,** help decide, be in on the decisions

participation NOUNS **partaking, sharing,** having a part *or* share *or* voice, contribution, association; **involvement,** engagement; complicity

particle NOUNS **bit,** little *or* wee *or* tiny bit <nonformal>, fragment, spot, **speck,** flyspeck, fleck, point, dot, jot, tittle, **iota,** ounce, **dab** <nonformal>, mote, **mite** <nonformal>; crumb, scrap, bite, snip, snippet, **morsel,** shard, potsherd

particular NOUNS 1 **instance, item, detail,** point, count, case, fact, matter, article, datum, element, part, ingredient, factor, facet, aspect, thing; **respect, regard,** angle
ADJS 2 **special,** especial, specific, express, precise, **concrete; singular, individual,** individualist *or* individualistic; **fixed,** definite, defined, distinct, different, different as night and day, determinate, certain, absolute

parting ADJS **departing,** leaving; last, final, farewell; valedictory; outward-bound

partisan NOUNS 1 **party member,** party man *or* woman; regular, stalwart, loyalist; wheelhorse, party wheelhorse; heeler, ward heeler, **party hack;** party faithful; **fan** *and* buff <both nonformal>, aficionado, **admirer**
ADJS 2 polarizing, **divisive,** factional, factious; **quarrelsome,** bickering, disputatious, wrangling, eristic, eristical, polemical; litigious, pugnacious, combative, **aggressive,** bellicose, belligerent; feisty <nonformal>, touchy, irritable, shrewish, **irascible**
3 **party;** bipartisan, biparty, two-party; **partial,** interested, involved, unneutral, **one-sided,** all on *or* way over to one side

partition NOUNS 1 **dividing wall,** division, separation, *cloison* <Fr>; **wall,** barrier; bulkhead; diaphragm; septum; **border, dividing line,** property line, party wall; **buffer,** bumper, mat, fender, cushion, pad, shock pad, collision mat; buffer state
VERBS 2 set apart, separate, divide, subdivide; **wall off,** fence off, screen off, curtain off, compartmentalize, segment; **apportion,** portion, parcel, part, divide, share; divide into shares, **share out** *or* **around,** divide up, divvy *or* divvy up *or* out <nonformal>, **split,** split up, carve, cut, slice, carve up, slice up, cut up, cut *or* slice the pie *or* melon <nonformal>

partner NOUNS pardner *or* pard <nonformal>, copartner, side partner, buddy <nonformal>, **sidekick** *and* sidekicker <both nonformal>; **mate; business partner,** general partner, special partner, silent partner, dormant *or* sleeping partner

partnership NOUNS **alliance,** hookup *and* tie-up *and* tie-in <all nonformal>; copartnership, copartnery <old>, cahoots <nonformal>; colleagueship, collegialism, collegiality

part-time ADJS **occasional,** casual, incidental; odd, sometime, extra, side, off, off-and-on, out-of-the-way, spare, sparetime

party NOUNS 1 **participator,** participant, partaker, player, sharer; **a party to,** accomplice, accessory; partner, copartner; cotenant; shareholder
2 **entertainment,** party time, **festivity,** celebration, fete, at home, housewarming, soiree, reception, **dance,** ball, prom, do <chiefly Brit>; **spree, bout, fling,** randy <Scots>; **carouse,** drinking bout

3 <nonformal> **brawl, bash,** blast, clambake, wingding, hoodang, blowout, shindig, shindy, do *and* bean-feast *and* knees-up *and* rave *and* rave-up <all Brit>

4 **political party,** major party, minor party, third party, splinter party; party in power, opposition party, loyal opposition
VERBS 5 **enjoy oneself,** have a good time, have the time of one's life

6 <nonformal> **throw a party; party,** have fun, live it up, have a ball, ball, boogie, jam, kick up one's heels, make whoopee, whoop it up

7 **dissipate,** plunge into dissipation, **debauch, wanton, carouse,** run riot, live hard *or* fast, squander one's money in riotous living, burn the candle at both ends, keep up a fast *or* killing pace, sow one's wild oats, have a fling

eat, drink, and be merry
BIBLE

ADJS 8 **partisan,** partial, interested; **factional,** sectional, sectarian, sectary, denominational

pass NOUNS 1 **narrow, narrows,** strait; gap, ravine
2 **complimentary ticket,** comp <nonformal>, free pass *or* ticket, paper <nonformal>, free admission, guest pass *or* ticket, Annie Oakley <nonformal>
VERBS 3 **transfer,** pass over, **hand over,** turn over, carry over, make over, consign, assign; pass on, pass the buck <nonformal>, hand forward, hand on, relay
4 **outdistance,** distance; surpass, overpass; **get ahead,** pull ahead, shoot ahead, walk away *or* off <nonformal>; **leave behind,** leave at the post, leave in the dust, leave in the lurch; **come to the front,** have a healthy lead <nonformal>
5 **ratify,** pass on *or* upon, give thumbs up <nonformal>; amen, say amen to
6 **succeed,** graduate, qualify, win one's spurs *or* wings, get one's credentials, be blooded; pass with flying colors; **stand the test,** stand up, hold up, hold up in the wash, **pass muster,** get by <nonformal>, make it *and* hack it *and* cut the mustard <all nonformal>, meet *or* satisfy requirements
7 be past, **be a thing of the past,** elapse, lapse, slip by *or* away, be gone, fade, fade away, be dead and gone, be all over, have run its course, have run out, have had its day; **disappear, go** *or* **pass by,** get *or* shoot ahead of; bypass

passable ADJS **acceptable,** admissible, **agreeable,** unobjectionable, unexceptionable, tenable, viable; **OK** *and* okay *and* all right *and* alright <all nonformal>; good enough, **mediocre,** middling, indifferent, fair, fairish, fair to middling <nonformal>, moderate, modest, medium, betwixt and between; respectable, **tolerable; so-so,** *comme ci comme ça* <Fr>

passage NOUNS **phrase,** musical phrase, strain, part, motive, motif, theme, subject, figure; leitmotiv; **movement**

passageway NOUNS **entrance,** corridor, companionway, hall, hallway, way; jetway, jet bridge; gangway, gangplank; **vestibule;** aisle, alley, lane; channel, conduit; opening, aperture; covered way, gallery, arcade, portico, colonnade, cloister, ambulatory

passé ADJS **past, gone,** by, **gone-by, bygone,** gone glimmering, bypast, ago, **over,** departed, passed, passed away, elapsed, lapsed, vanished, faded, no more, irrecoverable, never to return, not coming back; **dead,** dead as a dodo, expired, extinct, dead and buried, defunct, deceased; run out, blown over, finished, forgotten, wound up; **obso-**

lete, has-been, dated, antique, **antiquated,** extinct, outworn

passenger NOUNS **traveler,** fare, **commuter,** straphanger <nonformal>; transient

passion NOUNS 1 passionateness, strong feeling, powerful emotion; **fervor,** fervency, fervidness, impassionedness, **ardor,** ardency, *empressement* <Fr>, tender feeling *or* passion, warmth of feeling, **warmth, heat, fire,** verve, furor, **fury,** vehemence; heartiness, gusto, relish, savor; spirit, heart, soul; **liveliness;** zeal; excitement; predilection
2 **cause, principle,** interest, issue, burning issue, commitment, faith, great cause, lifework; reason for being, *raison d'être* <Fr>; **craze,** infatuation, enthusiasm, fascination, crazy fancy, bug <nonformal>

passionate ADJS **fiery, vehement,** hotheaded, **impetuous,** violent, volcanic, furious, fierce, **wild;** tempestuous, stormy, tornadic; simmering, volcanic, ready to burst forth *or* explode; **impassioned,** enthusiastic, **ardent, fervent,** burning, glowing, warm; urgent, stirring, exciting, stimulating, provoking

passive ADJS 1 **neutral,** standpat <nonformal>, **do-nothing;** *laissez-faire, laissez-aller* <both Fr>; **inert,** like a bump on a log <nonformal>, immobile, dormant, stagnant, stagnating, vegetative, vegetable, static, stationary, motionless, immobile, unmoving, paralyzed, paralytic; procrastinating; **inactive, idle**; quiescent; quietist, quietistic, contemplative, meditative; **submissive, compliant,** complying, **acquiescent,** consenting; supine, **unresisting**
2 **uninterested,** unconcerned, disinterested, uninvolved, **indifferent, apathetic,** impassive, stolid, phlegmatic, listless

password NOUNS **watchword,** countersign; token; open sesame; secret grip; shibboleth

past NOUNS 1 **the past,** foretime, former times, past times, times past, water under the bridge, **days** *or* **times gone by,** bygone times *or* days, yesterday, yesteryear; recent past, just *or* only yesterday; **history,** past history; dead past, dead hand of the past
ADJS 2 **gone,** by, **gone-by, bygone,** gone glimmering, bypast, ago, **over,** departed, passed, passed away, elapsed, lapsed, vanished, faded, no more, irrecoverable, never to return, not coming back; **dead**, dead as a dodo, expired, extinct, dead and buried, defunct, deceased; **passé, obsolete,** has-been, dated, antique, antiquated; **former,** previous, late, recent, **once, onetime,** sometime, **erstwhile,** then, quondam

pasta NOUNS **spaghetti,** spaghettini, ziti, fedellini, fettuccine, radiattore, vermicelli, **macaroni,** lasagne, linguine

paste NOUNS 1 **fake,** imitation, simulacrum, dummy; tinsel, *clinquant* <Fr>, pinchbeck, shoddy, junk
2 **pulp,** mash, mush, smash, squash, crush; tomato paste *or* pulp; cement, glue, mucilage
VERBS 3 **stick together,** cement, bind, colligate, glue, agglutinate, conglutinate, gum

pastime NOUNS **amusement,** entertainment, diversion, solace, divertisement, *divertissement* <Fr>, recreation, relaxation, regalement; *passe-temps* <Fr>

pastor NOUNS **clergyman,** clergywoman, man *or* woman of the cloth, divine, ecclesiastic, churchman, cleric, minister, parson, rector, curate

pastoral ADJS **rustic,** rural, country, provincial, farm, bucolic, Arcadian, **agrarian,** agrestic; agricultural; idyllic, eclogic

pastry NOUNS *patisserie* <Fr>; French pastry, Danish pastry; **tart;** turnover; timbale; **pie,** *tarte* <Fr>, fruit pie, tart; *quiche* or *quiche Lorraine* <Fr>; *vol-au-vent* <Fr>; dowdy, pandowdy; cream puff, croquembouche, profiterole; cannoli, cream horn; éclair, chocolate éclair

pat NOUNS 1 **caress; tap,** rap, dab, chuck, touch, tip; love-tap
VERBS 2 **caress,** pet, **fondle,** dandle, coddle, cocker, cosset; pat on the head *or* cheek, chuck under the chin; **tap,** rap, dab, chuck, touch, tip

patch NOUNS 1 **spot,** dot, polka dot, macula, macule, blotch, splotch, splash; **mottle,** dapple; speck, speckle, fleck, flick, flyspeck
2 **plot,** plot of ground *or* land, parcel of land, plat, **tract,** field
3 **scrap,** tatter, smithereen <nonformal>, **stitch, shred,** tag

patent NOUNS 1 **copyright,** certificate of invention, *brevet d'invention* <Fr>; **trademark, logo** *or* logotype, registered trademark, trade name, service mark
ADJS 2 **manifest,** apparent, evident,

self-evident, indisputable, **obvious, plain,** clear, perspicuous, distinct, palpable, tangible; **unquestionable,** unexceptionable, undeniable, axiomatic; indubitable, unarguable, incontestable, **irrefutable,** incontrovertible, irrefragable

paternal ADJS **loving,** fond, adoring, devoted; parental, parent; fatherly, fatherlike

paternity NOUNS **fatherhood,** fathership; natural *or* birth *or* biological fatherhood; fatherliness, paternalness; adoptive fatherhood

path NOUNS **track,** trail, pathway, footpath, footway, *piste* <Fr>; walkway, catwalk, skybridge *or* skywalk *or* flying bridge *or* walkway; **sidewalk,** walk, fastwalk, *trottoir* <Fr>, foot pavement <Brit>; boardwalk; hiking trail; towpath *or* towing path; bridle path *or* road *or* trail *or* way; bicycle path; beaten track *or* path, rut, groove; garden path

pathetic ADJS 1 **affecting,** touching, moving, emotive, saddening, poignant; comfortless, discomforting, uncomfortable; **pitiful,** pitiable, piteous, affecting, heartrending, grievous, doleful
2 **paltry, poor,** common, mean, sorry, sad, despicable, contemptible, beneath contempt, **miserable, wretched,** beggarly, vile, **shabby,** scrubby, scruffy, shoddy, crummy *and* cheesy <both nonformal>, **trashy,** cheap, worthless, valueless; tawdry, meretricious

pathological ADJS **unwholesome,** unhealthy, unsound, morbid, **infected,** contaminated, tainted, peccant, **poisoned,** septic

pathos NOUNS **woe,** sadness, sorrowfulness, mournfulness, lamentation, woefulness, poignancy; comfortlessness, discomfort, dreariness, cheerlessness, joylessness, dismalness, **depression,** bleakness

patience NOUNS **tolerance,** toleration, **acceptance; indulgence,** lenience, leniency; sweet reasonableness; **forbearance,** forbearing, forbearingness; **sufferance,** endurance; long-suffering, longsufferance, longanimity; **stoicism,** fortitude, self-control; patience of Job; waiting game, waiting it out; **perseverance**

a minor form of despair, disguised as a virtue
AMBROSE BIERCE

patient NOUNS 1 **sick person,** ill person, sufferer, victim; valetudinarian, **invalid, shut-in;** incurable, terminal case; **case;** inpatient, outpatient; **the sick,** the infirm
ADJS 2 armed with patience, with a soul possessed in patience, patient as Job, Job-like, Griselda-like; **tolerant,** tolerative, tolerating, accepting; understanding, **indulgent,** lenient; **forbearing;** philosophical; **long-suffering,** longanimous; **enduring,** endurant; disciplined, self-controlled; **persevering**

patina NOUNS **verdigris,** aerugo; patination; **polish,** gloss, glaze, burnish, **shine,** luster, finish; covering, **coat,** coating, veneer, film, membrane

patois NOUNS **jargon,** lingo <nonformal>, slang, cant, argot, patter, vernacular

patriarch NOUNS **old man,** elder, oldster <nonformal>; graybeard *or* greybeard, reverend *or* venerable sir; grandfather, grandsire; octogenarian, nonagenarian, centenarian; paterfamilias

patriarchal ADJS **ancestral,** ancestorial; **paternal,** paternalistic, patriarchic, patriarchical

patrician NOUNS 1 **aristocrat,** Brahmin, blue-blood, thoroughbred, member of the upper class, socialite, swell *and* upper-cruster <both nonformal>, grandee, grand dame, dowager, magnifico, lord of creation
ADJS 2 **upper-class,** aristocratic, upscale; gentle, genteel, of gentle blood; gentlemanly, gentlemanlike; ladylike, quite the lady; born to the purple, born with a silver spoon in one's mouth; **high-society,** socialite, hoity-toity <nonformal>, posh

to the manner born
SHAKESPEARE

patriot NOUNS nationalist; ultranationalist; **chauvinist,** chauvin, **jingo,** jingoist; patrioteer <nonformal>, flag waver, superpatriot, hard hat <nonformal>, hundred-percenter, hundred-percent American; hawk

patriotic ADJS **public-spirited,** civic; nationalistic; ultranationalist, ultranationalistic; overpatriotic, superpatriotic, flagwaving, **chauvinist,** chauvinistic, jingoist, jingoistic; hawkish

patriotism NOUNS love of country; **nationalism,** nationality, ultranationalism; **chauvinism,** jingoism, overpatriotism; patriotics, flag-waving; saber-rattling

patrol VERBS **police,** pound a beat <nonformal>, go on one's beat, reconnoiter, scout; **watch,** keep watch, keep guard, keep watch over, keep vigil, keep watch and ward; stand guard, stand sentinel; be on the lookout; mount guard; sweep, go *or* make one's rounds, scour, scour the country

patron NOUNS **contributor, subscriber,** supporter, backer, financer, funder, angel <nonformal>; subsidizer; patroness, Maecenas; **fan** *and* buff <both nonformal>; **customer,** client; patronizer <nonformal>, regular customer *or* buyer, regular

patronage NOUNS **fosterage,** tutelage, sponsorship, backing, auspices, aegis, coattails <nonformal>, care, guidance, **championing,** championship, seconding; interest, advocacy, encouragement, **backing,** abetment; **custom,** trade; **political patronage,** favors of office, pork *and* pork barrel <both nonformal>, plum, melon <nonformal>

patronize VERBS 1 **condescend, deign,** vouchsafe, stoop, descend, lower *or* demean oneself, trouble oneself, set one's dignity aside *or* to one side, be so good as to, so forget oneself, dirty *or* soil one's hands; deal with *or* treat *de haut en bas* <Fr, from high to low> or *en grand seigneur* <Fr, like a great lord>, talk down to, talk *de haut en bas*
2 **trade with,** deal with, traffic with, do business with, have dealings with, have truck with, transact business with; frequent as a customer, shop at, trade at, take one's business *or* trade to

patsy NOUNS trusting soul; **dupe;** sucker *and* easy mark *and* pushover<all nonformal>; scapegoat, fall guy <nonformal>

patter NOUNS 1 **rain,** rainfall, **shower,** sprinkle, flurry, pitter-patter, splatter
2 **jargon,** lingo <nonformal>, **slang,** cant, argot, patois, vernacular; vocabulary, phraseology; **sales talk,** sales pitch

pattern NOUNS 1 **gestalt,** figure, configuration, sensory pattern; figure-ground; **original,** archetype, prototype, **mold,** pilot model
2 **habit,** habitude, **custom,** second nature; stereotype; stereotyped behavior; force of habit; creature of habit; **knee-jerk** <nonformal>, automatism
3 **theme,** design, ornamental theme, ornamental *or* decorative composition; exemplar, epitome; **model,** standard, norm, mirror

paucity NOUNS **fewness,** infrequency, **sparsity,** sparseness, **scarcity,** scantiness, meagerness, miserliness, niggardliness, tightness, **dearth,** poverty; **rarity,** rareness, uncommonness

paunch NOUNS **abdomen; stomach,** belly <nonformal>, midriff; swollen *or* distended *or* protruding *or* prominent belly, *embonpoint* <Fr>, ventripotence

pauper NOUNS **poor man,** poorling, poor devil, down-and-out *or* down-and-outer, indigent, penniless man, hard case, starveling; homeless person, bag woman *or* lady, shopping-bag lady, shopping-cart woman *or* lady, homeless *or* street person; welfare client; charity case

pause NOUNS 1 **respite, recess, rest,** halt, stay, lull, **break,** surcease, suspension, interlude, **intermission,** spell <Australia>, letup <nonformal>, **time out** <nonformal>, time to catch one's breath; **breathing spell,** breathing time, breathing place, breathing space, breath; **breather**
2 **demur,** demurral, **scruple, qualm,** qualm of conscience, reservation, compunction; **hesitation,** hesitancy *or* hesitance, pause, boggle, **falter;** qualmishness, scrupulousness, scrupulosity; **stickling,** boggling; **faltering;** shrinking; shyness, **diffidence,** modesty, bashfulness; recoil; **protest, objection**
VERBS 3 **rest,** let up *and* take it easy <both nonformal>, **relax,** rest on one's oars; **recess,** take *or* call a recess; **take a break,** break, take ten

paw NOUNS 1 pad, pug, *patte* <Fr>; hand <nonformal>
VERBS 2 **touch, feel,** feel of, palpate; **handle,** palm; poke at, prod

pawn NOUNS 1 lightweight, follower, cog, flunky, yes-man, creature; **cat's-paw,** puppet, dummy, creature, minion, stooge <nonformal>; stalking horse; toy, plaything; dupe
VERBS 2 **pledge,** impignorate *and* handsel <both old>, **deposit,** stake, post, put in escrow, **put up,** put up as collateral, lay out *or* down; put in pawn, spout *or* put up the spout <both old>, **hock** *and* **put in hock** <both nonformal>

pay NOUNS 1 **payment,** remuneration,

compensation, total compensation, wages plus fringe benefits, financial package, pay and allowances, financial remuneration; rate of pay; **salary,** wage, wages, income, earnings
VERBS 2 **be profitable,** repay, pay off <nonformal>, yield a profit, show a percentage, be gainful, be worthwhile *or* worth one's while, be a good investment
3 **spend,** expend, disburse, pay out, fork out *or* over <nonformal>, shell out <nonformal>, **lay out,** outlay; **yield,** bring in, afford, **return**

4 <nonformal> **kick in, fork over,** pony up, pay up, cough up, stump up [Brit], come across, come through with, come across with, come down with, come down with the needful, plank down, plunk down, post, tickle *or* grease the palm, cross one's palm with, lay on one; pay to the tune of

payable ADJS **due,** owed, owing, receivable, redeemable, mature, **outstanding, unpaid,** in arrear *or* arrears, back, coming, **coming to**
payee NOUNS **recipient, receiver,** accepter, getter, taker, acquirer, obtainer, procurer; endorsee
payer NOUNS remunerator, compensator, recompenser; paymaster, purser, bursar, cashier, treasurer; defrayer; liquidator
payment NOUNS **paying,** paying off, paying up <nonformal>, payoff; **defrayment,** defrayal; paying out, doling out, **disbursal**; **discharge,** settlement, clearance, liquidation, amortization, amortizement, retirement, satisfaction; quittance; **debt service,** interest payment, sinking-fund payment; **remittance;** installment; **cash,** hard cash, spot cash, cash payment, cash on the nail *and* cash on the barrelhead <both nonformal>; pay-as-you-go; payment in kind
peace NOUNS *pax* <L>; **peacetime,** freedom from war, cessation of combat, exemption from hostilities, public tranquillity; **harmony,** accord
peaceful ADJS **pacific,** peaceable; tranquil, serene; idyllic, pastoral; halcyon, soft, piping, **calm, quiet,** restful, **untroubled,** orderly, **at peace;** concordant; bloodless
peacemaker NOUNS make-peace, reconciler, smoother-over; **pacifier,** pacificator; **conciliator,** propitiator, **appeaser**
peace of mind NOUNS **composure,** mental composure, calm of mind; peace of heart, peace of soul *or* spirit, peace of God

peace which passeth all understanding
Bible

peacock NOUNS 1 peafowl, peahen, bird of Juno
2 **strutter,** swaggerer, swash, swasher, **swashbuckler,** miles gloriosus
peak NOUNS 1 **summit,** top; **tip-top,** pinnacle; **summit,** mountaintop, point, topmost point *or* pinnacle, **crest,** tor, *pic* <Fr>, *pico* <Sp>; **limit,** extremity, extreme, **acme,** apogee, climax, **maximum,** ceiling, crown; **utmost,** uttermost, utmost extent, highest degree, nth degree *or* power, *ne plus ultra* <L>; **acme of perfection,** pink, pink of perfection, culmination, perfection, height
VERBS 2 **top,** top off, **crown, cap,** crest, **head,** tip, surmount; **culminate,** consummate, climax
peaked ADJS **haggard,** poor, puny, peaky <nonformal>, **pinched;** shriveled, withered; **wizened,** weazeny; **emaciated,** emaciate, emacerated, **wasted,** attenuated, worn to a shadow
peal NOUNS 1 **ring,** chime; toll, knell
VERBS 2 **ring,** tintinnabulate, sound; **toll,** knell, sound a knell; **chime**
peanuts NOUNS **petty cash,** pocket money, pin money, spending money, mad money, **change,** small change; nickels and dimes *and* chicken feed *and* chickenshit <all nonformal>
pearly ADJS **iridescent,** opalescent, nacreous, pearl-like, rainbowlike, mother-of-pearl; pearly-white, pearl-white;
peasant NOUNS **countryman,** countrywoman, **provincial,** son of the soil, tiller of the soil; *campesino* <Sp>, *Bauer* <Ger>, rustic; **peon,** hind, fellah, muzhik; hick *and* yokel *and* rube *and* hayseed *and* shit-kicker <all nonformal>, **bumpkin,** country bumpkin, clod, **clodhopper** <nonformal>, hillbilly *and* woodhick <both nonformal>
peculiar ADJS **odd, queer,** absurd, singular, curious, oddball <nonformal>, weird *and* kooky *and* freaky *and* freaked-out <all nonformal>, quaint, **eccentric,** gonzo <nonformal>; **strange,** outlandish, off-the-wall <informal>, surreal, not for real <nonformal>, passing strange

peculiarity NOUNS **eccentricity, idiosyncrasy,** idiocrasy, erraticism, erraticness, **queerness, oddity,** strangeness, singularity, freakishness, freakiness, quirkiness, crotchetiness, dottiness, crankiness, crankism, crackpotism; abnormality, anomaly, unnaturalness, irregularity, deviation, deviancy, differentness, divergence, aberration

peddler NOUNS **vendor,** huckster, hawker, butcher <old>, higgler, cadger <Scots>, colporteur, chapman <Brit>; coster *or* costermonger <both Brit>; sidewalk salesman

pedestal NOUNS **base; stand,** standard

pedestrian NOUNS 1 **walker,** walkist; foot traveler, foot passenger, hoofer <nonformal>, footbacker <nonformal>, ambulator, peripatetic
ADJS 2 **prosaic,** prosy, prosing; unpoetical, poetryless; **plain,** common, commonplace, ordinary, unembellished, mundane; **matter-of-fact,** unromantic, unidealistic, unimpassioned; **unimaginative,** insipid, vapid, flat; humdrum, tiresome, **dull**

pedigree NOUNS **genealogy,** stemma, *Stammbaum* <Ger>, genealogical tree, **family tree,** tree; genogram

peek NOUNS 1 **glance,** glance *or* flick of the eye, squiz <Australia>, slant <nonformal>, rapid glance, cast, side-glance; **glimpse,** flash, quick sight; **peep;** wink, blink, flicker *or* twinkle of an eye; casual glance, **half an eye;** *coup d'œil* <Fr>
VERBS 2 **pry, snoop,** peep, spy, nose, nose into, have a long *or* big nose, poke *or* stick one's nose in; meddle

peel NOUNS 1 peeling, rind; skin, epicarp; covering, **coat,** coating, veneer, film, patina, scum
VERBS 2 **pare,** skin, strip, flay, excoriate, decorticate, bark, denude

peer NOUNS 1 **equal, match,** mate, twin, fellow, **like, equivalent,** opposite number, counterpart, answer <nonformal>, vis à vis, equipollent, coequal, parallel, ditto <nonformal>; **compeer,** colleague, peer group; **nobleman,** noble, gentleman
VERBS 2 **look,** have a look, take a gander *and* take a look <both nonformal>, direct the eyes, turn *or* bend the eyes, cast one's eye, lift up the eyes; **look at,** take a look at, eye, **eyeball** <nonformal>, have a look-see <nonformal>, look on *or* upon, gaze at *or* upon; **watch,** observe, view, regard; keep one's eyes peeled *or* skinned, be watchful *or* observant *or* vigilant, keep one's eyes open

peerless ADJS **matchless, champion; unmatched,** unmatchable, unrivaled, unparagoned, unparalleled, immortal, **unequaled,** never-to-be-equaled, unpeered, unexampled, unapproached, unapproachable, **unsurpassed,** unexcelled; inimitable, **incomparable,** beyond compare *or* comparison, **unique;** in a class by itself, *sui generis* <L>, easily first, *facile princeps* <L>; second to none, *nulli secundus* <L>

peeve NOUNS 1 **complaint,** grievance, pet peeve, **groan; dissent,** protest; hard luck story <nonformal>, tale of woe; **grudge,** spite, crow to pick *or* pluck *or* pull, bone to pick
VERBS 2 **annoy,** irk, vex, nettle, provoke, pique, miff <nonformal>, distemper, **ruffle, disturb,** discompose, **roil,** rile, **aggravate,** make a nuisance of oneself, **exasperate,** exercise, try one's patience, try the patience of a saint

pellet NOUNS **sphere; ball,** orb, orbit, **globe,** rondure; **shot; bullet,** slug

pelt NOUNS 1 **fur, hide,** fell, fleece, vair <heraldry>
VERBS 2 **stone,** lapidate <old>, pellet; brickbat *or* egg <both nonformal>; **throw,** fling, sling, pitch, toss, cast, hurl, heave, chuck, chunk *and* peg <both nonformal>; **riddle, pepper,** pump full of lead <nonformal>; snipe, pick off

pen NOUNS 1 **enclosure,** close, **confine,** precinct, enclave, coop, fold; **penitentiary,** keep, penal institution
VERBS 2 **enclose,** close in, bound, include, **contain;** compass, encompass; **surround,** encircle; **shut in,** coop in, confine; coop, corral, cage, impound, mew; **imprison,** incarcerate, jail, lock up
3 **write, pencil,** drive *or* push the pen *or* pencil <nonformal>; take pen in hand; **put in writing,** put in black and white; author, **compose, indite,** formulate, produce, prepare

penalize VERBS put *or* impose *or* inflict a penalty *or* sanctions on; **punish; handicap,** put at a disadvantage

penalty NOUNS **sanctions,** penal *or* punitive measures; punishment; **reprisal,** retaliation, compensation, price; the devil to pay

penance NOUNS penitence, repentance;

penitential act *or* exercise, **mortification,** maceration, flagellation, lustration; **asceticism,** fasting; **purgation,** purgatory; **sackcloth and ashes;** hair shirt

penchant NOUNS **inclination,** partiality, fancy, favor, predilection, preference, propensity, proclivity, **leaning, bent,** turn, tilt, bias, **affinity**

pending ADJS **overhanging,** overhung, lowering, **impending,** impendent; pendent, dependent, depending, contingent, conditional, conditioned; **open,** in question, at issue, **in the balance,** up in the air, up for grabs <nonformal>, **in suspense,** in a state of suspense, suspenseful

penetrate VERBS **affect,** pierce, go through one, go deep; touch a chord, **touch a sympathetic chord,** touch one's heart, tug at the heart *or* heartstrings, go to one's heart, get under one's skin; **pervade,** permeate; **get over** *or* **across** <nonformal>, come through, register <nonformal>, sink in, soak in; **imbue,** imbrue, **infuse,** suffuse, transfuse, breathe, **instill,** infiltrate, **impregnate**

penetrating ADJS **piercing,** stabbing, cold, cutting, stinging, biting, keen, brisk, sharp, caustic, astringent, **striking,** incisive, trenchant, poignant, slashing, mordant, acid, corrosive; **sagacious,** discerning, acute, cogent

penis NOUNS **genitals,** phallus, *lingam* <Skt>; gonads

penitent NOUNS 1 confessor; **prodigal son,** prodigal returned; Magdalen
ADJS 2 **repentant;** penitential, penitentiary; **contrite,** abject, humble, humbled, **sheepish,** apologetic, touched, softened, melted

penitentiary NOUNS **prison,** prisonhouse, minimum- *or* maximum-security facility, pen <nonformal>, keep, penal institution, bastille, state prison, federal prison; maximum- *or* minimum-security prison

pen name NOUNS **nom de plume;** alias, pseudonym, anonym, **assumed name,** false *or* fictitious name

pennant NOUNS **flag, banner,** oriflamme, standard, gonfalon *or* gonfanon, guidon, *vexillum* <L>, *labarum* <L>; pennon, pennoncel, banneret, banderole, swallowtail, burgee, **streamer;** bunting

penniless ADJS **destitute,** broke *and* cleaned out *and* tapped out *and* wiped out <all nonformal>, down-and-out, in the gutter; moneyless, fortuneless, out of funds, **without a sou,** without a penny to bless oneself with, without one dollar to rub against another; insolvent, in the red, **bankrupt**

penny pincher NOUNS **niggard,** tightwad *and* cheapskate <both nonformal>, **miser,** hard man with a buck <nonformal>, **skinflint,** scrooge, pinchfist, churl, muckworm

pension NOUNS annuity; old-age insurance, retirement benefits, social security, remittance

pensive ADJS **wistful,** tristful; **thoughtful,** cogitative, **contemplative,** reflective, speculative, deliberative, meditative, ruminative, ruminant

peon NOUNS **peasant,** hind, fellah, muzhik

people NOUNS 1 **population, inhabitants,** habitancy, dwellers, **populace,** whole people, people at large, citizenry, folk, souls, living souls, body, whole body, warm bodies <nonformal>; **public,** general public; **family,** relatives, relations, folks <nonformal>
VERBS 2 empeople, **populate, inhabit,** denizen; colonize, **settle,** settle in, plant

the people NOUNS **the populace,** the public, the general public, people in general, everyone, everybody; **the population,** the citizenry, the whole people, the polity, the body politic; **common people,** ordinary people *or* folk, persons, folk, folks, gentry; the common sort, plain people *or* folks, the common run <nonformal>, the rank and file

pep NOUNS **liveliness,** life, spirit, verve, energy, adrenalin; moxie *and* oomph *and* pizzazz *and* piss and vinegar <all nonformal>, **vim**

peppy ADJS **spirited, lively,** gingery <nonformal>, racy, sparkling, vivacious; piquant, poignant, pungent

perceive VERBS **see, discern,** make out, descry; see the light, see daylight <nonformal>, wake up, wake up to, tumble to <nonformal>, come alive; **see through,** see to the bottom of, penetrate, see into, pierce, plumb; see at a glance, see with half an eye; understand, comprehend, fathom

perception NOUNS **sensation,** sense, feeling; sense impression, percept, sense perception; **vision,** sight, eyesight, seeing; power of sight, sense of sight, visual sense; discernment; perspicacity, perspicuity, sharp *or* acute *or* keen sight; **sagacity,** sagaciousness, **astuteness,** acumen

perceptive ADJS **discerning,** perspicacious, insightful; **astute,** judicious

perch NOUNS 1 **footing,** foothold, toehold, hold, perch, purchase; footrest
VERBS 2 **rest on,** stand on, repose on, **sit on,** ride, piggyback on; **straddle,** bestraddle, stride, bestride

percolate VERBS **trickle,** dribble, dripple, **drip,** drop, spurtle; **filter,** leach, lixiviate; distill, condense, sweat; seep, weep; **gurgle**

perennial ADJS 1 indeciduous, **evergreen,** sempervirent, ever-new, ever-young; ever-blooming, ever-bearing
2 **incessant,** constant, steady, stable, **ceaseless,** unceasing, **endless,** unending, never-ending, **interminable**

perfect VERBS 1 **touch up,** finish, put on the finishing touches, polish, fine down, fine-tune <nonformal>, tone up, **brush up, furbish,** furbish up, spruce, **spruce up,** freshen, vamp, vamp up, rub up, brighten up, polish, polish up, shine <nonformal>; retouch; **revive,** renovate; **repair,** fix
2 ADJS **ideal, faultless,** flawless, unflawed, not to be improved, **impeccable,** absolute; **just right;** spotless, stainless, taintless, unblemished, untainted, unspotted, immaculate, **pure,** uncontaminated, unadulterated, unmixed; sinless; chaste; indefectible, trouble-free; infallible; beyond all praise, irreproachable, unfaultable, *sans peur et sans reproche* <Fr>, **matchless,** peerless

perfectionist NOUNS precisian, precisianist, stickler, nitpicker <nonformal>, captious critic

perforate VERBS **pierce,** empierce, penetrate, puncture, punch, hole, prick; **tap,** broach; stab, stick, pink, run through; **transfix,** transpierce, fix, **impale,** spit, skewer; gore, spear, lance, spike, needle; **bore,** drill, auger; **ream,** ream out, countersink, gouge, gouge out; trepan, trephine; punch full of holes, make look like Swiss cheese *or* a sieve, **riddle,** honeycomb

perform VERBS **execute,** enact; transact; discharge, dispatch; conduct, **manage, handle;** dispose of, take care of, **deal with,** cope with; **make,** accomplish, complete; enact, dramatize; **act, play,** playact, tread the boards, strut one's stuff <nonformal>; appear, appear on the stage; **operate,** function, run, work

performance NOUNS **execution,** carrying out, enactment; **transaction; discharge,** dispatch; conduct, **handling,** management, administration; **achievement,** accomplishment, effectuation, implementation; commission, perpetration; completion; **master stroke,** *tour de force* <Fr>, exploit, adventure, gest, **enterprise,** initiative, production, track record <nonformal>; taking a role *or* part, theatrical performance, **show,** presentation, entertainment, stage presentation *or* performance

performer NOUNS **entertainer,** public entertainer; artist, artiste; impersonator, female impersonator; **vaudevillian,** vaudevillist; dancer, hoofer <nonformal>; song and dance man; chorus girl, show girl, chorine <nonformal>; coryphée; chorus boy *or* man; burlesque queen <nonformal>, **stripteaser,** exotic dancer, ecdysiast; **musician,** musico, **music maker,** professional musician

perfume NOUNS 1 **fragrance,** aroma, scent, redolence, balminess, **incense, bouquet,** sweet smell, sweet savor; odor; spice, spiciness; muskiness; fruitiness
VERBS 2 **scent,** cense, incense, thurify, aromatize, odorize, fumigate, embalm

peril NOUNS **danger,** endangerment, imperilment, jeopardy, hazard, risk, cause for alarm, **menace,** threat; **crisis,** emergency, hot spot, nasty *or* tricky spot, pass, pinch, strait, plight, predicament; powder keg, time bomb; gathering clouds, storm clouds

period NOUNS 1 **point, juncture,** stage; **interval,** lapse of time, time frame, space, span, timespan, stretch, time-lag, time-gap; **time,** while, **moment,** minute, instant, hour, day, **season;** psychological moment; pregnant *or* fateful moment, fated moment, kairos, moment of truth; **spell**
2 **menstruation,** menstrual discharge *or* flow *or* flux, catamenia, catamenial discharge, flowers <old>, **the curse** <nonformal>, the curse of Eve; **menses, monthlies,** courses, that time

periodic ADJS periodical, seasonal, epochal, **cyclic** *or* cyclical, serial, isochronal, metronomic; measured, steady, even, **rhythmic** *or* rhythmical; **recurrent,** recurring, reoccurring; **intermittent,** reciprocal, alternate

periodical NOUNS **serial, journal,** gazette; ephemeris; **magazine,** book *and* zine <both nonformal>; pictorial; review; organ, **house organ; trade journal,** trade magazine; daily, weekly, biweekly, bimonthly, fortnightly, monthly, quarterly; annual, yearbook; daybook, diary

peripheral ADJS **environing,** surrounding, encompassing, enclosing; **enveloping,** wrapping, enwrapping, enfolding, embracing; **encircling,** circling; bordering; circumjacent, circumferential, circumambient, ambient; circumfluent, circumfluous; circumflex; **roundabout,** suburban, neighboring

perish VERBS **expire,** succumb, die, cease, end, come to an end, go, pass, **pass away,** vanish, disappear, fade away, run out, peg *or* conk out <nonformal>, come to nothing *or* naught, be no more, be done for; be all over with, be all up with <nonformal>

perishable ADJS **impermanent,** unenduring, undurable, nondurable, nonpermanent; **passing,** fleeting, flitting, flying, fading, dying; fugitive, fugacious

perjury NOUNS **deceitfulness;** falseness; false swearing, oath breaking, forswearing, untruthfulness, credibility gap; **insincerity,** unsincereness, uncandidness, uncandor, unfrankness, disingenuousness; **prevarication,** equivocation

perky ADJS **lighthearted,** light, lightsome; **buoyant,** corky <nonformal>, resilient; **jaunty,** debonair, carefree, free and easy; **breezy,** airy

permanent ADJS **changeless,** unchanging, immutable, unvarying, unshifting; **unchanged,** unchangeable, unvaried, **unaltered,** inalterable, inviolate, undestroyed, intact; **constant, persistent,** sustained, fixed, firm, solid, steadfast, like the Rock of Gibraltar, faithful; unchecked, unfailing, unfading; **lasting, enduring,** abiding, remaining, staying, continuing; durable; perpetual; stable

permeate VERBS **pervade,** penetrate; **suffuse,** inform, transfuse, perfuse, diffuse, leaven, imbue; **fill,** extend throughout, leave no void, occupy; creep *or* crawl *or* swarm with, be lousy with <nonformal>, teem with; honeycomb

permission NOUNS **ratification,** endorsement, acceptance, approval, approbation, subscription, signing-off, imprimatur, **sanction,** the OK *and* the okay *and* the green light *and* the go-ahead *and* the nod <all nonformal>, **certification,** confirmation, validation, authentication, authorization, warrant; **stamp of approval**

permissive ADJS **indulgent,** compliant, complaisant, **obliging,** accommodating, agreeable, amiable, gracious, generous, benignant, affable, decent, kind, kindly, benign, benevolent; **hands-off** <nonformal>, overpermissive, overindulgent; **nonrestrictive,** unrestrictive

permit NOUNS 1 **license, warrant;** building permit, learner's permit; driver's license, marriage license, hunting license, fishing license, etc; nihil obstat, imprimatur

VERBS 2 **allow,** admit, let, give permission, give leave, make possible; **allow** *or* **permit of;** give *or* leave room for, open the door to; consent; **grant,** accord, vouchsafe; okay *and* OK *and* give the nod *or* go-ahead *or* green light *or* go sign <all nonformal>, say *or* give the word <nonformal>; **enable,** clear the road *or* path for, smooth the way for, open the way for, open the door to, open up the possibility of

perpetrate VERBS bring about, bring to pass, **bring off,** produce, deliver <nonformal>, **do the trick,** put across *or* through; swing *or* swing it *and* hack it *and* cut it *and* cut the mustard <all nonformal>; **achieve,** accomplish, realize; **inflict,** wreak, do to; **commit;** pull off <nonformal>; go and do, up and do *or* take and do <both nonformal>

perpetrator NOUNS **evildoer, wrongdoer,** worker of ill *or* evil, **malefactor,** malfeasant, malfeasor, misfeasor, malevolent, public enemy, **sinner, villain,** villainess, transgressor, delinquent; bad *or* bad guy *and* baddy *and* meany *and* wrongo *and* black hat <all nonformal>; **criminal,** outlaw, felon, **crook** <nonformal>, lawbreaker, perp <nonformal>

perpetual ADJS **everlasting,** everliving, ever-being, ever-abiding, ever-during, ever-durable, permanent, perdurable, indestructible; **eternal,** sempiternal, **infinite**, aeonian *or* eonian; dateless, ageless, timeless, immemorial; **endless,** unending, never-ending, without end, **interminable,** nonterminous, nonterminating; **continual,** continuous, steady, **constant, ceaseless,** nonstop, unceasing, never-ceasing, **incessant,** unremitting, unintermitting, uninterrupted

perpetuate VERBS **preserve,** preserve from oblivion, keep fresh *or* alive, perennialize, **eternalize,** eternize, **immortalize;** monumentalize; **sustain,** protract, prolong, extend, lengthen, spin *or* string out; **keep up,** keep going, keep alive, survive

perplex VERBS **baffle, confound,** daze, amaze <old>, maze, addle, fuddle, muddle, **mystify, puzzle,** nonplus, put to one's wit's end; keep one guessing, keep in suspense

persecute VERBS oppress, **torment,** victimize, play cat and mouse with, **harass,** get *or* keep after, get *or* keep at, harry, hound, beset; pursue, hunt

persevere VERBS 1 **persist, carry on,** go on, **keep on,** keep up, keep at, **keep at it,** keep going, keep driving, keep trying, try and try again, **keep the ball rolling,** keep the pot boiling, keep up the good work; not take 'no' for an answer; not accept compromise *or* defeat; **endure,** last, **continue**

2 <nonformal> **stick,** stick to it, stick with it, stick it, stick it out, hang on for dear life, hang in, hang in there, hang tough, tough it out, keep on trucking, keep in keeping on; **go the limit,** go the whole hog, go the whole nine yards, go all out, shoot the works, go for broke, go through hell and high water

persist VERBS **persevere,** keep at it, stick it out, stick to it, stick with it, never say die, see it through, hang in *and* hang tough *and* not know when one is licked <all nonformal>; press on; perseverate, iterate, reiterate, **harp,** go on about, chew one's ear off *and* run off at the mouth <both nonformal>, beat a dead horse

persistent ADJS **persevering,** perseverant, persisting, insistent; **enduring,** permanent, **constant,** lasting; continuing; resolute; **diligent,** assiduous, sedulous, industrious; dogged, plodding, slogging, plugging; **pertinacious,** tenacious, stick-to-itive <nonformal>; **unswerving,** unremitting, unabating, unintermitting, uninterrupted; **unfaltering,** unwavering, unflinching; relentless, **unrelenting; obstinate,** stubborn; **unrelaxing,** unfailing, **untiring,** unwearying, unflagging, never-tiring, **tireless,** weariless, **indefatigable,** undiscouraged, undaunted, indomitable, unconquerable, invincible, game to the last *or* to the end

person NOUNS **human, human being,** man, woman, child, member of the human race *or* family, Adamite, daughter of Eve; **mortal,** life, **soul,** living soul; **being,** creature, clay, ordinary clay; **individual,** personage, **personality,** personhood, individuality

personable ADJS **persuasive,** suasive, **winning,** magnetic, charming, enchanting, charismatic; **comely,** fair, good-looking, nice-looking, well-favored, presentable, agreeable, becoming, pleasing, goodly, bonny, likely <nonformal>, **sightly**

personal ADJS **individual,** private, peculiar, idiosyncratic; person-to-person, one-to-one, one-on-one; **intimate,** inmost, innermost, interior, inward

personality NOUNS 1 **psyche,** psychic apparatus, **self;** personage, **personhood,** individuality, personship, personal identity; **selfness,** selfhood, **egohood,** self-identity
2 **celebrity,** famous person, person of renown

personify VERBS **embody,** body forth, incarnate, personate, impersonate; **illustrate,** demonstrate, exemplify; metaphorize, similize; personalize; symbolize

personnel NOUNS **staff, employees,** human resources, help, hired help, the help, **crew, gang,** men, force, servantry, retinue

perspective NOUNS **vista,** view, horizon, prospect, outlook, survey; range, scan, scope; **outlook,** mental outlook; *Anschauung* <Ger>, **point of view,** viewpoint, standpoint, *optique* <Fr>; **frame of reference**

perspiration NOUNS **sweat,** water; exudation, exudate; diaphoresis, sudor; honest sweat, the sweat of one's brow; beads of sweat, beaded brow; cold sweat

perspire VERBS **sweat,** exude; break out in a sweat, **get all in a lather** <nonformal>; sweat like a trooper *or* horse, swelter, wilt

persuade VERBS **prevail on** *or* **upon,** prevail with, **sway,** convince, lead to believe, **bring round,** bring to reason, bring to one's senses; **win, win over,** win around, bring over, draw over, gain, gain over; **talk over, talk into,** argue into, out-talk <nonformal>; hook *and* hook in <both nonformal>, con *and* do a snow job on <both nonformal>, sell *and* sell one on <both nonformal>, **charm, captivate;** wear down, overcome one's resistance, arm-twist *and* twist one's arm <both nonformal>

persuasive ADJS persuading; wheedling, cajoling; hortative, hortatory; exhortative, exhortatory; **convincing,** convictional, well-founded, assuring, impressive, satisfying, satisfactory, confidence-building; decisive, absolute, conclusive, determinative

pert ADJS **impudent, impertinent,** saucy, flip <nonformal>, flippant, **cocky** *and* cheeky *and* **fresh** *and* facy *and* crusty *and* nervy <all nonformal>; **animated,** spirited, bubbly, ebullient, effervescent, **vivacious, sprightly,** chipper *and* perky <both nonformal>

pertinent ADJS **relevant,** appertaining, **germane, apposite,** cogent, material, admissible, applicable, applying, pertaining, belonging, involving, appropriate, **apropos,** *à propos* <Fr>, to the purpose, **to the point,** in point, *ad rem* <L>

perturb VERBS **agitate,** disturb, trouble, disquiet, discompose, discombobulate <nonformal>, unsettle, **stir, ruffle,** shake, shake up, shock, upset, make waves, jolt, jar, rock, stagger, electrify, bring *or* pull one up short, give one a turn <nonformal>; fuss <nonformal>, flutter, flurry, rattle, disconcert, **fluster**

peruse VERBS **study,** regard studiously, **read,** go over, have one's nose in a book <nonformal>; contemplate; **examine**; give the mind to; **pore over,** vet <nonformal>; **search into,** go into, delve into, dig into, poke into, pry into; **probe,** sound, plumb, fathom

pervade VERBS **permeate,** penetrate; **suffuse,** inform, transfuse, perfuse, diffuse, leaven, imbue; **fill,** extend throughout, leave no void, occupy; **overrun,** overswarm, overspread, bespread, run through, meet one at every turn, whelm, overwhelm; creep *or* crawl *or* swarm with, be lousy with <nonformal>, teem with

pervasive ADJS pervading, suffusive, perfusive, suffusing, all-pervading, ubiquitous, omnipresent, **universal**

perverse ADJS **contrary,** wrongheaded, wayward, froward, difficult, cross-grained, cantankerous, feisty, ornery <nonformal>; sullen, sulky, stuffy; irascible

pervert NOUNS 1 **degenerate,** sexual pervert; **deviant,** deviate, sex *or* sexual pervert, sex fiend, sex criminal, sexual psychopath; sodomist, sodomite, bugger; pederast; paraphiliac; zoophiliac; pedophiliac; sadist; masochist; sadomasochist, algolagniac; fetishist; transvestite *or* TV, cross-dresser; narcissist; exhibitionist; necrophiliac; coprophiliac; scotophiliac, voyeur; erotomaniac, nymphomaniac, satyr; rapist
VERBS 2 **falsify,** twist, garble, put a false construction upon, give a spin, give a false coloring, color, varnish, slant, strain, torture; put words in someone's mouth; **bias;** misrepresent, misconstrue, misinterpret, misrender, misdirect; misuse; send *or* deliver the wrong signal *or* message
3 **corrupt,** debase, degrade, degenerate, **deprave,** debauch, defile, violate, desecrate, deflower, ravish, ravage, despoil; warp, twist

pesky ADJS **annoying,** troublesome, bothersome, worrisome, bothering, troubling, disturbing, plaguing, plaguesome, plaguey <nonformal>, pestilent, pestilential, pesty *and* pestiferous <both nonformal>, pestering, plaguing, nagging, dunning

pessimist NOUNS **cynic,** malist, nihilist; killjoy, gloomy Gus *and* calamity howler *and* worrywart <all nonformal>, seek-sorrow, Job's comforter, prophet of doom, Cassandra, Eeyore; negativist; defeatist

one who is always building dungeons in the air
JOHN GALSWORTHY

pest NOUNS **nuisance, bother,** botheration <nonformal>, public nuisance, **trouble, problem,** pain <nonformal>, bore, crashing bore <nonformal>; **drag** *and* downer <both nonformal>; **pain in the neck** *or* **in the ass** <nonformal>; **blight**

pester VERBS **nag,** niggle, **carp at,** fuss at, fret at, yap *or* **pick at** <nonformal>, peck at, nibble at, **henpeck, pick on** *and* pick at <all nonformal>, bug *and* hassle <nonformal>

pesticide NOUNS **poison,** eradicant; systemic insecticide *or* systemic, fumigant, chemosterilant

pet NOUNS 1 **favorite,** preference; **darling,** idol, jewel, apple of one's eye, fair-haired boy, man after one's own heart; fondling, cosset, minion; spoiled child *or* darling, *enfant gâté* <Fr>; teacher's pet
VERBS 2 **stroke, caress,** fondle; **nuzzle,** nose, rub noses; feel up <nonformal>; rub, rub against, massage, knead
3 **pamper,** cosset, **coddle,** mollycoddle, make a lap dog of, **spoil;** spare the rod
ADJS 4 **beloved,** loved, dear, darling, precious; favorite; **cherished,** prized, treasured, held dear; **well-liked,** popular; **well-beloved,** dearly beloved, dear to one's heart, after one's heart *or* own heart, dear as the apple of one's eye

peter out VERBS be unproductive, **come to nothing,** come to naught, hang fire, flash in the pan, fizzle out

petite ADJS **little, small**, smallish; **slight,** exiguous; **puny, trifling,** poky, piffling *and* pindling *and* piddling *and* piddly <all nonformal>, **dinky** <nonformal>; pintsized <nonformal>, half-pint; knee-high, knee-high to a grasshopper; short

petition NOUNS 1 **request,** asking; the touch <nonformal>; desire, wish, expressed desire; petitioning, impetration, address; **application; requisition,** demand
VERBS 2 present *or* prefer a petition, sign a petition, circulate a petition; **pray,** sue; **apply to,** call on *or* upon; **supplicate,** invoke, make supplication, **implore, beseech**, obtest

pet peeve NOUNS **complaint,** grievance, peeve, **groan;** hard luck story <nonformal>, tale of woe

petrified ADJS 1 **terrified,** stunned, stupefied, paralyzed, frozen
2 **hardened,** lapidified <old>, fossilized

petty ADJS **insignificant,** inconsequential, negligible, unimportant, **trivial,** trifling, nugacious, nugatory, mean, niggling, picayune *or* picayunish, nickel-and-dime *and* penny-ante <both nonformal>; shallow, depthless, cursory, superficial, skin-deep; **ungenerous, illiberal,** small, little, paltry, mingy, **niggardly, stingy**

petulant ADJS **peevish,** pettish, **querulous, fretful,** resentful; **complaining,** faultfinding

peyote NOUNS

> <nonformal> bad seed, big chief, buttons, cactus, P, topi

phallic ADJS **genital;** penile, penial

phantom NOUNS 1 **phantasm,** phantasma, wraith, specter; shadow, shade; phantasmagoria; **fantasy,** wildest dream; **figment of the imagination**, phantom of the mind; **apparition,** appearance; vision, waking dream; shape, form, figure, presence; eidolon, idolum
ADJS 2 **spectral,** specterlike; **ghostly,** ghostish, ghosty, ghostlike; **spiritual,** psychic, psychical; **phantomlike,** phantomic *or* phantomical, phantasmal, phantasmic, **wraithlike,** wraithy, shadowy; etheric, ectoplasmic, astral, ethereal; incorporeal

pharmacy NOUNS **drugstore,** chemist *and* chemist's shop <both Brit>, apothecary's shop, dispensary, dispensatory

phenomenal ADJS **wonderful,** wondrous, marvelous, miraculous, fantastic, fabulous, **prodigious,** stupendous, unheard-of, unprecedented, extraordinary, exceptional, rare, unique, singular, **remarkable,** striking, **sensational;** incredible, inconceivable, outlandish, unimaginable, incomprehensible; **bewildering,** puzzling, enigmatic

phenomenon NOUNS **event,** occurrence, incident, episode, experience, adventure, hap, **happening,** happenstance, fact, matter of fact, reality, particular, circumstance, **occasion,** turn of events

philanderer NOUNS woman chaser, **ladies' man,** heartbreaker; masher, lady-killer, wolf, skirt chaser, man on the make *and* make-out artist <both nonformal>; libertine, lecher, cocksman <nonformal>, seducer, Casanova, Don Juan

philanthropic ADJS **benevolent,** charitable, beneficent, altruistic, humanitarian; **bighearted,** largehearted, greathearted, freehearted; **generous**; almsgiving, eleemosynary; giving, generous to a fault, liberal

philanthropist NOUNS **altruist,** benevolist, **humanitarian,** man of good will, **do-gooder,** bleeding heart <nonformal>, well-doer, power for good; Robin Hood, Lady Bountiful

philistine NOUNS 1 **vulgarian,** low *or* vul-

gar *or* ill-bred fellow, *épicier* <Fr>; Babbitt, bourgeois; **conventionalist**
ADJS 2 **uncultured,** uncultivated, unrefined, rude; nonintellectual, **unintellectual; lowbrow** *and* lowbrowed *and* lowbrowish <all nonformal>

philosopher NOUNS philosophizer, philosophe; philosophaster; **thinker,** speculator; casuist; metaphysician, cosmologist; sophist

philosophize VERBS reason, probe

philosophy NOUNS **ideology,** system of ideas, body of ideas, system of theories; world view, *Weltanschauung* <Ger>; ethos

phlegmatic ADJS **lethargic,** hebetudinous, **dull,** desensitized, sluggish, torpid, languid, slack, soporific, comatose, **languorous,** apathetic, logy, dopey <nonformal>, groggy, heavy, leaden, flat, slack, tame, **dead,** lifeless

phobia NOUNS **fear, fright,** affright; **dread,** unholy dread, **terror, horror,** horrification, mortal *or* abject fear; funk *or* blue funk <both nonformal>; **panic,** panic fear *or* terror

phone NOUNS 1 **telephone,** horn <nonformal>, telephone set; telephone extension, extension; wall telephone, desk telephone; dial telephone, touch-tone telephone, push-button telephone; coin telephone, pay station, pay phone; mobile telephone *or* phone <nonformal>, cellular telephone *or* phone <nonformal>
VERBS 2 **telephone, call,** call on the phone <nonformal>, put in *or* make a call, **call up, ring,** ring up, give a ring *or* buzz <nonformal>, buzz <nonformal>

phonic ADJS **acoustic,** acoustical, **sonic;** subsonic, supersonic, ultrasonic, hypersonic; transonic *or* transsonic, faster than sound

phony NOUNS **fake** *and* **fraud** <both nonformal>; affecter; mannerist; **pretender,** actor, playactor <nonformal>, performer; paper tiger, hollow man, straw man, man of straw, empty suit <nonformal>; **hypocrite,** sanctimonious fraud, pharisee
ADJS 2 **imitation,** mock, sham, copied, fake <nonformal>, counterfeit, forged, plagiarized, unoriginal, ungenuine; **pseudo,** synthetic, synthetical, ersatz, hokey *and* hoked-up <both nonformal>; **assumed,** put-on, pretended, simulated, feigned, counterfeited; spurious; hypocritical

phosphoresce VERBS **luminesce,** fluoresce; iridesce, opalesce

photograph NOUNS 1 **photo** <nonformal>, heliograph, **picture,** shot <nonformal>; **snapshot,** snap <nonformal>; black-and-white photograph; color photograph, color print, heliochrome; slide, diapositive, transparency; candid photograph; still, still photograph; photomural; montage, photomontage; **portrait;** pinup <nonformal>, cheesecake *and* beefcake <both nonformal>; police photograph, **mug** *or* mug shot <nonformal>, positive, negative, print, enlargement, contact print, photocopy
VERBS 2 **shoot** <nonformal>, take a photograph, **take a picture,** take one's picture; **snap,** snapshot, snapshoot; **film,** get *or* capture on film; **mug** <nonformal>

phrase NOUNS 1 **maxim,** aphorism, apothegm, epigram, dictum, adage, proverb, gnome, words of wisdom, **saw, saying,** witticism, sentence, expression, catchword, catchphrase, word, byword, mot, motto, moral; common *or* current saying, stock saying, pithy saying, wise saying *or* expression, oracle, sententious expression *or* saying
VERBS 2 express, find a phrase for, give expression *or* words to, **word,** state, **frame,** conceive, style, couch, **put in** *or* **into words,** clothe *or* embody in words, couch in terms, express by *or* in words, find words to express; put, present, set out; **formulate,** formularize

physical NOUNS 1 **checkup,** physical examination, physical checkup, health examination; self-examination; exploratory examination
ADJS 2 **carnal,** carnal-minded, **fleshly,** bodily; **corporeal,** corporeous, corporal, **bodily;** somatic, somatical, somatous; worldly, earthly, here-and-now, **secular,** temporal, **unspiritual,** nonspiritual

physician NOUNS **doctor,** doc <nonformal>, Doctor of Medicine *or* MD, medical practitioner, medical man, medico <nonformal>, leech <old>, croaker *and* sawbones <both nonformal>; **general practitioner** *or* **GP;** family doctor; country doctor; **intern; resident,** house physician, resident physician; medical attendant, attending physician; **specialist,** board-certified physician *or* specialist; health-care professional, health-care provider, therapist, therapeutist, practitioner

physique NOUNS **body,** the person, carcass, anatomy, frame, bodily *or* corporal *or* corporeal entity, physical self, physical *or* bodily structure, soma; **musculature,** build, body-build, somatotype, constitution, genetic makeup

piazza NOUNS **porch,** stoop, **veranda,** patio, lanai, gallery

picayune ADJS **detailed,** minute, full, particular, meticulous, fussy, finicky *or* finicking *or* finical, picky <nonformal>, nice <old>, precise, exact, specific; **petty,** puny, piddling, piffling, niggling, pettifogging, picayunish; small-beer

pick NOUNS 1 **choice,** selection, election, preference, decision, **choosing,** free choice
2 plectrum, plectron
3 **the best,** the very best, the best ever, the top of the heap *or* the line <nonformal>, the tops <nonformal>; **select,** elect, elite, *corps d'élite* <Fr>, chosen; **cream, flower,** fat; cream of the crop, *crème de la crème* <Fr>, salt of the earth
VERBS 4 **strum, thrum, pluck,** plunk, twang, sweep the strings
5 **choose, elect,** go with <nonformal>, opt, opt for, co-opt, make *or* take one's choice, make choice of, have one's druthers <nonformal>, use *or* take up *or* exercise one's option; pick and choose; handpick, **pick out, single out,** choose out, smile on, give the nod <nonformal>, jump at, seize on; **decide between,** cull, glean, winnow, sift; separate the wheat from the chaff, separate the sheep from the goats
6 **harvest, reap,** crop, **glean, gather,** gather in, bring in, get in the harvest, reap and carry

picket NOUNS 1 picketer, demonstrator, picket line; counterdemonstrator
VERBS 2 **march,** demonstrate, counterdemonstrate

pickle NOUNS 1 **predicament,** plight, pass, fix *and* jam *and* spot *and* bind *and* scrape *and* stew <all nonformal>; pretty pickle *and* fine kettle of fish *and* how-do-you-do *and* fine how-do-you-do <all nonformal>; **spot,** tight spot; squeeze, tight squeeze
VERBS 2 **preserve, cure,** season, salt, brine, marinate *or* marinade, corn

pickpocket NOUNS cutpurse, fingersmith *and* dip <both nonformal>; **purse snatcher;** light-fingered gentry

pickup NOUNS 1 **bracer, refresher,** reviver, tonic, hair of the dog *or* hair of the dog that bit one <nonformal>
2 **acceleration,** quickening; getaway; step-up, speedup; thrust, drive, impetus; **increase**, upgrade, upping *and* boost <both nonformal>

picky ADJS **selective,** choosy, choicy <nonformal>; **strict**, perfectionistic, precisianistic, puristic; **critical, faultfinding,** carping, nitpicky <nonformal>, caviling, quibbling, pettifogging, captious, cynical

picnic NOUNS **good time,** lovely time, pleasant time; big time *and* **high time** *and* high old time <all nonformal>, laughs *and* lots of laughs *and* ball <all nonformal>, great fun

picture NOUNS 1 **image, likeness,** representation, tableau; photograph; **illustration,** illumination; mental image, mental picture, visual image, vivid *or* lifelike image, eidetic image, concept, **conception,** mental representation *or* presentation, *Vorstellung* <Ger>

a poem without words
HORACE

VERBS 2 **describe, portray,** render, **depict,** represent, delineate, limn, **paint,** draw; evoke, bring to life, make one see; **visualize,** vision, envision, envisage, image, objectify; picture in one's mind, picture to oneself, **view with the mind's eye,** contemplate in the imagination, form a mental picture of

picturesque ADJS **pictorial,** pictural, graphic; picturable; **fancy,** chichi, pretty-pretty

piddling ADJS **petty, puny,** piffling, niggling, pettifogging, picayune, picayunish; small-beer

piece NOUNS 1 **particle,** bit, scrap, bite, **fragment, morsel, crumb,** shard, potsherd, snatch, snack; **cut,** cutting, clip, clipping, paring, shaving, rasher, snip, snippet, chip, slice, collop, dollop, scoop; **tatter,** shred, stitch; **splinter,** sliver; **shiver,** smithereen <nonformal>; **lump,** gob <nonformal>, gobbet, hunk, chunk
2 **sex object;** meat *and* piece of meat *and* ass *and* piece of ass *and* hot number <all nonformal>

piecemeal ADVS **separately,** severally, one by one; **apart,** adrift, asunder, **in two,** in twain; apart from, away from, aside from; abstractly, in the abstract, objectively, impersonally

pie in the sky ADJS **ideal, idealized;** utopian, Arcadian, Edenic, paradisal

pier NOUNS 1 **pillar, column,** post, pilaster; pier buttress, buttress pier; **shaft**, upright, post, jack, pole, staff, stanchion, pile *or* piling
2 **dock,** dockage, **wharf,** quay

pierce VERBS **penetrate,** interpenetrate, pass *or* go through, get through, get into, make way into, **stab, stick** <nonformal>, plunge in; **run through,** impale, spit, **transfix,** transpierce

piercing ADJS 1 **shrill, thin,** sharp, acute, argute, keen, keening, ear-piercing; **screechy,** screeching, shrieky, shrieking, **squeaky,** squeaking, screaky, creaky, creaking; **penetrating,** stabbing, cutting, stinging, biting, keen, brisk, sharp, caustic, astringent
2 **cold,** freezing cold, **raw,** bleak, keen, sharp, bitter, biting, pinching, cutting, penetrating

piety NOUNS **piousness,** pietism; **religion,** faith; religiousness, religiosity, religionism, religious-mindedness; theism; love of God, adoration; **devoutness,** devotion, devotedness, worship, worshipfulness, prayerfulness, cultism; faithfulness, dutifulness, observance, churchgoing, conformity; **reverence,** veneration

pig NOUNS 1 **swine, hog,** porker; **shoat,** piggy, piglet, pigling; sucking *or* suckling pig; gilt; **boar, sow;** barrow; wild boar, tusker, razorback; warthog, babirusa
2 **glutton,** greedy eater, **hog** *and* chow hound *and* khazer <all nonformal>; slob

pig out VERBS **overeat,** overgorge, **overindulge, make a pig** *or* **hog of oneself,** pork out *or* scarf out <nonformal>; stuff oneself

pigsty NOUNS **hovel,** dump <nonformal>, rathole, hole, sty, pigpen, tumbledown shack

pile NOUNS 1 **down, fluff,** flue, floss, fuzz, fur
VERBS 2 **pile on,** heap, stack, heap *or* pile *or* stack up; mound, hill, bank, bank up; rick; pyramid; drift

pilfer VERBS **steal,** thieve, purloin, appropriate, take, snatch, palm, **make off with,** walk off with, run off *or* away with, abstract, disregard the distinction between *meum* and *tuum;* have one's hand in the till; **filch;** shoplift; embezzle; defraud, swindle

pilgrim NOUNS **traveler,** wayfarer, journeyer, trekker; **palmer,** hajji

pilgrimage NOUNS **journey,** *jornada* <Sp>, peregrination, sally; **expedition,** hajj, quest

pill NOUNS bolus, tablet, capsule, lozenge, troche

the pill NOUNS **contraceptive,** birth control device, oral contraceptive, **birth control pill,** morning-after pill, abortion pill

pillage VERBS **plunder, loot,** sack, ransack, rifle, freeboot, spoil, spoliate, despoil, depredate, prey on *or* upon, **raid,** reive <Scots>, ravage, ravish, raven, sweep, gut; maraud, foray, forage

pillow NOUNS cushion, bolster

pilot NOUNS 1 **steersman,** helmsman, wheelman, wheelsman, boatsteerer; conner, sailing master; harbor pilot, docking pilot; river pilot, navigator, timoneer, steerman, steerer, coxswain, boatheader
2 **aviator,** airman, flier, air pilot, licensed pilot, private pilot, airline pilot, commercial pilot, aeronaut, flyboy *and* airplane driver *and* birdman <all nonformal>; captain, chief pilot; copilot, second officer; stunt flier
VERBS 3 helm, coxswain, **steer,** guide, be at the helm *or* tiller, direct, manage, handle, run, operate, **conn** *or* cond, be at *or* have the conn; **navigate,** shape *or* chart a course
4 control, be at the controls, **fly,** manipulate, drive <nonformal>, fly left seat; **copilot,** fly right seat; solo; fly blind, fly by the seat of one's pants <nonformal>; follow the beam, ride the beam, fly on instruments; fly in formation
ADJS 5 **experimental,** test, trial; testing, proving, trying; probative, probatory, verificatory; heuristic

pimp NOUNS 1 **procurer,** pander *or* panderer, *maquereau* <Fr>, mack *or* mackman, ponce <Brit nonformal>; **bawd;** procuress, **madam** <nonformal>; white slaver
VERBS 2 procure, pander

pimple NOUNS **pustule,** papule, papula, fester, hickey *and* zit <both nonformal>; **rising,** lump, bump

pin NOUNS 1 **brooch,** stickpin, breastpin,

scatter pin, chatelaine; tie clasp *or* clip, tie bar, tiepin *or* scarfpin, tie tack *or* tie tac; lapel pin *or* button
VERBS 2 **skewer,** peg, nail, nail up, tack, staple, toggle, screw, bolt, rivet; spread-eagle <nonformal>, pin down

pinch NOUNS 1 **squeezing,** compression, clamping *or* clamping down, tightening; **pressure,** press, crush; **squeeze,** tweak, nip
2 **crisis, critical point,** crucial period, climax, climacteric; **turning point,** hinge, turn, turn of the tide, cusp; **emergency, exigency,** juncture *or* conjuncture *or* convergence of events, critical juncture, crossroads; clutch *and* crunch <nonformal>, rub, push, pass, strait, extremity, spot <nonformal>, **predicament,** bind, pass, situation
VERBS 3 **pain,** give *or* inflict pain, **hurt,** wound, afflict, distress; nip, bite, tweak

pinched ADJS 1 **constricted,** strangled, strangulated, choked, choked off, coarcted, **squeezed,** clamped, nipped, pinched-in, wasp-waisted; puckered, pursed; knitted, wrinkled
2 **straitened,** reduced to dire straits, in desperate straits, sore *or* sorely pressed, **hard-pressed, hard up** <nonformal>, up against it <nonformal>; driven from pillar to post; **desperate,** in extremities, *in extremis* <L>, at the end of one's rope *or* tether

pinch-hit VERBS **substitute for,** sub for <nonformal>, subrogate; **act for,** double for *or* as, stand *or* sit in for, understudy for, fill in for, stand in the stead of, step into *or* fill the shoes of; **relieve,** spell *and* **spell off** <both nonformal>, cover for

pine VERBS **grieve,** sorrow; weep, mourn; be dumb with grief; pine away; **eat one's heart out,** break one's heart over; **agonize,** ache, bleed; **languish,** droop, flag, wilt; fade, fade away

pink NOUNS 1 **acme of perfection,** pink of perfection, culmination, perfection, height, top, acme, ultimate, summit, pinnacle, peak, highest pitch, climax, consummation, *ne plus ultra* <L>, **the last word,** a dream come true
ADJS 2 **pinkish,** pinky; pink-cheeked; fresh-faced, fresh as a daisy *or* rose, fresh as April

pink slip NOUNS **dismissal,** the bounce, the sack <Brit nonformal>; the boot *and* the gate *and* the ax <all nonformal>; walking papers *or* ticket <nonformal>

pinnacle NOUNS **limit,** extremity, extreme, **acme,** apogee, climax, **maximum,** max <nonformal>, ceiling, **peak,** summit, crown, top

pinpoint VERBS **locate,** put one's finger on, **fix,** assign *or* consign *or* relegate to a place; zero in on, home in on; find *or* fix *or* calculate one's position, triangulate, find a line of position, **get a fix on** *or* navigational fix, navigate; **pin on,** fix on *or* upon, attach to, accrete to, connect with, fasten upon, hang on <nonformal>, **saddle on** *or* **upon,** place upon, **father upon,** settle upon, saddle with

pinup NOUNS **photograph,** cheesecake *and* beefcake <both nonformal>; centerfold

pioneer NOUNS 1 **vanguard,** spearhead, advance guard, **cutting edge,** avant-garde, outguard; precursor; **settler,** *habitant* <Canadian & Louisiana Fr>; **colonist,** colonizer, colonial, immigrant, planter; **homesteader**
VERBS 2 **go before,** blaze *or* break the trail, break new ground, be in the van *or* vanguard; **lead,** lead *or* show the way; precede, **take the initiative,** take the first step, take the lead; **break the ice,** take the plunge, break ground, cut the first turf, lay the first stone
ADJS 3 **original,** novel, unprecedented; new, fresh; underived, **firsthand; avant-garde,** revolutionary; bellwether, trailblazing

pious ADJS **religious,** religious-minded; theistic; **devout,** devoted, worshipful, prayerful, cultish, cultist, cultistic; **reverent,** reverential, venerative, venerational, adoring, solemn; faithful, dutiful; affirming, witnessing, believing; **observant,** practicing

pipe NOUNS 1 tobacco pipe; corncob, corncob pipe, Missouri meerschaum; briar pipe, briar; clay pipe, clay, churchwarden <Brit>; meerschaum; water pipe, hookah, nargileh, kalian, hubble-bubble; peace pipe, calumet
2 **tube;** tubing, piping, tubulation; tubulure
VERBS 3 **channel,** put through channels; tube, pipeline, flume, **siphon, funnel,** tap
4 **blow a horn,** sound *or* wind the horn, sound, blow, wind, **toot,** tootle, tweedle

pipe dream NOUNS **airy hope,** unreal hope, dream, golden dream, bubble, chimera, fool's paradise, quixotic ideal, utopia

pipsqueak NOUNS **nonentity,** empty suit *and* nebbish <both nonformal>, an obscurity, a nothing, cipher; whipper-snapper *and* whiffet *and* squirt *and* shrimp *and* scrub *and* runt <all nonformal>

pique NOUNS 1 **huff,** pet, tiff, miff *and* stew <both nonformal>, fret, **fume,** ferment
VERBS 2 **annoy,** irk, vex, nettle, provoke, miff *and* peeve <both nonformal>, distemper, **ruffle, disturb,** discompose, **roil,** rile, **exasperate,** exercise, try one's patience, try the patience of a saint
3 **stimulate,** whet, sharpen, quicken, enliven, liven up, pick up, jazz up <nonformal>, animate, **exhilarate,** invigorate, galvanize, fillip, give a fillip to

pirate NOUNS **corsair, buccaneer, privateer,** sea rover, rover, picaroon; air pirate, airplane hijacker, skyjacker

pirouette NOUNS 1 **whirl,** wheel, reel, **spin, turn,** round
VERBS 2 **spin,** turn, round, **go round** *or* **around,** turn round *or* around; turn a pirouette

piss NOUNS 1 **urine,** water, number one, *pish* <Yiddish>, pee *and* pee-pee *and* wee-wee *and* whizz <all nonformal>, piddle, stale
VERBS 2 **urinate,** pass *or* make water, wet, stale, piddle, pee; pee-pee *and* wee-wee *and* whizz *and* take a whizz *and* number one <all nonformal>, spend a penny, pump bilge

pit NOUNS 1 **well, shaft,** sump; **chasm,** gulf, abyss, abysm; **excavation,** dig, diggings, workings; mine, quarry
2 **indentation,** indent, indention, indenture, **dent,** dint; pock, pockmark
3 **stone,** nut; pip; fruit; grain, kernel
VERBS 4 **indent,** dent, dint, **depress,** press in, stamp, tamp, punch, punch in, impress, imprint; pock, pockmark; dimple

pitch NOUNS 1 **tone, frequency,** audio frequency *or* AF; intonation
2 **incline,** inclination, **slope, grade,** gradient, **ramp,** rapid *or* steep slope; **extent, measure,** amount, ratio, proportion, stint, standard, height, reach, remove, compass, range, scale, scope, caliber
3 **sales talk,** sales pitch, patter; spiel *or* ballyhoo <both nonformal>
VERBS 4 **toss, tumble,** toss and tumble, pitch and toss, **plunge,** hobbyhorse, pound, **rear, rock,** roll, reel, swing, sway, lurch, yaw, heave, scend, **flounder, welter, wallow;** make heavy weather
5 **incline,** lean; slope, slant, rake, grade, bank, shelve; **tilt,** tip, list, cant, careen, keel, sidle, swag, sway
6 **proposition, come on to,** hit on, put *or* make a move on, make *or* throw a pass, george, **make a play for,** play footsie with, mash <old> <all nonformal>

pitfall NOUNS **trap,** trapfall, deadfall; baited trap; **booby trap,** mine; decoy

pithy ADJS **aphoristic,** proverbial, epigrammatic, epigrammatical; **sententious,** gnomic, pungent, succinct, terse, crisp, pointed

pittance NOUNS dole; drop in the bucket *or* the ocean; **mite,** bit; short allowance, half rations, cheeseparings and candle ends; mere subsistence, starvation wages; widow's mite

pitted ADJS **rough,** jolty, **bumpy,** rutty, rutted, pocky, potholed

pity NOUNS 1 **sympathy,** feeling, fellow feeling in suffering, **commiseration,** condolence, condolences; **compassion, mercy,** ruth, rue, humanity; **sensitivity; clemency,** quarter, reprieve, mitigation, relief, favor, grace; **leniency,** lenity, gentleness; **kindness,** benevolence; pardon, **forgiveness**; self-pity; **pathos**
VERBS 2 **be** *or* **feel sorry for,** feel sorrow for; **commiserate,** compassionate; open one's heart; **sympathize, sympathize with,** feel for, weep for, lament for, bleed, bleed for, have one's heart bleed for *or* go out to, condole with

pivot VERBS **turn round** *or* **around** *or* **about,** turn, make a U-turn, turn on a dime, turn tail, **come** *or* **go about,** put about, fetch about; **swivel,** pivot about, swing, round, swing round; wheel, wheel about, whirl, spin; heel, turn upon one's heel

pivotal ADJS **urgent, imperative,** imperious, **compelling, pressing,** high-priority, high-pressure, crying, clamorous, insistent, instant, exigent; crucial, critical, acute

pixie NOUNS **imp,** sprite, elf, puck, kobold, *diablotin* <Fr>, tokoloshe, poltergeist, **gremlin,** Dingbelle, Fifinella, **bad fairy,** bad peri; little *or* young devil, devilkin, deviling; erlking

pizazz NOUNS **liveliness,** animation, vivacity, vivaciousness, **sprightliness,** spiritedness, bubbliness, ebullience, effervescence, **briskness,** breeziness, peppiness <nonformal>; **life,** spirit, verve, energy, adrenalin; pep *and* moxie *and* oomph *and* piss and vinegar <all nonformal>, **vim**

placard NOUNS **poster, bill,** sign, show card, banner, *affiche* <Fr>

placate VERBS **pacify,** conciliate, propitiate, appease, mollify, dulcify; **calm,** settle, soothe, tranquilize; smooth, smooth over *or* out, smooth down, smooth one's feathers; cool <nonformal>, defuse; clear the air

place NOUNS 1 **location, situation,** position, spot, *lieu* <Fr>, placement, emplacement, stead; **whereabouts,** whereabout, ubicity; **locality,** locale, locus; abode; **site,** situs; **point,** pinpoint, exact spot *or* point, very spot *or* point; *locus classicus* <L>
VERBS 2 **locate, situate,** site, position; emplace, spot <nonformal>, **install,** put in place; **allocate,** collocate, dispose, deploy, assign; **localize,** narrow *or* pin down; **pinpoint,** zero in on, home in on; **recognize,** know, tell, distinguish, make out; identify, have

placement NOUNS **positioning,** emplacement, situation, location, siting, localization, **locating, placing,** putting; allocation, collocation, **disposition,** assignment, **deployment,** posting, stationing, spotting

placid ADJS **calm,** quiet, **tranquil, serene,** peaceful; **cool, coolheaded,** cool as a cucumber <nonformal>; unruffled, untroubled, stolid, stoic, stoical, impassive

plagiarize VERBS **pirate,** borrow *and* crib <both nonformal>, steal, appropriate; **pick one's brains;** infringe, infringe a copyright

plague NOUNS 1 **epidemic, pestilence,** pest, pandemic, pandemia, scourge; **infestation,** infestment; **invasion,** swarming, swarm, teeming, ravage; **bane, curse,** affliction, infliction, visitation, calamity, scourge, **torment,** open wound, running sore, grievance, woe, burden, crushing burden; disease; death; evil, harm
VERBS 2 **trouble,** beset; **bother,** pother, get one down, <nonformal>, disturb, perturb, irk, **torment,** drive one up the wall <nonformal>, give one gray hair, make one lose sleep; **harass,** vex, distress; inconvenience, **put out,** put out of the way, discommode; **concern,** worry; **puzzle,** perplex; give one a hard time *and* give one a bad time *and* make it tough for <all nonformal>

plain NOUNS 1 **plains,** flat country, flatland, **flats,** flat, level; champaign, champaign country, open country, **wide-open spaces; prairie,** grassland, sea of grass, **steppe, pampas,** *pampa* <Sp>, savanna, tundra, vega, campo, llano, sebkha; **veld,** grass veld, bushveld, tree veld; **plateau,** upland, tableland, table, **mesa,** mesilla; peneplain; coastal plain, tidal plain, alluvial plain, delta, delta plain; mare, lunar mare
ADJS 2 **distinct,** clear, obvious, evident, patent, unmistakable, not to be mistaken, much in evidence, plain to be seen, for all to see, showing for all to see, plain as the nose on one's face, plain as day, clear as day, plain as plain can be, big as life and twice as ugly; **definite,** defined, well-defined, well-marked, well-resolved, in focus; **clear-cut,** crystal-clear, clear as crystal; **simple,** bare, bare-bones *and* no-frills <both nonformal>, mere
3 **homely,** not much to look at, not much for looks, short on looks <nonformal>, hard on the eyes <nonformal>
ADVS 4 **absolutely,** perfectly, quite, right, stark, clean, sheer, plumb <nonformal>; irretrievably, unrelievedly, irrevocably

plaintive ADJS **sorrowful,** sorrowing, sorrowed, **mournful,** rueful, woeful, doleful, plangent; anguished; dolorous, **grievous,** lamentable, lugubrious; **tearful**

plan NOUNS 1 **scheme, design,** method, **program,** device, contrivance, game, envisagement, conception, enterprise, **idea, notion;** organization, rationalization, systematization, schematization; **planning,** calculation, figuring; long-range planning, long-range plan; **master plan,** the picture *and* the big picture <both nonformal>; approach, attack, plan of attack; way, procedure; **arrangement,** prearrangement, system, disposition, layout, setup, lineup; blueprint, **guideline, guidelines,** program of action; methodology; working plan, ground plan, tactical plan, strategic

plan; tactics, **strategy,** game plan <nonformal>; contingency plan
VERBS 2 **devise,** contrive, design, frame, shape, cast, concert, lay plans; organize, rationalize, systematize, schematize, configure, pull together, sort out; **arrange,** prearrange, make arrangements, set up, work up, work out; **schedule;** lay down a plan, shape *or* mark out a course; program; **project,** cut out, make a projection, plan ahead; intend

plant NOUNS 1 **vegetable; weed;** angiosperm, flowering plant; monocotyledon *or* monocot *or* monocotyl; dicotyledon *or* dicot *or* dicotyl; exotic, hothouse plant; ephemeral, annual, biennial, triennial, perennial; evergreen, deciduous plant; aquatic plant, hydrophyte
2 **shill,** decoy, **come-on man** <nonformal>, capper, stool pigeon, stoolie <nonformal>; *agent provocateur* <Fr>
3 **factory, works,** manufacturing plant, *usine* <Fr>; push-button plant, automated *or* cybernated *or* automatic *or* robot factory; assembly *or* production line; defense plant, munitions plant, armory, arsenal; **power plant**
VERBS 4 **set,** put in; **sow, seed,** seed down, seminate, inseminate; **disseminate,** broadcast, sow broadcast, scatter seed; drill; bed; dibble; **transplant,** reset, pot
5 **establish,** fix, site, pitch, seat; **found, base,** ground, lay the foundation; **cache,** stash <nonformal>, deposit; **bury**

plastic NOUNS 1 **thermoplastic;** thermosetting plastic; resin plastic; cellulose plastic; protein plastic; cast plastic, molded plastic, extruded plastic
2 **credit card,** plastic, plastic money *or* credit, gold card, charge card, charge plate; smart card, supersmart card
ADJS 3 **compliant,** pliant, complaisant, malleable, flexible, acquiescent, unmurmuring, other-directed, submissive, tractable, obedient

plate VERBS chromium-plate, copperplate, gold-plate, nickel-plate, silverplate; **electroplate, galvanize,** anodize

plateau NOUNS 1 **tableland,** high plateau, table, mesa, table mountain, butte, moor, fell <Brit>, hammada
2 **plane,** level

platform NOUNS 1 **stage,** estrade, dais, floor; **rostrum,** podium, pulpit, speaker's platform *or* stand, **soapbox** <nonformal>; hustings, **stump;** tribunal; emplacement; catafalque
2 party platform, **program,** declaration of policy

platitude NOUNS **cliché,** saw, old saw, commonplace, banality, bromide, **chestnut** <nonformal>, corn <nonformal>, tired phrase, trite saying, hackneyed *or* stereotyped saying, commonplace expression, *locus communis* <L>, **familiar tune** *or* **story,** old song *or* story, old song and dance <nonformal>, twice-told tale

platonic ADJS **continent;** abstemious, abstinent

plausible ADJS **believable,** credible; tenable, conceivable, colorable; **possible,** within the bounds *or* realm *or* range *or* domain of possibility, humanly possible; **conceivable,** conceivably possible, **imaginable,** thinkable, cogitable

play VERBS 1 **perform,** execute, render, do; interpret; make music; play by ear; play at, pound out *and* saw away at <both nonformal>
2 **sport,** disport; frolic, rollick, gambol, frisk, romp, caper, cut capers <nonformal>, lark about <Brit nonformal>, antic, curvet, cavort, caracole, flounce, trip, skip, dance; **cut up** <nonformal>, cut a dido <nonformal>, horse around <nonformal>, fool around, carry on <nonformal>
3 **gamble,** game, try one's luck *or* fortune; **speculate**

playboy NOUNS **dissipater,** free liver, high liver <nonformal>; nighthawk *and* nightowl <both nonformal>; partyer, partygoer, man-about-town

play down VERBS **minimize,** underplay, downplay, de-emphasize; **soften, subdue,** tame, hold in check, keep a tight rein, chasten, tone *or* tune down

player NOUNS 1 **participator,** participant, partaker, sharer; party, **a party to,** accomplice, accessory; **actor, actress,** stage player *or* performer, playactor, histrion, histrio, thespian, trouper; **instrumentalist,** instrumental musician; **athlete; gambler,** gamester, sport
2 **person** *or* **woman** *or* **man** of influence, a presence, a palpable presence, a mover and shaker <nonformal>, a person to be reckoned with, a player on the scene; heavyweight, big wheel *and* biggie *and* heavy *or* long-ball hitter *and* piledriver <all nonformal>, very important person *or* VIP <nonformal>

playful ADJS **sportive,** sportful; **frolicsome,** gamesome, rompish, larkish, capersome; waggish

plaza NOUNS **square,** *place* <Fr>, *piazza* <Ital>, *campo* <Ital>, **marketplace,** market, mart, rialto, forum, agora

plea NOUNS **entreaty, appeal,** bid, suit, call, cry, clamor, *cri du cœur* <Fr>, beseeching, impetration, obtestation; **supplication,** prayer, rogation, **beseechment,** imploring, imploration, obsecration, obtestation, adjuration, imprecation; **invocation,** invocatory plea *or* prayer; **defense,** pleading, **case,** *plaidoyer* <Fr>, brief

plead VERBS **enter a plea** *or* **pleading,** argue at the bar; **plead** *or* **argue one's case,** present one's case, make a plea, tell it to the judge <nonformal>

plead with VERBS **coax,** wheedle, cajole, blandish, sweet-talk *and* soft-soap <both nonformal>, **exhort,** call on *or* upon, advocate, recommend, put in a good word, buck for *and* hype <both nonformal>; insist, insist upon

pleasant ADJS **pleasing, pleasureful,** pleasurable; fair, fair and pleasant, **enjoyable,** pleasure-giving; felicitous, felicific; **likable, desirable,** to one's liking, to one's taste, to *or* after one's fancy, after one's own heart; **agreeable,** complaisant, harmonious, *en rapport* <Fr>, compatible; **blissful;** sweet, mellifluous, honeyed, dulcet; mellow; **gratifying,** satisfying, rewarding, heartwarming, grateful; **welcome,** welcome as the roses in May; genial, congenial, cordial, *gemütlich* <Ger>, affable, amiable, amicable, gracious; cheerful

please VERBS 1 **pleasure, give pleasure,** afford one pleasure, be to one's liking, sit well with one, meet one's wishes, take *or* strike one's fancy, feel good *or* right, strike one right; do one's heart good, warm the cockles of one's heart; **suit,** suit one down to the ground; **indulge,** humor, oblige; favor, gratify, satisfy, **cater to**

2 <nonformal> **hit the spot,** be just the ticket, be just what the doctor ordered, **make a hit,** go over big, go over with a bang

pleasure NOUNS **enjoyment;** quiet pleasure, euphoria, well-being, good feeling, **contentment,** content, **ease,** comfort; **gratification, satisfaction,** great satisfaction, hearty enjoyment, keen pleasure *or* satisfaction; **self-gratification,** self-indulgence; instant gratification; kicks <nonformal>, **fun,** entertainment, amusement; intellectual pleasure, pleasures of the mind; physical pleasure, creature comforts, bodily pleasure, sense *or* sensuous pleasure

pleat NOUNS 1 **pleating,** plait *or* plat; accordion pleat, box pleat, knife pleat
VERBS 2 **fold,** fold on itself, fold up; **plait,** plat <nonformal>; **tuck, gather,** tuck up, ruck, ruck up

plebeian NOUNS 1 **common man,** commoner, **average man,** ordinary man, typical man, **man in the street,** one of the people, man of the people, Everyman; pleb <slang>; ordinary *or* average Joe *and* Joe Doakes *and* Joe Sixpack <all nonformal>, John Doe, Jane Doe, John Smith, Mr *or* Mrs Brown *or* Smith
ADJS 2 **common, commonplace,** ordinary; homely, homespun; **general,** public, popular, pop <nonformal>

pledge NOUNS 1 **promise,** solemn promise, troth, plight, faith, parole, **word, word of honor,** solemn declaration *or* word; **oath,** vow; **assurance,** guarantee, warranty; **gage,** *pignus, vadium* <both L>; **earnest,** earnest money, god's penny, handsel; **bail,** bond, vadimonium; **hostage,** surety
VERBS 2 **deposit, stake,** post, put in escrow, **put up,** put up as collateral, lay out *or* down; **pawn,** put in pawn, **hock** *and* **put in hock** <both nonformal>; mortgage, hypothecate, bottomry, bond; **put up** *or* **go bail,** bail out; **subscribe,** put oneself down for; **obligate,** oblige, require, make incumbent *or* imperative, tie, **bind,** commit, saddle with, put under an obligation

plenty NOUNS 1 plenitude, plentifulness; myriad, myriads, numerousness; **amplitude,** ampleness; **abundance,** copiousness; **bountifulness,** bounteousness, liberalness, **liberality,** generousness, **generosity; lavishness,** extravagance, prodigality; luxuriance, fertility, teemingness, productiveness; **wealth,** opulence *or* opulency, richness, affluence; more than enough; maximum; **prevalence,** profuseness, **profusion,** riot; superabundance; no end of, great abundance, great plenty, as much as one could wish, more than one can shake a

stick at, lots, a fistful <nonformal>, **scads**
ADJS 2 **sufficient,** sufficing; **enough,** ample, substantial, **satisfactory,** adequate, decent, due; plenty good enough <nonformal>; sufficient for *or* to *or* unto, up to, equal to; **plentiful,** plenteous, plenitudinous, **ample,** all-sufficing; superabundant; a dime a dozen

pliable ADJS **pliant, flexible,** flexile, flexuous, **plastic,** elastic, tractile, **tractable,** yielding, giving, bending; adaptable, **malleable,** moldable, shapable, fabricable, fictile; compliant, submissive; like putty *or* clay

plight NOUNS **predicament,** spot of trouble, **strait,** straits, parlous straits, tightrope, knife-edge, thin edge; **pinch, bind,** pass, clutch, situation, emergency; **embarrassment,** embarrassing position *or* situation; **complication,** imbroglio; the devil to pay

plod VERBS **plug,** plug at, plug away *or* along; pound *or* hammer away; keep one's nose to the grindstone, struggle along, struggle on, work away

plodder NOUNS **drudge,** grub, hack, slave, galley slave, **workhorse,** beast of burden, slogger; grind *and* greasy grind <both nonformal>

plot NOUNS 1 plot of ground *or* land, parcel of land, plat, **patch, tract, field;** lot
2 **intrigue,** web of intrigue, **scheme,** deep-laid plot *or* scheme, game *or* little game <both nonformal>, trick, stratagem, finesse; **conspiracy,** confederacy, covin, cabal
VERBS 3 **map,** chart, **diagram,** graph; **sketch,** sketch in *or* out, draw up a plan; map out, plot out, **lay out,** set out, mark out; lay off, mark off
4 **scheme, intrigue,** be up to something; **conspire, connive,** collude, cabal; **hatch, hatch up,** cook up <nonformal>, brew, concoct, hatch a plot; counterplot, countermine

plow VERBS **cultivate,** culture, **work, till,** till the soil, dig, delve, spade; plow in, plow under, plow up, list, fallow, backset <W US>; **harrow**

ploy NOUNS **trick,** artifice, device, gambit, stratagem, **scheme,** design, *ficelle* <Fr>, **subterfuge,** blind, **ruse,** wile, **dodge,** artful dodge, sleight, pass, feint, fetch, chicanery

pluck NOUNS **spunk** <nonformal>, **mettle, backbone** <nonformal>, **grit,** true grit, spirit, **stamina,** guts *and* moxie <both nonformal>, pith <old>, bottom, **toughness** <nonformal>; pluckiness, spunkiness <nonformal>, **gameness,** feistiness <nonformal>, mettlesomeness; courage

plug NOUNS 1 **hydrant,** fire hydrant, water plug, fireplug
2 **stopper,** stop, **stopple,** stopgap; **cork,** bung, spike, spile, spigot
3 **publicity,** ballyhoo *and* hoopla <both nonformal>; **writeup,** puff <nonformal>, **blurb** <nonformal>; promo *and* hype <both nonformal>; commendation
VERBS 4 **stop up; obstruct,** bar, stay; **block,** block up; **clog,** clog up, foul; **choke,** choke up *or* off; **fill,** fill up; **stuff,** pack, jam; **congest,** stuff up; plug up
5 **publicize,** give publicity; promote, build up, cry up, sell, puff <nonformal>, **boost** <nonformal>, **ballyhoo** <nonformal>; make a pitch for *and* beat the drum for *and* thump the tub for <all nonformal>; recommend
6 keep doggedly at, **plod,** drudge, slog *or* slog away, soldier on, put one foot in front of the other, peg away *or* at *or* on; **plug at,** plug away *or* along; pound *or* hammer away; keep one's nose to the grindstone

plumage NOUNS **feathers,** feather, feathering; contour feathers; breast feathers; hackle; flight feathers; remiges, primaries, secondaries, tertiaries; covert, tectrices

plump VERBS 1 **fatten,** fat; **gain weight,** gather flesh, take *or* put on weight, become overweight
2 knead, plump up, fluff, fluff up, shake up
ADJS 3 **overweight,** fattish, buxom, *zaftig* <Yiddish>, pleasantly plump, full, huggy <nonformal>, **tubby** <nonformal>, roly-poly; **pudgy,** podgy

plunder NOUNS 1 **booty,** spoil, **spoils,** loot, swag <nonformal>, ill-gotten gains, haul, take, pickings, stealings, stolen goods, hot goods *or* items <nonformal>; **boodle** *and* squeeze *and* **graft** <all nonformal>
VERBS 2 **pillage,** loot, sack, ransack, rifle, freeboot, spoil, spoliate, despoil, depredate, prey on *or* upon, **raid,** ravage, ravish, raven, sweep, gut; **fleece**

plunge NOUNS 1 **dive,** pitch, drop, fall; free-fall; header <nonformal>; **swoop,**

pounce; **decline,** plummet, plummeting, nose dive *and* slump *and* sag <all nonformal>, free fall
VERBS 2 **dive,** pitch, plummet; swoop, swoop down, stoop, **pounce,** pounce on *or* upon; nose-dive, make *or* take a nose dive; **fall,** decline, drop, crash, head for the bottom, sag, slump; break, give way; reach a new low

plurality NOUNS pluralness; a greater number, a certain number; **several,** some, a few, more; the greater number

plus ADJS 1 **additional,** supplementary, supplemental; extra, further, **more,** new, **other,** another, ulterior; **surplus,** spare
ADVS 2 **additionally,** in addition, also, and then some, even more, more so, and also, and all <nonformal>, and so, **as well,** too, else, beside, **besides,** to boot, not to mention, let alone, into the bargain; on top of, over, above; **beyond**

plush ADJS **grandiose, sumptuous,** elegant, elaborate, luxurious, extravagant, deluxe; executive *and* posh *and* ritzy *and* swank *and* swanky <all nonformal>; **velvety,** plushy, soft as silk

pock NOUNS **furuncle,** boil, carbuncle, pustule; **pit,** pockmark; impression, impress; **blemish**

pocket VERBS 1 **retain, keep, save,** save up, hip-pocket <nonformal>; **maintain,** preserve; get into one's hold *or* possession; palm; draw off, drain off; skim *and* skim off *and* take up front <all nonformal>
ADJS 2 **miniature,** diminutive, **small-scale,** pocketsized, **vest-pocket;** handy, compact

pocketbook NOUNS **purse,** wallet, bag, handbag, poke <nonformal>, porte-monnaie, moneybag; money belt, money clip

pod NOUNS **hull,** shell, capsule, case, **husk, shuck; seed vessel,** seedcase, seedbox, pericarp; **capsule,** cod <nonformal>, seed pod

podium NOUNS **platform; stage,** estrade, dais, floor; **rostrum,** pulpit, speaker's platform *or* stand, **soapbox** <nonformal>; hustings, **stump**

poem NOUNS **verse, rhyme,** verselet, versicle; **thing of beauty,** vision, picture <nonformal>, eyeful <nonformal>, **sight** *or* **treat for sore eyes** <nonformal>

imaginary gardens with real toads in them
MARIANNE MOORE

poet NOUNS **poetess,** ballad maker, balladmonger; **bard, minstrel,** scop, fili, baird, skald, **jongleur, troubadour,** *trovatore* <Ital>, trouveur, *trouvère* <Fr>, *Meistersinger* <Ger>, minnesinger; **poet laureate;** occasional poet; **lyric poet;** epic poet; pastoral poet, pastoralist, idyllist, rhapsodist, rhapsode

poetic ADJS **poetical,** poetlike; **lyrical, narrative,** dramatic, lyrico-dramatic; bardic; runic, skaldic; epic, heroic; pastoral, bucolic, eclogic, idyllic

poetry NOUNS poesy, **verse,** song, rhyme

the rhythmic, inevitably narrative, movement from an overclothed blindness to a naked vision
DYLAN THOMAS

poignant ADJS **exquisite,** acute, sharp, **keen,** vivid, intense, extreme, excruciating; **pungent,** piquant; **deep-felt,** deep-going, from the heart, heartfelt, penetrating, penetrant, piercing, acute; **pathetic,** affecting, touching, moving, saddening

point NOUNS 1 pinpoint, pinhead, **dot; tip,** cusp; acumination, mucro; **nib,** neb
2 **meaning, significance,** signification, *significatum* <L>, *signifié* <Fr>, **sense,** idea, purport, import, where one is coming from <nonformal>; **particular,** instance, item, detail, count, case, fact, matter, article, datum, element, part, ingredient, factor, facet, aspect, thing
VERBS 3 **direct,** aim, turn, bend, train, fix, set, determine; point to *or* at, hold on, fix on, sight on; take aim, aim at, turn *or* train upon; give a push in the right direction; tend, tend to go, **incline,** head, lead, lean

point-blank ADJS 1 **directly,** to the point; candidly, frankly
ADVS 2 **exactly, precisely,** to a T, expressly; **just, dead,** right, straight, even, square, **plumb,** directly, squarely

pointless ADJS **useless,** of no use, no go <nonformal>; **aimless,** meaningless, **purposeless,** of no purpose, feckless; **unavailing,** of no avail, failed; ineffective, **ineffectual**; impotent; **superfluous**

point of view NOUNS **viewpoint,** standpoint, vantage, vantage point, point *or* coign of vantage, where one stands; bird's-eye view, worm's-eye view, fly on the wall; **outlook,** angle, angle of vision, *optique* <Fr>; mental outlook; **opinion,**

sentiment, feeling, sense, impression, reaction, **notion,** idea, thought, mind, thinking, **way of thinking,** attitude, stance, posture, position, mindset, **view,** sight, lights, observation, **conception,** concept, conceit, **estimation,** estimate, consideration, **theory**, assumption, presumption, **conclusion, judgment**, personal judgment

point out VERBS **call attention to,** direct attention to, **bring under** *or* **to one's notice,** hold up to notice, bring to attention, **mention,** mention in passing, touch on; **single out,** pick out, lift up, focus on, call *or* bring to notice, direct to the attention, **feature,** highlight; **direct to,** address to; **point to,** point at, put *or* lay one's finger on; **excite** *or* **stimulate attention,** drum up attention

poise NOUNS **equanimity,** equilibrium, equability, balance; **levelheadedness,** level head, well-balanced *or* well-regulated mind; aplomb, **self-possession,** self-control, self-command, self-restraint, restraint, possession, **presence of mind;** confidence, assurance, **self-confidence,** self-assurance

poison NOUNS 1 **venom,** venin, virus <old>, toxic, toxin, toxicant; eradicant, **pesticide; insecticide, herbicide,** defoliant, Agent Orange, paraquat, **weed killer;** fungicide; microbicide, germicide, antiseptic, disinfectant, antibiotic
VERBS 2 envenom; **contaminate,** confound, **pollute,** vitiate, infect, taint; **pervert,** warp, twist, distort

poisonous ADJS **toxic,** toxicant; **venomous,** envenomed, venenate, venenous; pollutive; **virulent,** noxious, malignant, malign, destructive, deadly; pestiferous, pestilential

poke NOUNS 1 **hit,** blow, stroke, knock, rap, pound, slam, bang, crack, **whack, smack,** thwack, smash, dash, swipe, swing, **punch, jab,** dig, drub, thump, pelt, cut, chop, dint, slog
VERBS 2 **go slow** *or* **slowly,** go at a snail's pace, take it slow, get no place fast <nonformal>; **poke along;** drag along, drag one's feet
3 **goad, prod,** nudge, prod at, goose <nonformal>, **spur,** prick, sting, needle; **punch,** jab, thwack, **smack,** clap, crack, swipe, **whack**

poky ADJS **slow, leisurely,** poking, slowpoky <nonformal>; slow as molasses *or* molasses in January, slow as death

pole NOUNS 1 **spar,** timber; **mast,** stick *and* tree <both nonformal>
2 **extremity, extreme; limit**, ultimacy, definitiveness, **boundary,** farthest bound, jumping-off place, Thule, *Ultima Thule* <L>

polemic NOUNS **argumentation,** argument, controversy, dispute, disputation, debate, eristic; war of words, verbal engagement *or* contest

police NOUNS 1 **police force,** law enforcement agency; **constabulary;** state police, troopers *or* state troopers, highway patrol, county police, provincial police
2 policeman, constable, officer, police officer, *flic* <Fr nonformal>, *gendarme* <Fr>, *carabiniere* <Ital>; peace officer, law enforcement agent, arm of the law; military policeman *or* MP; detective; policewoman, police matron; patrolman, police constable <England>; trooper, mounted policeman; reeve, portreeve; **sheriff, marshal;** deputy sheriff, deputy, bound bailiff, catchpole, beagle <nonformal>, bombailiff <Brit nonformal>; sergeant, police sergeant; roundsman; lieutenant, police lieutenant; captain, police captain; inspector, police inspector; superintendent, chief of police; commissioner, police commissioner; government man, federal, fed *and* G-man <both nonformal>; narc <nonformal>; **bailiff,** tipstaff, tipstaves <pl>; mace-bearer, lictor, sergeant at arms; beadle; traffic officer, meter maid

3 <nonformal> cop, copper, John Law, bluecoat, bull, flatfoot, gumshoe, gendarme, shamus, dick, pig, flattie, bizzy *and* bobby *and* peeler <all Brit>, Dogberry; the cops, the law, the fuzz; New York's finest; tec, op

VERBS 4 **watch, keep watch,** keep guard, keep watch over, keep watch and ward; stand guard; be on the lookout; patrol, pound a beat <nonformal>, go on one's beat
5 tidy, **tidy up,** neaten, trim, **put in trim,** trim up, **straighten up,** fix up <nonformal>, **clean up,** police up <nonformal>, groom, spruce *and* spruce up <both nonformal>, **clear up,** clear the decks

policy NOUNS 1 **polity,** public policy; line, **party line,** party principle *or* doctrine *or* philosophy, **position,** bipartisan policy; **prudence,** providence; **insurance policy,** certificate of insurance

polish NOUNS 1 **gloss, glaze,** burnish, **shine,** luster, finish; **patina; cultivation,** culture, refinement, civility; cultivation of the mind; **refinement,** finesse, refined *or* cultivated *or* civilized taste
VERBS 2 **shine,** burnish, furbish, sleek, slick, slick down, gloss, glaze, glance, luster; **rub,** scour, **buff;** wax, varnish; finish
3 **perfect,** touch up, finish, put on the finishing touches, fine-tune <nonformal>, tone up, **brush up,** furbish, furbish up, spruce, **spruce up,** freshen, vamp, vamp up, rub up, brighten up, polish up

polite ADJS **courteous,** civil, urbane, gracious, graceful, agreeable, affable, fair; complaisant; obliging, accommodating; **thoughtful,** considerate, tactful, solicitous; respectful, deferential, attentive

political ADJS **politic,** civil, civic; **official,** bureaucratic

politician NOUNS politico, political leader, professional politician; party leader, party boss *and* party chieftain <both nonformal>; machine *or* clubhouse politician, **political hack,** pol <nonformal>; old campaigner, war-horse; reform politician, reformer

politics NOUNS 1 polity, the art of the possible; practical politics, *Realpolitik* <Ger>; empirical politics; **party** *or* **partisan politics,** partisanism; politicization; reform politics; multiparty politics; power politics, *Machtpolitik* <Ger>; machine politics, bossism <nonformal>; **interest politics,** single-issue politics, interest-group politics, pressure-group politics, PAC *or* political action committee politics; consensus politics; pork-barrel politics; ward politics
2 **political science,** poli-sci <nonformal>, **government,** civics; political philosophy, political theory

pollute VERBS **corrupt,** contaminate, infect; taint, tarnish; vitiate, poison, pervert, warp, twist, distort; prostitute, misuse; **cheapen,** devalue; coarsen, vulgarize, drag in the mud; adulterate, alloy, water, water down

pollution NOUNS **corruption,** contamination, vitiation, **defilement,** fouling, befouling; **poisoning,** perversion, prostitution, misuse; denaturing, adulteration; environmental pollution, **environmental destruction,** ecocide, eco-catastrophe

Pollyanna NOUNS **optimist,** hoper, ray of sunshine <nonformal>, irrepressible optimist, Dr Pangloss <Voltaire>

poltergeist NOUNS **imp,** pixie, sprite, elf, puck, kobold, *diablotin* <Fr>, tokoloshe, **gremlin; specter,** ghost, spectral ghost, **spook** <nonformal>, **phantom,** phantasm, phantasma, **wraith, shade,** shadow, fetch, **apparition,** appearance, presence, shape, form, eidolon, idolum, revenant

pomade NOUNS **ointment, balm,** salve, lotion, cream, unguent, unguentum; **brilliantine,** pomatum, hairtonic

pommel VERBS **pound, beat,** hammer, maul, sledgehammer, **knock,** rap, bang, thump, **drub,** buffet, **batter,** pulverize, paste <nonformal>, patter, pummel, pelt, baste, lambaste

pomp NOUNS circumstance, pride, **state,** solemnity, formality; **pomp and circumstance,** heraldry

pompous ADJS **stuffy** <nonformal>, **self-important,** impressed with oneself, pontific, pontifical; **inflated,** swollen, bloated, tumid, turgid, flatulent, gassy <nonformal>, stilted; grandiloquent, **bombastic**; solemn, formal

pond NOUNS **pool,** lakelet, pondlet, dew pond, linn <Scots>, *étang* <Fr>; farm pond; fishpond; millpond, millpool; salt pond, salina, tidal pond *or* pool

ponder VERBS **consider,** contemplate, speculate, reflect, study, perpend, **weigh,** deliberate, debate, meditate, muse, brood, ruminate, chew the cud <nonformal>, digest; introspect, be abstracted; wrinkle one's brow; fall into a brown study, retreat into one's mind *or* thoughts

ponderous ADJS **heavy, massive,** massy, weighty, hefty <nonformal>, fat; **leaden,** heavy as lead; deadweight; heavyweight; overweight; **solemn,** grave; cumbersome, lumbering, hulking, hulky; **unwieldy**

pontificate VERBS **dogmatize,** lay down the law, oracle, oraculate, proclaim

pooch NOUNS **dog,** canine, bow-wow <nonformal>; **pup, puppy,** puppy-dog <nonformal>, **whelp;** bitch; toy dog, lap dog; working dog; watchdog, sheep dog, shepherd *or* shepherd's dog; Seeing Eye dog, guide dog

pooh-pooh VERBS **slight, ignore,** make

little of, dismiss, pretend not to see, disregard, overlook, neglect, pass by, take no note *or* notice of, look right through <nonformal>, pay no attention *or* regard to; sneer at, fleer, curl one's lip

pool NOUNS 1 **swimming pool,** plunge, plunge bath, natatorium; swimming hole; wading pool
2 **pot,** jackpot, stakes, kitty; bank; office pool

pool hall NOUNS **billiard parlor, poolroom**

pooped ADJS **worn-out, used up** <nonformal>, worn to a frazzle, frazzled, fit for the dust hole *or* wastepaper basket; **exhausted, tired,** fatigued, **spent,** effete, etiolated, played out, *ausgespielt* <Ger>, emptied; **run-down,** dragged-out <nonformal>, laid low, at a low ebb, in a bad way, far-gone, on one's last legs

poor ADJS 1 **ill off,** badly *or* poorly off, hard up <nonformal>, downscale, impecunious, **unmoneyed;** reduced, in reduced circumstances; **straitened,** in straitened circumstances, feeling the pinch, strapped, **financially embarrassed** *or* distressed, **pinched,** squeezed, at the end of one's rope, on the edge *or* ragged edge <nonformal>, on Queer Street; short, **short of money** *or* **funds** *or* **cash,** out-of-pocket; unable to make ends meet, unable to keep the wolf from the door
2 **paltry,** common, **mean,** sorry, sad, pitiful, pitiable, pathetic, **despicable,** contemptible, beneath contempt, **miserable, wretched,** beggarly, vile, **shabby,** scrubby, scruffy, shoddy, scurvy, scuzzy <nonformal>, scummy, **crummy** *and* cheesy <both nonformal>, **trashy,** rubbishy, garbagey <nonformal>, trumpery, gimcracky <nonformal>

pop NOUNS 1 **soft drink,** soda water, sparkling water, **soda,** soda pop, tonic
VERBS 2 **bulge,** bilge, **belly,** bag, balloon; **goggle,** bug <nonformal>; **swell,** swell up, dilate, distend, billow; swell out, **belly out,** round out
ADJS 3 **common,** commonplace, ordinary; plebeian; homely, homespun; **general,** public, popular; campy, high-camp, low-camp, kitschy
ADVS 4 **all of a sudden,** all at once: abruptly, sharp; precipitately, precipitantly, impulsively, impetuously, hastily; dash; smack, bang, slap, plop, plunk, plump

poppycock NOUNS **foolishness, folly,** foolery, foolheadedness, **stupidity,** asininity, *niaiserie* <Fr>; **inanity,** fatuity, fatuousness; **nonsense,** tomfoolery

populace NOUNS **population,** inhabitants, habitancy, dwellers, **people,** whole people, people at large, citizenry, folk, souls, living souls, body, whole body, warm bodies <nonformal>; **public,** general public

popular ADJS **desired, wanted,** coveted; **wished-for,** hoped-for, longed-for; in demand; prevalent, prevailing, widespread, obtaining, generally accepted, current; **general,** pop <nonformal>; **famous,** famed, honored, renowned, celebrated, acclaimed, much acclaimed, sought-after, hot *and* world-class <both nonformal>, **well-known,** on everyone's tongue *or* lips, talked-of, talked-about; **prevailing,** predominating

populate VERBS **people,** empeople, **inhabit,** denizen; colonize, **settle,** settle in, plant

population NOUNS **inhabitants,** habitancy, dwellers, **populace, people,** whole people, people at large, citizenry, folk, souls, living souls, body, whole body, warm bodies <nonformal>

porch NOUNS stoop, **veranda,** piazza <nonformal>, patio, lanai, gallery; sleeping porch; propylaeum

pore NOUNS 1 **outlet,** vent, ventage, venthole
VERBS 2 pore over, peruse; take a close *or* careful look; take a long, hard look; size up <nonformal>; take stock of

pornography NOUNS **obscenity,** dirtiness, bawdry, raunch <nonformal>, **ribaldry,** porno *and* porn <both nonformal>, hard-core pornography, soft-core pornography, salacity, **smut,** dirt, filth; lewdness, bawdiness, salaciousness, **smuttiness,** foulness, filthiness, nastiness, vileness, offensiveness; scurrility, fescenninity; pornographic art *or* literature; blue movie *and* dirty movie *and* porno film *and* skin flick <all nonformal>, adult movie, stag film <nonformal>, X-rated movie

porous ADJS porose; poriferous; like a sieve, sievelike, cribose, cribriform

port NOUNS 1 **harbor,** haven, seaport, port of call, free port, treaty port, home port; hoverport; harborage, **anchorage,** anchorage ground, protected anchor-

age, moorage, moorings; **roadstead,** road, roads
ADJS 2 **left, left-hand,** sinister, sinistral; near, nigh; **larboard**
ADVS 3 **leftward,** leftwards, leftwardly, **left, to the left,** sinistrally, sinister, sinistrad; on the left; larboard, aport

portable ADJS **transferable,** conveyable; transmittable, transmissible, transmissive, consignable, deliverable; **movable,** removable; portative; transportable, transportative, transportive

portent NOUNS **omen; augury,** auspice, soothsay, prognostic, prognostication; **ominousness,** portentousness, bodefulness, presagefulness, suggestiveness, significance, **meaning**, meaningfulness; **forewarning,** prewarning, **premonition,** precautioning; advance warning *or* notice, **foreboding**

porter NOUNS **bearer,** redcap, skycap; janitor

portfolio NOUNS **holdings,** investment portfolio; folder

portion NOUNS **share,** interest, part, stake, stock, **piece,** bit, segment; **bite** *and* **cut** *and* **slice** *and* **chunk** *and* slice of the pie *or* melon *and* piece of the action <all nonformal>, **allotment,** proportion, percentage, measure, quantum, **quota,** deal *or* dole <both old>, meed, moiety, mess, helping

portly ADJS **corpulent,** stout, fat, overweight, fattish, **obese,** adipose, gross, fleshy, beefy, meaty, hefty, porky, porcine; paunchy; imposing

portrait NOUNS **likeness, description,** portrayal, portraiture, **depiction,** rendering, rendition, **delineation,** limning, representation; **word painting** *or* **picture,** picture, image, photograph; portraiture, portrayal

portray VERBS **represent,** delineate, depict, render, characterize, **picture,** picturize, limn, draw, paint

pose NOUNS 1 **posing, posturing,** attitudinizing, attitudinarianism; peacockery, peacockishness; carriage, bearing, posture, poise, stance, way of holding oneself
VERBS 2 **posture, attitudinize,** peacock, strike a pose, strike an attitude, pose for effect; sit
3 **postulate,** predicate, posit, set forth, lay down, assert; advance, **propose,** propound

posh ADJS **sumptuous,** elegant, elaborate, luxurious, extravagant, deluxe; plush *and* ritzy *and* swank *and* swanky <all nonformal>, Corinthian; **high-society,** socialite, hoity-toity <nonformal>

position NOUNS 1 **job,** employment, gainful employment, situation, **office,** post, place, station, berth, billet, **appointment,** engagement, gig <nonformal>
2 **premise,** proposition, assumed position, sumption, **assumption,** supposal, presupposition, **hypothesis,** thesis, theorem, lemma, **statement,** affirmation, categorical proposition, assertion, basis, ground, foundation; **opinion,** sentiment, feeling, sense, impression, reaction, **notion,** idea, thought, mind, thinking, **way of thinking,** attitude, stance, posture, mindset
VERBS 3 **locate,** situate, site, place; **install,** put in place; **pinpoint,** zero in on, home in on

positive ADJS **emphatic,** decided, forceful, forcible; **emphasized,** stressed, accented, accentuated, punctuated, pointed

posse NOUNS **search,** searching, **quest, hunt,** hunting, stalk, stalking, still hunt, dragnet, search party; *posse comitatus* <L>; **vigilantes,** vigilance committee

possess VERBS 1 **have, hold,** have and hold, possess outright *or* free and clear, **occupy, fill, enjoy,** boast; have in hand, have in one's possession
2 **demonize,** devilize, diabolize; **obsess; bewitch,** bedevil

possessed ADJS 1 **owned,** held; **free and clear;** in one's possession, in hand, in one's grip *or* grasp, at one's command *or* disposal; on hand, by one, in stock, in store
2 possessed with a demon *or* devil, **pixilated, bedeviled,** demonized, devil-ridden, demonic, demonical, demoniacal; ghost-ridden; obsessed

possessive ADJS **avaricious,** greedy, grasping, graspy *and* grabby <both nonformal>, acquisitive; **individualistic,** personalistic, privatistic

possible ADJS within the bounds *or* realm *or* range *or* domain of possibility, in one's power, in one's hands, humanly possible; **conceivable,** conceivably possible, **imaginable,** thinkable, cogitable; plausible; **potential**

post NOUNS 1 **standard,** upright; newel; signpost, milepost; stanchion; hitching post, snubbing post, Samson post; **pillar,** column, pier, pilaster

2 **position, job,** employment, gainful employment, situation, **office,** place, station, berth, billet, **appointment**
VERBS 3 **pledge,** deposit, stake, put in escrow, **put up,** put up as collateral, lay out *or* down; **put up** *or* **go bail,** bail out
4 **mail,** dispatch, send; airmail

posterior NOUNS 1 **rear, rear end,** hind end, hind part, hinder part, afterpart, rearward, **behind,** breech, stern, tail, tail end, **buttocks, rump,** bottom, derrière
ADJS 2 **rear,** rearward, **back,** backward, retrograde, postern, tail; after *or* aft; **hind,** hinder; hindmost, **aftermost,** aftmost, rearmost

posterity NOUNS **progeny,** issue, offspring, fruit, seed, brood, breed, family; **descent,** succession; lineage, blood, bloodline; **descendants,** heirs, inheritors

postman NOUNS **mailman,** mail carrier, letter carrier; postmaster, postmistress; postal clerk

postmortem NOUNS **autopsy,** inquest, postmortem examination, ex post facto examination, necropsy, necroscopy

postpone VERBS **delay, defer,** put off, give one a rain check <nonformal>, hold off *or* up <nonformal>, prorogue, put on hold *or* ice *or* the back burner <all nonformal>, reserve, waive, **suspend,** hang up, stay, hang fire; **hold over,** lay over, stand over, let the matter stand, **put aside,** table, pigeonhole, **shelve,** put on the shelf

postscript NOUNS appendix; rider, allonge, codicil; **epilogue,** envoi, postlude, conclusion, peroration

postulate VERBS **predicate, posit,** set forth, lay down, assert; pose, advance, **propose,** propound

posture NOUNS 1 **look, air, mien,** demeanor, carriage, bearing, port, stance, poise, presence; pose, posing, attitudinizing; mannerism, affectation; opinion, attitude
VERBS 2 **pose, attitudinize,** peacock, strike a pose, strike an attitude, pose for effect

potbellied ADJS **obese,** abdominous, big-bellied, full-bellied, swag-bellied, pot-gutted *and* pussle-gutted <both nonformal>

potent ADJS **powerful,** powerpacked, **mighty,** irresistible, **vigorous,** vital, **energetic,** puissant, ruling, in power; **cogent,** striking, telling, effective, impactful, valid, operative; **virile,** viripotent; ultramasculine, **macho, he-mannish** *and* hunky <both nonformal>, two-fisted <nonformal>, broad-shouldered, hairy-chested

potentate NOUNS **sovereign,** monarch, ruler, prince, dynast, **crowned head,** emperor, *imperator* <L>, king-emperor, **king,** anointed king, majesty, royalty, royal, royal personage; **chief, chieftain,** high chief

potential NOUNS 1 **talent, flair,** power, ability, capability, capacity; the goods *and* the stuff *and* the right stuff *and* what it takes *and* the makings <all nonformal>; potentiality, virtuality
ADJS 2 **latent,** underlying, under the surface, submerged; unmanifested, virtual, possible

potion NOUNS **drink,** potation, libation; **nip,** draft, drop, spot, finger or two, sip, sup, suck, drench, guzzle, gargle, jigger

potpourri NOUNS **hodgepodge,** hotchpotch, hotchpot; **medley, miscellany,** mélange, pastiche, *pasticcio* <Ital>, **conglomeration,** assortment, assemblage, mixed bag, grab bag, olio, *olla podrida* <Sp>, **scramble,** jumble, **mix,** mishmash, **mess,** can of worms <nonformal>, rat's nest, hash, patchwork, salad, gallimaufry, salmagundi, stew, omnium-gatherum, **odds and ends,** everything but the kitchen sink <nonformal>

pottery NOUNS **ceramic ware,** ceramics; crockery

pounce VERBS **plunge,** dive, pitch, plummet, drop, fall; swoop, swoop down, stoop, pounce on *or* upon

pound NOUNS 1 **place of confinement,** close quarters, not enough room to swing a cat; pinfold *or* penfold; **cage; enclosure,** pen, coop; dog pound
VERBS 2 **beat,** hammer, maul, sledgehammer, **knock, rap,** bang, thump, **drub,** buffet, batter, pulverize, paste <nonformal>, patter, pommel, pummel, pelt, baste, lambaste

pour VERBS 1 **flow,** stream, issue, surge, run, course, rush, gush, flush, flood
2 **rain, precipitate,** stream, stream down, pour with rain, **pelt,** pelt down, drum, tattoo, come down in torrents *or* sheets *or* buckets *or* curtains, **rain cats and dogs** <nonformal>

pout NOUNS 1 **scowl,** frown, lower, **glower,** moue, mow, grimace, wry face; sullen looks, black looks, **long face**

VERBS 2 **look sullen,** look black, look black as thunder, gloom, pull *or* make a long face; **frown, scowl,** knit the brow, lower, **glower,** make a moue *or* mow, grimace, make a wry face, make a lip, hang one's lip, thrust out one's lower lip

poverty NOUNS poorness, impecuniousness, impecuniosity; **straits,** difficulties, **hardship**; financial distress *or* embarrassment, **embarrassed** *or* **reduced** *or* **straitened circumstances,** tight squeeze; genteel poverty; vows of poverty, voluntary poverty; **dearth,** paucity

powder NOUNS 1 **dust;** efflorescence; soot, smut; **particle, particulate,** particulates, airborne particles, air pollution; cosmic dust

VERBS 2 **pulverize,** comminute, triturate, contriturate, levigate, bray, pestle, reduce to powder *or* dust, grind to powder *or* dust, grind up; come *or* fall to dust, **crumble,** crumble to *or* into dust, **disintegrate**, fall to pieces, break up; effloresce

power NOUNS 1 potency *or* potence, prepotency, **force, might,** mightiness, **vigor,** vitality, vim, push, drive, charge; dint, virtue; powerfulness, forcefulness; cogence *or* cogency, validity, effect, impact, **effectiveness,** effectivity, effectuality, competence *or* competency; **authority**, weight; muscle power, sinew, might and main, beef <nonformal>, strong arm

2 **nation,** nationality, **state,** nation-state, sovereign nation *or* state, polity, **body politic;** superpower, world power

3 **governance,** authority, jurisdiction, control, command, rule, reign, regnancy, **dominion,** sovereignty, sway; **influence,** force, clout <nonformal>, potency

4 **personage,** important person, person of importance *or* consequence, **great man** *or* **woman,** man *or* woman of mark *or* note, **somebody, notable,** notability, figure

VERBS 5 **impel,** give an impetus, **set going** *or* agoing, put *or* set in motion, give momentum; **drive, move,** animate, actuate, forward; **thrust; propel;** motivate, incite; compel

power broker NOUNS **wire-puller;** influence peddler, four-percenter, fixer <nonformal>

the power elite NOUNS **the authorities,** the powers that be, ruling class *or* classes, the lords of creation, **the Establishment,** the interests, **the power structure; they,** them; the inner circle

powerful ADJS **vigorous,** strong, **forceful,** forcible, vital, driving, sinewy, sinewed, punchy *and* full of piss and vinegar *and* zappy <all nonformal>, **striking,** telling, effective, impressive

powerless ADJS **impotent,** forceless, out of gas <nonformal>; feeble, soft, flabby, **weak**, weak as a kitten, wimpy *or* wimpish <nonformal>; **ineffective,** ineffectual, inefficacious; **of no account,** no-account, without any weight, featherweight, lightweight

practical ADJS practicable, pragmatic *or* pragmatical, banausic; feasible, workable, operable, realizable; **efficient,** effective, **effectual**

practice NOUNS 1 **experience,** practical knowledge *or* skill, hands-on experience <nonformal>, field-work; rehearsal, exercise, drill

2 **observance,** performance, execution, discharge, carrying out *or* through; dutifulness, acquittal, ritual observance; **rite,** ritual, rituality

VERBS 3 **put into practice,** exercise, employ, use; carry on, conduct, prosecute, wage; follow, pursue; engage in, work at, devote oneself to, **do,** turn to, apply oneself to, employ oneself in; play at; **take up,** take to, undertake, tackle, take on, address oneself to, have a go at, turn one's hand to, **go in** *or* **out for** <nonformal>, follow as an occupation, set up shop

4 **rehearse,** go through, walk *or* run through, go over; go through one's part, read one's lines

pragmatic ADJS **realistic,** realist, **practical;** pragmatical, scientific, scientistic, positivistic; **unidealistic,** unideal, **unromantic,** unsentimental, practical-minded, sober-minded, sobersided, **hardheaded,** straight-thinking, **down-to-earth,** with both feet on the ground

prairie NOUNS **grassland,** range, grazing, grazing land; **savanna,** steppe, steppeland, **pampas,** pampa, campo, llano, **veld,** grass veld

praise NOUNS 1 **laudation,** laud; **glorification,** glory, exaltation, magnification, **honor; eulogy,** *éloge* and *hommage* <both Fr>, eulogium; **encomium,** accolade, kudos, panegyric; paean; **tribute,** homage; congratulation

VERBS 2 **applaud,** flatter, compliment, praise to the skies; scratch one's back; hand it to *or* take off one's hat to one <nonformal>, pay tribute, **glorify,** laud, exalt, extol, magnify, bless, celebrate; sing praises, sing the praises of, sound *or* resound the praises of

praiseworthy ADJS worthy, **commendable,** estimable, **laudable,** admirable, meritorious, creditable; exemplary, model, unexceptionable; deserving, well-deserving

prank NOUNS **trick,** practical joke, waggish trick, *espièglerie* <Fr>, antic, caper, frolic; **monkeyshines** *and* **shenanigans** <both nonformal>

prattle NOUNS 1 **chatter,** jabber, gibber, **babble,** babblement, prate, **prating,** palaver, chat, natter <Brit>, **gabble, gab** *and* jaw-jaw <both nonformal>, blab, **blabber,** blather, clatter, clack, cackle
VERBS 2 **talk nonsense,** twaddle, piffle, **blather,** blabber, babble, gabble, gibble-gabble, **jabber,** gibber, prate, rattle; talk through one's hat; gas *and* bull *and* **bullshit** *and* throw the bull *and* shoot off one's mouth *and* shoot the bull <all nonformal>

pray VERBS **supplicate,** invoke, petition, make supplication, *daven* <Yiddish>; **implore,** beseech, obtest; offer a prayer, send up a prayer, commune with God; **say one's prayers;** tell one's beads, recite the rosary; **say grace**

prayer NOUNS **supplication, invocation,** imploration, impetration, entreaty, beseechment, appeal, petition, suit, orison, obsecration, obtestation, rogation, **devotions**

prayer book NOUNS **psalter, psalmbook**

preach VERBS **admonish,** exhort, expostulate, remonstrate; Bible-thump *and* preachify <both nonformal>, **sermonize,** read a sermon

preacher NOUNS sermoner, sermonizer, sermonist, homilist; pulpiter, pulpiteer; predicant, predikant; preaching friar; television *or* TV preacher, telepreacher <nonformal>

precarious ADJS ticklish, touchy, touch-and-go, **critical, delicate;** slippery, slippy; on thin ice, on slippery ground; hanging by a thread, trembling in the balance

precaution NOUNS **forethought,** foresight, foresightedness; **providence,** provision, forearming; precautions, steps, measures, steps and measures; **safeguard,** protection, preventive measure, safety net, safety valve, sheet anchor; **insurance**

precede VERBS antecede, **come first,** come *or* go before, **go ahead of,** go in advance, stand first, stand at the head, **head,** head up <nonformal>, front, **lead**, take precedence, have priority

precedent NOUNS **precursor,** forerunner, **predecessor,** forebear, antecedent, ancestor

precept NOUNS prescript, **prescription, teaching;** instruction, direction, charge, commission, **injunction,** dictate; **order,** command; **a belief,** tenet, dogma, **principle,** principle *or* article of faith, canon, maxim, axiom; **doctrine,** teaching

precinct NOUNS **sphere,** orbit, **province,** department; **field,** pale, arena, place, locale, milieu, purlieu; **election district**

precious ADJS 1 **dear, valuable,** worthy, rich, golden, worth a pretty penny <nonformal>, worth a king's ransom, worth its weight in gold, good as gold; **priceless, invaluable,** inestimable, without *or* beyond price, not to be had for love or money
2 **pretentious,** mannered, artificial, unnatural, studied; *précieux, précieuse* <both Fr>, overnice, overrefined, overelegant, overelaborate, hyperelegant, etc

precipice NOUNS **cliff, sheer** *or* yawning cliff *or* precipice *or* drop, steep, bluff, wall, face, scar; scarp, **escarpment; palisade**

precipitate VERBS 1 **hasten,** hurry, accelerate, speed, speed up, **hurry up,** rush, quicken, hustle <nonformal>, bustle, bundle, forward
2 deposit, sediment, sedimentate
ADJS 3 precipitant; **sudden,** abrupt; **impetuous,** impulsive, rash; headlong, breakneck; breathless, panting, hasty, **overhasty,** too soon off the mark, too quick on the draw *or* trigger *or* uptake <nonformal>

précis NOUNS **abridgment,** *abrégé* <Fr>, condensation, condensed version, abbreviation, abbreviature, brief, digest, **abstract,** epitome, **capsule,** nutshell *or* capsule version, capsulization, encapsulation, **synopsis,** summary, résumé, summing up

precise ADJS **punctilious,** scrupulous, precisian, precisionist, precious, puristic; by-the-book; exact, meticulous;

detailed, minute, full, particular, fussy, finicky *or* finicking *or* finical, picayune, picky <nonformal>, nice <old>, specific

precision NOUNS **exactness,** exactitude, accuracy, preciseness, punctuality, correctness, prissiness; **strictness, rigor,** rigorousness, spit and polish

preclude VERBS **prohibit,** forbid; disallow, rule out *or* against; **bar,** debar, exclude, exclude from, shut out, shut *or* close the door on; **forestall,** foreclose, **obviate,** anticipate; rule out

precocious ADJS **premature,** too early, too soon, oversoon; forward, advanced, far ahead, born before one's time

precursor NOUNS **forerunner,** foregoer, *voorlooper* <Dutch>, vaunt-courier; pioneer, *voortrekker* <Dutch>, frontiersman, bushwhacker; trailblazer *or* trailbreaker, guide; **leader**, leadoff man *or* woman, bellwether, fugleman; **herald,** announcer, *buccinator* <L>, messenger, harbinger, stormy petrel; **predecessor,** forebear, precedent, antecedent, **ancestor; vanguard,** avant-garde, avant-gardist, innovator, groundbreaker

predecessor NOUNS forebear, precedent, antecedent, **ancestor**

predicament NOUNS 1 **plight,** spot of trouble, **strait,** straits, parlous straits, tightrope, knife-edge, thin edge; **pinch, bind,** pass, clutch, situation, emergency; pretty pass, fine state of affairs, sorry plight; **embarrassment,** embarrassing position *or* situation; the devil to pay

2 <nonformal> **pickle,** crunch, hobble, pretty pickle, fine kettle of fish, how-do-you-do, fine how-do-you-do; **spot, tight spot; squeeze, tight squeeze,** ticklish *or* tricky spot, hot spot, hot seat, sticky wicket <Brit>; **scrape, jam, hot water,** tail in a gate, tit in the wringer; **mess,** holy *or* unholy mess, mix, stew; hell to pay

predict VERBS make a prediction, **foretell, soothsay,** prefigure, **forecast,** prophesy, prognosticate, call <nonformal>, make a prophecy *or* prognosis, vaticinate, forebode, presage, see ahead, see *or* tell the future, read the future, see in the crystal ball

predictable ADJS **divinable,** foretellable, calculable, anticipatable; **foreseeable,** foreknowable, precognizable; **reliable,** dependable, sure, surefire <nonformal>, trustworthy, **to be depended** *or* **relied upon,** to be counted *or* reckoned on

predilection NOUNS **preference,** proclivity, bent, affinity, prepossession, predisposition, partiality, inclination, leaning, tilt, penchant, bias, tendency, taste; favor, fancy; personal choice, druthers <nonformal>; chosen kind *or* sort, style, one's cup of tea <nonformal>, type, bag *and* thing <both nonformal>

predominant ADJS **prevalent,** prevailing, common, popular, **current,** running; regnant, reigning, **ruling,** predominating, **dominant;** rife, rampant, pandemic, epidemic, besetting; **well-connected,** favorably situated, near the seat of power

preeminent ADJS **paramount,** principal, leading, foremost, main, chief, number one <nonformal>, premier, **prime, primary,** supreme; highest, uppermost, topmost, toprank, ranking, of the first rank, world-class, **dominant,** predominant, master, controlling, **overruling,** overriding, all-absorbing

preempt VERBS **appropriate, adopt, assume, usurp,** arrogate, accroach; preoccupy, prepossess

preen VERBS spruce up *and* gussy up *and* doll up *and* fix up <all nonformal>, **primp up,** prink up, prank up, trick up *or* out, deck out, fig out; primp, prink, prank; smarten, smarten up, dandify, titivate

prefer VERBS **favor, like better** *or* **best,** prefer to, set before *or* above, regard *or* honor before; **had** *or* **have rather,** choose rather, had rather *or* sooner, had *or* would as soon; see *or* think fit, think best, please; tilt *or* incline *or* lean *or* tend toward, have a bias *or* partiality *or* penchant

preferable ADJS of choice *or* preference, **better,** preferred, **to be preferred,** more desirable, favored; preferential, preferring, favoring

pregnant ADJS 1 *enceinte* <Fr>, knocked-up <nonformal>, **with child** *or* **young, in the family way** <nonformal>, gestating, breeding, teeming, parturient; heavy with child *or* young, great *or* big with child *or* young, wearing her apron high, in a delicate condition, gravid, heavy, great, big-laden; carrying; **expecting** <nonformal>, anticipating

and anticipating a blessed event <both nonformal>, infanticipating <nonformal>
2 **meaningful,** meaning, **significant,** significative; full of meaning, loaded *or* laden *or* fraught *or* freighted *or* heavy with significance; **pithy, meaty,** sententious, substantial, full of substance; pointed

prejudice NOUNS 1 prejudgment, forejudgment, **predilection, prepossession,** preconception; **bias,** bent, leaning, inclination, twist; **jaundice,** jaundiced eye; **partiality,** partisanship, favoritism, onesidedness
VERBS 2 prejudice against, prejudice the issue, prepossess, **jaundice, influence, sway, bias,** bias one's judgment; warp, twist, bend, distort

premature ADJS **too early, too soon,** oversoon; previous *and* a bit previous <both nonformal>; **untimely; precipitate,** hasty, **overhasty,** too soon off the mark, too quick on the draw *or* trigger *or* uptake <nonformal>; **unprepared,** unripe, impulsive, rushed, unmatured

premeditate VERBS **calculate,** preresolve, predetermine, preconsider, direct oneself, forethink, work out beforehand; plan; plot, scheme

premier NOUNS 1 **head of state,** chief of state; prime minister, chancellor, grand vizier, dewan <India>; doge
ADJS 2 **first,** foremost, front, up-front <nonformal>, **head,** chief, principal, **leading, main,** flagship

premiere NOUNS premier performance, debut

premise NOUNS **proposition, position,** assumed position, sumption, **assumption,** supposal, presupposition, **hypothesis,** thesis, theorem, lemma, **statement,** affirmation, categorical proposition, assertion, basis, ground, foundation; major premise, minor premise

premium NOUNS 1 **extra, bonus,** something extra, extra dash, extra added attraction, lagniappe, something into the bargain, something for good measure, baker's dozen; **interest**
ADJS 2 **expensive,** dear, costly, of great cost, dear-bought, high, high-priced, at a premium, top; big ticket <nonformal>, **fancy** *and* stiff *and* steep <all nonformal>, pricey

premonition NOUNS **forewarning,** prewarning, precautioning; presentiment, hunch *and* funny feeling <both nonformal>, **foreboding; portent**

warnings, and portents and evils imminent
Shakespeare

preoccupy VERBS **occupy the mind** *or* **thoughts,** engage the thoughts, monopolize the thoughts, fasten itself on the mind, seize the mind, fill the mind; **engross,** absorb, immerse, **occupy,** engage, involve, monopolize, exercise, take up

preparation NOUNS 1 **medicine,** medicament, medication, medicinal, theraputant, **drug, physic,** mixture
2 **training,** readying <nonformal>, **conditioning,** grooming, cultivation, development, improvement; sagacity, providence, discretion, provision, forehandedness, readiness, prudence

preparatory school NOUNS **secondary school,** middle school, **academy,** *Gymnasium* <Ger>; *lycée* <Fr>, lyceum; **high school,** senior high school, senior high <nonformal>; prep school <nonformal>, public school <Brit>, seminary

prepare VERBS **make** *or* **get ready,** prep <nonformal>, **ready, fix** <nonformal>; **make preparations** *or* **arrangements,** clear the decks <nonformal>, clear for action, settle preliminaries, tee up <nonformal>; mobilize, marshal, deploy, marshal *or* deploy one's forces *or* resources; **prepare** *or* **provide for** *or* **against,** forearm; **guard against, make sure against,** make sure, **look before one leaps;** see how the land lies *or* the wind blows, see how the cat jumps <nonformal>

preposterous ADJS **absurd, nonsensical,** insensate, ridiculous, laughable, ludicrous; **foolish,** crazy; cockamamie <nonformal>, fantastic, fantastical, grotesque, monstrous, wild, weird, **outrageous,** incredible, beyond belief, *outré* <Fr>, extravagant, **bizarre;** high-flown

prerequisite NOUNS **condition,** provision, proviso, stipulation, whereas; **requisite,** obligation; *sine qua non* <L>, *conditio sine qua non* <L>; **must,** must item; **essential,** indispensable

prerogative NOUNS **right, due,** droit; power, authority, prerogative of office; natural right, presumptive right, inalienable right; divine right; vested right *or* interest

preschool NOUNS infant school <Brit>, nursery, **nursery school;** day nursery, **day-care center,** day care, crèche; playschool; **kindergarten**

prescribe VERBS **require,** demand, dictate, impose, lay down, set, fix, appoint, make obligatory *or* mandatory; decide once and for all, carve in stone, set in concrete <nonformal>; authorize

presence NOUNS 1 being here *or* there, hereness, thereness, physical *or* actual presence, spiritual presence; **immanence,** indwellingness, **inherence;** whereness, **immediacy;** ubiety; availability, accessibility; nearness; **occurrence**, existence
2 **person** *or* **woman** *or* **man** of influence, an influential, an affluential, a presence, a palpable presence, a mover and shaker <nonformal>, a person to be reckoned with, a player *or* player on the scene; heavyweight, big wheel *and* biggie *and* heavy *or* long-ball hitter *and* piledriver <all nonformal>, very important person *or* VIP <nonformal>; power behind the throne, gray eminence, *éminence grise* <Fr>, hidden hand, manipulator, friend at *or* in court, kingmaker

present NOUNS 1 **gift,** presentation, *cadeau* <Fr>, **offering;** tribute, **award;** free gift, freebie *and* gimme <both nonformal>; oblation; handsel
ADJS 2 attendant; **on hand,** on deck <nonformal>, on board; **immediate,** immanent, indwelling, inherent, **available, accessible, at hand,** in view, within reach *or* sight *or* call, in place; **extant,** prevalent, current, in force *or* effect, afoot, on foot, under the sun, on the face of the earth
3 **immediate,** latest, current, running, extant, existent, **existing,** actual, topical, being, that is, as is, that be; **present-day,** present-time, present-age, **modern**, modern-day; **contemporary,** contemporaneous; up-to-date, up-to-the-minute, fresh, **new**

present VERBS 1 **give, donate,** slip <nonformal>, let have; **bestow,** confer, award, allot, render, bestow on; **issue,** dispense, administer; serve, help to; **distribute;** give out, deal out, dole out, mete out, hand *or* dish out <nonformal>, fork *or* shell out <nonformal>; make a present of, gift *or* gift with <nonformal>, give as a gift; **give generously,** give the shirt off one's back; be generous *or* liberal with, give freely
2 **introduce,** acquaint, make acquainted, give an introduction, give a knockdown <nonformal>, do the honors <nonformal>

presentable ADJS **tolerable,** goodish, fair, fairish, moderate, tidy <nonformal>, **decent,** respectable, good enough, **pretty good, not bad,** not amiss, not half bad, not so bad, **adequate,** satisfactory, all right, OK *or* okay <nonformal>; better than nothing; **acceptable,** admissible, **passable,** unobjectionable, unexceptionable; workmanlike; sufficient

presentiment NOUNS **hunch** <nonformal>, sense, **premonition,** preapprehension, intimation, foreboding; suspicion, **impression,** intuition, intuitive impression, **feeling,** forefeeling, vague feeling *or* idea, funny feeling <nonformal>, feeling in one's bones

preserve NOUNS 1 **sweets,** sweet stuff, **confectionery; sweet,** confection; **jelly,** jam, conserve
2 **reserve,** reservation; park, paradise; forest preserve *or* reserve; wilderness preserve; Indian reservation; **refuge,** sanctuary, game preserve *or* reserve, bird sanctuary, wildlife sanctuary *or* preserve
VERBS 3 **conserve,** save, spare; **keep,** keep safe, keep inviolate *or* intact; not endanger, not destroy; not use up, not waste, not expend; **guard,** protect; **maintain,** sustain, uphold, support, **keep up,** keep alive
4 **cure,** season, salt, brine, marinate *or* marinade, pickle, corn, **dry, dry-cure,** jerk, dry-salt; dehydrate, anhydrate, evaporate, desiccate; vacuum-pack; **smoke,** smoke-cure, smoke-dry, kipper; **refrigerate,** freeze, quick-freeze, blast-freeze; freeze-dry, lyophilize; irradiate
5 **perpetuate,** preserve from oblivion, keep fresh *or* alive, perennialize, **eternalize,** eternize, **immortalize;** monumentalize; freeze, embalm

preside VERBS **administer,** administrate; **officiate;** preside over, preside at the board; chair, chairman, occupy the chair; **administer justice,** administer, **sit in judgment**

president NOUNS prexy <nonformal>, chief executive officer, chief executive, managing director <Brit>; **head of state,** chief of state; the man in the White House

press NOUNS 1 **extractor,** separator; wringer; cider mill
2 **pressure,** press, crush; urgency; impulse, impulsion, compulsion; **drive,** push; constraint, exigency, stress, pinch
VERBS 3 **bring pressure to bear upon,** put pressure on, bear down on, bear against, bear hard upon; **importune, urge,** pressure <nonformal>, prod, prod at, apply *or* exert pressure, push, **ply;** dun; **beset,** buttonhole, besiege, take *or* grasp by the lapels

pressure NOUNS 1 **coercion,** intimidation, scare tactics, headbanging *and* arm-twisting <both nonformal>, **duress; the strong arm** *and* strong-arm tactics <both nonformal>, a pistol *or* gun to one's head, the sword, the mailed fist, the bludgeon, the boot in the face, the jackboot, the big stick, the club, *argumentum baculinum* <L>; **high pressure,** high-pressure methods
2 **urgency,** imperativeness, exigence *or* exigency; **press,** high pressure, **stress,** tension, **pinch;** clutch *and* crunch <both nonformal>; **crisis, emergency;** moment of truth, turning point, climax, defining moment
VERBS 3 **urge,** press, push, work on <nonformal>, twist one's arm <nonformal>; **insist,** push for, not take no for an answer, **importune,** nag, high-pressure, bring pressure to bear upon, throw one's weight around, throw one's weight into the scale, jawbone *and* build a fire under <both nonformal>, talk round *or* around

prestige NOUNS **authority,** influence, influentialness; **weight,** weightiness, moment, **consequence;** eminence, **stature,** rank, seniority, preeminence, priority, precedence; **importance,** prominence; **honor;** dignity; rank, standing, stature, high place, position, station, face, **status**

presume VERBS 1 **assume,** venture, hazard, dare, pretend, attempt, **make bold** *or* so bold, make free, **take the liberty,** take upon oneself, go so far as to
2 **suppose,** surmise, expect, **suspect,** infer, understand, gather, conclude, deduce, consider, reckon, divine, imagine, **fancy,** dream, conceive, **believe, deem,** repute, feel, **think,** be inclined to think, opine, say, be afraid <nonformal>; **think likely,** daresay, venture to say

presumption NOUNS assumption, **imposition; license,** licentiousness, undue liberty, liberties, familiarity, **presumptuousness,** freedom *or* liberty abused, hubris; **conjecture,** inference, surmise, guesswork; **probability,** likelihood, likeliness, **good chance;** presumptive evidence; reasonable ground *or* presumption

presumptuous ADJS presuming, assuming, overweening, would-be, self-elect, self-elected, self-appointed, self-proclaimed, *soi-disant* <Fr>; **insolent,** insulting; forward, pushy <nonformal>, obtrusive, pushy <nonformal>, familiar, impertinent

pretend VERBS **affect,** assume, put on, assume *or* put on airs, wear, **simulate,** counterfeit, sham, fake <nonformal>, **feign,** make out like <nonformal>, make a show of, play, playact <nonformal>, act *or* play a part, play a scene, put up a front <nonformal>, dramatize, lay it on thick <nonformal>

pretentious ADJS **ostentatious,** vaunting, **lofty,** highfalutin *and* highfaluting <both nonformal>, **high-flown,** high-flying; **high-toned,** tony <both nonformal>, **fancy,** extravagant

pretext NOUNS **pretense, pretension,** lying pretension, **show,** ostensible *or* announced *or* public *or* professed motive; **front,** facade, **sham; excuse,** apology, protestation, poor excuse, lame excuse

pretty ADJS **beautiful,** attractive, pulchritudinous, **lovely, graceful,** gracile; **cute;** pretty as a picture

prevail VERBS **excel,** surpass, **predominate,** preponderate; **outweigh,** overbalance, overbear; **persist,** run true to form *or* type, continue the same

prevail upon VERBS **persuade,** sway, convince, lead to believe, **bring round,** bring to reason, bring to one's senses; **win, win over,** win around, bring over, **talk over,** talk into, argue into, out-talk <nonformal>

prevalent ADJS **prevailing, common,** popular, **current,** running; rife, rampant, pandemic, epidemic, besetting

prevent VERBS **prohibit,** bar, **keep from;** deter, discourage, dishearten; **avert,** parry, keep off, ward off, stave off, fend off, fend, repel, deflect, turn aside; **preclude,** exclude, debar, **obviate,** anticipate; rule out

prevention NOUNS **stop,** stoppage, stopping; **determent,** deterrence, discouragement; forestalling, preclusion, obviation, foreclosure

previous ADJS **prior,** early, **earlier,** *ci-devant* or *ci-dessus* <Fr>, **former,** fore, prime, first, **preceding**, foregoing, above, anterior, **anticipatory,** antecedent; **preexistent**

prey NOUNS **sufferer,** victim, **wretch,** poor devil <nonformal>, object of compassion; **quarry,** game, venery, beasts of venery, victim, the hunted

price NOUNS 1 **quotation;** bid-and-asked prices, bid price, asked *or* asking *or* offering price; **odds**
VERBS 2 set *or* name a price, fix the price of; place a value on, **value, evaluate,** valuate, **appraise,** assess, rate, prize, apprize; quote a price

priceless ADJS **precious, invaluable,** inestimable, without *or* beyond price, not to be had for love or money, not for all the tea in China

prickly ADJS **touchy, tetchy,** miffy <nonformal>, ticklish, quick to take offense, **thin-skinned,** sensitive, high-strung, highly strung, temperamental

pride NOUNS proudness, pridefulness; **self-esteem, self-respect,** self-confidence; pardonable pride; obstinate *or* stiff-necked pride, stiff-neckedness; **vanity,** conceit; haughtiness, **arrogance**

priest NOUNS **father,** father in Christ, **padre,** cassock, presbyter; curé, parish priest; confessor, father confessor, spiritual father *or* director *or* leader

priesthood NOUNS **clergy, ministry,** the cloth; clerical order, clericals; presbytery; prelacy

prig NOUNS **prude,** priss, puritan, bluenose, goody-goody <nonformal>

prim ADJS **prudish,** priggish, prissy, smug, stuffy <nonformal>, old-maidish, **overmodest,** demure, **straitlaced,** stiff-necked, hide-bound, narrow, censorious, **puritanical**

primacy NOUNS **supremacy,** first place, height, acme, zenith, be-all and end-all, summit, top spot <nonformal>; **sovereignty,** rule, hegemony, control

prima donna NOUNS **leading lady, principal, star,** headliner; **diva,** singer

primal ADJS **original, primary,** primitive, pristine, primeval, aboriginal, elementary, elemental, **basic,** basal, **rudimentary,** crucial, central, radical, **fundamental**

primary ADJS **essential,** of the essence, **fundamental;** primitive, primal, elementary, elemental, simple, bare-bones *and* no-frills *and* bread-and-butter <all nonformal>, original, *ab ovo* <L>, **basic,** gut <nonformal>, basal, underlying

prime NOUNS 1 **the best, quintessence,** optimum, superlative; **cream,** flower, cream of the crop, *crème de la crème* <Fr>, salt of the earth
ADJS 2 **best,** very best, greatest *and* top-of-the-line <both nonformal>, optimum, optimal; **unsurpassed,** surpassing, unparalleled, unmatched, unmatchable, matchless, **peerless;** quintessential

primer NOUNS **schoolbook,** alphabet book, abecedary, abecedarium; gradus, **grammar,** reader

primitive ADJS **primeval,** primogenial, primordial, pristine; **aboriginal,** autochthonous; **original,** primary, primal, pristine

primp VERBS spruce up *and* gussy up *and* doll up *and* fix up <all nonformal>, **primp up,** prink up, prank up, trick up *or* out, deck out; prink, prank, preen

prince NOUNS *Prinz, Fürst* <both Ger>, knez, atheling, sheikh, sherif, mirza, khan, emir, shahzada <India>; crown prince, heir apparent; heir presumptive; prince consort; prince regent

princess NOUNS *princesse* <Fr>, *infanta* <Sp>, rani *and* maharani *and* begum *and* shahzadi *and* kumari *or* kunwari *and* raj-kumari *and* malikzadi <all India>; crown princess

principal NOUNS 1 **headmaster,** headmistress; **chief; lead,** leading man *or* lady, leading actor *or* actress
2 **capital, fund;** moneyed capital; corpus; fixed capital, working capital, equity capital, **risk** *or* **venture capital**
ADJS 3 **first, foremost,** front, up-front <nonformal>, head, chief, premier, **leading, main,** flagship

principle NOUNS **cause,** interest, issue, burning issue, commitment, faith, great cause, lifework; reason for being, *raison d'être* <Fr>; **a belief,** tenet, dogma, precept, **principle** *or* **article of faith,** canon, maxim, axiom; **doctrine,** teaching

print NOUNS 1 **imprint,** stamp, impression; **impact,** force, **repercussion,** reaction
VERBS 2 **imprint,** impress, stamp, engrave; **publish,** issue, put in print, bring out, put out, get out

prior ADJS **previous,** early, earlier, *ci-devant* or *ci-dessus* <Fr>, **former,** fore, prime, first, **preceding**, foregoing, above, anterior, **anticipatory,** antecedent; **preexistent**

priority NOUNS precedence, prerogative, privilege, right-of-way; antecedence *or* antecedency, anteriority, precession; preference, urgency; top priority; primacy, preeminence

prison NOUNS 1 correctional *or* correction facility, minimum- *or* maximum-security facility, **penitentiary,** pen <nonformal>, keep, bastille, state prison, federal prison; **jail, gaol** <Brit>, jailhouse, lockup; **military prison,** guardhouse, stockade, brig; dungeon, oubliette, black hole; **prison camp,** internment camp, detention camp, labor camp, forced-labor camp, gulag, **concentration camp;** penal settlement *or* colony

2 <nonformal> **slammer, slam, jug,** can, coop, cooler, hoosegow, stir, clink, pokey, nick *and* quod *and* chokey <all Brit>; **joint,** big house, big school, big cage, big joint, brig, tank

prisoner NOUNS **captive,** *détenu* <Fr>, **convict,** con <nonformal>; **jailbird** <nonformal>, gaolbird <Brit nonformal>, **internee; prisoner of war** *or* POW

prissy ADJS **prudish,** priggish, prim, smug, stuffy <nonformal>, old-maidish, **overmodest,** demure, **straitlaced,** stiff-necked, hide-bound, narrow, censorious, sanctimonious, **puritanical**

pristine ADJS **intact,** untouched, undamaged, all in one piece <nonformal>, unimpaired, virgin, unspoiled

privacy NOUNS retirement, isolation, sequestration, seclusion; incognito, anonymity; **confidentialness,** confidentiality

private ADJS **privy,** closed-door; intimate, inmost, innermost, interior, inward, **personal; priviliged,** protected; **secluded,** sequestered, isolated, withdrawn, retired; incognito, anonymous

privilege NOUNS **license,** liberty, freedom, immunity; favor, indulgence, **special favor,** dispensation

prize NOUNS 1 **award,** reward; first prize, second prize, etc; blue ribbon; consolation prize; booby prize; Nobel Prize, Pulitzer Prize; trophy, plum

VERBS 2 **value,** esteem, treasure, appreciate, **rate highly,** think highly of, think well of, **think much of,** set store by

probability NOUNS **good chance,** sporting chance, good opportunity, good possibility; odds-on, odds-on chance, **likelihood, possibility**, favorable prospect, well-grounded hope

probe NOUNS 1 **investigation,** research, legwork <nonformal>, inquiry into; data-gathering, gathering *or* amassing evidence; perscrutation, searching investigation, close inquiry, exhaustive study; police inquiry *or* investigation, criminal investigation, detective work, detection, sleuthing

VERBS 2 **sound out,** feel out, sound, get a sounding *or* reading *or* sense, **feel the pulse,** read

problem NOUNS **nuisance,** pest, bother, botheration <nonformal>, public nuisance, **trouble,** pain <nonformal>, difficulty, hot potato <nonformal>; puzzling *or* baffling problem, why; enigmatic question, **perplexity; puzzler,** poser, brain twister *or* teaser <nonformal>, sticker <nonformal>; mind-boggler; **issue,** topic, case *or* point in question, bone of contention, controversial point, riddle, conundrum, mystery, enigma

problematic ADJS **doubtful,** iffy <nonformal>; **in doubt,** *in dubio* <L>; dubitable, doubtable, **dubious,** questionable, problematical, speculative, conjectural, suppositional

proceed VERBS **take action,** take steps *or* measures; proceed with, go ahead with, go with, go through with; do something, go *or* swing into action, **do something about,** act on *or* upon, take it on, get with it <nonformal>

proceedings NOUNS **affairs,** concerns, matters, circumstances, relations, **dealings,** doings, goings-on <nonformal>

proceeds NOUNS **gain, profit,** percentage <nonformal>, **take** *or* take-in *and* piece *and* slice *and* end *and* rakeoff *and* skimmings <all nonformal>; **gains,** profits, earnings, winnings, return, returns, bottom line <nonformal>

process NOUNS 1 **procedure,** proceeding, course; **act,** step, measure, initiative, *démarche* <Fr>, move, maneuver, motion

VERBS 2 **prepare,** make *or* get ready, prep <nonformal>, **ready, fix** <nonfor-

mal>; convert; mill, machine; **mine,** extract, pump, smelt, **refine**

procession NOUNS **train,** column, line, string, cortege; cavalcade, caravan, motorcade; **parade,** pomp; dress parade; progression, rotation; **continuity**

proclaim VERBS cry, cry out, **promulgate,** give voice to; **herald,** herald abroad; **blazon,** blare, blare forth *or* abroad, thunder, declaim, shout, trumpet, trumpet *or* thunder forth, shout from the housetops

proclamation NOUNS **announcement,** annunciation, enunciation; decree, pronouncement, pronunciamento; **declaration,** statement; public declaration *or* statement, **notice,** notification, public notice; circular, encyclical, encyclical letter; manifesto, position paper; broadside; rationale; white paper, white book; ukase, edict; bulletin board, notice board

proclivity NOUNS **inclination,** penchant, partiality, fancy, favor, predilection, preference, propensity, **leaning, bent,** turn, tilt, bias, **affinity**

procrastinate VERBS be dilatory, hesitate, let something slide, hang, hang back, hang fire; **temporize,** gain *or* make time, **play for time,** drag one's feet <nonformal>, hold off <nonformal>; **stall,** stall for time, tap-dance <nonformal>

procrastinator NOUNS **slowpoke** *and* slowcoach <both nonformal>, plodder, slow goer, **lingerer,** loiterer, dawdler, **laggard,** foot-dragger, stick-in-the-mud <nonformal>, drone, slug, sluggard, lie-abed, goof-off <nonformal>, goldbrick <nonformal>

procure VERBS **acquire,** get, gain, obtain, secure; pimp, pander

prod VERBS **goad,** poke, nudge, prod at, goose <nonformal>, **spur,** prick, sting, needle; **importune,** urge, press, pressure <nonformal>, apply *or* exert pressure, push

prodigal NOUNS 1 **wastrel,** waster, **squanderer; spendthrift,** spender, spendall, big-time spender <nonformal>; prodigal son
ADJS 2 **extravagant,** lavish, profuse, **overliberal,** overgenerous, overlavish, **spendthrift,** wasteful, profligate, dissipative; pound-foolish, penny-wise and pound-foolish

prodigious ADJS **extraordinary,** exceptional, remarkable, noteworthy, **wonderful, marvelous,** fabulous, mythical, legendary; **stupendous,** stupefying, portentous, phenomenal

produce NOUNS 1 **vegetables; yield,** output, make, production; **proceeds,** product; **crop, harvest,** fruit, vintage, bearing
VERBS 2 **be productive,** proliferate, pullulate, fructify, be fruitful, **multiply,** spin off, engender, beget, teem; create, make, manufacture, form, formulate, evolve, mature, elaborate, fashion, fabricate; **adduce,** advance, present, bring to bear, **offer,** proffer, invoke, **bring forward,** bring on

product NOUNS **commodity,** ware, vendible, **article,** item, article of commerce *or* merchandise; **effect,** result, resultant, **consequence,** consequent

profane ADJS **unsacred,** nonsacred, **unholy,** unhallowed, unsanctified, unblessed; **secular,** temporal, worldly, fleshly, mundane; profanatory

profanity NOUNS **cursing,** cussing <nonformal>, swearing, profane swearing, foul *or* profane *or* obscene *or* blue *or* bad *or* strong *or* unparliamentary *or* indelicate language, vulgar language, vile language, colorful language, unrepeatable expressions, dysphemism, billingsgate, ribaldry, evil speaking, **dirty language** *or* **talk** <nonformal>, **obscenity,** scatology, coprology, **filthy language,** filth

profess VERBS **state, assert,** swear, swear to God <nonformal>, declare, **affirm,** avow, avouch, asseverate, confess, be under the impression, express the belief, swear to a belief

profession NOUNS **vocation,** walk of life, calling, mission, **practice,** pursuit, specialty, specialization, *métier* <Fr>

proficient ADJS **fitted,** adapted, adjusted, suited; qualified, fit, competent, able, capable, well-qualified, well-fitted, well-suited

profile NOUNS 1 **outline,** contour, delineation, lines, lineaments, silhouette; **characterization,** character, character sketch
VERBS 2 **outline,** contour; **delineate;** silhouette, limn

profit NOUNS 1 **gain,** percentage <nonformal>, **take** *or* take-in *and* piece *and* slice *and* end *and* rakeoff *and* skimmings <all nonformal>; **gains,** earnings, winnings,

return, returns, proceeds, bottom line <nonformal>
VERBS 2 **make** *or* **draw** *or* **realize** *or* **reap profit,** come out ahead, make money; gain by, **capitalize on,** cash in on *and* make a good thing of <both nonformal>, turn to profit *or* account, **realize on,** make money by, obtain a return, turn a penny *or* an honest penny

profitable ADJS **gainful,** productive, **remunerative,** remuneratory, lucrative, fat, **paying,** well-paying, high-yield, high-yielding; advantageous, worthwhile; banausic, moneymaking, breadwinning

profound ADJS **deep-felt,** from the heart, heartfelt, **deep,** pervasive, pervading, absorbing; penetrating, penetrant, piercing; **poignant,** keen, sharp, acute; **wise,** sage, sapient, seasoned, **knowing; learned**

profuse ADJS **plentiful,** plenty, **plenteous,** plenitudinous, profusive, effuse, diffuse

progeny NOUNS **posterity,** issue, offspring, fruit, seed, brood, breed, family; **descendants,** heirs, inheritors, sons, **children,** treasures, hostages to fortune, youngsters, younglings

prognosis NOUNS prognostication; diagnosis; **prediction,** foretelling, foreshowing, forecasting, presaging

program NOUNS 1 **plan,** scheme, design, method, device, contrivance, game, envisagement, conception, enterprise, **idea,** notion; **undertaking, venture,** project, proposition *and* deal <both nonformal>; **performance,** musical performance, musical program, program of music; **software,** computer program, source program, object program
VERBS 2 **inculcate,** indoctrinate, catechize, inoculate, **instill,** infuse, imbue, impregnate, **implant,** infix, impress; **impress upon the mind** *or* **memory,** condition, brainwash
3 **schedule,** line up <nonformal>, **slate,** book, book in, put on the agenda
4 **automate,** automatize, robotize; **computerize,** digitize

progress NOUNS 1 **progression,** going, going forward; **course,** career, **passage,** trend, **advance,** forward motion, going *or* moving on, momentum; **improvement, betterment,** bettering, change for the better; headway
VERBS 2 **advance,** proceed, go, go *or* move forward, step forward, go on, **go ahead,** go along, push ahead, pass on *or* along; move, travel; go fast; **make progress,** come on, **get along,** come along <nonformal>, **get ahead;** further oneself

progressive NOUNS 1 **liberal,** progressivist, **leftist,** left-winger
ADJS 2 progressing, advancing, proceeding, **ongoing,** oncoming, onward, forward, **forward-looking,** go-ahead <nonformal>; moving

prohibit VERBS **forbid; disallow,** rule out *or* against; deny, reject; **bar,** debar, preclude, exclude, exclude from, shut out, shut *or* close the door on, prevent; **ban,** put under the ban, **outlaw;** repress, suppress; **enjoin,** proscribe, inhibit, **interdict,** put *or* lay under an interdict *or* interdiction; taboo

prohibitive ADJS prohibitory, prohibiting, **forbidding;** inhibitive, inhibitory, **repressive,** suppressive; proscriptive, interdictive, interdictory; **exorbitant,** excessive, extravagant, inordinate, immoderate, undue, unwarranted, unreasonable, fancy, unconscionable, outrageous, out of sight <nonformal>

project NOUNS **task,** work, stint, job, labor, piece of work, **chore,** chare, odd job; **assignment,** charge, commission

project VERBS **overhang,** hang over, hang out, **impend,** impend over, project over, beetle, **jut,** beetle *or* jut *or* thrust over, stick out over; **protrude,** protuberate, extrude; stick out, jut out, poke out, stand out

proletarian NOUNS 1 **worker,** workman, working man, working woman, working girl, laboring man, toiler, stiff *and* working stiff <both nonformal>, member of the working class
ADJS 2 **working class,** blue collar, lower-class

proliferate VERBS **multiply,** increase, duplicate

prolific ADJS **productive,** proliferous, uberous, **teeming,** swarming, bursting, bursting out, plenteous, **plentiful,** copious, bountiful; creative

prolong VERBS **protract,** continue, **extend,** lengthen, lengthen out, **draw out,** spin out, drag *or* stretch out; linger on, dwell on; **keep up,** keep going, keep alive

prom NOUNS **dance, hop** <nonformal>, cotillion; promenade, <nonformal>, formal <nonformal>

promenade NOUNS 1 **path,** public walk, esplanade, alameda, parade, *prado* <Sp>, mall; review, march-past
VERBS 2 **go for a walk,** perambulate, take a walk, take one's constitutional <nonformal>, take a stretch, stretch the legs; *passeggiare* <Ital>, parade

prominent ADJS **conspicuous,** outstanding, stickout <nonformal>, much in evidence, to the front, in the limelight <nonformal>; **important,** consequential, significant

promiscuous ADJS indiscriminate, **wanton,** wayward, Paphian; **loose,** lax, slack, loose-moraled, of loose morals, of easy virtue, easy <nonformal>, whorish

promise NOUNS 1 **pledge,** solemn promise, troth, plight, faith, parole, **word, word of honor,** solemn declaration *or* word; **oath,** vow
VERBS 2 **suggest,** hint, imply, give prospect of, make likely, give ground for expecting, raise expectation, **lead one to expect,** hold out hope, have *or* show promise, **bid fair**
3 give *or* make a promise, hold out an expectation; **pledge,** plight, troth, **vow; give one's word,** pledge *or* pass one's word, give one's parole, **give one's word of honor**

promising ADJS of promise, full of promise, bright with promise, pregnant of good, best-case, **favorable,** looking up; **auspicious, propitious**

promote VERBS **advance, further,** forward, hasten, contribute to, foster, aid, facilitate, expedite, abet; build up, cry up, sell, puff <nonformal>, **boost** <nonformal>, **plug** <nonformal>, **ballyhoo** <nonformal>

promoter NOUNS **booster** <nonformal>, plugger <nonformal>; organizer, developer, expediter, facilitator, animator; **backer,** angel <nonformal>, rabbi <nonformal>; **patron,** Maecenas

prompt VERBS 1 **provoke,** evoke, elicit, call up, summon up, muster up, call forth, **inspire;** bring about, cause; prompt the mind, give the cue
ADJS 2 **punctual,** immediate, instant, instantaneous, **quick**, speedy, swift, expeditious, summary, decisive, apt, alert, **ready,** Johnny-on-the-spot <nonformal>

prone ADJS 1 **recumbent,** accumbent, procumbent, decumbent; **prostrate,** flat; **supine,** resupine
2 **disposed,** dispositioned, **predisposed,** inclined, given, bent, bent on, apt, likely, **minded,** in the mood *or* humor

pronounce VERBS announce, annunciate, enunciate, **proclaim; maintain,** have, **contend,** argue, **insist, hold,** submit, maintain with one's last breath; **pass judgment,** pronounce judgment, utter a judgment, deliver judgment

pronounced ADJS **conspicuous,** noticeable, notable, ostensible, **prominent,** bold, salient, in relief, in bold *or* high *or* strong relief, **striking, outstanding,** in the foreground

proof NOUNS **evidence,** reason to believe, grounds for belief; **ground, grounds,** material grounds, **facts, data,** premises, basis for belief; demonstration, ironclad proof, incontrovertible proof

prop VERBS **support,** lend support, give *or* furnish *or* afford support; reinforce, undergird, bolster, **bolster up,** buttress, shore, shore up, prop up

propaganda NOUNS indoctrination; brainwashing; **disinformation**

propagate VERBS **procreate,** generate, breed, beget, get, **engender; multiply;** proliferate

propel VERBS **set in motion,** move, actuate, motivate, push, shove, nudge, **drive,** impel

propellant ADJS **propulsive,** propulsory, propelling; **motive; driving,** pushing, shoving

proper ADJS **decorous,** decent, right, right-thinking, **seemly, becoming,** fitting, appropriate, suitable, meet, happy, felicitous; genteel; civil, urbane

property NOUNS 1 **real estate,** realty, real property, land, land and buildings, chattels real, tenements; immoveables; *praedium* <L>, **land,** lands, grounds, acres
2 **characteristic,** quality, attribute

prophecy NOUNS **prediction,** foretelling, forecasting, **prognosis,** prognostication, presaging; prophesying, vaticination

prophet NOUNS **predictor,** foreteller, prognosticator, seer, foreseer, foreshower, **forecaster;** prophesier, soothsayer, *vates* <L>

prophylactic NOUNS **preventive,** preventative, protective; **contraceptive,** birth control device; condom

proponent NOUNS **justifier,** vindicator; defender, pleader; **advocate,** successful advocate *or* defender, **champion; apologist,** apologizer, apologetic

proportion NOUNS **symmetry,** symmetricalness, proportionality, **balance**, equilibrium; **percentage,** measure, quantum, **quota; harmony,** order, concinnity

proportional ADJS **comparable,** proportionate, proportionable; **like,** homologous

proposal NOUNS **proposition,** suggestion, offer, instance; **motion,** resolution; marriage proposal, offer of marriage, popping of the question

proprietor NOUNS **owner;** *rentier* <Fr>; titleholder, deedholder; proprietress, proprietrix; **master, mistress, lord,** laird <Scots>; **landlord, landlady**

propriety NOUNS **decorum, decency,** good behavior *or* conduct, correctness, correctitude, rightness, properness, decorousness, goodness, goodliness, niceness, seemliness

propulsion NOUNS **pushing,** propelling; shoving, butting; **drive, thrust,** motive power, driving force, means of propulsion; **push, shove**

pro rata ADJS and ADVS **proportionate,** proportional; prorated, *pro rata* <L> <all adjectives>; **proportionately,** in proportion, *pro rata* <L> <all adverbs>

prosaic ADJS **prosy;** unpoetical, poetryless; **plain,** common, commonplace, ordinary, unembellished, mundane; **matter-of-fact,** unromantic, unidealistic, unimpassioned; pedestrian, **unimaginative**; insipid, vapid, flat; humdrum, tiresome, **dull**

proscribe VERBS **prohibit,** inhibit, **interdict,** put *or* lay under an interdict *or* interdiction; put on the Index; embargo, **lay** *or* **put an embargo on;** taboo, ban, outlaw

prosecute VERBS **sue, litigate,** go into litigation, **bring suit,** put in suit, sue *or* prosecute at law, **go to law,** seek in law, appeal to the law, seek justice *or* legal redress, implead, **bring action against,** prosecute a suit against, take *or* institute legal proceedings against; **put on trial,** take before the judge

proselytize VERBS **convince,** persuade, wean, bring over, sweep off one's feet <nonformal>, **win over;** proselyte, evangelize; convert

prospect NOUNS 1 **view,** scene, sight; outlook, lookout, vista, perspective; **expectation,** expectance *or* **expectancy,** state of expectancy; **anticipation,** outlook, probability, foresight, prevision
VERBS 2 **mine;** quarry; pan, pan for gold

prospective ADJS **expected,** in prospect, **coming,** forthcoming, imminent, approaching, nearing

prospectus NOUNS **proposal,** proposition; **scenario, game plan** <nonformal>

prosper VERBS enjoy prosperity, **fare well,** get on well, do well, have it made *or* hacked <nonformal>, have a good thing going, have everything going one's way, get on swimmingly, go great guns <nonformal>

prosperity NOUNS prosperousness, thriving *or* flourishing condition; success; **well-being,** weal, happiness, felicity; a chicken in every pot, a car in every garage

prosperous ADJS **successful,** affluent, wealthy; **comfortable,** comfortably situated, **easy;** on Easy Street *and* in Fat City *and* in hog heaven <all nonformal>, **in clover** *and* **on velvet** <both nonformal>

prostitute NOUNS 1 **harlot, whore,** *fille de joie* <Fr>, call girl *and* B-girl <both nonformal>, **scarlet woman,** unfortunate woman, painted woman, fallen woman, erring sister, **streetwalker,** hustler *and* **hooker** <both nonformal>, *poule* <Fr>, meretrix
VERBS 2 **misuse,** misemploy, abuse, misapply; divert, misappropriate, pervert; profane, violate, pollute

prostrate ADJS **disabled,** incapacitated; **on one's back,** on one's beam-ends, flat on one's back; prostrated, **forlorn;** desolated, **brokenhearted,** heartbroken

protect VERBS **guard, safeguard,** secure, keep, bless, make safe, **police,** enforce the law; keep from harm; **shelter,** shield, screen

protection NOUNS **guard,** shielding, safekeeping; policing, law enforcement; **shelter,** cover, shade, **defense**

protector NOUNS **keeper,** protectress, safekeeper; patron, patroness; tower, pillar, strong arm, tower of strength, rock; champion, **defender**

protégé NOUNS **dependent,** charge, ward, client, protégée, encumbrance

protest NOUNS 1 **complaint,** grievance, peeve, pet peeve, **groan;** objection, kick *and* **beef** *and* bitch *and* squawk *and* howl <all nonformal>, protestation;

remonstrance, remonstration, expostulation, **dissent**

VERBS 2 **object,** kick *and* beef <both nonformal>, put up a struggle *or* fight; bitch *and* **squawk** *and* howl *and* holler *and* put up a squawk *and* raise a howl <all nonformal>; exclaim *or* cry out against; yell bloody murder <nonformal>; **remonstrate,** expostulate; raise *or* press objections, raise one's voice against, enter a protest

protocol NOUNS **rule, guideline,** ground rule, rubric, working rule, working principle, standard procedure; **code, etiquette,** social code, rules *or* code of conduct; **formalities,** social procedures, social conduct, what is done, what one does

prototype NOUNS **original, model,** archetype, **pattern, mold,** pilot model; **innovation,** new departure

protract VERBS **prolong,** continue, **extend, lengthen,** lengthen out, **draw out, spin out,** drag *or* stretch out; linger on, dwell on; dawdle, procrastinate, temporize, drag one's feet

protrude VERBS **protuberate,** project, extrude; stick out, jut out, poke out, stand out, shoot out; **stick up,** bristle up, start up, cock up, shoot up

proud ADJS **prideful, self-esteeming,** self-respecting; proud as Punch, proud as Lucifer, proud as a peacock

prove VERBS **demonstrate, show,** afford proof of, prove to be, prove true; **establish,** fix, **determine, ascertain,** make out, remove all doubt; **verify,** confirm, test, validate

proven ADJS **proved,** demonstrated, shown; **established,** fixed, **settled,** determined, nailed down <nonformal>, ascertained; **confirmed,** substantiated, attested, **authenticated,** certified, validated, verified

proverb NOUNS **maxim,** aphorism, apothegm, epigram, dictum, adage, gnome, words of wisdom, **saw, saying,** phrase, catchphrase, motto, moral

provide VERBS **supply,** find, dish up *and* rustle up <both nonformal>, **furnish;** support, maintain, keep

provider NOUNS **supplier,** furnisher; donor; patron; **purveyor,** provisioner, **caterer,** victualer, sutler

provincial ADJS **rustic,** rural, country, farm, pastoral, bucolic, Arcadian, **agrarian,** agrestic; insular, parochial; **hidebound,** creedbound, **straitlaced,** stuffy <nonformal>

provision NOUNS **condition,** proviso, stipulation, whereas; **specification,** given, *donnée* <Fr>, **limitation,** limiting condition, boundary condition; **catch** *and* joker *and* kicker *and* string *and* a string to it <all nonformal>; sagacity, providence, discretion, preparation, forehandedness, readiness, prudence

provocative ADJS **provoking,** piquant, **exciting,** challenging, prompting, **rousing,** stirring, stimulating, stimulant, stimulative, stimulatory, energizing, electric, galvanizing, galvanic; **encouraging,** inviting, alluring; **tempting,** teasing, titillating, titillative, tickling; *provoquant* <Fr>; thought-provoking, thought-challenging, thought-inspiring; racy, juicy, spicy

provoke VERBS **incense,** arouse, inflame, embitter; **vex,** irritate, annoy, aggravate <nonformal>, **exasperate,** nettle, fret, chafe; **pique,** peeve *and* miff <both nonformal>, huff; **ruffle,** roil, rile <nonformal>, ruffle one's feathers, **rankle; sow dissension,** stir up trouble, make *or* borrow trouble; **alienate, estrange,** separate, divide, disunite, disaffect, come between

prowess NOUNS **skill,** skillfulness, **expertness,** proficiency, craft, **cleverness; dexterity,** dexterousness *or* dextrousness; **adroitness,** address, deftness, handiness, hand, practical ability; **facility,** mastery

prowl VERBS **wander,** roam, rove, knock around *or* about *and* bat around *or* about <all nonformal>; **sneak,** steal, steal along; slink, sidle, pad, nightwalk

prowler NOUNS **thief,** robber, crook <nonformal>; larcenist, larcener; sneak thief

proximity NOUNS **nearness,** closeness, nighness, propinquity, intimacy, immediacy; **vicinity,** vicinage, **neighborhood,** environs, surroundings

proxy NOUNS **deputy,** representative, substitute, vice, vicegerent, **alternate,** backup *and* stand-in <both nonformal>, alter ego, **surrogate,** procurator, secondary, understudy, pinch hitter <nonformal>; **ballot,** proxy ballot

prude NOUNS **prig,** priss, puritan, bluenose, goody-goody <nonformal>

prudent ADJS **judicious,** judicial, judgmatic, judgmatical, prudential, politic, careful, provident, **considerate,** circumspect, **thoughtful,** reflective, reflecting; **discreet;** discriminative, discriminating

prune VERBS **sever, dissever,** cut off *or* away *or* loose, shear off, hack off; **cut,** incise, carve, **slice,** pare, trim, trim away, resect, excise

pry VERBS 1 **snoop,** peep, peek, spy, nose, nose into, have a long *or* big nose, poke *or* stick one's nose in; meddle
2 prize, **lever,** wedge

psalm NOUNS **hymn,** hymn of praise, **doxology,** anthem, motet, canticle, chorale; hymnody, hymnology, hymnography, psalmody

pseudonym NOUNS **alias,** anonym, **assumed name,** false *or* fictitious name, *nom de guerre* <Fr>; pen name, stage name, *nom de théâtre* <Fr>, professional name

psyche NOUNS psychic apparatus, **personality,** self, personhood; **spirit,** spiritus, **soul,** *âme* <Fr>, **heart,** mind, anima, *anima humana* <L>

psychedelic ADJS **psychochemical,** psychoactive; ataractic; hallucinogenic, mind-expanding, psychotomimetic, consciousness-expanding, mind-expanding, mind-blowing <nonformal>

psyched up ADJS **prepared,** pumped up <nonformal>, eager, keen, champing at the bit; alert, vigilant; **set** *and* **all set** <both nonformal>, on the mark *and* teed up <nonformal>; primed, loaded, cocked, **loaded for bear** <nonformal>

psychic NOUNS 1 **spiritualist,** spiritist, **medium,** ecstatic, spirit rapper, automatist, psychographist; necromancer
ADJS 2 **psychical,** spiritual; spiritualistic, spiritistic; mediumistic; **clairvoyant,** second-sighted, clairaudient, clairsentient, **telepathic; extrasensory,** psychosensory

psycho NOUNS **psychotic,** mental, mental case, certifiable case, **psychopath,** psychopathic case

psychoactive drug NOUNS hallucinogen, psychedelic, psychedelic drug, psychoactive drug, psychoactive chemical *or* psychochemical, psychotropic drug, psychotomimetic drug, mind-altering drug, mind-expanding drug, mind-blowing drug

psychosis NOUNS psychopathy, psychopathology, psychopathic condition; certifiability

psychotic NOUNS 1 psycho <nonformal>, mental, mental case, certifiable case, **psychopath,** psychopathic case; psychopathic personality
ADJS 2 **psychopathic,** psychoneurotic, mentally ill, mentally sick, certifiable

psych out VERBS **unnerve,** unman, undo, unstring, unbrace, reduce to jelly, **demoralize,** shake, upset; **unriddle,** unscramble, undo, untangle, disentangle, untwist, unspin, unweave, **unravel,** ravel, ravel out; guess, divine, guess right

puberty NOUNS **adolescence,** maturation, maturement, pubescence, **sexual maturity,** nubility

public NOUNS 1 **population,** inhabitants, dwellers, **populace, people,** whole people, people at large, citizenry, folk, souls, living souls, body, whole body, warm bodies <nonformal>; general public
ADJS 2 **general,** common; communal, societal, social; civic, civil; pop <nonformal>; mass, grass-roots; notorious; known by every schoolboy; talked-about, **on everyone's tongue** *or* **lips**

publication NOUNS **publishing,** promulgation, evulgation, **propagation,** announcement, dissemination, diffusion, broadcast, broadcasting, spread, spreading, spreading abroad, **circulation,** ventilation, airing, noising, bandying, bruiting, bruiting about; **printing**

publicity NOUNS **notoriety,** fame, famousness, notoriousness, notice, public notice, **celebrity,** *réclame, éclat* <both Fr>; **limelight** *and* **spotlight** <both nonformal>, daylight, bright light, glare, public eye *or* consciousness, **exposure, currency,** common *or* public knowledge, widest *or* maximum dissemination

publish VERBS **promulgate,** propagate, circulate, circularize, **diffuse, disseminate,** distribute, **broadcast,** televise, telecast, videocast, air, **spread,** spread around *or* about, spread far and wide, publish abroad, **pass the word around,** bruit, **bruit about,** advertise, repeat, retail, put about, **bandy about,** noise about; **print;** issue, put in print, bring out, put out, get out

puerile ADJS immature, **childish;** childlike; **infantile,** infantine; **babyish**

pugnacious ADJS **belligerent,** truculent, bellicose, scrappy <nonformal>, full of fight; **aggressive,** antagonistic, **quarrelsome**

puke VERBS **gag,** retch, keck, heave, vomit, hurl *and* upchuck *and* barf <all nonformal>

pull NOUNS 1 **draw,** heave, haul, tug, a long pull and a strong pull, strain, drag; **attraction,** pulling power, magnetism
VERBS 2 **draw,** heave, haul, hale, lug, **tug,** tow, take in tow; **attract,** drag, pull *or* draw towards, have an attraction; **lure**

pull out VERBS 1 **retreat,** sound *or* beat a retreat, beat a hasty retreat, **withdraw,** retire, pull back, exfiltrate, advance to the rear, disengage; **fall back,** move back, go back, stand back; run back; withdraw one's support
2 **extract,** draw out, tear out, rip out, wrest out, pluck out, pick out, weed out, rake out; **pry out,** prize out, **pull up,** pluck up

pulsate VERBS **pulse,** beat, throb, not miss a beat; **palpitate,** go pit-a-pat; drum

pulse NOUNS **pulsation,** beat, throb; beating, throbbing; systole, diastole; **palpitation,** flutter, arrhythmia, pitter-patter, pit-a-pat; fibrillation, ventricular fibrillation, tachycardia, ventricular tachycardia <all medicine>; **heartbeat**

pulverize VERBS **powder,** comminute, triturate, contriturate, levigate, bray, pestle, disintegrate, reduce to powder *or* dust, grind to powder *or* dust, grind up; **fragment,** shard, shatter; **beat,** pound, mash, smash, crush, crunch, flail, squash, scrunch <nonformal>

pummel VERBS **whip,** give a whipping *or* beating *or* thrashing, **beat,** thrash, spank, whale; **smite,** thump, trounce, baste, pommel, **drub,** buffet, belabor, lay on

pump VERBS **draw off,** suck, suck out *or* up, **siphon off;** pump out

pumping iron NOUNS **weightlifting,** weight training, bench press

pun NOUNS **play on words,** *jeu de mots* <Fr>, paronomasia, *calembour* <Fr>, punning

punch NOUNS 1 **power,** force, vigor, vitality, vim, push, drive, charge, oomph *and* pizazz *and* bang *and* clout *and* steam <all nonformal>
2 **hit,** blow, stroke, knock, rap, pound, slam, bang, crack, **whack,** smack, thwack, smash, dash, swipe, swing, **poke, jab**
VERBS 3 **indent, dent,** dint, depress, press in, stamp, tamp, punch in, impress, imprint
4 **fight,** box, spar, mix it up <nonformal>, knock down, knock out, slug, maul

punctual ADJS **prompt,** immediate, instant, instantaneous, **quick**, speedy, swift, Johnny-on-the-spot <nonformal>

puncture NOUNS 1 **hole,** perforation, penetration, piercing, goring, boring, puncturing, punching, pricking, lancing, broach; acupuncture, trephining, trepanning
VERBS 2 **deflate,** let the air out of, take the wind out of; **perforate, pierce,** penetrate, punch, prick; explode, blow up, blow sky-high, shoot *or* poke full of holes, cut to pieces, cut the ground from under

pundit NOUNS **scholar,** learned man *or* woman, giant of learning, colossus of knowledge, mastermind, **savant**

pungent ADJS **piquant,** poignant; sharp, keen, piercing, penetrating, nose-tickling, stinging, **biting, acrid,** astringent, irritating, harsh

punish VERBS **chastise,** chasten, discipline, correct, castigate, penalize; take to task, bring to book, bring *or* call to account; **give one his desserts** *or* **just desserts,** teach *or* give one a lesson, make an example of

punishment NOUNS **reprisal,** requital, retribution; recompense, compensation, comeuppance <nonformal>, desserts, **just desserts,** what is merited, what's coming to one *and* a dose of one's own medicine <both nonformal>

puny ADJS **frail,** slight, delicate, dainty; trifling, poky, piffling *and* pindling *and* piddly <all nonformal>, **dinky** <nonformal>; **petty, piddling,** piffling, niggling, pettifogging, picayune

delicately weak
POPE

puppet NOUNS **marionette,** *fantoche* <Fr>, *fantoccino* and *fantoccio* <both Ital>, hand puppet, glove puppet

purchase VERBS **buy,** procure, make *or* complete a purchase, make a buy, make a deal for, blow oneself to <nonformal>; buy on credit, buy on the installment plan; buy sight unseen *or* blind

pure ADJS **faultless,** flawless, unflawed, **impeccable,** absolute; **just right;** spotless, stainless, taintless, unblemished, untainted, unspotted, immaculate, uncontaminated, unadulterated, unmixed; sinless; chaste

purgatory NOUNS living death, hell, hell upon earth; limbo; **purgation**

cold purgatorial fires
T S Eliot

purge NOUNS 1 **cleansing,** cleanout, cleaning out, purging, purgation, catharsis; **purification,** purifying, lustration; expurgation, bowdlerization; **laxative,** cathartic, physic, purgative, aperient, carminative; liquidation
VERBS 2 **clean, cleanse,** deterge, depurate; expurgate, bowdlerize; overthrow; **eliminate, get rid of,** rid oneself of, **get quit of,** get shut of <nonformal>, **dispose of, remove,** abstract, eject, expel, give the bum's rush <nonformal>, throw over *or* overboard <nonformal>; clear, clear out, clear away, clear the decks; liquidate, **do away with,** exterminate, annihilate

purify VERBS **refine, clarify,** clear, rectify, depurate; chasten, restrain; cleanse, wash one's sins away; distill

purist NOUNS dogmatist, positivist, bigot, fanatic; **pedant;** formalist, precisionist, precisian, *précieux* <Fr>, **bluestocking,** *bas bleu* <Fr>, *précieuse* <Fr fem>

purity NOUNS immaculacy, immaculateness, spotlessness, unspottedness; **chastity;** guiltlessness, innocence; cleanness, cleanliness, impeccability; clean hands, clean slate, clear conscience, nothing to hide; **virtue,** virtuousness, honor

purpose NOUNS **function,** use, role, part, end use, immediate purpose, ultimate purpose, operational purpose, operation; **intent,** intention, aim, object, design, plan

pursue VERBS **follow,** go after *or* behind, come after *or* behind, move behind; **shadow** *and* **tail** <both nonformal>, **trail,** trail after; **practice,** put into practice, exercise, employ, use; carry on, conduct, prosecute, wage; **elaborate,** develop, work out, enlarge, enlarge on *or* upon, amplify, **expand,** expand on *or* upon, detail, go into detail

pursuer NOUNS pursuant, **chaser,** follower; hunter, quester, **seeker**

pursuit NOUNS 1 pursuing, pursuance; **quest,** seeking, hunting, searching; **following,** follow, follow-up; tracking, trailing, tracking down, dogging, shadowing, stalking; **chase,** hot pursuit; hue and cry
2 **vocation,** occupation, business, work, line, line of work, walk, **walk of life,** calling, mission, **profession,** practice, specialty, specialization, *métier* <Fr>, **trade,** racket *and* game <both nonformal>

push NOUNS 1 **enterprise,** dynamism, initiative, **aggressiveness,** pushiness, drive, hustle, go, getup, **get-up-and-go** <nonformal>, go-ahead, go-getting
2 **thrust,** shove, boost <nonformal>; **pressure; stress**
VERBS 3 **propel,** impel, **shove,** thrust; **drive, move,** forward, advance; sweep, sweep along

pusher NOUNS **drug seller** *or* dealer, contact, connection

pushover NOUNS **weakling,** sissy *and* pansy *and* pantywaist <all nonformal>, lightweight; **wimp,** poor *or* weak *or* dull tool <nonformal>; trusting soul; **dupe;** sucker *and* patsy *and* easy mark <all nonformal>; **cinch** *and* snap <both nonformal>

pushy ADJS **insolent,** forward, obtrusive, familiar; self-assertive, self-asserting, importunate

pussyfoot VERBS **be cautious, tiptoe, go** *or* walk on tiptoe, walk on eggs *or* eggshells *or* thin ice; **shuffle,** dodge, shy, **evade,** sidestep, hedge, skate around <nonformal>, evade the issue; **beat about** *or* **around the bush**

put back VERBS **turn back, restore,** replace, return, place in *status quo ante;* **reestablish,** redintegrate, reenact, **reinstate,** restitute; **reinstall,** reinvest, revest, reinstitute, reconstitute, recompose, recruit, **rehabilitate,** redevelop; give back, hand back

put-down NOUNS **humiliation, abasement,** debasement, setdown, afront, dig <nonformal>, insult, slap *or* kick in the face

put down VERBS 1 **suppress,** subdue, quell, smash, **crush; quash,** squash *and* squelch <both nonformal>; **deprecate,** discommend, denigrate, **fault,** find fault with, pick holes in, pick to pieces; **ridicule**
2 **record,** write down, mark down, jot down, set down, take down

3 **pay over,** hand over; ante, **ante up,** put up; lay down, lay one's money down, show the color of one's money

put off VERBS 1 **offend,** give offense, **repel,** turn off <nonformal>, **revolt,** disgust, nauseate, sicken, make one sick, make one sick to *or* in the stomach
2 **not face up to,** hide one's head in the sand, not come to grips with, procrastinate, temporize, **postpone,** delay, defer, prorogue, put on hold *or* ice *or* the back burner <all nonformal>

put-on NOUNS 1 **gibe,** scoff, jeer, fleer, flout, mock, **taunt,** twit, quip, jest, jape, leg-pull <nonformal>, foolery
ADJS 2 **assumed, pretended,** simulated, **phony** *and* **fake** *and* **faked** <all nonformal>, feigned, counterfeited; spurious, sham; hypocritical

put out VERBS **inconvenience,** put to inconvenience, **discommode,** disoblige, **burden,** embarrass; trouble, bother, put to trouble, put to the trouble of, **impose upon;** harm, disadvantage

putrid ADJS **decayed,** decomposed; spoiled, corrupt, peccant, bad, **gone bad; rotten,** rotting, putrefied, foul

putter VERBS **trifle,** dabble, fribble, footle, potter, piddle, diddle, doodle; **dabble,** smatter

put together VERBS **join,** conjoin, **unite,** unify, bond, **connect,** associate, league, band, merge, **assemble,** accumulate; **gather,** mobilize, marshal, mass, amass, **collect,** conglobulate; fix together, lay together, piece together, clap together, tack together, stick together, lump together, roll into one

put-upon ADJS **distressed, afflicted,** beset, beleaguered; **troubled,** bothered, disturbed, perturbed, disquieted, discomforted, discomposed, agitated

put up with VERBS **endure,** bear, stand, support, sustain, **suffer,** tolerate, abide, bide, live with; persevere; **bear up under,** bear the brunt, bear with, stand for, tolerate, take the bitter with the sweet, hang in there

puzzle NOUNS 1 **enigma,** mystery, puzzlement; crossword puzzle, jigsaw puzzle; **problem,** puzzling *or* baffling problem, why; **perplexity;** knot, knotty point, crux, point to be solved; **puzzler,** poser, brain twister *or* teaser <nonformal>, sticker <nonformal>; mind-boggler
VERBS 2 **perplex,** baffle, confound, addle, fuddle, muddle, **mystify,** nonplus, put to one's wit's end; keep one guessing, keep in suspense

pyramid NOUNS **monument,** memorial; monolith, obelisk; **gravestone, tombstone;** memorial tablet, brass; headstone, footstone; mausoleum; cenotaph; cairn, mound, barrow, cromlech, dolmen, megalith, menhir, cyclolith; **shrine,** reliquary, tope, stupa

pyromaniac NOUNS **incendiary, arsonist,** torcher <nonformal>; firebug <nonformal>; pyrophile

Q

quack NOUNS 1 **charlatan,** quacksalver, quackster, **mountebank,** saltimbanco ADJS 2 **quackish;** charlatan, charlatanic; specious, meretricious

quadruple VERBS **quadruplicate,** fourfold, form *or* make four, multiply by four

quagmire NOUNS **marsh,** swamp, **morass,** mire, slough, quicksand

quail VERBS **cower,** cringe, crouch, skulk, sneak, slink; wince, blink, blench

quaint ADJS **odd,** queer, peculiar, absurd, **singular,** curious, oddball <nonformal>, weird *and* kooky *and* freaky *and* freaked-out <all nonformal>, **eccentric**

quake NOUNS 1 **earthquake,** temblor, diastrophism, epicenter, shock-wave; **shake,** quiver, quaver, falter, **tremor,** tremble, shiver, shudder
VERBS 2 **tremble,** shake, shiver, quiver, quaver; tremble *or* quake *or* shake in one's boots *or* shoes, tremble like an aspen leaf, shake all over

qualification NOUNS **limitation,** limiting, restriction, circumscription, **modification,** hedge, hedging; setting conditions, conditionality, provisionality, circumstantiality; specification; **mental reservation,** *arrière-pensée* <Fr>

qualify VERBS 1 **measure up,** meet the requirements, check out <nonformal>, have the credentials *or* qualifications *or* prerequisites; be up to *and* be just the ticket *and* fill the bill <all nonformal>
2 **limit,** hedge, hedge about, **modify,** restrict, restrain, circumscribe, set limits *or* conditions, box in <nonformal>, narrow

quality NOUNS **nature,** character, suchness; property, attribute; **goodness,** excellence, class <nonformal>

qualm NOUNS **compunction,** qualms, qualmishness, scruples, scrupulosity, scrupulousness, pang, pangs, **pangs of conscience,** throes, sting *or* pricking *or* twinge *or* twitch of conscience, **apprehension,** apprehensiveness, **misgiving,** funny feeling; qualm of conscience, reservation

quandary NOUNS **dilemma,** horns of a dilemma, double bind, damned-if-you-do-and-damned-if-you-don't, no-win situation, nonplus

quantify VERBS quantize, **count,** number off, enumerate, number, rate, fix; quantitate, **measure, gauge,** take the measure of, mensurate; compute, calculate

quantity NOUNS **numerousness**; quantities, much, abundance, copiousness, superabundance, superfluity, profusion, plenty, plenitude

quantum NOUNS **quantity,** amount, **whole**; mass, **bulk,** substance, matter, magnitude, amplitude, **extent, sum; percentage,** measure, **quota**

quarantine NOUNS 1 **isolation,** cordoning off, segregation, separation, sequestration, seclusion; walling in *or* up *or* off; sanitary cordon, *cordon sanitaire* <Fr>, cordon
VERBS 2 **isolate,** segregate, separate, seclude; **cordon, cordon off,** seal off, rope off; wall off, set up barriers, put behind barriers

quarrel NOUNS 1 open quarrel, dustup, **dispute, argument,** polemic, lovers' quarrel, **controversy,** altercation, **fight,** squabble, contention, strife, **tussle,** bicker, wrangle, snarl, **tiff, spat,** fuss; row, scrap, hassle
VERBS 2 **dispute,** oppugn, altercate, **fight, squabble,** tiff, spat, **bicker, wrangle,** spar, have words, set to, join issue, make the fur fly, make *or* kick up a row

quarter NOUNS 1 **district,** section, department, division; **neighborhood,** vicinity, vicinage, neck of the woods <nonformal>, purlieus
VERBS 2 **house,** domicile, domiciliate; **lodge,** put up, billet, room, bed, berth, bunk; stable
3 divide by four *or* into four; quadrisect

quarters NOUNS **living quarters; lodgings,** lodging, lodgment; diggings *and* digs <both Brit nonformal>, pad *and* crib <both nonformal>, **rooms,** berth, accommodations; **housing**, shelter

quartet NOUNS **four,** tetrad, quatern, quaternion, quaternary, quaternity, quadruplet, foursome

quash VERBS **cover up,** muffle up; **hush up, hush,** hush-hush, shush, hugger-mugger; **suppress,** repress, **stifle,** muffle, **smother,** squash, squelch, kill, sit on *or* upon, put the lid on <nonformal>; **censor,** black out <nonformal>

quaver NOUNS 1 **shake,** quake, quiver,

falter, **tremor,** tremble, shiver, shudder, twitter, didder, dither

VERBS 2 **shake,** tremble, quiver, cringe, cower, totter, teeter, dodder

queasy ADJS **nauseated,** nauseous, **squeamish,** qualmish, qualmy; **sick to one's stomach;** pukish *and* puky *and* barfy <all nonformal>; seasick, carsick, airsick

queer VERBS 1 **put out of order,** put out of commission <nonformal>, throw out of gear; bugger *and* bugger up *and* queer the works *and* gum up *or* screw up <all nonformal>, throw a wrench *or* monkey wrench in the machinery <nonformal>, sabotage, wreck

ADJS 2 **odd,** peculiar, absurd, **singular,** curious, oddball <nonformal>, weird *and* kooky *and* freaky *and* freaked-out <all nonformal>, quaint, **eccentric,** gonzo <nonformal>; queer in the head, strange, off, mentally deficient

3 **homosexual,** homoerotic, gay, limp-wristed *and* faggoty <both nonformal>; lesbian, sapphic, tribadistic

quell VERBS **subdue, master,** overmaster, **crush,** reduce, beat down, **break,** break down, overwhelm; cool

quench VERBS **gratify,** satisfy, sate, satiate; slake, appease, allay, assuage; pour *or* dash *or* throw cold water on, throw *or* lay a wet blanket on, damp, dampen, demotivate, **cool,** chill, blunt; **extinguish,** stanch, damp down, drown, kill

query NOUNS **question,** inquiry, interrogation, interrogatory

quest NOUNS **search,** searching, **hunt,** hunting, stalk, stalking, still hunt, dragnet, posse, search party

question NOUNS 1 **query,** inquiry, **interrogation,** interrogatory; interrogative; open question, question *or* point at issue, **moot point** *or* case; vexed *or* knotty question, burning question; leading question; feeler, trial balloon

VERBS 2 **inquire, ask,** query; make inquiry, take up *or* institute *or* pursue *or* follow up *or* conduct *or* carry on an inquiry, ask after, inquire after, ask about, ask questions, put queries; ask a question, put a question to, pose *or* set *or* propose *or* propound a question

3 **doubt,** be doubtful, be dubious, be skeptical, doubt the truth of, beg leave to doubt, **have one's doubts,** have *or* harbor *or* entertain doubts *or* suspicions, half believe, have reservations, **take with a grain of salt,** be from Missouri <nonformal>, **distrust, mistrust,** misgive, cross one's fingers; **query,** challenge, contest, dispute, cast doubt on, greet with skepticism, keep one's eye on, treat with reserve, bring *or* call into question, raise a question, throw doubt upon

questionable ADJS **doubtful,** iffy <nonformal>; dubitable, doubtable, **dubious,** problematic, problematical, speculative, conjectural, suppositional

questionnaire NOUNS **canvass,** survey, inquiry, questionary

queue VERBS **line up,** get in *or* get on line, queue up <Brit>, make *or* form a line, get in formation, **fall in,** fall in *or* into line

quibble VERBS **cavil, bicker,** boggle, chop logic, **split hairs,** nitpick, pick nits; Jesuitize; **equivocate,** mystify, obscure, prevaricate, tergiversate, doubletalk, doublespeak, tap-dance <nonformal>, palter, fence, parry, shift, **shuffle,** dodge, shy, **evade,** sidestep, hedge, pussyfoot <nonformal>, evade the issue

quick ADJS 1 **swift, speedy,** expeditious, snappy <nonformal>, celeritous, alacritous, **prompt,** ready, smart, sharp, quick on the draw *or* trigger *or* uptake <nonformal>; **agile,** nimble, spry

ADVS 2 **swiftly,** rapidly, quickly, snappily <nonformal>, **speedily,** with speed, **fast,** apace, at a great rate, at a good clip <nonformal>, **by leaps and bounds,** lickety-split <nonformal>

quid pro quo NOUNS **trade-off,** equivalent, consideration, something of value, tit for tat, give-and-take

quiet NOUNS 1 **silence,** silentness, **soundlessness,** noiselessness, **stillness, quietness,** quietude, quiescence, **still,** peace

VERBS 2 **silence,** put to silence, hush, hush one up, hush-hush, **shush,** quieten, **still**

ADJS 3 **silent, still,** stilly, quiescent, **hushed, soundless,** noiseless; **calm,** tranquil, peaceful, peaceable, pacific, halcyon; **placid**

quilt NOUNS **comforter,** down comforter, duvet, feather bed, eiderdown; patchwork quilt

quintet NOUNS fivesome, quintuplets, quints <nonformal>, cinquain, quincunx, pentad

quip NOUNS 1 **witticism, pleasantry,** conceit, bright *or* happy thought, **mot,**

bon mot, smart saying, stroke of wit, one-liner *and* zinger <both nonformal>; flash of wit, **sally,** flight of wit
VERBS 2 **joke,** jest, wisecrack *and* crack wise <both nonformal>, utter a mot, jape, josh <nonformal>, make fun, **kid** *or* **kid around** <both nonformal>

quirky ADJS **fanciful, notional,** fantastic *or* fantastical, maggoty, **crotchety,** kinky, harebrained, cranky, flaky <nonformal>

quit VERBS 1 **vacate,** evacuate, abandon, desert, turn one's back on, walk away from, leave to one's fate, leave flat *or* high and dry; leave *or* desert a sinking ship; **withdraw,** retreat, **beat a retreat,** retire, remove; walk away, abscond, disappear, vanish; **bow out** <nonformal>, make one's exit
2 **resign,** demit, leave, **vacate,** withdraw from; **retire,** superannuate, be superannuated, get the golden handshake *or* parachute <nonformal>; **tender** *or* **hand in one's resignation**

quiver NOUNS 1 **flutter,** flitter, flit, **flicker, waver,** dance; shake
VERBS 2 **shake,** tremble, quaver, cringe, cower, totter, teeter, dodder; **tremble,** shiver, quake, flutter, twitter, shake like an aspen leaf

quiz NOUNS 1 **examination,** school examination, **exam** <nonformal>, **test**
VERBS 2 **inquire,** ask, question, query; make inquiry, take up *or* institute *or* pursue *or* follow up *or* conduct *or* carry on an inquiry, ask after, inquire after, ask about, ask questions, put queries

quota NOUNS **part,** portion, fraction; percentage; **share,** parcel, dole, piece *or* piece of the action <nonformal>; cut *and* slice *and* vigorish <all nonformal>

quotation NOUNS 1 **price,** quoted price, price tag *and* ticket *and* sticker <all nonformal>
2 **citation,** reference, cross reference

quote VERBS **repeat,** repeat word for word *or* verbatim, quote chapter and verse

R

rabble NOUNS ragtag <nonformal>, **ragtag and bobtail; riffraff, trash,** raff, chaff, **rubbish,** dregs, **scum,** scum of the earth, dregs *or* scum **of society**

the tagrag people
SHAKESPEARE

rabble-rouser NOUNS **instigator,** inciter, exciter, urger; **provoker,** *provocateur* <Fr>, *agent provocateur* <Fr>; **agitator,** fomenter, inflamer; agitprop; rouser, **demagogue**

rabid ADJS **maniac** *or* **maniacal,** raving mad, stark-raving mad, **frenzied, frantic,** frenetic; **mad,** madding, wild, furious, violent; **amok, berserk,** running wild

race NOUNS 1 contest of speed *or* fleetness; derby; **horse race;** automobile race; boat race, yacht race, regatta
2 **people,** folk, family, house, clan, tribe, nation; **lineage,** line, blood, strain, stock, stem, species, stirps, **breed,** brood, kind; **ethnicity,** tribalism, clannishness
VERBS 3 **speed, go fast,** skim, **fly,** flit, fleet; go like lightning *or* a streak of lightning, go like greased lightning; **rush, tear,** dash, dart, shoot, hurtle, bolt, fling, **scamper, scurry,** scour, scud, scuttle, scramble, careen; **run**

racetrack NOUNS **track,** racecourse, turf, oval, course, strip

racial ADJS **ethnic,** tribal, national, family, clannish, totemic, **lineal; ethnic;** phyletic, phylogenetic, genetic

racing NOUNS 1 **track,** track sports; **horse racing**, the turf, the sport of kings; dog racing, automobile racing
ADJS 2 **flowing,** streaming, running, pouring, fluxive, fluxional, coursing, gushing, rushing, onrushing, surging, surgy, torrential, rough, whitewater

racism NOUNS **discrimination,** social discrimination, minority prejudice; xenophobia, know-nothingism; racialism, race hatred, **race prejudice,** race snobbery, racial discrimination

racist NOUNS 1 **bigot,** intolerant, illiberal; racialist, racial supremacist, white *or* black supremacist, pig <nonformal>
ADJS 2 **prejudiced,** prepossessed, biased, jaundiced; racialist, anti-Negro, antiblack, antiwhite; anti-Semitic

rack NOUNS **agony,** anguish, torment, torture, exquisite torment *or* torture, the rack, the iron maiden, excruciation, crucifixion, martyrdom, martyrization, excruciating *or* agonizing *or* atrocious pain; **strain,** straining, **stress,** stressfulness, **stress and strain,** taxing, tension, stretch

racket NOUNS 1 **noise,** loud noise, blast, **din,** clamor; outcry, **uproar,** hue and cry, noise and shouting
2 **cheating,** cheating scheme, cheating method, angle, con *and* grift *and* move *and* scam *and* sting <all nonformal>
3 **vocation,** occupation, business, work, line, line of work, line of business *or* endeavor, number <nonformal>, walk, **trade,** game <nonformal>

racketeer NOUNS gangster; **black marketeer,** gray marketeer; bootlegger, moonshiner <nonformal>; pusher *and* dealer <both nonformal>, narcotics *or* dope *or* drug pusher <nonformal>

racy ADJS **risqué,** risky, salty, spicy, **off-color,** suggestive, scabrous; **piquant,** lively, juicy, succulent, rich; readable

radar NOUNS radio detection and ranging; **radar set,** radiolocator <Brit>; radarscope; radar antenna; radar reflector

radial ADJS **radiating,** radiate, radiated; rayed, spoked; radiative

radiant ADJS **happy,** glad, joyful, joyous, flushed with joy, beaming, glowing, **bright, sunny,** sparkling

radiate VERBS 1 radiate out, ray, ray out, beam out, diffuse, emanate, spread, disperse, scatter
2 **shine,** shine forth, **glow,** beam, gleam, glint, luster, glance; **transmit,** send

radiation NOUNS radiant energy; ionizing radiation; **radioactivity,** activity, radioactive radiation *or* emanation, atomic *or* nuclear radiation; natural radioactivity, artificial radioactivity; **ray,** cosmic ray bombardment, electron shower; electron emission

radical NOUNS 1 **extremist,** ultra, ultraist; **revolutionary,** revolutionist; extreme left-winger, left-wing extremist, **red** <nonformal>; **anarchist,** nihilist; pink *and* parlor pink *and* pinko <all nonformal>
ADJS 2 **extreme, extremist,** extremistic, ultraist, ultraistic

3 revolutionary, revolutionist; ultraconservative; extreme left-wing, **red** <nonformal>; anarchistic, nihilistic, pink <nonformal>

radicle NOUNS **root,** radix; radicel, rootlet; **taproot,** tap; **rhizome,** rootstock

radio NOUNS 1 **radio receiver;** radio telescope; **radio set, receiver,** receiving set, **wireless** *and* wireless set <both Brit>, set
VERBS 2 **broadcast,** radiobroadcast, radiocast, simulcast, **wireless** <Brit>, radiate, **transmit,** send; narrowcast; shortwave
ADJS 3 **wireless** <Brit>; radiosonic; neutrodyne; heterodyne; superheterodyne; shortwave; radio-frequency, audio-frequency

radioactive ADJS activated, radioactivated, irradiated, charged, **hot; contaminated,** infected, poisoned; radioluminescent, autoluminescent

radioactive element NOUNS **radioelement; radioisotope; tracer, tracer element, tracer atom**

radio broadcasting NOUNS **broadcasting,** the air waves, radiocasting; commercial radio, public radio; AM broadcasting, FM broadcasting, shortwave broadcasting; **transmission,** radio transmission

radiology NOUNS radiography, radioscopy, fluoroscopy, magnetic resonance imaging, MRI, mammography

radius NOUNS **extent,** extension, expansion, expanse, square footage *or* yardage etc, **scope,** reach, range, ballpark <nonformal>, spread, coverage, area, cirumference, ambit, girth, diameter, boundary, border, periphery

raffle NOUNS **lottery,** drawing, sweepstakes *or* sweepstake *or* sweep

raft NOUNS **float;** balsa, balsa raft, Kon Tiki; life raft, Carling float

rag NOUNS 1 **material,** fabric, cloth, stuff; rags; **garment,** robe, frock, gown, togs *and* duds <both nonformal>
2 **newspaper,** paper, sheet <nonformal>
VERBS 3 **berate,** rate, tongue-lash, rail at, thunder *or* fulminate against, rave against, yell at, bark *or* yelp at

ragamuffin NOUNS **waif,** homeless waif, tatterdemalion; **gamin,** gamine, urchin, street urchin, dead-end kid <nonformal>, guttersnipe <nonformal>

rage NOUNS 1 **passion; fury,** furor; livid *or* towering rage *or* passion, blind *or* burning rage, raging *or* tearing passion, furious rage
2 **fad, craze;** infatuation, enthusiasm, wrinkle <nonformal>; novelty
VERBS 3 **storm,** rant, have a fit, rave, roar; **rampage,** ramp, **tear,** tear around; go *or* carry on <nonformal>

ragged ADJS **shabby,** raggedy, raggedy-ass <nonformal>, **tattered,** torn; patchy; **frayed,** in rags, in tatters, in shreds

raging ADJS **frenzied,** raving, roaring, bellowing, ramping, storming, howling, ranting, fulminating, frothing *or* foaming at the mouth; **wild,** hog-wild <nonformal>; **enraged; stormy,** tempestuous

rags NOUNS **tatters,** secondhand clothes, old clothes; worn clothes, **hand-me-downs** *and* reach-me-downs <both nonformal>; **refuse,** odds and ends, scraps

ragtime ADJS **syncopated;** ragtimey <nonformal>

raid NOUNS 1 **foray,** razzia; **invasion, incursion,** inroad, irruption; **air raid,** air strike, air attack, saturation raid; escalade, scaling, boarding
VERBS 2 foray, make a raid; **invade,** inroad, make an inroad, make an irruption into; escalade, scale, scale the walls, board; storm, take by storm, overwhelm, inundate; **plunder,** pillage, loot, sack, ransack, rifle, freeboot, spoil, spoliate, despoil, depredate, prey on *or* upon, reive <Scots>, ravage, ravish, raven, sweep, gut; maraud, forage

raider NOUNS **plunderer,** pillager, looter, marauder, rifler, sacker, spoiler, despoiler, freebooter, rapparee, reiver <Scots>, forager, ravisher, ravager

railroad NOUNS **railway,** rail, line, track, trackage, railway *or* railroad *or* rail line

railroad through VERBS **legislate,** make *or* enact laws, **put through,** jam *or* steamroller through <nonformal>, lobby through; bring pressure to bear upon; **ram,** ram through, bull, bulldoze, muscle, steamroller

rain NOUNS 1 **rainfall,** fall, **precipitation,** moisture, wet, rainwater; **shower, sprinkle,** flurry, patter, pitter-patter, splatter; streams of rain, sheet of rain, splash *or* spurt of rain; **drizzle,** mizzle; **mist,** misty rain, Scotch mist
VERBS 2 **precipitate,** rain down, fall; **shower,** shower down; **sprinkle,** spit *and* spritz <both nonformal>, spatter, patter, pitter-patter; **drizzle,** mizzle; **pour,** stream, stream down, pour with

rain, **pelt,** pelt down, drum, tattoo, come down in torrents *or* sheets *or* buckets *or* curtains, **rain cats and dogs** <nonformal>

rainbow NOUNS **halo,** nimbus, aura, **aureole,** circle, ring, glory; solar halo, lunar halo, ring around the sun *or* moon; white rainbow *or* fogbow

rainy ADJS **showery;** pluvious *or* pluviose *or* pluvial; **drizzly,** drizzling, mizzly, drippy; **misty,** misty-moisty; torrential, pouring, streaming, pelting, drumming, driving, blinding, cat-and-doggish <nonformal>

raise NOUNS 1 **increase, gain,** augmentation; **advance,** appreciation, rise, fattening *and* boost *and* hike <all nonformal>, **up** *and* upping <both nonformal>, buildup
VERBS 2 **elevate, rear,** escalate, up, boost *and* hike <both nonformal>; **erect,** heighten, lift, levitate, boost <nonformal>, **hoist,** heist <nonformal>, heft, heave
3 **breed,** rear, grow, hatch, feed, nurture, fatten; keep, run

raised ADJS **lifted,** elevated; upraised, **uplifted,** upcast; **reared,** upreared; rearing, rampant; erect, upright; high

rake NOUNS 1 **libertine,** swinger <nonformal>, **profligate,** rakehell, rip <nonformal>, **roué,** wanton, womanizer, cocksman <nonformal>, walking phallus, debauchee, rounder <old>, **wolf** <nonformal>, gay dog, gay deceiver, philanderer, lady-killer
VERBS 2 **comb,** curry, card, hackle *or* hatchel, heckle <nonformal>; harrow, weed

rally NOUNS 1 **recovery,** comeback <nonformal>, return; **recuperation,** convalescence
VERBS 2 come about *or* round, **take a favorable turn,** get over <nonformal>, take a turn for the better, gain strength; come a long way <nonformal>; **recuperate,** recover
3 **scoff,** jeer, gibe, **mock,** revile, rail at, chaff, **twit, taunt,** jape, flout, scout, have a fling at
4 **come together,** assemble, congregate, collect, come from far and wide, come *or* arrive in a body; league, ally; rally around

ram VERBS 1 **sail into,** run down, run in *or* into; collide
2 ram down, tamp, pile drive, jam, crowd, cram

ramble NOUNS 1 **walk,** amble, **hike,** tramp, traipse <nonformal>; **stroll,** saunter; **promenade;** jaunt, airing
VERBS 2 **wander,** wander off, rove, straggle, divagate, excurse, pererrate; meander, wind, twist, snake, twist and turn; **digress,** wander, get off the subject, wander from the subject, get sidetracked, excurse, maunder, stray, go astray

ramification NOUNS **complexity,** complication, involvement, complexness, involution, convolution, tortuousness, Byzantinism, *chinoiserie* <Fr>, tanglement, **entanglement,** perplexity, **intricacy,** intricateness, crabbedness, technicality, subtlety

ramp NOUNS **incline,** inclination, **slope, grade,** gradient, pitch, launching ramp, bank, talus, gentle *or* easy slope, glacis

rampage NOUNS 1 **commotion,** hubbub, Babel, tumult, turmoil, riot, **disturbance,** rumpus <nonformal>, ruckus *and* ruction <both nonformal>, **fracas, hassle**
VERBS 2 **rage,** storm, rant, rave, roar; ramp, **tear,** tear around; go *or* carry on <nonformal>; **destroy, wreck,** wreak havoc, ruin; sow chaos *or* disorder

rampant ADJS **prevalent,** prevailing, common, popular, **current,** running; **rife,** pandemic, epidemic, besetting; lousy with <nonformal>, teeming; **superabundant**; a dime a dozen

rampart NOUNS **fortification,** work, defense work, **bulwark,** fence, barrier

ramshackle ADJS **dilapidated,** decrepit, shacky, tottery, **tumbledown,** broken-down, run-down, in ruins, ruinous, ruined, derelict, gone to wrack and ruin, the worse for wear

ranch NOUNS **farmstead;** *rancho, hacienda* <both Sp>, rancheria; **cattle ranch;** dude ranch

rancher NOUNS **stockman,** stock raiser, stockkeeper <Austral>; cattleman, cow keeper, cowman, **rancher,** ranchman, ranchero

rancid ADJS **tainted,** off, blown; **sour,** soured, turned; **rank,** strong <nonformal>, **high,** gamy

rancor NOUNS **virulence,** venomousness, **venom,** vitriol, gall, **acrimony,** acerbity, asperity; **bitterness,** sourness

random ADJS **irregular,** haphazard, desultory, **erratic,** sporadic, spasmodic, fitful, promiscuous, indiscriminate, casual, frivolous, capricious, hit-or-miss, **aimless,** straggling, straggly; dysteleological, stochastic

range NOUNS 1 **scope,** compass, reach, stretch, expanse, radius, sweep, carry, fetch; **gamut,** scale, register, diapason; **spectrum**
2 **habitat,** home, stamping grounds, locality, native environment; grazing, grazing land
3 **mountain range,** massif; **mountain system, chain,** mountain chain, cordillera, sierra
VERBS 4 **extend,** reach, stretch, sweep, spread, run, cover, carry, lie; **reach** *or* stretch *or* thrust out; span, straddle, take in, encompass
5 **traverse,** cross, travel over *or* through, pass through, **go** *or* **pass over, cover,** measure, transit, track, range over *or* through, course

rank NOUNS 1 **standing,** level, footing, **status,** station; **position,** place, sphere, orbit, echelon; **order,** estate, precedence, condition; rate, rating
VERBS 2 **size,** adjust, grade, group, range, graduate, sort, match; gauge, **measure**, proportion; hierarchize
ADJS 3 **malodorous,** fetid, olid, **odorous,** stinking, reeking, reeky, nidorous, smelling, bad-smelling, **evil-smelling,** ill-smelling, strong, high, gamy
4 **luxuriant,** flourishing, **lush,** riotous, exuberant; overgrown, overrun; **weedy,** unweeded, weed-choked, weed-ridden

rankle VERBS **fester,** suppurate, matter, run, weep; **ruffle,** roil, rile <nonformal>, ruffle one's feathers

ransack VERBS **loot,** sack, rifle, despoil, depredate, prey on *or* upon, **raid,** reive <Scots>, ravage, ravish, raven, sweep, gut

ransom NOUNS 1 **redemption,** salvage, trover; **retrieval,** recovery
VERBS 2 **recover,** regain, retrieve, **get back,** come by one's own; **redeem,** reclaim

rant VERBS **rage,** storm, rave, roar, have a fit

rap NOUNS 1 **sentence,** judgment, punishment
2 **tap,** pat, dab, chuck, touch, tip
3 **trifle,** a hoot *and* a damn *and* a darn *and* a shit <all nonformal>, a tinker's damn
VERBS 4 **criticize;** pan *and* knock *and* slam *and* hit *and* take a rap *or* swipe at <all nonformal>, snipe at, strike out at, tie into *and* tee off on *and* rip into *and* open up on *and* plow into <all nonformal>
5 talk, **talk over,** hash over <nonformal>, talk of *or* about, comment upon, reason about, discourse about; **kick** *or* **knock around** <nonformal>
6 **tap,** pat, dab, chuck, touch, tip

rape NOUNS 1 **sexual possession,** taking; sexual assault, ravishment, violation, indecent assault, date rape *or* acquaintance rape, serial rape *or* gang bang <nonformal>; statutory rape
2 **plundering,** rapine, spoliation, depredation, **raiding,** reiving <Scots>, ravage, ravaging, ravagement, ravishment
VERBS 3 **possess sexually,** take; commit rape, commit date *or* acquaintance rape, ravish, violate, assault sexually, lay violent hands on, have one's will of

rapid ADJS **fast,** swift, speedy; staccato

rapport NOUNS **good terms,** good understanding, good footing, friendly relations; **harmony,** sympathy, fellow feeling

rapt ADJS **gripped,** held, fascinated, enthralled, spellbound, charmed, enchanted, mesmerized, **hypnotized,** fixed, caught, riveted, **arrested,** switched on <nonformal>

rapture NOUNS **happiness,** ravishment, bewitchment, **enchantment,** unalloyed happiness; elation, exaltation; **ecstasy,** ecstasies, transport; **bliss,** blissfulness

rare ADJS 1 **underdone,** undercooked, not done, *saignant* <Fr>
2 extraordinary, exceptional, unique, singular, **remarkable,** striking, sensational; *sui generis* <L, of its own kind>; **out of the ordinary,** out of this world, out-of-the-way, out of the common, out of the pale, **off the beaten track,** offbeat, breakaway
3 rarefied; **subtle; thin,** thinned, dilute, attenuated, attenuate

rascal NOUNS precious rascal, rogue, knave, **scoundrel,** villain, blackguard, **scamp, scalawag** <nonformal>, spalpeen <Ir>, rapscallion, **devil**

rash NOUNS 1 **skin eruption,** eruption, efflorescence, breaking out
ADJS 2 **brash,** incautious, overbold, **imprudent,** indiscreet, injudicious, improvident; **unwary,** unchary; overcareless; hubristic; temerarious

rasp VERBS **grate,** scratch, scrape, grind; provoke, **gall,** chafe, fret, grate, irritate

rat NOUNS 1 **informer, squealer** *and* preacher *and* **stool pigeon** *and* stoolie *and* **fink** <all nonformal>
VERBS 2 **betray,** inform, **inform on,** talk *and* peach <both nonformal>; stool *and* sing *and* squeal <all nonformal>, turn state's evidence

rate NOUNS 1 **velocity,** gait, pace, tread, step, stride, clip *and* lick <both nonformal>
2 **interest,** premium, price; interest rate, rate of interest, prime interest rate *or* **prime rate,** bank rate, lending rate, borrowing rate, the price of money; discount rate
VERBS 3 **deserve,** merit, earn, be in line for <nonformal>, **be worthy of,** be deserving, richly deserve
4 **rank,** count, be regarded, be thought of, be in one's estimation

rather ADVS 1 to a degree, to some extent, in a way, in a measure, in some measure; somewhat, kind of <nonformal>, sort of <nonformal>, pretty, quite, fairly; a little, a bit; slightly, scarcely, to a small degree; very, extremely, to a great degree
2 **instead,** *faute de mieux* <Fr>; in its stead *or* place; in one's stead, in one's behalf, in one's place, in one's shoes; by proxy; as an alternative

ratify VERBS **endorse,** sign off on, second, support, **certify,** confirm, validate, authenticate, accept, give the nod *or* the green light *or* the go-ahead *or* the OK <all nonformal>, give a nod of assent, give one's imprimatur, permit, give permission, **approve**

rating NOUNS 1 **berating,** tongue-lashing; **revilement, vilification,** blackening, execration, abuse, vituperation, invective, contumely, hard *or* cutting *or* bitter words
2 **estimate,** estimation; **evaluation,** evaluating, value judgment, evaluative criticism, analyzing, weighing, weighing up, gauging, ranking, rank-ordering

ration NOUNS 1 **portion,** clutch, share, issue, allotment, lot, deal; **allowance,** budget
VERBS 2 **budget;** put on an allowance

rational ADJS 1 **sane,** reasonable, sensible, **lucid,** normal, wholesome, clearheaded, clearminded, balanced, **sound,** mentally sound, of sound mind, *compos mentis* <L>, sound-minded, right in the head, **in one's right mind,** in possession of one's faculties *or* senses, together *and* all there <both nonformal>
2 **logical,** reasonable, cogent, sensible, sane, sound, well-thought-out, legitimate, just, justifiable, admissible

rationale NOUNS **reason,** reason why, reason for *or* behind, underlying reason, rational ground, **explanation,** the why, the wherefore, **the why and wherefore**

rationalize VERBS 1 **organize,** methodize, systematize, get *or* put one's house in order; **regularize,** routinize, normalize, standardize
2 logicalize, logicize; provide a rationale; intellectualize; explain away

rations NOUNS board, meals, commons <chiefly Brit>, mess, allowance, allotment, food allotment, tucker <Australia>; emergency rations; garrison *or* field rations

rat race NOUNS **futility,** vanity, emptiness, hollowness; **drudgery,** sweat, slavery, spadework; treadmill

rattle NOUNS 1 rattling, rattletybang; **clatter,** clitter, **clitterclatter,** chatter, clack, clacket <nonformal>; racket
VERBS 2 **clatter,** clitter, **chatter,** clack; rattle around, clatter about; **blather,** blabber, babble, gabble, gibble-gabble, **jabber,** gibber, prate, **prattle**
3 **agitate,** perturb, flutter, flurry, disconcert, **fluster**

raucous ADJS **harsh,** harsh-sounding; coarse, rude, rough, gruff, ragged; **hoarse, husky,** roupy <Scots>, cracked, dry; **guttural,** thick, throaty, croaky, croaking

raunchy ADJS **obscene,** lewd, adult, bawdy, ithyphallic, **ribald,** pornographic, salacious, lurid, **dirty,** smutty, blue, smoking-room, impure, unchaste, unclean, **foul,** filthy, nasty, vile, fulsome, offensive, unprintable, unrepeatable, not fit for mixed company

ravage NOUNS 1 **plundering,** rapine, spoliation, depredation, **raiding,** ravaging, ravagement, rape, ravishment
VERBS 2 **plunder,** pillage, loot, sack, ransack, rifle, freeboot, spoil, spoliate, despoil, depredate, prey on *or* upon, **raid,** reive <Scots>, raven, sweep, gut; **debauch,** ravish, ruin; **violate,** abuse; **rape,** force

rave VERBS 1 **be enthusiastic,** enthuse *and* be big for <both nonformal>; **rhapsodize,** carry on over *and* rave on <both nonformal>, make much of, **make a fuss over,** make an ado *or* much ado about, make a to-do over *and* take on

over <both nonformal>, rave about *and* whoop it up about <both nonformal>; go nuts *or* gaga *or* ape over <nonformal>
2 **rage,** storm, rant, roar; have a fit

ravenous ADJS **rapacious,** ravening, vulturous, vulturine, sharkish, **wolfish,** lupine, predacious, **predatory,** raptorial; **gluttonous,** greedy, voracious, edacious, insatiable, polyphagic, bulimic, hyperphagic, Apician

ravine NOUNS gorge, canyon, box canyon, *arroyo* <Sp>, barranca, bolson, coulee, gully, gulch, rift, rift valley, kloof, donga, graben, draw, wadi

ravish VERBS 1 **delight,** enravish, imparadise; transport, carry away
2 **possess sexually,** take; **rape,** commit rape, commit date *or* acquaintance rape, violate, assault sexually, lay violent hands on, have one's will of; deflower, deflorate, devirginate
3 **plunder,** pillage, loot, sack, ransack, rifle, ravage, raven, sweep, gut

raw ADJS 1 **sore;** smarting, tingling, **burning; irritated,** inflamed, tender, sensitive, fiery, angry, red; algetic; chafed, galled
2 **inexperienced,** unseasoned, unfledged, new-fledged, **callow,** unripe, ripening, unmellowed, **green,** vernal, dewy, juicy, sappy, budding, tender, virginal, intact, innocent, naive, ingenuous, **undeveloped**
3 **windblown,** blown; **windswept,** bleak, exposed
4 **crude; uncooked,** unbaked, unboiled; underdone, undercooked, rare, red
5 **coarse,** gross, rude, crude, crass, rough, **earthy;** ribald; raunchy <nonformal>, **obscene**

raw deal NOUNS **injustice,** wrong, injury, grievance, disservice; rotten deal *and* bad rap <both nonformal>; **bad luck,** ill luck, hard luck, **tough** *or* **rotten luck** <nonformal>

ray NOUNS **radiation,** sunray, radius, spoke; radiance, diffusion, scattering, dispersion, emanation; halo, aureole, glory, corona

raze VERBS rase, **fell, level,** flatten, smash, prostrate, raze to the ground *or* dust; steamroller, bulldoze; **pull down,** tear down, take down

razorback NOUNS **swine;** wild boar, tusker; warthog, babirusa

razzledazzle NOUNS **showiness, flashiness,** flamboyance, panache, dash, jauntiness; **gaudiness,** gaudery, glitz *and* gimmickry *and* razzmatazz <all nonformal>, **tawdriness,** meretriciousness

reach NOUNS 1 **earshot,** earreach, **hearing,** range, auditory range, carrying distance, **sound of one's voice**
2 **range,** scope, compass, stretch, expanse radius, sweep, carry, fetch
3 **knowledge,** knowing, knowingness, ken; **command**
VERBS 4 **move, touch,** affect, **soften,** unsteel, melt, melt the heart, appeal to one's better feelings; sadden, grieve
5 **extend, stretch,** sweep, spread, run, **go** *or* **go out,** cover, carry, **range,** lie; **reach** *or* stretch *or* thrust out; span, straddle, take in, hold, encompass, surround, environ
6 **arrive at,** come at, get at, arrive upon, **come upon,** hit upon, strike upon, fall upon, light upon, pitch upon, stumble on *or* upon
7 **communicate with,** get in touch *or* contact with, **make contact with,** raise, get to, get through to, get hold of, make *or* establish connection

reach out VERBS **stretch out,** extend, extend out, go *or* go out, range out, carry out; outstretch, outlie, outdistance, outrange

react VERBS **respond,** reply, answer, riposte, snap back, come back at <nonformal>; rise to the fly, take the bait; go off half-cocked *or* at half cock

reaction NOUNS **impact,** force, **repercussion,** backwash, backlash, reflex, recoil, response; **answer,** riposte, uptake <nonformal>, **retort,** rejoinder, return, **comeback** *and* **take** <both nonformal>

reactionary NOUNS 1 ultraconservative, arch-conservative, extreme right-winger, reactionist, diehard
ADJS 2 **conservative, right-wing,** right of center, ultraconservative, reactionist

reactive ADJS reacting, merely reactive; **responsive,** respondent, responding, antiphonal; **quick on the draw** *or* trigger *or* uptake

read VERBS peruse, go over, read up *or* read up on, have one's nose in a book <nonformal>; bury oneself in, wade through, plunge into; **dig** *and* **grind** *and* **bone** *and* bone up on <all nonformal>

ready VERBS 1 **prepare,** make *or* get ready, prep <nonformal>, **fix** <nonformal>; **make preparations** *or* **arrange-**

ments, put in *or* into shape; dress; treat, pretreat, process
ADJS 2 **eager,** agog, all agog; **avid,** keen, forward, prompt, quick, ready and willing, alacritous, bursting to, dying to, raring to
3 **handy,** convenient; available, accessible, **at hand,** to hand, **on hand,** on tap, on deck <nonformal>, on call, at one's call *or* beck and call, at one's elbow, at one's fingertips, just around the corner, at one's disposal

ready-made ADJS ready-formed, ready-mixed, ready-furnished, ready-dressed, ready-cooked; ready-to-wear, off-the-rack; cut-and-dried *or* cut-and-dry

real ADJS 1 **actual,** factual, veritable, for real <nonformal>, de facto, simple, sober, **hard;** established, inescapable, indisputable, undeniable; demonstrable, provable
2 **genuine,** authentic, veridic, veridical, **natural,** realistic, naturalistic, true to reality, **true to nature,** true to life, verisimilar, veristic

realistic ADJS **genuine,** authentic, veridic, veridical, **real,** natural, naturalistic, true to reality, **true to nature,** lifelike, true to life, verisimilar, veristic

reality NOUNS **actuality,** factuality, empirical *or* demonstrable *or* objective existence, the here and now; historicity; **authenticity;** sober *or* grim reality, hardball *and* the nitty-gritty <both nonformal>

realize VERBS 1 **externalize,** exteriorize, bring into the open, bring out, show, display, exhibit; **objectify,** actualize, project, realize
2 clear, **profit, make** *or* **draw** *or* **realize** *or* **reap profit,** come out ahead, make money; gain by, **capitalize on,** commercialize, make capital out of, **cash in on** *and* make a good thing of <both nonformal>, turn to profit *or* account, **realize on,** make money by, obtain a return, turn a penny *or* an honest penny
3 **understand,** comprehend, apprehend, have, **know, conceive,** appreciate, have no problem with, ken <Scots>, savvy <nonformal>, sense, make sense out of, make something of

realm NOUNS **sphere,** demesne, **domain,** dominion, jurisdiction, bailiwick; **kingdom, empire,** dominion, domain

ream VERBS **bore,** drill, auger; ream out, countersink, gouge, gouge out; **call down** *or* **dress down** <both nonformal>; give the deuce *or* devil, give hell

reap VERBS **harvest,** crop, glean, gather, gather in, bring in, get in the harvest, reap and carry; **acquire,** gain, earn, make

reappear VERBS **recur,** reoccur, return, repeat, **come again,** come up again, be here again, resurface, reenter, come round again, come in its turn

rear NOUNS 1 **rear end,** hind end, hind part, hinder part, afterpart, rearward, **posterior, behind,** breech, stern, tail, tail end; **afterpiece,** tailpiece, heelpiece, heel; **back,** back side, reverse <of a coin or medal>, tail <of a coin>; rear guard, rear area
VERBS 2 **pitch,** toss, tumble, toss and tumble, pitch and toss, **plunge,** hobbyhorse, pound, **rock,** roll, reel, swing, sway, lurch, yaw
3 **rise,** ramp, uprear, rear up, rise on the hind legs; upheave; sit up, sit bolt upright; jump up, spring to one's feet
4 **foster, nurture,** nourish, mother, care for, lavish care on, feed, parent, sustain, cultivate, cherish; **raise, breed,** grow, hatch, feed, nurture, fatten
ADJS 5 rearward, **back,** backward, retrograde, **posterior,** postern, tail; after *or* aft; **hind,** hinder; hindmost, hindermost, hindhand, posteriormost, **aftermost,** aftmost, rearmost

rearrange VERBS **reorganize,** reconstitute, **reorder,** restructure, reshuffle, rejigger <nonformal>, tinker *or* tinker with, tune, tune up, fine-tune; **shake up,** shake out; redispose, redistribute, reallocate, realign

reason NOUNS 1 reason why, rationale, reason for *or* behind, underlying reason, rational ground, **explanation,** the why, the wherefore, **the why and wherefore,** stated cause, pretext, pretense, excuse
2 **sanity, saneness,** sanemindedness, soundness, **soundness of mind,** sound-mindedness, sound mind, healthy mind, right mind <nonformal>, senses, **rationality,** reasonableness, lucidity, balance, wholesomeness; **sense,** common sense, sound sense, sweet reason, **logic**
VERBS 3 **discuss,** debate, deliberate, deliberate upon, exchange views *or* opinions, talk, **talk over,** hash over <nonformal>, talk of *or* about, reason about, discourse about, **consider, treat,** dissertate on, handle, deal with, **exam-**

ine, investigate, talk out, **analyze,** sift, **study,** review, pass under review, controvert, ventilate; **kick** *or* **knock around** <nonformal>

reasonable ADJS 1 **warrantable,** allowable, admissible, colorable, legitimate; **sensible,** logical, rational, cogent, sound, well-thought-out
2 **cheap, inexpensive,** unexpensive, low, low-priced, frugal, sensible, manageable, modest, moderate, affordable, to fit the pocketbook, budget, easy, economy, economic, economical

reassure VERBS **encourage,** hearten, embolden, nerve, pat *or* clap on the back, **assure,** bolster, support, cheer on, root for

rebate NOUNS **discount,** cut, deduction, slash, abatement, reduction, price reduction, price-cutting, price-cut, rollback <nonformal>; rebatement

rebel NOUNS 1 revolter; **insurgent,** insurrectionary, insurrecto, **insurrectionist;** malcontent, *frondeur* <Fr>; **mutineer,** rioter, brawler; maverick <nonformal>, troublemaker, refusenik <nonformal>; nonconformist
VERBS 2 **revolt,** kick over the traces, reluct, reluctate; **rise up,** rise, arise, rise up in arms, mount the barricades; mount *or* make a coup d'état; **mutiny**

rebellion NOUNS **revolt,** revolution, mutiny, insurrection, insurgence *or* insurgency, *émeute* <Fr>, **uprising,** rising, outbreak, general uprising, *levée en masse* <Fr>, **riot,** civil disorder; peasant revolt, *jacquerie* <Fr>; putsch, coup d'état; intifada

reborn ADJS **renascent,** redivivus, redux, resurrected, renewed, revived, resurgent, recrudescent, reappearing, phoenix-like; **redeemed, saved,** converted, regenerated, regenerate, justified, born-again

rebound NOUNS 1 **recoil,** resilience, repercussion, *contrecoup* <Fr>; backlash, backlashing, kickback, **kick,** a kick like a mule <nonformal>, ricochet, carom
VERBS 2 **recoil,** resile; **spring** *or* **fly back,** bounce *or* bound back, snap back; backlash, lash back; ricochet, carom

rebuff NOUNS 1 **repulse; dismissal,** cold shoulder, snub, spurning, brush-off, cut; kiss-off <nonformal>; turn-off <nonformal>; refusal
VERBS 2 **snub,** cut *or* cut dead <nonformal>, drop, repulse; cold-shoulder *or* turn a cold shoulder upon *or* **give the cold shoulder** <nonformal>, give *or* turn the shoulder <nonformal>, turn one's back upon

rebuke NOUNS 1 **reproof,** reproval, reprobation, a flea in one's ear; **reprimand,** reproach, reprehension, **scolding,** chiding, rating, **upbraiding,** objurgation
VERBS 2 **reprove,** reprimand, reprehend, put a flea in one's ear, **scold,** chide, rate, **admonish,** upbraid, objurgate, have words with, take a hard line with; **lecture,** read a lesson *or* lecture to

rebuttal NOUNS **counterstatement,** counterreply, counterclaim, counterblast, counteraccusation, countercharge, *tu quoque* <L, you too>, contraremonstrance; **rejoinder**

recalcitrant ADJS **defiant,** refractory, contumacious, obstreperous, unruly, restive, impatient of control *or* discipline; fractious, ornery *and* feisty <both nonformal>

recall NOUNS 1 **revocation,** retraction, recantation
2 **remembering,** remembrance, recollection, recollecting, exercise of memory, recalling
VERBS 3 **remember, recollect,** flash on *and* mind <both nonformal>; remember clearly, remember as if it were yesterday; have total recall, remember everything
4 **remind,** put in mind, refresh the memory of; **remind one of,** suggest, put one in mind of; take one back, carry back, carry back in recollection

recant VERBS **reject,** repudiate, abjure, forswear, **renounce**, disown, disclaim, retract; unwish

recap NOUNS 1 **summary,** résumé, recapitulation, rundown, run-through; **summation**
VERBS 2 **sum up,** summarize, recapitulate, rehash <nonformal>, **recount,** rehearse, recite, relate; detail, itemize, inventory

recede VERBS retrocede; **retreat,** retire, withdraw; **diminish,** decline, sink, shrink, dwindle, **fade, ebb,** wane

receipt NOUNS **reception,** taking in, receiving; **recipe; receiving,** receival, getting, taking; acquisition; **acknowledgment,** voucher

receipts NOUNS **income,** revenue, profits, earnings, returns, proceeds, **take,** takings, intake, take *or* take-in <nonformal>; gains; gate receipts, gate, box office; net receipts, net; gross receipts, gross

receive VERBS 1 **take in;** admit, let in, intromit, give entrance *or* admittance to; **welcome,** bid welcome, give a royal welcome, roll out the red carpet
2 **get,** gain, secure, have, come by, be in receipt of, be on the receiving end; **obtain,** acquire
3 **tune in,** pick up, spot, home on; pinpoint; identify, trigger; lock on

receiver NOUNS 1 **recipient,** accepter, getter, taker, acquirer, obtainer, procurer; payee, endorsee; addressee, consignee; holder, trustee; **hearer,** viewer, beholder, audience, auditor, listener, looker, spectator; the receiving end
2 **fence,** receiver of stolen goods, swagman *and* swagsman <both nonformal>, bagman, bagwoman
3 **radio,** radio receiver; **radio set,** receiving set, **wireless** *and* wireless set <both Brit>, set

recent ADJS 1 **late,** newly come, of yesterday; latter, later
2 **previous,** once, one time, former

receptacle NOUNS **container;** receiver, holder, vessel, utensil; basin, pot, pan, cup, glass, ladle, bottle; cask; box, case

reception NOUNS 1 **receiving,** receipt, getting, taking; acquisition; **assumption,** acceptance; **welcome,** welcoming
2 **social gathering, social,** at home, salon, levee, soiree

receptionist NOUNS **host,** mine host, hostess, greeter

receptive ADJS 1 recipient; welcoming, open, hospitable, cordial, inviting, invitatory; introceptive; **admissive,** admissory; receivable, receptible, admissible
2 **open-minded,** open, rational, admissive; **persuadable,** persuasible; **unopinionated,** unopinioned, unwedded to an opinion

recess NOUNS 1 **respite,** rest, pause, halt, stay, lull, **break,** surcease, suspension, interlude, **intermission,** spell <Australia>, letup <nonformal>, **time out** <nonformal>, time to catch one's breath
2 **nook,** corner, cranny, niche, cove, bay, oriel, alcove; cubicle, roomlet, carrel, hole-in-the-wall <nonformal>; **retreat,** hideaway; **sanctum,** inner sanctum, sanctum sanctorum
VERBS 3 **pause, rest,** let up *and* take it easy <both nonformal>, **relax,** rest on one's oars; take *or* call a recess; **take a break,** break, take ten

recession NOUNS 1 recedence, receding, retrocedence; **retreat,** retirement, withdrawing, withdrawal; retraction, retractation, retractility
2 **depression,** slump, economic stagnation, **bust** <nonformal>

recharge VERBS **reactivate,** revive, revivify, **renew,** reanimate, reinspire, **regenerate,** rejuvenate, revitalize, put *or* breathe new life into, restimulate

recidivism NOUNS **reversion,** reverting, retroversion, retrogradation, **retrogression,** retrocession, regress, **relapse, regression, backsliding,** lapse, slipping back, backing, recidivation

recipient NOUNS **receiver,** accepter, getter, taker, acquirer, obtainer, procurer; payee, endorsee; addressee, consignee

reciprocal ADJS **communal,** mutual, associated, **joint,** conjoint, **in common,** share and share alike; cooperative; reparative, compensatory, restitutive, recompensing, recompensive

reciprocate VERBS **correspond,** correspond to, respond to, answer, answer to, give in exchange, give and take, go tit-for-tat

recital NOUNS **narration,** narrative, relation, rehearsal, restatement, telling, retelling, recounting, recountal, review; **iteration,** reiteration, recapitulation, recap *and* wrapup <both nonformal>, rehash <nonformal>

recite VERBS **narrate,** tell, relate, recount, report, rehearse, give an account of; **iterate,** reiterate, recapitulate, rehash <nonformal>, **retell,** retail, **restate,** review

reckless ADJS devil-may-care; careless; **impetuous,** hotheaded; **hasty,** hurried, overeager, overzealous, overenthusiastic; precipitate, precipitant; headlong, breakneck; slapdash, slap-bang; accident-prone

reckon VERBS 1 **plan,** plan on, figure on, plan for *or* out, count on, figure out, calculate, calculate on, reckon *or* bargain on, bargain for, bank on *or* upon, make book on <nonformal>
2 **suppose,** assume, presume, surmise, expect, **suspect,** infer, understand, gather, conclude, deduce, consider, imagine, **fancy,** believe, deem, repute, feel, **think**

reckoning NOUNS **calculation,** computation, estimation, calculus; adding, casting, ciphering, totaling, count

reclaim VERBS **rehabilitate,** recondition, recover, restore, readjust

recline VERBS **lie, lie down,** repose, lounge, sprawl, loll, drape *or* spread oneself, splay, lie limply; **lie flat** *or* prostrate *or* prone *or* supine, lie on one's face *or* back, hug the ground *or* deck; prostrate, supinate

recluse NOUNS **loner,** solitaire, solitary, solitudinarian; **hermit,** eremite, anchorite, anchoret; hermitess, anchoress; **ascetic;** closet cynic; stylite, pillarist, pillar saint

recognition NOUNS **acknowledgment,** acceptance; appreciation; **identification,** reidentification, distinguishment; realization

recognize VERBS 1 **honor,** do honor, pay regard to, give *or* pay *or* render honor to; **know,** tell, distinguish, make out; identify, place, make <nonformal>
2 **know, perceive,** discern, see
3 **realize,** appreciate, understand, comprehend, be aware of, be conscious of

recoil NOUNS 1 **rebound,** resilience, repercussion, *contrecoup* <Fr>; **bounce,** bound, spring, bounce-back; **repulse,** rebuff; backlash, backlashing, kickback, **kick,** a kick like a mule <nonformal>, **backfire,** boomerang
VERBS 2 **rebound,** resile; **bounce,** bound, spring; spring *or* fly back, bounce *or* bound back, snap back; **kick,** kick back, kick like a mule <nonformal>, **backfire,** boomerang

recollect VERBS **remember,** recall, think of; **call** *or* **bring to mind,** recall to mind, call up, summon up, conjure up, evoke, recapture, call back, bring back

recommend VERBS 1 **advise,** counsel, suggest, advocate, propose, submit; **advance,** commend to attention, put forward, bring forward, put *or* set forth, put it to, put *or* set *or* lay *or* bring before
2 **advocate,** put in a word *or* good word for, support, back, lend one's name *or* support *or* backing to, make a pitch for <nonformal>

recompense NOUNS 1 **remuneration,** compensation; requital, requitement, quittance, **retribution,** reparation, redress, satisfaction, **atonement, amends,** return, restitution
VERBS 2 **compensate,** make compensation, make good, set right, restitute, pay back, rectify, **make up for; pay back,** repay, indemnify, cover; **trade off,** give and take; **retaliate**

reconcile VERBS bring to terms, **bring together,** reunite, heal the breach; bring about a détente; **iron** *or* **sort out,** adjust, settle, compose, accommodate, arrange matters, settle differences, resolve, compromise; **patch things up,** fix up <nonformal>

reconciliation NOUNS reconcilement, *rapprochement* <Fr>, **reunion,** shaking of hands, making up *and* kissing and making up <both nonformal>

recondition VERBS **rehabilitate,** reclaim, recover, restore, readjust; **renovate,** renew; refit, revamp, furbish, refurbish; refresh, face-lift

reconsider VERBS **reexamine,** review; revise one's thoughts, reappraise, revaluate, rethink; view in a new light, have second thoughts, think better of

reconstitute VERBS **rearrange,** reorganize, **reorder,** restructure, reshuffle, rejigger <nonformal>, tinker *or* tinker with, tune, tune up, fine-tune; redispose, redistribute, reallocate, realign

reconstruct VERBS **remake,** remodel, recompose, reconstitute, re-create, **rebuild,** refabricate, re-form, refashion, reassemble

record NOUNS 1 **phonograph record,** disc, wax, long-playing record *or* LP; transcription, electrical transcription, digital transcription, digital recording; compact disk *or* CD
2 **recording,** documentation, written word; **chronicle, annals,** history, story; roll, rolls, **register,** registry, rota, roster, scroll, catalog, inventory, table, list; **vestige,** trace
VERBS 3 put *or* place upon record; **inscribe,** enscroll; **register,** enroll, matriculate, check in; commit to *or* preserve in an archive, archive; **write,** commit *or* reduce to writing, put in writing, put in black and white, put on paper; **write down,** mark down, jot down, put down, set down, take down; note, note down, make a note, make a memorandum; put on tape, tape, tape-record; videotape; **chronicle,** write history, historify

recording NOUNS **record,** phonograph record, long-playing record *or* LP; transcription, electrical transcription, digital transcription, digital recording; wire recording, tape recording; tape, tape cassette, cassette; documentation, written word

recount NOUNS 1 election returns, **poll,** count, official count
2 **summation,** summary, summing, summing up, recounting, rehearsal, capitulation, **recapitulation,** recap *and* rehash <both nonformal>, statement, **reckoning,** count

recount VERBS **narrate,** tell, relate, report, **recite,** rehearse, give an account of; retell, **iterate,** reiterate, rehearse, recapitulate, rehash <nonformal>, restate

recoup VERBS **recover,** regain, retrieve, recuperate, **get back,** come by one's own; **repay,** pay back, restitute, **reimburse**

recourse NOUNS **resource,** resort; last resort *or* resource, *dernier ressort* and *pis aller* <both Fr>; **hope;** expedient

recover VERBS 1 **rally,** revive, get well, get over, pull through, pull round *or* around, come round *or* around <nonformal>, come back <nonformal>, make a comeback <nonformal>; get back in shape <nonformal>, be oneself again, feel like a new person
2 **regain,** retrieve, **recoup,** get back, come by one's own; **redeem,** ransom; reclaim; repossess, resume, reoccupy; **retake,** recapture, take back; replevin

recovery NOUNS **reclamation,** retrieval, salvage, salving; **rally,** comeback <nonformal>, return; **recuperation,** convalescence; **repossession,** resumption, reoccupation; reclaiming; upturn, uptick <nonformal>, expanding economy, **economic expansion**

recreation NOUNS **refreshment,** invigoration, reinvigoration, reanimation, revival, revivification, renewal; **relaxation,** regalement; **pleasure,** enjoyment

recruit NOUNS 1 **rookie** <nonformal>, **conscript,** draftee, inductee, selectee, enlistee, enrollee, trainee, boot <nonformal>; **raw recruit,** tenderfoot
VERBS 2 **employ, hire,** give a job to, take into employment, take into one's service, take on <nonformal>, headhunt <nonformal>, **engage,** sign up *or* on <nonformal>; **muster,** levy, raise

rectify VERBS **remedy,** correct, right, patch up, emend, amend, **redress,** make good *or* right, **put right,** set right, put *or* set to rights, put *or* set straight, set up, heal up, knit up, make all square

recuperate VERBS **get well, recover,** mend, be oneself again, feel like a new person, get back on one's feet, get over it

recur VERBS **repeat,** reoccur, **come again,** come round again, go round again, come up again, resurface, **return,** reappear, resume; resound, reverberate, echo; keep coming, come again and again, happen over and over; recur to the mind, return to mind, come back, reenter

redecorate VERBS **ornament,** decorate, adorn, dress, trim, garnish, array, **deck,** bedeck; prettify, **beautify;** refurbish, redo

redeem VERBS 1 **reclaim,** recover, retrieve; ransom; rescue; salvage, salve; recycle; win back, **recoup**
2 **pay in full,** meet one's obligations *or* commitments, redeem one's pledge, settle *or* square accounts; regenerate, **reform,** convert, save, give salvation

red flag NOUNS **warning sign,** premonitory sign, danger sign; **symptom,** early symptom, premonitory symptom, precursor; **red light**

red-handed ADJS 1 **guilty,** guilty as hell, peccant, criminal, to blame, at fault, faulty, on one's head; caught in the act *or* flatfooted *or* red-handed, caught with one's pants down *or* with one's hand in the till *or* with one's hand in the cookie jar <nonformal>
ADVS 2 red-hand, **in the act,** in the very act, *in flagrante delicto* <L>

red herring NOUNS **stratagem,** artifice, **ruse,** tactic, **maneuver, stroke,** gambit, **ploy,** dodge, artful dodge

redneck NOUNS 1 **vulgarian,** lout, yahoo; **ruffian,** roughneck <nonformal>, **rowdy,** hooligan
ADJS 2 rowdy, **rowdyish,** ruffianly, roughneck <nonformal>, hooliganish, raffish, raised in a barn

redo VERBS **remake,** make *or* do over, refashion, **reshape,** recast, rework, rejigger <nonformal>, **reconstruct,** rebuild, redesign, restructure, **revise;** redecorate, refurbish; **repeat,** do again, do a repeat

redress NOUNS 1 **reparation, recompense,** paying back, squaring <nonformal>; retribution, **atonement,** satisfaction, **amends,** making good, **requital**
VERBS 2 **remedy,** rectify, correct, right,

patch up, emend, amend, make good *or* right, **put right,** set right, put *or* set to rights, put *or* set straight, set up, heal up, knit up, make all square; pay reparations, requite, restitute, recompense, compensate, remunerate

red tape NOUNS **officialism,** bureaucracy; **red-tapism** *and* red-tapery <both nonformal>; bureaucratic delay, *paperasserie* <Fr>

reduce VERBS 1 **decrease,** diminish, lessen, take from; **lower,** depress, de-escalate, damp, dampen, **step down** *and* tune down *and* phase down *or* out *and* scale back *or* down *and* roll back *or* down <all nonformal>; **curtail,** retrench; **cut,** cut down *or* back, trim away, whittle away *or* down, pare
2 **conquer,** prostrate, fell, **flatten,** break, smash, crush, humble, bend, bring one to his knees; **impoverish,** pauperize, beggar

redundant ADJS **superfluous;** excess, in excess; unnecessary, unessential, nonessential, expendable, dispensable, **needless,** unneeded, gratuitous, uncalled-for; pleonastic, tautologous, tautological; verbose, prolix

reek VERBS **stink,** smell, smell bad, assail *or* offend the nostrils, smell to heaven *or* high heaven; **exude,** exudate, transude, transpire

reel NOUNS 1 **whirl,** wheel, **spin,** turn, round; spiral, helix, helicoid, gyre; pirouette; **swirl,** twirl, **eddy,** gurge, surge
VERBS 2 **whirl,** twirl, wheel, spin, spin like a top; **swirl,** gurge, surge, **eddy; flounder,** flounce, stagger, totter, roll, rock, lurch, careen, swing, sway

reel off VERBS **repeat,** rattle off, regurgitate; say again, repeat oneself, repeat word for word *or* verbatim, repeat like a broken record

reentry NOUNS **return,** homecoming, recursion; reentrance, remigration; Earth insertion; splashdown

refer VERBS **attribute,** assign, ascribe, impute, give, place, put, apply, attach; cite

referee NOUNS 1 **arbitrator,** arbiter, impartial arbitrator, third party, unbiased observer; **moderator; umpire,** judge
VERBS 2 **mediate,** intermediate, **intercede,** go between; **arbitrate,** moderate; **umpire,** judge

refer to VERBS **point to,** advert to, allude to, make an allusion to; **point out,** point at, put *or* lay one's finger on; **relate to,** apply to, bear on *or* upon, **concern,** involve, touch, affect, interest; **pertain to,** appertain, appertain to, belong to, fit

refine VERBS **clarify,** clear, purify, rectify, depurate, decrassify; try; **strain;** elute, elutriate; **filter,** filtrate; **process,** convert; mill, machine; extract, smelt

reflect VERBS 1 **image, mirror,** hold the mirror up to nature, figure; **embody,** body forth, incarnate, **personify,** personate, impersonate
2 **consider,** contemplate, speculate, study, ponder, perpend, **weigh,** deliberate, debate, meditate, muse, brood, ruminate, chew the cud <nonformal>, digest; introspect, be abstracted

reflection NOUNS 1 **stigma,** slur, reproach, censure, reprimand, imputation, aspersion, stigmatization; pillorying; disparagement
2 **consideration,** contemplation, speculation, meditation, musing, rumination, deliberation, lucubration, brooding, study, **pondering,** turning over in the mind
3 reflected *or* incident light; reflectance, albedo; blink, iceblink, ice sky, snowblink, waterblink, water sky

reflex NOUNS 1 conditioned reflex, conditioned response; simple reflex, unconditioned reflex; backwash, backlash, recoil, response; spontaneous reaction, unthinking response, knee-jerk <nonformal>
ADJS 2 **spontaneous,** unintentional, unintended, inadvertent, unwilled, **indeliberate,** undeliberate; **involuntary,** reflexive, knee-jerk <nonformal>, automatic

reform NOUNS 1 **reformation;** transformation; conversion; reformism, meliorism; **regeneration,** revival, reclamation, redemption, amendment, improvement, renewal, recrudescence, **rebirth,** renascence, new birth, change of heart; change of mind *or* commitment *or* allegiance *or* loyalty *or* conviction
VERBS 2 **improve, better,** change for the better, make an improvement; transform, transfigure; advance, promote, foster, favor, nurture, forward, bring forward; **lift,** elevate, **uplift,** raise, boost <nonformal>; put *or* set straight; reform oneself, turn over a new leaf, mend

one's ways, straighten out, straighten oneself out, go straight <nonformal>; get it together *and* get one's ducks in a row <both nonformal>

reformatory NOUNS **reform school,** correctional institution, industrial school, training school; borstal *or* borstal school *or* remand school <all Brit>

refrain NOUNS 1 **repeat,** repetend, bis, echo; **burden,** chant, undersong, chorus, bob
VERBS 2 **abstain,** hold, **spare,** forbear, forgo, keep from; hold *or* stay one's hand, sit by *or* idly by, sit on one's hands; **avoid,** shun, eschew, **pass up** <nonformal>, **keep from,** keep *or* stand *or* hold aloof from, have nothing to do with, take no part in, have no hand in, **let alone,** let well enough alone, **deny oneself,** do without, go without

refresh VERBS **freshen,** freshen up, fresh up <nonformal>; **revive,** revivify, **reinvigorate,** reanimate; **exhilarate,** stimulate, invigorate, fortify, enliven, liven up, animate, vivify, quicken; renew one's strength, put *or* breathe new life into, give a breath of fresh air, give a shot in the arm <nonformal>; renew, recreate, charge *or* recharge one's batteries <nonformal>

refreshment NOUNS refection, refreshing, **bracing,** exhilaration, stimulation, enlivenment, vivification, **invigoration,** reinvigoration, reanimation, revival, revivification, revivescence *or* revivescency, renewal, recreation; **tonic,** bracer, breath of fresh air, pick-me-up *and* a shot in the arm *and* an upper <all nonformal>

refrigerant NOUNS **coolant;** cryogen; Freon <trademark>, ether; liquid air, liquid oxygen *or* lox, liquid nitrogen, liquid helium, etc

refrigerate VERBS **cool,** chill; ice, ice-cool; water-cool, air-cool; **air-condition**

refuge NOUNS **sanctuary,** safehold, **asylum,** haven, port, harborage, **harbor;** harbor of refuge, port in a storm, snug harbor, safe haven; game sanctuary, bird sanctuary, preserve, forest preserve, game preserve

refugee NOUNS **emigrant,** émigré, outmigrant; defector; evacuee, boat person, *émigré* <Fr>; **displaced person** *or* DP, stateless person

refund NOUNS 1 **reparation,** recompense, paying back, squaring <nonformal>, repayment, reimbursement, remuneration, **compensation,** indemnification; kickback <nonformal>
VERBS 2 **recompense,** pay back, square <nonformal>, repay, reimburse, remunerate, kick back <nonformal>

refurbish VERBS **renovate,** renew; recondition, refit, revamp, furbish; refresh, face-lift; redecorate, redo

refusal NOUNS **unwillingness,** disinclination, nolition, **indisposition,** indisposedness, **reluctance,** renitency, renitence, grudgingness, grudging consent; **resistance,** dissent

refuse NOUNS **waste,** wastage, waste matter; leavings, sweepings, **scraps,** orts; **garbage,** slops, hogwash <nonformal>; dregs; deadwood; rags, bones, wastepaper, shard, potsherd; slag, culm, slack

refuse VERBS **be unwilling,** would *or* had rather not, not care to, not find it in one's heart to, not have the heart *or* stomach to; object to, draw the line at, be dead set against, **balk at;** grudge, begrudge; **disapprove,** decline, not consent, refuse consent, **reject, turn down** <nonformal>, decline to accept, not buy <nonformal>; put *or* set one's foot down, refuse point-blank *or* summarily; decline politely *or* with thanks, beg off

refute VERBS **confute,** confound, rebut, parry, answer, **answer conclusively,** dismiss, dispose of; argue down; silence, put *or* reduce to silence, shut up, stop the mouth of; take the wind out of one's sails; **contradict,** controvert, counter, run counter, **deny**

regal ADJS **stately,** imposing, grand, courtly, magisterial, aristocratic; **majestic,** royal, kingly, queenly; statuesque, fit for a king

regale VERBS 1 **feast, banquet,** eat heartily, lick the platter *or* plate, do oneself proud <nonformal>, put it away <nonformal>; refresh the inner man
2 **amuse,** cheer, entertain, divert, beguile, solace, recreate, refresh, enliven, exhilarate, put in good humor

regalia NOUNS **insignia,** ensign, **emblem,** badge, symbol, marking, attribute; badge of office, mark of office, chain, chain of office, collar; livery, uniform, mantle, dress, formal dress

regard NOUNS 1 **respect,** consideration, appreciation, favor; approbation, approval; **esteem,** estimation, prestige; **favor,** goodwill, good graces, mutual

regard, favorable regard, the good *or* right side of <nonformal>
2 **relevance,** pertinence, pertinency, cogency, relatedness, materiality, **appositeness,** germaneness; **connection,** reference, bearing, concern, concernment, interest, respect
VERBS 3 **cherish, hold dear,** hold in one's heart *or* affections, think much *or* the world of, prize, treasure; **admire,** esteem, revere; **adore, idolize,** worship, dearly love, think worlds *or* the world of, love to distraction
4 **care,** mind, heed, think, consider, pay heed to, take heed *or* thought of; **take an interest,** be concerned; pay attention
5 **contemplate,** look upon, view, see, view with the mind's eye, **envisage,** envision, visualize, imagine, image

regardless ADJS 1 **careless,** heedless, unheeding, unheedful, unsolicitous, uncaring; tactless, thoughtless, unthinking, inconsiderate, untactful, undiplomatic, mindless of, **unmindful,** forgetful, oblivious
ADVS 2 **anyhow,** anyway, anywise, in any way, **by any means,** by any manner of means; in any event, at any rate, in any case; **nevertheless,** nonetheless, however; at all, nohow <nonformal>

regards NOUNS **compliments,** respects, *égards, devoirs* <both Fr>; **best wishes,** one's best, good wishes, best regards, kind *or* kindest regards, love, best love; greetings

regent NOUNS ruler, governor; protector, prince regent, queen regent

regiment VERBS **hold** *or* **keep a tight hand upon,** keep a firm hand on, keep a tight rein on, rule with an iron hand, rule with a rod of iron, knock *or* bang heads together <nonformal>; discipline

region NOUNS **area,** zone, belt, **territory,** terrain; place; space; **setting,** locale, world, milieu

regional ADJS **territorial,** geographical, areal, sectional, zonal, topographic *or* topographical

register NOUNS 1 **range,** scope, compass, reach, stretch, expanse radius, sweep, carry, fetch; **gamut; spectrum**
2 **registration,** registry; **listing,** tabulation, cataloging, inventorying, indexing; **chronicle,** chronology, record
VERBS 3 be heard, **fall on the ear,** sound in the ear, catch *or* reach the ear, come to one's ear, make an impression, get across <nonformal>; **get over** *or* **across** <nonformal>, come through, **penetrate, sink in,** soak in; dawn on, be glimpsed
4 **represent,** delineate, depict, render, characterize, hit off, **portray,** picture, picturize, limn; convey an impression of
5 patent, copyright; **guard,** protect; **enroll,** matriculate, check in; impanel

regress VERBS go backwards, **recede,** return, revert; **retrogress,** retrograde, retroflex, retrocede; fall *or* get *or* go behind, lose ground, slip back; **backslide,** lapse, relapse, recidivate

regret NOUNS 1 **regrets,** regretting, regretfulness; **remorse,** remorsefulness, remorse of conscience; **shame,** shamefulness, shamefacedness, shamefastness; **sorrow,** grief; **contrition,** contriteness
VERBS 2 **deplore,** repine, be sorry for; rue, rue the day; **bemoan,** bewail; curse one's folly, **reproach oneself,** kick oneself <nonformal>, bite one's tongue, accuse *or* condemn *or* blame *or* convict *or* punish oneself, flagellate oneself, wear a hair shirt, make oneself miserable

regrettable ADJS much to be regretted; **deplorable,** lamentable, pitiful, pitiable, woeful, woesome <old>, grievous, sad

regular NOUNS 1 **customer,** client; patron, regular customer *or* buyer
ADJS 2 **habitual,** frequent, constant, persistent; **systematic** *or* systematical, methodical, ordered, orderly, regular as clockwork; **usual, customary,** accustomed, wonted, **normative,** standard, regulation, conventional

regularity NOUNS **constancy,** invariability, unvariation, undeviation, even tenor *or* pace, smoothness, clockwork regularity; **sameness, monotony,** undifferentiation, the same old thing <nonformal>, the daily round *or* routine, the treadmill

regulate VERBS **direct,** manage, conduct, carry on, handle, run <nonformal>; **control,** command, head, govern, boss *and* head up *and* pull the strings *and* mastermind *and* quarterback *and* call the signals <all nonformal>; **order,** prescribe; lay down the law, make the rules, call the shots *or* tune <nonformal>

regulation NOUNS 1 **direction,** directive, instruction, rule; prescript, prescription, **precept**; general order; **government,** governance, discipline

ADJS 2 **established,** received, accepted; set, prescribed, prescriptive; **standard,** regular, stock, **conventional**

regulatory ADJS **governing,** controlling, regulating, regulative, commanding

rehabilitate VERBS recondition, reclaim, recover, restore, readjust; **reeducate,** reinstruct; repatriate

rehash VERBS **paraphrase,** rephrase, reword, restate; **iterate,** reiterate, rehearse, recapitulate, recount, **recite,** retell, retail, review, run over

rehearse VERBS **practice,** go through, walk *or* run through, go over; go through one's part, read one's lines; study one's part

reign NOUNS 1 **governance,** authority, jurisdiction, control, command, power, rule, regnancy, **dominion, sovereignty,** empire, empery, raj <India>, imperium, **sway**
VERBS 2 **rule,** sway, wield the scepter, wear the crown, sit on the throne; rule over, govern

reigning ADJS **governing,** controlling, regulating, regulative, regulatory, commanding; ruling, sovereign, regnant; dominant, preponderant, **leading,** paramount, supreme, number one <nonformal>, hegemonic, hegemonistic

reimburse VERBS **repay,** pay back, restitute, recoup; pay in kind, pay one in his own coin, give tit for tat; **refund,** kick back <nonformal>

reinforce VERBS **intensify,** heighten, deepen, enhance, **strengthen,** beef up <nonformal>, aggravate, exacerbate; double, redouble, triple; bolster, back up, give *or* furnish *or* afford *or* supply *or* lend support; **corroborate,** bear out, buttress, **sustain,** fortify, undergird

reinforcements NOUNS **support, relief,** auxiliaries, reserves, reserve forces

reinstate VERBS **restore,** put back, replace, return, place in *status quo ante;* **reestablish,** redintegrate, reenact, restitute; **reinstall,** reinvest, revest, reinstitute, reconstitute, recompose, recruit, **rehabilitate,** redevelop

reiterate VERBS **repeat,** say again, do again; **iterate,** rehearse, recapitulate, recount, rehash <nonformal>, **recite, retell,** retail, **restate,** reword, review, run over, sum up, summarize, précis, resume, encapsulate

reject NOUNS 1 **discard,** throwaway, castaway, castoff, rejectamenta <pl>; **refuse**
VERBS 2 **repudiate,** abjure, forswear, **renounce,** disown, disclaim, recant; except, **exclude**, deselect, close the door on, leave out in the cold, cut out, blackball, blacklist; disregard; throw out *or* away, chuck *and* chuck out <both nonformal>, discard; categorically reject, disallow, not hear of; **turn thumbs down on** *and* thumb down <both nonformal>, ostracize, ban

rejoice VERBS jubilate, **exult,** glory, joy, delight, bless *or* thank one's stars *or* lucky stars, congratulate oneself, hug oneself, rub one's hands, clap hands; dance *or* skip *or* jump for joy, rollick, revel, frolic, caper, gambol, caracole, romp

rejoice in VERBS **delight in,** indulge in, luxuriate in, revel in, riot in, bask in, wallow in, swim in; groove on *and* get high on *and* freak out on <all nonformal>; feast on, gloat over *or* on; **relish,** appreciate, roll under the tongue, do justice to, savor, smack the lips; devour, eat up

rejuvenate VERBS **revive,** revivify, renew, **reanimate,** reinspire, regenerate, revitalize, put *or* breathe new life into, restimulate; **rekindle,** relight, reheat the ashes, stir the embers

relapse NOUNS 1 **lapse,** falling back; **reversion,** regression; reverting, retroversion, retrogradation, **retrogression,** retrocession, regress, **backsliding,** recidivism, recidivation
VERBS 2 **lapse,** backslide, slide back, lapse back, **slip back,** sink back, **fall back,** have a relapse, devolve, **return to,** revert to, yield again to, fall again into, recidivate; revert, regress; **fall,** fall from grace

relate VERBS **associate, connect,** interconnect, ally, link, link up, wed, marry, marry up, weld, bind, tie, couple, bracket, equate, identify; bring into relation with, bring to bear upon, apply; **parallel,** parallelize, draw a parallel; **interrelate,** relativize, **correlate**

related ADJS 1 **kindred, akin,** of common source *or* stock *or* descent *or* ancestry, agnate, cognate, enate, connate, connatural, congeneric *or* congenerous, consanguine *or* consanguineous, genetically related, related by blood, affinal
2 **connected; linked,** tied, coupled, knotted, twinned, wedded, wed, married *or* married up, welded, conjugate,

bracketed, bound, yoked, spliced, conjoined, conjoint, conjunct, joined

relate to VERBS **refer to, apply to, bear on** *or* **upon,** respect, regard, **concern, involve,** touch, affect, interest; **pertain, pertain to,** appertain, appertain to, belong to, fit; **have to do with,** have connection with, link with *or* link up with, connect, tie in with <nonformal>, deal with, treat of, touch upon

relation NOUNS **relationship, connection;** relatedness, connectedness, **association**, **affiliation,** filiation, bond, union, alliance, **tie,** tie-in <nonformal>, link, linkage, linking, linkup, liaison, **addition**, adjunct, junction, **combination**, assemblage; **positive** *or* **good relation,** affinity, rapport, mutual attraction, sympathy, accord; **closeness,** propinquity, **proximity,** approximation, contiguity, nearness, intimacy

relative ADJS **comparative,** relational; **relativistic,** indeterminate, uncertain, variable; **relating,** pertaining, appertaining, pertinent, referring, referable

relax VERBS unbend, unwind, slack, slacken, **ease; ease up, let up,** slack up, slack off, **ease off,** let down, **slow down,** take it slow, let up, take time to catch one's breath

relay VERBS **deliver**; pass on, pass the buck <nonformal>, hand forward, hand on

release NOUNS 1 **deliverance,** extrication, freeing, removal; suspension, intermission, respite, surcease, reprieve; discharge; catharsis, purging, purgation, purge, cleansing, cleansing away, emotional release
VERBS 2 **free, deliver,** reprieve, remove, free from; suspend, intermit, give respite *or* surcease; **relax,** decompress, ease, destress; act as a cathartic, **purge,** purge away, cleanse, cleanse away; give release, cut loose; **unhand,** let go, let loose, turn loose, cast loose, let out, let off, let go free; **discharge, dismiss;** let out on bail, grant bail to, go bail for <nonformal>; parole, put on parole; release from prison, spring <nonformal>; demobilize, separate from the service

relent VERBS **yield, give,** relax, bend, unbend, give way; submit

relentless ADJS **unyielding,** unbending, inflexible, hard, hard-line, inelastic, impliable, ungiving, **firm,** stiff, rigid, rigorous, stuffy; implacable, inexorable, unrelenting

relevant ADJS **pertinent,** appertaining, **germane, apposite,** cogent, material, admissible, applicable, applying, pertaining, belonging, involving, appropriate, **apropos,** *à propos* <Fr>, to the purpose, **to the point,** in point, *ad rem* <L>

reliable ADJS **dependable,** sure, surefire <nonformal>, **trustworthy,** trusty, to be depended *or* relied upon, to be counted *or* reckoned on; predictable, calculable; **secure,** solid, sound, firm, fast, **stable,** substantial, staunch, steady, **steadfast,** faithful, unfailing; true to one's word

relic NOUNS **memento,** remembrance, token, trophy, souvenir, keepsake, favor, token of remembrance; *memento mori* <L>

relief NOUNS **lightening,** easing, easement, alleviation; disburdening, disencumberment, unburdening, **unloading,** unlading, unsaddling, untaxing, unfreighting; **aid,** help, assistance, support, succor, comfort, ease, remedy

relieve VERBS 1 give relief; **ease,** ease matters; **relax,** slacken; **alleviate,** mitigate, palliate, soften, pad, cushion, assuage, allay, defuse, lay, appease, mollify, subdue, soothe; **dull, deaden,** dull *or* deaden the pain, numb, benumb, anesthetize; **lighten**
2 **substitute for,** subrogate; stand *or* sit in for, understudy for, fill in for, change places with, stand in the stead of, fill the shoes of; spell <nonformal>, cover for

relieve of VERBS **take from,** take away from, **deprive of,** do out of <nonformal>, disburden of, lighten of, ease of; **deprive,** bereave, divest

religion NOUNS religious belief *or* faith, **belief, faith,** teaching, doctrine, creed, credo, theology, orthodoxy; system of beliefs; tradition

religious ADJS 1 **pious,** pietistic; religious-minded; theistic; **devout,** devoted; **reverent,** reverential, venerative, venerational, adoring, solemn; faithful, dutiful; affirming, witnessing, believing; **observant,** practicing; **sacred, holy,** numinous, sacrosanct, spiritual
2 **conscientious,** scrupulous, punctilious, meticulous, strict

relinquish VERBS **give up,** surrender, yield, cede, hand *or* turn over; take one's hands off, loose one's grip on; **forgo,** do without, get along without, forswear, abjure, **renounce,** swear off; **part with,** give away, dispose of, rid oneself of, get rid of, see the last of, dump

relish NOUNS 1 **taste,** gusto, *goût* <Fr>; **flavor,** sapor; **smack,** tang; savor, sapidity; palate, tongue, tooth, stomach; taste in the mouth; sweetness, sourness, bitterness, bittersweetness, saltiness; aftertaste; savoriness
VERBS 2 **savor,** like, love, be fond of, be partial to, enjoy, delight in, have a soft spot for, appreciate, roll under the tongue, do justice to, smack the lips

reluctant ADJS **grudging,** renitent, loath; backward, laggard, dilatory, slow, slow to; unenthusiastic, unzealous, indifferent, apathetic, perfunctory; balky, balking, restive

rely on VERBS **trust,** confide in, depend on, repose, place trust *or* confidence in, have confidence in, **trust in**, trust utterly *or* implicitly, deem trustworthy, think reliable *or* dependable, take one's word, take at one's word

remain VERBS 1 **be left** *or* **left over,** survive, subsist, rest
2 **stay,** keep, hold, endure, stand, prevail, last long, hold out; defy *or* defeat time; live to fight another day; live on, live through; wear, wear well

remainder NOUNS **surplus,** surplusage, leftovers, plus, **overplus,** overstock, **overage,** overset, overrun, overmeasure, oversupply; **balance,** leftover, extra, spare, something extra *or* to spare

remains NOUNS **corpse,** dead body, mortal *or* organic remains, bones, skeleton, dry bones, relics, reliquiae

remark NOUNS 1 **statement,** earful *and* crack *and* one's two cents' worth <all nonformal>, **word,** say, **saying,** utterance, observation, reflection, expression; **assertion,** averment, allegation, affirmation, pronouncement, position, dictum; **declaration**
VERBS 2 **comment,** observe, note; mention, let drop *or* fall, say by the way, make mention of; refer to, allude to, touch on, make reference to, call attention to; muse, reflect

remarkable ADJS **outstanding,** extraordinary, **superior**, marked, of mark, signal, conspicuous, **striking; marvelous,** wonderful, formidable, exceptional, uncommon, astonishing, appalling, fabulous, fantastic, incredible, egregious

remedial ADJS **curative,** therapeutic, healing, corrective, alterative, restorative, analeptic

remedy NOUNS 1 **cure, corrective,** alterative, remedial measure, sovereign remedy; healing agent; restorative, analeptic; specific, specific remedy
VERBS 2 **rectify,** correct, right, patch up, emend, amend, **redress,** make good *or* right, **put right,** set right, put *or* set to rights, put *or* set straight, set up, heal up, knit up, make all square; **cure,** work a cure, **heal,** restore to health

remember VERBS **recall, recollect,** think of, call *or* bring to mind, recall to mind, call up, summon up, conjure up, evoke, recapture, call back, bring back

call back yesterday, bid time return
Shakespeare

remind VERBS **put in mind,** remember, put in remembrance, bring back, bring to recollection, refresh the memory of; **jog the memory,** awaken *or* arouse the memory, flap the memory, give a hint *or* suggestion; **prompt,** give the cue, nudge

reminder NOUNS **remembrance,** remembrancer; **prompt,** prompter, tickler; prompting, cue, hint; jogger <nonformal>

reminisce VERBS rake *or* dig up the past; **remember,** look back, reflect, think of, evoke, recapture, look back upon things past

remiss ADJS **lax,** slack, loose, relaxed; imprecise, sloppy <nonformal>, careless, slipshod; negligent; work-shy

remission NOUNS 1 **pardon,** excuse, sparing, **amnesty,** indemnity, exemption, immunity, reprieve, grace; **absolution,** shrift, remission of sin; redemption; **exoneration,** exculpation; **restitution,** restoration, restoring, giving back, sending back, remitting, **return**
2 **decline,** declension, **subsidence,** dwindling, wane, ebb; downturn, downtrend, retreat; modulation, **abatement, mitigation,** diminution, **reduction,** lessening

remit VERBS 1 **pay,** render, tender; **recompense,** remunerate, compensate, reward, guerdon, indemnify, satisfy
2 **ease up,** ease off, abate, mitigate; **slacken,** slack, slake, slack off, slack up

remittance NOUNS **payment,** paying, paying off, paying up <nonformal>, payoff; paying out, **disbursal**; installment

remnant NOUNS **remainder,** remains,

residue, residuum, **rest, balance;** holdover

remodel VERBS **re-form,** reshape, refashion, recast; rehabilitate

remorse NOUNS **regret,** remorsefulness, remorse of conscience; **ruth,** ruefulness, guilty conscience, guilt feelings; onus, burden

remorseless ADJS **unregretful,** unregretting, **unremorseful,** unsorry, unsorrowful, unrueful; **merciless,** unmerciful, without mercy, unruing, **ruthless,** heartless, steely, flinty

remote ADJS 1 **distant,** distal, **removed,** far, far-off, away, **faraway,** way-off, at a distance, exotic, separated, apart, asunder; out-of-the-way, in a backwater; **unfrequented,** unvisited, off the beaten track
2 **aloof,** standoffish, distant, **detached,** Olympian, withdrawn; **cool,** cold, coldfish, frigid, chilly, icy, frosty; inaccessible, unapproachable
3 **farfetched,** strained, forced, dragged in, neither here nor there, brought in from nowhere; improbable

remove VERBS 1 **move,** relocate, shift, send, shunt; displace, delocalize, dislodge; **take away,** cart off *or* away, carry off *or* away; set *or* lay *or* put aside, put *or* set to one side, side
2 **murder,** commit murder; assassinate; **purge,** liquidate, eliminate, get rid of
3 **detach,** disengage, take *or* lift off, doff; **unfasten,** undo, unattach, unfix; **free,** release, liberate, loose, unloose, unleash, unfetter; **dismiss,** discharge, expel, cashier, drum out, separate forcibly *or* involuntarily, **lay off,** suspend, make redundant, turn out, let go, let out, give the pink slip

removed ADJS **aloof,** standoffish, offish, standoff, **distant, remote,** withdrawn; isolated, shut off, insular, **separate,** separated, **apart,** detached

remunerate VERBS **pay,** render, tender; **recompense,** compensate, reward, guerdon, indemnify, satisfy

renaissance NOUNS **revival,** revivification, **renewal,** resurrection, resuscitation, restimulation, reanimation, resurgence, recrudescence; renascence, **rebirth,** new birth; **rejuvenation,** rejuvenescence

render VERBS 1 **translate,** transcribe, transliterate, put *or* turn into, transfuse the sense of; construe
2 **describe,** portray, picture, **depict,** represent, delineate, limn, **paint,** draw; evoke, bring to life, make one see; **characterize,** character; **express,** set forth, give words to; **play,** perform, execute, do; interpret; make
3 **give, bestow,** confer, award, allot, bestow on; **deliver,** hand, pass, reach, forward, put into the hands of; transfer
4 **melt,** melt down, liquefy; refine

rendezvous NOUNS 1 **tryst,** assignation, meeting; trysting place, meeting place, place of assignation; assignation house; love nest <nonformal>
VERBS 2 **meet,** date; **couple,** copulate, link

renegade NOUNS 1 **apostate,** defector, turncoat, traitor, deserter
ADJS 2 **apostate,** recreant, tergiversating, tergiversant; **treasonous,** treasonable, traitorous, forsworn; collaborating; faithless, **disloyal**

renege VERBS **repeal,** revoke, rescind, reverse, strike down, abrogate; renig *and* go back on *and* welsh <all nonformal>; **be unfaithful,** not keep faith *or* troth, go back on <nonformal>, **fail,** break one's word *or* promise, go back on one's word <nonformal>, break faith

renew VERBS **revive,** revivify, **reanimate,** reinspire, regenerate, rejuvenate, revitalize, put *or* breathe new life into, restimulate; refresh; **renovate,** recondition, refit, revamp, furbish, refurbish; face-lift, recast, revamp <nonformal>, change over

renounce VERBS **swear off,** forswear, **give up,** abandon, stop, discontinue; take the pledge, get on the wagon *or* water wagon <nonformal>; **kick** *and* kick the habit <both nonformal>, dry out; relinquish

renovate VERBS **renew;** recondition, refit, revamp, furbish, refurbish; refresh, face-lift

renown NOUNS **repute,** reputation; **fame,** famousness, **kudos,** report, **glory;** éclat, **celebrity,** popularity, recognition, a place in the sun; **acclaim,** public acclaim, réclame; **notoriety,** notoriousness, talk of the town

the bubble reputation
SHAKESPEARE

rent NOUNS 1 **crack, cleft,** cranny, chink, check, craze, chap, **crevice,** fissure,

scissure, incision, notch, score, cut, gash, slit, split, **rift**
2 **rental,** lease, let <Brit>; sublease, sublet; charter
VERBS 3 **cleave, crack,** check, incise, craze, **cut, cut apart,** gash, slit, **split,** rive, rip open
4 **lease,** let <Brit>, hire, job, **charter; sublease,** sublet

reorganize VERBS **rearrange,** reconstitute, **reorder,** restructure, reshuffle, rejigger <nonformal>, tinker *or* tinker with, tune, tune up, fine-tune; **shake up,** shake out; redispose, redistribute, reallocate, realign

repair VERBS **mend, fix,** fix up <nonformal>, do up, put in repair, put in shape, set to rights, put in order *or* condition; **condition,** recondition, service, overhaul; patch, patch up

reparation NOUNS **recompense,** paying back, squaring <nonformal>, repayment, reimbursement, refund, remuneration, **compensation,** indemnification; retribution, **atonement,** redress, satisfaction, **amends,** making good, **requital**

repartee NOUNS **conversation,** verbal intercourse, conversational interchange, interchange of speech, give-and-take, cross-talk, rapping <nonformal>, backchat; clever *or* ready *or* witty reply *or* retort

repast NOUNS **meal,** feed *and* sit-down <both nonformal>, mess, spread <nonformal>, table, board, meat, *repas* <Fr>; **refreshment,** refection

repay VERBS pay back, restitute, **reimburse,** recoup; **requite,** quit, **atone,** make amends, make good, make up for, make up to, make restitution, make reparation; pay in kind, pay one in his own coin, give tit for tat

repeal VERBS **revoke,** rescind, reverse, strike down, abrogate; countermand, counterorder; **abolish,** do away with; **annul,** nullify, disannul, withdraw, **invalidate,** void, vacate, make void, declare null and void

repeat NOUNS 1 ditto <nonformal>, echo; **refrain,** burden, chant, undersong, chorus, bob; **encore,** repeat performance, **reprise;** replay, replaying
VERBS 2 **redo,** do again, do over, do a repeat, **reproduce,** duplicate, reduplicate, double, redouble, ditto <nonformal>, **echo,** parrot, reecho; come again *and* run it by again <both nonformal>, say again, repeat oneself, **quote,** repeat word for word *or* verbatim, repeat like a broken record
3 **recur,** reoccur, **come again,** come round again, go round again, come up again, resurface, reenter, **return,** reappear, resume; revert, turn *or* go back; keep coming, come again and again, happen over and over

repeatedly ADVS **frequently, commonly,** usually, ordinarily, routinely, habitually; **often,** oftentimes; **again and again,** time after time; **in quick** *or* **rapid succession;** often enough, not infrequently, not seldom, unseldom

repel VERBS 1 **disgust,** turn one's stomach, nauseate; make one's gorge rise; gross one out <nonformal>; **offend,** give offense, put off, turn off <nonformal>, **revolt,** horrify, appall, shock; make the flesh creep *or* crawl, make one shudder
2 **repulse,** rebuff, shut *or* slam the door in one's face, turn one away; **drive back,** put back, push back

repellent ADJS 1 **offensive,** objectionable, odious, repulsive, rebarbative, **repugnant,** revolting, forbidding; **disgusting,** sickening, loathsome, beastly <nonformal>, **vile,** foul, nasty, nauseating
2 **resistant,** resistive, resisting, renitent, up against, withstanding

repent VERBS **think better of,** change one's mind, have second thoughts; **plead guilty,** own oneself in the wrong, humble oneself, **apologize**, beg pardon *or* forgiveness, throw oneself on the mercy of the court; **do penance**

repentant ADJS **penitent,** penitential, penitentiary, repenting; **contrite,** abject, humble, humbled, **sheepish,** apologetic, touched, softened, melted

repercussion NOUNS **impact,** force, reaction; backwash, backlash, reflex, recoil, response; **recoil,** rebound, resilience, *contrecoup* <Fr>

repertoire NOUNS repertory, stock-in-trade; stock

repetition NOUNS **reproduction,** duplication, reduplication, doubling, redoubling; **recurrence,** reoccurrence, cyclicality, return, reincarnation, rebirth, reappearance, renewal, resumption; iteration, reiteration, echoing

repetitive ADJS **repetitious,** repetitional *or* repetitionary, repeating; **duplicative,** reduplicative; **imitative**, parrotlike;

echoing, reechoing, echoic; **iterative,** reiterative, reiterant; battological, tautological *or* tautologous, redundant

replace VERBS 1 **restore,** put back, return, place in *status quo ante;* **reestablish,** redintegrate, **reinstate,** restitute; **reinstall,** reinvest, revest, reinstitute, reconstitute, recompose, reintegrate, reconvert, reactivate; refill, replenish

2 **supplant,** supersede, succeed, **remove,** displace, supplant, oust; **dismiss,** take the place of, crowd out, cut out <nonformal>

replacement NOUNS **successor,** backup, backup man *or* woman, substitute, stand-in, **substitution,** succedaneum

replay NOUNS **encore,** repeat performance, repeat, **reprise;** replaying, return match

replenish VERBS **complete,** bring to completion *or* fruition, mature; **fill in, fill out,** piece out, top off, eke *or* eke out, round out; **make up,** make good, refill; fill up, restock

replete ADJS **full,** filled, plenary, capacity, flush, round; **ample,** well-filled, running over, overflowing; **profuse,** profusive, effuse, diffuse; **surfeited,** gorged, glutted; cloyed, jaded

replica NOUNS **reproduction,** duplication, imitation, **copy,** dummy, mock-up, facsimile, representation, approximation, model, version, knockoff <nonformal>

reply NOUNS 1 **answer, response,** responsion, replication; riposte, uptake <nonformal>, **retort,** rejoinder, reaction, return, **comeback** <nonformal>, short answer, back talk; **repartee,** snappy comeback <nonformal>

VERBS 2 **answer,** acknowledge; reply by return mail; **defend,** offer *or* say in defense, allege in support *or* vindication, **support,** uphold, sustain, maintain, assert; respond, riposte, counter

report NOUNS 1 **bulletin,** brief, statement, account, accounting; notice, **write-up** <nonformal>; **rumor,** unverified *or* unconfirmed report, **hearsay,** *on-dit* <Fr>, **scuttlebutt** *and* latrine rumor <both nonformal>; common talk, town talk, **talk of the town,** topic of the day, *cause célèbre* <Fr>; **grapevine**

2 **explosion,** discharge, blowout, blowup, detonation, fulmination, blast, burst

VERBS 3 give a report, give an account of, tell, relate; write up, make out *or* write up a report; gather the news, newsgather; **narrate,** tell, recount, **recite,** give an account of

reporter NOUNS **journalist,** newspaperman, newspaperwoman, newsman, newswoman, inkstained wretch, newswriter, gentleman *or* representative of the press; newshawk *and* newshound <both nonformal>; leg man <nonformal>; investigative reporter; cub reporter; correspondent, foreign correspondent, war correspondent, special correspondent, own correspondent, stringer

repository NOUNS **storehouse,** storeroom, stock room, lumber room, store, storage, **depository,** reservoir, depot, supply depot, supply base, magazine, *magasin* <Fr>, warehouse; **archives,** library, stack room

reprehensible ADJS **blameworthy,** blamable, to blame, at fault, much at fault; censurable, reproachable, reprovable, open to criticism *or* reproach; **culpable,** chargeable, impeachable, accusable, indictable, arraignable, imputable

represent VERBS 1 **describe,** portray, picture, render, **depict,** delineate

2 **act for,** act on behalf of, substitute for, appear for, answer for, speak for, be the voice of, give voice to, be the mouthpiece of <nonformal>, hold the proxy of, hold a brief for, act in the place of, stand in the stead of, serve in one's stead, pinch-hit for <nonformal>

representation NOUNS **description,** portrayal, portraiture, **depiction,** rendering, rendition, **delineation,** limning; **characterization,** character, character sketch, profile

representative NOUNS 1 **deputy,** proxy, substitute, **alternate,** backup *and* stand-in <both nonformal>, alter ego, **surrogate,** procurator, secondary, understudy, pinch hitter <nonformal>; exponent, advocate, pleader, paranymph, attorney, champion; lieutenant; **legislator,** lawmaker, solon, lawgiver; **congressman,** congresswoman, Member of Congress; **senator**

ADJS 2 **model,** exemplary, precedential, typical, paradigmatic, standard, normative, classic

repress VERBS **cover up,** muffle up; **hush up,** hush, hush-hush, shush, hugger-mugger; **suppress,** stifle, muffle, **smother,** squash, quash, squelch, kill, sit on *or* upon, put the lid on <nonformal>; **censor,** black out <nonformal>; **enjoin,** put under an injunction, issue an injunction against, issue a prohibitory injunction; **proscribe,** inhibit

reprieve NOUNS 1 **pardon,** excuse, sparing, **amnesty,** indemnity, exemption, immunity, grace; respite
VERBS 2 **release,** free, deliver, remove, free from; pardon, remit, forgive; respite, give *or* grant a reprieve

reprimand NOUNS 1 **reproof,** reproval, reprobation, a flea in one's ear; **rebuke,** reproach, reprehension, **scolding,** chiding, rating, **upbraiding,** objurgation; **admonition; correction,** castigation, chastisement, spanking, rap on the knuckles; lecture, lesson
VERBS 2 **reprove,** rebuke, reprehend, put a flea in one's ear, **scold,** chide, rate, **admonish,** upbraid, objurgate, have words with, take a hard line with; **lecture,** read a lesson *or* lecture to; **correct,** rap on the knuckles, **chastise,** spank, turn over one's knees

3 <nonformal> **call down** *or* **dress down, speak** *or* **talk to, tell off,** tell a thing or two, pin one's ears back, **give a piece** *or* **bit of one's mind, rake** *or* **haul over the coals,** rake up one side and down the other, give it to, let one have it, let one have it with both barrels, trim, come down on *or* down hard on, jump on *or* all over *or* down one's throat; give one a hard time *or* what for; **bawl out,** give a bawling out, chew, **chew out,** chew ass, ream, ream out, ream ass, cuss out, jack up, sit on *or* upon, lambaste, give a going-over, tell where to get off; give the deuce *or* devil, give hell, give hail Columbia

reprisal NOUNS **requital,** retribution; recompense, compensation, **reward,** comeuppance <nonformal>, desert, deserts, **just deserts,** what is merited, what is due *or* condign, what's coming to one *and* a dose of one's own medicine <both nonformal>

reprise NOUNS **encore,** repeat performance, repeat; replay, replaying

reproach NOUNS 1 **rebuke,** reprimand, reprehension, **scolding,** chiding, rating, **upbraiding,** objurgation
VERBS 2 **disgrace,** dishonor, discredit, reflect discredit upon, bring into discredit, cast reproach upon, be a reproach to

reproduce VERBS **remake,** make *or* do over, **re-create,** regenerate, resurrect, revive, re-form, refashion, **reshape,** recast, rework, rejigger <nonformal>, redo, **reconstruct,** rebuild, redesign, restructure, **revise;** reprint, reissue; repeat, restore; **copy,** replicate, **duplicate,** clone; **be productive,** proliferate, fructify, be fruitful, **multiply,** engender, beget

reproduction NOUNS 1 **procreation,** generation, begetting, breeding, engenderment; **propagation,** multiplication, proliferation
2 **duplication,** imitation, copy, dummy, mock-up, **replica,** facsimile, representation, paraphrase, approximation, model, version, knockoff <nonformal>

repudiate VERBS **recant,** retract, withdraw, take back, unswear, renege, welsh <nonformal>, **abjure,** disavow, disown; **deny,** disclaim, unsay, unspeak; **renounce,** forswear, eat one's words, eat crow, eat humble pie; **back down** *or* **out,** climb down, crawfish out <nonformal>, backwater, weasel
2 **not pay;** dishonor, disallow, protest, stop payment, refuse to pay; **default,** welsh <nonformal>, levant
3 **reject,** blackball *and* turn thumbs down on <both nonformal>, read *or* drum out, ease *or* freeze out *and* leave *or* keep out in the cold <all nonformal>, ostracize, wave off *or* aside

repugnant ADJS **offensive,** objectionable, odious, repulsive, repellent, rebarbative, **revolting,** forbidding; **disgusting,** sickening, loathsome, **vile,** foul, nasty, nauseating; fulsome, **contemptible,** despicable, detestable, execrable, beneath *or* below contempt, **base,** ignoble

repulse VERBS **rebuff,** repel, kiss one off *and* slap one in the face *and* kick one in the teeth <all nonformal>, send one away with a flea in one's ear, give one short shrift, shut *or* slam the door in one's face, turn one away; cut, **snub**

repulsive ADJS **offensive,** objectionable, odious, repellent, rebarbative, **repugnant,** revolting, forbidding; **disgusting,** sickening, loathsome, gross *and* yucky *and* grungy *and* scuzzy <all nonformal>, beastly <nonformal>; fulsome, mephitic, miasmal, miasmic, malodorous, stinking, fetid, noisome, noxious

reputable ADJS highly reputed, **estimable,** esteemed, much *or* highly esteemed, **honorable,** honored; **meritorious,** worth one's salt, noble, worthy, creditable; respected, respectable, highly respectable; **well-thought-of,** highly regarded, held in esteem, in good odor, in favor, in high favor

reputation NOUNS **notability,** prestige, esteem, repute, honor, glory, renown, dignity, **fame**

repute NOUNS 1 prestige, esteem, reputation, honor, glory, renown, dignity, fame
VERBS 2 **suppose,** assume, presume, surmise, expect, **suspect,** infer, understand, gather, conclude, deduce, consider, reckon, divine, imagine, **fancy,** dream, conceive, **believe,** deem, feel, **think,** be inclined to think, opine, say, daresay

request NOUNS 1 asking; desire, wish, expressed desire; **petition,** petitioning, impetration, address; application; requisition; demand
VERBS 2 **ask,** make a request, **beg leave,** make bold to ask; **desire,** wish, wish for, express a wish for, crave; **ask for,** order, put in an order for, call for, trouble one for; **requisition,** make *or* put in a requisition; make application, **apply for,** file for, **put in for;** demand

requiem NOUNS **dirge,** funeral *or* death song, coronach, keen, elegy, epicedium, monody, threnody, threnode, knell, death knell, passing bell, funeral *or* dead march, muffled drums; eulogy, funeral *or* graveside oration

require VERBS **need, want,** feel the want of, have occasion for, be in need of, be hurting for <nonformal>, stand in need of, not be able to dispense with, not be able to do without; **call for,** cry for, cry out for, clamor for

requirement NOUNS **requisite,** requisition; **necessity,** need, want, occasion; need for, **call for,** demand, demand for; desideratum, desideration; necessities, necessaries, essentials, bare necessities

requisition NOUNS 1 **demand,** requirement, request, stated requirement, order, rush order; requisite, **prerequisite,** prerequirement; **must,** must item
VERBS 2 **request, ask,** make a request, make *or* put in a requisition; make application, **apply for,** file for, **put in for;** demand

rescind VERBS **repeal,** revoke, reverse, strike down, abrogate; countermand, counterorder; **abolish,** annul, nullify, withdraw, **invalidate,** void, vacate, make void, declare null and void; **overrule,** override

rescue NOUNS 1 **deliverance,** delivery, **saving;** lifesaving; **extrication,** release, freeing, liberation; **bailout; salvation,** salvage, redemption, ransom; **recovery,** retrieval
VERBS 2 come to the rescue, **deliver, save,** be the saving of, **redeem,** ransom, **salvage; recover,** retrieve; **free,** set free, **release,** extricate, extract, **liberate**; snatch from the jaws of death; save one's neck *or* ass *and* bail one out <all nonformal>

research NOUNS 1 **investigation,** legwork <nonformal>, inquiry into; data-gathering, gathering *or* amassing evidence; **probe,** searching investigation, close inquiry, exhaustive study
VERBS 2 **experiment,** make an experiment, **run an experiment; test,** try, essay, cut and try <nonformal>, **test** *or* **try out,** have a dry run *or* dummy run *or* rehearsal *or* test run; put to the test, **put to the proof,** prove, verify, validate, substantiate, confirm, put to trial, bring to test, make a trial of, give a trial to

researcher NOUNS **experimenter,** experimentist, experimentalist, bench scientist, research worker, R and D worker; **tester,** analyst, analyzer

resemble VERBS be like, bear resemblance; put one in mind of <nonformal>, remind one of, bring to mind, be reminiscent of, suggest, evoke, call up, call to mind; **look like,** favor <nonformal>, mirror; **take after,** have all the earmarks of, have every appearance of, have all the features of, have all the signs of, have every sign *or* indication of; **approximate,** approach, near, come near, come close; **compare with,** stack up with <nonformal>

resent VERBS be resentful, feel *or* harbor *or* nurse resentment, feel hurt, smart, feel sore *and* have one's nose out of joint <both nonformal>; bear *or* hold *or* have a grudge

reservation NOUNS 1 **preserve,** reserve; **refuge, sanctuary**, game preserve *or* reserve, bird sanctuary, wildlife sanctuary *or* preserve
2 **stipulation,** provision, proviso, condi-

tion; exception, qualification, question, question in one's mind

reserve NOUNS 1 **restraint, constraint,** backwardness, retiring disposition; low key, low visibility, low profile; reservedness, **detachment,** withdrawal
2 **preserve,** reservation; park, **refuge,** sanctuary, game preserve *or* reserve, wildlife sanctuary *or* preserve
VERBS 3 keep *or* hold back, save, save up, sock *or* squirrel away, tuck away, put under the mattress, hoard; keep in hand, have up one's sleeve; restrict to, restrict

reside VERBS live, **live in,** dwell, lodge, stay, remain, abide, hang *or* hang out <nonformal>, domicile, domiciliate

residence NOUNS **abode,** habitation, place, dwelling, dwelling place, abiding place, place to live, where one lives *or* resides, where one is at home, roof, roof over one's head, place of residence, **domicile,** *domus* <L>

resident NOUNS 1 **inhabitant,** inhabiter, habitant; **occupant,** occupier, **dweller, tenant, denizen,** inmate; resider; writer- *or* poet- *or* artist- *or* composer-in-residence; incumbent, *locum tenens* <L>; sojourner; physician
ADJS 2 residentiary, **in residence;** residing, living, dwelling, commorant, lodging, **staying,** remaining, abiding, living in; cohabiting, live-in
3 **inherent,** implicit, immanent, indwelling

residential ADJS residentiary; domestic, domiciliary, domal; **home,** household

residue NOUNS **remainder,** remains, remnant, residuum, **rest,** balance; **leavings,** leftovers, oddments; **debris,** detritus, ruins; vestige, trace, hint, shadow, afterimage, afterglow

resign VERBS **quit,** leave, **vacate,** withdraw from; **retire,** superannuate, be superannuated, be pensioned *or* pensioned off, be put out to pasture, get the golden handshake *or* parachute <nonformal>; retire from office, stand down, stand *or* step aside, give up one's post; **tender** *or* **hand in one's resignation,** send in one's papers, turn in one's badge *or* uniform; **abdicate,** renounce the throne, give up the crown

resilient ADJS **elastic,** springy, bouncy; **stretchable,** stretchy, stretch; extensile; **flexible**; flexile; **adaptable,** adaptive, responsive; buoyant; lively

resist VERBS **withstand;** stand; endure; **stand up,** bear up, hold up, hold out; defy, tell one where to get off <nonformal>, throw down the gauntlet; bear up against; **repel;** repulse, rebuff

resistance NOUNS 1 immunity, nonproneness *or* nonsusceptibility to disease
2 withstanding, countering, renitence *or* renitency, repellence *or* repellency; **defiance; opposing,** opposition; stand; repulsion, repulse, rebuff; **objection, protest,** remonstrance, **dispute,** challenge, demur; dissent; **reluctance;** passive resistance, noncooperation
3 **irregular,** casual; **guerrilla,** partisan, franctireur; underground, maquis; underground *or* resistance fighter

resolute ADJS **resolved,** determined, bound *and* bound and determined <both nonformal>, **decided,** decisive, **purposeful;** devoted, dedicated, committed, single-minded, relentless, persistent, tenacious, persevering

resolution NOUNS 1 **adjustment,** accommodation, composition of differences, compromise, arrangement, settlement, terms
2 resoluteness, tenaciousness, tenacity, pertinaciousness, pertinacity, bulldog courage

resolve NOUNS 1 **intention,** intent, mindset, purpose, set *or* settled *or* fixed purpose; resolution, mind, will; determination
VERBS 2 **determine,** decide, will, purpose, make up one's mind, make *or* take a resolution, make a point of; **settle,** settle on, fix, seal; conclude, come to a determination *or* conclusion *or* decision, determine once for all; **solve,** find the solution *or* answer, **clear up,** get, get right, do, work, **work out, find out,** figure out

resonate VERBS **vibrate,** oscillate, librate, nutate, pulse, throb; snore

resort NOUNS 1 **haunt,** purlieu, hangout <nonformal>, **stamping ground** <nonformal>; gathering place, rallying point, meeting place, clubhouse, club; casino, gambling house; health resort; **spa,** baths, springs, watering place
2 **recourse,** resource; last resort *or* resource, *dernier ressort* and *pis aller* <both Fr>; **hope**

resound VERBS **reverberate,** sound, **rumble,** roll, boom, echo, reecho, rebound, bounce back, be reflected, be sent back, echo back, send back, return

resource NOUNS **reserve,** reserves, reservoir; **resort,** recourse; answer, solution

resourceful ADJS **ingenious,** daedal, Daedalian; **adaptable,** adjustable, flexible, ready

respect NOUNS 1 **regard,** consideration, appreciation, favor; approbation, approval; **esteem,** estimation, prestige; **reverence,** veneration, awe; **deference,** deferential *or* reverential regard; great respect, high regard, **admiration;** courtesy, respectfulness
VERBS 2 entertain respect for, accord respect to, **regard, esteem,** hold in esteem *or* consideration, favor, **admire,** think much of, think well of, think highly of, have *or* hold a high opinion of; **revere, reverence,** hold in reverence, **look up to,** defer to, bow to, exalt, put on a pedestal, **worship,** hero-worship, deify, apotheosize

respectable ADJS **reputable,** estimable, esteemed, much *or* highly esteemed, **honorable,** honored; **meritorious,** worth one's salt, noble, worthy, creditable; respected, highly respectable; **decent,** presentable, **adequate,** satisfactory, all right

respectful ADJS **regardful,** attentive; **deferential,** conscious of one's place, dutiful, honorific, ceremonious, cap in hand; courteous, **thoughtful,** considerate, tactful, solicitous

respects NOUNS **regards,** *égards* <Fr>; duties, *devoirs* <Fr>; attentions

respite NOUNS **recess, rest,** pause, halt, stay, lull, **break,** surcease, suspension, interlude, **intermission,** spell <Australia>, letup <nonformal>, **time out** <nonformal>, time to catch one's breath; **breathing spell,** breathing time, breathing place, breathing space, breath

respond VERBS 1 **react,** be moved, be affected *or* touched, be inspired, echo, catch the flame *or* infection, be in tune; **respond to,** warm up to, take *or* lay to heart, open one's heart to, be turned on to <nonformal>, feel in one's breast; enter into the spirit of, be imbued with the spirit of; empathize with, identify with, relate to emotionally, dig *and* be turned on by <both nonformal>
2 **answer,** make *or* give answer, **reply,** say in reply; **retort,** riposte, **rejoin,** return; come back *and* come back at *and* come right back at <all nonformal>, answer back *and* talk back *and* shoot back <all nonformal>

respondent NOUNS 1 **accused,** defendant, codefendant, corespondent, libelee, suspect, prisoner
ADJS 2 **answering,** replying, responsive, responding; rejoining, returning; echoing, echoic, reechoing

response NOUNS **answer,** reply; **reaction,** gut reaction <nonformal>; echo, chord, sympathetic chord, vibrations, vibes <nonformal>; **empathy,** identification

responsibility NOUNS incumbency; **liability, accountability,** accountableness, answerability, answerableness, amenability; product liability; **responsibleness,** dutifulness, duteousness, devotion *or* dedication to duty, sense of duty *or* obligation

responsible ADJS 1 **answerable; liable,** accountable, amenable, unexempt from, chargeable, on one's head, at one's doorstep, on the hook <nonformal>; responsible for
2 **trustworthy,** trusty, trustable, faithworthy, **reliable,** dependable, straight <nonformal>, sure, to be trusted, **to be depended** *or* **relied upon,** to be counted *or* reckoned on, as good as one's word

responsive ADJS **sensitive,** sympathetic, compassionate, amenable, receptive; empathic, empathetic; **impressionable,** impressible, susceptible; **adaptable,** adaptive

rest NOUNS 1 **repose,** ease, relaxation, slippered *or* unbuttoned ease, decompression <nonformal>; **comfort**; restfulness, quiet, tranquility; inactivity; sleep
2 **remainder,** remains, remnant, residue, residuum, **balance**
VERBS 3 **repose,** take rest, take one's ease, **take it easy** <nonformal>, rest from one's labors, take life easy; **pause,** relax, rest on one's oars; **take a break,** break, take ten

restaurant NOUNS eating place, eating house, dining room; eatery *and* beanery *and* hashery *and* hash house *and* greasy spoon <all nonformal>; fast-food restaurant

restful ADJS **comfortable, easy,** easeful; reposeful, peaceful, **relaxing,** relaxed; **calm,** quiet, **untroubled,** orderly, at peace; **soothing**

restitution NOUNS **compensation, recompense,** repayment, payback, indemnity, indemnification, measure for measure, rectification, **reparation;** reinstatement, restoration

restless ADJS **bustling,** fussing, fussy; **fidgety,** fretful, jumpy, unquiet, unsettled; **agitated,** turbulent

restore VERBS **put back,** replace, return, place in *status quo ante;* **reestablish,** redintegrate, reenact, **reinstate,** restitute; **reinstall,** reinvest, revest, reinstitute, reconstitute, recompose, recruit, **rehabilitate,** redevelop

restrain VERBS **constrain,** control, govern, guard, contain, keep under control, put *or* lay under restraint; **inhibit, curb,** check, arrest, bridle, get under control, rein, snub, snub in; **hold** *or* **keep in check,** hold at bay; **moderate,** keep within bounds; modulate, mitigate

restraint NOUNS 1 **reserve, constraint,** backwardness, retiring disposition; low key, low visibility, low profile; **reticence** *or* reticency; control, discipline; composure, possession, aplomb; restrainedness, **understatement,** unobtrusiveness, quietness, subduedness, quiet taste
2 **confinement,** locking-up, lockup, lockdown, caging, penning, putting behind barriers, impoundment, restriction; self-control, self-restraint

restrict VERBS **limit,** narrow, confine, tighten; ground, restrict to home; circumscribe; keep in *or* within bounds, keep from spreading, localize; **cage in,** hem, hem in, box, box in *or* up; **cramp,** stint; qualify

restricted ADJS **limited,** confined; circumscribed, hemmed in, hedged in *or* about, boxed in; shut-in; cramped, stinted; cloistered, enclosed

restructure VERBS **rearrange,** reorganize, reconstitute, **reorder,** reshuffle, rejigger <nonformal>, tinker *or* tinker with, tune, tune up, fine-tune; **shake up,** shake out; redispose, redistribute, reallocate, realign

result NOUNS 1 **effect,** resultant, **consequence,** consequent, sequent, sequence, sequel, sequela, sequelae; **upshot,** outcome, logical outcome; **product**, fruit, derivative
VERBS 2 **ensue,** issue, follow, attend, accompany; **turn out,** come out, fall out, redound, **work out,** pan out <nonformal>, fare; **eventuate,** terminate, end; **end up,** wind up

resume VERBS **recommence,** rebegin, **renew,** reestablish; **revive,** resuscitate, recrudesce; reenter, reopen, **return to,** go back to, begin again, take up again, make a new beginning, make a fresh start, have another shot *or* crack *or* go <nonformal>

résumé NOUNS **summary,** recapitulation, recap <nonformal>, rundown, run-through; summation; **curriculum vitae,** vita

resurrect VERBS **revive,** revivify, renew; **reanimate,** reinspire, regenerate, rejuvenate, revitalize, put *or* breathe new life into, restimulate; **refresh;** bring back, call back, recall to life, raise from the dead

resuscitate VERBS **revive,** revivify, renew, **reanimate,** reinspire, regenerate, rejuvenate, revitalize, put *or* breathe new life into, restimulate; bring to, bring round *or* around; rally, reclaim, restore

retain VERBS **keep, save,** save up, pocket *and* hip-pocket <both nonformal>; **maintain,** preserve; keep *or* hold in, bottle *or* cork up <both nonformal>, suppress, repress, inhibit; **keep in memory,** bear in mind, keep *or* hold in mind, hold *or* retain the memory of, **keep in view,** have in mind, hold *or* carry *or* retain in one's thoughts, store in the mind

retainer NOUNS 1 dependent, follower; myrmidon, yeoman; vassal, liege, liege man, feudatory, homager; inferior, **underling, subordinate,** understrapper
2 **fee,** stipend, retaining fee

retaliate VERBS **retort,** counter, **strike back,** hit back at <nonformal>, give in return; **reciprocate,** give in exchange, give and take; **revenge,** avenge, take *or* exact revenge, even the score, get even with

retard VERBS **delay, detain,** make late, slacken, lag, drag, drag one's feet *and* stonewall <both nonformal>, slow down, **hold up** <nonformal>, hold *or* keep back, check, **stay, stop,** arrest, impede, **block,** hinder, obstruct, throw a monkey wrench in the works <non-formal>

retch VERBS **feel disgust,** be nauseated, sicken at, choke on, have a bellyful of <nonformal>; **gag,** keck, heave, vomit, puke, hurl *and* upchuck *and* barf <all nonformal>

reticence NOUNS reticency; **reserve,** reservedness, restraint, low key, **constraint;** guardedness, discreetness, discretion; suppression, repression; subduedness; backwardness, retirement, low profile

retire VERBS 1 **go to bed;** lay me down to sleep; bed, bed down

2 <nonformal> go night-night, go bye-bye, go beddy-bye; **hit the hay, hit the sack,** crash, turn in, crawl in, flop, sack out, sack up, kip down *or* doss down <both Brit>

3 **dismiss,** discharge, expel, cashier, drum out, **lay off,** make redundant, turn out, give the pink slip; put on the retired list; pension off, superannuate, put out to pasture; read out of

retired ADJS in retirement, superannuated, on pension, pensioned, pensioned off, emeritus, emerita <fem>; **secluded,** seclusive, withdrawn

retiring ADJS **reserved,** restrained, constrained; quiet; low-keyed, keeping low visibility *or* a low profile; **backward,** shrinking

retort NOUNS **answer,** reply, response, responsion; riposte, uptake <nonformal>, **rejoinder,** reaction, return, **comeback** *and* **take** <both nonformal>, back talk; clever *or* ready *or* witty reply *or* retort, snappy comeback <nonformal>

retouch VERBS **touch up,** finish, put on the finishing touches, polish, fine down, fine-tune <nonformal>, tone up, **furbish,** furbish up, spruce, **spruce up**

retract VERBS **draw** *or* **pull back,** pull out, draw *or* pull in; **recant,** repudiate, withdraw, take back, unswear, renege, welsh <nonformal>, **abjure,** disavow, disown; **deny,** disclaim, unsay, unspeak; **eat one's words,** eat one's hat, swallow, eat crow, eat humble pie; **back down** *or* **out,** weasel

retreat NOUNS 1 **withdrawal,** strategic withdrawal, exfiltration; **fallback,** pullout, pullback; advance to the rear; disengagement; **backing down** *or* **off** *or* **out** <all nonformal>; reneging, copping *or* weaseling out <nonformal>

2 **sanctum,** sanctum sanctorum, holy of holies; **den,** sanctuary, refuge; **hideaway,** ivory tower, lair, inner sanctum

VERBS 3 sound *or* beat a retreat, beat a hasty retreat, **withdraw, retire,** pull out *or* back, exfiltrate, advance to the rear, disengage; **fall back,** move back, go back, stand back; **draw back,** back out *or* out of *and* back off *and* back down <all nonformal>

retrenchment NOUNS **curtailment,** cut, cutback, drawdown, rollback, scaleback, pullback, truncation; **economizing,** reduction of expenses

retribution NOUNS **reprisal,** requital; recompense, comeuppance <nonformal>, desert, deserts, **just deserts,** what's coming to one *and* a dose of one's own medicine <both nonformal>; retributive justice, nemesis; reparation, redress, satisfaction, **atonement, amends,** return

retrieval NOUNS **reclamation,** recovery, salvage, salving; redemption, salvation

retrieve VERBS **recover,** regain, recuperate, **recoup,** get back, come by one's own; **redeem,** ransom; **repossess,** resume, reoccupy; **retake,** recapture, take back

retroactive ADJS **back,** backward, into the past; retrospective, retroactionary, *ex post facto* <L>, *a priori* <L>

retrospect NOUNS 1 retrospection, hindsight, looking back

VERBS 2 **think back,** go back, **look back,** carry one's thoughts back, look back upon things past, use hindsight, **see in retrospect,** hark back, retrace; review in retrospect

return NOUNS 1 **homecoming,** recursion, returning; reentrance, **reentry;** remigration; **recovery,** rally, comeback <nonformal>

2 **gain, profit,** earnings, winnings, returns, proceeds, bottom line <nonformal>; receipts; **fruits,** pickings, gleanings; net profit, clean *or* clear profit, net; dividend; interest; **yield,** return on investment, payout, payback

VERBS 3 **restore,** put back, replace; give back, restitute, hand back; **recur,** repeat, reappear, **come again,** come up again, be here again, resurface, reenter, **come round** *or* **around,** come round again, come in its turn; **revert,** retrovert, **regress,** retrogress, reverse, return to the fold; backslide, slip back, recidivate, lapse, lapse back, relapse

4 **reflect,** echo, bounce back

returns NOUNS 1 election returns, **poll,** count, official count

2 **receipts,** income, revenue, profits, earnings, proceeds, **take,** takings, intake, yield, fruits

reunion NOUNS **reconciliation,** reconcilement, *rapprochement* <Fr>, shaking of hands, making up *and* kissing and making up <both nonformal>; gathering, get-together <nonformal>; family reunion

revamp VERBS **renovate,** renew; recondition, refit, furbish, refurbish; refresh, face-lift

reveal VERBS **disclose,** let out, show, impart, discover, **leak,** let slip out, let the cat out of the bag *and* spill the beans <both nonformal>; manifest; bring into the open, get out in the open, bring out of the closet; **expose, show up; bare,** strip *or* lay bare, blow the lid off *and* blow wide open *and* rip open *and* crack wide open <all nonformal>; **bring to light,** bring into the open, hold up to view

revealing ADJS **disclosive,** revelatory, revelational; **disclosing,** showing, exposing, betraying; show-through, see-through, peekaboo; **diaphanous,** sheer, thin; **gossamer,** filmy, gauzy

reveille NOUNS **awakening,** wakening, rousing, arousal; rude awakening, rousting out <nonformal>; waking time, get-up time <nonformal>; **bugle call**

revel VERBS **make merry,** roister, jolly, lark <nonformal>, skylark, **make whoopee** <nonformal>, let oneself go, **blow** *or* **let off steam;** cut loose, let loose, let go, let one's hair down <nonformal>, whoop it up, **kick up one's heels;** celebrate; **go on a spree,** go on a bust *or* toot *or* bender *or* binge *or* rip *or* tear <all nonformal>; **carouse**

revelation NOUNS 1 **disclosure,** disclosing; revealment, revealing, making public, publicizing, broadcasting; exposure, exposition, **exposé**

2 **divine revelation;** inspiration, afflatus, divine inspiration; theophany, theophania, epiphany; **prophecy,** prophetic revelation, apocalypse

revenge NOUNS 1 **vengeance,** avengement, sweet revenge, getting even, evening of the score; revanche, revanchism; **retaliation,** reprisal; vendetta, feud, blood feud

VERBS 2 **avenge, take** *or* **exact revenge,** have one's revenge, wreak one's vengeance; **retaliate,** even the score, get even with; launch a vendetta

revenue NOUNS **receipts,** receipt, income, profits, earnings, returns, proceeds, **take**

reverberate VERBS **resound,** sound, **rumble,** roll, boom, echo, reecho, rebound, bounce back, be reflected, be sent back, echo back, send back, return

reverence NOUNS **respect,** regard, consideration, appreciation, favor; **veneration,** awe; **deference,** deferential *or* reverential regard; **honor, homage,** duty; adoration, breathless adoration, worship; deification, apotheosis; **obeisance,** genuflection, kneeling, bending the knee; prostration

reverie NOUNS **dream;** daydream, pipe dream <nonformal>; brown study, trance

reverse NOUNS 1 **reversal,** reversing, reversion; **backing,** backing up, backup; **about-face,** *volte-face* <Fr>, about-turn, turnaround, turnabout; tergiversation, tergiversating; **change of mind;** second thoughts, better thoughts, afterthoughts

2 opposite side, other side, the other side of the picture *or* coin, other face; **inverse,** obverse, converse

3 reversal of fortune, **setback,** check, severe check, backset *and* throwback <both nonformal>; **comedown,** descent, down

VERBS 4 go into reverse; **back, back up,** backpedal, back off *or* away; **backwater,** backtrack, reverse one's field; have second thoughts, think better of it, cut one's losses

5 **repeal,** revoke, rescind, strike down, abrogate; **annul,** nullify, disannul, withdraw, **invalidate,** void, vacate, make void, declare null and void; **overrule,** override; transpose, flip <nonformal>

revert VERBS **regress,** retrogress, retrograde, retrocede, **return,** return to the fold; backslide, slip back, recidivate, lapse, lapse back, relapse

review NOUNS 1 **criticism,** critique, *compte-rendu critique* <Fr>, analysis; critical review, **report,** notice, write-up <nonformal>; commentary

2 **study,** studying, application, conning; restudy, restudying, brushing up, boning up <nonformal>; grind *and* grinding *and* boning <all nonformal>, **cramming** *and* cram <both nonformal>

3 **reexamination,** recheck, reappraisal, revaluation, rethinking, revision, second *or* further look

VERBS 4 **brush up,** refresh the memory, restudy, **brush up,** polish up *and* bone up <both nonformal>, get up on; **cram** <nonformal>

5 **reconsider, reexamine,** revise one's thoughts, reappraise, revaluate, rethink; view in a new light, have second thoughts, think better of
6 **criticize,** critique; **censure**, pick holes in, pick to pieces; comment upon, annotate; moralize upon; pontificate

reviewer NOUNS **critic,** interpreter, exegete, analyst, explicator

revise VERBS redact, recense, **revamp,** rewrite, redraft, **rework,** work over; **emend,** amend, emendate, **rectify,** correct; **edit,** blue-pencil

revive VERBS revivify, **renew,** recruit; **reanimate,** reinspire, regenerate, rejuvenate, revitalize, put *or* breathe new life into, restimulate; **resuscitate,** bring to, bring round *or* around; **resurrect,** bring back, call back, recall to life, raise from the dead

revoke VERBS **repeal,** rescind, reverse, strike down, abrogate; renege, renig *and* go back on *and* welsh <all nonformal>; **waive,** set aside; countermand, counterorder; **annul,** nullify, withdraw, **invalidate,** void, vacate, make void, declare null and void

revolt NOUNS 1 **rebellion,** revolution, mutiny, insurrection, insurgence *or* insurgency, *émeute* <Fr>, **uprising,** rising, outbreak, general uprising, *levée en masse* <Fr>, **riot,** civil disorder; peasant revolt, *jacquerie* <Fr>; putsch, coup d'état; intifada
VERBS 2 **rebel,** kick over the traces, reluct, reluctate; **rise up,** rise up in arms, mount the barricades; mount *or* make a coup d'état; **mutiny; riot,** run riot; secede, break away

revolting ADJS **offensive,** objectionable, odious, repulsive, repellent, rebarbative, **repugnant,** forbidding; **disgusting,** sickening, loathsome

revolution NOUNS 1 **radical** *or* **total change,** violent change, striking alteration, sweeping change, clean sweep, clean slate, square one <nonformal>, tabula rasa; revolutionary war, war of national liberation; bloodless revolution, palace revolution; **revolt**
2 **rotation,** roll, **gyration,** spin

revolutionary NOUNS 1 **rebel**; anarchist, anarch, syndicalist, criminal syndicalist, terrorist; subversive
ADJS 2 **rebellious,** rebel, breakaway; **mutinous,** mutineering; **insurgent, insurrectionary,** riotous, turbulent; factious, **seditious,** seditionary; **radical,** extreme, extremist
3 **original,** novel, unprecedented; unique, *sui generis* <L>; **avant-garde,** trail-blazing

revolve VERBS **rotate,** spin, turn, round, **go round** *or* **around,** turn round *or* around; circumrotate, circumvolute; **swivel,** pivot, wheel

reward NOUNS 1 **incentive,** inducement, encouragement, carrot; payment; meed, guerdon; honorarium
VERBS 2 **pay,** render, tender; **recompense,** remunerate, compensate, guerdon, indemnify, satisfy

rhapsodize VERBS **be enthusiastic,** rave, enthuse *and* be big for <both nonformal>; get stars in one's eyes, **carry on over** *and* rave on <both nonformal>, make much of, **make a fuss over,** make an ado *or* much ado about; **idealize,** utopianize, quixotize

rhythm NOUNS **beat, meter,** measure, number *or* numbers, movement, **lilt, swing;** rhythmic pattern *or* phrase; tempo

rich ADJS **wealthy,** affluent, moneyed *or* monied, in funds *or* cash, **well-to-do,** well-off, well-situated, prosperous, comfortable, provided for, well provided for, fat, **flush,** flush with *or* of money, abounding in riches, worth a great deal, frightfully rich, rich as Croesus

rickety ADJS **unsteady, shaky,** ricketish, teetering, teetery, tottery, tottering, doddering, tumbledown, ramshackle, dilapidated, rocky <nonformal>

rid ADJS **quit,** clear, free, free of, clear of, quit of, rid of, shut of, shed of <nonformal>

riddle NOUNS **conundrum,** charade, rebus; logogriph, anagram; **matter of ignorance,** sealed book, enigma, mystery, puzzle

ride NOUNS 1 **drive;** spin *and* whirl <both nonformal>; joyride <nonformal>; Sunday drive; airing; lift <nonformal>, pickup <nonformal>
VERBS 2 **go for a ride** *or* **drive;** go for a spin <nonformal>, take *or* go for a Sunday drive; **drive,** chauffeur
3 **ridicule, deride,** make a laughingstock *or* a mockery of; roast <nonformal>, insult; **make fun** *or* **game of,** poke fun at, make merry with, put one on *and* pull one's leg <both nonformal>

ride for a fall VERBS **court danger,** mock

or defy danger, go in harm's way, thumb one's nose at the consequences, **tempt fate** *or* **the gods** *or* **Providence,** tweak the devil's nose, bell the cat, play a desperate game

ridge NOUNS ridgeline, *arête* <Fr>, chine, spine, horst, kame, esker, cuesta, serpent kame, Indian ridge, moraine, terminal moraine

ridicule NOUNS 1 **derision,** mockery, raillery, rallying, chaffing; panning *and* razzing *and* roasting *and* ragging <all nonformal>, **scoffing,** jeering; **banter**
VERBS 2 **deride,** ride <nonformal>, make a laughingstock *or* a mockery of; roast <nonformal>, **insult**; **make fun** *or* **game of,** poke fun at, make merry with, put one on *and* pull one's leg <both nonformal>

ridiculous ADJS **absurd,** nonsensical, insensate, laughable, ludicrous; **foolish,** crazy; preposterous, cockamamie <nonformal>, fantastic, **outrageous,** incredible, beyond belief, *outré* <Fr>, extravagant, **bizarre**

rid oneself of VERBS **give up,** leave off, **abandon,** drop, stop, discontinue, kick *and* shake <both nonformal>, throw off; **part with,** give away, dispose of, get rid of, see the last of, dump, be finished with

rifle NOUNS 1 **gun,** firearm; shoulder weapon *or* gun *or* arm; gun make
VERBS 2 **plunder,** pillage, loot, sack, ransack, freeboot, spoil, spoliate, despoil, depredate, prey on *or* upon, **raid,** reive <Scots>

rift NOUNS **falling-out,** breach of friendship, parting of the ways, bust-up <nonformal>; **breach,** break, rupture, schism, split, cleft; open rupture

rigamarole NOUNS **twaddle,** twiddle-twaddle, fiddle-faddle, fiddlesticks, **blather, babble,** babblement, **gabble,** gibble-gabble, **blabber,** gibber, jabber, prate, **prattle,** palaver, rigmarole, galimatias, skimble-skamble, drivel, drool

right NOUNS 1 rightfulness, rightness; what is right *or* proper, what should be, what ought to be, the seemly, the thing, the right *or* proper thing, the right *or* proper thing to do, what is done
2 **prerogative,** due, droit; power, authority, prerogative of office; faculty, appurtenance; **claim,** proper claim, demand, **interest, title,** pretension, pretense, prescription; birthright; natural right, presumptive right, inalienable right; divine right
VERBS 3 **remedy,** rectify, correct, patch up, emend, amend, **redress,** make good *or* right, **put right,** set right, put *or* set to rights, put *or* set straight, set up, heal up, knit up, make all square; **arrange,** order, reduce to order, **put** *or* **get** *or* **set in order,** put first things first, get one's ducks in a row <nonformal>
ADJS 4 rightful; fit, suitable; **proper,** correct, decorous, good, decent, seemly, **due, appropriate,** fitting, condign, **right and proper,** as it should be, as it ought to be, *comme il faut* <Fr>
ADVS 5 **rightward,** rightwards, rightwardly, **to the right,** dextrally, dextrad; on the right, dexter
6 **exactly, precisely,** to a T, expressly; **just,** dead, straight, even, square, **plumb,** directly, squarely, point-blank
PHRS 7 that's right, that is so, amen, that's it, *c'est ça* <Fr>; right you are, right as rain

PHRS 8 <nonformal> **right on!,** you better believe it!, you've got something there, I'll say, I'll tell the world, I'll drink to that, righto, quite, rather!, you got it!, you said it, you said a mouthful, now you're talking, you can say that again, you're not kidding, that's for sure, ain't it the truth?, you're damn tootin', don't I know it?, you're telling me?, you're not just whistling Dixie, bet your ass *or* sweet ass *or* bippy *or* boots *or* life *or* you bet the rent, fucking ay, fucking ay right

righteous ADJS **honest,** upright, **upstanding,** erect, right, **virtuous,** clean, squeaky-clean <nonformal>, decent; rightminded, right-thinking

rightful ADJS condign, appropriate, proper; fit, becoming; **fair,** just; **legal,** legitimate, legit *and* kosher <both nonformal>, **licit, lawful,** according to law, within the law

the right stuff NOUNS **qualifications;** talents, powers, parts; the goods *and* the stuff *and* what it takes *and* the makings <all nonformal>

the right thing NOUNS **right,** rightfulness, rightness; what is right *or* proper, what should be, what ought to be, the seemly, the thing, the proper thing, the right *or* proper thing to do, what is done

rigid ADJS **firm, rigorous,** rigorist, rigoristic, stiff, **hard,** iron, steel, steely, hard-shell, obdurate, **inflexible,** ironhanded, inexorable, dour, **unyielding,** unbending, impliable, **relentless,** unrelenting, procrustean; **uncompromising**

rigor NOUNS 1 **adversity,** adverse circumstances, difficulties, hard knocks *and* rough going <both nonformal>, **hardship,** trouble, troubles, vicissitude, stress, pressure
2 **rigidity,** rigidness, **firmness,** renitence *or* renitency, nonresilience *or* nonresiliency, inelasticity

rile VERBS **annoy,** irk, vex, nettle, provoke, pique, miff *and* peeve <both nonformal>, **ruffle,** disturb, discompose, **roil,** aggravate, make a nuisance of oneself, **exasperate,** exercise, try one's patience, try the patience of a saint

ring NOUNS 1 band, wedding band, engagement ring, mood ring, signet ring, school *or* class ring, circle, earring, nose ring
2 **clique,** coterie, set, circle, junto, junta, cabal, camarilla, **clan,** group
3 **halo,** nimbus, aura, **aureole,** circle, glory
VERBS 4 tintinnabulate, **peal,** sound; **toll,** knell, sound a knell; **tinkle,** tingle, **jingle,** ding, dingdong, dong; ring changes *or* peals; ring in the ear
5 **encircle, circle,** ensphere, belt, belt in, zone, cincture, encincture; **girdle,** gird, begird, engird; band

ringleader NOUNS **instigator,** inciter, **troublemaker,** mischief-maker

rinse VERBS **wash,** bathe, rinse out, flush, flush out, irrigate, sluice, sluice out

riot NOUNS 1 **uprising,** rising, outbreak, general uprising, *levée en masse* <Fr>, civil disorder; **free-for-all,** brawl, broil, melee, scrimmage, **fracas**
VERBS 2 **roister,** roil, carouse; **create a disturbance,** make a commotion, make trouble, cause a stir *or* commotion, create a riot, **cut loose,** run wild, run riot, run amok, go on a rampage, go berserk

ripe ADJS **mature,** matured, maturated, seasoned; blooming, abloom; **mellow,** full-grown, fully developed

ripen VERBS **mature,** maturate; bloom, blow, blossom, flourish; come to fruition, bear fruit; **mellow;** grow up, reach maturity, reach its season; bring to maturity, bring to a head

rip off VERBS

> <nonformal> **swipe, pinch,** bag, lift, hook, crib, **cop,** nip, snitch, snare, boost, burn, clip; **knock off** *or* **over,** tip over

rip-off NOUNS **hoax,** deception, spoof <nonformal>, **humbug,** flam, fake *and* fakement, **sham;** mare's nest

ripple NOUNS 1 **splash; crinkle,** crankle, rimple, wimple
VERBS 2 **agitate,** shake, disturb, perturb, shake up, perturbate, **disquiet,** discompose, upset, trouble, unsettle, stir, swirl, flurry, flutter, fret, roughen, ruffle, rumple, convulse

rise NOUNS 1 **ascent,** ascension, levitation, **rising,** uprising, **uprise,** uprisal; **uplift,** elevation; **uptick** <nonformal>, increase
VERBS 2 **arise,** mount, uprise, **rise up, get up,** get to one's feet; **stand up,** stand on end; jump up, spring to one's feet; **levitate,** ascend; hover, **rise in the world,** work one's way up, step up, come *or* move up in the world, claw *or* scrabble one's way up, mount the ladder of success, pull oneself up by one's bootstraps

risk NOUNS 1 **investment, venture,** plunge <nonformal>, speculation
2 **gamble,** chance, risky thing, hazard; **precariousness,** danger, riskiness
VERBS 3 take a chance, run a risk, push *or* press one's luck, lay one's ass on the line *and* put one's money where one's mouth is <both nonformal>, **gamble, bet**; risk one's neck *and* shoot the works *and* go for broke <all nonformal>

risqué ADJS risky, **racy,** salty, spicy, **off-color,** suggestive, scabrous

rite NOUNS **ritual,** rituality, **liturgy,** holy rite; order of worship; **ceremony,** ceremonial; observance, ritual observance

ritual NOUNS 1 **ceremony,** ceremonial; **rite,** formality; solemnity, service, function, office, **observance,** performance
ADJS 2 **ceremonious,** ceremonial; ritualistic; hieratic, hieratical, sacerdotal, liturgic

rival NOUNS 1 **contestant,** contender, competitor
VERBS 2 **equal,** match, correspond, be even-steven, be tantamount to, be equal to; **keep pace with,** keep step with, run abreast; vie, vie with

rivalry NOUNS **competition,** vying, emulation; cutthroat competition; **sportsmanship,** gamesmanship, lifemanship, one-upmanship

riveted ADJS **fixed,** fastened, anchored; **gripped,** held, fascinated, enthralled, rapt, spellbound, charmed, enchanted, mesmerized, **hypnotized,** caught, **arrested,** switched on <nonformal>

riveting ADJS **engrossing,** absorbing, consuming, **gripping,** holding, **arresting,** engaging, attractive, **fascinating,** enthralling, spellbinding, enchanting, magnetic, hypnotic, mesmerizing, mesmeric; obsessing

roam VERBS **wander, rove,** range, nomadize, **gad,** gad around *or* about, follow the seasons, wayfare, flit, traipse <nonformal>, gallivant, knock around *or* about *and* bat around *or* about <all nonformal>, prowl, **drift, stray,** float around, straggle, **meander, ramble,** stroll, saunter, jaunt, peregrinate

roar NOUNS 1 **noise,** loud noise, **racket,** din, clamor; outcry, **uproar,** hue and cry, noise and shouting; howl; thunder, thunderclap
VERBS 2 **be noisy,** make a noise *or* racket, raise a clamor *or* din *or* hue and cry, noise, racket, **clamor,** clangor; **bawl,** bellow, roar *or* bellow like a bull; cachinnate, roar with laughter

roast VERBS **ridicule,** deride, ride <nonformal>, make a laughingstock *or* a mockery of; **insult**; make fun *or* game of, poke fun at; **castigate,** flay, skin alive <nonformal>, scorch, blister, trounce

rob VERBS 1 commit robbery; pick pockets, jostle; hold up; **burglarize;** burgle <nonformal>; **steal,** appropriate, **make off with,** pilfer, filch, have one's hand in the till

2 <nonformal> **swipe, pinch,** bag, **lift,** hook, crib, **cop,** nip, snitch, snare, boost, annex, borrow, burn, clip, **rip off,** nick *and* nobble <both Brit>; **heist, knock off** *or* **over,** tip over; **stick up; mug;** roll, jackroll; hijack

robber NOUNS **holdup man** *and* stickup man <both nonformal>; highwayman, highway robber, footpad, road agent, bushranger <Austral>

robbery NOUNS 1 **theft,** robbing; bank robbery; highway robbery; **armed robbery,** holdup; jostling; hijacking; purse snatching

2 <nonformal> **heist, stickup,** job, stickup job, bag job, boost, burn, knockover, **ripoff**

robe NOUNS frock, mantle, gown, cloak

robot NOUNS **automaton,** mechanical man; cyborg; bionic man, bionic woman

robust ADJS **hale, hearty,** hale and hearty, robustious, robustuous, vital, **vigorous, strong,** strong as a horse *or* an ox, stalwart, stout, sturdy, **rugged,** rude, hardy, lusty, bouncing, well-knit

rock NOUNS 1 **rock-and-roll,** rock music, rock 'n' roll, hard rock, acid rock, folk rock, country rock, full-tilt boogie
2 **stone,** igneous rock, volcanic rock, granite, basalt, sedimentary rock, metamorphic rock, schest, gneiss, crag, bedrock
VERBS 3 **agitate,** perturb, disturb, trouble, disquiet, discompose, unsettle, **stir,** ruffle, shake, shake up, shock, upset, make waves, jolt, jar, stagger, electrify, bring *or* pull one up short, give one a turn <nonformal>
4 **oscillate, vibrate,** librate, nutate; pendulate; **swing,** sway, swag, dangle, **reel,** lurch, roll, careen, toss, pitch; **wag,** waggle; **calm,** calm down, tranquilize, pacify, mollify, appease, dulcify; **quiet,** hush, still, rest, compose, **lull,** soothe, gentle, cradle, rock to sleep
5 **pitch,** toss, tumble, pitch and toss, **plunge,** pound, **rear, rock,** reel, swing, sway, lurch, yaw, heave, scend, **flounder, welter,** wallow

rocket NOUNS 1 **missile;** ballistic missile, guided missile; torpedo; projectile rocket, ordnance rocket, combat *or* military *or* war rocket; bird <nonformal>
VERBS 2 **shoot up,** upshoot, upstart, upspring, upleap, upspear, **skyrocket**

rocketry NOUNS rocket science *or* engineering *or* research *or* technology; **missilery,** missile science *or* engineering *or* research *or* technology

rocket scientist NOUNS **talent,** gifted person, prodigy, natural <nonformal>, **genius,** mental genius, intellectual genius, intellectual prodigy, mental giant; brain surgeon <nonformal>

rock the boat VERBS **not conform,** nonconform, not comply; **get out of line** *and* make waves <all nonformal>, upset the apple cart, break step, break bounds; protest

rocky ADJS 1 **unsteady,** shaky, rickety, teetery, tottery, tottering, doddering, tumbledown, ramshackle, dilapidated; groggy, wobbly, staggery; **sickish,** seedy <nonformal>, **under the weather, out of sorts** <nonformal>, below par <nonformal>, off-color, off one's feed <nonformal>
2 **rugged,** ragged, harsh; **craggy,** cragged; gravelly, stony; **unreliable,** undependable, untrustworthy, treacherous, **insecure,** unsound, unstable

rod NOUNS 1 **scepter, staff,** wand, staff *or* rod *or* wand of office, baton, mace, truncheon, fasces; stick, switch
2 **gun, firearm;** shooting iron *and* gat *and* heater *and* convincer *and* piece <all nonformal>

rogue NOUNS **mischief-maker,** mischief, **devil,** knave, **rascal,** rapscallion, scapegrace, **scamp;** wag

role NOUNS 1 **function,** use, purpose, part, end use, immediate purpose, ultimate purpose, operational purpose, operation; work, duty, office; part, capacity, character

role model NOUNS **paragon,** person to look up to, *chevalier sans peur et sans reproche* <Fr>, **good example,** shining example; exemplar, epitome; **model,** pattern, standard, norm

roll NOUNS 1 **roster,** scroll, rota; **roll call,** muster, **census,** nose *or* head count <nonformal>
2 **swing,** swinging, **sway,** swag; **rock,** lurch, reel, careen; wag, waggle; wave, waver
VERBS 3 **reverberate, resound,** sound, **rumble,** boom, echo, reecho, rebound, bounce back, be reflected, be sent back, echo back, send back, return
4 **run smoothly,** go like clockwork *or* a sewing machine; present no difficulties, give no trouble, be painless, be effortless; flow, glide, slide, coast, sweep, sail

roll back VERBS **retrench,** cut down, cut *or* pare down expenses, curtail expenses; cut corners, tighten one's belt, cut back, slow down

rolling stone NOUNS **wanderer,** rover, roamer, gadabout <nonformal>, runabout, go-about <nonformal>; **itinerant,** peripatetic, bird of passage, visitant; **drifter** *and* **floater** <both nonformal>

roly-poly NOUNS 1 **fat person,** fatty *and* fatso <both nonformal>, **tub, tub of lard,** blimp <nonformal>, hippo <nonformal>
ADJS 2 **stout, obese,** adipose, gross, fleshy, beefy, abdominous, big-bellied, full-bellied, potbellied, **tubby** <nonformal>

romance NOUNS **love affair, affair,** affair of the heart, amour, romantic tie *or* bond, something between, thing <nonformal>, liaison, entanglement, intrigue; fiction, figment, **myth,** fable

romantic NOUNS 1 dreamer, daydreamer, dreamer of dreams, castle-builder, lotus-eater, **wishful thinker;** romanticist, romancer
ADJS 2 **loving,** lovesome, fond, adoring, devoted, affectionate, demonstrative, **sentimental, tender,** soft <nonformal>, melting; romanticized, romancing, romanticizing; **impractical,** unpractical, unrealistic; starry-eyed, dewy-eyed; with one's head in the clouds

romp NOUNS 1 **frolic,** play, rollick, frisk, gambol, caper, dido <nonformal>
VERBS 2 **play,** frolic, rollick, gambol, frisk, caper, cut capers <nonformal>, antic, cavort, caracole, flounce, trip, skip, dance; **cut up** <nonformal>, cut a dido <nonformal>, horse around <nonformal>

roof NOUNS roofing, roofage, top, **housetop,** rooftop

rook VERBS **cheat,** pluck *and* skin <both nonformal>

rookie NOUNS **novice,** novitiate *or* noviciate, **tyro,** abecedarian, alphabetarian, **beginner**, entrant, **neophyte,** tenderfoot *and* greenhorn <both nonformal>, freshman, **fledgling;** catechumen, initiate, debutant; **recruit,** raw recruit, inductee, yardbird<nonformal>

room NOUNS 1 **latitude,** swing, play, way; spare room, room to spare, room to swing a cat <nonformal>, **elbowroom,** margin, leeway
2 **chamber,** *chambre* <Fr>, *salle* <Fr>, four walls
VERBS 3 bunk, crash <nonformal>, berth; **lodge,** quarter, put up, billet, bed, bunk

roomer NOUNS **lodger,** paying guest; **boarder,** board-and-roomer, **transient,** transient guest *or* boarder; **renter,** tenant

roomy ADJS **spacious,** sizable, commodious, capacious, ample

roost NOUNS 1 perch, roosting place; eyrie
VERBS 2 **settle, settle down,** sit down, locate, park <nonformal>, ensconce, ensconce oneself; perch, nest, hive, burrow

root NOUNS 1 radix, radicle; rootlet; **tap-root,** tap; **rhizome,** rootstock; **tuber,** tubercle; **bulb,** bulbil, corm, earthnut
2 **source, origin,** genesis, original, origination, **derivation,** rise, beginning, conception, inception, commencement, etymon, primitive, radical
VERBS 3 **take root,** strike root; **stick,** stick fast
4 **cheer;** root for <nonformal>, cheer on; cheer *or* applaud to the very echo
5 look for, look around *or* about for, look for high and low, look high and low, search out, **search for,** seek for, **hunt for,** cast *or* beat about for

rooter NOUNS **booster** <nonformal>, applauder, *claqueur* <Fr>; claque; fan *and* buff <both nonformal>, adherent

root out VERBS **exterminate,** eliminate, eradicate, deracinate, **extirpate,** annihilate; wipe out <nonformal>; cut out, root up *or* out, uproot, pull *or* pluck up by the roots, cut up root and branch, strike at the root of

rope NOUNS 1 **cord,** line, wire, braided rope, twisted rope, **cable,** wire cable
2 **hanging,** the gallows, the rope *or* noose; **lynching,** necktie party; **hangman's rope,** noose
VERBS 3 **catch,** take, **trap,** lasso, noose; **bind,** tie, brace, truss, **lash,** leash, strap, lace, wire, chain

rope off VERBS **circumscribe,** bound; mark off *or* mark out, stake out, lay off; **cordon, cordon off,** seal off; set up barriers, put behind barriers

roster NOUNS **roll,** scroll, rota; **roll call,** muster, **census,** nose *or* head count <nonformal>; checkroll, checklist

rosy ADJS **optimistic,** upbeat <nonformal>, bright, sunny; cheerful; roseate, rose-colored, *couleur de rose* <Fr>

rot NOUNS 1 **rottenness,** foulness, putridness, putridity, rancidness, rancidity, rankness, **putrefaction,** putrescence, spoilage, decay, decomposition; dry rot, wet rot
VERBS 2 **decay,** decompose, disintegrate; go *or* fall into decay, go *or* fall to pieces, break up, crumble, crumble into dust; **spoil,** corrupt, go bad; putrefy, putresce

rotary ADJS **rotational,** rotatory, rotative; trochilic, vertiginous; circumrotatory, circumvolutory, circumgyratory

rotate VERBS **revolve,** spin, turn, round, **go round** *or* **around,** turn round *or* around; circumrotate, circumvolute; **swivel,** pivot, wheel, swing; pirouette, turn a pirouette

rotten ADJS **decayed,** decomposed; spoiled, corrupt, peccant, bad, **gone bad; rotting,** putrid, putrefied, foul; putrescent, **mortified,** necrosed, necrotic, sphacelated, gangrened, gangrenous; rotten at *or* to the core

rough ADJS 1 **unsmooth; uneven,** ununiform, unlevel, inequal, **broken,** irregular, textured; jolty, **bumpy,** rutty, rutted, pitted, pocky, potholed; **coarse,** gross, unrefined, coarse-grained; abrasive
2 **undeveloped, unfinished,** crude, unpolished, unrefined; uncultivated, uncultured

rough-and-ready ADJS **unarranged,** unorganized, haphazard; makeshift, **extemporaneous,** extemporized, improvised, ad-lib *and* off the top of one's head <both nonformal>; wild-and-woolly

roughhouse NOUNS 1 **misbehavior,** misconduct, **rowdiness,** rowdyism, riotousness, ruffianism, hooliganism; horseplay; helter-skelter, pell-mell, **rough-and-tumble**
VERBS 2 **misbehave,** cut up <nonformal>, horse around <nonformal>, cut up rough <nonformal>

rough it VERBS **camp,** go camping, camp out, sleep out

roughly ADVS approximately, nearly, some, about, circa; more or less, *plus ou moins* <Fr>, by and large, upwards of, **to the amount of,** to the tune of <nonformal>; as much as, all of <nonformal>, no less than

roughneck NOUNS 1 **vulgarian,** low *or* vulgar *or* ill-bred fellow, guttersnipe <nonformal>, *épicier* <Fr>; rough, **ruffian, rowdy,** hooligan; vulgarist, ribald

2 <nonformal> **tough,** bruiser, mug, mugger, bimbo, bozo, ugly customer, **hoodlum, hood, hooligan,** gorilla, ape, plug-ugly, strong-arm man, muscle man, **goon;** gun, gunsel, trigger man, rodman, torpedo, hatchet man; hellion, terror, holy terror, shtarker, ugly customer

rough up VERBS **mistreat,** maltreat, ill-treat, ill-use, abuse, injure, **molest;** do violence to, do one's worst to; mishandle, manhandle; buffet, batter, bruise, **savage,** manhandle, maul, knock about, rough

round NOUNS 1 **revolution,** rotation, cycle, circle, wheel, circuit
ADJS 2 **circular,** rounded, circinate, annular, annulate ring-shaped, ringlike; annulose; disklike, discoid

rouse VERBS **arouse,** raise, raise up, **waken, awaken,** wake up, turn on <nonformal>, charge *or* psych *or* pump up <nonformal>, stir, **stir up,** set astir, **pique**

rout NOUNS 1 **retreat,** *reculade* <Fr>, **withdrawal,** withdrawment, strategic withdrawal, exfiltration; **retirement,** fallback, pullout, pullback
VERBS 2 **overwhelm,** whelm, snow under <nonformal>, overbear, defeat utterly, deal a crushing *or* smashing defeat; **put to rout,** put to flight, scatter, stampede, panic

route NOUNS **path,** way, itinerary, course, track, run, line, road; trajectory, traject, *trajet* <Fr>; circuit, tour, orbit; walk, beat, round; trade route, **sea lane, air lane,** flight path

routine NOUNS 1 **act,** scene, number, turn, bit *and* shtick <both nonformal>
2 **order,** even tenor, standard operating procedure; **peace,** quiet, quietude, tranquillity; **round,** cycle, rotation, the daily grind <nonformal>, recurrence, periodicity, endless round; gamut, spectrum
ADJS 3 **habitual, regular,** frequent, constant, persistent; repetitive, recurring, recurrent; stereotyped; nine-to-five, workaday, well-trodden, well-worn, beaten; trite, hackneyed, **ordinary,** normal, average, usual, standard, par for the course <nonformal>

rove VERBS **stray,** go astray, lose one's way, err; take a wrong turn *or* turning; drift, go adrift; **wander,** wander off, ramble, straggle, divagate, excurse, pererrate

row NOUNS 1 **train,** range, rank, **file,** line, string, thread, queue, bank, tier; windrow, swath; single file, Indian file
VERBS 2 **paddle,** ply the oar, **pull,** scull, punt

row NOUNS 1 **commotion,** scrap, hassle <nonformal>, **brawl,** free-for-all <nonformal>, ruckus, rhubarb <nonformal>, rumpus <nonformal>, donnybrook *or* donnybrook fair, broil, embroilment, melee, scramble; helter-skelter, pell-mell, **roughhouse,** rough-and-tumble
VERBS 2 **be noisy, make a noise** *or* **racket,** raise a clamor *or* din *or* hue and cry, noise, racket, **clamor,** roar, clangor; brawl, rumpus; **make an uproar,** kick up a dust *or* racket, kick up *or* raise a hullabaloo, raise the roof

rowdy NOUNS 1 **ruffian,** rough, bravo, **thug;** bully, bullyboy, bucko; hell-raiser
ADJS 2 **noisy, boisterous,** rip-roaring, strepitous, strepitant, obstreperous; **disorderly,** disruptive, rowdyish, **ruffianly**

royal ADJS **sovereign; regal,** majestic, purple; **kinglike,** kingly

every inch a king
SHAKESPEARE

royalty NOUNS 1 **sovereignty,** regnancy, **majesty,** kingship, kinghood; queenship, queenhood; the throne, the Crown, the purple
2 **dividend; commission,** rake-off *and* cut <both nonformal>

rub NOUNS 1 **bone of contention,** apple of discord, sore point, tender spot, delicate *or* ticklish issue, beef <nonformal>; **crux,** hitch, pinch, snag, catch, joker <nonformal>, where the shoe pinches
NOUNS 2 **friction,** rubbing, frottage; **resistance,** frictional resistance
VERBS 3 **stroke,** pet, caress, fondle; **nuzzle,** nose, rub noses; feel up <nonformal>; rub against, massage, knead; frictionize; polish

rubber NOUNS 1 **elastic;** elastomer; gum elastic; **eraser,** India rubber
2 **contraceptive,** birth control device, prophylactic; condom
ADJS 3 **rubbery,** rubberlike; rubberized

rubberneck NOUNS 1 **rubbernecker** <nonformal>; watcher, Peeping Tom, voyeur, scopophiliac
VERBS 2 keep one's eyes open, keep one's eye on, stare, gape, peer, gawk, rubber <nonformal>

rubbish NOUNS **rubble, trash,** junk <nonformal>, shoddy, riffraff, **scrap,** debris, litter, lumber; **nonsense,** stuff and nonsense, pack of nonsense, **folderol,** balderdash, *niaiserie* <Fr>, flummery, trumpery

rub elbows with VERBS **associate with,** assort with, sort with, consort with, hobnob with, fall in with, go around with, **mingle with,** mix with, touch elbows *or* shoulders with

rub out VERBS 1 **obliterate,** expunge, efface, erase, blot, sponge, **wipe out,** wipe off the map, **blot out,** sponge out, wash away
2 kill, waste *or* zap <both nonformal>

rub the wrong way VERBS **ruffle,** wrinkle, corrugate, crinkle, crumple, **rumple;** bristle; go against the grain, set on edge

ruckus NOUNS **commotion,** hubbub, Babel, tumult, turmoil, **uproar, racket,** riot, **disturbance,** rumpus <nonformal>, ruction <nonformal>, **fracas, hassle,** rampage

ruddy ADJS **red-complexioned,** ruddy-complexioned, warm-complexioned, red-fleshed, red-faced, ruddy-faced, apple-cheeked, rubicund, **florid,** sanguine, full-blooded

rude ADJS **impudent,** impertinent, pert, flip <nonformal>, flippant, cocky *and* cheeky *and* fresh *and* facy *and* crusty *and* nervy <all nonformal>; **disrespectful,** derisive, brash, bluff; **coarse,** gross, crude, crass, raw, rough, **earthy**

rudimentary ADJS **original,** primary, primal, primitive, pristine, primeval, aboriginal, **elementary,** elemental, **basic,** basal, crucial, central, radical, **fundamental;** embryonic

rue VERBS **regret,** deplore, repine, be sorry for; rue the day; **bemoan,** bewail; curse one's folly, **reproach oneself,** kick oneself <nonformal>, wear a hair shirt, make oneself miserable

ruffian NOUNS rough, bravo, **rowdy, thug;** bully, bullyboy, bucko; hell-raiser

ruffle NOUNS 1 **flurry,** bustle, stir, swirl, swirling, whirl, vortex, eddy, hurry, hurry-scurry, hurly-burly
2 **tuck,** gather; frill, ruche, ruching; flounce
VERBS 3 **agitate,** perturb, disturb, trouble, disquiet, discompose, discombobulate <nonformal>, unsettle, **stir, shake,** shake up, shock, upset, make waves, jolt, jar, rock, stagger, bring *or* pull one up short, give one a turn <nonformal>; **fluster,** rub the wrong way, go against the grain, set on edge
4 wrinkle, corrugate, crinkle, crumple, **dishevel,** rumple; tousle <nonformal>, muss *and* muss up <both nonformal>, mess *and* mess up <both nonformal>; disarrange

rug NOUNS 1 **carpet,** floor cover *or* covering; carpeting, wall-to-wall carpet *or* carpeting
2 **wig,** peruke, toupee, hairpiece, divot *and* doormat <both nonformal>; **periwig**

rugged ADJS 1 ragged, harsh; rugose, rugous, wrinkled, crinkled, crumpled, corrugated; **scratchy, abrasive,** rough as a cob <nonformal>
2 **sturdy,** stable, **solid,** sound, firm, steady, tough, stout, strong; **durable,** lasting, enduring; **well-made,** well-constructed, well-built, well-knit

ruin NOUNS 1 **fall, downfall,** collapse, smash, crash, **undoing,** debacle, derailing, derailment; **destruction,** perdition, total loss, dead loss
VERBS 2 **destroy,** deal *or* unleash destruction, bring to ruin, lay in ruins, play *or* raise hob with; **devastate,** desolate, waste, **lay waste,** ravage, havoc, wreak havoc, despoil, depredate
3 **bankrupt, break,** bust *and* wipe out <both nonformal>; put out of business, drive to the wall, scuttle, sink; impoverish
4 **seduce,** betray, deceive, mislead, lead astray, lead down the garden *or* the primrose path; **debauch,** ravish, ravage, despoil, deflower

ruined ADJS 1 **destroyed, wrecked,** blasted, undone; broke, bankrupt; spoiled

2 <nonformal> **shot, done for,** done in, finished, *ausgespielt* <Ger>, kaput; gone to pot, gone to the dogs, gone to hell in a handbasket, phut, belly up, blooey, kerflooey, dead in the water, washed up, all washed up, history, **dead meat, down the tube** *or* **tubes,** zapped, nuked, tapped out, wiped out

ruins NOUNS **wreck,** ruin, total loss; hulk, carcass, skeleton; mere wreck, wreck of one's former self; **remains,** vestige

rule NOUNS 1 **norm,** procedure, **common practice,** the way things are done, form, prescribed *or* set form; common *or* ordinary run of things, matter of course, par for the course <nonformal>
2 **law,** canon, maxim, dictum, moral, moralism; ordinance, imperative, **regulation,** *règlement* <Fr>; **principle,** principium, settled principle, general principle *or* truth, tenet, convention; **guideline,** ground rule, rubric, protocol, standard procedure

3 **government,** governance, discipline, regulation; **regime,** regimen; **sway,** sovereignty, reign, regnancy
VERBS 4 **command, lead,** possess authority, have the authority, have the say *or* the last word, have the whip hand *and* hold all the aces <both nonformal>; **take precedence,** precede; **come** *or* **rank first,** outrank, rank, rank out <nonformal>
5 **sway, reign,** bear reign, have the sway, wield the scepter, wear the crown, sit on the throne; rule over, overrule

rulebook NOUNS **rule, law,** principle, standard, criterion, canon, code, code of practice, maxim, prescription, guideline, the book <nonformal>

rule out VERBS **make impossible,** disenable, disqualify, close out, **bar,** prohibit, put out of reach, leave no chance

ruler NOUNS 1 **straightedge, rule;** square, T square, triangle
2 **potentate,** sovereign, monarch, prince, dynast, **crowned head,** emperor, *imperator* <L>, king; **chief,** chieftain, high chief

ruling NOUNS 1 **verdict,** decision, **determination,** finding, holding; **decree,** consideration, order, **pronouncement,** deliverance; dictum
ADJS 2 **prevalent,** prevailing, common, popular, **current,** running; regnant, reigning, **predominant,** predominating, **dominant**

rumble NOUNS 1 **reverberation,** resounding; rumbling, thunder, thundering, boom, booming, growl, growling, grumble, grumbling, reboation; **talk,** whisper, buzz, bruit, cry
2 **fight, fistfight,** punch-out *and* duke-out <both nonformal>, punch-up <Brit nonformal>; street fight
VERBS 3 **reverberate, resound,** sound, roll, boom, echo, reecho, rebound, bounce back, be reflected, be sent back, echo back, send back, return

ruminate VERBS **consider,** contemplate, speculate, reflect, study, ponder, perpend, **weigh,** deliberate, debate, meditate, muse, brood, chew the cud <nonformal>, digest

rummage VERBS **grope,** grope for, **feel for,** fumble, grabble, scrabble, feel around, poke around, pry around

rumor NOUNS **report,** flying rumor, unverified *or* unconfirmed report, **hearsay,** *on-dit* <Fr>, **scuttlebutt** *and* latrine rumor <both nonformal>; idea afloat, news stirring; **common talk,** town talk, **talk of the town,** topic of the day, *cause célèbre* <Fr>

rumple VERBS **disarrange,** derange, misarrange; **disorder,** disorganize, throw out of order, put out of gear, dislocate, upset the apple-cart, **disarray; dishevel,** ruffle

rumpus NOUNS **commotion, hubbub,** Babel, tumult, turmoil, **uproar,** racket, riot, **disturbance,** ruckus *and* ruction <both nonformal>, **fracas,** hassle

run NOUNS 1 **sprint; dash,** rush, plunge, headlong rush *or* plunge, **race,** scurry, scamper, scud, scuttle, **spurt,** burst, burst of speed
2 **journey,** trip, progress, course; **voyage,** ocean *or* sea trip, **cruise,** sail; **passage; crossing; flight,** trip, hop *and* jump <both nonformal>
3 **burrow,** tunnel, earth, couch, lodge
4 **stream,** brook, branch; kill, bourn, **creek,** crick <nonformal>; **rivulet,** rill
5 **freedom, license,** the run of <nonformal>
6 **series,** succession, **sequence,** consecution, progression, course, gradation
VERBS 7 **fester,** suppurate, matter, rankle, run, weep
8 **extend,** reach, stretch, sweep, spread, **go** *or* **go out,** cover, carry, **range,** lie; **reach** *or* stretch *or* thrust out
9 **flee,** fly, take flight, take wing, fugitate, **cut and run** <nonformal>, make a precipitate departure, **run off** *or* **away,** run away from, bug out <nonformal>, decamp, **take to one's heels,** make off, **depart**, do the disappearing act, make a quick exit
10 **flow,** stream, issue, pour, surge, course, rush, gush, flush, flood
11 **direct,** manage, regulate, conduct, carry on, handle
12 **run for office,** throw *or* toss one's hat in the ring <nonformal>, announce for, enter the lists *or* arena
13 **operate,** function, work, act, perform, go, be in action *or* operation *or* commission

run amok VERBS **go berserk,** go on a rampage, cut loose, run riot, run wild

the runaround NOUNS **avoidance,** shunning; **evasion,** elusion; side-stepping, evasive action, buck-passing *and* passing the buck <both nonformal>

runaway NOUNS 1 **fugitive,** fleer, person

on the run, runagate, **bolter,** skedaddler <nonformal>
ADJS 2 **fugitive,** in flight, on the lam <nonformal>, hot <nonformal>; disappearing

run away VERBS **run off,** run along, flee, take to flight, fly, take to one's heels, cut and run *and* hightail *and* make tracks *and* absquatulate <old> <all nonformal>

run-down ADJS 1 **unhealthy,** frail; weakened, with low resistance, reduced, reduced in health
2 **dilapidated,** ramshackle, decrepit, **tumbledown,** in disrepair, broken-down, in ruins, ruinous

run into VERBS 1 **collide,** come into collision, be on a collision course, **clash,** meet, encounter, confront each other, impinge; bump into, bang into, slam into, **crash into,** impact, smash into
2 **come across,** run across, meet with, meet up with <nonformal>, fall in with, **encounter,** bump into <nonformal>, come *or* run up against <nonformal>; **chance on** *or* **upon,** happen on *or* upon *or* across, **stumble on** *or* **upon**

runner NOUNS **messenger,** message-bearer, courier, diplomatic courier, carrier; **smuggler,** contrabandist; drug smuggler; gunrunner, rumrunner

running start NOUNS **advantage,** start, head *or* flying start; **edge,** bulge *and* jump *and* drop <all nonformal>

runny ADJS exudative, exuding, transudative; percolative; porous, permeable, pervious, oozy, weepy, leaky

run-of-the-mill ADJS **ordinary,** average, normal, **common,** commonplace, garden *and* garden-variety <both nonformal>, **unexceptional,** unremarkable, unnoteworthy, unspectacular, no great shakes <nonformal>, no prize package, no brain surgeon, no rocket scientist

runt NOUNS **shrimp** <nonformal>, diminutive, wisp, chit, slip, snip, snippet, **peanut** *and* **peewee** <both nonformal>

run-through NOUNS **summary,** résumé, recapitulation, recap <nonformal>, rundown

runway NOUNS **taxiway,** strip, landing strip, **airstrip,** flight strip, take-off strip; run

rupture NOUNS 1 **break,** breakage, **breach,** burst, **fracture; crack,** cleft, **fissure,** cut, split, slit; slash, slice; **gap, rift,** rent, rip, tear
VERBS 2 **breach,** break open, force *or* pry *or* prize open, crack *or* split open, rip *or* tear open; break into, break through; break in, burst in, bust in <nonformal>, stave *or* stove in, cave in

rural ADJS **pastoral,** arcadian, bucolic, rustic, country

ruse NOUNS **trick,** artifice, device, ploy, gambit, stratagem, **scheme,** design, *ficelle* <Fr>, **subterfuge,** blind, **wile,** dodge, artful dodge, sleight, pass, feint, fetch, chicanery, gimmick <nonformal>, **red herring,** tactic, **maneuver, stroke,** master stroke, **move,** coup

rush NOUNS 1 **thrill, sensation,** titillation; **tingle,** tingling; quiver, shiver, shudder, tremor, tremor of excitement, kick *and* charge <both nonformal>; flush, rush of emotion, surge of emotion
2 **torrent,** gush, spate, cascade, spurt, jet, rapids; precipitation, haste, hastiness, **overhastiness,** impulse, impulsivity, impulsiveness
VERBS 3 **make haste, hasten,** festinate, **hurry,** hurry up, run, post, **rush,** chase, tear, dash, spurt, leap, plunge, **scurry,** hurry-scurry, scamper, scramble, scuttle, hustle <nonformal>, bundle, bustle; do on the run *or* on the fly

rust NOUNS 1 **blight,** blast; canker, cancer; mold, fungus, mildew, smut, must
VERBS 2 **oxidize; corrode,** erode, eat, gnaw, eat into, eat away, nibble away, gnaw at the root of; canker

rustic ADJS **rural,** country, provincial, farm, pastoral, bucolic, Arcadian, **agrarian,** agrestic; **agricultural**

rustle NOUNS 1 rustling, froufrou

a little noiseless noise among the leaves
KEATS

VERBS 2 crinkle; **swish,** whish
3 **steal,** thieve, purloin, appropriate, take, snatch, palm, **make off with;** poach

rustler NOUNS cattle thief, abactor, **cattle rustler** <nonformal>

rustle up VERBS **cook,** prepare food, prepare, do, cook up, fry up, boil up; make up, whip up, run up, whomp up <nonformal>, slap up *or* together *and* throw *or* slap together <all nonformal>; **provide, supply,** find, dish up <nonformal>, **furnish**

rusty ADJS **corroded,** eroded, eaten; rust-eaten, rust-worn, rust-cankered; **out of**

practice, out of training *or* form, soft <nonformal>, out of shape *or* condition, stiff; **stale,** fusty, musty, dusty, moldy; gone to seed

rut NOUNS **furrow, groove,** ruck <nonformal>, wheeltrack, well-worn groove; **routine,** track, beaten path *or* track

ruthless ADJS **merciless,** unmerciful, without mercy, unruing, dog-eat-dog; **heartless,** hard, hard as nails, steely, flinty, harsh, savage, **cruel;** remorseless, unremorseful

S

sabotage VERBS **disable,** disenable, unfit, **incapacitate,** put out of order, put out of commission <nonformal>, throw out of gear; bugger *and* bugger up *and* queer *and* queer the works *and* gum up *or* screw up <all nonformal>, throw a wrench *or* monkey wrench in the machinery <nonformal>, wreck

saboteur NOUNS **subversive;** fifth columnist, crypto

sack NOUNS 1 **plundering,** pillaging, looting, sacking, freebooting, ransacking, rifling, spoiling, **despoliation,** despoilment, despoiling; **pillage,** plunder
2 **bundle,** bindle <nonformal>, **pack,** package, **parcel,** fardel <nonformal>, bag, poke <nonformal>
VERBS 3 **plunder,** pillage, loot, ransack, rifle, freeboot, spoil, spoliate, despoil, depredate, prey on *or* upon, ravage, ravish, raven, sweep, gut; tackle; **fire** <nonformal>
4 **bundle,** bundle up, **package,** parcel, parcel up, **pack,** bag, truss, truss up; bale

sack out VERBS

<nonformal> **snooze,** get some shuteye, get some sack time, flake out, crash, catch forty winks *or* some zs, pound the ear

sacrament NOUNS **rite, ritual,** rituality, **liturgy,** holy rite; order of worship; sacramental, mystery

sacred ADJS **holy,** numinous, **sacrosanct,** religious, spiritual, heavenly, divine; **venerable,** awesome, awful; inviolable, **inviolate,** untouchable; **ineffable,** unutterable, unspeakable, inexpressible, inenarrable

sacred cow NOUNS **idol; fetish,** totem, joss; **graven image,** golden calf; devil-god; little tin god, tin god

the god of my idolatry
SHAKESPEARE

sacrifice NOUNS 1 **oblation,** offering, immolation, incense; peace offering, sacramental offering, sin *or* piacular offering, whole offering; human sacrifice, self-sacrifice, self-immolation
VERBS 2 **martyr,** martyrize; immolate; make a sacrifice; **give away,** dispose of, part with; **propitiate,** make propitiation; appease; **offer sacrifice,** make sacrifice to, immolate before, offer up an oblation

sacrilege NOUNS **blasphemy,** blaspheming, impiety; **profanity,** profaneness; sacrilegiousness, blasphemousness; **desecration,** profanation; tainting, pollution, contamination

sad ADJS 1 **unhappy, uncheerful,** uncheery, **cheerless, joyless, unjoyful,** unsmiling; mirthless, unmirthful, humorless, infestive; funny as a crutch <nonformal> **grim; out of humor,** out of sorts, in bad humor *or* spirits; **sorry,** sorryish; discontented; **wretched, miserable;** pleasureless
2 saddened; sadhearted, **sad of heart;** heavyhearted, heavy; dejected, depressed, downhearted, down, in low spirits; oppressed, weighed upon, weighed *or* weighted down, bearing the woe of the world, burdened *or* laden with sorrow
3 **disgraceful,** shameful, pitiful, deplorable, opprobrious

sadden VERBS darken, cast a pall *or* gloom upon, weigh *or* weigh heavy upon; **deject,** depress, oppress, crush, press down, hit one like a ton of bricks <nonformal>, **cast down,** lower, lower the spirits, get one down <nonformal>, take the wind out of one's sails, **discourage,** dishearten, take the heart out of, **dispirit**

saddle NOUNS 1 **ridge,** hogback, hog's-back, saddleback, horseback; **helm,** driver's seat <nonformal>; seat, **chair,** bench
VERBS 2 **burden,** load, load down *or* up, lade, cumber, **encumber,** charge, freight, tax, handicap, hamper; **oppress,** weigh one down, weigh on *or* upon, weigh heavy on, bear *or* rest hard upon, lie hard *or* heavy upon

saddle with VERBS **obligate,** oblige, require, make incumbent *or* imperative, tie, **bind,** pledge, commit, put under an obligation; **encumber,** cumber, **burden,** weigh *or* weight down, press down; hang like a millstone round one's neck

safe NOUNS 1 **strongbox,** money chest, coffer, locker, chest; piggy bank; **vault,**

strong room; safe-deposit *or* safety-deposit box *or* vault
ADJS 2 **secure,** safe and sound; **protected**; on the safe side; unthreatened, unmolested; unhurt, unharmed, unscathed, intact, untouched, with a whole skin, undamaged

safeguard NOUNS 1 **guard; shield,** screen, aegis; umbrella, protective umbrella
VERBS 2 **protect,** guard, secure, keep, bless, make safe, **police, enforce the law;** keep from harm; **insure,** ensure, guarantee; **shelter,** shield, screen, cover, cloak

safekeeping NOUNS **protection,** guard, shielding; policing, law enforcement; **safeguarding,** security, **shelter,** cover, refuge; preservation

safety NOUNS safeness, **security,** assurance; risklessness, immunity, clear sailing; **protection,** safeguard

safety valve NOUNS **precaution,** precautiousness; **forethought,** foresight, foresightedness, forehandedness, forethoughtfulness; **safeguard,** protection, preventive measure, safety net

sage NOUNS 1 **wise man,** wise woman, sapient, man *or* woman of wisdom; great soul, mahatma, guru, rishi; **intellect,** person of intellect; mandarin, **intellectual**; savant, scholar
ADJS 2 **wise,** sapient, seasoned, **knowing;** learned; **profound,** deep; wise as an owl *or* a serpent, wise as Solomon

sail NOUNS 1 **canvas,** muslin, cloth, rag <nonformal>; **full** *or* **plain sail,** press *or* crowd of sail; **voyage,** ocean *or* sea trip, **cruise,** run, passage; crossing
VERBS 2 **navigate, cruise,** steam, run, **seafare,** voyage, ply, go on shipboard, go by ship, go on *or* take a voyage

go down to the sea in ships
BIBLE

3 **run smoothly,** work well, work like a machine, go like clockwork *or* a sewing machine; present no difficulties, give no trouble, be painless, be effortless; flow, roll, glide, slide, coast, sweep

sailor NOUNS **mariner,** seaman, **navigator,** seafarer, seafaring man, bluejacket, sea *or* water dog <nonformal>, crewman, shipman, jack-tar, **tar,** salt <nonformal>, windsailor, windjammer

saint NOUNS God-fearing man, pietist, religionist, theist; **disciple,** follower, servant, faithful servant

sake NOUNS **intention,** intent, mindset, **aim,** effect, meaning, view, study, animus, **point,** purpose, function, set *or* settled *or* fixed purpose

salaam NOUNS 1 **obeisance,** reverence, homage; **bow,** nod, bob, bend, inclination, inclination of the head, **curtsy,** kowtow, scrape, bowing and scraping, making a leg; **genuflection,** kneeling, bending the knee; prostration
VERBS 2 **bow,** bend, kneel, genuflect, bend the knee, **curtsy,** make a low bow, make a leg, make a reverence *or* an obeisance, bob, duck; **kowtow,** prostrate oneself

salary NOUNS **pay,** payment, remuneration, compensation, total compensation, wages plus fringe benefits, financial package, pay and allowances, financial remuneration; rate of pay; **wage,** wages, income, earnings, hire

sale NOUNS closing-out sale, going-out-of-business sale, inventory-clearance sale, distress sale, fire sale; bazaar; rummage sale, white elephant sale, garage sale, flea market; tax sale

sales NOUNS selling, market, **marketing,** merchandising, retail, retailing, wholesale, wholesaling

salesmanship NOUNS **promotion, advertising,** Madison Avenue, hucksterism <nonformal>; **selling,** sales talk, hard sell, high pressure, hawking, huckstering

salesperson NOUNS **salesman,** seller, salesclerk; **saleswoman,** saleslady, salesgirl; **clerk,** shop clerk, store clerk, shop assistant

salient NOUNS **conspicuous,** noticeable, notable, ostensible, **prominent,** bold, pronounced, in relief, in bold *or* high *or* strong relief, **striking,** outstanding, in the foreground, sticking *or* hanging out

salivate VERBS ptyalize; **slobber,** slabber, slaver, **drool,** drivel, dribble; **expectorate,** spit, spit up; spew

sallow ADJS **pale,** pallid, wan, fallow; **pasty,** mealy, waxen

salt NOUNS 1 **saltiness,** salinity, brininess; brackishness; **brine**
2 **mariner,** seaman, sailor, sailorman, navigator, seafarer, seafaring man, bluejacket, sea dog <nonformal>, jack-tar, **tar,** hearty, *matelot* <Fr>
3 **wit, humor,** pleasantry, *esprit* <Fr>; Attic wit *or* salt, Atticism

VERBS 4 **preserve,** cure, season, brine

salt of the earth NOUNS **the best,** the very best, the best ever, the tops <nonformal>; cream of the crop, *crème de la crème* <Fr>

salute NOUNS 1 **obeisance,** reverence, homage; salutation; **greeting**
VERBS 2 **do** *or* **pay homage to,** show *or* demonstrate respect for, pay respect to, pay tribute to; **eulogize,** panegyrize, pay tribute, hand it to one <nonformal>; make one's salutations

salvage NOUNS 1 **reclamation,** recovery, retrieval, salving; redemption, salvation
VERBS 2 **redeem,** reclaim, recover, retrieve; ransom; rescue; salve; recycle; win back, **recoup**

salvageable ADJS **remediable,** curable; **reparable,** repairable, mendable, fixable; restorable, recoverable, retrievable, reversible, reclaimable, recyclable, redeemable

salvation NOUNS **redemption,** redeemedness, conversion, regeneration, new life, reformation, adoption; spiritual purification *or* cleansing

salve NOUNS 1 **ointment,** balm, lotion, cream, unguent, unguentum, inunction, inunctum, unction, chrism
VERBS 2 **alleviate,** mitigate, palliate, soften, pad, cushion, assuage, allay, defuse, lay, appease, mollify, subdue, soothe; pour balm into, pour oil on

salvo NOUNS **volley,** burst, spray, **fusillade,** drumfire, **cannonade,** cannonry, **broadside,** enfilade

Samaritan NOUNS **benefactor,** benefactress, **benefiter,** succorer, befriender; ministrant, ministering angel; **good Samaritan; helper,** helping hand; good person

same ADJS **identical,** selfsame, one, **one and the same,** all the same, all one, of the same kidney; **indistinguishable,** without distinction, without difference, undifferent, undifferentiated; wall-to-wall, back-to-back

sample NOUNS 1 **specimen;** piece, taste, swatch; **cross section,** random, sampling
VERBS 2 **taste,** taste of, sample; **savor,** savor of; sip, roll on the tongue; assay
ADJS 3 **typical,** typic, typal; exemplary

sanctify VERBS **hallow; purify,** cleanse, wash one's sins away; **bless,** beatify; **glorify,** exalt, ensky; **consecrate,** dedicate, devote, set apart

sanctimonious ADJS sanctified, **pious,** pietistic, pietistical, self-righteous, pharisaic, pharisaical, **holier-than-thou; false,** insincere, hypocritical; canting, sniveling, unctuous

sanction VERBS **ratify, endorse,** sign off on, second, support, certify, confirm, validate, authenticate, accept, give one's imprimatur, permit, give permission, **authorize,** warrant, accredit

sanctioned ADJS **authorized,** empowered, entitled; **warranted,** licensed, privileged; chartered, patented; franchised, enfranchised; accredited, certificated

sanctity NOUNS sanctitude; **sacredness,** holiness, hallowedness, numinousness; sacrosanctness, sacrosanctity; heavenliness, transcendence, divinity, divineness; venerableness, **venerability,** blessedness

sanctuary NOUNS **holy of holies,** sanctum, sanctum sanctorum, adytum, sacrarium; **refuge,** safehold, **asylum,** haven, safe haven; game sanctuary, bird sanctuary, preserve, forest preserve, game preserve

sanctum NOUNS **sanctum sanctorum,** holy of holies, adytum; **den,** retreat, **hideaway,** cell, ivory tower, inner sanctum

sand NOUNS 1 grain of sand; sands of the sea; sand pile, sand dune, sand hill; sand reef, sandbar
VERBS 2 **buff,** burnish, polish, rub up, sandpaper, smooth, dress, shine, furbish, sandblast

sandwich NOUNS 1 *canapé* <Fr>, *smörgåsbord* <Swed>; club sandwich, dagwood; hamburger, burger; submarine *or* sub *or* hero *or* grinder *or* hoagy *or* poorboy
VERBS 2 **interpose,** interject, interpolate, intercalate, interjaculate; **intervene;** put between, **insert in,** stick in, introduce in, insinuate in, sandwich in, slip in

sandy ADJS **granular,** grainy, granulate, granulated; gritty, sabulous, arenarious, arenaceous

sane ADJS sane-minded, **rational,** reasonable, sensible, **lucid,** normal, wholesome, clearheaded, clearminded, balanced, **sound,** mentally sound, right in the head, **in one's right mind,** in possession of one's faculties *or* senses, together *and* all there <both nonformal>

sanguine ADJS 1 sanguineous, **blood-red,** blood-colored, bloody-red, bloody, gory, red as blood

2 **cheerful, cheery,** of good cheer, in good spirits; **hopeful,** hoping, full of hope, in good heart, of good hope, of good cheer; optimistic

sanitary ADJS **hygienic,** prophylactic; sterile, aseptic, antiseptic, **uninfected;** disinfected, decontaminated, sterilized

sanity NOUNS **saneness,** sanemindedness, soundness, **soundness of mind,** sound mind, healthy mind, right mind <nonformal>, senses, reason, **rationality,** reasonableness, lucidity, balance, wholesomeness

sans PREP absent, lacking; void of, empty of, free of, **without,** minus, less

Santa Claus NOUNS **Santa, Saint Nicholas, Saint Nick, Kriss Kringle, Father Christmas**

sap NOUNS

1 <nonformal> **chump, boob,** booby, prize sap, klutz, basket case, dingbat, ding-a-ling, **ninny,** nincompoop, mutt, jerk, goof, schlemiel, gonzo, dumbo, dweeb, nerd, twerp, yo-yo

VERBS 2 **weaken,** enfeeble, debilitate, unnerve, rattle, shake up <nonformal>, **devitalize, enervate,** sap the strength of, exhaust; **undermine,** mine, sap the foundations of, honeycomb

sapling NOUNS **sprout,** seedling, sucker, shoot, slip; **twig,** sprig, scion

sarcasm NOUNS **irony,** cynicism, satire, satiric wit *or* humor, invective, innuendo; causticity

sardonic ADJS **sarcastic,** ironic, ironical, cynical, Rabelaisian, dry; caustic

sass NOUNS 1 **sauce** *and* lip <nonformal>, **back talk,** backchat <nonformal>
VERBS 2 **sauce** <nonformal>, **talk back,** answer back, lip *and* give one the lip <both nonformal>, provoke

sassy ADJS **impudent,** impertinent, pert; **rude,** disrespectful, derisive, brash, bluff; **saucy,** smart-alecky <nonformal>, smart-ass *or* wise-ass <nonformal>

Satan NOUNS 1 **demon, fiend,** fiend from hell, **devil,** bad *or* evil *or* unclean spirit
2 Lucifer, Old Ned *or* Old Harry <nonformal>, the Angel of Darkness, the archenemy, the Devil, the Evil Spirit, the Temptor

satanic ADJS **diabolic,** diabolical, devilish, demonic, demoniac, demoniacal, Mephistophelian; **fiendish,** fiendlike

sate VERBS **gratify, satisfy,** satiate; slake, appease, allay, assuage, quench

sated ADJS **satiated,** satisfied, slaked, allayed; **surfeited, gorged,** replete, engorged, **glutted; cloyed,** jaded

satellite NOUNS 1 **hanger-on,** adherent, dangler, appendage, **dependent,** follower, cohort, retainer, tagtail
2 puppet regime *or* government; dependency *or* dependent state, client state, satellite state, puppet government, creature
3 **moon; artificial satellite**, unmanned satellite, sputnik; communications satellite, weather satellite, orbiting observatory, geophysical satellite, navigational satellite, geodetic satellite, research satellite

satire NOUNS **burlesque,** lampoon, squib, **parody,** farce, mockery, imitation, wicked imitation *or* pastiche, takeoff <nonformal>, **travesty,** caricature

satirist NOUNS **lampooner,** lampoonist, ironist, pasquinader

satirize VERBS **lampoon,** pasquinade; parody, send up <nonformal>; dip the pen in gall, **burlesque**

satisfaction NOUNS **gratification,** great satisfaction, hearty enjoyment, keen pleasure *or* satisfaction; **self-gratification,** self-indulgence; entire satisfaction, fulfillment; **redress,** making *or* setting right, amends, compensation, **recompense**

satisfactory ADJS 1 **satisfying;** pleasant, agreeable
2 **sufficient**, sufficing, **adequate,** enough, commensurate, proportionate, proportionable, ample, equal to, suitable, good enough

satisfy VERBS 1 **gratify,** sate, satiate; slake, appease, allay, assuage, quench; do one's heart good, warm the cockles of the heart; put *or* set at ease, set one's mind at ease *or* rest
2 **pay in full,** pay off, pay up <nonformal>, **discharge,** settle, square, **clear,** liquidate, amortize; **atone,** atone for, propitiate, expiate, compensate, restitute, recompense, redress, redeem

satisfying ADJS **gratifying,** rewarding, heartwarming, grateful; **welcome;** pleasant, pleasing, pleasureful, to one's liking, *en rapport* <Fr>

saturate VERBS **imbue,** imbrue, **infuse,** steep, decoct, brew; soak, drench, supersaturate, supercharge

saucy ADJS **impudent,** impertinent, pert,

sassy <nonformal>, cheeky <nonformal>
saunter VERBS walk, ramble, **stroll,** amble, jaunt, peregrinate
sauté VERBS **brown,** embrown, infuscate; fry, braise, sear, blacken, brown
savage NOUNS 1 **barbarian,** brute, beast, animal, tiger, shark, hyena; wild man; cannibal, man-eater, anthropophagite
ADJS 2 **fierce,** ferocious, vicious, murderous, cruel, **atrocious,** mindless, brutal, brutish, **bestial,** mindless, insensate, monstrous, inhuman, pitiless, ruthless, merciless, bloody, sanguinary; feral, **barbarous,** barbaric
savanna NOUNS **grassland,** prairie, steppe, steppeland, **pampas,** pampa, campo, llano, **veld,** grass veld
savant NOUNS scholar, connoisseur, maven <nonformal>; **intellect,** person of intellect; mandarin, intellectual; **learned man,** man of learning, giant of learning, colossus of knowledge, mastermind, pundit
save VERBS 1 **reserve,** conserve, keep, retain, husband, husband one's resources, keep *or* hold back, withhold; **keep in reserve,** keep in store, keep on hand, keep by one; preserve; **set** *or* **put aside,** put *or* lay *or* set by; save up, save to fall back upon, keep as a nest egg, **save for a rainy day,** provide for *or* against a rainy day
2 **rescue,** come to the rescue, **deliver,** be the saving of, **redeem,** ransom, salvage
savings NOUNS **reserve,** reserves, **nest egg,** sinking fund; proved reserves; life savings
savior NOUNS **redeemer,** deliverer, **liberator,** rescuer, freer, **emancipator,** manumitter
savory ADJS **delectable,** delicious, luscious; tasty, flavorsome; juicy, succulent
savvy NOUNS **smartness,** braininess, smarts <nonformal>, mental alertness, nous, **sharpness,** keenness, acuity, acuteness
saw NOUNS 1 **platitude,** cliché, old saw, commonplace, banality, bromide, **chestnut** <nonformal>, corn <nonformal>, tired phrase, trite saying, hackneyed *or* stereotyped saying, commonplace expression
VERBS 2 **sever, dissever,** cut off *or* away *or* loose, shear off, **cleave,** sunder
say NOUNS 1 **remark, statement,** earful *and* crack *and* one's two cents' worth <all nonformal>, **word,** saying, utterance, observation, reflection, expression
VERBS 2 **state,** declare, assert, aver, affirm, asseverate, allege; make a statement, send a message
saying NOUNS **maxim,** aphorism, apothegm, epigram, dictum, adage, proverb, gnome, words of wisdom, **saw,** witticism, expression, phrase
scab NOUNS 1 **crust,** incrustation, scale, eschar
2 **strikebreaker,** rat *and* fink *and* scissorbill <all nonformal>, **blackleg** <Brit>
scald VERBS **burn, scorch,** parch, **roast,** toast, cook, bake, fry, broil, boil, seethe
scale NOUNS 1 **extent, measure,** amount, ratio, proportion, stint, standard, height, pitch, reach, remove, compass, range, scope, caliber
2 **flake,** flock, floccule, flocculus; **scurf,** dandruff
3 **gamut,** register, compass, range, diapason; diatonic scale, chromatic scale
VERBS 4 **flake,** scale *or* flake off, desquamate, exfoliate
5 **climb,** climb up, upclimb, **mount,** clamber; escalade, scale the heights; climb over, surmount
scalp VERBS 1 **peel,** pare, skin, strip, flay, excoriate, decorticate, bark
2 **trade,** speculate, resell
scam NOUNS 1 **cheating,** cheating scheme, cheating method, angle, con *and* grift *and* move *and* racket *and* sting <all nonformal>; deception
VERBS 2 **trick,** dupe, gammon, **gull,** pigeon, play one for a fool *or* sucker, bamboozle *and* snow *and* hornswoggle *and* diddle <all nonformal>
scamp NOUNS **mischief-maker,** mischief, **rogue,** devil, knave, **rascal,** rapscallion, scapegrace, precious rascal
scamper VERBS **rush, tear,** dash, dart, shoot, hurtle, bolt, fling, **scurry,** scud, scuttle, scramble, **race,** careen
scan NOUNS 1 **study,** look-through, run-through
VERBS 2 **browse,** skim, dip into, thumb over *or* through, run over *or* through, glance *or* run the eye over *or* through, turn over the leaves, have a look at, hit the high spots
scandal NOUNS **dirt** <nonformal>, **malicious gossip;** character assassination, **slander**; whispering campaign; **disgrace,** humiliation

gossip made tedious by morality
Oscar Wilde

scandalize VERBS **incur disgrace,** make oneself notorious, put one's good name in jeopardy; compromise oneself; raise eyebrows, cause tongues to wag

scant ADJS **sparse,** scanty, exiguous, **infrequent,** scarce, scarce as hen's teeth <nonformal>, poor, piddling, thin, slim, **meager**

scanty ADJS **scarce,** sparse, in short supply, at a premium; not to be had for love or money, not to be had at any price

scapegoat NOUNS **goat** <nonformal>, fall guy *and* can-carrier *and* patsy *and* catch dog <all nonformal>, **whipping boy**

scar NOUNS 1 **mark,** cicatrix, scarification, cicatrization, keloid, cicatrix; flaw, defect, fault
VERBS 2 **mark,** score, scratch, gash, scotch, scarify, cicatrize, disfigure, deface, **flaw, mar**

scarce ADJS **sparse,** scanty; in short supply, at a premium; **rare,** uncommon; scarcer than hen's teeth <nonformal>; not to be had for love or money, not to be had at any price

scarcity NOUNS scarceness; **sparsity,** sparseness; **scantiness,** scant sufficiency; **dearth,** paucity, poverty; **rarity,** rareness, uncommonness

scare NOUNS 1 **fear,** fright, affright; **alarm,** consternation, dismay; dread, unholy dread; **panic,** panic fear *or* terror
VERBS 2 **frighten,** frighten *or* scare out of one's wits

3 <nonformal> spook, scare one stiff *or* shitless *or* spitless, scare the life out of, scare the pants off of, scare hell out of, scare the shit out of; scare one to death, scare the daylights *or* the living daylights *or* the wits out of

scarecrow NOUNS **figure,** woman *or* man of straw; gargoyle, monster, **monstrosity,** teratism

scary ADJS **frightening,** frightful; scaring, chilling; **alarming,** startling, disquieting, dismaying, disconcerting; **unnerving,** daunting

scathing ADJS **acrimonious,** acrid, acidulous, acid, **bitter,** tart, **caustic,** mordant *or* mordacious; **cutting,** biting, stinging, stabbing, **piercing,** penetrating, edged, double-edged

scatter VERBS **disperse,** diffract; **distribute,** broadcast, sow, disseminate, propagate; scatter to the winds; **disband,** separate, part, break up, split up; **part company,** dispel

scatterbrain NOUNS **rattlebrain,** rattlehead, rattlepate, **harebrain,** featherbrain, shallowbrain, **flibbertigibbet**

scenario NOUNS 1 **script,** screenplay, motion-picture play *or* script, treatment, original screenplay

2 <nonformal> scheme, design, program, plan, idea, strategy

scene NOUNS **view,** scape; landscape; waterscape, riverscape, seascape; exterior, interior; scenery

scenery NOUNS decor; **scene; drop,** drop scene, drop curtain, scrim, cloth; **backdrop**

scent NOUNS 1 **fragrance,** perfume, aroma, redolence, balminess, **incense, bouquet,** sweet smell, sweet savor; **odor**; spice, spiciness; muskiness; fruitiness
2 **track,** trail, path, course, *piste* <Fr>, line, wake; **spoor,** signs, traces
VERBS 3 catch the scent of, sniff, smell, get a whiff of <nonformal>, **get wind of;** sniff *or* scent *or* smell out, nose out; be on the right scent, have a fix on

schedule NOUNS 1 **program,** programma, **bill,** card, **calendar,** docket, slate; schedule *or* program of operation, **order of the day,** things to be done, **agenda,** list of agenda; laundry list *and* wish list <both nonformal>
VERBS 2 **line up** <nonformal>, **slate,** book, book in, bill, program, calendar, docket, budget, put on the agenda

scheduled ADJS **slated,** booked, billed, booked-in, to come

scheme NOUNS 1 **plan,** design, method, **program,** device, contrivance, game, envisagement, conception, enterprise, **idea,** notion; **intrigue,** web of intrigue, **plot,** deep-laid plot *or* scheme, trick, stratagem; **scheming,** schemery, plotting; finagling <nonformal>, **machination,** manipulation, **maneuvering,** engineering, rigging
VERBS 2 **plot,** intrigue, be up to something; **conspire,** connive, collude, cabal; **hatch,** cook up <nonformal>, brew,

concoct, hatch *or* lay a plot; **maneuver,** machinate, finesse, operate <nonformal>, engineer, rig, wangle <nonformal>, angle, finagle <nonformal>

scholar NOUNS 1 **student,** pupil, learner, studier, educatee, trainee, *élève* <Fr>
2 **learned person,** man of learning, giant of learning, colossus of knowledge, mastermind, **savant,** pundit; **mine of information,** walking encyclopedia; **academician,** schoolman; classicist, classicalist, Latinist, humanist

scholarship NOUNS **erudition,** eruditeness, **learnedness,** reading, letters; **intellectuality,** intellectualism; **culture,** literary culture, high culture, book learning, booklore; **bookishness,** bookiness, pedantry, pedantism, donnishness <Brit>; classicism, classical scholarship, humanism, humanistic scholarship; **fellowship**

school NOUNS 1 **educational institution,** teaching institution, academic *or* scholastic institution, teaching and research institution, **institute,** academy, seminary, *Schule* <Ger>, *école* <Fr>, *escuela* <Sp>; alternative school; magnet school
2 **system of belief; cult,** ism, ideology, *Weltanschauung* <Ger>, world view; political faith *or* belief *or* philosophy; **creed, credo,** credenda
VERBS 3 **teach, instruct,** give instruction, give lessons in, **educate; edify,** enlighten, civilize, illumine; **direct,** guide; **ground,** teach the rudiments *or* elements *or* basics; catechize

schooled ADJS **informed,** enlightened, instructed, versed, well-versed, educated, taught; **up on,** up-to-date, abreast of, *au courant* <Fr>

science NOUNS **art,** craft; skill; **study,** discipline; **field,** field of inquiry, concern, province, domain, area, arena, sphere, branch *or* field of study, branch *or* department of knowledge, specialty, academic specialty; natural science; applied science, pure science, experimental science; Big Science

scientific ADJS **exact, precise,** express; **strict,** close, severe, **rigorous,** rigid; scientifically exact; pragmatic, pragmatical, scientistic, positivistic

scientist NOUNS person of science; practical scientist, experimental scientist, theoretical scientist; scholar; authority, expert, researcher

scintillating ADJS 1 **glittering,** glimmering, shimmering, twinkling, blinking, glistening, glistering; **sparkling,** scintillant, scintillescent, coruscating, coruscant
2 **smart,** brainy <nonformal>, bright, brilliant; sharp-witted, keen-witted, needle-witted, **quick-witted,** quick-thinking, steel-trap, nimble-witted, quick on the trigger *or* uptake <nonformal>; smart as a whip, sharp as a tack <nonformal>

scoff VERBS **jeer,** gibe, **mock,** revile, rail at, rally, chaff, **twit,** taunt, jape, flout, scout, have a fling at, cast in one's teeth

scold NOUNS 1 **shrew,** vixen, virago, common scold; kvetch, **complainer**
VERBS 2 **reprove,** rebuke, reprimand, reprehend, put a flea in one's ear, **chide,** rate, **upbraid,** objurgate; **take to task,** call on the carpet, read the riot act, give one a tongue-lashing, tonguelash

scoop NOUNS 1 **cavity,** concavity, concave; **hollow,** hollow shell, shell; depression, dip, pocket; scoopful
2 **information,** info <nonformal>, facts, data, knowledge; **intelligence;** the dope *and* the goods *and* the scoop <all nonformal>; **news item,** article, story, piece; beat <nonformal>, exclusive; **the facts,** the information, the particulars
VERBS 3 **ladle,** dip; bail, bucket; **excavate,** dig, dig out, scoop out

scope NOUNS **range,** compass, reach, stretch, expanse radius, sweep, carry, fetch; **spectrum**

scorch VERBS **burn,** parch, scald, torrefy, sear, singe; **darken,** blacken; **cauterize,** brand, burn in

score NOUNS 1 **notch, nick,** cut, cleft, **gash,** hack, blaze, scotch, kerf, crena, depression; **furrow, groove,** scratch, crack, cranny, chase, chink, striation, stria, gouge
2 reckoning, **tally, aggregate, amount,** quantity; box score <nonformal>
3 musical score *or* copy, **music,** notation, musical notation, written music, transcript, transcription, arrangement
VERBS 4 **notch,** nick, cut, incise, gash, slash, chop, crimp, scotch, blaze, jag, scarify; **furrow,** groove, scratch, incise, cut, striate, streak, gouge
5 **score a success,** be successful, notch one up <nonformal>, hit it, hit the mark, ring the bell <nonformal>, turn up trumps, hit the jackpot <nonformal>

6 **calculate,** compute, estimate, reckon, figure, reckon at, put at, cipher, cast, tally

scorn NOUNS 1 **contempt, disdain,** contemptuousness, disdainfulness, superciliousness, snottiness, sniffiness, scornfulness, contumely
VERBS 2 **disdain, despise,** hold in contempt, contemn, vilipend, disprize, misprize, rate *or* rank low, be contemptuous of, feel contempt for, **hold in contempt,** hold cheap, look down upon, think little *or* nothing of, hold beneath one *or* beneath contempt, look with scorn upon, view with a scornful eye, give one the fish-eye *or* the beady eye <nonformal>

scot-free ADJS free as the wind, free as a bird, at large, **free**

scoundrel NOUNS **rascal,** precious rascal, rogue, knave, villain, blackguard, **scamp,** scalawag <nonformal>, spalpeen <Ir>, rapscallion

scour VERBS **scrub; grope,** grope for, **feel for,** fumble, grabble, scrabble, feel around, poke around, grope in the dark; sweep, scour the country

scourge NOUNS **epidemic,** plague, pestilence, pest, pandemic, pandemia; **bane,** curse, affliction, infliction, visitation, calamity, **torment,** burden, crushing burden

scout NOUNS 1 **vanguard,** point, point man; **spearhead,** advance guard, outguard; pathfinder, explorer, trailblazer *or* trailbreaker, guide
VERBS 2 **reconnoiter,** get the lay of the land

scowl NOUNS 1 **frown,** lower, **glower, pout,** moue, mow, grimace, wry face; sullen looks, black looks, **long face**
VERBS 2 **frown,** knit the brow, lower, **glower, pout,** make a moue *or* mow, grimace, make a wry face, make a lip

scrabble VERBS 1 **creep, crawl,** scramble, grovel, **go on hands and knees,** go on all fours
2 **excavate, dig,** dig out, **scoop,** scoop out, **gouge,** gouge out, grub, shovel, spade, dike, delve, scrape, scratch; **scribble,** scratch, scrawl

scram INTERJ 1 go away!, begone!, get you gone!, go along!, get along!, **run along!, get along with you!,** away!, away with you!, **off with you!,** off you go!, on your way!, go about your business!, be off!, **get out of here!,** get out!, clear out!, leave!, *allez!* <Fr>, *allez-vous-en!* <Fr>, *va-t'-en!* <Fr>, *raus mit dir!* <Ger>, *heraus!* <Ger>, *¡váyase!* <Sp>, *via! or va' via!* <Ital>, shoo!, scat!, git! <nonformal>

stand not on the order of your going, but go at once
SHAKESPEARE

go and hang yourself
PLAUTUS

2 <nonformal> **beat it!,** buzz off!, bug off!, shoo!, skiddoo!, skedaddle!, vamoose!, cheese it!, make yourself scarce!, **get lost!,** take a walk!, take a hike!, go chase yourself!, go play in the traffic!, get the hell out!, push off!, shove off!, take a powder!, blow!

scramble NOUNS 1 **haste,** hurry, scurry, rush, race, dash, drive, scuttle, scamper, hustle <nonformal>, **bustle,** flutter, **flurry,** hurry-scurry, helter-skelter; no time to be lost
2 **jumble,** tumble, snarl-up, mess, bloody *or* holy *or* unholy *or* god-awful mess <nonformal>, **turmoil,** welter, mishmash, hash, helter-skelter, farrago, crazy-quilt, higgledy-piggledy
VERBS 3 **hustle** <nonformal>, **drive,** drive oneself, push, go all out <nonformal>, **make things hum,** step lively <nonformal>, make the sparks *or* chips fly <nonformal>
4 **make unintelligible,** jumble, garble; mix up, hash, stir up, conglomerate, shuffle, **jumble,** jumble up, mingle-mangle

scrap NOUNS 1 tatter, smithereen <nonformal>, patch, **stitch, shred,** tag; snip, **snippet,** snick, chip, nip; **morsel,** *morceau* <Fr>, crumb
2 fight; **row, rumpus,** ruckus, ruction, brannigan, set-to, run-in, **hassle,** rhubarb <all nonformal>
VERBS 3 **junk** <nonformal>, consign to the scrap heap, throw on the junk heap <nonformal>, discard, throw away, chuck, **get rid of,** dispense of, dump
4 **row, hassle,** make *or* kick up a row; mix it up, lock horns, bump heads <all nonformal>

scrape NOUNS 1 **rasp, scratch,** grind; burr, chirr, buzz; fix *and* jam *and* pickle *and* stew <all nonformal>; perturbation,

disturbance, upset, bother, pother
VERBS 2 **grate,** rasp, scratch, grind; **brush,** sweep, graze, brush by, glance, skim
3 **bow,** make obeisance, kowtow, **bow and scrape;** fall down before, fall at the feet of, prostrate oneself, kiss the hem of one's garment
4 **scrimp,** skimp <nonformal>, scrape and save; live frugally, get along on a shoestring, get by on little, eke out

scrappy ADJS **contentious,** quarrelsome; **argumentative,** argumental; on the warpath, looking for trouble

scraps NOUNS **leavings,** leftovers; refuse, odds and ends, rags, **rubbish,** waste

scratch NOUNS 1 **rasp,** scrape, grind; **furrow,** groove, crack, cranny, chase, chink, score, **cut,** gash, striation, streak, stria, **gouge,** slit, incision; sulcus, sulcation; **abrasion,** scuff
VERBS 2 **grate,** rasp, scrape, grind; **furrow,** groove, score, incise, cut, carve, chisel, gash, striate, streak, gouge, claw

scrawl NOUNS 1 **scribble,** scrabble, scratch, *barbouillage* <Fr>; *pattes de mouche* <Fr>, hen tracks *and* hen scratches <both nonformal>
VERBS 2 **scribble,** scrabble, scratch, make hen tracks *or* hen *or* chicken scratches <nonformal>

scrawny ADJS **skinny** <nonformal>, **gaunt,** lank, lanky; mere skin and bones, all skin and bones, nothing but skin and bones; twiggy

scream NOUNS 1 **screech,** shriek, squeal, shrill, keen, squeak, squawk, skirl; waul, caterwaul
VERBS 2 **screech,** shriek, squeal, shrill, keen; waul, caterwaul

screen NOUNS 1 **veil,** curtain, cover; fig leaf; **wraps** <nonformal>; disguise; **pretext,** smoke screen, stalking-horse, **blind;** guise, semblance; **shade,** light shield
VERBS 2 **cover,** cover up; **veil,** shield, screen off, mask, cloud, obscure, fog, befog, fuzz; block, eclipse, occult; **conceal,** hide, ensconce
3 **sort,** sort out, classify, select; **separate,** divide; **sift,** size, sieve, bolt, riddle

screw up VERBS 1 **bungle,** blunder; spoil, ruin, play havoc with

2 <nonformal> foul up, fuck up, bitch up, **blow,** louse up, queer, snafu, snarl up, balls up <Brit>, bugger, bugger up, gum up, ball up, bollix, bollix up, **mess up,** hash up, muck up; play hob with, play hell with, play merry hell with, play the devil with, rain on one's picnic *or* parade; upset the apple cart, cook, sink, shoot down in flames; **total**

scribble NOUNS 1 illegibility, unreadability; undecipherability, indecipherability; scrawl, **hen track** <nonformal>; scrabble, **scrawl,** scratch, *barbouillage* <Fr>; *pattes de mouche* <Fr>, hen tracks *and* hen scratches <both nonformal>
VERBS 2 scrabble, **scratch,** scrawl, make hen tracks *or* hen *or* chicken scratches <nonformal>, doodle

scribbler NOUNS **writer,** penman, pen, penner; pen *or* pencil driver *or* pusher <nonformal>, word-slinger, **inkslinger** *and* ink spiller *and* inkstained wretch <all nonformal>, knight of the plume *or* pen *or* quill <nonformal>; **hack writer,** hack, literary hack, potboiler <nonformal>

scrimmage NOUNS **free-for-all,** knock-down-and-drag-out <nonformal>, **brawl,** broil, melee, **fracas**

scrimp VERBS **stint,** skimp, scamp, scant, screw, **pinch,** starve, famish; **pinch pennies,** rub the print off a dollar bill, rub the picture off a nickel; live upon nothing; grudge, begrudge

script NOUNS 1 **handwriting,** hand, chirography, **calligraphy,** autography; **manuscript,** autograph, holograph; **penmanship,** stylography
2 **screenplay,** motion-picture play *or* script, shooting script

scripture NOUNS **scriptures,** sacred writings *or* texts, bible; canonical writings *or* books, sacred canon

Scripture NOUNS **Bible,** Holy Bible, the Scriptures, Holy Scripture, Holy Writ, the Book, the Good Book, the Book of Books, the Word, the Word of God

scroll NOUNS 1 **coil,** whorl, roll, **curl,** curlicue, ringlet, pigtail, **spiral,** helix, volute, volution, involute, evolute, gyre
2 **document,** official document, legal document, legal paper, legal instrument, **instrument,** writ, **paper,** parchment

scrooge NOUNS **niggard,** tightwad *and* cheapskate <both nonformal>, **miser,** hard man with a buck <nonformal>, **skinflint,** penny pincher, pinchfist, curmudgeon <old>

scrounge VERBS 1 beg, **cadge**

2 <nonformal>mooch, bum, panhandle; hit, hit up, touch, put the touch on, make a touch

scrub NOUNS 1 **brush,** bush, **brushwood,** shrubwood, scrubwood
VERBS 2 **wash, clean,** bathe, scrub up *or* out, **swab,** mop, mop up; **scour**
3 **discontinue,** terminate, abort, cancel, scratch <nonformal>, hold, **quit,** stay, belay <nonformal>

scruffy ADJS **dirty,** grimy, grubby, grungy <nonformal>, smirchy, dingy, messy <nonformal>; slovenly, untidy, **shabby,** scrubby, shoddy, scurvy, scuzzy <nonformal>, scummy, **crummy** *and* cheesy <both nonformal>

scrumptious ADJS **tasty,** finger-lickin' good <nonformal>, **savory,** palatable, toothsome, **luscious;** for the gods, ambrosial, nectarous, nectareous; fit for a king, yummy <nonformal>

scruple NOUNS 1 **compunction, qualm,** qualms, qualmishness, scruples, scrupulosity, scrupulousness, pang, pangs, **pangs of conscience,** throes, sting *or* pricking *or* twinge *or* twitch of conscience
2 **modicum,** whit, ace, hair, groat, farthing, pittance, trifling amount, **smidgen** *and* skosh *and* smitch <all nonformal>, pinch

scrupulous ADJS **punctilious, precise,** precisian, precisionist, precious, puristic; by-the-book; exact, meticulous; **orderly,** methodical; **conscientious,** careful

scrutinize VERBS **survey, eye,** contemplate, look over, give the eye *or* the once-over <nonformal>; **ogle,** ogle at, **leer,** leer at, give one the glad eye; examine, vet, inspect; **pore,** take a close *or* careful look; take a long, hard look; size up <nonformal>

scrutiny NOUNS overview, **survey,** contemplation; **examination,** inspection, the once-over <nonformal>, visual examination, a vetting

scuffle NOUNS **struggle,** fight, tussle, wrestle, hassle <nonformal>

sculptor NOUNS sculptress, sculpturer; figurer, *figuriste* <Fr>, **modeler,** molder, wax modeler, clay modeler

sculpture NOUNS 1 **figure,** bust, statue, statuette, statuary; portrait bust *or* statue; glyph; marble, bronze, terra cotta; mobile, stabile
VERBS 2 sculp *or* sculpt <nonformal>, insculpture <old>

scum NOUNS 1 **slime,** slop, sludge, slush; glop *and* gunk <both nonformal>, **muck,** mire, ooze; **offal,** slough, offscourings, scurf, riffraff, scum of the earth; off-scum, foam, froth; **film,** skin, scale

scuttle VERBS 1 **rush, tear,** dash, dart, shoot, hurtle, bolt, fling, **scamper, scurry,** scour, scud, scramble, **race,** careen
2 **sink,** send to the bottom, send to Davy Jones's locker; **founder, go down,** go to the bottom, sink like lead, go down like a stone; cook one's goose *and* cut one down to size *and* cut one off at the knees *and* pull the plug on *and* pull the rug out from under <all nonformal>

scuttlebutt NOUNS **report, rumor,** flying rumor, unverified *or* unconfirmed report, **hearsay,** *on-dit* <Fr>, latrine rumor <nonformal>

sea NOUNS **ocean,** great *or* main sea, *thalassa* <Gk>, **main** *or* ocean main, the bounding main, tide, salt sea, salt water, blue water, deep water, open sea, **the brine,** the briny *and* the big pond <both nonformal>, the briny deep

seam NOUNS 1 **joint,** join, joining, suture, closure; boundary, interface
2 **deposit,** mineral deposit, pay dirt; **vein,** lode

seamless ADJS **unvaried,** unruffled, undiversified, undifferentiated, unchanged; **unbroken,** serried, **uniform**, undifferentiated, wall-to-wall *and* back-to-back <both nonformal>, jointless, gapless, smooth

seamstress NOUNS **sewer,** needleworker, sempstress, needlewoman; dressmaker, modiste

sear VERBS **shrink,** shrivel, wither, parch, dry up; scorch, singe; **burn**

search NOUNS 1 searching, **quest, hunt,** hunting, stalk, stalking, still hunt, dragnet, posse, search party
VERBS 2 **seek, hunt,** look for high and low, look high and low, search out, **search for,** seek for, **hunt for,** cast *or* beat about for

season NOUNS 1 time of year, season of the year, **period,** annual period

the measure of the year
KEATS

VERBS 2 **flavor,** savor; mellow, temper, come of age, come into its own, mature, ripen, evolve
3 stiffen, work-harden, **temper,** strengthen

seasonable ADJS **timely,** well-timed, opportune, convenient, in the nick of time

seasonal ADJS in *or* out of season, off-season; early-season, mid-season, late-season; **periodic,** cyclic *or* cyclical, serial

seasoned ADJS **ripe,** mature, matured, maturated; **experienced,** practiced, tried, well-tried, tried and true, **veteran,** an old dog at <nonformal>; **toughened,** hardened, tempered, annealed

seasoning NOUNS **flavoring,** flavor, flavorer; seasoner, **relish,** condiment, spice, condiments

seat VERBS **place,** put, set, lay, pose, posit, site, stick <nonformal>, **station,** post; park, plump down <nonformal>

secede VERBS **defect, bolt,** break away; pull out <nonformal>, withdraw one's support; turn one's back on; apostatize

secluded ADJS **seclusive,** retired, withdrawn; isolated, shut off, insular, **separate,** separated, **apart,** detached, removed; **remote,** out-of-the-way, outback *and* back of beyond <both Austral>; **unfrequented,** unvisited, off the beaten track; untraveled

seclusion NOUNS reclusion, **retirement,** withdrawal, retreat, recess; **sequestration,** separation, detachment, apartness; **isolation**

splendid isolation
SIR WILLIAM GOSCHEN

second NOUNS 1 **instant,** moment, split second, millisecond, microsecond, nanosecond, half a second, **trice,** twinkle, twinkling *or* twinkle of an eye
VERBS 2 **ratify,** endorse, sign off on, support, **certify,** confirm, validate, authenticate, accept, give the nod *or* the green light *or* the go-ahead *or* the OK <all nonformal>, give a nod of assent, give one's imprimatur; take the part of, take up *or* adopt *or* espouse the cause of, **go to bat for** <nonformal>, side with, align oneself with

secondary ADJS **unessential,** subsidiary, subordinate; **incidental,** circumstantial, contingent; collateral, indirect

secondhand ADJS **used,** worn, previously owned, **unnew,** not new, pawed-over; hand-me-down *and* reach-me-down <both nonformal>

second thoughts NOUNS **irresolution,** change of mind, tergiversation, better thoughts, afterthoughts, mature judgment; **afterthought,** *arrière-pensée* <Fr>

secrecy NOUNS secretness, airtight secrecy, close secrecy; crypticness; **secretiveness,** closeness

secret NOUNS 1 **confidence;** private *or* personal matter, trade secret; confidential *or* privileged information *or* communication; deep *or* profound secret, sealed book, mystery of mysteries; skeleton in the closet *or* cupboard
ADJS 2 close, closed, closet; cryptic, dark; unuttered, unrevealed, undivulged, undisclosed, unspoken, untold; **unrevealable,** undivulgable, undisclosable, untellable, unwhisperable, unbreatheable, unutterable; arcane, esoteric, occult, cabalistic, hermetic; enigmatic, mysterious; *in petto* <L>

secretary NOUNS 1 amanuensis; **minister,** secretary of state, undersecretary, cabinet minister, cabinet member
2 *secrétaire* <Fr>, escritoire, **desk,** writing table

secrete VERBS 1 produce, give out; excrete; water; lactate; weep, tear
2 **hide away,** keep hidden, put away, store away, stow away, file and forget, bottle up, lock up, seal up, put out of sight; keep secret; **cache,** stash <nonformal>, deposit, plant <nonformal>; **bury;** squirrel away

sect NOUNS **faction,** division, wing, **caucus,** splinter, splinter group, breakaway group, offshoot; **school,** class, order; **denomination,** communion, confession, faith, church

sectarian ADJS **factional,** sectary, denominational, schismatic, schismatical

secular ADJS **unsacred,** nonsacred, **unholy,** unhallowed, unsanctified, unblessed; profane, **temporal, worldly,** fleshly, mundane, temporal; **unspiritual,** secularist; secularistic

secure VERBS 1 **guarantee,** guaranty, warrant, assure, insure, ensure, bond, **certify; sponsor,** be sponsor for, sign for, sign one's note, **back,** stand behind *or* back of, stand up for
2 make sure *or* secure, tie, tie off *or* up, chain, tether; make fast, fasten, fasten down; **anchor,** moor; batten *and* batten

down; **protect,** guard, safeguard, keep, make safe

build one's house upon a rock
BIBLE

ADJS 3 **fast,** fastened, fixed, firm, close, tight, set; **safe,** safe and sound; **protected;** on the safe side; unthreatened, unmolested; unhurt, unharmed, unscathed, intact, untouched, with a whole skin, undamaged

security NOUNS **surety,** indemnity, **guaranty,** guarantee, warranty, insurance, warrant, assurance; **stability,** firmness, soundness, substantiality, solidity; **safety,** safeness

sedate VERBS 1 narcotize, drug, dope <nonformal>; anesthetize, put under; tranquilize, deaden, dull, blunt, obtund, take the edge off, take the sting *or* bite out
ADJS 2 **staid,** sober, sober-minded, **serious,** grave, solemn, sobersided

sedative NOUNS 1 **sedative hypnotic,** depressant; sleeping pill *or* tablet *or* potion; **calmative,** tranquilizer
ADJS 2 **calmative,** calmant, depressant, **soothing,** tranquilizing, quietening; narcotic, opiatic; hypnotic, soporific, somniferous, somnifacient, sleep-inducing

sedentary ADJS **inert,** inactive, static, dormant, passive; **quiescent,** motionless

sediment NOUNS **deposit;** detritus, debris; settlings, deposits, deposition

seduce VERBS **betray,** deceive, mislead, lead astray, lead down the garden *or* the primrose path; **debauch,** ravish, ravage, despoil, ruin; deflower, pop one's cherry <nonformal>; **defile,** soil, sully; **violate,** abuse

seductive ADJS **attractive,** taking, winning, sexy <nonformal>, **provocative,** tantalizing, exciting; appetizing, tempting, toothsome, mouth-watering; seducing, **beguiling,** enticing, inviting, come-hither <nonformal>

see VERBS **behold,** observe, view, witness, perceive, discern, spy, espy, **sight,** have in sight, make out, pick out, descry, spot <nonformal>, discover, notice, take notice of, have one's eye on, distinguish, recognize, **catch sight of,** get a load of <nonformal>, take in, get an eyeful of <nonformal>, look on *or* upon, cast the eyes on *or* upon, **set** *or* **lay eyes on; glimpse,** get *or* catch a glimpse of; see at a glance, see with half an eye; see with one's own eyes

seed NOUNS 1 **sperm,** spermatozoa, semen, milt
2 **stone,** pit, nut; pip; fruit; **grain,** kernel, berry; flaxseed, linseed; bird seed
VERBS 3 **plant,** set, put in; **sow,** seed down, seminate, inseminate; **disseminate,** broadcast, sow broadcast, scatter seed; drill

seedy ADJS **shabby,** shoddy, scruffy, **tacky** <nonformal>, dowdy, tatty, ratty; **ragged,** tattered, torn; **frayed,** frazzled; **out at the elbows**

seek VERBS **quest,** quest after, seek out, look for, hunt, search, dig up, dig around for, nose out, nose around for

seem VERBS appear to be, seem to be, **appear, look,** feel, sound, look to be, appear to one's eyes, have *or* present the appearance of, give the feeling of, strike one as, come on as <nonformal>; have every appearance of, have all the earmarks of, have all the features of, show signs of, have every sign *or* indication of

seemly ADJS **appropriate,** fit, fitting, **proper,** correct, comely; **felicitous,** happy, **apt,** well-chosen; well-put, well-expressed, inspired

seep VERBS ooze, percolate; exude; sweat; secrete

seesaw VERBS **fluctuate,** vary; alternate, vacillate, oscillate, pendulate, blow hot and cold <nonformal>; go through phases, waver, shuffle, swing, sway, wobble, wobble about, flounder, stagger, teeter, totter, **teeter-totter**

seethe VERBS **boil, fume,** foam, simmer, stew, ferment, stir, churn; **mill,** mill around *or* about, stir, roil, moil, be turbulent

see to VERBS **attend to,** look to, advert to, be aware of; **pay attention to,** pay regard to, give mind to, pay mind to <nonformal>, not forget, spare a thought for, **give heed to;** occupy oneself with, concern oneself with, give oneself up to, be absorbed *or* engrossed in, be into <nonformal>; **care for,** take care of, **look after,** see after

segment NOUNS **portion,** share, interest, part, stake, stock, **piece,** bit

segregate VERBS **separate,** separate out *or* off, differentiate, demark, divide, cordon, cordon off; **isolate,** insulate, seclude; **set apart,** keep apart

seize VERBS take *or* get hold of, **lay hold of,** catch *or* grab hold of, glom *or* latch on to <nonformal>, **get** *or* **lay hands on,** clap hands on <nonformal>, put one's hands on, get into one's grasp *or* clutches; get one's fingers *or* hands on; **kidnap,** abduct, snatch <nonformal>

seizure NOUNS **attack,** access, visitation; arrest; **stroke,** ictus, apoplexy; **spasm,** throes, fit, paroxysm, convulsion, eclampsia, frenzy; **usurpation,** arrogation, assumption, taking over

seldom ADVS **infrequently,** unfrequently, rarely, uncommonly, scarcely, hardly, **scarcely** *or* **hardly ever,** not often, only now and then, at infrequent intervals

select NOUNS 1 **choice,** pick, elect, elite, *corps d'élite* <Fr>, chosen; **cream,** flower, cream of the crop, *crème de la crème* <Fr>, salt of the earth; *pièce de résistance* <Fr>; nonesuch, paragon, nonpareil
VERBS 2 make a selection; **pick,** handpick, **pick out, single out,** choose out, smile on, give the nod <nonformal>, jump at, seize on; **decide between,** choose up sides <nonformal>, cull, glean, winnow, sift
ADJS 3 **exclusive,** selective, elect, elite; **choice,** picked, handpicked; **prize,** champion

selection NOUNS 1 **choice,** election, preference, decision, **pick,** choosing, free choice; **specification,** naming, nomination, pointing, fingering <nonformal>, picking out
2 **excerpt, extract,** extraction, excerption, snippet; passage, selected passage

self NOUNS **ego; oneself,** I, me, myself, my humble self, number one <nonformal>, yours truly <nonformal>; the self

self-confidence NOUNS **pride,** proudness, pridefulness; **self-esteem,** self-respect, self-reliance, face, independence, self-sufficiency

self-control NOUNS **self-command,** self-possession, self-mastery, self-government, self-domination, **self-restraint,** self-conquest, self-discipline, **self-denial;** composure, possession, aplomb

self-esteem NOUNS **pride,** proudness, pridefulness; **self-respect,** self-confidence, self-reliance, face, independence, self-sufficiency; pardonable pride

selfish ADJS **self-seeking,** self-serving, self-advancing, self-promoting, self-advertising, ambitious for self, **self-indulgent,** self-pleasing, hedonistic, self-jealous, self-sufficient, **self-interested,** self-absorbed, wrapped up in oneself; possessive; **avaricious,** greedy, grasping, graspy *and* grabby <both nonformal>, acquisitive

self-reliance NOUNS **independence,** self-direction, autarky, autarchy, self-containment, self-sufficiency; self-dependence; inner-direction

self-respect NOUNS **self-esteem,** self-reliance, self-consequence, face, independence, self-sufficiency; pardonable pride; positive self-image

self-righteous ADJS **sanctimonious,** sanctified, pious, pietistic, pietistical, pharisaic, pharisaical, holier-than-thou

self-sufficient ADJS self-confident, self-reliant, **independent;** self-complacent, **smug,** complacent, self-contained

sell VERBS 1 **merchandise, market,** move, turn over, sell off, make *or* effect a sale; convert into cash, turn into money; **retail,** sell retail, sell over the counter; **wholesale,** sell wholesale, job, be jobber *or* wholesaler for; sell like hotcakes
2 **convince; win over,** lead one to believe, bring over, bring round, talk over, talk around, bring to reason, bring to one's senses, **persuade,** lead to believe, give to understand; sell one on <nonformal>

sell out VERBS **betray,** double-cross *and* two-time <both nonformal>, sell down the river <nonformal>, turn in; inform on

seminar NOUNS **discussion, panel,** panel discussion, open discussion, joint discussion, symposium, colloquium, conference; proseminar

send VERBS send off *or* away, send forth; **dispatch,** remit, consign, forward; **mail,** post, dispatch; **transmit,** radiate, beam

send for VERBS **summon, call,** demand, preconize; call for, send after, bid come; **cite,** subpoena, summon forth, call out

send-off NOUNS **leave-taking,** leave, parting, departure, congé; Godspeed; **adieu,** one's adieus, **farewell,** aloha, **good-bye;** valedictory address, valedictory, valediction, parting words; parting *or* Parthian shot; swan song; viaticum

senile ADJS decrepit, doddering, doddery; **childish,** childlike, in one's second childhood, **doting**

senior NOUNS 1 **superior,** higher-up

<nonformal>, principal, big shot <nonformal>; Sr, *senex* <L>, **elder,** dean, *doyen* <Fr>, *doyenne* <Fr>
ADJS 2 ranking, older, elder, dean; **oldest,** eldest

senior citizen NOUNS **old man,** old woman, elder, oldster <nonformal>; golden-ager, geriatric; old chap, old party, old codger <nonformal>, geezer *and* old geezer <both nonformal>, old duffer <nonformal>, old-timer <nonformal>, dotard, veteran

seniority NOUNS **eldership,** deanship, primogeniture; eminence, **stature,** rank, preeminence, priority, precedence

sensation NOUNS **sense, feeling;** sense impression, sense-datum *or* -data, percept, perception, sense perception; experience, sensory experience; **thrill,** titillation; astonishment, amazement, wonderful thing, nine days' wonder, amazing *or* astonishing thing, quite a thing, really something

sensational ADJS **lurid,** yellow, **melodramatic,** Barnumesque; spine-chilling, eye-popping <nonformal>; **wonderful,** wondrous, marvelous, miraculous, fantastic, fabulous, phenomenal, **prodigious,** stupendous, unheard-of, unprecedented, extraordinary, exceptional, rare, unique, singular, **remarkable,** striking

sense NOUNS 1 **meaning,** significance, signification, *significatum* <L>, *signifié* <Fr>, point, idea, **purport,** import, where one is coming from <nonformal>; **sensibleness,** reasonableness, reason, rationality, sanity, saneness, **soundness;** good *or* common *or* plain sense, **horse sense** <nonformal>
VERBS 2 **feel,** experience, **perceive,** apprehend, be sensible of, be conscious *or* aware of, apperceive; taste, smell, see, hear, touch; be sensitive to; **understand,** comprehend, apprehend, **know,** conceive, realize, appreciate, make sense out of, make something of; **intuit,** feel intuitively, **feel** *or* **know in one's bones** <nonformal>, **have a feeling,** have a funny feeling <nonformal>, **get** *or* **have the impression,** have a hunch <nonformal>, just know, know instinctively

sensible ADJS **reasonable,** rational, logical; practical, pragmatic; philosophical; commonsense, commonsensical <nonformal>; **levelheaded,** balanced, coolheaded, cool, **sound,** sane, sober, **sober-minded,** well-balanced

sensitive ADJS 1 responsive, sympathetic, compassionate; empathic, empathetic; delicate, tactful, considerate, courteous, solicitous, refined; **oversensitive,** thin-skinned; sensible, receptive; susceptible, impressionable; **tender,** soft, tender-hearted, softhearted, warmhearted
2 irritable, edgy, touchy, prickly

sensual ADJS **lascivious,** lecherous, sexy, salacious, carnal, animal, **sexual,** lustful, ithyphallic, **hot,** horny *and* sexed-up *and* hot to trot <all nonformal>; prurient, itching, itchy <nonformal>; concupiscent, lickerish, libidinous, randy, horny <nonformal>, lubricious; erotic, fleshly

sensuous ADJS **captivating,** irresistible, ravishing, enravishing; **winning,** winsome, taking, fetching, heart-robbing; inviting, tempting, tantalizing; voluptuous, zaftig <nonformal>

sentiment NOUNS 1 **love,** affection, attachment, devotion, fondness, warm feeling, soft spot in one's heart, weakness <nonformal>, like, **liking,** fancy, shine <nonformal>; **passion,** tender feeling *or* passion, **ardor,** ardency, fervor, heart, flame; **regard,** admiration
2 **opinion,** feeling, sense, impression, reaction, **notion,** idea, thought, mind, attitude, stance, posture, position, mindset, **view,** point of view

sentimental ADJS sentimentalized, soft, **mawkish, maudlin,** cloying; sticky *and* gooey *and* schmaltzy *and* sappy *and* soppy <all nonformal>, bathetic

sentry NOUNS **watchman,** watch, watcher; watchkeeper; **sentinel,** picket

separate VERBS 1 **divide,** disjoin, disunite, draw apart, dissociate, disassociate, grow apart, **disjoint,** disengage, disarticulate, disconnect; **part,** cut the knot, **divorce,** estrange; **alienate, segregate,** separate off, factor out, sequester, isolate, curtain off, shut off, set apart *or* aside, split off, cut off *or* out *or* loose *or* adrift; **part company,** split up, disband, scatter, **disperse,** break up, break it up <nonformal>, **go separate ways,** diverge
ADJS 2 **distinct,** discrete; unjoined, unconnected, unattached, unaccompanied, unattended, unassociated; **apart,** asunder, **in two;** discontinuous, noncontiguous, divergent; **isolated,** insular,

detached, detachable, free-standing, free-floating, autonomous; **independent,** self-contained, stand-alone <nonformal>; separated, alienated, withdrawn, aloof, standoffish, detached, removed

sequel NOUNS sequela *or* sequelae, sequelant, sequent, sequitur, consequence; **continuation,** continuance, follow-up *or* follow-through <nonformal>; consequent, sequent, sequence, eventuality, eventuation, **upshot,** outcome

sequence NOUNS **series,** succession, run, consecution, progression, course, gradation; **subsequence,** posteriority, following, supervenience, supervention

sequester VERBS **reserve,** conserve, retain, husband, keep *or* hold back, withhold; **keep in reserve,** keep in store, keep on hand, keep by one; put in escrow; confiscate, sequestrate, impound

seraph NOUNS **angel,** celestial, celestial *or* heavenly being; seraphim <pl>, angel of love

serendipity NOUNS **discovery,** accidental *or* chance discovery, happening *or* stumbling upon, tripping over, casual discovery; good luck *or* fortune, happy chance, dumb luck <nonformal>; **fortuity,** randomness, fortuitousness

serene ADJS **calm,** placid, quiet, **tranquil,** peaceful, untroubled, at peace; **cool,** coolheaded, cool as a cucumber <nonformal>; philosophical

serf NOUNS esne; helot, villein; peon

serial NOUNS 1 installment, *livraison* <Fr>; **periodical,** journal, gazette; ephemeris; daytime serial, soap opera *or* soap <nonformal>
ADJS 2 **periodic** *or* periodical, seasonal, epochal, **cyclic** *or* cyclical, isochronal, metronomic; continuing

series NOUNS **succession,** run, **sequence,** consecution, progression, course, gradation; **continuum,** plenum

serious ADJS **sedate, staid,** sober, sober-minded, grave, solemn, sobersided; temperate, moderate; **earnest,** thoughtful, sincere, weighty; moving, inspiring

sermon NOUNS **lesson,** teaching, instruction, lecture, harangue, **discourse,** disquisition, exposition, **talk,** homily, preachment; **moral,** morality, moralization, moral lesson

serum NOUNS serous fluid, blood serum; **antitoxin,** antitoxic serum; **antivenin;** antiserum

servant NOUNS 1 servitor, help; **domestic,** domestic help, domestic servant, house servant; live-in help, day help; scullion
2 **believer, disciple,** follower, faithful servant

serve VERBS 1 **lend** *or* **give oneself,** render service to, do service for, labor in behalf of; minister to, cater to; attend; pander to; do duty; **work for,** be in service with, serve one's every need
2 **suffice, do,** just do, **answer;** work, be equal to, **avail;** answer *or* serve the purpose, do the trick *and* fill the bill <both nonformal>, **suit**

service NOUNS 1 **act of kindness,** kindness, favor, mercy, **benefit,** benefaction, benevolence, benignity, blessing, turn, break <nonformal>, **good turn,** good *or* kind deed, good *or* kind offices, obligation, grace, act of grace, courtesy, kindly act, labor of love
2 **military service;** active service *or* duty; military obligation; selective service, national service <Brit>; branch of the service
3 servanthood, servitude <old>, servitorship, *servitium* <L>; **ministry,** ministration, attendance, tendance; divine service, public worship, **liturgy**, office, duty, exercises, **devotions;** church service
VERBS 4 **repair,** mend, fix, fix up <nonformal>, do up, doctor <nonformal>, put in repair, put in shape, set to rights, put in order *or* condition; **condition, recondition,** commission, put in commission, ready; **overhaul**

serviceable ADJS **useful,** employable, of use, of service, **functional,** utilitarian, of general utility *or* application

servile ADJS **slavish,** subservient, **menial,** base, mean; submissive, obsequious

servitude NOUNS **subjection,** compulsory *or* involuntary servitude, servility, bond service, indentureship

session NOUNS **meeting;** sitting, sit-down <nonformal>, séance; semester, trimester, term, academic year

set NOUNS 1 **clique,** coterie, circle, ring; **suit,** suite, series, outfit *and* kit <both nonformal>; group, matching pair *or* set, his and hers <nonformal>, couple, pair, twins, look-alikes, two of a kind, birds of a feather, peas in a pod
2 inclination, mind, **tendency,** grain, vein, mental set, mindset, **leaning,** propensity, proclivity, predilection, preference, predisposition

VERBS 3 **place,** put, lay, pose, posit, site, seat, stick <nonformal>, **station,** post; park, plump down <nonformal>;
4 **solidify,** conglomerate, agglomerate, conglobate; **congeal,** coagulate, clabber <nonformal>, **clot**
ADJS 5 **demarcated,** delimited, defined, definite, determined, determinate, specific, stated, fixed, **established,** stabilized, **entrenched,** vested, firmly established; **confirmed,** inveterate; settled

setback NOUNS **disappointment,** comedown, **letdown** <nonformal>; failure, fizzle <nonformal>, fiasco; **reverse,** reversal, devolution

setting NOUNS **background,** backdrop, ground, surround, field, scene, arena, theater, locale; stage, stage setting, stage set, *mise-en-scène* <Fr>; **environment,** environing circumstances, context, frame, surround, surrounding conditions; hardening, solidification

settle VERBS 1 **settle down,** sit down, locate, park <nonformal>, ensconce, ensconce oneself; take up one's abode *or* quarters, make one's home, **reside,** inhabit; **colonize,** populate, people
2 **sink, set; decline,** lower, **subside,** give way, lapse, cave, cave in; **light; land,** perch, come to rest; **arrange,** compose, patch up, adjust, straighten out, bring to terms *or* an understanding; make peace
3 **pay in full,** pay off, pay up <nonformal>, **discharge,** square, **clear,** liquidate, amortize, retire; pay the bill; settle the matter

settlement NOUNS 1 **peopling,** peoplement, empeoplement, **population,** inhabiting; **colonization,** plantation
2 **adjustment,** accommodation, resolution, composition of differences, compromise, arrangement, terms; **endowment,** investment, foundation; **dowry,** *dot* <Fr>, portion, marriage portion; **discharge,** clearance, liquidation, amortization, satisfaction

settler NOUNS **colonist,** colonizer, colonial, immigrant, planter; **homesteader;** *habitant* <Canadian & Louisiana Fr>; **squatter,** pioneer

set up VERBS **establish,** fix, plant, site, pitch, seat, set; found, base, ground, lay the foundation; **build,** put up; **install,** invest, vest; **inaugurate,** institute

set upon VERBS **attack, fall on** *or* upon, **descend on** *or* upon, come down on, swoop down on; pounce upon; lift *or* raise *or* lift a hand against

seventh heaven NOUNS **bliss,** blissfulness; paradise, heaven, cloud nine

sever VERBS **dissever,** cut off *or* away *or* loose, shear off, hack through, hack off, ax, amputate; **cleave,** split, fissure; sunder, cut in two, dichotomize, halve, bisect; **tear, rend,** rive, rend asunder

several ADJS divers, **sundry,** various; some five or six, etc; upwards of

severe ADJS 1 **harsh,** fierce, **rigorous,** rough, stringent, astringent, strident, **sharp, keen,** sharpish, cruel, dour, grave, incisive, trenchant, **cutting,** biting, stinging, **scathing,** stabbing, **piercing, poignant,** penetrating, edged, double-edged
2 **inornate,** unornate, **unelaborate,** unfancy, unfussy; austere, monkish, cloistral, stark, Spartan

sew VERBS **stitch,** needle; stitch up, sew up; **tailor**

sewer NOUNS **gutter,** pit, sink, sink of corruption; den of iniquity, den, **fleshpots,** hellhole; hole *and* joint *and* the pits <all nonformal>; Sodom, Gomorrah, Babylon; **brothel**

sex NOUNS 1 gender; maleness, masculinity, femaleness, femininity; **genitals,** genitalia
2 **copulation,** sex act, having sex, having intercourse, *le sport* <Fr>, coupling, mating, coition, **coitus,** pareunia, venery, **intercourse, sexual intercourse,** cohabitation, commerce, sexual commerce, congress, sexual congress, sexual union, sexual relations, relations, marital relations, marriage act, sleeping together *or* with

making the beast with two backs
SHAKESPEARE

ADJS 3 **sexual,** sexlike, gamic, coital, libidinal; **erotic,** sexy, amorous; nuptial; venereal; **carnal, sensual,** voluptuous, fleshly

sex appeal NOUNS **sexual attraction** *or* attractiveness *or* magnetism, sexiness

sexist NOUNS 1 male chauvinist, male chauvinist pig *or* MCP <nonformal>, manist, masculist, feminist, female chauvinist, womanist
ADJS 2 **man-hating,** misandrist; **woman-hating,** misogynic, misogynis-

tic, misogynous; male- *or* female-chauvinistic

sexless ADJS **unsexual,** unsexed; asexual, **neuter,** neutral; castrated, emasculated, eunuchized; **cold,** frigid; impotent

sex object NOUNS sex queen, sex goddess; stud <nonformal>; piece *and* meat *and* piece of meat *and* ass *and* piece of ass *and* hot number <all nonformal>

sex organs NOUNS **genitals,** genitalia, reproductive organs, pudenda, private parts, privy parts, privates <nonformal>; **male organs; penis,** phallus, *lingam* <Skt>; gonads; **testes,** testicles, balls *and* nuts *and* rocks *and* ballocks *and* family jewels <all nonformal>; scrotum, bag *and* basket <both nonformal>, cod <old>; **female organs; vulva,** *yoni* <Skt>, cunt <nonformal>; **vagina;** clitoris; labia, labia majora, labia minora, lips, nymphae; ovary; uterus, womb

sexual ADJS 1 gametic, gamic; **spermatic,** spermic, **seminal,** spermatozoal, spermatozoan, spermatozoic; sporal, sporous, sporoid; sporogenous
2 **lascivious,** lecherous, sexy, salacious, carnal, animal, **lustful,** ithyphallic, **hot,** horny *and* sexed-up *and* hot to trot <all nonformal>; prurient, itching, itchy <nonformal>; concupiscent, lickerish, libidinous, randy, horny <nonformal>, lubricious; **sensual,** fleshly; goatish, satyric, priapic, gynecomaniacal; **amorous,** amatory, amative, erotic

sexual desire NOUNS **sensuous** *or* carnal desire, bodily appetite, **biological urge,** venereal appetite *or* desire, sexual longing, **lust,** desire, lusts *or* desires of the flesh, itch, lech <nonformal>; **craving,** coveting, hunger, thirst, appetite

sexual intercourse NOUNS **copulation,** sex act, coupling, mating, coition, **coitus,** pareunia, venery, cohabitation, commerce, sexual commerce, congress, sexual congress, sexual union, sexual relations, relations, marital relations, marriage act, act of love, sleeping together *or* with; **lovemaking,** dalliance, amorous dalliance

sexy ADJS 1 **lustful,** prurient, hot, steamy, concupiscent, lickerish, libidinous, **salacious,** passionate, hot-blooded, itching, **horny** *and* hot to trot *and* sexed-up <all nonformal>, randy, goatish
2 **alluring,** fascinating, captivating, attractive, **seductive,** seducing, **beguiling,** enticing, inviting, come-hither <nonformal>; flirtatious, coquettish; **provocative,** *provoquant* <Fr>; appetizing, mouth-watering, piquant; **irresistible**

shabby ADJS **shoddy,** seedy, scruffy, **tacky** <nonformal>, dowdy, tatty, ratty; **niggardly,** niggard, pinchpenny, penurious, **grudging,** mean, mingy, sordid

shack NOUNS **hut,** hutch, **shanty,** crib, hole-in-the-wall <nonformal>, **shed;** lean-to

shackle NOUNS 1 restraint, **restraints,** fetter, hamper, trammel, trammels, **manacle,** gyves, bond, **bonds,** irons, chains, Oregon boat; electronic ankle bracelet *and* offender's tag *and* monitor
VERBS 2 **bind,** restrain, tie, tie up, put the clamps on, **strap,** lash, leash, pinion, fasten, secure, make fast; **fetter,** manacle, gyve, **put in irons; handcuff,** tie one's hands; tie hand and foot, hogtie <nonformal>; **hamper,** impede, cramp, embarrass; hobble, hamstring

shade NOUNS 1 **shadow,** shadiness; thick *or* dark shade, gloom; mere shadow; **phantom,** phantasm; nuance

the shadow of a shade
AESCHYLUS

VERBS 2 **screen,** veil, curtain, shutter, draw the curtains, put up *or* close the shutters; cover; **shadow**

shading NOUNS **gradation,** graduation, grading, staging, phasing, tapering, shadowing, overshadowing, **clouding,** overclouding, obnubilation, gathering of the clouds, overcast

shadow NOUNS **shade,** shadiness; umbra, umbrage, umbrageousness; thick *or* dark shade, gloom; penumbra; silhouette

shady ADJS 1 **disreputable,** discreditable, dishonorable, unsavory, up to no good, **seamy,** sordid; unrespectable, ignoble, ignominious, infamous, inglorious; notorious
2 **shadowy,** shadowed, shaded, darkling, umbral, umbrageous; overshadowed, overshaded, obumbrate, obumbrated; penumbral; screened, veiled, curtained

shaft NOUNS 1 air passage, air duct, airway, air shaft, **air hole,** air tube; **vent,** venthole, ventage, ventiduct; **ventilator,** ventilating shaft

2 **pit,** well, sump; **excavation,** dig, diggings, workings
3 **pillar,** stele *or* stela, column, memorial column, rostral column, manubial column; upright

shaggy ADJS **hairy,** bushy, tufty, shagged; matted, tomentose; mopheaded, burrheaded, shockheaded, unshorn; **nappy,** pily; nubby *or* nubbly; uncombed, matted

shake NOUNS 1 **quake,** quiver, quaver, falter, **tremor,** tremble, shiver, shudder, twitter, didder, dither; wobble
VERBS 2 tremble, quiver, quaver, cringe, cower, totter, teeter, dodder
3 **agitate,** disturb, perturb, shake up, perturbate, **disquiet,** discompose, upset, trouble, unsettle, stir, flutter the dovecote, fret, convulse; shake in one's boots *or* shoes

shakedown NOUNS 1 **extortion, blackmail,** bloodsucking, vampirism; protection racket; badger game
2 **tryout,** workout, **rehearsal,** practice; pilot plan *or* program; **dry run,** dummy run; *Gedankenexperiment* <Ger>; **trial run,** practical test; shakedown cruise

shaken ADJS **agitated,** perturbed, disturbed, troubled, disquieted, upset, unsettled, **discomposed, flustered,** ruffled

shakeout NOUNS **sorting,** sorting out, assortment, sifting, screening, triage, culling, selection, winnowing

shake up VERBS 1 **agitate,** perturb, disturb, trouble, disquiet, discompose, discombobulate <nonformal>, unsettle, **stir,** ruffle, shake, shock, upset, make waves, jolt, jar, rock, stagger, electrify, bring *or* pull one up short, give one a turn <nonformal>
2 **rearrange,** reorganize, reconstitute, **reorder,** restructure, reshuffle, tinker with; redistribute, reallocate, realign

shaky ADJS 1 **unsteady,** rickety, teetering, teetery, tottery, tottering, doddering, rocky <nonformal>; **tremulous,** trembling, trepidant, shivery
2 **insecure, unsound, infirm,** unsolid, **unstable,** unsubstantial, insubstantial, **unsteadfast,** desultory

shallow NOUNS 1 **shoal,** shallows, shallow *or* shoal water, flat, shelf
ADJS 2 **depthless,** not deep, unprofound; **surface,** on *or* near the surface, merely surface; **superficial,** cursory, slight, light, cosmetic, merely cosmetic, thin, jejune, trivial; unprofound; shallow-witted, shallow-minded, shallow-brained, shallow-headed, shallow-pated; **frivolous,** flighty, light, volatile, frothy, featherbrained, birdwitted, birdbrained

sham NOUNS 1 **hoax,** deception, spoof <nonformal>, **humbug,** flam, **fake** *and* fakement, **rip-off** <nonformal>; false front
VERBS 2 **pretend,** simulate, counterfeit, fake <nonformal>, **feign,** make out like <nonformal>, make a show of, play, playact <nonformal>, act *or* play a part, put up a front <nonformal>
ADJS 3 **imitation,** mock, copied, fake *and* phony <both nonformal>, counterfeit, forged, plagiarized, unoriginal, ungenuine, spurious; hypocritical

shamble NOUNS **leisurely gait,** snail's *or* tortoise's pace; slouch, shuffle, plod

shame NOUNS 1 **chagrin,** distress; embarrassment, abashment, discomfiture, egg on one's face <nonformal>, discomposure; **humiliation,** shamefacedness, mortification, disgrace, red face; dirty shame *and* low-down dirty shame <both nonformal>, crying *or* burning shame
VERBS 2 **disgrace,** put to shame, hold up to shame; hold up to public shame *or* public scorn *or* public ridicule, pillory, bring shame upon

shameful ADJS **disgraceful,** pitiful, deplorable, opprobrious, sad, sorry, too bad; degrading, debasing, demeaning, beneath one, beneath one's dignity, *infra dignitatem* <L>, infra dig <nonformal>, unbecoming, unworthy of one

shameless ADJS **brazen,** brazenfaced, boldfaced, barefaced, brassy <nonformal>, **bold,** bold as brass <nonformal>, unblushing, unabashed, aweless, dead *or* lost to shame; **blatant,** flagrant, lurid, extravagant, sensational, **spectacular,** glaring, flaring, flaunting, screaming <nonformal>, obtrusive, vulgar, crude; meretricious

shanghai VERBS **seize, kidnap,** abduct, snatch <nonformal>, carry off

shanty NOUNS **shack,** crib, hole-in-the-wall <nonformal>, **shed;** lean-to

shape NOUNS 1 **form,** figure; figuration, **configuration;** formation, **conformation;** structure; **build,** make, frame, **physique,** body-build
VERBS 2 **form,** formalize, **fashion,** tailor, frame, figure, **lick into shape** <nonformal>; work, knead; take form, **shape up,** take shape

3 **plan,** devise, contrive, design, frame, cast, concert, lay plans

shapeless ADJS **formless,** featureless, characterless, nondescript, inchoate, lumpy, lumpish, baggy <nonformal>, inform; amorphous, **chaotic,** orderless, disorderly, unordered, unorganized, confused, anarchic, inchoate

shapely ADJS **well-shaped,** well-proportioned, well-made, **well-formed,** well-favored; comely; trim, trig <old>, neat, spruce; well-built, built, stacked *or* well-stacked <both nonformal>, curvaceous, curvy <nonformal>, amply endowed, built for comfort *or* built like a brick shithouse <both nonformal>, callipygian, callipygous; Junoesque, statuesque

shard NOUNS **piece,** particle, bit, scrap, bite, **fragment,** morsel, crumb, potsherd

share NOUNS 1 **portion,** interest, part, stake, stock, **piece,** bit, segment; **bite** *and* **cut** *and* **slice** *and* **chunk** *and* slice of the pie *or* melon *and* piece of the action <all nonformal>, **allotment, proportion, percentage,** measure, quantum, **quota**
VERBS 2 **share in,** come in for a share, **go shares,** be partners in, have a stake in, have a percentage *or* piece of <nonformal>, **divide with,** divvy up with <nonformal>, halve, go halves; **share and share alike**

shared ADJS **mutual,** commutual, **common,** joint, communal, sharing, conjoint; respective, two-way

sharing NOUNS **apportionment,** apportioning, portioning, division, **partition,** repartition, partitionment, partitioning, parceling, budgeting, rationing, **dividing**

shark NOUNS **expert,** adept, proficient; sharp *or* sharpy *and* no slouch *and* tough act to follow <all nonformal>; vulture, **skillful gambler,** sharp, sharper, dean *and* professor *and* river gambler *and* dice gospeller *and* sharpie <all nonformal>; **cardsharp** *or* cardshark, cardsharper

sharp ADJS 1 **acrimonious, harsh,** fierce, **rigorous,** severe, rough, stringent, astringent, strident, **keen,** incisive, trenchant, **cutting,** biting, stinging, **scathing,** stabbing, **piercing,** poignant, penetrating, edged, double-edged; sharp as a razor *or* needle *or* tack
2 **steep,** precipitous, bluff, plunging, abrupt, bold, **sheer,** rapid; vertical
3 **alert,** quick, agile, nimble, quick on the trigger *or* draw *or* uptake <all nonformal>; **smart,** bright, keen; **wily,** crafty; calculating, scheming
4 **smart,** elegant; spiffy *and* classy *and* nifty *and* snazzy <all nonformal>
ADVS 5 **punctually,** precisely, exactly; **on time,** on the minute *or* instant, to the minute *or* second, **on the dot** <nonformal>

sharpen VERBS 1 **stimulate,** whet, pique, provoke, quicken, enliven, liven up, pick up, jazz up <nonformal>, animate, **exhilarate,** invigorate, galvanize, fillip, give a fillip to; infuse life into, give new life to, revive, renew, resuscitate
2 **edge,** acuminate, aculeate, spiculate, taper; **whet,** hone, oilstone, file, grind; strop, strap; **point;** file to a point

shatter VERBS **splinter,** shiver, break to *or* into pieces, fragmentize, break to *or* into smithereens <nonformal>; **smash,** crush, crunch, squash, make mincemeat of, make hamburger of <nonformal>

sheath NOUNS **case,** casing, encasement; sheathing

sheathe VERBS **clothe,** wrap, enwrap, lap, envelop, shroud, enshroud; wrap *or* bundle *or* muffle up; swathe, swaddle

sheen NOUNS **shine,** shininess, **luster,** gloss, glint; **glow,** gleam, flush, sunset glow

sheep NOUNS 1 jumbuck <Australia>; **lamb,** lambkin, yeanling; teg <Brit>; **ewe,** ewe lamb; **ram,** tup <Brit>, wether; bellwether; mutton
2 **conformist,** conformer, trimmer, parrot, yes-man, organization man

sheepish ADJS **contrite,** abject, humble, humbled, **apologetic,** touched, softened, melted

sheer ADJS 1 **steep,** precipitous, bluff, plunging, abrupt, bold, sharp, rapid; **mere,** stark, bare, bare-bones, plain, simple, unadorned, unenhanced
ADJS 2 **transparent,** transpicuous, light-pervious; show-through, see-through, peekaboo, revealing; **diaphanous,** thin; **gossamer,** gossamery, filmy, gauzy
ADVS 3 **perpendicularly,** up and down, **straight up and down;** plumb, *à plomb* <Fr>; at right angles
4 **absolutely,** perfectly, quite, right, stark, clean, plumb <nonformal>, plain

shelf NOUNS **ledge,** shoulder, corbel,

beam-end; mantel, mantelshelf, mantelpiece
shell NOUNS 1 seashell, lorication, lorica, conch; test, testa, episperm, pericarp, elytron, scute, scutum; **protective covering,** cortex, thick skin *or* hide
2 **cartridge,** cartouche, ball cartridge; blank cartridge, dry ammunition
VERBS 3 **husk,** hull, pod, shuck
4 **bombard,** blast, strafe, cannonade, mortar, barrage, blitz; rake, enfilade; pour a broadside into; cannon
shellacking NOUNS **utter defeat,** total defeat, overwhelming defeat, crushing defeat, smashing defeat, decisive defeat; no contest; **smearing** *and* **pasting** *and* creaming *and* **clobbering** *and* whomping <all nonformal>; whitewash *or* **whitewashing** <nonformal>, **shutout**
shelter NOUNS 1 **quarters,** living quarters; lodgings, lodging, lodgment; housing, **cover,** covert, coverture; concealment
VERBS 2 **protect,** guard, safeguard, secure, **shield,** screen, cover, cloak
sheltered ADJS **protected, guarded,** safeguarded, defended; safe; **shielded,** screened, covered, cloaked; cloistered, sequestered, sequestrated, isolated, secluded
shelve VERBS **put away,** lay away, **put aside,** lay *or* set *or* wave *or* cast *or* push aside, sideline <nonformal>, put *or* lay *or* set by; **pigeonhole,** put on the shelf, put in mothballs; put on ice <nonformal>
shenanigans NOUNS horseplay; monkey tricks *and* monkeyshines <both nonformal>
shepherd NOUNS 1 **herd,** herdsman, **herder,** drover, herdboy; shepherdess, **sheepherder,** sheepman
VERBS 2 **escort,** conduct, have in tow <nonformal>, marshal, **usher,** guide, lead; ride herd on <nonformal>
shield NOUNS 1 **cover,** covering, coverage, covert, coverture, housing, hood, cowl, cowling; **screen,** aegis, shroud, veil, pall, mantle, curtain, hanging, drape, drapery; **armor,** mail
VERBS 2 **defend,** guard, screen, secure, guard against; **safeguard,** protect; stand by the side of, flank; **shelter,** cover, cloak, shroud <old>
shift NOUNS 1 **moving,** removal, movement, relocation; **displacement,** delocalization, transition, **modulation,** qualification
2 work shift, **tour,** tour of duty, stint, bit, **watch, trick,** time, **turn,** relay, spell *or* turn of work; day shift, night shift, swing shift, graveyard shift <nonformal>, dogwatch, anchor watch; lobster trick; split shift
VERBS 3 **deviate,** depart from, vary, diverge, divaricate, branch off, angle, angle off; **digress,** divagate, turn aside, go out of the way, detour, take a side road; **swerve,** veer, sheer, curve, **turn,** trend, bend, heel, bear off; change horses in midstream, **change; change over,** switch over <nonformal>, switch
shifting ADJS **inconstant,** changeable, changeful, changing, uncertain, inconsistent; **shifty,** unreliable, undependable; **variable,** deviable, whimsical, **capricious,** fickle, off-again-on-again; **erratic,** eccentric, freakish; volatile, **fluctuating,** vacillating, wavering
shiftless ADJS **improvident,** thriftless, unthrifty, uneconomical; **feckless,** thoughtless, heedless; negligent, **unenterprising**
shifty ADJS **tricky,** trickish, cute, finagling, chiseling <nonformal>; **evasive,** slippery, slippery as an eel; **cunning,** crafty, artful, wily, devious, unstraightforward
shill NOUNS decoy, **come-on man** <nonformal>, plant, capper, stool pigeon, stoolie <nonformal>
shillelagh NOUNS **staff,** stave; **cane,** stick, walking stick, handstaff
shimmer NOUNS 1 **glitter,** glimmer, twinkle, blink; sparkle, spark; **scintillation,** scintilla; coruscation
VERBS 2 **glitter,** glimmer, twinkle, blink, spangle, tinsel, coruscate; **sparkle,** spark, **scintillate; glisten,** glister
shindig NOUNS **dance,** hop <nonformal>, dancing party, shindy <nonformal>; **party,** festivity, fete, brawl <nonformal>
shine NOUNS 1 shininess, **luster, sheen, gloss,** glint; **glow, gleam,** flush, sunset glow; lambency; **incandescence,** candescence
VERBS 2 shine forth, **burn, give light,** incandesce; **glow,** beam, gleam, glint, luster, glance; **buff,** burnish, polish, rub up, furbish
shining ADJS **illustrious,** lustrous, glorious, brilliant, splendid, splendorous, splendrous, splendent, resplendent, bright; **luminous,** incandescent, candescent; **radiant,** shiny, burning, lamping,

streaming; **glossy,** glassy, *glacé* <Fr>, bright as a new penny, **polished,** burnished, shined

shining example NOUNS **paragon,** ideal, beau ideal, nonpareil, person to look up to, *chevalier sans peur et sans reproche* <Fr>, **good example,** role model, **hero,** superhero

shirk VERBS **slack,** lie *or* rest upon one's oars, not pull one's weight; **lie down on the job** <nonformal>; soldier, duck duty, **goof off** *and* dog it <both nonformal>, goldbrick <nonformal>; **malinger**

shiver NOUNS 1 **tingle,** tingling; quiver, shudder, tremor, tremor of excitement, rush <nonformal>; **shake,** quake, quaver, falter, **tremor, tremble,** twitter, didder, dither
VERBS 2 **tremble,** shake, quake, quiver, quaver; tremble *or* quake *or* shake in one's boots *or* shoes, tremble like an aspen leaf, shake all over

shock NOUNS 1 **trauma; start,** jar, jolt, turn; **concussion,** impact, crunch, smash; **blow,** hard *or* nasty *or* staggering blow
VERBS 2 **offend,** give offense, **repel,** put off, turn off <nonformal>, **revolt,** disgust, nauseate, sicken, make one sick; **horrify,** appall; **shake up,** upset, jolt, jar, rock, stagger, electrify, bring *or* pull one up short, give one a turn <nonformal>; **startle,** electrify, **give one a turn** <nonformal>, give the shock of one's life, make one jump out of his skin

shocking ADJS **astonishing**; eye-opening, eye-popping <nonformal>; **startling,** electrifying, staggering, stunning, jarring, jolting; **scandalous,** outrageous

shod ADJS shoed, booted, *chaussé* <Fr>

shoddy ADJS **shabby,** seedy, scruffy, **tacky** <nonformal>, dowdy, tatty, ratty; **slovenly, sloppy** <nonformal>, schlocky <nonformal>, lumpen, chintzy, grubby <nonformal>, **frowzy,** blowzy, tacky <nonformal>

shoo-in NOUNS sure success, foregone conclusion, sure-fire proposition <nonformal>; **winner** *and* **natural** <both nonformal>; sure thing *and* sure bet *and* cinch *and* lead-pipe cinch <all nonformal>

shook ADJS **startled,** shocked, electrified, jarred, jolted, shaken, staggered, **given a turn** *or* **jar** *or* **jolt,** taken aback, bowled down *or* over <nonformal>, struck all of a heap <nonformal>, able to be knocked down with a feather

shoot NOUNS 1 **rapids,** white water; chute, sault
2 **offshoot,** offset, **branch,** sprout, filiation; sucker, slip
VERBS 3 **fire,** fire off, let off, let fly, **discharge,** eject; **riddle,** pepper, pelt, pump full of lead <nonformal>; snipe, pick off; potshot, take a potshot

shoot up VERBS 1 **spring up,** jump up, **leap up,** vault up, start up, fly up, pop up, bob up; float up, surface, break water; **gush, jet,** spurt, fountain; **inject,** mainline <nonformal>
2 **inject,** mainline; jab *or* get off <nonformal>

shop NOUNS 1 **office;** store, boutique, specialty shop
VERBS 2 **market,** go shopping, go marketing; **shop around;** window-shop, comparison-shop, **browse**

shore NOUNS 1 **coast,** *côte* <Fr>; **strand,** *playa* <Sp>, beach, beachfront, beachside shingle, plage, lido, riviera; waterside, **waterfront;** shoreline, coastline; **seashore,** coast, seacoast, seaside, seaboard
ADJS 2 **coastal,** littoral, seaside, shoreside; oceanfront, oceanside; seaside, seafront, shorefront, shoreline; beachfront

shore up VERBS **strengthen,** invigorate, fortify, beef up <nonformal>, brace, buttress, prop, support, undergird; reinforce, undergird, bolster, **bolster up,** shore, prop up

short ADJS 1 **brief,** abbreviated, abbreviatory; concise; **curt,** curtate, decurtate; **succinct,** summary, synoptic, synoptical, compendious, compact; **little**

short and sweet
THOMAS LODGE

2 **financially embarrassed** *or* distressed, **pinched,** feeling the pinch, squeezed, on the edge *or* ragged edge <nonformal>, down to bedrock, **short of money** *or* **funds** *or* **cash,** out-of-pocket
ADVS 3 **abruptly,** suddenly, all of a sudden

shortage NOUNS **want,** lack, need, deficiency, deficit, shortfall, **incompleteness,** defectiveness, shortcoming, imperfection

shortcoming NOUNS **imperfection,** imperfectness; **unperfectedness; fault-**

iness, defectiveness, defectibility; **deficiency,** lack, want, shortage, **inadequacy,** inadequateness; **weakness,** frailty, infirmity, failure, **failing,** foible

shortcut NOUNS cut, cutoff; shortest way; **beeline**

shorten VERBS **abridge,** condense, reduce, compress, cut, clip; capsule, capsulize, encapsulate; **put in a nutshell**

shortfall NOUNS **want,** lack, need, deficiency, deficit, shortage, wantage, **incompleteness,** defectiveness, shortcoming, imperfection

short-lived ADJS **transient,** transitory, transitive; **temporary,** temporal; **impermanent,** unenduring, undurable, nondurable, nonpermanent; **ephemeral,** evanescent, volatile, **momentary**

short shrift NOUNS **repulse,** rebuff, peremptory *or* flat *or* point-blank refusal, summary negative; kiss-off *and* slap in the face *and* kick in the teeth <all nonformal>

shortsighted ADJS **nearsighted,** myopic; **undiscerning,** unperceptive, imperceptive, impercipient, insensible, purblind, unapprehending, uncomprehending; unforseeing, unseeing

short temper NOUNS **irascibility,** irritability, excitability, quick temper, short fuse <nonformal>; **crankiness,** testiness, crustiness, huffiness, huffishness, churlishness, bearishness, snappishness, waspishness; **hotheadedness,** hot blood

short-term ADJS **brief,** short, short-time, quick, brisk, swift, fleet, speedy

shot NOUNS 1 **dose,** draft, potion, portion, injection; booster, booster shot; **snort,** jolt, snifter
2 discharge; ejection; detonation; gunfire
3 **guess,** conjecture, unverified supposition, surmise, educated guess; guesstimate *and* hunch *and* stab <all nonformal>; rough guess, wild guess, bold conjecture, shot in the dark <nonformal>
ADJS 4 **unnerved,** unmanned, unstrung, undone, reduced to jelly, unglued <nonformal>, **demoralized,** shaken, upset, dashed, stricken, **crushed;** shot to pieces; **done for** *and* done in *and* finished *and ausgespielt* <Ger> *and* kaput <all nonformal>

shoulder VERBS **support,** bear, carry, **hold,** sustain, maintain, bolster, reinforce, back, back up, give *or* furnish *or* afford *or* supply *or* lend support

shout NOUNS 1 **cry,** call, yell, hoot; war cry, battle cry, war whoop, rallying cry; cheer
VERBS 2 **cry,** call, yell, holler <nonformal>, hoot; **cheer,** give a cheer, give three cheers
3 **proclaim, herald,** trumpet, shout from the housetops

shove NOUNS 1 **thrust,** push, boost <nonformal>; pressure
VERBS 2 **push,** propel, impel, thrust; **drive,** forward, advance; sweep, sweep along; butt

show NOUNS 1 **display,** demonstration, showing; presentation, showing forth, presentment, ostentation <old>, **exhibition,** exhibit, exposition, retrospective; **showcase,** showcasing, unveiling, exposure
2 **pretext,** pretense, pretension, lying pretension, ostensible *or* announced *or* public *or* professed motive; **front,** facade, sham
3 theatrical performance, **performance,** production, entertainment, stage presentation *or* performance; premiere, premier performance, debut
VERBS 4 shine out *or* through, **surface,** appear, **be visible,** be seen, be revealed, be evident, be noticeable, meet the gaze, impinge on the eye, present to the eye, meet *or* catch *or* hit *or* strike the eye
5 **prove,** demonstrate, afford proof of, prove to be, prove true; follow, follow from, follow as a matter of course

show business NOUNS show biz <nonformal>, the entertainment industry; **the theater,** the footlights, the stage, the boards, the bright lights, Broadway, the Great White Way

showdown NOUNS **confrontation,** standoff, Mexican standoff <nonformal>, clashing, collision, cross-purposes, conflict

show off VERBS **grandstand** *and* hotdog *and* showboat <all nonformal>, play to the gallery *or* galleries <nonformal>, please the crowd; exhibit *or* parade one's wares <nonformal>, strut one's stuff <nonformal>, go through one's paces, show what one has

show-off NOUNS **exhibitionist,** flaunter; **grandstander** *or* grandstand player *or* hot dog *or* **hotshot** *or* showboat <all nonformal>

showpiece NOUNS **model,** pattern, standard, criterion, classic example, rule, mirror, paradigm; **classic,** masterwork, masterpiece, *chef d'œuvre* <Fr>

showstopper NOUNS **smash, hit,** smash hit, gas, gasser, blast, boffo, barnburner, howling *or* roaring success, one for the book, wow, sensation, overnight sensation, phenom, sockeroo <all nonformal>

show up VERBS 1 **arrive,** make *or* put in an appearance, turn up, **surface,** pop *or* bob up *and* make the scene <all nonformal>; **overshadow,** eclipse, throw into the shade, top; put to shame, put one's nose out of joint, put down <nonformal>
2 **disprove,** invalidate, disconfirm, discredit, prove the contrary, belie, give the lie to, **expose**

showy ADJS **flaunting, flashy,** snazzy, flashing, glittering, **jazzy** *and* **glitzy** *and* gimmicky *and* splashy *and* splurgy <all nonformal>; exhibitionistic, showoffy <nonformal>, bravura; **frilly,** flouncy, frothy, chichi

shred NOUNS 1 **scrap,** tatter, smithereen <nonformal>, patch, **stitch,** tag
VERBS 2 **tear** *or* **rip apart,** take *or* pull apart, **pick** *or* **rip** *or* **tear to pieces,** tear to rags *or* tatters, rip to shreds

shrew NOUNS **bitch** <nonformal>, **vixen,** virago, termagant, brimstone, fury, witch, beldam, cat, tigress, she-wolf, she-devil, spitfire; fishwife; **scold,** common scold; battle-ax <nonformal>

shrewd ADJS **artful,** cunning, knowing, crafty, wily, guileful, canny, slick, sly, smart as a fox, foxy *and* crazy like a fox <both nonformal>; devious, Byzantine, calculating

shriek NOUNS 1 **screech,** scream, squeal, shrill, keen, squeak, squawk, skirl; waul, caterwaul
VERBS 2 **screech,** screak, squeak, squawk, **scream,** squeal, shrill, keen; waul, caterwaul

shrill ADJS **thin,** sharp, acute, argute, keen, keening, **piercing,** penetrating, ear-piercing; **screechy,** screeching, shrieky, shrieking, **squeaky,** squeaking, screaky, creaky, creaking; strident, harsh, raucous, grating

shrine NOUNS holy place, dagoba, naos; sacrarium, delubrum; tope, stupa; reliquary, *reliquaire* <Fr>

shrink NOUNS 1 **psychotherapist,** therapist, **psychiatrist, psychoanalyst,** analyst; headshrinker *and* shrinker <both nonformal>
VERBS 2 **flinch,** shy, shy away from, draw back, recoil, funk <nonformal>, **quail,** cringe, wince, blench, blink, say *or* cry uncle
3 get smaller, **diminish,** decline, sink, dwindle, **fade, ebb,** wane

shrivel VERBS **shrink,** wither, sear, parch, dry up; **wizen,** weazen, wrinkle; consume, waste, waste away, attenuate, emaciate

shroud NOUNS 1 **screen,** shield, veil, pall, mantle, curtain, hanging, drape, drapery; **coat,** cloak, mask, guise; **graveclothes,** winding sheet, cerecloth, cerements; pall
VERBS 2 **wrap,** enwrap, wrap up, wrap about *or* around; **envelop,** surround, encompass, lap, smother, enfold, embrace, invest; swathe, swaddle; **screen,** cloak, veil, screen off, curtain, blanket, enshroud, envelop; **disguise,** camouflage, mask, dissemble; hide one's light under a bushel

shrunk ADJS shrunken; **shriveled,** shriveled up; **withered,** sear, parched, corky, dried-up; **wasted,** wasted away, consumed, emaciated, emacerated, thin, attenuated

shuck VERBS **husk,** hull, pod, **shell**

shudder NOUNS 1 **shake,** quake, quiver, quaver, falter, **tremor,** tremble, shiver, twitter, didder, dither
VERBS 2 **shake,** quake, vibrate, jactitate; **tremble,** quiver, quaver, falter, **shiver,** twitter, didder, chatter; shake in one's boots *or* shoes

shuffle NOUNS 1 **slow motion,** leisurely gait, snail's *or* tortoise's pace; slouch, plod, shamble
VERBS 2 **stroll,** saunter, *flâner* <Fr>; scuff, scuffle, straggle, shamble, slouch; riffle; **dance,** shake

shun VERBS **avoid,** fight shy of, shy away from, keep from, keep away from, circumvent, keep clear of, avoid like the plague, **steer clear of** <nonformal>, **give a wide berth,** keep remote from, stay detached from; **abstain,** abstain from, refrain, **refrain from,** eschew, **pass up** <nonformal>, have nothing to do with, take no part in, have no hand in

shut VERBS 1 **close,** occlude; close up, shut up, contract, constrict, strangle, strangulate, choke, choke off, squeeze,

squeeze shut; **turn off,** shut off, shut down
ADJS 2 **closed,** unopen, unopened; unvented, unventilated; **ruled out,** barred

shutdown NOUNS **closure,** closing, shutting, shutting up, occlusion; shutting down; **exclusion**, shutting out, **ruling out;** blockade, embargo

shut down VERBS **close up** *or* **down,** shut up, shut up shop, go out of business, shutter, put up the shutters; jump on *and* crack down on *and* clamp down on <all nonformal>, put *or* keep the lid on <nonformal>; bottle up, cork, cork up; **strike,** walk out, call a strike, go *or* go out on strike

shut-in NOUNS **sick person,** ill person, sufferer, victim; valetudinarian, **invalid,** bedridden invalid

shutter VERBS **shade,** screen, veil, curtain, draw the curtains, put up *or* close the shutters; cover

shuttle NOUNS 1 **train,** railroad train; shuttle train; **air shuttle,** shuttle service, shuttle trip; **spacecraft,** space shuttle
VERBS 2 **alternate,** go to and fro, **come and go,** ebb and flow; shuttlecock

shut up VERBS 1 **confine, shut in,** shut away, coop in, hem in, fence in *or* up, wall in *or* up, rail in; **coop up, pen up,** box up, mew up, bottle up, cork up, seal up, **impound**

2 <nonformal> keep one's trap *or* yap shut, button up, button one's lip, dummy up, clam up, not let out a peep, play dumb, stonewall, say nothing

shy ADJS 1 **timid,** timorous, **bashful,** shamefaced, shamefast, pudibund *and* verecund *and* verecundious <all old>; **coy, demure,** skittish, mousy
2 **incomplete,** uncompleted, deficient, defective, unfinished, imperfect, unperfected, **inadequate; short,** scant

shyster NOUNS 1 **trickster,** shady character; horse trader, Yankee horse trader; **swindler**

2 <nonformal> **mouthpiece, ambulance chaser,** lip, fixer, legal eagle, Philadelphia lawyer

sibling NOUNS agnate, enate; kinsman, kinswoman, sib, brother, sister

sick ADJS **ill,** ailing, unwell, indisposed, taken ill, down, bad, on the sick list; **sickish,** rocky <nonformal>, **under the weather,** out of sorts <nonformal>, below par <nonformal>, off-color, off one's feed <nonformal>; **sick at heart,** heartsick, soul-sick, heartsore

sicken VERBS **deteriorate,** worsen, get *or* grow worse, get no better fast <nonformal>, disimprove, **degenerate**

sickly ADJS **unhealthy,** healthless, in poor health; **infirm,** unsound, invalid, valetudinary, valetudinarian, debilitated, cachectic, enervated, exhausted, drained; peaky *or* peaked <nonformal>; **feeble,** frail; **run-down,** reduced in health

sickness NOUNS **disease,** illness, malady, ailment, indisposition, **disorder,** complaint, morbidity, *morbus* <L>, **affliction,** affection, **infirmity**

side NOUNS 1 aspect, **facet,** angle, viewpoint, slant *and* twist *and* spin <all nonformal>
2 **party,** interest, camp; interest group, pressure group, ethnic group; minority group, vocal minority
ADJS 3 **lateral;** flanking, skirting; **beside,** to the side, off to one side; **alongside,** parallel; next-beside; extra, off, spare, sparetime, **part-time**

sideburns NOUNS **whiskers,** burnsides, **muttonchops**

sidekick NOUNS **henchman,** co hort, hanger-on, buddy <nonformal>; **partner,** side partner, sidekicker <nonformal>; companion

sideline NOUNS **avocation,** hobby, side interest, pastime, spare-time activity; amateur pursuit, amateurism; unpaid work, volunteer work

sidestep VERBS **go sideways,** sidle, lateral, lateralize, **edge,** veer, angle, slant, skew; go crabwise; **sideslip,** skid; pull away *or* clear; pull back, shrink, recoil; step aside; hedge, skate around <Brit nonformal>, pussyfoot <nonformal>, evade the issue

sideswipe VERBS impinge, bump up against, hit; osculate; **graze,** caress, kiss, nudge, rub, brush, glance, scrape, skim, skirt, shave; **collide,** smack into, crash into, impact, smash into, dash into; **carom**

sideways ADVS **laterally,** laterad; sideway, **sidewise,** sidewards, sideward, sidelong, aside, crabwise; side-to-side; **edgeways,** edgeway, edgewise

side with VERBS take sides with, **unite with; join,** join with, join up with *and* get together with *and* team up with <all nonformal>, strike in with <old>; **throw in with** *and* string along with *and* swing in with <all nonformal>, **go along with; line up with** <nonformal>, align with, align oneself with, range with, range oneself with, stand up with, stand in with; **close ranks with,** fall in with, make common cause with, pool one's interests with

sidle VERBS **go sideways,** lateral, lateralize, **edge,** veer, angle, slant, skew, sidestep; go crabwise; **sideslip,** skid

siege NOUNS **besiegement,** beleaguerment; encompassment, investment, encirclement, envelopment; blockading, blockade; cutting of supply lines

sieve NOUNS screen, strainer, colander, riddle, cribble, net; **separator,** centrifuge

sift VERBS **refine,** separate, sieve, **screen,** bolt, winnow; cull, glean; separate the wheat from the chaff, separate the sheep from the goats; discriminate

sigh NOUNS 1 **sighing,** moaning, sobbing, whining, soughing
VERBS 2 **moan,** sob, whine, sough; **whimper**

sight NOUNS 1 **vision,** eyesight, seeing; **sightedness; look,** the eye *and* a looksee *and* a gander <all nonformal>, eye, regard; leer, leering look
2 sighthole; finder, viewfinder; panoramic sight; bombsight; peep sight, open sight
3 **view,** scene, prospect, outlook, lookout, vista, perspective; **spectacle,** exhibit, **exhibition,** exposition, **show,** stage show, **display,** presentation, representation
4 **eyesore,** blot, blot on the landscape, blemish, **fright,** horror, mess, no beauty, no beauty queen, ugly duckling

sightly ADJS **comely,** fair, good-looking, nice-looking, well-favored, **personable,** presentable, agreeable, becoming, pleasing, goodly, bonny, likely <nonformal>; pleasing to the eye, lovely to behold

sightsee VERBS see the sights, take in the sights; **rubberneck** <nonformal>; go on a tour, join a tour

sign NOUNS 1 telltale sign, sure sign, tipoff <nonformal>, **index,** indicant, **indicator,** measure; **symptom; mark,** earmark, hallmark; **signal; high sign** *and* the wink *and* the nod <all nonformal>
2 symbol, significant, significant, type, token, icon; **miracle,** signs and portents, prodigy, wonder, wonderwork
VERBS 3 **shake hands** *or* shake <nonformal>, affix one's John Hancock <nonformal>, seal, formalize, make legal and binding, solemnize; **endorse;** sign, cosign, **underwrite,** undersign, subscribe to; confirm, attest

signal NOUNS 1 **sign;** high sign *and* the wink *and* the nod <all nonformal>; wink, flick of the eyelash, glance, leer; **implication,** insinuation, innuendo; broad hint, gesture, nod, look, nudge, kick, prompt
VERBS 2 signalize, sign, give a signal, make a sign; speak; flash; **give the high sign** *or* **the nod** *or* a high five <all nonformal>; nod; nudge, poke, kick, dig one in the ribs, touch; wink, glance, raise one's eyebrows

signature NOUNS **ratification,** endorsement, acceptance, approval, approbation, subscription, subscribership, signing-off, imprimatur, **sanction,** permission, the OK *and* the okay *and* the green light *and* **the go-ahead** *and* the nod <all nonformal>, **certification,** confirmation, validation, authentication, authorization, warrant; **subscription,** autograph, John Hancock <nonformal>; countersignature

significant ADJS **important,** major, consequential, momentous, considerable, substantial, material, **great,** grand, big

significant other NOUNS **lover,** admirer, adorer, amorist; infatuate, paramour; escort, companion, date *and* steady <both nonformal>; live-in lover, POSSLQ *or* person of opposite sex sharing living quarters

signify VERBS **betoken,** stand for, identify, differentiate, speak of, talk, **indicate,** be indicative of, be an indication of, be significant of, connote, denominate, argue, bespeak, be symptomatic *or* diagnostic of, symptomize, **characterize, mark,** highlight, be the mark *or* sign of, give token, **denote,** mean

sign up VERBS **join,** join up <nonformal>, **enter,** go into, come into, get into, make oneself part of, swell the ranks of; **enlist,** enroll, affiliate, sign on <nonfor-

mal>, take up membership, take out membership

silence NOUNS 1 **quiescence,** *or* quiescency, **stillness,** quietness, **quiet,** quietude; **taciturnity,** untalkativeness, unloquaciousness

lucid stillness
T S Eliot

VERBS 2 **put to silence,** hush, hush one up, hush-hush, **shush, quiet,** quieten, **still; soft-pedal,** put on the soft pedal; squash, squelch <nonformal>, stifle, choke, choke off, throttle, put the kibosh on <nonformal>, put the lid on *and* shut down on <both nonformal>, put the damper on <nonformal>, **gag, muzzle,** muffle; strike dumb

silent ADJS **still, quiet,** quiescent, hushed, soundless, noiseless; **inaudible,** quiet as a mouse, mousy; silent as a post *or* stone, silent as the grave *or* tomb, still as death; **taciturn,** untalkative, unloquacious, indisposed to talk; **speechless,** wordless, mum

silhouette NOUNS **outline, profile; broad lines,** vignette; shadow figure; **shadow**

silky ADJS **smooth;** satiny, velvety, smooth as silk *or* satin *or* velvet, smooth as a billiard ball *or* baby's ass <nonformal>; **sleek,** slick, glossy, shiny, gleaming; silken, gossamer, gossamery, flossy; silklike, sericeous, soft as silk

silly ADJS **nonsensical,** poppycockish <nonformal>; **foolish,** absurd; twaddling, twaddly; rubbishy, trashy; skimble-skamble; Pickwickian; **fatuous,** fatuitous, inept, **inane,** empty, vacuous; trite, vapid

silver NOUNS 1 **tableware,** dining utensils; **silverware,** silver plate, stainless-steel ware; **flatware,** flat silver
ADJS 2 **eloquent,** silver-tongued; well-spoken, articulate; **glib, smooth,** smooth-spoken, smooth-tongued, slick

similar ADJS **like, alike,** something like, not unlike; **resembling,** resemblant, following, favoring <nonformal>, savoring *or* smacking of, suggestive of, **on the order of;** something of the sort *or* to that effect

simmer VERBS **seethe,** sizzle, smoke, smolder, steam; **fume,** stew <nonformal>, boil, fret, chafe; **foam,** froth, froth up; **boil,** ferment, stir, churn

Simon Legree NOUNS **oppressor,** hard master, driver, **slave driver;** martinet, disciplinarian, stickler

simpatico ADJS **amiable,** congenial, *simpático* <Sp>, *sympathique* <Fr>, pleasant, agreeable, favorable, well-affected, well-disposed, well-intentioned, well-meaning, well-meant; sociable; kind

simple ADJS 1 **plain,** ordinary, nondescript, common, commonplace, prosaic, prosy, **matter-of-fact,** homely, homespun, everyday, workday, workaday, household, garden, common- *or* garden-variety; pure, **pure and simple,** chaste, classic *or* classical, Attic; natural, homey, down-home *and* folksy <both nonformal>; **unaffected,** unassuming
2 **ignorant,** nescient, empty, empty-headed, blankminded, vacuous, inane, unintelligent; **green,** callow, innocent, ingenuous, gauche, awkward, naive, unripe, raw; **gullible,** dupable, ingenuous, unsophisticated, green, naive

simpleminded ADJS **artless,** simple-hearted; **ingenuous,** *ingénu* <Fr>; childlike, born yesterday; simplewitted, simple, simpletonian; **idiotic,** moronic, imbecile, imbecilic, cretinous, cretinistic

simpleton NOUNS **idiot,** imbecile, moron, half-wit, natural, natural idiot, born fool, natural-born fool, mental defective, defective

simplicity NOUNS **purity,** simpleness, **plainness,** no frills, starkness, severity; **unadulteration,** unsophistication, unspoiledness, intactness, fundamentality, elementarity, primitiveness *or* primitivity, primariness; **ingenuousness,** unsophistication; greenness, naïveness, **naïveté,** naivety; uncomplexity, uncomplicatedness

simulate VERBS **imitate,** counterfeit, fake <nonformal>, hoke *and* hoke up <both nonformal>; **parody,** pastiche; **affect, pretend, sham, feign,** make out like <nonformal>, make a show of, play, playact <nonformal>

sin NOUNS 1 **iniquity, evil,** bad, wrong, error, obliquity, villainy, knavery, reprobacy, peccancy, **abomination,** atrocity, infamy, shame, disgrace, scandal, unforgivable *or* cardinal *or* mortal sin
VERBS 2 **do wrong,** misbehave, misdemean *and* misdo <both old>, **err,** offend; commit sin; **transgress,** trespass

sincere ADJS **candid,** frank, genuine, honest, ingenuous, frankhearted; **open,** openhearted, transparent, open-faced; artless; **straightforward,** direct, upfront *and* straight <both nonformal>, **forthright,** downright, straight-out <nonformal>

sinful ADJS **wrongdoing,** evildoing, malefactory, malfeasant; **wrong,** iniquitous, wicked; **ungodly,** godless, **irreligious,** unrighteous, unholy, unsaintly, unangelic, unangelical; impious

sing VERBS **vocalize,** carol, descant, lilt, troll, line out *and* belt out *and* tear off <all nonformal>; **warble,** trill, tremolo

singe VERBS **burn,** torrefy, scorch, parch, sear; swinge; **blister,** vesicate; **cauterize,** brand, burn in

singer NOUNS **vocalist,** vocalizer, voice, songster, songbird, warbler, lead singer, caroler, melodist, minstrel, cantor; songstress, cantatrice, chanteuse, song stylist, canary <nonformal>; chanter, chantress

single ADJS 1 **unmarried,** unwedded, unwed, sole, spouseless, wifeless, husbandless; **bachelorly,** bachelorlike; **spinsterly,** spinsterish, spinsterlike; maiden, maidenly; virgin, virginal
2 **one,** singular, individual, sole, unique, a certain, **solitary, lone;** exclusive

singular ADJS 1 **wonderful,** wondrous, marvelous, miraculous, fantastic, fabulous, phenomenal, **prodigious,** stupendous, unheard-of, unprecedented, extraordinary, exceptional, rare, unique, **remarkable,** striking, sensational
2 **odd,** queer, peculiar, absurd, **curious,** oddball <nonformal>, weird *and* kooky *and* freaky *and* freaked-out <all nonformal>, quaint, **eccentric,** gonzo <nonformal>

sinister ADJS **ominous,** dark, black, gloomy, somber, dreary; **threatening,** menacing, lowering; bad, evil, ill, untoward; dire, baleful, baneful, **ill-fated,** ill-starred, evil-starred, star-crossed; shady <nonformal>, up to no good, not kosher <nonformal>, unsavory, insidious, indirect, slippery, devious, tricky, shifty, evasive

sink NOUNS 1 **washbasin,** washbowl, kitchen sink; sump; **sewer, hole,** pit, depression, dip; **basin,** trough, **bowl**
VERBS 2 **go down,** sink down, submerge; **set, settle,** settle down; **decline,** lower, **subside,** give way, lapse, cave, cave in; **slump,** slump down; founder; diminish, lessen; abate; shrink, wane, wither, ebb, ebb away, dwindle, languish; **deepen,** lower, depress
3 **scuttle,** send to the bottom, send to Davy Jones's locker; **founder, go down,** go to the bottom, sink like lead, go down like a stone; **slip,** go downhill, be on the skids <nonformal>

sinner NOUNS **wrongdoer,** malefactor, transgressor, delinquent; malfeasor, misfeasor, nonfeasor; misdemeanant, misdemeanist

sip NOUNS 1 **nip,** draft, drop, spot, finger or two, sup, suck, drench, guzzle, gargle, jigger
VERBS 2 **drink,** quaff, sup, bib, swig *and* swill *and* guzzle *and* pull <all nonformal>; **taste,** taste of, sample; **savor,** savor of; roll on the tongue

sire VERBS **engender,** beget, procreate; **give birth to,** bear, birth, bring to birth; father, mother

siren NOUNS 1 **tempter,** seducer, enticer, inveigler, **charmer,** enchanter, fascinator, tantalizer, teaser; coquette, flirt; **temptress,** enchantress, seductress; **vampire,** vamp <nonformal>, *femme fatale* <Fr>
2 **warning signal,** alert, red alert; klaxon, tocsin

sissy NOUNS 1 **milksop,** namby-pamby, mollycoddle, mama's boy, mother's boy, mother's darling, teacher's pet; pansy *and* pantywaist <both nonformal>, **wimp,** poor *or* weak *or* dull tool <nonformal>
ADJS 2 **weak-kneed, chicken** <nonformal>, afraid of one's shadow; weak, soft; **wimpy** *or* wimpish <nonformal>, unmanly, unmanful, sissified; milksoppy, milksoppish

sister NOUNS **nun,** *religieuse* <Fr>, clergywoman, conventual; abbess, prioress; **mother superior,** lady superior, superioress, the reverend mother, holy mother; novice, postulant

sit VERBS set <nonformal>, **sit down, be seated,** remain seated; perch, roost

site NOUNS 1 **arena,** scene of action, scene, setting, background, **field, ground,** terrain, sphere, place, locale, milieu, precinct, purlieu
VERBS 2 **situate,** place, position; emplace, spot <nonformal>, **install,** put in place; **pinpoint,** zero in on, home in on; find *or* fix *or* calculate one's posi-

tion, triangulate, find a line of position, **get a fix on**

sitter NOUNS **baby-sitter,** baby-minder <Brit>

sit tight VERBS **hold on** <nonformal>, hold one's breath; wait a minute *or* second, wait up; **wait and see,** bide the issue, see which way the cat jumps, see how the cookie crumbles *or* the ball bounces <nonformal>

situate VERBS **locate,** site, place, position; emplace, spot <nonformal>, **install,** put in place

situation NOUNS 1 **placement,** positioning, emplacement, location, siting, **locating,** placing, putting; **status,** status quo *or* status in quo, position, standing, footing, bearings, spot
2 **position,** job, employment, gainful employment, **office,** post, place, station, berth, billet, **appointment,** engagement, gig <nonformal>

size NOUNS **largeness,** bigness, greatness, vastness, vastitude, **magnitude,** order of magnitude, amplitude; mass, bulk, **volume,** body; **dimensions,** proportions, dimension, caliber; **measure,** measurement, gauge, **scale; extent,** scope, reach, range; depth, breadth, width

skeleton NOUNS 1 **frame,** framing; **framework,** fabric, cadre, chassis, shell, armature; lattice, latticework, infrastructure
2 **corpse,** dead body, dead man *or* woman, dead person, **cadaver,** carcass, body; *corpus delicti* <L>; **remains,** mortal *or* organic remains, bones, dry bones, relics, reliquiae

skeptic NOUNS doubter, dubitante, **doubting Thomas,** scoffer, cynic, pooh-poohler, nay-sayer, unbeliever

sketch NOUNS 1 **description,** portrayal, portraiture, **depiction,** rendering, rendition, **delineation,** limning, representation; vignette, cameo; **characterization,** character, character sketch, profile; **drawing;** line drawing; **draft**
VERBS 2 **describe,** portray, picture, render, **depict,** draft, represent, delineate, limn, draw; outline, sketch out, trace; **characterize,** character; **express,** set forth, give words to; **write**

sketchy ADJS **imperfect,** defective, faulty, inadequate, deficient, short, not all it's cracked up to be <nonformal>, lacking, wanting, found wanting; **unsound,** incomplete, unfinished, partial, patchy, uneven, unthorough; makeshift

skew NOUNS 1 **bias,** bend, bent, **crook,** warp, twist, turn, **veer,** sheer, **swerve,** lurch
VERBS 2 **unbalance,** disbalance, disequilibrate, overbalance, overcompensate, **throw off balance,** upset

skewer VERBS **pierce,** penetrate, puncture, punch, hole, prick; **tap,** broach; stab, stick, pink, run through; **transfix,** transpierce, fix, **impale,** spit; crucify; **disparage,** defame

ski VERBS run, schuss, traverse, turn, check

skid NOUNS 1 **slide; slip,** slippage; **glide,** coast, glissade; slither; sideslip
VERBS 2 **glide,** coast, skim, sweep, flow; **slide,** slip, skitter, sideslip, slither, glissade; sideslip

skid row NOUNS **slum** *or* **slums,** blighted area *or* neighborhood *or* section; tenderloin, red-light district, Bowery, skid road <nonformal>

skill NOUNS skillfulness, **expertness,** expertise, proficiency, craft, **cleverness; dexterity,** dexterousness *or* dextrousness; **adroitness,** address, **adeptness,** deftness, handiness, hand, practical ability; **competence,** capability, capacity, ability; **facility,** prowess; **craftsmanship,** workmanship, artisanship; **know-how** *and* savvy *and* bag of tricks <all nonformal>; **technique,** touch, technical brilliance, technical mastery

skillful ADJS **expert,** proficient; dexterous, **adroit,** deft, adept, coordinated, well-coordinated, **apt,** no mean, **handy;** masterly, masterful; authoritative, professional; **virtuoso,** bravura, technically superb; workmanlike

skim VERBS 1 **touch lightly,** touch upon; kiss, **brush,** sweep, graze, brush by, glance, scrape; **speed,** go fast, **fly,** flit, fleet, wing one's way, outstrip the wind; **scratch the surface,** hardly touch, skim over, hit the high spots *and* give a lick and a promise <both nonformal>, cut corners; slight
2 **cheat,** shortchange, shortweight, skim off the top; **pocket,** palm

skimp VERBS **stint,** scrimp, scamp, scant, screw, **pinch,** starve, famish; **pinch pennies,** live on nothing; **economize, scrape,** scrape and save; put something aside, save for a rainy day, have a nest egg

skimpy ADJS **meager, slight,** scrimpy, skimp, exiguous; scant, **scanty,** spare; miserly, niggardly, stingy, parsimonious, mean

skin NOUNS 1 dermis; **cuticle; rind; flesh;** bare skin *or* flesh, the buff; integument, tegument, tegmen, tegmentum; epicarp; bark
VERBS 2 **peel,** pare, strip, flay, excoriate, decorticate, bark; scalp

skinny ADJS **lean,** lean-looking, fleshless, lean-fleshed, thin-fleshed, **spare,** meager, **scrawny,** scraggy, **gaunt,** lank, lanky; twiggy; **underweight,** undersized, undernourished, spidery

skip NOUNS 1 **leap,** jump, hop, spring, bound, bounce
VERBS 2 **leave undone,** leave, **let go,** leave half-done, pretermit, jump, **miss,** omit, pass over, pass up <nonformal>, abandon; **slack,** shirk, malinger, goof off *and* goldbrick <both nonformal>
3 **leap,** jump, vault, spring, hop, bound, bounce; **gambol,** gambado, **frisk,** flounce, **trip,** bob, jump about

skirmish NOUNS **fight,** battle, fray, affray, combat, action, conflict, embroilment; **clash;** brush, scrimmage

skirt VERBS **border,** edge, bound, rim, hem, hem in, befringe, lap, list, margin, marge, marginate, verge; **graze,** caress, kiss, nudge, rub, brush, glance, scrape, sideswipe, skim, shave; **evade,** elude, **get out of,** shuffle out of, **get around** <nonformal>, circumvent

skittish ADJS **frisky,** antic, coltish, rompish, capersome; **jittery** <nonformal>, **jumpy,** twittery, skittery, trigger-happy <nonformal>, gun-shy; **coy,** demure, mousy

skulduggery NOUNS **chicanery,** chicane, **trickery,** dodgery, pettifogging, pettifoggery, *supercherie* <Fr>, **artifice,** sleight, machination; **sharp practice,** underhand dealing, connivery, connivance, conspiracy

skulk VERBS **sneak,** slink, prowl, nightwalk, **steal,** creep, pussyfoot <nonformal>, gumshoe <nonformal>, tiptoe; **cower,** quail, cringe, crouch

sky NOUNS **the heavens,** heaven, **firmament;** empyrean, welkin, *caelum* <L>; **the blue,** blue sky, azure, cerulean, the blue serene; **ether,** air

skyrocket VERBS **shoot up,** spring up, jump up, **leap up,** vault up, start up, fly up, pop up, bob up; upshoot, upstart, upspring, upleap, upspear, rocket, make rapid strides, take off <nonformal>

slab NOUNS plank, deal <Brit>, slat, tablet, table; puncheon

slack ADJS 1 **dilatory,** procrastinative, remiss, lax; **negligent,** neglectful, neglecting, derelict, culpably negligent; relaxed, laid-back <nonformal>, unrigorous, permissive, overly permissive; work-shy
2 **loose,** lax, relaxed, easy

slacker NOUNS **shirker,** shirk, **goldbricker,** goldbrick <nonformal>; clock watcher; **malingerer**

slake VERBS **satiate,** sate, satisfy, allay; **surfeit,** glut, gorge, engorge; **cloy,** jade, pall

slam NOUNS 1 **hit,** blow, stroke, knock, rap, pound, bang, crack, **whack,** smack, thwack, smash, dash, swipe, swing, **punch,** poke, jab, dig, drub, thump, pelt, cut, chop, dint, slog
2 **criticism;** knock *and* swipe *and* rap *and* hit <all nonformal>
VERBS 3 **crack,** clap, crash, wham, **bang,** clash
4 criticize; pan *and* knock *and* hit *and* rap *and* take a rap *or* swipe at <all nonformal>

slammer NOUNS

<nonformal> **slam, jug,** can, coop, cooler, hoosegow, stir, clink, pokey, **joint,** big house, brig, tank

slander NOUNS 1 **scandal,** libel, traducement; calumny, calumniation; backbiting, cattiness *and* bitchiness <both nonformal>; character assassination; whispering campaign
VERBS 2 **libel;** calumniate, traduce; stab in the back, backbite, speak ill of behind one's back

slang NOUNS **jargon,** cant, argot, patois, patter, vernacular; **colloquialism,** localism

slant NOUNS 1 aspect, look, view; facet, side, angle, viewpoint, twist *and* spin <both nonformal>; obliquity, bias, skew; **inclination,** leaning, **bent,** turn, tilt, cast, warp; way of looking at things, slant on things
VERBS 2 **incline,** lean; slope, rake, pitch, grade, bank; **tilt,** tip, list, cant, careen, keel, sidle, swag, sway
3 **pervert,** falsify, twist, garble, put a false construction upon, give a spin,

give a false coloring, color, varnish, put a spin on, twist the meaning of

slap NOUNS 1 smack, whack, whomp, **cuff, box,** buffet, belt; blow; **rap on the knuckles,** box on the ear, slap in the face; slap on the wrist, token punishment
VERBS 2 smack, whack, whomp, **cuff, box,** buffet; strike; slap the face, box the ears, give a rap on the knuckles

slapstick NOUNS 1 **comedy;** comic relief, comedy relief; sock, coxcomb, cap and bells, motley, bladder, buffoonery
ADJS 2 **comic** *or* **comical;** farcical, broad; burlesque

slash NOUNS 1 **wound,** injury, lesion; **cut,** incision, scratch, gash; **laceration,** mutilation; run, **rip,** rent, **tear**
2 **diagonal,** oblique, transverse, oblique line, **slant,** virgule, scratch comma, separatrix, solidus
VERBS 3 cut, cut *or* slant across, cut crosswise *or* transversely *or* diagonally, catercorner, diagonalize, slash across; **gash,** chop, crimp, scotch, **score,** blaze, jag, scarify; slit, scratch
4 **attack,** assail; castigate, flay, skin alive <nonformal>, **excoriate,** fustigate, scarify, scathe
5 **mark down,** cut prices, cut, shave, trim, pare, underprice, knock the bottom out of <nonformal>

slat NOUNS **strip,** lath, batten, spline, strake, plank

slate NOUNS 1 **ballot,** ticket; **schedule,** program, programma, **bill,** card, **calendar,** docket
VERBS 2 **schedule,** line up <nonformal>, **book,** book in, bill, program, calendar, docket, budget, put on the agenda

slaughter NOUNS 1 **butchery,** butchering, shambles, occision, slaughtering, hecatomb, holocaust
VERBS 2 **butcher,** massacre, decimate, commit carnage, depopulate, murder *or* kill *or* slay en masse; commit mass murder *or* destruction, murder wholesale, commit genocide

slaughterhouse NOUNS abbatoir, butchery <Brit>, shambles; stockyard; gas chamber, concentration camp, death camp, killing fields

slave NOUNS 1 **drudge,** grub, hack, fag, plodder, galley slave, **workhorse,** beast of burden, slogger
VERBS 2 **work hard;** scratch *and* hustle *and* sweat <all nonformal>, **sweat and slave** <nonformal>, slave away, toil away; work one's head off <nonformal>, work one's fingers to the bone, break one's back; work like a slave *or* galley slave, **work day and night,** burn the midnight oil; lucubrate, elucubrate

slavery NOUNS **subjection,** subjugation; **bondage,** captivity; thrall, thralldom, enthrallment; enslavement, master-slave relationship; **servitude; serfdom,** serfhood, villenage, **vassalage;** helotry, helotism; **peonage;** drudgery

slay VERBS 1 **kill,** put to death, deprive of life, take the life of, take one's life away, **do away with,** make away with, put out of the way, put to sleep, end, **put an end to,** end the life of, **dispatch,** do for, finish, finish off, kill off, **dispose of,** exterminate, destroy, annihilate; euthanatize; **execute**
2 **make one laugh,** strike one as funny, convulse; wow *and* knock dead *and* kill *and* break one up *and* crack one up *and* fracture one <all nonformal>; have them rolling in the aisles; keep them in stitches

sled NOUNS **sleigh,** *traîneau* <Fr>; snowmobile, Sno-Cat, weasel, Skimobile; toboggan

sleep NOUNS 1 **slumber; repose,** silken repose, *somnus* <L>, the arms of Morpheus; light sleep, fitful sleep, **doze,** drowse; beauty sleep <nonformal>; bedtime, sack time <nonformal>
VERBS 2 **slumber,** rest in the arms of Morpheus; **doze,** drowse; nap, catnap, take a nap, catch a wink, sleep soundly, **sleep like a top** *or* **log,** sleep like the dead
3 **fall asleep, go to sleep, drop off, retire,** doze off, drowse off, drift off, close one's eyes

sleepy ADJS **drowsy,** slumberous, slumbery, dreamy; **half asleep,** asleep on one's feet; sleepful, sleep-filled; heavy, **heavy-eyed,** heavy with sleep, sleep-swollen; **somnolent,** soporific; **lethargic,** comatose, narcose *or* narcous, stuporose *or* stuporous, in a stupor, out of it <nonformal>

sleet NOUNS 1 glaze, glazed frost, verglas, freezing rain
VERBS 2 **hail, frost,** ice, ice up, ice over, glaze, glaze over

slender ADJS **narrow,** narrowish, narrowy; **close,** near; **tight,** strait, isthmic, isthmian; **restricted,** limited, circumscribed, **confined,** constricted; **meager,** scant, scanty; **thin,** slim, gracile; **svelte,** slinky, sylphlike, willowy

slew NOUNS

<nonformal> **heap,** batch, pile, **stack,** loads, lots, **raft,** whole slew, spate, wad; **oodles,** gobs, scads, **mess**

slice NOUNS 1 **portion,** share, interest, part, stake, stock, **piece,** bit, segment; slice of the pie *or* melon *and* piece of the action <both nonformal>; **cut,** cutting, clip, clipping, paring, shaving, rasher, snip, snippet, collop
VERBS 2 **cut,** incise, carve, pare, prune, trim, trim away, resect, excise; slit, snip, lance, scissor

slick ADJS 1 **sleek,** glossy, shiny, gleaming; varnished, lacquered, shellacked, glazed, *glacé* <Fr>; **glassy,** smooth as glass; **slippery,** slippy, slithery *and* sliddery <both nonformal>, slippery as an eel; lubricious, lubric, oily, oleaginous, greasy, buttery, soaped; lubricated, oiled, greased
2 **cunning,** crafty, artful, wily, guileful, **sly,** insidious, **shifty,** arch, **smooth,** slick as a whistle <both nonformal>, **slippery,** snaky, serpentine; devious, Byzantine, calculating

slide NOUNS 1 **slip,** slippage; **glide,** coast, glissade; glissando; slither; **skid,** sideslip; **landslide,** mudslide, landslip, subsidence; **snowslide,** avalanche
VERBS 2 **slip,** slip *or* slide down; **glide,** skim, coast, glissade; **slither; skid,** sideslip; avalanche
3 **decline,** sink, fail, fall, fade, die, wane, **go downhill,** fall away, fall off, go off <nonformal>, slump, take a nosedive <nonformal>, go into a tailspin, hit the skids <nonformal>

slight NOUNS 1 **snub,** rebuff, repulse; humiliation, spurning, spurn, disregard, the go-by <nonformal>; cut, **the cold shoulder** <nonformal>; sneer, snort, sniff; contemptuous dismissal, kiss-off <nonformal>; **rejection**
VERBS 2 **ignore,** make little of, dismiss, pretend not to see, disregard, overlook, neglect, pass by, pass up *and* give the go-by <both nonformal>, leave out in the cold <nonformal>, take no note *or* notice of, look right through <nonformal>
3 **flout,** disregard, treat with contempt, snap one's fingers at; thumb one's nose at, cock a snook at, bite the thumb at; **disparage,** depreciate, belittle, degrade, debase, **run** *or* **knock down** <nonformal>, **put down** <nonformal>
ADJS 4 **frail,** delicate, dainty; puny; light, lightweight; **fragile,** unsubstantial, flimsy, **small**, smallish; **meager,** scrimpy, skimp, skimpy, exiguous

slim ADJS 1 **thin,** slender, gracile, thin-bodied, thin-set, narrow- *or* wasp-waisted; **svelte,** slinky, sylphlike, willowy; girlish, boyish; thinnish, slenderish, slimmish
ADJS 2 **meager,** scrimpy, skimp, skimpy, exiguous; scant, **scanty,** spare

slime NOUNS **filth,** muck, mess, sordes, foul matter; mucus, snot <nonformal>; **slop,** scum, sludge, glop *and* gunk <both nonformal>, ooze

slimy ADJS **filthy,** foul, vile, mucky, **nasty,** icky *and* yecchy *and* yucky *and* gross *and* grungy *and* scuzzy <all nonformal>; **odious,** repulsive; scummy <nonformal>; fulsome, slobbery, gushing, protesting too much, smarmy <nonformal>, insinuating, oily, **unctuous,** smooth, bland; **fawning,** sycophantic, obsequious

slink VERBS **lurk,** couch; **lie in wait,** lay wait; **sneak,** skulk, prowl, nightwalk, **steal,** creep, pussyfoot <nonformal>, gumshoe <nonformal>

slinky ADJS 1 **svelte,** sylphlike, willowy
2 furtive, stealthy, privy, backstairs, **sly, shifty, sneaky,** sneaking, skulking, slinking, feline

slip NOUNS 1 slipup *and* miscue <both nonformal>; **lapse,** *lapsus* <L>, **oversight,** omission, inadvertence *or* inadvertency, loose thread; **misstep,** trip, stumble, false *or* wrong step, wrong *or* bad *or* false move; false note; **slip of the tongue,** *lapsus linguae* <L>; **slip of the pen,** *lapsus calami* <L>
VERBS 2 **sink,** founder, go down, go under <nonformal>; go downhill, be on the skids <nonformal>; **fall,** lapse, trip; **err,** fall into error, **go wrong,** go amiss, go astray, go *or* get out of line, go awry, stray, get off-base <nonformal>, **deviate,** wander

slippery ADJS 1 slippy, **slick,** slithery <nonformal>, slippery as an eel; lubricious, lubric, oily, oleaginous, greasy, soaped; lubricated, oiled, greased

2 **fraudulent,** sharp, guileful, insidious, **shifty,** tricky
3 **precarious,** ticklish, touchy, touch-and-go, **critical,** delicate; on thin ice

slipshod ADJS **slovenly,** sloppy *and* messy *and* half-assed <all nonformal>, sluttish, untidy; **clumsy,** bungling; **haphazard,** promiscuous, hit-or-miss, hit-and-miss

slit NOUNS 1 **break,** breakage, **breach,** burst, **rupture,** fracture; crack, cleft, **fissure,** cut, split; **gap,** rift, rent, rip, tear
VERBS 2 **cut,** cut apart, gash, **split,** rive, rent, rip open; cut open, cleave; tear open, rent, tear, dispart, separate; slash, scratch

slither VERBS **slide,** slip, slip *or* slide down; **glide,** skim, coast, glissade

sliver NOUNS **scrap,** tatter, smithereen <nonformal>, patch, snip, **snippet,** snick; splinter, shiver; **morsel,** *morceau* <Fr>, crumb

slob NOUNS **slattern,** sloven, frump <nonformal>, Sloppy Joe, schlep, schlump, *Strüwelpeter* <Ger>; drab, **slut,** trollop; pig, swine; **litterbug**

slobber NOUNS 1 **saliva,** spittle, sputum, spit, expectoration; salivation, ptyalism, sialorrhea, sialagogue, slabber, slaver, **drivel,** dribble, drool; gush, smarm *and* smarminess <both nonformal>
VERBS 2 slabber, slaver, **drool, drivel,** dribble; dither, blither, blather, maunder, dote, burble

slogan NOUNS **catchword,** catch phrase, shibboleth, cry; **motto,** watchword, tag line; epithet

slope NOUNS 1 **declivity,** steep, versant, incline, rise, talus, brae <Scots>, mountainside, hillside, bank, gentle *or* easy slope, glacis, angle of repose, steep *or* rapid slope, fall line
VERBS 2 **incline,** lean; slant, rake, pitch, grade, bank, shelve; **tilt,** tip, list, cant, careen, keel, sidle, swag, sway

sloppy ADJS **slipshod,** slipshoddy, **slovenly, messy** *and* half-assed <both nonformal>, sluttish, untidy; **clumsy,** bungling; **haphazard,** promiscuous, hit-or-miss, hit-and-miss; half-assed <nonformal>

slot NOUNS **opening,** aperture, hole, hollow, orifice; split, crack, check; position

sloth NOUNS **apathy,** indifference, unconcern; **lethargy,** hebetude, sluggishness, languor, languidness; acedia, noonday demon; **indolence,** laziness, slothfulness, bone-laziness

slouch NOUNS 1 **bungler, blunderer,** blunderhead, boggler, slubberer, bumbler, **fumbler,** botcher; **lout,** oaf, gawk, boor, **clown**
VERBS 2 **droop,** sag, swag; **lie around,** lounge around, loll around, moon, sit on one's ass *or* butt *or* duff <nonformal>, **loiter about** *or* **around,** slouch around

slovenly ADJS **slipshod,** careless, loose, slack, nonformal, negligent; **untidy,** unsightly, **unkempt; messy** <nonformal>, mussy <nonformal>, **sloppy** <nonformal>, scraggly, poky, seedy <nonformal>, **shabby,** shoddy, chintzy, grubby <nonformal>, **frowzy,** blowzy, tacky <nonformal>

slow VERBS 1 **slow down** *or* **up,** let down *or* up, ease off *or* up, slack off *or* up, slacken, relax, moderate, taper off, lose speed *or* momentum; **decelerate,** retard, delay, **detain,** impede, obstruct, arrest, stay, **check,** curb, **hold up,** hold back
ADJS 2 **leisurely,** slack, moderate, gentle, **easy,** deliberate, go-slow, unhurried, relaxed, gradual, circumspect, tentative, cautious, reluctant, foot-dragging <nonformal>; poking, poky, slow-poky <nonformal>; **sluggish,** languid, languorous, lazy, slothful, indolent, idle, slouchy; slow as slow, slow as molasses *or* molasses in January, slow as death
ADVS 3 **slowly,** leisurely, unhurriedly, relaxedly, easily, moderately, gently; pokingly, pokily; **sluggishly,** languidly, languorously, lazily, indolently, idly, deliberately, with deliberation, circumspectly, tentatively, cautiously, reluctantly; in low gear

slowdown NOUNS 1 **slowing,** retardation, retardment, **slackening,** flagging, slowing down; slowup, **letup,** letdown, slack-up, slack-off, ease-off, ease-up; **delay**, detention, setback, holdup <nonformal>
2 **job action;** rulebook slowdown, sick-in *and* sickout <both nonformal>; work-to-rule, rule-book slowdown

slug NOUNS 1 **slowpoke** <nonformal>, plodder, slow goer, slow-foot, **lingerer,** loiterer, dawdler, dawdle, **laggard,** procrastinator, foot-dragger, stick-in-the-mud <nonformal>, drone, sluggard, lie-abed, goof-off <nonformal>, goldbrick <nonformal>
2 **shot; ball,** cannonball, rifle ball, minié ball; **bullet,** pellet

3 **token,** counter
4 **dose,** portion; shot *and* nip *and* snort *and* dram <all nonformal>
VERBS 5 **fight,** punch, spar, mix it up <nonformal>, knock down, knock out, maul

sluggish ADJS **languid,** languorous, listless, lifeless, inanimate, enervated, debilitated, **pepless** <nonformal>, lackadaisical, slow, wan, **lethargic,** logy, phlegmatic, hebetudinous, apathetic, dopey <nonformal>, nodding, droopy, **dull,** heavy, leaden, lumpish, torpid

slum NOUNS **slums,** the other side *or* the wrong side of the tracks, blighted area *or* neighborhood *or* section, run-down neighborhood, tenement district, shanty-town, hell's kitchen *or* half-acre

slump NOUNS 1 **sinkage,** lowering, **decline,** subsidence, submergence, lapse, decurrence; **droop,** sag; downturn, downtrend, retreat, remission; **descent,** downward trend, downturn, depreciation, **decrease,** drop, fall; **depression,** recession, economic stagnation, **bust** <nonformal>
VERBS 2 **decline,** sink, fail, fall, slip, fade, die, wane, ebb, subside, lapse, **run down,** go down, **go downhill,** fall away, fall off, go off <nonformal>, slide, take a nose dive <nonformal>, go into a tailspin, take a turn for the worse

slur NOUNS **aspersion,** remark, reflection, imputation, **insinuation,** suggestion, sly suggestion, innuendo, whispering campaign; disparaging *or* uncomplimentary remark

slurp VERBS **lap up,** sponge *or* soak up, lick, lap; snuff, snuffle, sniff, sniffle, snuff in *or* up

slut NOUNS **strumpet,** trollop, wench, hussy, jade, baggage, *cocotte* <Fr>, grisette; **tart** *and* **chippy** *and* **floozy** *and* broad <all nonformal>, drab, trull, quean, harridan, Jezebel, wanton, whore <nonformal>, bad woman, **loose woman,** easy woman <nonformal>, easy lay <nonformal>, woman of easy virtue, frail sister

sly ADJS **shrewd,** artful, cunning, knowing, crafty, wily, guileful, canny, slick, smart as a fox, crazy like a fox <both nonformal>; insinuating, insidious, devious, Byzantine, calculating

smack NOUNS 1 **slap,** flap; **box,** cuff, buffet; **spank**
VERBS 2 **slap,** whack, whomp, **cuff,** box, buffet; strike; slap the face, box the ears, give a rap on the knuckles
3 **kiss,** osculate, buss, smooch <nonformal>
ADVS 4 **suddenly,** precipitately, impulsively, impetuously, hastily; dash; bang, slap, plop, plunk, plump, pop; **unexpectedly**, out of a clear blue sky

small ADJS 1 **little,** smallish; **slight,** exiguous; **puny, trifling,** poky, piffling *and* pindling *and* piddling *and* piddly <all nonformal>, **dinky** <nonformal>; one-horse, two-by-four <nonformal>; pint-sized <nonformal>, half-pint; knee-high to a grasshopper; petite; short
2 **ungenerous,** illiberal, unchivalrous, mean, little, paltry, mingy, petty; **niggardly,** stingy; **narrow-minded,** small-minded, mean-minded, mean; uncharitable
ADVS 3 little, **slightly**, fractionally; **on a small scale,** in a small compass, in a small way, on a minuscule *or* infinitesimal scale; in a nutshell

smart ADJS 1 **brainy** <nonformal>, bright, brilliant, scintillating; **clever,** apt, **gifted,** talented; **sharp,** keen; **quick,** nimble, adroit, dexterous; **sharp-witted,** quick-witted, quick-thinking, nimble-witted, quick on the trigger *or* uptake <nonformal>; smart as a whip, sharp as a tack <nonformal>
2 **fashionable,** in fashion, in style, in vogue; all the rage, all the thing; **up-to-date,** up-to-the-minute, with-it <nonformal>, trendy <nonformal>

smart aleck NOUNS **braggart**, know-it-all *or* know-all, smart-ass *and* wise-ass <both nonformal>

smash NOUNS 1 **whack,** smack, thwack, swipe, swing, **punch,** poke, jab
VERBS 2 **demolish,** wreck, total *and* rack up <both nonformal>, undo, unbuild, unmake, dismantle; **disintegrate,** fragment, break to pieces, make mincemeat of, reduce to rubble, atomize, pulverize, shatter

smattering NOUNS **slight knowledge,** vague notion, imperfect knowledge, a little learning, glimmering, **smattering of knowledge,** smattering of ignorance, half-learning, sciolism

smear NOUNS 1 **defamation,** vilification, revilement, defilement, blackening, denigration; character assassination, *ad hominem* <L> *or* personal attack
VERBS 2 **vilify,** revile, defile, sully, soil,

smirch, besmirch, bespatter, tarnish, **blacken,** denigrate, blacken one's good name, give a black eye <nonformal>; **muckrake,** throw mud at, mudsling, heap dirt upon, drag through the mud

smell NOUNS 1 **odor,** scent, aroma, savor; **essence,** redolence, effluvium, emanation, exhalation, fume, breath, subtle odor, whiff, trace, detectable odor; trail, spoor; fragrance; stink, stench
VERBS 2 **scent,** nose; **sniff,** snuff, snuffle, inhale, breathe, breathe in; get a noseful of, smell of, catch a smell of, get *or* take a whiff of, whiff
3 **stink,** smell bad, assail *or* offend the nostrils, smell to high heaven, **reek;** smell up, stink up; stink out

smelly ADJS **malodorous,** fetid, olid, **odorous,** stinking, reeking, reeky, nidorous, smelling, bad-smelling, **evil-smelling,** stenchy; **foul,** vile, putrid, fulsome, noisome, fecal, feculent, excremental, offensive, repulsive, noxious, sulfurous

smile NOUNS 1 smiling; bright smile, gleaming *or* glowing smile, beam; silly smile *or* grin; **grin,** grinning
VERBS 2 crack a smile <nonformal>, break into a smile; **grin,** grin like a Cheshire cat *or* chessy-cat <nonformal>

smirk NOUNS 1 scornful laugh *or* smile, snicker, snigger, sardonic grin, leer, fleer, **sneer,** snort
VERBS 2 **smile,** crack a smile <nonformal>; simper

smitten ADJS **enamored,** charmed, becharmed, **fascinated, infatuated,** infatuate; heartsmitten

smooch VERBS **kiss, osculate,** buss, smack; blow a kiss

smooth VERBS 1 flatten, plane, planish, **level,** even, equalize; **dress,** dub, dab; smooth down *or* out, lay; plaster, plaster down; roll, roll smooth; harrow, drag; grade
2 **pacify,** smooth over *or* out, smooth down, smooth one's feathers; allay, pour oil on troubled waters, pour balm on; cool <nonformal>, defuse; clear the air
ADJS 3 **talkative, voluble, fluent; glib,** flip <nonformal>; gregarious, sociable
4 **even,** smoothened, smoothed out; table-like; flat, level, horizontal; velvety, smooth as silk *or* satin *or* velvet, smooth as a billiard ball *or* baby's ass <nonformal>
5 **suave,** smug, bland, **unctuous,** oily, oleaginous, fulsome, ingratiating, disarming

smother VERBS 1 **suppress,** repress, keep under, stifle, choke *or* hold back, fight down *or* back, inhibit; **suffocate,** stifle, asphyxiate, stop the breath
2 **extinguish,** quench, snuff out, put out, stamp *or* trample out, trample underfoot; **quash,** squash *and* squelch <both nonformal>, **quell,** put down

smudge NOUNS 1 **soil,** soilure, soilage, smut; **smirch,** smutch, smear, **spot,** blot, blotch, **stain**
VERBS 2 **darken,** smutch, **smirch,** besmirch, murk, blotch, blot, dinge; **smear,** blacken one's name *or* reputation, give one a black eye, tear down

smug ADJS **complacent,** self-complacent, self-satisfied, self-content, self-contented; **prudish,** priggish, prim, prissy, stuffy <nonformal>

smuggler NOUNS contrabandist, runner; drug smuggler, mule <nonformal>; gunrunner, rumrunner

smut NOUNS 1 **blackening,** denigration; **smudging,** smutching, smirching; smudge, smutch, smirch
2 **obscenity, ribaldry, pornography,** porno *and* porn <both nonformal>, salacity, **dirt,** filth; lewdness, bawdiness, salaciousness, **smuttiness,** foulness, filthiness, nastiness, vileness, offensiveness

snack NOUNS 1 **light meal,** refreshments, light repast, light lunch, nosh <nonformal>, **bite** <nonformal>
VERBS 2 nibble, pick, nosh <nonformal>; pick at, peck at <nonformal>, eat like a bird

snag NOUNS 1 **crux,** hitch, pinch, rub, catch, joker <nonformal>, where the shoe pinches
VERBS 2 **catch,** take, catch flatfooted, land *and* nail <both nonformal>, hook, **snare,** sniggle, spear, **bag,** trap, entrap

snake NOUNS 1 **serpent,** ophidian; **viper,** pit viper; sea snake; plumber's snake; snake in the grass
VERBS 2 convolve, **wind,** twine, twirl, **twist,** turn, twist and turn, meander, crinkle; serpentine, slink, worm; pluck, wrench

snappy ADJS **quick,** swift, speedy, expeditious, celeritous, alacritous, **prompt,** ready, smart, sharp, quick on the draw *or* trigger *or* upswing <nonformal>; **agile,** nimble, spry

snare NOUNS 1 springe, trap; noose, lasso, lariat; bola; **net,** trawl, dragnet, seine; cobweb; **meshes,** toils
VERBS 2 **catch, take,** catch flatfooted, land *and* nail <both nonformal>, hook, **snag,** sniggle; ensnare, enmesh, entangle, tangle, foul, tangle up with; **net,** bag, trap, entrap; lasso, rope, noose

snarl NOUNS 1 **grimace,** wry face, wry mouth, rictus
2 **fight,** squabble, contention, strife, **tussle,** bicker, wrangle, **tiff,** spat, fuss
3 **tangle,** tangled skein, mess *and* snafu *and* fuck-up <all nonformal>, ravel, snarl-up; can of worms <nonformal>, snake pit
VERBS 4 **growl,** gnarl, **snap,** show one's teeth, spit; **glower,** lower, scowl, **glare,** frown, give a dirty look <nonformal>, look daggers

snatch VERBS **seize,** snatch up, nip, nail <nonformal>, **clutch,** claw, clinch, clench; **kidnap,** hold for ransom; skyjack; **shanghai,** impress

sneak NOUNS 1 **dastard,** craven, poltroon, recreant, caitiff, arrant coward
VERBS 2 **creep,** steal, steal along; pussyfoot *and* gumshoe <both nonformal>, slink, sidle, pad, prowl, nightwalk; **cower,** quail, cringe, crouch, skulk

sneaky ADJS **underhanded;** furtive, stealthy, privy, backstairs, **sly,** shifty, sneaking, skulking, slinking, slinky; **cowering,** quailing, cringing

sneer NOUNS 1 scornful laugh *or* smile, snicker, snigger, **smirk,** sardonic grin, leer, fleer, snort
VERBS 2 **scoff,** jeer, **mock,** revile, **twit,** taunt, jape, flout, scout, have a fling at, cast in one's teeth; cut at; **sneer at,** fleer, curl one's lip

snicker NOUNS 1 scornful laugh *or* smile, snigger, **smirk,** sardonic grin, leer, fleer, **sneer,** snort
VERBS 2 chortle; cackle, crow; snigger, snort; laugh up one's sleeve, laugh in one's beard

snide ADJS **hostile,** antagonistic, repugnant, antipathetic, set against, spiteful, malicious, malevolent, malignant

snip NOUNS 1 **scrap,** tatter, smithereen <nonformal>, patch, **stitch,** shred, tag; **snippet,** snick, chip, nip
VERBS 2 **cut,** slit, lance, scissor

snit NOUNS **dither,** tizzy <nonformal>, swivet, foofaraw, **flutter,** fluster, **fret,** fuss, pother, bother, lather *and* stew <both nonformal>, flap

snitch NOUNS **informer,** betrayer, double-crosser <nonformal>, snitcher <nonformal>; whistle-blower <nonformal>; **tattler,** tattletale, telltale, talebearer; blab *or* blabber *or* blabberer *or* blabbermouth <all nonformal>; **squealer** *and* preacher *and* **stool pigeon** *and* stoolie *and* **fink** *and* rat <all nonformal>

sniveling ADJS **tearful,** weepy <nonformal>; lachrymal, lachrymose, lacrimatory; blubbering, whimpering; canting, unctuous, mealymouthed

snob NOUNS **prig;** elitist; highbrow *and* egghead <both nonformal>, Brahmin, mandarin; name-dropper

snobbish ADJS snobby, **priggish,** snippy <nonformal>; snooty *and* snotty *and* sniffy <all nonformal>; high-hat *and* high-hatted *and* high-hatty <all nonformal>

snoop NOUNS 1 **meddler,** intermeddler; **busybody,** pry, Paul Pry, prier, Nosey Parker *or* nosey Parker *or* Nosy Parker <all nonformal>, snooper, backseat driver <nonformal>
VERBS 2 **pry,** peep, peek, spy, nose, nose into, have a long *or* big nose, poke *or* stick one's nose in; meddle

snort NOUNS 1 **drink,** jolt, **shot,** snifter, wet; quickie
2 scornful laugh *or* smile, snicker, snigger, **smirk,** sardonic grin, leer, fleer, **sneer**
VERBS 3 snicker, snigger
4 **use,** be on; **sniff,** blow, toot, one and one <nonformal>

snotty ADJS **contemptuous,** disdainful, supercilious, sniffy, toplofty, toploftical, **scornful,** sneering, withering, contumelious; snobbish, snobby, priggish

snow job NOUNS **inducement,** coaxing, wheedling, working on <nonformal>, cajolery, cajolement, conning, smoke and mirrors <nonformal>, blandishment, sweet talk *and* soft soap <both nonformal>

snub NOUNS 1 **rebuff,** repulse; **slight,** humiliation, spurning, spurn, disregard, the go-by <nonformal>; cut, **the cold shoulder** <nonformal>; contemptuous dismissal, **dismissal,** kiss-off <nonformal>; **rejection**
VERBS 2 **rebuff,** cut *or* cut dead <nonformal>, drop, repulse; **high-hat** *and* upstage <both nonformal>; **look down**

one's nose at, look cool *or* coldly upon; cold-shoulder *or* turn a cold shoulder upon *or* **give the cold shoulder** <nonformal>
ADJS 3 **shortened, curtailed,** cut short, short-cut, **docked,** bobbed, sheared, shaved, trimmed, clipped, snubbed, nipped

snug ADJS **cozy,** snug as a bug in a rug; friendly, warm; **homelike,** homey *and* down-home <both nonformal>, homely, lived-in, intimate; **compact,** fast, shut fast

snuggle VERBS **nestle,** cuddle, cuddle up, curl up; nest, nuzzle; bundle; snuggle up to

soak VERBS 1 **overprice,** hold up *and* stick *and* sting *and* clip <all nonformal>, **make pay through the nose,** gouge
2 **drench,** imbrue, **souse,** sop, sodden; **saturate,** water-soak, waterlog; **steep,** seethe, macerate, infuse, imbue, impregnate

soap NOUNS **cleanser,** detergent, synthetic detergent, abstergent

soapbox NOUNS **platform; rostrum,** podium, pulpit, speaker's platform *or* stand; hustings, **stump**

soar VERBS 1 **fly,** be airborne, drift, hover; zoom, plane, kite, fly aloft
2 **tower,** rear, spire, outsoar

sob NOUNS 1 **cry,** *cri du coeur* <Fr>, outcry, scream, **howl,** yowl, bawl, yawp, keen, ululation
VERBS 2 **weep,** cry, **bawl,** boo-hoo; **blubber,** whimper, snivel, keen, whine, wail; shed tears, drop a tear; break down and cry, turn on the waterworks <nonformal>; cry one's eyes out

sober ADJS 1 **sedate,** staid, sober-minded, **serious,** grave, solemn, dignified, unsmiling, sobersided; temperate, moderate; **levelheaded,** balanced, coolheaded, cool, **sound,** sober-minded
2 in one's right mind, in possession of one's faculties; clearheaded; **unintoxicated,** uninebriated, uninebriate; cold *or* stone sober <nonformal>, **sober as a judge;** able to walk the chalk mark *or* line <nonformal>; dry, straight, temperate

sociable ADJS **social,** social-minded, fit for society, fond of society, **gregarious,** amiable, **friendly;** civil, urbane, courteous

social NOUNS 1 **social gathering,** social affair, social hour, hospitality hour, affair, gathering, get-together <nonformal>
ADJS 2 **communal,** common, general, public, collective, popular, societal; sociable

socialism NOUNS collective ownership, collectivization, public ownership; **collectivism;** state socialism, *Staatsozialismus* <Ger>; Fabian socialism, Fabianism; utopian socialism; Marxian socialism, Marxism

socialite NOUNS **aristocrat,** patrician, Brahmin, blue-blood, thoroughbred, member of the upper class, swell *and* upper-cruster <both nonformal>, grandee, grand dame, magnifico, lord of creation

socialize VERBS 1 **civilize,** acculturate, enlighten, edify; **educate**
2 **collectivize,** communize, communalize; nationalize, expropriate

society NOUNS 1 *société* <Fr>, fashionable society, **polite society, high society,** high life, *beau monde, haut monde* <both Fr>, good society; **smart set** <nonformal>; the Four Hundred, **upper crust** *and* upper cut <both nonformal>
2 **community,** commonwealth; **kinship group,** clan, totemic *or* totemistic group, phyle, phratry *or* phratria, gens, caste, subcaste, endogamous group; **class, social class**, economic class
3 **company,** association, consociation; guild, organization, fellowship, professional organization, union

soda NOUNS **beverage,** drink, thirst quencher; **soft drink,** nonalcoholic beverage; cold drink; carbonated water, soda water, sparkling water, pop, soda pop, tonic

sodden ADJS **soaked, drenched,** soused, bathed, steeped, macerated; **water-soaked,** waterlogged; soaking, sopping; wringing wet, soaking wet, sopping wet, wet to the skin, like a drowned rat; soppy, **soggy,** dripping wet

sodomy NOUNS **anal sex,** anal intercourse, buggery <nonformal>

soft ADJS 1 **faint, low,** gentle, subdued, dim, feeble, weak, faint-sounding, low-sounding, soft-sounding
2 **sentimental,** sentimentalized, **mawkish,** maudlin, cloying; sticky *and* gooey *and* schmaltzy *and* sappy *and* soppy <all nonformal>, oversentimental, oversentimentalized, bathetic
3 nonresistive, nonrigid; whisper-soft,

soft as putty *or* clay *or* dough, etc, soft as a baby's bottom

soft as sinews of the new-born babe
SHAKESPEARE

soften VERBS 1 **extenuate,** mitigate, palliate, lessen, diminish, **ease,** mince; **soft-pedal;** subdue, tame, hold in check, keep a tight rein, chasten, underplay, play down, downplay, de-emphasize, tone *or* tune down
2 **cushion,** absorb the shock, **soften the blow,** break the fall, deaden, damp *or* dampen, suppress, neutralize, offset
softhearted ADJS **tender,** soft, tender-hearted, warmhearted; kindhearted, warm, **sympathetic,** sympathizing, **compassionate**, merciful
softy ADJS **weakling,** weak *or* meek soul, weak sister <nonformal>, hothouse plant, softling, **jellyfish,** invertebrate, gutless wonder <nonformal>; **wimp,** poor *or* weak *or* dull tool <nonformal>
soggy ADJS **soaked,** drenched, soaking, sopping; **sodden,** soppy, soaky
soil NOUNS 1 soilage, smut; **smirch,** smudge, smutch, smear, **spot,** blot, blotch
2 **land, ground,** landmass, earth, **sod,** clod, **dirt,** dust, clay, marl; arable land; topsoil, subsoil
VERBS 3 **vilify,** revile, defile, sully, smear, smirch, besmirch, bespatter, tarnish, **blacken,** denigrate, blacken one's good name, give a black eye <nonformal>; **muckrake,** throw mud at, mudsling, heap dirt upon, drag through the mud; **stigmatize,** brand
soiree NOUNS **social gathering,** social; **reception,** at home, salon, levee
sojourn NOUNS temporary stay; **stay,** stop; **stopover,** stopoff, stayover, layover
solace NOUNS **consolation,** solacement, easement, heart's ease; support, **comfort,** crumb *or* shred of comfort; condolence, sympathy

surcease of sorrow
POE

soldier NOUNS 1 **military man** *or* **woman,** serviceman, servicewoman, navy man *or* woman; air service-man *or* -woman

2 <nonformal> **grunt, dogface,** foot-slogger, paddlefoot, doughfoot, blister-foot, crunchie, line doggie, ground-pounder

3 defender, champion, advocate; upholder; guardian angel, supporter; vindicator, apologist; **protector; guard;** paladin; guard dog, attack dog, junkyard dog
sole ADJS **unique,** singular, absolute, unrepeated, **alone,** lone, **only,** only-begotten, **one and only,** first and last; celibate
solemn ADJS 1 **dignified,** sober, grave, unsmiling, weighty, **somber,** frowning, **grim; sedate,** staid; **serious,** earnest, thoughtful; straight-faced, long-faced, grim-faced, stone-faced
2 **lofty,** elevated, sublime, grand, majestic, noble, stately; **reverent,** reverential, venerative, venerational, adoring
solicit VERBS **canvass; court,** woo, address, sue, sue for, pop the question <nonformal>; **seek,** bid for, look for; **fish for,** angle for; **make advances,** approach, **make an overture,** solicit, importune
solicitor NOUNS 1 **petitioner,** supplicant, suppliant, suitor; **applicant,** solicitant, claimant; **aspirant,** seeker; canvasser
2 **lawyer,** attorney, attorney-at-law, barrister, **counselor,** counselor-at-law, **counsel,** legal counsel *or* counselor, legal adviser, legal expert, **advocate,** pleader; member of the bar, legal practitioner, officer of the court
solicitous ADJS **considerate,** thoughtful, mindful, heedful, attentive, tactful, mindful of others; **helpful,** agreeable, **obliging,** indulgent, tolerant, lenient
solid NOUNS 1 solid body, body, mass; lump, clump, cluster; block, cake; node, knot
ADJS 2 **firm,** sound, stout, sturdy, hard, tough, hard-boiled <nonformal>, **staunch,** stable; sound as a dollar, solid as a rock, firm as Gibraltar, made of iron
3 **unanimous,** consentaneous, **with one voice;** agreeing, in agreement, like-minded, of one mind, of the same mind; of a piece, **at one,** at one with; **complete,** whole, total, global, **entire,** intact
4 **valid,** sound, well-grounded, well-founded, conforming to the facts *or* the data *or* the evidence *or* reality, hard, substantial
solidarity NOUNS **community,** harmony, concordance, concord, fellowship, fel-

low feeling, concert, **teamwork,** team spirit, esprit, *esprit de corps* <Fr>; solidity

solidify VERBS **cohere,** set, conglomerate, agglomerate, conglobate; **congeal,** coagulate, clabber <nonformal>, **clot; cluster,** mass, bunch; **integrate,** coalesce, come together, make one, unitize

soliloquy NOUNS monology, self-address; **monologue;** aside; monodrama; apostrophe

solitary ADJS **alone; in solitude,** by oneself, all alone; **lonely,** lonesome, lone; **one,** single, singular, individual, sole, unique; reclusive, antisocial

solution NOUNS 1 resolution, **answer,** reason, explanation; **finding,** conclusion, determination, ascertainment, verdict, judgment; **outcome,** upshot, denouement, **result,** issue, end, end result; **happy ending** *or* outcome, the answer to one's prayers, the light at the end of the tunnel; possible solution, **scenario**
2 decoction, infusion, mixture; chemical solution; lixivium, leach, leachate; **suspension,** colloidal suspension; **emulsion,** gel, aerosol

solve VERBS **resolve,** find the solution *or* answer, **clear up,** get, get right, do, work, **work out,** find out, figure out, dope *and* dope out <both nonformal>; **straighten out,** iron out, sort out, puzzle out; **get to the bottom** *or* **heart of,** fathom, plumb

solvent ADJS 1 **sound,** substantial, solid, good, sound as a dollar, creditworthy; **able to pay,** good for, unindebted, out of the hole *or* the red
2 dissolvent, resolvent, resolutive, thinning, cutting, diluent; alkahestic

somber ADJS **gloomy,** dismal, murky, bleak, grim, sombrous, **solemn,** grave; sad, *triste* <Fr>, **funereal,** funebrial, crepehanging <nonformal>, saturnine; sinister, dark, black, dreary; **lackluster, dull,** deadened, lifeless, **drab,** wan

somebody NOUNS **personage,** important person, person of importance *or* consequence, **great man** *or* **woman,** man *or* woman of mark *or* note, **notable,** notability, figure; **celebrity,** famous person, person of renown, personality

something NOUNS **object,** article, thing, material thing, affair; whatsit <nonformal>, what's-its-name; something or other, *etwas* <Ger>, *eppes* <Yiddish>, *quelque chose* <Fr>; artifact

sometime ADJS 1 **former,** past, fore, **previous,** late, recent, **once,** onetime, **erstwhile,** then, quondam; **occasional,** casual, incidental; off-and-on, spare, sparetime, **part-time**
ADVS 2 **someday,** some of these days, one of these days, some fine day *or* morning, sometime or other, somewhen, **sooner or later**

somewhat ADVS **to a degree,** to a certain extent, to some degree, in some measure, to such an extent, *pro tanto* <L>; **moderately,** mildly, detectably, just visibly, modestly, appreciably, visibly, **fairly,** tolerably, **partially,** partly, part, in part, incompletely

son NOUNS **offspring,** child, scion; son and heir, a chip of *or* off the old block, sonny; stepson, foster child

song NOUNS lay, *Lied* <Ger>, *chanson* <Fr>, carol, **ditty,** canticle, lilt; **ballad,** ballade, *ballata* <Ital>; *canzone* <Ital>; canzonet, *canzonetta* <Ital>

soon ADVS **presently,** directly, shortly, in a short time *or* while, **before long,** ere long, in no long time, in a while, **in a little while,** after a while, by and by, anon, betimes, *bientôt* <Fr>, in due time, in due course, at the first opportunity; in a moment *or* minute, *tout à l'heure* <Fr>

soot NOUNS **dirt,** grime; dust; smut

soothe VERBS **quiet,** quieten, **lull,** quiesce, **calm,** calm down, tranquilize, pacify, passivize, pour oil on troubled waters; mollify, dulcify; **settle,** smooth over *or* out, smooth down, smooth one's feathers

soothing ADJS **palliative,** lenitive, alleviative, assuasive, balmy, balsamic, demulcent, emollient; **sedative,** calmative, calmant, depressant, tranquilizing, **relaxing,** pacifying

sooty ADJS **dingy,** grimy, smoky, fuliginous, **smudgy,** smutty, blotchy, dirty, **muddy,** murky, smirched, besmirched

sophisticated ADJS 1 **worldly,** worldly-wise, wise in the ways of the world, knowing, cosmopolitan, cosmopolite, blasé, dry behind the ears, not born yesterday, long in the tooth
2 nice, fine, delicate, dainty, **subtle,** discriminating, fastidious

sorcerer NOUNS **necromancer,** wizard, wonder-worker, warlock, theurgist; warlock, male witch; thaumaturge, thaumaturgist; **conjurer**, diviner

sorceress NOUNS shamaness; **witch,** witchwoman <nonformal>, witchwife <Scots>, **hex, hag,** lamia

sordid ADJS **squalid,** wretched, shabby; **disreputable,** discreditable, dishonorable, unsavory, shady, **seamy**

sore NOUNS 1 pustule, papule, papula, fester; sore spot, tender spot, lesion
ADJS 2 **raw;** smarting, tingling, **burning; irritated,** inflamed, tender, sensitive, fiery, angry, red; algetic; chafed, galled; **festering; painful,** harsh, bitter, sharp

sorrow NOUNS sorrowing, **grief,** care, **woe;** heartgrief, heartfelt grief; **anguish,** misery, agony; **lamentation**

sorry ADJS 1 **regretful,** remorseful, full of remorse, **ashamed,** shamefaced, **rueful,** repining, unhappy about; **self-reproachful,** self-reproaching, self-condemning, self-convicting
2 **disgraceful,** shameful, pitiful, deplorable, opprobrious, sad; degrading, debasing, demeaning; **paltry,** poor, common, **mean,** pitiable, pathetic

sort NOUNS 1 **kind,** ilk, type, breed of cat <nonformal>, lot <nonformal>, **variety,** species, genus, *genre* <Fr>, phylum, denomination, designation, description, style, manner, **nature, character,** persuasion, the like *or* likes of <nonformal>
VERBS 2 **distinguish,** draw *or* make distinctions, secern, **separate,** separate out, divide, analyze, subdivide, **set apart,** sift, sift out, sieve, sieve out, winnow, screen, screen out, classify, sort out

so-so ADJS 1 **middling, ordinary,** usual, routine, common, mediocre, merely adequate, passing, banal
ADVS 2 **mediocrely,** middlingly, fairly, fairishly, middling well, fair to middling <nonformal>, moderately, modestly, **indifferently;** passably, **tolerably**

soul NOUNS 1 person, persona, body, warm body <nonformal>; **individuality,** personhood
2 **psyche,** spirit, spiritus, *âme* <Fr>, **heart, mind,** anima, *anima humana* <L>; *atman* and *purusha* and *buddhi* and *jiva* and *jivatma* <all Skt>; *ba* and *khu* <both Egyptian myth>; *ruach* and *nephesh* <both Hebrew>; spiritual being, inner man

the Divinity that stirs within us
ADDISON

soul-searching NOUNS self-analysis, examination of conscience

sound NOUNS 1 sonance, acoustic, acoustical *or* acoustic phenomenon; auditory phenomenon *or* stimulus, auditory effect; noise
2 **inlet, cove,** arm of the sea, arm, armlet, **bay,** fjord, bight
VERBS 3 make a sound *or* noise, give forth *or* emit a sound; **reverberate,** resound, **rumble,** roll, boom, echo
4 **take soundings,** make a sounding, heave *or* cast *or* sling the lead, **fathom, plumb,** plumb-line, plumb the depths
ADJS 5 whole, wholesome; unimpaired; sound of mind and body, sound in wind and limb, sound as a dollar <nonformal>
6 **stable,** substantial, firm, solid, stabile; solid as a rock, built on bedrock; **logical,** reasonable, rational, cogent, sensible, sane, justifiable, admissible; well-argued, well-founded, well-grounded, **valid**

sound bite NOUNS **excerpt,** extract, selection, extraction, excerption, snippet; selected passage; **clip** <nonformal>, film clip, outtake

sour VERBS 1 turn sour *or* acid, **acidify,** acidulate, acetify; acerbate, exacerbate; **embitter,** bitter, envenom
ADJS 2 soured, sourish; **tart,** tartish; crab, **crabbed;** acerb, acerbic, acerbate
3 **complaining,** faultfinding, grumbling, growling, **peevish,** petulant, sulky; **sour-tempered,** prune-faced <nonformal>

source NOUNS **origin,** genesis, original, origination, **derivation,** rise, beginning, conception, inception, commencement, **head;** provenance, provenience, background; **informant,** informer, teller, interviewee, enlightener

souvenir NOUNS **memento,** remembrance, token, trophy, keepsake, relic, favor, token of remembrance; *memento mori* <L>; **memorabilia** <pl>

sovereign NOUNS 1 **potentate,** monarch, ruler, prince, dynast, **crowned head,** emperor, *imperator* <L>, king-emperor, **king,** anointed king, majesty, royalty, royal, royal personage
ADJS 2 **governing,** controlling, regulating, regulative, regulatory, **commanding; ruling,** reigning, regnant; self-governing

sow VERBS **seed,** seed down, seminate,

inseminate; **disseminate,** broadcast, sow broadcast, scatter seed

spa NOUNS **health resort,** watering place, baths; mineral spring, warm *or* hot spring

space NOUNS 1 **extent,** extension, spatial extension, uninterrupted extension, space continuum, continuum; **expanse,** expansion; accommodation, room, measure; **margin,** clearance, open space *or* field, elbowroom, breathing space, **leeway** <nonformal>, sea room, wide berth
2 **outer space,** cosmic space, empty space, ether space, pressureless space, celestial spaces, interplanetary *or* interstellar *or* intergalactic *or* intercosmic space, metagalactic space, **the void**
VERBS 3 **interspace,** make a space, set at intervals, dot, scatter, **space out,** separate, split off, part, dispart, set *or* keep apart
ADJS 4 **spatial,** dimensional, proportional; **extraterrestrial,** extramundane, alien

spacecraft NOUNS **spaceship,** space rocket, rocket ship, manned rocket, interplanetary rocket; orbiter; **shuttle,** space shuttle; **capsule,** space capsule, ballistic capsule

spacious ADJS **sizable,** roomy, commodious, capacious, ample; spreading, **vast,** vasty, broad, **wide,** deep, high, voluminous

span NOUNS 1 **extent,** length, space, **reach,** stretch, range, compass, stride, haul, a way
2 **arch,** vault, vaulting, concameration, camber; ogive; apse; **bridge,** viaduct
3 **interval,** lapse of time, time frame, space, timespan, stretch, time-lag, time-gap
VERBS 4 **extend,** reach, stretch, sweep, spread, run, **reach** *or* stretch *or* thrust out; straddle, take in, hold, encompass, surround, environ

spangled ADJS **illuminated,** bespangled, tinseled, studded; star-spangled, star-studded

spank VERBS **correct,** rap on the knuckles, **chastise,** turn over one's knees; **whip,** give a whipping *or* beating *or* thrashing, **beat,** thrash, flog

spar VERBS **quarrel,** dispute, oppugn, altercate, **fight,** box, squabble, tiff, spat, **bicker,** wrangle, spar, broil, have words, set to, join issue, make the fur fly

spare VERBS 1 **forgive,** pardon, excuse, give *or* grant forgiveness; **abstain,** refrain, forgo, forbear, waive; **preserve,** conserve, save; **give away,** dispose of, part with, sacrifice
ADJS 2 **reserved,** preserved, saved, conserved, put by, kept, retained, held, withheld, held back, kept *or* held in reserve
3 **economical,** thrifty, frugal, economic, unwasteful, conserving, **saving,** economizing, **sparing; austere,** chaste, unadorned, uncluttered, stark, severe; scant, **scanty**

spark NOUNS 1 **inspiration,** infusion, infection; fire, firing, sparking; **immediate cause,** proximate cause, trigger; sparkle, **glitter,** glimmer, shimmer, twinkle, blink
VERBS 2 **kindle,** enkindle, **fire,** spark off, trigger, trigger off, touch off, set off, light the fuse, **enflame,** set afire *or* on fire
3 **originate,** give origin to, give occasion to, **give rise to,** spark off, set off, trigger, trigger off; **squire,** swain

sparkle NOUNS 1 **bubbling,** bubbliness, effervescence, spumescence, frothiness, frothing, foaming; **fizz,** fizzle, carbonation; ebullience, **spirit,** liveliness, vivacity, dash, verve, vividness
VERBS 2 **effervesce,** fizz, fizzle; scintillate, be brilliant, coruscate; **glitter,** glimmer, shimmer, twinkle, blink, spangle

sparse ADJS scant, **scanty,** exiguous, **infrequent,** scarce, scarce as hen's teeth <nonformal>, poor, piddling, piddly, thin, slim, meager

Spartan ADJS stoic, stoical, disciplined, self-controlled; austere, monkish, cloistral, severe, stark, ascetic, bare

spasm NOUNS **convulsion,** cramp, **paroxysm,** throes; **seizure,** grip, attack, **fit,** access, ictus

spastic ADJS **spasmodic,** paroxysmal, jerky, herky-jerky <nonformal>, eclamptic, orgasmic, convulsive

spat NOUNS **quarrel,** bicker, wrangle, snarl, **tiff,** fuss

spatter VERBS splatter, splash, **bespatter,** dabble, bedabble, spot, splotch; **sprinkle,** besprinkle, asperge

spawn VERBS **lay,** deposit, drop; breed, engender, beget, hatch; bring forth, give rise to, give being to, bring *or* call into being

speak VERBS **talk,** use language, communicate orally *or* verbally; use nonformal speech *or* style, colloquialize, vernacularize; jargon, jargonize, cant; patter

speaker NOUNS **talker,** public speaker, speechmaker, speecher, speechifier <nonformal>, spieler *and* jawsmith <both nonformal>; after-dinner speaker; **spokesman,** spokeswoman

speak up VERBS **speak out,** speak one's piece *or* one's mind, pipe up, open one's mouth, open one's lips, say out, say loud and clear, say out loud, sound off, lift *or* raise one's voice, break silence, find one's tongue; **have one's say,** put in one's two cents worth <nonformal>

spear NOUNS 1 throwing spear, javelin, assegai
VERBS 2 lance, poniard, bayonet, saber, sword, put to the sword; **catch,** take, land *and* nail <both nonformal>, hook, **snag,** snare, sniggle, harpoon

special ADJS **particular,** especial, specific, express, precise, **concrete; singular,** individual, individualist *or* individualistic; **distinguished,** noteworthy, **exceptional,** extraordinary

specialty NOUNS speciality, **line,** pursuit, pet subject, business, line of business, **field,** area, main interest; **forte,** métier, strong point, long suit

species NOUNS **kind,** sort, ilk, type, breed of cat <nonformal>, **variety,** genus, *genre* <Fr>, phylum, denomination, designation, description, style, manner, **nature, character,** persuasion, the like *or* likes of <nonformal>

specific ADJS **particular,** express, precise, **concrete; singular,** individual, individualist *or* individualistic

specification NOUNS **designation,** stipulation, specifying, designating, stipulating, singling-out, featuring, highlighting, focusing on, denomination; **allocation,** attribution, fixing, selection, assignment, pinning down

specify VERBS **designate;** denominate, name, denote; **itemize,** circumstantiate, particularize, **spell out,** detail, go *or* enter into detail, descend to particulars, give full particulars, atomize, anatomize; **call attention to,** direct attention to, **bring under** *or* **to one's notice,** hold up to notice, bring to attention, **mention,** mention in passing, touch on; **single out,** focus on, call *or* bring to notice, direct to the attention, **feature,** highlight

specimen NOUNS **sample,** taste, taster, little bite, little smack; **representative,** representation, **type,** typification, embodiment, **example**, exemplar; exemplification

specious ADJS **spurious, ostensible,** hypocritical, **fallacious,** colorable, plausible, hollow, superficially *or* apparently sound; deceptive, illusive, empty

speck NOUNS **dot;** mote, fleck, flyspeck, jot, tittle, iota, **trace,** trace amount, suspicion, *soupçon* <Fr>; **particle,** crumb, scrap, bite, snip, snippet; **blotch,** patch, speckle

speckle VERBS **spot,** bespot, **blot,** blotch, speck, bespeckle; freckle; **spatter,** splatter, splash, splotch

spectacle NOUNS **sight;** exhibit, **exhibition,** exposition, **show,** stage show, **display, presentation,** representation; **pageant,** pageantry; parade, pomp

spectacular ADJS extravagant, sensational, glaring, flaring, flaunting, screaming <nonformal>, obtrusive, vulgar, crude

spectator NOUNS **witness,** eyewitness; **bystander,** passerby

specter NOUNS **ghost,** phantom, revenant; **phantasm,** phantasma, wraith; **apparition,** appearance; shape, form, figure, presence; eidolon, idolum

spectrum NOUNS **range,** scope, compass, reach, stretch, expanse radius, sweep, carry, fetch; **gamut**

speculate VERBS **consider,** contemplate, reflect, study, ponder, perpend, **weigh,** deliberate, debate, meditate, muse, brood, ruminate, chew the cud <nonformal>, digest; **bet,** bet on, gamble

speculator NOUNS adventurer, operator; big operator, smart operator; **plunger,** gunslinger; **arbitrager** *or* arbitrageur; **gambler,** venturer; **theorist,** theorizer, **theoretician**

speech NOUNS **talk,** the power *or* faculty of speech, the verbal *or* oral faculty, talking, speaking, **discourse,** oral communication, vocal *or* voice *or* viva-voce communication, communication; rhetoric; oration, address, declamation, harangue

a faculty given to man to conceal his thoughts
TALLEYRAND

speechless ADJS **taciturn,** untalkative, **silent,** wordless, **mum; mute**, dumb, quiet; **closemouthed,** tight-lipped

speed NOUNS 1 **rapidity,** celerity, swiftness, fastness, **quickness,** snappiness <nonformal>, **speediness; dispatch,** expedition, promptness, promptitude, instantaneousness
2 stimulant; Adrenalin <trademark> *or* adrenaline <Brit> *or* epinephrine <US>, aloes; amphetamine sulphate, aromatic spirits of ammonia, caffeine, dextroamphetamine sulfate *or* Dexedrine <trademark>, digitalin *or* digitalis, methamphetamine hydrochloride *or* Methedrine <trademark>, smelling salts *or* salts
VERBS 3 **go fast,** skim, **fly,** flit, fleet, wing one's way, outstrip the wind; go like greased lightning; **rush, tear,** dash, dart, shoot, hurtle, bolt, fling, **scamper, scurry,** scour, scud, scuttle, scramble, **race,** careen; **hasten,** haste, **hurry,** accelerate, speed up, **hurry up,** quicken, hustle <nonformal>, bustle, bundle, precipitate, forward

4 <nonformal> **barrel,** tear along, thunder along, breeze along, tear up the road, rip, whiz, go full tilt, step on it, put the pedal to the metal, make tracks, go like blazes, get the lead out

speedy ADJS **quick,** swift, expeditious, snappy <nonformal>, celeritous, alacritous, dispatchful <old>, **prompt,** ready, smart, sharp, quick on the draw *or* trigger *or* upswing <nonformal>; **hasty,** hurried, festinate, **quick,** flying

spell NOUNS 1 magic spell, **charm,** glamour; evil eye, *malocchio* <Ital>, whammy <nonformal>; **hex,** jinx, curse
2 **interval,** lapse of time, time frame, space, span, timespan, stretch; course, series, **bout,** turn
VERBS 3 orthographize; spell *or* respell phonetically; spell out; spell backward; outspell, spell down
4 **substitute for,** relieve, cover for; ghost, **take the place of**

spellbound ADJS fascinated, captivated, under a charm, beguiled, enthralled, enraptured, enravished, enchanted, entranced, bewitched, hypnotized, mesmerized, stupefied, lost in wonder *or* amazement

spend VERBS 1 consume, expend, **pass,** employ, **put in;** devote, bestow, give to *or* give over to, devote *or* consecrate *or* dedicate to; dissipate, **exhaust,** use up
2 **expend,** disburse, pay out, fork out *or* over <nonformal>, shell out <nonformal>, **lay out,** outlay; loosen *or* untie the purse strings *and* throw money around <both nonformal>, splurge, spend money like a drunken sailor *and* spend money as if it were going out of style <both nonformal>

spendthrift NOUNS **prodigal,** wastrel, waster, **squanderer;** wastethrift, spender, spendall, big-time spender <nonformal>; Diamond Jim Brady; prodigal son

spent ADJS **devitalized,** drained, exhausted, sapped, burned-out, used up, played out, *ausgespielt* <Ger>, effete, etiolated; **wasted,** squandered, dissipated, consumed, used, lost; **gone to waste,** run *or* gone to seed; down the drain *or* spout *or* rathole <nonformal>

spew VERBS **erupt,** burst forth *or* out, break out, blow out *or* open, eruct, belch, **vomit,** spout, disgorge, **discharge,** eject, throw *or* hurl forth

sphere NOUNS 1 orb, **orbit,** ambit, circle; **realm,** demesne, **domain,** dominion, jurisdiction, bailiwick; **province,** precinct, **field,** arena
2 **ball,** globe, rondure; **pellet;** boll; **gob,** glob <nonformal>, blob, gobbet; **balloon,** bladder, bubble

spice NOUNS **flavoring,** flavor, flavorer; **seasoning,** seasoner, **relish,** condiment, condiments; **tang,** nip, bite; punch, snap, zip, ginger

spicy ADJS **zestful,** zesty, **nippy,** snappy, **tangy,** with a kick; spiced, seasoned, high-seasoned; curried, **peppery,** hot, burning, hot as pepper; musky; **risqué,** risky, **racy,** salty, **off-color,** suggestive, scabrous; piquant, lively, juicy, succulent

spiel NOUNS **sales talk,** sales pitch, patter; **pitch** *or* ballyhoo <both nonformal>

spill NOUNS 1 **overturn,** upset, overset, **overthrow,** upturn, turnover; **capsizing,** capsize, capsizal, turning turtle; **overflow,** spillage, spillover, overflowing, overrunning, alluvion, alluvium
VERBS 2 **run over,** well over, brim over, pour out *or* over, **slop, slosh,** spill out *or* over

spin NOUNS 1 **misrepresentation,** perversion, distortion, deformation, garbling, twisting, slanting; **coloring,** miscoloring, false coloring; falsification, spin control, disinformation; **slant,** angle

2 **whirl,** wheel, reel, **turn,** round; dizzy round, rat race
VERBS 3 **whirl,** whirligig, twirl, **wheel, reel,** spin like a top *or* teetotum, whirl like a dervish; **swirl,** eddy; **braid,** twist

spindly ADJS **unsteady,** shaky, rickety, spidery, teetering, teetery, tottery, tottering; gangling *and* gangly <both nonformal>, gawky, **spindling; underweight,** undersized, undernourished

spineless ADJS **weak-willed,** wimpy *or* wimpish <nonformal>, feeble, fainthearted, **frail,** faint, infirm; invertebrate; without a will of one's own

spin-off NOUNS **outgrowth,** offshoot, offspring, issue, aftermath, legacy; derivative

spinster NOUNS **single** *or* unmarried woman, spinstress, **old maid,** maid, maiden, bachelor girl, single girl, single woman, lone woman, maiden lady, feme sole

spiny ADJS **barbed,** tined, pronged; **spined,** spinous, hispid, acanthoid, acanthous

spiral NOUNS 1 **coil,** whorl, roll, **curl,** curlicue, ringlet, pigtail; helix, volute, volution, involute, evolute, gyre, scroll
ADJS 2 spiroid, volute, voluted; **helical,** helicoid, helicoidal; verticillate, whorled, scrolled; cochlear, cochleate

spire NOUNS **tower; turret,** *tour* <Fr>; campanile, bell tower, belfry; church spire

spirit NOUNS 1 **animation,** spiritedness, **briskness,** perkiness, pertness, **life,** life force, *élan vital* <Fr>; **zeal,** ardor, ardency, fervor, fervency, fervidness, warmth, fire, heat, heatedness, **passion;** soul, indwelling spirit, force of life, living force, *vis vitae* or *vis vitalis* <both L>, **vital force** *or* energy, vital principle, **vital spark** *or* **flame**
2 **familiar spirit,** familiar; **genius, good genius,** daemon, demon, *numen* <L>, totem; **guardian,** guardian spirit, guardian angel, angel, good angel, ministering angel, **fairy godmother**

spirited ADJS sprightly, **lively,** animated, vivacious, vital, zestful, zippy <nonformal>, **exuberant,** hearty; **active,** bubbly, ebullient, effervescent, chipper *and* perky <both nonformal>

spirits NOUNS **liquor,** intoxicating liquor, adult beverage, **hard liquor, whiskey,** firewater, spiritus frumenti, usquebaugh <Scots>, schnapps, **intoxicant,** toxicant, inebriant, strong drink, alcoholic drink *or* beverage, **booze** <nonformal>

spiritual ADJS 1 **godly,** godlike; God-fearing; righteous, holy
2 **ghostly,** ghostlike; **psychic,** psychical; **occult,** supernatural, astral

spite NOUNS spitefulness, despite, despitefulness, **malice,** malevolence, malignity, cattiness; grudge

splash NOUNS 1 **lap,** swash, wash, slosh, plash
VERBS 2 **spatter,** splatter, **bespatter,** dabble, bedabble, spot, splotch

splay VERBS **diverge,** divaricate; spread, **spread out,** outspread, fan out, deploy

splendid ADJS **magnificent,** splendiferous, tremendous, immense, **wonderful,** glorious, divine, heavenly, terrific, sensational; sterling, golden; **bright,** brilliant, vivid, **resplendent,** bright and shining

splendor NOUNS **luster,** resplendence *or* resplendency, refulgence, splendidness, **brilliance,** brightness, radiance, radiant splendor

splice NOUNS 1 **fastening,** attachment, affixation; bond, fastener
VERBS 2 **fasten, bind, tie,** brace, truss, **lash,** leash, rope, strap, lace

splinter NOUNS 1 **piece,** bit, scrap, bite, sliver; **shiver,** smithereen <nonformal>
VERBS 2 **shatter,** shiver, break to *or* into pieces, fragmentize, break to *or* into smithereens <nonformal>

split NOUNS 1 **breach,** break, rupture, schism, rift, cleft, splinter, **disunity,** disunion, disruption, separation, cleavage, divergence, division, dividedness
VERBS 2 **cleave,** slit, rive, rent, rip open; breach, break, fracture, rupture, sunder; **clear out,** make oneself scarce
3 **apportion,** portion, parcel, partition, part, divide, share; **split up,** carve, cut, slice, carve up, slice up, cut up, cut *or* slice the pie *or* melon <nonformal>; divide *or* split fifty-fifty

splurge VERBS **spend,** throw money around <nonformal>, go on a spending spree, spend money like a drunken sailor *and* spend money as if it were going out of style <both nonformal>, **squander**

spoil VERBS 1 **mar,** botch, **ruin,** wreck, blight, play havoc with; destroy, corrupt, canker; **butcher,** murder, make sad work of; **plunder,** pillage, loot, sack, spoliate, despoil

2 <nonformal> **screw up, foul up,** fuck up, bitch up, **blow,** louse up, queer, snafu, snarl up, balls up <Brit>, bugger, bugger up, gum up, ball up, bollix, bollix up, **mess up,** hash up, muck up; play hob with, play hell with, play merry hell with, play the devil with, rain on one's picnic *or* parade; upset the apple cart, cook, sink, shoot down in flames; **total**

3 **decay,** decompose, disintegrate; go *or* fall into decay, **go bad;** rot, putrefy, putresce; mold, molder, molder away, rot away, rust away, mildew
4 **indulge, cater to; give way to,** yield to, let one have his own way; **pamper,** cosset, **coddle,** mollycoddle, pet, make a lap dog of; spare the rod

spoken ADJS **vernacular,** colloquial, conversational, unliterary, nonformal, demotic, vulgar, vulgate

spokesperson NOUNS **spokesman,** spokeswoman, spokespeople, official spokesman *or* -woman *or* -person, press officer, speaker, **voice,** mouthpiece <nonformal>

sponge NOUNS 1 **parasite,** barnacle, leech; **sponger,** freeloader <nonformal>, smell-feast; beat *and* deadbeat <both nonformal>
VERBS 2 **sponge on** *and* **sponge off of** <both nonformal>; feed on, fatten on, batten on, live off of, use as a meal ticket, freeload

sponsor NOUNS 1 **financer,** backer, funder, **patron,** supporter, angel <nonformal>, Maecenas; cash cow *and* staker *and* grubstaker <all nonformal>, meal ticket <nonformal>
VERBS 2 **finance,** back, fund, patronize, support, provide for, capitalize, provide capital *or* money for, pay for, bankroll <nonformal>, angel <nonformal>, put up the money; **stake** *or* **grubstake** <both nonformal>

spontaneous ADJS **unpremeditated,** unmeditated, **uncalculated,** undeliberated, **undesigned,** unstudied; **involuntary,** automatic, impulsive; **instinctual,** libidinal

spoof NOUNS 1 **hoax, deception,** humbug, flam, fake *and* fakement, **rip-off** <nonformal>, sham; mare's nest
VERBS 2 **fool,** make a fool of, **pull one's leg,** make an ass of; **trick; kid** *and* put one on <both nonformal>; **play a trick on,** play a practical joke upon, send on a fool's errand

sporadic ADJS **irregular, haphazard,** desultory, **erratic,** fitful, promiscuous, indiscriminate, spasmodic, casual, frivolous, capricious, random, hit-or-miss

sport NOUNS 1 **banter,** badinage, persiflage, **raillery,** rallying, good-natured banter, harmless teasing
2 **dandy, fop,** coxcomb, macaroni, gallant, dude *and* swell <both nonformal>, jackanapes, clotheshorse, fashion plate
3 **fun,** funmaking, fun and games, **play,** game; **good time,** lovely time, pleasant time; **sports, athletics,** athletic competition, sports activity

spot NOUNS 1 **location,** situation, place, position, *lieu* <Fr>, placement, emplacement, stead
2 **stain, blot,** blur, **blotch,** patch, speck, speckle, fleck, flick, flyspeck
3 **tight spot;** squeeze, tight squeeze, hot spot, hot seat; **scrape,** jam, hot water, tit in the wringer; **mess,** holy *or* unholy mess; hell to pay <all nonformal>
VERBS 4 **locate,** situate, site, place, position; emplace, **install,** put in place; **dot,** blotch, splotch, dash, **speck,** speckle, fleck, freckle; **detect,** see, lay eyes on, catch sight of, **spy,** espy, descry, sense, pick up, notice, discern, **perceive,** make out, recognize, distinguish, identify

spotless ADJS stainless, taintless, **unblemished,** unspotted, untainted, unsoiled, unsullied, undefiled; pure, clean, **immaculate,** impeccable, squeaky-clean <nonformal>, **chaste,** virtuous

spotlight NOUNS 1 **celebrity,** *réclame, éclat* <both Fr>; **limelight** <nonformal>, bright light, public eye *or* consciousness
VERBS 2 **stress,** lay emphasis *or* stress upon, feature, highlight, place emphasis on, give emphasis to

spotty ADJS 1 **sporadic,** patchy, scrappy, snatchy, choppy, **broken,** disconnected, discontinuous; **intermittent,** desultory, fluctuating; **scattered,** sprinkled, few and far between
2 **spotted,** maculate, maculated, macular, blotched, **blotchy,** splotched, splotchy

spouse NOUNS **mate,** yokemate, partner, consort, **better half** <nonformal>

bone of my bones, and flesh of my flesh
Bible

sprawl VERBS **recline,** repose, lounge, loll, drape *or* spread oneself, splay, lie limply

spread NOUNS 1 **meal, repast,** feed *and* sit-down <both nonformal>, mess, table, board, *repas* <Fr>; **refreshment,** refection, treat
2 **divergence,** spreading, spreading out, splaying, fanning, fanning out, deployment; ripple effect; **enlargement,** amplification, growth, development, widening, roadening, **extension,** aggrandizement
3 **coverlet,** robe, buffalo robe, **afghan,** bedspread; bedcover; **comforter,** duvet, **quilt,** patchwork quilt
VERBS 4 spread out, outspread, outstretch; **expand,** extend, widen; open, **open up,** unfold; **flare,** flare out, broaden out, splay; spread like wildfire; overrun, overgrow

spree NOUNS **drinking bout,** bout, **carouse,** carousal, drunken carousal *or* revelry; bacchanal, bacchanalia, bacchanalian; debauch, orgy

sprightly ADJS **active,** lively, animated, spirited, bubbly, ebullient, effervescent, **vivacious,** chipper *and* perky <both nonformal>, pert; **agile,** nimble, spry, fleet; clever, brilliant, scintillating, sparkling

spring NOUNS 1 springtide, **springtime,** seedtime *or* budtime, Maytime, Eastertide; *primavera* <Ital>, prime of the year
2 **leap,** jump, hop, skip, bound, bounce; **elasticity,** resilience *or* resiliency, **give;** snap, bounciness

spring up VERBS **shoot up,** jump up, **leap up,** vault up, start up, fly up, pop up, bob up; **originate, arise,** crop up; burst forth, break out, erupt, irrupt

sprinkle NOUNS 1 **spray,** sparge, shower; spindrift, spume, froth, foam; **splash,** plash, swash, slosh; **splatter,** spatter
VERBS 2 **shower,** spatter, patter, pitter-patter; **drizzle,** mizzle; besprinkle, asperge, splash; **dot,** spot, speck, speckle, stud

sprout NOUNS 1 **seedling,** set; sucker, shoot, slip; **twig,** sprig, scion, sapling
VERBS 2 **grow, shoot up,** sprout up, upshoot, burgeon, blossom, germinate, pullulate; **flourish,** thrive, grow like a weed

spry ADJS **agile, nimble,** sprightly, fleet, featly, peart <nonformal>, light, graceful, nimble-footed, light-footed, sure-footed

spunk NOUNS **pluck,** mettle, backbone <nonformal>, **grit,** true grit, spirit, **stamina,** guts *and* moxie <both nonformal>, bottom, pluckiness, spunkiness <nonformal>, **gameness,** feistiness <nonformal>, mettlesomeness

spur NOUNS 1 **goad,** prod, prick <old>, sting, **gadfly;** oxgoad; rowel
2 **offshoot,** ramification, scion
VERBS 3 **goad,** prod, poke, nudge, prod at, goose <nonformal>, prick, sting, needle; whip, lash, urge

spurious ADJS **false,** untrue, truthless, not true, void *or* devoid of truth, contrary to fact, in error, **fallacious,** erroneous; unfounded

spurn VERBS **turn up one's nose at,** scorn to receive *or* accept, not want any part of; spit upon, **disdain,** scorn, **turn one's back upon,** not give one the time of day <nonformal>; **blackball,** turn thumbs down on, snub, cut, give the cold shoulder

spur-of-the-moment ADJS **extemporaneous,** extemporary, extempore, **impromptu,** unrehearsed, **improvised,** ad-lib, *ad libitum* <L>; **ad-hoc,** stopgap, makeshift, jury-rigged; **offhand,** off the top of one's head *and* off-the-cuff <both nonformal>, **quick and dirty** <nonformal>

spurt NOUNS **burst,** fit, spasm; **torrent,** rush, gush, spate, cascade; outpour, jet, spout, squirt

spy NOUNS 1 **secret agent,** operative, cloak-and-dagger operative, **undercover man,** inside man <nonformal>; espionage agent; counterspy, double agent; **intelligence agent** *or* **officer;** spy-catcher <nonformal>, counterintelligence agent
VERBS 2 **see,** behold, observe, view, witness, perceive, discern, espy, **sight,** make out, pick out, descry, spot <nonformal>, notice, take notice of, have one's eye on, **catch sight of,** get a load of <nonformal>, get an eyeful of <nonformal>, **glimpse,** get *or* catch a glimpse of; **pry, snoop,** peep, peek, nose into

squabble NOUNS 1 **quarrel,** dispute, argument, **fight,** contention, strife, **tussle,** bicker, wrangle, snarl, **tiff, spat,** fuss

VERBS 2 **quarrel,** dispute, oppugn, **fight,** tiff, spat, **bicker, wrangle,** spar, have words, set to, make the fur fly

squalid ADJS **sordid,** wretched, shabby; slumlike, slummy

squall NOUNS **storm,** tempest, line squall; stormy weather, rough weather, foul weather, dirty weather; rainstorm

squander VERBS **lavish,** slather, blow <nonformal>, play ducks and drakes with; **dissipate,** scatter to the winds; **run through,** go through; throw one's money away, throw money around, **spend money like water,** spend like a drunken sailor

square NOUNS 1 **plaza,** *place* <Fr>, *piazza* <Ital>, *campo* <Ital>, **marketplace,** market, mart, rialto, forum, agora
ADJS 2 **banal,** trite, unoriginal, platitudinous, **stereotyped,** stock, set, **commonplace,** common, truistic, twice-told, **familiar,** bromidic <nonformal>, old hat <nonformal>, back-number; corny *and* square-John *and* Clyde <all nonformal>
3 **straight,** foursquare, straight-arrow <nonformal>, honest and aboveboard, right as rain; **old-fogyish,** fogyish, old-fogy; fuddy-duddy, cornball <nonformal>; **stuffy,** stodgy
4 even, quits, zero-sum, even steven <nonformal>
ADVS 5 **exactly,** precisely, to a T, expressly; **just, dead,** right, straight, even, **plumb,** directly, squarely, point-blank

square one NOUNS **new start,** new beginning, fresh start, clean slate, tabula rasa

squash VERBS **suppress, repress,** stultify; **keep down,** hold down, keep under; close *or* shut down; **subdue,** quell, put down, smash, crush; mash

squat VERBS 1 **crouch,** stoop, bend, stoop down, squat down, get down, hunker *and* hunker down *and* get down on one's hunkers <all nonformal>; hunch down, hunch over, scrooch *or* scrouch down <nonformal>
ADJS 2 **stubby,** stumpy <nonformal>, dumpy; squatty, squattish; flat, short, runty

squawk NOUNS 1 **screech,** shriek, scream, squeal; **objection,** kick *and* beef *and* bitch *and* howl <all nonformal>, protestation
VERBS 2 **screech,** shriek, scream, squeal; **object,** kick *and* beef <both nonformal>, put up a struggle *or* fight; bitch *and* howl *and* holler *and* put up a squawk *and* raise a howl <all nonformal>; exclaim *or* cry out against, make *or* create *or* raise a stink about <all nonformal>; yell bloody murder <nonformal>

squeamish ADJS **nauseated,** nauseous, **queasy,** qualmish, qualmy; sick to one's stomach; **demurring,** boggling, stickling, hedging, **hesitant,** hesitating, faltering

squeeze NOUNS 1 **embrace,** hug, fond embrace, embracement, clasp, enfoldment, bear hug <nonformal>; **tight squeeze** *and* hot spot *and* hot water <all nonformal>
VERBS 2 **embrace,** hug, clasp, press, fold, **enfold,** press to the bosom
3 compress, clamp, cramp, cramp up, tighten; roll *or* wad up, roll up into a ball, ensphere; **press,** high-pressure <nonformal>, pressurize, crush, lean on <nonformal>; **exact,** extort, blackmail

squelch VERBS **cover up,** muffle up; **hush up, suppress,** repress, **stifle,** muffle, **smother,** squash, quash, kill, sit on *or* upon, put the lid on <nonformal>, **muzzle,** gag; bleep *or* bleep out <nonformal>, silence

squirm VERBS **fidget,** have the fidgets *and* have ants in one's pants <both nonformal>; twist and turn, wriggle, wiggle, writhe; **chafe,** fret, fuss

stab NOUNS 1 **wound,** puncture, stab wound; flesh wound; **thrust,** pass, lunge, swing, cut; home thrust
2 **try;** whack, fling, shot, crack, bash, <all nonformal>
VERBS 3 **stick** <nonformal>, **pierce,** plunge in; **run through,** impale, spit, **transfix,** transpierce

stabilize VERBS **firm,** firm up <nonformal>; **steady,** balance, counterbalance, ballast; **immobilize,** freeze, keep, retain; **transfix,** stick, hold, pin *or* nail down <nonformal>

stable ADJS **substantial,** firm, solid, sound, stabile; solid as a rock; **steady,** unwavering, steadfast; **balanced,** in equilibrium, in a stable state; **imperturbable,** unflappable <nonformal>, unshakable, **cool** <nonformal>, impassive, stolid, stoic; **reliable,** predictable

staccato ADJS **drumming,** thrumming,

beating, pounding, thumping; throbbing; palpitant, fluttering; **rapid,** stuttering, chattering

stack NOUNS 1 **chimney, flue,** stovepipe, smokestack
VERBS 2 **load, lade,** pile, heap, heap up, mass; heap *or* pile *or* stack up; mound, hill, bank, bank up

stadium NOUNS **arena, amphitheater,** circus, **hippodrome,** coliseum, colosseum, **bowl**

staff NOUNS 1 stave; pilgrim's staff, pastoral staff, shepherd's staff, crook; pikestaff, alpenstock; quarterstaff
2 **personnel, employees,** help, hired help, the help, **crew, gang,** force, retinue

stage NOUNS 1 **period,** point, juncture; interval
2 **platform;** the boards; estrade, dais, floor; **rostrum,** podium, pulpit, speaker's platform *or* stand
VERBS 3 **dramatize, present,** produce, mount, put on, put on the stage; put on a show

stagger VERBS 1 **astonish,** amaze, astound, surprise, startle, **bewilder,** perplex, flabbergast <nonformal>, confound, overwhelm, **boggle,** boggle the mind
2 **flounder,** flounce, totter, stumble, falter, blunder, wallop; **struggle,** labor; **wallow,** welter

staggering ADJS 1 **astonishing,** amazing, surprising, startling, **astounding,** confounding, stunning <nonformal>, eye-opening, breathtaking, overwhelming, mind-boggling *or* -numbing
2 **wobbly,** wobbling, weaving, lurching, careening

stagnant ADJS **inert,** inactive, static, dormant, passive, sedentary; sleeping, slumbering, smoldering; **standing,** foul, stagnating, vegetative

staid ADJS **sedate,** sober, sober-minded, **serious,** grave, solemn, sobersided; temperate, moderate; **stuffy** <nonformal>; stolid

stain NOUNS 1 **taint, tarnish;** mark, brand, **stigma; smirch,** smudge, smutch *or* smouch, smut, **smear;** splotch, splash, splatter, spatter
VERBS 2 **soil,** besoil; black, **blacken; smirch,** besmirch, sully, **smudge,** smear; **spot**

stainless ADJS **spotless,** taintless, unblemished, unspotted, **untainted,** unsoiled, unsullied, undefiled; pure, clean, immaculate, impeccable, pure as driven snow, squeaky-clean <nonformal>, chaste

stake NOUNS 1 **portion,** share, interest, part, stock, **piece,** bit, segment; **grubstake** <nonformal>; **bet,** wager, hazard, ante
VERBS 2 **finance,** back, fund, grubstake <nonformal>; subsidize; **bet,** wager, gamble, hazard, punt, lay, lay down, put up, **make a bet,** plunge <nonformal>; ante, ante up

stale ADJS **fusty, musty,** rusty, dusty, moldy, mildewed; **moth-eaten,** moldering, gone to seed

stalemate NOUNS **tie,** deadlock, wash *and* toss-up <both nonformal>, standoff *and* Mexican standoff <both nonformal>

stalk VERBS **hunt,** prowl after, **search out,** hunt out, spy out, scout out, **ferret out,** fish out, root out

stall NOUNS 1 **booth,** stand; newsstand, kiosk, news kiosk
VERBS 2 lose power; flame out; stick, die, go dead, **conk out** <nonformal>, sputter and stop, run out of gas *or* steam, come to a dead stop
3 **temporize,** gain time, **play for time,** drag one's feet <nonformal>, hold off <nonformal>; stall off, **stall for time,** stall *or* stooge around *and* tap-dance <all nonformal>; filibuster

stalwart NOUNS 1 **tower of strength,** muscle man, piledriver, bulldozer, hunk <nonformal>; **hero,** heroine; brave, gallant, valiant, man *or* woman of courage *or* mettle; support, **mainstay,** standby <nonformal>
ADJS 2 **courageous,** plucky, brave, bold, valiant, valorous, gallant, intrepid, doughty, **hardy,** stout, stouthearted, lionhearted; heroic

stamina NOUNS **pluck,** spunk <nonformal>, **mettle,** backbone <nonformal>, **grit,** true grit, spirit, guts *and* moxie <both nonformal>, bottom, **toughness** <nonformal>; endurance, staying power

stammer NOUNS 1 **stammering,** stuttering, hesitation, faltering, traulism, dysphemia, *balbuties* <L>; palilalia; stutter
VERBS 2 **stutter,** stammer out; hesitate, falter, halt, stumble

stamp NOUNS 1 seal, sigil, signet; postage stamp
VERBS 2 **impress upon,** bring home

to, make it felt; stamp on, etch, engrave, engrave on; mint
3 seal, punch, impress, imprint, **print,** engrave
4 stomp <nonformal>, trample, tread, drub, clump, clop

stampede VERBS **panic,** send scuttling, throw blind fear into; **rout, put to rout,** put to flight, scatter

stance NOUNS **attitude,** position, posture; **way of thinking; feeling, sentiment,** the way one feels; opinion

stanch VERBS **suppress, extinguish,** quench, damp down, pour water on, dash *or* pour cold water on, drown, kill

stand NOUNS 1 **station,** status, **standing,** standpoint; **viewpoint,** *optique* <Fr>, point of reference, reference-point, angle, perspective, distance; position
2 **growth,** crop; plantation, planting; **clump,** tuft, tussock, hassock
3 **engagement,** playing engagement, booking; **run;** one-night stand *or* one-nighter; date
4 **booth,** stall; newsstand, kiosk, news kiosk
VERBS 5 **endure,** bear, support, sustain, **suffer, tolerate,** abide, bide, live with; **bear up under,** put up with, stand for, brook, brave, brave out, hang in there, keep it up
6 **stand erect,** stand up, stand upright, stand up straight, be erect, be on one's feet; stand at attention *and* stand at parade rest <both military>

standard NOUNS 1 **yardstick,** norm, canon, **criterion,** test, touchstone, check; **model,** pattern, mirror; **rule,** law, principle, code, maxim, prescription, guideline, rulebook
2 **flag, banner,** oriflamme, gonfalon *or* gonfanon, guidon, *vexillum* <L>, *labarum* <L>
ADJS 3 **model,** exemplary, typical, paradigmatic, representative, normative, classic; ideal
4 **usual,** regular; customary, habitual, accustomed, wonted, **normative,** prescriptive, regulation, conventional; interchangeable, stereotyped, uniform

standardize VERBS **make uniform,** homogenize, assimilate, stereotype; **systematize,** methodize, routinize; **normalize,** regularize; codify

stand by VERBS **be prepared,** be ready, stand ready, hold oneself in readiness, keep one's powder dry

put your trust in God, my boys, and keep your powder dry
CROMWELL

stand for VERBS **suffer,** countenance, have, **tolerate,** condone, brook, endure, stomach, bear, bear with, put up with, hear of *and* go along with <both nonformal>; **signify, betoken,** identify, differentiate, **indicate,** be indicative of, be an indication of, connote, denote, mean

stand-in NOUNS **deputy,** proxy, representative, substitute, **alternate,** backup <nonformal>, alter ego, surrogate; **understudy,** standby

standing NOUNS **rank,** level, footing, **status,** station; **position,** place, sphere, orbit, echelon; **prestige,** honor; dignity; stature, high place

standoff NOUNS **impasse,** corner *and* box *and* hole <all nonformal>, cleft stick; **stalemate,** deadlock; stand, standstill, halt, stop

star NOUNS 1 **winner,** star in the firmament, success, superstar *and* megastar <both nonformal>; phenom *and* comer <both nonformal>; cult figure; **lead,** leading man *or* lady, leading actor *or* actress, principal, headliner, headline *or* feature attraction
2 **quasar,** quasi-stellar radio source; **pulsar,** pulsating star, eclipsing binary, X-ray pulsar
VERBS 3 **act,** perform, play the lead, get top billing, have one's name in lights
ADJS 4 **predominant,** topflight, highest-ranking, ranking; superstar, stellar, world-class

stare NOUNS 1 **gaze,** gape, goggle; sharp *or* piercing *or* penetrating look; **ogle,** glad eye, come-hither look <nonformal>, bedroom eyes <nonformal>; **glare,** glower, glaring *or* glowering look
VERBS 2 **gaze,** fix one's gaze, fix *or* fasten *or* rivet one's eyes upon, **eye, ogle;** stare at, stare hard, look, goggle, **gape,** gawk *or* gawp <nonformal>, gaze openmouthed

stark ADJS **sheer,** bare, bare-bones, **plain,** simple, **unadorned,** unenhanced; austere, monkish, cloistral, severe, Spartan

start NOUNS 1 shock, jar, jolt, turn
2 starting, start-off, setoff, setout, takeoff *and* getaway <both nonformal>; the starting gun *or* pistol; break; the green light; **point of departure,** starting place

or point, takeoff, **base,** baseline, basis; starting line *or* post *or* gate, starting blocks; head *or* flying *or* running start; **edge,** bulge *and* jump *and* drop <all nonformal>
VERBS 3 startle, **jump,** jump out of one's skin, jump a mile, leap like a startled gazelle; **shy,** fight shy, start aside, boggle, jib; **panic,** stampede, skedaddle <nonformal>
4 **set out** *or* **off,** be off, be on one's way, **start out** *or* **off,** strike out, get off, get away, get off the dime <nonformal>; get the green light, break; set sail; **begin,** commence; start up, kick *or* click in <nonformal>; **kick off** *and* **start the ball rolling** <both nonformal>; get off the ground *or* off the mark, **launch**

startle VERBS **shock,** electrify, jar, jolt, shake, stun, **stagger,** give one a turn <nonformal>, give the shock of one's life, make one jump out of his skin, take aback, take one's breath away, strike all of a heap <nonformal>; frighten

starve VERBS **hunger,** hunger for, feel hungry; be ravenous, raven; famish; not know where one's next meal is coming from, **live from hand to mouth,** eke out *or* squeeze out a living

stash NOUNS 1 **hiding place, cache**; drop
VERBS 2 **secrete,** hide away, **cache,** deposit, plant <nonformal>; **bury,** bury away

state NOUNS 1 **country,** land; **nation,** nationality, nation-state, sovereign nation *or* state, polity, body politic
2 mode, modality; **status,** situation, status quo *or* status in quo, position, standing, footing, location, bearings, spot; condition, circumstance
VERBS 3 **declare, assert,** aver, affirm, asseverate, allege; **say,** make a statement, send a message; **announce,** tell the world; **relate,** recite; proclaim, nuncupate

stately ADJS **dignified,** imposing, grand, courtly, magisterial, aristocratic; **noble,** lordly, princely; **majestic,** regal, royal, kingly, queenly; worthy, **august,** venerable; statuesque; **sedate,** solemn, sober, grave

statement NOUNS 1 **remark,** earful *and* crack *and* one's two cents' worth <all nonformal>, **word,** say, **saying,** utterance, observation, reflection, expression; **assertion,** averment, allegation, affirmation, pronouncement, position, dictum; **declaration,** statement of facts, *procès-verbal* <Fr>
2 **bill,** itemized bill, bill of account, **account,** reckoning, invoice

state-of-the-art ADJS **newest, latest,** the very latest, up-to-the-minute, last, most recent, newest of the new, most advanced

statesman NOUNS stateswoman, solon, public man *or* woman, national leader; elder statesman

a successful politician who is dead
THOMAS B REED

static ADJS **inert,** inactive, dormant, passive, sedentary; **quiescent,** motionless

station NOUNS 1 status, **stand,** standing, standpoint; **rank,** level, footing; **position,** place, sphere, orbit, echelon; **job,** employment, gainful employment, situation, **office,** post, berth, billet
2 **terminal,** stopping point

stationary ADJS **immovable,** unmovable, **immobile,** immotile, unmoving, frozen, not to be moved, at a standstill, on dead center

stationery NOUNS **paper,** paper stock, stock; sheet, leaf, page

statistics NOUNS **mathematical probability,** statistical probability, predictability; **figures,** indexes *or* indices; vital statistics

statue NOUNS **sculpture,** bust, statuette, statuary; portrait bust *or* statue; carving, wood carving; figurehead

statuesque ADJS **giant**, gigantic, colossal; Junoesque, goddess-like

stature NOUNS **prestige,** authority, influence; **weight,** weightiness, moment, **consequence;** eminence, rank, seniority, preeminence, priority, precedence

status NOUNS **social status,** economic status, socioeconomic status *or* background, standing, footing, prestige, rank, ranking, place, station, position, level, degree, stratum; state, status quo *or* status in quo

status quo NOUNS **state,** status, situation, status in quo, position, standing, footing, location, bearings, spot; **circumstances,** total situation, existing conditions *or* situation, set of conditions, terms of reference

statutory ADJS **preceptive,** official, authoritative, canonical, rubric, rubrical, protocolary; **enforceable,** legally binding; statutable

staunch ADJS **firm,** standup <nonformal>, fixed, settled, steady, steadfast, constant, reliable, flinty, steely; unshaken, not to be shaken, unflappable <nonformal>; undeflectable, **unswerving,** not to be deflected; immovable, unbending, inflexible, **unyielding**; true, loyal

stay NOUNS 1 **sojourn,** sojourning, sojournment, temporary stay; stop; **stopover,** stopoff, stayover, layover; abeyance, drop, lull, lapse; truce, cease-fire, stand-down
2 **curb, check,** countercheck, arrest, **stop,** damper, holdback
VERBS 3 **stop, halt,** bring to a stop, put a stop *or* end to, bring to a shuddering *or* screeching halt <nonformal>; **block,** stall, stymie, deadlock; nip in the bud

steadfast ADJS **devoted,** dedicated, committed, **fast,** constant, faithful, staunch; tried, true, **tried and true,** true-blue, tested

steady ADJS **reliable,** dependable, sure, surefire <nonformal>, **trustworthy,** trusty; predictable, calculable; **secure,** solid, sound, firm, fast, **stable, substantial,** staunch, steady, **faithful,** unfailing; true to one's word

steal VERBS **thieve,** purloin, appropriate, take, snatch, palm, **make off with,** walk off with, run off *or* away with, abstract, disregard the distinction between *meum* and *tuum;* have one's hand in the till; **pilfer,** filch

stealth NOUNS stealthiness, **furtiveness,** clandestine behavior, **surreptitiousness,** covertness, slyness, shiftiness, sneakiness, slinkiness, underhand dealing, undercover *or* underground activity, **covert activity** *or* **operation**

steamy ADJS **heated,** passionate, warm, hot, red-hot, flaming, **burning,** fiery, glowing, fervent, fervid; seething, boiling, boiling over, steaming

steep ADJS 1 **precipitous,** bluff, plunging, abrupt, bold, **sheer,** sharp, vertical
2 **expensive,** dear, costly; fancy *and* stiff <both nonformal>, pricey; upmarket, upscale <nonformal>

steer VERBS **direct to,** give directions to, lead *or* conduct to, point out to, show, **show** *or* **point the way,** put on the track, put on the right track; **pilot,** helm, coxswain, guide, **navigate**

stellar ADJS **celestial,** heavenly, empyrean, empyreal; **astral,** starry; all-star, star quality

stem VERBS **put a stop to,** call a halt to; block, brake, dam, stem the tide *or* current; bring up short, cut short, check in full career; checkmate

stench NOUNS **stink,** funk, malodor, fetor, foul odor, offense to the nostrils

step NOUNS 1 **pace,** stride; footstep, footfall, tread
2 **means,** means to an end, **measure,** action, **move,** maneuver, demarche, course of action
VERBS 3 **tread,** pace, stride, pad; foot, foot it; leg, leg it; hoof it

sterile ADJS 1 **sanitary,** aseptic, antiseptic, **uninfected;** disinfected, decontaminated, sterilized
2 arid, barren, blank, jejune; **unproductive,** infertile, unfruitful; **impotent,** gelded; ineffectual

stern ADJS **strict,** exacting, grim, dour, unsparing; austere, rugged, **tough** <nonformal>

stew NOUNS 1 olla, olio, *olla podrida* <Sp>; meat stew, *étuvée* <Fr>; Irish stew, mulligan stew *or* mulligan <nonformal>; goulash, Hungarian goulash; ragout; *bouillabaisse* <Fr>, *paella* <Catalan>, oyster stew, chowder
2 **dither, fret, fuss,** pother, bother, lather *and* sweat *and* snit <all nonformal>, flap; **huff,** pique, pet, tiff, miff <nonformal>, ferment; **fix** *and* jam *and* pickle *and* scrape <all nonformal>
VERBS 3 **fret,** fuss, chafe, fret and fume, sweat, get into a dither; bite one's nails, walk the floor, go up the wall <nonformal>, be on tenterhooks *or* pins and needles; **seethe,** simmer, sizzle, smoke, smolder, steam

steward NOUNS **attendant,** flight attendant, stewardess, hostess; major-domo, house steward; **custodian,** keeper, caretaker

stickler NOUNS **perfectionist,** precisian, precisianist, nitpicker <nonformal>, captious critic

the sticks NOUNS **the country,** the tall corn *and* yokeldom *and* hickdom <all nonformal>; the boondocks *and* the boonies <both nonformal>; nowhere

sticky ADJS **adhesive, tenacious,** clingy; **tacky,** gluey, gummy, **viscid,** glutinous

stiff ADJS **stilted,** prim, prissy, rigid, starch, starchy, starched; **rigid,** firm, renitent, incompressible; nonresilient, inelastic

stifle VERBS **suppress, repress,** keep under, smother, choke *or* hold back, fight down *or* back, inhibit; muffle, **smother,** squash, quash, squelch, kill, sit on *or* upon, put the lid on <nonformal>; suffocate, asphyxiate, strangle, throttle, choke off, **muzzle,** gag

stigma NOUNS stigmatism, onus; **brand,** badge of infamy; **slur,** reproach, censure, reprimand, imputation, aspersion, reflection, stigmatization; pillorying; **black eye** <nonformal>, black mark; **stain,** taint, tarnish

stigmatize VERBS **brand; stain,** besmirch, smirch, tarnish, taint, **blacken,** smear, **sully,** soil, defile, vilify, **slur,** cast a slur upon, **disparage,** defame; **give a black eye** <nonformal>

still ADJS **silent,** quiet, quiescent, **hushed,** soundless, noiseless; **at rest,** resting, reposing; **fixed,** stationary, static, at a standstill; **stock-still,** dead-still

stimulant NOUNS **energizer, stimulus,** stimulator, vitalizer, arouser, needle <nonformal>, restorative; tonic; **antidepressant**

stimulate VERBS **whet, sharpen,** pique, provoke, quicken, enliven, liven up, pick up, jazz up <nonformal>, animate, **exhilarate,** invigorate, galvanize, energize, spark

stimulus NOUNS **energizer,** stimulator, vitalizer, arouser, needle <nonformal>, restorative; **cause,** occasion, grounds

stingy ADJS **illiberal,** ungenerous, chintzy, miserly, cheap *and* tight *and* narrow <all nonformal>, **closefisted,** tightfisted, penny-pinching

stint NOUNS 1 **task,** work, job, labor, piece of work, **chore,** odd job; **restriction,** limitation
VERBS 2 **scrimp,** skimp, scamp, scant, screw, **pinch,** starve, famish; grudge, begrudge

stipulate VERBS stipulate for, specifically provide, set conditions *or* terms, make reservations; **make conditional,** make contingent; **specify,** designate, determine, single out, feature, highlight, focus on, select

stir NOUNS 1 **bustle,** fuss, flurry, flutter, fluster, scramble, ferment, stew; **commotion,** hubbub, hullabaloo, hoo-ha *and* foofaraw *and* flap <all nonformal>, ado, to-do <nonformal>
VERBS 2 **awake,** open one's eyes; **excite,** impassion, arouse, rouse, **stir up,** work up, work up into a lather <nonformal>, whip up; **ruffle,** shake up, shock, upset, make waves
3 **move,** budge; **bustle,** fuss, make a fuss, stir about, rush around *or* about, tear around, run *or* go around like a chicken with its head cut off

stock NOUNS 1 **lineage,** line, blood, strain, species, stirps, **breed,** brood, kind; ethnicity
2 **merchandise, consumer goods,** consumer items, retail goods, goods for sale; **stock-in-trade;** staples; inventory
VERBS 3 gather *or* procure materials; **store,** stock up, lay in, restock
ADJS 4 **stereotyped,** set, **commonplace,** truistic, twice-told, **familiar,** bromidic <nonformal>, old hat <nonformal>; **standard,** regular, regulation; **conventional,** common, commonplace, ordinary, average, everyday, mediocre, household

stockpile NOUNS 1 **reserve, reserves,** reservoir, resource; **cache,** backup, reserve supply, something in reserve *or* in hand
VERBS 2 **store up,** lay up, put up; **accumulate,** cumulate, collect, amass; backlog

stocky ADJS **stubby,** thickset, blocky, **chunky** <nonformal>

stodgy ADJS **dull,** stuffy, wooden, stiff; **old-fogyish,** fuddy-duddy, square *and* corny *and* cornball <all nonformal>

stoic ADJS **imperturbable,** unflappable <nonformal>, unshakable, **cool** <nonformal>, impassive, stolid; without nerves, without a nerve in one's body, unflinching

stoke VERBS **ignite;** feed the fire, stoke the fire, add fuel to the flame; poke *or* stir the fire

stolen ADJS pilfered, purloined; pirated, plagiarized; hot <nonformal>

stolid ADJS **inexcitable,** imperturbable, unflappable <nonformal>; stoic, stoical; even-tempered; impassive, laid-back <nonformal>; **staid,** stuffy <nonformal>

stomach NOUNS 1 **abdomen, belly,** paunch

2 <nonformal> goozle, guzzle; tum, tummy, tum-tum, breadbasket, **gut,** bulge, fallen chest, corporation, spare tire, bay window, **pot,** potbelly, potgut,

beerbelly, German *or* Milwaukee goiter, pusgut, swagbelly; **guts,** tripes, stuffings

stomp VERBS **stamp,** trample, tread, drub, clump, clop

stone NOUNS 1 **jewel,** bijou, **gem,** precious stone; rhinestone
2 **monument,** marker, **tablet,** boundary stone, memorial stone; **gravestone,** tombstone; headstone, footstone

stonewall VERBS **delay,** retard, stall, drag one's feet <nonformal>, slow down, **hold up** <nonformal>, hold *or* keep back, check, **stay, stop,** arrest, impede, **block,** hinder, obstruct, throw a monkey wrench in the works <nonformal>

stooge NOUNS **hanger-on,** dangler, adherent, appendage, dependent, parasite, flunky; cat's-paw, puppet, dummy, pawn, creature, minion, figurehead

stool pigeon NOUNS **informer, betrayer,** double-crosser <nonformal>, snitch *and* snitcher <both nonformal>; **squealer** *and* preacher *and* stoolie *and* **fink** *and* rat <all nonformal>

stoop NOUNS 1 **porch,** veranda, piazza <nonformal>, front steps
2 **crouch,** bend, squat; **bow,** genuflection, kneeling, kowtow, kowtowing
VERBS 3 **condescend,** deign, vouchsafe; descend, lower *or* demean oneself, trouble oneself, set one's dignity aside *or* to one side; **grovel,** crawl, creep, cower, cringe, crouch, kneel, bend the knee, fall on one's knees, prostrate oneself, throw oneself at the feet of, **kowtow,** bow, bow and scrape

stop VERBS 1 **stop up; obstruct,** bar, stay; **block,** block up; **clog,** clog up, foul; **plug,** plug up; come to a stop *or* halt, **halt,** stop in one's tracks, skid to a stop, stop dead; bring to a stop, put a stop *or* end to, bring to a shuddering *or* screeching halt <nonformal>
INTERJS 2 **cease!, stop!, halt!,** *halte!* <Fr>, hold!, freeze!, stay!, desist!, quit it!; **let up!,** easy!, take it easy!, relax!, get off it!, **leave off!,** *arrâtez!* <Fr>, stop it!, forget it!, no more!, have done!, *tenez!* <Fr>, **hold everything!, hold it!,** hold to!, hold on!, whoa!, that's it!, that's enough!, that will do!, enough!, enough is enough!, all right already!, *basta!* <Ital>

3 <nonformal> **cut it out!,** cool it!, bag it!, chill out!, call it quits!, can it!, turn it off!, chuck it!, stow it!, drop it!, lay off!, all right already!, come off it!, **knock it off!,** break it off!, break it up!

stopgap NOUNS 1 **improvisation,** temporary measure *or* arrangement, *pro tempore* measure *or* arrangement, **makeshift,** ad hoc measure, **fix** *and* **quick fix** <both nonformal>, jury-rigged expedient
ADJS 2 **makeshift,** band-aid <nonformal>, improvised, improvisational, **jury-rigged;** ad hoc; quick and dirty <nonformal>; temporary, provisional

stoppage NOUNS **delay,** jam *and* logjam <both nonformal>, obstruction, tie-up *and* bind <both nonformal>, **block,** blockage, **hang-up** <nonformal>; **stop,** halt, stay, arrest, check, cutoff <nonformal>

stopper NOUNS 1 stop, **stopple,** stopgap; **plug, cork,** bung, spike, spill, spile, tap, faucet, spigot, valve, check valve, cock, sea cock, peg, pin
VERBS 2 **plug,** plug up; stopple, **cork,** bung, spile; put the lid on

storage NOUNS **stowage;** cold storage, cold store, dry storage, dead storage; storage space; **depository,** repository, depot, supply depot, warehouse; bonded warehouse, entrepôt

store NOUNS 1 **hoard, treasure,** treasury; plenty, plenitude, abundance, cornucopia; **market,** mart, shop, salon, boutique, wareroom, emporium
VERBS 2 **stow,** lay in store; **lay in,** lay in a supply *or* stock *or* store, store away, stow away, **put away,** lay away, put *or* lay by, pack away, bundle away, lay down, stow down, salt down *or* away *and* sock away *and* squirrel away <all nonformal>

storm NOUNS 1 **tempest,** squall, line squall, **tornado,** cyclone, hurricane, tropical cyclone, typhoon, tropical storm; stormy weather, rough weather, foul weather, dirty weather
VERBS 2 **rage,** rant, rave, roar; **rampage,** ramp, **tear,** tear around; go *or* carry on <nonformal>; come in like a lion; **destroy,** wreck, wreak havoc, ruin; **attack,** assault, batter, savage, mug, maul, hammer

stormy ADJS **turbulent,** tumultuous, raging, chaotic, hellish, anarchic, **storming,** tempestuous, **frenzied,** wild, wild-eyed, frantic, furious

story NOUNS **tale,** yarn, account, narrative, narration, chronicle; trumped-up story, fabrication

stout ADJS **corpulent,** fat, overweight, fattish, **obese,** adipose, gross, fleshy, beefy, meaty, hefty, porky, porcine; **sturdy,** stable, **solid,** sound, firm, steady, tough, strong, rugged; **durable,** lasting, enduring

stouthearted ADJS **courageous,** plucky, brave, bold, valiant, valorous, gallant, intrepid, doughty, **hardy,** stalwart, stout, lionhearted; heroic

stove NOUNS **heater,** warmer; **furnace;** cooker, cookery

stow VERBS **put away,** lay away, **put aside,** put *or* lay *or* set by; store

straddle VERBS **extend,** reach, stretch, sweep, spread, span, take in, encompass; step over, overstride

strafe VERBS **bombard,** blast, shell, cannonade, mortar, barrage, blitz; rake, enfilade

straggle VERBS **bring up the rear,** come last, **follow,** come after; trail, trail behind, lag behind, fall behind, fall back

straight ADJS 1 dead straight, straight as an edge *or* a ruler, ruler-straight, even, right, true, straight as an arrow; **direct,** undeviating, unswerving, unbending, undeflected
2 **square,** foursquare, straight-arrow <nonformal>, honest and aboveboard, right as rain; **square-dealing,** square-shooting, straight-shooting, **on the up-and-up** *and* **on the level,** *and* on the square <all nonformal>; **aboveboard,** open and aboveboard; undiluted, unfortified
3 **conformist, conventional**, bourgeois, plastic *and* square *and* white-bread *and* button-down *and* buttoned-down <all nonformal>
ADVS 4 unswervingly, undeviatingly, **directly;** straight to the mark; in the groove *and* on the beam *and* on the money <all nonformal>; **exactly,** precisely, to a T; **dead,** right, even, square, **plumb,** squarely, point-blank

straightforward ADJS **unaffected, unpretentious,** unpretending, unassuming, unfeigning, direct, honest, candid; **uncomplicated,** uninvolved, simple

strain NOUNS 1 **lineage, extraction,** derivation, birth, **blood,** breed, **family,** house, **stock,** race, stirps, seed
2 straining, **stress,** stressfulness, **stress and strain,** taxing, **tension,** stretch, rack; **overwork,** overexertion, overstrain
VERBS 3 **tense,** stress, stretch, tax, press, rack; take on too much, spread oneself too thin, overexert, overstrain, overextend; drive *or* whip *or* flog oneself

strait NOUNS narrow, **narrows; bottleneck,** chokepoint; isthmus; **pinch,** clutch <nonformal>, rub, pass, extremity, spot <nonformal>; **predicament,** plight, spot of trouble

straitlaced ADJS **rigorous,** inflexible, **unyielding,** unbending, impliable, **relentless,** unrelenting, procrustean; ironbound, hidebound; puritanical

stranded ADJS **grounded,** aground, **on the rocks,** high and dry; **stuck,** stuck *or* set fast; castaway, marooned, shipwrecked

strange ADJS **extraneous,** foreign, alien, exotic, foreign-looking; **outlandish,** off-the-wall <informal>, surreal, not for real <nonformal>, passing strange; **unfamiliar**

stranger NOUNS **outsider,** non-member, the other, they; **foreigner,** alien; not our sort, not the right sort

strangle VERBS garrote, **throttle,** choke, burke; **suffocate,** stifle, smother, asphyxiate, stop the breath

stranglehold NOUNS **hindrance,** impediment, restriction, restraint; **obstruction,** blocking, blockage, clogging, occlusion; constriction, squeeze, stricture, cramp

strapping ADJS **sturdy,** hunky *and* husky *and* hefty *and* beefy <all nonformal>, doughty <nonformal>, **hardy,** robust, lusty

stratagem NOUNS **artifice,** craft, wile, **device,** wily device, **contrivance,** expedient, design, scheme, trick, cute trick, **ruse,** red herring, tactic, **maneuver,** stroke, master stroke, gambit, **ploy,** dodge, artful dodge

strategic ADJS **canny,** shrewd, acute, astute, clever; **Machiavellian,** politic, tactical

strategist NOUNS **tactician;** maneuverer, machinator, manipulator, wire-puller <nonformal>; calculator, schemer, intriguer; wheeler-dealer <nonformal>; behind-the-scenes operator, gray eminence, *éminence grise* <Fr>, power behind the throne, kingmaker <nonformal>

strategy NOUNS **plan,** scheme, design, long-range planning, long-range plan; program of action; methodology; working plan, strategic plan; tactics, game plan <nonformal>

stratum NOUNS **social class,** economic class, **social status,** economic status, socioeconomic status *or* background, standing, footing, prestige, rank, ranking, place, station, position, level, degree; **grade,** rank, rating, status, estate

stray NOUNS 1 **waif,** homeless waif, dogie, waifs and strays
VERBS 2 go astray, lose one's way, err; take a wrong turn *or* turning; drift, go adrift; **wander,** wander off, ramble, rove, straggle, divagate, excurse, pererrate; **digress,** wander, **get off the subject,** get sidetracked, excurse, maunder; **go wrong,** err, deviate from the path of virtue, leave the straight and narrow

streak NOUNS 1 **ray,** beam, gleam, **stream,** ray of light, beam of light; string of losses *or* victories
2 **disposition, tendency,** grain, vein, set, mental set, mindset, **leaning,** animus, propensity, proclivity, predilection, preference, predisposition; **bent,** turn, bias, slant, cast, warp, twist; strain
VERBS 3 **stripe,** striate, band, bar, vein; marble, marbleize

stream NOUNS **current,** run, rush, onrush, ongoing; **wash,** wake, **exhaust,** jet exhaust, **vapor trail,** condensation trail, contrail; **streak,** ribbon, ribbon of light, streamer, stream of light

streamline VERBS **simplify,** reduce, reduce to elements *or* essentials; **modernize,** update, **bring up to date,** move with the times

streetcar NOUNS **trolley** *or* trolley car, **tram** *or* tramcar <both Brit>; trolley bus, trackless trolley; cable car, grip car

street person NOUNS homeless person; bag woman *or* lady, shopping-bag lady, shopping-cart woman *or* lady

streetwalker NOUNS **prostitute,** whore, hustler *and* **hooker** <both nonformal>

strength NOUNS strongness; **robustness,** vigorousness, ruggedness, **vitality,** lustiness, hardiness, vigor; **might,** mightiness, power, intensity; **strong-mindedness,** strength of mind, strength *or* fixity of purpose, fortitude, moral fiber

strengthen VERBS **invigorate, fortify,** beef up <nonformal>, brace, buttress, prop, shore up, support, undergird, brace up; **toughen,** temper, **reinforce; reinvigorate,** refresh, revive, recruit one's strength; **intensify,** heighten, deepen, enhance

strenuous ADJS **laborious,** toilsome, arduous, painful, effortful, operose, troublesome, onerous, oppressive, burdensome

stress NOUNS 1 **pain,** distress, grief, stress of life, suffering, passion, dolor; **anxiety,** apprehension, apprehensiveness, misgiving, foreboding, suspense, strain, tension, nervous strain *or* tension;
2 **accent,** accentuation, stress accent; **emphasis,** word stress
VERBS 3 **strain,** tense, stretch, tax, press, rack
4 **emphasize,** lay emphasis *or* stress upon, feature, highlight, place emphasis on, give emphasis to, **accent,** accentuate, punctuate, point up

stretch NOUNS 1 **range,** scope, compass, reach, expanse, radius, sweep, carry, fetch; **extent,** length, span, stride, haul
2 **interval,** lapse of time, space, span, timespan, time-lag, time-gap; **time,** while; **term,** tenure, **enlistment,** hitch <nonformal>, tour; prison term
VERBS 3 **extend,** reach, sweep, spread, run, cover; **reach** *or* stretch *or* thrust out; span, straddle, take in, hold, encompass, surround, environ
4 distend, dilate, swell, swell up, swell out, puff up, puff out, pump up, bloat, tumefy, balloon, fill out
5 **lengthen,** prolong, prolongate, **elongate,** extend, produce, **protract,** continue; draw *or* drag *or* stretch *or* string *or* spin out
6 **exaggerate,** hyperbolize; stretch the truth, stretch the point, draw the longbow

stricken ADJS **wretched,** miserable; crushed, heartsick; desolate, disconsolate; shaken, upset, dashed, crushed

strict ADJS 1 **exacting,** exigent, demanding, not to be trifled with, **stringent,** astringent; disciplined, spit-and-polish; **severe,** harsh, dour, unsparing; Spartan
2 scripturalistic, evangelical; hyperorthodox, puritanical, purist *or* puristic, straitlaced; creedbound; **dogmatic,** fundamentalist, precisianist *or* precisianistic, literalist *or* literalistic

strident ADJS stridulant, stridulous; strident-voiced; shrill, harsh, raucous, grating

strife NOUNS **contention,** contest, contestation, combat, **fighting,** conflict, war, struggle, blood on the floor, cut and thrust

strike NOUNS 1 **attack, assault,** assailing, assailment; **offense,** offensive; surgical strike, first strike, **preemptive strike;** blitzkrieg, blitz, lightning attack, lightning war, panzer warfare, sudden *or* devastating *or* crippling attack, deep strike
2 **walkout** *or* tie-up <both nonformal>, industrial action <Brit>, **job action;** work stoppage, sit-down strike, sit-down, wildcat strike, outlaw strike; sympathy strike; general strike
VERBS 3 **slap,** smack, whack, whomp, **cuff, box,** buffet; slap the face, box the ears, give a rap on the knuckles; **bump,** hit, knock, bang

4 <nonformal> **belt,** bat, clout, bang, slam, bash, biff, paste, wham, whop, clump, bonk, wallop, clip, cut, plunk, swat, soak, sock, slog, slug, yerk <old>, clunk, clonk

5 **go on strike,** go out, walk, walk out; hit the bricks <nonformal>, shut it down
6 **impress,** make an impression, grab <nonformal>, hit; **sink in** <nonformal>

strikebreaker NOUNS **scab** *and* **rat** *and* **fink** *and* scissorbill <all nonformal>, **blackleg** <Brit>

striking ADJS **remarkable,** outstanding, extraordinary, **superior**, marked, of mark, signal, conspicuous, **outstanding,** in the foreground

stringent ADJS **strict,** exacting, exigent, demanding, not to be trifled with, astringent; **severe,** harsh, dour, unsparing; **stern,** grim, austere, rugged, **tough** <nonformal>; **hard-line,** authoritarian

strip NOUNS 1 **runway,** taxiway, landing strip, **airstrip,** flight strip, take-off strip
2 **strap,** strop; **band,** bandage, fillet, fascia, taenia; **tape,** tapeline, tape measure
VERBS 3 **divest,** strip away, remove; uncover, uncloak, unveil, **expose,** lay open, bare, lay *or* strip bare, **denude,** denudate; fleece, shear; pluck
4 **undress,** unclothe, undrape, disarray; **disrobe;** unsheathe, discase, uncase; strip to the buff <nonformal>, do a strip-tease
5 **peel,** pare, skin, flay, excoriate, decorticate, bark; scalp

strive VERBS **endeavor,** struggle, strain, sweat, sweat blood, labor, get one's teeth into, come to grips with, take it on, make an all-out effort, move heaven and earth, **exert oneself,** apply oneself, use some elbow grease <nonformal>

stroke NOUNS 1 **seizure, attack,** access, visitation; arrest; blockage, stoppage, occlusion, thrombosis, thromboembolism; ictus, apoplexy
VERBS 2 **pet,** caress, fondle; **encourage,** hearten, embolden, give encouragement, pat *or* clap on the back; **soft-soap,** butter, honey, **butter up,** soften up; massage the ego <nonformal>

stroll NOUNS 1 **leisurely gait,** snail's *or* tortoise's pace; **walk,** ramble, amble, saunter
VERBS 2 **go slow** *or* **slowly,** saunter, amble, waddle, ramble, meander, *flâner* <Fr>

stroller NOUNS **baby carriage,** baby buggy <nonformal>, perambulator, pram <Brit>; walker

strong ADJS 1 **forceful,** forcible, **mighty,** powerful, potent; **robust,** vigorous, hearty, nervy, **lusty,** bouncing, full- *or* red-blooded
2 strong-smelling, strong-scented; **pungent,** penetrating, nose-piercing, sharp; reeking, reeky

strong-arm VERBS use force, get tough <nonformal>, muscle *and* manhandle <both nonformal>

stronghold NOUNS hold, safehold, fasthold, strong point, **fastness,** keep, ward, **bastion,** donjon, **citadel,** castle, tower, tower of strength, strong point; refuge, sanctuary

structure NOUNS 1 **building,** edifice, construction, construct, erection, establishment, fabric; **plan,** architecture, architectonics, scheme, design; **syntax,** syntactic structure, word order, word arrangement
VERBS 2 **construct,** build; organize, shape, shape up; form, configure, array, pull it together, get *or* put one's ducks in a row <nonformal>, line up, set up, lay out

struggle NOUNS 1 **fight,** battle, tussle, scuffle, wrestle, hassle <nonformal>
VERBS 2 **strive,** contend, fight, battle, buffet, scuffle, tussle, wrestle, hassle <nonformal>, work *or* fight one's way,

agonize, huff and puff, grunt and sweat, sweat it <nonformal>, make heavy weather of it

strut NOUNS 1 **swagger,** swank <nonformal>, bounce, brave show; swaggering, strutting; peacockishness, peacockery
VERBS 2 **swagger,** swank <nonformal>, prance, stalk, peacock

stub NOUNS **extremity,** extreme; tail, **tail end,** butt end, tag, tag end, fag end; stump, butt

stubborn ADJS **obstinate,** pertinacious, restive; willful, self-willed, strong-willed, hardheaded, **headstrong,** strongheaded, *entêté* <Fr>; **dogged,** bulldogged, **tenacious,** persevering; **pigheaded,** mulish <nonformal>, stubborn as a mule; **unyielding**, ungiving

stuck ADJS **fast,** stuck fast, **fixed,** transfixed, caught, fastened, tied, chained, tethered, anchored, moored, held, inextricable; **jammed,** impacted, congested, packed, wedged; seized, seized up, frozen; **baffled,** perplexed, bewildered, mystified, stumped <nonformal>, stymied

stuck-up ADJS **conceited,** self-conceited, immodest, **puffed up,** chesty <nonformal>; aggressively self-confident, obtrusive, bumptious

studded ADJS **knobbed,** knobby, knoblike, nubbled, nubby, nubbly, torose; **knotty,** knotted; **ornamented,** decorated, embellished; **peppered,** spotted, dotted, powdered, dusted, specked, speckled; thronged, bristling, rife

student NOUNS **pupil,** scholar, learner, studier, educatee, **trainee,** *élève* <Fr>; tutee; **learned man,** person of learning, giant of learning, colossus of knowledge, mastermind, **savant,** pundit

studied ADJS **reasoned,** advised, considered, calculated, meditated, contemplated, deliberated, weighed, thought-out; **pretentious,** mannered, artificial, unnatural

studio NOUNS *atelier* <Fr>; gallery; **workplace,** workroom, worksite, workshop, shop; radio station

study NOUNS 1 branch of learning; **discipline,** subdiscipline; **field,** specialty, academic specialty, area; **studying,** application, conning; **reading,** perusal
2 **retreat,** sanctum, **den,** lair, mew; **ivory tower;** library
VERBS 3 regard studiously, apply oneself to, crack a book *and* hit the books <both nonformal>; **read, peruse,** go over, read up *or* read up on, have one's nose in a book <nonformal>; **grind** *and* **bone** *and* bone up on <all nonformal>, lucubrate, elucubrate, **burn the midnight oil**

stuff NOUNS 1 **matter,** material, materiality, **substance**
VERBS 2 **gorge**, pig out <nonformal>, engorge, glut, guttle, cram, eat one's fill, stuff *or* gorge oneself, gluttonize; **fill,** pack, load; **pad,** wad, **cram,** jam, jampack, fill to the brim, overfill, make burst at the seams, surfeit

stuffed ADJS **full,** packed, jammed, jampacked, like sardines; stuffed to the gills <nonformal>; **congested,** stuffed up; **surfeited,** glutted, gorged, overfed, bloated, replete, swollen, **satiated**, overstuffed

stuffy ADJS 1 **airless,** breathless, breezeless, windless; **close,** oppressive, stifling, suffocating, sultry
2 **pompous,** self-important, impressed with oneself, pontific, pontifical; **inflated,** swollen, bloated, tumid, turgid, flatulent, gassy <nonformal>, stilted; **hidebound,** straitlaced

stumble VERBS **topple,** lurch, pitch, stagger, totter, careen, list, trip, flounder, **slip,** trip, trip over one's own feet, get in one's own way, miss one's footing, miscue; commit a *faux pas,* commit a gaffe; **botch,** mar, **spoil,** butcher, murder, make sad work of

stump NOUNS 1 **platform; rostrum,** podium, pulpit, speaker's platform *or* stand, **soapbox** <nonformal>; hustings
VERBS 2 **electioneer,** campaign; take the stump *and* take to the stump *and* stump the country *and* take to the hustings *and* hit the campaign trail *and* whistle-stop <all nonformal>
3 **thwart, disconcert, baffle,** nonplus, perplex

stun VERBS **deaden,** numb, benumb, blunt, dull, obtund, desensitize; **stupefy,** bedaze, besot; knock unconscious, knock senseless, **knock out,** KO *and* kayo *and* lay out *and* coldcock *and* knock stiff <all nonformal>; **startle,** shock, electrify, jar, jolt, shake

stunning ADJS **astonishing,** amazing, surprising, startling, **astounding,** confounding, staggering, eye-opening, breathtaking, overwhelming, mind-boggling *or* -numbing; **eye-filling** *and* long on looks *and* raving *and* devastating *and* killing <all nonformal>

stunted ADJS **undersized,** undergrown, runty, pint-size *or* -sized *and* sawed-off <all nonformal>; shrunk, shrunken, wizened, shriveled; meager, scrubby, scraggy

stupefy VERBS **stun,** bedaze, besot; knock unconscious, paralyze, **deaden,** anesthetize, drug, narcotize, anesthetize, petrify, strike dumb

stupendous ADJS **prodigious,** unheard-of, unprecedented, extraordinary, exceptional, rare, unique, singular, **remarkable,** striking, sensational

stupid ADJS 1 **dumb,** doltish, blockish, klutzy *and* klutzish <both nonformal>, cloddish, lumpish, oafish, **dense,** thick <nonformal>, opaque, bovine, thick-headed

2 <nonformal> **blockheaded,** wooden-headed, stupidheaded, dumbheaded, dunderheaded, blunderheaded, clueless *or* jolterheaded *or* joltheaded *or* jingle-brained <all Brit>, chowderheaded, chuckleheaded, beetleheaded, nitwitted, numskulled, cabbageheaded, pumpkin-headed, sapheaded, lunkheaded, muttonheaded, meatheaded, fatheaded, boneheaded, knuckleheaded, clodpated; dead from the neck up, dead above *or* between the ears, muscle-bound between the ears; featherheaded, airheaded, bubbleheaded, out to lunch, lunchy, dufus, dufus-assed, spastic, spazzy, three bricks shy of a load, without brain one, not playing with a full deck

stupidity NOUNS 1 stupidness, *bêtise* <Fr>, **dumbness** <nonformal>, doltishness, **density,** denseness, opacity; **obtuseness,** sluggishness, slowness, **dim-wittedness,** thick-wittedness, thick-headedness

2 **blunder,** faux pas, gaffe, solecism; indiscretion; botch, bungle

stupor NOUNS **coma,** swoon, **trance;** narcosis, narcohypnosis, narcoma, narcotization, narcotic stupor *or* trance; **unconsciousness,** senselessness; nothingness, oblivion, obliviousness, nirvana; torpor, torpidity, stupefaction

sturdy ADJS stable, **solid,** sound, firm, steady, tough, stout, **strong,** rugged; **durable,** lasting, enduring; **well-made,** well-constructed, well-built, well-knit; **well-founded,** well-established, well-grounded

stutter NOUNS 1 **stammering, stuttering,** hesitation, faltering, traulism, dysphemia, *balbuties* <L>; palilalia; stammer

VERBS 2 **stammer,** stammer out; hesitate, falter, halt, stumble

style NOUNS 1 **fashion,** mode, vogue, trend, prevailing taste; proper thing, ton, bon ton; custom; convention; height of fashion; the season's look; high fashion, *haute couture* <Fr>

2 **kind,** sort, ilk, type, manner, **nature,** character, persuasion, the like *or* likes of <nonformal>

stylish ADJS **modish,** voguish, vogue; dressy <nonformal>; *soigné* or *soignée* <both Fr>; *à la mode* <Fr>, in the mode

stymie VERBS **stop,** stay, halt, bring to a stop, put a stop *or* end to, bring to a shuddering *or* screeching halt <nonformal>; **block,** stall, deadlock; nip in the bud

suave ADJS **smooth,** smug, bland, **glib,** unctuous, oily, oleaginous, fulsome, ingratiating, disarming; fine-spoken, fair-spoken, smooth-tongued, oily-tongued, honey-tongued

subconscious NOUNS 1 **inmost mind,** inner recesses of the mind, mind's core, deepest mind, center of the mind; inner man; subconscious mind

ADJS 2 **unconscious;** subliminal, extramarginal

subdue VERBS **master,** overmaster, **quell,** crush, reduce, beat down, **break,** break down, overwhelm; tread underfoot, trample on *or* down, trample underfoot, trample in the dust; **suppress**; make one give in *or* say 'uncle' <nonformal>, bring low, **bring to terms,** humble, humiliate, take down a notch *or* peg, bend, **bring one to his knees,** bend to one's will

subject NOUNS 1 **vassal,** liege, liege man, liege subject, homager

2 **topic,** matter, subject matter, what it is about, **concern,** focus of interest *or* attention, discrete matter, category

subjective ADJS **introverted,** introvert, introversive, **ingoing,** inner-directed; esoteric, private, secret, internal

subjugate VERBS **subject,** subordinate; dominate; **enslave,** enthrall, hold in thrall, make a chattel of; **hold in sub-**

jection, hold in bondage, hold captive, hold in captivity; **hold down,** keep down, keep under; **keep** *or* **have under one's thumb,** vassalize, make dependent *or* tributary

sublime ADJS **lofty,** elevated, grand, majestic, noble, stately, grave, solemn, dignified; moving, inspiring; **gorgeous,** ravishing; glorious, heavenly, divine

submarine NOUNS **sub,** submersible, underwater craft; **U-boat,** *U-boot* or *Unterseeboot* <both Ger>, pigboat <nonformal>; nuclear *or* nuclear-powered submarine; Polaris submarine; Trident submarine; hunter-killer submarine

submerge VERBS submerse, **immerse,** immerge, merge, **sink,** bury, engulf, **inundate,** deluge, drown, overwhelm, whelm; **dip,** duck, dunk <nonformal>, douse, souse, plunge in water; baptize

submissive ADJS **compliant,** complaisant, complying, **acquiescent,** consenting; subservient, abject, **obedient**; servile; **resigned,** uncomplaining; unassertive; **passive,** supine, unresisting, deferential, self-abnegating

submit VERBS 1 **comply,** take, accept, go along with <nonformal>, suffer, bear, brook, **acquiesce,** be agreeable, accede, assent; **succumb,** resign, resign oneself, give oneself up, not resist; take one's medicine, face the music; bite the bullet; knuckle under
2 **propose,** prefer; **suggest,** recommend, **advance,** commend to attention, **propound,** pose, put forward, bring forward, put *or* set forth, put it to, put *or* set *or* lay *or* bring before, dish up *and* come out *or* up with <both nonformal>

subordinate NOUNS 1 **junior,** secondary, second-in-command, lieutenant, **inferior; underling,** understrapper, low man on the totem pole <nonformal>, assistant, personal assistant, helper; **servant,** employee
ADJS 2 **inferior,** subaltern, **secondary; junior,** minor; **subservient,** subject, servile, **lowly,** humble, modest; **lesser,** less, lower; subsidiary

subscribe VERBS 1 **contribute,** chip in *and* kick in *and* pony up *and* pay up <all nonformal>, give one's share *or* fair share; contribute to, give to, donate to
2 **belong,** hold membership, be a member, be on the rolls, be inscribed, be in <nonformal>; hold a subscription

subsequent ADJS **after, later,** after-the-fact, *post factum* and *ex post facto* <both L>, posterior, **following, succeeding,** successive, lineal, ensuing, attendant

subservient ADJS **deferential,** obeisant; obsequious, servile; crouching, prostrate, prone, on one's belly, on one's knees, on bended knee; **assistant,** auxiliary, adjuvant, subsidiary, ancillary, accessory

subside VERBS **cease**, wane, ebb, run *or* die down, die off, dwindle, molder; **give way,** lapse, cave, cave in; **decline,** shrink, ebb away, languish, sink, sag, die down *or* away, wind down, taper off *and* trail off *or* away *and* tail off *or* away <all nonformal>

subsidiary ADJS **secondary,** subordinate; **incidental,** circumstantial, contingent

subsidize VERBS **finance,** bankroll *and* greenback <both nonformal>, fund; angel <nonformal>; **aid,** assist, support, help, pay the bills, pick up the check *or* tab *and* spring for *and* pop for <all nonformal>

subsidy NOUNS subvention, subsidization, support; **grant,** grant-in-aid, bounty; **allowance,** stipend, allotment

substance NOUNS 1 **sum and substance,** stuff, material, matter, medium, building blocks, fabric; **essence,** quintessence, elixir, distillate, distillation, distilled essence; sine qua non, irreducible *or* indispensable content
2 **meaning, gist,** pith, spirit, essence, gravamen, last word, name of the game *and* meat and potatoes *and* bottom line <all nonformal>

substandard ADJS **below par,** below standard, below the mark <nonformal>, **not up to scratch** *or* snuff *or* the mark <nonformal>

substantiate VERBS **confirm,** affirm, **attest,** warrant, **authenticate,** validate, certify, ratify, verify; **corroborate,** bear out, support, buttress, **sustain,** fortify, bolster, reinforce, undergird, strengthen; materialize

substitute NOUNS 1 sub <nonformal>, **substitution,** replacement, backup, deputy; locum tenens, **relief,** fill-in, **stand-in,** understudy, pinch hitter
VERBS 2 **exchange, change,** take *or* ask *or* offer in exchange, switch, ring in <nonformal>, **put in the place of,** change for, make way for, give place to
ADJS 3 **alternate, alternative,** other,

tother <nonformal>, equivalent, token, dummy, pinch, utility, backup, secondary; **proxy;** reserve, **spare,** stopgap, temporary, provisional

subterfuge NOUNS **secrecy,** secretness, concealment; **secretiveness,** closeness; **evasiveness,** evasion; **deception,** calculated deception, **deceptiveness,** gimmickry *or* gimmickery, trickiness; blind, **ruse,** wile, **dodge,** artful dodge, chicanery

subtle ADJS **nice,** dainty, delicate, *délicat* <Fr>, fine, refined, exquisite, **sophisticated,** discriminating, fastidious

subtract VERBS **deduct,** subduct, take away, take from, **remove,** withdraw, abstract; **reduce,** shorten, curtail, retrench, lessen, **diminish, decrease,** phase down, impair, bate, abate

subversive NOUNS 1 **saboteur,** fifth columnist, crypto; security risk; **revolutionist,** revolutionary, revolutionizer
ADJS 2 revolutionary, revolutional; traitorous, treasonable; vandalish, vandalistic; subversionary

subway NOUNS *métro* <Fr>, tube, underground <Brit>; shuttle train, shuttle

succeed VERBS 1 **prevail,** be successful, be crowned with success, meet with success, do very well, do famously, deliver, come through *and* make a go of it <both nonformal>; prosper; **make a hit** <nonformal>, click *and* connect <both nonformal>, **catch on** *and* take <both nonformal>, catch fire, have legs <nonformal>; **go over** *and* go over big *or* with a bang <all nonformal>; pass, graduate, qualify, win one's spurs *or* wings, pass with flying colors
2 **come** *or* **follow** *or* **go after,** follow, follow on *or* upon, replace, take the place of, displace, overtake, supervene; **step into** *or* **fill the shoes of,** don the mantle of, assume the robe of

succession NOUNS 1 **accession;** rightful *or* legitimate succession; **usurpation,** arrogation, assumption, taking over, seizure; line of succession, mode of succession, law of succession; primogeniture, ultimogeniture; **lineage,** line, bloodline, descent, descendancy, line of descent, ancestral line; devolution, reversion
2 **series,** run, **sequence,** consecution, progression, course, gradation

successive ADJS **consecutive,** successional, back-to-back <nonformal>; **serial,** ordinal, seriate, catenary; sequent, **sequential;** linear, lineal, inline

successor NOUNS **follower,** next in line; **replacement,** backup, backup man *or* woman, substitute, stand-in; **descendant,** posterity, **heir,** inheritor

succinct ADJS **pithy,** laconic, **sententious,** gnomic, pungent, terse, crisp, pointed

succulent ADJS **palatable,** delicious, dainty; **savory,** savorous, toothsome, sapid, delightful, delectable, exquisite; juicy, fleshy, **luscious,** for the gods, ambrosial, nectarous, nectareous

succumb VERBS 1 **perish,** expire, die, cease, end, come to an end, go, pass, **pass away, vanish, disappear,** fade away, run out, peg *or* conk out <nonformal>, come to nothing *or* naught, be no more, be done for; be all over with, be all up with <nonformal>
2 **submit,** relent, resign, resign oneself, give oneself up, not resist; take one's medicine, swallow the pill, face the music

sudden ADJS **abrupt,** precipitant, **precipitate; hasty,** headlong, impulsive, impetuous; speedy, swift, quick; **unexpected**, unanticipated, unpredicted, unforeseen, unlooked-for; **surprising**, startling

suddenly ADVS **abruptly,** all of a sudden

sue VERBS **litigate,** prosecute, go into litigation, **bring suit,** go to law, seek in law, appeal to the law, seek justice *or* legal redress, implead, **bring action against,** prosecute a suit against, take *or* institute legal proceedings against; take to court, bring into court, bring before a jury, bring to justice, bring to trial

suffer VERBS **feel pain,** feel the pangs, anguish; **hurt,** ache, have a misery <nonformal>, ail; **agonize,** writhe; **endure,** bear, stand, support, sustain, **tolerate,** bear up under, bear the brunt, bear with, put up with, brook, brave, hang in there, keep it up; **countenance,** condone, stomach; **be punished,** suffer for, **suffer the consequences** *or* **penalty,** get it *and* catch it <both nonformal>, **get one's desserts** *or* **just desserts**

sufficient ADJS sufficing; **enough,** ample, substantial, **plenty,** satisfactory, adequate, due

suffocate VERBS **stifle,** asphyxiate, stop

the breath; **smother,** choke, strangle, throttle

suggest VERBS 1 **promise,** hint, imply, give prospect of, make likely, give ground for expecting, raise expectation, **lead one to expect,** hold out hope, make fair promise, have a lot going for, have *or* show promise, **bid fair,** stand fair to; **advise,** counsel, recommend, advocate, propose, submit
2 **resemble,** put one in mind of <nonformal>, remind one of, bring to mind, be reminiscent of, evoke, call up, call to mind; savor *or* smack of, be redolent of; **have all the earmarks of,** have every appearance of

suggestion NOUNS **hint,** *soupçon* <Fr>, suspicion, intimation; **proposal,** proposition, instance; **remark,** reflection, imputation, **insinuation,** sly suggestion, innuendo, disparaging *or* uncomplimentary remark

suit NOUNS 1 suit of clothes, rig <nonformal>, **costume,** habit, bib and tucker <nonformal>
2 **lawsuit,** suit in *or* at law; countersuit; **litigation,** prosecution, action, legal action, proceedings, legal proceedings, legal process; legal remedy; **case,** court case, cause, legal case
VERBS 3 **outfit;** equip, **accouter,** uniform, caparison, rig, rig out *or* up, fit, **fit out,** turn out, **costume,** habit
4 fit, suit *or* fit to a tee, fit like a glove, **qualify, do,** serve, answer, be OK <nonformal>, do the job *and* do the trick *and* fill the bill *and* cut the mustard <all nonformal>

suitable ADJS **eligible,** qualified, fit, fitted, acceptable, admissible, worthy, desirable; **seemly,** becoming, fitting, meet, happy, felicitous; **apt,** apposite, appropriate; **expedient,** befitting; feasible, doable, swingable <nonformal>

suitor NOUNS **wooer,** pursuer, follower; escort, companion, date *and* steady <both nonformal>; significant other; **petitioner,** supplicant, suppliant

sulk VERBS **mope,** mope around; grump *and* grouch *and* bitch <all nonformal>, **fret;** get oneself in a sulk

sullen ADJS **morose,** mopish, mopey, uncommunicative; disobedient, recalcitrant, refractory, fractious, sulky, indocile

sully VERBS soil, defile; **corrupt,** seduce, deceive, **debauch, ravish,** ravage, despoil, ruin; **violate,** abuse

sultry ADJS **stifling,** suffocating, stuffy, close, oppressive; **humid,** sticky <nonformal>, muggy

sum NOUNS **total,** sum total, sum and substance, **the amount,** whole *or* gross amount, grand total; amount of money; round sum, lump sum; summation

summarize VERBS **restate,** reword, review, run over, sum up, précis, encapsulate; **recapitulate,** recap *and* rehash <both nonformal>, **recount,** rehearse, recite, relate; **sum up,** sum, summate, say it all <nonformal>

summary NOUNS **résumé,** rundown, runthrough; **summation,** summing up, recounting, capitulation, **recapitulation,** recap *and* rehash <both nonformal>; sum, substance, sum and substance, wrap-up

summer NOUNS **summertime,** summertide, good old summertime; growing season; midsummer; **dog days,** canicular days; Indian summer

summit NOUNS top; **tip-top,** peak, pinnacle; **crest,** brow; **supremacy,** primacy, paramountcy, **first place,** height, acme, zenith, top spot <nonformal>; **culmination,** perfection, top, ultimate, consummation, *ne plus ultra* <L>

summon VERBS **call,** demand, preconize; call for, send for *or* after, bid come; **invite,** ask, call in; **convoke,** call together

sumptuous ADJS **grandiose,** grand, magnificent, splendid, **elegant,** elaborate, luxurious, extravagant, deluxe

sun NOUNS orb of day, daystar

the glorious lamp of Heav'n,
the radiant sun
DRYDEN

sundry ADJS **diversified,** varied, assorted, heterogeneous; **various,** many and various, divers <old>, diverse, **several,** many; of all sorts *or* conditions *or* kinds *or* shapes *or* descriptions *or* types

sunglasses NOUNS colored glasses, sunspecs <nonformal>, dark glasses, shades <nonformal>

sunk ADJS **depressed,** lowered, debased, reduced, **fallen; sunken,** submerged; downcast, low, at a low ebb

sunny ADJS **bright,** fair, mild, balmy; halcyon, **radiant,** riant, sparkling, beaming, glowing, sanguine, optimistic, hopeful

sunrise NOUNS **dawn,** the dawn of day, dawning, daybreak, **sunup,** cockcrow, light, first light, daylight, aurora; **break of day,** peep of day, crack of dawn

sunset NOUNS **eventide,** vesper; **close of day,** decline *or* fall of day, shut of day, when day is done; **nightfall, sundown,** setting sun, going down of the sun, the cool of the evening

superb ADJS super <nonformal>, **exquisite; magnificent,** splendid, splendiferous, tremendous, immense, **marvelous,** wonderful, glorious, divine, heavenly, terrific, sensational

superficial ADJS **shallow,** unprofound; shallow-minded, **frivolous,** flighty, light, volatile, frothy, fluffy, **featherbrained,** birdbrained

superfluous ADJS **redundant;** excess, in excess; unnecessary, unessential, nonessential, expendable, dispensable, **needless,** unneeded, gratuitous, uncalled-for; pleonastic, tautologous, tautological

superintendent NOUNS **supervisor,** foreman, monitor, **head,** headman, taskmaster; **overseer,** inspector, proctor; **straw boss** <nonformal>

superior NOUNS 1 **chief,** head, boss, honcho <nonformal>, commander, **leader,** dean, *primus inter pares* <L, first among equals>, **master**; higher-up <nonformal>, senior, principal, big shot <nonformal>

ADJS 2 **greater,** better, finer; **higher,** upper, over, super, above; ascendant, in the ascendant, in ascendancy, coming <nonformal>; **surpassing,** exceeding, excellent, **excelling,** rivaling, eclipsing, capping, topping, **transcending,** transcendent *or* transcendental; **ahead,** a cut *or* stroke above, one up on <nonformal>

superiority NOUNS **preeminence,** greatness, **lead,** transcendence *or* transcendency, ascendancy *or* ascendance, prestige, favor, prepotence *or* prepotency, preponderance; predominance *or* predominancy, hegemony; **excellence**, virtuosity, inimitability, incomparability; **seniority,** precedence, deanship; success, accomplishment

superlative ADJS **supreme,** greatest, best, highest, veriest, maximal, maximum, topmost, **uppermost,** tip-top, top-level, top-echelon, top-notch *and* top-of-the-line <both nonformal>, **first-rate,** first-class, of the first water, top of the line; sublime

supernatural ADJS supranatural, **preternatural; supernormal,** hypernormal, preternormal, **paranormal; superhuman,** preterhuman, unhuman, nonhuman; **unearthly,** unworldly, otherworldly, eerie; fey; psychical, **spiritual,** occult; transcendental; mysterious, arcane, esoteric

supersede VERBS **supplant,** succeed, **replace,** displace, **take the place of,** crowd out, cut out <nonformal>

superstar NOUNS **first-rater,** topnotcher, world-beater; wonder, prodigy, genius, virtuoso, **star,** luminary, leading light, one in a thousand *or* a million; hard *or* tough act to follow <nonformal>

superstitious ADJS **credulous,** unthinking, uncritical, unskeptical

supervise VERBS **superintend,** boss, oversee, overlook, ride herd on <nonformal>, stand over, keep an eye on *or* upon, keep in order; **direct,** manage, administer, discipline

supplant VERBS **remove,** displace, outplace, replace; **supersede,** succeed, **take the place of,** crowd out, cut out <nonformal>

supple ADJS **adaptable,** adjustable, pliant, flexible, resourceful; limber, lithe, willowy, lithesome, lissome

supplement NOUNS 1 **adjunct,** addition, increase, **increment,** augmentation, supplementation, complementation, *additum* <L>, addendum, addenda <pl>, complement, continuation, extrapolation, extension

VERBS 2 **add to,** augment; **reinforce,** strengthen, fortify, beef up <nonformal>

supply NOUNS 1 **fund,** resource, resources; means, assets, liquid assets; **materials,** material resources *or* means; store

VERBS 2 **provide,** find, dish up *and* rustle up <both nonformal>, **furnish;** contribute, kick in <nonformal>, yield, present; make available; stock, store; provide for, make provision *or* due provision for; fill, fill up; replenish, restock

support NOUNS 1 **maintenance,** sustainment, sustentation, **sustenance,** subsistence, provision, total support, meal ticket <nonformal>; **keep,** upkeep; livelihood, living, meat, bread, daily

bread; **nurture,** fostering, nurturance, nourishment, **care,** caring, care-giving, tender loving care *or* TLC <nonformal>
VERBS 2 **back** *and* **back up** <both nonformal>, come out for, **endorse;** go with the party, follow the party line; **get on the bandwagon** <nonformal>; **finance,** fund, sponsor, patronize, provide for, provide capital *or* money for, bankroll <nonformal>, angel <nonformal>, put up the money; **stake** *or* **grubstake** <both nonformal>; subsidize
3 **corroborate,** bear out, buttress, **sustain,** fortify, bolster, back, back up, reinforce, undergird, strengthen; **document;** prove

supporter NOUNS **upholder,** maintainer, sustainer; support, **mainstay,** standby <nonformal>, stalwart, reliance, dependence; **backer,** promoter, angel <nonformal>, rabbi <nonformal>; **champion,** defender, apologist, **advocate,** exponent; **fan** *and* buff <both nonformal>, aficionado, **admirer**

suppose VERBS **assume,** presume, surmise, expect, **suspect,** infer, understand, gather, conclude, deduce, consider, reckon, divine, imagine, **believe,** deem, repute, feel; **think likely,** daresay, venture to say

suppress VERBS **repress,** keep under, choke *or* hold back, fight down *or* back, inhibit; **cover up,** hush up, stifle, muffle, **smother,** squash, quash, squelch, kill, sit on *or* upon, put the lid on <nonformal>; **conquer,** vanquish, quell, **put down,** subdue, subjugate, put under the yoke

supremacy NOUNS **primacy,** paramountcy, **first place,** height, acme, zenith, be-all and end-all, summit, top spot <nonformal>; **dominance,** dominion, domination; preeminence, superiority; **ascendance** *or* **ascendancy;** upper *or* whip hand, sway; **priority,** precedence

supreme ADJS **superlative,** greatest, best, highest, **uppermost,** first-rate, first-class, of the first water, top of the line; **governing,** preeminent, leading, **superior, peerless;** quintessential

sure ADJS 1 **certain,** sure-enough <nonformal>; bound; **positive,** absolute, definite, perfectly sure, apodictic; decisive, conclusive; clear, clear as day, clear and distinct, unequivocal, unmistakable, unambiguous, nonambiguous; **confident,** secure, **assured,** reassured, decided, determined; **convinced,** persuaded, positive, **cocksure; unhesitating,** unfaltering, unwavering; **self-confident,** self-assured, self-reliant, sure of oneself; poised; unafraid
ADVS 2 **surely, to be sure,** sure enough, for sure <nonformal>; sure thing *and* surest thing you know <both nonformal>

surf NOUNS **spray,** breakers, white water, spoondrift *or* **spindrift,** roller, curler, comber, whitecap, white horse

surface NOUNS 1 **exterior,** external, outside; superficies, covering, skin, outer skin *or* layer, epidermis, integument, envelope, crust, cortex, rind, shell; veneer, gloss
VERBS 2 **be revealed,** become known, come to light, appear, manifest itself, come to one's ears, transpire, **leak out,** get out, come out, out, come home to roost, come out in the wash, break forth, show its face; comes out of the closet <nonformal>, stand revealed; blow one's cover <nonformal>
ADJS 3 **apparent,** appearing, **seeming,** ostensible; outward, superficial; cosmetic, merely cosmetic; on *or* near the surface, merely surface, **nominal**

surge NOUNS 1 **flow,** course, onward course, **gush,** rush, onrush, spate, run, race; **upturn,** uptick <nonformal>, uptrend, upsurge, upswing; **leap,** jump; flood; **swirl,** twirl, **eddy,** gurge
VERBS 2 **flow,** stream, issue, pour, run, course, rush, flush, flood; **gush,** well, **swirl,** gurge, **eddy**

surly ADJS **sullen,** sulky, morose, dour, mumpish, dumpish, **glum,** grum, grim; **moody,** moodish; **mopish,** mopey <nonformal>, moping; crusty, bearish, beastly, churlish

surmise VERBS **suppose,** assume, presume, expect, **suspect,** infer, understand, gather, conclude, deduce, consider, reckon, divine, imagine, **fancy,** dream, conceive, **believe,** deem, repute, feel, **think,** be inclined to think, opine, daresay, be afraid <nonformal>

surmount VERBS **overcome,** overpower, overmaster, overmatch; overcome oneself, master oneself; kick the habit <nonformal>

surpass VERBS **excel,** outdo, pass, do *or* go one better; challenge comparison, make the most of

surplus NOUNS 1 leftovers, plus, overstock, **overage,** overset, overrun, **overmeasure,** oversupply; **remainder,** balance, leftover, extra, spare, something extra *or* to spare
ADJS 2 overplus; **remaining,** unused, **leftover;** over, over and above; extra, spare, supernumerary, as a bonus

surprise NOUNS 1 **astonishment;** surpriser, startler, shocker, **blow,** eye-opener, revelation; **bolt out of** *or* **from the blue,** thunderbolt, thunderclap; **bombshell,** earthshaker; sudden turn *or* development, *peripeteia* <Gk>; surprise package; surprise party; **surprise attack**
VERBS 2 **take by surprise,** do the unexpected, spring a surprise <nonformal>, **open one's eyes,** give one a revelation; **catch** *or* **take unawares,** catch *or* take short, take aback, pull up short, raise some eyebrows, **catch off-guard**, cross one up <nonformal>; throw a curve <nonformal>, **blindside** <nonformal>; **astonish**

surreal ADJS **strange,** outlandish, off-the-wall <informal>, not for real <nonformal>, passing strange

wondrous strange
SHAKESPEARE

surrender NOUNS 1 **capitulation;** renunciation, giving over, abandonment, relinquishment, **cession;** giving up *or* in, backing off *or* down <nonformal>, retreat, recession, recedence
VERBS 2 **give up,** capitulate, acknowledge defeat, **cry quits,** say 'uncle' <nonformal>, **throw in the towel** *or* **sponge** <nonformal>, show *or* wave the white flag; renounce, abandon, relinquish, **cede,** give over, hand over

surreptitious ADJS **covert,** clandestine, unobtrusive, **undercover,** underground, under-the-counter, under-the-table, **cloak-and-dagger,** backdoor, underhand, **underhanded; furtive,** stealthy, privy, backstairs, **sly,** shifty, sneaky, sneaking, skulking, slinking, slinky

surrogate NOUNS **deputy,** proxy, representative, substitute, vice, vicegerent, **alternate,** backup *and* stand-in <both nonformal>, alter ego, procurator, secondary, understudy, pinch hitter <nonformal>, utility man *or* woman, the bench <nonformal>; locum tenens

surround VERBS **environ,** compass, encircle, **encompass,** enclose, close; go round *or* around, compass about; **envelop,** enfold, lap, wrap, enwrap, embrace, enclasp, embosom, embay, involve, invest; **bound,** circumscribe, limit, girdle

surveillance NOUNS shadowing, following, trailing, tailing <nonformal>, 24-hour surveillance, observation, stakeout <nonformal>; **spying,** espionage, espial; wiretap, wiretapping, bugging <nonformal>, electronic surveillance

survey NOUNS 1 **scrutiny,** overview, contemplation; **examination,** inspection, scrutiny, the once-over <nonformal>, visual examination, a vetting <Brit nonformal>, ocular inspection, eyeball inspection <nonformal>; **discourse,** discussion, disquisition, descant, exposition, screed
2 **canvass,** inquiry, questionnaire, questionary; exit poll; **poll,** public-opinion poll, opinion poll *or* survey, statistical survey, opinion sampling, voter-preference survey; consumer-preference survey, market-research survey; consumer research, market research
VERBS 3 **scrutinize,** eye, contemplate, look over, give the eye *or* the once-over <nonformal>; examine, vet <Brit nonformal>, inspect; **watch,** put under surveillance, stake out <nonformal>

survive VERBS **remain,** be left *or* left over, rest; **keep alive,** keep body and soul together, endure, persist, last, last out, hang on, hang in <nonformal>, be spared; cheat death; **subsist,** cope, eke out, make out, scrape along, manage, get by; **recover,** pull through, pull round *or* around, come round *or* around <nonformal>, come back <nonformal>, make a comeback <nonformal>; weather the storm; outlive

survivor NOUNS heir, successor; **widow,** widower, relict, war widow, **orphan**

susceptible ADJS **exposed,** at risk, overexposed, open, like a sitting duck, **vulnerable**; liable, nonimmune

suspect VERBS 1 distrust, mistrust, doubt, misdoubt; surmise, **infer,** understand, gather, conclude, deduce, smell a rat *and* see something funny <both nonformal>; greet with skepticism, raise a question, throw doubt upon, awake a doubt *or* suspicion
ADJS 2 suspected, **under suspicion,**

under a cloud; **discredited,** exploded, rejected, **suspicious,** open to question *or* doubt; in question, in dispute, at issue

suspend VERBS **hang,** hang up, put up, fasten up; **interrupt,** intermit, **break,** break off, take a break <nonformal>, cut off, break *or* snap the thread; **lay off,** surplus, furlough

suspenders NOUNS pair of suspenders, braces <Brit>, galluses <nonformal>

suspense NOUNS state of suspense, cliff-hanging *and* nail-biting <both nonformal>; uncertainty, nervous expectation; **anxiety,** dread, pessimism, apprehension; abeyance, latency

suspicion NOUNS **suspiciousness,** doubt, misdoubt, mistrust, distrust, distrustfulness; **impression,** inkling, intuition, **feeling,** funny feeling <nonformal>, feeling in one's bones; wariness, leeriness, guardedness, skepticism

suspicious ADJS **incredulous,** suspecting, shy, wary, leery, cautious, guarded; suspect, funny; open to question *or* doubt

sustain VERBS **protract,** prolong, extend, perpetuate, lengthen, spin *or* string out; **maintain,** keep, hold, retain, preserve; **keep up,** keep going, keep alive, **survive**

sustenance NOUNS **nutriment,** nourishment, nurture; **support,** maintenance, sustainment, sustentation, **subsistence,** provision, total support, meal ticket <nonformal>

svelte ADJS **slender,** slinky, sylphlike, willowy

swag NOUNS **booty,** spoil, **spoils,** loot, ill-gotten gains, **plunder,** prize, haul, take, stolen goods, hot goods *or* items <nonformal>

swagger NOUNS 1 **strut,** side, swank <nonformal>, bounce, brave show; swaggering, strutting; peacockishness, peacockery
VERBS 2 **strut,** swank <Brit>, prance, stalk, peacock

swallow VERBS **ingest,** imbibe, drink; devour, ingurgitate; **gulp,** gulp down, swill, swill down, wolf down, gobble; **believe,** credit, trust, accept, buy <nonformal>

swamp NOUNS 1 **marsh,** marshland, swampland, fen, fenland, **morass,** bog, mire, quagmire
VERBS 2 **overflow,** inundate, engulf, sweep, whelm, overwhelm, **flood,** deluge, submerge

swanky ADJS **sumptuous,** elegant, elaborate, luxurious, extravagant, deluxe; plush *and* posh *and* ritzy *and* swank <all nonformal>

swap NOUNS 1 **trade,** horse trade <nonformal>; even trade, even-steven trade, **switch;** barter
VERBS 2 **interchange, exchange,** change, counterchange; **trade,** switch

swarm NOUNS 1 **invasion,** swarming, teeming, ravage, plague; **overrunning,** overswarming, overspreading
VERBS 2 **come together, throng, crowd,** teem, hive, surge, seethe, mill, stream, horde; **infest,** beset, invade, ravage, plague; **overrun,** overswarm, overspread

swarthy ADJS **dark,** dark-colored, **darkish,** darksome, blackish; nigrescent

swashbuckler NOUNS **blusterer, swaggerer,** swasher, fanfaron, bravo, **bully,** bullyboy, bucko, roisterer, cock of the walk, vaporer, blatherskite <nonformal>

sway NOUNS 1 **swing,** swinging, swag; **rock,** lurch, roll, reel, careen
VERBS 2 **rear,** rock, roll, reel, swing, lurch, yaw, heave, scend, **flounder,** welter, wallow
3 **induce,** prompt, move one to, influence, incline; **persuade,** prevail on *or* upon, convince, lead to believe, **bring round,** bring to reason, bring to one's senses

swear VERBS 1 **give one's word,** pledge *or* pass one's word, give one's parole, **give one's word of honor,** cross one's heart *and* cross one's heart and hope to die <both nonformal>; **vouch,** warrant, take one's oath, acknowledge, avow
2 **curse,** cuss <nonformal>, blaspheme, execrate, take the Lord's name in vain; swear like a trooper, cuss like a sailor; **talk dirty** <nonformal>, scatologize, coprologize, dysphemize, use strong language

sweat NOUNS 1 **perspiration,** water; exudation, exudate; diaphoresis, sudor; honest sweat, the sweat of one's brow; beads of sweat, beaded brow; cold sweat; **lather,** swelter, streams of sweat; sudoresis
VERBS 2 **perspire,** exude; break out in a sweat, **get all in a lather** <nonformal>; sweat like a trooper *or* horse, swelter, wilt; **fear,** break out in a cold sweat, sweat bullets <nonformal>; **stew,** get into a dither, get into a stew <non-

formal>, work oneself into a lather *or* sweat <nonformal>; wait impatiently, sweat it out <nonformal>
3 **work hard;** scratch *and* hustle <both nonformal>, **slave,** sweat and slave <nonformal>, slave away, toil away; work one's head off <nonformal>, work one's fingers to the bone, break one's back, bust one's hump *or* ass <nonformal>

sweep VERBS 1 sweep up *or* out, **brush,** brush off, whisk, broom; **graze,** brush by, glance, scrape, skim; go *or* make one's rounds, **scour,** scour the country
2 **glide,** coast, skim, flow; **drive,** move forward, advance; sweep along

sweepstakes NOUNS **lottery,** drawing, sweepstake *or* sweep; **raffle; state lottery,** Lotto, Pick Six, Pick Four; **numbers game** *or* **policy,** Chinese lottery <nonformal>; tontine

sweet NOUNS 1 **sweetness,** sweetishness, saccharinity; **sugariness,** syrupiness; oversweetness, mawkishness, cloyingness, sickly-sweetness
ADJS 2 sweetish, sweetened; sacchariferous; **sugary,** sugared, candied, **honeyed,** syrupy; mellifluous; honeyed, dulcet; sugarsweet, honeysweet, sweet as sugar *or* honey; sugar-coated; bittersweet
3 **endearing,** lovable, likable, adorable, admirable, **lovely,** lovesome, winning, winsome; caressable, kissable; cuddlesome, cuddly

sweetheart NOUNS 1 **loved one,** love, beloved, darling, dear, dear one, truelove, **object of one's affections,** light of one's eye *or* life, light of love

2 <nonformal> **sweetie, honey,** honeybunch, honey-bunny, honeypie, hon, main squeeze, sweetie-pie, sweet patootie, tootsie, tootsie-pie, tootsywootsy, dearie, baby, dreamboat, heartthrob, poopsy, poopsy-woopsy, sugar, sugar-bun, sweets

swell VERBS 1 **din;** surge, rise, crescendo, loudness
2 **billow,** surge, heave, lift, rise, send, scend, toss, popple; **bulge,** bilge, bouge <nonformal>, **belly,** bag, balloon, pouch; **swell up,** dilate, distend, swell out, **belly out,** round out

swelter VERBS **roast,** toast, cook, bake, fry, broil, boil, seethe, simmer, stew; **sweat,** break out in a sweat, **get all in a lather** <nonformal>; sweat like a horse, wilt

swerve VERBS **veer,** sheer, curve, **shift,** turn, trend, bend, heel, bear off; alter one's course, angle off *or* away, veer off, slant off, go off on a tangent

swift ADJS **quick,** speedy, expeditious, snappy <nonformal>, celeritous, alacritous, quick on the draw *or* trigger <nonformal>; **brief,** short, brisk, fleet; summary, decisive

swig NOUNS 1 **drink,** potation, potion, libation; draft, dram, drench, swill *and* guzzle <both nonformal>, quaff, **sip,** sup, suck, tot, bumper, snort *and* slug <both nonformal>, pull <nonformal>, lap, gulp, slurp <nonformal>; nip, peg
VERBS 2 **drink,** drink in, **imbibe,** wet one's whistle <nonformal>; **quaff,** sip, sup, bib, swill *and* guzzle *and* pull <all nonformal>; drink off *or* up, toss off *or* down, drain the cup; tipple, booze

swill NOUNS 1 **refuse,** waste, waste matter, **garbage,** pig-swill, slop, slops, hogwash <nonformal>; **mud,** muck, mire, slush, slosh, sludge, slime; slop
VERBS 2 **drink,** quaff, sip, sup, bib, swig *and* guzzle *and* pull <all nonformal>; toss off *or* down, drain the cup; tipple, **booze**

swim NOUNS 1 aquatics, **swimming,** bathing, natation, balneation, bathe <Brit>
VERBS 2 **bathe,** go in swimming *or* bathing; skinny-dip

swim suit NOUNS **swimwear; bathing suit,** tank suit, tank top, *maillot* or *maillot de bain* <Fr>, two-piece suit; bikini, string bikini *or* string

swindle NOUNS 1 **hoax,** cheat, fraud; **imposture; imposition,** cheating, cozenage, dodge, fishy transaction, piece of sharp practice; **graft** <nonformal>, grift <nonformal>; bunco
VERBS 2 **cheat,** victimize, gull, pigeon, fudge, **defraud,** practice fraud upon, euchre, **con,** finagle, **fleece,** mulct, **bilk,** cozen, cheat out of, do out of; bunco, play a bunco game; sell gold bricks <nonformal>

swine NOUNS 1 **pig,** hog, porker; **shoat,** piggy, piglet, pigling; gilt; **boar,** sow; **beast,** animal
2 bad person, animal, cur, reptile, snake

swing NOUNS 1 **rhythm,** beat, meter, measure, number *or* numbers, movement, **lilt;** play, range, scope, sweep

VERBS 2 **turn round** *or* **around** *or* **about,** swivel, pivot, pivot about, swing round; wheel, wheel about, whirl, spin; brandish, flourish, flaunt, shake, wield
3 **be promiscuous,** sleep around <nonformal>; **debauch, wanton,** rake, womanize, sow one's wild oats
4 **syncopate,** play jazz, jive <nonformal>

swinger NOUNS **libertine,** profligate, rake, **roué,** wanton, womanizer, debauchee

swirl NOUNS 1 **flurry,** ruffle, bustle, stir, swirling, whirl, vortex, eddy, hurry, hurry-scurry, hurly-burly
VERBS 2 **agitate,** unsettle, stir, flurry, flutter, fret, ruffle, rumple, ripple, ferment, convulse

switch NOUNS 1 **substitution,** exchange, change, switcheroo <nonformal>, commutation, subrogation; **replacement,** displacement; superseding, supersession
VERBS 2 **substitute,** exchange, change, take *or* ask *or* offer in exchange, ring in <nonformal>, **put in the place of,** change for, make way for, give place to

swivel VERBS **turn round** *or* **around** *or* **about,** pivot, pivot about, swing, round, swing round; wheel, wheel about, whirl, spin; heel, turn upon one's heel

swollen ADJS **distended,** dilated, inflated, sufflated, **blown up,** puffed up, swelled, **bloated,** turgid, tumid, plethoric, incrassate; **surfeited,** glutted, gorged, overfed, replete; overblown

swoon NOUNS 1 **unconsciousness,** senselessness; **faint,** blackout, syncope, athymia, lipothymy *or* lipothymia; semiconsciousness, grayout
VERBS 2 **faint,** drop, succumb, keel over <nonformal>, fall in a faint, fall senseless, pass *or* zonk out <nonformal>, go out like a light; gray out

swoop VERBS **plunge,** dive, pitch, plummet, drop, fall; plump, plunk, plop; swoop down, stoop, **pounce,** pounce on *or* upon

sword NOUNS **blade,** good *or* trusty sword; steel, **cold steel;** Excalibur

sworn ADJS **affirmed,** asserted, asseverated, avouched, avowed, averred, declared; **deposed,** warranted, **attested,** certified, vouched, **vouched for,** vowed, pledged, sworn to

sylvan ADJS **woodland,** forest, forestal; **wooded,** timbered, forested, arboreous; **woody,** woodsy, bosky, bushy, shrubby, scrubby; copsy, braky

symbol NOUNS **emblem,** icon, token, type; **representative,** exponent; **exemplification,** illustration, demonstration, explanation

symbolic ADJS symbolical, allegoric, allegorical, figural, figurative, tropological, **metaphoric,** metaphorical, anagogic, anagogical

symmetrical ADJS **symmetric,** balanced, balanced off, proportioned, eurythmic, harmonious; coequal, coordinate, equilateral; **well-balanced**

symmetry NOUNS **harmony,** proportion, concord, **balance,** equilibrium, order, orderedness, measure, measuredness, concinnity; **correspondence,** equivalence, equipollence, coequality

sympathetic ADJS **sensitive,** responsive, receptive; **comforting,** consoling, consolatory, of good comfort; condoling, condolent, condolatory; sympathizing, **compassionate**, merciful; empathic, empathetic; **congenial,** *en rapport* <Fr>, compatible, affinitive

sympathy NOUNS **fellow feeling,** sympathetic response, responsiveness, relating, warmth, **caring,** concern; response, echo, chord, sympathetic chord, vibrations, vibes <nonformal>; **empathy,** identification; **condolence,** condolences, **consolation,** comfort, balm, soothing words, **commiseration,** sharing of grief *or* sorrow; **compassion,** sensitivity

symposium NOUNS **forum,** conference, discussion group, **round table,** panel, panel discussion, seminar; open forum, colloquium

symptom NOUNS **warning sign,** premonitory sign, danger sign; preliminary sign *or* signal *or* token; early symptom, premonitory symptom, prodrome, prodroma, prodromata <pl>; precursor

synagogue NOUNS **temple,** fane; tabernacle; *shul* <Yiddish>; house of worship

synchronized ADJS **synchronous,** synchronic *or* synchronal, in sync <nonformal>; **in time,** in step, in tempo, in phase, with *or* on the beat

syndicate NOUNS commercial enterprise; **trust,** cartel, combine, pool, consortium; crime family, crime organization

syndrome NOUNS **signs,** symptoms, pathology, symptomatology, symptomology

synergy NOUNS **cooperation,** collaboration, coaction, concurrence, synergism; symbiosis, commensalism

synopsis NOUNS **abridgment,** condensation, short *or* shortened version, condensed version, abbreviation, **abstract,** epitome, **précis,** capsule, nutshell *or* capsule version, capsulization, encapsulation, conspectus

synthesis NOUNS **identification,** likening, unification, coalescence, combination, union, fusion, merger, blending, melding; syneresis, syncretism

synthetic NOUNS 1 **plastic;** thermoplastic, thermosetting plastic; resin plastic; cellulose plastic; protein plastic; synthetic fabric *or* textile *or* cloth
ADJS 2 **imitation,** synthetical, ersatz, hokey *and* hoked-up <both nonformal>, mock

system NOUNS **discipline,** method, methodology, methodicalness, systematicness; **frame of reference,** intellectual *or* ideational frame of reference, framework, arena, world, universe, world *or* universe of discourse, reference system

systematic ADJS **orderly,** ordered, **regular,** well-regulated, well-ordered, methodical, formal, regular as clockwork, uniform, symmetrical; businesslike, routine, steady, normal, habitual, usual

T

tab NOUNS **bill,** itemized bill, bill of account, **account,** reckoning, check, *l'addition* <Fr>, score <nonformal>

table NOUNS 1 **plateau,** tableland, high plateau, mesa, butte, moor, hammada
2 board, **stand; bench,** workbench; **counter,** bar, buffet; **lectern,** reading stand, ambo, reading desk
VERBS 3 **postpone,** delay, defer, put off, hold off *or* up <nonformal>, prorogue, put on hold *or* ice *or* the back burner <all nonformal>; **hold over,** lay over, stand over, let the matter stand, **put aside,** lay *or* set *or* push aside, lay *or* set by, pigeonhole, **shelve,** put on the shelf, put on ice <nonformal>

tableau NOUNS **spectacle,** sight; **show,** display, presentation, representation; tableau vivant; **picture;** image, likeness, representation

tabloid NOUNS **newspaper,** paper, sheet *or* rag <both nonformal>

taboo NOUNS 1 **exclusion,** ban, bar, injunction; prohibition
ADJS 2 **prohibited,** forbidden, *verboten* <Ger>, barred; banned, tabooed, untouchable

tabulate VERBS **file,** index, **catalog,** calendar, **list,** enumerate, itemize, tally

tacit ADJS **wordless,** unspoken, unuttered, unexpressed, unsaid; **implicit,** implied, understood, taken for granted

taciturn ADJS **untalkative,** unloquacious, indisposed to talk; **silent,** speechless, wordless, **mum;** close, **closemouthed,** close-tongued, tight-lipped; close-lipped, **laconic,** curt, brief, terse, brusque, short, concise, **sparing of words,** economical of words, of few words

tackle NOUNS 1 **harness,** caparison, trappings, **tack; impedimenta,** luggage, dunnage, baggage, bag and baggage, traps, apparatus, truck, gear, kit, outfit, duffel
VERBS 2 **take up,** take to, **undertake,** take on, address oneself to, have a go at, turn one's hand to, **go in** *or* **out for** <nonformal>, make it one's business, follow as an occupation, set up shop; **deal with,** cope with, come to grips with, contend with; **plunge into,** dive into; light into *and* wade into *and* tear into *and* sail into <all nonformal>

tacky ADJS 1 **shabby,** shoddy, seedy, scruffy, dowdy, tatty, ratty; **untasteful,** tasteless, in bad *or* poor taste, chintzy *and* Mickey Mouse <both nonformal>; meretricious
2 **sticky,** tenacious, adhesive, clingy, clinging, tough; gluey, gluelike, glutinous, glutenous, glutinose

tact NOUNS **considerateness,** sensitivity, tactfulness; **diplomacy,** *savoir-faire* <Fr>; **thoughtfulness,** consideration, **solicitousness,** solicitude

tactic NOUNS **maneuver,** demarche, course of action; **device,** contrivance, artifice, stratagem, shift; gimmick *and* dodge *and* trick <all nonformal>

tactile ADJS tactual; touchable, **palpable,** tangible

tag NOUNS 1 **label,** ticket, tally; stub, counterfoil; **token,** check; **name,** brand name, trade name, trademark
2 **afterpart,** afterpiece; **wake,** trail, train, queue; **tail,** tailpiece, rear, rear end; **tail end,** butt end, tag end
VERBS 3 **label,** tab, ticket; **brand,** earmark; hallmark; bar-code; name, **designate,** call, term, style, dub; nickname

tail VERBS 1 **follow,** move behind; **pursue,** shadow <nonformal>, **trail,** trail after, follow on the trail of, camp on the trail of
ADJS 2 **rear,** rearward, **back,** backward, retrograde, **posterior,** postern; after *or* aft; **hind,** hinder; hindmost, hindermost, hindhand, posteriormost, **aftermost,** aftmost, rearmost
3 caudal, caudate, caudated, tailed; taillike, caudiform

tailor NOUNS 1 tailoress, *tailleur* <Fr>, sartor; fitter; busheler, bushelman
VERBS 2 **form,** formalize, **shape, fashion,** frame, figure; adapt, fit, measure, proportion, adjust to, trim to, cut to, gear to, key to

taint NOUNS 1 **stain,** tarnish; mark, brand, **stigma**
VERBS 2 **stigmatize,** brand; stain, besmirch, smirch, tarnish, blot, **blacken, smear,** bespatter, **sully,** soil, defile, vilify, **slur,** cast a slur upon

take NOUNS 1 **gain, profit,** percentage <nonformal>, take-in *and* piece *and* slice *and* end *and* rakeoff *and* skimmings <all nonformal>; **gains,** profits,

earnings, winnings, return, returns, proceeds, bottom line <nonformal>
2 **catch,** bag, capture, seizure, **haul;** booty
VERBS 3 **pocket,** swallow, down, stomach, eat, digest, disregard, turn a blind eye, ignore; swallow an insult, turn the other cheek, take it lying down
4 **transport, convey,** freight, conduct; **carry, bear,** pack, tote *and* lug <both nonformal>, manhandle
5 **interpret,** diagnose; construe, put a construction on, understand, **understand by,** take to mean, take it that; **read into,** read between the lines
6 possess, take possession; **get,** get into one's hold *or* possession; pocket, palm; draw off, drain off; skim *and* skim off *and* take up front <all nonformal>; **steal,** thieve, purloin, appropriate, snatch

take back VERBS **recant,** retract, repudiate, withdraw, unswear, renege, welsh <nonformal>, **abjure,** disavow, disown; **deny,** disclaim, unsay, unspeak; **renounce,** forswear, eat one's words, eat crow, eat humble pie; **back down** *or* **out,** climb down, crawfish out <nonformal>, backwater, weasel; **apologize,** beg pardon, ask forgiveness, beg indulgence, express regret

take on VERBS 1 **undertake, assume,** accept, **take upon oneself,** take in hand, take upon one's shoulders, take up, go with, **tackle,** attack; engage *or* contract *or* obligate *or* commit oneself; **contend against,** strive against, struggle against, labor against, grapple with, join battle with, go to the mat with <nonformal>, **fight,** buck <nonformal>, counter
2 **employ, hire,** give a job to, take into employment, take into one's service, recruit, **engage,** sign up *or* on <nonformal>

take out VERBS 1 **extract,** get out, **withdraw,** remove; **exclude,** except, cancel, cancel out, censor out, bleep out <nonformal>, rule out, bar, ban
2 **escort, conduct,** have in tow <nonformal>, marshal, **usher,** shepherd, **guide,** lead; **squire,** esquire, **attend,** date, wait on *or* upon

take over VERBS **take command,** take charge, take the helm, take the reins of government, take the reins into one's hand, get the power into one's hands, gain *or* get the upper hand, take the lead; **take possession,** appropriate, take up, make one's own, move in *or* move in on <nonformal>, annex; buy out; **succeed,** take the mantle of, step into the shoes *or* place of

tale NOUNS **story,** yarn, account, narrative, narration, chronicle; anecdote

talent NOUNS **flair,** strong flair, **gift,** endowment, natural gift *or* endowment, **genius,** instinct, **faculty,** bump <nonformal>; **talented person,** man *or* woman of parts, gifted person, prodigy, natural <nonformal>, **child prodigy,** wunderkind, whiz kid *and* boy wonder <both nonformal>

talented ADJS **gifted,** endowed, with a flair; **clever,** apt

talisman NOUNS **charm,** amulet, fetish, periapt, phylactery; **voodoo,** hoodoo, juju, obeah, mumbo jumbo

talk NOUNS 1 **palaver,** speech, words; confabulation, **confab** <nonformal>; chinfest *and* chinwag *and* talkfest *and* bull session <all nonformal>; **dialogue,** duologue, trialogue; idle talk, small talk
VERBS 2 **speak,** use language, communicate orally *or* verbally; patter *or* gab *or* wag the tongue <all nonformal>; mouth; chatter; converse; declaim; **gossip,** talk over the back fence <nonformal>

3 <nonformal> **yak,** yap, yakkety-yak, gab, spiel, chin, jaw, shoot off one's face *or* mouth, shoot *or* bat the breeze, beat *or* bat one's gums, bend one's ear, make chin music, rattle away, talk a blue streak, talk someone's ear *or* head off, flap one's jaw, natter <Brit>, spout off, sound off

talkative ADJS **wordy,** verbose; **prolix,** windy <nonformal>, **long-winded,** longiloquent

talk into VERBS **persuade,** prevail on *or* upon, **sway,** convince, lead to believe, **bring round,** bring to reason, bring to one's senses; **win, win over,** win around, bring over, draw over, gain, gain over; **talk over,** argue into, out-talk <nonformal>

talk of the town NOUNS **report,** rumor, **common talk,** town talk, topic of the day, *cause célèbre* <Fr>; **notoriety,** notoriousness

tall ADJS **long,** lengthy; longish, longsome; **rangy,** lanky, lank, tall as a maypole;

gangling *and* gangly <both nonformal>; **long-legged,** long-limbed, leggy

tally NOUNS 1 **returns,** census report *or* returns, election returns; **account,** reckoning, rendering-up, score
2 **agreement,** correspondence, coincidence, intersection, overlap, parallelism, symmetry, equivalence
VERBS 3 **coincide,** correspond, agree, chime with, match, go hand in glove with, jibe
4 **list,** enumerate, itemize, tabulate, catalog
5 **calculate,** compute, estimate, reckon, figure, reckon at, put at, cipher, cast, score

tame VERBS 1 **domesticate,** break, bust *and* gentle <both nonformal>, break in, break to harness; **soften,** subdue, hold in check, keep a tight rein, chasten, underplay, play down, downplay, tone *or* tune down
ADJS 2 **domesticated,** tamed, broken; **subdued,** chastened, housebroken, domesticated; lamblike, gentle as a lamb, dovelike; **mild,** soft, bland, gentle

tamp VERBS **depress,** press in, stamp, punch, punch in, impress, imprint

tamper with VERBS **adulterate,** corrupt, contaminate, **debase,** denaturalize, pollute, denature, bastardize, **doctor** *and* doctor up <both nonformal>; **fortify,** spike <nonformal>, lace; **dilute,** cut <nonformal>, water, water down <nonformal>

tang NOUNS **taste,** *goût* <Fr>; **flavor,** sapor; **smack,** savor, relish, sapidity; **spice,** relish

tangent ADJS **in contact,** contacting, **touching,** meeting, contingent; impinging, impingent; tangential

tangible ADJS touchable, **palpable,** tactile; **obvious,** plain, clear, perspicuous, distinct, patent, sensible, appreciable

tangle NOUNS 1 **complex,** tangled skein, **mess** *and* snafu *and* fuck-up <all nonformal>, ravel, snarl, snarl-up; knot, Gordian knot; **maze,** meander, Chinese puzzle, labyrinth
VERBS 2 **snag, snare,** sniggle, ensnare, enmesh, entangle, foul, tangle up with; **snarl,** snarl up, ravel, knot, tie in knots

tank NOUNS **well,** cistern, vat

tantalizing ADJS **appetizing,** mouthwatering, tempting, piquant; **provocative**, provoking, teasing; **titillating,** tickling, inviting, exciting

tantrum NOUNS **fit,** fit of anger, fit of temper, rage, temper tantrum; duck *or* cat fit *and* **conniption** *or* conniption fit *and* snit <all nonformal>, paroxysm, convulsion

tape NOUNS 1 **strip,** strap, strop; **lace,** thong; **band,** bandage, fillet, fascia, taenia; **belt,** girdle; **ribbon,** ribband; tapeline, tape measure
2 magnetic tape, videotape
VERBS 3 **put together,** concatenate, articulate, agglutinate; glue, cement
4 **record,** put on tape, tape-record

taps NOUNS **funeral, burial,** burying; dead march, muffled drum, last post <Brit>; dirge; decease

tardy ADJS **late,** belated, slow, slow on the draw *or* uptake *or* trigger <all nonformal>, **behindhand,** never on time, backward, back, **overdue,** long-awaited, untimely; unpunctual, unready

target NOUNS **objective,** object, aim, end, goal, destination, mark, object in mind, **end in view,** telos, final cause, ultimate aim; butt, bull's-eye, quintain; quarry, prey, game

tarnish VERBS **stigmatize,** brand; stain, besmirch, smirch, taint, blot, **blacken, smear,** bespatter, **sully,** soil, defile, vilify, **slur,** cast a slur upon, blow upon; dirty, **soil**

tarry VERBS **dawdle,** linger, loiter, delay, dally, dillydally, shilly-shally, lollygag, waste time, **take one's time,** take one's own sweet time; goof off *or* around <nonformal>; **live on,** continue to be, subsist, exist

tart NOUNS 1 **pastry,** turnover; timbale; **pie,** *tarte* <Fr>, fruit pie; *quiche* or *quiche Lorraine* <Fr>
2 **strumpet,** trollop, wench, hussy, slut, jade, baggage, *cocotte* <Fr>, grisette; **chippy** *and* **floozy** *and* broad <all nonformal>
ADJS 3 **sour,** soured, sourish; tartish; acerb, acerbic, acerbate; acescent; **acrimonious,** acrid, acid, acidic, acidulous, acidulent, **bitter,** sharp

task NOUNS **work,** stint, job, labor, piece of work, **chore,** chare, odd job; **assignment,** charge, project, **duty,** service, exercise

taste NOUNS 1 **sample,** taster, little bite, little smack; **relish,** gusto, gust <Scots>; **passion, weakness** <nonformal>
2 **elegance,** tastefulness, good taste; discriminating taste, aesthetic *or* artistic

judgment; palate, fine *or* refined palate
VERBS 3 taste of, sample; **savor,** savor of; sip, roll on the tongue

tasteful ADJS **in good taste,** in the best taste; excellent, of quality, of the best, of the first water; **aesthetic,** artistic, pleasing, well-chosen, choice, of choice; **elegant,** graceful, **polished,** finished, round

tasteless ADJS **insipid,** flavorless, bland, spiceless, **savorless,** sapless, unsavory, unflavored, flat; **untasteful,** in bad *or* poor taste, tacky *and* chintzy *and* Mickey Mouse <all nonformal>; **offensive,** offensive to gentle ears

tasty ADJS fit to eat *and* finger-lickin' good <both nonformal>, good-tasting, **savory,** savorous, **palatable,** toothsome, sapid, **delicious,** delightful, delectable, exquisite; fit for a king, gourmet; scrumptious *and* yummy <both nonformal>

tatter NOUNS **scrap,** smithereen <nonformal>, patch, **stitch,** shred; snip, **snippet,** sliver, shiver

tattle VERBS **give away** *and* give the show away *and* give the game away <all nonformal>, betray a confidence, tell secrets, reveal a secret; have a big mouth <nonformal>, **blab** *or* blabber <nonformal>; babble, tell *or* tattle on, tell tales, tell tales out of school; tittle-tattle

tattletale NOUNS **snitch** *and* snitcher <both nonformal>; whistle-blower <nonformal>; **tattler,** telltale, talebearer; blab *or* blabber *or* blabberer *or* blabbermouth <all nonformal>

taught ADJS **informed,** enlightened, instructed, versed, well-versed, educated, schooled

taunt NOUNS 1 **gibe,** scoff, jeer, fleer, flout, mock, barracking <Brit>, **twit,** quip, jest, jape, put-on *and* leg-pull <both nonformal>, foolery
VERBS 2 **scoff,** jeer, gibe, barrack <Brit>, **mock,** revile, rally, chaff, **twit,** jape, flout, scout, have a fling at, cast in one's teeth; hold in contempt, ridicule, deride

taut ADJS **tense,** tensed-up, uptight <nonformal>, **strained,** stretched tight, unrelaxed, under a strain; **tight,** unrelaxed; nonresilient, inelastic

tawdry ADJS **gaudy,** garish, loud <nonformal>, **flagrant,** shameless, **brazen,** brazenfaced, lurid, extravagant, sensational, obtrusive, vulgar, crude; meretricious, **trashy,** rubbishy, cheap

tax NOUNS 1 **charge,** duty, task; **burden,** weight, freight, cargo, load, onus
VERBS 2 **strain,** tense, stress, stretch, press, rack; **burden,** load, load down *or* up, lade, cumber, **encumber,** charge, freight, handicap, hamper, saddle; **oppress,** weigh one down, weigh on *or* upon, weigh heavy on, **overburden,** overtax, overload
3 **charge,** demand, ask, require; **exact,** assess, levy, impose; assess a tax upon, slap a tax on <nonformal>, lay *or* put a duty on, make dutiable, subject to a tax *or* fee *or* duty, collect a tax *or* duty on

taxi NOUNS **cab,** taxicab, hack <nonformal>, medallion cab, gypsy cab <nonformal>; hired car, limousine, limo *and* stretch limo <both nonformal>

taxing ADJS **demanding,** exacting, exigent; draining, exorbitant, extortionate, grasping

taxpayer NOUNS **good** *or* **respectable citizen,** excellent *or* exemplary citizen, good neighbor, burgher, **pillar of society,** salt of the earth

teach VERBS **instruct,** give instruction, give lessons in, **educate,** school; edify, enlighten, civilize, illumine; **direct,** guide; inform; **show,** show how, show the ropes, demonstrate; teach a lesson, give a lesson to; **ground,** teach the rudiments *or* elements *or* basics; catechize; teach an old dog new tricks

teacher NOUNS **instructor,** educator, preceptor, mentor; master, maestro; **pedagogue,** pedagogist, educationist; **schoolteacher,** schoolmaster; **professor,** academic; don <Brit>, fellow; guide, docent

tear NOUNS 1 **rip,** rent, slash; fissure, cut, split, slit; slash, slice; **gap,** rift, rent
2 **binge,** drunk, bust, **bender,** toot, bat, jag, guzzle <all nonformal>
VERBS 3 **cut,** chop, hew, hack, slash, rip, cut, slit; gash, **rend,** rive, rend asunder

tear down VERBS 1 **raze,** pull down, take down, bring down, bring down about one's ears, bring tumbling *or* crashing down; **disassemble,** take apart *or* down; **dismantle,** demolish
2 **find fault,** pick holes, pick *or* pull *or* tear apart; carp, cavil, quibble, nitpick; **slur,** cast a slur on, do a number *or* a job on <nonformal>

tearful ADJS teary, **weepy** <nonformal>; lachrymal, lachrymose, lacrimatory; **weeping,** sobbing, crying; **in tears,** with tears in one's eyes, bathed *or* dissolved in tears

like Niobe, all tears
SHAKESPEARE

tears NOUNS **weeping,** sobbing, crying, bawling; blubbering, whimpering, sniveling; flood of tears, fit of crying; cry *and* good cry <both nonformal>; **tearfulness,** weepiness <nonformal>, lachrymosity, melting mood

tease NOUNS 1 **tormentor,** torment; teaser; annoyer, harasser, harrier, badgerer, heckler
VERBS 2 pick on <nonformal>, tweak the nose, pluck the beard, give a bad time to <nonformal>; **plague,** beset, beleaguer; **twit,** chaff, **jest,** jape, haze; **needle,** devil, get after *or* get on <nonformal>, bedevil

technical ADJS **specialized,** specialist, specialistic; **insignificant**, inconsequential, immaterial; nonessential, unessential, inessential, not vital, negligible

technicality NOUNS **intricacy,** intricateness, ramification, crabbedness, subtlety; **a nothing,** nothing in particular, nothing to speak *or* worth speaking of, nothing to think twice about, nothing to write home about, thing of naught; mere technicality

technician NOUNS **specialist,** technical expert, techie <nonformal>, nerd <nonformal>

technique NOUNS **approach,** attack, tack; **procedure,** process, proceeding, course, practice; technical skill, touch, technical brilliance, technical mastery; technology

technology NOUNS **technique,** technic, **technics,** technical knowledge *or* skill, technical know-how <nonformal>; **mechanics,** mechanism; high technology, high-tech *or* hi-tech <nonformal>

tedious ADJS **monotonous,** humdrum, singsong, jog-trot, treadmill, unvarying, invariable, uneventful, broken-record, parrotlike, harping, everlasting, too much with us <nonformal>; **dreary,** drearisome, dry, dryasdust, dusty, dull, lackluster; insipid, vapid; protracted, prolonged; prolix, long-winded

teeming ADJS **swarming,** crowding, thronging, overflowing, overcrowded, overwhelming, bursting, **crawling, alive with,** lousy with <nonformal>, crowded, packed, jammed, jam-packed, thronged, rife, superabundant, **profuse,** in profusion, thick with; **productive,** fertile, fecund, prolific, seminal, germinal, pregnant

teeter VERBS **shake,** tremble, quiver, quaver, cringe, cower, totter, dodder; **vacillate,** waffle <nonformal>, fluctuate, pendulate, oscillate, wobble, wobble about, dither; **seesaw,** teeter-totter

teetotaler NOUNS **abstainer,** abstinent; teetotalist; Rechabite, hydropot, nondrinker

telepathy NOUNS **mental telepathy,** mind reading, thought transference, telepathic transmission; telepathic dream, telepathic hallucination

telephone NOUNS 1 **phone** *and* horn <both nonformal>, telephone set; telephony, telephonics
VERBS 2 **phone** <nonformal>, **call,** call on the phone <nonformal>, put in *or* make a call, **call up,** ring, ring up, give a ring *or* buzz <nonformal>, buzz <nonformal>

televise VERBS **telecast,** videocast; colorcast; simulcast

television NOUNS **TV, video,** telly <Brit nonformal>; the small screen *or* the tube <both nonformal>, the boob tube <nonformal>; **network television,** free television; the dream factory; subscription television, pay TV; cable television, cable TV; closed-circuit television *or* closed circuit TV; public-access television *or* public-access TV

tell VERBS **inform,** apprise, **advise,** advertise, advertise of, **give word,** mention to, **acquaint,** enlighten, familiarize, brief, verse, give the facts, give an account of, give by way of information; **narrate,** relate, recount, report, **recite,** rehearse, give an account of

telling ADJS **cogent,** effective, impactful, valid, operative, in force; impressive, striking; effectual, efficacious; material, convincing, weighty; **conclusive,** determinative, **decisive,** salient

temper NOUNS 1 **hot temper,** quick *or* short temper, irritable temper, warm temper, fiery temper, fierce temper, short fuse <nonformal>, pepperiness, feistiness *and* spunkiness <both nonformal>, **hotheadedness,** hot blood; dan-

der *and* Irish <both nonformal>; bad temper
2 **mood,** humor, feeling, feelings, frame of mind, state of mind, morale, vein; mind, heart, spirit *or* spirits
VERBS 3 **moderate, alleviate,** assuage, allay, lay, lighten, palliate, extenuate, lenify; **damp,** dampen, bank the fire, reduce the temperature, throw cold water on, throw a wet blanket on
4 **harden,** indurate, firm, toughen; anneal, oil-temper, heat-temper, **case-harden,** steel; season

temperament NOUNS **disposition,** character, nature, temper, mettle, constitution, makeup, stamp, type, stripe, kidney, make, mold; **turn of mind,** inclination, mind, grain, vein, set, mental set, mindset

temperate ADJS 1 **moderate,** sober, frugal, restrained, **sparing,** stinting, measured
2 **cool,** coolish; **fresh,** brisk, crisp, bracing, sharpish, **invigorating,** stimulating

tempest NOUNS **windstorm,** big *or* great *or* fresh *or* strong *or* stiff *or* high *or* howling *or* spanking wind, storm, stormy winds, tempestuous wind; **outburst,** outbreak, **flare-up,** explosion, eruption, irruption, upheaval, convulsion, spasm

temple NOUNS fane; tabernacle; synagogue, *shul* <Yiddish>; **mosque,** masjid; dewal, girja; pagoda; kiack; pantheon

tempo NOUNS **time, beat,** time pattern, timing; **rhythm**

temporal ADJS **secularist,** secularistic, worldly, earthly, earthy, terrestrial, **mundane; unspiritual,** profane, carnal, **secular;** humanistic, secular-humanistic; worldly minded, earthly minded, carnal-minded

temporary NOUNS 1 temporary employee, office temporary, temp <nonformal>
ADJS 2 **transient,** transitory, transitive; temporal; **impermanent,** unenduring, undurable, nondurable, nonpermanent; **short-lived,** ephemeral, fly-by-night, evanescent, volatile, momentary; **expedient**, ad-hoc, stopgap, provisional, tentative

tempt VERBS **attract,** interest, appeal, engage, impress, charismatize, catch *or* get one's eye, command one's attention, rivet one, attract one's interest, be attractive, take *or* tickle one's fancy; **tantalize,** titillate, tickle, **tease,** whet the appetite, make one's mouth water, dangle before one

temptress NOUNS **tempter,** seducer, enticer, inveigler, **charmer,** enchanter, fascinator, tantalizer, teaser; coquette, flirt; enchantress, seductress, **siren;** *femme fatale* <Fr>

tenacious ADJS **persevering,** perseverant, **persistent,** persisting, insistent; **diligent,** assiduous, sedulous, industrious; dogged, plodding, slogging, plugging; **pertinacious,** stick-to-itive <nonformal>; **unswerving,** unremitting, unabating, unintermitting, uninterrupted; **unfaltering,** unwavering, unflinching; relentless, unrelenting

tenant NOUNS 1 **occupant,** occupier, incumbent, **resident; lodger,** roomer, paying guest; **renter,** subtenant; squatter
VERBS 2 **inhabit, occupy,** move in *or* into, take up one's abode, make one's home; rent, **reside,** live, live in, dwell, lodge, stay, remain, abide

tend VERBS 1 have a tendency, **incline,** be disposed, **lean,** trend, have a penchant, set, verge, turn, warp, tilt, bias, bend to, work *or* gravitate *or* set toward; show a tendency *or* trend *or* set *or* direction, swing toward
2 **care for,** take care of; **look after,** see after, attend to, minister to, look *or* see to, keep an eye on *or* upon, **watch over,** keep watch over, **watch,** mind

tendency NOUNS **inclination,** leaning, penchant, proneness, conatus, weakness, susceptibility; liability, readiness, willingness, eagerness, aptness, aptitude, **disposition,** proclivity, propensity, predisposition, **predilection,** a thing for <nonformal>, affinity, prejudice, **liking,** delight, soft spot

tender VERBS 1 **offer,** proffer, present, offer up, **put up,** submit, extend, **hold out,** hold forth, place in one's way, lay at one's feet, put *or* place at one's disposal, put one in the way of
ADJS 2 **sensitive,** sensible, emotionable, delicate; responsive, sympathetic, receptive; susceptible, impressionable; **soft,** tenderhearted, softhearted, warmhearted; affectionate, demonstrative, **romantic,** sentimental

tenement NOUNS **apartment house,** flats; duplex, duplex house; apartment complex; high-rise apartment building *or* high rise

tenet NOUNS **a belief,** dogma, precept, **principle,** principle *or* article of faith, canon, maxim, axiom; **doctrine,** teaching

tenor 1 alto; male alto, countertenor; falsetto; lyric tenor, operatic tenor, heldentenor *or* heroic tenor *or* Wagnerian tenor
2 **trend,** tone, the general tendency *or* drift, the main course, the course of events, the way the wind blows, **the way things go,** trend of the times, spirit of the age *or* time, time spirit, *Zeitgeist* <Ger>

tense ADJS tensed-up, uptight <nonformal>, **strained,** stretched tight, taut, unrelaxed, under a strain; **on edge,** with bated breath, with muscles tense, quivering, keyed-up, biting one's nails

tension NOUNS tenseness, tautness, **strain, stress,** stress and strain, mental strain, nervous tension *or* strain, pressure; personal conflict

tent NOUNS canvas; top, whitetop, round top, big top; tentage

tentacles NOUNS **clutches,** claws, talons, pounces, unguals; **nails,** fingernails; **pincers,** nippers, chelae

tentative ADJS **hesitant,** hesitating, pikerish; faltering; diffident, timid, cautious; trial, experimental; unprecipitate, cool; stopgap, temporary, provisional

tenuous ADJS **thin,** subtile, subtle, evanescent, fine, overfine, refined, rarefied; **ethereal,** airy, windy, spirituous, vaporous, gaseous; **chimerical,** gossamer, gossamery, gauzy, shadowy, phantomlike; dreamlike, illusory, unreal

tenure NOUNS **term,** time, duration; spell; continuous tenure, tenure in *or* of office

tepid ADJS **indifferent,** halfhearted, perfunctory, fervorless; **cool,** lukewarm, Laodicean; neither hot nor cold, neither one thing nor the other

term NOUNS 1 **word,** phrase, utterance, lexical form *or* item, linguistic form, semantic *or* semiotic *or* semasiological unit
2 time, duration, **tenure;** spell

terminal NOUNS 1 **destination,** end of the line, terminus, terminal point; stop, stopping place, last stop; **airport,** air terminal
ADJS 2 **past hope,** incurable, cureless, remediless, immedicable, beyond remedy; **dying,** expiring, going, slipping, slipping away, sinking, sinking fast, low, despaired of, given up, given up for dead, not long for this world

terminate VERBS **end,** determine, close, close out, close the books on, phase out *or* down, **finish,** conclude, finish with, resolve, finish *or* wind up <nonformal>; **put an end to,** put a period to, put paid to <Brit>, put *or* lay to rest, **make an end of,** bring to an end, bring to a close *or* halt; **kill**, extinguish, scrag *and* waste *and* take out *and* zap <all nonformal>, **give the quietus**

terminology NOUNS **nomenclature,** orismology; onomatology, onomastics; vocabulary, nomenclator

terrace NOUNS **balcony,** gallery; step terrace, deck

terrain NOUNS **land,** ground, **field,** sphere, place, locale, milieu, precinct, purlieu

terrestrial ADJS **earth,** earthly, telluric, tellurian; earthbound; **secularist,** secularistic, worldly, earthy, **mundane,** temporal

terrible ADJS terrific, tremendous; **horrid,** horrible, horrifying, horrific, horrendous; **dreadful,** dread, dreaded; **awful;** awesome, awe-inspiring; **shocking,** appalling, astounding; **dire,** direful, fell

terrific ADJS **superb,** super <nonformal>, **superexcellent, supereminent,** superfine, **exquisite; magnificent,** splendid, splendiferous, tremendous, immense, **marvelous, wonderful,** glorious, divine, heavenly, sensational

terrified ADJS terror-stricken, terror-struck, terror-smitten, terror-ridden; **horrified,** horror-stricken, horror-struck; **appalled,** astounded, aghast; frightened out of one's wits *or* mind, **scared to death,** scared stiff *or* shitless *or* spitless <nonformal>; unnerved, unstrung, unmanned, undone, **cowed,** awed, **intimidated; stunned,** petrified, stupefied, paralyzed, frozen

territory NOUNS **region,** area, zone, belt, terrain; **sphere of influence,** orbit, ambit; bailiwick, vantage, stamping ground, footing, turf, home turf, constituency, **power base**

terror NOUNS **fear,** fright, affright; **scare,** alarm, consternation, dismay; dread, unholy dread, awe; horror, horrification, mortal *or* abject fear; holy terror

terrorism NOUNS **terrorization,** terrorizing, horrification, scaremongering, panic-mongering, scare tactics; terror *or* terroristic tactics, *Schrecklichkeit* <Ger>, rule by terror, reign of terror

terrorist NOUNS 1 **revolutionist,** revolutionary, revolutionizer; rebel; anarchist, anarch, syndicalist, criminal syndicalist; subversive
ADJS 2 **revolutionist,** revolutionary, anarchic *or* anarchical, syndicalist, terroristic

terrorize VERBS **intimidate,** put in bodily fear, use terror *or* terrorist tactics, pursue a policy of *Schrecklichkeit,* systematically terrorize; threaten; hold a pistol to one's head, sow terror, barbarize, brutalize

terse ADJS **laconic,** curt, brief, brusque, short, concise, **sparing of words,** economical of words, of few words; **sententious,** pithy, gnomic, pungent, succinct, crisp, pointed

test NOUNS 1 **trial,** try; assay; crucial test; acid test, litmus *or* litmus-paper test; ordeal, crucible; test case
VERBS 2 **try,** essay, cut and try <nonformal>, **test** *or* **try out,** have a dry run *or* dummy run *or* rehearsal *or* test run; run it up the flagpole and see who salutes <nonformal>; put to the test, put to trial, bring to test, make a trial of, give a trial to; **verify,** confirm, prove, audit, **check,** check up *or* on *or* out <nonformal>, check over *or* through, **double-check,** triple-check, cross-check, check and doublecheck
ADJS 3 **experimental,** trial; testing, proving, trying; probative, probatory, verificatory; empirical; trial-and-error, hit-or-miss, cut-and-try

testament NOUNS **will,** last will and testament; **bequest,** bequeathal, **legacy,** devise

testify VERBS **attest,** give evidence, witness, witness to, **give** *or* **bear witness;** disclose; **vouch,** state one's case, **depose,** depone, **warrant, swear,** take one's oath, acknowledge, avow, **affirm,** avouch, aver, allege, asseverate, **certify,** give one's word

testimonial NOUNS 1 **celebration,** tribute; testimonial banquet *or* dinner; salute
2 **recommendation,** reference, credential, letter of reference, voucher; character reference, character, certificate of character, good character

testimony NOUNS **attestation,** witness; **deposition,** legal evidence, sworn evidence *or* testimony; *procès-verbal* <Fr>; affidavit, sworn statement; instrument in proof, *pièce justificative* <Fr>

test run NOUNS **tryout,** workout, **rehearsal,** practice; pilot plan *or* program; **dry run,** dummy run; road test; **trial run,** practical test; shakedown, shakedown cruise, bench test; flight test, test flight; audition, hearing

testy ADJS **irascible,** irritable, excitable, flappable <nonformal>; **cross,** cranky, disagreeable; perverse, fractious, cross-grained

tête-à-tête NOUNS 1 **chat,** cozy chat, friendly chat *or* talk, **little talk,** coze, causerie, **visit** <nonformal>, **heart-to-heart talk** *or* heart-to-heart; pillow-talk, intimate discourse
ADJS 2 **intimate,** familiar, cozy, chatty; man-to-man, woman-to-woman

tether NOUNS 1 **shackle,** restraint, **restraints,** fetter, hamper, trammel, trammels, **bonds,** irons, chains; spancel, leash, lead
VERBS 2 **secure,** make sure *or* secure, tie, tie off *or* up, chain

textile NOUNS **material,** fabric, cloth, textile fabric, texture, tissue, stuff, weave, weft, woof, web, goods

texture NOUNS surface texture; **surface; finish,** feel; **grain,** granular texture, fineness *or* coarseness of grain

thank VERBS **extend gratitude** *or* **thanks,** bless; give one's thanks, **express one's appreciation;** offer *or* give thanks, tender *or* render thanks, return thanks; acknowledge, make acknowledgments of, credit, recognize, give *or* render credit *or* recognition

thankful ADJS **grateful,** appreciative, appreciatory, sensible; **obliged,** much obliged, beholden, indebted to, crediting, under obligation, acknowledging, cognizant of

thankless ADJS **disliked,** unappreciated, misunderstood; unsung, unwept, unlamented, unmourned, undeplored, unmissed, unregretted; **ungrateful,** unappreciative, unmindful

thanksgiving NOUNS **thanks,** praise, laud, hymn, paean, benediction; grace, prayer of thanks; **acknowledgment,** cognizance, **credit,** crediting, recognition; thank offering, votary offering

thaw NOUNS 1 **melting,** liquefaction, liquefying, liquescence, running; **thawing**
VERBS 2 **melt,** melt down, liquefy; **run,**

colliquate; thaw out, unfreeze; defrost, deice

theater NOUNS **the theater,** the footlights, the stage, the boards, the bright lights, Broadway, the Great White Way; **playhouse,** house, theatron, odeum; **amphitheater;** circle theater, arena theater, theater-in-the-round; vaudeville theater; burlesque theater; **little theater,** community theater; open-air theater, outdoor theater

theatrical ADJS **theatric,** stagy, dramatic, histrionic, thespian; **spectacular; melodramatic;** overacted, overplayed, milked <nonformal>

theatrics NOUNS **emotionalism,** theatricality, histrionics, dramatics, hamminess *and* chewing up the scenery <both nonformal>; **sensationalism, melodrama,** melodramatics, blood and thunder; theatricism, theatricalism, staginess

theft NOUNS **thievery,** stealing, thieving, **purloining;** swiping *and* lifting *and* snatching *and* snitching *and* pinching <all nonformal>; **pilfering,** pilferage, filching; sneak thievery; shoplifting, boosting <nonformal>; **robbery,** robbing

theme NOUNS **motif,** pattern, design, ornamental theme; **essay,** pandect; excursus; **paper,** research paper, term paper; **subject,** topic

then ADJS 1 **former,** past, fore, **previous,** late, recent, **once,** onetime, sometime, **erstwhile,** quondam; **ancient,** immemorial, early, primitive, primeval, prehistoric; **old,** olden
ADVS 2 thereat, thereupon, **at that time,** at that moment *or* instant, in that case *or* instance, on that occasion; **again,** at another time, at some other time, anon; **subsequently,** after, afterwards, after that, after all, **later,** next, since; **thereafter,** thereon, therewith

theological ADJS **religious; divine;** doctrinal, doctrinary; canonic *or* canonical

theology NOUNS **religion,** religious belief *or* faith, **belief,** faith, teaching, doctrine, creed, credo, orthodoxy; system of beliefs

theoretical ADJS **hypothetical,** hypothetic; postulatory, notional; **speculative,** conjectural; impressionistic, intuitive; general, generalized, abstract, ideal; merely theoretical, academic, moot; impractical, armchair

theory NOUNS theorization, *theoria* <Gk>; **hypothesis,** hypothecation, hypothesizing; **speculation,** mere theory; analysis, **explanation,** abstraction; theoretical basis *or* justification; body of theory, theoretical structure *or* construct; unified theory

therapeutic ADJS **remedial,** curative, healing, corrective, disease-fighting, alterative, restorative, analeptic, sanative, sanatory; all-healing, panacean; adjuvant

therapist NOUNS **psychotherapist,** psychotherapeutist; clinical psychologist; licensed psychologist, psychological practitioner; **psychoanalyst,** analyst; shrink *and* headshrinker *and* shrinker <all nonformal>; **counselor,** psychological counselor; therapeutist

therapy NOUNS **therapeutics,** therapeusis, **treatment,** medical care *or* treatment, medication; noninvasive *or* nonsurgical therapy *or* treatment; disease-fighting, healing; healing arts; psychotherapy; **cure,** curing, remedy

thereabouts ADVS **there,** thereat, in that place, in those parts; thereabout, in that vicinity *or* neighborhood; **thither,** thitherward, thitherwards, to that place; **near** *or* **close at hand**

thereafter ADVS **subsequently,** after, afterwards, after that, after all, **later,** next, since; thereon, thereupon, therewith, **then;** *ex post facto* <L>

thereby ADVS herewith, therewith, wherewith, wherewithal; whereby, hereby

therefore ADVS **accordingly,** in that case, in that event, at that rate, that being the case, such being the case, that being so, **under the circumstances,** the condition being such, as it is, as matters stand, as the matter stands, **consequently,** as a result, as a consequence, in consequence, in the event, **hence,** thence, *ergo* <L>, for which reason

therein ADVS **in,** inside, within; herein, wherein

thermal ADJS **warm,** thermic; **toasty** <nonformal>, warm as toast

thermometer NOUNS thermal detector; mercury, glass; thermostat

thermonuclear reaction NOUNS **fusion,** nuclear fusion, fusion reaction, thermonuclear fusion, laser-induced fusion, cold fusion

thesaurus NOUNS Roget's, storehouse *or* treasury of words; word list, lexicon, glossary

thesis NOUNS 1 **treatise,** treatment, handling, tractate, tract; disquisition, descant, exposition, screed; dissertation, essay, **monograph,** research monograph
2 **supposition,** supposal, supposing; **presupposition,** presupposal; **assumption,** presumption, conjecture, inference, surmise, guesswork; **postulate,** postulation, *postulatum* <L>, set of postulates; **proposition,** premise

they NOUNS **the authorities,** the powers that be, ruling class *or* classes, the lords of creation, **the Establishment,** the interests, the power elite, **the power structure;** them; the inner circle

thick ADJS 1 three-dimensional; **thickset, heavyset,** thick-bodied, broad-bodied, thick-girthed; **massive, bulky**, corpulent; coarse, heavy, gross
2 **luxuriant,** flourishing, **rank, lush,** riotous, exuberant; dense, impenetrable, overgrown, overrun; **profuse,** in profusion, thick with; **teeming,** swarming, crowding, thronging, overflowing, overcrowded, overwhelming, bursting, **crawling**
3 **familiar,** intimate, close, near, inseparable, on familiar *or* intimate terms; just between the two, hand and glove *or* hand in glove; **thick as thieves** <nonformal>
4 **stupid, dumb,** doltish, blockish, klutzy *and* klutzish <both nonformal>, cloddish, **oafish,** boobish, lamebrained, dense
ADVS 5 **densely,** compactly, **close,** closely, thickly, heavily; solidly, firmly

thicken VERBS grow thick, thick; incrassate, inspissate; fatten; **congeal,** condense, coagulate, clot, set, concrete; gelatinize, gelatinate, jelly, jellify, **jell,** gel; **curdle,** curd, clabber, lopper <nonformal>; cake, lump, clump, cluster, knot

thicket NOUNS thickset, **copse,** coppice; bosket <old>, boscage; covert

thief NOUNS **criminal,** outlaw, felon, **crook** <nonformal>, lawbreaker, perpetrator, perp <nonformal>

thin VERBS 1 thin down, thin away *or* off *or* out; **rarefy,** subtilize, **attenuate;** dilute, water, water down, weaken; **emaciate**
ADJS 2 **slender, slim,** gracile; thin-bodied, thin-set, narrow- *or* wasp-waisted; **slight,** frail, delicate, light, airy, wispy, lacy, gauzy, papery, gossamer, diaphanous, insubstantial, ethereal, misty, vague, flimsy, wafer-thin, **fine; tenuous,** subtle, rare, **rarefied;** attenuated, attenuate, **watery, weak,** diluted, watered *or* watered-down

imperially slim
E A Robinson

3 **sparse,** scant, **scanty,** exiguous, **infrequent,** scarce, scarce as hen's teeth <nonformal>, poor, piddling, piddly, **meager**

thing NOUNS 1 **object,** article, material thing, affair, something; whatsit <nonformal>, what's-its-name; something or other, *etwas* <Ger>, *eppes* <Yiddish>, *quelque chose* <Fr>; artifact
2 **affair,** concern, matter, concernment, interest, **business,** job <nonformal>, **transaction,** proceeding, doing; **lifestyle,** way of life, preferences; cup of tea *and* bag *and* weakness <all nonformal>

things NOUNS **belongings,** appurtenances, trappings, paraphernalia, appointments, accessories, perquisites, appendages, appanages, choses local; material things, mere things; **personal effects,** chattels personal, movables, choses transitory

think VERBS 1 **cogitate,** cerebrate, put on one's thinking *or* considering cap <nonformal>, intellectualize, ideate, conceive, conceptualize, form ideas, entertain ideas; **reason;** use one's head, use one's noodle *or* noggin <nonformal>, use *or* exercise the mind, set the brain *or* wits to work, have something on one's mind, have a lot on one's mind
2 **opine,** be of the opinion, be persuaded, be convinced; be afraid <nonformal>, **have the idea,** have an idea, **suppose,** assume, presume, judge, **guess,** surmise, suspect, have a hunch <nonformal>, have an inkling, expect <nonformal>, have an impression, conceive, **imagine,** fancy, daresay; **deem,** esteem, hold, regard, consider, maintain

thinker NOUNS **intellectual,** intellect; brainworker, **brain** *and* rocket scientist *and* brain surgeon <all nonformal>; **reasoner,** ratiocinator; sophist; philosopher, speculator

thin-skinned ADJS **touchy,** tetchy, miffy <nonformal>, ticklish, prickly, quick to take offense, **sensitive,** oversensitive, hypersensitive, high-strung, highly strung, temperamental; squeamish, susceptible

third world NOUNS **unaligned** *or* nonaligned nation, third force; underdeveloped nation, depressed area, chronic poverty area

thirst NOUNS thirstiness, dryness; polydipsia; **yen,** appetite, instinct *or* feeling for, sensitivity to

thirsty ADJS thirsting, athirst; **dry,** arid, parched, droughty <nonformal>; bibulous, imbibitory, soaking, blotting

thorn NOUNS **bramble,** brier, nettle, burr, prickle, sticker <nonformal>; **spine;** bristle; **affliction,** infliction, visitation, **torment,** grievance, woe, thorn in the flesh *or* side, pea in the shoe; bugbear, **bête noire,** bogeyman, nemesis

thorny ADJS **prickly,** muricate, echinate, acanaceous, aculeolate; brambly, briery, nettly, bristly; **difficult,** knotty, spiny, set with thorns; delicate, ticklish, tricky, sticky <nonformal>, critical, exacting, demanding; intricate, complex

thorough ADJS **thoroughgoing,** exhaustive, intensive, broad-based, A-to-Z, comprehensive, all-embracing, all-encompassing, sweeping; **unmitigated,** unqualified, unconditional, unrestricted, unreserved, **all-out,** wholesale, whole-hog <nonformal>; **utter,** absolute, total

thought NOUNS **thinking, cogitation,** cerebration, ideation, noesis, mentation, intellection, intellectualization, ratiocination; reasoning; **brainwork,** headwork, mental labor *or* effort, mental act *or* process, act of thought, mental *or* intellectual exercise; conceptualization; abstract thought, imageless thought; **idea;** mental *or* intellectual object, **notion,** concept, conception, conceit, fancy; consideration, mind

thoughtful ADJS **considerate,** mindful, heedful, regardful, solicitous, delicate, tactful, mindful of others; respectful, deferential, attentive; **prudent,** politic, careful, provident, circumspect, reflective, reflecting

thoughtless ADJS **inconsiderate,** unthoughtful, unmindful, heedless, respectless, mindless, unthinking, **tactless,** insensitive; **unhelpful,** unaccommodating, unobliging, uncooperative

thought-provoking ADJS **interesting,** stimulating, provocative, provoking, thought-challenging, thought-inspiring

thrash VERBS **whip,** give a whipping *or* beating *or* thrashing, **beat,** spank, flog, scourge, flagellate, flail, whale

thread NOUNS **filament;** fiber; **strand,** suture; filature; **string,** continuum, queue; gamut, spectrum

threadbare ADJS **worn,** well-worn, deep-worn, worn-down, the worse for wear, dog-eared; **worn ragged,** worn to rags, worn to threads; bare; **hackneyed,** hackney; **stale,** musty, fusty; timeworn, moth-eaten, **worn thin**

threat NOUNS **menace,** promise of harm, knife poised at one's throat, arrow aimed at one's heart, sword of Damocles; imminent threat, powder keg, timebomb, imminence; **intimidation**, arm-twisting <nonformal>; veiled *or* implied threat, idle *or* hollow *or* empty threat; **danger,** peril, endangerment, imperilment, jeopardy, hazard, risk, cause for alarm

threaten VERBS **menace,** bludgeon, bulldoze, put the heat *or* screws *or* squeeze on <nonformal>, lean on <nonformal>; hold a pistol to one's head, terrorize, **intimidate,** twist one's arm *and* arm-twist <both nonformal>; utter threats against; hold over one's head; **lower,** spell *or* mean trouble, look threatening, loom, loom up

threshold NOUNS **boundary line,** borderline, division line, interface, limen, limit, boundary, line of demarcation; **sill,** doorsill

thrift NOUNS **economy,** thriftiness, **frugality,** frugalness; tight purse strings; **prudence,** providence; **husbandry,** management, good management *or* stewardship, custodianship, prudent *or* prudential administration

thrifty ADJS **economical,** frugal, conserving, **saving,** economizing, spare, sparing; **prudent,** prudential, provident, careful; scrimping, skimping <nonformal>, penny-wise; parsimonious

thrill NOUNS 1 **sensation,** titillation; **tingle,** tingling; quiver, shiver, shudder, tremor, **tremor of excitement,** rush <nonformal>; flush, rush of emotion, surge of emotion
VERBS 2 **tickle,** thrill to death *or* to pieces, give a thrill, **give one a kick** *or* boot *or* charge *or* bang *or* lift <nonformal>; intoxicate, fascinate, titillate, take

one's breath away; tingle, **tingle with excitement,** shiver, quiver, quaver, quake, flutter, twitter

thrive VERBS **flourish,** boom; blossom, bloom, flower; batten, fatten, grow fat; be fat, dumb, and happy <nonformal>

throb VERBS **pulsate,** pulse, beat, not miss a beat; **palpitate,** go pit-a-pat, pitter-patter

throes NOUNS **seizure,** attack, **spasm,** fit, paroxysm, convulsion, eclampsia, frenzy; **pain,** pang, wrench, cramp; **pangs of conscience,** sting *or* pricking *or* twinge *or* twitch of conscience, touch of conscience, **voice of conscience**

throng NOUNS 1 **multitude, horde,** host, heap <nonformal>, army, panoply, legion; flock, cluster, galaxy; **crowd,** press, crush, mass; **mob,** rabble, rout, ruck, jam, *cohue* <Fr>, everybody and his uncle *or* his brother <nonformal>
VERBS 2 **crowd,** swarm, teem, hive, surge, seethe, mill, stream, horde

throttle VERBS **strangle,** garrote, **choke,** burke; **suffocate,** stifle, smother, choke off, asphyxiate, stop the breath; muzzle, gag

throw NOUNS 1 **toss,** fling, sling, cast, hurl, chuck, chunk <nonformal>, lob, **heave,** shy, **pitch,** peg <nonformal>; **flip;** put, shot-put
VERBS 2 **fling,** sling, pitch, toss, cast, hurl, heave, chuck, chunk *and* peg <both nonformal>, lob, shy, fire, burn, pepper <nonformal>, launch, dash, let fly, let go, let rip, let loose
3 **discompose,** throw into confusion, perturb
4 **fix,** rig, go in the tank, hold a boat race <all nonformal>
5 **stump,** stick, floor, beat, beat the shit out of <all nonformal>

throw away VERBS **discard,** throw out, chuck *or* chuck away *and* shit-can *and* eighty-six <all nonformal>, **get rid of,** dispose of, slough, **ditch** <nonformal>, jettison, throw *or* heave *or* toss overboard, deep-six <nonformal>; **squander,** blow <nonformal>, throw one's money away

throwback NOUNS **reversion,** regression; **reversal,** backward deviation, devolution; **return,** recurrence, renewal, recrudescence; atavism; **setback,** check, severe check, backset

throw out VERBS **eject,** expel, discharge, extrude, obtrude, detrude, exclude, **reject,** cast, remove; **oust,** bounce *and* give the hook <both nonformal>, **put out,** turn out, thrust out; run out <nonformal>, cast out, chuck out, toss out, heave out, kick *or* boot out <nonformal>; give the bum's rush *or* give the old heave-ho *or* throw out on one's ear <all nonformal>; defenestrate; jettison, throw overboard, discard, junk, throw away

thrust NOUNS 1 **push,** shove, boost <nonformal>; **pushing,** propulsion, propelling; shoving, butting; **drive,** motive power, driving force, means of propulsion; **rocket propulsion,** reaction propulsion, jet propulsion, blast propulsion
VERBS 2 **push,** shove, boost <nonformal>; press, stress, **bear,** bear upon, bring pressure to bear upon; **drive,** force, run

thud NOUNS **thump,** flump, crump, clop, clump, clunk, plunk, tunk, plump, bump, dull thud

thug NOUNS **murderer,** man-killer, bloodletter, Cain; **assassin,** assassinator; **cutthroat,** desperado, gorilla <nonformal>, gunman; professional killer, hired killer, hit man *or* button man *or* gun *or* trigger man *or* torpedo *or* gunsel <all nonformal>; hatchet man; **bandit,** dacoit; gangster *and* mobster <both nonformal>; **hoodlum,** ruffian, rowdy; goon <nonformal>

thump NOUNS 1 **punch,** poke, jab, dig, drub, pelt, cut, chop, dint, slog
VERBS 2 **drum,** thrum, beat, pound, thump out, roll; palpitate, flutter; **throb,** pulsate

thunder NOUNS 1 thundering, clap *or* crash *or* peal of thunder, **thunderclap,** thundercrack, thunderstroke
VERBS 2 **din,** boom; **resound,** blast the ear, pierce *or* split *or* rend the ears, rend *or* split the eardrums, split one's head; rock the sky, fill the air, shake *or* rattle the windows; **peal,** rumble, grumble, growl, **roll,** roar

thunderstruck ADJS **dumbfounded,** dumbstruck, staggered, overwhelmed, unable to believe one's senses *or* eyes; wonder-struck, wonder-stricken, awestricken, awestruck, struck all of a heap <nonformal>

thwart VERBS **frustrate,** foil, cross, balk; spike, scotch, checkmate; **throw a monkey wrench into the works** <nonformal>; spike one's guns, put one's nose out of joint <nonformal>, upset one's applecart

tiara NOUNS crown, royal crown, coronet, diadem

tic NOUNS twitching, vellication; **jerk,** twitch, grimace, rictus; **fixation,** complex, fascination

ticket NOUNS 1 **permission,** permission to enter, admission, ticket of admission; **certificate,** certification; **summons,** parking ticket
2 **ballot,** slate; straight ticket, split ticket
3 **price,** quotation, quoted price, price tag *and* **sticker** <both nonformal>

tickle NOUNS 1 tickling, **titillation,** pleasant stimulation, **ticklishness,** tickliness
VERBS 2 **titillate,** delight, delectate, **thrill,** enrapture, enthrall, enchant, entrance, fascinate, captivate, bewitch, **charm,** becharm; transport, carry away; tickle pink *or* to death <nonformal>, tickle the fancy

tickled ADJS **pleased,** delighted; **thrilled;** tickled to death *and* tickled pink <both nonformal>, exhilarated; **gratified,** satisfied; pleased with, taken with, favorably impressed with, sold on <nonformal>; pleased as Punch

ticklish ADJS 1 tickling, tickly, **titillative**
2 **precarious,** touchy, touch-and-go, **critical,** delicate; on thin ice, on slippery ground; hanging by a thread, trembling in the balance; tricky, sticky <nonformal>, easier said than done, exacting, demanding

tidal ADJS estuarine, littoral, grallatorial; **coastal,** seaside, shore, shoreside; tideland, wetland

tidbit NOUNS 1 **delicacy,** dainty, goody <nonformal>, treat, kickshaw, titbit; **morsel,** choice morsel, *bonne bouche* <Fr>
2 **scandal,** dirt <nonformal>, **malicious gossip;** juicy morsel, choice bit of dirt <nonformal>

tide NOUNS tidal current *or* stream, tidal flow *or* flood, tide race; **riptide,** rip, tiderip, overfalls; **spring tide; high tide,** high water, full tide; **low tide,** low water; **neap tide,** neap; lunar tide, solar tide; **flood tide,** ebb tide

tidy VERBS 1 **tidy up,** neaten, **straighten up,** fix up <nonformal>, **clean up,** police *and* police up <both nonformal>, groom, spruce *and* spruce up <both nonformal>, clear up
ADJS 2 **trim,** natty, neat, spruce, sleek, slick *and* slick as a whistle <nonformal>, smart, **shipshape,** well-kept, well-cared-for, neat as a pin <nonformal>

tie NOUNS 1 **intermediary,** link, **connecting link,** connection, **go-between,** liaison; **allegiance,** bond, attachment
2 dead heat, draw, wash <nonformal>
VERBS 3 **bind,** restrain, tie up, put the clamps on, **tie one's hands; tie hand and foot,** hog-tie <nonformal>; straitjacket; **obligate,** oblige, require, make incumbent *or* imperative, pledge, commit, saddle with; **connect,** interconnect, ally, link, link up, wed, marry, marry up, weld, couple, bracket, equate
4 **equal,** match, rival, correspond, be even-steven, be tantamount to, be equal to; **keep pace with,** measure up to, come up to, stack up with <nonformal>, match up with

tie-in NOUNS **affiliation,** hookup *and* tie-up <both nonformal>, filiation, bond, union, alliance, **tie,** link, linkage, linking, linkup, liaison

tier NOUNS **layer,** thickness; **level,** stage, story, floor, step, ledge, deck; **stratum,** seam, *couche* <Fr>, belt, band

tie up VERBS 1 **bind,** restrain, tie, put the clamps on, **strap,** lash, leash, pinion, fasten, secure, make fast; **hamper,** trammel, entrammel; **shackle,** fetter, manacle, gyve, **put in irons; handcuff,** tie hand and foot, hog-tie <nonformal>; hobble, put on a lead <chiefly Brit>, spancel; tether
2 **monopolize,** hog *and* grab all of *and* gobble up <all nonformal>, have exclusive possession of *or* exclusive rights to; engross, forestall, corner *and* get a corner on *and* corner the market <all nonformal>
3 **wrap up,** do *or* bind up

tiff NOUNS **quarrel,** open quarrel, dustup, **dispute,** argument, lovers' quarrel, **spat,** fuss

tight ADJS 1 **narrow,** strait, isthmic, isthmian; close-fitting; **restricted,** limited, circumscribed, confined, constricted; **cramped,** cramp; incapacious, incommodious, crowded
2 **stingy,** illiberal, ungenerous, chintzy, miserly, **cheap** <nonformal>, near, close, closefisted, tightfisted, penny-pinching; miserly, niggardly
ADVS 3 **securely,** firmly, fast; **inseparably,** indissolubly

tightwad NOUNS **niggard, cheapskate** <nonformal>, **miser,** hard man with a buck <nonformal>, **skinflint,** scrooge, penny pincher

till VERBS **cultivate,** culture, **dress,** work, till the soil, dig, delve, spade; **plow,** plow under, plow up

tilt NOUNS 1 **leaning,** bent, turn, bias, **affinity;** mutual affinity *or* attraction; **tip,** pitch, **list, cant,** swag, sway
VERBS 2 **incline,** lean; slope, slant, pitch, grade, bank; **tip,** list, cant, careen, keel, sidle, swag, sway
3 **tend,** have a tendency, **incline,** be disposed, lean, trend, have a penchant, turn, warp, bend to; show a tendency *or* trend *or* set *or* direction

timber NOUNS **woodland,** timberland; stand of timber, **forest,** forest land, forest cover, forest preserve, state *or* national forest

time NOUNS 1 **tempo,** beat, time pattern, timing; **duration,** *durée* <Fr>, lastingness, continuity, term, while, tide, space, spell
2 **age,** generation, day, date, cycle
VERBS 3 **fix** *or* **set the time,** mark the time; **keep time,** mark time, measure time, beat time; **clock** <nonformal>

timeless ADJS **perpetual, everlasting,** dateless, ageless, immemorial; **endless,** unending, never-ending, without end, **interminable**

timely ADJS **well-timed,** seasonable, opportune, convenient; **expedient,** meet, fit, fitting, befitting, suitable, sortable, appropriate; **propitious,** ripe, auspicious, lucky, providential, heaven-sent, fortunate, happy, felicitous

time off NOUNS **lull,** quiet spell, resting point, point of repose, plateau, letup, relief, vacation, holiday, off-time; respite

time-out NOUNS **respite,** recess, rest, pause, halt, stay, lull, **break,** time to catch one's breath; **breathing spell,** breather; coffee break, tea break, cigarette break

timepiece NOUNS timekeeper, **timer, chronometer,** ship's watch; horologe, horologium; **clock,** Big Ben, ticker <nonformal>, **watch,** turnip

timetable NOUNS **plan, schedule,** time-scheme, time frame; timeline, time schedule, time chart; time scale

timid ADJS **fearful,** fearing, fearsome; **timorous,** shy, mousy <nonformal>, afraid of one's own shadow; **shrinking,** bashful, diffident; **hesitant,** hesitating, tentative, cautious

timing NOUNS **tempo,** time, beat, time pattern; synchronism, sync <nonformal>; **chronology,** timekeeping, clocking, horology

timorous ADJS **afraid,** fearful; timid, overtimorous, overtimid; **fainthearted,** weakhearted, chicken-hearted, lily-livered <nonformal>; **weak-kneed,** chicken <nonformal>, afraid of one's shadow; daunted, dismayed, unmanned, cowed, intimidated

tinge NOUNS 1 **hint,** *soupçon* <Fr>, **suspicion,** suggestion, intimation; **trace,** touch, dash, cast, **smattering,** sprinkling; tincture; coloration, undertone, overtone, undercurrent, more than meets the eye *or* ear, something between the lines, intimation, touch, nuance, innuendo
VERBS 2 **imbue,** imbrue, **infuse,** suffuse, transfuse, breathe, **instill,** infiltrate, **impregnate, permeate,** pervade, penetrate, leaven; **tincture,** entincture, temper, color, dye, flavor, tone, slant, impart spin

tingle NOUNS 1 tingling, thrill, buzz; **prickle,** prickles, prickling, pins and needles; **sting,** stinging, urtication
VERBS 2 thrill; **itch;** scratch; **prickle,** prick, sting; **tingle with excitement,** glow; thrill to; **throb,** palpitate, go pit-a-pat; **tremble,** shiver, quiver, quaver, quake, flutter, twitter

tinker VERBS **putter,** potter, **piddle; dabble,** smatter; toy with, fiddle with, fool with, play with

tinny ADJS **inferior,** poor, punk <nonformal>, **base,** mean, common, coarse, cheesy *and* tacky <both nonformal>; cheap, Mickey Mouse <nonformal>, paltry

tint NOUNS 1 **color,** hue; tinct, tincture, **tinge,** shade, tone, cast; key; **coloring,** coloration; **touch,** dash, smack, **trace,** vestige, hint, inkling
VERBS 2 **color,** hue, lay on color; **tinge,** tinct, **tincture,** tone, complexion; pigment; **stain,** dye, imbue

tiny ADJS teeny *and* teeny-weeny *and* eentsy-weentsy <all nonformal>, wee *and* peewee <both nonformal>, bitty *and* bitsy *and* little-bitty *and* little-bitsy *and* itsy-bitsy *and* itsy-witsy <all nonformal>; **minute,** fine

tip NOUNS 1 **summit,** top; **tip-top,** peak, pinnacle; **crown,** cap, cusp, point, spire,

apex, acme, *ne plus ultra* <Fr>, **zenith, climax,** apogee, pole
2 **tilt,** pitch, **list, cant,** swag, sway
3 piece of advice, **word of advice,** word to the wise, *verbum sapienti* <L>, verb *or* verbum sap <nonformal>, **hint,** broad hint, flea in the ear <nonformal>, a few words of wisdom, one's two cents' worth <nonformal>, intimation, insinuation
4 **gratuity,** largess, bounty, liberality, donative, sportula; consideration, *pourboire* <Fr>, *Trinkgeld* <Ger>, sweetener, inducement; grease *and* salve *and* palm oil <all nonformal>
VERBS 5 **careen,** list, heel, cant; **tilt,** dip, fall off *or* away, **go downhill**
6 tip off *and* **give one a tip** <both nonformal>, alert; **give a pointer to** <nonformal>; **let in on,** let in on the know <nonformal>; let next to *and* put next to *and* **put on to** *and* put on to something hot <all nonformal>

tipple VERBS **drink,** nip; **imbibe,** have a drink *or* nip *or* dram *or* guzzle *or* gargle, soak, bib, quaff, sip, sup, lap, lap up, take a drop, slake one's thirst, cheer *or* refresh the inner man, drown one's troubles *or* sorrows; **down,** toss off *or* down, knock back, throw one back, drink up, drink bottoms-up, drink deep

tipsy ADJS **intoxicated, inebriated,** inebriate, inebrious, **drunk,** drunken, *shikker* <Yiddish>, **in one's cups,** under the influence, the worse for liquor; **tiddly,** dizzy, muddled, addled, flustered, reeling; mellow

tiptoe VERBS 1 **be cautious,** make haste slowly; feel one's ground *or* way; pussyfoot, go *or* walk on tiptoe, walk on eggs *or* eggshells *or* thin ice
ADJS 2 **on tiptoe,** on tippytoe, tiptoeing, tippytoe

tip-top ADJS **A-1, A number one,** primo, top-notch, topflight, top-drawer, tops; topping *or* top-hole <both Brit> <all nonformal>

tirade NOUNS **speech,** screed, **diatribe,** jeremiad, philippic, invective

tire VERBS 1 **fatigue,** weary, exhaust, wilt, flag, jade, harass; **wear,** wear on *or* upon, **wear down; tire out,** wear out, burn out; wind, put out of breath; weaken, enervate, weary *or* tire to death

2 <nonformal> **beat, poop,** frazzle, fag, tucker; fag out, tucker out, knock out, do in, do up; **poop out,** peter out

tired ADJS 1 **weary, fatigued,** wearied, weariful, jaded, run-down, good and tired; in need of rest, ready to drop; drooping, droopy, wilting, flagging, sagging; worn to a frazzle, **exhausted, spent,** effete, etiolated, played out, *ausgespielt* <Ger>, emptied, drawn, worn, wan

2 <nonformal> **beat, pooped, bushed,** poohed, paled, frazzled, bagged, fagged, tuckered, plumb tuckered, done, done in, all in, dead, dead beat, dead on one's feet, gone; **pooped out,** knocked out, wiped out, tuckered out, played out, fagged out; run ragged; used up, done up, beat up, washed-up

3 **cliché,** banal, trite, platitudinous

tireless ADJS **industrious,** assiduous, diligent, sedulous, **hardworking;** unfailing, **untiring,** unwearying, unflagging, never-tiring, weariless, **indefatigable,** game to the last *or* to the end

tiresome ADJS **vexatious,** vexing, irking, **irksome,** wearisome; **wearying,** wearing, tiring; pedestrian, **unimaginative**; insipid, vapid, flat; humdrum, **dull**

titanic ADJS **gigantic,** mountainous, colossal, mammoth, Gargantuan, gigantesque, monster, monstrous, outsize, sizable, larger-than-life, overgrown; **monumental,** heroic, heroical, epic, epical, towering

titillate VERBS **delight,** delectate, tickle, thrill, **enrapture,** enthrall, enchant, entrance, fascinate, captivate, bewitch, **charm,** becharm; intoxicate, fascinate, take one's breath away; **tempt,** tantalize, **tease,** make one's mouth water, dangle before one; **pique,** tickle one's fancy, **provoke,** stimulate, arouse, excite, pique one's interest, turn one on <nonformal>

title NOUNS 1 **ownership,** *dominium* <L>, proprietorship, proprietary, **property right** *or* rights; **claim,** proper claim, demand, **interest,** pretension, pretense, prescription
2 **honorific,** honor, title of honor; **handle** *and* handle to one's name <both nonformal>; courtesy title; **caption,** heading, head, superscription, rubric
VERBS 3 **name,** denominate, nominate, **designate,** call, term, style, dub; define, identify; entitle; **label,** tag; nickname; christen; caption, subtitle

titled ADJS **named,** called, yclept <old>, **styled,** denominated, known as, known by the name of, designated, termed, dubbed, identified as; christened, baptized; **noble,** of rank, high, exalted; aristocratic

TLC NOUNS **tender loving care,** consideration, solicitude, caring, loving care, caregiving

toady NOUNS 1 **sycophant,** flatterer, toadeater, lickspit, lickspittle, **yes-man,** truckler, creature, ass-kisser *and* brownnose *and* bootlicker <all nonformal>
VERBS 2 **fawn,** truckle; flatter; toadeat; **bootlick** <nonformal>, lickspittle, lick one's shoes, lick the feet of; kiss one's feet, kiss the hem of one's garment, make a doormat of oneself; **kowtow,** bow, bow and scrape

to and fro ADVS **back and forth,** backward and forward, backwards and forwards, in and out, seesaw, from side to side, from pillar to post

toast VERBS 1 **drink to,** pledge, drink a toast to, drink *or* pledge the health of, give you

INTERJ 2 <toasts> *skoal!*, *skl!* <Norw>, *prosit!* or *prost!*, *à votre santé!* <Fr>, *¡salud!* <Sp>, *l'chaim!* <Heb>, *slàinte!* <Ir>, *salute!* <Ital>, *na zdorovye!* <Russ>, *nazdrowie!* <Pol>, to your health!, long life!, to life!, cheerio!, cheers!, down the hatch!, bottoms up!, here's how!, here's to you!, here's looking at you!, here's mud in your eye!, here's good luck!, here's to absent friends!, confusion to our enemies!

today NOUNS 1 **the present,** presentness, present time, the here and now; **now,** the present juncture *or* occasion, the present hour *or* moment, this instant *or* second *or* moment; **the present age,** this day, this day and age
ADVS 2 **now,** at present, at this point, at this juncture, at this stage *or* at this stage of the game, on the present occasion, **at this time,** at this moment *or* instant, at the present time; this day, in these days, **in this day and age,** in our time, nowadays

to-do NOUNS **agitation,** perturbation, ferment, **commotion,** disturbance, ado, *brouhaha* <Fr>; **bustle,** fuss, flurry, flutter, fluster, **stir,** hubbub, hullabaloo, hoo-ha *and* foofaraw *and* flap <all nonformal>; **trouble,** bother, pother

together ADJS 1 **composed,** collected, levelheaded; poised, equanimous, **balanced,** well-balanced; **self-possessed,** self-controlled, self-restrained; confident, assured, **self-confident,** self-assured; **like-minded,** akin, of the same mind, of one mind, at one, united
ADVS 2 **collectively, mutually,** jointly, unitedly, in conjunction, conjointly, *en masse* <Fr>, communally, corporately, **in a body,** all at once, *ensemble* <Fr>; simultaneously, coincidentally, concurrently, synchronously; **connectedly,** cumulatively

toil NOUNS 1 **work, labor,** industry, moil, travail, toil and trouble, sweat of one's brow; **drudgery,** sweat, slavery, spadework; dirty work, grunt work *and* donkey work *and* shit-work *and* scutwork <all nonformal>
VERBS 2 **work,** labor; **drudge,** grub, moil, toil and moil, travail, **plod,** slog, peg, plug <nonformal>, plug away *or* along <nonformal>, hammer away, pound away, struggle along, work away; keep one's nose to the grindstone

toilet NOUNS **latrine,** water closet; john *and* johnny *and* can *and* crapper <all nonformal>; commode, potty-chair <nonformal>; **chamber pot,** chamber, pisspot <nonformal>, potty <nonformal>; throne <nonformal>; **bathroom,** lavatory, washroom, **rest room,** comfort station; head <nautical>

token NOUNS 1 **symbol,** emblem, icon; **counter,** slug; **memento,** remembrance, trophy, souvenir, keepsake, relic, favor, token of remembrance
ADJS 2 **substitute,** alternate, alternative, other, tother <nonformal>, equivalent, dummy, pinch, utility, backup, secondary; ad hoc, provisional; makeshift, reserve, **spare,** stopgap, temporary, tentative

tolerable ADJS **goodish,** fair, fairish, moderate, **decent,** respectable, presentable, good enough, **pretty good,** not bad, not half bad, not so bad, **adequate,** satisfactory, all right, OK *or* okay <nonformal>; better than nothing; **acceptable,** admissible, **passable,** unobjectionable, unexceptionable

tolerance NOUNS **indulgence,** lenience *or* leniency, condonation, lenity; **forbearance,** patience, long-suffering; permissiveness; **compassion**, sympathy; sensitivity

tolerate VERBS **endure,** bear, stand, support, sustain, **suffer,** abide, bide, live with; **bear up under,** put up with, stand for, brook, brave, hang in there, bear with; **countenance,** condone, stomach, indulge; shut one's eyes to, **wink at,** blink at, overlook; **accept,** shut one's eyes to, look the other way

toll NOUNS 1 **ringing,** tintinnabulation, **pealing,** chiming, **tolling,** knelling; clangor, clanking, clanging; **ring,** peal, chime; knell
2 **fee,** charge, charges, demand, exaction, exactment; user fee; **levy,** impost, imposition
VERBS 3 **ring,** tintinnabulate, **peal,** sound; knell, sound a knell; chime

tomb NOUNS **sepulcher; grave,** gravesite, burial; resting place, last home, long home, narrow house, house of death; **crypt,** vault, burial chamber; ossuary *or* ossuarium; **mausoleum; catacombs;** mastaba; cist grave, box grave, passage grave, shaft grave, beehive tomb; pyramid, mummy chamber; burial mound, tumulus, barrow, cist, cromlech, dolmen

tome NOUNS **book,** volume; **work,** opus; **classic,** magnum opus, great work, scholarly work, standard work, definitive work

tomorrow NOUNS 1 **the future,** future, futurity, what is to come, imminence, subsequence, eventuality, **hereafter,** aftertime, afteryears, **time to come;** the morrow, the morning after, *mañana* <Sp>; **immediate** *or* **near future,** time just ahead, immediate prospect, offing, next period
ADVS 2 **in the future,** afterward *or* afterwards, **later,** at a later time, after a time *or* while, anon; **by and by,** in the sweet by-and-by <nonformal>; *mañana* <Sp>, the day after tomorrow; **in the near** *or* **immediate future,** just around the corner, **imminently**, soon, before long

tone NOUNS 1 **tint,** tinct, tincture, **tinge,** shade, cast
2 **fitness,** condition, shape, trim, fettle, aerobic fitness, anaerobic fitness, cardiovascular fitness, cardiorespiratory fitness; tonus, tonicity
3 **feeling,** emotional coloring *or* shade *or* nuance, feeling tone, note, overtone, undertone; **tone of voice; tenor,** mood, humor, feelings, temper, frame of mind, state of mind, morale, note, vein

tone down VERBS **muffle,** mute, dull, soften, deaden, subdue, **soft-pedal; moderate,** tame, hold in check, keep a tight rein, chasten, underplay, play down, downplay, de-emphasize

tongue NOUNS **language,** speech, *lingua* <L>, spoken language, natural language; **utterance,** voice

tongue-in-cheek ADJS **joking,** jesting, jocose; facetious, joshing <nonformal>; satiric, **satirical,** sarcastic, ironic, ironical

tongue-tied ADJS **speechless,** wordless, breathless, at a loss for words, choked up; inarticulate; dumbstruck, dumbstricken, stricken dumb, dumbfounded; **tight-lipped;** close-lipped, word-bound

tonic NOUNS 1 **bracer,** cordial, restorative, analeptic, roborant, **pick-me-up** <nonformal>; shot in the arm <nonformal>; **refresher,** reviver, hair of the dog *or* hair of the dog that bit one <nonformal>
ADJS 2 **stimulating,** bracing, invigorating, reviving, refreshing, restorative, analeptic, strengthening, roborant; remedial, **curative**

tool NOUNS **instrument,** implement, utensil; apparatus, device, mechanical device, contrivance, contraption <nonformal>, gadget, gizmo, gimcrack, gimmick <nonformal>, means, mechanical means

tooled ADJS enchased, inscribed, incised, marked, lined, creased, cut, carved, glyphic; grooved, furrowed

too much NOUNS 1 **superabundance,** overabundance, superflux, **plethora,** redundancy, overprofusion, too many, too much of a good thing
2 ADJS **insufferable,** intolerable, insupportable, unendurable, unbearable, excessive, past bearing, not to be borne *or* endured, for the birds <nonformal>, a bit much <nonformal>, overmuch, more than flesh and blood can bear

toot NOUNS 1 tootle, **honk,** beep, blat, trumpet

2 <nonformal> **binge,** drunk, bust, tear, **bender,** bat

VERBS 3 tootle, sound, peal, wind, blow, blat; pipe, trumpet; **honk,** honk *or* sound *or* blow the horn, beep

top NOUNS 1 top side, upper side, upside; topside *or* topsides; **peak,** summit, pinnacle, crown, perfection, height, acme, ultimate
2 **cover,** lid, cap, screw-top; stopper; **tent,** big top
3 **toy,** spinning top, teetotum
VERBS 4 top off, **crown,** cap, crest, **head,** tip, peak, surmount; have the top place *or* spot, over-arch; **culminate,** consummate, climax; ice, frost <a cake>; fill, top up; **overshadow,** eclipse, throw into the shade; **rise above,** tower above *or* over
ADJS 5 topmost, **uppermost,** upmost, overmost, **highest;** tip-top, tip-crowning, **maximum,** maximal, ultimate; **head,** headmost, capital, chief, paramount, supreme, preeminent; **top-level,** highest level, top-echelon, top-flight, top-ranking, top-drawer <nonformal>

topic NOUNS **subject,** matter, subject matter, what it is about, **concern,** focus of interest *or* attention, discrete matter, category; **theme,** burden, matter in hand, **question,** problem, issue; point in question, main point, gist; item on the agenda

topical ADJS 1 **local, localized**
2 present, immediate, **latest, current, running, extant, existent,** existing, **actual;** contemporary, **up-to-date, up-to-the-minute, fresh; thematic**

topless ADJS 1 **unclad,** undressed, half-clothed; low-necked, low-cut, décolleté, strapless; **seminude,** scantily clad
2 headless, crownless; **towering,** towery, soaring, monumental, colossal

top-notch ADJS **superlative,** top, topmost, **uppermost,** tip-top, top-level, top-echelon, top-of-the-line <nonformal>, **first-rate,** first-class, of the first water, highest-quality

topple VERBS **tumble,** fall, fall down; **fall over,** topple down *or* over; lurch, pitch, **stumble,** stagger, totter, careen, list, tilt, trip, flounder

tops ADJS

> <nonformal> **A-1, A number one,** primo, first-chop, tip-top, top-notch, topflight, top-drawer; topping *or* top-hole <both Brit>

topsy-turvy ADJS **upside-down,** ass over elbows *and* ass over tincups *and* arsy-varsy <all nonformal>; **confused,** chaotic, **muddled,** jumbled, scattered, helter-skelter <nonformal>, in a mess; **screwed up** <nonformal>, mucked up <nonformal>

torch NOUNS 1 flaming torch, flambeau, cresset; **flare,** signal flare, fusee; beacon
VERBS 2 **set fire to,** fire, set on fire, kindle, enkindle, inflame, **light,** light up, strike a light, touch off, **burn,** conflagrate

toreador NOUNS **bullfighter,** *torero* <Sp>; banderillero, picador, matador

torment NOUNS 1 **torture,** excruciation, crucifixion, passion, laceration, clawing, lancination, flaying, excoriation; **worry,** worriedness; **worries,** troubles, concerns; worrying, fretting; harassment
2 **tormentor,** torturer; **nuisance,** pest, pesterer, pain *and* pain in the neck *or* ass <nonformal>, nag, public nuisance; **tease,** teaser; annoyer, harasser, harrier, badgerer, **heckler,** plaguer, persecutor
VERBS 3 **torture,** rack, put to torture, put *or* lay on the rack, **agonize, harrow,** crucify, martyr, martyrize, excruciate, wring, twist, contorse, convulse
4 **persecute,** oppress, victimize, play cat and mouse with, **harass,** get *or* keep after, get *or* keep at, harry, hound, beset; **disturb, perturb,** irk, plague, drive one up the wall <nonformal>, give one gray hair, make one lose sleep

torn ADJS **impaired,** lacerated, mangled, cut, split, rent, slit, slashed, mutilated, chewed-up; raggedy, raggedy-ass <nonformal>, **ragged,** tattered; **alienated,** estranged, disaffected, separated, divided, disunited

tornado NOUNS **storm,** tempest, squall, line squall, **cyclone,** hurricane, tropical cyclone, typhoon, tropical storm

torrential ADJS **pouring,** streaming, pelting, drumming, driving, blinding

torrid ADJS **hot,** heated, sweltering, sweltry, canicular; **burning,** parching, scorching, searing, scalding, blistering, baking, roasting, toasting, broiling, **boiling,** seething, ebullient; hot as hell *or* blazes, hot as the hinges of hell, so hot you can fry eggs on the sidewalk <nonformal>, like a furnace *or* an oven

tortuous ADJS **distorted,** contorted, warped, twisted, crooked; labyrinthine, buckled, sprung, bent, bowed; irregular, deviative, anamorphous; sinuous, serpentine, mazy, meandering; convoluted, overelaborate, overinvolved

torture NOUNS 1 **torment,** excruciation, crucifixion, passion, laceration, clawing, lancination, flaying, excoriation; **agony**
VERBS 2 **torment,** agonize, harrow, savage, **rack,** scarify, crucify, impale, excruciate, lacerate, claw, rip, bloody, lancinate, macerate, convulse, wring; prolong the agony, kill by inches, make life miserable *or* not worth living; martyr, martyrize; put on *or* to the rack; dismember, tear limb from limb; draw and quarter, break on the wheel, keelhaul

toss NOUNS 1 **throw,** fling, sling, cast, hurl, chuck, lob, **heave,** shy, **pitch,** peg <nonformal>; flip
2 **even chance,** even break *and* fair shake <both nonformal>, even *or* square odds, level playing field, **half a chance,** fifty-fifty; **tossup,** standoff <nonformal>
VERBS 3 **pitch,** tumble, toss and tumble, pitch and toss; **flounder,** welter, wallow; make heavy weather
4 **throw,** fling, sling, pitch, cast, hurl, heave, chuck, lob, fire, launch, dash, let fly, let go, let rip, let loose; **flip,** snap, jerk

tossup NOUNS **gamble,** guess, piece of guesswork, estimate, guesstimate *and* ball-park figure <nonformal>; **coin-toss** <nonformal>, **touch and go;** contingency, double contingency, possibility upon a possibility

total NOUNS 1 **sum,** sum total, sum and substance, **the amount,** whole *or* gross amount, grand total
VERBS 2 **compute,** add up; sum, totalize, total up, tote *and* tote up <nonformal>, tally; **amount to,** come to, run to *or* into, mount up to, add up to, tote *or* tote up to <nonformal>, aggregate to
3 **demolish,** wreck, rack up <nonformal>, **fragment,** break to pieces, make mincemeat of, reduce to rubble, atomize, pulverize, **smash,** shatter
ADJS 4 **thorough,** thoroughgoing, complete; **unmitigated,** unqualified, unrelieved, unspoiled, undeniable, unquestionable, unequivocal; **unmitigated,** unabated; unmixed, unalloyed
5 **cumulative,** accumulative, overall, without omission *or* exception; blanket, omnibus, across-the-board; **whole,** entire, aggregate, gross, all

totaled ADJS **wrecked,** ravaged; worthless

totter NOUNS 1 **flounder,** flounce, stagger, stumble, falter
VERBS 2 **flounder,** flounce, **stagger,** stumble, falter, blunder, wallop; **struggle,** labor; **wallow,** welter

touch NOUNS 1 **contact,** touching, *attouchement* <Fr>, taction, tangency, contingence; gentle *or* tentative contact, caress, brush, glance, nudge, kiss, rub, graze; impingement, impingence
2 **knack,** art, hang, trick, way; feel
VERBS 3 **feel,** feel of, palpate; **finger,** pass *or* run the fingers over, feel with the fingertips, thumb; **handle,** palm, paw; **manipulate,** wield, ply; poke at, prod; tap, flick; come in contact
4 **affect,** move, stir; melt, soften, melt the heart, choke one up, give one a lump in the throat; **penetrate,** pierce, go through one, go deep; touch a chord, **touch a sympathetic chord,** touch one's heart, tug at the heart *or* heartstrings, go to one's heart, get under one's skin; **touch to the quick,** smart, sting

touch and go NOUNS **even chance,** even break *and* fair shake <both nonformal>; **half a chance,** toss, toss-up, standoff <nonformal>

touched ADJS 1 **affected,** moved, impressed; impressed with *or* by, penetrated with, seized with, imbued with, devoured by, obsessed, obsessed with *or* by; **contrite,** abject, humble, humbled, **sheepish,** apologetic, softened, melted
2 **unbalanced,** unsettled, distraught, sick *or* soft in the head, not right, not in one's right mind, touched in the head, **out of one's mind,** out of one's senses *or* wits, bereft of reason, irrational, deprived of reason, senseless, witless

touch on VERBS **call attention to,** mention, specify, mention in passing, cite, **refer to,** allude to

touch up VERBS **perfect,** finish, put on the finishing touches, polish, fine-tune <nonformal>, tone up, **brush up,** furbish, furbish up, spruce, **spruce up,** freshen, brighten up, polish, polish up, shine <nonformal>

touchy ADJS 1 **tetchy,** ticklish, prickly, quick to take offense, **thin-skinned,** sensitive, oversensitive, hypersensitive, high-strung, highly strung, temperamental
2 **precarious,** ticklish, touch-and-go, **critical,** delicate; on thin ice, hanging by a thread, trembling in the balance

tough ADJS **resistant;** shockproof, shock-resistant, impact-resistant; stubborn, stiff; hard *or* tough as nails; **strong,** hardy, vigorous; cohesive, **tenacious,** viscid; **durable,** lasting; untiring

tough break NOUNS **bad luck,** hard luck, **rotten luck** <nonformal>, raw deal <nonformal>, bad *or* tough *or* rotten break <nonformal>, devil's own luck; **ill fortune,** evil fortune, evil star, ill wind, evil dispensation; frowns of fortune

toupee NOUNS **wig,** peruke, hairpiece, rug *and* divot *and* doormat <all nonformal>; **periwig**

tour NOUNS 1 **shift,** work shift, tour of duty, stint, bit, **watch,** trick, time, **turn,** relay, spell *or* turn of work; day shift, night shift, swing shift, graveyard shift <nonformal>; lobster trick *or* tour, sunrise watch
2 **term,** time; **tenure,** continuous tenure, tenure in *or* of office; **enlistment,** hitch <nonformal>
3 **sight-seeing,** rubbernecking <nonformal>; walking tour, bus tour, sightseeing tour *or* excursion, rubberneck tour <nonformal>
VERBS 4 **journey, travel,** make *or* take *or* go *or* go on a journey, **take** *or* **make a trip,** gad around *or* about, junket, go on a junket; campaign, go overseas, go on an expedition, go on safari; go on a sight-seeing trip, sight-see, rubberneck <nonformal>

tourist NOUNS **traveler,** sightseer, excursionist, rubberneck *or* rubbernecker <nonformal>

tournament NOUNS tourney, gymkhana, **field day;** rally; **regatta**

tout NOUNS 1 **booster** <nonformal>, puffer, promoter; plugger *and* touter <both nonformal>; pitchman, barker, spieler; **tipster** <nonformal>, dupester <nonformal>
VERBS 2 boost *and* give a boost to <both nonformal>, puff, promote, cry up; plug *and* hype; pour *or* spread *or* lay it on thick <all nonformal>; make a pitch for <nonformal>

tow VERBS **pull,** draw, heave, haul, hale, lug, **tug,** take in tow

tower NOUNS 1 **turret,** *tour* <Fr>; campanile, bell tower, belfry; **spire,** church spire; **lighthouse,** light tower; martello, martello tower; observation tower, fire tower; antenna tower; water tower, standpipe; Texas tower
VERBS 2 **soar,** spire; **rise,** uprise, ascend, mount, rear

town NOUNS 1 township; market town <Brit>; small town; twin town; boom town, ghost town
ADJS 2 **urban,** metropolitan, municipal, metro, burghal, **civic,** oppidan; small-town; boom-town

toxic ADJS **poisonous,** toxicant; **venomous,** envenomed, venenate, venenous; veneniferous, toxiferous; **virulent,** noisome, noxious, malignant, malign, destructive, deadly; mephitic, miasmal, miasmic, miasmatic

toy NOUNS 1 **plaything,** bauble, knickknack, gimcrack, gewgaw, kickshaw, whim-wham, folderol
ADJS 2 **miniature,** diminutive, minuscule, minuscular, mini, micro, miniaturized, subminiature, **small-scale,** minimal; pony, bantam

trace NOUNS 1 **essence,** definite odor, redolence, effluvium, emanation, exhalation, fume, breath, subtle odor, whiff, detectable odor; trail, spoor; **hint,** *soupçon* <Fr>, suspicion, suggestion, intimation, vestige; **touch,** dash, **smattering,** sprinkling; tinge, tincture
VERBS 2 **represent,** delineate, limn, draw; trace out, trace over; **sketch,** draft, outline
3 **search out,** hunt out, spy out, scout out, **ferret out,** fish out, pry out

track NOUNS 1 **trail,** path, course, *piste* <Fr>, line, wake; vapor trail, contrail, condensation trail; **spoor,** signs, traces, **scent**
VERBS 2 **traverse,** cross, travel over *or* through, pass through, **go** *or* **pass over,** cover, measure, transit, range, range over *or* through, course, peregrinate, overpass, go over the ground; patrol, reconnoiter, scout; sweep, go *or* make one's rounds, scour, scour the country
3 **hunt,** go hunting, hunt down, chase, run, shikar <India>, sport; trail; **stalk,** prowl after, still-hunt; hound, dog; **follow** *or* **go after, follow up,** trail, come close on *or* tread on the heels of, dog the footsteps of

track record NOUNS **qualification,** qualifiedness, credentials, record

tract NOUNS 1 **plot,** plot of ground *or* land, parcel of land, plat, **patch,** field; lot; section <square mile>, forty <sixteenth of a section>; real estate
2 **booklet,** pamphlet, brochure, chapbook, leaflet, folder; **treatise,** piece, treatment, handling, tractate

traction NOUNS **pulling,** drawing, draft, dragging, heaving, tugging, towing; **purchase,** hold, **foothold,** toehold, footing

trade NOUNS 1 **vocation,** occupation, business, work, line, line of work, line of business *or* endeavor; racket *and* game <both nonformal>
2 **trading,** doing business, trafficking; horse trading <nonformal>, **dealing,** deal-making, wheeling and dealing <nonformal>
VERBS 3 **deal,** traffic, truck, buy and sell, do business; barter; speculate, venture, operate, **play the market,** buy *or* sell *or* deal in futures; arbitrage; **swap** <nonformal>, **switch**
ADJS 4 **commercial,** business, trading, **mercantile,** merchant; commercialistic, mercantilistic

tradition NOUNS **custom,** immemorial usage; ancient wisdom, ways of the fathers; traditionalism *or* traditionality; lore, folklore

traditional ADJS **legendary,** unwritten, oral, handed down; true-blue, tried and true; **prescriptive,** customary, conventional, understood, admitted, recognized, acknowledged, received; **hallowed,** time-honored, immemorial; **venerable,** hoary, worshipful; **longstanding,** of long standing, long-established, established, fixed, inveterate, rooted; folkloric

traffic NOUNS **commerce,** trade, truck, intercourse, **dealing,** dealings; **business,** business dealings *or* affairs *or* relations, commercial affairs *or* relations

tragedy NOUNS 1 tragic drama; tragic flaw; buskin, cothurnus; tragic muse, Melpomene
2 **disaster,** calamity, catastrophe, meltdown, cataclysm; **shock,** blow, hard *or* nasty *or* staggering blow; **accident,** casualty, collision, crash, plane *or* car crash; **wreck,** shipwreck; smash *and* smashup *and* crack-up *and* pileup <all nonformal>

tragic ADJS **disastrous,** calamitous, catastrophic, cataclysmic, cataclysmal, **ruinous,** fatal, dire, black, woeful, sore, baneful, grievous; destructive

trail NOUNS 1 **path,** track, pathway, footpath, footway, *piste* <Fr>; **course,** line, wake; vapor trail, contrail, condensation trail; **spoor,** signs, traces, **scent**
VERBS 2 **follow,** go after *or* behind, come after *or* behind, move behind; **pursue,** shadow *and* tail <both nonformal>, trail after, follow on the trail of, follow *or* tread *or* step on the heels of, follow in the steps *or* footsteps *or* footprints of, tread close upon, breathe down the neck of, sit on the tail of, tailgate <nonformal>, bring up the rear, eat the dust of, take *or* swallow one's dust; tag *and* tag after *and* tag along <all nonformal>; **dog,** bedog, **hound,** chase, get after, take out *or* take off after
3 **bring up the rear,** come last, **follow,** come after; trail behind, lag behind, draggle, **straggle;** fall behind, fall back, fall astern

train NOUNS 1 railroad train; choo-choo *and* choo-choo train <both nonformal>; passenger train; aerotrain, bullet train, *train de haute vitesse* <Fr>; local, way train, milk train; express train, express; lightning express, flier, cannonball express <nonformal>; monorail; streamliner; rolling stock
2 **afterpart,** afterpiece; **wake,** trail, queue; body of retainers
VERBS 3 **drill,** exercise; practice, rehearse; keep in practice, keep one's hand in; **prepare,** ready, **condition,** groom, fit, put in tune, form, **lick into shape** <nonformal>; **discipline,** take in hand; put through the mill *or* grind <nonformal>; break, break in, housebreak

trained ADJS 1 **conditioned,** seasoned; experienced, **familiarized,** broken-in, oriented, orientated; acclimated, acclimatized; inured, hardened, case-hardened; adapted, adjusted, accommodated; housebroken, potty-trained
2 **skilled,** accomplished; practiced; coached, prepared, primed, finished; at one's best; posted, briefed, primed

trainee NOUNS **recruit,** rookie <nonformal>, enrollee, boot <nonformal>; **raw recruit,** tenderfoot; **apprentice,** learner

traipse VERBS **go slow** *or* **slowly,** poke, poke along; drag along, drag one's feet, walk, mosey <nonformal>; **saunter,** stroll, amble, waddle, toddle <nonformal>; ambulate

trait NOUNS **characteristic,** peculiarity, singularity, particularity, specialty, individualism, **character,** nature, quirk, point of character, bad point, good point, saving grace, redeeming feature, mannerism, keynote, trick, **feature,** distinctive feature

traitor NOUNS treasonist, **betrayer,** quisling, rat <nonformal>, serpent, snake, cockatrice, **snake in the grass,** double-crosser <nonformal>, double-dealer; Judas, Judas Iscariot, Benedict Arnold, Quisling, Brutus; **apostate,** turncoat, turnabout, **recreant,** renegade, **defector,** tergiversator, **deserter,** turntail, fifth columnist, collaborationist, collaborator

tramp NOUNS 1 **walk,** ramble, amble, **hike,** traipse <nonformal>; slog, trudge, schlep <nonformal>; **stroll,** saunter
2 **bum,** derelict; **good-for-nothing,** good-for-naught, ne'er-do-well, wastrel; drifter, vagrant, hobo, vagabond, stiff *and* bindlestiff <both nonformal>, swagman *or* sundowner <both Austral>
VERBS 3 **plod,** peg, shamble, **trudge,** stump, lumber; plod along, plug along <nonformal>, schlep <nonformal>; **hike,** backpack

trample VERBS **run over,** overrun; **ride over,** override, **run down,** ride down; **trample on** *or* **upon,** trample down, tread upon, step on, walk on *or* over, trample underfoot, ride roughshod over

trance NOUNS **daze,** stupor; catatonic stupor, catalepsy; cataplexy; dream state, reverie, daydreaming; somnambulism, sleepwalking; hypnotic trance; **ecstasy,** ecstasis, transport, mystic transport; meditation, contemplation; **rapture;** yoga trance, dharana, dhyana, samadhi; hypnosis

tranquil ADJS **calm,** halcyon, pacific, peaceable, placid, quiet, **serene,** peaceful; **cool,** coolheaded, cool as a cucumber <nonformal>; reposeful

tranquilizer NOUNS **sedative,** sleeping pill *or* tablet, knockout drop *and* Mickey Finn <both nonformal>; drug, dope <nonformal>, narcotic, opiate, calmative

transact VERBS **execute,** complete, promulgate, make; **discharge,** fulfill, render, administer; **carry out,** carry through, put through, prosecute; effect, effectuate, set in motion, implement

transaction NOUNS business *or* commercial transaction, **deal,** business deal, operation, turn; package deal; **execution,** completion

transcend VERBS **excel,** surpass, exceed, get *or* have the ascendancy, get *or* have the edge, have it all over <nonformal>, overcome, overpass, best, **better,** improve on, perfect, go one better <nonformal>; **predominate,** prevail, preponderate; **outweigh,** go beyond, overbalance, overbear

transcribe VERBS **write,** copy out, engross, make a fair copy, copy; **adapt,** make an adaptation; transpose

transfer NOUNS 1 transference; **conveyance,** conveyancing; **giving**; **delivery,** deliverance; **assignment,** assignation; **consignment,** consignation; **exchange,** barter, trading
VERBS 2 **transmit,** transpose, translocate, metathesize, switch; **transplant,** translate; **pass,** pass over, **hand over,** turn over, carry over, make over, consign, assign; deliver; communicate, diffuse, disseminate, spread, impart; transfuse, perfuse, transfer property *or* right

transfix VERBS 1 **stab,** stick, pink, run through; transpierce, fix, **impale,** spit, skewer; gore, spear, lance, spike, needle
2 **immobilize,** freeze, keep, retain; stick, hold, pin *or* nail down <nonformal>; captivate, engross, enthrall, fascinate, spellbind

transform VERBS **transfigure,** transmute, transmogrify; **translate;** transubstantiate, metamorphose; **do over,** redo, make over, rejigger <nonformal>; **change,** change into, turn into, become, resolve into, assimilate to, bring to, reduce to

transgress VERBS **violate,** break, breach; infringe, overstep, overstep the bounds, trespass, contravene, trample on *or* upon; **do wrong,** misbehave, **err,** offend; **sin,** commit sin; disobey the law, offend against the law, flout the law, make a mockery of the law, fly in the face of the law

transient NOUNS 1 transient guest *or* boarder, temporary lodger; **sojourner;** passer, passerby; **wanderer; vagabond,** drifter, derelict, homeless person, tramp, hobo, bum <nonformal>
ADJS 2 **transitory,** transitive; **temporary,** temporal; **impermanent,** unenduring, undurable, nondurable, nonpermanent; frail, brittle, fragile, insubstantial; changeable, **mutable,** unstable, inconstant; capricious, fickle, impulsive, impetuous; **short-lived,** ephemeral, fly-by-night, evanescent, volatile, momentary; **passing,** fleeting, flitting, flying, fading, dying; fugitive, fugacious; perishable, mortal

transition NOUNS **change,** switch, switchover, changeover, turn, turnabout, about-face, **reversal,** flip-flop <nonformal>; apostasy, defection, change of heart; **shift,** modulation, qualification; transit, passage

translate VERBS **render,** transcribe, transliterate, put *or* turn into, transfuse the sense of; construe; **transform,** transfigure, transmute, transmogrify; transubstantiate, metamorphose

translation NOUNS 1 transcription, transliteration; **paraphrase,** loose *or* free translation; decipherment, decoding; amplification, restatement, rewording; literal *or* verbal *or* faithful *or* word-for-word translation; **pony** *and* trot *and* crib <all nonformal>; interlinear, interlinear translation, bilingual text *or* edition
2 **apotheosis,** resurrection, gathering, **ascension,** the Ascension; **assumption,** the Assumption; removal to Abraham's bosom

translucent ADJS lucent, translucid, lucid, pellucid; semitranslucent, semipellucid

transmission NOUNS **transferal,** transfer; transference, transmittal, transmittance; translocation, **transplantation,** translation; communication, spread, spreading, dissemination, diffusion; transduction, conduction, convection; transfusion, perfusion; **radio broadcasting,** AM broadcasting, FM broadcasting, shortwave broadcasting; **gearbox,** automatic transmission, standard transmission, stick shift; synchronized shifting, synchromesh

transmit VERBS **transfer,** transpose, translocate, transplace, metathesize, switch; **pass,** pass over, **hand over,** turn over, carry over, make over, consign, assign; deliver; pass on, hand forward, relay; communicate, diffuse, spread, impart; **dispatch,** remit, consign, forward; expedite; **convey,** send, send word, deliver *or* send a signal *or* message, **disseminate,** broadcast, **pass on** *or* **along,** hand on; report, render, make known, get across *or* over

transparent ADJS transpicuous, perspicuous, translucent, light-pervious, luminous; show-through, see-through, peekaboo, revealing; **lucid,** pellucid, **clear,** limpid; **crystal-clear,** clear as crystal; **diaphanous,** sheer, thin; **gossamer,** gossamery, filmy, gauzy

transpire VERBS 1 **exude,** exudate, transude, reek; **emit, discharge,** give off
2 **occur,** happen, eventuate, **take place,** come *or* go down <nonformal>, go on, be realized, come, **come off** <nonformal>, **come about,** come true, **come to pass,** pass, pass off, go off, fall, **befall,** betide

transplant NOUNS 1 **insertion,** introduction, insinuation, injection, infusion, perfusion, inoculation, intromission; graft, grafting, engrafting, transplantation; infixing, implantation, embedment
VERBS 2 **transfer,** transmit, transpose, translocate, transplace, metathesize, switch; translate; **implant,** infix; fit in, **inlay**

transport NOUNS 1 **transportation,** conveyance, carrying, bearing, packing, toting *and* lugging <both nonformal>; **hauling,** haulage, portage, porterage, waft, waftage; **shipment,** shipping, transshipment
2 **trance,** ecstasy, ecstasis, mystic transport; **rapture;** yoga trance, dharana, dhyana, samadhi
VERBS 3 **convey,** freight, conduct, **take; carry, bear,** pack, tote *and* lug <both nonformal>, manhandle; lift, waft, whisk, wing, fly
4 **fascinate,** captivate, charm, becharm, spell, spellbind, cast a spell, put under a spell, **beguile,** intrigue, enthrall, infatuate, **enrapture,** enravish, entrance, enchant, witch, **bewitch;** carry away, sweep off one's feet, turn one's head, knock one's socks off <nonformal>

transpose VERBS **reverse,** convert; put the cart before the horse; turn into the opposite, turn about, turn the tables, turn the scale *or* balance; rotate, revolve, pronate, supinate, resupinate; **interchange,** exchange, change, counterchange

transsexual NOUNS **intersex,** epicene; hermaphrodite, pseudohermaphrodite; androgyne, gynandroid

transverse NOUNS 1 **crosspiece,** traverse, transversal, transept, transom; diagonal; **crossbar,** crossarm; oblique, bias, bend <heraldry>, oblique line, slash
ADJS 2 transversal, traverse; **across,** cross, crossway, **crosswise** *or* crossways, thwart, athwart, overthwart; oblique, **diagonal,** catercorner *or* **cater-cornered** *or* cattycorner *or* catty-cornered *or* kittycorner *or* kittycornered;

slant, bias, biased, biaswise *or* biasways
ADVS 3 **crosswise** *or* crossways *or* crossway, decussatively; **cross,** criss-cross, across, thwart, thwartly, thwartways, **athwart,** athwartwise, overthwart; traversely; transversely, transversally; obliquely; **sideways** *or* sidewise

trap NOUNS 1 **ambush,** ambushment, **ambuscade,** *guet-apens* <Fr>; surveillance, shadowing; lurking hole *or* place; blind, stalking-horse; booby trap, gin; pitfall, trapfall, deadfall; **booby trap,** mine; decoy
VERBS 2 entrap, gin, catch, catch out, catch in a trap; **ensnare,** snare, hook, **hook in,** sniggle, noose; inveigle; net, mesh, enmesh, ensnarl, wind, tangle, entangle, entoil, enweb; trip, trip up; **set** *or* **lay a trap for,** bait the hook, spread the toils; **lure,** allure, **decoy**

trappings NOUNS **harness,** caparison, **tack,** tackle; **belongings,** appurtenances, paraphernalia, appointments, accessories, perquisites, appendages, appanages; **finery,** frippery, gaudery, trumpery, folderol, trickery, festoons, superfluity; **frills,** frills and furbelows, bells and whistles *and* gimmickry *and* Mickey Mouse *and* glitz <all nonformal>

trash NOUNS 1 **rubbish, junk,** refuse, waste; **nonsense,** stuff and nonsense, pack of nonsense, **folderol,** balderdash, *niaiserie* <Fr>, flummery, trumpery, vaporing, rant, claptrap, fustian, rodomontade, bombast, absurdity
VERBS 2 **censure,** reprehend; **blame,** lay *or* cast blame upon; **bash** *and* rubbish <both nonformal>; **reproach,** impugn; **denounce,** denunciate, accuse, **decry,** cry down, impeach, arraign, indict, call to account, exclaim *or* declaim *or* inveigh against, raise one's voice against, raise a hue and cry against, reprobate, hold up to reprobation

trauma NOUNS **wound,** injury, hurt, lesion; **laceration,** mutilation, abrasion, scuff, scrape, chafe, gall; **psychological stress,** stress; psychological *or* emotional trauma, traumatism, mental *or* emotional shock

traumatic ADJS **impaired,** damaged, hurt, injured, harmed; deteriorated, worsened, cut to the quick, aggravated, exacerbated, irritated, embittered; **damaging,** injurious, degenerative

travel NOUNS 1 traveling, going, journeying, touring, moving, **movement,** motion, locomotion, transit, progress, passage, course, crossing; world travel, globe-trotting <nonformal>; junketing; **tourism,** touristry
VERBS 2 **go,** move, pass, fare, wayfare, fare forth, fetch, flit, hie, sashay <nonformal>; progress; move on *or* along, go along; wend, **wend one's way;** betake oneself, direct one's course, bend one's steps *or* course; course, run, flow, stream; **journey,** make *or* take *or* go *or* go on a journey, **take** *or* **make a trip,** navigate, trek, jaunt, peregrinate; junket, go on a junket; tour

travesty NOUNS **exaggeration, burlesque,** lampoon, squib, **parody,** satire, farce, mockery, imitation, wicked imitation *or* pastiche, takeoff <nonformal>, **caricature**

treacherous ADJS **perfidious,** false-hearted; **shifty,** slippery, tricky; **double-dealing,** double, ambidextrous; two-faced; **unsafe,** unhealthy <nonformal>; **unreliable,** undependable, untrustworthy, **insecure,** unsound, unstable, unsteady, shaky, tottery, rocky

treachery NOUNS treacherousness; **perfidy,** perfidiousness, falseheartedness, two-facedness, doubleness; **duplicity,** double-dealing, foul play, dirty work *and* dirty pool *and* dirty trick *and* dirty game <all nonformal>

tread NOUNS 1 **gait,** pace, walk, stride; **step,** stair, footstep, rest, footrest, steppingstone
VERBS 2 **walk,** ambulate, **step,** pace, stride, pad; **stamp,** stomp <nonformal>, trample, clump, clop

treason NOUNS petty treason, misprision of treason, high treason; lese majesty, sedition; fifth-column activity; collaboration; apostasy, renunciation, **defection, desertion,** crossing-over, abandonment

treasure NOUNS 1 **wealth,** riches, opulence *or* opulency, luxuriousness; **fortune,** handsome fortune; full *or* heavy *or* well-lined *or* bottomless *or* fat *or* bulging purse, deep pockets <nonformal>; money to burn <nonformal>; substance, **assets,** resources, total assets, worth, net worth, **pecuniary resources,** means, available means *or* resources *or* funds, cash flow, wherewithal, command of money

2 **good thing,** a thing to be desired; gem, jewel, diamond, pearl; boast, pride, pride and joy
VERBS 3 **value, esteem,** prize, appreciate, **rate highly,** think highly of, think well of, **think much of,** set store by; give *or* attach *or* ascribe importance to; make much of, make a fuss *or* stir about, make an ado *or* much ado about; hold up as an example

treasury NOUNS **treasure house;** depository, repository; storehouse; **strongbox,** safe, money chest, coffer, locker, chest; **public treasury,** public funds, taxpayer funds *or* money, pork barrel, public crib *or* trough *or* till <nonformal>

treat NOUNS 1 **delicacy,** dainty, goody <nonformal>, kickshaw, **tidbit,** titbit; **morsel,** choice morsel, *bonne bouche* <Fr>; **regalement,** regale; **feast,** banquet, Lucullan feast; feast *or* banquet of the soul; **standing treat,** picking up the check *or* tab <nonformal>; paying the bills
VERBS 2 **doctor,** minister to, care for, give care to, physic; nurse; **cure,** remedy, heal; **handle,** manage, use, **deal with, cope with,** come to grips with, take on, tackle <nonformal>, contend with, do with
3 treat to, **stand treat,** go treat, pick up the check *or* tab <nonformal>, pay the bill, set up, blow to <nonformal>; stand drinks; maintain, support; subsidize

treatise NOUNS piece, treatment, handling, tractate, tract; examination, survey, **discourse,** discussion, disquisition, descant, exposition, screed; dissertation, **thesis;** pandect; excursus; **study,** lucubration, étude; **paper,** research paper; monograph

treatment NOUNS 1 medical treatment *or* attention *or* care; **cure,** curative measures; medication; **regimen,** regime, protocol; **usage,** handling, management; way *or* means of dealing; processing
2 **discussion,** consideration, investigation, **examination,** study, analysis, logical analysis; **technique,** draftsmanship, brushwork, painterliness

treaty NOUNS international agreement, *entente, entente cordiale* <both Fr>, concord, concordat, cartel, convention, paction, capitulation; **alliance,** league; nonaggression pact, mutual-defense treaty

trek NOUNS 1 **journey,** trip, *jornada* <Sp>, peregrination, sally; migration, transmigration
VERBS 2 **journey,** travel, make *or* take *or* go *or* go on a journey, **take** *or* **make a trip,** migrate, transmigrate

tremble NOUNS 1 **quiver,** quaver, shiver, shudder, twitter, tremble, flutter
VERBS 2 **shake,** quake, shiver, quiver, quaver; tremble *or* quake *or* shake in one's boots *or* shoes, tremble like an aspen leaf, shake all over

tremendous ADJS **huge,** immense, vast, enormous, astronomic, astronomical, humongous *and* jumbo <both nonformal>, prodigious, stupendous; magnificent, splendid, splendiferous, **marvelous,** wonderful, glorious, divine, heavenly, terrific, sensational

tremor NOUNS **shake,** quake, quiver, quaver, falter, **tremble,** shiver, shudder, twitter, didder, dither; **shock,** jolt, jar, jostle; **bounce,** bump

trench NOUNS **trough,** channel, ditch, entrenchment, fosse, **canal,** cut, gutter; moat; sunk fence, ha-ha; slit trench

trend NOUNS 1 **fashion,** style, mode, vogue, prevailing taste; current *or* stream of fashion; height of fashion; the new look, the season's look; high fashion, *haute couture* <Fr>
2 **drift,** course, current, *Tendenz* <Ger>, flow, stream, mainstream, main current, movement, glacial movement, motion, run, **tenor,** tone, **the way things go,** trend of the times, spirit of the age *or* time, time spirit, *Zeitgeist* <Ger>; the way it looks

trendy ADJS **fashionable,** in fashion, smart, in style, in vogue; all the rage, all the thing; **popular,** prevalent, current; **up-to-date,** up-to-datish, up-to-the-minute, switched-on *and* hip *and* with-it <all nonformal>, **in the swim;** sought-after, much sought-after; **faddish,** faddy <nonformal>

trespass VERBS **encroach,** infringe, impinge, trespass on *or* upon, invade, infiltrate; **transgress,** disobey the law, flout the law, **overstep,** intrude, break bounds, overstep the bounds, go too far, know no bounds

trial NOUNS 1 **tribulation,** trials and tribulations; **ordeal,** fiery ordeal, the iron entering the soul; cross, curse, blight, **affliction**; plight, predicament
2 **test,** *concours* and *rencontre* <both

Fr>; **experiment,** experimentation; testing, trying, trying-out

3 **jury trial,** trial by jury, trial at the bar, **hearing,** inquiry, inquisition, inquest, assize; court-martial

ADJS 4 venturesome, willing; determined, resolute; **experimental,** test; testing, proving, trying; probative, probatory, verificatory; **tentative,** provisional; empirical; trial-and-error, hit-or-miss, cut-and-try; heuristic

tribe NOUNS **race,** people, **folk,** family, house, clan, nation; strain, line; patriclan, matriclan, deme, sept, gens, phyle, phratry, totem

tribunal NOUNS **forum,** board, curia, Areopagus; judicature, judicatory, judiciary; council; inquisition, the Inquisition

tribute NOUNS 1 **praise,** homage, meed of praise; congratulation; adulation, lionizing, hero worship; **citation,** eulogy, kudos, **accolade**

2 **tax,** taxation, duty, taxes, rates <Brit>, contribution, **assessment,** revenue enhancement, cess <Brit>, **levy,** toll, impost, imposition

trick NOUNS 1 **artifice,** device, ploy, gambit, stratagem, **scheme,** design, *ficelle* <Fr>, **subterfuge,** blind, ruse, wile, **dodge,** artful dodge, sleight, pass, feint, fetch, chicanery; **knack,** art, hang, way; **prank,** practical joke, waggish trick, *espièglerie* <Fr>, antic, caper, frolic; monkeyshines *and* shenanigans <both nonformal>

2 **shift,** work shift, **tour,** tour of duty, stint, bit, **watch,** time, **turn,** relay, spell *or* turn of work; day shift, night shift, swing shift, graveyard shift <nonformal>, dogwatch, lobster trick

VERBS 3 **play a practical joke,** play tricks *or* pranks, **play a joke** *or* **trick on,** make merry with; spoof *and* kid *and* put one on <all nonformal>; **clown around,** pull a stunt *or* trick; pull one's leg <nonformal>

trickle NOUNS 1 tricklet, **dribble,** drip, dripping, drop, spurtle; percolation, leaching, lixiviation; seeping, seepage; **handful,** scattering, sprinkling

VERBS 2 **dribble,** dripple, **drip,** drop, spurtle; **filter,** percolate, leach, lixiviate; seep, weep

tricky ADJS 1 **fraudulent,** sharp, guileful, insidious, slippery, slippery as an eel, **shifty,** trickish, cute, finagling, chiseling <nonformal>; **cunning,** artful, gimmicky <nonformal>, **wily,** crafty; calculating, scheming

2 **difficult,** difficile; **not easy,** no picnic; wicked *and* mean *and* hairy <all nonformal>, **formidable;** delicate, ticklish, sticky <nonformal>, critical, easier said than done, like pulling teeth; exacting, demanding

trifle NOUNS **triviality,** oddment, bagatelle, fribble, **gimcrack,** gewgaw, frippery, **trinket,** bibelot, curio, **bauble,** gaud, toy, **knickknack,** knickknackery, kickshaw, folderol; hill of beans <nonformal>, molehill

trifle with VERBS show disrespect for, **show a lack of respect for,** be disrespectful, treat with disrespect, be overfamiliar with; make bold *or* free with, take a liberty, take liberties with, play fast and loose with

trigger NOUNS 1 **immediate cause,** proximate cause, spark; ultimate cause, immanent cause, causing cause, *causa causans* <L>; provocation, **last straw,** straw that broke the camel's back

VERBS 2 **cause,** be the cause of, **give rise to,** spark, spark off, set off, trigger off

trill VERBS **ripple,** babble, burble, bubble, **gurgle,** guggle, purl; **warble,** sing, call; chirr, roll; **twitter,** tweet, twit, chatter, chitter

trim NOUNS 1 **ornamentation,** decoration, **adornment,** embellishment, embroidery, elaboration; trimming

VERBS 2 **ornament,** decorate, adorn, dress, garnish, array

3 **mark down,** cut prices, cut, slash, shave, pare, underprice, knock the bottom out of <nonformal>

4 **shorten,** abbreviate, cut short, **crop,** prune, dock, shear, mow, clip

ADJS 5 **shapely,** well-shaped, well-proportioned, well-made, **well-formed,** well-favored; neat, spruce, clean, clean-cut, clean-limbed

6 **tidy,** natty, neat, spruce, sleek, slick *and* slick as a whistle <nonformal>, smart, snug, tight, **shipshape,** well-kept, well-cared-for, well-groomed; neat as a button *or* pin <nonformal>

trinket NOUNS gewgaw, **knickknack** *or* nicknack, knack <old>, **gimcrack,** kickshaw, whim-wham, **bauble,** fribble, bibelot, toy, gaud

trip NOUNS 1 **journey,** *jornada* <Sp>, peregrination, sally, trek; **tour,** grand tour; **conducted tour,** package tour *or*

holiday; **excursion,** jaunt, junket, outing, pleasure trip; sight-seeing trip *or* tour; day-trip; **cruise,** package cruise, cruise to nowhere
VERBS 2 **tumble,** fall, fall down, come *or* fall *or* get a cropper <nonformal>, take a fall *or* tumble, take a flop *or* spill <nonformal>, precipitate oneself; fall over, tumble over, trip over; **take a header** <nonformal>; fall prostrate, fall flat, fall on one's face, fall flat on one's ass <nonformal>; **stumble,** stagger, totter, careen, flounder

trite ADJS corny *and* square *and* square-John *and* Clyde <all nonformal>, fade, **banal,** unoriginal, platitudinous, **stereotyped,** stock, set, **commonplace,** common, truistic, twice-told, **familiar,** bromidic <nonformal>, old hat <nonformal>, back-number, bewhiskered, warmed-over, **cut-and-dried;** hackneyed, **stale,** musty, fusty; **worn,** time-worn, well-worn, moth-eaten, threadbare, **worn thin**

triumph NOUNS 1 **great success,** resounding triumph, brilliant success, striking success, meteoric success; **victory,** conquest, subduing, subdual; a feather in one's cap <nonformal>
VERBS 2 **prevail, be victorious,** come out ahead, come out on top <nonformal>, clean up; **win** *or* **carry** *or* **gain the day,** win the battle, come out first, finish in front, make a killing <nonformal>; **win the prize,** win the palm *or* laurels, take the cake <nonformal>
3 **exult,** glory, delight, joy, jubilate; **crow** *or* crow over, **gloat,** gloat over

triumphant ADJS **victorious,** triumphal, **winning,** prevailing; conquering, vanquishing, defeating, overcoming; ascendant, in the ascendant, in ascendancy, sitting on top of the world *and* sitting pretty <both nonformal>, dominant; flushed with success *or* victory

trivial ADJS **insignificant,** inconsiderable, inconsequential, negligible, no great shakes; unimportant, no skin off one's nose *or* ass; trifling, nugacious, nugatory, petty, mean, niggling, picayune *or* picayunish, nickel-and-dime *and* penny-ante *and* Mickey-Mouse *and* chickenshit <all nonformal>

trolley NOUNS **streetcar,** trolley car, **tram** *or* tramcar <both Brit>; electric car, electric <nonformal>; trolley bus, trackless trolley; horsecar

trollop NOUNS **strumpet,** wench, hussy, slut, jade, baggage, *cocotte* <Fr>, grisette; **tart** *and* **chippy** *and* **floozy** <all nonformal>, drab, trull, harridan, Jezebel, wanton, whore <nonformal>, **loose woman,** easy woman <nonformal>, easy lay <nonformal>, woman of easy virtue, frail sister

trophy NOUNS 1 laurel, **laurels,** bays, palm, palms, crown, chaplet, wreath, garland, **feather in one's cap** <nonformal>; prize, plum; **cup,** loving cup, pot <nonformal>; **belt,** championship belt, black belt, brown belt, etc; banner, flag
2 **memento,** remembrance, token, souvenir, keepsake, relic, favor, token of remembrance

troubadour NOUNS **minstrel,** ballad singer, balladeer, **bard,** rhapsode, rhapsodist; wandering *or* strolling minstrel, trovatore, trouveur, *trouvère* <Fr>, minnesinger, *Meistersinger* <Ger>, scop, gleeman, jongleur

trouble NOUNS 1 **inconvenience,** bother; encumbrance, cumbrance; difficulty; **the matter;** headache <nonformal>, problem, besetment, **inconvenience,** disadvantage; the bad part, the downside <nonformal>
VERBS 2 beset; **bother,** pother, get one down, <nonformal>, **disturb,** perturb, irk, plague, **torment,** drive one up the wall <nonformal>, give one gray hair, make one lose sleep; inconvenience, **put out,** put out of the way, discommode; **concern,** worry; **puzzle,** perplex; give one a hard time *and* give one a bad time *and* make it tough for <all nonformal>; be too much for

troublemaker NOUNS **instigator,** inciter, **provoker,** *provocateur* <Fr>, *agent provocateur* <Fr>, catalyst; **agitator,** fomenter, inflamer; agitprop; **rabble-rouser,** firebrand, incendiary; seditionist, seditionary; mischief-maker, ringleader

troubleshooter NOUNS **mender, fixer,** doctor <nonformal>, restorer, renovator, repairer, **repairman, repairwoman,** maintenance man *or* woman, **serviceman, servicewoman;** trouble man <nonformal>; Mr Fixit *and* little Miss Fixit <both nonformal>

trough NOUNS **trench,** channel, ditch, fosse, **canal,** cut, gutter

trounce VERBS **best,** beat, beat out, defeat; beat all hollow <nonformal>, clobber *and* take to the cleaners *and* smoke *and* skin *and* skin alive <all nonformal>, worst, whip *and* lick *and* have it all over *and* cut down to size <all nonformal>; **smite,** thump, baste, **pummel,** pommel, **drub,** buffet, belabor, lay on

troupe NOUNS **company,** acting company; repertory company, stock company; circus troupe

trousers NOUNS **pants,** pair of trousers *or* pants, **breeches,** britches <nonformal>, breeks <Scots>, **pantaloons,** jeans, slacks

trousseau NOUNS **wardrobe,** wedding clothes, bridal outfit

trove NOUNS **find,** finding, **discovery;** *trouvaille* <Fr>; treasure trove, buried treasure; **windfall,** windfall money, found money, money in the bank

truce NOUNS **armistice,** peace; pacification, suspension of hostilities, **cease-fire,** stand-down, breathing spell, cooling-off period; temporary arrangement, *modus vivendi* <L>; hollow truce, *pax in bello* <L>

truck NOUNS 1 lorry <Brit>, *camion* <Fr>; trailer truck, truck trailer, tractor trailer, semitrailer, rig *and* semi <both nonformal>; eighteen-wheeler <nonformal>
2 **dealings,** dealing, traffic, social intercourse; **commerce,** trade, intercourse, business, business dealings *or* affairs *or* relations, commercial affairs *or* relations

true ADJS **truthful;** in conformity with the facts *or* the evidence *or* reality, on the up-and-up *or* strictly on the up-and-up <nonformal>; gospel, **hard,** cast-iron; **factual,** actual, effectual, **historical,** documentary; objectively true; **certain,** undoubted, unquestionable; unrefuted, unconfuted, undenied; categorically true

trumpet VERBS **proclaim,** cry, cry out, **promulgate,** give voice to; blare forth *or* abroad, thunder, declaim, trumpet *or* thunder forth, shout from the housetops; celebrate, sing the praises of

trust NOUNS 1 investment company; investment trust, holding company; trust fund; blind trust
2 **belief,** credence, credit, faith
VERBS 3 **believe,** credit, accept, receive, buy <nonformal>; give credit *or* credence to, give faith to, put faith in, take stock in *or* set store by <nonformal>, take to heart, attach weight to; **confide in,** rely on, depend on, repose, place trust *or* confidence in, have confidence in, **trust in**, trust utterly *or* implicitly, deem trustworthy, think reliable *or* dependable, take one's word, take at one's word

trustworthy ADJS **trusty,** trustable, faithworthy, **reliable,** dependable, responsible, straight <nonformal>, sure, to be trusted, **to be depended** *or* **relied upon,** to be counted *or* reckoned on, as good as one's word; tried, true, **tried and true,** tested, proven

truth NOUNS 1 **trueness, verity,** veridicality, conformity to fact *or* reality *or* the evidence *or* the data, simple *or* unadorned truth, very truth; historical truth, **objective truth,** actuality, historicity, impersonality; **fact,** actuality, reality, the real world, the truth

2 <nonformal> **what's what,** how it is, how things are, like it is, where it's at, dinkum oil <Austral>, the straight of it, the straight goods *or* skinny *or* scoop, the honest-to-God truth, God's truth, the real thing, the very model, the genuine article, the very thing, it, the article, the goods, the McCoy, the real McCoy, chapter and verse, the gospel, the gospel truth, the lowdown, the skinny

try NOUNS 1 **test,** trial; essay; acid test, litmus *or* litmus-paper test; ordeal, crucible; probation
VERBS 2 **attempt,** essay; try one's hand *or* wings; **undertake**, approach, come to grips with, engage, take the bull by the horns; venture, venture on *or* upon, chance
3 try a case, conduct a trial, **hear,** give a hearing to, sit on; **judge,** sit in judgment

trying ADJS **oppressive,** burdensome, crushing, onerous, heavy, weighty; **harsh,** wearing, wearying, exhausting, grueling

tryout NOUNS workout, **rehearsal,** practice; **dry run,** dummy run; road test; **trial run,** practical test; shakedown, shakedown cruise, bench test; flight test, test flight *or* run; audition, hearing

tryst NOUNS **rendezvous,** assignation, meeting; trysting place, meeting place, place of assignation; assignation house; love nest <nonformal>

tub NOUNS **bath,** bathtub; bidet; washtub, washpot, washing pot, wash boiler

tube NOUNS **pipe; tubing,** piping, tubulation; tubulure

tubular ADJS tubate, tubiform, tubelike, pipelike; cylindrical; tubed, piped; tube-shaped

tuft NOUNS **flock,** fleck; forelock, widow's peak, quiff <Brit>, fetlock, cowlick; goatee; **crest,** topknot; panache; **clump,** tussock, hassock

tug NOUNS 1 **pull,** draw, heave, haul, a long pull and a strong pull, strain, drag
VERBS 2 **pull,** draw, heave, haul, hale, lug, **tow,** take in tow; **drag,** man-haul, draggle, snake <nonformal>; troll, trawl

tumble NOUNS 1 **fall,** *culbute* <Fr>, cropper *and* **spill** <both nonformal>, **flop** <nonformal>; **header** <nonformal>; sprawl; pratfall <nonformal>; **stumble,** trip; **dive,** plunge
VERBS 2 **fall,** fall down, take a fall *or* tumble, take a flop *or* spill <nonformal>, precipitate oneself; fall over, tumble over, trip over; **sprawl,** sprawl out, take a pratfall <nonformal>, spread-eagle <nonformal>, fall headlong, **take a header** <nonformal>; fall on one's face, fall flat on one's ass <nonformal>; **fall over,** topple down *or* over; **topple,** lurch, pitch, **stumble,** stagger, totter, careen, list, tilt, trip, flounder

tumor NOUNS **growth,** neoplasm; intumescence; benign tumor, nonmalignant tumor; malignant tumor, malignant growth, metastatic tumor, **cancer,** sarcoma, carcinoma

tumult NOUNS **commotion,** hubbub, Babel, turmoil, **uproar,** racket, riot, **disturbance,** rumpus <nonformal>, ruckus *and* ruction <both nonformal>

tune NOUNS 1 **air,** aria, **melody,** line, melodic line, refrain, note, **song,** lay, descant, lilt
VERBS 2 **tune up,** attune, atone, chord, **put in tune;** voice, string; tone up, tone down

tunnel NOUNS 1 **burrow,** earth, run, couch, lodge, warren; railroad tunnel, vehicular tunnel
VERBS 2 **dig,** excavate, **drill;** pierce to the depths; **trench,** burrow; drive sink, lower; **mine,** sap; drill, bore

turbulent ADJS **tumultuous,** tempestuous, boisterous, clamorous, uproarious; **agitated;** raging, chaotic, hellish, anarchic; **turbid,** roily

turf NOUNS 1 **sod,** sward, greensward
2 **field,** sphere, profession, province, bailiwick, area, discipline, orb, orbit, realm, arena, home turf, stamping ground, territory, domain, walk

turkey NOUNS 1 gobbler, turkey gobbler; turkey-cock, tom, tom turkey; hen turkey
2 failure, **flop** *and* bomb <both nonformal>

turmoil NOUNS **disorderliness,** unruliness, **disorder,** disruption, confusion, chaos; **commotion,** hubbub, Babel, tumult, disturbance

turn NOUNS 1 **start,** shock, jar, jolt
2 **crook,** warp, twist, skew, slue, **veer,** sheer, **swerve,** lurch
3 **aptitude,** bent, propensity, **leaning,** inclination, **turn of mind,** mind, **tendency,** grain, vein
VERBS 4 **turn round** *or* **around** *or* **about,** make a U-turn, turn on a dime, turn tail, **come** *or* **go about,** put about, fetch about; veer, veer around; **swivel,** pivot, pivot about, swing, round, swing round; wheel, wheel about, whirl, spin; heel, turn upon one's heel; **rotate,** revolve, **go round** *or* **around,** spiral, gyrate, gyre; circumrotate, circumvolute; circle

turn down VERBS **refuse,** decline, refuse consent, **reject,** decline to accept, **not have,** not buy <nonformal>; vote down, **turn thumbs down on;** turn one's back on, turn a deaf ear to, set oneself against, harden one's heart, resist entreaty *or* persuasion; **repudiate,** disallow, disclaim

turning point NOUNS **crisis,** critical point, crunch, crucial period, climax, climacteric; hinge, turn, turn of the tide, cusp; decisive moment, defining moment, **moment of truth,** when push comes to shove <nonformal>

turn off VERBS **offend,** give offense, **repel,** put off, **revolt,** disgust, nauseate, sicken, make one sick; distract, put off <nonformal>; **shut off,** shut, shut down, close; **phase out,** phase down, taper off, wind up *or* down; **kill, cut,** cut off short, switch off

turn on VERBS 1 **rouse, arouse,** raise, raise up, **waken, awaken,** wake up, charge *or* psych *or* pump up <nonformal>, stir, **stir up,** set astir, **pique**
2 **depend,** hang, rest, hinge; **depend on** *or* **upon,** hang on *or* upon, rest on *or* upon, stand on *or* upon, be based on, be contingent on

turnout NOUNS **attendance,** frequenting, frequence; number present; box office *and* draw <both nonformal>

tutor NOUNS 1 tutorer; **coach,** coacher; **private instructor,** *Privatdocent, Privatdozent* <both Ger>
VERBS 2 **coach; prime,** cram <nonformal>, cram with facts, stuff with knowledge

TV NOUNS **television,** video, telly <Brit nonformal>; television set, the small screen *or* the tube <both nonformal>, the boob tube <nonformal>, idiot box <nonformal>

twang NOUNS **accent,** regional accent, brogue, burr, drawl, broad accent

tweak NOUNS 1 **twitch,** pluck, hitch, wrench, snatch, start, bob
VERBS 2 **twitch,** pluck, snatch, hitch, wrench, snake <nonformal>

twig NOUNS sprig, scion, sapling; switch; branch, imp, bough

twilight NOUNS 1 **dusk,** evening twilight, crepuscule, crepuscular light, gloam, **gloaming,** glooming; **foredawn,** morning twilight, half-light, glow, first light, **the small hours;** alpenglow

the dawn's early light
FRANCIS SCOTT KEY

ADJS 2 **evening,** evensong, vesper, vespertine *or* vespertinal; twilighty, crepuscular; **dusk,** dusky, duskish

twin NOUNS 1 **the same,** selfsame, **duplicate,** double, clone *and* cookie-cutter copy <both nonformal>, *Doppelgänger* <Ger>, very image, look-alike, dead ringer <nonformal>, the image of, the picture of, spitting image *and* spit and image <both nonformal>, carbon copy; **equal,** match, mate, fellow, **equivalent,** opposite number, counterpart, coequal, parallel
ADJS 2 **identical,** identic; **same,** selfsame, one, **one and the same,** all the same; **alike,** all alike, like, just alike, exactly alike, like two peas in a pod; **duplicate,** reduplicated, of the same hue *or* stripe

twine NOUNS **cord,** line, rope, **string**

twinge NOUNS 1 **pang,** twitch, wrench, jumping pain; crick, kink, hitch, cramp *or* cramps; **nip,** thrill, pinch, tweak, bite, prick, **stab,** stitch
VERBS 2 **suffer,** feel pain, feel the pangs, **hurt,** ache, have a misery <nonformal>, ail; **smart,** tingle; thrill, twitch

twinkle NOUNS 1 **glitter,** glimmer, shimmer, blink; sparkle, spark; **scintillation,** scintilla; coruscation
2 **instant,** moment, second, **trice,** twinkling, twinkling *or* twinkle of an eye, **wink,** bat of an eye <nonformal>, two shakes of a lamb's tail *and* two shakes *and* shake *and* half a shake *and* **jiffy** *and* jiff *and* half a jiffy <all nonformal>
VERBS 3 **glitter,** glimmer, shimmer, blink, spangle, tinsel, coruscate; **sparkle,** spark, scintillate

twins NOUNS pair of twins <nonformal>, identical twins, fraternal twins, exact mates, look-alikes, dead ringers <nonformal>; Tweedledum and Tweedledee, Siamese twins

twirl VERBS convolve, **wind,** twine, **twist,** turn, twist and turn; **whirl,** whirligig, **wheel,** reel, spin, spin like a top *or* teetotum, whirl like a dervish

twist NOUNS 1 **bias,** bend, **crook,** skew, slue, **veer,** sheer, **swerve,** lurch; **quirk,** kink, crank, quip, trick, mannerism, **crotchet,** conceit, whim, bee in one's bonnet *or* head <nonformal>; **bent,** turn, slant, cast, warp; idiosyncrasy, eccentricity, individualism; strain, streak
VERBS 2 angle, **angle off,** swerve, shoot off at an angle, **veer,** sheer, sway, slue, **skew,** turn, bend, bias; wind, screw, crank
3 **pervert,** falsify, garble, put a false construction upon, give a spin, give a false coloring, color, varnish, slant, strain, torture; put words in someone's mouth; warp, bend, distort
4 **deform,** misshape, torture, disproportion

twisted ADJS **distorted,** contorted, warped, crooked; tortuous, labyrinthine; **falsified,** perverted, garbled, slanted, doctored, biased, strained, tortured; misrepresented, misquoted; influenced, swayed

two-faced ADJS **deceitful,** false; **false-hearted,** treacherous; sneaky; **cunning,** artful, gimmicky <nonformal>, **wily,** perfidious; **shifty,** slippery, tricky; double-dealing, duplicitous, hypocritical

two-timer NOUNS **cheat,** cheater; **traitor,** betrayer, quisling, Judas, double-dealer, **deceiver**

two-way ADJS **mutual,** commutual, common, joint, communal, shared, sharing, conjoint; respective

tycoon NOUNS **businessman,** businesswoman; big businessman, magnate, baron, king, top executive, business leader; **industrialist,** captain of industry; banker, financier; robber baron

type NOUNS 1 **example,** exemplar; **representative,** symbol, emblem, exponent; **exemplification,** illustration, demonstration, explanation; **kind,** sort, ilk, breed of cat <nonformal>, lot <nonformal>
VERBS 2 transcribe, copy out, engross, make a fair copy, copy
3 **classify,** class, assign, designate; **categorize,** put down as, **pigeonhole,** place, **group,** arrange

typhoon NOUNS **cyclone,** tornado, twister, rotary storm, *baguio* <Sp>, hurricane, tropical cyclone, tropical storm

typical ADJS typic, typal; exemplary, sample; **characteristic,** distinctive, distinguishing, quintessential; **natural,** normal, usual, regular, par for the course <nonformal>; **true to type,** true to form, the nature of the beast <nonformal>; paradigmatic, representative, standard, normative, classic

typify VERBS **designate,** specify; denominate, name, denote; **symbolize,** stand for, be taken as

tyranny NOUNS **despotism,** fascism, domineering, domination, oppression; heavy hand, high hand, iron hand, iron heel *or* boot

tyrant NOUNS **despot,** warlord; **autocrat,** autarch; absolute ruler *or* master *or* monarch, omnipotent *or* all-powerful ruler; **dictator,** duce, führer, commissar, pharaoh, caesar, czar; **oppressor,** hard master, driver, **slave driver,** Simon Legree <Harriet B Stowe>

U

ubiquitous ADJS **omnipresent,** all-present, everywhere; **pervasive,** all-pervading, universal; **returning,** reappearing, revenant

UFO NOUNS unidentified flying object; **flying saucer**

ugly ADJS **unsightly,** unattractive, unhandsome, unpretty, unlovely, uncomely, inelegant; ugly as sin, ugly as hell; **uglified,** disfigured, defaced, blotted, blemished, marred, spoiled

ulterior ADJS 1 **thither,** yonder, yon; **farther,** further, remoter, more distant; **latent,** concealed, hidden

ultimate NOUNS 1 **acme of perfection,** pink, pink of perfection, culmination, perfection, height, top, acme, summit, pinnacle, peak, highest pitch, climax, consummation, *ne plus ultra* <L>, **the last word,** a dream come true
ADJS 2 **farthest, furthest,** farthest off, furthermost, extreme, remotest, most distant; **last,** final, terminal; **eventual,** coming

ultimatum NOUNS last *or* final word *or* offer, firm bid *or* price, sticking point

umbrage NOUNS **offense,** pique; glower, scowl, angry look, dirty look <nonformal>, glare, frown

umbrella NOUNS **shade,** shader, **screen,** light shield, curtain, drape, drapery, blind, veil; **awning,** sunblind <Brit>; **sunshade,** parasol, beach umbrella; cover; shadow; protection

umpire NOUNS 1 **judge,** judger, adjudicator, justice; arbiter; referee
VERBS 2 **sit in judgment,** hold the scales, hold court; **hear,** give a hearing to; try; **referee,** officiate; arbitrate

unabashed ADJS **brazen,** brazenfaced, boldfaced, barefaced, brassy <nonformal>, **bold,** bold as brass <nonformal>, unblushing, aweless, **shameless,** dead *or* lost to shame; **undaunted,** undismayed, uncowed, unintimidated, unawed

unabated ADJS **undiminished,** unreduced, unrestricted, unretarded, unmitigated; unquenched, unextinguished

unable ADJS **incapable, incompetent,** inefficient, ineffective; **unqualified,** inept, unendowed, ungifted, untalented, **unfit,** unfitted; **outmatched,** out of one's depth, in over one's head, outgunned; **inferior**

unabridged ADJS uncondensed, unexpurgated; complete

unacceptable ADJS inadmissible, unsuitable, undesirable, **objectionable,** exceptionable, impossible, untenable, indefensible; intolerable, not to be thought of, beyond the pale, **unwelcome,** unwanted

unaccustomed ADJS **new,** disaccustomed, **unused,** unwonted; **unused to,** unfamiliar with, unacquainted with, unconversant with, unpracticed, new to, a stranger to

unadulterated ADJS **unpolluted,** nonpolluted, untainted, **undefiled;** pure, unspoiled, untouched, intact, virgin, uncorrupted, unsophisticated, unalloyed, untinged, undiluted, unfortified

unaffected ADJS 1 **unmoved, untouched,** dry-eyed, unimpressed, unstruck, **unstirred,** unruffled, unanimated, uninspired; **uninfluenced,** unswayed
2 **natural,** inartificial, unartificial; **unpretentious,** unpretending, unassuming, unfeigning, direct, straightforward, honest, candid; innocent, naive

unafraid ADJS **unfearing,** unfearful; unapprehensive, undiffident; **confident,** fearless, dauntless, aweless, dreadless; **unfrightened,** unscared, unalarmed, unterrified; **untimid,** untimorous, unshy, unbashful

unambiguous ADJS **clear,** crystal-clear, clear as day, clear as the nose on one's face; explicit, express; unmistakable, unequivocal, univocal, unconfused; **loud and clear** <nonformal>

unanimous ADJS **solid,** consentaneous, **with one consent** *or* **voice;** unchallenged, uncontroverted, uncontested, unopposed; **of one accord;** like-minded, of one mind, of the same mind; of a piece, **at one,** at one with

unannounced ADJS **unexpected,** out of the blue, out of left field *and* from out in left field <both nonformal>; without warning, unheralded

unanticipated ADJS **unexpected,** unlooked for, unhoped for, unprepared for, undivined, unguessed, unpredicted, **unforeseen;** without warning, unheralded; **surprising**, startling, electrifying, shocking, nerve-shattering

unappealing ADJS **unpleasant,** unpleasing, unenjoyable; displeasing, disagreeable; unlikable, dislikable; **abrasive,** wounding, hostile, unfriendly; **undesirable,** unattractive, unengaging, uninviting, unalluring; **distasteful,** unpalatable

unappetizing ADJS **unsavory,** unpalatable, untasteful, untasty, ill-flavored, foul-tasting, **distasteful,** dislikable, unlikable, uninviting, unpleasant, unpleasing, displeasing, disagreeable

unappreciated ADJS **disliked,** unvalued, unprized, misprized, undervalued; **despised,** lowly, spat-upon, untouchable; **unpopular,** out of favor, gone begging; misunderstood; unsung, thankless; unwept, unlamented, unmourned

unapproachable ADJS 1 **peerless,** matchless, champion; unmatched, unmatchable, unrivaled, unparalleled, **unequaled,** never-to-be-equaled, **unsurpassed,** unexcelled; inimitable, **incomparable,** beyond compare *or* comparison, **unique;** without equal *or* parallel, *sans pareil* <Fr>; in a class by itself, *sui generis* <L>, easily first, *facile princeps* <L>; second to none, *nulli secundus* <L>; **unbeatable,** invincible
2 **out-of-the-way,** godforsaken, back of beyond, upcountry; **out of reach,** forbidding, inaccessible, untouchable, hyperborean, antipodean

unarguable ADJS **obvious,** patent, unquestionable, indubitable, indisputable, incontestable, **irrefutable,** unrefutable, incontrovertible, irrefragable, unanswerable, unimpeachable, absolute

unarmed ADJS **unprotected,** unshielded, unsheltered, **unguarded,** undefended, unattended, unwatched, unfortified; barehanded, weaponless; **defenseless,** helpless

unashamed ADJS **immodest,** unmodest; exhibitionistic; **shameless,** unembarrassed, unabashed, unblushing, **brazen,** brazenfaced, brassy; **forward,** bold, pert, bumptious

unassuming ADJS **natural,** unaffected, unpretending, unpretentious, unfeigning, undisguising, undissimulating, undissembling, undesigning; simple

unattached ADJS **free;** at liberty, at large, on the loose, unengaged, disengaged, detached, uncommitted, uninvolved, clear, in the clear, footloose, footloose and fancy-free; **separate,** distinct, discrete; unjoined, unconnected, unaccompanied, unattended, unassociated

unattainable ADJS **impracticable,** unachievable; unrealizable, insurmountable, unsurmountable, insuperable; **beyond one,** beyond one's power, beyond one's control, out of one's depth, too much for; **unobtainable,** unavailable, unprocurable, unsecurable, not to be had, **not to be had for love or money**

unauthorized ADJS **prohibited,** forbidden, *verboten* <Ger>, barred; beyond the pale, off limits, out of bounds; **unsanctioned,** unlicensed; banned, under the ban, **outlawed,** contraband; taboo, tabooed, untouchable; **illegal,** unlawful, illicit

unavailable ADJS **inaccessible,** unaccessible; **unreachable,** beyond reach, out of reach; **impenetrable,** impervious; closed to, denied to, lost to, closed forever to; **unobtainable,** unattainable, unprocurable, unsecurable, not to be had, **not to be had for love or money**

unavoidable ADJS **inevitable,** necessary, **inescapable,** unpreventable, ineluctable, irrevocable, indefeasible; relentless, inexorable, unyielding, inflexible; **certain,** fateful, **sure,** sure as fate, sure as death, sure as death and taxes; **destined,** fated

unaware ADJS **unconscious,** insensible, unknowing, incognizant; mindless, witless; **unmindful,** unwitting, unsuspecting; unperceiving, impercipient, unaware of, in ignorance of, unconscious of, unmindful of, insensible to, out of it <nonformal>, not with it <nonformal>; **blind to,** deaf to, dead to, a stranger to; **off one's guard,** caught napping, caught tripping

unbalanced ADJS 1 **ill-balanced,** overbalanced, off-balance, tippy, listing, heeling, leaning, canted, top-heavy; **unstable,** unsteady
2 **insane,** of unsound mind, **demented,** deranged, deluded, disoriented, unhinged, unsettled, distraught, wandering, mazed, crackbrained, brainsick, sick *or* soft in the head, not right, not in one's right mind, bereft of reason, irrational, senseless, witless

unbearable ADJS **insufferable,** intolerable, insupportable, unendurable, for the birds <nonformal>, **too much** *or* a bit much <nonformal>, more than flesh and blood can bear, enough to drive one mad, enough to try the patience of Job; **flagrant,** arrant, shocking, shattering, egregious, unconscionable, glaring, stark-staring, **rank,** crass, gross

unbeatable ADJS **irresistible; invincible,** indomitable, unconquerable, unsubduable, unyielding, incontestable, more than a match for; overpowering, overwhelming; **peerless,** matchless, champion

unbecoming ADJS **indecent,** indelicate, inelegant, indecorous, improper, inappropriate, **unseemly,** indiscreet

unbefitting ADJS **inexpedient,** undesirable, inadvisable, counterproductive, impolitic, impolitical, unpolitic, not to be recommended, contraindicated; **ill-advised,** ill-considered, unwise; **unfit,** unfitting, **inappropriate,** unsuitable, unmeet, inapt, inept, unseemly

unbelievable ADJS **incredible,** unthinkable, **implausible,** unimaginable, inconceivable, not to be believed, **hard to believe,** beyond belief, unworthy of belief, not meriting *or* not deserving belief, tall <nonformal>; **defying belief,** staggering belief, passing belief; **mind-boggling,** preposterous, absurd, ridiculous, unearthly, ungodly

unbiased ADJS **unprejudiced,** unprepossessed, unjaundiced; impartial, even-handed, **fair,** just, equitable, objective, dispassionate, impersonal, detached, disinterested; indifferent, neutral

unburden VERBS **lighten,** unload, unfreight, disencumber, disembarrass, ease one's load; **set one's mind at ease** *or* **rest,** set at ease, take a load off one's mind, let one's hair down, pour one's heart out, talk it out, let it all hang out *and* go public <both nonformal>, get it off one's chest

uncalled-for ADJS **unwelcome,** unasked, unbidden, uninvited, unasked-for; **disrespectful,** derisive, brash, bluff; **unsolicited,** needless, gratuitous

uncanny ADJS **creepy,** spooky, eerie, weird, unearthly, macabre

uncaring ADJS **apathetic,** indifferent, unconcerned, **uninterested; careless,** heedless, unheeding, unheedful, disregardful, unsolicitous; tactless, respectless, **thoughtless,** unthinking, inconsiderate, untactful, undiplomatic, mindless of, **unmindful,** forgetful, oblivious

uncertain ADJS **unsure; doubting,** agnostic, **skeptical,** unconvinced, unpersuaded; chancy, dicey <Brit>, touch-and-go; **equivocal,** polysemous, inexplicit, imprecise, ambiguous; unpredictable, doubtful, dubious

unchanging ADJS **unchangeable,** not to be changed, changeless, unchanged, unvarying, unvariable, **unalterable,** unaltered, unalterative, **immutable,** incommutable, inconvertible, unmodifiable; lasting, unremitting, permanent

uncharitable ADJS **unbenevolent,** unbeneficent, unphilanthropic, unaltruistic, ungenerous

uncharted ADJS **unknown,** uninvestigated, unexplored; unidentified, unclassified, unfathomed, unplumbed, virgin, untouched; **unfamiliar,** strange

unchecked ADJS **unrestrained,** unconstrained, unforced, uncompelled, uncoerced; **uncurbed,** unbridled, unmuzzled; **unreined,** uncontrolled, ungoverned, **unruly;** out of control, out of hand, out of one's power; **abandoned,** intemperate, immoderate, **incontinent,** licentious, loose, wanton, rampant, riotous, wild; irrepressible; lax

uncivilized ADJS **barbarous,** barbaric, unchristian; **inhuman,** inhumane, unhuman; fiendish, fiendlike; demoniac *or* demoniacal, diabolic, diabolical, devilish, satanic, hellish, infernal; **unrefined,** unpolished, uncouth, unkempt, uncombed, unlicked; noncivilized

unclad ADJS **undressed,** unclothed, unattired, disrobed, ungarmented, undraped, ungarbed, unrobed, unappareled, uncased; half-clothed, *en déshabillé* <Fr>, in dishabille, nudish; low-cut, décolleté, strapless, topless; scantily clad

unclassified ADJS **unordered,** orderless, disordered, unorganized, random, entropic, unarranged, ungraded, unsorted; unidentified, uncharted, unfathomed, unplumbed

unclear ADJS **indeterminate,** indefinite, undefined, indecisive, vague, misty, hazy, fuzzy, blurred *or* blurry, obscure; opaque, muddy, **clear as mud** *and* clear as ditch water <both nonformal>; **illegible,** unreadable, undecipherable, indecipherable

unclog VERBS **unstop,** unblock, clear, unfoul, free; **unplug,** uncork, uncap; crack; **unlock,** unlatch, undo; **purge,** clean *or* scour out, clear off *or* out *or* away, flush out, blow, blow out, sweep out; **open up,** unjam, unbar, loose

uncomfortable ADJS **distressed,** afflicted, put-upon, beset, beleaguered; **troubled,** bothered, disturbed, perturbed, disquieted, discomforted, discomposed, agitated; uneasy, ill at ease

uncommitted ADJS **neutral,** noncommitted, uninvolved; neither one thing nor the other, neither hot nor cold; **on the fence** *or* **sidelines** <nonformal>, in the middle of the road, centrist, moderate, midway; **independent,** nonpartisan; unaligned, nonaligned; **impartial**

uncommon ADJS **marvelous,** wonderful, formidable, exceptional, astonishing, appalling, fabulous, fantastic, incredible, egregious; strange, unusual, almost unheard-of, seldom met with, seldom seen, few and far between; **rare,** scarcer than hen's teeth <nonformal>; not to be had for love or money, not to be had at any price

uncomplicated ADJS **uninvolved,** incomplex, straightforward; plain, **simple,** Mickey Mouse <nonformal>, simple as ABC <nonformal>, easy as pie *and* easy as falling off a log <both nonformal>, downhill all the way, like shooting fish in a barrel, like taking candy from a baby

uncomplimentary ADJS **disapproving,** disapprobatory, unapproving, **unfavorable,** low, poor, **opposed,** opposing, against, agin <nonformal>, dead set against, death on, down on; unappreciative

uncompromising ADJS **unyielding,** unbending, inflexible, hard, hard-line, inelastic, impliable, ungiving, **firm,** stiff, rigid, rigorous, stuffy; **adamant,** adamantine; **immovable,** not to be moved; **unalterable,** unchangeable, immutable; **intransigent,** irreconcilable, hard-shell *and* hard-core <both nonformal>; implacable, inexorable, **relentless,** unrelenting; stern, grim, dour

unconcerned ADJS **uninterested,** turned-off, **dispassionate,** insouciant, **careless,** regardless; easygoing; incurious; mindless, **unmindful,** heedless, inattentive, disregardful; **devil-may-care,** reckless, negligent; unsolicitous, unanxious; pococurante, **nonchalant,** inexcitable; **blasé** undiscriminating, casual; **listless,** lackadaisical, sluggish; bovine; numb, **apathetic**

unconditional ADJS **unqualified,** unconditioned, **unrestricted,** unhampered, **unlimited,** uncircumscribed, unmitigated, **categorical,** straight, **unreserved,** without reserve; **explicit,** express, unequivocal, clear, unmistakable; **peremptory,** indisputable, **without exception,** admitting no exception; **positive,** absolute, flat, definite, definitive, determinate, decided, decisive, fixed, final, conclusive; **utter,** perfect, downright, outright, out-and-out, straight-out <nonformal>, all-out, flat-out <nonformal>

unconfirmed ADJS **unproved,** not proved, unproven, **undemonstrated,** not shown; **untried,** untested; **unsubstantiated,** unattested, **unauthenticated,** unvalidated, uncertified, **unverified; uncorroborated,** unsustained, **unsupported,** unsupported by evidence, **groundless,** without grounds *or* basis, unfounded; **inconclusive,** indecisive; **moot**

unconscionable ADJS **flagrant,** arrant, shocking, shattering, egregious, intolerable, unbearable, glaring, stark-staring, **rank,** crass, gross; **conscienceless,** shameless, without shame *or* remorse, **unscrupulous,** unprincipled, unethical, immoral, amoral; **exorbitant,** undue, outrageous, **unreasonable**

unconscious NOUNS 1 **subconscious,** subconscious *or* unconscious mind, submerged mind, subliminal, subliminal self; collective unconscious, racial unconscious
ADJS 2 **senseless,** oblivious, comatose, asleep, dead, **dead to the world,** cold, out, **out cold;** half-conscious, semiconscious; drugged, narcotized; **subliminal,** extramarginal; preconscious, foreconscious, coconscious; **unpremeditated,** spontaneous, undesigned, unstudied; **unaware,** insensible, unknowing, incognizant

uncontested ADJS **unanimous,** uncontradicted, unchallenged, uncontroverted, unopposed; **undoubted,** unquestioned, undisputed

uncontrollable ADJS **ungovernable,** unmanageable, indomitable, untamable, **intractable,** refractory; **recalcitrant,** contumacious; obstreperous, **unruly,** restive, wild, fractious; beyond control, out of hand; **beside oneself,** like one possessed; unstoppable; relentless, inexorable, unyielding, inflexible

unconventional ADJS **unorthodox, eccentric,** gonzo <nonformal>, heterodox, heretical; unfashionable, offbeat <nonformal>, way out *and* far out *and* kinky *and* out in left field <all nonformal>, fringy, breakaway, out-of-the-way; original, maverick, Bohemian, beat, hippie, counterculture

unconvinced ADJS **uncertain,** unsure; doubting, agnostic, **skeptical,** unpersuaded, unconverted; **hesitant,** hesitating; **indecisive,** incredulous, irresolute; **unbelieving,** disbelieving, nonbelieving

uncooperative ADJS **insubordinate,** unsubmissive, indocile, **uncompliant,** noncooperative, noncooperating, intractable; **unhelpful,** unaccommodating, unobliging, disobliging

uncoordinated ADJS **clumsy,** awkward, maladroit, unhandy, left-hand, left-handed, heavy-handed, ham-handed <nonformal>, butterfingered <nonformal>, **all thumbs,** fingers all thumbs, with a handful of thumbs

uncouth ADJS **unpolished,** uncultivated, uncultured, unrefined; **ungainly,** ungraceful, graceless, inelegant, *gauche* <Fr>; unrefined; **vulgar,** barbarous, barbaric, rude, **crude,** outlandish

uncover VERBS **unearth,** dig up, disinter, exhume, excavate; **disclose,** expose, reveal, blow the lid off, crack wide open, **bring to light;** turn up, root up, ferret out, pry out

uncut ADJS **complete,** whole, total, global, **entire,** intact, solid; **full,** full-fledged, full-dress, **full-scale;** unabbreviated, undiminished, unexpurgated

undaunted ADJS **undismayed,** uncowed, unintimidated, unappalled, unabashed, unawed; **unflinching,** unshrinking, unquailing, uncringing, unwincing, unblinking

undecided ADJS **irresolute,** irresolved, unresolved; **indecisive,** undetermined, unsettled, infirm of purpose; dubious, **uncertain**; at loose ends, at a loose end; **of two minds,** in conflict, double-minded, ambivalent; changeable, mutable; capricious, mercurial, fickle; **pending,** depending, contingent, conditional, conditioned; **open,** in question, at issue, **in the balance,** up in the air, up for grabs <nonformal>, **in suspense,** in a state of suspense, suspenseful

undeclared ADJS **unexpressed,** unpronounced, **unsaid,** unspoken, unuttered, unvoiced, wordless, silent; **unmentioned,** untalked-of, **untold,** unsung, unproclaimed, unpublished; unwritten, unrecorded

undefeated ADJS **unbeaten,** unvanquished, unconquered, unsubdued, unquelled, unbowed

undemanding ADJS **unstrict,** unexacting; unsevere, unharsh; lenient; **permissive,** overpermissive, overindulgent, **soft;** easy, easygoing, laid-back <nonformal>; **flexible,** pliant, yielding; **uncritical,** uncriticizing, nonjudgmental

undeniable ADJS **obvious,** patent, unquestionable, unexceptionable, self-evident, axiomatic; indubitable, unarguable, indisputable, incontestable, **irrefutable,** unrefutable, incontrovertible, irrefragable, unanswerable, unimpeachable, absolute; admitting no question *or* dispute *or* doubt *or* denial; **demonstrable,** verifiable, testable, confirmable; well-founded, well-established, well-grounded

underbrush ADJS **undergrowth,** underwood, copsewood, undershrubs, boscage

undercover ADJS 1 **covert,** clandestine, quiet, unobtrusive, hugger-mugger, **surreptitious,** underground, under-the-counter, under-the-table, **cloak-and-dagger,** backdoor, underhand, **underhanded; furtive,** stealthy, privy, backstairs, **sly,** shifty, sneaky, sneaking, skulking, slinking, slinky, feline
ADVS 2 **secretly,** in secret; in the closet; nobody the wiser; **covertly,** *à couvert* <Fr>, under the cloak of; **behind the scenes,** in the background, in a corner, in the dark; *sub rosa* <L>, under the rose; underground; *sotto voce* <Ital>, under the breath, with bated breath, in a whisper

undercurrent NOUNS **implication,** connotation, import, latent *or* underlying *or* implied meaning, ironic suggestion *or* implication, more than meets the eye, what is read between the lines; **suggestion,** allusion; coloration, tinge, undertone, overtone, more than meets the eye *or* ear, something between the lines, intimation, touch, nuance, innuendo; **inference,** supposition, presupposition, assumption, presumption; undermeaning, undermention, subsidiary sense, subsense, **subtext**

undercut VERBS **disprove, invalidate,**

disconfirm, discredit, prove the contrary, belie, give the lie to; **expose,** show up; explode, blow up, blow sky-high, **puncture,** deflate, shoot *or* poke full of holes, cut to pieces, cut the ground from under; knock the props *or* chocks out from under, cut the ground from under one's feet, not leave a leg to stand on

undergarments NOUNS **underclothes,** underclothing, bodywear, **underwear,** undies <nonformal>, skivvies, body clothes, smallclothes, unmentionables <nonformal>, **lingerie,** linen, underlinen

undergo VERBS **experience,** have, know, feel, taste; **encounter,** meet, meet with, meet up with <nonformal>, run up against <nonformal>; **go through,** pass through, be subjected to, be exposed to, stand under, labor under, **endure,** suffer, sustain

underground NOUNS 1 **irregular,** casual; **guerrilla,** partisan, franctireur; resistance, maquis; *maquisard* <Fr>, underground *or* resistance fighter; fifth column; underground route, underground railroad
ADJS 2 **subterranean,** subterraneous, buried, deep-buried
3 **covert,** clandestine, surreptitious, undercover, **stealthy,** sneaky, sneaking, skulking, slinking, slinky, feline; **concealed,** hidden, under cover, under wraps <nonformal>
ADVS 4 beneath the sod, six feet under <nonformal>; at rest, resting in peace
5 **secretly,** in secret, **covertly,** under the cloak of; in the dark, in darkness, behind the veil of secrecy

underhanded ADJS **fraudulent,** sharp, guileful, insidious, slippery, slippery as an eel, **shifty,** tricky, trickish, cute, finagling, chiseling <nonformal>; underhand, **furtive,** surreptitious, indirect; **dishonest,** dishonorable; **unscrupulous,** unprincipled, unethical, immoral, amoral; **corrupt,** corrupted, rotten; **crooked,** criminal, felonious, shady <nonformal>, up to no good, unsavory, dark, sinister, devious

underling NOUNS **inferior,** understrapper <Brit>, **subordinate,** subaltern, **junior;** secondary, second fiddle *and* second stringer *and* third stringer *and* benchwarmer *and* low man on the totem pole <all nonformal>, understrapper, errand boy, flunky, gofer <nonformal>

underlying ADJS **latent,** lurking, **hidden,** obscured, obfuscated, veiled, muffled, covert, **under the surface,** submerged; **between the lines;** hibernating, sleeping, dormant; **basic,** gut <nonformal>, basal

undermine VERBS **weaken,** enfeeble, debilitate, soften up <nonformal>, unbrace, unman, unnerve, rattle, shake up <nonformal>, **devitalize,** enervate, eviscerate; **sap,** sap the strength of, exhaust, gruel, take it out of <nonformal>; blunt, dull, damp *or* dampen, take the edge off; mine, sap the foundations of, honeycomb; sabotage, throw *or* toss a monkey-wrench in the works <both nonformal>; subvert, **overthrow,** overturn, overwhelm, upset, subvert, defeat, demolish

underprivileged ADJS **indigent,** poverty-stricken; needy, necessitous, **in need,** in want, disadvantaged, deprived, **impoverished,** depressed, pauperized, starveling

underrated ADJS **underestimated,** undervalued, on the low side; unvalued, unprized, misprized

underscore VERBS **underline,** emphasize, stress, lay emphasis *or* stress upon, feature, highlight, place emphasis on, give emphasis to, **accent,** accentuate, punctuate, point up, bring to the fore, put in the foreground; prioritize; **highlight,** spotlight; **star,** italicize; make a big deal *or* Federal case of <nonformal>

understand VERBS 1 **comprehend,** apprehend, have, **know,** conceive, realize, appreciate, have no problem with, make sense out of; **fathom,** follow; grasp, seize, get hold of, grasp *or* seize the meaning, **take in,** catch, **catch on,** get the meaning of, get the hang of; **suspect,** infer, gather, conclude, deduce, consider, reckon, divine

2 <nonformal> **read one loud and clear,** read, read one, dig, get the idea, be with one, be with it, get the message, get the word, get the picture, get up to speed, get into *or* through one's head *or* thick head, get, get it, catch *or* get the drift, have it taped, have it down pat, see where one is coming from, hear loud and clear, hear what one is saying, grok, have hold of, have a fix on, know like the back *or* palm of one's hand, know inside out

understanding NOUNS 1 entente; mutual *or* cordial understanding, consortium, *entente cordiale* <Fr>; **compact**
2 **intelligence,** comprehension, apprehension, intellection, prehension; conception, conceptualization, ideation; **grasp,** mental grasp, grip, **command,** mastery
ADJS 3 **patient,** armed with patience, with a soul possessed in patience, patient as Job; **tolerant,** tolerative, tolerating, accepting; **indulgent,** lenient; **pitying,** sympathizing, commiserative, condolent; **compassionate,** merciful, ruthful, rueful; lenient, forbearant; charitable, empathic, empathetic
4 **sagacious, astute,** discerning, penetrating, incisive, acute, trenchant, cogent, piercing; **perspicacious,** perspicuous; **perceptive,** percipient, apperceptive, appercipient, insightful

understated ADJS **tasteful,** in good taste, in the best taste; **restrained,** unobtrusive, quiet, subdued, simple, unaffected

understudy NOUNS **alternate,** backup *and* stand-in <both nonformal>, alter ego, **surrogate,** procurator, secondary, pinch hitter <nonformal>; locum tenens; **relief,** fill-in

undertake VERBS **assume,** accept, **take on,** take upon oneself, take upon one's shoulders, take up, go with, **tackle,** attack; engage *or* contract *or* obligate *or* commit oneself; **put** *or* **set** *or* **turn one's hand to,** engage in, devote oneself to, apply oneself to, address oneself to, give oneself up to; pitch into <nonformal>, plunge into, fall into, **launch into** *or* **upon;** go at, set at, have at <nonformal>, knuckle *or* buckle down to; put one's shoulder to the wheel

undertaker NOUNS **mortician,** funeral director; embalmer; gravedigger; sexton

undertone NOUNS **significance,** emotive *or* affective meaning, overtone, coloring; **drift,** tenor; **secondary meaning,** connotation, implied meaning, implication; **suggestion,** allusion; coloration, tinge, undercurrent, more than meets the eye *or* ear, something between the lines, intimation, touch, nuance, innuendo

underwear NOUNS **underclothes,** underclothing, undergarments, bodywear, **undies** <nonformal>, skivvies, body clothes, unmentionables <nonformal>, **lingerie,** linen, underlinen; woolies <nonformal>; long johns <nonformal>

underworld NOUNS 1 **depths,** deeps, bowels, bowels of the earth; bottomless pit; infernal pit, hell, nether world; dark *or* unknown *or* yawning *or* gaping depths, unfathomed deeps
2 **the underworld,** gangland, organized crime, gangsterism

underwrite VERBS **secure,** guarantee, guaranty, warrant, assure, insure, ensure, bond, **certify; sponsor,** insure, be sponsor for, sign for, sign one's note, **back,** stand behind *or* back of, stand up for; sign, cosign, subscribe to; confirm, attest

undeserved ADJS **unmerited,** unearned; **unwarranted,** unjustified, unprovoked; unentitled, undeserving, unmeriting, nonmeritorious, unworthy; preposterous, outrageous

undesirable NOUNS 1 bad person, bad man *or* woman *or* child, unworthy *or* disreputable person, unworthy, disreputable, *persona non grata* <L>, unacceptable *or* unwanted *or* objectionable person
ADJS 2 unattractive, unappealing, unengaging, uninviting, unalluring; unwelcome, thankless; **distasteful,** untasteful, **unpalatable,** unsavory; **unacceptable,** inadmissible, unsuitable, **objectionable,** exceptionable, impossible, untenable, indefensible; **intolerable**

undetectable ADJS **imperceptible,** unperceivable, **indiscernible,** undiscernible; behind the curtain *or* scenes; disguised, camouflaged, hidden, **concealed;** undisclosed, unrevealed, *in petto* <L>; latent, unrealized, submerged

undeveloped ADJS **unfinished,** unlicked, unformed; unfashioned, unwrought, unlabored, unworked, unprocessed, untreated; **underdeveloped;** backward, arrested, stunted; **crude,** rude, coarse, unpolished, unrefined; uncultivated, uncultured; rough, roughcast, roughhewn, **in the rough;** rudimentary

undignified ADJS **vulgar,** inelegant, indelicate, indecorous, indecent, improper, unseemly, unbeseeming, unbecoming, unfitting, inappropriate, unsuitable, ungenteel; **untasteful,** tasteless, in bad *or* poor taste, tacky *and* chintzy *and* Mickey Mouse <all nonformal>; **offensive,** offensive to gentle ears

undiminished ADJS unabated, unreduced, unrestricted, unretarded, unmitigated; complete, unreduced

undisciplined ADJS **ungoverned,** unrestrained; insubordinate, mutinous, disobedient; **uncontrolled,** uncurbed, unbridled, unchecked, rampant, untrammeled, unreined, reinless, anything goes; irresponsible, fast and loose

undisputed ADJS **unquestioned,** uncontested, uncontradicted, unchallenged, uncontroverted, uncontroversial; **doubtless,** beyond a shade *or* shadow of doubt, past dispute, beyond question

undivided ADJS uncut, unsevered, unclipped, uncropped, unshorn; **undiminished,** unreduced, complete; unseparated

undo VERBS 1 **take off,** remove, doff, slip *or* step out of, slip off, slough off, cast off, throw off, drop

2 **unnerve,** unman, unstring, unbrace, reduce to jelly, **demoralize,** shake, upset, psych out <nonformal>, dash, knock down *or* flat, **crush,** overcome, prostrate

3 **do for,** fix <nonformal>, settle, sink, cook *and* cook one's goose *and* cut one down to size *and* cut one off at the knees *and* pull the plug on *and* pull the rug out from under <all nonformal>, scuttle, put the kibosh on *and* put the skids under <both nonformal>, do in, poleax, torpedo, knock out, KO <nonformal>, deal a knockout blow to, zap *and* shoot down *and* shoot down in flames <all nonformal>

4 **abolish,** nullify, void, abrogate, annihilate, annul, tear up, repeal, revoke, negate, negative, invalidate, **cancel,** cancel out, bring to naught, put *or* lay to rest

undoing NOUNS **destruction,** ruin, ruination, **dissolution,** disintegration, breakup, disruption, disorganization, lysis; **neutralization,** nullification, annulment, cancellation, voiding, invalidation, vitiation, frustration, thwarting

undress NOUNS 1 **dishabille,** *déshabillé* <Fr>, something more comfortable; **negligee,** *négligé* <Fr>; **wrap,** wrapper; bareness, baldness, **nakedness,** nudity, beauty unadorned

VERBS 2 **unclothe,** undrape, **disrobe; strip,** strip to the buff <nonformal>, do a strip-tease

undying ADJS **immortal,** everlasting, **deathless,** never-dying, **imperishable,** incorruptible, amaranthine; **continuous**, ceaseless, unceasing, unending, endless, incessant, unremitting, steady, sustained, protracted, indefatigable

unearthly ADJS **deathly,** deathlike, deadly; **weird,** eerie, uncanny, unworldly; **otherworldly,** extraterrestrial, extramundane, transmundane, not of the earth, not of this world; weird, passing belief; **mind-boggling,** preposterous, absurd, ridiculous, ungodly; supernatural

uneasy ADJS **restless,** restive, unquiet, unsettled, unrestful, tense; **fidgety,** antsy <nonformal>, fussy, fluttery; **troubled,** bothered; perturbed, disturbed, disquieted, agitated; **apprehensive,** qualmish, nail-biting, white-knuckle <nonformal>, nervous as a cat; unpeaceful

uneconomical ADJS **improvident,** thriftless, unthrifty; **shiftless,** feckless, thoughtless, heedless; happy-go-lucky; negligent

uneducated ADJS **unlearned, inerudite,** unerudite, unschooled, uninstructed, untutored, unbriefed, untaught, unedified, unguided; **lowbrow** *and* lowbrowed *and* lowbrowish <all nonformal>

unemotional ADJS **unfeeling,** emotionless, affectless, emotionally dead *or* numb *or* paralyzed, anesthetized, drugged, narcotized; passionless, **spiritless,** heartless, soulless; **unresponsive,** unresponding, unsympathetic; **impassive,** impassible; immovable, untouchable; **inexcitable**

unemployed ADJS **idle,** fallow, otiose; **unoccupied,** disengaged, *désœuvré* <Fr>, **jobless,** out of work, out of a job, out of harness; free, available, at liberty, at leisure; at loose ends

unending ADJS **incessant,** constant, steady, stable, **ceaseless,** unceasing, **endless,** never-ending, **interminable,** perennial, without end

unenlightened ADJS **ignorant,** nescient, unknowing, uncomprehending, **know-nothing; ill-informed,** uninformed, unilluminated, unapprized, unposted <nonformal>, clueless <Brit nonformal>; **unacquainted,** unconversant, unversed, uninitiated, **unfamiliar,** strange to

unequaled ADJS **peerless,** matchless, champion; unmatched, unmatchable, unrivaled, unparalleled, immortal, never-to-be-equaled, unapproached, unapproachable, unsurpassed, unexcelled; unsurpassable; inimitable, **incomparable,** beyond compare *or* comparison, **unique;** without equal *or* parallel, *sans pareil* <Fr>; in a class by itself, *sui generis* <L>

unequivocal ADJS **certain,** sure, sure-enough <nonformal>; **positive,** absolute, definite, perfectly sure, apodictic; decisive, conclusive; clear, clear as day, clear and distinct, unmistakable, unambiguous, univocal

unessential ADJS inessential *or* nonessential, unnecessary, nonvital, superfluous; **accessory,** extra, collateral, auxiliary, supernumerary; adventitious, appurtenant, adscititious; **additional,** supplementary, supplemental, superadded, supervenient, make-weight; **accidental,** chance, fortuitous, casual, aleatory; extraneous, extrinsic; incidental, parenthetical

unethical ADJS **unconscientious,** unconscienced, conscienceless, unconscionable, shameless, without shame *or* remorse, **unscrupulous,** unprincipled, immoral, unmoral, amoral, nonmoral; **corrupt,** corrupted, rotten

uneven ADJS **unbalanced,** discriminatory, uneven; **inconstant,** unsteady, rough, unequal, uncertain, unsettled; **variable,** deviative, heteroclite; **capricious,** erratic, off-again-on-again, eccentric; **incomplete,** unfinished, partial, patchy, sketchy, unthorough; makeshift

uneventful ADJS **uninteresting,** unexciting; uninspiring; **tedious,** monotonous, humdrum, invariable; **dreary,** dry-as-dust, **dull**

unexceptional ADJS **ordinary,** average, normal, **common,** commonplace, garden *and* garden-variety <both nonformal>, run-of-the-mine *or* -mill; **unremarkable,** unnoteworthy, unspectacular, nothing *or* nobody special *and* no great shakes <all nonformal>, no prize package, no brain surgeon, no rocket scientist

unexpected ADJS **unanticipated,** unlooked for, unhoped for, unprepared for, undivined, unguessed, unpredicted, **unforeseen;** unforeseeable, unpredictable, off-the-wall <nonformal>; **improbable**; contrary to expectation, beyond *or* past expectation, more than expected, more than one bargained for; out of the blue, out of left field *and* from out in left field <both nonformal>; without warning, unheralded, unannounced; sudden

unexplained ADJS unascertained; uninvestigated, unexplored; undiscovered, untraced, untracked; unaccounted for, unsolved

unexplored ADJS **unexamined,** unstudied, unconsidered, unsearched, unscanned, unweighed, unsifted, uninvestigated, unindagated, unconned

unfailing ADJS **persevering,** unrelenting; **unrelaxing,** untiring, unwearying, unflagging, never-tiring, **tireless,** weariless, **indefatigable,** unwearied, unsleeping; undrooping, unnodding, unwinking, sleepless; undiscouraged, undaunted, indomitable, unconquerable, steadfast, invincible, game to the last *or* to the end; **patient,** patient as Job

unfair ADJS not fair; **unsporting,** unsportsmanly, unsportsmanlike, not done, not kosher <nonformal>, not cricket <Brit nonformal>; **dirty** <nonformal>, foul, below the belt

unfaithful ADJS faithless, of bad faith, trothless; **inconstant,** unsteadfast, fickle; **disloyal,** unloyal; false, **untrue,** not true to; disaffected, recreant, derelict, barratrous

unfamiliar ADJS **novel,** original, unique, different; strange, unusual; unheard-of; **first,** first ever; **uncustomary,** unwonted, **uncommon,** atypic *or* atypical, *recherché* <Fr>; **out of the ordinary,** out of this world, out-of-the-way, off the beaten track, offbeat; uninitiated, strange, strange to

unfashionable ADJS **old-fashioned,** old-fangled, **dated,** out, out-of-date, outdated, **outmoded,** out of style *or* fashion, out of use, disused, out of season, styleless, **behind the times,** of the old school, old hat *and* back-number *and* has-been <all nonformal>

unfavorable ADJS **unpropitious,** unpromising, unfortunate, unlucky; untoward, dire, baleful, baneful, **ill-fated,** ill-starred, evil-starred, star-crossed; **adverse,** detrimental

unfeeling ADJS **unemotional,** nonemotional, emotionless, affectless, emotionally dead *or* numb *or* paralyzed, anesthetized, drugged, narcotized; **unpassionate,** dispassionate, unimpassioned, **objective;** passionless, **spiritless,** heartless, soulless; **unaffectionate,** unloving; **unresponsive,** unresponding, unsympathetic; **impassive,** immovable, untouchable; **callous,** obdurate, indurated; **unmerciful**

unfinished ADJS **undeveloped,** unlicked, unformed; unfashioned, unwrought, unlabored, unworked, unprocessed, untreated; **underdeveloped;** backward, arrested, stunted; **crude,** rude, coarse, unpolished, unrefined; uncultivated, uncultured; rough, roughcast, rough-hewn, **in the rough**

unfit VERBS 1 **disable,** disenable, **incapacitate,** drain, de-energize; enfeeble, debilitate, weaken; cripple, maim, lame, hamstring, knee-cap, defang, pull the teeth of <nonformal>; wing, clip the wings of; **put out of order,** put out of commission <nonformal>, throw out of gear; bugger *and* bugger up *and* queer *and* queer the works *and* gum up *or* screw up <all nonformal>

ADJS 2 **incompetent,** incapable, unable, inadequate, unequipped, unqualified, ill-qualified, out of one's depth, outmatched, **unfitted,** unadapted, not equal *or* up to, not cut out for <nonformal>; ineffective, **ineffectual;** unadjusted, maladjusted

unflappable ADJS **inexcitable,** imperturbable, undisturbable; **unirritable,** steady; stoic, stoical; **even-tempered;** impassive, stolid; unshaken, not to be shaken, undeflectable, **well-balanced;** unshakable, **cool** <nonformal>, without nerves, without a nerve in one's body, unflinching

unflattering ADJS unexaggerated, undistorted; unvarnished, uncolored, unqualified

unflinching ADJS **unhesitating,** unhesitant, **unfaltering,** unshrinking; unquailing, uncringing, unwincing, unblinking; without nerves, without a nerve in one's body

unfold VERBS **unclose,** unwrap, unroll, open; **uncover,** uncase, unsheathe, unveil, undrape, uncurtain; **disclose,** expose, reveal, bare, take the lid off, **manifest,** show, exhibit, demonstrate, display, breathe, develop; **amplify,** expatiate, dilate, expand, enlarge, **enlarge on,** expand on, elaborate; **develop,** open out, fill in, flesh out, evolve, work out, explicate

unforeseen ADJS **unexpected,** unanticipated, unlooked for, unhoped for, unprepared for, undivined, unguessed, unpredicted; contrary to expectation, beyond *or* past expectation, more than one bargained for; out of the blue, without warning, unheralded, unannounced

unforgettable ADJS **never to be forgotten,** never to be erased from the mind, **indelible,** indelibly impressed on the mind, fixed in the mind; haunting, persistent, recurrent, nagging, plaguing, rankling, festering; obsessing, obsessive; **memorable,** striking, telling, salient

unforgivable ADJS **unjustifiable,** unwarrantable, unallowable, unreasonable, indefensible; **inexcusable,** unconscionable, **unpardonable,** inexpiable, irremissible

unfortunate ADJS **unlucky,** unprovidential, unblessed, **unprosperous,** sad, unhappy, hapless, fortuneless, misfortuned, luckless; **out of luck,** short of luck; **down on one's luck** <nonformal>, badly *or* ill off, down in the world, in adverse circumstances; ill-starred, evil-starred, born under an evil star, star-crossed

unfounded ADJS **baseless,** groundless, ungrounded, **without foundation,** not well-founded, built on sand, **unsupported,** unsustained, without basis *or* sound basis; **untenable,** unsupportable, unsustainable; **unwarranted,** idle, empty, vain

unfriendly ADJS **inimical,** unamicable; uncordial, unamiable, ungenial, incompatible; cool, cold, chill, chilly, frosty, icy; inhospitable; unsociable

unfurl VERBS unfold, unroll, unwind, unreel, uncoil, reveal, reveal *or* expose gradually

ungainly ADJS uncouth, **ungraceful,** graceless, inelegant, *gauche* <Fr>; **gawky,** gawkish; clumsy, clunky <nonformal>

unglued ADJS **unnerved,** unmanned, unstrung, undone, reduced to jelly, **demoralized,** shaken, upset, dashed, stricken, **crushed;** neurasthenic, prostrate, prostrated, overcome

ungodly ADJS 1 godless, **irreligious,** unrighteous, unholy, unsaintly, unangelic, unangelical; impious; **wicked,** sinful, **execrable,** damnable

2 **mind-boggling,** preposterous, absurd, ridiculous, unearthly

ungrateful ADJS **unthankful,** unthanking,

thankless, unappreciative, unappreciatory, unmindful, unrecognizing

unhappy ADJS **uncheerful,** uncheery, **cheerless,** joyless, unjoyful, unsmiling; mirthless, unmirthful, humorless; funny as a crutch <nonformal>; **grim;** out of humor, out of sorts, in bad humor *or* spirits; **sorry,** sorryish; discontented; **wretched,** miserable; unpropitious; infelicitous

unhealthy ADJS in poor health; **infirm,** unsound, invalid, valetudinary, valetudinarian, debilitated, cachectic, enervated, exhausted, drained; **sickly,** peaked <nonformal>; **feeble,** frail; weakened, with low resistance, **run-down,** reduced in health; **unwholesome,** unsound, morbid, diseased, pathological

unheard-of ADJS **unrenowned,** renownless, nameless, inglorious, **unnotable,** unnoted, unnoticed, unremarked, **undistinguished,** unfamed, uncelebrated, unsung, unhonored, unglorified, unpopular; little known, obscure, *ignotus* <L>

uniform NOUNS 1 **livery,** mantle, outfit, dress, monkey suit <nonformal>
ADJS 2 **equable,** equal, **even; level,** flat, smooth; **regular,** constant, steadfast, persistent, continuous; **unvarying,** undeviating, unchanging, steady, stable; cloned *or* clonish *and* cookie-cutter <all nonformal>; **consistent,** consonant, correspondent, accordant, homogeneous, **alike,** all of a piece, monolithic

unify VERBS reduce to unity, unitize, make one; **integrate,** unite, bond, link, yoke

unimpeachable ADJS **faultless,** flawless, impeccable, reliable, unexceptionable; **believable,** credible

unimportant ADJS **of no importance,** of little *or* small importance, of no great importance, **of no account,** of no significance, of no concern, of no matter, of little *or* no consequence, no great shakes <nonformal>; **inferior,** secondary, of a low order of importance, low-priority, expendable; marginal

unimpressed ADJS **unaffected,** unmoved, untouched, dry-eyed, **unstirred,** unruffled, unanimated, uninspired

unimpressive ADJS **insignificant**, inconsequential, immaterial; unnoteworthy; **inconsiderable,** inappreciable, negligible

uninformed ADJS **unsuspecting,** unaware, unwarned, unforewarned, unadvised, unadmonished; off one's guard; **ill-informed,** unenlightened, unilluminated, unapprized, unposted <nonformal>

uninhabitable ADJS **unhabitable,** nonhabitable, unoccupiable, untenantable, **unlivable,** unfit to live in, not fit for man or beast

uninhibited ADJS **unsuppressed,** unrepressed, unreserved, exuberant; **uncurbed,** unchecked, unbridled, unmuzzled; **unreined,** uncontrolled, **unruly;** out of control, out of hand; **abandoned,** intemperate, immoderate, **incontinent,** licentious, loose, wanton, rampant, riotous, wild; irrepressible

uninspired ADJS **unaffected,** unmoved, untouched, dry-eyed, unimpressed, unstruck, **unstirred,** unruffled, unanimated; arid, barren, infertile, infecund; **unoriginal,** undaring, unaspiring, uninventive

uninterrupted ADJS **continuous,** continued, **continual,** continuing; **unintermittent,** unintermitted, featureless, unrelieved, monotonous; **connected, joined**, linked, chained, concatenated, catenated, articulated; unremitting, **incessant,** constant, steady, stable, **ceaseless,** unceasing, **endless,** unending, never-ending, **interminable,** perennial

uninvolved ADJS **uncomplicated,** straightforward; **uninquisitive,** uninquiring; bored; inattentive; **uninterested,** unconcerned, **indifferent,** apathetic, passive, impassive, stolid, phlegmatic, listless; aloof, detached, distant, withdrawn, reclusive, sequestered, eremitic

union NOUNS 1 **affiliation,** alliance, allying, alignment, association, consociation, combination, unification, **coalition,** fusion, merger, coalescence, amalgamation, **league,** federation, confederation, confederacy, consolidation, incorporation, inclusion, integration; labor union; hookup *and* tie-up *and* tie-in <all nonformal>
2 **joint,** join, joining, **juncture, connection,** link, connecting link, **coupling,** interface

unique ADJS inimitable, **incomparable,** beyond compare *or* comparison, *sui generis* <L>; **novel,** original, different; strange, unusual, uncommon; unfamiliar, unheard-of; **first,** first ever, **sole,** singular, absolute, unrepeated, **alone,** lone, **only,** only-begotten, **one and only,** first and last

unit NOUNS **individual,** single, integer, entity, singleton, **item,** article, point, module

unite VERBS **converge,** come together, approach, run together, **meet,** connect, merge; fall in with, link up with; **join,** band, league, **associate,** affiliate, ally, **combine,** fuse, coalesce, amalgamate, federate, confederate, consolidate; hook up *and* tie up *and* tie in <all nonformal>; **close ranks,** make common cause, throw in together <nonformal>, unite efforts, join in; **integrate,** form a unity

United States of America NOUNS **United States,** US, USA, US of A <nonformal>, **America,** Columbia, the States, Uncle Sugar *and* Yankeeland <both nonformal>, Land of Liberty, the melting pot

unity NOUNS **oneness,** homogeneity, consubstantiality; **completeness,** totality; wholeness, entireness, **entirety; integrity,** integrality, undividedness, intactness, untouchedness, unbrokenness; solidity, solidarity; **indivisibility,** inseparability, impartibility, infrangibility, cohesion, coherence

universal ADJS cosmic *or* cosmical, heaven-wide, galactic, planetary, worldwide, transnational, planet-wide, **global;** catholic, **all-inclusive,** all-including, **all-embracing,** all-encompassing, all-comprehensive, all-comprehending

universe NOUNS **world,** cosmos; creation, created universe, created nature, all, **all creation,** all tarnation <nonformal>, all *or* everything that is, all being, totality, totality of being, sum of things; wide world, whole wide world; **macrocosm; frame of reference,** intellectual *or* ideational frame of reference, framework, arena, world *or* universe of discourse, system, reference system

world without end
BIBLE

university NOUNS institution of higher education *or* learning, degree-granting institution; graduate school, postgraduate school; academe, academia, the groves of Academe, **the campus,** the halls of learning *or* ivy, ivied halls; alma mater

unjust ADJS **inequitable,** unequitable, iniquitous, **unbalanced,** discriminatory, uneven, unequal; **wrong,** wrongful, unrightful; **undue,** unmeet, undeserved, unmerited

unkempt ADJS **unrefined,** unpolished, uncouth, uncombed, unlicked; **untidy,** unsightly, unneat, slobby *and* scuzzy <both nonformal>, **messy** <nonformal>

unkind ADJS **unkindly,** ill; **unbenign,** unbenignant; **unamiable,** disagreeable, **uncordial,** ungracious, inhospitable, **ungenial,** unaffectionate, unloving; **unsympathetic,** unsympathizing, uncompassionate, uncompassioned; malevolent

unknown ADJS unbeknown <nonformal>, **unheard-of,** unapprehended, unapparent, unperceived, unsuspected; uninvestigated, unexplored; unidentified, unclassified, uncharted, unfathomed, unplumbed, virgin, untouched; **undisclosed,** unrevealed, undivulged, undiscovered, unexposed, sealed; **unfamiliar,** strange

unlawful ADJS **illegal,** illegitimate, illicit, nonlicit, nonlegal, lawless, wrongful, fraudulent, creative <nonformal>, **against the law; unauthorized,** unallowed, impermissible, unwarranted, unwarrantable, unofficial; **criminal,** felonious; outlaw, outlawed

unlike ADJS **dissimilar,** unsimilar, unresembling, unresemblant; unidentical; **disparate,** diverse, divergent, **contrasting,** different; nonuniform; scarcely like, hardly like, a bit *or* mite different; **incomparable,** incommensurable, not to be compared, of different orders; apples and oranges

unlikely ADJS **improbable,** unpromising, hardly possible, logic-defying, scarcely to be expected *or* anticipated; statistically improbable; **doubtful,** dubious, **questionable,** dubitable, more than doubtful; **implausible,** incredible; unlooked-for, unexpected, unpredictable

unlimited ADJS **unrestricted,** unconfined, uncircumscribed, unbound <old>, unbounded, unmeasured; limitless, illimitable; unqualified, unconditioned, **unconditional,** without strings, no strings, no strings attached; open-ended, open, **wide-open** <nonformal>; decontrolled, deregulated; **infinite,** boundless, unbounded, undefined, omnipresent, ubiquitous

unlivable ADJS unhabitable, **uninhabitable,** nonhabitable, unoccupiable, untenantable, **unfit to live in,** not fit for man or beast

unload VERBS off-load, unlade, unpack, disburden, unburden, **discharge,** dump; **disembarrass,** disencumber, relieve, disburden, unhamper, get out from under; throw on the market, **liquidate**

unlock VERBS **explain,** decipher, crack, find the key to, unravel, read between the lines, read into, solve; **get to the bottom** *or* **heart of,** fathom, plumb; **unlatch,** unbolt, unbar

unloved ADJS unbeloved, uncherished, loveless; **lovelorn,** forsaken, **rejected,** jilted, thrown over <nonformal>, spurned, crossed in love

unlucky ADJS **unfortunate,** unprovidential, unblessed, **unprosperous,** sad, unhappy, hapless, fortuneless, misfortuned, luckless; **out of luck,** short of luck; **down on one's luck** <nonformal>, badly *or* ill off, down in the world, in adverse circumstances; ill-starred, evil-starred, born under a bad sign, star-crossed; **in a jam** *and* in a pickle *or* pretty pickle *and* in a tight spot *and* between a rock and a hard place <all nonformal>, between the devil and the deep blue sea; up a tree *and* up the creek *or* up shit creek without a paddle *and* up to one's ass in alligators <all nonformal>

unmanageable ADJS **unwieldy,** unhandy; inconvenient, impractical; **awkward,** clumsy, cumbersome, unmaneuverable; contrary, perverse, crosswise; ponderous, bulky, hulky, hulking

unmarked ADJS **unheeded,** unobserved, unnoticed, unnoted, unperceived, unseen, undiscerned, undescried, unremarked, unregarded, unminded, unconsidered, unthought-of, unmissed; **unmarred,** unscarred, unscratched, undefaced, unbruised; none the worse for wear

unmarried ADJS **unwedded,** unwed, single, sole, spouseless, wifeless, husbandless

unmentionable ADJS **indescribable,** ineffable, inexpressible, unutterable, unspeakable, undefinable, unnamable, unwhisperable; **atrocious,** monstrous

unmistakable ADJS **express,** explicit, not to be mistaken, open-and-shut <nonformal>; **unequivocal,** unambiguous, unconfused; **loud and clear** <nonformal>; **lucid,** pellucid, limpid

unnatural ADJS **heartless,** unfeeling, unresponsive, insensitive; **artificial,** insincere; **abnormal,** irregular, divergent, deviative, deviant, different, exceptional

unnecessary ADJS **unessential,** inessential *or* nonessential, nonvital, superfluous; **superfluous,** redundant; excess, in excess; expendable, dispensable, **needless,** unneeded, gratuitous, uncalled-for

unnerving ADJS **nerve-racking,** nerve-rending, nerve-shaking, nerve-jangling, nerve-trying, nerve-stretching; jarring, grating

unobtainable ADJS **inaccessible,** unattainable, unavailable, unprocurable, unsecurable; not to be had, **not to be had for love or money;** undiscoverable, unascertainable

unoccupied ADJS 1 **available,** open, free, unfilled, **uninhabited,** unpopulated, unpeopled, untaken, untenanted, tenantless, untended, unmanned, unstaffed; **deserted,** abandoned, forsaken, godforsaken <nonformal>
2 idle, free, open, spare; retired, semiretired

unofficial ADJS **unauthoritative,** unauthentic, nonofficial, apocryphal; **uncertified,** unverified, unchecked, unconfirmed, uncorroborated, unauthenticated, unvalidated, unattested, unwarranted

unopposed ADJS **unanimous,** solid, consentaneous, **with one voice;** uncontradicted, unchallenged, uncontroverted, uncontested, carried by acclamation

unorganized ADJS amorphous, **chaotic,** orderless, disorderly, unordered, confused, anarchic; **unarranged,** haphazard; makeshift, rough-and-ready, **extemporaneous,** extemporized, improvised, ad-lib *and* off the top of one's head <both nonformal>; **random,** entropic, unarranged, ungraded, unsorted, unclassified

unorthodox ADJS nonorthodox, **heterodox,** heretical; **unauthoritative,** unauthentic, unaccepted, unreceived, unapproved; **nonconformist,** individualistic, inner-directed, perverse; **unconventional,** eccentric, original, maverick, Bohemian

unpardonable ADJS **inexcusable,** unconscionable, **unforgivable,** inexpiable, irremissible; shameful, disgraceful, scandalous, **infamous,** improper, reprehensible, blamable, blameworthy, unworthy

unplanned ADJS **unintentional,** unintended, **unmeant,** undesigned, unpurposed, unthought-of; **unpremeditated,** unprompted, unguided, unguarded; **unwitting,** unthinking, unconscious, involuntary

unpleasant ADJS **unpleasing,** unenjoyable; displeasing, disagreeable; unlikable, dislikable; **abrasive,** wounding, hostile, unfriendly; unwelcome, thankless; **distasteful,** uncongenial; **not to one's taste,** against the grain, uninviting; unlovable; **abhorrent,** odious; **intolerable**

unpopular ADJS **disliked,** out of favor, gone begging; **unappreciated,** misunderstood; unsung, thankless; **undistinguished,** unfamed, uncelebrated, unsung, unhonored; **unknown,** little known, obscure, unheard-of, *ignotus* <L>

unprecedented ADJS **original,** novel; unique, *sui generis* <L>; new, fresh; underived, firsthand; **unimitated,** uncopied, **unduplicated,** unparalleled, unreproduced, unexampled; **archetypal,** archetypical, archetypic, prototypal

unpredictable ADJS **unexpected,** unanticipated, unlooked for, unhoped for, unprepared for, unpredicted, **unforeseen;** unforeseeable, off-the-wall <nonformal>; out of the blue, dropped from the clouds; incalculable, uncountable, unreckonable, unaccountable, undivinable; **fickle,** capricious, whimsical, **erratic,** variable

unprejudiced ADJS **unbiased,** unprepossessed, unjaundiced; impartial, evenhanded, **fair,** just, equitable, **objective,** dispassionate, impersonal, detached, disinterested

unprepared ADJS **unsuspecting,** unaware, uninformed, unwarned, unforewarned, unadvised, unadmonished; unready, off one's guard; **unskilled,** unaccomplished, untrained, untaught, unschooled, untutored, uncoached, unimproved, uninitiated, unprimed, unfinished, unpolished

unpretentious ADJS **modest,** meek; humble; unpretending, **unassuming,** unpresuming, unpresumptuous, **unostentatious,** unobtrusive, unimposing, unboastful; unambitious, unaspiring; **unaffected,** genuine, inartificial, unartificial, unadorned, unvarnished, unembellished

unprincipled ADJS **dishonest,** dishonorable; unconscionable, shameless, **unscrupulous,** unethical, immoral, amoral; **corrupt,** corrupted, rotten

unprintable ADJS **obscene,** foul, filthy, nasty, vile, fulsome, offensive, unrepeatable, not fit for mixed company; scurrilous, scurrile, fescennine

unproductive ADJS nonproductive *or* nonproducing; **infertile,** sterile, unfertile, **unfruitful,** unfructuous, infecund, unprolific; **barren,** arid, dry, dried-up, sere, exhausted, drained, leached, sucked dry, wasted, gaunt, **waste,** desolate, jejune

unprofessional ADJS **amateurish,** unbusinesslike, semiskilled

unprofitable ADJS **fruitless,** gainless, profitless, bootless, otiose, unremunerative, nonremunerative; **unrewarding,** worthless, useless; sterile, futile, unproductive

unprovoked ADJS **undeserved,** unmerited, unearned; **unwarranted,** unjustified; preposterous, outrageous

unpublished ADJS **unmentioned,** untalked-of, **untold,** unsung, unproclaimed; unwritten, unrecorded

unqualified ADJS 1 **incapable,** incompetent, inefficient, ineffective; inept, unendowed, ungifted, untalented, **unfit,** unfitted; disqualified

2 **unmitigated,** unrelieved, unspoiled, undeniable, unquestionable, unequivocal, unvarnished, uncolored; **flagrant,** arrant, shocking, shattering, egregious, intolerable, unbearable, unconscionable; total, utter

3 <nonformal> **no ifs, ands, or buts; no strings attached,** no holds barred, no catch *or* joker *or* kicker, no joker in the deck, no small print *or* fine print, no fine print at the bottom; downright, that's that, what you see is what you get

unquestionable ADJS **unmitigated,** unqualified, unrelieved, unspoiled, undeniable, unequivocal; **inalienable,** unalienable, uninfringeable, unchallengeable, unimpeachable, unexceptionable; **obvious,** patent, self-evident, axiomatic; **certain,** undoubted, categorically true

unravel VERBS **disentangle,** untangle, **unscramble,** unsnarl, unknot, untwist, unbraid, unweave, untwine, unwind, uncoil, unthread, ravel; **unclutter,** clarify, clear up, disambiguate, sort out, get to the core *or* nub *or* essence; **solve, resolve,** find the solution *or* answer, **clear up,** work out, find out, figure out, dope *and* dope out <both nonformal>

unreadable ADJS **illegible,** unclear; undecipherable, indecipherable

unready ADJS **unprepared,** unprimed; surprised, caught short, caught napping, caught with one's pants down <nonformal>, taken by surprise, taken aback, taken unawares, blindsided <nonformal>, caught off balance, caught off base <nonformal>, tripped up

unreal ADJS unrealistic, unactual, not real; merely nominal; immaterial; unsubstantial; **imaginary,** imagined, fantastic, fanciful, fancied; illusory

unrealistic ADJS **visionary,** idealistic, quixotic; romantic, romanticized, romancing, romanticizing; **impractical,** unpractical, starry-eyed, dewy-eyed; in the clouds, with one's head in the clouds

unreasonable ADJS 1 **capricious,** whimsical; **arbitrary,** motiveless; **moody,** temperamental, petulant; **unjustifiable,** unwarrantable, unallowable, indefensible; **inexcusable,** unconscionable; **unsound,** unsensible, senseless, insensate, reasonless, **irrational,** reckless, inadvisable

2 **overpriced,** grossly overpriced, **exorbitant,** excessive, extravagant, inordinate, immoderate, undue, unwarranted

unrecognizable ADJS **indistinct,** unclear, **indefinite,** undefined, ill-defined, ill-marked, **faint,** pale, feeble, weak, **dim,** dark, **shadowy,** vague, obscure, indistinguishable

unrelated ADJS **unconnected,** unallied, unlinked, **unassociated,** unaffiliated *or* disaffiliated; disrelated, disconnected, dissociated, detached, discrete, disjunct, removed, **separated,** segregated, apart, other, independent, marked off, bracketed; **foreign,** alien, strange, exotic, outlandish; extraneous

unrelenting ADJS **unyielding,** unbending, inflexible, hard, hard-line, inelastic, impliable, ungiving, **firm,** stiff, rigid, rigorous, stuffy; **unalterable,** unchangeable, immutable; **uncompromising,** intransigent, irreconcilable, hard-shell *and* hard-core <both nonformal>; implacable, inexorable, **relentless**

unreliable ADJS **undependable,** untrustworthy, unfaithworthy, treacherous, **unsure,** not to be depended *or* relied on; **insecure,** unsound, infirm, unsolid, **unstable,** unsubstantial, insubstantial, **unsteadfast,** unsteady, desultory, shaky; **precarious,** hazardous, dangerous, perilous, risky, ticklish; **unauthentic** *or* **inauthentic,** unauthoritative

unresolved ADJS **remaining,** outstanding, unmet; **irresolute,** irresolved, **undecided,** indecisive, undetermined, unsettled, at loose ends; changeable, mutable; capricious, mercurial, fickle

unresponsive ADJS **unfeeling,** emotionless, affectless, emotionally dead *or* numb *or* paralyzed, anesthetized, drugged, narcotized; **coldhearted,** cold-blooded, cold as charity; **unaffectionate,** unloving; unresponding, **unsympathetic; impassive,** dull, obtuse; **heartless,** unnatural, insensitive; **uninfluenceable,** unswayable, unmovable

unrest NOUNS **agitation,** perturbation, **malaise,** unease, restlessness; **disquiet,** disquietude, inquietude, discomposure; **turmoil,** turbulence, **disorder**

unripe ADJS **immature,** underripe, unripened, impubic, **raw, green,** callow, wet behind the ears, cub, cubbish, unfledged, fledgling, unseasoned, unmellowed

unruly ADJS **disorderly,** obstreperous; **unbridled;** restive, riotous, fractious, out of control, wild, rampant

unsafe ADJS unhealthy <nonformal>; **unreliable,** undependable, untrustworthy, treacherous, **insecure,** unsound, unstable, unsteady, shaky, tottery, rocky

unsaid ADJS **tacit,** wordless, unspoken, unuttered, unexpressed; **implicit**

unsanitary ADJS **unhealthful,** unhealthy, insalubrious, unsalutary, unwholesome, peccant, bad, **bad for;** noxious, noisome, injurious, baneful, harmful; **polluted,** contaminated, tainted, foul, septic; unhygienic, insanitary; morbific, pathogenic, pestiferous

unsatisfactory ADJS **unsatisfying,** ungratifying, unfulfilling; **displeasing**; disappointing, disheartening, not up to expectation, not good enough; **inadequate,** incommensurate, insufficient

unsavory ADJS 1 **unpalatable,** unappetizing, untasteful, untasty, ill-flavored, foul-tasting, **distasteful,** dislikable, unlikable, uninviting, unpleasant, unpleasing, displeasing, disagreeable
2 **disreputable,** discreditable, dishonorable, shady, **seamy,** sordid

unscrupulous ADJS 1 **unmeticulous,** unexacting, unpainstaking, unrigorous, **unconscientious,** unpunctilious, unpunctual, **unparticular,** unfussy, unfinical, uncritical
2 **dishonest,** dishonorable; conscienceless, unconscionable, shameless, without shame *or* remorse, **unprincipled,** unethical, immoral, amoral; **corrupt,** corrupted, rotten

unseat VERBS **dislodge,** unplace; evict; depose, unsaddle

unseemly ADJS **indecent,** indelicate, inelegant, indecorous, improper, inappropriate, **unbecoming,** indiscreet

unseen ADJS **unheeded,** unobserved, unnoticed, unnoted, undetected, unperceived, undiscerned, undescried, unmarked, unremarked, unregarded, unspied, unminded, unconsidered

unsightly ADJS **ugly,** unattractive, unhandsome, unpretty, unlovely, uncomely, **inelegant; disfigured,** defaced, blotted, blemished, marred, spoiled

unskilled ADJS **unaccomplished,** untrained, untaught, unschooled, untutored, uncoached, unimproved, uninitiated, **unprepared,** unprimed, unfinished, unpolished; **untalented,** ungifted, unendowed; amateurish, unprofessional, unbusinesslike

unsophisticated ADJS **artless,** simple, plain, **guideless;** simplehearted, simpleminded; **ingenuous,** *ingénu* <Fr>; **naive,** childlike, born yesterday; **innocent;** trustful, trusting, unguarded, unwary, unreserved, confiding, unsuspicious; **uncomplex,** uncomplicated, uncorrupted

unsound ADJS **infirm,** unfirm, **unstable,** unsubstantial, unsturdy, unsolid, decrepit, crumbling, fragmented, fragmentary, disintegrating; rotten, rotten at *or* rotten to the core; **unwholesome,** unhealthy, morbid, diseased, pathological; **insolvent,** indebted; **unreasonable,** unsensible, senseless, insensate, reasonless, **irrational,** reckless, inadvisable

unsparing ADJS **harsh,** severe, **stringent,** astringent, hard, stern, dour, grim, inclement; **unremitting,** relentless, zealous, ardent, fervent, vehement; **unstinting,** stintless, unstinted

unspeakable ADJS **indescribable,** ineffable, inenarrable, inexpressible, unutterable, noncommunicable, incommunicable, indefinable, undefinable, unnamable, unwhisperable, unmentionable; execrable, damnable; disgraceful, scandalous, **infamous,** unpardonable, unforgivable

unspoiled ADJS **natural,** naturelike, native; in the state of nature; primitive, primal, pristine, untainted, uncontaminated; **unaffected,** unassuming, unpretending, unpretentious, unfeigning, undisguising, undissimulating, undissembling, undesigning; **intact,** untouched, undamaged, all in one piece <nonformal>, unimpaired, virgin

unspoken ADJS **tacit,** wordless, unuttered, unexpressed, unsaid; **implicit**

unsportsmanlike ADJS **unfair,** not fair; **unsporting,** unsportsmanly, not done, not kosher <nonformal>, not cricket <Brit nonformal>; **dirty** <nonformal>, foul, below the belt

unstable ADJS **unsound,** infirm, **unsubstantial,** unsturdy, unsolid, decrepit, crumbling, fragmented, fragmentary, disintegrating; changeable, **mutable,** inconstant; **insecure,** unsound, insubstantial, **unsteadfast,** unsteady, desultory, shaky

unsteady ADJS 1 **shaky,** rickety, spindly, spidery, teetering, teetery, tottery, tottering, doddering, tumbledown, ramshackle, dilapidated, rocky <nonformal>, unstable; groggy, wobbly, staggery
2 **inconstant,** uneven, unrhythmical, unmetrical, rough, unequal, uncertain, unsettled; **variable,** deviative, heteroclite; **capricious,** erratic, off-again-on-again, eccentric

unsuccessful ADJS successless, failing; failed, *manqué* <Fr>; unfortunate; fruitless, bootless, no-win <nonformal>, futile, useless; lame, **ineffectual,** ineffective, inefficacious, of no effect; malfunctioning

unsuitable ADJS **unacceptable,** inadmissible, undesirable, unfit, **objectionable,** exceptionable, impossible, untenable, indefensible; intolerable; improper, **unbecoming,** unseemly

unsung ADJS **unexpressed,** unpronounced, **unsaid, unspoken, unuttered,** undeclared, unbreathed, unvoiced, wordless, silent; **unmentioned,** untalked-of, **untold,** unproclaimed, unpublished; unwritten, unrecorded; **unrenowned,** nameless, inglorious, **unnotable,** unnoticed, unremarked, **undistinguished,** uncelebrated, unhonored, unglorified, unpopular

unsure ADJS **uncertain,** doubting, agnostic, **skeptical,** unconvinced, unpersuaded; **unconfident,** unassured, insecure, unsure of oneself; unself-confident, unself-assured, unself-reliant

unsurpassed ADJS **best,** very best, greatest *and* top-of-the-line <both nonformal>, **prime,** optimum, optimal; **supreme,** paramount, surpassing, unparalleled, unmatched, unmatchable, matchless, **peerless;** quintessential

unsuspecting ADJS **unaware,** unconscious, insensible, unknowing, incognizant; **unmindful,** unwitting, **trusting,** trustful, **confiding,** unsuspicious, without suspicion; credulous; unwarned

unsymmetrical ADJS unsymmetric, **asymmetric,** asymmetrical, nonsymmetric, nonsymmetrical; **irregular,** deviative, anamorphous; ununiform *or* **nonuniform,** disproportionate, misshapen

unsympathetic ADJS uncompassionate; unconcerned, unsolicitous, non-caring; **unperceptive,** imperceptive, impercipient, blind; **unfeeling,** apathetic, affectless; callous; **unresponsive,** unresponding, unsympathizing, **uncompassionate,** uncompassioned

untalented ADJS **unqualified,** inept, unendowed, ungifted, **unfit,** unfitted; **amateurish,** unprofessional

untangle VERBS **extricate,** free, release, clear, get out; **disengage,** disentangle, unsnarl, unravel, disentwine, disinvolve, unknot, disembarrass, disembroil; **solve,** resolve, find the solution *or* answer, **work out,** figure out, dope *and* dope out <both nonformal>; **unriddle,** unscramble, untwist, unspin, unweave; **decipher,** decode, decrypt, crack

untenable ADJS **unacceptable,** inadmissible, unsuitable, undesirable, **objectionable,** exceptionable, impossible, indefensible; **unsupportable,** unsustainable

unthinkable ADJS **unbelievable,** incredible, **implausible,** unimaginable, inconceivable, not to be believed, **hard to believe,** hard of belief, beyond belief, unworthy of belief, not meriting *or* not deserving belief, tall <nonformal>; **defying belief,** staggering belief, passing belief

untidy ADJS **slovenly,** slipshod, careless, loose, slack, nonformal, negligent; **unsightly,** unneat, unkempt; **messy** <nonformal>, sloppy <nonformal>, scraggly, poky, seedy <nonformal>, **shabby,** shoddy, schlocky <nonformal>, lumpen, chintzy, grubby <nonformal>, **frowzy,** blowzy, tacky <nonformal>

untimely ADJS **unseasonable,** inopportune, ill-timed, ill-seasoned, mistimed, unripe, unready, ill-considered, too late *or* soon, out of phase *or* time *or* sync; **inconvenient,** unhandy; **inappropriate,** irrelevant, improper, out of line, off-base, unsuitable, **inexpedient,** unfitting, unbefitting, untoward, malapropos, *mal à propos* <Fr>, intrusive

untoward ADJS **adverse,** detrimental, unfavorable; sinister; hostile, antagonistic, inimical; contrary, counter, counteractive, conflicting, opposing, opposed, opposite, in opposition; **difficult,** troublesome, troublous, hard, trying, rigorous, stressful

untried ADJS **unproved,** not proved, unproven, **undemonstrated,** unshown, not shown; untested

untrue ADJS **unfaithful,** faithless, of bad faith, trothless; **inconstant,** unsteadfast, fickle; **disloyal,** unloyal; false, not true to; **erroneous,** not true, **not right**

unusable ADJS **unserviceable,** unemployable, inoperative, inoperable, unworkable; out of order, out of whack *and* on the blink *and* on the fritz <all nonformal>, in disrepair; inapplicable; unsuitable, unfit; functionless, nonfunctional, otiose

unused ADJS unutilized, **unemployed,** unapplied, unexercised; in abeyance, suspended; waived; **unspent,** unexpended, unconsumed; held back, held out, put by, put aside, saved, held in reserve, in hand, spare, to spare, extra, reserve; untapped; **new,** original, pristine, fresh, fresh off the assembly line, mint, in mint condition, factory-fresh

unusual ADJS unordinary, **uncustomary,** unwonted, **uncommon,** unfamiliar, atypical, *recherché* <Fr>; **rare,** out of the ordinary, out of this world, out-of-the-way, **off the beaten track,** offbeat, breakaway

unveil VERBS **uncover,** uncase, unsheathe, undrape, uncurtain; **disclose**, expose, reveal, bare, take the lid off, manifest, ventilate, take the wraps off, lift *or* draw the veil, raise the curtain, let daylight in, unshroud, unwrap

unwanted ADJS unwished, undesired; **unwelcome,** unasked, unbidden, uninvited, uncalled-for, unasked-for

unwarranted ADJS **baseless,** groundless, ungrounded, **unfounded,** ill-founded, unbased, **unsupported,** unsustained, **without foundation,** without basis *or* sound basis; **untenable,** unsupportable, unsustainable; idle, empty, vain

unwavering ADJS **confident,** sure, secure, **assured,** reassured, decided, determined; **convinced,** persuaded, positive, cocksure; **unhesitating,** unfaltering

unwelcome ADJS **unwanted,** unwished, undesired; **unagreeable,** undesirable, unacceptable; **uninvited,** unasked, unbidden, uncalled-for, unasked for

unwilling ADJS **disinclined,** indisposed, not in the mood, averse; unconsenting; dead set against, opposed; resistant; disobedient, recalcitrant, refractory, fractious, sullen, sulky, indocile, mutinous; **involuntary,** forced

unwind VERBS 1 **relax,** unbend, slack, slacken, **ease; ease up,** let up, slack up, slack off, **ease off,** let down, **slow down,** take it slow, take time to catch one's breath; lay back *and* kick back *and* decompress <all nonformal>
2 unfold, unroll, unfurl, unreel, uncoil, reveal, reveal *or* expose gradually

unwise ADJS injudicious, **imprudent,** unpolitic, impolitic, contraindicated, **counterproductive;** indiscreet; inconsiderate, thoughtless, mindless, witless, unthoughtful, unthinking, unreflecting, unreflective; **unreasonable,** unsound, unsensible, senseless, insensate, reasonless, **irrational,** reckless, inadvisable

unwitting ADJS **unintentional,** unintended, **unmeant,** unplanned, undesigned, unpurposed, unthought-of; **unpremeditated,** unmeditated, unprompted, unguided, unguarded; **unthinking,** unconscious, involuntary

unworkable ADJS **impracticable,** impractical, unpragmatic, unfeasible; unperformable, inoperable, undoable, unnegotiable, unbridgeable

unwritten ADJS **traditional; legendary,** oral, handed down; **customary,** conventional, understood, admitted, recognized, acknowledged, received; **hallowed,** time-honored, immemorial, long-established, established, fixed, inveterate, rooted; folk, of the folk, folkloric

upbeat ADJS **optimistic,** bright, sunny; cheerful; **rosy,** roseate, rose-colored, *couleur de rose* <Fr>

update VERBS **modernize,** streamline; **bring up to date,** keep *or* stay current, move with the times

upgrade VERBS **promote,** advance, boost <nonformal>, elevate, jump; kick *or* bump upstairs <nonformal>; **raise;** exalt, aggrandize

upheaval NOUNS **convulsion,** cataclysm, catastrophe, disaster; **revolution, break,** break with the past, sudden change, radical *or* revolutionary *or* violent *or* total change, catastrophic change, overthrow, **quantum jump** *or* **leap,** sea change; **uplift,** upcast, upthrust

uphill ADJS 1 **laborious,** toilsome, arduous, strenuous, painful, effortful, operose, troublesome, onerous, oppressive, burdensome; **heavy,** hefty <nonformal>, tough <nonformal>, **backbreaking,** grueling, punishing, crushing, killing, Herculean; hard-fought, hard-earned
ADVS 2 **slantingly,** slopingly, aslant, aslope, atilt, rakingly, tipsily, slantwise, on *or* at a slant; slaunchwise *and* slaunchways <both nonformal>; off plumb *or* the vertical; **upgrade**

uphold VERBS **buoy,** buoy up; **sustain,** hold up, bear up, upbear, uplift, upraise; **maintain,** support, **keep up,** keep alive; **defend,** offer *or* say in defense, allege in support *or* vindication, assert; **confirm,** affirm, **attest,** warrant, **substantiate,** authenticate, validate, certify, ratify, verify; **corroborate,** bear out, buttress, bolster

upkeep NOUNS **preservation,** conservation, saving, salvation, salvage, **keeping,** safekeeping, maintenance, support

uplift VERBS **elate,** exalt, elevate, lift; **buoy,** buoy up; **sustain,** hold up, bear up, uphold, upbear, upraise; raise, boost <nonformal>; **ennoble,** aggrandize, magnify, exalt to the skies

upper class NOUNS **upper classes,** aristocracy, patriciate, ruling class, ruling circles, elite, elect, the privileged, the classes, the better sort, upper circles, upper cut *and* upper crust *and* cream <all nonformal>, gentry, lords of creation; **high society,** high life, the Four Hundred, *haut monde* <Fr>

upper crust NOUNS **society,** fashionable society, **polite society,** high society, high life, *beau monde, haut monde* <both Fr>; **smart set** <nonformal>; the Four Hundred, upper cut <nonformal>; **cream of society,** *crème de la crème* <Fr>, elite, carriage trade; café society, jet set, beautiful people, in-crowd, the glitterati <nonformal>

upper hand NOUNS **advantage,** leg up *and* inside track *and* pole position <all nonformal>; whip hand; start, head *or* flying *or* running start; **edge,** bulge *and* jump *and* drop <all nonformal>, trump card

uppermost ADJS **paramount,** principal, leading, foremost, main, chief, number one <nonformal>, premier, **prime,** primary, preeminent, **supreme,** cardinal; highest, topmost, toprank, ranking, of the first rank, world-class, **dominant,** predominant, master, controlling

uppity ADJS **insolent,** insulting; **presumptuous,** presuming, overpresumptuous, overweening; **audacious,** bold, assured, hardy, bumptious; **contemptuous**, contumelious; **disdainful**, arrogant, uppish <nonformal>; forward, pushy <nonformal>, obtrusive, familiar

upright ADJS **honest,** uprighteous, **upstanding,** erect, right, **righteous,** virtuous, good, clean, squeaky-clean <nonformal>, **decent; honorable,** full of integrity, **reputable,** estimable, creditable, worthy, noble, sterling, manly, yeomanly; **respectable,** highly respectable; **ethical,** moral; principled, high-minded, right-minded; **erect**

uprising NOUNS **revolt,** rebellion, revolution, mutiny, insurrection, insurgence *or* insurgency, *émeute* <Fr>, rising, outbreak, general uprising, *levée en masse* <Fr>, **riot,** civil disorder

uproar NOUNS **commotion,** hubbub, Babel, tumult, turmoil, **racket,** riot, **disturbance,** rumpus <nonformal>, ruckus *and* ruction <both nonformal>, **fracas,** hassle, rampage

upscale ADJS **expensive,** dear, costly, **high-priced,** premium, at a premium, top; big ticket <nonformal>, **fancy** *and* stiff *and* steep <all nonformal>, pricey; upmarket, rich, sumptuous, executive *and* posh <both nonformal>, **luxurious**, gold-plated; **prosperous,** high-income, well-heeled <nonformal>; **affluent,** wealthy

upset NOUNS 1 **distress,** trouble, vexation, unease; **uneasiness,** perturbation, disturbance, **agitation,** disquiet, disquietude, inquietude, unquietness; **defeat**
2 **dislodgment;** unplacement, **unseating,** unsaddling, unhorsing; **overturn,** overthrow, **turnover,** spill <nonformal>; **capsizing,** capsize, capsizal, turning turtle
VERBS 3 **chagrin,** embarrass, abash, discomfit, disconcert, discompose, confuse, throw into confusion *or* a tizzy, confound, cast down, mortify, put out, put out of face *or* countenance; **distress,** afflict, trouble, burden, load with care, **bother,** disturb, perturb, disquiet, discomfort, agitate; **worry,** give one gray hair, vex, fret, agitate, get to <nonformal>, **harass,** harry
4 **unnerve,** unman, undo, unstring, unbrace, reduce to jelly, **demoralize,** shake, psych out <nonformal>, dash, knock down *or* flat, **crush,** overcome, prostrate
5 **overthrow,** overturn, overwhelm; upend, **subvert,** throw down *or* over; undermine, honeycomb, **sap,** sap the foundations, weaken; **disorder,** disarrange, disorganize, **confuse**, sow confusion; **discompose**, destabilize, unsettle, **disturb,** perturb
ADJS 6 **agitated,** perturbed, disturbed, troubled, disquieted, antsy <nonformal>, unsettled, **discomposed,** flustered, ruffled, shaken, **overcome,** overwhelmed, overpowered, overmastered; *bouleversé* <Fr>

upside-down ADJS **inverted,** topsy-turvy, ass over elbows *and* ass over tincups *and* arsy-varsy <all nonformal>; **capsized,** head-over-heels; **mixed up,** balled *or* bollixed up <nonformal>, screwed up <nonformal>, mucked up <nonformal>, **fouled up** *and* fucked up *and* snafu <all nonformal>

upstage VERBS **snub,** rebuff, cut *or* cut dead <nonformal>, drop, repulse; **high-hat** <nonformal>; **look down one's nose at,** look cool *or* coldly upon; steal the show, steal the spotlight

upstart NOUNS **parvenu,** adventurer,

sprout <nonformal>; *bourgeois gentilhomme* <Fr>, would-be gentleman; *nouveau riche* <Fr>, *arriviste* <Fr>, **newly-rich,** pig in clover <nonformal>; **social climber,** climber, name-dropper, status seeker

an upstart crow beautified in our feathers
ROBERT GREENE

upsurge NOUNS 1 **surge,** upsurgence, upleap, upshoot, uprush; **gush,** jet, spurt, spout, fountain; uptick <nonformal>, **increase,** uptrend, upswing
VERBS 2 **surge,** rise, rise up, upheave; **rear,** rear up, **tower,** loom; increase

uptight ADJS **tense,** tensed-up, **strained,** stretched tight, taut, unrelaxed, under a strain; pedantic, **stuffy** *and* hidebound <both nonformal>

up-to-date ADJS 1 **fashionable,** in fashion, smart, in style, in vogue; all the rage, all the thing; abreast of the times, up-to-the-minute, switched-on *and* hip *and* with-it <all nonformal>, trendy <nonformal>, modern, contemporary, newfashioned, new; **in the swim;** sought-after, much sought-after
2 **informed, enlightened, instructed,** versed, well-versed, educated, schooled, **taught;** posted, briefed, primed, trained; **up on,** abreast of, *au courant* <Fr>

upturn NOUNS **uptrend,** uptick <nonformal>, upcast, upsweep, upbend, upsurge; **increase,** gain, augmentation, **advance,** appreciation, ascent, mounting, crescendo, waxing, snowballing, **rise** *or* raise, buildup

urban ADJS **metropolitan,** municipal, metro, **civic,** oppidan; citywide; citified; downtown, uptown, midtown; **inner-city,** core, core-city, ghetto

urbane ADJS **courteous,** polite, civil, gracious, graceful, agreeable, affable, fair

urge NOUNS 1 urgency; impulse, impulsion, compulsion; press, **pressure,** drive, push; sudden *or* rash impulse
VERBS 2 **press,** push, work on <nonformal>, twist one's arm <nonformal>; **insist,** push for, not take no for an answer, **importune,** nag, pressure, high-pressure, bring pressure to bear upon, jawbone *and* build a fire under <both nonformal>, talk round *or* around; **lobby; coax,** wheedle, cajole, blandish, plead with, sweet-talk *and* soft-soap <both nonformal>, **exhort,** call on *or* upon, advocate, recommend, put in a good word, buck for *and* hype <both nonformal>; insist upon

urgent ADJS **imperative,** imperious, **compelling,** pressing, high-priority, high-pressure, crying, clamorous, insistent, instant, exigent; crucial, critical, pivotal, acute

urinate VERBS **pass** *or* **make water,** wet, stale, **piss** <nonformal>, piddle, pee; pee-pee *and* wee-wee *and* make *or* do *or* go number one <all nonformal>

usable ADJS **utilizable;** applicable, appliable; practical, operable; **reusable; exploitable;** manipulable, pliable, compliant

usage NOUNS 1 **custom,** convention, use, standard usage, standard behavior, **wont,** wonting, **way,** established way, time-honored practice, **tradition,** standing custom, **folkway,** manner, **practice,** praxis, prescription, **observance,** ritual, consuetude, mores
2 **treatment,** handling, management; way *or* means of dealing
3 **diction,** words, wordage, verbiage, word usage, *usus loquendi* <L>, use *or* choice of words, formulation, way of putting *or* couching, word garment, word dressing; **rhetoric,** speech, talk <nonformal>; **language,** dialect, parlance, locution, expression, grammar; **idiom**

use NOUNS 1 **employment,** utilization, usage; exercise, exertion, active use; good use; ill use, wrong use, misuse; hard use, hard *or* rough usage; **application,** appliance; expenditure, expending, using up, exhausting, dissipation, dissipating, **consumption**
2 **function,** purpose, role, part, end use, immediate purpose, ultimate purpose, operational purpose, operation; work, duty, office
3 **wear,** hard wear; wear and tear
VERBS 4 **utilize,** make use of, do with; **employ,** practice, ply, work, manage, handle, operate, **wield,** play; have *or* enjoy the use of; exercise, exert; **exploit,** take advantage of, **use for one's own ends;** make a paw *or* cat's-paw of, sucker *and* play for a sucker <both nonformal>; **manipulate,** work on, work upon, stroke, play on *or* upon; play both ends against the middle; use ill, ill-use, abuse, misuse

used to ADJS **accustomed,** wont, wonted; **familiar with,** conversant with, **at home in** *or* **with,** no stranger to, an old hand at, **habituated,** *habitué* <Fr>; **in the habit of,** never free from; in a rut

useful ADJS employable, of use, of service, **serviceable,** good for; **helpful,** of help; **advantageous,** to one's advantage *or* profit, profitable, beneficial, fructuous, worthwhile, worth one's while; **practical,** banausic, pragmatical, **functional,** utilitarian, of general utility *or* application; fitting, proper, appropriate, expedient; well-used, well-thumbed

useless ADJS of no use, no go <nonformal>; **aimless,** meaningless, **purposeless,** of no purpose, **pointless,** feckless, futile; **unavailing,** of no avail, failed; ineffective, **ineffectual,** inefficacious, of no effect; malfunctioning, worthless, unrewarding

user NOUNS 1 employer; **consumer,** enjoyer
2 **drug user,** drug abuser, junkie *and* head *and* druggy *and* doper *and* toker *and* fiend *and* freak *and* space cadet <all nonformal>

user-friendly ADJS **handy,** wieldy, **manageable,** maneuverable; **convenient,** foolproof, goofproof <nonformal>, practical, untroublesome

usher NOUNS 1 **attendant,** tender, usherer, usherette; ostiary
VERBS 2 **escort,** conduct, have in tow <nonformal>, marshal, shepherd, **guide,** lead; convoy, guard; **attend,** wait on *or* upon; **chaperon**

usual ADJS **regular; customary,** habitual, accustomed, wonted, **normative,** prescriptive, standard, regulation, conventional; **common,** commonplace, ordinary, average, everyday, mediocre, familiar, household, vernacular, stock; **prevailing,** predominating, current, popular; **universal**

usurp VERBS **arrogate,** seize, grab *and* latch on to <both nonformal>, **appropriate,** assume, adopt, take over, arrogate to oneself, pretend to, infringe, encroach

usury NOUNS **lending,** loaning; moneylending, lending at interest; loansharking *and* shylocking <both informal>; excessive *or* exorbitant interest

utilize VERBS **use,** make use of, do with; **employ,** practice, ply, work, manage, handle, manipulate, operate, **wield,** play; **have** *or* **enjoy the use of;** exercise, **exert**

utmost ADJS **superlative,** supreme, greatest, best, highest, maximal, maximum, most, outstanding, stickout <nonformal>; top, topmost, uppermost, damndest <nonformal>

utopia NOUNS Utopia <Sir Thomas More>, **paradise,** heaven, **heaven on earth;** land of dreams, land of enchantment, land of heart's desire, wonderland, cloudland, fairyland, Eden, Garden of Eden; the Promised Land, land of promise, land of plenty, land of milk and honey

utopian ADJS perfectionist, millenarian, chiliastic; **ideal,** idealized; Arcadian, Edenic, paradisal; pie in the sky <nonformal>

utter VERBS 1 **say,** breathe, sound, **voice,** vocalize, phonate, **articulate,** enunciate, pronounce, lip, give voice, give tongue, give utterance; **express,** give expression, verbalize, put in words, find words to express; **tell,** communicate; **convey,** impart, disclose; **issue,** deal out, retail, dispense
ADJS 2 **downright,** outright, out-and-out; **absolute,** perfect, consummate, superlative, surpassing, the veriest, positive, definitive, classical, pronounced, decided, profound, stark; **thorough,** thoroughgoing, **complete,** total

V

vacancy NOUNS vacuity, voidness, **emptiness,** blankness, hollowness, inanition; **bareness,** barrenness, desolateness, bleakness, desertedness; **nonoccupancy,** nonoccupation, nonresidence; job vacancy, **opening,** open place *or* post, vacant post

vacate VERBS **quit,** evacuate, abandon, desert, turn one's back on, walk away from, leave to one's fate, leave flat *or* high and dry; **withdraw,** retreat, **beat a retreat,** retire, remove; walk away, abscond, disappear, vanish; **bow out** <nonformal>, make one's exit; **resign,** demit, leave, withdraw from; **abdicate,** renounce the throne, give up the crown

vacation NOUNS 1 holiday <Brit>; **time off;** day off, week off, month off, etc; paid vacation, paid holiday <Brit>; **leave,** leave of absence, furlough; **sabbatical,** sabbatical leave *or* year; weekend; busman's holiday; package tour *or* holiday
VERBS 2 **get away from it all,** holiday, take a holiday; **take a leave of absence,** take leave, go on leave, go on furlough, take one's sabbatical; weekend

vacillate VERBS **waver,** waffle <nonformal>, **fluctuate,** pendulate, oscillate, wobble, wobble about, teeter, totter <old>, dither, swing from one thing to another, **shilly-shally,** back and fill, keep off and on, keep *or* leave hanging in midair; blow hot and cold; **equivocate**, fudge; change one's mind, tergiversate; shift, change horses in midstream, **change**

vacuum NOUNS **void,** blank, emptiness, empty space, inanity; **nothingness;** *tabula rasa* <L>, clean slate; nothing; **omission,** gap, hiatus, hole, break, lacuna, discontinuity, interval; **vacuity,** vacuousness, vacancy, mental void, blankness, hollowness, inanity, vapidity, jejunity

vagabond NOUNS 1 **vagrant,** bum *or* bummer <nonformal>, loafer, wastrel, *lazzarone* <Ital>; **tramp,** turnpiker, piker, knight of the road, easy rider, **hobo** *or* bo <nonformal>, rounder <nonformal>, stiff *or* bindlestiff <nonformal>; landloper, sundowner *or* swagman *or* swagsman <all Australian nonformal>; beachcomber, idler; ski bum, beach bum, surf bum, tennis bum; **wanderer;** drifter, derelict, homeless person
ADJS 2 **wandering,** roving, roaming, ranging, **rambling,** meandering, strolling, **straying,** straggling, shifting, flitting, landloping, errant, **transient,** transitory, fugitive; **vagrant,** vagabondish; **footloose,** footloose and fancy-free

vagrant NOUNS 1 **bum,** stiff <nonformal>, derelict, skid-row bum, Bowery bum, *lazzarone* <Ital>; beachcomber; **good-for-nothing,** good-for-naught, **ne'er-do-well,** wastrel; drifter, hobo, tramp
ADJS 2 **inconstant,** irregular, spasmodic; **desultory,** rambling, roving, wanton, wayward, wandering, afloat, adrift; **unrestrained,** undisciplined, irresponsible, uncontrolled, fast and loose

vague ADJS **indefinite,** indecisive, indeterminate, indeterminable, **undetermined,** unpredetermined, undestined; **random,** stochastic, entropic, **chance,** chancy <nonformal>, dicey *and* dodgy <Brit nonformal>, aleatory *or* aleatoric, hit-or-miss; indefinable, undefined, ill-defined, **unclear,** unplain, **indistinct,** fuzzy, **obscure,** confused, hazy, shadowy, misty, foggy, fog-bound, murky, blurred, blurry, veiled; **loose,** lax, inexact, inaccurate, imprecise; nonspecific, unspecified; **broad,** general, sweeping; amorphous, shapeless, inchoate, disordered, orderless, chaotic, incoherent

vain ADJS 1 **vainglorious,** conceited, overproud, overweening; **self-important,** self-esteeming, self-assuming, **self-admiring,** self-delighting, self-worshiping, self-loving, self-infatuated, narcissistic; **self-satisfied,** self-content, self-contented, self-approving, self-congratulating, self-congratulatory, self-complacent, **smug,** complacent, self-sufficient
2 **futile,** hollow, empty, idle; absurd; inane, fatuous, fatuitous; **unwarranted**

weary, stale, flat, and unprofitable
SHAKESPEARE

valentine NOUNS **love letter,** billet-doux, mash note <nonformal>

valet NOUNS **man,** manservant, serving man, gillie <Scots>, **boy,** *garçon* <Fr>, houseboy, houseman; butler; *valet de* *chambre* <Fr>, gentleman, gentleman's gentleman

valiant ADJS **courageous,** plucky, brave, bold, valorous, gallant, intrepid, doughty, **hardy,** stalwart, stout, stouthearted, ironhearted, lionhearted, greathearted, bold-spirited, bold as a lion; **heroic,** chivalrous, chivalric, knightly, knightlike, soldierly, soldierlike; **manly,** manful, virile, macho

valid ADJS **sound,** well-grounded, well-founded, conforming to the facts *or* the data *or* the evidence *or* reality, hard, solid, substantial; consistent, self-consistent, logical; **good,** just, sufficient; **cogent,** weighty, authoritative; legal, lawful, legitimate, **binding**

validate VERBS **confirm,** affirm, **attest,** warrant, **substantiate,** authenticate, certify, ratify, **verify; corroborate,** bear out, support, buttress, **sustain,** fortify, bolster, back, back up, reinforce, undergird, strengthen; **document;** probate, prove

valley NOUNS vale, dale, dell, dingle; **glen,** bottom, bottoms, bottom glade, intervale, wadi, grove; trench, trough, lunar rill; gap, pass, ravine

valor NOUNS **courage,** nerve, pluck, **bravery,** braveness, **boldness,** valorousness, valiance, valiancy, **gallantry,** conspicuous gallantry, gallantry under fire *or* beyond the call of duty, gallantness, **intrepidity,** intrepidness, **prowess,** virtue; **heroism,** military *or* martial spirit, soldierly quality *or* virtues; **manliness,** manfulness, **manhood,** virility, machismo

valuable ADJS of value, all for the best, all to the good, **profitable,** yielding a return, well-spent, **worthwhile,** rewarding; gainful, remunerative; **precious,** dear, worthy, rich, golden, of great price <old>, worth a pretty penny <nonformal>, worth a king's ransom, worth its weight in gold, good as gold, precious as the apple of one's eye; **priceless,** invaluable, inestimable, without *or* beyond price, not to be had for love or money, not for all the tea in China

value NOUNS 1 **benefit,** use, service, avail, profit, advantage, percentage *and* mileage <all nonformal>, what's in it for one <nonformal>, convenience; worth, **preciousness,** dearness, high *or* great value, extraordinary worth, **pricelessness,** invaluableness

VERBS 2 **esteem,** treasure, prize, appreciate, **rate highly,** think highly of, think well of, **think much of,** set store by; give *or* attach *or* ascribe importance to; make much of, make a fuss *or* stir about, make much ado about; hold up as an example

vamp NOUNS 1 **flirt,** coquette, gold digger <nonformal>; **courtesan,** adventuress, **seductress,** femme fatale, vampire, temptress

VERBS 2 **charm,** becharm, **infatuate,** hold in thrall, command one's affection, **fascinate,** attract, allure, grow on one, strike *or* tickle one's fancy, **captivate,** bewitch, enrapture, carry away, sweep off one's feet, turn one's head, inflame with love; **seduce,** draw on, tempt, tantalize

3 **improvise,** wing it <nonformal>, fake <nonformal>, play by ear <nonformal>

vampire NOUNS **frightener,** scarer, hairraiser; **ogre,** ogress, **monster,** harpy, werewolf, ghoul, bête noire; incubus, succubus, nightmare; **ghost,** specter, phantom, revenant; bloodsucker; living dead

vandalism NOUNS **destruction,** ruin, ruination, rack, **rack and ruin; desolation;** dissolution, disintegration, depredation, spoliation, despoliation, despoilment

vanguard NOUNS **forefront,** cutting edge, front line; **predecessor,** forebear, precedent, antecedent, **ancestor; avant-garde,** avant-gardist, innovator, groundbreaker; advance guard, van

vanilla ADJS **unadorned,** undecorated, unornamented, unembellished, ungarnished, unfurbished, unvarnished, untrimmed, plain; back-to-basics, no-frills, no-nonsense, plain-vanilla *and* white-bread *or* white-bready <all nonformal>

vanish VERBS **disappear,** vanish from sight, do a vanishing act <nonformal>, depart, fly, **flee**, go, be gone, **go away,** pass, pass out *or* away, pass out of sight, exit, pull up stakes <nonformal>, leave the scene, clear out, pass out of the picture, pass from sight, become lost to sight, be seen no more; **perish, die,** die off; die out *or* away, dwindle, wane, fade, **fade out** *or* **away,** do a fade-out <nonformal>; dematerialize, evaporate, evanesce, **vanish into thin air,** go up in smoke; **cease to be;** leave no trace

vanity NOUNS **vainness;** overproudness, overweening pride; **self-importance,** consequentiality, consequentialness, **self-esteem,** high self-esteem *or* self-valuation, **self-admiration,** self-love, *amour-propre* <Fr>, self-infatuation, narcissism, **self-satisfaction,** ego trip <nonformal>, self-approbation, self-congratulation, **smugness,** complacency, self-sufficiency; vainglory, vaingloriousness

an itch for the praise of fools
ROBERT BROWNING

vapid ADJS **insipid,** inane, superficial; **flat,** tasteless; characterless, colorless, pointless; **dead,** lifeless, spiritless, bloodless, pale, pallid, etiolated, effete; **dreary,** drearisome, dismal; **heavy,** leaden, ponderous, elephantine; inexcitable; **vacuous,** vacant, empty, hollow, inane, jejune, blank, airheaded *and* bubbleheaded <both nonformal>; **rattlebrained,** rattleheaded; scatterbrained

vapor NOUNS volatile; **fume,** reek, exhalation, breath, effluvium; fluid; **miasma,** mephitis, fetid air; **smoke,** smudge; **damp,** chokedamp, blackdamp, firedamp, afterdamp; **steam,** water vapor; **cloud**

variable ADJS **inconstant,** inconsistent, varying, **changeable,** changing, mutable, capricious, impulsive, mercurial, erratic, spasmodic, sporadic, wavery, wavering, **unstable,** unsteady; **multiform,** diversiform, versatile; **protean;** deviative, heteroclite; **capricious,** off-again-on-again, eccentric; checkered, ever-changing, many-sided, kaleidoscopic

variation NOUNS **inconstancy,** instability, changefulness, unstableness, **unsteadiness,** unsteadfastness, unfixedness, unsettledness, rootlessness; **variability,** variety, restlessness, deviability; unpredictability, irregularity; flightiness, impulsiveness, mercuriality, moodiness, whimsicality, **capriciousness,** fickleness; **changing,** fluctuation, vicissitude, oscillation, vacillation

varied ADJS **diversified,** assorted, heterogeneous; **various,** many and various, divers <old>, diverse, sundry, **several,** many; of all sorts *or* conditions *or* kinds *or* shapes *or* descriptions *or* types; **conglomerate,** pluralistic, multiracial, multicultural, multiethnic, multinational, **miscellaneous,** medley, motley, dappled, patchy

variety NOUNS 1 **miscellany,** miscellanea, collectanea; **assortment,** medley, mixture; hodgepodge, conglomerate, **conglomeration,** omnium-gatherum <nonformal>; **sundries,** oddments, odds and ends; **multiformity,** multifariousness, nonuniformity, **diversity,** diversification, variation, variegation, variability, versatility, proteanism, manifoldness, multiplicity, heterogeneity, pluralism
2 **kind,** sort, ilk, type, breed of cat <nonformal>, lot <nonformal>, denomination, designation, description, style, manner, **nature,** character, persuasion, the like *or* likes of <nonformal>

various ADJS **diversified,** varied, assorted, heterogeneous; many and various, divers <old>, diverse, sundry, **several,** many; of all sorts *or* conditions *or* kinds *or* shapes *or* descriptions *or* types; pluralistic

vary VERBS **differ,** diverge, stand apart, be distinguished *or* distinct; **deviate from,** diverge from, divaricate from, depart from; **disagree with,** disaccord with, conflict with, contrast with, clash with, jar with; not be like, bear no resemblance to, not square with, not accord with; **diversify,** variegate, waver, mutate; change, intermit, **fluctuate,** shift, lack regularity, go by fits and starts

vast ADJS **huge,** immense, enormous, astronomic, astronomical, humongous *and* jumbo <both nonformal>, tremendous, prodigious, stupendous, macro, mega, giga; great big, larger than life, Homeric, mighty, **titanic,** colossal, monumental, heroic, towering, mountainous; profound, abysmal, deep as the ocean; **mammoth,** gigantic, giant; **infinite**

vault NOUNS 1 **jump,** spring, saltation, leap; pole vault
2 **compartment,** chamber, space, enclosed space, **crypt,** burial chamber; arch, **span,** vaulting, concameration, camber; **dome,** cupola, geodesic dome, igloo, concha; arched roof, ceilinged roof

veer VERBS **swerve,** sheer, curve, **shift,** **turn,** trend, bend, heel, bear off; turn right, turn left, hang a right *or* left <nonformal>; alter one's course, make a course correction; **go sideways,** sidle, **edge,** angle, slant, skew, sidestep; go crabwise; **sideslip,** skid

vegetable ADJS 1 vegetal, vegetative, vegetational, vegetarian; **plantlike; herbaceous,** herbal, herbous, herbose, herby; leguminous, leguminose, leguminiform
ADJS 2 **passive;** standpat <nonformal>, do-nothing; **inert,** like a bump on a log <nonformal>, immobile, dormant, stagnant, stagnating, vegetative, static, stationary, motionless, immobile, unmoving, paralyzed, paralytic; **inactive,** idle; quiescent, torpid, comatose; phlegmatic, numb

vegetarian NOUNS 1 lactovegetarian, vegan, fruitarian, plant-eater, **herbivore,** phytophagan, phytophage; grass-eater, graminivore; grain-eater, granivore
ADJS 2 vegetable-eating, lactovegetarian, veganistic, fruitarian; plant-eating, **herbivorous,** phytivorous, phytophagous; grass-eating, graminivorous; grain-eating, granivorous

vegetate VERBS 1 **grow;** germinate, pullulate; **burgeon,** sprout, shoot; **bud,** gemmate, put forth *or* put out buds; flourish, luxuriate, riot, grow rank *or* lush
2 **stagnate,** merely exist, just be, pass the time; sleep, slumber, idle

vegetation NOUNS 1 **plants; flora,** plant life, vegetable life; **vegetable kingdom,** plant kingdom; herbage, flowerage, verdure, greenery, greens; **growth;** germination, pullulation; burgeoning, sprouting; budding, luxuriation
2 **mere existence,** simple existence, **vegetable existence,** mere tropism; **stagnation,** stagnancy, apathy, indolence, languor, torpor

vehement ADJS emphatic, **passionate,** impassioned, enthusiastic, **ardent,** fiery, **fervent,** burning, glowing, warm; urgent, stirring, exciting, stimulating, provoking

vehicle NOUNS **conveyance,** carrier, means of carrying *or* transporting, means of transport, medium of transportation, carriage; watercraft, aircraft; **instrument,** tool, implement, appliance, device; contrivance, lever, mechanism; organ; agent; medium, mediator, intermedium, intermediary, intermediate, interagent, liaison, go-between

veil NOUNS veiling; *yashmak* <Turk>, *chador* <Iranian>; mantilla; curtain, pall, **cover,** screen, wraps; fig leaf; **wraps** <nonformal>; cover, disguise; **veil of secrecy,** iron curtain, bamboo curtain; wall *or* barrier of secrecy; guise, semblance; mask, cloak, cover-up, cover story, alibi

vein NOUNS 1 **duct,** vessel, canal, passage; blood vessel, jugular vein, vena cava, pulmonary vein; portal vein, varicose vein; venation; veinlet, veinule, venule
2 **style; mode,** manner, strain; **way,** habit, tenor, cast, hue, tone, grain, streak, stripe, mold, brand, stamp; **mood,** humor, feeling, feelings, temper, frame of mind, state of mind, morale, note
3 **deposit,** mineral deposit, pay dirt; **lode,** seam, dike, ore bed

velocity NOUNS **speed; rapidity,** celerity, **swiftness,** fastness, quickness, speediness; **rate,** gait, pace, tread, step, stride, clip *and* lick <both nonformal>

velvet NOUNS 1 **comfort,** ease, security, well-being; clover <nonformal>, bed of roses; luxury, lap of luxury, life of ease; solid comfort
2 **smoothness**, down, **downiness,** fluff, fluffiness, velvetiness; satin, satininess; silk, silkiness; softness

venal ADJS **corruptible,** bribable, purchasable, on the take *and* on the pad <nonformal>, mercenary, hireling; **corrupt,** bought and paid for, in one's pocket

vendetta NOUNS **feud,** blood feud, **bad blood,** ill blood

vendor NOUNS supplier, salesman; **peddler,** huckster, hawker, butcher <old>, colporteur, chapman <Brit>; coster *or* costermonger <both Brit>; sidewalk salesman

veneer NOUNS **coating,** coat, gloss; **facing,** veneering, revetment; pellicle, **film,** skin, patina, scum, membrane; slick, oil slick; **lamina,** lamella; **sheet,** leaf, *feuille* <Fr>, foil

venerable ADJS **reverend,** estimable, honorable, worshipful, august, awe-inspiring, awesome, awful, dreadful; respected, respectable, highly respectable; revered, venerated, worshipful; time-honored, **aged,** elderly, old, hoary, grown old in years, along *or* up *or* advanced *or* on in years, **at an advanced age,** ancient, geriatric, gerontic; old as Methuselah *or* as God *or* as the hills; patriarchal

venereal disease NOUNS **VD, sexually-transmitted disease** *or* STD, social disease, Cupid's itch *or* Venus's curse, dose <nonformal>; chancre, chancroid; gonorrhea *or* clap *or* the clap *or* claps <nonformal>; syphilis *or* syph *or* the syph *or* the pox <nonformal>

vengeance NOUNS **revenge,** avengement, sweet revenge, getting even, evening of the score; **wrath;** revanche, revanchism; **retaliation,** reprisal; vendetta, feud, blood feud; the wrath of God

venom NOUNS **poison,** venin, toxic, toxin, toxicant; **bitterness,** sourness, **rancor,** acrimony, gall, virulence, vitriol, **animosity,** animus; **ill will,** ill feeling, bitter feeling, **hard feelings,** no love lost; **bad blood**

vent NOUNS 1 **outlet,** ventage, venthole, port; venting, discharge; **emission,** emitting, giving forth, giving out; emanation
VERBS 2 **reveal,** make known, tell, breathe, utter, ventilate, air, give vent to, **give out,** let out <Brit>, let get around, out with <nonformal>, come out with; **exhaust,** drain

ventilate VERBS 1 **air,** air out, cross-ventilate, refresh, freshen
2 **disclose,** reveal, let out, show, impart, **leak,** let slip out, let the cat out of the bag *and* spill the beans <both nonformal>; **uncover,** unveil, take the lid off <nonformal>, take the wraps off, lift *or* draw the veil, raise the curtain, let daylight in, **make public,** go public with <nonformal>; bring *or* lay *or* drag before the public, **display,** take one's case to the public, **give** *or* **put out,** give to the world, **make known;** divulge, bring into the open, get out in the open, open up, broach, give vent to

venture NOUNS **undertaking,** enterprise, operation, work, **project,** proposition *and* deal <both nonformal>; **program,** plan; **affair,** business, matter, task, concern, interest; **initiative,** effort, attempt; **investment,** risk, flutter, flier, plunge <nonformal>, speculation

verbalize VERBS **express,** give expression, put in words, find words to express; **word,** formulate, put into words, couch, phrase

verbatim ADJS 1 **genuine,** verisimilar, veristic; **literal,** following the letter, letter-perfect, *au pied de la lettre* <Fr>, true to the letter; word-perfect, word-for-word; **original,** unimitated, uncopied; unexaggerated, undistorted; unvarnished, uncolored, unqualified; unadulterated
ADVS 2 **exactly,** precisely, to a T, expressly; **literally,** *literatim* <L>, word for word, word by word, word for word and letter for letter, *verbatim et litteratim* <L>, in the same words, *ipsissimis verbis* <L>, to the letter, according to the letter, *au pied de la lettre* <Fr>; **faithfully,** strictly, rigorously, rigidly

verbiage NOUNS **diction,** words, wordage, word-usage, **usage,** *usus loquendi* <L>, use *or* choice of words, formulation, way of putting *or* couching; **rhetoric,** speech, talk <nonformal>; **language,** dialect, parlance, locution, expression, grammar; **wordiness,** verbosity, verbalism, verbality

verdict NOUNS **decision,** resolution <old>, **determination,** finding, holding; **pronouncement,** deliverance; **award,** action, sentence; condemnation, doom; acquittal; dictum; **judgment,** landmark decision

verify VERBS **confirm,** test, prove, audit, **collate,** validate, **check,** check up *or* on *or* out <nonformal>, check over *or* through, **double-check,** triple-check, cross-check, recheck, check and doublecheck, check up and down, check over and through, check in and out; **audit,** take stock, inventory

make assurance double sure
SHAKESPEARE

veritable ADJS **real,** actual, factual, for real <nonformal>, de facto, simple, sober, **hard; absolute,** positive; accepted, conceded, stipulated, given; admitted, well-known, **established,** inescapable, indisputable, undeniable; demonstrable, provable; empirical, **objective,** historical; **true,** honest-to-God <nonformal>, genuine, card-carrying <nonformal>, **authentic**

vermin NOUNS 1 parasite; **louse,** head louse, body louse, grayback, cootie <nonformal>; crab, crab louse; weevil
2 **riffraff,** trash, raff, chaff, **rubbish,** dregs, sordes, offscourings, off-scum, **scum,** scum of the earth, dregs *or* scum *or* off-scum *or* offscourings of society, swinish multitude

vernacular NOUNS **nonformal language**

or **speech,** nonformal standard speech, **spoken language,** colloquial language *or* speech, vernacular language *or* speech; colloquialism, colloquial usage, ordinary language *or* speech; nonformal English, conversational English, colloquial English, English as it is spoken; **jargon,** lingo <nonformal>, **slang,** cant, argot, patois, patter

versatile ADJS **handy,** convenient; available, accessible, **ready, at hand,** to hand, **on hand,** on tap, on deck <nonformal>, on call, at one's call *or* beck and call, at one's elbow, at one's fingertips, just around the corner, at one's disposal; adaptable; **ambidextrous,** all around <nonformal>, broad-gauge, **well-rounded,** many-sided, generally capable; adjustable, flexible, resourceful

verse NOUNS stanza; **poem,** rhyme; verselet, versicle

imaginary gardens with
real toads in them
MARIANNE MOORE

version NOUNS **rendering,** rendition; reading, lection, variant, variant reading; **edition,** critical *or* scholarly edition; variorum edition *or* variorum; conflation, composite reading *or* text; **draft,** first draft, second draft, etc, recension

versus ADJS vs, **opposed to,** adverse to, counter to, **in opposition to,** in conflict with, at cross-purposes with; **against,** agin <nonformal>, dead against, athwart

vertical ADJS **upright,** bolt upright, ramrod straight, **erect,** upstanding, standing up, stand-up; rearing, rampant; **upended,** upraised, upreared

vertigo NOUNS **dizziness,** vertiginousness, spinning head, swimming, swimming of the head, **giddiness,** wooziness <nonformal>, **lightheadedness;** Ménière's syndrome

verve NOUNS **vim,** fire, adrenalin, **dash,** drive; **liveliness,** vivacity, vitality, life, **animation,** spiritedness, spirit, esprit, élan, **sprightliness,** high spirits, zestfulness, zest, zip <nonformal>, vigor, gusto, **exuberance,** heartiness

vessel NOUNS 1 **duct,** canal, passage; blood vessel
2 **ship,** craft, bottom, bark, argosy, hull, hulk, keel, watercraft
3 **container,** receptacle; receiver, holder, utensil; basin, pot, pan, cup, glass, ladle, bottle

vest NOUNS 1 **waistcoat,** weskit <nonformal>, down vest, bulletproof vest
VERBS 2 **endow,** invest; endow with, favor with, bless with, grace with, vest with; **settle on** *or* **upon;** dower
3 **delegate,** devolute, devolve, devolve upon, invest; depute, **deputize**

vested interest NOUNS **pressure group,** interest group, special-interest group, political action committee *or* PAC, single-issue group; **special interest;** vested right

vestige NOUNS **remainder,** remains, remnant, residue, residuum, **rest,** balance; **leavings,** leftovers, oddments; survival, trace, hint, shadow, afterimage, afterglow, **spoor,** scent, whiff

veteran NOUNS 1 vet <nonformal>, seasoned *or* grizzled veteran, **old pro** <nonformal>; **old hand,** old-timer <nonformal> one of the old guard; old campaigner, war-horse *or* old war-horse <nonformal>; salt *and* old salt *and* old sea dog <all nonformal>, shellback <nonformal>
ADJS 2 **experienced,** practiced, mature, matured, ripe, ripened, **seasoned,** tried, well-tried, tried and true, **old,** an old dog at <nonformal>

veto VERBS put one's veto upon, decide *or* rule against, **turn thumbs down on** <nonformal>, negative, kill; **reject,** categorically reject, disallow, not hear of; vote down, exclude, ostracize, blackball, ban; say no to; **pocket**

vex VERBS **irk,** annoy, aggravate, exasperate; **trouble,** worry, give one gray hair, plague, harass, bother, hassle; **provoke,** incense, arouse, distress, inflame, embitter; **irritate,** annoy, nettle, fret, chafe; **pique,** peeve *and* miff <both nonformal>, huff; **ruffle,** roil, rile <nonformal>, ruffle one's feathers, rankle; **stir up,** work up, stir one's bile, stir the blood

via PREPS **through,** by, passing by *or* through, **by way of,** by the way of; over, around, round about, here and there in, all through

viable ADJS 1 **acceptable,** admissible, **agreeable,** unobjectionable, unexceptionable, tenable; **practicable,** feasible, practical
2 **living,** alive, having life, live, very much alive, alive and well, alive and

kicking <nonformal>, conscious, breathing, quick <old>, **animate,** animated, **vital,** zoetic, instinct with life, imbued *or* endowed with life, vivified, enlivened, inspirited; tenacious of life; capable of life *or* survival

vibrant ADJS **energetic,** vigorous, strenuous, forceful, forcible, strong, dynamic, kinetic, intense, acute, keen, incisive, trenchant, vivid; **resonant,** reverberant, sonorous, plangent, rolling

vibrate VERBS **resonate,** pulse, throb; **oscillate,** librate, nutate; **shake,** quake, jactitate; **tremble,** quiver, quaver, falter, **shudder,** shiver, twitter, didder, chatter

vicarious ADJS ersatz, **mock,** phony *and* fake *and* bogus <all nonformal>, counterfeit, imitation; **proxy**

vice NOUNS viciousness; criminality, **wrongdoing**; **immorality,** unmorality, evil; amorality; **unvirtuousness,** ungoodness; **unrighteousness,** ungodliness, unsaintliness, unangelicalness; **uncleanness,** impurity, unchastity, fallenness, fallen state, lapsedness; delinquency, moral delinquency; peccability; **weakness,** weakness of the flesh, **flaw,** moral flaw *or* blemish, **frailty,** infirmity; failing, failure; weak point, weak side, foible; bad habit, besetting sin; **fault,** imperfection

vice versa ADJS **inversely,** conversely, contrarily, contrariwise, the other way around, **backwards,** turned around; **reciprocally,** back and forth, backward and forward, backwards and forwards, alternately, seesaw, to and fro; counter, topsy-turvy, upside down, arsy-varsy <nonformal>, **on the other hand,** *per contra* <L>, **on** *or* **to the contrary,** *tout au contraire* <Fr>

vicinity NOUNS **nearness,** closeness, nighness, **proximity,** propinquity, intimacy, immediacy; approximation, approach, convergence; a rough idea <nonformal>; vicinage, **neighborhood,** environs, surroundings, surround, setting, grounds, purlieus, confines, precinct; neck of the woods <nonformal>

vicious ADJS **savage,** ferocious, feral, mean *and* mean as a junkyard dog <both nonformal>, fierce, **atrocious,** truculent, fell; **wicked,** evil, bad, naughty, wrong, sinful, iniquitous, peccant, reprobate; **malignant,** malign, malevolent, malefic

victim NOUNS 1 **sufferer,** prey; **wretch,** poor devil <nonformal>, object of compassion; martyr
2 **quarry,** game, prey, venery, beasts of venery, the hunted; **dupe,** john *and* lamb *and* mark *and* monkey *and* patsy *and* sucker <all nonformal>

victimize VERBS **cheat,** gull, deceive, pigeon, fudge, **swindle,** defraud, practice fraud upon, euchre, **con,** finagle, **fleece,** mulct, **bilk,** cozen, chouse, **cheat out of,** do out of, chouse out of, beguile of *or* out of; **persecute,** oppress, **torment,** harass, get *or* keep after, get *or* keep at, harry, hound, beset

Victorian ADJS **prudish,** priggish, prim, prissy, smug, stuffy <nonformal>, old-maidish, **overmodest,** demure, **strait-laced,** stiff-necked, hidebound, narrow, censorious, sanctimonious, **puritanical**

victorious ADJS **triumphant,** triumphal, **winning,** prevailing; conquering, vanquishing, defeating, overcoming; ahead of the game, ascendant, in the ascendant, in ascendancy, sitting on top of the world *and* sitting pretty <both nonformal>, dominant; successful; flushed with success *or* victory

victory NOUNS **triumph,** conquest, subduing, subdual; a feather in one's cap <nonformal>; total victory, grand slam; **championship,** crown, laurels, cup, trophy, belt, blue ribbon, first prize

video NOUNS **television,** TV, telly <Brit nonformal>; the small screen *or* the tube <both nonformal>, the boob tube <nonformal>

vie VERBS **compete,** contend, **compete with** *or* **against,** vie with, challenge, enter into competition with, give a run for one's money, **meet;** try *or* test one another; **rival,** emulate, outvie; keep up with the Joneses

view NOUNS 1 **intention,** intent, intendment, mindset, **aim,** effect, meaning, study, animus, **point,** purpose, function, set *or* settled *or* fixed purpose; **estimate,** estimation; opinion; **assessment,** assessing, **appraisal,** appraisement, appraising, appreciation, reckoning
VERBS 2 **look,** peer, have a look, take a gander *and* take a look <both nonformal>, direct the eyes, turn *or* bend the eyes, cast one's eye, lift up the eyes; **look at,** take a look at, eye, **eyeball** <nonformal>, have a look-see <nonformal>, look on *or* upon, gaze at *or* upon; **watch,** observe, regard; **contemplate,**

look upon, regard, view with the mind's eye, **envisage,** envision, **visualize**, imagine, image

viewpoint NOUNS **standpoint,** point of view, vantage, vantage point, point *or* coign of vantage, where one stands; bird's-eye view, worm's-eye view, fly on the wall; **outlook,** angle, angle of vision, *optique* <Fr>; mental outlook, perspective

vigil NOUNS **watchfulness,** watching, observance, surveillance; watch, lookout; *qui vive* <Fr>; **sharp eye,** weather eye, peeled eye, watchful eye, eagle eye, lidless *or* sleepless *or* unblinking *or* unwinking eye; all-night vigil, lidless vigil, *per vigilium* <L>

vigilant ADJS **wary,** prudent, **watchful,** lidless, sleepless, observant; **on the lookout,** *aux aguets* <Fr>; **on guard,** on one's guard; with open eyes, with one's eyes open, with one's eyes peeled *or* with a weather eye open <both nonformal>; alert, sharp-eyed, Argus-eyed, eagle-eyed, hawk-eyed; all eyes, all ears, **all eyes and ears**

vigor NOUNS **force,** power, strength, vitality, drive, sinew, sinewiness, nervousness, nervosity, vigorousness, forcefulness, effectiveness, impressiveness, pizzazz *and* punch *and* clout <all nonformal>; incisiveness, trenchancy, cuttingness, poignancy, bitingness, bite, mordancy; strong language

thoughts that breathe and words that burn
THOMAS GRAY

vile ADJS **low,** base, mean, ignoble, scurvy, sorry, scrubby, beggarly; low-minded, base-minded; **dirty,** smutty, raunchy <nonformal>, blue, smoking-room, impure, unchaste, unclean, **foul,** filthy, nasty, fulsome, offensive, unprintable, unrepeatable, not fit for mixed company

vilify VERBS **revile,** defile, sully, soil, smear, smirch, besmirch, bespatter, tarnish, **blacken,** denigrate, blacken one's good name, give a black eye <nonformal>; **call names,** give a bad name, give a dog a bad name, stigmatize; **muckrake,** throw mud at, mudsling, heap dirt upon, drag through the mud; engage in personalities

village NOUNS **hamlet;** country town, crossroads, wide place in the road

villain NOUNS **malefactor,** malfeasant, malfeasor, misfeasor, malevolent, public enemy, **sinner,** villainess, transgressor, delinquent; **scoundrel,** blackguard, **scamp,** scalawag <nonformal>, spalpeen <Ir>, rapscallion, devil

vim NOUNS **verve,** fire, adrenalin, **dash, drive; aggressiveness,** enterprise, initiative, proactiveness, thrust, spunk; **eagerness**, zeal, heartiness, keenness, gusto; **liveliness,** vivacity, vitality, life, **animation,** spiritedness, spirit, esprit, élan, **sprightliness,** high spirits, zestfulness, zest, zip <nonformal>, vigor

vindicate VERBS **justify,** do justice to, make justice *or* right prevail; get off the hook <nonformal>, exculpate; **clear,** clear one's name *or* one's good name, purge, destigmatize, reinstate, restore, rehabilitate; **acquit,** exonerate, absolve, give absolution, bring in *or* return a verdict of not guilty

vindictive ADJS **revengeful,** vengeful, avenging; vindicatory; revanchist; **wrathful,** rancorous, grudgeful, irreconcilable, unappeasable, implacable, unwilling to forgive and forget, unwilling to let bygones be bygones; **retaliatory**

violate VERBS 1 **corrupt,** debase, degrade, degenerate, **deprave,** debauch, defile, desecrate, deflower, ravish, ravage, despoil; **possess sexually,** take; **rape,** abuse, commit rape, commit date *or* acquaintance rape, assault sexually, lay violent hands on, have one's will of; 2 **break** *or* **violate the law,** breach the law, infringe, contravene, infract, **transgress,** trespass, disobey the law, offend against the law, flout the law, make a mockery of the law, fly in the face of the law, circumvent the law, disregard the law, **take the law into one's own hands,** commit a crime

violence NOUNS **cruelty,** brutality, mindless *or* senseless brutality, brutalness, **brutishness,** bestiality, animality, beastliness; **savagery,** viciousness, fiendishness

VIP NOUNS **very important person, somebody;** important person, standout <nonformal>, personage, one in a hundred *or* thousand *or* million etc; cynosure, model, very model, ideal type; popular hero, folk hero; luminary, celebrity

viper NOUNS **serpent,** snake, ophidian; pit viper; **reptile,** vermin, varmint <non-

formal>, hyena; **swine,** pig; **skunk,** polecat; insect, worm

virgin NOUNS 1 virgo intacta, cherry <nonformal>; vestal, vestal virgin
ADJS 2 **natural,** native, in a state of nature, in the raw; inartificial, artless; virginal, pristine, untouched, unsullied; maidenly, vestal, intact; **undamaged,** unharmed, unhurt, uninjured, unscathed, **unspoiled,** inviolate, unimpaired

virile ADJS **potent,** viripotent; ultramasculine, **macho,** he-mannish *and* hunky <both nonformal>, two-fisted <nonformal>, broad-shouldered, hairy-chested; **manly,** manful

virtual ADJS **potential,** unmanifested, possible

virtue NOUNS **virtuousness,** goodness, righteousness, rectitude, right conduct *or* behavior, the straight and narrow, the straight and narrow way, the right thing; probity; **morality,** moral fiber *or* rectitude *or* virtue, morale; **saintliness,** saintlikeness; **chastity,** honor; **purity,** cleanness, cleanliness; **immaculacy,** immaculateness, spotlessness, stainlessness, taintlessness, blotlessness; uncorruptness; sexual innocence, innocence

virtuoso NOUNS **first-rater,** topnotcher, world-beater; wonder, prodigy, genius, **star,** superstar; luminary, leading light, one in a thousand *or* a million; hard *or* tough act to follow <nonformal>

virtuous ADJS **good,** moral; upright, honest; **righteous,** just, straight, right-minded, right-thinking; **angelic,** seraphic; **saintly,** saintlike; **chaste,** pure, purehearted, pure in heart; **immaculate,** spotless, blotless, stainless, taintless, white, snowy, pure *or* white as driven snow; **unsoiled,** unsullied, undefiled, untarnished, unstained, unspotted, untainted, unblemished; sexually innocent, innocent

virulent ADJS 1 **acrimonious,** acrid, acidulous, acid, **bitter,** tart, caustic, mordant *or* mordacious, rancorous, **violent,** vehement, vitriolic; **noxious,** malignant, malign, destructive, deadly
2 **infectious,** infective, contagious, communicable, catching, pernicious; toxic, noisome

virus NOUNS **infection,** contagion, contamination, taint; filterable virus, nonfilterable virus, adenovirus, echovirus, reovirus, rhinovirus, enterovirus, picornavirus, retrovirus

visa NOUNS entry visa, exit visa, *visé* <Fr>; **clearance,** clearance papers

viscous ADJS **viscid,** viscose, slabby; **thick,** heavy, stodgy, soupy, thickened, inspissated, incrassated; curdled, clotted, grumous, coagulated, clabbered *and* loppered <both nonformal>; **sticky,** tacky, tenacious, adhesive, clingy, clinging, tough; gluey, gluelike, glutinous, glutenous, glutinose; **gummy,** gummous, gumlike, syrupy; **gelatinous,** jellylike, jellied, jelled; tremelloid *or* tremellose

vise NOUNS contractor, constrictor, clamp, compressor, pincer, squeezer; thumbscrew

visible ADJS visual, **perceptible,** perceivable, **discernible,** seeable, viewable, witnessable, beholdable, observable, detectable, noticeable, recognizable, to be seen; **in sight,** in view, in plain sight, in full view, before one's eyes, under one's eyes, open, naked, outcropping, hanging out <nonformal>, exposed, showing, open *or* exposed to view; **evident,** in evidence, **manifest,** apparent; revealed, disclosed, unhidden, unconcealed, unclouded, undisguised

vision NOUNS 1 **sight,** eyesight, seeing; **sightedness;** eye, power of sight, sense of sight, visual sense; **perception,** discernment; perspicacity, perspicuity, sharp *or* acute *or* keen sight, visual acuity, quick sight
2 **apparition,** appearance, phenomenon; **image,** shape, form, figure, presence; false image, mirage, specter, **phantom,** phantasm, phantasma, wraith, specter; **dream;** reverie, daydream, pipe dream <nonformal>; **nightmare,** incubus, bad dream
3 **thing of beauty,** picture <nonformal>, poem, eyeful <nonformal>, sight *or* treat for sore eyes <nonformal>

visit NOUNS 1 **social call,** call; formal visit, duty visit, required visit; exchange visit; flying visit, look-in; visiting, visitation; round of visits; social round, social whirl, mad round
VERBS 2 make *or* pay a visit, **call on** *or* **upon,** drop in, run *or* stop in, look in, look one up, see, stop off *or* over <nonformal>, drop *or* run *or* stop by, drop around *or* round; exchange visits

visitor NOUNS **guest,** visitant; **caller,** company; invited guest, invitee; frequenter, habitué, haunter; uninvited guest, gate-crasher <nonformal>; moocher *and* freeloader <both nonformal>

vista NOUNS **view,** scene, sight; prospect, outlook, lookout, perspective; scenery, scenic view; panorama, sweep; bird's-eye view, worm's-eye view

visual ADJS **ocular,** eye, eyeball <nonformal>; **sighted,** seeing, having sight *or* vision; **optic,** optical; ophthalmic; revealed, disclosed, unhidden, unconcealed, unclouded, undisguised

visualize VERBS vision, **envision,** envisage, picture, image, objectify; picture in one's mind, picture to oneself, **view with the mind's eye,** form a mental picture of, represent, **see,** just see, have a picture of; **call up,** summon up, conjure up, **call to mind,** realize

vital ADJS **all-important,** crucial, of vital importance, life-and-death *or* life-or-death; earth-shattering, epoch-making; **essential,** fundamental, indispensable, basic, substantive, bedrock, material; **central,** focal; bottom-line *and* meat-and-potatoes *and* gut <all nonformal>

vitality NOUNS **energy,** vigor, force, power, strenuousness, **intensity,** dynamism, demonic energy; potency; strength; vim, push, drive, charge, puissance <old>; virility; **haleness,** heartiness, robustness, vigorousness, ruggedness, lustiness, hardiness; **liveliness,** life, vivacity, élan, spirit, animation

vitriolic ADJS **acrimonious,** acrid, acidulous, acid, **bitter,** tart, **caustic,** mordant *or* mordacious, **virulent,** violent, vehement; **rancorous; venomous,** venenate, envenomed

vivacious ADJS **active,** lively, living, **animated,** spirited, go-go <nonformal>, brisk, bright-eyed and bushy-tailed <nonformal>, hearty, enthusiastic, mettlesome, zesty, zestful, impetuous, spanking, smacking; pumped *and* pumped up *and* jazzed-up *and* charged up *and* switched on <all nonformal>, snappy *and* zingy *and* zippy *and* peppy <all nonformal>; vital, **exuberant,** frisky, antic, skittish, coltish, rompish, capersome; **full of beans** *and* **feeling one's oats** <both nonformal>

vivid ADJS **expressive,** graphic, suggestive, imaginative; well-turned; eidetic, fresh, green, alive; **bright,** brilliant, splendid, splendorous, splendent, **resplendent,** bright and shining; fulgent, effulgent, refulgent

vocation NOUNS **occupation,** business, work, line, line of work, line of business *or* endeavor, number <nonformal>, walk, **walk of life,** calling, mission, **profession,** practice, pursuit, specialty, specialization, *métier* <Fr>, **trade,** racket *and* game <both nonformal>; **career,** lifework, life's work; **the ministry,** call, sacred calling

vociferous ADJS vociferant, vociferating; **clamorous,** blatant; obstreperous, brawling; **noisy;** yelping, yapping, yappy, yammering; loud-voiced, loud-mouthed, openmouthed, stentorian

vogue NOUNS **fashion,** style, mode, trend, prevailing taste; custom; the swim <nonformal>, current *or* stream of fashion; height of fashion; the new look, the season's look; high fashion, *haute couture* <Fr>

voice NOUNS *voce* <Ital>; *voce di petto* <Ital>, chest voice; *voce di testa* <Ital>, head voice; **soprano,** mezzo-soprano, dramatic soprano, soprano spinto, lyric soprano, coloratura soprano; boy soprano; male soprano, castrato; alto, contralto; tenor, lyric tenor, operatic tenor, heldentenor *or* heroic tenor *or* Wagnerian tenor; baritone, light *or* lyric baritone; **bass,** basso, basso profundo, basso cantante *or* lyric bass, basso buffo *or* comic bass; treble, falsetto

void NOUNS 1 **vacuum,** blank, emptiness, empty space, inanity; **nothingness;** *tabula rasa* <L>, clean slate; nothing; **gap,** gape, **abyss,** gulf, chasm

VERBS 2 **abolish,** nullify, abrogate, annihilate, annul, tear up, repeal, revoke, negate, negative, invalidate, **undo,** cancel, cancel out, bring to naught, put *or* lay to rest

3 **evacuate,** eliminate, remove; **empty,** empty out, deplete, **exhaust,** vent, drain; **clear,** purge, clean *or* scour out, clear off *or* out *or* away, clear, unfoul, unclog, flush out, blow, blow out, sweep out, make a clean sweep, clear the decks; defecate

ADJS 4 **vacant,** empty, hollow, inane, **bare,** vacuous, without content, with nothing inside, devoid, null, null and void; **repealed,** revoked, rescinded, struck down, set aside; **invalid**

volatile ADJS **capricious,** fickle, off-again-on-again; **erratic,** eccentric, freakish;

giddy, dizzy, scatterbrained, mercurial, moody, flighty, impulsive, impetuous; mercurial; volatilizable; **vaporable,** vaporizable, vaporescent; **evaporative,** evaporable

volcanic ADJS **warm,** burning, heated, hot, red-hot, fiery, flaming, glowing, ablaze, afire, on fire, boiling over, steaming, steamy; emotionally unstable; explosive, eruptive, inflammable; **impetuous,** violent, furious, fierce, **wild;** tempestuous, stormy, tornadic; simmering, ready to burst forth *or* explode; **hot-tempered,** hotheaded, passionate, peppery, feisty, combustible

volley NOUNS **salvo,** burst, spray, **fusillade,** drumfire, **cannonade,** cannonry, **broadside,** enfilade; **barrage,** artillery barrage

volume NOUNS 1 **loudness,** intensity, amplitude, fullness; sonorousness, sonority; surge of sound, surge, crescendo, swell, swelling; loudishness
2 **capacity,** content, holding capacity, cubic footage *or* yardage etc, accommodation, room, space, measure, limit, burden; gallonage, tankage; poundage, tonnage, cordage; stowage; **quantity**
3 **tome; edition,** issue; library edition; back number; **trade edition,** subscription edition, subscription book; school edition, text edition

voluminous ADJS **capacious,** generous, ample, copious, broad, wide, extensive, expansive, comprehensive; **spacious**

voluntary ADJS **volunteer;** ex gratia, gratuitous; spontaneous, free, freewill; **discretionary,** discretional, nonmandatory, **optional; unsought,** unasked, unrequested, **unsolicited,** uninvited, unbidden; unprompted, uninfluenced; **elective;** volitional, volitive

volunteer VERBS do voluntarily, do ex gratia, **do of one's own accord,** do of one's own volition, **do of one's own free will** *or* **choice;** do independently, **come** *or* **step forward,** offer *or* proffer *or* present oneself, not wait to be asked, not wait for an invitation, need no prodding

voluptuous ADJS **carnal,** sensual, sensualist, sensualistic, fleshly; zaftig <nonformal>; luxurious; sensuous; luxurious

vomit NOUNS 1 vomitus, **puke** *and* barf <both nonformal>, spew, egesta; the dry heaves <nonformal>; vomiturition; **vomiting,** vomition, disgorgement, **regurgitation,** egestion, emesis, the pukes *and* the heaves <both nonformal>; **retching,** heaving, gagging; nausea
VERBS 2 spew, disgorge, **regurgitate,** egest, **throw up,** bring up, be sick, cast *or* heave the gorge; **retch,** keck, heave, gag; reject; be seasick, feed the fish

3 <nonformal> **puke,** upchuck, chuck up, urp, oops, oops up, shoot *or* blow *or* toss one's cookies *or* lunch, barf, ralph, ralph up, blow grits

voodoo NOUNS 1 voodooism, hoodoo, wanga, juju, jujuism, obeah, obeahism; shamanism; fetishism
2 **shaman,** shamanist; voodooist, wangateur, **witch doctor,** obeah doctor, **medicine man,** mundunugu, isangoma

voracious ADJS **gluttonous,** greedy, ravenous, edacious, rapacious, insatiable, polyphagic, bulimic, hyperphagic, Apician; **piggish,** hoggish, swinish; **gorging,** cramming, glutting, stuffing, guzzling, wolfing, bolting, **gobbling,** gulping, gluttonizing

vote NOUNS 1 voting, **suffrage,** franchise, enfranchisement, voting right, right to vote; **voice,** say; **poll,** polling, canvass, canvassing, counting heads *or* noses; **ballot,** balloting, secret ballot, Australian ballot; ballot-box, voting machine; **plebiscite,** plebiscitum, referendum; endorsement
VERBS 2 **cast one's vote,** ballot, cast a ballot; have suffrage, be enfranchised, have a say *or* a voice; hold up one's hand, exercise one's suffrage *or* frachise, stand up and be counted; **poll,** canvass

voter NOUNS elector, **balloter;** registered voter; fraudulent voter, floater, repeater, ballot-box stuffer; proxy

vow NOUNS 1 **promise, pledge,** solemn promise, troth, plight, faith, parole, **word, word of honor,** solemn declaration *or* word; **oath;** avouchment; assurance, guarantee, warranty
VERBS 2 **promise,** give *or* make a promise, hold out an expectation; **pledge,** plight, troth; **give one's word,** pledge *or* pass one's word, give one's parole, **give one's word of honor,** plight one's troth *or* faith, pledge *or* plight one's honor; cross one's heart *and* cross one's heart and hope to die <both nonformal>, **swear;** vouch, avouch,

warrant, guarantee, assure; underwrite, countersign

voyage NOUNS ocean *or* sea trip, **cruise,** sail; course, **run,** passage; crossing; shakedown cruise

voyeur NOUNS **Peeping Tom,** watcher, scopophiliac, scoptophiliac

vulgar ADJS 1 **inelegant,** indelicate, indecorous, indecent, improper, unseemly, unbeseeming, unbecoming, unfitting, inappropriate, unsuitable, **ungenteel,** undignified; **untasteful,** tasteless, in bad *or* poor taste, tacky *and* chintzy *and* Mickey Mouse <all nonformal>; **offensive,** offensive to gentle ears; barbarous, barbaric, rude, **crude, uncouth,** Doric, outlandish; low, gross, **coarse**

2 **vernacular,** colloquial, conversational, unliterary, nonformal, demotic, spoken, vulgate; unstudied, familiar, common, everyday; **substandard,** nonformal, uneducated; dysphemistic

vulnerable ADJS **pregnable,** penetrable, expugnable; assailable, attackable, surmountable; conquerable, beatable <nonformal>, vincible; weak, **exposed,** susceptible, at risk, overexposed, open, like a sitting duck; **in debt, indebted,** financially burdened, heavily committed, overextended

W-X-Y-Z

wacky ADJS

> **kooky, goofy,** birdy, funny, kinky, loopy, goofus, haywire, screwy, screwball, nutty, flaky, oddball, wacko, out to lunch, nobody home, weird

wad NOUNS **accumulation,** agglomeration, conglomeration, conglomerate, agglomerate; **aggregation,** aggregate; **mass,** lump, gob <nonformal>, chunk *and* hunk <both nonformal>

waddle VERBS **go slow** *or* **slowly,** go at a snail's pace, take it slow, get no place fast <nonformal>; **drag,** creep, crawl; poke, **poke along;** shuffle *or* stagger *or* totter *or* toddle along; drag along, drag one's feet, toddle <nonformal>; limp, hobble, claudicate

waffle VERBS **vacillate,** waver, **fluctuate,** pendulate, oscillate, wobble, dither, swing from one thing to another, **shilly-shally,** back and fill, keep *or* leave hanging in midair; blow hot and cold; **equivocate,** fudge; change one's mind, tergiversate; shift, change horses in midstream; **evade,** evade the issue, duck the issue *and* **cop out** <both nonformal>

wag NOUNS 1 **funnyman,** comic, *bel-esprit* <Fr>, life of the party; **joker,** jokester, gagman <nonformal>, **jester,** quipster, wisecracker *and* gagster <both nonformal>; wagwit; zany, madcap, cutup <nonformal>; prankster
VERBS 2 **wiggle,** wriggle; waggle; **writhe,** squirm

wager NOUNS 1 **bet,** stake, hazard, lay, play *and* chunk *and* shot <all nonformal>; cinch bet *or* sure thing, mortal cinch *and* mortal lock *and* nuts <all nonformal>; long shot
VERBS 2 **bet,** gamble, hazard, stake, punt, lay, lay down, put up, **make a bet,** lay a wager, give *or* take *or* lay odds, get a piece of the action <nonformal>; plunge <nonformal>; **bet on** *or* **upon,** back; play *or* follow the ponies <nonformal>; parlay

wagon NOUNS 1 wain; haywagon, milkwagon; dray, van, caravan; covered wagon, prairie schooner, Conestoga wagon
2 **police car,** patrol car; prowl car, squad car, cruiser; **police van,** patrol wagon; paddy wagon *and* Black Maria <both nonformal>

waif NOUNS homeless waif, dogie, stray, waifs and strays; ragamuffin, tatterdemalion; **gamin,** gamine, urchin, street urchin, dead-end kid <nonformal>, mudlark, guttersnipe <nonformal>

wail NOUNS 1 **lament,** plaint, *planctus* <L>; **moan,** groan; whine, whimper; wail of woe; **sob,** *cri du coeur* <Fr>, **cry,** outcry, scream, **howl,** yowl, bawl, yawp, keen, ululation
VERBS 2 ululate; **moan,** groan; howl, yowl; **cry,** squall, bawl, yawp, **yell,** scream, shriek; cry out, make an outcry; bay at the moon; whine, keen, blubber, sob

wait NOUNS 1 **delay,** stoppage, jam *and* logjam <both nonformal>, obstruction, tie-up *and* bind <both nonformal>, **block,** blockage, **hang-up** <nonformal>; **retardation** *or* retardance, slowdown *and* slow-up <both nonformal>, slowness, lag, time lag, lagging, dragging, dragging one's feet *and* foot-dragging <both nonformal>; **halt,** stay, stop, downtime, break, pause, interim, respite; reprieve, stay of execution; moratorium
VERBS 2 **await,** wait for, wait on *or* upon, stay *or* tarry for; wait around *or* about, watch and wait; **bide one's time,** bide, abide, **mark time;** cool one's heels <nonformal>; **wait up for,** stay up for, sit up for; **be patient,** forbear, bear with composure, wait it out, play a waiting game, wait one's turn, watch for one's moment, keep one's shirt *or* pants on <nonformal>; contain oneself, possess oneself, possess one's soul in patience

waiter NOUNS **waitress;** carhop; counterman, soda jerk <nonformal>; busboy; headwaiter, *maître d'hôtel* <Fr>, maître d' <nonformal>

wait on VERBS **toady to,** truckle to, pander to, cater to; **wait upon,** wait on hand and foot, dance attendance, do service, fetch and carry, do the dirty work of, do *or* jump at the bidding of; **look after,** take care of

waive VERBS **give up,** relinquish, surrender, yield, yield up, **forgo,** resign, renounce, **abjure,** forswear, give up on, have done with, hand over, lay down, wash one's hands of; **not use,** do without, dispense with; prorogue, put on hold *or* ice *or* the back burner <all nonformal>, reserve, **suspend,** set aside, ease, lift temporarily, pull one's punches <nonformal>

waiver NOUNS special permission, charter, patent, **dispensation,** release; zoning variance, variance; suspension; waiving, setting aside

wake VERBS **awake,** awaken, wake up, get up, rouse, come alive <nonformal>; open one's eyes, stir <nonformal>; stir up, set astir, stir the feelings, stir the blood, cause a stir *or* commotion, play on the feelings; **work up,** work into, work up into a lather <nonformal>, lather up, whip up, **key up,** steam up; foment, incite; turn on <nonformal>

walk NOUNS 1 ramble, amble, **hike,** tramp, traipse <nonformal>; slog, trudge, schlep <nonformal>; **stroll,** saunter; **promenade,** *passeggiata* <Ital>; jaunt, airing; **constitutional,** turn; **march,** forced march, route march; parade

2 **path,** track, trail, pathway, footpath, footway, *piste* <Fr>; walkway, catwalk, skybridge *or* skywalk *or* flying bridge *or* walkway; **sidewalk,** *trottoir* <Fr>, foot pavement <Brit>; boardwalk; public walk, promenade, esplanade, alameda, parade, *prado* <Sp>; beaten track *or* path, rut, groove; garden path

3 **walk of life,** calling, mission, **profession,** practice, pursuit, specialty, specialization, *métier* <Fr>, **trade,** racket *and* game <both nonformal>

VERBS 4 ambulate, peripateticate, pedestrianize, traipse <nonformal>; **step,** tread, pace, stride, pad; foot, foot it; leg, leg it; hoof it, ankle, heel and toe, ride shank's mare <nonformal>, ride the shoeleather *or* hobnail express, stump it <nonformal>; peg *or* jog *or* shuffle on *or* along; perambulate; circumambulate; jaywalk; power walk, exercise walk, speed walk, race walk

5 **go free,** breathe the air of freedom; be freed, be released; be exonerated, go *or* get off scot-free

6 **strike,** go on strike, go out, walk out; hit the bricks <nonformal>, shut it down

wall NOUNS **fence,** boundary, **barrier;** stone wall; paling, palisade; **partition,** dividing wall, separation, *cloison* <Fr>; **dividing line,** property line, party wall

wallop NOUNS 1 **sock,** bang, bash, bat, belt, bust, clip, clout, duke, swat, larrup, paste, lick, biff, whop, slam, slug <all nonformal>

VERBS 2 **beat up,** rough up, clobber, work over, lick, larrup, whop, beat one's brains out, whale, whale the tar out of, beat *or* kick the shit out of, beat to a jelly, **beat black and blue,** knock one's lights out, nail, lather, **hide,** tan, **tan one's hide,** kick ass, knock heads together; **paddle;** lambaste, take it out of one's hide *or* skin <all nonformal>

wallow VERBS **pitch,** toss, tumble, toss and tumble, pitch and toss, **plunge,** pound, **rear,** rock, roll, reel, swing, sway, lurch, yaw, heave, scend, **flounder,** welter; make heavy weather, grovel

Wall Street NOUNS **stock exchange,** exchange, **stock market,** bourse, board; the Exchange, the Big Board; **financial district,** the Street

wan ADJS tired-looking, weary-looking, tired-eyed, tired-faced, haggard, hollow-eyed, ravaged, drawn, cadaverous, worn, zombiish <nonformal>; **pale,** dim, weak, **faint; pallid,** sallow; pale *or* blue *or* green around the gills; **pasty,** mealy, waxen; **ashen,** ashy, ashen-hued, cinereous, cineritious, gray, griseous; **lackluster,** dull, dead, deadened, **lifeless,** somber, drab

wander VERBS **roam,** rove, range, nomadize, **gad,** gad around *or* about, follow the seasons, wayfare, flit, traipse <nonformal>, gallivant, knock around *or* about *and* bat around *or* about <all nonformal>, prowl, **drift,** stray, float around, straggle, **meander,** ramble, stroll, saunter, jaunt, peregrinate, pererrate, divagate; **digress,** get off the subject, wander from the subject, get sidetracked, excurse, maunder, stray, go astray, woolgather, **daydream**

wanderer NOUNS **rover,** roamer, rambler, stroller, straggler, mover; **itinerant,** peripatetic, rolling stone, peregrine, peregrinator, bird of passage, visitant; **drifter** *and* **floater** <both nonformal>; **exile,** outcast, refugee, émigré displaced person *or* DP, *déraciné* <Fr>

wane VERBS **decline,** sink, fail, fall, slip, fade, die, ebb, subside, lapse, **run down,** go down, **go downhill,** fall away, fall off, slide, slump, hit a slump, take a nose dive <nonformal>, go into a tailspin

wangle VERBS **maneuver,** manipulate, pull strings *or* wires; **machinate,** contrive, angle <nonformal>, **jockey,** engineer; play games <nonformal>; **plot,** scheme, intrigue; finagle

want NOUNS 1 **lack,** need, deficiency, deficit, shortage, shortfall, wantage, **incompleteness,** defectiveness, shortcoming, imperfection; **absence**, omission; **destitution,** impoverishment, beggary, deprivation
VERBS 2 **desire,** desiderate, be desirous of, **wish,** lust after, bay after, kill for *and* give one's right arm for <both nonformal>, die for <nonformal>, **have a mind to,** choose <nonformal>; fancy, take to, **take a fancy** *or* a shine to, have a fancy for; tilt toward, have a penchant for, have a weakness *or* soft spot in one's heart for; set one's cap for, have designs on; wish very much; **lack**, want for; fall short; **require,** need, feel the want of, have occasion for, be in need of, be hurting for <nonformal>, stand in need of, not be able to dispense with, not be able to do without

wanted ADJS **desired,** coveted; **wished-for,** hoped-for, longed-for; in demand, popular; **welcome,** welcome as the roses in May; **called for,** indicated

wanton ADJS **wayward,** Paphian; **loose,** lax, slack, loose-moraled, of loose morals, of easy virtue, easy <nonformal>, **light,** no better than she should be, promiscuous; **desultory,** rambling, roving, vagrant, wandering, afloat, adrift; **unrestrained,** undisciplined, irresponsible, uncontrolled

war NOUNS 1 **warfare,** warring, warmaking, combat, fighting, *la guerre* <Fr>; armed conflict, armed combat, military operations, the sword, arbitrament of the sword, appeal to arms *or* the sword, resort to arms, force *or* might of arms, bloodshed; **state of war,** hostilities, belligerence *or* belligerency, open war *or* warfare *or* hostilities; **hot war,** shooting war; total war, all-out war; holy war, jihad

a conflict which does not determine who is right—but who is left
ANON

politics with bloodshed
MAO TSE-TUNG

VERBS 2 **wage war,** make war, carry on war *or* hostilities, engage in hostilities, wield the sword; battle, **fight;** spill *or* shed blood

warden NOUNS **jailer,** gaoler <Brit>, correctional *or* correction *or* corrections officer; **keeper,** warder, prison guard, **turnkey,** bull *and* screw <both nonformal>; custodian, guardian; **game warden,** gamekeeper

wardrobe NOUNS furnishings, things, accouterments, trappings; **outfit,** livery, harness, caparison; turnout *and* getup *and* rig <all nonformal>; wedding clothes, bridal outfit, trousseau; clothes closet

warehouse NOUNS 1 **storehouse,** storeroom, storage, **depository,** repository, depot, supply depot, supply base, magazine, *magasin* <Fr>, godown; bonded warehouse, entrepôt
VERBS 2 **store,** stow, lay in store; **lay in,** lay in a supply *or* stock *or* store, store away, stow away, **put away,** lay away, put *or* lay by, pack away, bundle away, lay down, stow down, salt down *or* away *and* sock away *and* squirrel away <all nonformal>; **deposit,** reposit, lodge; **cache,** stash <nonformal>

wares NOUNS **merchandise,** commodities, goods, effects, vendibles; **consumer goods,** consumer items, retail goods, goods for sale; **stock,** stock-in-trade; **line,** line of goods

warfare NOUNS **contention,** contest, contestation, combat, **fighting,** conflict, strife, war, struggle, blood on the floor, cut and thrust; armed conflict, armed combat, military operations, resort to arms, force *or* might of arms, bloodshed; **state of war,** hostilities, open war *or* warfare *or* hostilities

warhead NOUNS **payload;** nuclear *or* thermonuclear warhead, atomic warhead; multiple *or* multiple-missile warhead

warm VERBS 1 **heat,** raise *or* increase the temperature, warm up, fire, fire up, stoke up; take the chill off; preheat; **reheat,** warm over; mull
ADJS 2 **heated,** passionate, hot, red-hot, flaming, **burning,** fiery, glowing, fervent, fervid; feverish, febrile, hectic, flushed
3 **kind, kindly,** kindly-disposed; **benign,** benignant; good as gold, **good,** nice, decent; gracious; kindhearted,

warmhearted, softhearted, tenderhearted, tender, loving, affectionate; **cordial,** genial, hearty, ardent, warm-hearted, affable; hospitable

warmonger NOUNS **militarist,** war dog *or* hound, war hawk, **hawk** <nonformal>; **chauvinist,** jingo, jingoist

warn VERBS **caution,** advise, admonish; give warning, give fair warning, utter a caveat, address a warning to, put a flea in one's ear <nonformal>, have a word with one, say a word to the wise; tip *and* tip off <both nonformal>; notify, put on notice, give notice *or* advance notice *or* advance word; tell once and for all; issue an ultimatum; **threaten; alert,** warn against, put on one's guard, warn away *or* off; **give the high sign** <nonformal>; **put on alert,** cry havoc, sound the alarm

warning NOUNS **caution,** caveat, **admonition,** monition, admonishment; **notice,** notification; **word to the wise,** *verbum sapienti* <L>, verbum sap, enough said; tip-off <nonformal>; **lesson,** object lesson, **example,** deterrent example, warning piece; alarm; final warning *or* notice, ultimatum; **threat**

warp NOUNS 1 **bias, bend,** bent, **crook,** twist, turn, skew, slue, **veer,** sheer, **swerve,** lurch; **distortion,** unsymmetry, disproportion, lopsidedness, imbalance, irregularity, deviation; idiosyncrasy, **eccentricity,** individualism; strain, streak
VERBS 2 bias, twist, distort, contort, torture, skew; put in a false light, **pervert,** garble, wrench, slant, put a spin on, twist the meaning of; **color,** mis-color, **give a false coloring,** put a false construction *or* appearance upon, falsify; **deform,** kink

warrant NOUNS 1 **ratification,** endorsement, acceptance, approval, approbation, subscription, signing-off, imprimatur, **sanction,** permission, the OK *and* the okay *and* the green light *and* the go-ahead *and* the nod <all nonformal>, license, nihil obstat, **certification,** confirmation, validation, authentication, authorization; **oath,** vow, **word,** assurance, guarantee, solemn oath *or* affirmation *or* word *or* declaration; pledge
2 **summons,** subpoena, writ of summons; **writ**
VERBS 3 **authorize,** sanction, give official sanction *or* warrant, legitimize, validate, legalize; empower, give power, enable, entitle; **license;** charter, patent, enfranchise, franchise
4 **state,** assert, swear, swear to God <nonformal>, declare, **affirm,** vow, avow, avouch, asseverate, confess, be under the impression, profess, express the belief, swear, swear to a belief; depose, make an affidavit *or* a sworn statement

warranty NOUNS **security,** surety, indemnity, **guaranty,** guarantee, insurance, assurance; **obligation**, full faith and credit; **bond,** tie; **authorization,** authority, sanction, licensing, countenance, **warrant,** fiat

warrior NOUNS **military man** *or* **woman,** serviceman, servicewoman, **soldier,** brave, fighting man, legionary, hoplite, **man-at-arms,** Amazon

wary ADJS **chary,** cagey <nonformal>, **leery** <nonformal>, **suspicious,** suspecting, distrustful, mistrustful, shy

wash VERBS **bathe,** bath <Brit>, shower, lave; **launder;** wash up *or* out *or* away; **rinse,** rinse out, flush, flush out, irrigate, sluice, sluice out; ritually immerse, baptize; **sponge,** sponge down *or* off; **scrub,** scrub up *or* out, **scour,** holystone; hose out *or* down

washout NOUNS **debacle,** disaster, **breakdown,** collapse; total loss

waste NOUNS 1 **refuse,** wastage, waste matter, **leavings,** sweepings, scraps, orts; **garbage,** swill, slops, lees, **dregs**; **consumption;** wasting, wasting away, atrophy, wilting, emaciation
2 **prodigality,** profligacy, **extravagance,** pound-foolishness, recklessness, reckless spending *or* expenditure; **wastefulness,** dissipation, squandering; conspicuous consumption *or* waste
VERBS 3 **waste away, wither away,** atrophy, consume, consume away, erode away, emaciate, pine away
4 **deplete, depreciate,** dissipate, wear, wear away, erode, ablate, consume, drain, **shrink,** dribble away; **spend,** expend, use up, exhaust; lose; spill, pour down the drain *or* rathole; pour water into a sieve, cast pearls before swine, kill the goose that lays the golden egg, throw out the baby with the bath water
ADJS 5 **unproductive,** nonproductive *or* nonproducing; **unfruitful,** infecund, unprolific *or* nonprolific; ineffectual; **barren,** desert, arid, dry, dried-up, sere,

exhausted, drained, leached, sucked dry, gaunt, **desolate,** jejune

wasteful ADJS **devastating, desolating,** ravaging, wasting, spoliative, depredatory; vandalic, vandalish, vandalistic; **prodigal,** extravagant, lavish, profuse, **overliberal,** overgenerous, overlavish, **spendthrift,** profligate, dissipative

wasteland NOUNS **waste,** desolation, barren *or* **barrens,** barren land; heath; **desert,** karroo <Africa>, badlands, dust bowl, salt flat, Death Valley, lunar waste *or* landscape

watch NOUNS 1 **vigil,** lookout; *qui vive* <Fr>; invigilation, proctoring, monitoring; **sharp eye,** weather eye, peeled eye, watchful eye, eagle eye, lidless *or* sleepless *or* unblinking *or* unwinking eye
2 **shift,** work shift, **tour,** tour of duty, stint, bit, **trick,** time, **turn,** relay, spell *or* turn of work
3 **timepiece,** timekeeper, **timer,** chronometer, ship's watch; horologe, horologium; **clock,** Big Ben, ticker <nonformal>, turnip
VERBS 4 **look, peer,** have a look, take a gander *and* take a look <both nonformal>, direct the eyes, turn *or* bend the eyes, cast one's eye, lift up the eyes; **look at,** take a look at, eye, **eyeball** <nonformal>, have a look-see <nonformal>, look on *or* upon, gaze at *or* upon; **observe,** view, regard; keep one's eyes peeled *or* skinned, be watchful *or* observant *or* vigilant, keep one's eyes open; keep in sight *or* view, hold in view; look after
5 **keep watch,** keep guard, keep watch over, keep vigil; stand guard, stand sentinel; be on the lookout; **police,** patrol, pound a beat <nonformal>, go on one's beat

watchful ADJS **vigilant,** wary, prudent, lidless, sleepless, observant; **on the lookout,** *aux aguets* <Fr>; **on guard,** on one's guard, guarded; alert, aware, with open eyes, with one's eyes open, with one's eyes peeled *or* with a weather eye open <both nonformal>; all eyes, all ears, **all eyes and ears;** custodial

watchword NOUNS **password,** countersign; catchword, catchphrase, slogan; shibboleth

water NOUNS 1 **fluid,** liquid; **juice,** sap; **body fluid,** semiliquid
VERBS 2 **dilute,** cut <nonformal>, water down, adulterate, irrigate *and* baptize <both nonformal>; **weaken,** attenuate, extenuate

watery ADJS **waterish, aqueous,** aquatic; liquid; **splashy,** plashy, sloppy; hydrous, hydrated; hydraulic

wave NOUNS 1 **billow,** surge, **swell,** heave, undulation, lift, rise, send, scend; trough, peak; **sea,** heavy swell, ocean swell, ground swell; **roller,** roll; **comber,** comb; **tidal wave,** tsunami; **whitecap,** white horse; standing wave
VERBS 2 **signal,** give the high sign *or* the nod <both nonformal>; wave the hand, wave a flag, **flag,** flag down
3 **undulate; brandish,** flourish, flaunt, shake, swing, wield; **flap,** flutter; wag, wigwag

waver VERBS **vacillate,** waffle <nonformal>, **fluctuate,** pendulate, oscillate, wobble, wobble about, teeter, dither, swing from one thing to another, **shilly-shally,** back and fill, keep off and on, keep *or* leave hanging in midair; blow hot and cold; **equivocate**, fudge; shift, change horses in midstream, **change**

wavy ADJS **undulant,** undulatory, undulative, undulating, undulate, undulated; **billowy,** billowing, surgy, rolling; **wavering,** wavery, flitting, flickering, guttering, fitful, shifting, shuffling

way NOUNS 1 **route,** path, itinerary, course, track, run, line, road; **scope, room,** range, maneuvering space *or* room, room to swing a cat <nonformal>
2 **manner,** wise, **means,** mode, modality, **fashion,** style, tone; **method,** methodology, system; **approach,** attack, tack; **technique,** procedure, process, proceeding, course, practice; *modus operandi* <L>, mode of operation *or* MO, manner of working; **habit,** tenor, cast, grain, vein, streak, stripe, mold, brand, stamp

wayward ADJS 1 **disobedient,** transgressive, uncomplying, violative, lawless, froward, naughty; **undisciplined,** ill-disciplined, indisciplined; **desultory,** rambling, roving, vagrant, wanton, wandering, afloat, adrift
2 **unvirtuous,** virtueless, ungood; fleshly, carnal, wanton, prodigal; erring, **fallen, lapsed,** postlapsarian

weak ADJS 1 weakly, **feeble,** debilitated, imbecile; **strengthless,** sapless, marrowless, pithless, sinewless, listless, out of gas <nonformal>, nerveless, lustless; **impotent,** powerless; spineless, lily-liv-

ered, whitelivered, wimpy *and* wimpish *and* chicken *and* gutless <all nonformal>, cowardly; dull, slack; **languorous,** languid, **drooping,** droopy, pooped <nonformal>; asthenic, anemic, bloodless, effete, etiolated
2 <comparisons> a kitten, a reed, thread, matchwood, a rope of sand; a house of cards, a house built on sand, a sand castle; water, milk and water, gruel, dishwater, cambric tea

weak as water
Bible

3 **faint,** low, soft, gentle, subdued, dim, feeble, faint-sounding
4 attenuated, attenuate, **watery,** diluted, watered *or* watered-down

weaken VERBS 1 grow weak *or* weaker, go soft <nonformal>; **languish,** wilt, faint, **droop,** drop, **sink, decline,** flag, pine, fade, tail away *or* off, fail, fall *or* drop by the wayside; crumble, go to pieces, disintegrate; give out, have no staying power, run out of gas <nonformal>, conk *or* peter *or* poop *or* peg *or* fizzle out <nonformal>; come apart, come apart at the seams, come unstuck *or* unglued <both informal>
2 **enfeeble,** debilitate, unstrengthen, unsinew, undermine, soften up <nonformal>, unbrace, unman, unnerve, rattle, shake up <nonformal>, **devitalize,** enervate, eviscerate; **sap,** sap the strength of, exhaust, gruel, take it out of <nonformal>; dilute, water, water down, attenuate, extenuate

weakling NOUNS **weak** *or* meek soul, weak sister <nonformal>, hothouse plant, softy <nonformal>, softling, **jellyfish,** invertebrate, gutless wonder <nonformal>, **baby,** big baby, crybaby, chicken <nonformal>, Milquetoast, sop, **milksop,** namby-pamby, mollycoddle, mama's boy, mother's boy, mother's darling, teacher's pet; sissy *and* pansy *and* pantywaist <all nonformal>, pushover <nonformal>, lightweight; **wimp,** poor *or* weak *or* dull tool <nonformal>; doormat *and* empty suit *and* nebbish *and* sad sack <all nonformal>

wealth NOUNS 1 **opulence** *or* opulency, richness, affluence; **prosperity,** prosperousness, thriving *or* flourishing condition

2 <nonformal> **bundle, big bucks,** megabucks, gigabucks, big money, serious money, gobs, heaps, heavy lettuce, heavy jack, heavy money, important money, pot, potful, power, mint, barrel, raft, load, **loads,** pile, wad, wads, nice hunk of change, packet <Brit>

wealthy ADJS 1 **rich,** affluent, moneyed *or* monied, in funds *or* cash, **well-to-do,** well-off, well-situated, prosperous, comfortable, provided for, well provided for, fat, **flush,** flush with money, abounding in riches, worth a great deal, frightfully rich, rich as Croesus; privileged, born with a silver spoon in one's mouth

2 <nonformal> **loaded, well-heeled, filthy rich,** warm <Brit>, in the money *or* dough, well-fixed, made of money, **rolling in money,** rolling *or* wallowing in it, disgustingly rich, big-rich, rich-rich, oofy, lousy rich, upscale

wean VERBS **disaccustom,** cure, break off, stop; **convince,** persuade, bring over, sweep off one's feet <nonformal>, win over

wear NOUNS 1 use, hard wear; **wear and tear;** erosion, weathering, ablation, ravages of time
VERBS 2 **have on,** be dressed in, affect, sport <nonformal>
3 **wear away,** wear down, wear off; abrade, fret, whittle away, rub off; fray, frazzle, tatter, wear ragged; **wear out;** weather, erode, ablate

wear out VERBS **fatigue,** tire, weary, exhaust, wilt, flag, jade, harass; **wear,** wear on *or* upon, wear down; **tire out,** burn out; use up; weaken, enervate, debilitate

weary ADJS **weariful; tired,** wearied, irked; good and tired, tired to death, weary unto death; **sick and tired of;** jaded, satiated, palled, fed up <nonformal>; **listless,** dispirited

weasel VERBS **equivocate,** waffle <nonformal>, tergiversate, evade, dodge, sidestep, say in a roundabout way, parry, duck, weasel out <nonformal>, palter; renege

weather NOUNS 1 **climate,** clime; **the elements,** forces of nature; microclimate, macroclimate

VERBS 2 **weather the storm,** ride, ride out, ride out a storm; erode, ablate

weather-beaten ADJS **weatherworn,** weathered; eroded; **faded,** washed-out

weave VERBS loom, tissue; **interweave,** interlace, intertwine, interknit, intertissue, intertwist; **braid,** plait, pleach, **wreathe,** raddle, **knit,** twist, mat, wattle

web NOUNS **cobweb,** gossamer, spider *or* spider's web

wed VERBS **marry,** join, unite, hitch *and* splice <both nonformal>, couple, match, match up, make *or* arrange a match, join together, **unite in marriage,** join *or* unite in holy wedlock, tie the knot, tie the nuptial *or* wedding knot, make one

wedding NOUNS **marriage,** marriage ceremony, nuptial mass; church wedding, civil wedding, civil ceremony; espousement, bridal; **nuptials,** spousals, hymeneal rites

wedge VERBS **jam,** seize; make fast, fasten, fasten down

weed VERBS **cultivate,** weed out, hoe, cut, prune, thin, thin out

weep VERBS **sob,** cry, **bawl,** blubber, whimper, snivel; shed tears, drop a tear; give way to tears, melt *or* dissolve in tears, break down, break down and cry, turn on the waterworks <nonformal>; cry one's eyes out; **drip,** seep

weepy ADJS **tearful,** teary; lachrymal, lachrymose, lacrimatory; in the melting mood, on the edge of tears, ready to cry; **weeping,** sobbing, crying; blubbering, whimpering, sniveling; oozy, runny, leaky

weigh VERBS **heft** <nonformal>, balance, weigh in the balance, strike a balance, hold the scales, put on the scales; **consider,** contemplate, speculate, reflect, study, ponder, **deliberate,** debate, meditate, muse, brood, ruminate, chew the cud <nonformal>

weight NOUNS 1 **heaviness,** weightiness, ponderousness, heftiness *and* heft <both nonformal>; body weight, avoirdupois <nonformal>, fatness, beef *and* beefiness <both nonformal>; poundage, tonnage; **solemnity,** gravity, moment, consequence, importance, eminence; cogency, force, persuasiveness

2 paperweight, letterweight; sinker, lead, plumb, plummet, bob; sash weight; sandbag

weight-watching NOUNS **reducing,** slenderizing, slimming down, dieting; calorie-counting

weird ADJS **eerie,** eldritch, **uncanny,** unearthly, macabre; **spooky** *and* spookish *and* hairy <all nonformal>; **absurd,** preposterous, fantastic, fantastical, grotesque, monstrous, wild, **outrageous,** incredible, beyond belief, *outré* <Fr>, extravagant, **bizarre**

welcome NOUNS 1 welcoming, **reception,** *accueil* <Fr>; cordial *or* warm *or* hearty welcome, pleasant *or* smiling reception, the glad hand <nonformal>, **open arms;** welcome mat

VERBS 2 make welcome, bid one welcome, make one feel welcome *or* at home *or* like one of the family, give one the freedom of the house, hold out the hand, extend the right hand of friendship; glad-hand *and* give the glad hand *and* glad eye <all nonformal>; **receive** *or* **welcome with open arms;** give a warm reception to, roll out the red carpet, give the red-carpet treatment

kill the fatted calf
Bible

ADJS 3 welcome as the roses in May, wanted, desired, wished-for; **agreeable,** desirable, acceptable

weld VERBS **fuse, solder,** braze; **stick together,** cement, bind, colligate

welfare NOUNS **well-being,** weal, happiness, felicity; quality of life; comfortable *or* easy circumstances, **comfort,** ease, security; **welfare work,** social service, social welfare, social work; commonweal, public welfare; public assistance, relief, the dole, social security <Brit>

well NOUNS 1 **pit,** deep, depth, hole, hollow, **cavity,** shaft, sump; oil well; wellspring, wellhead, **spring,** fountain, fount, font, *fons et origo* <L>

ADJS 2 **unailing,** unsick, unsickly, unfrail; all right, doing nicely, up and about, sitting up and taking nourishment, alive and well

ADVS 3 **ably,** capably, competently, adequately, effectively, effectually, efficiently; to the best of one's ability, as lies in one's power, so far as one can, as best one can; **successfully,** to some purpose, to good purpose; **skillfully,** expertly, proficiently, excellently

well-being NOUNS **health,** fitness, health and fitness, physical fitness; bloom, flush, glow, rosiness; euphoria; happiness; **comfort,** ease, contentment

well-bred ADJS highbred, **well-brought-up;** cultivated, cultured, polished, refined, genteel, gentle; gentlemanly, gentlemanlike, ladylike

well-built ADJS **sturdy,** stable, **solid,** sound, firm, steady, tough, stout, **strong,** rugged; **durable,** lasting, enduring; **well-made,** well-constructed; **shapely,** built, well-proportioned, well-formed, stacked *or* well-stacked <both nonformal>, curvaceous, curvy <nonformal>, amply endowed, built for comfort *or* built like a brick shithouse <both nonformal>, buxom

well-known ADJS **well-understood, well-recognized, widely known,** commonly known, universally recognized, generally *or* universally admitted; **familiar,** common, current; proverbial; public, notorious; **on everyone's tongue** *or* **lips;** commonplace, trite, hackneyed, platitudinous, truistic

well-rounded ADJS **versatile,** all-around <nonformal>, broad-gauge, **many-sided,** generally capable; **adaptable,** adjustable, flexible, resourceful, supple

well-to-do ADJS **wealthy,** well-situated, prosperous, comfortable, provided for, well-off, well provided for; independent, independently rich, independently wealthy; privileged, higher-income, upper-income

welsh VERBS **repudiate,** renege, dodge, duck; **not pay;** dishonor, **default,** levant <Brit>

wet NOUNS 1 **moisture,** damp; **dampness,** moistness, moistiness, **wetness,** soddenness; mistiness, fogginess; rainfall

VERBS 2 **moisten,** dampen, moisturize, damp, wet down; humidify, **water,** sprinkle, besprinkle, **spray,** spritz <nonformal>, sparge, asperge; **swash,** slosh, splatter, spatter, bespatter

ADJS 3 **moist,** moisty; **damp,** dampish; wettish; **humid,** dank, muggy, dewy, bedewed; rainy

wet blanket NOUNS **spoilsport,** killjoy, grouch, grinch *and* sourpuss <both nonformal>, malcontent, **dog in the manger** <nonformal>

whammy NOUNS **curse,** anathema, fulmination; hex, evil eye, jinx, *malocchio* <Ital>

wheedle VERBS **coax,** cajole, blandish, flatter, palaver, plead with, sweet-talk *and* soft-soap <both nonformal>

wheel NOUNS steering wheel; **potter's wheel,** kick wheel, pedal wheel, power wheel; **big shot** *and* big wheel *and* big-time operator *and* **bigwig** *and* big man *and* big gun *and* high-muck-a-muck *and* big man on campus *or* BMOC

wheeler-dealer NOUNS operator *and* finagler *and* **wire-puller** <all nonformal>; **person** *or* **woman** *or* **man** of influence, a presence, a palpable presence, a mover and shaker <nonformal>, a person to be reckoned with, a player *or* player on the scene; influencer, powerbroker

whereabouts NOUNS 1 **location,** place, position, spot, *lieu* <Fr>, placement, emplacement, stead; whereabout, ubicity

ADVS 2 **where,** in what place, in which place

whereas NOUNS **condition,** provision, proviso, stipulation

wherewithal NOUNS **means,** ways, **ways and means,** means to an end; funds; **resources,** disposable resources, capital; **assets,** total assets, worth, net worth, **pecuniary resources,** available means *or* resources *or* funds, cash flow, command of money

whet VERBS **stimulate,** sharpen, pique, provoke, quicken, enliven, excite, stir, liven up, pick up, jazz up <nonformal>, animate; infuse life into, give new life to, revive, renew, resuscitate; **hone,** oilstone, file, grind; strop

while NOUNS **time,** duration, *durée* <Fr>, lastingness, continuity, term, tide, space; **meantime,** meanwhile, the while

while away VERBS **fritter away,** fool away, fribble away, dribble away, drivel away, **trifle away,** dally away, potter away, piss away <nonformal>, muddle away, diddle away <nonformal>, squander in dribs and drabs; idle away

whim NOUNS **caprice,** humor, **whimsy,** freak, whim-wham; **fancy,** fantasy, **conceit, notion,** flimflam, toy, freakish inspiration, crazy idea, fantastic notion, fool notion <nonformal>, harebrained idea, brainstorm, **vagary,** megrim; **quirk,** twist, kink, crank, quip, trick, mannerism, **crotchet,** maggot, maggot in the brain, bee in one's bonnet *or* head <nonformal>

whimper VERBS **blubber,** snivel; shed

tears, drop a tear; give way to tears, melt *or* dissolve in tears, break down, break down and cry, turn on the waterworks <nonformal>

whimsical ADJS **capricious,** freakish, humorsome, vagarious; **fanciful,** notional, fantastic *or* fantastical, maggoty, kinky, harebrained, cranky, flaky <nonformal>, quirky; **droll,** quizzical; **fickle,** erratic, variable, wavering, **changeable**

whine NOUNS 1 **lament,** plaint, *planctus* <L>; **whimper;** cry
VERBS 2 **whimper,** yammer <nonformal>, pule, grizzle <chiefly Brit nonformal>; nasalize, **speak through one's nose,** snuffle

whip NOUNS 1 **lash,** scourge, flagellum, strap, thong, rawhide, cowhide, blacksnake, kurbash, sjambok, belt, razor strap; knout; bullwhip, bullwhack; horsewhip; crop; quirt; cat, cat-o'-nine-tails
VERBS 2 give a whipping *or* beating *or* thrashing, **beat,** thrash, spank, flog, scourge, flagellate, flail, whale; **smite,** thump, trounce, baste, **pummel,** pommel, **drub,** buffet, belabor, lay on; **lash,** lace, cut, stripe; horsewhip; knout; **strap,** belt, rawhide, cowhide; **switch,** birch, give the stick; pistol-whip

whippersnapper NOUNS **brat,** urchin; minx, **imp,** puck, elf, gamin, little monkey, young whippersnapper, *enfant terrible* <Fr>, little terror, holy terror; spoiled brat; snotnose kid <nonformal>; punk *and* punk kid <both nonformal>; pipsqueak *and* squirt *and* shrimp *and* scrub *and* runt <all nonformal>

whir NOUNS 1 **turning,** whirling, swirling, **spinning,** wheeling, reeling
VERBS 2 **hum,** thrum, **drone,** buzz, whiz, burr, purr

whirl NOUNS 1 **eddy,** swirl, twirl; **bustle,** fuss, flurry, flutter, fluster, scramble, ferment, stew, sweat, vortex, maelstrom, **stir,** hubbub, hullabaloo, hoo-ha *and* foofaraw *and* flap <all nonformal>, ado, to-do <nonformal>; **round of pleasure,** mad round, merry-go-round, the dizzy rounds
VERBS 2 **eddy,** gurge, **swirl,** purl, reel, spin; **swivel,** pivot, pivot about, swing, round, swing round; wheel, wheel about, go round *or* around, circle, rotate, gyrate

whiskey NOUNS **spirits,** liquor, intoxicating liquor, **hard liquor,** firewater, spiritus frumenti, usquebaugh <Scots>, schnapps, ardent spirits, strong waters, **intoxicant,** toxicant, inebriant, **drink, strong drink,** strong liquor, alcoholic drink *or* beverage, **alcohol,** aqua vitae, water of life, **grog,** social lubricant, nectar of the gods; **booze** <nonformal>; **rum,** the Demon Rum, John Barleycorn; the cup that cheers

whisper NOUNS 1 whispering, stage whisper, breathy voice, sussuration; **hint,** gentle hint, **intimation,** indication, suggestion, **suspicion,** inkling, **glimmer,** glimmering; **implication,** insinuation, innuendo; **report,** rumor, flying rumor, unverified *or* unconfirmed report, **hearsay,** *on-dit* <Fr>, scuttlebutt *and* latrine rumor <both nonformal>; **talk,** buzz, rumble, bruit, cry; common talk, town talk, **talk of the town,** topic of the day, *cause célèbre* <Fr>
VERBS 2 **tell confidentially,** tell for one's ears only, mention privately, **breathe,** whisper in the ear; tell one a secret; confide, take aside, see one alone, talk to in private, speak in privacy; say under one's breath, **put a bug in one's ear** <nonformal>

white NOUNS **whiteness,** whitishness; albescence; **lightness,** fairness; paleness, chalkiness

white elephant NOUNS **impediment,** handicap, disadvantage, inconvenience, penalty; **burden,** imposition, cross, weight, deadweight, ball and chain, millstone around one's neck

white flag NOUNS **truce, surrender;** truce flag, flag of truce; offer of parley; calumet, peace pipe, **pipe of peace;** downing of arms, empty hands, hand of friendship, outstretched hand

white lightning NOUNS **bootleg liquor, moonshine** <nonformal>; hooch *and* shine *and* mountain dew <all nonformal>, white mule <nonformal>

whitewash VERBS **excuse, absolve,** vindicate, clear, exculpate, exonerate, give absolution; justify; **discharge,** release, dismiss, free, set free, let off <nonformal>, let go; quash the charge *or* indictment, withdraw the charge; clear the skirts of, shrive, purge; wipe the slate clean; **decontaminate,** destigmatize

whittle VERBS **shape, fashion,** carve, cut, hew, hew out; trim, pare down, gash

whiz NOUNS 1 **ace,** star, superstar, crack-

erjack, great, all-time great, topnotcher, first-rater, flash, hot stuff, pistol, no slouch, world-beater, hot rock, the one who wrote the book <all nonformal>
VERBS 2

<nonformal> **barrel,** clip, tear *or* tear along, bowl along, thunder along, breeze *or* breeze along, tear up the track *or* road, eat up the track *or* road, scorch, sizzle, rip, zip, nip, zing, highball, pour it on, shake *or* get the lead out, give it the gun, skedaddle, scoot, step on it, step on the gas, hump *or* hump it, hotfoot, hightail, make tracks, step lively, step along, carry the mail, hop along, get, git, go like a bat out of hell, run like a scared rabbit, run like mad, go at full blast, go all out, go flat out, run wide open, go at full tilt *or* steam, let her out, open her up, go hell-bent for election *or* leather, give it the gas, go like blazes *or* blue blazes, floor it, make tracks

whole NOUNS 1 **totality, entirety,** collectivity; complex; integration, embodiment; **unity,** integrity, wholeness; organic unity, oneness
ADJS 2 **sound,** wholesome; unimpaired; sound of mind and body, sound in wind and limb, sound as a dollar <nonformal>
3 **complete,** total, global, **entire,** intact, solid; full-grown, mature, matured, ripe, developed; **uncut,** unabbreviated, undiminished, unexpurgated

wholehearted ADJS **resolute,** resolved, determined, bound *and* bound and determined <both nonformal>, **decided,** decisive, purposeful; **earnest,** serious, sincere; devoted, dedicated, committed; single-minded, relentless, persistent, tenacious, persevering

wholesome ADJS **healthful,** healthy, salubrious, salutary, health-preserving, health-enhancing, life-promoting, **beneficial,** benign, good, **good for; hygienic,** hygienical, hygeian, sanitary; constitutional, for one's health; conditioning; bracing, refreshing, invigorating, tonic; **sound,** whole; **sane,** sane-minded, **rational,** reasonable, sensible, **lucid,** normal, clearheaded, clear-minded, balanced

whopper NOUNS 1 thumper *and* lunker *and* whale *and* jumbo <all nonformal>; monster, hulk
2 **monstrous lie,** consummate lie, deep-dyed falsehood, out-and-out lie, gross *or* flagrant *or* shameless falsehood, **barefaced lie,** dirty lie <nonformal>; the big lie

whore NOUNS 1 **prostitute,** harlot, *fille de joie* <Fr>, daughter of joy, call girl *and* B-girl <both nonformal>, **scarlet woman,** unfortunate woman, painted woman, fallen woman, erring sister, **streetwalker,** hustler *and* **hooker** <both nonformal>, strumpet, woman of the town, *poule* <Fr>, stew, meretrix, Cyprian, Paphian
VERBS 2 **be promiscuous,** sleep around *and* swing <both nonformal>; **debauch,** wanton, fornicate, **cheat,** commit adultery, get a little on the side <nonformal>

whorehouse NOUNS **brothel,** house of prostitution, house of assignation, house of joy *or* ill repute *or* ill fame, bawdyhouse, massage parlor, sporting house, disorderly house, **cathouse,** bordello, bagnio, stew, dive, den of vice, den *or* sink of iniquity, crib, joint

whorl NOUNS 1 **coil,** roll, **curl,** curlicue, ringlet, pigtail, **spiral,** helix, volute, volution, involute, evolute, gyre, scroll; screw, corkscrew; tendril, cirrus; whirl, swirl, vortex
VERBS 2 convolve, **wind, twine,** twirl, **twist, turn,** twist and turn, meander, crinkle; serpentine, snake, slink, worm; screw, corkscrew; whirl, swirl; scallop; intort; contort

why NOUNS 1 **enigma,** mystery, puzzle, puzzlement; **problem,** puzzling *or* baffling problem; question, question mark, vexed *or* perplexed question, enigmatic question, sixty-four dollar question <nonformal>; **perplexity; puzzler,** poser, brain twister *or* teaser <nonformal>, sticker <nonformal>; mind-boggler, **hard** *or* **tough nut to crack**
ADVS 2 whyever, how come <nonformal>, how is it that, **wherefore,** what for, for which, **on what account,** on account of what *or* which, for what *or* whatever reason, from what cause, *pourquoi* <Fr>

wicked ADJS 1 **evil,** vicious, bad, naughty, wrong, sinful, iniquitous, peccant, reprobate; dark, black; **base,** low, vile, foul, rank, flagrant, arrant, nefarious, **heinous,** villainous, criminal, up to no good, knavish, flagitious; abominable,

atrocious, monstrous, unspeakable, execrable, damnable; shameful, disgraceful, scandalous, **infamous,** unpardonable, unforgivable; **improper,** reprehensible, blamable, blameworthy, unworthy
2 **difficult,** difficile; **not easy,** no picnic; **hard,** tough *and* rough *and* rugged <all nonformal>, rigorous, brutal, severe; mean *and* hairy <both nonformal>, **formidable; arduous,** strenuous, toilsome, laborious, operose, Herculean; knotty, knotted; thorny, spiny, set with thorns; easier said than done, like pulling teeth; exacting, demanding; intricate, complex; abstruse

wide ADJS 1 **voluminous,** capacious, generous, ample, copious, broad, extensive, expansive, comprehensive; **spacious;** wide-scale, wide-ranging, exhaustive, in-depth; widespread
ADVS 2 **clear;** wide of the mark, abroad, all abroad, astray, afield, far afield

widen VERBS 1 **broaden,** stretch, distend, dilate, swell, inflate, sufflate, **blow up,** puff up, huff, puff, bloat; **expand,** extend, extend to the side *or* sides; **spread**, spread out *or* sidewise *or* sideways, outspread, outstretch
2 **generalize,** universalize, catholicize, ecumenicize, globalize, internationalize; make a generalization, deal in generalities *or* abstractions

widespread ADJS 1 **customary,** wonted, consuetudinary; traditional, time-honored; **normative,** normal; prevalent, prevailing, obtaining, generally accepted, popular, current; conventional; conformist, conformable
2 **dispersed,** scattered, distributed, disseminated, strown, strewn, broadcast, **spread,** dispread; diffuse, discrete, sparse; far-spread, **far-reaching,** far-ranging, **far-flung,** wide-flung, wide-reaching, wide-ranging

width NOUNS **breadth,** broadness, wideness, fullness, amplitude, latitude, distance across *or* crosswise *or* crossways, extent, **span, expanse, spread;** beam

wield VERBS **use,** utilize, make use of, do with; **employ,** practice, ply, work, manage, handle, manipulate, operate, play; **have** *or* **enjoy the use of;** exercise, exert; **brandish,** flourish, flaunt, shake, swing

wieldy ADJS **handy,** wieldable, handleable; tractable; **manageable,** maneuverable; **convenient,** foolproof, goofproof <nonformal>, practical, untroublesome, user-friendly; adaptable

wife NOUNS **married woman,** wedded wife, goodwife <old>, squaw, woman, lady, matron, old lady *and* old woman *and* little woman *and* ball and chain <all nonformal>, feme, feme covert, **better half** <nonformal>, **helpmate,** helpmeet, rib, wife of one's bosom; common-law wife

wig NOUNS **peruke,** toupee, hairpiece; rug *and* divot *and* doormat <all nonformal>; periwig

wiggle NOUNS 1 **wriggle;** wag, waggle; writhe, **squirm**
VERBS 2 **wriggle;** wag, waggle; **writhe, squirm,** twist and turn; have ants in one's pants <nonformal>

wild NOUNS 1 **wilderness,** howling wilderness, wilds
ADJS 2 **furious,** fierce, savage, untamed; raving mad <nonformal>, **rabid,** foaming *or* frothing at the mouth; **fuming,** in a fume; **enraged,** raging, raving, ranting, storming
3 **unrestrained,** unconstrained, unforced, uncompelled, uncoerced; unmeasured, **uninhibited,** unsuppressed, unrepressed, unreserved, boisterous, exuberant; **uncurbed,** unchecked, unbridled, unmuzzled; **unreined,** uncontrolled, unmastered, unsubdued, ungoverned, **unruly;** out of control, out of hand, out of one's power; **abandoned,** intemperate, immoderate, **incontinent,** licentious, loose, wanton, rampant, riotous, rowdy

wilderness NOUNS **wasteland,** waste, desolation, barren *or* **barrens,** barren land; howling wilderness, wild, wilds

will NOUNS 1 **resolution,** resolve, resolvedness, **determination,** decision, fixed *or* firm resolve, purpose; **resoluteness,** determinedness, decisiveness, **purposefulness;** single-mindedness, relentlessness, persistence, tenacity, perseverance; self-will, obstinacy; **moral fiber; iron will,** will of iron *or* steel; a will *or* mind of one's own, the courage of one's convictions, moral courage
2 **testament,** last will and testament; **bequest,** bequeathal, **legacy,** devise; inheritance
VERBS 3 **wish,** see *or* think fit, think good, think proper, **choose to,** have a mind to; have half a mind *or* notion to;

choose, determine, decide; **desire; resolve,** purpose, make up one's mind, make *or* take a resolution, make a point of
4 **bequeath,** will and bequeath, **leave,** devise, will to, hand down, hand on, pass on, transmit; make a bequest, write one's last will and testament, write into one's will

willful ADJS 1 **obstinate,** stubborn, pertinacious, restive; self-willed, strong-willed, hardheaded, **headstrong,** strongheaded, *entêté* <Fr>; **dogged,** bulldogged, tenacious; bullheaded, bulletheaded, **pigheaded,** mulish <nonformal>, stubborn as a mule; set, **set in one's ways,** case-hardened, stiff-necked
2 **intentional,** intended, proposed, purposed, telic, **projected,** designed, of design, aimed, aimed at, **meant,** purposeful, purposive, voluntary, deliberate

willing ADJS **willinghearted,** ready, game <nonformal>; **disposed,** inclined, minded, willed; **well-disposed,** well-inclined, favorably inclined *or* disposed; predisposed; **favorable,** agreeable, cooperative; compliant, **acquiescent,** consenting; in the mood *or* vein *or* humor *or* mind, receptive, responsive; amenable, tractable, docile, pliant

will power NOUNS **will,** volition; choice, determination, decision; **free choice,** one's own will *or* choice *or* discretion *or* initiative, **free will**; conation, conatus; **resolution**

wilt VERBS **languish,** pine, droop, flag; fade, fade away; **wither,** shrivel, shrink, diminish, wither *or* die on the vine, **dry up,** desiccate, wizen, wrinkle, sear

wily ADJS **shrewd,** artful, cunning, knowing, crafty, guileful, canny, slick, sly, smart as a fox, foxy *and* crazy like a fox <both nonformal>; insinuating, insidious, devious, Byzantine, calculating

wimp NOUNS **weakling,** jellyfish, milksop, milquetoast; poor *or* weak *or* dull tool <nonformal>, sissy

wimpy ADJS **weak,** spineless, lily-livered, whitelivered, wimpish *and* chicken *and* gutless <all nonformal>, cowardly; weak as a kitten, wimpish <nonformal>, fainthearted

win NOUNS 1 **victory,** triumph, conquest, subduing, subdual; a feather in one's cap <nonformal>; **championship,** crown, laurels, cup, trophy, belt, blue ribbon, first prize
VERBS 2 **triumph,** prevail, be victorious, come out ahead, come out on top <nonformal>; **gain,** capture, carry; win out <nonformal>, **win through,** carry it, carry off *or* away; **win** *or* **carry** *or* **gain the day,** win the battle, come out first, finish in front; **win the prize,** win the palm *or* bays *or* laurels, take the cake <nonformal>, win one's spurs *or* wings
3 **acquire,** get, gain, obtain, secure, procure; score; **earn,** make; **reap,** harvest; take, catch, capture; come *or* enter into possession of, **come into,** come by, come in for, be seized of

wince VERBS **flinch,** shrink, shy, shy away from, draw back, recoil, funk <nonformal>, **quail,** cringe, blench, blink, say *or* cry uncle

wind NOUNS 1 current, **air current,** current of air, **draft,** movement of air, stream, stream of air, flow of air; updraft, uprush; downdraft, downrush, microburst; fall wind, gravity wind, katabatic wind, head wind, tail wind, following wind; jet stream, upper-atmosphere *or* upper-atmospheric wind
2 **breath,** breath of air; pant, puff; gasp, gulp; **artificial respiration,** kiss of life, mouth-to-mouth resuscitation
3 **fart** <nonformal>, flatulence *or* flatulency, flatuosity, flatus, gas; **belch,** burp <nonformal>, belching, eructation

wind VERBS **wander,** meander, curl, twist, snake, twist and turn; screw, crank, wind up

windbag NOUNS **chatterer,** chatterbox, babbler, jabberer, prater, prattler, gabbler, gibble-gabbler, **gabber** <nonformal>, **blabberer,** blatherer, patterer, word-slinger, *moulin à paroles* <Fr>; gasbag *and* windjammer *and* hot-air artist *and* motor-mouth *and* ratchet-jaw <all nonformal>; big talker <nonformal>, spendthrift of one's tongue

windfall NOUNS **windfall money, windfall profit, found money, money in the bank, bonus,** gravy <nonformal>; godsend

winding ADJS **convolutional,** twisting, twisty, **turning; meandering,** meandrous, mazy, labyrinthine; **serpentine,** snaky, anfractuous; roundabout, circuitous, ambagious, circumlocutory; labyrinthine; **tortuous,** torsional

windup NOUNS **completion,** completing, **finish,** finishing, conclusion, end, ending, **termination,** terminus, **close,**

rounding off *or* out, topping off, wrapping up, wrap-up, finalization

windy ADJS **blowy; breezy,** drafty, airy, airish; brisk, fresh; **gusty,** blasty, puffy, flawy; **squally;** blustery, blustering, blusterous; aeolian, favonian, boreal; ventose

wine NOUNS *vin* <Fr>, *vino* <Sp & Ital>; vintage wine, nonvintage wine; red wine, white wine, rosé wine, pink wine; dry *or* sweet wine, heavy *or* light wine, full *or* thin wine, rough *or* smooth wine, still wine, sparkling wine; jug wine, plonk <Brit>

wing NOUNS 1 **addition,** annex, extension, ell *or* L; **branch,** organ, division, arm, offshoot, affiliate; **offshoot,** ramification, scion, spur; pinion
2 **protectorship,** guardianship, stewardship, custodianship; **care,** charge, keeping, nurture, nurturing, nurturance, custody, fostering, fosterage; hands, safe hands

wing it VERBS **1 improvise,** extemporize, improv *and* tapdance *and* talk off the top of one's head <all nonformal>, speak off the cuff, think on one's feet, make it up as one goes along, depart from the prepared text, throw away the speech, scrap the plan, **ad-lib** <nonformal>, **do offhand,** fake <nonformal>, play by ear <nonformal>
2 **do easily,** make short work of, do with one's hands tied behind one's back, do with both eyes shut, do standing on one's head, sail *or* dance *or* waltz through

wink NOUNS 1 casual glance, **half an eye;** flick of the eyelash, glance, leer; **hint,** broad hint, signal, nod, look; blink
2 **instant,** moment, **trice,** twinkle, twinkling, twinkling *or* twinkle of an eye, twink, bat of an eye <nonformal>
VERBS 3 **blink,** nictitate, bat the eyes <nonformal>; **signal,** give a signal, make a sign; glance, raise one's eyebrows

winner NOUNS 1 **victor,** victress, victrix, triumpher; **conqueror,** defeater, **vanquisher,** subduer, subjugator, *conquistador* <Sp>; top dog <nonformal>; champion, champ *and* number one <both nonformal>; easy winner, sure winner, shoo-in <nonformal>; **star,** success, superstar
2 **good thing,** a thing to be desired; no slouch *and* nothing to sneeze at <both nonformal>; catch, find <nonformal>

winning NOUNS 1 **acquisition,** gaining, getting, getting hold of <nonformal>, coming by, **acquirement, obtainment,** obtention, **attainment,** securement
ADJS 2 **victorious,** triumphant, triumphal, prevailing; conquering, vanquishing, defeating, overcoming; ahead of the game, ascendant, in the ascendant, in ascendancy, sitting on top of the world *and* sitting pretty <both nonformal>, dominant; successful
3 **delightful,** winsome, taking, fetching, heart-robbing; inviting, tempting, tantalizing; **attractive,** sexy <nonformal>, **seductive,** provocative, exciting; **endearing,** lovable, likable, adorable, admirable, **lovely,** magnetic, charming, enchanting, charismatic

winnings NOUNS **gains,** cut *and* take <both nonformal>, **profits,** earnings, return, returns, proceeds, bottom line <nonformal>, makings; **fruits,** pickings, gleanings; **booty,** spoils

winnow VERBS **select,** make a selection; **pick,** handpick, pick out; **decide between,** choose up sides <nonformal>, cull, glean, sift; separate the wheat from the chaff, separate the sheep from the goats

winsome ADJS **endearing,** lovable, likable, adorable, admirable, **lovely,** lovesome, sweet, winning; **charming;** caressable, kissable; **pleasant,** genial, irrepressible, prepossessing

wintry ADJS **cold,** freezing, freezing cold, **crisp,** brisk, nipping, **nippy,** snappy <nonformal>, **raw,** bleak, keen, sharp, bitter, biting, pinching, cutting, **piercing,** penetrating; **wintery,** winterlike, winterbound, hiemal, brumal, hibernal

wipe VERBS **wipe up** *or* out, wipe off; rub, swab, brush; towel

wipe out VERBS 1 **exterminate,** eliminate, eradicate, deracinate, **extirpate,** annihilate; **liquidate,** purge; remove, sweep away, wipe off the map, rub out
2 **bankrupt,** ruin, break, bust <nonformal>; put out of business, drive to the wall, scuttle, sink, impoverish; **cancel,** delete, expunge

wire NOUNS 1 **cable,** electric wire, electric cord, cord, power cord, power cable; **telegram,** telex; **cablegram,** day letter, night letter
VERBS 2 **electrify,** wire up; **telegraph,** telegram, send a wire <nonformal>, telex; cable

wiretap NOUNS 1 **surveillance,** wiretapping, bugging <nonformal>, electronic surveillance
VERBS 2 **listen in;** eavesdrop, tap, intercept, bug <nonformal>

wiry ADJS **well-built,** thewy, sinewy; **stringy,** ropy, fibrous

wisdom NOUNS ripe wisdom, seasoned understanding, mellow wisdom, wiseness, sageness, sapience, good *or* sound understanding; **profundity,** intelligence, profoundness, depth; **conventional wisdom,** received wisdom, prudential judgment, prudence

wise ADJS **sage,** sapient, seasoned, **knowing;** learned; **profound,** deep; wise as an owl, wise as Solomon; wise beyond one's years, in advance of one's age

wisecrack NOUNS 1 **witticism,** pleasantry, *plaisanterie, boutade* <both Fr>; **crack** *and* smart crack <both nonformal>; **mot,** bon mot, smart saying, stroke of wit, one-liner *and* zinger <both nonformal>; **sally,** flight of wit; **repartee,** backchat, retort, riposte, snappy comeback <nonformal>; **gibe,** dirty *or* nasty crack <nonformal>; persiflage
VERBS 2 **joke,** jest, crack wise <nonformal>, utter a mot, **quip,** jape, josh <nonformal>, fun <nonformal>, make fun, **kid** *or* **kid around** <both nonformal>; make a funny <nonformal>; **crack a joke,** get off a joke; **make fun of,** gibe at, fleer at, mock, scoff at

wise guy NOUNS **wiseacre,** wisehead, wiseling, **witling,** wisenheimer *or* weisenheimer <nonformal>, smart ass <nonformal>; **gangster,** hoodlum

wise man NOUNS **sage,** wise woman, sapient, man *or* woman of wisdom; **philosopher,** thinker, lover of wisdom; elder, wise old man, elder statesman; seer; mentor; **intellect,** man of intellect; mandarin, **intellectual**; savant; brain *and* rocket scientist *and* brain surgeon <all nonformal>; **pundit,** Brahmin, mandarin, egg-head *and* pointy-head <both nonformal>; **highbrow** <nonformal>

wish NOUNS 1 **desire,** wanting, **want,** need, desideration; **hope;** fancy; will, mind, pleasure, will and pleasure; heart's desire; **inclination,** disposition, liking, appetence, appetency, espressed desire
VERBS 2 **desire,** desiderate, be desirous of, ewish for, express a wish for, crave, lust after, bay after, kill for *and* give one's right arm for <both nonformal>, die for <nonformal>, **want,** have a mind to, choose <nonformal>; **like,** have *or* acquire a taste for, fancy, take to, **take a fancy** *or* a shine to, have a fancy for; lean toward, tilt toward, have a penchant for, have a weakness *or* soft spot in one's heart for

wishful thinking NOUNS **fantasy,** fantasizing, escape into fantasy, dreamlike thinking, autistic *or* dereistic thinking, autism, dereism; **wistfulness,** wishfulness, **nostalgia;** sheep's eyes, longing *or* wistful eye; daydream, daydreaming; **credulity,** credulousness, inclination *or* disposition to believe, ease of belief, will *or* willingness to believe, wishful belief

wishy-washy ADJS tasteless, bland, **insipid,** vapid, neutral, watery, milktoast, milky, milk-and-water, mushy; halfhearted, infirm of will *or* purpose, **indecisive,** irresolute, changeable; **unsteady,** spineless, shapeless, amorphous, blowing hot and cold <nonformal>, like a feather in the wind, unsteadfast

wistful ADJS **wishful; longing,** yearning, yearnful, **hankering** <nonformal>, **languishing,** pining, honing <nonformal>; **nostalgic,** homesick; **pensive,** tristful

wit NOUNS 1 **humor,** pleasantry, *esprit* <Fr>, salt, spice *or* savor of wit; Attic wit *or* salt, Atticism; ready wit, quick wit, nimble wit, agile wit, pretty wit; dry wit, subtle wit; **sense,** mother wit, natural *or* native wit, **intelligence,** intellect, understanding
2 **humorist,** funnyman, comic, *bel-esprit* <Fr>, life of the party; **joker,** jokester, gagman <nonformal>, **jester,** quipster, wisecracker *and* gagster <both nonformal>; wag, wagwit; epigrammatist; satirist, ironist; burlesquer, caricaturist, parodist, lampooner

witch NOUNS **hag,** vixen, hellhag, hellcat, she-devil, virago, brimstone, termagant, grimalkin, Jezebel, beldam, she-wolf, tigress, wildcat, bitch-kitty <nonformal>, siren, fury; **sorceress,** shamaness; witchwoman <nonformal>, witchwife <Scots>; witch of Endor

witchcraft NOUNS **sorcery,** necromancy, magic, sortilege, **wizardry,** theurgy, rune, glamour; spellcraft, spellbinding, spellcasting; **witchery,** witchwork, bewitchery, enchantment

witch hunt NOUNS **persecution,** oppression, harrying, hounding, tormenting, bashing <nonformal>, harassment, victimization; **witch-hunting,** redbaiting <nonformal>, McCarthyism; fishing expedition, inquisition

withdraw VERBS 1 **retreat,** sound *or* beat a retreat, beat a hasty retreat, **beat a retreat,** remove; **retire,** pull out *or* back, exfiltrate, advance to the rear, disengage; **fall back,** move back, draw back, back out *or* out of *and* back off *and* back down <all nonformal>
2 **retract,** draw *or* pull back, pull out, draw *or* pull in; draw in one's claws *or* horns; defer, take a back seat, play second fiddle; **shrink,** wince, cringe, flinch, shy, fight shy, duck
3 **stand alone,** stand *or* move *or* keep apart, keep oneself to oneself, alienate *or* seclude *or* sequester *or* isolate oneself, feel out of place

withdrawal NOUNS 1 **retreat,** *reculade* <Fr>, strategic withdrawal, exfiltration; **retirement,** removal, fallback, pullout, pullback; advance to the rear; rout; disengagement; **backing down** *or* **off** *or* **out** <all nonformal>; reneging, copping *or* weaseling out <nonformal>, **recantation,** disavowal, denial, **repudiation,** retraction
2 **aloofness,** standoffishness, distance, remoteness, **detachment,** reclusiveness, solitariness; **inaccessibility,** unapproachability; introversion; **alienation,** standing *or* moving *or* keeping apart, **isolation**
3 **resignation,** demission, **abdication,** voluntary resignation; forced resignation, deposal; relinquishment

wither VERBS **shrink,** shrivel, sear, parch, dry up; **wizen,** wrinkle, weazen; consume, waste, waste away, attenuate, thin, emaciate

withhold VERBS hold back, hold out on <nonformal>, **refrain from,** forbear, forgo, spare, **avoid,** shun, eschew, **pass up** <nonformal>, **keep from,** keep *or* stand *or* hold aloof from, have nothing to do with, take no part in, have no hand in, **let alone,** let well enough alone, let go by, **deny oneself,** do without, go without, make do without, not *or* never touch, keep hands off

witness NOUNS 1 **eyewitness,** spectator, earwitness; **bystander,** passerby; **deponent,** testifier, attestant, attester, attestator, voucher, swearer; **informant,** informer; character witness; cojuror, compurgator
VERBS 2 **see,** behold, observe, view, perceive, discern, spy, espy, **sight,** have in sight, make out, pick out, descry, spot <nonformal>, discover, notice, take notice of, have one's eye on, distinguish, recognize, ken <nonformal>, **catch sight of,** get a load of <nonformal>, take in, get an eyeful of <nonformal>, look on *or* upon, cast the eyes on *or* upon, **set** *or* **lay eyes on,** clap eyes on <nonformal>; **glimpse,** get *or* catch a glimpse of; see with one's own eyes
3 bear witness, affirm, **believe**; keep the faith, fight the good fight, let one's light shine, praise and glorify God, walk humbly with one's God; be observant, follow righteousness

wits NOUNS **senses,** faculties, parts, capacities, intellectual gifts *or* talents, mother wit; consciousness

witticism NOUNS **pleasantry,** *plaisanterie, boutade* <both Fr>; play of wit, *jeu d'esprit* <Fr>; **crack** *and* smart crack *and* **wisecrack** <all nonformal>; **quip, mot,** bon mot, smart saying, stroke of wit, one-liner *and* zinger <both nonformal>; epigram, turn of thought, aphorism, apothegm; flash of wit, scintillation; **sally,** flight of wit

witty ADJS **amusing,** humorous, comic, comical, farcical; **funny; jocular,** joking, jesting, jocose, tongue-in-cheek; facetious, joshing <nonformal>, **whimsical,** droll, humorsome; smart, clever, brilliant, scintillating, sparkling, sprightly; keen, sharp, rapier-like, pungent, pointed, biting, mordant; satiric, **satirical,** sarcastic, ironic, ironical; **keen-witted,** quick-witted, nimble-witted

wizard NOUNS **sorcerer,** necromancer, wonder-worker, theurgist; warlock, male witch; thaumaturge, thaumaturgist; alchemist; conjurer; diviner; dowser, water witch, water witcher; diabolist

wobble VERBS **fluctuate,** pendulate, oscillate, wobble about, teeter, dither, flounder, stagger, **seesaw,** teeter-totter, wamble

woe NOUNS **wretchedness,** despair, bitterness, infelicity, **misery,** anguish, agony, woefulness, bale, balefulness; **heartache,** aching heart, heavy heart, bleeding heart, broken heart, agony of mind *or* spirit; **despondency,** despond; **desolation,** prostration; **curse,** distress, grievance, **sorrow,** *tsuris* <Yiddish>

wolf NOUNS 1 timber wolf, lobo <W US>, brush wolf, prairie wolf, coyote, medicine wolf <W US>
2 masher, lady-killer, skirt chaser, man on the make *and* make-out artist <both nonformal>, gay deceiver, philanderer; libertine, lecher, cocksman <nonformal>, seducer, Casanova, Don Juan
VERBS 3 **gobble,** gulp, bolt, gobble *or* gulp *or* bolt *or* wolf down; **gorge,** engorge, glut, cram, **stuff,** batten, guttle, **devour,** raven, eat like a horse, stuff oneself *and* hog it down *and* eat one's head off *and* fork *or* shovel it in <all nonformal>, eat one out of house and home

woman NOUNS 1 **womankind,** women, femininity, **womanhood,** womenfolk *or* womenfolks <nonformal>, the distaff side; **the female sex;** the second sex, **the fair sex,** the gentle sex, the softer sex, **the weaker sex,** the weaker vessel

2 <nonformal> **gal, dame,** hen, biddy, skirt, jane, broad, doll, babe, chick, wench, bird <Brit>, tomato, bitch, minx, momma, mouse, sister, squaw, toots

3 **wife,** married woman, wedded wife, goodwife <old>, squaw, lady, matron, old lady *and* old woman *and* little woman *and* ball and chain <all nonformal>, feme, feme covert, **better half** <nonformal>, **helpmate,** helpmeet, rib, wife of one's bosom; wife in name only; wife in all but name, common-law wife; **mistress,** kept woman, kept mistress, paramour, concubine, doxy, playmate, spiritual *or* unofficial wife; live-in lover <nonformal>

the female of the human species, and not a different kind of animal
G B Shaw

O fairest of creation! last and best of all God's works
Milton

womanizer NOUNS **libertine,** swinger <nonformal>, **profligate,** rake, rakehell, **roué,** wanton, cocksman <nonformal>, debauchee, **wolf** <nonformal>, woman chaser, skirt chaser <nonformal>, gay dog, gay deceiver, gallant, philanderer, lover-boy <nonformal>, Lothario, Don Juan, Casanova

wonder NOUNS 1 wonderment, sense of wonder, marveling, marvel, **astonishment,** amazement; **surprise;** beguilement, fascination; bewilderment, puzzlement
2 **marvel,** prodigy, miracle, phenomenon, phenom <nonformal>; **sensation,** rocker *and* stunner <both nonformal>; one for the book *and* something to brag about *and* something to shout about *and* something to write home about *and* something else <all nonformal>; **rarity,** nonesuch, nonpareil, exception, one in a thousand, **first-rater,** topnotcher, worldbeater; hard *or* tough act to follow <nonformal>
VERBS 3 **marvel,** be astonished *or* amazed *or* astounded, be seized with wonder; **gaze,** gape, drop one's jaw, look *or* stand aghast *or* agog, gawk, **stare,** stare openmouthed, open one's eyes, rub one's eyes, hold one's breath
4 **be uncertain,** feel unsure; doubt, have one's doubts, **question,** puzzle over, agonize over; wonder whether, wrinkle one's brow; not know what to make of, not be able to make head or tail of

wonderful ADJS **wondrous,** marvelous, miraculous, fantastic, fabulous, phenomenal, **prodigious,** stupendous, unheard-of, unprecedented, extraordinary, exceptional, rare, unique, singular, **remarkable,** striking, sensational

woo VERBS **court,** sue, press one's suit, **pay court** *or* **suit to,** cozy up to <nonformal>, eye up *and* chat up <Brit nonformal>, pay one's court to, fling oneself at; **pursue,** follow; chase <nonformal>; set one's cap at *or* for <nonformal>; spark <nonformal>, squire

wood NOUNS **woodland,** woods, timberland; **timber,** stand of timber, **forest,** forest land, forest cover, forest preserve, state *or* national forest; **firewood,** stovewood; **kindling,** kindling wood; brush, brushwood; log, backlog, yule log *or* yule clog <old>; **lumber,** forest-product; hardwood, softwood

wooded ADJS **sylvan,** woodland, forest, forestal; timbered, forested, arboreous; **woody,** woodsy, bosky, bushy, shrubby, scrubby; copsy, braky

wooden ADJS **inexpressive,** unexpressive, impassive, uncommunicative; **expressionless; vacant,** empty, blank; glassy, glazed, glazed-over, deadpan, poker-faced <nonformal>

woolly ADJS **fleecy,** lanate, lanated, flocky, flocculent, floccose; bushy, tufty, **shaggy,** shagged; fuzzy

woozy ADJS **dazed,** mazed, **dazzled,** bedazzled, in a daze; **silly,** knocked silly, cockeyed <nonformal>; **groggy** <nonformal>, dopey <nonformal>; **punch-drunk** *and* punchy *and* slaphappy <all nonformal>

word NOUNS 1 **oath,** vow, assurance, guarantee, warrant, solemn oath *or* affirmation *or* word *or* declaration; pledge; **promise,** solemn promise, troth, plight, faith, parole, **word of honor**
2 **report,** message, presentation, account, **statement,** mention; **news,** tidings, intelligence, information, advice; parol, the spoken word; vocable

wordy ADJS **verbose;** talkative; **prolix,** windy <nonformal>, **long-winded,** longiloquent; **protracted,** extended, *de longue haleine* <Fr>, lengthy, long, **long-drawn-out,** spun-out, endless, unrelenting; padded

work NOUNS 1 **composition,** opus, production, literary production, literary artifact *or* artefact, lucubration, brainchild; essay, article; poem; play; novel, short story; **work of art,** object of art, objet d'art, art object, art work, artistic production, piece, **study,** design; creation, brainchild
2 **occupation,** job, employment, business, employ, **activity,** function, enterprise, undertaking, **affairs,** labor; thing *and* bag <both nonformal>; **task,** stint, job, piece of work, **chore,** odd job
VERBS 3 **labor;** busy oneself; turn a hand, do a lick of work, earn one's keep; do the chores; **operate,** function, act, perform, go, run, be in action *or* operation *or* commission; be effective, go into effect, have effect, take effect, militate; **accomplish,** achieve, **deliver,** realize, engineer, effectuate, **bring about,** bring to fruition *or* into being, cause; be productive
4 **suffice,** do, just do, serve, **answer;** be equal to, **avail;** answer *or* serve the purpose, do the trick <nonformal>, suit; **satisfy,** meet requirements; **pass muster,** make the grade *or* the cut *and* hack it *and* cut the mustard *and* **fill the bill** <all nonformal>; get by *and* scrape by <both nonformal>, do in a pinch, **pass,** pass in the dark <nonformal>
5 **cultivate,** culture, **dress,** till, till the soil, dig, delve, spade

workable ADJS **operable,** operatable, **performable,** actable, doable, manageable, compassable, negotiable, maneuverable; **practicable,** feasible, practical, viable

workaday ADJS **routine,** nine-to-five, well-trodden, well-worn, beaten; **matter-of-fact,** homely, homespun, everyday, household, garden, common- *or* garden-variety, prosaic

workaholic NOUNS **hustler** *and* self-starter <both nonformal>, bustler; go-getter *and* ball of fire *and* live wire *and* powerhouse *and* human dynamo *and* spitfire <all nonformal>; overachiever; beaver, busy bee, **eager beaver** <nonformal>

worker NOUNS **workman,** working man, working woman, working girl, proletarian, laborer, laboring man, toiler, stiff *and* working stiff <both nonformal>, artisan, mechanic, industrial worker, factory worker

workhorse NOUNS **drudge,** grub, hack, fag, plodder, slave, galley slave, beast of burden, slogger; grind *and* greasy grind <both nonformal>

hewers of wood and drawers of water
BIBLE

2 **draft horse,** dray horse, cart horse, plow horse

working class NOUNS **lower class,** lower classes, lower orders, plebs, workers, working people, proletariat, laboring class *or* classes, toilers, toiling class *or* classes, the other half, low-income group, wage-earners, hourly worker, blue-collar workers

working-class ADJS **blue-collar,** proletarian, lower-class, born on the wrong side of the tracks

workmanlike ADJS **skillful,** good, goodish, excellent, **expert,** proficient; dexterous, **adroit,** deft, adept, coordinated, well-coordinated, **apt,** no mean, **handy; ingenious,** resourceful, well-done; **passable,** unobjectionable, unexceptionable

workmanship NOUNS **skill,** skillfulness, **proficiency,** craft, **craftsmanship,** artisanship; **know-how** *and* savvy *and* bag of tricks <all nonformal>; technical skill, **technique,** touch, **mastery,** command, control, grip

works NOUNS 1 **benevolences,** philanthropies, charities; **good works,** public service
2 **complete works,** oeuvre, canon, literary canon, author's canon
3 **plant,** factory, manufacturing plant, *usine* <Fr>
4 **mechanism,** machinery, **movement,** movements, **action,** motion, workings, inner workings, what makes it work, innards, what makes it tick; clockworks, watchworks, servomechanism

world NOUNS 1 **outlook,** mental outlook; *Anschauung* <Ger>, **point of view,** viewpoint, standpoint, **perspective,** *optique* <Fr>; slant, way of looking at things, slant on things, where one is coming from <nonformal>; **frame of reference,** intellectual *or* ideational framework, arena, universe, world *or* universe of discourse, system, reference system
2 **universe,** cosmos; creation, created universe, created nature, all, **all creation,** all tarnation <nonformal>, all *or* everything that is, all being, totality, totality of being, sum of things; omneity, allness; nature, system; wide world, whole wide world; **macrocosm**

world without end
BIBLE

worldly ADJS 1 **experienced,** practiced, mature, matured, ripe, ripened, **seasoned,** tried, well-tried, tried and true, **veteran,** old, an old dog at <nonformal>; **worldly-wise,** wise in the ways of the world, knowing, **sophisticated,** cosmopolitan, cosmopolite, blasé, dry behind the ears, not born yesterday, long in the tooth
2 **unsacred,** nonsacred, **unholy,** unhallowed, unsanctified, unblessed; profane, **secular,** temporal, fleshly, mundane; unsaved, unredeemed, unregenerate, reprobate; **secularist,** secularistic, earthly, earthy, terrestrial, **materialistic,** material, Philistine

worn ADJS 1 **wasted, rundown,** worn-out, worn to a frazzle <nonformal>, worn to a shadow, reduced to a skeleton; tired-looking, weary-looking, haggard, hollow-eyed, ravaged, drawn, cadaverous, wan; dissipated, **eroded,** consumed, ablated; worn-down, the worse for wear, dog-eared; timeworn; **threadbare,** bare
2 **secondhand,** used, previously owned, **unnew,** not new, pawed-over; hand-me-down, reach-me-down <Brit nonformal>

worry NOUNS 1 worriment <nonformal>, worriedness; **worries,** worries and cares, troubles, concerns; worrying, fretting; harassment, torment
VERBS 2 **upset,** vex, fret, agitate, get to <nonformal>, **harass,** harry, **torment,** dog, hound, plague, persecute, haunt, beset; worry oneself, worry one's head about, worry oneself sick, trouble one's head *or* oneself, lose sleep; **fuss,** chafe, stew *and* take on <both nonformal>, fret and fume; bite one's nails, walk the floor, go up the wall <nonformal>, be on tenterhooks *or* pins and needles <nonformal>

worrywart NOUNS **worrier,** killjoy, nervous Nellie *and* gloomy Gus *and* calamity howler <all nonformal>, seek-sorrow, Job's comforter, prophet of doom, Cassandra

worse ADJS **aggravated,** worsened, worse and worse, exacerbated, embittered, soured, deteriorated; **intensified,** heightened, stepped-up, **increased,** worse off, the worse for, all the worse for; **degenerate,** unmitigated

worsen VERBS get *or* grow worse, take a turn for the worse; go from push to shove, **go from bad to worse;** jump out of the frying pan and into the fire, avoid Scylla and fall into Charybdis; **deteriorate,** sicken, get no better fast <nonformal>, disimprove, **degenerate;** slip back, **retrogress,** retrograde, regress, relapse, fall back

sow the wind and reap the whirlwind
BIBLE

worship NOUNS 1 worshiping, **adoration,** devotion, homage, veneration, reverence; idolatry
VERBS 2 **adore,** reverence, venerate, revere, honor, do *or* pay homage to, pay divine honors to, do service, lift up the heart, bow down and worship, humble oneself before; idolize

worst ADJS flagrant, **scandalous,** shameful, **shocking,** infamous, **notorious,** arrant, **egregious; odious,** disgusting, repulsive, loathsome, **abominable,** detestable, despicable, contemptible, beneath contempt, hateful; as bad as they come, as bad as they make 'em <nonformal>, as bad as bad can be; worthless

worth NOUNS 1 **preciousness,** dearness, value, high *or* great value, extraordinary worth, **pricelessness,** invaluableness; **assets,** resources, total assets, net worth, **pecuniary resources,** means, available means *or* resources *or* funds, cash flow, wherewithal, command of money
2 **goodness,** excellence, quality, class <nonformal>; **virtue,** grace; **merit,** desert; **fineness,** virtuousness

worthless ADJS **valueless,** good-for-nothing, good-for-naught, no-good *or* NG <nonformal>, no-account <nonformal>, dear at any price, not worth a dime *or* a red cent *or* a hill of beans *or* shit <nonformal>, not worthwhile, not worth having, not worth mentioning *or* speaking of, not worth a rap *or* a continental *or* a damn, of no earthly use; unworthy, unprofitable, profitless, unrewarding, useless

worthwhile ADJS **valuable,** of value, all for the best, all to the good, **profitable,** fructuous, rewarding, worth one's while; gainful, remunerative, advantageous

worthy ADJS **warranted,** justified, entitled, qualified; **deserved,** merited, richly deserved, earned, well-earned; **reputable,** highly reputed, **estimable,** esteemed, much *or* highly esteemed, **honorable,** honored; **meritorious,** worth one's salt, noble, creditable; respected, respectable, highly respectable; **well-thought-of,** held in esteem, in good odor, in favor, in high favor

would-be ADJS **presumptuous,** presuming, assuming, overweening, self-elected, self-appointed, self-proclaimed; **so-called,** *soi-disant* <Fr>; **self-called,** self-styled, self-christened

wound NOUNS 1 **trauma,** injury, hurt, lesion; **cut,** incision, scratch, gash; puncture, stab, stab wound; flesh wound; **laceration,** mutilation; **bruise,** contusion, ecchymosis
VERBS 2 **pain,** give *or* inflict pain, **hurt,** afflict, bruise, distress; pierce, prick, stab, cut, lacerate; **grieve,** aggrieve, anguish; hurt one's feelings; wound *or* sting *or* cut to the quick; **injure,** draw blood, traumatize

wow NOUNS 1 belly laugh, rib tickler, sidesplitter, thigh-slapper, howler, scream, riot, panic
VERBS 2 **make one laugh,** raise a smile *or* laugh, convulse, be the death of; slay *and* knock dead *and* kill *and* break one up *and* crack one up *and* fracture one <all nonformal>; have them rolling in the aisles; keep them in stitches

wrangle NOUNS 1 **quarrel,** open quarrel, **dispute,** argument, polemic, lovers' quarrel, **controversy,** altercation, **fight,** squabble, contention, strife, **tussle,** bicker, snarl, **tiff,** spat, fuss; words, sharp words, war of words, logomachy
VERBS 2 **quarrel,** dispute, oppugn, altercate, **fight,** squabble, tiff, spat, **bicker,** spar, have words, set to, join issue, make the fur fly; **be quarrelsome** *or* contentious, be thin-skinned, be touchy *or* sensitive, get up on the wrong side of the bed

wrap NOUNS 1 **dishabille,** *déshabillé* <Fr>, undress, something more comfortable; **negligee,** *négligé* <Fr>; **wrapper,** wrapping, gift wrapping
VERBS 2 enwrap, lap, envelop, sheathe, shroud, enshroud; wrap *or* bundle *or* muffle up; swathe, swaddle; **package,** pack, parcel; box, case, encase, crate, carton; shrink-wrap; do *or* tie *or* bind up

wrath NOUNS **anger,** ire, *saeva indignatio* <L>; angriness, irateness, wrathfulness; vials of wrath, grapes of wrath; the wrath of God

wreck NOUNS 1 **nervous wreck,** a bundle of nerves; wrack, shipwreck; total loss; **accident,** casualty, collision, crash, plane *or* car crash, smash *and* smashup *and* crack-up *and* pileup <all nonformal>
VERBS 2 **spoil,** mar, botch, **ruin,** blight, play havoc with; **demolish,** total *and* rack up <both nonformal>; **take apart,** tear apart, tear asunder, rend, take *or* pull *or* pick *or* tear to pieces, tear to shreds *or* rags *or* tatters; **disintegrate,** fragment, break to pieces, make mincemeat of, reduce to rubble, atomize, pulverize, **smash,** shatter

wrench NOUNS 1 **pang,** throe, throes; seizure, spasm, paroxysm; **twinge,** jumping pain; **pain,** distress, grief, stress, stress of life, suffering, passion,

dolor; ache, aching; shock, blow, hard *or* nasty blow
2 **jerk,** yank <nonformal>, quick *or* sudden pull; **twitch,** tweak, pluck, hitch, snatch, start; tool
VERBS 3 **twist,** turn, screw; **wrest,** wring, **rend,** rip; **force from,** wrest from, wrench from, wring from, tear from, rip from, rend from, snatch from, pry loose from

wrestle VERBS **struggle,** strive, contend, fight, battle, buffet, grapple, grapple with, go to the mat with, scuffle, tussle, rassle <nonformal>, hassle <nonformal>, work *or* fight one's way, agonize, huff and puff, grunt and sweat, sweat it <nonformal>, make heavy weather of it

wretch NOUNS mean *or* miserable wretch, beggarly fellow, **beggar;** devil, **poor devil,** *pauvre diable* <Fr>, poor creature, *mauvais sujet* <Fr>; **sad case,** sad sack <nonformal>; **good-for-nothing,** good-for-naught, no-good <nonformal>, **ne'er-do-well,** wastrel, *vaurien* <Fr>, worthless fellow

wretched ADJS **miserable;** woeful, woebegone; crushed, stricken, **cut up** <nonformal>, heartsick, heart-stricken, heart-struck; deep-troubled; desolate, disconsolate; **lamentable,** deplorable, regrettable, pitiable, piteous, rueful, **sad,** sorrowful, mournful, **depressing,** depressive; **pathetic,** affecting, touching, moving, saddening, poignant; **squalid,** sordid, shabby; beggarly, vile

wring VERBS **agonize,** harrow, crucify, martyr, martyrize, excruciate, twist, contorse, convulse; **squeeze** *or* **press out,** express, wring out; **wrest,** wrench, **rend,** rip; **wrest from,** wrench from, rip from, rend from, snatch from, pry loose from

wrinkle NOUNS 1 **corrugation,** crease, crimp, ruck, pucker; **crinkle,** crankle, rimple, ripple, wimple; crumple, rumple; crow's-feet
2 **fad,** craze, rage; new take <nonformal>; novelty; fillip
VERBS 3 **corrugate,** shirr, ridge, **furrow,** crease, crimp, crimple, cockle, cocker, **pucker,** purse; knit; ruck, ruckle; **crumple,** rumple; **crinkle,** rimple, ripple, wimple
4 **age, grow old,** senesce, get on *or* along, **get on** *or* **along in years,** wither, shrivel, wizen, shrink, diminish, wither *or* die on the vine, **dry up,** desiccate, sear

writ NOUNS **document,** official document, legal document, legal paper, legal instrument, **instrument,** paper, parchment, scroll, roll, **writing,** script, scrip; **summons,** subpoena, writ of summons; warrant

write VERBS **pen,** pencil, drive *or* push the pen *or* pencil <nonformal>; spill ink <nonformal>, **scribe;** take pen in hand; **put in writing,** put in black and white; **draw up,** draft, write out, make out; **write down,** record; author, **compose,** indite, formulate, produce, prepare; dash off, knock off *or* out <nonformal>, pound *or* crank *or* grind *or* churn out; **correspond,** correspond with, **communicate with,** write to, write a letter, send a letter to, send a note, **drop a line** <nonformal>

writer NOUNS **author,** composer, inditer; authoress, penwoman; **creative writer,** *littérateur* <Fr>, literary artist, literary craftsman *or* artisan *or* journeyman, belletrist, man of letters, literary man; free lance, free-lance writer; ghostwriter, ghost <nonformal>; scribbler <nonformal>, penman, pen, penner; pen *or* pencil driver *or* pusher <nonformal>, wordslinger, **inkslinger** *and* ink spiller *and* inkstained wretch <all nonformal>, knight of the plume *or* pen *or* quill <nonformal>; writer's cramp, graphospasm

writing NOUNS 1 scrivening <old>, inscription, lettering; pen, **pen-and-ink;** inkslinging *and* ink spilling <both nonformal>, pen *or* pencil pushing <nonformal>; secret writing, cryptography
2 **composition,** the art of composition, inditing, inditement; **creative writing,** literary art, verbal art, literary composition, literary production, verse-writing, short-story writing, novel-writing, playwriting, drama-writing; essay-writing; expository writing

wrong NOUNS 1 **misdeed,** misdemeanor, misfeasance, malfeasance, malefaction, criminal *or* guilty *or* sinful act, **offense,** injustice, injury, **iniquity,** evil, peccancy, *malum* <L>; tort; **error,** fault, breach; **impropriety,** slight *or* minor wrong, venial sin, **indiscretion,** peccadillo, misstep, trip, slip, lapse; **transgression,** trespass; **sin,** cardinal *or* deadly *or* mortal sin
ADJS 2 **wrongful;** improper, incorrect, indecorous, undue, unseemly; unfit,

unfitting, inappropriate, unsuitable; **evil,** sinful, wicked, unrighteous; not the thing, hardly the thing, not done, **off-base** *and* **out-of-line** *and* **off-color** <all nonformal>
3 **erroneous,** untrue, not true, **not right;** unfactual, all wrong; peccant, perverse, corrupt; **false,** fallacious, self-contradictory; illogical; unproved; **faulty,** faultful, flawed, defective, **at fault;** wide of the mark, beside the mark; amiss, awry, askew, deviant, deviative, deviational; erring, errant, aberrant; mistaken, in error, erring, **all wet** <nonformal>; in the right church but the wrong pew
ADVS 4 **wrongly,** wrongfully; **improperly,** incorrectly, indecorously; **erroneously,** falsely, by mistake, fallaciously; **mistakenly;** amiss, astray, on the wrong track

X-rated ADJS **lascivious,** lecherous, sexy, salacious, carnal, animal, **sexual,** lustful, ithyphallic; prurient, itching, itchy <nonformal>; **lewd,** bawdy, adult, hard, pornographic, porno <nonformal>, **dirty,** obscene; erotic, **sensual,** fleshly

yacht NOUNS **sailboat,** sailing vessel, sailing boat, ragboat <nonformal>, sailing yacht, sailing cruiser, sailing ship, tall *or* taunt ship, sail, sailer, **windjammer** <nonformal>, windship, windboat; pleasure boat, a hole in the water into which one pours money <nonformal>

yank NOUNS 1 **jerk,** quick *or* sudden pull; wrench, snatch
VERBS 2 **jerk,** snatch, wrench

Yankee NOUNS **Northerner,** northlander; Northman; New Englander, Down-Easter Yankee

yard NOUNS 1 **enclosure,** close, **confine,** precinct, enclave, pale, paling, list, cincture; park, court, courtyard, curtilage, toft
2 yards, railroad yard, brickyard, shipyard, dockyard, boatyard

yawn NOUNS 1 **gap,** gape, hiatus, lacuna, gat, space, interval; **chasm,** gulf; **gaping, yawning,** oscitation, oscitancy, dehiscence, pandiculation; the gapes
VERBS 2 **gape,** oscitate, dehisce, hang open

yell NOUNS 1 **cry,** call, shout, hoot; **whoop,** holler <nonformal>; **cheer,** hurrah; howl, yowl; bawl, bellow, roar; **scream, shriek,** screech, squeal, squall, caterwaul; yelp, yap, yammer, yawp, bark; war cry, battle cry, war whoop, rallying cry
VERBS 2 **cry,** call, shout, holler <nonformal>, hoot; whoop; **cheer; howl,** yowl, yammer; squawk, yawp; **bawl,** bellow, roar, roar *or* bellow like a bull; cry *or* yell *or* scream bloody murder *or* blue murder; **scream, shriek,** screech, squeal, squall, waul, caterwaul; yelp, yap, bark; give a cheer, give three cheers, yell oneself hoarse

yellow ADJS 1 **sensational,** lurid, **melodramatic,** Barnumesque; spine-chilling, eye-popping <nonformal>; **jealous,** jaundiced, jaundice-eyed, yellow-eyed
2 **cowardly,** coward; **afraid,** fearful; timid, timorous, overtimorous, overtimid, rabbity *and* mousy <both nonformal>; **fainthearted,** weakhearted, chicken-hearted, yellow-bellied *and* with a yellow streak <both nonformal>; **chicken** <nonformal>, afraid of one's shadow; panicky, panic-prone, funking *and* funky <both nonformal>; daunted, dismayed, unmanned, cowed, intimidated

yelp NOUNS 1 **cry,** call, shout, yell, hoot; screech, squeal, squall, caterwaul; yap, yammer, yawp, bark
VERBS 2 **cry,** screech, squeal, squall, waul, caterwaul; yap, bark; **grumble,** murmur, mutter, growl, clamor, croak, grunt

yen NOUNS **yearning,** longing, desiderium, **hankering** <nonformal>, **pining,** aching; lech <nonformal>, hunger, thirst; instinct *or* feeling for, sensitivity to

yeoman NOUNS 1 **retainer,** dependent, follower; myrmidon; vassal, liege, liege man, feudatory, homager; **attendant,** tender, usher, squire; guardsman; yeoman of the guard *or* beefeater, gentleman-at-arms
2 **agriculturist,** agriculturalist; **farmer,** granger, husbandman, cultivator, tiller, sodbuster, **tiller of the soil**

yes INTERJS 1 yes, yea, aye, *oui* <Fr>, *sí* <Sp>, *da* <Russ>, *ja* <Ger>; yes sir, yes ma'am; why yes, *mais oui* <Fr>; **indeed,** yes indeed; **surely, certainly,** assuredly, most assuredly, **right, right you are,**

exactly, precisely, just so, absolutely, positively, really, truly, rather <Brit>, quite, to be sure; **all right, right, good,** well and good, good enough, **very well,** *très bien* <Fr>; naturally, *naturellement* <Fr>; **of course,** as you say, **by all means,** by all manner of means; **amen;** hear hear <Brit>

2 <nonformal> **yeah,** yep, yup, uh-huh; yes sirree, same here, likewise, indeedy, yes indeedy, sure, sure thing, sure enough, surest thing you know; right on!, righto!; OK, okay, Roger, Roger-dodger; fine; you bet!, bet your ass!, you can bet on it!, you can say that again!, you said it!, you better believe it

yes-man NOUNS 1 sycophant; lightweight, follower, pawn, cog, flunky, creature, lacky, hanger-on; toady, jackal, minion, myrmidon; ass-kisser *and* brown-nose *and* bootlicker <all nonformal>
2 **conformist,** conformer, sheep, trimmer, parrot, organization man

yesterday NOUNS 1 **the past,** past, foretime, former times, past times, times past, water under the bridge, **days** *or* **times gone by,** bygone times *or* days, yesteryear; recent past, just *or* only yesterday; **history,** past history; dead past, dead hand of the past

a bucket of ashes
CARL SANDBURG

ADVS 2 **formerly,** previously; **earlier,** before, before now, erenow, **hitherto,** heretofore, aforetime, beforetime, **in the past,** in times past; then; only yesterday, recently; **historically,** in historic *or* prehistoric times

yet ADVS 1 **additionally,** in addition, also, and then some, even more, more so, and also, and all <nonformal>, and so, **as well,** too, else, beside, **besides,** to boot, not to mention, let alone, into the bargain; on top of, over, above; **beyond,** plus; **more,** moreover, *au reste* <Fr>, *en plus* <Fr>, thereto, farther, further, **furthermore,** at the same time, then, again; similarly, likewise, by the same token, by the same sign
2 **until now,** hitherto, till now, thitherto, **hereunto,** heretofore, until this time, by this time, **up to now,** up to the present, up to this time, to this day, to the present moment, to this very instant, **so far,** thus far, **as yet,** to date, already, still, now *or* then as previously
ADVS, CONJ 3 **notwithstanding,** but, still, even; **however,** nevertheless, nonetheless; **although,** when, though; albeit; **at all events,** in any event, in any case, at any rate; **be that as it may,** for all that, even so, **on the other hand,** rather, again, at the same time, all the same, just the same; after all, after all is said and done

yield NOUNS 1 **output,** make, production; **proceeds,** produce, product; **crop,** harvest, fruit, vintage, bearing; bumper crop; **interest; return,** return on investment, payout, payback
VERBS 2 **give up,** relinquish, surrender, yield up, waive, **cede,** give way, give ground, back down, give up, give in, cave in <nonformal>, withdraw from *or* quit the field; **cease,** desist from, leave off, give over; cry quits, acknowledge defeat, **throw in the towel** *or* **sponge**
3 **bear,** produce, furnish; **bring forth,** usher into the world; fruit, **bear fruit,** fructify; **give,** relent, relax, bend, unbend, give way; bounce, spring, spring back

yokel NOUNS 1 **oaf,** lout, boor, lubber, **gawk,** gawky, **lummox,** rube, hick, hayseed, bumpkin, clod, clodhopper
ADJS 2 **hick,** hicky, hickified, from the sticks, rube, hayseed, down-home, shitkicking, hillbilly, redneck <all nonformal>

yonder ADJS 1 yon; **farther,** further, remoter, more distant
ADVS 2 yon; **in the distance,** in the remote distance; **in the offing,** on the horizon, in the background

young NOUNS 1 **young people,** youth, **younger generation,** rising *or* new generation, young blood, young fry <nonformal>; **children,** tots, childkind; small fry *and* kids *and* little kids *and* little guys <all nonformal>
ADJS 2 youngling, youngish, **juvenile,** juvenescent, **youthful,** youthlike, in the flower *or* bloom of youth, blooming, florescent, flowering, dewy, fresh-faced; fresh as a daisy, fresh as the morning dew

youngster NOUNS **young person, youth,** juvenile, youngling, young'un <nonformal>; **stripling,** slip, sprig, sapling; fledgling; hopeful, young hopeful;

minor, infant; **adolescent,** pubescent; **teenager,** teener, teenybopper <nonformal>

youth NOUNS 1 **youthfulness,** juvenility, juvenescence, tenderness, tender age, early years, school age, *jeunesse* <Fr>, prime of life, flower of life, salad days, springtime *or* springtide of life, seedtime of life, flowering time

my green age
DYLAN THOMAS

2 **youngster,** young person, **juvenile,** youngling, young'un <nonformal>; **stripling,** slip, sprig, sapling; fledgling; hopeful, young hopeful

yowl NOUNS 1 **howl,** yawl <Brit nonformal>; bawl, bellow, roar; **cry,** caterwaul, outcry, scream, yawp, keen, ululation
VERBS 2 **howl,** yammer, ululate, yawl <Brit nonformal>; squawk, yawp; **bawl,** bellow, roar, roar *or* bellow like a bull; cry *or* yell *or* scream bloody murder *or* blue murder; **scream,** shriek, screech, squeal, squall, caterwaul; yelp, yap, bark

yummy ADJS 1 **tasty,** good, fit to eat *and* finger-lickin' good <both nonformal>, good-tasting, **savory,** savorous, **palatable,** toothsome, sapid, good to eat, nice, agreeable, likable, pleasing, to one's taste, **delicious,** delightful, delectable, exquisite; for the gods, ambrosial, nectarous, nectareous; fit for a king, gourmet, of gourmet quality; scrumptious <nonformal>
2 **fun,** kicky, chewy, dishy, drooly, sexy <all nonformal>

yuppie NOUNS **conventionalist,** Babbitt, Philistine, middle-class type, button-down *or* white-bread type <nonformal>, **bourgeois,** plastic person *and* clone *and* square <all nonformal>, three-piecer <nonformal>

zap VERBS **annihilate,** exterminate, eradicate, extirpate, **eliminate,** liquidate, **wipe out,** stamp out, waste *and* take out *and* nuke <all nonformal>, put an end to, **end, terminate,** bring to an end, bring to a close *or* halt; **dispose of,** polish off <nonformal>; put the kibosh on <nonformal>, put the skids under <nonformal>; **kill,** extinguish, **give the quietus,** put the finisher *or* settler on <nonformal>, knock on the head, knock out <nonformal>, kayo *or* KO <both nonformal>, shoot down *and* shoot down in flames <both nonformal>, wipe out <nonformal>; **cancel, delete,** expunge, censor, censor out, blank out, erase

zeal NOUNS **ardor,** ardency, fervor, fervency, fervidness, spirit, warmth, fire, heat, heatedness, **passion,** passionateness, impassionedness, heartiness, intensity, **abandon,** vehemence; intentness, resolution; **devotion,** devoutness, devotedness, dedication, commitment, committedness; **earnestness, seriousness,** sincerity; loyalty, faithfulness, faith, fidelity; **zealousness,** zealotry, fanaticism

zealot NOUNS **enthusiast,** infatuate, energumen, rhapsodist; faddist; hobbyist, collector; **fanatic;** visionary, fundamentalist, militant; **devotee,** votary, aficionada, aficionado, **fancier,** admirer, **follower; disciple,** worshiper, idolizer, idolater; devotionalist

zenith NOUNS **apex,** vertex, acme, *ne plus ultra* <Fr>, **climax,** apogee, pole; **culmination; extremity,** maximum, limit, upper extremity, highest point; **supremacy,** primacy, paramountcy, **first place,** height, be-all and end-all, summit, top spot <nonformal>

zero NOUNS **nothing,** nil, *nihil* <L>, *nichts* <Ger>, *nada* <Sp>, **naught,** aught, nullity; cipher; nothing whatever, nothing at all, nothing on earth *or* under the sun, no such thing; **nonentity,** nobody *and* nonstarter *and* nebbish <all nonformal>, nonperson, unperson, hollow man; flash in the pan, dud <nonformal>

zero hour NOUNS **crucial moment,** critical moment, loaded *or* charged moment, decisive moment, defining moment, turning point, climax, **moment of truth,** crunch *and* when push comes to shove <both nonformal>; H-hour, D-day, A-day, target date, deadline

zest NOUNS **animation,** vivacity, liveliness, **ardor,** glow, keen desire, **appetite,** savor, relish; warmth, enthusiasm, lustiness, robustness, mettle, zestfulness, **sprightliness,** high spirits, vim, zip <nonformal>, vigor, verve, **exuberance,** heartiness, **gusto,** élan, *joie de vivre* <Fr>, *brio* <Ital>, spiritedness, vitality; **briskness,** perkiness, pertness, **life,** spirit

zigzag NOUNS 1 zig, zag; zigzaggedness, flexuosity, **crookedness,** crankiness; switchback, hairpin, dogleg; wandering *or* twisting *or* zigzag *or* shifting course *or* path; **divergence,** divarication, branching off, divagation, declination, aberration, aberrancy
VERBS 2 zig, zag, **stagger,** wind in and out, **go to and fro,** to-and-fro, **come and go,** pass and repass, back and fill; **bend,** curve, pull, crook, dogleg, hairpin; **digress**
ADJS 3 **digressive,** discursive, excursive, **circuitous;** devious, indirect, errant, erratic, dogleg *or* doglegged, **wandering,** rambling, roving, winding, twisting, meandering, snaky, serpentine; **crooked,** zigzagged, zigzaggy <nonformal>, jagged, serrate, sawtooth *or* sawtoothed

zilch NOUNS

<nonformal> **zip,** zippo, nix, goose egg, diddly, diddly squat, bubkes, beans, a hill of beans, a hoot, a rat's ass

zip NOUNS **zest,** zestfulness, zestiness, **briskness,** liveliness, raciness; **nippiness,** tanginess, snappiness; **spiciness,** pepperiness, hotness, fieriness; **tang,** spice, relish; **nip,** bite; punch, snap, ginger; **sprightliness,** high spirits, vim, vigor, verve, gusto, **exuberance,** heartiness

zodiac NOUNS **band,** belt, cincture, cingulum, **girdle,** girth, girt, zone, fascia, fillet; ecliptic, equator, great circle; **orbit,** circle, trajectory; circle of the sphere, great circle, small circle; ecliptic; **signs of the zodiac**

zombie NOUNS **apparition,** appearance, presence, shape, form, eidolon, idolum, revenant, larva; **spirit;** unsubstantiality, immateriality, incorporeal, incorporeity, incorporeal being *or* entity; **walking dead man**

zone NOUNS 1 **region,** area, belt, **territory,** terrain; space; **country**, land, territoriality; territorial waters, air space; **district,** quarter, section, department, division; salient, corridor; neck of the woods <nonformal>, purlieus; confines, precincts, environs, milieu; **orbit,** circle
2 postal zone, zip code *or* zip, postal code <Canada>, postcode <Brit>

zoo NOUNS **menagerie,** *Tiergarten* <Ger>, zoological garden *or* park

zoom VERBS **speed,** skim, **fly,** flit, fleet, wing one's way, outstrip the wind; **ascend,** climb, gain altitude, mount; **soar,** plane, kite, fly aloft, chandelle